MW01094708

With warm
wishes and
planting the thought
for Umeligo to
organize a wine safari

for your wine club to
South Africa
Cheers, Melissa

Platter's

BY **Diners Club INTERNATIONAL**

—2024—
SOUTH AFRICAN
WINE
GUIDE

John Platter SA Wine Guide (Pty) Ltd
www.wineonaplatter.com

EDITOR

Philip van Zyl

ASSOCIATE EDITORS

Cathy van Zyl & Tim James

TASTERS

Winnie Bowman, Greg de Bruyn, Tim James, Nomonde Kubheka, Malu Lambert, Angela Lloyd, Cathy Marston, Fiona McDonald, Christine Rudman, Penelope Setti, Dave Swingler, Cathy van Zyl & Meryl Weaver

Associates: Ndabezinhle Dube, Keize Mumba

Previous editions: David Biggs, David Clarke, Hennie Coetzee, Christian Eedes, Joanne Gibson, Higgo Jacobs, Ingrid Motteux, Khuselo Mputa, Gregory Mutambe, Jörg Pfützner, James Pietersen & Samarie Smith

COPYWRITERS

Greg de Bruyn, Tim James, Angela Lloyd, Fiona McDonald, Christine Rudman & Cathy van Zyl

COORDINATORS

Ina de Villiers (information); Amanda Ferreira (wine & tasting)

DATABASE & QR CODES

Sean de Kock, Ben van Rensburg (Modern Web Presence)

TYPESETTING & MAPS

Gawie du Toit

ADVERTISING, SALES & ADMINISTRATION

Philip van Zyl ▪ T +27 (0)82-896-9685 ▪ office@wineonaplatter.com

© John Platter SA Wine Guide (Pty) Ltd 2024
PO Box 788, Constantia 7848
T +27 (0)82-896-9685 ▪ office@wineonaplatter.com

Wineonaplatter.com
Facebook.com/wineonaplatter
Twitter.com/wineonaplatter ▪ @wineonaplatter
Instagram/wineonaplatter ▪ @wineonaplatter

All rights reserved. All rights attached in and to this book are, unless the context clearly indicates otherwise, the property of John Platter SA Wine Guide (Proprietary) Limited. They are protected under local and international laws and treaties. No part of this book may be reproduced, adapted or transmitted in any form or by any means (including, but not limited to, photocopying, recording, or by any information storage and retrieval system) without express written permission from the author/publisher.

All reasonable care has been taken in the preparation of this book, but the publishers and authors accept no liability whatsoever for any consequences, or loss, damages, whatsoever and howsoever incurred, or suffered resulting or arising from the use of the book or any information contained therein.

We receive numerous requests for lifting rights and, when these are for non-commercial, non-profit activities, we will assess and oblige same in writing at our sole discretion. Those wishing to quote from the book for commercial and advertising purposes, however, should make prior written arrangements with the editor, who, if permission is granted, will request a donation be made to a suitable education programme.

ISBN 978-0-6397-7566-1

Printed and bound in the Republic of South Africa by ABC Press, Cape Town

Contents

A Warm Welcome From Diners Club

Diners Club is proud to introduce the 44th edition of *Platter's by Diners Club South African Wine Guide*.

Globally respected, South African wines continue to perform remarkably at an international level, garnering significant results at competitions and professional tastings, a heartening outcome for local wine producers who work meticulously and innovatively on their wines.

Platter's by Diners Club remains the definitive guide for the broad spectrum of South Africa's wines. As Diners Club, we are delighted that the quality of wines presented in the 2024 edition has remained consistently high. Diners Club proudly supports South African wine through our flagship initiatives: *Platter's by Diners Club*, the annual Diners Club Winemaker and Young Winemaker of the Year awards, and the Diners Club Winelist award.

We also take great pride in our CSI programme, Dine for Change, which aims to positively impact wine and agriculture by upskilling and empowering young women in those sectors.

Diners Club wishes all the growers and wineries continued success in the year ahead, and sincerely thanks all who keep the flag of South African wines flying high.

For more on how Diners Club can enhance your wine, food and travel experiences, please visit www.dinersclub.co.za.

Esh Naidoo
Managing Director
Diners Club South Africa

How To Use This Guide

Our Track-Record-Based Rating System

General rating   ★★★★ **Caldera**
For 4-star or better wines, we give the 'track-record rating' over two or more vintages in the margin. Wines rated 4½ stars or more are set in red type

Vintage-specific rating   06 (★★★☆)
Any differences from the general rating are noted in brackets beside the particular vintage

★★★★★	95–100 / 18–20 pts	Superlative. A South African classic
★★★★☆	90–94 / 17–17.5 pts	Outstanding
★★★★	86–89 / 16–16.5 pts	Excellent
★★★☆	83–85 / 15.5 pts	Very good/promising
★★★	80–82 / 15 pts	Good, for early drinking
★★☆	77–79 / 14.5 pts	Average, with some appeal
★★	73–76 / 14 pts	Pleasant enough
★☆	70–72 / 13 pts	Plain and simple
★	65–69 / 12 pts	Unexciting
★	60–64 / 11 pts	Very ordinary
No star	50–59 / 10 pts	Somewhat less than ordinary

Symbols

Winery symbols

- (Ⓠ) Open for tasting (no fee unless noted)
- (🍴) Restaurant/refreshments
- (🏠) Accommodation
- (📷) Other tourist attractions/amenities on the property
- (🧺) Bring your own (BYO) picnic
- (👶) Child friendly
- (♿) Wheelchair friendly
- (NEW) New winery

Wine symbols

- (88) Rating on 100-point scale (see above)
- (✓) Good value
- (☺) Superquaffer
- (NEW) New wine
- (Ⓧ) Wine still selling, not retasted
- (Ⓥ) Organic
- (◎) Biodynamic
- (Ⓣ) Hidden gem
- (🏅) From vines officially 35 years or older*
- (🏆) Worth cellaring 8-10 years (reds, fortifieds), 4-6 years (whites)

* See oldvineproject.co.za

Abbreviations

% alc	Percentage alcohol by volume	MW	Master of Wine
1stB	First bottled vintage	NLH	Noble Late Harvest
BEE	Black Economic Empowerment	NV	Non-vintage. Year of harvest
BYO	Bring your own (wine, picnic)		not stated on label
Cs	Cases	RS	Residual sugar
CWG	Cape Winemakers Guild	SLH	Special Late Harvest
CWM	Cape Wine Master	Veritas	SA National Bottled Wine Show
Est	Date established	WIETA	Wine & Agricultural Ethical
g/L	Grams per litre		Trade Association
IPW	Integrated Production of Wine	WO	Wine of Origin
IWC	International Wine Challenge	cabernet/cab	cabernet sauvignon
IWSC	International Wine & Spirit	pinot	pinot noir
	Competition	tinta	tinta barocca
LBV	Late Bottled Vintage	touriga	touriga nacional
Malo	Malolactic fermentation	chenin	chenin blanc
MCC	Méthode cap classique	sauvignon/sauv	sauvignon blanc

How to use this Guide

Note: The example text used here is illustrative and not complete or up to date. See A–Z for full details.

Producer's name

Our track-record-based rating system
See page 5 for an explanation

Listings of wines available during the currency of the book

Wine name, vintage, colour & style

Location: nearest major centre to winery, vineyard, head office

Map & grid reference: see Maps section for winery's position

WO: Wine of Origin geographical unit, region, district or ward; wines described/rated bear the first-mentioned WO certification unless noted

Unless noted, red wines wooded; whites unoaked

Symbols
See page 5 for a complete list

Other attractions or activities available on the property

Bartinney Private Cellar

Perched high on the slopes of the Helshoogte Pass lie
owned by Michael and Rose Jordaan who are increa
plantings interspersed with native fynbos on steep, u

★★★★ **Cabernet Sauvignon** Elegant & understa
fruit tempered by savoury Marmite hints, olive tapen
lengthy finish. 12-18 months French oak, 50% new.

★★★★☆ **Elevage** Poised & polished **10** oozes cla
Stellenbosch fruit shows minty notes on nose giving
balanced grippy tannins. Shades of dark chocolate or

★★★★☆ **Chardonnay** Classically styled **13** conti
citrus on nose before palate glides delicately into pla
ity & lengthy finish.

★★★★☆ **Sauvignon Blanc** Peaches & cream **14**
green figs & quinces below. Good depth & length bu

Location/map: Stellenbosch ▪ WO: Banghoek/Stellenbo
10-4 ▪ Closed all pub hols ▪ Cellar tours by appt ▪ Bartin
Stellenbosch) ▪ Owner(s) Rose & Michael Jordaan ▪ Wir
Ryno Maree (Oct 2010) ▪ 27ha/±17ha (cab, chard, sau
BWI champion ▪ Postnet Suite 231 Private Bag X5061 S
bartinney.co.za ▪ F +27 (0)21-885-2852 ▪ **T +27 (0)2**

Barton Vineyards

Barton is a 200-ha working farm in the hills overlook
offering a range of activities, farm produce and luxur
stylish wines is still boutique in scale, critical acclaim
having to expand the cellar facilities to vinify other p

★★★★☆ **Winemakers Reserve** Maiden **11** mer
elegance & balance than barrel sample. Understated,
nuance. So tailored & sleek, belies its youthful intensi

★★★★ **Shiraz-Cabernet Sauvignon** Youthful, h
with garrigue scrub, pepper & a touch of cab's clean h

Rouge 🌿 ⊘ ★★★★ 4-way blend **12**, shiraz dom
ture, & merlot & malbec plump out fruit-filled interes
Blanc 13 ★★★★ **Sauvignon Blanc 13** ★★★★ **B**

Location: Bot River ▪ Map: Elgin, Walker Bay & Bot Riv
ing, sales & cellar tours Mon-Fri 9–5 Sat 10–4 ▪ Clos
olive oil, marinated olives & proteas ▪ Barton Villas ▪
winemaker(s)/viticulturist(s) PJ Geyer (Oct 2010) ▪ 2(
raz, chenin, sauv, sem) ▪ 120t/20,000cs own label 4C
River 7185 ▪ info@bartonvineyards.co.za ▪ www.bartor
▪ F +27 (0)28-284-9776 ▪ T +27 (0)28-284-9283

Symbols
See page 5 for a complete list

s Bartinney Private Cellars, a boutique wine estate
ing their bio-diversity credentials with new
nterraced slopes.

Brief introduction/news update

ed **11** (★★★★★) improves on **10** with refined black
de, vanilla & spice. Delightfully gritty texture & clean

All wines dry unless noted

s & distinction. Cab-led Bordeaux blend from
vay to plushy black fruit with herbal hints & nicely
lengthy finish.

Abbreviations
See page 5 for a list of abbreviations

Taster/s initials

ues form of **12** showing oatmeal, cream & yellow
with pineapples & tropical fruit, balancing oak/acid-

Tastings, sales & cellar tour times (closed
Saturdays & Sundays but open public holidays
unless noted)

★★★★) preview moves on to flinty minerality with
lacks concentrated appeal of **13**. — CM

sch ▪ Est 2006 ▪ 1stB 2008 ▪ Tasting & sales Mon-Fri
ney Wine Bar Mon-Sat 11.30-9 (cnr Church & Bird Str,
emaker(s) Ronell Wid (consultant) ▪ Viticulturist(s)

Names of owner, winemaker, viticulturist &
consultant/s; year/month of appointment in
brackets

) ▪ 118t/4,000cs own label 70% red 30% white ▪

Production, in tons and/or 6-bottle cases (cs)
and red:white ratio

ellenbosch 7599 ▪ info@bartinney.co.za ▪ www.
1-885-1013

Postal & email address, website
(see www.wineonaplatter.com for social media
details)

ng the Bot River Valley, rich in biodiversity and
accommodation. Though the own portfolio of
is resulting in French-trained winemaker PJ Geyer
oducers' wines on contract.

T = Telephone number

ot-led Bordeaux blend, now bottled, shows more
refined core of inky red fruit & violets with cedary
y, will age with distinction.

rmonious **11** blend has a sappy texture, infused
erbaceousness. Supple structure enhanced by oak.
inates though equal part cab adds pliable struc-
t. Also tasted: **Shiraz Rosé 13** ★★★ **Chenin**
anc ⊘ **13** ★★★★ — MW

Date established

er ▪ WO: Walker Bay ▪ Est 2001 ▪ 1stB 2003 ▪ Tast-
d Easter Sun, Dec 25 & Jan 1 ▪ Lavender products,
)wner(s) Peter J Neill ▪ Cellarmaster(s)/
)0ha/30ha (cab, malbec, merlot, mourv, pinot, shi-
% red 50% white 10% rosé ▪ IPW ▪ PO Box 100 Bot
vineyards.co.za

Total hectares/hectares under vine (not necessarily in production); main varieties planted

Some Trends In South African Wine

There's a bit of good news for South African wine producers, adding to the profound satisfaction of good winter rainfall. In a world where, nearly everywhere, wine consumption has been on a downward path for half a decade and more, in 2022 not only had local consumption recovered to pre-Covid (and pre-liquor ban) times, but more wine was drunk than ever before.

This (possible) trend interestingly complements two others. First, wine exports have been going down (even taking Covid-inspired problems into account), again, an international trend consequent on reduced consumption. Any improvement in local sales must help. Secondly, the South African vineyard continues to shrink. By the end of 2022, the total area under vines had slipped below 90,000 hectares — a decade earlier it had been over 100,000. The most notable recent level of uprooting has been in the warm, irrigated Northern Cape and the similarly mostly volume-orientated Olifants River.

Again, this planting reduction is an international phenomenon to some extent, bringing the world's supply of wine closer to its lower consumption level. South Africa's annual harvest, though, had for many years not kept pace with the fewer vines; presumably, the remaining vineyards were being worked harder. But that seems to be changing. Tonnage in 2022 was down on 2021, and 2023 looks likely to have been one of the smallest in over a decade.

If these trends continue — improved consumption and reduced production — it bodes well for a better balance in the industry. We must hope that the uprooted vineyards have given room to some better-rewarded and arguably more useful agricultural pursuits.

The continuing rise of single-vineyard wines

Decline in vineyard and production is of most relevance to cheaper wines where, we can note, sweet and semi-sweet whites, rosés and reds overwhelmingly lead the local market. At the top end of wine buying, it would be hard to overestimate the importance of a simple-seeming but long-demanded change in wine legislation that finally happened 20 years back. Given the role of single vineyards in the Cape's modern fine-wine scene, it's hard to believe that until 2004 the very word 'vineyard' could not appear on a bottle of

wine, to protect the concept of the 'estate', as the then-smallest unit in the Wine of Origin scheme.

The change in legislation, allowing the invocation of an individual vineyard as a wine's origin, was an important impetus in the great modern revolution in South African fine wine, itself kick-started by the social changes marked by the first democratic elections of ten years earlier.

The European ideal of 'terroir' (meso- and micro-climate, soil, slopes, etc) has internationally grown in significance through this century, trumping the New World cult of the winemaker and even challenging, at wine's grander levels, the primacy accorded grape variety. Terroir expression depends on delimiting a vineyard or block of vines. The tiny discriminations in origin found in areas like Burgundy, Rheingau and Piedmont have increasingly inspired the most ambitious winegrowers everywhere, not least in South Africa, and similarly inspired winelovers looking for uniqueness in a homogenising world market.

This trend persists. Here it also encouraged new generations of ambitious but cash-poor winemakers to buy in grapes from good vineyards for a few wines with comparatively little investment, especially if they were sharing winery facilities. A brilliant element has been added through the formal categorising of old vineyards, especially thanks to the efforts of the Old Vine Project, whereby an authenticated vineyard planting-date appears on a special seal.

Another sign of this trend has been winemakers offering a few or more subtly different versions of wines made from the same grape, all made in essentially the same (restrained) way. Any differences can then be ascribed to the vineyard. This has long been common for chardonnay and pinot noir in Burgundy (and riesling in Germany and nebbiolo in Piedmont, for example), and it first started happening here with those grapes too, especially pinot.

More recently though, the commonest expression of this trend in South Africa has been with chenin blanc. Based on the international success and prestige of serious Cape chenin, an increasing number of producers are advancing the grape's claim to greatness by showing just how terroir-reflective it can be, by offering a number of different chenins distinguished not by style or winemaking practices, but by origin. Expect this trend to persist.

Grape varieties

Some trends are less strongly marked than the interest in wine origins. But even when one looks at statistics that show more stability than change, a little digging reveals interesting developments, mostly positive. Varieties for example. The top ten list has remained much the same for a good long while. Chenin blanc is still at its head, something increasingly to be celebrated, as the workhorse of old is ever more convincingly proving to be the country's signature grape, internationally recognised as making many of the world's best dry examples. Some of them are very expensive now by local standards, but there are swathes of middle-priced excellence and even pretty cheap, eminently drinkable chenins.

Given the continued shrinkage of the total vineyard area, it is unsurprising that plantings of chenin and, in fact, most varieties are lower than they were a decade back. Sauvignon blanc is alone in the top ten list as having increased its footprint, leaping over colombard, cabernet sauvignon and shiraz to claim the second spot in the rankings. Pinotage is now in sixth position, having overtaken chardonnay. They are followed by merlot, ruby cabernet and cinsaut.

It is down the list that there's more of interest and perhaps portents of the future. The numbers are comparatively small but significant for many varieties whose plantings have grown appreciably over the decade, often from zero. There's been spectacular growth in grenache, both noir and blanc. The black version has grown from 245 ha ten years ago to 552 ha at the end of 2022; the white one from 65 to 148 ha. Even more impressive has been the performance of durif (more often known as petite sirah): from 38 to 409 ha.

And there are some tinier plantings, risen from nowhere, some essentially still experimental, of, particularly, Mediterranean varieties. But some of the names are likely to be tripping off the (happily tingling) tongues of curious winelovers in another ten years: like agiorgitiko, albariño, assyrtiko, nero d'avola, marselan, vermentino, marsanne, counoise, bourboulenc… Much of the impetus behind this experimentation is the hoped-for suitableness of these varieties in a hotter, drier future. Very different reasons, connected with the grape's role in the Cape's viticultural past, lie behind the re-entry of pontac onto the list, thanks to the planting of cleaned-up, virus-free material.

Into the cellar

The interest in terroir and experimentation with new and potentially useful varieties are part of an improvement in viticulture, something that crucially underpins the leap in quality at the higher end. The best winemakers demand the best possible grapes, and it is no coincidence that many of them are as deeply involved in their vineyards (including leased or jointly developed ones, the latter an important if minor development) as they are in their production cellars.

There, trends that have become established are continuing. In the physical environment of the cellar, good old concrete has firmly found its place again, now often in the egg-shaped tanks referred to frequently in this guide, along with clay pots (generally called amphoras) of varying shape and size. And while new oak barrels will always have a place in the making of fine, long-lived wines, they are increasingly supplemented with larger-format vessels (foudres, mostly) and older barrels, all of which reduce the flavour effect of oak in maturation while retaining the oxidative element that helps brings texture into play. 'Non-intervention' and 'minimalist' appear ever more often in this guide – frequently accompanied with the somewhat undermining but honest phrase 'as much as possible'.

Freshness, less extreme ripeness, and a general 'lightening up', then, continue as a fundamental trend in Cape wine. Most notably in reds, whose general international reputation seems to be growing and perhaps even catching up with that of the country's white wines. The number of significantly lighter reds, with modest alcohol levels (sometimes very modest), comparatively little extraction, and an avoidance of new oak, keeps growing. As more and more pinotages are made in this style, complementing the splendours of the grander ones, an interesting effect could be the further enhancement of that grape's reputation internationally, where it has long been pretty unfashionable.

Rosés too have been changing in response to demand from international and sophisticated local consumers. For them, rosé must be properly dry, with a savoury element at least as much as a fruity one. And the paler the blush, the better.

Editor's Note

Since we switched to a somewhat more lively colour for our annual cover in 2002, speculation has run high in the run-up to launch about the next shade. After last year's long-requested and well-received white livery, we've opted for something a touch richer, in tune with the more indulgent times. We hope you like the look as much as we do.

This is the 44th edition of our guide, and as ever we've extensively revised and updated it. In the process we've been reminded of one of the intentions of the guide's founders, John and Erica Platter, to not merely sit in judgement over the wines being reviewed, but to understand and convey, via the tasting notes and winery overview, the winegrower's intention and how it relates to the soil, climate and terrain of the vine, and ultimately to the wine in the glass.

We've also not deviated from the original goal of tasting, rating and describing as many as possible South African-made wines, available locally and overseas during the currency of the book.

That said, participation in the guide remains voluntary, and a limited number of producers, for a variety of reasons, elect not to enter wines or opt to be omitted entirely. Other wineries are not yet ready to be featured, and we look forward to including them next time.

Sampling thousands of wines can only be a team effort, and our remarkable crew again showed muscle, backbone and unflagging persistence through to the finish. We'd like to thank them for their hard work and enthusiasm. The team members are (in no particular order):

Wine judges Winnie Bowman (WB), Greg de Bruyn (GdB), Tim James (TJ), Nomonde Kubheka (NK), Malu Lambert (ML) Angela Lloyd (AL), Cathy Marston (CM), Fiona McDonald (FM), Christine Rudman (CR), Penelope Setti (PS), Dave Swingler (DS), Cathy van Zyl (CvZ) and Meryl Weaver (MW). You'll note their initials below the wines or spirits they reviewed. There's a brief biography of each at the end of this section of the guide.

Huge thanks are also due to associate editors Cathy van Zyl (also copywriter) and Tim James (also copywriter and proofreader); copywriters Greg de Bruyn, Angela Lloyd, Fiona McDonald and Christine Rudman; information coordinator Ina de Villiers; the logistics and data capture team of Beyers Pape, Carli Basson, Cephas Basopo, Emily Klue, Hendrik du Plessis, Hijke Coetzee, Irene Nel, Karla Viljoen, Lizelle Crous, Tracy Bougard, Wilmarie Coetzee and Zanna Hugo; software engineer Sean de Kock; map-maker and typesetter Gawie du Toit; fact-checker Lauren de Kock; and financial administrator Margie Barker.

And to Lara Philp and Johan Rademan of Vineyard Connection for the use of their excellent facilities; Mark Whyte and XtraSmile Couriers; Ben van Rensburg and Modern Web Presence for the QR code; and the ever-helpful industry bodies SAWIS and Vinpro.

A particular word of thanks to the wine producers. We much appreciate their cooperation.

On a personal note, I'm deeply grateful to my family, son Luke and his wife Vicky, and my incredible wife Cathy, who saved the day.

In closing, it's worth noting that our ratings are the considered opinion of wine experts who understand the responsibility of giving a rating to a product as changeable as wine. Even so, because of the subjective element associated with wine assessment, we recommend you view our rankings as adjuncts to the tasting notes rather than oracular pronouncements.

Philip van Zyl

Our Method And The Accolades We Award

Platter's is one of the few wine guides in the world that aims to taste and rate every wine from every South African vintage – and it's been doing so since 1980. In this endeavour, Platter's uses two judging methods: label-sighted assessment as well as blind tasting (with no label showing).

As Platter's is primarily a wine guide and not a wine competition, our expert tasters initially assess the wines sighted to have access to vital contextual details such as site, climate and style. Since Platter's not only rates wines, but also provides rich editorial content, this information enables our team to understand (and editorialise) the intent of the producer and the wine's back-story.

Annually Platter's assesses a potential 9,000 wines. Those rated 93-points or more by the sighted judges are all entered into a second round of blind tasting. Here, a single taster assesses the wines within a category (for example, Syrah/Shiraz) without sight of the label to verify the sighted tasting score. If the category has a large number of wines rated 93-points or more, it will be divided into flights, each flight tasted on a different day but by the same single taster. Should this blind verification taster strongly disagree with the sighted taster about a wine's score, the change in score is referred back to the blind taster for ratification.

The wines regarded as superlative in a South African context are awarded the guide's highest rating, namely five stars, which equates to 95–100 points.

Our Wines of the Year are the highest-scoring five-star wines within each tasting category. In the case of two or more wines being tied at a five-star highest score, the wine that is noted as the 'favourite' by the blind verification taster and/or the second-opinion taster is selected as 'category best'.

Another noteworthy group is the wines which rated 94 points, just under the five-star cut but extremely fine and collectable in their own right. They are listed under the heading Highly Recommended.

The Top Performing Winery of the Year is awarded to the winery that achieves the most five-star results after the annual final tasting round. In the case of an overall five-star tie, this award goes to the winery that then has the most 94-point wines, and so on, until the year's Top Performer is identified.

The Newcomer Winery of the Year is awarded to a producer who debuted in Platter's this year and achieved the highest ratings at the Five Star tasting, or the highest scores (should the wines not have reached the Five Star round).

The Editor's Award Winery of the Year recognises a winegrowing team (or teams) who, based on performance in the current edition as well as their track record, are ambassadors par excellence for South African wine.

Implicit in both the Five Star and Highly Recommended categories is the potential that the wines will improve with further bottle-maturation: 8–10 years, perhaps more in the case of reds and fortified wines, and around 4–6 years for the whites. (Proper storage is, of course, vital for sound maturation.) However, during the sighted tasting cycle, our team identified a number of bottlings, over and above the Five Stars and Highly Recommended, which show particular potential for cellaring. These age-worthy wines are listed under the heading Buy Now, Drink Later.

Also included in our Wines of the Year listing is a small selection of the wines which tasters feel are particularly worthy of note – interesting, attractive, unusual, unique, representative of an important trend, etc. Look out for these Hidden Gems in the A–Z directory; they are highlighted with the 'jewel' icon.

Further details about wines pertaining to all awards and categories mentioned above will be found under the names of the relevant producers in the A–Z directory.

Honours Roll

These are the past recipients of our highest accolades, Winery of the Year (awarded since 2008), and Editor's Award of the Year and Newcomer Winery of the Year (both given each year since 2019). The accompanying notes are from earlier editions of the guide, when the respective awards were made.

Top Performing Winery of the Year

2023 – Mullineux
'Andrea and Chris's track record is astounding – the Guide's best-performing winery in 2014, 2016, 2019, 2020 and 2023 – and almost numberless five-star wines.'

2022 – Sadie Family Wines
'A focus on the Cape's old vineyards is just one of the significant areas in which Eben Sadie has been a pioneer and leader for nearly two decades.'

2021 – Kleine Zalze
'Of its seven top ratings, three are from the new Project Z, two others are for on-trend chenin, with one each for more mainstream cab and sauvignon.'

2020 – Mullineux
'Yet more success for Mullineux, with five five-star ratings, including Shiraz of the Year.'

2019 – Mullineux
'Andrea and Chris Mullineux triumphed in 2014 and 2016. Now they have five top ratings and a Wine of the Year.'

Editor's Awards Winery of the Year

2023 – Savage Wines
'Arguably the hardest-working winegrower in South Africa and undoubtedly one of the Cape's foremost winemakers.'

2022 – Spier
'It is rare for a producer to be known for excellence at both the rarefied and volume ends of the market.'

2021 – Rall Wines
'Refined, harmonious and gracefully elegant wines reflecting a unifying aesthetic.'

2020 – Boekenhoutskloof Winery
'Produces quality in large enough quantities to be extremely significant, something rare in SA.'

2019 – Newton Johnson Vineyards
'Wines combining precision, respect for terroir and joy.'

Newcomer Winery of the Year

2023 – Trade Winds
'An auspicious beginning for a team in it for the long-haul.'

2022 – The Vineyard Party
'Jolette Steyn's wines place her squarely amongst the avant garde , and testify to the depth of her winemaking intelligence and understanding.'

2021 – Pilgrim Wines
'The splendid Chenin particularly caught our eye and tastebuds, coming within a point of five stars.'

2020 – Pieter Ferreira Cap Classique
'Bubbly king' Pieter Ferreira, with the highest score this guide has awarded a sparkling wine.'

2019 – Erika Obermeyer Wines
'Two debut wines achieved our highest rating, a third just one point shy. A great achievement.'

Winery of the Year

2018 – Raats Family Wines
'Five wines received our highest rating this year, an altogether remarkable success.'

2017 – Nederburg Wines
'Nederburg plays a crucial role in SA wine.'

2016 – Mullineux
'A great and dynamic wine partnership.'

2015 – Sadie Family Wines
'Producers of superlative wines which help set the bar for SA.'

Honours Roll *(continued)*

2014 – Mullineux

'In the league of the greatest modern-era wineries.'

2013 – Cape Chamonix Wine Farm

'This must now be among SA's top winegrowers.'

2012 – Boekenhoutskloof Winery

'We salute Boekenhoutskloof's remarkable 14 five-star ratings since 2000.'

2011 – Nederburg Wines

'A phenomenal quintet of five-star ratings this edition.'

2010 – Sadie Family Wines

'Continue to set the benchmarks and retain their status as a true Cape icon.'

2009 – Kanonkop Estate

'A 'first growth' with consistent, focused and classic wines.'

2008 – Cape Point Vineyards

'Exciting, site-revealing wines of stellar quality."

Wineries Of The Year

Top Performing Winery of the Year 2024

SADIE FAMILY WINES

For over two decades at the heart of the Swartland – and indeed the South African – wine revolution, Eben Sadie's winery won its latest (at press time at least!) major international award, as the 2023 Golden Vines Best Rising Star. Not to our surprise. Three times already Sadie has been our highest-achieving winery, and this edition is so again, with seven five-star ratings amongst a remarkable line-up of terroir-eloquent wines. One of them is a newcomer to the Old Vine Series, Rotsbank, a chenin blanc off the Paardeberg home-farm, expanded in recent years, and with mostly youthful vineyards, organically farmed. The Sadie team (including winemaker Paul Jordaan and viticulturist Morné Steyn) ranges widely for grapes, and Rotsbank is the first bottling from vines they own. On the estate, a new cellar is rising, adding to the already splendid array of winery buildings where 20 years ago there was scrub and eucalyptus. But nearby, testifying to history, is the thick-walled old shed where the early wines were made (if not the maiden Columella 2000, which, of course, won five stars on its first outing), and where the barrels of the young red blend still rest.

Editor's Award Winery of the Year 2024

BOSMAN FAMILY VINEYARDS

If any wine concern is entitled to invoke 'family' in its name, this 8th-generation business – with Petrus Bosman the current CEO – certainly is. Based in Wellington, they've been growing winegrapes for over two centuries. Not content with over 300 ha of vineyards (where organic farming is increasingly important), more recently including holdings in Hemel-en-Aarde, they've been bottling wines under their own name for two decades now. Corlea Fourie, cellarmaster for some 18 years, more recently with protégé Natasha Williams under her wing (now gratefully flown off), has been responsible for an increasingly impressive range of wines, including the Cape's first from nero d'Avola. And not content even with that, Bosman Adama is Africa's largest vine nursery. This is a giant in the industry (much more could be adduced), a softly-spoken, confident but unassertive and unalarming one. And ethically motivated too. In 2009, in an unprecedentedly large reform transaction, 26% of the business was ceded to 260 permanent employees as the Adama Trust. Spearheading social projects in the community is continuous. The multi-meaning motto on the Bosman website, 'Dedicated to better', is no exaggeration, and for that we are proud to make this award.

Newcomer Winery of the Year 2024

EDOUARD LABEYE

The name of Frenchman Edouard Labeye is hardly new to South Africa. Notably, he has long been involved with Radford Dale, for some time as cellarmaster, now as a viticulturist as well as part-owner. His name even briefly headlined the label on a Pinot Noir there. This didn't prevent his being also a well-regarded consultant and winemaker in the south of the France and the Rhône. And there, apart from anything else, he became deeply acquainted with grenache. It is fine examples of two forms of that variety that Edouard offered as the maiden wines under his own label: Grenache Blanc (which our reviewers particularly admired) and Grenache Noir, both from organically farmed Swartland vines. It is a particular pleasure, if slightly ironical, to welcome this old friend of Cape wine as our Newcomer of the Year.

Wines Of The Year 2024

These are the highest-scoring five-star wines within each category, tasted during our annual Wines of the Year blind tasting. Where wines tied at the same rating, the taster responsible for each category and/or second-opinion taster decided which wine deserved this accolade. Please refer to the A–Z section for the rating and tasting note for each wine.

Cabernet Franc
☐ Raats Eden High Density Single Vineyard 2021

Cabernet Sauvignon
☐ Beyerskloof Eerste Ry 2019

Cinsault
☐ Savage Follow The Line 2022

Grenache Noir
☐ Kleine Zalze Project Z 2022

Merlot
☐ Simelia Fluvius Single Vineyard 2019

Petit Verdot
☐ Thelema Sutherland Reserve Emily 2021

Pinotage
☐ L'Avenir Single Block 2020

Pinot Noir
☐ Shannon RocknRolla 2021

Shiraz/Syrah
☐ Savage CWG Auction Syrah 2021

Red Blends, Cape Bordeaux
☐ Vondeling Philosophie 2019

Red Blends, With Pinotage
☐ Beyerskloof Faith 2020

Red Blends, Shiraz/Syrah-Based
☐ Fairview Cyril Back 2020

Red Blends, Other
☐ Alto Estate Blend 2020

Albariño
☐ Botanica Flower Girl 2023

Chardonnay
☐ Delaire Graff Terraced Block Reserve 2022

Chenin Blanc
☐ Stellenrust Old Bushvine 2022

Grenache Blanc
☐ The Foundry 2022

Roussanne
☐ Saronsberg 2021

Sauvignon Blanc
☐ Diemersdal The Journal 2022

Semillon
☐ Steenberg 2022

Semillon Gris
☐ Mullineux CWG Auction The Gris Old Vine 2022

Viognier
☐ Lourensford Limited Release 2022

White Blends, Cape Bordeaux
☐ Steenberg Magna Carta 2021

White Blends, Other
☐ Beaumont New Baby 2022

Cap Classique
☐ Babylonstoren Sprankel 2018

Dessert Wine, Fortified
☐ Orange River Omstaan Rooi Muskadel XO NV

Dessert Wine, Unfortified
☐ Alvi's Drift Muscat Nectarinia 2017

Natural Sweet
☐ Klein Constantia Vin de Constance 2020

Noble Late Harvest
☐ Delheim Edelspatz 2021

Vin de Paille
☐ Savage Not Tonight Josephine 2022

Port-Style
☐ KWV Cape Tawny NV

Five Stars

These are the wines achieving the guide's highest rating, five stars, or 95 and above points. Refer to the A–Z section for the rating and tasting note for each wine.

Cabernet Franc
- ☐ Beaumont Ariane 2021
- ☐ De Trafford 2021
- ☐ Hogan Mirror For The Sun 2022
- ☐ Raats Eden High Density Single Vineyard 2021
- ☐ Raats CWG Auction Stella Nova 2019
- ☐ Raats Family 2021

Cabernet Sauvignon
- ☐ Beyerskloof Eerste Ry 2019
- ☐ Boekenhoutskloof Stellenbosch 2021
- ☐ Cederberg Five Generations 2021
- ☐ David Finlayson GS 2021
- ☐ Diemersdal The Journal 2021
- ☐ Hartenberg CWG Auction 2021
- ☐ Kanonkop 2019
- ☐ Le Riche 2021
- ☐ Mooiplaas Tabakland 2020
- ☐ MVH Signature 2021
- ☐ Nederburg Two Centuries 2019
- ☐ Stellenrust Reserve 2019
- ☐ The High Road Reserve 2019
- ☐ Thelema 2020

Cinsault
- ☐ ArtiSons The Basket Child 2021
- ☐ Eenzaamheid 2022
- ☐ Savage Follow The Line 2022
- ☐ Van Loggerenberg Lotter 2022

Grenache Noir
- ☐ Elemental Bob Cosmic Flower The Turkish 2022
- ☐ Kleine Zalze Project Z 2022

Merlot
- ☐ Simelia Fluvius Single 2019
- ☐ Villiera Monro 2021

Petit Verdot
- ☐ Benguela Cove Vinography 2021
- ☐ Thelema Sutherland Reserve Emily 2021

Pinotage
- ☐ Fairview Primo 2021
- ☐ Francois van Niekerk 2021
- ☐ Kanonkop Black Label 2021
- ☐ Kanonkop 2021
- ☐ Lanzerac Commemorative 2019
- ☐ L'Avenir Single Block 2020
- ☐ Survivor Reserve 2021

Pinot Noir
- ☐ Crystallum Bona Fide 2022
- ☐ David Finlayson Camino Africana 2021
- ☐ Iona Kloof 2020
- ☐ Kara-Tara Reserve 2021
- ☐ Shannon RocknRolla 2021
- ☐ Storm Ignis 2022

Shiraz/Syrah
- ☐ ArtiSons Blueberry Hill Shiraz 2021
- ☐ Boschkloof Epilogue 2021
- ☐ De Grendel Elim Shiraz 2021
- ☐ Diemersdal Reserve Syrah 2022
- ☐ Driehoek Syrah 2021
- ☐ La Bri Limited Release Syrah 870 2021
- ☐ Metzer & Holfeld Shiraz 2022
- ☐ Mullineux Syrah 2021
- ☐ Oldenburg Stone Axe 2021
- ☐ Patatsfontein Sons of Sugarland Syrah 2022
- ☐ Sakkie Mouton Dawn Of The Salty Tongues Syrah 2022
- ☐ Savage CWG Auction Syrah 2021
- ☐ Saxenburg Private Collection Syrah 2021
- ☐ Van Loggerenberg Graft 2022

Red Blends, Cape Bordeaux
- ☐ Babylonstoren Nebukadnesar 2021
- ☐ Bacco Red Blend 2020
- ☐ Constantia Glen Five 2020
- ☐ Diemersdal Private Collection 2021
- ☐ Ernie Els Signature 2017
- ☐ Jordan Cobblers Hill 2020
- ☐ Keet First Verse 2020
- ☐ Marianne Desirade 2020
- ☐ Meerlust Rubicon 2021
- ☐ Rainbow's End Family Reserve 2020
- ☐ Remhoogte Sir Thomas Cullinan 2019
- ☐ Ridgeback Signature C 2019
- ☐ Rustenberg John X Merriman 2021
- ☐ Vondeling Philosophie 2019

Red Blends, With Pinotage
- ☐ Beaumont Vitruvian 2019
- ☐ Beyerskloof Faith 2020
- ☐ Beyerskloof Faith 2019
- ☐ Nuiba Third Post 2019
- ☐ Opstal Carl Everson Cape Blend 2021

Red Blends, Shiraz/Syrah-Based
- ☐ Boekenhoutskloof The Chocolate Block 2022

Red Blends, Shiraz/Syrah-based *(continued)*

☐ Fairview Cyril Back 2020
☐ Fairview Caldera 2021
☐ Rall Red 2021
☐ Ridgeback Signature S 2019
☐ Savage Are We There Yet? 2022
☐ Sijnn Free Reign 2018

Red Blends, Other

☐ Alto Estate Blend 2020
☐ Anysbos Tesame 2021
☐ Boschendal Nicolas 2019
☐ De Trafford Elevation 393 2017
☐ Hogan Divergent 2022
☐ Leeu Passant 2020

Albariño

☐ Botanica Flower Girl 2023

Chardonnay

☐ Bartinney Hourglass 2021
☐ Cap Maritime 2022
☐ Capensis Fijnbosch 2019
☐ Creation Reserve 2022
☐ David Finlayson Shale Terraces 2022
☐ Delaire Graff Terraced Block Reserve 2022
☐ Draaiboek Kinkel 2022
☐ Draaiboek Onskuld 2022
☐ GlenWood Vigneron's Selection 2022
☐ Haskell Anvil 2022
☐ Hogan The Galvanised 2022
☐ Kershaw Kogelberg Sandstone CY76 2021
☐ Kershaw Kogelberg Iron Stone CY548 2021
☐ La Bri Barrel Select 2022
☐ Lanzerac Mrs English 2022
☐ Leeu Passant Radicales Libres 2017
☐ Leeu Passant Stellenbosch 2021
☐ MVH Signature 2022
☐ Oak Valley Groenlandberg 2022
☐ Oldenburg 2022
☐ Paul Clüver Estate 2021
☐ Plaisir Grand Plaisir White 2022
☐ Restless River Ava Marie 2021
☐ Storm Ridge 2022
☐ Storm Vrede 2022

Chenin Blanc

☐ Ahrens Koffieklip OVC 2021
☐ ArtiSons The Mothership 2022
☐ Asara Amphora 2022
☐ Beaumont Hope Marguerite 2022
☐ Bellingham The Bernard Series Old Vine 2022
☐ Bosman Optenhorst 2022
☐ Botanica Mary Delany 2022
☐ Carinus Polkadraai Heuwels 2022

☐ Cederberg Five Generations 2022
☐ Charla Haasbroek 2022
☐ City On A Hill Earth 2022
☐ Daschbosch Mossiesdrift Steen 2022
☐ David & Nadia CWG Veiling 2022
☐ David & Nadia Plat'bos 2022
☐ DeMorgenzon Reserve 2022
☐ Eenzaamheid 2021
☐ Huis van Chevallerie Bergskilpad Old Vine 2022
☐ Ken Forrester The FMC 2022
☐ Leeuwenkuil White 2022
☐ Metzer & Holfeld Maritime 2022
☐ Mullineux Granite 2022
☐ Mullineux Schist 2022
☐ Rijk's Reserve 2021
☐ Sadie Mev. Kirsten 2022
☐ Sadie Rotsbank 2022
☐ Sadie Skurfberg 2022
☐ Sakkie Mouton Revenge Of The Crayfish 2022
☐ Savage Never Been Asked To Dance 2022
☐ Stark-Condé Monk Stone 2022
☐ Stellenbosch Vineyards Credo 2022
☐ Stellenrust 58 Barrel Fermented 2022
☐ Stellenrust Old Bushvine 2022

Grenache Blanc

☐ Riebeek Valley Raar Small Batch 2022
☐ The Foundry 2022

Roussanne

☐ Saronsberg 2021

Sauvignon Blanc

☐ Anthonij Rupert Altima 2023
☐ Bartho Eksteen CWG Auction Vloekskoot 2022
☐ Buitenverwachting Maximus 2021
☐ Buitenverwachting Hussey's Vlei 2022
☐ Cederberg David Nieuwoudt Ghost Corner Wild Ferment 2022
☐ Die Kat Se Snor 2023
☐ Diemersdal The Journal 2022
☐ Diemersdal Wild Horseshoe 2022
☐ Diemersdal Reserve 2023
☐ Hasher Fat Lady 2022
☐ Klein Constantia Metis 2020
☐ Klein Constantia Perdeblokke 2022
☐ Lomond Pincushion 2022
☐ Neil Ellis Amica 2021
☐ Strandveld Pofadderbos 2022
☐ The Giant Periwinkle Wind Scorpion 2022
☐ Thorne & Daughters Snakes & Ladders 2022
☐ Waterkloof 2022
☐ Zevenwacht Z–Collection 2022

Semillon
- [ ] Benguela Cove Catalina 2021
- [ ] Old Road Grand-Mère 2021
- [ ] Opstal The Barber 2022
- [ ] Rickety Bridge Pilgrimage Old Vine 2021
- [ ] Sadie Kokerboom 2022
- [ ] Shannon Triangle Block 2021
- [ ] Steenberg Semillon 2022
- [ ] Super Single Vineyards Pella White Granite 2021
- [ ] Wildeberg White 2022

Semillon Gris
- [ ] Mullineux CWG Auction The Gris Old Vine 2022

Viognier
- [ ] Lourensford Limited Release 2022

White Blends, Cape Bordeaux
- [ ] Constantia Glen Two 2021
- [ ] Delaire Graff White Reserve 2021
- [ ] Groot Constantia Gouverneurs Reserve 2021
- [ ] Kershaw Cape South Coast Sauvignon Blanc-Semillon 2021
- [ ] Steenberg Magna Carta 2021

White Blends, Other
- [ ] Ahrens The WhiteBlack 2021
- [ ] Beaumont New Baby 2022
- [ ] Brookdale Sixteen 2022
- [ ] Fairview Beryl Back 2022
- [ ] Mullineux Old Vines White 2022
- [ ] Rall White 2022
- [ ] Sadie Palladius 2021
- [ ] Sadie Skerpioen 2022
- [ ] Sadie 'T Voetpad 2022
- [ ] The Grapesmith Mediterraneo 2021
- [ ] Thelema Sutherland Viognier-Roussanne 2022
- [ ] Thorne & Daughters Rocking Horse 2022

Cap Classique
- [ ] Anthonij Rupert L'Ormarins Blanc de Blancs 2018
- [ ] Babylonstoren Sprankel 2018
- [ ] Graham Beck Extra Brut 157 2009
- [ ] Graham Beck Blanc de Blancs Brut 2018
- [ ] Silverthorn The Green Man Magnum 2017

Dessert Wine, Fortified
- [ ] Orange River Omstaan Rooi Muskadel XO NV

Dessert Wine, Unfortified
- [ ] Alvi's Drift Muscat Nectarinia 2017

Natural Sweet
- [ ] Klein Constantia Vin de Constance 2020
- [ ] Klein Constantia Vin de Constance 2019

Noble Late Harvest
- [ ] Boschendal Vin d'Or 2021
- [ ] Delheim Edelspatz 2021

Vin de Paille
- [ ] Mullineux Straw Wine 2022
- [ ] Savage Not Tonight Josephine 2022

Port-Style
- [ ] De Krans Cape Vintage Reserve 2021
- [ ] Delaire Graff Cape Vintage 2021
- [ ] KWV Cape Tawny NV

Brandy
- [ ] Boplaas Potstill Reserve 20 Years
- [ ] KWV Cellar Reserve XO Potstill
- [ ] KWV Centenary
- [ ] KWV Nexus
- [ ] KWV 20 Year Old
- [ ] KWV 15 Year Old Alambic
- [ ] KWV 12 Year Old Barrel Select
- [ ] KWV 10 Year Old Vintage
- [ ] Tokara XO Potstill
- [ ] Van Ryn 20 Year Old Potstill
- [ ] Van Ryn 15 Year Old Potstill
- [ ] Van Ryn 12 Year Old Potstill

Husk Spirit
- [ ] Dalla Cia 10 Year Old Celebration Cabernet Sauvignon-Merlot

Highly Recommended

These are wines of exceptional merit, scoring 94 points. See the A–Z directory for ratings and notes.

Cabernet Franc
- [ ] Chamonix Reserve 2021
- [ ] David Finlayson Camino Africana 2021
- [ ] Hermanuspietersfontein Swartskaap 2019
- [ ] Jordan Insiders Wine Club Private Collection 2021
- [ ] KWV The Mentors 2020
- [ ] Leeu Passant CWG Auction Franschhoek Hillside 2021
- [ ] Rainbow's End Limited Release 2021
- [ ] Van Loggerenberg Breton 2022

Cabernet Sauvignon
- [ ] Anthonij Rupert 2019
- [ ] Bartinney 2019
- [ ] Bartinney Skyfall 2018
- [ ] Black Elephant Amazing Grace 2018
- [ ] David Finlayson 2021
- [ ] David Finlayson GS 2020
- [ ] De Trafford 2020
- [ ] Delaire Graff Reserve 2020
- [ ] Delaire Graff Laurence Graff Reserve 2020
- [ ] Glen Carlou Gravel Quarry 2020
- [ ] La Bri Limited Release 2021
- [ ] Leeu Passant Stellenbosch 2021
- [ ] Miles Mossop Sam 2020
- [ ] Miles Mossop CWG Auction Maximilian 2020
- [ ] Muratie Martin Melck 2020
- [ ] Oldenburg 2021
- [ ] Peter Falke Kailani 2019
- [ ] Plaisir 2019
- [ ] Restless River Main Road & Dignity 2020
- [ ] Rickety Bridge Paulina's Reserve 2021
- [ ] Simonsig The Garland 2018
- [ ] Stony Brook Ghost Gum 2020
- [ ] Super Single Vineyards Pella Granietbult 2018
- [ ] Vergelegen V 2017
- [ ] Waterford 2019
- [ ] Webersburg Shobi 2019

Carignan
- [ ] ArtiSons Villain Vines 2021

Cinsault
- [ ] Bellevue 1952 2021
- [ ] Bosman Twyfeling 2021
- [ ] Darling Old Bush Vines 2021
- [ ] Rall 2022
- [ ] Scions of Sinai Heldervallei 2022
- [ ] Van Loggerenberg Geronimo 2022

Grenache Noir
- [ ] Lourens Lua Ilse 2022
- [ ] Momento 2021
- [ ] Neil Ellis Piekenierskloof 2019
- [ ] Savage Thief In The Night 2022
- [ ] Vriesenhof 2022

Malbec
- [ ] Winshaw 2022

Merlot
- [ ] De Trafford 2019
- [ ] Diemersdal The Journal 2021
- [ ] Longridge Organic Misterie 2019
- [ ] Marianne 2020
- [ ] Plaisir 2020
- [ ] Shannon The Shannon Black 2019
- [ ] Shannon Mount Bullet 2020
- [ ] Super Single Vineyards Pella Verlatenkloof 2019
- [ ] Thelema Reserve 2021

Mourvèdre
- [ ] Beaumont Far Side 2020

Petit Verdot
- [ ] Stellenbosch Vineyards 2018

Pinotage
- [ ] Anura Signature 2020
- [ ] Beeslaar 2021
- [ ] Beyerskloof Diesel 2021
- [ ] Bruce Jack Flag of Truce 2021
- [ ] Bruwer Vintners Liberté 2021
- [ ] Diemersfontein Carpe Diem 2021
- [ ] KWV The Mentors 2020
- [ ] Longridge Organic Maandans 2019
- [ ] Neil Ellis Bottelary Hills 2020
- [ ] Rijk's Reserve 2018
- [ ] Wildekrans Barrel Select 2021
- [ ] Wolf & Woman 2022

Pinot Noir
- [ ] Bosman Hermanus 2022
- [ ] Bouchard Finlayson Tête de Cuvée 2021
- [ ] Catherine Marshall Pinot Noir On Clay Soils 2021
- [ ] Catherine Marshall Finite Elements 2019
- [ ] Cirrus 2022
- [ ] Creation Emma's Pinot Noir 2022
- [ ] Creation Reserve 2022
- [ ] Creation The Art of Pinot Noir 2022
- [ ] Crystallum Cuvée Cinéma 2022
- [ ] Crystallum Mabalel 2022

Highly Recommended, Pinot Noir *(continued)*

- ☐ De Grendel Op Die Berg 2022
- ☐ Hamilton Russell 2022
- ☐ Kershaw Elgin Clonal Selection 2021
- ☐ Litigo 2022
- ☐ Oak Valley Groenlandberg 2022
- ☐ Paul Clüver Seven Flags 2020
- ☐ Restless River Le Luc 2021
- ☐ Saurwein Om 2022
- ☐ Saurwein Nom 2022
- ☐ Shannon Rockview Ridge 2021
- ☐ Storm Ridge 2022
- ☐ Storm Vrede 2022

Shiraz/Syrah

- ☐ Anthonij Rupert Syrah 2018
- ☐ Arcangeli Syracuse Syrah 2020
- ☐ Beau Constantia Stella 2021
- ☐ Bellingham The Bernard Series Basket Press Syrah 2020
- ☐ Black Pearl Shiraz 2021
- ☐ Blackwater Cultellus Syrah 2021
- ☐ Boekenhoutskloof Syrah 2021
- ☐ Boschendal Grande Syrah 2019
- ☐ Boschkloof 2021
- ☐ Bruce Jack Clean Slate Shiraz 2020
- ☐ Carinus Polkadraai Syrah 2022
- ☐ Cederberg David Nieuwoudt Ghost Corner Syrah 2020
- ☐ Creation Reserve Syrah 2021
- ☐ De Op Die Berg Syrah 2022
- ☐ De Grendel Shiraz 2021
- ☐ De Trafford Syrah 393 2021
- ☐ Dewaldt Heyns Weathered Hands Shiraz 2020
- ☐ Eagles' Nest Shiraz 2020
- ☐ Ernie Els Proprietor's Syrah 2017
- ☐ Fairview Eenzaamheid Shiraz 2021
- ☐ Flagstone Dark Horse Shiraz 2019
- ☐ Gabriëlskloof Syrah On Shale 2021
- ☐ Harry Hartman Somesay 2022
- ☐ JC Wickens Swerwer 2022
- ☐ Joostenberg Klippe Kou Syrah 2021
- ☐ Keermont Topside Syrah 2018
- ☐ Kleine Zalze Vineyard Selection Shiraz 2021
- ☐ Kleine Zalze Family Reserve Shiraz 2020
- ☐ Kloovenburg Riebeekberg Syrah 2021
- ☐ Leeuwenkuil Syrah 2019
- ☐ Lievland Heart's Ease Syrah 2020
- ☐ Lomond Cat's Tail Syrah 2020
- ☐ Michaella Shiraz 2022
- ☐ Mullineux Iron 2021
- ☐ Mullineux Schist 2021

- ☐ Nico Van Der Merwe Syrah 2020
- ☐ Radford Dale Syrah 2021
- ☐ Rall Ava Syrah 2022
- ☐ Rall Syrah 2022
- ☐ Remhoogte Reserve Syrah 2019
- ☐ Reyneke Biodynamic Syrah 2021
- ☐ Rust en Vrede Syrah 2021
- ☐ Saronsberg Shiraz 2021
- ☐ Savage Girl Next Door 2022
- ☐ Savage Red 2021
- ☐ Scions of Sinai Swanesang 2022
- ☐ Stellenbosch Vineyards Credo 2021
- ☐ Tamboerskloof John Spicer Syrah 2017
- ☐ Tamboerskloof Syrah 2019
- ☐ The Fledge & Co Nest Egg Syrah 2020
- ☐ The Foundry Syrah 2021
- ☐ Tokara Reserve Syrah 2020
- ☐ Tokara Reserve Syrah 2019
- ☐ Vergelegen Reserve Shiraz 2019
- ☐ Wolf & Woman Syrah 2022

Tinta Barocca

- ☐ Momento 2021

Red Blends, Cape Bordeaux

- ☐ Alto MPHS 2017
- ☐ Anthonij Rupert Optima 2020
- ☐ Benguela Cove Collage 2021
- ☐ Buitenverwachting Christine 2016
- ☐ Chamonix Troika 2021
- ☐ Constantia Glen Three 2020
- ☐ Delaire Graff Botmaskop 2021
- ☐ Delheim Grand Reserve 2020
- ☐ Dornier Donatus Red 2019
- ☐ Eikendal Classique 2020
- ☐ Epicurean Red 2017
- ☐ Fleur du Cap Laszlo 2020
- ☐ Groot Constantia Gouverneurs Reserve 2019
- ☐ Hartenberg The Mackenzie 2019
- ☐ Haskell IV 2021
- ☐ Hermanuspietersfontein Kleinboet 2019
- ☐ Jordan Sophia 2018
- ☐ Jordan CWG Auction Sophia 2021
- ☐ Kanonkop Paul Sauer 2020
- ☐ Koelenhof The Legacy 2019
- ☐ KWV The Mentors Orchestra 2020
- ☐ Miles Mossop Max 2020
- ☐ Mitre's Edge Sholto 2020
- ☐ Mulderbosch Estate Blend 2021
- ☐ Mvemve Raats MR de Compostella 2020
- ☐ Nederburg The Brew Master 2020

Highly Recommended, Red Blends, Cape Bordeaux *(continued)*

- ☐ Nico van der Merwe Merlot-Cabernet Sauvignon-Cabernet Franc 2021
- ☐ Noble Hill Estate Reserve 2021
- ☐ Spier Creative Block Five 2020
- ☐ Steenberg Catharina 2020
- ☐ Stellenbosch Reserve Vanderstel 2021
- ☐ Stellenrust Timeless 2020
- ☐ Super Single Vineyards The King & I 2018
- ☐ Taaibosch Crescendo 2020
- ☐ Thelema Rabelais 2021
- ☐ Van Biljon Cinq 2019
- ☐ Warwick Trilogy 2020
- ☐ Waterkloof Boreas 2020
- ☐ Winshaw Bill Winshaw 2019

Red Blends, With Pinotage

- ☐ Spier Creative Block Eight 2020
- ☐ Springfontein Whole Lotta Love 2018
- ☐ Springfontein Gadda Da Vida 2018

Red Blends, Shiraz/Syrah-Based

- ☐ Anthonij Rupert Riebeeksrivier Southern Slopes 2018
- ☐ Anthonij Rupert Riebeeksrivier Western Slopes 2018
- ☐ ArtiSons JJ Handmade Eight Pillars 2020
- ☐ Bartho Eksteen Groepsdruk 2021
- ☐ Bellingham The Bernard Series The Maverick SMV 2020
- ☐ Black Pearl The Mischief Maker 2022
- ☐ Boschendal Black Angus 2020
- ☐ Boschendal Black Angus 2019
- ☐ Erika Obermeyer CWG Auction Silver Linings 2021
- ☐ Hermanuspietersfontein Skoonma 2021
- ☐ Joostenberg Bakermat 2020
- ☐ KWV Dr Charles Niehaus 2020
- ☐ Mullineux Roundstone Red 2021
- ☐ Neil Ellis Rodanos 2020
- ☐ Olifantsberg The Bull 2019
- ☐ Saronsberg Full Circle 2021
- ☐ Sijnn Red 2020
- ☐ Strandveld The Navigator 2020

Red Blends, Other

- ☐ Ahrens Paarl Rooiwijn 2021
- ☐ Charla Haasbroek Grenache Noir-Carignan 2022
- ☐ Fairview Homtini 2020
- ☐ Haskell II 2018
- ☐ Ken Forrester The Gypsy 2018
- ☐ Ken Forrester Three Halves 2017

- ☐ Leopard's Leap Pardus 2021
- ☐ Marianne Floréal 2020
- ☐ Nederburg The Motorcycle Marvel 2020
- ☐ Spice Route Chakalaka 2021
- ☐ Thistle & Weed Nastergal 2021
- ☐ Waterford The Jem 2016
- ☐ Wines Of Brocha One Man Band 2019

Rosé

- ☐ Ken Forrester The Silver Rose 2023

Alvarinho

- ☐ Kleine Zalze Project Z 2022

Chardonnay

- ☐ Almenkerk 2021
- ☐ Asara Terroir 2022
- ☐ Baleia Limitados 2021
- ☐ Benguela Cove 2022
- ☐ Benguela Cove Vinography 2022
- ☐ Boschendal Elgin 2021
- ☐ Callender Peak 2022
- ☐ Chamonix Reserve 2021
- ☐ Creation Glenn's Chardonnay 2022
- ☐ Crystallum Ferrum 2022
- ☐ DeMorgenzon Reserve 2021
- ☐ Die Kat Se Snor 2022
- ☐ Doolhof Morestond 2019
- ☐ Epicurean 2022
- ☐ Glenelly Estate Reserve 2022
- ☐ GlenWood Grand Duc 2021
- ☐ Hamilton Russell 2022
- ☐ Iona Fynbos 2021
- ☐ Iona Kloof 2021
- ☐ Jordan CWG Auction 2022
- ☐ Joubert-Tradauw Barrel Fermented 2022
- ☐ Kershaw Lake District Bokkeveld Shale CY95 2021
- ☐ Kershaw Lake District Bokkeveld Shale CY96 2021
- ☐ Kershaw Elgin Clonal Selection 2021
- ☐ Kleine Zalze Vineyard Selection 2022
- ☐ La Vierge Apogée 2020
- ☐ Lourensford Kleipot 2020
- ☐ Mooiplaas Roos Family 2022
- ☐ Natasha Williams Lelie Van Saron 2022
- ☐ Paul Clüver CWG Auction The Wagon Trail 2022
- ☐ Paul Clüver Seven Flags 2022
- ☐ Paul Wallace Reflection 2022
- ☐ Quoin Rock 2020
- ☐ Shannon Oscar Browne 2022

Highly Recommended, Chardonnay *(continued)*

- ☐ Stellenbosch Vineyards Credo 2022
- ☐ Thelema Sutherland Reserve Anna 2018
- ☐ Tokara Reserve Collection 2022
- ☐ Trizanne Benede-Duivenhoksrivier 2022
- ☐ Vergelegen Reserve 2022
- ☐ Vriesenhof 2021
- ☐ Whalehaven Seascape 2020

Chenin Blanc

- ☐ Ahrens Hometown OVC 2021
- ☐ Ahrens Kwarts Van Die Paarl OVC 2021
- ☐ Alheit Cartology 2022
- ☐ Alheit Fire By Night 2022
- ☐ Alheit Huilkrans 2022
- ☐ Alheit Nautical Dawn 2022
- ☐ Angus Paul On A Flight Of Furious Fancies 2022
- ☐ Belle Rebelle Intrepid 2022
- ☐ Bellingham Old Vine 2022
- ☐ Brookdale Old Vine 2021
- ☐ Carinus Rooidraai 2022
- ☐ Catherine Marshall Fermented In Clay 2022
- ☐ City On A Hill Wine Old Vine 2022
- ☐ David & Nadia 2022
- ☐ David & Nadia Hoë-Steen 2022
- ☐ David & Nadia Skaliekop 2022
- ☐ David Finlayson Camino Africana 2022
- ☐ De Trafford Reserva 2021
- ☐ De Trafford Skin Macerated 2022
- ☐ Dewaldt Heyns Weathered Hands 2021
- ☐ Gabriëlskloof Elodie 2022
- ☐ illimis 2022
- ☐ JC Wickens Tiernes 2021
- ☐ Jordan Timepiece 2022
- ☐ Kaapzicht Kliprug 2022
- ☐ Keermont Riverside 2020
- ☐ Ken Forrester Old Vine Reserve 2022
- ☐ Kleine Zalze Family Reserve 2022
- ☐ Kleine Zalze Project Z 2022
- ☐ KWV The Mentors 2021
- ☐ Leeuwenkuil 2021
- ☐ Lievland Old Vine 2022
- ☐ Lourens Skuinskap Steen 2022
- ☐ McFarlane Monday's Child 2022
- ☐ Metzer & Holfeld Montane 2022
- ☐ Miles Mossop Chapter Three Stellenbosch 2022
- ☐ Opstal Bergsteen 2022
- ☐ Paulus Bartas 2022
- ☐ Paulus Bosberaad 2022
- ☐ Piekenierskloof Bergendal 2022
- ☐ Pilgrim 2022
- ☐ Raats CWG Auction The Fountain 2022
- ☐ Raats Eden High Density Single Vineyard 2022
- ☐ Raats Old Vine 2022
- ☐ Rall Ava 2022
- ☐ Rall Noa 2022
- ☐ Scions of Sinai Granietsteen 2022
- ☐ Thistle & Weed Brandnetel 2022
- ☐ Thistle & Weed Duwweltjie 2022
- ☐ Van Wyk 2022
- ☐ Wildekrans Barrel Select Reserve 2022
- ☐ Zevenwacht Old Vine 2022

Grenache Blanc

- ☐ De Kleine Wijn Koöp Die Posman Wit 2022
- ☐ Edouard Labeye 2021

Grenache Gris

- ☐ Momento 2022

Riesling

- ☐ Saurwein Chi 2022

Roussanne

- ☐ The Foundry 2022

Sauvignon Blanc

- ☐ Benguela Cove Vinography 2022
- ☐ Callender Peak Winterhoek 2022
- ☐ Cape Point Reserve 2022
- ☐ Constantia Glen 2022
- ☐ Diemersdal 8 Rows 2023
- ☐ Eagles' Nest 2022
- ☐ Fryer's Cove Hollebaksstrandfontein 2022
- ☐ Hermanuspietersfontein Kat Met Die Houtbeen 2022
- ☐ Iona Wild Ferment 2022
- ☐ Jasper Raats Organic Driefontein Blanc 2023
- ☐ Klein Constantia Block 382 2020
- ☐ Kleine Zalze Family Reserve 2022
- ☐ Lomond Ben Nevis 2022
- ☐ Oak Valley Fountain Of Youth 2023
- ☐ Spier 21 Gables 2023
- ☐ The Giant Periwinkle Blanc Fumé 2021

Semillon

- ☐ Alheit Monument 2022
- ☐ De Kleine Wijn Koöp Road to Santiago 2022
- ☐ Elemental Bob White Gold 2022
- ☐ Gabriëlskloof Magdalena 2022
- ☐ Highlands Road 2020
- ☐ Leeu Passant Franschhoek 2021
- ☐ Radford Dale Revelation 2022
- ☐ The Garajeest Jim 2020
- ☐ Thorne & Daughters Paper Kite 2022

Verdelho

- ☐ Stellenbosch Vineyards 2022

Vermentino

☐ Ayama 2022

White Blends, Cape Bordeaux

☐ Beau Constantia Pierre 2022
☐ Cape Point Isliedh 2022
☐ Cape Point Elixirr 2022
☐ Cederberg David Nieuwoudt Ghost Corner The Bowline 2022
☐ Nitida Coronata Integration 2022
☐ Savage White 2022
☐ Tokara Director's Reserve White 2020
☐ Wade Bales Constantia White 2022
☐ Wildeberg Coterie Semillon-Sauvignon Blanc 2022

White Blends, Other

☐ Alheit Hemelrand Vine Garden 2022
☐ Alvi's Drift CVC 2021
☐ Anysbos Disdit 2022
☐ Ashbourne Sandstone 2022
☐ David & Nadia Aristargos 2022
☐ De Grendel Winifred 2023
☐ Keermont Terrasse 2022
☐ Kumusha The Flame Lily 2022
☐ Lourens Lindi Carien 2022
☐ Maanschijn Cape White 2022
☐ Miles Mossop Saskia 2021
☐ Momento Chenin Blanc-Verdelho 2022
☐ Mullineux Roundstone White 2022
☐ Naudé Soutbos 2023
☐ Olifantsberg The Matriarch 2020
☐ Sijnn White 2022
☐ Stark-Condé The Field Blend 2022
☐ Swartberg Miracle Bush White 2022
☐ The Fledge & Co Vagabond 2021
☐ The Grapesmith Die Kluisenaar 2020
☐ Thistle & Weed Khakibos 2022
☐ Van Niekerk Vintners Sonwater 2022
☐ Van Wyk Olivia Grace 2021
☐ Vondeling Babiana 2022
☐ Vuurberg White 2022

Cap Classique

☐ Anthonij Rupert L'Ormarins Private Cuvée 2015
☐ Black Elephant Chardonnay Blanc de Blancs 2013
☐ Black Elephant Chardonnay Brut NV
☐ Bon Courage Jacques Bruére Brut Reserve 2014
☐ Bon Courage Jacques Bruére Cuvée Brut Rosé 2014
☐ Canto Chardonnay 2020
☐ Colmant Absolu Zero Dosage NV
☐ Colmant Cap Blanc de Blancs NV
☐ Graham Beck Cuvée Clive 2018
☐ Haute Cabrière Pierre Jourdan Blanc de Blancs 2018
☐ Jordan Blanc de Blancs 2018
☐ La Bri Sauvage La Bri Blanc de Blancs 2017
☐ Le Lude Venus Brut Nature Millésime Magnum 2014
☐ Noble Hill Blanc de Blancs Brut Nature 2020
☐ Paul René 2019
☐ Pieter Ferreira Blanc de Blancs 2017
☐ Pieter Ferreira Rosé 2016
☐ Silverthorn CWG Auction Big Dog VIX 2018
☐ Silverthorn Jewel Box 2018
☐ Silverthorn The Green Man 2020
☐ Steenberg Lady R 2018
☐ Tokara 2016
☐ Villiera Monro Brut 2016
☐ Waterford Brut 2015
☐ Woolworths Signature Vintage Reserve Brut 2016

Méthode Ancestrale

☐ Vondeling Rurale 2019

Dessert Wine, Fortified

☐ Daschbosch Gevonden Hanepoot 2017
☐ Orange River Omstaan Wit Muskadel XI NV
☐ Thelema Gargantua Muscadel NV

Natural Sweet

☐ Groot Constantia Grand Constance 2018
☐ Stellenrust Chenin d'Muscat 2021

Noble Late Harvest

☐ Boschendal Vin d'Or 2020

Vin de Paille

☐ De Trafford Straw Wine 2021
☐ Keermont Fleurfontein 2021
☐ Tierhoek Straw Wine NV

Port-Style

☐ Boplaas Cape Tawny Single Harvest 2007
☐ Boplaas Cape Vintage Reserve 2021

Sherry-Style

☐ Klein Amoskuil Perpetual Reserve Under Flor NV

Brandy

☐ Oude Molen XO
☐ The Inventer XO Rosso
☐ The Inventer XO Blanco

Husk Spirit

☐ Dalla Cia Single Cultivar Moscato

Hidden Gems

This is a small selection of wines we think are exceptionally interesting or particularly good value for money. Please look for the 'jewel' icon ⊕ in the A–Z directory for other wines receiving this distinction.

Cabernet Sauvignon
☐ Landskroon 2021

Cinsault
☐ Woolworths Cherry 2021

Merlot
☐ Badsberg 2021
☐ De Wet 2021

Petit Verdot
☐ KWV Classic 2022

Pinotage
☐ Wellington Duke 2021

Shiraz/Syrah
☐ Aan de Doorns Shiraz 2021
☐ Cape Fold Breedekloof Shiraz 2021
☐ Guardian Peak Shiraz 2022
☐ Klawer Shiraz 2022
☐ Mile High The Bald Ibis Shiraz 2022
☐ Neil Joubert Shiraz 2019
☐ Renegade CanCan Limited Edition Syrah 2021
☐ Walker Bay Llyswen Syrah 2022
☐ Windfall Shiraz 2021

Zinfandel
☐ Idiom 2018

Red Blends
☐ Delheim Shiraz-Cabernet Sauvignon 2021
☐ Skilpadvlei ML Joubert 2020
☐ Grape Grinder Blue Moose Cabernet Sauvignon-Shiraz 2021
☐ Kloovenburg Stamboom The Village Red Blend 2022

Rosé
☐ Allesverloren Tinta 2022
☐ Arra Blanc de Noir 2023
☐ Ken Forrester Petit 2023
☐ Raka 2022

Colombard
☐ Goedverwacht Crane White 2023

Chardonnay
☐ Cape Wine Crafters Collectibles 2022
☐ Meerhof 2023
☐ Merwida 2022
☐ Rietvallei Calcrete 2023
☐ Under Oaks 2022

Chenin Blanc
☐ Babylon's Peak 2023
☐ Chameleon 2023
☐ Eerste Hoop 2022
☐ Fat Bastard 2023
☐ Groot Phesantekraal 2023
☐ Pulpit Rock Brink Family Vineyards 2023
☐ Rickety Bridge 2022
☐ Simonsig 2023

Clairette Blanche
☐ Wrightman & Sons 2022

Grenache Blanc
☐ KWV Classic 2023

Pinot Grigio
☐ Anthonij Rupert Protea 2023

Sauvignon Blanc
☐ Botha Sjanter 2023
☐ Darling Cellars Reserve Bush Vine 2023
☐ False Bay Windswept 2023
☐ Zevenwacht 7even 2023

White Blends
☐ Saxenburg Guinea Fowl White 2023

Cap Classique
☐ Bemind Wyne Brut Cinsault 2020

Sparkling Wine
☐ Stettyn Babelki Sparkling Rosé Brut NV

RIO LARGO

OLIVE ESTATE

BEST OF SHOW

Proudly South African
Internationally recognised
Consistently winning awards since 2010

www.riolargo.co.za

Pork and fennel meatballs with tomato sauce

This is a welcome, fresh update from your regular, popular beef meatball recipe. Serve these hearty meatballs with pasta, mashed potato or with crusty bread.

www.sapork.co.za

Buy Now, Drink Later

This is a selection of wines we think will reward cellaring for a few years. Please look for the Buy Now, Drink Later icon 🐝 in the A–Z section for these and other wines receiving this distinction.

Cabernet Franc
☐ Gabriëlskloof Landscape 2021
☐ Keermont Pondokrug 2018
☐ Marklew 2021
☐ Wildekrans Barrel Select

Cabernet Sauvignon
☐ Atlas Swift Shelter 2020
☐ Groot Phesantakraal 2021
☐ MVH Signature Vine & Co Dryland 2021

Carignan
☐ Ayama 2022

Cinsault
☐ Metzer & Holfeld 2022

Malbec
☐ Diemersfontein Carpe Diem 2022
☐ Doolhof Limietberg Bloedklip 2020
☐ Glen Carlou 2018
☐ Yerden Nosotros 2022

Merlot
☐ Canto 2020
☐ Dornier 2020

Nebbiolo
☐ Morgenster The Giulio Nabucco 2019
☐ Steenberg 2018

Petit Verdot
☐ Le Bonheur Reserve 2021
☐ Post House Stormy Hope 2021
☐ Zorgvliet 2021

Pinot Noir
☐ Villiera Punchion 2022
☐ Vriesenhof 2022

Pinotage
☐ Cecilia 2021
☐ Dewaldt Heyns Weathered Hands 2021
☐ Lanzerac 2022
☐ Southern Right 2022
☐ Survivor Terroir 2021
☐ Windmeul 2019

Shiraz/Syrah
☐ Babylonstoren Shiraz 2021
☐ Hartenberg Shiraz 2020
☐ Jean Daneel Autograph Syrah 2018
☐ Stellenbosch Vineyards Shiraz 2021
☐ Waterkloof Circumstance Syrah 2021

Red Blends
☐ Aslina Umsasane 2021
☐ Great Heart Swartland Red 2020
☐ Holden Manz Proprietors' Blend 2017
☐ Mooiplaas Rosalind 2020
☐ Perdeberg Endura Winemaker's Selection Cape Blend 2020
☐ Rietvallei Estéanna Cabernet Sauvignon-Cabernet Franc 2019
☐ Stellekaya Orion 2021

Chardonnay
☐ Arendsig A15 2022
☐ Highlands Road 2022
☐ Kara-Tara 2022
☐ Van Loveren Christiena Trousseau 2022

Chenin Blanc
☐ Groenland Ou Bosstok Steen 2022
☐ Mullineux Kloof Street Old Vine 2020
☐ Wolvenhoek Impisi Old Vine 2022

Clairette Blanche
☐ Ghost In The Machine 2022

Riesling
☐ Fledge & Co Constantia 2022

Sauvignon Blanc
☐ Groot Constantia 2022
☐ La Motte Pierneef 2022

White Blends
☐ Brookdale Bradbourne 2022
☐ Creation Sauvignon Blanc-Semillon 2022
☐ Flagstone Treaty Tree Reserve 2022
☐ The Kitchen Sink White 2022

Cap Classique
☐ KWV Laborie Blanc de Blancs 2017
☐ Maison 2016
☐ Weltevrede Philip Jonker Brut Entheos NV

Vin de Paille
☐ Foothills Monogram 2017

Fortified Desserts
☐ Darling Cellars Wildflower Hanepoot Jerepigo NV
☐ Pulpit Rock Dessert Wine 2021

Port-Style
☐ Allesverloren Fine Old Vintage 2018
☐ Stettyn Cape Vintage 2017

Superquaffers

This is a selection of wines we think are exceptionally drinkable and well priced. Please look for the Superquaffer icon ☺ in the A–Z section for these and other wines noted as such.

Cabernet Sauvignon
☐ Leopard's Leap 2021

Merlot
☐ Ken Forrester Petit 2021

Pinotage
☐ Imbuko Van Zijl Family Vintners Coffee 2022
☐ Boland Cellar Cappupino Ccinotage 2023

Sangiovese
☐ Koelenhof Koelenbosch 2022

Shiraz
☐ Namaqua 2022

Red Blends
☐ Ashton Cabernet Sauvignon-Merlot 2021
☐ Bonnievale The River Collection Cabernet Sauvignon-Merlot 2021
☐ Klawer Shiraz-Malbec 2022
☐ Robertson Chapel Dry Red 2022
☐ Truter Taste Shiraz-Cabernet Sauvignon 2021
☐ Val Du Charron Aphaea Red 2022

Rosé
☐ Blake 16 Mile Beach Rooipan 2023
☐ Cape Wine Crafters She Chardonnay-Pinot 2023
☐ Darling Cellars Pyjama Bush 2023
☐ Kumusha Cinsault Rosé 2023
☐ Steenberg Classic Ruby Rosé 2023
☐ Stettyn Chardonnay-Pinot Noir 2023

Bukettraube
☐ Swartland Winery Winemakers Collection 2023

Chardonnay
☐ Du Toitskloof Heritage 2023

Colombard
☐ Rooiberg 2023

Chenin Blanc
☐ Boland Cellar Classic 2023
☐ O'Connell's Private Selection 2022
☐ Perdeberg Cellar Collection 2023
☐ Slanghoek Vinay NV

Grüner Veltliner
☐ Niel Joubert 2023

Sauvignon Blanc
☐ Badsberg 2023
☐ Cloof The Duckitt Collection 2023
☐ Stellenbosch Hills Polkadraai 2023
☐ Yonder Hill Benjamin 2023

White Blends
☐ Aan de Doorns Route 43 Crisp White 2023
☐ Flagstone Noon Gun Chenin Blanc-Sauvignon Blanc-Viognier 2023
☐ Riebeek Valley Klein Kasteelberg Chenin Blanc-Grenache Blanc 2022
☐ Waboomsrivier Kaapse Wit 2023

Cap Classique
☐ Van Loveren Blanc de Blanc 2023

Sparkling Wine
☐ Grape Grinder Cape Fynbos Bubbly Chardonnay NV
☐ House of BNG Nectar Blanc NV

Tasters For This Edition

Winifred Bowman

Introduced to wine at a young age, through a thimbleful of sweet muscadel with Sunday lunch, Winnie's immersion in the fruit of the vine deepened during her student days at Stellenbosch University and later through frequent travels to international winegrowing areas, and widened to include brandy and husk spirit. A qualified physiotherapist and biomedical scientist, and holder of a PhD in Education, she is a Cape Wine Master, and regular judge at several local and international wine and spirit competitions. Winnie also loves books, opera, travel and long dinner parties.

Greg de Bruyn

Greg is an architect by day, and a wine devotee after hours. A casual interest in winetasting at a social club snowballed, leading him to qualify as a wine judge in 1996 and a Cape Wine Master in 2000. He was runner-up in Wine Magazine's inaugural New Wine Writer competition, after which he contributed regularly to that and other wine publications. In 1999, Greg settled in the Cape, first to establish a new wine estate in Hermanus, and later as a specialist consultant in winery construction. He has judged for Veritas, Diners Club Winemaker of the Year, Nederburg Auction and several magazine panels, lectured at Diploma level for the Cape Wine Academy and has been a taster for this guide since 2010.

Ndabezinhle Dube

Wine, Ndaba says, found him, instead of the other way round. It was at the Vineyard Hotel in 2009, when management tapped the then resident barman to take on the role of maître d' with a key focus on wine at the Square Restaurant, one of the first in Cape Town to emphasise fine-wine and -food pairing. Ndaba's palate, acumen, gregariousness and passion for top-notch service ensured the success of this residency, paving the way for elevation to senior restaurant manager. A sojourn as food and beverage manager at Blaauwberg Beach Hotel was followed by a move to the four-star President Hotel, where Ndaba has been F&B operations manager since 2019. He is a graduate (with distinction) of the Michael Fridjhon Wine Judging Academy, holds the WSET Level 3 diploma and currently judges mostly for Wine Magazine. He joins Platter's team this edition as an associate taster.

Tim James

Tim, a Cape Wine Master, is an established and multiple award-winning winewriter, contributing freelance to local and international publications and websites, most frequently nowadays to Winemag.co.za but also a regular column to the London-based World of Fine Wine magazine. He is also SA consultant to the World Atlas of Wine. Tim's book, Wines of the New South Africa: Tradition and Revolution, was published in 2013. He has been a taster and associate editor for this guide for many years.

Nomonde Kubheka

It was Nomonde's father, involved in cellar equipment manufacture, who suggested winemaking as a possible career to his recently matriculated daughter. Never exposed to wine or its production, Nomonde's natural curiosity and appetite for a new challenge were piqued, and she enrolled in the Viticulture & Oenology programme at Stellenbosch University, graduating in 2003. The same year she joined powerhouse producer KWV as winemaker and, in 2015, the wine-industry research, development and innovation coordinating body, Winetech, as facilitator and educator. Currently she's an independent wine educator with a particular involvement with the Pinotage Youth Development Academy where she provided technical skills for its recently launched uLutsha wine brand. Nomonde has served on Wine & Spirit Board tasting panels and several wine competitions, including the International Wine & Spirit Competition and Diners Club Winemaker of the Year.

Malu Lambert

Malu fell in love with wine while working as a waiter to pay for her studies, and the allure of the vine has since drawn her into a many-sided career, notably as a writer and judge. Winner of the Veritas Young Wine Writer 2015 and Louis Roederer International Emerging Wine Writer 2019 awards, Malu contributes to numerous local titles and has written internationally on South African wine for

Jancis Robinson, Club Oenologique, Decanter, Falstaff and more. She also recently co-authored an awarded book on Klein Constantia. The avowed wine-geek is a graduate of the Michael Fridjhon Wine Judging Academy and currently enrolled in the WSET Level 4 Diploma programme. She judges on many high-profile competitions, locally and overseas, and is a panel member of Wine-of-the-Month Club. Away from wine, Malu runs Fable, a story-telling, social media and copywriting company, and occasionally helps her husband in their craft spirit distillery in Cape Town.

Angela Lloyd

Wine was a hobby Angela readily took to soon after her arrival from the UK in 1970. Encouraged by her husband, Mark, her interest bloomed into a professional career spanning a remarkable four decades. After running a wine centre in the early 1980s, she turned to freelance wine-writing and -judging, receiving innumerable commissions both locally and abroad. Travel to the world's winelands from her Cape Town base has increased her knowledge and fascination for all types of wine. In 2022 she was honoured by the Veritas Awards as a Living Legend. This edition is her 38th as a member of Platter's tasting team.

Cathy Marston

Following an English degree at Cambridge University, Cathy fully intended to go into theatre production but travelled the world instead, gaining her both a husband and a love of wine. After working at Adnams Wine Merchants in Suffolk, UK, where she earned the Wine & Spirit Education Trust (WSET) Level 4 Diploma, she ended up in Cape Town, owning and running The Nose Restaurant & Wine Bar for several years. Selling this in 2009 left her free to concentrate on writing, judging and, increasingly, teaching WSET courses. She went on to become the first WSET Approved Programme Provider in Africa and, in 2015, WSET Educator of the Year. Her teaching has since taken her to locations such as Qatar, United Arab Emirates, Mauritius and the Maldives. Cathy continues studying and is currently a Stage 2 Master of Wine (MW) student.

Fiona McDonald

Travel is said to broaden the mind, and Fiona, former editor of Wine magazine for eight years, has had her wine mind broadened by having been a long-serving jury president of several international wine competitions: International Wine Challenge, International Wine & Spirit Competition, Concours Mondial de Bruxelles and, more recently, Decanter World Wine Awards' regional panel chair for South Africa. Initially trained as a news journalist, she got into wine by happy accident, helping to organise The Mercury Wine Week in between reportage and newsroom management as the night news-editor on that Durban broadsheet. Currently freelancing, Fiona edits Cheers magazine, and contributes to a range of publications and websites.

Keize Mumba

The dream of a role in the movie industry as a screenwriter led Keize to leave his home in Zambia and enrol in a course at South Africa's leading film, TV and performance school, AFDA. But in a plot twist, while working part-time at a hotel he discovered a new passion - the world of wine - and along with it a 'pool of stories that are yearning to be told'. To better tell those tales, he left film school and immersed himself in wine studies, completing the Wine & Spirit Education Trust (WSET) Level 3 programme. Currently he is finishing Level 4 and working as sommelier at Grub & Vine, chef Matt Manning's refined bistro restaurant on Cape Town's trendy Bree Street. Keize is an associate taster for this guide.

Christine Rudman

Zambia-born Christine's love affair with wine started when she joined the then Stellenbosch Farmers'Winery after a Johannesburg FMCG marketing career. Enrolling in the Cape Wine Academy, she achieved her Cape Wine Master qualification in 1986, then chaired the Institute of CWMs for nine years. She left SFW to run the CWA and, since her retirement in 2002, has been occupied with consultancy work, wine-judging, -lecturing and -writing. Christine writes on wine in Die Burger newspaper, and has published two editions of A Guide to the Winelands of the Cape. She travels widely, and has done tastings and wine training on various luxury liners. The recipient of three wine industry awards, Frans Malan Cap Classique trophy, Veritas Living Legend and, in 2022 at the Wine Harvest Commemoration Event, for Wine Appreciation and Advancement, Christine serves as judge and chair on local and international juries, and has been a taster for this guide since the 2003 edition.

Penelope Setti

Wine drew Penny into its orbit while waiting on tables at an upmarket Italian restaurant in Eastern Cape province in the 2000s. The then freshly graduated Political Science major was handed a nugget of advice by the maître d, 'You can't sell something you don't know', along with a tasting glass of wine so alluring, it changed the course of her life. Now based in Cape Town, and still boundlessly passionate about the vine, Zambia-born Penny is a sommelier, consultant and owner of her own wine bar, Penny Noire, set to re-open at the time of writing after a short break. Penny is furthering her education with the Wine & Spirit Education Trust (WSET) Level 4 Diploma, has been a judge on various tasting panels, and is a prominent promoter of women in wine.

Dave Swingler

A taster for this guide for over two decades, Dave has consulted to restaurants, game lodges and convention centres, taught wine courses and contributed to radio, print and other media. He is co-author of One Hundred Wines – An Insider's Guide to South African Wine, and drinks contributor to Posh Nosh. A long-standing member of the International Wine & Food Society and the South African consultant for its Annual Vintage Chart, Dave is currently Cellarmaster of the Cape Town branch. A psychiatrist by day, he's intrigued by language in general, and the lexicon of wine in particular.

Cathy van Zyl

Cathy became the first Master of Wine on the African continent when she passed the notoriously difficult and prestigious MW examination in 2005. Previously chair of the Institute of Masters of Wine's education committee and a member of its Council for six years, she became chair of the IMW in September 2022. Cathy lectures and judges locally and internationally, occasionally contributes to wine journals and websites around the world, but spends most of her wine-time as associate editor of this guide. In 2019, she was named Institute of Cape Wine Masters' Personality of the Year for her passionate promotion of South African wine.

Meryl Weaver

Bacchus and the Cape winelands lured Meryl away from her Gauteng legal career more than 30 years ago. She remains happily under their spell, having qualified as a Cape Wine Master and graduated with distinction from the Michael Fridjhon Wine Judging Academy. She has conducted wine presentations abroad on behalf of Wines of South Africa, lectures for the Cape Wine Academy and judges for various wine competitions. Meryl has been associated with this guide for over 20 years, initially as wine coordinator and, since 2007, copywriter and taster. Food and travel continue to inspire her, and she and husband Alex regularly venture out in their camper van to explore the many wild and beautiful places in southern Africa.

A–Z of South African Producers

AA Badenhorst Family Wines
'Some changes that are taking place within the company' meant new vintages were unavailable for tasting from the pioneering and internationally hailed Kalmoesfontein estate of Adi Badenhorst and cousin Hein. We look forward to sampling them next time.

Location: Malmesbury ▪ Map: Swartland ▪ Map grid reference: C8 ▪ Est 2007 ▪ 1stB 2006 ▪ Tasting & tours Wed & Fri by appt ▪ Farm lunches Mon-Fri from 12.30-1.30, prior booking essential ▪ Closed all pub hols & weekends ▪ Conferences ▪ Function venue for 130 people ▪ Conservation area ▪ Guest cottages ▪ Owner(s) Adi, Cornelia & Hein Badenhorst ▪ Winemaker(s) Adi Badenhorst (2006) ▪ Viticulturist(s) Hannes Coetzee (2018), Pierre Rossouw (Jan 1975) ▪ 150ha (cinsaut, grenache, shiraz, chard, chenin, rouss) ▪ 50,000cs own label 40% red 60% white ▪ PO Box 1177 Malmesbury 7299 ▪ wynbefok@icloud.com ▪ www.aabadenhorst. com ▪ T +27 (0)82-373-5038/+27 (0)22-125-0116 (office)

Aaldering Vineyards & Wines
When Fons and Marianne Aaldering unveiled the debut vintage simultaneously in SA and their native Netherlands almost fifteen years ago, the wine they showcased was a pinotage. The locally developed variety remains the cornerstone, with a half-dozen bottlings in the line-up, including a rare blanc de noir. Youngest daughter Jacqueline and husband Gert-Jan manage the Devon Valley home-farm, with its luxury lodges and recently completed facility for bottle-ageing in ideal conditions for four years before release.

Aaldering range
★★★★ **Lady M** Unwooded pinotage, nice comparison with sibling. **22** ⑧⑧ not lesser in any way, dark berries, a cocoa seam giving it richness & interest. Enough grape tannin for definition, ageing.

★★★★ **Pinotage** Plush dark ripe fruit backed by 18 months in barriques, 25% new, rest 2nd fill (as other reds, unless noted), **20** ★★★★★ ⑨⑩ was made to impress & does. More powerful than **18** ⑧⑦, with interwoven layers of spice & cocoa, enough succulence to enjoy now but the best lies ahead, has deep musculature. Also in 1.5 & 3L. **19** sold out untasted, as Cab-Merlot.

★★★★ **Shiraz** ⓐ Full-ripe **20** ⑧⑧'s oaking tames the opulence, adds spicing, the tannins a firm backbone in the luscious fruit. Long life ahead.

★★★★ **Cabernet Sauvignon-Merlot** Cab at 58% dominates but merlot brings its part: **20** ⑧⑨ a good meld of cassis & plums, tobacco & chocolate, the oaking serious enough to give structure for cellaring.

★★★★ **Pinotage Blanc** Pale in colour but not personality, **23** ⑧⑧ showcases varietal fruit, has lovely food-friendly texture, verges on savoury. Impressive. **22** untasted.

★★★★ **Chardonnay** Deftly combining stonefruit & orange perfume with oat biscuit savouriness, **22** ⑧⑧ then springs the surprise of zesty saline acidity to finish. Spent 9 months in barrel, 25% new.

★★★★☆ **Sauvignon Blanc** Staying in **21** ⑨⑩'s style & quality, **22** ⑨⑩'s grapefruit pithiness sets it apart, adding to the fennel & greengage core, giving interest, length & ageability.

Pinotage Rosé ★★★★ Bright pink, with prominent berry styling, **23** ⑧⑤ is fresh & dry, piquant & flavourful. Also in magnum. Not tasted: **Noble Late Harvest Sauvignon Blanc**.

Florence by Aaldering range
★★★★ **Winemakers Selection Cape Blend** ⓟ Cellarmaster has free rein here, so blend can vary. A fraction more pinotage than cab in **20** ⑧⑥, 7% merlot, packed with dark berry fruit, definite tannin tug & hint of char from 10% new oak.

Chenin Blanc ★★★★ Sleek & fruity **22** ⑧⑤ has enough fresh apple & pear perfume & flavours for tasty, youthful enjoyment. **Sauvignon Blanc-Chardonnay** ★★★★ Sauvignon leads at 80% in **21** ⑧⑤, so that's the first impression: fresh, with some green notes, but chardonnay contributes palate weight & citrus in the flavours. Not tasted: **Pinotage Rosé**. — CR

Location/map/WO: Stellenbosch ▪ Map grid reference: D4 ▪ Est 2004 ▪ 1stB 2007 ▪ Tasting & sales Mon-Thu 10-5 Fri 10-4 Sat (Oct-Apr) 10-3 ▪ Closed all pub hols ▪ Cellar tours by appt ▪ 3 luxury lodges (TGCSA 5 star) ▪ Owner(s) Marianne & Fons Aaldering ▪ Winemaker(s) Jaco Parson (Oct 2023) ▪ Viticulturist(s) Conrad Schutte (Vinpro) ▪ 27ha/19.7ha (cab, merlot, ptage, shiraz, chard, sauv) ▪ ±120t/±18,300cs own label 50%

red 50% white ▪ IPW ▪ PO Box 1068 Stellenbosch 7599 ▪ estate@aaldering.co.za ▪ www.aaldering.co.za ▪ **T +27 (0)21-865-2495**

Aan de Doorns Cellar

A big year for the 27 shareholder-growers: the 70th anniversary of their collaboration, centred on production facilities and visitor venue near Worcester, and fanning out over a substantial 1,600 ha of vineland. Export titan FirstCape remains the primary channel for the ±30,000-ton crop, but the own-labels are carefully made & curated by the team under veteran cellarmaster Johan Morkel, and priced like it was 1954.

Vintage range

★★★★ **Red Muscadel** Ⓐ As always, **21** ⑧⑦ fortified muscat stands out for combining a feeling of fresh lightness with fully sweet, raisiny-fruity intensity & richness.

. . . .

Shiraz ⊘ ⊛ ★★★★ Enjoyable **21** ⑧③ charms with red plum & cherry fruit edged with smoked ham from new oak, part American. **Chenin Blanc** ⊘ ⊛ ★★★★ Apples & pineapples on **23** ⑧③, showing excellent depth of flavour & fresh acid balance. An over-deliverer of note.

. . . .

Cabernet Sauvignon Ⓐ ★★★ Ripe fruitiness with desired toast & spice from wooding on **21** ⑧①, but green note on palate too, along with some sweetness. **Pinotage** ⊘ ★★★ Decent typicity on **21** ⑧② in its ripe black fruit; tarry overtone, smoky tannin & sweet vanilla finish added by oak staves, 10% American. **Doornroodt** Ⓐ ★★★★ Cherry & plum on **20** ⑧③ from ruby cab & merlot, pleasantly flaunting vanilla oak too. Full, juicy & undemanding. **Sauvignon Blanc** ⊘ ★★★ Tutti-frutti **23** ⑧⓪ mingles peach, granadilla & lime for carefree alfresco enjoyment. **Cape Ruby** Ⓐ ★★★★ An approachable 'port' matured in big old wood vats, from tinta barocca in **20** ⑧④. Sweetly delicious, smooth & cheering.

Route 43 range

Crisp White ☺ ★★★ Properly dry **23** ⑦⑨ sauvignon & colombard duo hits the spot with bright grapefruit notes, lively freshness, fire sale price. Keep some chilled for a happy summer.

. . . .

Deep Red Ⓐ ★★★ Ripe & fruity **21** ⑦⑧ from shiraz & pinotage in bottle & 3L box. Not dumbed down with sugar, just tasty, juicy & balanced, for straightforward quaffing. **Fruity White** ★★ Semi-sweet **23** ⑦⑤ from colombard shows light limy fruit but more needed for real interest. — CM

Location/map/WO: Worcester ▪ Map grid reference: B4 ▪ Est 1954 ▪ Tasting & sales Mon-Fri 9-5 Sat 9-1 ▪ Olive/olive oil & wine pairing by appt ▪ Closed all pub hols ▪ Tours during harvest by appt ▪ Wedding/function venue ▪ Owner(s) 27 shareholders ▪ Cellarmaster(s) Johan Morkel (Nov 1993) ▪ Winemaker(s) Gert van Deventer (Sep 1997) & Chris Geldenhuys (Sep 2016) ▪ Viticulturist(s) Pierre Snyman ▪ 1,600ha (cab, ptage, chard, chenin, cbard) ▪ 29,000t/33,253cs own label ▪ PO Box 235 Worcester 6849 ▪ info@aandedoorns.co.za ▪ www.aandedoorns.co.za ▪ **T +27 (0)23-347-2301**

Aan't Vette Wine Estate

With his small, sustainably farmed block of shiraz beside the Vette River in Riversdale, Pieter Steyn is following in his 19th-century forebears' winegrowing footsteps. An engineer and founder of Cranefield College, Pieter is also owner of De Doornkraal Vinotel and Aan't Vette Country Kitchen. The wines are crafted by a consultant using modern equipment tucked into a 150-year-old converted barn, with metre-thick walls.

Louis Meurant Syrah Ⓐ ★★★ With its juicy mix of blackcurrants & raspberries, & meaty-spicy notes from year in oak, 20% new, **19** ⑧① drinks easily & well now & for next year/2. **17** ⑧② also still available. Not tasted: **Divine Rouge Syrah**, **Divine Blush Syrah Blanc de Noir**. — ML

Location: Riversdale ▪ Map: Klein Karoo & Garden Route ▪ Map grid reference: C6 ▪ WO: Cape South Coast ▪ Est 2009 ▪ 1stB 2012 ▪ Tasting & cellar tours by appt only ▪ Sales online ▪ Closed all pub hols ▪ Meals/refreshments (arranged by the hotel) by appt only ▪ Conference venue (max 20 pax) ▪ Aan't Vette Country Kitchen ▪ De Doornkraal Vinotel (4-star hotel) ▪ Owner(s) Pieter Steyn ▪ Winemaker(s) Petri de Beer (consultant) ▪ Viticulturist(s) Pieter Steyn & Theo Geldenhuys (consultant) ▪ 1.2ha (shiraz) ▪ ±10-12t own label 90% red 10% blanc de noir ▪ kelder@dedoornkraal.com ▪ www.dedoornkraal.com ▪ **T +27 (0)28-713-3838/+27 (0)82-772-5734**

Abbottshill   🍷 🍽 🏠 📷

Since returning to their Swartland farm, Hillcrest, and making the first vintage after an extended break, Cameron and Dianne Bain have added a dedicated ferment area to the boutique cellar which, like the vineyard, they run along the lines of 'keep it simple, stupid' and organic where possible.

Cabernet Sauvignon ★★★☆ Returns to the guide after a break, as Shiraz. Previewed **22** ⑧⑤'s whiffs of violets introduce a herby flavour profile & still somewhat austere tannins. Needs more time to settle & meld. WO Swartland. Older oak, 12–18 months for these. **Shiraz** ⊘ ★★★☆ Natty 2L bag-in-box suggests picnics, & **22** ⑧⑤ a perfect fit: fresh plum & forest-floor berry fruit, hint of smoked bacon, lipsmacking dryness. Not tasted: **Shiraz-Cabernet Sauvignon**. — DS

Location: Malmesbury ▪ Map: Swartland ▪ Map grid reference: B7 ▪ WO: Malmesbury/Swartland ▪ Est/1stB 2004 ▪ Tasting, sales & tours by appt ▪ BYO picnic ▪ Guest house ▪ See website for wine tours & other activities offered from the farm ▪ Owner(s) Dynadeals One (Pty) Ltd ▪ Winemaker(s)/viticulturist(s) CA Bain ▪ PO Box 433 Malmesbury 7299 ▪ cameron@empa.co.za ▪ www.abbottshill.com ▪ **T +27 (0)83-645-6038**

☐ **Absolute Zero** *see* Van Loveren Family Vineyards

Accolade Wines South Africa

Part of Accolade Wines, one of the big five international wine businesses, whose portfolio includes some of the best-known New World wine labels, Accolade Wines South Africa's winemaking operation, based in Somerset West, is responsible for the global Kumala, Fish Hoek Fairtrade-accredited range of single varieties and, listed separately, highly regarded Flagstone pinnacle wines.

Location: Somerset West ▪ Tasting & sales at Flagstone Winery ▪ Winemaker(s) Gerhard Swart (group winemaker), Juan Slabbert & Chandré Davey ▪ 2.6m cs own label ▪ PO Box 769 Stellenbosch 7599 ▪ flagstone. wines@accoladewines.com ▪ www.accoladewines.com ▪ **T +27 (0)21-852-5052**

☐ **Adama** *see* Bosman Family Vineyards

Adama Wines

The three stakeholders uniting to further women's empowerment in the winelands are fronted by 'an ambitious, all-female, all-black team that combines skillsets to offer a unique proposition - a wine brand women can be proud of.' Based on a Paarl farm, with Praisy Dlamini as cellarmaster and prime mover, and Ruth Faro as viticulturist, they collaborate on wines commissioned by wholesalers as well as their own brands: the original Her Wine Collection, which has been 'flying off shelves', and its UK sibling, Amandla, which won Drinks Business' Launch of the Year award the past year on a 'minuscule' marketing budget.

Her Wine Collection

★★★★ **Shiraz** ⊘ Lightly oaked **22** ⑧⑦ shows better fruit ripeness & concentration than unwooded **21** ★★★★ ⑧⑤, spicy-aromatic black cherry, delicate scrub scent, sleek tannins. 10% durif.

★★★★ **Chenin Blanc** ⊘ Cheerful, sunny & supple, **23** ⑧⑥ is pure everyday pleasure, delivers a generous rush of tropical fruit, satisfying lees weight & grip. Unwooded, with 15% pinot gris. Step up from **22** ★★★★ ⑧④.

Pinotage ⊘ ★★★★ Exuberance of **22** ⑧⑤'s wild black berries tempered by 15% malbec, tiny brush of oak. Light-bodied, sweetly ripe, poolside appeal. **Sauvignon Blanc** ⊘ ★★★★ Fresh & crisp, with succulently ripe passionfruit & gentle herb wafts, multi-region **23** ⑧⑤ upbeat & appealing, for anytime enjoyment.

Amandla range (NEW)

Shiraz-Zinfandel ★★★★ Rare appearance of Croatian grape made famous by California, only 14% of the **22** ⑧③ blend but enough to add wild berry highlights to solid cherry & plum fruit core. **Sauvignon Blanc** ★★★★ From far-flung vineyards, including Orange River, **23** ⑧⑤ exotic aromatics, juicy granadilla fruit, linear acid & mineral seam. — GdB

Location: Paarl ▪ WO: Western Cape/Greater Cape ▪ Est 2005 ▪ 1stB 2019 ▪ Owner(s) Adama Wines (Pty) Ltd (shareholders Bosman Adama, Dynasty Trust, Adama Appollis Investments) ▪ Cellarmaster(s)/winemaker(s) Praisy Dlamini (Jun 2019) ▪ Viticulturist(s) Ruth Faro (Jan 2017) ▪ 293ha/80ha (cab, cinsaut, merlot, ptage, shiraz, chard, chenin, cbard, sauv) ▪ 1,800t ▪ Brands for clients: Woolworths ▪ WIETA ▪ Schoon Organic

Wine Farm & Cellar, Windmeul 7630 ▪ info@herwinecollection.co.za, praisy@adamawines.co.za ▪ www. herwinecollection.co.za ▪ **T +27 (0)21-873-3170**

Aden's Star

Johannesburg wine entrepreneur Jason Neal is the owner of this limited-quantity, best-years-only label, made by consultant James McKenzie from multiple terroirs and released when ready for drinking.

The Golden Fleece ★★★ From cab franc, spent 15 months in barriques, 70% new, so **20** ⑧⑴'s profile includes savoury spice & tannins, both compatible with the plummy fruit. — CR

Location: Johannesburg ▪ WO: Western Cape ▪ Est 1997 ▪ 1stB 2012 ▪ Closed to public ▪ Owner(s) Jason Neal ▪ Winemaker(s) James McKenzie ▪ Viticulturist(s) James McKenzie (2012) ▪ 4,400cs own label 100% red ▪ PO Box 1659 Jukskei Park 2153 ▪ jason@nicholsonsmith.co.za ▪ www.nicholsonsmith.co.za ▪ **T +27 (0)11-496-2947**

AD Wines ⓠ

Picking a tiny parcel of Darling fruit to craft naturally and respectfully into an ethereal and pure expression of cinsault has been the after-hours pursuit of Cape Town legal man Adrian Dommisse for most of the past ten years. Much of the attraction has been the involvement of his family at harvest time, so it's especially pleasing that daughter Hannah additionally is taking over the sales function, and son James logistics.

★★★★ Skylark Cinsault In usual light & dry style (just 11% alc), aged in older oak. **22 ★★★★** ⑧⑶ delightful floral-fruit fragrance, like **21** ⑧⑺, but medicinal, slightly bitter hints among the flavour.— TJ

Location: Cape Town ▪ WO: Darling ▪ Est 2013 ▪ 1stB 2014 ▪ Tasting by appt only ▪ Owner(s)/winemaker(s) Adrian Dommisse ▪ 2t/150cs own label 100% red ▪ PO Box 13225 Mowbray 7705 ▪ adriandommisse@gmail. com ▪ www.adwines.co.za ▪ **T +27 (0)71-674-4316**

☐ **Africa Five** *see* Stellenview Premium Wines
☐ **African King** *see* Zidela Wines

African Pride Wines

The current team at African Pride have been working together for 20 years, their overseas-orientated wine business having been formed in Constantia in 2002. Mike Graham, shareholder, winemaker since inception and 40+ harvest veteran, continues to style the wines, not tasted this edition.

Location: Stellenbosch ▪ Est 2002 ▪ 1stB 2003 ▪ Closed to public ▪ Owner(s) Privately owned ▪ Cellarmaster(s)/winemaker(s) Mike Graham (Jan 2002) ▪ 100,000cs 50% red 47% white 3% rosé ▪ BRC, IFS, IPW ▪ Bosmans Crossing, Distillery Rd, Stellenbosch 7600 ▪ info@africanpridewines.co.za ▪ www. africanpridewines.co.za ▪ **T +27 (0)21-887-2204**

☐ **African Roots** *see* Seven Sisters Vineyards
☐ **African Sun Wines** *see* Mara Wines

Afrikaans ⓠ

Sibling to esteemed Rust en Vrede in the Jean Engelbrecht portfolio, this wine pair pays tribute to one of South Africa's eleven official languages and its 'culture, history and sense of belonging'. It's styled at another Engelbrecht winery, Guardian Peak, to be accessible, welcoming and exuberant, and suit every occasion.

★★★★☆ Cabernet Sauvignon-Cinsault Highly successful version of traditional Cape red blend. **21** ⑨⑴ adds lipsmacking red-fruited cinsault (20%) to deliciously fragrant black-fruited cab. Year in large, old oak barrels adds just the right amount of tobacco & spice.

★★★★ Chenin Blanc-Chardonnay Bright, fruity **22** ⑧⑺ ups chardonnay to 35%, giving creamy length to zingy pineapple & peach. Lees time adds weight, as do 15% new oak & portion in concrete 'egg'.— CM

Location: Stellenbosch ▪ WO: Stellenbosch-Piekenierskloof ▪ Est/1stB 2016 ▪ Tasting & sales at Guardian Peak Wines ▪ Owner(s) Jean Engelbrecht ▪ Winemaker(s) Duran Cornhill (Dec 2021) ▪ own label 50% red 50% white ▪ IPW ▪ PO Box 473 Stellenbosch 7599 ▪ info@drinkafrikaans.com ▪ www.drinkafrikaans.com ▪ **T +27 (0)21-881-3881**

☐ **Agaat** *see* Truter Family Wines

☐ **A Glass of Wine** *see* Duma Wines
☐ **Ahrens Family** *see* The Ahrens Family
☐ **Akkedisberg** *see* Southern Treasures

Akkerdal Wine Estate ⓨ ⌂

Despite the challenging conditions and outlook for the industry, Pieter Hanekom continues to quote his slogan - 'dream, believe, achieve' - and find positives to celebrate, like the 'exceptional' 2023 harvest on his Franschhoek estate, and the fact that wine and its making has been part of his family's heritage and culture for 300 years and 'an essential part of the good life'.

Limited Release range

★★★★ **Malbec** ⓨ Intense sour cherry & spice appeal, **15** ⑧⑦ skilfully reins in fruit generosity to finish with elegance & focus. Attractive dinner companion, with sufficient heft to partner hearty food.

★★★★ **Kallie's Dream** ⓨ Rhône-style **15** ★★★★☆ ⑨① engages on many levels, not least the unusual co-ferment of all components: shiraz (48%), mourvèdre, grenache, carignan & viognier. Fruit rich, yet plenty of tannic oomph & freshening acidity; lingering pure-fruited farewell. Worth waiting since **10** ⑧⑦.

★★★★ **TDT** ⓨ Creative blend tempranillo, durif & tannat has intriguing dark perfumed fruit & supple tannins. **12** ⑧⑦ succulent, balanced but still youthful, with potential. Step up previous.

★★★★ **Wild Boar** ⓨ Five-part Bordeaux blend including dab of rarely seen carmenère in **18** ⑧⑧. Succulent, with array of dark fruit, creamy tannins & earthy, savoury farewell. Older oak, 2 years.

★★★★ **SG Blush** ⓨ Luminous salmon **21** ⑧⑧ from grenache noir opens with rosepetal & lavender perfume, followed by savoury strawberry compote. Smooth, balanced & rounded, a lovely dry grip to end.

★★★★☆ **Chardonnay** ⓨ Poised & refined **20** ⑨⓪, complex melange baked apple, cantaloupe & tangerine nicely accented by salt on the finish. Beautifully balanced, oak simply there to support the fruit.

★★★★ **Semillon** ⓨ Wild-fermented **20** ⑧⑧'s initial green apple & green bean aromas give way to melon & just-ripe pineapple, palate given breadth by 8 months in older, larger barrels.

Not tasted: **Kallie's Dream Rosé**, **Sauvignon Blanc**. — WB

Location/map/WO: Franschhoek ▪ Map grid reference: C4 ▪ Est 2000 ▪ 1stB 2001 ▪ Tasting & sales Mon-Fri 10-4 by appt only ▪ Closed all pub hols ▪ Self-catering chalet ▪ Owner(s)/cellarmaster(s)/winemaker(s)/viticulturist(s) Pieter Hanekom ▪ 18ha (barbera, cab f, carignan, carmenère, durif, grenache n/b, malbec, merlot, mourv, p verdot, roobernet, shiraz, tannat, tempranillo, chard, chenin, macabeu, nouvelle, rouss, sauv, sem, verdelho, viog) ▪ 6,000cs own label 95% red 4% white 1% rosé ▪ IPW, WIETA ▪ PO Box 36 La Motte 7691 ▪ wine@akkerdal.co.za ▪ www.akkerdal.co.za ▪ **T +27 (0)21-876-3481/+27 (0)82-442-1746**

Akkerdraai ⓨ ⓞ

Sad news from the small winery on the Helderberg's Annandale Road is the passing of its owner and co-winemaker, Salie de Swardt. Happier tidings are that son Stephan and his family are running with the philosophy of modern, soft but ageworthy cabernet-based wines 'hopefully with the same pleasure and love' as the founder. They offer the current vintage, Salie's second-last, with his favourite saying: 'Enjoy!'

Cabernet Sauvignon ⊘ ★★★☆ Everything about **21** ⑧⑤ geared for smooth, satisfying everyday drinking (including bargain price): ripe plums with dried herb & black tea extras, gentle older-oak ageing. Last tasted was **19** ★★★★ ⑧⑦. In abeyance: **Cabernet Sauvignon-Merlot**. — WB

Location/map/WO: Stellenbosch ▪ Map grid reference: E8 ▪ Est 1956 ▪ 1stB 2007 ▪ Tasting by appt only ▪ Fee R25, waived on purchase ▪ Closed all pub hols ▪ Walks/hikes ▪ Winemaker(s) Ronell Wiid (consultant), with Salie de Swardt (Jan 2013 - Sep 2022) ▪ Viticulturist(s) Ronell Wiid (consultant) ▪ 1.5ha (cab) ▪ 12t 100% red ▪ PO Box 22 Lynedoch 7603 ▪ plaasakkerdraai@gmail.com ▪ **T +27 (0)73-507-6140**

Alexanderfontein

Meant to enhance 'enjoyment of the simpler aspect of life', this range is made by Ormonde Wines in Darling. The Cabernet, Merlot, Shiraz, Chardonnay, Chenin and Sauvignon not ready for tasting this edition.

Alheit Vineyards

The husband-and-wife team of Chris and Suzaan Alheit founded their now internationally renowned boutique winery in 2010 with the aim of crafting 'wine with a very clear Cape identity, heritage wine from dry-farmed old bushvine sites, made carefully and simply, with no manipulation of the must at all'. Their debut release, Cartology, described their search for suitable sites across the winelands on the label and website, and presented the results in a stellar chenin-based wine. That variety remains the mainstay of the current, expanded range of mainly single-site expressions. While still working from Hemelrand cellar in Hemel-en-Aarde Ridge, the Alheits continue to place emphasis on the farming on Nuwedam, their property on Swartland's Paardeberg, where more pontac has been planted, for a total of 3.5 ha. Release date of the first wine from the parcel is uncertain, as is the roll-out schedule for 'something we have brewing in Ceres'.

★★★★★ **Cartology** (Ⓐ) (Ⓦ) Distinguished old-vine chenin from diverse vineyards. **22** (94) ex 7 parcels from Citrusdal Mountain to False Bay, plus usual splash 8% Franschhoek semillon. As with **21** ★★★★★ (95), lengthy lees contact gives a salt edge to peach fruit, croissant & orange blossom highlights. Wholebunch press, natural ferment, only older vessels, also in 1.5L magnums, as all.

★★★★☆ **Fire By Night** (Ⓐ) (Ⓦ) Chenin from venerable Swartland bushvines planted 1974-1985. Perfumed **22** (94) has talcum powder & fynbos notes with savoury lees, the acid integrated. **21** ★★★★★ (95) a slow starter; both should improve & give pleasure many years. 60% cement eggs & mix old barrels & large foudre, on lees a year.

★★★★☆ **Hereafter Here** Young-vine chenin from four diverse sites spotlights bright, fresh peachy fruit & lemon zest acid in **22** (90), creamy & nutty thanks to year older oak.

★★★★☆ **Huilkrans** (Ⓐ) (Ⓦ) From Citrusdal Mountain, **22** (94) rich, honeyed, displaying stonefruit & rooibos tea, beautiful balance between peaches-&-cream texture & lime acidity. Exceptionally low yields of 1.5-2 t/ha, 80% in 2,000L Austrian foudre, rest in barrel. Last made was **19** (93).

★★★★☆ **Nautical Dawn** (Ⓐ) (Ⓦ) Wonderfully rich & succulent yet restrained cool-fruit tones of pear & yellow plum on **22** (94) from Stellenbosch maritime single-site chenin. Toasted oats & cream notes balance racy acid & freshness at salty finish. Austrian foudres & barrels.

★★★★☆ **Monument Semillon** (Ⓐ) (Ⓦ) From venerable single vineyard on granite & quartz in Franschhoek, 'La Colline'. Ripe, candied citrus fruit is countered by orange pith & wild thyme nuances in **22** (94), more complex than **21** (94), similar creamy texture from old oak & limy acid balance. Beautiful finish.

★★★★★ **Hemelrand Vine Garden** (Ⓐ) Chardonnay leads **22** ★★★★★ (94) Hemel-en-Aarde Ridge 'field' blend, with co-grown roussanne, chenin, verdelho & touch of muscat wholebunch pressed, wild yeast fermented & old-oaked 18 months to add complex layers (peach, orange, quince) to gently spiced oak. Steely oak ties it all together on the finish, beyond which the flavours echo endlessly as in **21** (95).

Not tasted: **Magnetic North**. Discontinued: **Lost & Found**. — DS

Location: Hermanus ▪ WO: Western Cape/Swartland/Citrusdal Mountain/Stellenbosch/Franschhoek/ Hemel-en-Aarde Ridge ▪ Est 2010 ▪ 1stB 2011 ▪ Closed to public ▪ Wine club ▪ Owner(s) Chris & Suzaan Alheit ▪ Cellarmaster(s) Chris Alheit ▪ Winemaker(s) Chris Alheit & Suzaan Alheit, with Gabriel du Bois (Jun 2020) ▪ 150t/±7,000cs own label 100% white ▪ PO Box 711 Hermanus 7200 ▪ office@alheitvineyards.co.za ▪ www. alheitvineyards.co.za

Allée Bleue Wines   (Ⓨ) (Ⓟ) (Ⓐ) (Ⓞ) (Ⓑ)

The avenue of imposing bluegums in rural Franschhoek that inspired the brand name leads to a German-owned wine and lifestyle estate where refurbishments to the ca 1690 manor, tasting lounge and bistro were underway at press time. The diverse visitor offering is a strong focus, and constantly updated, lately with pairings of pinotage and biltong, and cap classique and local confectionery. Fruit for the tiered ranges is sourced as far away as Piekenierskloof, and vinified by Van Zyl du Toit and team 'to reflect a true sense of the wine, and project it such that it enhances the drinking experience. The key is knowing when to intervene'.

Black Series

★★★★☆ **Old Vine Pinotage** (Ⓐ) (Ⓦ) What could have been a blockbuster - ripe plummy fruit lavished with 100% new oak, 16 months - handled with restraint, so **20** (93) shows variety's freshness & elegance as well as perfumed mocha & liquorice opulence. From venerable Piekenierskloof bushvines.

★★★★☆ **Single Vineyard Syrah** Delicious **18** ⑨①, as dark & rich as last, from certified single-vineyard, enjoys 80% new oak, 16 months. Generous dark chocolate & mulberry flavours are enveloped in a plush texture, dry tannins keep ripeness in check.

★★★★☆ **L'Amour Toujours** ⊘ ⊛ Delicate fragrance & dark-fruited power create a riveting tension in stunning cab franc blend with cab, merlot & soupçon petit verdot, from Banghoek vines. Serious oak, 60% new, 18 months, but long skin contact ensures perfumed fruit flavours remain the focus of **18** ⑨③. Lifted freshness veils 14.5% alc, as it did on **17** ★★★★★ ⑨⑤.

★★★★ **Isabeau Chardonnay** Golden hue reflects gravitas of quince- & citrus-toned **21** ⑧⑨, recently 100% chardonnay, previous included dashes semillon, viognier. Reined-in 10% new oak retains rich aromas & beautiful balance.

Premium range

★★★★☆ **Pinotage** ⊘ Subtle spiced plum & fragrant tobacco from home-farm & old-vine Piekenierskloof grapes in **20** ⑨⓪. Firm yet supple structure layers spice with overt oak, 50% new, 16 months, 5% American. A trifle rustic but understated, satisfying food partner.

★★★★ **Sauvignon Blanc** ⊘ Ripe **22** ⑧⑥ ex Darling offers powerful fig & gooseberry flavours, waxy overlay from splash of semillon, fine balance. Previous, without semillon, from Walker Bay.

★★★★ **Méthode Cap Classique Brut** ⊘ Dry **19** ⑧⑨ sparkler interleaves textured pinot noir & elegant chardonnay for green apple, honey & smoky almond profile. 36 months on lees add buttered toast opulence, best with food. No **18**, **17**.

Shiraz ★★★★ Familiar red-fruit profile elevated by savoury nuance in **20** ⑧⑤. Dry, spicy tannins offer piquant farewell. **Shiraz Rosé** ★★★ Softly dry, salmon pink **23** ⑧① fleshed out by splash semillon. Strawberry notes & gentle acid for effortless sunset sipping, well chilled. Not tasted: **Chenin Blanc**, **Méthode Cap Classique Brut Rosé**.

Starlette range

Shiraz Rosé ★★★ Dashes semillon & sugar lend plumpness to **23** ⑧⓪. Balanced quaffing, with savoury red berry flavours & crisp finish. **Blanc** ★★★ Lively, tropical-toned sauvignon & chenin in accessible, eminently drinkable **23** ⑧②. Value for money crowd-pleaser. In abeyance: **Pinotage**, **Rouge**. — DS

Location/map: Franschhoek ▪ Map grid reference: C6 ▪ WO: Franschhoek/Piekenierskloof/Banghoek/ Piekenierskloof-Franschhoek/Darling ▪ Est 1690 ▪ 1stB 2001 ▪ Tasting & sales Mon–Fri/pub hols 9-5 Sat 10-5 Sun 10-4 ▪ Tasting fee: Signature tasting R115pp/5 wines, Estate tasting R75pp/5 wines ▪ Bistro Allée Bleue ▪ Picnics seasonal (booking required) ▪ Tour groups by appt ▪ Conferences ▪ Weddings ▪ Allée Bleue accommodation: Kendall Cottage & Manor House Suites ▪ Owner(s) DAUPHIN Entwicklungs-und Beteiligungs GMH (Germany) ▪ Winemaker(s) Van Zyl du Toit (Jul 2009), with Armand Hartzer (Dec 2019) ▪ Viticulturist(s) Douw Willemse (Sep 2008) ▪ 210ha/31ha (ptage, pinot, shiraz, chard, chenin, sauv, sem, viog) ▪ 450t/30,000cs 45% red 50% white 5% MCC ▪ IPW ▪ PO Box 100 Groot Drakenstein 7680 ▪ info@alleebleue. com ▪ www.alleebleue.co.za ▪ **T +27 (0)21-874-1021**

Allesverloren   ⊘ 🍴 🅐 ♿

There will almost certainly be a popping of corks at Allesverloren this year, as the Malan family celebrate the 320th anniversary of their estate on the slope of Swartland's Kasteelberg. At least some of the stoppers are likely to be from their ever-popular Fine Old Vintage 'port', the modern incarnation of the sweet fortified wine made by forebear Daniël Francois, who arrived at the mostly wheat-producing estate in 1872, found vines there, and developed a market for his wine. Today's 100,000 cases are produced by 5th-generation cellarmaster Danie and wife Juanita, son and farm manager Fanie, and daughter and marketer Danielle.

★★★★ **Cabernet Sauvignon** Ripe redcurrants & raspberries & on **20** ⑧⑧, generous 14.6% alc in balance with brisk acid & core of sweet fruit. 18 months in oak, 30% new, for extra grip & cigarbox nuance.

★★★★ **Shiraz** ⊘ Subtle, beguiling, carefully oaked **19** ★★★★★ ⑨⓪ regains elegance of **17** ⑧⑦ after ripe but tight **18** ⑧⑥. Fresh berry flavours laced with woodsmoke, lovely silky tannins soften the texture. Only 20% spent year in oak, just 5% new.

★★★★ **Tinta Barocca** From 1958 & 1996 dryland vineyards, **19** ⑧⑧ edges ahead of previous with charcuterie, spice & deep black fruit, enlivening acid & charming rusticity to layered, juicy tannins. Mix old & new oak, 8 months.

★★★★☆ **Três Vermelhos** Characterful unfortified blend 3 port grapes: souzão, tinta & touriga. **20** ⑨⓪ full-bore black cherry & spiced plum, pot-pourri & orange zest. Smooth tannins, 18 months oak, 20% new, barely noticeable. Plush, but leaves dry impression.

★★★★ **Fine Old Vintage** Ⓐ Harvest-dependent melange tintas barocca, amarela & francisca, tourigas nacional & franca, souzão, pontac. **18** ★★★★★ ⑨⓪ vivacious red fruit & cinnamon from 20 months in old oak. Finer balance than last-tasted **16** ⑧⑧, bold acid keeping 18.7% alc & 126 g/L sugar in check.

Tinta Rosé ⑰ ★★★★ From Portuguese grapes (tinta & 3 others), a rarity in SA. Now bottled, **22** ⑧⑤ retains generous strawberry & peach flavours, appealing medium feel & dryness, keen acid-fruit balance.

Chenin Blanc Ⓔ ★★★★ Sunny, fresh tropical & citrus tones on **22** ⑧⑤, pineapple, mango & grapefruit, appealing soft texture from 3 months lees contact. Not tasted: **Red Muscadel**. In abeyance: **Touriga Nacional, Fanie Malan Reserve**. Discontinued: **1704 Red**. — ML, CvZ

Location: Riebeek West ▪ Map/WO: Swartland ▪ Map grid reference: D6 ▪ Est 1704 ▪ Tasting & sales Mon-Fri 9-5 Sat/Sun/pub hols 10-3 ▪ Tasting R50/5 wines ▪ Closed Good Fri, Dec 25 & Jan 1 ▪ Cellar tours by appt ▪ Pleasant Pheasant restaurant T +27 (0)22-461-2170 Wed-Sat 9-3 & 6-10 Sun 9-4 ▪ Facilities for children ▪ Owner(s) Malan Boerdery Trust ▪ Cellarmaster(s) Danie Malan (Nov 1987) ▪ Winemaker(s) Wilhelm de Vries (Jan 2016) ▪ 227ha/115ha (cab, shiraz & various port varieties) ▪ 100,000cs own label 90% red 10% white ▪ PO Box 23 Riebeek West 7306 ▪ info@allesverloren.co.za ▪ www.allesverloren.co.za ▪ **T +27 (0)22-461-2589**

Almenkerk Wine Estate   Ⓠ Ⓜ Ⓐ Ⓘ

This small family estate in Elgin was established by Joris and Natalie van Almenkerk two decades ago. It was an apple farm when they bought it, and some orchards remain, though the painstakingly established vineyards are the core of their concern. In the state-of-the-art cellar whose building Joris oversaw, Cameron Corney has joined him as winemaker. The core range of single-vineyard, largely naturally fermented wines is supplemented by the Lace line-up – the name alluding to the family's Belgian origins - and a Flemish Masters series, paying 'tribute to the painters of our home country'. These have not been tasted by us.

★★★★ **Merlot** Flavourful **21** ⑧⑨, first since **18** ⑧⑦, has some cool-climate herbal notes along with varietal fruitcake ones. Well balanced, light-feeling, bright & well structured. Natural ferment; 18 months oak starting to integrate well.

★★★★☆ **Chardonnay** Ⓐ Citrus & tropical notes on **21** ⑨④, with a nutty contribution to the complexity from oak (nearly half new) - all barrels assessed as the wine matures for 8- 11 months. Youthful & vibrant, with fresh acidity & a light phenolic grip; fairly restrained but sufficiently intense & satisfying.

★★★★☆ **Sauvignon Blanc** Panoply of tropical, floral & blackcurrant notes on forwardly fragrant, flavourful & rather gorgeous **22** ⑨②. Partly naturally fermented in older oak. Lees contact adds to the textured richness, but freshness dominates.— TJ

Location/map/WO: Elgin ▪ Map grid reference: B2 ▪ Est 2004 ▪ 1stB 2009 ▪ Tasting, sales & cellar tours Tue-Sat 10-4 ▪ Open pub hols except on Sun/Mon ▪ Meals/picnics by prior booking (min 12 pax), or BYO picnic ▪ CrossFit hiking trail 'Active@Almenkerk'; & 5km trail through orchards, vineyards & wild parts of estate ▪ Conservation area ▪ Heliport ▪ Boule court ▪ Wine club ▪ Owner(s) Van Almenkerk family ▪ Cellarmaster(s) Joris van Almenkerk ▪ Winemaker(s) Cameron Corney (Aug 2022), with Danver van Wyk (Feb 2009) ▪ Viticulturist(s) Michael Keown (Jan 2014) ▪ 104.2ha/15ha (cabs s/f, malbec, merlot, mourv, p verdot, shiraz, chard, sauv, viog) ▪ 100t/5,000cs own label 65% red 30% white 5% rosé ▪ Brands for clients: Pot Luck Club ▪ SIZA, WWF-SA Conservation Champion ▪ Viljoenshoop Rd, Grabouw 7160 ▪ info@almenkerk.co.za ▪ www.almenkerk.co.za ▪ **T +27 (0)21-848-9844**

☐ **Almost Zero** *see* Van Loveren Family Vineyards
☐ **Alpha Bravo Charlie** *see* Lieben Wines

Alto Wine Estate   Ⓠ Ⓘ

In the hands since 2020 of German businessman Hans von Staff-Reitzenstein (also sole- or part-owner of nearby Stellenzicht and Ernie Els), this historic top-end winery in Stellenbosch's 'golden triangle' is understood to be the oldest red-wine-only producer in SA, with another distinction of having only 5 winemakers in more than a century of production. Presiding over the latest harvest was incumbent Bertho van der Westhuizen, whose predecessors, including his father Schalk, lend their initials to the pinnacle wine.

★★★★☆ **Cabernet Sauvignon** Noble & consistent, typifying the wines of Stellenbosch's 'golden triangle', previewed **19** Ⓝ inky & robust yet has innate vibrancy & freshness. Liquorice & wet earth nuances to tight-packed blackcurrant fruit, burnished 18 months in seasoned barriques. Mouthcoating tannins need more time, but already approachable.

★★★★☆ **Shiraz** Bold & concentrated, with tannins to match, **19** Ⓝ has ripe, rounded cherry & currant fruit, scrub & pepper from part wholebunch ferment, sweet spice from 18 months in small-oak, none new.

★★★★☆ **MPHS** Ⓐ Assured, aristocratic flag-bearer exudes class in **17** Ⓝ, cab with 10% cab franc, a change from 50/50 in **16** ★★★★★ Ⓝ. Impossibly dense & sumptuous black fruit, layered with truffle, tobacco & spice, partly from 18 months in new barrels, all set to unfurl over the next decade.

★★★★☆ **Estate Blend** Ⓐ Shift in style & blend in **20** ★★★★★ Ⓝ sees cab leading 30% shiraz & dab cab franc. Extraordinary extract & intensity of plump, ripe black fruit is balanced & supported by a suede tannin structure, 18 months in 70% new oak provide platform for the long haul. Last **18** Ⓝ was 4-way Bordeaux blend.

★★★★ **Rouge** Ⓥ Ubiquitous, high-volume Cape classic delivers customary quality & value in **21** Ⓝ, a 5-way cab-led Bordeaux blend. Cassis pairs with signature liquorice-iodine gravitas, gains refined oak spicing from 14-16 months in barriques, 20% new.

Not tasted: **Fine Old Vintage**. — GdB

Location/map/WO: Stellenbosch ▪ Map grid reference: E8 ▪ Est 1693 ▪ 1stB 1922 ▪ Tasting & sales Mon-Sun 10-5; Restaurant Wed-Sun 10-5 (seasonal hours); Sunset Rouge evenings - every Friday (Nov-Apr) ▪ Fee R50-R120/wine tasting ▪ Closed Good Fri, Dec 25 & Jan 1 ▪ Biltong & wine pairing, advance booking required ▪ MTB track ▪ Owner(s) Hans von Staff-Reitzenstein ▪ Cellarmaster(s) Bertho van der Westhuizen (May 2015) ▪ Viticulturist(s) Bertho van der Westhuizen & Danie van Zyl ▪ 191ha/92ha (cabs s/f, malbec, merlot, p verdot, shiraz) ▪ 800t/100,000cs own label 100% red ▪ PO Box 286 Stellenbosch 7599 ▪ info@altowines.co.za ▪ www.alto.co.za ▪ **T +27 (0)21-881-3884**

Alvi's Drift Private Cellar   Ⓠ Ⓒ

A vast family agribusiness, based on 6,000 ha of Breede River Valley land, 450 ha of which planted with vines. These and the cellar are the responsibility of former medical doctor and namesake of the founder, Alvi van der Merwe, his brother Johan tasked with running the mixed farming. They claim sustainability but walk their talk. There's conversion to solar energy, more efficient lighting and cooling technologies, sophisticated waste management and natural pest control, to name a few examples. The wine range is diverse and creative, and concrete fermenters and foudres recently added to the cellar will help keep it so. Evidence that Alvi and team are doing things right lies in both ongoing critical success and the 330,000 cases that traverse the low-water bridge that names the brand, on their way to winelovers around the world.

Flagship wine

★★★★☆ **Verreaux Pinotage** Ⓐ Pinotage taken to a more serious level than before. Traditional open tank ferment & punch downs for maximum extraction, then all-new French & American oak, 18 months. Deep ruby, a complex mix of red & dark berries in **20** Ⓝ, shot through with savoury spice, including white pepper, tannins amenable, a hidden muscle tone for cellaring.

Icon range

★★★★☆ **Albertus Viljoen Bismarck** Ⓖ Bold, opulent **19** Ⓝ from 43% shiraz, with pinotage, cab & 5 others. Bright, clean fruit & spicy tobacco, all winningly coddled with some sweetness in firm structure.

★★★★☆ **Albertus Viljoen Chardonnay** Full treatment, wholebunch, wild ferment/year 70% new oak, & **21** Ⓝ repays the attention with intense citrus & stonefruit, oat biscuit threaded throughout. Showy, back on track after **20** ★★★★ Ⓝ, there's richness, opulence. Zesty acid gives lift, vibrancy, a future.

★★★★☆ **Albertus Viljoen Chenin Blanc** Ⓐ Combo wild & cultured yeast, ferment/year 70% new barrels. **21** Ⓝ is Lemon Cream biscuit-scented with a lime overlay, strengthening in the flavours. There's concentration & intensity, mouthwatering zestiness promising a long life. Still youthfully taut.

Reserve range

★★★★☆ **Drift Fusion** Ⓥ Ⓐ Cape Blend, pinotage, cab, 3 others, vinified separately in closed/open tank or barrel to best suit: then year oak, part American, 33% new. **20** Ⓝ glossy dark-toned berries, mixed spice overlay including vanilla, black pepper. Backbone of firm but ripe tannins, supple texture. More impressive than **19** ★★★★ ⑧⑧.

★★★★ **Chardonnay** ⊘ Tank & barrel ferment gives **21** ⑧⑧ fruit-forward styling, mixed citrus, becoming more lemony in the flavours, oak's seasoning a buttered toast note. Well-balanced fruit & freshness, zippy acid to keep it in good condition for years to come.

★★★★☆ **Muscat Nectarinia** Dessert from 25-40 year old muscat blanc à petit grains, extended skin contact to extract sugar & juice from dried berries, long & slow wild ferment to 15.7% alc, 4 years old barrels. Amber-hued **17** ★★★★★ ⑨⑦ intense honey & raisin sweetness (375 g/L) yet astonishingly drinkable, an apricot freshness stops it being syrupy. Sumptuous & ageworthy step up on **16** ⑨⓪. 375 ml.

★★★★☆ **Sauvignon Blanc** ⊘ Small new barrels 6 months, but **22** ⑨⓪'s fruit still shines through, watermelon & greengage, a delicate smoky nuance the only evidence of oaking. Zinging freshness adds vibrancy, promises a future.

★★★★☆ **CVC** ⊘ 67% chenin with viognier & chardonnay, mainly barrel ferment/11 months, 30% new, varieties handled separately, then selection for blending, there's serious intent in **21** ⑨④. Perfume leaps from the glass, peach & melon, oak adding nicely rounded body, melba toast note in the flavours. Crisp finish promises ageability, food compatibility.

221 range

★★★★ **Chenin Blanc** ⊘ Only 25% oaked to highlight primary fruit, forthcoming stonefruit & Bosc pear. Dry **22** ⑧⑧ has individual character, doesn't follow the herd. Palate tangy, a fruit-acid interplay, nice crisp finish. Back on track after **21** ★★★★ ⑧⑤.

★★★★ **Sauvignon Blanc** ⊘ Quarter oaked, 4 months, rest tank, to showcase grape's essence. **22** ⑧⑨ less fruity than Reserve, more green notes, lemongrass & pea, suggestion of flintiness, all following through to palate, ending fresh. Lovely focus & precision.

Pinotage ⊘ ★★★★ Wild ferment, barrel ageing for 30%, rest tank, to showcase **21** ⑧④'s fruit & create different style to Verreaux. Plush blueberries, juicy & smooth, easy tannin grip at the end. **Special Cuvée** ⊘ ★★★☆ Shiraz with cab & 5 others, made separately, partly in tank, some wild ferment, then selection for bright berries, spice highlights. **21** ⑧④ texture streamlined, smooth & juicy.

Sparkling range

★★★★ **Brut Rosé** Pinot noir & 45% chardonnay, pale salmon **NV** ⑧⑥ bubbly had lees contact, but essentially fresh-fruity styled as aperitif. Apple & strawberry, a tangy note from perfectly judged acid & sugar, finishes dry. More to offer than last.

★★★★ **Brut Blanc de Blanc** Fruit rules in **NV** ⑧⑥ sparkling from chardonnay; citrus aromas, some crunchy apple, no lees effect, this is about freshness. Elegant & dry, another perfect aperitif.

Cap Classique range

★★★★ **Brut** ⊘ Chardonnay with 30% pinot noir, 24 months on lees, **NV** ⑧⑦ doesn't have a shy bone in its body. Powerful stonefruit & barley sugar scents, good rounded texture despite the slim 12.5% alc (as next), ends dry & fruity-fresh.

★★★★☆ **Brut Nature** Consistent handling: wild ferment, 36 months on lees, no dosage. Medium-gold **NV** ⑨③ ex chardonnay & 30% pinot noir, honeyed preserved citrus & melon, toasted brioche aromas, lively mousse & freshness. Lovely dry elegance on extended lemony finish.— CR

Location/map/WO: Worcester ▪ Map grid reference: B5 ▪ Est 1928 ▪ 1stB 2004 ▪ Temporarily closed for renovations, plse phone ahead ▪ Sales Mon-Fri 9-5 ▪ Closed all pub hols ▪ Farm produce ▪ Wine club ▪ Owner(s) Alvi & Johan van der Merwe ▪ Cellarmaster(s) Riaan Marais ▪ Winemaker(s) Alvi van der Merwe, Wim Viljoen & Bernard Louw ▪ Viticulturist(s) Jan du Toit ▪ 6,000ha/420ha (22 varieties, mostly ptage, shiraz, chard, chenin) ▪ ±7,500t/330,000cs own label ▪ IPW, WIETA ▪ PO Box 126 Worcester 6849 ▪ admin@alvisdrift.co.za ▪ www.alvisdrift.co.za ▪ **T +27 (0)21-905-0653**

☐ **Amandla** see Adama Wines
☐ **Amatra** see Catherine Marshall Wines
☐ **Ama Ulibo** see Goedverwacht Wine Estate

Ambeloui Wine Cellar

A quarter-century of specialising in premium cap classique was greeted last year with the best possible celebration - more top-class bubbly, in the form of a new standout Brut that continues the tradition of naming wines and vintages for members of the Christodoulou family. 'Miranda' honours daughter Miranda Green who latterly took the reins as winery owner and cellarmaster, working alongside her father Nick and brother Alexis in the Hout Bay cellar and ambeloui (Cypriot for 'small vineyard').

★★★★☆ **Méthode Cap Classique Brut Miranda** (NEW) (🐝) Celebratory sparkling is 60% pinot noir with chardonnay. **NV** (93) brut styled but bursting with ripe apple, honey & zesty citrus, subtly but richly underscored by toasted nut & brioche from lengthy 72 months on lees. Harmonious, fresh & refined.

★★★★☆ **Méthode Cap Classique Brut Rosé Rosanna** (❡) Reliably superior sparkler, 60/40 pinot noir & chardonnay in sumptuous **NV** (92), generous red berry fruit, subtle brioche. Ready now but good for years to come. Small portion oaked, 36 months on lees.

★★★★☆ **Méthode Cap Classique Brut** (❡) Four vintages of stylish dry pinot noir & chardonnay bubbly still available: **19** (93) 'Anne', 54% pinot, 36 months on lees, most balanced & structured, refined & long lived. **18** (90) 'Ceri', 53% chardonnay, 48 months, ripe & even more supple than **17** (90) 'Martin', 52% chardonnay, 60 months, very fresh but leaner, more savoury. **16** ★★★★ (88) 'Luvuyo', 60% pinot noir, 24 months, fruity & fresh, clean & precise. 10% oaked, year, as all.

★★★★ **Méthode Cap Classique Brut Nicholas** (❡) Fresh, versatile **NV** (88) bubbly from 64% chardonnay, pinot noir. Just 24 months on lees but ample almond & brioche, rich & appealing. — MW

Location: Hout Bay ▪ WO: Western Cape ▪ Est 1994 ▪ 1stB 1998 ▪ Open for sales on 1st weekend of Nov annually ▪ Annual harvest festival (March) ▪ Owner(s)/cellarmaster(s) Miranda Green ▪ Winemaker(s) Nick Christodoulou (1994) & Alexis Christodoulou (2009), with Miranda Green (2020) ▪ Viticulturist(s) Miranda Green (2020), Alexis Christodoulou (2009) ▪ 1ha/0.5ha (pinot noir/meunier, chard) ▪ 15t/3,000cs own label 100% MCC ▪ PO Box 26800 Hout Bay 7872 ▪ wine@ambeloui.co.za ▪ www.ambeloui.co.za ▪ **T +27(0)71-850-0376**

Amperbo (NEW)

The vines on Pieter and Michelle Smit's sloping farm reach higher and higher, till they're 'Almost At The Top' of the Bottelary Hills. Viticulturist Pieter's lifelong dream was an own wine brand and, in a basic on-site cellar housed in two converted garages, in 2020 he crafted his first wine - which promptly won gold at a local competition. Encouraged to 'reach for the stars', they've added wines while focusing on the original unusual pinotage blend to develop it into the flagship. 'Work with nature and look after him' is their motto.

Amperbo range

★★★★ **Infinitum** 5-part Bordeaux blend with cab in charge at 83%, & **21** (86) does it proud. Expressive cassis, lovely cocoa savouriness from 22 months in small barrels (as all reds), quarter new. Streamlined texture, despite 15% alc, there's succulence coating the tannins.

Pinotage-Tempranillo ★★★★ 80% pinotage in **21** (85), voluptuous with dark fruit & chocolate, the oak adding a serious tone. Tannins firm, dry, but not harsh, there's current enjoyment but the best lies ahead.

Fantasia range

Merlot ★★★★ Herbaceous top note, with underlying red berries, **22** (83) has easy drinkability, the tannins smooth, accessible, whiff of mint in the flavours. **Pinotage** ★★★★ Burly (15% alc), loaded with savoury spice from 20% new barrels, **22** (83) demands attention. Dark-toned fruit, cocoa & salty liquorice, it's still an infant, tannins firm, ending dry. **Dry Red** (✓) ★★★★ Eclectic 6-part blend, cab-led at 30%, seasoned barrels only, **NV** (83) shows plummy fruit threaded through with savoury spice, nice palate appeal from fresh, fruity flavours, supple tannins. **Malbec Rosé** ★★★ Pale pink, slender (11% alc) **23** (78), bright fruited, red berries & cherries but only in perfume, the flavours more muted, even a mineral note. — CR, CvZ

Location: Stellenbosch ▪ WO: Coastal ▪ Est 2020 ▪ 1stB 2021 ▪ Closed to public ▪ Sales online ▪ Owner(s) Amperbo Boerdery Bk ▪ Cellarmaster(s)/winemaker(s) Pieter Smit (Jan 2020) ▪ Viticulturist(s) Pieter Smit (Jan 2010) ▪ 68ha/5oha (cab, merlot, ptage, tempranillo) ▪ 350t/842cs own label 93% red 7% rosé ▪ WIETA ▪ PO Box 6025 Stellenbosch 7612 ▪ wines@amperboplaas.co.za ▪ www.amperbowines.co.za ▪ **T +27 (0)82-784-3208**

Andreas Wines

These fine syrahs are grown on a small 18th-century property in Wellington, latterly owned by UK share-holders, and crafted the past seven years by cellarmaster Shaun Meyeridricks, who recently took delivery of additional French barrels and installed a backup power supply, among 'numerous other enhancements to the farm and cellar'. Luxury accommodation is offered in elegantly restored Cape Dutch surrounds.

Andreas range

★★★★ **Syrah** Attractive stemmy spice from 30% wholebunch ferment overlays rich & generous **20** ⑧⑧'s plum & fresh prune tones. Decently dry, with refined structure of tannin & 18 months oak, 10% new.

Lithic Whisperer range

★★★★☆ **Syrah** ⑦ 30% wholebunch for **19** ★★★★ ⑧⑨, with berries & earthy pomegranate fragrance, toasty spice from 18 months in oak. Crisp & crunchy on palate, just the right touch of juicy mulberry on finish to match the good, dry grip. Smidgen less intensity than **18** ⑨⓪.— ML

Location/map: Wellington ▪ Map grid reference: C3 ▪ WO: Bovlei ▪ Est 2003 ▪ 1stB 2004 ▪ Tasting & sales by appt Mon-Fri 9-5 ▪ Closed all pub hols ▪ Cellar tours by appt ▪ Luxury accommodation ▪ Owner(s) Andreas Wine Trading Incorporated (England) ▪ Cellarmaster(s)/winemaker(s) Shaun Meyeridricks (Dec 2017) ▪ 6ha/4.5ha (mourv, shiraz) ▪ 43t/4,688cs own label 100% red ▪ PO Box 892 Wellington 7654 ▪ info@andreas.co.za ▪ www.andreas.co.za ▪ **T +27 (0)21-873-2286**

André van Rensburg Artisan Wines

Celebrated former Vergelegen cellarmaster André van Rensburg in 2023 released a small parcel of Bordeaux-style wine and saw it snapped up by eager fans. We hope to taste the follow-up releases next time.

Location: Sir Lowry's Pass ▪ Private tastings only by prior arrangement (min 4, max 8 persons) ▪ Owner(s)/winemaker(s) André van Rensburg ▪ 87 High Riding Estate, Sir Lowry's Pass Village, Somerset Wes 7130 ▪ andrewynmaker@gmail.com ▪ **T +27 (0)72-415-3788**

☐ **Angels Tears** *see* Grande Provence Heritage Wine Estate

Angus Paul Wines

Chenin and pinotage remain the focus, says Angus Paul, with his new cinsault (from a leased old block of vines originally destined for blending) being 'a nice refrain' within his range of somewhat mysteriously named wines. He's humorously described his minimalistic winemaking as 'undogmatic but always with a frugality of input', now adding that he is 'still cheaping out and not paying for yeast'. This admirable restraint happens at the communal Karibib Wine Craft cellar in Stellenbosch, also the continued focus of his explorations for grapes.

★★★★ **Diapsalmata Cinsault** ㊉ Pure red-fruit fragrance & flavour, with savoury hint, on charming **22** ⑧⑨. Fresh & lively balance, with a bit of grip. Light-feeling 12.5% alc; a touch thin on mid-palate. Maturation in neutral 8-year-old barrels, like all these, for textural benefit.

★★★★ **Transient Lands Pinotage** ㊐ A good example of the new-wave fresh & comparatively light, elegant pinotages (13.1% alc here). Aromatic **22** ★★★★☆ ⑨③ even more attractive than **21** ⑧⑨. Brightly vivacious & flavourful though not overstated & more than simply fruity. Fine tannin adds to the succulent grip. 15% wholebunch. All wines bar Cinsault also in magnum.

★★★★☆ **Barbary Fictions Chenin Blanc** ㊐ Chenin from a cool, 1972 Bottelary hilltop vineyard. **22** ⑨③ rounder, showing more yellow peachy fruit, less bracing than Flight version; but also a fine acidity, here rather lemony, with a stony & savoury quality on its lengthy finish.

★★★★☆ **On A Flight Of Furious Fancies Chenin Blanc** ㊐ Usual core of restrained but luscious sweet fruit on **22** ⑨④, along with scrubby hillside notes, & a hint of salt on the long finish. At 12.6% alc, a little lighter-feeling than Barbary; the acidity a bit more succulently pronounced & grippy, but in harmony. Polkadraai Hills origin. These whites also in older oak.

Not tasted: **Mesas Pinotage**. In abeyance: **Hespers**. — TJ

Location: Stellenbosch ▪ WO: Western Cape/Bottelary/Polkadraai Hills ▪ Est 2020 ▪ 1stB 2021 ▪ Tasting & sales Wed-Sat 11-7 Sun 11-3 at Tasting Room at Karibib Wine Craft ▪ Closed Dec 25 & Jan 1 ▪ Owner(s) Angus Paul ▪ Cellarmaster(s)/winemaker(s) Angus Paul (Jan 2020) ▪ 12t/1,100cs own label 50% red 50% white ▪ Karibib

Wine Craft, Polkadraai Rd, Stellenbosch 7600 ▪ angus@anguspaulwines.com ▪ www.anguspaulwines.com ▪
T +27 (0)76-132-2864

☐ **Anker** *see* Scali
☐ **Annabelle** *see* KWV Wines

Annandale Wines

Hempies du Toit, rugby Springbok legend and veteran Helderberg winegrower-owner, opened the doors of his craft winery on Annandale Road 28 years ago with a now voguish low-and-slow approach, letting natural processes run their course, which included very long maturation cycles. There have been some earlier releases lately, but all are still red, and grown on the estate, where deli cheese and meat platters are offered.

★★★★ **Cabernet Sauvignon** ⓐ First since **12** ★★★☆ ⑧③, rustic but appealing **20** ⑧⑦, solid black fruit spiced with roast nuts & leather. Though oaked 2 years, as Cavalier, tannins still bold, need time.

★★★★☆ **Shiraz** ⓐ First since **05** ⑨⓪, **18** ⑨⓪ spent 3 years in 300L barrels, shows supple body & texture with brooding black cherry & plum fruit elevated by hints of pepper & scrub. Poised & elegant.

★★★★ **Cavalier** ⓐ Atypically youthful release, **20** ⑧⑧ cab, merlot & shiraz blend has well-formed & solid black fruit with attractive earthy notes, smooth, ripe tannins. First tasted since **07** ⑧⑧.

Not tasted: **Charlbert Merlot**, **CVP**. In abeyance: **Cabernet Franc**. — GdB

Location/map/WO: Stellenbosch ▪ Map grid reference: E8 ▪ Est/1stB 1996 ▪ Tasting & sales Mon-Sat 9-5 ▪ Closed Easter Fri-Mon, Ascension day & Dec 25 ▪ Farm produce ▪ Deli cheese & meat platters ▪ Wine club ▪ Owner(s) Hempies du Toit ▪ Winemaker(s)/viticulturist(s) Hempies du Toit (1996) ▪ 72ha/45ha (cabs s/f, merlot, shiraz) ▪ 250t/10,000cs own label 100% red ▪ PO Box 12681 Stellenbosch 7613 ▪ info@annandale. co.za ▪ www.annandale.co.za ▪ **T** +27 (0)21-881-3560

Anthology Wines

It's been ten years since Cape-born, Gauteng-based business analyst Christian Naudé crafted the openers to his vinous anthology in the cellar on De Goede Sukses, home of Marklew Family Wines: small batches of chardonnay and cabs sauvignon and franc from single blocks on the Stellenbosch farm. His approach, source and materials are unchanged, the vintage tasted for this guide made 'as we watched the pandemic roll in'.

★★★★ **Cabernet Sauvignon** ⓐ Brawny, super-ripe **17** ⑧⑨ followed by laudably restrained **19** ⑧⑥, leaner, tauter, with well-judged oak, blackcurrant fruit & attractive leathery tannins. WO Stellenbosch.

★★★★☆ **Cabernet Franc** Robust **20** ★★★★ ⑧⑦ shows good typicity: leafiness, minerality & taut black fruit. Tannins & smoky oak-spices still touch apart, the whole not quite as well-assembled as last **18** ⑨①.

★★★★ **Chardonnay** ⓐ Smooth & polished **NV** ⑧⑦ blends wines from 2018, 2019 & 2020 vintages. Nicely dry & just 12% alc, salty-savoury lick to lemon-lime fruit from deft partial oaking, 50% new.— GdB

Location: Stellenbosch ▪ WO: Simonsberg-Stellenbosch/Stellenbosch ▪ Est/1stB 2014 ▪ Closed to public ▪ Sales online ▪ Owner(s) Christian Naudé ▪ Winemaker(s) Christian Naudé (Feb 2014) ▪ 55ha/±40ha (cabs s/f, merlot, ptage, shiraz, chard, sauv) ▪ 2,250cs own label 66% red 34% white ▪ De Goede Sukses, R44 Muldersvlei Stellenbosch 7600 ▪ info@anthologywines.co.za ▪ www.anthologywines.co.za ▪ **T** +27 (0)83-238-5887

Anthonij Rupert Wyne

International businessman Johann Rupert's model wine enterprise, named after his late brother, has 18th-century Franschhoek estate L'Ormarins as its exquisite, mountain-silhouetted home. The venture encompasses an internationally awarded sextet of brands, and upscale visitor attractions such as the remarkable, 100+ year retrospective Franschhoek Motor Museum, linked to the two tasting venues by specially built trams. Grapes are sourced from own prime vineyards in Darling, Swartland, Elandskloof and the home farm, as well as exceptional vineyard sites, including old-vine parcels around the winelands. Vinification is done by specialist winemakers in custom facilities, such as the Cape Of Good Hope Cellar, devoted to the eponymous range, with on-trend, Italian amphora-shaped concrete tanks.

Anthonij Rupert range

★★★★☆ **Cabernet Sauvignon** ⓐ Ripe & modern, with cab's firm tannins & vanilla sheen of 50% new oak embracing deep bramble fruit, **19** ⑨④ structured for cellaring, as all these. Wild yeast ferment, 18-24 months in barrique, unfined/filtered, as range. No **18**.

★★★★☆ **Cabernet Franc** ⊛ Statuesque tannins & oak cushioned by morello cherry & liquorice-nuanced black plum fruit, though **18** ⑨③ less fleshy than varietal siblings, shows more verve. Franschhoek WO, rest Coastal unless noted. No **17**.

★★★★☆ **Merlot** Oystershell, iodine & exotic charcuterie complexity to **18** ⑨①'s plush plum & mulberry fruit. Tannins less tight than last **16** ⑨①, form aided & mocha added by half new oak. Also in 1.5L & 3L, as all unless noted.

★★★★☆ **Syrah** ⊛ From home-farm block with echalas/staked-vine training system. Beautifully fragrant - pepper, fynbos, red plums & berries, vanilla - **18** ⑨④ as attractive on palate. Deeply concentrated, shaped & toned for development, oak in support. No **17**.

★★★★☆ **Anthonij Rupert** Careful selection & precise attention to detail, plus luxury of time, go into flagship Bordeaux red. Magnificent vintage **15** ⑨② still dark & intensely fruity, sweet vanilla from 80% new oak integrated & adding to allure. Cab, cab franc & merlot (41/32/27), similar blend to last **13** ⑨⓪.

★★★★☆ **Optima** ⊛ Venerable brand, consistently superior quality given the quantity. Cape Bordeaux, merlot with cab, cab franc & petit verdot in **20** ⑨④. Brambly forest floor hints, clean leather & dark fruit with spearmint accent, tannins firm but sweet & ageworthy. No **19**. 1.5L, 3L & 5L options.

Cape Of Good Hope range

★★★★☆ **Parel Vallei Merlot** Small Helderberg suburban vineyard produces deeply rich fruit enlivened by crisp acid, sustained dry finish. **18** ⑨⓪'s plump palate laced with mocha & graphite from ferment/2 years in barrique, 30% new. Would benefit from time to settle.

★★★★☆ **Sneeuwkrans Pinot Noir** ⊘ From ±700-m Elandskloof vines, picked in 2 stages according to elevation, ripeness & clone, lightly brushed with older oak. Damp-leaf aromas mask delicate raspberry & cherry fruit of **20** ⑨⓪ in youth, may resolve with few years cellaring which availability of 1.5L encourages.

★★★★☆ **Basson Pinotage** Swartland-grown **19** ⑨⓪ quintessential plummy, meaty, woodsmoke character, in contrast to lighter-styled, bone-dry & deftly balanced **18** ⑨⓪. No new oak, tempered 2 years in bottle before release.

★★★★ **Riebeeksrivier Syrah** ⊘ Shale & clay vine (south & west aspects at 450-m elevation) on the Swartland property, daubs grenache noir, carignan, mourvèdre & viognier. **18** ★★★★☆ ⑨⓪ savoury but with plump mulberry fruit, added appeal of seamless tannin & oak, 18 months, all older, with greater sense of accomplishment than **17** ⑧⑨.

★★★★☆ **Riebeeksrivier Southern Slopes** ⊘ ⊛ 'Slopes' pair aim to show aspect/soil influence; here higher clay content of the Malmesbury shale. Confident **18** ⑨④'s white pepper whiffs from shiraz, spice & savoury extras from splashes mourvèdre, viognier, & 16-18 months seasoned oak.

★★★★☆ **Riebeeksrivier Western Slopes** ⊘ ⊛ Shale/schist soils give enticing floral lift, tensioned structure to **18** ⑨④, 64% shiraz with grenache noir & dab carignan. Impressive cassis & blackberry core woven with tannin & freshened by thrilling acid. For the long haul.

★★★★☆ **Serruria Chardonnay** Integrated **21** ⑨② from 2 elevated Elandskloof vineyards on decomposed shale. Scintillating acid permeating elegant & cool lemon fruit, creamy texture & subtle oak vanilla from only 30% in barrel, 30% new, vs 80% oaked, 25% new, last vintage.

★★★★☆ **Riebeeksrivier Chenin Blanc** ⊘ Vinous rather than fruity expression of chenin, typically with lively acid, uncompromising dryness & length. Lovely **22** ⑨⓪ has fynbos & earthy minerality, subtle dried apple note. Wild yeast ferment, 51% in barrel, 10% new, year on lees.

★★★★☆ **Van Lill Chenin Blanc** ⊛ ⊛ Expressive & thrilling Citrusdal Mountain version fruitier than Riebeeksrivier sibling, as poised & vibrant. **22** ⑨③'s soft peach & apricot has wet earth, nut & khaki bush nuances, a crystalline acid. Weight & texture from 57 year old bushvines & time in seasoned oak.

★★★★★ **Altima Sauvignon Blanc** ⊘ ⊛ Arresting **23** ⑨⑤ excites with seamless fantail of aromas & flavours from staggered picking of cool south-west facing Elandskloof vines. Excellent weight ex 4 months on lees, restrained 13% alc, exceptional persistence on the smooth farewell.

★★★★★ **Laing Groendruif Semillon** ⊛ ⊛ Deeply rich, supple & smooth gift of old vines on Citrusdal Mountain. **23** ★★★★★ ⑨③ embodies the best of the grape: thatch spine, lanolin sheen & chalky depth; quince & lemon thyme extras, waxy roundness, invigorating mineral acid. Like last tasted-2021, half old-oaked, 2 months, but lighter 12.5% alc.

★★★★☆ **Riebeeksrivier Caroline** ⊘ Sophisticated Swartland white blend, marsanne & roussanne seasoned with chenin piquepoul blanc & dash viognier in **21** (90). Third old-oaked, adding attractive savouriness to floral, perfumed fruit. Fresh, salty finish for sipping at table or solo.

Occasional release: **Serruria Reserve Chardonnay**.

Jean Roi range

★★★★☆ **Cap Provincial Rosé** Honours the Huguenot founder, from Lourmarins in Provence, which French region inspired the light blush & bone-dry styling of **23** (90). Mostly grenache noir, dabs mourvèdre, cinsault & shiraz, brush of seasoned oak for a brilliant savoury aperitif, also in 1.5L. WO Swartland. No **22**.

L'Ormarins range

★★★★☆ **Die Ou Bosstok Chenin Blanc** 🐝 😊 Tiny volume off Paardeberg vines planted 1964, saved & transplanted to Franschhoek 44 years later. **22** (93) epitome of balance, intensity & length. Light toned despite weight & density of white peach & macadamia flavour thanks to salty minerality. Fermented in mix 50/50 steel & old 225L barrels. **21** untasted.

★★★★ **Brut Classique Rosé** Pale coral **NV** (89) cap classique, 51/49 pinot noir & chardonnay. Lipsmacking lemon tang & dryness to strawberries-&-cream character yet not too spirited for solo sipping.

★★★★☆ **Brut Rosé Vintage** ⊘ 🐝 Delightfully feisty **18** (93) cap classique from 51% pinot noir & chardonnay. Provençal paleness gives no clue to richness & weight of 2 years on lees, creaminess of mousse or echoing persistence of piquant raspberry & lemon. Oozes style & joie de vivre.

★★★★★ **Private Cuvée** 🐝 Exceptional cap classique from home-vine chardonnay & 31% pinot noir, indulged up to 84 months on lees. Poised **15** ★★★★☆ (94) pale onion skin hue, languid bead, developed bakery whiffs & touch of wood in classy mouthful, seamlessly woven, ready. **14** (96) also notably elegant.

★★★★★ **Blanc de Blancs** ⊘ 🐝 Exquisite **17** (95) chardonnay cap classique took the racy bubbles, frangipani & lemon sorbet features to the next level. **18** (95) keeps it there with elegant richness from 30% cask ferment of basewine, depth from 48 months on lees, beautifully finesse.

★★★★ **Brut Classique** Fine mousse, refined oystershell & apple nuances light up vivacious **NV** (89) cap classique from chardonnay, 23% pinot noir adding vinosity & palate weight. Minimum 24 months on lees.

★★★★ **Cape Vintage Reserve** Fine 'port' from Franschhoek touriga & souzão, 2 years in older barrique. Like **20** (86), fruitier than Douro template but **21** ★★★★☆ (90) balances that with firm tannin & convincing 20% alc fire. Winter's night friend now & for good few years.

★★★★☆ **Sagnac** 🥃 First SA brandy produced in original Armagnac alambic still from Robertson & Franschhoek colombard. Elegant **09** (93) alluring golden hue, delicate flavours finishing smooth, with creamy vanilla nuance. 500 ml.

Terra Del Capo range

★★★★ **Sangiovese** ⊘ Tangy aperitif or dinner mate. Earthy **21** (86) marked by variety's sour cherry character, dry tannin & acid bite. 15 months in cask.

★★★★ **Arné** Unusual co-ferment of half each sangiovese & merlot from Groenekloof, year in oak, 15% new. **20** (86) compelling, as dry as red sibling, less piquant, with softer, more pliable palate.

Pinot Grigio ⊘ ★★★☆ Signature macadamia nougat character mingled with yellow apple flavour & Granny Smith acid. Brief sojourn on lees for extra palate weight on **23** (85).

Protea range

. . . .

Dry Rosé ⊘ 🍷 ★★★☆ Perky pink **23** (83) offers strawberries & cranberries, subtle earthiness & good dry farewell. Mostly cinsault & 6 Bordeaux & Rhône partners. Also in 1.5L for extra conviviality. **Pinot Grigio** ⊘ 🍷 ★★★☆ Tasty alternative to the same-old white varieties. Crunchy green apple & lemongrass, added body & texture from lees ageing in **23** (83).

. . . .

Cabernet Sauvignon ⊘ ★★★☆ Textbook cassis & blackberry tones of **21** (83) unfettered by charry oak-stave notes & stern tannins of previous, old casks smooth the sweet fruit. These in distinctive, eye-catching & upcyclable bottles, each a different design, closed with 'twist & tipple' cork. **Merlot** 🍷 ★★★ Soft & smooth courtesy dab sugar, **20** (80) juicy plum fruit & faintest nudge of tannin. **Shiraz** ★★★ Mulberry fruit in undemanding **20** (82) has pleasant savoury spice & brush of tannin. **Chardonnay** ⊘ ★★★☆ Abundant citrus & winter melon flavours in **23** (83) get breadth from touch of oak, balance from crisp acid for easy enjoyment. **Chenin Blanc** ⊘ ★★★☆ Trademark thatch & thorntree aromas of bright, unassuming **23** (85) gain a yellow apple finish, palate weight & delicious creaminess from lees contact. **Sauvignon Blanc** ★★★ Anywhere, anytime sipper appeals with plump fresh fig, nettle & pear in balanced, crisp & dry **23** ⑧②. — DS, WB

Location/map: Franschhoek ▪ Map grid reference: C5 ▪ WO: Western Cape/Riebeeksrivier/Coastal/Franschhoek/ Elandskloof/Swartland/Citrusdal Mountain/Stellenbosch/Groenekloof ▪ Est 1714 ▪ 1stB 1982 ▪ Operating hours Mon-Sun 10-4.30 ▪ Two tasting rooms: Anthonij Rupert & Terra del Capo, both by appt only ▪ Fee R35-R150 per flight of 3-4 wines ▪ Closed Good Fri & Dec 25 ▪ Antipasti Bar serving local artisanal produce ▪ Black Angus biltong, truffles, olive oil & honey ▪ Franschhoek Motor Museum by appt only T +27 (0)21-874-9002; admittance R80pp, seniors & motor club members R60pp & children (3-12 yrs) R40pp ▪ Two specially built trams travel between the motor museum & tasting rooms ▪ Wine club ▪ Owner(s) Johann Rupert ▪ Winemaker(s) Dawie Botha (Jan 2005), Zanie Viljoen (Jan 2007), Vernon van der Hoven (2012) & Mark van Buuren (2013) ▪ 4 farms: total ±1,100ha/±210ha (cabs s/f, carignan, cinsaut, grenache, marsanne, merlot, mourv, pinot, sangio, shiraz, chard, chenin, pinot grigio, rouss) ▪ ISO 14001:2015, WWF-SA Conservation Champion ▪ PO Box 435 Franschhoek 7690 ▪ tasting@rupertwines.com ▪ www.rupertwines.com ▪ **T +27 (0)21-874-9074/+27 (0)21-874-9041 (tasting)**

Anura Vineyards   ⓛ ⑪ ⑩ ⑤

Extensive work is underway at the Bouma family estate near Paarl to upgrade and enlarge the cellar and its equipment. Included is a new hospitality area, with a tasting lounge and restaurant that will overlook, and give access to, both the cellar and the vineyards. This will join existing facilities like the deli-farm shop and cheesery, which welcome visitors as well as residents of the on-site luxury estate, Vini Fera. The wine and vine team led by Lance Bouma say their passion is red wine (more than a dozen planted varieties attest to that) and their goal 'to handcraft wines for individuals looking for something unique and distinctive'.

Signature Series

★★★★ **Cabernet Sauvignon** ⓧ Long skin contact (as all these reds), along with 24 months mainly French oak, give **17** ⑧⑧ depth & structure. Voluptuous, for early enjoyment, yet ageable. Last was **14** ⑧⑥.

★★★★ **Merlot** ⓧ Shows intense cassis, touch of mint chocolate in **17** ★★★★★ ⑨⓪, supple tannins with enough hidden strength to promise a future. More power & concentration than last-tasted **15** ⑧⑨.

★★★★ **Nebbiolo** ⓧ Gymnastic litheness apparent on red fruit- & cinnamon-toned **14** ⑧⑦, dry & lean, with leashed power. Polished 2 years in barrel, 20% new, same in bottle.

★★★★ **Pinotage** ⓐ Change in direction for supercharged **20** ★★★★☆ ⑨④ barrel selection, using some French oak, 60% new, vs all-American **19** ⑧⑦. Smoky dried herbs, dense black fruit & touch of raisin, wrapped in velvet tannins & supported by great power & intensity. Long evolving finish.

★★★★ **Sangiovese** ⓧ 15% cab for structure, but **16** ⑧⑧ is variety true. Full ripe, black cherry & plum, dusty overlay from 18 months older barrels. Smooth texture, tannins friendly. Last was **14** ⑧⑨.

★★★★☆ **Layla Blaire** ⓧ 4-part Cape Bordeaux, cab led, **18** ⑨③ is seriously made, shows impressive power & polish, fruit as intense as you'd expect, resting on master-crafted tannins, supple but muscled.

★★★★ **Cape Cuvée** ⓧ French/American oak, **18** ★★★★★ ⑨⓪'s pinotage complemented by 30% each cab for structure, shiraz for plushness, all contributing scents, flavours. More heft & layers than **17** ⑧⑦. Not tasted: **Syrah**. Discontinued: **Carignan**, **Grenache**.

Reserve range

★★★★ **Cabernet Sauvignon** ⓥ Return to touch more classic styling for **19** ★★★★★ ⑨⓪, replacing **18** ⑧⑧'s American oak with French, 30% new. Still big, powerful wine, strong vanilla tone, yet shows good bones & some refinement in lavender lift, dusty tannins.

★★★★☆ **Malbec** ⓥ Bold, confident **21** ⑨⓪, now bottled, shows rich black fruit, pot-pourri florals & creamy vanilla from 24 months in oak, half American, 45% new. Firm tannins & rich texture rein in hefty 14.5% alc with ease. A conversation stopper of note.

★★★★ **Merlot** ⓧ Sorting table & some whole berries, as most reds. Vividly perfumed **20** ★★★★★ ⑨⓪'s 22 months in barrel ensure an ageing foundation but tannins supple enough for current enjoyment. More layered than last-tasted **18** ⑧⑧.

★★★★ **Petit Verdot** ⓧ Rare single bottling. 30% American barrels in **17** ⑧⑨'s 22-month maturation emphasises vanilla spicing, well matched to the deep, dark-toned, smoothly curvaceous fruit.

★★★★ **Pinotage** ⓧ Fruit leaps out of glass in hedonistic display of concentration & power. Masterly tannin, lithe strength for a future but already accessible. More on offer in **20** ★★★★★ ⑨⓪ than last **18** ⑧⑦.

★★★★ **Shiraz** Earthy overtone of **22** ⑧⑥ frames black cherry fruit & velvet tannins, adds spicy funk to rich, rounded wine. Vanilla thanks to 30% new oak, 14 months, tad shorter duration than last-tasted **20** ⑧⑨.

★★★★☆ **Syrah-Mourvèdre-Grenache** ⊘ Now shiraz-led, **22** ⑨⓪ reverts to grenache portion after last-reviewed **20** ⑨⓪'s carignan substitution, making red, plummy fruit the star. Better alc balance (13.5% vs 15%) leaves space for delicate spice, sweet meaty tang, fresh lengthy finish. 14 months French oak.

★★★★ **Méthode Cap Classique Brut** ⑧ Some tweaking for **15** ★★★★☆ ⑨⓪ bubbly, now pinot noir leads chardonnay, 5 years in bottle. Powerful scents, palate a citrus concentration, very long finish. Touch sugar but zesty acid balances. More presence & personality than **14** ⑧⑧. WO W Cape.

Not tasted: **Chardonnay**, **Chenin Blanc**.

Estate range

★★★★ **Cabernet Sauvignon** ⊘ Brightness of black & blue fruit on **20** ⑧⑦ aided by 15% petit verdot added at bottling. Juicy & soft, refreshing herbal note mid-palate & lick of vanilla spice at finish. 2 years mostly French oak, 20% new.

★★★★ **Pinotage** ⊘ Warm Xmas spices light up **22** ⑧⑦'s dark plum fruit, touch of raisin, chocolate & orange peel. Smoky oak, some American, 35% new, adds dimension to already layered & accomplished wine, step up from last-tasted **19** ★★★★ ⑧④.

★★★★ **Tempranillo** ⊘ Smart winemaking tames **20** ⑧⑥'s brawn with enerising wholeberry portion, only old oak to smooth tannins & splash young grenache noir, enhancing red cherry-berry notes in mainly black-plum wine. Enjoyable drinking, fresher than **19** ★★★★ ⑧⑤.

★★★★ **Legato** ⊘ 40% merlot, cab & dab petit verdot radiate easy-drinking friendliness & warmth on **20** ⑧⑧, which majorly over-delivers. Cassis & blackberry flavour, cinnamon & clove extras thanks to 2 years mostly old oak, 20% American.

★★★★ **Symphony** ⑧ Half grenache, with shiraz, mourvèdre, **19** ⑧⑧ is about drinking pleasure, berry rich in both perfume & flavour, oaking subservient, just adding spice & supple tannin.

Grenache Noir ⑧ ★★★★ Style change since last **16** ★★★ ⑦⑧, now 100% grenache, 18 months seasoned barrels, & **19** ⑧④ rewards that with much better expression of the variety. **Merlot** ⑧ ★★★★ Small barrels 24 months, quarter new, & **20** ⑧⑤ preview returns that care with spice-dusted plush fruit, suave tannins & succulent drinkability. Also in 375ml, 1.5L. **Pinotage-Shiraz** ⊘ ★★★★ Ups new wood, some American, in **22** ⑧⑤ equal blend to 40% from **19** ★★★★ ⑧⑦, slightly overpowering sappy red-berried fruit. Tarry, savoury notes mix with smoky meat at finish. **Arpeggio** ⊘ ★★★★ Shiraz-led old-oaked **22** ⑧⑤ Rhône blend uses smidge viognier to lift smoky red-berried fruit, adding perfume & delicacy to generally meaty, salami-spice tone. **Rosé** ⑧ ★★★ From grenache noir, 6 months on lees, pale pink **21** ⑧② cranberry scents but palate more earthy mineral, reminiscent of southern France. Ideal food partner. **Chardonnay** ⊘ ★★★★ Unpretentious, fruit-forward enjoyment in **23** ⑧③. Tropical base with peach & banana, creamy texture from oaked portion & 5 months on lees. **Pinot Grigio** ★★★ Plenty of pears & pear drops on straightforward, fresh **23** ⑧②, showing lighter, poolside-quaffing side of this grape (12.4% alc). **Sauvignon Blanc** ⊘ ★★★★ Greenpeppers & grapefruit shine forth strongly on **23** ⑧④, offering delicious typicity & freshness. 3 months on lees add pleasing breadth to palate. — CM

Location/map: Paarl ▪ Map grid reference: C7 ▪ WO: Simonsberg-Paarl/Western Cape ▪ Est 1990 ▪ 1stB 2001 ▪ Tasting & wine sales Mon-Sat 9-5 Sun 9-4 ▪ Closed Dec 25 & Jan 1 ▪ Fee R70/cheese & wine, R50/wine only ▪ Farm produce & Forest Hill cheese ▪ Tour groups ▪ The Cooperage events venue (40-300 guests seated & up to 850 cocktail style) ▪ Owner(s) Bouma family ▪ Cellarmaster(s) Lance Bouma (2007) ▪ Winemaker(s) Stander Maass (2017) & Lance Bouma (Jan 2007) ▪ Viticulturist(s) Quintus van Wyk (Oct 2019) ▪ 240ha/120ha (cab, carignan, grenache, malbec, merlot, mourv, nebbiolo, p verdot, ptage, pinot, sangio, shiraz, tempranillo, chard, chenin, nouvelle, pinot gris, sauv, verdelho) ▪ 750t/60,000cs own label 80% red 17% white 2% rosé 1% fortified ▪ PO Box 244 Klapmuts 7625 ▪ info@anura.co.za ▪ www.anura.co.za ▪ **T +27 (0)21-875-5360**

Anwilka ⑧

The warmer-climate twin of Klein Constantia, merged with its business model and prestigious international ownership, Anwilka has had its own personality, composition and flavour profile since inception, varying portions of syrah/shiraz differentiating it from its Estate Blend cousin. Mutual winemaker Matt Day readied the latest Anwilka releases in his cellarmaster debut in 2019, delighting in the return of cabernet primacy following vine replanting. As always, the wines are released when deemed ready. Arjen Rijpstra joins Matt as vine minder, and the estate joins the Stellenbosch Wine Route as an attraction on its False Bay border.

★★★★☆ **Anwilka** (🐝) Ample power, plushness in **19** (93), cab & syrah (70/30) styled for long term. Deeply concentrated blackcurrant, cocoa, touch liquorice lifted by pepper spice. Firm ripe tannins aided by charry oak, 50% new, 20 months. 14.9% alc shows at lengthy finish, just needs a little more time to settle.

★★★★ **Petit Frère** (🍷) Little brother also a syrah & cab blend, **19** (89) spotlights spicy black fruit & silky tannins, reflects gentle vinification. Only half oaked in larger barrels. Dabs petit verdot & malbec.— CM

Location/WO: Stellenbosch ▪ Est 1997 ▪ 1stB 2005 ▪ Tasting & sales at Klein Constantia ▪ Owner(s) Zdenek Bakala, Charles Harman, Bruno Prats & Hubert de Boüard ▪ CEO Pascal Asin ▪ Winemaker(s) Matthew Day (Jan 2021) ▪ Viticulturist(s) Arjen Rijpstra (May 2023) ▪ 48ha/±39ha (cab, malbec, p verdot, shiraz) ▪ 250t/±28,000cs own label 100% red ▪ PO Box 5298 Helderberg 7135 ▪ info@kleinconstantia.com ▪ www. kleinconstantia.com ▪ **T +27 (0)21-794-5188**

Anysbos   (🍷)

Celebrated film producer Johan Heyns with his wife Sue arrived on the Bot River home-farm in 2007 and enthusiastically planted vines, mostly Rhône varieties, as well as olives for farming, and brought in goats to provide milk for a cheesery. Highly regarded Marelise Niemann, winemaker since inception, latterly has crafted her own Momento boutique collection here and is delighted that upgrades to cellar are almost complete. 'It's now so big, we need a new forklift!' Visitors to the property will also be welcomed at a new tasting venue, where they can sample the wines that are crafted with a light and deft hand.

★★★★★ **Tesame** (✓) (🐝) Enticing purity, lightness & energy in **21** (95), where grenache, shiraz & cinsaut align with depth & harmony. Wild red berries & a touch of liquorice, associated with local shrub anysbos, bring flavour distinction. Lively tannins, not out of sync for current enjoyment, will also allow for many more years. Older oak, 20 months.

★★★★☆ **Disdit** (🐝) Chenin increased to 69% in **22** (94); Rhône varieties, mainly roussannne & marsanne with grenache blanc a strong influence on weight, textural breadth. Full peach flavours need time to emerge from light oak spicing, 8% new, when promise usual excellence & pleasure. Wholebunch, spontaneously fermented, 10 months oaked.— AL

Location/WO: Bot River ▪ Map: Walker Bay & Bot River ▪ Map grid reference: C3 ▪ Est 2010 ▪ 1stB 2018 ▪ Tasting, sales & cellar tours by appt ▪ Owner(s) Anysbos Olywe BK ▪ Winemaker(s) Marelise Niemann (2016) ▪ Viticulturist(s) Quintus le Roux (2012) ▪ 380ha/18ha (cinsaut, grenache n/b, shiraz, chenin, marsanne, rouss) ▪ PO Box 550 Bot River 1785 ▪ hello@anysbos.co.za ▪ www.anysbos.co.za ▪ **T +27 (0)82-601-1067**

☐ **Aphaea** see Val du Charron
☐ **Apogée** see La Vierge Private Cellar
☐ **Arabica** see Cape Wine Company

Arbeidsgenot Wines   (🍷) (🍴) (📷)

With business partner and namesake Jaco Olivier, Jaco Brand is indulging his 'absolute passion' for winemaking under a boutique own-label whose name translates as 'work is pleasure'. It was previously listed in this guide under Meerhof, where Jaco was cellar chief. He's now working from custom crush facilities in nearby Riebeek-Kasteel, sourcing grapes around Swartland, and selling locally and in Namibia and Europe.

Premium range

★★★★ **Grenache Noir** In footsteps of light-textured & piquant predecessor, **21** (86) engaging raspberry & strawberry notes, commendably dry & fruit-filled but not -sweet, cola nuance from oak.

★★★★ **Shiraz** Brawny 15.5% alc deftly handled: no heat or harshness, though **22** (88)'s red & black fruit shade less fresh than **21** ★★★★★ (90)'s. Like Grenache, year 40% new oak; whites & rosé 6 months 20% new. 50% American barrels for all.

★★★★ **Grenache Blanc** Lemon thyme-scented **22** (89) almost flamboyant in its mouthfilling richness. Less mineral acid & savouriness than **21** ★★★★★ (91), so few grams sugar seem more obviously sweet.

★★★★ **Roussanne** (NEW) Thyme & tarragon on a base of pear & macadamia, **22** (88) has flavour & character aplenty, owes its substantial body & weight to fruit rather than sugar, acid uplift ensuring balance.

★★★★ Verdelho Locally rare Portuguese grape an absolute charmer in **22** ⑧⑦, also shows real complexity in its apple, quince, pear & nut array. Varietal acid adds verve, house's 'combo' oak regime lends texture & weight.

Grenache Rosé (NEW) **★★★** Dry & savoury, emphatically 'un-pretty', **22** ⑧② recalls Rioja's Vina Tondonia's oxidative expression. Intriguing suggestion of frangipani. — CvZ

Location: Riebeek-Kasteel ▪ Map/WO: Swartland ▪ Map grid reference: D6 ▪ 1stB 2018 ▪ Tasting & sales Wed-Fri 11-5 Sat 11-6 Sun 11-2 ▪ Tasting R20/glass ▪ Closed Dec 25 & Jan 1 ▪ Meals/refreshments Wed-Sat 11-8 Sun 11-3 ▪ Tour groups ▪ Brewery ▪ Owner(s) Jaco Brand & Jaco Olivier ▪ Winemaker(s) Jaco Brand ▪ 3,000cs own label 40% red 50% white 10% rosé ▪ IPW, WIETA ▪ PO Box 93 Riebeek Kasteel 7307 ▪ cornel@ arbeidsgenotwines.co.za ▪ **T +27 (0)84-589-9255**

☐ **Arboretum** see Botanica Wines

Arcangeli Vineyards

Identifying as a 'bespoke family concern focused on making low-intervention wines', Arcangeli has built on the accomplishments of the last owners, the brothers De Andrade, with roots in Feiteiras on Portuguese Madeira, who helped pioneer verdelho locally. Current owners Allesandro and Fabio Arcangeli have an Italian heritage, and the wine names reflect that also. Krige Visser brings creativity and a vigorous natural-winemaking approach, using only old wood, adding stalks for structure and harvesting early.

★★★★☆ Syracuse Syrah ⊘ 🍇 Restraint & freshness bring extra class to lovely **20** ⑨④. Cool-climate purity pervades gently spiced dark fruit & silky flow, both focused by finest tannin into effortless harmony. Good for a few more years, but why wait?

★★★★☆ Pellegrini Merlot-Cabernet Sauvignon Pure fruit & natural freshness bring sense of lightness to **20** ⑨⓪. Merlot (53%) delivers sweet fleshy flavours, cab adding effective, unharsh support. The reds fermented wholebunch, 50-70% older-oak aged, 8 months, rest in PVC 'egg', 13.5-14% alc.

★★★★ Vesta Semillon No frills in its earthy herb & lemon flavours, weighty texture & bone-dry grip. Yet **22** ⑧⑨ has balance, more so than last **18** ⑧⑧, & authentic if individual varietal character. Natural ferment (as all) in PVC 'egg', half with some stems. Modest 12% alc. WO Cape South Coast.

Not tasted: **Romulus Nebbiolo, Merlot-Petit Verdot-Cabernet Sauvignon, Feiteiras Verdelho.** — AL

Location: Bot River ▪ Map: Walker Bay & Bot River ▪ Map grid reference: C3 ▪ WO: Bot River/Cape South Coast ▪ Est/1stB 2015 ▪ Tasting & sales by appt ▪ Restaurant ▪ Luxury guest cottages ▪ Owner(s) Roodeheuvel Boerdery cc (directors Allesandro & Fabio Arcangeli) ▪ Winemaker(s) Krige Visser ▪ 16.2ha/4.2ha (cab, merlot, mourv, p verdot, shiraz, verdelho) ▪ 3,500cs own label 70% red 30% white ▪ PO Box 234 Bot River 7185 ▪ info@arcangeliwines.com ▪ www.arcangeliwines.com ▪ **T +27 (0)82-412-7795**

☐ **Arco Laarman** see Laarman Wines

Arendsig Handcrafted Wines

Great excitement on the Van der Westhuizen family's Robertson farm, where the focus has been exclusively on single-site varietal bottlings, to see the evolution of the wines made from the first crop of the 'field blend' vineyards. Planted in 2019, one block with Bordeaux grapes, cab, cab franc, merlot and malbec, the other Rhône, shiraz, mourvèdre, grenache noir and viognier, were harvested and vinified separately to get a feel for how each variety performs. The intention is for the next harvest to be co-fermented.

Inspirational range

★★★★ Batch 10 Merlot From single-vineyard, as most. **21** ⑧⑨ well-judged fruit & tannin ripeness without big alc or residual sugar. Like last, enlivened by bright acid but oak more restrained, 15% new, 14 months, hence absence of overt sweet vanilla.

★★★★☆ Batch No 3 Chenin Blanc Nectarine, orange & macadamia ripeness & cream are aided by barrel ferment, full malo & few grams sugar, yet **22** ⑨① 's burst of tangy apricot acid ensures seamless, fresh entry, middle & finish.

Discontinued: **Batch No 2 Grenache.**

OUTSTANDING!

Add **Westfalia Fruit Avocado Oil** to every meal. It's perfect for any cooking method & bursting with healthy fats. Be an **#AVOEXPERT**

SCAN
FOR
RECIPES

BIG 5 SAFARI & SPA

Real Africa. Real Close To Cape Town.
Over 10 000-hectares of Big 5 conservancy.

4-STAR ACCOMMODATION | SPA
GAME DRIVE | HORSEBACK & QUAD BIKE SAFARI

At the award-winning Aquila Private Game Reserve and Spa, guests will get the opportunity to experience a Big 5 safari, together with outstanding service; it just does not get any better than this. With game drives, quad bike and horseback safaris situated just 2 hours' drive from Cape Town, it's the closest you will get to real Africa, in the lap of luxury.

The world-class spa at Aquila adds to the already exceptional facilities and services on offer. It is a masterpiece of luxury, defined by its serenity and creative use of natural elements.

THE
LILIZELA
TOURISM AWARDS

FACILITIES & ACTIVITIES
4-STAR ESTABLISHMENT | PREMIER, FAMILY & LUXURY COTTAGES | LODGE ROOMS | DAY TRIP SAFARI | HORSEBACK SAFARI | QUAD BIKE SAFARI | STAR SAFARI | OVERNIGHT SAFARI | FLY-IN SAFARI | INDOOR & OUTDOOR RESTAURANTS | OUTDOOR POOL | WET BAR | CONFERENCE CENTRE | SPA | CURIO SHOP | CHILDREN'S FACILITIES & JUNIOR RANGER PROGRAMME

www.aquilasafari.com   **f** AquilaSafari   **⊙ ⊘** AquilaSafaris

+27 (0)21 430 7260 or RES@AQUILASAFARI.COM

Arendsig Estate range

★★★★☆ **Cabernet Sauvignon A9** (🐝) Vines deliver their usual ripeness at moderate alc of 12.8% in lean but well-built **21** (91). Cassis & raspberry, graphite top note, fine but present tannin. 12-14 months older foudre & barrel for these reds.

★★★★ **Pinotage A19** (NEW) Rum-&-raisin ice cream & maraschino cherry sweetness & persistence on smartly oaked (10% new) **22** (86). Neatly dry, too, with an enlivening aloe lift.

★★★★ **Shiraz A12** Despite name, **22** (86) more French than Australian in style. Treads lightly with pleasing stemmy freshness & reined-in red fruit & alc (13.6%). Spontaneous ferment, as most.

★★★★☆ **Chardonnay A15** (🐝) The varied ferment & ageing vessels, including wood & concrete, contribute more to creamy texture & weight than aroma of **22** (90). Peach & Granny Smith apple emerge with time, exit with subtle pithy grip.

★★★★☆ **Sauvignon Blanc A10** (🌿) Classy, sleek & confident at last, bone-dry & subtle. **22** (90) not overtly fruity or sharp, just impressively vinous at modest 12.5% alc. Lovely grapefruity acid & pithiness. 8 months on lees in concrete.

★★★★ **1000 Vines Viognier** Less than 1,000 bottles from 1,000 vines in mature vineyard. **22** (87) not as showy on nose as variety can be, with faint pear & peach nuances, more expressive on palate, which is also richer than last.

Not tasted: **Pinot Noir, Colombar**. — CvZ

Location/map/WO: Robertson ▪ Map grid reference: C4 ▪ Est/1stB 2004 ▪ Tasting & cellar tours by appt ▪ Self-catering accommodation available (up to 16 pax) ▪ Farm walks, bird watching, hiking & running trails, river kayak ▪ Owner(s) Lourens van der Westhuizen ▪ Cellarmaster(s)/viticulturist(s) Lourens van der Westhuizen (2004) ▪ 30ha (cab, grenache, merlot, mourv, ptage, shiraz, chard, chenin, cbard, sauv, viog) ▪ 100t/13,000cs own label 60% red 40% white ▪ PO Box 147 Robertson 6705 ▪ info@arendsig.co.za ▪ www.arendsig.co.za ▪ T +27 (0)84-200-2163/+27 (0)23-616-2835

Arendskloof-New Cape Wines (🔱)

These wines are crafted by Christiaan Groenewald, owner/winemaker at separately listed Eagle's Cliff and twice Diners Club Winemaker of the Year, for cognoscenti, hence some rare varieties and unusual blends.

Voetspore range

★★★★ **Petit Sirah** (🔱) One of few single-variety bottlings (drops 'e' off 'petite'). **NV** (87) change in style from vintaged **16** ★★★★☆ (90); riper, spice-infused, fruit pastille richness, dried herbs. Tasty but lesser.

★★★★ **Shiraz** (🌿) Opulent & generous (15% alc), **21** (87) is intensely fruit-driven, offering black & red berry compote, honeyed & rich. Powdery, ripe tannins & well-judged acid add to appeal, as does spicy lift from 18 months in barrel. Improves on last **17** ★★★★ (85).

★★★★ **Tannat** (🌿) Rare example of French variety, **21** (87) packed with spicy black fruit & tarry minerality. Mouthcoating tannins vie with assertive acid, begging time to integrate. 75% barrel matured, 60% new, 18 months. Last was **16** (86).

★★★★ **Shiraz-Tannat** (🌿) Unusual pairing works well, heft & power of tannat complementing juicy black fruit, spice & aromas of shiraz. **21** (88) is 68% of latter, 75% in 50% new barrels, some American.

Pinot Noir (🌿) ★★★★ Light bodied & fragrantly fruity, **22** (84) has touch of oak but focuses on juicy berries, offering youthful refreshment. **Pinot Noir Rosé** ★★★ Soundly made, juicy & appealing **22** (82) offers raspberry cordial fruit, food-friendly acid lift. **Wooded Chardonnay** ★★★★ Lean & mineral, **22** (85) has well-judged body, perky acid & delicate lemon zest notes. 50% spent 6 months in new French & American oak. Shade off fuller **20** ★★★★ (87). **Unwooded Chardonnay** (NEW) ★★★★ Cheerful, energetic **22** (84) offers supple body, brisk acid & ample citrus flavour. Perfect picnic fare. **Sauvignon Blanc** ★★★★ Light, mild-mannered **22** (83) delivers easygoing sipping enjoyment with appealing lime cordial fruit, bright acid, modest 12% alc. **Pinot Noir Méthode Cap Classique** (🔱) ★★★★ Youthful **21** (84) bubbly gets no colour from pinot noir but shows the variety in its red berry styling. Elegant (10% alc) & fresh, a touch of citrus on finish making it an attractive aperitif. WO Breede River Valley, as Petit Sirah, rest Worcester. Not tasted: **Cabernet Sauvignon, Pinotage, Chardonnay Méthode Cap Classique**. Occasional release: **Tannat-Syrah, Chenin Blanc**. — GdB

☐ **Are We Having Fun Yet?** *see* Wine Village-Hermanus

Aristea Wines

This long-distance partnership between three friends, Cape Town consultant winemaker Matthew Krone, UK Bordeaux vineyard owner Martin Krajewski and Bordeaux oenologist Florent Dumeau, sources fruit from leading growers in Stellenbosch, Elgin and Hemel-en-Aarde to showcase the ancient soils of the Cape.

★★★★☆ **Cabernet Sauvignon** Ⓥ Assured, seamless & restrained expression of cab. Classic cassis, graphite & rockpool notes, focused tannins, commendable dryness. **19** ⑨④, like more concentrated **18** ★★★★★ ⑨⑤, drinks well early, also has oak support (18 months, 33% new) for good few years cellaring.

★★★★ **Pinot Noir** Ⓥ Wholeberry ferment, just 10% new oak for refined **20** ⑧⑧ from Hemel-en-Aarde Ridge. Sweet fruit & svelte body laced with zesty raspberry acid, all wrapped in supple tannin.

★★★★☆ **Chardonnay** Ⓥ Complex vinification, inter alia some bunch-pressing & part natural ferment plus deft barreling, 35% new, contribute to **20** ⑨⓪'s subtle nutty nuance & fine detail. 'Cool' citrus fruit is steelier, more focused than last-tasted **18** ★★★★ ⑧⑨.

★★★★☆ **Sauvignon Blanc-Semillon** Ⓥ Fine Bordeaux white from Elgin, **19** ⑨③ 75% sauvignon & bone-dry, shows green fig & white stonefruit, pebbly minerality. Richer, more intense & vivacious than last.

★★★★ **Méthode Cap Classique Rosé** Ⓥ Deliciously dry, sophisticated blush **17** ⑨⓪ with tiny streaming bubbles, creamy texture from 2 years on lees. Well-defined citrus & red berry flavours reflect chardonnay & pinot noir make-up, latter variety also providing palate weight & depth.

★★★★ **Méthode Cap Classique Blanc** Ⓥ Refined, pale gold **17** ⑨③ from chardonnay (66%) & pinot noir. Almost 4 years on lees provide brioche aromas & creamy richness, scintillating acid & oystershell minerality lift the elegant lemon & apple fruit. Beautifully dry & light-footed.— CvZ

Location: Constantia ▪ WO: Stellenbosch/Hemel-en-Aarde Ridge/Elgin ▪ Est 2014 ▪ 1stB 2015 ▪ Closed to public ▪ Owner(s) Martin Krajewski, Florent Dumeau & Matthew Krone ▪ Cellarmaster(s)/winemaker(s) Matthew Krone (2014) ▪ 1,000cs per wine ▪ 13 Sillery Estate, Constantia 7806 ▪ matthew@matthewkronewines.co.za ▪ www.aristeawines.com

Arniston Bay Fairtrade

Carefree seaside holidays are evoked by the name of Stellenbosch Vineyards' long-running collection of affordable easy-drinkers, endorsed by Fairtrade and The Vegan Society, and sourced from Coastal vines.

Shiraz ★★★ Wholebunch crushed, older 300L barrels 10 months, giving **22** ⑧② a spicy red fruit expression, supple tannin seam for food or some ageing. **Rosé** ★★★ Fresh berry profile, **23** ⑧② is dry & zesty, perfect summertime fare. **Sauvignon Blanc** ⊘ ★★★★ Care taken in the making to preserve flavours, vivid passionfruit & lime, **23** ⑧④ vibrates with life & freshness. — CR

Arno Smith Wine Company   Ⓥ ◎

Arno Smith's Jack Russell terrier Saartjie lent her name to a wine collection previously housed under Hillcrest Estate, where Arno Smith is consultant winemaker. He's now acquired the brand and added it to this standalone signature label, along with the first of a new collection of experimental wines which reflect his belief that every winemaker is an artist, with a unique style and flavour profile. Both ranges are made in the Hillcrest cellar in Durbanville, and available for tasting and sale there, along with a variety of craft items.

Artist Selection ⒩🅴🅆

★★★★ **Kromtak Grenache Noir** Pretty, refined **22** ⑧⑨, fragrant, juicy red berries & racy acid adding tang, solid body & ripe tannins, smoothed by year in seasoned barrels.

★★★★ **Kronkelpad Verdelho** Variety-true tingly acid, viscous texture & palpable tannin grip alongside spicy baked apple & pear notes on **22** ⑧⑦, natural yeast fermented (as red sibling), 9 months older barrels.

Saartjie Single Vineyard Selection

Not tasted: **Cabernet Franc, Malbec, Petit Verdot, Semillon.** — GdB

Location: Durbanville ▪ Map: Durbanville, Philadelphia & Darling ▪ Map grid reference: C7 ▪ WO: Stellenbosch ▪ Est 2021 ▪ 1stB 2023 ▪ Tasting & sales Tue-Sat 10-5 Sun 11-4 ▪ Fee R80 ▪ Seasonal pairings ▪ Closed Dec 25 & Jan 1 ▪ Olive oil & olive products, coffee beans, tea, nougat, chocolate, wine bags & aprons ▪ Owner(s) Arno Smith ▪ Cellarmaster(s)/winemaker(s) Arno Smith (Nov 2021) ▪ 2,150cs own label 85% red 15% white ▪ WIETA ▪ Private Bag X3 Durbanville 7550 ▪ info@arnosmithwine.co.za ▪ www.arnosmithwine.co.za ▪ **T +27 (0)84-591-7480**

Arra Vineyards

These Paarl slopes of Klapmuts Hill are planted with French and South African grapes, mostly black-skinned, including rare ruby cab. John Jacobs and Carami Lanser are their care givers, Carami also looking after the cellar since hopping over the rise from Warwick four years ago. The sole white variety, viognier, helps the winemaker cover the bases, from dry to sweet to occasional fortified, sparkling being the exception for now.

★★★★ **Cabernet Sauvignon** First tasted since **18** ⑧⑧, big, ripe **21** ⑧⑥ (15.4% alc) delivers classic cassis aroma & flavour, firm grip of tannin, faint whiff of green herbs. 2 years in oak, 20% new, bring spice.

★★★★ **Shiraz** Red fruit cosseted by chalky tannins in **21** ⑧⑥, gentle savouriness & spice added by 2 years in old oak, high 15% alc integrated with the fleshy body. First since **18** ⑧⑥.

★★★★ **Viognier** ⑧ Single parcel continues to impress. Bunch-pressed **22** ⑧⑥ has youthful stonefruit on a seam of mineral freshness, backbone of satiny lees. Judicious combo tank & 20% old barrel.

Blanc de Noir ⑨ ★★★★ Pinotage & shiraz marry harmoniously in **23** ⑧⑤ for a delicious peaches-&-cream pink sipper. Nicely dry & moreish at modest 12.7% alc.

Pinotage ★★★☆ Berry-perfumed **20** ⑧④ fresh & primary, sweet, juicy fruit supported by firm acid & partial oaking, just 20%, 20 months, none new. **Cape Blend** ★★★★ 50/30/20 mix of cab, pinotage & merlot offers plums & mulberries, 10% smidgen new oak, 18 months, lends texture. Acid tad apparent on **21** ⑧③, missing **20** ★★★★ ⑧⑥'s fine balance. **Shiraz-Cabernet Sauvignon** ⊘ ★★★ 60/40 blend for improved **21** ⑧② Mix older barrels & oak chips, 16 months, gives cherries noticeable vanilla spicing & tannin grip. **Natural Sweet Red Blend** ⑧ ★★★ Modestly sweet **20** ⑦⑨'s equal cab & merlot bring supple berries, dark chocolate & liquorice with spicy grip from wood chips & 6 months in old oak. **Natural Sweet Viognier** ⑧ ★★★ Clean & balanced **22** ⑧① trumps previous. Peach blossom, pineapple & fresh honey achieved from same grape source & by same process as dry wine, ferment stopped at desired sugar of 28 g/L. Not tasted: **Shiraz-Mourvèdre-Viognier.** Occasional release: **Cape Vintage.** — ML

Location/map/WO: Paarl ▪ Map grid reference: C8 ▪ Est 1998 ▪ 1stB 2001 ▪ Tasting & sales Mon-Sun 10-4.30 ▪ Owner(s) Arra Vineyards (Pty) Ltd ▪ Winemaker(s) Carami Lanser ▪ Viticulturist(s) John Jacobs & Carami Lanser ▪ 72ha/26.12ha (cab, merlot, ptage, ruby cab, shiraz, viog) ▪ 20,000cs ▪ PO Box 298 Klapmuts 7625 ▪ admin@arrawines.com ▪ www.arrawines.com ▪ **T +27 (0)21-875-5363**

☐ **Art Collection** *see* Rascallion Wines

ArtiSons

A blend of craftsmanship and artistry, in service of expressing the uniqueness of select parcels of grapes, many from vines advanced in age, sets this range apart from the standard line-up from the Stellenrust cellar, presided over by Tertius Boshoff, with Herman du Preez as co-winemaker. Tertius references the words attributed to Picasso: 'Learn the rules like a pro so you can break them like an artist'. In that spirit, Herman mooted a white cinsault, a novelty that won him Diners Club Young Winemaker of the Year - twice. It's about attention to detail, traditional, even old-fashioned winemaking and taking time to harness the special gifts of old vines. Their well-considered labours have gained consumer and critical acclaim around the world.

ArtiSons range

★★★★★ **JJ Handmade Eight Pillars** ⊛ Mesmerising, supple-textured **20** ★★★★☆ ⑨④ a refined, harmonious blend of 8 varieties, shiraz leading 4 Rhône, 3 Bordeaux & pinotage, as in **19** ⑨⑤. Nuanced, layered, blue & black fruit in a sleek, succulent body gently spiced from 24 months in oak, 20% new. 30+ year old vines in Stellenbosch, Swartland & Voor Paardeberg.

SeriesRARE range

★★★★☆ **La Dolce Vita Cabernet Sauvignon** ⊛ Second release of this homage to Amarone. **18** ⑨③ grapes dried on bamboo racks to accentuate the spice, rooibos tea & cherry vibrancy. Few grams sugar enlivened by bright acid & firm tannin grip for a long, satisfying dry finish. Two years in new oak.

★★★★☆ **Villain Vines Carignan** ⊛ Layered, complex & elegant **21** ⑨④ is compelling in its generous succulence, cranberry crunch & herby spice before a good squeeze of tannin. Complex construction of grapes off old Swartland dryland bushvines, third cluster-fermented in open vessel & basket pressed. Older oak, 16 months, lends structure.

★★★★★ **The Basket Child Cinsault** (NEW) Ⓐ Exceptional **21** ⑨⑤ shows almost ethereal delicacy & purity of fruit from natural wholebunch ferment & soft basket pressing. Also a persuasive underlying power & concentration of raspberry, cherry & spice notes on intricate, silky, poised palate from year in barrel.

★★★★☆ **The Phantom Grenache** Ⓐ Shows vintage influence in refinement & dried herb overlay. **21** ⑨③ rose florality on enveloping black cherry fruit with savoury nuance. 49 year old Voor Paardeberg bushvines, 43% bunch fermented before 16 months older barrels. Confident, assured, with layered charms.

★★★★☆ **After Eight Shiraz** Ⓐ Engaging appeal of cherry, cocoa & mint to **20** ⑨③ from 0.2-ha eucalyptus-lined Bottelary site. Plush, rewarding & gently spicy yet also dry & structured. Natural ferment & 18 months in oak, 30% new, lend poise, stature & harmony to elegantly long mouthful.

★★★★☆ **Blueberry Hill Shiraz** Ⓐ Violets, spice & trademark blueberries on rounded, engaging **21** ★★★★★ ⑨⑤. Textured yet rich with dry, cedary press of tannin. As with **20** ⑨④, 62% bunch fermented, softly basket pressed then into combo French, American & Hungarian oak (95/3/2). Long, sleek & seamless.

★★★★☆ **The Mothership Chenin Blanc** Ⓐ Vibrant lime edge to rich **22** ★★★★★ ⑨⑦ echoes **21** ⑨④ in its freshness & honeyed stonefruit notes. Chalky mouthfeel & breadth courtesy of skin contact, natural ferment in foudre, year lees-ageing in concrete 'egg'. Complex, focused & pure, with restraint & thrilling acid (7.2 g/L) adding to the sophisticated.

★★★★☆ **The White Cinsault** Ⓐ Ⓦ Old Bottelary cinsaut block with mutated vines giving 'white' & light pink bunches. **22** ⑨③ naturally fermented in older oak, 9 months on lees, leaving bright & vivacious 7 g/L acid intact but adding creamy lees note, balance & body.

Discontinued: **Under My Skin Gewürztraminer.** — FM

Location/map: Stellenbosch ▪ Map grid reference: C3 ▪ WO: Stellenbosch/Coastal/Swartland/Voor Paardeberg ▪ Est/1stB 2013 ▪ Tasting, sales & cellar tours by appt only ▪ Closed all pub hols ▪ Owner(s) Tertius Boshoff & Kobie van der Westhuizen ▪ Cellarmaster(s) Tertius Boshoff (Jan 2005) ▪ Winemaker(s) Tertius Boshoff (Jan 2005) & Herman du Preez (Jan 2016) ▪ Viticulturist(s) Kobie van der Westhuizen (Jan 2000) ▪ 20ha/4ha (cabs s/f, carignan, cinsaut, grenache, merlot, ptage, shiraz, chenin) ▪ 10t/600cs own label 70% red 30% white ▪ PO Box 26 Koelenhof 7605 ▪ artisonswine@gmail.com ▪ **T +27 (0)82-455-6431**

☐ **Art Series** *see* Seven Springs Vineyards

Arumdale Cool Climate Wines ⓧ

Mark Simpson's Huguenot ancestors were from a renowned wine region, the Loire, so it's appropriate that he's deeply invested in wine, as both a brand owner - of this more serious range, and the meal partners, Robin Hood Legendary Wine Series, listed separately - and as a merchant, via his outlet in Grabouw town.

★★★★ **St Andrew's Blend** ⓧ Cab (60%), merlot & shiraz **14** ⑧⑦ improves on last-tasted **12** ★★★★ ⑧④ in texture, depth & concentration of black fruit, supple, silky integrated tannin. Long rich finish.

Pink Shiraz ⓧ ★★★ Pomegranate pink hue to bright, tangy dry **15** ⑧① rosé. Fun, light bodied & easy.

Special LYC Sauvignon Blanc ⓧ ★★★ Maintains form with nectarine, white pepper & rich lees breadth, **15** ⑧① pleasant acid tang & dry finish. — FM

Location/map/WO: Elgin ▪ Map grid reference: B1 ▪ Est 1962 ▪ 1stB 2003 ▪ Tasting & sales Mon-Fri 10-4; pub hols by appt only ▪ No tasting fee if purchasing ▪ Closed Easter Fri-Mon, Dec 25/26 & Jan 1 ▪ Online sales ▪ Owner(s) Mark Simpson ▪ Cellarmaster(s)/winemaker(s) Christo Versfeld (Villiersdorp Cellar) ▪ (cab, merlot, shiraz, sauv) ▪ PO Box 2 Elgin 7180 ▪ royalwine@arumdale.co.za ▪ www.arumdale.co.za ▪ **T +27 (0)21-859-3430**

Asara Wine Estate & Hotel ⓧ Ⓟ ⌂ ⓞ ⓐ

The sea of vines circling the luxe boutique hotel and facilities on the Asara wine and lifestyle estate in Stellenbosch is the focus of a multi-year replanting plan overseen by long-term viticulturist Alan Cockcroft. The aim is to remove virused material while making wine from the best-performing remaining blocks, thereby continuing to benefit from substantial recent work, guided by a top consultant, specifically around the Terroir range and its spotlight on the farm's rare gamay noir vines and other special parcels. Winemaker since 2021 Michiel du Toit will keep steering the grapes into bottle in a manner that 'combines tradition with modern thinking and our experience to create elegant wines with complexity and personality'.

Terroir range

★★★★ Gamay Noir ⊘ Fine Beaujolais-style **21** ⑧⑧ with succulent poached fruit, respectable dry farewell, brush of oak & fresh acid ensuring a vibrancy, inviting the next sip. No **20**.

★★★★ Passione Pinotage ⊘ Deep, concentrated & complex barrel selection. Spicy berry vibrancy supported by new oak, 16 months. **17** ⑧⑨ improves on **16** ★★★★☆ ⑧⑤ in subtlety & restraint.

★★★★☆ Chardonnay (NEW) ⊛ Clean lime, white peach & some delicate white flowers in elegantly styled **22** ⑨④. Pervasive freshness, subtle brush of toasted hazelnut from 3 months in older barrels, polished by a further 8 in bottle. Effortlessly balanced & graceful. Delicious solo or at the table.

★★★★☆ Amphora Chenin Blanc ⊛ Continues in fine & flavoursome style in **22** ★★★★★ ⑨⑤. Fermented in amphora & aged 3 months in older oak, lees contact providing mouthfilling richness to array of apple, citrus, green papaya, toasted nuts. Structured & wonderfully fresh, lingering & ageworthy. Last tasted was **18** ⑨②. WO W Cape, as all range whites tasted the edition.

★★★★☆ Granite Chenin Blanc ⊘ Creamy cashew & oatmeal breadth on **18** ⑨⓪, stonefruit vivacity is sufficient to counter it. Structured & long, the wine is refined & elegant, worth cellaring.

★★★★☆ Viognier Lovely intensity & freshness in **22** ⑨⓪, mouthfilling rich & tangy stonefruit infused with variety's floral notes. Tank ferment & less time in oak, 3 months vs 11, yet enough to add some plush breadth. A delicious glassful, perfect with spicy Asian fare. **20**, **21** not tasted.

★★★★☆ CVC ⊘ Chenin (68%) leads unoaked chardonnay & viognier in confident **18** ⑨⓪. Creamy, spicy apricot with gentle acid freshness followed by textured, persistent mouthful. Oak will knit in time.

Speciality Collection

★★★★☆ The Bell Tower ⊛ Cab leads again in this youthful 4-way Bordeaux blend, even more authoritative & restrained in cooler **19** ⑨①. Tightly coiled core of dark fruit in dry, firm tannin framework. Further inky intensity & minerality from 18 months in oak. Built for the long haul, deserves time to show full potential. **17**, **18** not made. WO W Cape, as next.

★★★★ Avalon Staggered harvesting of vine-dried pinotage & shiraz, **17** ⑧⑦ one of few SA Amarone-style wines. Compact tannin structure balances alc strength (15.6%), sweetness & layers of flavour: dried prune, polished leather, aromatic spice. Individual components in new oak 12 months, blend further 24, then lengthy bottle sojourn. **14** & **16** not made, **15** untasted.

★★★★ Méthode Cap Classique As tangy & arrestingly fresh in bone-dry **18** ★★★★ ⑧⑤ sparkler from chardonnay as **17** ⑧⑥. Hints lemon & green apple woven with subtle 15 months lees enrichment. Bottle aged 2-4 years, but still tighter than lightly oaked last, & best paired with food. Also in 1.5L.

★★★★ Carillon ⊘ Noble Late Harvest from chenin, old-oak aged. Deep gold **14** ⑧⑦ attractive stone-fruit & rooibos aromas, bracing acid to balance the apricot richness, uncloying marmalade conclusion.

★★★★ Vine Dried Sauvignon Blanc ⊘ Bottle-aged **14** ⑧⑧ just 10% alc yet packed with flavour & decadent richness, 198 g/L sugar well tucked in. Raises bar on earlier-released **16** ★★★☆ ⑧④. 375 ml.

The Red Cab ⊘ ★★★ Leafy freshness in **19** ⑧② from cabernet sauvignon contrasts with ripe cassis & dark chocolate, all in a chunky tannin embrace from 4 months on oak staves. **The White Cab** ⊘ ★★★ Unusual white from cabernet. Gentle tang of raspberry, light body & soft acid on **19** ⑧② summertime sipper.

Vineyard Collection

★★★★ Cabernet Sauvignon ⊘ **18** ⑧⑦ improves on **17** ★★★☆ ⑧⑤ in intensity, depth, but retains light succulence. Approachable & rounded, 90% had 18 months in 10% new oak, rest unoaked.

★★★★ Merlot ⊘ Quite structured & more serious in **19** ⑧⑦. Compact dark-berried fruit, dusting of dry firm tannins from year in older oak. Bottle ageing 2 years hones this youthful tablemate, even better if given more time. Step up on lighter **18** ★★★★ ⑧⑤. WO W Cape.

★★★★ Pinotage ⊘ Ripe berry fruit abundance of **18** ⑧⑦ tempered by chalky texture & dry tannin from 14 months in French barrels, third new. Structured yet rounded & rewarding. WO Coastal.

★★★★ Shiraz ⊘ Perky blueberry brightness to ripe, fresh **19** ⑧⑦. Rounded & fleshy, with herb nuance & inky depth. Good structure & body from 85% oaked portion, 15% new, 15 months.

★★★★ Sauvignon Blanc ⊘ Tangy & bright **22** ⑧⑦ more exuberant than last-tasted **20** ★★★★ ⑧⑤. Ample fig & passionfruit flavour, mouthfilling succulence & lingering farewell.

Pinotage Rosé ⊘ ★★★☆ Bright & breezy **22** ⑧③, appealing cranberry & pomegranate flavours, balancing acid. Marginally riper & plumper than last, still fits the poolside sipping bill, with aplomb. **Chardonnay**

Lightly Wooded Ⓥ ★★★☆ Plenty of charm in **20** (85) with ripe pear & twist of lime. Subtle toasty enhancement from 30% oaked portion. Ample & flavoursome tablemate. **Chenin Blanc** Ⓥ ★★★★ Rich-&-ripe styled **22** (85) is rounded, with baked apple & almond, complete with the cream for texture. Just enough acid for balance. Shade off last-tasted **20** ★★★★ (86).

Cape Fusion range
★★★★ **White** Ⓥ Ripe & juicy **20** (86) blend of oaked chenin & chardonnay (53/37), unwooded sauvignon. Stonefruit, almond & pear, toasted hazelnut & just enough freshening lime to streamline opulence. **Red** Ⓥ ★★★☆ **17** (85) sees cab join shiraz, pinotage & malbec in 4-way blend. Light, succulent, red & black berry charm in spades. WO Coastal. **Rosé** Ⓥ ★★★ Unfussy **20** (81) pre-bottling sample abounds with easy cherry, berry freshness. Light, bright & gluggable. Mostly malbec & merlot. — MW

Location/map: Stellenbosch ▪ Map grid reference: D6 ▪ WO: Stellenbosch/Western Cape/Coastal ▪ Est/1stB 2001 ▪ Tasting Mon-Sat 11-5 Sun/pub hols 11-4 ▪ Tasting fee R60-R75 ▪ Closed Dec 25 ▪ Tasting centre ▪ Cellar tours by appt Wed-Fri ▪ Tour groups ▪ 5-star TGCSA hotel ▪ Raphael's ▪ Sansibar bistro ▪ Deli ▪ Function & banqueting facilities ▪ Conferences ▪ Weddings ▪ Vineyard walks ▪ Winemaker(s) Michiel du Toit (2021) ▪ Viticulturist(s) Alan Cockcroft (2013) ▪ 180ha/102ha (cab, malbec, merlot, p verdot, ptage, shiraz, chard, chenin, sauv) ▪ 1,000t/125,000cs own label 70% red 30% white ▪ IPW, WIETA ▪ PO Box 882 Stellenbosch 7599 ▪ winesales@asara.co.za ▪ www.asara.co.za ▪ **T +27 (0)21-888-8000**

Ashbourne Ⓥ ⓘ

Owners Anthony and Olive Hamilton Russell's stately residence in Hemel-en-Aarde Valley gives this boutique label its name. Though produced by the Hamilton Russell Vineyards team in their cellar, Ashbourne has its own home nearby, with a vineyard (the only grape source) and a large conserved area. There are just two labels in the portfolio, a pinotage and a sauvignon blanc-based white, both showing 'restrained, classic styling while being quintessentially South African', crafted in minuscule quantity. Sauvignon gris, a pink-skinned mutation, is being planted to add 'an interesting textural component' rather than an aromatic one.

★★★★☆ **Pinotage** Ⓑ Shows serious intent in brooding dark fruit & savoury notes of tapenade & spice. **21** (93) full, rounded, with layers that unfold on the nose & palate, smooth & succulent to the last powdery drop. Well-judged oaking, 40% new barrel & foudre, 20 months. Also in magnum.

★★★★★ **Sandstone** Ⓑ Site-driven white, vines on sandstone, 51% sauvignon with chardonnay & semillon in **22** (94) shows lovely harmony of crème brûlée opulence & restraint courtesy piquant citrus at finish. Bunch pressed, naturally fermented/5 months on lees in amphora, 'egg' & older barrel for a persistent, moreish mouthful.— WB

Location: Hermanus ▪ WO: Hemel-en-Aarde Valley ▪ Est 1996 ▪ 1stB 2001 ▪ Tasting & sales at Hamilton Russell Vineyards ▪ Fynbos reserve, 2 wetlands, 3 biodiversity corridors ▪ Owner(s) Anthony & Olive Hamilton Russell ▪ Winemaker(s) Emul Ross (2014) ▪ Viticulturist(s) Johan Montgomery (2005) ▪ 64ha/24.35ha (ptage, sauv, sem) ▪ 700cs own label 40% red 60% white ▪ WWF-SA Conservation Champion ▪ PO Box 158 Hermanus 7200 ▪ info@ashbournewines.com ▪ www.ashbournewines.com ▪ **T +27 (0)28-312-3595**

Ashton Winery Ⓥ Ⓜ Ⓑ Ⓓ

Much pride here about the unveiling of the flagship blend, Lift The Eye, a tribute to the Ashton Arch, an engineering marvel and the first bridge of its kind in Africa. A portion of sales of the wine supports three local charities via a foundation run by the winery, which produces 15-million litres of wine and grape juice concentrate annually. An important 3% is bottled under the 45 shareholders' own label, and offered for tasting and sale at the venue in Ashton town, with special tastings and facilities available for children.

Reserve range
Roodewal Reserve ★★★★ Shiraz (36%) alongside cab & pinotage, dashes cab franc & merlot in **18** (85), showing just enough freshness to balance ripe prune & rum-&-raisin flavours, pleasing tannin bite & length. **Chardonnay Limited Release** ★★★★ Bright **22** (85) opens with peach, grapefruit & lemon meringue pie aromas, follows with fairly intense lemon-lime flavours & harmonious creamy oak from 70% new 500L barrels. **Angels Grace Morio Muscat** ★★★★ Fortified dessert wine from rare aromatic grape variety. **NV** (83) attractive deep straw hue, fresh grape & smoke aromas, luscious sweetness of 248 g/L sugar. Special bottling in memory of winery director Willem Viljoen's young daughter Winé. 500 ml. Not tasted: **Pinotage Winemaker's Reserve, Red Muscadel**.

Ashton range

★★★★ Lift The Eye Cape Blend (NEW) Attractive packaging, elegant modern styling for this pinotage (45%) blend with equal cab franc & merlot, splash shiraz, lavished with 50% new 300L oak. **19** (87) nice dryness at just 2 g/L sugar, vibrant acid & satisfying savoury overlay.

....

Cabernet Sauvignon-Merlot ☺ **★★★** Friendliest red in the line-up. **21** (82)'s oak spice mingles with black plum & berry compote, gentle tannins for ready drinkability.

....

Cabernet Sauvignon ★★★ Charry top note & grippy tannins from brief sojourn on new oak staves (like other reds unless noted) on **20** (79) matched with fresh blackberry flavours & acid for pleasant everyday drinking. **Merlot ★★★** Uncomplicated sipper with or without food, **20** (77)'s red & black fruit has a pleasing piquant lift. **Pinotage ★★★** Plum tones overlaid with olive tapenade & vanilla whiff from 20% American-oaked portion. **20** (77) moderate 12.5% alc for easy enjoyment. **Shiraz ★★** Red plums embraced by firm tannins on **20** (74), nice touch of black pepper in the background. **Chenin Blanc ★★★** Mid-2023, **23** (78) still shows guava ferment note & muted varietal character. **Sauvignon Blanc** ✓ **★★★** Tropical tones with pronounced granadilla & some guava accents on **23** (80), tart citrus acid to balance a few grams of sugar. Not tasted: **Satynrooi**, **Satynrosé**, **Chardonnay Unwooded**, **Satynwit**, **Satynperlé**, **Sauvignon Blanc Sparkling Brut**.

Joy range

Not tasted: **Juicy Red**, **Rosé**, **Crisp White**, **Sparkling Rosé**, **Sweet Red**. — NK, CvZ

Location: Ashton ▪ Map/WO: Robertson ▪ Map grid reference: B4 ▪ Est 1962 ▪ 1stB 1970 ▪ Tasting & sales Mon-Fri 8-5 Sat/pub hols 10-2 ▪ Closed Good Fri & Dec 25/26 ▪ Facilities for children ▪ Tour groups ▪ Picnic baskets by appt ▪ Gourmet sandwiches & cheese platters ▪ Owner(s) 45 shareholders ▪ Cellarmaster(s) Sterik de Wet (Oct 2009) ▪ Winemaker(s) Heinrich Coetzee (Sep 2013) & Willie Conradie (Nov 2021) ▪ 1,280ha (cab, merlot, ptage, ruby cab, shiraz, chard, chenin, sauv) ▪ 24,041t/15m L total: 3% under own label 56% bulk & 41% grape juice concentrate ▪ Other export brands: Joy, Nine Fields ▪ ISO 22000, HACCP, IPW, WIETA ▪ PO Box 40 Ashton 6715 ▪ info@ashtonwinery.com ▪ www.ashtonwinery.com ▪ **T +27 (0)23-615-1135**

Aslina Wines   ℗

Widely celebrated as an inspiration and role model, Ntsiki Biyela was raised in rural Kwa-Zulu Natal and won a scholarship to study Oenology & Viticulture, graduating in 2003 and joining Stellekaya. She established this boutique brand in 2016, honouring the biggest influence in her life, her grandmother Aslina. Since last edition, she's welcomed two new team members, and opened a tasting venue in Stellenbosch. 'A deep respect for the land, commitment to quality and celebration of African heritage' guide her winemaking.

★★★★ Cabernet Sauvignon Dark & dense **21** (88) packed with bright black fruit, pencil shavings & dark chocolate. 15% petit verdot & 18 months in older French barrels (as Umsasane) add backbone & firm tannin, needing time to unfurl.

★★★★☆ Umsasane (🐝) Understated **21** (90) blend from cab, cab franc & petit verdot (70/18/12) impresses with pristine blackcurrant, bramble, graphite & a violet perfume. Rounded & layered, delicious tannin & lively berry grip giving structure & build to last.

★★★★ Chardonnay More complexity in **22** (87) than 21 **★★★★** (85), baked apple, buttered toast & gentle vanilla richness tempered by fresh acidity. Flavourful yet elegant, lengthy grapefruit pith finish. Grapes from Stellenbosch (vinified in stainless steel) & Elgin (fermented in older barrels & lees aged).

★★★★ Skin-Contact Chenin Blanc Stonefruit & bruised apple, & a pithy, fleshy texture are well balanced, rich & supple in **22** (86). Simonsberg fruit fermented & left on skins in tank 7 days give this trademark style. Firm grip on exit makes it an excellent food wine.

Sauvignon Blanc ★★★★ Bright apple & tropical fruit leap out the glass in **22** (85) for a satisfying, zippy mouthful. Lees ageing adds complexity. WO W Cape. — WB

Location/map: Stellenbosch ▪ Map grid reference: D3 ▪ WO: Stellenbosch/Western Cape/Simonsberg-Stellenbosch ▪ 1stB 2013 ▪ Tasting strictly by appt ▪ Online shop ▪ Wine club ▪ Owner(s)/winemaker(s) Ntsiki Biyela ▪ 2,000cs own label 50% red 50% white ▪ Unit 1, Ground Floor, Building 4, Alberto Dr, Devonbosch, Bottelary Rd Stellenbosch 7605 ▪ info@aslinawines.com ▪ www.aslinawines.co.za ▪ **T +27 (0)71-924-9920**

☐ **Astraeus** *see* Waterkloof

☐ **Ataqua** *see* PaardenKloof
☐ **At Botha Wyn** *see* At se Wyn
☐ **Atlantic Slopes** *see* Hillcrest Estate
☐ **Atlantikas** *see* Scions of Sinai

Atlas Swift Ⓠ Ⓟ Ⓒ

A richly detailed 'atlas' of the winelands, highlighting the chosen sites and offering salient details, accompanies these terroir wines by boutique vignerons Martin and Welma Smith. They work in the Atlas cellar near Franschhoek (Martin also vinifies the Paserene label there), striving for 'a balance between winemaker and mother nature'. The promised red wines have been released, volumes are up and exports have begun.

Shelter range

★★★★☆ **Cabernet Sauvignon** (NEW) ⓐ Paarl grapes produce youthfully ruby-hued **20** ⑨⓪ showing textbook blackcurrant, tomato & tealeaf in a well-structured body, tannins supple & polished in older oak. Balanced, with graphite minerality on the expansive farewell.

★★★★ **Tempranillo** (NEW) Rare single bottling, Cederberg-grown **21** ⑧⑨ juicy, fruity & lipsmacking array of savoury aromas & smooth flavours - black cherry, tar, pot-pourri & vanilla from seasoned oak.

★★★★☆ **Red Blend** ⓐ Ageworthy Cape Bordeaux, **21** ⑨⓪ chiefly merlot & cab franc (56/20), 2 others, off Paarl & Wellington vines. Generous & typical blueberry & blackcurrant accented with fynbos & dried herbs. Pliant tannins & 22 months oaking allow for lengthy ageing. No **20**.

Not tasted: **Chardonnay**.

Atlas Swift range

★★★★☆ **Cape South Coast Chardonnay** ⓐ Evocatively packaged wines identically made to reveal terroir: spontaneous ferment & malo in small Burgundy barrel, year aged. **22** ⑨⓪ on limestone & chalk, preserved lemon & orchard fruit, smooth, rounded, salty minerality on finish.

★★★★ **Franschhoek Chardonnay** ⓐ Burst of tropical fruit introduces **22** ⑧⑨, followed by creamy roast cashew, & white flower perfume in a silky body with good weight, depth & length.

★★★★☆ **Robertson Chardonnay** ⓐ Limestone-based **22** ⑨① most expressive of the quintet. Golden Delicious, baked pie crust, lemongrass & light orange marmalade are all layered with passionfruit & ginger spice, delightful grapefruit tang at the end. Worth keeping, as all these.

★★★★ **Wellington Chardonnay** ⓐ Most generous of the range, rich & rounded, shows a panoply of tropical flavours in **22** ⑧⑧'s medium body. Fruit, acid & oak in good balance, cleansing lime zing on finish.

★★★★ **Wine of Origin Cederberg Chardonnay** ⓐ Cool-climate **22** ★★★★☆ ⑨⓪ bright & steely as expected, delicately jasmine perfumed, restrained yet with good depth & unfolding layers of citrus & creamy baked apple, long toasted almond farewell. Harmonious & less lean than **21** ⑧⑧. — WB

Location/map: Franschhoek ▪ Map grid reference: C3 ▪ WO: Western Cape/Cape South Coast/Franschhoek/Robertson/Wellington/Cederberg ▪ Est 2021 ▪ 1stB 2019 ▪ Tasting, sales & cellar tours Mon-Sun 10-4.30 & Tue-Sun (winter) ▪ Tasting from R160 ▪ Closed Dec 25 ▪ Tasting platters ▪ Farm produce ▪ Motor museum ▪ Wine Club ▪ Owner(s) Martin & Welma Smith ▪ Cellarmaster(s)/winemaker(s) Martin Smith ▪ Own label 20% red 80% white ▪ R45, Franschhoek 7690 ▪ welma@atlasswift.co.za ▪ www.atlasswift.co.za ▪ **T +27 (0)71-349-1773**

At se Wyn Ⓠ

Artist At Botha lives and works in the West Coast village of Paternoster, and his love for art, culture, wine and food inspired him to work with boutique vintner Christa von La Chevallerie on a small range of fresh, convivial wines, with labels that speak of his joie de vivre, while expressing Swartland character.

★★★★ **At se Wit** Ⓠ Charming & high-spirited blend of chenin & 4 others. **21** ⑧⑦ lipsmackingly dry, very easy to like. Paardeberg fruit certified as WO W Cape.

At se Rooi Ⓠ ★★★★ Savoury cherries & plums, dusty tannins & tealeaf lift, nice dry finish. **18** ⑧⑤ pinotage for current drinking. **At se Rosé** Ⓠ ★★★★ Pale salmon pink **21** ⑧③ sunset sipper from pinotage. Dry & light, with friendly raspberry & nectarine aromas & flavours, tad unlingering farewell. — CvZ

Location: Riebeek-Kasteel ▪ WO: Swartland/Western Cape ▪ Est/1stB 2020 ▪ Tasting & sales by appt only ▪ Fee R50pp ▪ Owner(s) At Botha, Stephan Niehaus, Christa von La Chevallerie ▪ Cellarmaster(s)/viticulturist(s) Christa von La Chevallerie ▪ Winemaker(s) Christa von La Chevallerie, with tasters Stephan Niehaus & At Botha

• 35t/600cs own label 30% red 40% white 30% rosé ▪ Huis van Chevallerie/At Se Wyn, 32 Main Str, Riebeek-Kasteel 7307 ▪ christa@huisvanchevallerie.com ▪ www.huisvanchevallerie.com ▪ **T +27 (0)72-237-1166**

☐ **Aubergine** *see* Migliarina Wines

Audacia Wines

Veteran winemaker Michael Dobrovic has joined part-owner Trevor Strydom and the Audacia team at the Stellenbosch cellar, noted for pioneering the use of the natural antioxidants in refined (i.e. de-flavoured and fully dissolvable) tannins derived from indigenous fynbos as a substitute for sulphur. Benefits include enhanced flavour, Trevor believes, and 'none of the allergens or irritations linked with sulphur-added wines'.

Naturally Preserved, No Sulphur Added range

★★★★ **Cabernet Sauvignon** ⓥ Herbaceous & rather meaty **21** ⑧⑥, with same solid dark fruit & firm tannins, but more depth, breadth & interest than **20** ★★★★ ⑧⑤.

★★★★ **Shiraz** ⊘ Continuing recent improved form, **21** ⑧⑥ similar harmonious sweet black fruit & tannin frame, latter touch less forthright. New oak now just 15%, 11 months, as other reds tasted this year.

★★★★ **Premium Red Blend** ⊘ Mulberry-fruited **21** ★★★★ ⑧⑤ followed by **NV** ⑧⑥, from malbec & merlot, showing improved structure & flavour, cassis & an attractive savouriness that invites a Sunday roast.

Merlot ⓥ ★★★★ Fruit-forward **21** ⑧④ has appealing ripe blueberry tone & full body, crunchy texture with chewy tannin. **Codebreaker** ★★★★ Decipher the creative label - Ant-I-Ox-ID-Ant - to break the code. Now **NV** ★★★★ ⑧④, from shiraz & malbec, similar opulent berry fruit & oak tannins needing time. Not tasted: **Ant-Ox Merlot Can**. Occasional release: **Chenin Blanc**. — DS

Location/map/WO: Stellenbosch ▪ Map grid reference: E8 ▪ Est 1930 ▪ Tasting by appt; sales Mon-Fri 10-3 ▪ Closed pub hols ▪ Owner(s) Strydom & Harris families ▪ Cellarmaster(s)/winemaker(s)/viticulturist(s) Michael Dobrovic (Jun 2023) ▪ 24ha/17ha (cabs s/f, malbec, merlot, p verdot, roobernet, shiraz) ▪ 120t/18,000cs own label 100% red ▪ IPW ▪ PO Box 12679 Die Boord 7613 ▪ info@audacia.co.za ▪ www.audacia.co.za ▪ **T +27 (0)21-881-3052**

Aufwaerts Co-operative

Breedekloof family enterprise Aufwaerts produces wine mostly for the trade but also markets a limited range under its own label, unavailable for us to taste this time.

Location: Rawsonville ▪ Map: Breedekloof ▪ Map grid reference: B6 ▪ Tasting by appt ▪ Winemaker(s) Hennie de Villiers ▪ PO Box 51 Rawsonville 6845 ▪ hanepoot39@gmail.com ▪ **T +27 (0)82-349-4001**

Aurelia Wines

Groote Post winemaker Lukas Wentzel drew on family for inspiration in naming his personal cap classique specialist brand: the wife of the first Wentzel at the Cape, Aurelia Stafforinus. Recently he's delighted to have help, marketing wise especially, from son Wian, for the thimblefuls of bubbly intended to be both consistent in style and reflective of the same Darling Hills vines that have supplied the grapes almost since inception.

★★★★ **Brut Rosé** ⊘ Pinot noir leads chardonnay 61/39 on **21** ⑧⑥. Strawberry & lemon zest vivacity, good dryness & gentle bread note from 15 months on lees. Crisp & refreshing, lingering aftertaste. These bubblies are Vegan Society endorsed.

★★★★ **Brut** ⊘ Varieties & proportions as Rosé, 14 months on lees. **21** ⑧⑦ is zippy & taut with green apple, lime sherbet & vivid, almost nervy acidity. Gentle, persistent mousse.— FM

Location/WO: Darling ▪ Est 2010 ▪ 1stB 2008 ▪ Closed to public ▪ Owner(s)/cellarmaster(s)/winemaker(s) Lukas Wentzel ▪ 3t/600cs own label ▪ WIETA ▪ PO Box 103 Darling 7345 ▪ lukas@grootepost.co.za ▪ **T +27 (0)22-492-2825/+27 (0)82-306-7373**

☐ **Autumn Harvest Crackling** *see* Heineken Beverages

Avontuur Estate

Endowed with prime Helderberg viticultural land, and now guided by awarded veteran wine-man Kevin Arnold, the 'home of fine wines and fast horses' is set on a new course, away from volume toward ultra-premium. With Kevin in the cellar, the accent is on Bordeaux varieties, shiraz and chardonnay, while some 45 ha of vines are being replanted with advice from big-name viticulturists Francois Hanekom and Heinie Nel. Meanwhile the Taberer family owners will 'heavily focus' on tourism and leisure offerings on the estate.

Premiere Collection

★★★★☆ **Talk Of The Town Cabernet Sauvignon Reserve Premium** Layered, confident **19** ⑨⓪ echoes enhanced form of **18** ⑨①. Richly fruited & ripe but with beautiful gentle texture. Fine tannin balance & backbone from 16 months in 30% new oak.

★★★★ **Baccarat** ⓩ Petit verdot leads on brambly, spicy **17** ⑧⑧, improving on merlot-accented **14** ⑧⑥ version of the Bordeaux blend. Squeeze of dry tannin is from 80% oaking in older casks, 24 months.

Not tasted: **Legal Eagle Cabernet Franc Reserve**, **Dominion Royale Shiraz Reserve**, **Luna de Miel Chardonnay Reserve**. Discontinued: **Minelli Pinot Noir Reserve**, **Sarabande Sauvignon Blanc Reserve**.

Estate Collection

Cabernet Sauvignon-Merlot ★★★☆ Savoury, succulent **21** ⑧⑤ near-equal blend has splash shiraz, is gently dry with subtle brush of tannin. Accessible & easy, ideal for Tuesday night pasta. **Rosé** ★★★ Bright, raspberry-toned **22** ⑧② is light, fresh & unfussy. Summertime poolside quaffing from pinot noir & pinotage. **Sauvignon Blanc** ★★★ Delivers tropical stonefruit with light lemon zest nuance. **22** ⑧② fresh, rounded & succulent, soft rather than crisp. **Brut Cap Classique** ★★★☆ Pinot noir amped up to 42% on **NV** ⑧⑤ dry sparkler with chardonnay. Lively, brisk, with crunchy green apple notes & rounded finish from year on lees. Discontinued: **Pinotage**.

Private Collection

★★★★★ **10 Year Old Potstill** ⓩ Robustly impressive brandy ⑨⓪ from chenin. Less blatant fruitiness than many but deeply flavourful; silky, rich & rather gorgeously ingratiating.— FM, TJ

Location/WO: Stellenbosch ▪ Map: Helderberg ▪ Map grid reference: C2 ▪ Est 1850 ▪ 1stB 1984 ▪ Tasting & sales Mon-Fri 8.30-5 Sat/Sun 9-4; pub hols 8.30-4 ▪ Fee R100/5 wines ▪ Closed Good Fri, Dec 25 & Jan 1 ▪ Wine pairing experiences ▪ Tour groups ▪ Avontuur Estate Restaurant ▪ Function/wedding venue ▪ Thoroughbred stud ▪ Self-guided farm walks ▪ Seasonal events ▪ Wine club ▪ Luxury accommodation in historic Avontuur Manor House ▪ Owner(s) Taberer family ▪ Winemaker(s) Kevin Arnold (Jan 2023, consultant) ▪ Viticulturist(s) Francois Hanekom & Heinie Nel ▪ 110ha/40ha (cabs s/f, merlot, shiraz, chard) ▪ 250t 70% red 30% white ▪ PO Box 1128 Somerset West 7129 ▪ info@avontuurestate.co.za ▪ www.avontuurestate.co.za ▪ **T +27 (0)21-855-3450**

Axe Hill   ⓩ 🍴

Since the change of ownership in the late 2000s, prime mover Mike Neebe has retained the port-style made famous by the late boutique winery founder Tony Mossop, while adding unfortified varietal wines and blends chiefly using Portuguese varieties, plus chenin and some rarities like palomino. Though a new site is available, 'the jury is out' on new plantings mooted last time. Better news is the granting of a liquor licence for Die Bakhuis farmstall, which shares the farm near Calitzdorp town with the tiny vineyard and cellar.

Axe Hill range

★★★★ **Touriga Nacional** ⓩ Like last, hearty **19** ⑧⑥ shows good typicity in its deep purple colour, dark prune & plum aromas with orange rind nuance, firm ripe tannins. Just a tad less juice on palate.

★★★★ **Machado** Touriga with 14% tinta roriz delivers more flavour, complexity than other reds. **19** ⑧⑥'s red fruit topped with pot-pourri & orange zest, lifted by punchy tannins. Worth keeping year/2.

★★★★ **Cape Vintage** Opaque **20** ⑧⑨ blends tempranillo & touriga with 17% souzão, offers plenty of glacé cherry & mince pie interest, commendable dryness (for 'port') & integrated spirit; shade less 'heart' than last **16** ★★★★★ ⑨①, just misses the tannin structure for lengthy cellaring. Now in 750 ml, was in slender 500-ml bottle.

....

Distinta 🍃 ★★★☆ Similarly piquant **21** ⑧⑤ the first since nicely savoury **17** ★★★ ⑧②. Mostly touriga but 14% grenache noir ups the fruit flavour & complexity, ensures satisfying balance & grip.

....

Tinta Roriz 🆕 ★★★★ Redcurrant & plum fruit, pleasant meaty whiff & firm grape tannins in a tangy but ripe - not sweet - body in **21** ⑧⑤. No new oak, as all tasted this edition. Not tasted: **Ambientem**, **Cape Late Bottled Vintage**, **Cape Ruby**, **Cape Tawny**, **Cape White**. Occasional release: **Shiraz**, **'Cellar Red'**.

Gatos range

Cinsault ② ★★★☆ Less of a cherry-berry fruit bomb than previous, slightly more vinous at 11.8% alc. **21** ⑧③ still savoury, bone-dry & delicious. **Baksteen** ★★★☆ From chenin, 24 hours on skins before free-run & some press juice is barrel-fermented; overwinters on its lees, bottled unfined/filtered. Step-up **22** ⑧④ white peach & apple (bruised, skin) nuances, bracing acid. **Kanna** ★★★☆ Now WO Calitzdorp, **22** ⑧⑤ drops chenin to become 50/50 viognier & palomino combo. As broad as expected (these being low-acid varieties) & easy (3.6 g/L sugar), friendly tug of tannin aiding drinkability.

Lenie's Hof range

Red ② ★★★ Soft floral fragrance on **20** ⑧⓪ contrasts with rather stern palate, robust tannins of touriga & tinta roriz (63/37). **Tant Lenie** ★★★☆ Barrel-fermented, unfiltered typically more 'white wine' than 'viognier'. **22** ⑧③ no exception, with subtle varietal apricot & peach on nose & palate, smooth finish. — CvZ

Location/WO: Calitzdorp ▪ Map: Klein Karoo & Garden Route ▪ Map grid reference: B5 ▪ Est 1993 ▪ 1stB 1997 ▪ Tasting, sales & cellar tours Mon-Sat by appt ▪ Die Bakhuis farmstall - separate from the cellar on the R62, serving wood-fired pizza, baking bread, grilling on an open fire, & more - www.bakhuis.co.za - disabled access & toilet facilities ▪ Owner(s) Axe Hill Winery (Pty) Ltd ▪ Cellarmaster(s)/winemaker(s) Mike Neebe (Oct 2007) ▪ Viticulturist(s) Mike Neebe ▪ ±60ha/1.8ha (cinsaut, grenache, souzão, tinta barocca, tinta roriz, touriga nacional, chenin, viog) ▪ ±5t/±1,000cs own label 60% red 40% white ▪ Wesoewer Rd, Calitzdorp 6660 ▪ info@axehill.co.za ▪ www.axehill.co.za ▪ **T +27 (0)11-447-3900/+27 (0)83-676-3000**

Axle Wines

Stellenbosch vintner and cycling enthusiast Alex Milner credits his own team, as well as Darling grower Albé Truter and his crew for aiding the goal of 'keeping the link between grape and bottle as close as humanly possible' for this chenin-focused terroir project. Alex wishes the tiny old Natte Nalleij cellar could produce more of the wine that's mostly exported, to Australia inter alia, 'which is a bit like winning a test match!'

★★★★☆ **Chenin Blanc** ⓐ ⊛ Darling old dryland bushvine fruit, naturally fermented in old oak, aged 9 months on fine lees for sumptuous mouthful of pineapple, apple pie, honeydew melon. **22** ⑨③ balanced & rounded, suggestion of ginger persisting on finish.— WB

Location: Stellenbosch ▪ WO: Darling ▪ Est 2018 ▪ 1stB 2019 ▪ Closed to public ▪ Owner(s)/winemaker(s) Alexander Milner ▪ 6t/550cs ▪ PO Box 4 Klapmuts 7625 ▪ wine@nattevalleij.co.za ▪ **T +27 (0)84-643-3600**

Ayama Wines   ② ⑪ ⌂ ◎ ⑧

For almost 20 years, historic Slent Farm on the Voor Paardeberg slope has been in the hands of 'proudly South African, truly Italian' investors who celebrate the connections between the two countries, and forge new ones, like sourcing and planting material from Sardinia to 'bring the vermentino grape into SA ampelography'. They also adopt exotics like petite sirah to the farm's original chenin and pinotage, and extend Italian inspiration beyond wine into the farm garden and deli, with produce like olive oil and artichokes.

Premium range

★★★★☆ **Carignan** ⓐ Redcurrant & ripe strawberry, dialed-down new oak, from 50% to 30%, allows **22** ⑨② 's savoury freshness & round, fruit-coated tannins to shine. **21** untasted.

★★★★☆ **Vermentino** ⓥ ⓐ Sardinian specialty has a happy home here. **22** ⑨④ bunch pressed, fermented in tank & aged in old barrels, giving distinct salty-leesy character to peachy fruit.

Ayama range

★★★★ **Nero d'Avola** ⑯ Previewed **23** ⑧⑦ 's fragrant raspberries dusted with woody cinnamon, light feel enhanced by restrained oaking in large older barrels, 6 months. WO W Cape.

★★★★ **Grenache Blanc** ⓥ Good fruit typicity on clean & lithe **23** ⑧⑦ unwooded tank sample. Bottled in spring & has that season's fresh feel & fragrance, lime blossom & sliced pear, appealing lemony dryness.

★★★★ **Vermentino** Tank ferment/ageing for early-drinking **23** ★★★★ ⑧⑤. Lemony & peachy, few grams sugar contrast with its pithy freshness. Misses salty nuance of **22** ⑧⑥.

Chenin Blanc ⑰ ⊛ ★★★ Good tropical fruit & weight to **23** ⑧② , pineapple, mango & squeeze of lemon, tangy, lively acid & benign 13% alc.

Cabernet Sauvignon ⊛ ★★★ A leaner, red-fruited (rather than black-) take on the classic grape. **23** ⑧② barrel sample's oak regime (partial ferment, further 6 months ageing in new wood) lends marked tannin grip. **Merlot** ⑫ ★★★★ 6 months in older, larger barrels provide a stage for **21** ⑧⑤ to express its red plum, cherry & raspberry character. Pure pleasure, soft tannins melting into chocolaty finish. **Petite Sirah** ★★★★ Inky garnet hue hints at grape's often brooding character. Pre-bottling, **23** ⑧④ smoky blackberries, smooth finish from 6 months on fine lees in older barrels. **Pinotage** ⑫ ★★★★ Improving on previous, **22** ⑧⑤ unwooded to show off vibrancy & fruit. Alluring, variety-true berry perfume & some less usual pepper spice. **Shiraz** ⑫ ★★★ Aged year+ in steel tank, **19** ⑧② preview vinified with freshness in mind. Plummy & juicy, with touches of sweet tobacco & spice. **Viognier** ★★★ Spicy white blossoms & clean peach on **23** ⑧②, shot through with vigorous acidity, improves on last.

Discontinued: **Leopard Spot range.** — ML

Location/map: Paarl ▪ Map grid reference: B2 ▪ WO: Voor Paardeberg/Western Cape ▪ Est 2005 ▪ 1stB 2006 ▪ Tasting & sales Mon-Sun 10-4; pub hols (seasonal) please call ahead ▪ Meals/refreshments ▪ Deli with fresh farm produce, olive oil, wines, artichokes & much more ▪ Walking trail ▪ Child friendly ▪ Dog friendly ▪ Conservation area ▪ Guesthouse ▪ Owner(s) Slent Farms (Pty) Ltd ▪ Director & marketing manager Giuseppe Di Benedetto ▪ Cellarmaster(s)/winemaker(s) Chiara Fabietti (2021) ▪ Viticulturist(s) Eugene Taylor (2021) ▪ 210ha/65ha (cab, carignan, grenache n/b, merlot, nero d'avola, petite sirah, ptage, shiraz, chenin, sauv, vermentino, viog) ▪ 300t/40,000c own label 40% red 58% white 2% rosé ▪ WIETA ▪ Suite 106 Private Bag X3041 Paarl 7620 ▪ ayama@ayama.info ▪ www.ayama.info ▪ **T +27 (0)21-869-8313**

☐ **Azania** see Germanier Wines
☐ **Baba Yetu** see Wolvenhoek Vineyards
☐ **Baboon Rock** see La Petite Ferme Winery

Babylon's Peak Private Cellar   ⑫ ⊚ ♿

Bushvines planted by previous generations in granitic soils are the pride of owner and cellarmaster Stephan Basson and wife Inalize on their expansive estate high on Swartland's Paardeberg. The focus is on Rhône varieties, chenin and pinotage, and, after two years' preparation, a new ultra-premium range featuring certified heritage vineyards is set to launch this year. Meanwhile the cellar is being significantly expanded.

Babylon's Peak range

★★★★ **Cinsault** ⑫ Enticing **19** ⑧⑦ steps up on **18** ★★★★ ⑧⑤. Textured, but packed with cherry & cranberry succulence, framed by judicious oak, 10 months. Good body & length.

★★★★ **Pinotage** ⑫ Refined **20** ⑧⑥ is on the black-fruit spectrum (cherries, blackberries), hints liquorice & fennel framed by super-soft tannins & just the faintest grip from 10 months in old oak.

★★★★ **Shiraz-Carignan** ⑫ Mediterranean bedmates shiraz (60%) & carignan harmonise in **20** ⑧⑧. Redcurrants & spiced dates with gentle acid & fine, fruity tannins, burnished 10 months in old oak.

★★★★ **SMG** ⑫ Savoury **18** ⑧⑨ pliable & textured, shows good depth & 14-month oak support. Near-identical blend to last, 50/40 syrah & mourvèdre, dab grenache for seasoning.

★★★★ **Viognier-Roussanne** ⑫ Barrel-fermented viognier (56%) & roussanne in total harmony on enchanting **21** ★★★★★ ⑨⓪, latter adding flesh & stonefruit to jasmine & earthy note. Old oak, 8 months. Improves on last **17** ⑧⑨.

....

Chenin Blanc ⊘ ⊛ ★★★★ Sunshiny **23** ⑧⑤ as delicious as ever. Unwooded, with tropical bounce & lemony verve, supported by line of creamy lees.

....

The Wedge range
Not tasted: **Grenache, Pinotage, Shiraz-Mourvèdre-Viognier, Chenin Blanc, Chenin Blanc-Roussanne.** — ML

Location: Malmesbury ▪ Map/WO: Swartland ▪ Map grid reference: C8 ▪ Est/1stB 2003 ▪ Tasting & sales by appt only ▪ Conservation area ▪ Owner(s) Stephan Basson ▪ Cellarmaster(s)/winemaker(s)/viticulturist(s) Stephan Basson (Jan 2003) ▪ 580ha/350ha (carignan, grenache, mourv, ptage, shiraz, chenin, rouss, viog) ▪ 30,000c own label 65% red 35% white ▪ PO Box 161 Malmesbury 7299 ▪ info@babylonspeak.co.za ▪ www.babylonspeak.co.za ▪ **T +27 (0)21-300-1052**

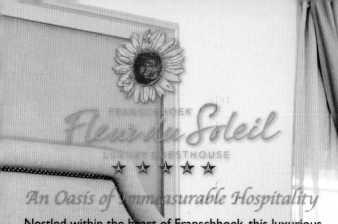

FRANSCHHOEK
Fleur du Soleil
LUXURY GUESTHOUSE
★ ★ ★ ★ ★

An Oasis of Immeasurable Hospitality

Nestled within the heart of Franschhoek, this luxurious sanctuary guarantees more than just personalised hospitality.

Here, you can experience an exclusive rejuvenation of self and reclamation of precious time.

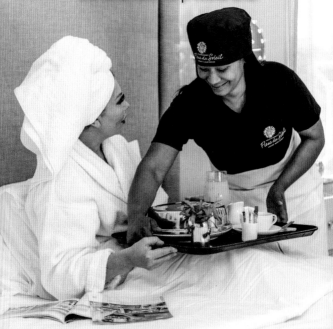

📍 7A Van Riebeeck Street, Franschhoek, 7690

✉️ bookings@fleur-du-soleil.com

🌐 www.fleur-du-soleil.com

📞 +27 60 808 8905

f fleurdusoleilguesthouse   fds_luxury   fds_luxury

2023
Travelers'
Choice
Tripadvisor
Best of the Best

FALK FAMILY

CANETSFONTEIN

EST 1781

BAINSKLOOF · WELLINGTON

Just as the roots of the vines
are embedded in these
ancient mountain soils,
so wine making lives in our soul.

www.canetsfontein.com | social media: @canetsfonteinwines

Canetsfontein, Bovlei Rd, Wellington, Western Cape, South Africa
tel: 021 204 5845 | email: info@canetsfontein.com
gps: 33° 38'21"S 19°03'58"E

CLIFFHANGER

by

CANETSFONTEIN

So extreme we named a wine after it

organic wine · mtb

AWARD WINNING CRUISE SPECIALISTS

Whitestar Cruise & Travel are **award-winning Cruise Operators** representing selected Premium Cruise Lines: **Cunard, Seabourn, P&O Cruises, Norwegian Cruise Line, Celestyal Cruises, Hurtigruten** & **Viva River Cruises.**
WHERE WILL YOUR SEAFARING ADVENTURE UNFOLD?

WHITESTAR
CRUISE & TRAVEL

🌐 www.whitestar.co.za
📞 +27 11 463 3293
✉ info@whitestar.co.za

Babylonstoren

In a previous guide we noted Babylonstoren and its multifarious allures as 'a buffet, tucked into a cornucopia, served on a smorgasbord', and a visit since confirmed this as something of an understatement, with yet more features added and several in train, such as a heritage-farm development in an adjacent valley, complete with period costumes for the people working there, and the incorporation of neighbour land and buildings acquired from the Back family. It's not just the jaw-dropping variety of amenities available on Koos Bekker and wife Karen Roos' 17th-century Cape Dutch home-farm on the Paarl side of Simonsberg that impresses, but also the attention to detail, reflected in the unique wine to be offered to wine club members, a debut pinot noir from their highest vineyard, with attached invitation-only deck that, at the owner's request, includes Table Mountain in the view, without which the experience would be deemed incomplete.

★★★★ **Cabernet Sauvignon** ⓐ Deep ruby colour already attests to ripeness & fruit quality: **21** ⑧⑨ oaked 18 months (as Shiraz), 40% new, giving dark chocolate seasoning to cassis & plums. Good tannin foundation for ageing but already accessible, the body nicely curvaceous.

★★★★ **Shiraz** ⓐ Standout plush fruit, berries & plums, reflects **21** ★★★★★ ⑨⓪'s ripeness, which allowed the oaking, 70% new. Spice & charcuterie savoury tones, tannins supple, texture succulent but a lithe strength for ageing. Hedonistic, level up from **20** ⑧⑨.

★★★★ **Nebukadnesar** ⓐ Estate's flagship always Bordeaux styled: cab, merlot, 3 others, all made separately. Seriously oaked, 2 years, 85% new. Inky coloured **21** ★★★★★ ⑨⑤ has layered depths, plush berries & plums, tobacco & cocoa dusting, yet a smooth-textured, luscious partner for the firm but ripe tannins. Distinguished future, the best lies ahead, as with **20** ⑨②.

★★★★ **Babel** Shiraz with cab & 9 others (aptly named!), barrel & foudre fermented, total year in oak. **22** ⑧⑧ is dark toned, brambly, smoky, with scrub note, attractively accessible palate, tannins amenable, with lithe strength for ageing.

★★★★☆ **Chardonnay** Cellar attention: wholebunch, tank ferment completed in barrel, 4 months on lees, then 6 in oak, 35% new. Intense citrus in **22** ⑨⓪, a melba toast top note, marmalade flavours, a function of ripeness, fruit & oak. Ends dry, zesty. Also in 1.5L, as Cab & Nebukadnesar.

★★★★ **Viognier** Combo tank (70%), older oak barrels & foudre, 7 months on lees, care taken to preserve **22** ⑧⑧'s fruit, which shows best in the perfume. Peach, fresh, dried & kernel, some honeysuckle aromatics, the flavours fruity-fresh.

★★★★ **Candide** ⊘ Blend of all white varieties on farm: chardonnay plus chenin, semillon, 2 others, all made separately: combo barrel ferment, tank, concrete 'egg' & clay amphora, 4 months on lees. **23** ⑧⑨ wonderfully perfumed, floral notes & stonefruit, body & freshness, heaps of flavour.

★★★★☆ **Sprankel** ⓐ Cap classique sparkler, chardonnay with 5% pinot noir. No effort spared in **18** ★★★★★ ⑨⑦'s making: 7 months on primary lees, then 55 months in bottle for 2nd ferment; no oak, unlike **17** ⑨④. Clementine & ruby grapefruit, vibrant acid keeping it in prime condition. Only clue to age is on palate, a preserved lemon top note. Taut, nervy, admirably pure & focused.

. . . .

Mourvèdre Rosé ⓥ ★★★★ Official rosé of 2023 Chelsea Flower Show. Among handful of SA pinks from this grape: very pale colour but **23** ⑧④ makes up for it in scent, prominent red berries. Elegant, softly rounded palate, finishes fresh & dry. **Chenin Blanc** ⓥ ★★★★ Unwooded **23** ⑧④, 10% in concrete 'egg' & clay amphora, intensifying baked apple scent, adding a lemon essence refinement to the flavour. — CR

Location: Simondium ▪ Map: Franschhoek ▪ Map grid reference: B8 ▪ WO: Simonsberg-Paarl ▪ Est 1692 ▪ 1stB 2011 ▪ Wine tasting & sales daily 10-5 (winter)/10-6 (summer) ▪ Cellar tours daily at 10, 1 & 4 (2 hrs) - please email enquiries@babylonstoren.com to book ▪ Tour groups by appt ▪ Farm shop, Lekker Room, Meat Room, Milk Room & Scented Room open daily 9-5 ▪ Online shop ▪ Guided garden tours at 10 daily ▪ Special collection tours at 11.30 daily ▪ Babylonstoren Farm Hotel ▪ Bakery dinners: Italian inspired evenings Mon & Fri 6-9 ▪ Babel Restaurant: breakfast Mon-Sun 8-9.30, lunch Wed-Sun from 12-3.30, dinner Mon-Sun from 6-8.30; The Greenhouse Restaurant Mon-Sun 9-5 (winter)/9-6 (summer) ▪ Garden Spa 8-5 ▪ Spice Garden open for group bookings at 12 ▪ Olive oil and balsamic vinegar tours daily at 11, 1 & 3 ▪ Mampoer distillery ▪ The Story of Wine museum ▪ Wine club ▪ Cellarmaster(s) Charl Coetzee ▪ Winemaker(s) Klaas Stoffberg, with Jeanne Pienaar ▪ Viticulturist(s) Ian de Villiers ▪ Babylonstoren Farm, Klapmuts-Simondium Rd, Simondium 7670 ▪ cellar@babylonstoren.com ▪ www.babylonstoren.com ▪ **T** +27 (0)21-863-3852

Bacco Wine Estate   ⓠ ⑪

Nathan Jankelowitz's Tuscan-accented homage to the god of wine on the Simonsberg-Paarl foothills has opened its doors to the public, with a lounge and restaurant offering tastings paired with canapés and Italian-style small-plate meals paired with the wines, plus further options for private tasting groups. In the cellar, by leading designer Gerard de Villiers, the philosophy is 'perfection takes time', and Nathan says he's inspired by the Supertuscans in the 'gentle fermentation and long maturation of at least two years in barrel and one in bottle before release'. Julia Blaine is now responsible for styling 'classic but true-to-terroir wines'.

Bacco range

★★★★ Cabernet Sauvignon-Malbec ⓧ Ageworthy **19** ⑧⑧ blend, 28% malbec provides subtle meaty overlay to dominant variety's attractive cassis, lead pencil & tobacco notes. Fleshy palate given form & solid grip by all-new oak, 22 months. Paarl WO.

★★★★★ Red Blend ⓝⓔⓦ ⓥ ⓐ With striking packaging **20** ⑨⑤ is a cab-led (61%) Bordeaux blend, bunch & berry sorted for the best fruit expression, 22 months in barrel. Classic lead pencil, blackcurrant & plum, a herbal whiff, but main attraction is the palate: streamlined, luscious fruit in charge, tannins fine.

★★★★ Rosé One of a kind, from distinctive bottle to malbec, syrah & vermentino blend, to year in neutral barrel. Salmon pink **22** ⑧⑨ is complex, with fresh strawberry, rosepetal & white peach in an elegant body. Dry, with a fresh lift giving vibrancy. Wow!

★★★★ Chardonnay ⓝⓔⓦ Partial wild ferment/12 months small barrels give **22** ⑧⑨ classic chardonnay styling: citrus preserve & Lemon Cream biscuit, nice roundness, a tangy finish. Sleek, taut racehorse lines.

★★★★ Vermentino Care taken to extract maximum varietal expression: skin contact, use of neutral barrels. Distinctive, **22** ⑧⑨'s profile is pithy grapefruit, touch of lime, strengthening in the crisp finish. Classy, one of a handful on the market. Moved from Prelude line-up, as Rosé.

Prelude By Bacco range

★★★★ Red Blend Changed composition, now near-equal malbec & cab, deep colour attesting to cellar extraction processes. More oak (22 months) than still-available **19** ⑧⑥, **20** ⑧⑧ is dense & dark toned, with hints of green brush, but gets the tannin right, supple support that gives strength without intruding.

Syrah ★★★★ Handling change in **20** ⑧⑤, increased to 18 months in older barrels. Brambleberry & dried herb, a touch of fynbos, lovely savoury note in the flavour. — CR

Location: Paarl ▪ Map: Franschhoek ▪ Map grid reference: A8 ▪ WO: Simonsberg-Paarl/Paarl ▪ Est 2016 ▪ 1stB 2019 ▪ Tasting, sales & cellar tours 10-5 daily ▪ Fee R120 ▪ Cicchetti-style meal offerings, patisserie, coffee & tea bar in tasting room ▪ Closed Jan 1 ▪ Tour groups ▪ Owner(s) Bacco Estate (Pty) Ltd - shareholder Nathan Jankelowitz ▪ Cellarmaster(s) Martin Smith (Jun 2018, consultant) ▪ Winemaker(s) Julia Blaine (Oct 2022) ▪ Viticulturist(s) Johan Wiese (Jun 2015, consultant) ▪ 60ha/15ha (cabs s/f, malbec, merlot, sangio, shiraz, chard, vermentino) ▪ 100t/14,500cs own label 80% red 10% white 10% rosé ▪ PO Box 651253 Benmore 2010 ▪ info@baccoestate.co.za ▪ www.baccoestate.co.za ▪ **T +27 (0)63-296-2147**

Backsberg Family Wines   ⓠ ⑪ ⓒ ⓖ

Latterly under DGB custodianship, with production facilities and memorabilia-filled visitor locale relocated to Franschhoek, the venerable and much-loved Backsberg label continues on its accessible path, the aim being 'to provide enjoyment in each and every glass'. Basic concerns under the previous Back family ownership, notably care for the environment, remain, evidenced by carbon-neutral certification for some of the wines. Sibling brands Sydney Back Kosher Wines, Unorthodox and Tread Lightly not tasted this edition.

The Patriarch range

★★★★☆ Cabernet Franc ⓧ 'Best secret vineyard' in Stellenbosch the provenance of alluring **21** ⑨③, perfumed, fresh & light footed despite 14% alc. A youthful, graceful & ageworthy gem. Stellenbosch WO.

The Family Tree range

★★★★ Pumphouse Shiraz Streamlined **22** ⑧⑥ has minuscule splashes mourvèdre & viognier. Properly ripe, well made & complete, with approachable tannins, juicy red fruit & savoury notes; oak well judged, now 12 months, 25% new. Better balanced than last-tasted **20 ★★★★** ⑧⑤.

★★★★ John Martin Cabernet Sauvignon-Malbec-Cabernet Franc-Petit Verdot Honours former stalwart farm manager. Tweaked blend touch riper in **18** ⑧⑨ though similar dark berries & dry cedar spice from melded oak, 25% new, 18 months. Retains freshness, accessible balance & potential for growth. WO Paarl.

★★★★ **Smuggled Vines Chardonnay** Name alludes to early 1970s arrival of variety to SA. Continues zesty styling in tablemate **22** ⑧⑧, similar piquancy to citrus, nectarine & marzipan scents & flavours, subtle oak support.

The Fifth Generation range

★★★★ **Four Pillars Cabernet Sauvignon** ⊘ More balance & juicy ripe plum & cassis flavours in **20** ⑧⑦, buffed by well-melded vanilla oak spicing, 12 months, 15% new. Dry & deliciously drinkable.

Plum Valley Merlot ★★★★ More approachable in riper **20** ⑧⑤. Shows namesake dark fruit notes, hint of mint & some dry spiced tannins from a year in oak. Bright, with fresh acid lift, will make a good food partner. **Blueberry Row Pinotage** ⑫ ★★★★ Aptly named **20** ⑧③ adds Turkish delight-scented flavours to the advertised berries. Slightly fuller yet still fresh, poised, farewell is dry, spicy from brush of oak. Not tasted: **Old Cellar Dry Red, Ella Pinotage Rosé, Summer Berry Rosé, Citrus Hill Chardonnay, Gravel Road Chenin Blanc, Hillside Sauvignon Blanc.**

Fortified range

Not tasted: **Pinneau.**

Brandy range

Not tasted: **Sydney Back First Distillation, Sydney Back 15 Year, Sydney Back 10 Year.** — MW

Location/map: Franschhoek ▪ Map grid reference: C2 ▪ WO: Coastal/Stellenbosch/Paarl ▪ Est 1916 ▪ 1stB 1970 ▪ Tasting Wed–Sun 10–6; pub hols (seasonal) please call ahead ▪ Cellar tours ▪ Selection of pairings, both sweet and savoury; grazing-boards; picnics in summer ▪ Historic memorabilia on display ▪ Wine club ▪ Owner(s) Backsberg Family Wines ▪ Winemaker(s) Alicia Rechner (Jun 2012) ▪ 900t/160,000cs own label 65% red 30% white 5% rosé ▪ Other export brands: Unorthodox, Sydney Back ▪ Certified carbon neutral PAS 2060:2014 ▪ Main Rd R45, Franschhoek 7690 ▪ backsbergwine@dgb.co.za ▪ www.backsberg.co.za ▪ **T +27 (0)21-876-2086**

☐ **Bad Brothers** see Goedverwacht Wine Estate
☐ **Badenhorst Family Wines** see AA Badenhorst Family Wines

Badger & Mountain ⑫

Adrian Strydom's young brand, with the Cape honey badger as its emblem, has a home on Swartland's Paardeberg, and it's in that vicinity that the grapes for his new release were sourced and allowed to ferment with native yeasts, in line with his preference for making 'fresh and honest' wine as naturally as possible.

★★★★ **Grenache Rock** ⓝⓔⓦ Whole bunch, wild ferment, 10 months in small barrels, **22** ⑧⑧ offers grenache noir's drinkability, prominent red berries in perfume & flavour. The oak spicing adds to the attraction, tannins are harmonious, the texture plush. Nicely made.

Not tasted: **Syrah Mantra, Cape Red Blend, Holiday Rosé, Chenin Heaven, Cape White Blend.** — CR

Location: Malmesbury ▪ Map/WO: Swartland ▪ Map grid reference: C8 ▪ Est/1stB 2019 ▪ Tasting, sales & cellar tours Mon–Sat by appt only ▪ Fee R50 ▪ Closed all pub hols ▪ Wine club ▪ Owner(s) Adrian Strydom ▪ Winemaker(s) Lisa Gerber & MC Stander (both Jun 2019, consultants) ▪ ±5ha (cinsaut, grenache, ptage, shiraz, chenin, sem) ▪ 40,000 L own label 80% red 10% white 10% rosé ▪ IPW ▪ 33 Lismore Ave, Tokai, Cape Town 7945 ▪ adrian@greenhillwines.co.za ▪ www.badgermountain.co.za ▪ **T +27 (0)82-589-1371**

☐ **Badlands** see Thor Vintners

Badsberg Wine Cellar ⑫ ⑪ ⓸ ⓑ ⓕ

On the foot of the Badsberg, the namesake winery has been in production for over 70 years, and today brings a substantial 43,000 tons from 18 shareholders into its cellar near Rawsonville. Cellarmaster Willie Burger and his colleagues carefully select parcels for the proprietary range, which retains the historical sweeter styles alongside the unfortified/dry bottlings that do so well at the Young Wine Show in particular, winning the competition's top prize, the General Jan Smuts Trophy, on multiple occasions.

★★★★ **Ruby Cabernet Generaal Smuts** ⓥ Remarkable poise & focus from variety that typically adds succulence to quaffing blends. **20** ⑧⑨ dense & concentrated yet fine textured & well extracted. Light years from a jolly trolley filler, it has intriguing prospects - try age some.

★★★★ **Belladonna** ⓥ Revamped blend in **20** ⑧⑦ sees near-equal cab, merlot & petit verdot with shiraz, cab franc & durif - diverse yet cohesive & more satisfying than last-tasted **18** ★★★★ ⑧⑤.

★★★★ **Barrel Fermented Chenin Blanc** ⊘ Fermented/8 months in small barrels, 70% new, 70% American, **22** ⑧⑧ offers peaches & custard on a leesy texture, rich, rounded body with pronounced vanilla oak that needs time to settle & meld.

★★★★ **Chardonnay-Colombar Generaal Smuts** ⓥ Unusual **21** ⑧⑥ blend offers satisfying spiced tropical fruit with powerful American oak aromas, supple body & lively acid.

★★★★☆ **Badslese** Rich & luscious Natural Sweet from chenin & splash hanepoot, **21** ⑨① billows sultana & honeysuckle along with melon & apricot, charming bitter twist to finish. Piercing acid tames 135 g/L sugar for pinpoint balance. First since **12** ⑨② , worth the wait. 500 ml.

★★★★☆ **Noble Late Harvest** ⓥ Abundant jasmine allure on **17** ⑨⓪ botrytis dessert. Penetrating sweetness (196 g/L sugar) balanced by harmonious acid; good intensity, body & length with clean dry finish. Low alc. Unwooded chenin & muscat d'Alexandrie (80/20), like last **09** ★★★★ ⑧⑦. 375 ml.

★★★★ **Red Muscadel** Super-sweet, honeyed & fragrant **22** ⑧⑥ midwinter comforter has concentrated raisin & plum pudding fruit, gentle yet effective spirit grip at 15.4% alc. Occasional release, **20** ⑧⑥ was last.

★★★★ **Cape Vintage** ⓥ Richly sweet 'port' with raisined nutty notes, **17** ⑧⑦ improves on last-reviewed **13** ★★★☆ ⑧③. Focused, dry-seeming thanks to well-judged harmonious fire from 16.7% alc.

. . . .

Merlot ⊘ 🍷 ★★★★ What merlot lovers want: easy-flowing fruit (blackcurrant & cherry), hints of earth & spice from 10% oaked portion, **21** ⑧④ adds the bonus of a bargain price. **Chenin Blanc** ⊘ 🍷 ★★★★ Light, refreshing & fruit-forward **23** ⑧③ has generous melon & pineapple flavour, perky, well-judged acid.

. . . .

Sauvignon Blanc ☺ ★★★ Light, zippy & unpretentious **23** ⑧① delivers ample lime & green fig flavours, finishes on attractive salty note. Also in 3L pack for summer parties, as Chenin.

. . . .

Pinotage Reserve ★★★ Light & spicy **21** ⑧② has vibrant bramble & cranberry fruit, insistent acid & tannins suggesting braai matching. **Perlé Moscato Pink** ⊘ ★★★ Frizzante **23** ⑧① from red muscat de Frontignan is semi-sweet, with modest 9.5% alc, grapey overtones & raspberry nuance adding an appealing tang. **Chardonnay Sur Lie** ★★★★ Butterscotch & vanilla custard foremost on **22** ⑧⑤, despite only 10% being oaked. Good body, with lemon curd on finish. **Perlé Moscato White** ⊘ ★★★ Pétillant semi-sweet **23** ⑧⓪ has vivid muscat fruit & scent, offers light & breezy drinkability thanks to low 9.5% alc. **Vin Doux** ⓥ ★★★ Sweetness restrained by acid in **21** ⑧⓪ carbonated fizz from muscat d'Alexandrie, showing fragrant sultana fruit. **Hanepoot Jerepigo** ★★★★ With honey-laced muscat fruit, solid 206 g/L sugar & alc fortification nudging 16%, **22** ⑧④ is perfect fireside fare. Also good over ice cream. **Red Jerepigo** ⓥ ★★★★ Hedonistic fortified winter warmer, **21** ⑧④ has grapey muscat-like fruit (though variety/ies undeclared), appealing spirit nip. 16% alc, 204 g/L sugar. Discontinued: **Pinotage Generaal Smuts**. — GdB

Location: Rawsonville ▪ Map/WO: Breedekloof ▪ Map grid reference: B5 ▪ Est 1951 ▪ 1stB 1958 ▪ Tasting & sales Mon-Fri 9-5 Sat/pub hols 10-3; pub hols (seasonal) please call ahead ▪ Tasting R30pp/5 wines ▪ Cellar tours by appt ▪ Facilities for children ▪ Farm produce ▪ Cheese platters ▪ Soup platters ▪ Conservation area ▪ Owner(s) 18 members ▪ Cellarmaster(s) Willie Burger (1998) ▪ Winemaker(s) Henri Swiegers (2002), Jaco Booysen (Jan 2007), Cobus Kruger (2022) ▪ ±1,500ha (ptage, shiraz, chenin, cbard) ▪ 43,000t 20% red 65% white 10% rosé 5% fortified ▪ ISO 22000:2018, IPW, WIETA ▪ PO Box 72 Rawsonville 6845 ▪ info@badsberg. co.za ▪ www.badsberg.co.za ▪ **T +27 (0)23-344-3021**

☐ **Bain's Kloof** *see* Bergsig Estate
☐ **Bakenkop** *see* Mellish Family Vineyards
☐ **Balance** *see* Overhex Wines International
☐ **Bald Ibis** *see* Mile High Vineyards

Baleia Wines

Much excitement at the Joubert family's farm in the maritime Lower Duivenhoks appellation, where a tiny parcel of vines shares 1,000 ha of hard, wind-buffeted land with grain fields, olive groves (and luxury accommodation): the first picks of alicante bouschet, grenache noir and mourvèdre, and grenache blanc, roussanne and verdelho, the former destined for the red blend, and latter to spice up the Sauvignon and possibly form a future Mediterranean white with semillon. More amphoras have been brought into the cellar, some kilometres distant in Riversdale town, beside the tasting lounge and airstrip for fly-in visitors.

Limitados range

★★★★ **Amphora Syrah** (NEW) Lots happening on **20** (88): big aromas of flowers, tar, plums, prunes, pure fruit & nice earth-tinged texture from year in clay. Low sulphur, so drink early while fresh & appetising.

★★★★☆ **Syrah** Lovely **21** (90) shows toasty edge from 14 months in barrel, 40% new, to mix of red & black fruit, firm yet velvet tannin & fresh, lively acid. Cool-climate elegance & restraint epitomised.

★★★★ **Tempranillo** (NEW) Classic notes of dried strawberry, crunchy cranberry & smoky earth to amphora-aged **21** (89), all laced with crisp acid & firm tarry tannins. Very expressive; potential for keeping.

★★★★☆ **Chardonnay** (🐝) Barrel fermented, 50% new, aged 11 months, seamlessly integrating the oak & fruit of brilliant **21** (94). Balances fresh, zesty orange citrus with warm oak notes of smoke & nuts, honey & oatmeal complete the lengthy finish.

Baleia range

★★★★ **Pinot Noir** (✓) Array of aromas on **22** (86), floral, pot-pourri, cranberry & raspberry plus hints of floor polish & mint. 11 months in old foudres. Garnet hue suggests not for keeping but very enjoyable now.

★★★★ **Vinho Rochas** (✓) Near-even syrah & tempranillo, **22** (86) lively & juicy, bursts with perfumed red berries & violets, savouriness from year old oak. Excellent everyday drinking with x-factor that raises bar on **21** ★★★★ (85). Cape South Coast WO, as Deborah & Sauvignon.

★★★★ **Sauvignon Blanc** Ripe tropical fruit combines with furry texture & richness in **23** (86) to deliver punchy yet elegant flavour, tiniest amount coming from smidgen of oak. Satisfying & crowd pleasing.

Deborah Rosé ★★★★ Smorgasbord of varieties led by pinot noir & sauvignon, pale pink **23** (83) zestily dry with fresh fruit-salad flavours & brisk acid. Cape South Coast WO, as Rochas & Sauvignon. **Chardonnay** ★★★☆ Peaches & cream **21** (84) mingled with soft spice from 50% oak treatment plus texture from amphora component. Racy acid leaves impression at fresh finish. Discontinued: **Tempranillo Port**. — CM

Location: Riversdale ▪ Map: Klein Karoo & Garden Route ▪ Map grid reference: C6 ▪ WO: Lower Duivenhoks River/Cape South Coast ▪ Est 2010 ▪ 1stB 2011 ▪ Tasting, sales & cellar tours Mon-Fri 9-5 Sat/pub hols 10-3 ▪ Wine, olive oil, coffee ▪ Facilities for children ▪ Picnic area available ▪ Pet-friendly area ▪ Videira Country House, luxury self-catering accommodation ▪ Hiking, biking & bird watching ▪ Airstrip next to cellar for easy access ▪ Owner(s) Jan-Hendrik & Lindi Joubert ▪ Winemaker(s) Gunter Schultz ▪ 1,000ha/9.5ha (pinot, shiraz, tempranillo, chard, sauv) ▪ 8ot/600cs own label 60% red 40% white ▪ PO Box 268 Riversdale 6670 ▪ admin@baleiawines.com ▪ www.baleiawines.com ▪ **T +27 (0)28-713-1214**

☐ **Bales Choice** *see* Wade Bales Wine Co
☐ **Bamboes Bay** *see* Fryer's Cove Vineyards
☐ **Banks Brothers** *see* Renegade Wines
☐ **Barber's Wood** *see* Celestina

Barista

With quantities nudging 150,000 cases, Vinimark's Barista Pinotage is available in 50+ countries and 'the biggest-selling coffee-style pinotage in the world'. Bertus Fourie created the wine almost 15 years ago and, with Barbara Melck, is still making it and the newer, more luxurious premium incarnation, Barista Black.

★★★★ **Barista Black** (2) Oak flavours dominate, but **20** (86) avoids the overt mocha styling of sibling. Pleasant plummy fruit, medium body & attractive sweet spices, ripe, smooth tannin structure.

Barista Pinotage ★★★ Billed as 'a modern take on SA's signature grape', **22** (77)'s emphatic coffee-essence styling & medium body will please its extensive fan base. — GdB

Location: Robertson ▪ WO: Western Cape ▪ Est/1stB 2009 ▪ Closed to public ▪ Online shop ▪ Owner(s) Vinimark ▪ Winemaker(s) Bertus Fourie & Barbara Melck ▪ 146,000c's own label ▪ PO Box 6223 Paarl 7620 ▪ info@vinimark.co.za ▪ www.baristawine.co.za ▪ **T +27 (0)21-883-8043**

☐ **Barony** see Rosendal Wines
☐ **Barrel Selection 008** see Imbuko Wines

Bartho Eksteen Estate Wine Ⓥ Ⓜ ◎ Ⓐ

Bartho Eksteen, the 'sage of sauvignon blanc', built his reputation and affinity for the variety in and around the Cape South Coast before launching his own brand in 2015. Latterly with a small vineyard and cellar in Hemel-en-Aarde Valley, he and son Pieter Willem, sharing the winemaking responsibilities, still rely on fruit from that region for the three excellent 'savage whites' featured below, plus another listed separately under Wijnskool. 'The longer, cooler season allows the grapes to ripen without the dangers inherent to the heatwaves often experienced inland, resulting in wines that are extremely elegant and persistent.'

Flagship range

★★★★ **Fluister** Pinot noir from Hemel-en-Aarde Valley. Lavender-toned **22** ⑧⑧ has smoky oak on lifted berries, subtle undergrowth note. Firm acid & stemmy grip somewhat ruffle otherwise silky texture & persistent flavour flow.

★★★★☆ **Professore** Ⓐ Nodding to SA viticultural history, **21** ⑨① blends 3 local crosses, pinotage, roobernet (70/20) & white grape nouvelle. Narrower shouldered than last at 13.5%, with 30% new oak (vs all older), treads lighter & with added barrel perfumes of liquorice & light char.

★★★★☆ **Groepsdruk** Ⓐ Single barrel of standout wine each vintage, typically light-feeling despite 14.5% or higher alc. **21** ⑨④ mostly red fruit from 70% syrah, equal mourvèdre & grenache noir, dash viognier, vibrant but still tightly swaddled in 50% new oak's sweet vanilla & tannin.

★★★★☆ **Houtskool** Ⓐ Sauvignon flies solo in **22** ⑨③ after **21** ★★★★★ ⑨⑥ added smidgen semillon. Signature freshness & minerality, usual cool 'green' perfume accented by wisps smoke. Tad uncompromising, missing the subtle padding. Barrel fermented/11 months older oak. WO Cape South Coast.

CWG Auction range

★★★★★ **Vloekskoot** Ⓐ Similar make-up, treatment & WO to Houtskool. In this **22** ⑨⑤ the barrel's influence more nuanced & integrated. Elegant, with restrained granadilla & grapefruit, succulent acid from start to fantail finish.

Signature range

★★★★ **Ouskool** Though different vintage, same blend & fruit origin for **20** ⑧⑧ as Groepsdruk. Rum-&-raisin fruit bound by firm yet yielding tannin. Generous but slightly more rustic than **19** ★★★★★ ⑨⓪. 30% new oak.

★★★★☆ **Blom** Pale pink dry rosé, always smartly done & serious. **23** ⑨① bracingly fresh with vivacious red berry fruit, dusty top note & mouthfeel from added handful oak chips during ferment. Less presence (& alc) than standout **22** ⑨③. 70% grenache noir with mourvèdre, syrah & viognier.

★★★★☆ **Meester** Sauvignon inoculated with 3 yeasts for wide array aromatics, flavours. **22** ⑨⓪ myriad green & tropical tones, rounded palate with pinpoint acid offsetting fruit sweetness. Unlike last, no wooded semillon for extra heft. WO Cape South Coast.

★★★★☆ **Dom** Walker Bay chardonnay, pinot noir & meunier (47/47/6) star in expressive **20** ⑨② cap classique sparkler. Lemon tone with toasty note from 11 months on lees after primary ferment, further 24 on lees in the bottle. Nicely dry, added mid-palate heft from the black grapes.

★★★★ **Soetmuis** Noble Late Harvest from Elgin sauvignon, **22** ⑧⑦ fermented in tank rather than usual barrel. Revisited mid-2023, faint apricot botrytis notes, delicate rather than rich sweetness, lovely bitter almond on mango & papaya finish.

★★★★ **Bedjie Toe** ⊘ New bottling ⑨⓪ of water-k-white husk spirit steps up with gorgeous violet, lavender & fynbos fragrances, smooth, warming palate with berries, creamy peach melba, nuts & oriental spice. For espresso & almond biscotti, then beddy-byes. 82% sangiovese, dabs roobernet, viognier, sauvignon, 43% alc, 375 ml.

Experimental range

★★★★ **Grrrrenache** 'A vineyard practice experiment. No irrigation, vigorous crop control' of Upper Hemel-en-Aarde grenache noir. Energetic sweet strawberries & raspberries, meaty top note, **22** ⑧⑥'s finish lifted by spirited acid.— CvZ, WB

Location: Hermanus ▪ Map: Walker Bay & Bot River ▪ Map grid reference: A3 ▪ WO: Western Cape/Cape South Coast/Hemel-en-Aarde Valley/Walker Bay/Elgin/Upper Hemel-en-Aarde Valley ▪ Est/1stB 2015 ▪ Tasting & sales Mon-Sat 10-4 ▪ Tasting fees differ from wine to wine ▪ Closed Good Fri, Dec 16/25 & Jan 1 ▪ Cellar tours by appt ▪ Maná Fresh deli/bistro Mon-Sat 10-4 ▪ In-season farm to table locally produced delicacies ▪ Facilities for children ▪ Tour groups by prior arrangement ▪ Functions & events ▪ Hiking & MTB trails ▪ Historic building ▪ Husk spirit ▪ Owner(s) Eksteen family ▪ Winemaker(s) Bartho Eksteen (Jan 2015) & Pieter Willem Eksteen (Jan 2015), with Dewald Grobler (May 2022) ▪ Viticulturist(s) Johan Viljoen ▪ 5ha total ▪ 4,540cs own label 34% red 37% white 19% rosé 10% cap classique ▪ PO Box 1999 Hermanus 7200 ▪ bartho@hermanus.co.za, sune@hermanus.co.za ▪ www.barthoeksteen.co.za ▪ **T +27 (0)82-920-7108 (Bartho), +27 (0)72-323-5060 (Suné)**

Bartinney Private Cellar

The boutique winery owned by architect Rose Jordaan and venture capitalist husband Michael continues its successful specialisation in cabernet and chardonnay, and production of 'world-class wine that reflects the unique vineyard sites' on the upper reaches of Botmaskop in Banhoek Valley. Heinright Prins, farm manager, and Ronell Wiid, a Diners Club Winemaker of the Year, work side by side on an estate that's a fixture on WWF-SA's roster of conservation champions for ongoing preservation efforts within the Banhoek Conservancy. Visitors will find guest cottages and extensive trails reflecting Rose's flair and love of mountain biking, and a renovated tasting lounge with more outside seating and a view that's truly magnificent.

Reserve range

★★★★☆ **Skyfall Cabernet Sauvignon** ⑧ Superb **18** ⑨④, elegant & sophisticated, with deep, unfolding layers of flavour, blackcurrant, blackberry, mocha, baking spice, black olive & vanilla. Specific parcels on home-farm, including 2 highest), 18 months in 70-80% new oak. Tannins still tight, decant now, confidently keep a decade, as **17** ★★★★★ ⑨⑤.

★★★★★ **Hourglass Chardonnay** ⑧ Triumphant selection from best sites of 2 blocks on estate, **21** ⑨⑤ floral & apple intensity & brightness, baked stonefruit & balancing citrus lift on unflagging finish. Complex, rounded, with outstanding texture from barrel ferment/11 months, 50% new. Statement wine, for keeping.

Bartinney range

★★★★☆ **Cabernet Sauvignon** ⑧ Younger sibling from selective picking of only healthiest grapes is the other's equal in **19** ⑨④. Refined, with presence, intensity & persistence for ageing, bolstered by fine structure from 15-18 months in 50% new barrels. Decant in youth to experience plum, dark chocolate, fynbos & polished leather nuances.

★★★★☆ **Chardonnay** Barrel-fermented **22** ⑨⓪ deep fruited & fragrant, fynbos & herb aromas, apple & pear crumble, perfectly balanced acid & oak structure, 33% new, 11 months. Polished, with poise & firm backbone for keeping good few years. Stellenbosch WO.— WB

Location/map: Stellenbosch ▪ Map grid reference: H5 ▪ WO: Banghoek/Stellenbosch ▪ Est 2006 ▪ 1stB 2008 ▪ Tasting & sales Mon-Thu 10-5 Fri 10-8 Sat 10-5 Sun 11-4 ▪ Various tasting experiences offered; cheese & charcuterie platters ▪ Closed Dec 25/26/31 & Jan 1 ▪ Bartinney Wine & Champagne Bar Mon-Sun 1-10 (T +27 (0)76-348-5374, 5 Bird Str Stellenbosch) ▪ MTB trails ▪ Annual trail run events ▪ Vineyard guest cottages ▪ Craft beer & gin ▪ Wine club ▪ Owner(s) Rose & Michael Jordaan ▪ Winemaker(s) Ronell Wiid ▪ Farm manager Heinright Prins ▪ 27ha/±17ha (cab, chard) ▪ 100t/4,000cs own label 70% red 30% white ▪ WWF-SA Conservation Champion ▪ Postnet Suite 231 Private Bag X5061 Stellenbosch 7599 ▪ info@bartinney.co.za, tastingshed@bartinney.co.za ▪ www.bartinney.co.za ▪ **T +27 (0)21-885-1013/+27 (0)76-328-6793**

☐ **Basson Collection** *see* Ormonde Wines

Bayede!

The traditional salute to the Zulu king, Bayede! is also a majority black-owned brand, believed to be the first local royal-signature 'by appointment' label. The venture is focused on empowering women and creating sustainable jobs, exemplified by the beadwork that adorns each bottle, crafted by women in rural areas. The wines and spirits are available for tasting and sale at The Wine Arc in Stellenbosch and Vendôme in Paarl.

7 Icon Wines
★★★★☆ **Cabernet Sauvignon** ⓐ Age is part of **15** ⑨⓪'s appeal, yet still shows vivid cassis, with spice & violet nuances. Tannins now well integrated, the texture succulent, lithe & curvaceous.

★★★★ **Merlot** ⓐ Lively dark fruit, fruitcake & spice on mellow, made-for-food **15** ⑧⑧. Well structured, silky, savoury farewell from oak, quarter new. Stellenbosch WO.

★★★★ **Shiraz** ⓐ Differs from other Shiraz, 100% French oak, year, further bottle-ageing has brought tannin integration. **17** ⑧⑧ dark chocolate, black plums & spice array, smooth & streamlined.

Discontinued: **Pinotage Reserve**, **Chardonnay**, **Chenin Blanc**, **Sauvignon Blanc**.

King & Queen range
King Goodwill Shiraz ⓐ ★★★★ Dark toned, liquorice & spice, black plum, **19** ⑧④ is ripe & generous, year French & American oak giving cellaring potential. **King Goodwill Jubilee** ⓐ ★★★ Cab, merlot, petit verdot in sweet, dark-fruited **18** ⑧① from Robertson vines. Juicy & uncomplicated for everyday drinking. In abeyance: **Queen Nandi Méthode Cap Classique Brut Rosé**.

King Shaka-Zulu range
Pinotage ★★★ Dark plum & briar notes framed by firm oak tannins in **21** ⑧⓪. Acid adds succulence & resolved dry finish. **Chenin Blanc** ⓐ ★★☆ Light textured for early drinking, **21** ⑦⑧ tank sample is fresh & fruity.

B Royal range
Pinotage ⓐ ★★★ Better wood use than previous, toning down toastiness in **21** ⑧①. Mulberries & blueberries, a smoky seam in the flavours, tannins ripe, accessible. Not tasted: **Chenin Blanc**.

Prince range
Cabernet Sauvignon ⓐ ★★★☆ Only red to receive new oak treatment, a change from last vintage, taking **21** ⑧④ to another level. Cassis & cigarbox, texture juicy & smooth, tannins a hidden strength. **Merlot** ⓐ ★★★ Only brief oaking to keep the texture plush & round, **20** ⑧① celebrates fruit, berries & plums, enhanced by a light spice dusting. Occasional release: **Pinotage**.

Royal range
Jubilee Merlot ⊘ ★★★ Mulberry & tomato-leaf herbaceous nuance to retasted **21** ⑧②. Somewhat dry, with tannin grip edging out fruit. Good persistence though. **Reserve Syrah** ⊘ ★★★★ Dark-fruited **19** ⑧⑤, revisited, shows dried herbs & fresh succulence, firm yet supple tannin squeeze from time in oak. Inky breadth & depth make it a good food partner. Not tasted: **Jubilee Sauvignon Blanc**.

Cape Brandy range
Not tasted: **XO Royal Cape Brandy**.

Discontinued: **Princess range**. — FM

Location/map: Paarl ▪ Map grid reference: E6 ▪ WO: Western Cape/Stellenbosch/Robertson ▪ Est 2009 ▪ Tasting & sales at Vendôme, Paarl, by appt; or at The Wine Arc, Stellenbosch, Tue-Fri 9-4 Sat-Sun 9-5 pub hols (seasonal) please call ahead ▪ Tour groups by appt ▪ Brandy tasting/tour by prior arrangement ▪ 60% red 30% white 10% rosé ▪ PO Box 7362 Northern Paarl 7623 ▪ marketing@bayede.co.za, admin@bayede.co.za ▪ www.bayede.co.za ▪ **T +27 (0)21-863-3406/+27 (0)83-650-3585**

☐ **Bayten** see Buitenverwachting
☐ **BC Wines** see Brandvlei Cellar

Bé a Daisy ⓐ ⓘ
A year of expansion for the hive in Midrand, with increased direct sales and followers, additional team members helping drive volumes, and new boutique wines. The venture continues to operate as a 'wine farm that isn't a farm', sourcing across the Western Cape, and blending and bottling there. The branded wines are intended as 'fun, easy-drinking', while bespoke wines for the on-trade and private use are also on the menu.
Cabernet Sauvignon ⊘ ★★★★ Deep ruby attesting to youth & good fruit, **23** ⑧④ shows cassis & cedar, palate smoothly rounded & succulent, ending with grip of tannin. **Rosé** ⓝⓔⓦ ★★★ Fresh strawberries, fairly shy on nose but **23** ⑧⓪'s flavours make up for it, watermelon, ending dry & fresh. From mourvèdre. **Chenin**

Blanc ★★★ Apple & quince with a herbal edge, **23** ⑧② perked up by salty acidity, ending tangy-fresh.
Sauvignon Blanc ⊘ **★★★★** Green apple & pear styling, **23** ⑧③'s acidity giving lift & length. **Hexagon Brut** (NEW) ⊘ **★★★★** Citrus with some stonefruit on nose, **19** bubbly has toasted brioche from time on lees. Flavours are more citrus, with satisfying finishing freshness. Not tasted: **Unwooded Chardonnay**. — CR

Location: Midrand ▪ Est/1stB 2020 ▪ Tasting Mon-Fri 10-4 ▪ Fee R160pp ▪ Sales Mon-Fri 8-5 ▪ Closed all pub hols ▪ Wine club ▪ Office & boardroom facilities ▪ Owner(s) Els & Be (Pty) Ltd - 1 shareholder ▪ Cellarmaster(s) Craig Bester (Sep 2020) ▪ Winemaker(s) Elsabe Bester (2013) ▪ 24,166cs own label 44% red 40% white 16% rosé + 8,000cs for clients ▪ Brands for clients: Cradle Boutique Hotel & Spa, Doppio Zero, Life Grand Café, Potato Shed ▪ 112 Richards Dr, Midrand, Gauteng 1685 ▪ craig@elsabe.co.za ▪ www.bevino.co.za ▪ **T +27 (0)84-507-2988**

☐ **Beast Wine Collection** *see* The Beast Wine Collection

Beau Constantia   ⓠ ⑪ ⊚

Megan van der Merwe, winemaker-viticulturist the past five years, now joined by farm manager Braam Storm, believes 'we need to spend most of our time in the vineyards' and 'purely preserve the fruits of our labour in the cellar'. They're adding pinot noir to the mostly Bordeaux varieties at the family-owned boutique estate, tourist destination and winery atop Constantia Nek, and, hospitality wise, continuing to collaborate with varying local brands on a food truck that supplements the acclaimed on-site restaurant.

Beau Constantia range
★★★★★ Stella (&) Expressive, complex, elegant & long **21** ⑨④, syrah & splash co-fermented viognier, shows vibrant mulberry & violet scent, savoury herbs wrapped in sleek tannins. Natural ferment & 18 months in wood, as other range reds; 40% wholebunch, 54% new oak.

★★★★ Lucca (&) Cab franc & merlot (57/47) in melange of dark plum, blackberry, graphite & a leafy coolness. **19 ★★★★★** ⑨⓪ is bold, structured with aid of 68% new oak, sturdy tannined. Like **18** ⑧⑨, needs time to reveal full charm.

★★★★★ Aidan (&) Fruit, spice & fragrant herbs announce **19** ⑨① from syrah & petit verdot (39/36), rest cab. Succulent, generously berry fruited & fragranced with violet, lead pencil & a smooth coat of vanilla from 79% new oak. Lovely spicy conclusion. For the long haul.

★★★★★ Cecily Viognier delightful as ever, textured & balanced for a satisfying mouthful of orchard blossom, peach melba & exotic spice in **22** ⑨⓪. Only 76% oaked, 8 months, 17% new, rest concrete 'egg'.

★★★★★ Pierre (&) Classic, cellarworthy cool-climate blend, **22** ⑨④ full yet elegant, layered. Great intensity of citrus fruit, gentle vanilla & wax overlays, salty wet pebble farewell. Intricately vinified sauvignon & 7% semillon from 5 windswept blocks, including skin- & co-ferment, amphora & barrel ageing. Not tasted: **Karin**.

Pas de Nom range
★★★★ Creative Batch Multi-region, -technique & -vessel **22** ⑧⑨ is 65% chenin, dashes roussanne, colombard, clairette & viognier. Vivacious, inviting, lush fruited, juicy lemon squeeze on long finish.— WB

Location: Constantia ▪ Map: Cape Peninsula ▪ Map grid reference: B3 ▪ WO: Constantia/Western Cape ▪ Est 2002 ▪ 1stB 2010 ▪ Tasting & sales Tue-Thu 11-6 Fri-Sun 11-7 ▪ Fee R100-R160, waved according to purchase ▪ Closed Good Fri & Dec 24/25 ▪ Amphitheatre for concerts & outdoor events ▪ Chefs Warehouse Restaurant ▪ Wine club ▪ Owner(s) Apostax (Pty) Ltd ▪ Farm manager Braam Storm (May 2022) ▪ Winemaker(s)/viticulturist(s) Megan van der Merwe (2019) ▪ 22ha/±11ha (cabs s/f, malbec, merlot, p verdot, pinot, shiraz, sauv, sem, viog) ▪ 40t/4,000cs own label 80% red 20% white ▪ 1043 Constantia Main Rd, Constantia 7806 ▪ winesales@beauconstantia.com ▪ www.beauconstantia.com ▪ **T +27 (0)21-794-8632**

Beau Joubert Wines   ⓠ

On a millennium family visit from Wisconsin, Andrew Hilliard fell in love with the Cape and winemaking, joining forces with the Joubert family on their 17th-century farm in Stellenbosch to form a rare US-SA wine venture. Now MD, with co-owner Lydia Afonso, he strives to 'showcase the consistent quality of SA wine to an international market' while supporting winelands non-profit Pebbles Project with every bottle sold.

Beau Joubert range

★★★★ **The Ambassador** Merlot leads cab franc & cab in classically styled **21** (87), with a pleasing fragrance to the blackcurrant fruit. Restrained tannic grip & 20% new oak well balanced.

★★★★ **The Potter's Wheel** ⊘ The part oaking doesn't show on **22** (86) chenin, as it did in **21** ★★★★ (84), except in added broadness & the component in clay pot brings a stony focus. Restrained but persistent peachy fruit triumphs in overall good balance. WO W Cape.

★★★★ **The Genesis** ⊘ Citrus & blackcurrant leaf on **23** (86) sauvignon as well as tropical notes, but the fruitiness is nicely restrained, & the whole is well balanced, with a succulent freshness. Time on lees adds to the weight. From Elgin.

Jacob's Cab ★★★★ Good varietal character on **21** (85), also with cab's firm underpinning of the modestly flavoured palate. Well-judged oak. 13.3% alc. **Fat Pig** ★★★★ As lightly delightful as ever, **19** (85) port-style shiraz from Breedekloof is clean & fresh, if not profound. Fortified with brandy to just under 20% alc, moderately sweet, quite lightly structured & generously flavoured. 500 ml. Occasional release: **Christmas Cabernet**. Discontinued: **JC Visser MCC**.

Oak Lane range

Otto Make You Smile ⊘ ★★★ Cab-merlot blend off older bushvines. Forward ripe fruit (though just 13% alc) on unoaked **22** (80), but a little dilute & short. **The Wild West** ⊘ ★★★ Ready to drink unoaked **21** (81) from shiraz & cab, with sweet fruitcake notes & a gentle grip. Not tasted: **Everyday Reneé**. — TJ

Location: Stellenbosch ▪ WO: Stellenbosch/Western Cape/Breedekloof ▪ Est 1695 ▪ 1stB 2000 ▪ Tasting by appt only ▪ Owner(s) Andrew Hilliard (MD); Lydia Afonso (marketing & sales) ▪ Winemaker(s) Catherine Marshall & Andrew Hilliard ▪ 1377 Polkadraai Rd, Stellenbosch 7603 / PO Box 1114 Stellenbosch 7599 ▪ andrew@ beaujoubert.com ▪ www.beaujoubert.com ▪ **T +27 (0)82-641-7040 (RSA) & +1 920-360-7700 (USA)**

Beaumont Family Wines

(ⓒ icons) 🍷 🍴 🏠 📷 👤 ♿

It's 50 years since Raoul and Jayne Beaumont bought historic Compagnes Drift in Bot River. There followed replanting of vineyards, upgrading of the wine cellar and, after Raoul's passing, selling the farm to son Sebastian, winemaker and viticulturist, who is proud to say most of the key vineyards are as old as he. Jayne helps on the hospitality side, which now has so much to offer visitors that she jokes it should be renamed 'Bot Riviera'. She has never lost her interest in wine and crafts a namesake range, listed separately. With the mantra of 'elegance over power', Sebastian clearly understands the terroir he and assistant Chelsea Gibson work with, particularly suited to chenin, pinotage and Rhône varieties, making up most of the range.

Beaumont range

★★★★★ **Ariane Cabernet Franc** ⊘ (icon) 100% cab franc since last **19** (93), previously 5-part Bordeaux blend. **21** ★★★★★ (95) spent 14 months older barriques (just 2 produced) & has everything you'd want in a fine wine: classic red fruit, graphite, polish, nothing overt. Masterly tannin structure, fine grained, a lithe seam promising a distinguished future. Has finesse, grace.

★★★★★ **Far Side Mourvèdre** (icon) Few single bottlings, named for winemaker's favourite surf break. **20** (94) dark toned, dry scrub, charcuterie note, enough tannin for definition & ageing but without edges to bar current access. 20 months in barriques. Has personality & latent power.

★★★★ **Jackals River Pinotage** (icon) Blueberries & salty liquorice, **21** (89)'s 16 months in barrel added spice, buffed the firm but ripe tannin structure. Still tight, youthful, with good potential.

★★★★ **Dangerfield Syrah** (icon) Wild ferment, some wholebunch, 16 months barriques, **20** (93) classic syrah: pepper, brambleberry, smoky spice, dried scrub, mix of fruity & savoury, captured in succulent frame, ending very long. Just enough tannin to provide support, structure.

★★★★★ **Raoul's Red Blend** ⊘ (icon) Honours the late Raoul Beaumont, winemaker Sebastian's father. Changed blend for **22** (93) preview, syrah 47% with mourvèdre, 3 others. Brambly fruit, dried herbs, spice array from 16 months oak. Forthcoming perfume, packed with flavour despite its sleekness (13% alc), rests on bed of amenable tannins. Also in 1.5L. Does Raoul justice.

★★★★★ **Vitruvian** (icon) Eclectic flagship in best vintages only 'to capture best of Beaumont in a blend'. 5 varieties in **19** (95), shiraz, mourvèdre, pinotage, 2 others, 2 years small-oak, 25% new. Lithe (12.5% alc) but fruit carries it: raspberries & cherries, fresh & vibrant, tannin seam promising a future but already delicious. Wonderful finesse.

★★★★★ **Hope Marguerite** (⊛) (⊛) Benchmark chenin, from low-yield single-vineyard planted 1974-1978, given deserved cellar respect. 26th vintage, **22** (95) wild fermented/11 months mainly older oak, ensuring expected richness & complexity: bruised apple & barley sugar, preserved quince. Packs lots of power into trim body, lifted by crisp acid, ending long. Like **21** ★★★★★ (94), great presence & character.

★★★★ **Chenin Blanc** In contrast to Hope Marguerite, no oak, **23** (89) is about varietal purity, focus. Crunchy apple & pear, hint of fennel, zinging freshness, sparks with life, vitality. WO Cape South Coast.

★★★★ **Chenin Blanc Demi-Sec** Occasional release. Off-dry **22** (88) slender (11.5% alc) but plenty to offer: expressive fruit, apple & pear, underpinned by crisp acid, 15 months older barrels a subtle biscuit note, especially in the flavours. Touch sugar fits perfectly, ending tangy & long. Step up on **21** ★★★★ (84).

★★★★★ **New Baby** (⊛) Blend change in **22** (96), still chenin in lead, with sauvignon & colombard, from old vines (1974, 1983, 1988 respectively). No semillon. 11 months seasoned oak but fruit holds centre stage; lemon & lime, some thatch & quince, taut & intense, especially on palate & finish. Mouthwateringly zesty.

★★★★☆ **Goutte d'Or** (⊛) Occasional release, Noble Late Harvest chenin requiring right growing conditions. **22** (93) has vivid fruit expression, dried stonefruit & pineapple, overlay of honeyed botrytis, savoury notes from 16 months in barrel. But real magic lies in racy acidity, lifting the sweetness. Irresistible. 375 ml.

★★★★☆ **Cape Vintage Foot Stomped** (⊛) 'Port' from pinotage, syrah & petit verdot, lengthy ageing (2 years old oak) per Vintage tradition. Previewed **20** (91) less ripe than **19** ★★★★ (88) & better for it, just 56 g/L sugar, rich fruitcake, oak tannins a factor, as they should be, designed for cellaring. 375 ml.

Not tasted: **Cape White**. Occasional release: **R&B**.

The Kin range

★★★★ **Grenache Noir** Just 2 barrels, bottled after 11 months, **22** (89) admirable typicity: red fruit, vivid cranberries & cherries, lightly spice-dusted, overall impression of tightly packed flavours & structure, still in prime of youth. Tannins present but supple, fruit's the hero. No **21**.

★★★★☆ **Colombar** (⊛) Vines planted 1988. Occasional release, last was **19** (93), which **22** (93) emulates. Light years from cheap & cheerful varietal renditions, this i elegant & stylish. Apple & white peach, lovely purity & focus, touch sugar fitting like a glove, plumping slim lines (12% alc), finishing tangy. 11 months barrel regime not evident.

Occasional release: **Semillon**. — CR

Location: Bot River ▪ Map: Walker Bay & Bot River ▪ Map grid reference: C2 ▪ WO: Bot River/Cape South Coast ▪ Est 1750 ▪ 1stB 1994 ▪ Tasting & sales Mon-Fri 9.30-4 Sat/Sun 10-3; pub hols 10-3 (seasonal) please call ahead ▪ Tasting fee ▪ Closed Good Fri, Dec 25/26/31 & Jan 1 ▪ Kitchen & Deli with café-style menu, frozen meals, farm produce ▪ Facilities for children ▪ Private functions ▪ MTB route ▪ Walking/hiking trails ▪ Conservation area ▪ 250-year-old watermill ▪ 3 historic self-catering guest cottages ▪ Wine club ▪ Owner(s) Beaumont family ▪ Winemaker(s) Sebastian Beaumont (Jun 2003), with Chelsea Gibson (Jun 2021) ▪ Viticulturist(s) Sebastian Beaumont (Jun 1999) ▪ 500ha/31ha (mourv, ptage, shiraz, chenin) ▪ 180t/22,000cs own label 40% red 60% white ▪ IPW ▪ PO Box 3 Bot River 7185 ▪ info@beaumont.co.za ▪ www.beaumont. co.za ▪ **T +27 (0)28-284-9194/book via WhatsApp +27 (0)66-251-8155**

☐ **Bee Conscious** see Germanier Wines

Beeslaar Wines

A 'love affair' with pinotage prompted Abrie Beeslaar to create this signature label a dozen years ago with his wife Jeanne, supported by children Ben and Emma. The grape source is a single Simonsberg bushvine parcel on shale soil, crafted 'to make wine that represents the vineyard.' As cellarmaster since 2003 of Kanonkop Estate, with its unrivalled local and international repute for pinotage, he brings an enormous amount of experience and talent to the task, and his soupçons of world-class wine are eagerly awaited.

★★★★☆ **Pinotage** (⊛) Opulent layers of pleasure characterise **21** (94), from chocolate-dipped black cherry to gentle vanilla & tobacco smoke on the endless finish. Satin tannin & perfectly judged oak, 50% new, 20 months make for a complete, ageworthy wine. As impressive in youth as **20** ★★★★★ (95).— WB

Location: Stellenbosch ▪ WO: Western Cape ▪ Est 2011 ▪ 1stB 2012 ▪ Closed to public ▪ Owner(s) Abrie & Jeanne Beeslaar ▪ Cellarmaster(s)/winemaker(s) Abrie Beeslaar (Jul 2011) ▪ Viticulturist(s) Abrie Beeslaar ▪ 8t/750cs own label 100% red ▪ PO Box 93 Elsenburg 7607 ▪ info@beeslaar.co.za ▪ www.beeslaar.co.za ▪ **T +27 (0)83-663-3256/+27 (0)84-255-8686**

Bein Wine Cellar ⚲

Not long after deciding in the 1990s to trade veterinary practice in their native Switzerland for boutique winegrowing in Stellenbosch, Ingrid and Luca Bein opted to put all their varietal eggs in one basket and focus on merlot. With this specialisation and a limited scale - they farm just 2 ha - the couple set themselves the challenge of producing a full range of styles: still, rosé, dried-grape and most recently, sparkling. The secret lies in working with the differences within the vineyard, says Luca, a task made easier by precision viticulture aided by remote sensing technology and multispectral imagery from drones and satellites.

★★★★ **Little Merlot** ⚲ Fruit-filled, as usual, with hallmark char & spice from French oak, signature dry finish; ripeness (14.7% alc) adds whisper of cherry liqueur in **21** ⑧⑥.

★★★★☆ **Merlot** 🐝 Flagship **22** ⑨③ elegant & complex, fynbos & subtle iodine overlaying intense black plum & berry fruit. Less plush & heady than **20** ⑨②, bright acid & 30% new oak provide support & springboard for long ageing. Also in 1.5L. No **21**.

★★★★ **Merlot Forte** From partly dried grapes, 2 years in seasoned oak, intended to be concentrated rather than sweet. **21** ⑧⑥ succeeds thanks to piquant blackthorn & dried Italian herb nuances, restrained 11 g/L sugar, pleasing bitter twist. Unfined. 16% alc. 375 ml. Occasional release, last was **16** ⑧⑥.

★★★★☆ **Merlot Reserve** ⚲ From very best vineyard portions, **20** ⑨③ as rich & stylish as siblings, more tightly wound & structured from 2 years in new oak. Very dry, will reward 5+ years cellaring. No **19**.

Pink Merlot ★★★★ A rosé that smells & tastes of fruit (instead of boiled sweets) worth seeking out. With splash of floral muscat d'Alexandrie, **23** ⑧⑤ in usual fine, crisp, berry- & pomegranate-toned form. **Merlot Cap Classique Brut Rosé** ★★★★ 2nd vintage of this sparkling 'wine to celebrate life', **22** ⑧⑤ fruity strawberry & plum bouquet & palate, on sweeter side of brut but dry enough for aperitif enjoyment. — CvZ

Location/map/WO: Stellenbosch ▪ Map grid reference: B6 ▪ Est/1stB 2002 ▪ Tasting, sales & cellar tours Mon-Sat by appt only ▪ Owner(s)/cellarmaster(s)/winemaker(s) Luca & Ingrid Bein ▪ Viticulturist(s) Luca Bein ▪ 3ha/2ha (merlot) ▪ 16t/2,400cs own label 70% red 30% rosé ▪ IPW ▪ PO Box 3408 Matieland 7602 ▪ lib@beinwine.com ▪ www.beinwine.com ▪ **T +27 (0)21-881-3025**

Bellascene

Interest shown in South African wine on trips to the Democratic Republic of Congo prompted entrepreneurial diamond trader Nomalungelo Stofile to launch this brand seven years ago. It's been in the care of MD Marilyn Sili latterly, with the wines featured here made in Wellington by the team at Mischa Estate.

Manindzi Shiraz ⚲ ★★★★ Big & ripe **15** ⑧④ shiraz has full-on aroma & fruit-rich flavour, with some tobacco/spice oakiness (25% new barrels). Marked by some sweetness on the finish, enhanced by warm 14.2% alc. **Cabernet Sauvignon-Merlot** ⚲ ★★★★ Fruitcake, dark choc & cigarbox notes with a herbal touch on balanced, firmly structured but approachable **16** ⑧⑤. Plenty of flavour. — TJ, CvZ

Location: Wellington ▪ WO: Western Cape ▪ Est 2016 ▪ 1stB 2014 ▪ Closed to public ▪ Sales online ▪ Owner(s) Marilyn Sili (MD) ▪ Winemaker(s) Andrew Barns, Gary Barns (Mischa Estate) ▪ Oakdene Rd, Wellington 7655 ▪ info@bellascenewines.com ▪ www.bellascenewines.com ▪ **T +27 (0)84-500-9967/+27 (0)83-310-4460**

☐ **Bella Vino** see Nicholson Smith

Belle Rebelle ⚲ 🍴 📷 👤

It's only a dozen years since the first bottling, yet this boutique winery owned by the Stofberg and Coetzee families is already well established as a leader in Breedekloof Valley, with a reputation for quality and terroir expression, notably of chenin and semillon, plus a penchant, per the brand name, for touches of nonconformity. Hence the rare solo bottling of pinot blanc and, inspired by the success of Italy's Prosecco, recent emphasis by co-founder/owner and winemaker Mariëtte Stofberg-Coetzee on Charmat-method sparkling, a niche which she hopes will grow into an area speciality under the generic banner of CapeSecco.

Rebelle range

★★★★☆ **Intrepid Chenin Blanc** ⊘ 🐝 Switch from last time, **22** ⑨④ lighter, more elegant than Solitude, freshening acid lifting apple pie fruit. Dried pineapple & herbs round out palate to a lengthy finish in very lovely wine. Fermented in old barrel, smidgen on skins, 9 months on lees, as Solitude & Bird.

★★★★☆ **Solitude Chenin Blanc** ⊘ From Swartland dryland bushvines, **22** ⑨① shows green pineapple & bruised apple notes on nose but palate slightly shyer than last, culminating in toffee apple finish. Delightful acid & lovely texture.

★★★★☆ **A Bird In The Hand Semillon** ⊘ Highly individual **22** ⑨⓪ from registered single-vineyard (as Intrepid & Mariëtte Chenin) planted 1997 gives interesting & rather unusual flavours of litchi, banana & mango in delicious fruit salad mix. Gentle old-oak, part Hungarian, adds some richness & spice.

CapeSecco Rosé ⑧ ★★★★ Vivacious pink bubbly using Charmat method (2nd ferment in tank, as Chenin sibling), **21** ⑧⑤ from pinot noir (70%) & chenin. Modest 10.18% alc but vivid flavour, just-dry & beautifully presented. **CapeSecco Chenin Blanc** ⊘ ★★★★ Delicious fusion of Italian style & SA chenin, **21** ⑧⑤ froths with fruit (apple & pear), light bubbles & touch of biscuit from 12 weeks on lees. Gram sugar rounds out perfect brunch sparkler. Occasional release: **Butcher Bird Sauvignon Blanc**.

Mariëtte range

★★★★ **Cabernet Sauvignon** Combines ripe blackcurrant jam fruit with distinct green herbaceous edge, giving freshness but also slight stalkiness. **18** ⑧⑧ concentrated palate & crisp acid but less harmonious than standout **17** ★★★★★ ⑨④. 36 months older oak.

★★★★☆ **Syrah** Serious spice on succulent **18** ⑨② gives fragrance & perfume to lush black plum fruit. Velvet tannins & lively acid lead to a dark chocolate & liquorice finish. Smidgen juice bled off to aid concentration, as for Cabernet.

★★★★ **Chenin Blanc** Bruised apple & apple pie entry on **21** ★★★★ ⑧⑦ gives way to tropical pineapple fruit with creamy spice from 9 months old oak, 20% new. A little more focus at finish wouldn't go amiss, bringing it more in line with **20** ⑨③.

★★★★☆ **Pinot Blanc** From 31 year old vines, rare bottling of this variety. **21** ★★★★ ⑧⑥ shows good typicity with pear & honey, barrel ferment adds toffee & caramel hints. Just-dry styling (5.2 g/L sugar) adds breadth but more intensity needed throughout to match **20** ⑨①'s appeal.

★★★★ **Cap Classique Brut Rosé** ⑧ Salmon-hued sparkler from pinot noir (57%) & chardonnay, 40 months on lees. **18** ⑧⑦ smooth brioche, cranberry & savoury flavours, vivaciously balanced for solo or mealtime enjoyment.

★★★★☆ **Cap Classique Chardonnay** 2nd disgorgement of **16** ⑨① feeling the benefit of additional time on lees, giving real richness & texture to very elegant wine. Clean, fresh, with still-lively bubbles & crisp acid. Excellent drinking now & for the next few years.

Mía range

Shiraz ★★★★ Strong menthol overtone to fresh **20** ⑧⑤, spicy blackcurrant lozenge with some salami & leather notes from 18 months in old oak. Less alc (14%) than **19** ★★★★ ⑧⑦. **Chenin Blanc** ⑧ ★★★★ Ripe & crunchy red apple & hint of almond in unwooded **22** ⑧⑤. Silky smooth texture & zesty finish make it a super-quaffing summer treat. — CM

Location: Rawsonville ▪ Map: Breedekloof ▪ Map grid reference: C5 ▪ WO: Breedekloof/Swartland ▪ Est 2011 ▪ 1stB 2012 ▪ Wine & gin tasting at Ou Stokery restaurant ▪ Private winetasting with winemaker by appt only - subject to availability - R150pp minimum 4 people ▪ Cellar tours by appt ▪ Closed Dec 25 & Jan 1 ▪ Ou Stokery Restaurant, admin@oustokery.co.za ▪ Play area for children ▪ Craft gin/brandy distillery ▪ Wine club ▪ Owner(s) PJD Stofberg, M Stofberg-Coetzee & GJN Coetzee ▪ Cellarmaster(s)/winemaker(s) Mariëtte Stofberg-Coetzee (Nov 2011) ▪ Viticulturist(s) Pieter Jacobus Daniël Stofberg (Jan 1981) & Gideon Jacobus Nicolaas Coetzee (Nov 2011) ▪ ±102ha ▪ 42.5t 19% red 25% white 12% MCC 9% rosé 35% brandy ▪ PO Box 298 Rawsonville 6845 ▪ info@bellerebelle.co.za ▪ www.bellerebelle.co.za ▪ **T +27 (0)82-867-6958 (cellar); +27 (0)23-004-0540 (restaurant)**

Bellevue Estate Stellenbosch ⑨ ⑪ ⑧ ⑧

Blessed with some magnificent old vines, including the stokkies that produced the first commercial pinotage, the Morkel family estate strives to 'create site-specific wines that are a true reflection of the terroir of each vineyard'. The cinsault making its debut is a classic example, being from the original block on the Bottelary property and delivering beautiful varietal fruit along with the gravity characteristic of old vines. Attaining a high standard of quality in this wine and across the board stems from investment in the best barrels for each wine, and the expertise of the head of winemaking, Wilhelm Kritzinger, whose remarkable tenure covers all but three of the 25 years of bottling wine under the Bellevue label.

Flagship range

★★★★☆ **1952 Cinsault** (NEW) (🍇) (🍷) Impressive debut for this old vines bottling, **21** (94) showing significantly more body & heft than Estate sibling. Full-frontal red berry attack is tempered by delicate rosepetal scent, velvet tannins. Subtle & integrated, should reward good few years in bottle.

★★★★★ **1953 Pinotage** (🍇) (🍷) From Cape's first commercially producing pinotage block, showing its lighter, more gracious side, **19** (95) has violet perfume, spicy spicy red berry fruit, svelte tannins after 23 months' polishing in 60% new barrels.

Reserve Collection

★★★★☆ **Cabernet Sauvignon** After leaner **20** (90), returns to muscular form in **21** (92). Solid & dense, with earthy blackcurrant, hint of iodine & massive ripe tannins, all in sync, promising decade or longer cellaring. 23 months in small-oak, 67% new.

★★★★☆ **Pinotage** (🍇) Extracted **20** (93) has brooding black berry & plum fruit, dense ripe tannins, all kept vibrant by acidity, burnished by 22 months in barrel, 50% new. Imposing now & for many years.

★★★★ **Tumara** Bordeaux-style 5-way blend is 60% cab in **20** (88), equal parts other 4, showing a dark earthiness underlain by salty minerality. 22 months in 50% new barrels have added polish, but blackcurrant fruit currently rather sullen, tannins mouthcoating, need more time for incipient plushness to develop.

★★★★ **Chardonnay** Full bodied & expressive, **22** (88)'s generous citrus-marmalade fruit is laced with nutty notes, lees richness & lively acid. Prominent oak from ferment/year in small barrels, 50% new, should settle & integrate with time.

★★★★ **Eselgraf Single Vineyard Chenin Blanc** (🍷) Hands-off approach allows fruit from 1976 vines to take centre stage. **23** ★★★★☆ (90)'s succulent yellow peach, vivid acid & sweet mixed spices enhanced by lightly oaked portion. Fine varietal form improves on also-impressive **22** (87).

Estate range

★★★★ **Cinsaut** (✓) Lipsmacking, sappy **21** (86) alluring floral scents, crunchy raspberry fruit & tingling acid. Light, delicate, yet showing body & tannin texture, sweet spice from year in French & American oak.

★★★★ **Malbec** (✓) Lighter & juicier than last, **21** (86) bursts with crushed red berry & cassis, tangy raspberry on finish. Gentle, ripe tannins lend texture & backbone, year in 25% new oak adds spice & body.

★★★★ **Pinotage** (✓) Succulent & distinctive, with vivacious bramble & mulberry fruit, **19** (86) supple, with gentle tannins, firm acid & char-vanilla notes from year in American oak, 50% new.

★★★★ **Atticus Cape Blend** (✓) Mostly pinotage & cab, dash petit verdot, **21** (87) is opaque & muscular, with big chalky tannins overshadowing black cherry & currant fruit 50% American oak adds sweet vanilla to the mix. All should coalesce with time in bottle.

★★★★ **Méthode Cap Classique Pinot Noir Brut Rosé** Grape variety now reflected in the bubbly's name - & the pale onion skin hue. **20** (89) pleasing acid grip, sweet brioche & shortbread wafts, baked apple & strawberry fruit. Creamy, fine mousse enlivens the generous body. 30 months on lees. WO W Cape.

Shiraz (✓) ★★★★ Pleasantly light & upbeat, with prominent acid, **21** (85) sour black cherry fruit & aromatic tobacco note from year in barrel. **Sauvignon Blanc** ★★★★ Strikingly pungent nettle & gunflint on **23** (85) mask juicy granadilla fruit, appealing grass & dusty pebble nuances. Discontinued: **Rosé.** — GdB

Location/map: Stellenbosch ▪ Map grid reference: C3 ▪ WO: Bottelary/Western Cape ▪ Est 1701 ▪ 1stB 1999 ▪ Wine tasting room: Mon-Thu 10-5 Fri-Sun 10-6; Platters Tue-Sun, Pizza's Thu-Sun ▪ Kiddies play area ▪ Functions ▪ Wine club ▪ Owner(s) Bellevue Landgoed (Pty) Ltd ▪ Winemaker(s) Wilhelm Kritzinger (Feb 2002) ▪ Viticulturist(s) Dirkie Morkel (Jan 1979) ▪ 291ha/100ha (cabs s/f, cinsaut, malbec, merlot, p verdot, ptage, shiraz, chenin, sauv) ▪ ±450t/±30,000cs own label 90% red 10% white ▪ Brands for clients: Woolworths ▪ IPW, WIETA ▪ PO Box 458 Durbanville 7550 ▪ info@bellevue.co.za ▪ www.bellevue.co.za ▪ **T +27 (0)21-865-2055**

Bellingham

(🍷) (🍴) (📷) (👤)

Grapes that tell a story of old vines and unique sites are sought out by Richard Duckitt and Ricardo Cloete, winemakers, and Heinie Nel, viticulturist, for this brand established in the years after WW2 by Bernard Podlashuk, innovative vintner and reviver, with wife Freda, of its home-farm Belle en Champ. The team members then focus on preserving that specialness through the farming and winemaking, for example fermenting with wild yeasts, using neutral vessels such as amphoras and concrete tanks, and reducing sulphite content. Tastings of the DGB-owned line-up are offered at the brand home in Franschhoek town.

The Founders Series

★★★★☆ Pod (NEW) (🏵) A fitting salute to house's creator, Bernard Podlashuck. Shiraz (60%) & pinotage carefully selected from berry to barrel, only best three casks chosen. Sensational **20** (93) has spicy interest to feisty plum fruit, measured oak, half new, 16 months, lifts doesn't mask pure Bottelary & Darling fruit.

★★★★☆ Quintessential Couple (ⓥ) (🍸) This luxury rosé one of SA's best pink wines. Old-vine Stellenbosch & Franschhoek semillon deliver immensely focused & concentrated fruit flavours, wonderful freshness in **22** (90).

★★★★★ Freda (ⓥ) Best 4 barrels of chenin, semillon & grenache blanc ex 3 regions. Exceptional **21** (95) shows tremendous depth of ripe flavour & balance, beautifully firm texture & structure.

The Bernard Series

★★★★☆ Bush Vine Pinotage (⊘) Styled for the long haul from Darling & Stellenbosch fruit, **20** (91) opens with heady mix of dark plum & mulberry leading to toasty 40% new oak & ripe, supple tannin. As rich & juicy as last, tethered by fresh acid.

★★★★☆ Basket Press Syrah (⊘) (🏵) Thrilling aromas announce **20** (94)'s elegant, ripe black fruit balanced by crisp acid. Stellenbosch, Darling & Paarl grapes are 20% wholebunch fermented before year in 300L barrel, 30% new, & 2,500L foudre to showcase variety's alluring spice. No new wood last time.

★★★★☆ The Maverick SMV (⊘) (🏵) Voor-Paardeberg syrah & dash viognier, co-fermented, 25% mourvèdre, 14 months in 33% new oak, producing great intensity of blackberry & blackcurrant flavour in **20** (94), just reined in by toasty oak, aromatic black pepper & pliable tannins.

★★★★☆ Old Vine Chenin Blanc (⊘) (🏵) (🍸) From single parcel of Durbanville bushvines planted 1983, concentrated **22** ★★★★★ (97)'s ample citrus notes edged with sweet spice from small barrels & foudres (30%), third new. Ripe, cream-textured, with an elegant acid balance that improves on **21** (93)'s.

★★★★☆ Old Vine Chenin Blanc Limited Release (⊘) (🏵) (🍸) Stunning **22** (94) again combines Stellenbosch & Durbanville parcels, & complex vinification: wild yeast ferment in 2,500L foudre, concrete tank & amphora for the early picked component, 300L barrel for the riper one, lees stirred monthly. Rich, toasted oat, poached peach & toffee apple notes on a gloss-textured palate.

Discontinued: **Hand Picked Viognier**.

Homestead Series

★★★★ Pinotage (ⓥ) Excellent drinking pleasure from Stellenbosch vines. Potent perfume of ripe black fruit on juicy **20** (88), soft tannins & fresh vanilla from year in oak, 6% new.

★★★★ Shiraz (⊘) Maintains improved form in **20** (88), an aromatic beauty from Paarl grapes showing arresting whiffs of violets & pan-fried spice over pimento & black pepper. Pleasingly priced, as all ranges.

★★★★☆ Red Blend (⊘) Cape Bordeaux from near-equal merlot & cab. **20** (90) endowed with dark plum, blackcurrant & graphite in lithe tannin frame. Understated & unassuming yet highly satisfying. WO W Cape. No **19**.

★★★★ Chardonnay (⊘) Previewed **22** (87) from Stellenbosch reflects hallmark careful crafting in its vivid peach & cantaloupe flavour, fresh lemon-lime acid, oatmeal richness from 50% old-oaked portion, fine length.

★★★★ Old Orchard Chenin Blanc (⊘) Plump summer melon on ex-cask **23** (86), gains creamy vanilla note from 10% wooded component, which also adds weight & richness before a fresh, clean finish. Coastal WO. **22** skipped.

Sauvignon Blanc (⊘) ★★★★ Vibrant **23** (85) offers generous guava & passionfruit with a nettle top note, integrated acid. Perfect aperitif & picnic accompaniment. WO Cape Town. — DS

Location/map: Franschhoek ▪ Map grid reference: C2 ▪ WO: Coastal/Paarl/Cape Town/Stellenbosch/Western Cape ▪ Est 1693 ▪ 1stB 1947 ▪ Tasting & sales at Bellingham cellardoor, located at Franschhoek Cellar: Mon-Thu 10-6 Fri/Sat 10-9 Sun 10-5; pub hols (seasonal) please call ahead ▪ Closed Easter Fri/Sun, Dec 25/26 & Jan 1 ▪ Alfresco-style food daily ▪ Kiddies play area ▪ Events venue (seat 300 pax) ▪ Online shop ▪ Owner(s) DGB (Pty) Ltd ▪ Winemaker(s) Richard Duckitt (Nov 2017) & Ricardo Cloete (Jun 2021) ▪ Viticulturist(s) Heinie Nel (Jul 2018) ▪ 4,000t/560,000cs own label 50% red 49% white 1% rosé ▪ ISO 9001:2000, HACCP, IPW, WIETA ▪ PO Box 52 Franschhoek 7690 ▪ bellingham@dgb.co.za ▪ www.bellinghamwines.com ▪ **T +27 (0)21-876-2086**

Bellpost ⓠ

As primarily grape suppliers to others, the Thiart family - owner Lollies and sons Nico (viticulturist) and Koos (winemaker) - are especially mindful of the need to keep renewing vineyards with virus-free material and varieties better adapted to the challenges of climate change. Their Vredendal-area farms Bellevue and Buitepos also feed their own boutique winery, where they focus on small batches and minimal intervention. **Merlot** ⊘ ★★★★ Gentle texture & black fruit on **19** ⑧⑷, mild & pleasant after year in oak, just 10% new. Raises bar on previous. **Ruby Cabernet** ⊘ ★★★★ Approachable in its bramble-fruited ease, **21** ⑧⑸ amiable braai companion improves on last. **Shiraz** ★★★ Plum & herb typicity to light, succulent **18** ⑧②. Unfussy, with gentle texture & savoury finish. **Chardonnay** ⊘ ★★★★ Light & bright, unoaked **21** ⑧③ is citrus toned & fresh. Uncomplicated & easy to like. **C'est La Vie** ★★★ Golden-hued **18** ⑧② chardonnay & viognier mix delivers tangy lemon flavour on creamy oak backing, oxidative & nutty notes too. — FM

Location: Vredendal ▪ Map: Olifants River ▪ Map grid reference: B3 ▪ WO: Western Cape ▪ Est/1stB 2005 ▪ Tasting, sales & cellar tours by appt; tasting & sales also at Thi Art Restaurant, Vredendal ▪ Owner(s) Lollies Thiart ▪ Winemaker(s) Koos Thiart (Jan 2005) ▪ Viticulturist(s) Nico Thiart (Jan 2005) ▪ 5ha/2ha (merlot, ruby cab, shiraz, chard, viog) ▪ 12t/1,800cs own label 80% red 20% white ▪ PO Box 39 Vredendal 8160 ▪ bellpost@starmail.co.za ▪ www.bellpost.co.za ▪ **T +27 (0)27-213-2562/+27 (0)82-619-2428 (cellar); +27 (0)76-792-0806 (Thi Art restaurant)**

Bemind Wyne deur Ilse Schutte ⓠ ⑪

A convivial visitor experience has been key to Ilse Schutte since she launched her small-parcel venture 'from the heart' (hence the brand name 'Beloved Wines'), in a cellar and self-designed venue on McGregor village's main road. Hence the inviting aromas of traditional savoury vetkoek that now fill the courtyard, paired with wines that roam free in terms of both source and approach, Ilse's main guide being 'fruit dictates style'.
★★★★ **Shiraz** Hint of smoke, coriander & ripe red strawberries on **21** ⑧⑹ ex local-area grapes, tannins from extended 2-week maceration & 15 months in old barrels soft & tastily fruit-coated.

★★★★ **Chenin Blanc** Unwooded, like **21** ⑧⑹, yet **22** ★★★★ ⑧⑷ has buttery nuance from 9 months on lees, also touch salt to generous tropical fruit, finishing dry. Both vintages have rare Theewater certification.
....
Méthode Cap Classique Brut Cinsault ⑦ ★★★ Unusual variety for bottle-fermented sparkling, **20** ⑧② rosé also notable for crown cap (not cork), holding back explosion of strawberries, melon & nectarine. Just 10% alc & nicely dry, goes down easily.
....
Cinsault ★★★★ Ex 46 year old bushvines, **22** ⑧⑷ has settled since last time, shows good density of sappy red fruit at just 12.8% alc. 50% oaked portion adds to mouthfeel along bright line of acid. **Méthode Cap Classique Brut** ⓠ ★★★ Sparkler shows McGregor chenin's lemon, green apple flavours & tangy acidity. **NV** ⑧① invigoratingly tart, clean & bone-dry. Not tasted: **Cabernet Sauvignon**. — ML

Location: McGregor ▪ Map: Robertson ▪ Map grid reference: D6 ▪ WO: Breedekloof/McGregor/Theewater ▪ Est 2015 ▪ Garagiste winery: Tasting, sales & cellar tours Wed-Fri 10-4 Sat 10-2; pub hols (seasonal) please call ahead ▪ Fee R30/3 wines, waived on purchase ▪ Closed Easter Fri-Sun, Pentecost, Dec 25/26 & Jan 1 ▪ Food & wine pairing on request (4-15 pax/group) ▪ Owner(s) Ilse Schutte ▪ Cellarmaster(s)/winemaker(s) Ilse Schutte (Jan 2015) ▪ 10-15t/±850cs own label 50% red 30% white 20% MCC ▪ IPW ▪ PO Box 446 McGregor 6708 ▪ ilse@bemindwyne.co.za ▪ www.bemindwyne.co.za ▪ **T +27 (0)83-380-1648**

Benguela Cove Lagoon Wine Estate ⓠ ⑪ ⊚ ⑧ ⑤

In their ongoing quest to produce 'site-specific, cool-climate and authentic wines', the awarded cellar team of Johann Fourie and Michelle Waldeck, and viticulturist Jaco Mouton continue to show their skill in playing to the strengths of the Benguela Cove site, on a windy hill at the very edge of the Atlantic, and 'marginal as far as grape growing goes'. The property is the centrepiece of the Benguela Collection of luxury lifestyle assets, here and in Britain, owned by Penny Streeter OBE and her family. Also on this property is a tourist venue with a possibly uniquely extensive and diverse array of attractions, many taking advantage of the Bot River lagoon setting and nearby prime whale-watching locations. In the UK, sibling winegrowing projects at Penny's Mannings Heath and Leonardslee estates are also in Johann's seasoned and steady hands.

Icon range

★★★★★ **Catalina Semillon** (🍇) Textbook stuff: expressive, with real refinement to the lemon & lime flavours, dewy orchard fruit in a waxy coat of integrated creamy vanilla & spice. **21** (95) complex, stylish & built to give years of pleasure. Freshness from 20% tank component, remainder barrel fermented/10 months in half new oak; similar regime to **20** ★★★★★ (94).

Vinography range

★★★★☆ **Cabernet Sauvignon** (🍇) Following exceptional **19** ★★★★★ (96), **20** (93) has similar effortless complexity & sophistication. Perfumed plum, blackcurrant, graphite & polished leather flavours & scents. Impeccable structure from 40% new barrels, 20 months, layered & fine powdery tannins. Dark chocolate on endless finish. Will reward 10+ years ageing.

★★★★★ **Petit Verdot** (🍇) Relatively rare solo bottling, from a tiny block. **21** (95) restrained, yet with impressive length, depth & intensity of black fruit & warm sweet spice. Exemplary structure from 22 months in combo small & large barrels, all older, harmonious & savoury.

★★★★☆ **Chardonnay** (🍇) Single-vineyard bottling shows its trademark clementine nuance in characterful **22** (94), rich yet vivacious with long finish. Complex & rewarding flavours of strudel, lemon cream & cinnamon spice on a steely backbone courtesy no malo. Wholebunch natural ferment in large, older barrel/11 months with lees stirring.

★★★★☆ **Sauvignon Blanc** (🍇) Fruit ex 1-ha parcel, intricately vinified: 8 hours skin contact, into large, older barrel halfway through inoculated ferment, on lees 10 months. **22** (94) excellent expression of the variety: fragrant, creamy yet crisp, terrific depth, breadth & texture. No **21**.

Occasional release: **Cabernet Franc, Pinot Noir, Syrah, Semillon-Sauvignon Blanc.**

Estate range

★★★★☆ **Cabernet Sauvignon** (🍇) Younger sibling as impressive & ageworthy (& tad more plentiful). **21** (93) 22 months in 40% new barrel for silky smoothness to the vibrant plum, dark chocolate, tealeaf & tomato aromas & tastes. Fine concentration, complexity & polish, luxurious touch of cocoa on the finish.

★★★★☆ **Pinot Noir** (✓) Light-footed **22** (92) finishes with a delicious cranberry crunch, after an array of intense red berries, cherries & delicate florals on the palate & nose. 10% whole bunches in the gentle vinification; fine, well-integrated oak, 35% new, 11 months.

★★★★ **Syrah** (🍷) Same power & muscularity as **19** (89) in **20** ★★★★☆ (91), with more restraint & refinement, light tannin grip. Nuanced palate, herb brushed after 18 months in oak, 30% new.

★★★★☆ **Collage** (🍇) Still taut, but this perfectly constructed Bordeaux blend will reward patience. Cab, malbec, petit verdot & merlot (41/23/19/17), richly flavoured with fruitcake, leather, exotic spice & graphite in harmony with fine tannin & 45% new oak, 18 months, giving backbone, texture & depth in **21** (94).

★★★★☆ **Chardonnay** (🍇) Harmony & impressive complexity the result of hyper-oxidation & reductive handling of different portions, 11 months in half new oak. **22** (94), from 2 different clones, delights with vibrant & perfumed apple & grapefruit. Elegant & delicious, bright citrus finish.

★★★★☆ **Sauvignon Blanc** (✓) A punchy, joyful & memorable mouthful, excellent **22** (92) gains a firm structure from portion barrel fermented & 9 months in 25% new oak, rest on lees in amphora & stainless tank. A burst of lemongrass, lemon zest & green apple, creamy texture aided by 14% semillon.

★★★★☆ **Joie de Vivre Brut** Aptly named cap classique from 54% chardonnay with pinot noir, **19** (91) green apple sherbet & preserved lemon borne on endless strings of fine bubbles, creamy mouthfeel after 36 months on lees, long salty finish. Already harmonious, will improve with cellaring.

★★★★☆ **Noble Late Harvest** (🍷) Rich yet beautifully poised & fresh **20** (91) dessert wine from botrytised sauvignon blanc, unoaked. Textured & long, defined clean finish. 10% alc. 375 ml.— WB

Location: Hermanus ▪ Map: Walker Bay & Bot River ▪ Map grid reference: B2 ▪ WO: Walker Bay ▪ Est 2004 ▪ 1stB 2007 ▪ Trading hours: Mon-Sun 10-8 (summer)/10-6 (winter) ▪ Wine tasting ▪ Chocolate/cheese/oyster/charcuterie & wine pairing ▪ Various platters ▪ Moody Lagoon Restaurant; private dining (vinoteque); Blackbeards Diner; picnics; deli ▪ Art gallery ▪ Shops ▪ Tour groups ▪ Facilities for children ▪ Splash pad ▪ Helicopter whale watching ▪ Heli-flips ▪ Birding ▪ Walks ▪ E-bike trails ▪ Kayak tours ▪ Pirate Adventure Golf course ▪ Vineyard safaris, winery tours, guided wine walks, wine blending & pontoon cruises on the lagoon ▪ Luxury Villas ▪ Wedding venue ▪ Conferencing facilities ▪ Wine club ▪ Owner(s) Benguela Cove Investments (Pty) Ltd (Penny Streeter OBE) ▪ Winemaker(s) Johann Fourie (Sep 2016), with Michelle Waldeck (Feb 2017)

▪ Viticulturist(s) Jaco Mouton ▪ 206ha/66ha (cabs s/f, malbec, merlot, p verdot, pinot, shiraz, chard, sauv, sem) ▪ 400t/50,000cs own label 50% red 50% white ▪ WWF-SA Conservation Champion ▪ PO Box 327 Bellville 7535 ▪ info@benguelacove.co.za ▪ www.benguelacove.co.za ▪ **T +27 (0)87-357-0637**

☐ **Berg en Dal** see Wine-of-the-Month Club

Bergheim ⓦ

Paarl general practitioner Edwin Jordaan since the millennium has crafted small batches of mostly shiraz- and -blends after hours, intervening as little as possible in the process of making 'wines for drinking'. There's no follow-up release on the chenin as lower yield meant there wasn't enough fruit available at the source.

★★★★ **Frisgewaagd** ⊘ Name means 'taking bold risk' in switching from solo shiraz to blend with mourvèdre (80/20). Continues to pay off in full-flavoured **21** ⑧⑦, good depth of dark cherry fruit & savoury nuances, firm, supple tannins & some old-oak backing. Robust but well made, with good future.

Hoeksteen ⓦ ★★★★ Ripe & rounded, with just enough acid for balance in **22** ⑧③ unoaked chenin. Creamy oatmeal, apple cider & peach nuances, enjoyable solo or with a meal. Wellington WO. — MW

Location/map: Paarl ▪ Map grid reference: E6 ▪ WO: Western Cape/Wellington ▪ Est/1stB 2000 ▪ Tasting by appt ▪ Owner(s) Edwin Jordaan ▪ Cellarmaster(s)/winemaker(s) Edwin Jordaan (Jan 2000) ▪ 4-6t/1,000cs own label 66% red 34% white ▪ PO Box 6020 Paarl 7622 ▪ drjordaan@gmail.com ▪ **T +27 (0)82-923-3115**

Bergsig Estate ⓦ ⑪ ⌂ ◉ ⓐ ⓖ

Experience accumulated over a remarkable 180 years of Lategan family farming underpins these ranges, produced by 6th-generation owners and brothers Plum and Louis (viticulturists) and De Wet (cellarmaster) on the feet of the Langerug mountains. The sloping location and geological faulting mean there are many soil types on Bergsig, unlike the mostly alluvials of the Breedekloof Valley, and the challenge for the siblings and future custodians is to determine 'what does best on which parts of the farm'. A love for cycling brings a scenic new off-road route through vineyards and fynbos, with a technical stage that ascends to 270 m.

Lategan range

★★★★☆ **Oom Prop Cabernet Sauvignon** ⓦ Less oak in **19** ⑨③ than last, but fruit remains king, coating the tannins. Lithe, succulent, in perfect drinking condition. A template for the variety.

★★★★ **Tant Anna Chardonnay** ⓦ More wood than Estate sibling, which **21** ⑧⑧ displays as savoury oatmeal flavours, perfect for food pairing. Has character, individuality, like wine's namesake.

★★★★ **Patmos Chenin Blanc Reserve** ⓦ From one block, **21** ⑧⑦ fermented/9 months in barrel, on lees 60 days for fuller mouthfeel. Stonefruit & vanilla biscuit perked up by lively acid. WO W Cape.

Bergsig Estate range

★★★★☆ **Icarus Red** ⓦ Cab with touriga in **20** ⑨③. Cassis & plum, lovely cedar note, some smoked meat, backed by fruit-driven palate with freshness adding to appeal. Delicious. Last made was **18** ⑨①.

★★★★ **Weisser Riesling** ⓦ From 38 year old over-grafted vines. Clean freshness in **20** ⑧⑥, aromatic allure & tangy acid balancing fruit sweetness, touch of cream adds to appeal. Step up on **19** ★★★★ ⑧⑤.

★★★★☆ **Icarus White** ⓦ Golden colour & overt toasty honey flavours on **17** ★★★★ ⑧⑨ reflect generous barrelling & some age on chardonnay blend with chenin & riesling. May settle with time.

Cabernet Sauvignon ⓦ ★★★★ Less new oak than last, but still 2 years in barrel, so expect structure & a savoury overlay to the plums. Tannins ripe, seamed in the fruit, there's harmony in **19** ⑧④. **Pinotage** ⓦ ★★★ Smoky mulberry flavours in **20** ⑧①, sweet vanilla backing from mostly American older oak. Full body & tannin nip, one for the BBQ. **Touriga Nacional** ⊘ ★★★★ Unfortified & dry version of traditional port variety. With fruitcake scents & flavours, **22** ⑧⑤ spent year in older barrels, streamlined & juicy, tannins supple. Last tasted was **15** ⑧④. **Chardonnay** ★★★★ Barrel fermented/matured, mainly American, which accounts for big & bold **22** ⑧⑤'s vanilla spicing to forthcoming citrus, giving heady flavour richness. Nice limy finish. **Chenin Blanc** ⊘ ★★★ From a single block, unoaked, dry **23** ⑧② shows crunchy apple & pear flavours, acid providing lift & crisp finish. **Gewürztraminer** ⊘ ★★★★ Packs lovely flavour & perfume into a slender body (12% alc), Turkish delight among the aromatic notes, **23** ⑧⑤'s touch of sugar in support. **Sauvignon Blanc** ⊘ ★★★★ Different altitude vineyards harvested to build flavour plus freshness. Gooseberry & litchi in **23** ⑧④, whiff of lemongrass, the racy acid giving vitality. Also in 1.5L. Not tasted:

Rose Gold Rosé, Cape Late Bottled Vintage. Occasional release: **Weisser Riesling Late Harvest, Gewürztraminer Edel Laatoes, Cape Ruby, Cape Vintage**. Discontinued: **The Family Friend**.

Bain's Kloof range
Not tasted: **Merlot**. — CR

Location: Wolseley ▪ Map: Breedekloof ▪ Map grid reference: A3 ▪ WO: Breedekloof/Western Cape ▪ Est 1843 ▪ 1stB 1977 ▪ Tasting & sales Mon-Fri 8-5 Sat/pub hols 9-4 ▪ Various food-&-wine pairing, winetasting options ▪ Closed Good Fri, Dec 25 & Jan 1 ▪ Cellar tours by appt ▪ Bergsig Bistro ▪ Facilities for children ▪ Die Kelderhuis accommodation ▪ Cycling route ▪ Farm produce ▪ Conferences ▪ Self-guided birdwatching route ▪ MTB ▪ Conservation area, visits by appt ▪ Lategan family history & historical artefacts on display ▪ Gravel & Grape (Oct) ▪ Owner(s) Lategan family ▪ Cellarmaster(s) De Wet Lategan (Jan 1989) ▪ Winemaker(s) Chris du Toit (Jul 2003) ▪ Viticulturist(s) Louis & Plum Lategan (1991) ▪ 253ha (cab, ptage, shiraz, touriga, chard, chenin, sauv) ▪ 3,200t ▪ BRC, IPW, WIETA ▪ PO Box 15 Breërivier 6858 ▪ info@bergsig.co.za ▪ www.bergsig.co.za ▪ **T +27 (0)23-355-1603**

☐ **Bernard Series** *see* Bellingham
☐ **Berrio Wines** *see* The Berrio Wines

Berry Wines

With a surname like Berry, it's only fitting that winemaker Thian (helicopter pilot and 'business enthusiast') and Elmarie (entrepreneur and food stylist) have realised a dream of making their own wine, sourcing small pockets of grapes across Stellenbosch for ripe and generous reds, which we hope to taste next time.

Location: Stellenbosch ▪ Est/1stB 2017 ▪ Closed to public ▪ Owner(s) Thian & Elmarie Berry ▪ Winemaker(s) Thian Berry ▪ 800cs own label 100% red ▪ info@berrywines.co.za ▪ www.berrywines.co.za ▪ **T +27 (0)82-510-8321/+27 (0)79-211-4657**

Bertha Wines   Ⓨ Ⓨ Ⓐ Ⓞ Ⓐ

Birdwatching has joined the impressively long and varied list of allures at Weltevreden, the once derelict property on the Stellenbosch foothills of Simonsberg nurtured since 2012 by André Bezuidenhout and family into a destination and home to Bertha Wines. Consultant Jaco Engelbrecht nurtures the ±8 ha of vines, and the teams at Dornier and Zorgvliet craft the boutique wines that salute the owners' late mother and gran.

★★★★ **Semillon** Barrel-fermented 22 ★★★ ⑧② is light bodied & lean, with buttery oak-spice, roasted nuts & baked apple fruit. Misses opulence of **20** ⑧⑥.

Shiraz Ⓨ ★★★ Bold 14.9% alc shows on **20** ⑧① 's palate as warmth & slipperiness, along with full-ripe fruit & robust tannins for winter sipping. **Rosé** ★★★ Pale salmon pink **23** ⑧⓪ from merlot is dry, with very gentle acid, muted strawberry fruit. **Sauvignon Blanc** ★★★ Fresh & zesty, still showing some fermentation high-tones, **23** ⑧① has cheerful fig & grassy notes, dusty finish. — GdB

Location/map/WO: Stellenbosch ▪ Map grid reference: E4 ▪ Weltevreden Estate 1692 ▪ Bertha Wines Est/1stB 2020 ▪ Tasting Mon-Sun & pub hols 11-6.30 (Oct-Apr)/11-4.30 (May-Sep) ▪ Fee R80pp/4 wines; R150pp/4 wines & macarons; R250pp/4 wines & small plates ▪ 4 different small plate/macaroon & wine pairing options ▪ Jonkershuis Restaurant ▪ Facilities for children ▪ Tour groups ▪ Conferences ▪ Weddings & functions ▪ Art collection ▪ Guest house, stay@weltevredenestate.com ▪ Walks/hikes ▪ Conservation area ▪ Birding self-guided tours ▪ Owner(s) Weltevreden Retief Residence (Pty) Ltd ▪ Cellarmaster(s)/winemaker(s) Bennie Booysen, Bernard le Roux & Philip van Staden (Mar 2019, consultants) ▪ Viticulturist(s) Jaco Engelbrecht (Feb 2019, consultant) ▪ 11ha/7.8ha (merlot, shiraz, sauv, sem) ▪ 50t/2,184cs own label 52% red 32% white 16% rosé ▪ WIETA ▪ info@berthawines.co.za ▪ www.weltevredenestate.com, www.berthawines.co.za ▪ **T +27 (0)72-432-4778**

Bester Family Wines   Ⓨ

Veteran winemaker Zakkie Bester's boutique signature label, from select grapes in top Swartland vineyards, reflects family roots in the area dating from the 1700s, when forebear Andreas Bester settled in Malmesbury. For the current release of his chenin, Zakkie was 'privileged' to ferment and age a portion in a clay amphora.

★★★★☆ **Bester Family Red** ⊘ 60% unoaked cinsaut with shiraz, aged in older barrels 10 months, pre-bottled 22 ⑨⓪ honours both varieties: bright cranberries, some white pepper & scrub, lovely texture. Sleek, with juicy freshness, has 'drink me' written all over it. Not for long ageing, no hardship. No **21**.

★★★★ **Chenin Blanc** Half tank ferment, rest 25% each wild ferment amphora & older barrels, 10 months on the lees, all designed for quality expression. **22** ⑧⑨ shows grapefruit & lime, some mineral nuances, good palate weight with integrated tannins, oak spice subtle. Complex, polished.— CR

Location: Riebeek-Kasteel ▪ WO: Swartland ▪ Est/1stB 2016 ▪ Tastings for max 8 pax by appt (48 hrs notice required) ▪ Owner(s) Zakkie Bester ▪ Winemaker(s) Zakkie Bester (2016) ▪ 1,400cs own label 50% red 50% white ▪ PO Box 292 Riebeek-Kasteel 7307 ▪ zakkie@besterwines.com ▪ www.besterwines.com ▪ **T +27 (0)82-805-5586**

☐ **Bethani** *see* Cathedral Peak Wine Estate

Beyerskloof　　　　　　　　　　　　　　　ⓠ ⑪ ◎ ⑤

Into its fifth decade, this internationally acclaimed Stellenbosch venture was founded by leading pinotage advocate and exponent Beyers Truter, and has been in the capable hands of son Anri for some years now. Very much his own man, Anri says there's no need to reinvent the wheel, but is proud to have added two wines to the range: a single-vineyard Pinotage from the Kriekbult farm bought in 2018, and an estate Cabernet Sauvignon from, as its name suggests, the original vines planted by Beyers in 1988/9 and historically part of the Field Blend, recently discontinued. While the big price tags might be attached to the small-volume pinotages at the top end, the everyday one remains affordable and an outstanding commercial success, with global sales now topping 100,000 cases. So, while seven hectares of vineyard were uprooted the past year, another five were planted - including a dash of pinotage, of course.

★★★★★ **Eerste Ry Cabernet Sauvignon** ⑨ẼⱲ ⑧ Alluring **19** ⑨⑦ is textured & harmonious, offers cassis & hedgerow fruit with fragrant spices framed by dry, fine, integrated tannin, the result of 2 years in new barriques. Layered, supple & restrained, made for the long haul.

★★★★★ **Diesel Pinotage** ⑧ Meticulous barrel selection for this pinnacle pinotage. **21** ⑨④ complex, layered yet rounded & instantly appealing blue & black fruit & spice. Has the generous 15% alc but it's assimilated into a refined structure which includes 20 months in new oak & a supple, dry tannin backbone. As always, will reward patience.

★★★★☆ **Kriekbult Pinotage** ⑨ẼⱲ ⑧ From new single-site bushvine fruit source, impressive **20** ⑨③ is concentrated & powerful yet contained, the blackberry, liquorice & spice richness matched with good tannin grip. 18 months in oak, half new, add sleekness & extend the length.

★★★★☆ **Pinotage Reserve** ⑧ Serious **20** ★★★★ ⑧⑧ has depth & concentration but also lightness in its vivacious red & blue berry fruit. Care as ever taken with oaking, reduced from **19** ⑨⓪'s 20% new to just 5%, same 14 month duration, & still intended to improve over at least a decade.

★★★★☆ **Winemakers Reserve Pinotage** ⑧ A limited release, just 650 cases of **21** ⑨⓪, to keep 6-10 years. Silky smooth & confident, poised & fresh, with enduring flavours of cassis, plum & spiced berry, harmonious 18 months oaking in support. Sleek & rewarding.

★★★★★ **Faith** ⑧ Floral nuance adds some delicacy to **20** ⑨⑦ Cape Blend, near-equal pinotage, cab & merlot. Like **19** ⑨⑤, also tasted, velvety soft with seamless, sustained cocoa-tinged fruitcake notes & firm spine of all-new oak, 22 months, showing serious intent. Regal, statuesque & rewarding. Usual tiny quantity (700 cases each) built to age decade-plus.

★★★★☆ **Synergy Cape Blend** ⊘ Vintage conditions in **21** ★★★★ ⑧⑧ saw pinotage dropped to 45%, with cab, merlot, shiraz, cinsaut & pinot noir in support. Like **20** ⑨⓪, plump & supple body of ripe hedgerow berries in harmony with dry tannin & just 5% new oak, 13 months. Earlier ready, but could be cellared several years.

★★★★☆ **Traildust** Multiple Cape Blends but each differentiated; this a trio with pinotage (44%) & its parents cinsaut & pinot noir. **21** ★★★★ ⑧⑦ trademark cheer & freshness, good cohesion of components & concentration too. Older oak, like **20** ⑨⓪, 12 months.

★★★★ **Lagare Cape Vintage** Underlining pinotage's versatility is this 'port', traditional in most other ways, notably a heart of black fruit, tea & fiery 18% alc in **21** ⑧⑨. Vibrant, spicy & richly rewarding in its harmony & sweet seduction. 500 ml.

Pinotage ★★★★ Still wows the crowds with friendly medium body & ripe red & blue fruit, **21** ⑧⑤'s succulence undimmed by only 10% of the wine seeing oak staves in tank. Also in 250ml, 1.5L, 3L & 5L.

Cabernet Sauvignon-Merlot ★★★★ Merlot (43%) takes bigger role in **21** ⑧⑤ than last, when just 14%. Retains friendly persona, smooth & gentle body, cedar- & tobacco-edged fruitcake flavour to enjoy every day. Oak staves in tank. WO Coastal. **Pinotage Dry Rosé ★★★★** Strawberry & pomegranate succulence & brightness on charming **23** ⑧④ summertime companion. Light squeeze of lemon on dry finish. **Chenin Blanc-Pinotage ★★★★** Trim **22** ⑧③ is light, easy, with subtle citrus seam to pear fruit in unusual varietal combo. WO W Cape, as Pinotage & Rosé. — FM

Location/map: Stellenbosch ▪ Map grid reference: E3 ▪ WO: Stellenbosch/Western Cape/Coastal ▪ Est 1988 ▪ 1stB 1989 ▪ Tasting & sales Mon-Fri 9-4 Sat 9.30-4 Sun 10-3.30 ▪ Closed Easter Fri-Mon, Dec 25/26 & Jan 1 ▪ Cellar tours by appt ▪ Red Leaf Restaurant ▪ Conferences (30 pax) ▪ Wine club ▪ Owner(s) Beyers Truter, Jan Morgan, Barnie van Straten & Anri Truter ▪ Cellarmaster(s) Beyers Truter (Jan 1988) ▪ Winemaker(s) Anri Truter (Jan 2004), with Buddy Hendricks (Jan 2010) & Elsa du Plessis (Aug 2017) ▪ Viticulturist(s) Christo Hamman (Apr 2023) ▪ 193ha/125ha (cab, cinsaut, merlot, ptage, pinot, shiraz, chenin, sauv) ▪ 950t/280,000cs own label 96% red 2% white 2% rosé + 10,000cs for clients ▪ Brands for clients: Pick's Pick, Woolworths ▪ IPW, WIETA ▪ PO Box 107 Koelenhof 7605 ▪ enquiries@beyerskloof.co.za ▪ www.beyerskloof.co.za ▪ **T +27 (0)21-865-2135**

Bezalel Wine & Brandy Estate ⓆⓎⓖⓞⓐ

Martiens Bezuidenhout, winemaker, distiller and MD of this family venture on the Orange River in Northern Cape, inaugurated a new, more comfortable tasting venue inside the distillery, where the twin handcrafted copper stills are on display, and the roof is supported by pillars made from granite bedrock removed to make space for the vineyards. We hope to taste the bottlings emanating from this atmospheric setting next time.

Location: Upington ▪ Map: Northern Cape, Free State & North West ▪ Map grid reference: B8 ▪ Est 1949 (farm)/1997 (cellar) ▪ 1stB 1998 ▪ Tasting, sales & cellar tours Mon-Fri 8.30-5.30 Sat 8.30-3 ▪ Fee R50-R100pp ▪ Large groups by appt ▪ Closed Easter Fri/Mon & Dec 25 ▪ Garden Café: breakfast, lunch & platters ▪ Venue for conferences & weddings ▪ Accommodation ▪ Craft beer ▪ Owner(s) Bezuidenhout family ▪ Winemaker(s) Martiens Bezuidenhout (2015) ▪ Viticulturist(s) Inus Bezuidenhout (1989) ▪ 60ha/44ha (cab, cornifesto, merlot, pinot, sangio, shiraz, touriga, cbard, gewürz, sauv, viog) ▪ ±1,000cs own label 40% red 60% white ▪ IPW ▪ PO Dyasonsklip 8805 ▪ marketing@bezalel.co.za ▪ www.bezalel.co.za ▪ **T +27 (0)54-491-1325/+27 (0)83-257-4736**

Bezuidenhout Family Wines Ⓠⓖ

Wijnand Leenders, from The Hague's Bezuidenhout neighbourhood, later head gardener of the Dutch East India Company and early Cape vinegrower/winemaker is the 17th-century ancestor remembered in the vinous stories told by Cape Wine Master Francois Bezuidenhout. From a Stellenbosch base, he crafts 'Rhône-style wines with South African flair', and offers luxury accommodation, tastings and winemaker's dinners.

Leenders range

★★★★ Sielverkoper Silky Rhône red, 60% syrah & 3 partners in **21** ⑧⑦. Year older oak adds lustre to plums & fennel, gram sugar balanced by vibrant freshness & delicate weave of tannin. Also in 1.5L.
Not tasted: **Armosyn, Baviaan**.

Reserve range

Not tasted: **Soetdoring, Skietkraal**. — ML

Location/map: Stellenbosch ▪ Map grid reference: E5 ▪ WO: Breedekloof ▪ Est/1stB 2018 ▪ Tasting & sales by appt only ▪ Accommodation ▪ Owner(s) Francois Bezuidenhout ▪ Winemaker(s) Francois Bezuidenhout (Apr 2018) ▪ 8,300cs own label 30% red 50% white 20% rosé ▪ Stellenbosch Landbougenootskap, R44, Stellenbosch 7600 ▪ francois@bezfamily.com ▪ www.leenderswine.com ▪ **T +27 (0)84-668-8500**

☐ **Big Easy** *see* Ernie Els Wines
☐ **Bigfeet Africa** *see* Meerendal Wine Estate
☐ **Big Flower** *see* Botanica Wines
☐ **Big Mouth** *see* Overhex Wines International
☐ **Birkenhead Estate & Brewery** *see* Walker Bay Estate

Birthmark of Africa Wines

Prominent in the branding of this venture co-owned and -run by Miranda Abrahams are a bunch of grapes and the African continent, silhouettes of which correspond to the shapes of two birthmarks on the Cape Town-based vigneronne, who understandably feels she was born to be in wine.

★★★★ **Premium Heritage Red Blend** ⓥ Excellent balance on **17** ⑧⑧ from syrah, mourvèdre & carignan (36/36/28). Dark fruit with silk texture & savoury veneer. Has matured well, ready to drink.

★★★★ **Méthode Cap Classique Chardonnay Brut** ⓥ On the lees 15-18 months, giving brioche richness & a smooth, creamy texture to delicious **NV** ⑧⑧, while retaining chardonnay's citrus zing.

Bordeaux Blend ⓥ ★★★★ Soft & supple **18** ⑧⑤, dark berries, hint of dried herbs on a light tannin frame buffed 18 months in older oak. Mostly cabernet (52%), with cab franc, petit verdot & merlot. — WB

Location: Cape Town ▪ WO: Western Cape ▪ Closed to public ▪ Sales 8–5/online orders ▪ Winemaker(s)/ viticulturist(s) various ▪ 600cs own label 50% red 50% white ▪ info@birthmarkofafricawines.com ▪ www. birthmarkofafricawines.com ▪ **T +27 (0)78-494-9464**

Bitou Vineyards ⓥ ⑾

'Balanced and elegant wines' is the brief given by Ireland-born owner Ronald Leacy to cellarmaster Anton Smal, working in an on-site cellar with grapes grown on former polo fields beside the Bitou River in the relatively young Plettenberg Bay winegrowing area. We look forward to sampling the wines next time.

Location/WO: Plettenberg Bay ▪ Map: Klein Karoo & Garden Route ▪ Map grid reference: C1 ▪ Est 2009 ▪ Tasting, sales & restaurant Tue-Sun 11-5; pub hols (seasonal) please call ahead ▪ Owner(s) Ron Leacy - Leacy Property (Pty) Ltd ▪ Cellarmaster(s) Anton Smal (Jan 2020) ▪ 13.5ha (malbec, chard, sauv, sem) ▪ 56t/5,000cs ▪ info@bitouvineyards.co.za ▪ www.bitouvineyards.co.za ▪ **T +27 (0)44-004-0369**

Bizoe Wines

When he started his boutique venture in 2008, Rikus Neethling sought to honour his family by naming the wines for them: mother Henriëtte, father Tiny and wife Estalét, twin sons Retief and André, who communicate in their own private idioglossia, and their brother, Genant. Now he's created a lifestyle range under his own name, aiming for 'excellent quality at an affordable price'. All the wines are widely sourced and crafted in the Croydon Estate cellar near Somerset West, where Rikus is resident consultant winemaker.

Bizoe range

★★★★ **Idioglossia Malbec** ⓥ Bold & sturdily built, **19** ⑧⑥'s sweet, silky mulberry fruit shines through even the insistent tannin layers. Combo small & larger oak, all older, 19 months.

★★★★☆ **Estalét Syrah** ⓥ From Wolseley grapes, **19** ⑨⓪ generous dark fruit & spice on richly textured palate, secured by silky tannin web; lengthy, savoury finish. Older oak, 15 months.

★★★★ **Genant Shiraz-Grenache-Mourvèdre** ⓥ Flavoursome, rich & rounded, **20** ⑧⑦ enough freshness to maintain satisfying approachability. Darling & Stellenbosch grapes, older oak, 7 months.

★★★★ **Idioglossia Chardonnay** ⓥ Elegant & composed, **21** ⑧⑧ from Franschhoek has quiet citrus fruit expanded by creamy lees & acid. To enjoy now & a few more years. Amphora/barrel ferment & ageing.

★★★★☆ **Henriëtta** ⓥ Franschhoek's graceful semillon refreshed with Elgin sauvignon. Lemony accent enlivens & focuses **20** ⑨⓪, leaving intense aftertaste. Older-oak ferment/7 months for semillon.

Occasional release: **Tiny Noble Late Harvest**.

Semillon Collection

★★★★★ **Morningstar** ⓥ Three clones each add nuance to fruit of Darling sandy loam soils. Compelling **20** ⑨④'s deeply rich lanolin profile & thrilling acid make it a food wine.

★★★★☆ **Robertsvlei Road** ⓥ Revered Franschhoek vines, single 'green-fruit' GD1 clone, **18** ⑨⓪ a very grassy expression. **19** ⑨⓪ though riper, fuller, remains within the greenpepper spectrum.

★★★★☆ **Crossroad** ⓥ Franschhoek & Darling grapes fermented with champagne yeasts, **18** ⑨⓪, labelled as 'Kruispad', is lemon & lime toned; **19** ⑨⓪, renamed for trademark reasons, freshly cut grass. These terroir wines are unoaked, with modest 10.5-12% alc. All will age.

Rikus Neethling range ⓃⒺⓦ

★★★★ **Red Blend** ⓥ Rhône-inspired blend, half mourvèdre, equal shiraz, grenache, plus 10% malbec. Delicious **22** ⑧⑧ rich & full of dark fruit, spice & liquorice, fresh lift & smooth tannins, long & savoury.

★★★★ **Chenin Blanc** Fresh, juicy, **22** ⑧⑥ also has density in the earthy, red apple flavours, enhanced & lengthened by a fine mineral thread & firm finishing grip. Concrete 'egg' ferment; 10% skin contact.

Sauvignon Blanc ★★★ Fresh but unaggressive **22** ⑧⓪, modest tropical fruit & some creamy lees. — AL

Location: Somerset West ▪ WO: Western Cape/Darling/Franschhoek/Franschhoek-Darling/Stellenbosch ▪ Est/1stB 2008 ▪ Closed to public ▪ Wine club ▪ Owner(s)/cellarmaster(s)/winemaker(s)/viticulturist(s) Rikus Neethling ▪ 2,000cs ▪ Unit 189, Croydon Vineyard Estate, Somerset West 7130 ▪ info@bizoe.co.za ▪ www. bizoe.co.za ▪ **T +27 (0)21-843-3307**

Blaauwklippen Vineyards   ⓟ ⑪ ◎ ⑧ ⑤

One of Stellenbosch's oldest winefarms, company-owned Blaauwklippen prides itself on innovation when entertaining its many visitors. Hence the new Tasting House, which has not the usual single venue but several locales offering different styles of wine-and-food pairing, all orchestrated by the winemaker herself, Narina Cloete. Resident since 2016, she's just completed the first vintage in the renovated cellar, made the first wooded chardonnay here in decades, and has plans for premium-quality cabernet and malbec.

Blaauwklippen range

★★★★ **Malbec** ⓥ Savoury, with sturdy body underpinned by sleek tannins, meaty aromas, cherry & prune fruit. **21** ⑧⑧ wholeberry fermented/year in oak, 22% new. Follows exceptional **20** ★★★★☆ ⑨⓪.

★★★★ **Shiraz** ⓥ Ripe & robust, **20** ⑧⑦ displays more heft than **19** ★★★★ ⑧⑤ in its solid tannins & 14.5% alc. Fruit more forthcoming too - black cherry, plum & mulberry. 18 months in oak, 27% new.

★★★★ **Zinfandel** ⓥ One of only 2 solo bottlings in the guide, **19** ⑧⑥ shows telltale intense bramble-berry fruit in a pleasingly modest body. Soft, supple tannins & juicy drinkability add to appeal.

★★★★ **De Blaauwe Klip** ⓥ Cab-led 5-way Bordeaux blend, **18** ⑧⑧ more oak presence than **17** ★★★★☆ ⑨①, generous black cherry & currant fruit, cedar spicing & imposing tannins, demanding time.

★★★★ **Winning Blend** ⊘ Blending competition's 39th victor, **21** ⑧⑥ is 40% each cab & malbec, rest merlot, but better than the sum of its parts. Generously fruity, with pronounced spice from 16 months in 20% new barrels. **20** ★★★★ ⑧④ was mostly cab franc. Only in magnum.

★★★★ **Chardonnay** ⑭ First since mid-1990s, from neighbours' grapes. Plump & buttery, **22** ⑧⑦ shows finessed oak (11 months in barrique, 22% new), lending heft without intruding on charming citrus.

Cabernet Sauvignon ★★★★ Plush & juicy, **21** ⑧⑤ reins in oak influence despite 16 months in 40% new barrels, showcasing appealing cassis fruit, modest tannins. **Merlot** ⑭ ★★★★ Solid black fruit core, underpinned with cocoa & charred oak. Creamy texture lends appeal to **21** ⑧⑤. **Blush Rosé** ★★★★ Pretty coral pink **23** ⑧③ from zinfandel & malbec shows delicate floral scent, bright acid & vibrant red berry fruit. **Chenin Blanc** ⓥ ★★★★ Fresh & fruity, unwooded **22** ⑧⑤ has lees richness, well-rounded summer fruit, pleasing mineral-salty finish. **Sauvignon Blanc** ★★★★ Youthful & zesty **23** ⑧⑤ ramps up the herbal aromas, needs time for exaggerated khaki bush note to settle & meld with granadilla fruit.

Limited Releases

★★★★ **Cabernet Franc** ⓥ Hint of leafy minerality, musty & earthy notes on **19** ⑧⑥ alongside cassis & leathery tannins. Trendily lighter bodied, with good length. Supportive 17 months in 29% new barrels.

Specialities

★★★★☆ **10 Year Reserve Potstill Brandy** New bottling of 100% potstill ⑨② from chenin & colombard has light amber-gold glints, shows similar harmony of floral, baked apple & roast nut perfumes. Subtle texture & length, lovely intensity with luxurious chocolate, vanilla & exotic spice extras. 500 ml.

Cap Classique Zinfandel Brut ★★★★ Unique bubbly, **22** ⑧③ is fresh & frothy, shows minimal lees influence, hint of varietal wild-berry fruit. **Before & After Aperitif** ★★★★ Extravagantly packaged NV ⑧⑤ appetite whetter from botrytised malbec & shiraz, fortified to 16.3% alc. Ruby port-like, ultra-sweet (212 g/L sugar) & intense. 500 ml. — GdB, WB

Location/map: Stellenbosch ▪ Map grid reference: E7 ▪ WO: Stellenbosch/Elgin ▪ Est 1682 ▪ 1stB 1974 ▪ Tasting & sales Mon-Sat 10-6 (summer)/10-5 (winter) Sun/pub hols 10-6 ▪ Wine tasting; chocolate & wine pairing; macaron & wine pairing; tapas & wine pairing ▪ Closed Dec 25 & Jan 1 ▪ Wine blending on request ▪ Cellar tours daily, booking advised ▪ Family market every Sat & Sun 10-4 ▪ Restaurant ▪ Facilities for children ▪ Weddings/functions ▪ Walks/hikes & MTB ▪ Gin & brandy ▪ Owner(s) Blaauwklippen Agricultural Estates (Pty) Ltd ▪ Winemaker(s) Narina Cloete (Jun 2016) ▪ Viticulturist(s) Jaco van der Westhuizen (Jun 2019) ▪ 52ha ▪ 460t/35,000cs wine & 13,000cs (x4-btl) brandy ▪ IPW ▪ PO Box 54 Stellenbosch 7599 ▪ info@ blaauwklippen.com ▪ www.blaauwklippen.com ▪ **T +27 (0)21-880-0133**

☐ **Black Bird** see Zidela Wines

☐ **Black Box** *see* Wineways Marketing

Black Elephant Vintners

It's really something to strike a balance between wide and adventurous sourcing of grapes, making wines that not only reflect their terroir but also impress the critics - and having fun while doing it. The three owners of Franschhoek-based Black Elephant Vintners set out to break free from wine industry conformity, which shows in the quirky wine monikers and label art, as well as the winery name, referencing Kevin Swart (his surname is 'black' in Afrikaans), Raymond Ndlovu ('elephant' in the Nguni languages) and 'vintner' Jacques Wentzel. And success has come: besides wider local distribution, exports are expanding into the US's eastern seaboard; their UK focus is now on-consumption sales; and they have targeted Singapore.

Black Elephant range

★★★★☆ **Amazing Grace Cabernet Sauvignon** ⓐ Inclusion of young vines refreshes heretofore power-packed wine, crafted for longevity. Vivid cassis, some mocha chocolate notes, resting on a palate succulence already accessible & delicious, but dry finish reveals **18** ⑨④ geared for further ageing.

★★★★ **The Power Of Love Chenin Blanc** ⊘ Swartland old dryland bushvines, **23** ⑧⑧ more fruit expressive than last, apple, pear & melon throughout; still elegant but lots of texture, length & appeal. Crisply fresh, some palate weight from 2 months on lees.

★★★★ **Two Dogs, A Peacock & A Horse Sauvignon Blanc** Sauvignon tasted ex tank, **23** ⑧⑨ same style as last, a nervy focus proclaiming cooler-area provenance: gooseberry & kiwi, limy freshness, some interwoven mineral notes. WO W Cape.

★★★★☆ **The Dark Side Of The Vine Semillon** ⓐ Wild ferment/2 years in one old barrel, no fining, filtration. So many layers, hard to pin down: citrus, stonefruit, preserved melon, roasted nuts, beeswax, **20** ⑨③ unfolds in glass. Acid the foundation for long ageing, adding fresh piquancy to the flavours. From 1905 vines, like **19** ★★★★★ ⑨⑤.

★★★★ **Pinot Noir Brut Rosé MCC** Single parcel, primary ferment/6 months old barrels, 12 months in bottle. Pale salmon, fruit-forward **NV** ⑧⑨ boasts vivid red berries & cherries seamed with freshness, gentle biscuit note in the flavours. Early drinking, no hardship.

★★★★☆ **Chardonnay Blanc de Blancs MCC** ⓐ Single block of chardonnay, 6 months lees, 72 months in bottle. Fruit leaps out of glass, intense citrus preserve, also lemony notes, a honeyed, nutty overlay, toasted brioche richness. **13** ⑨④ dry, elegant (12% alc) yet huge fruit & flavour concentration. Seam of acid ensures balance, access, enhances the styling.

★★★★☆ **Chardonnay Brut MCC** ⓐ Simonsberg-Paarl vines, lees contact then in bottle 40 months, substantial style & origin change from last. Medium gold, intense citrus, preserve & zest, there's richness & depth in **NV** ⑨④, piercing lemon acid adding spark of life, promising a future. In perfect condition, impressive crafting, bold but not to excess.

★★★★☆ **Chardonnay Zero Dosage MCC** ⓐ Single Elgin vineyard, lees contact then bottle 100 months. Breathtaking concentration, honeyed citrus with nutty nuance; overall impression of deeply layered intensity, achieved without dosage, just the effect of fruit & bottle development. Yet elegant **NV** ⑨③'s palate reveals there's limy freshness, finishing very long. Admirable.

★★★★☆ **Chardonnay-Pinot Noir Brut MCC** Wonderfully elegant (12% alc), fresh & vibrant 75/25 blend, 36 months on lees, up on last. Mostly citrus in **NV** ⑨⓪, intense & focused, lemon & grapefruit, palate showing richness, a honeyed baked apple flavour.

The Fox & Flamingo Rosé ★★★★ From pinotage, **23** ⑧④ offers variety of fruit notes, part of attraction for early enjoyment. Light (12% alc) & zesty, some salty freshness at the end. Simonsberg-Paarl grapes. Not tasted: **The Power Of Love Cabernet Sauvignon**, **Three Men In A Tub With A Rubberduck Red Blend**. Discontinued: **The Honey Thief Natural Sweet**.

The Back Roads range

★★★★☆ **Anderkant Die Berg Chenin Blanc** ⓝⓔⓦ Impressive debut for previewed **22** ⑨⓪, cellar's other take on chenin, from Breedekloof, as new sibling. Melon & stonefruit, especially apricot, has weighty texture, lovely full body, great length. Balanced freshness, there to highlight fruit. Wholebunch, wild ferment/year old barrels, unfined/filtered.

★★★★ **Unknown Pleasures Pinot Blanc** Rare variety. Same winemaking as oaked chenin, **22** (88)'s greengage scents & flavours have pronounced melba toast savoury notes, but the fruit handles it. Nice freshness gives lift, extends the flavours.

Not tasted: **Bakenshoek Grenache Noir**, **Matoppie Petite Sirah**. In abeyance: **Bo Lamotte Viognier**.

Yes, You Can range

Not tasted: **Pinot Noir**, **Rosé**, **Sauvignon Blanc**. — CR

Location/map: Franschhoek ▪ Map grid reference: C1 ▪ Map: Franschhoek ▪ WO: Franschhoek/Breedekloof/Simonsberg-Paarl/Western Cape/Elgin/Swartland ▪ Est 2013 ▪ 1stB 2012 ▪ Tasting Mon-Fri 11-4 ▪ Music & wine pairing sessions Saturdays 11-2 by appt only ▪ Owner(s) Kevin Swart, Raymond Ndlovu & Jacques Wentzel ▪ Winemaker(s) Jacques Wentzel (Jan 2013) ▪ 140t/18,000cs own label 30% red 70% white ▪ IPW ▪ PO Box 686 Franschhoek 7690 ▪ sales@bevintners.co.za, jacques@bevintners.co.za, online@bevintners.co.za ▪ www.bevintners.co.za ▪ **T +27 (0)21-876-2903**

☐ **Black Granite** see Darling Cellars
☐ **Black Korhaan** see Rockbelt Ridge
☐ **Black Marble Hill** see Rhebokskloof Wine Estate

Black Oystercatcher Wines

Having decided to focus on syrah, semillon and sauvignon blanc, owner-cellarmaster Dirk Human the past year was gratified to receive recognition for not just the distinct character of his sauvignon, in particular, but also its ability to age with benefit, courtesy naturally high acid and low pH. More of the variety has been planted in the quartzite, iron ferricrete and broken shale soils of his Moddervlei farm near Elim at the southern tip of Africa. Crafting 'with the least possible interference, in symbiosis with nature' is his approach, and he's 'trying new methods like carbonic maceration and adding skin ferments to the range'.

★★★★ **Triton** Smoky, savoury dark-fruited profile in **20** (88) shiraz, though as juicy & flavoursome as last-tasted **17** (88) thanks to part carbonic maceration. Lengthy 24 months well-melded oaking in support.

★★★★ **Sauvignon Blanc** Consistently shows cool-climate minerality & freshness in range of green to tropical flavours, from harvesting at 3 ripeness levels. **23** (89) elegantly balanced, dry & flinty, with some leesy breadth. Also in 250-ml can.

★★★★☆ **White Pearl** (2) **19** (92) has 59% wooded semillon, its wax & lemon prominent, unoaked sauvignon's blackcurrant emerging more on palate, adding complexity. Likely to develop over a few years.

★★★★ **Méthode Cap Classique Brut Rosé** (2) Mid-gold **17** (86) merlot sparkler tasted from a later disgorgement (not noted on label). Ripe, bruised apple adding to notes of brioche & berry. Dry & clean.

Cabernet Sauvignon (2) ★★★★ Cool-climate herbal notes on **17** (85), with firm tannins & firmer acidity. Modest 13% alc; only older oak used. Good dry finish. Not tasted: **Rosé**. Discontinued: **Cabernet Sauvignon-Merlot**, **Semillon Wild Ferment**. — MW

Location/WO: Elim ▪ Map: Southern Cape ▪ Map grid reference: B3 ▪ Est 1998 ▪ 1stB 2003 ▪ Tasting & sales Tue-Sat 10-4; pub hols (seasonal) please call ahead ▪ Tutored tastings by appt ▪ Closed Good Fri, Dec 24/25 & Jan 1 ▪ Farm shop, platters on booking ▪ Facilities for children ▪ Tour groups ▪ Conferences ▪ Conservation area ▪ Peak season programme & other activities throughout the year ▪ Visit website/social media or call regarding updates on trading hours in case of private functions or public holidays ▪ Accommodation (stay@blackoystercatcher.co.za) ▪ Owner(s)/cellarmaster(s)/viticulturist(s) Dirk Human ▪ Winemaker(s) Dirk Human, with Willem Pietersen ▪ 1,200ha/11ha (shiraz, sauv, sem) ▪ ±110t/±13,000cs own label 20% red 60% white 20% rosé ▪ IPW, WIETA ▪ PO Box 199 Bredasdorp 7280 ▪ wine@blackoystercatcher.co.za, orders@blackoystercatcher.co.za ▪ www.blackoystercatcher.co.za ▪ **T +27 (0)28-482-1618**

Black Pearl Wines

Due for release at press time were three vintages of a reserve shiraz by Mary-Lou Nash, winemaker-viticulturist and co-owner of Black Pearl boutique winery. Another limited bottling, a 5-clone cabernet seeing its first release, will follow later this year. A recent Cape Nature stewardship award for outstanding contribution to biodiversity speaks of the road taken since Mary-Lou's father Lance bought Rhenosterkop Farm atop Paarl Mountain in 1995 and set aside a reserve that now features a 'beautiful' hiking trail. Mary works with own and select low-yield, unirrigated vines to elicit 'intense and exotic flavours' and, in the cellar, interferes as little as possible for near-bargain priced 'wines of distinction' that drink well young and can be cellared.

★★★★☆ **Cabernet Sauvignon** ⓥ Outstanding definition of ripe black berry & cherry fruit on **21** ⑨③, woven into rich dark-chocolate & liquorice from year in seasoned oak. Always a big wine (14.5% alc) but 'people friendly' & consistent top seller at Disney in the US.

★★★★☆ **Shiraz** ⊘ ⓐ Four barrels of brilliance from this 'madcap outfit' crafting its gems 'the good old fashioned way'. Lifted spice & black fruit of captivating **21** ⑨④ melded with tarragon & sage perfume, refined body aided by 10% new oak, 18 months. Beautiful balance bodes well. **20** untasted. WO Paarl.

★★★★☆ **The Mischief Maker** ⊘ ⓐ Plush **22** ⑨④ blend syrah, grenache & the mischief maker, mourvèdre (80/10/10), showing forward fruit yet a serious intent. Reprises **21** ⑨②'s year in oak, 10% new; vanilla, baking spices & white pepper add to dark & fresher red berries, whisper of sweetness on finish. Paarl & Swartland vines, as Cabernet.

★★★★☆ **Chenin Blanc** ⓥ From 17 year old Swartland bushvines, unwooded **22** ⑨⓪ has penetrating intensity of yellow fruit (nectarine, pineapple, Cape gooseberry) & creamy, near guava-like texture, all balanced by lively acid. Accessible early, can age, like all.

Occasional release: **Mourvèdre**. — DS

Location/map: Paarl ▪ Map grid reference: D5 ▪ WO: Coastal/Paarl/Swartland ▪ Est 1998 ▪ 1stB 2001 ▪ Tasting, sales & tours just about anytime but phone ahead ▪ Closed Dec 25 ▪ Hiking trail ▪ Lapa & camping facilities; self catering cottage ▪ Conservation area ▪ Owner(s) Lance & Mary-Lou Nash ▪ Winemaker(s)/viticulturist(s) Mary-Lou Nash CWM ▪ 24oha/2.7ha (cab, shiraz) ▪ ±5,000cs own label 80% red 20% white ▪ IPW ▪ PO Box 609 Suider-Paarl 7624 ▪ info@blackpearlwines.com ▪ www.blackpearlwines.com ▪ **T +27 (0)83-297-9796 (wine)/+27 (0)83-395-6999 (lapa & camping)**

☐ **Black Swan** *see* Hout Bay Vineyards
☐ **Black Tie** *see* Wineways Marketing

Blackwater Wine   ⓥ

Muddy brown, rather than dark waters that named his brand, presented a challenge to small-batch winemaker and consultant Francois Haasbroek. A trickling stream became a raging torrent with 100-year-high rainfall in winter cutting off access to the Tulbagh Mountain Vineyards home-farm, where Francois is cellar chief. He moved stock, barrels and cans a year ago (he's a partner in tinned-wine business Renegade). Grapes are still sourced widely, and the approach remains minimalist, the focus on structure, classically dry tannins and acid, eschewing overt ripeness and power. With his main market in the US, a Top 100 spot in Wine Enthusiast's annual list is well-deserved recognition and a substantial fillip.

★★★★☆ **Omerta Carignan** ⊘ Inky **20** ⑨⓪ retains Tulbagh origin. Herb & plum delicacy on nose, with liquorice touch, the core & body somewhat robuster. 40% wholebunch fermented naturally, 18 months in older oak, further 12 in bottle.

★★★★☆ **Zeitgeist Cinsaut** ⊘ Vibrant, spicy **21** ⑨⓪ is agile & somewhat leaner than last **19** ⑨① despite shared Darling origin. House-style wild ferment with 80% wholebunch but oaking upped to half, all older 500L, rest concrete vessels, 14 months.

★★★★☆ **Daniel Grenache** ⊘ Nimble **21** ⑨① shows cranberry brightness & verve with good density. Delicate chalky texture & fine dry tannin after 14 months in seasoned large-format barrels. Bot River grapes naturally fermented, half as whole clusters. No **20**.

★★★★☆ **Cuvee Terra Lux Pinot Noir** ⊘ Ethereal delicacy to dry, restrained **22** ⑨⓪ from Robertson. Subtle purity of red-berried fruit with good concentration & density. Sinuous & supple. Natural ferment, 30% wholebunch, 18 months seasoned wood. Last-tasted **19** ⑨⓪ was from Elgin.

★★★★☆ **Cultellus Syrah** ⓐ Black cherry & fynbos on **21** ⑨④. Like last **19** ⑨②, naturally fermented but wholebunch portion upped to 60%. Muscular yet refined with good restraint, poise & dry tannin firmness.

★★★★ **Fox & Boxer** ⊘ Syrah (90%) leads grenache & mourvèdre in alluring **22** ⑧⑦. Dry but succulent red cherries & plums. Harmonious, with good fruit concentration & density. Natural ferment, 20% wholebunch, 15 months in seasoned oak. First tasted since **18** ⑧⑦. WO W Cape, as Sophie.

★★★★★ **Sophie Cabernet Franc-Cinsaut** ⓐ Cinsaut upped to 35% with destemmed cab franc at 65% in **22** ★★★★★ (93). Xmas pudding & herb sheen marry with ink & cocoa depth. Taut, savoury, with leashed power, firm tannin spine. Like **21** (95) seriously conceived & suitably oaked, 50% new, 18 months.

★★★★★ **Picquet Chenin Blanc** ⓐ Savoury spice with baked apple & quince on **20** (93) from Piekenierskloof. Bunch pressed & fermented in barrel, so oak frames fruit beautifully, lending texture & length. Rich, ripe finish but fresh too.

★★★★ **The Underdog Chenin Blanc** ⓥ Result of concrete & stainless tank ferment, 8 months on lees, **22** (87) elderflower & quince brightness with clean, crisp exit & modest 12.5% alc.

★★★★☆ **Pleasure Garden Palomino** ⓥ Composed & structured rare solo bottling, **21** (91) ex venerable Robertson vines. Tarte tatin & cinnamon liveliness with broad, textured palate & distinct weight from 20% skin ferment. Impressive length. 50/50 concrete & older oak ageing, 14 months.

★★★★ **Highroller Sauvignon Blanc** ⓥ Nettle & white pepper typicity on restrained **22** (87) from Stellenbosch. Grapefruit zest & succulent acid. Lees-time down from 9 months to 3.

★★★★ **Chaos Theory Blanc** Blend streamlined to 70% chenin & palomino for **18** (88). Barrel ferment/8 months on lees before blending, then equal time in older oak. Succulent, broad & crunchy, a light nectarine & cashew creaminess, dry limy farewell. Like **17** ★★★★☆ (90), very tasty.— FM

Location: Paarl/Tulbagh ▪ Map: Tulbagh ▪ Map grid reference: C6 ▪ WO: Swartland/Robertson/Western Cape/Tulbagh/Darling/Bot River/Stellenbosch ▪ Est/1stB 2010 ▪ Tasting by appt only ▪ Wine club ▪ Owner(s) Blackwater Wines & Vines ▪ Cellarmaster(s)/winemaker(s)/viticulturist(s) Francois Haasbroek (Feb 2010) ▪ (carignan, cinsaut, pinot, shiraz, chenin, palomino, sauv) ▪ 30t/5,000cs own label 70% red 30% white ▪ Rose Str Paarl 7646 ▪ info@blackwaterwine.com ▪ www.blackwaterwine.com ▪ **T +27 (0)82-329-8849**

Blackwood Spirits ⓥ ⓐ

Fanciers of a good after-dinner spirit, grappa especially, Helene and Guido Zsilavecz were inspired to turn their hand to distilling. A hobby turned into a small business, with grape pomace sourced from local Hout Bay wineries, double-distilled in a small copper vessel, bottled and labelled, all in a converted home storeroom. Husk spirit being seasonal, they diversified into gin and other spirits.

★★★★ **Husk Spirit Pinot Noir** ⓥ These are more sophisticated than many locals. This (88) the more complex & intensely flavourful of the pair, with slippery fire. Both previewed in 500 ml, 43% alc.

★★★★ **Husk Spirit Pinot Noir-Chardonnay** ⓥ A little lighter, less intense than the straight Pinot, this digestif (86) also aromatic & refined, smooth & elegant. A charming lemony edge to the flavour.— TJ

Location/WO: Hout Bay ▪ Map: Cape Peninsula ▪ Map grid reference: A3 ▪ Est 2017 ▪ 1stB 2019 ▪ Tasting & distillery tours Mon-Fri 9-5 Sat 9-1 by appt only ▪ Tasting fee R120/2 x husk spirtis, 2 x gins and snacks, waived on purchase ▪ Sales Mon-Fri 9-5 Sat 9-1 ▪ Closed all pub hols ▪ Distillery: husk spirits (grappa), gins, schnapps & liquors ▪ Owner(s) Helene & Guido Zsilavecz ▪ Distiller(s) Helene & Guido Zsilavecz (Jul 2017) ▪ 7 Blackwood Dr, Hout Bay 7806 ▪ helene@blackwoodspirits.com ▪ www.blackwoodspirits.com ▪ **T +27 (0)83-629-7885**

Blake Family Wines ⓥ ⓘ

'You have to bring your A game, because there's only once chance a year to make a good wine,' say Andries and Marinda Blake, who live and handcraft in West Coast resort Yzerfontein, blessed with the longest uninterrupted sand beach in South Africa. The cellar they renovated there has a tasting and dining venue attached, which they've just upgraded and enlarged. Weekend live music sessions remain a popular feature.

Blake's range

★★★★ **Malbec Single Vineyard** ⓥ Like last-tasted **20** (87), **22** (86) from Philadelphia vines. Redcurrants & plums, fairly brief 6 months in oak, 30% new, for coat of vanilla spice.

★★★★ **Amethyst** ⓥ Sweet-fruited pinotage (50%) plus few savoury notes ex shiraz & cab. **18** ★★★★ (84) built to allow for early drinking, best while fruit holds off 15% alc. Not quite up to **17** (86).

★★★★ **Single Vineyard Chenin Blanc** ⓥ Exuberant melon, peach & pineapple on **23** (88), only 30% oaked in older barrels, 6 months, yet vanilla-spice seasoning more obvious than on last-sampled **21** (86).

★★★★ **Tourmaline** ⓥ 49% chenin with chardonnay & viognier in **21** (87). Handles 51% new oak well, allowing peach, melon & pineapple to speak clearly while providing texture, form & savouriness.

16 Mile Beach range

Blomtuin ☺ ★★★ Amiable quaffer, 60% pinotage, with shiraz & malbec in **22** ⑦⑨. Red berries dressed with chocolate & spice from ferment with staves. WO W Cape. **Rooipan Rosé** ☺ ★★★ Pinotage's juicy berry fruit is full & textured in **23** ⑧②, dry lemony finish & modest 12.9% alc improve on last.

Swemgat ★★★ Equal chenin & sauvignon in **23** ⑦⑦ deliver punchy passionfruit & guava on soft acid backdrop. To sip by the swemgat. Cape West Coast WO, as Rooipan. — ML

Location: Yzerfontein ▪ Map: Durbanville, Philadelphia & Darling ▪ Map grid reference: A1 ▪ WO: Swartland/ Cape West Coast/Cape Town/Western Cape ▪ Est 2013 ▪ 1stB 2011 ▪ Tasting room & restaurant/deli Wed-Sat 11-6 Sun 11-4; pub hols (seasonal) please call ahead ▪ Sales via website, selected wine shops & cellardoor facility ▪ Wine club ▪ Owner(s) Andries & Marinda Blake ▪ Cellarmaster(s)/winemaker(s) Andries Blake ▪ 10t/6,000cs own label 40% red 60% white ▪ Other export brand: Blake's ▪ PO Box 626 Yzerfontein 7351 ▪ info@blakefamilywines.com ▪ www.blakefamilywines.com ▪ **T +27 (0)22-451-2701**

☐ **Blake's** *see* Blake Family Wines
☐ **Bloemcool** *see* Fairview

Bloemendal Wine Estate

Company-owned Bloemendal is among the oldest and largest wine properties in Durbanville, covering north-facing slopes on Tierberg and southerly ones on Kanonberg, the latter also the vantage point for a tasting lounge, restaurant and social café overlooking Table Bay. The vines are tended by Andri Hanekom, also GM and cellarmaster, and the wines made by Boetman Langevelt in a low-intervention boutique cellar.

Estate range

★★★★ **Cabernet Sauvignon** ⊘ Impressive extract & focus on **19** ⑧⑧, earthy mineral seam through dense blackcurrant & plum fruit. Body & texture from solid but ripe tannins. Outpaces last-tasted **17** ★★★★ ⑧⑤. 18 months oak, 30% new, as all reds.

★★★★ **Merlot** ⊘ Meaty-savoury **20** ⑧⑥ has better fruit definition than **19** ★★★★ ⑧③, black berry compote with hints of cocoa & creamy caramel from barrel ageing. Chewy tannins should settle with time.

★★★★ **Shiraz** ⊘ Inky, concentrated **19** ⑧⑦ has morello & plum fruit with smoked meat, cinder & tobacco nuances. Robust, muscular, heftily tannined, suggesting cellar time.

★★★★☆ **Tyger Syrah** Was 'Tierberg'. Sleek, well-balanced **17** ⑨② shows quality of vintage in expressive black cherry fruit, velvet tannins, exotic herbal highlights. 18 months in barrel, 58 in bottle lend harmony & nuance. Drinks well now & for several years.

★★★★ **Chardonnay** Inclining towards classic style, **20** ⑧⑧ elegant, integrated, with primary mineral seam, muted lime citrus & satisfying leesy breadth, all honed & spiced by ferment/year new oak. No **19**.

★★★★☆ **Suider Terras Sauvignon Blanc** ⊘ From cool, windy site, benefits from, & is among few sauvignons to undergo, long ageing in bottle at cellar. **17** ⑨② full & textured, with body & structure from ferment/11 months in new oak.

★★★★☆ **Semillon** Seriously conceived **17** ⑨① barrel fermented/year in new oak. Ripe & generously rounded, tertiary development adding detail to typical asparagus & lanolin notes on fine-textured palate.

★★★★ **Kanonberg** ⊘ Substantial, aromatic **17** ⑧⑧ sauvignon & semillon (60/40) has developed elegantly. Forthcoming nettle, lanolin & lemon zest notes, spiced by 50% new-oak ferment & ageing.

★★★★ **Noble Late Harvest** ⊘ Botrytis dessert from equal sauvignon & semillon in **20** ⑧⑥, oaked 12 months, shows high-toned spice with roast hazelnut on plump, mega-sweet palate. Last-made **15** ⑧⑧ was 40% sauvignon. 500 ml.

Malbec ★★★★ Aromatic, rather unmeshed **20** ⑧⑤ shows prominent oak spice over tanned leather & stewed prune notes. **Pinotage** ★★★★ Massive extract & super-ripe black fruit on **19** ⑧④, intimidating tannins & raw earthiness, near 15% alc. Not for the faint-hearted. **Merlot Rosé** ★★★★ Pretty pale coral **23** ⑧③ is dry & refreshing, shows sunny strawberry fruit, appealing palate weight, gentle acid grip. **Sauvignon Blanc** ★★★★ Herbaceous, floral-scented **23** ⑧④ tank sample has pleasantly ripe passionfruit, hints of greenpepper, light, supple body. **Méthode Cap Classique Blanc de Blancs** ★★★★ Unusual sauvignon-semillon NV ⑧④ sparkler shows cool provenance in tinned pea pyrazine notes, scything acidity, dusty pebble mineral underpin. WO Cape Town, as Merlot & Tyger. — GdB

Location: Durbanville ▪ Map: Durbanville, Philadelphia & Darling ▪ Map grid reference: C7 ▪ WO: Durbanville/Cape Town ▪ Est 1702 ▪ 1stB 1987 ▪ Tasting & sales Mon-Sat 10-5 Sun/pub hols 11-3; pub hols (seasonal) please call ahead; larger groups by appt ▪ Tasting fee R60pp ▪ Wine & nougat/ice cream pairing ▪ Kiddies pairing with grape juice & ice cream ▪ Closed Dec 25/26 & Jan 1 ▪ Bon Amis @ Bloemendal ▪ 360° Wine Lounge ▪ MTB ▪ Owner(s) Spirito Trade 82 (Pty) Ltd ▪ Cellarmaster(s)/viticulturist(s) Andri Hanekom (2017) ▪ Winemaker(s) Boetman Langevelt (2006) ▪ Cab, malbec, merlot, ptage, shiraz, chard, sauv, sem ▪ 120t ▪ PO Box 466 Durbanville 7551 ▪ winetasting@bloemendalwines.co.za ▪ www.bloemendalwines.co.za ▪ **T +27 (0)66-340-8392**

Blue Crane Vineyards

Opening an on-site tasting lounge at the Crabbia family farm and boutique winery in Tulbagh has been delayed, but crafting by cellarmaster Zia Fox of small batches of wine from selected grapes grown by her husband Chris continues, as does the intensive focus on extra virgin olive oil production and distribution. **Pinotage** ★★★★ Familiar soft plum fruit of 21 (84) shaded by spicy oak, 20% new, some American. Needs time for components to meld. **Shiraz** ★★★★ Continues the ripe & fruity theme with plump mulberries & generous meaty, campfire characters, but alc more beneficially below 14% & sweet oak a more modest 10% new in 21 (85). **Full Flight** ★★★★ A Cape Blend & a bold one too. Shiraz in charge in 21 (85) with pinotage & mourvèdre in a succulent, fruity body lifted by spice & finished by a dry chalky grip. Pinotage & cab were in the lead previously. **Chardonnay-Pinot Noir** (NEW) ★★★ A 'blush' rendition of this popular combo, co-fermented 22 (81) has a candyfloss/confectionary flavour profile but finishes brisk & bone-dry. **Pinot Noir Rosé** ⊘ ★★★★ More overtly pink than new sibling, 22 (84) has a delicate hue that belies the ample red berry flavours that raise the drinkability. Shares zippy balance of previous's fruit & acid, for summer party fun. **First Flight** ⊘ ★★★★ Fleshy stonefruit & lemon attractions of 22 (84) chenin (67%) blend with sauvignon, medium weighted for wide appeal. Unoaked, unlike last, which has splash viognier & was less rich than its predecessor. Occasional release: **SMV, Chenin Blanc, Sauvignon Blanc, Viognier**. — DS

Location/WO: Tulbagh ▪ Est 2001 ▪ 1stB 2004 ▪ Closed to public ▪ Sales via website & Takealot ▪ Olive oil ▪ Cellarmaster(s)/winemaker(s) Zia Fox ▪ Viticulturist(s) Chris Fox ▪ 138ha/9ha (mourv, ptage, pinot, shiraz, chard, chenin, sauv, viog) ▪ 4,000cs own label 50% red 50% white ▪ PO Box 306 Tulbagh 6820 ▪ sales@bluecrane.co.za, wines@bluecrane.co.za ▪ www.bluecrane.co.za ▪ **T +27 (0)60-980-0384/+27 (0)82-495-8512/+27 (0)82-498-0069**

☐ **Blue Moose** *see* The Grape Grinder

Blue Owl Wines ⓠ

The Allée Bleue winemakers who craft this affordable trio, inspired by a resident owl family on the old Franschhoek farm Riversmeet, strive for drinkability without loss of flavour, substance or enjoyment. **Merlot** (ⓠ) ★★★★ Exudes drink-me appeal & over-delivers on value for money, as Chardonnay. 21 (83) black cherry, sweet spice & bright seam of acid, splash cab for supple support & drop viognier for charm. **Chardonnay** ⊘ ★★★★ Plump ripe pear & a twist of fresh lime define previewed 23 (83). Unoaked, poised, with creamy lees appeal, ready to enjoy. Franschhoek WO. Not tasted: **Pinotage**. — DS

Location: Franschhoek ▪ WO: Coastal/Franschhoek ▪ 1stB 2015 ▪ Tasting at Allée Bleue Wines ▪ Winemaker(s) Van Zyl du Toit, with Armand Hartzer (Dec 2019) ▪ PO Box 100 Groot Drakenstein 7680 ▪ info@alleebleue.com ▪ www.alleebleue.com ▪ **T +27(0) 21-874-1021**

☐ **Bob's Your Uncle** *see* Nicholson Smith

Boekenhoutskloof Winery ⓠ ♿

It started 30 years ago with the acquisition of Boekenhoutskloof, the idyllic farmstead in Franschhoek, and founding of the namesake wine brand, and expanded with offspring labels Porcupine Ridge, The Chocolate Block, The Wolftrap and Porseleinberg, as well as ventures in Stellenbosch (Helderberg Winery), Hemel-en-Aarde (Cap Maritime) and Swartland (Porseleinberg and Goldmine, boosted by the recent purchase of a property west of Malmesbury, where replanting and grafting are underway). New plantings of cabernet on both the Franschhoek and Helderberg farms, coupled with the Swartland purchase underline the overall quality ambitions while highlighting the value of own-fruit holdings for maintaining growth aspirations for The Chocolate Block, in particular. Marc Kent, first as winemaker, latterly cellarmaster, has looked after the brands' vinous fortunes. In this he's aided by Gottfried Mocke, Eben Meiring, Johan Nesenberend and Heinrich Hugo, the stalwart senior winemakers who make the critical day-to-day and harvest decisions.

★★★★☆ **Franschhoek Cabernet Sauvignon** (🐝) Signature sweet cassis & blue fruit on generous **21** (93) from home farm (30%) & long-term partner vineyard. Leafy top note from 12% cab franc, tad larger body than last (14.9% alc vs 14.6) & more new oak (95% vs 80). Still satisfyingly dry, stern tannin frame for decade ageing. Spontaneous ferment in concrete tank, as all reds unless noted.

★★★★☆ **Stellenbosch Cabernet Sauvignon** (🐝) Rings the changes in **21** (95), 4 parcels in Helderberg & Polkadraai (no long-standing Faure contribution), no usual dab cab franc. Less rich than sibling despite similar build (14.8% alc) but more graphite & rockpool nuance, echoing lithe **19** (97) more than brooding **20** ★★★★☆ (93). Fine linear tannin supported by 22 months in oak, 60% new.

★★★★☆ **Syrah** (🐝) Unshowy & confident **21** (94)'s succulent red plum & cherry fruit overlaid with white pepper, fynbos & charcuterie. Graceful, with vibrant acid seam, focused tannins & rousing stemmy grip. Fruit from own Swartland farms Porseleinberg (90%) & Goldmine, 65% wholebunch ferment, 18 months older & larger oak.

★★★★☆ **The Chocolate Block** (✓) (🐝) One of SA's international big hitters with nearly 200,000 cases made, excluding smaller (375 ml) & larger bottle formats. From Swartland, **22** ★★★★★ (95) seamless syrah-led Rhône-ish blend (dab of cab), wholeberry ferment in concrete & steel, 5% new oak, down from 10% in **21** (94), mostly barrique. Juicy red & black fruit seasoned with fresh herbs, fynbos & earth.

★★★★ **Helderberg Winery Reserve** (NEW) (🐝) Intended as a Stellenbosch heritage blend, cab based with dashes cinsaut & syrah, **21** (86) sweet-fruit bouquet & entry (cassis, strawberry jam) but savoury & dry finish. 14.8% alc neatly handled, inter alia by some wholebunch freshness. 30% new oak.

★★★★☆ **Semillon** (🐝) (🍷) Iconic example ex old vines, semillon dating from 1902, 1936 & 1942, most of splash muscat d'Alexandrie from 1902. **21** (93) notes of lime, yuzu, quince & muesli; part barrel-ferment, 70% new, rest concrete 'egg' & amphora give depth & breadth; linear persistence, as **20** ★★★★★ (95).

★★★★☆ **Noble Late Harvest** (🍂) (🐝) Exceptional botrytised semillon dessert, fermented/3 years in new barrique. Distinctive marzipan & apricot notes, succulent green-citrus acid lifting **20** (93)'s 157 g/L sugar, extending the fantail finish. Follows standout **19** (93). 375 ml. Certified vegan, as all. — CvZ

Location/map: Franschhoek ▪ Map grid reference: D1 ▪ WO: Franschhoek/Stellenbosch/Swartland ▪ Est 1994 ▪ 1stB 1996 ▪ Tasting by appt only ▪ Closed all pub hols ▪ Wines also available to purchase or enjoy on-premise at inVINcible Wine Shoppe & Wine Bar in Franschhoek ▪ Owner(s) Boekenhoutskloof Winery (Pty) Ltd ▪ Cellarmaster(s) Marc Kent (1994) ▪ Winemaker(s) Gottfried Mocke, Eben Meiring, Johan Nesenberend & Heinrich Hugo ▪ Boekenhoutskloof: 71ha/9ha (cabs s/f, sem); Porseleinberg: 135ha/90ha (cinsaut, grenache, shiraz); Goldmine: 65ha/40ha (cinsaut, grenache, shiraz, chenin) ▪ 60% red 39% white 1% rosé ▪ BRC, HACCP, IPW ▪ PO Box 433 Franschhoek 7690 ▪ info@boekenhoutskloof.co.za ▪ www.boekenhoutskloof.co.za ▪ T +27 (0)21-876-3320

Boland Cellar   (♀)

An extensive, long-established winery near Paarl, with 30 producing shareholders, more than 1,500 ha of vines and over 200,000 annual cases of own-label wine, Boland Cellar says it takes its custodianship of nature 'very seriously'. Hence a range of initiatives designed to enable sustainable grape production, such as water-saving strategies, a focus on soil preparation and health, and biological pest control, to name a few. Through its involvement with Greenpop, and donation of proceeds from certain wines, Boland is working to preserve the habitat of honeybees through reforestation 'to ensure the future viability of agricultural crops'.

Reserve range

★★★★ **Cabernet Sauvignon** (♀) Lively cassis & plum intertwined with graphite, cigarsmoke & dried herb on the finish from 20 months in oak, 60% new. **19** (89) young yet already showing good integration.

★★★★ **Merlot** (♀) Christmas cake & warm spice on **19** (88), layered with mocha & supple tannin after 16 months in 40% new oak. Succulent & tasty now, yet enough structure to keep for later.

★★★★ **Shiraz** (♀) Blackcurrant, raspberry flavours & hint of liquorice are in harmony with **19** (89)'s understated oak tannin (only 60% in older barrels, 18 months), spicy & savoury finale.

★★★★ **Chardonnay** (♀) Citrus, baked pastry & roasted nut entice in part-oaked **21** (89). Silky, with tangy lemon curd finish. Lovely focus & expression. Could keep year/2.

★★★★ **Chenin Blanc** ⓧ Crisp & dry **21** ⑧⑨, part wooded this vintage, adding to cream texture imparted by lees ageing. Nice interplay between fresh tropical fruit & savoury herbs, long spicy finish.

One Formation range

★★★★ **Grenache Noir** ⓧ Lovely intensity & layering of ripe, dark berry & bramble fruit with spicy, savoury & peppery notes in **20** ⑧⑨. Only 50% oaked, 16 months, for excellent balance & length.

★★★★ **Shiraz-Grenache-Viognier** ⓧ Complex **20** ⑧⑨, succulent & smooth, dash of spice augmented by 70% portion aged in new oak. **19** untasted.

★★★★ **Chenin Blanc-Sauvignon Blanc-Grenache Blanc** ⓥ Now bottled, **22** ⑧⑨ harmonious, rounded & delicious. Fragrant lemongrass intro, orchard fruit palate, creamy vanilla from the oaked portion.

Discontinued: **Shiraz**, **Chenin Blanc**.

Boland Cellar range

Cappupino Ccinotage ☺ ★★★ Pinotage made in the 'coffee' style, with roast bean, cream & vanilla to the fore. **23** ⑧② adds juicy plums to the mix for an easy-drinker that will keep its many fans smiling.

Discontinued: **Méthode Cap Classique**.

Classic Selection

Chenin Blanc ☺ ★★★ Copious tropical fruit salad aromas & flavours on delightful **23** ⑧②, with lipsmacking citrus zest aftertaste. Friendly, happy & cracking value.

Cabernet Sauvignon ⓧ ★★★★ Over-delivers on price & palate appeal in **21** ⑧⑤, with good depth of cassis flavour, supple tannin, lovely fresh finish. Similar oaking to Merlot. Worth seeking out. **Merlot** ⓧ ★★★ Fruit-forward **21** ⑧② preview is easy & juicy, with ripe plums, hints of vanilla & warm spice to finish. 60% wooded, mostly older barrels. **Chardonnay** ★★★ Fresh ripe apple & lemon flavours on partly older-barrel-fermented **23** ⑧②, rounded & easygoing. **Sauvignon Blanc** ★★★ Sleek, green-toned **23** ⑧⓪, grass, herbs & greengage flavours, a lemony finish that will pair well with creamy pasta. WO W Cape.

Melita range

Pinotage ⓧ ★★★ Dark berries, spiced by touch oak, juicy **19** ⑦⑨ is light & smooth. Low alc (±8%) for these. **Chenin Blanc** ⓧ ★★★ Tank sample **22** ⑦⑨ delicate, just-dry, with melon & papaya wafts. — WB

Location/map: Paarl ▪ Map grid reference: E4 ▪ WO: Coastal/Paarl/Western Cape ▪ Est/1stB 1941 ▪ Tasting & sales Mon-Fri 9-5 Sat/pub hols 10-3 ▪ Closed Easter weekend, Dec 25/26 & Jan 1 ▪ Wine club ▪ Owner(s) 30 producing shareholders ▪ Winemaker(s) Handré Barkhuizen (2009) & Bernard Smuts (2001), with Monique de Villiers (2015), Rosco Lewis (2016) & Rynard Muller (2020) ▪ Viticulturist(s) Spekkies van Breda (2016) ▪ 1,548ha (cab, merlot, ptage, shiraz, chard, chenin, nouvelle, sauv, viog) ▪ 16,439t/205,000cs own label 48% red 50% white 2% rosé + 129,000cs for clients ▪ Other export brands: Flutterby, Lindenhof, Lionsway, Montestell ▪ WIETA, WWF-SA Conservation Champion ▪ PO Box 7007 Noorder-Paarl 7623 ▪ info@boland-kelder.co.za ▪ www.bolandkelder.co.za, www.bolandcellar.co.za ▪ **T +27 (0)21-872-1766**

☐ **Boland Kelder** *see* Boland Cellar

Bon Courage Estate   ⓧ ⓜ ⓐ ⓑ ⓒ

The late André Bruwer may have been channelling his family's French heritage when in 1983 he registered the Robertson familial farm Goedemoed as 'Bon Courage Estate' estate, giving rise to the winery's slogan 'The courage to craft quality wines'. And perhaps a Gallic muse sparked the love for crafting champagne-method sparkling in his son and current owner-cellarmaster Jacques while still a student at Elsenburg. What's certain is the strong work ethic that underlies the production of an extensive range, with enviable consistency, and a keenness to embrace new technology and techniques, evidenced by the recent cellar makeover that's making harvests 'so much more efficient and cost-effective'.

Inkará range

★★★★ **Cabernet Sauvignon** ⓐ Cab's cassis character to the fore in fruit-driven **19** ⑧⑨, overlaid with vanilla from portion American oak. Careful raising in new wood provides structure for long cellaring; well-managed grape tannins add slight 'green stick' bitterness which enlivens the palate.

★★★★ **Merlot** ⓥ Lovely fruit on **16** ⑧⑧, plums & berries, 18 months oaking a dark chocolate overlay plus a firm backbone for cellaring. Already accessible, enjoyable, but designed for a rewarding future.

★★★★ **Shiraz** Whisper black pepper & fynbos on **21** ⑧⑨'s pure black & red fruit, sweet notes from new American oak. Supple & approachable now, crafted to improve in bottle.

Pinot Noir ⓥ ★★★★ More restraint in **16** ⑧⑤ than last, closer to variety's character: raspberry, some earthy notes, elegant, smooth textured. Mainly older French barrels, 24 months, provide svelte tannins.

Jacques Bruère Cap Classique Sparkling range

★★★★☆ **Cuvée Brut Rosé** ⓐ Myriad tiny bubbles rise through **14** ⑨④ pale pink glassful, explode on palate to enhance distinct raspberry & lemon flavours ex 80/20 pinot noir & chardonnay. Elegant modest sugar & alc (5.5 g/L, 11%), satisfying weight from 10% barrel-fermented portion & 48 months on lees.

★★★★☆ **Blanc de Blancs** ⓥ Venerable **12** ⑨④ sparkling from chardonnay spent 5 years on lees, 3 further on cork gaining creamy richness. Savoury & complex, lengthy finish. Delicious now & for several more years.

★★★★☆ **Brut Reserve** ⓐ Exceptionally well-judged **14** ⑨④ sparkling has incredible fruit & richness, weight from 10% oaked portion & 8 months on lees in tank, 48 in bottle. Array of apple tones (fresh, baked, dried & caramelised), racy acidity & thrilling, near-austere dryness. 60/40 pinot noir & chardonnay.

Bon Courage range

★★★★☆ **Noble Late Harvest** ⓥ Unoaked botrytis dessert from riesling treads lightly in **23** ⑨⓪ at just 10.9% alc, charms with jasmine & honeysuckle detail on apricot fruit, which is both sweet & tart. 375 ml.

★★★★☆ **White Muscadel 22** ⑨⓪ more delicate version than most of this fortified dessert, with palest yellow hue, modest spirit adjustment (just 15.5%). Full-sweet though, with honeysuckle & fresh/dried apricot tones. Wonderfully rich but shade less flavorsome, freshness, overall presence than **21** ⑨④.

Lady of the House Pinotage Rosé ⓥ ⓥ ★★★★ Sunset pink & nicely dry, plenty of boiled sweet & strawberry flavour. At nearly 14% alc, **23** ⑧⑤ perhaps too much fun for lunch - better for at-home dinner?

Cabernet Sauvignon ★★★★ Vibrant cassis fruit spiced with year new oak leads **22** ⑧④ work-in-progress; variety's signature acid backbone & grippy tannins up its refreshment score. **The Mulberry Bush Merlot** ★★★ Previewed **23** ⑦⑨ fruity but a little gruff & hot at 14.9% alc. **Pinotage** ★★★ Pre-bottling, **22** ⑧② promises to be as enjoyable as previous, thanks to piquant cranberry fruit, brush vanilla, supple tannins. **The Pepper Tree Shiraz** ★★★★ Lots of love shown to **22** ⑧④, including wholeberry ferment & 20% new oak. Abundant black & red berry fruit nicely seasoned with black pepper, tannins ultra-soft & round. Rating provisional, as all previewed wines. **Estate Blend Cabernet Sauvignon-Shiraz** ⓥ ★★★★ Same 60/40 mix in **21** ⑧③ as last. Unexpected (for the varieties) sweet-sour fruit, pleasant acid nip & good support from year in older oak. **Chardonnay Prestige Cuvée** ★★★★ Smooth & nutty-creamy from 8 months lees ageing in older barrels, **22** ⑧③ has blue orange ripeness to lemon & lime fruit, yet easy to drink & enjoy. **Chardonnay Unwooded** ★★★ Banana- & peach-toned **23** ⑦⑧ unchallenging everyday tipple; relies on viscosity from 13.8% alc to add weight & extend the finish. **André's Fame Colombard** ⓥ ★★★★ Lively & balanced, **23** ⑧③ drinks well with dash sugar curtailing piercing acid. More of variety's 'sweaty' side than last, but still plenty fresh guava, citrus. **Gewürztraminer Dry** ⓥ ★★★★ Pre-bottling sample **23** ⑧④ flush with varietal Turkish delight & frangipani tones, silky texture, fruity but dry finish. Always a pleasing expression of this rare grape. **The Gooseberry Bush Sauvignon Blanc** ★★★ Cool green grass & fig, subtle Cape gooseberry appeal on **23** ⑧⓪ party starter. **Estate Blend Colombard-Chardonnay** ⓥ ★★★★ Stalwart unwooded white, usual 70/30 combo in ex-tank **23** ⑧③. Chardonnay's lime & yellow citrus attractive foil for colombard's guava; undemanding, zippy & fresh sipping. **Blush Vin Doux** ★★★ Rosepetal & Turkish delight on fragrant, sunset pink **NV** ⑦⑧ carbonated sparkler from red muscadel. Frothy, with grapey tastes & sweet finish. **Gewürztraminer Special Late Harvest** ★★★★ Year later, **22** ⑧⑤ Turkish delight & litchi aromas, flavours, have intensified somewhat. Spot-on acid-sugar balance this producer's signature. Best sipped chilled, like **21** ★★★★ ⑧⑥. **Red Muscadel** ★★★★ Palest garnet hue, berries & rooibos tea, full-sweet grapey palate & delicate 16% spirit, **23** ⑧⑤ fortified muscat ticks the winter fireside sipping boxes. **Cape Vintage** ⓥ ★★★★ Cask sample of **22** ⑧⑤ 'port' from usual tinta, touriga & souzão combo. Xmas spice, glacé cherries & orange zest top notes to blue-black fruit. Persistent, with tempting sweetness & decent spirit integration.

Like Father Like Son range

Merlot-Cabernet Sauvignon ★★ Fruity, softly dry **22** ⑦⑥, unoaked easy-quaffing 60/40 blend with light raisin nuance. WO W Cape, as all these. **Pinotage Rosé** ⊘ **★★★** Palest of sunset hues, **23** ⑦⑦ ex tank delivers cherry, raspberry & strawberry bonbon aromas & flavours, sweet farewell. **Chenin Blanc ★★★** Soon after bottling, **23** ⑦⑦ still quite estery, with little varietal character. Just-dry & zesty. — CvZ

Location/map: Robertson ▪ Map grid reference: B5 ▪ WO: Robertson/Western Cape ▪ Est 1927 ▪ 1stB 1983 ▪ Tasting & sales Mon-Fri 8-5 Sat/pub hols 9-3; pub hols (seasonal) please call ahead ▪ Fee R40pp/5 wines; booking essential for groups of 10+ ▪ Closed Good Fri, Dec 25 & Jan 1 ▪ Café Maude T +27 (0)82-898-9592 ▪ Facilities for children ▪ Olive oil ▪ Owner(s)/viticulturist(s) Jacques Bruwer ▪ Winemaker(s) Jacques Bruwer, with Phillip Viljoen (Jan 2015) ▪ 150ha (cab, pinot, shiraz, chard) ▪ 40% red 50% white 10% rosé ▪ Export brand: Three Rivers ▪ PO Box 589 Robertson 6705 ▪ wine@boncourage.co.za ▪ www.boncourage.co.za ▪ **T +27 (0)23-626-4178**

☐ **Bonfire Hill** *see* Bruce Jack Wines
☐ **Bonne Esperance** *see* KWV Wines

Bonnievale Wines ⓠ ⊚ ⓖ

An upbeat report from the 110 owner-growers, with headquarters outside Bonnievale town: 'record sales and authoritative awards', for wines styled by five winemakers from an extensive ±1,500 of vines, with 'purity, freshness and elegance' foremost in mind. With just short of 75 years of heritage, Bonnievale Wines prides itself on using 'the latest technology that allows us to single out the fruit behind our very best wines of every vintage'. If it all sounds a tad corporate, visitors can expect a personal welcome at the gabled venue.

Limited Release range

★★★★ Cabernet Sauvignon Carefully nurtured top-performing rows produce the flagship. **21** ⑧⑧ fresher, purer than last, 18 months older oak, 33% American, well judged, allowing fruit to shine.

★★★★ Chardonnay ⊘ Few grams sugar leave the good balance undisturbed, contribute to smooth seamlessness of **22** ⑧⑥. Peach more than citrus this vintage, smart staving adds subtle spice & structure.

The River Collection

Cabernet Sauvignon-Merlot ☺ **★★★** Step-up **21** ⑧⓪ a vibrant & engaging everyday companion. Indian spice on red & black fruit, light & neatly dry.

Cabernet Sauvignon ★★★ As last, **21** ⑧②'s gruff tannins tamed by few grams sugar, black rather than red fruit with farmyard nuance. Deft oak staving for hint of spice & complexity, as all these reds. **Merlot** ⓠ **★★★** Vivacious & quaffable **21** ⑧② has crisp acid, piquant black plum fruit & slight salty lift at the end. **Pinotage** ⓠ **★★★** Tannins on **21** ⑦⑨ a tad strong for its light blackberry fruit. Best with a braai. **Shiraz** ⓠ **★★★** Nice shiraz characteristics of fynbos, spice & black pepper on **21** ⑧⓪, feisty tannins for a meal. **Cinsault Rosé** ⓠ **★★★** Pale pink, off-dry **22** ⑦⑨ has restrained red berry & pomegranate appeal, lightly flavoured & bouncy. **Rosé Moscato Perlé ★★** Was 'Dusk' in Nature range. If well chilled, full-sweet, sunset-hued **NV** ⑦③ rosé glides smoothly, charms with rooibos & ginger nuances, low 9% alc. WO Robertson, as Chenin & Sauvignon. **Chardonnay ★★★** Decently dry & lightly oaked, **23** ⑧② has apple & peach attractions, creamy finish from some lees contact. **Chenin Blanc** ⊘ **★★★★** Starts with sauvignon-like grassy whiffs, opens to more typical white & yellow peach, some Golden Delicious richness. Smidgen sugar ups palate appeal on **23** ⑧④. **Sauvignon Blanc ★★★** Not the explosion of greenness of previous, **23** ⑦⑧ instead idiosyncratic banoffee pie & ripe papaya, very soft & rounded. Best well chilled. **Sweet Shiraz ★★★** Plenty of red & black fruit, some fynbos on latest **NV** ⑧⓪. Needs, & has, firm tannin to counter generous sugar.

Neat range

De-Alcoholised Shiraz ⓠ **★★** Red berry & pomegranate fruit on **20** ⑦③, aged with staves 6 months. Combo brisk acid & gentle tannin ensure drier palate than the norm. **De-Alcoholised Sauvignon Blanc ★★★** Flavoursome **23** ⑦⑦, varietally true Cape gooseberry & greenpepper, commendably broad palate at less than 0.5% alc but needs tad more freshness.

The Vale range

Cinsault Rosé Brut ★★ Light pink hue, lazy bubbles, pleasing strawberry lollipop character, **NV** ⑦⑥'s sweet touch lifted by raspberry tang. Carbonated, as sibling. **Sauvignon Blanc Brut** ★★ Palest straw **NV** ⑦④ frothy & grassy, as expected, adds guava hint to ever so slightly sweet palate.
Discontinued: **Nature range**. — CvZ

Location: Bonnievale ▪ Map: Robertson ▪ Map grid reference: D3 ▪ WO: Bonnievale/Robertson ▪ Est 1950 ▪ 1stB 1977 ▪ Tasting & sales Mon-Fri 9-5 Sat/pub hols 10-1 ▪ Closed Good Fri, Dec 25/26 & Jan 1 ▪ Tour groups ▪ Conferences (12 pax) ▪ Spring market ▪ Wine club ▪ Online shop ▪ Owner(s) 110 members ▪ Winemaker(s) Marthinus Rademeyer (Dec 2009), Edwin Mathambo (Dec 2012), Jean Slabber (Jun 2017), Tinus le Roux (2017) & Chris van Reenen (2020) ▪ Viticulturist(s) Sakkie Bosman (Nov 2006) ▪ 1,490ha (cab, cinsaut, merlot, ptage, shiraz, chard, chenin, cbard, sauv) ▪ ISO 22 000, IPW, WIETA ▪ PO Box 206 Bonnievale 6730 ▪ info@ bonnievalewines.co.za ▪ www.bonnievalewines.co.za ▪ **T +27 (0)23-616-2795**

Boplaas Family Vineyards   ⓠ ⓞ ⓑ

A familial winery this certainly is, the industrious Nel family working from cellars on Saayman Street in Calitzdorp, with 6th-generation members in key roles: Margaux and Rozanne, winemaker and marketer respectively, and Daniel, distiller and co-marketer, paterfamilias Carel as cellarmaster. Their longtime focuses are awarded 'port' and unfortified wines from port grapes, widening latterly to include other Mediterranean varieties, hence the debuting albariño. Conservation minded, the Nels protect 5,000ha of Klein Karoo veld, where carbon-sequestering spekboom occurs naturally. Ever welcoming, they've opened a new tasting lounge at Red Berry Farm outside George on the Garden Route, the venue at Klein Brak River having closed.

Heritage Reserve range

★★★★★ **White Muscadel** ⓠ Limited bottling in exceptional years. **14** ⑨③ exudes marmalade, honey, candied ginger. Mouthfilling, complex & rich, with clean fresh finish. Will reward ageing. W Cape WO.

Family Reserve range

★★★★ **Cabernet Sauvignon** ⓠ Cassis & leafy tomato typicity on velvety **20** ⑧⑦ from Stellenbosch. Like **17** ⑧⑨, & following house style, open ferment in traditional kuip with 12 months in 1st & 2nd fill oak.

★★★★★ **Touriga Nacional** ⓠ Three vineyards blended after 18 months in oak. **19** ⑨⓪ offers vivacious fruit flavour, dry tannin & impressive concentration. Less brooding than last **16** ⑨①.

★★★★ **Ring of Rocks** Red blend made in best years only. Impressive 9 varieties, Portuguese & French, in **21** ⑧⑧, showing fruit purity & spice in cohesive whole, well rounded after 14 months in barrel.

★★★★★ **Gamka** Refined blend of touriga nacional & tinta barocca (55/8), 2 (French) others, **21** ⑨⓪ vivid plum, fynbos & spice, light cedary grip from year in barrels, good persistence.

★★★★ **Bobbejaanberg Sauvignon Blanc** ⓠ From high-altitude, windswept vines plagued by baboons. **22** ⑧⑥ bright, fresh & tropical, defined dry finish. As with **19** ★★★★★ ⑨①, skin & lees contact. WO Coastal, rest of these WO W Cape. No **20**, **21** untasted.

★★★★★ **Gamka Branca** Chardonnay holds sway over chenin, verdelho & 4 others in distinctive **22** ⑨①. Bright, fresh, lemongrass & stonefruit matched by broad creamy cashew notes. Like last-tasted **20** ⑨①, fermented in oak, chenin with own yeast, aged 9 months before blending.

★★★★ **Alvarinho** ⓝⓔⓦ One of only a handful from this Iberian grape, **23** ⑧⑥ shows grapefruit, lemon & stonefruit zip on taut, pithy palate. Bright, lively, gains good texture from 4 months on lees.

Boplaas range

★★★★ **Touriga Nacional** ⓥ Friendly cherry appeal of **22** ⑧⑦ inches bar higher on last release. Bright, lively, with aromatic five-spice & light tannin grip from 10 months in seasoned oak.

★★★★★ **The 1932 Block Hanepoot** ⓠ Exceptional fortified from small, very low-yield parcel planted in 1932. **15** ⑨② wonderful freshness & a lemon zest finish balance intense, opulent fruit & floral flavours. 500 ml.

★★★★ **Red Muscadel** ⓠ Jasmine & brûlée seduction on **22** ⑧⑥ along with tealeaf & typical muscat florality. Sweet & rich yet lovely poise & balance, too, finishes clean. **21** untasted. WO Klein Karoo.

★★★★ **White Muscadel** ⓠ Powerfully sweet & concentrated yet balanced **22** ⑧⑨. Grilled apricot, honeysuckle & sundried pineapple unctuousness, deftly fortified for a light & clean impression.

★★★★☆ **Cape Ruby** ⊘ Seductive plum, blueberry, raisin & spice appeal of **NV** ⑨⓪ 'port' improves on previous. Lovely balance of fiery spirit & sweetness. Vibrant but smooth & restrained, dry tannin from year seasoned 'pipes'. Alc 17%.

★★★★☆ **Cape Tawny** ⓧ Rich, nutty **NV** ⑨③ 'port' from mostly tinta barocca with touriga nacional & souzão, 10-12 years in barrel adding layers of flavour, salty nuance. Creamy yet vibrant. Alc 19.7%. This, sibling tawnies & Chocolate WO W Cape.

★★★★☆ **Cape Tawny Single Harvest** ⓐ Complex melange of flavours: butterscotch, toffee, hazelnut, citrus zest & anise on elegant **07** ⑨④ 'port'. Tinta barocca & touriga nacional (70/30), 16 years in large barrels, as last **05** ★★★★★ ⑨⑤. Effortless ease & poise, thanks to balance of fruit & 17% alc, vibrant freshness to the last sip. Richly rewarding, like last-made **05** ★★★★★ ⑨⑤. WO W Cape.

★★★★☆ **Cape Tawny Vintners Reserve Bin 1880** ⓧ Concentrated 'port' with many flavour layers, raisined fruit, wonderful oak/alc integration & unflagging finish. **NV** ⑨④ from tinta barocca (85%) & touriga nacional, aged minimum 10 years. 375 ml.

★★★★☆ **Cape Vintage** Jasmine & violet delicacy on **20** ⑨① 'port' from touriga nacional, old-vine tinta barocca & souzão. Spice & blueberry-cherry ripeness add allure. Oak is forward but dry, framing fruit well. Good alc fire & year in seasoned 'pipes' lend longevity. Touch less intense than **19** ⑨③.

★★★★★ **Cape Vintage Reserve** ⓐ Deep, dense, inky **21** ★★★★★ ⑨④ 'port' impresses with spice & richness of blue & black berries, fruitcake & roasted nuts. Dry grip of fine tannin is balanced by superbly judged 17.3% alc. Made traditionally & aged in large-format oak, it's complex, layered & elegant. Touriga nacional with 10% each tinta barocca & souzão, unlike **20** ⑨⑤ which had touriga franca too.

★★★★ **Cape Vintage The Chocolate** Tinta barocca (70%) & touriga nacional vines selected for chocolate flavour. **20** ⑧⑨ improves on last **18** ★★★★ ⑧⑤ in balance of fruit, alc (17.7%) & fine dry tannins. Cocoa from year seasoned barrels on long clean finish. 375 ml.

Cabernet Sauvignon ★★★★ Fruitcake & spice notes of **22** ⑧⑤ are framed by subtle wood from 10 months in/with older barrels & oak alternatives. Supple & approachable. WO W Cape, as Pinotage & Tinta Barocca. **Merlot** ★★★★ Gentle, rounded black fruit with touch of graphite on **21** ⑧⑤, pliable & light bodied. Fresh & typical of the grape. **Pinotage** ★★★★ Blueberry & raspberry notes of **21** ⑧⑤ retain light succulence & spine of oak from 9 months in older barrels. Ideal braai companion. WO W Cape. **Tinta Barocca** ⊘ ★★★★ Redcurrant & raspberry with spicy vivacity on bright, gentle **21** ⑧⑤, subtle dry tannin from 10 months in seasoned barrels. Easy to like. **Dry Shiraz Rosé** ★★★★ Strawberries & plums vie for prominence on tangy, light & fresh **23** ⑧③. Uncomplicated & easy for summertime enjoyment. **Stoepsit Sauvignon Blanc** ★★★★ Granadilla, lemon zest & fig on succulent, light-bodied **23** ⑧④. Ultra-quaffable poolside fare. **Cape Portuguese Collection Verdelho** ★★★★ Improves marginally on last in tang & citrus zip, apple & pear ripeness for balance. **23** ⑧⑤ juicy & appealing. **Pinot Noir Brut Sparkling** ★★★★ Coral pink hue to pomegranate- & strawberry-toned **23** ⑧⑤. Piquant & light, crisply dry end. **Hanepoot** ★★★★ Barley sugar richness on **22** ⑧④ fortified muscat from 30+ year old vines. Floral sweetness matched by spirit, balanced & long. **Pink Moscato Frizzante** ⓃⒺⓌ ★★★ Fun, not overtly sweet pink sparkler from white & red muscadel. **23** ⑧② juicy raspberries, strawberries & floral overtone, good bubble & piquancy for summer. **White Moscato Frizzante** ⓃⒺⓌ ★★★ Jasmine florality on **23** ⑧② white muscadel sparkler. Fresh, tangy, sweetness matched by acid. Light & unfussy for easy enjoyment. Low alc, as sibling. Not tasted: **Ouma Cloete Straw Wine**.

Brandy range

★★★★★ **Potstill Reserve 20 Years** ⓧ Gold colour, with hint of olive green on rim of this exceptional spirit ⑨⑦. Array of fruit flavours mingle with smooth vanilla on super-complex, elegant & silky palate - both delicate & penetrating - gorgeous long finish.

★★★★★ **Single Harvest Potstill** Single-vintage brandies, especially older ones, are rare, as **05** ⑨② from colombard, after 17 years in oak, is remarkably fresh as well as characterful. The aromas & flavours are fine & complex (florals, herbs & subtle apricot), texture smooth, finish more elegantly dry than most. Just the unusually high 46% alc throws it a little off balance.

Not tasted: **Potstill Reserve 15 Years, Potstill Reserve 12 Years, Potstill Reserve 8 Years, Carel Nel Reserve 5 Years**. — FM, TJ

Location: Calitzdorp ▪ Map: Klein Karoo & Garden Route ▪ Map grid reference: B5 ▪ Map: Klein Karoo & Garden Route ▪ Map grid reference: C3 ▪ Map: Klein Karoo & Garden Route ▪ Map grid reference: C1 ▪ WO: Calitzdorp/Western Cape/Stellenbosch/Coastal/Klein Karoo ▪ Est 1880 ▪ 1stB 1982 ▪ Tasting & sales Mon-Fri

9–5 Sat 9–4 Sun 10–3 ▪ Fee R70pp ▪ Closed Good Fri & Dec 25 ▪ Cellar tours by appt ▪ Facilities for children ▪ Gifts ▪ Farm produce ▪ Walks/hikes ▪ Conservation area ▪ Ring of Rocks ▪ Spirits tasting incl brandy, gin & whisky ▪ Distilling lounge ▪ Owner(s) Carel Nel ▪ Cellarmaster(s) Carel Nel (1982) ▪ Winemaker(s) Margaux Nel (Dec 2006) ▪ Distiller(s) Daniel Nel ▪ Viticulturist(s) Danie Strydom ▪ 5,000ha/70ha (cab, ptage, shiraz, tinta, touriga, chard, cbard, sauv) ▪ 55% red 45% white ▪ IPW ▪ PO Box 156 Calitzdorp 6660 ▪ info@boplaas. co.za ▪ www.boplaas.co.za ▪ **T +27 (0)44-213-3326**

☐ **Born of Fire** *see* Julien Schaal

Boschendal Wines   ⓠ ⑪ ⓐ ⓞ ⓢ ⓛ

This DGB-owned brand has been ubiquitous on shelves and in cellars for so many years, and maintained so enviable a standard of quality, it seems to spring into bottle spontaneously. Of course that's not the reality, and there's an extensive, slightly tweaked team that makes it all happen: cellarmaster and red/rosé maker Jacques Viljoen, Danielle Coetsee styling the sparklers, and newcomer Charl Schoeman taking charge of the white wines, with Stephan Joubert as group winemaker. 'Utmost care' is taken to select the sites best suited to the chosen varieties, and viticulturist Heinie Nel is especially pleased with the maturing managed vineyards in the Helderberg. Visitors to the three-century-old, mountain-edged Franschhoek home continue to be royally catered for, themed tastings, eateries, shops and luxury accommodation being just a few of the available options. WWF-SA Conservation Champion status highlights the concern for sustainability.

Heritage Collection

★★★★☆ **Grande Syrah** ⓑ From Stellenbosch fruit, in a great year, **19** ⑨④ packaged to impress, its modern styling deftly handled. Deep blue & black fruit cosseted by a streamlined oak structure & freshened by crisp acid. Firm tannin, dry persistence.

★★★★☆ **Black Angus** ⓑ Evolution of the 1980s Grand Reserve pinnacle label, shiraz with Bordeaux varieties as for Nicolas, but exclusively from Helderberg vines. Two vintages tasted, both peppery with firm tannin grip reining in generous savoury red & black fruit, bright acid adding lift. **20** ⑨④ concentrated & robust, **19** ⑨④'s stunning stunning balance allowing enjoyment now & for many years.

★★★★☆ **Vin d'Or** ⓑ Noble Late Harvest from riesling &/or viognier, depending on harvest. **19** ⑨④ was the former, as is **20** ⑨④ ex Elgin; arresting perfumes of jasmine, quince & honey unfurling on cornucopia of fruit flavours. Powerfully sweet, it lacks the piquancy & uber-brisk acid to ensure thrilling cleanout on stellar **21** ★★★★★ ⑨⑤, riesling & viognier. No oak for either, 11% alc, 375 ml.

Special Cuvée range

★★★★☆ **Nicolas** ⊘ ⓑ Named for founder Nicolas de Lanoy, a luxury blend of shiraz & the 5 Bordeaux varieties, showing rounded black fruit balanced by overt tannins. Multiple vintages tasted: **21** ⑨② brightly berried with mocha warmth, **19** ★★★★★ ⑨⑤ the most beautifully balanced, **18** ⑨⓪ a bit leaner. **20** ⑨⓪, reviewed last edition, for earlier drinking. Also in 1.5L.

★★★★ **Suzanne** Old-barrel-fermented Elgin semillon & sauvignon (54/46), aged 6 months, **22** ⑧⑨'s herb intensity joins white pepper nuance in a taut body showing persistent lively mineral acid & waxy undertone. Last was **19** ⑧⑨.

Not tasted: **Chardonnay-Pinot Noir**.

Appellation Series

★★★★☆ **Stellenbosch Cabernet Sauvignon** ⓑ Herbaceous scrub tones accompany cassis fruit in a tarry graphite frame. **19** ⑨② is tight but not hard, has classic cedar overlay from French oak, 34% new, 16–18 months. Like last, all in place for a fine future, just needs time.

★★★★☆ **Elgin Pinot Noir** ⊘ Trademark vivid, moreish cherry & raspberry fruit of the cool climate, **21** ⑨⓪'s year in oak, 10% new, adds savouriness & smooths the tannin to perfectly counter-weigh the rich palate for a flavour-packed experience without heaviness.

★★★★☆ **Elgin Chardonnay** ⓑ Refined **21** ⑨④ another lesson in restraint & precision. Citrus fruit infused with subtle oak spice & supported by succulent acid. Elegant but with powerful length of flavour. 22% new barrels, 11 months. Usual reined-in 13.5% alc.

★★★★ **Elgin Sauvignon Blanc** Lightly oaked, just 5 months in old cask, **22** ⑧⑨ thrills with nettle, fresh-cut grass & dusty khaki bush character, hint of blackcurrant. Appealing, fresh & bright before or during the meal. **21** untasted.

A global community of professional
and non-professional members
whose focus is brotherhood, friendship,
camaraderie and sharing a passion
for the culinary arts.

Please email us for membership details.

La Chaîne des Rôtisseurs
Association Mondiale de la Gastronomie

https://southafrica.chainedesrotisseurs.com
baillidelegue@chaine.co.za

INVERDOORN
PRIVATE GAME RESERVE
WESTERN CAPE CHEETAH CONSERVATION

CAPE TOWN
BIG 5 SAFARI

10 000-Hectare Private Game Reserve

Inverdoorn Private Game Reserve is situated just under 2.5 hours from Cape Town, in the vastness of the majestic Ceres Karoo. With thick wooded Acacia river beds and magnificent golden mountains on the horizon, Inverdoorn provides the ultimate tranquil Big 5 day trip and overnight safari experience.

+27 (0)21 422 0013 | WWW.INVERDOORN.COM
BIG 5 SAFARI 2.5 HOURS FROM CAPE TOWN

@INVERDOORN

1685 range

★★★★ **Merlot** Smoked bacon lead-in to medium-bodied **20** ⑧⑥, expressive blueberry palate, soft & accessible but far from frivolous. More satisfying & complete than **19** ★★★★ ⑧⑤.

★★★★ **Chardonnay** Wide appeal of **22** ⑧⑥ ensured by typicity of citrus flavour & nutty buttered toast nuances from deft oaking, 12% new. Satisfyingly dry, impressively weighty & long.

★★★★ **Sauvignon Blanc Grande Cuvée** ⊘ Invariably lively, engaging & well priced. Peppery note to asparagus & tropical fruit, **23** ⑧⑥ spent 5 months on lees for weight & texture. **22** ⑧⑥ & previous added a dash semillon for same purpose.

Shiraz ★★★★ White pepper & scrub lift red-berried fruit of **20** ⑧⑤, touch firmer tannins but sufficiently mellow after year in 20% new oak for pleasurable drinking, solo or with food. **Chenin Blanc** ★★★ Preview of **23** ⑧② loses gram sugar for a bone-dry profile, promises pithy fruit flavour lifted by fresh acid. Coastal WO.

Méthode Cap Classique Collection

★★★★ **Brut Rosé** Pale pink **NV** ⑧⑨ dry bubbly, now pinot noir-led with chardonnay & dab pinotage. Satisfying chalky berry flavour & texture, palate weight enlivened by lemon acid, oystershell nuance & finessed bubbles. WO W Cape, as all these unless noted.

★★★★ **Brut** Ever-dependable dry sparkler from customary mix chardonnay (65%) & pinot noir. **NV** ⑧⑨ retains wide appeal based on texture & complex structure, usual pleasure-boosting touch sugar.

★★★★☆ **Grande Cuvée Brut** ⓐ Sophisticated gold-flecked **16** ⑨③ sparkler from 62% pinot noir & chardonnay. Long 56 months on lees add depth to balanced core of red berry fruit, shot through with brilliant acid on a mineral backbone. Perfect now & over next year/2. Off Elgin vines, as next.

★★★★☆ **Jean Le Long Prestige Cuvée** ⓐ Showing compelling maturity, stylish, premium-priced **12** ⑨③ extra-brut sparkling from chardonnay has intense brioche & umami character from 10 years ageing on lees. Rich lemon biscuit is lifted by bone-dryness & vibrant acid.

Luxe Nectar ★★★★ Popular semi-sweet **NV** ⑧⑤ fizz from chardonnay & pinot noir offers seamless drinkability, from its lemon cake & honey aromas to its upholstered palate.

Cape Brandy range

★★★★ **XO Brandy** ⓠ Latest bottling of 10 year old potstill ⑧⑨ touch more refined & elegant than last. Lightly rich, with usual dried fruit, spice & sandalwood. From chenin & colombard.— DS, TJ

Location/map: Franschhoek ▪ Map grid reference: D6 ▪ WO: Cape Coast/Elgin/Stellenbosch/Western Cape/Coastal ▪ Est 1685 ▪ 1stB 1975 ▪ Tasting & sales daily 10-6 (Oct-Mar) & 10-5 (Apr-Sep) ▪ Online shop ▪ Chocolate & wine pairing ▪ Brandy tasting ▪ Signature experiences, presented in private room, incl Historic tasting, 5 wines representing Boschendal history; Connoisseur tasting, 5 limited releases ▪ Closed Good Fri & Dec 25 ▪ Cheese platters on request R125ea ▪ The Werf Restaurant ▪ Farm shop & deli ▪ Weddings & functions ▪ Facilities for children ▪ Tour groups ▪ Gifts ▪ 23 luxury Werf & Orchards cottages ▪ Owner(s) DGB (Pty) Ltd ▪ Group winemaker Stephan Joubert ▪ Cellarmaster(s) Jacques Viljoen (Aug 2018) ▪ Winemaker(s) Jacques Viljoen (reds & rosé, 2018), Danielle Coetsee (MCC, 2021) & Charl Schoeman (whites, 2022) ▪ Viticulturist(s) Heinie Nel (Jul 2018) ▪ 2,240ha/200ha (shiraz, sauv) ▪ 3,100t/500,000cs own label 32% red 43% white 14% rosé 11% sparkling ▪ WIETA, WWF-SA Conservation Champion ▪ Private Bag X03 Groot Drakenstein 7680 ▪ cellardoor@boschendal.co.za ▪ www.boschendalwines.com ▪ **T +27 (0)21-001-3150**

☐ **Boschenheuwel** *see* Wine-of-the-Month Club

Boschheim   ⓠ

Stellenbosch polymer scientist and Cape Wine Master Andy Roediger's recent strategy of sourcing grapes more widely for his boutique label continues, with a new malbec from Breedekloof joining the Ceres Plateau shiraz which launched last edition. The compact but fully equipped Devon Valley cellar in which Andy works is shared with Mark Philp, longtime friend and owner of separately listed small-batch brand Muse.

★★★★ **Cabernet Sauvignon** ⓠ Ever-improving label, **20** ⑧⑦ has ample currant fruit elegantly held in the variety's firm structure, 10% merlot adds pleasing balance in the finish. Last was **18** ★★★★ ⑧④.

★★★★ **Malbec** ⓝⓔⓦ ⊘ Bold perfume on **22** ⑧⑥ from Breedekloof matched by bright, succulent blueberry & spice. Compact yet agile, squeeze of tannin from year in third new barrels.

★★★★ **Merlot** ⓠ Refined **20** ⑧⑥ lovely combo of floral & spice aromas, smoky berry fruit & supportive oak, 14.8% alc kept in check. Last tasted was **08**.

★★★★ **Shiraz** ⓥ From cool-climate Ceres Plateau (but certified W Cape), **21** ★★★★★ ⑨⓪ is lithe, athletic, with fragrant spice; touch more successful than meaty-savoury **20** ⑧⑨ ex Stellenbosch, which also still selling ex cellar. Both year in barrique, roughly third new.

★★★★ **Chenin Blanc** ⓥ Sunshiny, spice-dusted apple & pineapple flavours on **22** ⑧⑥, similar leesy dimension as last, same duration in oak, year, but only third new vs half.

Rosé ⓥ ★★★ Salmon pink **22** ⑦⑨ uses saignée method to bleed off juice from shiraz, cab & 2 others. Delicious dryness, noticeable but pleasant dustiness from time in oak. In abeyance: **Ella Marie.** — FM

Location/map: Stellenbosch ▪ Map grid reference: E5 ▪ WO: Stellenbosch/Western Cape/Breedekloof ▪ 1stB 2003 ▪ Tasting & sales by appt ▪ Owner(s)/winemaker(s) Andy Roediger ▪ 1,800cs own label 90% red 10% white ▪ PO Box 3202 Matieland 7602 ▪ andy@roedigeragencies.co.za ▪ **T +27 (0)21-887-0010**

☐ **Boschheuvel** *see* Zidela Wines

Boschkloof Wines

When Jacques Borman and his wife Marina established this winery near Stellenbosch, the purchase was prompted by Jacques having worked with syrah grapes from nearby Reyneke Wines in his previous cellar, opening his eyes to the area's potential - since realised by both Jacques and Reenen, his son and present winemaker, in wines like Epilogue, a syrah from a single parcel planted in 1996, classically styled, with perfume and texture the goals. It's a regular top performer in this guide and elsewhere. With disease claiming 8% of these vines, a new block is being established with a new clone. Other plantings include three hectares of cabernet and one of grenache noir, for a future total of 24 hectares under vine.

Boschkloof range

★★★★ **Cabernet Sauvignon** Classic cab scents of ripe blackberries & cassis, accessorised with cedar, yield to soft, sweet fruit harnessed by resistant tannins. **21** ⑧⑦ full bodied but structured, fruit & freshness create satisfying balance for medium-term benefits. Older oak.

★★★★★ **Epilogue** ⓐ Always one of SA's best syrahs. Freshness of **21** ⑨⑦ lends initial impression of delicacy & lightness, with beguiling spice & floral fragrance. Greater density & concentration than Syrah sibling never at expense of finesse in suppleness or fine tannins. The flavours grow, leaving memorable savoury length. 60% wholebunch, 60% aged in concrete, rest new oak. 13.7% alc.

★★★★☆ **Syrah** ⓐ Cool-vintage fragrance & delicate, fresh feel characterise **21** ⑨④. Spice & florals, with more savoury features in the silky, supple texture, yet to reveal their full dimension. Natural balance & squeeze of forming grip suggest development in store. Portion wholebunch, oak aged, 15% new.

★★★★ **Cabernet Sauvignon-Merlot** ⓥ Strikes happy balance in its 72/28 partnership in **22** ⑧⑦; cab's cassis fleshed out by plummy merlot, sweet fruit firmly braced by ripe grape tannins. Older oak.

★★★★☆ **Conclusion** ⓥ Greater than sum of its parts, **20** ⑨① cab & merlot with 18% each cab franc, syrah, none dominating. Ripe red fruit & savoury edge, smooth & mouthfilling, lifted by a mineral thread. Tannins, firm yet rounded, allow for current & future enjoyment. Oak, 40% new, stylish enhancement.

★★★★ **Chardonnay** Bright citrus zest accompanied by a little oak spice, underpinned by leesy weight, **23** ⑧⑧ makes for harmonious youthful enjoyment with a few years to go. Mix seasoned wood & tank ferment. WO W Cape. **22** untasted.

★★★★ **Sauvignon Blanc** ⓥ Understated yet persuasive figgy flavours comfortably weighted by lees ageing, **23** ⑧⑧ departs with zing. **22** untasted.

Discontinued: **Merlot**.

Kottabos range

★★★★☆ **Grenache-Syrah** Maintains flavoursome grenache (80%), syrah partnership in **22** ⑨⓪, with more red fruit, spice to fore & touch more grip than last. All capture freshness, energy for current & future pleasure. Grenache wholebunch, unwooded; syrah destemmed, older oak.

★★★★☆ **Chenin Blanc** Individual in a crowded field. Elegant & detailed, **22** ⑨① delicate honeyed earthy tones & peachy richness; light, grainy tannins both firm & add energy to upbeat, fantail farewell. Tank fermented, 5 days on skins; older-oak aged 10 months. **21** untasted.— AL

Location/map: Stellenbosch ▪ Map grid reference: C6 ▪ WO: Stellenbosch/Western Cape ▪ Est/1stB 1996 ▪ Tasting, sales & cellar tours Mon-Fri 9–5; pub hols (seasonal) please call ahead ▪ Fee R50 ▪ Closed Easter Fri-Sun, Dec 25

& Jan 1 ▪ Cheese & charcuterie platters ▪ BYO picnic ▪ Owner(s)/cellarmaster(s) Jacques Borman ▪ Winemaker(s) Reenen Borman (Jun 2010) ▪ Viticulturist(s) Jacques Borman, with Reenen Borman ▪ 30ha/19ha (cabs s/f, merlot, shiraz, chard) ▪ ±100-150t/6-8,000cs own label 90% red 10% white ▪ PO Box 1340 Stellenbosch 7599 ▪ orders@boschkloofwines.com ▪ www.boschkloofwines.com ▪ **T +27 (0)66-396-2689**

Boschrivier Wines - NJT de Villiers   (ⓦ) (ⓜ) (ⓐ) (ⓖ) (ⓞ) (ⓚ)

On twin farms at the foot of the Klein River mountains, inherited from family in the 1990s, Theo 'Ficky' de Villiers planted vines and, with consultants, produced his first shiraz just over 20 years ago. Though the visitor amenities near Stanford since have grown significantly, and lately there has been a dedicated winemaker, winegrowing is still small in scale and essentially a weekend passion for the Worcester paediatrician.

Rosé (ⓦ) ★★★ Bold reddish pink hue on dry **21** (78) from undisclosed variety/ies, offers succulent strawberry & raspberry flavours. **Sauvignon Blanc** (ⓦ) ★★★ Shows variety's lemon notes in uncomplicated **21** (78), juicy if lacking cohesion. Cape South Coast WO. In abeyance: **Cabernet Sauvignon**, **Shiraz**. — FM

Location: Stanford ▪ Map: Walker Bay & Bot River ▪ Map grid reference: C8 ▪ WO: Klein River/Cape South Coast ▪ Est 1998 ▪ 1stB 2002 ▪ Tasting & sales Mon-Sat 8-5 Sun (Sep 1 to Mar 31) 10-3 ▪ Closed Dec 25 ▪ Restaurant ▪ BYO picnic ▪ Gift shop ▪ Farm produce ▪ Conferences/functions (100 pax) ▪ Wedding venue ▪ Walking/hiking & 4x4 trails ▪ 5 self-catering farmhouses ▪ Owner(s)/viticulturist(s) Theodore de Villiers ▪ Winemaker(s) Mike Dobrovic ▪ 14ha (cab, shiraz) ▪ 7t/ha ±3,300cs own label 68.5% red 21% white 10.5% rosé ▪ Remhoogte, Caledon 7230 ▪ boschrivierwines@gmail.com ▪ www.boschrivierwines.co.za ▪ **T +27 (0)23-347-3313/2 ext 3; +27 (0)82-420-4267; +27 (0)28-008-5031 (tasting)**

Bosjes   (ⓜ) (ⓐ) (ⓞ) (ⓐ)

With a breathtaking curvilinear-roofed chapel at its centre, the Stofberg family's mountainside farm in Breedekloof is an internationally awarded food, accommodation and wedding destination, with small parcels of branded wines by local winemakers adding to the lustre. Environmental concern sees a new solar farm power the entire property, and botanist Leon Kluge assist with rehabilitating their renosterveld reserve.

Reserve range (NEW)
Merlot ★★★★ Full-bodied **20** (85) ripe & plummy, sweet flesh firmed by rounded tannins. High acid slight detraction from pleasing succulence. Older oak, 8 months. Not tasted: **Shiraz**, **Chardonnay**.

Bosjes range
Cinsault Rosé (NEW) ★★★★ Full, spicy red fruit flavours, softish & sappy, **23** (83) also dry, pleasingly modest 11.7% alc, perfect as aperitif & with variety of dishes. **Riesling** (NEW) ★★★ Shows development in both colour & hint of kerosene on spicy limes. **21** (77) lowish acid with clean, fruity finish. **Sauvignon Blanc** ★★★ Crisp & dry **23** (77) is lightish, its high acid offset by juicy green apple flavours. — AL

Location: Worcester ▪ Map/WO: Breedekloof ▪ Map grid reference: B3 ▪ Est 2017 ▪ 1stB 2018 ▪ Sales Wed-Sun 8.30-5 ▪ Closed Mon/Tue & Dec 25 ▪ Bosjes Kombuis & Spens Wed-Sun 9-3 ▪ Custom designed playground; special menu for children ▪ Garden & farm tours: groups to book in advance ▪ Olive oil ▪ Weddings & events ▪ Small conference/meeting venue (12 pax) ▪ Hiking trails in enclosed Bergkamp with various antelope; rare & endangered flowers ▪ Chapel - an architectural masterpiece ▪ 7-bedroomed boutique guesthouse ▪ Owner(s) Stofberg Family Trust ▪ 10ha newly planted vines ▪ WIETA ▪ PO Box 13 Botha 6857 ▪ carlen@bosjes. co.za ▪ www.bosjes.co.za ▪ **T +27 (0)23-004-0496**

Bosman Family Vineyards   (ⓦ) (ⓜ)

The wide-ranging achievements, on a large scale, of this Wellington-based, family-based business make it a worthy winner of our Editor's Award Winery of the Year 2024. The family has been involved in wine production for over two centuries - and this year celebrate 20 years of bottling it under their own label with great success. Not only have landholdings at home increased, there's also a farm in Hemel-en-Aarde (see Bosman Hermanus listing). Recently, the focus has shifted to organic viticultural practices, with the Twyfeling and Optenhorst vineyards fully certified. A significant moment in ownership came in 2009, when more than a quarter of the overall business was ceded to employees through the Adama Workers Trust; this social investment has been extended with schools, housing, sports and education programmes. Bosman Adama is now the largest wine nursery in the country, and since 2014 includes the Ernita vine improvement programmes. In the winery, cellarmaster Corlea Fourie last year said a regretful farewell to winemaker Natasha Williams who's landed a fine job at Hasher, but welcomed Maryke Botha.

Adama range

★★★★☆ **Red** ⊘ Supple, accomplished blend of 62% shiraz with 7 others, **21** ⑨⓪ is sweet-spiced, ripe & rewarding. Appealing mix of red berries & stewed prunes, with lacework of tarry tobacco, vanilla & cured meat. Year in mostly seasoned oak, 20% American. WO W Cape. Both these Fairtrade.

★★★★ **White** ⓦ ⊘ Leading the journey to full organic status, **21** ⑧⑨ chenin-grenache blanc blend is succulently fruity, plump & rounded, with savoury-spicy notes from chenin's ferment & 7 months in oak.

Creative Space range

★★★★☆ **Twyfeling Cinsaut** ⓐ Delightfully floral & charming, **21** ⑨④ from organic vines is supple, juicy & weightless. Scented red berries borne on satin tannins & pinpoint acid, offering pure drinking pleasure. Small portions wholebunch & stem fermented, adding detail, burnished year in mostly older oak.

★★★★★ **Openhorst Chenin Blanc** ⓐ ⓦ Structured & linear, with great concentration & layered complexity, **22** ⑨⑥ from 1952 dryland bushvines (4th oldest in Cape) exudes class & charm. Succulent stonefruit with notes of mulled honey, citrus zest & white nuts, all beautifully integrated. Wild yeast ferment in 50/50 concrete tank & older barrels.

★★★★☆ **Fides Grenache Blanc** ⓦ Radical take on organic vines, **20** ⑨⓪ 3 weeks tank-fermented on skins with wild yeast, 9 months in older barrels. Rich & textured, with prominent tannins. For the initiated.

★★★★ **Loose Cannon** ⓦ Old-vine varietal chenin fruit shines through in **21** ⑧⑦ cap classique spark-ling, sunny notes of pineapple & peach lightly spiced by oak but not intruding. Primary ferment in barrel, sun-dried chenin in dosage, 12 months on lees in bottle. No **20**.

Nero range

★★★★ **Nero d'Avola** SA's 1st solo bottling. Latest **20** ⑧⑨ typical of Sicilian variety: light body but supple & juicy, vibrant berries, hints of anise & maraschino. Cries out for tomato-based dishes. 18 months oak.

Signature range

★★★★★ **Erfenis** ⓦ Blend tweak in **17** ⑨③, cab, cinsaut & nero d'avola giving lighter body, more aromatic fragrance than **16** ⑨④ pinotage blend. Lithe, with subtle savoury spice. 2 years oak, 30% new.

Generation 8 range

★★★★ **Merlot** ⊘ Notable earthy-tarry focus, hints of leaf & solid black plum fruit on **22** ⑧⑥. Weightier than siblings, satisfying tannin grip. 10% in new oak adds more spicy appeal than **21** ★★★☆ ⑧⑤.

★★★★ **Rosé** ⊘ Early-harvested exclusively for rosé, **22** ⑧⑥ cinsault charmer offers floral red-berry fruit rush, pleasant textured dry mouthfeel, modest 12.5% alc. Built for poolside refreshment.

★★★★ **Chenin Blanc** ⊘ Cheery & ripe, with impressive tropical fruit concentration, unoaked **23** ⑧⑥ repeats winning formula: 1.5% sun-dried grapes, 3% skin contact, 5% grenache blanc, 3% viognier.

Cabernet Sauvignon ⊘ ★★★☆ Unpretentious, with honest cassis fruit, **23** ⑧⑤'s gentle tannins & lush body promise everyday enjoyment. Range labelled Fairtrade in some markets. **Shiraz** ⊘ ★★★☆ Fresher, more focused berry fruit on **22** ⑧⑤ than last. Supple, spicy, lightly oaked, with smooth tannins. — GdB

Location/map: Wellington ▪ Map grid reference: C3 ▪ WO: Wellington/Western Cape ▪ Est 1699 ▪ 1stB 2004 ▪ Wine tasting & cellar tours preferably by appt ▪ Snack platters ▪ Tasting fee R150pp/standard, R200pp/premium ▪ Open Mon-Sat 9-4 ▪ Closed Sun, Good Fri & Dec 25 ▪ Wine club ▪ Owner(s) Bosman Adama (Pty) Ltd ▪ Cellarmaster(s) Corlea Fourie (Nov 2006) ▪ Winemaker(s) Maryke Botha (Jul 2023) ▪ Viticulturist(s) Dan Swart ▪ 335ha (24 varieties r/w) ▪ 6,000t/25,000cs own label 57% red 42% white 1% rosé ▪ Brands for clients: Sainsbury Supermarkets, The Cooperative ▪ BBBEE certificate (level 6), Fairtrade accredited, certain accredited organic vineyards ▪ Lelienfontein Farm, Hexberg Rd, Wellington 7655 ▪ taste@bosmanwines.com ▪ www.bosmanwines.com ▪ T +27 (0)21-873-3170/+27 (0)63-052-5352

Bosman Hermanus ⓦ ⓘ ⓒ

Wellington's Bosman family of vinegrowers (see Bosman Family Vineyards listing) purchased the 270-ha Upper Hemel-en-Aarde mountainside farm De Bos in 2001, and now have 42 different grape varieties planted on 54 ha, along with proteas and other indigenous flowers. The wines are made, 'gently and sensitively', in the Wellington cellar, but visitors to the farm, with vistas over Walker Bay, are hosted in the wooden Frame House for curated tastings, food pairings and more. A commitment to farming regeneratively sees, inter alia, more than half the farm given over to fynbos and wildlife, earning WWF Conservation Champion status and, most recently, first place in the Best of Wine Tourism & Ambassador Awards category for Sustainable Wine Tourism Practices.

★★★★☆ Magnum Opus Pinot Noir ⓦ Savoury-earthy **18 ★★★★** ⑧⑧ from same Oudam single high-density vineyard, similar treatment, but misses expressive **17** ⑨③'s intensity & perfume.

★★★★☆ Pinot Noir ⊘ ⓐ Beautiful expression of this exceptional area, **22** ⑨④ continues impressive recent form, including fine **21 ★★★★★** ⑨⑤. Perfumed & delicate, ethereal floral wafts, plump & ripe red berries alongside rhubarb & pomegranate, all grounded in earthy truffles, wrapped in silky tannins. 8 months in Burgundian oak, 15% new, perfectly judged.

★★★★☆ Chardonnay Barely perceptible oak influence - just 15% in ceramic-toasted new barrels - allows fine fruit expression, retains suppleness in **22** ⑨⓪. Waves of marmalade & fresh citrus rind, hints of honeyed lemon curd, all elegantly cloaked in leesy minerality.

★★★★☆ Sauvignon Blanc ⊘ Impressive body & structure of **22** ⑨② echoes previous vintages, complex herbal & mineral array spicing succulent tropical fruit. Layered & lingering, masterly balance & grace. Laudably modest price, too.— GdB

Location: Hermanus ▪ Map: Walker Bay & Bot River ▪ Map grid reference: B3 ▪ WO: Upper Hemel-en-Aarde Valley ▪ Est 2001 ▪ 1stB 2009 ▪ Wine tasting & tapas-style food ▪ Tasting fee R100pp ▪ Open Tue-Fri 9-5 Sat 10-4 Sun 10-3; pub hols (seasonal) please call ahead ▪ Closed Mon, Good Fri & Dec 25 ▪ Nature trails, wine tasting, food, coffee, reserved picnics available ▪ Family friendly ▪ Indigenous flowers & proteas ▪ Wine club ▪ Owner(s) Bosman Adama (Pty) Ltd ▪ Cellarmaster(s) Corlea Fourie (Nov 2006) ▪ Winemaker(s) Maryke Botha (July 2023) ▪ Viticulturist(s) Dan Swart ▪ 54ha (42 varieties r/w) ▪ 120t/17,500cs own label 40% red 60% white ▪ BBBEE certificate (level 6), WWF-SA Conservation Champion ▪ De Bos Farm, Karwyderskraal Rd, Upper Hemel-en-Aarde, Hermanus 7200 ▪ taste@bosmanhermanus.com ▪ www.bosmanhermanus.com ▪ **T +27 (0)76-300-0819**

Botanica Wines

By Stellenbosch standards, this is a small vineyard, just 5 ha, but there are also cut flowers grown here, a tradition dating from the 1940s, when, it is believed, the Protea Heights home-farm in Devon Valley became the first in SA to commercially cultivate indigenous proteas. It's the inspiration for the flower-themed labels and names chosen by owner and self-taught winemaker Ginny Povall, formerly a New York corporate consultant, who crafts wines she likes to drink: 'fresh, nuanced and vibrant'. With the exception of the flagship chenin, all grapes are home-grown and organically farmed. Ginny plans to reopen the tasting venue, shut since Covid, and extend the gardens to provide a more attractive visitor experience.

Mary Delany Collection

★★★★☆ Pinot Noir ⊘ Small portion wholebunch, small barrels 7 months, designed to highlight bright red fruit yet allow some seasoning. **22** ⑨⓪ captures variety's elegance. **20** & **21** untasted.

★★★★★ Chenin Blanc ⓐ ⓦ From Citrusdal Mountain, the only grapes not home-grown. Follows in footsteps of previous - why change something that works so well? - **22** ⑨⑤ marries quince & stonefruit to savoury tones imparted through oak & concrete 'egg', entrenching texture & mouthfeel. Elegant (12.5% alc), adding to the quality perception, finishing citrus-fresh & long. Wonderful finesse.

★★★★☆ Fire Lily Straw Wine ⓦ Dessert wine from air-dried, old-oaked viognier, **NV** ⑨⓪ blend of 4 vintages shows delicate fruit (apple, pear, pineapple & melon), muted acid but sugar in balance, light body. Sales support Urban Caracal Project. 375 ml.

Discontinued: **Three Barrels Pinot Noir**, **Chardonnay**, **Semillon**.

Arboretum range

★★★★ Arboretum ⓦ Rich, plush **17 ★★★★☆** ⑨③ a barrel selection of cab, cab franc, merlot (53/23/21) & splash petit verdot, seamless after 11 months in mostly older oak to show off ripe dark fruit, more complex than **16** ⑧⑨ with leafy & floral aromas.

Big Flower range

★★★★ Cabernet Sauvignon Quite complex perfume, the expected cassis but also violets, Provençal herbs & nutmeg, all draw you in. **22** ⑧⑨'s tannins are present but supple, texture streamlined, ending dry.

★★★★☆ **Cabernet Franc** (Ⓐ) Again, a vintage impressing with its polish & restraint, **21** (93) has a classic profile: graphite, red berries, herbaceous whiff. Tannins finely judged, just 11 months in seasoned barrels, providing backbone, supple support. A class act. **20** ★★★★★ (95) first showed breakthrough quality.

★★★★☆ **Merlot** House-style ripeness & depth, curvaceous **21** (90) shows more oak than last (18 months small barrels), pepper & allspice, a bed of fine tannins with musculature for cellaring. But there's enough fruit to balance, layered blackcurrant & plum, showing admirable crafting.

★★★★ **Petit Verdot** One few single bottlings in SA, occasional release. Deep ruby, **20** (87) is power-packed with berries & plums, oak's spicing a seam of graphite & earth. Has heft & texture, could develop other nuances over time. More serious than **19** ★★★☆ (85).

Petit Verdot Rosé ★★★★ Not discontinued as we thought. Uncommon rosé parent, giving dry **23** (84) a just-pink hue, wild brush & brambleberry profile suitable for food matching.

Flower Girl range

★★★★☆ **Albariño** (Ⓐ) Iberian variety, rare in SA. No oak, to highlight the fruit: pithy grapefruit, some floral whiffs, different profile to usual whites. Sleek **23** ★★★★★ (95)'s crisp acid creates a tautness, linear structure, there's purity & focus here. Admirable typicity, as in **22** (93).

Discontinued: **Blanc de Noir Méthode Cap Classique, Cabernet Franc Pétillant Naturel, Petit Verdot Pétillant Naturel.** — CR

Location/map: Stellenbosch ▪ Map grid reference: D4 ▪ WO: Stellenbosch/Citrusdal Mountain ▪ Est/1stB 2008 ▪ Tasting by appt only ▪ Wine sales daily 8-5 ▪ Flower sales ▪ Conferences ▪ Walks/hikes ▪ MTB trail ▪ Refreshments offered at Sugarbird Manor guest house ▪ Wine club ▪ Owner(s) Virginia C Povall ▪ Winemaker(s) Virginia Povall (Jan 2008) ▪ Viticulturist(s) Francois Viljoen ▪ 21.6ha/5ha (cabs s/f, merlot, p verdot, pinot, albariño) ▪ PO Box 12523 Die Boord 7613 ▪ ginny@botanicawines.com ▪ www.botanicawines.com ▪ **T +27 (0)76-340-8296/+27 (0)79-478-1515**

Botha Wine Cellar (Ⓨ)(Ⓧ)(Ⓒ)(Ⓐ)(Ⓖ)

The farmer-shareholders welcome all ages to their Breedekloof venue 'circled by beautiful mountains', hence not one but two kiddies' pairings and a play park, plus cheese boards and food-and-wine matches for the grown-ups, among other enticements. 'Innovation, quality and creativity' is the motto, and the new Sjanter branding (meaning 'to guide, manoeuvre, keep the flow moving') being introduced adds the intended novelty to the 17,000 cases of own-label wines that constitute a tiny but carefully nurtured portion of output.

Inspired Selection

★★★★ **Turoc Unify** (Ⓨ) Youthful **19** (89) Cape Blend from selected barrels of pinotage (34%), equal cab & shiraz. Alluring dark fruit & spice, full body, structured dry tannins after 18 months in oak, 25% new.

★★★★ **Amyah Chenin Blanc** Golden **22** (89)'s well-judged ripeness a fruit-sweet foil for enlivening acid & spicy new oak, 34%, 10 months. Peaches - dried & fresh, white & yellow - to the fore. No **21**.

★★★★ **Mijmere Charmat Method** Sparkling **NV** (86) from chenin really done well. Immediate lemon sherbet appeal followed by apricot & peach, lovely dry impression despite few grams sugar courtesy inspired touch of quince astringency.

Amyah Chardonnay (Ⓨ) ★★★★ Barrel fermented/aged, 25% new, **18** (85) richly textured, full of preserved citrus & butterscotch. Crisp acidity adds lift, vibrancy.

Valley Selection

Sjanter Chenin Blanc (✓)(Ⓣ) ★★★ New name & striking label, as Sauvignon. **23** (81) soft peach & apple tones. No bells & whistles, just drinks very well. **Sjanter Sauvignon Blanc** (Ⓣ) ★★★ Array of both green & tropical aromas & flavours on light (12.5% alc) & zippy **23** (81). Pleasant subtle pithiness at the end.

Cabernet Sauvignon ★★★ Satisfying everyday drinking in briefly wooded, pliable & red berry-toned **20** (82). Like Pinotage, 50% American oak adds barest hint of sweet vanilla to spice & cedar of the French. **Merlot** (Ⓨ) ★★★★ Bursts with rich & ripe berry fruit, plush tannin & dusting of cocoa in **19** (83). Brush of oak adds toasty appeal to this crowd pleaser. **Pinotage** ★★★ Sweet-sour mulberry fruit dusted with icing sugar & malleable tannins the attractions in **21** (79). Not unpleasant charry whiff on finish. **Shiraz** (Ⓨ) ★★★ Touch mocha to dark fruit in full-ripe (15% alc) **19** (79). Oaking adds savoury sheen to a meal mate. **Red Jerepigo** (Ⓨ) ★★★ Fortified shiraz, **16** (78) preview is salty liquorice scented, with wild berries

& a minty note, but palate has power-packed fruit, almost jammy sweetness. **Hanepoot Jerepigo** ★★★ Light, fresh **22** ⑧⑪ fortified sweetie for solo enjoyment or the cheese board. Raisins, florals & citrus notes, gentle flush of 16% alc. **Late Bottled Vintage** ⓥ ★★★★ Spicy toffee, mocha flavours in **16** ⑧③ port-style shiraz, 36 months in old mixed-origin oak. A supple winter warmer, though spirit a tad obvious.

Social range

Dassie's Rood ⓥ ★★ Unoaked BBQ buddy, **21** ⑦⑥ has cinsaut's red-berry jam note, ruby cab's thatch nuance & cab's freshening verve. Also in 3L pack. **Blanc de Noir** ★★ Pale pink **23** ⑦④ from pinotage, lightish (12.4% alc), softly dry & lively, for uncomplicated enjoyment.

3L range

Dassie's Blanc ★★ Pear & apple mingle quietly in pale **23** ⑦④ chenin in party-perfect bag-in-box. — CvZ

Location: Worcester ▪ Map/WO: Breedekloof ▪ Map grid reference: B3 ▪ Est 1949 ▪ 1stB 1974 ▪ Tasting & sales Mon-Fri 9-5 Sat/pub hols 10-3 ▪ Closed Easter Fri/Sun, Dec 25/26 & Jan 1 ▪ Cellar tours by appt ▪ Play area for children ▪ Food & wine pairings ▪ Kiddies pairings ▪ Cheese platters ▪ Conferences ▪ Conservation area ▪ Owner(s) Botha Wynkelder (Edms) Bpk ▪ Production manager Johan Linde (Nov 1996) ▪ Cellarmaster(s) Gerrit van Zyl (Nov 2007) ▪ Winemaker(s) Michiel Visser (Nov 1999) & Annamarie van Niekerk (Dec 2008), with Stefan Joubert (Nov 2016) ▪ Viticulturist(s) Jan-Carel Coetzee (Nov 2010) ▪ 1,969ha (cab, merlot, ptage, shiraz, chard, chenin, cbard, sauv) ▪ 41,320t/17,000cs own label 61% red 25% white 14% fortified ▪ IPW, ISO 22000:2009, WIETA ▪ PO Box 30 PK Botha 6857 ▪ admin@bothakelder.co.za ▪ www.bothakelder.co.za ▪ **T +27 (0)23-355-1740**

☐ **Bottega Family Wines** *see* Idiom Wines

Bouchard Finlayson

This eminent Hemel-en-Aarde Valley winery this edition records 35 years since establishment by Peter Finlayson, joined shortly after by a Burgundian partner, reflected in the dual name. Ownership today is with the hotelier Tollman family. Chris Albrecht, winemaker since 2010, took over from Peter as cellarmaster in 2022. New initiatives start in the vineyards, where viticulturist Stefan Hartmann is introducing regenerative practices, initially focusing on composting all cellar waste and recycling it back into the soil. Birds, a perennial problem, are being managed with netting, already resulting in improvements in bunch health. Chris' mantra of paying attention to detail, and not rushing the process, is producing fresher, more focused wines.

★★★★☆ **Galpin Peak Pinot Noir** ⊘ Brighter, light-of-foot style, **21** ⑨② attracts with red cherry & raspberry perfume, supple flesh. Appropriately firm yet fine tannin bite & oak, 30% new, for future development. 7 separately vinified vineyards; 14% wholebunch. 13% alc. Also in 1.5 & 3L.

★★★★☆ **Tête de Cuvée Pinot Noir** ⓐ Barrel selection from farm's 7 vineyards. **21** ⑨④ quality vintage but slow starter, will require patience. Bigger than Galpin, full richness of silky, sweet fruit yet to emerge from insistent tannins. Oak, 50% new, an enhancement. 13.2% alc.

★★★★☆ **Hannibal** Blend of Italian & French varieties with its own fan base. **21** ⑨② headed by sangiovese, nebbiolo, shiraz & pinot noir, dabs barbera & mourvèdre. Rich in flavour, berries & spice, light footed with mouthwatering acid, zesty grip. Promises greater complexity & savouriness with age. Oak, 23% new, year. 13.2% alc.

★★★★☆ **Kaaimansgat Crocodile's Lair Chardonnay** Follows previous expressive, cool lemon purity from celebrated high-lying Elandskloof vineyard in **22** ⑨⓪. Oak spice, 23% new, needs time to meld with fruit, lees-enriched creaminess; has balanced structure, taut acid to warrant laying down. Wholebunch spontaneous ferment in 23% new oak.

★★★★☆ **Missionvale Chardonnay** ⓐ From three older home vineyards. Familiar toasty, nutty, citrus tones woven into creamy texture, sound spine in support. **22** ⑨③ already harmonised, ensuring future complexity. 92% barrel fermented, 28% new; rest amphora.

★★★★ **Sans Barrique Chardonnay** ⊘ Cool-climate lemon intensity from mainly Elandskloof vineyard shines distinctively in **21** ★★★★☆ ⑨⓪. Purity, precision & steely tension are subtly lees-weighted, producing a more compelling unoaked chardonnay than **20** ⑧⑧.

★★★★ **Sauvignon Blanc** Sauvignon's more penetrating 'sauvage' features curbed by broadening effect of 10% barrel-fermented semillon. **23** ⑧⑦ still maintains vibrancy, fig & lemongrass freshness. Will benefit from short rest. WO Walker Bay. **22** untasted.

★★★★ **Blanc de Mer** ⊘ Unusual & popular unoaked blend. **23** ⑧⑧ captures riesling's spicy pizazz, flavoursome extras from viognier & chardonnay, culminating in mouthwatering dry finish. Cape Coast WO.

★★★★ **Aurum Straw Wine** From riesling bunches dehydrated 90 days under cover. Honey gold colour, **20** ★★★★★ ⑨② honey-spiced aromas too which permeate intense sweetness (410 g/L sugar). Scintillating acid rescues this elixir from any cloy, ensures lengthy pleasure. Greater concentration than **19** ⑧⑦. Fermented in tank. 8.6% alc. 375 ml.— AL

Location: Hermanus ▪ Map: Walker Bay & Bot River ▪ Map grid reference: B4 ▪ WO: Hemel-en-Aarde Valley/Elandskloof/Cape South Coast/Walker Bay/Cape Coast ▪ Est 1989 ▪ 1stB 1991 ▪ Tasting, sales & cellar tours Mon-Fri 9-4.30 Sat/Sun & most pub hols 10-4 ▪ Fee between R85-R350pp ▪ Wine pairings ▪ Grazing platter ▪ Gift shop ▪ Conservation area ▪ Self-guided nature walks ▪ Owner(s) The Tollman Family Trust ▪ Winemaker(s) Chris Albrecht (Nov 2010), with Shannon Morse (Oct 2021) ▪ Viticulturist(s) Stefan Hartmann (2021) ▪ 125ha/22ha (barbera, nebbiolo, pinot, sangio, chard, riesling, sauv) ▪ 250t/30,000cs own label 30% red 70% white ▪ IPW, WWF-SA Conservation Champion ▪ PO Box 303 Hermanus 7200 ▪ info@bouchardfin-layson.co.za ▪ www.bouchardfinlayson.co.za ▪ **T +27 (0)28-312-3515**

☐ **Boutinot** see Wildeberg Wines
☐ **Bowwood** see Vondeling
☐ **Braai** see Cape Classics
☐ **Brahms** see Domaine Brahms Wineries

Brampton ⓥ ⓞ

DGB's long-established easy-drinking range, named for a champion Jersey bull and made by the Boschendal team, targets younger winelovers with an exhortation to 'Just B' - live spontaneously and creatively. The theme underpins the facilities and events on offer at the brand home in central Stellenbosch.

Roxton Black ★★★★ Only wine tasted this edition is also named for a pedigree bull, a **20** ⑧⑤ cabernet, suitably muscular & powerful, oozing ripe black berry fruit, coffee & spice from 30% new oak, chewy tannins best with a barbeque or aged few years. — DS

Location/map/WO: Stellenbosch ▪ Map grid reference: F5 ▪ Opening hours Mon-Thu 9-9 Fri 10-9 Sat 11-9 Sun/pub hols 10-6; pub hols (seasonal) please call ahead ▪ Craft beer ▪ Owner(s) DGB (Pty) Ltd ▪ Winemaker(s) Boschendal Cellar ▪ Viticulturist(s) Heinie Nel (Jul 2018) ▪ WIETA ▪ 11 Church Str, Stellenbosch 7600 ▪ brampton@dgb.co.za ▪ www.brampton.co.za ▪ **T +27 (0)21-883-9097**

☐ **Break A Leg** see Van Loggerenberg Wines
☐ **Bredell's** see JP Bredell Wines

Breëland Winery - Marais Family Wines ⓥ ⓐ ⓞ

Lizelle Marais' family has owned the 1,500-ha home-farm in Breedekloof since 1825, and grown grapes and made wine there since the late 19th century. Building on that heritage are extensive current investments in cellar equipment, including 20 small steel tanks for the white wines, and open barriques for Wickus Erasmus to ferment the reds. Plus a new vat cellar, visible through glass walls. All this added to the recently unveiled tasting area, offering 'an exceptional panorama of the Slanghoek mountains and Breëland's natural beauty'.

Breëland range

Cabernet Sauvignon ⓥ ★★★ Off-dry **19** ⑧② emphasises ripe red-berry fruit, with firm tannin structure, youthful freshness. **Pinotage** ★★★ Plumper than last, **21** ⑧⓪ attractive notes of wax & berries, core of sweet fruit & soft tannins from 18 months in old barrels. Breedekloof WO. **Chardonnay** ⓥ ★★★★ Peaches-&-cream & lemon curd on silky **22** ⑧③, richness from lees ageing on wood & good few grams sugar, freshened by zippy acid & moderate alc. **Chenin Blanc** ⓥ ★★★ Tropical-toned **22** ⑧② bursts with sunshiny fruit, guava, pineapple unencumbered by wood. **Sauvignon Blanc** ⊘ ★★★★ More tropical, less steely in **23** ⑧④, guava, mango & lime, 3 months on lees with stirring add silky mouthfeel. **Vin Doux Sparkling** 🆕 ★★★ Natural Sweet sauvignon blanc & semillon with the prickle of bubbles, **NV** ⑦⑨ shows keen balance between sugar, racy freshness & modest alc. **Perlé Moscato** ★★★ Naturally sweet rosé with gentle bubbles, **NV** ⑦⑨ from muscadel & pinotage, latter adds colour & ups fruitiness on zippy, balanced wine offering lime, orange cordial & rose flavours. Not tasted: **Hanepoot**. Discontinued: **Hope range**. — ML

Location: Rawsonville ▪ Map: Breedekloof ▪ Map grid reference: A5 ▪ WO: Slanghoek/Breedekloof ▪ Est 1825 ▪ 1stB 2010 ▪ Tasting & sales Mon-Fri 9-5 Sat 10-3 pub hols (seasonal) please call ahead ▪ Cellar tours by appt ▪ Closed Easter Fri-Mon, Ascension day, Dec 25 & Jan 1 ▪ MTB & 4x4 trails ▪ Conservation area ▪ Weddings/functions ▪ Self-catering guest accommodation ▪ Owner(s) Lizelle Marais ▪ Cellarmaster(s)/winemaker(s) Wickus Erasmus (Dec 2008) ▪ Viticulturist(s) Wickus Erasmus ▪ 1,500ha/110ha (cab, cinsaut, merlot, nebbiolo, ptage, shiraz, tannat, chenin, cbard, hanepoot, pinot gris, sauv, sem) ▪ 3,500t/500cs own label 30% red 70% white + 500cs for clients ▪ PO Box 26 Rawsonville 6845 ▪ tasting@maraiswines.co.za ▪ www.maraiswines.co.za ▪ T +27 (0)23-344-3129

☐ **Brendel Collection** see Le Manoir de Brendel

Brew Cru ⓠ

Now owned by Jesse Balsimo and Brian Norman of US wine importer Truvino, this small venture crafts wines from cool-grown marginal vineyards on the Cape south coast to showcase a 'somewhereness'.

★★★★★ **Black Label Pinot Noir** ⓠ Almost playful entry then deeper concentration of black fruit cloaked with spice & oak. Structured & smooth, **21** ⑨② subtler & less brooding than last.

★★★★ **Pinot Noir** ⓠ Walker Bay fruit for this expression. Supple, succulent & bright **21** ⑧⑧ emulates **19** ⑧⑨ in red-fruited appeal. Sleek, spicy but a tad lighter in body. Follows standout **20** ★★★★★ ⑨⓪.

★★★★★ **Chardonnay** ⓠ Light-footed but serious **21** ⑨⓪ from Elgin has orange cream breadth from year in 35% new barrels mingling with taut, crisp acid. Poised, fresh & long.— FM

Location: Hermanus ▪ WO: Hemel-en-Aarde Ridge/Walker Bay/Elgin ▪ Est/1stB 2017 ▪ Tasting by appt only ▪ Owner(s) Jesse Balsimo, Brian Norman ▪ Winemaker(s) Johann Fourie ▪ 3.5ha (pinot, chard) ▪ 10t/1,300cs own label 60% red 40% white ▪ IPW, WIETA ▪ us@truvino100.com ▪ www.brewcru.wine ▪ T +1 (208) 649-4046

☐ **Brink Family Vineyards** see Pulpit Rock Winery
☐ **Britz Brothers** see Under Oaks
☐ **Brocha** see Wines of Brocha
☐ **Broken Barrel** see Fairview
☐ **Broken Stone** see Slaley

Brookdale Estate ⓠ ⑪ ⌂ ◎

Owner of this rising star, UK businessman Tim Rudd, and his team deserve some time off, given their extraordinary achievements since acquiring the run-down Paarl property in 2015. They cleared 67 ha of alien vegetation and liberated overgrown vines, rehabilitated a nearly 40-year-old block of chenin, established 27 ha of vines, launched the first wines by Kiara Scott (to rave reviews), and built a new cellar and tasting lounge. They also planted indigenous vegetation and gardens, restored the manor and opened it for luxury stays, and built and opened an 80-seat bistro with alfresco seating and a fine panorama.

Brookdale range

★★★★★ **Chenin Blanc Old Vine** ⓐ ⓦ Fine **21** ⑨④ from vineyard planted in decomposed granite & shale adds 'Old Vine' to its name. Complex winemaking, including fractional picking & wholebunch wild ferment, yields confident array quince, apple, peach, thrilling acid extends the finish. 11 months seasoned barrel & foudre more than a whisper mid-2023, but don't detract from effortless elegance.

★★★★★ **Bradbourne White Blend** ⓝⓔⓦ ⓐ Mostly grenache blanc with dabs roussanne, marsanne & rare piquepoul, fermented/aged in older 500L barrels. **22** ⑨② smooth, lighter & cooler feel than others, with attractive essential oil citrus notes.

★★★★★ **Sixteen Field Blend** ⓐ Same 16 bushvine interplanted white varieties, but in **22** ★★★★★ ⑨⑤ harvested in 2 stages rather than together to address different ripening dates. Incredibly perfumed - white florals, fresh herbs, various stonefruit, simply kissed with older oak - & rich yet expertly balanced with piquant citrus acid. Full malo, unlike range siblings. **21** ⑨④ was the first. Also in 375 ml, 1.5L & 3L.

Mason Road range

★★★★ **GSM** ⓝⓔⓦ ⓥ Red & black berries, fynbos abound on **22** ⑧⑥. More complexity - from both the grenache noir- & syrah-dominated blend & winemaking - than red sibling, more depth & plushness.

★★★★ **Chenin Blanc** ⊘ Offers more on palate than nose: fresh & dried peach, peach stone & green apple; **22** ⑧⑥ well-judged weight & cream from 11 months on lees. 85% tank fermented, rest older oak.

Syrah ★★★★ Skin contact, stems, 8 months in older barrels & foudre deliver harmony, refreshment & sweet berries in **22** ⑧⑤, with enough tannin to attract, & hold, attention. **Serendipity Rosé** ★★★★ Pale sunset hue on dry & gently wooded **22** ⑧④ from syrah, grenache noir & cinsault. Tad shy but no wallflower, with lovely vinosity & dried herb finish. 1.5L also available. — CvZ

Location/map/WO: Paarl ▪ Map grid reference: G5 ▪ Est 2016 ▪ Tasting & sales Tue-Sun 11-5; pub hols (seasonal) please call ahead ▪ Bistro @ Brookdale: lunch Tue-Sun 12-3.30; dinner Fri & Sat 6-9 - booking advised ▪ Brookdale Manor House ▪ Weddings/functions ▪ Owner(s) Rudd Farms Limited (Tim Rudd) ▪ GM Yvonne & Gary Coetzee ▪ Winemaker(s) Kiara Scott (Jan 2019), advised by Duncan Savage (Oct 2016, consultant), with Alessio Ballerini ▪ Viticulturist(s) Adam Dirkse (Oct 2016), with Jaco Engelbrecht (Oct 2018, consultant) ▪ 67ha/27ha under vine ▪ 40% red 60% white ▪ Hawequa Forest Rd, Klein Drakenstein, Paarl 7646 ▪ enquire@brookdale-estate.com ▪ www.brookdale-estate.com ▪ **T +27 (0)76-400-0229**

☐ **B Royal** *see* Bayede!

Bruce Jack Wines

A dynamic label, created in the mid-2000s by Bruce Jack while winemaker and prime mover for Flagstone, Bruce Jack Wines was listed recently in the world's Top 50 Most Admired Wine Brands for the fourth year in a row, making it the only SA-based wine brand to have achieved this distinction to date. With wines from Chile, Spain and the US, as well as South Africa in the portfolio, BJW collaborates with businesses who also believe in the importance of outstanding quality, value and provenance, as well as responsible consumption and reducing complexity for customers. The venture continues to support projects in social upliftment, environmental sustainability and carbon neutrality, and believes 'wine should add joy to life'.

Heritage Collection

★★★★☆ **Flag Of Truce Pinotage** (NEW) (🐝) Subtlety defines **21** ⑨④. Pure fruit, poised ripeness, chalky grip on layered, nuanced palate. Serious intent but raspberry vibrancy & lifted spice ensure interest & drinkability. Natural ferment, 2 years in small, mostly old barrels.

★★★★☆ **Clean Slate Shiraz** (🐝) Tiny parcel on shattered slate, barrelled 18 months, 20% new, portion American. **20** ⑨④ mimics last **18** ⑨③ in nuance, velvet texture & squeeze of tannin that supports sappy plum & spice. Elegant, confident & composed, for the long haul. WO Overberg, as Chenin.

★★★★☆ **Hard Day Chardonnay** Blood orange & elderflower appeal on **22** ⑨①. Like last **20** ⑨⓪, combo natural & commercial yeast ferment & softly creamy baked notes from 8 months in seasoned oak. Partial malo retains lime freshness on broad, dry finish. Modest 12.8% alc. WO Overberg, as Shiraz.

★★★★☆ **Boer Maak 'n Plan Chenin Blanc** Complex & serious, **22** ⑨① broad, rich palate balanced by a taut lime acid that focuses & invigorates. Harmonious & layered, with grip from slow ferment (natural & inoculated) in old barrels, 8 months ageing. No **21**.

Discontinued: **Heartbreak Grape Pinot Noir**.

Reserve Collection

★★★★ **Pinotage** ⊘ (🐝) Black Forest gateau appeal on **21** ⑧⑨, cherry, cocoa, creamy richness. Softly rounded with a subtle tannin nuance from just 8 months in barrel & tank with staves. Balanced, succulent, like supple **20** ★★★★★ ⑨①.

★★★★ **Chardonnay** ⊘ Light but structured, creamy & generous mouthful. Tangerine & vanilla from year's oaking & extended lees contact on **22** ⑧⑧.

★★★★ **Sauvignon Blanc** Cool Darling & Elim origins on **22** ⑧⑨ apparent in gooseberry, fig & leafy notes. Fresh, taut & focused, with gravel base to lively citrus. Good texture & length.

★★★★ **Viognier** (NEW) Peaches-&-cream richness on **22** ⑧⑨ from single site. Delicate & precisely textured thanks to subtle oaking. Goldilocks wine: everything is just right, fruit, wood & acid in harmony.— FM

Location: Stanford ▪ Map: Walker Bay & Bot River ▪ Map grid reference: B6 ▪ WO: Breedekloof/Overberg/Western Cape ▪ 1stB 2005 ▪ Tastings at Stanford Wine Bar ▪ Wine sales via website ▪ Owner(s) Bruce Jack ▪ Winemaker(s)/viticulturist(s) Various ▪ IPW, WIETA ▪ PO Box 174 Rawsonville 6845 ▪ wineadventures@brucejack.com ▪ www.brucejack.com ▪ **T +27 (0)21-180-3668**

Brunia Wines

Firmly committed to the most ambitious new-wave wine-growing, young Wade Sander has one overriding aim: 'to translate the uniqueness of our vineyards sites and make authentic wines'. On the substantial family estate in the cool Sunday's Glen ward near Stanford (it has large tracts of indigenous fynbos, but fruit, vegetables and flowers are also produced) the approach is regenerative, with a concentration on organic methods. In the cellar, indigenous yeasts are used, with 'minimal additives and other unnecessary interventions'. The farm's own production facility is nearing completion as we go to press. But no new wines for us to taste this year.

Location: Stanford ▪ Map: Southern Cape ▪ Map grid reference: B2 ▪ Est 2005 ▪ 1stB 2009 ▪ Tasting & sales by appt only ▪ Tasting R100pp ▪ Closed all pub hols ▪ Self-guided hiking trails ▪ Mountain biking ▪ Conservation area ▪ Owner(s) Sander family ▪ Winemaker(s)/viticulturist(s) Wade Sander ▪ 417ha/17ha (pinot, shiraz, chard, sauv, sem) ▪ 30t own label 20% red 80% white, balance sold ▪ Sandies Glen Rd, Sondagskloof, Stanford 7210 ▪ info@bruniawines.co.za ▪ www.bruniawines.co.za ▪ **T +27 (0)28-341-0432**

Bruwer Vintners Vine Exploration Co

The brand offers the shared name of cousins Bruwer Raats and Gavin Bruwer Slabbert (both also of high-flying Raats Family and Mvemve Raats, listed separately). Their explorations for this label have come to focus on Stellenbosch vineyards, with wines from varieties quintessentially South African - the Haarlem to Hope name celebrating grapes brought to the Cape by the pioneering 17th-century Dutch settlers. Semillon, which dominated the Cape in the 19th century, now gets a varietal wine as well as the blend. Like the others, it evidences the light touch and elegant restraint that is these vintners' hallmark.

★★★★☆ **Lone Wolf Cinsault** Not as light & simply charming as some of the new-wave examples of the variety, **22** ㉜ as usual at the more serious end. There's fragrance & juiciness, but also lightly grippy tannins to match the fresh acid, & fruit depth & vinous weight at 12.5% alc. From old Bottelary Hills vines.

★★★★☆ **Liberté Pinotage** ⓐ Very satisfactorily poised between the hipster ultra-light style & the powerful traditional one, this a fine alternative example, at 13% alc. Ripe, pure & fragrant fruit on **21** ㉟, silky, elegant, bright & fresh, structured for approachability as well as development over a good many years.

★★★★ **Lone Wolf Semillon** ⓝⓔⓦ Notes of honeyed beeswax & lemon on **22** ㉘. Lightly balanced & fresh at 11.5% alc with fair texture & good flavour, but not much in the way of concentrtion or length.

★★★★☆ **Haarlem to Hope** Blends 2 historic varieties, chenin & semillon. 81% of former in **22** ㉛, with minuscule oak influence. Light, bright, dry & fresh at 12.5% alc, with some intensity; there's a lemony twist but sweet, a peachy chenin core. Supple & not without concentration, but touch off last.— TJ

Location/map/WO: Stellenbosch ▪ Map grid reference: B6 ▪ Est/1stB 2014 ▪ Tasting Mon-Fri 9-5 by appt ▪ Fee R500 (2-10 pax) ▪ Closed all pub hols ▪ Owner(s)/cellarmaster(s) Bruwer Raats & Gavin Bruwer Slabbert ▪ Own label 50% red 50% white ▪ PO Box 2068 Dennesig 7601 ▪ office@raats.co.za ▪ www.raatswines.co.za ▪ **T +27 (0)21-881-3078**

☐ **Buchu Trail** see Swanepoel Wines

Buitenverwachting

There's a wide range of wines made on this historic, visitor-welcoming farm. Not all are produced every year, and some are held back for release until readier for drinking (meanwhile leapfrogged by more approachable vintages). The specialisation is constant, however: sauvignon blanc dominates the white wine offering, and the Bordeaux varieties make up most of the red range - the five main grapes feature in the latest release of the flagship, Christine. That wine is named for Christine Mueller, of the German family that bought the run-down estate in 1981 and rehabilitated it, an important moment in Constantia's modern revival. Son and co-owner Lars Maack has long run the property. Further ensuring continuity, Brad Paton has been in the cellar for 20 years.

Buitenverwachting range

★★★★☆ **Christine** ⓐ Showing some useful savoury development, **16** ㉞ beneficially less ripe & powerful than **15** ㉞ & (tasted out of sequence) **18** ㉛. 14.1% alc much down, allowing for some classic elegance. Latest blends cab (55%), cab franc, merlot & dashes malbec, petit verdot. All-new oak still evident, but deep, dense, ripe fruit more so, & firm but rounded tannic structure gives good support & will help ensure longer-term development.

★★★★☆ **Meifort** ⊘ Similar varietal blend to Christine, also with classic Bordeaux-style aromas of blackcurrant, cedar, spice. **20** ⑨⓪ bigger, richer & riper than that, though still balanced, with savoury refinement more than obvious fruitiness. The older oak less intrusive (which some will prefer), bigger 14.5% alc. Drinks very well now, & at a bargain price for a rather grand wine.

★★★★☆ **Chardonnay** Less about subtle refinement than hugely flavourful approachability. **22** ⑨⓪ usual forward aromas lime, nuts & toast, latter 2 from 10 months oak, 30% new. Richly textured, with modest acidity & few enriching grams sugar making for easygoing softness. Lingering depth of flavour. Confident & engaging.

★★★★★ **Hussey's Vlei Sauvignon Blanc** ⊘ ⊛ Piercing passionfruit purity, but also hinting at ripe stonefruit, on **22** ⑨⑤ from single special site. Intense aroma & flavour. Supple, charming & long-lingering, soft but lively, though off-dry balance not allowing for real elegance. On lees 9 months, adding to weight & texture. 12.5% alc. Same wonderful precision & focus as last-tasted **20** ⑨⑦.

★★★★ **Sauvignon Blanc** ⊘ Citrus mingling with the tropical fruit character on **23** ⑧⑧. Core of ripe sweetness, held in place by refined, dry minerality & firm structure that doesn't preclude estate's soft-textured styling. More demanding, but no less enjoyable, than Buiten Blanc version.

★★★★ **Sauvignon Blanc-Chardonnay** ⊘ Just 17% oaked chardonnay in **22** ⑧⑥, adding some citric complexity as well as breadth & texture, with blackcurrant & passionfruit freshness from sauvignon. Gentle grippiness, pleasingly dry. More impressive than **21** ★★★★ ⑧⑤.

★★★★★ **1769** ⓩ Noble Late Harvest from muscat de Frontignan, **20** ⑨⑤ has expected sweetness, richness, oak an underpin, not masking standout fruit. Ageless, timeless, a classic. 500 ml. Last was **17** ⑨⑤.

Rosé ★★★ From the 2 cabs & merlot, deeper & pinker than fashionable pale salmon. Lots of fruity flavour on **23** ⑧②, fresh & dry. **Buiten Blanc** ⊘ ★★★★ Forward, exuberant aromas, mostly tropical, on **23** ⑧⑤ from sauvignon. Full of ripely sweet flavour, neatly balanced for uncomplicated but satisfying drinking. Like **22** ★★★★ ⑧⑥, WO W Cape. In abeyance: **Cabernet Sauvignon**.

Limited Release range

★★★★☆ **Cabernet Franc** ⊛ Great bonus to have a serious red released with this maturity, **15** ⑨③ out of sequence after tasting **19** ⑨⓪ last year. While adding to sandalwood fragrance, all-new oaking has largely integrated with flavours of ripe fruit, now more savoury. Firm, rounded & succulent tannins in support of sweetly lingering flavours on dry finish. Powerful version of the grape, but lighter-feeling, more elegant than 14.6% alc would suggest.

★★★★ **Restless** ⊘ Pure, clean strawberry aromas touched with earthiness on **22** ⑧⑦ pinot noir. More robust than delicate, & structured more through acidity than tannin, the plentiful red fruit supported by only older oak. First since **19** ⑧⑦.

★★★★ **Double Cab** ⓩ Cab just 22% with cab franc but brings cassis & cedar to the fore on impressive **17** ⑨④. Massive, ripe-fruited yet fairly lively. Strong, fine, dry tannins; many years to go.

★★★★ **MPV** Equal blend merlot & petit verdot in **20** ⑧⑨. Fruitcake notes, some dried & fresh herbs. Bright, full, ripely sweet flavours; rather dry tannins will benefit from few years in bottle. For now, less harmonious & substantial than Rough Diamond version with malbec. 2 years in oak, 15% new. 14.3% alc.

★★★★ **Rough Diamond** ⊛ Blend of malbec & petit verdot; 62% of former in **19** ★★★★☆ ⑨②. Overly heavy oaking (26 months, all new) gives notable spice & tobacco notes & makes tannins somewhat drying. But there's suppleness & lingering fruity juiciness too, as well as density & intensity, holding promise for the future. At 13.7% alc, perhaps more refined than last **17** ⑧⑧.

★★★★☆ **Pioneer Chenin Blanc** ⓩ Only tiny plantings in Constantia. Characterful **21** ⑨⓪ has intriguing limy note & bright mineral focus hinting at cooler origins. Old oak adds to texture & savouriness.

★★★★ **G** ⓩ A rarity, oaked dry gewürztraminer, without losing **20** ⑧⑧'s aromatics, just tamed, made more food friendly. Turkish delight scented, with citrus & stonefruit freshness in the flavours.

★★★★☆ **Maximus** ⊛ Amongst range of sauvignons, this occasional release the only oaked version, 18 months in barrel, 50% new. But wood not too obvious on **21** ★★★★★ ⑨⑤, adding spicy complexity & subduing grape's overt fruitiness, though passionfruit lingers, along with stonefruit. Pleasingly dry & fresh, with satisfying chalky bite. 14% alc. Last was **19** ⑨③.

★★★★ **3rd Time Lucky** ⓥ Shows how individual & good viognier can be. Bold, aromatic **20** ★★★★★ ⑩'s 10 months in oak & acacia a gentle savoury seam. More personality than **19** ⑧⑧. WOW Cape, as G.

Occasional release: **Gracious**. In abeyance: **The Phoenix**. — TJ

Location: Constantia ▪ Map: Cape Peninsula ▪ Map grid reference: B3 ▪ WO: Constantia/Western Cape ▪ Est 1796 ▪ 1stB 1985 ▪ Tasting & sales Mon-Fri 9-5 Sat 10-5 ▪ Closed all pub hols ▪ Selection of platters available in tasting room ▪ Deli & coffee shop ▪ Conferences ▪ Gin, brandy & whisky ▪ Owner(s) Sieglinde (Christine) Mueller & Lars Maack ▪ Cellarmaster(s) Brad Paton (Dec 2004) ▪ Winemaker(s) Brad Paton (Dec 2004), with Stephan Steyn ▪ Viticulturist(s) Peter Reynolds (Jan 2001) ▪ 78.3ha under vine (Bordeaux varieties, chard, sauv) ▪ 25% red 75% white ▪ PO Box 281 Constantia 7848 ▪ info@buitenverwachting.com ▪ www. buitenverwachting.com ▪ **T +27 (0)21-794-5190/1**

☐ **Bukhosi** *see* House of Hlela Royal Wines

Bundu Brands   ⓥ ⑭

The brand celebrates, they say, the 'medley of culture and landscapes of our country' - most notably, on its all-Afrikaans bottles, its wildlife. The pair of brandies, named for and featuring the wildebeest, was inaugurated back in 2019 with Swart, primarily intended for mixing; the more ambitious Kamoefleer, a pure potstill brandy, followed. On the horizon is a longer-matured potstill 'and perhaps a brandy liqueur'. Already, there's also a herbal liqueur, Bobbejaan. All can be sampled at Kelkiewyn in Villiersdorp.

Wildebeest Brandewyn range

★★★★ **Kamoefleer** VS potstill brandy ⑧⑥, 3 years matured, with elegantly refined, though not complex stonefruit flavours. Balanced, smooth & dry, demanding thoughtful sipping. Screwcapped bottle features the wildebeest (& a rousing poem, in Afrikaans like the rest of these labels) against the eponymous camouflage pattern. 40% alc.

Swart ⊘ ★★★☆ Powerful blended brandy ⑧③, minimum 30% potstill, strongly flavourful enough to welcome a mixer, but sufficiently smooth & dry to be savoured neat while admiring the stylish label - or the wildlife. 43% alc. From colombard & chenin, as Kamoefleer. — TJ

Location/map: Villiersdorp ▪ Map grid reference: C1 ▪ WO: Western Cape ▪ Est 2019 ▪ Office Mon-Fri 8-5 ▪ Kelkiewyn tasting room Tue-Thu 8-5 Fri 8-7 Sat 8-5 Sun 8-3; pub hols (seasonal) please call ahead ▪ Owner(s) Bundu Brands (Pty) Ltd ▪ PO Box 171 Villiersdorp 6848 ▪ info@bundubrands.co.za ▪ www. bundubrands.co.za ▪ **T +27 (0)79-498-8005**

Burgershof

The speciality of Robertson's Klaasvoogds area is muscat de Frontignan, and though the Reynecke family of Burgershof, one of the area's original farms, lately have focused on modern, in-demand varietal and blended wines, they happily acknowledge that fortified muscat is their heritage and biggest strength.

★★★★ **Red Muscadel** ⓥ Premium-priced & -packaged **16** ⑧⑦ is complex, light footed & balanced. Gorgeous flavour array of peach through tealeaf to ginger. 375 ml intended as a gift for someone special.

Merlot ⓥ ★★★ A crowd pleaser with its plummy tone, juicy flavours & downy texture. **17** ⑦⑨ does it again. Not tasted: **Pinotage, Cabernet Sauvignon-Shiraz, Chardonnay, Sauvignon Blanc**. — WB

Location/WO: Robertson ▪ Est 1864 ▪ 1stB 2000 ▪ Closed to public ▪ Sales at La Verne Wine Boutique & Ashton Wine Boutique ▪ Owner(s) Hennie Reynecke ▪ Cellarmaster(s)/winemaker(s)/viticulturist(s) Hennie Reynecke (Jan 1979) ▪ 70ha (cab, merlot, muscadel r/w, ptage, ruby cab, shiraz, chard, chenin, cbard, sauv) ▪ IPW, WIETA ▪ PO Box 72 Klaasvoogds River 6707 ▪ burgershof@barvallei.co.za ▪ www.burgershof.com ▪ **T +27 (0)23-626-5433**

☐ **Bushgirl** *see* Bushmanspad Estate

Bushmanspad Estate   ⓥ ⑪ ⊖ ⌂ ⊚

Much excitement among the members of the team about their new winemaking colleague, Neil Marais, who's moved from Tempel Wines in Paarl to this also Belgian-owned (with Norwegian partnership) estate in Robertson. His brief is to craft 'more-natural wines with minimal intervention, that showcase our exceptional terroir' - the latter dominated by a stretch of mountain rising dramatically above the vines and cellar.

Bushmanspad Estate range

★★★★ **Cabernet Sauvignon** Cassis appeal of **20** ⑧⑧ improves on last-made **18** ★★★★ ⑧⑤ in velvet texture. Tobacco & spice nuances retained, along with ripe tannin from 18 months in oak, 10% new.

★★★★ **Cabernet Franc** Swarthy, chunky **20** ⑧⑦ a notch above **19** ★★★★ ⑧④ in inky intensity & density. Cherry brightness balanced by muscularity, power & grip of tannin on dry finish.

★★★★ **The Menno** ⓥ Flagship produced every third year, **18** ⑧⑧ dense, fruity & stylish malbec & shiraz-led 6-way blend. Sweetly ripe mulberries with savoury-spicy tobacco notes, silky tannins.

Malbec ★★★★ Pliable **20** ⑧⑤ follows form. Berry compote, tealeaf & spice, with fresh acid & light frame from 18 months in 10% new oak. **Shiraz** ⓥ ★★★★ Ferment with stems amps up shiraz spice in **18** ⑧⑤, lush dark fruit elegantly framed by 20% new oak, 15 months, savoury, concentrated finish. **Cabernet Sauvignon-Merlot** ⓥ ★★★★ Plush **18** ⑧③ is an indulgence, with choc-dipped strawberry & baked plum flavours, coated chewy tannin. Some malbec & cab franc. **Red Gold Blend** ⓥ ★★★★ Red-berried & friendly, **18** ⑧④ touch more rustic than last. 4 Bordeaux grapes & 2 others, dash 2017 cab franc, 18 months mostly old oak & FlexCube. **Merlot Rosé** ⓥ ★★★ Merlot replaces malbec from **21** ⑧⓪, plenty of ripe strawberry fruit & lemon thyme notes. **Sauvignon Blanc** ⓥ ★★★ Crisp **21** ⑧② tastily straddles ripe fruit & lemony herbs. Perfect as an aperitif. In abeyance: **Grand Reserve Merlot**.

Bushgirl Méthode Ancestrale Sparkling range

★★★★ **Chardonnay Skin Contact** ⓥ Delightful line-up of single-ferment bubblies. Fragrant **22** ⑧⑦ bursts with white flowers, peaches & candied lemons. Mousse is lush, buoyant & super-crisp.

★★★★ **Chardonnay-Pinot Noir** Cloudy coral hue on **23** ★★★★ ⑧⑤, tweaked to 70/30 in favour of chardonnay, up from **22** ⑧⑥'s 67/33. Good bubble & citrus zing, lively & fresh, gentle yeasty farewell. **Cabernet Sauvignon** ★★★★ Dark pink hue & vivid fizz on sparkly **23** ⑧⑤. Plums & cherries abound with light sourdough & lees to balance. Decent depth & intensity, dry conclusion. **Chenin Blanc** ⓝⓔⓦ ★★★★ Melon & quince effervescence on **23** ⑧④, fresh & vibrant, broad lemony body & focused dry finish. **Colombard** ⓝⓔⓦ ★★★ Fizzy & bright **23** ⑧②, lemon sherbet with zesty tang on dry finish. Unfussy alternative to cap classique. **Grenache Noir** ⓥ ★★★★ Light & invigorating **22** ⑧④ makes the perfect summer companion. Juicy Ribena-like fruit shot through with lemony verve. **Malbec** ⓝⓔⓦ ★★★ Cherries & berries with bubblegum brightness on ruby-hued **23** ⑧②. Exuberant foam but with tinge of leafiness on medium body. **Merlot** ★★★★ Cherry pink **23** ⑧③ melds red & blue fruit with a fynbos herb note. Light, vibrant bubbles with an almost sour piquancy. Not tasted: **Chardonnay**, **Pinot Noir**, **Shiraz**. In abeyance: **Merlot-Cabernet Franc**, **Shiraz-Cabernet Franc**. — FM

Location: Bonnievale ▪ Map/WO: Robertson ▪ Map grid reference: C1 ▪ Est 2000 ▪ 1stB 2006 ▪ Tasting & sales Mon-Fri 9-4 ▪ Fee R50/5 wines ▪ Closed all pub hols ▪ Cheese platters by appt ▪ BYO picnic ▪ Walks/hikes ▪ Self-catering cottages ▪ Owner(s) see intro ▪ Winemaker(s) Neil Marais ▪ 52ha (cabs s/f, malbec, merlot, mourv, shiraz, sauv) ▪ 400t own label 80% red 15% white 5% rosé ▪ PO Box 227 Bonnievale 6730 ▪ info@ bushmanspad.co.za ▪ www.bushgirl.estate ▪ **T +27 (0)23-616-2961**

☐ **Butcher Shop & Grill** see The Butcher Shop & Grill

☐ **B Vintners Vine Exploration Co** see Bruwer Vintners Vine Exploration Co

☐ **Cabrière** see Haute Cabrière

☐ **Café Culture** see KWV Wines

Cage Wine @ AA Badenhorst Family Wines   ⓥ

Cage is the nickname of Keiji Sato, chef and promoter of wine culture in his native Japan, and for some years now harvest assistant at esteemed AA Badenhorst Wines in Swartland. For this own-label he's been working on 'more possibilities of what the region is' and looking forward to showing his 'new babies' next time.

★★★★ **Grenache Noir** Majority wholebunch treatment amplifies lovely berry & floral fragrance, adds stemmy spice to **22** ⑧⑦. Ferment in old vat, 11 months in large old barrel for satin grip. Improves on last.

★★★★ **Chenin Blanc** This Swartland charmer just gets better. Hint of flint, bright apple & pear, creamy mouthfeel on **22** ⑧⑧ from wholebunch barrel ferment/11 months on these. Moderate 11.5-13% alc on these.

★★★★ **Cape White Blend** ⓥ Compelling trio of chenin (45%), semillon & clairette, some wholebunch in older oak, **21** ⑧⑨ shows a textured stonefruit richness along with mouthcoating persistence.

★★★★ **Pet-Nat** Light, refreshing single-ferment sparkling, **22** ⑧⑥ sweet-fruited limy bubbles touched with lemon verbena. Mostly grenache blanc & clairette, enlivening burst of colombard.— ML

Location: Malmesbury ▪ Map/WO: Swartland ▪ Map grid reference: C8 ▪ Est/1stB 2017 ▪ Tasting & cellar tour by appt ▪ Fee R100pp ▪ Owner(s) Keiji Sato (brand), AA Badenhorst Family (farm) ▪ Cellarmaster(s)/viti-culturist(s) Adi Badenhorst (2008) ▪ Winemaker(s) Keiji Sato (2017) ▪ 300cs own label 20% red 40% white 40% pet-nat ▪ Off R45, Jakkalsfontein Rd, Malmesbury ▪ keiji.or@gmail.com ▪ **T +81-80-5545-8280**

Calitzdorp Cellar ⓠ ◎ ⑤

Carlo Sciocatti has settled into the general manager-winemaker role at the winery on the hill in Calitzdorp town, and is guiding the process of 'extracting as much flavour from the grapes as possible while keeping the wine easy to drink and elegant'. A modest 3,000 cases are sold under the own label of the 28 grow-er-owners, and a new team member has been recruited to assist with digital branding and marketing.

★★★★ **Golden Jerepigo** Delightful NV ⑧⑥ fortified pudding wine reflects perfume, intensity & complexity of hanepoot & white muscadel, delivers unctuous sweetness with texture & flair.

Cabernet Sauvignon ⊘ ★★★☆ New bottling of **21** ⑧③ handled differently, oak chips replace barrels, a little chunkier yet retains accessibility & typical cassis fruit profile. **Pinotage** ★★★ Ample succulent red fruit of **22** ⑦⑨ framed by light brush of oak, masking a few grams sugar. Klein Karoo WO, as previous & next. **Shiraz** ⊘ ★★★★ Sweet mulberry fruit of soft, gentle **21** ⑧③ gets grip from subtle oaking, year in old barrels. **Tinto** ★★★ Chewy **22** ⑧② blend of tinta (45%), ruby cab & merlot shows dry, spicy tannins which vie with ripe cherry & plum flavour. Older barrels. **Blanc de Noir** ⊘ ★★★ From pinotage, pale coral **23** ⑧①'s floral, plum & peach fruit woven with bright acid. Good dry body & length. **Chardonnay** ⓠ ★★★☆ Gentle cream, vanilla & orange appeal on light, juicy **21** ⑧③. Good for everyday enjoyment. **Chenin Blanc** ★★★ Pear drop & melon accents on tropical **23** ⑧①, fresh & vibrant, dry finishing. For summertime quaffing. **Limited Edition** ⓠ ★★★ Faint floral nuance on slightly sparkling NV ⑧② from muscat d'Alexandrie. Balanced, so palate gently succulent rather than sweet, finish is clean. Uncertified. **Sauvignon Blanc** ⊘ ★★★★ Litchi, guava & pear on **23** ⑧③. Tangy, with typical zest on good body broadened by lees contact. Nicely balanced. WO W Cape. **Muscat Delight** ⑩ⓐ ★★★ Natural Sweet pool-party starter **23** ⑧⓪ has abundant sugar but also gentle fizz & freshness for a clean finish, inviting the next grapey sip. **Red Muscadel** ★★★★ Touch lighter, less lipsmacking than previous, yet **23** ⑧⑤ fortified dessert retains alluring cherry blossom & plum aromas, balanced sweetness & spirit. WO Klein Karoo. **Cape Ruby** ★★★★ Undisclosed varieties in NV ⑧⑤ 'port'. Delivers good punch of alc, blue-black fruit & spice on rich, sweet chocolaty palate. Supple, nutty finish from 6 months in old oak. **Cape Vintage** ⓠ ★★★★ - Fynbos edge to prune- & spice-toned **19** ⑧⑤ 'port'. Gentle fire & tannin grip from 2 years in old oak improve on previous, long peppery ending. Not tasted: **Merlot, Tinta Barocca, Touriga Nacional, Hanepoot, White Muscadel.** — DS

Location: Calitzdorp ▪ Map: Klein Karoo & Garden Route ▪ Map grid reference: B5 ▪ WO: Calitzdorp/Klein Karoo/ Western Cape ▪ Est 1928 ▪ 1stB 1976 ▪ Tasting & sales Mon-Sat 9-5 Sun 11-3; pub hols (seasonal) please call ahead ▪ Closed Good Fri & Dec 25 ▪ Conferences ▪ Owner(s) 28 members ▪ Winemaker(s) / GM Carlo Sciocatti (May 2022), with Abraham Pretorius ▪ 150ha (10 varieties, r/w) ▪ 2,800t/3,000cs own label ▪ IPW ▪ PO Box 193 Calitzdorp 6660 ▪ info@calitzdorpwine.co.za ▪ www.calitzdorpwine.co.za ▪ **T +27 (0)44-213-3301**

Callender Peak

The Jeffery and MacDonald families' vines, some ungrafted and thus very rare, grow at 850 m altitude in Ceres Plateau among mountains dusted with winter snow. The grapes from this special site are handled as carefully and naturally as possible by Donovan Rall of Rall Wines 'to express only the fruit and soil'.

★★★★☆ **Callender Peak Chardonnay** ⑧ Graceful **22** ⑨④ unfurls white florals, orange blossom & fresh pear. Bunch pressed, wild fermented in barrel with 10 months in old oak for a gentle, pure expression enhanced further by light chalky grip.

★★★★☆ **Winterhoek Sauvignon Blanc** ⊘ ⑧ Purity without sharpness a hallmark of this cool-grown sauvignon. From ungrafted vines, **22** ⑨④'s juicy green fruit (limes, figs, nettles) tempered with regular lees stirring for full mouthfeel, balanced by a clean dry finish.— ML

Location: Ceres ▪ WO: Ceres Plateau ▪ Est/1stB 2007 ▪ Closed to public ▪ Owner(s) MacDonald & Jeffery families ▪ Cellarmaster(s)/winemaker(s) Donovan Rall ▪ 2ha (chard, sauv) ▪ 5t/500cs own label 100% white ▪ donovanrall@yahoo.com

Camberley Wines

John and Gaël Nel welcome walk-in visitors to their small wine and hospitality farm in Banhoek Valley, but recommend making an appointment ahead of time to ensure a personal tasting experience. John's handcrafted wines offer ample character and flavour, with one or two experiments added for interest, like the pink chenin that's now a fixture due to popular demand. Most bottlings are high in alcohol because their maker likes the slight sweetening effect. 'Anything below 14.5% gets a zero score from me,' he chortles.

Camberley range

★★★★ **Cabernet Sauvignon** Plush, soft & silky **15** ⑧⑦ has 7% merlot tucked into gentle body with ample berry, plum & black cherry appeal. Shows good evolution, finishes spicily dry.

★★★★ **The 5th Element** Blueberry & spice attractions on **20** ⑧⑥ pinotage, restrained but bright with lively succulence & rich, accommodating texture.

★★★★ **Shiraz** Trim body of **21** ★★★★ ⑧⑤ still delivers plum, earth & dried herb typicity. Somewhat leaner than last-tasted **17** ⑧⑦ but retains house's generous 15% alc.

★★★★ **Cabernet Sauvignon-Merlot** Supple & generous **20** ⑧⑥ shows authentic Bordeaux-style fruitcake, tealeaf & bright baking spice, good core & backbone supporting lush fruit & soft texture.

★★★★ **Charisma** More idiosyncratic Bordeaux blend, **21** ★★★★ ⑧④ light bodied with boldly ripe blue & black fruit, resinous nuance. Star anise vibrancy & signature 15% alc lift the palate. Last tasted was **08**.

★★★★ **Philosopher's Stone** Cab blend, **21** ★★★★ ⑧⑤ shows trademark tealeaf & cassis with fine tannin grip. Supple & rounded, pleasantly dry, with moderate 13.5% alc. Previous was **NV** ★★★★ ⑧⑦.

Pinotage ★★★★ Compote of prunes & spice on **19** ⑧⑤. Ripe, raisined, with alc of 16.5% & subtle liquorice nuance, light oak grip on a nutty farewell. Uncertified, as all. **Responsibly** ⑩ ★★★★ Pear, melon & apricot make up the **22** ⑧④ fruit salad bowl from chenin. Fresh, juicy & easy to like with its lively lemon zip. Not tasted: **Cabernet Franc, Illusion, Shiraz Méthode Cap Classique**. Discontinued: **Elm Tree Merlot, Elixir Fortified Red**.

Noisy Grape range

★★★★ **Pet-Nat** ⑩ Lively **NV** ⑧⑥ méthode ancestrale makes sparkling debut with coral pink hue, toasty strawberry bubbles, preserved lemon aftertaste. Undisgorged, so touch cloudy from lees presence.

Pink Chenin Blanc ⊘ ★★★★ Plump & delicious mix of chenin with a dash of shiraz. **22** ⑧④ pear, quince & leesy nectarine made for summer enjoyment. Not tasted: **Méthode Cap Classique**.

Prohibition range

Red ⊘ ★★★★ Dark fruit, prune & spice on **NV** ⑧④ blend. Medium bodied, rounded, with yielding oak frame & star anise nuance. **White** ⊘ ★★★★ Apple blossom intro to **NV** ⑧③ summer sipper, flinty note to grapefruit & apple succulence that leads to a dry finish. Not tasted: **Méthode Cap Classique**. — FM

Location/map: Stellenbosch ▪ Map grid reference: H4 ▪ Est 1990 ▪ 1stB 1996 ▪ Tasting & sales Mon-Sun 10.30-5; pub hols (seasonal) please call ahead ▪ Tasting fee depending on wine of choice ▪ Closed Dec 25 & Jan 1 ▪ 3 self-catering guest cottages ▪ Wine club ▪ Online sales ▪ Owner(s) John & Gaël Nel ▪ Winemaker(s) John Nel ▪ Viticulturist(s) Bennie Booysen ▪ 6ha (cabs s/f, merlot, p verdot, ptage, shiraz, touriga) ▪ ±35t/6,400cs own label ▪ PO Box 6120 Uniedal 7612 ▪ john@camberley.co.za ▪ www.camberley.co.za ▪ **T +27 (0)82-808-0176**

☐ **Camino Africana** see David Finlayson Wines

☐ **CanCan** see Renegade Wines

Canetsfontein Wine Estate

A mountainside boutique winery in Wellington producing organic and no-sulphur-added wines, this venture focuses on Bordeaux-style blends and varietal wines under the Canetsfontein and Cliffhanger brands, the latter taking its name from one of the mountain biking trails on the property - 'certainly not for the faint hearted!' (There's a photograph of it between pages 60 and 61 of this guide.) The wine portfolio, which we look forward to tasting next time, is from grapes from the farm and selected Coastal organic vines.

Location: Wellington ▪ Est 1996 ▪ 1stB 2017 ▪ Currently no tasting room ▪ Conservation area ▪ MTB by appt ▪ Winemaker(s) Frank Meaker (Jan 2022), with Dirk Sameuls (Jan 2000) ▪ 1,000cs own label 100% red ▪ Organic (Ecocert), WIETA ▪ PO Box 207 Wellington 7655 ▪ info@canetsfontein.com ▪ www.canetsfontein.com ▪ T +27 (0)21-204-5845

Canto Wines   Ⓠ Ⓨ Ⓞ Ⓐ

'Consumer friendly, but also serious enough to command respect', Canto's boutique wines are crafted by winemaker since inception Anneke Potgieter from vines on a 22-ha portion of Durbanville's Meerendal Estate. Local winelover Marinus Neethling acquired the land in the mid-2010s, and built a cellar and venue focused on cap classique. The portfolio has since grown, but much else is unchanged, including emphasis on a convivial visitor experience, now including the Longtable craft workshops and wine dinners.

Canto Wines range

★★★★ **Merlot** ⊘ Ⓐ Seriously conceived, with dense blackcurrant & cherry fruit, liquorice-toned earthiness & hint of aromatic tobacco, **20** ★★★★☆ ⑨① is assured & textured, a step up from **19** ⑧⑧. Still young & taut after 16 months in 50% new barriques, built to age.

★★★★ **Pinotage** ⊘ Ⓐ Bold, confident **21** ⑧⑨ has concentrated wild berry core, sweet spices from 17 months in seasoned oak, appealing acid tang. Tannins ripe & full, should settle with time.

★★★★☆ **Chardonnay** 100% barrel-matured **21** ⑨⓪ has more prominent oak than previous, but counters with generous marmalade fruit, rich lees texture & steely mineral thread, finishing with chalky lime. Begs rich seafood partners.

Sauvignon Blanc ★★★☆ First from 100% own grapes. Steely, vibrant **23** ⑧⑤ has prominent gunflint & mown grass aromas, engagingly austere granadilla & greengage fruit.

Méthode Cap Classique range

★★★★ **Pinot Noir** Pretty, onion skin-shaded **20** ⑧⑨ has plenty of savoury heft from 30 months on lees, baked apple & quince, salty mineral finish. Firm but well-judged acid & vigorous mousse add racy charm. Better balanced than last.

★★★★ **Shiraz** Fuller, more savoury than siblings, **20** ★★★★☆ ⑨① is deeper-hued & -flavoured than pale rosé **19** ⑧⑨, shows more defined brioche & strudel notes from 26 months on lees. Fine, rapid bubble, piercing acid add to appeal.

★★★★☆ **Chardonnay Brut** Ⓐ Accomplished blanc de blancs sparkler, 26 months on lees. **20** ⑨④ exudes finesse & charm. Baked apple, buttery shortbread & subtle hints of citrus rind & marzipan borne on smooth, creamy mousse. Continues upward trajectory of zero-dosage **19** ⑨①.

Not tasted: **Pinot Noir-Chardonnay**. — GdB

Location/WO: Durbanville ▪ Map: Durbanville, Philadelphia & Darling ▪ Map grid reference: C7 ▪ Est/1stB 2015 ▪ Tasting & sales Tue–Thu 11–5 Fri/Sat/pub hols 10–6 Sun 11–5 ▪ First Fizzy Thursday (1st Thursday of every month) we will stay open until 7pm ▪ Wine tasting R65pp; MCC tasting R75pp; macaroon & MCC pairing R140pp; non-alcoholic macaron pairing R100pp; gin infused tasting R140pp – tasting fees may change ▪ Pizza & picnics from Wed–Sun ▪ Closed Good Fri, Dec 25 & Jan 1 ▪ Deli products to build your own platter, available daily ▪ Picnics ▪ Big lawn & cricket pitch for children ▪ Functions & weddings ▪ Owner(s) Marinus Neethling ▪ Winemaker(s) Anneke Potgieter (Sep 2015, consultant) ▪ 22ha/18ha (merlot, chard, sauv) ▪ 8–10t/3,500cs own label 40% red 30% white 30% MCC ▪ info@cantowines.co.za ▪ www.cantowines.co.za ▪ T +27 (0)21-492-2821

Capaia Wine Estate   Ⓠ Ⓨ Ⓞ Ⓐ

Transformed around the turn of the millennium from a wheat farm into a showpiece vineyard and cellar, with a then-avant garde array of large oak fermenters, and a hilltop setting with endless vistas over the Philadelphia wine-ward, Capaia today is owned by the founders' daughter, Mariella von Essen, and wine-consultant since inception, Stephan von Neipperg. Investments in renewables, notably solar, aim for eventual 'power independence', and tweaks to the deck area make those views 'even more memorable'.

★★★★ **Shiraz** Ⓩ Firm, feisty **19** ⑧⑦ preview, with dry, dusty tannins. Needs time, decant in youth. Naturally fermented in large foudre, then ±12 months in barrique, as Capaia. Seasoned wood only.

★★★★ **Capaia** (Ⓐ) Flagship reverts to original name after several years as 'One'. **20** ⑧⑨ cab & shiraz (43/21) with 3 other Bordeaux grapes produce ample succulent black fruit, some fynbos & meat spice accents. Smooth, well-balanced structure seamlessly assimilates 50% new oak. Also in 1.5L, 3L & 5L.

Cabernet Sauvignon-Merlot (Ⓥ) ★★★★ Juicy plums & hints of graphite & savouriness, easy & food friendly. **19** ⑧⑤ includes splashes cab franc, petit verdot & shiraz; 18 months in older barrels. **Rosé** ★★★★ Summery & fun, salmon pink **23** ⑧⑤ from shiraz is appealingly fruit-forward yet nice & dry for food matching. **Sauvignon Blanc** ★★★★ Ripe, generous tropical fruit gains touch of cream from 4 months on lees, **23** ⑧⑤ hint of citrus cleanses & revives the finish. — WB

Location/WO: Philadelphia ▪ Map: Durbanville, Philadelphia & Darling ▪ Map grid reference: C5 ▪ Est 1997 ▪ 1stB 2003 ▪ Tasting, sales & cellar tours Mon-Fri 8-1; Sat/Sun tasting & sales at Mariella's; pub hols (seasonal) please call ahead ▪ Tour groups ▪ Mariella's Restaurant T +27 (0)21-972-1103/+27 (0)72-770-9695, mariellas@capaia. co.za ▪ Deli Olivia ▪ Facilities for children ▪ Picnic baskets in summer ▪ MTB & trail running routes ▪ Owner(s) Mariella von Essen & Stephan von Neipperg ▪ Cellarmaster(s) Bernabé Strydom (Oct 2006), assisted by Stephan von Neipperg ▪ Viticulturist(s) Derrick Steyn (Aug 2016) ▪ 140ha/60ha (cabs s/f, merlot, p verdot, shiraz, sauv) ▪ 260t/26,000cs own label 85% red 15% white ▪ IPW ▪ PO Box 131 Melkbosstrand 7437 ▪ info@capaia.co.za ▪ www.capaia.co.za ▪ **T +27 (0)21-972-1081 (winery)/+27 (0)21-972-1103 (restaurant)**

☐ **Cape Bay** *see* FirstCape Vineyards
☐ **Cape Beach Collection** *see* Fortes Family Wines
☐ **Cape Chamonix** *see* Chamonix Wine Farm

Cape Classics (Ⓠ)

Founded in 1992 by André Shearer and now helmed by CEO Robert Bradshaw, Cape Classics is the leader in the South African wine category in the US, importing one in every three bottles, including the proprietary brands featured here. The company operates from a warehouse and office complex near Somerset West, and recently added top Stellenbosch label Taaibosch to its portfolio. Indaba is the original own-brand and a long-time supporter of social progress in the winelands; newer Jam Jar caters for the non-dry drinker with, among others, a new red bubbly, untasted by us; and youngest label Braai celebrates SA's national pastime.

Indaba range
Merlot ★★★★ Red fruited & smooth for easy sipping. **22** ⑧③ just a hint of spice on the finish from 1% oaked portion. **Mosaic** ★★★★ Juicy dark fruit mingles with creamy vanilla oak in **21** ⑧⑤ cab-led Bordeaux blend. Rounded for everyday enjoyment. **Chardonnay** ★★★★ Easygoing **22** ⑧③ shows bright apple & citrus flavours, filled out by brush of oak. **Chenin Blanc** ★★★★ Rush tropical fruit on **22** ⑧③, vibrant pine-apple & melon gain breadth from 13% oak & lees ageing. Also-tasted **23** ⑧③ in same vein, with a lemon lift as it exits. **Sauvignon Blanc** ★★★ Mellow **21** ★★★★ ⑧③ has ripe yellow plum & savoury herb flavour. **22** ⑧②, also tasted, much fresher, greenpepper in a lean body. Both best enjoyed soon.

Braai range
Cabernet Sauvignon ★★★★ Get the fire started with amiable **21** ⑧③, smooth & easy, dab malbec adds some complexity, 25% oaked portion lends spice & roundness. **Pinotage** ★★★★ Gluggable & moreish **22** ⑧③ brings rich dark plums to the party, 13 months in small barrels give the savoury seasoning.

Jam Jar range
Sweet Blush ★★★ Light florals from muscat, pretty pinkness & spice ex shiraz on not over-sweet **NV** ⑦⑧. Chill well, as all these. **Sweet White Moscato** ★★★ Billows of muscat fragrance, ripe apple flavour & well-managed sugar make **23** ⑧② oh-so-easy to sip. **Sweet Red Blend** ★★★ Sweet blueberry & smoke mingle with soft vanilla in **22** ⑧⓪ from cab & shiraz union that will please the fans. **Sweet Shiraz** ★★★ Sweet, yes, but also vibrant & juicy, so the dark berries & spice on **22** ⑧② are smooth & uncloying. — WB

Location: Somerset West ▪ Map: Helderberg ▪ Map grid reference: F4 ▪ WO: Western Cape ▪ Est 1992 ▪ 1stB 1996 ▪ Tasting by appt only ▪ Winemaker(s) Bruwer Raats (Indaba & Cape Classics ranges, May 2010), Clayton Christians (Indaba & Cape Classics ranges, Jan 2019) ▪ 154,000cs ▪ 15 Blend Cres, Firgrove Ind. Business Estate 7130 ▪ info@capeclassics.com ▪ www.capeclassics.com, www.indabawines.com, www.jamjarwines.com, www.braaiwines.com ▪ **T +27 (0)21-847-2400**

Cape Collective

Via their Cape Collective portal, specialist wine negotiant Dane Raath and designer Janneman Solms invite winelovers to 'explore outside their comfort zone' with 'great, mould-breaking but approachable' bottlings, made by a Cape wine elite. Born of Covid necessity, the wrapper packaging has proved a hit with critics.

The Wrapper Series

★★★★☆ **Staunch Stellenbosch Cabernet Sauvignon** ⓧ Mint & dried tomato among array of aromas & flavours on **18** ⑨⓪, staunch tannins from 21-day ferment on skins. To pair with 'any lekker vleisie'.

★★★★ **Cabernet Franc** ⓧ From Polkadraai & Bottelary vines, leafy **20** ⑧⑨ shows typicity as well as complexity, a tobacco nuance & velvet tannin from 16 months in barrique.

★★★★ **Pinotage** (NEW) ⊘ Radiant plum hue of **21** ⑧⑦ matched with a light feel at 12.5% alc. Fennel & green herbs on sappy berry palate, barest touch of oak tannin from year in older barrels. WO Montagu.

★★★★☆ **Rad Red** ⓧ Perfumed **21** ⑨① is bright, vivacious, eclipses **20** ★★★★ ⑧⑧ with its fine tannins & savoury edge. 50% cinsaut with Stellenbosch pinot noir & pinotage, brief 7 months in old oak.

★★★★ **Cape Claret** ⊘ Modern take on classic cab & cinsaut blend (50/50), wholeberry wild fermented, year in older oak. **22** ⑧⑥ shows lightly expressed black & red cherries on a bed of velvet. Raises the bar on **18** ★★★★ ⑧⑤, a 5-way Bordeaux red.

★★★★☆ **Epic White** ⓧ Chenin from Stellenbosch, Slanghoek & Elgin, 7-12 months in older oak. **21** ⑨① gorgeous almond & fresh green-apple joined by creamed white nuts on palate. Improves on **20** ★★★★ ⑧⑨, also chenin but seasoned with 4 others.

★★★★☆ **Elgin Riesling** ⓧ Fantastic typicity, tension & delicacy on **21** ⑨⓪ from cool-grown vines. Aromas of lime & green apple, taut balance between sugar & acid (5 & 7.6 g/L).

★★★★ **Wit Mossel** ⓧ Idiosyncratic but deft expression of riesling from Darling. **21** ⑧⑧ bunch-pressed into older barrel for ferment, matured 7 months, giving notes of slate, green pineapple, touch of mango.

★★★★ **Coltamino** ⓧ From Montagu, unique mix of old-vine colombard (57%), sultana & dash palomino; **21** ⑧⑧ grapey aromas, then yellow apple & orange flavours, smooth, savoury texture.

- -

Ayé Ayé Rosé ⓥ ★★★★ Attractive peachy pink **22** ⑧⑤ lightly pressed from Stellenbosch cab, variety's grape tannin lending a fine dry structure to strawberries & pomegranate. Impresses more than last.

- -

Syrah ⓧ ★★★★ Violet, bramble, white pepper & touch of smoke on appealing **20** ⑧⑤ from mix of Polkadraai, Bottelary & Devon Valley grapes, chalky tannins that could age a few years. **Mauve** ⓧ ★★★★ Widely sourced shiraz, grenache noir & dab cinsaut aged 10 months in older oak. **20** ⑧③ red cherry, black pepper & a meaty note, wrapped in lively tannins. Not tasted: **Seeboei Sauvignon Blanc**. In abeyance: **Capitán**, **Cape Coast Chardonnay**. Discontinued: **Tinta Barocca**. — ML

Location: Cape Town ▪ WO: Stellenbosch/Western Cape/Montagu/Elgin/Darling ▪ Est 2020 ▪ 1stB 2018 ▪ Closed to public ▪ Wine club ▪ Owner(s) Janneman Solms & Dane Raath ▪ Winemaker(s)/viticulturist(s) Lucinda Heyns, Gunter Schultz, Johann Fourie, Bruwer Raats ▪ 3,500cs own label 65% red 35% white ▪ 1 Perth Str, off Queen Victoria Str, Cape Town 8001 ▪ drink@capecollective.co.za ▪ www.capecollective.co.za ▪ **T** +27 (0)72-200-4700/+27 (0)82-492-4327

☐ **Cape Cult** see Darling Cellars

☐ **Cape Discovery** see Stellenview Premium Wines

Cape Dreams Wine ⓧ

Entrepreneur Bunty Khan in the late 2000s aspired to promote local enfranchisement and development by creating an internationally recognised wine brand. With a presence in over 20 countries, she's realised her dream through a competitive price-quality ratio, consistency of supply and focus on consumer tastes and preferences, the latter leading her to add more labels to the Ayah pinnacle line-up of small-batch wines.

Ayah Family Super Premium Collection

★★★★ **Matriarch Cape Blend** From Paarl fruit, **19** ⑧⑧ mixes pinotage with cab, shiraz & malbec for full-throttle mouthful of meat, leather, spice, copious blackberry & bramble fruit. Coffee & smoky oak from 18 months old barrels add definition to very enjoyable wine.

★★★★ Wooded Chenin Blanc (NEW) Rich & ripe **21** (88) from Paardeberg presents enticing mouthful of apricot jam, cooked apple & honey. Equal portions aged in amphora, old oak & stainless steel, gaining both texture & spice. Needs a little more freshness to be truly top tier.

Grande Dame Pinot Noir Rosé Méthode Cap Classique (NEW) ⊘ **★★★★** A burst of red appleskin fruit greets on **NV** (85) before toasty biscuit & fresh-baked bread weigh in on well-rounded palate, aided by few grams sugar. Crisp acid, clean, zesty finish. Excellent breakfast fizz. 18 months on lees; Paardeberg WO.

Cape Dreams Wine Collection

Cabernet Sauvignon ★★★ Juicy blackcurrant jam flavour **22** (81) with slight charry smoke accent from old barrels & staves (as for all these reds). **Pinotage ★★★** Soft, smooth **22** (82) aided by dab sugar filling out black & red plum jam notes. Not quite the character of previous but enjoyable everyday drinking. **Shiraz** ⊘ **★★★★** Step-up **22** (83) shows good varietal correctness with plum, prune, leather & pepper spice. Smoked meat & soft tannins at finish. More oomph than last. **Pinotage Rosé** ⊘ **★★★** Pretty in palest pink **23** (82) teems with pomegranate, bubblegum & cherry, touch of sugar nicely balances crisp acid. **Chardonnay** ⊘ **★★★** A breakfast punch wine, with peach, banana & granadilla in lightweight mouthful. Slightly warm finish in unoaked **23** (80). **Chenin Blanc** ⊘ **★★★★** Big mouthful of pink grapefruit on **23** (84), fresh & fruity, with crisp acid & clean finish. Ideal summer all-day wine, shade more exciting than last. **Natural Sweet Red ★★★** From pinotage & cab (60/40), with modest sugar, **22** (80)'s black fruit confection seems drier thanks to tarry grip of soft tannins. **Natural Sweet Blanc** ⊘ **★★★★** From muscadel, remarkably fresh & lively **22** (83) has light grape & white flower appeal, zesty acid & clean finish. Delightful summer wine. Not tasted: **Merlot**, **Colombar**, **Sauvignon Blanc**.

Discontinued: **Reserve range**. — CM

Location/map: Robertson ▪ Map grid reference: A6 ▪ WO: Robertson/Paardeberg/Paarl ▪ Tasting & cellar tours by appt ▪ Owner(s) Bunty Khan ▪ Cellarmaster(s) André van Dyk ▪ Winemaker(s) Andre Schriven ▪ (cab, merlot, ptage, shiraz, chard, chenin, cbard, sauv) ▪ 60% red 40% white ▪ BEE, HACCP, IPW, ISO 9001, WIETA ▪ sales@capedreamswine.co.za ▪ www.capedreamswine.co.za ▪ **T +27 (0)83-792-7638/+27 (0)83-780-9428**

☐ **Cape Elements** *see* Nico van der Merwe Wines
☐ **Cape Fern** *see* Truter Family Wines
☐ **Cape Five** *see* Stellenview Premium Wines

Cape Fold ⌂

The Droomer family work with consultant winemaker Sheree Nothnagel from their farm Rouzelle near Wolseley to showcase pockets along the Cape Fold Belt, whose ancient mountain ranges inform and beautify much of wine country. Striking and original labels adorn the wines, intended to be 'serious enough for fine-dining but fun enough for a braai'. A tasting lounge is planned, to join the hewn-stone guest cottage.

Breedekloof Shiraz (map) **★★★★** Prominent red berries & cherries, **21** (85) is ripe & fleshy, oak's influence showing in the vanilla spice. Silky & round, a delicious mouthful.

Farm Blend (NEW) **★★★** Shiraz 62% plus 4 others, & it works. **21** (82) is dark toned, sweet spiced, whiff of pepper, enough tannin for backbone but essentially styled to enjoy the luscious palate at its youthful best. **Breedekloof Chenin Blanc ★★★** Just-sliced green apple throughout, dry **22** (85) has supporting acid adding vitality, giving an overall impression of tasty freshness. Not tasted: **Cinsaut**, **Swartland Cape Blend**, **Swartland Chenin Blanc**. — CR

Location: Wolseley ▪ WO: Breedekloof ▪ 1stB 2020 ▪ Closed to public ▪ Online sales ▪ Die Kliphuisie guest cottage ▪ Owner(s) Droomer family ▪ Winemaker(s) Sheree Nothnagel (2020, consultant) ▪ 100ha/68ha (cab, merlot, ptage, ruby cab, shiraz, chenin) ▪ 40t/1,000cs own label 78% red 22% white ▪ WIETA ▪ wine@dreem.co.za ▪ wine.dreem.co.za ▪ **T +27 (0)82-774-6841**

☐ **Cape Fusion** *see* Asara Wine Estate & Hotel
☐ **Cape Fynbos** *see* The Grape Grinder
☐ **Cape Georgians** *see* Marklew Family Wines
☐ **Cape Haven** *see* Pulpit Rock Winery

Capelands Estate

'Mineral and elegant wines' are styled for Italians Johann Innerhofer and Laura Mauri by top consultants from bought-in grapes and cabernet from a rare walled vineyard on the estate near Somerset West. The small parcel is overlooked by a guest house and restaurant, where pre-booked tastings are presented.

★★★★☆ **CR1 Redstone** Mostly cab with 5% splash malbec, **19** ⑨⓪'s rich blackcurrant & plum fruit styling reined in by tight linear tannins & leading variety's bright acidity. Like more elegant **18** ⑨③, dusted with cedar & dried herbs. 30 months in oak, some new.

★★★★ **Klein Redstone** ⓥ 100% cab in **17** ⑧⑧ yet approachable early. Perfumed blueberry, plum & cassis seamlessly melded with creamy vanilla from same 30 months in barrel as CR1. Last-tasted **12** ★★★★ ⑧⑤ had dash malbec. Also in 1.5L, as next.

★★★★ **CR1 Redstone Special Reserve** ⓝⒺⓌ From malbec, flavoursome **20** ⑧⑦ already shows subtle forest floor development on its characteristic blueberry bouquet & palate, along with savoury hint of charcuterie. Very firm tannins extend the finish, broaden the shoulders.

★★★★ **CR1 Redstone Reserve** ⓥ From tiny 3 ha parcel. **15** ★★★★★ ⑨③ harvested early, shows in freshness & tight tannins, beautifully pure fruit - cassis, sour cherry, blueberry abound. 77% cabernet, rest malbec; only 7,000 bottles. Follows sumptuous **14**.

★★★★ **Whitestone Viognier** ⓥ Delicate **22** ⑧⑥ is softly dry, with trademark peach blossom & apricot kernel. Smooth & supple, showing orchard fruit & apple brûlée flavours, exotic spice on exit.

★★★★☆ **Whitestone Reserve** Substantial **22** ★★★★ ⑧⑧, same blend of chenin & 10% each chardonnay, viognier, similar sweet Golden Delicious apple tones along with noticeable vanilla from 9 months in oak. Touch of bitter quince freshens & lifts, but tad less so than in **21** ⑨①. WO W Cape, as Viognier

Not tasted: Whitestone Chardonnay, Whitestone Chenin Blanc, Whitestone Sauvignon Blanc. — CvZ

Location: Somerset West ▪ Map: Helderberg ▪ Map grid reference: F7 ▪ WO: Stellenbosch/Western Cape ▪ Est 2004 ▪ 1stB 2010 ▪ Tasting by appt ▪ Capelands Restaurant open for lunch & dinner Thu-Mon ▪ Guest house ▪ Online shop ▪ Owner(s) Capelands Resort Estate (Pty) Ltd ▪ Winemaker(s) Abé Beukes (consultant) ▪ Viticulturist(s) Francois Hanekom (Feb 2009, consultant) ▪ 12.5ha/3ha (cab) ▪ 6t/2,500cs own label 100% red ▪ 3 Old Sir Lowry's Pass Rd, Somerset West 7130 ▪ capelands.booking@gmail.com ▪ www.capelands.com ▪ T +27 (0)71-400-2073

☐ **The Capeman** see Darling Cellars
☐ **Capeman** see Darling Cellars

Cape Moby Winery

Unlike its parent, Springfontein, which emphasises SA-bred grapes, this 17-year-old scion's subjects are mostly cultivars from overseas, typically France, and yields from two of these in 2021 and 2022 were enough to allow for debut solo bottlings. Quality is the major goal here, says Mariska Kammies, who shares winemaking duties with a team that's proud and excited to be moving into an own home on the mother estate.

★★★★ **Sauvignon Blanc** ⓝⒺⓌ Extravagantly perfumed **21** ⑧⑥, with an almost frangipani character & intensity making it somewhat unusual. Flavours equally intense; the balance crisp & dry.

★★★★ **White** ⓥ Much improved **22** ⑧⑥ adds a little chardonnay to the semillon-sauvignon blend of last-made **20** ★★★☆ ⑦⑧, which was oaked, unlike this. At 35%, aromatic sauvignon noticeable, but more muted in previous. Lively & fresh, flavourful. At 12% alc, more convincing than previous.

Pinot Noir ⓥ ★★★ Nicely perfumed aromas on **20** ⑧① though the palate is more savoury than fruity. Rather lean, with dry tannins. Matured in old oak, as Red. WO Springfontein Rim. **Red** ⓥ ★★★★ Exuberantly fruity **17** ⑧③ is from pinotage, merlot & 3 others; characterful if not concentrated, with modest tannic grip. WO W Cape. **Chardonnay** ★★★☆ Quietly expressive aromas on **21** ⑧⑤, lime & stonefruit notes, but flavours more intense. Light (12% alc) but not insubstantial; balanced & lively. Old-oak fermented & matured. Indigenous yeast, as for all. **Semillon** ⓝⒺⓌ ★★★★ An unoaked version, **22** ⑧③ picked early (just 11% alc) to add a green freshness to the lanolin-tinged fruit. Dry, very light, unlingering. — TJ

Location: Stanford ▪ Map: Walker Bay & Bot River ▪ Map grid reference: B5 ▪ WO: Walker Bay/Springfontein Rim/Western Cape ▪ Est/1stB 2007 ▪ Ulumbaza Wine Bar(n): bistro & winetasting/sales 11am-9pm daily; pub hols (seasonal) please call ahead ▪ Klein River cruises & tasting onboard African Queen of Springfontein and the River Rat cruises ▪ Owner(s) Springfontein family, friends & employees ▪ Winemaker(s) Jeanne Vito with Mariska Kammies-Bantom et al ▪ 5,000cs own label 80% red 20% white ▪ PO Box 71 Stanford 7210 ▪ info@ capemoby.co.za ▪ www.capemoby.co.za ▪ **T +27 (0)28-341-0651**

Capensis ⓠ

Meaning 'From the Cape', this chardonnay-only boutique venture co-founded and now wholly owned by Barbara Banke, also owner of California's Jackson Family Wines, pays homage to the Western Cape, one of the world's oldest winemaking regions, and the diversity of its winegrowing potential. The home-farm is high-lying Fijnbosch, in Stellenbosch's Banhoek Valley, where visitors are welcomed by appointment at Kliphuis, an entertainment area built of material sourced on the property. South African Graham Weerts, winemaker since inception and previously in California, crafts individual wines of balance and complexity.

★★★★☆ **Capensis Chardonnay** Classically styled **20** ⑨② sees subtle yet effective interplay of yellow citrus flavours, oak spice, silky texture, lees influence & sustained freshness. Seamless, refined & elegant, with usual distinctive salty length. From several sites; barriques only & 11 months (as Fijnbosch), 38% new.

★★★★★ **Fijnbosch Chardonnay** ⓐ Biggest of these in power, breadth & structure, but perfectly proportioned to avoid heaviness. Oak (50% new) also important part of whole. Full expression of usual dried orange peel, lees-enriched complexity yet to emerge but **19** ⑨⑤ driven by intensity to resounding length. A grand future beckons.

★★★★☆ **Silene Chardonnay** ⓐ From Fijnbosch & 3 other Stellenbosch sites, impressive **21** ⑨③ bright & fresh; citrus, spice & toasty notes form lively, intricate aromas. Lemony flavours are ripe & juicy, lees adding a serious tone & deeper silky texture. On-point structure & balance portend long future. Supportive oak, 30% new, some foudre; 10% ceramic pot ferment textural extra.— AL

Location/map: Stellenbosch ▪ Map grid reference: H5 ▪ WO: Stellenbosch/Western Cape ▪ 1stB 2013 ▪ Private tastings by appt, contact Anzel Rheeder +27 (0)84-501-9472, anzel.rheeder@capensiswines. com ▪ Owner(s) Barbara Banke (owner of Jackson Family Wines USA) ▪ Winemaker(s) Graham Weerts ▪ Farm manager Cedrick Delport ▪ 2,000cs own label 100% white ▪ concierge@capensiswines.com ▪ www. capensiswines.com/za ▪ **T +27 (0)84-501-9472**

☐ **Cape of Good Hope** see Anthonij Rupert Wyne

Cape Point Vineyards ⓠ ⑪ ⓐ ⓑ ⓒ

Sauvignon blanc has been a cornerstone of the vineyard and wine portfolio since Sybrand van der Spuy founded Cape Point Vineyards, the first estate on the Cape Peninsula's southern tip, close to 30 years ago. Thus it's not surprising there's been much interest here in sauvignon gris, a pink-berried mutation. 2022 saw the first crop off young vines brought into the cellar by viticulturist Steffan Lochner and, while he's planting more rows, winemakers Anzette and Riandri Visser are preparing to release the first varietal bottling and blend. Sauvignon (blanc), the sisters note, in the right hands can reach 'incredible' heights, the key is 'to know the terroir well enough to unlock its possibilities'. Semillon, sauvignon's historical partner here as in Bordeaux, is not neglected, and its footprint is set to expand as part of a replanting project.

★★★★ **Cape Town Chardonnay** Not yet bottled, **22** ⑧⑨ mid-2023 gorgeously open lemon butter & warm toast aromas, intense, pure, bright & fresh flavours. Seasoned oak adds complexity. Last **20** ⑧⑨ saw 30% new wood. Durbanville vines.

★★★★☆ **Sauvignon Blanc Reserve** ⓐ Built for ageing, **22** ⑨④ gets full treatment: own grapes bunch-pressed, wild yeast fermented in older oak, 14 months on lees, giving creamy richness to tight, stony flavours, more blackcurrant-tinged than Noordhoek.

★★★★☆ **Noordhoek Sauvignon Blanc** ⊘ With usual touch semillon (as Reserve), previewed **23** ⑨② range of intense riper, less green flavours, kernel of sweet peachy fruit to its brightly succulent dryness. 15% barrel fermented, on lees 10 months for texture & breadth.

★★★★ **Sauvignon Blanc** ⊘ Unwooded version adds Elgin to Durbanville & home grapes for pre-bottled sample **23** ⑧⑦. Pungent lemon drop & herbaceous notes but ripe, a bright succulence & breadth from 14% semillon, 4 months on fine lees.

★★★★☆ **Isliedh** ⓐ Veteran benchmark for Cape Bordeaux white category with distinctive aromatic profile & finessed fruit. Own windswept vines, **22** ⑨④ adds dash sauvignon gris to sauvignon & semillon

(66/27), bunch pressed & spontaneously fermented/16 months in 25% new oak, adding savoury complexity without muting blackcurrant flavours. For ageing.

★★★★☆ **Elixirr** Sibling to flagship Isliedh, for co-owner Stephen Newton & named for consultancy he founded. Stunning **22** (94) debut, richly textured, deeply flavoured & beautifully balanced. Finishes with echoing length. Also has splash sauvignon gris joining sauvignon & semillon (72/24), bunch pressed & spontaneously fermented but only in old oak, 14 months on lees.

Occasional release: **Noble Late Harvest**. — DS

Location: Noordhoek ▪ Map: Cape Peninsula ▪ Map grid reference: B4 ▪ WO: Cape Town/Western Cape ▪ Est 1996 ▪ 1stB 2000 ▪ Tasting & sales Mon-Tue 12-4 Wed-Sun 12-6; pub hols (seasonal) please call ahead ▪ Fee R50-R80 ▪ Tasting room menu available during tasting hours ▪ Restaurant, lunch & dinner Wed-Sun 12-3 ▪ Picnics (weather permitted) 12-4 & outside courtyard Thu-Sun 12-6.30 pm ▪ Weddings & events ▪ Weekly Thu evening food markets ▪ Child friendly ▪ Conservation area ▪ Wine club ▪ Owner(s) Sybrand van der Spuy ▪ Winemaker(s) Riandri Visser (Jul 2014), with Anzette Visser (Feb 2021) ▪ Viticulturist(s) Steffan Lochner (May 2016) ▪ 22ha (sauv blanc/gris, sem) ▪ 25,000cs own label 100% white ▪ Brands for clients: Woolworths ▪ IPW, Farming for the Future ▪ PO Box 100 Noordhoek 7979 ▪ info@cape-point.com ▪ www.capepointvineyards.co.za ▪ **T +27 (0)21-789-0900**

☐ **Cape Portrait** *see* Durbanville Hills

Cape Rock Wines

Unlike most wineries in Olifants River, the critically acclaimed venture of Willie Brand and son Gavin is modest in scope: just 11 ha under vine and ±2,000 cases made annually. Still, co-winemaker and marketer Gavin reports that with 'many young vines coming online, we are focused on developing new wines and finding more international niche markets'. Other differentiators are the choice of rare varieties like counoise and vermentino to season the mostly blended wines, and the policy of working 'in the simplest, most unadulterated way', using, inter alia, neutral vessels for 'a true and honest product, reflecting a specific place'.

★★★★ **Grenache** Gentle, warm-hearted & aromatic **22** ★★★★ (85) has a svelte texture from old-oak ageing, some grip though not the freshness of **21** (86). An easy-drinking winter warmer, or lightly chilled summer refresher. Naturally fermented, as all.

★★★★☆ **Red** ⊘ A hedonistic but serious blend of mostly syrah (86%), drops mourvèdre & viognier, co-fermented before year older French barrels. **17** (94) spice, plum & pomegranate tones, more complex than last-tasted **14** ★★★★ (88).

★★★★ **Amnesty** Style & blend change in **21** ★★★★ (85) to equal mourvèdre & syrah, splash carignan. Sombre, savoury, with dark spice; dry, leaner tannins from part wholebunch ferment. Fuller bodied & still quite taut in youth; less balanced & deep than **20** (89).

★★★★ **Asylum** Succulent & waxy new blend in **22** ★★★★ (85) of grenache blanc (85%), aromatic splash viognier & zesty vermentino. Lighter (11.9% alc), accessible style, has a brush of oak, but less verve than **21** (89). WO W Cape, as for Amnesty.

Not tasted: **Carignan**, **White**. Occasional release: **Syrah**, **Rosé**. Discontinued: **Cabernet Sauvignon**. — MW

Location: Vredendal ▪ Map: Olifants River ▪ Map grid reference: B4 ▪ WO: Olifants River/Western Cape ▪ Est 2001 ▪ 1stB 2002 ▪ Tasting, sales & cellar tours by appt ▪ Closed Good Fri, Dec 25 & Jan 1 ▪ BYO picnic ▪ Owner(s) Willie Brand ▪ Cellarmaster(s) Willie Brand (Jan 2001) ▪ Winemaker(s) Willie Brand (Jan 2001) & Gavin Brand ▪ 13ha/11ha (cab, carignan, counoise, grenache, mourv, shiraz, chenin, cbard, marsanne, rouss, vermentino, viog) ▪ 40t/2,100cs own label 60% red 40% white ▪ PO Box 261 Vredendal 8160 ▪ caperockwines@gmail.com ▪ www.caperockwines.co.za ▪ **T +27 (0)27-213-2567**

☐ **Cape to Cairo** *see* Rogge Cloof

Cape Town Wine Co

In this more recent sibling venture to vaunted Cape Point Vineyards, owner Sybrand van der Spuy and family recall 18th-century forebear and Cape Town wine trader Meldt van der Spuy. The wine-making Visser sisters at CPV and their viticulturist colleague Steffan Lochner source and vinify grapes from vines in the wider Cape Town Wine of Origin district with the objective of producing 'wines of great quality at an affordable price'.

★★★★ **Sauvignon Blanc** ⊘ Fynbos note woven with citrus, stonefruit & hint of bubblegum on **23** ⑧⑥ ex tank. Tight & steely-dry grip leavened on lingering finish by 8% unoaked semillon & 4 months on lees. **Cabernet Sauvignon-Merlot-Cabernet Franc** ⓧ ★★★★ Cab's (56%) ample cassis is the lead-in to the **20** ⑧⑤ blend, vanilla from oak staves then takes centre stage. Has a decently firm structure yet is easy to drink. **Rosé** ★★★ 15% merlot gives a gentle fruitiness to lively sauvignon, now bottled & rerated **22** ⑦⑧ flavoursome & delectably dry. Discontinued: **Shiraz**, **Chardonnay**, **Méthode Cap Classique Pinot Noir**, **Méthode Cap Classique Brut**. — DS

Location/WO: Cape Town ▪ Map: Cape Peninsula ▪ Map grid reference: A4 ▪ Est/1stB 2017 ▪ Tasting & sales Mon-Tue 12-4 Wed-Sun 12-6; pub hols (seasonal) please call ahead ▪ Owner(s) Sybrand van der Spuy ▪ Winemaker(s) Riandri Visser (Jul 2014), with Anzette Visser (Feb 2021) ▪ Viticulturist(s) Steffan Lochner (May 2016) ▪ PO Box 100 Noordhoek 7979 ▪ marketing@capetownwine.com ▪ www.capetownwinecompany.com ▪ T +27 (0)21-789-0900

☐ **Cape Venture Wine Co** see Lubanzi Wines
☐ **Cape View** see Kaapzicht Wine Estate
☐ **Cape West** see Namaqua Wines

Cape Wine Company ⓠ

The portfolio of Paarl-based Erlank Erasmus includes multiple wine, spirit and non-alcoholic brands, the newest, named The Nature Reserve, being certified-organic wines and reflective of the winemaker-entrepreneur's goal of organic compliance across the board. Deadline pressures meant we weren't able to taste it or some of its sibling ranges, notably the long-established, fruit-forward, good-value Juno collection.

Erasmus Family range

★★★★ **Grenache Noir** Sampled ex barrel, where it spent a year, soft-textured **22** ⑧⑦ is generous & ripe, with subtle squeeze of tannin, liquorice & herb nuances. Reminiscent of last **20** ⑧⑧.

★★★★ **Shiraz** Previewed **22** ⑧⑨ eschews 15% petite sirah on last **19** ⑧⑧. Inky depth to succulent plum & black fruit. Structured & sturdy (15% alc) but fresh, a salty note on balanced long finish.

★★★★☆ **Reserve** Last a preview, **21** ⑨⓪ has settled & improved, shows ample succulent plum fruit, dry fine tannin from 14 months in third new oak. Seamless & elegant 4-way Rhône blend led by carignan.

Arabica range

Pinotage ★★★ Soft, juicy **21** ⑧② now bottled & showing appealing mocha overlay & light freshness, black & blue fruit still centre stage. Coastal WO.

Nieuwe Haarlem range

★★★★ **Chenin Blanc** Citrus vivacity on **22** ★★★★ ⑧⑤ counters a honeyed ripeness from 15% viognier. Lively, pleasant nectarine & peach notes, dry finish. Last-tasted **20** ⑧⑥ had dab roussanne.

Pinotage ★★★★ Supple, trim **22** ⑧⑤ pre-bottling sample is juicy, a light tannin nuance countering raspberry ebullience. Certified vegan, as Arabica. WO Paarl, like Chenin.

Juno range

Not tasted: **Grenache Noir**, **Merlot**, **Pinotage**, **Shiraz**, **Shiraz-Mourvèdre-Viognier**, **Rosé**, **Chenin Blanc**, **Sauvignon Blanc**.

The Merchant range

Occasional release: **Cabernet Sauvignon-Merlot**.

The Nature Reserve

Not tasted: **Organic Cabernet Sauvignon-Merlot**, **Organic Chenin Blanc-Chardonnay**. — FM

Location: Paarl ▪ WO: Swartland/Paarl/Coastal ▪ Est/1stB 2010 ▪ Tasting by appt only ▪ Online shop ▪ Owner(s)/winemaker(s) Erlank Erasmus ▪ 20,000cs own label 60% red 40% white ▪ BEE, Fairtrade, Organic, WIETA ▪ hello@capewinecompany.co.za ▪ www.capewinecompany.co.za ▪ T +27 (0)21-863-2450

Cape Wine Crafters ⓠ ⓜ ⓞ ⓐ

The wines featured here are grown and made by the Weltevrede Estate team, and the brand home - with its own tasting lounge - is sited on that estate in Bonnievale. Owner and cellarmaster Philip Jonker aims to offer something for everyone, and invites winelovers to 'come and find your favourite'.

smart **GasDetection** Technologies

GAS DETECTION SOLUTIONS FOR WINEMAKING

Contact us to discuss the ideal solutions for your business.

CO$_2$ alarm
Leave the room

M21

0-50 ppm SO$_2$

GMA400

GMA400   EC22   G888   G999

GfG (Pty.) Ltd.
7 Voortrekker Road | Mindalore North - Krugersdorp
P. O. Box 6004 | ZA-Westgate 1734
Phone: +27 11 955-4862
E-mail: info@gfg.co.za

GfGsafety.com

FEATURING
THE UNDERGROUND CELLAR

SITE OF
CONSERVATION SIGNIFICANCE

The CAVERN
EST. 1941
NORTHERN DRAKENSBERG - KZN

THE GREAT OUTDOORS

036 438 6270 | 083 701 5724
info@cavern.co.za | www.cavern.co.za

Simplicity Collection

Cherrychoc Merlot ★★ Mix of red & black cherry aromas on **22** ⑦⑥, palate adds chocolate, plum & fynbos, going savoury on finish. Misses previous' juiciness. **Cigarbox Shiraz** ★★★ Proffers black pepper, espresso, choc-dipped cherries in **21** ⑦⑨, the spicy-sweet fruit continues on palate, accessible & generous. **Turkish Delight Rosé** ★★ Now mix of gewürztraminer & muscat, giving **23** ⑦⑥ hallmark rosewater fragrance. Fruity & semi-sweet, good partner for spicy foods. Dash pinking shiraz. **Vanilla Chardonnay** ★★★ Abundant aromas of fresh lime on **22** ⑦⑧ party starter, heaped with signature vanilla from specially treated white American oak. **Lemon Zest Unwooded Chardonnay** ★★★ Piquant by name & nature: appealing **23** ⑦⑨ crisp lemon & lime with bright apple core. Good density for unwooded chardonnay. Not tasted: **Blueberry Cabernet Sauvignon**.

She range ⑭⑮

Chardonnay-Pinot Noir Rosé ☺ ★★★ Elegantly packaged to show off attractive hue. **23** ⑦⑧ softly dry with ample Pink Lady apple & strawberry flavour, energy & freshness. 77/22 combo joined by splash shiraz.

Collectibles range

Chardonnay ⑦ ★★★★ In established style, creamy **22** ⑧④ enchants with glacé pineapple & crème brûlée; rich yet balanced by vibrant limy acid. Offers pleasure & drinkability.

Cabernet Sauvignon ⑦ ★★★★ Toasty spice (allspice, aniseed, clove) on savoury **19** ⑧④. Plush, with berries & black cherries, supported by faint grip of tannin. **Shiraz** ★★★★ Gently chewy tannins buoy ripe red plums & pepper. 9 months in oak, 50% new, add extra spice & grip to **21** ⑧③.

Terroir Collection

Bedrock Black Syrah ⑦ ★★★★ From a single block on near-solid rock. **21** ★★★★ ⑧④ unfurls menthol, pepper, black tea & charcuterie, year oak, 80% new, contributes mocha to otherwise savoury styling, freshened by orange-toned acid. Last tasted was **18** ⑧⑥.

Heritage range

★★★★ **Ouma se Wyn** Redolent of ouma Lisbeth Jonker's sweets drawer, **20** ★★★★ ⑧④ fortified dessert crafted 'as in old days' from white muscadel. Citrus, honeysuckle & ginger allures, well judged at 199 sugar g/L & modest 15% alc. **18** ⑧⑧ was last tasted. 375 ml, as Oupa.

Oupa se Wyn ★★★★ 1926 red muscadel bushvines give **23** ⑧③ fortified dessert its pomegranate, apricot, allspice & sultana fragrances, hint bitter toffee balances 197 g/L sugar & gentle acid. 16% alc. — ML

Location: Bonnievale ▪ Map/WO: Robertson ▪ Map grid reference: D3 ▪ Est/1stB 2020 ▪ Tasting, sales & cellar tours Mon-Sat 8.30–5 ▪ Fee R50 ▪ Closed Good Fri, Dec 25/26 & Jan 1 ▪ Kapokbos restaurant ▪ Facilities for children ▪ Deli ▪ Walking/hiking trails ▪ Owner(s) Philip Jonker ▪ Cellarmaster(s)/winemaker(s) Philip Jonker (Jan 2020) ▪ 45% red 45% white 10% rosé ▪ WIETA ▪ info@capewinecrafters.com ▪ www.capewinecrafters.com ▪ **T +27 (0)23-616-2141**

Cap Maritime

It's cellarmaster Gottfried Mocke's style to let his wines do the talking (though on occasion he can make wine chemistry sound like a love story), and this small Burgundy-inspired collection in the Boekenhoutskloof portfolio speaks oh so eloquently of finesse, flair and stellar quality, with five stars this edition for the Upper Hemel-en-Aarde Chardonnay, repeating last year's rating for the Pinot Noir from the same ward. These 'grands vins' are from partner grapes till the home vines, also in Upper H-e-A, come on-stream. The pair of newcomers, as well as Gottfried's Cape Winemakers Guild wines, are from further afield.

Cap Maritime range

★★★★☆ **Pinot Noir** ⊘ ⑧ Pedigreed **22** ⑨③ confidently reflects Upper H-e-A's signature mineral acidity, threading through piquant sour cherry & raspberry fruit, fine-grained grape tannins. Approachable & delicious, has dense core & supportive oak, 14 months, 60% new, for good few years cellaring. 40% wholebunch. Follows standout **21** ★★★★★ ⑨⑥.

★★★★ **Coastal Pinot Noir** ⑭⑮ ⊘ For earlier enjoyment, still with serious intent & typicity. **22** ⑧⑧ fermented in concrete, 25% wholebunch, year older oak. Earth & herb accents, pliable but present tannins reining in smooth & succulent red cherry fruit. WO Cape South Coast, as Coastal Chardonnay.

★★★★☆ **Chardonnay** ⓐ Taut, dry **22 ★★★★★** ⑨⑤ marches to a different drum, its beauty derived not from perfection but unwavering reflection of terroir. Like **21** ⑨④, emphatically unfruity, with paired-back green citrus & preserved lemon, just a whisper of spice from natural ferment/14 months in foudre & 70% new barrique.

★★★★☆ **Coastal Chardonnay** ⓝⓔⓦ ⊘ Racy, courtesy feisty 6.1 g/L acid & 30% unoaked portion, yet **22** ⑨⓪ far from lean: abundant yellow & lime citrus with umami overlay, weight & light vanilla & cardamom spicing from ferment/year in barrique, 20% new.— CvZ

Location: Hermanus ▪ WO: Upper Hemel-en-Aarde Valley/Cape South Coast ▪ Est/1stB 2017 ▪ Closed to public ▪ Owner(s) Boekenhoutskloof Winery (Pty) Ltd ▪ Cellarmaster(s) Gottfried Mocke ▪ Winemaker(s) Gottfried Mocke & Eben Meiring (Jan 2017) ▪ Viticulturist(s) Petrus Bothma, with consultant Rosa Kruger ▪ 36ha ▪ 3,000cs own label 30% red 70% white ▪ BRC, BSCI, IPW, WIETA ▪ PO Box 433 Franschhoek 7690 ▪ info@capmaritime.co.za ▪ www.capmaritime.co.za ▪ **T +27 (0)21-876-3320**

☐ **Captured Reflections** *see* Kindred Coast

Caravel Wines

These once-off limited releases are like a mixtape of wine, art and design, says Cape Town brand owner Kyle Martin. Small batches, occasionally blends, are chosen for flavour, personality and interest, and packaged such that each of the six bottles in a carton carries a different label on a theme, unique to the release.

Golden Phoenix vs The White Lotus ⓝⓔⓦ ★★★★ Some maturity adds interest to **NV** ⑧⑤ sauvignon & oaked semillon; ripe, waxy richness lifted by brisk acidity for balanced, ready enjoyment. — AL

Location: Cape Town ▪ WO: Durbanville ▪ Closed to public ▪ Winemaker(s) various ▪ info@cabo-esp.com ▪ **T +27 (0)72-449-6070**

Carinus Family Vineyards

Danie Carinus and his distantly related namesake, Hugo, are based respectively on Stellenbosch's Polkadraai Hills and in Swartland, farming animals and growing crops other than grapes, selling much of the latter to some high-profile producers. They chose chenin and syrah for their own label 'to show the specific terroir and not a particular wine style. The wines are so different yet alike in their honesty'. They believe their respective areas are presently SA's most exciting, with the two varieties playing a key role in the exhilaration. The wines are made by two of those high-flying producers: Chris Alheit of Alheit Vineyards handling the Polkadraai Hills chenin, and Lukas van Loggerenberg of the eponymous brand the rest.

★★★★☆ **Polkadraai Syrah** ⊘ ⓐ Has an established reputation, confirmed in **22** ⑨④ after lesser **21 ★★★★** ⑧⑨. Fine floral, white spice, freshness & echoing length speak of elevated growing conditions. Delicious now with substance & structure for cellaring. 35% stems added to ferment; older oak, 10 months.

★★★★☆ **Chenin Blanc** From Swartland farm Rooidraai, **22 ★★★★** ⑧⑧ toned down on generous, energetic **21** ⑨①; quiet dried peach, warm earth aromas, palate's juicy freshness bringing them to life for pleasurable early drinking. Older oak, 30% tank ferment, 10 months.

★★★★★ **Polkadraai Heuwels Chenin Blanc** ⓐ Complete contrast to Swartland version. **22 ★★★★★** ⑨⑤ cool-climate Polkadraai Hills has exhilarating intensity to its steely core & reverberating dry finish. A little grip adds to structure, allowing for ripe red apple flavours to fully emerge over time. Wholebunch press, 75% concrete 'egg', rest year older oak, like **21** ⑨③.

★★★★☆ **Rooidraai Chenin Blanc** ⓐ More personality & reflective of Swartland sunshine than sibling, **22** ⑨④ from dryland bushvines has plenty of bounce & depth in its juicy, ripe peach flavours. These are freshened & intensified by lively fruity acidity, leaving a long memory. Older oak, 10 months.— AL

Location: Stellenbosch ▪ WO: Stellenbosch/Swartland ▪ Est 2016 (cellar) ▪ 1stB 2011 ▪ Closed to public ▪ Owner(s) Hugo Carinus & Danie Carinus ▪ Winemaker(s) Lukas van Loggerenberg (Dec 2015) & Chris Alheit (2018, Polkadraai chenin) ▪ Viticulturist(s) Danie & Hugo Carinus ▪ 25t/1,650cs own label ▪ Fransmanskraal Farm, Devon Valley, Stellenbosch 7600 ▪ danie@carinusvineyards.co.za, hugo@carinusvineyards.co.za ▪ www.carinusvineyards.co.za ▪ **T +27 (0)72-249-3599**

☐ **Carpe Diem** *see* Diemersfontein Wines

Carstens Wines

Director of winemaking at top-flight Leeuwenkuil, Pieter Carstens for this small private project achieves his sought-after 'complexity, with many layers of fruit, maturation character and weight' with Leeuwenkuil grapes and a solera-like system, where the components are aged separately, then pass an evaluation before being blended. The resulting non-vintage releases therefore always contain a fraction of the oldest wine, and are multi-variety assemblies of varying proportions.

★★★★ **V4 Red** ⓒ Changing blend, still shiraz-led but latest **NV** ⑧⑨ partnered with cab, cinsaut & grenache from 4 vintages. Older foudre, 12 months, more fruit than last, plums & berries, a woodsmoke top note. Tannins perceptible, a dry finish, but ripe, no hindrance to current enjoyment.

★★★★★ **V4 White** ⓒ Now chenin-led with sauvignon & chardonnay, 4-vintage blend. Wholebunch, foudre ferment/ageing 10 months for a preserved citrus character, ending mineral, savoury. Everything working harmoniously; well-crafted & original **NV** ⑨⓪.

Discontinued: **Shiraz.** — CR

Location: Paarl ▪ WO: Swartland ▪ Est 2015 ▪ 1stB 2020 ▪ Closed to public ▪ Owner(s) Pieter Carstens ▪ Winemaker(s) Pieter Carstens (Jan 2015) ▪ 500cs own label 60% red 40% white ▪ pieter@leeuwenkuilfv. co.za ▪ **T +27 (0)84-510-1265**

☐ **Casa da Baleia** *see* Baleia Wines
☐ **Casa Simelia** *see* Simelia Wines
☐ **Cathedral Cellar** *see* KWV Wines

Catherine Marshall Wines ⓒ

Cathy Marshall makes these acclaimed boutique wines in rented space at Lavinia Farm in Polkadraai outside Stellenbosch from hand-picked vineyards in cool climates. Her distinguished career includes early stints at Ken Forrester and Ridgeback, and several harvests abroad before co-founding this venture (formerly Barefoot Wine Company) and bottling the first vintage 27 years ago. She also had a close association with and mentorship role in the garagiste movement. Son and surfer Jonathan Oxenham joined the team in 2011 and since 2017 looks after day-to-day winemaking operations. For many years the sourcing of grapes has centred on Elgin, though other areas supply special parcels as needed.

Fine Art Collection

★★★★★ **Grenache** ⓐ Pale garnet hue belies concentration & body in **22** ⑨③, gushing with crushed berry fruit on a silken tannin carpet, laced with fragrant floral wafts. Wholeberry, wild yeast ferment of Swartland grapes, 10 months in older oak.

★★★★★ **Pinot Noir Finite Elements** ⓐ Exemplifies Elgin's elegance & nuance. Svelte & poised, with rosepetals on ripe raspberry fruit, lingering perfume & earthiness. **19** ⑨④ tiny 2-barrel production: new 300L & seasoned 225L, spontaneous ferment/10 months aged.

★★★★★ **Peter's Vision** ⓒ Most robust wine in range, **17** ⑨② from 60% merlot, cab franc. Forward aromas & sweet fruit on substantial palate, which should meld harmoniously with a few years in bottle.

★★★★★ **Chenin Blanc Fermented In Clay** ⓐ Precise, succulent rendering of 85% Elgin fruit, wild yeast fermented in stoneware amphoras, balance ex Stellenbosch, made in small barrels, **22** ⑨④ follows lofty form of **21** ★★★★★ ⑨⑤, with layer upon layer of tropical & stonefruit flavour, beautifully cosseted in rich lees texture. Wholesome, generous & delicious.

Catherine Marshall range

★★★★★ **Pinot Noir On Clay Soils** ⓥ ⓐ An exercise in soil effects, granitic clay delivering savoury, earthy notes with hint of truffle, woven into delicate flower-scented cherry & raspberry fruit. **21** ⑨④ has firm, ripe tannins, lithe, well-rounded body. WO Cape South Coast, as Sandstone.

★★★★★ **Pinot Noir On Sandstone Soils** ⓥ More fragrantly floral than sibling, **21** ⑨② offers violet-toned red berry compote on delicate, silky tannins. Sleek & elegant, lingering. Like Clay, polished by 10 months in older barrels.

★★★★★ **Riesling** ⓥ One of SA's best. Concentrated citrus fruit, vivid acid & aromatic presence make **22** ⑨① exceptional. Pure, refined & linear, heightened by perfectly balanced 8 g/L sugar. 12% alc.

★★★★☆ **Sauvignon Blanc** ⊘ Confident, forthright **22** ⑨⓪ expresses cool-climate vibrancy in its herbaceous aromatics, lifted passionfruit, tingly acid. Palate fleshed out by extended lees contact. **21** untasted.

Amatra range

★★★★ **The Oreads** ⊘ Reinvented as merlot & cab franc blend, **21** ⑧⑦ solid, well-proportioned & satisfying, offering upfront blackcurrant fruit, appealing earthy & leafy notes, touch of spice from 10 months in older barrels. **20** ⑧⑨ was 100% merlot; both WO Stellenbosch, as is Jono.

★★★★ **Jono's Wave Chenin Blanc** Delectably showing region's typical yellow stonefruit, barrel-fermented **22** ⑧⑧ is rich, buttery, with light vanilla & lees weight. 10 months in mostly older barrels & a clay amphora. WO Stellenbosch.— GdB

Location/map: Stellenbosch ▪ Map grid reference: B6 ▪ WO: Elgin/Cape South Coast/Stellenbosch/Swartland/Western Cape ▪ 1stB 1997 ▪ Tasting, sales & cellar tours Mon-Fri 10-4 ▪ Closed Easter Fri-Sun, Dec 25 & Jan 1 ▪ Owner(s) / directors Catherine Marshall, Greg Mitchell, Alphan Njeru ▪ Cellarmaster(s) Catherine Marshall (Oct 1996) ▪ Winemaker(s) Jonathan Oxenham (2017) ▪ Viticulturist(s) various ▪ 9st own label 43% red 57% white ▪ IPW ▪ PO Box 13404 Mowbray 7705 ▪ cathy@cmwines.co.za ▪ www.cmwines.co.za ▪ **T +27 (0)83-258-1307**

Cavalli Wine & Stud Farm

Manicured paddocks and a colt-statued entrance on the R44 between Stellenbosch and Somerset West beckon visitors to the equine-themed wine and lifestyle estate owned by the Smith family. Such numbers accept the invitation that the tasting terrace, with vistas of lawns, fynbos gardens and mountains, is being extended. An array of other diversions is offered, along with wine, now crafted by vaunted Rianie Strydom.

Premium Collection

★★★★ **Cabernet Sauvignon** Inky & powerful **20** ★★★★☆ ⑨① strides confidently ahead of **19** ⑧⑧. Firm core of oak, 30% new, lends backbone but is well-knit with dark fruit after 2 years. Supple & refined, with good restraint & spicy allure.

★★★★☆ **Warlord** Evolution of 3-way Bordeaux blend continues in **21** ⑨①. Cab's dominance reduced from 63% to 50% with petit verdot & malbec nearly equal. Spicy fruitcake flavours, elegance & silky texture remain, while oaking held steady at 18 months, slightly reduced 35% new.

★★★★☆ **Reserve Chardonnay** Complex construction, including 3 harvest dates & batch ferments in barrel, 25% new. Result is rich, creamy, polished **22** ⑨⓪, with spicy citrus notes. More complex, elegant than last-tasted **18** (listed without 'Reserve' in name, as Chenin). Maturation, with bâtonnage, down to 10 months from 18.

★★★★ **Reserve Chenin Blanc** Improves on last in brightness & tang yet retains creamy breadth from barrel ferment/6 months. **22** ⑧⑨ balanced & long, with stonefruit verve matched by dry, spicy finish.

★★★★☆ **Cremello** 4-way chenin-led **22** ⑨② improves on **21** ⑨⓪ in structure, body & vitality. Supportive oak (26% new, 6 months) just one component in intricate gestation: bunch pressing, separate ferments, partial malo. Long, dry, complex & rewarding.

★★★★ **Capriole Méthode Cap Classique** New disgorgement of **20** ⑧⑧ balanced, rich all-chardonnay bubbly offers fine bead, lime verve & brightness. 27 months on lees add creamy breadth to a long toasty finish, as on **19** ★★★★ ⑧⑤.

Lifestyle Collection

Shiraz ★★★★ Smoky blueberry & cherry appeal & freshness to **22** ⑧⑤. Dry & unfussy, subtle oak influence from older barrels & staves. Ideal barbecue companion. **Unoaked Chenin Blanc** ★★★★ Crunchy, bright & juicy **23** ⑧④ is undemanding & easy to enjoy, with nectarine & apricot attractions. — FM

Location/WO: Stellenbosch ▪ Map: Helderberg ▪ Map grid reference: C1 ▪ Est/1stB 2008 ▪ Wine tasting & sales Wed-Sun 10-6 ▪ Closed Dec 26 & Jan 1 ▪ Cavalli Restaurant lunch & dinner Wed-Sat 10-10pm Sun 10-6 ▪ Picnics in summer ▪ Sport & music memorabilia ▪ Art gallery ▪ Fashion boutique ▪ Conferences ▪ Banqueting facility (350 seater) ▪ Conservation area ▪ Equestrian centre: stable tours & out-rides by appt ▪ Wine club ▪ Owner(s) Smith family ▪ Winemaker(s) Rianie Strydom (Aug 2023), with Eric Frieslaar (Oct 2020) ▪ Viticulturist(s) Rianie Strydom (Aug 2023) ▪ 110ha/27ha (cab, malbec, p verdot, shiraz, chard, chenin, verdelho, viog) ▪ 140t/6,500cs own label 45% red 55% white ▪ IPW, WIETA, WWF-SA Conservation Champion ▪ PO Box 102 Somerset West 7129 ▪ orders@cavalliestate.com, winemaker@cavalliestate.com ▪ www.cavalliestate.com ▪ **T +27 (0)21-855-3218**

☐ **CCM** *see* Tulbagh Winery

Cecilia Wines ⓠ

Trained concert pianist and winemaker Cerina van Niekerk's boutique brand has a strong familial element: Cecilia is a family name (and that of the patron of musicians), and a recent household relocation sees her working from new facilities in Breedekloof. The key source vineyards for the terroir range, mostly heritage certified and dryland, and her minimalist approach are unchanged. Newer Wind Band is an affordable range for everyday, the labels representing sound waves 'to add to the atmosphere of any meal'.

Cecilia range

★★★★☆ **Pinotage** ⓐ ⓦ Elegant & accomplished **21** ⑨⓪ from bushvines (a West Coast rarity) on Citrusdal Mountain, mostly wholeberry, wild yeast fermented, lending spice & texture to succulent black berry & currant fruit. Concentrated yet sleek from 15 months in barrel, all older, as both ranges unless noted.

★★★★☆ **Syrah** ⊘ Ex cask, where it spent year, **22** ⑨⓪ taut & youthful but showing promise as sumptuous black cherry fruit emerges from oak mantle, tannins present but already smooth, refined. Darling bushvines, as last **20** ⑨⓪.

★★★★☆ **Chenin Blanc** ⓦ Gnarled Piekenierskloof vines impress in **23** ⑨⓪ preview with silky, lees-rich texture, focused acid & dense fruit - dried apricot & pineapple, hint honeyed caramel. Ferment completed in large barrel, 6 months on lees. No **22**.

Wind Band range

★★★★ **Rococo Red** ⊘ As elegant & appealing as namesake musical genre, gentle **21** ⑧⑥ shiraz & dab grenache noir has a lovely light feel to its fine, ripe red berry fruit, tannins buffed by part oaking.

Wah-Wah White ⊘ ★★★★ Fresh, healthy tropical fruit prevails in unoaked **23** ⑧⑤ chenin, tasted ex tank. Cheerful citrus acid, easy lees texture. Not tasted: **Pastiche Rosé**. — GdB

Location: Rawsonville ▪ Map: Breedekloof ▪ Map grid reference: C6 ▪ WO: Western Cape/Citrusdal Mountain/Darling/Piekenierskloof ▪ Est 2010 ▪ 1stB 2013 ▪ Tasting & sales by appt ▪ Owner(s) Cerina van Niekerk ▪ Cellarmaster(s)/winemaker(s) Cerina van Niekerk (2010) ▪ 3,000cs own label 70% red 30% white & rosé ▪ info@ceciliawines.co.za ▪ www.ceciliawines.co.za ▪ **T +27 (0)82-334-9422**

Cederberg Private Cellar ⓠ ⓐ ⓐ

Five generations of Nieuwoudts have farmed this remote, idyllic tract, 250 km north of Cape Town and over 1,000 m above sea level in the Cederberg mountain range, providing a unique viticultural mesoclimate. The area attracts nature and mountaineering tourists, not least for the rugged terrain, floral kingdom reserve, stunning trails and charming guest accommodation at the Sanddrif Resort. In pursuit of other cool climates, incumbent owner, cellarmaster and CWG member David Nieuwoudt has established a parallel operation at Elim near the southern tip of Africa, where grapes for the Ghost Corner brand are grown, and partnered with friends in the Walker Bay-sourced Escape label launched this edition. He also produces the Driehoek range for the Du Toit family neighbours (see listings).

Five Generations range

★★★★★ **Cabernet Sauvignon** ⓐ Massive, concentrated, statement wine, **21** ★★★★★ ⑨⑤ intense cassis with truffle & iodine accents. Despite boldness, muscularity, shows nuance & refinement in delicate rose perfume, delightful forest floor earthiness, suede tannins. Like **20** ⑨③, 18 months mostly new oak.

★★★★★ **Chenin Blanc** ⓐ Ripe, luscious & indulgent, **22** ⑨⑤ retains fine focus & balance, with layered stone & citrus fruit complexity, rich, creamy texture & vivid acid. Slow, wild yeast barrel ferment/10 months mostly seasoned oak round out palate without intruding. Delicious now & for several years.

David Nieuwoudt Ghost Corner range

★★★★☆ **Pinot Noir** ⊘ Slick, elegant **22** ⑨② has delicious crushed raspberry fruit, exotic perfume & earthy truffle notes, all neatly rounded & polished. Velvet tannins lend structure to generously full body. 10 months in barriques, 20% new. WO Elim, as all these. **21** untasted.

★★★★☆ **Syrah** ⓝⓔⓦ ⓐ Cool-climate **20** ⑨④ has impressive extract & weight, shows tobacco-spiced aromas & smoked meat, elegantly scented with sweet fynbos. Plush, rounded, with satin tannins after 15 months in seasoned oak.

★★★★★ **Wild Ferment Sauvignon Blanc** ⊛ Very special fumé-style flagship sauvignon, **22** ⑨⑤ barrel fermented/10 months in oak, 13% new, yet character is all dusty-mineral, lime & lees. Impressive concentration of passionfruit, wild herb aromatics, pitch-perfect acid seam.

★★★★☆ **Sauvignon Blanc** ⊛ Attention-grabbing **23** ⑨③ has distinctive oystershell-seaweed min-erality, great depth & layered fruit & herbs. Grapefruit & lemon marmalade confection marries elegantly with leesy lime-accented juiciness. No winemaking tricks, just exceptional fruit.

★★★★☆ **Semillon** Still taut & introverted, **22** ⑨② shows promise of last-made **19** ⑨④, already develop-ing beeswax & lanolin character, with textured body. 30% portion slow-fermented in oak, 30% new, adds heft & sleekness. Will reward time in bottle.

★★★★☆ **The Bowline** ⊛ Refined, elegant Cape Bordeaux white, **22** ⑨④ delivers customary lipsmack-ing fruit, linearity & wholesome body. 67% sauvignon tank fermented, 33% semillon wild-yeast barrel fermented, both on lees 10 months.

Old Ways range ⓃⒺⓌ

★★★★☆ **Sauvignon Gris** Unique mutation, vinestock from ancient Chilean strains, **22** ⑨⓪ has little in common with blanc cousin. Plump & rounded, with well-moderated acid, subtler aromatics, gaining lees weight & texture from wild yeast ferment & 5 months older oak.

Cederberg Private Cellar range

★★★★☆ **Cabernet Sauvignon** Ripe, robust & structured **21** ⑨② has precise focus & varietal definition. Mineral-earth platform, refined tannins, ethereal choc-mint & rosepetal nuances to core of blackcurrant fruit. 15 months in 40% new oak.

★★★★☆ **Shiraz** ⊘ Aromatic **20** ⑨② is an elegant, accomplished creation showing ripe, supple tannins, generous yet accessible weight, precise lingering finish. Best tucked away in the cellar.

★★★★ **Merlot-Shiraz** ⊘ Merlot leads in **21** ⑧⑥ with earthy leanness, blackcurrant & cherry fruit, firm but ripe tannins. Year in seasoned barrels adds shape & polish. **20** ⑧⑦ was near-equal blend.

★★★★ **Bukettraube** ⊘ Increasingly rare variety. Semi-sweet **23** ⑧⑥ is perfect for spicy fare. Aromatic notes on bright citrus & apricot fruit, held in balance by 7.8 g/L acid. Notch above **22** ★★★★ ⑧④.

★★★★ **Chenin Blanc** ⊘ With heightened pyrazines from reductive handling, tangy, herbaceous **23** ⑧⑥ follows familiar form. Crisp, bright & fresh, showing gooseberry & passionfruit, a fine food match.

★★★★ **Sauvignon Blanc** Racy, vibrant & satisfying, **23** ⑧⑧ gooseberry & lime spiced with heady, wild aromas of flint, nettle & lemon-grass. Full & generous, with lees contact adding palate weight.

★★★★☆ **Blanc de Blancs Brut** Svelte & sophisticated chardonnay cap classique, **19** ⑨⓪ spent 37 months on the lees, reflected in rich baked bread yeastiness, fine, vigorous bubble. Extra-dry, with delectable apple strudel notes, salty minerality on finish.

Sustainable Rosé ⊘ ★★★★ Pert & pretty tinsel-pink **23** ⑧⑤ shiraz is pure summery refreshment, with tangy raspberry fruit, leesy fullness & fine-tuned acid. — GdB

Location: Citrusdal ▪ Map: Olifants River ▪ Map grid reference: D7 ▪ WO: Cederberg/Elim/Western Cape ▪ Est 1973 ▪ 1stB 1977 ▪ Tasting Mon-Sat/pub hols 9-4.30 ▪ Fee R100 (R50 Five Generations) ▪ Closed Good Fri & Dec 25 ▪ Sales Mon-Sat 8-5; Sun/pub hols 9-12 & 4-6 ▪ Sanddrif Holiday Resort self-catering cottages; camping ▪ Walks/hikes ▪ MTB ▪ Conservation area ▪ Rock climbing ▪ Sport climbing ▪ Observatory ▪ Craft beer brewery ▪ Wine club ▪ Owner(s) Nieuwoudt family ▪ Cellarmaster(s) David Nieuwoudt (Jan 1997) ▪ Winemaker(s) Jean Nel, Thinus Botha & Gwen Marais, with Jerome van Rooi ▪ Viticulturist(s) Dirk de Bruyn ▪ 5,500ha/74ha (cab, shiraz, bukettraube, chenin, sauv) ▪ 900t/90,000cs own label 40% red 60% white ▪ WWF-SA Conservation Champion ▪ PO Box 84 Clanwilliam 8135 ▪ info@cederbergwine.com ▪ www. cederbergwine.com ▪ **T +27 (0)27-482-2827**

Celestina

Top Cape Town wine merchant Caroline Rillema and husband Ray established their small Celestina vineyard at Baardskeerdersbos on the cool South Coast in 2004. Recently they realised another dream - an own cellar beside the rows of sauvignon and semillon. Lack of cooling equipment meant the first 'proper crush' in the new facility had to wait a year. Now, with an amphora and barrel also added, all is set to 'harness the gorgeous aroma and flavour from the grapes grown in our tiny mesoclimate just 8 km from the ocean'.

★★★★☆ **Sauvignon Blanc-Semillon** Reverts to customary 50:50 blend in **22** ⑨, as usual nicely & effectively expressing the blackcurrant notes of cool-climate sauvignon & citrus & waxy ones of semillon. With a green, limy core, it's vibrant & silky. Old-oak matured; 13.5% alc makes it a touch richer than last. In abeyance: **Semillon**. — TJ

Location: Baardskeerdersbos ▪ WO: Cape Agulhas ▪ Est 2004 ▪ 1stB 2009 ▪ Closed to public ▪ Owner(s) Caroline Rillema ▪ Winemaker(s) Dirk Human (Black Oystercatcher) ▪ Viticulturist(s) Caroline & Ray Kilian ▪ 3.4ha/1.85ha (sauv, sem) ▪ 6t/600cs own label 100% white ▪ c/o Caroline's Fine Wine Cellar, Forest Glade House, Tokai Rd, Tokai, Cape Town 7945 ▪ carowine2@mweb.co.za ▪ www.carolineswine.com ▪ **T +27 (0)21-712-2258**

☐ **Cellar Door** *see* Namaqua Wines

Chameleon

Previously listed under the banner of its owner, Jordan, this flavourful, affordable and easy-drinking range celebrates the native Cape dwarf chameleon, which makes the estate's vineyard its home. Worldwide sales provide funds to study and conserve the endearing little animal, classified as near-threatened.

★★★★ **Cabernet Sauvignon-Merlot** ⊘ Characterful **21** ⑧⑥ steps up on **20** ★★★★ ⑧⑤ with ripe blackcurrant fruit, crunchy acid & silk texture. Dab shiraz adds verve & spice to near-equal blend, rounded 16 months in mostly older French oak.

. . . .

Chenin Blanc ⊘ ⑦ ★★★☆ Crisp, clean **23** ⑧⑤'s unwooded freshness frames melange of cheery apple, pineapple & guava, making for delicious al fresco enjoyment.

. . . .

No Added Sulphur Merlot ⊘ ★★★★ Plums & prunes with light smoky char from 10 months on staves, two-thirds American, softly gripping tannins & fresh herbal finish on **22** ⑧③. To drink soon. **Syrah** ⊘ ★★★★ Plush, plummy **22** ⑧⑤ has hints of dark chocolate, cinnamon & pepper, velvet-soft tannins after year old oak for easy-drinking pleasure. **Sauvignon Blanc** (NEW) ⊘ ★★★★ Burst of flavour on welcome addition to range: sherbet lemon, white blossom & hint of lime. **23** ⑧④ bright acid padded with some richness from 6 months on lees. Not tasted: **Sauvignon Blanc-Chardonnay**. Discontinued: **Rosé**. — CM

Chamonix Wine Farm   ⑦ ⑪ ⑭ ◎

This Franschhoek estate, originally part of La Cotte, granted to Huguenot refugees in 1688, lies on mountain slopes overlooking the town, benefiting from less vigorous soils and cooler temperatures than obtain in the valley below. It was bought a few years back by a Norwegian real estate mogul, Ivar Tollefsen, with great ambitions for Chamonix. These focus initially on vineyards and wines. Large swathes of vines have been uprooted, and new plantings are well advanced; the cellar, to be enlarged, has received new equipment. Replanting with virus-free material means that from vintage 2023 most of the wines will, for a while, be made from grapes sourced elsewhere, but primarily Franschhoek, by winemaker-viticulturist Neil Bruwer, to be vinified in the elegant style well exemplified by the cap classique, returned to the range after many years.

Reserve range

★★★★☆ **Cabernet Franc** ⊛ Usual dry leaf, berry & tobacco fragrance on **21** ⑨④. Ripely sweet fruit supported by modest oaking (18 months, 10% new) & balanced structure, with rounded tannins, leading to a lingering finish. Altogether a feeling of restraint, even elegance. 14.2% alc.

★★★★☆ **Pinot Noir** Cherry fruit but more savoury aromas on **21** ★★★★ ⑧⑨. There is some intensity of flavour, but with a lean element to any richness - it's less generous than **20** ⑨② & less ripe at just 12.5% alc. 30% wholebunch ferment; 16 months in oak, half new.

★★★★☆ **Troika** ⊛ Cab franc-led blend, with cab plus merlot & petit verdot in **21** ⑨④. Unshowy but persuasive, giving sweet, ripe fruit, with an edge of franc's herbal note supporting the pleasing element of noble austerity that complements the succulent fruit & cushioned tannins. Well balanced; 14% alc, 30% new oak. Still youthful, deserving time in bottle.

★★★★☆ **Chardonnay** ⊛ **21** ⑨④ offers richer, more forthcoming aromas than standard version, with tropical notes added to the citrus. The 40% new oak for 75% of the grapes is spicy but well integrated; 25% was in concrete 'egg' for freshness & purity. Lingering full fruit, but the impression of elegance remains, thanks to the fine line of acidity. Beneficially less sweet than previous.

★★★★☆ **Old Vine Steen** ⊛ Subtle dried peach notes on **22** ⑨⑨ chenin, with some pithy citrus on the palate. Balanced & ripe, with a core of sweet fruit. Some stony grip partly from the firm acidity (there's a touch of apple sourness), reinforced by the 30% portion in concrete 'egg', remainder in older oak.

★★★★☆ **Estate White** ⊛ **21** ⑨③ reverts to majority sauvignon (52%), contributing floral & black-currant notes, with wax & lanolin - & a lemony edge on the palate - from semillon. Restrained refinement should gain a little more flesh as the wine matures. 75% oaked (Austrian barrels; 25% new), remainder in concrete 'egg'. 13.5% alc.

Chamonix range

★★★★ **Feldspar Pinot Noir** As with Reserve version, **21** ★★★★ ⑧⑤ rather lighter & leaner than **20** ⑧⑦; 12.5% alc. Light-feeling, with red fruit & a herbal note; quite firmly tannined. Not a lot of charm, but pleasingly fresh. 10% new oak well absorbed.

★★★★☆ **Greywacke Pinotage** ⊘ For a different take on the grape, complex winemaking includes a component of partly dried grapes added after 14 days for a 2nd fermentation. Characterful **20** ⑨② has lightly perfumed aromas leading to a balanced, generous yet restrained palate - velvety, but less voluptuous than 14.5% alc suggests. The tight dry tannins should melt & meld in time. No **19**.

★★★★☆ **Chardonnay** Oak (20% new barrels) brings spicy complexity to **21** ⑨⓪ without diminishing or outweighing the citrusy fruit contribution. Fresh, lightly rich & with the house elegance - an impressive 2nd-level wine but less concentrated & lingering than the Reserve. 13.5% alc part of the good balance.

★★★★ **Chardonnay Unoaked** From a mix of Franschhoek & Stellenbosch grapes, **23** ⑧⑥ offers lovely pure aroma & full-fruited flavour. Softly textured but with succulent acidity for a lively grip. Even more appealing than fully home-grown **22** ★★★★ ⑧⑤.

★★★★ **Sauvignon Blanc 23** ⑧⑥ tasted pre-bottling & too unfinished to rate, but fruit intensity & bright balance seem likely to push it to its established level. No oaked element, unlike previous.

★★★★ **MCC Blanc de Blancs** Characterful aromas include apple & brioche on **21** ★★★★★ ⑨⓪ from mostly-oaked chardonnay. 18 months before disgorgement adding interest. Crisply bone-dry, but any austerity is very satisfying, given the great balance with stonefruit flavours & a savoury, stony tug. The first made since **06**.

Rouge ⊘ ★★★★☆ Cheerfully packaged blend in **21** ⑧④ led by cab, with merlot, petit verdot & malbec. Ripe fruitcake & lightly cedary aromas & flavours. Not without seriousness, including a decent tannic grip, but made for early fruity readiness. **Pinot Noir Rosé** ★★★★☆ Delightful salmon-coloured **23** ⑧⑤ from Stellenbosch grapes. Refined, bone-dry & well-balanced pleasure, with subtle fruitiness. — TJ

Location/map: Franschhoek ▪ Map grid reference: C1 ▪ WO: Franschhoek/Stellenbosch/Stellenbosch-Franschhoek ▪ Est 1991 ▪ 1stB 1992 ▪ Tasting & sales Mon-Sun 8.30-5 ▪ Selection of tasting options from R60-R170 ▪ Closed Dec 25 & Jan 1 ▪ Cellar tours by appt ▪ Arkeste restaurant ▪ Conservation area ▪ Marco Polo Lodge, Waterfall Lodge, Forest Suites & fully equipped self-catering cottages ▪ Winemaker(s)/viticulturist(s) Neil Bruwer (Jun 2019) ▪ 234ha/45ha (cabs s/f, merlot, p verdot, pinot, chard, chenin, sauv, sem) ▪ 220t/20,000cs own label 50% red 50% white ▪ IPW ▪ PO Box 28 Franschhoek 7690 ▪ bernard@chamonix. co.za, winemaker@chamonix.co.za ▪ www.chamonix.co.za ▪ **T +27 (0)21-876-8400**

Chantelle ⓠ

On boutique Franschhoek property La Ferme Chantelle, British owners Robert and Michele Bowman revived a small 19th-century cellar and parcel of chardonnay to create their beloved blanc de blancs style of bubbles with the aid of a consultant. Latterly focused on enhancing soil health, using earthworm compost among other strategies, they've seen 'a drastic change' for the better in fine-root growth and general plant health.

★★★★ **Méthode Cap Classique Blanc de Blancs Brut Reserve** Showing pleasing evolution, retasted **15** ★★★★★ ⑨⓪ sparkler has classic brioche & umami undertone from 5 years on lees. Bracing lemon freshness balanced by subtle breadth from small oaked portion. Raises the bar on **14** ⑧⑥. — DS

Location/map/WO: Franschhoek ▪ Map grid reference: C2 ▪ Est 2005 ▪ 1stB 2008 ▪ Tasting, sales & cellar tours by appt only ▪ Owner(s) Chantelle Collection Ltd (shareholders Robert & Michele Bowman) ▪ Winemaker(s) Michael van Niekerk (Mar 2017) ▪ 0.5ha (chard) ▪ 6t/700cs own label 100% white ▪ PO Box 53001 Kenilworth 7745 ▪ rjeb@plot20.com ▪ www.chantelle-winery.co.za ▪ **T +27 (0)73-145-0046**

☐ **Chapel** *see* Robertson Winery

Charla Haasbroek Wines

As winemaker for the Sijnn boutique venture near Malgas on the Cape South Coast for the past decade, Charla Bosman (née Haasbroek) has had access to that estate's unique and varied fruit and, since 2016, crafted tiny parcels of acclaimed wine for her own account. She aims to translate what's grown in the vineyards into bottle while staying true to the vintage, using natural processes and least interference without compromising quality. A '23 chardonnay and semillon from other lesser-known wards will debut next time.

★★★★☆ **Grenache Noir-Carignan** With its convincing blackcurrant & plum fruit on silky tannins, **22** ⑨④ ably expresses both varieties, in a surprisingly dense & concentrated body. Partly bunch-fermented with wild yeast, year in seasoned barrels, unfined/filtered, it typifies the sensitive & artisanal winemaking here.

★★★★☆ **Chenin Blanc** ⑧ Near-austere minerality defines elegant, poised **22** ★★★★★ ⑨⑤, underlying satisfyingly pure apple & stonefruit, vivid acid. Single 400L older barrel, wild yeast ferment & extended lees contact, no fining/filtration all contribute to authenticity & precise varietal expression. Follows exceptional **21** ⑨④.

Occasional release: **Cabernet Sauvignon, Trincadeira, Syrah-Grenache, Viognier**. — GdB

Location/WO: Malgas ▪ Est/1stB 2016 ▪ Closed to public ▪ Winemaker(s) Charla Bosman (née Haasbroek, Sijnn) ▪ Lemoentuin Farm, 342 Malgas ▪ charlahaasbroek@gmail.com ▪ **T +27 (0)82-782-5875**

Charles Fox Cap Classique Wines

Just one of Charles and Zelda Fox's portfolio of exceptional boutique bubblies was ready for us to taste this edition, regrettably, but it's business as usual on the hilly Elgin property the couple bought in the mid-2000s after exhaustive research and developed, with a focus on 'uncompromising quality', into one of South Africa's top specialist cap classique estates. Under Charles' direction, more meunier and pinot noir 115 clone will be planted, and the cellar extended, enabling the panoramic outside patio, a visitor favourite, to be enlarged.

★★★★☆ **Reserve Brut** ⊘ Golden colour & red appleskin perfume from pinot & meunier (41/35), chardonnay adding cooked apple & limy acidity. Quietly elegant **NV** ⑨⓪ shows gentle bubbles & good length, fresh biscuit & almond notes thanks to 40 months on lees.

Not tasted: **Prestige Cuvée Cipher Blanc de Noir, Prestige Cuvée Blanc de Blancs, Reserve Rose, Reserve Gold, Vintage Brut Rosé, Vintage Brut**. Occasional release: **Prestige Cuvée Coeur de Cuvée**. — CM

Location/map/WO: Elgin ▪ Map grid reference: C3 ▪ Est 2007 ▪ 1stB 2010 ▪ Tasting, sales & cellar tours Mon-Fri 10-5 pub hols 10-4 ▪ Fee applicable ▪ Closed Dec 25 & Jan 1 ▪ Play area for children ▪ Owner(s) Charles & Zelda Fox ▪ Cellarmaster(s) Charles Fox (2010) ▪ Viticulturist(s) Kevin Watt (2008, consultant) ▪ 33.4ha/9ha (pinots noir/meunier, chard) ▪ 6,000cs own label 100% MCC ▪ PO Box 105 Elgin 7180 ▪ charlesfoxmcc@gmail.com ▪ www.charlesfox.co.za ▪ **T +27 (0)82-569-2965/+27 (0)82-471-3444**

Chateau Libertas

Launched in 1932 and since produced near-continuously, Heineken Beverages' 'Chateau Lib' is a local icon, still styled for affordable ready drinking with potential for cellaring.

Chateau Libertas ⊘ ★★★ Stalwart of many a braai, continues to please crowds in **22** ⑧① with easy-drinking black fruit, juicy palate & smoky oak. Mainly cab with others. Also in 2L. WO W Cape. — CM

Chennells Wines

Overlooked by Helderberg Mountain, owners Jeremy and Colleen Chennells, with sons Matt and Jack, strive to farm responsibly and holistically, and are intimately involved in the crafting of their single-block wines.

★★★★ **The Journey** Cabernet with 45% shiraz, of which portion underwent carbonic maceration, giving red fruit of **20** ⑧⑥ an attractive lift, enhanced by careful oaking, 30% new, 18 months. Step up on last-tasted **17** ★★★★ ⑧④.

Saudade ★★★★ Naturally fermented (as all) **20** ⑧⑤ cabernet is better balanced & fresher-feeling than last, cool-toned cassis fruit wrapped in gentle tannin & oak, 30% new, 19 months. **A Handful of Summers** ★★★ Soft, supple viognier, 10 months in oak, 33% new, adding smooth coat of vanilla to litchi, pear & peach fruit of **21** ⑧②. Not tasted: **Cabernet Sauvignon, Shiraz, Viognier**. — ML

Location/WO: Stellenbosch ▪ Map: Helderberg ▪ Map grid reference: C2 ▪ Est 2004 ▪ 1stB 2008 ▪ Tasting, sales & cellar tours Mon-Sun 9-5 by appt ▪ Closed all pub hols ▪ Owner(s) Jeremy & Colleen Chennells ▪ Cellarmaster(s)/winemaker(s) Jeremy Chennells & Chris Keet (Jul 2009, consultant) ▪ Viticulturist(s) Francois Hanekom, Chris Keet & Colleen Chennells ▪ 5ha/3.2ha (cab, shiraz, viog) ▪ 42t/500cs own label 85% red 15% white ▪ Cordoba Winery Rd, Helderberg, Somerset West 7130 ▪ chennell@iafrica.com ▪ www.chennellswines.com ▪ T +27 (0)21-855-3905/+27 (0)82-555-2829

☐ **Chip Off The Old Block** *see* Ormonde Wines
☐ **Chocoholic** *see* Darling Cellars
☐ **Chris Keet** *see* Keet Wines
☐ **Christiena** *see* Van Loveren Family Vineyards
☐ **Christine-Marié** *see* Niel Joubert Estate
☐ **Chrysalis** *see* Lourensford Wine Estate
☐ **Cilliers Cellars** *see* Stellendrift - SHZ Cilliers/Kuün Wyne

---

Cilmor Winery ⓠ

An early 20th-century vegetable and poultry farmer, Cecil Morgan, has a special significance at this substantial Fairtrade-certified winery in the Worcester area, as it was the urban development by the Cilmor Trust of his Kuils River farms that made the winegrowing endeavours here possible. Up to 12 million litres of bulk wine can be produced from 23 varieties in surrounding vineyards, but more emphasis is being placed on the packaged ranges, cellarmaster Quintin van der Westhuizen says, with a shift to bottling premium wines only.

Winemaker's Selection

★★★★ **Cape Red** ⓠ Sumptuous Cape Blend from pinotage & shiraz (60/20), 2 others, juicy notes of plum, toast, chocolate & fynbos in 21 ⑧⑦. Balanced oak allows the fruit to shine.

★★★★ **Sauvignon Blanc** ⓠ Abundant tropical flavours on 21 ⑧⑨ in perfect harmony with a creamy structure from lees contact, seasoned by vanilla. Well-structured & -balanced to the last lemony drop.

★★★★ **Cape White** ⓠ Citrus, stonefruit & peach blossom are layered with creamy oak for complexity & rounded mouthfeel in 21 ⑧⑧. Harmonious combo of 60% chenin with splashes sauvignon, semillon, chardonnay & viognier, 50% oaked with mixed-origin staves.

★★★★☆ **Sauvignon Blanc-Semillon** ⓠ Remarkable balance in 75/25 Bordeaux-style blend. 21 ⑨③ immediate appeal of herbal blackcurrant, gooseberry & nectarine supported by creamy vanilla spice. Finely weighed, with long, crisp mineral finish. Half in French, American & Hungarian barrels.

Limited Edition range

Shiraz-Pinotage-Malbec ⓠ ★★★★ Energetic 21 ⑧⑤ shows red berries, plums, touch of leather & dried herbs, earthy hint on the finish. Well constructed & food friendly. **Chenin Blanc** ⓠ ★★★★ Flavourful 21 ⑧⑤ is packed with orchard fruit, ripe apple & white blossom, combines richness with texture & a clean zippy farewell. 100% oak-staving brings harmony. **Sauvignon Blanc** ⓠ ★★★☆ Good varietal expression, from green herby to ripe tropical flavours. 21 ⑧⑤ has palate weight from staving & lees contact.

Premium Collection

Pinotage ⓠ ★★★ Easygoing juicy & fruity 21 ⑧①, dark plums over cappuccino, a gluggable braai bro. Lightly oaked, as next 2. **Shiraz** ⓠ ★★★ Mulberry & earthy spice lead the way in 21 ⑧② to a savoury liquorice finish. Smooth & approachable. **Chardonnay** ⓠ ★★★ Ripe apple flavour on zesty & dry 20 ⑧⓪, delightful honeyed fruit on the finish. **Chenin Blanc** ⓠ ★★★★ Unoaked 21 ⑧③ offers bright tropical flavours, silk texture from lees ageing, slips down easily. **Sauvignon Blanc** ⓠ ★★★ Gets a round texture in 21 ⑧② from lees stirring yet remains crisp & zingy-fresh, appealing lime squeeze at the end. — WB

Location/map/WO: Worcester ▪ Map grid reference: B4 ▪ Est 1997 ▪ 1stB 2015 ▪ Tasting & sales Mon-Fri 9-4.30 Sat/Sun by appt ▪ Fee R50 ▪ Closed all pub hols ▪ Owner(s) Cilmor Trust ▪ Cellarmaster(s)/winemaker(s) Quintin van der Westhuizen (Dec 2012) ▪ Viticulturist(s) Rudi du Toit (July 2008) ▪ ±2,000ha/377.2ha (cab, cinsaut, malbec, merlot, p verdot, ptage, roobernet, shiraz, chard, chenin, cbard, hanepoot, nouvelle, pinot gris, sauv, sem, viog) ▪ 9,300t/±8,000cs own label 40% red 60% white ▪ Fairtrade, FSSC 22000, IPW, WIETA ▪ PO Box 479 Worcester 6850 ▪ info@cilmorwines.com ▪ www.cilmorwines.com ▪ T +27 (0)23-340-4141

☐ **Cinsault Collective** *see* Natte Valleij Wines

☐ **Circle of Life** *see* Waterkloof
☐ **Circumstance** *see* Waterkloof

Cirrus Wines

A respected Jean Engelbrecht brand, latterly showcasing own vineyards on cool-climate farm Rietfontein high on the Ceres Plateau. The stellar wine featured here is the first of an envisaged series, made by Duran Cornhill at Guardian Peak in Stellenbosch, and available for tasting and sale there.

★★★★☆ **Pinot Noir** ⊘ ⊛ Delightfully fresh bouquet, a cherry-berry confection from 70/30 wholeberry/bunch ferment, **22** ⑨④ gains gravitas with classic flavours of earth, wet leaves & cumin spice, tied together with soft, charry oak & crisp acid. Step up on **21** ⑨③, New World pinot at its best. 14 months in seasoned 500L barrels.— CM

Location: Stellenbosch ▪ WO: Ceres Plateau ▪ Est 2002 ▪ 1stB 2003 ▪ Tasting & sales at Guardian Peak Wines ▪ Owner(s) Jean Engelbrecht ▪ Winemaker(s) Duran Cornhill (Dec 2021) ▪ 14.6t/1,200cs own label 100% red ▪ IPW ▪ PO Box 473 Stellenbosch 7599 ▪ info@cirruswines.com ▪ www.cirruswines.com ▪ **T +27 (0)21-881-3881**

City on a Hill Wine Company

Critically acclaimed low-intervention boutique vintner André Bruyns' portfolio has undergone 'a serious re-think and -structure', specifically around a critical assessment of the quality of the fruit he works with and, based on eight years of Swartland experience, the varieties that 'I honestly think to be the best for the region, given increasingly dry and challenging circumstances'. A factor playing into his deliberations was his decision to take care of the 43 ha of vines on the Johannes family's Lammershoek property, which in turn prompted a scaling back of volumes of his beautifully crafted wines to around 10,000 bottles.

★★★★ **Song of Ascents** ⒩ Minimalist winemaking for all. Reds naturally fermented, varying portions wholebunch, basket pressed, year older barrels. **22** ⑧⑥ single Malmesbury parcel (as Hills) of cinsaut on weathered granite, delicate strawberry & raspberry fruit, subtle tug of tannin (50% wholebunch), lengthy dry finish. On trend, & ready to be enjoyed now & few years.

★★★★ **Thousand Hills** ⒩ Grenache noir planted 2000 on ferricrete, 100% wholebunch, youngest of all the vines. **22** ⑧⑦ serious expression but quiet, subtly fruited. Incredibly slender at just 1.5 g/L sugar & so well-balanced, 14% alc drinks like 13.

★★★★ **Sk'windjiesvlei** ⒩ Tinta barocca, made dry like many Douro examples (±2 g/L sugar) but **22** ⑧⑨ lighter (hue & alc), restrained, (older-) oaked only for fruit support. Just 15% wholebunch confidently done. 61 year old vines on clay-rich granite. Paardeberg site, as Earth & Sky.

★★★★★ **Exodus** ⒩ Near-equal grenache noir & syrah with ±12% each cinsaut, carignan & tinta in jewel-like, floral- & fynbos-scented **22** ⑨⓪. Unlike varietal siblings, expressive hedgerow fruit, ample flavour & house's signature dryness, lowish alc, present but not obvious grip.

★★★★★ **Earth** ⒩ ⊛ Stellar expression of oldest of the chenin blocks, mix of granite, sandstone & quartz, aptly named **22** ⑨⑧ dusty terracotta nuance to quince & white peach fruit. Beautifully dry, with satisfying quince tart/bitter accent, seamless length. Like white siblings, simple wholebunch press, natural ferment/10 months older barrels.

★★★★☆ **Old Vine Chenin blanc** ⒩ ⊛ Blend of fruit from vines planted 1968-1981. **22** ⑨④ leads the chenin trio in richness & extroversion. Peach & apricot - fresh, dried & stewed - on nose & layered on palate, satin's weight & texture.

★★★★☆ **Sky** ⒩ Chenin on granite is ethereal, barest whiff of white flowers & fynbos, exquisitely balanced acidity & salty minerality. **22** ⑨② study in understatement & purity.

Discontinued: **Syrah, Tinta das Baroccas, Red, Chenin Blanc, Muscat d'Alexandrie, White.** — CvZ

Location: Malmesbury ▪ Map/WO: Swartland ▪ Map grid reference: C8 ▪ Est/1stB 2015 ▪ Tasting Mon-Fri by appt only ▪ Owner(s) André Bruyns ▪ Winemaker(s) André Bruyns (2015) ▪ 1,500cs own label 55% red 45% white ▪ andre@cityonahillwine.co.za ▪ www.cityonahillwine.co.za ▪ **T +27 (0)84-252-5500**

☐ **CL** *see* Oldenburg Vineyards

Clairvaux Cellar Ⓟ 🍴 ♿

Wouter de Wet owns the cellar on Robertson town's main road and multiple farms on various soil types in the area, providing manager/winemaker Jaco van der Merwe with the building blocks for his 'clean and fruit-driven' wines, smidgens of which are bottled. Replacement of unproductive chardonnay, chenin and sauvignon, among others, reflects the team's positive outlook on agriculture 'despite all the challenges'.

★★★★ **Hanepoot** ⊘ Was 'Good Night Irene'. Fortified muscat d'Alexandrie, grape & sultana richness, mouthfilling sweetness, but **23** ⑧⑦ is neither unctuous nor simple, has a delicious extended finish. In the same class as the other fortified wines; has an edge on last-tasted **21** ★★★★ ⑧④.

★★★★ **Red Muscadel** ⊘ The muscadels & hanepoot all have 200+ g/L sugar but are so well made, with such depth of flavour, they're remarkably drinkable. **23** ⑧⑧ pale red, raisiny, full bodied & mouthcoatingly rich, a lovely fresh tang at the end.

★★★★ **White Muscadel** ⊘ Was 'Madonna's Kisses'. Fortified & full-sweet, with raisin & sultana flavours, not over the top, **23** ⑧⑦ aided by fresh notes on the finish. Powerful, concentrated, very long finish.

Cabernet Sauvignon ⊘ ★★★★ Just French oak, no American this time, 18 months, ex-barrel **22** ⑧③'s spicing more savoury than last, white pepper, shows more cab authenticity, plums & berries, supple tannin. **Shiraz** ★★★ Ripe & generous, previewed **22** ⑧② in same mode as previous, smoky notes from oak, but in harmony with plummy fruit. Nice freshness at the end. **Sauvignon Blanc** ★★★ Greengage & kiwi, **23** ⑧②'s green notes a good example of the variety. Zesty acid makes it spark with life. **Cape Vintage** ⊘ ★★★ 'Port' from shiraz, 30 months in older barrels. Fruitcake richness, sweet **21** ⑧① pre-bottling sample is well spiced, without grippy tannins, drinks smoothly. Discontinued: **Straw Wine**. — CR

Location/map/WO: Robertson ▪ Map grid reference: B6 ▪ Est/1stB 2000 ▪ Tasting & sales Mon-Fri 9-5 ▪ Closed all pub hols ▪ Cellar tours by appt ▪ BYO picnic ▪ Sales (at cellar price) also from La Verne Wine Boutique T +27 (0)23-626-4314 Mon-Fri 9-5.30 Sat 9-3 ▪ Owner(s) Wouter J de Wet ▪ Winemaker(s) / manager Jaco van der Merwe (Oct 2011) ▪ 300ha (cab, merlot, ptage, shiraz, chard, chenin, cbard, hanepoot, muscadel, sauv) ▪ 6,000t/4.5m L bulk ▪ PO Box 179 Robertson 6705 ▪ info@clairvauxcellar.co.za ▪ www.clairvauxcellar.co.za ▪ **T +27 (0)23-626-3842**

☐ **Clear Streams** see Friesland Wines

Cloof Wine Estate Ⓟ 📷 🍷 ♿

WWF-SA Conservation Champion status speaks of the emphasis on sustainability and preservation at this extensive company-owned farm in Darling, with both an expanse of set-aside land and eco/game drives on the menu of visitor amenities. The vineyard, cared for by Duckitts Peter and Charles, and the output, in the hands of Hennie Huskisson, are large in scope, too, with 460 ha under vine and 100,000 own-label cases made, plus bottlings for private clients. The Winemakers and Duckitt ranges are terroir wines, showing 'the true character of the unique berries in the Darling area', while Signature responds to 'market-related trends'.

The Winemakers Selection

★★★★ **Cloof Pinotage** Best barrels from estate's top block, as all these reds. Previewed **22** ⑧⑥ bright berries & black cherries, year in oak, 20% new, 4% American, adds just the right amount of grip to silky smoothness. Last tasted was **18** ⑧⑥.

★★★★ **Cloof Syrah** Satisfying **22** ⑧⑨ barrel sample's cool plum & cherry fruit finessed by year in oak, 20% new, tightening the seams of the satin tannins. Nicely dry, too.

★★★★ **Cloof Lynchpin** Ⓖ Addition of cab (19%) to usual cab franc (51%) & merlot blend raised **19** ⑧⑧ a notch above last **14** ★★★★ ⑧③. Polish & poise, with violet perfume, defined structure & ripe fruit.

Discontinued: **Cloof Chenin Blanc**.

Duckitt Reserve range 🆕

★★★★ **Cabernet Sauvignon** ⊘ Cassis & forest berry flavours & scents on fragrant, fresh **19** ⑧⑧. Smart ageing - combo 25% tank & year older oak - aids drinkability, but enough concentration & structure for good few years.

★★★★ **Pinotage** Deep crimson **22** ⑧⑥ vibrant mix of red & black berries, fine-grained oak tannins from year in barrique, 20% new. Perfect with roast pork belly.

★★★★ **Syrah** Cured meat, cherry liqueur & woody spice on **22** ⑧⑨ pre-bottling sample. Gentle balance between freshness & dryness; year oak, 20% new, enhances smokiness & gives form to fruity tannins.

The Signature range
★★★★ The Very Sexy Shiraz Ⓥ Gorgeous plum colour on **20** ㊻, fragranced with black pepper & violets. Good density of fruit & layered silky tannins. Year in small oak. Fantastic value.

Inkspot ⊘ ㊧ **★★★★** Imaginative 5-way blend again led by pinotage & including drop viognier in **22** ㊻ delivers plum, brambleberry & tangy cranberry flavours, freshness aided by 15% tank ageing. Silk texture & generous fruit improve on last.

The Dark Side Ⓥ **★★★★** Satisfyingly savoury & spicy **19** ㊸, with its juicy ripe red fruit & hint of grip, is the perfect braai companion. Cab & dab shiraz, 50% tank matured.

The Duckitt Collection
Sauvignon Blanc ☺ **★★★** Zippy, tropical **23** ㊵ tank sample the perfect lunchtime companion, with modest 12.5% alc enhancing the light, carefree tone.

Merlot ★★★ Sweet plum & mocha fragrance echoed in the flavours on step-up **22** ㊿'s velvet body. 50/50 combo barrel & tank, as the other reds here. **Pinotage** ⊘ **★★★★** Freshness intended & achieved with unoaked portion, **22** ㊺ uses 10% fruity shiraz to add plumpness & berry generosity. Also in 1.5L.
Cabernet Sauvignon-Merlot-Cabernet Franc ★★★ Just a 2% dash cab franc, enough to lend a herbal perfume to **21** ㊿. Dark fruit & touch of sweet vanilla oak. Not tasted: **Cabernet Sauvignon Reserve**. Discontinued: **Chardonnay**, **Chenin Blanc**.

Iconic range
Not tasted: **Crucible Shiraz**.
Discontinued: **The Bush Vines range**, **Darling Wine In A Can range**. — ML

Location/WO: Darling ▪ Map: Durbanville, Philadelphia & Darling ▪ Map grid reference: B3 ▪ Est/1stB 1998 ▪ Cellar tours & tastings by appt ▪ Wine sales during office hours ▪ Conservation area ▪ Game & eco drives by appt ▪ Child friendly ▪ Owner(s) Cloof Wine Estate (Pty) Ltd ▪ Winemaker(s) Hennie Huskisson (Sep 2017) ▪ Viticulturist(s) Peter Duckitt (May 2004), with Charles Duckitt (2021) ▪ 4,100ha/461ha (cabs s/f, merlot, ptage, shiraz, chard, chenin, viog) ▪ 700t/100,000cs own label 88% red 12% white ▪ WWF-SA Conservation Champion ▪ PO Box 269 Darling 7345 ▪ info@cloof.co.za ▪ www.cloof.co.za ▪ **T +27 (0)22-492-2839**

☐ **Closilo** see Mont Blois Wynlandgoed

Clos Malverne Ⓥ ㊙ 🏠 📷 🅰 ♿
Proudly Stellenbosch's smallest cellar when it launched commercially over 35 years ago, the Pritchard family's venture has grown substantially and acquired a slew of visitor enticements. Now responsible for the day to day running is Suzanne Coetzee, involved here for many years, latterly as head of sales. She's clearly pleased that a solar array puts an end to outages, and that the new owners of the restaurant have made it child-friendlier. The plan is to trim and focus the wine range, while retaining the Cape Blend as the flagship.

Reserve range
★★★★ Pinotage Ⓥ Appealing strawberry & candyfloss on nose & palate of **20** ㊻, fair structure aided by year in French barrique but near 15% alc slightly warming. Misses dash & verve of last-made **17** ㊻, which saw 20% American oak.

★★★★☆ Auret Ⓥ The flagship, a Cape Blend, mostly cab in **20 ★★★★** ㊻, splash merlot, 30% pinotage adding strawberry & tar to bouquet. Palate's mulberry & plum sweetness countered by bright acidity, subtly supported by year in 10% new barrels, but overall not as well-structured or persistent as last **18** ㊼.

Cabernet Sauvignon Ⓥ **★★★★** Subtle cassis & graphite introduction to **18** ㊺, juicy berry palate enlivened by variety's lively tannins. Light veneer of oak, just 10% new. **Ellie Cap Classique Shiraz Rosé ★★★★** From single block on coldest site, pale copper **19** ㊺ 36 months on lees, like **18** ㊺, variety shows in wild strawberry scents & flavours, gentle tannin finish. Nicely done, not just about exuberant fruit.

Clos Malverne range
Merlot ★★★★ Back to darker fruit, **20** ㊸ spicy, with cocoa note. Palate provides a fresh underpin, extending the length. **Le Café Pinotage ★★★★** In popular 'mocha' style, **21** ㊸ spent 9 months in older French/American barrels (vs 20% new for **20** ㊸), giving full-ripe berry fruit the requisite coffee flavouring.
Cabernet Sauvignon-Merlot Ⓥ **★★★** Commendably dry **19** ㊿ has spearmint, earth & clean leather

whiffs to its ripe berry fruit. Balanced & ready to drink. **Cabernet Sauvignon-Shiraz** ⓥ ★★★ Opulent styling for richly fruited **16** ⑧⑴, well spiced, designed for enjoyment. Nice defining grip on the finish. **Chardonnay** ⓥ ★★★ Back after two-vintage hiatus. **21** ⑧⑴ attractive peach & Golden Delicious apple scents & tastes, light oak dusting from 9 months in older barriques. WO W Cape, as Honeydew. **Sauvignon Blanc** ★★★ Going the extra mile, **22** ⑧⓪ had skin contact before pressing & 6 months on post-ferment lees giving palate weight. Reductive winemaking ensured asparagus & capsicum fruit intensity. **Sauvignon Blanc Brut** ★★★ Crunchy green apples, a herbaceous nuance, lively-bubbled **NV** ⑧⓪ makes a tasty aperitif. **Honeydew** ★★★ Rare riesling Natural Sweet. Latest **NV** ⑧⓪ showing expressive stonefruit, apricot & peach, sweetness fitting the character. Soft, rounded palate, bit lacking in freshness.

Devonet range

Shiraz ⓥ ★★★ Leather, white pepper & black fruit tick the typicity boxes, tannins are gritty & rustic but in a good way, making **19** ⑧② easy to like. **Merlot-Pinotage** ⓥ ★★★ Ripe black plums, prunes & a definite mocha chocolate overtone to **17** ⑧⑴, smooth & round for current drinking. **Dry Rosé** ⓥ ★★☆ Pale pink **20** ⑦⑧ shows crushed strawberries, ends dry & fresh. **Sauvignon Blanc** ⓥ ★★★ With green apple & chopped herbs, fresh & vibrant **20** ⑧② wakens the taste buds. — CR

Location/map: Stellenbosch • Map grid reference: D4 • WO: Stellenbosch/Western Cape • Est/1stB 1986 • Tasting & sales Mon-Fri 10-4.30 Sat/Sun 10-1 pub hols 10-5 • Fee R135 for ice cream & wine pairing, R75/4 wines or R100/6 wines (premier tasting) • Closed Dec 25 & Jan 1 • Cellar tours Mon-Fri (booking essential) • The Restaurant @ Clos Malverne • Tour groups • Weddings/functions • Wellness day spa • Accommodation: 9 x 4-star rooms & 1 self-catering unit • Wine club • Facilities for children • Owner(s) Seymour & Sophia Pritchard • Cellarmaster(s) IP Smit (Jul 1997) • Winemaker(s) Mynhardt Hitchcock • 7ha (merlot, ptage, shiraz, sauv) • 150t/10,000cs own label 60% red 40% white • PO Box 187 Stellenbosch 7599 • info@ closmalverne.co.za • www.closmalverne.co.za • **T** +27 (0)21-865-2022

☐ **Cloud Haven** see Elgin Vintners

Clouds Wine Estate   ⓥ ⑪ ⑯

At their Stellenbosch luxury boutique hotel, acquired in the early 2010s, Dutch nationals Paul Burema and Jolanda van Haperen have placed a strong emphasis on the wine from the on-site vines, so much so, Paul latterly has been hands-on in the crafting, working alongside top-ranked winemaker and mentor Donovan Rall in a recently completed boutique cellar. The promised blanc de noir has arrived and, like all the wines in their eye-catching, orange-accented packaging, it's intended to 'delight its drinker with every sip'.

★★★★☆ **Pinot Noir** ⓐ Picked at different ripeness levels to capture spectrum of aromas & flavours, from strawberry to earth & truffle. **22** ⑨③'s 50% wholebunch ferment & combo vat & small-barrel ageing deftly done, so tannins & oak are only the lightest brush.

★★★★ **Shiraz** Cornucopia floral & berry aromas on bunch-fermented Swartland grapes. **21** ⑧⑥'s ripe mulberry & blueberry palate given savoury appeal by hints olive & salt, fruit tannins complemented by 10 months in older foudre.

★★★★ **Field Blend** 'Bordeaux Blend' renamed to reflect interplanted Banhoek vineyard. **21** ⑧⑨ cab, merlot (53/33%) & petit verdot, red & black cherries, soft & juicy, smoothness enhanced by 18 months oaking, gentle 10% new.

★★★★☆ **Chardonnay Reserve** Bunch press, spontaneous ferment in vat & concrete 'egg', 10 months in same vessels magnify **22** ⑨⑴'s steely freshness. Gunflint & greengage aromatic detail, creamy citrus & smidgen sweetness up attraction.

★★★★ **Chardonnay Unwooded** Unfettered by oak, **22** ⑧⑦'s lime character present on nose & palate, also in the limy tang of the acid. Mix tank & concrete 'egg', 6 months on lees for savoury-salty edge. No **21**.

★★★★ **Chenin Blanc** Notably dry & light **22** ⑧⑥ emphasises texture & grip in its grapefruit pith & lemon preserve notes. Clever vinification & ageing in combo amphora & concrete 'egg' heighten the lipsmacking austerity. WO W Cape, as Sauvignon.

★★★★ **Sauvignon Blanc** Zippy **22** ⑧⑥ offers punchy grapefruit & orange zest flavours. Fruit-forward, thanks to stainless tank ferment & ageing, touch salty lees from regular stirring.

★★★★ **Méthode Cap Classique** Elegant & satisfying sparkling aperitif from chardonnay. **21** ⑧⑨ bright apple & lime, biscuit nuance from 21 months on the lees, creamy yet bone-dry, persistent finish.

Blanc de Noir ★★★☆ Was 'Pink Sauvignon Blanc-Syrah', now co-fermented shiraz (70%), carignan & grenache. 6 months lees-ageing give heft to otherwise light-textured, tangy & red-berried dry **22** (84). — ML

Location/map: Stellenbosch ▪ Map grid reference: H5 ▪ WO: Stellenbosch/Western Cape/Swartland ▪ Est/1stB 1993 ▪ Tasting, sales & cellar tours by appt ▪ Breakfast, lunch & dinner - booking essential ▪ Hotel & villas ▪ Owner(s) Paul Burema & Jolanda van Haperen ▪ Cellarmaster(s) Donovan Rall (Jan 2014, Vuurberg) ▪ Winemaker(s) Donovan Rall (Jan 2014, Vuurberg), with Paul Burema (Jan 2012) ▪ 4.5ha/2.7ha (cab, carignan, grenache, merlot, p verdot, pinot, shiraz, chard) ▪ 24t/2,500cs own label 50% red 50% white ▪ PO Box 540 Stellenbosch 7599 ▪ info@cloudsestate.co.za ▪ www.cloudsestate.co.za ▪ **T +27 (0)21-885-1819**

☐ **Cluster Series** see Laarman Wines
☐ **Cocoa Hill** see Dornier Wines
☐ **Cold Mountain** see Brunia Wines
☐ **Collection** see Roos Family Vineyards

Colmant Cap Classique & Champagne

From the first boutique bottling in 2006, Belgian Jean-Philippe Colmant was uncompromising about quality and time on lees at his specialist sparkling-wine house in Franschhoek. The intervening years have seen the addition of portions of both wooded and reserve wines, as well as grapes from Robertson, Elgin, Hemel-en-Aarde and Bonnievale. All play a role in increasing consistency and reputation. Cellar chief Paul Gerber, a maths teacher in a previous life, knows the impact of small fractions on the greater whole. With consultant Pieter Ferreira, the fizz obsessives are steadfast in their pursuit of the perfect bubble, be it in zero-dosage or increasingly popular sweetish 'nectar' style, always non-vintage because of the reserve portion.

★★★★☆ **Brut Rosé** Pale blush intro to vivid, crunchy citrus & apple flavours on **NV** (91) from 75% pinot noir with chardonnay. Crisp & tangy but also toasty, resolved, after 24 months on lees.

★★★★☆ **Absolu Zero Dosage** (84) Vivacious, taut, bone-dry & complex **NV** (94) from chardonnay. Composed & cohesive, intricately crafted from oaked reserve wine (15%) & 85 months under crown cap. Zippy lime tang with refined creamy breadth on palate that's structured & long, set to age well.

★★★★☆ **Blanc de Blancs** (84) Sherbet, apple & sea air allure of all-chardonnay **NV** (94). Vivacious & bright, taut acid matched with cracker & toast richness from 45 months on lees. Seamless composition includes 48% oaked portion & 20% reserve.

★★★★☆ **Brut Reserve** Oystershell & lemon sherbet tied with ripe apple & autumn leaves on **NV** (92), rich & creamy from pinot noir dominance (52%, with chardonnay) & 30 months on lees before disgorgement. House-style reserve (15%) & wooded components in the brisk & energetic mix.

★★★★☆ **Délice Nectar** Gentle sweet edge to grapefruit notes of **NV** (90), 52/48 pinot noir & chardonnay. Rounded yet piquant & fresh, it had 24 months on lees after standard 15% of reserve was blended in. Structured, finishes beautifully clean.— FM

Location/map: Franschhoek ▪ Map grid reference: C1 ▪ WO: Western Cape ▪ Est 2005 ▪ 1stB 2006 ▪ Tasting & sales Mon-Sat 11-1; or by appt; pub hols (seasonal) plse call ahead ▪ Fee R35 per ½ glass MCC, R75 per ½ glass Champagne ▪ Cellar tours on request ▪ Owner(s) / proprietor Jean-Philippe Colmant ▪ Oenologist & winemaker Paul Gerber (Mar 2019) ▪ Wine consultant Pieter Ferreira ▪ 5ha/3ha (pinot, chard) ▪ 8,800cs own label 100% MCC ▪ PO Box 602 Franschhoek 7690 ▪ info@colmant.co.za ▪ www.colmant.co.za ▪ **T +27 (0)83-778-8874**

Commando

One of the Cape's oldest drinks brands, this brandy has been produced under the Commando label since 1915. Now owned by Heineken Beverages, it has minimum 30% potstill, aged in oak at least three years.
Commando (84) ★★★ A good & versatile mixer (82), vibrant fresh peach & prune flavours, hint of caramel, spirited bite on the finish from 43% alc. — WB

Compagniesdrift

Set in a large, modern facility among vineyards and farmland on Stellenbosch's Eerste River, Compagniesdrift provides wine storage, labelling and rework services to the industry. Since 2015, it also produces a range of bespoke wines for the local market and export. A recently opened farm shop offers deli platters to accompany on-site tastings, plus a selection of locally crafted preserves to enjoy at home.

★★★★ **Albertus** Charm of muscat d'Alexandrie is forefront in delicious unfortified Natural Sweet. Mostly 2021, though labelled **NV** ⑧⑧, had wholeberry open ferment with 2 days on skin, small portion 18 months in barrel. Luscious & honeyed yet delicate, with modest sugar & alc (107 g/l, 10.4%). 500 ml.

Cabernet Sauvignon-Merlot ★★★★ Previewed **22** ⑧⑤ shows promise, honest, concentrated blackcurrant fruit & solid tannin underpinning. 10 months in small oak. **Chardonnay-Pinot Noir** ★★★★ Barely discernable blush on chardonnay with 1% pinot to tint, **23** ⑧③ off Robertson vines has striking macadamia aroma, ripe berry fruit. **Chardonnay** ★★★★ Unwooded **23** ⑧④ has appealing lime & beeswax notes, fresh acid core. Touch of sugar, 4 months on lees add body & texture. WO W Cape. — GdB

Location: Stellenbosch ▪ WO: Stellenbosch/Western Cape ▪ Est 2010 ▪ 1stB 2015 ▪ Tasting by appt only during weekends ▪ Sales Mon-Fri 9-4 ▪ Closed all pub hols ▪ Wine club ▪ Wine & farm shop ▪ Cheese/meat platter; locally produced preserves ▪ Owner(s) Meerlust Workers' Trust ▪ Winemaker(s) Altus Treurnicht (Nov 2018) ▪ 10% red 90% white ▪ PO Box 7121 Stellenbosch 7599 ▪ info@compagniesdrift.com ▪ www.compagniesdrift.com ▪ **T +27 (0)21-843-3902/913/916**

☐ **Compagnies Wijn** *see* Swanepoel Wines
☐ **Condé** *see* Stark-Condé Wines
☐ **Conservation Coast** *see* Whalehaven Wines

Constantia Glen ⓠ ⑪

Founded around the millennium on the steep slopes of Constantia Nek Pass, the internationally hailed Waibel family property is registered as an 'estate' and produces only Bordeaux-style whites and reds, and sauvignon blanc. Cellarmaster Justin van Wyk and viticulturist Etienne Southey, now joined by winemaker Georgina Wilkinson believe the farm has ideal conditions to grow and optimally ripen the chosen seven varieties, and they aim to produce a style that is 'elegant, fresh and clearly demonstrates not only the cool climatic conditions of the region but also our unique meso-climate'. Especially for the reds, later-afternoon sunlight allows for the ripening of anthocyanins and tannins, and complex flavour development, they note, producing the aimed-for intensity of flavour, texture and balance.

★★★★★ **Constantia Glen Five** ⓐ Elegant **20** ⑨⑤ combines a cool herbal fragrance with dark plum, blackcurrant, vanilla & tobacco in concentrated blend of cab franc, cab, merlot, petit verdot & malbec (28/24/21/17/10), 19 months in 72% new barriques. Textured, with fine mouthcoating tannins, well structured &, like **19** ★★★★★ ⑨③, prepped for the long haul. 1.5L-12L bottles available.

★★★★☆ **Constantia Glen Three** ⓐ Merlot-dominant sibling Bordeaux blend is voluptuous yet bright, fresh, ends with a lingering savouriness. **20** ⑨④'s array of plum, dark chocolate, dried herbs & cedar is expertly framed by 18 months in 25% new small-oak. A joy & a keeper; best decanted in youth. Merlot, cab & cab franc (65/25/10), also in magnum.

★★★★☆ **Sauvignon Blanc** ⓐ Exceptionally concentrated in lime-hued **22** ⑨④, tropical, lemongrass & citrus intensity matched with mouthwatering acid & long precise finish. Refined & balanced, a touch of unoaked semillon & 5 months' lees-ageing adding dimension & palate weight.

★★★★★ **Constantia Glen Two** ⓐ Complex flavours & vinification result in exceptional **21** ⑨⑤ blend of sauvignon (73%) & semillon. Lime leaf, white flower & subtle hay allures on nose lead to layered palate of stonefruit & citrus, unflagging mineral conclusion. Barrel ferment, then year on lees in wood (Austrian oak, French oak & acacia) & clay pot. A beauty that will give years of drinking pleasure.— WB

Location/WO: Constantia ▪ Map: Cape Peninsula ▪ Map grid reference: B3 ▪ Est 2000 ▪ 1stB 2005 ▪ Tasting & sales: in season Mon-Sun 10-8; out of season Sun-Thu 10-6 Fri/Sat 10-8 ▪ Tasting fees from R130, waived according to purchase ▪ Closed Dec 25 & Jan 1 ▪ Various platters; gourmet flammkuchen; salads; delectable main courses; desserts; soups during winter months ▪ Wine club ▪ Owner(s) Waibel family ▪ Cellarmaster(s) Justin van Wyk (Dec 2011) ▪ Winemaker(s) Georgina Wilkinson (Oct 2022) ▪ Viticulturist(s) Etienne Southey (Sep 2012, farm manager) ▪ 60ha/28.5ha (cabs s/f, malbec, merlot, p verdot, sauv, sem) ▪ 200t/25,000cs own label 65% red 35% white ▪ PO Box 780 Constantia 7848 ▪ wine@constantiaglen.com ▪ www.constantiaglen.com ▪ **T +27 (0)21-795-5639**

Constantia Nectar ⓠ

On the Huis-in-Bos property, part of the historic Nova Constantia estate owned since 1950 by Peter Rawbone-Viljoen, a parcel of muscat de Frontignan contributes to a recreation of Constantia's world-famous

18th/19th-century sweet wines. The lyrebird on the label alludes to Peter's (and his sons') career in audio, the farm being home to Digital Forest Studio. We look forward to tasting the new release next time.

Location: Constantia ▪ Est 2007 ▪ 1stB 2009 ▪ Tasting by appt ▪ Owner(s) Peter Rawbone-Viljoen Trust ▪ Viticulturist(s) Kevin Watt (Aug 2006, consultant) ▪ 4.5ha/2.5ha (muscat de F) ▪ 9t/1,600cs own label 100% natural sweet ▪ Huis-in-Bos, Klein Constantia Rd, Constantia 7806 ▪ charmaine.l.kelly@gmail.com ▪ www. constantianectar.co.za ▪ **T +27 (0)82-788-5771**

Constantia Royale

Roger Burton, winemaker and, now, MD of Lynn Rowand's Constantia winery is keen to develop the Bordeaux white in the small portfolio into a world-class blend and 'premium showcase' for the valley, through 'terroir-specific plantings and methodical farming and winemaking'. Established in 1997 but bottling only since 2015, the venture sits on twin farms, Zonnestraal and Nova Zonnestraal. A strong, possibly unique drawcard is the venue, inside a tunnel that links the sibling properties under the M3 expressway.

★★★★ **Sauvignon Blanc** ⊘ Forward aromas & flavour (mostly tropical, with a good limy edge) on balanced, fresh & lively **22** ★★★★★ ⑨⓪, in line with **21** ⑧⑧ but a touch more impressive. Time on lees & 10% old-oaked component add richness & texture to the satisfying whole.

★★★★☆ **Don's Reserve** Has 40% semillon added to the sauvignon, both wild-fermented & 8 months in oak - the latter adding a spicy, savoury dimension but should fully integrate soon. **22** ⑨① more restrained than the Sauvignon but deeper, with a ripe tangerine note. Rich, firm acidity.— TJ

Location/WO: Constantia ▪ Map: Cape Peninsula ▪ Map grid reference: B3 ▪ Est 1997 ▪ 1stB 2015 ▪ Tasting by appt only ▪ Closed all pub hols ▪ Owner(s) Lynn Marais Rowand ▪ MD/winemaker Roger Burton (Oct 2013) ▪ Viticulturist(s) Joseph van Wyk Contractors (Nov 2013) ▪ 16ha/7.5ha (sauv, sem) ▪ 50t/3,000cs own label 100% white ▪ Suite 193 Private Bag X16 Constantia 7848 ▪ wine@constantiaroyale.co.za ▪ www.constantiaro-yale.co.za ▪ **T +27 (0)21-794-4841**

Constantia Uitsig

The list of visitor attractions here is so long that it's (almost) possible to overlook the growing line-up of wines, mostly white, now including a brilliant Natural Sweet muscat d'Alexandrie inspired by Constantia Valley's stellar dessert-wine heritage, and the fact that Constantia Uitsig belonged to Cape governor Simon van der Stel's original landholding in the 1700s, and therefore is part of the tradition. The lowest-lying farm in the valley, it's both somewhat protected from the south-easterly winds and the beneficiary of the cooling influence of False Bay. The focus remains on growing wine as naturally and environmentally responsibly as possible. On-site are a coffee shop, deli, restaurant and beautiful heritage gardens that not only supply flowers for purchase but also host rose-growing demonstrations, plus much more to beguile and entertain.

Constantia Uitsig range

★★★★☆ **Constantia Red** ⊛ Layered, refined Cape Bordeaux, cab & merlot joined by other 3 reds in **20** ⑨①. Abundant cassis & spicy fruitcake on a velvet cushion, 20% new oak, 15 months, perfectly judged.

★★★★☆ **Chardonnay Reserve** Elegant, alluring **22** ⑨② shows hallmark harmony of fruit, acid & oak. Rounded citrus in lovely density & concentration, restrained creaminess ex 10 months in 33% new barrels.

★★★★☆ **Sauvignon Blanc** ⊘ Fig & lime zest vivacity of **22** ⑨① reminiscent of taut **21** ★★★★ ⑧⑨. White pepper & flint notes comingle with lively acid & lees breadth. 11% splash of (unoaked) semillon.

★★★★☆ **Semillon** Taut lemon & lime vibrancy of **22** ⑨② countered by broad mouthfeel enhanced by touch of cream. Gravity & presence provided by oak, just 10% new, 10 months, same duration as **21** ⑨⓪.

★★★★☆ **Natura Vista** All change for Cape Bordeaux white, as tank-fermented sauvignon (60%) takes baton from barrelled semillon in focused, taut & cohesive **22** ⑨①. Gooseberry & lime tang with richness of oak from 6 months in barrel.

★★★★☆ **Gravitas** 🆕 Confident debut of **20** ⑨⓪ Constantia dessert wine from white muscat de Frontignan. Picks at various stages of raisining deliver a rose, jasmine & ginger delicacy, apricot piquancy countering 159 g/L sugar for balanced & clean palate, polished 25 months in seasoned barrels. 500 ml.

In abeyance: **Méthode Cap Classique**.

Ex Oppido range

★★★★☆ **Red Horizon** (Ⓨ) Spicy blueberry & plum on approachable **21** ★★★★ **(88)**. As sleek as **20** **(90)**, also shiraz driven, but new oak hiked to 20% for year. WO W Cape unless noted.

★★★★ **Red Tableau** Cab franc joins cab & merlot (44/34) on smooth, juicy **21 (89)**. Spicy, dark fruit with cedar & tobacco interest. Soft yet intense with good length from year in oak, 20% new. WO Stellenbosch.

★★★★ **Chardonnay** (Ⓨ) Pre-bottled **22 (86)** is pleasantly tart, juicy & fresh, with nectarine & orange notes. Light bodied, unwooded, with enticing zip of acid.

★★★★ **Mensis XII** (NEW) (✓) Vivid interplay of apple tarte tatin, brioche & zingy grapefruit on **NV (89)** cap classique sparkler from chardonnay & pinot noir (80/20). Complex, broad, yeasty & rich, but 7 g/L acid keeps it fresh after year on lees. WO W Cape.

Rosé ★★★☆ Fragrant cherry & strawberry abundance on juicy, fresh **23 (85)** from 6 grapes, mostly shiraz & cab franc. Light, friendly but with a bit of pizzazz. Ideal for summer. WO Cape Town. — FM

Location: Constantia ▪ Map: Cape Peninsula ▪ Map grid reference: B3 ▪ WO: Constantia/Western Cape/ Stellenbosch/Cape Town ▪ Est 1980 ▪ 1stB 1988 ▪ Wine sales at the Wine Shop Wed-Sun 10-6 ▪ Closed Good Fri, Dec 25/26 & Jan 1 ▪ Hanepoot grapes (red & white) sold annually ▪ Block House Kitchen ▪ La Grotto Ristorante ▪ Chris Nixon Cycling Academy ▪ Heritage Market: Kristen's Kick-Ass Ice Cream, Nest Deli, Sushi Box, Fishermans Cottage, Four & Twenty ▪ Owner(s) Constantia Uitsig Holdings (Pty) Ltd ▪ Winemaker(s) Estian de Wet (Jul 2023) ▪ 60ha/18ha (cabs s/f, shiraz, chard, muscat d'F, sauv, sem) ▪ 130t/20,000cs own label & 170t/28,000cs Ex Oppido; 10% red 90% white ▪ PO Box 32 Constantia 7848 ▪ info@uitsig.co.za ▪ www.uitsig.co.za

☐ **Constitution Road** see Robertson Winery
☐ **Continental** see Super Single Vineyards

Contreberg Wines   (Ⓨ) (⌂) (◎)

One of still relatively few wineries in the Darling vicinity, the Pretorius family's young venture aims to produce 'wines true to the area', with local speciality sauvignon blanc as the centrepiece. The home-farm boasts various amenities, and the owners strive to meet visitors in person and offer an authentic experience.

Cabernet Sauvignon (Ⓨ) ★★★☆ Big, bold but balanced by ripe dark berry aromas/flavour & firm structure in **19 (85)**. Older oak for both reds, 18 months. **Shiraz** (✓) ★★★★ Admirers will recognise the friendly forward power & fullness of smoky, fruity flavour on pleasingly rustic **20 (85)**, released ready to enjoy, the tannins supportive but tame. Juicy, with a sweet edge. **Sauvignon Blanc** (✓) ★★★★ Restrained but flavourful **22 (85)** is poised & refreshing, with just enough lively citric acidity in its good balance. — TJ

Location/WO: Darling ▪ Map: Durbanville, Philadelphia & Darling ▪ Map grid reference: A2 ▪ Est/1stB 2018 ▪ Tasting Mon-Fri by appt, Sat/Sun 10.30-3; pub hols (seasonal) please call ahead ▪ Weddings/functions ▪ Accommodation ▪ Owner(s) Michael Pretorius ▪ Winemaker(s) Bernard Smuts (Jan 2022, consultant) ▪ 352ha/45ha (cab, shiraz, sauv) ▪ 18t own label 35% red 65% white ▪ Contreberg Farm Box 20493 Big Bay 7441 ▪ eleanor@contreberg.co.za ▪ www.contreberg.com ▪ **T +27 (0)72-717-1607**

☐ **Cooperative** see Bosman Family Vineyards

Copeland Spirits

Small-scale Cape Town distiller James Copeland's pisco is made from juice and skins sourced from Vondeling in Voor Paardeberg, where his brother Matthew is winemaker. Cold fermented on skins, then half single-distilled 'for character and body', the rest double-distilled 'for finesse and aroma'.

★★★★ **Pisco** (Ⓨ) Delightfully smooth & fragrant brandy **(89)**, notes of passionfruit, melon, wax & almonds. From of aromatic varieties, year in tank (not oak) for fruit purity. 43% alc. — WB

Location: Cape Town ▪ Est/1stB 2018 ▪ Closed to public ▪ Owner(s) James Copeland ▪ Cellarmaster/distiller James Copeland (Jan 2018) ▪ Postnet Suite 416 Private Bag X4 Sun Valley Cape Town 7985 ▪ jamesacopeland@gmail.com ▪ **T +27 (0)76-481-9302**

☐ **Copper Pot** see Thorne & Daughters Wines
☐ **Coral Reef** see Wineways Marketing
☐ **Cosmic Hand** see Elemental Bob
☐ **Coterie by Wildeberg** see Wildeberg Wines

Coucou Vino

Renche van Aarde's boutique brand combines her love of design with a desire to offer 'unpretentious, good-quality and palate-friendly dry wines' with an aesthetic touch. Husband and star winemaker Nic guides the winecrafting in Stellenbosch. We look forward to tasting the new releases next time.

Location: Stellenbosch ▪ Est/1stB 2020 ▪ Closed to public ▪ Online store ▪ Owner(s) Renche van Aarde ▪ 12t/1,700cs own label 66% white 33% rosé ▪ WIETA ▪ PO Box 2246 Dennesig 7601 ▪ info@coucoucollections. com ▪ www.coucoucollections.com ▪ **T +27 (0)79-102-0100**

☐ **Coutelier** *see* Domaine Coutelier
☐ **Covenant** *see* Croydon Vineyard Residential Estate
☐ **Cradle Boutique Hotel & Spa** *see* Bé a Daisy
☐ **Craft 3** *see* Land of Hope
☐ **Craft & Origin** *see* Origin Wine

Creation Wines

Endowed with immense natural beauty, Creation in Hemel-en-Aarde Ridge ward is owned by Swiss-born Jean-Claude Martin and wife Carolyn (née Finlayson) with business partner Jonathan Drake. JC is also cellarmaster and chief viticulturist, Carolyn looks after public relations locally and abroad, staff training and hospitality, which includes wine-and-food matching, for which Creation is famous. Recent changes include an upgrade of the restaurant and tasting area, making it lighter, more open, with plant features. The team belongs to various research bodies to keep abreast of the latest international trends in climate change, clonal development and other areas that could affect vineyard health and cellar regimes, the aim being to build a business for future generations. Their son and daughter are already involved, Glenn making his own chardonnay and Emma a pinot noir, both part of the pinnacle Art range, with ratings to match.

Art range

★★★★☆ **Emma's Pinot Noir** ⓐ Limited release, by daughter Emma Martin. Same winemaking as Art, except 30% wholebunch, 40% new barrels. Prominent fruit in **22** ⓐ(94), red berries & cherries, the oak spicing making its appearance in the flavours, smoky, savoury, ending dry, with lithe, youthful tannins for cellaring. Still tightly held, decant before serving.

★★★★★ **The Art of Pinot Noir** ⓐ Single site & barrel selection, pinot noir flagship, designed to reveal the variety's essence. 60% wholebunch, wild ferment in large foudre, year in barrique, 33% new, give lovely balance between red fruit & spice, there's harmony & polish in **22** ★★★★☆ (94). Tannins supple yet with hidden strength for the long haul, as in **21** (96).

★★★★☆ **Glenn's Chardonnay** ⓐ By Glenn Martin, 4th-generation winemaker. Wild ferment/10 months in half new oak, unfined/filtered, **22** (94) richest, most expressive of the 4 chardonnays: toasted almond, lemon preserve, orange zest, with palate weight. Has cellar's signature racy acid, providing foundation for long ageing, keeping flavours fresh & ideal for fine dining. **21** ★★★★★ (95) also boldly styled.

★★★★☆ **The Art of Chardonnay** ⓐ Flagship, specific site within single vineyard, & as name suggests, **22** (93) aiming to best express variety's soul. Same winemaking & oaking as Reserve, except for 50% wild ferment. Citrus toned, seamed with Lemon Cream biscuit savoury note, there's restraint, polish, precision. Signature lemon-lime freshness underpin for health, vibrancy & a future.

Reserve range

★★★★☆ **Pinot Noir** ⊘ ⓐ Vineyard selection, designed to age without losing pinot's seductive side. **22** (94) 50% wholebunch, fermented in large foudre, then year in barrique, 25% new, giving tobacco & peppery tones to the red berry & cherry fruit. Well-crafted tannins, have strength for long ageing yet accessible. There's power here, weight, concentration & serious intent.

★★★★☆ **Syrah** ⓐ Portion wholebunch, wild ferment, long skin contact, 18 months in small barrel, 25% new, **21** (94) follows trend set by last few vintages, with similar result. Muscular styling, savoury spices, scrub & pepper; there's intensity with power-packed flavours, tannins still firm, will meld over time.

★★★★★ **Chardonnay** ⓐ Same winemaking as Estate, with 30% new oak, but spice subservient to fruit, lemon & ruby grapefruit, becoming more limy in the flavours. Piercing freshness, fitting the fruit style, promising longevity. **22** (95) shows noteworthy tautness, reflecting its cool provenance. Gentle savoury note on palate adds another layer. WO Cape South Coast, as **21** ★★★★★ (94).

In abeyance: **Merlot**. Discontinued: **Sumac Grenache**.

Estate range

★★★★☆ **Merlot** (Ⓐ) Barrel aged 14 months, 30% new, giving lightly spice-dusted perfume, an even stronger showing in the flavours: savoury, almost meaty, with cocoa nuance to cassis & plum of **21** (90). Layered, lots to hold the attention, including firm but ripe tannins promising good cellaring.

★★★★☆ **Pinot Noir** (✓) Wild ferment, 10 months in barrique, just 10% new, **22** (92) showcases varietal fruit: glossy red berries, hint of forest floor, the spicing an overlay of white pepper. Tannins lithe, perceptible on dry finish yet allowing current access. WO Cape South Coast.

★★★★☆ **Syrah-Grenache** 75/25 blend, fermented in large foudre & tank, barrel aged 14 months, 25% new. Spice a part of **22** (92)'s character, woodsmoke & scrub, white pepper notes, threaded through the hedgerow fruit. Bold personality, tannins firm but ripe, end dry but without barrier to current access, though best served with rich dishes. **21** untasted.

★★★★☆ **Rosé** Shiraz with 45% grenache, pale salmon-hued & light textured (12.5% alc) yet no shortage of personality. **23** (89)'s just-picked strawberries vie with mineral scents & palate, there's enough freshness to give pleasure, match food. WO Cape South Coast, as Chardonnay.

★★★★☆ **Chardonnay** Most approachable of the 4 siblings but still admirable. Lees aged 10 months in barrique, 10% new. Melba toast savoury note fits **22** (90)'s citrus profile perfectly, there's harmony yet richness of flavour. Ends with racy limy acidity, making it eminently drinkable, adding vibrancy to the wine.

★★★★☆ **Old Vine Chenin Blanc** (NEW) (✿) Wholebunch fermented in concrete 'egg' to showcase the vineyard, planted 1984 in Swartland. Melon & thatch, some quince, a dry scrub nuance, **22** (90) perked up by brisk acidity, adding a limy note. Has palate weight, balance & interest.

★★★★☆ **Sauvignon Blanc-Semillon** (Ⓐ) 80/20 blend, barrel fermented/10 months, 20% new for sauvignon. Core of minerality, some leafy nuances, **22** (90)'s fruit shows more on palate, gooseberry & citrus, zinging fresh & long. Spicing is subtle, this is about freshness & flavours.

★★★★☆ **Roussanne-Grenache Blanc** (NEW) Equal blend, fermented in concrete 'egg', **22** (90) for early enjoyment. Ripe, showcases varietal aromatics, florals, stonefruit, especially white peach & nectarine, flavours revealing some minerality, an earthy finish. Zesty, like all the whites. Admirable debut. WO Overberg.

Not tasted: **Cabernet Sauvignon-Merlot-Petit Verdot**, **Cool Climate Chenin Blanc**, **Sauvignon Blanc**, **Viognier**, **Viognier-Roussanne**. — CR

Location: Hermanus ▪ Map: Walker Bay & Bot River ▪ Map grid reference: C4 ▪ WO: Walker Bay/Cape South Coast/Western Cape/Overberg ▪ Est 2002 ▪ 1stB 2006 ▪ Tasting, sales & cellar tours daily 10-5; pub hols 9.30-5 (seasonal) please call ahead ▪ Closed Dec 25 & Jan 1 ▪ Six-course pairing experience; à la carte menu; breakfast menu; wine & chocolate pairing; tea pairing; harvest platters; kids menu ▪ Owner(s) Jean-Claude & Carolyn Martin, Jonathan Drake ▪ Cellarmaster(s) Jean-Claude Martin (Jan 2006) ▪ Winemaker(s) Jean-Claude Martin (Jan 2006), with Gerhard Smith (Dec 2017) ▪ Viticulturist(s) Jean-Claude Martin & Gerhard Bruwer (2020) ▪ 50ha (cab, grenache noir, merlot, p verdot, pinot, shiraz, chard, chenin, grenache blanc, rouss, sauv, sem, viog) ▪ EnviroWines, IPW, WWF-SA Conservation Champion ▪ PO Box 1772 Hermanus 7200 ▪ info@creationwines.com ▪ www.creationwines.com ▪ **T +27 (0)28-212-1107**

☐ **Creative Block** *see* Spier
☐ **Creative Space** *see* Bosman Family Vineyards
☐ **Credo** *see* Stellenbosch Vineyards
☐ **Cross Collection** *see* Dieu Donné Vineyards

Croydon Vineyard Residential Estate (Ⓨ)(◎)(Ⓐ)(Ⓖ)

Since inception 20 years ago, winegrowing has been part of the lifestyle on this exclusive residential estate - fittingly, given its setting on Helderberg viticultural land. Grapes from the own vines, overseen by consultant Rikus Neethling, are supplemented with some brought-in fruit and vinified by Rikus and aide Jannie Alexander in the on-site cellar. The wine lounge on the property now has a deli serving 'delicious lunches'.

Covenant range

★★★★ **Pinotage** Fresh, lighter-style **22** (88) has juicy mulberry, plummy fruit, its ripe flavour persisting through refined if dense tannins. Harmonised in older oak, 14 months. Moderate 13% alc. No **21**.

★★★★ **Chenin Blanc** Sprightly & fresh 22 ⑧⑦ has delicate apple flavours supported by creamy breadth from ferment/8 months in concrete 'egg'. A crisp, fantail finish adds to its attraction.

Merlot ★★★★ Modest dark fruit on softish 22 ⑧③, short on complexity & structure for long ageing but carefully judged tannin & older oak, 14 months, provide pleasant current drinking. **Shiraz** ★★★☆ Softish 22 ⑧⑤, smooth, simple dark berry fruit, mere whisper of spice, held by squeeze of tannin. Lighter, less concentrated than last-tasted 19 ★★★★ ⑧⑧. **Sauvignon Blanc** (⊘) ★★★★ Refreshing 21 ⑧⑤ shows pungent grass & white pepper, maintains raised quality of previous. Not tasted: **Cabernet Sauvignon**, **Méthode Cap Classique Brut**.

Title Deed range

Cape Blend ★★★★ Shiraz (57%) in harmony with pinotage & cab franc in 22 ⑧⑤. Sappy fruitcake & spice trimmed by fine, freshening tannins. Attractive, easy to drink. Older oak, 15 months. **Rosé** ★★★★ Unusual pinotage, grenache noir, chardonnay mix, 23 ⑧③ zestily fresh & dry. Punchy spice & red berry flavours, broadened by underlying creaminess, linger pleasantly. Not tasted: **Cape Blend White**. — AL

Location: Stellenbosch ▪ Map: Helderberg ▪ Map grid reference: A3 ▪ WO: Stellenbosch/Western Cape ▪ Est/1stB 2004 ▪ Tasting & sales Mon-Fri 9-5; pub hols 10-5 (seasonal) please call ahead ▪ Cellar tours by appt ▪ Facilities for children ▪ Tour groups ▪ Conferences ▪ Events ▪ Weddings ▪ Owner(s) Croydon Vineyard Estate ▪ Winemaker(s) Rikus Neethling (consultant), with Jannie Alexander ▪ Vineyard manager Rikus Neethling ▪ 9ha (cabs s/f, malbec, merlot, ptage, shiraz, chenin) ▪ 65t/4,000cs own label 95% red 5% white ▪ Unit 1, Croydon Vineyard Estate, Somerset West 7130 ▪ operations@croydon-vineyards ▪ www.croydon-vineyards.com ▪ **T +27 (0)21-843-3610**

Crystallum

This internationally reputed team took to social media last year to tease the release in '2025-ish' of a cap classique made with Thorne & Daughters, one of the nature-friendly craft producers sharing cellar space at Gabriëlskloof, where Crystallum co-founder and CWG member Peter-Allan Finlayson is cellarmaster and part-owner. All will be revealed, but for now small batches of chardonnay and pinot noir are the exclusive Crystallum focus, and grapes are still sourced from Hemel-en-Aarde valleys and ridges, and lately Overberg, for classic-styled wines that consistently represent the finest SA expressions of Burgundy's flagship grapes.

★★★★★ **Bona Fide Pinot Noir** (⬩) From Hemel-en-Aarde Valley, 22 ⑨⑤ showcases earthy truffle notes with herbal lift. Crushed raspberry palate with smooth tannin grip & lengthy savoury finish. 60% wholebunch. Natural ferment, 10 months in barrique for all pinots.

★★★★★ **Cuvée Cinéma Pinot Noir** (⬩) Hemel-en-Aarde Ridge vines for this expression, 22 ★★★★★ ⑨④ displays hallmark refined decadence in its aromatic mix of raspberry, dark chocolate, smoke & spice. All contained in an elegant structure, with velvet tannins & taut acidity, earthy richness at finish reflecting 21 ⑨⑤. Freshness from half each whole bunches & whole berries, power & drive from 20% new oak.

★★★★★ **Mabalel Pinot Noir** (⬩) Cellar-worthy (as all the wines) bottling from elevated Elandskloof vineyard. Fragrant tobacco & new leather notes surround crunchy, perfumed red cherry of 22 ★★★★★ ⑨④, which 100% destemmed, 36 days on skins. Spiced complexity lifts soft tannins in smoky finish. Like 21 ⑨⑤, 20% new oak.

★★★★☆ **Peter Max Pinot Noir** (⊘) Wider sourced sibling, refined & distinguished yet notably drinkable in youth, courtesy yielding tannins & fresh acid vein. 22 ⑨⓪ echoes previous in its supple strawberry & raspberry fruit, attractive earth & wild game extras, spice from only older oak this vintage.

★★★★☆ **Clay Shales Chardonnay** (⬩) Hemel-en-Aarde Ridge vines for outstanding 22 ⑨③, showing customary leesy breadth & enlivening seam of lemon & lime acidity. Touch new oak yields fine, buttered-toast notes. Naturally fermented in 228l & 300L barrel, 10 months aged, as all chardonnays.

★★★★☆ **Ferrum Chardonnay** (⬩) From iron soils in Overberg, richly ripe 22 ⑨④'s tropical scents & flavours seamlessly melded with limy acid & subtle, supportive oak. Pure, focused, gathers energy through the palate to lengthy finish. 20% new barrels, as Clay Shales.

★★★★☆ **The Agnes Chardonnay** Fruit from various W Cape vineyards combine for signature elegance & restraint in 22 ⑨①, delicious savoury nuance to creamy citrus palate, texture & freshness from bunch pressing, as all the chardonnays. Deft oak, barrel & foudre, none new, supple finish. — DS

Location: Bot River ▪ WO: Hemel-en-Aarde Ridge/Western Cape/Hemel-en-Aarde Valley/Elandskloof/Overberg ▪ Est 2006 ▪ 1stB 2007 ▪ Closed to public ▪ Owner(s) Crystallum Coastal Vineyards (Pty) Ltd ▪

Winemaker(s) Peter-Allan Finlayson (2006) ▪ 60t/7,000cs own label 60% red 40% white ▪ PO Box 857 Hermanus 7200 ▪ info@crystallumwines.com ▪ www.crystallumwines.com

---

☐ **Culemborg** see DGB (Pty) Ltd
☐ **Culinaria Collection** see Leopard's Leap Family Vineyards

CvD Wines

Christopher van Dieren's nearly 30 years in the wine industry, latterly in the Darling area, enable him to select the best fruit from various areas to vinify at contract facilities for this boutique venture, owned with Olwethu Sotiya. The first releases will be followed by a shiraz and sauvignon blanc. Sales of the wines help support Is'thatha, an awarded Cape Town contemporary dance group, of which Olwethu is artistic director.

Merlot-Cabernet Sauvignon-Cabernet Franc-Petit Verdot ⓥ ★★★★ Plush mint-tinged **19** ⑧⑤ Bordeaux blend has ripe fruit on solid tannins, savoury finish & spiciness from 18 months in combo French & American oak. 50% merlot; WO Franschhoek. **Chardonnay Brut Méthode Cap Classique** ⓥ ★★★★ Upbeat, happy-occasions bubbly with citrus freshness & hint of lemon curd borne on fine, vigorous dry mousse. **18** ⑧⑤ well priced, too, as sibling. — GdB, CR

Location: Cape Town ▪ WO: Franschhoek/Western Cape ▪ Est 2020 ▪ 1stB 2021 ▪ Closed to public ▪ Owner(s) Christopher van Dieren & Olwethu Sotiya ▪ Winemaker(s) Christopher van Dieren ▪ 2,000cs own label 90% red 10% MCC ▪ 46 Rhodes Ave, Cape Town 7925 ▪ christophervandieren1@gmail.com ▪ T +27 (0)83-656-8548

☐ **Da Capo Vineyards** see Idiom Wines

DA Hanekom Familie Wyne   ⓥ

Between managing Bloemendal, helming its cellar and tending its vines, Andri Hanekom makes time for this hobby turned small business, owned with wife Yvette. Their quartet of low-intervention terroir wines is available for tasting by appointment and sale at 360° Skye Lounge Restaurant on the Durbanville estate.

★★★★ **Langrug Malbec** Plump & supple, **21** ⑧⑧ offers stewed fruit with leather & cocoa, full but ripe tannins, subtle oak notes from 18 months in seasoned barrels (as Putfontein) add to appeal. **20** untasted.

★★★★ **Putfontein Pinotage** Vibrant hedgerow berry fruit has notes of cocoa & tar in **19** ⑧⑥, sweet spice & tobacco aromas, notably powerful tannins given wine's age. **18** sold out untasted.

★★★★ **Witteberg Chenin Blanc** ⓥ Grapes from Swartland's Piketberg, fermented/9 months in old oak. **19** ⑧⑨ hints of wild scrub in generously ripe tropical fruit mix, grainy minerality following to finish.

★★★★ **Klipmuur Sauvignon Blanc** Striking herbal & sweet spice aromatics, hint of menthol from ferment/year in seasoned barrels. **20** ⑧⑦ still somewhat unsettled after standout **19** ★★★★★ ⑨⓪, but ripe, wholesome, with good fruit concentration.— GdB

Location: Durbanville ▪ Map: Durbanville, Philadelphia & Darling ▪ Map grid reference: C7 ▪ WO: Durbanville/ Swartland ▪ Est/1stB 2016 ▪ Tasting by appt only ▪ Wine available for sale 10-5 daily at 360°Wine Lounge, Bloemendal Wine Estate ▪ Owner(s) Andri & Yvette Hanekom ▪ Cellarmaster(s) Andri Hanekom (Jan 2016) ▪ 4t/580cs own label 50% red 50% white ▪ WIETA ▪ andri@dahfamiliewyne.com ▪ www.dahfamiliewyne. com ▪ T +27 (0)66-189-3371

Dainty Bess   ⓥ

A favourite rose in the garden of Klein Optenhorst, her parents' former Wellington home, inspired the branding of Jane Ferreira-Eedes' extra-dry sparkler, unready for tasting this edition. She selects parcels in Elgin, Robertson and Overberg, and a consultant styles the wine to her spec, ageability being a consideration.

Location: Cape Town ▪ Est/1stB 2016 ▪ Tasting by appt only ▪ Owner(s) Jane Ferreira-Eedes ▪ Winemaker(s) Corné Marais (consultant) ▪ See intro for grape sources ▪ 100% MCC ▪ 44 Liesbeek Rd, Rosebank, Cape Town 7700 ▪ daintybesswine@gmail.com ▪ www.daintybess.co.za ▪ T +27 (0)83-324-6855

Dalkeith

This boutique brand is owned by esteemed California winery Jackson Family Wines. Dalkeith, a watering hole in the Kgalagadi Transfrontier Park, was named in 1914 by another Jackson, a Scot with first name Rodger, while surveying beacons in the area. A red wine is planned to join the current pair of chenins.

Graham Weerts, winemaker at JFW for many years and now back permanently in South Africa, vinifies the wines in the company's cellar at Simonsvlei near Paarl. A tasting room at this venue is also on the cards.

★★★★☆ **Kalmoesfontein Chenin Blanc** ⓥ Textured **21** ⑨③, soft summer fruits enfolded in plump flesh. Minerality & freshening grainy finish enhance dimension & individuality. Ends on savoury-salty note.

★★★★☆ **Koplandsteen Chenin Blanc** ⓐ ⓦ Instant appeal of expressive ripe red apple aromas on **22** ⑨③; full flavour curtailed in youth by intense steely core, firm build. Bone-dry, mouthwatering fantail conclusion. Will reward more with year/2. Ex Bottelary Hills; wild yeasts; older oak & ceramic vessels.— AL

Location: Paarl ▪ WO: Swartland/Stellenbosch ▪ 1stB 2019 ▪ Closed to public ▪ Owner(s) Jackson Family Wines ▪ Cellarmaster(s) Graham Weerts ▪ Viticulturist(s) Adi Badenhorst (Kalmoesfontein), Jacques DuBois (Koplandsteen) ▪ 400cs own label 100% white ▪ JWE, Simonsvlei, Old Paarl Rd, R101, Paarl 7646 ▪ ann.ferreira@dalkeithwines. co.za ▪ www.jacksonfamilywines.com, www.dalkeithwines.co.za ▪ **T +27 (0)82-909-1116 (Ann Ferreira)**

Dalla Cia Wine & Spirit Company

Twenty years ago, Giorgio Dalla Cia was persuaded by his son George to join him in this family wine-and-spirit venture, based in Stellenbosch's Bosman's Crossing area. Three decades before, Giorgio and his family had left northern Italy for the Cape and, as cellarmaster for esteemed Meerlust Estate for a quarter century, he helped pioneer Bordeaux-style blends and, later, artisanal husk spirits in South Africa. Giorgio's father Vittorio had been a distiller since the 1920s, and his heritage is reflected in the collection that now includes the term 'grappa' in its name, after being registered as part of the Dalla Cia trademark in South Africa ('Dalla Cia Acquavitae' in European markets). Joining the grappas is a salute to the fabled muscats of Constantia.

Dalla Cia Wine range

★★★★☆ **Classico** ⓐ Cabernet sauvignon & 10% petit verdot. Refinement personified, **20** ⑨⓪ is subtle, cohesive & charming in its cigarbox, cassis & herb classicism. Backbone & grip from 18 months in half new oak. Rewarding & long. Unlike no-holds-barred **19** ★★★★ ⑧⑧, alc a reasonable 12.5%.

★★★★ **Pinot Noir** Forest fruit, violet & cherry abundance on suave, succulent **19** ★★★★☆ ⑨②. Harmonious & supple, its light, powder-fine tannin reflects the 18 months in new oak. Will reward patience. Improves on both **17** ★★★★ ⑧⑤ & **15** ⑧⑦; **18** not made, **16** not tasted.

★★★★☆ **Giorgio** ⓥ Full-throttle Bordeaux blend intended for decade cellaring. **19** ⑨⓪'s sweet fruit a foil for its 80% new oak, neatly balanced by a feisty acid. 67% cab, merlot & petit verdot.

★★★★☆ **Teano** ⓥ French & Italian grapes meet in **17** ⑨④ blend. Flavours effortlessly assimilate 100% new oak, multiply & evolve through to lengthy finish. Last tasted was **14** ⑨②. Also in 1.5L, as Giorgio.

★★★★ **Chardonnay** ⓥ Just 5% barrel-fermented portion in atypically reticent **21** ⑧⑨. Whispers of spicy oak, lemon & fennel, more animated palate shows satisfying smooth persistence. **20** not made.

★★★★ **Sauvignon Blanc** Not your typical sauvignon: fleshy, broad, with pear, fig & light lemon succulence. Finish is resolved, with peppery aftertaste. **22** ★★★★ ⑧⑤, like **21** ⑧⑦, well judged.

Bullicante Sparkling Pinot Grigio Brut ★★★★☆ Named for bubbles in Murano glassware, **NV** ⑧⑤ bright & vivacious, fun & fizzy, acid balancing pear & melon ripeness. Just 9 g/L sugar. WO W Cape, as Teano.

Dalla Cia Grappa range

★★★★★ **10 Year Old Celebration Cabernet Sauvignon-Merlot** ⓥ Limited release marks family's Stellenbosch distillery's 10th anniversary. Rich, with a velvet texture, delightfully mellow. Long-lasting sipper ⑨⑤ to be savoured. 500 ml, stylishly packaged.

★★★★ **Cabernet Sauvignon-Merlot Premium Selection** ⓥ Slight straw tinge to this more refined, less aggressive Premium (lightly barrelled) version ⑧⑦ of the standard husk spirit from these varieties. Supple, gently unctuous palate, lingering finish.

★★★★ **Pinot Noir-Chardonnay** ⓥ Fresh aromas of fruit & nuts; some delicacy, focus & refinement evident on a delightfully textured, smooth & balanced spirit ⑧⑦.

★★★★☆ **Single Cultivar Moscato** ⓝⓔⓦ ⓥ ⓐ Exquisite expression ⑨④ from Constantia muscat de Frontignan. Water white, with delicate rosepetal & orange blossom perfume, green apple, ripe pineapple accents. Complex, smooth, refined & warming (43% alc), long tropical finish. The perfect digestif. 500 ml.

★★★★ **Single Cultivar Organic Merlot** ⓥ ⓨ High-toned note gives magnificent lift to red berry & floral aromas; sweet spice & some citrus buoy spirity finish (43% alc) of this elegant bottling ⑧⑦.

Cabernet Sauvignon-Merlot ② ★★★★ Robust aromas & flavours, husk-y, quiet berry hint. This unmatured bottling ⑧④ smooth enough, but with some rusticity. Not tasted: **Limited Edition Pinot Noir**.

Brandy range

★★★★ **H&G Fine & Rare Potstill Brandy** ② Potstill ⑧⑥ aged 9 years. Rich & rounded, with waxy plum & orchard fruit flavours in harmony with oak. Sleek & long. From semillon & shiraz.— FM, WB

Location/map: Stellenbosch ▪ Map grid reference: E5 ▪ WO: Stellenbosch/Western Cape ▪ Est 2004 ▪ Tasting, sales & traditional Italian meals at Pane E Vino Food & Wine Bar, Mon-Sat 10–5 ▪ Closed all pub hols ▪ Grappa distillery by appt Mon-Fri 10–4 ▪ Wine club ▪ Owner(s) George Dalla Cia ▪ Winemaker(s) Giorgio Dalla Cia & George Dalla Cia ▪ 15,000cs ▪ 7A Distillery Rd, Bosman's Crossing, Stellenbosch 7600 ▪ info@dallacia.com ▪ www.dallacia.com ▪ T +27 (0)21-888-4120

Dalsig Wines

Seasoned wine man Ansgar Flaatten and wife Lee-Zanne created this boutique brand in 2022 'to celebrate the small wins in life', like returning to Ansgar's hometown Stellenbosch that year, specifically the leafy neighbourhood of Dalsig, after a decade away. The vision is an expanded line-up which 'reflects the great wine regions and celebrates their lifestyles', made as naturally and 'close to the soil' as possible.

★★★★☆ **Chardonnay** Expressive **22** ⑨⓪ pear, apple & yellow citrus notes on interesting & captivating palate. Impressive depth, with texture & richness from 'egg' ferment. Nicely dry & savoury conclusion, the whole enlivened by salty acidity.— CR, CvZ

Location/WO: Stellenbosch ▪ Est/1stB 2022 ▪ Closed to public ▪ Winemaker(s) Adam Mason & Ansgar Flaatten (Jun 2022) ▪ 1,000cs ▪ ansgar@dalsig.com ▪ www.dalsig.com ▪ T +27 (0)82-729-0602

☐ **Daredevils' Drums** *see* Springfontein Wine Estate

D'Aria Winery

Much that's new and refreshed at the company-owned, music-named and -themed D'Aria estate on Durbanville's Tygerberg Hills. Elizabeth Meyer has joined as wine/brandy-maker and viticulturist, with a philosophy of 'maintaining the integrity of the vineyard in the cellar as far as possible', and plans to release a new red wine; the Premium labels have been refreshed, to be followed by the Music series; and key visitor attractions have been extensively redone, including the guest cottages, tasting lounge and function venue.

Reserve range

★★★★ **The Soprano Shiraz** ⓐ Top-tier red shows class & sophistication in **22** ★★★★☆ ⑨① , muscle & spice reined in, allowing supple ripe fruit to take centre stage. Elegant & nuanced, with exotic scrub & dried herbs, all borne on powdery tannins. Stellenbosch vines. Improves on last-tasted **20** ⑧⑨.

★★★★☆ **The Songbird Sauvignon Blanc** ⊘ Showing region's pyrazine highlights, **22** ⑨⓪ has impressive concentration at modest 11.6% alc, vibrant herbal & mineral aromas, appealing salty finish. Fresh & youthful, should age with grace.

Premium Cape range

★★★★ **Shiraz** Plush, fruit-forward **22** ⑧⑦ shows some heft & muscle, solid leathery tannins, black cherry & plum pudding fruit, tempered by fragrance from 7% viognier. Stellenbosch fruit.

★★★★ **Cabernet Sauvignon-Merlot** ⊘ Earthy, tarry **22** ⑧⑥ has sombre black fruit with appealing anise & rosepetal highlights. Fruit from Piekenierskloof & Stellenbosch (as Merlot), cab upped to 85%, delivers intensity & weight, textured tannins.

Merlot ★★★★ Medium bodied, with upfront cherry & plum fruit, **22** ⑧⑤ shows firm but ripe tannins, oaky aromas, good juiciness. **Blush** ★★★ Mild-mannered, light **23** ⑧② has restrained strawberry cordial flavour, tangy acid for summer refreshment. **Sauvignon Blanc** ⊘ ★★★★ Prominent greenpepper high tones, fig & gooseberry fruit, ensure reductively handled **23** ⑧③ bursts with freshness. Durbanville WO, as Blush. Discontinued: **Lullaby Noble Late Harvest**.

Music by D'Aria range

Winter Ballad ⊘ ★★★★ Name changed from 'Shiraz-Cab-Merlot' but same varieties used for light, pliable **22** ⑧④. Black plum & cherry fruit, cocoa & mint accents, gentle tannins. **Summer Anthem** ⊘

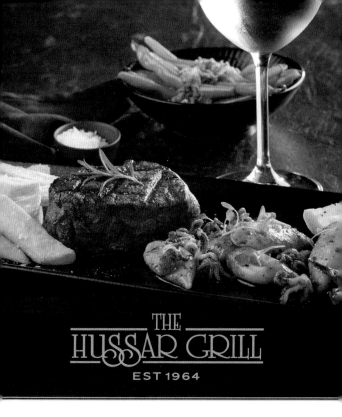

Excellence. Always.

Western Cape Camps Bay | Century City | Durbanville
Franschhoek | George | GrandWest | Hermanus
Mouille Point | Paarl | Rondebosch | Somerset West
Steenberg | Stellenbosch | Willowbridge | Worcester
Gauteng Blueberry | Forest Walk | Harvest Place
Montecasino Morningside | Silverstar Casino | Waterfall
KZN Kloof | Oceans | **Eastern Cape** Walmer
Northern Cape Kimberley

www.hussargrill.co.za | @TheHussarGrill **f** ⓘ

Alcohol Not For Persons Under The Age Of 18.

Smile
POWER

A BRIGHT, WHITE SMILE IS A GREAT CONFIDENCE BOOSTER.

Zoom Whitening is very effective in removing stains and you will **get radiant results in just one office visit.**

N°1
patient-requested
whitening
brand

PHILIPS

ZOOM!

FOR LOCATIONS OF DENTISTS OR FURTHER DETAILS: **+27 21 418 1561**

INFO@ZOOMWHITENING.CO.ZA
WWW.ZOOMWHITENING.CO.ZA

A **BALTIMORE INTERNATIONAL PTY LTD** COMPANY

★★★★ Was blend of sauvignon & chenin, **22** (83) re-named & -cast as varietal sauvignon plus dab chenin, showing appealing ripeness of tropical fruit, refreshing, well-judged acid.

Sparkling range
Love Song Sparkling Pinot Noir ★★★ Carbonated **NV** (82) has tart raspberry fruit & savoury overtone, fine, vigorous bubble. Not tasted: **Pop Song Sparkling Sauvignon Blanc**. Discontinued: **Rock Song Sparkling Shiraz**.

Artisan range
Not tasted: **The Wild Thing Sauvignon Blanc**. Discontinued: **Cape Minstrel**, **The Following Sauvignon Blanc**.

Brandy range
Not tasted: **The Piccolo 9 Year Old Potstill**. — GdB

Location: Durbanville ▪ Map: Durbanville, Philadelphia & Darling ▪ Map grid reference: C7 ▪ WO: Western Cape/Durbanville ▪ Est/1stB 2007 ▪ Tasting & sales Mon-Fri 10-6 Sat 10-5 Sun/pub hols 11-5 ▪ Fee R100pp/5 wines ▪ Closed Dec 24/25 & Jan 1 ▪ Cheese platters, gourmet burgers, oysters, kiddies cookie tasting ▪ Kiddies play area ▪ Venue @ D'Aria T +27 (0)21-975-0421: conferences/events/weddings ▪ Restaurants: The Terrace at D'Aria, Patina Steak House, Botany Cocktail Bar ▪ Trail running & MTB ▪ 3-star guest cottages ▪ Craft gin ▪ Wine club ▪ Owner(s) Barinor Holdings ▪ Production manager Rolene Schonken-Moon ▪ Farm foreman Christiaan Ras (Jul 2023) ▪ Brandy master Elizabeth Meyer (Jan 2023) ▪ Winemaker(s)/viticulturist(s) Elizabeth Meyer (Jan 2023) ▪ 80ha/63ha (cab, carignan, grenache, merlot, ptage, shiraz, sauv, sem, viog) ▪ M13 Tyger Valley Rd Durbanville 7550 ▪ info@daria.co.za ▪ www.dariawinery.co.za ▪ **T +27 (0)21-801-6772**

Darling Cellars   (♀)(♍)(◎)(♨)(♿)

A dynamic, substantial and five-star awarded winery, with facilities (including function venue and restaurant serving light meals and platters) near the eponymous West Coast town, and an extensive, well-priced and ever-expanding wine portfolio that tracks consumer preferences and industry trends. Examples include the surging no-low alcohol and bag-in-box categories. In the cellar, newly promoted (to white-wine maker) Bertrum Titus and colleagues have installed a third amphora, started renewing old floor areas and vinified the first crops of young merlot, pinotage, shiraz and chardonnay.

Old Bush Vines range
★★★★☆ **Cinsaut** (✓)(♨)(♞) Excellent varietal rendition, from vine age to cellar handling, which includes 22 months in mainly seasoned barrels. **21** (94) has depth & harmony, fruit & oak spice equal partners, enough firm dry tannin for definition, ageing. There's sleek muscle tone, latent power.

★★★★☆ **Chenin Blanc** (♀)(♞) More overtly flavourful & opulent than Amphora sibling, also higher acid, sugar & alc at 13.14%. **21** (93) again a barrel selection showing tangy dried peach, apple & almond flavours from 43 year old bushvines. New-oak portion further reduced, highlighting fruit purity.

Cinsaut Rosé (♀) ★★★ Unusual style, savoury, with a salty nuance to its dryness. **21** (80) delicate yet persistent in a lighter frame (11.78% alc). A canapé partner.

Hannuwa range
★★★★ **Amphora Chenin Blanc** (♨) Fermented in ceramic amphora, then 8 months on lees, which **22** (88) rewards with bruised apple & almond tones, textural richness on the palate. Nothing flashy, just seductive & classy, with long ageing potential.

★★★★ **Amphora Sauvignon Blanc** (NEW)(♨) Same handling as chenin, lees contributes to palate weight, integration of fruit. Quietly confident, **22** (89) has gentle green notes, pithy grapefruit, acidity in support. Refined, unshowy, with built-in credentials for a long life.

Darling Heritage Collection
★★★★ **Sir Charles Darling** (♀) Polished flagship Bordeaux blend, in **19** ★★★★★ (95) is 73% cab with merlot. Dark-fruit intensity a foil for serious but integrated oaking, 22 months, 70% new, ensures firm dry tannin framework & augurs well for development. Sophisticated step-up on softer, smoother **18** (87).

★★★★ **The Old Grain Silo** Shiraz with 32% pinotage, **20** (88) is voluptuous, a ripe style given 22 months in 60% new barrels, portion American. Heaps of dark fruit, vanilla spiced, the smoothly rounded curves seamed with supple tannins.

Lady Ann Darling ★★★★ White Bordeaux blend of sauvignon with 25% semillon, **21** ⑧⑤ barrel fermented/9 months, 60% new. Sauvignon holds its own in perfume as leafy, limy tones but, as with **20** ⑧⑤, the savoury oak contribution dominates the flavours. Elegant (12.5% alc) & dry. Not tasted: **Lime Kilns**.

Gustus range

★★★★ **Cabernet Sauvignon** ② Pencil shavings, cedar & black fruit on **19** ⑧⑧, more seriously structured & oaked (22 months, 50% new barrels, as next) than Reserve sibling. Velvet tannin integration, full body, opulent & youthful though already tempting. WO W Cape, as in the range.

★★★★ **Pinotage** ⊘ Dark berries & liquorice. **20** ⑧⑧'s fruit has easily assimilated the oaking (some American, as next), leaving a palate succulence, smoothly curvaceous lines. Delicious.

★★★★ **Shiraz** ⊘ Similar oak handling to pinotage, 60% new, creating an unashamedly opulent wine. Plush ripe fruit, brambleberries & mulberries, coated with vanilla, **21** ⑧⑦'s palate curvy, yet with a dry finish, the tannins promising some cellaring potential.

★★★★ **Sauvignon Blanc** ⊘ Pure sauvignon in **21** ⑧⑧, without semillon, reductively made to showcase fruit, but 6 months on lees giving palate weight, enriching the winter melon & litchi. Lovely finish, salty acid's vibrancy. Lots going on, all of it good.

Skattie ★★★★ Afrikaans for 'sweetie/darling'. Dessert wine from pinotage, vine dried, which accounts for the high sugar, raisined character. No oak but **NV** ⑧⑤'s fruit so concentrated, seems to be smokiness in it. Ultra smooth. Lovely distinctive 375-ml bottle. Not tasted: **Chenin Blanc**. Discontinued: **Bukettraube**.

Winemaker's Selection

Occasional release: **Bukettraube**, **Sauvignon Blanc-Chenin Banc**.

Reserve range

Bush Vine Sauvignon Blanc ⊘ ⑦ ★★★★ Winemaking locks in the fruit, giving **23** ⑧⑤ admirable intensity, focus: kiwi & passionfruit, brisk acid lends vitality. Sleek (12.5% alc) & packed with flavour.

Pyjama Bush Rosé ☺ ★★★ Sauvignon & 4% grenache noir for delicate pink colour, **23** ⑧① forthcoming perfume, gooseberries & kiwi, a whiff of minerality. Palate is crisp, while touch sugar gives a tangy effect.

Terra Hutton Cabernet Sauvignon ⊘ ★★★★ Named for the vineyard soil. **21** ⑧⑤ a touch more elegant than last, but admirable styling remains cassis & choc mint. Has supple dry tannin from 9 month stave oaking, some American, as all reds unless noted. **Eveningstar Cinsault** ② ★★★ Gentle, with ample plummy, perfumed fruit & smooth texture, but still fresh & bright. Less serious style than Old Vine cousin, just a whisper of tannin, but **19** ⑧⓪ a step up on last. **Six Tonner Merlot** ★★★ Named for the modest crop yield. Piquant berries, lightly oak spiced, **21** ⑧② has appealing juiciness, drinkability, gentle grip for food matching. **Chocoholic** ② ★★★ Popular semi-dry, easy-drinking quaffer from pinotage. **22** ⑧②'s dark berry flavours get decadent mocha-choc coating from 9-month oak-stave treatment. Includes 10% vine-dried bunches. Also in magnum & 2L bag-in-box. **Old Blocks Pinotage** ⊘ ★★★★ Ripe & fleshy, some vanilla tones from 40% American oak, **21** ⑧④ is pinotage at its most succulent, berry fruited, a whiff of salty liquorice. Has personality. **Black Granite Shiraz** ⊘ ★★★★ Good typicity in **21** ⑧⑤, brambly fruit & smoky spice from oak, there's fleshy ripeness, amenable tannin. Lovely drinkability. Also in magnum. **SMG** ⊘ ★★★ Different label design to rest of range. Equal shiraz & unusually, malbec, with 20% grenache, blend proportion changed in **22** ⑧①. Dark-toned fruit, spicing courtesy of oak, the overall effect smooth, flavourful. WO W Cape. **Quercus Gold Chardonnay** ⊘ ★★★★ Lees contact 3 months then new oak 4 months, which **23** ⑧④ integrates with stonefruit & citrus in the flavours. Nice palate weight, a gentle biscuit nuance, appealing zestiness. **Arum Fields Chenin Blanc** ⊘ ★★★ Reductively made (as all whites) to preserve the fruit, **23** ⑧② has a limy character, perfect fit for the zesty acid, leaves the mouth refreshed.

Classic range

Cabernet Sauvignon-Merlot ⊘ ★★★ Unwooded, fruit the main attraction, rich berries, hint of cassis, **22** ⑧⓪'s tasty freshness brightening the flavours. More to offer than the last. Also in 500 ml & WO W Cape for all these. **Merlot Rosé** ② ★★ Easy sundowner-styled tipple with gentle strawberry notes. Dry & lighter (12.3% alc) in **22** ⑦⑤. **Chenin Blanc-Sauvignon Blanc** ⊘ ★★★ Now an 80/20 combo, slender (12.5% alc) but zesty-fresh **23** ⑧⓪ showcases chenin's crunchy apple tones, sauvignon's fennel nuance.

2L Bag-in-Box range

Chocoholic ⊘ ★★★ Small portion vine-dried bunches added for richness, NV ⑧② pinotage with 9% cinsaut is easy to love. French & American staves impart mocha-choc decadence to the fruit; touch sugar furthers the appeal. Also in magnum. **Black Granite Shiraz** ⊘ ★★★★ Good typicity in NV ⑧⑤, brambly fruit & smoky spice from oak, there's fleshy ripeness, amenable tannin. Lovely drinkability. Also in magnum. **Pyjama Bush Rosé** ⊘ ★★★ Sauvignon plus 4% grenache for delicate pink colour, NV ⑧① has ample perfume, gooseberries & kiwi, a mineral nuance. Palate is crisp, touch sugar gives a tangy effect. **Bush Vine Sauvignon Blanc** ⊘ ★★★★ Svelte (12.5% alc) & packed with flavour, NV ⑧⑤ has admirable intensity, focus: kiwi & passionfruit, brisk acid giving vitality.

Méthode Cap Classique range

★★★★ **Blanc de Blancs Brut** ⊘ Toasted brioche woven through the chardonnay fruit from 16 months on lees; some roasted nut & honey notes in the flavours, a touch of sugar. Elegant **20** ⑧⑧ doesn't have a shy bone in its body.

★★★★ **Old Bush Vines Brut** ⓧ Golden hue from oaked reserve portion, rich honey, ripe peach zested with lemon acid from chardonnay in **18** ⑧⑧ bubbly. Creamy brioche undertone from lees enrichment, both pre-bottle ferment (6 months) & in bottle (36 months). Notch up on **16** ★★★★ ⑧⑤. **17** untasted.

★★★★ **Nectar** ⊘ New name for Demi Sec but style unchanged: from chenin, elegant (10.5% alc) **20** ⑧⑥'s 16 months on lees add a honeyed seam to the appley fruit. Sweet, but the bubbles provide lift, vibrancy.

Brut Rosé ⊘ ★★★★ From grenache noir, 16 months on lees, **20** ⑧⑤'s delicate pink colour & light structure (11.5% alc) belie the characterful appeal: vivid cranberries, glacé cherries throughout, the touch of sugar offset by brisk acid.

Sweet Darling range

Sweet Rosé ⊘ ★★★ Delicate pink NV ⑦⑨ from mainly bukettraube, dash of red, offers forthcoming floral & muscat scents & flavours. Blend change to its benefit, fits the sweetness. These all WO W Cape. **Sweet White** ★★★ From bukettraube, light alc (as all these) but NV ⑦⑦'s sweetness gives texture, fullness. Aromatic, would enhance spicy dishes. **Sweet Red** ⊘ ★★★ Unspecified blend, no oak, for early drinking. NV ⑦⑦ mix of berries & plums, has smooth, sleek appeal, the sweetness upping texture & flavour.

Wildflower range

★★★★ **Hanepoot Jerepigo** ⓐ Outstanding muscat grapiness, threaded with barley sugar, NV ⑧⑥'s perfume leaps out the glass. Rich in flavour & sweetness, hedonistic, trumps the last one. WO Swartland. **Muskadel** ★★★★ Sweetest of this range, fortified (as rest) NV ⑧③ has muscatty, raisiny fruit, a barley sugar top note, mouthfilling sweetness. Rich & powerful. WO W Cape. **Cape Ruby** ⊘ ★★★★ 3-part blend of Portuguese varieties led by tinta barocca, NV ⑧④ 'port' fermented in small lagares, aged 12 months in large old vats, everything done to create a classic Ruby style. Fruit forward, smoothly sweet, tannins subservient. WO Calitzdorp.

DC De-alcoholised range

Shiraz ★★ French & American barrels & staves part of NV ⑦④'s winemaking process, give a spiciness to the red berries. Sweetness apparent, counterbalancing the tannins. Alc under 0.5% for all. **Rosé** ★★ Vinified conventionally, then alc removed with 'spinning cone' technology, as all. Pale pink NV ⑦⑥ doesn't lack character: sauvignon giving the leaf & gooseberry tones, 4% grenache the colour. Plumping sweetness aids the appeal. **Sauvignon Blanc** ★★★ With just a touch of semillon, NV ⑦⑦ not disadvantaged by the low alc, all of sauvignon's character showing, ending limy-fresh. Sugar plumps the body, gives tanginess to the flavours. **Sparkling Rosé** ⓧ ★★ Sauvignon with soupçon grenache noir in salmon-hued NV ⑦② fizz. Hint of cranberry, 23 g/L sugar & lifted bubbly freshness. — CR

Location: Darling ▪ Map: Durbanville, Philadelphia & Darling ▪ Map grid reference: B2 ▪ WO: Darling/Western Cape/Swartland/Calitzdorp ▪ Est 1948 ▪ 1stB 1981 ▪ Tasting & sales Mon-Thu 9-5 Fri 9-4 Sat 10-3; pub hols (seasonal) please call ahead ▪ Closed Good Fri, Dec 25 & Jan 1 ▪ Cellar tours by appt ▪ Light meals & cheese platters ▪ Facilities for children ▪ Bottling services offered ▪ Wine club ▪ Function venue (150 pax) ▪ Owner(s) 20 shareholders ▪ Winemaker(s) Pieter-Niel Rossouw (Sep 2014-Oct 2023), Anthony Meduna (Oct 2011), Maggie Immelman (Jun 2014), Bertrum Titus (May 2023) ▪ 980ha (barbera, cab, carignan, cinsaut, durif, grenache, malbec, merlot, mourv, ptage, roobernet, shiraz, bukettraube, chard, chenin, cbard, riesling, sauv, sem) ▪ 7,000t/450,000cs own label 60% red 30% white 10% rosé ▪ Other export brands: Black Granite, Cape

Cult, Capeman, Chocoholic ▪ PO Box 114 Darling 7345 ▪ info@darlingcellars.co.za ▪ www.darlingcellars.co.za ▪ **T** +27 (0)22-492-2276/+27 (0)82-226-8769

☐ **Darling Wine In A Can** *see* Cloof Wine Estate

Daschbosch   ⓠ ⓑ

In past editions we've reflected on the importance of wineries that are able to excel at both ends of the volume spectrum, and Daschbosch's 55 grower-shareholders and their team in Breedekloof the past number of years have proved themselves adept at achieving this challenging goal. On the one hand the impressive numbers attached to the standard bottlings, 200,000 cases made for the own label, 750,000 for clients; on the other, the tiny parcels of 'elegant artisanal wines' in the heritage collection, some from 1960s and 1970s vines, that this edition earn a maximum 5-star rating, an achievement all concerned should be proud of.

Daschbosch Heritage range

★★★★ The Mill Cinsault (NEW) Lightly perfumed & savoury **22** (86), satisfyingly dry & with greater presence, palate weight than 12% alc would suggest. 6 months older oak add support, not flavour.

★★★★☆ Mossiesdrift Steen ⓑ ⓦ Precise & elegant **22** ★★★★★ (95) from chenin bushvines over 60 years old, partly wild-yeast fermented/10 months in old oak. Impressive concentration & breadth of white peach, quince & honey, lingering sweet-salty finish. Beautifully realised & ageworthy, raises the bar on **21** ★★★★ (89) & **20** (91).

★★★★☆ Avon Clairette Blanche ⓑ ⓦ Arguably one of the most interesting bottlings in SA's vinous firmament, simultaneously restrained & assured, subtle & expressive. Just 222 cases, thus hard to find. Old-oak ferment, 6 months on thick lees provide texture & weight in **22** (93).

★★★★☆ Gevonden Hanepoot ⓑ ⓦ Acclaimed fortified from muscat d'Alexandrie bushvines planted in 1900. Also lightly brushed with old oak, **17** (94) as full-sweet & hedonistic as **16** (94). Thrill lies in the contrast between mouthcoating apricot & marzipan richness, delicate yet effective spirit heat (17.7% alc). 375 ml.

Daschbosch Experimental range

★★★★☆ Skin Contact Arresting label art for back-to-form **23** (90), same 50/50 chenin & muscat d'Alexandrie partnership but on skins for just 3 months after ferment vs 6 on last-tasted **19** ★★★★ (86). Bracingly dry, with gentle tannin tug & muscat florality to the fore; peach pip, dried peach, attractive bitter quince complexity.

Not tasted: **Méthode Ancestrale Verdelho**.

Daschbosch Popular Premium range

★★★★ The Gift ⓠ Alluring depth to **20** (87) pinotage (48%), shiraz & petit verdot. Textured, plush & appealing, with plum, cocoa & peppery spice. Impressive length aided by 10 months oaking. **Cabernet Sauvignon** ⓠ ★★★★ Violet perfume & berry compote on **21** (85). Lightly oaked, as Merlot, shows good concentration & depth. **Merlot** ⓠ ★★★★ Herb-brushed fruitcake appeal on **21** (84), light grip & dryness on finish. **Sauvignon Blanc** ⓠ ★★★★ Echoes previous in lemon zest & tropical fruit but **22** (85) improves in bright acid & mineral grip. Succulent, with good length & palate weight. WO W Cape. **Méthode Charmat Rosé** (NEW) ⓥ ★★★★ From chenin & pinotage, pale salmon & gently sweet **NV** (83) is frothy & light (10.6% alc), with intense berry aromas & flavours. **Sauvignon Blanc Brut Sparkling** (NEW) ★★★ Feisty **NV** (82) revels in its apple sherbet & cut grass characters, easy-to-enjoy sweetness.

Meander range

Malbec ⓠ ★★★ Plump cherry exuberance on **21** (82), tank fermented with oak staves. Ripe yet light bodied & approachable. **Pinotage** ⓠ ★★★ Cherry & plum simplicity to **21** (82), succulent & bright but a tad slight. **Shiraz** ⓠ ★★★★ Supple **21** (83) styled for everyday quaffing (as all these), spent time in tank with staves, offers herb-dusted black fruit & juicy appeal. **Chenin Blanc** ⓥ ★★★ Slightly dusty but neatly dry finish on vibrant & satisfying **23** (81). **Sauvignon Blanc** ⓠ ★★★ Trademark grapefruit zest on succulent **21** (81), dab sugar balances acid for comfortable poolside sipping. **Moscato Pink** ★★★ Slightly sparkling, low-alc **NV** (81) from muscat d'Alexandrie & merlot. Sunset hue, ripe strawberry & grape aromas & flavours. Refreshing when chilled despite overt sweetness. **Moscato White** ★★★ Tad less joie de vivre than Pink, perlé **NV** (79) from muscat d'Alexandrie has faint Turkish delight & muscat florality, low 5.5% alc, noticeable sweetness.

Meander 3L range

Merlot ⊘ ★★★ Mulberry succulence on **21** ⑧②, light squeeze of tannin from time in tank with staves, pleasant dry conclusion. **Sauvignon Blanc** ⊘ ★★★ Forthcoming grenadilla & other tropical fruits, hint of sweetness, zippy acid: **23** ⑧⓪ ticks the summer party boxes.

Palesa Fairtrade range

Pinotage ⊘ ★★★☆ Blueberry & raspberry exuberance of **21** ⑧③ also shows a deeper core. Gentle grip of tannin & cohesive body, good length. More complex than previous. **Chenin Blanc** ⊘ ★★★ Ripe fig & guava of **22** ⑧② countered by tang of acid. Fresh, lively & structured. Ups the bar on last.

Discontinued: **Goudini Lifestyle range**. — CvZ

Location: Rawsonville ▪ Map: Breedekloof ▪ Map grid reference: C6 ▪ WO: Breedekloof/Western Cape ▪ Est/1stB 2007 ▪ Tasting & sales at Sneeukop facility on Goudini premises: Mon-Fri 9-5 Sat 9-3 Sun closed ▪ Closed Good Fri, Dec 25/26 & Jan 1 ▪ Fully licensed ▪ Owner(s) 55 shareholders ▪ Head(s) of winemaking Willem Visagie (2010, branded) & Johan Lotz (bulk) ▪ Head of resources Nicolaas Rust (2008) ▪ Senior winemaker(s) Schalk van der Merwe (2007), Jaco van Niekerk (2022), Pieter van Wyk (2016) & Etienne le Roux (2021) ▪ Winemaker(s) Ruan Stander (2012), Nicolaas du Toit (2017) & Lamees Isaacs (2017) ▪ Viticulturist(s) Nicholas Bruyns (2013) ▪ 3,000ha (cab, cinsaut, merlot, ptage, shiraz, chard, chenin, cbard, sauv) ▪ 65,000t/200,000cs own label 50% red 50% white + 750,000cs for clients ▪ ISO 22000:2008, Fairtrade, IPW, WIETA ▪ PO Box 174 Rawsonville 6845 ▪ info@uniwines.co.za, hello@sneeukop.co.za ▪ www.uniwines.co.za ▪ T +27 (0)23-349-1110

☐ **Dassie's** see Botha Wine Cellar

David & Nadia ⊘

David and Nadia Sadie are one of the clutch of pioneering and now internationally renowned producers based on the Paardeberg. They lead a close team, with Nadia, a qualified soil scientist and viticulturist, taking primary responsibility for the home-farmed grapes and those that are brought in from elsewhere in their 'beloved Swartland'. They collaborate closely with other farmers, taking ever more responsibility for the vineyards they work with. Continuing cellar improvements - to sorting and other equipment for example, and increased attention paid to individual batches - are also directed at boosting quality. The focus is on chenin blanc and grenache noir. There are now four chenins in the Single Vineyard range - and two blended versions, one for the CWG Auction and one in the David & Nadia range. All are naturally fermented, as are the reds, and made in a light, fresh and supremely elegant style.

CWG Auction range ⑭ℰⓦ

★★★★★ **Veiling Chenin Blanc** ⊛ ⊛ Light-feeling **22** ⑨⑥ blended from 4 heritage vineyards. Especially pale & delicately refined, but with forward fruit richness controlled by tense balance & light phenolic grip. Soft, almost velvety, despite a more prominent succulent acidity than on the other chenins here.

Single Vineyard range

★★★★☆ **Hoë-Steen Chenin Blanc** ⊛ ⊛ Like all these chenins, matured 11 months in neutral oak barrels, none new, and minimalistically handled. **22** ⑨④ has subtle earthiness to its harmonious profundity. Acidity moderate but very telling in the taut balance, making for youthful tightness yet not precluding approachability. Citrus element on the finish, not uncommon aspect of this vintage.

★★★★★ **Plat'bos Chenin Blanc** ⊛ ⊛ Paler gold than, say, Hoë-Steen, & more exuberant aromas. **22** ⑨⑤ nervy & vibrant, with subtle stoniness complementing the long-lingering intensity of flavour. 12% alc, the lowest in the range of chenins; bone-dry like all.

★★★★☆ **Rondevlei Chenin Blanc** ⊛ ⊛ Less stony-taut & a little richer-feeling than some of these, **22** ⑨③'s deep intensity delicately expressed, fruit tinged with thatchy dried herb notes. Third aged in concrete 'egg', unlike the others. Typical bright acidity does not preclude accessibility, hallmark of this vintage.

★★★★★ **Skaliekop Chenin Blanc** ⊛ ⊛ Not untypically for all these chenins, stoniness (even an earthiness) underlines the comparatively assertive pure fruit of **22** ★★★★☆ ⑨④ & richness of texture, complemented by succulent freshness also seen in **21** ⑨⑥. Long-lingering finish. Like the other chenins, rather more open in youth this vintage, but this will not affect at least their mid-term maturity prospects.

David & Nadia range

★★★★☆ **Grenache Noir** Lovely varietal fragrance on **22** (92), with bright red fruit. Some flavour power but overall feeling is of slightly austere lightness, though it does open with aeration. Fine tannins; firm dryness on finish. Matured in mix of old oak barrels & concrete tanks, as Elpidios. 13% alc. Less intense than **21** ★★★★★ (95). Also in magnum, as all these.

★★★★☆ **Elpidios** (🐝) At 54%, grenache more dominant than usual in **21** (93), with syrah & carignan & mere drops pinotage & cinsaut. Perfumed aroma leads to full-fruited yet elegantly restrained palate with early complexity. Succulent, with unassertive but important tannic presence. Lingering finish. 13.5% alc.

★★★★☆ **Chenin Blanc** (🐝) (🍃) From various old vineyards. **22** (94) notably well balanced, with bright but ripely rich acidity, & core of sweet fruit & harmonious charm that makes it particularly ready for early but refined drinking. As **21** ★★★★★ (95), mix of concrete & old barrels for the vinification & maturation.

★★★★☆ **Aristargos** (🐝) From nearly half chenin with 8 other varieties in **22** (94), same cellar regime as other white. Fuller fruit aroma & flavour than the straight chenins, complex character including floral, citrus, stonefruit; intense yet still light-feeling, with long fantailing finish. Silky texture shot through with vibrant acidity. 12.5% alc. Like **21** ★★★★★ (95), should have a great future.— TJ

Location: Malmesbury ▪ Map/WO: Swartland ▪ Map grid reference: C8 ▪ Est/1stB 2010 ▪ Tasting by appt only ▪ Closed all pub hols ▪ Owner(s)/viticulturist(s) David & Nadia Sadie ▪ Winemaker(s) David & Nadia Sadie, Corrien Basson (Nov 2020) ▪ Carignan, cinsaut, grenache, ptage, shiraz, chenin, clairette, cbard, marsanne, rouss, sem, viog ▪ 100t/12,000cs own label 40% red 60% white ▪ Old Vine Project member; Swartland Independent Producers (2011) ▪ info@davidnadia.com ▪ www.davidnadia.com ▪ **T +27 (0)22-001-0025**

David Finlayson Wines   (Ⓛ)

Truly a life of wine. David Finlayson was born into the industry, with vintages at, among others, Château Margaux and Peter Lehmann Wines, and locally a long residency at Glen Carlou, before focusing on once rundown hillside estate Edgebaston just north of Stellenbosch's suburbs, bought by his family in 2004. He personally oversaw the planting of all 24 ha, with mostly classic French varieties carefully matched to soils and aspects. A member of the esteemed Cape Winemakers Guild, lately he's also sought out unique parcels in the broader winelands for the Camino Africana label. These days, winemaking in the cellar on the farm is in the hands of Pieter van der Merwe. See also Sanniesrust listing.

Camino Africana range

★★★★☆ **Cabernet Franc** (🐝) Complex, concentrated, with dark, dense core of cassis & minerality, tightly structured in **21** (94), from a 1983 vineyard. Natural ferment & 2 years in 30% new oak enhance & harmonise the tannins for a long & rewarding life. All elements in place, already streamlined & sophisticated in youth. Deserves lengthy cellaring, as **20** ★★★★★ (95).

★★★★★ **Pinot Noir** (✓) (🐝) Two vintages tasted. Translucent ruby **21** ★★★★★ (95) from mature Stellenbosch Mountain vineyard (clone 667) shows effortless grace & balance. Delicate yet persistent fruit intensity as alluringly perfumed red fruit & damp earth nuances unfurl. Tannins are fine-grained after 18 months in new oak, clean acid woven into sleek texture. **22** (92) similar age vines in Bottelary Hills, also natural ferment but only 12 months new oak, touch lower alc & acid, riper fruit but tad less perfume, finesse & silkiness. Still good depth of flavour & freshness, potential for further development.

★★★★★ **Shale Terraces Chardonnay** (🐝) Exhilarating in its burst of mouthfilling tangerine, ginger biscuit & toasted hazelnut flavours, **22** (95) as intense & complex as last. Natural ferment & year new barrels in harmony, infusing the complex layers of fruit with a creamy oatmeal richness. Fresh & piquantly balanced, lingering lemony farewell. Consistently impressive & world class.

★★★★☆ **Chenin Blanc** (🐝) Fruit from 1960s & 1980s vines, naturally fermented in barrel, similar finesse & balance as last. **22** (94) rich yet understated, subtle savouriness to clean greengage & lanolin notes, pervasive minerality & freshness from curtailed malo. Texture still alluringly silky & seductive, polished by year older oak, 10% in concrete 'egg'.

★★★★ **Cape Vintage** Preview of port-styled fortified **21** (88), equal touriga & tinta from dryland vines in Prince Albert Hamlet. Concentrated dark fruit compote with firm tannin backbone, befitting the style, not overly sweet (92 g/L sugar), though fiery spirit still not fully melded. 18.75% alc.

David Finlayson range

★★★★☆ **Cabernet Sauvignon** ⊘ ⊛ As sophisticated, though even more structured in **21** ⑨④ vintage of this flagship variety. Fine balance of intensity, elegance & finesse, with herbaceous nuance laced into tight core of blackcurrant fruit, in sync with oak, 18 months, 20% new. Youthful & ageworthy - handsome rewards in store.

★★★★☆ **GS Cabernet Sauvignon** ⊛ A double bill of these pure, distinguished tributes to George Spies' legendary 1960s wines. **20** ⑨④ more generous & opulent in its richly layered dark fruit & supple tannins. Like sibling, 2 years in new oak, suitable foil for opulence. **21** ★★★★★ ⑨⑥ shows vintage's expressive restraint. Lovely intensity & complexity, similar fruit profile but finer tannins & structure for the long haul, while debonaire sibling entertains.

★★★★☆ **Pinot Noir** ⊘ Lively red fruit with some savoury notes in **22** ⑨⓪, supple structure & fresh acid, 10 months in oak. Modern, accessible style, touch less serious than Camino siblings though no less respectable or flavourful. WO Coastal, as Cab Et Al & Pepper Pot.

★★★★☆ **Cab Et Al** ⓃⒺⓌ ⊘ Cab-led Bordeaux blend with merlot (52/26), cab franc, malbec & petit verdot reflects sheathed power of classic **21** ⑨① vintage. Coiled & muscular structure restrains dark-fruited core; cocoa-dusted nuance to the dry tannins, older oak, 14 months, in sync. Ageworthy, though tempting.

★★★★ **The Pepper Pot** Drier & more savoury in **21** ★★★★ ⑧⑤ than **20** ⑧⑥. Aromatic spice attractions subtler, though similar blend syrah & grenache noir (54/24) with mourvèdre & tannat. All in balance, oak well integrated, needs time to unfurl.

★★★★☆ **Chardonnay** ⊘ Harvesting at different ripeness levels ensures freshness & balance in **22** ⑨①. Still rich & elegant, with similar vinification to previous: ferment in mostly seasoned barrels, partly with wild yeast. Vibrant citrus & honeysuckle nuances, creamy shortbread substrate from lees contact.

★★★★ **Sauvignon Blanc** ⊘ Burst of fresh & tangy gooseberry, lime & nettle flavours in **23** ⑧⑥. Splash unoaked semillon & some lees enrichment add to creamy mid-palate appeal. Pocket-friendly, bright summer staple.

Merlot ★★★★ Drops 'Berry Box' from name. Balanced & approachable but not as intense in **22** ⑧⑤, plush dark berry fruit streamlined by inclusion of dabs petit verdot & cab franc. Drier, cinnamon-infused farewell. In abeyance: **Syrah**, **The Berry Box White**. — MW

Location/map: Stellenbosch ▪ Map grid reference: E3 ▪ WO: Stellenbosch/Coastal ▪ Est/1stB 2004 ▪ Tasting by appt only ▪ Wine club ▪ Owner(s) David Finlayson ▪ Cellarmaster(s) David Finlayson (Jan 2004) ▪ Winemaker(s) Pieter van der Merwe (Jan 2016) ▪ 30ha/24ha (cab, shiraz, chard, sauv) ▪ 300t/60,000cs own label 60% red 40% white ▪ PO Box 2033 Dennesig 7601 ▪ admin@edgebaston.co.za ▪ www.edgebaston. co.za ▪ **T +27 (0)83-263-4353**

☐ **David Nieuwoudt** *see* Cederberg Private Cellar

Dawn Patrol Wines

For this mostly exported boutique label, keen surfer and accomplished vigneronne Trizanne Barnard of Cape Town-based Trizanne Signature Wines celebrates the 'inspiring and uplifting' ritual of rising early to find the day's perfect swell. To support marine ecology protection, she sponsors Voice of the Ocean, a youth education programme involving Hout Bay's Sentinel Ocean Alliance, coordinated by non-profit Ocean Pledge.

Dawn Patrol range

Syrah ⓥ ★★★★ Light-footed **21** ⑧⑤ raised in older, larger oak to preserve plum scents & succulent flavour. **Cinsault Rosé** ⓥ ★★★★ Appealing dry **22** ⑧④ is juicy, with bright acid & berry flavours, ideal for summer. **Chenin Blanc** ⊘ ★★★★ Lively apricot & nectarine allure to **22** ⑧③. Breadth & texture from natural ferment in foudre & tank. **Sauvignon Blanc** ⊘ ★★★★ Lemon & granadilla typicity on **22** ⑧③ with subtle floral extra. Tangy, fresh & lively, light lees element. WO W Cape, as Slimline version.

Slimline Can range

Cinsault ★★★ Lively & berry-licious as ever, **22** ⑧② with subtle frame & texture from open-top natural ferment & 4 months oak treatment. **Syrah** ★★★★ Friendly herb-dusted plum & blueberry on **22** ⑧③ from older vines. Supple & lithe, gentle grip from year seasoned oak. **Cinsault Rosé** ⓥ ★★★★ Berry & plum verve of **22** ⑧④ promises much alfresco enjoyment in its tasty, fresh appeal. **Chenin Blanc** ★★★★ Offers stonefruit brightness in **22** ⑧③. Fresh, good mouthfeel & body from natural ferment in foudre & tank.

Sauvignon Blanc ★★★★ Tangy lemon zip & leafy fig typicity on juicy **23** (83). Gentle body & breadth from few months on lees. 250 ml, as all these. — FM

Location: Cape Town ▪ WO: Swartland/Western Cape ▪ Est 2015 ▪ Wine sales via website ▪ Owner(s) Trizanne Barnard ▪ Winemaker(s) Trizanne Barnard & Madré van der Walt ▪ 6,000cs ▪ info@trizanne.co.za ▪ www. dawnpatrolwines.com ▪ **T +27 (0)82-383-6664**

☐ **DC De-alcoholised** *see* Darling Cellars

Deep Rooted Wines

Stanford craft vintner Mark Stephens emphasises the wellness aspect of wine, seen in his management of, and sourcing from organic or regenerative vineyards, including some new ones. He also has most wines certified as 'alternative', thus assuring low sulphur levels. After a growth spurt, he's focused 'just on quality'.

★★★★☆ **Hinterlands** (NEW) (✓) Masterly expression of cool-climate syrah, **22** (91) slowly reveals subtle violet tones, reined-in red & black fruit, elegant length. Fine graceful tannins courtesy clever balance 20% wholebunch ferment & 11 months older oak.

★★★★☆ **Journey To The Centre Of The Universe** (🐝) Spontaneously fermented sauvignon blanc, on lees in older oak 11 months. **22** (93) as restrained but more refined than last, with succulent acid & an effortless glide to a persistent, dry, faintly tannic finish. Cape South Coast WO.

★★★★☆ **Touch Me** Inspired if idiosyncratic expression of Portugal's verdelho, given partial carbonic ferment/11 months in old barrels. **22** (90) boasts variety's crunchy green apple & racy acid with nutty aromas & flavours & pithy apple grip. No **21**.

★★★★ **Free The Bubble** Méthode ancestrale (single-ferment) sparkler, hence crown cap, from chardonnay & pinotage. Hue of antique lace, raw biscuit dough & ginger aromas, berry flavours. **23** (88) frothy with captivating dryness & energy.— CvZ

Location: Stanford ▪ Map: Walker Bay & Bot River ▪ Map grid reference: B6 ▪ WO: Walker Bay/Cape South Coast ▪ Est/1stB 2018 ▪ Tasting, sales & cellar tours by appt ▪ Owner(s) Mark Stephens ▪ Winemaker(s)/ viticulturist(s) Mark Stephens (2018) ▪ Bought-in grapes ▪ 8t/1,200cs own label 33% red 33% white 33% bubbles ▪ Weltevrede Farm, Stanford 7210 ▪ taste@deeprooted.wine ▪ www.deeprooted.wine ▪ **T +27 (0)82-222-6129**

Definitum Wines

Becoming recognised as the definitive producer of the particular variety or blend being bottled was the goal of Somerset West financial planner Fritz van der Merwe and a friend in launching this after-hours boutique label in the late 2000s. Later the idea of using unusual varieties was added, hence petit verdot in the line-up.

★★★★ **Petit Verdot Reserve** (♀) Like Arbalest, a preview last time, **19** (87)'s edges since smoothed & spiciness integrated, massive structure tempered by velvet tannins. Step up on last **17** ★★★★☆ (84).

★★★★ **Arbalest** (♀) Cab (60%) with merlot & petit verdot, **19** (86) sleeker after extra year's ageing, oak subservient to plum fruit; generous body & ripe, full tannins. Up a notch on last **17** ★★★★ (84).

In abeyance: **Benevolence**. — GdB

Location: Somerset West ▪ WO: Stellenbosch ▪ Est/1stB 2009 ▪ Closed to public ▪ Owner(s) Fritz van der Merwe ▪ 1,625cs own label 100% red ▪ 55A Pienaar Str, Somerset West 7130 ▪ definitumwines@gmail.com ▪ www.definitumwines.com

De Grendel Wines

Owned by De Villiers Graaff, this expansive Tygerberg Hills property overlooking Cape Town's Table Mountain and Table Bay has been farmed since the early 18th century, cattle and sheep studs joined from 2000 by classic grape varieties and a modern cellar captained from the outset by Charles Hopkins, now with former assistant Morgan Steyn elevated to winemaker. More tanks were added in 2023 to accommodate a bigger crop, raising overall capacity to 800 tons. Maritime vineyards are supplemented from Graaff-owned parcels and contracted blocks in areas such as Faure, Ceres Plateau, Elim and Darling, with vine renewal a constant. Completion of a 3-year conversion saw the first organic viognier bottled. New opportunities and markets continue to be explored, the goal being an equal split among exports, direct to consumer and retail. The De Grendel winemaking approach?'We are not aspiring towards quality, we are completely obsessed with it.'

Heritage range

★★★★☆ **Op Die Berg Pinot Noir** ✓ ⊛ 'Op Die Berg' name given to wines from high-altitude Ceres Plateau vines. **22** ⑨④ as pleasing & characterful as last. Exotic nutmeg & anise detail on strawberry & fynbos, fresh tannins, piquant fantail finish.

★★★★☆ **Amandelboord Pinotage** ⊛ Shade less rich, deeply fruited than previous but **22** ⑨③ still a showy wine, exotic curry leaf nuance on sugared mulberry nose & palate. Commendable tannin tug at the end adds lift.

★★★★★ **Elim Shiraz** ⊛ Coastal expression vs continental Op Die Berg sibling. **21** ⑨⑤'s tight tannins embrace elegant & precise raspberry & red plum core of fruit, enhance the grip from well-judged oak regime, 13 months, 5% new. Only in magnum, invites & deserves cellaring.

★★★★☆ **Op Die Berg Syrah** ⊛ Refined **22** ⑨④'s cool origin evident in pepper top note, more delicate fruit profile & leaner body than coastal sibling. Violet & subtle blood orange complexity, restrained oaking, 6% new, year, impressive dry persistence. **21** ★★★★★ ⑨⑥ silky & lush.

★★★★☆ **Op Die Berg Chardonnay** ⊘ Very expressive, with compelling tautness & minerality that give elegant freshness to **22** ⑨③. Persistent apple, quince & citrus woven around creamy core of vanilla & spice from brief 4.5 months in 30% new barrels, with lees stirred.

★★★★☆ **Winifred** ⊛ Numerous vessel types, including clay amphora, ceramic 'egg' & older barrels, plus some skin & lees contact for unusual, successful blend semillon, chardonnay & viognier (60/25/15). **23** ⑨④ tasty, compelling, with considerable gravitas given wine's youth, dryness (below 2 g/L sugar) & modest 13% alc.

★★★★☆ **Proposal Hill Brut Rosé** From pinot noir, which lends **20** ⑨⓪ celebratory sparkler its pale salmon hue & gossamer red berry fruit, 30 months on lees add the energetic bubbles. Exquisitely dry (just 1.3 g/L sugar, technically brut nature) but not quite as long-lingering as last **18** ⑨②.

Not tasted: **Rubáiyát, Sir David Graaff First Baronet, Koetshuis Sauvignon Blanc**.

De Grendel range

★★★★ **Merlot** Plums, red & black, with cocoa & Indian spices in nicely rounded **21** ⑧⑥. Plumped with 9% petit verdot & treated to year in oak, 33% new, ends with slight green walnut bitterness.

★★★★☆ **Shiraz** ✓ ⊛ Fruit forward & succulent, **21** ⑨④'s red & black fruit perfumed with black pepper & charry oak, embroidered with savoury herbs. Masterly tannins & 13 months in 20% new oak contribute to decade cellaring potential. WO Coastal, like Rosé.

★★★★ **Rosé** ✓ Equal cab & pinotage star in neatly dry, flavoursome & pale pink **23** ⑧⑦. Bright acid, pronounced strawberry-lime tang & pleasant subtle tannin nudge.

★★★★ **Sauvignon Blanc** ✓ Water-white **23** ⑧⑦ gains decent palate heft from 6% unoaked semillon & 80 days on lees, yet not sharing much in terms of aromas or flavours; shade less personality than **22** ⑧⑨. WO Cape Town.

★★★★ **Viognier** ⊘ Previewed **23** ⑧⑨ quite compact & bracingly dry, with quiet peach & almond tones. Well rounded from the 30% that saw oak, 20% new, for 4 months, lingering orange essential oil suggestion at finish.

★★★★ **Méthode Cap Classique Brut** From chardonnay & 25% pinot noir, **21** ⑧⑦'s trails of elegant bubbles, soft mousse & intense toasty brioche aromas from 14 months sur lie. Ripe pineapple nuance with white variety's lemon acid & burst of freshness. No **20**.

★★★★☆ **Sauvignon Blanc Noble Late Harvest** ⊘ Preview of **22** ⑨② botrytis dessert wine oozes honeyed flavours layered with marmalade & nutty complexity. Perfect acid balance, for a fresh, long citrus crème finish. 375 ml. — CvZ

Location: Durbanville ▪ Map: Durbanville, Philadelphia & Darling ▪ Map grid reference: C8 ▪ WO: Durbanville/ Ceres Plateau/Coastal/Elim/Cape Town ▪ Est 1720 ▪ 1stB 2004 ▪ Tasting & sales Mon-Sat 9-5 Sun 10-4; pub hols (seasonal) please call ahead ▪ Gourmet snack selection available in tasting room ▪ Closed Dec 25 ▪ Cellar tours by appt ▪ Conferences ▪ De Grendel Restaurant ▪ Three Spades Cider ▪ Wine club ▪ Owner(s) De Villiers Graaff ▪ Cellarmaster(s) Charles Hopkins (Oct 2005) ▪ Winemaker(s) Morgan Steyn (Jan 2023) ▪ Viticulturist(s) Pierre Carstens (Jul 2021) ▪ 800ha/75ha (cab f, merlot, p verdot, ptage, pinot, shiraz, chard, sauv, sem, viog) ▪ 700t/55,000cs own label 35% red 50% white 15% rosé ▪ WWF-SA Conservation Champion ▪ Plattekloof Rd, Panorama 7500 ▪ info@degrendel.co.za ▪ www.degrendel.co.za ▪ **T +27 (0)21-558-6280**

deKaap Vineyards   (ⓘ) (🍴) (◎)

William Wilson's winery near McGregor village is proudly 'boutique' in its footprint and approach, with just over a hectare of vines, and the wines handcrafted by limited-release specialist Lourens van der Westhuizen.

Edel Rouge ★★★ Subtle dark berries & herbaceous notes on cab with 25% each malbec, cab franc. Coiled fruit & oak tannins in **21** ⑧②, unyielding, need time & a hearty meal. Not tasted: **Blanc de Noir**. — MW

Location: McGregor ▪ Map: Robertson ▪ Map grid reference: C5 ▪ WO: Western Cape ▪ Est 2019 ▪ 1stB 2020 ▪ Tasting & sales Mon-Sun 12-3 ▪ Fee R50 ▪ Closed all pub hols ▪ Cheese platters ▪ Farm produce ▪ Art gallery ▪ Owner(s) Caimee Properties cc (sole member William John Wilson) ▪ Winemaker(s) Lourens van der Westhuizen (2010, Arendsig) ▪ 1.8ha/1.2ha (cabs s/f, grenache noir, malbec) ▪ 1,600cs own label 75% red 25% blanc de noir ▪ PO Box 512 McGregor 6708 ▪ dekaap@netactive.co.za ▪ www.dekaapvineyards.co.za ▪ **T +27 (0)87-550-3369/+27 (0)82-904-3130**

☐ **Dekker's Valley** see Mellasat Vineyards

De Kleine Wijn Koöp   (ⓘ)

Lately in the care of minimal-intervention winemaker Wynand Grobler and wife Anya, 'The Small Wine Co-op' retains its boutique scale, serious-yet-unpretentious spirit and wide sourcing from 'prestigious and somewhat mysterious' vineyards. The couple have added personal touches, like The First XI, conceived with a who's who of professional cricket, and crafting private labels for local celebrities. After a recent move, they're working from a cellar on Twyfeling Farm in Wellington, where they welcome visitors by appointment.

De Kleine Wijn Koöp range

★★★★☆ Die Posman Rooi (NEW) ⊘ From Voor Paardeberg carignan, **22** ⑨① needs some aeration to reveal its spicy strawberries & ripe raspberries, burnished 15 months in older barrique. Nicely dry & worth seeking out - not many solo bottlings of the grape locally.

★★★★☆ Kreatuur ⊘ Say hello to 'Die Razmasaunache', latest incarnation of this changing Mediterranean blend. **22** ⑨① pips previous with more shiraz (53%), layering meaty spice with the berries of mourvèdre & grenache, & touch juicy cinsaut. Purity encouraged by wholebunch wild ferment & older oak ageing, year.

★★★★☆ Die Posman Wit ⊘ (🐝) Grenache blanc ex cool Cape Agulhas exudes limy freshness, 9 months on lees giving a salty hint to its green apple, cucumber & litchi flavours. **22** ⑨④ bunch pressed & wild fermented, half in old barrels, rest tank.

★★★★★ Debutant White ⊘ (🐝) Some skin-ferment & 6 months ageing in old oak for **22 ★★★★☆** ⑨③ semillon from original Franschhoek clone, GD1. Like **21** ⑨⑤, delivers outstanding lemony weight & length at low 11% alc, crystalline acidity & barest hint of lemon creams on the finish.

★★★★☆ Road to Santiago (🐝) Same (semillon) site as Debutant yet expression is more orange- than lemon-toned, thanks to varied picking dates. **22** ⑨④ mandarin & kumquat, zesty acidity & modest 11.5% alc offer refreshment aplenty, as did **21 ★★★★★** ⑨⑤, also only 100 cases.

Not tasted: **Heimwee**, **Ou Treffer**, **Me. Bonthuys**, **Ronkedoor**. In abeyance: **Debutant Red**.

Hoendertande range
Not tasted: **Grenache Noir**, **Pinot Noir**.

The First XI range
★★★★ The Belter Spicy shiraz gets generous splash of fruity cinsaut for **21** ⑧⑧ (vinfied separately, then blended). Extra time in old oak (15 months) elevates from **20** ⑧⑥. WO Cape Coast.

Not tasted: **The Centurion**, **The Partnership**.

Klipkers range
Not tasted: **Red**, **Rosé**, **White**. — ML

Location/map: Wellington ▪ Map grid reference: C3 ▪ WO: Cape Coast/Franschhoek/Cape Agulhas/Voor Paardeberg ▪ Est/1stB 2011 ▪ Tasting by appt ▪ Sales via website ▪ 10,000cs own label ▪ Twyfeling Farm, Bovlei Rd, Bovlei ▪ sales@infinitywines.co.za ▪ www.dekleinewijnkoop.co.za ▪ **T +27 (0)82-451-8010**

☐ **De Knolle Fonteyn** see Rogge Cloof

De Krans Wines

Brothers Boets and Stroebel Nel are joined by director René Oosthuizen in this awarded Calitzdorp venture, marking its 60th anniversary as historic emphasis on family deepens to include a new generation. Viticulturist Stroebel's son Chris is assisting with ongoing vine care, planting of pinotage and cab, and completing the restoration of blocks impacted by severe drought, while MD-cellarmaster Boets' daughter Annemi now looks after local marketing and some exports. Diners Club-lauded Christoff de Wet's exceptional 'ports' and unfortified Portuguese varieties continue their winning ways at competitions and professional tastings. Also doing well are the wine club, the on-site bistro, and the tradition of inviting winelovers to pick their own grapes and apricots in season. See also Garden Route Wines.

Terroir range

★★★★★ **Touriga Nacional** ⊘ Among the early unfortified solo bottlings (in **00**) of this port grape. The dark-toned fruit is the star in **21** (90), with surprisingly svelte tannins for this muscular variety. Streamlined yet expressive, showing restraint & balance. Older-oak matured.

★★★★★ **Tritonia Red** Subtitled 'Calitzdorp Blend', barrel selection of touriga (78%) with 2 tintas, after year in mixed-age oak. **21** (90) not as plush as last **18** (92), with cleaner lines, more red fruit, some violets & a dusting of oak spice. Elegantly structured, still a tad reticent, should unfurl with age.

★★★★★ **Tritonia Verdelho** Not many solo bottlings of this white grape known for retaining vibrant acid & aromatic profile in warmer climes. **22** (90) hallmark florality & piquant stonefruit flavours, underpinned by creamy shortbread texture from lees ageing 12 months in barrel. Delicious now & for the next few years.

......

A Twist of Fate ⊘ ⊕ ★★★★ Juicy **21** (85) blend of tintas amarela & barocca. Supple tannins & pleasingly moderate 12.7% alc. Flavoursome fruit & spice, dry & even more deliciously drinkable than last.

......

Not tasted: **Tinta Roriz**.

Classic range

......

Wild Ferment Unwooded Chardonnay ⊕ ★★★★ Lovely clean lines in more appealing **22** (85), exudes pure fruit flavours of ripe pear, apple & tangy lime. Light & balanced, with subtle creamy butterscotch base from 6 months on lees in tank.

......

Basket Press Cabernet Sauvignon ⊘ ★★★ Similar rich fruitcake notes in **22** (82) with a toasty mocha nuance from oak staves. Full bodied, a good nip of tannin, approachable but with a hearty meal. WO W Cape, as most of these. **Pinotage Rosé** ★★★ Delicate floral notes with some red berry piquancy, crisp & dry, **23** (81) is perfect as an aperitif or sunset tipple. **Free Run Unwooded Chenin Blanc** ⊘ ★★★ Ample melon & passionfruit in **23** (82) with a twist of lime as counterpoise. Quite plump, but as pleasant a summer quaffer as ever. **Premium Moscato Perlé Red** ★★★ Carbonated muscats give these 3 lightly sparkling wines their grapey, aromatic profile. All with attractive labels & clear bottles to show the wine colours. **23** (80) is pale ruby from 15% pinotage, also giving an earthiness. Bubbles lift the sweetness. Just 9% alc for all in this style. **Premium Moscato Perlé Rosé** ★★★ Splash pinotage gives the pinkish hue to **23** (80), otherwise similar pétillance, low alc & delicate sweetness, muscat perfume & raisiny flavours. **Premium Moscato Perlé White** ★★★ Tangy, aromatic, sweet & light in **23** (80). This uncomplicated fizz, like its siblings, is for carefree summer quaffing.

Fortified range

★★★★★ **Muscat Blanc** Richest & sweetest of these dessert wines, **23** (92) even more so than previous with 221 g/L sugar, from fortified unfermented white muscadel juice. Ample raisin, honeysuckle & litchi flavours & aromas with some enlivening acidity. Though tad softer & less vibrant than **22** ★★★★★ (95), as inviting. WO Klein Karoo.

★★★★★ **Cape Tawny Limited Release** ⊛ Occasional release, latest decadently delicious **NV** (93) 'port' is from 3 traditional grapes. Wild ferment (as all the ports except Pink) in old barriques, blend of 5-15 vintages. Classic tawny hue, complex bouquet: dried fruit, orange peel, toasted hazelnut & caramel, all following through to palate. Intense, persistent & opulently seductive.

★★★★ **Cape Vintage** ⊗ Classic blend of 5 port varieties, previewed **19** ★★★★★ (90) made in traditional way, 24 months aged, half time in concrete tank, then older barrels. Violet, fruitcake & cocoa-rich chocolate, for drinking earlier than Reserve, what a pleasure! 18.5% alc, 93 g/L sugar. Step up on **18** (88).

★★★★★ **Cape Vintage Reserve** Among finest 'ports' in this style, **21** ⑨⑥ shows exceptional class & complexity. As **20** ★★★★★ ⑨④, a vineyard & row selection of touriga with tintas roriz (71/23) & barocca, 20 months in large vats. 19% alc beautifully meshed, in unobtrusive support of dense core of rich, dark-berried fruit & chocolate, authoritative dry & firm tannins. Powerful & polished, clean farewell. Augurs well for long & rewarding future: 3 decades or more, cellarmaster predicts.

★★★★ **Premium Cape Ruby** Latest **NV** ⑧⑦ from 4 traditional port varieties, stylistically true, with rich dark fruit as the star, oak & tannins the supple understudies, ensuring earlier drinkability. Spirit well-judged & -integrated for a respectable drier farewell.

The Original Cape Pink ★★★ First in SA of this blush 'port'. Made from traditional varieties with brief skin contact. Delicious solo on crushed ice or with a mixer, this **NV** ⑧⓪ for sweet-toothed fans. Discontinued: **The Original Espresso**. — MW

Location: Calitzdorp ▪ Map: Klein Karoo & Garden Route ▪ Map grid reference: B5 ▪ WO: Calitzdorp/Western Cape/Klein Karoo ▪ Est 1964 ▪ 1stB 1977 ▪ Wine tasting, sales & deli Mon-Sun 9-5 ▪ Tasting fee R70pp ▪ Bistro (indoor/outdoor seating) Mon-Sun 10-4 ▪ Wine tasting daily 9-4 (booking advised for groups) ▪ Closed Good Fri & Dec 25 ▪ Pick your own: apricots last week Nov-1st week Dec; hanepoot grapes whole month of Feb ▪ Children's playground ▪ Walking trail ▪ Wine club ▪ Owner(s) De Krans Wines (MD Boets Nel & directors Stroebel Nel, René Oosthuizen) ▪ Winemaker(s) Christoff de Wet (Aug 2019) ▪ Viticulturist(s) Stroebel Nel (Jan 1988) ▪ 78ha/32ha (cab, ptage, tinta barocca/roriz, touriga nacional, chard, chenin & muscats) ▪ 500t/60,000cs own label 20% red 45% white 10% rosé 25% fortifieds ▪ IPW ▪ PO Box 28 Calitzdorp 6660 ▪ dekrans@mweb.co.za ▪ www.dekrans.co.za ▪ **T +27 (0)44-213-3314/64**

Delaire Graff Estate

The sensory experience starts at the drive onto the estate at the top of Helshoogte Pass outside Stellenbosch, through fynbos gardens dotted with sculptures, to two outstanding restaurants with breathtaking views, and a third, Japanese, just opened. The extensively refurbished hotel and spa provide luxury accommodation and pampering; the continent's only Graff boutique sells jewellery; and the Capri store offers perfume and designer clothing. Owner and London diamantaire Laurence Graff's 400+ African original artworks are displayed throughout. The wine side is as impressive, Delaire being judged a Top 50 winery by World's Best Vineyards. Grapes are sourced by Kallie Fernhout from home blocks with varied aspects, as well as select parcels elsewhere, and vinified by Morné Vrey and team, their cellar visible behind a glass wall.

Icon range

★★★★☆ **Cabernet Sauvignon Reserve** Barrel selection, heavyweight bottle already proclaims this as a serious wine. Long post-ferment skin contact, 16 months in 80% new barriques, **20** ⑨④ is opulent, boasts deeply rich cassis & dark plum, cigarbox spicing. Texture is plush, curvaceous, tannins amenable but deeply muscled for cellaring. Banghoek WO, as Laurence Graff.

★★★★☆ **Laurence Graff Reserve** Flagship, oaked 18 months, 80% new, selection of best 5 barrels from Reserve cab. Equally ripe but less showy, **20** ⑨④ exudes class & polish. Dark fruit, cocoa & spice brushed, texture streamlined, sinewy tannin as foundation for long ageing. Has succulence, freshness & presence. No **19**.

★★★★ **Banghoek Reserve Merlot** Full-ripe **21** ⑧⑧ had extended post-ferment skin contact, 16 months in 70% new barrels, so expect a bold showing. Berries & plums, chocolate coated, texture smoothly rounded, plush. Tannins firm but ripe, promise a future but already very appealing.

★★★★☆ **The Banghoek** Another take on Cape Bordeaux: cab franc at 60% with cab & 2 others, 18 months in 60% new oak after wholeberry ferment. **19** ⑨③ smoky, with dark chocolate scent, red & black berries, a nuance of glacé violets. Streamlined texture, with lovely fresh smoothness. An individual, shows intensity & gravitas, like still-available **18** ⑨④.

★★★★★ **Terraced Block Reserve Chardonnay** Same vinification & oaking as Premium sibling, but **22** ⑨⑥ is (Banghoek) single-vineyard, has more forceful personality. Roasted nut & shortbread vie with forthcoming citrus, lemon, lime & grapefruit, seamed with thrilling trademark enlivening acidity, promising a long distinguished future.

★★★★★ **White Reserve** Sauvignon with 27% semillon, which was bunch pressed. Barrel ferment for both, oak aged 10 months, adding gentle oat biscuit tone to the classic fruit profile of this partnership: green fig & lemongrass with waxy-lanolin overlay, the brisk acid fitting perfectly. **21** ⑨⑤ fresh, focused, has style & verve. WO Coastal.

★★★★ **Sunrise Brut Méthode Cap Classique** Named for the 118-carat Delaire Sunrise. Chenin leads with chardonnay, dab cab franc, not a usual sparkling pairing but works. Apple & citrus in **NV** (88), gentle brioche nuance from 15 months on lees, elegant (12.5% alc) & dry, zippy acidity keeping it lively.

★★★★ **Sunburst Noble Late Harvest** (②) Charming & complex **21** (87) botrytis dessert wine from sauvignon, barrel fermented/12 months, 30% new. Rich sweetness enlivened by energetic acid, litchi nuance on finish. First since **15** (87). WO W Cape, as Sunrise.

★★★★★ **Cape Vintage** (⊛) Tinta with 20% touriga, inky-hued **21** ★★★★★ (96)'port' has depth & heft, fruitcake richness, the expected sweetness & tannin structure. Older oak, year, allows immediate consumption but clearly it's crafted for cellaring. **20** (94) similar blend.

Premium range

★★★★☆ **Botmaskop** (⊛) Cab-led Bordeaux blend with 3 others, **21** (94) had plenty of cellar attention: grape sorting, 70% berry ferment, long post-ferment skin contact, 16 months 40% new oak. All designed to showcase fruit & build an ageing platform, succeeds on both counts. Cassis & plum compote, cinnamon & nutmeg spices, lusciously smooth texture, with tannin grip at the end. Also in 1.5L.

★★★★☆ **Chardonnay Banghoek Reserve** Barrique fermented/10 months, 40% new, no lees stirring or malo, designed to extract maximum freshness in **22** (90). White peach, lemon & ruby grapefruit, layered fruit shot through with biscuit savouriness, all given tensile strength & vibrancy by the brisk acid.

★★★★☆ **Coastal Cuvée Sauvignon Blanc** With 6% oaked semillon, **23** (90) spent 5 months on lees, contributing palate weight, fleshing out the green fig & capsicum scents & flavours. Vibrantly fresh, a salty note at the end.

★★★★ **Banghoek Chardonnay Eau de Vie de Marc** (②) A grand & suitably sophisticated name for this potstill husk spirit (89). Perfumed & refined, with less of the rustic 'husky' character & more fruit suggestiveness, the alc fire (43%) finer than last bottling.

Luxury range

★★★★ **Cabernet Franc Rosé** Pale coral with variety's red berries, herbaceous whiff, smooth-textured **23** (86) is zesty-fresh, for drinking solo or at table. More serious rosé than most, thanks to cab franc.

★★★★ **Summercourt Chardonnay** (②) To drink earlier than sibling chardonnays, **21** (86) buttered toast top note on upfront citrus. Creamy & quite delicate. Ferment started in tank, completed in old barrels, 10 months on lees.

Shiraz (⑰) ★★★★ To drink sooner than other reds & priced accordingly, **21** (85) smoky dark fruit from 10 months seasoned oak, peppery highlights, smoothly appealing plush texture, tannins integrated. Classic shiraz styling. — CR, TJ

Location/map: Stellenbosch ▪ Map grid reference: H5 ▪ WO: Stellenbosch/Banghoek/Western Cape/Coastal ▪ Est 1983 ▪ 1stB 1984 ▪ Tasting & sales Mon-Sat 10-5 Sun 10-4 ▪ Fee R75/3 wines, R100/4 wines, R125/5 wines, R350/Icon range wine ▪ Cellar tours by appt before 12 (no tours during harvest) ▪ Gifts ▪ Farm produce ▪ Walks/hikes ▪ Art collection ▪ Delaire Graff & Indochine Restaurants ▪ 5-star lodges & spa ▪ Wine club ▪ Owner(s) Laurence Graff ▪ Winemaker(s) Morné Vrey (Jul 2009) ▪ Viticulturist(s) Kallie Fernhout (Jun 2010) ▪ 42ha/20ha (cabs s/f, merlot, p verdot, chard, sauv) ▪ 480t/30,000cs own label 36% red 48% white 16% rosé ▪ PO Box 3058 Stellenbosch 7602 ▪ info@delaire.co.za ▪ www.delaire.co.za ▪ **T +27 (0)21-885-8160**

Delaire & Hammel ⓃⒺⓌ

This collaborative celebration of riesling and family sees Christoph Hammel, 9th-generation winemaker at Weingut Hammel in Germany's Pfalz region return to Delheim on the Stellenbosch slopes of Simonsberg, where he gained experience as a youngster in the 1980s in the cellar then run by patriarch Spatz Sperling.

Staying Alive Riesling ★★★★ Heady floral aromas of **22** (85) matched with delicate, scented fruit flavours on palate marked by racy acid & bone-dry finish. Very youthful, give it time. — DS

Delheim Wines (②) (⑪) (◎) (⑤)

'Look after nature and it will look after you' is one of the pillars of the Sperling family's welcoming wine and hospitality venture, founded over 50 years ago on the high Simonsberg-Stellenbosch slopes by the late paterfamilias Michael 'Spatz' Sperling - regenerative farming and WWF-SA awarded conservation efforts being but two outflows of this guiding principle. Under current custodians and siblings, Nora Thiel and Victor Sperling, other underpinnings of the venture include a 'holistic approach to community, land, good business practice and winemaking', the latter in the hands of cellarmaster Roelof Lotriet and winemaker Nongcebo Langa. In a few years, they will have estate-grown cabernet to add to their palette, as the variety is being re-established after a break. See also Delheim & Hammel listing.

★★★★ **Cabernet Sauvignon** Muscular **20** ⑧⑥ reflects Stellenbosch in its firm yet ripe tannin structure & cassis fruit, tobacco & herb nuances, 33% new oak adding spice. Up a notch up on **19** ★★★★ ⑧⑤. Both need year/2 to fully unfurl.

★★★★☆ **Vera Cruz Pinotage** ⑧ Delightful **20** ⑨③ from estate's best block offers cassis, herbs & dark chocolate notes wrapped in charry oak, 40% new, 18 months. Quintessential old-vine pinotage, intensely concentrated, much to love, as in **19** ⑨②.

★★★★☆ **Grand Reserve** ⑧ A worthy flagship & consistent top performer. Classic Stellenbosch cab notes of blackcurrant & dried herbs carried through from **18** ⑨③ to super **20** ⑨④. Elegant, ripe tannins give firm support, helped by sturdy 18 months oaking. Delicious acid freshens focused intensity with seductive hint of vanilla at finish. Splashes cab franc & petit verdot with dab merlot. No **19**.

★★★★☆ **Chardonnay Sur Lie** Elegantly full-flavoured **22** ⑨⓪ balances oatmeal richness from 9 months on lees with zinging acidity threaded through soft stonefruit cocktail of flavours. Barrel ferment, 15% new, adds appealing savoury notes to the finish.

★★★★☆ **Chenin Blanc Wild Ferment** ⊘ ⊛ From farm's oldest chenin vines, naturally fermented in old oak, 9 months on lees for texture. **20** ★★★★ ⑧⑨ walked thrilling line between acid zest & pineapple softness. **22** ⑨⓪ & **21** ⑨⓪, tasted this edition, fuller, more sumptuous. Both a step up.

★★★★★ **Edelspatz Noble Late Harvest** ⑧ ⊛ Numerous pickings & relentless selection deliver this consistently gorgeous botrytis dessert from riesling. **21** ⑨⑥'s classic bouquet & flavours of marmalade, apricot, rye bread & honey are richly unctuous, but 8 g/L acid ensures a balanced finish. As satisfying as **20** ⑨⑤, also fermented/9 months in older oak. 12% alc. 375 ml.

. . . .

Shiraz-Cabernet Sauvignon ⑦ ★★★★ Accessible, affordable, quaffable! **21** ⑧⑤ has shiraz (77%) tastily to the fore, adding pepper & meaty notes to the black cherry, coffee & chocolate mix. Subtle oak completes a clever package.

. . . .

Merlot ★★★★ Like previous, **20** ⑧⑤ is bold & ripe, has crisp black & red fruit mingled with toasty oak (third new, year), velvet tannin underpin. Gives immediate pleasure plus substance for a further few years. **Pinotage** ★★★★ Enjoyable everyday drinking, as always, in **20** ⑧③. Abundant spiced plum aromas, satin texture & pleasantly grippy tannins. **Pinotage Rosé** ★★★ Another spot-on vintage of this delicious raspberry-toned pink, for summer parties, picnics or simply solo. **23** ⑧② technically dry but plump & moreish thanks to deft dabs of grapey muscat & sugar. Perfectly judged 12.5% alc. **Gewürztraminer** ★★★★ Litchi & lime highlights the soft peach & pear notes on elegantly off-dry **22** ⑧⑤, 12 g/L sugar offset by sappy acidity. An excellent food partner - try Vietnamese spring rolls. **Sauvignon Blanc** ★★★★ Pops with tropical aromas, stonefruit centre & limy freshness. Nimble **23** ⑧④ will be life & soul of any party. WO Coastal, as Shiraz-Cab & Rosé. Not tasted: **Blanc de Blancs Brut**, **Spatzendreck**. — DS

Location/map: Stellenbosch ▪ Map grid reference: F2 ▪ WO: Simonsberg-Stellenbosch/Coastal ▪ Est 1971 ▪ 1stB 1956 ▪ Tasting & sales Mon-Sun 9-5 ▪ Premium tasting R85/5 wines & Reserve tasting R150/5 wines ▪ Wine & Fynbos cupcake pairing ▪ Closed Easter Fri/Sun, Dec 25 & Jan 1 ▪ Delheim Restaurant serving breakfast & lunch; Delheim cheese & meat platters since 1976 ▪ Gifts ▪ Conferences ▪ Events: see website for schedule ▪ Wine club ▪ Owner(s) Delheim Trust ▪ Cellarmaster(s) Roelof Lotriet (Dec 2018) ▪ Winemaker(s) Nongcebo Langa (May 2022) ▪ 375ha/130ha (cab, merlot, ptage, chard, chenin, gewürz, riesling, sauv) ▪ Brands for clients: Woolworths ▪ IPW, WIETA, WWF-SA Conservation Champion ▪ PO Box 210 Stellenbosch 7599 ▪ info@delheim.com ▪ www.delheim.com ▪ **T +27 (0)21-888-4600**

☐ **De Liefde** *see* Mountain Ridge Wines
☐ **Delisa** *see* House of Hlela Royal Wines

Delphin Wines

Boutique vintner Colin Snyman is gratified to have brought in the first crops from rehabilitated vines on his cool-climate Greyton farm Heuningkloof: chardonnay, of a quality that may obviate the need to buy in fruit; and shiraz, from a higher, rockier site than the current block, with a more delicate fruit profile suggesting it be labelled 'syrah'. Sauvignon is the other focus variety, brought in from also-cool Elgin and unwooded.

★★★★ **La Mez** ⓃⒺⓌ ⊘ Shiraz (67%) with grenache, long skin contact & 13 months in barrel, **22** ⑧⑧ preview proudly displays its fruit, intense berries, easily accommodating the smoky oak spice, adding to the appeal. Elegant structure, tannins fine, there's harmony here, freshness, polish.

SMG ★★★★ Shiraz at 56%, with grenache (co-fermented) & mourvèdre, long skin contact & 12 months oaked. **22** ⑧④ shows red berries & cherries, a charcuterie tone, the palate unexpectedly fresh & succulent. A pleasure to drink. **Chardonnay** ★★★★ Change from **22** ⑧④'s unwooded style, **23** ⑧④ fermented/5 months in oak, giving sleek pre-bottling sample a gentle Lemon Cream biscuit tone, fitting the citrus flavours. Enough acid backing to make it spark with life. **Sauvignon Blanc** ⊘ ★★★★ Elgin fruit for pre-bottled **23** ⑧⑤, ripe & expressive, kiwi & gooseberry, yet zinging fresh, adding vibrancy. Repays care taken in the making, slow cool ferment, 4 months on lees. Not tasted: **Wheatlands Shiraz**, **Le Mélange**. — CR

Location: Greyton ▪ Map: Southern Cape ▪ Map grid reference: A7 ▪ WO: Western Cape/Elgin ▪ Est 2016 ▪ 1stB 2019 ▪ Tasting, sales & cellar tours Mon-Sun 9-4; pub hols by appt ▪ Tasting R75pp ▪ Closed Dec 25 & Jan 1 ▪ Cheese platter ▪ Owner(s) Colin Snyman ▪ Winemaker(s) Colin Snyman (Jul 2016) ▪ 54ha/2.5ha (shiraz, chard) ▪ 1,000cs own label 55% red 45% white ▪ PO Box 350 Greyton 7233 ▪ info@delphinwines.co.za ▪ www.delphinwines.co.za ▪ **T +27 (0)87-551-2771**

☐ **Delucius** *see* Simelia Wines
☐ **Delush** *see* Orange River Cellars

DeMorgenzon

The symbolism of the brand name, 'The Morning Sun', is not lost on owners Wendy and Hylton Appelbaum, heavyweights in the business and social empowerment communities, as they see every new day as an opportunity to explore new ideas and directions. This ethos has been enthusiastically embraced by cellar-master and CEO Alastair Rimmer, now firmly settled in and hitting his straps. The lofty and stately estate near the top of Stellenboschkloof strives for classical purity in the wines, and hope and harmony in the lives of those who live and work there. In the cellar, the ranges are getting a makeover, and the arrival of the first terracotta amphoras keeps them on-trend. The extensive vegetable garden project provides weekly food hampers for the staff as well as ingredients for platters available to visitors.

Reserve range

★★★★★ **Syrah** ⓐ Immensely concentrated & proudly New World, **20** ⑨③ from high-density echalas/staked-vine parcel, 19 months in oak, 30% new. Black fruit embellished with cocoa & white pepper, powerful extraction & leathery tannins suggest years of cellaring.

★★★★☆ **Chardonnay** ⓐ With heady aromas of roast nut & citrus rind, subtle flavour richness, **21** ⑨④ combines refinement of **20** ⑨③ & showiness of **19** ⑨④. Lemon curd with touches of oak spice, shaped & rounded by 10 months in barrel, 30% new. Measured 13.4% alc.

★★★★★ **Chenin Blanc** ⓐ Aristocratic, assured, brimming with generously ripe stonefruit, **22** ⑨⑦ follows impressive form. Seamless & focused, with brilliant acid seam, lees fatness, minimal oak influence despite barrel ferment & maturation.

★★★★★ **The Divas Chenin Blanc** ⓠ ⓦ Selection of top-performing vines in oldest vineyard, made when Reserve can do without. More new oak (40%) than its sibling in **20** ⑨⑥, unobtrusive in layers of understated complexity. Supremely elegant, an SA chenin classic. No **18**, **19**.

★★★★☆ **Méthode Cap Classique Chenin Blanc** Elegant, ultra-dry **21** ⑨① changes tack, basewine now unoaked, with wild yeast primary ferment showcasing honeysuckle & dried peach fruit. Fine, vigorous bead & tingly acid add to freshness & appeal. 18 month on lees.

Occasional release: **Vinedried Chenin Blanc**.

Maestro range

★★★★☆ **Blue** Inky, robust blend of 72% syrah with durif, mourvèdre, grenache noir & malbec, 18 months in foudre & concrete. **21** ⑨⓪ spiced berry compote, hints of scrub & smoke. Bold, weighty, with powdery tannins begging time in bottle. Shade off **19** ⑨②. **20** held back.

★★★★☆ **Red** ⊘ ⑱ Pinpoint Bordeaux-like earthiness in cab-led blend with cab franc, petit verdot & splash durif, 18 months oaked. **19** ⑨③ nervous poise, focus & energy, with graphite, iodine & liquorice highlights, sombre but expressive blackcurrant fruit. **18** held back.

★★★★☆ **White** Hearty, satisfying Rhône-style blend of roussanne, marsanne, grenache blanc, with 15% chenin, **21** ⑨② is rich & satin-textured, with mineral-laced sweet melon fruit. Wild yeast barrel-fermented & 14 months on lees in concrete & barrel.

DMZ range

★★★★ **Grenache Noir** ⊘ Showing riper, fuller cherry & raspberry fruit, **21** ⑧⑦ outperforms leaner **19** ★★★★ ⑧⑤. Heightened aromatic notes from 30% wholebunch ferment, better focus from foudre & concrete maturation. No **20**.

★★★★ **Syrah** ⊘ Solid, dependable, better than everyday fare, **20** ⑧⑥ fruit driven & smooth, with suede tannins, juicy red berries, plums & cherries, brushed by fynbos & sweet confection spices.

★★★★ **Chardonnay** Barrel- & foudre-fermented **22** ⑧⑦ is voluptuously rounded & sleek, with lemon curd note delicately spiced & plumped by lees contact. Finishes focused & dry, with mineral twist.

★★★★ **Chenin Blanc** Spicy, vibrant & totally delicious, **23** ⑧⑥ has typical Stellenbosch yellow peach, pineapple & melon fruit. 90% barrel fermented/6 months, yet still fruit forward, generous & sunny.

★★★★ **Sauvignon Blanc** Previewed **23** ⑧⑦ shows notable shift to fruit purity, tangy granadilla to the fore. Vibrant & taut, with commendable lees texture & lingering finish, promising good things once settled.

Rosé ⑫ ★★★★ Unpretentious & generous **21** ⑧④, eminently satisfying, floral scents highlighting ripe red-berry fruit. Grenache & 4 other grapes, mostly Rhône. — GdB

Location/map: Stellenbosch ▪ Map grid reference: C5 ▪ WO: Stellenbosch/Western Cape ▪ Est 2003 ▪ 1stB 2005 ▪ Tasting & sales daily 10-5 ▪ Fee R30-R125 ▪ Closed Good Fri, Dec 25 & Jan 1 ▪ Delicious platters, home-made preserves, pickles & fresh produce ▪ Cellar tours on request ▪ Conservation area ▪ Owner(s) Wendy & Hylton Appelbaum ▪ CEO Alastair Rimmer ▪ Cellarmaster(s) Alastair Rimmer (Jun 2021), with junior winemaker Anthony Sanvido (Dec 2019) ▪ Viticulturist(s) Danie de Waal (Dec 2014) ▪ 91ha/50ha (cabs s/f, durif, grenache n/b, malbec, merlot, mourv, p verdot, shiraz, chard, chenin, marsanne, rouss, sauv, sem) ▪ 500t/40,000cs own label 40% red 50% white 10% rosé ▪ IPW, WWF-SA Conservation Champion ▪ PO Box 1388 Stellenbosch 7599 ▪ info@demorgenzon.com ▪ www.demorgenzon.com ▪ **T +27 (0)21-881-3030**

☐ **Den** see Painted Wolf Wines

Denneboom ⑫ ⌂ ◎

An on-site private game reserve speaks of the eco-concern of the De Waal family, farmers in Voor Paardeberg for more than 140 years. This winegrowing venture was launched just over two decades ago, with grapes from mostly own vines replanted in the 1990s. Tasting is by appointment at the farm.

Denneboom range

★★★★ **Black Harrier Shiraz** ⑫ Plush dark fruit backed by firm but ripe tannins, ending dry. **19** ⑧⑨ built to age but accessible now, there's enough fruit succulence.

Chenin Blanc ⊘ ★★★☆ Thatch & bruised apple, nice typicity in **22** ⑧④, perked up by zesty, limy acidity. Mouthwatering freshness, good length, drink solo or at table.

Emmara range

Mourvèdre Rosé ★★★ Handsome glass-stoppered bottle, **22** ⑧② has personality; forthcoming berries in the scents & flavours, well-judged acid lifting the fruit, refreshing the dry palate. — CR

Location/map/WO: Paarl ▪ Map grid reference: C2 ▪ 1stB 2003 ▪ Tasting by appt at the farm ▪ 4-star self-catering cottages ▪ Private game reserve open to staying guests ▪ Wine club ▪ Owner(s) De Waal family ▪ GM Willem de Waal ▪ Winemaker(s) Handré Barkhuysen (consultant) ▪ Viticulturist(s) Willem de Waal ▪ 199ha/±60ha (cab, mourv, ptage, shiraz, chenin, nouvelle, sauv, viog) ▪ 800t/10,000cs own label 60% red

40% white ▪ IPW, WIETA ▪ PO Box 2087 Windmeul 7630 ▪ info@denneboompaarl.co.za ▪ www.denneboom-vineyardsandwildlife.co.za ▪ **T** +27 (0)21-869-8072

☐ **De Oude Opstal** *see* Stellendrift - SHZ Cilliers/Kuün Wyne

De Trafford Wines ⓠ

Being sited on the high slopes of Stellenbosch Mountain, surrounded by 192 ha of fynbos has its benefits, says David Trafford, architect and co-owner of this acclaimed boutique winery. The 5 ha of vines experience a cool, gentle spring and a hot summer ripening period, giving wines of great power and intensity while retaining elegance and balance because of the altitude. The vines are also exposed to wildfires and, in 2022, most (1.35 ha) of the acclaimed Syrah 393 vineyard was lost. Replanting is underway, following the system proven best for the site: relatively narrow (1.8 m) rows and high density (5,000 vines/ha).

★★★★☆ **Belfield Cabernet Sauvignon** (NEW) (🐝) From mature Elgin vines, **21** ⑨③ reflects cool season in bright, succulent acid, ripe but still tight grape tannin structure. Pleasantly savoury, piquant, 15% merlot from same site & 25% new oak providing a little padding to bracingly dry finish. Bottled by hand unfiltered, like all.

★★★★☆ **Cabernet Sauvignon** (🐝) Pure blackcurrant/berry profile of **20** ⑨④ distinctly sweeter than Elgin solo bottling but smartly balanced with masterly tannins & complexity from graphite minerality & spice from oak, 35% new, 22 months. Also in 1.5L & 3L.

★★★★★ **Cabernet Franc** ⓥ From Stellenbosch mountain slope overlooking False Bay. Liquorice-toned **21** ⑨⑤, first since equally superb **15** ⑨⑤, for the long haul, 19 months in oak, 35% new, providing well-judged support for densely packed dark berries & soft-leaf herbs.

★★★★☆ **Merlot** (🐝) Firm but not drying tannins give shape & serious structure to **19** ⑨④'s variety-true fresh, baked & sugar-dusted plums. Thanks to gentle, slow ripening, more refined & brighter at roughly same alc (14.6%) as broad-shouldered **18** ⑨③.

★★★★☆ **Petit Verdot** ⓠ Off Keermont vines. Weighty richness & breadth in **14** ⑨②, with good structure & poise, the fruit well-knit with the supple tannins & 30 months in 30% new barrels.

★★★★☆ **Blueprint Syrah** Most accessible of syrah trio, **21** ⑨① ready now & good for a few years. Faint black pepper highlight on sweet dark fruit, supple tannin & elegant oak detail, 21 months, older barrels.

★★★★☆ **CWG Auction Glen Rosa Syrah** (NEW) (🐝) Just one seasoned barrel from 20 year old Tip Top Mont Fleur vineyard planted with Côte Rôtie clone 470. Fynbos- & cardamom-spiced **21** ⑨③ confidently harmonises succulent cassis fruit with sleek but compact tannin, beautiful dryness on fantail finish.

★★★★☆ **Syrah 393** (🐝) Purer, more focused & detailed than Blueprint; **21** ⑨④ trimmer, too, than **20** ⑨③ with 14% alc vs 15% but less savoury than CWG. In fine form for decade-plus cellaring, with precise tannin lattice, deep cassis fruit & knife-edge acid balance. Also in 1.5L, as Elevation.

★★★★★ **Elevation 393** (🐝) Includes cab franc in **17** ⑨⑤ incarnation of respected single-site cab, merlot & syrah blend. Achieves impressive fruit depth & weight without sacrificing vineyard's characteristic stern tannin frame or piquancy. As most reds, promises to reward cellaring.

★★★★☆ **Chenin Blanc** Multi-vineyard mix of bought-in grapes, natural ferment in various size barrels, 10% new, 8 months on lees. Floral **22** ⑨② intricate weave of citrus, pear & white peach, vivacious acid & hallmark seamless farewell which a tad briefer than usual. Also in 1.5L, 5L.

★★★★☆ **Chenin Blanc Reserva** (🐝) 'Reserva' a reference to nearly 2 years in older oak. **21** ⑨④ in similar savoury vein as previous with captivating salty, nutty & umami conclusion. Same fruit source as skin contact & standard versions.

★★★★☆ **Skin Macerated Chenin Blanc** (🐝) Pea shoot & ginger top notes from skin ferment of **22** ⑨④ underpinned by subtle white peach note, gentle tannin tug on almond-toned finish. More austere than chenin siblings but less than **21** ⑨③. Confident & adroit expression.

★★★★☆ **Straw Wine** (🐝) 24th bottling of richly ripe dessert from chenin, its creator's 'treasured wine'. **21** ⑨④, tasted while we wait for **20**, air-dried under 70% shade for 3 weeks, fermented/19 months in 50% new barrel. Array of tropical, citrus & dried stonefruit, sweetness shot through with livening limy acid, long satin farewell. 375 ml.

Occasional release: **Cinsaut**, **The Drawing Board**. — CvZ

Location/map: Stellenbosch ▪ Map grid reference: G8 ▪ WO: Stellenbosch/Elgin ▪ Est/1stB 1992 ▪ Tasting, sales & tours Mon-Fri by appt only; Sat 10–3 ▪ Private tasting (current releases) R250pp weekdays/Sat, waived on purchase; Vintage tasting (6 wines from library selection) incl. an optional vineyard walk R500pp; The Sijnn Experience R250pp - all to be booked in advance ▪ Closed all pub hols ▪ Owner(s) David & Rita Trafford ▪ Winemaker(s) David Trafford & Hendry Hess, with Fred Fismer ▪ Viticulturist(s) Etienne Terblanche (Vinpro) ▪ 200ha/5ha (cabs s/f, merlot, shiraz) ▪ 71t/7,000cs own label 70% red 30% white ▪ PO Box 495 Stellenbosch 7599 ▪ info@detrafford.co.za ▪ www.detrafford.co.za ▪ **T +27 (0)21-880-1611**

Deux Frères Wines

A 'beautifully designed' new tasting area, with a veranda under old palm trees, and longer opening hours on Saturdays, is the main update from Retief and winemaker Stephan du Toit on their property Le Present. It's Stellenbosch's smallest registered 'estate', and the brothers believe its Simonsberg foothills terroir is a gift to be farmed responsibly, with least intervention. Some mature shiraz has been grafted over to cab franc for the Tribute blend, crafted, as all the reds, to show a balance between fruit and acid, with soft, ripe tannin.

Deux Frères range
★★★★☆ **Cabernet Sauvignon** Maintains quality, rich fruitcake appeal & suppleness in **20** ⑨⓪. Ripe yet layered, composed & elegant. Oak regime amended: now French only, just 12% new, lends smooth texture & length. No **19**.

★★★★ **Mourvèdre** Echoes of **20** ⑧⑥ in spicy, light-bodied **21** ⑧⑦. Juicy hedgerow fruit with rounded mouthfeel & easy appeal. Time in old 500L oak reduced to 12 months from 18.

★★★★☆ **Tribute** ⓐ 'Best wines in cellar' in **19** ⑨⓪ are 3 Bordeaux varieties plus shiraz, latter relinquishing **18** ⑨②'s lead role. Touch brooding but melded & poised, shows dark & spicy fruit with density & fine tannin after 2 years in mainly older oak. Impressively long. Will cellar well.

Blanc de Noir ★★★ Cherries & plums on all-mourvèdre **23** ⑧① preview from Darling vines. Dry, lively & succulent, it's ideal for summer. Discontinued: **Liberté, Fraternité**.

Heritage Old Vines range
Sauvignon Blanc ⊛ ★★★ Rounded & soft **22** ⑧② offers gentle guava & subtle lemon zest but misses the freshness & punch of zippy, crisp **21** ★★★★ ⑧⑦. — FM

Location/map: Stellenbosch ▪ Map grid reference: E3 ▪ WO: Stellenbosch/Darling ▪ Est 2008 ▪ 1stB 2012 ▪ Tasting, sales & cellar tours Mon-Sat 11–5; pub hols (seasonal) please call ahead ▪ Closed Easter Fri-Mon, Dec 25 & Jan 1 ▪ Tasting platters & picnics to be pre-booked ▪ Guest accommodation ▪ Wine club ▪ Owner(s) Stephan & Retief du Toit ▪ Cellarmaster(s)/viticulturist(s) Stephan du Toit (Jan 2008) ▪ 3.5ha (cabs s/f, malbec, mourv, p verdot, sauv) ▪ 5,000cs own label 75% red 15% white 10% rosé ▪ PO Box 209 Koelenhof 7605 ▪ stephan@dfwines.co.za ▪ www.dfwines.co.za ▪ **T +27 (0)21-889-9865/+27 (0)82-371-4770**

De Villiers Wines

Villiers de Villiers, based on the family farm in Paarl, makes wine under contract to buyers in various international markets, and for his own, eponymous label, distributed by Wineways Marketing, listed separately.

Cabernet Sauvignon ⊘ ★★★ Cassis expression of typical cab, unoaked (as rest) **22** ⑧② has nice freshness in the juicy body. **Merlot** ⊘ ★★★ Forthcoming red berries & plums, smooth-textured **22** ⑧⓪ is youthfully appealing. **Pinotage** ⊘ ★★★ With blueberry authenticity, **22** ⑧① designed for early drinking, plush yet streamlined (12.5% alc) & sleek. **Classic Red** ⊘ ★★★ Fruit-forward unspecified **NV** ⑧⓪ blend, semi-sweet styling guarantees rounded & undemanding drinkability. — CR

Location: Paarl ▪ WO: Western Cape ▪ Est/1stB 1688 ▪ Closed to public ▪ Owner(s) De Villiers Family Trust ▪ Cellarmaster(s)/winemaker(s)/viticulturist(s) Villiers de Villiers (1980) ▪ 50,000cs own label 80% red 20% white ▪ PO Box 659 Suider-Paarl 7624 ▪ info@devillierswines.com ▪ www.devillierswines.com ▪ **T +27 (0)21-863-2175**

☐ **Devonet** see Clos Malverne

DeWaal Wines

Pieter de Waal, owner of this wine brand on home-farm Uiterwyk, draws inspiration from the fact that family member Charl Theron ('CT') de Waal was the first to make wine from pinotage in 1941. Hence the four versions of the grape, produced with winemaker/viticulturist brothers Chris and Daniël. Uiterwyk in

Stellenboschkloof has been cultivated by De Waals since 1864, and pride of place goes to a gnarled-vine block named Top of the Hill, planted in 1950 and the high point of a themed tasting at the farm venue.

★★★★ **Cabernet Sauvignon 21** ⑧⑨ improves marginally on also-tasted **18** ⑧⑦. Both are dark fruited, structured from 18 months in 25% new oak. Light grip & long, dry finish add interest. No **19** or **20**.

★★★★☆ **CT de Waal Pinotage** ⑨ Brooding plum, fine herbs & supple tannin, **15** ⑨⓪ characterful, juicy & harmonious, more accessible on release than TOTH sibling of same vintage yet built to last. Last-tasted **13** ★★★★ ⑧⑨ also had 60% new-oak support & complexity.

★★★★☆ **Top Of The Hill Pinotage** ⓐ ⓦ Jewel in the crown from 73 year old heritage vines. Low yield saw just 300 cases of **18** ⑨①, fewer than tad more impressive **15** ⑨③. Ripe, spicy, inky black fruit but with succulence & dry grip from 18 months in new oak. Lithe & complex, made to last. No **16** & **17**.

★★★★ **Signal Rock** ⑨ Estate's signature pinotage joined by cab in **19** ⑧⑥, replacing the merlot of **17** ⑧⑧; unchanged are liquorice, blueberry & spice on light palate, & 18 months ageing in 225L barrels.

Merlot ★★★★ Succulent, spicy, cocoa-dusted plum on **19** ⑧⑤, supple body courtesy of brief 3 months in older barrels. Lifts bar on previous. **Pinotage** ⑨ ★★★★ Improves on last, **20** ⑧⑤ generous dark fruit & spice remain, but 6 months in oak add breadth, texture & length. **Shiraz** ★★★★ Return of **21** ⑧⑤ echoes last-made **17** ⑧⑤ in savoury, supple & easy blue & black-fruited mouthful. **Chenin Blanc** ★★★ Fresh, undemanding & light **23** ⑧② has nectarine & quince flavours for good summertime sipping. **Sauvignon Blanc** ★★★★ Tropical verve of **23** ⑧③ shows bags of unfussy citrus appeal. Improves on lighter, more floral **22** ★★★ ⑧①, also tasted this edition. — FM

Location/map/WO: Stellenbosch ▪ Map grid reference: C5 ▪ Est 1682 ▪ 1stB 1972 ▪ Tasting & sales Mon-Sat & pub hols 10-4.30 ▪ Tasting R50/standard & R100/premium ▪ Closed Sun, Easter weekend, Dec 25/26 & Jan 1 ▪ Owner(s) Pieter de Waal ▪ Winemaker(s)/viticulturist(s) Chris de Waal & Daniël de Waal (whites/reds, both consultants) ▪ 800t 50% red 50% white ▪ IPW, WIETA ▪ Stellenboschkloof Rd, Vlottenburg 7604 ▪ admin@dewaal.co.za ▪ www.dewaal.co.za ▪ **T +27 (0)21-881-3711**

Dewaldt Heyns Family Wines ⑨

For this small signature collection, CWG member and one of South Africa's most awarded winemakers Dewaldt Heyns strives to consistently and respectfully express the unique character of 'stark yet beautiful' Swartland, through wines sourced from mature vines in Hutton soils just north of Malmesbury, and old parcels in decomposed granite on Paardeberg, where his father Cecil acquired the calluses that name the range.

Weathered Hands range

★★★★☆ **Pinotage** ⓐ Very old Paardeberg dryland vines combine rich, spicy cherry fruit & abundant red blossoms in a velvet texture, poise & length in **21** ⑨②. 10% wholebunch ferment/18 months 40% new barrels provide structure for a long life.

★★★★☆ **Shiraz** ⓐ Ageworthy knockout from mature dryland vines by a shiraz maestro. Portions whole-bunch & -berry, 20 months 60% new oak. Part natural ferment, as all. **20** ⑨④ understated, balanced & refined notes of dark fruit, smoky minerality & classic black pepper, long persistent savoury finish.

★★★★☆ **Chenin Blanc** ⓐ Fruit from old dryland Paardeberg bushvines fermented/11 months large barrels, 40% new, for **21** ⑨④. Mouthfilling, concentrated flavours of honeyed yellow fruit & crème brûlée, textured palate & enduring mineral finish. Track record for ageing decade or more.— WB

Location/WO: Swartland ▪ Est/1stB 2006 ▪ Tasting by appt ▪ Owner(s) Dewaldt Heyns Family Wines ▪ Cellarmaster(s)/winemaker(s)/viticulturist(s) Dewaldt Heyns ▪ (ptage, shiraz, chenin) ▪ 1st/1,100cs own label 60% red 40% white ▪ dewaldt@dewalttheyns.com ▪ www.dewalttheyns.com ▪ **T +27 (0)82-441-4117**

De Wet Cellar ⑨ ⑪ ⊜ ◎ ⑤

Though co-owner of major export brand FirstCape, this grower-owned winery near Worcester's own label is no afterthought. A significant 35,000 cases are carefully considered and made by a long-standing team, with recent emphasis on site 'to give an identity to each wine'. An example is the current chardonnay release, from vines planted in virgin soil on a 900m-high farm near the border of Klein Karoo and Koo Valley.

De Wet range

★★★★ **Cabernet Sauvignon** ⊘ Like last-tasted **18** ⑧⑧, ambitious **21** ⑧⑥ spent year in 30% new oak, adding dark chocolate & olive savouriness, smoky nuance to ripe black fruit, integrating the tannins.

★★★★ Chardonnay ⊘ Assertive **22 ★★★★** ⑧⑤ ups new oak to 50%, adding banana-vanilla confected note to peach & mango fruit. Shows good intensity throughout. A bold wine, tad less sophisticated than last **20** ⑧⑦. WO Klein Karoo.

★★★★☆ Leyland Chenin Blanc ⊘ Excellent concentration & depth on **23** ⑨⓪, peach, pineapple & apple fruit spiced up by 6 months in oak, third new. Lovely length & freshness, intriguing minty finish.

★★★★ Red Muscadel ⑳ Fortified muscat a talent here & **19** ⑧⑨ confirms it: dried stonefruit scents, but the taste's the real pleasure, richly sweet, like drinking raisins. No **18**. 500 ml, as next.

★★★★ White Muscadel ⑳ Sultanas & beeswax, some citrus peel, fortified **21 ★★★★★** ⑨⓪ layered & packed with favour, nudges ahead of **19** ⑧⑧. Intensely sweet, so best served chilled. Long life ahead.

Merlot ⑲⑰ ⊘ ⑰ **★★★★** Cheerful **21** ⑧④ has super-soft tannins enfolding ripe black cherries, tweak of fresh mint & dark chocolate finish. Very pleasant braai partner. Stave aged, as other reds unless noted.

Shiraz ⊘ **★★★** Cooked red plums & raisins on **22** ⑧⓪, spicy top notes mixed with smoky oak & soft tannins. **Merlot-Cabernet Sauvignon** ⊘ **★★★** New blend (70/30) of **21** ⑧⓪ is slight & soft, with liquorice-edged raisin fruit. Lacks bounce of previous, drink soon. **Petillant Rosé** ⑳ **★★☆** Lightly sparkling **NV** ⑦⑧'s touch of strawberry sweetness, modest alc & fine bubbles make it a party pleaser. **Chenin Blanc** ⊘ **★★★** Fruity little number **23** ⑧②, differently styled to its sibling, unwooded & for current drinking; crisp & dry. **Petillant Fronté ★★** Semi-sweet & lightly frothy **NV** ⑦③ from white muscadel shows grapes & flowers in light mouthful. **Sauvignon Blanc ★★☆** Light tropical notes on **23** ⑦⑨, bone-dry & crisp mix of yellow fruit. **Special Late Harvest** ⊘ **★★★** From chenin, **21** ⑧① semi-sweet sipper with fresh appley acid & shortish finish. Lacks intensity of previous. **Hanepoot** ⑳ **★★★** Impresses with its essence of grape character, **21** ⑧① pure muscat perfume & flavour. Fortified, richly sweet but tangy, vibrant. **Cape Ruby** ⑳ **★★★☆** For drinking rather than cellaring, **NV** ⑧④ 'port' a fruitcake delight; enough spice, not too sweet, satisfyingly round. Occasional release: **Cravate**. Discontinued: **Cabernet Sauvignon-Merlot, Cape Blend**.

Vintage Mashup range

★★★★ Red ⊘ Eclectic mix of petit verdot with shiraz, cab & merlot, **22 ★★★★** ⑧④'s minty chocolate surrounds somewhat shy fruit. Lightly oaked with staves, unlike unwooded **20** ⑧⑥.

Chardonnay-Pinot Noir-Grenache Noir ⑳ **★★★☆** Tangerine-hued **21** ⑧⑤ dry rosé offers pleasing fruity aromas & gravelly texture. Not tasted: **White, Sauvignon Blanc-Chenin Blanc-Semillon**. — CM

Location/map: Worcester ▪ Map grid reference: B3 ▪ WO: Worcester/Klein Karoo ▪ Est 1946 ▪ 1stB 1964 ▪ Tasting & sales Mon-Fri 9-5 Sat 10-3 ▪ Closed all pub hols ▪ Cellar tours by appt ▪ Cheese platters ▪ BYO picnic ▪ Wedding/function venue for hire ▪ MTB trail ▪ Six Dogs gin available on premises ▪ Owner(s) 25 members ▪ Manager Tertius Jonck ▪ Winemaker(s) Tertius Jonck (Sep 2007) & Phillip Vercuiel (Dec 2007) ▪ Viticulturist(s) Hennie Visser (Jul 2008, Vinpro) ▪ 1,000ha (cab, shiraz, chard, chenin, sauv) ▪ 25,000t/35,000cs own label 29% red 36% white 5% rosé 30% fortified + 10m L bulk ▪ ISO 22000, SABS, WIETA ▪ PO Box 16 De Wet 6853 ▪ admin@dewetcellar.co.za ▪ www.dewetcellar.co.za ▪ **T +27 (0)23-341-2710**

☐ **De Wit Family** *see* Signal Gun Wines

DGB (Pty) Ltd

Well-established producer with a strong portfolio of premium brands including Backsberg Family Wines, Bellingham, Roschendal, Brampton, Franschhoek Cellar, Fryer's Cove and Old Road Wine Company, listed separately in this guide.

Location: Wellington/Franschhoek ▪ Est 1942 ▪ Closed to public ▪ Owner(s) Capital Works & Tim Hutchinson ▪ Winemaker(s)/viticulturist(s) see under Backsberg, Bellingham, Boschendal, Brampton, Franschhoek Cellar, Fryer's Cove ▪ PO Box 79 Groot Drakenstein 7680 ▪ info@dgb.co.za ▪ www.dgb.co.za ▪ **T +27 (0)21-001-3150**

☐ **Diamond Collection** *see* Lutzville Vineyards

Dickens Family Wines ⑲

With a famous family name and a history spanning centuries, including great-grandfather George Alfred Dickens' move from England to South Africa, brand owner and marketer Heloise Dickens and winemaker

Lionel tell their familial story through their wines. Based in Paarl, they source grapes widely to 'supply our buyers with a taste of the entire industry' in 'classic wines with strong flavours but an elegant French style'.

★★★★ **Four Novels** ⊘ Lots of care taken with this Bordeaux blend, including 18 months in small barrels. 86% cab, 3 others in **18** ⑧⑦, fruitcake richness, well spiced, a touch of mint chocolate in the flavours. Has structure for further ageing, but already drinking well, a function of bottle age.

Tale of Three Wines ★★★★ 85% shiraz, dabs mourvèdre & viognier, **18** ⑧⑤'s 18 months in barrel produce a smoky top note, spicy, peppery perfume & flavours. Fruit is mellow from maturation, berries & plums, smooth textured for current enjoyment. **Unexpected** ★★★★ From chardonnay, **22** ⑧③ fresh pear & grapefruit, year in oak a butterscotch note on the nose & palate. Quite expressive, easy to like. — CR, CvZ

Location: Paarl ▪ WO: Coastal ▪ Est 2008 ▪ 1stB 2005 ▪ Closed to public ▪ Owner(s) Heloise Dickens ▪ Winemaker(s) Lionel Dickens ▪ 15,000t 50% red 50 % white ▪ info@dickenswines.co.za ▪ www.dickenswines.co.za ▪ **T +27 (0)84-655-3340**

Die Kat se Snor

Underpinning the playful brand name, 'The Cat's Whiskers', and moustachioed feline on the label is the serious intent to create, with minimal intervention, small batches showing texture and focus. The boutique crafter is Gerhard Smith, assistant winemaker at reputed Creation. As his current releases illustrate, he ranges beyond home-base Hemel-en-Aarde for interesting parcels that enable his No. 1 attribute, 'lekker to drink'.

★★★★ **Cinsault** ⊘ Ex-barrel, bunch pressed, wild fermented/6 months in seasoned oak, **23** ⑧⑨ thus handled to give the fruit & elegant structure the best chance to express varietal character. And succeeds: red berries, smooth & freshly succulent. What a pleasure! WO Bottelary.

★★★★ **Grenache Noir** (NEW) From Swartland, medium hued & trim figured (12.5% alc), **22** ⑧⑧ nevertheless has personality & appeal. Brambly berries & dry heath, tobacco notes from 9 months in barrel, fresh & streamlined palate, the tannins supple.

★★★★ **Pinot Noir** ⊘ Forthcoming red berries & cherries on nose & palate, lovely freshness adding a spark. **20** ⑧⑨'s youthful appeal reinforced by some oak spice - but the fruit's in charge, & reflective of its cool Overberg provenance.

★★★★☆ **Chardonnay** ⊘ 🍇 Bunch pressed, 10 months wild fermented/matured in French barriques, this care taken to highlight **22** ⑨④'s fruit. Vivid lemon & lime, even more pronounced in the flavours, underlined by racy acidity. Gentle oat crunchie savouriness peeks through, but overshadowed by the citrus. Has power & presence.

★★★★★ **Sauvignon Blanc** ⊘ 🍇 **23** ⑨⑤ continues the stellar styling of **22** ★★★★★ ⑨④: lemon & lime intensity, a seam of minerality in the flavours & extended racy finish. It couldn't be more classic.— CR

Location: Hermanus ▪ WO: Overberg/Bottelary/Swartland ▪ Est/1stB 2014 ▪ Closed to public ▪ Owner(s) Gerhard Smith ▪ Winemaker(s)/viticulturist(s) Gerhard Smith (Jan 2014) ▪ Own label 60% red 40% white ▪ katsesnorwines@gmail.com ▪ **T +27 (0)76-254-0294**

☐ **Die Laan** see Stellenbosch University Welgevallen Cellar

Die Mas van Kakamas Ⓠ Ⓟ Ⓗ Ⓞ Ⓐ

'Something for everyone' is the approach at family-owned Die Mas estate near Kakamas on the Orange/Gariep River, and it applies equally to the ranges of wine and brandy styled by André Landman, and the cornucopian amenities and allures available to visitors, from biking to conferencing to camping.

Die Mas range

Pinot Noir Rosé ⊘ ★★★ Previewed **23** ⑧⓪ touch riper than last yet still bone-dry, with plum compote & mulberry scents & flavours. **Chardonnay** ★★★ Toasted nuts & honeyed brioche on pre-bottling **23** ⑧②. Tropical toned, mango & pineapple with cinnamon & clove accents from few months on staves. **Sauvignon Blanc** ★★ Ex-tank **23** ⑦⑤ more oxidative in style than last. Baked apple & pear, refreshed somewhat by brisk acidity. Not tasted: **Cabernet Sauvignon**, **Merlot**, **Pinotage**, **Shiraz**. In abeyance: **Kalahari Klassiek Méthode Cap Classique**.

Rooi Kalahari range

★★★★ **Rooi Muskadel** Hints of blood orange, rosepetal & allspice on **NV** ⑧⑧ fortified muscat, tasted pre-bottling. Translucency belies ample sweetness & red fruit flavour, to become more complex with time.

Not tasted: **Cape Vintage**.

Goue Kalahari range

★★★★ **Wit Muskadel** Delicious NV ⓐ⁹ muscat dessert improves on last with quince, apricot & orange on nutty, salted caramel. Keenly balanced, 16% alc fortification adding spice to nascent complexity.

Not tasted: **Hanepoot**.

Brandy range

★★★★ **Braai Brandewyn** ⓥ Amber-tinged blended brandy ⑧⁷ is fiery at 43% alc yet delectably sweet & smooth. Mixes well. For braais & good enough for more sophisticated occasions.

★★★★☆ **Die Kalahari Truffel** ⓥ Involving, deep & complex, 5-6 year old potstill ⑨⁰ unfurls layers of ripe fruit, toasted nut, candied lemon & dark chocolate on full, rounded palate which is subtly earthy. 500 ml, like XO. Equal colombard & chenin, as all these.

★★★★☆ **Die Kalahari XO** ⓥ 10 year old potstill ⑨⁰ has plenty of smoky oak, fresh & smooth, with a little caramel sweetness adding to rich texture, though integrated spirit means light-feeling at 38% alc.

★★★★ **Vêr In Die Ou Kalahari** ⓥ Blended brandy ⑧⁸, with 30% potstill content aged 3 years (as Braai), draws you in with vibrant stonefruit & freshness, perfect for mixing.

Die Kalahari Fynetjie ⓥ ★★★★☆ Blended brandy ⑧³, 40% potstill component aged 5-6 years. Specially for women, they say, light in feeling, sweetish, softer & less fiery than 43% alc suggests. — ML, TJ

Location: Kakamas ▪ Map: Northern Cape, Free State & North West ▪ Map grid reference: B8 ▪ WO: Northern Cape ▪ Est/1stB 2005 ▪ Tasting, sales & cellar tours Mon-Fri 8-5 Sat/pub hols 10-4 ▪ Closed Good Fri & Dec 25 ▪ Facilities for children ▪ Tour groups ▪ Gift shop ▪ Farm produce ▪ Conferences ▪ Walks/hikes ▪ MTB trail ▪ Conservation area ▪ Camping facilities, 4 self-catering chalets & large lapa/bush pub ▪ Craft gin ▪ Die Koker Kombuis @ Die Mas Wynkelder Wed-Sat 11-10, reservation required T +27 (0)66-378-7034 ▪ Owner(s) Die Mas Boerdery (Pty) Ltd ▪ Cellarmaster(s)/winemaker(s) André Landman (Apr 2016) ▪ 36ha (cab, merlot, muscadel r/w, p verdot, pinot, ptage, sangio, shiraz, souzão, tinta, touriga, chard, chenin, cbard, sauv, viog) ▪ 150t/6,000cs own label 25% red 15% white 30% brandy 30% gin ▪ PO Box 193 Kakamas 8870 ▪ wine@ diemas.co.za ▪ www.diemas.co.za ▪ **T +27 (0)54-431-0245/+27 (0)71-015-7131**

Diemersdal Estate ⓥ ⑪

For the Louw family on their estate on the cool slopes of Dorstberg in Durbanville, the past year was bracketed by the first harvest in a satellite cellar in Darling, acquired mostly for producing their substantial contribution to the Woolworths wine portfolio, but raising the possibility of West Coast wines for the own ranges; and the 70th birthday of their paterfamilias and 5th-generation owner, Tienie, who was wished a day as smooth as aged Bordeaux and vibrant as sauvignon blanc on social media, neatly namechecking their vinous calling cards. It's the aforementioned white grape that continues to particularly dazzle and captivate Diemersdal's legion of fans, and win critical praise, but the stellar ratings below speak of deftness with multiple styles and varieties, including still very rare Austrian grape grüner veltliner. Less visible, but on-trend, is the work with Cape Nature to preserve critically endangered Swartland Shale Renosterveld.

The Journal range

★★★★★ **Cabernet Sauvignon** ⓐ Barrel selection of cool-climate cab a flagship; same 22 months in oak but only half new in 21 ★★★★★ ⑨⁵ vs 100% in 20 ⑨³ - makes for better balance, & gives graphite grip to rich, succulent cassis fruit, ensuring a great future; also buffs tannin frame & finesses texture.

★★★★★ **Merlot** ⑭ ⓐ Extended maceration aids body & flavour before 2 years in 50% new barriques, only the best of which made the cut for 21 ⑨⁴. Smoky, meaty aromas & ripe mulberry flavour, broad shouldered at 14.5% yet not without refinement.

★★★★★ **Pinotage** ⓐ Savoury expression of 3 decade old vines, 21 ⑨³ balances opulent dark fruit with freshness, coriander spice & tapenade nuance from 22 months in half new oak. Natural food match.

★★★★★ **Sauvignon Blanc** ⓐ Still embracing trendy fumé style, the 30-plus year old vines dial back oaking from 50% new to just 20%, 11 months in 10, & eschew wood for 10% of the wine, resulting in stunning 22 ⑨⁷, with next-level elegance & vinosity with no diminution of fruit intensity or lemon cream opulence. Unquestionably the pinnacle of estate's remarkable sauvignon line-up.

Reserve range

★★★★☆ **Pinotage** ⊘ ⊛ Juicier & more vivacious than Journal sibling, **22** ⑨③ has choc-mocha sheen to ripe red berries, big tannins & alc (14.8% alc) plus similar liquorice & spice from deft oaking, 30% new, for appeal & balance.

★★★★★ **Syrah** ⓝⓔⓦ ⊛ Aromatic shows enviable typicity & restraint in its white pepper & pimento spicing, mulberry profile & medium body (13.5% alc). Black olive piquancy adds lift to dense fruit & tight tannins that will give **22** ⑨⑤ a decade's lifespan, suggest decanting in youth.

★★★★★ **Private Collection** ⊘ ⊛ Deep-flavoured & persistent **21** ★★★★★ ⑨⑤ a concentrated yet focused 5-way cab-led Bordeaux blend, like **20** ⑨③. Dark graphite-laced fruit, refined tannins & serious 30% new oak are true to style & augur well. Cellar 3-5 years, then enjoy the controlled athletic power unleash over the following half-decade.

★★★★★ **Wild Horseshoe Sauvignon Blanc** ⊛ Less mainstream version hitting its stride with running double of maximum ratings. **22** ⑨⑤'s extended wild-yeast skin-ferment in older oak delivers hallmark biscuit richness & lemon curd texture, offset with quince & grapefruit pithiness on lingering farewell.

★★★★☆ **8 Rows Sauvignon Blanc** ⊛ Literally 8 rows in an old block, dry-farmed, as all estate's vines, **23** ⑨④ yields just 5,000 bottles. Lively orchard fruit & stony minerality well & vividly expressed, as ever, need no oak embellishment. WO Cape Town, rest of these Durbanville.

★★★★☆ **Sauvignon Blanc** ⊘ ⊛ Bounty of riches for sauvignon lovers in the portfolio. Unoaked/filtered, from estate's highest site, exceptional **23** ★★★★★ ⑨⑤ captures the essence of the place & region. Intense, poised, the slate character brushed with oatmeal from time on lees. Follows complex **22** ⑨④.

★★★★☆ **Winter Ferment Sauvignon Blanc** ⊛ Intricate handcrafting sees grape-must chilled ±4 months to intensify flavour, lees-aged 4 months post ferment for palate breadth. **23** ⑨③ evinces expected concentration of flavour (gooseberry, tropical) around mineral core, acid balancing glossy lanolin texture.

★★★★☆ **Noble Late Harvest Sauvignon Blanc** ⓨ Gorgeous part-oaked botrytis dessert with distinctive ethereality from low alc (10% in latest **21** ⑨③) yet ample honeyed tropical flavour, concentration & texture, thrilling acid cleanout inviting another sip. 375 ml.

Diemersdal range

★★★★ **Pinotage** ⊘ Succulent, appetising mulberry & plum fruit balanced by yielding tannin structure. **22** ⑧⑥ fragrant dried herb nuance from sympathetic oak, year, 10% new, as Shiraz.

★★★★ **Chardonnay Unwooded** ⊘ Green apple & winter melon, touch of spice adds lift to creamy mouthfeel from lees contact. Salty tang in lingering aftertaste of **23** ⑧⑥.

★★★★ **Sauvignon Blanc** ⊘ Pea & crushed green herb fragrances on **23** ⑧⑥, fresh tropical flavours zested with lemon. Unoaked bottling never fails to over-deliver.

Malbec ★★★★ Generous, fragrant **22** ⑧⑤ is table friendly, with fynbos, dark fruit & toasted coconut, black pepper on the finish. 20% new oak, 16 months. Cape Town WO unless noted. **Merlot** ★★★★ Sappy blackberries in a firm but accessible structure, spice & hint vanilla from year in seasoned cask on **22** ⑧④. **Shiraz** ★★★★ BBQ-friendly styling, with spice, cured meat & compote of dark berries in **22** ⑧④. Generous, textured, tang of pomegranate keeps you reaching for more. **Cabernet Sauvignon-Merlot** ⊘ ★★★★ Succulent dark berries & layers of spice linger in affable, easy-drinking **22** ⑧④, 71/29 blend raised in seasoned oak. WO W Cape. **Sauvignon Rosé** ★★★ Mixes estate's signatures, sauvignon blanc & cab sauvignon, for vibrantly pink, dry & zesty **23** ⑦⑨, for picnics & patio parties. Not tasted: **Grüner Veltliner**. Occasional release: **Viognier**. Discontinued: **Sparkling Sauvignon Blanc**.

Prospect range

Not tasted: **Cabernet Sauvignon, Pinotage, Shiraz.** — DS

Location: Durbanville ▪ Map: Durbanville, Philadelphia & Darling ▪ Map grid reference: D7 ▪ WO: Durbanville/Cape Town/Western Cape ▪ Est 1698 ▪ 1stB 1976 ▪ Tasting & sales Mon-Sat/pub hols 9-5 Sun 10-3; pub hols (seasonal) please call ahead ▪ Closed Good Fri, Dec 25 & Jan 1 ▪ Diemersdal Farm Eatery ▪ Wine club ▪ Owner(s) Tienie Louw ▪ Winemaker(s) Thys Louw & Mari Branders, with Juandre Bruwer & Janeke Beck ▪ Viticulturist(s) Gerrit Visser (2019) ▪ (cab, grenache, malbec, merlot, p verdot, ptage, shiraz, chard, grüner veltliner, sauv) ▪ 50% red 50% white ▪ BRC, HACCIP, WWF-SA Conservation Champion ▪ PO Box 27 Durbanville 7551 ▪ info@diemersdal.co.za ▪ www.diemersdal.co.za ▪ **T +27 (0)21-976-3361**

Diemersfontein Wines

Under the care of third-generation owners David and Susan Sonnenberg, the family retreat in Wellington since the millennium has been developed into a landmark destination, with this acclaimed wine range, an array of attractions, sustainability emphasis and flourishing empowerment venture, Thokozani, listed separately. The wine emphasis is firmly on reds, specifically pinotage, and coincidentally it and chenin were the stars of the most recent harvest, the 20th for Diemersfontein veteran Francois Roode, who works alongside Lauren Hulsman in the cellar, and solo among the vines. New on the estate is chef Dylan Smith, who's moved from KwaZulu-Natal to run the restaurant, renamed Hope, offering contemporary bistro fare.

Carpe Diem Reserve range

★★★★☆ **Malbec** ⊛ Similar dark fruit compote & savoury profile to **21** ★★★★ (88), though **22** (90) richer & broader, adroitly reined in by chalky dry fruit & wood tannins from 14 months in barriques, 50% new. Youthful & ageworthy.

★★★★☆ **Pinotage** ⊛ Flagship more restrained in cooler **21** (94) vintage, though pedigree is clear. Usual fine dry tannins, clove & cedar nuances from 16 months in oak, 50% new, hold the dark fruit in a firm embrace. Should unfurl & reveal more after some deserved cellaring.

★★★★☆ **The Clockmaker** ⊛ ⊛ Fitting tribute to Italian craftsman & prisoner of war, Cesare Zanardi, who lived on the farm. Grapes from 38 year old chenin, fermented/year in 25% new oak. Complex layers of flavour: dried peach, quince, honey & citrus unspool in **22** (93), woven into the creamy opulence.

Diemersfontein range

★★★★ **Cabernet Sauvignon** ⊘ Preview of **21** (87) shows characteristic cassis & some fresh leafiness, year older oak (as Shiraz) in supple support. Well structured & already harmoniously integrated, ends respectably dry. Potential step up on **20** ★★★★☆ (85).

★★★★ **Shiraz** Big-boned **22** ★★★★ (85) adds good pepperiness to savoury dark fruit. Partly checked by dry tannins, but still tad chunky, less harmonious than **20** (86) & needing time to meld. **21** untasted.

★★★★ **Sweet Sue** ⊘ Seductively aromatic & flavoursome **NV** (89) dessert wine from vine-dried viognier, fermented & matured in old oak. Touch tangier & even lower sugar (114 g/L vs 135), but ample apricot, peach & jasmine appeal. 375 ml.

Pinotage ★★★ Preview of **23** (82) bursts with varietal wild berry, banana flavours & sweet mocha-vanilla spicing from oak stave treatment. In ever-popular, supple & easy-drinking style. **The Prodigy** ★★★ Unwooded pinotage. Plumper & more pleasing ample dark plum & cherry flavours in **22** (82). Supple, juicy, ready to enjoy solo or with a light meal. **Harlequin** ⊘ ★★★ Consistent style & blend, 70% shiraz with pinotage in **21** (81) preview. Fruit a touch brighter, more of a foil for mocha-caramel oak flavours. WO W Cape, as Sauvignon. **Rosé** ★★★ More savoury styled in **23** (80), just a hint of red berries. Dry, with a pithy twist. Mostly mourvèdre plus grenache & cinsaut. **Chenin Blanc** ★★★ Still plump & waxy, but apple pie & ripe pear flavours touch fresher in **23** (80). Smooth & affable. **Sauvignon Blanc** ⊘ ★★★★ Remains delightfully fresh, juicy & quaffable in **23** (84), exudes ripe pineapple & fresh herbaceous notes.

Brandy range

★★★★☆ **10 Year Old Potstill** ⊛ Strikingly packaged new blend (93) from chenin & crouchen blanc, only 120 cases of 500 ml. Vivid amber hue hints at richness of apricot & pear fruit, dark chocolate & toasted almond, melded with warming 40% alc in a brandy of great elegance & harmony.— MW, WB

Location/map: Wellington ▪ Map grid reference: B4 ▪ WO: Wellington/Western Cape ▪ Est 2000 ▪ 1stB 2001 ▪ Tasting & sales daily 10-5 ▪ Closed Dec 25 ▪ Cellar tours by appt ▪ Wine & biltong/artisanal sweets pairings ▪ Hope restaurant serving lunch & dinner Tue-Sun ▪ Tour groups ▪ Conferences ▪ Weddings ▪ Amphitheatre, contact them for upcoming events ▪ Walks/hikes ▪ 3-star Diemersfontein Country House ▪ Wine club ▪ Owner(s) David & Susan Sonnenberg ▪ Winemaker(s) Francois Roode (Sep 2003) & Lauren Hulsman (Nov 2011) ▪ Viticulturist(s) Francois Roode (Jul 2021) ▪ 180ha/45ha (cabs s/f, grenache, malbec, mourv, p verdot, ptage, roobernet, shiraz, chenin, viog) ▪ 600t/80,000cs own label 86% red 11% white 3% rosé ▪ HACCP, IPW, WIETA ▪ PO Box 41 Wellington 7654 ▪ tastingroom@diemersfontein.co.za ▪ www.diemersfontein.co.za ▪ T +27 (0)21-864-5050

☐ **Die Tweede Droom** *see* Groot Parys Estate

A Tide of Pure Style

Experience...

the Best Classical &

Contemporary Cuisine,

Rare Wine Vintages,

Breathtaking Views,

Unsurpassed Service,

..ward winning Wines,

the Finest Cultivars...

A Combination so

freshingly Satisfying,

it should be Savoured,

Every Day...

Victoria Wharf • V&A Waterfront • Cape Town
Tel: 021 421-0935/6/7 • baiarestaurant@wol.co.za
www.baiarestaurant.co.za

BAIA
SEAFOOD RESTAURANT

WWW.DINERSCLUB.CO.ZA

Experience And Belong

DINERS CLUB, IT'S WHERE YOU BELONG

Apply online or scan the QR code to become a member and enjoy the finest Travel, Lifestyle, and Entertainment experiences.

Dieu Donné Vineyards Ⓨ ⑪ ⌂ ◎

Established 40 years ago, the Maingard family's wine and hospitality estate lies on steep slopes overlooking Franschhoek town, the altitude and rocky, weathered granite soils combining to produce wine with a different profile to that from vines on mostly alluvials on the valley floor. Hospitality historically has been an emphasis, and additional luxury accommodation has come on-stream, with a tasting room update to come.

The Cross Collection

★★★★☆ **Shiraz-Viognier** Ⓨ Sleek, supple & seductive **16** (93), captivating interplay of soft plum, inky blue & black berries with fine dry tannin from 22 months in new French oak. Lovely integration & length, exotic note from the 2% viognier.

★★★★☆ **Merlot-Cabernet Sauvignon** Ⓨ Only the best barrels selected for this range. Rewarding & complex **16** (91) has cab (14%) supporting merlot in a poised, fresh & restrained blend, rounded from 24 months in new French oak. Rich, deep & long.

Dieu Donné range

★★★★ **Cabernet Sauvignon** Ⓨ Pleasing berry character on **19** (87), supported by 18 months oak, half new, adding chalky tannic grip to the fruit-derived structure. Modest 13% alc. Genuinely dry finish - an attraction on all these reds.

★★★★ **Merlot** Ⓨ Varietal fruitcake, with herbal note & tobacco on big (14.7% alc) **19** ★★★★ (84). Ripely rounded, firm tannins. 50% new oak adds cocoa to palate. Briefer than **18** (86).

★★★★ **Shiraz** Ⓨ Black plum fruit, tobacco & spice on **19** (86). Some depth of sweet fruit, though dry. Well structured; shapely acid & tannin. 50% new American oak; 14.1% alc.

Cabernet Sauvignon-Shiraz ⊘ ★★★★ Warm-hearted & full-fruited **21** (84), with a light grippiness that's much friendlier than on last-made **19** ★★★ (82). Balanced & pleasingly dry. **Blanc de Noir** ★★★ Attractive berried aromas on **22** (82) from merlot. Softly textured, bone-dry & pleasant enough, but the acidity a touch assertive. **Chardonnay** ★★★★ **22** (85) first tasted since **19** (84). This has more buttery richness along with the limy citrus fruit. Oaked, the 50% new barrels giving toastiness. Pleasing & easy, but no real depth or concentration. **Chardonnay Unwooded** ★★★ **23** (82) tasted very young, but promising the usual modest flavourfulness, dry drinkability, with easy 12.5% alc. As with Sauvignon, no **22** made. **Sauvignon Blanc** ★★★★ A happily typical fresh, dry & tropical-toned example in **23** (85) off high-lying, unirrigated vines. **Méthode Cap Classique Brut Rosé** Ⓨ ★★★★ A little cab imparts a faint rosiness to the gold of **20** (83) sparkling from chardonnay. Dry enough, but an ingratiating sweetness to the lemony freshness & modest flavour. 2 years on lees. **Méthode Cap Classique Brut Blanc de Blancs** Ⓨ ★★★★ Usual 2 years on lees give lemon-cream biscuit note & richness to **19** (85) bubbly from chardonnay. Flavourful & satisfying. In abeyance: **Henriette Viognier**. — TJ

Location/map/WO: Franschhoek ▪ Map grid reference: C1 ▪ Est 1984 ▪ 1stB 1986 ▪ Tasting & sales Mon-Fri 9–5 Sat/Sun 10.30–5; pub hols Mon-Fri 10.30–4 Sat 10.30–5 Sun 10.30–4 ▪ Fee R80 ▪ Closed Dec 25 & Jan 1 ▪ Cellar tours Mon-Fri by appt ▪ Cheese platters ▪ Grand Country restaurant ▪ Boutique hotel ▪ Wine club ▪ Owner(s) Maingard family ▪ Cellarmaster(s)/winemaker(s) Gregory Siebrits (Sep 2018) ▪ Viticulturist(s) Hennie du Toit (Apr 1988) ▪ 40ha (cab, merlot, shiraz, chard, sauv) ▪ ±280t/33,000cs own label 60% red 32% white 3% rosé 5% MCC ▪ PO Box 94 Franschhoek 7690 ▪ sales@dieudonnevineyards.com ▪ www.dieudonnevineyards.com ▪ **T +27 (0)21-224-0667**

❏ **Die Waghuis** *see* Org de Rac
❏ **Dig This!** *see* Stellar Winery
❏ **Distell** *see* Heineken Beverages
❏ **Diversity** *see* Douglas Green
❏ **DMZ** *see* DeMorgenzon

Domaine Coutelier Ⓨ ⌂ ◎

Rare grape carmenère forms part of Briton Quint Cutler's small vineyard on a ridge in Devon Valley, the other varieties, cabernet and merlot, also being associated with Bordeaux; fruit for the white wines in the 'Home of Cutler' portfolio is brought in. On-site wedding, function and accommodation facilities are available.

Reserve range

★★★★☆ **Cabernet Sauvignon** Ⓨ Slightly riper in **14** (90), same melded oak as last (100% French, 2 years), though not quite as complex or fresh. Polished & svelte, ready to savour over next few years.

★★★★ **Merlot** ⓥ Ripe & dense in **14** ⑧⑨, but perfectly balanced between fruit & supple but firm tannins. More modern, fruit-forward style, also more new oak (85%) than sibling. Also in magnum.

Coutelier range

★★★★ **Cabernet Sauvignon** ⓥ Slow-evolving **15** ⑧⑨ much firmer than last. 2 years in oak, 55% new, bolster firm dry tannins. Deserves decade in the cellar to show its full potential.

★★★★ **Merlot** ⓥ Dark berries & cedar aromas, but **15** ⑧⑥ still tightly buttoned, almost austere, with very dry chalky fruit & oak tannins (45% new, 24 months), needing many years to unfurl.

★★★★ **Chardonnay** ⓥ Elgin & Durbanville grapes for **16** ★★★★ ⑧⑤. Shows bottle age, also distinct earthy note. Oak adds mellow sheen. Just enough limy acidity to lift. Ready to enjoy, but shade off **15** ⑧⑧.

Méthode Cap Classique ⓥ ★★★★ Honey, subtle brioche, salt & earthy notes on **NV** ⑧④ dry sparkler from chardonnay & pinot noir (70/30). Some leesy breadth from 2 years on lees. WO W Cape.

Festin range

★★★★ **Red Blend** ⓥ Merlot with cab (70/30), **15** ⑧⑥ quite firmly bound up in tannins & oak, 2 years, all old. Better than **14** ★★★★ ⑧⑤, will be a fine table wine but needs some time to meld.— MW

Location/map: Stellenbosch ▪ Map grid reference: D4 ▪ WO: Stellenbosch/Western Cape ▪ Est/1stB 2012 ▪ Tasting, sales & cellar tours by appt ▪ Closed all pub hols ▪ Weddings/functions ▪ Two self-catering cottages ▪ Wine club ▪ Owner(s)/winemaker(s) Quint Cutler = 4ha/3.5ha (cab, carmenère, merlot) ▪ ±21t/2,300cs own label 70% red 10% white 10% rosé 10% MCC ▪ 45 Blumberg Dr, Devon Vale, Stellenbosch 7600 ▪ quint. cutler@domainecoutelier.com ▪ www.domainecoutelier.com ▪ **T +27 (0)79-498-0772**

Domaine des Dieux ⓥ ⑪ ⓢ

The family-owned small vineyard and cellar in Hemel-en-Aarde Ridge are aptly named, given the splendid site on the Babylonstoren foothills. A tiny 0.4 ha of Champagne-clone chardonnay is set to be planted this year, as part of an increased focus on cap classique in a portfolio which is notable for the age of most of the wines, due to a policy of extended bottle-maturation at cellar. Latterly in some cases a younger vintage is released simultaneously 'for those seeking something fresher and more lively'.

★★★★☆ **Josephine Pinot Noir** ⊘ Retains savoury mushroom & red berry profile & sympathetic oaking, & gains some acid piquancy in **21** ⑨②. Also-tasted, simultaneously released **17** ⑨② similar character plus barnyard nuance acquired over 66 months in bottle.

★★★★ **Sangiovese** Rare solo bottling has **16** ⑧⑧'s brooding quality in **17** ⑧⑧, still tense & tannic, quality fruit yet to unfold. Contrast with **15** ⑧⑥, accessible young. 22 months old oak.

★★★★ **Syrah-Mourvèdre-Grenache** ⓥ Distinct Rhône-like scrub aroma in pungent, savoury **18** ⑧⑧, tannins smoothed by 43 months' rest in bottle. Walker Bay WO. Also in 1.5L, as Pinot Noir, Chardonnay & the bubblies.

★★★★ **Chardonnay** Highlights house's penchant for long bottle-ageing at cellar, here 4 years. **19** ⑧⑧ fresh bakery aromas balance citrus verve, adding oatmeal touch from barrel ferment/9 months, 25% new.

★★★★ **Sauvignon Blanc Reserve** 5 months in seasoned oak add complexity to this individual sauvignon, & bolsters lengthy rest in bottle, 45 months in **19** ⑧⑦. Shares amplified green fruit character with previous, inviting food partnering.

★★★★☆ **Rose of Sharon Cap Classique Brut Rosé** ⓥ From 60/40 pinot noir & chardonnay, extraordinary 101 months on lees, **13** ⑨⓪ palely blushing bubbly has classic berried brioche profile, textured finish & fine racy acid. Mature & still vibrant, in same class as last-tasted **11** ⑨⓪.

★★★★☆ **Claudia Cap Classique Brut** Six years on lees for **17** ⑨⓪ add brioche breadth & savoury gravitas with restrained freshness, hallmark of these bubbles. 80/20 chardonnay with pinot noir, as last-tasted **15** ⑨⓪. WO Cape South Coast, like Sharon.

Petit Rose ★★★★ Grenache noir & mourvèdre meld well with syrah in tasty **22** ⑧⑤ rosé that finishes blissfully dry. 80% in old oak 7 months. WO Walker Bay. First reviewed since **16** ★★★★ ⑧⑥. **Sauvignon Blanc** ★★★★ Latest **NV** ⑧⑤ softer, gentler, less intense flint & gunsmoke than last, milder acid too. WO Cape South Coast. — DS

Location: Hermanus ▪ Map: Walker Bay & Bot River ▪ Map grid reference: C4 ▪ WO: Hemel-en-Aarde Ridge/ Walker Bay/Cape South Coast ▪ Est 2002 ▪ 1stB 2006 ▪ Tasting & sales at the vineyards: Tue-Sat 11-5 Sun 11-4; pub hols (seasonal) please call ahead ▪ Closed Easter Fri/Sun, Dec 25 ▪ Cheese & meat platters; refreshments

• Child-friendly • Owner(s) Domaine des Dieux (Pty) Ltd • Winemaker(s) Megan Mullis & consultants
• Vineyard manager(s) Shane Mullis & Leonore Kroukamp • Viticulturist(s) Kevin Watt (consultant) •
28ha/20ha under vine (pinot, mourv, shiraz & other Bordeaux & Italian red varieties, chard, sauv) • 10,000cs
own label 25% red 25% white 50% MCC • PO Box 2082 Hermanus 7200 • info@domainedesdieux.co.za •
www.domainedesdieux.co.za • T +27 (0)28-313-2126

☐ **Dombeya** see Haskell Vineyards

Domein Doornkraal ⓠ ⑪ ⓐ ⓞ

The Le Roux family remain passionate about the Klein Karoo and their farm Doornkraal, its terroir and warm
welcome, despite many challenges. As a practical demonstration, their farm shop near De Rust has been
reorganised to showcase the full spread of regional wines, in addition to craft produce. Plus, of course, their
own boutique bottlings by paterfamilias Swepie, now with updated labels for the Kannaland pair.

Domein Doornkraal range

★★★★ Kaptein ⓠ Deep brown NV ⑧⑨ fortified from red muscadel thrills with toast, coffee, caramel
& raisin notes. Xmas spices & roasted nuts round off delicious mouthful to warm the cockles in winter.
Tickled Pink ⓠ ★★★ Light (9% alc) & gently sweet NV ⑦⑨ rosé fizz from muscat. Fresh & floral, to
serve chilled as welcome drink or fun dessert partner. **Kuierwyn** ⓠ ★★★ Natural Sweet from colombard,
'made for pleasant people'. NV ⑦⑦ has dried pear & pineapple tones, slides down effortlessly. **Majoor**
ⓠ ★★★★ Plenty of lemon on NV ⑧⑧ fortified muscat d'Alexandrie - dried, glacé & spiced. Nice balance
between sweetness & acid, good length. **Jerepigo** ⓠ ★★★ Clean grapey aromas on NV ⑧① fortified,
with raisins & coffee adding depth & interest. Warming alc suggests enjoying with food. **Luitenant** ⓠ
★★★★ Oxidative toffee, coffee, nutty aromas & flavours on NV ⑧③ red jerepiko. Try with baked camembert
cheese. **Pinta** ⓠ ★★★ Raisins & coffee on NV ⑧⓪ 'port' followed by lashings of blackberry jam & hint
toffee. Tad more acid would improve. **Tanige Port** ⓠ ★★★★ Unusual vintage-dated tawny 'port' from
tinta & touriga, 8 years in barrel. **92** ⑧④ prune & wild honey aromas, savoury/toasty tastes. Very sweet, long
almost malty finish. Klein Karoo WO.

Swepie Selection

Kannaland Merlot ★★★★ Rustic in the most pleasant way, **21** ⑧③ ripe plum & prune fruit, fresh & clean,
just enough tannin to get your attention. Under screwcap for easy access. **Kannaland Chenin Blanc**
★★★ Apples - both fresh & stewed - baking spices & some earth, **23** ⑧① bright & undemanding. — CvZ
Location: De Rust • Map: Klein Karoo & Garden Route • Map grid reference: B3 • WO: Western Cape/Klein
Karoo • Est 1880 • 1stB 1973 • Tasting & sales at Doornkraal Padstal Mon-Fri 8-5 Sat 8-3 Sun 10-2; pub hols
(seasonal) please call ahead • Closed Dec 25 & Sun (mid term) • Light refreshments • Farm & regional
produce • Small selection of brandy, gin & whiskey • Gifts • Function venue on farm • Self-catering farm
cottage & lodge • Online shop • Picnics on the farm with or without horse riding excursions • Owner(s)
Swepie le Roux & family • Cellarmaster(s) Swepie le Roux (Apr 2011) • Winemaker(s) Swepie le Roux •
Viticulturist(s) Celia le Roux • 5ha (cab, merlot, muscadel, chenin) • 110t/4,500cs own label 15% red 15%
white 70% fortified • PO Box 14 De Rust 6650 • wyn@doornkraal.co.za • www.doornkraal.co.za • T +27
(0)82-895-5009/+27 (0)82-763-5296 (farm stall)

☐ **Donatus** see Dornier Wines

Donegal Wine Estate ⓠ ⑪ ⓐ ⓐ

Carl Ahlström and Ansua Steyn-Ahlström made a shiraz from their vines in Swartland in 2017, added a blend
in 2018 on the basis of good reviews, and the same year moved to Victoria Bay on the Garden Route, opening
visitor and maturation spaces there. Niel Bester crafts the wines to 'make a new memory with every sip'.
★★★★ Grenache ⓠ From low-yield Swartland site, bright & fragrant **21** ★★★★ ⑧⑤ redolent of hibiscus, red cherry & spice. Pleasant sipping, with good varietal character, though touch lighter than **20** ⑧⑥.
★★★★ Shiraz ⓠ Powerful **19** ⑧⑧ from registered single-vineyard in Swartland has a lovely raspberry
& cherry clarity, good tannin that frames the fruit to a spicy finish. Top note of vanilla from judicious oak,
part American, 14 months, 30% new. Improves on **18** ★★★★ ⑧⑤.
★★★★ Chardonnay ⓠ From Paarl, **20** ⑧⑥ spent 11 months on lees in oak, 45% new, resulting in a
classic, creamy rendition with appetising flavours of baked lemon & clove-studded apple.

Vic Bay Red Ⓧ ★★★★ Satisfying blend keeps syrah & cab in **20** ⑧₃, adds dabs grenache noir & petit verdot for a fleshy palate with fruity tannins, added spice from oak-staving 10 months in FlexCube. — ML

Location: George ▪ Map: Klein Karoo & Garden Route ▪ Map grid reference: C3 ▪ WO: Coastal/Paarl ▪ Est 2016 ▪ 1stB 2017 ▪ Tasting, sales & cellar tours Tue-Sat 10-5; pub hols (seasonal) please call ahead ▪ Closed Easter Sun, Dec 25 & Jan 1 ▪ Cheese platters ▪ BYO picnic ▪ Jungle gym ▪ Tour groups ▪ Owner(s) Carl Robert Ahlström & Ansua Steyn-Ahlström ▪ Cellarmaster(s) Carl Robert Ahlström ▪ Winemaker(s) Niel Bester ▪ 1,5ha/1ha (shiraz) ▪ 5t/4,000 litres 100% red ▪ Donegal Estate, Victoria Bay, George 6529 ▪ carl@donegal.co.za, ansua@donegal.co.za ▪ www.donegal.co.za ▪ **T +27 (0)83-448-8869/+27 (0)83-388-1345**

Donkiesbaai   Ⓧ

Vigneron Jean Engelbrecht, also owner of top-ranked Rust en Vrede, here offers a paean to Piekenierskloof, whose 'climate and deep sandy soils allow for the production light-bodied, elegant wines with finesse'. All are styled to enhance the cuisine of the West Coast, where four Engelbrecht generations have holidayed. Vinification, tasting and sales are at another Engelbrecht property, Guardian Peak, in the Helderberg.

★★★★ **Cinsault** Ⓧ Now with Heritage Vineyard seal (as Steen), textbook **22** ⑧₉ mingles ripe cherry & strawberry with fragrant rosemary & oregano. Lively acid, soft tannin & touch of earth at finish. 20% bunch ferment; year large old barrels unless noted. Follows weighty **21** ★★★★ ⑨₁.

★★★★ **Grenache Noir** Charming (wine & label) **22** ⑧₉ pleases with riot of perfume, white pepper, florals & earth. Cooked strawberry fruit backed by loose-knit tannins, spicy pepper finish. Shade more needed for **21** ★★★★ ⑨₁'s rating. 25% wholebunch.

★★★★☆ **Suiderkruis** Ⓧ Greater than sum of its (4) parts, Rhône blend from grenache & cinsault (45/42), splash grenache blanc, but **20** ⑨₃ ups syrah, showing strongly in dark berry-plum core, firm yet pliable tannins. Exotic spice at lingering finish completes very satisfying wine. Combo wholebunch/berry.

★★★★☆ **Steen** Thoughtful **22** ⑨₂ shows classic honey & wool notes overlaying green pineapple & ripe apple fruit. Salty & steely, with quiet acid thread, needs time to open & show off its charms. 75% fermented in oak, 12% new, rest concrete 'egg'.

★★★★☆ **Grenache Blanc** Excellent example of increasingly popular grape, **22** ⑨₂ shines brightly with pear & peach notes, soft baking spices & marvellous grainy pearskin texture from amphora & concrete 'egg' ferment. Freshening acid & intriguing, lingering finish. 20% in old oak.

★★★★☆ **Hooiwijn** Ⓧ Luscious straw wine from chenin, **22** ⑨₃ oozes flavour & loveliness. Honey & apricot, pineapple & light florals, all paired with lively acid to balance 205 g/L sugar. Delightful palate weight, aided by 6 months in old oak, rich but not at all cloying. Masterly winemaking. 375 ml. — CM

Location: Stellenbosch ▪ WO: Piekenierskloof ▪ Est 2010 ▪ 1stB 2011 ▪ Tasting & sales at Guardian Peak Wines ▪ Owner(s) Jean Engelbrecht ▪ Winemaker(s) Duran Cornhill (Dec 2021) ▪ ±38t/6,000cs own label 30% red 70% white ▪ IPW ▪ PO Box 473 Stellenbosch 7599 ▪ info@donkiesbaai.com ▪ www.donkiesbaai.com ▪ **T +27 (0)21-881-3881**

Doolhof Wine Estate   Ⓧ Ⓧ Ⓧ Ⓧ Ⓧ

International investment and involvement continue to energise the 'Labyrinth' estate in the mountains above Wellington town, where a new sorter has been introduced to further raise quality, more chenin planted and new labels for the Single Vineyard range rolled out. Gielie Beukes, winemaker the past decade, uses 'very traditional methods' to style mostly red wines from multiple microclimates on the steep-sloped land, also home to a conserved area and many visitor allures, including a 5-star country house and luxury AfriCamps.

Limietberg Exclusives range

★★★★☆ **Bloedklip Malbec** Ⓧ Hand-picked grapes from registered single-vineyard (as both ranges), 18 months in 300L barrels, 100% new. Mulberry, cherry fruit with lick of chocolate, shaped by glossy tannins. **20** ⑨₁ touch toastier than last **18** ⑨₃, will mellow with age.

★★★★☆ **Morestond Chardonnay** Ⓧ Bunch-pressed fruit from 1996 low-crop vines on granite soil delivers an expressive **19** ⑨₄, loaded with pear, lemon & honeysuckle. 8 months older oak (some Hungarian, as all except Chenin) & regular bâtonnage add richness, balanced by characteristic bright acid.

★★★★☆ **Riviersteen Chenin Blanc** Same regime of ferment/8 months older oak with regular lees stirring, yet gently savoury **19** ⑨ has a broader palate than **18** ⑨: fresh yellow apple, sliced pear, apricot kernel cosseted in a creamy texture, hint of sweet nuts on finish.

Single Vineyard range

★★★★ **Cabernet Sauvignon** Fragrant cassis aroma impresses on **20** ⑧, plum fruit follows with spice ex 30% new oak, some American, year, body nicely sculpted by tannins. Improves on last **18** ★★★★ ⑧.

★★★★ **Cabernet Franc** Hand-picked & -sorted grapes for **20** ⑧, perfumed with wild herbs & loaded with plums. Delicate tannins overlaid with spice whisper from year in oak, 30% new, dab American.

★★★★ **Malbec** Ripe strawberries & plums ride a wave of cocoa & spice ex year in oak, 30% new; **21** ⑧'s sweet-sour pull on palate begs for food, good tight acid refreshes too.

★★★★ **Pinotage** ⓥ Flavourful & intense **20** ⑧ has variety's red & purple berries, hallmark cranberry acid. Fresh & seamless, if tad brief. Like Cabernet & Merlot, from mature vines planted 1996.

★★★★ **Jacques Potier** (NEW) Hint of earth, crushed-rock minerality & ink on savoury **21** ⑧ Cape Bordeaux, 60/40 merlot & cabernet franc, showing elegant blackcurrant fruit & exotic juniper nuance, harmonious oak, year, 25% new.

....

Chenin Blanc (NEW) ⑦ ★★★★ Clean aromas of melon, yellow apple & lime describe **22** ⑧. Touch oak (staves) buoys tropical & grapefruit on palate, energetic lemony acid freshens & revives.

Merlot ⓥ ★★★★ Engaging plum, dried mint & floral bouquet, **18** ⑧ shows all the richness & concentration expected of the Bordeaux variety, good savoury finish. Just misses complexity & length of siblings. Discontinued: **Malbec Blanc de Noir, Chardonnay Unwooded, Sauvignon Blanc.** — ML

Location/map: Wellington ▪ Map grid reference: D3 ▪ WO: Limietberg ▪ Est 1712 ▪ 1stB 2003 ▪ Tasting & sales Mon-Fri 8-5 Sat 9-4 Sun 10-3; pub hols 10-4 ▪ Fee R100/5 wines, R150/Limietberg exclusive range ▪ Closed Good Fri, Dec 25/26 & Jan 1 ▪ Cellar tours by appt ▪ Mila Restaurant: breakfast & light lunches Wed-Sun 9-3; picnics by appt ▪ Walks/hikes ▪ MTB trails ▪ 5-star Grand Dédale Country House; AfriCamps luxury accommodation (www.africamps.com) ▪ Craft gin ▪ Owner(s) PR Richards ▪ Winemaker(s) Gielie Beukes (Aug 2014) ▪ Viticulturist(s) Walter Schlomms (Mar 2022) ▪ 380ha/30ha (cabs s/f, grenache, malbec, merlot, p verdot, ptage, shiraz, chard, chenin, sauv) ▪ 250t/25,000cs own label 70% red 28% white 2% rosé ▪ IPW, WIETA ▪ PO Box 157 Wellington 7654 ▪ wine@doolhof.com ▪ www.doolhof.com ▪ **T +27 (0)21-873-6911**

☐ **Doppio Zero** see Bé a Daisy

Doran Vineyards ⑨ 🏠 ⓞ ♿

Vineyards planted from the early 2010s on the Voor Paardeberg home-farm by Irish owner Edwin Doran are being redeveloped under a five-year plan supervised by vine-wine man Piet Kleinhans. The emphasis remains on Mediterranean varieties, with 'a South African touch of chenin and pinotage'. The first estate plantings mean that the sauvignon debuting this edition will be made from own grapes in a few years.

★★★★ **Grenache Noir** ⓥ Light bodied **18** ⑧, pronounced pomegranate & raspberry fruit, gentle tannins & spicy oak highlights, suggesting Mediterranean food matches. Paarl WO.

★★★★ **Incipio** ⓥ Mimicking Rhône technique, shiraz co-fermented with 10% chenin, **19** ⑧ athletic & juicy, appealing scrub, bright red cherry & currant fruit. First tasted since **15** ⑧.

★★★★ **Chenin Blanc** Similar minerality though riper fruit in **22** ★★★★ ⑧. Baked apple & quince, sheen from oak at odds with feisty acid. Warm farewell despite modest 13.5%. Less balance than **21** ⑧.

Pinotage ⓥ ★★★★ Honest & wholesome, with vibrant red berry fruit, **19** ⑧ has loads of unforced, light-textured enjoyment, enhanced by seasoned oak. **Honor D** (NEW) ⊘ ★★★★ Savoury, dark spiced berries & some sweet thatch in **21** ⑧ shiraz & grenache noir duo (75/25). Ripe, full & smooth, with 14.5% alc that calls for a hearty meal. **Rosie D** ⊘ ★★★★ A touch plumper but as flavoursome as last, **23** ⑧ rosé from grenache noir shows ample strawberry cordial flavour & refreshing brisk finish. **Sauvignon Blanc** (NEW) ★★★ Light, zesty lemon & guava notes in **23** ⑧, ends with fresh pithiness. One for the summer picnic basket. **Arya** ⊘ ★★★★ Chenin (90%) with dashes grenache blanc & sauvignon in **22** ⑧, unoaked & exudes ripe yellow cling peach & tropical flavours. Lithe textured & fleshier than last, but as pleasing & quaffable. WO W Cape, as Sauvignon. Not tasted: **Iosa, The Romy D, Grenache Blanc.** In abeyance: **Roussanne.** Discontinued: **Chenin Blanc Reserve.** — MW

Location/map: Paarl ▪ Map grid reference: C1 ▪ WO: Voor Paardeberg/Western Cape/Paarl ▪ Est 2010 ▪ 1stB 2012 ▪ Tasting Mon-Sat by appt ▪ Closed Good Fri, Dec 25/26 & Jan 1 ▪ Function venue ▪ Accommodation ▪ Owner(s) Edwin Doran ▪ Winemaker(s)/viticulturist(s) Piet Kleinhans ▪ 170ha/40ha (cab, merlot, ptage, shiraz, chenin, grenache blanc/noir, rouss, sauv) ▪ 50t/5,000cs own label ▪ PO Box 2143 Windmeul 7630 ▪ monique@doranvineyards.co.za ▪ www.doranvineyards.co.za ▪ **T +27 (0)83-340-4478**

☐ **Doring Bay** *see* Fryer's Cove Vineyards

Dornier Wines

Plans made under the recent ownership of local businessman Jan Rupert and his family are swiftly taking shape: more than 37,000 vines, mostly cabernet, have been established and virused blocks removed, with more plantings envisaged this year and next. Additional export channels have been opened, and the domestic share has been expanded 'significantly'. Known for bold, intense and ageworthy wines, the extensive Dornier estate in Stellenbosch's Blaauwklippen Valley boasts non-vinous allures like a showpiece cellar with reflecting pool, designed by Swiss artist and winery founder Christoph Dornier, and a Herbert Baker homestead, both doubtless to feature in the imminent relaunch of Dornier's hospitality facilities.

Founders range
★★★★☆ **CMD** Ⓨ Bordeaux flagship equal petit verdot & malbec, 14% cab franc in **16** ㉔. As usual, all in excess yet harmonising beautifully. Firm but succulent tannins suggest improvement for 5+ years.

Donatus range
★★★★★ **Red** ⓐ Built for cellaring, **19** ㉔ five-way cab-led Bordeaux blend, 18 months in oak, third new. Streamlined & intense, signature freshness enlivening solid tannin, lifting fleshy dark fruit.
In abeyance: **White**.

Dornier range
★★★★☆ **Equanimity Cabernet Sauvignon** ⊘ Back in linear form after tad riper **18** ★★★★ ㉙. 30% new oak wraps **19** ㉚'s reined-in cassis fruit, polished grape tannins. Lovely savoury finish.

★★★★ **Malbec** One of SA's more characterful bottlings. Fresh Italian herbs & meaty nuances on **19** ㉘'s dense black fruit, hallmark seductive spice & vanilla from 30% new wood, 18 months.

★★★★ **Merlot** ⓐ Always more pronounced black plum & cherry varietal notes, greater presence than Cocoa Hill sibling. Subtly oaked **20** ㉘ a step up on last, with lovely shape & length.

★★★★ **Petit Verdot** Ⓨ Fine & elegant expression, with enlivening graphite edge. **18** ㉙ densely ripe black cherry fruit, refined tannins supported by two years in oak. Notch above last-tasted **16** ★★★☆ ㉕.

★★★★ **Pinotage** All Swartland fruit in **19** ㉚ (vs just over a third in **18** ㉚), partly fermented/16 months in barrel, 10% new, for just a nudge of tannin, lighter mulberry fruit extraction.

★★★★☆ **Siren Syrah** ⊘ Expected heady mix of aromas (pepper, fynbos & smoked meat) on **19** ㉚ but overall more restrained than last. Curvy rather than Rubenesque blackberry body, integrated spicy oak, 20% new, 15 months. Notch above sturdier **18** ★★★★ ㉙.

★★★★ **Moordenaarskloof Tinta Barocca** From Swartland fruit, as before, **21** ㉙ similar flavour profile with shade more freshness. Pot-pourri & orange zest aromas, black plum flavours & good tannins.

★★★★ **Cabernet Sauvignon-Merlot** Ⓨ Twice as much cab as merlot in **18** ㉖, firm tannin structure & bright acid to offset the sweet black fruit. 25% new oak, 18 months, adds subtle spice complexity.

★★★★★ **Moordenaarskloof Chenin Blanc** Emphasis on texture & palate weight in **22** ㉚ without sacrificing freshness. Silkier, richer than many courtesy ferment in oak, 10% new, & near 4 g/L sugar. Lots of white peach appeal, interesting wet terracotta nuance.

★★★★☆ **Semillon** Less toasty than previous (only 10% new oak vs 20%) but similarly more expressive on palate than nose, **22** ㉚ subtly lemon & gooseberry toned, satin textured & bright.
Not tasted: **Tempranillo Reserve**. Occasional release: **Leda**, **Scarlette**, **Froschkönig Natural Sweet**.

Cocoa Hill range
Merlot ★★★ Goes up a notch with appealing savoury edge to typical bright fruit. **21** ㉛ smooth & supple, fresh too thanks to 20% unoaked portion. **Ruby Red** ★★★★ Near-equal merlot & shiraz with Bordeaux extras a bit four-square in **21** ㉝, still provides pleasant everyday drinking. 80% oaked, none new. WO W Cape. **Cabernet Sauvignon Rosé** ★★★ Uncomplicated & a little short but **22** ㉛ a satisfyingly dry, pale

pink aperitif. **Chenin Blanc ★★★** Pineapples & nuts, ripe **22** (82) blends Swartland & Stellenbosch fruit, 40% of it old-oak fermented, for laidback enjoyment. **Sauvignon Blanc ★★★** Undeniably sauvignon, **22** (80) intensely fruity & fruit-sweet. Marries Elgin & Stellenbosch grapes, shows more ripe passionfruit & papaya than fig & grass this vintage. — CvZ

Location/map: Stellenbosch ▪ Map grid reference: F7 ▪ WO: Stellenbosch/Swartland/Western Cape/Elgin-Stellenbosch ▪ Est 1995 ▪ 1stB 2002 ▪ Tasting & sales daily 9-6 ▪ Closed Dec 25 ▪ Cellar tours by appt ▪ Art ▪ Conservation area ▪ Wine club ▪ Owner(s) Jan Rupert family ▪ Winemaker(s) Philip van Staden (Oct 2015) ▪ Viticulturist(s) Arjen Rijpstra (Nov 2017) ▪ 180ha/41ha (cabs s/f, malbec, merlot, p verdot, ptage, shiraz, tempranillo, chenin, sauv, sem) ▪ 380t 78% red 16% white 6% rosé ▪ PO Box 7518 Stellenbosch 7599 ▪ info@ dornier.co.za ▪ www.dornier.co.za ▪ **T +27 (0)21-880-0557**

☐ **Dorper** *see* Holder Vineyard & Wines
☐ **Dorp Street** *see* Barnardt Boyes Wines

Dorrance Wines (Ⓠ) (🍴)

Launch of their attractively priced debut pinot noir met with such demand that Christophe and Sabrina Durand are increasing production 'significantly'. They searched many years for the perfect site, and found it in Franschhoek. Just 222 cases were released. Based in a heritage building in central Cape Town, they continue to focus on French grapes and chiefly varietal wines, 'concentrating on picking perfect grapes at the right time, with high acids and low pH, working minimalistically in the cellar with mostly bunch pressing'.

★★★★ Rouge ⊘ Bushvine cinsault for **22** (86). Wild fermented (as most) & aged in part tank & wood. Mix red & black fruit works nicely with 20% new oak, giving light tannin tug while cosseting freshness. Betters **20 ★★★★** (85).

★★★★ Pinot Noir Cuvée Monrache La Culotte ⊘ Refined **22** (89) again from Franschhoek grapes. Elegant dark fruit gently shaped in barrique, 20% new, 14 months, adding layers of spice to gossamer tannins. Quite tightly wound, will develop gracefully.

★★★★☆ Syrah Cuvée Ameena Light-footed, fragrant **22** (92) displays all the virtues of cool-grown Elgin grapes, notably the mineral acidity winding through the red cherries & plums. 11 months in oak, 20% new, highlight variety's spice & gorgeous dry finish. Step up from **21** (90).

★★★★ Rosé From cinsault, with alluring Provençal hue on **22** (87). 10% spent 3 months in old oak, adding fullness to generous peach & strawberry palate, notable for appetising dryness & modest 12.5% alc. Trumps **20 ★★★★** (84).

★★★★☆ Chardonnay Cuvée Anaïs Ethereal **22** (92) from Robertson has touch slighter body than last at 12.5% yet equally beautifully realised & alluring, with marzipan from 11 months in oak, 20% new, crushed stone & white citrus, & a grapefruit pithiness & brisk acid controlling the finish.

★★★★ Blanc ⊘ Complementary chenin & viognier (70/30) from Swartland bushvines, wild fermented without oak thus magnifying **22** (88)'s sense of place. Supple acid backbone supports stonefruit, pineapple & litchi in a vibrant wine that improves on last.

Not tasted: **Chenin Blanc Cuvée Kama**. — ML

Location: Cape Town ▪ Map: Cape Peninsula ▪ Map grid reference: B1 ▪ WO: Swartland/Franschhoek/Elgin/ Western Cape ▪ Est/1stB 2000 ▪ Tasting, sales & cellar tours Mon-Fri 11-6 or by appt; pub hols 10.30-3.30 ▪ Wine shop ▪ Bouchon bistro & wine bar Mon-Fri from 4-11, www.bouchon.co.za ▪ Owner(s) Christophe & Sabrina Durand ▪ Cellarmaster(s)/winemaker(s) Christophe Durand ▪ 26ha ▪ 30t/4,666cs own label ▪ Fairtrade ▪ 95 Hout Str Cape Town 8001 ▪ christophe@dorrancewines.com ▪ www.dorrancewines.com ▪ **T +27 (0)21-422-0695/+27 (0)83-409-7071**

☐ **Double Door** *see* La Bri Wines
☐ **Douglas Green** *see* DGB (Pty) Ltd
☐ **Douglas Wine Cellar** *see* Landzicht Wine Cellar
☐ **Down to Earth** *see* Villiera Wines

Draaiboek Wines

The 'Screenplay' wines crafted for a globally dispersed group of Stellenbosch University friends by Thistle & Weed's acclaimed Stephanie Wiid has met with 'a level of success well beyond our expectations', prompting another doubling of the volume and the debut of a third chardonnay, from a different cool-climate source to the original Onskuld, but as stunning. We look forward to their next 'exciting and interesting' episode.

★★★★★ **Kinkel Chardonnay** 🆕 🐝 Cool-grown Elgin fruit delivers a stellar debut, **22** ⑨⑤ with precise & focused citrus aromas & flavours in a gentle nougat frame from 25% new oak. Beautifully structured, bright & intense, perfectly balanced for the long haul. Delectable salty farewell.

★★★★★ **Onskuld Chardonnay** 🐝 Graceful, poised **22** ⑨⑤, from Hemel-en-Aarde Ridge fruit, aged 10 months in 45% new barrels. Gorgeous depth, breadth & layering of pure lemon & lime, creamy vanilla & fragrant white flowers, pithy grapefruit farewell. Superbly balanced & made to last, decant in youth.

Not tasted: **Waagmoed Pinot Noir, Kripnota Chardonnay**. — WB

Location: Paarl ▪ WO: Hemel-en-Aarde Ridge/Elgin ▪ Est 2018 ▪ 1stB 2019 ▪ Closed to public ▪ Online sales ▪ Owner(s) Vijf Investments (Pty) Ltd (5 shareholders) ▪ Cellarmaster(s)/winemaker(s) Stephanie Wiid (Jan 2019, consultant) ▪ 1,600cs own label 25% red 75% white ▪ Klein Drakenstein Rd, Paarl 7646 ▪ hello@draaiboek.wine ▪ www.draaiboek.wine

---

Dragonridge

On Fynbos Estate, between granite peaks Dragonridge and Sonkop on Swartland's Paardeberg, Dragonridge boutique winery produces natural wines with no additives, apart from a brush of sulphur, from vines tended by co-owner Johan Simons. Johan and consultant Andy Kershaw make a diversity of mostly small bottlings, usually fresh, pure and dry, sometimes quirky. Tourist allures include 270 ha of pristine reserve.

★★★★ **Dark Star** 🐝 Unusual blend of mourvèdre (67%) & pinotage, riotous berries of the varieties on full display in **22** ⑧⑥ preview, just 7 months in old oak to tame them. More arresting than **21** ★★★★ ⑧④.

★★★★ **Aquila** 🐝 Again a sangiovese (60%) & cab blend in **22** ★★★★ ⑧④ pre-bottling sample, presenting a touch more rustic than **21** ⑧⑥. Yet the energy & intrigue that characterise this blend persist.

Cygnus 🐝 ★★★★ Fresh & vital **22** ⑧④ chenin blanc has typical Swartland sunny exuberance in its youthful, oak-brushed body. Tropical & slightly funky, it may not be for everyone but it certainly is a style. Tasted pre-bottling. **Orion's Belt** 🐝 ★★★ From chardonnay, **18** ⑧② offers citrus & stonefruit, but savoury thanks to 2 days skin contact before a year in old oak. Lightish 12.5% alc, serious acidity, silky texture. **Rigel** 🐝 ★★★ Faint marzipan, apricot & honey notes on oaked **15** ⑧① straw wine from chenin. Oxidative & rich, broad textured, with high acid countering huge sugar level. Clean finish. Not tasted: **Capella, Viognier, Galaxy**. In abeyance: **Pinotage, Cosmos, Orion, Supernova**. — ML

Location: Malmesbury ▪ Map/WO: Swartland ▪ Map grid reference: C8 ▪ Est 2004 ▪ 1stB 2006 ▪ Tasting, sales & cellar tours by appt ▪ Fee R80, R40 off on purchase of 3 btls ▪ Closed Good Fri, Dec 25/26 & Jan 1 ▪ Country meals by arrangement for groups of 10+ ▪ Facilities for children ▪ Farm produce ▪ Weddings/functions ▪ Conferences ▪ Walks/hikes ▪ Simson-Simons Contract Nature Reserve ▪ Guest houses: 6-bedroom, 2 x 4-bedroom & 2 x 2-bedroom cottages ▪ De Perdestal Restaurant open for Sunday lunch (bookings only groups of 10+) ▪ Owner(s) Fynbos Estate (3 partners) ▪ Cellarmaster(s) Johan Simons (Jan 2004) ▪ Winemaker(s) Johan Simons (Jan 2004), Andy Kershaw (2015, consultant) ▪ Viticulturist(s) Johan Simons (Jun 1997) ▪ 320ha/13ha (cab, mourv, ptage, sangio, shiraz, chard, chenin, viog) ▪ 35t/1,400cs own label 40% red 45% white 5% rosé 10% méthode ancestrale ▪ Swartland Independent Producers ▪ P O Box 526 Malmesbury 7299 ▪ info@fynbosestate.co.za, info@dragonridge.co.za ▪ www.dragonridge.co.za, www.fynbosestate.co.za ▪ **T +27 (0)22-487-1153**

☐ **Drakenskloof** *see* Spier

Driehoek Wines

The small parcel of mature, mostly red-wine varieties on the Du Toit family farm in the Cederberg Conservancy have been tended since planting by Dawie Burger, with advice from neighbour and winemaker David Nieuwoudt of Cederberg Private Cellar. Among South Africa's highest-lying vines, they deliver top-quality cool-climate fruit with purity and power. A multitude of accommodation options and leisure activities are available to suit all ages and fitness levels.

★★★★☆ **Mieke Pinot Noir** ⊘ Supple, rounded **21** ⑨② more charming & less earthy than last. Heady rosepetal perfume, plush & juicy berry fruit, creamy powdery tannins. Generous body smoothed & polished from 10 months in barriques, 20% new.

★★★★☆ **Syrah** ⊘ ⊛ Expressive **21** ★★★★★ ⑨⑤ less forceful than **20** ⑨②, its elegance evident in fine plum & cherry fruit, aromatic tobacco, scrub & pepper highlights, suede-textured tannin wrapping. 18 months oak, 31% new.

★★★★ **Ludic Sauvignon Blanc** ⊘ Extroverted, reductively made **23** ⑧⑦ has flinty, salty minerality, nettle & khaki bush aromatics, ripe gooseberry fruit. Firm & vibrant, for early drinking.

Not tasted: **Cria Rosé**. — GdB

Location: Citrusdal • Map: Olifants River • Map grid reference: D6 • WO: Cederberg • Est/1stB 2009 • Sales Mon-Sat 8-12 & 2-6 Sun/pub hols 9-11 & 3-5 • Closed Good Fri & Dec 25 • Facilities for children • Gift shop • Walking/hiking & MTB trails • Horse riding • Bird watching • Fishing • Bushman paintings • Conservation area • Self-catering cottages & camping • Owner(s) Du Toit family • Cellarmaster(s)/winemaker(s) David Nieuwoudt (Jan 2008, Cederberg) • Viticulturist(s) Dawie Burger (Jun 2006), advised by David Nieuwoudt • 375ha/5ha (pinot, shiraz, sauv) • 3,500cs own label 60% red 40% white • PO Box 89 Clanwilliam 8135 • driehoekcederberg@gmail.com • www.cederberg-accommodation.co.za • **T +27 (0)27-482-2828**

☐ **Drie Kleine Leeuwen** *see* Leeuwenberg
☐ **Drie Papen Fontein** *see* Fairview
☐ **Drift** *see* The Drift Estate

Drostdy-Hof Wines

Launched over half a century ago, this Heineken Beverages range recalls De Oude Drostdy, a heritage site in Tulbagh and for a time the brand home. The fruit-forward wines are styled and priced for everyday drinking.

Core range

Merlot ⊘ ★★★ Earthy spice on appealing **22** ⑧⓪, black fruit is lightly framed, as only half the wine had oak-stave treatment (like red sibling). WO W Cape unless noted. **Shiraz-Merlot** ⊘ ★★★ Briar & smoke intro to **22** ⑧①, slim hipped but ripe, juicy & plum toned. Touch sweet but subtle grip from oak ensures balance. **Chardonnay** ⊘ ★★★ Retains 10% colombard & light oak treatment for two-thirds of **23** ⑧⓪. Fresh, lively citrus & stonefruit, trim & bright. **Sauvignon Blanc** ⊘ ★★★ Crisp & zesty **23** ⑧⓪ shows typical lemon tang & flint. Has 10% colombard & touch of sugar to offset vivid acid. Moderate alc, as all. Not tasted: **Pinotage**, **Claret Select**, **Shiraz Rosé**, **Chenin Blanc**, **Adelpracht**. Discontinued: **Chardonnay-Viognier**, **Premier Grand Cru**.

Light range

Not tasted: **Extra Light Rosé**, **Extra Light White**.

Natural Sweet range

Not tasted: **Red**, **Rosé**, **White**. — FM

☐ **Duckitt Collection** *see* Cloof Wine Estate

Duikersdrift Winelands Country Escape   ⊕ ⑪ ⌂ ⊙ ⊗ (ᴺᴱᵂ)

After acquiring the Duikersdrift farm in Tulbagh in 2017, Trevor and Caroline Carnaby tapped the expertise of Dirk Swanepoel to nurture the tiny 2006 shiraz vineyard and craft an own-label wine in the nearby Swanepoel Wines cellar (formerly Oude Compagnies Post). Harvest 2020 was followed by a larger crop, allowing for a blend and a fortified, and from 2022 chenin was brought in from Citrusdal. The wines are sold at the on-site restaurant, and lodges and restaurants in Limpopo province. See also Schotia listing.

★★★★ **Syrah** Red & black fruit seasoned with pepper, **22** ⑧⑥ attractively lean & tight, auguring well for development. Also-tasted **21** ★★★★ ⑧③ more open & expressive, tannins more resolved. Both 10 months in older barrels, as all unless noted.

★★★★ **Cabernet Sauvignon-Shiraz** Same 67/33 proportions for both vintages tasted. **21** ⑧⑥ good depth of blue & black fruit & ripe-fruit finish, lighter (12.5% alc vs 14%) than **22** ★★★★ ⑧⑤, which has fresh leafy top note, less fruit-sweetness but some warmth.

★★★★ **Chenin Blanc** From old mountain bushvines, natural older-barrel ferment/6 months on fine lees with regular stirring. **22** ⑧⑦ quietly impressive, subtle scents & flavours & a body that's streamlined but not austere (14% alc), thrilling acid for food pairing. WO W Cape.

Cape Ruby ★★★★ From shiraz, generous Xmas cake fruit & spice, as per this port style, notes of almond & green walnut on both vintages tasted. **21** ⑧⑤ fierier heart (20% alc vs 18.5%), not sugary thanks to good grip of tannin. **22** ⑧⑤ younger & thus firmer, less obviously sweet. — PS, CvZ

Location/map: Tulbagh ▪ Map grid reference: B5 ▪ WO: Tulbagh/Western Cape ▪ Est 2018 ▪ 1stB 2021 ▪ Tasting Mon-Fri 11-4.30 Sat 11-4 Sun 11-4.30 ▪ Fee R15 per wine ▪ Sales Mon-Fri 9-8 Sat 9-5 Sun no sales ▪ Restaurant Tue-Sat 12.30-9.30 lunch & dinners Sun 9.30-5.30 breakfast & lunch; closed Mondays ▪ Deli & shop ▪ Playground ▪ Duikersdrift Parkrun ▪ MTB ▪ Luxury guesthouse/B&B (no self-catering), comprising 4 cottages ▪ Owner(s) Trevor & Caroline Carnaby ▪ Cellarmaster(s) Oude Compagnies Post / Swanepoel Wines (Jan 2019) ▪ Winemaker(s)/viticulturist(s) Dirk Swanepoel (Jan 2019, consultant) ▪ 34ha/1ha (shiraz) ▪ 5t/400cs own label 100% red ▪ PO Box 158 Tulbagh 6820 ▪ info@duikersdrift.com ▪ www.duikersdrift.com ▪ **T +27 (0)66-236-4122**

☐ **Duke** *see* Wellington Wines

Duma Wines   ⓥ ⓘ

Based in KwaZulu-Natal, Siphakamiso Blessing Duma fell under the vine's spell while working in the wine section of a chain store. After wine courses and retail experience, he launched this personal brand in collaboration with Seven Springs Vineyards, with wines of 'premium quality, lighter in style, with clean and pure fruit'. A new approach and strategy, coupled with multiple business and media nominations and awards for his start-up helping raise awareness, he's looking to expand his audience and grow the fledgeling venture.

A Glass of Wine range
Syrah Rosé ★★★★ Expressive strawberries perked up by finishing freshness, **21** ⑧③ has easy appeal & drinkability. **Unoaked Chardonnay ★★★** A slight honeyed seam from bottle aging, with underlying stonefruit. **18** ⑧⓪ good palate weight & for food matching. Not tasted: **Sauvignon Blanc.** — CR

Location: Hermanus ▪ WO: Overberg ▪ Est 2021 ▪ 1stB 2017 ▪ Tasting Sat 8-5 Sun 10-1 ▪ Online shop ▪ Tour groups ▪ Experiences offered: food & wine pairing; walking/hiking trails; MTB and 4x4 trails offered as exclusive packages; museum tours ▪ Wine club ▪ Owner(s) Siphakamiso Blessing Duma ▪ SAWISA, WIETA ▪ 40 Hilltop Rd, Wyebank, Pinetown 3610 ▪ info@dumawines.co.za ▪ www.dumawines.co.za ▪ **T +27 (0)73-736-4144**

Dunstone Winery   ⓥ ⓘ ⌂ ⓘ ⓘ ⓘ

A luxury guest house, bistro and scenic setting at the foot of Wellington's Bainskloof Pass are some of the attractions of the farm recently acquired by Dirk and Natascha Vaeye, who plan to 'continue as before', with the boutique wines, all from Rhône varieties, crafted by Gielie Beukes in the on-site cellar. The Vaeyes have imported, inter alia, top SA wine into Europe for over a decade, and through their extensive network, the first Dunstone pallets have already been shipped overseas.

Roots range
★★★★☆ Grenache Noir ⓥ This & single variety sibling move here from Dunstone range. Extroverted **21 ★★★★** ⑧⑦ shows youthful aromas of raspberries, sweet plums & perfumed flowers; the palate is juicy & fresh though not quite as restrained & elegant as **20** ⑨③.
★★★★ Shiraz ⓥ Spicier, richer than last, **19** ⑧⑨ offers a seamless drinking experience with lovely red fruit detail underpinned by subtle oaking, 8 months, all older.
Not tasted: **QV Grenache Noir-Syrah-Mourvèdre**.

Dunstone range
Shiraz Rosé ⓥ **★★★★** Generous & well-rounded **22** ⑧⑤ an appealing, iridescent pink, delivers on promise of bright berry fruit with hint of dessert peach on dry finish.

Reserve range
In abeyance: **Grenache Noir**, **Shiraz**, **Shiraz-Mourvèdre-Viognier**, **Viognier**. — FM

Location/map/WO: Wellington ▪ Map grid reference: C3 ▪ Est/1stB 2006 ▪ Tasting upon reservation at the GH lounge & sales ▪ Fee R50pp, waived on purchase ▪ The Stone Kitchen Restaurant ▪ Playground inside & outside for children ▪ Dunstone Country House luxury B&B guest house & self-catering cottage ▪ Owner(s) Dirk & Natascha Vaeye ▪ Winemaker(s) Gielie Beukes (Jan 2022) ▪ Viticulturist(s) Walter Schloms (Jan 2022)

▪ 5ha (grenache, mourv, shiraz, viog) ▪ 30t/3,300cs own label 70% red 20% white 10% rosé ▪ Bovlei Rd Wellington 7655 ▪ wine@dunstone.co.za ▪ www.dunstone.co.za ▪ **T +27 (0)76-351-7315**

☐ **Du Plevaux** *see* Imbuko Wines

Du Preez Estate ⓠ ♿

Built over the past century by three generations of the Du Preez family, this venture near Rawsonville in Breedekloof strives for 'clean, fruity, New World wines' while 'keeping things simple'. With 350 ha under vine, and the equivalent of 360,000 cases to process, the to-do list is long, and present custodians Hennie snr, Jean and Janette must simply have overlooked the fact that 15 years slipped by without a label refresh, something they're rectifying, starting with the pair of new wines and the sauvignon.

Hendrik Lodewyk range
★★★★ Méthode Cap Classique ⓠ Classic baked biscuit & apple pie richness on **NV** ⑧⑥ bubbly, 70% chardonnay with pinot noir, 15 months on lees. Steps up on last but at peak, best enjoyed soon. Also in 1.5L
Petit Verdot ★★★★ Change in style, **21** ⑧③ preview drier than last **16 ★★★** ⑧②, just 6 months oaked with chips. Dark-toned fruit, smoky, savoury spice, smooth albeit best with food to offset the prominent wood flavours. Not tasted: **Cabernet Sauvignon**.

Du Preez Private Cellar range
★★★★ Hanepoot ⓠ Latest fortified is copper-gold **NV** ⑧⑧. Sweetness well balanced by 16.5% alcohol (not fiery) to give the barley sugar & marmalade character a clean & fresh gloss. Last-tasted lemon-gold **15 ★★★★★** ⑨③ was big step up on **11 ★★★★** ⑧④.
Merlot ⓠ **★★★** Typical leafiness in **20** ⑧⓪, slightly bigger body than last, older-oak spice to redcurrant fruit. **Shiraz** ⓠ **★★★** Year older oak accounts for the smoky aromas on **20** ⑧⓪, sour cherry fruit the tang on palate, overall savoury character & leathery tannins. **Polla's Red** ⓥ **★★★★** Tasted from magnum but mostly sold in 750 ml, pinotage 49% with shiraz, 3 Bordeaux grapes, on staves 3 months, just enough to add savoury notes to **21** ⑧④'s berry fruit. Texture smooth, tannins supple, this is for enjoying, not ageing. **Chardonnay** ⓝⓔⓦ ⓥ **★★★** Salad of apple & pear, underlying citrus, unwooded **23** ⑧② has notable freshness, lively palate appeal. **Chenin Blanc** ⓝⓔⓦ ⓥ **★★★★** Freshness abounds in **23** ⑧④, just-sliced apple & pear, some thatch in the flavours, giving palate fullness, adding to the appeal. **Sauvignon Blanc** ⓥ **★★★★** Showing good typicity, slender (13% alc) **23** ⑧⑤ prominent grass aromas, kiwi, crunchy green apple, flavours tangy from fruit-acid interplay. Not tasted: **Cabernet Sauvignon**. — CR

Location: Rawsonville ▪ Map/WO: Breedekloof ▪ Map grid reference: B6 ▪ Est 1916 ▪ 1stB 1998 ▪ Tasting & sales Mon-Fri 8-5 Sat 10-1 ▪ Closed all pub hols ▪ Cellar tours by appt, 1-day prior notice required ▪ Tour groups (max 40 pax), 1-day prior notice required ▪ Owner(s) Du Preez family ▪ Winemaker(s) Jaco Marais (Nov 2020) ▪ Viticulturist(s) Jean du Preez ▪ 350ha (cab, merlot, p verdot, ptage, shiraz, chard, chenin, cbard, nouvelle, sauv) ▪ 6,000t ▪ IPW, WIETA ▪ PO Box 12 Route 101 Rawsonville 6845 ▪ info@dupreezestate.co.za ▪ www.dupreezestate.co.za ▪ **T +27 (0)23-349-1995**

Durbanville Hills ⓠ ⑪ ◎ ⓐ ♿

One of SA wine's great characters, Martin Moore was at this winery 'since brick number 1' and his 25 harvests here, latterly as cellarmaster, undoubtedly were instrumental in the success of the venture. His sudden passing was met with sadness across the industry. Ex-Darling Cellars Pieter-Niel Rossouw has been tapped to fill the role, joining the established team of Kobus Gerber and Wilhelm Coetzee, assisted by newcomer Jenna Higgins, with the long-standing brief of making 'high-quality wine in a consistent style that over-delivers on price'. New at the hillside venue is a visitor centre providing information about the vineyards, winemaking and ranges, and general insights on one of the winery's focus areas, sustainability.

Tangram range
★★★★☆ Bordeaux Blend Cab-based flagship has positive attributes of past vintages, well-controlled fruit sweetness & deft 2 years new oak. More classic than Collectors reds, with considerable complexity from other 4 grapes. **20** ⑨② just a touch less balanced, burlier at 14.7% alc than **19** ⑨③.
★★★★☆ Sauvignon Blanc-Semillon Impressive fruit richness under delicate smoky oak veil on **22** ⑨②, stylish barrel-fermented/aged Cape Bordeaux white. Mostly sauvignon, with reined-in cool green characters & white floral/fruit accents, 12% semillon adding subtle wax on finish.

Collectors Reserve range

★★★★ **The Castle of Good Hope Cabernet Sauvignon** Hallmark generous alc slightly checked in **21** ⑧⑦ (14.8% vs 15% in **20** ⑧⑦) but not so the vanilla sheen of 40% new oak, 16 months, coating the dark fruit. Bone-dry & racy but impression of sweetness lingers.

★★★★☆ **The Lighthouse Merlot** Overtly plummy, slick & modern **21** ⑨⓪ ticks the boxes. Dark chocolate, dense fruit under cloak of savoury spice, slight herbaceous nuance. Complex & structured, has heft (14.6% alc) & same dry palate as last.

★★★★ **The Promenade Pinotage** Broad shouldered at 14.6% alc, variety true blackberry & mulberry body & bouquet, **21** ⑧⑧ is the mirror image of **20** ⑧⑨.

★★★★ **The High Noon Shiraz** Very appealing **21** ⑧⑧, dried herbs & black pepper, fresh meaty tone & dense red fruits, lightly coated in vanilla & coconut from 5% American oak. Better balanced than **20** ⑧⑦ at 14% alc vs 15%.

★★★★ **The Cape Garden Chenin Blanc** Fine display of depth & length variety can deliver. Portion of **22** ⑧⑨ barrel fermented/10 months, 33% new, for structure & spice, rest amphora & stainless steel to help maintain freshness of peach, nectarine & hint bitter quince.

★★★★ **The Cape Mist Sauvignon Blanc** Unfussy cellar handling - tank fermented/10 months on lees - consistently delivers appetising results, with mouthfeel & some weight from nearly 14% alc, usual rounded acid in **22** ⑧⑦.

Not tasted: **The Cableway Chardonnay**.

Durbanville Hills range

★★★★☆ **Méthode Cap Classique Blanc de Blancs** White-gold **21** ★★★★ ⑧⑦ from chardonnay, frothy with lemon sherbet acidity seaming green, red & toffee apple palate. Less rich than last-tasted **18** ⑨⓪, but beautifully fruited for early drinking.

★★★★ **Cape Honey Bee Noble Late Harvest** Unoaked botrytis dessert from sauvignon. **23** ★★★★ ⑧⑤ litchi, mango &, yes, honey, all energised by burst of succulent acid; like **22** ⑧⑦, only light noble rot character. 375 ml.

Cabernet Sauvignon ★★★★☆ Subtle cassis, smoother than others in this line-up, **21** ⑧⑤ a neatly dry & pleasant companion. For early drinking, as all these; pleasant tarry note from oak staves, like all the reds. **Merlot** ★★★★ Red & black plums, firm tannin grip, **21** ⑧③ simple, slightly green & very fresh quaffing. **Pinotage** ★★★ Translucent cerise hue, soft **21** ⑧② 's effortless smoothness aided by 14.7% alc, bone-dry finish offset by sweet red fruit. **Shiraz** ★★★★ Driest of these reds but, like others, **21** ⑧⑤ doesn't show as austere. Oak well integrated with supple tannins & vibrant red berry fruit. **Merlot Rosé** ★★★ Pinkish orange **23** ⑧⓪ a pleasing tannin grip, decent berry flavours & mouthfeel from 14% alc. Chill well. **Chardonnay** ★★★ Small portion oak-stave ferment/6 months adds strong vanilla overlay on **22** ⑧① 's nose & palate of lemon, lime & sweet apple. **Chenin Blanc** ★★★★ Textbook example of the unoaked, fruity style at a wallet-friendly price. **23** ⑧④ good acid balance & appealing peach stone grip. **Chenin Blanc Light** ★★★ Water white & still slightly estery, just-bottled **23** ⑦⑧ doesn't shout the variety but is vinous, fresh & just 9.8% alc. **Sauvignon Blanc** ★★★ Durbanville's characteristic dusty top note on **23** ⑧① 's grass & apple. A shopping list stalwart (200,000 cases) that glides down easily. Discontinued: **Shiraz Light**.

Cape Portrait range

Not tasted: **Red Blend, White Blend**.

Sparkling range

Rosé ★★★ Carbonated **NV** ⑧① from cab, shiraz & merlot puts its party foot forward. Happy orange-pink hue, rosepetal & strawberry tones, frothy mousse from start to finish, satisfyingly dry. Not tasted: **Sauvignon Blanc, Honeysuckle Demi-Sec**.

Brandy range

★★★★☆ **Merlot Potstill Brandy** Unusual both in being from merlot & vintaged. **11** ⑨① potstill ex Durbanville grapes & aged 10 years in Durbanville Hills Merlot barrels. Still fresh, but development brings a savoury, cedary quality to ripe fruit, sense of refinement augmented by drier finish than is common. Lovely sipping at 38% alc.— CvZ, TJ

Location/WO: Durbanville ▪ Map: Durbanville, Philadelphia & Darling ▪ Map grid reference: C7 ▪ Est 1998 ▪ 1stB 1999 ▪ Tasting & sales Mon 12-6 Tue-Fri 10-6 Sat/pub hols 10-4 Sun 11-4 (bar & kitchen close 1hr earlier) ▪ Closed Dec 25 & Jan 1 ▪ Fee starting at R100/5 wines ▪ Range of tasting options include chocolate/biltong/cheese & wine pairings ▪ Tasting room menu available daily ▪ Sparkling wine cocktails available Fri-Sun & pub hols ▪ Cellar tours Mon-Fri (bookings 24 hrs in advance) Mon at 3 Tue-Fri at 11 & 3 ▪ The Tangram restaurant: breakfast 8.30-11 & lunch 12-3 daily; dinner Wed-Sat 6-10 ▪ Facilities for children ▪ Conferences ▪ Weddings/functions ▪ Wine club ▪ Owner(s) Heineken Beverages & 9 farmers & staff trust ▪ Cellarmaster(s) Pieter-Niel Rossouw (Nov 2023) ▪ Winemaker(s) Wilhelm Coetzee (reds, Sep 2008) & Kobus Gerber (whites, Jul 2015), with assistant Jenna Higgins ▪ Viticulturist(s) Henk van Graan (consultant) ▪ 770ha ▪ 6,000t/300,000cs own label 40% red 58% white 2% rosé ▪ FSSC 2200, ISO, ISO 45001, ISO 9000-1, ISO 14000-1, HACCP, IPW, WIETA ▪ PO Box 3276 Durbanville 7551 ▪ info@durbanvillehills.co.za ▪ www.durbanvillehills.co.za ▪ **T +27 (0)21-558-1300**

Du'SwaRoo (2) (◎)

There's a sense of exuberant individuality here in Calitzdorp, starting with the brand name, juxtaposing key places in the life of the previous owner, Durban, South West Africa/Namibia and Klein Karoo, and current proprietor (and everything else) Kallie Calitz clearly having a grand time making his micro-batches and giving some fun names. There's more: the first tannat and petit verdot from baby vines. Keep watching.

★★★★ Cape Vintage Reserve ⊘ 'Port' from touriga & 33% tinta, 2 years older oak for chocolate nuance to Xmas cake fruit & spice. Good grip & warmth from judicious 19% alc. **20** ⑧⑦ more interesting, better balanced than **19 ★★★** ⑧①.

Ruby Cabernet (⑨) ★★ California variety rarely bottled on its own in SA. Unwooded **21** ⑦⑥ engaging fushia hue, sappy tannin grip. **Shiraz** ⊘ ★★★★ A repeat of previous: more mulberries & currants than variety's hallmark pepper & spice, but **20** ⑧③ balanced & fresh, tasty. Attractive & well-priced pick of the reds. **Tinta Barocca ★★★** Continuing the lighter styling, translucent ruby **22** ⑧① offers bright strawberry fruit that won't mind light chilling. **Touriga Nacional ★★★** More body & obvious oak (18-24 months) on **21** ⑧② than Portuguese sibling, reprises distinct & unusual minty top note. **Karoo Spoor** (NEW) ★★★ 'Karoo Footprint' celebrates the land with earthy cinsault & tinta blend, unoaked. **23** ⑦⑧ chunky, crunchy, satisfying in a rustic way. **Kolskoot!** ★★★ Calizdorp Blend of touriga & tinta, co-fermented, **22** ⑦⑧ hits the easy-drinking spot with ripe plum & tang of orange zest, gentle 6 months' old-oaking. **Chardonnay ★★** Highlights citrus fruit in **23** ⑦③, fresh & clean, notch up on previous retsina-like bottling. **Chenin Blanc ★★★** Melon & stewed quince pepped by decent acid vibrancy in **23** ⑦⑦. Modest 11.6% alc. **Tant Annie Muscat d'Alexandrie ★★★** Rare unfortified solo bottling named for Calitz matriarch. **23** ⑦⑧ lovely sweet-ripe grape bouquet that contrasts appealingly with a bone-dry palate. Bonus of low 9% alc. **Verdelho ★★** Unusual solo bottling, **23** ⑦⑤ has a confected character with evident tannins from oak chips. Restrained 10.7% alc. **Grumpy** (NEW) ★★★ How you'll feel if you miss this 400-bottle fruity blend of near-equal char-donnay, chenin & verdelho. **23** ⑧⓪ for drinking without too much thinking. **Hanepoot ★★★** Sunshine in a glass, **23** ⑧⓪ redolent of sultanas & raisins, fortified with gentle 17% alc. Touch drier than last & better for it. Was 500 ml, now 750. **Red Muscadel** (NEW) ★★★ Old gold fortified elixir, **23** ⑧⓪ offers honey & Turkish sweets to delight the sweet toothed. Klein Karoo WO. **Cape Ruby** (⑨) ★★★ For early sipping, per the Ruby port style, **21** ⑧⓪ near-equal shiraz, tinta & ruby cab, unoaked. Not too sweet, with decent 17% spirit kick. **Cape Pink ★★** Early-drinking 'port', **23** ⑦③ prettily pink & sweetly delicious, vanilla ice cream nuance to shy berry aromas & flavours. Touriga & shiraz, unoaked. 375 ml. Not tasted: **JMC Pinotage, Tannat, Shiraz Rosé**. In abeyance: **Petit Verdot**. Discontinued: **Cinsaut, Mooiloop**. — DS

Location: Calitzdorp ▪ Map: Klein Karoo & Garden Route ▪ Map grid reference: B5 ▪ WO: Calitzdorp/Klein Karoo ▪ Est/1stB 2008 ▪ Tasting, sales & cellar tours Mon-Sat 10-4 ▪ Closed Sundays, Good Fri & Dec 25 ▪ Farm produce & deli products ▪ Owner(s)/cellarmaster(s)/winemaker(s)/viticulturist(s) Kallie Calitz ▪ 1.2ha (p verdot, shiraz, tannat, tinta barocca, touriga nacional, chard); 1.5ha/20t hanepoot - majority delivered to Calitzdorp Cellar ▪ 8,000cs own label 60% red 30% white 10% port ▪ PO Box 279 Calitzdorp 6660 ▪ kallie@duswaroo.co.za ▪ www.duswaroo.co.za ▪ **T +27 (0)44-213-3055/+27 (0)82-826-2419**

Du Toitskloof Winery (2) (¶¶) (◎) (⑤)

A milestone in 2023 for the extensive and welcoming winery near Rawsonville in Breedekloof Valley: the 60th anniversary of the first crush, following the founding by six winefarmers in 1962. Du Toitskloof remains one of the smaller producer cellars by number of owners, with 13 members farming 985 ha of vines. The winery's three principles, delivering utmost quality, consistently and without compromising ethically, in

2005 saw it become one of the first in South Africa to participate in the Fairtrade social responsibility project, to date benefiting over 3,000 individuals. Conveniently situated close to the major south-north highway, it's a must-stop for the large local fan base, offering a new tasting room, art exhibitions, bakery and, for MTB and trailing enthusiasts, modern ablution facilities. The substantial 800,000-case production is also shared around the world for equally loyal fans. See also separate listings for the Quest and Land's End brands.

Legacy range

★★★★ Nebbiolo ⓥ Attractive true-to-type tar & violet aromas on **20 ★★★★** ⑧⑤, agreeable freshness too. On softish, approachable side of variety. First since better-structured **16** ⑧⑥.

★★★★ Dimension ⓥ Tasty **18** ⑧⑥ headed by shiraz & merlot for plush feel; freshness, structure & greater interest from partners cab franc, mourvèdre, cab & petit verdot. No pinotage, like in **17 ★★★★** ⑧④.

★★★★ Old Vine Sauvignon Blanc ⊛ From 1985 Breedekloof single block, **22** ⑧⑥ in quieter tropical mode yet showing concentration & weight. Balanced acid lends form without dominating. Good now & for year/2. Part barrel fermented/6 months. **21** untasted.

Heritage range

★★★★ Hanepoot Jerepigo ⓥ Intense yet refined fresh grape, nut & hint orange citrus on **21** ⑧⑨ fortified muscat d'Alexandrie. Full sweetness balanced by purity, sufficient acid. Moreish golden nectar!

★★★★ Red Muscadel ⓥ Flame-licked red hue on **20** ⑧⑨ fortified, full-sweet & rich in raisins, dried fruit, including figs; concentrated & with delicious persistence. Superb winter fireside sipping.

. . . .

Chardonnay ☺ **★★★** Bouncy **23** ⑧① has plentiful lightly oak-spiced lemon flavours, cheerful fruity finish. **Chenin Blanc** ☺ **★★★** Delicate yet pure pear scents, nicely sustained on plump, juicy texture with a little sweetness & crisp finish. **23** ⑧② offers notably good drinking & value. **Sauvignon Blanc** ☺ **★★★** Effusive tropical & passionfruit on bright & breezy **23** ⑦⑨, few grams sugar prolong the pleasure. **Moscato** ⓝⓔⓦ ☺ **★★★** Medley of classic flavours from muscats d'Alexandrie & morio with Hungarian partner irsai olivér. **23** ⑧② floral & Turkish delight succulence, enough zip to balance good few grams sugar.

. . . .

Cabernet Sauvignon ⓥ **★★★** Plenty fresh blackcurrant on youthful **20** ⑧①, sweet fruit restrained by still-firm grip. Better with food or after 6/12 months. **Merlot** ⊘ **★★★★** Full-bodied **21** ⑧④ has perfectly ripe, plummy-rich fruit, freshened by melded tannin grip. French oak injects further class. Will convert many nonfans. **Pinotage** ⊘ **★★★★** Plums & mulberries with vanilla hint on smooth, gently fresh **20** ⑧③. Rounded finish allows for ready enjoyment. **Shiraz** ⊘ **★★★★** Plentiful white pepper spice, floral & berry attractions on **20** ⑧⑤; creamy, with gentle freshness & upbeat vanilla-spiced finish ex portion American oak. **Pinotage-Merlot-Ruby Cabernet** ⓥ **★★★** Red-berry succulence on full-bodied **21** ⑦⑧, good freshness with fruit-extending few grams sugar. For youthful enjoyment. Also in 3L bag-in-box, as Rosé. **Cabernet Sauvignon-Shiraz** ⓥ **★★★** Complementary 60/40 partnership, **21** ⑧⓪ has lively spice & dark berries with light oak dusting. Comfortably rounded for ready enjoyment. **Cape Sugarbird** ⓝⓔⓦ **★★★** Cab & shiraz combo packs in pepper, berries & cherries in **22** ⑧①, glides down easily, handling good few grams sugar & vanilla from part-American oaking with aplomb. **Pinotage Rosé** ⊘ **★★★** Soft red berries-&-cream attractions on fruity **23** ⑧① all the way to tangy finish. **Brut ★★★** Tropical flavours brightened by pinprick bubble on carbonated **NV** ⑧⓪. Latest 100% sauvignon, previous included chardonnay. Discontinued: **Cape Ruby**. — AL, CvZ

Location: Rawsonville ▪ Map: Breedekloof ▪ Map grid reference: B6 ▪ WO: Western Cape/Breedekloof ▪ Est 1962 ▪ Tasting & sales Mon-Fri 8-5 Sat/Sun/pub hols 9-4 ▪ Closed Dec 25 & Jan 1 ▪ Cellar tours by appt ▪ Ou Meul Bakery ▪ Art exhibitions ▪ MTB & trail running ▪ Owner(s) 13 members (22 farms) ▪ Cellarmaster(s) Shawn Thomson (Oct 1999) ▪ Winemaker(s) Tiaan Loubser (Nov 2016) & Willie Stofberg (Feb 2011), with Derrick Cupido (Jan 1993) ▪ Viticulturist(s) Leon Dippenaar (Jan 2005, consultant) ▪ 900ha (cab, merlot, ptage, shiraz, chard, chenin, cbard, sauv) ▪ 16,500t/±800,000c own label 45% red 55% white ▪ Fairtrade ▪ PO Box 55 Rawsonville 6845 ▪ info@dtkwines.com ▪ www.dutoitskloof.co.za ▪ **T +27 (0)23-349-1601**

DuVon & DeVries Vintners ⓥ ⌂ ⌾

Changes at this small-scale venture on Robertson's visitor-friendly Little Italy farm see DuVon owners Armand du Toit and his uncle Alex von Klopmann join forces with Izak de Vries in a new entity, with Izak as cellarmaster and winemaker-in-chief. Their first wines, unready for tasting by us, are a chenin blanc and sauvignon blanc, with plans for a cabernet, chardonnay and cap classique.

Location/map: Robertson ▪ Map grid reference: B7 ▪ Est/1stB 2023 ▪ Tasting, sales & cellar tours by appt ▪ Conferences ▪ Weddings ▪ Guest house ▪ Owner(s) Armand du Toit, Alex von Klopmann & Izak de Vries ▪ Cellarmaster(s) Izak de Vries ▪ Winemaker(s) Izak de Vries & Armand du Toit ▪ Viticulturist(s) Armand du Toit ▪ 20ha (cab, ruby cab, shiraz, chenin, cbard, sauv) ▪ 400t/1,000cs own label 40% red 60% white ▪ PO Box 348 Robertson 6705 ▪ armand@duvon.co.za ▪ www.duvon.co.za ▪ **T +27 (0)72-514-4204**

☐ **Dwyka Hills** see Eagle's Cliff Wines-New Cape Wines
☐ **Dyasonsklip** see Bezalel Wine & Brandy Estate

Eagle's Cliff Wines-New Cape Wines   ⓠ ⑪ ◎ ⑤

Supported latterly by sons Jacques and Nicholas, Christiaan Groenewald grows 'nature-friendly, early-drinking yet ageable' wine on the Worcester grape farm where he was raised and, in the early 2000s, added a cellar and later a visitor venue. The latter has now been upgraded with, among others, facilities for participants in MTB weekends and trail runs, plus an enlarged patio with a pond added to the panorama.

Eagle's Cliff range

Pinotage ⓠ ★★★ Savoury notes of mocha chocolate from light oaking, which **20** ⑧⑵'s dark fruit matches, the whole succulent & softly rounded. **Shiraz-Pinotage** ⓠ ★★★★ Oak-brushed **21** ⑧③ equal blend but shiraz in charge of the perfume, smoky scrub & hedgerow fruit; pinotage works its magic on the palate, smoothly rounded, juicy, fresh note at the end. **Chardonnay-Pinot Noir** ⓠ ★★★ Increasingly popular varietal pairing for rosé, **22** ⑧⑵ is 50/50. Pale salmon, strong citrus & piquant red berries plus freshness showing the partnership works. **Chenin Blanc** ⊘ ★★★ Generous yellow peach fruit in a firm acid grip, pleasant salty twist on **23** ⑧⓪. **Pinot Grigio** ⓠ ★★★ Italian variety, still quite rare locally, styled mostly for everyday enjoyment, which is the template for **22** ⑧⑵: perky freshness, green & red apples, a quince highlight. **Sauvignon Blanc** ⊘ ★★★ Light hearted, crisp & fresh, **23** ⑧⓪ has tingling acidity, herbal notes to sunny fruit salad flavours. Also in 3L pack, as Shiraz-Pinotage. In abeyance: **Shiraz Rosé**. Discontinued: **Cabernet Sauvignon-Merlot**.

Dwyka Hills range

Shiraz ⓠ ★★★ Fresh, fruity, with salty olive nuances, **18** ⑧⑵ is tasty but lacks depth of previous. 20% oaked 6 months.

Hoeks Rivier range

Cabernet Sauvignon ⓠ ★★★☆ Differs from last, **20** ⑦⑧ now lightly oaked, which adds a toasty note to the fruit, making it more food friendly. — GdB

Location/map: Worcester ▪ Map grid reference: A6 ▪ WO: Breede River Valley ▪ Est 2000 ▪ Tasting & sales Mon-Thu 9-3 Fri 9-2 ▪ Closed all pub hols ▪ Cheese & meat platters (reservation only) ▪ Bistro for functions/ birthdays/anniversaries (reservation only) ▪ Function venue ▪ Black Eagle Coffee Roasters ▪ New Cape Nuts ▪ Owner(s)/winemaker(s) Christiaan Groenewald ▪ 600ha/80ha under vine ▪ 40% red 60% white ▪ PO Box 898 Worcester 6849 ▪ christiaan@ncw.co.za ▪ www.eaglescliff.co.za ▪ **T +27 (0)23-340-4112**

Eagles' Nest   ⑤

Having built an internationally respected winery from the ashes of a millennium wildfire, the Mylrea family have handed the keys to the Constantia eyrie to German-owned company Elleke Harvest & Hospitality. Kobus Jordaan, viticulturist since 2008, is overseeing the replanting of portions of the 12-ha vineyard, planted in rocky terraces on what's understood to be the steepest commercially farmed land in the Cape. Just three varieties are grown, merlot, shiraz and viognier, all well-suited to the cool False Bay breezes and altitude of up to 400 m - above which, in the nearby nature reserve, the name-giving Verreaux's eagles reside. Craig Barnard does the handcrafting 'of a small range of wines that are truly expressive of their origin'.

★★★★☆ **Merlot** Smoky green nuance dominates **20** ★★★★ ⑧⑥, taking edge off bright red-berry fruit. 18 months in barrels, third new, add coffee & chocolate to generally cool-toned fruit with dark twist at finish. Lacks richness of last **16** ⑨③.

★★★★☆ **Shiraz** ⑧ Wonderfully poised **20** ⑨④ confidently walks the finest of lines between restraint & exuberance, ethereal perfume & meaty undertones, red fruit sweetness & savoury, smoky oak (18 months, 35% new). Selected from 11 blocks of altitudes up to 400m. First since **16** ⑨④.

★★★★ **Sauvignon Blanc** ⊛ Very confident 22 ★★★★★ ⑨④ uses different picking times & yeast strains to create highly complex wine, further lifted by 65% older-barrel ferment & time on lees. Result is multifaceted, exciting mouthful of tropical fruit & fresh hay, with creamy acid & bright citrus finish. Constantia fruit clearly an improvement over last-tasted 20 ⑧⑧'s brought-in grapes.

★★★★☆ **Viognier** Dialled-back & elegant 21 ★★★★ ⑧⑨ shows change in style from last 19 ⑨③'s powerful structure. Delicate white peach fruit, subtle oak (just 10% new barrels for the ferment) & lower alc all make for enjoyable drinking, though a little more varietal oomph wouldn't harm. — CM

Location/WO: Constantia ▪ Est 2001 ▪ 1stB 2005 ▪ Closed to public ▪ Wine club ▪ Owner(s) Elleke Harvest & Hospitality (Pty) Ltd ▪ Cellarmaster(s)/winemaker(s) Craig Barnard (Jan 2022) ▪ Viticulturist(s) Kobus Jordaan (2008) ▪ 38ha/12ha (merlot, shiraz, viog) ▪ 100t/15,000cs own label 85% red 15% white ▪ info@ eaglesnestwines.com ▪ www.eaglesnestwines.com ▪ **T +27 (0)21-794-3359**

☐ **Earth Beneath Our Feet** *see* The Earth Beneath Our Feet
☐ **Ecology** *see* PaardenKloof
☐ **Edenhof** *see* Schalkenbosch Wines
☐ **Edgebaston** *see* David Finlayson Wines

Edouard Labeye ⓥ

Bringing the 'French touch' to locally grown Rhône varieties is Edouard Labeye, Radford Dale shareholder and viticulturist, veteran of well over 60 vintages in his home country and SA, and now owner of an own boutique label. Working sustainably, he sources grapes from organically grown vines, and intervenes as little as possible in the cellar. Unready for review last time, his bottlings are fine additions to two trendy categories. While Edouard himself is no newcomer, these wines win for him our award for Newcomer Winery of the Year.

★★★★ **Grenache Noir** ⑲⑤ Ripe aromatic fragrance & flavour on 21 ⑧⑦. Full bodied & with some richness. 10 months in oak, none new, supportive. Fine, firm tannins to balance the 14.5% alc, but this latter does warm the finish.

★★★★☆ **Grenache Blanc** ⑲⑤ ⊛ There's a fine stony quality to characterful 21 ⑨④, underlining light & delicate structure & complementing plentiful flavour. Just 12.5% alc, with beautifully balanced acidity & dryness. Fermented in barrel & 10 months on lees in older oak for extra dimension & interest. — TJ, AL

Location: Elgin ▪ WO: Swartland ▪ Est 2003 ▪ 1stB 2021 ▪ Tasting by appt at cellardoor of Radford Dale; sales Mon-Fri 9-5 ▪ Closed all pub hols ▪ Wine club ▪ Owner(s) Edouard Labeye ▪ Cellarmaster(s) Edouard Labeye (Jan 2003) ▪ 400cs own label 50% red 50% white ▪ WIETA ▪ thirsty@radforddale.com ▪ **T +27 (0)21-855-5528**

Eendracht Brandewyn ⓥ ⑪ ⓒ

Devon Hofmeyr and Nikita Joubert's brandy was born in quiet Elgin's Oude Molen distillery but lives upcountry in livelier surroundings: Eendracht Pub & Grill in Cullinan, and Ketelkraal Brewing & Distilling Co in Centurion. New products have been added, and we look forward to sampling them next time.

★★★★ **VSOP** ⑫ Savoury edge to the nuts, citrus & dried stonefruit on sweetly flavourful potstill ⑧⑦, aged 4-10 years. It's smooth, the 40% alc in balance, encouraging neat sipping. Notably good value.— TJ

Location: Cullinan ▪ Est 2022 ▪ Tasting & sales Wed-Fri 10-6 Sat/Sun 9-6 at Eendracht Pub & Grill, Cullinan ▪ Live music on weekends ▪ Ketelkraal Mon-Fri 9-late Sat 9-5 pub hols (seasonal) please call ahead, Unit 6 Edison Bell Park, Bell Cres, Hennopspark, Centurion ▪ Owner(s) Devon Hofmeyr & Nikita Joubert ▪ 80 Oak Ave, Cullinan, Pretoria 1000 ▪ nikita@eendrachtbrandewyn.co.za ▪ www.eendrachtbrandewyn.co.za ▪ **T +27 (0)60-867-0857/+27 (0)66-270-9153**

Eenzaamheid ⓥ ⓒ

Encouraged by critical acclaim for wines made from their dryland-grown grapes by third parties, the Briers-Louw family, Christo and Karina and Elsenburg-trained son Janno, just short of 15 years ago began crafting small batches under the banner of their 17th-century Agter Paarl farm, named 'Solitude' because of its remove from Cape Town. Now MD of the extensive estate and a Cape Wine Master, Janno is hitting the high notes with wines that 'express terroir and vintage character through minimal intervention in the cellar'.

★★★★☆ **Cinsaut** ✓ 🏵 Lipsmackingly delicious **22** ★★★★★ 95 is light-toned yet shows old-vine intensity of fruit & perfume, red cherry, pomegranate & rosepetal among the notes, underpinned by earthy spice & gentle tannins, lingering sweet-sour farewell. Lightly chill & enjoy now or keep a few years. From 1989 bushvines; older oak, 11 months. **21** 91 for earlier drinking.

★★★★ **Pinotage** 🏵 Full bodied, with great concentration of black & red berries, leather & warm exotic spice, **21** ★★★★☆ 93 packed with flavour to the last drop. Harmonious & well structured for long ageing. Improves on last **17** ★★★★ 85 & **16** 89.

★★★★☆ **Shiraz** 🏵 Full-throttle **21** 93 runs the gamut of hedgerow fruit, fragrant fynbos, cured meat spice, liquorice, tapenade & hint of dust. Rich, rounded, with presence & precision, well-judged oak (10% new, 11 months, as Pinotage) making the fruit shine. For the long haul.

★★★★ **Cinsaut Rosé** NEW Coral pink **22** 89 fermented wholebunch & lees stirred for a full-bodied, intensely flavoured blush - spicy strawberry, watermelon & perfumed rose on a creamy base, rounded & lively with grapefruit at the finish.

★★★★★ **Chenin Blanc** 🏵 🏵 Janno Briers-Louw's signature wine, from low-yield bushvines, now Old Vine Project certified, bunch pressed, 11 months in barrel, 10% new, tour de force **21** 95 near-carbon copy of last vintage's opulent elegance, with ripe yellow orchard fruit, melon, toasty almond & vanilla held in a perfectly judged structure that will carry the wine for many years.

★★★★★ **Vin Blanc** Unoaked **22** 89 from bushvine chenin, grenache blanc & viognier is delightfully fresh & fragrant, mixing tropical fruit, peach melba & apricot for a tasty summer sipper. Bunch pressed, fermented naturally & lees aged.

Not tasted: **Cuvée**. — WB

Location/map: Paarl ▪ Map grid reference: B5 ▪ WO: Agter Paarl ▪ Est 1693 ▪ 1stB 2010 ▪ Tasting by appt only ▪ Functions ▪ Conferences ▪ Owner(s) Christo & Karina Briers-Louw ▪ Winemaker(s) Janno Briers-Louw (Apr 2008) ▪ Viticulturist(s) André Coetzee (Sep 2003) ▪ 1,185ha/400ha (cinsaut, malbec, ptage, shiraz, chenin) ▪ 3,000t/6,000cs own label 50% red 50% white ▪ Fairtrade, WIETA ▪ PO Box 22 Klapmuts 7625 ▪ info@eenzaamheidwines.co.za ▪ www.eenzaamheidwines.co.za ▪ **T +27 (0)82-493-9930**

Eerste Hoop Wine Cellar

Tucked into the mountains between Bot River and Villiersdorp, the site of a 17th-century Cape governor's hunting lodge is thriving in the care of consultant winemaker Susan Erasmus. Tweaks in vineyard and cellar are raising wine quality year on year, she believes, and while chardonnay remains the flagship in terms of both focus and sales, pinot noir (red and pink) is performing well too. Adding impetus, trained process engineer Aimée Calasse has signed up permanently as assistant winemaker and farm manager.

Lemahieu range

★★★★ **Lady Brigitte** Enticing peppery aromas on **21** 88, shiraz & grenache, with mourvèdre, dash viognier, give way to juicy black & red fruit, leathery whiffs & smoky finish courtesy 15-18 months Hungarian oak, dab new. Highly drinkable & enjoyable.

★★★★ **Lodewijkx** Fresh, elegant **22** 89's bright pineapple fruit & zesty acid from chenin blanc enhanced with rounded chardonnay, enlivened with viognier spice. Some barrel ferment, portion new.

Eerste Hoop range

★★★★ **Pinot Noir** ✓ Perfumed **22** 87 suffused with aromatic Indian spices & fresh raspberry fruit. Mere touch of old oak adds nutmeg & cinnamon to light & dashing summer red.

★★★★ **Shiraz** Light, supple **21** 86 charms with black cherry & berry fruit spiced up with coffee & liquorice, aided by 12-18 months in Hungarian oak. Part wholebunch adds to freshness & easy drinking pleasure.

★★★★ **Chardonnay** Showing clean, lively appeal of the range, **22** 87 adds softest kiss of oak, small portion new, textural interest from lees contact. Peach & citrus fruit with creamy floral finish.

Chenin Blanc 🏵 ★★★★ Cut above your everyday chenin, gentle oaking (60% barrel ferment) adding touch of richness & creamy spice to pineapple & mandarin fruit in **22** 85.

Blushing Bride ★★★★ Delightfully fruity rosé from pinot noir, red cherry core & fragrant seasoning. **23** 85 crisp & dry with bouncy acid verve. **Rosé** ✓ ★★★★ Cheery pink from shiraz **23** 85 moves from

Witklip range but same fresh & zesty appetite for life. Sappy strawberry, fresh cherry conclusion. Not tasted: **Cabernet Sauvignon**, **Viognier**.

Witklip range

. . . .

Misses Louise Chardonnay ⊘ 🍷 ★★★★ Riot of fruit salad flavours on chirpy unwooded **23** ⑧③. Zesty acid & a pineapple & mango finish add up to perfect summer sipping.

. . . .

Sir Vital Shiraz ⊘ ★★★★ Spectacular colour on previewed **21** ⑧③ showcases equally showy black fruit, pepper & floral notes. Touches liquorice & spice from light oaking bode well for bottled version. — CM

Location/map: Villiersdorp ▪ Map grid reference: A2 ▪ WO: Theewater ▪ 1stB 2009 ▪ Tasting, sales & cellar tours by appt only ▪ Owner(s) Lodewijk Lemahieu (Belgium) ▪ Winemaker(s) Susan Erasmus (Jun 2020, consultant), with Aimeé Calasse (Oct 2022, also farm manager) ▪ 24.5ha/11ha (cab, grenache, mourv, pinot, shiraz, chard, chenin, viog) ▪ 85t/14,000cs 40% red 45% white 15% rosé ▪ wine@eerstehoop.co.za ▪ www.eerstehoop.co.za ▪ **T +27 (0)28-841-4190/+27 (0)82-754-4408**

☐ **Eight Feet** see Kloovenburg Wine & Olives
☐ **Eighth Wonder** see VinGlo Wines

Eikehof Wines　　　　　　　　　　　　　　Ⓟ ⑪ ◎

Elize Malherbe says husband, brand owner and winemaker Francois is a man of few words but cares deeply about his craft and their oak-shaded Franschhoek farm, on which the 1903 cellar where his great-grandfather worked still proudly stands. Hands-on, from running the venture to selling the wines, the family value the opportunity afforded by the Wine Tram to be discovered by winelovers from around the world.

Merlot Ⓟ ★★★★ Red plums spiced with wood & baking spices, **18** ⑧③'s modest sweet, juicy fruit is limited by all-new oak's bold tannins. Needs year/2 to harmonise. **Semillon** Ⓟ ★★★ Semillon's waxy tones, silky texture given slight lemony lift by 13% sauvignon on **21** ⑧①. Extra shoulder from small portion older-oaked semillon. Not tasted: **Cabernet Sauvignon**, **Shiraz**, **Rosé**, **Chardonnay**, **Sauvignon Blanc**, **Bush Vine Semillon**, **Cape Ruby**. — AL

Location/map/WO: Franschhoek ▪ Map grid reference: C3 ▪ Est 1903 ▪ 1stB 1992 ▪ Tasting & sales Mon-Sun 10-4 ▪ Closed Dec 24/25/31 & Jan 1 ▪ Cheese platters ▪ Functions ▪ Franschhoek Wine Tram ▪ Owner(s)/cellarmaster(s)/winemaker(s) Francois Malherbe ▪ 15ha (cab, merlot, shiraz, chard, sauv, sem) ▪ 28t/3,000cs own label 60% red 40% white ▪ PO Box 222 Franschhoek 7690 ▪ info@eikehof.com ▪ www.eikehof.com ▪ **T +27 (0)83-232-6223**

Eikendal Vineyards　　　　　　　　Ⓟ ⑪ �🏠 ◎ ⓐ ⓑ

Owned for over 30 years by the Swiss Saager family, this welcoming estate lies on the Helderberg's low slopes, not far from False Bay, and is largely planted to red-wine varieties, plus the chardonnay for which it is well known. In an interesting take on the no/low-intervention mantra repeated across the winelands, the team here say 'if we can produce even better wines with some intervention, we try and help our grapes achieve this goal without changing their character'. Tasked with making the generous, accessible but classically conceived wines is incoming winemaker Aldert Nieuwoudt, aided by Christo Hanse and farm manager Willem van Kerwel; responsible for marketing and selling them is fellow newcomer Eonay Terblanche.

Eikendal range

★★★★☆ **Cabernet Sauvignon** ⊘ Classic Stellenbosch cab, **21** ⑨② ripe & bold, blackcurrant fruit, firm chewy tannins & freshening acid. Delicious spice & vanilla from 18 months chiefly old oak give definition & depth before lengthy finish.

★★★★ **Cabernet Sauvignon-Merlot** Ⓟ Poised happily between seriousness & approachability, equal blend **21** ⑧⑨'s structure is firm but fairly easygoing, older oak allows fruit purity. Charming, with hints of savoury depth.

★★★★☆ **Classique** 🍇 4-way Cape Bordeaux, **20** ⑨④ ups merlot to 70%, adding lashings dark plum, rich juicy texture, tethered by robust tannins & cedary oak, 18 months, 20% new. Slightly warm at finish (14.4% alc) but should settle brilliantly with time.

★★★★☆ **Charisma** ⊘ Eclectic pairing of 67% shiraz & petit verdot (plus 1% sangiovese!) crams huge amount of blackberry-plum flavour into the glass. Nice chewy texture, aided by touch oak. Plenty to love. **21** ⑳ back to **19** ⑳'s form after **20** ★★★★ ⑧⑨.

★★★★ **Rosé** Pleasing **23** ★★★★ ⑧⑤, wholebunch freshness & bouncy strawberries, crisp acid & grain sugar complete enjoyable summer sipper. Grenache noir, mourvèdre & cinsaut, as last-tasted **20** ⑧⑨.

★★★★☆ **Chardonnay** As always, lavished with care & attention, e.g. only part malo for freshness, gentle 20% new oaking. Hence **21** ⑳ up to usual lofty standard yet fruit vies for attention with so many layers - nut, honey, hay, vanilla cream - begs a tad more space.

★★★★☆ **Mon Désir Chardonnay** ⓥ Oystershell minerality & delicate wood spice add intrigue to **18** ⑳'s panoply of citrus flavours. From Elgin, CY277 clone, more usually associated with sparkling wine.

★★★★ **Janina Unwooded Chardonnay** ⊘ Fresh, zesty entry to unoaked **22** ⑧⑦ broadens out to creamy yellow apple & apricot flavours with excellent acid bite. An all-day, everyday white from gently pressed wholebunch fruit. WO W Cape, like wooded sibling.

★★★★ **Sauvignon Blanc** From Elgin, grassy elegance on **23** ⑧⑥ gives way to pineapple & peach, lively acid seam running through fuller mid-palate from lees contact in concrete 'eggs'. **22** untasted.

Discontinued: **Merlot**.

Infused by Earth range
Occasional release: **Cabernet Franc**, **Chardonnay**. — CM

Location: Stellenbosch ▪ Map: Helderberg ▪ Map grid reference: C1 ▪ WO: Stellenbosch/Western Cape/Elgin ▪ Est 1981 ▪ 1stB 1984 ▪ Tasting & sales Tue-Sun 11-7 (Sep-Apr)/9-5 (May-Aug) ▪ Fee R70/5 wines; cheesecake pairing R170 (Sep-Apr) ▪ pizza pairing R170 (May-Aug) - booking essential; kiddies cookie tasting R75 ▪ Closed Good Fri, Dec 25/26 & Jan 1 ▪ Cucina di Giovanni @ Eikendal Tue-Sat lunch & dinner, Sun lunch only ▪ Facilities for children ▪ Tour groups ▪ Tractor rides (weekends Sep-Apr) ▪ Walks/hikes ▪ Eikendal Lodge ▪ Owner(s) Substantia AG ▪ Winemaker(s) Aldert Nieuwoudt (2012), with Christo Hanse (2012) ▪ Farm manager Willem van Kerwel (2012) ▪ 78ha/±41ha (cabs s/f, cinsaut, grenache, malbec, merlot, mourv, p verdot, sangio, shiraz, chard) ▪ 250t/40,000cs own label 50% red 50% white ▪ IPW ▪ PO Box 2261 Stellenbosch 7601 ▪ info@eikendal.co.za ▪ www.eikendal.com ▪ **T +27 (0)21-855-1422, +27 (0)21-855-5033 (Restaurant)**

☐ **Electos** see Nico Vermeulen Wines

Elemental Bob

It's 20 years since Craig Sheard blended his nickname, Farmer Bob, for his interest in agriculture, and his love of all the elements that go into making wine, to name this creative, individual and often stellar micro-batch brand. Now based in Hermanus, and sourcing chiefly from cool slopes around Walker Bay, his approach remains on 'making different wines from vintage to vintage, seeking out new vineyards and interesting cultivars'. Production is 'kept to a minimum', with mostly one barrel of each characterful and expressive wine.

My Cosmic Hand range
★★★★☆ **My Delight** ⓐ Bunch pressed, spontaneously fermented, 10 months in older 300L barrel, as both ranges unless noted. **22** ⑳ is 53% shiraz with grenache noir & barbera, red fruit of crystal clarity with wild herb edge. Oak adds detail to fine, dry tannins.

★★★★☆ **The Wild Child** Gently foamy single-ferment sparkling from chenin, **21** ★★★★ ⑧⑤ has vivid acid, silky weight from barrel ageing of Upper Hemel-en-Aarde basewine. First since **15** ⑨①.

Occasional release: **Somersault Cinsault**. Discontinued: **My Stonefields Moon**.

Cosmic Flower range
★★★★☆ **The Turkish** ⓝ ⓐ From Walker Bay single-site grenache noir. Translucent **22** ★★★★★ ⑨⑤ generously aromatic, with rhubarb, raspberry, candied musk & spice all in the mix, sappy tannins smoothed by oak, exuberant fruit nipped by trenchant dryness.

★★★★☆ **A Grape In The Fog** ⓝ ⓐ From nebbiolo, **22** ⑳ startlingly complex: savoury-leafy tomato & smoky perfume, rust & sanguine among the notes. Precise balance of umami & freshness, oak providing support & house's dryness the perfect finishing touch.

★★★★ **My Panache Spice** Stellenbosch gewürztraminer exudes signature litchi & rose in **22** ⑧⑨. Exotic spice seasoning for pear & lemon flavour, gentle fruity acid invites sip after sip.

★★★★ **Cosmic Angle** (NEW) Oaked, unusually for riesling, yet **22** (87)'s aromas unimpeded, burst with apple & limy freshness of cool-grown fruit. Good balance between freshness, richness & fine, dry finish.

★★★★☆ **Green Gold** (NEW) (🍃) From semillon. Green lime, apple & lemon preserve on **22** (91)'s delicately textured palate. Gentle acidity coats light & lifted fruit, oak (here 225L barrel) in support. Quiet & contemplative personality fascinating contrast with assertive White.

★★★★☆ **White Gold** (NEW) (🍃) Same semillon parcel as Green sibling, completely different expression. **22** (94) impressive harmony between waxy, lemony texture & vibrant freshness, white pear & peach depth & complexity. Just 28 cases.

Occasional release: **Over There Pinot Noir**. Discontinued: **Graveyard Tinta Barocca**.

Retro Series

Occasional release: **The Turkish**. — ML

Location: Hermanus ▪ WO: Hemel-en-Aarde Ridge/Upper Hemel-en-Aarde Valley/Stellenbosch/Walker Bay ▪ Est/1stB 2004 ▪ Closed to public ▪ Owner(s)/winemaker(s) Craig Sheard ▪ 600cs own label 50% red 50% white ▪ elementalbob@gmail.com ▪ www.elementalbob.co.za ▪ **T +27 (0)82-265-1071**

☐ **Elements** see Paserene
☐ **Elgin Highlands** see Iona Vineyards

Elgin Vintners
(💲) (🍴) (🏠) (◎)

A year under the lead of Burgundy-trained cool-climate specialist Gus Dale has touched all facets of this venture, owned by James Rawbone-Viljoen and Max Hahn, with Derek Corder, this year marking two decades since the first bottling. A vineyard focus and hands-on involvement sees the introduction of cover crops and a series of other improvements. In the cellar, wild yeasts are the new norm, and a steam machine aids water-use reduction. Pinot noir and chardonnay now are the mainstay bottlings, the others made in slightly lower volumes. All are lighter styled for cool-climate elegance. Luxury game lodges in SA, and markets in Europe, Asia and the US are being targeted. The tasting room features a new spacious wooden deck with a view, and the guest house is gearing up to accommodate more weddings and functions.

Site-Specific range

★★★★ **Oudebrug Merlot** (💲) Selected vines of single clone (348) for promising **20** (89), violet aroma turning savoury on palate, polished tannins. Natural wholebunch ferment, as Pinot & Syrah.

★★★★ **Ponthuis Pinot Noir** (💲) Pair of clones for **21** (89), 50% in new oak, 9 months. Cherry & raspberry aromas, spicy & savoury palate, fine tannins & tangy acid support a deep berry core, long finish.

★★★★ **Ironstone Syrah** (💲) Portion wholeberry ferment of clone SH9, 20 months oak, giving spice to **20** ★★★★☆ (90)'s vibrant plums & cherries aromas. Elegant, nimble & aromatic, improves on last **17** (88).

★★★★☆ **Sandstone Sauvignon Blanc** (💲) Fruit of clone 315 on sandstone, wild fermented in 500L barrel, part new. Fig, kiwi & pear intensity marks **21** (94), which ramps up quality & interest from **20** (91).

Elgin Vintners range

★★★★ **Merlot** (💲) Delicious **19** (88), dark choc/cedar over redcurrant & herb profile, satin tannins, full body & lingering berried farewell. Much better than last-tasted **16** ★★★★ (85). Also in 1.5L, 3L.

★★★☆ **Pinot Noir** (🌿) Part wholeberry ferment in wooden vats then 11 months in 20% new oak for polished structure. Deceptively light-hued **22** ★★★★☆ (90) cranberry & sour cherry bouquet before a complex, sensual palate of fruit & velvet tannin. As suave as **21** (89), longer lingering.

★★★★ **Syrah** (💲) Intense ripe mulberries & plums in **20** (87) lead to violets, white pepper & clove spice. 20% bunch pressing & subtle oaking assure elegance, soft tannins & juiciness.

★★★★ **Chardonnay** Delicious consistency epitomised in **22** (87), carbon copy of previous in its engaging peach, pear & apple pie persistence, roast nut & honey extras. 100% oaked, more new (25%), for subtle butter & oatmeal enrichment.

★★★★ **Sauvignon Blanc** (💲) Alluring dried fig, kiwi & pear fruit intensity marks **22** (88). Skin & lees contact amplify sauvignon focus. Concrete 'eggs' replace barrels used for last-tasted **20** (88).

★★★★ **The Century** (💲) Signature tropical & lemon notes remain while semillon-sauvignon blend switches from usual unoaked to lightly wooded in **21** (89). Still well knit & pleasing, fresh & bone-dry.

Belle Amie Blanc de Noir 🍷 ★★★★ Last **21** ⑧⑤ mostly from merlot, **23** ⑧⑤ is 100% syrah. Sampled pre-filtration, promises sweet-sour succulence, strawberry seduction. Wholebunch press, wild yeasts, 5 months on lees.

T'Kane Ouwe Straw Wine ⓥ ★★★★ Viognier, air-dried on straw mats, gives dried apple & mango in **20** ⑧⑤ dessert wine, crème brûlée & spice undertones. Sugar balanced by fresh acid & 15% alc. 500 ml.

Cloud Haven range
★★★★ **Sauvignon Blanc** Racy acid & green-spectrum flavours - gooseberry, nettle & lime - given breadth by 14.5% alc in **22** ⑧⑥. Notch up on **21** ★★★★ ⑧⑤. Wild & cultured yeasts, concrete & steel tanks.

Merlot-Shiraz ⓥ ★★★★ Soft & juicy **20** ⑧⑤ has dark fruit & spicy-savoury nuances from 6 months oaking. 72/28 blend is ready, but no hurry to drink up.

Fynbos Lite range
Premium Red ⓥ ★★★ Light-hearted **20** ⑦⑧ offers red fruit, subtle spice & low 8.5% alc. Same varieties & proportions as Cloud Haven red, similar succulence & easy drinkability. **Premium White** ⓥ ★★★ Tropical fruit salad tones on **20** ⑦⑨ mix of sauvignon & 3 others, dry & light at 8.5% alc. Only in attractive 300 ml aluminium can, as Red.

Discontinued: **Mirra range**. — DS

Location/map/WO: Elgin ▪ Map grid reference: B2 ▪ Est 2003 ▪ 1stB 2004 ▪ Tasting & sales Wed-Sun 10-4; pub hols (seasonal) please call ahead ▪ Cheese platters, food & wine pairings, pizzas ▪ Function facility ▪ Fynbos walks ▪ Birding ▪ Vineyard tours ▪ 4-star guest house ▪ Wine club ▪ Owner(s) / shareholder(s) James Rawbone-Viljoen & Max Hahn (majority), with Derek Corder ▪ Winemaker(s) & business manager Augustus Dale (Oct 2022) ▪ ±50ha (merlot, pinot, shiraz, chard, sauv, sem) ▪ 150t/12,000cs own label ▪ IPW ▪ PO Box 121 Elgin 7180 ▪ info@elginvintners.co.za ▪ www.elginvintners.co.za ▪ **T +27 (0)21-848-9587**

Ellerman House Hotel & Villas
ⓥ 🍴 🏠 ◎

The Ellerman is the first 'house wine' commissioned by luxury boutique hotel Ellerman House on Cape Town's Atlantic seaboard, and forms part of the 9,000-bottle on-site gallery of the world's finest wines. The syrah blend is made by Erika Obermeyer Wines, this guide's Newcomer Winery of the Year in 2019.

★★★★★ **The Ellerman** ⓥ Blending partners, widely sourced syrah (67%), grenache noir, cinsaut & cab, had individual attention in the cellar, resulting harmonious, deeply complex & involving **20** ⑨⑤. Despite its current allure, will reward cellaring, especially in the larger bottle sizes on offer. — CR

Location: Cape Town ▪ Map: Cape Peninsula ▪ Map grid reference: B1 ▪ WO: Coastal ▪ Est 1992 ▪ 1stB 2018 ▪ Daily complimentary winetastings for hotel guests ▪ Restaurant ▪ Boutique shop ▪ Meetings & events facilities ▪ Art gallery ▪ Wine gallery ▪ Owner(s) Harris family ▪ Winemaker(s) Erika Obermeyer (consultant) ▪ Own label 100% red ▪ 180 Kloof Rd, Bantry Bay, Cape Town 8005 ▪ reception@ellerman.co.za ▪ www. ellerman.co.za ▪ **T +27 (0)21-430-3200**

☐ **Embrace** see Stellenrust
☐ **Emineo** see Rogge Cloof
☐ **Emmara** see Denneboom

Enfin Wines
ⓥ

Franschhoek attorney Susan van Aswegen marks 10 years of after-hours boutique winecrafting with a heartfelt return to the magical days when the cellar was her 'playground of the imagination' and the place of 'innovation and experimentation'. With French poodles still her mascot and inspiration, she's adopting 'play' as the central theme and guiding principle, and grenache noir as the lead variety and 'blank canvass on which to paint the brand's unique narrative' over the second decade of her brand.

Location/map: Franschhoek ▪ Map grid reference: C1 ▪ Est/1stB 2014 ▪ Tasting by appt only ▪ Owner(s)/ winemaker(s) Susan van Aswegen ▪ 6t 90% red 10% white ▪ 4 Huguenot Str, Franschhoek 7690 ▪ info@ enfinwines.co.za ▪ **T +27 (0)83-310-1679**

Epicurean Wines

Mutle Mogase, Mbhazima Shilowa and Moss Ngoasheng, epicureans and leaders in finance, economics and politics, entered the third decade of bottling their luxury boutique wines with celebrations that included tastings of the debut vintages. Both the Bordeaux blend and more recent chardonnay are available online.

★★★★☆ **Red** (ⓐ) Harmonious & restrained **17** (94) usual majority merlot (70%), equal cab & cab franc, dab malbec for complexity, structure. Less sensuous & curvy than last **15** (91), drinks well now with pleasant undergrowth notes, will hold good few years. Mostly Stellenbosch grapes.

★★★★☆ **Chardonnay** (ⓐ) Quietly confident **22** (94) showcases Elgin's cool conditions in array of citrus fruit (green to orange) & succulent acidity. Poise & freshness of previous, plus hazelnut, honey & almond complexity with brush of oak for support. Also in magnum, as Red.— CvZ

Location: Sandton ▪ WO: Stellenbosch/Elgin ▪ Est 2001 ▪ 1stB 2003 ▪ Closed to public ▪ Online store ▪ Wine club ▪ Owner(s) Epicurean Wine (Pty) Ltd ▪ Cellarmaster(s) Mutle Mogase, Mbhazima Shilowa, Moss Ngoasheng ▪ Winemaker(s) Consultants ▪ 1,500cs own label 67% red 33% white ▪ WIETA ▪ 6 Benmore Rd, Sandton 2196 ▪ info@epicureanwine.co.za ▪ www.epicureanwine.co.za ▪ **T +27 (0)11-568-3100**

Equitania   (ⓥ)

A former private home, Equitania latterly has been the premises of the Institute of Mine Seismology, with its own small parcel of cabernets franc and sauvignon. This is carefully tended and the wine made with top consultants using organic and regenerative principles to be 'true to our terroir at the foot of the Helderberg'.

★★★★ **Cabernet Franc-Cabernet Sauvignon** (✓) (ⓐ) Juicy & generous 57/43 blend in **20** (87), succulent cassis, cigarbox & leafy-scrubby flavours, tannins smoothed 13 months in 50% new barriques. Moreish yet will keep good few years.

Not tasted: **Chenin Blanc**. — WB

Location/WO: Stellenbosch ▪ Map: Helderberg ▪ Map grid reference: C3 ▪ Est 2000 ▪ 1stB 2008 ▪ Tasting & sales by appt; see website for details ▪ Closed all pub hols ▪ Owner(s) Institute of Mine Seismology ▪ Winemaker(s) Ronell Wiid (consultant) ▪ Viticulturist(s) Francois Hanekom (consultant) ▪ 4.65ha/1.38ha (cabs s/f) ▪ 10.54t/12,000cs own label 100% red ▪ Postnet Suite #854 Private Bag X15 Somerset West 7130 ▪ kobus@equitania.co.za ▪ www.equitania.co.za ▪ **T +27 (0)21-809-2070**

☐ **Erasmus Family** see Cape Wine Company
☐ **Erica** see Raka

Erika Obermeyer Wines

Recently inducted CWG member Erika Obermeyer launched her first Auction wine, and was tremendously gratified and proud to have it received enthusiastically by critics and winelovers alike. The name she chose for the debut is a 'daily reminder that no matter how hard or challenging the last 5 years at times were, there many silver linings to be grateful for and to celebrate'. Her 'pint-sized boutique winery' is homed beside the Eerste River in Stellenbosch, where she has perfect conditions, tools and equipment to take her 'special grape parcels through the process and turn them into even more special wines'. All the vines are farmed with precision, and handcrafted with minimum intervention 'to reflect a true sense of place'.

CWG Auction range (NEW)

★★★★☆ **Silver Linings** (ⓐ) Serious, subtle & beguiling blend of syrah, grenache noir & cinsaut - stiffened with dash cab - from 'perfect' **21** (94) vintage embodies elegance & finesse, intense perfumed & layered complexity, power without force. Widely sourced grapes receive hands-off care, portion wholebunch, 90% in oak, 60% new, 18 months, rest in concrete 'egg'.

Erika O range

★★★★☆ **Cabernet Sauvignon** (ⓩ) Luscious blackcurrants on **19** (95) a match for the embedded tannins; 26 months 85% new barrels give earthy herb tones, complex layers hold one's interest but it's the overall balance & latent power that impresses, as did **18** ★★★★☆ (94). A keeper, already seductive.

★★★★☆ **Syrah** (ⓩ) Ocean-influenced Firgrove vines (as Cab), elegant **19** (94) shows syrah's restraint, finesse & precision. Deeply complex, dark-toned fruit with interwoven cocoa, salty liquorice & scrub. Streamlined & polished. Tiny production. In larger bottle sizes, as Cab & blend.

★★★★★ **Syrah-Grenache Noir-Cinsault** Ⓥ Light styled but always deeply flavourful, compatible & stylish blend. Firgrove syrah dictates **20** ★★★★★ ⑨③'s smoky red fruit & fynbos profile, charcuterie savouriness & lithe strength, Wellington grenache noir & Agter Paarl cinsault add to svelte texture, lovely freshness. Still-available **19** ⑨⑤ also excellent.

★★★★☆ **Chenin Blanc** Ⓥ Grapes off 48 year old Agter Paarl bushvines on shale. Cool **21** ⑨③ harvest gets 5 hours of skin contact, ferment in 30% new oak, 10 months on lees, creating delicious bed of creamy oatmeal for crisp, complex array of tropical fruits, finishing lipsmackingly dry.

★★★★☆ **Sauvignon Blanc** Ⓥ Dryland 22 year old Groenekloof vineyard, grapes fermented in half each tank & barrel, latter 50% new. **21** ⑨④ retains cool-climate green tones, touch of thatch & an almond seam that adds richness, texture & heft. Ends savoury, mineral. No **20**.

★★★★☆ **Meticulous Sauvignon Blanc** Ⓥ Unoaked sibling, from same cool-climate area, which **21** ⑨① expresses as crushed herbs, green asparagus, capsicum, a nervy tension taking it to a crisply fresh, taut, dry conclusion. Same styling as last **19** ⑨②.

Flabbergast Cinsault Ⓥ ★★★☆ Agter Paarl old dryland bushvines given cellar respect. Half each older barrels & concrete 'eggs', & **19** ⑧⑤ celebrates red fruit, touch of fynbos & standout drinkability. — DS
Location: Stellenbosch ▪ WO: Stellenbosch/Coastal/Groenekloof/Paarl/Agter Paarl ▪ Est 2016 ▪ 1stB 2015 ▪ Closed to public ▪ Owner(s)/winemaker(s) Erika Obermeyer ▪ 30t/4,000cs own label 80% red 20% white ▪ Stellenbosch Agri-Park, Baden Powell Dr, Stellenbosch 7600 ▪ info@erikaobermeyerwines.co.za ▪ www. erikaobermeyerwines.co.za ▪ **T +27 (0)82-940-3499**

☐ **Erika O** *see* Erika Obermeyer Wines

Ernie Els Wines

Ⓠ ⑾ ◎ Ⓖ

This top-rated Helderberg Mountain venture was founded 25 years ago on a site chosen specifically for its suitability to grow the finest cabernet and -blends. The vineyard was nurtured and extended, soon producing acclaimed wines under Louis Strydom, winemaker since inception and latterly cellarmaster. With co-investment since 2015 by German businessman Hans von Staff-Reitzenstein, the cellar was refurbished and, with great pride, a stylish new visitor area unveiled. It features a tasting lounge, restaurant and trophy room displaying the impressive silverware of South African co-owner, international golf's 'Big Easy', Ernie Els.

Ernie Els Signature Wine
★★★★★ **Ernie Els Signature** ⓐ Distinguished packaging & return to form for **17** ⑨⑤ flagship 5-way Bordeaux blend. Like **16** ★★★★☆ ⑨③, majority cab & merlot (60/25), but fresher, touch lighter alc (14.7%) & more classically styled. Lovely intensity & complexity, 18 months in oak, 60% new, providing harmonious framework for dark core of cassis, cigarbox & savoury spice. Infanticide even after 5 years in the bottle, deserves decade or more in the cellar. Also in 1.5L.

CWG Auction Wine
★★★★☆ **Ernie Els** ⓐ Consistent blend of cab, shiraz & cinsaut (60/30/10) but more opulent in riper **20** ⑨① vintage. Full, succulent dark cherry & berry flavours just reined in by dry cocoa & cedar spicing from 18 months in oak (as most of the reds), this 70% new, further 20 months in bottle. Tad less gravitas than previous, though will provide flavoursome drinking pleasure for many years.

Ernie Els Proprietor's range
★★★★☆ **Syrah** ⓐ Pure syrah in **17** ⑨④, svelte & streamlined, seductively charming, released after lengthy 5 years in bottle. Full (14.9% alc) but balanced, as deftly wooded as viognier-dabbed **16** ⑨③ (both 50% new oak), including some American barrels. Even more vibrant.

★★★★☆ **Proprietor's Blend** Ⓥ Similar cab-led blend with shiraz (60/20) & 4 others in **18** ⑨①. Riper & more sombre dark berry, earthy tones, all slightly muted by 35% new oak's dry, dusty tannins. Less fruit intensity & gravitas than previous.

Ernie Els Major Series
★★★★☆ **Cabernet Sauvignon** ⓐ Pure cab in **21** ⑨② from selected parcels of different clones, individually vinified & blended after ageing. Quite brooding, with concentrated dark berries & some savouriness bound up in firm, cedary oak framework, 30% new. Youthful, handsome rewards in time. Last-tasted **18** ⑨② had dashes syrah & petit verdot.

★★★★ **Merlot** Even fresher & more nervy in cooler **21** (87). More new oak though less time in wood (20%, 16 months) holding piquant red berry, cherry fruit in a firm, dry tannic embrace. Shade leaner than last-tasted **19** ★★★★★ (90), bottle-aged 10 months but needs more time to reveal its charms.

Big Easy range

★★★★ **Cabernet Sauvignon** ⊘ Some leafiness to the red-berried flavours in **21** (86), which includes 15% splash cinsaut. Matured mostly in mixed-origin older barrels; 20% unoaked. Juicy & poised, sleek tannins make for earlier broaching; also a good tablemate. **20** untasted.

★★★★ **Red Blend** Similar dapper blend in **21** (87), mostly shiraz & cab (60/19) with 4 others. Supple structure, mostly older oak, aptly reflects the range description: 'delivering full flavour but gentle approach-ability'. Also in 1.5L.

Chenin Blanc ★★★ A little brisker than previous, but unoaked **23** (82) still has plenty of crunchy apple flavours for a light summer lunch. WO W Cape. Not tasted: **Cabernet Sauvignon Rosé**. — MW

Location/map: Stellenbosch ▪ Map grid reference: E8 ▪ WO: Stellenbosch/Western Cape ▪ Est 1999 ▪ 1stB 2000 ▪ Tasting room Mon-Sun 10-5 ▪ Restaurant: lunch Wed-Sun 12-3.30; dinner Thu-Sat 6.30-9, bookings essential ▪ Closed Good Fri, Dec 25 & Jan 1 ▪ Winemaker's Table ▪ Outdoor Grillworks (seasonal) ▪ Tour groups ▪ Gift shop ▪ MTB trail ▪ Ernie Els' Trophy Room ▪ Vinotéque ▪ Owner(s) Ernie Els & Baron Hans von Staff-Reitzenstein ▪ Cellarmaster(s)/winemaker(s) Louis Strydom (Dec 1999) ▪ Viticulturist(s) Leander Koekemoer (2015) ▪ 72ha/45ha (cab, merlot, shiraz) ▪ 430t/55,000cs 85% red 15% white ▪ PO Box 7595 Stellenbosch 7599 ▪ marketing@ernieelswines.com ▪ www.ernieelswines.com ▪ **T +27 (0)21-881-3588**

Ernst Gouws & Co Wines

With daughter Ezanne Gouws-Du Toit latterly at their side, Stellenbosch vintner Ernst Gouws and wife Gwenda for more than 20 years have selected mostly Stellenbosch grapes for traditional vinification and export around the world. Ernst strives for wines that are 'pure and typical of the variety, and remarkably approachable for their underlying complexity and depth'. Based at Koelenhof Winery, they offer tastings and sales of the namesake range, as well as the golf-themed brand, 19th Wines, unreviewed by us this edition.

Ernst Gouws range

★★★★ **Family Reserve Cabernet Sauvignon** Riper dark-fruited profile from Swartland grapes in **20** (88). Full bodied, quite dense though smooth, year old oak polishes the whole for rich & satisfying drinkability. Pair with fillet steak, suggests cellarmaster.

★★★★ **Merlot** ⊘ Riper & more robust in **20** ★★★ (82). Dark baked fruit, firm tannins & a toasty nuance despite no new oak used in 12-month maturation. Less balanced & refined than **19** (87).

Pinot Noir ★★★★ Similar savoury, sour cherry flavours in **22** (85), quite fresh, with dry chalky tannins. Part ageing in older oak buffs the edges, though still a table partner rather than solo entertainer. **Pinotage** ★★★★ Vivid red fruit is the focus in unoaked **21** (83), poised, straightforward & ready to quaff, tastes lighter than 14.5% alc. **Chenin Blanc** ★★★ Cheerful apple & tropical flavours in **23** (82), with plush leesy breadth. Well-weighted & fresh summer quaffer at modest 12.5% alc. Not tasted: **Chardonnay**. Discontinued: **Shiraz**.

19th Wines

Not tasted: **Pinotage, Cabernet Sauvignon-Merlot, Chenin Blanc, Sauvignon Blanc**. — MW

Location/map: Stellenbosch ▪ Map grid reference: D1 ▪ WO: Stellenbosch/Swartland ▪ Est 2003 ▪ Tasting & sales at Koelenhof Winery Mon-Thu 9-5 Fri 9-4 Sat/pub hols 10-4 ▪ Closed Easter Fri/Sun, Ascension day, Dec 25/26 & Jan 1 ▪ Facilities for children ▪ Owner(s) Gouws family ▪ Cellarmaster(s) Ernst Gouws snr ▪ 50 000cs Ernst Gouws & Co and The 19th wines ▪ ezanne@ernstgouws.co.za ▪ www.ernstgouws.co.za ▪ **T +27 (0)82-371-3633**

Escape Wines

Four friends and winelovers in 2017 bought Afdaksrivier Farm in prime Walker Bay terroir, and changed the focus from oats and wheat to proteas and vines. Recognising the potential, latterly cool-climate specialist, CWG member and Cederberg Private Cellar prime mover David Nieuwoudt joined as sharehold-er-wine-maker. The site, overlooking Sandown Bay and the Bot River lagoon, is influenced by the namesake rivercourse, bringing in oceanic air and ensuring water supply, and the Onrus mountains, a shield against excessive rainfall. 'Unique and revolutionary wines, and a novel experience for our customers' is the aim.

★★★★ **RAZ Shiraz** Indian spice & vanilla, from 10 months in older barrels, & varietal black pepper complement **22** (88)'s lively red plums & cherries. 15% wholebunch ferment lends stemmy grip but the structure is supple & the wine accessible now with legs for good few years.

★★★★ **SAV Sauvignon Blanc** Crossover style, some early-picked green notes & riper tropical for overall 'cool' profile in **23** (86), subtle cream from time on lees, citrus finish. Lovely solo & will grace a dinner table.

★★★★ **Reserve Sauvignon Blanc** Fuller, weightier than SAV thanks to barrel-fermented portion & lengthy lees ageing, **23** (89) also different flavour spectrum, white citrus & iodine, plus sibling's creamy texture, inviting freshly shucked oysters.

RZE Grenache Rosé ★★★★ Barely pink, **23** (85)'s paleness matches low 9.5% alc but belies generosity of pure (rather than boiled sweet) berry flavour, fresh acid, proper dryness. Also in 1.5L. — GdB, CvZ

Location: Hermanus ▪ Map: Walker Bay & Bot River ▪ Map grid reference: B2 ▪ WO: Walker Bay ▪ Est 2018 ▪ 1stB 2022 ▪ Tasting Mon-Sat by appt only ▪ Vineyard & farm tours by appt ▪ Owner(s) Afdaksrivier (Pty) Ltd (5 shareholders) ▪ Winemaker(s) David Nieuwoudt (Jan 2022), with Jean Nel (Jan 2022, consultant) ▪ Viticulturist(s) Johan Viljoen (Aug 2019, consultant) ▪ 50.9ha/13.494ha (grenache, mourv, pinots noir/meunier, shiraz, chard, sauv) ▪ 120t/4,600cs own label 11% red 45% white 16% rosé 28% cap classique ▪ Postnet Sandbaai, Suite 378, Private Bag X16, Hermanus 7200 ▪ info@escwines.com ▪ www.escwines.com

☐ **Eskdale** *see Frater Family Wines*

Esona Boutique Wine Estate

'We are small, but we are many,' say Rowan and Caryl Beattie about the substantial number of wines in their portfolio ('something for everyone') and contrastingly modest volumes. Charmaine Arendse has been the crafter since 2017, working 'in harmony with nature and embracing artistry in winemaking' in the modern cellar. At the old one nearby, converted cement tanks offer a private tasting area, while upstairs a public tasting lounge, bistro and shop give way to a lovely view of their Robertson stretch of the Breede River.

Single Vineyard range
★★★★ **Pinot Noir** ⊘ Raspberry & forest fruit on **21** (86) tempered by light spice & smoke courtesy year in older barrels. Structured yet fresh, improves on last **17** ★★★★ (85).

★★★★ **Shiraz** Light-bodied, supple & fresh **21** ★★★ (82) has ample black fruit with dry grip on finish from year older oak. Pronounced saltiness on entry, missing from better-balanced **19** (89).

★★★★☆ **Chenin Blanc** (♀) Continues succulent, ripe tropical styling, subtle vanilla fragrance in **19** (90). Pleasure to drink now & into next decade. Official single-vineyard, as all these.

Chardonnay ★★★★ Lightly oaked **22** (85) vat sample follows previous form in creamy softness & gentle citrus. Ideal for summertime. **Colombar** ★★★ Previewed **22** (82) has subtle lemon & shy stonefruit, faint cream note from stay in older casks. **Pinot Gris** (NEW) ★★★★ Fresh, lively **22** (83) impresses with zip & tang of lemon sherbet. Gentle lees nuance adds some breadth. **Sauvignon Blanc** ★★★ Unfussy lemon zest to **23** (81) tank sample. Light, juicy, with subtle herbaceous note, it's a good everyday quaffer. **Viognier** (NEW) ★★★★ Shy floral fragrance to typical stonefruit on unoaked **22** (84). Pleasant succulence, body & dry grip.

Esona Estate range
★★★★ **Stories** Shiraz (80%) leads grenache noir on **21** (86) blend & improves on last **19** ★★★★ (84). Peppery blue & black fruit with trace of salt. Sappy & fresh, a great BBQ companion.

★★★★ **Méthode Cap Classique** (♀) Salmon hue adds visual appeal to **18** (88) bubbly from equal pinot noir & chardonnay. Taut, tangy red fruit balanced by sourdough richness from 36 months on lees. **Barbera** (NEW) ★★★★ Vibrant **22** (84) pre-bottling sample shows decent intensity of black cherry & plum fruit. Light spice nuance to dry finish from year older oak. **Grenache Noir** ★★★★ Floral dimension to raspberry & cherry fruit on **22** (85). Light bodied & juicy, gentle finish, made for daytime enjoyment. **Mourvèdre** (NEW) ★★★★ Tasted before bottling, supple & spicy **22** (84) is cherry fruited, pleasantly bright & nimble. Year in older barrels, like other reds in range. **Sangiovese** (NEW) ★★★★ Affable cask sample **22** (84), typical lively but light cherry & spice with attendant dryness. Succulent & accessible, finishing dry. **Frankly My Dear Grenache Blanc de Noir** ★★★ Plum, strawberry & raspberry ripeness matched by lifted acid on ex-tank **23** (80). Fresh, undemanding, for poolside sipping. — FM

Location/map/WO: Robertson ▪ Map grid reference: C4 ▪ Est 2002 ▪ 1stB 2010 ▪ Tasting & sales Mon-Fri 9-5 Sat/pub hols 10-4 ▪ Closed Dec 25 & Jan 1 ▪ Std tasting; Taste-the-Difference tasting (between 2 vintages of 3 cultivars); fruit preserve/chocolate/music & wine/art pairing ±55 min, essential to book ▪ Caryl's Bistro ▪ Caryl's Little Shoppe ▪ Owner(s) Rowan & Caryl Beattie ▪ Winemaker(s) Charmaine Arendse (Jan 2017) ▪ 17ha/9.83ha (barbera, grenache, mourv, pinot, sangio, shiraz, chard, chenin, cbard, sauv) ▪ ±250t/6,000cs own label 34% red 66% white ▪ PO Box 2619 Clareinch 7400 ▪ info@esona.co.za ▪ www.esona.co.za ▪ T +27 (0)76-343-5833

☐ **Essay** see MAN Family Wines
☐ **Essence du Cap** see Fleur du Cap

Excelsior Estate ⓨ ⑭ ⓐ ◎ ⑧

Five generations have made wine on the Robertson home-farm over the past 170 years, building a substantial business whose 320,000 cases are exported to over 20 markets, the US being the biggest and Excelsior its leading SA supplier. Current custodians Freddie de Wet and son Peter are planting blending varieties like petit verdot, malbec and viognier for their 'accessible, approachable and non-pretentious wines for all occasions.' They are proud of innovations such as helping introduce drip irrigation to the industry, progressive environmental moves such as switching 50% of the winery's power needs to solar, and the plethora of initiatives to enrich employees and their families, including more than 20 ha of citrus 90% owned by staff.

Excelsior Reserve range

★★★★☆ **Evanthius Cabernet Sauvignon** ⊘ Named for imported hackney horse, **20** ⑨⓪ shows good form of last **17** ⑨③. Cassis, herb & spice appeal matched by cohesive structure & freshness. Good interplay of fruit & oak, long rewarding finish.

★★★★ **Gondolier Merlot** ⑧ In even finer fettle than **18** ⑧⑥, **19** ★★★★☆ ⑨⓪ redolent of violets & abundant blackberry fruit, balanced, deftly oaked, 25% new, year, completing a delicious performance.

★★★★ **San Louis Shiraz** ⊘ Powerful **20** ★★★★☆ ⑨⓪ echoes **19** ⑧⑧ in dark-berried density & concentration. Generous & flavourful with good succulence. Year in oak, 10% new, lends grip & raises stature.

Norah Chardonnay ⑧ ★★★★ Sprightly tangerine & vanilla on light, fresh, supple **21** ⑧③. Combo French & American oak is unclassic but balanced, doesn't mask fruit.

Excelsior Classic range

Cabernet Sauvignon ⊘ ★★★★ Ripe **21** ⑧⑤ is approachable & bright in its cassis & tealeaf typicity. Spicy oak - French & American, as all these reds - lends body while retaining affability. **Merlot** ⊘ ★★★★ Ticks boxes for merlot fans in **21** ⑧④: succulent plum & black fruit, supple body with soft tannins from 45% briefly oaked portion. **Paddock Syrah** ⊘ ★★★★ Ripe prune fruit with slight creaminess on **22** ⑧③. Light body & feel despite 30% portion being oaked for 8 months. **Caitlyn Rosé** ⊘ ★★★ Coral pink **23** ⑧② from shiraz offers crisp plum refreshment. Light & bright, finishes dry. **Chardonnay** ★★★ Retains citrus typicity & fresh vibrancy in **23** ⑧②. Despite 25% portion fermented in oak, wood is virtually indiscernible. **Sauvignon Blanc** ★★★ True to form, **23** ⑧② is tangy with typical granadilla profile & zesty freshness. **Viognier** ⊘ ★★★★ Peach & quince notes of **23** ⑧⑤ show influence of late-harvested portion in richer, honeyed nuance. Nice definition & body, with acid restraining few grams of sugar.

Purebred range

Malbec-Merlot ⑲ ★★★ Malbec 75% holds sway over partner in **22** ⑦⑨. Plum- & red-berry appeal on unfussy, light-bodied palate. Not tasted: **Sauvignon Blanc**. Discontinued: **Shiraz-Merlot**. — FM

Location/map/WO: Robertson ▪ Map grid reference: C4 ▪ Est 1859 ▪ 1stB 1990 ▪ Tasting & sales Mon-Fri 10-4 Sat 10-3; pub hols (seasonal) please call ahead ▪ Deli serving light lunches (closed Sun/Mon) ▪ Picnics available on request ▪ Facilities for children ▪ Pet friendly ▪ Conferences ▪ 4-star Excelsior Manor Guest House ▪ Wine club ▪ Owner(s) Freddie & Peter de Wet ▪ Cellarmaster(s)/winemaker(s) Johan Stemmet (Aug 2003) ▪ Viticulturist(s) Freddie de Wet (1970) ▪ 320ha/220ha (cab, merlot, p verdot, shiraz, chard, sauv) ▪ 2,200t/320,000cs own label 75% red 25% white ▪ Other export brand: Stablemate ▪ BRC ▪ PO Box 17 Ashton 6715 ▪ barry@excelsior.co.za ▪ www.excelsior.co.za ▪ T +27 (0)23-615-1980

Excelsior Vlakteplaas ⓨ

The Schoeman family has grown grapes on Vlakteplaas estate near De Rust village in Klein Karoo since the 1930s. Their Excelsior venture is based in the old cellar, where winemaker Jan-Jurie produces the fortified muscat pair featured here alongside a larger volume for their primary clients in the bulk-wine sector.

His Master's Choice range
★★★★ **Red Muscadel** Ⓥ House's traditional labelling for this version of its fortified muscat. **21** ⑧⑥ immediate fresh red-berry attraction, honey & rooibos tea nuances, interesting black coffee note.

New Generation range
Red Muscadel Ⓥ ★★★★ Only touch less sugar & alc on this bottling (191 g/L vs 211, 16.9% vs 17.4), yet **21** ⑧⑤ feels much lighter. Similar rooibos & honey tones plus subtle ginger & nut, hint of tannin. — CvZ

Location: De Rust ▪ Map: Klein Karoo & Garden Route ▪ Map grid reference: B3 ▪ WO: Klein Karoo ▪ Est 1934 ▪ 1stB 1998 ▪ Tasting & sales by appt only ▪ Closed Easter Fri-Mon, Ascension day, Dec 16/25/26 & Jan 1 ▪ Owner(s) Danie Schoeman ▪ Winemaker(s) Jan-Jurie Schoeman ▪ 31ha (merlot, ptage, ruby cab, chenin, muscadel r/w) ▪ 300t/1,000cs own label 100% red ▪ PO Box 112 De Rust 6650 ▪ excelsiorwinery@gmail.com ▪ **T +27 (0)72-532-0015**

☐ **Ex Oppido** see Constantia Uitsig
☐ **Fable Mountain Vineyards** see Tulbagh Mountain Vineyards
☐ **Fairhills** see Origin Wine
☐ **Fair Karoo** see Rogge Cloof

Fairvalley Wines ⓥ
Fairvalley was one of South Africa's first black-owned wine brands. The current shareholders are farm and cellar staff of Fairview, where the well-priced, mostly exported line-up is produced by Awie Adolf and offered for sale. We hope to taste the chenin, their launch wine in 1998, and the other bottlings next time.

Location: Paarl ▪ Est 1997 ▪ 1stB 1998 ▪ Tasting by appt only ▪ Fee R25 ▪ Closed Good Fri, Dec 25 & Jan 1 ▪ Sales at Fairview ▪ Owner(s) Fairvalley Farmworkers Association ▪ Cellarmaster(s)/winemaker(s) Awie Adolf (2018) ▪ 20,000cs own label 50% red 50% white ▪ Fairtrade ▪ PO Box 6219 Paarl 7620 ▪ wine@fairvalley.co.za ▪ www.fairvalley.co.za ▪ **T +27 (0)21-863-2450**

Fairview Ⓥ ⑪ ◎ ⑤
It's half a century since the first wine went into a bottle labelled 'Fairview', the brand name somewhat more lovely than that on the Paarl Mountain farm's 1693 title deed, 'Cauliflower Fountain'. Charles Back is the current, third-generation owner, and he's been hands-on with the wine and farm for all but four of the 50 years, having worked alongside his father Cyril since 1978 and taking the rein in 1995. A transformative vision and entrepreneurial approach have seen the portfolio extended and orientated to Mediterranean grapes, the inspired goat-themed branding introduced, sibling labels added (see separate Goats do Roam and La Capra listings) and production ramped up to 330,000 cases, with much innovation along the way to maintain consumer interest, and quality and value always non-negotiable. A significant contributor to success is Anthony de Jager, in the cellar for close to 30 years, latterly as its captain. On-trend, sustainability is a major emphasis for both the wine and cheese sides of the business, while the visitor experience, centered on the tasting area, the famous goats and their climbing tower, and Goatshed eatery, is ever fresh and compelling.

Regional Revival range
★★★★☆ **Caldera** ⊘ ⊛ One of SA's 1st Rhône-inspired blends & consistent performer since **03** debut in the guide. Sprightly **21** ★★★★★ ⑨⑤ separately vinified/9 months aged grenache, shiraz & mourvèdre (50/40/10). Scented fruit & buchu perfume in a svelte tannin framework. As harmonious, flavoursome & ageworthy as **20** ⑨③.

★★★★★ **Extraño** ⊘ ⊛ Continues as Rioja-inspired blend in **20** ⑨③, 86% tempranillo giving dark plum, cherry flavours lifted by perfumed freshness from part bunch-fermented grenache noir. 2 years French & American barrels, 20% new for tempranillo, add sweet spice & polish the firm tannins.

★★★★★ **Homtini** ⊘ ⊛ References mountain pass near Knysna with links to cellarmaster's Italian forebears. Blend tweaked in **20** ⑨④, sangiovese & cab (40/35), dabs merlot, shiraz. Rich, juicy, still fresh but riper red fruit & some earthiness & plusher texture from 2 years oak. Balanced, though likely peaking earlier than standout **19** ★★★★★ ⑨⑤. WO Darling.

★★★★ **Charles Back Brut** Unusual dry cap classique from Paarl grenaches blanc & noir (59/41). **20** ⑧⑦ pale hue, energetic bead & limy acid zesting silky succulence, clean green apple & greengage. 29 months on lees add waxy breadth. Enjoyable solo or with a light meal. **19** untasted.

Limited Releases

★★★★☆ **Stok by Paaltjie Grenache Noir** Elegant & charming but much lighter 22 ★★★★ ⑧⑨ from high-lying vine-by-post (echalas) block on Paarl Mountain. Scented red fruit & sprinkle pepper main attraction, nicely fresh from 20% wholebunch, tannins supple & balanced, 9 months older oak in support. Touch less structure & gravity than 21 ⑨②.

★★★★☆ **Primo Pinotage** ⑧ Powerhouse of ripe, spicy wild berries, rich & dark fruits & some salty liquorice in more concentrated 21 ★★★★★ ⑨⑤ from dryland bushvines (known in-house as Primo) on home-farm. As 20 ⑨③, foudre ferment/18 months in barrel, 40% new, further bolster solid but suave structure. Sheathed power, layers of flavour, already balanced & tempting but deserves time.

★★★★☆ **Eenzaamheid Shiraz** ⑧ Opulent & concentrated in fine 21 ⑨④ from Paarl dryland vineyard on shale soil. Billows alluring fynbos scrub, white pepper & fragrant lily. Supple, well structured tannin support from open-foudre ferment, 22 months in barrel, 25% new. 19 & 20 not made.

★★★★☆ **The Beacon Shiraz** ⑧ Even more refined & restrained in cooler 19 ⑨③ from 29 year old Swartland dryland bushvines. Streamlined, with graceful tannins from oak ferment & ageing 20 months, 40% new, all in sync with pure fruit & dusting of signature white pepper. One to savour over many years. 18 sold out.

★★★★☆ **Cyril Back** ⑧ Leashed power & elegant concentration in 20 ★★★★★ ⑨⑥ flagship red, barrel selection from best shiraz sites in Swartland (88%) & Darling, latter also source of dab cab, aiding structure & giving lifted freshness to dense black & blue berry fruit. Like last 18 ⑨③, 66% new oak, 22 months, in harmony, allows pristine fruit to shine. Balanced, sophisticated & ageworthy.

★★★★☆ **Beryl Back** ⑧ Exceptional white blend honouring late matriarch. 22 ★★★★★ ⑨⑥ chenin & viognier (50/33), verdelho & roussanne ex home-farm's top vines. Intricate vinification to showcase best varietal traits & terroir includes ferment/ageing in amphora & barrel. Rewarded with complex layers of flavour, viognier's spiced peach woven with lemon & stonefruit, pervasive freshness. More harmonious than 21 ⑨④; even more charming in a few years.

Discontinued: Pegleg Carignan.

Fairview range

★★★★ **Cabernet Sauvignon** ⊘ Familiar cassis & herbaceous notes in 20 ⑧⑦, structured though tannins more supple & open textured. Fermented in half each foudre & tank, aged in oak barrels, 18 months, 20 % new. Still ageworthy though tad less heft & longevity than 19 ★★★★★ ⑨⓪.

★★★★ **Grenache Noir** ⊘ Classic varietal perfumed red fruit & silky tannin structure echoed in 22 ⑧⑥. Slightly riper, touch less substance, retains freshness & balance. Less seriously than Limited Release sibling. Refined & approachable. WO W Cape.

★★★★ **Merlot** ⊘ Same Stellenbosch & Darling sources, more classic styling in 21 ⑧⑧. Piquant red fruit & dry chalky tannin. Portion foudre ferment/year in 15% new barrel adds some complexity, but still tight, needing time.

★★★★☆ **Petite Sirah** ⊘ ⑧ Very fine example of French variety, first bottled solo in SA by Fairview in 07 ★★★★. 21 ⑨③ more structured & streamlined than last-tasted 18 ★★★★ ⑧⑨, yet not lacking layers of savoury olive & inky dark fruit, variety's sturdy tannins further bolstered by years oak, 40% new. Still tight but already balanced, with long, rewarding future. WO Paarl.

★★★★ **Pinotage** ② Firm 21 ⑧⑧ has smoky berry flavours in dry tannin framework from fruit & oaking. Less new wood & ageing than Primo. Fresh balance & potential to age. 20 untasted.

★★★★ **Shiraz** ⊘ White pepper, fynbos & subtle red berries in 21 ⑧⑧ from Paarl, Swartland & Darling. Ferment/20 months mostly in oak, 20% new, in sync with concentrated fruit, firm dry tannin providing platform for development.

★★★★☆ **Chardonnay** ⊘ Only Paarl fruit in 22 ⑨⓪, though same winemaking & appeal as 21 ⑨⓪: 60% fermented/10 months on lees in mix of older oak barrels, giving silky breadth & texture to zesty citrus, pear & apricot, lingering mineral finish.

★★★★ **Chenin Blanc** ⊘ Vivacious 23 ⑧⑦ from dryland Darling & Paarl vines improves on 22 ★★★★ ⑧⑤. Varying ripeness levels & mostly tank ferment ensure freshness; tangy nectarine & passionfruit with some creamy lees enrichment perfect solo or with meals.

★★★★☆ **Grenache Blanc** ⊘ Home-farm & Darling bushvines for **22** ⑨⓪. Tad muted, waxy & fuller bodied, not quite as vibrant as last, but balanced & with similar clean stonefruit & citrus filled out by 20% oaked portion.

★★★★ **Darling Riesling** ⊘ Echoes previous deliciously piquant flavours in **23** ⑧⑦ from same unirrigated vines at 300m altitude. Semi-dry styling spotlights white peach & floral notes, finely balanced acid ensures lift.

★★★★ **Darling Sauvignon Blanc** ⓠ Provenance shines through in inviting dusty, wet pebble & tangy tropical notes on **22** ⑧⑦. Crisp, bright, with some creamy breadth & fine mineral seam.

★★★★ **Viognier** Another cultivar pioneered in SA by Fairview, noting suitability to climate. Mostly oak-fermented & aged Paarl fruit (64%) in **22** ⑧⑨, riper, more viscous though well balanced by fresher tank-vinified Darling portion. Lemon acid pervades hallmark peach aromas & flavours.

Rose Quartz ⓠ ★★★★ Rose gold hue to **22** ⑧⑤ rosé inspired by source site's pink quartz minerals. Unoaked grenache, cinsaut (49/43) & splash wooded carignan, light, dry & very quaffable. **Fizzy Verdelho** ★★★ Light (8.4% alc) carbonated local version of spritzy vinho verde. Much more neutral in **22** ★★★ ⑦⑧, just a hint of green apple & sherbet, zesty & refreshing. WO Paarl. Not tasted: **Bushvine Cinsault**.

Sweet Wines range

★★★★ **Sweet Red** Winter-warming port-style **22** ⑧⑥ from petite sirah & tempranillo, oak aged 10-12 months, splash souzão in reserve wine. Fruitcake, prune & spiced tobacco sweetness checked by brandy spirit for more balance & appeal than last.

La Beryl Rouge ⓠ ★★★★ Occasionally released, unconventional oak-aged straw wine from black grape tannat, **21** ⑧④ has dense core of black, aromatic fruit, scrub & salty liquorice. 500 ml. Not tasted: **La Beryl Blanc**. — MW

Location/map: Paarl ▪ Map grid reference: D6 ▪ WO: Coastal/Paarl/Darling/Western Cape/Swartland ▪ Est 1693 ▪ 1stB 1974 ▪ Tasting & sales Mon-Sun & pub hols 9-5, last tasting 30min before closing ▪ Standard/ Master tasting (applicable fees apply) ▪ Closed Dec 25 & Jan 1 ▪ The Goatshed Restaurant ▪ Shop & Deli: artisanal cheeses, cured meats, preserves & fresh farm breads ▪ Owner(s) Charles Back ▪ Winemaker(s) Anthony de Jager (Dec 1996), with Annette van Zyl (2014) ▪ 300ha under vine (grenache n/b, merlot, mourv, petite sirah, ptage, shiraz, tempranillo, chenin, marsanne, rouss, sauv, viog) ▪ 2,200t/330,000cs own label 65% red 30% white 5% rosé ▪ BRC, Fairtrade, HACCP, IPW, WIETA ▪ PO Box 583 Suider-Paarl 7624 ▪ info@ fairview.co.za ▪ www.fairview.co.za ▪ **T +27 (0)21-863-2450**

False Bay Vineyards

Though mostly high-volume, these well-priced 'non-estate' ranges are crafted by the same hands, and in the same non-interventionist spirit as their British-owned Waterkloof counterparts, and each has a defined style, personality and story: Last Of The First, sole remaining pinotage block on Schapenberg Hill (on which Waterkloof is sited), elegant and perfumed; On Borrowed Time, wind-pummelled vines, yield so small, viability in question; Peacock, earlier drinking yet refined; False Bay, value for money, for everyday enjoyment.

Last Of The First range

★★★★★ **Pinotage** ⓠ From 28 year old single-vineyard. **21** ★★★★★ ⑨③ as beguiling as **20** ⑨⑥. Tad riper scents, youthfully resistant but still refined structure, fantail finishing charm. Will reward patience.

On Borrowed Time range

★★★★ **Chardonnay** Touch new oak added to delicate fruit of tiny Helderberg parcel in **22** ⑧⑥, giving toasty marmalade & toffee apple notes. Impossibly low yield (1.5 t/ha) delivers concentration but fruit shaded by wood mid-2023, may simply need more time.

Peacock Wild Ferment range

★★★★ **Chenin Blanc** ⊘ Plenty of drinking pleasure from now-unwooded **23** ⑧⑦, featuring ripe, vibrant yellow apple, pear & pineapple. Zesty acid, excellent concentration & greater than expected length lifts it above others in this price bracket.

★★★★ **Sauvignon Blanc** ⊘ Slow starter **23** ⑧⑧ opens to riotous fruit flavours (granadilla & peach), interesting wild herb & wet stone texture. Deft winemaking (wild yeast, time on lees) adds richness & flavour to superior summer sipper.

Cabernet Sauvignon ⓧ ★★★ Honest, undemanding **20** ⑧② sound, sweet fruit & structure well-melded for current & short-term enjoyment. **Merlot** ⓥ ★★★★ Plump **22** ⑧⑤ beguiles with black cherries & plums, soft tannins & floral top note. Plenty of carefree quaffing to be had here. 10 months old oak. **Syrah** ⓥ ★★★★ Fresh, bouncy **22** ⑧⑤ glassful swirls red plums & cherries with mulberries, pepper & violets. Rich, satisfying, creamy spice tweak at finish, aided by year in large old oak.

False Bay range

★★★★ **Whole Bunch Cinsault-Mourvèdre** ⓧ Serious dry rosé, onion-skin-hued **22** ⑧⑥ maintains house's purity & gentle touch. Persistent savoury-toned herb & berry flavours. WO Coastal as all these.

Windswept Sauvignon Blanc ⓥ ⓟ ★★★★ Perfect summer imbibing in crisp & brisk **23** ⑧⑤. Grassy aromas give way to granadilla ripeness & a talcum powder finish. Happy days.

Bushvine Pinotage ⓥ ★★★★ Juicy **22** ⑧④ improves on previous, shows dark berries, tar & tobacco supported by soft tannins & snappy acid. Easy to like. Seasoned oak, 10 months. **Old School Syrah** ⓥ ★★★ Jammy & hammy **22** ⑧① has cheery ripe black fruit & soft structure, supported by year in old large oak. **Crystalline Chardonnay** ★★★ Dialled-back unwooded **23** ⑧② shows soft apple & white flower notes with fresh acid & gentle finish. Lacks intensity of previous. **Slow Chenin Blanc** ⓧ ★★★★ Quieter than last, **22** ⑧⑤ still displays purity in pear & apple flavours, supported by comfortably dry finish. — CM

Location: Somerset West ▪ WO: Stellenbosch/Coastal ▪ Est/1stB 2000 ▪ Tasting lounge closed ▪ Owner(s) Paul Boutinot ▪ Cellarmaster(s) Nadia Langenegger (Jan 2013) ▪ 250,000cs own label 30% red 65% white 5% rosé ▪ IPW, WIETA ▪ PO Box 2093 Somerset West 7129 ▪ info@waterkloofwines.co.za ▪ www.falsebayvine-yards.co.za ▪ T +27 (0)21-858-1292

Fat Bastard

During a 1990s blending session, Franco-British wine partners Thierry Boudinaud and Guy Anderson found a barrel of delicious lees-aged chardonnay that tasted like a fat version of Bâtard-Montrachet, leading to a globally exported wine range with a smiley hippo as its logo, made in South Africa by Robertson Winery.

★★★★ **Golden Reserve** Juicy & rounded cab-merlot blend, **22** ★★★★ ⑧④ bright blackberry & raspberry fruit, grippy tannins smoothed by sprinkle of sugar. Very drinkable but lacks nuance of **21** ⑧⑥.

Pinotage ⓟ ★★★★ Fresh **22** ⑧③ steals the red-wine show with black & red cherries edged with tobacco & tar courtesy time in old oak. Supple & moreish. **Chenin Blanc** ⓟ ★★★★ Oodles of bright grapefruit & pineapple mingled with subtle vanilla oak on **23** ⑧④ raises the bar on previous.

Cabernet Sauvignon ★★★ Abundant perfume & sunshiny ripeness on **21** ⑧②, blackberry jam fruit, hint of cassis & savoury overlay. Dry tannins balance grain sugar at finish. WO Robertson, as all these. **Merlot** ★★★ Cherry-choc confection on bright & cheery **22** ⑧② with soft tannins & leathery finish. **Shiraz** ★★★ Nice little tweak of American oak spices up **21** ⑧②'s red & black plummy fruit, adding smoked meat note & tarry conclusion. **Rosé** ★★★ Pretty pink from cinsaut, **23** ⑧① pops with strawberry & cherry fruit, zingy acid cleaning up just-dry finish. Perfect poolside sipping. **Chardonnay** ★★★ Creamy peach & cantaloupe fruit on **22** ⑧① received light oaking to add some ginger & nutmeg. Soft acid, rounded finish thanks to dab of sugar. **Sauvignon Blanc** ★★★★ Happy summer drinking in **23** ⑧⑤, kiwi & gooseberry then quince & grapefruit, snappy, sappy acid & bone-dry finish. — CM

- ☐ **First Sighting** *see* Strandveld Wines
- ☐ **First Stone** *see* Spier
- ☐ **Fish Hoek Wines** *see* Accolade Wines South Africa
- ☐ **Fishwives Club** *see* The Fishwives Club Boutique Winery
- ☐ **Five Cellars** *see* FirstCape Vineyards
- ☐ **Five Generations** *see* Cederberg Private Cellar
- ☐ **Five's Reserve** *see* Van Loveren Family Vineyards
- ☐ **Flagship** *see* Stellenbosch Vineyards

Flagstone Winery 　　　　　　　　　　(?) (?) (?)

Set in a converted glycerine refinery near Somerset West, Accolade-owned Flagstone is one of the Cape's early 'wineries without a vineyard'. Recently increased sourcing from blocks around Stellenbosch by head winemaker Gerhard Swart and his team means more vintages are certified Coastal or Cape Coast, with some wines being more area specific. This also means less diesel is used to get the grapes to the cellar, boosting Flagstone's emphasis on sustainability. In this arena the biggest project is a solar installation, set to reduce the carbon footprint by a remarkable 25%. Tasting room renovations are complete, and food-and-wine pairings every last and first weekend of the month have been added, along with a veranda so visitors can enjoy the fresh ocean breeze. Note: the sibling Kumala and Fish Hoek wines not tasted by us this edition.

Super Premium range

★★★★★ **Time Manner Place Pinotage** (?) Heaps of sex appeal ex Breedekloof single-vineyard, tiny parcel of **17** (97) on par with stellar **14** (95); plush fruit with cool minty edge & authoritative oak (all new, **16** ★★★★☆ (93) only 50% new). Compact tannins to unfurl pleasurably over next decade. No **15**.

★★★★★ **Velvet Red Blend** (?) Luxury packaging (& price) for sumptuous wine from 67% shiraz with mourvèdre & cinsaut. **17** (93) billows mulberry fruit laced with vanilla (mainly American oak, 50% new) in pliable tannic frame, sweet feel (not heat) from alc on the finish.

★★★★ **Paradigm Reserve Chenin Blanc** (?) From 1979 Agter Paarl bushvines, **23** ★★★★★ (91)'s purity kept intact with judicious wooding, only 65% in oak, half new. Sunshiny apple, pear, pineapple & crushed stone with delicate grip & brisk freshness. Last was **20** (89).

★★★★ **Free Run Reserve Sauvignon Blanc** A showcase for cool-grown Darling fruit. Green gooseberry, cucumber & fig on **22** ★★★★★ (90). Steps up from **20** (89) with pinpoint balance between acid, tiny grain sugar & vinosity of 14% alc.

Premium range

★★★★☆ **Music Room Cabernet Sauvignon** (?) Rich, ripe & spicy **20** (91) has all the oomph of previous, though missing its muscular structure. Black & red berries given clove detail by mix American, French (64/35) & Hungarian oak (as most of these reds, here 16-18 months, 30% new).

★★★★☆ **Writer's Block Pinotage** (?) Power & freshness combine in assertive **21** (93). Swartland fruit includes 14% durif, lending ink & texture to opulent tannins. Impressive structure from 18 months in oak, 25% new. Unapologetically bold at 14.8% alc. Intended to go the distance.

★★★★☆ **Dark Horse Shiraz** (?) Some wholeberry ferment & 13% durif in rich, rewarding **19** (94). Full & savoury, with roast meat & olive notes. Empathetically oaked, 12-18 months in barrique, 20% new, to cosset & amplify inherent spice. WO Cape Coast, as Music Room.

Core range

★★★★ **Fiona Pinot Noir** (?) From Darling fruit. 16-18 months in older barrels a delicate enhancement to **22** (86)'s bright berries & plums. Gentle acid & slightly chewy fruit tannins extend the finish. Mix French, American & Hungarian oak for all range reds unless noted.

★★★★ **Treaty Tree Red Blend** (?) Touch smoke on 4-way Bordeaux blend, from 12-18 months in older oak, hint of spice ex 10% new. **21** (87) fennel & damson notes, 50% cab gives structure to rich berries. Riper, broader than last at 14.9% alc.

★★★★ **Dragon Tree Cape Blend** (?) Delightful well-harmonised pinotage, shiraz, cab, 2 others in **20** (89). Cherry pie, forest berries & baked plums, 10% new oak, 16-18 months, adding curves in right places.

★★★★☆ **Tributary Chenin Blanc** Fresher **22** ★★★★ (89), just 22% wooded, 60% new vs 100% in **21** (91). Confident spice weaves through yellow plums & apples, zesty orange acid assists persistence.

★★★★ **Free Run Sauvignon Blanc** Salt & white pepper seasoning for tropical fruit on **22** ⑧⑨, thrillingly fresh & mineral, with lovely length. Certified by Vegan Society SA, as all wines tasted this edition. Like **21** ★★★★★ ⑨⓪, WO Cape Coast.

★★★★☆ **Word of Mouth Viognier** ⊘ Well-judged **22** ⑨① has gorgeous sweet fruit (peaches, honeyed pears) yet is bone-dry with acid brightness. 30% in combo French & Hungarian oak, 6 months, no American this vintage. Stellenbosch grapes.

★★★★☆ **Treaty Tree White Reserve** ⊘ ⓐ Vibrant Darling sauvignon & 35% semillon marry harmoniously in **22** ⑨②, laced with blackcurrant, fresh pineapple & passionfruit. 6 months in oak give a bright structure, 30% new component adds smoky appeal. Last **19** ⑨① from Elim.

★★★★☆ **Ice Vine Dried Sauvignon Blanc** ⓧ Stunning **16** ⑨③ nectar from vineyard-desiccated Stellenbosch grapes, intended to be poured over ice. Old-gold sheen, tangerine vies with fig, mango & honey in a fruit cornucopia braced by almost startling acidity. 375 ml (notably svelte wax-sealed bottle).

Truth Tree Pinotage ★★★★ Wholeberry portion & dab tempranillo aid showy **21** ⑧④'s exotic aroma of juniper & pot-pourri, plus lashings of vanilla-spice from 10% new oak, which also smooths & softens effect of 14.7% alc. WO Coastal, as Treaty Tree. **Two Roads Chardonnay** ★★★★ Part wholebunch for lemony **22** ⑧③, tank & 35% new barrel ageing add spice to peaches-&-cream flavour. Very dry but 14.5% alc lends a cushion. Coastal WO, as Chenin. Not tasted: **Longitude**.

Lifestyle range

Noon Gun Chenin Blanc-Sauvignon Blanc-Viognier ☺ ★★★ Crowd pleaser **23** ⑧①, unoaked & radiating tropical verve & refreshment, bit like a glass of mango sorbet. **22** not tasted.

Poetry range

Cabernet Sauvignon ⊘ ★★★★ Floral, piquant aroma on **22** ⑧④, mostly unoaked to show off cab's lighter side. Juicy, fresh, barest touch of tannin. 10% aged briefly with staves, 1% new, as all range reds. **Merlot** ★★★ Plumped with red berries, dusted with sweet vanilla, **22** ⑧② tad less structured than last but tasty, easy to drink. **Pinotage** ★★★ Heroes pinotage's bouncy berries in **22** ⑧②, gram sugar (as red siblings) & 14% alc give pleasing palate weight. **Cinsault Rosé** ⊘ ★★★★ Offers refreshment value in spades at modest 12.5 alc. **23** ⑧④'s lively acid complements the sweet berries, adding some brightness for food pairing too. **Chardonnay** ★★★ Accessible, flavoursome **23** ⑦⑨ is packed with lemons & pears. Unwooded this vintage & without dab chenin. Not tasted: **Chenin Blanc, Sauvignon Blanc**. — ML

Location: Somerset West ▪ Map: Helderberg ▪ Map grid reference: B6 ▪ WO: Western Cape/Coastal/Darling/Cape Coast/Stellenbosch/Breedekloof/Agter Paarl/Swartland ▪ Est 1998 ▪ 1stB 1999 ▪ Tasting & sales Mon-Fri 10-4 Sat/pub hols 10-3 ▪ Fee R80-R100pp for 5 wines ▪ Food and Wine pairings every last & first Friday & Saturday - please book ahead ▪ Closed Good Fri, Dec 25/26 & Jan 1 ▪ Cellar tours by appt ▪ Wine club ▪ Owner(s) Accolade Wines South Africa ▪ Winemaker(s) Gerhard Swart (head, Sep 2007), with Mia Boonzaier (Jan 2007) & Willene Roelofse (Jun 2014) ▪ 55% red 45% white ▪ WR Quinan Blvd, Paardevlei, Somerset West 7130 ▪ flagstone.wines@accoladewines.com ▪ www.flagstonewines.com ▪ **T +27 (0)21-852-5052**

☐ **Flatrock** *see* Rhebokskloof Wine Estate
☐ **Fledge & Co** *see* The Fledge & Co
☐ **Fleet** *see* Steenberg Vineyards
☐ **Flemish Masters** *see* Almenkerk Wine Estate
☐ **Fleur de Vie** *see* Fleur du Cap

Fleur du Cap

Owned by Heineken Beverages, Fleur du Cap is a venerable corporate-owned brand, dating from the 1960s as a Distillers/Bergkelder label. The incumbent sisterly team of Tamsyn Claasen, Isabel Habets and Isabel Teubes believe a key to success is having 'unrestricted access to the widest geography of vineyards in SA', allowing for rigorous selection and the making of wines that 'exemplify regional excellence'. The range is topped by a Cape Bordeaux honouring late cellarmaster and pioneer of small-barrel ageing, Julius Laszlo.

Flagship range

★★★★★ **Laszlo** (🐝) Tribute blend **20** (94) a sumptuous feast of stonefruit, berries & graphite, underpinned by a serious but supple tannin structure. Harmonious 5-part ensemble of mostly cab & cab franc (44/29) made for 10+ years cellaring. 2 years in small-oak, 30% new, like exceptional **19** ★★★★★ (96).

Series Privée Unfiltered

★★★★★ **Merlot** (⊘) Bold yet crafted & expressive **20** (91) has complex, deep & fragrant aromas & flavours, lingering chocolate & spice finish. Tannin & oak, 18 months, 50% new, for the long haul.

★★★★☆ **Chardonnay** (⊘) A long honeyed farewell preceded by aromatic palate where apple & citrus fruit is in harmony with vanilla from 35% new barrels, 8 months. **22** (92) rich, rounded & spicily flavourful to the end. Will keep a few years. WO Stellenbosch for these.

Discontinued: **Cabernet Sauvignon**.

Essence du Cap range

Cabernet Sauvignon (⊘) ★★★★ Now bottled, **21** (84) has settled & delivers glassful of dark berries edged with vanilla from combo barrels & staves (as Merlot). For delicious everyday drinking, also in magnums. **Merlot** (⊘) ★★★★ Red plums, dark chocolate & cinnamon spice makes for easy sipping in **21** (83). **Chenin Blanc** ★★★ Dry, unadorned by oak, **23** (81) shows tropical fruit with a lemon tang, to which lees ageing adds some weight. **Sauvignon Blanc** ★★★ Easy, breezy **23** (81) mixes lemons & limes with some gooseberry for a zippy, picnic-friendly drink. Also in 2L. Not tasted: **Chardonnay**. Discontinued: **Rosé**.

Fleur de Vie range

Natural Light Chenin Blanc ★★★ Dryish **23** (79) is light in tone, texture & alc at 9.7%, offers gentle citrus & melon flavours best served chilled. — WB

Location: Stellenbosch ▪ WO: Coastal/Stellenbosch/Western Cape ▪ Closed to public ▪ Owner(s) Heineken Beverages ▪ Winemaker(s) Tamsyn Claasen (Aug 2021) ▪ Viticulturist(s) Isabel Habets / Isabel Teubes ▪ ±870t/±128,300cs own label 18% red 82% white ▪ ISO 14001, ISO 9001, BRC, HACCP, IFS ▪ www.fleurducap.co.za

---

Flight of the Fish Eagle

Untraditionally packaged brandy, the dark green, squared-off bottle with label featuring the eponymous raptor in full flight more likely to summon up images of whisky. Heineken Beverages' direct appeal here is to new categories of drinkers, as is that of the style of the brandy itself.

★★★★ **Natural Potstill Brandy** (🥃) Light in colour & freshly fruity, with hint of smoky oak. At 38% alc, the brandy (87) is delicate & smooth. Good on a rock or two, mixers not needed. — TJ

☐ **Flippenice** see Tulbagh Winery
☐ **Florence by Aaldering** see Aaldering Vineyards & Wines
☐ **Flower Girl** see Botanica Wines
☐ **Flutterby** see Boland Cellar
☐ **Focal Point** see Laarman Wines
☐ **Foodbarn Restaurant** see Migliarina Wines

Foothills Vineyards   (🍷) (🍴) (🏠) (📷)

On Raithby Road in the Helderberg foothills, Glenn Hesse and Tim Featherby's Klein Welmoed estate is home to a luxury guest house, self-catering cottages, olive groves and a vineyard giving rise to this collection of boutique wines, made off-site by consultants 'to reflect the unique terroir and delight every palate'.

Monogram Collection

★★★★ **Shiraz** (🥃) Spicy & aromatic **18** (89) barrel sample follows form of previous, tobacco & scrub-floral notes, intense black cherry fruit. Full but supple body textured with ripe, powdery tannins.

★★★★★ **Semillon** (⊘) Retasted year later, lightly oaked **19** (90) continues to impress: a fruity-savoury partnership, ripe melon & greengage, with varietal wax, perfume top note of barley sugar. Sleek (13% alc) yet bold & full-flavoured.

★★★★★ **Straw Wine** (🐝) Unusually, from viognier. Traditional straw mat drying of grapes, **17** (90) differs from unoaked **16** ★★★★ (86) in spending 2 years in older barrels. Amber-gold, glacé pineapple & dried apricot scents & flavours, caramelised sweetness, notable richness & length. Back on track. 375 ml.

Not tasted: **Méthode Cap Classique**.

Foothills range

★★★★ Syrah ⊘ Brambly berries dusted with pepper, spicy notes from 16 months older oak, now-bottled **20** ⑧⑧ has depth & succulence, the tannins supple. For enjoying, not long ageing.

Pinot Noir ⑧ **★★★★** Light, rather attenuated **20** ⑧④ is fresh & racy, with satin texture, raspberry cordial fruit, hints of spice from year in barrel. **Dry Rosé ★★★★** Syrah with 10% each viognier & semillon, pale salmon-hued **22** ⑧④ has perked-up aromatics, a floral highlight to the cherries & red berries. Crisply fresh & appetising. **Sauvignon Blanc ★★★★** Citrus & passionfruit, with grass nuance on the palate, **22** ⑧④ has lively freshness, good typicity. Not tasted: **Viognier**. In abeyance: **Chardonnay**, **The Partners**, **Sparkling Sauvignon Blanc**. — CR

Location/WO: Stellenbosch ▪ Map: Helderberg ▪ Map grid reference: B1 ▪ Est 2008 ▪ 1stB 2012 ▪ Tasting & sales by appt only - please contact Loriane on +27 (0)71-288-5994 to book a personalised tasting experience ▪ Fee R100pp ▪ Meals/refreshments by appt ▪ Olive oil ▪ Conferences ▪ 4-star luxury guest house (B&B), info@kleinwelmoed.co.za ▪ Wine club ▪ Owner(s) Glenn Hesse & Tim Featherby ▪ Winemaker(s) Bernard le Roux ▪ Viticulturist(s) Bennie Booysen ▪ 39ha/19ha (pinot, shiraz, chard, sauv, sem, viog) ▪ 8,000cs own label 25% red 70% white 5% rosé ▪ IPW ▪ PO Box 647 Somerset Mall 7137 ▪ info@foothillsvineyards.co.za ▪ www. kleinwelmoed.co.za ▪ **T +27 (0)21-842-0045**

☐ **Forager** *see* African Pride Wines
☐ **Force Celeste** *see* Mother Rock Wines
☐ **Forresters** *see* Ken Forrester Wines

Fortes Family Wines   ⑧ ⊖ ⌂

With France's Sancerre region as inspiration, international businessman Neil Fortes continues to specialise in sauvignon blanc, sourced partly from the small family vineyard in cool-climate Napier, where there have been limited new plantings. Conrad Vlok of nearby Strandveld Wines co-crafts the wines for mostly export by Neil's son Toby. Airbnb facilities overlooking the vines on the home-farm are now available.

Fortes Single Vineyard range

★★★★ Sauvignon Blanc Same Napier registered vineyard & winemaking in **22** ⑧⑥, mostly aged in old barrels, 5 months vs 6 for **21** ⑧⑦. Touch riper, plusher, less acid & linearity though retains lemony freshness offset by oaking's nutty, rich texture.

Cape Beach Collection

★★★★ Camps Bay Sauvignon Blanc ⑧ Dusty nettle & herb flavours in **21** ⑧⑥ from Napier & Elim, creamy undertone from barrel ferment/ageing in old, mostly French oak. Balanced, dry & zesty.— MW

Location: Napier ▪ Map: Southern Cape ▪ Map grid reference: B2 ▪ WO: Coastal/Napier ▪ Est 2005 ▪ 1stB 2016 ▪ Tasting, functions & cellar tours by appt only ▪ Sales Mon-Sat 10-5 ▪ Closed all pub hols ▪ BYO picnic ▪ Airbnb facility (4 persons), with horse riding available for guests ▪ Owner(s) The Trojan Trust ▪ Cellarmaster(s)/ winemaker(s) Neil Fortes & Conrad Vlok (Jun 2006, consultants) ▪ Viticulturist(s) Neil Fortes (Jun 2006, consultant) ▪ 3.5ha/2ha (sauv) ▪ 5t/800cs own label 100% white ▪ PO Box 208 Napier 7270 ▪ info@wineguru. ca ▪ www.forteswines.com ▪ **T +27 (0)71-223-9927/+1 613 661 2223 (Canada); +44 7824 633 484 (sales & marketing); +1 289 771 1744 (WhatsApp)**

☐ **Fortress Hill** *see* Fort Simon Wine Estate
☐ **Foundation Stone** *see* Rickety Bridge Winery
☐ **Foundry** *see* The Foundry
☐ **Four Cousins** *see* Van Loveren Family Vineyards

Four Paws Wines

Rob Meihuizen, Anne Jakubiec and winemaker-viticulturist Gerda Willers in the mid-2000s created this wine brand to express their fondness for felines. Now, in support of bigger, wild cats threatened with extinction, they're giving a portion of proceeds from their bottlings to the cheetah conservation project of Selati Wilderness Foundation, based near the Kruger National Park. The wines' new names reflect the historic farmlands on which the foundation operates. A code on the labels allows customers to donate to the cause.

★★★★ **Huja** ⊘ Same cab-led 4-way blend as **14** ★★★★ (84), listed as 'Red Blend', **15** (87) more characterful, bursts with ripe berries & spice, freshness belying its age, some old oak & bottle age adding cigarbox & leather for very pleasurable drinking. Splashes old Piekenierskloof bushvine cinsaut & grenache.

Lillie ★★★★ Was 'White Blend', **22** (85) similar chenin, grenache, roussanne (60/30/10) co-fermented melange, all from same 1-ha block. As pretty, tad more expressive, clean starfruit, honey & almond flavours.

Champurrs Méthode Cap Classique (⊗) ★★★★ From chardonnay, **17** (85) dry sparkler has steely acidity, lively bubbles & pleasant yeasty brioche for 18 months on lees. — MW

Location: Franschhoek ▪ WO: Franschhoek/Western Cape ▪ Est 2005 ▪ 1stB 2006 ▪ Closed to public ▪ Email orders to sam@fourpawswines.com ▪ Owner(s) Rob Meihuizen, Gerda Willers & Anne Jakubiec ▪ Winemaker(s) Gerda Willers (2005) ▪ Viticulturist(s) Gerda Willers ▪ 2ha (shiraz, chenin, grenache b, rouss) ▪ 20t/3,000c own label 70% red 30% white ▪ PO Box 69 Simondium 7670 ▪ sam@fourpawswines.com ▪ www.fourpawswines.com

☐ **4th Street** *see* Heineken Beverages
☐ **Foxtrot** *see* Whiley Wines

Fram Wines ⊗

From his recent vantage atop Piketberg Mountain in Swartland, boutique vintner Thinus Krüger sallies forth (like the 19th-century Norwegian ship Fram) to discover and harvest fruit around the winelands for his 'fine wines of exploration', now crafted in an on-site cellar. Planting mooted last year is taking place, the choice of cabernet sauvignon evoking his days as red-wine maker at Fleur du Cap. The new red typifies the Fram style of overt fruit tempered by a savoury-mineral element, the interplay being a compelling experience.

Fram range

★★★★★ **Cinsault** (⊗) Pleasing vinosity & weight (13.6% alc) in **21** (90), pure & linear but offers more than simple fruitiness. Slightly more grip than last from 10% pinotage & year in older oak.

★★★★★ **Grenache Gris** ⊘ Voor Paardeberg grapes of rare mutation of grenache noir. Coppery hue from pale red skins, **22** (90) maverick among traditional rosés. Savoury toned, with spice & earth, some tannin grip & lingering umami finish.

★★★★ **Dark Days** (NEW) Unwooded pinotage, near black in the glass, dark plum & berry fruit, brooding welder's arc whiff, yet **23** (88) surprisingly succulent on palate, refreshed with grape tannin, nice salty finish. Winemaker's 'ode to Eskom & loadshedding' from Citrusdal Mountain vines.

★★★★★ **Pinotage** (⊗) Plummy fragrance with dried herb complexity on **17** (92), but fresher & lighter seeming than ripeness & 14% alc might suggest. Dry tannins control the fruit on lingering finish; oaking doesn't obscure the purity of the flavour.

★★★★★ **Shiraz** ⊘ Smooth but present tannins give form to **22** (90)'s appetising red fruit, laced with white pepper & fynbos. Satisfying & unforced feel, courtesy 30% unoaked portion, rest older wood only. Dabs cinsaut & grenache noir; Swartland vines.

★★★★ **Chardonnay** ⊘ Fruit of **23** (86) given extra appeal by 10% chenin & sippably modest 12% alc. Decent weight from extended lees contact rather than oaking - only 10% saw barrels, & they're a venerable 12 years old! Robertson vines, like **22** ★★★★ (85).

★★★★ **Chenin Blanc** Old-foudre-matured **22** (89) rich & flavoursome without excess. Ripe fruit - cling peach & hint papaya - full malo & higher alc (13.5% vs 12.3%) give sweeter impression than in **20** ★★★★★ (90). WO Piekenierskloof. No **21**.

★★★★ **Carmelina** Was 'Dry White Wine', still **NV** (87) & mostly palomino, 20% splash undisclosed others conjure complex deciduous fruit flavours, jasmine & spice attractions. Dry, delicate, but more substance than 12% alc would suggest.

Regional range (NEW)

Chenin Blanc ★★★★ From Voor Paardeberg & Piekenierskloof vines, intended as lighter alternative to single-site sibling. **23** (85) sleek & svelte, 10% old-oak portion adding a little breadth, zesty acid & lowish 12.5% alc ensuring freshness. — CvZ

Location: Piketberg ▪ WO: Citrusdal Mountain/Voor Paardeberg/Swartland/Robertson/Piekenierskloof/Western Cape ▪ Est/1stB 2012 ▪ Tasting by appt only ▪ Online shop ▪ Owner(s) Thinus Krüger ▪

Cellarmaster(s)/winemaker(s) Thinus Krüger (Dec 2012) ▪ 45t/3,000cs own label 45% red 55% white ▪ PO Box 657 Riebeek West 7306 ▪ thinus@framwines.co.za ▪ www.framwines.co.za ▪ **T +27 (0)72-545-4959**

☐ **Francois le Vaillant** *see* Lutzville Vineyards

Francois van Niekerk Wines

For this small private label, Wellington Wines CEO Francois van Niekerk combines his original training in forestry, an abiding fascination with vinifying unforgiving pinotage and an intimate knowledge of two particular blocks - 'perfectly formed', low-yield bushvines on shale in Agter Paarl and Wellington - which he vinifies 'traditionally but precisely' and ages in Tronçais oak.

★★★★★ **Pinotage** The pinotage whisperer coaxes another stellar performance from his vines, **21** (97) sleek, harmonious, with a polished tannin structure & 2 years 70% new oak supporting unfolding layers of flavour: plums, hedgerow fruit, scrub, spice & whiff of sweet cigar. 'Gaan baie mooi verouder', minimum 10 years, especially in magnum.— WB

Location: Wellington ▪ WO: Coastal ▪ Est 2018 ▪ 1stB 2019 ▪ Closed to public ▪ Sales online ▪ Owner(s) Francois van Niekerk ▪ Winemaker(s)/viticulturist(s) Francois van Niekerk (Jul 2018) ▪ 10t/±1,000cs own label 100% red ▪ BRC, IPW, WIETA ▪ info@francoisvanniekerk.co.za ▪ www.francoisvanniekerk.co.za ▪ **T +27 (0)82-067-6679**

Franki's Vineyards

After a brief pause, winemaking at the Swartland home-farm (also site of a pioneering commercial solar array) resumed in 2022 and the result, a Rhône-style blend, is selling from select wine boutiques and the on-site tasting lounge, with its attached wedding venue and guest lodge. After older wines sell out, Erica Joubert plans to make only the blend and sell off the rest of the fruit from the 22 ha of goblet-trained vines.

★★★★ **Grenache** Shy cranberry scent on **16** (89) gives way to intense, fresh palate showing fine structure & red-berry fruit, improving on **15** ★★★☆ (84). Year old oak.

★★★★ **Viognier Barrel Fermented** Slowly fermented in seasoned wood, **18** (86) peaches-&-cream flavours with a spicy farewell. Minuscule production, as all these.

Next Generation ★★★☆ Mourvèdre at 68%, with shiraz & grenache noir, small yield, 10 months in barriques, which **22** (85) rewards with spice & dried herbs in the dark fruit. Lovely texture, plush, the tannin structure supple, accessible.

Mourvèdre Rosé ★★★ Pleasant, dry **18** (82), enticing summer fruits led by strawberry & just a touch of spice. Not tasted: **Joubert Red Blend**. — CR

Location: Malmesbury ▪ Map: Swartland ▪ Map grid reference: A6 ▪ WO: Swartland/Western Cape ▪ Est 2004 ▪ 1stB 2007 ▪ Tasting, sales & cellar tours Mon-Fri 8-5 by appt ▪ Closed all pub hols ▪ BYO picnic ▪ Franki's Guest Lodge ▪ Functions ▪ Small wedding venue (±30 pax) ▪ Owner(s) Franco Afrique Technologies (Pty) Ltd ▪ Winemaker(s) Erica Joubert (Jan 2004) ▪ 700ha/22ha (grenache, mourv, viog) ▪ ±160t ▪ PO Box 972 Malmesbury 7299 ▪ erica.joubert@cropspec.co.za ▪ www.frankisvineyards.co.za ▪ **T +27 (0)82-888-3702**

☐ **Franschhoek 1688** *see* La Couronne Wines

Franschhoek Cellar

Part of the Franschhoek townscape for almost 80 years, DGB's venerable winery produces multiple ranges, mostly untasted by us, including Reserve, Cap Classique and Village Walk, the latter inspired by local landmarks and monuments, and styled for 'easy and casual enjoyment'. The brand home at the town entrance beckons all ages to try the wines, enjoy a meal outdoors or stay in the luxury cottages beside the cellar.

Franschhoek Cellar range

★★★★☆ **The Last Elephant** Aptly named 4-way Bordeaux blend has power & dimension in spades. **20** (91) swaps merlot for cab as lead variety, shows great depth of succulent black fruit enrobed in ripe tannins & spice that will meld & develop over a decade.— DS

Location/map: Franschhoek ▪ Map grid reference: C2 ▪ WO: Stellenbosch ▪ Est 1945 ▪ Tasting & sales Mon-Sat 10-6 Sun 10-5 ▪ Wine pairing: 6 wines with 6 cheeses, or with assorted chocolates ▪ Closed Good Fri & Dec 25 ▪ Alfresco dining daily ▪ Supervised play area for children ▪ Weddings ▪ Conferences ▪ Events venue (seat

300 pax) ▪ Rose & Protea cottages ▪ Online shop ▪ Owner(s) DGB (Pty) Ltd ▪ Winemaker(s) Ryan Puttick (Nov 2017) ▪ Viticulturist(s) Heinie Nel (Jul 2018) ▪ 300ha (cab, merlot, shiraz, chard, chenin, sauv, sem) ▪ 30,000t 49% red 50% white 1% rosé ▪ ISO 9001:2001, IPW ▪ PO Box 52 Franschhoek 7690 ▪ fhccellardoor@dgb.co.za ▪ www.franschhoekcellar.co.za ▪ **T +27 (0)21-876-2086**

☐ **Frans K Smit** *see* Spier

Frater Family Wines

The Scottish Frater family settled on De Zoete Inval in Paarl 146 years ago, and it's the 5th generation, John-Robert, with wife Eulalia, who today crafts wines in open fermenters with minimal intrusion to be 'modern & ripe, with Old World charm', and currently targets African export markets. A one-stop private label service matches wine with customer requirements, and assists with label design and execution.

Cabernet Sauvignon Limited Release (NEW) ★★★★ Opens with vanilla & chocolate tones from year in new Siberian oak, **21** (85) follows with opulent body of morello cherry & liquorice. Present but unaggressive tannins give shape & length. **Cape Vintage** ★★★ A different take on Vintage 'port'. **22** (82) more fresh cherry & plum character than expected Xmas cake & dried fruit, much lower sugar (65 g/L), barely noticeable tannin & alc. From shiraz, year in old oak. For current enjoyment. Not tasted: **Pinotage, Shiraz, Cab Sauvignon-Malbec-Petit Verdot, Shiraz-Mourvèdre-Grenache**. — NK, CvZ

Location/WO: Paarl ▪ Est 1878 ▪ 1stB 1976 ▪ Closed to public ▪ Owner(s) DZI Agricultural Investments cc (John Robert & Eulalia Frater) ▪ Cellarmaster(s)/winemaker(s) John Robert Frater (1999) ▪ Viticulturist(s) Robert Frater ▪ 80ha/20ha (cab, grenache, malbec, mourv, p verdot, shiraz, chard) ▪ 200t/16,000cs own label 50% red 50% white ▪ Other export brands: Eskdale, Safari ▪ PO Box 591 Suider-Paarl 7624 ▪ info@fraterfamily-wines.co.za, sales@fraterfamilywines.co.za ▪ www.fraterfamilywines.co.za ▪ **T +27 (0)82-731-3898**

☐ **Free To Be** *see* Remhoogte Wine Estate
☐ **Friesland** *see* Kaapzicht Wine Estate

Friesland Wines   (②) (⑪)

'An outstanding year with exponential growth' is the upbeat summation of De Bruyn Steenkamp, lawyer, wine advisor, Cape Wine Master and winery owner, citing local success in targeting mostly wine clubs and the direct-to-consumer segment through an online shop, and international expansion via several new ranges exported around the globe. The venture operates and sources from Stellenbosch, and promotes what De Bruyn sees as 'the unique Stellenbosch style, clean, fruit-driven wines with elegance, class and finesse'.

Friesland Wines range

★★★★☆ **M-Klas Cabernet Sauvignon** (②) Flagship from old vines impresses, **18** (91) has real presence & varietal muscle along with delicate fragrant & earthy notes. One to watch.

★★★★ **Broer & Suster Shiraz-Grenache** (✓) Shiraz at 91% dictates **21** (88)'s style, with blackberry & mulberry spiced with cloves, pepper, dried herbs. Tasty & involving, tannins supple, structure sleek. No **20**.

★★★★ **Berg & See Chenin Blanc** (✓) Single high-altitude vineyard planted 1987. Barrel ageing 9 months & long lees contact have rounded **22** (89)'s fruit without losing the citrus freshness. Enough personality & substance to age well. **21** not made.

★★★★ **Sauvignon Blanc** (✓) Elevated vines plus reductive handling to highlight the cool styling: cucumber & fennel, some herbaceous notes in the flavours. Ex-tank **23** (86) tightly knit with zinging freshness; wakens the taste buds. Improves on **22** ★★★★ (84).

Merlot-Cabernet Sauvignon (✓) ★★★★ Oak a noticeable component in **21** (85) (different age barrels), while avoiding harshness: spicy aromas, tannin backbone for ageing, all mirrored by plummy fruit.

Welgelegen Bush Vine range

Not tasted: **Pinotage, Chenin Blanc**. — CR

Location/map/WO: Stellenbosch ▪ Map grid reference: B3 ▪ Est 2018 ▪ 1stB 2017 ▪ Tasting for groups Mon-Sat/pub hols by appt only ▪ Meals by prior arrangement only ▪ Wine club ▪ Online shop ▪ Owner(s) De Bruyn Steenkamp ▪ Production Stefan Truter (Jul 2020) ▪ Viticulturist(s) Piet Steenkamp (Jan 2001, Groenland) ▪ 36.5ha (cab, merlot, shiraz, chenin, sauv) ▪ 20,000cs own label 60% red 40% white ▪ IPW, WIETA ▪ Friesland

Farm, Fischers Rd, Bottelary, Stellenbosch 7600 ▪ debruyn@frieslandwines.com ▪ www.frieslandwines.com
▪ T +27 (0)79-598-5274

☐ **Frisia** *see* Friesland Wines
☐ **Frozen Wines** *see* Spioenkop Wines

Fryer's Cove Vineyards   ⓵ ⓾ ◎ ⓧ ⓛ

Born 25 years ago with the planting of vines at Strandfontein on the West Coast - their toes almost touching the cold Atlantic - Fryer's Cove is now part of premier-wine company DGB's collection, and homed on the dock at Doring Bay, where tasting, cellar tours and The Jetty eatery's traditional regional food are all on offer, along with the caw of seagulls. The Bamboes Bay wines are from the original vineyard, still the only one in the eponymous wine-ward; the other bottlings are from the wider 'wild, desolate and extraordinary' area.

Bamboes Bay range

★★★★☆ **Hollebaksstrandfontein** 🕸 Bracing briny tang on **22** ⑨④ which improves on last-tasted **20** ⑨①. Taut grapefruit & fig with richer, fleshier body that unfurls from 50/50 ferment in 1,500L Austrian oak & clay pot. Nuanced, focused, bright & thrilling. Will reward patience.

★★★★☆ **Sauvignon Blanc** Trademark nettle, flint & sea air on tangy **22** ★★★★ ⑧⑨. Zippy & linear, with grapefruit vibrancy. Not as racy as **21** ⑨② but still refreshing, with light pithy finish.

Not tasted: **Pinot Noir**.

Fryer's Cove range

★★★★ **Grenache-Cinsault** ⊘ Gentle floral edge to cranberry crunch on agile, energetic **22** ⑧⑦. Juicy, with subtle inky core, the fruit pure & unencumbered as there's no oak influence.

★★★★ **Chenin Blanc** Pre-bottling sample of **23** ★★★★ ⑧⑤ has gentle, soft melon, quince & apple fruit with subtle frame from the 10% portion oaked for 5 months. Touch less expressive than **22** ⑧⑧.

★★★★ **Sauvignon Blanc** Previewed **23** ★★★★ ⑧⑤ shows typical cool-climate fig, leaf & grapefruit in light, zesty package. Unlike taut, precise **22** ⑧⑦, more of a summer sipper.

Doring Bay range

Not tasted: **Dry Pinot Noir Rosé**, **Sauvignon Blanc**. — FM

Location: Doring Bay ▪ Map: Olifants River ▪ Map grid reference: A4 ▪ WO: Cape West Coast/Bamboes Bay ▪ Est 1999 ▪ 1stB 2002 ▪ Tasting, sales & cellar tours Mon-Sun 10-6; pub hols (seasonal) please call ahead ▪ Child friendly ▪ The Jetty restaurant open 10-4, bookings on weekends & pub hols ▪ West Coast walking trail ▪ Online wine sales ▪ Owner(s) DGB (Pty) Ltd ▪ Winemaker(s) Liza Goodwin (2021) ▪ Viticulturist(s) Jan van Zyl (Apr 1999) ▪ 6ha (pinot, sauv) ▪ 70t/5,000cs own label 20% red 80% white ▪ PO Box 93 Vredendal 8160 ▪ admin@fryerscove.co.za ▪ www.fryerscove.co.za ▪ T +27 (0)27-215-1092 **(office & tasting)**

☐ **Full Moon** *see* Alphabetical

Fuselage Wines   ⓵

This exciting young aviation-themed boutique brand is owned by Danie Morkel, whose father and name-sake founded Diemerskraal Airfield, sited on the family farm near Wellington. The converted milkshed where Danie crafts the wines (and the separately listed Roodekrantz ones) is so near the action, you can 'hear the novice parachutists tame their vertigo'. We look forward to tasting the new releases next time.

Location: Wellington ▪ Map: Paarl ▪ Map grid reference: D1 ▪ Est/1stB 2020 ▪ Tasting & cellar tour by appt ▪ Spittooners loyalty club ▪ Owner(s) Danie Morkel ▪ Winemaker(s) Danie Morkel (Jan 2020) ▪ Viticulturist(s) Philip Morkel & Anton Laas ▪ 2,500cs own label 60% red 30% white 10% rosé ▪ PO Box 338 Wellington 7655 ▪ info@fuselagewines.com ▪ www.fuselagewines.com ▪ T +27 (0)76-038-5495

☐ **Future Eternal** *see* L'Avenir Wine Estate

Fynbos Distillery   ⓵ ⓾ ◎ ⓧ

At this family distillery, which visitors are welcome to tour, Werner Viljoen and Armand du Plessis craft a remarkable variety of products, including the three grape-based spirits noted below, plus an Oaked Witblits which we look forward to taste next time. All are offered with a food pairing at the venue in Stanford town.

Husk Spirit ★★★★ Attractively rustic husk character on latest (84), forceful & fiery, but plenty of balancing flavour deriving from cab's dark berries. 43% alc on all these. **Oaked Husk Spirit** ★★★ Mid-gold husk spirit (82) from cab has a sophisticated perfumed element, but a slightly smoky-rubbery shading to the nutty husk quality adds a note of discord. **Plain Witblits** ★★★★ Unmatured spirit is distilled from chenin, which gives suggestion of dried peach. Clean & fresh, focused & flavourful. — TJ

Location/WO: Stanford ▪ Map: Walker Bay & Bot River ▪ Map grid reference: B6 ▪ Est/1stB 2014 ▪ Tasting, sales & distillery tours Wed-Sun 9-5 ▪ Fee R10 per tasting ▪ Closed Dec 25 ▪ Jolly Rooster restaurant ▪ Facilities for children ▪ Conferences/small weddings (up to 55 pax) ▪ Gifts ▪ Stanford heritage video & show ▪ Craft gin, mampoer, witblits & liqueurs ▪ Owner(s) Gigi Sipple & Mike Crole ▪ Master distiller Werner Viljoen (Jan 2022) ▪ Distiller(s) Armand du Plessis (Mar 2022), with Dani Crole (Jun 2014) ▪ 5,000 btls own label ▪ 32 Kleine Str, Stanford Business Park, Stanford 7210 ▪ info@fynbosdistillery.co.za ▪ www.fynbosdistillery.co.za ▪ **T +27 (0)28-007-0398/+27 (0)76-320-3092**

☐ **Fynbos Lite** *see* Elgin Vintners

Gabriel & Gysbert

(NEW)

Generations of family and fellow farmers on the eastern edge of Robertson have grown top-quality fruit anonymously, and Elsenburg-trained Pieter Rossouw believes the time has come to showcase it and the shale terroir, ideal for chardonnay especially. On returning in 2017 from years making wine abroad, he started identifying the best blocks and launched the debut wines in 2021 under a banner honouring his grandfathers and, via the label artwork, a childhood quilt made by his mother. 'Less is more' and 'patience pays' are his watchwords, the latter also applicable to those who buy the wines, intended for ageing at least 5 years.

★★★★ **Kwartskop Cabernet Sauvignon** Only 480 bottles of **22** (86), fruit-sweet sugared plums, an icing sugar note, lighter styled & fresh, nice stemmy grip, balanced, interesting & attractive.

★★★★ **Ijsland Chardonnay** Two vintages tasted, both from opposing windswept slopes. **21** ★★★ (82) lemon & lime with aniseed nuance, harmonious oak & more restraint than **22** (86), which riper & more expressive, a honeydew & lemon meringue pie profile, plenty of buttery bâtonnage character.

Welville Old Vine Chenin Blanc ★★★★ Ambitious, rich & oaky style, **22** (83) forward ripe cling peach & nectarine, vein of acid enlivening the whole. — CR, CvZ

Location/WO: Bonnievale ▪ Est 2020 ▪ 1stB 2021 ▪ Closed to public ▪ Owner(s) Dawid Rossouw ▪ Winemaker(s) Pieter Rossouw (2020) ▪ Viticulturist(s) Dirk Rossouw (2014) ▪ 244ha/42ha (cab, chard, chenin) ▪ 800t/420cs own label 30% red 70% white ▪ Welville Farm, Gelukshoop Rd, Bonnievale 6730 ▪ pieter@gabrielgysbert.com ▪ www.gabrielgysbert.com ▪ **T +27 (0)76-256-9445**

Gabriëlskloof

The visual serenity of Gabriëlskloof, with its hilltop setting and perfectly symmetrical grid of vines at its feet, reveals little of the hive-like activity in the cellar or the labour on the Bot River land that go into maintaining the enviably high standards maintained by shareholder, cellarmaster and CWG member Peter-Allan Finlayson and the vineyard team of Adriaan Davids and Chris Keet jnr. The latter have completed the chenin blanc planting referenced last edition, bringing the total hectares under the variety to 3.3, and are planning high-density blocks of cab franc and syrah. Peter-Allan, with Anmar Sprong assisting, works with the home-farm and brought-in pockets of fruit, using minimal intervention to express terroir - as do the high-powered group of new-wave winemakers who rent space in the large, modern facilities for their small-batch production. Peter-Allan also crafts the acclaimed Crystallum pinot noirs and chardonnays here.

Landscape Series

★★★★☆ **Cabernet Franc** Consistent, food-cordial styling showcases the variety's herbaceous character partnered with black fruit, firm oak (year, some new) & matching tannin. **21** (90)'s robust structure & pervasive freshness invite lengthy cellaring. Natural ferment, as all ranges.

★★★★☆ **Syrah on Sandstone** Natural ferment in smaller vessel, 30-50% whole bunches, then year in older 225-500L barrels, giving **21** (92) its peppery perfume, smoky oak note, supple red fruit & firm but tailored tannins. Deeply satisfying & charming, as ever. Just ±800 cases each of this & Shale.

★★★★☆ **Syrah on Shale** ⊛ Same vinification & ageing, yet piquant 21 ⑨④ has more zip & grip than Sandstone sibling, along with the familiar mix of black berry fruit, liquorice spice & appealing meatiness. Delicious now & will improve over next few years. Graceful Niel Jonker artwork for this range.

★★★★☆ **Elodie** ⊛ ⊛ Bot & Olifants River added to Swartland source in 22 ⑨④ old-vine chenin, which maintains impressive form & alluring styling: ripe, honeyed apple with savouriness, texture & spice from ferment/9 months older barrels. Underlying citrus freshness assures balance & lengthens flavours.

★★★★☆ **Magdalena** ⊛ Semillon from Swartland, Franschhoek & Olifants River, fermented in mostly older large barrels, giving rich lanolin texture & grip to 22 ⑨④'s greengage fruit in youth, but concentration & structure will allow it to develop & unfurl beautifully in time. Follows stellar 21 ★★★★★ ⑨⑤.

Projects range

★★★★☆ **Whole Bunch Syrah** ⊘ Label design a play on 'wholebunch', the style of ferment that happens in steel tank for this wine, aiding soft tannins & a cornucopia of flavours & aromas: summer berries, liquorice, pepper & violets. Paired, in 22 ⑨⓪, with moderate 13% alc & fresh acid.

★★★★☆ **Amphora Sauvignon Blanc** Olifants River joins own fruit in clay amphora of various sizes up to 850L, adding detail & texture to 22 ⑨⓪. This ferment/ageing choice adds cream to palate, restrains fruitiness for a more linear (citrus) flavour profile, retains lively acid for elegance & food compatibility.

★★★★ **Madame Lucy's Méthode Cap Classique** The elegant & bone-dry sparkler is now mostly chardonnay, pinot noir down to 17%, 21 months on lees, tad longer than last. 21 ⑧⑦ fresher, better balanced, still with oystershell saltiness & crunchy biscuit nuances. WO W Cape.

Discontinued: **Broken Stem Late Harvest**.

Estate range

★★★★ **Syrah** ⊘ Made to enjoy now & cellar a few years, 22 ⑧⑧'s dark fruit & savoury spice succulent & tempting as ever, fresh & pleasantly firm tannins perfectly fit the style. 21 untasted.

★★★★☆ **The Blend** ⊘ Stylish & well-priced Cape Bordeaux, cab, cab franc, merlot & petit verdot, 21 ⑨⓪ deftly seasoned 18 months in older oak for classic cedar & spice overlay to fresh cassis & blackberry. All trimmed with enough ripe tannin to age good few years. 20 untasted.

★★★★ **Chenin Blanc** Home vines combine with 3 other districts for flavour-packed 22 ⑧⑦. 40% portion fermented/9 months older oak adds usual nut & honey dimension to vibrant stonefruit.

Sauvignon Blanc ★★★★ Restrained & elegant mouthful of cut grass flavour, 22 ⑧⑤ tingles with well-integrated acid. Crisp, appetising & persistent. WO W Cape, as Chenin. Not tasted: **Rosebud**. — DS

Location: Bot River ▪ Map: Walker Bay & Bot River ▪ Map grid reference: C3 ▪ WO: Bot River/Western Cape ▪ Est 2002 ▪ 1stB 2007 ▪ Tasting & sales Mon-Sun 9-5 ▪ Fee R60 for Gabriëlskloof range, R150 for Landscape range, waived on purchase ▪ Closed Dec 24/25 ▪ Cellar tours by appt ▪ Farro Restaurant ▪ Child friendly; dogs welcome ▪ Owner(s) Bernhard Heyns, Peter-Allan Finlayson & Nicolene Finlayson ▪ Winemaker(s) Peter-Allan Finlayson (Jul 2014), Anmar Sprong (Dec 2021) ▪ Viticulturist(s) / farm manager(s) Adriaan Davids (2003) & Chris Keet jnr (2018) ▪ 66ha (cabs s/f, malbec, merlot, mourv, p verdot, pinot, shiraz, chenin, sauv, sem, viog) ▪ IPW, WIETA, WWF-SA Conservation Champion ▪ PO Box 499 Kleinmond 7195 ▪ info@gabrielskloof.co.za ▪ www.gabrielskloof.co.za ▪ **T +27 (0)28-284-9865**

☐ **Game Reserve** see Rooiberg Winery
☐ **Garajeest** see The Garajeest

Garden Route Wines

Small parcels, cool-grown at ±550-700 m altitude, on a south-facing hill in Upper Langkloof ward on the Garden Route, and the Kammanassie mountain range near De Rust in Klein Karoo, are taken to De Krans Wines in Calitzdorp, 100 km distant, for vinification. Tasting and sales are at De Krans.

★★★★ **Shiraz** More tightly structured in 21 ⑧⑨, also a barrel selection after 12 months in older oak. Appealing cool-fruited character of red berries, nutmeg & fragrant white pepper. Lithe tannins, fresh, elegant & ageworthy.

★★★★☆ **Sauvignon Blanc** ⊘ Preview of 23 ⑨⓪ from Upper Langkloof just as confident as last in its zesty freshness & feisty combination of green, herbaceous & tropical guava flavours. Crisp & crunchy, with some food-pairing breadth & weight from 6 months lees ageing.— MW

Location: Calitzdorp/Waboomskraal ▪ Map: Klein Karoo & Garden Route ▪ Map grid reference: C3 B5 ▪ WO: Klein Karoo/Upper Langkloof ▪ Est/1stB 2008 ▪ Tasting & sales at De Krans, Calitzdorp (see entry) ▪ Owner(s) Boets Nel ▪ Winemaker(s) Christoff de Wet (Aug 2019) ▪ Viticulturist(s) Boets Nel (2008) ▪ 6ha (shiraz, sauv) ▪ 20t/±2,700cs own label 25% red 75% white ▪ PO Box 28 Calitzdorp 6660 ▪ dekrans@mweb.co.za ▪ **T +27 (0)44-213-3314**

☐ **Gatos** *see* Axe Hill

GD1 Project

Semillon is becoming increasingly associated with Franschhoek, this project (the initials refer to the original clone of groen druif ('green grape' aka semillon), being a noteworthy contributor. A group of 10 winemakers vinify fruit from a single parcel, following a set of standard methods, this year including less-aromatic yeasts and low-temperature ferments. The goal is a modern style: vibrancy and freshness in youth but the ability to mature gracefully. The first two vintages have developed secondary characteristics of nuttiness and honey sooner than anticipated, but citrus remains a major component. The participants are excited by the 'fantastic' consumer response, and that more are aware of the variety and its link with the area.

★★★★ **Semillon** Greater expression every vintage, even some complexity in **22** ⑧⑨'s lemony, waxy flavours, layered texture; all focused, lengthened by steely acidity. Tank ferment, no malo. 11% alc.— AL

Location/WO: Franschhoek ▪ Est 2018 ▪ 1stB 2019 ▪ Closed to public ▪ Owner(s) 10 members/winemakers ▪ 100cs own label 100% white ▪ info@gd1project.com ▪ www.gd1project.com ▪ **T +27 (0)84-510-1496**

☐ **Gecko Ridge** *see* Thor Vintners

Gedeelte Wines ⑨

Brakkuil farm is near St Helena Bay on the West Coast, 3-4 km from the cold Atlantic, its vineyards planted in virtual sea-sand over limestone. That is rare enough, but so is John Bouwer's winemaking on the family farm. It focuses on maturing the wines (to a greater or lesser degree) under a protective veil of flor yeast, particularly recalling traditional, artisanal wines from France's Jura region. The wine cellar dates from 1948, and now also hosts a small tasting venue, and a house from the 1800s is being renovated (and surrounded by newly planted chardonnay) to allow a welcome for more visitors.

★★★★ **Authentic 23 Barbarossa** Light red retasted after further year in bottle. Fresh, charming red & rosepetal fruit aroma & flavour remain, but **21** ⑧⑥ palate beneficially shows touch more flesh, weight & structure. Unique contribution to SA wine: 1978 vines planted to French table grape danugue (aka gros guillaume), called barbarossa here.

★★★★☆ **Deel 23 Palomino** Veil of flor gives usual subtle nutty, salty tang on **22** ⑨⓪, the fruit character rather neutral. Light elegance at 11% alc, but also real presence & character, with savoury, stony & succulent dryness - this should be a great food wine.

★★★★☆ **Deel 6 Sauvignon Blanc** As usual, flor veil over maturing wine (prior to further maturation in old oak) means typical varietal notes are downplayed on **22** ⑨⓪, but result is fascinatingly different. Bone-dry, nutty, savoury & flavourful, with fruit character less forward than on previous. Bright, grippy acidity.

★★★★ **Vin John** ⑫ Previously noted as 'Johra', **18** ⑧⑧ bottled after sauvignon blanc had 3½ years biological ageing in oak under flor, giving intense, powerful nutty, umami, sherry/Jura character. Acid now better integrated than when previewed; satisfying mineral, salty dryness. 500 ml.— TJ

Location: Velddrif ▪ Map: Olifants River ▪ Map grid reference: B7 ▪ WO: St Helena Bay ▪ Est 2008 ▪ 1stB 2018 ▪ Tasting by appt only ▪ Owner(s)/cellarmaster(s) John Bouwer ▪ 850ha/8ha (barbarossa, palomino, sauv) ▪ 70t/1,800cs own label 60% red 40% white ▪ Brands for clients: Hermanus Wine Village; Wolfgat ▪ john@gedeeltewines.co.za ▪ www.gedeeltewines.co.za ▪ **T +27 (0)82-678-9273**

☐ **Generation 8** *see* Bosman Family Vineyards

Genevieve Méthode Cap Classique ⑨

Since 2009, Melissa Genevieve Nelsen has crafted consistently excellent cap classique, starting with a chardonnay brut, then adding a chardonnay brut nature and most recently a non-vintage brut rosé. Latterly based in Bot River, and using dedicated production facilities in Paarl, she and longtime viticulturist Leon

Engelke want each vintage to 'express itself from grape to bottle' and to this end they apply 'vigilant attention in the vineyard and minimal but concise intervention in the cellar'. We hope to taste her bubblies next time.

Location: Bot River ▪ Map: Walker Bay & Bot River ▪ Map grid reference: C2 ▪ Est 2009 ▪ 1stB 2008 ▪ Tasting Wed-Sat 10-4 ▪ Function venue ▪ Wine club ▪ Owner(s) Melissa Nelsen ▪ Viticulturist(s) Leon Engelke (2008) ▪ 16t/1,650cs own label 100% MCC ▪ PO Box 122 Elgin 7180 ▪ melissa@genevievemcc.co.za ▪ www. genevievemcc.co.za ▪ **T +27 (0)83-302-6562**

☐ **Gentis** *see* Thor Vintners
☐ **Geographica** *see* The Foundry

Germanier Wines

Environmental care has been a feature of this Paarl-based pioneer (as 'African Terroir') of sustainable wine-farming in SA since inception over three decades ago. Now Sophie Germanier, daughter of the late founder and head of the local venture since 2014, is partnering with Stanford nonprofit Honeybee Heroes to channel revenue from the Bee Conscious range into setting up hives on farms and private reserves countrywide.

Organic Wine by Sophie Germanier
Cabernet Sauvignon (NEW) ⊘ ★★★ Fresh smoky cassis & blue fruit on **21** (82), texture softened by oaking of 20% of the wine. Certified vegan by Proveg, as both ranges. **Pinotage** (NEW) ⊘ ★★★ Bright, juicy raspberries on **21** (82) matched by a lively acidity. Also-tasted **22** (81) easy, soft blueberry flavour, light, sappy & not as dry. Both unoaked. **Shiraz-Mourvèdre-Viognier** (🅥) ⊘ ★★★★ Bold black fruit on **21** (85) with shiraz dominant at 70%. Inky depth & good concentration, light squeeze of tannin from small sea-soned-oak portion. **Shiraz-Viognier** (NEW) ⊘ ★★★★ Pepper on **21** (85) shows shiraz dominance (97%), fynbos & herbs mingle with pronounced oak notes, but 18 months in new barrels will do that. **Cabernet Sauvignon-Merlot-Shiraz** (🅥) ⊘ ★★★ Tar top note, **20** (79) positively brims with sweet fruit, ends with pillow-soft tannins. WO W Cape. **Rosé** (NEW) ⊘ ★★★ Pale coral hue from dab mourvèdre on **22** (82) from sauvignon. Light, succulent & crisp with a flint nuance. Ideal for summer. **Chardonnay** ⊘ ★★★★ Upbeat & well-fruited **22** (84) has a gentle honeyed cream note on the finish from 9 months in old oak. **Sauvignon Blanc-Semillon** ⊘ ★★★ Elderflower & citrus mingle on tangy **22** (81) in which sauvignon at 90% leads the way. Well padded & brisk with subtly ripe conclusion.

Bee Conscious range (NEW)
Cabernet Sauvignon-Merlot-Shiraz ⊘ ★★★★ Merlot & shiraz at 20% each share second billing to cab on soft, approachable **21** (85) blend. Unfussy & light for everyday. **Sauvignon Blanc-Semillon** ⊘ ★★★ Sweet & sour tang to 90/10 mix on **22** (82). Easygoing, with dust & flint notes to lemongrass & elderflower succulence. — FM

Location/map: Paarl ▪ Map grid reference: C1 ▪ WO: Coastal/Western Cape ▪ Est/1stB 1991 ▪ Tasting by appt ▪ Owner(s) Sophie Germanier ▪ Brands: Azania, Jacques Germanier, Organic Wine by Sophie Germanier ▪ IPW, Organic, WIETA ▪ PO Box 2029 Windmeul Paarl 7630 ▪ admin@germanier.co.za ▪ www.organicbysg.com ▪ **T +27 (0)21-204-0562**

☐ **Get Lost** *see* Overhex Wines International
☐ **Ghost Corner** *see* Cederberg Private Cellar

Ghost In The Machine

In this strikingly presented small-batch collection, entrepreneurial winegrower Bruce Jack celebrates 'the enduring light of human imagination and the art of winemaking' to transcend machines and AI to 'find solutions and create something truly special'. See also The Drift Estate and Bruce Jack Wines listings.

★★★★ **Cabernet Franc** (NEW) Lithe, supple **21** (87) shows hedgerow fruit, graphite & spice in a gentle frame. Succulent, bright, with leashed power & concentration. Dabs grenache noir & petit verdot.

★★★★ **Shiraz** (NEW) Pepper & herb accents to dark fruit on **21** (88). Lively & juicy from wholebunch carbonic ferment of 12% grenache noir component. Suave, composed, with a firm core & fine tannin from same 17 months oaking as blended sibling. WO W Cape, as all unless noted.

★★★★ **Malbec-Viognier** (NEW) Novel varietal pairing, naturally co-fermented, resulting in cranberry vibrancy & charcuterie savouriness on **21** (88), perky, with dry berried palate framed by oak.

★★★★ **Chardonnay** (NEW) Vibrant, fresh yet chalk-textured **22** (88), skin fermented/6 months in neutral oak. Citrus & marmalade with lime cordial zip, gentle vanilla caramel at poised & dry end.

★★★★☆ **Chenin Blanc** Textured, broad & smooth **22 ★★★★** (86) from Swartland & Breedekloof vines. Quince, oatmeal & nutty nuance balanced by lively acid freshness. Natural ferment, 7 months in oak, some American, for harmonious & rewarding glassful, like **19** (91), tasted earlier as 'Ghost In The Machine' under The Drift label.

★★★★ **Clairette Blanche** (NEW) (🌿) Rare solo bottling of relic grape. **22** (87) waxy stonefruit & zesty lemon the result of old-vine fruit skin-fermented & basket pressed. Structure & texture from 6 months in seasoned oak. Balanced & persistent. Should age interestingly.

★★★★ **Sauvignon Blanc** (NEW) Flint & nettle typicity touched with cream on **22** (86) with dab semillon. Skin ferment, completed in barrel with 40% through malo, 8 months ageing, lend mouthfeel & body with no loss of vivacity. WO Elim. — FM

☐ **Giant Periwinkle** *see* The Giant Periwinkle
☐ **Glass Collection** *see* Glenelly Estate

Glen Carlou

(🍷) (🍴) (📷) (👤) (♿)

Owned since 2016 by a local family consortium, the substantial 145-ha Glen Carlou property on the Simonsberg-Paarl foothills is planted with some 50 ha of vines, mostly French varieties, covering diverse slopes and aspects. Each vineyard block is farmed individually to maximise potential, and small-batch harvested to allow greater control and selection of incoming fruit, aiding head winemaker Johnnie Calitz's goal of limited intervention in the cellar processes, with some wines allowed to ferment naturally. The brand has a long-standing international reputation, not least for a multifaceted experience that includes an impressive contemporary art collection and memorable views from the high-ceilinged thatch-and-stone visitor centre.

Glen Carlou Wines

★★★★ **Cabernet Sauvignon** Stern grape tannins of **21** (86) countered by opulent black fruit & older oak. Lingering sweetness from nearly 15% alc & 5 g/L sugar overlaid with pencil shavings. Paarl WO.

★★★★☆ **Gravel Quarry Cabernet Sauvignon** (🌿) From registered single-vineyard (as Quartz Stone), **20** (94) head & shoulders above range partners this year. Glossy, powerful, as last, sweet fruited & high in alc (as most of the reds), yet better focused & defined, a welcome savoury nuance to its succulence.

★★★★ **Syrah** Commands attention with plum jam & tomato paste intro, **21 ★★★★** (84) then delivers effortless mouthful of flavour touched, like more serious **20** (87), with vanilla from part American oak.

★★★★☆ **Grand Classique** (🌿) Consistent & respected cab-led 5-way Bordeaux blend. Chocolate top note from oak, 18 months, 50% new, contrasts attractively with **21** (90)'s softly spiced fruit, walnut whiff; satisfying tannin hold extends the finish. WO Coastal.

★★★★☆ **Quartz Stone Chardonnay** (🍷) Hallmark elegance in **21** (92), pared-back fruitiness, seamless dry finish. Subtle vanilla from ferment in new oak, 10% concrete 'egg' portion aids creamy texture.

★★★★ **Méthode Cap Classique Blanc de Blancs** From chardonnay, 30 months on lees. With pronounced oxidative waft, **20** (88) for fans of bubbly showing some age. Engaging, too, is its toast & Golden Delicious apple bouquet, bracingly dry strudel palate. WO W Cape.

★★★★ **Natural Sweet Chenin Blanc** (🍷) Unoaked **17** (89) has zesty citrus notes & lively acid offsetting substantial sugar. Honeyed pineapple & lipsmacking finish make for dessert delight. 375 ml. Paarl WO.

Merlot ★★★★ Raspberry- & sherbet-toned **21** (85) decently dry, smooth, with only a slight tug of tannin. Step up on somewhat gruff predecessor. **Pinot Noir** (✓) ★★★★ Jewel-like translucence, red pastille fruit & malleable tannins on wallet-friendly (for pinot) **22** (84). Older oak aids pleasurable sipping on release. **Chardonnay ★★★★** Consumer favourite from 15 different Simonsberg-Paarl sites. **22** (85)'s cordial-like lemon & lime aromas, flavours & acid smoothed by creamy, buttery notes from ferment in 25% new barriques. **Sauvignon Blanc ★★★★** From Durbanville vines, **23** (83) prominent grassy, green, pyrazine characters, faint passionfruit tastes & grenadilla pith texture. Tad less substance & life than last.

The Glen Carlou Collection

★★★★☆ **Malbec** (🌿) Sugar plum- & mulberry-nuanced **18** (90) released after **19** (90). As full & broad, with a light savoury lift, plenty of ripe, rich fruit to buttress variety-true firm tannin.

★★★★ Pinotage From Swartland fruit aged year in new barriques, **21** ⑧⑧ has a vanilla & oak-spice sheen to its herb-tinged blue & black fruit. Confident & harmonious.

★★★★ Muscat d'Alexandrie Just handful of dry varietal bottlings. Old oceanside vines at St Helena Bay, wild fermented in older oak, **22** ⑧⑨ oozes fresh grape, musk & floral charm, dialled up by racy acid & variety's natural pithy texture.

Occasional release: **Cabernet Franc**, **Grenache Noir**, **Merlot**, **Petite Sirah**, **Tannat**, **Red Blend**, **Chenin Blanc**, **Verdelho**, **Sauvignon Blanc-Semillon**, **White Blend**. — CvZ

Location/map: Paarl • Map grid reference: D7 • WO: Simonsberg-Paarl/Paarl/Coastal/Cape Town/Western Cape/Swartland/St Helena Bay • Est 1985 • 1stB 1988 • Tasting & sales Mon-Fri 9-5 Sat/Sun & pub hols 10-4 • Fee R50-R150 • Closed Good Fri, Dec 25 & Jan 1 • Cellar tours by appt • Restaurant • Facilities for children • Tour groups • Gifts • Weddings • Conferences • Conservation area • Gallery • Wine club • Owner(s) Pactolus Consortium (chair Wayne Pitout) • Winemaker(s) Johnnie Calitz (head, Oct 2016) • Viticulturist(s) Marius Cloete (2000) • 145ha/48ha (cabs s/f, malbec, merlot, mourv, p verdot, pinot, shiraz, chard, viog) • ±850t/100,000cs own label • Simondium Rd, Klapmuts 7625 • hello@glencarlou.co.za • www.glencarlou. com • T +27 (0)21-875-5528

Glenelly Estate   ⚲ 🍴 📷 ♿

Although Glenelly's vision is to produce authentic South African wines reflecting terroir and vintage in the Simonsberg-Stellenbosch ward, one cannot help but be aware of the French connection. Owner is May-Eliane de Lencquesaing, ex Château Pichon Longueville in Bordeaux, the CEO is her grandson Nicolas Bureau, the restaurant chef is French, and on display, with Gallic flair, is a world-class glass collection, including 1st-century pieces, collected over the years by Madame, and the inspiration for a wine range. The portfolio is elegant, of course, maintaining classic European traits, no commercial yeasts are used, and the vines are tended as naturally as possible. Prompted by last year's 20th anniversary, there are long-term replanting plans in place, aided by the latest technology, in particular to substantially expand the cabernet vineyards.

Lady May range

★★★★★ Lady May ⓥ Estate flagship, cab-led (85%) Bordeaux red with 3 others. Built for the long haul, with meticulous care taken: **18** ⑨⑤ spent 2 years in 75% new barrels, then 4 years in bottle before release. Has depth & concentration, fine tannins in a polished body, deep muscle tone.

Estate Reserve range

★★★★☆ Red ⓥ Hand grape sorting for **17** ⑨④ & 18 months in barrel, 30% new. Cab (64%), 3 Bordeaux varieties plus 15% syrah - not the expected Left Bank blend but works supremely well. Plush dark fruit, cigarbox throughout, compact tannins for a distinguished future. Larger bottle formats, as Lady May.

★★★★☆ Chardonnay 🍇 Both chardonnays vinified with wild yeast, but lots more cellar attention to craft this **22** ⑨④. Wholebunch barrel ferment, extended lees contact, year oak, portion new, give blanched almond savoury seam, citrus core, taut, sleek freshness. Also in 1.5L.

Glass Collection

★★★★☆ Cabernet Sauvignon ⊘ 🍇 Unless noted, all reds same treatment: crushed berries, wild ferment in tank, post-ferment extended skin contact, then to barrel for a year, small fraction new. Classic lead pencils & blackcurrant, **21** ⑨⓪ has a Bordeaux-inspired refinement, enough ripe tannin for cellaring.

★★★★ Cabernet Franc ⓥ Ticking all the boxes, **20** ★★★★★ ⑨⓪ displays lead pencils, dried & crushed herbs, red berries & plums, is proudly cab franc. Structure is streamlined, carrying the firm but ripe tannins, fruit-enfolded for earlier access. Very nicely done, with spot-on styling, improves on **19** ⑧⑧.

★★★★ Merlot ⓥ Mixed berries & dark chocolate, **20** ⑧⑨'s tannin backbone promises ageing ability though already drinking well. Good typicity, enough crafting to reinforce why merlot remains so popular.

★★★★ Syrah ⊘ Different to other reds, wholebunch maceration, wild ferment, extended skin contact, year seasoned barrels, all designed to give **21** ★★★★☆ ⑨⓪ admirable fruit intensity, plush texture. White pepper spicing to add to the attraction. Improves on **20** ⑧⑨. Lovely!

★★★★ Unoaked Chardonnay With fruit good enough to not need oak, **22** ⑧⑥ vibrates with citrus & apple freshness, is stylish & pure.— CR

Location/map/WO: Stellenbosch • Map grid reference: F4 • Est/1stB 2003 • Tasting Tue & Wed 10-6 Thu-Sat 10-7 Sun 10-3 (please phone to confirm times as they may change for winter) • Closed Easter Fri/Sun, Dec 25

& Jan 1 ▪ Cellar tours by appt ▪ Glass museum Tue-Sat 10-5 Sun 10-3 ▪ Restaurant: lunch Tue-Sun 12-3; dinner Thu-Sat 6.30-8.30 (last order), in winter Fri & Sat only ▪ Wine club ▪ Owner(s) May-Eliane de Lencquesaing ▪ CEO Nicolas Bureau ▪ Cellarmaster(s) Dirk van Zyl (Aug 2022) ▪ Viticulturist(s) Heinrich Louw (2003) ▪ 123ha/57ha (cabs s/f, merlot, p verdot, shiraz, chard) ▪ 500t/55,334cs own label 90% red 10% white ▪ PO Box 1079 Stellenbosch 7599 ▪ tasting@glenelly.co.za ▪ www.glenellyestate.com ▪ **T +27 (0)21-809-6440**

Glen Heatlie Wines

Paarl part-time vintner Joan-Marie Heatlie has completed her articles at the audit firm where she's worked the past four-plus years, and is set to join the family business. The possibility exists to convert the 19th-century cellar where an ancestor produced brandy into a production space for her small batches of wine. A chardonnay single-ferment bubbly made with Huis van Chevallerie will be the next release.

★★★★☆ **The Frontier** From grenache blanc, showcases richness variety can show when fermented in oak, without sacrificing freshness or elegant dryness. **22** ⑨⓪ subtle Golden Delicious apple & baking spice tones. Bunch fermented/8 months in barrel, 25% new. No **21**.

Not tasted: **Petnat**. In abeyance: **Ruptura**. — PS, CvZ

Location: Paarl ▪ WO: Piekenierskloof ▪ Est 2006 ▪ Tasting by appt only ▪ Owner(s)/winemaker(s) Joan Heatlie ▪ 225cs ▪ joan@glenheatlie.co.za ▪ **T +27 (0)82-364-4702**

☐ **Glenrosa Vineyards** see Stettyn Family Vineyards

GlenWood

The GlenWood philosophy is 'simple, natural, quality', and it's the second element that's spotlit in the latest addition to the visitor experience, pre-booked Wine & Fynbos tours. Owner Alastair Wood has set aside one-fifth of his Franschhoek land to encourage fynbos regeneration and return of animal life, earning his winery WWF-SA Conservation Champion recognition. The new tour offers the opportunity to explore this pristine reserve on foot or in a 4x4 vehicle, a high point being a tasting (with optional accompaniment by the on-site sushi kitchen) at Nature's Window, the venue on the mountain overlooking the cellar.

Grand Duc range

★★★★☆ **Syrah** Trademark opulent style made irresistible by ultra-smooth texture & full-bore spicing via all-new barrels, 24 months, portion American. **21** ⑨① 's vanilla & nutmeg notes pair with plush dark fruit for tempting drinkability but, like **20** ⑨③, has tannin backbone for those who can wait.

★★★★★ **Chardonnay** ⊛ The flagship has remarkable presence & gravity, both packaging & wine. **21** ★★★★★ ⑨④, like previous, bunch pressed, wild fermented, 2 years on lees in new oak, & echoes the toasted brioche richness & density while retaining a lovely citrus freshness & finesse. **20** ⑨⑤ had remarkable presence.

★★★★☆ **Noblesse** ⊛ Now **NV** ⑨③ - last was **17** ★★★★★ ⑨⑤ - still 100% semillon Noble Late Harvest, as perfectly balanced, the enjoyment unimpaired. Wild yeast fermented/36 months in older oak. Honeysuckle, candied citrus, apricot, with enough exhilarating acidity to offset the richness. 375 ml.

Vigneron's Selection

★★★★ **Shiraz** ⊘ Shaped to enjoy earlier than Syrah, a more streamlined texture & touch of sugar the keys, but **21** ★★★★★ ⑨⓪ has a svelte structure ramping up its quality. Same vibrancy of cherry & berry fruit as **20** ⑧⑧, harmonious underpin of 18-month oaking.

★★★★★ **Chardonnay** ⊛ Less barrel time than Grand Duc & 30% less new oak, but stellar **22** ⑨⑤ as arresting, perhaps better balanced. Careful styling balances toast & candied nut decadence with lime & lemon freshness through to the lingering finish. Wholebunch, wild yeast ferment, 8 months on lees.

GlenWood range

★★★★ **Merlot** Crafted for early drinking while respecting the grape's character; **22** ⑧⑦ smooth & juicy as ever, reflects the mocha-toned berry scents & flavours of the variety.

★★★★ **Chardonnay** Proving chardonnay can charm without oak, **23** ⑧⑧ offers a focused mix of citrus, vibrant & fresh, to enjoy in youth. Easiest of cellar's varietal trio.

Sauvignon Blanc ★★★★ Returns to the guide after an extended break. Crisp **23** ⑧⑤ packed with cut-grass aroma & flavour unfettered by oak, a greengage tension on palate ensures zip & zing. Discontinued: **Sauvignon Blanc-Semillon**. — DS

Location/map/WO: Franschhoek ▪ Map grid reference: C2 ▪ Est/1stB 2002 ▪ Tasting & sales Tue-Sun 11-4; pub hols (seasonal) please call ahead ▪ Closed Easter Fri/Sun, Dec 25 & Jan 1 ▪ Tasting R105 & R200 ▪ Wine & Fynbos tour daily by appt only, min 2 persons ▪ Gourmet sushi restaurant open for lunch Tue-Sun 11-4 ▪ Wine club ▪ Owner(s) Alastair G Wood ▪ Cellarmaster(s)/viticulturist(s) DP Burger (Apr 1991) ▪ Winemaker(s) Natasha Pretorius (Dec 2018) ▪ 49ha/30ha (merlot, shiraz, chard, sauv, sem) ▪ 150t/16,000cs own label 50% red 50% white ▪ IPW, WIETA, WWF-SA Conservation Champion ▪ PO Box 204 Franschhoek 7690 ▪ info@ glenwoodvineyards.co.za ▪ www.glenwoodvineyards.co.za ▪ T +27 (0)21-876-2044

☐ **Glorious** see Stellenbosch Family Wines

Goats do Roam Wine Company ⓥ

Fairview's take on Rhône blends, launched in 1998, ruffled feathers and tickled funny bones in equal measure with its gentle satire and whimsical branding. Latterly with Italian flavour and many export markets added, the wines remain expressive, approachable and good value. See also listing for sibling La Capra.

★★★★ **Goats do Roam Red** ⊘ Even juicier in riper **22** ⑧⑥ shiraz blend with 6 others. Spicy red berries & dusting of pepper & sweet cinnamon from light oaking. Silky tannins, balanced freshness & grip, ready to entertain. More to give than **21** ★★★★ ⑧⑤, also shiraz-led but a five-way mix.

★★★★ **The Goatfather** ⊘ Sterner **21** ★★★★ ⑧⑤ than **20** ⑧⑥, with sangiovese's (50%) Italianate dried tomato character blended with cab & merlot. Drier tannins, 15 months oaking adding dusting of cocoa to fennel, red & black berry flavours. The Don calls for an antipasto platter. WO Coastal, rest W Cape.

Goats do Roam Rosé ⓥ ★★★★ Bright & juicy grenache noir & cinsaut pairing in **22** ⑧④. Piquant cranberry freshness, light & dry, a summery delight. **Goats do Roam White** ⓥ ★★★★ Flavoursome & aromatic **22** ⑧④ an unoaked blend of mostly viognier & grenache blanc with marsanne & roussanne from Fairview home-farm. Plump, succulent & dry. Also in 3L bag-in-box, as Red. — MW

Goedverwacht Wine Estate ⓥ 🍷 ◎

A dream of growing wine spurred civil engineer Gabriël du Toit to switch careers in the 1960s. The venture he founded has grown substantially under his son Jan and, latterly, grandson Gawie, and the 1950s cellar, extensively modernised and enlarged, now produces well over 2-m litres of mostly exported wine from 220 hectares of own vines around Bonnievale. The crane in the logo and some wine names is SA's national bird.

Maxim range

★★★★ **Cabernet Sauvignon** ⓥ Classic cab, cassis & spice, good tannin foundation from 2 years mainly older oak, but **19** ⑧⑦ already drinking well, smooth & streamlined. Last tasted as **15** ⑧⑥.

★★★★ **Chardonnay** Now bottled, **22** ⑧⑧ affirms elegant balance & freshness of preview. Rich almond seam from 6 months in barrel (double that of Expectations sibling) to complement zesty citrus & ripe pear. Lingering farewell. No **20**, **21**.

Great Expectations range

★★★★ **Sauvignon Blanc** ⊘ Piquant gooseberry & greenpepper notes with touch ruby grapefruit in vivaciously fresh **23** ⑧⑦. Body & structure perfect for food pairing, a long lemony & salty conclusion.

....

Crane White Colombar ⊘ 🍷 ★★★★ Ever fresh & lively, **23** ⑧⑤ with signature fennel, greengage & lemon notes. A plush, creamy texture adds to the appeal.

....

Great Expectations Crane Red Merlot ★★★ Tangy red berries & spicy oak (barrels & staves, 8 months, as all these reds) in preview of **22** ⑧②. Juicy & light, for easy, uncomplicated summer quaffing. **Shiraz** ⊘ ★★★★ White pepper dusting to dark berries in **23** ⑧④, oak in supple support. Less rounded than last, but fresh, balanced, one for the table. **Triangle** ⊘ ★★★★ Flavoursome, juicy blend cab, merlot & petit verdot in **22** ⑧⑤. Same wooding as last, well melded, lithe & accessible. Not serious but a dapper everyday staple. **Shiraz Rosé** ⊘ ★★★ Flamingo pink, bright & breezy **23** ⑧② has mix of savoury & red berry flavours. Plumped by some sugar but still dry, light at 12% alc & refreshing. **Chardonnay** ★★★ Crunchy apple freshness woven with ripe peach & pear in amiable **23** ⑧②, given some breadth by brush of oak. **Chenin**

Blanc ⊘ ★★★ Similar apple & pear flavour profile in **23** ⑧ & identically made to Bad Brothers sibling. Crisp & lively alfresco sipper. **Sparkling Rosé Demi-Sec** ⊘ ★★★ Carbonated shiraz bubbly, pale pink & packed with strawberries. **22** ⑧'s sweetness fits the style, goes down oh so easily.

Bad Brothers range

Pinotage ⊘ ★★★ Savoury, farmyard nuances to dark plummy fruit in unwooded **22** ⑦. A tad rustic, ripeness spars with edgy tannins, better with a BBQ. **Rosé** ⊘ ★★★ Pale pink **22** ⑧ shiraz tank sample welcomes you with strawberry scents, a slender, fruity dry body. **Chenin Blanc** ⊘ ★★★ Easy-drinking, affable style (despite the label) in **23** ⑧. Quite creamy though still fresh, with ripe pears & crunchy apples.

J&G range

Cabernet Sauvignon ★★★ Styled for ready drinking, **22** ⑧ dry, with hint of juicy berries, brush of oak (staves) & gentle nip of tannin. Could even chill it. In abeyance: **Chardonnay, Chenin Blanc.** — MW

Location: Bonnievale ▪ Map/WO: Robertson ▪ Map grid reference: C4 ▪ Est 1960s ▪ 1stB 1994 ▪ Tasting, sales & cellar tours Mon–Fri 8.30-4.30; pub hols (seasonal) please call ahead ▪ Closed Easter Fri/Sun, Dec 25/26 & Jan 1 ▪ BYO picnic ▪ Tour groups ▪ Conservation area ▪ Owner(s) Jan du Toit & Sons (Pty) Ltd ▪ Winemaker(s) Christiaan van Tonder (Sep 2016) ▪ Viticulturist(s) Jan du Toit, advised by Francois Viljoen ▪ 220ha/150ha (cabs s/f, merlot, p verdot, shiraz, chard, chenin, cbard, sauv) ▪ 4,000t/2.7m L 15% red 80% white 5% rosé ▪ Other export brands: Ama Ulibo, Soek die Geluk ▪ BEE, GlobalGAP, IPW, WIETA ▪ PO Box 128 Bonnievale 6730 ▪ info@goedverwacht.co.za ▪ www.goedverwacht.co.za ▪ **T +27 (0)23-616-3430**

☐ **Gôiya** see Namaqua Wines
☐ **Golden Kaan** see KWV Wines
☐ **Good Natured Organic** see Spier
☐ **Goose Wines** see The Goose Wines
☐ **Gottfried Mocke Wine Projects** see Cap Maritime
☐ **Goudini Lifestyle** see Daschbosch
☐ **Goue Kalahari** see Die Mas van Kakamas
☐ **Gouverneurs** see Groot Constantia Estate
☐ **GPS Series** see Kershaw Wines
☐ **Graça** see Heineken Beverages

Graham Beck   ⊘ ⑪ ⑤

Established in the early 1980s by visionary entrepreneur Graham Beck, and latterly run by his son Antony, the namesake winery has been at the forefront of the development and growth of bottle-fermented bubbly in SA. After deciding in 2016 to focus on cap classique exclusively, the team have pursued the goal of consistently producing among the best sparkling wine in the world. With Pieter Ferreira, driving force for over 30 vintages, as chief operating officer, and his mentee Pierre de Klerk helming the substantial Robertson cellar, their goal is 'elegance, freshness and balance, always in pursuit of the perfect bubble'. To this end they continue to harvest all estate-grown grapes in the cold of night, and conduct R&D that will see 'intriguing releases' in the Artisan range. The Vintage Collection and Cuvée Clive are now available in magnum format.

Icon Collection

★★★★★ **Cuvée Clive** ⑤ Sublime flagship, **18** ⑭ now extra brut & from mainly Robertson estate chardonnay, only 5% pinot noir. Scintillating bubbles surge through crisp apple & lemon fruit, barrel-fermented portion & 58 months on lees add creamy brioche & biscuit complexity through to lengthy, tingly finish. Still an infant, everything in place for outstanding development. **17** ⑭ had 40% pinot.

Artisan Collection

★★★★★ **Extra Brut 157** (NEW) ⑤ Thoroughly intriguing **09** ⑨ sparkler a triumph of patience & skilled winemaking, from near-equal chardonnay & pinot noir. Starts with toasted marshmallow, hint of Marmite umami then settles in glass with cooked apple & touch of cranberry fruit. Open hour before serving, even decant to get full benefit of 157 months on lees.

Discontinued: **Yin, Yang, Extended Lees Ageing.**

Vintage Collection

★★★★☆ **Pinot Noir Rosé** From various sites, 10% chardonnay addition, **18** ⑨① shows textbook earthy, savoury edge to pristine red appleskin fruit. Hints of smoke, raspberry & leaf, then tangy baked goods & yeast, laced throughout with lively bubbles from 4 years on lees. To enjoy with food.

★★★★☆ **Blanc de Blancs Brut** (醸) Ripeness & elegance hand-in-hand in **18** ★★★★★ ⑨⑤ from Robertson estate chardonnay, mixing peach with quince & green apple in persistent mouthful of flavour. Toast & brioche add to the mid-palate from 4 years on lees, fine seam of acid & integrated bubbles lead to crisp, refined finish. Like **17** ⑨④, 50% barrel aged, 7% new, for even greater complexity.

★★★★☆ **Ultra Brut** Sweet white peach entry to **17** ⑨① gives way to flinty minerality & biting acid in bone-dry style. Ripe apple, smoke & tiny bubbles carry through to good length at finish. Two-thirds chardonnay, rest pinot noir, portion old-oaked then 62 months on lees. WO Robertson.

Non-Vintage Collection

★★★★ **Brut Rosé** Touch drier than Brut, **NV** ⑧⑦'s perfume & whiffs of toast & biscuit mingle with bright raspberry & red appleskin fruit. Brighter acid clinches satisfying improvement on last. Also in 375 ml.

★★★★ **Bliss Nectar Rosé** Slightly less lees-time on latest **NV** ⑧⑦ off-dry sparkler, & all the better for really lovely berry & cherry fruit shining through. Balanced acid & touch of yeast from 12 months in bottle.

★★★★ **Brut** Ever-reliable & -popular **NV** ⑧⑥ from near-equal chardonnay & pinot noir (as Rosé & Bliss Nectar) is all brightness & bounce, with fine bubbles, zesty acid & green apples. Light toast & brioche at finish. Also in halves & magnums.

Bliss Nectar ★★★★ Similar blend & same ageing as pink cousin yet latest **NV** ⑧⑤ softer & slighter. Gentle lemons, apples & almonds, just enough acid to balance semi-dry 26.9 g/L sugar.

Magnum Collection

★★★★☆ **30th Celebratory Magnum** (Ⓕ) Celebrating 30 years since inception of the brand, **15** ⑨④ beautifully balanced, refined & lingering. Chardonnay (75%) & pinot noir, widely sourced, 5 years on lees. Intricate vinification includes some perpetual reserve initiated 3 decades ago. Magnum bottlings of Pinot Noir Rosé, Blanc de Blancs, Brut, Cuvée Clive & Ultra Brut also still available. — **CM**

Location/map: Robertson ▪ Map grid reference: B6 ▪ WO: Western Cape/Robertson ▪ Est 1983 ▪ 1stB 1991 ▪ Tasting & sales Mon-Fri 9-5 Sat/Sun 10-4 ▪ Closed on selected public holidays ▪ Tasting options: Non-Vintage R80; Vintage R120; Deluxe 'A Glass Act' R180; Sparkle & PoP gourmet popcorn & Cap Classique tasting R180; Olive oil & Cap Classique tasting R170 ▪ Cheese & charcuterie platters on request ▪ The Society wine club ▪ Owner(s) Beck Family Estates ▪ COO Pieter Ferreira (Aug 1990) ▪ Cellarmaster(s) Pierre de Klerk (Oct 2010) ▪ Viticulturist(s) Pieter Fouché ▪ Robertson 120ha ▪ 1,690t/120,000cs cap classique ▪ ISO 14001, IPW, SABS 1841, WIETA, WWF-SA Conservation Champion ▪ PO Box 724 Robertson 6705 ▪ market@grahambeck.com ▪ www. grahambeck.com ▪ **T +27 (0)23-626-1214/+27 (0)21-874-1258 (marketing)**

☐ **Grand Domaine** *see* Le Grand Domaine
☐ **Grand Duc** *see* GlenWood

Grande Provence Heritage Wine Estate ⓕ ⓕ ⓐ ⓪ ⓢ ⓑ

Belgian and Dutch-owned Grande Provence draws visitors in with its gorgeous Cape Dutch manor, sea of vines and dramatic Franschhoek mountain backdrop, keeps them spellbound with an array lifestyle features, including restaurant, art and luxury accommodation in a lush garden setting. Equally varied is the wine portfolio, in the care of consultant Philip Costandius, the common theme being 'elegance and balance'.

Flagship range

★★★★☆ **The Grande Provence Red** (醸) Cab-based blend suitably grandly packaged & built for the long haul. **20** ⑨① with petit verdot & cab franc packed with berry fruit still in a tight grip of tannin & graphite minerality. Allow few years to open & reveal charms. Also-tasted **19** ★★★★ ⑧⑨, without cab franc, more yielding. 2 years in oak. Coastal WO.

Grande Provence Premium range

★★★★ **Cabernet Sauvignon** With 14% petit verdot, **20** ⑧⑧ shows good typicity in its cassis & graphite profile, deserves few years to show at its best. 21 months oak, as for cab-only **19** ⑧⑧ which had splash of 2018 to make for earlier pleasure. Coastal WO, as Shiraz.

★★★★ **Shiraz** Wisps of white pepper & woodsmoke precede succulent blue & black berries in **21** (89), followed by firm but not harsh dry grip from 21 months in oak & power from 14.8% alc.

★★★★ **Chardonnay** Stave-fermented **21** (87) was quiet when previewed last time, but has since broadened & become smooth, offering creamy oatmeal depth along with trademark elegance.

★★★★☆ **Amphora** Last was **17** (92), chenin & 7.5% muscat d'Alexandrie, peach-filled **20** (92) loses latter variety, maintains textured, chalky appeal, rich spice & honey brightened by a clean freshness. 1982 Coastal vines, naturally fermented on skins, 8 months in clay amphora.

★★★★☆ **White** (ℚ) Scintillating **19** (93), smooth & broad, with textured richness given elegance by appealing twist of citrus zest. Chenin (76%) supported by viognier, 18 months older oak. Franschhoek WO.

Merlot ★★★★ Pliable **20** (85)'s spiced cherry & mulberry fruit is supported by integrated 21 months oaking. Combo Franschhoek & Stellenbosch grapes. **Chenin Blanc** (✓) ★★★★ Sunny peach-, pear- & quince-toned **22** (83) gets breadth & depth from dab seasoned oak. Moreish & ideal for a picnic. **Sauvignon Blanc** ★★★★ Careful, cool handling retains green grassy profile of lively **22** (84) from Durbanville & Franschhoek. Brisk & refreshing. Not tasted: **Méthode Cap Classique Rosé Brut**, **Méthode Cap Classique Brut**.

Angels Tears range

Pinotage (ℚ) ★★★ Cheerful **20** (80), a pleasant country red that's not too serious. **Fruity Red** ★★★ Merlot & cab lead the 4-way blend in now-bottled **20** (80). Approachable, portion oak-staved for body, finishes firmly dry. Fruity too. **Fruity Red 3L Bag-in-Box** (NEW) (✓) ★★★ Very fruity **20** (80) blend with touch of oak is accessible & friendly, finishes firmly dry for pizza, pasta & braai partnering. **Rosé** ★★★ Cheerful dry pink has blue- & red-fruit appeal with fresh acid. **22** (82) blended from black & white grapes. **Sauvignon Blanc** ★★★ Tangy citrus simplicity to **22** (80), bright & refreshing. **Sauvignon Blanc 3L Bag-in-Box** (NEW) (✓) ★★★ Zippy grapefruit ease & freshness, **22** (80) in a convenient easy-carry pack, as Red. **Moscato-Chenin Blanc** ★★★★ White muscadel & chenin medley billows sweet grapey appeal. Fresh & fun **22** (83) is light & balanced, would pair well with variety of foods. — DS

Location/map: Franschhoek ▪ Map grid reference: C2 ▪ WO: Western Cape/Coastal/Franschhoek ▪ Est 1694 ▪ 1stB 2004 ▪ Tasting & sales Mon-Sun 10-5 (winter) & 10-6 (summer) ▪ Fee R120-R180 ▪ Group tastings under oak tree in summer and during winter in cathedral extension of art gallery (seat up to 80 pax) ▪ Cellar & gallery tours by appt ▪ Wine blending sessions by appt ▪ Picnics (seasonal) ▪ The Restaurant at Grande Provence ▪ The Bistro at Grande Provence ▪ Deli at Grande Provence ▪ Tour groups ▪ Gift shop ▪ Conferences, weddings & year end functions ▪ Art gallery ▪ Harvest festival ▪ The Owner's Cottage & La Provençale Villa in the Vineyard at Grande Provence ▪ On Franschhoek Wine Tram route, express wine tram tasting option for R120/5 wines ▪ Wine club ▪ Owner(s) Dutch & Belgium consortium ▪ Winemaker(s) Philip Costandius (consultant) ▪ 32ha/22ha (cab, merlot, chard, sauv) ▪ Grande Provence: 80t/6,444cs own label 40% red 60% white; Angels Tears: 160t/15,000cs own label 45% red 45% white 10% rosé ▪ PO Box 102 Franschhoek 7690 ▪ logistics@grandeprovence.co.za ▪ www.grandeprovence.co.za ▪ **T** +27 (0)21-876-8600

☐ **Grand Vin de Stellenbosch** *see* Le Grand Domaine

Grangehurst

(ℚ) (⌂)

The Walker family's long-dreamed-of new tasting lounge has opened its doors, an airy multi-volume struc-ture that takes full advantage of the views across False Bay from the site on the lower Helderberg slopes. Welcoming visitors 'with warm hospitality' is venue manager Liz Lombard, also new sales and marketing chief, whose portfolio is unusual in being weighted to mature wines as current releases (as distinct from archive specials). It's aligned with acclaimed prime mover Jeremy Walker's 'handcrafted, traditional and unhurried' principle, applied since he started crafting boutique wine in the converted on-site squash court over 30 years ago. See also Wavescape Wines listing for Jeremy's collaboration with fellow surfer Steve Pike.

★★★★☆ **Cabernet Sauvignon Reserve** (ℚ) Care taken, 50% wholeberry ferment, 26 months oak, no fining/filtration et al. **09** (93) shows it, tannins integrated, silky yet end grip invites more time in cellar.

★★★★☆ **Pinotage** (⌂) A masterclass in classic pinotage-making. **11** (93)'s sweet oak (15% American, 28 months) provides solid backbone for cooked red fruit, time adds leather & spice complexity, moulding still-firm tannins into highly complex mouthful with endless finish. Old school in very best way. No **10**.

★★★★ **Pinotage Reserve** (ℚ) With 13% cab, 30 months older barriques, **15** (88)'s tannin structure muscular but still accessible, everything else in place, plush fruit, a spice array, great length.

★★★★☆ **Cabernet Sauvignon-Merlot** ② Lengthily mellowed wine in perfect condition - what a pleasure. Complex, involving **09** ⑨① on track after **08** ★★★★ ⑧⑧. Vivid cassis seamed with leafy tomato.

★★★★☆ **Nikela** ② Cab with pinotage, shiraz, 2 others, same handling as Cab Reserve. Highly complex **09** ⑨① smooth & round, but can be cellared further. Notch above **08** ★★★★ ⑧⑨. Also in 1.5L, as all above.

Not tasted: **Grangehurst, Daylea Red, Cape Rosé**. In abeyance: **Reserve Blend**. Discontinued: **The Reward, 350 Pinotage Reserve**. — CM

Location/WO: Stellenbosch ▪ Map: Helderberg ▪ Map grid reference: C1 ▪ Est/1stB 1992 ▪ Tasting & sales Wed-Sat 11-5 but refer to website/facebook for updates or phone to enquire ▪ Closed Easter Fri-Mon, Dec 25/26 & Jan 1 ▪ Self-catering guest cottages ▪ Owner(s) Grangehurst Winery (Pty) Ltd ▪ Cellarmaster(s) Jeremy Walker (Jan 1992) ▪ Winemaker(s) Jeremy Walker (Jan 1992), with Gladys Brown (Jan 2002) ▪ ±13ha/6ha own (cab) + 7ha bought in grapes (merlot, p verdot, ptage, roobernet, shiraz) ▪ 80t/8,000cs own label 90% red 10% rosé ▪ PO Box 206 Stellenbosch 7599 ▪ sales@grangehurst.co.za ▪ www.grangehurst.co.za ▪ **T +27 (0)21-855-3625**

☐ **Grinder** see The Grape Grinder
☐ **Grapesmith** see The Grapesmith
☐ **Great Expectations** see Goedverwacht Wine Estate
☐ **Great Five** see Stellenview Premium Wines

Great Heart Wines ⚲

Seeking a sustainable way to realise equity and meaningful transformation, Chris and Andrea Mullineux's vision came to life five years ago in this venture, owned by the employees of Mullineux & Leeu Family Wines, with profits from sales of all wines going directly to them as shareholders. It has an own sales and by-appointment tasting venue, Great Heart Wine Boutique, at Le Quartier Français in Franschhoek. Supported by Andrea, also viticulturist, Gynore Fredericks vinifies grapes sourced from select, sustainably farmed vines to the lofty standard Mullineux is known for.

★★★★☆ **Stellenbosch Cabernet Sauvignon** ② Ageworthy **20** ⑨① shows an exciting pairing of currant fruit & shrubby olive savouriness in a complex, dense yet refined wine. 10% new oak, year in 500L barrel, then 11 months in 5,000L foudre.

★★★★☆ **Franschhoek Cabernet Franc** (NEW) ⚲ From a deep, loamy slope, raised 11 months in older barrels, **21** ⑨③ well-structured & balanced for a long life, though already lithe & delicious. Well-expressed varietal character: pristine blackcurrant, grippy graphite, violet & fragrant crushed green herbs.

★★★★☆ **Elgin Pinot Noir** (NEW) ⊘ A lipsmacking, spice-laced farewell before forest floor dustiness & liquidised strawberry & raspberry flavours on delicate, elegant **22** ⑨①. High-lying vines on sandstone, grapes naturally fermented wholebunch, 6 months in only older barrels to conserve inherent freshness.

★★★★☆ **Swartland Red Blend** ⊘ ⚲ Dryland bushvine grapes styled to age good few years, tweaked blend is 82% cab & syrah, naturally fermented, half wholebunch, 18 months older oak. Modern, lavender-scented **20** ⑨① well-constructed, supple, with moreish savoury bramble & cassis fruit.

★★★★☆ **Stellenbosch Chardonnay** Highly attractive **20** ⑨⓪ followed by mouthfilling & intense yet refined **22** ⑨⓪, naturally wholebunch fermented, 6 months aged in older barrel. Complexity of apple, citrus blossom & lemongrass aided by lees ageing, which also adds to texture. Polkadraai granite soils.

★★★★ **Swartland Chenin Blanc** ② Naturally wholebunch-fermented **21** ★★★★★ ⑨⓪ is unoaked, showcasing delicate fruit & fragrance. Concentrated & full, with grapefruity acid & long salty conclusion. Notch above partly wooded **20** ⑧⑧.— WB

Location/map: Franschhoek ▪ Map grid reference: C1 ▪ WO: Stellenbosch/Swartland/Franschhoek/Elgin ▪ Est 2019 ▪ 1stB 2020 ▪ Tasting (by appt only) & sales at the Great Heart Wine Boutique, Franschhoek ▪ Closed Good Fri, Dec 25 & Jan 1 ▪ Owner(s) The employees of Mullineux & Leeu Family Wines ▪ Cellarmaster(s) Chris & Andrea Mullineux (Jan 2019) ▪ Winemaker(s) Gynore Fredericks (Jun 2020) ▪ Viticulturist(s) Andrea Mullineux (Jan 2019) ▪ 4-6t/ha 15,000cs own label 50% red 50% white ▪ IPW, WIETA ▪ PO Box 369 Riebeek-Kasteel 7307 ▪ info@greatheartwines.com ▪ www.greatheartwines.com ▪ **T +27 (0)21-569-3010**

Groenland ⚲ ♿

Owner Piet Steenkamp has been making wine on the Bottelary Hills family farm for over 20 years, mostly reds. For the new exceptional chenin, he harvested a small parcel from a heritage block on Groenland and, 'to ensure only the best wine ends up in the bottle', delivered the grapes to neighbour, friend and 'exceptional winemaker and specialist in the making of chenin', Kaapzicht's Danie Steytler, to work his magic.

Steenkamp range

★★★★☆ **Steenkamp** 🐝 Bold **18** ㉒ Cape Bordeaux repeats previous' equal cab-merlot composition & year in new oak. Full body of black fruit & pencil shavings shows considerable power yet balance & harmony too. Will reward further cellaring.

★★★★☆ **Ou Bosstok Steen** ⓃⒺⓌ 🐝 🦋 Richly impressive debut of **22** ㉙ from chenin planted 1981. Ripe vanilla & caramel flavours leavened by elderflower & lime acid. Though structured from 10 months in half new oak, it remains light-footed & bright.

Premium range

★★★★☆ **Cabernet Sauvignon** ✓ 🐝 Cassis, cedar & spice on **19** ㉙ matches previous in polish & refinement. Structured, layered & balanced, it has fine dry tannins from year in 75% new oak.

★★★★☆ **Merlot** ✓ Lithe & supple **21** ㉙ mimics last **19** ㉙ in capturing vintage quality. Tomato seam to black fruit, but succulent & lively, with cocoa nuance & long dry finish. Same ageing as Cab.

★★★★☆ **Syrah** ✓ Was 'Shiraz'. Melange of blue & black fruit, spice, violets & dry herbs on ripe, textured **18** ㉒. Plushness amplified by American oak being upped to 80%, of which 75% new, yet retains elegance & harmony. Aged year each in barrel & bottle. Improves on **17** ★★★★ ㉙.

Classic range

★★★★ **Cabernet Sauvignon** ✓ Structured yet supple **20** ㊆ improves on **19** ★★★★ ㊅. Typical cassis fruit & tealeaf note, backed by succulence & light feel despite 14.7% alc. Approachable & rewarding. Also in 1.5, 3 & 5L, as red siblings & Premium Merlot.

★★★★ **Antoinette Marié** ✓ Shiraz leads cab & merlot on **20** ㊆, unlike **19** ★★★★ ㊅ where latter held sway. Blue fruit & liquorice, plum note with svelte spiciness, rounded & fresh with good definition.

Shiraz Ⓩ ★★★★ Touch more red-berry fruity than Premium sibling, but **19** ㊃ maintains elegance while showing some of its year in seasoned oak. Food friendly. **Pinotage Rosé** ✓ ★★★ Light, bright & juicy **22** ㊁ pink dedicated to matriarch Heléne Steenkamp. Raspberry crispness & verve, balanced dry finish.

Sauvignon Blanc ✓ ★★★★ Guava tropicality vies with lemon zest on tangy, peppery **23** ㊃. Gentle structure but lively freshness makes it ideal for summer.

Landskap range

Shiraz-Merlot ✓ ★★★ Cocoa sheen to vivacious blue fruit on **22** ㊁ 70/30 blend. Light chalky grip & vanilla nuance courtesy of few months in older American oak. Good braai partner. **Chenin Blanc** ✓ ★★★ Melon, pineapple & lemon ease of **23** ㊁, unfussy & charm, unwooded for freshness. — FM

Location/map: Stellenbosch ▪ Map grid reference: B3 ▪ WO: Bottelary ▪ Est 1975 ▪ 1stB 1997 ▪ Tasting & sales Mon-Fri 10-4 Sat 10-1 ▪ Fee R45pp ▪ Closed Good Fri, Dec 25/26 & Jan 1 ▪ Cellar tours by appt ▪ Owner(s) Piet Steenkamp ▪ Winemaker(s)/viticulturist(s) Piet Steenkamp (Jan 2001) ▪ 190ha/150ha (cab, merlot, ptage, shiraz, touriga nacional, chard, chenin, sauv) ▪ 1,500t/±13,000cs own label 80% red 20% white ▪ IPW, WIETA ▪ PO Box 4 Kuils River 7579 ▪ steenkamp@groenland.co.za, wines@groenland.co.za ▪ www.groenland.co.za ▪ **T +27 (0)21-903-8203**

☐ **Groenlandberg** see Oak Valley Estate

Groot Constantia Estate Ⓟ 🍴 📷 ♿

Danie Keulder assisted here from 2009 to 2014, and it's with pleasure that the team welcome him back as winemaker at this extensive, high profile and historic estate. It's South Africa's oldest wine-producing farm, with a three-century heritage, and all concerned are aware of working in a very special space, and focused on 'translating that uniqueness into the bottle, with minimum intervention in the vineyards and cellar'. Groot Constantia is one of Cape Town's six biggest tourist attractions, visited by about 450,000 people from around the world, and much emphasis is being placed on beautifying the estate, with renovations in both restaurants as well as the wine and gift shop. In the cellar, Danie and his colleagues strive to cater for all tastes, including fine brandy, in an output that's large enough to supply one case for every visitor.

Gouverneurs Reserve range

★★★★☆ **Red** 🍷 Flamboyant & wonderfully complex Cape Bordeaux, **19** ⑨④ mostly cab & merlot, with cab franc & petit verdot, 15 months in 75% new oak. Classic cassis & blackberry, touches of liquorice, leaf & exotic spic, rich & weighty with poised acid & fine structure. Should age 10+ years, like stellar **18** ★★★★★ ⑨⑤. Also in 1.5L, as Lady.

★★★★★ **White** 🍷 Elegant Bordeaux white, sauvignon & semillon (61/29), vinified separately, 10 months in 50% new barrels. **21** ⑨⑤ luscious orchard fruit, light spice & hint of vanilla in a substantial structure, with a waxy texture & long savoury finish. A wine of great finesse that will reward the patient, like last-tasted **19** ★★★★☆ ⑨④.

Groot Constantia range

★★★★☆ **Cabernet Sauvignon** 🍷 Regal **20** ⑨③ spent 14 months in 34% new oak gaining structure to last a decade or more. Classy, fragrant blackcurrant, graphite, leather & dark chocolate, layered & broad, with pristine fruit & fine powdery tannins. Endless farewell has delicious, bright berry grip.

★★★★☆ **Merlot** 🍷 Round, velvety plums, cherries & warm spice on **20** ⑨② amply supported by supple, textured tannins & oak, 15 months, 35% new. As delectable last-tasted **18** ⑨② for keeping as many years.

★★★★☆ **Pinotage** 🍷 As all the reds, styled for long-term cellaring. A riot of dark fruit mingles with plum, chocolate & fragrant fynbos in **21** ⑨① creamy vanilla from year in 40% new barrels adds to complexity on firm, long, expansive palate, best decanted in youth.

★★★★☆ **Shiraz** 🍷 Savoury & fragrant dried herbs & cured meat mix with dark bramble & mulberry in **20** ⑨③. Intense, pure fruit is matched with smooth tannins & well-judged combo of barrel (25% new) & large vat. Perky twist of black pepper on never-ending finish.

★★★★☆ **Lady of Abundance** ⊘ 🍷 Name says it all: plentiful luscious dark fruit, in harmony with scrub & savoury spice notes, fine tannin structure & restrained oaking, just 10% new, for a juicy, satisfying mouthful. **19** ⑨⓪ is shiraz & pinotage (42/40), dash grenache for silkiness.

★★★★ **Rosé** Perfumed red plum & cherry, rosepetal & crunchy apple flavours & aromas make **23** ⑧⑥ a pink delight. Mostly sauvignon blanc & merlot end crisp & dry. **21** ⑧⑦ was last tasted.

★★★★☆ **Chardonnay** 🍷 Built-in longevity here, too, & good few years' cellaring recommended to allow **22** ⑨③ full expression. Impeccably structured, deep & long, it's rich & intense, with ripe fruit, creamy brûlée, salty & nutty notes. 30% natural ferment/10 months in 35% new oak. Decant in youth. **21** untasted.

★★★★☆ **Sauvignon Blanc** ⊘ 🍷 Excellent varietal expression in **22** ⑨② enriched with 9% unwooded semillon & extended lees ageing, resulting in complex, intense melange of tropical fruit, beeswax & freshly crushed herbs, citrusy farewell.

★★★★☆ **Grand Constance** 🍷 Perfect balance, length & depth in luscious Natural Sweet dessert wine from red & white muscat de Frontignan. Luminescent amber **18** ⑨④'s thrilling complexity includes honey, wildflower, musk, dried apricot, preserved fig & pineapple. Sweetness tempered with fine acid backbone & savoury spice from 2 years in older oak. 375 ml in exquisite 'vintage' packaging.

★★★★☆ **Cape Ruby** Full marks for typicity in vibrant, youthful **21** ⑨⓪ 'port'. Fresh dark plum compote, spice & a warming buzz of 17% alc. Balanced, bite of red cherry on the finish. 100% touriga naçional, like last-reviewed **19** ⑨⓪, old-barrelled 18 months.

Not tasted: **Méthode Cap Classique Brut Rosé**. Discontinued: **Constantia Rood**.

Cape Brandy range

★★★★☆ **VSOP Cape Brandy** 🥃 Gorgeous dried pear & ripe apricot fragrance on 8 year old potstill ⑨① from 50/50 sauvignon & pinotage. Luscious & deep, with cinnamon, caramel & nuts on the lingering velvety finish. Stylish 375 ml packaging. — WB

Location/WO: Constantia • Map: Cape Peninsula • Map grid reference: B3 • Est 1685 • 1stB 1688 • Tasting & sales daily 9-6 • Closed Good Fri & Dec 25 • Cellar tours 10-4 on the hour, every hour • Simon's Restaurant; Jonkershuis Restaurant • Tour groups • Wine & Gift shop • Conferences • Walks/hikes • Conservation area • Iziko Museum, Manor House, historic buildings • Wine club • Owner(s) Groot Constantia Trust NPC RF • Winemaker(s) Daniel Keulder (Jul 2023), with Elzaan Bosman • Vineyard manager Floricius Beukes • 170ha/±90ha (cab, merlot, ptage, pinot, shiraz, chard, muscat, sauv, sem) • 650t/450,000cs • WWF-SA

Conservation Champion ▪ Private Bag X1 Constantia 7848 ▪ enquiries@grootconstantia.co.za ▪ www.grootconstantia.co.za ▪ T +27 (0)21-794-5128

☐ **Groot Eiland** *see* Daschbosch

Groote Post Vineyards Ⓟ Ⓜ Ⓐ Ⓒ Ⓖ

Dairy farming's loss was winegrowing's gain when the Pentz family gave up their Holsten cows in 2001 to focus exclusively on the vines they'd planted a few years earlier, in the process helping put Darling on the viticultural map. The 3,000 ha home-farm, just 8 km from the Atlantic and mostly given over to threatened renosterveld, was once on the postal route, hence the name. Cooling oceanic influence makes the area ideal for sauvignon blanc, the majority variety in their consumer hit, Seasalter. Featuring a riper fruit profile and hints of salt and oak, it was joined at press time by a similarly styled chardonnay sibling, Pinch of Salt. Visit wise, conservation is combined with wine, food and activities for the whole family, for a rewarding day out.

Flagship range

★★★★☆ **The Inheritance Merlot** Ⓐ Special bottling for wineclub members, **21** ⑨⓪ is rich & ripe, with pillowy plum fruit. Graphite undertone with concentration & balance, 17 months in new oak aid silky texture & complexity. Made to last.

★★★★ **The Inheritance Pinot Noir** ⓃⒺⓌ Pretty, light & succulent debut for **22** ⑧⑦ wineclub exclusive. Red-fruited & floral delicacy & pliability shows deft handling, including year in 500L barrel.

★★★★☆ **Salt of the Earth** Tweak in **20** ⑨⓪ shiraz & cinsaut blend to 56/40, along with 15 months in oak, 50% new, a change from robust, savoury **19** ⑨② . Latter grape's vibrant cherry succulence & spice in harmony with muscle & good grip of former.

★★★★☆ **Seasalter** ⊘ Top-tier sauvignon (with 10% semillon) continues form in **22** ⑨① . Crisp, fresh, textured, citrus & salty notes but also gravel grip. Touch of oak adds palate weight not flavour. Focused & precise, impressively lengthy.

Varietal range

★★★★ **Merlot** Cocoa-dusted plum allure to **21** ⑧⑦ . Opulent & generous but balanced by a good backbone of tannin & oak, dab American, 20% new, 15 months.

★★★★☆ **Shiraz** Polished **21** ★★★★ ⑧⑨ less muscular than **20** ⑨⓪ but not lacking herb-scented blue-fruit ripeness, freshness & squeeze of tannin. Identical oaking: 15 months in new & seasoned barrels. Also in 1.5L, like Merlot.

★★★★ **Riesling** Balanced **22** ⑧⑥ maintains improved form of previous. Sugar dialled down to technically dry 6.2 g/L but in harmony with crisp limy acid. Precise, zesty citrus conclusion.

★★★★☆ **Sauvignon Blanc** ⊘ Grapefruit, grass & pepper typicity of both variety & Darling origin on **23** ★★★★ ⑧⑧ . Like stellar **22** ⑨⓪ , fresh, crisp, tangy & rewarding. Light & appealingly flinty exit.

Pinot Noir Rosé Limited Release ★★★★ Previewed **23** ⑧⑤ matches previous in appealing cherry & strawberry freshness. Light, succulent & ideal poolside in summer. Endorsed by The Vegan Society, as all wines tasted this edition. **Chenin Blanc** ★★★★ Lively quince & apple flavour on dry, unwooded **23** ⑧⑤ tank sample. Perky acid & gentle body make for pleasant anytime drink. WO W Cape. Discontinued: **Unwooded Chardonnay**, **Riesling Barrique**.

The Old Man's Blend range

★★★★ **The Old Man's Blend Red** ⊘ Crowd pleasing anytime/place wine honouring patriarch Peter Pentz. **22** ⑧⑥ near-equal merlot, cab & shiraz improves on **21** ★★★★ ⑧⑤ in fruitcake appeal backed by spice & light muscle flex from 70/30 French/American oak, none new.

The Old Man's Blend White ★★★★ Chenin portion upped to a third in ever-reliable blend with sauvignon. **23** ⑧④ granadilla mingles with flint on undemanding fresh palate. Crisp & dry to the end. WO Coastal & also in 1.5L, as Red.

Perdebee range

Not tasted: **Shiraz**.

Méthode Cap Classique range

★★★★ **Brut Rosé** Pink fizz offers raspberry & grapefruit tang that vies with creamy biscuit note from 14 months on lees. **NV** ⑧⑧'s fresh acid balances the richness, ending clean & dry with good focus. Less pinot noir than last, chardonnay up to 40%.

★★★★ **Brut** Dominance switched in latest **NV** ⑧⑥ sparkler, 61/39 pinot noir to chardonnay. Taut, piquant lemon & apple with leesy breadth from 13 months before disgorgement. Fresh, bright & juicy, ending dry.

Discontinued: **Kapokberg range.** — FM

Location: Darling ▪ Map: Durbanville, Philadelphia & Darling ▪ Map grid reference: A3 ▪ WO: Darling/Coastal/Western Cape ▪ 1stB 1999 ▪ Tasting, sales & cellar tours Mon-Sun & pub hols 10-4 ▪ Tasting fee R45/6 wines ▪ Closed Good Fri, Dec 25/26 & Jan 1 ▪ Hilda's Kitchen open for lunch Wed-Sun, booking essential ▪ Facilities for children ▪ Conferences ▪ Walks/hikes ▪ Game drives to be pre-booked; fee on request ▪ Conservation area & bird hide ▪ Wine club ▪ Owner(s) Peter & Nicholas Pentz ▪ Winemaker(s) Lukas Wentzel (Nov 2000) ▪ Viticulturist(s) Jannie de Clerk (1999) ▪ 3,000ha/100ha (cabs s/f, merlot, pinot, shiraz, chard, chenin, riesling, sauv, sem) ▪ 580t/64,000cs own label ▪ PO Box 103 Darling 7345 ▪ wine@grootepost.co.za ▪ www.grootepost.co.za ▪ **T +27 (0)22-492-2825**

Groot Parys Estate ⓠ

The 17th-century Groot Parys property on the edge of Paarl town was acquired in the early 2000s by boutique vignerons Eric Verhaak and Mariëtte Ras, and formed the base for the bottlings that helped pioneer natural winemaking locally, with then-radical wild ferments and ageing in amphora. The estate is home to parcels senior enough to be included in the Old Vine Project, and 'a tremendous amount of work' to revitalise them is paying dividends. Olifantsberg's Elizma Visser crafts the wine such that 'the grapes speak'.

Die Tweede Droom range

★★★★ **Chenin Blanc Vatgegis** ⊘ ⊛ Wild ferment, 78% in seasoned barrels, rest amphora with skin contact. Baked apple richness with ginger biscuit tones, **22** ⑧⑧ finishes zesty, fresh & long. Chenin with personality & ability to age.

★★★★ **Chenin Blanc Wellustig Vatgegis** Wild ferment in barrel, then a barrel selection for best expression of terroir. Baked apple, savoury seamed. Like sibling, **22** ⑧⑨ has palate weight & richness, fresh length & ageability.

Not tasted: **Chenin Blanc Dopkontak**, **Chenin Blanc Amfora Gegis**. In abeyance: **Pinotage**, **Chenin Blanc Spontane Gisting**. — CR

Location/map/WO: Paarl ▪ Map grid reference: E5 ▪ Est 1699 ▪ 1stB 1709 ▪ Tasting & sales by appt ▪ Owner(s) Eric Verhaak & Mariëtte Ras ▪ Winemaker(s) Elizma Visser (consultant) ▪ Viticulturist(s) Donevine Boois ▪ 81ha/22ha (ptage, ruby cab, chard, chenin, cbard) ▪ 100t 90% white 10% rosé ▪ PO Box 82 Huguenot 7645 ▪ grootparys@wam.co.za ▪ www.grootparys.co.za ▪ **T +27 (0)76-567-8082**

Groot Phesantekraal ⓠ ⑪

A former livestock and grain farm founded in the 17th century, owned by the Brink family since just before the turn of the 20th, this hospitable Durbanville estate strives to capitalise on its ocean proximity by producing 'elegant, cool-climate wines through intervening as little as possible in the natural flow'. Two concrete vessels being added to the cellar will aid this ambition while increasing capacity to cater for rising volumes.

Reserve range

★★★★☆ **1897** ⓐ Was 'Arend Brink Family Reserve' when we tasted last **18** ⑨① , a Cape Blend. Stately **21** ⑨② 100% cab, celebrates acquisition 4 generations ago. Concentrated, linear & focused yet showing freshness of cool origin, cassis succulence, iodine minerality. Minuscule 65 cases raised in a new 300L barrel.

★★★★ **Berliet** Pinotage recalling classic car owned by André Brink's late father. Supple, plush **21** ★★★★★ ⑨① first since **17** ⑧⑧. Gets modern, vibrant styling, with wholebunch/berry ferment adding elegant aromatic lift to mixed berry fruit resting on gentle, cosseting tannins. Also in 1.5L, as Cabernet.

★★★★☆ **Anna De Koning** Classy barrel-fermented **22** ⑨① chenin has generous wholesome body with 20% new-oak-spiced stone & citrus fruit, fine acid grip & lingering finish. 11 months' lees fatness & texture add to attractiveness. Durbanville WO.

★★★★☆ **Marizanne** Statement sauvignon blanc, **22** (90) is 70/30 barrel & amphora fermented, emphasising minerality, showing in flint & struck match notes, salty finish, complementing the luscious stonefruit at its centre.

Estate range

★★★★ **Cabernet Sauvignon** ⊘ (🏵) Well-judged & -weighted **21** ★★★★★ (90) shows better varietal focus than **20** (87). Satisfyingly taut & earthy, tempered by blackcurrant fruit. After 14 months in 20% new oak, tannins still sturdy, should meld with cellar time.

★★★★ **Pinotage** (🍾) More restraint in **21** (88), revealing sweetly spiced cherry & plum fruit with supple, juicy body. Fresh & vibrant, a welcome change from robust **19** (87), the last made.

★★★★ **Syrah** ⊘ Supple & ripe, with tobacco-spiced black fruit, **22** (89) offers great drinkability without sacrificing structure or form. Silky tannins burnished by judicious oaking, same regime as Cab.

★★★★ **Sauvignon Blanc** ⊘ Retains signature wild nettle aromas in **23** ★★★☆ (85), but lighter, leaner than **22** (87). Tart gooseberry fruit & tangy acid.

★★★★ **Cap Classique** From chardonnay, **21** (89) austere, with cream of tartar grip, steely acid on energetic bead. Baked apple & biscuit notes lend appeal, as does savouriness from 24 months on lees. No **20**.

....

Chenin Blanc ⊘ (🍇) ★★★★ Zesty, youthful **23** (85) still showing ferment hint of guava along with generous tropical fruit & well-judged acid. Crisp & satisfying, typically sunny chenin.

....

Cape Francolin Red (NEW) ⊘ ★★★★ Juicy, quaffable blend of syrah, pinotage, cab & petit verdot, **22** (84) fruity, no-frills braai wine. **Syrah Rosé** ⊘ ★★★★ Pale coral, sprightly **23** (84) has attractive frangipani-scented red berries, pronounced acid. Last was from pinotage. — GdB

Location: Durbanville ▪ Map: Durbanville, Philadelphia & Darling ▪ Map grid reference: D7 ▪ WO: Cape Town/Durbanville ▪ 1stB 2005 ▪ Tasting Mon-Fri 11-6 Sat/Sun 9-5 ▪ Fee R80/estate, R100/reserve ▪ Restaurant Tue-Fri 8-4.30 Sat 9-4.30 ▪ Closed Dec 25 ▪ Owner(s) André & Ronelle Brink ▪ Winemaker(s) Richard Schroeder (Nov 2020) ▪ Viticulturist(s) André Brink ▪ 65ha (cab, ptage, shiraz, chard, chenin, sauv) ▪ 41,666cs own label ▪ PO Box 8 Durbanville 7551 ▪ restaurant@phesantekraal.co.za, functions@phesantekraal.co.za, wines@phesantekraal.co.za ▪ www.grootphesantekraal.co.za ▪ **T +27 (0)21-825-0060**

☐ **Groot Tulbagh** see Tulbagh Winery

Group CDV

Cape Dutch Vignerons is a large Netherlands-owned, Somerset West-based group supplying SA wines especially to European supermarkets, packaged locally or at CDV facilities in France. The offering includes own-brand Vry Burgher, overseen by veteran Nicky Versfeld, whose namesake label is listed separately.

Vry Burgher range

Cabernet Sauvignon (🍾) ★★★ Unfussy everyday drinking. **18** (78) previews red cherry & berry fruit, ripe but leanish in effect, with a spicy finish. **Chardonnay** ★★★★ Fresher greengage, kiwi & citrus flavours in unwooded **23** (84). Light bodied & subtly leesy, pleasant summer quaffer ends with dry, pithy twist. From Swartland; last-made & still-available **20** (83) from Robertson. — MW

Location: Somerset West ▪ WO: Western Cape/Swartland ▪ Est/1stB 2006 ▪ Closed to public ▪ Owner(s) Groupe LFE South Africa ▪ Cellarmaster(s) Nicky Versfeld (consultant) ▪ 1.2m cs own label 60% red 35% white 5% rosé ▪ PO Box 88 Somerset Mall 7137 ▪ rob@groupcdv.co.za ▪ www.groupcdv.co.za ▪ **T +27 (0)21-850-0160**

Grundheim Wines

(🍾) (📷) (♿)

Six generations of Grundlings have farmed near Oudtshoorn, making them something of an institution in Klein Karoo grape/winegrowing and distilling. The latter, due to drought, was the focus for several years, but welcome recent rain will hopefully result in us having wine to taste next time.

Brandy range

Boegoe (🍾) ★★★ Buchu-infused brandy (78) with 35% matured potstill component. Chartreuse colour; minty, wild herbal character. Palate less obviously attractive - but this is intended medicinally, after all (though refreshing with the right mixer). 375 ml, as next. **Gemmer** (🍾) ★★★★ Natural ginger infusion works beautifully with the brandy ⑧③, giving it a rich, sweet charm - there's a herbal element too. Remarkably sippable. 5-year matured potstill component, 35%. **Kuipers** ⓥ ★★★ Blended brandy ⑧⓪, with 5-year-matured 45% potstill component. Deliciously idiosyncratic, with pungent pine & herbs to complement the prune & dried apricot. **Potstill 12 Year Old** ⓥ ★★★★ Characterfully individual ⑧⑤, with herbal, gingery & sherry-like interest, complexity from the oak maturation. Clean & lively, not lacking smooth refinement, with a nicely dry finish. 40% alc vs the others at 43%. These all from chenin.

Grundheim range
In abeyance: **Stasiemeester Shiraz**. — TJ

Location: Oudtshoorn ▪ Map: Klein Karoo & Garden Route ▪ Map grid reference: B4 ▪ Est/1stB 1995 ▪ Tasting & sales Mon-Fri 9-4.30 Sat by appt (please book on a Fri before 4, Elana +27 (0)83-632-7496/Ena +27 (0)63-345-7400); pub hols 10-3 (seasonal) please call ahead ▪ Fee R40pp ▪ Closed Easter Fri/Sun, Dec 25 & Jan 1 ▪ Craft gin & brandy distillery ▪ Owner(s) Danie Grundling ▪ Manager/marketer Elana Grundling ▪ 10ha (muscadel r/w, ruby cab, tinta, touriga, cbard) ▪ 10t own label ▪ PO Box 400 Oudtshoorn 6620 ▪ grundheim@ absamail.co.za ▪ www.grundheim.co.za ▪ **T +27 (0)44-272-6927**

Guardian Peak Wines   ⓥ ⑪ ◎ ⓖ

This Jean Engelbrecht venture's tag line is 'Live with wine' and its branding built on the belief that 'wine and food should be inseparable in our daily diet'. Hence the grill restaurant atop the cellar, and appetite-rousing styling by winemaker Duran Cornhill. Beside the meal service area, overlooking the Stellenbosch Mountain outcrop that inspired the winery name, is a venue where sibling Engelbrecht labels can be tasted.

★★★★ **SMG** Mainly shiraz, third mourvèdre & fresh tweak of grenache, part-wholebunch **21** ⑧⑦ has drinkability in spades. Red fruit, perfume & tobacco ex 18 months old oak, elastic tannins & floral finish. Happy everyday enjoyment with tad more style than siblings.

Shiraz ⓦ ★★★★ Everything you could want in a shiraz. **22** ⑧④ fresh & juicy with plenty of sweet black cherry fruit & meaty, savoury finish. Braai wine par excellence.

Cabernet Sauvignon ★★★ Straightforward but succulent **22** ★★★ ⑧② gives flavours of black cherry ice cream with touch of lavender at just-dry finish. **Merlot** ★★★ Mouthful of sweet ripe blackberries, **22** ⑧② follows in footsteps of previous with gentle tannins & dash of spice. **Chenin Blanc** ★★★ Unwooded **23** ⑧② shows soft yellow fruit with thread of limy citrus, shade less cheerful personality than last. **Sauvignon Blanc** ★★★ Tropical **23** ⑧② vibrates with guava, granadilla, peach & hay over clean bouncy acidity. Pop in an (optional) ice cube & summer's sorted. — CM

Location/map: Stellenbosch ▪ Map grid reference: E8 ▪ WO: Western Cape ▪ Est 1997 ▪ 1stB 1998 ▪ Tasting & sales Mon-Sun 9-5 ▪ Various tasting options - fee waived on purchase ▪ Closed Good Fri & Dec 25 ▪ Guardian Peak Grill ▪ Merchandise available ▪ Owner(s) Jean Engelbrecht ▪ Winemaker(s) Duran Cornhill (Dec 2021) ▪ ±600t/90,000cs own label 85% red 15% white ▪ IPW ▪ PO Box 473 Stellenbosch 7599 ▪ info@guardianpeak. com ▪ www.guardianpeak.com ▪ **T +27 (0)21-881-3899**

Guillaumé   ⓥ

Better news from advertising executive Johan Giliomee about his quest to produce South Africa's best artisan wine from mostly Bordeaux red varieties. After skipping 2022, he was able to secure premium grapes in harvest 2023 and bring them into the little cellar he's fitted out in a gap under his Cape Town home.

★★★★ **Cabernet Sauvignon** Dabs merlot & petit verdot, but cab is in charge. **20** ⑧⑦ back on track after leaner **19** ★★★★ ⑧⑤, no shortage of ripe fruit, dark plums & cassis, cedar spiced by 22 months in barrel, 54% new. Oak & winemaking techniques ensure a bed of firm but ripe tannin, no edges, so cellaring is also possible. Like Phenix, also in 1.5L.

★★★★ **Jong Hugenoot** ⓥ Like Phenix, a merlot-led (87%) Bordeaux red, **20** ⑧⑧ unashamedly opulent but gloriously so, red-fruited tangy exuberance lifting sweet raspberry & maraschino cherry, hint of wood spice from 22 months in older barrels. Balanced by tug of tannin on the finish.

★★★★ **Le Phenix** ⓥ Merlot (50%) dominates in **20** ★★★★☆ ⑨⓪ 4-part Bordeaux blend, showing silky plum compote, forest berries & mulberries, light tannins & smooth cinnamon spice from 22 months in older oak. **19** ⑧⑨ was mostly cabs franc & sauvignon.

Not tasted: **Rosé**. — CR

Location: Cape Town ▪ WO: Stellenbosch ▪ Est 2016 ▪ 1stB 2015 ▪ Tasting by appt only ▪ Owner(s)/winemaker(s) Johan Giliomee ▪ 1t/67cs own label 90% red 10% rosé ▪ giliomee1@icloud.com ▪ **T +27 (0)82-902-4917**

☐ **Guinea Fowl** *see* Saxenburg Wine Farm

Gun Bay Wines & Spirits

Cape Town negociant Andrew Ing's brand name was carefully chosen to sound like 'cheers!' in Mandarin, while hinting at something authentically local, the daily firing of the noon cannon over Table Bay. Asia remains in his sights, with recent new orders from there, plus Africa and the UK. An imminent social media campaign targets SA winelovers looking for 'great-value wines with quality and sustainability at the core'.

★★★★ **Shiraz** ⊘ Adds varietal pepper & spice to plummy fruit in **20** ⑧⑥, a line of acid refreshes while a tannin tug & year in old oak contribute just the right amount of structure for solo or with food. **Cabernet Sauvignon-Merlot-Cabernet Franc** (NEW) ★★★ A bold & lush blend for **21** ⑧②, main partners seasoned with just 2% cab franc. Rich & sweetly ripe dark fruit matched with glossy tannins from 12 months oaking, half new. **Sauvignon Blanc** ★★★ Nettle, asparagus & freshly squeezed lemon on **22** ⑧⓪. From cool-grown coastal grapes, their racy acid making for a vibrant mouthful. In abeyance: **Cabernet Sauvignon, Pinotage, Cabernet Sauvignon-Merlot Reserve, Smoothbore Red**. — ML

Location: Cape Town ▪ WO: Darling ▪ Est/1stB 2019 ▪ Sales Mon-Sun 8-5 ▪ Owner(s) Andrew Ing ▪ Winemaker(s) Hennie Huskisson (Cloof Wine Estate) ▪ 70% red 30% white ▪ andrew@gunbay.co.za, admin@gunbay.co.za ▪ www.gunbay.co.za ▪ **T +27 (0)72-266-8208**

☐ **Guru** *see* Hoopenburg Wines
☐ **Gustus** *see* Darling Cellars
☐ **Habata** *see* Le Grand Chasseur Estate

Hamilton Russell Vineyards ⓠ ⓞ

Expressing a single 52-ha, clay- and iron-rich monopole on the 170-ha estate in the Hemel-en-Aarde Valley, through a classically styled, ageworthy single red and a single white, which happen to be pinot noir and chardonnay as the varieties with the most beautiful expression of the site, is the focus here. And, as co-owner Anthony Hamilton Russell notes, 'there is a kind of comfort in knowing that the essence of what Hamilton Russell Vineyards does, remains unchanged. Refinements continue as always, but the aim remains the same'. Feeling a duty to nurture the estate, its people and broader valley ecology, Anthony is working with the Hemel-en-Aarde Conservancy 'to create a contiguous ring of privately conserved Cape mountain fynbos around the entire Hemel-en-Aarde. Within this ring will be conserved wetlands, biodiversity islands and corridors, managed bee-friendly forest and some renosterveld'.

★★★★☆ **Pinot Noir** ⓐ Understated, fresh & elegant, styled for long keeping. Naturally fermented **22** ⑨④ complex, unfurling layers of cherries, berries & spice in a tight tannin structure with wet stone finish. Grapes destemmed, not crushed; 36% new barrique, 10 months. In various bottle formats.

★★★★☆ **Chardonnay** ⓐ Wholebunch fermented with some indigenous yeast inoculation, **22** ⑨④ pristine apple & citrus fruit dabbed with fragrant cinnamon & warm pastry from 9 months on lees in barrel, 23% new. Rounded, packed with flavour & very long. Excellent focus, substance & harmony for ageing, like **21** ★★★★★ ⑨⑥. Also in 250ml & 1.5L. — WB

Location: Hermanus ▪ Map: Walker Bay & Bot River ▪ Map grid reference: B4 ▪ WO: Hemel-en-Aarde Valley ▪ Est 1975 ▪ 1stB 1981 ▪ Tasting & sales Mon-Fri 9-5 Sat 10-2 ▪ Closed Easter Fri/Mon, Dec 25/26 & Jan 1 ▪ Tours by appt ▪ Fynbos reserve, 2 wetlands & 2 biodiversity sites ▪ Owner(s) Anthony and Olive Hamilton Russell ▪ Winemaker(s) Emul Ross (2014) ▪ Viticulturist(s) Johan Montgomery (2005) ▪ 170ha/52ha (pinot, chard) ▪ 12,900cs own label 40% red 60% white ▪ WWF-SA Conservation Champion ▪ PO Box 158 Hermanus 7200 ▪ info@hamiltonrussellvineyards.com ▪ www.hamiltonrussellvineyards.com ▪ **T +27 (0)28-312-3595**

☐ **Hannuwa** *see* Darling Cellars
☐ **Harold's Cape Knight** *see* M'hudi Wines

Harry Hartman Wines

The circle of 'wine-obsessed' owners and friends who created this brand to share extraordinary SA bottlings, stories and personalities report 'no big changes except for growing steadily, locally and all over the world'. Accenting refinement in both wine and packaging, and aiming to offer something out of the ordinary, 'Harry' has launched Succo Marcio, a 'grappa' (untasted by us) from the husk of his five-star Somesay Syrah.

★★★★★ **Myst** (NEW) Pinot noir ex some of Elgin's highest vines. **21** (88) appealingly piquant rather than pretty, slightly earthy fynbos- & raspberry-toned fruit. Sleek & decently dry, tailored tannin frame.

★★★★☆ **Somesay** (❀) From widely sourced fruit, mostly Stellenbosch & Cederberg, nuanced, refined & **22** (94) same top league as **21** ★★★★★ (96). Restrained oaked in only older barriques & foudres, 11 months, & light-footed at 13% alc, pleasingly juxtaposes succulence, vibrancy & bone-dryness.

★★★★☆ **Coracle** (②) (❀) Bordeaux blend from Stellenbosch, **20** (91) as polished & modern as last. 40% cab & taut, coiled, for cellaring decade or more.

★★★★★ **Mosi Harry Hartman** (②) Smooth, fine & delectably dry **20** (92) Bordeaux blend, 82% cab, a collaboration with Joseph Tongai Dhafana, sommelier, owner of wine-brand Mosi Wines & a star of documentary Blind Ambition.

★★★★★ **Finn** (NEW) Harry's 'home wine', intended to enjoy fireside, beloved cat on lap. **22** (87) blend syrah, grenache & cinsault styled accordingly: bright, pepper-accented raspberry fruit on a rug of laidback tannins. WO W Cape.

★★★★★ **Church Stellenbosch** Poised **22** ★★★★★ (90) repeats **21** (89)'s yellow peach, white flower & sweet pineapple features; steps up with greater richness (from slightly higher sugar) & persistence. Same older oak, juicy acid in support.

★★★★☆ **Church Swartland** (❀) Slightly less ripe than sibling, with a fine acid, yet **22** (93) still the more sensual, with lingering fruity depths. Thyme & earth nuances add complexity, as does older oak.

★★★★★ **Summer** Sauvignon blanc from Elgin, 6 months 'stone aged' (per the label) in concrete tanks. **22** (87) delicate & cool glassful of green melon, grapefruit & lime, spirited acid, hint flintiness. — CvZ

Location: Somerset West ▪ WO: Stellenbosch/Elgin/Western Cape/Swartland ▪ Est 2019 ▪ 1stB 2020 ▪ Closed to public ▪ Wine club ▪ Owner(s) Sean Harrison, Marcel Hartman, Stan Contat, Jen Yates & Simon Garnham ▪ Winemaker(s) Consultants & collaborators ▪ 3,700cs own label 76.25% red 23.75% white ▪ info@harryhartman.com ▪ www.harryhartman.com ▪ **T +27 (0)83-928-8900**

Hartenberg Estate   (②) (🍴) (◎) (③) (⑤)

The buzzword at this highly respected Bottelary estate is 'regenerative', with extensive projects underway to farm with diversity and respect for nature. The process - before it had a name - was set in motion soon after the MacKenzie family acquired the hillside farm in 1986. Extensive indigenous conservation areas, including 65 ha of wetlands, encourage fauna populations which help control vineyard pests, while a cattle herd, introduced in 2017, substitutes for mowers in the fallow land and cover crops. In the cellar, veteran cellarmaster and CWG member Carl Schultz maintains tried-and-trusted vinification techniques, true to his mantra of 'wine doesn't like change', which translates into consistency and incremental improvement. The estate warmly welcomes visitors with a busy tasting room, restaurant and pre-packed picnic hampers.

Ultra Premium range

★★★★☆ **Gravel Hill Syrah** (❀) Apex label of exceptional line-up deserves its place. Multifaceted **19** (93) plum, rhubarb & cherry fruit plus delightful strands of pepper, tobacco & smoked meat, heady floral & fynbos scents. Dense & robust yet surprisingly approachable, polished by 18 months in 50% new barriques.

Super Premium range

★★★★☆ **The Stork** (❀) Monumental heft & muscle in **20** (93) shiraz, augmented with waves of tar & tobacco, all balanced & focused by elegant detailing, spice & vivacious black cherry & plum fruit. Deserves decade to integrate & express itself fully, as with rich & intense **19** ★★★★★ (95). Also in 1.5L.

★★★★☆ **The Mackenzie** (❀) Statuesque, muscular & immensely classy, **19** (94) is 97% cab, splash cab franc. Poised & defined, with delicate nuances of earth, iodine minerality & liquorice woven into compelling blackcurrant fruit core. 12 months in 60% new oak, 36 in bottle. **17** ★★★★★ (95) was last reviewed.

★★★★ **The Megan** Change in style & make-up in **19** ★★★★★ ⑨⑴ sees blend of 65% grenache noir with shiraz, bringing freshness & elegance to complex berry compote fruit. Refined & structured, promises good cellaring. **18** ⑧⑧ was 81% shiraz, dabs mourvèdre & grenache.

★★★★★ **The Eleanor** ⊛ Richly textured, assured flag-bearer chardonnay, **21** ⑨③ generous & nuanced citrus fruit, hints of hazelnut, zest & beeswax, tapering to long, elegant finish. Barrel ferment/11 months in barriques, 35% new. **20** untasted.

CWG Auction range

★★★★☆ **Cabernet Sauvignon** ⊛ Stunning & exclusive, **21** ★★★★★ ⑨⑤ brilliant varietal expression, with impossibly dense black fruit, earth, cocoa & iodine notes, velvet tannins. Brawny & assertive yet retaining typical nervous energy. Splash cab franc. Built to last - a collector's item. **18** ⑨③ was last tasted.

Premium range

★★★★☆ **Cabernet Sauvignon** ⊛ Classically styled **20** ⑨⓪ combines power & finesse, offering concentrated black cherry & currant fruit, typical mineral undertone & robust tannins. 18 months in 45% new oak add polish & depth. Also in 1.5L.

★★★★★ **Merlot** ⊘ ⊛ Deep, concentrated & tarry, showing the serious side of merlot, **20** ⑨⓪ vibrant black cherry & damson fruit, forest floor earthiness & full, ripe tannins. 14 months oak, 30% new.

★★★★ **Doorkeeper Shiraz** ⊘ Like previous, **21** ⑧⑥ impresses & over-delivers with its opulently ripe black fruit wrapped in ripe, powdery tannins. Full yet supple, promises rewarding early drinking with potential for few years.

★★★★ **Shiraz** ⊛ Parcels unused for Gravel Hill or Stork for this bottling, quality therefore assured, no more so than in bold & assured **20** ★★★★★ ⑨⑴. With muscles to spare, offers intense black fruit woven with subtle scrub & sweet spices. After 19 months in barrique, 25% new, tannins still robust, need time. Tops lighter **19** ⑧⑧.

★★★★ **Chardonnay** Stylish, characterful **21** ⑧⑧ has refined, complex citrus mix, hints of marmalade & zest overlaid with hazelnut, nutmeg & vanilla. Rich & wholesome, burnished by 10 months oak, 20% new.

★★★★ **Doorkeeper Chardonnay Unwooded** ⊘ Light, fresh & supple, **23** ⑧⑥ has lemon blossom scent with pear & fig fruit aromas. Satisfying everyday fare at friendly price. WO Coastal. **22** untasted.

★★★★ **Riesling** Ripe & sunny, with commendable extract & body, **21** ⑧⑥ has floral-scented tropical & citrus fruit, wafts of honey nougat nuttiness. Dry & bracingly fresh, firm, focused acid.

Doorkeeper Merlot-Malbec ★★★★ Unusual pairing, **21** ⑧⑤ is 86% merlot, shows plush red & black cherry & plum fruit, appealing savoury notes, sleek tannins. **Doorkeeper Shiraz-Mourvèdre-Grenache** ★★★★ Well-rounded, fruit-driven Rhône-style blend, **21** ⑧⑤ supple & juicy. Includes splash grenache. **Cabernet Sauvignon-Shiraz** ★★★★ Large-volume stalwart, **21** ⑧⑤ unpretentious but generous, delivers honest, ripe & bright berry-currant fruit. WO W Cape. **Sauvignon Blanc** ★★★★ Riper, more rounded fruit-acid balance in **23** ⑧⑤, offering solid, convincing tropical mix, toned-down but present herbal aromas. Occasional release: **Occasional Riesling, Riesling Noble Late Harvest**.

Tenacity range

★★★★☆ **Cabernet Sauvignon** ⓃⒺⓦ ⊛ Limited edition (92 cases) from cellar's archives, **16** ⑨③ impresses with poise, intensity & sleek integration, showing benefits of bottle ageing. Perfect now, but could go few more years. 18 months in 77% new oak.

Occasional release: **Malbec, Mourvèdre, Semillon**. — GdB

Location/map: Stellenbosch ▪ Map grid reference: C4 ▪ WO: Stellenbosch/Western Cape/Coastal ▪ Est/1stB 1978 ▪ Tasting & sales Mon–Fri 9–5 Sat 9–4 Sun 10–4 ▪ Closed Good Fri, Dec 25 & Jan 1 ▪ Tasting fee waived on purchase ▪ Cellar tours by appt ▪ Picnics & lunches 12–3 Tue–Sun (summer); lunches Wed–Sun (winter) ▪ Light snacks, charcuterie & cheese platters ▪ Facilities for children ▪ Walks/hikes ▪ Bird watching ▪ Bottelary Renosterveld Conservancy ▪ Owner(s) Hartenberg Holdings ▪ Cellarmaster(s) Carl Schultz (Nov 1993) ▪ Winemaker(s) Patrick Ngamane (Jan 2001), with Oscar Robyn (Nov 2003) ▪ Viticulturist(s) Wilhelm Joubert (May 2006) ▪ 187ha/85ha (cab, merlot, shiraz, chard, riesling, sauv) ▪ 550t/60,000cs own label 80% red 20% white ▪ IPW, WWF-SA Conservation Champion ▪ PO Box 12756 Die Boord 7613 ▪ info@hartenbergestate.com ▪ www.hartenbergestate.com ▪ **T +27 (0)21-865-2541**

Hasher Family Estate

The name derives from contracting and combining the surnames of Belgian couple Frederik Herten and Céline Haspeslagh, who acquired the old Sumaridge estate in Upper Hemel-en-Aarde Valley in 2021 and have since been expending energy and capital on their grand ambitions. The main concern has been the vineyards, with innovations directed at rejuvenation and improved quality. Ten hectares of new vines have already been planted, mostly pinot noir and chardonnay. These grapes will be the estate focus but, as two new releases witness, not exclusively, with bottlings off the estate's well-established pinotage and cabernet franc vines. Into the cellar comes the light touch of winemaker Natasha Williams (ex Bosman and with her own Lelie van Saron label), with Hannes Storm, greatly experienced in the Hemel-en-Aarde, as an advisor.

★★★★ Cyriel Cabernet Franc (NEW) Fruitcake notes & some fragrance on **22** (88), lightest herbal touch. Juicy soft ripeness (14.3% alc), understatedly firm tannic structure. Still young, will benefit from bottle age.

★★★★☆ Ernest Pinot Noir From a range of estate vineyards in **22** (92), previously just one block. Well-integrated oak, 20% new, 11 months in total, & supportive of the red & darker fruit. Elegant rather than plush styling, with structure & depth. 13.5% alc.

★★★★☆ Batrachella Pinotage (NEW) Lovely pure fruit aromas & flavours on **22** (90), but it is more than just pretty. Well structured, with tannins firmly controlled, modestly extracted, & the whole in balance. 10% new oak; 13.6% alc - somewhere between older & newer stylings of the grape. Properly dry, like all these wines. Part spontaneous ferment, as for Pinot.

★★★★ Marimist Chardonnay Toasty oak evident on youthful **22** (88), though only 20% new barrels for 70% of wine (remainder in stainless steel for freshness & pure fruit), & it should integrate over a few years. Ripe citrus flavours, with an enlivening acid vein. No **21** made.

★★★★☆ Fat Lady Sauvignon Blanc ⊘ (leaf) Forward mix of tropical & cooler blackcurrant notes on **22** ★★★★★ (95). Light-feeling & fresh at 13.5% alc, with lees contact & some old-oak influence adding weight & texture; ripe, succulent acidity nicely controls the richness. **21** (93) a touch lighter at 12.5% alc.

Not tasted: **Pinot Nouveau**. — TJ

Location: Hermanus ▪ Map: Walker Bay & Bot River ▪ Map grid reference: B4 ▪ WO: Upper Hemel-en-Aarde Valley ▪ Est 2021 ▪ 1stB 2022 ▪ Tasting Thu-Sat 10-4 ▪ Group tastings (up to 10 pax) to be booked in advance ▪ MTB trail, permit holders only ▪ Conservation area ▪ Owner(s) Herten & Haspeslagh families ▪ Winemaker(s) Natasha Williams (Jun 2022), advised by Hannes Storm (Dec 2022) ▪ Viticulturist(s) Kevin Watt (Sep 2021, consultant) ▪ 180ha/25ha (cab f, ptage, pinot, chard, sauv) ▪ 86t/5,375cs own label 50% red 50% white ▪ IPW, WWF-SA Conservation Champion ▪ info@hasherfamilyestate.co.za ▪ www.hasherfamilyestate.co.za ▪ **T +27 (0)28-008-5107**

Haskell Vineyards

This small property on the northern Helderberg slope was, until 2002, the fruit farm Dombeya, also known for its hand-woven wool products, when it was bought by American Preston Haskell IV. He hired top-ranked Rianie Strydom as GM and winemaker, and she quickly established Haskell Vineyards as a premier brand with many awards. Now a lease agreement with celebrated neighbour Rust en Vrede sees that team taking over the care of the vineyards and crafting of the Haskell ranges. The cellardoor no longer offers tastings but the wines may be purchased during office hours on weekdays. Conversion from conventional farming the past few years results in the Haskell Rosé certified organic from the 2023 vintage.

Haskell range

★★★★☆ Pillars Syrah (leaf) Smoky, seductive & supple **18** (92) shows finely judged heft & texture. Hint of almond in maraschino & baked plum fruit, elegantly laced with white pepper, nutmeg & scrub. Only three 500L barrels, one new.

★★★★☆ Haskell IV (leaf) Sublime Cape Bordeaux red, 65% cab with cab franc, merlot & petit verdot in standout **21** (94), which caps long succession of excellent releases. Plush, svelte black fruit is woven with tarry liquorice, gentle violet & leafy herbal whiffs.

★★★★☆ Haskell II (leaf) Harmonious, smooth & elegant blend of 60% shiraz & cab, **18** (94)'s hallmark rich black fruit has earthy mineral vein, hint of liquorice, lovely gloss to the ripe tannins from 22 months in 35% new small barrels.

★★★★ **Rosé** (NdA) ⊘ Pale rose, bone-dry **23** (86) from merlot has noteworthy weight & texture, dainty raspberry, shortbread & floral notes. One of estate's two certified organic wines from vintage. **22** untasted.

★★★★☆ **Anvil Chardonnay** (⊛) Poised & stately, with prominent minerality enlivening a rich texture, **22** ★★★★★ (95) ticks many boxes. Beautifully ripe citrus melange toned with bitter grapefruit & nutty highlights, elegantly spiced by year in oak, 35% new. **21** (93) also had impressive length.

Dombeya range

★★★★ **Fenix** (⊛) Now 100% cabernet, streamlined **21** (88) eschews typical 'golden triangle' power, emphasises finesse in its fine-tuned blackcurrant fruit, tar & tilled earth notes borne on leathery tannins. **20** (88) was cab-led Bordeaux blend.

★★★★ **Merlot** (⊘) Gravitas & complexity in **20** (89), firm structure, deep & rich flavours provide drinking pleasure now & for a decade. 35% new oak, year. **18, 19** untasted.

★★★★ **Boulder Road Shiraz** Loaded with ripe black fruit, **21** (87) is plump & rounded, substantial yet easygoing, with silky tannin texture, savoury accents of tobacco & tanned leather.

★★★★ **Chardonnay** Barrel-fermented **22** (86) has striking citrus fruit notes, vibrant acid & satisfying texture & weight from 11 months on lees. Fresh, youthful, showing potential to age beneficially.

★★★★ **Sauvignon Blanc** (⊘) From Elgin, Franschhoek & Stellenbosch, **22** (87) is stylish & precise, with abundant ripe, lively tropical fruit & herbaceous punch. No oak or lees contact this vintage.

Discontinued: **Lily Rosé**. — GdB

Location: Stellenbosch • WO: Stellenbosch/Western Cape • Est 2002 • 1stB 2008 • Wine sales Mon-Fri 9-5 • Closed all pub hols • 25ha/14ha (cabs s/f, merlot, shiraz, chard) • ±80t/10,000cs own label 80% red 20% white • PO Box 12766 Die Board 7613 • info@haskellvineyards.com • www.haskellvineyards.com • T +27 (0)21-881-3895

Haute Cabrière   (⊘) (⊕) (⊚) (⊛)

Remarkable consistency since the establishment by Achim and Hildegard von Arnim more than 40 years ago has seen an unwavering focus on Burgundy's most famous grapes, pinot noir and chardonnay. Latterly, under the lead of son Takuan, 'innovation and colouring outside the lines' has brought different vinification techniques, styles and price points, yet always within the tried-and-true paradigm. The newest example is the 'low in alcohol, big on taste' rosé sparkling. And a parcel of chardonnay, Burgundy clone CY 95 planted the year after the founding, is their entrée to the ranks of certified heritage vineyards via the Old Vine Project, making the winery one of only four OVP-certified chardonnay producers, and the only one in Franschhoek.

Haute Collection

★★★★☆ **Pinot Noir** ⊘ From early 1990s high-density mixed-clone parcel, back on track **21** (90) same trim body as **20** ★★★★ (88) (12% alc), more tangy berry, sweet cherry generosity & complexity, better oak integration. 10% wholebunch, 11 months oak, 50% new. Single-vineyard, as all these.

★★★★ **Chardonnay** (⊛) Off 1983 vines; fermented/aged in half-half new-old barrel & 30% amphora. **21** (89) sweet lime & Golden Delicious, fair acid tension, satin texture, pleasing savoury thread throughout.

★★★★☆ **Amphora Chardonnay** (⊛) (⊛) Same vines as sibling, this fermented/11 months in terracotta vessels, various sizes. **21** (93) compact, composed, wild honey & beeswax overlaying its restrained citrus fruit, arresting crystalline quality to its acidity, lengthy savoury conclusion.

★★★★☆ **Amphora Semillon** (⊛) Just 11% alc but satisfying & thrilling, **22** (93)'s acid effortlessly pierces lemon-quince richness, adding lift & vivacity. Inspired by GD1 Project, raising profile of Franschhoek semillon (GD1 being the original clone).

Haute Cabrière range

★★★★ **Pinot Noir Réserve** Appealing earthiness, subtle Indian spice over intense red berry fruit & thyme. **20** (88) older oak, 11 months, for earlier drinkability but will hold a few years.

★★★★ **Armin Family Réserve** Unusual but successful blend 80% syrah & pinot noir. Glacé plum & sage, **20** (87) packs plenty of flavour, spice from 18 months oak, 10% new, bright acid for solo or mealtimes.

★★★★ **Chardonnay Réserve** Very dry & light (1.5 g/L sugar, 12.5% alc) but not austere, **22** (87) lemon blossom, tangerine & charred pineapple precede long, creamy finish. 60% new oak so well-judged, it's just a kiss. Franschhoek WO, as Réserve siblings, rest W Cape.

Pinot Noir Unwooded ⊘ ★★★★ Joyful pinot, ferment begins on skins, pressed off midway-ish for completion in tank. **23** ⑧④ sage top note to red berries, crunchy acid smoothed by smidgen sugar. **Pinot Noir Rosé** ★★★★ Versatile companion at table & beyond. Pale Provençal hue yet full red-berry flavour, **23** ⑧④ decently dry & zingy, pleasingly vinous courtesy well-judged 12.5% alc. **Chardonnay Unwooded** ★★★ White peach & guava, **23** ⑧② sweet-fruited & fresh, uncomplicated & with modest 12.5% alc for satisfying alfresco sipping. **Chardonnay-Pinot Noir** ★★★★ Shows its popular appeal in soft peach & citrus flavours, gentle 12.5% alc in **23** ⑧⑤, 70/30 split ensuring nice balance between freshness & heft.

Pierre Jourdan range

★★★★ **Belle Rose** ⊘ Pinot noir flies solo in salmon-hued, raspberry-toned **NV** ⑧⑦ sparkler. Creamy, from 20 months on lees, fruity, with vibrant acid.

★★★★☆ **Blanc de Blancs** ⊛ A Cape classic sparkler from own chardonnay, carefully done. 60% of **18** ⑨④ oaked for extra weight & richness, 60 months lees-aged for autolytic complexity, minimal dosage for those who savour interplay between richness & dryness.

★★★★ **Brut** ⊘ Perennial favourite, latest **NV** ⑧⑥ reverses proportions for 75/25 pinot noir & chardonnay partnership, reflected in extra heft & some red apple character without loss of chardonnay's brightness.

★★★★ **Belle Nectar** ⊘ Pinot noir leads chardonnay in semi-sweet party-starting **NV** ⑧⑦ rosé, 18 months on lees & packed with piquant wild & sweet strawberries. Sugar well-judged so it's nectarous yet uncloying. WO W Cape, as Brut.

Tranquille ⊘ ★★★★ 60/40 pinot noir & chardonnay **NV** ⑧④ rosé a firm summer favourite. Faintest pink glow, delicate sweet strawberries & zesty raspberries, appeal upped by restrained 11.5% alc. **Tranquille Sparkle** ⊛ ★★★ Bottle-fermented & briefly aged, with the colour of sunset, **NV** ⑧② from pinot noir & chardonnay (60/40) offers tasty sweet fruit, soft dryness & slow bubbles. **Ratafia** ★★★★ Heady aperitif/ dessert from chardonnay grape juice fortified with aged brandy. **NV** ⑧⑤ shows more complexity in its sweet lime-bitter marmalade combo, almond nougat & warm honey notes. Warming 18% alc. 375 ml. — CvZ

Location/map: Franschhoek ▪ Map grid reference: C1 ▪ WO: Franschhoek/Western Cape ▪ Est 1982 ▪ 1stB 1984 ▪ Open Mon-Sun & pub hols ▪ Tasting, sales & cellar tours - refer to website for hours ▪ Private tasting/ tour to be pre-booked ▪ Restaurant ▪ Events ▪ Wine club ▪ Owner(s) Clos Cabrière (Pty) Ltd ▪ Cellarmaster(s) Takuan von Arnim (2005) ▪ Winemaker(s) Tim Hoek (2014) ▪ 30ha (pinot, chard) ▪ 40% red 60% white ▪ PO Box 245 Franschhoek 7690 ▪ info@cabriere.co.za ▪ www.cabriere.co.za ▪ **T +27 (0)21-876-8500**

Havana Hills   ⓠ

Farm manager Rudi Benn has been custodian of the vines on Havana Hills almost since inception in the late 1990s, when friends and business partners Kobus du Plessis and Nico Vermeulen's vision of a cool-climate terroir spurred them to convert 65 ha of wheatfields to vineyards in the Philadelphia area north of Cape Town. Rudi is now re-joined by Paul Engelbrecht, winemaker from 2005 to mid-2008, on the site with the 'world's most beautiful vista' of Table Mountain, Robben Island and the cooling Atlantic only 8 km away.

Kobus range

★★★★☆ **Red** ⓠ Generous oak, some American, 60% new, 2 years, easily assimilated by **18** ⑨⓪'s fruit. Still cab-driven (53%), cassis & cigarbox, with plum & leafy tomato notes from merlot & dash cab franc. Approachable now, with New World opulence in well-structured but less svelte body than previous.

★★★★ **Chardonnay** ⓠ Forthcoming & engaging **20** ⑧⑧'s lemon- & ginger-tones sit comfortably on toasty oak from 8 months in 50% new barrels. Usual bright acid refreshes, elegantly extends the finish.

Havana Hills range

★★★★ **Cabernet Sauvignon** ⓠ Solid core of cassis & plum supported by firm tannin, enlivened by bright acid. **18** ⑧⑥ well-composed & -integrated, 30% new oak, dab American, adds chocolate appeal.

★★★★ **Merlot** ⓠ Fresh plum nose & palate, decent ripe tannin grip, **18** ⑧⑥ satisfying glassful for now & few years. Same oaking as Cabernet, similar chocolate overtone.

★★★★ **Pinot Noir** ⓠ First since **15** ★★★★ ⑧⑤, **20** ⑧⑥ shows more power & structure than most SA pinots in its opacity, savoury-toned black fruit, very present tannin grip. Yet a satisfying wine & good value.

★★★★ **Shiraz** ⓠ Ripe, generous & fruity, some black pepper & savoury spice. 20% American barrels add less sweet veneer, more char. **18** ⑧⑧ easy to like, has potential to develop.

Sangiovese Ⓥ ★★★ Friendly styling for **16** ⑧②, with year in old wood. Fresher, brighter than last unoaked vintage. Equally pleasant solo or as antipasto partner. **Chardonnay-Pinot Noir** Ⓥ ★★★★ Plenty of savoury, spiced cranberry appeal in **20** ⑧④ rosé. Onion skin hue & twist of tannin from 10% pinot, dry & flavoursome, piquant farewell. **Méthode Cap Classique** Ⓥ ★★★★ Pinot noir at 75% leads **19** ⑧④ sparkler, but chardonnay's apple & lemon dominate pleasingly, notes of nut & butter from 11 months on lees. Vibrant & light (12% alc), bone-dry. **Natural Sweet** Ⓥ ★★★★ Subtle dried-hay & high-toned notes on **19** ⑧③ vine-dried sauvignon (56%) & viognier with touch of oak. Lowish 12.3% alc, sweetness well contained, tastes much drier. 375 ml. Not tasted: **Sauvignon Blanc, Sauvignon Blanc Sparkling.**

Lime Road range

Cabernet Sauvignon Rosé Ⓥ ★★★★ Quite buxom but well-balanced **20** ⑧③, soft texture & few grams sugar neatly tucked into freshening acidity, red-fruited flavours & dry finish. Not tasted: **Cabernet Sauvignon-Merlot-Cabernet Franc, Shiraz-Mourvèdre-Viognier, Sauvignon Blanc.** — CvZ
Location/WO: Philadelphia ▪ Map: Durbanville, Philadelphia & Darling ▪ Map grid reference: C5 ▪ Est 1999 ▪ 1stB 2000 ▪ Tasting, sales & cellar tours by appt only ▪ Owner(s) Xinxing Pang ▪ Winemaker(s) Paul Engelbrecht (Oct 2023) ▪ Farm manager Rudi Benn (Jan 2001) ▪ 260ha/60ha (barbera, cabs s/f, merlot, mourv, sangio, shiraz, sauv) ▪ 70,000cs own label 70% red 30% white ▪ IPW ▪ PO Box 451 Melkbosstrand 7437 ▪ sales@havanahills.co.za ▪ www.havanahills.co.za ▪ **T +27 (0)21-972-1110**

Hawksmoor at Matjieskuil   Ⓨ ⑪ ⌂ ◎

Between Paarl and Stellenbosch, Matjieskuil has been a working farm for more than 300 years. Notable among the current crops are grapes from ±23 ha of vines, some, like the chenin bottled under the Saint Anne label, sufficiently aged to qualify for the Old Vine Project's Heritage Vineyard certification. Consultants generally make small batches of wine, buying in from neighbours as needed to widen the range. Sales are typically via tasting lunches for groups like the Rolls-Royce Enthusiasts' Club. Accommodation is offered in the restored Cape Dutch werf, and riding lessons, stabling and trails at and around the equestrian centre.

Signature range

★★★★ Buurman ⊘ Cabernet from neighbour, hence 'Buurman'. **20** ⑧⑥ bold yet well-built, 15% alc & few grams sugar hidden among the blackcurrants. Fine complexity & concentration, cedar perfume from 18 months oaking on lengthy finish. Only older barrels for all unless noted.

★★★★ Cabernet Franc Ⓥ Inky depth to **18** ⑧⑦, which improves on last-tasted **15** ★★★ ⑧②. Dense black fruit & cocoa with integrated spicy wood, 14 months. Fresh & appealing, long lingering.

★★★★ Saint Botolph ⊘ Range, name & blend change from 'Cab Franc-Mourvèdre' under Limited Releases. Now shiraz & mourvèdre (60/40), **20** ⑧⑦ dark berried with savoury tones over smooth tannins, pleasing juicy mouthfeel. Combo barrels & staves. WO Coastal. No **18, 19.**

Shiraz 'Bastille' Ⓥ ★★★★ Bottling day (14 July) gives name to supple & light **18** ⑧⑤, succulent fruit & dry conclusion from 27 months in tank with oak staves. Not tasted: **Mourvèdre, Algernon Stitch, Saint Alfege, Edward Goodge.**

Limited Releases

★★★★ Cabernet Franc Ⓥ Brooding, dark-fruited **17** ⑧⑦, vivid spice & good succulence. Layered, structured & deep, a rich, balanced mouthful. Year in barrel.

★★★★ Saint Anne ⊛ Own gnarled vines produce creamy, mouthfilling yet precise & balanced **21** ⑧⑧. Bags of stonefruit & baked apple on a citrus base, nutty glacé pineapple on just-dry exit. Wholebunch natural ferment/10 months in small-oak.

★★★★ Méthode Cap Classique Now vintaged, **19** ⑧⑨ from Walker Bay chardonnay, 44 months on lees. Minuscule 184 cases showing lovely balance of citrus verve & creaminess from stirring of base wine, delightful strings of tiny bubbles.

Shiraz Ⓥ ★★★★ Light & fruity **20** ⑧④ offers plums, chocolate & a brush of oak from staves for 16 months. Fresh grip on the finish. Stellenbosch WO. **Magdalen** Ⓥ ★★★★ Rosé from cab franc, **19** ⑧⑤ shows body & breadth to gentle but lively red-berry fruit. Good concentration & dryness. Not tasted: **Mourvèdre, Triginta, Saint George.**

Classic range
Magdalen Cabernet Franc Rosé ⓥ ★★★★ Very dry salmon pink **21** ⑧⑤ shows dried rosepetal, plum & leafy notes, firm grip for food partnering. **Serliana** ⓥ ★★★ Fleeting apple & lemon notes on lean **21** ⑧② unoaked chenin. Not tasted: **Pinotage Lightly Oaked, Vanbrugh Pinotage Unoaked**. — WB

Location/map: Paarl ▪ Map grid reference: A7 ▪ WO: Paarl/Stellenbosch/Coastal/Walker Bay ▪ Est 1692 ▪ 1stB 2005 ▪ Tasting by appt 10-4 daily ▪ Fee dependent on number of people/wines tasted ▪ Sales by appt daily ▪ Specialise in group tastings (8-25 pax), option of lunch in Cape Dutch manor house, prior arrangement essential ▪ Closed Easter Fri-Sun, Dec 25/31 & Jan 1 ▪ Luxury guest house ▪ Wedding & function venue ▪ On site Equestrian Centre (silver-mistec.office@gmail.com, www.silvermistec.co.za): horse riding lessons, horse trails & events ▪ Owner(s) Brameld Haigh ▪ Winemaker(s) various ▪ Viticulturist(s) Paul Wallace (2004) ▪ Farm manager Jan Lategan ▪ ±23ha (cab f, mourv, ptage, shiraz, chenin) ▪ ±130t/1,000cs own label 65% red 25% white 10% rosé ▪ PO Box 9 Elsenburg 7607 ▪ wines@hawksmoor.co.za, reservations@hawksmoor.co.za ▪ www.hawksmoor.co.za ▪ **T +27 (0)21-884-4587**

Hazendal Wine Estate   ⓠ ⑪ ⌂ ⊚ ⑧ ⑥

German settler Christoffel Hazenwinkel was the founder in 1699, but Russian businessman Mark Voloshin, owner since 1994, and his family are the ones who've transformed the Bottelary Hills estate into a destination offering remarkable attractions 'encompassing culture, cuisine, adventure and entertainment for the entire family' and, due to open at press time, luxury lodgings. Russian ways and traditions are celebrated, but wine is central, and its making is now in the hands of Neil Strydom, also vine caregiver with Hugo Vlok.

Hazendal range
★★★★☆ **Cabernet Sauvignon** Continues **17** ⑨① 's classic styling in **18** ★★★★ ⑧⑦, supportive 30% new oak, moderate 13.5% alc & convincing black fruit. Adds herbaceous notes & tertiary leather & forest floor ones, too, plus nudge of acid suggesting drinking rather than keeping.

★★★★ **Carignan** ⓥ Bright, lively **17** ⑧⑨ ex Wellington, almost belying big (but balanced) 14.5% alc, but palate near jammy in its tastiness. Rounded, ripe tannins. Just one delightful barrel, sadly.

★★★★ **Pinotage** Welcoming as a favourite armchair & ready to enjoy, **18** ★★★★ ⑧⑤'s sweet mulberry fruit matched with tangy varietal freshness & supple tannins. Same mellow 13% alc as **17** ⑧⑥.

★★★★ **Syrah** Violet-toned **18** ★★★ ⑧⓪'s plum fruit seasoned lightly with 30% new oak, down from **17** ⑧⑧'s 50%, though acid on younger vintage more than just a counterpoint, will need monitoring if keeping. Not tasted: **Pinot Noir, Chardonnay, Chenin Blanc, Semillon-Sauvignon Blanc**. In abeyance: **Roussanne**.

Heritage range ⓝⒺⓦ
★★★★ **White Blend** ⊘ Sauvignon at 30% leads chenin, 3 others in lightly oaked **22** ⑧⑥. Forthcoming salad of citrus & tropical fruit, beautifully dry, strikes right balance of freshness & richness.

Red Blend ★★★★ Subtle high-toned aroma to medley of fruits in **19** ⑧④, 60% pinotage with cab & shiraz. Some choc-mint notes from 30% new oak, zippy acid rounded by few grams sugar. **Blanc de Noir** ★★★ Pale salmon hue, quiet red berry tones, **22** ⑧① briskly dry & fresh with satisfying vinosity at 13% alc, fleeting farewell. Undisclosed variety/ies.

Cap Classique range ⓝⒺⓦ
★★★★ **Blanc de Noir** Exceptionally pale blush on **20** ⑧⑦ from pinot noir. Effusive strawberry & red apple tones with almond & hazelnut overlay, smooth mousse & good length.

Blanc de Blanc ★★★★ Chardonnay provenance evident in lemony froth & mostly citrus flavours; faint toasty note speaks of the time spent on lees by pleasingly dry **20** ⑧⑤.

Discontinued: **Christoffel Hazenwinkel range, Hazendal 23.5 Range**. — NK, CvZ

Location/map: Stellenbosch ▪ Map grid reference: B3 ▪ WO: Stellenbosch/Wellington ▪ Est 1699 ▪ 1stB 1996 ▪ Wine tasting Tue-Sun 9-5; pub hols 8-5 ▪ Cellar tours by appt ▪ Craft vodka distillery ▪ Russian tea experience ▪ Babushka deli & picnics ▪ Pivnushka beer garden ▪ The Glasshouse ▪ Wonderdal children's edutainment centre ▪ Conferences, weddings & functions ▪ Jazz club ▪ Marvol art gallery ▪ Antique cars showroom ▪ 18 hole par 3 golf course; The Burrow driving range; Kleine Hazen adventure putting park ▪ The Homestead guesthouse ▪ The Hazendal Hotel & Spa ▪ Owner(s) Mark Voloshin ▪ Cellarmaster(s)/winemaker(s) Neil Strydom (2023) ▪ Viticulturist(s) Neil Strydom & Hugo Vlok ▪ 145ha/12ha (cab, carignan, carménère, ptage, pinot, shiraz, chard, chenin, marsanne, rouss, sauv, sem) ▪ 100t/26,000cs own label 50% red 50% white ▪ Bottelary Rd Stellenbosch 7600 ▪ bookings@hazendal.co.za ▪ www.hazendal.co.za ▪ **T +27 (0)21-903-5034**

☐ **HB Vineyards** *see* Hout Bay Vineyards
☐ **Heaven on Earth** *see* Stellar Winery
☐ **Hedgehog** *see* Orange River Cellars

Heineken Beverages

Heineken Beverages SA is the premier producer and marketer of fine wines, spirits, ciders and ready-to-drink beverages in South Africa. From its Sandton HQ, the company produces some of SA's most successful and enduring marques. The premium- and fine-wine portfolio includes the following brands: Durbanville Hills, Fleur du Cap, Nederburg, Pongrácz and Zonnebloem. Other Heineken Beverages wine labels are Autumn Harvest Crackling, Chateau Libertas, Drostdy-Hof, 4th Street, Graça, Monis (producing sherry-style wines), Overmeer, Paarl Perlé, Sedgwick's, Ship, Tassenberg, The House of JC le Roux and Two Oceans. The group's brandy labels include Commando, Flight of the Fish Eagle, Klipdrift, Olof Bergh Solera, Richelieu, Van Ryn and Viceroy. Heineken Beverages also manages The Vinoteque (www.vinoteque.co.za), an online shop for premium and well-matured wines as well as brandies, with the option of having purchases stored in perfect cellar conditions. See separate entries for most of the above brands.

Location: Sandton ▪ Closed to public ▪ Winemakers/viticulturists: see individual brand entries ▪ PO Box 184 Stellenbosch 7599 ▪ info@heineken.com ▪ www.heinekenbeverages.co.za ▪ **T +27 (0)10-226-5000**

☐ **Hendrik Lodewyk** *see* Du Preez Estate
☐ **Herbarium Collection** *see* Maanschijn
☐ **Heritage Heroes** *see* Nederburg Wines

Hermanuspietersfontein Wynkelder

With its cellar, hospitable tasting venue and Saturday market at The Village lifestyle hub, this family winery proudly honours its home-base of Hermanus, and the resort town's founding father, Hermanus Pieters, in its brand and wine names. But the core of the venture is its vineyard, which lies a little further along the coast, in the cool-climate ward of Sunday's Glen. 'Expressing a sense of the place' is the aim of winemaker/MD Wilhelm Pienaar and his team, through wines of 'balance, elegance, freshness, drinkability and longevity'.

★★★★☆ **Swartskaap** ⓐ Cab franc **19** ⑨④ thrillingly restrained, dark plum & cassis mingling harmoniously with crushed herbs, cocoa & graphite, succulent acid & powdery tannin from oaking. 24 months in barrel (as all unless noted), half new. Also in magnum. Some **18** ⑨③ available too.

★★★★☆ **Kleinboet** ⓐ Sumptuous yet balanced & focused 5-way Bordeaux blend, **19** ⑨④ deeply dark-fruited, pencil shaving & violet aromas & touch of tapenade. Supple tannin with good breadth on palate, persistent savoury finish. 51% cab, combo barrels & 6,000L foudre.

★★★★ **Skoonma** ⓐ Complex, textured & ageworthy syrah (87%) & grenache, **21** ★★★★☆ ⑨④ juicy, fresh & succulent blackberries, dark plums & cured-meat spice, unending savoury finish. Tannin structure finely honed in older oak. **16** ⑧⑧ was last tasted.

★★★★☆ **Kat Met Die Houtbeen** ⓐ Excellent expression of cool-climate sauvignon & 15% semillon, intense, deep, with perfectly judged oak, 40% new, 12 months. **22** ⑨④ pinpoint greengage, citrus & passionfruit, exotic spice & herbs to wrap up with. Some **21** ⑨④ still available.

Not tasted: **Posmeester, Bloos, Kaalvoet Meisie**. — WB

Location: Hermanus ▪ Map: Walker Bay & Bot River ▪ Map grid reference: A3 ▪ WO: Sunday's Glen ▪ Est 2005 ▪ 1stB 2006 ▪ Tasting & sales Mon-Fri 10-4 Sat 10-1; pub hols (seasonal) please call ahead ▪ Closed Easter Fri/Sun, Dec 25/26 & Jan 1 ▪ Cellar tours on request ▪ Self-catering cottages ▪ Owner(s) The Pretorius Family Trust ▪ Winemaker(s) / MD Wilhelm Pienaar (Dec 2014) ▪ Viticulturist(s) Lochner Bester (Nov 2012) ▪ 320ha/±65ha (cabs s/f, malbec, merlot, p verdot, sauv, sem) ▪ 350t/35,000cs own label 60% red 25% white 15% rosé ▪ Hemel-en-Aarde Village Suite 47 Private Bag X15 Hermanus 7200 ▪ kelder@hpf1855.co.za ▪ www.hpf1855.co.za ▪ **T +27 (0)28-316-1875**

Hermit on the Hill Wines

The recluse said to have tended vines on the Rhône's famed Hermitage slope named Pieter and Lohra de Waal's winery, and that spirit the couple are 'hiding on their hill in Cape Town's northern suburbs', crafting tiny batches only when there's 'time and inspiration' - which there was in 2023, when they bottled and disgorged the current releases. Their other stamping ground is Slovenia, where to date they've made a skin-ferment dry white, using their favoured 'low-fi', minimalistic approach. See also Mount Abora listing.

★★★★ **Syrah** ⊘ 80% Durbanville, balance Swartland grapes for **22** ⑧⑥. Expressive red berries & white pepper. Sweet fruity succulence energised by lively & refreshing tannins, which further enhance current & medium-term drinking enjoyment. 20% older oak, year. 13% alc. Last was **15**, untasted by us.

★★★★ **Méthode Cap Classique Knights In Tights** (NEW) Bubbly from unusual chardonnay & sangiovese (50/50) partnership has ripe citrus spiced with red berries & a little brioche, fine persistent bead, bone-dry finish. **20** ⑧⑨ unconventional in nature, delicious in character. Uncertified, as Syrah.— AL

Location: Cape Town ▪ Map: Durbanville, Philadelphia & Darling ▪ Map grid reference: C8 ▪ Est/1stB 2000 ▪ Tasting & sales by appt ▪ Owner(s)/cellarmaster(s) Pieter de Waal & Lohra de Waal ▪ (sangio, shiraz, chard, chenin) ▪ 10t/1,000cs own label 40% red 60% white ▪ 65 Broadway Str, Bellville 7530 ▪ pieter@dw.co.za ▪ www.hermitonthehill.co.za ▪ T +27 (0)83-357-3864

Herold Wines   ⓥ ⑪ ⌂ ⊚ ⑧ ⑤

Winemaker-viticulturist Nico Fourie follows a minimum-intervention approach on the large farm he owns with wife Maureen, high in the Outeniqua mountains on the Garden Route. The compact vineyard, whose fruit was first bottled just over 20 years ago, is exposed to mist, icy frosts and snow in winter, just the ticket for the cool-climate-loving varieties planted. An extended growing season benefits all the vines.

★★★★ **Pinot Noir** ⓥ Subdued **17** ★★★ ⑧① has a soft core with modest dark-berry fruit, soon falls away under glow of 15% alc. Best opened over next year/2. **16** ⑧⑦ was brightly sweet-fruited.

★★★★ **Pinot Noir 'Screwcap'** ⓥ Label depicts sheep, one black, reference to rebellious wine when young, redeeming itself with age, which **16** ⑧⑥ has more than done. Seductive dark cherry, undergrowth & subtle oak; texture both supple & fresh, firm & dry. **15** ★★★★ ⑧③ delightful but simpler.

★★★★ **John Segon** ⓥ Fresh, lively **16** ⑧⑦ merlot, pinotage & shiraz, none of them stands out; nor does 14% alc. No great intensity but far from trivial, with good structure of acid & tannin. Old oak.

★★★★ **Riesling** ⓥ Captures variety's vitality, mouthwatering lime & spice freshness with a peachy note in its delicious concentration. **19** ⑧⑧ balanced & refreshingly dry. **18** ★★★★ ⑧③ off-dry.

★★★★ **Sauvignon Blanc** ⓥ Green apple freshness tuned down somewhat in **19** ★★★★ ⑧⑤, acidity dialled up, still some fruit persistence thanks to sweetish finish. Not as balanced as **18** ⑧⑨.

Syrah ⓥ ★★★☆ Just a whisper of spice on full-bodied **17** ⑧③. Tannins nicely judged to highlight supple texture but finishes touch short, with bit of an alc glow. **Red Men** ⓥ ★★★★ Named for rock paintings found on estate. Harmonious shiraz, merlot & cab full of sweet berry fruit, spice & herbal tang on savoury finish. Firm but comfortable, **17** ⑧⑤ tasty now & few more years. **Pinot Noir Rosé** ⓥ ★★★ Copper-tinged **19** ⑧②, dry, zippy natural acid gives bit of lift to rather sombre fruit. **Semillon** ⓥ ★★★★ Invigorating natural freshness blends well with semillon's textured feel. Light honey, tangerine flavours, pinch oak spice add character to tasty **19** ⑧⑤. Not tasted: **Pinot Noir Reserve**, **Private Collection Pinot Noir Reserve**, **Schaam Schaap**, **Laatlammetjie Natural Sweet**. — AL

Location: George ▪ Map: Klein Karoo & Garden Route ▪ Map grid reference: C3 ▪ WO: Outeniqua ▪ Est 1999 ▪ 1stB 2003 ▪ Tasting, sales & cellar tours Mon-Sat 10-4 ▪ Fee R50, waived on purchase ▪ Closed Easter Sun & Dec 25 ▪ Light refreshments/cheese platters during opening hours ▪ Picnic baskets/farm lunches with 2 days prior notice ▪ Facilities for children ▪ Tour groups ▪ Gifts ▪ Farm produce ▪ Conferences ▪ Walks/hikes ▪ MTB ▪ Conservation area ▪ Self-catering cottages ▪ Owner(s) Nico & Maureen Fourie ▪ Winemaker(s)/viticulturist(s) Nico Fourie (Jul 2011) ▪ 324ha/8ha (cab, merlot, pinot, shiraz, chard, riesling, sauv, sem) ▪ 45t/5,400cs own label 55% red 25% white 20% rosé ▪ PO Box 10 Herold 6615 ▪ info@heroldwines.co.za ▪ www.heroldwines. co.za ▪ T +27 (0)72-833-8223/+27 (0)83-653-5770

☐ **Her Wine Collection** see Adama Wines

Hidden Valley Wines   ⓥ ⑪ ⌂ ⊚ ⑤

High on the Helderberg, in Stellenbosch's prime 'golden triangle', with vines, olive groves, cellar and tasting lounge set among lush mountain fynbos, Hidden Valley is 'leaving no stone unturned in unlocking the full potential of this multifaceted winefarm' after its recent acquisition by industrialist Patrice Motsepe. Overseen by farm manager Louis Horn, a complete technology-assisted replant has commenced, with cabernet as main focus 'to add a versatile and rewarding component' to Annalie van Dyk's restrainedly fruit-driven wines. The restaurant and tasting centre will be upgraded, and world-class experiences added 'to become a sought-after highlight on any visitor's itinerary'.

★★★★☆ **Petit Verdot** (NEW) Only 4 barrels (one new) selected after 2 years. **18** (90) sleek & svelte, quite austere black berry fruit with firm but yielding tannin support that's likely to soften with time, though enjoyable at table now.

★★★★★ **Hidden Gems** (ᗺ) Scintillating melange of cab & petit verdot (61/32), splash merlot. **19** (93) opulent & well integrated after 16-18 months in barrique, 25% new, then 2 years in bottle at cellar - the latter contributing to enhanced gravity & style.

★★★★★ **Hidden Secret** Rich, finely textured **18** (90) has powerful intensity of spicy dark-fruit with cocoa & coffee nuances. 24% tannat yet enough of partner shiraz to ensure a supple tannin frame. New small-oak upped from 25% to 35%, same 18 months as last.

★★★★ **Sauvignon Blanc** (Ⓥ) Herbaceous & leafy notes, racy acid & reductive winemaking give laser focus to **21** (86), waxy undertone courtesy six months lees contact. A half-yard off **20** (88).

★★★★ **Méthode Cap Classique Brut Rosé** (Ⓥ) Same careful handling of Brut sibling goes into this pink sparkler, **18** ★★★★★ (90) equal chardonnay & pinot noir. Gains quiet oomph, colour & balance from small dosage, creamy breadth from 2 years on lees, refreshment from acid. More interest than **17** (86).

★★★★ **Méthode Cap Classique Brut** (Ⓥ) Dry oystershell, lemon & green apple nuances on **18** ★★★★★ (90) bubbly from equal chardonnay & pinot noir. Refreshing acid, with some creamy breadth from ±2 years on lees. More promise than **17** (86).

Hidden Treasure (Ⓥ) ★★★★ Salmon hue to **22** (85) rosé, bone-dry but plenty of lipsmacking, piquant & juicy red berries, sweet spice & subtle creaminess from few months on lees. Mostly merlot, splashes cab & shiraz. Not tasted: **Merlot**. Discontinued: **Sauvignon Blanc-Viognier**. — DS

Location/map/WO: Stellenbosch ▪ Map grid reference: E8 ▪ Est/1stB 1995 ▪ Tasting & sales Mon-Sun 9-6 (summer)/9-5 (winter) ▪ Fee R100pp ▪ Open pub hols, but closed Dec 25 & Jan 1 ▪ Cellar tours by appt ▪ The Deck at Hidden Valley ▪ The Restaurant at Hidden Valley Wines ▪ Cheese/chocolate platters ▪ Picnics, to be pre-booked ▪ Tour groups by appt ▪ Boardroom & conference facilities ▪ Functions ▪ Bush Lodge luxury accommodation ▪ Nature walk ▪ Conservation area ▪ Wine club ▪ Owner(s) Patrice Motsepe ▪ Winemaker(s) Annalie van Dyk (Nov 2014) ▪ Viticulturist(s) Louis Horn (Nov 2021) = 40ha/8ha (cab, merlot, p verdot, sauv) ▪ 150t/24,000cs own label 70% red 30% white ▪ WWF-SA Conservation Champion ▪ PO Box 786136 Sandton Gauteng 2146 ▪ winetasting@hiddenvalleywines.co.za ▪ www.hiddenvalleywines.co.za ▪ **T +27 (0)21-880-2646**

Highlands Road Estate
(Ⓥ) (Ⓨ) (◎) (ᗺ) (ᗺ)

Believing that the finesse associated with Elgin wine is 'obtained in the vineyard, and a reflection of the balance between a healthy canopy, root structure and fruit-carrying capacity', Michael White and his team are tapping the extensive regional knowledge of top viticultural adviser Kevin Watt. Under his guidance a sampling project is underway to provide data on what needs to be done to gain and maintain soil health. A science-based approach is followed in the cellar, too, with winemaker Vanessa Simkiss 'trying new approaches when research information is available and adapting the vinification to produce the best possible expression of each vintage'.

★★★★ **Pinot Noir** (✓) Intense pulped berry fruit on **21** ★★★★★ (90), subtle spice from well-judged oaking, 30% new, 18 months. Light, yet with good concentration & texture. Notch up on last-tasted **18** (89).

★★★★☆ **Syrah** (✓) Excellent cool-climate expression, **20** (90) fragrant fynbos & leafy green herb intro, pepper on the finish, ripe blackberries in-between. Generous flavour & depth, plus good oak structure, 18 months, 28% new, augur well. **19** untasted.

★★★★☆ **Chardonnay** (ᗺ) Elegant & poised **22** (91) naturally fermented/year in barrel, 30% new, lovely melange of baked apple, citrus tart & white blossom, creamy texture from lees ageing, freshening lime on the finish. Made to last.

★★★★☆ **Sauvignon Blanc** (✓) Part-oaked sibling no shrinking violet. Pre-bottling sample **22** (90) vivacious citrus & apple crunch to balance creaminess from 20% oaked portion, 50% new, 18 months. Long finish with wet stone minerality for pleasurable seafood partnering.

★★★★☆ **Sauvignon Blanc White Reserve** ⓐ Excellent structure & seriousness on previewed **21** ⑨②, thrilling complexity & depth of citrus & tropical flavour overlaid with vanilla & spice. Creamy texture from ferment/18 months on lees in barrique. Styled for the long haul, like last **19** ⑨②.

★★★★☆ **Semillon** ⓐ Now bottled, **20** ⑨④ has settled & improved. Layered & finely structured in 33% new barrique, 18 months, to support fruit intensity & preserve the myriad nuances that help make the wine so attractive: apricot, honey, beeswax, honeysuckle, hay & baked apple.

★★★★☆ **Sine Cera** Harmonious, classically styled Bordeaux white from 60% sauvignon with semillon, just 18% portion aged in new oak 18 months. Tasted from barrel, **22** ⑨② reveals remarkable complexity, from baked apple to toasted nut, honeydew melon, beeswax & touches dark honey & vanilla. No **20**, **21**.

★★★★☆ **Noble Late Harvest** ⓐ Always-excellent botrytis dessert wine from sauvignon, undergoes 50% new-oak ageing in previewed **21** ⑨⓪ having been unoaked last time. Silky, with tropical fruit flavours & sweet spice, the palate is weightier yet retains a delicious grapefruit tang & freshness.

Occasional release: **Pinot Noir Rosé**. — WB

Location/map/WO: Elgin ▪ Map grid reference: C3 ▪ Est 2005 ▪ 1stB 2007 ▪ Tasting, sales & cellar tours Wed-Sun 10-4; pub hols (seasonal) please call ahead ▪ Cheese & charcuterie platters to be pre-booked ▪ Facilities for children ▪ Boule court ▪ Owner(s) Michael White ▪ Winemaker(s) Vanessa Simkiss ▪ 28ha/10ha (pinot, shiraz, chard, sauv, sem) ▪ 70t/4,500cs own label 35% red 65% white ▪ PO Box 94 Elgin 7180 ▪ info@ highlandsroadestate.co.za ▪ www.highlandsroadestate.co.za ▪ **T +27 (0)71-271-0161/+27 (0)82-652-3004/+27 (0)72-260-5566**

☐ **High Road** see The High Road

Hill & Dale Wines

Launched 21 years ago as an offshoot of Stellenzicht, this standalone label is now owned by Iwayini, the South African subsidiary of French wine company GCF. The wines maintain their Stellenbosch origin, and continue to be crafted as 'affordable options for easy enjoyment'.

Merlot ⊘ ★★★★ Oodles of blue & mulberry fruit on offer in **22** ㊶'s soft mouthful. Unoaked, it's as appealing as last. **Pinotage** ⊘ ★★★★ Showing a wild robustness, **22** ㊴ contrasts with the cranberry & raspberry juiciness of the previous vintage. No less drinking pleasure, however. **Cabernet Sauvignon-Shiraz** ⊘ ★★★★ Textured **22** ㊵ shows ample dark-fruit body & concentration, retains its all-occasions compatibility without the oak that supported previous. **Dry Rosé Merlot** ⊘ ★★★ Pomegranate-hued **23** ㉛ carries its full body through to a bone-dry finish. Quaffable young, but some leesy grip will see it through to next summer. **Chardonnay** ⊘ ★★★★ Bright & zesty **23** ㊵ shows trademark lively citrus with appealing succulence, not needing wood for lipsmacking enjoyment. **Chenin Blanc** ⊘ ★★★★ 'Versatile anytime drinking interest' we said last time, '& satisfaction well above the price tag.' Ditto in **23** ㊴, light & crisp, with lively nectarines & melons. **Sauvignon Blanc** ★★★ Tropical coconut & fleshy grapefruit flavours on **23** ㉟, its body & length given extra zip by brisk acidity. **Sparkling Brut Rosé** ⊘ ★★★★ Cheerful, light (8.8% alc) & fun, but coral-hued **NV** ㊳ also offers substance, character & lingering flavour at a modest price. Carbonated, as next. **Sparkling Brut** ★★★ Uncomplicated **NV** ㊷ has lime verve & zest in trim body, merry bubbles & modest ±11% alc for easy enjoyment. — DS

Location/WO: Stellenbosch ▪ Est 2003 ▪ 1stB 2001 ▪ Closed to public ▪ Online wine shop ▪ Owner(s) Iwayini Company (Pty) Ltd ▪ 50,000cs own label 40% red 40% white 20% rosé ▪ IPW, WIETA ▪ PO Box 104 Stellenbosch 7599 ▪ info@hillanddale.co.za ▪ www.hillanddale.co.za ▪ **T +27 (0)21-883-8988**

Hillcrest Estate ⓘ ⓘ ⓘ

Rich in visitor allures, including fishing in the old on-site quarry, the Durbanville hilltop home-farm was acquired by executives in the construction business who planted vines, and later olives, and, after a period supplying grapes on contract, made branded wine from 2002. Recently resident wine-and-vine man Arno Smith became the consultant winemaker, leasing part of the cellar space for a namesake, separately listed label which includes the Saartjie Selections. He's also adviser to farm manager Marickus Brand.

Atlantic Slopes range

★★★★ **Quarry Merlot** Shows bottle development & integration in smoothed tannins, stewed prune fruit & savoury core on **18** ㊶. Appealing oak-spice & cocoa notes from 18 months in barrel.

★★★★☆ **Hornfels** Cape Bordeaux red named for vineyard's shale soil. Now merlot led, dropping previous malbec component. Sumptuous berry compote, earthy truffle & hint of iodine minerality, **17** ⑨② mature & ready to enjoy, as Quarry.

★★★★☆ **Sauvignon Blanc** ⓥ Signature gooseberry fruit on **21** ⑨⓪, with vanilla & exotic chocolate highlights from oak, 10% new, ratcheted up from last **19** ⑨③.

Hillcrest Estate range

★★★★ **Robbenzicht** ⓥ Unpretentious merlot & cab franc blend, **20** ⑧⑥ brings best of both grapes & their 12 months in 10% new oak. Restrainedly concentrated, with ripe leathery tannins. Improves on last **18** ★★★★ ⑧③.

★★★★ **Sauvignon Blanc** ⓥ Mild-mannered, fruit-driven **22** ⑧⑦ has sweetly ripe granadilla fruit, herbal & mown grass aromas, hint of dusty pebble.

Rosé ⓥ ★★★ Easygoing **22** ⑧② from cabernet has generous berry fruit, light body, silky texture. — GdB
Location: Durbanville ▪ Map: Durbanville, Philadelphia & Darling ▪ Map grid reference: C7 ▪ WO: Cape Town ▪ Est/1stB 2002 ▪ Tasting & sales Tue-Sat 10-5 Sun 11-4 ▪ Tasting fees: estate range R50, Saartjie range R80, flagship range R70, white wine tasting R55, red wine tasting R110 ▪ Nougat & wine pairing; biltong & wine pairing ▪ Olive platter ▪ Summer pairing ▪ Closed Dec 24/25/26/31 & Jan 1 ▪ Cellar tours by appt ▪ Hillcrest Restaurant T +27 (0)21-975-2346 open Tue-Sun for b'fast & lunch; dinner Fri & Sat (kitchen close at 9) ▪ Outdoor beer garden ▪ Farm produce ▪ MTB ▪ Fishing ▪ Conservation area ▪ Wine club ▪ Owner(s) Rick Haw ▪ Winemaker(s) Arno Smith (Jan 2014, consultant) ▪ Viticulturist(s) Marickus Brand, advised by Arno Smith ▪ 25ha (cabs s/f, malbec, merlot, p verdot, sauv) ▪ 60t/±6,000cs own label 45% red 55% white ▪ Private Bag X3 Durbanville 7551 ▪ info@hillcrestfarm.co.za, sales@hillcrestfarm.co.za ▪ www.hillcrestfarm.co.za ▪ **T +27 (0)21-970-5800**

Hillock Wines   ⓥ ⑪ ⌂ ◉

Now advised by Duan Brits, former surgeon Andy Hillock with wife Penny crafts characterful small batches on their Klein Karoo grape-growing guest farm Mymering, overlooked by dramatic 'cleft' mountain Towerkop. Visitor allures include an eatery serving light meals, for which the style of wine is ideally suited.

★★★★ **Méthode Cap Classique Penelope Ann Chardonnay** Short time on bottle lees, 12 months, but **22** ⑧⑦ bubbly showing honey notes in the appley citrus scents & flavours. Elegant (12.4% alc), sparks with life, the acid balance giving lift & ageability.

Merlot ★★★ Unwooded **NV** ⑧② shows its berry & plummy fruit upfront, as intended, this is for earlier consumption, with nice freshness in the succulence. WO W Cape, as Sauvignon. **Shiraz** ★★★ Brambly berries, mixed spice & white pepper dusted from 15 months new/2nd-fill barrels, previewed **22** ⑧⓪ is supple, tannins amenable. **Blanc de Noir** ⒩ₑw ★★★ From shiraz, **22** ⑦⑨ onion skin hued, strawberry scented, a confected note throughout, the touch of sugar giving palate weight. **Sauvignon Blanc** ★★★ Gooseberries vie with meadow grass notes, which become more pronounced in the flavours. Water-white **23** ⑦⑨ trim (12% alc) & zesty. **Méthode Cap Classique Hedonist Chenin Blanc** ⒩ₑw ★★★ Rather an unusual take on sparkling chenin, with green tea, fynbos & cardamom on nose, apple & peach on palate. **22** ⑧② dry, with a bite of acid. Not tasted: **Mile High**. Discontinued: **Black Poodle Reserve Chardonnay**, **Chenin Blanc**, **Fergalicious MCC**. — CR, CvZ

Location: Ladismith ▪ Map: Klein Karoo & Garden Route ▪ Map grid reference: B6 ▪ WO: Klein Karoo/ Western Cape ▪ Est 2010 ▪ 1stB 2011 ▪ Tasting, sales & cellar tours daily 10-5; pub hols 10-3 ▪ Closed Dec 25 ▪ Light lunches 12-3 daily ▪ Tour groups ▪ Gifts ▪ Farm produce ▪ Guided hikes & vineyard tours ▪ Mountain biking ▪ 4-star guest house (sleeps 20), Mymering Estate www.mymering.com ▪ Owner(s) Andy & Penny Hillock ▪ Winemaker(s) Andy Hillock, Duan Brits (consultant) ▪ Viticulturist(s) Riaan Steyn ▪ 400ha/50ha (shiraz, chard, chenin) ▪ 24t/3,600cs own label 50% red 50% white ▪ PO Box 278 Ladismith 6655 ▪ penny@ mymering.com ▪ www.hillockwines.com, www.mymering.com ▪ **T +27 (0)28-551-1548**

☐ **Hill of Enon** see Zandvliet Wine Estate
☐ **Hills** see The Hills
☐ **Hilton Vineyards** see Richard Hilton Vineyards

Hirst Wines

Retailer Vino Pronto in central Cape Town has hipster bottlings, hidden gems and top mainstream brands in its 600-wine portfolio, plus the eponymous labels of owner and rugby enthusiast Luke Hirst, which offer quality and satisfaction at friendly prices. The Chenin and Riverhorse red are temporarily out of stock.

The Front Row range

★★★★ **Shiraz** ⓥ Confident **18** ★★★★☆ ⑨⓪ is harmonious & well structured, with depth from 27 year old vines. Evolves impressively in the glass, should do same in bottle. **14** ⑧⑦ was last tasted.— PS

Location: Cape Town ▪ WO: Olifants River ▪ Est/1stB 2013 ▪ See website for sales hours ▪ Owner(s) Luke Hirst ▪ PO Box 12066 Hout Bay 7872 ▪ lukeh@vinopronto.co.za ▪ www.vinopronto.co.za ▪ **T +27 (0)82-751-8169**

☐ **His Master's Choice** see Excelsior Vlakteplaas
☐ **Hlela Royal Wines** see House of Hlela Royal Wines
☐ **Hoeks Rivier** see Eagle's Cliff Wines-New Cape Wines
☐ **Hoendertande** see De Kleine Wijn Koöp

Hofstraat Kelder ⓥ ⑪ ⓐ

Born on Hof Street in Swartland's Malmesbury town, Wim and Karin Smit's boutique winery was later moved to a nearby smallholding named Myrtledene, where today they are partnered by Wim's sibling and chef Lawrence in an on-site café-restaurant, serving book-ahead meals inside the cellar on Friday evenings.

Renosterbos range

★★★★ **Nebbiolo** Rare-in-Cape bottling. Breedekloof-sourced **22** ⑧⑥ ups bar on **21** ★★★★ ⑧⑤ in lithe structure, spice & pure cherry brightness. Lovely textured dryness, grip & length. Tad warmth (15.5% alc) on farewell only quibble.

★★★★ **Myrtledene** Tinta (53%) holds sway in **22** ⑧⑨ blend with pinotage & shiraz. Deep, spicy & dry, with plum & graphite notes. Succulent, with grip & backbone from 9 months oak. Improves on **21** ⑧⑦.

Tinta Barocca ★★★★ Spice-dusted berries on **22** ⑧④ which improves on previous in flavour & texture. Good structure & tannin squeeze. Not tasted: **Barbera**, **Cabernet Sauvignon**, **Pinotage**, **Shiraz**.

Oesland range

Not tasted: **Cabernet Sauvignon**. — FM

Location: Malmesbury ▪ Map: Swartland ▪ Map grid reference: C7 ▪ WO: Swartland/Breedekloof ▪ Est 2002 ▪ 1stB 2003 ▪ Tasting, sales & tours by appt ▪ Dine at the cellar on Fri evenings ▪ Functions (up to 80 pax) ▪ Café Myrtledene T +27 (0)60-329-1668 open Mon-Fri 5-10 ▪ Swartland Wine & Olive Route ▪ Owner(s) Wim & Karin Smit ▪ Cellarmaster(s)/winemaker(s) Wim Smit ▪ 4t/505cs own label 100% red ▪ PO Box 1172 Malmesbury 7299 ▪ renosterbos@cornergate.com ▪ **T +27 (0)83-270-2352**

Hogan Wines

Having her wines sampled by no fewer than six Masters of Wine at a UK trade tasting is a recent highlight for boutique vigneronne Jocelyn Hogan Wilson, who launched her brand just over ten years ago and developed it into a model of careful consideration and crafting of the highest order, with an interestingly composed portfolio setting it apart. She sources from mostly home-base Stellenbosch, and in Swartland and Overberg, and though disappointed that the Polkadraai Hills cabernet block used for Divergent has been uprooted, feels its replacement, a younger Helderberg bushvine pocket, is a 'move in the right direction' (and, given the wine's maximum rating, clearly another inspired selection on her part). She's been applying regenerative practices in her source vineyards, and starting to see the benefits in the wines. 'Really exciting' is her verdict on trials with chenin blanc from a site in Banhoek, just below the parcel she uses for her chardonnay.

★★★★★ **Mirror For The Sun Cabernet Franc** ⓐ Exceptional expression of the variety. **22** ★★★★★ ⑨⑤ vivacious berries & cherries perfumed with rose & fresh green herbs. Fine tannin structure for support & texture. Seamless, balanced & long, made for the long haul, decant in youth. Helderberg grapes, naturally fermented (as all), 10 months all-older barrels, **21** ⑨③ included some new.

★★★★★ **Divergent** ⓐ Regal, precise & harmonious blend, more cab (50%) **22** ⑨⑤, with carignan (both Stellenbosch) & cinsault (Wellington), fragrant violet, wild berry, earthy fynbos & spice on nose &

flawless palate. Pure fruit in perfect harmony with 10 months older oak, long, lifted savoury finish. Last tasted was **19** ⑨⑤.

★★★★☆ **The Galvanised Chardonnay** ⓐ Back to Kaaimansgat (56%) & Banhoek grapes in textbook **22** ★★★★★ ⑨⑤. Elegant, understated lemon, lime & apple aromas & flavours, subtle older-oaking adds lightly roasted nut & pie crust nuances. Great depth & breadth on palate deserve good few years to fully unfurl. **21** ⑨③ only Banhoek fruit.

★★★★☆ **Chenin Blanc** ⓐ From Swartland grapes, wholebunch fermented/10 months older barrels, adding delicate vanilla scent to lemon blossom & hay in **22** ⑨③. Good citrus & baked apple concentration, rounded & harmonious, wet pebble note in endless farewell.

Occasional release: **The Lift**. — WB

Location: Stellenbosch ▪ WO: Stellenbosch/Coastal/Banghoek/Swartland ▪ Est 2013 ▪ 1stB 2014 ▪ Closed to public ▪ Owner(s) Jocelyn Hogan Wilson ▪ Winemaker(s) Jocelyn Hogan Wilson (Nov 2013) ▪ 1st/1,100cs own label 44% red 56% white ▪ PO Box 2226 Dennesig 7601 ▪ jocelyn@mweb.co.za ▪ www.hoganwines.co.za ▪ **T +27 (0)21-885-1275**

Holden Manz Wine Estate

Gerard Holden and Migo Manz lovingly restored and developed their boutique estate in a quiet, mountain-backed corner of Franschhoek, their care for the environment evident in, among others, the use of solar energy and natural winemaking. Bordeaux University graduate Thierry Haberer, who's worked with renowned guru Michel Rolland, runs the cellar, with Elsenburg-trained Annamarie Fourie at his side since 2015. They use own as well as brought-in grapes, overseen by viticulturist Mynhardt le Roux and consultant Marko Roux. The farm also has a luxury guest lodge and many other allures, such as the owners' highly rated collection of contemporary African art, displayed on-site and in their gallery in the town centre.

Reserve range

★★★★☆ **Cabernet Franc** ⓐ Berry-laden **20** ⑨③, wild yeast fermented in 80% new barrels, aged 2 years, for a substantial yet supple frame for mouthfilling, fynbos- & herb-scented flavours & house's generous 15% alc. Needs many years to reveal full charm.

★★★★☆ **Merlot** ⓐ Luxuriously rich **20** ⑨③ entices with bouquet & palate of black cherry, spice cake, mulberry & dark chocolate, following to lingering dusty finish. Well-knit tannins & 70% new oak, 22 months, help disguise powerful 15.5% alc. Keep decade, decant in youth. Also in 1.5L, as Cab Franc & Hiro.

★★★★☆ **Syrah** ⓐ 20% whole bunches aid the spicy, savoury & peppery nuances that offset the 15% alc boldness of **18** ⑨③. Refined, with a beautiful silky texture to the ripe black cherry & blackcurrant fruit. 70% new barrels, some larger format. Like **17** ⑨⓪, seriously made for the long haul.

★★★★ **Hiro Rosé** 80% grenache noir with cinsaut combine for striking, seriously styled Provençal pink. **22** ⑧⑧ red cherries, earth & fragrant dried herbs on full, dry palate leavened with cream from 9 months' lees stirring. Wellington & Stellenbosch grapes.

★★★★☆ **Chardonnay** ⓐ Franschhoek & Stellenbosch grapes fermented/10 months in 70% new barrels, **21** ⑨③ rounded & bountiful yet refined, with good texture & long finish lifted by cinnamon & preserved citrus nuances. Keep some for future drinking pleasure.

★★★★☆ **Chenin Blanc** ⓟ ⓐ House style lets the fruit speak, oaking minimal (here 20%), main focus texture, style & longevity. **20** ⑨④'s profile is ruby grapefruit & quince, becoming more citrus at the end. Has nervous energy, vibrates with life, promises a long future. Fruit ex Swartland & Stellenbosch.

★★★★☆ **Semillon** ⓟ Mineral & textured, the classic weight of Franschhoek semillon balanced by freshness. **21** ⑨③ understatedly offers wax, honeyed notes, hay & candied lemon peel scents & flavours. Only 25% oaked, 20% new barrel, 8 months. Like **20** ⑨④, worth cellaring.

Contemporary range

★★★★☆ **Cabernet Sauvignon** ⓐ Styled for decade's cellaring, **21** ⑨③ well-structured & -endowed with bramble, cassis, graphite, polished leather flavours & scents. Depth & richness supported by powdery tannins & firm scaffold of oak, 30% new, 23 months (as Syrah).

★★★★☆ **Syrah** ⓐ Concentrated dark berry & hedgerow fruit, cured meat spice & fragrant lavender, a sleek body with a liquorice nuance on the finish of **20** ⑨①. Good future, decant if broaching now.

★★★★ **Proprietors' Blend Red** Cab & 33% shiraz combine in **17** ★★★★★ ⑨⓪, opulent, with plum & berry fruit, leather & savoury herb finish. Structured & balanced, drinks well now, but worth saving some a few years. 15% new oak, 22 months, 15% portion barrel-fermented. More characterful than **16** ⑧⑧.

★★★★☆ **Chenin Blanc** Sibling off Stellenbosch & Wellington vines is serious, too, & seductive, with a cream texture from 20% barrel-fermented portion buoyed with lively apple, melon & pineapple fruit. **22** ⑨① delicious now & for several years.

★★★★☆ **Proprietors' Blend White** Ageworthy near-equal chenin, semillon, chardonnay & viognier from 3 regions, just 30% oaked, all older barrels, 8 months, giving curves & dried herb savouriness to **22** ⑨③. White flowers, apple, preserved lemon & warm hay perfumes on rich, integrated body.

Avant Garde range

★★★★☆ **Big G** Aptly named & seriously constructed Cape Bordeaux, 66% cab with merlot & cab franc, 30% new oak 23 months, 10% barrel-fermented. **19** ⑨① plums & mulberries, Xmas cake & tapenade nuances, good succulence & sturdy tannin structure promise longevity. Also in 1.5L.

★★★★ **Visionaire** Blend tweak sees merlot lead the 3 Bordeaux varieties in **19** ⑧⑨, 20% syrah adding to a sumptuous & complex wine with array of aromas & flavours in a sleek body with suave tannins & oak, 20% new, 24 months. Ready & will keep good few years.

★★★★ **Chardonnay** Keeping to style, expressive, showy **20** ⑧⑨'s vibrant citrus is partnered by savoury notes from year small-barrel ageing, half new. Zesty, fresh, in perfect condition. WO W Cape.
Not tasted: **Good Sport Cape Vintage**.

Modern range

★★★★ **Vernissage** Earlier drinking **20** ⑧⑧ sibling of Visionaire, with merlot, cab, syrah, cab franc aged 18 months in older oak. Rounded, fruit forward, with smooth tannins & black pepper twist.
Not tasted: **Rothko Rosé**. — WB

Location/map: Franschhoek ▪ Map grid reference: D1 ▪ WO: Franschhoek/Western Cape/Coastal ▪ Est 2010 ▪ 1stB 2005 ▪ Tasting & sales daily 10–5 ▪ Fee R30 ▪ Cellar tours by appt ▪ Franschhoek Kitchen ▪ Spa ▪ Picnic area ▪ Holden Manz Country House ▪ Owner(s) Gerard Holden & Migo Manz ▪ Winemaker(s) Thierry Haberer (Dec 2014), with Annamarie Fourie (Apr 2015) ▪ Viticulturist(s) Mynhardt le Roux (Apr 2023) & Marko Roux (Oct 2016, consultant) ▪ 20ha/16ha (cabs s/f, merlot, shiraz) ▪ 110t/13,332cs own label 50% red 26% white 23% rosé 1% port ▪ IPW ▪ PO Box 620 Franschhoek 7690 ▪ info@holdenmanz.com ▪ www.holdenmanz.com ▪ T +27 (0)21-876-2738

Holder Vineyard & Wines

Reg Holder, seasoned in some prestigious Stellenbosch cellars, established this own-label in 2017, working with viticulturist Etienne Terblanche, as well as introducing the Lautus range of de-alcoholised wines, listed separately. Stellenbosch remains his focus - it is the source of grapes and the 'dorp' (town in Afrikaans) alluded to in the name. The approach is modern, minimalistic, and understatedly and deliciously elegant.

★★★★ **Dorper Pinotage** Beautifully balanced **21** ★★★★★ ⑨② is structured but already offering much pleasure. There's a perfumed intro, pure fruit on nose & palate untrammelled by 10 months in older oak, which does, however, add to the texture. Gently firm tannins, 13.5% alc, easy acidity, genuinely dry finish. Even trumps elegant **20** ⑧⑨.

★★★★ **Dorper Chenin Blanc** At 12.7% alc, old-oaked **22** ⑧⑨ is light-feeling but without richness, with a core of sweet fruit as well as some scrubby herbal notes. Balanced, textured & dry; modest in the best sense & eminently drinkable in youth, though no hurry.— TJ

Location/WO: Stellenbosch ▪ Est/1stB 2017 ▪ Tasting only by prior arrangement ▪ Closed all pub hols ▪ Owner(s) Holder Vineyard & Wines (Pty) Ltd ▪ Winemaker(s) Reg Holder (2018) ▪ 1st ▪ reg@holderwines.co.za ▪ T +27 (0)83-678-9598

☐ **Holism** *see* Swartberg Wingerde
☐ **Homestead Series** *see* Bellingham

Hoopenburg Wines

A north Stellenbosch stalwart for more than three decades, guided by general manager Anton Beukes for almost half that time, the Schmitz family estate has welcomed a new winemaker, Gizelle Coetzee, bringing

fresh plans for 'making smaller batches of interesting cultivars, as well as applying new techniques to reproduce what we taste in the vineyard in the bottle'.

Integer range

★★★★ **Cabernet Sauvignon-Cabernet Franc-Petit Verdot-Merlot** ⊘ Dense core of dark fruit an equal match for substantial oak (60% new, 18 months), in **18** ★★★★★ ⑨⓪ from similar blending partners to **17** ⑧⑨, matured in 2nd-fill barrels. Powerful, flexing muscular tannins & 15% alc, deserves cellar time.

★★★★ **Syrah-Mourvèdre-Carignan** More integrated in **19** ⑧⑨, with near-equal blend partners (39/31/30), 18 months in older oak. Balanced, juicy & savoury, firm, supple structure & respectable dry finish. Still youthful, potential to improve.

★★★★ **Chardonnay** Plump & succulent stonefruit & pear in **22** ⑧⑦. Richer & more curvaceous than sibling, but less verve than previous, shorter oaking (year, older barrels) providing the creamy base. Ready to entertain. WO Stellenbosch.

★★★★ **Méthode Cap Classique Brut** ⊘ Latest **NV** ⑧⑦ similar style to previous, also from chardonnay. Dry, but plenty of baked apple & almond flavour; subtle creaminess despite only 12 months on lees. Versatile, balanced & ready to celebrate. WO W Cape.

Méthode Cap Classique Rosé ⊘ ★★★★ Another disgorgement of **20** ⑧④ sparkler from 3% pinot & chardonnay. Tad smoother from extra lees time, but more savoury, bone-dry styling make this a definite canapés partner rather than solo sipper. Occasional release: **Pinot Noir**, **Late Harvest**.

Hoopenburg Bush Vine range

★★★★ **Cabernet Sauvignon** ⊘ Ticks the varietal boxes with cassis & cedar/cigarbox notes in more structured **19** ⑧⑧. Quite fresh & elegant, most poised & complete of these reds, all with 18 months in oak, this 20% new, well integrated.

★★★★ **Pinot Noir** ⊘ Similar svelte texture, savoury-earthy notes with some polished leather in **19** ⑧⑦. Lifted freshness, with respectable structure & ageing in combo barrel & FlexCube well integrated. Satisfying drinking. WO Stellenbosch, as the other still wines.

Merlot ★★★★ Piquant red cherry fruit reined in by firmer acid & tannins in **19** ⑧③. Partially tempered by old-barrel ageing, but needing a few years to harmonise. **Shiraz** ★★★★ More accessible in riper **20** ⑧⑤. Pliant structure & less oak influence, with ample spicy dark fruit for flavoursome engagement, albeit shade off peppery **19** ★★★★ ⑧⑥. **Chardonnay** ★★★★ Ripe, pear seamed with citrus nuance in unoaked **22** ⑧④. Clean & balanced for attractive easy drinking, solo or with a light meal. **Blanc de Noir Sparkling** ★★★ Sunset pink, light-hearted (11 % alc) picnic bubbles from cabernet, latest dry carbonated **NV** ⑧⓪ showing both savoury & fruity/strawberry notes. Not tasted: **Pinotage**, **Rosé**, **Chenin Blanc**, **Sauvignon Blanc**.

Guru range

Merlot ★★★ Ample red berry flavours restrained in **21** ⑦⑨ by firmer acid & heavily spiced oaking (chips, as for next), that also impart some tannic grip. A BBQ partner. **Cabernet Sauvignon-Merlot** ★★★ Hearty 75/25 duo in **20** ⑧⓪, ripe mixed-berry fruit & a toasty infusion from oak. Chunky & cheerful, good for chilly nights & hearty fare. **Sauvignon Blanc** ★★★ Zesty acidity cuts through riper tropical, almond & dried grass flavours in **22** ⑦⑨. Both plump & tart, better with food. — MW

Location/map: Stellenbosch ▪ Map grid reference: E1 ▪ WO: Coastal/Stellenbosch/Western Cape ▪ Est/1stB 1992 ▪ Tasting, sales & cellar tours Mon-Fri 9-4; pub hols (seasonal) please call ahead ▪ Fee R30/6-8 wines ▪ BYO picnic ▪ Conferences ▪ Guest house T +27 (0)21-884-4534 ▪ Owner(s) Gregor Schmitz ▪ GM Anton Beukes (Aug 2009) ▪ Winemaker(s) Gizelle Coetzee (Jan 2023) ▪ Viticulturist(s) Gert Snyders ▪ 70ha/30ha (cab, merlot, ptage, pinot, shiraz, chard, chenin) ▪ 180t/40,000cs own label 80% red 18% white 2% MCC ▪ PO Box 1233 Stellenbosch 7599 ▪ info@hoopenburg.com ▪ www.hoopenburgwines.co.za ▪ **T +27 (0)21-884-4221**

☐ **Hope** see Breëland Winery - Marais Family Wines
☐ **Horsemen** see The Horsemen

House of BNG

The 'ambassador and leading lady' of this young sparkling-wine specialist brand is media personality, actress and businesswoman Bonang Matheba, whose exuberant style and sobriquet ('Queen B') inspired the tone and luxurious 'honeycomb' packaging of the line-up, made by consultant and leading fizz exponent Jeff

Grier. Since last in the guide, the trio of cap classiques has gained a pair of demi-sec perlé siblings, cleverly presented in 250-ml cans and matching 'purse' in which to carry multiple serves with style.

★★★★ **Méthode Cap Classique Brut Rosé** Gloriously presented (as all), pale onion skin **NV** ⑧⑦ spent 18 months on lees adding toasty & savoury notes to red appleskin flavour from roughly equal pinot noir, chardonnay & pinotage, tweak of meunier. Crisp acid balances mere touch of sugar to delicious effect.

★★★★ **Méthode Cap Classique Brut** Classic chardonnay entry of yellow apples & flowers on **NV** ⑧⑧, alongside marzipan creaminess acquired over 18 months on lees. 30% pinot noir bolsters zesty overall feel, thimbleful sugar adds hint of toffee sweetness at the end.

★★★★☆ **Méthode Cap Classique Prestige Reserve Brut** Lots of elegance & interest on **13** ⑨⓪, ripe peach & apple with creamy, nutty texture & zingy citrus finale. House's luxe just-dry styling, but vibrancy too, for a very satisfying bubbly from mostly chardonnay, dabs pinot noir & meunier, 6 years on lees.

. . . .

Nectar Blanc ☺ ★★★ Superior festival fizz in a can, **NV** ⑧② surprises & delights with plenty of classic chardonnay flavours, a goodly dollop of sugar nicely offset by lively acid.

. . . .

Nectar Rosé 🆕 ★★★ Semi-sweet NV ⑦⑨ lightly sparkling pink wine packaged in sleek cans for enjoyable everyday drinking. Carbonated, as sibling, from pinot noir, red fruit & florals. — CM

Location/WO: Stellenbosch ▪ Est 2019 ▪ 1stB 2018 ▪ Closed to public ▪ Cellarmaster(s) Julian Brewer (consultant) ▪ Winemaker(s) Jeff Grier (consultant) ▪ 50,000cs own label MCC & sparkling wine ▪ sparkle@ houseofbng.com ▪ www.houseofbng.com

☐ **House of GM & Ahrens** *see* The House of GM&AHRENS

House of Hier

Here Arendsig owner and small-batch winemaker Lourens van der Westhuizen collaborates with IT entrepreneur Jaco Pienaar on premium wines from special sites they find and that fit their philosophy, which encompasses rigorous grape selection, staggered picking, low yields, spontaneous ferments and limited quantities, among others. Crafting happens at Arendsig in Bonnievale and, while the current parcels are local and elsewhere in Robertson Valley, wider sourcing is a possibility as the portfolio grows.

★★★★ **Cinsaut** Ⓥ On-trend styling for **21** ⑧⑧: fragrant raspberry, strawberry, earth & pot-pourri; lovely fresh acid, beautifully austere dryness, satisfying vinosity at just 11% alc. 25% aged in old 300L barrel, rest concrete 'egg', 9 months.

★★★★ **Hadassah Pinot Noir** Ⓥ Was just 'Pinot Noir' when we tasted **21** ⑧⑥. Berry, cherry & wax aromas, a quiet bouquet relative to siblings' but palate more expressive, black cherry imparts sweet ripeness to near bone-dry finish. Single-vineyard, as Chenin; wholeberry fermented in concrete 'egg', 9 months old barrique.

★★★★☆ **Chenin Blanc** Ⓥ At 14.5% alc, **20** ⑨① broad shouldered with personality to match. Crams ripe peach & nectarine, tangy apple & lemon into the bouquet, along with savoury fynbos & wet stone; packs leesy complexity & dried-fruit piquancy onto the palate. From 28 year old vines, stage picked, 10 months in old oak. WO Robertson.— ML, CvZ

Location: Robertson ▪ WO: Bonnievale/Robertson ▪ Est 2021 ▪ 1stB 2020 ▪ Tasting by appt at Arendsig, or in Cape Town ▪ Online sales; available at selected establishments ▪ Owner(s) Jaco Pienaar ▪ Winemaker(s) Lourens van der Westhuizen (Arendsig) ▪ 657cs own label 70% red 30% white ▪ info@hier.co.za ▪ www.hier. co.za ▪ **T +27 (0)81-048-2153**

House of Hlela Royal Wines

Based in the Netherlands, Gugulethu Hlela with husband Igor Milovanovic owns the wine business named House of Hlela Royal Wines, which represents the wine brands Delisa and recently launched Bukhosi ('Royalty') in Europe. Gugulethu's aunt, princess Ntombifuthi Zulu, owns the two brands, having lived overseas for decades and acquired a taste and love for wine. Her highness and daughter Thandiwe Ngubane also run SA's first winefarm owned by royal Zulu women, Groot Droom, situated in the Paarl area. On the estate are parcels of old vines, including chenin blanc planted in 1976 and 1983, that are Old Vine Project certified.

Bukhosi Royal Wines

Pinotage ★★★★ Unfettered by oak, **21** ⑧⑤ fresh, youthful mulberry & brambleberry fruit, easy to drink & vivacious even at 14.5% alc, enlivening aloe tweak on the finish for interest. **Chenin Blanc** ⊛ ★★★★ Satisfying varietal flavours from vines planted in 1976, supported by 10% older-oak ageing. **21** ⑧③ a little shy but decently dry & vinous, may gain more complexity with time. Fairtrade certified, as Pinotage. Not tasted: **Sauvignon Blanc**. — NK, CvZ

Location: Paarl ▪ WO: Western Cape ▪ Owner(s) Ntombifuthi Zulu ▪ Winemaker(s) consultants ▪ Groot Droom Royal Farm, Vryguns Road, Windmeul, Paarl ▪ info@hlelaroyalwines.com ▪ www.hlelaroyalwines.com ▪ T +31-85-203-1333

☐ **House of JC le Roux** *see* The House of JC le Roux
☐ **House of Krone** *see* Krone

House of Mandela

Celebrating 'the life and spirit of a great African soul', the late SA statesman and Nobel laureate Nelson Mandela, this portfolio is owned by daughter and businesswoman Makaziwe Mandela, with her daughter Tukwini. Together, they have plans to 'diversify the portfolio and be truly a holistic beverage brand'. This, in the near future, will see the inclusion of spirits and beer. The wines, meanwhile, are made with Durbanville's D'Aria Winery and available for tastings there by appointment.

King Vusani range
★★★★ **Cabernet Sauvignon** ② Concentrated black fruit with oak spices on **18** ⑧⑦, also tarry liquorice after 13 months in 90% new barrels. Full & forceful, with grainy tannin structure, suggesting cellaring. **Shiraz** ② ★★★★ Opulent, as befits nobility, but **17** ⑧⑤ perhaps touch too sweet & clove spiced. Less balanced, structured than **16** ★★★★ ⑧⑥, ready now.

Phumla range
Pinotage ② ★★★★ Wild savoury aromas on **18** ⑧④, which had 30% new oak vs 20% last time. Bold, full bodied, with intense black fruit. **Chenin Blanc** ② ★★★ Unoaked this vintage, **20** ⑦⑧ is unassuming, light bodied & easy to drink (noting the high 14.8% alc).

Thembu range
Cabernet Sauvignon ⊘ ★★★★ From Citrusdal vines, improved **21** ⑧④ has black fruit, decent heft & ripe tannins, buffed 13 months in oak. **Shiraz** ⊘ ★★★★ Appealing scrub & floral notes introduce variety-true **21** ⑧⑤, showing black cherry fruit, gentle tannins. **Sauvignon Blanc** ② ★★★ Light & undemanding, **22** ⑧② has a dusty-grassy centre & pleasing gooseberry tang from mix of cooler areas, Durbanville & Lutzville. — GdB

Location: Durbanville ▪ Map: Durbanville, Philadelphia & Darling ▪ Map grid reference: C7 ▪ WO: Western Cape ▪ Est 2009 ▪ Tasting by appt ▪ Owner(s) Makaziwe & Tukwini Mandela ▪ Winemaker(s)/viticulturist(s) Elizabeth Meyer (D'Aria Winery) ▪ 80% red 20% white ▪ capewinematch.portia@gmail.com ▪ www.thehouseofmandela.com

Hout Bay Vineyards

Having hewn vineyard terraces from a Hout Bay mountainside and planted ±14,000 vines, fashioned a boutique cellar from stone, and taught themselves about winegrowing from scratch, Peter and Catharine Roeloffze accurately describe their venture as 'completely hands-on'. They farm 'in the most practical, eco-friendly manner' and craft 'in the noblest of ways', unusually using acacia wood for some of the varieties.
★★★★ **Shiraz** Touch rustic **21** ★★★★ ⑧⑤ has barnyard aromas, misses spicy red fruit of **20** ⑧⑧; both show fair amount of the 18 months in oak, 50% new in latest, with serious dry tannin & piquant acid.
★★★★ **Petrus** Mostly grenache noir in **19** ⑧⑦, plus mourvèdre & 35% shiraz (80% in **18** ⑧⑧, which also had dab viognier). Spicily perfumed, richly fruited, firmly built & dry. Aged in oak & acacia, half new.
★★★★ **Klasiek by Catharine** Chardonnay cap classique bubbly with splashes pinots noir & meunier, bone-dry, balanced & flavourful in **20** ⑧⑧, freshness balancing the richness of the fruit. 30 months on lees.
★★★★ **Black Swan Cape Vintage** More 'Late Bottled Vintage' in style & gestation, having spent decade in old oak. **13** ⑧⑥'s fresh fruitcake depth, brisk clean finish improve on **12** ★★★★ ⑧⑤. Both from equal parts of 5 port grapes & WO W Cape; very similar ±95 g/L sugar, 19% alc.

Merlot ★★★★ Friendly **21** (83) loses earthiness of previous, retains pleasing fruitcake character. Dry tannin but enough fruit to balance it & 13.7% alc. 18 months old oak. **Blush** (Ⓥ) ★★★★ Dry rosé from chardonnay plus pinots meunier & noir. Aromatic **22** (83) preview combines charm with an austere touch; balanced, fresh & light (11.3% alc). **Rosé** (Ⓥ) ★★★★ Pre-bottling, elegant **22** (85) partridge eye hued, but not pale; like **21** ★★★★ (86), from Wellington grenache, whose aromas are more complex from ferment/5 months in new acacia barrel, also giving grip. **Sauvignon Blanc** (Ⓥ) ★★★★ Flavourful **22** (84) tank sample bursts out of the blocks with fresh tropicality, ends with racy lemon freshness. — DS

Location: Hout Bay ▪ Map: Cape Peninsula ▪ Map grid reference: A3 ▪ WO: Hout Bay/Western Cape ▪ Est 2001 ▪ 1stB 2004 ▪ Tasting, sales & cellar tours by appt ▪ Fee R100pp (min R500) ▪ Facilities for children ▪ Owner(s) Peter & Catharine Roeloffze ▪ Cellarmaster(s)/winemaker(s)/viticulturist(s) Peter & Catharine Roeloffze (both Jan 2004) ▪ 4ha (merlot, pinots meunier/noir, shiraz, chard, sauv, viog) ▪ 28.7t/4,100cs own label 49% red 19% white 11% rosé 21% MCC ▪ Other brand: HB Vineyards ▪ PO Box 26659 Hout Bay 7872 ▪ cathy@4mb.co.za ▪ www.houtbayvineyards.co.za ▪ **T +27 (0)83-790-3303**

Hughes Family Wines ⓥ

Argentina-born engineer-turned-vigneron Billy Hughes and daughter Kiki own the certified-organic Swartland home-farm and boutique brand, and now also craft the wines in the underground cellar along low-intervention lines to 'express the full sense of the place'. They're looking to further improve quality through, inter alia, trials with various ferments, and creative responses to unusual rain and weather patterns. The vineyard will see added biodynamic practices and alternative approaches to harvesting times.

Nativo range
★★★★☆ **Red Blend** (Ⓥ) (☺) Lovely brightness to creative & involving **18** (90), mourvèdre (38%), shiraz, grenache noir, tempranillo & pinotage. Fresh wild berries, earthy spice with just-right tannin grip. Also still available, **17** (90) same varieties, rich dark fruit & earthy touch, firm tannin grip.

★★★★☆ **White Blend** (☺) (🐝) Blossoms & honey on consistently excellent 'Swartland white', again chenin-led (52%) in **22** (93) with grenache blanc (32%), viognier & roussanne, appetisingly bone-dry. All fermented separately in older barrels, 'eggs' & tanks; half matured 10 months in barrel.

Nativo Varietal range
★★★★☆ **Tempranillo** (☺) Violet bouquet, blackberry palate & chalky tannins, **21** (91) also gently refreshing & decently dry. As all in range, combo tank, barrel, 'egg' for ferment, then 10 months older oak.

★★★★ **The Bees** (☺) Previewed **22** (88) has 10% dash of racy, tropical chenin added to classic peachy viognier. Maturation perfectly preserves elegant freshness (12.5 alc), supports gossamer texture & weight.

★★★★☆ **Amarillo** (☺) (🐝) Peach melba & honey melon, to which are added nuts & honey from prolonged (10-12 days) skin contact. Exciting contrast brisk stony acid, chalky texture & bracing dryness. Just 11% alc in **21** (93) for lunchtime sipping. From chenin, roussanne & grenache blanc.

★★★★☆ **Field Blend** (☺) Chenin, grenache blanc & roussanne vinified separately, half unoaked in pre-bottling sample of **22** (90) to showcase melon & quince fruit, penetrating acid & bone-dry finish, all in pinpoint balance.

Not tasted: **Mourvèdre, Pinotage, Shiraz, Zero, The Birds**. — ML

Location: Malmesbury ▪ Map/WO: Swartland ▪ Map grid reference: C6 ▪ Est 2000 ▪ 1stB 2004 ▪ Tasting by appt ▪ Owner(s) Billy & Kiki Hughes ▪ Cellarmaster(s) Billy Hughes ▪ Winemaker(s) Kiki & Billy Hughes ▪ Viticulturist(s) Kevin Watt (Jul 2005, consultant) ▪ 52ha/27ha (grenache n/b, mourv, ptage, tempranillo, shiraz, chenin, rouss, viog) ▪ 180t total 25t/3,600cs own label 50% red 50% white ▪ Organic & Biodynamic PGS ▪ 6 Riverstone Rd, Tierboskloof, Hout Bay 7806 ▪ billy@nativo.co.za ▪ www.nativo.co.za ▪ **T +27 (0)83-270-2457**

☐ **Huis Te Merwede** see Merwida Wines (Huis Te Merwede)

Huis van Chevallerie ⓥ ⓒ

Despite selling her Paardeberg land a while back, and bringing in some grapes from beyond Swartland for the current releases, Christa von La Chevallerie and her naturally crafted boutique brand remain firmly rooted in the region, and are based in the town at its heart, Riebeek-Kasteel. She's immensely gratified that, just as she thought she'd have to scale back production of her beloved bubbles, they sold out faster than World Cup rugby tickets. While she's 'taking a good look' at how to raise both her sparklings and stillwines to the next level, perhaps the five-star rating this edition for her chenin will bring joy and food for thought, while she contemplates the future in the smallgame-frequented town garden she calls 'my new farm'.

★★★★ **Pegasus Old Vine Pinotage** Translucent, with light 11% alc, yet **22** ⑧⑥ not at all trivial. Satisfying dry persistence, supple almost silky tannins, refined fruit. Clarity of expression & precision, too.

★★★★ **Klein Bakoor Old Vine Pinotage Rosé** Similar tawny hue in **22** ⑧⑦ but less spice because no barrels are new; dry, savoury, noticeable tannin tug. House's modest alc (11.5%). 'Ready for anything: braai, pizza, hamburgers, biltong or just block of ice.'

★★★★★ **Bergskilpad Old Vine Chenin Blanc** ⊛ Same Kasteelberg & Paardeberg origin yet **22** ★★★★★ ⑨⑤'s mango & yellow peach subtle departures from usual pear & white peach. Old vines do exert on palate with all expected substance, weight & complexity. Hallmark lipsmacking finish. Older oak, as all. No **21**; last tasted was **19** ⑨④.

★★★★ **Grenache Blanc** From Piekenierskloof, like last, **22** ⑧⑧ as well-balanced, pineapple & floral tones touch more expressive, bright acid that seams the rounded richness from 10 months oak (as all, unless noted) more thrilling.

★★★★☆ **Spookberg Old Vine Palomino** Winemaker's signature low alc & near-austere dryness shine in **22** ⑨②, where aromatic bay leaf, almond & cream notes abound. Shade broader than last, equally captivating. Half of the Piekenierskloof fruit bunch-pressed, few days on skin before wild (as all) ferment.

★★★★ **Springhaas Vin Blanc** Verdelho leads chenin & viura (26/28) in lively combo. **22** ⑧⑧ whiffs white peach & pear, satisfying fruity mid-palate, finish seasoned with hint of salt. WO Coastal. **21** untasted.

★★★★ **Filia Chenin Blanc Kaap Klassiek** ⊗ ⊛ Zero dosage cap classique from old-vine chenin shows more vivacity & elegance in **18** ★★★★★ ⑨⓪ than last-tasted **15** ⑧⑦. Arresting oystershell finish & persistence. 2 years on lees.

Not tasted: **Hummingbird Brut**, **Circa Pinotage Brut Rosé**. Occasional release: **Filia Chenin Blanc Kaap Klassiek Reserve**. — CvZ

Location: Riebeek-Kasteel ▪ WO: Swartland/Piekenierskloof/Coastal ▪ Est 1956 ▪ 1stB 2011 ▪ Tasting by appt only ▪ Pub hols by prior arrangement ▪ Tours & tastings in the Swartland available by appt ▪ Owner(s)/winemaker(s) Christa von La Chevallerie ▪ Viticulturist(s) Christa von La Chevallerie & several consultants ▪ Bought in grapes: ptage, chenin, grenache b, palomino, verdelho, viura ▪ 60% MCC 40% still wines ▪ 32 Main Str, Riebeek-Kasteel 7307 ▪ info@huisvanchevallerie.com ▪ www.huisvanchevallerie.com ▪ **T +27 (0)72-237-1166**

Hunneyball Wines   ⓥ ⌂ ◎

Jim Hunneyball and Swedish wife Marie manage a luxury guest house on a winefarm in Swartland, facilitating activities such as harvesting and blending. They also offer private guided winetasting tours with an emphasis on Swartland and other top-echelon wines. With the Bain family of Abbottshill, they additionally craft boutique wines from local grapes. We look forward to tasting their handiwork next time.

Location: Malmesbury ▪ Map: Swartland ▪ Map grid reference: B7 ▪ Est 2012 ▪ 1stB 2011 ▪ Tasting by appt ▪ Guided winetasting tours of Cape winelands; wine activities such as blending & harvesting ▪ Accommodation ▪ Winemaker(s) Jim & Marie Hunneyball ▪ 5t 100% red ▪ PO Box 795 Stellenbosch 7599 ▪ jim@africaninvite.com ▪ www.africaninvite.com ▪ **T +27 (0)71-674-9379**

☐ **IBN Negociants** see O'Connell's
☐ **Idelia** see Swartland Winery
☐ **Ideology** see Spier

Idiom Wines   ⓥ ⑴ ◎

The Bottega family's estate on the mountainside high above Sir Lowry's Pass Village is home to a panoramic tasting and events venue, restaurant and library housing an impressive range of Italian wines, as well as a collection of Italian varieties in the vineyards. Different aspects, the cooling effect of altitude and prevailing winds, and other factors allow for cultivation of many other grapes, too, and the owners have embraced the opportunity since the first plantings in 1999. The wines are made near Hermanus in the Bottega-owned Whalehaven cellar (see listing), where Reino Thiart uses some Idiom grapes to produce the sibling portfolio.

246 · IDIOM WINES

Idiom Collection

★★★★ **Sangiovese** Classic leafy tomato with dried basil & thyme notes on **19** ⑧⑨, first tasted since **16** ⑧⑨. Sweet-sour acid creates tension on sour cherry palate, year in older oak, mostly French, contributes chalky tannins & hint tobacco.

★★★★☆ **Bordicon** ⓐ Whiffs incense & clove on 5-way cab-led Bordeaux blend. Improving on **18** ⑨①, **19** ⑨②'s 14 months oaking delivers finely crafted tannin frame for juicy blackcurrant core. High percentage new barrels tightens & lengthens the body, aids cellaring potential.

★★★★ **Cape Blend** Well-balanced 5-way pinotage blend, 14 months in oak, 45% new, for toast, cocoa & vanilla notes in **19** ⑧⑦. Cab's 23% portion evident as blackberry seam through the full-fruited whole.

★★★★ **Rodanico** Rhône blend, **18** ⑧⑧ & **19** ★★★★★ ⑨⓪ identical fractions syrah (74%), mourvèdre & teeny drop viognier. Smartly juggles density with light-footed energy, melds 70% new oak generosity with vibrant red plum flavour, spice & florals.

★★★★ **Iberico** Alluring Iberian quartet, equal grenache noir & carignan, 17% each mourvèdre & tempranillo in **19** ⑧⑥. Goes notch up on **18** ★★★★ ⑧⑤ in harmony of plush fruit, dry finish & firm tannins. Moreish notes of roast fennel & baking spices from oak, 12-14 months, 30% new.

★★★★ **Sauvignon Blanc** ⊘ Elderflower prettiness & perfume on **20** ★★★★★ ⑨⓪ helps elevate it above **19** ⑧⑧. Silky pear & peach borne on vivid acid, oak ageing, year, 15% new, adds smoky nuance to flinty, light-feeling palate (12.7% alc).

★★★★ **Semillon** Intriguing aromatics on **20** ⑧⑥ - cardamom, dried grass & green apple - very attractive, as is trim body (12.5 alc) & subtle spice from oak, 10 months, 15% new.

★★★★☆ **Viognier** ⊘ Variety's peach & other stonefruit on **20** ⑨②'s lush palate, along with blossoms & high 14.8% alc, latter deftly tucked away in the structure of fruit & restrained oak, 20% new, for only half the wine.

. . . .

Zinfandel ⓥ ★★★★ 40% new French & American (20%) barrels help to round the chewy tannins, smooth the plum fruit & add cigarbox spice in **18** ⑧③, giving more luxurious feel than last **16** ⑧③.

Barbera ★★★★ Full-bodied, slightly evolved **19** ⑧⑤ exudes ripe pomegranate & dark berries. Polish & firm tannin frame from mix French, American & European oak, 2 years, 45% new. Occasional release: **Malbec, Merlot-Cabernet Sauvignon-Cabernet Franc-Petit Verdot-Malbec, The Works**.

900 Series

★★★★☆ **Nebbiolo** Convincing & fragrant aromas of pot-pourri zested with orange open elegant **19** ★★★★ ⑧⑨, vivid red fruit & dried tomato shaped by tangy acid & perfectly dry tannins. Diminishing new oak influence: 40% vs last-tasted **16** ⑨⓪'s 45% & **15** ⑨①'s 50%.

Occasional release: **Barbera, Cabernet Sauvignon, Cabernet Franc, Merlot, Mourvèdre, Pinotage, Sangiovese, Syrah**.

Heritage Series

★★★★ **Bianco di Stellenbosch** ⊘ From pinot grigio, as before, touches kerosene & honey to pear drop & lemon cream on balanced, slightly evolved **21** ⑧⑥, dab sugar well-married with racy acid. Weightier than **20** ★★★☆ ⑧⑤.

. . . .

Rosso di Stellenbosch ⊘ ⓥ ★★★☆ Seldom-seen sangiovese & 9% of even rarer barbera in **19** ⑧⑤. Unwooded, fresh, spicy, with typical blood orange note & racy acid. Deliciously drinkable, just add antipasti. — ML

. . . .

Location: Sir Lowry's Pass ▪ Map: Helderberg ▪ Map grid reference: H7 ▪ WO: Stellenbosch ▪ Est 1999 ▪ 1stB 2003/4 ▪ Tasting & sales Mon-Sun 10-5; Restaurant open for breakfast/brunch & lunch Mon-Sun 9-5 (see website for extended hours in summer) ▪ Open for exclusive events & weddings in evenings ▪ Signature wine tasting & canapé experience; informative food & wine pairings; contemporary dining multi-course menus or à la carte ▪ Imported Vinotria Italian wine library & Fynbos garden ▪ Owner(s) Bottega family ▪ Winemaker(s) Reino Thiart ▪ 39ha (barbera, cabs s/f, grenache, merlot, mourv, nebbiolo, p verdot, ptage, primitivo, shiraz, tempranillo, sauv, sem, viog) ▪ 85% red 15% white ▪ PO Box 3802 Somerset West 7129 ▪ wine@idiom.co.za, reservations@idiom.co.za ▪ www.idiom.co.za ▪ **T +27 (0)21-858-1088 (restaurant & wine tasting centre)/+27 (0)21-852-3590 (distribution/sales)**

Idun

The Elgin boutique winemaking project prodded by a late midlife crisis is working out well for Mauritius-born Albert Rousset, who is adding the 11th country to his export list and planning three new releases later this year. With co-owner wife Joanne, he's still experimenting with varieties and learning from past vintages, but 'sticking to my guns' as regards the basic style, which he describes as 'sexy and elegant'.

Poetique range

★★★★ Confession ⟨Ⓩ⟩ From spicy & earthy grenache noir, **21** ⟨89⟩ shows good expression of berries & perfumed fynbos. Elegant, with lovely depth & length. Year in 20% new oak, will age several more. No **20**.

★★★★ Crepuscule ⟨Ⓩ⟩ Very youthful & bright pinot noir, **21** ⟨88⟩ delicate & characterful, fresh cranberry, undergrowth & earthy spice in balanced structure. 9 months in 25% new oak give foundation for ageing.

★★★★☆ Nuit Eternelle Multi-layered **20** ⟨90⟩ syrah showcases cool climate in its brightness, perfume & subtle white pepper spicing. Gentle but ample tannins allow keeping several years. Natural ferment (as most Poetiques tasted this year), 40% wholebunch, 15% new barrels, 14 months.

★★★★ Charismatique ⟨⧆⟩ Similar blend to **20** ⟨89⟩, 55% cinsault with syrah & mourvèdre, but **21** ★★★★☆ ⟨91⟩ improves in structure & depth of sweet fruit. Smooth, balanced & very easy to like. Exotic spice & pot-pourri fragrance on long farewell. Year in 15% new oak.

★★★★ Renaissance ⟨Ⓩ⟩ Rich baked apple, nectarine & crème brûlée in opulent **20** ⟨88⟩ chardonnay. Weighty, with spice from 20% new oak, harmonised by lemony freshness for a smoothly satisfying drop.

★★★★☆ Cabriole ⟨✓⟩ Bright & vibrant **22** ⟨90⟩, sauvignon with 5% semillon displays tropical fruit with a waxy coat & orange marmalade richness on broad finish. 10% oaked portion gives extra depth & texture. Bot River WO, as Confession & Charismatique.

★★★★ L'Imperatrice Brut Nature Light, elegant cap classique, **19** ⟨89⟩ pinot noir with 40% chardonnay, delicate berry & citrus on bone-dry palate, persistent mousse & stony minerality make the perfect aperitif.

★★★★ L'Intemporelle Brut Touch sweeter than sparkling sibling, from chardonnay & pinot noir with percentages reversed, both 34 months on lees. **19** ⟨89⟩ fine, smooth mousse showing lovely orchard fruit, citrus rind & cashews, rounded & generous.

Discontinued: **Jouvence**.

Reverie range

★★★★ Trois Cailloux Scrumptious Rhône-style blend, 62% syrah, equal grenache & mourvèdre, **21** ⟨88⟩ voluptuous dark berry fruit, earthy tones, cured meat spice & lavender in a succulent body. Older oak, 16 months (as other red) deftly judged.

★★★★☆ Four Pebbles Mostly merlot & malbec (39/31), dabs cab & syrah combine in generous mouthful of black plums & Xmas spice, supple & savoury to the last drop. **20** ★★★★ ⟨89⟩ touch less complex than **19** ⟨91⟩ but drinks well & early.

★★★★ Seul Amour Sauvignon Blanc ⟨✓⟩ Well-made, lively & bright **22** ⟨88⟩, greengage, grass & capsicum joined by fragrant flowers, lemon curd on tasty finish. WO Cape South Coast for these.— WB

Location: Elgin ▪ WO: Elgin/Bot River/Cape South Coast ▪ 1stB 2017 ▪ Closed to public ▪ Owner(s) Albert & Joanne Rousset ▪ Winemaker(s) Albert Rousset, Kobie Viljoen (consultant) ▪ info@idun.co.za ▪ www.idun.co.za

iL Geco   (NEW)

'One-woman show' Clarise Sciocatti-Langeveldt blends Italian heritage with her 'favourite little critter, shy but resilient and adaptable' in her boutique venture based in Klapmuts. Trial vintages 2014 and 2015 of her sparkling were praised by critics, as was 2017, the first meaningful production, prompting her to add a pair of stillwines and, from 2023, focus full-time on crafting wines that are 'moreish' on palate but 'less' in terms of intervention and artifice: 'I don't want to turn wine into something it is not'. Exports are a to-do.

iL Geco range

★★★★ Sangiovese Sweet & sour cherries, bay leaf & rosemary - nuances of the old country on **22** ⟨86⟩. Palate commendably dry, tannins firm, fruit not overworked, variety well expressed. WO Simonsberg-Paarl.

Pinot Gris ★★★★ **22** ⟨83⟩ full, fragrant peach, lanolin & geranium bouquet, weighty, rounded palate. Individual & characterful take on variety, doesn't need food. WO Stellenbosch.

Cap Classique range

Brut ★★★★ Pinot noir & chardonnay sparkler, **17** ⑧⑤ more savoury than creamy, alluring toastiness with brioche from 61 months on lees. Delicious rich-dry interplay; just needs tad more persistence. — CR, CvZ

Location: Paarl ▪ WO: Tulbagh/Simonsberg-Paarl/Stellenbosch ▪ Est/1stB 2017 ▪ Closed to public ▪ Owner(s) Clarise Sciocatti-Langeveldt ▪ Winemaker(s)/viticulturist(s) Clarise Sciocatti-Langeveldt (2017) ▪ 6t/600cs own label 30% red 30% white 40% cap classique ▪ IPW ▪ il Geco (Pty) Ltd, 50 Rozenmeer Estate, Klapmuts 7625 ▪ info@ilgeco.co.za ▪ www.ilgeco.co.za ▪ **T +27 (0)84-909-9723**

illimis Wines

Stellenbosch small-batch vigneronne Lucinda Heyns hopes her unusual Latin brand name, meaning 'clarity', conveys her process of stepping aside as much as possible and letting the wine be a window to the vineyard, and the vineyard a reflection of the wine. She avoid additives, save for a touch of sulphur, and uses very old oak to not sully the pristine fruit flavours. She's always worked with the same single parcels, chosen to allow gentleness in the crafting, so there's also a 'golden thread' of seasonality expressed in the wines.

★★★★☆ Cinsault ⊘ Beguilingly perfumed Turkish delight, sweet silage & spicy, savoury notes in **22** ⑨② Quite plush yet retains hallmark lower alc (12%), svelte texture & balance. Minimalistic winemaking, as for all these wines: mostly bunch pressed, naturally fermented, old neutral oak 7 months.

★★★★☆ Grenache Noir Similar juicy raspberry character from the same Wellington fruit source in **22** ⑨①. Dances nimbly across the palate at lower (13.5%) alc. All elements well integrated, retains fruit purity while half bunch-pressing ensures freshness. Eminently drinkable, with clean dry farewell.

★★★★★ Pinotage ⑧ Polkadraai Hills vines consistently show this wine's hallmark: pinotage's pinot noir character & parentage. **22 ★★★★☆** ⑨③ similar light handling, allows fruit purity to shine, delicate yet intense (at modest 12% alc), perfumed, with subtle savouriness & pervasive fresh seam of acidity. A shade off **21** ⑨⑤ but still a class act.

★★★★☆ Chenin Blanc ⑧ Two components contribute to richly textured **22** ⑨④: Elgin's cool structure, Stellenbosch's flesh. Natural ferment/7 months on lees in neutral oak give dimension & breadth to ripe pear & almond flavours; lovely restraint & focus, clean limy farewell. WO Cape Coast.

In abeyance: **Riesling**. — MW

Location/map: Stellenbosch ▪ Map grid reference: B6 ▪ WO: Darling/Wellington/Polkadraai Hills/Cape Coast ▪ Est/1stB 2015 ▪ Tasting Wed-Sat 11-7 Sun 11-3 at Somm & Co at Karibib Wine Craft, Polkadraai Rd, Stellenbosch ▪ Owner(s)/winemaker(s) Lucinda Heyns ▪ 1,500cs ▪ lucinda@illimiswines.com ▪ www. illimiswines.com

Imbuko Wines

'Consumer-friendly wine that's acceptable to the entire market and offers value for money at all price levels' is their tried-and-true recipe 'and we stick to it', say the Van Zyl family on their farm Uitkyk in Wellington. Cellarmaster Theunis van Zyl and his team produce more than half a million cases, mostly for export, and countries where they don't yet have a presence are being targeted. Locally, a logistics company now handles storage and distribution in four key provinces, speeding delivery and reducing cost to the customer.

Van Zijl Reserve range

★★★★ Red Ink Shiraz Barrel selection, as all these, **21** ⑧⑧ is opulently perfumed, spice, including pepper, dark berries, the velvet tannins making it irresistible. Last was **17** ⑧⑥. WO Paarl.

★★★★ Blue Ink Cabernet Sauvignon-Merlot Makes a statement, starting with the heavyweight bottle, then its contents: **21** ⑧⑨ is packed with fruit, luscious cassis, well-spiced by French oak. There's enough tannin for some ageing, but the balance is right for earlier consumption, smoothly round. **17 - 20** not made. WO Swartland.

Not tasted: **Blue Ink FB Van Zyl Rhône Blend**.

Du Plevaux Private Collection

Jean Prieur Pinotage ★★★★ Full-ripe & packed with fruit, **21** ⑧⑤ tasted as preview last time, now bottled (as for range), lovely silky texture, just a touch of tannin at the end from stave oaking, promising some ageing. WO Paarl for all. **Daniël Johannes Shiraz ★★★★** Year later, **21** ⑧⑤'s dark-toned fruit seductive, well spiced, tannins integrated, giving smooth & juicy enjoyment. **Madeleine Menanteau Sauvignon**

Blanc ★★★★ Distinctive, differs from other range versions, **22** ⑧⑤ comes across as cool-grown/early picked, a mineral & nettle character, cucumber in the flavours. Slender (12% alc) but no shortage of appeal.
Elizabeth Albertha Chenin Blanc-Viognier ★★★★ Floral notes & apple, stonefruit flavours, **22** ⑧③ is ripe & generous, the slight sweetness fitting like a glove, giving appetite appeal.

Van Zijl Family Vintners range

Pink Sauvignon Blanc ⑦ ★★★ Just 1% pinotage is all it takes for the delicate rosé colour, but **23** ⑧②'s character is pure sauvignon: kiwi & litchi, its flavours refreshed by limy acidity. Delicious.

Coffee Pinotage ☺ ★★★ Expressive mocha chocolate-scented from stave oaking, some American, **22** ⑧② is smooth & juicy, no tannins showing; tasty, easy, friendly.

Cabernet Sauvignon ⊘ ★★★★ Year later, the oak (French & American staves) & fruit have melded, leaving a plush texture with cassis & cherries, **21** ⑧③'s smoky, meaty notes adding interest. **Pinotage** ★★★ Same oaking as Coffee Pinotage, but **21** ⑧②'s scents & flavours less mocha, more fruit-driven, dark berries; smooth textured, succulent. Was preview, now bottled, as next. **Shiraz-Mourvèdre** ⊘ ★★★★ Shiraz in charge, smoky, spicy, dark toned, fits the profile. Palate juicy, nice fresh seam, **21** ⑧⑤ has grip but it's supple, without edges. For food or ageing. **Chenin Blanc** ★★★ Trim figured (12.5% alc) but **23** ⑧① makes up for it in crunchy apple flavours, refreshing dryness. **Sauvignon Blanc** ⊘ ★★★★ Mineral notes fit **23** ⑧⑤'s slender frame (12.5% alc), has focus & precision, nice contrast to other sauvignons. Ends salty-fresh. Not tasted: **Elizabeth Francoinette Méthode Cap Classique**.

Imbuko range

Cabernet Sauvignon ⊘ ★★★ Affordably priced range of everyday drinking wines. **21** ⑧② vanilla spiced from 30% American staves, cassis fruit compatible, resulting in richness of flavour, despite a structural sleekness. Was preview, now bottled, as next. **Merlot** ⊘ ★★★ Oak better integrated year later, vanilla more subdued, in sync with **21** ⑧①'s cassis & plummy fruit. Still firm but tannins are ripe. **Chenin Blanc** ⊘ ★★★ Fruity-fresh **23** ⑧⓪'s apple & pear styling coupled with the brisk acid has 'drink me' written all over it. **Sauvignon Blanc** ⊘ ★★★★ Year later, **23** ⑧③ shows as a good rendition of the variety, crunchy greengage, a lemon-lime finish. Exudes freshness. **Iswithi Pinotage** ★★★ Not commonly found, semi-sweet pinotage, unoaked, but **22** ⑦⑧'s fruit is there, blueberries & fruit pastilles, a smooth touch of grape tannin at the end.

Shortwood range

Winemakers Red Blend ★★★ Cinsaut, ruby cab & pinotage plus 2 others, **NV** ⑧⓪ retasted year later; designed for early drinking, no oak, just plush fruit, smooth texture. **Rosé** ⊘ ★★★ Well priced for the quality, pale pink **23** ⑦⑧'s just-picked strawberry scents & flavours fit the touch of sugar without it being sweet. **Chenin Blanc** ⊘ ★★★ Nice fruity-freshness, lime & crunchy apple, **23** ⑧②'s elegance (12.5% alc) part of the drinking appeal.

Pomüla range

Not tasted: **Berry Vanilla, Moscato Spumante, Pomegranate Marula, Passion Fruit**. — CR

Location/map: Wellington ▪ Map grid reference: B4 ▪ WO: Western Cape/Paarl/Swartland ▪ Est/1stB 2004 ▪ Tasting Mon-Fri 9-5 Sat/pub hols 9-3 ▪ Fee R60/5 wines ▪ Sales 9-5 ▪ Closed Good Fri, Dec 25 & Jan 1 ▪ Cellar tours by appt only ▪ Pie & wine pairing - booking essential ▪ Farm produce ▪ Child friendly ▪ Owner(s) Imbuko Wines (Pty) Ltd ▪ Cellarmaster(s) Theunis van Zyl (2004) ▪ Viticulturist(s) Jan-Louw du Plessis ▪ 60ha (cab, cinsaut, merlot, mourv, ptage, shiraz, chenin, sauv, viog) ▪ 570,000cs own label 60% red 40% white ▪ Other export brands: Barrel Selection 008, Fat Barrel, King Shaka, Kleine Kaap, Makulu, Rebourne Fairtrade & Releaf Organic ▪ Fairtrade, IPW, ISO, Organic ▪ PO Box 810 Wellington 7654 ▪ info@imbuko.co.za ▪ www.imbuko.co.za ▪ T +27 (0)21-873-7350

☐ **Immortal Souls** *see* Origin Wine
☐ **Imoya** *see* KWV Brandies
☐ **Impressions of Nature** *see* Olivedale Private Vineyards
☐ **Imprint** *see* Wellington Wines

Imvini Wethu

'High enthusiasm', notably among sommeliers, greeted an initiative by a group of German business owners, importers, and trade and wine industry professionals to support SA's Covid-impacted wine industry by marketing a special heritage-vine wine in their country and donating most of the proceeds to selected projects. The success of the wine, made in association with the CWG Protégé Programme and the Old Vine Project, has motivated the partners to continue the project and its prominent social responsibility component.

Old Vine Cinsault-Pinotage ⓥ ⓦ ★★★★ Pretty florals & berries but subtle, not showy; really nice fruity-fresh palate with tiny stemmy grip, **20** ⑧⑤ 70/30 blend seems more for good drinking than contemplation, & nothing wrong with that. — CR, CvZ

WO: Western Cape ▪ Est/1stB 2020 ▪ Closed to public ▪ Owner(s) German based partners ▪ Winemaker(s) CWG Protégé Programme ▪ 9,600 btls own label 100% red ▪ Certified Heritage Vineyards ▪ andre@oldvine-project.co.za, info@oldvineproject.co.za, pm@pm-kommunikation.de ▪ www.imviniwethu.com

☐ **Indaba** *see* Cape Classics
☐ **Infused by Earth** *see* Eikendal Vineyards
☐ **Inkará** *see* Bon Courage Estate
☐ **Integer** *see* Hoopenburg Wines
☐ **Intulo** *see* Kumala

Iona Vineyards

ⓥ ⓒ

Claiming to be the coolest winefarm in the Cape, the Gunn family's Elgin property sits 420 m above sea level, on an exposed ridge just 4.5 km from the Atlantic. The philosophy here is to express each vintage and the uniqueness of each site as best as possible, without too much interference in the cellar. The harshness of the climate, myriad soils and numerous slopes are reflected in the profound 'monopole' (single-site) wines, while the Highlands wines, mostly multi-vineyard, are different, equally true expressions of Iona. Mr P is that vinous rare bird: good, affordable pinot noir. Responsibility for guiding these into bottle rests on the collective shoulders of winemaker Werner Muller and Iona's loyal and dedicated vineyard team, which executes tasks with pride and attention to the smallest detail.

Single Vineyard range

★★★★★ **Kloof Pinot Noir** ⓐ Single-vineyard (as all these) on clay-based silica quartz, north-facing & offering respite from the wind. Undergrowth accent on **20** ⑨⑤'s red berry perfume, 20% new oak just a whisper, like Kroon & Highlands. Signature tightly packed tannins give impressive form & shape, longevity, as in **19** ★★★★★ ⑨④.

★★★★☆ **Kroon Pinot Noir** ⓐ Compact **20** ⑨③ expresses its alluvial (sandstone & ferricrete), clay-underlain & south-facing site in its more forthright character & savoury, sanguine tones. Same winemaking, wholeberry natural ferment in open tanks, malo & 11 months in oak, 20% new, for these & Highlands sibling.

★★★★☆ **Fynbos Chardonnay** ⓐ 21 year old north-facing clay-underlain sandstone site named for its surroundings; fruit (as all from this variety) bunch pressed, natural ferment/11 months in oak, 20% new. Stylish & more savoury than Kloof with soft-leaf herb accents, **21** ⑨④ long, subtly spiced end.

★★★★☆ **Kloof Chardonnay** ⓐ Like namesake pinot, sheltered from the wind. Expressive **21** ⑨④ complex lemon, lime, mandarin, yuzu notes & beautiful dryness, 20% new oak playing supporting role to fruit purity, tangy acid.

Elgin Highlands range

★★★★☆ **Nebbiolo d'Elgin** ⓝⓔⓦ ⓐ Co-owner Andrew Gunn's current passion project, tiny vineyard precariously balanced on narrow spine of Bokkeveld shale with sheer drop into gorge below. Satisfyingly dry & savoury **19** ⑨⓪ a fine example, with variety's red cherry & floral scents, tight, big tannins.

★★★★☆ **Pinot Noir** ⓥ ⓐ From slower-ripening sites, **20** ⑨⓪ takes time to open to similar yet subtle earthy tones, piquant fruit as single-site siblings. Elegant & long, tobacco top note, satisfying structure.

★★★★☆ **Chardonnay** Intense lime & lemon flavours & scents, more obvious toasty oak richness on **21** ⑨② than uni-parcel bottlings, yet still vibrant with rapier acid & a certain delicacy.

★★★★☆ **Wild Ferment Sauvignon Blanc** ⍟ Dialled-back version of younger sibling, **22** ⑨④ natural ferment/11 months in 500L older oak. Richer, with enlivening greengage & starfruit, smoky note, succulent acidity.

★★★★☆ **Sauvignon Blanc** ⟢ With 10% unoaked semillon replacing **21** ⑨①'s tiny wooded portion, **23** ⑨① seems touch less complex but wine's pedigree & signatures are present: bone-dryness, racy acid & grassy pungency, pleasing vinosity & thrilling length. **22** untasted.

Mr P range

★★★★ **Mr P Pinot Noir** ⟢ Mr P certainly knows how to tick the early-accessible pinot boxes. Pre- & post-ferment macerations give **22** ⑧⑧ lively raspberry fruit & grape tannin grip, older oak supports both, subtle herb & earthy tones for complexity.

NLH range

★★★★☆ **Noble Late Harvest** ⍟ Botrytis dessert wine from sauvignon, **17** ⑨① delicate & piquantly sweet, clean limy farewell. Natural ferment, half each in tank & older oak. 12.8% alc, 375 ml.— CvZ

Location/map/WO: Elgin ▪ Map grid reference: C4 ▪ Est 1997 ▪ 1stB 2001 ▪ Tasting, sales & tours Mon-Fri 9-4 Sat by appt ▪ Closed all pub hols ▪ Walks/hikes ▪ MTB ▪ Conservation area ▪ Owner(s) Andrew Gunn, Workers Trust ▪ Winemaker(s) Werner Muller (May 2011) ▪ Vineyard manager(s) Joseph Sebulawa ▪ Viticulturist(s) Kevin Watt (consultant) ▪ 100ha/40ha (pinot, chard, sauv, sem) ▪ 350t/30,000cs own label 20% red 80% white ▪ PO Box 527 Grabouw 7160 ▪ orders@iona.co.za ▪ www.iona.co.za ▪ **T +27 (0)28-284-9678**

☐ **Island View** *see* Orange River Cellars
☐ **Italian Collection** *see* Morgenster Estate

Izak van der Vyver Wines

Elgin GP Izak van der Vyver annually downs his stethoscope and dons his after-hours vintner's boots to craft a tiny batch of sauvignon in the cellar of his friend Paul Cluver, aiming to capture the cool climate while building mouthfeel through extended lees ageing. The current release includes grapes from a younger block.

★★★★ **Limited Release Sauvignon Blanc** ⟢ Flinty nettle & granadilla on **22** ⑧⑧, reflects cool origins in vibrant acid merged with bold, generously proportioned fruit. Broad & textured, offering better than everyday refreshment.— GdB

Location/WO: Elgin ▪ 1stB 2002 ▪ Closed to public ▪ Owner(s) Izak van der Vyver ▪ Cellarmaster(s) Andries Burger (Paul Cluver Wines) ▪ Winemaker(s) Izak van der Vyver (Jan 2002) ▪ 1.4t/±166cs own label ▪ PO Box 42 Grabouw 7160 ▪ drs@telkomsa.net ▪ **T +27 (0)21-859-2508**

Jacaranda Wine & Guest Farm   ⍟ ⍟ ⍟

On what's understood to be SA's smallest registered wine estate, just outside Wellington town, 'what you taste in the vineyard is what you'll taste in the wine', with vintage variations also expressed as clearly as possible through natural farming and handcrafting of the wines, with minimum interference, wild ferments, light filtrations and low sulphur levels throughout. Owners and founders René and Birgit Reiser are proud that the same team that tended the vines and cellar at the outset 15 years ago, continue to do so today, and still personally present tastings on the rustic veranda under the jacaranda or at the kitchen table.

Reserve range

★★★★ **Shiraz No. 47** Elegant **19** ⑧⑧ smartly oaked (year, 10% new) to allow fruit to shine. Liquorice nuance on nose echoed on palate of blackberry, mulberry & red plum, silky tannins extend satisfyingly dry finish. Charming now, few years' potential.

★★★★ **Salt Old Vine Chenin Blanc** From 40 & 60-year-old low-yielding vines, named for distinct salty line that runs through palate. **18** ⑧⑧ popcorn & caramelised nut smells/tastes from 2 days' skin contact, lengthy ferment/10 months in older wood. Rich citrus bouquet & body, engaging tug of texture. Not tasted: **Down-to-Earth Cabernet Sauvignon-Merlot**.

Artisanal range

The Rebel Shiraz-Viognier ★★★★ Smattering American oak (10%) partners with French (mostly old) to add vanilla to spicy character of **18** ⑧⑤ 88/12 combo. Pink peppercorns from the first variety, florals from the second, zippy acidity & bone-dry. **Incognito Viognier-Chenin Blanc** ★★★★ Wild-yeast barrel-ferment of near-equal viognier & chenin exceedingly pretty, with white flower, ripe peach & apricot appeal, butter biscuit accent. 10 months old oak smooths **19** (85)'s palate, full & satisfying courtesy 14% alc.

Harvest range
Night Shift ★★★ Petit verdot, merlot & cab, near-equal portions, & just 5% new oak, 15 months, ensure **19** (82) thrills with racy red primary fruit & steely backbone. Not tasted: **Horizon Chenin Blanc**.

Jacaranda range
Not tasted: **Early Bird Mourvèdre Rosé**. — ML, PS

Location/WO: Wellington ▪ Map: Paarl ▪ Map grid reference: F1 ▪ Est/1stB 2009 ▪ Tasting & sales Mon-Sat 10-4 (last tasting starts at 4pm) ▪ Fee R80/6-8 wines (depending on availability), served with olives & bread ▪ Closed Easter Fri/Sun, Dec 25 & Jan 1 ▪ Mediterranean/cheese platters by appt ▪ 2 self-catering cottages, each sleeping 4 guests ▪ Owner(s) René & Birgit Reiser ▪ Cellarmaster(s)/winemaker(s)/viticulturist(s) René Reiser (Jun 2009) ▪ 3.2ha (mourv, shiraz, chard, chenin, viog) ▪ 15t/6,000cs own label 50% red 40% white 10% rosé ▪ PO Box 121 Wellington 7654 ▪ info@jacarandawines.co.za ▪ www.jacarandawines.co.za ▪ **T +27 (0)72-432-6716**

☐ **Jack Parow Brandy** *see* Parow Brandy
☐ **Jackson Wine Estates (South Africa)** *see* Dalkeith
☐ **Jacoline Haasbroek Wines** *see* My Wyn
☐ **Jacquéren** *see* Nabygelegen Private Cellar
☐ **Jacques Bruére** *see* Bon Courage Estate
☐ **Jacques Germanier** *see* Germanier Wines
☐ **Jacques Mouton** *see* La Couronne Wines
☐ **Jade** *see* Natasha Williams Signature Wines
☐ **Jailbreak** *see* Mountain Ridge Wines
☐ **Jakkalskloof** *see* Wine-of-the-Month Club

Jakkalsvlei Private Cellar   (♀) (♟) (◎) (♟)

Development and expansion continue at Jantjie Jonker's wine, lifestyle and craft beer estate near Herbertsdale on the Garden Route to keep pace with unswerving growth, which should see volumes reach a remarkable 1-million bottles. Viticulturist Hennie Kotze is planting a further 8 ha of vines, mostly red and white muscadel, and cellarmaster Louis van der Riet, who also crafts his boutique Le Sueur collection here, is installing new tanks and equipment to support the goal of 'creating quality wines from the Garden Route'.

Lord Jackal range
★★★★ **Cabernet Franc** Good core of red & black cherry, aromatic spice in firm but fine dry framework of both fruit tannin & year older oak in **22** (89). Variety's piquancy ensures freshness. Less alc (13.8%) than last, but similar call for time to unfurl, show full potential.

★★★★ **Pinot Noir** (⊘) Riper **22** (87) more expressive than **21** ★★★★ (85). Similar raspberry, red plum & some sweet-spiced rooibos tea, supported by smooth, supple tannins from year older oak. Fresh acid befitting the variety, perfumed farewell.

★★★★☆ **Chardonnay** Rounder, more succulent in riper **22** (90), rich lemon cream flavours & subtle toasted almond underpin. Wild ferment/10 months older oak add further polish to lees-enriched texture. Less vibrant than last, but balanced & very appealing. WO Klein Karoo, as sparkling.

★★★★ **Méthode Cap Classique Limited Release Pinot Noir** (NEW) Burst of bright citrus & florality in rose gold **21** (87). Super-crisp & tangy-fresh, subtle cream from lees-aged base wine & 18 months in bottle partly temper vibrant acid. One for the canapé platter, though may develop interestingly. Just 200 cases.

★★★★ **Cape Vintage Reserve** More structure in **21** (89) 'port' from touriga gives more tannin grip, befitting style, though tad sweet. Ample dark fruit, leather & stewed prune reined in - just - by good, fiery 18.8% alc. Harmonised year in old oak, should meld further in bottle. WO W Cape, as reds in all ranges.

Jakkalsvlei range
★★★★ **Cabernet Sauvignon** Ticks varietal boxes with dark berries, firm lithe tannins & fresh herbal touch in previewed **22** (88). Older oak, 18 months, adds brush of cedar spice. Ready to enjoy, solo or with a meal.

★★★★ **Mount Cuvée** Pinotage with 49% shiraz in **22** (88), more fruity than savoury with mulberry, plum & some lighter aromatic notes. Nicely fresh, melded, infused with dry chalky tannins. Less serious than **21** ★★★★☆ (90) but lots to like.

★★★★ **Chenin Blanc** ⊘ Freshness & flavour from younger Outeniqua Mountain vines & some depth & minerality from older Swartberg vineyard contribute to **23** (86)'s bright, balanced & tangy stonefruit & lime. Vinified separately & lees aged pre-bottling, adding breadth.

★★★★ **Sauvignon Blanc** ⊘ Harvesting at different ripeness levels ensures both freshness & juicy ripe citrus & tropical flavours in **23** (86). Lees provides plumpness & texture. Good-value summer staple.

★★★★ **River Cuvée** ⊘ Klein Karoo gem & very creditable Rhône white from shale soils in a Kammanassie Mountain valley. Individually vinified roussanne in new oak, grenache blanc & chenin (41/10) in tank. Delicious, lipsmacking **23** (88) succulent white peach & pear, waxy texture, shot through with clean acid.

★★★★☆ **Hanepoot** ⊘ Well-balanced fortified muscat, decadently rich but, like last, uncloying in **23** (90). Ruby grapefruit & grapey flavours, melded 15.7% alc & drier farewell make this a delightful chilled aperitif or one to pair with spicy Asian food.

★★★★ **Red Muscadel** Retains luscious sweetness in **23** (86) fortified, ample perfumed Earl Grey tea & raisined charm, acid on softer side. Seductive dessert/chilled aperitif for the sweeter toothed.

Merlot ★★★ Touch richer in **22** (82), better balanced & riper plummy fruit, dab sugar too in more supple tannin framework, enhanced by old-oak ageing. **Pinotage** ★★★ Continues in crowd-pleasing style. Coffee, toffee oak nuances from barrels & staves to variety's plummy flavours, semi-dry **22** (79) ends with fresh acid twist. **Pinotage Rosé** ★★★ Retains friendly, quaffable style in **23** (82) anytime wine. Crisp, flavoursome rosepetals & summer berries, fruity & dry.

Moscato range

Red (Ⓧ) ★★ Piquant pomegranate & sweet muscat on **22** (76) from red muscadel & 15% pinotage. Gentle effervescence, juicy sweetness. Not tasted: **Pink, White**. — MW

Location: Herbertsdale ▪ Map: Klein Karoo & Garden Route ▪ Map grid reference: C5 ▪ WO: Herbertsdale/ Western Cape/Klein Karoo ▪ Est 1987 ▪ 1stB 2008 ▪ Tasting & sales Mon-Sun 10-4; pub hols (seasonal) please call ahead ▪ Food & wine pairing options ▪ Restaurant ▪ Deli ▪ Conferences ▪ Functions/weddings ▪ Facilities for children ▪ Walks/hikes ▪ Pick your own hanepoot (mid Feb-mid Mar) ▪ Music festival ▪ MTB & trail run event ▪ Craft beer: Jackal Lager & Wolf Ale ▪ Owner(s) Jantjie Jonker ▪ Cellarmaster(s)/winemaker(s) Louis van der Riet (Sep 2019) ▪ Viticulturist(s) Hennie Kotze (Jun 2022) ▪ 50ha/30ha (cabs s/f, merlot, muscadel r, ptage, pinot, shiraz, touriga nacional, chenin, grenache b, hanepoot, rouss, sauv) ▪ 45ot/140,000cs ▪ PO Box 79 Herbertsdale 6505 ▪ info@jakkalsvlei.co.za ▪ www.jakkalsvlei.co.za ▪ **T +27 (0)44-333-0222**

Jakob's Vineyards (Ⓧ)

'Elegant, finely nuanced cabernet that reflects the cool area terroir' is what André and Yvonne de Lange envisaged when they established their small single-vineyard on a hillside in Hemel-en-Aarde Ridge, still circled by conserved renosterveld. Top consultants have grown and styled the wine accordingly, using a low-intervention and sustainable approach, and classic French barrique ageing.

★★★★☆ **Cabernet Sauvignon** Cool provenance delivers perfumed cassis & hint of herbaceousness in tighter **19** (91) vintage. Natural ferment of whole berries ensures sappy, youthful & bright flavours, subtly supported by 24 months in oak, 30% new. Deserves & will reward cellaring to show full potential. Raises the bar on softer **18** ★★★★ (89).— MW

Location: Hermanus ▪ Map: Walker Bay & Bot River ▪ Map grid reference: C4 ▪ WO: Hemel-en-Aarde Ridge ▪ Est 2002 ▪ 1stB 2006 ▪ Tasting by appt ▪ Wine & olive products available via online shop ▪ Owner(s) André & Yvonne de Lange ▪ Farm manager & viticulturist Peter Davison (Jun 2003) ▪ Winemaker(s) Peter-Allan Finlayson (2010, consultant) ▪ 5ha/1ha (cab) ▪ 5t/±500cs own label 100% red ▪ 51 Belvedere Ave Oranjezicht 8001 ▪ info@jakobsvineyards.co.za ▪ www.jakobsvineyards.co.za ▪ **T +27 (0)82-781-5858/+27 (0)82-371-5686**

☐ **Jam Jar** *see* Cape Classics
☐ **J&G** *see* Goedverwacht Wine Estate

Jan Harmsgat

This extensive estate on the Langeberg foothills near Robertson has had a colourful history since its founding by Jan Harmansz in the 18th century. Vines account for a little over 16 ha, and their fruit is part of a much larger agricultural production, just as wine (made by Francois Haasbroek of Blackwater Wine and untasted by us this edition) is but one attraction - there's also luxury accommodation and a restaurant, to name a few.

Location: Bonnievale ▪ Map: Robertson ▪ Map grid reference: C2 ▪ Est 1723 ▪ Tasting & sales Mon-Sun 8-5 ▪ Fee R40 ▪ Open all year round ▪ 5-star Country Guest Lodge & Restaurant ▪ Gift shop ▪ Farm produce ▪ Conferences ▪ Walks/hikes ▪ MTB trail ▪ Heritage property ▪ Vineyard tours; farm & nature 4x4 tour ▪ Owner(s) AH Kleinhans-Curd ▪ Winemaker(s) Francois Haasbroek (consultant) ▪ Viticulturist(s) Kowie Smit (Dec 2012, consultant) ▪ 625.05ha/16.35ha (cab, ptage, pinot, shiraz, chard, sauv, viog) ▪ 260t/3,300cs own label 65% red 35% white ▪ IPW, GlobalGAP, Siza, WIETA ▪ PO Box 161 Swellendam 6740 ▪ wine@janharmsgat.com ▪ www.janharmsgat.com ▪ **T +27 (0)23-616-3407**

JAN Wines

South African Michelin-star chef Jan Hendrik van der Westhuizen's own wine bears the name of his lifestyle portfolio of restaurants, food publications, online learning initiatives and homeware. The Zevenwacht team in Stellenbosch recently became his collaborators in the current pair of blends, and are planting more mourvèdre for the red and chenin for the white. The latter will also benefit from newly acquired amphora.

★★★★☆ **Shiraz-Mourvèdre-Grenache** ✓ Rhône-like black pepper & scrub, wild berry scents, **19** (90) is complete, seamless, the elements merging to present a wine of class & finesse. Smooth textured & long, the tannins a hidden muscle tone. It's the total experience that seduces.

★★★★ **Chardonnay-Chenin Blanc-Roussanne-Viognier** No semillon in **22** (89), it's the stonefruit & aromatically perfumed varieties, 80% oaked for 9 months, which bring a shortbread richness. Persistent & flavourful, acidity adding a lift.— CR

Location: Kuils River ▪ WO: Stellenbosch ▪ Tasting & sales available at Zevenwacht cellar door Mon-Fri 8.30-5 Sat/Sun/pub hols 9.30-5 ▪ Closed Dec 25 ▪ Tasting fee: executive R70pp/6 wines ▪ Winemaker(s) Hagen Viljoen, with Charles Lourens (Zevenwacht) ▪ Viticulturist(s) Eduard van den Berg (Zevenwacht) ▪ info@zevenwacht.co.za ▪ www.janonline.co.za, www.zevenwacht.co.za ▪ **T +27 (0)21-900-5700**

☐ **Jardin** *see* Jordan Wine Estate
☐ **Jason's Creek** *see* Jason's Hill Private Cellar

Jason's Hill Private Cellar

Headline news from the winery on the Du Toit family's grape-growing estate, Jasonsfontein, is the release of what's understood to be the first all-chenin cap classique in the Breedekloof district. A limited release of 660 cases, it joins a portfolio made by daughter Ivy, who in the early 2000s converted a farm garage into a mini-cellar and produced the first wine, going on to gain Diners Club Young Winemaker among other titles.

Reserve range

★★★★ **Izak** Cab franc-led 5-way Cape Bordeaux is classically styled & seriously oaked. Though generous & full bodied, **18** (89) shows refinement & restraint in its convincing cassis fruit, powdery tannins.

★★★★ **Arrois Cap Classique** (NEW) From chenin, **18** (86) has satisfying yeasty savouriness from 42 months lees contact. Taut & austere, with green apple & persimmon fruit on refined mousse.

Not tasted: **Beatrix**.

Jason's Hill range

★★★★ **Cabernet Sauvignon** Full-bodied **18** ★★★★ (84) has high-toned blackcurrant fruit, hint of dark chocolate, chalky tannins, shade less focus than last-made **16** (86).

★★★★ **Merlot** Lean yet juicy **18** (86) has herbaceous red berry fruit, earthy minerality, good varietal focus. 14 months in 25% new French oak lend breadth & polish. Better form than **17** ★★★ (81).

Cinsault Unwooded ★★★ Pale hued & light bodied, **21** (78) has hints of cherry & almond. **Petit Verdot** ★★★★ A little sullen, **18** (83) shows malty notes, dark chocolate & plums. Big but ripe tannins need time to settle. **Shiraz** ★★ Pervasive smoked meat & cinder notes shade the fruit of **18** (74).

Jason's Creek range

Classic Red ② ★★★☆ Sleek shiraz & pinotage, **18** ⑧④ has honest black fruit, gentle oak nudge. — GdB

Location: Rawsonville ▪ Map/WO: Breedekloof ▪ Map grid reference: A5 ▪ Est/1stB 2001 ▪ Tasting & sales Mon-Fri 8-5 Sat/pub hols 10-3 ▪ Shop ▪ Facilities for children ▪ Weddings/functions ▪ 6,6km hiking trail ▪ Owner(s) Du Toit family ▪ Cellarmaster(s) Ivy du Toit (Jan 2001) ▪ Viticulturist(s) Alister Oates (Jan 2004) ▪ 100ha ▪ 45% red 55% white ▪ PO Box 14 Rawsonville 6845 ▪ info@jasonshill.co.za ▪ www.jasonshill.co.za ▪ **T +27 (0)23-344-3256**

Jasper Raats Wines ⑨

In this small-scale, often single-site signature collection, Longridge cellarmaster Jasper Raats combines his 'ultra-natural' winecrafting with an adventurous streak for 'the highest expression of terroir possible, always with balance and elegance'. His Cape Blend supports a non-profit in its fight against crime.

★★★★☆ **Die Plêk Cinsault** ⑳ From 1974 heritage dryland bushvines, **20** ⑨⓪ like last has weight & intensity along with a summery quality, aided by soft tannins & acid adding vibrancy to the spiced cherry fruit. Oak, year, none new this time, in balance.

★★★★☆ **Cuvée Rika Pinot Noir** ⊘ Named for Raats matriarch, **21** ⑨② achieves a delicate balance between cherry fruit & soft baking spices from ±14 months in older oak. Beneficially less muscular than last. Recent vintages ex Stellenbosch, previous from Elgin.

★★★★ **The Silk Weaver Sangiovese** Tribute to Italian immigrants from Como who farmed & weaved silk in Knysna mid-1800. **21** ★★★★ ⑧⑤ again bold & burly, even a touch wild & rustic, mirroring **20** ⑧⑥ in its red fruit & tealeaf note backed by sweet cherry oak.

★★★★☆ **Driefontein Syrah** Ripe red & black plum paired with dialled-down oak (none new, year) in **22** ⑨① still shows sensational savoury profile demanding attention. A pleasure now but more in store. **21** untasted. **20** ⑨② had 20% new oak, 22 months.

★★★★ **Skebenga** Name changed from 'Skollie' but remains a Cape blend of pinot noir, cinsaut & their 'Naughty Child' pinotage. **21** ⑧⑧ continues in lighter styled, fruit-forward mode, brushed with seasoned oak & rustic charm. **20** untasted.

★★★★☆ **Organic Concrete & Clay Chardonnay** As name suggests, **22** ⑨① raised in egg-shaped concrete tanks & clay amphora. As tasty as previous, showing admirable gravitas & texture; a lemony acidity energises the layers of succulent tropical peach & pine flavour.

★★★★☆ **Organic Driefontein Blanc** ⑨ ⑱ Hands-off vinification of sauvignon blanc - bunch pressing, wild-yeast ferment in old oak, no fining or filtration - results in arresting length of flavour along with textured earthy grip in **23** ⑨④, sampled pre-bottling. Ex registered single-vineyard (as Olindo).

★★★★ **Organic Olindo Verdelho** ⑨ Excellent version of locally scarce Portuguese grape. **22** ★★★★☆ ⑨⓪ delivers liquid lemon meringue pie - citrus curd, creamy mallow, ginger biscuit - supported by older oak, even more delicious than previewed last time. **21** untasted. **20** ⑧⑦ was the first sampled by us. — DS

Location/WO: Stellenbosch ▪ Map: Helderberg ▪ Map grid reference: C1 ▪ Est 2010 ▪ 1stB 2011 ▪ Tasting & sales Mon-Tue 10-5 Wed-Sat 10-6 Sun 10-3.30 ▪ Tasting fee applicable ▪ Closed Good Fri & Dec 25 ▪ Owner(s) Vigneron Consulting Ltd ▪ Winemaker(s)/viticulturist(s) Jasper Raats (2010) ▪ 5.5ha (cinsaut, pinot, sangio, shiraz, sauv, verdelho) ▪ 17t/2,300cs own label 60% red 40% white ▪ info@jasperraats.co.za ▪ www. jasperraats.co.za ▪ **T +27 (0)76-752-5270**

☐ **Jasper Wickens** see JC Wickens Wines

Jayne's ⑨

Beaumont Family Wines' historic home-farm in Bot River is the birthplace of artist Jayne Beaumont's Burgundy-inspired signature wines, both from a small, young vineyard beside the old watermill, specially planted for her by son, viticulturist and BFW co-owner Sebastian. She crafts a single barrel of each, from grapes selected on the vine and traditionally handled. This year sees a unique anniversary: Jayne's 50th year on Compagnes Drift and Sebastian's big 5-0, having been born a few months after the farm was purchased.

★★★★☆ **Pinot Noir** ⊘ To preserve intrinsic varietal character, part wholebunch, wild ferment, basket press, year 2nd-fill barrique, which **21** ⑨⓪ rewards with plush berries, cigarbox & white pepper, a hint of forest floor. Classic styling, has elegance & finesse, appealing freshness. Enjoy at its youthful best. No **20**.

★★★★☆ **Electrique Chardonnay** ⓐ Sleek but not shy, **22** ㉜ bunch pressed, 11 months in barrique yet vivid citrus holds centre stage. Enough savoury edging to add a layer, season the flavour. Admirable extended length. Has polish & style.— CR

Location/WO: Bot River ▪ Est/1stB 2011 ▪ Tasting & sales at Beaumont Family Wines ▪ Owner(s)/winemaker(s) Jayne Beaumont ▪ PO Box 3 Bot River 7185 ▪ jayne@beaumont.co.za ▪ www.beaumont.co.za ▪ **T +27 (0)82-928-2300/+27 (0)28-284-9194**

☐ **JC le Roux** *see* The House of JC le Roux

JC Wickens Wines   ⓛ

Another think-on-your-feet vintage in 2023 for Jasper Wickens, owner with viticulturist wife Franziska of this Paardeberg boutique venture focused on varietal purity and terroir expression through low intervention. An 'impressive' early season yielding 'beautiful fruit and finesse' turned trickier, with spells of wet weather and cool conditions till the end. There was however opportunity for the customary harvest trials, notably extended skin contact and submerged cap on shiraz, and the crafting of a single-ferment sparkling for export. The winter planting programme included grenache blanc, verdelho and colombard.

Swerwer range

★★★★☆ **Shiraz** ⓐ Gentle handling shows in smooth-textured tannins, sweet-scented black cherry fruit, delicate floral nuances. **22** ㉞ partial wholebunch, wild yeast ferment, year in old barrels. Supple, youthful & elegant, with charming scrub & herbal notes, enduring finish.

★★★★☆ **Touriga Nacional** Exotic mix of blueberry, bramble & mulled plum redolent of port origins, yet **22** ㉛ has full cred as natural table wine. Sprightly & youthful, with succulent juiciness & fine tannins. Vinification & ageing as Shiraz; modest alc, as all, mostly 13%.

★★★★☆ **Swartland Red Blend** Fragrant, juicy **22** ㉚ is old bushvine cinsault & splash tinta, reflecting Swartland's viticultural heritage, plus younger grenache noir on very rocky slope. Svelte, with honest red berry fruit, light body & supple tannins, just missing wow-factor of **21** ㉞.

★★★★★ **Chenin Blanc** From 4 granite parcels, 10 to 60-plus years, **22** ★★★★☆ ㉜ is plump & ripe, with complex tropical, stonefruit & citrus melange, hints of honey & eucalyptus. Wild yeast ferment & year in very old barrels. Shade less intensity, tautness than **21** ㉟.

★★★★☆ **Rooi-Groen Semillon** Unique semillon gris block, propagated over 20 years by mass selection, **22** ㉜ has character & charm. Full & textural, with beeswax & mulled honey, heightened aromatics from skin contact & 5-day carbonic maceration. Year on lees in old barrels.

Single Vineyards range

★★★★☆ **Tiernes Chenin Blanc** ⓐ From 1983 vines on granite, **21** ㉞ curvaceous, creamy, with mineral-lees breadth, sweet-scented stonefruit, fine-tuned acid. Natural ferment & year in old barrels lend shape & structure.

★★★★☆ **Wolwekop Semillon** Rich & complex, with tertiary nuances from wild yeast ferment, **21** ㉜ from 1963 organically farmed single-vineyard has thought-provoking presence, subtle savoury & mineral notes, satisfying weight & texture, polish from year in very old barrels.— GdB

Location: Malmesbury ▪ Map/WO: Swartland ▪ Map grid reference: C8 ▪ Est 2012 ▪ Tasting strictly by appt only ▪ Owner(s)/winemaker(s) Jasper Wickens ▪ Viticulturist(s) Franziska Wickens ▪ 2,000cs ▪ jcwickens@gmail.com ▪ www.swerwerwines.com ▪ **T +27 (0)72-461-4249**

☐ **JD Initial Series** *see* Jean Daneel Wines

Jean Daneel Wines   ⓘⓘ

Jean Daneel has made wine in some large and grand Cape wineries but now he's contentedly based in a small, recently built cellar in the Overberg hamlet of Napier, between the family home and spouse Renée's bistro. There he immerses himself in his craft, working mostly alone, with wifely help when needed, using 'simple French techniques that create a closer and more intimate relationship between wine-making and -maker'. Visits have been discontinued but the wines are on the eatery's winelist and in its shop/deli.

Signature Series

★★★★ Red Blend 🍇 Harmonious Bordeaux blend from cab, cab franc & merlot, 2 years in 20% new oak, **18 ★★★★★ ⑨⓪** steps up from **16 ⑧⑨** with complex flavours of blackcurrant, graphite & crushed green herbs supported by a ripe, well-knit tannin structure. No **17**.

★★★★☆ Chenin Blanc 🍇 Smooth, mouthfilling **22 ⑨③** delights with tropical & orchard fruit mingling with warm exotic spice, citrus & rich vanilla. Excellent varietal expression, depth of flavour & persistence.

★★★★ Méthode Cap Classique Brut ⊘ From chenin, **14 ⑧⑦** is mature yet still fruit-forward, showing baked apple & stewed quince flavours overlaid with brioche. Fine bubbles give extra texture. No **12, 13**.

Directors Signature Series

★★★★☆ Red Blend 🍇 Another take on Cape Bordeaux, this cab franc-led with variety's perfume foremost on **18 ⑨①**, dark plum, mulberry & Xmas spice following on to rich palate with robust tannin framework, lengthy farewell. 50% new oak, 2 years. No **17**.

Not tasted: **Chenin Blanc**.

Autograph Series

★★★★☆ Syrah 🆕 🍇 Alluring, impeccably balanced **18 ⑨①**, perfumed aromatics of dark flowers & spice, bright, juicy flavours of black fruit & dried herbs, smooth, harmonised tannins after 24 months in older oak, further 30 in bottle. Many more to go.

★★★★☆ White Blend 🍇 Was 'Autograph'. Generous 80% sauvignon & chenin partnership delivers punchy flavours of Golden Delicious apple, orchard fruit & citrus in **22 ⑨③**, combo 500L & 225L barrels adds gentle vanilla, spice & creamy richness, ending with a lemon lift. Last was **17 ⑨③**.— WB

Location: Napier ▪ WO: Western Cape ▪ Est/1stB 1997 ▪ Tastings & tours: see intro ▪ JD Bistro ▪ Owner(s) Jean & Renée Daneel ▪ Winemaker(s) Jean Daneel ▪ 20t 40% red 60% white ▪ 1 Bo Dorp Str Napier 7270 ▪ reneedaneel@gmail.com ▪ www.jdwinesandbistro.co.za ▪ T +27 (0)82-577-7041

☐ **Jean Roi** see Anthonij Rupert Wyne
☐ **Jemma** see Painted Wolf Wines
☐ **JHG Wine Collection** see Jan Harmsgat
☐ **Jikken Barrels** see The Fledge & Co
☐ **Joachim Scholtz** see Rogge Cloof
☐ **John Montagu** see Montagu Wine & Spirits Co

Joostenberg Wines 🍷 🍽 📷 🏠

The Myburgh family acquired Paarl estate Joostenberg in 1879, and made both wine and brandy until 1947, thereafter selling their grapes until brothers Tyrrel and Philip, current custodians and 5th-generation farmers, revived the tradition 52 years later, with Tyrrel as winemaker and viticulturist. Their focus has been on shiraz and chenin, coupled with natural winemaking and environmental accountability (full organic status achieved in 2012). Understandably, today's challenge is identifying varieties that work best in a changing climate, and the performance of newly planted pontac, verdelho and petit manseng will be eagerly watched. See Myburgh Bros listing for another facet of Tyrrel and new assistant Mia Burger's boutique crafting.

Estate range

★★★★☆ Philip Albert Cabernet Sauvignon ⊘ 🍃 🍇 Restrained **20 ⑨③** repeats merlot splash of previous, ups new oak from 15% to 20%. Similar subtle fennel nuance, slightly more savoury edge to crystalline blackcurrant fruit. Beautifully dry, with fine tannin structure for cellaring.

★★★★☆ Klippe Kou Syrah ⊘ 🍃 🍇 Easy-to-like **21 ⑨④** more robust & less perfumed than previous, as dry, with similar steely core though higher alc (14%) adds a rustic touch. 11 months in half-half concrete 'egg' & barrel.

★★★★☆ Bakermat 🍃 🍇 Like all reds from this respected organic producer, **20 ⑨④** underpinned by appetising savouriness that aids freshness & drinkability without sacrificing ageability. Inky, sleek & seductive; very dry & fine. Syrah with 30/20 cab & mourvèdre, 30% bunch ferment, 22 months in 500L cask, 15% new.

★★★★ Family Blend ⊘ 🍃 Mostly syrah, year in older mixed-size barrels (previous had some staves), **21 ⑧⑦** gets orange zest note from drop touriga, meaty tone from dab mourvèdre. Satisfying now & next ±5 years.

★★★★☆ **Die Agteros Chenin Blanc** ⊘ ⊛ Combination old-vine provenance, wild-yeast ferment & multiple maturation vessels gives **22** ⑨⓪ complexity & detail. Like previous, some richness despite bracing dryness, pleasantly challenging quince tartness & bitterness.

★★★★☆ **Fairhead** ⊘ ⊛ Always an interesting & satisfying drink; roussanne & chenin (50/36), with equal dashes viognier & albariño in **22** ⑨③. White peach & floral bouquet, nutty richness threaded with appetising saltiness. Usual old-oak & amphora ferment/10 months on lees.

★★★★☆ **Chenin Blanc Noble Late Harvest** ⊘ Electrifying botrytis dessert, **21** ⑨② with fresh & dried apricot, honey & macadamia nut complexity, brilliant acid lift. Same 6% new oak & similar uncloying sugar (125 g/L) as previous. 375 ml.

Not tasted: **Chenin Blanc**.

Small Batch Collection

★★★★ **No. 22 Mourvèdre** ⓩ ⊘ Second bottling of **20** ⑧⑥ deep-flavoured & gutsy; full, with 14.5% alc, linear tannin & wonderfully savoury finish.

Not tasted: **No. 23 Grenache**. Occasional release: **No. 7 Lightweight Syrah**, **No. 10 Touriga Nacional**, **Early Bird Chenin Blanc**. — CvZ

Location/map/WO: Paarl ▪ Map grid reference: A7 ▪ Est/1stB 1999 ▪ Tasting & sales Sat-Sun 10-4; weekdays by appt at Joostenberg Wines ▪ The Kraal Restaurant open for lunch Sat & Sun - booking essential ▪ Sales daily 7.30-5 at the Joostenberg Deli & Bistro on Klein Joostenberg Farm ▪ Closed Dec 25 & Jan 1 ▪ Joostenberg Bistro ▪ Facilities for children ▪ Tour groups ▪ Gifts ▪ Farm produce ▪ Conferences ▪ Ludwig's Rose Nursery ▪ Owner(s) Philip & Tyrrel Myburgh ▪ Cellarmaster(s) Tyrrel Myburgh (1999) ▪ Winemaker(s) Tyrrel Myburgh (1999), with Mia Burger (2022) ▪ Viticulturist(s) Tyrrel Myburgh (1999), with Jaco Lourens (2023) ▪ 30ha (cab, merlot, mourv, pontac, shiraz, touriga nacional, alvarinho, chenin, petit manseng, rouss, verdelho, viog) ▪ 120t/6,000cs own label 35% red 50% white 15% NLH ▪ PO Box 82 Elsenburg 7607 ▪ winery@joostenberg. co.za ▪ www.joostenberg.co.za ▪ **T +27 (0)21-200-9903 (Joostenberg Wines/The Kraal); +27 (0)21-884-4141 (Joostenberg Deli & Bistro)**

Jordan Wine Estate   ⓠ ⑾ ⌂ ⊙ ⓑ

It's a tempting prospect: living like an owner of one of the Cape's most celebrated wineries, in hilltop luxury with views to tomorrow. Renovated Ted's Villa on the Jordan estate in Stellenboschkloof is now part of the accommodation offering and intended for long-term stays, so there'll be plenty of time to get to know the famous neighbour, the Nine Yards Chardonnay vineyard, and sample the delights of chef Marthinus Ferreira's restaurant, recently remodelled to maximise the panorama. Plus of course tour the internationally awarded winery, with Sjaak Nelson resident for over 20 years and still making exceptional terroir wines (the Chameleon easy-drinkers now listed separately in this guide), here and in the UK, where cellarmasters and co-proprietors Gary and Kathy Jordan own a country estate with a vineyard. Knowledge gained since the founding in 1983 informs ongoing winemaking tweaks, such as adding concrete vessels to the cellar, and doing carbonic maceration in amphora for syrah and merlot for 'the best expression the fruit is giving us'.

CWG Auction range

★★★★☆ **Sophia** ⊛ Slow-burning cab-led Cape Bordeaux, **21** ⑨④ needs & deserves time to fully reveal considerable charms. Elegant, restrained blackcurrant & cherry fruit with subtle vanilla & smoke, despite 81% new oak, 2 years, backed by firm, ripe tannins. Everything is leashed power & poise, keep for a decade or more. Last was **18** ★★★★★ ⑨⑤.

★★★★☆ **Chardonnay** ⓝⓔⓦ ⊛ Exceptional **22** ⑨④'s massive fruit intensity (orange, peach, quince) soaks up 85% new-oak barrel ferment in style. Wild yeast adds toasty oatmeal note while year in oak with barrel rolling adds texture & depth at surprisingly modest 12.5% alc.

Premium range

★★★★★ **Sophia** ⊛ Straight from Bordeaux's Left Bank, remarkable **18** ★★★★★ ⑨④ puts its age to excellent effect with complex ripe blackcurrant fruit, liquorice & lead pencil surrounded by lovely chalky tannins, delicate vanilla oak brush at the lengthy finish. Very complete, very satisfying. 4-way blend, cab at 72%. 61% new oak, 31% American, 18 months. **17** ⑨⑥ effortlessly sublime.

Timepiece range

★★★★☆ **Chenin Blanc** ⓐ ⓦ Very fresh & lovely **22** ⑨④ subtly laces together lots of deft wine-making, some wild ferment in old barrels, portion in amphora, full malo plus 9 months on lees for added richness. Result is a broad yet detailed wine with cooked yellow fruit, wildflowers & honey joined with notes of cream & ginger biscuit.

★★★★ **Riesling** ⓝⓔⓦ ⓦ Late Harvest-style **22** ⑧⑧ shows lovely floral bouquet with apricot & honey giving way to touches rye bread & petrol. Lovely acid-fruit balance, on-point finish for perfect spicy food partnering. 375 ml.

★★★★☆ **Sauvignon Blanc** ⓦ Incredibly textured **22** ⑨② from 39 year old vines, 55% fermented/9 months in older oak with barrel rolling, 37% in amphora, tweak of tank-vinified wine for freshness. Shows great concentration & power, with papaya, gooseberry & hay top notes, lively acid & creamy length.

Reserve range

★★★★★ **Cobblers Hill** ⓐ New World yet still entirely classic 3-part, cab-led Bordeaux blend, **20** ⑨⑤ needs time to open up, allow the ripe blackberry & plum fruit to mesh with smoky mocha oak, 18 months, 25% American, none new. Grows in the glass, suggesting decanting or further ageing will bring even greater drinking pleasure. No **19**.

★★★★☆ **Nine Yards Chardonnay** ⓐ Slightly reductive start to **22** ⑨③, unfurls to cooked apple, peach & tangerine in balance with vanilla & toffee oak from barrel ferment/9 months, 77% new. Like **21** ★★★★★ ⑨⑤, elegant, but feels like it's holding back, plenty of structure to wait until it's ready.

★★★★☆ **Méthode Cap Classique Blanc de Blancs** ⓐ Tiny, lively bubbles lift elegant apple & citrus fruit in graceful **18** ⑨④ from chardonnay. Bracing acid & bone-dry austerity rounded out by 51 months on lees, adding toasted marshmallow complexity & honeyed length.

★★★★☆ **Mellifera Natural Sweet** ⓐ Honey, dried herbs & golden sultana notes on unoaked **22** ⑨③ from raisined riesling grapes. Modest 93 g/L sugar superbly balanced by zesty acid suggests excellent match for cheese more than sweet desserts. 375 ml.

Jordan Estate range

★★★★☆ **The Long Fuse Cabernet Sauvignon** Concentrated rather than rich & ripe, **21** ⑨⓪ exudes elegance & refinement. Blackberries & touch of herbaceousness offset by fresh acid & delicate vanilla & cedar oak, 15% American, 14% new, down from 70% in **20** ⑨②.

★★★★☆ **Black Magic Merlot** ⓥ Cherry & chocolate cake in a glass, **21** ⑨⓪ entices with soft tannins framing nicely ripe black fruit, smooth succulent finish. 20 months older oak, portion American.

★★★★☆ **The Prospector Syrah** Highly enjoyable combination of richness & freshness on **21** ⑨② velvet tannins & texture - aided by some carbonic wholebunch ferment in amphora - highlighting dark plums & pepper spice. Lively acid carries through to floral finish.

★★★★ **Assyrtiko** Exciting future for this white grape associated with Greece's Santorini, enjoying interest in the Cape. **23** ⑧⑥ from young vines showing resinous character with oranges & flinty minerality. Still to grow into itself, for now it's tangy & fresh for summer.

★★★★ **Barrel Fermented Chardonnay** 21% new oak showing strongly on **22** ⑧⑥, smoky, charry notes added to apple pie & orange zest fruit. A welcome 5% of tank-fermented wine adds freshness at the end.

★★★★ **Unoaked Chardonnay** Abundant fruit on **23** ⑧⑦, mixing apple, peach & a touch of floral talcum powder. 4 months on lees add some savoury notes & pleasing palate breadth.

★★★★ **Inspector Péringuey Chenin Blanc** Eminently drinkable **22** ⑧⑧ shows pineapple & apple fruit freshness from stainless steel element with subtle spices from older-barrel-fermented portion. Creamy texture from splash of amphora fruit adds interest at finish.

★★★★ **The Real McCoy Riesling** Technically dry, **22** ⑧⑨ achieves excellent acid-sugar balance, giving crisp, clean mouthful of lilies, limes & suggestion of smoke. Vibrant & lively deliciousness. WO W Cape.

★★★★ **The Outlier Sauvignon Blanc** ⓥ Complex, layered **22** ★★★★★ ⑨⓪ steps up on **21** ⑧⑧ with delicate balance of nettle & woody herbs given richness & mouthfeel from toasty oak (just over half barrel-fermented in mix of old & new). Tinned grapefruit & mandarin zest complete very satisfying wine.

★★★★ **Cold Fact Sauvignon Blanc** Bursting with fresh fruit, **23** ⑧⑥ uses short skin contact & 6 months on lees to add breadth & interest to tangy grapefruit, green apple & lemon flavours.

Dry Rosé ★★★★ Tank sample **23** (85) from equal merlot & shiraz is bone-dry, with vibrant strawberry, raspberry fruit & fresh fynbos herbs. Stunning purplish pink colour too.

Insiders Wine Club Private Collection

★★★★☆ **Cabernet Franc** (Ⓐ) Textbook Stellenbosch cab franc, **21** (94) shows rich blackberry fruit, dried herbs & graphite minerality before perfume & spice from 18 months in old oak. Full & rich but with freshening acid carrying through to lengthy conclusion.

Not tasted: **Petit Verdot**. Discontinued: **Amphora Chardonnay**.

Discontinued: **Checkers range**. — CM

Location/map: Stellenbosch ▪ Map grid reference: C5 ▪ WO: Stellenbosch/Western Cape ▪ Est 1982 ▪ 1stB 1993 ▪ Tasting & sales daily 9-4.30 ▪ Tasting fee from R20pp ▪ Cellar tours by appt Mon-Sun 11 ▪ Pre-booking required for: tasting & cellar tour from R245pp; speciality tasting from R425pp; exclusive vineyard & cellar wine safari from R645pp ▪ The Restaurant at Jordan (seasonal hours) ▪ The Cellar Door 8-4 daily ▪ Conferences (30 pax) ▪ Mountain biking ▪ Conservation area ▪ Jordan Luxury Suites ▪ Wine club ▪ Owner(s) Jordan family ▪ Cellarmaster(s) Gary & Kathy Jordan (1993) ▪ Winemaker(s) Sjaak Nelson (Jan 2002), with Jacobus van Zyl (Aug 2020) ▪ Viticulturist(s) Gary Jordan (1983), Robert Stolk (2021) ▪ 160ha/105ha (cab, merlot, shiraz, chard, chenin, riesling, sauv) ▪ 750t/80,000cs own label 45% red 54% white 1% rosé ▪ Other export brand: Jardin ▪ PO Box 12592 Die Boord Stellenbosch 7613 ▪ info@jordanwines.com ▪ www.jordanwines.com ▪ **T +27 (0)21-881-3441**

Joseph Barry Distillery

(Ⓟ) (◎)

This premium boutique Cape Brandy portfolio is owned by top spirit producer Oude Molen and crafted by a team led by master distiller Kobus Gelderblom in the Klein Karoo town named for 19th-century English émigré, entrepreneur and brandy enthusiast Joseph Barry. Wines from the area are distilled in traditional copper pots and aged underground in French barrels 3-10+ years before hand-bottling and -embellishing with elegant antique-style labels. The tasting lounge is conveniently sited right alongside the R62 arterial.

Cape Brandy range

★★★★☆ **Joseph Barry XO** (Ⓑ) Dark fruit notes of prune, dried pear & stonefruit with vanilla & cedar oak on latest potstill (93), aged minimum 10 years. Sweetly smooth & intense. Attention to detail on appropriately fine packaging: bottling date & lot no. included.

★★★★ **Joseph Barry VSOP** (Ⓑ) All potstill, aged 5-9 years. Latest (88) has more power & rounded, supple elegance than VS, with good fruit essence & toasty wood overtones, the 40% alc in balance. Like all, from Klein Karoo & (except Muscat), chenin & colombard.

★★★★ **Joseph Barry Muscat** (Ⓑ) Totally delightful potstill (88), aged 6-9 years, the grapey muscadel perfume very obvious, & on the softly sweet-fruited palate too. Not really complex, but a unique & welcome contribution to Cape brandy. Tiny volumes made; 500 ml bottles.

Joseph Barry VS (Ⓑ) ★★★☆ Fruity aromas with wood overtones on latest bottling (85). More fiery than expected at 40% alc, but pleasingly clean & fresh. — TJ

Location: Barrydale ▪ Map: Klein Karoo & Garden Route ▪ Map grid reference: C7 ▪ Tasting & sales Mon-Fri 10-5 Sat 10-4 Sun 10-3; pub hols (seasonal) please call ahead ▪ Fee R80pp ▪ Barrydale Hand Weavers retail section ▪ MD Andre Simonis ▪ Brandy master(s) Kobus Gelderblom (Jun 2013, consultant) ▪ info@josephbarry.co.za ▪ www.josephbarry.co.za ▪ **T +27 (0)28-572-1012**

Joubert Family Wines

(Ⓟ) (Ⓨ) (☺) (◎) (Ⓐ) (NEW)

Directly opposite a famous Stellenbosch estate, Simonsig, the Joubert family's 17th-century Koelenhof Farm has its own rich heritage, with winegrowing a feature since 1940, when paterfamilias Pierre began producing in bulk. The first bottled wine came only in 2001, a cabernet-cinsaut released by Attie Joubert and son Hentas. Now, after 21 years, Hentas, wife Elizna and son Attie jnr are delighted to offer a small bottled collection, made on-site, where tastings are available along with facilities for families and businesspeople.

Cabernet Sauvignon ★★★ Briefly oaked, sleek **22** (82) is crafted for earlier drinking, shows berries & plums, juicy texture, bit of plumping sugar, a grip of tannin at the end. **Rosé** (✓) ★★★ Provençal pale & slender (11% alc), with a touch of sweetness, berry-fruited **22** (79) is designed for early enjoyment. **Sauvignon Blanc** ★★★ With flinty styling, winter melon & fresh pear, **22** (82)'s acidity adds freshness, nice drinkability. — CR, CvZ

Location/map/WO: Stellenbosch ▪ Map grid reference: E2 ▪ Est 1681 ▪ 1stB 2022 ▪ Tasting & sales Mon-Fri 8-5 Sat 8-3 ▪ Closed all pub hols ▪ Play area for children ▪ BYO picnic ▪ Conference facility ▪ Owner(s) Hentas, Elizna & Attie Joubert ▪ Cellarmaster(s) Attie Joubert (Dec 2014) ▪ Winemaker(s) Jehan de Jongh (May 2023) ▪ Viticulturist(s) Ruan Mitchell (Jun 2022) ▪ 170ha/110ha under vine ▪ 1,500t/1,760cs own label 20% red 75% white 5% rosé ▪ IPW, WIETA ▪ Koelenhof Boerdery (Pty) Ltd, PO Box 3, Kromme Rhee, Koelenhof 7605 ▪ winemaker@joubertfamilywines.com ▪ www.joubertfamilywines.com ▪ **T +27 (0)21-879-3407**

Joubert-Tradauw Wingerde & Kelder

Varietal wines are the speciality at the small Joubert family winery near Barrydale in Tradouw Valley, the sole blend named by the major tourist route that brings visitors to taste and buy Meyer Joubert's bottlings. These are traditionally crafted to 'capture the magic of this beautiful and unique terroir', and matured till deemed ready. Wife and award-winning cookbook author Beate adds her own magic at on-site Deli Alfresco.

★★★★☆ **Reserve Cabernet Franc** ⓧ Tantalising, complex entry on **17** ⑨④ followed by layered fruit that's vibrant, subtly lifted & seamlessly oaked. Compelling single-vineyard wine, better than **16** ⑨①.

★★★★ **Syrah** Previewed last edition, **17** ⑧⑧'s thyme- & rosemary-scented savoury styling improves on previous, 2 years oak refines dark cherries & plums, wraps them in silk. Pinpoint dry finish deftly done.

★★★★ **R62** Delectably mellow fireside red, merlot & dabs cab franc & syrah, **16** ⑧⑦ has texture like velvet yet spiced plum & cherry fruit still sappy, vital. Tasted out of sequence, shows better than **18** ⑧⑥.

★★★★☆ **Chardonnay Barrel Fermented** ⓐ Smoky oystershell opens **22** ⑨④, then tangerine, blossom & toast ex 13 months oak, 25% new. Balanced, both rich & tangy-fresh. Preserved lime & lemon pith further wake up the appetite. WO W Cape. Last was **18** ⑨③.

Discontinued: **Redfin Pinot Noir**. — ML

Location: Barrydale ▪ Map: Klein Karoo & Garden Route ▪ Map grid reference: C7 ▪ WO: Tradouw/Western Cape ▪ Est/1stB 1999 ▪ Tasting, sales & cellar tours Mon-Fri 9-5 Sat 10-2; pub hols (seasonal) please call ahead ▪ Closed Easter Fri/Sun & Dec 25 ▪ R62 Deli Alfresco Mon-Sat 10-3 lunches & Klein Karoo tapas ▪ Walks/hikes ▪ MTB ▪ Conservation area ▪ Lentelus B&B (www.lentelus.co.za) ▪ Owner(s) Joubert-Tradauw Agri ▪ Cellarmaster(s)/winemaker(s)/viticulturist(s) Meyer Joubert (1999) ▪ 1,100ha/20ha (cabs s/f, merlot, shiraz, chard) ▪ 8,000cs own label 70% red 30% white ▪ PO Box 1 Barrydale 6750 ▪ info@joubert-tradauw. co.za ▪ www.joubert-tradauw.com ▪ **T +27 (0)28-125-0086/+27 (0)82-815-3737/+27 (0)71-656-1230**

Journey's End Vineyards

In Gabb family hands since the mid-1990s, Journey's End focuses on producing delicious premium wines ethically and sustainably. It was one of the first Cape wineries to convert to solar, and in 2021 gained WWF-SA Conservation Champion status. Vineyards in mostly granite soils on the Hottentots Holland foot-hills, influenced by False Bay breezes, produce elegant, high-quality wines, the winemakers seeing their role as 'merely guiding the fruit into the bottle'. Supporting the local Sir Lowry's Pass Village community is also key. In 2020, a foundation was launched which now provides over 30,000 meals a week to those in need.

Precision range

★★★★☆ **The Griffin Syrah** ⓧ Continues improved form & perfumed styling in **18** ⑨②, portion American oak adds smokiness to stylish, persistent wine, with potential for ageing few years.

★★★★☆ **Cape Doctor** ⓐ Pinnacle label a 5-part Bordeaux blend named for prevailing wind. **18** ⑨③ has 55% cab, abundant class. Opulently ripe yet focused & linear, with earthy gravitas, heavenly black fruit, richly textured body honed by 22 months in mostly new oak. **17** untasted.

★★★★ **Destination Chardonnay** Top-tier **22** ★★★★★ ⑨② has ample charm & appeal. Rich, creamy texture from ferment/year in barrel, 20% new, overlaying convincing & pure citrus core, bolstered by pinpoint acid. Outshines **19** ⑧⑧, the last tasted.

Vineyard Series

★★★★ **V4 Cabernet Sauvignon** ⊘ Rebranded & reworked **19** ★★★★☆ ⑨⓪ places emphasis on ripe, healthy fruit, showing in succulent blackcurrant woven with liquorice, wrapped in solid, leathery tannins. Now only French oak, 17 months, 30% new, lends polish & weight without intruding. Upstages **18** ⑧⑦.

★★★★ **V5 Cabernet Franc** ⊘ Supple middleweight with intense varietal character: blackcurrant & blueberry fruit laced with leafy herbs, pencil shavings & iodine-infused liquorice. **21** ★★★★★ ⑨①'s hefty tannins need time, but should settle. 14 months seasoned oak. Last-tasted **19** (89) listed without 'V number', as most of these.

★★★★ **V2 Merlot** Brooding **19** (86) has tarry-savoury tertiary development, dried prune fruit, bone-dry finish. Lithe, with melded tannin & acid. 16 months in 30% new oak, some American. For current drinking.

★★★★ **V3 Shiraz** Aromatic **20** (88) has appealing smoked meat, tobacco & scrub-flower notes, high-toned perfume from 10% carbonic maceration & 15% new oak, third American. Gentle, juicy & appealing, improves on last-tasted **18** (86).

★★★★ **V1 Chardonnay** Rich, creamy barrel-fermented (with 20% concrete 'egg' & clay amphora) **22** (88) offers fine citrus fruit, waft of baking spice, decent heft & length. Portion wholebunch, only free-run juice.

★★★★ **V6 Sauvignon Blanc** Seriously aromatic **22** (86), khaki bush & nettle notes, intense pyrazines from reductive handling, rich texture ex skin & lees ageing. Concentration shade off last-reviewed **19** (87).

Tale Series
The Huntsman Shiraz-Mourvèdre-Grenache ★★★★ With shiraz at 73%, **21** (85) offers lovely ripe plummy fruit alongside savoury & aromatic hints. Medium bodied & smooth. **Haystack Chardonnay** ★★★★ Pleasantly limber & lean, **22** (85) has scented tangerine notes lightly brushed by oak, lees weight to palate. WO Coastal, as next. **Weather Station Sauvignon Blanc** ★★★ Mild-mannered, light-hearted **22** (82) has lemon & gooseberry fruit, gentle acid. Not tasted: **Pastor's Blend**. — GdB

Location: Sir Lowry's Pass ▪ Map: Helderberg ▪ Map grid reference: G7 ▪ WO: Stellenbosch/Coastal ▪ Est 1995 ▪ 1stB 2001 ▪ Tasting & sales by appt only ▪ Closed Easter Fri-Mon, Dec 25 & Jan 1 ▪ Walks/hikes ▪ Horse riding ▪ MTB ▪ Conservation area ▪ Owner(s) Gabb family ▪ Cellarmaster(s) Leon Esterhuizen (Jun 2006) ▪ Winemaker(s) Leon Esterhuizen (Jun 2006) & Mike Dawson (Jun 2015) ▪ Viticulturist(s) Lodewyk Retief (Jun 2011) ▪ 50ha/30ha (cabs s/f, malbec, merlot, mourv, p verdot, shiraz, chard, sauv, sem, viog) ▪ 300t/30,000cs own label 60% red 40% white ▪ Fairtrade, HACCP, IPW, WIETA, WWF-SA Conservation Champion ▪ PO Box 3040 Somerset West 7129 ▪ info@journeysend.co.za ▪ www.journeysend.co.za ▪ **T +27 (0)21-858-1929**

☐ **Joy** *see* Ashton Winery

JP Bredell Wines (Ⓠ)

Based on a mountainside farm at Zeekoegat in the Langeberg-Garcia ward near Riversdale, Anton Bredell and wife Lynne enjoy the challenges of 'micro producing' wines from their own tiny vineyard and grapes brought in. She loves chardonnay, he shiraz, so that's what they're focused on. We hope to taste next time.

Location: Riversdale ▪ Map: Klein Karoo & Garden Route ▪ Map grid reference: C5 ▪ 1stB 1991 ▪ Tasting & sales by appt only ▪ Owner(s) Helderzicht Trust ▪ Winemaker(s)/viticulturist(s) Anton Bredell (1988) ▪ 2ha (port cultivars & some other experimentals) ▪ 500cs own label ▪ antonbredellwines@gmail.com ▪ **T +27 (0)82-550-0684**

Julien Schaal (Ⓠ)

Former sommelier and peripatetic winemaker Julien Schaal came under the spell of the Cape 20 years ago working the vintage in Hemel-en-Aarde. Latterly he and winemaker wife Sophie have pursued a seasonal commute between Alsace, where they produce grand cru riesling, and Elgin, where they've built on an enviable reputation for regionally expressive, elegant wines. The chardonnays are from Paul Clüver Wines in Elgin; the debut Born of Fire pair from Leeuwenkuil in Agter Paarl, certified organic by Control Union. They celebrate the Cape's fynbos and the centrality of fire in ensuring its propagation and survival.

Julien Schaal range
★★★★☆ **Evidence Chardonnay** More sophisticated & better balanced in **22** (91) than sibling, extra barrel-ageing partly buffing the seriously feisty acidity, hallmark of Elgin's cooler climate. Tangy lime & citrus peel on subtle hazelnut cream base from year in oak, 20% new, & natural ferment (as all the wines). Deserves a dinner date & some ageing.

★★★★☆ **Mountain Vineyards Chardonnay** Similar green/tart spectrum: starfruit, angelica & green-gage, though noticeably zestier in **22** ★★★★ (89), showcasing Elgin's elevated vines. Similar ferment/oak to Evidence. Less balanced than **21** (92), better with a meal, best with some cellar time to meld.

Sophie Schaal range

★★★★☆ **Born of Fire Syrah** ⊘ ⊛ Meaty, savoury impression develops into appealing aromatic red-fruit intensity in **21** ⑨⓪. 300L barrels, 20% new, 10 months add touch of spice. Juicy, firm tannins show potential but already tempting in youth. WO Cape Coast, as Chenin.

★★★★☆ **Born of Fire Chenin Blanc** ⊘ ⊛ Kiwi & stonefruit flavours in **21** ⑨①, with some spicy beeswax from the deftly integrated 30% oaked portion (20% new, 10 months). A persistent limy thread freshens, succulent, flavoursome & lingering.— MW

Location: Elgin ▪ WO: Elgin/Cape Coast ▪ Est 2004 ▪ 1stB 2005 ▪ Tasting by appt only ▪ Owner(s) Julien Schaal ▪ Winemaker(s) Sophie & Julien Schaal ▪ 28t/4,000cs own label 20% red 80% white ▪ c/o PO Box 48 Grabouw 7160 ▪ julien@vins-schaal.com ▪ www.julienschaal.com ▪ **T +33 (0)6-10-89-72-14**

☐ **Juno** see Cape Wine Company

Kaapse Liqueurs & Cape Spirits

Cape Town founder-owner Carol Mills since 2014 has been partnering with local businesses to produce a brandy, among other spirits, for sale nationally through markets, events, restaurants and the web. Being preservative-, additive- and colourant-free, as well as fynbos infused, the brandy holds particular appeal for health- and eco-conscious consumers. It's now available in both 750 ml and the original 375 ml.

★★★★ **Cape XO Buchu Brandy** ⊛ 10 year old potstill brandy ⑧⑦ with twigs of indigenous 'miracle herb' Agothosma betulina infusing in the bottles. Medicinal properties aside, shows obvious herbal influence, with suggestion of apricot. Finely fiery structure. 40% alc.— TJ

Location: Cape Town ▪ Est 2014 ▪ 1stB 2021 ▪ Closed to public ▪ Online sales ▪ Owner(s) Carol Mills ▪ Brandy master(s) Oude Molen ▪ 47 Silwood Rd, Rondebosch, Cape Town 7700 ▪ kaapseliqueurs@gmail.com ▪ www.kaapseliqueurs.com ▪ **T +27 (0)83-473-5038**

Kaapzicht Wine Estate   ⓠ ⓞ

Kaapzicht, the 4th-generation Steytler family farm on Stellenbosch's Bottelary Hills, largely faces north-west, which provides the intense sunlight that gives its wines a generosity of fruit. Yet the cooling ocean breezes from Table and False bays, coupled with low cloud cover, deliver freshness. 'It's this juxtaposition of generosity and restraint that is our fingerprint,' says current custodian, Danie jnr. He and his team are proud of the abundance of senior vines on the property - including the 2nd-oldest chenin in SA, planted in 1947 - and believe in farming the young vines to grow old. 'We are always learning from our vineyards. The exciting part is that we're nowhere near our full potential. Hopefully, my kids, or even their kids, will be a step closer.'

Steytler range

★★★★☆ **Pinotage** ⓠ Vintage's best pinotage, paying homage to George & Zelda Steytler who farmed Kaapzicht for 33 years. Vivacious **20** ★★★★★ ⑨⑤ more refined than **18** ⑨⓪, yet, with 85% new oak, 20 months (as the other reds), crafted to reward long cellaring. No **19**, as red siblings.

★★★★☆ **Pentagon** ⓠ Barrel-selected Bordeaux blend whose power & concentration are cleverly contained by an intricate frame of fine tannin, bright acid & plush cab fruit in **20** ⑨③. Just 24% of the other 4 varieties, 70% new oak.

★★★★☆ **Vision** ⓠ Cape Blend styled for the long haul. **20** ⑨② near-equal pinotage & cab, liberal splash merlot provide the plush core of mulberry & blackberry fruit, 89% new oak the stern grip. Stellenbosch WO, as all these flagship wines.

★★★★☆ **The 1947 Chenin Blanc** ⓐ ⓦ From SA's 2nd-oldest chenin. White stonefruit, pear & quince - hallmarks of the variety here, especially the heritage vines - highlighted in **22** ⑨③ by the dryland 1.1-ha vineyard's natural acid. Silky, with obvious vanilla & spice from 10 months in larger barrels, light-feeling despite fruit/oak richness thanks to modest 13% alc.

Terroir range

★★★★ **Skemerlig Cabernet Sauvignon** Broad-shouldered (14.9% alc) & very ripe, yet **20** ⑧⑥ hasn't lost its varietal markers, dark fruit & tobacco, as well as terroir succulence. Tannins firmer than last, need few years to yield.

★★★★☆ **Skuinsberg Cinsaut** ⊘ Translucent ruby hue & light 12% alc belie depth of flavour, subtle yet effective tannins & overall presence of **22** ⑨⓪. From 1991 single bushvine parcel on estate's steepest slope, expressive cherry & red berry fruit, rousing stemmy freshness & piquant finish. 10 months older oak.

★★★★ **Rooiland Pinotage** Ⓟ Traditionally styled, from 20+ year old dryland bushvines. Fynbos-toned **20** ⑧⑦ also has berry scents & flavours, variety's zesty acid, form-giving tannin aided by 15% cab. Portion in new oak.

★★★★ **Skraalhans Pinotage** Surprising & pleasing steeliness to **22** ⑧⑥ brings it back from the edge of being easy-fruity. Brighter & lighter (12.5% alc) than sibling yet no pushover. 10 months older barrels.

★★★★☆ **Kliprug Chenin Blanc** ⓐ ⓨ 40 year old vines on rocky ridge, **22** ⑨④ slightly fleshier than **21** ★★★★★ ⑨⑤, same pear & subtle spice from 80% old-oaked portion, & signature tight acid. Takes time to open in glass, worth decanting in youth.

Suidooster Shiraz ★★★★ Namesake south-easterly wind results in small berries & relatively thick skins, giving brooding character & berry intensity of **21** ⑧④. Lovely black pepper note, hallmark tannic firmness.

Bottelary Hills Estate Blend Ⓟ ★★★★ Medley of red & black fruits on six-way **20** ⑧⑤ Bordeaux-shiraz combo. Impressive fruit-packed centre, with just-present tannins for early enjoyment. Occasional release: **Cabernet Franc**.

Family range

Kaleidoscope Red Ⓟ ★★★★ Fruity & easy **20** ⑧③, shiraz & cab, petit verdot & merlot aged in barrel for smooth sipping. **Pinotage Rosé** ★★★ Pale salmon **23** ⑧② alfresco sipper with faint berry fruit, some breadth from sojourn on lees, well-judged dry finish. **Chenin Blanc** ★★★★ Everyday tipple with decent depth, vinosity & pithy texture. Floral top note to white & yellow peach on **23** ⑧⑤. **Sauvignon Blanc** ★★★★ Pungent **23** ⑧③ grassy aromas & flavours, energetic acid adding freshness & length. Chill & enjoy.

Brandy & Husk Spirit range

Grape Husk Spirit Ⓟ ★★★★ Fresh & persistent spirit ⑧④ from aromatic varieties gewürztraminer & riesling, giving a gentle fragrant quality, the nuttiness touched with grape & raisin notes. 375 ml. Not tasted: **15 Year Potstill Brandy**, **20 Year Old Cape Brandy**. — (vZ, TJ)

Location/map: Stellenbosch ▪ Map grid reference: B4 ▪ WO: Bottelary/Stellenbosch ▪ Est 1946 ▪ 1stB 1984 ▪ Tasting & sales Mon-Sat 9-4 ▪ Closed Good Fri, Dec 24/25/26 & Jan 1 ▪ MTB trail ▪ Conservation area ▪ Postill brandy & grappa ▪ Wine club ▪ Owner(s) Kaapzicht Landgoed (Pty) Ltd ▪ Cellarmaster(s) Danie Steytler jnr (Jan 2009) ▪ Winemaker(s) Kayleigh Hattingh (Nov 2018) ▪ Viticulturist(s) Callie Hefer (Apr 2019) ▪ 190ha/130ha (cabs s/f, cinsaut, malbec, merlot, p verdot, ptage, shiraz, chard, chenin, hanepoot, rouss, sauv, sem, verdelho) ▪ 1,100t/60,000cs own label 70% red 30% white + 20,000cs for clients ▪ Other export brands: Cape View, Friesland, Schneider Rooi Olifant ▪ PO Box 35 Koelenhof 7605 ▪ carin@kaapzicht.co.za ▪ www.kaapzicht.co.za ▪ **T +27 (0)21-906-1620**

☐ **Kadette** *see* Kanonkop Estate
☐ **Kakamas** *see* Orange River Cellars
☐ **Kalkveld** *see* Zandvliet Wine Estate
☐ **Kanah Winery** *see* Twelve Apostles Winery
☐ **Kannaland** *see* Domein Doornkraal

Kanonkop Estate   Ⓟ ⓜ ⊕ ⊚ ⓖ

Now in the sixth decade of bottling under its own label, the debut being the 1973 Cabernet Sauvignon, the iconic Stellenbosch estate owned by the Krige family keeps growing in international prestige for its top wines, and in appreciative admiration for the consistent quality and value of its Kadette range. Despite the 'first growth' status, there has always been a refreshing and praiseworthy welcome extended to visitors, and recent upgrades make the experience yet more comfortable and appealing, with a new deck under leopard trees for outdoor tastings, and a lounge with fireplace 'for those red-wine days'. A vinoteque offers a selection of older vintages, all with perfect provenance, and there's a new private tasting area in the barrel cellar for groups of up to 20. Continued striving for excellence sees a regenerative agricultural plan being implemented across the Simonsberg property, part of which involves a rewilding project where species propagated from the estate's own stretches of fynbos are used to establish corridors between the vineyards.

Kanonkop Estate range

★★★★★ **Cabernet Sauvignon** Ⓐ Beguiling Old World nuance on **19** ⑨⑤'s cassis: savoury spices & old books. At 13.7% alc, lighter than **18** ⑨⑤ (14.8%) though in no way lacking fruit, oak (2 years, 50% new) adding aroma & flavour, & contributing to intricate tannin structure, bright acid adds nervy freshness. Deserves ample time to integrate & unfurl, released later than others in range.

★★★★★ **Black Label** Ⓐ Standout expression of old-vine pinotage, testimony to variety's potential. Arresting blackcurrant & smoke fragrance on **21** ⑨⑥, succulent fruit & flawless dry finish. Dense, compact core soaks up all-new oak, 18 months, adding to already powerful, layered grape tannins, enhancing the whole's stateliness. Like siblings, for decade-plus cellaring.

★★★★☆ **Pinotage** Ⓐ Power & precision align in pitch-perfect **21** ★★★★★ ⑨⑤, step up on refined **20** ⑨③. From the grape, violets, cherries, forest berries & juicy tannins; from the barrique (18 months, 80% new), ash, toast, spice & deft structure; all enlivened by well-judged acidity. Impressive now, will reward patience. Available in many bottle sizes, as all except Black Label.

★★★★☆ **Paul Sauer** Ⓐ Perfumed **20** ⑨④ Cape Bordeaux most expressive & aromatically complex of the quartet: wax, crème de cassis, violets, graphite, cedar shavings & plums. New oak, 2 years, contributes subtle fine-grained tannin framework. Harmonious, a sense of lightness courtesy moderate 13.5% alc, vivacious acidity. 69% cab with near-equal cab franc & merlot.

Kadette range

★★★★ **Cabernet Sauvignon** Ⓥ Only older oak, year, for **21** ⑧⑨ vs **20** ★★★★☆ ⑨⓪'s 75% new for accessible take on classic grape. Ripe, plummy, with blackcurrant, elderberry & hint liquorice, lifted with bright acid. Like sibling reds, includes fruit from wider Stellenbosch, approachable early but will improve.

★★★★ **Pinotage** Ⓥ Lovely expression of estate's flagship grape. Clean-cut **21** ⑧⑧ is vibrant, modern & juicy, neatly dry. Raised year in older oak. In magnum, too.

★★★★ **Cape Blend** Ⓥ Pleasing balance of fleshy fruit, freshness & tailored dry finish elevate **21** ⑧⑧ over **20** ⑧⑥. 39% pinotage gives that tell-tale lift; merlot, cab & dabs cab franc & petit verdot add dark berry character; year older oak in support. Available in larger bottle formats.

★★★★ **Pinotage Dry Rosé** Ⓥ Salmon pink **23** ⑧⑥ spotlights pinotage's ripe red berries & strawberries, is fruit forward with good density, lip-smacking dry finish. WO Coastal.— ML

Location/map: Stellenbosch ▪ Map grid reference: F2 ▪ WO: Simonsberg-Stellenbosch/Stellenbosch/Coastal ▪ Est 1910 ▪ 1stB 1973 ▪ Tasting & sales Mon-Fri 9-5 Sat 9-3 pub hols 10-4 ▪ Fee R70 ▪ Closed Good Fri, Dec 25 & Jan 1 ▪ Cheese platters in summer; traditional snoek barbecues by appt (min 15 people); or BYO picnic ▪ Conservation area ▪ Art gallery ▪ Wine club ▪ Owner(s) Johann & Paul Krige ▪ Cellarmaster(s) Abrie Beeslaar (Jan 2002) ▪ Winemaker(s) Christelle van Niekerk, Ruan van Schalkwyk ▪ Viticulturist(s) Ryno Maree (May 2016) & Annelie Viljoen (2017) ▪ 120ha/100ha (cabs s/f, merlot, ptage) ▪ 3,000t/500,000cs own label 98% red 2% rosé ▪ WIETA ▪ PO Box 19 Elsenburg 7607 ▪ wine@kanonkop.co.za ▪ www.kanonkop.co.za ▪ **T +27 (0)21-884-4656**

Kanu Wines　　　　Ⓨ Ⓜ ◎ Ⓖ

Few Cape visitor locales offer putt-putt or fishing, but corporate-owned Kanu presents both at its hillside venue and cellar in the Koelenhof area, along with many other attractions, following a recent redevelopment and upgrade. A mythical African bird of promise inspired the winery name and stylised branding.

Ultra Premium range

★★★★ **Pinotage** Ⓟ Plums & blueberries, with savoury spice from 22 months in barrel, **20** ⑧⑨ has moved on from **19** ⑧⑥'s restraint, balances structure & fruit for current enjoyment as well as ageing.

★★★★ **Sapphyr** Ⓟ 8-part blend of French, Italian & Spanish grapes, 28 months in new oak, so expect something different in **18** ⑧⑧. Impressive fruit array; cedar-dusted scents; flavours more savoury, clove & pepper, finishing grainy. Long life ahead, or enjoy with rich food. WO Coastal, as Pinotage.

★★★★☆ **Old Vine Chenin Blanc** Ⓟ Ⓦ Rich, ripe **19** ⑨⓪ has tangy lime to freshen stonefruit opulence. Creamy palate with fruit cradled by oak. Everything in harmony. Stellenbosch WO.

Cabernet Sauvignon Ⓟ ★★★★ Stern, powerful & dry **18** ⑧④ shows tannin grip over cherry fruitcake note. Oak is prominent, as on last-tasted **15** ⑧⑤.

Premium range

★★★★ **Shiraz** ⓥ Hedgerow fruit, scrub, leather & woodsmoke, **19** ⑧⑧ wears its typicity proudly. Crafted for ageing, the 33 months in barrel, 77% new, a firm foundation.

★★★★ **Keystone** ⓥ Classic 5-variety Bordeaux blend, cab-led in **18** ⑧⑨, 3 years in new oak. Improves on **17** ★★★★ ⑧⑤ with plush styling, harmony & polish. Beautifully crafted. Coastal WO, as Shiraz.

★★★★ **Nu Era** ⓥ Seductive **17** ⑧⑥ shiraz & mourvèdre deliver blackcurrant pliability with gentle tannin grip & vibrant spice. Nuanced, succulent & with few grams sugar, will age well.

★★★★ **KCB Chenin Blanc** ⓥ Wholebunch, wild ferment/10 months in mainly older barrels, **18** ⑧⑨ an enriched chenin, the vanilla overlay & touch of sugar matched by limy acid, creating a tangy effect.

★★★★ **Viognier** ⓥ Creamy lees provides platform for typical peach & nectarine flavours & aromas on **20** ⑧⑥ from Franschhoek grapes. Structured, with good body.

★★★★ **Giselle Méthode Cap Classique** ⓥ Change in latest **NV** ⑧⑦ bubbly, now 100% chardonnay, 32 months on lees bringing out the citrus flavours, a good fit with the sleekness (12% alc) & bright acid.

Merlot ★★★ Extended stave oaking gives a toasty character to **20** ⑧⓪'s perfume & flavours, dominating the fruit. Best served with rich dishes or cellared a few years. WO Stellenbosch, as Sauvignon Blanc, Angelina & Noble Late Harvest. **Pinotage Rosé** ⓥ ★★★ Perky candyfloss & strawberry on **21** ⑧⓪. Juicy, fresh & easy to like. **Chenin Blanc** ⓥ ★★★★ Improves on last in stonefruit appeal, bright acid twist on **21** ⑧⑤ adds freshness for poolwatering enjoyment. **Sauvignon Blanc** ⓥ ★★★★ No mistaking **22** ⑧③'s variety, gooseberry & kiwi scents, slight touch of sugar compatible with fruitiness. Lees contact 8 months gives palate weight, length. **Angelina Méthode Cap Classique** ⓥ ★★★★ Pink sparkler from pinot noir with coconut marshmallow attraction. **NV** ⑧④ balanced & dry, with green apple tang after year on lees. **Sauvignon Blanc Noble Late Harvest** ⓥ ★★★★ Brûléed pineapple & mango sweetness on **15** ⑧④ wooded botrytis dessert. Piquant acid offsets richness & sugar effectively. 375 ml.

Black Label range
Not tasted: **Rifle Range Red, Rifle Range White, Natural Sweet Shiraz**. — CR

Location/map: Stellenbosch ▪ Map grid reference: E3 ▪ WO: Western Cape/Stellenbosch/Coastal ▪ Est/1stB 1998 ▪ Tasting & sales Wed-Sun 9-4 ▪ Fee R75pp ▪ DuVin restaurant Wed-Fri 12-9 Sat/Sun 9-4 ▪ Curio shop ▪ Putt-putt course ▪ Fishing ▪ Owner(s) ABC GROUP & Caratex (Pty) Ltd ▪ Cellarmaster(s)/winemaker(s) Johan Grimbeek (Jan 2002) ▪ 48ha/20ha (cab, merlot, chard, sauv) ▪ 200t/60,000cs own label 50% red 45% white 5% rosé ▪ WIETA ▪ PO Box 548 Stellenbosch 7599 ▪ info@kanu.co.za ▪ www.kanu.co.za ▪ **T +27 (0)21-865-2488**

☐ **Kapokberg** see Groote Post Vineyards

Kara-Tara ⓥ

Craft vintner Rüdger van Wyk was raised in the town of George on the Garden Route, also home to the Karatara River. A harvest in France kindled a love for Burgundian varieties, so it was natural that this personal project would focus on chardonnay and pinot noir. He sources grapes in cool climates and makes the wines carefully and gently in the Stark-Condé cellar in Stellenbosch, where he has worked since 2017.

★★★★ **Pinot Noir** ⓥ Fresh & light feeling, **22** ⑧⑨ from Elgin, Overberg & Durbanville, 20% bunch fermented, 10% new-oak aged. Smooth pulpy berries, touches clove & black pepper on lingering farewell.

★★★★★ **Pinot Noir Reserve** ⓐ Great depth, complexity & harmony to the last mineral drop, **21** ⑨⑤ from small, isolated Overberg site, carefully barrel selected. Smooth, savoury, gains vibrancy from 30% wholebunch portion. Well-judged year in oak, 20% new, preserves pristine strawberry & red cherry fruit.

★★★★☆ **Chardonnay** ⓐ Elegant & sophisticated, **22** ⑨② styled for the long haul from Overberg, Elgin & Stellenbosch grapes. Mouthwatering tropicals & citrus, exquisite balance between vibrant fruit & lemon crème brûlée richness, dabs clove & nutmeg from barrel ferment & 9 months lees stirring.— WB

Location: Stellenbosch ▪ WO: Western Cape/Overberg ▪ Est/1stB 2017 ▪ Tasting at Stark-Condé Wines ▪ Owner(s) Kara-Tara (Pty) Ltd ▪ Winemaker(s) Rüdger van Wyk (2017) ▪ 5,000cs own label ▪ PO Box 389 Stellenbosch 7599 ▪ sales@karataratawines.co.za ▪ **T +27 (0)21-861-7700**

☐ **Karate Water** see Parow Brandy
☐ **Karen Zoid Collection** see Twin Wine Collective

Karo Brandy

In a tarot reading many years ago, astrologer Rod Suskin saw a fine future for the few rows of colombard owned by Gerald Phillips and wife Carol on their small Klein Karoo farm, Karoolkie. It's come to pass, in a single-origin brandy crafted at Oude Molen. Tasting is by appointment in Stellenbosch's Bosman's Crossing.

★★★★ **Cape Brandy XO** ⓥ Superb label for this striking 10 year old potstill **(89)**. Delicate spice to the dried peach, pear drop & toasted almond, a fiery heart of 40% alc yet delightfully smooth. 500 ml. — WB

Location/map: Stellenbosch ▪ Map grid reference: E5 ▪ Est/1stB 2019 ▪ Online sales - www.kinshipspirits. co.za/shop ▪ Tasting available at Kinship Spirits Distillery, Stellenbosch, by mailing info@kinshipspirits. co.za for appointment ▪ Owner(s) Kinship Spirits (Pty) Ltd ▪ Brandy master Kobus Gelderblom (Oude Molen Distillery) ▪ 6ha/2ha (cbard) ▪ 500cs ▪ 13 Distillery Rd Stellenbosch 7700 ▪ cath@kinshipspirits.co.za ▪ www. kinshipspirits.co.za ▪ **T +27 (0)84-265-6682**

☐ **Karoobossie** *see* Teubes Family Wines
☐ **Kasteelberg** *see* Riebeek Valley Wine Co

Kay & Monty Vineyards

A craft label from only the 2nd farm in Plettenberg Bay to plant vines, the brand name a santé to grandparents Kay and Monty who loved their glass of chilled 'champu' at sundown. Founded in the 2000s by the late property developer John Legh as a polo estate, it's now run by his family, and the wines grown and made by farm manager Lloyd Kasimbi and consultant winemaker Anton Smal, working in a recent on-site cellar.

★★★★ **The Chick** Previewed as 'SMG Blend', now honours winery founder 'Chick' Legh. **21** ★★★★ **(85)** 1st crop off young shiraz, mourvèdre & grenache more muted than last, still shows promise. More savoury, black pepper spice than fruit, ready to drink.

★★★★ **SAV** ⓥ Fig & pear appeal on bright, zesty **21** **(87)** sauvignon blanc. Improves on still-available **20** ★★★★ **(83)** in lees breadth & rounded body. Good integration & length.

★★★★ **Champu Blanc de Blancs** ⓥ All-chardonnay **17** ★★★★★ **(90)** sparkler steps up on **16** **(86)** in focus, complexity & verve courtesy of ultra-crisp acid (7.7 g/L). Persistent lime flavour overlain by a biscuit tone from 54 months on the lees.

Pretty Polly Rosé ★★★ Unready for tasting last time. Mostly shiraz, dashes chardonnay & pinot noir. **22** **(79)** perky cranberry notes, racy acid & dry finish, calling for canapés. Occasional release: **Champu Brut**. — MW

Location/WO: Plettenberg Bay ▪ Map: Klein Karoo & Garden Route ▪ Map grid reference: C1 ▪ Est 2009 ▪ 1stB 2012 ▪ Tasting & restaurant Wed-Sun 11-4 ▪ Restaurant ▪ Weddings & events (200-seat venue) ▪ Self-catering house ▪ Owner(s) Steph Legh ▪ Cellarmaster(s)/winemaker(s) Anton Smal (2012, consultant) ▪ Viticulturist(s) Lloyd Kasimbi ▪ 163ha/7.09ha (carignan, grenache, mourv, pinot, shiraz, chard, sauv) ▪ PO Box 295 The Crags 6602 ▪ hello@kayandmonty.com ▪ www.kayandmonty.com ▪ **T +27 (0)79-965-9779**

☐ **KC** *see* Klein Constantia Estate

Keermont Vineyards

Last edition's induction of Alex Starey into the CWG has seen him add mentor (to Kaylin Willscott, as part of the guild's Protégé Programme) to his roles of winemaker and viticulturist since inception at this high-altitude venture in the fold between the Stellenbosch and Helderberg mountains. The Wraith family acquired two abutting pieces of steep-sloped land after moving from Gauteng just over 20 years ago, and their and Alex's vision of terroir wine, 'grown, made and bottled on the estate', using gentle, traditional and sustainable methods remains unchanged. They've had to part with some rows of their 'grande dame', the chenin heritage vineyard on the riverside, but 2.4 ha remain and, on the terraces, more chenin, chardonnay and sauvignon have been added for the blend. In the cellar, a 2,000L French foudre was 'a new toy for Alex'.

Single Vineyard Series

★★★★★ **Pondokrug Cabernet Franc** ⓐ Open, expressive raspberries, cherries & signature herby-rosemary nuance on **18** ★★★★ **(89)**, from 1.8 ha of low-yield vines on exposed ridge. Sappy core is flavourful & dense, 15.34 % alc well handled. Also in 1.5L, as **17** **(91)** & all wines unless noted.

★★★★☆ **Steepside Syrah** ⊛ Pretty detailing on **18** ⑨③: lavender perfume, incense & hibiscus, moving gracefully to super-smooth red cherry & plum, all shaped gently by careful handling. Range from registered single-vineyards, aged in older oak.

★★★★☆ **Topside Syrah** ⊛ Barrel selection, as all these reds; this consistently excellent bottling from a steep-sided block. Savoury charcuterie & hint lily on **18** ⑨④, muscular grip to rich plummy fruit, woven with gentle acidity to spicy finish. Follows scented **17** ★★★★★ ⑨⑤.

★★★★☆ **Riverside Chenin Blanc** ⊛ ⊛ Aromas of talc & oystershell on distinctive **20** ⑨④. Best-years-only bottling from gnarled vines dating from 1970 & 1973. Creamy texture zested with yellow apple & kumquat, full yet fresh. Tiny quantity, as all these.

Annual Release range

★★★★☆ **Cabernet Sauvignon** ⊛ Classic cab styling elevates **20** ⑨② from previous: cedar, graphite & 6% cab franc leafy perfume woven seamlessly with blackcurrant & plum, smooth fruity tannins & a black cherry finish.

★★★★☆ **Merlot** ⊛ Rich & moreish **20** ⑨⓪ seasoned with estate's other 4 red grapes. Powerful red & black fruit in easy but present grip of powdery tannins that will go the distance.

★★★★☆ **Syrah** Silky, smoky **18** ⑨② has splash mourvèdre, adding bright mulberries & forest berries to spiced plum of shiraz (no cab franc this vintage). Good freshness magnifies juicy fruit in estate's careful frame. 22 months in barrel & bottled unfiltered, as all these reds.

★★★★☆ **Amphitheatre** 5 Bordeaux grapes plus heft of shiraz melded harmoniously in barrel, 5% new oak magnifies shiraz spice, while black cherry nods to the Bordeaux varieties. **17** ⑨① drinking beautifully. Endorsed by VeganSA, as both ranges.

★★★★☆ **Terrasse** ⊛ Named for farm's terraced blocks where 6 white varieties are planted & blended according to vintage. Fragrant **22** ⑨④ ups chenin to 46% from **21** ★★★★★ ⑨⑤'s 36%, partnering chardonnay, sauvignon, roussanne, marsanne & viognier, year older oak. Abundant stonefruit, chiefly peach & pear, zippy lime-toned acid, minerality at the end.

★★★★☆ **Fleurfontein** ⊛ Name celebrates farm's water source, apt given the gush of flavour on vine-dried **21** ⑨④: quince, pear, apple, peach, ginger & more. Last was **NV** ★★★★☆ ⑨②, still a blend of sauvignon & roussanne (24%), fermented/year older oak for an intense, complex dessert wine, balanced by lead variety's natural freshness. 375 ml. — ML

Location/map/WO: Stellenbosch ▪ Map grid reference: G8 ▪ Est 2003 ▪ 1stB 2007 ▪ Office Mon-Thu 8-5 Fri 8-3.30 ▪ Tasting room Fri & Sat 10.30-1.30 or any other time by appt ▪ Tasting fees apply ▪ Closed all pub hols ▪ Cellar tours by appt ▪ Luxury self-catering accommodation ▪ Companion Club ▪ Owner(s) Wraith family ▪ Winemaker(s)/viticulturist(s) Alex Starey (Jan 2005) ▪ 156ha/±28ha (cabs s/f, malbec, merlot, mourv, p verdot, shiraz, chard, chenin, marsanne, rouss, sauv, viog) ▪ ±90t/10,000cs own label 65% red 33% white 2% dessert ▪ IPW, VeganSA ▪ PO Box 21739 Kloof Str Cape Town 8008 ▪ info@keermont.co.za ▪ www.keermont.co.za ▪ T +27 (0)21-880-0397

Keet Wines   ⓛ

'There's nowhere to hide with a one-wine portfolio,' Chris Keet notes, yet he continues to resist any temptation to make more than one wine for his eponymous boutique label, saying it's 'to maintain the focus and attention to detail required to produce premium-quality wine'. His Bordeaux blend is sourced from top sites across Stellenbosch, proportions of the various components differing in response to the vintage. He works in the Van Biljon cellar on the Polkadraai Hills, where he is co-winemaker, intervening thoughtfully in the vineyards and the wine to 'combine the classicism of the Old World and generosity of the New'.

★★★★★ **First Verse** ⊛ Consistently superior Cape Bordeaux, slightly more cab franc than cab in **20** ⑨⑤, near-equal merlot & petit verdot, dab malbec, from prime Stellenbosch sites, 18 months oak, 15% new. At 14.5% alc, touch more heft but retains signature freshness, compelling fruit intensity & almost weightless powdery tannins. — CvZ

Location/WO: Stellenbosch ▪ Est 2008 ▪ 1stB 2009 ▪ Tasting by appt ▪ Owner(s) Christopher Keet ▪ Cellarmaster(s)/winemaker(s)/viticulturist(s) Christopher Keet (Oct 2008) ▪ 1t/2,000cs own label 100% red ▪ PO Box 5508 Helderberg 7135 ▪ chris@keetwines.co.za ▪ www.keetwines.co.za ▪ T +27 (0)82-853-1707

☐ **Keimoes** see Orange River Cellars

☐ **Keldermeester Versameling** *see* Lanzerac Wine Estate

Ken Forrester Wines ⓠ ⓟ ⓑ

Energetic, innovative and tireless in his promotion of chenin blanc, former Johannesburg restaurateur Ken Forrester launched himself into the Cape wine business in the 1990s. With Helderberg farm Scholtzenhof as base, he, wife Teresa and mentor winemaker Martin Meinert built one of the Cape's top wineries, since 2016 with French wine company AdVini's shareholding and support for Ken's emphasis on sustainable viticulture and, lately, regenerative soil strategies. With Louw Strydom coming in as general manager, and young Shawn Mathyse elevated to winemaker, the specialisation in chenin and Rhône blends and varietal wines continues. New collection The Misfits is Shawn's 'personal expression, targeting winelovers and sommeliers'.

Icon range

★★★★★ **The Gypsy** ⓐ Threaded with rose perfume & meaty nuance, **18** ⑨④ lively barrel-selected Rhône blend is on song, its opulent blackberry & plum fruit, fresh, chalky tannins & 2 years oaking, 35% new, well-meshed & drinking deliciously. Shiraz with 35% old vine grenache.

★★★★★ **The FMC** ⓦ Internationally celebrated chenin, mostly 1974 low-yield Stellenbosch vines, naturally fermented, 10-12 months in oak, then barrel selected. **22** ★★★★★ ⑨⑦ brilliantly combines & balances fruit richness, minerality, acid & sugar (6.4 g/L, 7.9 g/L) to express a sense of place. Trumps excellent **21** ⑨③ with exquisite poised dryness, fine typicity.

★★★★☆ **'T' Noble Late Harvest** ⓠ Simply glorious **20** ⑨④ dessert wine from 40-45 year old vines. Delicate & fresh, select pickings of botrytised chenin fermented & aged in new 400L barrel for moreish notes of creamy vanilla & honeyed nuts. Enduring, with piercing freshness. 375 ml. Stellenbosch WO.

Occasional release: **FMC Première Sélection Moelleux**.

Cellar Exclusives range

★★★★☆ **Three Halves** ⓐ Released every 2nd vintage. Usual mourvèdre, syrah, grenache noir in **17** ⑨④, former (57%) giving blueberry & earth, equal portions of latter lending spice, plum & blackberry. Oak, 18 months, 2nd fill, buffs sinewy tannin.

★★★★☆ **The Silver Rose** ⓐ Pale pink **23** ⑨④ shows how fine rosé can be in the right hands. 100% grenache noir from single parcel, free-run juice only for strawberry, watermelon & melon purity. 4-5 months on lees in tank add texture & freshness. Delights more than last-tasted **21** ⑨⓪.

★★★★☆ **Terre Noire Chenin Blanc** ⓦ Our first taste of impressive chenin from small Swartland parcel. **21** ⑨⓪ wild fermented & aged on lees in barrel, 30% new, for a silky body with ripe pear fruit & grapefruit pith grip inviting a 2nd sip.

★★★★☆ **Roussanne** ⓐ Rare varietal bottling, from Stellenbosch vines on granite. **22** ⑨③ white pear & peach fruit, blossom & litchi fragrance, fine-spun texture. Wild ferment & lees ageing in oak, 10% new, adding light grip.

★★★★ **Sparklehorse** ⓦ Seductive **20** ⑧⑧ bubbles from 1975 chenin bushvines reserved for crafting cap classique. Vivid apple, pear & peach juxtaposed with delicate creaminess from 2 years on lees, vivid acid lifts & focuses Stellenbosch fruit.

★★★★ **Stained Glass Méthode Ancestrale** Rosé pet-nat from Stellenbosch grenache noir bottled while still fermenting for fragrant, spicy **21** ⑧⑧. Richness from 18 months on lees, weight from bold-for-style 14% alc, refreshment from crisp acidity & bone-dryness. Improves on last-tasted **NV** ★★★★ ⑧⑤.

Reserve range

★★★★☆ **Renegade** One of Cape's first Rhône-style blends. Shiraz, near-equal partner with 2 others in last-tasted **18** ⑨⓪, at 58% now leads grenache noir & mourvèdre. **21** ⑨② undergrowth, mulberry & cherry flavours & scent, light nudge from 18 months older oak.

★★★★☆ **Old Vine Chenin Blanc** ⓐ Weightless intensity on always-excellent expression of select gnarly vineyards around Stellenbosch. Tank & barrel ferment/8 months, 20% new, build delicate scaffold for tangy pineapple, grapefruit & pear in **22** ⑨④, ending with pleasant quinine lift.

★★★★ **Sauvignon Blanc** Free-run juice for mineral-toned tropicality on **22** ⑧⑥ from Stellenbosch vines. Extended 8 weeks lees contact add cream to stony, flinty palate, shot through with green-apple acid.

Not tasted: **Pat's Garden**.

The Misfits range (NEW)

★★★★ **Cinsault Met Sonder Stingels** Afrikaans part of quirky name, 'With Without Stalks', references partial stem-ferment for **20** ⑧⑧'s small Piekenierskloof crop. Resultant peppery lift marries tastily with bouncy red berries & super-smooth tannins from 9 months in old oak.

★★★★☆ **Grenache Noir** 'Misfit', perhaps, in having both power & perfume. Perfectly pitched **20** ⑨① gets cooler, more floral notes from Piekenierskloof, flesh & density from Stellenbosch. Red fruited & juicy, strawberries & raspberries buffed by year older wood.

★★★★ **Syrah** Unoaked, setting it apart, **20** ⑧⑥ showcases mature, low-yield Stellenbosch vineyards, delivering peppery plums on soft, fruity tannins. Tempting now, will keep a few years.

Petit range

Rosé ⑦ ★★★★ Dry, fruity **23** ⑧④ from grenache noir & viognier improves & hits the right spot with strawberry freshness & easy drinkability.

Merlot ☺ ★★★ Well-balanced, amiable **21** ⑧⓪ has variety's black cherries & plums in plentitude. Unwooded, as Pinotage. **Sauvignon Blanc** ☺ ★★★ Even brighter than last, **23** ⑧② delivers vibrant citrus & gooseberry alongside nettle & an appetising acid tang.

Cabernet Sauvignon ★★★ Soft & fruity, with frisson of spice, **22** ⑧⓪ intended for early enjoyment, like siblings. **Pinotage** ★★★★ Fruit forward, **22** ⑧③'s character cosseted by cold ferment & light skin contact for a juicy berry bonanza. WO Stellenbosch. **Chardonnay** ★★★ Creamy apples & pears, with pinch of salt from lees contact in stainless tank, **22** ⑧② balanced by limy acid. **Chenin Blanc** ★★★ Earlier picked for freshness, **23** ⑧② packs green apples & citrus into a steely, crisp body. Not tasted: **Natural Sweet**. — ML

Location: Stellenbosch ▪ Map: Helderberg ▪ Map grid reference: C2 B2 ▪ WO: Western Cape/Stellenbosch/Piekenierskloof/Swartland ▪ Est/1stB 1994 ▪ Tasting & sales on home farm, cnr R44 & Winery Rd: Mon-Fri 9-5 Sat/pub hols 10.30-4 ▪ Tasting options: Petit R60/5 wines; Reserve R80/4 wines; Chenin R100/5 wines; Icon R150/4 wines ▪ Closed Good Fri, Dec 25 & Jan 1 ▪ Sundays & after hours tasting available at 96 Winery Rd Restaurant (pre-booked) ▪ Owner(s) Forrester Vineyards Pty Ltd ▪ Cellarmaster(s) Ken Forrester (1994) ▪ Winemaker(s) Ken Forrester (1994) & Shawn Mathyse ▪ Viticulturist(s) Pieter Rossouw (Oct 2009) ▪ (grenache, merlot, mourv, shiraz, chenin) ▪ 1,150t 45% red 55% white ▪ Other export brand: Marks & Spencer Classics Chenin Blanc ▪ Brands for clients: Woolworths ▪ ISO 9001:2000, HACCP, SEDEX, WIETA ▪ PO Box 1253 Stellenbosch 7599 ▪ info@kenforresterwines.com ▪ www.kenforresterwines.com ▪ **T +27 (0)21-855-2374**

Kershaw Wines ⑨

Since 2012, Elgin Valley has been home to UK-born winemaker, trained chef and Master of Wine Richard Kershaw (his listing in this guide previously under 'Richard Kershaw Wines'). His goal, to capture the unique qualities of 'the coolest climate in South Africa', is pursued on several fronts but with the same classic cool-climate varieties, chardonnay, pinot noir and syrah. The three Clonal Selection wines head the list; the Deconstructed range reflects its creator's geeky side, focusing on site, soil and clone; and Smuggler's Boot offers an easier-drinking style. Beyond Elgin, the GPS range is directed to unusual sites. While his emphasis is on the vineyard, Richard believes in the cellar, 'the maturation cycle plays a proportionately important role'. His many other activities include lecturing, mentoring MW students, consulting and judging on panels.

Clonal Selection

★★★★☆ **Elgin Pinot Noir** ⑳ Purity & precision in **21** ⑨④, beguiling in its red cherry perfume, silky texture & waves of ripe fruit, all secured by vibrant, fine tannins & Elgin's cool freshness. There's power without heaviness; oak, 25% new, added refinement. A charmer. Also in 1.5 & 3L, as all these.

★★★★☆ **Elgin Syrah** Attracts with ruby translucence, **20** ⑨⓪ palate supple & fleshy, ripe dark spice & truffly flavours augmented by dash toasty oak, 43% new. Rumble of grainy tannins will benefit from short ageing, but probably ready sooner than **19** ⑨④.

★★★★★ **Elgin Chardonnay** ⑳ Steely backbone on **21** ★★★★☆ ⑨④ confident support to sleek, citrus-toned flavours, lees-weighted undertones. Energy, intensity lead to rousing, resonant length. Oak, 53% new, completes a vintage for the patient. Malo discouraged to preserve acid, as **20** ⑨⑤ & all chardonnays.

Kershaw Deconstructed range

★★★★ Kogelberg Sandstone Pinot Noir PN777 ⓧ Dark cherry fruit of **19** ⑧⑨ pure & well defined, whiff toasty 25% new oak adds interest. Freshness & fine tannin alleviate riper features though alc glow & sweet impression notable.

★★★★☆ Kogelberg Sandstone PN115 Pinot Noir ⓧ Bright-fruited **20** ⑨⓪, sweet red cherry juiciness & touch of spice, balancing substance & frame of fine tannin. Judicious oak, 33% new, further enhancement. Good now, promise of further interest.

★★★★☆ Valley Ridge Gravel Over Clay Pinot Noir PN777 ⓧ Same clone & ripeness as Kogelberg, different soil; **19** ⑨④ elegant, balanced, palate supple, fragrant red fruit still held in resolute grip. Patience will be rewarded. Oak 25% new, 10 months.

★★★★☆ Groenland Bokkeveld Shale SH22 Syrah ⓧ Offers plentiful floral aromas, sweet red berry substance & lick of spice. **19** ⑨⓪ more energetic than last, needing time to settle & fully absorb 17 months in 75% new oak, up from 50%.

★★★★☆ Groenland Bokkeveld Shale SH9C Syrah ⓧ More composed & harmonious of the two syrah clones. **19** ⑨④ charming example of cool-climate syrah; perfectly ripe, with freshness & plenty of room to grow. Oak 75% new, up from 40%, in sync.

★★★★☆ Lake District Cartref SH9C Syrah ⓧ Brighter red fruit & floral scents on **18** ⑨① than partner SH9C of that vintage; plenty of energy & freshness, less weight but showing more toasty oak, 50% new. May grow in harmony & interest.

★★★★★ Kogelberg Iron Stone CY548 Chardonnay ⓐ Already showing complexity in its citrus, nutty concentration, layered on a creamy texture, invigorated by taut acid. Oak, 100% new seamless enhancement. **21 ★★★★★** ⑨⑤ better integrated, harmonious in youth than **20** ⑨⓪, similar bright future.

★★★★★ Kogelberg Sandstone CY76 Chardonnay ⓐ Cool-grown classic. Fragrant lemon blossom aromas, citrus fruity acids are delicate & pure but also persuasive thanks to textural depth of lees ageing, extra dimension of oak, 50% new. Thrilling tension & energy lead to lengthy, resounding conclusion, suggest rewarding future for **21** ⑨⑤.

★★★★☆ Lake District Bokkeveld Shale CY95 Chardonnay ⓐ Expressive nutty, earthy flavours broadened by creamy, lees-enriched texture on **21** ⑨④; steely backbone, firm structure in sound support, augurs well for greater complexity over several years. New oak, 11 months seamlessly integrated.

★★★★☆ Lake District Bokkeveld Shale CY96 Chardonnay ⓐ Same site & vinification, different persona to CY95. **21** ⑨④ racy & taut, flavoursome rather than fruity, cleansing citrus-toned acid currently dominating lees-rich undertones. Oak, 100% new, prominent, will resolve with time.

Kershaw GPS Series

★★★★☆ Walker Bay Pinot Noir ⓧ Purity & freshness hallmarks of **20** ⑨①, sweet, dark cherry succulence lifted by bright acid & framed by fine tannins. Oak, 24% new, for structure rather than flavour. Enough concentration should see greater harmony with time. Ex Hemel-en Aarde Ridge.

★★★★☆ Klein River Syrah ⓧ Exuberant & with plentiful juicy substance, cool-climate **19** ⑨⓪ backed by equally lively tannins. These & floral & red fruit features will benefit from time to settle, fully integrate oak, 33% new.

★★★★★ Lower Duivenhoks River Chardonnay ⓧ Full of energy, bracing acid, offset by creamy core, exceptional **20** ⑨⑤ strikes great unity between textural lightness & weight. Strong salty thread through & beyond citrus & hazelnut features, 63% new oak spice a further enhancement. More harmonious than **19 ★★★★★** ⑨②.

★★★★☆ Cape South Coast Sauvignon Blanc-Semillon ⓐ Distinctive 56/44 partnership from excellent **21 ★★★★★** ⑨⑤; sea breeze-fresh tangerine peel & lemongrass flavours, semillon adding breadth & weight, sauvignon verve & intensity, memorable length. Will reward with a few years, as in **20** ⑨①. 22% new oak.

Smuggler's Boot range

★★★★ Pinot Noir ⓥ Quality individual, **21** ⑧⑧ has much charm in its dark cherry fragrance, supple texture. Freshening acid & lively tannin form complementary structure that doesn't hinder early-drinking pleasure. Wholeberry ferment in 50% plastic 'egg', ageing in older oak. Cape South Coast WO.

★★★★ **GSM Blend** ⊘ Grenache noir & syrah with dab mourvèdre adding savouriness to spice & sweet strawberry on **19** ⑧⑦. Part older-oaked for complexity, rounded tannins. Tasty drinking from Paardeberg.

★★★★ **Chardonnay** Offers quiet creamy, lemony notes on textured palate. **22** ⑧⑦'s partial oaking, 16% new, sprightly acid in harmony for easy drinking. WO W Cape. No **21**.

★★★★ **Sauvignon Blanc** Cape South Coast sourced **22** ⑧⑥ quiet fruit, gentle freshness, a little breadth from short lees-ageing. Less dramatic than last, which included drop semillon. Only inoculated ferment, all others tasted this edition spontaneous.

Discontinued: **Cabernet Blend**. — AL

Location/map: Elgin ▪ Map grid reference: B2 ▪ WO: Elgin/Cape South Coast/Western Cape/Walker Bay/Klein River/Lower Duivenhoks River ▪ Est/1stB 2012 ▪ Tasting by appt ▪ Closed all pub hols & weekends ▪ Wine club ▪ Owner(s) Richard Kershaw ▪ Winemaker(s) Richard Kershaw (2012) & Dudley Wilson (2016) ▪ ±6,000cs own label 50% red 50% white ▪ PO Box 77 Grabouw 7160 ▪ info@richardkershawwines.co.za ▪ www.kershawwines.com ▪ **T +27 (0)21-200-2589**

☐ **Kevin King** *see* South Hill Vineyards
☐ **KFK Reserve** *see* Stellenview Premium Wines

Khayelitsha's Finest Wines ⓥ

Based in the historically black residential area of Khayelitsha in Cape Town, Lindile Ndzaba has a mission to foster the culture of wine enjoyment there, as well as to take his brand beyond. He has now partnered with Saxenburg, the eminent Stellenbosch winery, to not only produce the wines but to build up distribution. For a 'wine tasting with an African twist' in Khayelitsha, contact Lindile (two weeks in advance).

★★★★ **White Blend** Exuberant aromatic & flavour profile of **23** ⑧⑥ owes much to sauvignon's passionfruit & guava, though chenin dominates blend (75%). Some of latter & dollop semillon spontaneously fermented & briefly aged in oak, helps give depth & breadth. Fresh & dry, with succulent lemony acidity.

Red Blend ★★★★ Different blend to previous (as White), now syrah (60%) & cab, offering pleasing ripe berry aroma & flavour. **22** ⑧⑤ fairly rich, though not imposing at 14.2% alc, balanced, with smooth but structuring tannins. Only older oak to keep fruit freshness. Discontinued: **Pinot Noir**. — TJ

Location: Cape Town ▪ WO: Polkadraai Hills ▪ Est 2018 ▪ Tasting in Khayelitsha ▪ Owner(s) Lindile Ndzaba ▪ Winemaker(s) Brendan Smith (Saxenburg Wine Farm) ▪ Viticulturist(s) Donovan Diedericks (Saxenburg Wine Farm) ▪ 750-1,000cs own label 50% red 50% white ▪ Mbolwa Cres, Khayelitsha Cape Town 7784 ▪ khayelitshawinegems@gmail.com ▪ **T +27 (0)73-081-3691**

Khulu Fine Wine 📷 (NEW)

IsiZulu for 'great' or 'extravagant', Khulu was created in 2021 to be a 'bold and luxurious' wine brand that represents the personal tastes and preferences of CEO Kwanele Nyawo and her co-founders, while shining the spotlight on the various wine regions of the Western Cape. A further ambition is to increase diversity in the winemaking sphere, inter alia by creating a co-working space on home-farm Kunnenburg in Paarl 'where winemakers of various backgrounds can come and make their very own special wine'. Plans also include planting more vines. In the interim the boutique wines are crafted from select grapes by consultants.

Izigidi Cap Classique ★★★★ Classy **NV** ⑧⑤ from chardonnay exudes nougat & all manner of apple (green, red, toffee) on bouquet & palate. Bone-dry at less than 3 g/L sugar but rich & creamy, with izigidi ('million') honeyed bubbles slipping down oh so easily. — PS, CvZ

Location: Paarl ▪ WO: Western Cape ▪ Est 2021 ▪ 1stB 2022 ▪ Currently not offering tastings ▪ Sales online ▪ Events venue ▪ Owner(s) Mzansi Craft Wine ▪ 24ha/4ha under vine ▪ 500cs own label 70% red 30% white ▪ kwanelenyawo@gmail.com ▪ kwanele@mzansicraftwine.com ▪ **T +27 (0)72-497-8363**

Kindred Coast (NEW)

Stellenbosch-trained winemaker Stuart Botma gained seasoning in Australia, France and the US before settling in Hermanus and in 2021 embarking on his 'viniferous voyage along the southern coast of Africa'. The plan is to develop the core pair while adding bottlings from select vineyards to portray the wider region in wines that are 'honest and expressive', and made pragmatically, with intervention only when needed.

Captured Reflections range

★★★★ **Red Blend** Flavoursome & satisfying Rhône blend successfully treads tightrope between lightness & substance. 21 ⑧⑦'s succulence tempered by near bone-dry finish & just right amount of grip. Mourvèdre & grenache noir (45/33), splash syrah, naturally fermented, 23% wholebunch.

★★★★☆ **White Blend** Confident blend of sauvignon (55%), with semillon, viognier & nouvelle. On paper, 21 ⑨⓪ bracingly dry with piercing acid; in the glass, elegantly balanced & graceful. Faintly floral notes, whispers citrus, nuanced smoke & flint. Barrel fermented/±4 months on lees. — PS, CvZ

Location: Hermanus ▪ WO: Cape South Coast ▪ Est/1stB 2021 ▪ Closed to public ▪ Owner(s) Kindred Coast Wine (Pty) Ltd ▪ Winemaker(s) Stuart Botma (Jan 2021) ▪ 450cs own label 45% red 55% white ▪ PostNet Suite #318 Private Bag X29 Somerset West 7129 ▪ stu@kindredcoastwine.co.za ▪ www.kindredcoastwine.co.za

Kingna Distillery

At the boutique home-farm on the Kingna River near Montagu, the brandy master has been crafting colombard grapes into premium brandies since 2007, using a 2,000L still and French/American oak barrels. A new VSOP was debuting as we went to press. Tastings and tours are available at the distillery, along with weddings, functions and conferences.

Location: Montagu ▪ Map: Klein Karoo & Garden Route ▪ Map grid reference: C8 ▪ Est 2007 ▪ 1stB 2012 ▪ Tasting, sales & distillery tours by appt Mon-Fri 10-5 Sat 10-11pm Sun 10-4 ▪ Closed Easter Sat/Sun, Dec 25/26 & Jan 1 ▪ Tour groups ▪ Conferences ▪ Weddings/functions ▪ Owner(s) Norbert Engel, Esti Haupt & Willrich Cadle ▪ Brandy master Fransie Mouries (since 2020) ▪ Winemaker(s) Damien Cadle ▪ 12ha under vine ▪ 150t/112,500L ▪ PO Box 395 Montagu 6720 ▪ cadlecraft1@gmail.com ▪ www.cadlecraft.co.za, www.tahliafarm.co.za ▪ **T +27 (0)74-173-0599**

☐ **King & Queen** *see* Bayede!
☐ **King Shaka** *see* Imbuko Wines
☐ **King Shaka-Zulu** *see* Bayede!

Kings Kloof Vineyards

The Newton-Kings bought part of an old farm high on the Somerset West side of Helderberg Mountain in 1936, and family women managed it for many years. Today there are 11 ha of vines, mostly supplying grapes to Spier, to be joined by a terraced parcel of pinot noir. Tiny batches are made for this label by Johan Jordaan and team, including the chenin featured here, off a 1-ha block just six years old, showing terrific potential.

Family Reserve range

★★★★ **Merlot** ⊘ Ripe-fruit style, cassis & black plums, with 40% new oak for 18 months. Well-integrated tannins, 21 ⑧⑨'s overall effect is of luscious drinking pleasure. Last-tasted was 17 ⑧⑨, as next.

★★★★ **Syrah** ⊘ Showing typicity & heaps of character, 21 ⑧⑨ has hedgerow fruit well-spiced by 10 months' oaking. Texture succulent & streamlined, already deliciously drinkable.

★★★★☆ **Chenin Blanc** ⊘ Not ready last time, 22 ⑨① sleek, compact, tightly knit, there's concentration & depth of appley fruit from extended lees contact. Lovely purity, shows the essence of chenin.

★★★★ **Sauvignon Blanc** ⊘ Last tasted was 19 ⑧⑨, but 22 ⑧⑨ worth the wait. Gooseberry & passionfruit, becoming mineral on the finish. Captures the house-style nervous acid tension.

In abeyance: **Semillon**. — CR

Location: Somerset West ▪ Map: Helderberg ▪ Map grid reference: E4 ▪ WO: Stellenbosch ▪ Est 1939 ▪ 1stB 1986 ▪ Tasting by appt ▪ Owner(s) Newton-King family ▪ Cellarmaster(s) Johan Jordaan (2020, Spier) ▪ Winemaker(s) Johan Jordaan & Spier winemaking team ▪ Viticulturist(s) Bennie Liebenberg (Spier) ▪ 73ha/11ha (merlot, shiraz, chenin, sauv, sem) ▪ 120t/600cs own label 40% red 60% white ▪ WIETA ▪ PO Box 2 Somerset West 7129 ▪ richardnk@kingskloof.co.za ▪ www.kingskloof.co.za

Kirabo Private Cellar

A preview last time, and too unformed to rate, the Verdelho has been bottled and retasted, and shows the enhanced quality and character that Ronald le Roux has achieved across the board since taking the reins of the cellar and vines five years ago. He's added more interesting wines to showcase at the multi-attraction venue on the Breedekloof family farm Watervalkloof, whose boutique brand's name means 'Gift From God'.

Winemaker's Collection

★★★★ **Sidouws Reserve** Ⓥ Petit verdot (60%), equal pinotage & shiraz, bunch fermented then 2 years in older oak, during which power-packed **19** ⑧⑥ lost some of its tannin edge but none of its dense colour or intense maraschino cherry flavour. **18** ★★★ ⑧① was 'Sidouws Red'.

★★★★ **She Awoke** Slightly riper & plumper in **22** ⑧⑦ but as expressive & engaging, just enough acid to counter rich dried-peach & -pear flavours, breadth from long lees-ageing. From gnarled 1981 block, naturally fermented & aged in old oak, unfiltered/fined, as all these.

★★★★☆ **Sauvignon Blanc** ⓃⒺⓌ Delicious **21** ⑨① green fruit & herb flavours with creamy lemon curd undertone from 2 years on lees in older oak. Latter gives subtle hazelnut polish, pervasive fresh seam ensures vivacious persistence.

★★★★☆ **Verdelho** Alluring, scented white flower, greengage & kiwi aromas in **22** ⑨⓪, one of few single bottlings of this variety. Sleek texture & mouthfilling weight (14% alc), though freshness & length retained. Only one barrel made of this interesting, emphatic wine, to pair with food.

Kirabo range

★★★★ **Petit Verdot** Ⓥ Intense & glossy plum fruit, richness freshened by crisp acid, inky **19** ⑧⑥ similar profile to **18** ★★★★ ⑧⑤ but lifts the bar with pleasing dryness & promise of fruitful ageing. **Merlot** ★★★★ Similar plums & dark cherries in **20** ⑧⑤, quite rich (14% alc) yet with variety's piquant acidity, partly buffed by 2 years in old oak. Flavoursome rather than complex, good with Italian toma-to-based cuisine. **Shiraz** ★★★★ A fireside sipper for fans of hearty reds. Big-boned & deep-fruited **20** ⑧② has distinctly sweet impression from hefty 15.5% alc, less expressive than last but reined in by 2 years in old oak. Discontinued: **Barrels End**.

Family Wines range

Petrus Red Blend ★★★ Last was vintage dated (**20** ⑧①), latest a **NV** ⑧① mix of petit verdot & merlot (72/28). Old oak melds the gentle tannins, juicy dark-berried fruit provides warm-hearted (14% alc), undemanding quaffability. **Girlie Rosé** ⓃⒺⓌ ★★ Pale only in hue, **23** ⑦⑥ from shiraz is technically dry but unashamedly ripe, 14.5% alc & low acid giving mouthfilling warmth & sweetness. **Rachel Chenin Blanc** ⓃⒺⓌ ★★★ Crunchy Granny Smith apple flavours in **23** ⑧⓪, perky twist of lime on finish. Light (12% alc) & summery, slimmer's delight. **Dario Cupcake** Ⓥ ★★★ If dulcet reds are your thing, Dario's your name. **20** ⑧① appealing sugared plum flavours, sweetness (ex grape concentrate) controlled by gentle tannins. — MW

Location: Rawsonville ▪ Map/WO: Breedekloof ▪ Map grid reference: C6 ▪ Est 2002 ▪ 1stB 2003 ▪ Tasting, sales & cellar/vineyard tours Tue-Fri 11-4 Sat 11-3; closed Sun/Mon ▪ Light meals ▪ Facilities for children ▪ Tour groups ▪ Farm produce ▪ Walking/hiking trails ▪ Weddings/functions ▪ Conservation area ▪ Owner(s) Karen, Ronald & Andries le Roux ▪ Winemaker(s) Ronald le Roux (2019) ▪ Viticulturist(s) Ronald le Roux ▪ 21t/3,000cs own label 90% red 10% white ▪ IPW ▪ PO Box 96 Rawsonville 6845 ▪ info@kirabocellar.co.za ▪ www.kiraboprivatecellar.com ▪ **T +27 (0)71-681-9019**

☐ **Kitchen Sink** see The Kitchen Sink
☐ **Klaasenbosch** see Wine-of-the-Month Club

Klawer Wine Cellars   Ⓠ Ⓖ Ⓛ

'Nature's best' is what winelovers should expect from a bottle or resealable pouch of wine by this significant Olifants River producer, with a pair of cellars, at Klawer and Trawal, receiving grapes from over 2,000 ha belonging to more than 80 growers. The bulk trade is the primarily outlet, but the team long led by Andries Blake and Pieter van Aarde vinify selections for the winery's own substantial 50,000-case proprietary labels, value-priced Klawer, outdoorsy Vino Sacci and premium Villa Esposto.

Villa Esposto range

★★★★ **Chenin Blanc** Ⓦ Grapes from Citrusdal Mountain for **23** ★★★★ ⑧⑤. Good tension between racy acid & sweet pear & apple, just missing **22** ⑧⑦'s density of fruit. Modest 12.6% alc.

★★★★☆ **Straw Wine** ⊘ Ⓦ Exceptional unoaked dessert wine from sun-dried muscat d'Alexandrie, light-footed at just 8% alc yet great concentration of quince, sultana & apricot aromas, apple, peach & lemon flavours. Electric acid easily scythes through 260 g/L sugar. 54 year old vines planted by legendary grower, the late Basie van Lill, making **21** ⑨① even more special. 375 ml.

Pinotage Rosé ✓ 🏵 ★★★☆ Provençal pink **23** ⑧⑤ is loaded with melon & strawberry, zested with orange acid. Great drinkability & value.

. . . .

Sauvignon Blanc 🆕 ☺ ★★☆ Bouncy gooseberries & passionfruit, vein of gentle, refreshing acid. Carries newer Nieuwoudtville WO certification, seldom seen on a bottle, more reason to seek out **23** ⑦⑧.

. . . .

Pinotage ★★★☆ Now bottled, **21** ⑧⑤ realises the promise of last year's preview in its berries, plums & spicy core, lifted with crisp acid. **Cabernet Sauvignon-Merlot** 🉐 ★★★☆ Mouthfilling fruit on exuberant **21** ⑧⑤ from Citrusdal Mountain, chocolate-drizzled plums, cherries cosseted in fine tannins. Some American oak.

Klawer range

★★★★ **Hanepoot** 🉐 Bursting with pineapple, lemon rind & litchi, flavoursome & spicy **20** ⑧⑨ is well balanced by warming fortification, tapers to long, luscious finish with hint of dried pear. No **19**.

★★★★ **African Ruby Rooibos** Fortified dessert wine from red muscadel infused with rooibos. **NV** ⑧⑨ much like a cup of the aromatic tea, plus extras like red berry & ginger, & comforting warmth of 16.9% alc.

★★★★ **Red Muscadel** 🉐 Complex, inviting fortified dessert wine. **21** ⑧⑦ has flavours of Xmas cake, raisin & spice, a tangy pomegranate freshness running through. Lightly chill for the best experience.

★★★★ **White Muscadel** 🉐 Dried figs, lemon blossoms & syrupy peaches of **20** ★★★★ ⑧⑤ are wrapped in a soft, lush body with gentle acid. Not as vibrant as last-tasted **18** ⑧⑧.

. . . .

Shiraz ✓ 🏵 ★★★☆ Keeps getting better. **22** ⑧④ saw no oak, so the fresh, lifted spice, plum & crushed herb flavours & scents are the unembellished grape.

. . . .

Shiraz-Malbec ☺ ★★★ Unusual & compatible blend, generous with the cherry & spice flavour, less so with the alc at just 12.8%, making **22** ⑧② all the more quaffable. **Sauvignon Blanc** ☺ ★★★ Deliciously drinkable balance between tropical ripeness, nicely judged weight & acid crispness on **23** ⑦⑨ at smile-inducing price.

Cabernet Sauvignon 🉐 ★★★ Musk & berry fragrances on youthful **21** ⑦⑨. Slips down easily. **Merlot** 🉐 ★★★ Smooth & approachable **21** ⑧① layers mocha-chocolate on juicy plums, spicy dates & seam of ripe tannins. **Pinotage** 🉐 ★★★ A balanced mouthful of dark berries & creamy chocolate in delicious, almost gluggable **20** ⑧②. **Rosé** ★★★ Litchis & strawberries on delightfully aromatic semi-sweet **NV** ⑦⑧ blush. Fresh, uncloying, bonus of modest 10.5% alc. Uncertified. **Chardonnay** ★★★ Vanilla, blossom, pear drop & Lemon Cream biscuit on **23** ⑦⑨, unoaked, with touch of sweetness. **Chenin Blanc** ✓ ★★★ Punchy, unwooded **23** ⑧③ piles on the fruit, adding gooseberry & melon to mango, pineapple & lime. **Michelle Sparkling** 🉐 ★★★ Red muscadel's blush, petals & red berries on **NV** ⑦⑧ frothy, light (10% alc) carbonated sparkler. Chill well & start the party. **Cape Vintage** 🉐 ★★★ Shiraz given 'port' treatment in **19** ⑧②, amplified spice from American oak complements savoury character.

Vino Sacci range

Not tasted: **Merlot**, **Chenin Blanc**. — ML

Location: Klawer ▪ Map: Olifants River ▪ Map grid reference: B4 ▪ WO: Olifants River/Citrusdal Mountain/ Nieuwoudtville ▪ Est 1956 ▪ Tasting & sales Mon-Fri 8-5 Sat 9-1; pub hols 9-5 (seasonal) please call ahead ▪ BYO picnic ▪ 4 wine pairing options & kiddies pairing ▪ Owner(s) 87 members ▪ Manager Andries Blake ▪ Cellarmaster(s) Pieter van Aarde ▪ Winemaker(s) Roelof van Schalkwyk, Werner Barkhuizen & Sean de Necker, with Christo Beukes ▪ Viticulturist(s) Johannes Mellet ▪ 2,095ha (cab, merlot, ptage, shiraz, chard, chenin, hanepoot, muscadel, sauv) ▪ 34,000t/50,000cs own label 40% red 40% white 5% rosé 15% other ▪ ISO 22000:2009, Organic, DLG, IPW ▪ PO Box 8 Klawer 8145 ▪ ontvangs@klawerwyn.co.za ▪ www. klawerwine.co.za ▪ T +27 (0)27-216-1530

Klein Amoskuil

Klein Amoskuil in Swartland was acquired in 1997 by Fairview and Spice Route owner Charles Back and run, with long-term winemaker Charl du Plessis, along low-intervention and sustainable lines. These culminated in organic certification of the farm and cellar, and release of the first of the small-batch wines to be accredited by Ecocert, the '22 Sauvignon. To follow are a shiraz, grenache noir and carignan single-ferment sparkling. Some 400 ha in size, Klein Amoskuil's ±80 ha of vines are dry-farmed and the grapes vinified in traditional concrete kuipe, older barrels and, since 2018, Georgian earthenware for the Obscura wines.

Obscura by Klein Amoskuil

★★★★ **White Blend** Equal sauvignon, chenin, viognier & semillon in **22** ⑧⑥. Golden hue from 6 weeks on skins after ferment in qvevri. Earth, lanolin & nuts with flor sherry-like freshness. Richer waxy under-tone & long savoury farewell. Unusual but less quirky than **21** ★★★ ⑧⓪. Fairtrade, as all tasted this edition.

Red Blend ★★★★ Different 3-way blend in **22** ⑧⑤, 44% shiraz with grenache noir, carignan, naturally fermented (as White), 3 months on skins in buried qvevri, further 9 for smoothness. Dry, with charcuterie & sweet thatch nuances. For gentle contemplative sipping. Not tasted: **Grenache Rosé**, **Orange**.

The Amos Block by Klein Amoskuil

★★★★ **Sauvignon Blanc** ⓥ ⓥ ⓥ Oldest (1965) block of sauvignon in SA. Tiny 3 t/ha yield shows concentrated nettle, kiwi & dried fig flavours with some minerality in **22** ⑧⑨. Part oaking adds silky sheen, all integrated & unshowy in lightish frame. WO Swartland for these.

★★★★★ **Perpetual Reserve Under Flor** ⓥ ⓥ Rivetingly fresh & bone-dry, fino sherry-styled **NV** ⑨④ from SA's oldest sauvignon block. Exudes flor character in its orange peel & rich, nutty texture. Annual solera components since 2014 naturally fermented in old barrels before flor inoculation. Just 400 attractive 500-ml bottles per year.— MW

Location: Malmesbury ▪ WO: Coastal/Swartland ▪ Est 2022 ▪ Closed to public; tasting by appt only ▪ Owner(s) Charles Back ▪ Winemaker(s) Charl du Plessis (Dec 2001), with Licia Solomons (Jan 2006) ▪ 400ha/80ha (carignan, durif, grenache, mataro, mourv, ptage, shiraz, tannat, sauv) ▪ 45t/4,216cs ▪ Fairtrade, IPW, Organic (Ecocert), WIETA ▪ ruan@kleinamoskuil.co.za ▪ www.kleinamoskuil.co.za ▪ **T +27 (0)61-704-0321**

Klein Constantia Estate

Incoming CEO Pascal Asin dons the custodian's mantle of this Constantia jewel and heirloom as a new chapter begins in the story of its globally famous sweet wine, Vin de Constance. A project 15 years in the making has seen muscat de Frontignan vines from the mother block, dating from 1982, mass-selected and propagated, and the soil is now being prepared for the planting of a new vineyard to this unique clone. With sustainability top of mind, viticulturist Craig Harris and winemaker Matt Day are using precision technology to work proactively, 'applying organic products and biodynamic principles as much as possible'. Stellenbosch sibling winery Anwilka has been fully integrated with the larger business ('no longer the stepchild'), and the rest of the Estate range looks as fresh and smart as the Sauvignon Blanc after a new label roll-out.

Estate range

★★★★☆ **Estate Red Blend** Richly fruited, from mainly cab with malbec & drop petit verdot, **20** ⑨②'s classic blackcurrant core adds chocolate from 40% new oak, 15 months, with fresh acid & supple tannins. Opulent, lengthy finish.

★★★★☆ **Chardonnay** Lively citrus notes of orange & lime, **21** ⑨⓪ balanced by crisp acid, aided by blocked malo, & seamed through with lovely smoky oaking, 60% new, 9 months. Touch of caramel now showing on **20** ★★★★ ⑧⑧, also tasted.

★★★★☆ **Riesling** ⓥ Weighty yet elegant **18** ⑨⓪ shows pleasing development of petrol & dried apricot, with lime marmalade tang & perfect balance between grain sugar & mouthwatering acid. Naturally fermented in tank after 4 days on skins.

★★★★☆ **Clara Sauvignon Blanc** Intriguing perfume on **22** ⑨②, blossom, apricot, mango & guava, barrel ferment (40% new) adds vanilla & spice to tropical fruit flavours. Fresh & enticing, with balance & length. Doubles the new oak component from **21** ⑨⓪, also tasted.

★★★★☆ **Metis Sauvignon Blanc** ⓥ Focused & concentrated **20** ★★★★★ ⑨⑤ dazzles with dialled-back freshness of blackcurrant, lemon & dusty greenpepper. Natural ferment, partial oak, 12 months, all older, same time on lees, all add breadth & length to lingering finish. Purer fruited than also-tasted **19** ⑨②.

★★★★☆ **Perdeblokke Sauvignon Blanc** ⓥ Distinctive tangy apricot nose on stellar **22** ★★★★★ ⑨⑤ gives way to pink grapefruit palate edged with subtle smoky oak, 25% new. Naturally fermented, 9 months on lees soothes vibrant acidity at lengthy finish. **21** ⑨②, also tasted & excellent, just not quite the purity & concentration. From high-lying single-vineyard.

★★★★☆ **Sauvignon Blanc** Benchmark **22** ⑨⓪ detailed & precise, with orange zest & crunchy granadilla fruit, steely acidity racing through broad mid-palate given texture by 6 months lees & small portion (10%) barrel-fermented in old oak.

★★★★☆ **Sauvignon Blanc Block 382** ⓐ Majestic single-vineyard **20** ⑨④ made up of multiple layers of flavour - grass, nettle & hay with oatmeal, lemon curd & subtle spice notes from 20 months in single, old 500L barrel. Hyperoxidised fruit ensures longevity, added to seamless acidity & long finish. One for keeping.

★★★★☆ **Méthode Cap Classique Brut Blanc de Blancs** Elegant bone-dry **19** ⑨② from chardonnay spent 36 months on lees after 9 months in old oak, both adding creamy toast notes to vibrant apple & lemon with zesty acidity. Touch of Marmite & brioche broaden lengthy finish.

★★★★★ **Vin de Constance** ⓐ World-renowned & highly individual Natural Sweet from muscat de Frontignan, **20** ⑨⑦ picked over 19 separate occasions, creating contrasting layers of white flowers, perfume & fresh acid with richer litchi & apricot flavours culminating in a pith & peel finish. 50% new oak, some Hungarian, 18 months, then old foudres, same duration. Also-tasted **19** ⑨⑤ starting to show some development but both are wines for the ages.

Occasional release: **Sauvignon Blanc Block 371**, **Sauvignon Blanc Block 381**, **Brut Méthode Cap Classique Reserve**.

KC range
Cabernet Sauvignon-Merlot ⊘ ★★★★ Mainly cab with merlot & tweaks of malbec, petit verdot & syrah. **20** ⑧③ clean blackberry fruit, touches tar & tobacco, greenleaf finish. WO W Cape for these. **Sauvignon Blanc** ★★★★ Pea aroma on **21** ⑧⑤, easy-drinking style, pineapple & guava fruit with brisk acid & dry finish. — CM

Location: Constantia ▪ Map: Cape Peninsula ▪ Map grid reference: B3 ▪ WO: Constantia/Western Cape ▪ Est 1823 ▪ 1stB 1824 ▪ Tasting & sales Mon-Sun 10-5 ▪ Closed Good Fri & Dec 25 ▪ Tasting from R150 ▪ The Bistro @ Klein Constantia Mon-Sun 12-3 (winter hours apply) ▪ Gift shop ▪ Vineyard tours (bookings in advance) ▪ Collection of original Constantia bottles on display ▪ Wine club ▪ Owner(s) Zdenek Bakala, Charles Harman, Bruno Prats & Hubert de Boüard ▪ CEO Pascal Asin ▪ Winemaker(s) Matthew Day (2009) ▪ Viticulturist(s) Craig Harris (Oct 2013) ▪ 146ha/64ha (cab, malbec, p verdot, shiraz, chard, muscat de F, riesling, sauv, sem) ▪ 500t/80,000cs own label 30% red 70% white ▪ WIETA, WWF-SA Conservation Champion ▪ PO Box 375 Constantia 7848 ▪ info@kleinconstantia.com ▪ www.kleinconstantia.com ▪ **T +27 (0)21-794-5188**

Klein DasBosch   Ⓠ ⑰

These wines are grown on the banks of Stellenbosch's Blaauwklippen River, on the farm Klein DasBosch, owned by James 'Whitey' Basson, former CEO of retail giant Shoprite. Latterly two big names, Chris Keet and Adam Mason, have been involved as consultants in styling the wines, which remain limited in quantity and points of sale, the most attractive by far being nearby Mont Marie Restaurant, also the official tasting venue.

Mont Marie range
★★★★ **Directors Reserve** Assured Cape Bordeaux is half cab with merlot, petit verdot & cab franc, latter adding varietal leafy lift to **22** ⑧⑨'s deep cassis fruit. Light dusting of savoury spices from oak.

Klein DasBosch range
★★★★ **Cabernet Sauvignon** ⊘ Fresh **22** ⑧⑧ showcases variety's black fruit & fine tannin structure, additional pleasure provided by attractive graphite detail, satisfying grip & savoury farewell. 16 months in barrel, as Reserve; 12 months for Merlot.

★★★★ **Chardonnay** Well-composed & restrained **22** ⑧⑨, white blossom, peach & lemon tones, pleasing breadth from 38% oaked portion shot through with brilliant acidity, fantail finish.

Merlot ★★★★ Plummy **22** ⑧⑤ bright & engaging, needs time to unfurl full charm, very present - slightly herbaceous - tannins tightly wrapped around dense fruit. Older oak only, as both ranges. **Maude's Selection Rosé** ⊘ ★★★★ From mourvèdre, **23** ⑧⑤ dry & satisfyingly vinous, tangy berry scents & flavours, zesty acidity, decent heft from few months in oak. — NK, CvZ

Location/map/WO: Stellenbosch ▪ Map grid reference: F7 ▪ Tasting & sales at Mont Marie Restaurant, Stellenbosch T +27 (0)21-880-0777 - phone ahead as tasting hours are subject to change ▪ Owner(s) James Wellwood Basson ▪ Viti/vini consultant Chris Keet ▪ Winemaker(s) Adam Mason (consultant) ▪ ±25ha ▪ 90% red 10% white ▪ PO Box 12320 Stellenbosch 7613 ▪ mia@kleindasbosch.com ▪ www.kleindasbosch.co.za, www.montmarie.co.za ▪ **T +27 (0)21-880-0128/+27 (0)71-859-1773 (office)/+27 (0)21-880-0777 (tasting/sales)**

☐ **Kleine Kaap** *see* Imbuko Wines
☐ **Kleine Rust** *see* Stellenrust
☐ **Kleine Vesting** *see* Friesland Wines

Kleine Zalze Wines Ⓨ ⓞ ⓖ

Top Performing Winery of the Year in the 2021 edition of this guide, Kleine Zalze has evolved from a neglected Stellenbosch property into an upmarket lifestyle estate, golf course, lauded restaurant, guest house and multi-award winning winery. The transition from family ownership to the burgeoning SA stable of French specialist wine company AdVini was seamless, and the ship remains steady in the hands of long-term cellar chief RJ Botha and his team. Though just a few years old, the Project Z test bed for alternative vessels and techniques has borne fruit, the trickle-down effect increasingly seen in the various tiers. The Family Reserve wines now boast either skin-fermented or amphora-aged components, grenache noir is a fixture in the Vineyard Selection line-up, and new concrete and more terracotta vessels form part of the winemaking toolkit. The winery's robust presence in world markets remains the envy of many.

Family Reserve range

★★★★☆ **Cabernet Sauvignon** ⓐ Refined, silky **20** ㉝, confident & composed, with fruitcake, violet & cedar generosity, underlying power & sleek muscularity beautifully restrained. Nuance, structure & length aided by 18 months in oak, 70% new. Worth keeping, as all these.

★★★★☆ **Shiraz** ⓐ Peppery notes amplified on rich, plum-fruited **20** ㉞ by 15% stem return during ferment. Complex, savoury, with concentration but also pliability & succulence. Herbs & liquorice add depth to lengthy finish. Bold yet harmonious oak & alc, 65% new, 15.5%.

★★★★☆ **Chenin Blanc** ⓐ ⓦ Subtle lily & elderflower aromas on **22** ㉞, nectarine & pineapple richness has bright acid & chalky texture to counter, cohesive & composed from ferment/8 months on lees in old oak, terracotta amphora &, a first, concrete 'egg'. Lovely mineral tautness & length.

★★★★☆ **Sauvignon Blanc** ⓐ Granadilla, fig & flint on cerebral & engaging **22** ㉞, crafted with 50% reductive portion using skin contact in tank, plus wholebunch fraction in new oak & amphora for 6 months. Crisp & lively, taut yet curvaceous & supple too. Fruit from Darling & Durbanville.

Discontinued: **Pinotage**.

Project Z range

★★★★☆ **Cabernet Sauvignon** ⓝ ⓐ Herb brush to typical cassis & violet on **22** ㉝. Ripe, silky fruit with pleasant textural dryness from ferment in cement tanks & 8 months in amphora. Compact yet still succulent, refreshing & rewarding.

★★★★★ **Cinsault** Ⓩ Berry & rose perfume of unoaked **21** ㉟ leads to dry, taut black cherry & liquorice palate. Both generous & juicy, it has backbone to balance. 3 months in amphora, followed by 15 in bottle.

★★★★☆ **Grenache** ⓐ Rosepetal & cranberry on **22** ★★★★★ ㉞ echo last-tasted **20** ㉝'s aromatic profile. Energetic & lively, with deeper blueberry & liquorice concentration. Fresh & well composed after ferment in stainless tank (25% wholebunch), 8 months in terracotta amphora. Long lavender farewell. WO Darling.

★★★★★ **Shiraz** Ⓩ Whole berries (25%) covered by crushed/destemmed fruit in tank lend **21** ★★★★☆ ㉝ a heady violet & blueberry compote allure. Refined yet concentrated & powerful. Dry, fine tannin from seasoned oak & amphora, 9 months. Follows lithe & sleek **17** ㉟.

★★★★☆ **Alvarinho** ⓝ ⓐ Among handful of solo bottlings, **22** ㉞ fermented/6 months in amphora, preserving the vivacious green apple, lemon & spice notes on crisp, bright palate. 8.8 g/L acid ensures focus & precision. Textured, broad & long, with years ahead of it.

★★★★☆ **Chenin Blanc** ⓐ Thrilling **22** ㉞ shows bright, almost peppery stonefruit in a tight structure from ferment & 9 months in 30% amphora & concrete 'egg'. Yet to reveal its full charms, it teases apricot ripeness & breadth. Deserves time.

★★★★☆ **Chenin Blanc Skin Contact** Linear, individual style, leaner than its sibling. Spicy pear & apple on **22** ㉛ taut & nervy palate, textured dry grip from week on skins in amphora, 9 months ageing in same terracotta vessel. Modest 12% alc.

★★★★☆ **Riesling** Ⓡ Taut, zingy green apple & lime on amphora-fermented **21** ⑨② from Elgin. Thrillingly dry & nervy, with vivid 8.9 g/L acid, it will reward patience as it evolves.

★★★★★ **Sweet Fortified** Ⓡ Deliciously different fortified **NV** ⑨④ dessert made in 'solera-style' system, comprising sauvignon, chenin, viognier from multiple vintages. Sweet toffee richness tempered by bright acid & spirit.

Occasional release: **Sauvignon Blanc**. Discontinued: **Grenache**.

Vineyard Selection

★★★★☆ **Cabernet Sauvignon** ⓥ ⓐ Shows trademark refinement & typicity in its fruitcake & cigarbox notes. **21** ⑨③ complex, layered, with lovely succulence & harmony of fruit & oak, slightly upped to 40% new & 20 months.

★★★★★ **Grenache** ⓥ Vibrant **22** ⑨⓪ from Darling is luscious & tasty, with plump red & black berries from 20% wholebunch ferment. Light squeeze from mostly fruit tannin as only older oak & amphora used for 10 months ageing.

★★★★★ **Syrah** ⓥ ⓐ Was 'Shiraz'. Restrainedly rich **21** ⑨④ repeats previous dry herb nuance to black fruit, shows impressive density & concentration along with balance. Separately vinified parcels, harmonised 18 months in 30% new oak. **20** untasted.

★★★★ **Shiraz-Mourvèdre-Viognier** Ⓡ Some Swartland fruit for soft, plush & spicy **19** ⑧⑨, with appealing plum & violet scents. Gentle oak frame, as the red grapes had 14 months in older wood, the white one 10 months in tank.

★★★★☆ **Chardonnay** ⓥ ⓐ Adds portion Robertson grapes in **22** ⑨④, rounded but bright & lively, with creamy breadth & lovely dry end to the tangerine & oatmeal flavours. Oak, 60% new, 8 months, effortlessly integrated & supportive, as in **21** ★★★★ ⑧⑨.

★★★★☆ **Chenin Blanc** ⓥ ⓐ ⓦ Pineapple & quince appeal on **22** ⑨③, hint of sweetness braced by fresh 6.9 g/L acid. Textured from brief skin contact & small portion wholebunch pressed. Fermented/7 months in combo amphora & older barrels for poised & rewarding glassful.

★★★★☆ **Sauvignon Blanc** ⓥ Grapefruit zest & granadilla succulence mingle on **23** ⑨⓪, tangy & light with a taut, focused core. Reductively made, with Durbanville & Darling fruit adding gravel & flint notes to riper Stellenbosch. Brief 2 months on the lees.

Cellar Selection

★★★★ **Cabernet Sauvignon** ⓥ Black cherry, tobacco & cocoa notes on soft, supple **21** ⑧⑦. Gentle grip but good spine & cohesion after year in older oak. WO Coastal for all unless noted.

★★★★ **Merlot** ⓥ Blueberry & plum compote on lively, juicy & soft **21** ⑧⑥. Tasty & approachable, with soft body, light chalky grip & elegant length. Year in older oak, 10% unwooded for freshness.

★★★★ **Pinotage** ⓥ Packed with raspberry cheer & gentle grip from open ferment in concrete & tank. Grapes for **21** ⑧⑥ from Stellenbosch & Durbanville aged year in seasoned oak.

★★★★ **Cabernet Sauvignon-Merlot** ⓥ 80% cab in **21** ⑧⑥, up from 58% last vintage yet same inky hedgerow fruit, herb & cocoa from 14 months in seasoned barrels on gently muscular body. Ideal fireside companion, braai or kaggel.

Cinsault Rosé ⓥ ★★★★ Bright, perky **23** ⑧④ has signature plump strawberry, blueberry & raspberry appeal. Light, dry & fun. **Chardonnay Unwooded** ⓥ ★★★★ Gentle loquat on **23** ⑧④ which brings Swartland & Bonnievale grapes into the mix. Dry, tangy & bright, chalky mouthfeel & light lees breadth. Ideal for everyday. WO W Cape, as Sauvignon. **Chenin Blanc Bush Vines** ⓥ ★★★★ Crisp quince, melon & pear on temptingly fresh & vibrant **23** ⑧⑤. Light-feeling, with good body & length from 2 months on lees. **Sauvignon Blanc** ⓥ ★★★★ Fig, tropical fruit & lemon on sappy **23** ⑧④, gravel nuance courtesy portions Darling & Durbanville grapes. As always, deftly styled for everyday sipping.

Méthode Cap Classique Sparkling range

★★★★ **Cape Nectar Rosé** ⓃⒺⓌ ⓥ Pinot noir (64%) leads chardonnay on **NV** ⑧⑥ pink bubbly. Cherry nuance to fruit salad vibrancy & tang on gently sweet palate (42.6 g/L sugar). Good body & concentration, gentle lees nuance from 18 months in bottle. WO W Cape for these.

★★★★ **Brut Rosé** Ⓡ Pale salmon hue to **NV** ⑧⑧ from pinot noir & 40% chardonnay. Berry aroma gives way to citrus on taut palate, riper red fruit & toasty notes emerging along with breadth from 18 months on the lees.

★★★★ **Brut** ⊘ Melange of citrus on bright **NV** (87) sparkler from chardonnay & pinot noir (60/40). Focused, with rich, ripe, rounded palate & sourdough flavour. Light, refreshing finish. On lees 10 months.

★★★★ **Vintage Brut** Fine strings of bubbles on **17** (89) from chardonnay & pinot noir (64/36). Bracing sea air, yeast & marmalade, repeating on dry, vibrant & focused palate. Lovely precision with some breadth & richness from 72 months on lees. Portion Robertson grapes, like all these. Exceptional **15** ★★★★★ (90) was last tasted.

Cape Nectar Blanc (NEW) ⊘ ★★★★ Chardonnay leads pinot noir 64/36 on **NV** (85) bubbly. Sweet-sour orange piquancy with subtle caramel & toast notes, gentle sweetness of 43.6 g/L sugar but bright acid to balance. Low 10.5% alc adds to appeal. — FM

Location/map: Stellenbosch ▪ Map grid reference: E7 ▪ WO: Stellenbosch/Western Cape/Coastal/Darling/ Elgin ▪ Est 1695 ▪ 1stB 1997 ▪ Tasting & sales Mon-Sat 9-6 Sun/pub hols 11-6; pub hols (seasonal) please call ahead ▪ Closed Good Fri, Dec 25 & Jan 1 ▪ De Zalze Golf Course ▪ Wine club ▪ Owner(s) AdVini South Africa ▪ Cellarmaster(s) RJ Botha (Dec 2012) ▪ Winemaker(s) L Geldenhuys, N Botha, H Ferreira ▪ Viticulturist(s) H Retief (May 2006) ▪ 2,300t/350,000cs own label 40% red 50% white 10% rosé ▪ PO Box 12837 Die Boord 7613 ▪ quality@kleinezalze.co.za ▪ www.kleinezalze.co.za ▪ **T +27 (0)21-880-0717**

☐ **Klein Friesland** see Friesland Wines

Klein Goederust Boutique Winery

A whirlwind year for this team, with inclusion in both Time and the New York Times, showing their wines at Vinexpo America, winning a top wine tourism award, and selling out of two vintages of their sparkling - the latter perhaps the proudest achievement for winery co-owner Paul Siguqa, as the wine is named for his mother. Raised on a Cape winefarm, he developed a successful business in Gauteng but was drawn back to the winelands, where in 2019 he found run-down Klein Goederust in Franschhoek, dating from 1905, and carefully restored it. Seasoned Rodney Zimba does the winecrafting, with equally experienced Johan Viljoen advising on the vine side, including young home-farm blocks. Attention is now turning to an on-site cellar.

★★★★ **Cabernet Sauvignon** Dense & inky-hued, **20** (86) spent 18 months in 60% new barriques. Dark fruited, with meaty tones, it's sturdy & broad-shouldered, with a long life ahead.

★★★★ **Shiraz** Smoky, savoury-spiced from 14 months in oak, **21** (87) ticks a lot of boxes. Dark-fruited & plush, has curvaceous appeal.

★★★★ **Nomaroma Méthode Cap Classique** Fermented/11 months older barrel, then 36 months on lees, yet **20** (87) shows lovely youthful freshness. Classic chardonnay & pinot noir citrus & red berries, toasted brioche & savouriness adding to the attraction. Characterful & delicious.

Chardonnay ★★★ Stonefruit, with a subtle dusting of biscuit from 50% wooded portion, **22** (80) has rounded texture, mellow flavours. **Chenin Blanc** ★★★ Bushvines, barrel fermented/10 months giving **23** (83) appealing richness, preserved quince & melon, lifted by zesty freshness. — CR

Location/map: Franschhoek ▪ Map grid reference: C2 ▪ WO: Western Cape ▪ Est 1905 ▪ 1stB 2019 ▪ Tasting & sales Mon-Sun 10-4.30 ▪ Tasting fee R200 ▪ Closed Dec 25 ▪ Cheese platters, lamb & cheese platters, beverages ▪ Conference/meeting room (seats 8 pax) ▪ Owner(s) Ntsikelelo Paul Siguqa, Beauty Makhosazana Zwane-Siguqa ▪ Winemaker(s) Rodney Zimba (Sep 2019) ▪ Viticulturist(s) Johan Viljoen (Sep 2019, consultant) ▪ 10ha/6.5ha (mourv, pinot, shiraz, chard, chenin, sem) ▪ 1,500cs own label 63% red 37% white ▪ WIETA ▪ R45 Main Rd, Franschhoek 7690 ▪ info@kleingoederust.co.za ▪ www.kleingoederust.co.za ▪ **T +27 (0)66-483-4549/+27 (0)10-494-7985**

Klein Gustrouw Estate

Klein Gustrouw dates from the 19th century but vines on the property in Stellenbosch's Jonkershoek Valley found their way into bottle under this boutique label only 30 years ago. Latterly the estate passed into the hands of businessman Jannie Mouton, who extensively restored and replanted it, appointing CWG member Warren Ellis of Neil Ellis Wines to make the wines, available for on-site tasting by special arrangement.

★★★★ **Reserve** ⊘ Four-way Cape Bordeaux blend with cabernet at 60% in **16** (89). Handles riper vintage well through lead variety's fresh leafiness lifting dark berry flavours. Supple, polished tannins, 17 months oak, 60% new, in harmony. With merlot, cab franc & petit verdot (20/10/10).

Not tasted: **Sauvignon Blanc**. — MW

Location: Stellenbosch ▪ WO: Jonkershoek Valley ▪ Est 1817 ▪ 1stB 1993 ▪ Private tastings by special arrangement only ▪ Owner(s) Jannie Mouton, Klein Gustrouw (Pty) Ltd ▪ Winemaker(s) Warren Ellis (2006)

▪ Viticulturist(s) Pieter Smit (consultant) ▪ ±23ha/±14ha under vine ▪ 70% red 30% white ▪ PO Box 6168 Uniedal 7612 ▪ info@kleingustrouw.co.za ▪ **T +27 (0)21-882-8152/+27 (0)72-584-5314**

☐ **Klein Kasteelberg** *see* Riebeek Valley Wine Co
☐ **Kleinkloof** *see* Niel Joubert Estate
☐ **Kleinood** *see* Tamboerskloof Wine - Kleinood Farm
☐ **Klein Optenhorst** *see* Dainty Bess

Klein Roosboom Boutique Winery ⓠ ⑪ ⓞ ⓐ ⓖ

Durbanville's De Villiers family's debut premium bubblies were still selling at press time, the next vintage held back for later launch from their 'Little Rose Bush' boutique estate, with its welcoming venue and 'tasting cave' set in old concrete fermenters. They've formed a wine circle to give fans the inside track on news and events, planted more Bordeaux varieties, and have plans for limited-release stillwines to meet demand.

My Way range

★★★★ **Brut Rosé Méthode Cap Classique** ⓠ Generously berry-fruited **19** ⑧⑨ from 30% pinot noir, with chardonnay, mouthfilling mousse, red apple & salted caramel nuances. Same time on lees as sibling.

★★★★☆ **Brut Méthode Cap Classique** ⓠ Cool-climate zing on **19** ⑨③ sparkler from chardonnay (72%) & pinot noir. Crisp green apple, pearskin & zesty lemon magnify refreshment appeal, 33 months lees contact add a creamy-salty element. Finish is precise & bone-dry.

Not tasted: **Barrel Selection Red**, **Sauvignon Blanc Reserve Single Vineyard**.

Klein Roosboom range

★★★★ **Marné Brut Méthode Cap Classique** Super-zippy & appley **NV** ⑧⑦ bubbly from 80% chardonnay with pinot noir, basewine oaked, spent year on lees for creaminess to balance brisk acid.

Marianna Roos Rosé ★★★ Coral-hued **23** ⑦⑨ again mostly merlot with enlivening shot of zippy sauvignon to offset strawberry fruit-sweetness. **Dear Diary Chardonnay** ★★★★ Yellow apple, butterscotch & stonefruit on medium-bodied **23** ⑧④. Unwooded, the palate weight comes from 6 months lees contact. **Jéan Sauvignon Blanc** ★★★★ 5 months on lees with regular stirring adds silky texture to improved **23** ⑧④, nicely complementing fig & lime fruit, appetising dryness. Not tasted: **Johan Cabernet Sauvignon**, **Nicol Merlot**, **Janét Shiraz**. — ML

Location/WO: Durbanville ▪ Map: Durbanville, Philadelphia & Darling ▪ Map grid reference: C7 ▪ Est 1984 ▪ 1stB 2007 ▪ Tasting & sales Tue-Sun 10-4.30; pub hols (seasonal) please call ahead ▪ Fee R80pp, waived on purchase (6 wines) ▪ Wine tasting in a 'cave' ▪ Closed Good Fri, Dec 25/26 & Jan 1 ▪ Jéan Deli Tue-Sun 9-4.30 ▪ Facilities for children ▪ Party Bike ▪ Owner(s) Jéan de Villiers Trust ▪ Cellarmaster(s) Karin de Villiers (2007) ▪ Winemaker(s) Piti Coetzee (2016) ▪ Viticulturist(s) Nicol de Villiers (2018) ▪ 26oha/15oha (cab, merlot, p verdot, shiraz, chard, chenin, sauv, sem) ▪ 8,500cs own label 30% red 70% white ▪ Postnet Suite #3 Private Bag X19 Durbanville 7551 ▪ tastingroom@kleinroosboom.co.za, info@jeanrestaurant.co.za, bookings@kleinroosboom.co.za ▪ www.kleinroosboom.co.za ▪ **T +27 (0)860-572-572 (tasting & deli)**

Klein Sering ⓠ ⑪

The deft hands that heal hearts also look after the health of the soils and tiny parcel of vines at Klein Sering, vintner, prominent Cape Town cardiac surgeon and farmer-at-heart Willie Koen being invested in an ongoing project to introduce compost from vineyard vegetation deep into the ground. He's already seeing better soil analyses and berry quality, boosting his goal of showcasing coastal Noordhoek's 'unique fruity tastes'.

★★★★ **Sauvignon Blanc** Gentle, fresh **22** ★★★★ ⑧④ has ripe pear & delicate whiteflower nuances, plush texture, smooth & friendly drinkability. Tad softer than last **20** ⑧⑥.

★★★★ **Sauvignon Blanc Reserve** For fans of generously oaked whites, toastiness on **22** ⑧⑥ dominates gentler pear, kiwi & greengage. Fine creamy texture, some freshness & long nutty farewell. No **21**.

★★★★ **Semillon** Variety's delicate waxy lanolin flavours overlaid by more dominant oaking in **22** ⑧⑥. Retains bright, lemony acid, some pithiness & breadth. One for the table. **21** skipped.

★★★★ **Semillon-Sauvignon Blanc** Harmonious 60/40 blend & most balanced wine here. **22** ⑧⑧ unoaked sauvignon complemented by old-oak-fermented semillon charms with succulent blackcurrant leafiness & fragrant green fruit, long citrus-toned finish. No **21**. — MW

Location/WO: Cape Town ▪ Est 2013 ▪ 1stB 2016 ▪ Tasting & vineyard tours by private pre-arrangement only ▪ Sales online ▪ Closed all pub hols ▪ Meals/refreshments by pre-booking ▪ Owner(s) Willie Koen family ▪ Winemaker(s) Riandri Visser, with Anzette Visser (Cape Point Vineyards) ▪ Viticulturist(s) Willie Koen (2013) ▪ 2ha/1.2ha (sauv, sem) ▪ 10t/±1,000cs own label ▪ PO Box 10 Noordhoek 7979 ▪ info@kleinsering.co.za ▪ www.kleinsering.co.za ▪ **T +27 (0)60-687-0875/+27 (0)82-925-5922**

☐ **Klein Simonsvlei** see Niel Joubert Estate
☐ **Klein Tulbagh** see Tulbagh Winery
☐ **Klein Welmoed Wine & Olive Estate** see Foothills Vineyards
☐ **Kleipot** see Lourensford Wine Estate

Klipdrift

In 1938, the first drops of Klipdrift brandy were, so the story goes, distilled at 8.02 pm - the time reflected on the clock face on the label of Klipdrift Export. It grew into an iconic South African brand (best known mixed with cola), joined later by a Premium version. By Heineken Beverages. In various formats, 50ml to 1L.

Export ⓥ ★★★☆ Blended brandy (83), with standard 30% potstill component. Destined for mixing, the fiery apricot flavours offer little complexity, but balanced & smooth & lingering enough for small neat sips.
Premium ⓥ ★★★★ 30% potstill component aged 5 years, so this brandy (84) is richer, more intense & interesting than Export, tobacco, nutty notes from oak. — TJ

☐ **Klipkers** see De Kleine Wijn Koöp
☐ **Klippenkop** see Robertson Winery
☐ **Kloof Street** see Mullineux

Kloovenburg Wine & Olives   ⓥ ⑪ ◎ ⑧ ⑤

Pieter and Annalene du Toit's substantial estate in Swartland has unveiled changes to the tiers and new wines. Excitingly included is SA's first commercial bottling of lledoner pelut, from what's understood to be the first such vines to be planted locally, in 2018. The variety is a mutation of grenache, chiefly from France's Languedoc-Roussillon and Spain's Catalonia, named 'pelut' ('poilu' or furry in French) for the downy under-side of the leaves. Joining the line-up at press time was another first for the enterprising estate, a debut cap classique. Visitors will find not one but two venues, the original one on the home-farm, and newer Eight Feet Village a little further outside Riebeek-Kasteel, both showcasing Annalene's famous olive products.

Riebeekberg range
★★★★☆ **Syrah** ⓑ Usual quiet fynbos bouquet, vibrant fruit & scintillating brightness, along with fine grape/oak tannins, augur well for **21** (94)'s future. No new oak, so there's a real sense of fruit purity, 40% whole cluster ferment for subtle grip.

Estate range
★★★★ **Grenache Noir** A gentle tannic tug on translucent **22** ★★★★ (85) courtesy 60% bunch ferment; very little of the strawberry fragrance, flavour & vivacity of **21** (88).

★★★★ **Lledoner Pelut** ⓝⓔⓦ Packed with red berry fruit, enlivened by zesty acid, **22** (87) unchallenging yet characterful summer red.

★★★★ **Merlot** ⊘ Plum & blackberry, subtle spice from older oak, **21** (86)'s richness restrained &, like all the reds, commendably savoury rather than fruit-sweet. No **20**.

★★★★ **Shiraz** Rounded, more approachable in youth than Riebeekberg sibling, shade less refreshing than **19** ★★★★☆ (90), **20** (88)'s red fruit overlain with olive tapenade & dried Mediterranean herbs.

Barrel Fermented Chardonnay ★★★★ No wallflower, orange- & lime-toned **22** (84) intensely toasty & buttery, with leesy richness, its cordial-like fruit overwhelmingly sweet. Fermented in older barrel & tank with staves. Not tasted: **Carignan**.

Eight Feet range
★★★★ **Red** Appealing shiraz-led combo with significant portions grenache & mourvèdre, drop carignan, for drinking now & over next few years. **21** (89) complex herb, spice, red & black melange, tight tannins.

★★★★☆ **White** Mostly grenache blanc, roussanne, verdelho & chenin (23/20/16) in support in **22** ⑨⓪. White flowers & dusty earth notes, good vinosity & weight at modest 12.5% alc. Touch less showstopping than **21** ⑨① but appetising & satisfying nonetheless.

Stamboom range

The Village Red Blend ⑭ ⊘ ⑰ ★★★★ Engaging grenache, shiraz & mourvèdre trio lightly oaked in **22** ⑧④ for easy enjoyment. Welcoming grape tannin tug, lifted acid completes the package.

Unwooded Chardonnay ★★★☆ Quick-quaff **23** ⑦⑨ has barely there lemon aromas & flavours, nicely dry (1.6 g/L sugar) with some vinosity. **Sauvignon Blanc** ★★★ Bright & breezy **23** ⑦⑨ more vinous than aromatic or flavour packed, tart dry finish. **Grenache Blanc de Noir Brut Sparkling** ⊘ ★★★★ Salmon pink NV ⑧④ a fruit-filled & fun carbonated tipple. Plenty of strawberry candyfloss & sherbet flavours, pleasingly dry conclusion. — CvZ

Location: Riebeek-Kasteel ▪ Map: Swartland ▪ Map grid reference: D6 ▪ Map: Swartland ▪ Map grid reference: D6 ▪ WO: Swartland/Riebeekberg ▪ Est 1704 ▪ 1stB 1998 ▪ Tasting & sales Mon-Fri 9-4.30 Sat 9-4 Sun 10-4; pub hols (seasonal) please call ahead ▪ Closed Good Fri, Dec 25/26 & Jan 1 ▪ Wine & olive pairing/tasting options: to be booked online by selecting 'book an experience' ▪ Gift shop ▪ Farm produce/olive products ▪ 'Build your own picnic' from a wide selection of products ▪ Kringe Inni Bos restaurant Fri-Sun; playground ▪ Conservation area ▪ Wine club ▪ Eight Feet Village venue, Botmaskloof Pass: Kloovenburg shop (wine & olive sales) ▪ Curio shop ▪ Mura restaurant (fine dining) Tue-Sun 12-late, to book online www.muraeightfeet. co.za/#reservations; Eight Feet village restaurant (outdoor) open daily, www.eightfeet.co.za/eight-feet-village/; both restaurants can be booked for functions ▪ Owner(s) Pieter du Toit ▪ Cellarmaster(s) Pieter du Toit (Jan 1998) ▪ Winemaker(s) Duncan Stuart (Jan 2021) ▪ 300ha/130ha (carignan, grenache n/b, lledoner pelut, merlot, mourv, shiraz, chard, chenin, rouss, sauv, verdelho) ▪ 200t/12,000cs own label 55% red 40% white 4% rosé 1% sparkling ▪ WWF-SA Conservation Champion ▪ PO Box 2 Riebeek-Kasteel 7307 ▪ info@ kloovenburg.com ▪ www.kloovenburg.com ▪ **T +27 (0)22-448-1635**

Knorhoek Wines   ⑨ ⑪ ⑩ ⑩ ⑧ ⑧

On the Stellenbosch slopes of Simonsberg, where Cape lions once made the ravines reverberate with their 'knor', the home-farm, its facilities and wine brand were acquired by private investors in 2019. This was some years after purchasing Quoin Rock, set on adjoining high-altitude land. Both terroirs are farmed and vinified by viticulturist Nico Walters and winemaker Schalk Willem Opperman, who believe the weathered granite soil and direct sea influence impart structure and elegance as well as forward fruit, a combination they seek to express along with 'differences from vintage to vintage, instead of manipulating them in the cellar'.

★★★★ **Cabernet Sauvignon** Both vintages tasted were fermented in combo barrel, tank, foudre & concrete, then 20 months in small & large barrel. Ripe **19** ⑧⑦ gaining gentle savouriness, fresh acid still in balance with red fruit, dusty tannins & oak. **20** ⑧⑨ touch more classic in both alc (13.8% vs 14.5) & herby cassis flavour profile, firmer tannin grip black fruit core.

★★★★ **Chenin Blanc** ⑭ Exuberant aromas of pear & blossom on **22** ⑧⑦, builds complexity while balancing richness & freshness via combo foudre, tank, concrete 'egg' & oak, 23% new, 11 months.

Discontinued: **Méthode Cap Classique Brut**. — ML

Location/map: Stellenbosch ▪ Map grid reference: F3 ▪ WO: Simonsberg-Stellenbosch ▪ Est 1827 ▪ 1stB 1997 ▪ Tasting & sales Tue-Sun 10-4 ▪ Closed Good Fri, Dec 25 & Jan 1 ▪ Knorhoek Restaurant Tue-Sun 10-4 Wed-Sat 10-10; Sat/Sun booking essential ▪ Facilities for children ▪ Tour groups ▪ Weddings/conferences ▪ Hiking trail ▪ 3-star guest house & self-catering cottages ▪ Owner(s) Knorhoek Farms (Pty) Ltd ▪ Winemaker(s) Schalk Willem Opperman (Aug 2020) ▪ Viticulturist(s) Nico Walters (Mar 2019) ▪ ±60ha ▪ PO Box 23 Elsenburg 7607 ▪ info@knorhoek.co.za ▪ www.knorhoek.co.za ▪ **T +27 (0)21-865-2114**

☐ **Kobus** *see* Havana Hills
☐ **Koelenbosch** *see* Koelenhof Winery

Koelenhof Winery   ⑨ ⑪ ⑩ ⑧ ⑧

A Stellenbosch institution with close to 85 vintages, Koelenhof Winery vinifies select parcels for its substantial own labels, smaller batches for clients, plus a large quantity for the bulk trade. Longtime general manager Andrew de Vries and team are determined to dispel 'the unfair perception that high-volume wineries can't consistently produce world-class wines', hence the Stellenbosch 1679 pinnacle bottlings.

Stellenbosch 1679 range

★★★★☆ **Cabernet Sauvignon** Plush, rewarding **20** ⑨⑴ gains power & stature from 2 years new oak. Fruitcake abundance & spice add to richness, as does layered, supple palate. Good freshness to long finish.

★★★★☆ **Single Vineyard Old Vine Pinotage** ⊛ Retains 'old-school hedonistic' styling from venerable vines in **21** ⑨⑴. Ripe (15.2% alc) dark-berry fruit with light dry tannin grip & cedar from 16 months new oak. Inky & intense, yet as seductive as last.

★★★★☆ **The Legacy** ⊛ Retains 50% cab with other 4 Bordeaux varieties in equal parts in **19** ⑨⑷, but raises the bar on **18** ⑨⑵. Opulent & satisfying mouthful of spicy berries & plums yet nothing overplayed. Harmonious, broad & supple, a controlled finish courtesy 2 years in new oak.

★★★★☆ **Single Vineyard Bush Vine Chenin Blanc** ⊘ ⊛ Keen sugar-acid tension on old-vines **20** ⑨⑷, thrilling complexity too, new oak adding its own nuances. Depth of fruit promises future pleasure.

Koelenbosch range

★★★★☆ **Director's Reserve Pinotage** Confident & boldly styled **21** ⑨⓪ matches previous in chalky grip from 14 months new oak without sacrificing cherry & blueberry vivacity & appeal. Integrated & long.

★★★★ **Nineteenfortyone** ⊘ Switches to pinotage as lead variety with 3 others in **20** ⑧⑻, luxurious black-fruit styling & generous 14.9% alc offset with sappy freshness & 18 months oaking.

★★★★ **Single Vineyard Noble Late Harvest** ⊘ ⊛ Botrytised bushvine chenin, 2 years in old oak, shows fantastic sugar-acid balance, energising the flavours of **19** ⑧⑼. 14.6% alc not out of kilter. 375 ml.

....

Sangiovese ☺ ★★★ Among handful of SA varietal bottlings. Previewed **22** ⑧⑵ offers light, bright delicious cherry-berry succulence.

....

Merlot ⊘ ★★★☆ Plum, tealeaf & cocoa appeal on **21** ⑧⑷. Bright fruitiness plays off gentle tannin grip from 18 months in seasoned oak. Moderate 13.2% alc. **Pinotage** ⊘ ★★★☆ Full-flavoured charm of **21** ⑧⑷ all about lively berry fruit bolstered by gentle tannin grip from 18 months in old oak. Alc (14.9%) is high but in sync. **Shiraz** ⊘ ★★★☆ Peppery bite to rounded, plump **21** ⑧⑸, made more interesting by liquorice & salt nuances. 18 months seasoned oak frames fruit without contributing flavour. **Dry Pinotage Rosé** ★★★ Raspberry & strawberry flavours on **23** ⑧⑵ dry pink, invigorated by good acid. **Chenin Blanc** ★★★ Fresh & light **23** ⑧⑴ an everyday crowd-pleaser with its unfussy melon & quince verve. **Sauvignon Blanc** ★★★ Waxy lemon zest typicity to sappy & bright **23** ⑧⑴. Uncomplicated & easy. **Pinotage Rosé Méthode Cap Classique** ⊘ ★★★ Strawberry sherbet appeal to **22** ⑧⑵ pink bubbly. Dry, tangy, with zip & gentle breadth from year on lees. **Chardonnay Méthode Cap Classique** ⊘ ★★★☆ Taut, focused **22** ⑧⑷ bottle-fermented sparkler improves on last in concentration. Bright lime & apple with fresh acid balance, some breadth from year on lees.

Koelenhof range

Pinotage ⊘ ★★★ Bouncy berries on **21** ⑧⑵, their juiciness complemented with dabs vanilla & spice from oak staving. **Koelenberg** ⊘ ★★★ Merlot (62%) leads shiraz on **21** ⑧⑵. Pliable, juicy & fresh, it had 6 months in tank with oak staves, lending gentle support. **Koelenhoffer** ⊘ ★★★ All-sauvignon **23** ⑧⑴ improves on previous in rounded lees breadth but retains grapefruit tang & typicity. Pleasant dry exit. **Pinotage Rosé Vin Sec** ★★★ Lightly sparkling **23** ⑦⑼ is easy to like in its perky semi-sweet strawberry brightness. **Sauvignon Blanc Vin Sec** ★★★ Tangy granadilla sweetness of **23** ⑦⑼ is ideal for fun times with friends. Light, fresh & frothy, it finishes clean & dry from judicious acid. **Pinorto** ⊘ ★★★ Pinotage 'port', **20** ⑧⑵ unctuous & chocolaty, soft tannined after year in old oak. Not tasted: **Koelnektar**. — FM

Location/map/WO: Stellenbosch ▪ Map grid reference: D1 ▪ Est 1941 ▪ 1stB 1970's ▪ Tasting & sales Mon-Thu 9-5 Fri 9-4 Sat/pub hols 10-4 ▪ Guided cellar tours daily ▪ Closed Easter Fri/Sun & Dec 25 ▪ Facilities for children ▪ Picnics to be pre-booked; fresh roosterkoek available daily ▪ Koel-Tainer deli ▪ Conference/function venue ▪ Wine club ▪ Owner(s) 67 shareholders ▪ GM Andrew de Vries (2006) ▪ Winemaker(s) Nicholas Husselman (Oct 2017), with Handré Visagie (Jan 2018) ▪ 16,500t/55,000cs own labels 45% red 45% white 8% rosé 2% fortified + 2,000cs for clients & 100,000L bulk ▪ Other export brands: Stellenbosch Gold ▪ IPW ▪ PO Box 1 Koelenhof 7605 ▪ koelwyn@mweb.co.za ▪ www.koelenhof.co.za ▪ **T +27 (0)21-865-2020/1**

Koelfontein

Owned by the Conradie family for seven generations, extensive Koelfontein is planted with 185 ha of decid-uous fruit orchards, with a further 750 ha given over to conservation, earning WWF-SA Champion status. Just 6 ha is vineyard - but enough to make the farm an exception in cool-climate Ceres Valley. The own-label line-up, in its third decade, is vinified off-site for owner Handri Conradie by distinguished consultants.

★★★★ Shiraz Voluptuous & sweet fruit of **21** ⑧⑨ balanced & enhanced by savoury-spicy tones of cured meat, coriander & scrub. Good firm texture aided by 20 months in 80% new 300L barrels.

★★★★ Chardonnay Ripe-fruited yet poised & svelte **22** ⑧⑦'s Golden Delicious, vanilla & lime curd fra-grances & flavours deftly supported by oaking, 9 months, 20% new. Natural wholebunch ferment.— WB

Location: Ceres ▪ Map: Tulbagh ▪ Map grid reference: H5 ▪ WO: Western Cape ▪ Est 1832 ▪ 1stB 2002 ▪ Tasting & sales Mon-Fri 11-4 Sat by appt ▪ Closed all pub hols ▪ Farm produce ▪ Hikes ▪ Conservation area ▪ Die Kloof self-catering historic house (sleeps 6) ▪ Owner(s) Handri Conradie ▪ Winemaker(s) Dewaldt Heyns & John Secombe (current releases) ▪ Viticulturist(s) Hennie van Noordwyk ▪ 950ha/±6ha (shiraz, chard) ▪ ±24t/2,400cs own label 50% red 50% white ▪ WWF-SA Conservation Champion ▪ PO Box 4 Prince Alfred's Hamlet 6840 ▪ wine@koelfontein.co.za ▪ www.koelfontein.co.za ▪ **T +27 (0)23-313-3304/+27 (0)76-181-5626**

Konkelberg

The brand name means 'Connivance Corner', and the backstory has a whiff of 17th-century extra-legal activity not far from the present-day Longridge cellar, adding piquancy to wines made by recent appointee Lucilia Ramos to be fruity, refreshing and easy on the palate and pocket.

Rouge ★★★★ Blend changes each vintage, curvaceous body & soft, juicy tannins stay the same, create a delicious fruity everyday red in **20** ⑧⑤, 73% cab with pinotage. **Sauvignon Blanc ★★★** Previewed **23** ⑧② attractive & easy to drink; appeal, character & interest enhanced by natural winemaking, as Rouge. — DS

Location/WO: Stellenbosch ▪ Map: Helderberg ▪ Map grid reference: C1 ▪ Est 2011 ▪ Tasting & sales Mon-Tue 10-5 Wed-Sat 10-6 Sun 10-3.30 ▪ Tasting fee applicable ▪ Closed Good Fri & Dec 25 ▪ Owner(s) Phinimal Farms ▪ Winemaker(s)/viticulturist(s) Lucilia Ramos (2022) ▪ 20ha/18ha (cabs s/f, merlot, sauv) ▪ 100t/7,800cs own label 60% red 40% white ▪ Suite 116 Private Bag X4 Die Boord 7613 ▪ info@konkelberg. co.za ▪ www.konkelberg.co.za ▪ **T +27 (0)21-855-2005**

Koopmanskloof Vineyards

Winemaking at 'Trader's Ravine' on Stellenbosch's Bottelary Hills dates from the 1770s, and bottling to the 1970s when the label was established by Stevie Smit. Now company managed, the extensive venture includes just under 450 ha of sustainably farmed vines across six properties, one of which is staff-owned and -run, plus a large private nature reserve with hiking trails. Winemaker Stephan Smit aims for excellent quality at an affordable price, with good balance and 'clever use of oak on the reds'.

Reserve range

Peacock Vine Cabernet Sauvignon ⑧ **★★★★** Juicy dark fruit with integrated spicing from 15 months in 60% new barrels plus some staves & blocks (70/30 French/American, as Pinotage). **21** ⑧⑤ has structure, fruit depth & freshness for beneficial development. This range tasted pre-bottling. **Peacock Vine Pinotage** ⑧ **★★★★** More time than Koopmanskloof reds (15 months vs 8) & 55% new oak barrels, with staves & blocks, affords more integration, gravitas & a dry spicy impression in **21** ⑧⑤.

Koopmanskloof range

Cabernet Sauvignon ⑦ **★★★** Slightly riper in **22** ⑧② than previous, dark berries with a subtler herby nuance. Dry tannins & toasty top note from oak staves & blocks. Fairtrade accredited, as both ranges. **Merlot** ⑧ **★★★** Like previous, smoky savoury nuance to dark-fruited **21** ⑧① from oak treatment. Ripe, plush texture gives smooth & satisfying drinkability. **Pinotage** ⑧ **★★★** Oaking imparts a sternness to plummy red fruit, less rounded in **21** ⑦⑨, but a good barbecue partner. **Shiraz** ⑧ **★★★★** Most balanced of these reds. Riper in **22** ⑧④, but with similar toasty mocha tone to savoury dark berries. French & American blocks & staves also give grip & some spice, but better melded for early accessibility. **Pinotage Rosé** ⑦ **★★★** Pleasing on the eye, palate & (as all these wines) pocket. Flamingo pink, with a dry savou-riness balancing the cranberry in **23** ⑧② tangy sunset sipper. **Chardonnay** ⑦ **★★★★** Caramel/vanilla nuance underpins ample ripe pear & citrus on improved **23** ⑧③. Quite plush & mouthfilling yet fresh, finish-ing with a perky acid twist that calls for a lunch date. Oaked, unlike last. **Chenin Blanc** ⑦ **★★★★** Bright

& flavoursome, **23** (83) even friendlier than previous. Smooth lemon cream texture freshened with crunchy apple acidity. Your everyday staple for carefree sipping. **Sauvignon Blanc** ⊘ ★★★ Crisp lemon barley & a hint of tropical in **23** (82) poised & easy-drinking quaffer. In abeyance: **Mocha Pinotage**. — MW

Location/WO: Stellenbosch ▪ Est 1801 ▪ 1stB 1970 ▪ Closed to public ▪ Private nature reserve ▪ Owner(s) Managed by Koopmanskloof Wingerde (Pty) Ltd ▪ MD Rydal Jeftha ▪ Winemaker(s) Stephan Smit ▪ Viticulturist(s) Japie de Villiers ▪ 440ha (cab, carignan, merlot, ptage, roobernet, ruby cab, shiraz, chard, chenin, sauv, sem) ▪ ±3,700t/±2.5m L 50% red 50% white ▪ Other brand(s): The Fair Trade ▪ Fairtrade, IPW, WIETA ▪ PO Box 19 Koelenhof 7605 ▪ info@koopmanskloof.co.za ▪ www.koopmanskloof.co.za ▪ **T +27 (0)21-842-0810**

☐ **Kottabos** see Boschkloof Wines

Kranskop Wines

The only WO Klaasvoogds wines in the guide, these well-priced bottlings are made by former Nederburg cellarmaster Néwald Marais, working in a small cellar on the side of the rocky hill that lends its name to the venture. After more than 20 vintages, he still finds it 'invigorating' to be crafting in hands-on, traditional fashion. Visitors are welcome to taste the wines over a cheese platter out on the deck and savour the view.

★★★★ **Cabernet Sauvignon** ⓟ Marked upswing in **19** (86) from previewed **17** ★★★☆ (84). Bolder structure & fruit, appealing earth & leaf notes. Single-vineyard, as Pinot, Chardonnay & Sauvignon. No **18**.

★★★★ **Pinot Noir** ⓟ Appealing violet scent with silken tannins & bright raspberry fruit on pre-bottling **21** (86), showing emphatic improvement on near-austere **20** ★★★ (80).

★★★★ **Beekeeper's Block Shiraz** ⓟ Commendable effort in **19** (87) outshines last **17** ★★★☆ (85), savoury core enlivened with black cherry fruit, supported by 18 months in 33% new barriques.

★★★★ **Tannat** ⊘ Grape seldom seen in SA. Year in seasoned barriques, **21** (86) has convincing depth of spicy red & black fruit, solid body & tannins.

★★★★ **MCT Selection** ⓟ Exotically aromatic merlot, cab & tannat blend, **21** (86) juicy & supple, with subtle oak spicing, 33% new, ripe, gentle tannins.

★★★★ **Chardonnay** ⊘ Follows form, with orange blossom fragrance, vanilla-spiced mixed citrus flavour & satisfying texture & heft in **22** (86). 50% barrel fermented, 6 months on lees. Very appealing.

★★★★ **Viognier Noble Late Harvest** ⊘ Fine acid-sugar balance, striking peach & citrus fruit make **22** ★★★★★ (91) unoaked botrytis dessert wine exceptional. Honeyed, focused, shows real class & obvious staying power at modest 10% alc. Upstages last-tasted **20** (88). 375 ml.

Merlot ⓟ ★★★★ Light & leafy, with pretty plum fruit, single-vineyard **20** (83) preview offers undemanding everyday enjoyment. **Shiraz** ★★★★ Riper, better-balanced **21** (85) shows black cherry fruit with tarry, earthy notes, appealing oak-spice lift. **Shiraz-Viognier Rosé** ⊘ ★★★★ Equal parts co-fermented for dry, leesy **23** (85), offering primary red berry fruit, satisfying texture & body, tingly acid. **Sauvignon Blanc** ⊘ ★★★☆ Pleasing weight & texture, with solid gooseberry & passionfruit core & zesty acid in **23** (85). Not tasted: **Chenin Blanc, Viognier**. — GdB

Location/map: Robertson ▪ Map grid reference: B4 ▪ WO: Klaasvoogds ▪ Est 2001 ▪ 1stB 2003 ▪ Tasting, sales & tours Mon-Fri 10-4.30 Sat/pub hols 10-2 ▪ Closed Good Fri & Dec 25 ▪ Cheese platters ▪ Owner(s)/viticulturist(s) Néwald Marais ▪ Cellarmaster(s)/winemaker(s) Néwald Marais (2008) ▪ 43ha/27.5ha (cab, merlot, pinot, shiraz, tannat, chard, chenin, sauv, viog) ▪ 240t/3,000cs own label 75% red 25% white ▪ IPW, WIETA ▪ PO Box 49 Klaasvoogds 6707 ▪ newald@kranskopwines.co.za, info@kranskopwines.co.za ▪ www.kranskopwines.co.za ▪ **T +27 (0)23-626-3200**

Krone

A collection of premier cap classique sparklers, made in Tulbagh at dedicated, specialist facilities, and differentiated by being vintage-dated 'to show the characteristics of the year without having to meet a set mould'. Additions to the portfolio reflect on-trend natural winemaking and a terroir focus inspired by the French grower champagne movement, plus a praiseworthy degree of seriousness in the burgeoning nectar (semi-dry) category. On 18th-century brand-base Twee Jonge Gezellen (see listing), restored gracious Cape Dutch buildings house a tasting lounge and modern-art gallery, lately with an artist residency programme.

★★★★☆ **Amphora Blanc De Blancs** ⓐ Stellar **21** (93) leads newly extended line of chardonnay sparklers, this one unique in clay pot ferment/ageing, 6 months, before 24 on lees in bottle; unfiltered, with zero dosage. Ex Tulbagh, it's richly textured, with layers of lemon cream, ginger shortbread & toasted nuts. A bold, deeply delicious wine balanced by brisk acid. Previously from Elandskloof vines.

★★★★☆ **Kaaimansgat Blanc De Blancs** (🐝) Showcases famed vineyard, 700 m altitude in cool Elandskloof; first of the site-specific chardonnay sparklers from this house. Six months in 2,500L foudre before 30+ on lees. **20** (93) shows brioche complexity, very pure, focused & flinty fruit, with great balance & oystershell minerality. Last was **16** (93).

★★★★☆ **Koelfontein Blanc de Blancs** (NEW) Spotlights high-lying (600 m) Ceres Plateau site, slight easterly (cooler) aspect. **20** (91) fascinating in its emphasis on fruit rather than savoury character, vinosity than brioche richness, even after ferment/6 months in foudre & 30 on lees. Thus not classic but undoubtedly top quality, something different. Should age interestingly.

★★★★☆ **Twee Jonge Gezellen Blanc de Blancs** (NEW) (🐝) From Tulbagh vineyards, **20** (93) the antithesis of Koelfontein sibling: quintessential freshly baked bread aromas, with depth of savoury umami flavour. Full but elegant, grippy yet refreshing. Layers unfurl satisfyingly now, will amplify over time.

★★★★☆ **Night Nectar Blanc de Blancs** (🐝) In new livery ('Demi-Sec' dropped from name), **20** (93) chardonnay bubble is from Tulbagh, carries plush 33 g/L sugar with aplomb. Its 6.2 g/L acid freshens & lengthens the flavours without sacrificing poise, invites dessert at table. Last was **18** (93).

★★★★☆ **RD** (🐝) Prestige sparkling, recently disgorged after remarkable ten years on lees. Vivacious mousse of **13** (93) delivers complex array of scents & flavours - umami yeast extract, toasted nut, honey & nutmeg - courtesy of 65% chardonnay with pinot noir. Deliciously austere for age, bracing & bone-dry.

★★★★ **Rosé Vintage Cuvée Brut** (✓) Salmon pink **21** ★★★★★ (90) dry bubbly from 74% pinot noir, rest chardonnay, has vibrant cranberry & juicy pomegranate notes in textured, full body. Fresh, with hint of toasted hazelnut after 13 months on lees, beautifully rounded finish. Notch up on **19** (89); no **20** made.

★★★★ **Borealis Vintage Cuvée Brut** A Cape institution. Dry, steely sparkler, **21** (88) with crunchy apple & ginger notes that will get more complex with time, but great to drink now. Splash pinot blanc joined by chardonnay & pinot noir (49/45). Also in 375 ml & magnum, as Rosé Brut & the Demi-Secs.

★★★★ **Night Nectar Rosé Demi-Sec** Carnival pink & with liquidised strawberries & cream flavour, **21** (89) gains sufficient gravitas from 74% pinot noir & fresh acid to balance 43 g/L sugar, sustain its velvet mousse. No **20**.

★★★★ **Night Nectar Demi-Sec** Deservedly popular (100,000 cases), carefully made semi-sweet version of Borealis (42 g/L sugar). Luxurious **21** (86) offers lemon tart rather than fresh citrus notes, indulgent yet refined thanks to gossamer mousse & bright acid. 15 months on lees, like Demi-Sec sibling.

★★★★☆ **Night Nectar Blanc de Noir** (NEW) Heft of pinot noir gives fruit density & grip to sweet **21** (90) sparkler, clean acid sweeps through for a balanced & crisp finish. Year on lees. WO Franschhoek.— DS

Location/map: Tulbagh ▪ Map grid reference: F4 ▪ WO: Western Cape/Tulbagh/Elandskloof/Ceres Plateau/Franschhoek ▪ Est 1710 ▪ 1stB 1937 ▪ Tasting & sales Mon-Sat 10-4 ▪ Tasting fee R70pp/discovery, R15opp/premium, R100pp/vintage-only ▪ Closed all pub hols ▪ Cellar tours Mon-Sat at 11 ▪ Annual festival: Christmas in Winter (Jun) ▪ Art gallery ▪ Owner(s) TJG Estate (Pty) Ltd ▪ Winemaker(s) Stephan de Beer (2008), with Lizette Stander (2021) ▪ Viticulturist(s) Rosa Kruger ▪ PO Box 16 Tulbagh 6820 ▪ info@kronecapclassique.co.za ▪ www.kronecapclassique.co.za ▪ T +27 (0)23-230-0680

Kronendal Boutique Winery   (♿)

'Interesting but reserved' wine is what Magdaleen Kroon strives to produce under her and husband Pieter's handcrafted Durbanville label Kronendal, and she uses ambient yeasts, gentle basket-pressing and avoidance of additives among other low-tech strategies 'to portray terroir and vintage as authentically as possible'.

★★★★☆ **Mirari** (🍷) Characterful Mediterranean blend brings tempranillo back into the mix with shiraz (83%), mourvèdre, viognier in **17** (90). Naturally fermented, like **15** (90), the red-berried flavours accessible partly due to less new oak, 30% vs 50%. Various large-format bottles on offer. **16** held back for now.— DS

Location: Durbanville ▪ Map: Durbanville, Philadelphia & Darling ▪ Map grid reference: C7 ▪ WO: Cape Town ▪ Est 2003 ▪ 1stB 2006 ▪ Currently online sales only ▪ Wine club ▪ Owner(s) Pieter & Magdaleen Kroon ▪ Winemaker(s) Magdaleen Kroon ▪ 0.6ha (mourv, shiraz, viog) ▪ 4t/520cs own label 100% red ▪ PO Box 4433 Durbanville 7551 ▪ info@kronendalwine.co.za ▪ www.kronendalwine.co.za ▪ T +27 (0)82-499-0198

☐ **Kruger Family** *see* Stellenview Premium Wines

Kruger Family Wines

Johan Kruger and Belgian wife Sofie have happily seen the dust settle on their new building in Somerset West, with 'wine storage space, offices, a blending/operational section, as well as a tasting room' (the latter open by appointment). The local wine portfolio is focused on chardonnay, pinot noir and old vines, as this, says Johan, is 'where our passion lies'. Something of an outlier (in many ways, but not in terms of that passion) is the new Syrah from high-altitude Sutherland-Karoo. Like the rest of the range, it shows Johan's elegant, 'soft-handed' restraint in the winery. A chardonnay from the area will be following 'shortly'. The range made for Naked Wines is also substantial, the wines mostly going to UK 'angels', but some to the US.

Kruger Family Wines range

★★★★ **Old Vines Cinsault** ⊛ Understated, lightly perfumed aroma on **22** ⑧⑥ introduces palate with delicate, shallow fruitiness & edge of tartness. Very gentle tannin & modest 12% alc in balance. Only older oak, as for most. From Wellington.

★★★★ **Old Vines Grenache** ⊘ ⊛ The lifted perfume of **20** ★★★★★ ⑨⑥ made more complex by earthy note. Good depth of fruit, with fine texture, smoothly mouthcoating tannins, succulent acidity & 13% alc all in balance. Impresses more than **19** ⑧⑥. Delicious drinking now, should develop.

★★★★☆ **Pearly Gates Pinot Noir** ⊘ Fragrance (accentuated by 30% wholebunch ferment) & touch of earthiness to the dark cherry fruit on elegant, refined **22** ⑨② from Upper Hemel-en-Aarde Valley. Lively balance, with succulent acidity, a little ripe tannin & 13.5% alc.

★★★★☆ **Karoo Syrah** ⑱⑲ ⊛ Natural ferment, 30% wholebunch, on **22** ⑨③ from Karoo-Sutherland vines, 'highest & coldest in Cape'. Gorgeous, subtle perfume followed by palate with Kruger's signature restraint, subtlety & elegance combined with red & darker fruit charm. Fine but firm structural balance; good dry & persistent length. Just 13% alc.

★★★★☆ **Klipkop Chardonnay** Recognised single-vineyard (as most tasted this edition), **22** ⑨① delicate & light-feeling at 12.5% alc, quietly aromatic & complexly flavourful without intensity. Pleasing dry stoniness. Older oak, 10 months. 30% wholebunch, as Old Vines sibling.

★★★★☆ **Old Vines Chardonnay** From cooler Stellenbosch slopes, old-oaked **22** ⑨② quietly lovely, pure aromas & equally attractive flavours on creamy palate. Acid less strong than on previous, but adequate for balance. Appealing liquorice hint on good lemony finish. 13% alc.

★★★★ **Sans Chêne Chardonnay** ⊘ Light **21** ⑧⑥ no great intensity, but some flavourful charm & lipsmacking lemon-lime freshness. Natural ferment in stainless steel & concrete, as **20** ★★★★ ⑧⑤.

★★★★☆ **Old Vines Chenin Blanc** ⊛ From 1962 vines, **22** ⑨① most incisive as well as most generous & fruit-rich of vintage's, though lighter-feeling (at 12.5% alc) than last. Usual fragrant aroma, good acidity in balance, with some sweet fruit at core. Natural ferment in concrete 'egg'.

★★★★ **Old Vines Palomino** ⊛ Notably light-feeling **22** ⑧⑥ does have forward & expressive aroma & flavour despite not much vinosity at 11.5% alc. Oaking adds some breadth, the whole pleasantly balanced.

★★★★ **Old Vines Sauvignon Blanc** As always, **22** ⑧⑥ attractively understated, from gently fragrant aromas on, with old oak taming grape's showiness. Restrained, balanced, with good integrated acidity. Ex 1988 Stellenbosch parcel.

Brut Rosé Méthode Cap Classique ⊘ ★★★★ Upper Hemel-en-Aarde pinot noir gives pale salmon blush, creamy mousse & quiet cherry notes on refreshing, truly dry **19** ⑧⑤. Older-oak ferment, 9 months add further dimension. Not tasted: **Western Cape Pinot Noir**. Discontinued: **Elandskloof Pinot Noir**, **Grenache Rosé, Walker Bay Chardonnay**.

Naked Wines range

★★★★ **Cabernet Sauvignon** ⊘ Ripe, full-fruited **21** ⑧⑥, rich & showy, but also not immodest with 13.5% alc & restrained oaking. Decent firmness but juicy & approachable. **19** ★★★★ ⑧⑤ was last tasted.

★★★★ **Old Vines Cinsault** ⊛ Beguiling fragrance on **22** ⑧⑨ from vines not far off their half-century. But also something deeper than fresh & fruity charm, & touch of ripe richness, easy tannic tug to the bright lightness. 6 months older oak; 13% alc.

★★★★ **Merlot** Dark, ripe berries aplenty on **21** ★★★★☆ ⑨② with dark chocolate & tobacco. Touch tannic severity to textured elegance, which works well as counterpoint to succulent, quite intense sweet fruit. 20% new oak in support. 14.5% alc in balance. Impresses more than **20** ⑧⑦, also from Stellenbosch.

★★★★ **Old Vines Tinta Barocca** 🌱 Modest dark berry aromas on **22** ㊇, mulberry fruitiness continuing, if not intensely, to variety's big dry tannins, though these quite restrained, & the whole more light-seeming than dense at 13.5% alc. 10 months older oak. From 1974 Wellington bushvines.

★★★★ **Cabernet Sauvignon-Merlot** 🏵 Cab in slight majority in neatly structured, deft **21** ㊅, adding cedar to fruitcake tones. Fresh & balanced, easily accessible young though will keep. WO W Cape.

★★★★ **Elements** 🏵 Cab at around 60%, **21** ㊅ unusually big & rich for this range, alc 14.5%. Ripe, spicy fruit character. Bit fresher in feeling than last, cleaner & brighter, more convincing. WO Coastal.

★★★★ **Maxime Reserve** 🏵 Shiraz with 21% grenache, 11% cinsaut, latter 2 giving pretty, fruity perfume of **21** ㊅. Easygoing & ready for early drinking, but in touch with dry, classic styling. WO W Cape.

★★★★ **Chardonnay** Widely sourced **22** ㊅ has full-fruited charm, 25% new oak infusing some nutty notes into lemon & lime. Well balanced, with good fresh acidity & house's elegance, albeit at 13.5% alc. Touch more impressive than **21** ★★★★ ㊄.

★★★★☆ **Old Vines Chardonnay** 🌱 From Swartland block that's probably Cape's oldest at ±36 years. **22** ㊉, part old-oaked, part concrete 'egg', fresh & surprisingly delicate despite warm origins, a mineral stoniness on dry finish. 13.5% alc.

★★★★☆ **Old Vines Chenin Blanc Coastal** 🌱 Light-footed **22** ★★★★ ㊈ has some complexity in its delicacy, but feels touch dilute despite 13.5% alc indicating ripeness. Soft textured & supple, acid standing a little apart. WO Coastal; more generous **21** ㊈ ex Wellington.

★★★★☆ **Old Vines Chenin Blanc Swartland** 🌱 This version goes to the US. **22** ★★★★ ㊈ from 1982 Swartland vines. Light & refined at just 12% alc, with scrubby hillside, stony notes infused with dried peach. Old oak & 25% concrete 'egg' ageing. Nicely balanced, but quieter & softer than **21** ㊈.

★★★★ **Nieuwoudtville Sauvignon Blanc** 🏵 From high, cool vines, gently aromatic **22** ㊇ preview has understated tropicality, is lively & fresh. May reveal more intensity once bottled. For Naked Wines US.

Pinotage 🏵 ★★★★ Forwardly ripe, rather rustic charm on **21** ㊄. Bright acidity, velvet texture, some sweet fruit depth; variety's tannins much under control. Old oak only. WO Coastal, as next. **Unoaked Chardonnay** 🏵 ★★★★ Ex Franschhoek, **22** ㊄ tasted very young (as Sauvignon), needed to settle, but already with forward varietal aromas & flavour, expressed with charm & balance. **Sauvignon Blanc** 🏵 ★★★★ Still a bit raw, but **22** ㊄ seems short of **21** ★★★★ ㊅, though it does have good tangy freshness, juicy brightness. WO Stellenbosch. **Angels Selection** ★★★★ Lightly oaked **22** ㊂ from the accustomed blend of chenin with chardonnay & colombard. Aromatic, softly rounded & dry, pleasingly & easily approachable. Not tasted: **Matteo Reserve**. — TJ

Location: Somerset West ▪ WO: Piekenierskloof/Stellenbosch/Coastal/Western Cape/Wellington/Upper Hemel-en-Aarde Valley/Swartland/Franschhoek/Nieuwoudtville/Sutherland-Karoo ▪ Est/1stB 2015 ▪ Tasting by appt only ▪ Owner(s) Johan & Sofie Kruger ▪ Cellarmaster(s)/winemaker(s) Johan Kruger (Sep 2015) ▪ 80t/25,000cs own label 50% red 50% white + 40,000cs for clients ▪ Brands for clients: Naked Wines (UK), Naked Wines (USA) ▪ WIETA ▪ johan@krugerfamilywines.co.za ▪ www.krugerfamilywines.co.za ▪ T +27 (0)83-411-0757

☐ **Kumala** see Accolade Wines South Africa

Kumusha Wines

Following a Cape Town sommelier career, Zimbabwean Tinashe Nyamudoka moved to Johannesburg to expand his interests, including this wine label, which he also successfully and creatively markets. The name means 'home' or 'roots' in Shona, and the brand has seen rapid growth since the debut 2016 bottling, also in terms of the number of wines on offer. The grapes are widely sourced, with some specific to a site, and the wines made by Opstal Estate's winemaker, Attie Louw, who shares the belief that wine's primary attribute must be drinkability. Exports now include America, the UK and a number of African countries.

★★★★ **Pinotage** ⃠ Sleek (13% alc) **22** ㊅, ex Swartland, wild fermented (as all except Hurudza), displays oak-influenced liquorice & smoky spice, the glossy dark berries giving succulence & length. Enough tannin grip for a few years.

★★★★ **Hurudza** Classic Bordeaux blend, 85% cab with 3 others, **21** ★★★★☆ ㊉ flagship from Stellenbosch fruit, the most generously oaked of all reds, 18 months, 60% new. Deep colour hints at ripeness & concentration: vivid cassis, cedar & spice perfumes, palate seamed with firm but ripe tannin. Has potential but also accessible earlier. Step up on **20** ㊇. Also in 1.5L.

★★★★ **Cabernet Sauvignon-Cinsault** ⊘ Blend 75/25, 8 months older barrels plus concrete tank, **22** ⑧⑦ designed for earlier drinking, light texture, fruity fresh, tannins amenable. It's as if cinsaut leads, there's a delicacy in the red fruit & texture.

★★★★☆ **Sondagskloof Sauvignon Blanc** ⊘ From tiny ward (aka Sunday's Glen) in Cape South Coast region. In contrast to sibling, **22** ⑨⓪ is 10% oaked, giving light savoury tone to the passionfruit & greengage perfume, the flavours more mineral. Layered, involving, zesty finish imparts vibrancy.

★★★★☆ **The Flame Lily** ⓐ Roussanne 62% with chenin, 2 others, 10 months oaked, unfiltered **22** ⑨⓸ is melon-toned, some stonefruit, all follow through to palate, backed by crisp acid. Good combo fruit & oak, both play their part, the wood tannins a hidden support. Also in 1.5L.

. . . .

Cinsault Rosé ☺ ★★★ Pale pink & slender (12% alc), **23** ⑧② has drink-me written all over it. Red berries & cherries, balancing freshness, an appealing quaffer.

. . . .

Cabernet Sauvignon ⊘ ★★★☆ Bright fruited, berries & plums, light spice dusting from year older barrels, **22** ⑧④'s texture plush, smoothly round. Designed for drinking on release, what a pleasure. WO W Cape, as Sauvignon Blanc. **Chenin Blanc** ★★★★ 20% oak component takes **23** ⑧④ out of the fruit-driven mode: Lemon Cream biscuit & crunchy apple & pear scents, becoming more mineral in the flavours. Streamlined, fresh & dry. WO Breedekloof, as Rosé. **Sauvignon Blanc** ★★★★ Greener notes than last but still spot-on sauvignon: fennel & lemongrass, **23** ⑧④ perky lemony freshness. Wakens the taste buds. — CR

Location: Johannesburg ▪ WO: Slanghoek/Western Cape/Swartland/Stellenbosch/Breedekloof/Sunday's Glen ▪ 1stB 2016 ▪ Closed to public ▪ Owner(s)/cellarmaster(s) Tinashe Nyamudoka ▪ Winemaker(s) Attie Louw (Opstal) ▪ c/o Opstal Estate Rawsonville 6845 ▪ tinashe@kumushabrands.com ▪ **T +27 (0)83-432-5400**

Kusafiri Organic Wines ⓠ ⓗ

Having made a leap a few years back from Vredendal to Voor Paardeberg, Klaas Coetzee's latest move is a short hop over Paarl Mountain to Dal Josafat and its Mooi Bly winery, where he rents space to craft his 'organic, no-sulphur-added, vegan-friendly wines' in partnership with Swiss national Sandro Bertuol.

Kusafiri range

★★★★ **Cabernet Sauvignon** ⓠ ⊘ Compact (13.4% alc), refined & balanced **21** ⑧⑨ is laudably free of the need to impress, almost easy-drinking yet has ample substance & interest to offer.

Shiraz ⓠ ⊘ ★★★★ Previewed mid-2022 & retasted year later, **21** ⑧④ still generous, with plump fruit & sweet vanilla from 10% American oak, tad softer & delightfully fragrant. **Sauvignon Blanc** ⊘ ★★★★ Celebrating the kukumakranka flower on its label, **23** ⑧③ offers a profusion of summer fruit tightened by fresh acid. Reined-in 12.5% alc for everyday quaffing. **Viognier** ⓝⓔⓦ ⊘ ★★★★ Opulent & showy but not over the top thanks to bone-dry finish & controlled 12.8% alc. Just 50% of **22** ⑧④ brushed with oak. Not tasted: **Merlot, Pinotage, The Spice Of Life Shiraz, Cabernet Sauvignon-Merlot, White Blend.**

Cans range

Organic Red ⓠ ⊘ ★★☆ No sulphites added to **21** ⑦⑨ pinotage in convenient 250-ml can. **Sauvignon Blanc** ⓠ ⊘ ★★★★ Fresh, sunshiny fruit & restrained 12% alc, **22** ⑧④ has added appeal of certified-organic wine in a tin, as Red. — DS

Location/map: Paarl ▪ Map grid reference: F4 ▪ WO: Coastal ▪ Est/1stB 2020 ▪ Tasting, sales & cellar tours by appt only ▪ Guest house ▪ Owner(s) Kusafiri Wines (Pty) Ltd ▪ Cellarmaster(s)/winemaker(s)/viticulturist(s) Klaas Coetzee (Jan 2020) ▪ 40t/6,000cs own label 100% red ▪ Organic (Control Union) ▪ 27 Flambeau Str, Courtrai, Paarl 7646 ▪ klaas@kusafiriwines.co.za ▪ www.kusafiriwines.co.za ▪ **T +27 (0)82-801-3737**

KWV ⓠ ⓨ ⓐ ⓑ

Founded in 1918, KWV has evolved into a producer of over 100 products represented in more than 100 markets globally. The company's enduring reputation for quality is reflected in its fine and much-awarded wines and fortifieds, as well as its brandies (see separate listings). Visitors to HQ in Paarl are greeted by venerable production facilities transformed into modern and memorable tourist spaces: the House of Fire, originally the distilling cellar for KWV's brandies, and the imposing, vaulted Cathedral Cellar, built in 1930.

Location/map: Paarl ▪ Map grid reference: E6 ▪ KWV Wine Emporium: Kohler Str, T +27 (0)21-807-3007/8 F +27 (0)21-807-3119, wineemporium@kwv.co.za, www.kwvemporium.co.za ▪ Tasting & sales Mon-Fri 9-4

Sat 9-3 Sun 9-1 ▪ Several food & wine pairings available ▪ Cellar tours: Eng & Ger available - book @ info@ kwvemporium.co.za ▪ Tour groups by appt ▪ Closed Good Fri, Dec 25 & Jan 1 ▪ KWV House of Fire: Kohler Str, contact details same as for KWV Wine Emporium, or houseoffire@kwv.co.za ▪ House of Fire tour & brandy tasting: Eng Mon-Fri 11.30 & 2.30 reservations essential (max 14 persons per tour), regret no under 18s allowed ▪ Owner(s) Warshay Investment (Pty) Ltd t/a KWV ▪ Chief winemaker Justin Corrans ▪ Senior winemaker(s) Izele van Blerk, Kobus van der Merwe, James Ochse ▪ Winemaker(s) Carla Cutting, Sacha Muller ▪ Viticulturist(s) Marco Ventrella, Anneke du Plessis & Oursula Lenee ▪ PO Box 528 Suider-Paarl 7624 ▪ customer@kwv.co.za ▪ www.kwv.co.za ▪ **T +27 (0)21-807-3911 (office)**

KWV Brandies

KWV has been producing quality spirit - potstill brandy in particular - since 1918, garnering a worldwide reputation and many prestigious awards including multiple Best Brandy Producer trophies. Any new release by master distiller Pieter de Bod and his team therefore is something to savour, and this edition's unveiling of not one but two new brandies is very special indeed. The portfolio is showcased at a venue named House of Fire, part of the KWV Wine Emporium in Paarl. See KWV 'corporate' listing for details.

★★★★★ **Centenary** ⓧ Just 100 hugely expensive bottles of this magnificent brandy ⑨⑨ to celebrate 100 years of KWV. SA's oldest, with portion distilled in 1926 & average ageing period 37 years. Combines ethereal, elegant delicacy with subtle intensity. Mellow & deeply satisfying, reverberating endlessly.

★★★★★ **Nexus** ⓧ Superb packaging featuring individually crafted bottle & wooden case sets the scene for this 30 year old ⑨⑤: fine floral notes, wafts of soft spice, dried pears & apple follow on to intense fruit on the palate. Elegant, regal & oh so smooth, with a dry lingering citrus bite. Astounding quality.

★★★★★ **20 Year Old** ⓧ Exquisite aromas - sandalwood, apricot, scented flowers, hints spice & oxidative maturity. Rich & full, yet ultra-refined & delicate. This ⑨⑥ touch less forceful than 15YO, but more grace. Beautifully balanced, with supreme oak support. Long, mellow, mature notes carry to sweetish finish.

★★★★ **Imoya Fine Potstill** ⓧ Modern, beautifully presented brandy ⑧⑧. Fresh fruity aromas & flavours; elegant, rich balance, subtle texture with nutty, spicy oak in support, lifted with a fresh spirity finish. 100% potstill of up to 20 years.

★★★★★ **15 Year Old Alambic** ⓧ Attractive honey, soft spice & dried fruit with floral backing & some fine oak on this brandy ⑨⑦. Smooth, fine texture & good balance; great complexity from a range of citrus & rich fruitcake flavours. Mellow & mature, with everlasting finish.

★★★★★ **12 Year Old Barrel Select** ⓧ A triumph ⑨⑤. Rich, robust with caramelised nuts, sun-dried peaches, pear drop on the nose. The palate is that & more. Layers of cashew nut flavours melt in the mouth, honey, dark chocolate & fine sprinkling of spice.

★★★★★ **Cellar Reserve XO Potstill** ⓝⓔⓦ ⓐ Intense pot-pourri aromas on rich, weighty 10 year old potstill ⑨⑤, with candied fruit, pear drop & spice on long, velvet finish. Perfectly balanced, rounded & full bodied. Fruitier than sibling 10 year old, differently oaked & matured.

★★★★★ **10 Year Old Vintage** ⓧ Exquisite 100% potstill ⑨⑤. Jewel bright & delicate, with citrus aromas, dried apple, spice & dark chocolate on the palate. Rounded & full bodied, long mellow finish.

★★★★ **5 Year Old Superior** ⓧ Notes of sweet caramel, fruit, nuts & vanilla. Excellent balance, clean & lightly fiery on sweet-tinged finish. Blended brandy ⑧⑨; could compete with pure potstills on their turf!

★★★★☆ **Signature Release VS** ⓝⓔⓦ Moreish 4 year old potstill ⑨② is fresh & very fruity, with Golden Delicious, ripe apricot, cinnamon & creamy vanilla aromas & flavours. Good palate intensity yet effortlessly elegant, a lingering citrus bite on the finish. Mostly chenin & colombard, & 40% alc, as XO.

3 Year Old Finest Blend ⓧ ★★★★ This ⑧④ less aggressive than many young blended brandies - sippable neat. Fruity nose with caramel, dark molasses, tealeaves. Sufficiently complex, balanced. — WB

KWV Wines

Established in 1918, KWV today is a globally recognised, award-winning wine and spirit company, and a fixture on Drinks International magazine's list of the world's most admired wine brands. A highlight this edition is the 75th anniversary of Roodeberg, one of KWV's best-known and -loved brands, present in over 50 countries. All the ranges are created under the leadership of chief winemaker Justin Corrans, with 'drinkability first' as mantra and the goal of 'elegant, balanced and fresh wines of high quality'. Tastings and sales of the wines and separately listed brandies are at KWV's Wine Emporium in Paarl. See KWV 'corporate' entry.

The Mentors range

★★★★☆ **Cabernet Franc** (🏵) Ripe & full bodied yet lithe & precise, **20** (94) has pinpoint typicity: leafy herbal notes, tilled earth, graphite & concentrated blackcurrant fruit, firm leathery tannins. Laudable complexity aided by 18 months in oak, 70% new. WO Stellenbosch, as Petit Verdot & Pinotage; all other wines W Cape unless noted.

★★★★☆ **Petit Verdot** (🏵) Dense & inky, as last, with tarry minerality, earthy nuance & massive blackcurrant whack on **20** (93). Big suede tannins add structure, rounded & tamed by same oaking as Cab Franc.

★★★★☆ **Pinotage** (🏵) A paragon of consistency, with exquisite plush red fruit, **20** (94) maintains form & class. Full & rich, with fine tannins, judiciously spiced & polished by 18 months in older barrel, 15% American adding aromatic notes.

★★★★☆ **Orchestra** (🏵) Refined 5-way, cab-led Cape Bordeaux, **20** (94) remains supple & sleek despite formidable heft & plushness. Red & black berry fruit laced with minerals & iodine, borne on full, savoury tannins, suggesting beneficial ageing. Seasoned oak only.

★★★★☆ **Perold** (🏵) Pinnacle label commemorates pioneer viticulturist who developed pinotage. **20** (93) contains 40%, with shiraz, cab, petite sirah & malbec in deep & imposing Cape Blend. Succulent blackcurrants, cherries & wild berries spiced with fine oak, cloaked in velvet tannins, all in perfect harmony. On track after **19** (94). WO Coastal.

★★★★☆ **Canvas** (🏵) Classy, sumptuously fruity shiraz blend with variable partners, **20** (92) includes petite sirah, carignan, tempranillo & mourvèdre. Dark & intense yet fragrantly spicy, with delicate tobacco highlights & tannins built to last.

★★★★☆ **Chenin Blanc** (✓) (🏵) Characterful & concentrated **21** (94) ex Swartland has delightful spicy baked stonefruit & pineapple, aromatic oak & cedar notes. Full & lush yet supple, with brightening tingly acid, inviting creamy food partners. Barrel ferment, 50% wild yeast, 9 months on lees.

★★★★☆ **Grenache Blanc** (✓) (🏵) Forthright, assertive **21** (93) has personality & presence, with terpene-tinged lemon & lime fruit, creamy lees texture, delicate spice nuances from ferment/9 months in older barrels. WO Coastal.

Discontinued: **Cabernet Sauvignon Darling**, **Cabernet Sauvignon Stellenbosch**, **Shiraz**.

Cathedral Cellar range

★★★★ **Cabernet Sauvignon** (✓) Earthy, visceral take on variety, **21** ★★★★★ (90) tarry black fruit, hints of tobacco & anise, iodine & leafy herbs among the brooding scents. Solid & unyielding, demands & will reward cellar time, more so than **20** (88). 18 months oak, none new.

★★★★ **Pinotage** (✓) Inky **21** (86) has impressive extract & tannin grip, its fruit ultra-ripeness mirrored in 14.5% alc. Dense black berry & currant core spiced by 16 months in oak, 15% American.

★★★★ **Shiraz** (✓) Robust as ever, **20** (88) shows imposing extract, hefty but honed tannins & attractive meat, liquorice & tobacco aromas. Dabs sangiovese & tempranillo add nuance, as does mostly older oak.

★★★★☆ **Triptych** (✓) Respected Bordeaux-based but variable blend since **97** Finessed **20** (90) is majority cab with shiraz, malbec, petit verdot & petite sirah, offering generous, silk-textured black fruit & alluring sweet & oak spices.

★★★★ **Chardonnay** (✓) Graceful & focused **22** (88) follows dependable form, well-judged oak, 9 months, none new, adding roundness & polish to ripe, juicy mandarin & tangerine fruit with pretty honeyed notes. Great value too.

★★★★ **Sauvignon Blanc** (✓) Distinctive tinned pea & nettle aromatics on **22** (86), alongside riper tropical fruit & gooseberry. Lean, taut & mineral palate, fine acid, salty twist on finish.

Roodeberg range

★★★★☆ **Dr Charles Niehaus** (🏵) Honours Roodeberg's creator in 1949, **20** (94) equal cab & shiraz plus dabs malbec & petite sirah. Extroverted styling features dense, concentrated blackcurrant & morello fruit, perky acid & sleek tannins. House-style 18 months wooding, here only older barrels.

★★★★ **Red** (🍷) Cab-led allsorts blend, previewed **21** (86) follows reliable form, pumped up by durif & petit verdot components, shows dried red & black fruit, robust tannins. Year in barrel, 10% American.

★★★★ **Reserve** (NEW) (✓) Variation on the Charles theme, **20** (88) adds petit verdot for a 5-way blend showing sweetly ripe, somewhat jammy berry fruit with hints of caramel & tobacco, leathery tannins.

★★★★☆ **Roodeberg 1949** ⊛ Evolving blend, **20** ⑨② mostly cab franc with tempranillo & carignan among the parts, combining seamlessly to offer earthy minerality, plump ripe fruit & exotic mixed spice, borne on broad but toned shoulders. WO Stellenbosch.

★★★★ **White** ⊘ Sauvignon & chardonnay with others, older-oaked **22** ⑧⑥ is notably salty & savoury, baked apple & quince fruit in generously full body on a gentle bed of lees.

Black ⑭ ★★★★ Sibling to 1949, **21** ⑧⑤ cab blend is lighter, juicier, with distinct sweet edge, heightened fruit profile, less gravitas. **Rosé** ★★★ Pleasant Turkish delight & strawberry cordial notes to **23** ⑧① multi-part blend, dry, with refreshing acid lift.

Laborie range

★★★★☆ **Signature Shiraz** Bold & concentrated, **21** ⑨⓪ has plenty of grunt but also some refinement in its satin tannin, rounded body & sweetly ripe black cherry fruit. 18 months oak, portion American. First tasted since **17** ★★★★ ⑧⑧.

★★★★ **Cap Classique Brut Rosé** ⊘ Pretty salmon pink **NV** ⑧⑦, 60% pinot noir with chardonnay, dash pinotage. Dependably consistent, showing strawberry & apple fruit, hint of brioche & delicate bead.

★★★★★ **Cap Classique Blanc de Blancs** ⊘ ⊛ The thoroughbred of the pack, **17** ⑨① chardonnay spent 5 years on lees, reflected in rich, savoury-yeasty palate, baked apple & citrus fruit, lingering flavour on fine-spun, cream-textured mousse.

★★★★ **Cap Classique Brut** ⊘ Satisfying wafts of fresh-baked brioche & stewed apple on mostly chardonnay **NV** ⑧⑧ with pinot noir & pinotage. Elegantly textured, with gentle bubbles, vivid acid lance on dry finish. 24 months on lees.

★★★★ **Cap Classique Le Grande Nectar** ⊘ Similar cuvée & ageing to Brut, with 40 g/L sugar, latest **NV** ⑧⑥ is overtly sweet, with bright tropical fruit, hints of honey on vigorous bubble.

★★★★ **Pino de Laborie** Standard port-style formula **NV** ⑧⑥ sees 75% pinotage with petit verdot, fermented & fortified to 17% alc. Full-sweet at 125 g/L, with up-front cherry & plum fruit, hint of malt.

Cabernet Sauvignon ⊘ ★★★★ Convincing black fruit, cocoa & leafiness on previewed **22** ⑧⑤, seamed with sweet oak spices, hint of earthy minerality. **Merlot** ★★★ Restrained **22** ⑧⓪ barrel sample is light & tangy, layers plum & damson fruit with rather chalky tannins. **Shiraz** ⊘ ★★★★ Appealingly smooth & fruity, but lacking varietal definition, **22** ⑧③ is undemanding braai fare. **Merlot-Cabernet Sauvignon** ⊘ ★★★★ Mild-mannered & pleasant everyday drinking, pre-bottled **22** ⑧⑤ offers familiar juicy black fruit, well-judged tannins. 55/45 blend. **Rosé** ★★★ Tinsel pink, with rosepetal & marshmallow scents, **23** ⑧② is fragrant & delicate. From multiple varieties, chiefly mourvèdre & cab. **Chardonnay** ⊘ ★★★★ Tasted pre-bottling, **23** ⑧③ has pretty orange blossom scent, zesty acid & hint of vanilla from gentle kiss of oak. **Chenin Blanc** ⊘ ★★★★ Light bodied but substantial, **23** ⑧④ offers generous stonefruit, perky acid, gentle waft of oak from fraction on staves. **Sauvignon Blanc** ★★★☆ Lean & green, **23** ⑦⑨ has gooseberry with pungent nettle & nasturtium tang.

Classic Collection

★★★★★ **Cape Tawny** ⊘ ⊛ Perennial high-flying 'port' nails the style, with nutty raisined fruit, hints of molasses & malt, toffee & fine spirit twist. Totally consistent **NV** ⑨⑦ of undisclosed varieties with extended barrel maturation, one for the fans.

· ·

Petit Verdot ⊘ ⊚ ★★★★ Typically inky & sombre, previewed **22** ⑧④ ex Swartland offers impressive body & fruit weight at the price, leathery tannins that will keep a year/2. **Chenin Blanc** ⊘ ⊚ ★★★★ **23** ⑧③ has sweetly ripe stonefruit & pineapple, nice freshening acid, a cheerful personality with commendable body & enduring flavour. **Grenache Blanc** ⊘ ⊚ ★★★★ Very appealing **23** ⑧⑤ offers convincing pear & melon fruit, lees weight & texture. Clever oaking adds layer of exotic spice.

· ·

Cabernet Sauvignon ★★★ Lean & sinewy **22** ⑦⑧ has a green leaf tannin edge, attenuated fruit. **Merlot** ★★★ Light & leafy, with tangy plum & currant fruit, **22** ⑧① gets dash of tannat for hearty braai-side appeal. **Pinotage** ⊘ ★★★★ Authentic varietal expression in **22** ⑧③, with forthright brambleberry fruit, lean, steely underpin, hints of oak spice. **Shiraz** ⊘ ★★★★ Sweetly ripe, with juicy red berry fruit, firm tannins, **22** ⑧④ has well-rounded body, appealing scrub spicing. **Cabernet Sauvignon-Shiraz** ⊘ ★★★ With splash petit verdot, **22** ⑧① has ripe & generous black fruit, oak seasoning & modest tannin grip. Fresher, fuller than last. 2L bag-in-box. **Rosé** ⊘ ★★★ Light, breezy & softly dry **23** ⑧⓪ is mainly pinotage, offers tangy red berry fruit, plenty of refreshment at modest 12.5% alc. **Chardonnay** ⊘ ★★★★ Tasted before bottling, **23** ⑧③ all about sunny citrus fruit, juicy & plump, well balanced by acid. Lightly oaked, adding baking spices. **Moscato** ⊘ ★★★★ Rush of sultana fruit on typically fragrant semi-sweet muscat d'Alexandrie. **23** ⑧③ an obvious match with Indian or Thai spicy food. **Sauvignon Blanc** ⊘ ★★★★ Riper, more tropical than previous, **23** ⑧③ has pineapple & melon fruitiness, tempered acid for a crisp, refreshing summer sip. **Sparkling Cuvée Brut** ★★★ Fully dry **NV** ⑦⑨ from chenin has vigorous fizz, overt peach fruit. **Sparkling Demi-Sec** ★★★ Chenin carbonated **NV** ⑦⑦ bubbly is unabashedly sweet, frothy & fruity. **Red Muscadel** ★★★★ Always satisfying fortified fireside warmer, **NV** ⑧⑤ packs 222 g/L sugar, 17% alc, loads of spicy red raisin fruit. **Cape Ruby** ⊘ ★★★★ Current **NV** ⑧④ shiraz 'port' is unpretentious & uncomplicated, offers exuberantly ripe plum fruit & satisfying grip of 17.5% alc.

Café Culture range
Pinotage Ⓠ ★★ For lovers of mocha-toned wine, **22** ⑦③ tank sample shows typical charred oak & cocoa.

Contemporary range
Cabernet Sauvignon-Merlot ⊘ ★★★★ Unassuming, fruit-driven **22** ⑧③ mixes sweet-ripe cassis cordial with gentle tannins. Also under African Passion label.

Golden Kaan range
Cabernet Sauvignon ★★★ Slender & leafy, with chalky tannins, **22** ⑦⑨'s cassis & plum fruit is for current drinking, as all these. **Merlot** ★★★ Plum & red berry fruit, hint of sweet spice & toffee, **22** ⑦⑧ is easy-drinking, undemanding fare. **Shiraz** ★★★ Pleasantly plump, with ripe plum & cherry fruit, **22** ⑧⓪ offers satisfying everyday drinking. **Sauvignon Blanc** ★★★ Fresh & youthful, **23** ⑧⓪ has prominent acid, appealing pear & tropical fruit.

Bonne Esperance range
Red ★★ Enduring no-frills, quick-quaffing range. Pinotage & several others offer their piquant red berries on latest **NV** ⑦③. **White** ⊘ ★★★ Pocket-friendly dry summer refresher. Fruit-driven **NV** ⑧⓪ a chenin & muscat combo, with raisin & pineapple notes.

Pearly Bay range
Celebration Rosé ★★ Muscat-toned, lightly fizzy **NV** ⑦④ has a very generous 80 g/L sugar, modest 8% alc (as sibling). **Celebration White** ★★ Sweet **NV** ⑦④ bubbly from chenin & hanepoot has pronounced grapey fruit.

Annabelle range
Cuvée Sparkling Rosé ★★ Hanepoot-based sweet **NV** ⑦④ low-alc fizz with scented raisin fruitiness. **De-alcoholised Cuvée Sparkling Rosé** ★★ Extravagantly packaged, chenin-led **NV** ⑦④ bubbly with abundant sugar, under 0.5% alc. — GdB

Kyburg Wine Estate   Ⓠ ⌂

Still-available 2015 is the last red-wine vintage from this Devon Valley estate, but the chenin blanc continues, and Swiss nationals and owners Fred and Rosmarie Ruest are delighted that its crafting is now in the five-star-awarded hands of compatriot Wade Metzer of Metzer & Holfeld Family Wines, who will also look after marketing. Replanting of the 10 ha is complete, and the first young crops are expected next year.

★★★★ **Cabernet Sauvignon** Ⓠ Reflecting the fine vintage, **15** ⑧⑦ more savoury, meaty than previous **13** ⑧⑨ but focused & generously fruity, with inky-iodine minerality. Already evolved & ready to enjoy.

★★★★ **Merlot** Ⓠ Nutty, pithy **15** ⑧⑥ has abundant ripe plum fruit, with spiced meaty-savoury underpin. Ready to drink after 16 months in barrel &, like all the reds, 5 years in bottle.

★★★★ **Shiraz** Ⓠ Savoury **15** ⑧⑦ shows bottle development yet retains vibrancy in its scrub-spiced red fruit, silky texture. Hints of tobacco & smoke, better concentration than last **13** ★★★★ ⑧⑤.

★★★★ **33 Latitude** Ⓠ Cab-led blend with merlot & shiraz, **15** ⑧⑧ is refined & sleek, with dense black fruit, hints of aromatic spices from 16 months in 20% new oak. Also in 1.5L.

★★★★☆ **33 Latitude Select** Ⓠ Dark & brooding, fruit-driven & concentrated, **15** ⑨⓪ is 60% cab with merlot & shiraz. Sleek, smooth tannins, burnished by 28 months in new barrels, lend velvet texture & body. Ready, but could keep for several more years. No **14**.

★★★★ **Chenin Blanc** ⊘ Unoaked, sunny & fruity **20** ⑧⑦ succeeded by **21** ★★★★★ ⑨⓪, wild-yeast fermented in older 300L oak, on lees 9 months. Change of style sees richer, creamier & more integrated wine with serious aspirations, offering honeyed stonefruit, gentle nudge of acid, lingering finish. Stellenbosch WO.— GdB

Location/map: Stellenbosch ▪ Map grid reference: D4 ▪ WO: Devon Valley/Stellenbosch ▪ Est 1998 ▪ 1stB 2006 ▪ Tasting by appt ▪ Self-catering guest house (exclusive use, rental min 2 weeks) ▪ Owner(s) Fred & Rosmarie Ruest ▪ Winemaker(s) Jacques Fourie (Jan 2006) & Wade Metzer (2021) ▪ Viticulturist(s) Frans Snyman (Jul 2006, consultant) ▪ 28ha/6ha (merlot + 10ha replanted with cabs s/f, merlot, ptage, chard) ▪ 60t/2,000cs own label 90% red 10% white ▪ info@kyburgwine.com ▪ www.kyburgwine.com ▪ **T +27 (0)82-651-5688**

Laarman Wines

Arco Laarman's craft wines, strikingly and innovatively packaged under the Focal Point branding, are focused on cinsault and chardonnay from the cool-climate southern Cape coast, the area around the resort of Vermaaklikheid on the Duivenshok River estuary of particular interest. We hope to taste them next time.

Location: Hermanus ▪ Est 2016 ▪ 1stB 2017 ▪ Tasting by appt only ▪ Owner(s)/winemaker(s) Arco Laarman ▪ 5,000cs own label 40% red 60% white ▪ arco@laarmanwines.com ▪ www.laarmanwines.com ▪ **T +27 (0)83-546-1146**

☐ **Labeye** *see* Edouard Labeye
☐ **Laborie** *see* KWV Wines

La Bri Wines

Under recent ownership of the Von Kuenheim family, improvements to the tasting area are underway, vineyards will be replanted over the next few years and the bijoux Franschhoek farm will reduce its carbon footprint greatly by going solar. Unchanged are the veteran team of GM/winemaker Irene de Fleuriot, assistant Glen Isaacs and viticulturist Gerard Olivier, and focus on 'signature-styled wines created with passion'.

Limited Release range

★★★★☆ **Cabernet Sauvignon** (🐝) From estate's oldest red-wine block, planted 1999, **21** (94) 2 years in seasoned oak (previous was 100% new) gaining pliant, velvet texture which enfolds elegant cassis fruit & pencil shaving nuance. Promises to gain complexity with time. Last was **18** (93).

★★★★☆ **Syrah 870** (🐝) Name reflects number of bottles filled after barrel selection only in best years. Intensely spicy **21** ★★★★★ (95) offers sumptuous ripe berry fruit & dark choc sheen. Co-fermented with 3% viognier & 2 years in oak, as last-made **18** (93), but none new.

★★★★☆ **Chardonnay Barrel Select** (✓) (🐝) Delayed harvest of riper grapes from 30 year old block, bunch fermented then 10 months in 2nd-fill cask. Layer upon layer of fresh citrus & stonefruit mark **22** ★★★★★ (95), rich yet bright, focused & elegant, with a mineral finish. Last was **20** (93).

★★★★☆ **Viognier** (✓) Unequivocal but lovely, **22** (90) jasmine scent, ripe nectarine & apricot fruit, rich mouthfeel with a brightening line of acid that makes it slide down with alarming ease (& pair with food).

★★★★☆ **Sauvage La Bri Blanc de Blancs** (🐝) Zero-dosage cap classique from oldest chardonnay block, 6 years on lees after primary ferment in old oak, **17** (94) vibrates with lemon & grapefruit energy, joined by rich brioche character in the explosive mousse. 11.3% alc as elegant as last **15** (93).

Estate range

★★★★ **Merlot** Meaty **21** (89) redolent of smoked bacon & violets, offers ripe mulberry flavour with more grunt than last, though similar 18-20 months in oak, 10% new.

★★★★☆ **Syrah** (✓) Plumes of lavender, thyme & heady spice leap out of delicious **21** (90) glass. Wholeberry co-ferment with 3% viognier, 2 years in used oak for seamless, refined, satisfying drinking.

★★★★ **Affinity** Fine red blend, best years only. Plush **21** (89)'s ripe berries brushed with mocha on velvet palate. 71% cab leads merlot, petit verdot & cab franc. 24 months oak vs 18 for **20** (89), both 10% new.

★★★★☆ **Chardonnay** (✓) Orange blossom & hay scents herald vivacious lemons & limes of **22** (90), delicately framed by older oak, 10 months, which regime also adds creamy texture. Elegant mineral finish.

Double Door range

★★★★☆ **Petit Verdot** (✓) 'Not a 2nd label', but showcase for 'unusual, quirky wines'. Purple-edged **21** (90) whiffs of tar & wildflower, still-chewy tannins after 2 years in older oak. Big but supple, polished.

★★★★ **Red** ⓩ Well-priced **19** ⑧⑧ merlot-based Bordeaux blend with dark chocolate, dried thyme & mulberries, juicy & elegant. Vanilla sheen thanks to 20 months in older oak.

★★★★ **Roussanne** Listed as 'White' last edition, as **20** ⑧⑥ added 40% semillon. 100% varietal & aromatic **22** ⑧⑧ picked twice: 1st wholebunch fermented, 2nd skin contact for texture. 10 months older oak give good breadth & balance. No **21**.

Rosé ⓩ ★★★☆ Previewed **22** ⑧③ from merlot, bone-dry with sweetly spiced cranberry & rosepetal, added texture from oak. **Chardonnay-Viognier** (NEW) ★★★★ Crowd-pleasing **22** ⑧⑤ packed with ripe peach & citrus, sweet-fruited but bone-dry, brush older oak adds style. Not tasted: **Semillon**. — DS

Location/map/WO: Franschhoek ▪ Map grid reference: C1 ▪ Est 1694 ▪ Tasting & sales Mon-Sun 10-5 ▪ Fee varies ▪ Closed Good Fri, Dec 25 & Jan 1 ▪ Chocolate & wine pairing; biltong & wine experience; Turkish delight & wine pairing ▪ Cheese platters ▪ Bicycle friendly ▪ Part of Franschhoek Tram route ▪ Owner(s) Von Kuenheim family ▪ Winemaker(s) Irene de Fleuriot (Oct 2010), with Glen Isaacs (Jun 2009) ▪ Viticulturist(s) Gerard Olivier (Oct 2010) ▪ ±24ha/±14ha (cabs s/f, merlot, p verdot, shiraz, chard, viog) ▪ 100t/10,000cs own label 80% red 20% white ▪ PO Box 180 Franschhoek 7690 ▪ info@labri.co.za ▪ www.labri.co.za ▪ **T +27 (0)21-876-2593**

La Capra

Owner Charles Back here continues the caprine theme associated with his Fairview and Goats do Roam brands, listed separately. La Capra single-variety, well-priced wines are styled and presented with an invitation to 'let yourself indulge in the carnival spirit of fruit-driven, approachable wines, ideal to enjoy now'.

Merlot ⓥ ★★★ Spicy red & dark berries reined in by nip of tannin, brisk acid & toasty oak notes in **21** ⑧⓪. For pasta night with tomato-based sauces. WO Coastal, as Chenin, rest WO W Cape. **Pinotage** ⓥ ★★★★ Billows ripe mulberries in **21** ⑧③, adding sweet vanilla & cinnamon from older oak, tannins in succulent support. **Sangiovese** ⓥ ★★★★ Varietally correct, sappy & lively red fruit & dried tomato flavours in **22** ⑧③. Older oak adds polish & juicy tannins ensure friendliness, solo or with a meal. **Chenin Blanc** ⓥ ★★★ Plump peaches & nectarines in **23** ⑧⓪, not as fresh as previous but smooth textured for easy-drinking pleasure. **Pinot Grigio** ★★★ Subtle stonefruit, citrus & herbs on **23** ⑦⑨. Dry, lightish quaffing with a mineral seam. **Sauvignon Blanc** ⓥ ★★★ Appealing ripe fig, granadilla & some crisp greenpepper aromas & flavours in **22** ⑧②. — MW

☐ **La Cave** see Wellington Wines
☐ **Lace** see Almenkerk Wine Estate
☐ **La Colline** see Mont du Toit Kelder

La Couronne Wines

Continuing changes at 'The Crown' mountainside boutique winery in Franschhoek see the visitor amenities and website shut for now, though on-site sales of the wines, including new vintage releases, are available.

Franschhoek 1688 range

★★★★ **Malbec** Berries & dark plums, ripe & forward, **20** ⑧⑧ vanilla-spiced by 24 months in small barrels, 40% new, to create a bold, flavour-packed wine. Smoothly round, delicious. No **19**.

★★★★ **Shiraz** Seductively perfumed, plush berries & glacé cherries, saturated with vanilla spice (50% American small oak, 24 months, 30% new), **20** ⑧⑨ is shiraz in technicolour, hard to resist. Last was **16** ⑧⑧.

★★★★☆ **Chardonnay** ⓥ Changed cellar practice: bunch pressing, wild ferment/year in barrels of various sizes, origins & ages. Citrus array, especially lemon, fruit more pronounced than last, **21** ⑨⓪ ends tangy, lime-zesty. Oak's influence subtle biscuit.

Jacques Mouton range

★★★★ **Antoinette Special Reserve No.1** ⓩ Unusual malbec-led blend with shiraz (50/35) & splash petit verdot hits the balanced sweet spot in **20** ⑧⑨. Less time in oak (year) highlights brambleberry flavours & sprinkle of white pepper. Ready to enjoy.

★★★★ **Madeleine Chardonnay** ⓥ Named for French Huguenot pioneer/owner's daughter, who accompanied him to the Cape in 1699. Sleek **22** ⑧⑦ made with combo staves & barrels, 20% Hungarian. Citrus & melon fruit richness, Lemon Cream biscuit seam, fruity-fresh finish.

Catherine Cabernet Sauvignon ⓩ ★★★ Cooler vintage & less ripe black & red fruit shows austerity in **21** ⑧② from Stellenbosch, tannins needing time & hearty fare. **Marguerite Merlot** ⓩ ★★★☆ Switches back to tighter, more restrained style in cooler **21** ⑧⑤. Red cherry & berry fruit in dry tannic embrace. Older oak, year. Needs time. Less balance & fruit depth than **20** ★★★★ ⑧⑨. WO W Cape.

Signature Collection
Merlot Rosé ⊘ ★★★ Pale pink, trim-figured (11.5% alc), **22** ⑦⑧ shows the merlot fruit in a gentle way, ends crisp & dry. **Chenin Blanc** ⊘ ★★★ Golden Delicious apple profile, **23** ⑦⑧ has a touch of sweetness for an easy-drinking style. WO W Cape.

Premium Collection
In abeyance: **Muscadel**. — CR

Location: Franschhoek ▪ WO: Franschhoek/Western Cape/Stellenbosch ▪ Sales Mon-Fri 9-4.30 (tasting room closed until further notice) ▪ Winemaker(s) Henk Swart (May 2015) ▪ 13ha (malbec, merlot, p verdot, shiraz, chard, viog) ▪ 100t/±13,000cs own label 70% red 30% white ▪ sales@lacouronnewines.co.za ▪ **T +27 (0)21-876-3939**

☐ **Ladismith** *see Joseph Barry Distillery*

Ladybird Vineyards

Since acquisition last year by illustrious neighbour Kanonkop, and rebranding from Laibach Vineyards, the wine line-up of this local pioneer of organic winefarming has become more focused on merlot and chenin, which are 'the true specialities of this site' on the Simonsberg foothills. Michael Malherbe, viticulturist the past three decades, is replanting old and poorer-performing blocks, and working with Kanonkop colleagues on shared regenerative farming practices. Francois van Zyl, winemaker since 2000, is preparing to build a new cellar, in which some of the components of the top-selling Kadette range will be produced.

Reserve range
★★★★☆ **Claypot Merlot** ⊘ ⊛ Riot of fruit on **18** ⑨③: cooked black plum, damson, mulberry alongside vanilla & oak spice from 90% new barriques. 10% cab franc adds fresh herbal tweak to still very youthful wine, chewy grip of tannin suggests long, exciting future.
★★★★☆ **Chenin Blanc Sur Lie** ⊘ ⊘ As before, intricate ('crazy!') winemaking & considered stylistic choices reflected in **21** ⑨⓪, contrasting tropical fruit with soft baking spice & creamy dairy notes. Skin contact, carbonic maceration, wild ferment, concrete 'eggs' & old oak all add layers of complexity to possibly polarising but to us pleasing palate.

Ladybird range
★★★★ **Red** ⊘ ⊘ Highly drinkable merlot-led Cape Bordeaux, **20** ⑧⑨ cherry & almond, whiffs earth & dried herbs. Gently firm tannins, lashings of nutmeg & cinnamon from 14 months in mostly old oak.
★★★★☆ **White** ⊘ ⊘ Sophisticated **22** ⑨⓪, chardonnay & dab chenin, alluring aromatic array of orange citrus, cantaloupe, dried ginger & florals. 50% oaked, 10% new, adding texture to complex, engaging mouthful. Notable & versatile food partner.— CM

Location/map: Stellenbosch ▪ Map grid reference: F1 ▪ WO: Simonsberg-Stellenbosch ▪ Est 1994 ▪ 1stB 1997 ▪ Tasting & sales @ Kanonkop Wine Estate Mon-Fri 9-5 Sat/pub hols 9-3 ▪ Fee R50 ▪ Closed Good Fri, Dec 25 & Jan 1 ▪ Ladybird Vineyards Lodge ▪ Owner(s) Kanonkop Wine Estate ▪ Cellarmaster(s)/winemaker(s) Francois van Zyl (Jan 2000) ▪ Viticulturist(s) Michael Malherbe (Jun 1994) ▪ 50ha/37ha (cabs s/f, merlot, p verdot, ptage, chard, chenin) ▪ 300t/30,000cs own label 70% red 30% white + 15,000cs for Woolworths ▪ PO Box 19 Elsenburg 7607 ▪ wine@ladybirdvineyards.co.za ▪ www.ladybirdvineyards.co.za ▪ **T +27 (0)21-884-4511**

☐ **Lady Lillian** *see Du Toitskloof Winery*
☐ **Lady May** *see Glenelly Estate*
☐ **La Famille** *see Mischa Estate*
☐ **Lakehurst** *see Wine-of-the-Month Club*

Lammershoek Winery

This large estate on the Paardeberg (dating back to 1718) has been a significant player in the Swartland winemaking revolution this century. Ownership changes and some bad lack have been thwarting factors, most recently when ill-health obliged the Abold family to sell. But, promisingly, Lammershoek was purchased in 2023 by the Johannes family, who recently returned from an experiment in winefarming in Australia. Young Stefan Johannes (who had remained in the Cape, gaining winemaking experience, notably at BlankBOTTLE)

is now winemaker and CEO. 'It has its challenges,' he says, 'but, my-oh-my, this is an exciting place and adventure!' First concerns are the vineyards, which must be farmed sustainably, and the farm community, who 'must advance as we advance'. As for wine, it's all change, as Stefan plans to focus on just two from 2024 onwards, a red and a white as 'the epitome of what an estate in the Paardeberg can produce'.

Location: Malmesbury ▪ Map: Swartland ▪ Map grid reference: C8 ▪ Est 1718 ▪ 1stB 1999 ▪ Tasting, sales & cellar tours by appt only ▪ Tasting R100 ▪ Closed all pub hols ▪ Owner(s) Johannes family ▪ Cellarmaster(s)/ winemaker(s) Stefan Johannes (Dec 2022) ▪ Viticulturist(s) André Christiaan Bruyns (Jul 2022) ▪ 177ha/43ha (carignan, mourv, ptage, shiraz, tinta barocca, chard, chenin, hárslevelü, marsanne, viog) ▪ 200t/15,000cs own label 50% red 50% white ▪ PO Box 597 Malmesbury 7299 ▪ stefan@lammershoek.co.za ▪ www. lammershoek.co.za ▪ T +27 (0)22-482-2835

La Motte

$\textcircled{Y}$ $\textcircled{\dagger\dagger}$ $\textcircled{@}$ $\textcircled{\&}$

La Motte in Franschhoek has been in the hands of the Rupert family for over half a century, and since they launched a multifaceted wine tourism initiative in 2010, the estate has become one of SA's most awarded in terms of attractions, ranging from a museum with, inter alia, works by famed artist JH Pierneef, to heritage walks and guided hikes. Now a phased refresh of the experience aims to incorporate the historic buildings and ensure guests can enjoy more of the beautiful setting and gardens. First to be unveiled is the relaxed, family-friendly Artisanal Bakery & Garden Café, which dovetails with the continuing strong overall emphasis on cuisine and art. Sustainability in all spheres, creating opportunities in and for the local community, and a focus in the wine portfolio on syrah and sauvignon blanc also remain as drivers for the brand as a whole.

The Pierneef Collection

★★★★☆ **Syrah-Viognier** ⊛ Rhône-inspired blend from 3 regions, 2 years in 50% new oak. Fragrant black berry, hedgerow, cured meat, fynbos & a lifted violet perfume in **19** ⑨③. Well-structured & -integrated, a firm yet supple tannin backbone for a long life. Also in 1.5L.

★★★★☆ **Sauvignon Blanc** ⊘ ⊛ Only Elim fruit for **22** ⑨②, including 15% (unoaked) semillon to add breadth & complexity. Restrained & cool toned, greengage, gooseberry, greenpepper & hints of honey & wax, all in creamy body from 5 months lees ageing. Worth keeping some.

La Motte Collection

★★★★☆ **Syrah** ⊘ ⊛ Concentrated, with depth & breadth, aided by 14% durif in **19** ⑨⓪. Full spread of flavours & aromas, berries, currants, cigar smoke & earthy herbs, plus vanilla oak, 30% new, 14 months. Will age beneficially, also in magnum.

★★★★ **Chardonnay** Franschhoek grapes for this range. Elegant **22** ⑧⑨ marked by freshness from a third being unoaked, rest fermented in barrel, 20% new, on lees year, adding creamy, nutty vanilla to apple & quince fruit. No **21**.

★★★★☆ **Méthode Cap Classique Brut** Sophisticated **19** ⑨① from 68% chardonnay & pinot noir, 46 months on lees with 10% oaked portion from 2018 vintage. Baked apple, brioche & subtle strawberry flavour, never-ending creamy mousse to toast any occasion.

Classic Collection

★★★★ **Cabernet Sauvignon** Generously flavoured yet seriously intentioned **20** ⑧⑧'s ample tannin frame & 50% new oak, 2 years, effortlessly carry bright, ripe, minty plum & cassis fruit, & some graphite minerality, now & for good few years. Stellenbosch WO.

★★★★ **Millennium** ⊘ Ever-dependable over-deliverer, balanced & well integrated, smooth & savoury in **21** ⑧⑨. Dark berries, dried herbs, tealeaves & touch of leafy tomato all classic markers for Cape Bordeaux, mostly merlot & cab franc, 2 others, older-oaked, year, also bottled in magnum.

★★★★ **Rosé** ⊘ Mostly grenache noir, dabs mourvèdre, syrah & cinsault in delightful, fragrant, ballet pink **22** ⑧⑧, living up to its subtitle 'Vin de Joie' in its exuberant savoury, earthy & spicy scents & flavours.

Sauvignon Blanc ★★★★ Bright, breezy citrus & tropical fruit on **23** ⑧⑤, some complexity & texture from lees ageing & touch of semillon but essentially for easy, early enjoyment. Certified vegan, as all the ranges. — WB

Location/map: Franschhoek ▪ Map grid reference: C3 ▪ WO: Western Cape/Franschhoek/Cape South Coast/ Stellenbosch ▪ Est 1969 ▪ 1stB 1984 ▪ Tasting & sales Tue-Sun 9-5 ▪ Fee R60pp ▪ Booking essential for: group tastings 8-16 R70pp; themed tastings R250pp ▪ Closed Easter Fri/Mon & Dec 25 ▪ Artisanal Bakery & Garden Café, JAN Franschhoek, farm shop, hiking trail, guided hike, historic walk, sculpture walk, museum:

experiences could be closed during renovation period, please refer to website for regular updates ▪ 35ha conservation area ▪ Owner(s) Hanneli Rupert-Koegelenberg ▪ CEO Hein Koegelenberg ▪ Cellarmaster(s) Edmund Terblanche (Dec 2000) ▪ Winemaker(s) Edwin Grace (Oct 2019) ▪ Viticulturist(s) Jaco Visser (Oct 2007) ▪ 180ha/80ha (cab, merlot, pinot, shiraz, chard, sauv, sem) ▪ Brands for clients: Woolworths ▪ ISO 14001:2015, EnviroWines, Farming for the Future, HACCP, IPW, Vegan, WIETA, WWF-SA Conservation Champion ▪ PO Box 685 Franschhoek 7690 ▪ info@la-motte.co.za ▪ www.la-motte.co.za ▪ T +27 (0)21-876-8000

Land of Hope ⓦ

The cellar team at estimable Radford Dale in the Helderberg cuts no corners in delivering on this sibling brand's 'drink well, do good' promise, the goal being to assist the Land of Hope Trust's aim of long-term social upliftment of the community of RD employees (of previously disadvantaged individual status) by providing high-quality education, skills development and empowerment of successive generations of children.

Land of Hope Reserve range
★★★★ **Cabernet Sauvignon** ⓦ Pleasantly ripe, if rather one-dimensional, **20 ★★★★** ⑧⑤ also slender in build, tannin light enough to encourage current drinking. Shadow of **19** ⑧⑨.

★★★★ **Chenin Blanc** Modest ginger spice & bruised apple on softly dry **22 ★★★★** ⑧④. Balanced freshness, unintrusive oak, 10% new, provide pleasant, easy drinking if not as distinctive as **20** ⑧⑧. **21** untasted.

Not tasted: **Pinot Noir**. Discontinued: **Organic Sauvignon Blanc**.

Land of Hope Classic range
★★★★ **Syrah** Affords immediate pleasure in **22** ⑧⑧ with fresh, lithe feel & array of sweet ripe red berries, spice & new leather, rounded off with gentle tannin. Half in older oak adds class. **18** ⑧⑦ last tasted.

Chardonnay ★★★★ Bright citrus zest with creaminess from tiny barrel-fermented portion & 9 months on lees. Lightish & dry, **22** ⑧⑤ offers enjoyable early drinking.

Discontinued: **Craft 3 range**. — AL

Location: Stellenbosch ▪ WO: Stellenbosch/Coastal/Western Cape ▪ Est/1stB 1998 ▪ Tasting by appt at cellar door of Radford Dale; sales Mon-Fri 9-5 ▪ Closed all pub hols ▪ Owner(s) Alex Dale, Andy Openshaw, Robert Hill-Smith (Yalumba), Edouard Labeye, Cliff Roberson, Ben Radford, Heather Whitman, Kathleen Krone & Jacques de Klerk ▪ Director of viticulture & winemaking Jacques de Klerk ▪ Winemaker(s) Jacques de Klerk (Nov 2008), with Gerhard Joubert (Jun 2016) & Petroné Thomas (Oct 2021) ▪ Viticulturist(s) Edouard Labeye, Jacques de Klerk & Gerhard Joubert ▪ ±100ha (cab, carignan, cinsaut, gamay, grenache, mourv, ptage, pinot, shiraz, chard, chenin, clairette) ▪ 700t/40,000cs own label 60% red 40% white ▪ IPW, WIETA ▪ Postnet Suite 124 Private Bag X15 Somerset West 7129 ▪ hope@landofhope.co.za ▪ www.landofhope.co.za ▪ T +27 (0)21-855-5528

☐ **Landscape Series** see Gabriëlskloof

Land's End Wines

Bottled from the turn of the millennium, this boutique brand was the first from Cape Agulhas, created by a group of 'winelovers and pioneers' who saw the potential for exceptional sauvignon (and later shiraz) grown in this windswept maritime district. In the care of Du Toitskloof Winery since 2016, the line-up features a pair from Agulhas and Elim grapes exclusively, another from Agulhas and the wider Cape South Coast.

★★★★☆ **Cape Agulhas Syrah** Full-bodied, rich & savoury, some freshening tannins lend balanced drinking. **20 ★★★★** ⑧⑨ showing some development & missing complexity of **18** ⑨⓪, probably best over next year/2. Oaked 20 months, as Shiraz, 100% new. No **19**.

★★★★ **Cape South Coast Shiraz** ⊘ Wholesome **20** ⑧⑥ rich, full bodied with spice whisper & soft berries. Modicum of freshness & grip help balance but also suggest drinking soonish. Older oak. No **19**.

★★★★ **Cape Agulhas Sauvignon Blanc** ⓦ Quiet aromas but fine acid starting to awaken the cool-climate flavours on **21** ⑧⑦. Lees ageing & few grams sugar add balance & allow for beneficial ageing.

★★★★ **Cape South Coast Sauvignon Blanc** ⊘ Calm tropical purity, enlivening acid & gentle lees enrichment in **22 ★★★★** ⑧⑤ provide pleasant if not quite as characterful drinking as last **20** ⑧⑥.— AL

WO: Cape Agulhas/Cape South Coast ▪ Est 1996 ▪ 1stB 2000 ▪ Closed to public ▪ Owner(s) DTK Wines ▪ Cellarmaster(s) Shawn Thomson (2016) ▪ Winemaker(s) Shawn Thomson, with Tiaan Loubser (both 2016) ▪ Viticulturist(s) Leon Dippenaar (2016) ▪ info@dtkwines.com ▪ www.landsendwines.co.za ▪ T +27 (0)23-349-1601

☐ **Landskap** see Groenland

Landskroon Wines

Plans aplenty for the simultaneous celebration of a remarkable 175 years of De Villiers family farming on this western slope of Paarl Mountain, and 50 years of bottling under an own label, focused since inception on quality at affordable prices. Resolutely untrendy, they 'concentrate on what we do, and do it well', cellarmaster and 5th-generation Paul de Villiers says. However, he does note in passing that varieties now de rigueur, like cabernet franc and cinsaut, have been here since forever; in fact, cinsaut was the first variety bottled.

Paul de Villiers range

★★★★ Cabernet Sauvignon Textbook intro of cassis, cigarbox & cedar to 21 (89), rich yet refined, juicy brambles & plums in harmony with ripe tannins & oak, French & American (as all reds unless noted), 35% new. Lovely chocolate & lead pencil finish.

★★★★ Merlot Warm Xmas cake, ripe plum & exotic spice combine for succulent mouthful in 21 (88). Generous, silky, pleasing grip & fresh-ground coffee nuance at the end.

★★★★ Shiraz Dab cab adds backbone to powerful, mouthfilling 21 (89), raised in 48% new oak & intended for decade-plus ageing (as all these). Savoury toned, with cured meat, fynbos & lavender lacing blackberry & mulberry fruit. 8-12 months in barrique, as all reds unless noted.

★★★★☆ Reserve ⊘ 5-way Cape Bordeaux, cab & merlot leading an excellent, balanced melding of blackcurrant, polished leather, tealeaves & violet scent. 21 (90)'s structure still firm but given time will resolve & fully reveal the charm. 14% new oak. On par after robuster 20 ★★★★ (89).

Landskroon range

★★★★ Cinsaut ⊘ Previewed last time, 21 (86) now showing more of its lively redcurrant & cherry fruit, earthy spice & vanilla, mouthwatering cranberry crunch. Better expression than last-tasted 19 ★★★★ (85).

★★★★ Cape Vintage Traditional varieties for previewed 22 (88)'port'. Ripe plum, prune & hints of toasted nut & toffee on soft tannins, sweetness leavened by cleansing 19% alc. Just 10% oaked 12 months.

....

Cabernet Sauvignon 🏵 ★★★★ Now bottled, 21 (85) still friendly & filled with dark-fruited cheer, spiced with a little oak. Will raise many a smile. **Pinotage** 🏵 ★★★★ Moreish 21 (85) showcases plums, dried mixed herbs from 10% shiraz, chocolate ex 2% new wood. Rounded & a joy to drink now & soon. Pocket friendly, as the whole range.

....

Merlot ★★★★ Rounded, juicy & brimming with ripe plum & warm mulled-wine spice, silky 21 (84) slips down easily. Older oak, as Cab, Cinsaut & Hugo. **Shiraz** ★★★★ Tasty, approachable 21 (85) barrel sample is fruit-filled, savoury spiced & mellow. Perfect for a juicy burger. **Cabernet Franc-Merlot** ⊘ ★★★★ Leafy 22 (85) offers fragrant green herbs, ample red & black fruit & a graphite grip on the finish. Tasted ex barrel (French only, as Red). Over-delivers. **Cinsaut-Shiraz** ★★★ With dashes cab franc, petit verdot & malbec, 21 (82) is fruity & light footed, ends with a savoury dark-cherry tang. **Paul Hugo Red** ★★★ Gentle, fragrant & already well-padded with red berry fruit, 22 (82) gets extra plumpness from gram sugar for effortless everyday sipping. Cab franc, shiraz & merlot. **Pinotage Blanc de Noir Off-Dry** ★★★ Pale pink 23 (81) from free-run juice offers mixed red berries & similar citrus nuance as last. Chill well. **Chardonnay** ★★★ Unoaked 23 (81) generously fruited with ripe Golden Delicious apple, the gentle, clean body also includes subtle hay flavours & aromas. **Chenin Blanc** ⊘ ★★★★ Harvesting a little later gives 23 (83) some fullness as well as ripe tropical flavours, a limy tweak in the tail ensures balance. **Sauvignon Blanc** ★★★ Robertson grapes, as previous, & 23 (82) as lively & crisp as last, with green plum, gooseberry & apple in the refreshing mix. — WB

Location/map: Paarl ▪ Map grid reference: D6 ▪ WO: Paarl/Western Cape ▪ Est 1874 ▪ 1stB 1974 ▪ Tasting & sales Mon-Thu 8.30-5 Fri 8.30-4.30 Sat (Sep-Apr) 9.30-1 ▪ Closed Sun, Easter weekend, Dec 25 & Jan 1 ▪ Fee R50/5 wines ▪ Heritage food & wine pairing R115 ▪ Paul's food & wine pairing R190 ▪ Cellar tours by appt Mon-Fri 9-4 ▪ BYO picnic ▪ Play area for children ▪ Permanent display of Stone Age artefacts ▪ Self-catering cottage ▪ Owner(s) Paul & Hugo de Villiers Family Trusts ▪ Cellarmaster(s) Paul de Villiers (Jan 1980) ▪ Winemaker(s) Fanie Geyser (Nov 2021), with Kaylin Baxter (Dec 2021) ▪ Viticulturist(s) Hugo de Villiers (1995) ▪ 330ha/160ha (cab, cinsaut, merlot, ptage, shiraz, souzão, tinta amarela/barocca, touriga nacional, chenin, chard, sauv, viog) ▪ 86% red (incl port) 14% white ▪ IPW, WIETA ▪ PO Box 519 Suider-Paarl 7624 ▪ huguette@ landskroonwines.com ▪ www.landskroonwines.com ▪ T +27 (0)21-863-1039

Landzicht Wine Cellar

A crop decline of 40% can't be the update cellarmaster Sanmari Snyman would prefer to give, but she and her peers know they must deal with nature's increasingly unpredictable gifts, and 'very good-quality grapes' are one of those. Owner and major Northern Cape agribusiness GWK aims to 'satisfy all tastes', hence the spread of wine styles, plus Cape brandy and sherry, and craft gin for those moments only a G&T will do.

Winemakers Reserve range

★★★★ **Tannat** (NEW) ⊘ Inky black fruit on structured body, **19** (86) layered cocoa & herbs with dry tannin from 18 months in oak, third new. Further 2 years in bottle pre-release.

Cabernet Sauvignon (⊘) ★★★ Restrained maraschino cherry, slight medicinal nuance, bright acid & reined-in grip on pleasant, everyday **20** (80). WO Free State. **Merlot** (⊘) ★★★ Plum-toned **18** (81) sweet fruited & doused in vanilla, but has freshness from burst of acid & firm tannin. **Petit Verdot** (⊘) ★★★★ Very enjoyable **16** (83), appetising & supple, stewed black fruit, warm spices & coffee, great for a braai. **Shiraz** (NEW) ★★★★ Rounded plum & spice on **20** (84) preview, gentle oak support from 28 months in 20% new barrels. **Sauvignon Blanc** (⊘) ★★★ Appealing white asparagus & passionfruit, **21** (79)'s soft acid makes for smooth, easy sipping. WO W Cape.

Winemakers Selection range

Pinotage (NEW) ★★★ Supple, juicy raspberry & blueberry ease to unfussy **20** (82), made for early enjoyment. **Tannat** (NEW) ★★★ Uncomplicated & tasty **21** (82) charms with soft spice, cherry appeal & succulence. **Colombar** (⊘) ★★★ Semi-sweet but sugar-acid nicely balanced, makes **19** (80) a zesty partner for full-flavoured curries.

Landzicht range

Cabernet Sauvignon (⊘) ★★★ No rough edges, unoaked **21** (77) preview offers honest cassis & black-berry fruit, balanced tannin grip. WO W Cape. **Merlot** (⊘) ★★★ Plummy flavours, spice, friendly tannins & modest 13% alc push all the good-drinking buttons in **21** (78). **Rosenblümchen** (⊘) ★★★ Subtle spice & rosewater intro to **NV** (80) rosé from mostly colombard. Treads lightly with low alc & not-overdone sweetness. **Chenin Blanc** ★★★ Tank sample **23** (79) echoes previous in its atypical pear & grape nuances. Light body & gentle sweetness, alc a modest 11.5%. **Blümchen** (⊘) ★★★ Mere suggestion of aroma & fleeting flavour on **NV** (77) fully sweet colombard blend with low 8% alc. **#Fling** (NEW) ★★★ Pale coral low-alc (8.5%) sparkler. Candyfloss & strawberry tones, **NV** (78) ultra-light, sweet to the end. WO W Cape. **Hanepoot** (⊘) ★★★ Sultana & ripe pineapple attractions on **21** (81) fortified muscat, enough fire & fresh-ness to leaven sticky sugar. **Nagmaalwyn** (⊘) ★★ Cherries & orange zest perfume on **NV** (71) sacramental wine from red muscadel, usual lashings of sugar without balancing freshness. **Red Muscadel** (⊘) ★★★ Pleasing orange zest perfume, deft fortification to 16.6% alc to offset the sugar, ensure appetite appeal in **21** (82). **Red Jerepigo** ★★★ Richly sweet fortified dessert from merlot, ex-tank **22** (80) finishes clean, alc & roasted hazelnut element still vie for prominence, hopefully to settle & marry. **Cape Ruby** ★★★ 'Port' of undeclared grapes lengthily aged in seasoned oak, counter to style. **17** (79) generous Xmas cake, prune & spice but 19.5% alc jars a touch. **Oak Matured Full Cream** (⊘) ★★★ Full-sweet sherry-style fortified, **11** (80) dried fruit & molasses, proclaiming its richness, nut-toffee finish. Not classic, but flavourful. **Brandy** (⊘) ★★★ Potstill (81) from chenin & colombard, 3-5 years in oak. More nutty & leathery than fruity, with caramel hint. Fiery 43% alc best for mixing. 350 & 750 ml. Not tasted: **White Muscadel**. — FM, TJ & CR

Location: Douglas ▪ Map: Northern Cape, Free State & North West ▪ Map grid reference: C5 ▪ WO: Northern Cape/Western Cape/Free State ▪ Est 1968 ▪ 1stB 1977 ▪ Tasting & sales Mon-Fri 9-1 & 2-5 ▪ Closed all pub hols ▪ Cellar tours by appt ▪ Function/lapa venue (up to 60 pax) ▪ Gin & brandy ▪ Owner(s) GWK Ltd ▪ Cellarmaster(s)/winemaker(s) Sanmari Snyman ▪ Douglas + Landzicht GWK: 350ha (cab, merlot, p verdot, ruby cab, shiraz, tannat, chenin, cbard, sauv) ▪ 10,000cs own label 40% red 20% white 10% rosé 30% fortified ▪ PO Box 47 Douglas 8730 ▪ lisad@gwk.co.za ▪ www.gwk.co.za, www.landzicht.co.za ▪ T +27 (0)53-298-8314/5

☐ **Landzicht Wyn** *see* Landzicht Wine Cellar
☐ **Langtafel** *see* Mooiplaas Wine Estate & Private Nature Reserve

Langverwacht Wynkelder   ⓨ ⓰

Few Cape wineries can boast 70-plus years' accumulated experience in their core team, and fewer still have had the same leader for over half those years. And, speaking of continuity, grower-owned Langverwacht as an entity in 2024 celebrates seven decades of making wine near Bonnievale - still bulk-wine focused, with a small branded line-up intended to offer 'fruity, easy-drinking anytime wines at an affordable price'.

Cabernet Sauvignon ⊘ ★★★★ Smoky top note from oaking in FlexCube, resulting tannins accessible & smooth; 21 ⑧④ more than enough blackcurrant fruit to offer pleasant, complete wine experience. **Ruby Cabernet** ⓨ ★★★ Variety rarely bottled solo. Lightly oaked, enough to add savoury notes without detracting from 20 ⑧②'s juicy fruit. **4 Barrel Shiraz** ⓨ ★★★★ Started as four best barrels, switched to FlexCubes with oak contact from 18 ★★★★ ⑧⑦. 21 ⑧⑤ sweet-fruited, with shade less depth & intensity than the original. **Chardonnay** ⊘ ★★★★ Unwooded but holds its own, vibrant melon & stonefruit in 23 ⑧④. Lipsmacking zesty flavours, well priced for the quality. **Chenin Blanc** ⊘ ★★★ Crunchy summer fruit salad perfume & flavours, dry 23 ⑧② livened by brisk acidity. **Colombar** ⓨ ★★★★ Perennial lively, fruity bargain, 22 ⑧③ reprises litchi & guava aromas & flavours of previous. **Sauvignon Blanc** ⊘ ★★★ Grapefruit-fresh, with attractive green top note & salty finish, 23 ⑧② fits classic sauvignon profile. — CR

Location: Bonnievale ▪ Map: Robertson ▪ Map grid reference: D4 ▪ WO: Robertson/Bonnievale ▪ Est 1954 ▪ Tasting, sales & tours Mon-Fri 8-5 ▪ Closed all pub hols ▪ Online shop ▪ Owner(s) 25 members ▪ Cellarmaster(s) Johan Gerber (Dec 1986) ▪ Winemaker(s) Theunis Botha (Dec 2005) ▪ Viticulturist(s) Hennie Visser (Jul 2008) ▪ 600ha (cab, ruby cab, shiraz, chenin, chard, cbard, sauv) ▪ 12,600t/4,500cs own label 50% red 50% white ▪ IPW, WIETA ▪ PO Box 87 Bonnievale 6730 ▪ info@langverwachtwines.co.za ▪ www. langverwachtwines.co.za ▪ **T +27 (0)23-616-2815**

Lanzerac Wine Estate   ⓨ ⓜ ⓖ ⓞ ⓰

A deep sense of heritage permeates picture-perfect Lanzerac wine and luxury hospitality estate at the gateway to Stellenbosch's Jonkershoek Valley, with its Cape Dutch buildings and traditional werf edged by vines and mountains. Historical links, such as Lanzerac being the first commercial pinotage, launched in 1961, are reflected in the new range, while the Heritage wines acknowledge Mrs English, who bought the farm in 1920 and renamed it Lanzerac. The vineyard renewal project is mostly complete, the first cinsault crop adding youthful pep to the Kurktrekker which, like all new releases, is Jonkershoek certified, realising a long-term goal. Cellar tweaks by Wynand Lategan are ongoing and aimed at attaining 'balance and purity'. Sustainability focus even sees own microherbs grown for the kitchen and proteas for flower arrangements.

Commemorative range ⓝⓔⓦ

★★★★★ **Pinotage** ⓐ Celebrates diamond jubilee of first commercial pinotage release, 1959, from 1953 vines on Bellevue Estate in Stellenbosch's Bottelary. 19 ⑨⑤, from Lanzerac home-farm, delectable bramble & woodland berries with tobacco & tealeaf, velvet tannins & lingering finish. A measured, worthy tribute.

Heritage range

★★★★☆ **Pionier Pinotage** ⓐ From Jonkershoek single-vineyard, naturally fermented 20 ⑨③ concentrated & styled for long haul after 22 months in half new barrels. Yet no lack of refinement or freshness, tannins silky, finish lingering, wild black-berry fruit vibrant & sustained.

★★★★☆ **Le Général** ⓐ Honouring WW1 French hero Charles Lanrezac, sophisticated 20 ⑨③ Bordeaux blend is 60% cab with merlot, malbec & petit verdot. Intense, sweetly ripe blackcurrant & cherry fruit prevails, spiced with rosepetal & liquorice, wrapped in sleek, powdery tannins. 22 months in 50% new oak.

★★★★☆ **Mrs English** ⓐ Certified single-vineyard chardonnay named for owner who launched estate's winemaking. 22 ★★★★★ ⑨⑤ full, weighty & rich, prominent oak from ferment/year 40% new barrels, refined citrus marmalade & toasted nut finish. 21 ⑨③ also big, bold & aromatic.

Jonkershoek range

★★★★ **Cabernet Sauvignon** ⓐ Bold, forthright 19 ⑧⑨ has concentrated blackcurrant fruit, solid, leathery tannin structure & satisfying earthiness. 18 months in 25% new barrels will help it attain intended maturity a decade hence.

★★★★ **Merlot** ⓐ Dense, concentrated & sombre black fruit laced with tarry liquorice & thick tannins, 22 ⑧⑨ has abundant muscle & staying power. Year in barrel shows in aromatic spice.

★★★★ **Pinotage** (🐝) Not outshone by its siblings, **20** (88) shows sophistication & cellarworthiness in its bright wild-berry fruit, sweet aromatic scent, appealing spice, partly from 16 months in 25% new oak.

★★★★☆ **Reserve** (✓) (🐝) Impressive cab, shiraz & petit verdot blend, **20** (90) tad lighter than last, reflecting vintages. Dark, deep & noble, with earthy, savoury notes, liquorice-tinged black cherries & currants, ripe solid tannins. Judicious oaking ensures focus remains on fruit.

★★★★ **Chardonnay** Barrel ferment reined back to 50% in **22** (88), but still rich & leesy with appealing butter & lemon notes. Well balanced, elegant & characterful, should pair well with cream-based seafood.

★★★★ **Sauvignon Blanc** (✓) Fruit-forward **22** (86) juicy & refreshing, flinty minerality bolstering ripe gooseberry & granadilla. Extended skin contact adds to satisfying weight & mouthfeel.

★★★★ **Blanc de Blancs Brut** Youthful, vivacious chardonnay **NV** (87) cap classique has rich lemon cream confection with lime cordial highlight, well-judged acid & energetic mousse. Small portion lightly oaked, 18 months on lees.

Pinotage Rosé ★★★★ Coral-hued, just-dry **22** (85) has floral scent on cheerful raspberry fruit, satisfying lees texture, well-judged acid. Discontinued: **Syrah**.

Keldermeester Versameling

★★★★ **Kurktrekker** Now 100% cinsault, **22** ★★★★☆ (91) is delightfully supple, juicy & perfumed. Surprisingly full body, to which year in older barrels adds structure without intruding. Last **18** (88) had some alicante bouschet & cab franc.

★★★★ **Dok** Honouring rugby legend Danie 'Doc' Craven, single-site malbec **21** (88) supple & concentrated, with spicy mulberry & plum pudding fruit, delicate liquorice-anise note. 16 months seasoned barrels. Last was **19** (89).

★★★★ **Prof** Pinotage progenitors pinot noir & cinsault pair up in tribute to its creator, prof Abraham Perold. **22** ★★★★☆ (90), first since **17** (88), is unoaked, allowing dense, succulent fruit to shine, while ripe grape tannins add breadth & texture.

★★★★ **Bergpad** Pinot blanc, rare in SA. **22** (87), first since **18** (87), makes welcome return, with varietal fatness bolstered by ferment & year in clay amphora. Leesy richness is complemented by delicate floral & lemon notes, appealing mineral finish.

★★★★ **Bergstroom** First since **17** ★★★★☆ (84), current **22** (86) is 75% sauvignon with semillon, barrel fermented with year maturation. Creamy, mild-mannered & leesy, showing green apple fruit with tart, mineral finish. WO Cape Coast.— GdB

Location/map: Stellenbosch ▪ Map grid reference: G5 ▪ WO: Jonkershoek Valley/Cape Coast ▪ Est 1692 ▪ 1stB 1957 ▪ Tasting daily 8-7 (summer)/8-6 (winter) ▪ Sales daily 9-7 (summer)/9-6 (winter) ▪ Cellar tours on request ▪ Open all pub hols ▪ Deli platters; wine & chocolate tasting ▪ 5-star Lanzerac Hotel, Spa & Restaurants ▪ Conferences ▪ Weddings/functions ▪ Owner(s) Lanzerac Estate Investments ▪ Cellarmaster(s) Wynand Lategan (Jan 2005) ▪ Viticulturist(s) Philip le Roux (2020) ▪ 163ha/45ha (cab, cinsaut, malbec, merlot, ptage, shiraz, chard, pinot blanc, sauv) ▪ 500t/24-26,000cs own label 55% red 30% white 15% rosé ▪ PO Box 6233 Uniedal 7612 ▪ wine@lanzerac.co.za, winetasting@lanzerac.co.za ▪ www.lanzerac.co.za ▪ T +27 (0)21-886-5641

La Petite Ferme Winery (ⓧ) (🍴) (🏠) (📷)

Cellars with add-on restaurants are fairly common, but restaurants with their own cellar, vines and custodian are much less run-of-the-mill. Company-owned La Petite Ferme is one of the rarities, a convivial, verandaed eatery with a compact yet full-fledged winery, complete with an export network, under the same roof. Separate, but with a shared stellar vista over Franschhoek and its valley, are luxury guest suites.

La Petite Ferme range

★★★★ **Cabernet Sauvignon** Dark-berried **20** (89) supple & juicy, with cedary nuance from 14 months in oak, 20% new. Balanced & approachable but with respectable structure to last good few years.

★★★★ **Merlot** Black cherry & some savoury notes in **21** (87). Touch less new oak (20%, 14 months) than **20** (89), similar dry tannins but tad less generosity of fruit. Quite restrained in youth, begs time.

★★★★☆ **Shiraz** Savoury, earthy **20** (90) is plush & ripe with a lovely seam of fresh acid. Year in oak, 20% new, gives spice & bolsters the supple tannin structure. Seductive & approachable, with potential to age.

★★★★ **Barrel Fermented Chardonnay** Creamy butterscotch & oatmeal in **22** ⑧⑦, zested through with acid. Subtle oak presence from ferment/9 months in barrel, only 10% new, also adds a little padding. Medium bodied, elegant & structured for some ageing & mealtime enjoyment.

★★★★ **Viognier** Varietally true **22** ⑧⑧ is floral & peachy & has plenty of bright freshness for balance. Oaking changed to 8 months in old barrels, melds the whole & finds a sweet spot. Pleasurable solo, but as most of these wines, food friendly.

Rosé ★★★★ Delicate blush of pink on **23** ⑧③, with a flourish of racy acid. Perky cherry & berry notes, bone-dry finish. **Sauvignon Blanc** ★★★★ Bone-dry, flinty **23** ⑧④, with pervasive cool zest & a clean lemon & grapefruit tang, is one for the table.

Winemaker's Edition range

★★★★☆ **The Verdict** ⓥ Alluring fruitcake & subtle florality on **18** ⑨⓪ echo the previous blend though it changes from 'Cape' to 'Bordeaux' by the omission of pinotage from union of cabs sauvignon & franc. Somewhat slighter, less dense, but still spicy from 14 months in 35% new oak, & a pleasure to drink.

★★★★☆ **Variation** ⓥ Shiraz-led (54%) Rhône red loses viognier & ups grenache to 37% in **18** ★★★★ ⑧⑥, adds dab mourvèdre. Still darkly spicy & dry, but less fleshy & accessible than **17** ⑨⓪. Occasional release: **'White'**.

Baboon Rock range

★★★★ **Grenache** ⓥ Raising the bar on **19** ★★★★ ⑧④, lively & fresh **20** ⑧⑥ has ample red-berry appeal & is lithe & light-bodied. 10 months in older oak add subtly supportive structure.

Unwooded Chardonnay ⓥ ★★★★ Kumquat & orange zip on light, easy **22** ⑧④, as approachable & uncomplicatedly flavoursome as ever. WO W Cape. Occasional release: **Rosé**. — MW

Location/map: Franschhoek ▪ Map grid reference: C1 ▪ WO: Franschhoek/Western Cape ▪ Est 1972 ▪ 1stB 1996 ▪ Tasting daily at 10.30 by appt; pub hols (seasonal) please call ahead ▪ Fee R100pp ▪ Sales daily 8.30-5 ▪ Restaurant ▪ Guest suites ▪ Tour groups ▪ Gift shop ▪ Wine club ▪ Owner(s) The Nest Estate South Africa (Pty) Ltd, t/a La Petite Ferme ▪ GM Riaan Kruger ▪ Winemaker(s) Wikus Pretorius (Oct 2015) ▪ Viticulturist(s) Wikus Pretorius (Oct 2015) ▪ Farm manager Frans Malies ▪ 16ha/14ha (cabs s/f, grenache, merlot, shiraz, chard, sauv, viog) ▪ 60-70t/10,000cs own label 40% red 50% white 10% rosé ▪ PO Box 683 Franschhoek 7690 ▪ reception@lapetiteferme.co.za ▪ www.lapetiteferme.co.za ▪ T +27 (0)21-876-3016

La Petite Provence Wine Company   ⓥ

Wine as a lifestyle is what home owners of La Petite Provence in Franschhoek get to enjoy, with 3.5 ha of cabernet sauvignon and merlot as part of their residential estate. Wine is made and matured off-site, and enjoyed by residents, friends, family and customers in multiple countries.

Cabernet Sauvignon ⓥ ★★★★ Unfussy, bright **18** ⑧④ offers spicy cherry approachability. Like last, had oak staves in tank but upped to 18 months from 10. **Merlot** ⓥ ★★★★ Cocoa nuance to dark-berried fruit on **18** ⑧⑤, soft, light bodied & gentle. A crowd pleaser. Not tasted: **Cabernet Sauvignon-Merlot**. — FM

Location/WO: Franschhoek ▪ Est 2001 ▪ 1stB 2005 ▪ Tasting & sales Wed/Sat by appt ▪ Wine club ▪ Owner(s) La Petite Provence Wine Trust ▪ Winemaker(s) Helena Senekal (2017, Simonsvlei) ▪ 3.5ha (cab, merlot) ▪ 30t/900cs own label 100% red ▪ 2 Cabernet Dr, La Petite Provence, Franschhoek 7690 ▪ info@lapetite-provence.co.za ▪ www.lapetiteprovence.co.za ▪ T +27 (0)82-550-6495/+27 (0)83-236-4247

☐ **La Petite Vigne** see Black Elephant Vintners
☐ **La Polka** see Nico van der Merwe Wines

La RicMal   ⓥ ⓒ

Originally from KwaZulu-Natal, the Green family ventured into the wine industry in 2007 after eldest son Ricardo joined his entrepreneur father Malcolm in the family business. Headquartered in Stellenbosch's Bottelary Hills, the Greens 'value and strive for consistency and quality year on year'.

Suprême range

Merlot ⊘ ★★★ Range created for easy drinking at an affordable price. 12 months' oaking, otherwise same regime as Shiraz, **22** ⑧⓪'s plummy fruit is juicy, with a fresh seam. **Shiraz** ⊘ ★★★ Partial wooding on French & American staves, 8 months, touch of vanilla, **22** ⑧⓪'s tannins in harmony with prominent sappy red berries. Not tasted: **Cabernet Sauvignon**, **Sauvignon Blanc**.

Lerato range

Sweet Red ⊘ ★★★ Unoaked merlot & cab blend, trim (12.5% alc) but not apparent because of **NV** ⑦⑧'s smooth plumping sweetness. Not tasted: **Classic Red**, **Classic White**. — CR

Location: Stellenbosch ▪ WO: Western Cape ▪ Est 2007 ▪ 1stB 2008 ▪ Tasting & sales by appt only ▪ Olive oil ▪ Owner(s) Green family ▪ Winemaker(s)/viticulturist(s) various ▪ ±550t/±10,000cs own label 90% red 10% white ▪ WIETA ▪ rgreen@laricmal.com ▪ www.laricmal.com ▪ **T +27 (0)82-456-1430/+27 (0)84-888-0430**

☐ **Last Of The First** see False Bay Vineyards

Late Bloomer Boutique Winery   ⓠ (NEW)

Per the branding, Stephan Kruger was tardily out of the blocks but with great satisfaction and gusto, having always wanted to make wine. Opportunity called in 2016 while in Johannesburg, and he crafted the first wines in a literal garage. He's since relocated and upgraded, to a small converted brewery in Gordon's Bay, sourcing grapes widely and nimble enough to try something new or different. Tastings are among the barrels and tanks, so visitors should expect more than the usual noises off if sampling during season.

★★★★ **Fanie's Fusion** ⊘ 3-way split of cab, merlot & shiraz, different oaking here, only 14 months. Smoky cigarbox tones on **20** ⑧⑥, with berry-plummy fruit holding its own in perfume & flavour. Streamlined texture, silky finish, tannins amenable for current drinking. WO Coastal.

Hiraeth Cabernet Sauvignon ★★★★ Oaking as majority of reds, 18 months with French & American chips inserted into older barrels, giving **21** ⑧⑤ from Stellenbosch a pronounced savoury element to its nose & palate. Plummy fruit helps drinkability but tannins are dry on finish, need time. **The Day Dreamer Syrah** ★★★★ Same oaking as majority of the reds, but in **21** ⑧④ the 30% American's vanilla fits the syrah's plushness, will make many friends. Succulent texture adds to the appeal. **Oddity Pinot Noir-Syrah** ★★★ Certainly an unusual combo in **21** ⑧①. Syrah oaked per house style, 56% pinot noir unwooded, providing attractive berry profile, underpinned by savoury spicing, tannins supple. WO W Cape. **Je Ne Sais Quoi Syrah-Sauvignon Blanc** ★★★ Syrah with 17% sauvignon, pale coral hue. **22** ⑧⓪ rosé is strawberry scented, the white grape showing in the flavours, drinkability enhanced by crisp acid. **Cheninanigans Chenin Blanc** ★★★ Catchy name & blue-patterned label. From Franschhoek, apple & pair, some crushed herbs, **22** ⑧① has limy freshness, perking up the fruit. **Summer Sauvignon Blanc** ★★★ Winter melon- & yellow apple-scented **21** ⑦⑧'s racy acidity adds vitality, but perhaps too pronounced for the fruit? **The Lucky Old Man** ★★ From sauvignon & semillon, American oak chips 3 months give **21** ⑦③ coconut & vanilla styling, dominating the 66/34 blend's nose & palate. Some fruit salad flavours. Chill well. Not tasted: **Signature Cabernet Sauvignon**. — CR, CvZ

Location: Gordon's Bay ▪ WO: Elgin/Coastal/Franschhoek/Western Cape/Stellenbosch ▪ Est/1stB 2017 ▪ Tasting & sales Wed-Sun 10-5 ▪ Closed Mon-Tue, Easter Fri/Sun, Dec 25 & Jan 1 ▪ Owner(s) Kief Bru Holdings (Pty) Ltd ▪ Winemaker(s) Stephan Kruger (Jun 2017) ▪ 1st/200-600cs per cultivar/blend ▪ info@latebloomerwines. com ▪ www.latebloomerwines.com ▪ **T +27 (0)82-550-9351**

☐ **Lategan** see Bergsig Estate

Lautus De-Alcoholised Wines

A conventional winemaker by training and also in practice (see listing under Holder Vineyards), Reg Holder's prescience in launching this Stellenbosch specialist venture, a local pioneer of de-alcoholised wine, has seen volumes rise to a substantial 80,000 cases, a high-profile listing with retailer Woolworths under the De-Alc label, as well as exports, in only seven years. For the wines below, a 'spinning cone' removes and sets aside the aromatic 'essence of the wine' and then practically all the alcohol; after that, the 'essence' is added back.

Savvy Red ★★ Juicy NV ⑦⑤, mostly shiraz & pinotage, improves on previous with well-judged plums, berries & light kiss of oak. For all these, alc less than 0.5%, sugar 23-32 g/L, origin not certified. **Rosé** ★★★ Salmon-pink NV ⑦⑧ uses pinotage's bountiful berries for tasty, refreshing sipping. **Chardonnay** (NEW) ★★★ Body & brightness on NV ⑦⑦, vibrant acid lifts apples & pears, barest brush of oak. **Savvy White** ★★★ Switches to chardonnay from sauvignon for more a structured NV ⑦⑨ with backbone of lemony acid. **Sparkling** ★★★ Apples & pineapples on fruit-forward carbonated NV ⑦⑧ from chardonnay with racy-fresh mousse. — ML

Location: Stellenbosch ▪ Est 2017 ▪ Closed to public ▪ Owner(s) Holder Vineyard & Wines (Pty) Ltd ▪ Cellarmaster(s) Reg Holder (Jan 2018) ▪ 80,000cs own label 30% red 50% white 20% rosé ▪ Brands for clients: Woolworths ▪ 9 Markotter Ave, Uniepark, Stellenbosch 7600 ▪ info@drinklautus.com ▪ www.drinklautus.com ▪ **T +27 (0)83-678-9598**

L'Avenir Wine Estate

Just over 3 decades ago, Mauritian Marc Wiehe envisioned a different future for his grape-supplying farm on the Simonsberg foothills of Stellenbosch, and enlisted ex-pharmacist Francois Naudé as in-house winemaker to begin vinifying for own account. Pinotage, Francois' great love, is also the passion of his protégé and incumbent winemaker, Dirk Coetzee. The other focus variety was chenin blanc, L'Avenir being one of the first to produce a high-end version. Under the latter ownership of French specialist wine company AdVini, emphasis on both varieties continues, with milestones in 2023 for each: the 30th pinotage vintage, and 50th year of the chenin heritage block. 'Evolving the conversation around pinotage from extraction, oak and alcohol to site expression' is the aim with a new collection launched with the Le Sommet bottling. The team moreover firmly believes 'pinotage can have the fruit intensity of Argentinian malbec, the spice of Gigondas and the longevity of St Emilion. This is what we want to show to the world'.

Single Block range

★★★★ **Le Sommet Pinotage** (NEW) Pared-back expression from Bottelary grapes, **21** (88) has variety's candyfloss & iced vanilla biscuit top notes but little forward fruit. Pleasingly dry & approachable.

★★★★☆ **Pinotage** Change in oaking to just 20% new allows **20** ★★★★★ (98)'s fruit purity & firm ripe tannins centre stage. **19** (94) had 80% new. Black plum & mulberry, whiffs of dried & fresh herbs, the whole a pleasing contrast of elegance & power. Like Chenin, from registered single-vineyard.

★★★★☆ **Glenrosé** Sophisticated pale pink dry rosé from pinotage, named for Glenrosa vineyard soils. **23** (90) pure berry aromas & flavours alongside flint & salt, weight, depth & persistent subtle savoury undertone from 15% wooded portion, 2% new, down from 6% in **22** ★★★★ (89).

★★★★☆ **Chenin Blanc** Old-vine block once again delivers a feast of flavour in **21** (93): lemon, peach, apricot, hints of honey & rosemary, helped by two picking dates, supported by spicy oak (ferment in barrel, none new), enlivened by usual bright acid, quince flick on finish. Follows lovely **20** ★★★★★ (95).

Provenance range

★★★★ **Pinotage** Juicy red & black berry character overlaid with earthy, meaty tones & shot through with crisp acid. **21** (87) rounded & firm for satisfying mealtime sipping.

★★★★ **Stellenbosch Classic** Previewed **20** (87) departs from Bordeaux template with pinotage joining cab, cab franc & merlot (32/29/6). Unoaked portion (15%) aids freshness & drinkability.

★★★★ **Chenin Blanc** Obvious but pleasant bitter quince lift finish to confident lemon- & peach-toned **22** (86). Some oak, 20% new, adds richness, weight & attractive toasty complexity.

Merlot ★★★★ Less fruity than previous, with faint plum & mulberry whiffs, some iodine. **22** (83) also less obvious oak grip thanks to smaller portion new, 9% vs 20%.

Future Eternal range

★★★★ **Méthode Cap Classique Pinotage Brut Rosé** Coral-hued **19** (86) sparkler makes the most of pinotage's forward berry aromas & flavours to deliver a feisty dry aperitif or fruity dessert companion. 32 months on lees.

L'Horizon range

....

Pinotage ★★★★ Unoaked & vibrant, **22** (85) tank sample's appealingly gutsy tannins give form to exuberant mulberry & black plum fruit.

....

Rosé de Pinotage ★★★★ Silky, bone-dry & vinous, **23** (85) emphasises texture but also offers fruit & confectionary aromas & flavours for a very satisfying drink. **Chenin Blanc** ★★★★ Some lees stirring in tank adds weight & subtle grip to cheerful combo of citrus & stonefruit. **23** (83) nicely dry & lightish on its feet at 13.5% alc. **Sauvignon Blanc** ★★★★ **23** (83) mixes cool green fruits with slightly riper passionfruit & mango notes, bouncy acidity for easy enjoyment. — CvZ

Location/map: Stellenbosch ▪ Map grid reference: E3 ▪ WO: Stellenbosch/Bottelary ▪ Est/1stB 1992 ▪ Tasting & sales Mon-Sat 10-7 (Oct-Apr)/10-5 (May-Sep) Sun/pub hols 10-4 ▪ Fee based on tasting option selected ▪

Closed Good Fri, Dec 25 & Jan 1 ▪ Cellar tours by appt ▪ Light meals ▪ Child friendly ▪ Function venue ▪ Luxury 4-star Country Lodge ▪ Wine club ▪ Owner(s) AdVini ▪ Winemaker(s) Dirk Coetzee (Aug 2009), with Mattheus Thabo (Jan 2007) & Luke Giesler (Jan 2021) ▪ Viticulturist(s) Leigh Diedericks ▪ 64.9ha/37.05ha (cabs s/f, merlot, ptage, chenin, sauv) ▪ 300t/40,000cs own label 44% red 38% white 18% rosé ▪ IPW, WIETA ▪ PO Box 7267 Stellenbosch 7599 ▪ info@lavenir.co.za ▪ www.lavenirestate.co.za ▪ **T +27 (0)21-889-5001**

La Vierge Private Cellar Ⓟ 🍽 ⓥ

A pioneer of winegrowing in the cool-climate Hemel-en-Aarde area, La Vierge is situated at the gateway to the higher-lying appellations of Upper Hemel-en-Aarde and Hemel-en-Aarde Ridge. Its racy branding may raise a smile, but the chardonnay- and pinot noir-focused wines are seriously conceived, and intended to be 'variety- and terroir-expressive, and over-deliver on quality'. From its vantage at the crest of a steep slope, the visitor locale includes a restaurant and a patio area with 'sundowners' written all over it.

Icon range

★★★★☆ **Apogée Pinot Noir** ⊘ 🍸 Pinnacle label struts its self-assured stuff with intriguing red berry array - compote, essence & cordial - ripe, powdery tannins & complex weave of exotic spices in **19** ⑨③. Intense & concentrated, promising a long life, yet sleek & approachable. 16 months in oak, 20% new.

★★★★☆ **Apogée Chardonnay** 🍸 Summit of portfolio is suitably imposing, showing style as well as gravitas in **20** ⑨④. Full, opulently ripe & assured, with lime & orange marmalade, sweet vanilla biscuit & counterfeit of vibrant acid. Upfront spice from wild-yeast ferment/14 months in oak should integrate.

Ultra Premium range

★★★★☆ **Royal Nymphomane** 🍸 Classic 5-way, cab-led Bordeaux blend, **20** ⑨③ sumptuous & assertive, yet alluringly mineral too, with earthy & iodine notes spicing up cassis & plum fruit. Shows well now, but solid tannins supply legs for longer cellaring. First tasted since **18** ⑨③.

Premium range

★★★★☆ **La Vierge Noir** ⊘ Second tier of pinot quartet, 9 months in 20% new barriques, **19** ⑨⓪ offers solid drinking pleasure with fewer frills. Sweetly ripe red berry fruit, delicately laced with rosepetal & oak spice, smoothly ripe tannins.

La Vierge Collection

★★★★ **The Affair** ⊘ Fresh & youthful pinot noir, **22** ⑧⑦ showing impressive cherry & raspberry concentration, sweetly fragrant violet scent. Delicate brush of oak, mostly seasoned, 11 months, adds spice.

★★★★ **Satyricon** Wholesome, elegant rendering of sangiovese, **21** ⑧⑧ follows form, with tangy cherry & plum fruit, savoury tomato concentrate character, silk texture polished by year in older oak.

★★★★ **Anthelia** Pale garnet hued, lithe & lean, **21** ★★★★ ⑧⑤ is lighter than **20** ⑧⑧, delivers juicy cherry fruit, gentle tannins, modest scrub & oak spice.

★★★★ **Nymphomane** Textbook flavour & structure in **21** ⑧⑧ merlot & cab-led 5-way Bordeaux blend. Lean & earthy, with dark chocolate & some leafy nuances, intense cassis fruit & leathery tannins, rounded by year in mostly seasoned oak.

★★★★☆ **Jezebelle** ⊘ Barrel-fermented **22** ⑨② chardonnay is poised & confident, offering marmalade with citrus peel & hazelnut, spun through with delightful salty mineral thread. 9 months in seasoned Burgundian barrels subtly burnish & round out palate.

★★★★ **Redemption** ⊘ Unoaked & wild yeast fermented to express succulent citrus fruit, **22** ⑧⑥ chardonnay is undemanding yet rewarding, offering good palate weight & texture from 6 months on lees. Young & vivacious now, good for a few years. No **21**.

★★★★ **The Last Temptation** ⊘ Racy **20** ⑧⑥ riesling has flair & varietal character, spice & aromatics, with restrained terpene whiff, floral-scented grapefruit & green apple. Upstages last-tasted **17** ★★★★ ⑧④.

★★★★ **Original Sin** Ⓐ Distinctive, almost pungent herbal & scrub aromas on **22** ⑧⑥ sauvignon, with lime cordial-accented citrus fruit, hints of buchu & nettle. Leesy texture & vibrant acid rounded out by 11% unoaked semillon. **21** not tasted. WO Walker Bay, like the Nymphomanes.

Seduction ⊘ ★★★★ Unpretentious, fruit-driven **21** ⑧⑤ unwooded pinot noir is youthful & sprightly. Previewed last time, now offers tangy cherry fruit with hazel & almond highlights. — GdB

Location: Hermanus ▪ Map: Walker Bay & Bot River ▪ Map grid reference: B4 ▪ WO: Hemel-en-Aarde Ridge/Walker Bay ▪ Est 1997 ▪ 1stB 2006 ▪ Tasting & sales Mon-Sun 10-5 ▪ Closed Good Fri & Dec 25 ▪ La Vierge

Restaurant & Champagne Verandah ▪ Tour groups by appt ▪ Owner(s) La Vierge Wines (Pty) Ltd & Viking Pony Properties 355 (Pty) Ltd ▪ Winemaker(s) Christo Kotze (Jul 2017) ▪ Viticulturist(s) Neill Gellatly (Oct 2019), Kevin Watt (consultant) ▪ 44ha (cab f, p verdot, pinot, sangio, shiraz, chard, riesling, sauv, sem) ▪ 200t 60% red 40% white ▪ PO Box 1580 Hermanus 7200 ▪ admin@lavierge.co.za ▪ www.lavierge.co.za ▪ **T +27 (0)28-313-0130**

Lazanou Organic Vineyards Ⓠ ⑾ ⌂ ◎

The Bavaud family in 2020 moved from Switzerland and settled on their Wellington organic boutique estate, where pastures, olive groves and fruit trees border the vines, and ducks and hens dine on snails and harmful insects. Klaas Coetzee, co-owner of organic specialist Kusafiri, does the crafting on a consulting basis, aiming for 'exceptional quality in a sustainable and eco-responsible way'. We hope to taste the wines next time.

Location/map: Wellington ▪ Map grid reference: B2 ▪ Est 2002 ▪ 1stB 2006 ▪ Tasting & sales by appt ▪ Open days with wine & food pairing - booking required ▪ Tour groups ▪ Farm produce ▪ Cow Shed Cottage ▪ Owner(s) Xavier, Martine & Valentin Bavaud ▪ Winemaker(s) Klaas Coetzee (Jan 2021, consultant) ▪ Viticulturist(s) Johan Wiese (Jan 2006, consultant) ▪ 8.48ha/4.2ha (mourv, shiraz, chard, chenin, viog) ▪ 28t/3,600cs own label 40% red 60% white ▪ Certified organic by Ecocert ▪ PO Box 834 Wellington 7654 ▪ wine@lazanou.co.za ▪ www.lazanou.co.za ▪ **T +27 (0)61-502-4770**

☐ **Le Belle Rebelle** *see* Belle Rebelle

Le Bonheur Wine Estate Ⓠ

The name translates as 'happiness', and it describes the feeling of the team members resident at the storied property on Klapmuts Hill, and their counterparts at AdVini, the French wine-specialist company and estate owner, about the recent performance of the brand especially in Francophone countries, Canada being the standout. The concept on the industry's lips, regenerative viticulture, is 'the name of the game' here too, matched with conservation of ±80 ha of indigenous fynbos, and natural processes where possible in the cellar, with 'lower alcohol on the reds than typical for Stellenbosch' one of William Wilkinson's goals.

Reserve range

★★★★☆ **Cabernet Sauvignon** ⓐ Refined, complex, sleek & rewarding **20** ㊉. Composed & elegant, the spicy dark fruit is from smallest cab vineyard. Polished oak, 22 months, frames fruit seamlessly. Cohesive & poised, with freshness matched by deep concentration & long, dry finish.

★★★★☆ **Petit Verdot** ⓐ Bar inched up in **21** ㊉, showing light fynbos edge to vivid berry fruit & well-judged firm, chalky grip aided by 22 months in new oak.

★★★★☆ **Estate Barrel Selection** Ⓠ Handsome packaging (as range) & wine: 4-part Bordeaux blend led by cab & petit verdot. **19** ㊉ wonderfully perfumed & complex, sleek, with polished tannins & a strong core of fruit for long ageing. Stellenbosch WO.

★★★★ **Blanc Fumé** ⓦ Venerable vines - 2nd-oldest sauvignon in SA - meticulously treated. Granadilla & grapefruit typicity & succulence of **22** ㉙ has added texture, depth from year in 50% new oak. Matches previous in composure & elegance, lengthy finish.

Le Bonheur Estate range

★★★★☆ **Cabernet Sauvignon** ⊘ ⓐ Heady violet perfume & rich, ripe fruitcake flavours on **21** ㊉, layered with cocoa, ink & graphite after 18 months in third new oak. Taut, powerful & complex, with muscular dry tannin grip. Give it plenty of time.

★★★★ **The Manor Meander Merlot** ⊘ ⓦ 1984 heritage vineyard next to manor house. **21** ㉙ signature dark berry fruit with leafy tomato nuance & cedar spice. Previous was fully oaked, this reduced to half, just 10% new. Textured, with fine dry tannins.

★★★★ **Prima** ⊘ 4-part Bordeaux blend is led by petit verdot in **21** ★★★★★ ㊉, others in near-equal proportions. Smooth, soft & juicy, ample black berry fruit, spice & light veneer of oak, 30% new. Composed & cohesive, supple, it drinks well now & will age well, like **20** ㉙.

★★★★ **The Eagle's Lair Chardonnay** ⊘ From 3 vineyards on different soils, **23** ㉘ step up on **22** ★★★★ ㉕ in structure & intent. Marmalade & elderflower palate with delicious cream edge. Curvaceous yet fresh & juicy, nothing overplayed so overall impression is of harmony & poise.

★★★★☆ **The Weather Blocks Sauvignon Blanc** ⊘ ⊛ Ex 1977 high-altitude sites of 'weerstasie' (weather station) clone, consistently delivers zesty lime & white pepper flavour. 23 ★★★★ (89) matches 22 (90) in brisk acid & flint but oak reduced to 10% from a third, touch lighter as a result.— FM

Location/map: Stellenbosch ▪ Map grid reference: F1 ▪ WO: Simonsberg-Stellenbosch/Stellenbosch ▪ Est 1790s ▪ 1stB 1972 ▪ Tasting by appt only ▪ Owner(s) AdVini South Africa ▪ Winemaker(s) William Wilkinson (May 2017), with Francois Conradie (2020) ▪ Viticultural consultant Etienne Terblanche ▪ 163ha/75ha (cab, merlot, chard, sauv) ▪ 600t/60,000cs own label 40% red 60% white ▪ cellar@lebonheur.co.za ▪ www.lebonheur.co.za ▪ **T +27 (0)21-889-5001/+27 (0)21-875-5478**

Le Chant Wines ⓠ

Belief in the Polkadraai Hills' potential to produce top terroir wine sees the French Oddo family, owners of Taaibosch and Pink Valley elsewhere in Stellenbosch, and Taaibosch cellarmaster Schalk Willem Joubert consolidate four properties there. All face south or southeast, and benefit from cooling bay breezes. Farming is organic, official certification the goal. Currently 70 of the 100 ha are under vine, and a further 15 are being planted with black grapes. Tastings are at Le Chant Wine Bar in Stellenbosch town pending on-site facilities.

★★★★★ **Rouge** ⊘ Fruitcake, leafy tomato & violet on 20 (91) on creative blend of merlot, the 2 cabs & 4 others. Elegant & rewarding, with cassis & dry spice highlights. Supple body from 2 years in combo concrete & large & small wood, 5% new. Lingers long.

★★★★ **Blanc** Nectarine & pear vibrancy on all-chenin 22 (87). Ripe, rounded, good flesh balanced by acid & breadth from time on lees. 30% wooded for 11 months, all old.— FM

Location/map/WO: Stellenbosch ▪ Map grid reference: F5 ▪ Est 2018 ▪ 1stB 2019 ▪ Tasting by appt only ▪ Wine club ▪ Wines also available for tasting at Le Chant Wine Bar, 7 Church Str, Stellenbosch: phone ahead for opening hours ▪ Owner(s) Oddo Vins et Domaines & Joubert ▪ Winemaker(s) Petri Venter (Feb 2019) ▪ Viticulturist(s) Francois Hanekom & Takkies Cloete (Feb 2018) ▪ ±100ha/70ha (cabs s/f, merlot, shiraz, chenin) ▪ 98% red 2% white ▪ IPW, Organic (in conversion) ▪ PO Box 17 Vlottenburg Stellenbosch 7604 ▪ info@lechant.wine ▪ www.lechant.wine ▪ **T +27 (0)21-855-3744**

☐ **Leenders** see Bezuidenhout Family Wines

Leeu Passant ⓠ

The partnership of Andrea and Chris Mullineux with businessman Analjit Singh allow the pair to work with vineyards beyond the Swartland. The inspiration of much of the winemaking at the winery in Franschhoek is what Andrea calls 'a deconstruction, reconstruction of the incredible Cape wines from the middle of the last century'. Working in the cellar with Kelsey Shungking and in the vineyards (many old, one from 1900) with Chris, Andrea complements history with modern care in 'winemaking techniques that focus on terroir and express these extraordinary sites'. Two new wines this year, one a cabernet franc off the estate's own vines. The other typifies the whole enterprise, not just in its excellence: a naturally fermented wine off old semillon vines, a project they 'have been working on since 2015' and now consider worthy of a release.

★★★★☆ **Stellenbosch Cabernet Sauvignon** ⊛ Superb 21 (94) from Helderberg slopes adds origin to name. Brims with dark blackcurrant fruit, graphite, floral perfume & fynbos. Voluminous & powerful, yet finely textured with powdery tannins, great depth & long-lingering intensity. Built to develop 15+ years. Natural ferment; 23 months in 30% new barrel & 5,000L foudre. Also in magnum.

★★★★☆ **CWG Auction Franschhoek Hillside Cabernet Franc** (NEW) ⊛ Debut wine from first vineyard planted on hillside of Franschhoek property. For winemaker this wine 'an accumulation of love'. 21 (94) seduces with ripe plum, raspberry, cedar & a green herb & fynbos perfume. Bold & intensely deep with unflagging finish, but truly elegant & delicately textured. A single 500L barrel made.

★★★★☆ **Wellington Old Vines Basson Cinsault** ⊛ ⊛ From SA's oldest registered red-wine vineyard, named for original farmer (& now also for area). With appropriately gentle vinification, 21 (93) offers delicate violet, red cherry, raspberry & earthy aromas & flavours. Ripe tannins provide delicious grip on expansive farewell. Stunning expression of variety, as was 20 ★★★★★ (95). Older 500L barrels, 20 months. Also in 1.5L, as next.

★★★★★ **The Leeu Passant** ⊛ Flagship (was 'Dry Red') nods to famous mid-20th century red wines of the Cape, includes widely sourced fruit from some of its oldest vines - equal cab & cab franc with 10%

cinsaut. Elegant **20** (95) shows pure dark fruit & bergamot perfume, refined tannins in perfect harmony. Depth & intensity will reward the patient (15+ years). Year in 30% new barrel, another in 5,000L foudre.

★★★★★ **Radicales Libres** (ⓐ) Inspired by traditional Rioja winemaking, this spectacular - though certainly unusual - chardonnay from Barrydale fruit spends 5 years in 225L barrels after wholebunch, natural ferment in oak in an oxidative environment. **17** (95) intense, harmonious & impressive, notes of preserved citrus, beeswax & savoury dark honey. Unflagging length. Profoundly dry, like **16** ★★★★★ (94).

★★★★★ **Stellenbosch Chardonnay** (ⓐ) High-lying, cooler Helderberg site with maritime influence. **21** (95) expressively pure, bright notes of lemon, lemongrass, ginger & roasted hazelnut. Sleek & toned, with terrific balance, texture, depth, complexity & poise to the last ruby grapefruit & salty lick on finish. Year in 30% new oak. Unfiltered. Also in magnum.

★★★★☆ **Franschhoek Semillon** (NEW) (ⓐ) A fine debut from vines planted in the 1960s. Regal **21** (94) has floral perfume, dewy stonefruit, poached quince, cashew nut butter. Rounded & seamless with intensity, breadth & astonishing balancing acidity. Herby, lemongrass notes emerge on long finish. Natural ferment & year in smaller barrel, 8 months in concrete 'egg'.

Discontinued: Lötter Cinsault. — WB

Location/map: Franschhoek ▪ Map grid reference: C2 ▪ WO: Stellenbosch/Franschhoek/Wellington/Western Cape/Barrydale ▪ Est 2013 ▪ 1stB 2015 ▪ Tasting & sales Mon-Sun 10-5 at the Wine Studio, Leeu Estates, Franschhoek (booking recommended) ▪ Fee R110-R350 depending on tasting ▪ Closed Good Fri, Dec 25 & Jan 1 ▪ Wine club ▪ Owner(s) Mullineux & Leeu Family Wines (Pty) Ltd ▪ Winemaker(s) Andrea Mullineux, with assistant Kelsey Shungking (Jan 2023) ▪ Viticulturist(s) Andrea Mullineux, with Chris Mullineux ▪ 40t/3,000cs own label 75% red 25% white ▪ WIETA ▪ info@mlfwines.com ▪ www.mlfwines.com ▪ **T +27 (0)21-492-2455 (office)/+27 (0)21-492-2224 (Wine Studio)**

Leeuwenberg   ⓛ

German fine-wine merchant Frank Kastien has explored South Africa's winelands for over 20 years, and his boutique shop in Wiesbaden has an impressive range of local brands. Complementing these are an own-label named for his 'three young lions', Yannick, Ben and Raphael, and styled to 'enrich your culinary lifestyle'.

Drie Kleine Leeuwen range

★★★★ **Shiraz** (ⓛ) Ticks all-important drinkability box in **19** (86) with ample berry, cherry & pepper flavour. Shows a serious side too in complexity, well-judged tannin, good dry finish.

★★★★☆ **Chardonnay Barrel Selection** (ⓛ) Impresses with balance & concentration, **18** (93)'s 11 months on lees in 50% new oak result in melba toast, grapefruit & lime styling, long & mouthfilling finish.

★★★★ **Sauvignon Blanc** Was 'The White One' when we tasted last **20** (86). **23** ★★★★ (85) lively Granny Smith apple, guava & citrus, zesty acid & gram sugar for smoothness on a pleasing summer sundowner.

Merlot Barrel Selection (ⓛ) ★★★★ Very pretty & appealing **21** (85), pure & juicy plum fruit, lively tannin lift & good structure after year in older barrels. **Shiraz Rosé** ★★★★ For current enjoyment, **23** (85) pale pink sipper offers delicate berry & cherry fruit, zippy acid & subtle savouriness on the finish. **Chardonnay** (ⓛ) ★★★ Delicate lemon blossom aroma on unwooded **22** (81), full & rounded from 5 months on lees, fantail finish with citrus echoing. Not tasted: **The Red One**. — CvZ

WO: Franschhoek ▪ Est/1stB 2010 ▪ Tasting only in Wiesbaden, Germany Mon-Fri 11-7 Sat 10-6 ▪ Closed all pub hols ▪ Owner(s) Procellar Wines ▪ Winemaker(s) Frank Kastien ▪ 6,000cs own label 50% red 50% white ▪ PO Box 422 Franschhoek 7690 ▪ info@procellarwines.com ▪ www.procellarwines.com ▪ **T +49 (0)611-30-86-778**

Leeuwenkuil Family Vineyards

Last harvest saw the final pressing of grapes at the venerable Bottelary facility, and the birth of a new era of processing exclusively at the recently commissioned cellar in Agter Paarl. The scale of the bespoke structure and its robust temperature control, solar power source and water efficiency are designed to enable optimally ripe grapes, grown mostly in owners Willie and Emma Dreyer's Swartland vineyards, to be brought into a controlled environment with minimal delay, thereby maintaining cellarmaster Pieter Carstens' lofty quality standards while supporting the drive to work as simply as possible, with mostly natural ferments and minimal sulphur additions. Planting is ongoing, partly aimed at obtaining the best variety to soil matches.

Heritage series

★★★★☆ **Syrah** ⓐ Syrah taken to another level, wild ferment (for all unless noted), long skin contact, 2 years older small barrels, so well judged, oak doesn't overwhelm the fruit, nor is the style showy or structure burly. There's finesse in **19** ⑨④, polish, sleek muscle tone for long ageing. Classy, hard to fault.

★★★★☆ **Chenin Blanc** ⓐ Older barrels 14 months, trim (13% alc) **21** ⑨④ has no shortage of character. Melon preserve, apple pie scents but the real action is on the palate: flinty, mineral flavours, touch of lime, a thatch savouriness. Has weight from lees contact, this is chenin in masterly hands.

Reserve range

★★★★☆ **Red** ⊘ ⓐ Shiraz at 85% with 4 others, long skin contact post-ferment, then year seasoned foudre, which **21** ⑨③ rewards with full dark-toned fruit, cocoa, savoury spice including pepper, clove. Lots of layers, depth. Tannin perceptible on finish, firm but ripe, no barrier to current enjoyment. **20** untasted.

★★★★ **Rosé** ⊘ Handsomely packaged, copper-hued **23** ⑧⑦ from cinsaut retains house-style elegance & restraint in scents & flavours: red berries, a mineral note, some dry scrub, all underpinned by crisp acid. Lovely food wine. **22** untasted.

★★★★★ **White** ⊘ ⓐ Cellar handling designed to bring out the best in this chenin, wholebunch, half fermented/9 months in foudre, half stainless steel, **22** ⑨⑥ is multi-layered & impressive, yellow apple & watermelon, toasted almond savoury richness yet still allowing the fruit centre stage. Palate elegant & fresh with an unexpected linearity, mineral & salty.

Leeuwenkuil range

★★★★ **Shiraz** ⊘ Three versions of shiraz in this portfolio, this unoaked, gets to the essence of the variety. **22** ⑧⑧ brambly fruit, dried scrub, hint of fynbos, touch wildness in the flavours. Streamlined texture, for earlier enjoyment.

Chenin Blanc ⊘ ★★★★ Unwooded, in contrast to Heritage & Reserve versions, **23** ⑧⑤ lovely fruit purity, crunchy apple & ruby grapefruit. Freshness abounds, ends lemony & long. — CR

Location: Paarl • WO: Swartland • Est 2008 • 1stB 2011 • Open by appt only • Online shop • Owner(s) Willie & Emma Dreyer • Head winemaker Pieter Carstens (Aug 2008) • Winemaker(s) Bernard Allison (Jan 2012), Gerhard Augustyn (Sep 2021) & Madré van der Walt (Sep 2013) • Viticulturist(s) Koos van der Merwe (Dec 2008) • 2,500ha • 25,000t/18m L 70% red 30% white • Fairtrade, Fair for Life, Organic, WIETA • PO Box 2001 Windmeul 7630 • pieter@leeuwenkuilfv.co.za • www.leeuwenkuilfv.co.za

---

☐ **Legend Collection** see Windmeul Cellar
☐ **Legends** see Slanghoek Winery
☐ **Legends of the Labyrinth** see Doolhof Wine Estate

Le Grand Chasseur Estate   ⓠ ⓑ

Stretched along the Breede River, home to uber-hunter, the African fish eagle, extensive Le Grand Chasseur in Robertson is owned by Eastern Cape fresh produce enterprise Habata, and planted with both wine- and table-grape vines. From the former, Carel Botha crafts 'well-balanced wines, each with its own uniqueness'.

Habata Reserve Selection

★★★★ **Cabernet Sauvignon** ⓠ A sophisticated step up on **18** ★★★ ⑧② balanced & complex **19** ⑧⑦ has fine tannin & oak, 30 months, 50% new, long savoury finish that augurs well for good few years.

Pinotage ⓠ ★★★★ Less of previous spice-dusted maraschino cherry, **18** ⑧③ more savoury black olive & green walnut, good dry finish. 50% new oak still melding, give it time. **Shiraz** ⓠ ★★★★ Remains big & bold, at 15% alc, but **17** ⑧③ dials back new oak from 100% to zero, loses gram sugar. Tannins firm but offset by fresh plum fruit. Robertson WO.

Habata range

★★★★ **White Muscadel** ⓠ Balanced & moreish fortified **20** ⑧⑧ opens with classic grapey appeal & intensity, white flower, wax, marmalade & barley sweet complexities, clean, fiery finish. 500 ml.

Cabernet Sauvignon-Merlot ⓠ ★★★ Vibrant & fresh **20** ⑧② is fruit forward, offers succulent flavours of plum, cassis & dark chocolate (though unoaked), concludes with cranberry crunch. **Chardonnay Unwooded** ⓠ ★★★★ Easygoing **21** ⑧⑤ shows apple-dominated orchard fruit over spice & a creamy body courtesy 4 months lees ageing. **Sauvignon Blanc Tropical** ⓥ ★★★★ Pineapple, melon & granadilla abound on smooth **21** ⑧④, a fresh tropical fruit salad in a glass. — WB

Location/map: Robertson ▪ Map grid reference: B7 ▪ WO: Le Chasseur/Robertson ▪ Est 1881 ▪ 1stB 1999 ▪ Tasting by appt ▪ Closed all pub hols ▪ Owner(s) Hannes Joubert (Habata Boerdery) ▪ Cellarmaster(s)/wine-maker(s) Carel Botha (Jan 2011) ▪ Viticulturist(s) Jan Rabie (Sep 2015) ▪ ±1,300ha/220ha (cab, merlot, ptage, ruby cab, shiraz, chard, chenin, cbard, muscadel w, nouvelle, sauv) ▪ ±4,500t ▪ IPW ▪ PO Box 439 Robertson 6705 ▪ cellar@lgc.co.za ▪ www.habata.co.za ▪ **T +27 (0)23-626-1048**

Le Grand Domaine   ⓥ ⑪

Bernard Fontannaz, also founder-owner of Origin Wine, in this high-end venture focuses on creating 'tra-ditionalist and serious' wines in the Grand Vin range, and 'adventurist, always boundary-pushing' bottlings under The Pledge label. Debbie Thompson helms the wine team at the cellar in Devon Valley, where 15 ha of premium vines have been identified and added to the vineholding. A trial bushvine chenin proved successful enough to join the line-up, alongside a new 'sustainable' pair, Our Planet, certified organic and Fairtrade.

Grand Vin de Stellenbosch

★★★★☆ **Cabernet Sauvignon** ⓥ Inky graphite & cocoa powder complement the ripe hedgerow fruits on **20** ⑨④, velvet mouthfeel adds to stature & elegance of coherent, nuanced palate.

★★★★ **Cabernet Sauvignon-Merlot** ⓥ Barrel selection **20** ★★★★★ ⑨① improves on **19** ⑧⑨ in poise & dimension. Xmas pudding, spice & dark fruit on an oak platform, elegant & cohesive. Also in 1.5L.

★★★★☆ **Sauvignon Blanc** Vibrant & taut **22** ★★★★ ⑧⑧ shows bold grapefruit zest & flint typicity. Like **21** ⑨⓪, has good mouthfeel & density from extended lees contact & stirring.

★★★★☆ **Méthode Cap Classique Brut** Energetic, steady bubble on **21** ⑨⓪ pinot noir & chardonnay sparkler. Crisp lime entry, then broad, creamy mid-palate that unfurls to gentle toasty farewell. Balance of vivid acid, fruit & lees well judged.

Rosé ★★★★ Previewed **23** ⑧④ pink charmer from shiraz & clairette blanche. Fresh, lively & rounded, ample berry-toned summer appeal.

The Pledge range

★★★★☆ **Our Stellie Cabernet Sauvignon** ⊘ Rewarding **21** ⑨⓪ picks up where **20** ⑨⓪ left off in confidence, body & density. Cigarbox oak notes from year in older barrels matched by ripe, supple fruitcake & spice, harmonious & long.

★★★★ **Our Lekker Pinotage** ⊘ Aptly named **21** ⑧⑦ is lithe, rounded & juicy, offers friendly rasp-berry & youngberry flavour with everyday appeal. Less oak than last, just 12 months, all old. WO Coastal.

★★★★ **Our Planet Organic Red** ⓝⒺⓦ ⊘ ⓥ Liquorice & smoky blueberry on **21** ⑧⑧ blend of shiraz, mourvèdre & grenache noir. Ripe, sappy, with good backbone from complex gestation & 14 months in oak, 15% new. Fine concentration & body with dry finish. WO Swartland, as White.

★★★★ **Our Barrels Chardonnay** Amphora-aged portion joins 94% that had 13 months in new oak, creating more resolved & balanced **22** ⑧⑧ than oaky **21** ★★★★ ⑧⑤. Harmonious marriage of creamy oatmeal & orange flavours, fresh & lively yet with density & length.

★★★★ **Our Old Vine Chenin Blanc** ⓝⒺⓦ ⓦ Confident debut of **22** ⑧⑨ from 1983 bushvines. Broad, rich, yet also fresh & perky. Fruit salad flavour with added creamy note from year in 77% new oak. Well balanced, with prolonged finish.

★★★★☆ **Our Darling Sauvignon Blanc** Pungent capsicum & flint notes on **22** ★★★★ ⑧⑧ typical of cool origins. Lemon vivacity echoes that of **21** ⑨⓪ rather than tropical **20** ⑨①. Taut focused finish.

★★★★ **Our Origin Sauvignon Blanc** Three Coastal areas birthed bright, dry & lively **22** ⑧⑥, showing both tropical & nettle notes. Typical succulence but acid more rounded, less racy than **21** ⑧⑧. Time on (stirred) lees adds breadth.

★★★★ **Our Planet Organic White** ⓝⒺⓦ ⓥ Quince, nectarine & spice intrigue on **21** ⑧⑨ equal verdelho & roussanne, 12% chenin. Complex, broad & succulent, a toned body from non-Saccharomyces yeast ferment & part oaking in 300 & 500L barrels, some new.— FM

Location/map: Stellenbosch ▪ Map grid reference: D4 ▪ Map: Stellenbosch ▪ Map grid reference: F5 ▪ WO: Stellenbosch/Coastal/Swartland/Darling ▪ Est/1stB 2014 ▪ Tasting strictly by appt ▪ Sales Mon-Sat 10-5 ▪ Le Grand Domaine Enoteca wine bar & bistro, 9 Church Str Stellenbosch Tue-Sat 12-10 Sun 12-6 ▪ Owner(s)

Bernard Fontannaz ▪ Winemaker(s) Debbie Thompson, assisted by Juanita Lategan ▪ Viticulturist(s) Deon Joubert ▪ 40% red 50% white 10% rosé ▪ PO Box 7177 Stellenbosch 7599 ▪ feedme@granddomaine.co.za ▪ www.granddomaine.co.za ▪ **T +27 (0)66-398-6122**

☐ **Leipoldt 1880** *see* Wineways Marketing

Leipzig Winery

Winemaking on the Nuy home-farm near Worcester, ongoing since the 1890s and so successful, the British royalty requested the White Leipzig blend during their visit in the 1940s, was paused in 1963 after the opening of a large combine winery in the valley. About a decade ago, Francois and Lida Smit revived the brand, focusing on blends from selected winelands parcels and a sauvignon from their own small vineyard. With daughter Alida Bester and husband Vian as co-owners and managers, they're looking to add Rhône black varieties after releasing their first pinot gris sparkling and updating the visitor venue and experience.

★★★★ **Cabernet Sauvignon** ⊘ Leafier, fresher, more structured **19** (87) improves on **18** ★★★★ (85), both ex Stellenbosch & year older oak. Solid cassis fruit in firm but fine tannin framework.

★★★★☆ **Grand Master** Ⓩ Elegant Cape Bordeaux showing serious intent. **18** (90) cab (50%) & the 4 others from Stellenbosch & Malmesbury (as other Master), styled for decade's ageing, will reward patience.

★★★★ **Master Blend** More restrained Cape Blend in **19** (89), less pinotage, 21% each cab & merlot adding dry chalky tannins & brisk acid to plums & berries. Coiled, but should unwind & show its potential.

★★★★ **The Manor** ⊘ Tweaked **21** (89) blend unusually malbec-led (31%), 5 others, all giving full expression to vintage's dense fruit & savouriness, partly reined in by tannins & old oak though not achieving balance of **20** ★★★★★ (90), 15% alc glowing on exit. Fruit as for Heimat.

★★★★ **Heimat** Ⓩ Smooth, savoury & earthy Rhône blend, 70/23 shiraz & mourvèdre, dab viognier adds florals for truly delightful experience. **18** (87) ticks all the boxes, including easy 12.1% alc. Same fruit as Master plus bought-in Nuy.

★★★★ **Chenin Blanc** Rich oatmeal & baked apple pie in **21** (87) from Breedekloof. Ferment completed/9-12 months older oak for a creamy, succulent profile, ready to enjoy & few years in store.

★★★★ **White Leipzig** Same varieties but lead changes to chardonnay in sappy, aromatic **22** (88), 30% each chenin, viognier. Melded pear, peach & florals in creamy, lees-padded texture from part ferment & ageing in older oak. Fresher, better balanced. Stellenbosch, Durbanville & bought-in Nuy grapes.

Malbec (NEW) ★★★★ Stellenbosch vines give baked dark berries & very earthy, savoury notes in **20** (85). Supple but full, brooding, riper than 13.5% alc suggests, will show better with a meal. **Pinotage** Ⓩ ★★★★ Vibrant plum & blackberry underpinned by smooth tannins, good structure & varietal typicity in **20** (85). Robertson grapes, as Rosé. **Shiraz** ★★★ Riper berry aromas than last but tarter palate restrained by brisk acid & dry oak-stave tannins in **22** (81) from Malmesbury. **Pinotage Rosé** ★★★ Continues perfumed candyfloss & rosepetal styling, alluring salmon hue in **23** (82). Friendly, softly dry for carefree summer quaffing. **Sauvignon Blanc** ★★★ Less effusive in **23** (80) with earth & damp vegetation nuances. All Nuy fruit, plumper despite acid-retaining staggered harvest, for early drinking. Also in 1.5L, as Master Blend. Occasional release: **Viognier**. — MW

Location/map: Worcester ▪ Map grid reference: C3 ▪ WO: Western Cape/Stellenbosch/Robertson/Malmesbury/Breedekloof/Nuy ▪ Est/1stB 2013 ▪ Tasting, sales & cellar tours Tue–Fri 9-4 Sat 9-2 or by appt; pub hols (seasonal) please call ahead ▪ Closed Ash Wednesday, Easter Mon, Dec 25 & Jan 1 ▪ Cheese & charcuterie platters by appt, other meals as advertised ▪ Facilities for children ▪ Tour groups ▪ Conferences ▪ Weddings/functions ▪ Walks/hikes ▪ MTB trail ▪ Guided tours by appt: historic buildings & art ▪ Leipzig Country House ▪ Wine club ▪ Owner(s) Francois & Lida Smit, Vian & Alida Bester ▪ Winery manager Vian Bester ▪ Winemaker(s) Jacques Fourie & Wynand Pienaar (May 2018, consultants) ▪ 10ha/2ha (sauv) ▪ 30-40t own label 65% red 35% white ▪ PO Box 5104 Worcester 6849 ▪ winery@leipzig.co.za ▪ www.leipzig.co.za ▪ **T +27 (0)23-347-8422**

☐ **Lelie van Saron** *see* Natasha Williams Signature Wines

Le Lude Cap Classique

Exceptional sparkling wines that 'could turn the heads of the French' through their fresh, expressive and sophisticated styling were the inspiration for Nic and Ferda Barrow to establish their cap classique specialist house in Franschhoek. Key to achieving the aimed-for profile and quality are careful selection of vineyards that express specific terroir aspects, use of only the finest cuvées, and minimum 90 months maturation for the vintage wines to develop fullness of character. The Franschhoek brand home offers tastings with canapé and afternoon tea menus to enhance the experience. At on-site Orangerie restaurant, chef Nicolene Barrow crafts season-inspired dishes, and there's luxury accommodation on the estate, too, in Lily Pond guest villa.

★★★★★ **Agrafe** Cellarworthy **13** (96) bottle-fermented/aged under cork as opposed to usual crown cap, gives more harmonious, evolved wine. For fans of 'drier brut' (just 3.8 g/L sugar) with pleasing tension & minerality. Chardonnay & 36% pinot noir. Some Stellenbosch fruit, as Cuvées.

★★★★★ **Vintage Cuvée Magnum** Selection of best parcels in **13** (96), chardonnay with 36% pinot noir. Crisp acid well to fore, mineral & oystershell tone, nascent creaminess from extended lees contact will develop with ageing (longer than Cuvée).

★★★★☆ **Vintage Cuvée** Best parcels for assured **13** (94), same blend, very similar analysis to Agrafe. Most fruity of line-up, vivid freshness as expected with crown-cap ageing. Great energy & acid tension, creaminess to emerge with time.

★★★★☆ **Venus Brut Nature Millésime Magnum** (NEW) Exquisitely lean, lithe & focused, **14** (94)'s crackling acid amplifies its bracing zero-dosage dryness; both are a foil for the richness imparted by 96 months on the lees. Mostly chardonnay with pinot noir & meunier (27/2), 5% in old oak. Only in magnum.

★★★★☆ **Venus Brut Nature Millésime** New disgorgement of bone-dry **14** (93), now with 7 years on lees, similar well-managed balance of acid & sugar, pinpoint bubbles & enduring finish. Chardonnay, small fraction oaked, 27% pinot noir & drop meunier.

★★★★☆ **Brut Rosé Reservé** Pale antique rose **NV** (92) led by pinot noir (57%) with chardonnay, dab meunier. Savoury toned & neatly dry, faint hazelnut & charcuterie suggestions, satisfying richness & breadth from 40 months on lees.

★★★★☆ **Brut Reservé** Step-up **NV** (94) uses 36 months on lees to delicious effect, adding almond, brioche & lemon meringue pie, leading to long, salty finish. Well-integrated mousse. Chardonnay, small portion barrel fermented, 9% pinot noir.— CvZ

Location/map: Franschhoek ▪ Map grid reference: C1 ▪ WO: Western Cape ▪ Est 2009 ▪ 1stB 2012 ▪ Tasting, sales & cellar tours Mon-Sun & pub hols 10-5 ▪ Closed Dec 25/26 & Jan 1 ▪ Orangerie restaurant ▪ Lily Pond guest house ▪ Owner(s) Nic & Ferda Barrow ▪ Winemaker(s) Kalissa de Kok (Jul 2023) ▪ 6ha (pinot noir/meunier, chard) ▪ 120t/80,000 btls plus magnums own label 100% cap classique ▪ PO Box 578 Franschhoek 7690 ▪ info@lelude.co.za ▪ www.lelude.co.za ▪ **T +27 (0)21-876-3099/2961**

☐ **Lemahieu** *see* Eerste Hoop Wine Cellar

Le Manoir de Brendel

These are the own-label wines of the luxury Franschhoek hospitality venue owned by the Brendel family. Vinified by consultants from own and some brought-in grapes, all are ready to drink and some fully mature.

Le Manoir de Brendel Collection

Shiraz ★★★★ Full-ripe **22** (83) shows plum compote styling, savoury-spice dusted by 6 months on staves. Plush texture, nice grip at the end for food. Also in 1.5, 3, 6L. Last tasted was **05** ★★★ (81).

Brendel Collection

Cabernet Sauvignon ★★★ Rhubarb & prune notes, firm tannin for food pairing on **07** (81). **Merlot** ★★★ Tobacco, dried tomato & fruit-sweet edge to **NV** (78), was nearing drink-by date when last reviewed. **Pinotage** ★★★ Sweet fruit, spicy aromas & acetone whiffs on ready **NV** (78); handles 15% alc well. **Shiraz** ★★★ Engaging sweet-sour tang on meaty **NV** (78); soft textured, slips down easily. Discontinued: **Chardonnay, Chenin Blanc, Sauvignon Blanc, Sauvignon Blanc-Viognier**. — CR

Location/map/WO: Franschhoek ▪ Map grid reference: C3 ▪ Est/1stB 2003 ▪ Tasting daily 12-4; pub hols 10-3 (seasonal) please call ahead ▪ Fee R50pp, waived on purchase ▪ Sales daily 7.30-4 ▪ Open daily, closed when booked for weddings/conferences ▪ Facilities for children ▪ Gift shop ▪ Conferences: day package (60 pax)/overnight package incl 10 rooms & 2 private cottages ▪ Walks ▪ Weddings (up to 60 pax) with chapel ▪ 5-star guest house (10 suites) ▪ Owner(s) Christian & Maren Brendel ▪ 30ha/±23ha (cab, merlot, ptage, shiraz, chard, chenin, sauv, sem) ▪ ±150t ▪ PO Box 117 La Motte Franschhoek 7691 ▪ lmb@brendel.co.za ▪ www.le-manoir-de-brendel.com ▪ **T +27 (0)21-876-4525**

Lemberg Wine Estate   ⓠ ⑪ ⊖ ⌂ ◎ ⚐

Henk du Bruyn and Suzette Jansen van Rensburg continue to build on the legacy of estate founder Janey Muller, who in the 1980s pioneered Hungarian grape hárslevelü in SA and earned a reputation for boutique winecrafting. Under recent winemaker and co-viticulturist Anri Botha the premium wines retain their serious intent and styling, with a touch of informality in most being named for loved farm bulldogs. Visitors will find plenty to see, do and buy in this tranquil corner of Tulbagh, including a novel brandy from black grapes.

Premium range

★★★★ **Pinot Noir** Trim but succulent red fruit on subtle **22** (88). Gentle texture & lightly supportive frame from time in well-seasoned 500L oak will aid some cellaring.

★★★★☆ **Spencer** Cherry abounds on **18** ★★★★ (88) from pinotage with dab syrah. Herb & spice notes add interest to light body. New oak upped to 15% from 5% on **17** (92) but alc reduced to 13.4% from 14.5% for subtler power & density.

★★★★ **Nelson** Blue & black berries on light, lithe **18** (86) syrah, showing dried herb & savoury notes. Alc beneficially down from bold 15% to 13.2%, only 10% new oak, 15 months, for a perkier personality.

★★★★ **Louis** Syrah 51% leads **20** (88) blend with equal grenache & mourvèdre, dabs viognier & petite sirah. Rounded, succulent & lively with light tannin grip from 18 months in oak, 10% new. Cohesive & poised, like **19** ★★★★★ (90). WO Coastal.

★★★★☆ **Hárslevelü** (🍃) Unusual Hungarian white variety, Lemberg's calling card. **22** (93) remains individual with honeyed peach & spice liveliness. Like **21** ★★★★★ (95), natural ferment/6 months in older barrels. More delicate than powerful predecessor.

★★★★☆ **Lady** (✓) Retains 4-way hárslevelü blend with viognier, sauvignon & chenin in **22** (90). Wild ferment in 80% older oak, rest FlexCube, 6 months on lees. Vivacious chamomile, quince & stonefruit, light textural grip & body. Finishes clean & dry.

Ella (🍷) ★★★☆ Nine months in seasoned barrels respect **20** (84) grenache noir's cranberry & cherry fruit, adding gentle spice. Fleshy, rounded, has tannin definition for food pairing.

Lifestyle range

★★★★ **Cape Blend** (✓) Shiraz (42%) takes the lead from pinotage in **21** (86), with equal pinot noir & grenache. Bouncy & bright blueberry & raspberry with freshness & balance. Notch up on **20** ★★★ (82).

★★★★ **The House of Spencer Potstill Brandy** (🍷) Rather delicate & subtle 5-year potstill (87) has savoury notes as well as fruit. Unusual in coming from pinot noir & pinotage. Also drier than many; 38% alc part of the restrained elegance.

Pinotage (✓) ★★★★ Bright cranberry & plum vivacity in **21** (84). Touch of cedar & spice from 10 months in older oak. Ideal for everyday enjoyment. **Syrah** (✓) ★★★★ Peppery lift to savoury blue & black fruit on **21** (85) braai companion. Light, with soft grip courtesy 10 months seasoned casks. WO Coastal, as Pinotage. **Rosie's Blanc de Noir** ★★★ Pale blush on **23** (82) tank sample from syrah, pinot noir & grenache. Floral strawberry appeal to pleasant, lively quaffer, ideal for summer. **Chenin Blanc** (✓) ★★★★ Previewed **23** (84) yields vivid lemon & pear tang, the acid balanced by subtle lees width from 4 months contact post ferment. **Sauvignon Blanc** (✓) ★★★★ Typical flint nuance to elderflower & citrus zest on juicy **23** (83) pre-bottling sample. Light, with gentle breadth from time on lees. — FM, TJ

Location/map: Tulbagh ▪ Map grid reference: F5 ▪ WO: Tulbagh/Coastal ▪ Est 1978 ▪ Tasting, sales & cellar tours Mon-Fri 9-5 Sat 10-3.30 Sun 10-3; pub hols (seasonal) please call ahead ▪ Fee R50 ▪ Closed Dec 25 ▪ Cheese platters ▪ BYO picnic ▪ Table olives & olive oil; quince jelly ▪ Function venue (40 pax) ▪ 2 self-catering guest cottages (sleeps 4 & sleeps 2) ▪ Owner(s) Blowfish Investments 117 (Pty) Ltd ▪ Winemaker(s) Anri Botha ▪ Viticulturist(s) Lemberg team ▪ 21ha/9ha (grenache, ptage, pinot, shiraz, hárslevelü, sauv, viog) ▪ 70t/10,000cs own label 53% red 36% white 11% blanc de noir ▪ IPW ▪ PO Box 221 Tulbagh 6820 ▪ suzette@lemberg.co.za ▪ www.lemberg.co.za ▪ **T +27 (0)21-300-1130**

☐ **Lenie's Hof** *see* Axe Hill

Leopard's Leap Family Vineyards   ⓠ ⑪ ◎ ⑧

Hein and Hanneli Rupert-Koegelenberg's substantial portfolio celebrates the magic that can happen when wine meets food, in both the tiered ranges and the stylish Franschhoek brand-home, with its multiple culinary attractions and family-friendly amenities. 'Over-delivering on expectations and offering exceptional value for money, both from visitor experience and wine quality perspectives' is the longtime mantra, along with sponsorship of the Cape Leopard Trust, as part of the sustainability concern, specifically conservation.

Pardus range

★★★★☆ **Pardus** ⊘ 🐾 Restrained & elegant flagship celebrates the 'king of the mountains'. **21** ⑨④ repeats **20** ★★★★★ ⑨⑤'s near-equal blend of Stellenbosch & Darling merlot, cinsaut (35+ year old vines) & cab for pristine & delicious black & red fruit profile, supple tannin, supportive oak, 12–18 months, new & older. Will reward patience, decant in youth.

Culinaria Collection

★★★★ **Pinot Noir** ⊘ Cool-grown **21** ⑧⑧ bursts with fragrant strawberry & raspberry, subtle earthy spice, hint of smoke & lifted savoury finish. Light footed, its brightness undimmed by 14 months ageing in older oak. Elim vines.

★★★★☆ **Grand Vin** ⊘ Darling & Stellenbosch grapes for this Bordeaux blend, cab with the other 4. **21** ★★★★ ⑧⑧ has lean body (12.2% alc), offers vibrant red & black berries, wafts of cappuccino & smoke, supple tannin structure but not the gravitas of **20** ⑨⓪.

Pinot Noir-Chardonnay ★★★☆ Palest pink **23** ⑧⑤ dry rosé has 75% pinot & its mashed strawberry & cherry fruit, plus the other variety's crunchy apple & cleaning grapefruit bite. Fresh & breezy. **Brut Cap Classique** ★★★★ From chenin, **NV** ⑧⑤ is a riot of fresh apple & lemon on palate. Smooth, creamy mousse from 18 months on lees, squeeze of lime on dry finish. Not tasted: **Muscat**, **Chenin Blanc**.

Special Editions

★★★★ **Pinotage** ⊘ Mostly dryland Swartland vines impress in **22** ⑧⑨ with good structure, length & smooth drinkability. Luxe chocolate-dipped plums, balanced by spice from 14-16 months in 5% new oak.

★★★★ **Red Blend** ⊘ Merlot-led Cape Bordeaux **21** ⑧⑨ spent 16–18 months in 20% new barrels, shows serious intent. Cassis, dried tealeaves, roasted nuts & new leather notes in rounded, silky body with suave tannins. Majority Stellenbosch grapes. No **20**.

Family Collection

★★★★ **Heritage Blend** ⊘ Shiraz (85%), cinsault, grenache noir in richly perfumed **21** ⑧⑥ blend from Ceres & Paarl. Rounded mulberries, blackberries & cured meat spice from mostly old oak, all suffused with lavender. Delightful.

Classic range

....

Chenin Blanc ⊘ 🍷 ★★★★ Joyful glass of tropical fruit unobscured by oak, **23** ⑧③ beautifully balanced texture & lipsmacking freshness.

....

Cabernet Sauvignon ☺ ★★★ Amicable & oh-so-drinkable expression of cabernet. **21** ⑧② juicy black-currants & gentle tannins, subtle oak-stave ageing (as most of these reds) for spice & texture. **Pinotage** ☺ ★★★ Approachable & rounded, deep flavoured with plums & hints of latte & coriander, **21** ⑧② made for braais & burgers. **Shiraz** ☺ ★★★ Blackberries mingle with vanilla & savoury notes of spice & biltong in **22** ⑧②, deftly styled for flavourful early drinking. Excellent value too.

....

Merlot ★★★ Fun & fruity **22** ⑧② , fresh plums & juicy cherries, mild-mannered & easy. **Cabernet Sauvignon-Merlot** ★★★ Now in bottle, **20** ⑧⓪ as easy & appealing as last year's tank sample. Dark plum & cocoa, light body for relaxed drinking. **Chardonnay-Pinot Noir** ⊘ ★★★★ Just-dry, prettily pink **23** ⑧③ rosé sparks with freshness & cherry-strawberry flavour, piquant ruby grapefruit farewell. Will make a good sushi partner. **Unwooded Chardonnay** ★★★ Melon & fresh apricot flavours abound on lively **23** ⑧②, lees ageing adds to creamy mouthfeel. **Sauvignon Blanc** ★★★ Packed with gooseberry, crunchy apple & pineapple, **23** ⑧② ticks the ready drinkability box. Zippy & balanced for summer. **Chescato** ★★★ Vivacious, colour-splashed label for fragrant **23** ⑧① equal chenin & muscat with modest 10% alc. Smooth, semi-dry, perfect for Cape Malay fare. Chill well. **Sparkling Chardonnay-Pinot Noir** ★★★ Party-starting pink bubbles on upbeat **NV** ⑧② fizz, smooth & softly dry, with red fruit & apple flavours. Carbonated, as sibling. **Sparkling Cuvée Brut** ★★★ Gentle silky mousse on dry **NV** ⑧② from chenin & chardonnay, offering apple & citrus vibrancy for everyday enjoyment.

Lookout range

Cape Leopard Mountain Red ★★★ Unoaked **21** ⑦⑧ has gentle red berries & sprinkle sugar hitting the right notes. Mostly pinotage, shiraz, dabs cinsaut & cab. **Cape Leopard Mountain Rosé** ⊗ **★★★** Just-dry, light pink **22** ⑦⑨ from cinsaut offers undemanding candyfloss flavour & whiff of spice. **Cape Leopard Mountain White ★★★** Unoaked **23** ⑦⑨, mix of 90% chenin & chardonnay, animated lemon flavours & waft of pineapple. **Cape Leopard Mountain Semi-Sweet ★★★** Uncloyingly sweet **23** ⑦⑧ from mostly chenin & muscat, fragrant, fruity & trim (11% alc), for spicy food.

Natura range

De-Alcoholised Classic Red ★★★ Shy NV ⑦⑧ offers dark & red berries & soft spice in semi-sweet mix. Alc removed by spinning cone technology, as next. **De-Alcoholised Classic White ★★★** Demure, dry & perfumed **NV** ⑦⑧ from chenin & muscat has just 0.27% alc (as sibling). For a healthy lifestyle. — WB

Location/map: Franschhoek ▪ Map grid reference: C3 ▪ WO: Western Cape ▪ Est 2000 ▪ Sales Mon-Sun 9-5 ▪ Tasting Tue-Sun 9-4.30 ▪ Wine tasting R60/6 wines; private tasting R70/6 wines, booking essential ▪ Virtual wine tastings R60/60 minutes (not including wine or shipping cost) ▪ Closed Easter Fri/Mon & Dec 25 ▪ Rotisserie lunches Wed-Sun 11.30-4 ▪ South African Table as per schedule ▪ Family Table on request, booking essential ▪ Shop: lifestyle gifts, wine accessories, tableware, linen ware, kitchen utensils & equipment, food literature ▪ Child friendly ▪ Owner(s) Hein Koegelenberg & Hanneli Rupert-Koegelenberg ▪ Winemaker(s) Renier van Deventer (Nov 2014) ▪ PO Box 1 La Motte 7691 ▪ info@leopardsleap.co.za ▪ www.leopardsleap.co.za ▪ **T +27 (0)21-876-8002**

☐ **Leopard Spot** see Ayama Wines

Le Pommier Wines

As the name suggests, Johan and Melanie van Schalkwyk's Le Pommier was an apple farm, like many neighbours in Stellenbosch's Banhoek Valley. Now it's a lifestyle venue with many family amenities, plus an 'everyday range' made at nearby Zorgvliet 'that you can unwind with and easily pair with a good meal'.

★★★★ Angle Peur Cabernet Franc ⊘ French translation of 'Banghoek', the home appellation. **22** ⑧⑦ ample extract & weight but retains suppleness & drinkability, showcasing varietal minerality, earthiness & black fruit charm.

★★★★ Jonathan's Malbec Riper & sleeker than **21 ★★★★** ⑧⑤, **22** ⑧⑥ meaty black berry fruit, appealing tobacco overlay, gentle tannin grip. Year older barrels.

★★★★ Mac Cabernet Franc-Malbec ⊘ As previous, **22** ⑧⑥ is 68% cab franc, with steely, peppery blackcurrant fruit to the fore. Honest & forthright, muted oak spice adding appeal.

★★★★ Summercourt Chardonnay ⑧⑧ Lightly oaked **23** ⑧⑦ is refined & impressive, punches above its weight. Lithe, with textbook zesty citrus fruit, lime-mineral texture. Named for vineyard source.

Maraai Rosé ★★★ Light-bodied sauvignon with 2% cab franc for blush, **23** ⑧① is undemanding poolside refreshment. **Sauvignon Blanc ★★★** Appealing middleweight **23** ⑧② has grippy acidity with grassy & herbal aromas, lemon & gooseberry fruit. — GdB

Location/map: Stellenbosch ▪ Map grid reference: H4 ▪ WO: Banghoek ▪ Est/1stB 2003 ▪ Wine tasting Mon-Sun 11-5; pub hols (seasonal) please call ahead ▪ Facilities for children ▪ Picnics ▪ Le Pommier Restaurant Mon-Sat 8-11pm Sun 8-6 ▪ Country lodge & self-catering units ▪ Conferences & weddings ▪ Owner(s) Johan & Melanie van Schalkwyk ▪ Winemaker(s) Bernard le Roux (Zorgvliet) ▪ Viticulturist(s) Hannes Jansen van Vuuren ▪ 6.8ha (cab f, malbec, sauv) ▪ 6,500cs own label 45% red 55% white ▪ PO Box 1595 Stellenbosch 7599 ▪ gm@lepommier.co.za ▪ www.lepommier.co.za ▪ **T +27 (0)21-885-1269**

☐ **Lerato** see La RicMal

Le Riche Wines

The focus of this celebrated generational venture involving the Le Riche family is firmly on producing top-quality cabernet from Stellenbosch. To this end, cellarmaster Christo works with a multitude of vineyard sites and has built new open concrete vessels to enable separate ferments for each in the bespoke cellar on the Helderberg foothills. The team's prowess at expressing the district's terroir was affirmed by a Best in Show accolade for the Reserve '20 at a prestigious recent international competition. Christo is just as proud of his acceptance into the Cape Winemakers Guild, the organisation his father helped found in 1982.

★★★★★ **Cabernet Sauvignon Reserve** ⓐ 'Reserve' status kept for fruit & resultant wine of exceptional quality. **20** ★★★★★ ⑨③ opulent & generous with alluring cassis depth & length, enlivening acid, taut tannin frame. Mostly from older, lower-yield Helderberg vines with a single Simonsberg parcel, vinified separately, blended after year. Also in 1.5 & 3L. **19** ⑨⑥ was a knockout.

★★★★☆ **Cabernet Sauvignon** ⊘ ⓐ Same wards as Reserve plus Jonkershoek, masterly **21** ★★★★★ ⑨⑤ finer, leaner than **20** ⑨④, subtle hint of blackcurrant decadence, iodine & rockpool complexity. House's hallmark coiled intensity, shaped by 22 months in oak, 18% new, augurs well for cellaring.

★★★★★ **Vogelgezang Cabernet Sauvignon-Cinsaut** ⓃⒺⓌ Nod to ageability of cabernets of the late 60s & early 70s which typically included healthy portions cinsaut. **14** ⑨① drinking well, still fruit-filled, with undergrowth complexity, enlivening acid, commendable dryness & supple tannin frame.

★★★★★ **Richesse** ⊘ Cabernet with 13% each cinsaut & cab franc, ±9% each petit verdot & merlot in vibrant **21** ⑨⓪, fermented & aged separately in older oak 20 months, further 8 as blend. Bone-dry, as all reds, but more approachable tannins for a plusher feel.

★★★★☆ **Chardonnay** After taut **21** ⑨③, **22** ⑨② rich & satiny, perfumed with lemon & Seville orange, judiciously supported by ageing in mix ceramic pot & barrel, 25% new. Nicely dry.

Discontinued: **Mountain Cabernet Sauvignon, Ocean Cabernet Sauvignon, Steynsrust Cabernet Sauvignon.** — CvZ

Location/WO: Stellenbosch ▪ Map: Helderberg ▪ Map grid reference: B1 ▪ Est 1996 ▪ 1stB 1997 ▪ Tasting by appt Thu/Fri 9-12.30; sales Mon-Fri 9-4.30 ▪ Closed weekends & pub hols ▪ Wine club ▪ Owner(s) Le Riche Wines (Pty) Ltd ▪ Cellarmaster(s) Christo le Riche ▪ Winemaker(s) Christo le Riche (Jan 2010), with Mark Daniels (Sep 2000) ▪ 80t/10,000cs own label 90% red 10% white ▪ PO Box 5274 Helderberg 7135 ▪ wine@leriche.co.za ▪ www.leriche.co.za ▪ **T +27 (0)21-842-3472**

☐ **Les Coteaux** see Mont du Toit Kelder
☐ **Les Grandes Horizontales** see My Wyn

Less   ⓆⓎ

Seasoned Cape Town marketing communications practitioner Marlene Truter confounded conventional practice by launching a wine brand offering less - undesirable attributes, that is, like synthetic farm inputs and heavy bottles, and more that concerned winelovers want to see, like a new carbon-neutral cork from sugar cane. Now aiding her on the business development side is respected organic-wine maker Johan Delport.

Pinotage ⓆⒾ ★★★★ Generous **20** ⑧④ is big in most dimensions: burly 14.5% alc, firm acid tannins (the latter a common varietal character). To keep things evened out, there's plenty of sweet fruit too.

Chardonnay ★★★ Less variety-true than last, **22** ⑧① more asparagus on nose than citrus. Similar unshowy body, gentle acid-fruit-sugar interplay, pleasing weight from 6 months on lees in tank. — CvZ

Location: Hout Bay ▪ WO: Robertson ▪ Tasting by appt only ▪ Online shop ▪ Owner(s) Cape of Good Hope Wines ▪ Brand owner Marlene Truter ▪ Business development Johan Delport ▪ Winemaker(s) Fred Viljoen ▪ IPW, WIETA ▪ marlene@lessismorewine.com, johan@lessismorewine.com ▪ www.lessismorewine.com ▪ **T +27 (0)83-294-6060/+27 (0)83-233-1326**

Le Sueur Wines   ⓆⓎ

Emphasis the past year on marketing and brand building was rewarded with a good few listings, says Louis Le Sueur van der Riet, which hopefully will help boost volumes in coming years. Louis bottled his debut vintage ten years ago while making the wines of De Krans in Calitzdorp; he's now working from the Jakkalsvlei cellar near Herbertsdale, and crafting that farm's ranges alongside his own. Improving the image of Klein Karoo, and styling unique wines from forgotten vineyards or unsung parts of the region remain his focus. —

Le Sueur range

★★★★★ **Paradoks** ⊘ ⓐ Refined & balanced blend, equal pinot noir & old vine (1966) cinsaut from Calitzdorp & Langeberg-Garcia in **21** ⑨③. Brighter than last, cranberry, pomegranate flavours, clean forest floor note. Tannins more elegant, supple & dry from part ferment/year in old oak; 20% wholebunch cinsaut portion adds freshness. Unfiltered/unfined, as Kluisenaar.

★★★★☆ **Kluisenaar** ⊘ Graceful & lingering chenin from secluded 6-ha parcel on Meiringspoort mountain pass, hence name 'Hermit'. Slightly riper **22** ⑨② retains cool-climate freshness to balance gently spiced stonefruit & lees enrichment after natural ferment (as sibling) & ageing in large foudre.

Wild Card range

★★★★ **Sauvignon Blanc** ⊘ Grown on Outeniqua mountains 20km from the ocean, tank sample **23** ⑧⑥ sports bright tropical tones & some zesty acid. Lees ageing 5 months adds breadth. Fresher, more balanced & expressive than **22** ★★★★ ⑧④.

Queen of Hearts Merlot ★★★ Ample ripe spiced plum in previewed **22** ⑧②, though drier than last with distinct toasty nuance from oak staving during ferment. Tad unsettled, time should resolve. — MW

Location: Herbertsdale ▪ Map: Klein Karoo & Garden Route ▪ Map grid reference: C5 ▪ WO: Klein Karoo ▪ Est 1987 ▪ 1stB 2014 ▪ Tasting & sales at Jakkalsvlei, booking essential ▪ Owner(s)/winemaker(s) Louis van der Riet ▪ 15t/1,600cs own label 50% red 50% white ▪ PO Box 79 Herbertsdale 6505 ▪ louis@lesueurwines.co.za ▪ www.lesueurwines.co.za ▪ **T +27 (0)79-602-2161**

☐ **Letaba** see Rogge Cloof
☐ **L'Horizon** see L'Avenir Wine Estate
☐ **L'Huguenot Vineyards** see Val de Vie & Polo Club Wines

Libby's Pride Wines ⓠ

Entrepreneurial vintner Elizabeth 'Libby' Peterson, whose star sign is Leo, is focused on nurturing and developing her good-value 'pride', produced to her specs by a contracted winery.

Cabernet Sauvignon ⓠ ★★★ Unobtrusively oaked, so **19** ⑧② 's lively, fresh red & black fruit has the stage. Soft, honest & tasty. Enjoy soon. Darling WO. **Merlot** ⓠ ★★★ Only a quarter of **20** ⑦⑨ saw oak, because it's all about the fresh plum flavour, tannins are tailored accordingly. **Pinotage** ⓠ ★★★ Was 'A-Cutely Cheeky Pinotage' when we tasted **19** ⑧①, with oak influence dialled back to let the berries shine. Round & juicy, alc of 12.3% is reined in, too. **Shiraz** ⓠ ★★★ Fruit from Darling vines pops with red-berried brightness in **18** ⑧②, subtle spice on finish, cradled by year in old oak. **Sauvignon Blanc** ⓠ ★★★ In keeping with lighter styling, **20** ⑦⑨ restrained 12% alc, bright & bouncy. Not tasted: **Pinotage Rosé, Unwooded Chardonnay, Chenin Blanc, De-Cadently Sweet Wine, Sweet White, Sparkling Brut, Sweet Lullaby, Sweet Rosé.** — ML

Location: Riebeek-Kasteel ▪ WO: Swartland/Darling ▪ Visit by appt Mon to Fri only ▪ Owner(s) Elizabeth Petersen ▪ info@libbyspridewines.com ▪ www.libbyspridewines.com ▪ **T +27 (0)82-745-5550 / +27 (0)68-187-5298**

☐ **Liberator** see The Liberator

Lieben Wines ⓠ

Walker Bay-based Alwyn Liebenberg sources grapes widely for his terroir wines, including his beloved vintage-style 'port', made with minimal interference and bottled without fining or filtration.

Lieben Wines range

★★★★☆ **Pinot Noir** ⓠ Expressive **20** ⑨③ from Hemel-en-Aarde Valley fruit improves on **19** ★★★★ ⑧⑤ & previous with aroma & flavour array, delicious crispness & deft touch of oak, 20% new, 18 months.

★★★★☆ **Tannat** ⓠ Locally rare variety. **20** ⑨⓪ brooding, powerful (15% alc) but balanced, with solid fruit core & structure to age decade or more. Also in 1.5L.

Not tasted: **Chardonnay.** Discontinued: **Cabernet Franc, Chenin Blanc.**

Quinta do Sul range

★★★★☆ **Cape Vintage** ⓠ 'Port' 21 from Prince Albert tinta barocca, dense, sweet dark fruit & tobacco, reined in by firm peppery tannins & integrated spirit. Approachable, with potential.

Alpha Bravo Charlie range

★★★★ **Merlot** ⓠ Big, juicy **17** ⑧⑥ is dry but has Ribena-like sweet-fruitedness, contrasting dusty, tight tannins which will soften with time/decanting. 2 years old barrels.

Not tasted: **Chenin Blanc, Sauvignon Blanc.** — MW

Location: Hermanus ▪ WO: Stellenbosch/Western Cape/Prince Albert Valley ▪ 1stB 2012 ▪ Visits by appt ▪ Gin ▪ Owner(s) Alwyn & Beulah Liebenberg ▪ Cellarmaster(s)/winemaker(s) Alwyn Liebenberg (Jun 2005) ▪ 4 Petersen Str, Onrus 7201 ▪ alwyn@lieben.wine ▪ www.lieben.wine ▪ **T +27 (0)82-610-2279**

Lievland Vineyards ⓠ ⓘ ⓖ

'Even more vineyards' have been planted on Lievland, the historic estate on the Stellenbosch foot of Simonsberg Mountain rejuvenated since 2017 by Tyrrel Myburgh and José Conde of MAN Family Wines. High-end shiraz/syrah was co-pioneered here in the 1990s and, not coincidentally, it's the centrepiece of the refreshed and restyled line-up. There was much excitement at press time about welcoming visitors back to the tasting lounge in the gabled manor and a new restaurant in a farm building, both lovingly restored.

★★★★ **Cabernet Sauvignon** ⊘ ⓐ Bright, modern 21 ★★★★☆ ⑨⓪ has dabs syrah & petit verdot adding complexity & structure for ageing. Well-melded ripe chocolate-coated plums, tealeaves, meat spice, graphite minerality & firm but supple tannins. Stellenbosch vines mostly.

★★★★ **Bushvine Pinotage** Usual touch grenache noir brings an earthiness to juicy exuberance of 21 ⑧⑨ ex mature dryland vines in Agter Paarl. Lovely fresh plum, mulberry & savoury spice for pure drinking pleasure. 11 months oaked, 16 for red siblings. Drinking well, will reward some ageing.

★★★★☆ **Heart's Ease Syrah** ⓐ Flagship named for flower edging high-lying home-farm vines, 20 ⑨④ seamless, focused, dab mourvèdre again adds depth to meat-spiced dark plum & hedgerow fruit, all in harmony with supple oak, 11% new (15-16% for other reds). 20% wholebunch. Keep some for later.

★★★★ **Liefkoos Rosé** Provençal pale dryness on 23 ⑧⑨, intense yet lively & enduring red berry & cherry flavours, fresh lime finish. Handsome packaging for simply delicious pink from 51% syrah with mourvèdre & cinsault. WO Simonsberg-Stellenbosch.

★★★★☆ **Old Vine Chenin Blanc** ⓐ ⓦ Dry-farmed Paarl vines 38-45 years old, 22 ⑨④ intended to showcase variety's ageability. Extraordinary intensity & balance of ripe orchard & tropical fruit, warm spice & texture from brief lees ageing in tank & 32% neutral oak, endless slices & creamy vanilla finish.

★★★★☆ **Sauvignon Blanc** Textbook tropical, citrus & green grass aromas carry to mouthfilling palate in crisp, moreish 23 ⑨⓪ ex Elgin. Roundness from lees ageing balances freshness & zing in limy farewell.

Discontinued: **Cinsault Méthode Cap Classique.** — WB

Location/map: Stellenbosch ▪ Map grid reference: F1 ▪ WO: Paarl/Simonsberg-Stellenbosch/Coastal/Elgin ▪ Lievland tasting room: Mon-Sun 9-4 ▪ Lievland Café Wed-Sun 8-4 (open daily from Dec 2023) ▪ Closed Dec 25 & Jan 1 ▪ Owner(s) MAN Vintners (Pty) Ltd ▪ Winemaker(s) Riaan Möller, with Mahalia Kotjane ▪ Viticulturist(s) Theunis Bell ▪ 15,000cs own label ▪ PO Box 37 Klapmuts 7625 ▪ info@lievland.co.za ▪ www.lievland.co.za ▪ **T +27 (0)21-875-3079**

☐ **Life Grand Café** *see* Bé a Daisy
☐ **Lighthearted Low Alcohol** *see* Perdeberg Wines
☐ **Lighthouse Collection** *see* Benguela Cove Lagoon Wine Estate
☐ **Like Father Like Son** *see* Bon Courage Estate
☐ **Lime Road** *see* Havana Hills
☐ **Limestone Rocks** *see* Springfontein Wine Estate
☐ **Limietberg Site Exclusive** *see* Doolhof Wine Estate
☐ **Limitados** *see* Baleia Wines
☐ **Lindenhof** *see* Boland Cellar

Lingen ⓠ

A 2021 mountain fire is the reason for not having a vintage to taste of this delicious red blend, from a small block in Jonkershoek Valley owned by the Krige family. It's next to Stark-Condé Wines, and their team do the crafting, yet a different soil type, primarily vilafontes, gives the wine a distinct flavour profile and structure.

Location: Stellenbosch ▪ Est 2003 ▪ 1stB 2008 ▪ Tasting & sales at Stark-Condé Wines ▪ Owner(s) JD Krige Family Trust ▪ Cellarmaster(s) José Conde (2003) ▪ Winemaker(s) Rüdger van Wyk (2017) ▪ Viticulturist(s) Andrew Klinck ▪ 7ha/2ha (grenache, mourv, p verdot, shiraz) ▪ 14t/508cs own label 100% red ▪ PO Box 389 Stellenbosch 7599 ▪ info@stark-conde.co.za ▪ www.stark-conde.co.za ▪ **T +27 (0)21-861-7700**

☐ **Lion Hound** *see* Ridgeback
☐ **Lion's Drift** *see* Silkbush Mountain Vineyards

Lion's Kop by Château de Valcombe

Basile and Nicolas Ricome, 10th-generation owners of Château de Valcombe in the Rhône, have made wine in local cellars since the turn of the millennium. A merlot from vintage 2009 was the first under this proprietary branding, which references one of the peaks flanking Table Mountain. The wines below were made at L'Avenir in Stellenbosch and are marketed in France, as all before, and now also in Switzerland and Belgium.

Location: Stellenbosch ▪ Est/1stB 2009 ▪ Closed to public ▪ Order via email ▪ Owner(s) Ricome family ▪ Cellarmaster(s)/viticulturist(s) Dirk Coetzee (2011) ▪ Winemaker(s) Basile & Nicolas Ricome ▪ Bought-in grapes ▪ 5t/660cs own label 100% red ▪ Organic ▪ Château de Valcombe, 30510 Générac, France ▪ info@chateaudevalcombe.com ▪ www.chateaudevalcombe.com ▪ **T +33 4 66 01 32 20**

☐ **Lion's Pride** see Stellenrust
☐ **Lionsway** see Boland Cellar
☐ **Lisha Nelson Signature Wines** see Nelson Family Vineyards
☐ **Lithic Whisperer** see Andreas Wines

Litigo Wines

As hinted in the brand name, the law is the tad less romantic, perhaps, but vital underpin of trademark attorney Eben van Wyk's low-intervention, small-parcel crafting of pinot noir. He and Peter-Allan Finlayson of top-rated Burgundy specialist Crystallum are partners in an Overberg farm near Shaw's Mountain, and the wine featured here is the third single-site bottling from that pocket. It's also the 11th vintage release.

★★★★☆ **Pinot Noir** ⊛ Individual take on pinot noir, designed & structured to age. **22** ⑨④ follows **21** ⑨③ in partial wholebunch press, wild ferment, 11 months in barrel, 15% new. Great fruit in aromas & flavours, but no mistaking the ripe tannin seam. — CR

Location: Hermanus ▪ WO: Overberg ▪ Est 2011 ▪ 1stB 2012 ▪ Closed to public ▪ Owner(s) Eben van Wyk ▪ Winemaker(s) Eben van Wyk & Peter-Allan Finlayson (both 2011) ▪ 2t/200cs own label 100% red ▪ Postnet Suite 134 Private Bag X1005 Claremont 7735 ▪ info@litigowines.com ▪ www.litigowines.com ▪ **T +27 (0)82-803-4503**

☐ **Little J** see Myburgh Bros
☐ **Little Rock** see Mont Rochelle Hotel & Vineyard
☐ **Live-A-Little** see Stellar Winery

Liz Ogumbo Wines

Kenyan self-described 'multi-disciplinary creative entrepreneur' Liz Ogumbo added this wine brand to her palette five years ago. She's expanded her range, made by various cellars, and is looking at markets in Africa firstly, then 'the rest of the world one bottle at a time'. We hope to open the new bottles next time.

Location: Johannesburg ▪ Est/1stB 2018 ▪ Closed to public ▪ Owner(s) Liz Ogumbo ▪ Winemaker(s) various ▪ 70% red 30% white ▪ liz@lizogumbo.com ▪ www.lizogumbowines.com ▪ **T +27 (0)76-943-0396/+254 745694342**

☐ **Llyswen** see Walker Bay Estate

Lodestone Wines & Olives

The Lodestone wine, lifestyle and olive venture, on two fynbos-rich neighbour farms in the The Crags Valley near Plettenberg Bay, was recently acquired by a UK property investment company aiming to 'create one of the most pristine private wine estates in the valley'. A parcel of honeybush is making way for vines this summer, and while varieties were undecided at press time, 'new and exciting blends' were mooted. The visitor facilities remain temporarily closed but the new releases and oil can be shopped online.

★★★★ **Pinot Noir** ⊘ Origin-influenced 12% alc sleekness (as all), but pale-hued **22** ⑧⑦ doesn't lack fruit, piquant red berries, cherries. 10-month older-barrel ageing shows in the flavours, a savoury seam, supple tannins. Nice harmony, finesse.

Miss Lottie Rosé ★★★ Pinot noir with 15% chardonnay, **22** ⑧② previewed last time, now bottled. Pale blush, red berry scents, an intriguing baked apple savoury note, texture light & zesty-fresh. **Strandloper Sauvignon Blanc** ★★★★ Year later, **22** ⑧③ shows more gooseberry styling, variety-true whiffs of green grass, the palate freshness fitting the slender frame. Not tasted: **Stonechat Méthode Cap Classique Brut Rosé**. Occasional release: **The Jimdog**, **Chardonnay**, **Sauvignon Blanc-Semillon**. — CR

Location/WO: Plettenberg Bay ▪ Est 2012 ▪ 1stB 2014 ▪ Tasting room & restaurant currently closed ▪ Sales online ▪ Owner(s) UK property investment company ▪ Winemaker(s) Jaco van der Watt ▪ 4.3ha (pinot, chard, sauv, sem) ▪ 28t/3,000cs own label 15% red 35% white 15% rosé 35% MCC ▪ 9 Rondebosch Rd, The Craggs, Plettenberg Bay 6600 ▪ info@lodestonewines.com ▪ www.lodestonewines.co.za ▪ **T +27 (0)44-534-8015/+27 (0)84-404-0099**

Lokaia

With their third release, friends Craig McNaught (Stony Brook) and Clayton Reabow (Môreson) believe the fine-tuning of the wines is bearing fruit. Their aim is to capture the purity and freshness of Franschhoek's signature grapes, semillon, chardonnay and cabernet franc, with early picking for lower alcohol and no oak. Named for Ole Lukøje, giver of dreams of Scandinavian folklore, the small batches may be atypical ('don't think you'll be drinking regular wines') but they have captured winelovers worldwide, with 90% exported.

★★★★ **Call Of The Void** From cab franc, picked at different sugars. Perhaps more Loire than Bordeaux, but 22 ★★★★★ ⑨② is its own style. Perfumed sweet fruit - redcurrant with curry leaf spicing - & crystalline tannins create proper ripeness at low 10% alc. Mouthwatering & bone-dry. Wholeberry ferment & malo in amphora; 4 months on skins under olive oil layer. **21** untasted; **20** ⑧⑧ also had modest alc (11.5%).

★★★★☆ **The Sandman** From chardonnay, 22 ⑨⓪ focused on texture & purity, as all the wines. Delicate & suave, with cashmere tannins to broaden & frame unshowy leesy, biscuity notes. Harmonious, dry & full of verve. 12.8% alc more mainstream, yet light & fresh-feeling. Wholebunch in amphora; 3 months on skins under oil. **21** untasted.

★★★★☆ **Pound Of Flesh** From Bo-Hoek, acclaimed semillon stronghold. 22 ⑨② lights up the senses: dense, textured & taut, structured for ageing & development of characteristic waxy, lemony features. Wholebunch ferment in amphora; 4 months on skins under oil. A revelation at 10.5% alc. **21** untasted.— AL

Location/WO: Franschhoek ▪ Est 2019 ▪ 1stB 2020 ▪ Closed to public ▪ Sales online ▪ Owner(s)/cellarmaster(s)/winemaker(s)/viticulturist(s) Clayton Reabow & Craig McNaught ▪ 2.5t/300cs own label 30% red 70% white ▪ PO Box 22 Franschhoek 7690 ▪ info@lokaia.com ▪ www.lokaia.com ▪ **T +27 (0)83-415-0856/+27 (0)84-510-1496**

Lomond

An invigorating freshness characterises these wines from the wind-blown southern tip of Africa, their home terrain lying on the slopes of Ben Lomond in the Cape Agulhas appellation and forming part of the biodiverse Walker Bay Fynbos Conservancy. The Lomond estate revels in this extreme maritime climate and, while white grapes sauvignon, semillon and viognier are central, many soil types have allowed black-skinned varieties to share the limelight from the first bottling almost 20 years ago. Care for the vines is in the hands of Nicole Peltzer and newcomer Koos Groenewald, working alongside incoming winemaker Henk Swart.

Seven Rows range

★★★★ **Ben Lomond Merlot** ⑫ From youngest merlot vines, cool provenance evident in leafy nuance to the fruit. **19** ⑧⑧ good concentration & firmly gripping tannins, sensitive older-oaking.

★★★★☆ **Ben Nevis Sauvignon Blanc** ⑭ Tangerine & nougat aromas on 22 ⑨④ give way to limy citrus edged with smoky, creamy oak, 11 months, none new. Broad palate enlivened by zesty acid, smoky finish completes very lovely, confident wine from premium fruit of Pincushion & Sugarbush blocks.

★★★★☆ **Semillon** ⑫ Only the best rows, then best barrels. **20** ⑨⓪ reined-in cool-terroir expression, with vibrant acid & pervasive grassy tone, old-oak regime supportive without detracting from the fruit.

★★★★☆ **Snowbush** ⑭ Wild hedgerow flavours of nettle & dandelion on 21 ⑨③ from mainly sauvignon with semillon, no dab viognier, part barrel-fermented. Palate opens out to steely citrus & creamy spice laced together with thrilling acid drive. Dynamic & focused. Tiny 150-200 cases of these.

In abeyance: **Viognier.**

Single Vineyard range

★★★★☆ **Cat's Tail Syrah** ⑭ From ferricrete soils, **20** ⑨④ shows earthy, smoky side of syrah, adding interesting dimensions to crunchy redcurrant & red cherry fruit. Excellent oak integration (18 months, 50% new, as Conebush) gives subtle clove & cinnamon notes before lengthy finish.

★★★★☆ **Conebush Syrah** Shy **20** (92) opens out to red & black plum fruit with sweet spice & touch of fynbos, but needs time to relax & fully assimilate rather charry oak. Firm tannins & crisp acid should aid good few years development.

★★★★★ **Pincushion Sauvignon Blanc** Classic flavours of lemon, grapefruit & Granny Smith apple, **22** (95) vibrates with life & intensity. 8 weeks on lees add some breadth & length, vibrant acid races through to perfumed finish. Notch up on **21** ★★★★☆ (93) in concentration & focus.

★★★★☆ **Sugarbush Sauvignon Blanc** Steely minerality a hallmark of **22** (92), restrained green aromas moving to rich blackcurrant & flint on palate. Chalky texture & smoky finish (though unoaked, as sibling) conclude excellent wine, only a shade less focused than sibling.

Not tasted: **Phantom Pinot Noir**.

Winery Exclusives range

★★★★ **Candelabra Cabernet Sauvignon** Round & opulent **18** (89) delivers pure cassis aromas & flavours, fruit sweetness extending the finish, coating cab's tannins for a smooth glide. No **17**.

★★★★☆ **Belladonna SMV** Delicious **19** (92) from 75% shiraz, dab mourvèdre, splash viognier. Bright plum & red cherry fruit, lots of spice & pepper, pliable tannins & hint smoked meat courtesy 25% new oak, 14 months. Highly attractive, full of dash & verve.

★★★★ **Méthode Cap Classique Brut Rosé** Palest pink sparkler from Lomond pinot noir, **20** (86) creamy despite just 14 months on lees, lively acid, more savoury than fruity, softly dry finish.

★★★★ **Méthode Cap Classique Blanc de Blancs** (NEW) From chardonnay, **19** (89)'s lively bubbles lift rich apple pie fruit, 41 months on lees add honey, nougat & waxy intensity. Fresh, zesty finish. Perfect partner for south coast seafood.

★★★★ **Méthode Cap Classique Brut** From equal pinot noir & chardonnay, latter ex Stellenbosch, **19** (86) ups lees time to 41 months, shows lemon curd, honey & red apple flavour, vibrant mousse & dry finish.

In abeyance: **Noble Late Harvest**.

Estate range

★★★★ **Syrah** Plenty of cool-grown character on **20** (89), mixes plum, cherry & pepper with leather, smoke & meat in harmonious mouthful. Velvet tannins & appetising acid round off a lipsmacking syrah.

★★★★ **Sauvignon Blanc** Green & lean **23** (87) shows classic notes of grapefruit & capsicum plus concluding hint of litchi perfume. 8 weeks on lees round it out nicely, leaving sense of sapid freshness.

★★★★ **SSV** Usually reveals all charms after year/2 when semillon (with sauvignon, viognier) asserts its waxiness. Elegant **23** (88) preview follows pattern in restrained bouquet, yet already more weight & precision than last, hinting at good development.

Merlot ★★★☆ Red- & black-berried **21** (85) has fresh herbal tweaks overlaid with surprisingly charry notes from portion oaked 14 months. **Merlot Rosé** ★★★☆ Summer fruit delight **23** (84), strawberries, plums & cherries lifted by florals & pleasing dry grip at finish.

Rockpool range

★★★★ **Pinotage** From old dryland bushvines, light **18** (88) already integrated & beginning to overlay primary strawberry bouquet with tertiary forest floor aromas. Lovely dry finish & austere tannin grip.

★★★★ **Syrah-Mourvèdre** Riding wave of lighter reds, **21** (87) 50/50 combo picked early for higher acid, less plush fruit & lowish 12% alc, carbonic ferment ensures engaging fruitiness & tannin grip.

★★★★ **Chenin Blanc** Well-judged ripeness reflected in pre-bottled **22** (86)'s cool peach, pear & apricot tones, balanced by signature racy acid. Satisfying weight & length, time in barrel provides support not obvious flavour. Rung above **21** ★★★☆ (85).

★★★★ **Sauvignon Blanc-Semillon Co-Ferment** (NEW) Intriguing winemaking using wholebunch/carbonic then 11 months old oak. **22** (88) packed full of interest: orange peel, ginger biscuit, smoke & cream. Decant to get full gamut of flavour. Cape Agulhas WO.

Chardonnay ★★★☆ Fermented/9 months in barrel, **20** (85) brings together variety's blue orange, ripe tangerine fruit & enlivening acidity with woody spice. WO Stellenbosch for these unless noted. In abeyance: **Mourvèdre**. — CM, CvZ

Location: Gansbaai ▪ Map: Southern Cape ▪ Map grid reference: C8 ▪ WO: Cape Agulhas/Stellenbosch/Western Cape ▪ Est 1999 ▪ 1stB 2005 ▪ Tasting & sales Mon-Sun 10-4 ▪ Food platters ▪ Craft beer ▪ Part of Walker Bay Conservancy ▪ Cellarmaster(s) Anné van Heerden (Nov 2023) ▪ Winemaker(s) Henk Swart (Nov

2023) ▪ Viticulturist(s) Nicole Peltzer & Koos Groenewald ▪ 1,100ha/100ha (merlot, mourv, shiraz, nouvelle, sauv, sem, viog) ▪ 700t 60% red 40% white ▪ WWF-SA Conservation Champion ▪ PO Box 1269 Gansbaai 7200 ▪ info@lomond.co.za ▪ www.lomond.co.za ▪ **T** +27 (0)28-388-0095/+27 (0)82-908-0099

☐ **Long Mountain** see Thor Vintners

Longridge Wine Estate
⊘ ⊗ ⌂ ◎ ⊗ ⊗

To produce 'world-class wines that are healthy and amazing to drink', the Dutch Van der Laan and South African Raats family owners of certified-organic Longridge avoid all commercial yeasts, enzymes, fining agents and filtration, and use minimal sulphur, while working with international advisers to keep improving their farming practices with a special focus on soil health. Not to score marketing points, but 'let the vintage and Helderberg terroir reveal themselves through the wines.' See also Jasper Raats and Konkelberg listings.

Ultra Premium range

★★★★☆ **Organic Misterie** ⊘ ⊛ Deep, dark & handsome **19** (94) from cosseted best block of merlot makes an emphatic statement: dense black plum fruit backed by spicy oak notes of cinnamon & star anise (French barrels, 24 months). Like last **17** ★★★★★ (95), firm tannins & solid fruit core point to future rewards for the patient. Price as serious as the wine.

★★★★☆ **Organic Maandans** ⊘ ⊛ ⊛ From old-vine pinotage planted 1972, **19** (94) balances succulent, dark plummy fruit with fresh acid & firm tannins, aided by expert oaking, 50% new. Everything, including 14.9% alc, in place to continue improving decade or more.

★★★★☆ **Organic Ekliptika** ⊘ Fine-tuned flagship Bordeaux red, **20** (92) cab franc led (66%), showing attractive herb & greenpepper lift to ripe blackcurrant & black cherry in muscular frame. 18 months older oak ensure well-managed tannins to give structure & potential to age.

★★★★☆ **Organic Clos du Ciel** ⊘ ⊛ High-density, dry-farmed plantings of 9 different chardonnay clones nearly 30 years old deliver layer upon layer of complexity in **19** ★★★★★ (93). Opulent stonefruit & citrus mingle with creamy oatmeal & intense coconut character, though oaking in seasoned cask only, 18 months. Unique, seamless mouthful from official single-vineyard. Follows sumptuous **19** ★★★★★ (93).

★★★★☆ **Organic Ou Steen** ⊘ ⊛ ⊛ Heritage block of 1981 chenin, 'chaperoned' rather than 'made' in its natural passage to stellar, rich, deep-flavoured wine. **21** (93) semi-dry, like last-tasted **19** (93), but bright acid freshens the cantaloupe ripeness & creaminess from sensitive oaking.

Premium range

★★★★ **Organic Cabernet Sauvignon** ⊘ A preview last edition, bottled **20** (89) brims with blackcurrant fruit. Shows a tobacco note & spice from 18 months in French oak, none new. A more typical profile than previous, which had a floral nuance & Russian oak component.

★★★★ **Organic Merlot** ⊘ Weightier than Cabernet, now-bottled **20** (87)'s firm structure enfolds good depth of black plum fruit, with plenty of clove & nutmeg spice in well-balanced wine.

★★★★ **Pinotage** Elegant **20** (89) a step up on last, offers ripe strawberry & cherry fruit with plenty of smoky, toasty oak (though just 20% new). Now bottled, shows potential to develop interestingly.

★★★★ **Organic Chardonnay** ⊘ Ample creamy & malty notes on **21** (86), which emulates the previous release in its baked apple & lemon rind flavours, crisp acid & good length. Year older oak.

★★★★ **Organic Chenin Blanc** ⊘ Ten months in seasoned oak impart a leesy undertone to delicious **22** (86), delivering tangy apple & tropical melon flavours on a firm acid backbone.

★★★★ **Edelgoud** ⊘ Ginger & honey, fynbos & umami, oak-matured **16** (88) Noble Late Harvest from riesling is a more savoury, less sweet & weighty botrytis dessert style, underscored by light 11.4% alc.

The Emily Cuvée Classique ★★★★ Rosé named for 19th-century humanitarian Emily Hobhouse now **NV** (83), last was **21** (85). Ripe raspberry top note in bone-dry blend of chardonnay & dab oaked pinot noir. For summer salads. WO W Cape.

Méthode Cap Classique range

★★★★ **Organic Brut Vintage Reserve** ⊘ ⊘ 100% verdelho since **16** (89), bone-dry (zero dosage, as all these) with zesty acid running through apple fruit & toffee notes from 60 months on lees. Richness & freshness just balanced at finish. New disgorgement tasted.

Brut Rosé ★★★★ Creative pairing of pinot noir & verdelho (77/23) works well in **NV** (85) sparkler, resulting in earthy red-fruit flavours. Acid still crisp after oak ferment & 36 months on lees. WO W Cape. **Organic Blanc de Blancs Brut** ⊘ **★★★★** 'White from white' but **NV** (85) sparkling not chardonnay but unusually all-verdelho. Steely-savoury, with light apple fruit, to which 36 months on lees add some breadth. — DS

Location: Stellenbosch ▪ Map: Helderberg ▪ Map grid reference: C1 ▪ WO: Stellenbosch/Western Cape ▪ Est 1841 ▪ 1stB 1992 ▪ Tasting & sales Mon-Tue 10-5 Wed-Sat 10-6 Sun 10-3.30 ▪ Tasting fee applicable ▪ Booking essential for groups of 8+ ▪ Closed Good Fri & Dec 25 ▪ Cellar tours by appt ▪ Longridge Restaurant T +27 (0)21-855-4082, restaurant@longridge.co.za ▪ Tour groups ▪ Gift shop ▪ Child friendly ▪ Manor House (prices on request) ▪ Wine club ▪ Owner(s) Van der Laan & Raats families ▪ Cellarmaster(s) Jasper Raats ▪ Winemaker(s) Jasper Raats & Lucilia Ramos (2022) ▪ Viticulturist(s) Jasper Raats & Huey Janse van Rensburg ▪ 38ha (cab, merlot, ptage, chard, chenin) ▪ 21st/30,000cs own label 45% red 50% white 5% MCC ▪ Suite 116 Private Bag X4 Die Boord 7613 ▪ info@longridge.co.za ▪ www.longridge.co.za ▪ **T +27 (0)21-855-2005**

☐ **Lookout** *see* Leopard's Leap Family Vineyards

☐ **Lord Jackal** *see* Jakkalsvlei Private Cellar

Lord's Wines ⓛ ⑪ ◎ ⓐ

Owner, co-winemaker and viticulturist Jacie Oosthuizen's love for cricket prompted the name of his small-batch venture in the mountains above McGregor town in Robertson district. Marketing has topped the to-do list the past year, resulting in a series of wine-and-food matches by professional chefs at the panoramic visitor locale and, more widely, 'incredible feedback' from wine-festival goers around the country. Worth noting when tasting/drinking the wines are the low sugars. 'We believe in a dry style for Lord's wines.'

Limited Releases

★★★★ Three Barrel Shiraz ⓖ Curvaceous **18** (86) shows rich plum, black pepper, smoke & dark chocolate after 3 years in new oak. Firm tannins need time to soften & meld. Decant in youth.

Lord's range

★★★★ Chardonnay ⓖ Light footed, with apple & pear flavours & a fresh, zippy finish in lightly oaked **21 ★★★★** (83), a contrast with last **18** (86), which was rich & fat.

★★★★ Cap Classique Brut ⓖ Classic bone-dry **NV** (86) from chardonnay & pinot noir (72/28), 12 months on the lees. Shows orchard fruit, pie crust & buttered toast, good balance & persistent mousse.

★★★★ Cap Classique Brut Vintage ⓖ Gorgeous gold **12** (88) from chardonnay & pinot noir (74/26) shows plenty of life & brioche-laced flavours. Delicate & elegant, with fine bubbles & long savoury ending.

Pinot Noir ⓖ **★★★★** Signature floral notes of this wine - specifically violets in **20** (85) - along with darker-shaded berry flavours than last. Robust, 19 months on oak masking fruit a tad in youth. **Shiraz ★★★★** Lovely to drink now, **19** (85) improves on last with smoky plums & blackberries in a juicy body, smooth dried herb farewell. **Pinot Noir Rosé** ⓖ **★★★★** Cheery blush hue on **21** (83), dry & balanced, vibrant strawberry & raspberry flavours & light dusting of spice. Chill well. **Chenin Blanc** ⓖ **★★★★** Vibrant tropical fruit, vanilla biscuit & poached quince attractions on **20** (84). Nimble, with concluding citrus zip. WO W Cape. **Sauvignon Blanc ★★★** Very light, with some tropical wafts & a citrus conclusion, **22** (82) misses some of the dimension of previous. **Cap Classique Brut Rosé** ⓖ **★★★★** Light pink-gold **NV** (84) is lively & bright, red fruit & crunchy apple flavours, fine mousse rounding off a satisfying sip. — WB

Location: McGregor ▪ Map: Robertson ▪ Map grid reference: D7 ▪ WO: McGregor/Western Cape ▪ Est 2005 ▪ 1stB 2006 ▪ Tasting & sales Mon-Sun 9-4; pub hols (seasonal) please call ahead ▪ Breakfast from 9-11 & light meals 11-3 ▪ Function & wedding venue ▪ Child friendly ▪ Owner(s) Jacie Oosthuizen ▪ Cellarmaster(s) Jacie Oosthuizen (2006) ▪ Winemaker(s) Jacie Oosthuizen (2006), with Samuel Lekay (2006) ▪ Viticulturist(s) Jacie Oosthuizen (Jan 2003) ▪ 33ha/13ha (pinot, shiraz, chard, sauv) ▪ 90t/13,200cs own label 50% red 45% white 5% rosé ▪ PO Box 165 McGregor 6708 ▪ marketing@lordswinery.com, info@lordswinery.com ▪ www.lordswinery.com ▪ **T +27 (0)23-625-1265**

☐ **L'Ormarins** *see* Anthonij Rupert Wyne

Louis 57 Wines

Route 57 is the tasting HQ, shop and restaurant of this brand, in Mossel Bay on the Garden Route, not far from the golf course where Louis Oosthuizen scored a record-breaking low score of 57. The golf connection explains some of the names of the wines, made by the Bormans at Boschkloof in Stellenbosch.

★★★★ Jasoma Conclusion Ⓥ Blends cab & merlot with a little cab franc & less malbec. **18** ⑧⑦ dark berries & herbal edge; flavourful & juicy, with smooth but form-giving tannins. **17** untasted.

Not tasted: **King Louis Merlot**, **Open Champion Syrah**, **Fifty Seven Red Blend**, **Nelmari Rosé**, **Signature Sauvignon Blanc**. — TJ

Location: Mossel Bay • Map: Klein Karoo & Garden Route • Map grid reference: C4 • WO: Western Cape • Est/1stB 2009 • Tasting & sales Mon–Fri 11–5 at 12 Marsh Str, Mossel Bay • Sales also via www.louis57online. co.za • Route 57 Market • Fifty Seven Cellar • Gift shop • Craft brandy & gin • Owner(s) Louis 57 Group (Pty) Ltd • Winemaker(s) Jacques & Reenen Borman (Boschkloof) • marco@louis57.co.za • www.louis57wines. com • **T +27 (0)72-189-4599**

☐ **Louisa** see Pulpit Rock Winery

Louisvale Wines

Cabernet and chardonnay have long been the focus at this welcoming company-owned estate in Devon Valley, and old blocks of both varieties are being replaced with new material under the watch of viticulturist-winemaker Simon Smith. With a remarkable 27 years on Louisvale, he still sees his role as 'making the wine in the vineyard first', then gently aiding the ferment so the grapes express their character and terroir.

Louisvale range

★★★★☆ Five Barrels Cabernet Sauvignon Ⓥ Premium label accorded all-new barrique treatment, **20 ★★★★** ⑧⑧ boldly styled around a firm core of tannin, yet to integrate & fully reveal the fragrant fruit. **19** ⑨⓪ tad more complex & long lived.

★★★★ Limited Cabernet Sauvignon Bold & dense **20** ⑧⑧ shows dark black fruit, cigar smoke & dried herbs. Well-structured, smooth, long savoury farewell. 10% new oak, 12–18 months, as standard Cab & Boris. Delicious now, worth keeping some. No **19**.

★★★★☆ Boris Ⓐ Always-impressive Cape Bordeaux, mostly cabernet & the 4 others. Bold & full but **20** ⑨⓪ already drinks well thanks to rounded body & tannin. Pleasing typicity in the blackberry, graphite & dried tealeaf notes, long savoury herb finish. Will keep many years.

★★★★ Chardonnay For everyday enjoyment, vivacious just-dry **22 ★★★★☆** ⑧③ offers lemon curd, crunchy apple & crushed hazelnut in a curvy body. Like tad more serious **21** ⑧⑥, 30% new oak, 10–12 months.

★★★★ Méthode Cap Classique Rosé Brut Delightful salmon pink **NV** ⑧⑧'s fine strings of bubbles deliver a medley of fresh red berries in a round, generous & spicy mouthful. Chardonnay & 48% pinot noir.

★★★★ Méthode Cap Classique Brut Fresh & bright **NV** ⑧⑧ from chardonnay showcases pristine apple & lime fruit. The mousse is refined & soft, the flavours never ending. 18 months on lees, as sibling.

Cabernet Sauvignon ★★★ As easy & affable as last, abundant fresh blackcurrant, chocolate & fynbos in **21** ⑧②. **Merlot ★★★★** Seductive Xmas cake, warm spice & mocha on older-oaked **21** ⑧③, laid-back & friendly for early enjoyment. **Dominique ★★★★** Seasoned wood only for this sibling Bordeaux blend of cab, merlot & cab franc. **21** ⑧⑤ smooth, juicy black plums, milk chocolate & savoury herbs. Ticks the drinkability boxes. **Chavant ★★★** Subtly oaked (just 4 months, all old) sibling chardonnay **23** ⑧② has sprinkle of sugar rounding out the tropical fruit salad & nougat flavours. **Unwooded Chardonnay** Ⓥ **★★★★** Showcases bright fruit salad & lemon flavours in **22** ⑧③. Fresh, with a citrus tang in the farewell. **Sauvignon Blanc ★★★★** Vibrant **23** ⑧③ mixes leaf, gooseberry, yellow plum & capsicum, adds a citrus squeeze on the dry conclusion.

Stone Road range

Cabernet Sauvignon ★★★ Chocolate-dipped plum & hint of mocha on **21** ⑦⑨ easy sipper. Older oak for these reds. **Merlot ★★★** Plum pudding, cinnamon & nutmeg on juicy **21** ⑦⑧, slips down easily. **Shiraz** Ⓥ **★★★** Succulent & bouncy **20** ⑧② oozes fresh dark fruit, with savoury pepper & satisfying rounded finish. **Sauvignon Blanc ★★★** Lean & grassy **23** ⑧⓪ offers light pineapple & pithy lemon flavours. Chill well. Not tasted: **Cinsault Rosé**. — WB

Location/map/WO: Stellenbosch ▪ Map grid reference: D4 ▪ Est/1stB 1989 ▪ Tasting & sales Mon-Sat 10-4 Sun/pub hols (seasonal) please call ahead ▪ Fee R70-R150 ▪ Restaurant Mon-Sat 9-4 Sun (refer to website) 12-3 ▪ Closed on selected pub hols ▪ Wedding/function venue (150 pax) ▪ Owner(s) Louisvale Wines (Pty) Ltd ▪ Directors Altmann Allers, Hendrik Kluever, Johann Kirsten & Zane Meyer ▪ Winemaker(s)/viticulturist(s) Simon Smith (Jul 1997) ▪ 22ha ▪ 160t/16,000cs own label 50% red 50% white ▪ PO Box 542 Stellenbosch 7599 ▪ winery@louisvale.com ▪ www.louisvale.com ▪ **T +27 (0)21-865-2422**

Lourens Family Wines

Owner-winemaker of this boutique label, Franco Lourens, strives to make honest wines with a sense of place, which also tell a story about the place and the farmer tending the vines. He sources from single vineyards and old vines across the winelands, and adopts a minimalist approach in the cellar, eschewing yeast, acid, enzymes, fining agents and new oak. The 2022 vintage was his second in the Paarl facility owned by friend Lukas van Loggerenberg, and 'it feels like I'm starting to find my feet in the new space'.

★★★★☆ **Lua Ilse Single Vineyard Grenache Noir** ⊛ Dryland bushvines for refined **22** ⑭, an almost ethereal presence yet not without intensity born of layers of flavour, strawberry & white pepper, rather than upfront fruit. Also in magnum, as all.

★★★★☆ **Howard John Red Blend** ⊛ Fynbos & earth, kiss of stemmy tannin on southern Rhône-style **22** ⑬ blend. Grenache noir (44%) with equal cinsault & syrah, all ex Swartland. Subtle red cherry & plum fruit, similar refreshing grape tannin lift as last. Adds 'Red Blend' to name.

★★★★☆ **Skuinskap Steen Single Vineyard Chenin Blanc** ⊛ Now with 'Single Vineyard' on label to reference 46 year old source, **22** ⑭ very tight & lean but, with a little time in glass or decanting adds white peach & khaki bush, soft-leaf herb appeal to thrilling mineral acidity.

★★★★☆ **Lindi Carien White Blend** ⊛ Creamy texture a foil for piercing acid, remarkably intricate mix of florals & herbs, this one of SA's most accomplished white blends. Chenin regains lead role from verdelho (52/27) in **22** ⑭, splashes colombard, skin-contact grenache blanc & palomino, all ex mostly Swartland & Piekenierskloof. Now includes 'White Blend' on label. — CvZ

Location: Paarl ▪ WO: Piekenierskloof/Swartland/Western Cape ▪ Est/1stB 2016 ▪ Closed to public ▪ Owner(s) Franco Lourens ▪ Winemaker(s) Franco Lourens (Jan 2016) ▪ ±30t/±3,500cs own label 45% red 55% white ▪ Private Bag X3036 Postnet Suite 182 Paarl 7620 ▪ info@lourensfamilywines.co.za ▪ www.lourensfamilywines.co.za

Lourensford Wine Estate   Ⓟ Ⓜ ⊚ ⅇ

Covering a remarkable 4,000 hectares, ranging almost all the way up Helderberg Mountain, businessman Christo Wiese's estate at Somerset West embraces a large fynbos conservatory, forests, orchards and, centrally for winelovers, 100 ha of cool-grown vineyard, which the wine and vine team of Hannes Nel, Timothy Witbooi and Piet Uys sustainably nurture and draw upon for a globally exported portfolio, with certifications that underscore compliance with best environmental, ethical and safety practice. Adding spice are tiny batches for collectors and geeks, including a trio raised in clay pots. Plus a panoply of visitor amenities, from night markets to themed tastings to padel courts, all with the immense natural beauty of the site at its core.

Chrysalis range

★★★★☆ **Red** ⊛ Stately flag-bearer Bordeaux blend, 69% cab with merlot & cab franc in **18** ⑬, elegantly poised between power & finesse. Finely wrought black fruit & noble earthy minerality, 19 months in 64% new oak adding structure for ageing & intricately detailed spice.

★★★★☆ **White** Big-boned, distinctively aromatic, with dusty nettle & faint menthol notes from 69% sauvignon, chardonnay, viognier & dash roussanne, **19** ⑨⑪ commands attention. 8 months on lees in complex oaking regime, including barrels with acacia heads.

Estate range

★★★★☆ **Limited Release Shiraz-Mourvèdre-Viognier** Lithe, supple **21** ⑨⑪ is 93% shiraz lent succulence & dimension by dabs mourvèdre & viognier. Plummy red fruit has convincing scrub & pepper notes, 18 months in 35% new oak add silky tannins, aiding drinkability. Improves on **20** ★★★★ ⑧⑨.

★★★★☆ **Limited Release Chardonnay** Classy, lemon-scented single-vineyard **22** ⑨⑫ shows impressive varietal focus, generous body, silky lees texture & lingering citrus finish. 85% barrel fermented, rest amphora, 11 months on lees, lending unintrusive polish.

★★★★☆ **Limited Release Viognier** ✓ ⓐ Certified single-vineyard fruit for plump, luscious **22** ★★★★★ (95), showing pinpoint varietal definition in honeysuckle-scented peach & pear fruit. Similar gestation to **21** (94), 81% wild yeast ferment in barrel, rest plastic 'egg', 11 months on lees in oak, 35% new, but less bold & assertive.

★★★★ **Brut Rosé** ✓ Delicate onion skin hue of **19** ★★★★☆ (91) cap classique shot through with gold, adds dab meunier to 52% pinot noir with chardonnay, giving more prominent red berry fruit than **18** (89). 39 months on lees, charming shortbread note ex 13% lightly oaked basewine. WO Cape Coast.

★★★★☆ **Brut** ✓ Classy cap classique from 82% chardonnay with pinot noir, **18** (90) had 51 months lees contact, small portion lightly oaked. Heady savoury aromas, fresh-baked bread on palate, with appealing lemon-lime fruit, smooth, gentle mousse.

★★★★☆ **Brut Zero Cuvée** Ultra-long 124-month lees contact on **11** (90) chardonnay with 13% pinot noir translates to impressive tertiary development, showing seashell minerality with brioche, vibrant acid, lemon-lime citrus & white nuts. Vigorous fine mousse & bone-dry lingering finish. Fraction lightly oaked.

Not tasted: **Kurkbos Viognier Late Bottled Vintage**.

Kleipot range

★★★★ **Petite Sirah** This collection fermented & aged in clay amphora ('kleipot'), the vessels sealed in **20** (87) for carbonic maceration, lending floral perfume to otherwise dense wine, with powerful meaty-savoury undertones yet to integrate. Single-vineyard, as sibling.

★★★★☆ **Chardonnay** ⓐ From the best site, **20** (94) shows real substance & distinction. Wild yeast ferment/8 months on lees deliver impressive depth, structure & texture. Notes of lemon & butter, aromatic spice, extended finish & better focus than **19** (90). Tiny quantities of these, premium priced.

Not tasted: **Roussanne**.

The Dome range

★★★★ **Merlot** ⓨ Ripeness shows through on succulent, juicy **19** (88), yet enough bright acid to balance. Powdery tannins, hint of spice from 18 months in barrel, 28% new. Follows excellent **18** (88).

★★★★ **Pinot Noir** ✓ Dainty rosepetal scent mingles with raspberry cordial in **22** (87) from Elgin. Light & fresh, silky tannins & hints of earth & truffle, harmonious 22% new oak, 11 months.

★★★★ **Shiraz** ⒩ Selection from single-vineyard after 18 months in seasoned barrels. **21** (86) light hued & supple, gentle tannins cosseting bright red-berry fruit with grenache noir-like redolence.

★★★★ **Cabernet Sauvignon-Merlot** ⓨ Lighter & leaner **19** ★★★★ (85) near-equal blend, showing juicy redcurrant & plum fruit, piquant spicing from 18 months in oak. **18** (87), with 87% cab, had more heft.

★★★★ **Rosé** Unusual pinot noir, mourvèdre, meunier pairing. **22** ★★★★ (84) light & restrained, missing fruit ripeness of **21** (86) which added chardonnay. WO Cape Coast.

★★★★☆ **Chardonnay** ✓ Satisfyingly plump, **22** (90) has silky lees texture, vibrant acid & sweetly ripe lemon & orange fruit with hint of spice from 60% portion in barrels & foudres, 8 months.

★★★★ **Chenin Blanc** Toned-down oaking in **22** (88) brings better balance & expression of generous peachy tropical fruit, hint of honeysuckle. 60% barrel ferment/8 months, rest tank give appealing lemon-lime perk on finish.

★★★★ **Sauvignon Blanc** Less aromatic, more fruit-driven & restrained in **22** (86), supple body buoyed with acid, 25% barrel-fermented portion contributes spice & lees texture.— GdB

Location: Somerset West ▪ Map: Helderberg ▪ Map grid reference: F4 ▪ WO: Stellenbosch/Cape Coast ▪ Est 1999 ▪ 1stB 2003 ▪ Tasting, sales & cellar tours daily 10-6 ▪ Fee R95-R150 ▪ Closed Dec 25 ▪ Restaurant ▪ Tour groups ▪ Market ▪ Coffee Roastery ▪ Function hall ▪ Conservation area ▪ Craft beer ▪ Padel ▪ MTB ▪ Fly fishing ▪ Ghenwa's Culinary Club ▪ Artjamming ▪ Wedgewood ▪ Art Curator ▪ Persian Carpets ▪ Vinfari ▪ Putt Putt ▪ Spa ▪ Sidecar Safaris ▪ Owner(s) Christo Wiese ▪ Winemaker(s) Hannes Nel (Nov 2002), with Timothy Witbooi (May 2005) ▪ Viticulturist(s) Piet Uys ▪ 4,000ha/100ha (cab, merlot, pinot, shiraz, chard, sauv, viog) ▪ 1,200t/240,000cs own label 40% red 58% white 2% rosé ▪ BRCGS, HACCP, WIETA, WWF-SA Conservation Champion ▪ PO Box 16 Somerset West 7129 ▪ info@lourensford.co.za ▪ www.lourensford.co.za ▪ **T +27 (0)21-847-2333**

Lovane Boutique Wine Estate & Guest House   Ⓨ ⌂ ⓞ

Hennie and Theresa Visser have spent time and treasure making their wine and hospitality estate, one of Stellenbosch's smallest, as energy independent as possible, inter alia to ensure the crafting of their aimed-for 'high-quality, elegant wines' is free from disruption. They invite local and international visitors to stop by, or stay over, for a memorable tasting experience in their underground cellar.

Theresa Blanc de Noir ★★ From cab, pale pink **23** ⑦⑥ shows red berry perfume & flavour, the touch of sugar making it easily drinkable. **Sauvignon Blanc** ★★★ Expressive, passionfruit & gooseberry, **23** ⑧② has fruity-fresh flavours, finishing long. Not tasted: **Cabernet Sauvignon**, **Cabernet Franc**, **Isikhati**, **Pinotage-Petit Verdot**, **Méthode Cap Classique**, **Cape Ruby**. Occasional release: **Malbec**, **Petit Verdot**, **Shiraz**. — CR

Location/map/WO: Stellenbosch ▪ Map grid reference: D6 ▪ Tasting, sales & cellar tours Mon-Sun 10-5 ▪ Tasting fee R50, waived on purchase ▪ Conferences ▪ 4-star guest house (16 rooms) ▪ Owner(s) Hennie & Theresa Visser ▪ Winemaker(s)/viticulturist(s) Hennie Visser ▪ 3.6ha/2.5ha (cabs s/f, p verdot) ▪ PO Box 91 Vlottenburg 7604 ▪ info@lovane.co.za ▪ www.lovane.co.za ▪ **T +27 (0)21-881-3827**

☐ **Love Story Collection** *see* Matthew Krone Wines

Lowerland

There are just 9 ha of certified-organic vines on Lowerland, the substantial Coetzee family agribusiness in the semi-arid Prieska ward of the Northern Cape. Animal pasture and grain make up most of the 12,000 ha but Bertie Coetzee's belief that quality grapes can also be produced here has been proved over many of the past 17 years. High rainfall in 2022 compromised quality, which unfortunately meant there were no wines to submit for this edition. When better seasons produce the right quality, some of the fruit is cool-trucked to the Cape, where it is vinified with minimal interference by top-ranked winemakers.

Lowerland range
★★★★ **Koedoe Cabernet Sauvignon** ⓥ Precociously drinkable, with its sweet & juicy blackberry flavours & ripe tannins, but **21** ⑧⑥ also has form & firmness associated with variety, sufficient to benefit from short ageing. Also-tasted **20** ⑧⑧ has darker fruit, also sweet, with juicy acid in its firmer frame. Concentration & balanced freshness suggest a longer future.

★★★★☆ **Tolbos Tannat** ⓥ Rich & viscous, with full, ripe berry flavours, **21** ⑨④ gains form from a mineral tang & variety's dense but well-managed tannins. For all its substance & structure, at 12.8% alc (vs 14.2% in **20** ⑨④) it is approachable & intriguing. Fermented, aged older oak.

★★★★☆ **Dag In Die Wingerd** ⓥ Was 'Herd Sire Reserve' when we tasted **21** ⑨②. Wholesome & richly flavoursome blend of equal cab & tannat with 29% petit verdot. Generous, ripe dark fruit offer plenty of substance, backed by appropriate tannins. Sound acid brings balance & degree of approachability. Wholebunch natural ferment; 10 months older oak. No **20**.

Not tasted: **Vaalkameel Colombard**, **Witgat Viognier**. Occasional release: **Méthode Cap Classique**.

#WO Prieska range
★★★★ **Die Verlore Bokooi** ⓥ Spicy, sweet-fruited **21** ⑧⑦ blend of merlot, petit verdot, shiraz, tannat & cab. Satisfyingly rich, with freshness & ripely firm grip to balance. Pleasurable in youth, & for a few years.

★★★★ **Die Wonderdraai** ⓥ Whiff wild herb, taste of peach & apricot & creaminess lifted by perky acid, **21** ⑧⑦ an interesting, tasty blend of colombard, chenin & viognier. Older oak, on lees 5 months.— AL

Location/WO: Prieska ▪ Map: Northern Cape, Free State & North West ▪ Map grid reference: C6 ▪ Est 2000 ▪ 1stB 2006 ▪ Tasting & cellar tours by appt ▪ Owner(s) Lowerland (Pty) Ltd ▪ Winemaker(s) Lukas van Loggerenberg (Van Loggerenberg Wines), Stephanie Wiid (Thistle & Weed) & Paul Gerber (Colmant) ▪ Viticulturist(s) Bertie Coetzee (May 2013) ▪ 12,000ha/9ha (cab, merlot, p verdot, shiraz, tannat, chard, chenin, cbard, viog) ▪ 90t/1,994cs own label 76% red 23% white 1% other ▪ Organic vyd (Ecocert) ▪ PO Box 292 Lowerland Prieska 8940 ▪ bertie@lowerland.co.za, alette@lowerland.co.za ▪ www.lowerland.co.za ▪ **T +27 (0)83-349-9559/+27 (0)82-854-9109**

Lozärn Wines

The Smuts family, owners of an extensive agribusiness that includes this boutique winery, are marking a century of farming in Robertson Valley with new wines and the introduction of tiers for the portfolio crafted by Salómé Buys-Vermeulen. The Heritage range houses 'bold and outspoken' wines honouring family members, including Granny Kay, whose beloved flock of ducks is recalled in the striking label art; Elemental, varietal wines speaking of 'terroir and winemaking styles'; and Lifestyle, 'everyday enjoyable and easy sippers'. A notable feature is locally rare variety carmenère, which stole Salóme's heart 'at first sip' back in 2012.

Heritage range

★★★★☆ **Carmenère** ⓐ SA's first commercial solo bottling in 2016. Accomplished **21** ⑨③ repeats distinctive capsicum flavour, maraschino cherry note, sour cherry acidity of last-tasted **19** ⑨④. Decently dry, commendably moderate 13% alc, pleasingly lithe finish.

★★★★ **Kay's Legacy** Ripe tannins give grip & shape to succulent red & black fruit of **20** ⑧⑧ cab franc blend with cab, merlot, carmenère & malbec (20/18/12/10). House's signature dryness, firm acid & clean leather nuance up appeal.

★★★★ **Sebastian Chardonnay** This wine a departure from producer's penchant for sterner acid & leaner body. **22** ⑧⑥ soft, courtesy full malo, plenty of creamy oak (9 months, 44% new) overlaying lemon & honeydew melon fruit.

Elemental range

★★★★ **Cabernet Sauvignon** ⓝⓔⓦ Year in oak, 10% new, for **21** ⑧⑥, adding light spicing to plums & cassis on nose & palate. Good fruit, well handled.

★★★★☆ **Cabernet Franc** Sense of lightness on **22** ★★★★ ⑧⑧, unlike denser, more 'worked' **19** ⑨④, the last tasted. Focused freshness & distinct stemmy lift, attractive blue & hedgerow fruit. Restrained oaking aids positive stylistic direction for drinkers looking for piquancy & refreshment.

★★★★ **Malbec** ⓝⓔⓦ Another Bordeaux grape seeking to tread more lightly: reined-in 13% alc, modest 10% new oak. **22** ⑧⑨ engaging red fruit with floral & wood spice nuances, juicy, with brisk acid.

Merlot ⓝⓔⓦ ★★★★ Pure plum whiffs of variety, gentle savoury charcuterie overlay & softer tannins than siblings. Piercing acid in **21** ⑧⑤ may be overdone for some, for others the perfect foil for richer foods.

Lifestyle range

★★★★ **Shiraz-Carmenère** ⓝⓔⓦ Acidity the point in **22** ⑧⑥ distinctive 67/33 combo, & 33% new oak which adds mocha sheen to slightly earthy, bright, ripe red fruit. Grippy, interesting food wine.

Shiraz ★★★★ These wines for earlier drinking but not trivial. Aromatic **22** ⑧⑤ only older oak to preserve white pepper & fynbos complexity, smidgen sugar to aid sippability. **Carmenère Rosé** ★★★★ Pale pink & dry **23** ⑧③, smooth, supple & flavoursome, with decent vinosity & creamy finish thanks to brief time on lees. **Sauvignon Blanc** ★★★ Ticks the boxes for uncomplicated enjoyment in **23** ⑧② , mixing mango & papaya tropicality with green grass & blackcurrant & leafiness. — CvZ

Location: Bonnievale ▪ Map/WO: Robertson ▪ Map grid reference: D3 ▪ Est/1stB 2017 ▪ Tasting, sales & cellar tours by appt ▪ Owner(s) Smuts Brothers Agri (Pty) Ltd (Directors Grant & Juan Ivan Smuts) ▪ Winemaker(s) Salóme Buys-Vermeulen (Jun 2017) ▪ 12ha under vine (1.9ha carmenère) ▪ 55t/5,000cs own label 80% red 15% white 5% rosé ▪ PO Box 6 Robertson 6707 ▪ winemaker@lozarn.co.za ▪ www.lozarn.co.za ▪ **T +27 (0)82-576-8093**

Lubanzi Wines

'Taste good, do good' is the ethos informing the export-orientated venture owned by the American Brain and Walker families, the brand name recalling a canine companion named Lubanzi on a long-ago hike along South Africa's Wild Coast. Tasting good (presumably, as we've not sampled it) is 'Orange Is', a new Swartland wine that spent 'seven blissful days' on the skins. Doing good is their support for Stellenbosch-based winelands charity Pebbles Project, along with other social and environmental entities and programmes. Doing well is the expansion of their global footprint, with Ireland and three other export markets recently added.

★★★★ **Chenin Blanc** Honeyed & rich **23** ⑧⑥ improves on **22** ★★★★ ⑧③ in complexity & interest, partly via bunch pressing & natural ferment. Ripe peach & pineapple with vivid acid to balance. Unoaked.

Rosé Bubbles ★★★★ Lively froth on coral pink **NV** ⑧④ from cinsaut. Refreshingly crisp & dry with cranberry & blueberry tang. Modest alc, also in 259-ml can & Fairtrade, as Chenin. Not tasted: **Red Blend**, **Rainboat Pet-Nat**. — FM

Location: Cape Town ▪ WO: Swartland ▪ Est 2016 ▪ 1stB 2017 ▪ Closed to public ▪ Owner(s) Charles Brain, Cathi & David Brain, Walker Brown ▪ Winemaker(s) Trizanne Barnard (Sep 2017, consultant) ▪ 13,000cs own label 40% red 40% white 20% rosé bubbles ▪ Certified: B Corporation, Climate Neutral, Fair for Life; 1% For The Planet member ▪ 17 Exeter Ave, Fish Hoek, Cape Town 7975 ▪ hello@lubanziwines.com ▪ www.lubanziwines.com ▪ **T +27 (0)21-100-4840**

☐ **Luca & Ingrid Bein** *see* Bein Wine Cellar

Luddite Wines
Ⓥ ◎ ♿

The Verburg family, viticulturist Penny, winemaker and CWG member Niels, and daughter Alice, now indentured in the cellar, built their little farm on the Van der Stel Pass, overlooking the town of Bot River, with little more than grit, determination and buckets of talent. Specialising in shiraz and chenin, and eschewing technology, as the brand name suggests, they have fashioned an enviable product identity that expresses its origins without modern interventions. The more recent Saboteur blends, sourced around the area and innovatively packaged, present a lighter-hearted variation on the themes of handcrafting and naturalness.

★★★★★ **Shiraz** ⓐ Outstanding poise & intensity in **19** ⑨③ from miserly 1.6 t/ha yield, underscored by deliciously ripe, generous yet complex berry flavours. Silky dry tannin structure, polished 2 years in mostly older barriques, adds elegant texture & finish. Like **18** ⑨④, also in 375 ml, 1.5L & 3L.

★★★★☆ **Saboteur Red** Delightful Rhône-style shiraz blend with grenache, mourvèdre & dab cab, **20** ⑨② has heady pepper & scrub spicing up dainty floral berry fruit. Light & whimsical, yet showing poise & focus, with lingering dry finish. Year in barrel, 18% new. WO Cape South Coast, as White.

★★★★☆ **Chenin Blanc** Richly textured & elegant, with tannin grip from 22 days skin contact, **22** ⑨① offers complex melange of ginger nut, dried stonefruit & honeyed beeswax, sleek minerality adds lift to lingering finish. Wild yeast fermented & old-barrel aged. Modest 12% alc.

★★★★☆ **Saboteur White** Proudly artisanal, characterful **22** ⑨⓪ cocks a snook at convention. Chenin (71%), viognier & sauvignon blend has earthy, yeasty charm, with rich baked apple & quince preserve notes, meaty skin-ferment tannins. Pop the quirky crown cap & enjoy, now & over next few years.— GdB

Location: Bot River ▪ Map: Walker Bay & Bot River ▪ Map grid reference: D2 ▪ WO: Bot River/Cape South Coast ▪ Est/1stB 2000 ▪ Tasting & sales Mon-Fri 9-3 Sat/Sun/pub hols by appt only ▪ Cellar tours by appt ▪ Closed Dec 25 & Jan 1 ▪ Farm produce ▪ Walks/hikes ▪ Conservation area ▪ Owner(s) Verburg family ▪ Cellarmaster(s) Niels Verburg (2000) ▪ Winemaker(s) Niels Verburg (2000), with cellar assistant Alice Verburg (Jan 2017) ▪ Viticulturist(s) Penny Verburg (2000) ▪ 17ha/8.5ha (cab, grenache, mourv, shiraz, chenin) ▪ 80t ▪ Own label 60% red 40% white + 1,000cs for clients ▪ PO Box 656 Bot River 7185 ▪ info@luddite.co.za, niels@luddite.co.za ▪ www.luddite.co.za ▪ **T +27 (0)83-444-3537 (Niels Verburg)/+27 (0)72-055-8660 (Office Mon-Fri 9-2)**

Lutzville Vineyards
Ⓥ ⑪ ◎ ♿

With a winemaking heritage first noted in the late 1700s by French explorer François Le Vaillant - whose name lives on in the flagship range - company-owned Lutzville Vineyards is one of South Africa's largest wineries, crushing around 48,000 tons and bottling 400,000 cases for its own labels, 95% exported to more than a dozen markets. Its 2,100 ha of vines are planted on West Coast land 7 - 35 km from the cold Atlantic shore, enjoying an average temperature comparable with Durbanville's. Two viticulturists oversee fruit supply to a pair of lead winemakers, their work coordinated by one of still relatively few female cellarmasters.

Francois le Vaillant range

★★★★ **Pinotage** Approachably soft **20** ⑧⑥ barrel sample shows typical raspberries & cherries in light nutty frame, tangy & fresh. French (85%) & American oak, half new, same as for **19** ⑧⑧, previewed last year, now bottled & still in fine form.

Occasional release: **Noble Late Harvest**, **Cape Vintage**. In abeyance: **Cabernet Sauvignon**.

Diamond Collection

★★★★ **Cabernet Sauvignon** Leafy nuance to cassis on now-bottled **20** ⑧⑥, bright & accessible, round body & good length for drinking now & over next few years (as all these reds). Oak, half new, adds structure. Notch up on **19** ★★★★ ⑧④.

★★★★ **Shiraz** Pre-bottling, **21** ⑧⑦ maintains level of last **19** ⑧⑦. Plush, gentle, with spicy fynbos & black fruit. Oak, 50% new, portion American, 18-24 months, adds structure & polish.

★★★★ **Ebenaeser** Friendly Xmas cake flavours & succulence on **20** ⑧⑥ (variety/ies undisclosed). Dry grip from 18-24 months in seasoned French & 10% American oak. Good table companion.

★★★★ **Chardonnay** Ⓥ Naartjie & kumquat on gentle, textured **21** ⑧⑥. 8 months in oak, 30% new, lend a distinct vanilla & butterscotch breadth.

Sauvignon Blanc ★★★☆ Tank sample **23** (84) displays tropical granadilla & fig typicity plus taut acid lift. Night harvested, 8 months on lees. Reminiscent of **22** ★★★★ (86). Not tasted: **White Muscadel**. In abeyance: **Oaked Chenin Blanc**.

Lutzville range

Cabernet Sauvignon ★★★☆ Now bottled, **21** (84) perky & fresh, with ripe black fruit, inky depth & subtle tannin grip from year in combo staves & barrel. **Merlot** ★★★ Sampled before bottling, juicy yet structured **21** (82) shows bright mulberry & fruitcake notes, amenable light body. **Pinotage** ★★★ Combo French & American staves, 12 months, for work-in-progress **21** (82), displaying plush berries tinged with spice. Light & juicy, finishes dry. **Shiraz** ★★★ Pre-release, **21** (82) shows plum & black cherry sappiness. Fresh, light bodied with noticeable oak grip from 12-18 months in tank with staves, some American. **Shiraz Rosé** ★★★ Ex tank, **23** (81) offers vivacious & fresh cranberries & plums, is softly dry & easy for everyday enjoyment. **Chardonnay** ★★☆ Light-bodied **23** (79) is unoaked, delivers lively citrus & stonefruit flavours. **Chenin Blanc** ★★★ Gently expressive melon & pear on **23** (80). Juicy & fresh with subtle ripeness, finishes dry. **Sauvignon Blanc** ★★★ Unusual flint & celery combo on **23** (81). Crisp & succulent with granadilla vibrancy, light lees nuance adds breadth. **Sparkling Rosé** ★★☆ Hanepoot, chenin & dash ruby cab combine in **NV** (79) pink fizz. Signature jasmine with ample sweetness. Low alc (8-9%) for these sweet wines. **Natural Sweet Red** ★★☆ Pinotage leads latest **NV** (78) blend with chenin & dab ruby cab. Herb edge to gently sweet plum & berry caramel flavours. **Natural Sweet Rosé** ★★☆ Floral notes show hanepoot dominance on sweetish, cherry pink **NV** (79), with chenin & dash ruby cab. Uncomplicated, perky & light. **Natural Sweet White** ★★☆ Grapey pear on **NV** (79) from hanepoot & chenin. Uncomplicated sweetness with fresh acid to balance & clean the finish. — FM

Location/WO: Lutzville ▪ Map: Olifants River ▪ Map grid reference: B3 ▪ Est 1961 ▪ 1stB 1980 ▪ Tasting & sales Mon-Fri 8-5 Sat/pub hols 9-2 ▪ Closed Sundays, Good Fri, Dec 25 & Jan 1 ▪ Cellar tours by appt only ▪ Coffee shop & restaurant Mon-Fri 8-5 Sat/pub hols 9-2 (kitchen closes 30min earlier) ▪ Function/conference venue ▪ Owner(s) Lutzville Wingerde Beperk ▪ Cellarmaster(s) Brenda Thiart (Nov 2011) ▪ Winemaker(s) Christo Basson (Feb 2019 - Sep 2023) & Andries Eygelaar (Jan 2014) ▪ Viticulturist(s) Gideon Engelbrecht (Sep 2009) & Hugo Lampbrechts (Sep 2012) ▪ 2,100ha (cab, merlot, ptage, pinot, ruby cab, shiraz, chard, chenin, cbard, nouvelle, sauv, sem, viog) ▪ ±48,000t/400,000cs own label 15% red 85% white ▪ BRC, Fairtrade, IPW, WIETA ▪ PO Box 50 Lutzville 8165 ▪ catherine@lutzvillevineyards.com ▪ www.lutzvillevineyards.com ▪ **T +27 (0)27-217-1516**

☐ **Lycaon Pictus** *see* Painted Wolf Wines

Lyngrove

Company owned, the Lyngrove property on Stellenbosch's False Bay coast is home to a luxury country house, small conference facility and some 80 ha of vines, the latter cared for by André van den Berg, his colleague Danie van Tonder in charge of the cellar crew. Their substantial, widely exported output is carefully tiered, and styled for varietal typicity along with elegance and soft textures.

Platinum range

★★★★☆ **Cabernet Sauvignon** Impressive debut for **20** (91), showing plenty of muscle, intricate mineral nuances, earthy core, refined cassis fruit. Full & assertive, will reward cellaring.

★★★★ **Pinotage** Muscular & bold, **20** ★★★★☆ (90) packed with spicy black berry fruit but well rounded, with smooth tannins, balanced acid & lengthy finish. Step up from last **18** (88).

★★★★☆ **Latitude** Pinotage, cab & shiraz Cape Blend continues to impress, **20** (92) offering even better concentration & refinement. Plush, ripe red fruit, solid tannin structure, extended finish. No **19**.

★★★★ **Old Bush Vine Chenin Blanc** Barrel-fermented offering from 3-ha 1980 Helderberg parcel, **20** (89) enticing stonefruit, tangerine & sweet spice flavours, (older) oak should integrate with time.

Reserve range

★★★★ **Shiraz-Pinotage** Supple & sleek, with bright bramble & cranberry fruit, **20** (86) is 61% shiraz, 14 months in oak, 5% American adding vanilla spice & aromatics. Handles 14.8% alc with aplomb.

★★★★ **Chardonnay** Pleasantly plump & ripe, **22** (87) reins back barrel ferment to 30%, allowing better fruit expression than last. Rich, leesy, with gentle waft of sweet spice rounding out buttery citrus.

Not tasted: **Cabernet Sauvignon**.

Lyngrove Collection

Merlot ★★★☆ Ripe & generous black fruit on **22** ⑧⑤, well concentrated, tannin & 14.8% alc more obvious than last vintage. **Pinotage ★★★★** Unoaked, allowing better fruit definition in **22** ⑧④. Sleek, easygoing despite 14.5% alc. Enjoyable braai companion. **Shiraz** ⓥ **★★★** Juicy, uncomplicated **20** ⑧② is light, supple & appealing, with hints of black cherries, vanilla oak spice. **Shiraz Rosé ★★★** Light & youthful, with appealing floral scent, **23** ⑧⓪ has poolside appeal, modest 12.5% alc. **Chenin Blanc ★★★☆** Reductive pear & guava fruit notes on young, fresh & crisp **23** ⑧④, well-judged acid, leesy texture. **Sauvignon Blanc ★★★★** Tartly crisp granadilla fruit & pungent herbal whiff, appealing salty tang on finish of **23** ⑧③.

Lyngrove range

★★★★ Pinot Noir Brut ⓥ Accomplished **NV** ⑧⑧ cap classique has toasted nuts & brioche on the nose, apple strudel & strawberry shortbread on the palate. Elegant yet satisfyingly rich, with delicate bead.

Sparkling Brut ⓥ **★★★★** Appealing dry **NV** ⑧③ carbonated chenin bubbly has green apple fruit, lively mousse. Perfect summer sundowner. WO W Cape. — GdB

Location: Stellenbosch ▪ Map: Helderberg ▪ Map grid reference: B1 ▪ WO: Stellenbosch/Western Cape ▪ Est/1stB 2000 ▪ Tasting & sales by appt only ▪ Guest house ▪ Conferences (12 pax) ▪ Wine club ▪ Owner(s) Lyngrove Wine Estate (Pty) Ltd ▪ Winemaker(s) Danie van Tonder (2015) ▪ Viticulturist(s) André van den Berg ▪ 76ha (cab, cinsaut, merlot, p verdot, ptage, shiraz, chard, chenin, sauv) ▪ 100,000cs own label 70% red 20% white 10% rosé ▪ WIETA ▪ Postnet Suite 052 Private Bag X5071 Stellenbosch 7600 ▪ info@lyngrove.co.za ▪ www.lyngrove.co.za ▪ T +27 (0)21-300-0487

Lynx Wines   ⓥ ⑪ ⌂

With newcomer Saul du Plessis at his side in the cellar, and Frans Tolla assisting in the vineyard of the German-owned Franschhoek estate, Pierre Louw is happy to be back to pre-Covid volumes on the reds, and working with recently acquired amphoras and large-format barrels to add 'new elements' across the board. He's harvested the first 'estate' chardonnay for a stillwine and a cap classique, and planting chenin while grafting over some existing vines for a broader palette of white varieties. A tweaked oaking regime aims for bigger, fuller-bodied red wines 'with the unique velvet-like Lynx Wines finish'.

Ultra Premium range

★★★★☆ The Spirit of Lynx ⓐ Cape Bordeaux showing power & precision in **19** ⑨⓪, dominated by cab & cab franc (73/25), dabs merlot, petit verdot. New oak, 18 months, adds savoury-char & Xmas spice to redcurrant & plum fruit. Fleshy richness lifted by tangy acid.

Reserve range

★★★★☆ The Cabernet Sauvignon Redolent of mocha from 18 months in new oak, **20 ★★★★** ⑧⑥ ripe-fruited, with blackcurrant & baking spice, & decently dry, offers good drinking & vibrant cherry acid but misses **19** ⑨⓪'s keen focus.

★★★★☆ The Cabernet Franc Expressive mix red & black berries, **20 ★★★★** ⑧⑧ tad broader at 14.8% alc than **19** ⑨⓪. Succulent tannins, woven with vanilla spice from 18 months in oak, 25% new, buoy juicy fruit compote.

★★★★ The Shiraz Hedonistic tones of cinnamon, allspice, dates & cocoa on well-realised **20** ⑧⑥. Tightrope balance between ripeness & pomegranate-toned acid creates engaging mouthfeel.

★★★★ The Viognier Six months in new oak overlays vanilla & cardamom on variety's stonefruit in **20** ⑧⑨, racy orange zest acid adds nervy edge & pleasing vitality given wine's age.

Occasional release: **The Chardonnay**.

Lynx range

★★★★ Cabernet Franc Great focus & typicity on **21** ⑧⑨, leafy perfume over succulent blackcurrant palate, oak, 12 months, 30% new, lending well-judged support.

★★★★ Pinot Noir ⓥ Just the right amount of flesh & tannins on **20** ⑧⑥. Gentle oak, 2nd fill, accompanies damsons & forest berries to good, bone-dry conclusion, raising the bar on **19 ★★★** ⑧②.

★★★★ The Tinto ⓥ Cornucopia of varieties, cab, shiraz, mourvèdre & 4 others deftly moulded in oak, some American, year, 10% new. **20** ⑧⑦ generously fruited yet tapers easily to dryness at finish.

Blanc de Noir (?) ★★★★ Gently basket-pressed merlot in **23** (84), wild strawberry & melon aromas before sweet core of berry fruit, balanced by well-judged acid for satisfying dry sip.

Cabernet Sauvignon ★★★★ Year in older oak lifts mix of red & black fruit. Tangy cranberry-toned acid winds through **20** (85), refreshing ripe berry core. **Grenache** ★★★★ Ripe fruit handles big 15% alc well in **20** (85), soaks up 25% new oak, 12 months, allowing mulberries & blueberries to shine. **Shiraz** ★★★★ Brooding plums & berries layered with peppery spice on **20** (85), robust tannins tailored by year in barrique, mostly French. Ripe yet nicely dry. **Passion** ★★★★ 4-way Bordeaux blend led by cab in **20** (85). Vibrant acid freshens dense red fruit, year in mixed-origin small-oak, 22% new, adds a muscular structure. **Revolution** ★★★★ Smart 75% cab & cab franc blend, **20** (85)'s medley of red & black plums & forest berries smoothed, spiced & shaped by year in 2nd-fill oak. **SMG** ★★★★ Wisps of cocoa & sumac spice on classic pairing shiraz (67%), near-equal mourvèdre & grenache noir. **21** (85) shot through with cedar from year in 33% oak, lifted by zesty acid. **Viognier** ★★★★ Nutty nuance on **21** (85) from 40% fermented in new oak complements variety's peach & apricot, palate cut with racy acid for refreshment appeal. Not tasted: **Rosé, Chardonnay.** Discontinued: **Emotion, Vision.** — ML

Location/map/WO: Franschhoek ▪ Map grid reference: C4 ▪ Est/1stB 2002 ▪ Tasting, sales & cellar tours Mon-Sun 10-5; pub hols (seasonal) please call ahead ▪ Tasting R50/5 wines (Lynx), R90/4 wines (premium) ▪ Guest house ▪ Bistro ▪ Owner(s) Brigitte & Manuel Konen ▪ Winemaker(s) Pierre Louw (Apr 2018), with Saul du Plessis (Dec 2022) ▪ Viticulturist(s) Pierre Louw (Apr 2020), Frans Tolla (Sep 2020), with Luca Orcelli (consultant) ▪ 26ha/13ha (cabs s/f, grenache, merlot, mourv, p verdot, pinot, shiraz, chard, viog) ▪ 130t/8,000cs own label 46% red 13% white 41% rosé ▪ IPW ▪ PO Box 566 Franschhoek 7690 ▪ winemaker@ lynxwines.co.za ▪ www.lynxwines.co.za ▪ **T +27 (0)21-867-0406**

☐ **Lyra** *see* Orange River Cellars
☐ **Maankloof** *see* Mountain River Wines

Maanschijn   (?)

Upbeat Team Maanschijn, Paul Hoogwerf and Doug Mylrea, work in, and welcome phone-ahead visitors 'with open arms' to a renovated 1913 stable on Stonefields Farm overlooked by Maanschynkop near Stanford. Where once Oom Samie dried his fynbos cuttings, they craft their Herbarium Collection, meant to tell a story, embrace vintage variation and express the cool-climate Walker Bay area through selective sourcing and blending of multiple varieties and pockets. For 2022, both low-intervention wines were tweaked based on learnings since debut 2020, with 'engaging, honest and district-specific wines' still the overarching goal.

Herbarium Collection

★★★★☆ **Cape Red** Violets & plums on entry, lovely fruit purity supported by subtle oaking, 10 months, old barrels (as White), powdery tannins & gentle acid. **22** (90) again mostly pinotage (42%) with syrah, mourvèdre, touch fuller at 13.5% alc.

★★★★☆ **Cape White** (?) Changing blend goes from strength to strength, **22** (94) retains sauvignon, chenin, semillon, swaps hanepoot for chardonnay; remains aromatic, lemon blossom, white peach, grapefruit, with vivid palate & stony acid.— ML

Location: Stanford ▪ Map: Walker Bay & Bot River ▪ Map grid reference: B5 ▪ WO: Walker Bay ▪ Est 2017 ▪ Tasting, sales & tours by appt ▪ Winemaker(s) Douglas Mylrea & Paul Hoogwerf ▪ info@maanschijn.co.za ▪ www.maanschijn.co.za ▪ **T +27 (0)72-859-1093**

Maastricht Estate   (?) (?) (?)

High on Durbanville's cool-climate Tygerberg Hills, with a 'beautiful' view of the cooling Atlantic, Maastricht is owned and run by the Louw family: viticulturist 'Wheaty' and winemaker son Thys, the next generation 'still a bit young but will hopefully follow'. They're adding more of area speciality sauvignon to the 90 ha of vines, all farmed dryland, for their 'handcrafted and authentic wines'. The tasting lounge in a converted barn is increasingly popular, and memorabilia, seasonal cheese platters and traditional bitterballen accompani- ments all reflect the 18th-century founders' origins in the Dutch city of Maastricht.

★★★★ **Cabernet Sauvignon** (?) Thanks to masterly oaking, 16 months, 30% new, & control of substantial 14.9% alc, **21** (86) steps up on **20** ★★★★ (83), variety's cassis notes, bright acid backbone & fine tannins to the fore.

★★★★ **Pinotage** ✓ No new oak on lively & juicy **22** (86), so mulberry & red plum fruit shines through to the end. Also, playful grape tannin tug on finish & super balance elevate it above simpler, everyday drinking **21** ★★★★ (85).

★★★★ **The Contour Block Sauvignon Blanc** Very dry **22** (88) has a smoky, biscuity overlay from 50% barrel ferment mingling with white asparagus on nose & palate. Less complex than **21** ★★★★★ (90), but impressive fine-spun texture.

Merlot ⊘ ★★★★ Savoury, with cardamom, clove & curry leaf spicing up the pretty plum fruit, **21** (85) unforced, energetic & engaging, very satisfying drinking. **Pinotage Rosé** ★★★★ There's honest & pure - unconfected - berry character on pale salmon **23** (83)'s nose & palate. Bone-dry & with pleasing vinosity thanks to 13.4% alc. **Sauvignon Blanc** ✓ ★★★★ Intense Cape gooseberry whiff on mostly cool- & green-toned **23** (85) - capsicum, blackcurrant, cut grass. Lively acid, little rasp of grapefruit pith neatly counter hallmark generous 14% alc. **Méthode Cap Classique Brut Rosé** ★★★★ Onion skin hue, subtle charcuterie waft the immediate appeal of **NV** (84) from grenache. While brut in style, there is plenty of raspberry jam sweetness mid-palate, too, but little length. WO Darling. Not tasted: **Pinot Noir**. Discontinued: **Chardonnay**. — CvZ

Location: Durbanville ▪ Map: Durbanville, Philadelphia & Darling ▪ Map grid reference: C7 ▪ WO: Cape Town/ Darling ▪ Est 1702 ▪ 1stB 2009 ▪ Tasting & sales Mon-Sat 10-5 Sun/pub hols 10-3; pub hols (seasonal) please call ahead ▪ Closed Good Fri, Dec 25/26 & Jan 1 ▪ Platters ▪ Tasting room available for small functions/events ▪ Wine club ▪ Owner(s) Johannes Beyers Louw ▪ Cellarmaster(s) Thys Louw jnr (Jan 2009) ▪ Viticulturist(s) Johannes Beyers Louw (1986) & Thys Louw jnr ▪ 90ha (cab, ptage, pinot, sauv) ▪ ±1,000t/5,000cs own label 30% red 70% white ▪ info@maastricht.co.za ▪ www.maastricht.co.za ▪ **T +27 (0)21-976-1996**

☐ **Maestro** *see* DeMorgenzon
☐ **Magnetic Fields** *see* The Drift Estate

Maison   ⓠ ⑾ ⊚

Seb Ackerstaff and Jessie Verdonschot are palpably delighted to have taken this Franschhoek boutique winery and destination under their wing, savouring the beauty of its 'rolling vines surrounding the home-stead, and fruit orchards leading down the lane to the award-winning Chefs Warehouse', and adding their own touches aimed mostly at making the amenities more comfortable, appealing and outage free. They're particularly enthused by the current wine style and Antwan Bondesio's natural, handcrafted approach.

★★★★ **Malbec** Baton passes to young 2017 vineyard in **20** (86), touch lighter than last but delivers ample, satisfying mulberries & plums, takes 33% new oak in its stride & adds a gentle tug of tannin.

★★★★ **Shiraz** ⊛ 21-day skin contact extracts spice & freshening grape tannin in **19** (88), 15 months in oak, 35% new, hone expressive red fruit, dab viognier adds floral scent. Sophisticated step up on last.

★★★★ **Blanc de Noir** Watermelon & strawberry dusted with black pepper in **22** (86) from shiraz, shows finely tuned acid & dryness. Bunch pressed to old barrels for ferment & ageing brief 4 months. 21 untasted.

★★★★☆ **Chardonnay** ⊘ Fruit intensity & seamless bonding of tangy citrus & creamy oak impress in deeply layered **19** (93), showing exceptional balance. Fermented with 3 yeasts, 1 wild, 8 months in barriques, 30% new.

★★★★ **Single Vineyard Chenin Blanc** Vivacious & lifted **21** (89) showcases vivid citrus, lemon & tangy grapefruit. Regular lees stirring in tank gives just the right amount of body. From registered single block.

★★★★☆ **Single Vineyard Chenin Blanc Reserve** ⊛ Oaked version, **21** (92) bright grapefruit scent & flavours, creamy texture from 8 months on lees in barrel, 33% new. Broader & more savoury than last. Just 286 cases.

★★★★ **Viognier** Supreme balance raises **22** (89) above last-tasted **20** (87). Barrel ferment/6 months ageing subtly supports peaches & white florals.

★★★★☆ **Méthode Cap Classique** ⊛ Toasty & nutty nuances to stonefruit from barrel ferment/6 months ageing of basewine & 75 months on lees in bottle. Bone-dry **16** (92) from chardonnay, the grape's lemony fruit balancing & brightening the finish of this ageworthy zero-dosage sparkler.

In abeyance: **Straw Wine**. — ML

Location/map/WO: Franschhoek ▪ Map grid reference: C3 ▪ Est 2005 ▪ 1stB 2008 ▪ Tasting & sales Mon-Sun/ pub hols 10-5 ▪ Chefs Warehouse @ Maison open Thu- Mon for lunch 12-2.30 dinner 6-8 Sun lunch only -

booking advised ▪ Whiskey tastings ▪ Owner(s) Seb Ackerstaff & Jessie Verdonschot ▪ Winemaker(s)/viticulturist(s) Antwan Bondesio ▪ 11ha/4.5ha (malbec, shiraz, chard, chenin, viog) ▪ 50% red 50% white ▪ PO Box 587 Franschhoek 7690 ▪ info@maisonestate.com ▪ www.maisonestate.com ▪ **T +27 (0)21-876-2116**

Maison de Teijger   ⓠ

Aided by wife Danél and children Matthew and Elda-Marie, anaesthetist and Cape Wine Master Charl van Teijlingen crafts small parcels in his suburban garage in De Tyger Street, Durbanville, based on a particular theme each vintage. It's very hands-on, from approaching sympathetic estates about sourcing grapes, to making and ageing the creations, to marketing them through friends, wineclubs and tasting groups.

Méthode Cap Classique range

★★★★ **Pinot Noir** ⓠ Pinkish gold blush, stronger red fruit aromas with lees interest on **16** ⑧⑥. Hint of oxidation, in part offset by bright bubble, balanced dry finish. Zero dosage, as both. Aged 40 months.

★★★★☆ **Chardonnay** ⓠ Displays citrus, lees & brioche notes associated with blanc de blancs in **17** ⑨⓪. The bead is fine & persistent, adds to overall freshness. Bone-dry yet unaggressive thanks to balanced acidity. 38 months on crown cap.

Discontinued: **Pinot Noir-Chardonnay**.

Chenin Blanc range

Chenin Blanc Wooded ⓠ ★★★★ Ex 1986 Paarl bushvines. Quiet peachy tones; **19** ⑧⑤ short on intensity expected from older vines; firm, balanced acid; oak, all older, 8 months, unobtrusive support.

Chardonnay range

Not tasted: **Chardonnay Wooded**.

Sauvignon Blanc range

Occasional release: **Sauvignon Blanc Wooded, Sauvignon Blanc Unwooded**. — TJ, AL

Location: Durbanville ▪ Map: Durbanville, Philadelphia & Darling ▪ Map grid reference: D7 ▪ WO: Durbanville/ Paarl ▪ Est/1stB 2004 ▪ Tasting by appt only ▪ Owner(s) Charl van Teijlingen ▪ Cellarmaster(s) Charl van Teijlingen (2004) ▪ Winemaker(s) Charl van Teijlingen, with Danél van Teijlingen (both 2004), Matthew & Elda-Marie van Teijlingen (2016) ▪ 5-9t/±300cs own label 80% red 20% white ▪ PO Box 2703 Durbanville 7551 ▪ charlvanteijlingen@gmail.com ▪ **T +27 (0)83-456-9410**

☐ **Makulu** see Imbuko Wines
☐ **Malan Family** see Simonsig Wine Estate

Malanot Wines   ⓠ ♿

Marius Malan, vintner, consultant winemaker and Cape Wine Master, lives by the sea in Pringle Bay, and gives by-appointment tastings there, and works with minimal interference in Stellenbosch facilities for wines that 'respect the purity of the fruit' and 'always deliver more than the price suggests'.

Family Reserve range

★★★★ **Triton Syrah** ⓠ Gentle but powerful **19** ★★★★★ ⑨⓪, pure purple fruit & spice backed by fine tannins from 15 months in French oak, 15% new. Lithe & long. Ratchets up quality from **18** ⑧⑨.

In abeyance: **Chardonnay**.

Malanot range

★★★★ **Cabernet Sauvignon** ⓠ Trademark savoury succulence with cassis & violet hints in **19** ★★★★★ ⑨⓪, good frame of oak, 28 months, 50% new, for Elgin fruit. Improves on **18** ⑧⑦ in concentration & depth. Will reward patience.

★★★★★ **Cyclops Malbec** ⓠ Exotic nuance to dark-fruited, cocoa-toned **19** ⑨② from Paarl, chalky grip of tannin synonymous with the grape but smooth & supple. Serious & structured after 28 months in large barrels, half new, intended for long ageing.

★★★★ **Chenin Blanc** ⓠ Crisp & fresh **19** ⑧⑧ shows textured palate from natural ferment in older barrel. Creamy vanilla & citrus intermingle, balanced by lively acid. WO Bot River.

★★★★ **Non Boisé Chenin Blanc** ⓠ Was 'Bush Pig', **21** ⑧⑨ from Bot River vines has quince & melon tropicality & verve on balanced palate. 6 month lees contact with weekly bâtonnage supplies breadth & length. Improves on Paarl-sourced **20** ★★★★ ⑧⑤, also unoaked.

Occasional release: **Cherry Blossom**. In abeyance: **Rosé**, **Sauvignon Blanc**, **Flower Pot**. — FM

Location: Stellenbosch ▪ WO: Stellenbosch/Elgin/Coastal ▪ Est/1stB 2006 ▪ Tasting by appt at Bistro 365, Pringle Bay ▪ Sales online ▪ Owner(s) Malanot Wine Projects cc ▪ Cellarmaster(s)/winemaker(s)/viticulturist(s) Marius Malan (Jan 2006) ▪ 500t/40,000cs own label 80% red 20% white + 2,000cs for clients ▪ marius@malanot.com ▪ www.malanot.com ▪ **T** +27 (0)72-124-7462

☐ **Malkopbaai** *see* Teubes Family Wines

Mama Afrika Wines

Owner and co-winemaker Mpelo Sikhwatha dedicates this young boutique brand to his home community of Zwelethemba in Breede River Valley, where a mountain peak resembling an elephant was referred to as Mama Afrika for the 'togetherness, passion and hope' it inspired. In just a few years, a single label has grown to four, exported chiefly to the UK plus two other markets, with plans for expansion into several African countries. Wines that 'embrace and embody quality, precision, longevity, consistency and intimacy, while taking care of the planet by being green' are crafted alongside winemaker-viticulturist Aldert Nieuwoudt.

Nebbiolo ⊕ ★★★★ Rare solo bottling. Perfumed **20** ⑧⑤ well crafted to cushion variety's strong tannins & cranberry piquancy. Very drinkable & different. Breede Valley fruit, older oaked.

Malbec ★★★★ Rounded, fresh **20** ⑧④, just 14 months in old oak to preserve appealing black plum flavour & aroma. Easy tannins & few grams sugar for smooth, uncomplicated enjoyment. **Chardonnay** ★★★★ Year in oak, 20% new, gives previewed **22** ⑧④ gentle support & complexity. Subtle lemon & lime from entry to finish, bright acid for pleasurable sipping. Not tasted: **Pinot Noir**. — NK, CvZ

Location: Sandton ▪ WO: Western Cape ▪ Est/1stB 2019 ▪ Online shop ▪ Owner(s) 2 shareholders ▪ Winemaker(s) Aldert Nieuwoudt (Oct 2019), with Mpelo Sikhwatha (Oct 2019) ▪ Viticulturist(s) Aldert Nieuwoudt (Oct 2019) ▪ 15 La Garitta BC, 12 Mafusa Rd, Sunninghill, Sandton 2191 ▪ info@mawines.co.za ▪ www.mawines.co.za ▪ **T** +27 (0)61-315-1614

☐ **Mandela** *see* House of Mandela

MAN Family Wines

From a 'side-gig' in an old tractor shed to a significant business with 280,000 widely exported cases, the MAN Family's key to success is making 'high-quality wines that punch above their weight, challenging brands that are double the price tag'. Homed on Lievland estate in Stellenbosch, the team includes a grower's collective, with grapes sourced primarily from old-vine and dry-farmed vineyards in Agter Paarl.

Essay range

★★★★ **Red** ⊘ Name change from 'Syrah-Cinsault-Grenache-Mourvèdre' but varieties unchanged for **22** ⑧⑥, still a savoury, food-friendly blend, with smooth, long-lingering red & black fruit. WO Coastal.

★★★★ **White** ⊘ Same varieties previously in wine name keep ticking drink-me boxes in **23** ⑧⑦, 57% chenin, splash viognier for fragrance. Unoaked yet creamy, substantial, courtesy lees ageing & dab roussanne, grapefruit pith cleans & freshens.

MAN range

★★★★ **Bosstok Pinotage** ⊘ Extrovert expression of bushvines, **21** ⑧⑥ sees quaffable plums mingle with fresh-brewed coffee & hot chocolate. Dabs syrah, cinsault & grenache noir add seriousness.

★★★★ **Skaapveld Syrah** ⊘ Delicious current drinking with legs for few more years, thanks to supple tannin & polished oak structure. **21** ⑧⑥ hedgerow fruit with lavender, coriander & cured meat complexity.

★★★★ **Padstal Chardonnay** ⊘ Pure drinking pleasure on moreish **23** ⑧⑥. Gets clever aromatic boost from splash muscat; oaked portion gives toast & depth to rounded pineapple body. **22** untasted.

★★★★ **Free-Run Steen Chenin Blanc** ⊘ Light & utterly delicious, unoaked **23** ⑧⑥'s crunchy apple, biscuit & lime zest are bright & vibrant, lead to an expansive tropical fruit lift on exit.

★★★★ **Sparkling Chenin Blanc** Handsomely packaged **23** ⑧⑥ improves on last-tasted **21** ★★★★ ⑧⑤ in intensity, breadth & depth of tropical & citrus fruit. Gentle mousse shows a nice salty touch as it lingers.

Ou Kalant Cabernet Sauvignon ⊘ ★★★★ Fan favourite, the 'Old Rascal' is all dark fruit & toast from year in 30% new oak, **21** ⑧④ gets yet more deep tones from cocoa & coffee. **Jan Fiskaal Merlot** ⊘

★★★★ Dabs petit verdot & cab stiffen the body, but **22** ⑧⑤ remains an easy drinker, juicy, smooth plums & cherries throughout, unoaked fraction keeps it fresh. **Warrelwind Sauvignon Blanc** ⊘ ★★★★ From Agter Paarl & Elgin fruit, **23** ⑧④'s gooseberry & lime in harmony with sleek body & fresh acid bite. Good balance & body from usual 9% semillon & 3 months on lees in tank. — WB

Location: Stellenbosch/Paarl ▪ WO: Cape Coast/Coastal ▪ Est 2001 ▪ Tasting & sales at Lievland Vineyards (available online at wineman.co.za) ▪ Owner(s) MAN Vintners (Pty) Ltd ▪ Cellarmaster(s) Tyrrel Myburgh (2001) ▪ Winemaker(s) Riaan Möller, with Marcho Benjamin ▪ 280,000cs own label 60% red 40% white ▪ PO Box 37 Klapmuts 7625 ▪ info@manwines.com ▪ www.manwines.com ▪ **T +27 (0)21-874-1034**

Manley Private Cellar ⓟ ⓐ ⓞ

At the Tulbagh boutique wine and hospitality estate founded by the late David Manley Jordan and lately acquired by German business associates, winemaker-viticulturist Joshua van Blommestein focuses on 'depicting terroir in the best way possible', through wines with 'complex aromas and immense elegance'.

★★★★ **Cabernet Sauvignon** Retasted year later, 2 years older barrels' smokier scents confirm **20** ⑧⑥'s oak has melded with cassis & plummy fruit. Texture as succulent as first tasted, tannins a hidden strength.

★★★★ **Chenin Blanc Reserve** Handling change, compared with sibling, expressive **21** ⑧⑥ fully oaked 7 months, still allowing fruit to shine, boosted by dash viognier: apricot & gooseberry, light ginger biscuit spicing. Dry, with zesty acid underpin.

Pinotage ★★★★ Preview last time, now bottled, same oaking as Cab, comes to fore as spicy overlay to **20** ⑧⑤'s dark-toned berries, but tannins smoothly accessible. **Shiraz** ★★★★ Year later, **20** ⑧⑤ shows more typicity, smoky oak spice in dark-toned fruit, same smooth juicy texture that appealed before. 2 years older barrels, some American & Hungarian, as all reds. **Chenin Blanc** ⓥ ★★★★ Small portion briefly oaked but **21** ⑧④'s fruit remains in charge, citrus & stonefruit, exuding freshness & appetite appeal. Dash viognier. **Viognier** ★★★ Touch of sauvignon, unoaked **22** ⑧① better expression of aromatic fruit: honeysuckle alongside the peach, touch sugar adding palate weight, fitting style perfectly. In abeyance: **Rosé**. — CR

Location/map/WO: Tulbagh ▪ Map grid reference: B5 ▪ Est/1stB 2002 ▪ Tasting & sales Mon-Fri 9-4 Sat/pub hols 10-4 ▪ Fee R70, waived on purchase of R200 in value ▪ Cellar tours by appt ▪ Closed Good Fri, Dec 25 & Jan 1 ▪ B&B & self-catering accommodation ▪ Wedding & conference facilities ▪ Chapel ▪ Owner(s) Manley Wine Estate (Pty) Ltd ▪ Winemaker(s)/viticulturist(s) Joshua van Blommestein (Sep 2019) ▪ PO Box 318 Tulbagh 6820 ▪ booking@manleywineestate.co.za ▪ www.manleywineestate.co.za ▪ **T +27 (0)23-007-0009**

☐ **Manor House** *see* Nederburg Wines
☐ **Marais Family Wines** *see* Breëland Winery - Marais Family Wines

Mara Wines

These 'fruit-forward quality wines made in Africa by Africans' are adorned with traditional beadwork crafted by women who derive revenue, business-creation and skill-acquisition benefits. The range is a collaboration between African Sun, an exporter of South African wines to international markets, and local wineries.

Nyekundu ★★★ Swahili for 'red'. Unoaked cab & merlot, **22** ⑦⑨ generously fruited, appeal enhanced by some sweetness. For early drinking. **Tamu Rosé** ⓥ ★★ Tamu meaning 'sweet', **NV** ⑦⑥ has a pale sunset colour but there's nothing understated about its grapey muscat aroma or flavour. Gently fizzy, full-sweet yet clean & bright. **Nyeupe** ⊘ ★★★ 'White' in Swahili. **23** ⑧① tasted ex-tank (as Nyekundu), chenin's crunchy apple & pear flavours, beefed up by a bit of sugar, fitting the style. **Tamu Red** ⓥ ★★ Pale ruby-garnet **NV** ⑦⑥, frothy, sweet & easygoing, tasty party fare designed to please. Just 8.5% alc, as Rosé. — CR

Location: Paarl ▪ WO: Western Cape ▪ Est/1stB 2006 ▪ Closed to public ▪ Owner(s) Kalika Sahi Ruparelia (Director) ▪ Winemaker(s) Pieter Carstens (Aug 2019, consultant) ▪ 7,471cs (6x750ml) & 500cs (24x250ml) own label 65% red 35% white 5% rosé ▪ PO Box 351, Boschenmeer Estate, Paarl 7646 ▪ info@marawines. co.ke, elsabe@africansunwines.co.za ▪ www.marawines.co.za ▪ **T +27 (0)82-325-1288**

Marcology

The subject being studied in this boutique label based in Franschhoek is the husband of La Bri Estate winemaker Irene de Fleuriot. We know that Marc's first love is chardonnay, and the variety is already covered in the range, so we deduce this year's best-barrel selection is more to the taste of its 5-star-lauded creator. Beyond doubt is it fits the intended profile of 'classic wine that everyone can enjoy'.

★★★★ **Cabernet Sauvignon** (NEW) Most promising debut. **21** (88) an elegant, beautifully weighted package of blackcurrant fruit, grainy tannins & sensitive oak support, 2nd-fill barrique, 2 years. Will bloom over good few years.

★★★★ **Chardonnay** (♀) 2nd-fill oak for **20** ★★★★ (85) vs 100% new for **19** (86), thus younger wine fresher, more integrated, albeit honeyed flavours shade less intense. Touch drier, more vinous.— DS

Location/WO: Franschhoek ▪ 1stB 2019 ▪ Closed to public ▪ Owner(s) Marc & Irene de Fleuriot ▪ Winemaker(s) Irene de Fleuriot ▪ 65cs own label 100% white ▪ crystalagenciesza@gmail.com ▪ **T +27 (0)82-077-2099**

Maree Family Wines

A team of father and son, both named Jacques, based in Somerset West, working with the vineyards of handpicked partners 'to showcase the quality of Stellenbosch-area grapes and wines'. They 'usher in' the new vintage as naturally as possible but intervene when needed, for a compact range with charming labels.

★★★★ **Klein Jakkals** (✓) Changes since **20** (87), no splash of cab & French oak only, mostly older barriques, 18 months. Vivid black fruit still one of **21** (89)'s attributes, as is vanilla spicing; streamlined texture, tannins amenable. Already delicious, with potential.

★★★★ **Old Man Sam** Oaked chenin, **22** (89) 8 months seasoned barrels, giving thatch & ginger biscuit seasoning to the stonefruit & melon scents & flavours, perked up by brisk acidy. Lots going on, all good.

Not tasted: **Pieter & The Jackal**. — CR

Location: Somerset West ▪ WO: Stellenbosch ▪ Est/1stB 2016 ▪ Closed to public ▪ Owner(s) Maree Family Wines (Pty) Ltd (shareholders Jacques Maree snr & jnr) ▪ Winemaker(s) Jacques Maree (2016) ▪ Own label 80% red 20% white ▪ 94 Lourensford Rd, Somerset West 7130 ▪ jacques@mareefamilywines.com ▪ www.mareefamilywines.com ▪ **T +27 (0)82-925-9493**

Marianne Wine Estate   (♀) (¶) (⌂) (◎) (♨) (♿)

The Dauriac family owners, from Bordeaux and still with wine properties there, bought this Simonsberg estate 20 years ago, naming it for the fictional character who embodies the French Republic and its core ideals, liberty, brotherhood and equality. Current GM Charles Rodenbach was born and raised in France, winemaker Jos van Wyk spends time there, and consulting oenologist Thierry Haberer is a Bordeaux University graduate. More Gallic influence is seen in the stylish and engaging label designs, the varieties used for the ranges, all French with the exception of pinotage, and the motto 'terroir et savoir faire'.

Flagship range

★★★★★ **Desirade** (🍇) Merlot with 37% cab, lavished with attention, 28 months in barrel, 40% new (as this range), which **20** (96) shows as cedar/chocolate-coated cassis & plums, admirably opulent yet with enough tannin foundation to promise a future, give definition & support. Noteworthy.

★★★★☆ **Floréal** (🍇) Cab & merlot with 26% shiraz, treated with respect, 26 months in oak, but **20** (94)'s full-ripe glossy fruit easily handles it. A perfume array, spice, violets, charcuterie, the palate as special: berry intensity, plush texture, the tannins present but supple. Already delicious, though the best lies ahead. Near-equal varieties in **19** ★★★★★ (95) blend.

★★★★☆ **Germinal** (🍇) Changing blend, mourvèdre with shiraz, grenache. Wild berries, prominent dried scrub & meaty tones, heaps of savoury spice from 22 months oaking. Got the tannins right, firm but ripe, the texture streamlined with nice freshness in the flavours & finish. **20** (93) has a long future.

Estate range

★★★★☆ **Cabernet Sauvignon** (🍇) No effort spared in the making, **20** (93)'s generous oaking (same as Merlot) easily assimilated by the luscious berries & plums, but there's more on offer. A whiff of green scrub, lead pencils, a complex interweaving of its attributes. Tannins declare a distinguished future, no barrier to current access. WO Coastal.

★★★★☆ **Merlot** (🍇) **20** (94) spent 30 months in barrel, 40% new (as Pinotage), which shows as a dark chocolate overlay on vivid cassis. Texture is succulent, smoothly curvaceous, tannins a hidden strength, Admirable rendition.

★★★★ **Pinotage** Sumptuous & fleshy, as recent vintages have been, **21** ⑧⑨ dark fruited, with salty liquorice & savoury spice woven through the fruit. Smooth & round, with amenable tannins from 11 months in barrel. Has juicy appeal.

★★★★☆ **Shiraz** To allow full fruit expression, only 31% of **20** ⑨⓪ oaked, but still shares the spotlight, mocha & chocolate alongside plush dark berries & plums. Texture succulent, curvy, tannins ripe.

★★★★ **Cape Blend** ⓥ Deep & dark berries given spice & chocolate shading by 25% new barrels. **19** ★★★★☆ ⑨⓪ a smooth mouthful, seductively rich & concentrated. Outclasses **18** ⑧⑦. WO W Cape.

★★★★☆ **Sauvignon Blanc** ⓑ Blanc fumé style, **22** ⑨③ 11 months in oak & acacia, 30% new, well judged to allow varietal attributes their say. Pea & lemongrass aromas, gentle oat biscuit tone, crisp finish. Not overt, oozes class & finesse, wonderful precision. **21** ★★★★★ ⑨⑤ a standout. WO Coastal.

★★★★☆ **Viognier** Wholebunch, barrel fermented/11 months, bold & showy **22** ⑨⓪ is peach- & peach pip-scented, some floral notes. Stonefruit flavours brushed with savoury oak spice, tannins integrated.

Rosé ★★★ Mainly cinsaut with grenache, delicate pink **22** ⑧② offers cranberry scents & flavours, is bone-dry & food friendly. — CR

Location/map: Stellenbosch ▪ Map grid reference: G1 ▪ WO: Simonsberg-Paarl/Coastal/Western Cape ▪ Est/1stB 2004 ▪ Tasting, sales & cellar tours Mon-Sun & pub hols 11-5 ▪ Fee R100/5 wines; R150/wine & biltong pairing ▪ Cellar tour, barrel tasting & vertical tasting of flagship wines ▪ Meat & cheese platters ▪ Picnics ▪ Panoramic tasting deck ▪ Gift shop ▪ 4-star accommodation ▪ Owner(s) Dauriac family ▪ GM Charles Rodenbach ▪ Winemaker(s) Jos van Wyk, with Thierry Haberer (consultant) ▪ 36ha/±26ha (cabs s/f, cinsaut, grenache, merlot, mourv, ptage, shiraz, sauv, viog) ▪ 100t/16,000cs own label 90% red 5% white 5% rosé ▪ PO Box 7300 Stellenbosch 7599 ▪ info@mariannewinefarm.co.za, hospitality@mariannewinefarm.co.za ▪ www.mariannewines.com ▪ **T +27 (0)21-875-5040**

☐ **Marié** see Thiart Wines
☐ **Mariëtte** see Belle Rebelle

Mark le Roux Wines

Winemaker for over a decade at Waterford, Stellenbosch-based Mark le Roux uses the space afforded by this own-brand to 'explore the unknown' and thereby grow and learn without being bound to continuous or successive bottlings or releases. He sources grapes from growers with whom he has special relationships.

MARK. range

★★★★ **Re-mark-able Sauvignon Blanc** ⓥ Piquantly fresh & bursting with passionfruit, fresh herbs & lime in **21** ⑧⑦, showcasing Elgin's cooler provenance. 8 months on lees focus the flavours.

Not tasted: **Cabernet Sauvignon, Pinot Noir, Chenin Blanc.** — MW

Location: Stellenbosch ▪ WO: Elgin ▪ Est/1stB 2018 ▪ Closed to public ▪ Sales online ▪ Winemaker(s) Mark le Roux ▪ PO Box 12485 Die Boord Stellenbosch 7613 ▪ mark@marklerouxwines.co.za ▪ www.marklerouxwines.co.za ▪ **T +27 (0)72-101-1289**

Marklew Family Wines   ⓥ ◎

Auspiciously named De Goede Sukses on prime Simonsberg-Stellenbosch land is the home-farm of this mostly red-wine boutique collection, marking its 21st anniversary this year. Dirk Tredoux recently took over the crafting in the two-centuries-old, extensively modernised cellar, and he shares vineyard duties with Bill Marklew, who runs the estate with his sister Haidee, parents and co-owners Dudley and Lyn having retired.

Marklew range

★★★★ **Cabernet Sauvignon** ⓥ Rich, robust, with dark plum, cassis & chocolate on nose & palate of **21** ⑧⑧. Very dry, long savoury finish. 15% new oak, 18 months, as all reds. Last tasted was **18** ⑧⑧.

★★★★☆ **Cabernet Franc** ⓑ Understated & elegant yet with an underlying power & well-knit tannin structure for lengthy ageing. **21** ⑨⓪'s black fruit density offset with herbal undertone & black pepper nuance on the substantial finish. **20** untasted.

★★★★ **Merlot** ⓥ Improving on last-tasted **16** ★★★★ ⑧⑤, ruby-hued **21** ⑧⑦ rich & dark, supple & smooth, with good carry-through of black cherry, mulberry & dark chocolate to lingering spicy finish.

★★★★ **Cape Flora Pinotage** ⊘ Well-structured & -balanced **21** ⑧⑧ will keep a good few years, like last-tasted **17** ⑧⑧. Juicy, generously fruited with ripe berries & hint of mocha, tannins already integrated.

★★★★ **Family Reserve** ⑫ Forthright yet sophisticated mouthful of dark fruit, leather & fynbos couched in smooth tannins & judicious oak. **20** ⑧⑨ near-equal cab & merlot, dab cab franc made to age.

★★★★ **Sauvignon Blanc** ⊘ Zesty, fruit-forward & just-dry **23** ⑧⑨ shows tropical fruit tempered by a delicious balanced acidity. Fresh & more expressive than last-tasted **20** ★★★ ⑧⓪.

★★★★ **Méthode Cap Classique Brut Reserve** Vibrant citrus mixed with creamy lees from 36 months ageing on all-chardonnay **19** ⑧⑧. Very dry, broad palate & fine mousse, echoing lemon biscuit finish. Not tasted: **Shiraz Reserve**, **Celebration Chardonnay**.

Cape Georgians range

Reserve ⑫ ★★★★ Succulent equal mix merlot & cab with 14% cab franc slips down easily, **20** ⑧④ ripe plum & mulled dark berries with cocoa dusting from oak, 10% new. Not tasted: **Merlot**. — WB

Location/map: Stellenbosch ▪ Map grid reference: F1 ▪ WO: Simonsberg-Stellenbosch ▪ Est 1970 ▪ 1stB 2003 ▪ Tasting, sales & tours by appt ▪ Tour groups (max 20) ▪ Private/business functions for small groups ▪ Walks ▪ Mountain biking ▪ Conservation area ▪ Owner(s) Marklew family (Edward Dudley, Edward William, Lyn & Haidee) ▪ Winemaker(s) Dirk Tredoux (May 2022) ▪ Viticulturist(s) Billy Marklew (Jun 2001), with Dirk Tredoux (May 2022) ▪ 58ha/45ha (cabs s/f, merlot, ptage, shiraz, chard, sauv) ▪ ±300t/5,000cs own label 65% red 30% white 5% MCC ▪ IPW, WIETA ▪ PO Box 17 Elsenburg 7607 ▪ wine@marklew.co.za ▪ www.marklew.co.za ▪ **T +27 (0)21-884-4411**

☐ **Martindale** *see* Wine-of-the-Month Club
☐ **Mary Delany** *see* Botanica Wines

Mary Le Bow ⑫

Previously listed under Bruce Jack's The Drift Estate, this long-established brand remains in the portfolio of the entrepreneurial winegrower, taking its name from the London church where a distant ancestor of a Jack family friend is buried.

★★★★☆ **Red** ⑫ Supple **19** ⑨④ blend retains cab dominance (45%) in 3-way blend with cab franc & shiraz. Like **18** ⑨①, velvety, plush & effortless in its elegant fruitcake, spiced refinement but oak ramped up to 100%, 45% new, French & American for 25 months. Will age well. WO W Cape, as sibling.

★★★★☆ **Viognier** ⑫ Textured **20** ⑨⓪ shows signature peach & florals. Like **19** ⑨⓪, has dab chenin blanc (5%) to liven broad yet fresh palate. Good grip, body & length from natural ferment, French & American oak (only 15% new, 6 months) & lees contact. — FM

Maske Wines ⑫

Wellington vintners Erich and Janine Maske contract with various winemakers and viticulturists to produce a boutique portfolio for export. Locally, they're selling their '15 Cabernet and offering pre-booked tasting/sales.

Cabernet Sauvignon ⑫ ★★★★ Shy cedar & tobacco notes, savoury & earthy whiffs, fruitier on palate with dry tannins reining in the exuberance & lending structure. Drink **15** ⑧④ now & over 3+ years. — CvZ

Location/map/WO: Wellington ▪ Map grid reference: C4 ▪ Est/1stB 2000 ▪ Tasting & sales by appt only ▪ Closed Ash Wed, Easter Fri/Sun & Dec 25 ▪ Owner(s) Erich & Janine Maske ▪ Winemaker(s)/viticulturist(s) outsourced ▪ 7ha/sha (cab, merlot, shiraz, chenin) ▪ 80% red 20% white ▪ Klein Waterval PO Box 206 Wellington 7654 ▪ laureat@iafrica.com ▪ www.maskewines.co.za ▪ **T +27 (0)82-658-4584/+27 (0)21-020-1629**

☐ **Mason Road** *see* Brookdale Estate

Mason's Winery ⑫ ⑪

From a family long involved with stonemasonry, Derek Clift tends a small terraced block on Paarl Mountain, from which he handcrafts 'a typical Paarl shiraz for the discerning drinker'. We hope to taste it next time.

Location/map: Paarl ▪ Map grid reference: E6 ▪ Est/1stB 2001 ▪ Tasting & sales by appt at The Hussar Grill Paarl, next to cellar ▪ Owner(s) JA Clift (Pty) Ltd - Clift family ▪ Cellarmaster(s)/winemaker(s)/viticulturist(s) Derek Clift (2001) ▪ 47ha/4ha (shiraz) ▪ 30t/2,000cs own label 100% red ▪ Main Str Suider-Paarl 7646 ▪ masons@cliftgranite.co.za ▪ www.cliftgranite.co.za ▪ **T +27 (0)83-228-7855**

☐ **Masterpiece of Nature** *see* Olivedale Private Vineyards
☐ **Maties** *see* Stellenbosch University Welgevallen Cellar

Matthew Krone Wines

From a family of successful and innovative SA winemakers, 12th-generation Matthew Krone makes, consults and markets wine, and a particular focus and passion is champagne-method sparkling (see Aristea Wines listing for other styles he crafts). In this Constantia boutique venture, he selects from rows within ultra-premium vineyards for just two elegant bubblies, dedicated to his daughters and released only on 29 February.

The Love Story Collection

★★★★☆ **Méthode Cap Classique Amelia Rose** ⓥ Refined **17** ⑨③ rosé sparkler from pinot noir, expertly crafted, with fine, generous mousse, impressive weight & depth. Like sibling, 30 months on lees.

★★★★☆ **Méthode Cap Classique Alexandra de la Marque** ⓥ Silvery gold **17** ⑨③ from chardonnay & pinot noir delivers apple pie & brioche aromas, energetic mousse, focused creamy dryness.— CvZ

Location: Constantia ▪ WO: Coastal ▪ Est 2014 ▪ Closed to public ▪ Owner(s)/cellarmaster(s) Matthew Krone ▪ 1,000cs own label ▪ Brands for clients: Velvet Rope MCC ▪ matthew@matthewkronewines.co.za ▪ www.matthewkronewines.co.za

☐ **Matys** *see* Diemersdal Estate
☐ **Maxim** *see* Goedverwacht Wine Estate
☐ **Mbali** *see* Zidela Wines

McFarlane Wines ⓥ

With significant winery experience behind her, Alexandra McFarlane started her own brand in 2018. She sources in varied climates and soils across the winelands for her range of wines made from the heritage varieties she champions. Pinotage enters this year for the first time, as a varietal wine and as part of a blend, and there's also a new rosé from cinsault. All are fresh, light and pure, made in simple, hands-off fashion and as fine as they are unpretentious and irresistibly drinkable.

McFarlane Wines range

★★★★ **Tuesday's Child Cinsault** Widely sourced **22** ★★★★ ⑨② has 14% pinotage while **21** ⑧⑨ was pure cinsault. The change brings added depth, substance & structure, light but effective grip. Slightly higher alc now, at 12%, adding vinosity. No real loss of aromatic charm or freshness, but greater character. Cinsault 100% wholebunch, pinotage 30%.

★★★★☆ **Saturday's Child Pinotage** ⓝⒺⓦ From Stanford grapes, **22** ⑨② fine example of new-wave pinotage. Fresh & dry, fairly light at 12.5% alc but substantial, matured in old oak. Plenty of sweet varietal berry fruit on textured, well-balanced palate with gently firm but unpushy tannic structure that should help ensure good few years of development. Also in 1.5L, like both ranges.

★★★★☆ **Monday's Child Chenin Blanc** 🌿 From bunch-fermented Stellenbosch fruit matured in old oak, **22** ⑨④ has quietly expressive & lovely dried peach aromas & flavours, with scrubby herbs & a stony quality too. Firmly rounded, succulent & flavoursome, remarkably intense for just 12% alc. No **21**.

Not tasted: **Thursday's Child Chenin Blanc**.

Capitoline Wolf range

★★★★ **Red** ⊘ Forthcoming & very pretty perfume on widely sourced cinsault. **22** ⑧⑨ pure & clean, elegant & fresh at 12% alc, with bright acidity & touch of tannic grip. Wholebunch, old-oaked. More interesting than many new-wave & lighter versions. This range notably good value.

★★★★ **Rosé** ⓝⒺⓦ Unusual & effective blend in old-oaked **22** ⑧⑧: cinsault & 14% semillon, latter giving added weight. Aromatic & sophisticated (with fashionable light onion skin hue), dry & just 11.5% alc, delightful core of sweet berry charm.

★★★★☆ **White** ⊘ Rather more lemony semillon (75%) than previously on old-oaked **22** ⑨⓪ blend with peachy chenin. Perhaps even more delicious, for super early-drinking while the chenins mature a little in bottle. Pure, linear, fresh & irresistible. No **21**.— TJ

Location: Hermanus ▪ Map: Walker Bay & Bot River ▪ Map grid reference: C5 ▪ WO: Western Cape/Walker Bay ▪ Est 2018 ▪ 1stB 2019 ▪ Tasting & cellar tours by appt only ▪ Wine club ▪ Owner(s) Alexandra McFarlane &

Wayne van den Heuvel ▪ Winemaker(s)/viticulturist(s) Alexandra McFarlane (Jul 2018) ▪ 25t/650cs own label 50% red 50% white ▪ info@mcfarlanewines.com ▪ www.mcfarlanewines.com ▪ T +27 (0)82-783-4380

McGregor Winery

Two large and long-established grower-owned cellars in Robertson Valley, Roodezandt and McGregor, merged in 2020 to benefit from economies of scale. The focus remains on serving the needs of large corporate customers but the branded line-up of 'full, round, balanced and very nice' wine is consumer driven, appealingly priced and offered for tasting at two town venues, McGregor and Robertson. On a poignant note, cellar helmsman Christie Steytler has retired after a lifetime 43 years 'and will be sorely missed'.

McGregor range

Cabernet Sauvignon (NEW) ✓ ★★★☆ Affable debut for **22** (83) preview. Peppery, herb-brushed dark fruit notes & slight muscular power in unfussy, soft-textured body. Good braai accompaniment. **Elmo Pinot Noir** (NEW) ✓ ★★★ Light-bodied & juicy **22** (82)'s ripe, red-fruit nose is a tad confected, palate same. Gentle wood note courtesy of oak chips during ferment. **Pinotage** ✓ ★★★ Savoury black olive & plum on **22** (80). Inky & dark, with chalky dry grip from year in barrel, 30% new, mainly American. **Shiraz** ✓ ★★★☆ Improves on predecessor in verve & succulence of red & blue fruit. **22** (84) structured, with depth & light intensity. Year in small barrel, portion new, adds length. **Cabernet Sauvignon-Merlot** ✓ ★★★☆ Cab at 85% dominates plush, soft & accessible **22** (83). Fruitcake notes supported by light oak, house-style combo French & American, 12 months. **Chardonnay** ✓ ★★★ Light & dry, with easy tropical & citrus flavours. Fresh acid adds vigour to unwooded **23** (82). **Chenin Blanc** ✓ ★★★ Guava & lemon pepper liveliness to **23** (81). Light, juicy & fresh, ideal for summertime. **Colombard** ✓ ★★★ Lightweight & zesty **23** (81) offers lemony brightness & succulence. Uncomplicated & approachable. **Sauvignon Blanc** ✓ ★★★ Grapefruit & fig on tangy, energetic **23** (82). Light & easy to drink, will be most enjoyable poolside. **Red Muscadel** ★★★★ Heady jasmine perfume on richly sweet yet uncloying **22** (83) fortified dessert. Sultana flavour is light & straightforwardly appealing. **White Muscadel** (★) ★★★★ Pineapple, barley sugar & distinctive muscat aromas, **19** (83) fortified pudding wine is full-sweet, will make many friends. WO W Cape, as Red.
Discontinued: **Winemaker's Reserve range**. — FM

Location: Robertson/McGregor ▪ Map: Robertson ▪ Map grid reference: B5 ▪ Map: Robertson ▪ Map grid reference: D6 ▪ WO: McGregor/Western Cape ▪ Roodezandt premises: Tasting & sales Mon-Fri 9-5 ▪ McGregor premises: Tasting & sales Mon-Fri 9-5 Sat/pub hols 9-1 ▪ Closed Good Fri, Dec 25/26 & Jan 1 (subject to change) ▪ Facilities for children ▪ Owner(s) 45 family farms ▪ CEO Altus Theron ▪ Cellarmaster(s) Jean du Plessis (2012) ▪ Winemaker(s) Roodezandt premises: Hugo Conradie (2018), with Tiaan Blom (Oct 2005); McGregor premises: Prieur du Plessis (2022) ▪ Viticulturist(s) Jaco Lategan (Dec 2006) ▪ 2,300ha ▪ 42,000t/33m L ▪ HACCP, IPW, WIETA ▪ PO Box 164 Robertson 6705 ▪ info@roodezandt.co.za, info@mcgregorwinery.co.za ▪ www.mcgregorwinery.co.za ▪ T +27 (0)23-626-1160 (Robertson)/+27 (0)23-625-1741 (McGregor)

☐ **Meander** see Daschbosch

Meerendal Wine Estate

Durbanville's grande dame turns 322 this year, its substantial ±230 hectares, with vineyards, cellar and varied visitor amenities latterly under the custodianship of the Coertze family. Conversation to organic continues, with a block each of sauvignon and merlot set for certification this year, the full 54 ha hopefully completed by end-2028. Also due this year is opening of the new tasting venue, offering food pairings and including a chocolatier and deli. On the marketing front, Meerendal led the formation of First 14, an association marking 50 years since the first farms were granted 'estate' status under then-new Wine of Origin rules.

Prestige range

★★★★☆ **Heritage Block Pinotage** (★) (★) Official single-vineyard, 1955 bushvines, Durbanville's oldest. **17** (94) highly aromatic, spice & vanilla alongside blueberry fruit, there's richness & pleasure here.
★★★★☆ **Intensio** (★) Collaboration with Italian vintner Stefano Contini, Amarone-style vine-dried pinotage. **19** (93) intense plum/prune scent but palate surprisingly dry, smooth. Individual, memorable.
★★★★☆ **Cape Blend The Loft** (★) Half pinotage & 3 others. Despite oaking, **21** (90)'s fruit remains the hero, wonderfully succulent with freshness threaded through. Lovely curves & lithe tannins.

★★★★ **Heritage Reserve** Complex, restrained & refined blend, **22** ★★★★☆ ⑨ⓛ, like **21** ⑧⑨, led by merlot supported by cab & shiraz, dab pinotage. Inky black fruit seamlessly integrated with oak, 9 months, 44% new. Powerful yet accessible, supple & silky.

★★★★ **Méthode Cap Classique Brut** ⓥ Sparkler from pinot noir with chardonnay, 21 months on lees, a lot of citrus, **NV** ⑧⑧'s red berries a perfume highlight, enriching flavour note. Dry, with good weight.

★★★★ **Sauvignon Blanc Natural Sweet** ⓥ Vine-dried grapes with 20% botrytis portion, **18** ⑧⑨ unoaked dessert has apple & yoghurt-coated almond flavours, intensely sweet but fresh. 375 ml.

Discontinued: **Merlot Prestige, Merlot Reserve, The Pinotage Vine, Bin159 Shiraz, Estate Red Blend**.

Standard range

★★★★ **Merlot** ⓥ Agile, silky & rich **22** ⑧⑨ a notch above **21** ★★★★ ⑧④ in complexity, definition & concentration. Cherry, cocoa & graphite well knit with oak, 44% new, 9 months, lending stature & length.

★★★★ **Pinot Noir** ⓥ Welcome return by restrained & rewarding **23** ⑧⑨. Bright raspberry succulence with forest floor nuance, freshness & fruit retained by just 9 months oaking vs **20** ⑧⑦'s full year. Textured, with good density & length. **21** untasted, **22** not made.

★★★★ **Pinotage** ⓥ Savoury-edged **22** ⑧⑦ improves on **21** ★★★★ ⑧⑤ with lively red fruit & squeeze of light, fine dry tannin. Touch of tobacco & earthy density lend gentle power to medium-bodied whole.

★★★★ **Shiraz** ⓥ Olive tapenade joins plum & fynbos on succulent but structured **22** ⑧⑥. Tannins are supple & balanced, good body & enduring flavour.

★★★★☆ **Organic Sauvignon Blanc** ⓥ ⓥ Delicious **22** ⑨⓪ from Elgin & differently styled to sauvignon siblings, yellow apple & pear, even a melon note, impression is of richness of fruit in the flavours.

★★★★☆ **Sauvignon Blanc** ⓥ Chiselled **23** ★★★★ ⑧⑦ shows variety's trademark gooseberry & grapefruit vim & tang. Zesty, taut, with balanced acid & flinty end. **22** ⑨⓪ touch riper but still impressive.

Pinotage Blanc de Noir ★★★★ Cheery, berry-toned off-dry **23** ⑧④ is lively & vibrant, acid easily countering the sugar. Sappy & fresh, ideal for summer. **Pinotage Rosé** ★★★★ Gentle coral hue on **23** ⑧④ tank sample. Plum, cherry verve is bolstered by fresh acidity. Crisp, with firm dry finish. **Chenin Blanc** ★★★★ Preview of rewarding **23** ⑧⑤ shows pear & nectarine flavours in a brisk, fresh body. Subtle textural note from 29% barrel ferment. In abeyance: **Cabernet Sauvignon**. Discontinued: **Chardonnay Unwooded**. Discontinued: **Meerendal Moments range**. — FM

Location: Durbanville ▪ Map: Durbanville, Philadelphia & Darling ▪ Map grid reference: C7 ▪ WO: Cape Town/Elgin ▪ Est 1702 ▪ 1stB 1969 ▪ Tasting & sales Mon-Sun 10-6 summer/10-5 winter; pub hols (seasonal) please call ahead ▪ Closed Good Fri, Dec 25 & Jan 1 ▪ Cellar tours by appt ▪ Bossa Winelands Restaurant at Meerendal T +27 (0)21-008-5669, Mon-Sun 7am-10pm ▪ La Romantica Restaurant at Meerendal T +27 (0)28-008-5280, Mon-Fri 11am-10pm Sat/Sun 8am-10pm ▪ Facilities for children ▪ Tour groups ▪ Weddings/functions ▪ Walking/running/MTB trails ▪ Renosterveld conservation area ▪ Meerendal Wine Academy ▪ The Meerendal Boutique Hotel ▪ Wine club ▪ Owner(s) Coertze family ▪ Cellarmaster(s) Wade Roger-Lund (Jun 2022) ▪ Winemaker(s) Trudie Mulder (Jun 2022) ▪ Viticulturist(s) Zach Moolman (May 2023) ▪ 227ha/48ha (cab, merlot, ptage, pinot, shiraz, sauv) ▪ 400t/50,000cs own label 75% red 20% white 5% rosé ▪ IPW, WIETA ▪ Private Bag X1702 Durbanville 7551 ▪ info@meerendal.co.za ▪ www.meerendal.co.za ▪ **T +27 (0)21-975-1655**

Meerhof Wines ⓥ ⓥ ⓥ

Explorer Pieter van Meerhof pitched a tent on a slope outside today's Riebeek-Kasteel 363 years ago and, on reportedly the exact spot, guests are welcome to tie the knot, deliberate or let their hair down and have a good old party, courtesy of the hospitable Jansen van Rensburgs, Highveld farmers in a previous life, and Meerhof owners the past five years. Unlike most small-scale family vintners in Swartland, their wine range is wide, and includes Bordeaux varieties. Fans of the Arbeidsgenot wines will find them listed separately.

Premium range

★★★★☆ **Shiraz-Grenache** ⓥ Seductive **21** ⑨ⓛ incredibly fruity, with well-judged & -extracted flavour, intensity & weight. Pure, piquant & persistent, smooth finish neatly tweaked with lively acidity.

★★★★☆ **White Blend** ⊘ Splash viognier (10%) dominates the **23** ⑨② blend, equal chenin & chardonnay, 20% perfumed & satin-textured grenache blanc. Only old French oak (vs **21** ⑨④'s new French/American combo), shade less complex & fresh. No **22**.

Grenache Rosé ⑨ ★★★★ 8 months in new oak, half American, give palest pink **21** ⑧③ a different character to the Meerhof version, the wood a tad prominent this vintage.

Speciality Wines

★★★★★ **Mooistrooi** ⑨ Muscat d'Alexandrie air-dried on straw-lined racks, aged ±8 months in new barrels, half American in **22** ⑨④. Full-sweet yet buoyed by a brightening acid. Ever-evolving & involving. 500 ml. Last tasted was stellar **20** ★★★★★ ⑨⑤.

In abeyance: **Hanepoot Natuurlike Soet**, **Special Late Harvest**.

Meerhof range

· ·

Chardonnay ⊘ ⑨ ★★★★ Unoaked **23** ⑧③'s friendly acid nip enlivens lemon, straw & dried scrub flavours, extends the finish. **Chenin Blanc** ⊘ ⑨ ★★★★ Somewhat dusty **23** ⑧③ opens to white peach & intriguing khaki bush, fruit-sweet & vivacious for satisfying everyday drinking.

· ·

Merlot ⑨ ★★★ Slips down smoothly, **21** ⑧② showing true-to-variety ripe plums & black berries, sleek tannins. **Pinotage** ⑨ ★★★★ Steps up with nicely ripe blackberry fruit & neatly tucked-away 15% alc, variety's bright acid delivering fresh mouthful in **21** ⑧④. **Shiraz** ⑨ ★★★★ Barrel sample **21** ⑧④ very ripe maraschino cherry nuance, some fynbos & charcuterie complexity, attractive spiced vanilla tone. Bright acid adds verve. **Red Blend** ⊘ ★★★★ Pinotage & shiraz with dabs cab & merlot in **22** ⑧④. Red & black fruit melange, some fynbos & floral notes, orange zest & pleasant bitter tannin twist. **Grenache Rosé** ⑨ ★★★ Palest of pinks, dust & smoke accents (though unoaked), dry & brief in **22** ⑦⑧. Not tasted: **Cabernet Sauvignon**, **Sauvignon Blanc**. — CvZ

Location: Riebeek-Kasteel ▪ Map/WO: Swartland ▪ Map grid reference: D6 ▪ 1stB 2017 ▪ Tasting, sales & restaurant Wed-Fri 9-5 Sat 9-4.30 Sun 9-3; pub hols (seasonal) please call ahead ▪ Fee R100pp ▪ Closed from Dec 23rd ▪ Conferences ▪ Weddings ▪ Parties ▪ Conservation area ▪ Owner(s) Erik, Koos & Hestia Jansen van Rensburg ▪ PO Box 148 Riebeek-Kasteel 7307 ▪ info@meerhofwines.co.za ▪ www.meerhofwines.co.za ▪ **T** +27 (0)22-125-0422/3

Meerlust Estate ⑨ ⌂

The historic estate, with its fine Cape Dutch farmstead, on the Eerste River, just 5 km from Stellenbosch's False Bay coast, has been in the Myburgh family for 8 generations and over 250 years. Current owner and custodian, Hannes, has held the reins since 1988, by which time the wines were already achieving acclaim, and he has maintained the lofty standards with admirable consistency. Historically a red-wine specialist, with the lone chardonnay white, the similarity of the vineyards to the gently undulating geography and clay-gravel soils of Médoc is difficult to miss, as is the classic Bordeaux style of their flagship label, Rubicon. Their mentorship venture, Compagniesdrift, listed separately, provides wine storage and other services to the industry, and its branded wines are made at Meerlust by Altus Treurnicht.

★★★★☆ **Cabernet Sauvignon** 🍇 Classically structured & styled, **20** ⑨③ still taut & coiled but already shows pedigree. Dark chocolate, damp earth & iodine add highlights to intense, rich blackcurrant fruit. Like **19** ⑨③, dense tannins & concentration, begging time to settle & evolve. 18 months in oak, 50% new.

★★★★☆ **Merlot** 🍇 Bold & self-assured, **20** ⑨③ has typical blackcurrant & cocoa underpinning, with earth & mineral threads, solid tannins. Small dashes petit verdot & cab franc add breadth & appeal. As with last **18** ⑨③, serious oaking (18 months, 40% new) prepare it for the long haul.

★★★★☆ **Pinot Noir** ⊘ Showing fine varietal form, **22** ⑨② has enviable body & weight, violet-scented cherry fruit, meaty-savoury & mineral embroidery, satin tannins. 11 months in oak, 40% new, portion in foudre. Needs time to reveal its best.

★★★★☆ **Red** More pocket-friendly cousin to Rubicon, **21** ⑨⓪ cab franc, cab, merlot & petit verdot blend (36/25/25/14) not lacking in stature. Similarly styled, sumptuous black fruit on an earthy mineral platform. Though showing impressive extract & body, perhaps for earlier drinking.

★★★★☆ **Rubicon** 🍇 A Cape classic, pioneer cab & merlot-led Bordeaux blend, **21** ★★★★★ ⑨⑤ (48/46) typically bold, assertive & brawny yet precisely poised. Delightful earthy mineral core, with iodine & intense blackcurrant, graphite & delicate leafy highlights. 50% new oak, 18 months. Finer than **20** ⑨③; no **19**.

★★★★☆ **Chardonnay** Citrus fruit touch more prominent on **22** ⓟ, & deftly poised on solid, lees-rich foundation of buttered nuts & tempered spices from ferment/9 months in small-oak, 33% new. Full, ripe body enlivened with tingling acid to the commendable finish. — GdB

Location/map/WO: Stellenbosch ▪ Map grid reference: C8 ▪ Est 1693 ▪ 1stB 1975 ▪ Tasting & sales Mon-Fri 9-5 Sat 10-2 ▪ Fee R30 ▪ Closed all pub hols ▪ Cellar tours by appt ▪ Quarters self-contained cottage ▪ Wine club ▪ Owner(s) Hannes Myburgh ▪ Cellarmaster(s) Wim Truter (2020) ▪ Winemaker(s) Altus Treurnicht (2018) ▪ Viticulturist(s) Izak Basson (2020) ▪ 400ha/68ha (cabs s/f, merlot, p verdot, pinot, chard) ▪ 500t/60,000cs own label 90% red 10% white ▪ PO Box 7121 Stellenbosch 7599 ▪ info@meerlust.co.za ▪ www.meerlust.co.za ▪ T +27 (0)21-843-3587

Meinert Wines ⓠ

Meinert Wines, based on high-lying Devon Crest estate in Devon Valley, was founded by Martin Meinert in the 1980s. After he sold the venture a few years ago, Cape Wine Master Brendan Butler took on the roles of general manager, winemaker and viticulturist, with Martin as adviser. The home-farm is planted mostly with semillon, pinotage and three Bordeaux varieties; cabernet is on nearby Fleurbaix, home to Meinert owners Wilna and Werner van Rhyn. Wider-spread fruit comes from Swartland, and cooler Elgin and Upper Hemel-en-Aarde, a challenging mix for harvest 2023 and its late-season rain, but with attention to detail in vineyard and cellar, Brendan believes their philosophy of 'reflecting each site, with quality' will be upheld.

Meinert range

★★★★ **Cabernet Sauvignon** ⓠ Grapes from Stellenbosch sibling farm's granitic soil add perfume to estate's dark-berried fruit in **18** ⑧⑨. Naturally fermented (as most Meinert wines), elegantly balanced.

★★★★☆ **Merlot** ⓠ Piquant red-berry flavours from estate's iron-rich clay soils in **18** ★★★★ ⑧⑧, which has 4% pinotage. 30-40% new oak adds spice, though less depth of fruit & structure than **17** ⑨⓪.

★★★★ **Printer's Ink Pinotage** ⓠ Both maceration carbonique & conventional natural ferment of home-farm grapes contribute a perfumed fruitiness & richer mellowed tone to dry & supple **19** ⑧⑧.

★★★★☆ **Synchronicity** ⓠ The flagship, a barrel selection of vintage's best-performing varieties. Exceptional **17** ⑨③ a marriage of cab, merlot, petit verdot & pinotage. Complex & brooding, with a dense core of dark fruit & cocoa in a firm but velvety tannin embrace. Will handsomely reward cellaring.

★★★★ **The German Job Riesling** ⊘ Delicate lemon blossom, spicy lime purity set off by few grams sugar, sprightly acidity. Some skin contact enhances structure but **23** ⑧⑦ misses some of the tangy, sweet-sour tension of **22** ⑧⑧, both from Elgin.

★★★★ **Sauvignon Blanc** ⊘ Mainly from Elgin, **23** ⑧⑧ has precision & purity in its zesty lemongrass & blackcurrant flavours. Textural interest from portion barrel-fermented, home-farm semillon, distinction & potential for some ageing ex skin contact & oxidative vinification.

La Barry Red ⓠ ★★★★ Merlot (55%) & cab from home-farm. **NV** ⑧⑤ juicy, with supple tannins & integrated oak. Gracefully balanced for everyday enjoyment.

Limited Editions

★★★★ **The Graduate Syrah** Elegant red fruit, pepper spice & clean leather savoury tones reflect cool Upper Hemel-en-Aarde origin of **20** ⑧⑨. Supple, with frisson of freshening tannins, year older oak integrates, adds extra nuance. Youthful attractions promise to age as well.

★★★★ **The Italian Job White Merlot** ⓠ Unique mix of merlot without the skin-derived colour & splash Swartland old-vine chenin in **20** ⑧⑨. Oak adds creamy depth to Earl Grey & cranberry flavours.

★★★★☆ **Semillon Straw Wine** ⓠ Richly sweet **15** ★★★★ ⑧⑥ dessert wine from Devon Valley. Balanced acid ensures clean dry finish, as with memorable **14** ⑨③. Mostly in 375 ml.

La Barry Sauvignon Blanc ⓠ ★★★★ Elegant & crisp, unoaked **20** ⑧⑤ from Elgin has appealing white flower, herbaceous notes & smooth texture. Occasional release: **Pinot Noir**. — AL

Location/map: Stellenbosch ▪ Map grid reference: D4 ▪ WO: Stellenbosch/Devon Valley/Elgin/Western Cape/Upper Hemel-en-Aarde Valley/Coastal ▪ Est 1987 ▪ 1stB 1997 ▪ Tasting Mon-Sat strictly by appt only ▪ Closed all pub hols ▪ Owner(s) Hesticap (Pty) Ltd ▪ Cellarmaster(s) / winemaker / GM Brendan Butler CWM (Aug 2017); Martin Meinert (1997, consultant) ▪ Viticulturist(s) Brendan Butler CWM (Aug 2017) & Henk Marconi (Jan 1991) ▪ 19ha (cabs s/f, merlot, p verdot, ptage, shiraz, sem) ▪ 90t/10,000cs own label 67% red 33% white ▪ PO Box 375 Stellenbosch 7599 ▪ info@meinertwines.com ▪ www.meinertwines.com ▪ T +27 (0)21-865-2363

☐ **Melita** *see Boland Cellar*

Mellasat Vineyards ⓪ ⑪ ⓐ ⓞ ⓑ

Briton Stephen Richardson and family rejuvenated the small Paarl home-farm Dekkersvlei in the late 1990s and crafted a range of pinotage-accented terroir wines with minimal intervention for release when deemed ready. New owner Hugh Asher has appointed Jean van Rooyen as manager-winemaker, converted the manor into guest accommodation and at press time was preparing to open a restaurant.

Premium Exclusive Collection

★★★★ **'M' Cabernet Sauvignon** ⓪ Flag bearer, **16** ⑧⑥ intriguing bouquet of tobacco, mint, crushed berries & spices from lengthy 5 years in barrel. Solid currant palate with leafy notes, chewy tannins.

★★★★ **Tempranillo** ⓪ Varietal notes of cherry tobacco & dried rosepetal engage with raspberry & mulberry in previewed **18** ⑧⑧, tannins firm as expected but polished after 28 months in 70% new oak. Very enjoyable now but fit to keep many years.

★★★★ **Viognier** ⓪ Like previous, **18** ⑧⑥ carefully wooded to retain varietal character while adding layers of complexity. Soft acid on stonefruit finish. 11 months in mixed-origin barrels.

Not tasted: **Méthode Cap Classique White Pinotage.**

Mellasat range

★★★★ **Shiraz** ⊘ More focused than **18** ★★★★ ⑧⑤, with black cherries centre stage, **20** ⑧⑥ has appealing pepper & scrub spiciness, toned-down oak (seasoned barrels, 2 years). Supple & juicy, for everyday enjoyment. No **19**.

★★★★ **Chardonnay** Spicy buttered citrus to the fore on **19** ⑧⑦, oak less prominent, in welcome style change from wood-dominated **18** ★★★★ ⑧⑤. Medium-light body & subtle acid twist make for satisfying solo sipping or seafood accompaniment. 11 months in small barrels, 33% new.

Revelation ★★★ Unusual blend: 73% cab with tempranillo, splash pinotage, year in older barrels. Meaty, foursquare **21** ⑧⓪ has ripe black fruit & hint of iodine. WO Coastal. **Shiraz Rosé** ★★★ Coral hued, light & likeable, **23** ⑧② bursts with fresh red berry fruit underpinned by gentle acid. Unfussy everyday fare. **Chenin Blanc** ⑩ ★★★ Fresh & fruity **23** ⑧① has subtle honey overtone, rather muted acid. Unoaked, with brief lees contact. **'Sigma' White Pinotage** ⓪ ★★★★ Unusual white wine from black grapes, bunch-pressed & fermented in Romanian barrels, some new. Pre-bottling **19** ⑧⑤ fresher than previous, impresses with pear & yellow stonefruit whiffs, noticeable exotic starfruit on finish. Modest 11.5% alc. Discontinued: **Tuin Wyn.**
Discontinued: **Dekker's Valley range.** — GdB

Location/map: Paarl ▪ Map grid reference: G5 ▪ WO: Paarl/Coastal ▪ Est 1996 ▪ 1stB 1999 ▪ Tasting & sales Mon-Sat 10-5 Sun/pub hols 10-4 ▪ Closed Good Fri, Dec 25 & Jan 1 ▪ Cellar tours by appt ▪ Pop-up Synergy food & wine pairing ▪ Light lunches for groups/tours or private dinner functions by appt; picnics in summer; cheese platters; other food-based events ▪ Tour groups ▪ Wine club ▪ Guest house ▪ Owner(s) Hugh Asher ▪ Winemaker(s) Jean van Rooyen (Dec 2022) ▪ Viticulturist(s) Poena Malherbe (Sep 1996) ▪ 13ha/8ha (cab, ptage, shiraz, tempranillo, chard, chenin, viog) ▪ 50t/3,500cs own label 40% red 50% white 10% rosé ▪ IPW ▪ PO Box 7169 Paarl 7623 ▪ tastingroom@mellasat.com ▪ www.mellasat.com ▪ **T +27 (0)21-862-4525**

Mellish Family Vineyards

Flanked by regenerated renosterveld, and dating mostly from the early 2000s, the ±30 ha of vines on the Mellish family's Durbanville farm Welbeloond are a relatively recent addition. Only a few select pockets of their fruit are bottled for the own label, overseen by Andrew Mellish, the stylistic aim being 'freshness, poise, complexity and flavour depth that expresses the ancient, stony shale soils and coastal climate'.

Bakenkop range

★★★★ **Syrah** ⊘ **21** ★★★★☆ ⑨⓪ shows continued improvement, even more attractive than **20** ⑧⑦, from the vibrant, compelling aromas to the balanced, fresh & lively palate, with its gently firm grip. Drinks well now, but plenty of time ahead. Spontaneous ferment; old oak 5 months.

★★★★☆ **Blanc Fumé** Fresh, elegant at 12.5% alc, **21** ⑨② has plenty of blackcurrant-edged fruit given a savoury complexity by oak maturation: third each new, 2nd-fill & older barrels, 9 months. Skin-contact portion adds to succulent but restrained bite & texture. Should develop nicely for a few years.— TJ

Location/WO: Durbanville ▪ Est/1stB 2018 ▪ Closed to public ▪ Owner(s)/cellarmaster(s)/viticulturist(s) Andrew Mellish ▪ 36ha (cab, merlot, ptage, shiraz, chenin, sauv) ▪ 230t/350cs own label 50% red 50% white ▪ Welbeloond Farm, cnr Potsdam Rd & Malibongwe Dr, Cape Farms, Cape Town 8001 ▪ info@mellishvine-yards.com ▪ www.mellishvineyards.com

☐ **Mensa** see Overhex Wines International
☐ **Mentors** see KWV Wines
☐ **Mercia Collection** see Mooiplaas Wine Estate & Private Nature Reserve

Merwida Wines (Huis Te Merwede) ⊘ ⊘ ⊚ ⊛

Custodians of one of the Cape's largest private vineyards, cousins Schalk and Pierre van der Merwe paint a vivid picture of 'over 800 ha and 24 different varieties planted in fertile soils on a bed of riverstone 4 m deep'. It is farmed, and the combination bulk and bottled wines made under the direction of cellarmaster Magnus Kriel with eco and social responsibility in mind, the Papenkuils range spotlighting their work in conserving the namesake Breede River wetland. Schalk's daughter Lieza looks after marketing and the stylish visitor venue, a manor named Huis Te Merwede after the ancestral home beside the Merwede River in Holland.

Family Vintners range
★★★★ **Reserve Chenin Blanc** Oaked version, nice contrast with its sibling. Ferment halfway in tank, then barrel, only 60% matured further 9 months, all to preserve fruit: bruised apple & quince in **22** (89), gentle biscuit tone adding another layer, finishing with mouthwatering lemon zest flavours. Lots to offer.

Merwida range
★★★★☆ **Barbera** ⊘ Italian variety, just handful on market. Long skin contact, 12 months oaking for savoury spice, **21** (90) easily seduces with its fruit purity & freshness, luscious texture, supple tannins. Does barbera proud.

Chardonnay ⊘ ⊛ ★★★★ Portion barrel-aged 6 months, all French in **22** (85), unlike last. Vivid lemon & ruby grapefruit with oat biscuit seasoning, has heaps of flavour & personality.

Cabernet Sauvignon ⊘ ★★★ Oak a presence in **20** (80), smoky scents, firm tannin backbone, the plummy fruit more obvious in the flavours. Give another year to meld, or match with rich food. **Pinotage** ★★★★ Back in the guide, with more gravitas, showing plush dark berries, salty liquorice & peppery spice, **22** (84)'s year in barrel & ripe tannin seam give structure, definition. **Chenin Blanc** ⊘ ★★★★ Crunchy green apples, sleek **23** (84) vibrates with freshness & good health, vitality. Created for everyday enjoyment, solo or at table. **Sauvignon Blanc** ★★★ Passionfruit, with some herbal notes, **23** (82) ends refreshingly brisk, with lime peel flavours. **Cap Classique Blanc de Blancs** 🆕 ★★★★ Attractive packaging, **NV** (84) sparkler from chardonnay, 24 months on lees. Forthcoming citrus preserve perfume & flavour, dry, with zesty acidity. Lovely aperitif. WO Breedekloof, as Reserve Chenin Blanc. **Cuvée Brut** ⊘ ★★★ From sauvignon, **NV** (80) carbonated bubbly. Kiwi-toned, touch of sugar, goes down oh so easily. **White Muscadel** ⊘ ★★★★ Full-bodied & -sweet **21** (84) fortified dessert wine exudes muscat's raisiny floral charm in all its decadent deliciousness. Less delicate than **18** ★★★★ (86), now a feisty winter warmer (19.5% alc).

Papenkuils range
Vlei Vygie Pinotage Rosé ⊘ ★★★ Range named after Unesco- & WWF-recognised conservation wetland; individual wines after plants found there, shown on labels. Berry-rich **23** (80) offers bright-fruited, zesty drinking pleasure. WO Breedekloof, as next. **Kukumakranka Unwooded Chardonnay** ★★★ White peach, a hint of citrus, **23** (82) gets the fruit right; crisply dry, made to enjoy at its youthful best. **Waterblommetjie Pinot Grigio** ⊘ ★★★ Not many on the local market, Italian variety doesn't disap-point in **22** (82), floral scents, crunchy fresh palate, a herbal touch to make things interesting.

Huis Te Merwede range
Occasional release: **Rooi**, **Wit**. — CR

Location: Rawsonville ▪ Map: Breedekloof ▪ Map grid reference: C6 ▪ WO: Western Cape/Breedekloof ▪ Est 1963 ▪ 1stB 1975 ▪ Tasting & sales Mon-Fri 9-5 Sat/pub hols 10-3; pub hols (seasonal) please call ahead ▪ Cecile's Tea Room Tue-Fri 9-5 Sat 10-3 (times may vary on pub hols) ▪ Terroir-driven wine tastings, cheese platters, fresh baked goods, light lunches, barista ▪ Small conference facility ▪ For bookings at Huis Te Merwede: lieza@merwida.com/joel@merwida.com ▪ Owner(s) Schalk & Pierre van der Merwe ▪ Facility manager (Huis Te Merwede) Lieza van den Heever ▪ Cellarmaster(s) Magnus Kriel ▪ Winemaker(s) Magnus Kriel (Dec 2000) & Jéan Aubrey (Sep 2021), with Sarel van Staden (Aug 1982) & Nico Visser (Jan 2016) ▪ Viticulturist(s) Magnus Kriel ▪ 800ha (barbera, cab, merlot, shiraz, chard, chenin, sauv, sem, viog) ▪ 22,000t/25,000cs own label 40% red 60% white ▪ ISO 22000, Fairtrade, IPW, WIETA, WWF-SA Conservation Champion ▪ PO Box 4 Rawsonville 6845 ▪ wines@merwida.com ▪ www.merwida.com ▪ **T +27 (0)23-349-1144/WhatsApp +27 (0)67-361-3210 (bookings)**

☐ **Metafisika** *see* Osbloed Wines

Metanoia Permaculture Farm & Distillery ⓥ

Kenny Scheepers in 2015 bought a degraded piece of land near Barrydale in the Tradouw Valley to establish this venture 'based on regenerative agricultural principles, including permaculture, agroforestry and holistic management'. The name Metanoia suggests spiritual conversion and transformation. Unsurprisingly, perhaps, the distillery (producing a wide range of spirits from a hybrid copper potstill, including those tasted here) runs on gas and solar, and all water is harvested from rain or a waterfall in the mountain above the farm. There's a small block of colombard and chenin, from which an estate potstilled brandy should be bottled later this year. If the inaugural Heerlik blended brandy is a portent, it should be an exciting moment.

★★★★★ **Heerlik Brandy** (ⓝ) ⊘ Remarkable spirit ⑨⓪ in many ways. Rare thing - no colourant added, so the straw hue is from the (bought-in) 40% potstill component matured 5 years in oak. As rare, no added sweetness, the bone-dry palate giving delicate refinement uncommon for a blended brandy at 43% alc, though the finish is a touch hot. Deserves sipping unmixed (but doesn't insist!). Sense of great purity to the lovely flavours. Beautifully done.

★★★★ **Premium Husk Spirit** (ⓝ) From shiraz, pale straw thanks to 9 months in oak. This grappa ⑧⑦ touch more suave & smooth than sibling, rather unctuous even. A light fruitiness with a modestly perfumed quality. Both 43% alc, 'diluted to drinking strength with mountain water', like Heerlik. 500 ml.

★★★★ **Husk Spirit** (ⓝ) There's a little traditional grappa rusticity on these, but also a modern perfumed quality. This vigorous, appropriately fiery water-white version ⑧⑥ from chardonnay has a citrus note showing through. Grape husks for both ex Joubert-Tradauw.— TJ

Location: Barrydale ▪ Map: Klein Karoo & Garden Route ▪ Map grid reference: C7 ▪ Visits Thu-Sun 10-3 ▪ Online shop ▪ Owner(s) Kenny Scheepers ▪ (chenin, cbard) ▪ Op de Tradouw, Barrydale 6750 ▪ kenny@metanoiadistillery.co.za ▪ www.metanoiadistillery.co.za ▪ **T +27 (0)71-641-4869**

Metzer & Holfeld Family Wines ⓥ

The 2023 harvest, says Somerset West vintner Wade Metzer, will be remembered as two distinct vintages, before and after the rain. But, he phlegmatically adds, 'as winegrowers we always try and adhere to the old-timey saying: there's no such thing as bad weather, only the wrong clothes'. Expressing a sense of 'somewhere-ness' in his wine has been his long-standing pursuit, and the focus of his low-intervention crafting is now the Helderberg mountain slopes and foothills. Syrah is his first love, and the variety remains a pillar of the boutique winery he owns with Australia-born friend and fellow deep-sea fishing enthusiast Barry Holfeld. However, Wade's more recent bottlings, particularly the now trio of near-identically vinified and matured chenins, are exceptionally fine and collectible, too, and critically acclaimed.

★★★★★ **Cinsault** (ⓐ) (ⓦ) Boisterous red berry fruit on **22** ⑨②, from oldest bushvine parcel in the range, planted 1957. 30% wholebunch amplifies juiciness & chalky texture, shaped by 10 months old oak. Character kept intact by bottling unfined & unfiltered.

★★★★★ **Shiraz** (ⓐ) From two elevated Helderberg blocks, **22** ★★★★★ ⑨⑤'s radiant plum hue a clue to its intense fragrance of violets, incense & black cherries. Melting tannins on vibrant acid thread, some added stems aid texture, spice & structure, which gains savouriness from 11 months in oak, 10% new. Last made was **19** ⑨③.

★★★★★ **Mantra** Adds 20% bushvine cab ex Steynrust to **21** ⑨⓪'s Helderberg majority shiraz & Firgrove cinsault in **22** ⑨⓪. 11 months in old oak a platform for dainty floral aromas (roses, lilies) unwinding to palate of savoury intensity, complemented by crunchy tannins & stemmy spice from wholebunch component.

★★★★★ **Maritime Chenin Blanc** (ⓐ) Impressing even more than **21** ⑨③, stunning **22** ★★★★★ ⑨⑤ from same single parcel of 42 year old dryland bushvines near False Bay. Gorgeous & pure aromatics, lemon, pear & blossoms, lithe & long texture & palate. Older-barrel ferment/9 months on lees without stirring. A lift of salt on the finish.

★★★★☆ **Montane Chenin Blanc** ⓐ Flashes of mountain fynbos, ripe fig & lime on **22** ⑨④, broader, more immediately appealing than **21** ★★★★★ ⑨⑥. Elegant texture from 58 year old dryland bushvines, tantalising mineral acidity winds through. Oak as for Maritime.

★★★★☆ **Riverine Chenin Blanc** ⓝⓔⓦ From 1986 vineyard planted between 2 mountain streams on Helderberg foothills. Gently savoury **22** ⑨⓪ aged on the lees 10 months in older barrels, a delicate texture cushions peaches, pineapples & pears.

★★★★ **PetNat** Bright, bubbly & fruit-forward, **22** ⑧⑧ single-ferment sparkling a total joy. 100% chenin blanc, fermented in barrel, showcases grape's apple & pear vibrancy. Well-judged 4.6 g/L sugar appetisingly drier than **21** ⑧⑥. From 1981 single bushvine parcel by False Bay.

Not tasted: **Cabernet Sauvignon**. — ML

Location: Somerset West ▪ WO: Stellenbosch ▪ Est/1stB 2006 ▪ Tasting by appt ▪ Owner(s) Wade Metzer & Barry Holfeld ▪ Winemaker(s) Wade Metzer ▪ 30t/4,500cs 60% red 40% white ▪ info@mhfwines.co.za ▪ www.mhfwines.com ▪ **T +27 (0)72-279-7645**

M'hudi Wines

In the early 2000s, with little farming experience and limited wine knowledge, the upcountry Rangaka family bought a Stellenbosch vegetable, fruit and wine farm. 'A relentless pursuit of one's aspirations' has seen the wine business grow from a boutique 3,000 to a significant 160,000 cases a year. Recent visitor focus has brought renovations and extended opening hours, plus cheese boards and wood-fired pizzas, the goal being 'an inclusive, non-traditional and relaxed tasting room'. A bistro and accommodation will follow.

M'hudi Boutique Family Wines

★★★★ **Foro's Legacy** Blend & style change in **19** ★★★★ ⑧④, still mostly shiraz but with near-equal mourvèdre, grenache noir & cinsaut for engaging & approachable Rhône combo, showing rosemary & beef whiffs, some charry oak. **18** ⑧⑥ was partnered with Bordeaux varieties.

★★★★ **Barrel Fermented Chenin Blanc** Leading the pack, **21** ⑧⑥ apricot & straw prelude to rich, creamy palate, few grams sugar adding to the plushness. Drinks well now, crisp acid & structure from 20% new oak should ensure it keeps doing so for a few years. **19** ⑧⑧ was last tasted.

Cabernet Sauvignon ★★★★ Succulent & sweet berry tones of **20** ⑧⑤ mingle with dried herbs & vanilla from 35% new oak. Variety's tannin structure & bright acid well-managed to ensure current enjoyment.

Pinotage ★★★★ Quintessential ripe mulberry & subtle banana whiff, **20** ⑧⑤ is supple & friendly, tannins tad rustic by no means unpleasant. **Shiraz** ★★★ Not discontinued as thought. Savoury **19** ⑧② mixes clean leather, Indian spice & biltong, choc-dusted from 20% new oak, ends with a bitter twist.

Harold's Cape Knight Wines

Cabernet Sauvignon ⓥ ★★★★ Typical cassis & fruitcake on **19** ⑧③. Light frame & grip from 30% oaked portion. Ideal everyday red. WO W Cape for these. **Pinotage** ⓥ ★★★ Cocoa fringe to spicy cherry appeal of **19** ⑧②. Good succulence & textured softness. **Chenin Blanc** ⓥ ★★★★ Notch-up **20** ⑧③, ripe tropical fruit balanced by zesty vivacity. Perfect for summer. Discontinued: **Medley**. — NK, CvZ

Location/map: Stellenbosch ▪ Map grid reference: B1 ▪ WO: Coastal/Western Cape ▪ Est 2003 ▪ Tasting Tue-Fri 10-7; pub hols (seasonal) please call ahead ▪ Cheese boards ▪ Bistro 9-6 daily ▪ Owner(s) Rangaka family ▪ Winemaker(s) Albertus Louw (consultant) ▪ 160,000cs own label 90% red 10% white ▪ WIETA ▪ PO Box 30 Koelenhof 7605 ▪ malmsey@mhudi.com ▪ www.mhudiwines.co.za ▪ **T +27 (0)61-476-9365**

☐ **Mía** see Belle Rebelle

Michaella Wines

Eight years ago, Cape Town businessman Adrian Dix created an own brand and dedicated it to his young children Michael and Ella. To ensure only the highest quality represents them, he continues to tap the estimable Lukas van Loggerenberg of Van Loggerenberg Wines to craft the wine, in minuscule quantity, to be elegant and persuasive, with any vintage falling short of their stringent standard not released.

★★★★☆ **Shiraz** Fragrant & enticing **22** (94), energetic & elegant, with pure fruit. Harmonious fine balance, with fresh acidity & restrained tannic structure. Light-feeling but not without intensity. Drinking so deliciously as an infant, one wonders where it has yet to go. 13.2% alc. Last tasted was **17** (93).

★★★★☆ **Chenin Blanc** Characterful **22** (93) more sunny fynbos hillside than peach. Elegantly juicy, with good acidity. As usual, remarkable presence given low alc (11.8%). Lingering & fantailing fruit on stony dry finish. Only older oak, as Shiraz, adding to texture. Natural ferment for both. — TJ

Location: Paarl ▪ WO: Swartland ▪ Est/1stB 2016 ▪ Closed to public ▪ Owner(s) Adrian Dix ▪ Cellarmaster(s)/winemaker(s) Lukas van Loggerenberg (Jan 2016, consultant) ▪ 2t/280cs own label 70% red 30% white ▪ adrian@michaellawines.co.za ▪ www.michaella.co.za ▪ **T +27 (0)21-712-2978/+27 (0)83-230-1634**

☐ **Michelle d'Or** *see* Fort Simon Wine Estate

Micu Narunsky Wines Ⓥ

Micu Narunsky, Somerset West jazz pianist and winemaker, has been on a marketing drive, hence only one of his older vintages still available, to be joined by the '22 Chenin mooted last edition. He's seeking approval to make wine at his home 'and be a proper "garagiste", as the wine will be made very close to my garage'.

★★★★ **Iemanjá** Ⓥ First since **12** (86), **16** (86) is all-touriga (no tinta, souzão). Impeccably ripe mulberry & blueberry mingle with Xmas pudding & cherry tobacco, impressively downy tannins & spicy finish.

Not tasted: **Olodum, La Complicité, Tinta.** — GM

Location: Somerset West ▪ WO: Stellenbosch ▪ Est 2005 ▪ 1stB 2006 ▪ Tasting by appt ▪ Owner(s)/cellarmaster(s)/viticulturist(s) Micu Narunsky ▪ Winemaker(s) Micu Narunsky, advised by Francois Naudé ▪ 4.8t/450cs own label 85% red 15% white ▪ 3 De Hoop Cres, Somerset West 7130 ▪ micunarunsky@gmail.com ▪ www.micunarunsky.com ▪ **T +27 (0)73-600-3031**

Middelvlei Estate Ⓥ 🍴 🏠 ◎ 🅐 ♿

The Momberg family make the point that they've owned Middelvlei on the edge of Stellenbosch town for more than a century, and their winemaking philosophy isn't going to change overnight. Therefore expect 'quality that can age' in the Estate bottlings and 'quality at an affordable price' in the Rooster range. On which subject, 'rooster' is Afrikaans for gridiron, and a reference to one of the favourite visitor attractions here, traditional barbecues, with all trimmings including grilled sandwiches, aka braaibroodjies.

Estate range

★★★★☆ **Cabernet Sauvignon** Ⓥ Stellar harvest **19** (90) structured not to overpower pleasant tealeaf, blackberry fruit; fresh, integrated tannin further adds to elegant touch. Combo French & American oak, in house style, 12 months, 30% new. **18** ★★★★ (88) for earlier drinking.

★★★★☆ **Momberg Pinotage** Ⓥ Top-tier pinotage. Refined **18** (91) has ripe, unshowy raspberry features. Highly polished, the downy fruit is ably supported by fine tannin & lifted freshness. Oak, 60% new, needs year/2 to mesh, allow more savoury development.

★★★★ **Shiraz** Ⓥ Flavoursome dark berries & spice are ripe & welcoming, slide down easily. As in **18** (87), oak subtly aids approachability, but **20** ★★★★ (83) misses some of older vintage's complexity.

★★★★ **Momberg** Ⓥ Happily interwoven cab (59%), shiraz & pinotage. Elegance of **19** ★★★★★ (90) lends light touch to 14% alc, highlights bright, glossy fruit & gentle muscularity. Year oak, half new, & fine tannin need time to settle. **18** (89) tad less graceful.

Free Run Pinotage Ⓥ ★★★★ As name suggests, **20** (85) has no press juice, creating silky flow to juicy plum & mulberry fruit. Spice from older barrels evident but integrated. **Pinotage-Merlot** Ⓥ ★★★★ Usual happy partnership, in **20** (83) shared equally. Ripe mulberry & plum juiciness spiced with year in seasoned oak (70/30 French/American) for extra flavour without disturbing ready drinkability. **Cinsaut Rosé** Ⓥ ★★★ Brisk & fresh **22** (81), lighter bodied (11.5% alc) with wild strawberry & spice appeal extending to fruitily dry finish. WO W Cape, as Chardonnay & Rooster Merlot. **Chardonnay Unoaked** Ⓥ ★★★★ Bracingly fresh **22** (85), delicious, easy to drink, touch higher 13.5% alc no detraction. Very versatile.

Rooster range

Merlot Ⓥ ★★★☆ Tasty mouthful of rich, plummy flavours with fresh fillip. Moderate 13.5% alc in rounded, dry **20** (83). Unoaked. Not tasted: **Chardonnay, Sauvignon Blanc.** — DS

Location/map: Stellenbosch ▪ Map grid reference: E4 ▪ WO: Stellenbosch/Western Cape ▪ Est 1919 family farm/1941 cellar ▪ 1stB 1973 ▪ Tasting & sales daily 10-4.30 ▪ Fee R60pp/4 wines ▪ Closed Good Fri, Dec 25/26 & Jan 1/2 ▪ Cellar tours by appt ▪ Traditional lunchtime braai 7 days a week (booking advisable); evenings by prior arrangement for groups of 35 pax ▪ Tapas & wine pairing; 'braaibroodjie' & wine pairing ▪ Wine blending experience ▪ The Wine Barn function venue (150 pax) ▪ Facilities for children ▪ Conferences ▪ Walking/hiking & MTB trails ▪ 3 Cottages ▪ Owner(s) Momberg family ▪ Cellarmaster(s)/winemaker(s)/viticulturist(s) Tinnie Momberg (Feb 1992) ▪ 160ha/50ha (cab, merlot, ptage, shiraz, chard, sauv) ▪ 200t/30,000cs own label 95% red 5% white ▪ IPW, WIETA ▪ PO Box 66 Stellenbosch 7599 ▪ info@middelvlei.co.za ▪ www.middelvlei.co.za ▪ T +27 (0)21-883-2565

Midgard

Between vintages at press time, this 'good-quality sauvignon at a reasonable price for a good cause' aids adults with special care needs from all Western Cape communities at the Alta du Toit Aftercare Centre in Cape Town, through the profits of sales. Winemaker Riaan Oosthuizen crafts selected Durbanville grapes pro bono.

Location: Durbanville ▪ Est/1stB 2012 ▪ Closed to public ▪ Winemaker(s) Riaan Oosthuizen (Nomada Wines) ▪ 2-3t/±300cs own label 100% white ▪ PO Box 2703 Durbanville 7551 ▪ thetreehouse@mweb.co.za

Migliarina Wines

Carsten Migliarina's small but exciting portfolio comprises mostly single-variety wines, plus an experimental one from a different cultivar each year for 'complete artistic freedom' - the next is an albariño 'which I am super excited about'. The Somerset West-based, internationally experienced sommelier and winemaker's philosophy is well reflected in his creations: 'fruit-driven wines that represent the SA authenticity of the variety, and show the true flavours of the grape'. To this end he avoids fining, filtration and cold stabilisation.

Migliarina range

★★★★☆ **Grenache** Ⓥ Swaps Wellington source for Stellenbosch, **21** ⑨⓪ retains house's on-trend lighter styling, lithe tannin structure. Shade less generous raspberry & black cherry girth than last **18** ⑨⓪ but as satisfying, dry & savoury.

★★★★ **Syrah** Ⓥ A little darker toned, more brooding than siblings, with strong iodine & blackberry nuances, still delicious & accessible thanks to neatly tucked tannins. **20** ⑧⑧ from single Helderberg vineyard, like last **17** ★★★★☆ ⑨⓪. Mixed-provenance oak, 14 months.

★★★★ **Chenin Blanc** Ⓥ Impressive depth & weight from 40 year old bushvines in white peach- & nectarine-toned **20** ⑧⑨. Vinified, matured as Bush Vine Chardonnay; here the oak is barely noticeable.

Not tasted: **Chardonnay**.

Premium Range

★★★★ **Chardonnay Bush Vine** Ⓥ The plusher, more obviously wooded version. **20** ⑧⑧ concentrated, fully ripe yellow peach/orange citrus, buttered toast finish. (Uncertified) single vineyard bushvine fruit, bunch pressed, spontaneously fermented/aged in barrel, unfiltered/fined.

Not tasted: **Syrah-Cabernet Sauvignon Equilibrium**.

Creative range

Not tasted: **Luminosity Blanc de Noir**. — CvZ

Location: Somerset West ▪ WO: Stellenbosch ▪ Est 2001 ▪ 1stB 2002 ▪ Tasting by appt only ▪ Owner(s)/winemaker(s) Carsten Migliarina ▪ 4,000cs own label 40% red 60% white + 1,920cs for clients ▪ Brands for clients: Foodbarn Restaurant, Aubergine ▪ PO Box 673 Stellenbosch 7599 ▪ carsten@migliarina.co.za ▪ www.migliarina.co.za ▪ T +27 (0)72-233-4138

☐ **Miko** see Mont Rochelle Hotel & Vineyard

Mile High Vineyards

We've noted before, growing wine at altitude 1,680 m in eastern Free State province isn't for the faint of heart. Artisan vintners John and Trish Critchley use the words 'abnormally excessive' to describe the rain that fell at their Rose House guest farm near Fouriesburg in 2022 and 100-year-high 2023, resulting in just 2 tons each of pinotage and shiraz, with modest sugar and ripeness. Unfazed, they brought in Cape grapes to bottle separately and thus boost volumes for the fans of their never-say-die wines, available via online shop.

The Bald Ibis range

★★★★ **Estate Shiraz** Lighter touch for **22** ★★★ ⑧②, from barrel shows red currants & berries in a fresh, streamlined body (11.5% alc) that's tasty & easy to drink. Last reviewed was exceptional **19** ★★★★★ ⑨②.

Cabernet Sauvignon (NEW) ★★★ Previewed **22** ⑦⑨ quite closed, some cherry fruit & hint of graphite, should reveal more once bottled. Wellington grapes, as Shiraz. Fermented in open brick tank, basket pressed, aged in old barrique, as all. **Estate Pinotage** ★★★ Oak gives gentle shape to pre-bottling **22** ⑦⑧'s delicate fruit, adds spice to the fresh berries. Misses firmness of previous but makes an enjoyable lunchtime red. **Shiraz** (NEW) ★★★ Tasted before bottling, **22** ⑧① is deep-flavoured, with plums & cherries sprinkled with peppery spice, house's brisk acidity evident here too. Not tasted: **Pinot Noir**. In abeyance: **Shiraz-Pinotage**, **Shiraz-Tannat**. — ML

Location: Fouriesburg ▪ WO: Free State/Western Cape ▪ Est 2008/2009 ▪ 1stB 2013 ▪ Tasting & sales Tue-Sat 10-4; pub hols (seasonal) please call ahead ▪ Tasting fee ▪ Closed Easter Sun, Dec 25/26 & Jan 1 ▪ Winelovers should phone to order the wine, which can be couriered ▪ Cellar tours by appt ▪ Mile High Vineyards lunch venue 10-4 ▪ Farm produce ▪ Walking/hiking trails ▪ The Rose House: 2 garden suites & 2 barn cottages (self-catering) ▪ Owner(s)/cellarmaster(s)/winemaker(s) John & Trish Critchley ▪ Viticulturist(s) Johan Wiese (Aug 2008) ▪ ±460ha/1.5ha (ptage, pinot, shiraz) ▪ 6-8t/800cs own label 100% red ▪ PO Box 149 Fouriesburg 9725 ▪ critch@netactive.co.za ▪ www.milehighvineyards.com ▪ **T +27 (0)82-319-0722**

Miles Mossop Wines

Twenty years have passed since CWG member Miles Mossop began crafting small batches of wine, and naming them for family members, while still full-time in the Tokara cellar, building an international reputation for sustained excellence that's mirrored in this signature label. The number of wines has grown, and grape sourcing expanded beyond home-base Stellenbosch to include Swartland, among others, but the 'simple', tried-and-true approach is unchanged: 'Source grapes from exceptional vineyards, tend them best you can, pick the grapes at the correct time, and help guide them through the natural process of winemaking'. With no significant developments to report, it's a case of 'just trying to do the same things even better'.

CWG Auction range

★★★★☆ **Maximilian** ⑱ Seriously opulent in **20** ⑨④, but cab-merlot (87/13) blend as distinguished as predecessors. Most expressive & sumptuous of the high-end reds, with a dense core of cassis reined in by fine-grained tannins. Similar vinification: part wholeberry natural ferment, portion in oak, barrel matured 22 months. Already so harmonious but deserves a decade or more yet. **19** ★★★★★ ⑨⑥ also distinguished.

The Family range

★★★★☆ **Sam** ⑱ Cabernet (92%) provides the firm foundation for **20** ⑨④ that includes splashes cab franc & merlot. More serious styling & oak (51% new) than Max. Blackcurrant & some salty savouriness enveloped in firm but fine dry tannins. Like **19** ⑨④, quite sophisticated though youthfully restrained; augurs well for a rewarding future.

★★★★☆ **Max** ⑱ Confident Bordeaux blend, mostly cab plus merlot, petit verdot & cab franc (56/23/15/6), shows more opulent fruit depth in **20** ⑨④. Classic dark berries & pencil shavings, touch less new oak (22 vs 38%) is well integrated & supportive. Balanced, though still quite tightly structured, more drinking pleasure with time. In a range of bottle formats.

★★★★☆ **Saskia** ⑱ A few tweaks to **21** ⑨④ bottling of consistent charmer, but retains signature aromatic white peach & citrus from blend chenin (59%), clairette, grenache blanc, viognier & verdelho ex older Swartland vines. Wholebunch natural ferment & ageing, mostly in oak, 10% new, 19% in concrete 'egg' for clean piquancy fleshed out by leesy breadth. Merits ageing. Also in 1.5L.

Not tasted: **Kika**. In abeyance: **Tony's Cape Vintage Reserve**.

The Chapters range

★★★★ **Chapter One Swartland Cinsault** From low-crop bushvines, naturally fermented & matured in concrete 'egg'. **22** ⑧⑥ a little plusher & fuller at 12.5% alc than **21** ★★★★ ⑧⑤, reprises delicate scented fruit pastille & dried fynbos notes with refined, smooth tannins.

★★★★☆ **Chapter Three Stellenbosch Chenin Blanc** ⑱ ⊛ From 37 year old bushvines on Bottelary Hills shale. Tangy, ripe yellow peach flavours in **22** ⑨④ from natural ferment & oaking, 15% new. A fine food-pairer now, will unfurl beautifully in time. Brighter & crisper than Swartland sibling.

★★★★ **Chapter Four Stellenbosch Sauvignon Blanc** ⊛ As feisty & fresh in **22** (89), albeit a touch riper & rounder, from same 35 year old bushvines on shale. Naturally fermented & aged on lees in older oak, adding breadth to contrast with citrus rind (dried & fresh) & piquant gooseberry nuance. Quite mouthfilliing at 13.5% alc & shade off **21** ★★★★☆ (90), still a fine one for the table.

Not tasted: **Chapter Two Swartland Chenin Blanc**.

The Introduction range

★★★★ **Red** Cab (76%) plus cinsaut & splash merlot in **21** (86). Less forthcoming than previous, but smoky dark berry flavours & firmer, drier tannins would pair so well with a hearty roast. Well-melded oak backing to this mealmate & good introduction to the more serious reds.

★★★★ **Chenin Blanc** With splashes of clairette, grenache blanc, verdelho, viognier & sauvignon. **22** (87) is succulent, fresh & flavoursome: yellow peach, kiwi & citrus; partly aged in oak, rest concrete 'egg' & steel. WO Coastal, as Red.— MW

Location: Stellenbosch ▪ WO: Stellenbosch/Swartland/Coastal ▪ Est/1stB 2004 ▪ Closed to public ▪ Owner(s)/winemaker(s)/viticulturist(s) Miles Mossop ▪ 8ot/5,000cs own label 61% red 36% white 3% NLH ▪ PO Box 7339 Stellenbosch 7599 ▪ office@milesmossopwines.com ▪ www.milesmossopwines.com ▪ **T +27 (0)66-275-9637**

☐ **Milkwood** *see* The Grape Grinder
☐ **Millstream** *see* DGB (Pty) Ltd

Mimosa Wines

Multiple new releases by Bernhard Hess and Richard Weilers, owners of the boutique winery on the main road in Montagu, who work with Robertson consultant Lourens van der Westhuizen to produce 'terroir-driven, Old-World-style wines that showcase what nature offers'. Bespoke brandy has also been offered for some years now, and the XO debuting this edition is 'a welcome addition to the Mimosa stable'.

Reserve range

★★★★ **Natus MMX** Elegant, Cape Bordeaux, equal 40% cab & merlot, dabs malbec & petit verdot in **21** ★★★★☆ (90). Rich mulberry & cassis fruit in frame of supple tannins, well integrated. Notch up on cab-free, merlot-based **20** (88). Less oak, 30% new. WO W Cape, as next.

★★★★ **Solus Cape Blend** (NEW) Pinotage leads 4 Bordeaux grapes in enticing **22** ★★★★☆ (90), masterly melange of sweet plummy fruit, measured tannins & fine minerality ex petit verdot. Also-tasted **21** (88) has all 5 Bordeaux varieties, similar profile & character. Both vintages 15 months in 20% new oak.

★★★★ **Josef Chardonnay** (NEW) Limited release honours co-owner Bernhard Hess' father. Just 2.2 kg grapes cosseted into each bottle of **22** (86) for concentrated flavours, 11 months oak, half new, for oatmeal richness lifted by citrus acid. Enduring finish. Attractively moderate 12.4% alc.

★★★★ **Chenin Blanc** ⊛ **19** ★★★★ (85) tighter than **18** (88) & **17** ★★★★☆ (90), needs time for harmony; brief aromas, lightish body underpinned by zesty core, oak adds sweet note. WO W Cape.

★★★★ **Méthode Cap Classique Blanc de Noir Brut** ⊛ From pinot noir & chardonnay, 60 months on lees. 10% oak adds shoulder to modest lees, brioche tones of **15** ★★★★☆ (84). Brisk bubble, crisp & dry. Lighter than last **13** (86).

★★★★☆ **5 Year Old Alambic Potstill Brandy** Latest bottling of 5YO potstill (86) has better integrated spicy oak notes than previous. Dried fruit rather than the commoner ripe apricot makes for a more restrained, though still rich presence. Balanced & smooth.

★★★★★ **Alambic Potstill Brandy XO** (NEW) Lighter hued than most, a lovely rich gold, 10YO potstill (92) (using the international category) has more delicate, refined & complex bouquet than younger sibling. Floral hints come through, with fruit & strong notes of oak. Nuanced & subtly sweet palate continues the focus, making for elegant sipping. Distilled from Stellenbosch chenin. 40% alc.

★★★★ **Méthode Cap Classique Blanc de Blancs Brut** Deliciously mature & ready bubbly from chardonnay gains amazing depth & penetrating length of flavour from 6 years on lees. **15** (86) enticing nori, brioche & umami resonance, elegant palate weight. Last tasted was **13**.

Not tasted: **Pinotage**, **Natural Sweet**.

Mimosa range

★★★★ **Mysterium Rhône Blend** Shiraz (60%) with grenache, mourvèdre. Spicy, ripe & meaty **21** ⑧⑧ has usual neat tannin trim & freshness for satisfying early drinking. Older oak. Also in 1.5L. WO W Cape.

Cabernet Sauvignon ★★★★ Elegant, berry-toned **21** ⑧③ steps up in reined-in herbaceousness & use of oak, none new. Palate is supple, finish bone-dry, alc a modest 13%. **Shiraz** ★★★★ Dark berries & pepper spice attract; juicy, fleshy fruit, sound acid seam & grippy tannins up the allure. New oak complementarily raised to 30% in **22** ⑧⑤. **Chardonnay** ★★★ Pleasant current drinking in **22** ⑧①, quite complex floral aromas before creamy lemon flavours & hint of oak sweetness. Not tasted: **Sauvignon Blanc**. — DS, TJ

Location: Montagu ▪ Map: Klein Karoo & Garden Route ▪ Map grid reference: B8 ▪ WO: Robertson/Western Cape ▪ Est 2004 ▪ 1stB 2003 ▪ Tasting, sales & restaurant Wed-Sun 9-5; pub hols (seasonal) please call ahead ▪ Tour groups ▪ BluVines Restaurant ▪ Owner(s) Bernhard Hess & Richard Weilers ▪ Cellarmaster(s)/winemaker(s)/viticulturist(s) Lourens van der Westhuizen (consultant) ▪ 5ha/3ha (cab, shiraz, chard, sauv) ▪ 20t/2,480cs own label 70% red 30% white ▪ PO Box 323 Montagu 6720 ▪ bernhard@mimosa.co.za ▪ www.mimosawines.co.za ▪ **T +27 (0)23-614-1512**

☐ **Miracle Bush** *see* Swartberg Wingerde

Miravel Ⓠ

Zimbabwe expats Maarten and Janine van Beuningen still live on the Helderberg farm which originally housed their boutique brand, named for children Mark, Michael, Melanie and David. Latterly neighbours' grapes have been sourced and vinified by contractors, and the wines offered for tasting by appointment.

★★★★ **Cabernet Sauvignon** Cassis- & smoke-toned **20** ⑧⑥ more restrained than last-tasted **15** ★★★ ⑧⓪ (14.3% alc vs 15.5%), smoother & easier to drink. Body neatly perked up by fresh acid & pliable tannin.

★★★★ **Petit Verdot** Ⓠ The flavours of **16** ⑧⑥ are ripe & the tannin robust enough to outweigh 15% alcohol. A fruit purity, hint of scrub, lend a certain refinement, big-boned as this wine may be.

★★★★ **Nigma** Barrel-fermented sauvignon, **21** ⑧⑥ flavoursome & nicely dry with no rough edges, oak well-judged (none new), brief skin contact adding texture, extending the finish.

Ella Family Reserve Cabernet Sauvignon ★★★★ While **19** ⑧⑤ flagship delivers house's juicy blueberry & mulberry fruit & slight warmth (alc nudges 15%), a change to all-new oak adds 'woody' tannins & noticeable sweet vanilla. **1952 Family Blend** ★★★★ Port-like overtones of prune & ripe plum, firm tannins & 15% alc that mutes the freshness. **18** ⑧④ mostly cab, splashes merlot & petit verdot, 2 years older oak. **Sauvignon Blanc** ★★★★ Quite rare to see older-vintage sauvignon on current release, but tangy **21** ⑧④'s bottle age adds pleasing white asparagus to usual nettle & pea shoot. Discontinued: **Merlot**. — CvZ

Location/WO: Stellenbosch ▪ Map: Helderberg ▪ Map grid reference: A3 ▪ Est 2002 ▪ 1stB 2005 ▪ Tasting & sales Mon-Sat & pub hols by appt ▪ Closed Ash Wed, Easter Fri-Mon, Ascension day, Pentecost, Dec 25/26 & Jan 1 ▪ Owner(s) Maarten & Janine van Beuningen ▪ Winemaker(s) Schalk van der Westhuizen (whites since 2020, reds since 2019) & André Liebenberg (reds, 2018 vintage) ▪ 500cs own label 55% red 45% white ▪ PO Box 5144 Helderberg 7135 ▪ maarten@miravel.co.za ▪ www.miravel.co.za ▪ **T +27 (0)21-842-3154/+27 (0)72-212-4668**

Mischa Estate Ⓠ ⑪ ◎

'Minimum interventions and maximal net positive impact' continues to be the philosophy of the Barns brothers, Andrew and Gary (aka 'The Vine Guys'), who produce a range of boutique wines with assistance of a core team, and viticulture professor Kobus Hunter in an advisory role for the Ring Fence blend, while running their Wellington estate's four-decades-old vine nursery. Biodiversity efforts show increasingly positive results, the naturally made wines are now all vegan and vegetarian, and the by-appointment winetasting experience has been reopened. Selections from their portfolio (named for the Barns' great-great grandmother's Russian ballet partner) are available on popular local third-party platforms, in local gourmet and fine-dining establishments, and internationally via partner portals and direct-to-market stores.

Reserve range

★★★★☆ **Grenache** ⊛ Outstanding varietal expression. Voluptuous & generously fruited, rose-scented **22** ⑨③ offers sweet berry compote with delicate tobacco note, suede tannins & persistent finish. Mix of French, Hungarian & American oak barrels lends weight & finely judged spice. **21** ★★★★★ ⑨⑤ a standout.

★★★★☆ **Malbec** Bold, dense 22 ⑨ follows form in its massive tannins, opulently ripe black berry & cherry, plum pudding spice. Despite fruit ripeness, less rigorous extraction than 21 ⑨ aids drinkability & expression of varietal fragrance. Dabs petit verdot & cab franc.

★★★★ **Petite Sirah** Addition of 10% grenache noir lends vibrant fruit facets, tempers muscularity of 22 ★★★★☆ ⑨. Plush, ripe black berry & cherry, leathery tannins, brooding iodine & earthy notes need time, but hold great promise. 18 months in mixed barriques, 30% new. Tad more finessed than 21 ⑧.

★★★★☆ **Ring Fence** ⑧ Aspirationally priced flagship label, a Bordeaux blend of mostly cab franc in 20 ⑨, splashes merlot, cab & petit verdot. Sleek & refined, with suede tannins, medium-full body & voluptuous fruit-bowl of currants, black cherries & damsons.

Occasional release: **Merlot-Cabernet Sauvignon**, **Créer**.

Mischa Limited Edition-Heritage Collection

★★★★☆ **Cinsault** ⑧ ⑨ From 1974 Stellenbosch bushvine block, Die Dam, 21 ⑨ exudes character & charm, heady perfume, cherry & mulberry fruit. Full, grippy tannins, elegant body & lengthy farewell. An exceptional reincarnation of a once-workhorse grape in SA.

★★★★ **Chenin Blanc** ⑧ ⑨ From venerable 1977 Kliprug heritage vineyard in Voor Paardeberg, unoaked 22 ⑧ oozes charm & character. Svelte & rounded, with evolved dried peach fruit, spicy notes. Massive leap from 21★★★ ⑦.

Estate Limited Edition range

★★★★☆ **Cabernet Franc** Leafy, lean & nervous, with striking graphite & iodine minerality, 22 ⑨ shows quintessential varietal character. Herb-infused cassis mingles with damp earth & delicate oak spice, cossetted by ripe, solid tannins. Splashes merlot, petit verdot, 18 months in oak.

Estate range

★★★★ **Cabernet Sauvignon** ⑧ Young, vibrant 21 ⑧ has a signature blackcurrant, liquorice & iodine profile on four-square tannins. Full & earthy, with touches of leaf & tar, promises rewards for cellaring. 15 months in mixed oak.

★★★★ **Merlot** ⑧ Lean & focused 20 ⑧, with leafy notes, sweetly ripe black plum & cherry fruit, subtle oak spice (year mixed small barrels, 20% new) & gentle tannins. Follows mellower 19 ⑧.

★★★★ **Shiraz** ⑧ Ripe & full bodied, with convincing black cherry fruit, 21 ⑧ raises the bar from 20 ★★★★ ⑧. Year in mixed barriques creates a full toasty oak presence but big extract handles it with ease.

★★★★ **Roussanne** Wholeberry-fermented, barrel-matured 23 ★★★★☆ ⑨ is seductively perfumed, with frangipani & rosepetal notes, satisfying fullness on palate. Oak lends weight without intruding, vibrant but well-judged acid maintains poise & drinkability. 21 ⑧ was unwooded.

Mischa range

★★★★ **Sauvignon Blanc** Classy, elegant 22 ⑧ emphasizes tropical fruit core over aromatics, with appealing hints of liquorice & stony minerality on sleek, leesy platform.

Not tasted: **Accordance**.

La Famille range

Cabernet Sauvignon ⑧ ★★★★ Unpretentious & characterful 20 ⑧ shows cheerful cassis fruit on a medium body, with grippy tannins & oaky aromas. WO W Cape for these. **Merlot** ⑧ ★★★★ Emphasises primary fruit in 20 ⑧, hedgerow berries, plums & cherries. Well-judged, silken tannin.

The Vine Guys range

Occasional release: **Sauvignon Blanc**. — GdB

Location/map: Wellington ▪ Map grid reference: B2 ▪ WO: Groenberg/Western Cape/Stellenbosch/Voor Paardeberg ▪ Est/1stB 1999 ▪ Tasting, sales & tours (vine nursery in winter & cellar in summer) by appt Mon-Thu 8-1 & 2-5 Fri 8-1 & 2-4 Sat/Sun closed ▪ Fee R180pp, waived if purchase equals/exceed it ▪ Closed all pub hols ▪ Snacks by appt ▪ Walks ▪ MTB ▪ Online shop ▪ Owner(s) Andrew & Gary Barns ▪ Cellarmaster(s) Andrew Barns (Jan 1999) ▪ Winemaker(s) Johan Calitz (2019) ▪ Viticulturist(s) Mortimer Lee (2021) & Kobus Hunter ▪ 40ha (cabs s/f, malbec, merlot, mourv, p verdot, petite sirah, shiraz, rouss, sauv) ▪ 97t/4,000cs own label 75% red 25% white ▪ Oakdene Rd, Wellington 7654 ▪ andrew@mischaestate.com ▪ www.mischaestate.com ▪ **T +27 (0)21-864-1020**

☐ **Misfits** *see* Ken Forrester Wines

Miss Molly

This brisk-selling and remarkably well-priced collection is made by the Môreson team in Franschhoek, and references the Friedman family owners' characterful Weimaraner in the name and on the charming labels. In line with the house's strategic decision, all bubblies are featured here along with the two long-standing stillwines, Manor Born and Kitchen Thief; separately listed Môreson focuses on stillwines from chardonnay.

★★★★ **Petit Rosé** ⊘ Chardonnay (63%) resumes lead from pinot noir in latest **NV** ⑧⑥ pink cap classique sparkler. Crisp & tangy interplay of lime & berries, subtle toasty note from time on lees, vibrant yet pleasingly rounde on palate. WO Coastal, rest Franschhoek.

★★★★ **Bubbly** ⊘ Vivid apple aromas - blossom & baked - lend bright appeal to **NV** ⑧⑦ cap classique bubbly from chardonnay & 9% chenin. Crisp, pithy citrus flavour, light, taut, dry finish. Richness added by 10% wooded portion, plus dosage containing oaked & lightly carbonated chardonnay.

Kitchen Thief Sauvignon Blanc ⊘ 🍷 ★★★★ Zippy verve of grapefruit & blackcurrant on fresh **23** ⑧⑤. Cohesive, bright & succulent, good texture from time on lees.

Manor Born Chardonnay ⊘ ★★★★ Sherbety tang with light cream nuance on **22** ⑧⑤. Third oaked, 11% new, rest year on lees in concrete 'egg' for texture & length. Not tasted: **Blanc de Blancs**. — FM

Misty Mountains Estate ⑨ 🍴 🏠 ◎

The focus at this family estate near Stanford in the Walker Bay district - overseen by the Klein River mountains - is firmly on sauvignon blanc and syrah. There's a new example of each variety reported on below, and a Single Vineyard Syrah will soon complete the range. Meanwhile there's a rosé that, unusually, features both, and only the sparkling wine (vinified some years back) diverges.

★★★★ **AnaMae Barrel Fermented Sauvignon Blanc** Variety less important than 9 months on skins in barrel for **22** ⑧⑥, though it hints at tropical fruit along with more savoury, spicy notes. Nicely balanced, fresh & dry. Should be great with food. The 'orange wine' character more restrained than in 21 ★★★★ ⑧⑤.

★★★★ **High Terrace Bush Vine Sauvignon Blanc** (NEW) Slightly deeper straw hue on **23** ⑧⑧ than on Single Vineyard version & adding blackcurrant note to increase complexity. Acidity notably succulent & there's some phenolic grip to the suppleness. More characterful & interesting.

★★★★ **Single Vineyard Sauvignon Blanc** Good varietal character on aromatic **23** ⑧⑥, with tropical nose dominant but also citrus notes. Flavourful, balanced & fresh.

Family Reserve Syrah (NEW) ★★★ Smoky, charry notes dominate any ripe dark fruit on **19** ⑦⑦, though only older oak barrels. Heavy texture, a touch of sweetness. 14.5% alc. **Georgia Skin Fermented & Matured Syrah** (NEW) ★★★★ Good dark cherry character on pre-bottling sample of pleasantly rustic **22** ⑧⑤, along with hints of smoke & tobacco. Big & flavourful, softly & thickly textured but with firm ripe tannins. 20 months older oak. 14.5% alc. **Shiraz** ⊗ ★★★ Very ripe & big **19** ⑧① shows sweet fruit, but firm-tannined, dry & rather savoury, with the influence of older oak. **Pink Sauvignon Blanc With A Splash of Syrah** ★★★★ Syrah adds the colour to **23** ⑧③ rosé & a hint of berries to mingle with sauvignon's tropicality for something out of the ordinary. Dry, fresh & grippy. **Amrita Méthode Cap Classique** ★★★ Adds Amrita to name - last MCC was a **15** ⑧⓪ rosé. **17** ⑧② from chardonnay & pinotage shows no rosiness, & has a lemony citrus character. Little development despite 60 months on lees, but lacking real freshness. Not tasted: **Estate Sauvignon Blanc**. — TJ

Location: Stanford ▪ Map: Walker Bay & Bot River ▪ Map grid reference: B5 ▪ WO: Walker Bay ▪ Est 2004 ▪ 1stB 2008 ▪ Tasting & sales Mon-Sun 9-5; pub hols 10-5 ▪ Closed Good Fri, Dec 25 & Jan 1 ▪ Cellar tours by appt ▪ Conferences (±60 pax) ▪ Self-catering cottages ▪ Restaurant & farm stall ▪ Enduro MTB trails ▪ Craft beer, gin & cider ▪ Owner(s) Misty Mountains Estates (director A van Vuuren) ▪ Winemaker(s) Neil Moorhouse ▪ Viticulturist(s) Robert Davis ▪ 46ha/16ha (shiraz, sauv) ▪ PO Box 26 Stanford 7201 ▪ info@mistymountains. co.za ▪ www.mistymountains.co.za ▪ **T +27 (0)82-973-5943**

Mitre's Edge ⑨ 🏠 ◎

The 'small, dedicated and motivated team' on the Paarl border with Stellenbosch are co-owner and winemaker Lola Nicholls, whose father passed the land down to her in 1999, crafting mostly Bordeaux varietal wines and blends, 'slowly and gently'; husband and ex mechanical engineer Bernard, general manager with a focus on the farming activities; assistant winemaker Alex Shone, newly married to Megan, now handling most of the social media; vineyard manager Bertus de Clerk and viticultural adviser Danie Kritzinger, who maintained production levels during the difficult years through careful practices aided by technology.

Flagship range

★★★★☆ **Malbec** Sleek, velvet **20** ⑨⓪ is well integrated, adding depth to measured palate of blueberry & spice, woven with tannins & line of freshness. **19** ⑨⓪ improved on previous.

★★★★☆ **Sholto** (🍂) More complex of the Bordeaux blends, 60% cab with 3 others in deep & engaging **20** ⑨④. Allspice & plum intro, then unfolding layers of cherry, graphite & leather-bound book. House-style dry finish & subtle ageing, combo barrique & FlexCube, just 10% new wood, as The Mitre.

★★★★☆ **The Mitre** Varieties cut from 4 to 2 varieties (cab franc, 92%, & merlot) in **20** ⑨①. Leafier, sappier than notch-up **19** ⑨⓪. Same inviting cassis, roast fennel & black cherry on a mineral spine, with house's satin tannins.

Not tasted: **Cabernet Sauvignon**, **Cabernet Franc**, **Merlot**, **Petit Verdot**. Occasional release: **Merlot Reserve**.

Mitre's Edge range

★★★★ **Shiraz** Rich **20** ⑧⑥'s savoury & spicy profile well balanced by brightening acid & fruity ripe tannins. As confident & seemingly effortless as **19** ⑧⑥.

Cinsaut ★★★★ Understated wine from Wellington bushvines, only 'non-estate' bottling here. **22** ⑧③ oaked (year, 10% new) but shares unwooded **21** ★★★ ⑧⓪'s earthy varietal expression - rhubarb, redcurrant & tomato leaf - in gentle structure. Not tasted: **Viognier**. Occasional release: **Cabernet Sauvignon**, **Rosé**, **Chenin Blanc**.

ME range

★★★★ **nvME Classic Red** (✓) Shiraz leads cab, merlot & petit verdot in latest **NV** ⑧⑥, its silky structure, youthful black mulberry & cassis flavours, crunchy tannins & effortless freshness satisfy.— DS

Location/map: Paarl ▪ Map grid reference: C8 ▪ WO: Simonsberg-Paarl/Wellington ▪ Est 1999 ▪ 1stB 2004 ▪ Tasting & sales by appt Mon-Fri 9-5 Sat/Sun 9-4 ▪ Cellar tours by appt ▪ Online shop ▪ Olive oil ▪ Special events (max 50 pax) ▪ Guest house B&B ▪ Owner(s) Bernard & Lola Nicholls ▪ Winemaker(s) Lola Nicholls (2004), with Alex Shone ▪ Viticulturist(s) Danie Kritzinger (consultant) ▪ Vineyard manager(s) Bertus de Clerk ▪ 58ha/18ha (cabs s/f, malbec, merlot, p verdot, shiraz, chenin, viog) ▪ 33t/4,400cs own label 90% red 10% white ▪ IPW, WIETA ▪ PO Box 12290 Die Boord 7613 ▪ info@mitres-edge.co.za ▪ www.mitres-edge.co.za ▪ **T +27 (0)21-875-5960**

☐ **MM Louw** *see* Diemersdal Estate

MolenVliet Oosthuizen Family Vineyards ⓨ ⓐ ⓞ

The luxury MolenVliet Vineyards accommodation, wedding and conference estate in Stellenbosch's Banhoek Valley, where these wines are the house labels, is owned by former Springbok rugby prop Ockie Oosthuizen and wife Susan. Produced by a contract winemaker, the wines are also available via the online shop.

Private Collection

Cabernet Sauvignon (ⓨ) ★★★★ Firm tannins, prominent acid, modest oaking (just 10% new) give form to **14** ⑧④'s sweet berry fruitiness. **Merlot** (ⓨ) ★★★ Appealing confectionery sugar & black plum aromas, **14** ⑧⓪ drinks easily & well courtesy very soft tannins. **Proprietors Blend** (ⓨ) ★★★★ Cab franc, cab & merlot combo with very ripe rum-&-raisin profile lifted by cab franc's leafiness. **13** ⑧⑤ briefer, with sweeter impression than Selection. 10% new oak is well-judged. First tasted since **05** ★★★★ ⑧⑦. **Proprietors Selection** (ⓨ) ★★★★ Equal cab & merlot blend in **14** ⑧④. Rich & plummy, with nutmeg note, vibrant fantail conclusion. Judicious 10% new oak. Not tasted: **Duet**, **Quartet**, **Sauvignon Blanc**. — GM, CvZ

Location/map: Stellenbosch ▪ Map grid reference: H4 ▪ WO: Simonsberg-Stellenbosch ▪ Est/1stB 2005 ▪ Tasting only available to in-house guests ▪ Wedding/conference venue ▪ 5-star luxury accommodation ▪ Owner(s) Ockie & Susan Oosthuizen ▪ Winemaker(s) Barry van Niekerk ▪ 14ha/8ha (cab, merlot, shiraz) ▪ 13t/±2,500cs own label 100% red ▪ PO Box 6288 Uniedal 7612 ▪ info@molenvliet.co.za ▪ www.molenvliet.co.za ▪ **T +27 (0)21-206-0822**

Momento Wines

A visit to its home-country of Spain kindled Marelise Niemann's love for garnacha, aka grenache, and she's been working with the variety since the inception of her boutique brand 12 vintages ago. Her more recent line-up has added blush and white expressions to the original red one, and all show the benefit of learning to 'listen to the vineyards and they will produce magic'. She casts a wide net for her range, including the West Coast, and brings the select fruit to the Anysbos cellar in Bot River for crafting as naturally as possible.

★★★★★ **Grenache Noir** 🍃 Stalwart & favourite variety for Marelise Niemann since first **11** ★★★★ ⑧⑦. **21** ★★★★★ ⑨④ is light-footed & lithe, perfumed rosepetal & red berries taking centre stage. Secured by lively acid & fine tannin weave, its ageability isn't in doubt. As **20** ⑨⑤, from Swartland fruit.

★★★★★ **Tinta Barocca** 🍃 From 40+ year old vines in Stellenbosch, Darling & Swartland, **21** ⑨④ has focus & clarity in its fresh plum & earth scents. Juicy flesh with sound structural support & balance suggest a promising future. 15% wholebunch. 16 months oaked, as other red, rest 10 months. 13% alc.

★★★★★ **Grenache Gris** 🍃 From 9 year old Voor Paardeberg & SA's only grenache gris vineyard. Week's cold soak pre-ferment for pinkish-gold lights. **22** ⑨④ riveting in its acidity & intense spice & red apple flavours; needs some time to harmonise resistant grip. Natural ferment, older oak & no fining, as all.

★★★★★ **Grenache Blanc** 🍃 Layers of texture & flavour in **22** ⑨③ from Voor Paardeberg fruit, cold-soaked 3 days. Confidently & firmly built, there's also a richer, creamy core hosting hay, honey & green apple medley, underpinned by racy acidity. One of most expressive to date.

★★★★★ **Chenin Blanc-Verdelho** 🍃 Delivers concentration of Paardeberg old bushvine chenin with 34% verdelho ex Voor Paardeberg & Bot River in **22** ⑨④. Generous textural breadth reined in by taut core, layered with tropical flavours of peach, mango & lime, ending bracingly fresh & dry.— AL

Location: Bot River ▪ WO: Western Cape/Paardeberg/Voor Paardeberg ▪ 1stB 2012 ▪ Private tastings on request ▪ Owner(s)/winemaker(s) Marelise Niemann ▪ 4,000cs own label 50% red 50% white ▪ marelise@ momentowines.co.za ▪ www.momentowines.co.za ▪ T +27 (0)82-968-8588

☐ **Moments** *see* Meerendal Wine Estate

Monis Wines

Tuscan brothers Giuseppe and Roberto Moni's turn of the 20th century cheese, olive oil, pasta and wine trading company today is a fortifieds-only business based in Paarl. The team led by cellarmaster Cobus Viviers source locally and from Breede River, Calitzdorp and Stellenbosch for their sherry-style wines. The fortifying brandy spirit is from parent Heineken Beverages' own distilleries.

★★★★ **Full Cream** 🍷 Richest, sweetest of this fortified range, & yet **NV** ⑧⑧ tastes drier than it is. Red amber, concentrated dried fruit & nuts with savoury depths, a tealeaf note. Complex, involving & delicious. **Medium Cream** 🍷 ★★★★ Orange gold & sweet, but **NV** ⑧④ has plenty to offer: classic flor & nutty nose, candied fruit flavours, with an alcohol lift that makes it a perfect aperitif. **Pale Dry** 🍷 ★★★★ From chenin, matured under flor 3 years, then further 3 in solera (average barrel age 64 years!), like all these. Orange gold, touch sugar but **NV** ⑧④ tastes dry. Rock salt & tealeaf, underlying preserved citrus zest, ends savoury. Serve chilled, as aperitif. — CR

Location: Paarl ▪ Est 1906 ▪ Closed to public ▪ Owner(s) Heineken Beverages ▪ Cellarmaster(s) Cobus Viviers (Jul 2020) ▪ 35,000cs 100% fortified ▪ PO Box 266 Paarl 7620 ▪ jacobus.viviers@heineken.com ▪ www. moniswines.co.za ▪ T +27 (0)21-860-1624

☐ **Monogram Collection** *see* Foothills Vineyards

Montagu Wine & Spirits Co

The brothers Brink are thought to be first to make sweet fortified muscadel in the vicinity of Montagu in the 1930s, giving rise to a speciality of the area and of this winery, founded over 80 years ago and now owned by 12 shareholder-growers. Bulk wine is the calling card but winemaker Henk Wentzel sets aside 20,000 choice cases for the own label, available to taste and buy at the revamped venue just off the town centre.

John Montagu range

Shiraz ✅ ★★★ Spicy plum & fruitcake notes on **19** ⑧② . Soft textured, light bodied & unfussy for everyday enjoyment. Unwooded, as all tasted this edition. **Shiraz-Touriga Nacional-Merlot** ✅ ★★★★

Shiraz (51%) holds sway on **19** ⑧⑤, adding violet & ripe blueberry notes to soft, approachable blend. Gentle depth & good body with dry finish. **Muscadel Rosé** ⓠ ★★★ Pale salmon hue & shy floral, peach & berry notes on **21** ⑦⑦, gentle tang of acid & subtle sweetness. **Chenin Blanc** ⊘ ★★★ Improves on last in guava, melon & quince expression. **22** ⑧② light, succulent & uncomplicated, hint of honey at the end. **Red Muscadel** ★★★ Latest NV ⑧② fortified dessert improves on previous in balance of spirit & sugar, latter reduced from 214 g/L to 164. Typical jasmine, sultana & muscat notes but focused & uncloying, pleasantly light. **White Muscadel** ⓠ ★★★ Cohesion, body & concentration in NV ⑧⓪ fortified dessert. Ample mouthfilling honeysuckle & sultana charm, nice clean conclusion. **Cape Ruby** ⓠ ★★★ Dusty red fruitcake & spice on NV ⑦⑨ 'port' from equal touriga & ruby cabernet. Light hearted, the 16.8% spirit well integrated. Not tasted: **Merlot.** Discontinued: **Sauvignon Blanc.**

John Montagu 3L Box range
Chenin Blanc ⊘ ★★★ Tangy freshness to NV ⑧② any-occasion quaffer. Guava & citrus succulence with lively presence. Not tasted: **Shiraz.**

Uitvlucht range
★★★★ **VO Brandy** ⓠ Dark amber hue to blended 5 year old ⑧⑥ from chenin. Full, fruity, with dried peach, fresh pear, light caramel & hint of roast nut, 43% alc will give your favourite cocktail a pleasing kick. **Jerepico Red** ⓠ ★★★ Heady seduction on fortified NV ⑧② dessert from muscadel. Fiery spirit grip to brûléed berry & barley sugar flavours, richly sweet but balanced. 500 ml; also in 250 ml plastic (PET), & 1L, 2L, 5L glass bottles, as next. **Jerepico White** ⓠ ★★★ Golden NV ⑧⓪ fortified muscadel has touch less alc (16.5%) than sibling, bold sultana & honeysuckle sweetness, clean finish. 1L. — FM, WB

Location: Montagu ▪ Map: Klein Karoo & Garden Route ▪ Map grid reference: B8 ▪ WO: Western Cape ▪ Est 1941 ▪ Tasting & sales Mon-Thu 9-5 Fri 9-4 Sat 9-1; pub hols (seasonal) please call ahead ▪ Owner(s) 12 shareholders ▪ Winemaker(s) Henk Wentzel ▪ 140ha ▪ 2,000t/20,000cs 20% red 25% white 55% muscadel ▪ PO Box 332 Montagu 6720 ▪ wine@mwswine.co.za ▪ www.mwswine.co.za ▪ **T +27 (0)23-614-1340**

Mont Blois Wynlandgoed ⓠ ⓒ

The wall that encloses the silo on Mont Blois, lately depicted on some of the labels, was built from red clay and dates from 1948, but ownership by the Bruwers goes back another half-century, when the first of three Robertson properties was bought (the Loire town of Blois was the family home before leaving for SA). Now in the hands of 6th-generation Ernst, the estate supplies most of its grapes to top private cellars and large merchants, but top parcels are crafted for this small-batch line-up in the 1884 cellar by Raymond Kirby.

Mont Blois range
★★★★☆ **Bacchus Red Blend** ⓠ Cab & 18% petit verdot. **18** ⑨② ripely dark fruited, with herbal edge & generally modest demeanour - just 13% alc & only older oak. Like last-made **16** ⑨②, mingles charm & seriousness, with a savoury touch. Balanced, lively & light-feeling.

★★★★ **Hoog & Laag Chardonnay** ⓠ Always the richer, deeper of the pair, **19** ⑧⑧, off clay soils, has ripe stonefruit character (with touch of bruised apple), smooth texture shot through with fine acidity that balances the plush element. Unfiltered, as all.

★★★★☆ **Kweekkamp Chardonnay** ⓠ From a single-vineyard on limestone, **18** ★★★★ ⑧⑨ as previously the subtler, more focused of the chardonnays. With 12.5% alc, lighter & more obviously green-limy than **17** ⑨②, fresh & grippy, with some finesse but less depth & intensity than last.

★★★★☆ **Groot Steen Chenin Blanc** ⓠ Ripely forward, fruity charm balanced by a firm acidity marks **18** ⑨⓪, off 33 year old single-vineyard. The peachy sweetness marks it from more austere chenins but freshness & elegant structure redeem it, & deliciousness is the decider.

★★★★ **Keller Colombard** ⓠ Serious effort with unheralded heritage variety, barrel-matured **20** ⑧⑧ offers spice & minerality, delicate fennel & scented notes, impressive palate weight, salty finish. No **19**.

★★★★ **Grenache Blanc** ⓠ Bold, assertive **20** ★★★★☆ ⑨⓪ has strong oak presence (6 months older barrels), with poached stonefruit, limestone minerality & white nuts. Rich & leesy, with silk texture & impressive weight. Should reward cellaring. First since **18** ⑧⑥.

★★★★ **Kirby Sauvignon Blanc** ⓠ Named for long-serving staff member, now cellarmaster, distinctive & appealing **21** ⑧⑥ has piercing acidity highlighting greengage & granadilla fruit. Lean & linear, demanding seafood matches. **20** untasted.

★★★★☆ **Pomphuis Muscadel** ⓥ Signature mint humbug happily present on golden **17** ⑨②fortified dessert, along with a host of other aromas & flavours. As sweet & viscous as you like, yet poised & lively, everything harmoniously cooperating to give pleasure. Year in old oak. 500 ml.

★★★★☆ **Harpie Muscadel** ⓥ Second single-vineyard fortified, matured in oak. **16** ⑨② packed with multitudinous flavours, from raisin to marmalade & beyond. Silky texture, good, balanced acid keeping from cloy, the 16% alc not fiery. More refined than many examples.

Not tasted: **Tarentaalsdraai Pinotage**.

Closilo range

Kierie ⓥ ★★★★ Entry-level range for early & easy drinking. Unwooded cabernet, showing pure, ripe blackcurrants with convincing fruit tannins in **20** ⑧⑤. **Kopbeen** ⓥ ★★★★ From pinotage that saw no wood, **20** ⑧④ has typical high-toned fruit, metallic note. Juicy & approachable, with sleek ripe tannins. **Agterkop** ⓥ ★★★ Unoaked **21** ⑧① chenin has interesting floral & tropical fruit notes. Light & fresh, with modest aftertaste. **Sandland** ⓥ ★★★★ Crisp & breezy **21** ⑧④ colombard offers rush of tropical fruit with well-judged acidity, pleasant lees texture. **Poekel** ⓥ ★★★★ Bright, aromatic **21** ⑧⑤ sauvignon delivers generous passionfruit, crisp acidity & leesy texture, gunflint on finish. — GdB

Location/map/WO: Robertson ▪ Map grid reference: A5 ▪ Est 1869/1884 (farm/cellar) ▪ Tasting & sales by appt only ▪ Conservation area ▪ MTB trail ▪ Drinkwaterskloof trail run ▪ Owner(s) Ernst Bruwer ▪ Cellarmaster(s) Raymond Kirby (Jun 1984) ▪ Viticulturist(s) Rian Viljoen (2019) & Dean Kriel (Jul 2013) ▪ 288.79ha (cabs s/f, durif, muscadel r/w, p verdot, ptage, pinot, shiraz, cbard, chard, chenin, gewürtz, grenache b, sauv) ▪ Own label 20% red 80% white ▪ IPW, WIETA ▪ PO Box 181 Robertson 6705 ▪ info@ montblois.co.za ▪ www.montblois.co.za ▪ **T +27 (0)23-626-3872/+27 (0)82-561-4139**

Mont du Toit Kelder ⓥ ⊚ ♿

Stephan du Toit, scion of a wine-growing Huguenot family, bought the Wellington home-farm at the foot of Hawequa Mountain in 1996 to handcraft small quantities of international-standard wine modelled on the classics, hence the involvement of German vigneron Bernd Philippi, who continues to advise. A label revamp and upgrade rolling out at press time features the creativity of Iaan Bekker, designer of SA's coat of arms.

Mont du Toit range

★★★★☆ **Le Sommet** ⓥ Different, smooth & savoury blend in riper **18** ★★★★ ⑧⑨ with cab, merlot & petit verdot in the mix. Similar lithe structure, lengthy oaking (18 months, 25% new) in svelte support, but more rounded, showing less gravitas & fruit depth than **17** ⑨④ 4-way partnership.

★★★★ **Mont du Toit** The **17** ⑧⑧ blend has cab franc, cab, rare alicante bouschet & shiraz in undisclosed proportions. Components vary with vintage, yet admirably retain similar dark fruit & savoury profile, sleek tannins. 18 months mostly older oak buff the edges, tempt broaching, though there are a few years in store.

Hawequas ⓥ ★★★★ Touch more modest 4-way blend in **17** ⑧⑤ than **16** ★★★★ ⑧⑧. Earthy red fruit, supple tannins honed by oaking, 25% new, now 12 months vs 18. Balanced, approachable & well priced.

Discontinued: **Cabernet Sauvignon**, **Merlot**.

Les Coteaux range

★★★★ **Cabernet Sauvignon** ⓥ Though plush, rounded & approachable, **17** ⑧⑨ impresses more than **16** ★★★★ ⑧⑤. Succulent ripe black-fruit compote offset by dry, fine tannin balance & generous length.

★★★★ **Cabernet Franc** ⓥ Spiced poached plum & mulberry in riper **20** ⑧⑥. Lacks varietal perfumed lift, a tad brooding (14.5% alc), 18 months, 25% new oak providing drier structural support. No **18**, **19**.

★★★★ **Shiraz** ⓥ Unashamedly ripe & robust in **21** ⑧⑦, with smoky dark-fruit compote & sweet tobacco flavours. Full body (14.5% alc) with rich & velvety texture. Oak (12 months, 25% new) adds a vanilla sheen. Step up on last **15** ★★★★ ⑧⑤, but for hearty fare.

★★★★ **Sélection** ⓥ A rich, smooth & savoury mix of 5 varieties in **18** ⑧⑥. Balanced structure & refined tannins, less time in oak than last, 12 months vs 18, 25% new. Approachable styling. **17** untasted.

Merlot ⓥ ★★★★ Plush black fruit of **18** ⑧⑤ is layered & nuanced, backed by chalky grip from 18 months in 12% new oak & the same duration in bottle.

La Colline range

Cabernet Sauvignon Rosé ⓥ ★★★ Attractive coral hue to dry, fresh & succulent **21** ⑧①, offering cherry & berry appeal. **Sauvignon Blanc** ⓥ ★★★ Subtle lees nuance fleshes out bright, zesty palate of

21 ⑧. Ideal for summer. WO Paarl. **Viognier** ⊘ ★★★☆ Similar tangy nectarine & peach blossom notes in unwooded **22** ⑧. Richly textured, still light (13.2% alc), finishes with a pithy almond twist. — MW

Location/map: Wellington ▪ Map grid reference: C4 ▪ WO: Wellington/Paarl ▪ Est 1996 ▪ 1stB 1998 ▪ Tasting, sales & cellar tours by appt only ▪ Closed all pub hols ▪ Hiking trails ▪ Owner(s) Stephan du Toit ▪ Cellarmaster(s) Bernd Philippi (1997) ▪ Winemaker(s) Philip Costandius (2019), with Abraham Cloete (Jan 2005) ▪ ±40ha/±20ha (alicante bouschet, cabs s/f, merlot, mourv, p verdot, shiraz, tinta barocca) ▪ ±150t/±1,200cs own label mainly red, small volume viognier ▪ IPW, WIETA ▪ PO Box 704 Wellington 7654 ▪ kelder@montdutoit.co.za ▪ www.montdutoit.co.za ▪ **T +27 (0)21-873-7745**

Montegray Vineyards

Returning to the guide after a short break is this sibling label to Bartinney and Plaisir in the Jordaan family portfolio, this showcasing interesting vineyards in limited special bottlings. Previously ex a parcel in Banghoek Valley near the Bartinney home-farm, it's now made from vines in the Simonsberg-Paarl ward.

★★★★ **Syrah** Different fruit source & character to last-tasted **17** ⑧, bolder **22** ★★★★ ⑧ intense plum & spice on big tannin scaffold, finish touch warm at 15% alc. Wild ferment/14 months in older oak.— WB

Location: Stellenbosch ▪ WO: Simonsberg-Paarl ▪ Est 2014 ▪ 1stB 2015 ▪ Discover more & purchase Montegray wines via website ▪ Owner(s) Rose & Michael Jordaan ▪ Winemaker(s) Fred Fismer ▪ Viticulturist(s) Alec Versveld ▪ enquiries@montegray.co.za ▪ www.montegrayvineyards.co.za

☐ **Montestell** see Boland Cellar
☐ **Montino** see Riebeek Valley Wine Co
☐ **Mont Marie** see Klein DasBosch

Mont Rochelle Hotel & Vineyard ⊘ ⑪ ⌂ ◎

Part of UK entrepreneur Richard Branson's Virgin Limited Edition collection of exclusive retreats and hotels since 2014, Mont Rochelle's luxury facilities and on-site winery are scenically arrayed on a mountainside in Franschhoek. Winemaker-viticulturist Michael Langenhoven works with grapes from own vines and ranges further for some of his wines, such as the new Provence-inspired pink one, which is 'like summer in a glass'.

Miko range

★★★★☆ **Syrah** ⊛ 100% syrah in **16** ⑨, like **10** ⑨; last-tasted **12** ⑨ had cab & merlot, was labelled 'Red'. Mega-ripe (15% alc) yet slick & refined, red cherry & currant fruit on well-mannered tannins, serious oaking of 2 years, 80% new barrels, aids further ageing.

★★★★☆ **Chardonnay** ⊘ Barrel fermented/year in new oak, **17** ⑨ packs a fruit & spice punch, with quince & baked cinnamon apple flavours. Long, persistent & intense, with a slatey minerality. Built to last.

Mont Rochelle range

★★★★ **Cabernet Sauvignon** Leaner than last-tasted **18** ⑧, showing subtle oak & cedar, **20** ⑧ allows fruit to take centre stage. Juicy & plush, with well-managed tannins, hints leather & liquorice from 18 months in barrel, 20% new.

★★★★ **Syrah** Meaty, savoury **19** ⑨ has smoothly ripe tannin platform for luscious black core of cherry & baked plum. 18 months in 15% new oak adds finesse & elegant spicing. **17** ⑨ was last tasted.

★★★★ **Chardonnay** Since last-tasted **20** ⑧, oaking up to 85% for 8 months, shows in **22** ⑧'s heightened spicing to succulent citrus fruit. Sleek & fine textured, with wholesome body & spot-on acid.

★★★★ **Sauvignon Blanc** Fresh & fruity **23** ★★★★ ⑧ has striking nettle & nasturtium aromatic kick, firm but well-judged acid. Light, refreshing, just misses generosity of last-reviewed **21** ⑧. Durbanville vines for 50%, as Blanc.

Little Rock range

Rouge ⊘ ★★★★ Early-drinking cab with shiraz & cab franc, **21** ⑧ somewhat muted red berry fruit on well-judged tannins. Cape Agulhas grapes. **Rosé** 🆕 ★★★★ From Swartland grenache noir, **23** ⑧ pale blush, bone-dry, with fragrant rose-scented red berry fruit. **Blanc** ★★★★ Juicy, light & fresh, **23** ⑧ sauvignon with semillon, viognier & chardonnay provides undemanding summer sipping. — GdB

Location/map: Franschhoek ▪ Map grid reference: C2 ▪ WO: Franschhoek/Coastal ▪ Est 1994 ▪ 1stB 1996 ▪ Tasting & sales 10-7 daily; pub hols 10-6 (seasonal) please call ahead ▪ Fee available on request ▪ Wine tasting closed Dec 25 ▪ Cellar tours Mon, Wed, Fri at 11 (pre-booking required) ▪ Winemaker tutored tastings by appt only ▪ Miko Restaurant & The Country Kitchen ▪ Mont Rochelle Hotel & Vineyard ▪ Picnics ▪ Owner(s) Virgin Limited Edition ▪ Cellarmaster(s)/winemaker(s)/viticulturist(s) Michael Langenhoven (Nov 2021) ▪ 33ha/14.32ha (cabs s/f, shiraz, chard, nouvelle, sauv, sem) ▪ 90–120t/12,000cs own label 60% red 40% white ▪ PO Box 448 Franschhoek 7690 ▪ wine@montrochelle.virgin.com ▪ www.montrochelle.virgin.com ▪ **T** +27 (0)21-876-2770

Mooi Bly Winery

Caring for vines and wines at this Paarl venture owned by his Belgian in-laws is Erik Schouteden, a classicist in terms of winemaking approach, with a touch of the maverick in his use of feisty and locally rare tannat, and the rosé he made from chenin but tinted by ageing it in barrels previously used for malbec.

Cultivar range

★★★★ **Tannat** ⓩ Rare varietal bottling of famously tannic grape, though tannins on this **18** ⑧⑦ are firm & dry but well managed. Savoury note to the ripe fruit; the modest 13% alc adds to approachability.

★★★★ **Chenin Blanc Rosé** ⓩ Chenin matured in ex-Malbec barrels 4 months to add colour & some berry notes. Moderate flavour on **21** ★★★★ ⑧④, but softer & duller than **20** ⑧⑥.

Not tasted: **Cabernet Sauvignon, Malbec, Shiraz, Chardonnay, Chenin Blanc**. — DS

Location/map/WO: Paarl ▪ Map grid reference: F4 ▪ Est/1stB 2005 ▪ Tasting, sales & cellar tours by appt ▪ Fee R75pp ▪ Closed Dec 25 & Jan 1 ▪ Walks ▪ 6 self-catering cottages ▪ Owner(s) Wouters family ▪ Cellarmaster(s)/winemaker(s) Erik Schouteden (Jan 2005) ▪ Viticulturist(s) Erik Schouteden (Feb 2001) ▪ 32ha/18ha (cab, malbec, shiraz, tannat, chard, chenin) ▪ 70t/6,000cs own label 50% red 50% white ▪ PO Box 801 Huguenot 7645 ▪ info@mooibly.com ▪ www.mooibly.com ▪ **T** +27 (0)82-371-2299

Mooiplaas Wine Estate & Private Nature Reserve

Blessed with great natural beauty, Mooiplaas with its vineyards and extensive nature conservancy are owned and managed by Tielman and Louis Roos. The vines lie on steep slopes of ancient mineral-rich soils in the Bottelary Hills, overlooking Cape Town. The brothers produce a range of environmentally friendly wines rooted in tradition and artisan techniques to reflect the terroir. Tielman looks after viticulture, while cellarmaster Louis manages exports to 23 countries. Winemaker Bertus Basson, in the cellar seven years now, is especially excited about the chardonnay designed, as all the wines, 'to add joy to life'.

Mercia Collection

★★★★☆ **Tabakland Cabernet Sauvignon Reserve** ⓐ Refined **20** ★★★★★ ⑨⑤, now bottled, rewards patience. Long skin contact, barrel selection after 2 years (as Rosalind, Cab), 40% new, showing as a cedar dusting on the fruit, which is deep, dense & concentrated but feels effortless. Velvet mouthfeel & lovely harmony. Last was **18** ⑨⓪.

★★★★ **Watershed Pinot Noir** ⊘ Improving on last **19** ⑧⑧ in density & concentration, **22** ★★★★☆ ⑨⓪ pure red fruit, silky texture with depth & structure but deft lightness too. Aged in oak, 25% new, year.

★★★★☆ **Rosalind** ⓐ Only in standout years. Cab (50%) leads cab franc, merlot & petit verdot in **20** ⑨② Gears up on **19** ⑨⓪ in depth of Black Forest flavours, leashed power & elegance. Light-footed harmony & balance, with rich, savoury, smooth-textured palate. Made to last. Just 60 cases.

★★★★ **Houmoed Bushvine Chenin Blanc** ⓐ ⓦ Complex construction of fruit from 1972 dryland bushvines. **22** ★★★★☆ ⑨③ rich quince & stonefruit plus creamy nuance from year in oak, 20% new, 10% Hungarian. Tiny portion botrytis fleshes out lively, fresh palate. Gains on last **19** ⑧⑧ in composure & length.

★★★★ **Laatlam Noble Late Harvest** ⓩ Light & uncloyingly sweet **14** ⑧⑨, caramelised sugar flavours from botrytised sauvignon aged 48 months in old oak. Delicious dessert in a glass. 375 ml.

Duel Méthode Cap Classique ⓩ ★★★☆ Pinot noir leads **NV** ⑧⑤ sparkler at 66%, with chardonnay, soupçon meunier. Bruised apple, touch barley sugar, surprisingly rich effect given the slender body & shorter stay on lees than last.

Roos Family range

★★★★☆ **Cabernet Sauvignon** ⊘ Previewed **21** ⑨② inches the bar up on last. Plush but muscular, the spiced fruitcake abundance is checked by squeeze of oak tannin from time in 20% new barrels. Layered, complex & nuanced, it has a dab (10%) of petit verdot. Rewarding now, will improve.

★★★★ **Pinotage** ⊘ Supple vibrancy of **22** ㊇⑦ from bushvines improves on **21** ★★★★ ㊇④. Blueberry & raspberry with gentle spice lift & structure from year in mainly older barrels. Textured, with fine, dry tannin. Good focus & balance, precise finish.

★★★★☆ **Merlot-Cabernet Franc** ⊘ Merlot at 65% leads cab franc in **21** ㊉① preview. Intricate, nuanced, plush yet with musculature of concentrated dark fruit & 18 months oak, 10% new. Light graphite & herb note adds personality & interest to long, rewarding, textured mouthful.

★★★★☆ **Chardonnay** ⒩ⓔⓦ ⊘ ⓐ Confident debut by creamy yet vibrant **22** ㊉④. Peach & orange depth & body within a sound structure from barrel ferment, lees stirring & 11 months in oak, 15% new.

★★★★ **Chenin Blanc Bush Vines** ⓦ Planted in 1972. Cool nights pre-harvest allowed **23** ㊇⑨ to improve on **22** ★★★★ ㊇⑤ in zesty acid. Bright peach & quince on broad, creamy palate from half natural ferment & long lees contact in tank. Textured yet fresh & long.

★★★★ **Sauvignon Blanc** Peppery edge to fig typicity on **23** ㊇⑧ tank sample. Tangy, lively & fresh, racy acid balanced by structured body. Matches previous for interest & length.

Discontinued: **Langtafel range**. — FM

Location/map/WO: Stellenbosch ▪ Map grid reference: B4 ▪ Est 1806 ▪ 1stB 1995 ▪ Tasting & sales Mon-Fri 10-4.30 Sat/pub hols 10-5 Sun 10.30-3.30; closed Sundays from Jun-Aug ▪ Tasting R85/5 wines ▪ Closed Good Fri, Dec 25 & Jan 1 ▪ Gourmet picnic hampers & cheese platters, booking essential ▪ Private dinners/luncheons or tutored tastings in the manor house (a heritage site), by appt ▪ Accommodation ▪ Walks/hikes ▪ MTB ▪ Child friendly ▪ 70ha private nature reserve ▪ Wine club ▪ Owner(s) Louis & Tielman Roos ▪ Cellarmaster(s) Louis Roos (1983) ▪ Winemaker(s) Bertus Basson (2017) ▪ Viticulturist(s) Tielman Roos (1981) ▪ 240ha/90ha (cabs s/f, merlot, p verdot, ptage, pinot, shiraz, chard, chenin, sauv, viog) ▪ 650t/70,000cs own label 56% red 40% white 4% rosé ▪ IPW, WIETA, WWF-SA Conservation Champion ▪ PO Box 104 Koelenhof 7605 ▪ info@mooiplaas.co.za ▪ www.mooiplaas.co.za ▪ **T +27 (0)21-200-7493**

☐ **Moonlight Organics** *see* Stellar Winery
☐ **Môrelig Vineyards** *see* Wightman & Sons Wine Co

Môreson ⓠ ⓞ

At the Friedman family farm in Franschhoek, they continue to follow the plan devised in 2019, phasing out the red wines to focus exclusively on white-wine styles and varieties, chiefly sparkling wine under the Miss Molly label, listed separately, and stillwine under this original range. Marozanne Grobbelaar does the styling with the guidance of Clayton Reabow, Diners Club-lauded cellarmaster and GM.

★★★★☆ **The Widow Maker Pinotage** ⓠ Swansong from Stellenbosch dryland vines. **19** ㊉③ remarkable verve, succulent dark fruit, sprinkling dried leaves, sweet vanilla spice ex 30% new oak.

★★★★☆ **FYM** ⓠ From rare CY18 chardonnay clone. Flinty notes with stonefruit, fresh pineapple on barrel-fermented **20** ㊉④. Citrus & orange blossom, toasted nut from 11 months oak ageing, 33% new.

★★★★☆ **Mercator Chardonnay** ⓠ Orange blossom & lemon sherbet life to **21** ㊉① from single parcel. Rich & creamy from 10 months in oak, 25% new, but also focused & lively from vivid acid (7.1 g/L).

★★★★☆ **Dr Reason Why** ⓠ Unoaked chardonnay, bunch pressed, cool fermented in concrete 'egg' & clay amphora. **22** ㊉⓪ pineapple & lemon vivacity followed by textured breadth from 5 months on lees.

In abeyance: **The Fudge**. Discontinued: **Cabernet Franc**, **Magia**. — FM

Location/map: Franschhoek ▪ Map grid reference: C3 ▪ WO: Franschhoek/Stellenbosch ▪ Est 1983 ▪ 1stB 1994 ▪ Tasting by appt only ▪ Happy Valley Distillery: tasting by appt only ▪ Closed all pub hols ▪ Owner(s) One Happy Valley (Pty) Ltd ▪ Cellarmaster & GM Clayton Reabow ▪ Winemaker(s) Marozanne Grobbelaar (May 2020) ▪ 35ha/±18ha (chard) ▪ ±300t 10% white 90% MCC ▪ EuroGAP, IPW ▪ One Happy Valley Rd, Franschhoek 7690 ▪ hanrick@moreson.co.za ▪ www.moreson.co.za

Morgenhof Wine Estate ⓠ ⓨ ⓐ ⓞ ⓐ ⓑ

Rejuvenation and development continue at scenic 17th-century Morgenhof, owned since 2021 by a black empowerment venture aiming to transform the extensive Stellenbosch estate into 'a world-class destination for wine, food, music'. Purchased vineyards see an expanded line-up this edition, and winemaker Emil Kluge promising further releases. The central manor precinct, now an 'inclusive and diverse lifestyle retail cluster', has had two eateries and a cocktail kitchen added, and more attractions are on the way.

★★★★ **Cabernet Sauvignon** Inky plum compote & spice on **17** (86) preview, muscular & powerful with good fruit expression & length but also balancing firm grip from 2 years in barrels. Last was **15** ★★★★ (85).

★★★★★ **Malbec Vintage Select** (𝒱) Varietal characteristics well expressed on **14** (92). Older oak showcases dark, ripe & spicy fruit-laden profile. Modern, compact style, with smooth dry tannins. Already tempting but plenty of potential.

★★★★ **Merlot** Black cherry & chocolate on spicy **18** (86). Supple, rounded & harmonious balance of fruit & oak, just 20% new, 24 months. More appealing than **15** ★★★★ (85). No **16**, **17** sold out.

★★★★ **Merlot-Cabernet Franc** Near-equal blend in **15** ★★★★ (85) showing tertiary edge to hedgerow fruit & spice, with somewhat lean dry grip from 18 months in 20% new oak. Best enjoyed soon. (Appealing) bottle age also a feature of **14** (86) when tasted mid-2022.

★★★★ **Chenin Blanc** Ahead of bottling, **22** (86) has more to give than **21** ★★★★ (85): fresh, ripe quince & pear balanced by acid & subtle oak, 20% new, 9 months. Clean, crisp farewell.

★★★★ **Brut Reserve** (𝒱) Full, persistent mousse carries red pear flavours of bone-dry **10** (86) chardonnay, pinot noir cap classique sparkling. Couple of years on lees impart freshness & complexity.

★★★★ **Cape LBV** Alluring raisin & plum pudding richness on **05** ★★★★★ (90) 'port'. Nutty, sweet, yet harmonious thanks to well-judged spirit & appealing dry grip from 17 years in oak. Notch up on **04** (87).

Pinotage Rosé ★★★★ Vivid youngberry & plum appeal to **23** (85) tank sample. Lively, crisp, juicy & fun, with balanced fruit & acid. Ideal for summer. **Chardonnay** ★★★★ Rounded but lively **22** (85) improves on last with creamy citrus & oatmeal attractions. Subtle oak, just 20% new, 9 months, adds structure & body. **Unoaked Chardonnay** (NEW) ★★★★ Pre-bottling, **23** (85) displays vivid succulence & fleshy suppleness. Gently bright & smooth. No oak but shows benefit of 6 months on lees. **Gewürztraminer** (NEW) ★★★★ Gentle rosepetal typicity on ex-tank **23** (84) lightened by dry, tangy & juicy acid. Leesy breadth adds body & length. **Nouvelle** (NEW) ★★★ Dusty lemon & straw notes on **23** (82). Slight & mild, yet juicy with gentle freshness & body. None of variety's frequent pungency on tank sample. **Pinot Gris** (NEW) ★★★★ Bright & vivid **23** (85) ex tank is succulent, vibrant & crisp, peach & other stonefruit flavours balanced by tangy acid. A summer staple. **Sauvignon Blanc** ★★★★ Taut **23** (84) pre-bottling sample full of verve & vigour. Peppery & zesty, good body, length & balance. **Viognier** (NEW) ★★★★ Appealing interplay of nectarine & peach on lightly wooded **23** (85). Sampled before bottling, light but fleshy with good acid tang & definition. Occasional release: **The Morgenhof Estate.** Discontinued: **Cabernet Franc.** — FM

Location/map: Stellenbosch ▪ Map grid reference: F3 ▪ WO: Simonsberg-Stellenbosch ▪ Est 1692 ▪ 1stB 1984 ▪ Tasting & sales Mon-Fri 9-5.30 Sat/Sun 10-5 ▪ Fee R75pp ▪ Closed Good Fri, Dec 25 & Jan 1 ▪ Private cellar tours ▪ 1692 Bistro Mon-Sun 8-6 ▪ Bella Stella ▪ Cause & Effect Bar ▪ Meat Kraft @ Morgenhof ▪ Hiking, running, MTB & quad bike trails ▪ Kids playpark ▪ Conferences ▪ Weddings/functions ▪ Helipad ▪ Conservation area ▪ Boutique Villa Hotel ▪ Day spa ▪ Owner(s) Unipalm Investments ▪ Cellarmaster(s) Andries de Klerk (Jan 2012) ▪ Winemaker(s) Emil Kluge (Oct 2022) ▪ Viticulturist(s) Rohan Breytenbach (Dec 2017) ▪ 213ha/78ha (cabs s/f, carménère, malbec, merlot, nebbiolo, tempranillo, touriga, shiraz, chenin, chard, gewürtz, nouvelle, pinot gris, sauv, viog) ▪ 385t/20,000cs own label 32% red 60% white 8% rosé ▪ BBBEE, IPW, Vegan friendly ▪ marketing@morgenhof.com ▪ www.morgenhof.com ▪ **T +27 (0)21-001-9416**

Morgenster Estate   (𝒱) (🍴) (◎)

A slight tweak sees the collection of opera-themed wines in this esteemed portfolio honour the late Italian industrialist, Giulio Bertrand, who bought the historic Morgenster estate in the Helderberg in the early 1990s to restore it and make world-class wine and olive oil. A masterstroke was involving Pierre Lurton of Château Cheval Blanc as wine adviser, providing early big-name Bordeaux direction with black grapes such as merlot and cabernet franc. But the Italian tug was strong, hence nebbiolo, sangiovese and vermentino entering the repertoire, and latterly the pillars of Bordeaux blanc, sauvignon and semillon. All are guided into bottle 'with quality at the forefront, to beautifully showcase terroir, culture and passion'. The beautiful 'Morning Star' estate is in the care of Giulio's family and, led by daughter Federica, his legacy flourishes.

The Reserve Collection

★★★★☆ **Estate Reserve** (𝒱) Merlot-led, 4-way Bordeaux blend, **16** (94) more intense than Lourens River, powerful & sleek. Ageworthy, but so balanced & sumptuous it tempts broaching.

★★★★☆ **White Reserve** (🍇) Vintage blend, showcases best of each season. Mostly semillon with 30% sauvignon in **22** (93) classic white Bordeaux, ferment completed/8 months in oak, 25% new. More understated in its subtle herbaceous, citrus & beeswax nuances than arresting **21 ★★★★★** ⑨⑤. Deep, fresh core, leavened by semillon's waxy texture, will unfurl beautifully with cellaring.

Lourens River Valley range

★★★★☆ Lourens River Valley (🐝) Merlot (40%), plus equal parts cab & cab franc, dash petit verdot in more muscular & tightly coiled **19** ⑨②. Oak, 25% new, 18 months, provides cedary framework for concentrated dark fruit. Still youthful, handsome rewards in store.

The Giulio range

★★★★ Nabucco Nebbiolo (✓) (🐝) Shows lifted freshness along with variety's compact structure, dry tarry tannins in **19 ★★★★★** ⑨⓪. Yet not harsh, just concentrated & deeply contemplative in hallmark slow-evolving style. Just 5% new oak, 18 months. Raises bar on riper **18** ⑧⑨, though infanticide now, for broaching after a decade.

★★★★ Rigoletto Sangiovese From two complementary clones, **22** ⑧⑥ is brushed with oak, refreshingly dry & ticks all the varietal boxes: juicy aromatic fruit, herbs & dried tomato, svelte tannin framework. More appealing than **21 ★★★** ⑧①.

★★★★ Tosca Sangiovese Blend (✓) (🐝) The two cabs (31/4) are in the cast in **21 ★★★★★** ⑨①, franc's pervasive perfume & tannins almost steal the limelight from lead player sangiovese's smoky cherry & aniseed. Complex & engaging, balanced & fresh. Blended after partial ageing, total 12 months, 20% new. Even more enthralling than last **18** ⑧⑧. Deserves ageing.

★★★★☆ Vespri Vermentino (✓) Riveting freshness with a sweet-sour tang in **23** ⑨⓪ from Sicilian clone of this variety, still rare & different to other whites in SA. Unoaked, lipsmackingly dry, herbaceous lemon, pine & some floral top notes. Could age interestingly; best with a meal now.

Caruso Sangiovese Rosé ★★★★☆ Onion skin hue, citrus & savoury aromas, but much zestier in **23** ⑧③. Light (12.5% alc), bone-dry, with a bright piquancy that favours food pairing.

Single Varietal range

★★★★ Cabernet Sauvignon (✓) (🐝) Youthful, dense fruit in more structured **21** ⑧⑨, framed by fine dry tannins. Just 10% new oak, 16 months, as other range reds. All in place for development.

★★★★ Cabernet Franc (🐝) Shyer varietal perfume in **21** ⑧⑨ but more forthcoming flavour & a vibrant, leafy spice to the dark fruit & savouriness. Youthful & refined table mate.

★★★★ Merlot (✓) (🐝) Similar fully ripened grapes showcase the variety's fragrant dark-berried charm, but touch more structure & intensity in **21** ⑧⑧. Streamlined, bright & balanced.

★★★★ Sauvignon Blanc As racy & bright in **23** ⑧⑧, tingles with life. Mouthfilling, juicy herbaceous & passionfruit flavours. Succulent & zingy mouthful for solo or mealtimes.— MW

Location: Somerset West ▪ Map: Helderberg ▪ Map grid reference: F5 ▪ WO: Stellenbosch ▪ Est 1993 ▪ 1stB 1998 ▪ Tasting & sales Mon-Sat 9-5 Sun 9-4; pub hols (seasonal) please call ahead ▪ Tasting fee R60-R120pp wine/R75 olive oil & olive products ▪ Closed Good Fri & Dec 25 ▪ Restaurant Botanicum at Morgenster ▪ Owner(s) Bertrand family ▪ Winemaker(s) Yolande van Staden, mentored by Christopher Keet; Pierre Lurton (Nov 1997, member in the board of directors) ▪ 200ha/30ha (cabs s/f, merlot, nebbiolo, p verdot, sangio, sauv, sem, vermentino) ▪ 70% red 25% white 5% rosé ▪ IPW, SIZA ▪ PO Box 1616 Somerset West 7129 ▪ info@morgenster.co.za ▪ www.morgenster.co.za ▪ **T +27 (0)21-852-1738**

☐ **Mortons** see Wine-of-the-Month Club

Mosi Wines

'Those who want to know more about what we do or what we have done,' says Zimbabwean Joseph Dhafana, 'please watch Blind Ambition.' And indeed his role in that acclaimed 2022 documentary is central. Integral to his story is a desperate move to the Cape in 2010 with his wife, later tasting his first wine, making wine with top Swartland winegrowers, qualifying as a sommelier, and then launching this brand. Mosi relies simply, he says, on sourcing fruit from sustainable farms and 'converting that into delicious wine'.

★★★★ Flavian Syrah (🍇) Light perfume on **21 ★★★★★** ⑨⓪ brought out by 30% wholebunch ferment. Pure, ripe red & dark plum notes ally with silky texture, gently firm tannic & bright acid structure to produce early deliciousness. Judicious oaking, 15 months, 25% new. A finer presence than **20** ⑧⑧.

★★★★ **Tinashe Chenin Blanc** ⓐ Restrained aromas, fairly savoury, of dried peach & fynbos on **21** ⑧⑧. Light richness but mostly a fresh, understated elegance to the well-balanced palate, with the same modest 13% alc as **20** ★★★★ ⑧④ but more substance.

Not tasted: **Mapoporma Sauvignon Blanc**. — TJ

Location: Cape Town ▪ WO: Swartland ▪ Closed to public ▪ Sales online ▪ Owner(s) Dhafana family ▪ Winemaker(s) Joseph Dhafana ▪ info@mosiwinesandspirits.com ▪ www.mosiwinesandspirits.com ▪ **T +27 (0)73-421-9219/+27 (0)78-259-6392**

Mount Abora Vineyards ⓐ

Latterly homed at Arcangeli in Bot River, the boutique winery that invokes the imaginary landmark in Coleridge's poem 'Kubla Khan' will delight its fans with new releases of the celebrated cinsaut and chenin, after a few parched years. With co-founder Pieter de Waal and wife Lohra in the cellarmaster role, and Krige Visser the joint-founder and winemaker, the original vision of natural, authentic wines continues, using in-house-designed Zeppelin PVC 'eggs' to replace oak. By-appointment tastings are in Cape Town.

★★★★ **Saffraan** A pioneer of modern, fresh & light cinsauts. From Breedekloof, **22** ⑧⑨ unoaked yet with good substance, intensity of berry fruit, dryness & length at modest 12% alc. First since **17** ⑧⑨.

★★★★☆ **Koggelbos** ⊘ ⓐ Widely sourced fruit, skin fermented with 5% stems, aged in PVC 'egg' (as Saffraan). Textural **22** ⑨③ faintest white floral & wild honey tones, bracing dryness & umami finish. This is 'chenin unplugged', not a make-up box in sight. First since **19** ⑨③.

Discontinued: **The Abyssinian**. — CvZ

Location: Bot River/Cape Town ▪ WO: Breedekloof/Western Cape ▪ Est/1stB 2011 ▪ Tasting & sales by appt at MojoVino Wine Warehouse, Parow East Industrial ▪ Owner(s) Vinotage CC ▪ Cellarmaster(s) Pieter & Lohra de Waal ▪ Winemaker(s) Krige Visser ▪ 2,000cs own label 50% red 50% white ▪ 14A Duminy Str, Parow East Industrial 7501 ▪ wine@abora.co.za ▪ www.abora.co.za ▪ **T +27 (0)82-413-6719 (Krige)/+27 (0)83-357-3864 (Pieter)**

Mountain Ridge Wines ⓐ ⓐ ⓐ

Mountain Ridge has a heritage dating back to 1706, when Dutch settler Conraad Scheepers established the farm De Liefde. In 1950, that estate sent the first grapes to the grower-owned cellar known as Romansrivier in the Breedekloof town of Wolseley. Today the venture bills itself a 'boutique bulk producer', with 'quality the main objective no matter the quantity', and value for money a particular emphasis in the own-label wines.

Mountain Ridge range

Shiraz ⓐ ★★★★ Plum mingles with spice & herbs on **20** ⑧⑤, plush & succulent with good body & length. 85% wooded, 12 months, older barrels. Breedekloof WO, as next. **Pinotage Rosé** ★★★ Pleasant raspberry & strawberry fruit on crisp & juicy **22** ⑧② pink. Easy & approachable for summertime quaffing. **The Twins Chenin Blanc** ⊘ ★★★★ Grapefruit tartness on **23** ⑧③ preview leads to creamy caramel notes from 4 months oaking, combo French & American. **The Twins Sauvignon Blanc** ★★★ Granadilla & citrus tang on **23** ⑧② pre-bottling sample. Somewhat sharp acid, followed by creamy lees element. Not tasted: **Cabernet Sauvignon**, **Merlot**.

De Liefde range

Cabernet Sauvignon-Merlot ⊘ ★★★★ Cocoa overlay on dark-berried **NV** ⑧④ blend. Soft, juicy, gently brushed with sweetness from 6 g/L sugar. Good braai companion. **Chenin Blanc** ⊘ ★★★ Light succulence to latest **NV** ⑧②, boasting nectarine & peach notes. Unfussy summer poolside sipper. Breedekloof WO.

Romansrivier range

Occasional release: **Vin Rood**, **Steen**. Discontinued: **Cabernet Sauvignon Reserve**, **Shiraz Reserve**. Discontinued: **Jailbreak range**. — FM

Location: Wolseley ▪ Map: Breedekloof ▪ Map grid reference: A2 ▪ WO: Western Cape/Breedekloof ▪ Est 1949 ▪ Tasting & sales Mon-Fri 10-5 Sat 9-2 ▪ Closed some pub hols ▪ Cellar tours by appt only ▪ Wine & truffle pairings ▪ Wedding & function venue (140-160 pax) ▪ Owner(s) 15 members ▪ CEO Johan Schwartz (Jun 2020) ▪ Cellarmaster(s) Carel Hugo (Jul 2019) ▪ Winemaker(s) Carel Hugo (Jul 2019) & Hendrik Myburgh (Oct 2020) ▪ 400ha (cab, grenache, merlot, ptage, shiraz, chenin, sauv) ▪ 8,000t/10,000cs own label 37% red

48% white 15% rosé ▪ FSSC 22000, IPW, WIETA ▪ PO Box 108 Wolseley 6830 ▪ marketing@mountainridge. co.za ▪ www.mountainridge.co.za ▪ **T +27 (0)23-004-1492**

Mountain River Wines

Founded in the early 1990s when newly democratic South Africa's wine exports took off, and run from one of Paarl Main Street's elegantly restored homes, De Villiers Brits' merchant business carved a place for both bulk and bottled wines in markets around the world. We look forward to sampling the packaged ones next time.

Location: Paarl ▪ Est 1993 ▪ 1stB 1998 ▪ Closed to public ▪ Owner(s) De Villiers Brits ▪ Cellarmaster(s) De Villiers Brits, with consultants ▪ 1.2ha (shiraz) ▪ 80,000cs own label 60% red 40% white ▪ 146 Main Rd, Paarl 7646 ▪ dev@mountainriverwines.co.za, mattie@mountainriverwines.co.za ▪ www.mountainriverwines.co.za ▪ **T +27 (0)21-872-3256**

Mount Babylon Vineyards

Johan and Yolanda Holzhausen craft their boutique cap classiques with their neighbours in Hemel-en-Aarde Ridge, JC Martin and Gerhard Bruwer of Creation Wines. Local landmark Babylonstoren Peak forms part of the 'amazing views' from the Holzhausens' vineyard and venue, hosting private events and small weddings.

★★★★☆ **Elation Méthode Cap Classique** ⓠ Oaked chardonnay (40%) with pinot noir, 4 years on lees, pale onion skin **15** ⑨⓪ lovely combo of red berries & preserved citrus, brioche & wild honey richness. Self-assured, sleek & vibrantly fresh, bone-dry, some mineral notes with the lemon finish.

Not tasted: **Mount Babylon Méthode Cap Classique**. — CR, CvZ

Location: Hermanus ▪ Map: Walker Bay & Bot River ▪ Map grid reference: C4 ▪ WO: Cape South Coast ▪ Est 2002 ▪ 1stB 2007 ▪ By invitation only ▪ Exclusive events venue ▪ Owner(s) Johan Holtzhausen ▪ Winemaker(s) Jean-Claude Martin (2008, consultant), Johan & Yolanda Holtzhausen ▪ Viticulturist(s) Jean-Claude Martin & Gerhard Bruwer ▪ 65ha/16ha (pinot, shiraz, sauv, sem, viog) ▪ ±38t/±400cs own label 90% red 10% white ▪ PO Box 7370 Stellenbosch 7599 ▪ info@mountbabylon.co.za ▪ www.mountbabylon.co.za ▪ **T +27 (0)84-511-8180**

Mount Pleasant Vineyards

A tiny walled shiraz block in Darling on the West Coast is the source of this wine, produced in Malmesbury by Wim Smit of Hofstraat Kelder for Alfred Legner, former London banker, now an active music patron.

Darling Pascale's Shiraz ⓠ ★★★★ Cherries & berries, lovely perfume intensity, purity, oak mainly on **17** ⑧⑤'s palate, as white pepper thread. Sleek, polished. Last was **13** ⑧④. — CR

Location/WO: Darling ▪ Est 2009 ▪ 1stB 2011 ▪ Closed to public ▪ Owner(s) Legner family ▪ Winemaker(s) Wim Smit (Dec 2010, Hofstraat) ▪ Viticulturist(s) Alfred Legner (Jun 2006) ▪ 0.2ha/0.1ha (shiraz) ▪ 2t/ha 66cs own label 100% red ▪ 11 High Str, Darling 7345 ▪ info@darlingmusic.org ▪ **T +27 (0)72-015-1653**

☐ **Mount Sutherland Continental** *see* Super Single Vineyards

Mount Vernon Estate

Inspiration for the branding of this boutique winery on the Simonsberg-Paarl foothills near Klapmuts came from an old family name (coincidentally also the name of first US president George Washington's home). Debbie Hooper, brand owner with husband David, is also cellarmaster, joined by Philip du Toit as winemaker and viticulturist, striving for 'exceptional, handcrafted wines of the highest quality'.

★★★★ **Cabernet Sauvignon** Fermented partially in tank, then barrel (as all reds), **18** ⑧⑥ shows house-style mintiness in plush blackcurrant fruit. Same oaking as Malbec gives savoury layer, but texture is sleekly smooth, tannins harmonious. Fresher, more balanced than last-tasted **15** ★★★★ ⑧⑤.

★★★★ **Galileo** Bordeaux blend, petit verdot, merlot & malbec, 15 months in 75% new small barrels, half Hungarian, **18** ⑧⑦'s flavour is rich in berries & plums; tannins firm but ripe, coated by fruit, ensure a future but no barrier to current enjoyment. **17** untasted.

★★★★ **Chardonnay** Wholebunch, older small-barrel ferment/8 months, **20** ⑧⑥ has appealing, prominent citrus & buttered toast, roasted nut perfume & flavours. Richly textured, has power & concentration, a fresh lift at the end. More to offer than **15** ★★★★ ⑧③, the last tasted.

Malbec ★★★☆ Sharing the spotlight, full-ripe **20** ⑧⑤'s forthcoming cherry & cassis have tobacco savouriness. Tannins firm but ripe & buffed after 15 months in barrel, 30% new, promise some ageing. — CR

Location/map: Paarl ▪ Map grid reference: C7 ▪ WO: Simonsberg-Paarl ▪ Est 1996 ▪ 1stB 2005 ▪ Tasting by appt ▪ Owner(s) David & Debbie Hooper ▪ Cellarmaster(s) Debbie Hooper (Jan 2003) ▪ Winemaker(s) Philip du Toit (2019) ▪ Viticulturist(s) Philip du Toit (Jun 1997) ▪ 160ha/57.5ha (cab, malbec, merlot, p verdot, ptage, shiraz, chard) ▪ 210-225t/5,300cs own label 80% red 15% white 5% rosé ▪ PO Box 348 Klapmuts 7625 ▪ john@mountvernon.co.za ▪ www.mountvernon.co.za ▪ **T +27 (0)21-875-5073**

Mulderbosch Vineyards ⓨ ⑪ ⓞ ⓐ ⓖ

This significant and well-established winery on Stellenboschkloof slopes west of Stellenbosch town is owned by a private partnership based in the US. Its widely exported portfolio is grown in the own 45-ha vineyard as well as selected sites around the winelands. Ferdi Coetsee is the farm and vineyard manager, building on best viticultural practices aimed at minimising chemical usage, and implementing precision viticulture to invigorate the soils. Cellar chief Henry Kotzé and assistant winemaker Morne McGear have added a pair of wines, both from estate grapes, and continue improving and fine-tuning the production process, from grape intake to bottling. They are proud to have doubled cellar capacity 'without losing the ability to drill down to the finest oenological detail on all the parcels received'.

Single Vineyard range

★★★★★ Cabernet Franc ⓐ Will give years of drinking pleasure, this regal expression of the variety. **20 ★★★★☆** ⑨③ elegant, understated & harmonious, plum, graphite & fragrant herbs wrapped in velvet tannin. Well structured & textured, as **19** ⑨⑥, aided by 60% new oak. Also in 1.5L.

★★★★☆ Chenin Blanc Block W ⓐ ⓦ Fruit is the hero in this cellar-worthy expression of a single-vineyard (as Cab Franc), yet very restrained. Expert crafting, bunch ferment/10 months in seasoned 500L barrels & 1,500L foudre, allows full rein to **22** ⑨③'s luscious stonefruit, Golden Delicious apple & subtle vanilla to the layered, long, spiced finish.

Mulderbosch range

★★★★☆ Pinot Noir ⓝⒺⓦ ⊘ Only best barrels selected for light, delicate & fragrant **21** ⑨②, deftly oaked, 18 months in older barrels, to let the fruit shine. Good depth of cherry, strawberry & earth flavour, forest floor finish. Will age a few years.

★★★★☆ Estate Blend ⓝⒺⓦ ⓐ Flagship takes different angle on Cape Bordeaux, cab franc (44%) the star, accessorised with petit verdot & merlot. Shows serious intent in **21** ⑨④'s 35% new oak, 18 months. Rich, powerful & very impressive yet controlled, layers of ripe berries, plums & chocolate seamlessly melded & glossed with vanilla, ready for the long haul.

★★★★☆ Faithful Hound ⊘ ⓐ Consistently excellent 5-way Cape Bordeaux. **20** ⑨① mostly merlot, cab franc & cab, abundant red & black fruit, graphite & polished tannins, long savoury finish. 30% new oak, 16 months. 1.5L too. Also-tasted **21** ⑨① 30% cab, equal other 4. Similar profile yet fruitier, fresher & lighter with no lack of stuffing, only 6% new oak, 18 months. Both vintages worth ageing.

★★★★ Chardonnay Much drinking pleasure now & for some years in **22** ⑧⑨ with its delightful & mouthfilling orchard fruit, ripe apple & spicecake flavours, long citrus-kissed farewell. 10 months in 26% new 500L barrels & 1,500L foudre.

★★★★ Chenin Blanc Steen op Hout ⊘ Dependable part-oaked sibling satisfies in **22** ⑧⑧ with complexity & depth of flavour, fruit salad & lemon meringue, citrus freshness on the finish. 35% fermented in combo neutral barrel & 1,500L foudre.

★★★★ Sauvignon Blanc ⊘ Excellent value in **22** ⑧⑨, as ever. Structured & rounded from 33% oaked portion & lees-ageing 6 months. Melon, nettle & capsicum in harmony with cream texture & fresh acid.

★★★★☆ Méthode Cap Classique Brut ⊘ ⓐ Elegant, bright & ready for any celebration, **18** ⑨③ uses classic varieties for meticulous crafting: 42% pinot noir unoaked, chardonnay & 25% meunier fermented/9 months in barrel, the whole 36 on lees for explosive, creamy mousse accented with apple pie, strawberry compote & marmalade.

Cabernet Sauvignon Rosé ⓩ **★★★** At 200,000 cases, no afterthought in the range. Appealingly dry & fragrant **22** ⑧② has flower & berry aromas, lifted cranberry flavour, crunchy finish. Also in 1.5L glass, & 3L pack in Scandinavia. WO Coastal. **Sparkling Rosé** ⓩ **★★★★** From cab, specifically managed for rosé, as stillwine sibling. Dry, crisp & sassy, **21** ⑧③ perfumed rose & crunchy red-berry appeal. Perfect sundowner.

Sparkling Chenin Blanc ⓧ ★★★☆ Zesty & summery, with a creamy mousse, **21** ⑧④ oozes ripe apple, white peach & cinnamon, exits with a zesty lime flourish. Both bubblies carbonated & WO W Cape. — WB

Location/map: Stellenbosch ▪ Map grid reference: C5 ▪ WO: Stellenbosch/Western Cape/Coastal ▪ Est 1989 ▪ 1stB 1991 ▪ Summer: Wed-Thu 10-5 tasting & sales only, Fri-Sun 11-6 lunch, tasting & sales; Winter: Wed-Fri 10-5 tasting & sales only, Sat-Sun 11-6 lunch, tasting & sales ▪ Tasting fee R50/4 wines ▪ Closed Easter Fri/Mon, part of Jun/Jul (annual winter break), Dec 25 & Jan 1 ▪ Pizzas, burger with fries, cheese & charcuterie platter, wines, sodas ▪ Boules ▪ Kids play area ▪ Conservation area ▪ Owner(s) Private partnership based in the US ▪ Winemaker(s) Henry Kotzé (Jun 2020), with Morne McGear (Sep 2020) ▪ Farm manager(s) Ferdi Coetzee (Sep 2021) ▪ 80ha/45.2ha (cabs s/f, merlot, p verdot, shiraz, chard, chenin, sauv) ▪ IPW, WIETA ▪ PO Box 12817 Die Boord Stellenbosch 7613 ▪ info@muldersbosch.co.za ▪ www.muldersbosch.co.za ▪ **T +27 (0)21-881-8140**

Mullineux ⓠ

Andrea and Chris Mullineux's experience with Swartland fruit convinced them to move in 2007 to a region still not widely known for excellence, to establish their own label. With the 2008 Syrah, White Blend and Straw Wine (the last of those winning the pair the first of an almost uncountable number of five-star ratings) they inaugurated a massive contribution to SA wine. They established a new centre for the Swartland revolution, away from Paardeberg, by being based in Riebeek-Kasteel, where, after a few vintages elsewhere, they established a small cellar in 2010. The Mullineux aim to reflect the granite, schist and iron soils of Swartland, using shiraz and chenin as the lens in the varietal wines and crucial to the blends, has not wavered in all the growth and development since. A partnership with Indian businessman Analjit Singh (Peter Dart had long been a minor partner) came a decade ago, followed by the purchase of Roundstone farm on Kasteelberg, which they developed splendidly over succeeding years. With Andrea now chiefly responsible for vineyards as well as winemaking, they have planted, for example, rare blocks of assyrtiko and semillon gris, and are in the third year of 'regenerative organic conversion'. Two excellent blends coming entirely off the home-farm make their Platter's debut this year, joining the internationally applauded array that has made Mullineux the guide's best-performing winery five times. The Roundstone cellar is now complemented by a tasting space, open by appointment. See separate listings for Leeu Passant and Great Heart.

CWG Auction range

★★★★★ **The Gris Old Vine Semillon** ⓐ ⓦ Rare red-skinned mutation selected from 1960 semillon block, naturally fermented/11 months in 50% new oak. **22** ★★★★★ ⑨⑤ beautifully structured, shines with pure fruit, honeysuckle & rose, grapefruit & creamy texture with a unflagging wet stone finish. As sensational as **21** ⑨④.

Single Terroir range

★★★★★ **Granite Syrah** ⓐ Unwavering in its elegance & balanced power & restraint, **21** ★★★★☆ ⑨③ supple, concentrated, with dark fruit, spice & floral notes. Peppery element underlies gentle oak & long finish. From 1989 dryland Paardeberg vines. Needs time, as all these, decant in youth. Single-terroir Syrahs foot-crushed wholebunch, naturally fermented & gently plunged by hand; 11 months in seasoned 500L barrel, then year in 2,000L foudre. Follows powerful & regal **20** ⑨⑥.

★★★★☆ **Iron Syrah** ⓐ Grown on red iron-rich hill in Malmesbury, **21** ⑨④ oozes personality: rich & round with ripe plums & mulberry, charcuterie, dried herbs & pot-pourri. Perfectly balanced & harmonious, unfurling never-ending layers of fruit, powdery tannins & exotic spice. Ageworthy, like **20** ★★★★★ ⑨⑤. Available in magnums, as rest of range.

★★★★★ **Schist Syrah** ⓐ Showcases soil on Roundstone farm with dense & complex flavours of hedgerow fruit, fynbos, wisp of smoke & herbal notes on polished tannin base. Plush, with savoury herbs & sprinkling of black pepper on finish. **21** ★★★★★ ⑨④ as ageworthy as **20** ⑨⑤.

★★★★★ **Granite Chenin Blanc** ⓐ ⓦ Apple & citrus freshness on nose nicely concentrated with touches of pear, creamy oak on still-taut, well-structured palate, grapefruit bite on extensive finish. **22** ⑨⑦ from Paardeberg grapes. Same winemaking for all chenins to showcase terroir & varietal expression: bunch pressed, fermented naturally/11 months in older barrique, unfiltered. Made for the long haul.

★★★★☆ **Schist Chenin Blanc** ⓐ Vibrant & bright **22** ★★★★★ ⑨⑦ from bushvines on home-farm, producing smaller berries with higher skin:juice ratio, aiding tannin & texture. Lime, fennel, quince & fresh apple on finely balanced & layered palate. Excellent expression of terroir & craftsmanship. Keep some for later drinking pleasure, as with **21** (94).

Occasional release: **Iron Chenin Blanc**, **Quartz Chenin Blanc**.

Roundstone range (NEW)

★★★★☆ **Red** (⌾) Considered debut, as White, **21** (94) blend of 54% syrah, equal grenache noir & cinsault from producers' own Swartland farm. Bunch pressed, aged in 50% new oak 11 months, another year in neutral 'egg'. Luscious & fragrant, dark berries, violet & baked earth; intense, layered with dark fruit, fynbos & herbs. Super complex & long. Unfiltered.

★★★★☆ **White** (⌾) Another stunning debut from 57% macabeo, equal grenache blanc, clairette blanche & chenin. **22** (94) orchard fruit, white flower, honey & hint of spice. Seamless & pure, great depth & length. From bushvines, naturally barrel-fermented/11 months in older barrel.

Signature range

★★★★★ **Syrah** (⌾) Expression of the Swartland, blending the 3 soil types featured in the Single Terroir range. **21** (95) 90% bunch pressed, naturally fermented/11 months in 500L barrel, 20% new, year in 2,000/5,000L foudre. Expansive & impressive, with intense depth of black fruit, perfumed violet, dried herbs & exotic spice. Well structured, complex, built to last. Also in 1.5L, as White.

★★★★★ **Old Vines White** (⌾) (🍇) Mostly chenin (72%) in **22** (95), with clairette, grenache blanc, viognier, semillon gris & verdelho, flagship white since **08** ★★★★★. Generous stonefruit, apple blossom, quince & pear combine with harmonious silky oak, 20% new barrel & foudre, 11 months. Elegant, poised & precise. Unfiltered. Ageworthy.

★★★★☆ **Straw Wine** (⌾) Intense & very long, **22** ★★★★★ (95) from air-dried chenin is sophisticated, concentrated & textured, with sumptuous tropical fruit, pineapple & apricot & candied nut underlay, balanced by mouthwatering acidity. Naturally barrel fermented, 10% new, 11 months aged. Follows suave & viscous **21** (94).

Not tasted: **Assyrtiko**, **Essence Straw Wine**. Occasional release: **Carignan**, **Flora**, **Olerasay Straw Wine**.

Kloof Street range

★★★★ **Swartland Rouge** (✓) (⌾) Succulent & bright **21** ★★★★☆ (90) from 57% syrah with grenache noir, tinta, cinsault & carignan offers generous red & black berry fruit mingling with smooth tannins. Made for earlier drinking, but will keep. Very well-priced, like **20** (89). 50% in large, older oak, year.

★★★★ **Old Vine Chenin Blanc** (✓) (⌾) (🍇) A must for any chenin lover, from old vines in Swartland. **22** ★★★★☆ (90) notch up on **21** (89), fresh, with tropical fruit, hint of green herbs balanced by texture & spice from 2% portion in oak, 6 months. Also in magnum. Will reward ageing.— WB

Location: Riebeek-Kasteel ▪ Map: Franschhoek ▪ Map grid reference: C2 ▪ Map: Swartland ▪ Map grid reference: D6 ▪ WO: Swartland ▪ Est 2007 ▪ 1stB 2008 ▪ Tasting & sales Mon-Sun 10-5 at the Wine Studio, Leeu Estates, Franschhoek (booking recommended); Roundstone Farm, Riebeek-Kasteel Thu-Sat by appt only ▪ Wine club ▪ Owner(s) Mullineux & Leeu Family Wines (Pty) Ltd ▪ Cellarmaster(s) Andrea Mullineux (May 2007) ▪ Winemaker(s) Andrea Mullineux (May 2007), with assistant Gynore Fredericks (2019) ▪ Viticulturist(s) Andrea Mullineux, with Chris Mullineux ▪ 38ha (cinsaut, grenache, shiraz, chenin, clairette, sem gris, verdelho, viog) ▪ 160t/16,000cs own label 58% red 40% white 2% dessert ▪ PO Box 369 Riebeek-Kasteel 7307 ▪ info@mlfwines.com ▪ www.mlfwines.com ▪ **T +27 (0)21-492-2455 (office)/+27 (0)21-492-2224 (Wine Studio)**

Muratie Wine Estate   (♀) (🍴) (📷)

This uniquely atmospheric estate on the upper reaches of Stellenbosch's Simonsberg has a history stretching back 300-plus years, incorporating the ownership of a freed slave, Ansela van de Caab, and a bohemian artist, George Canitz, among many. The farm reverted to the Melck family in 1987. 'At Muratie, it's more than our historical buildings and artefacts, and the famous residents immortalised by our wines,' former medic and current custodian Rijk Melck says. 'It's the stories of traditions and relationships that have endured through centuries, and the values and team culture that are actively nurtured as part of our living heritage.'

Premium range

★★★★☆ **Martin Melck Cabernet Sauvignon** Violet delicacy to dark-fruited, supple & soft **18** ⑨. Nuanced & layered with fine dry tannin from 18 months in new barrels. Spicy & sustained.

★★★★☆ **Martin Melck Cabernet Sauvignon Family Reserve** ⍟ Full-throttle **20** ⑨④ continues stellar form. Spicy fruitcake notes with charming fresh, nuanced & layered palate. Silky texture & backbone from 22 months in new oak, year in bottle. Will reward patience. No **19** made.

★★★★ **George Paul Canitz Pinot Noir** ⍟ Vivacious **20** ⑧⑦ impresses with cranberry succulence. Supple, with light brush of spice & squeeze of tannin from 16 months in 20% new oak.

★★★★☆ **Ronnie Melck Family Selection Syrah** ⍟ ⍟ Bottling from low-crop single-vineyard last seen in **08**. **19** ⑨⓪ bold plum compote, spice & inky notes. Harmonious oak, 16 months, 100% new, supple & soft texture with a long peppery conclusion.

★★★★☆ **Ansela van de Caab** Cab leads merlot, cab franc & petit verdot in Cape Bordeaux blend. **20** ⑨⓪'s cocoa & cassis richness, gentle silky texture echo previous, which also had 22 months in 50% new oak. Good concentration, density & harmony.

★★★★ **Melck's Blended Red** ⊘ Blend changes from majority shiraz in last-tasted **18** ⑧⑥ to mostly merlot & cab in **20** ⑧⑦, retains unpretentious, approachable & appealing fruit-forward character, well spiced & easy to like. Also in 1.5L.

★★★★ **Isabella Chardonnay** Creamy citrus texture & tone of **22** ⑧⑧ mirrors that of last-tasted **20** ★★★★☆ ⑨⓪. Portion natural ferment, while oaking remains judicious, just 10 months in barrel. Rounded & rich but also fresh & vibrant courtesy good acid. Balanced & persistent.

★★★★ **Laurens Campher Blended White** Crisp, bright & lemony blend of ±45% chenin plus sauvignon blanc, verdelho & viognier. **22** ⑧⑧ gains structure & cream from 11 months in 50% new oak. Similar regime & effect in also-tasted **21** ⑧⑧, white pepper & flint nuances, fruit & oak well meshed. Both vintages supple & light, dry finishing.

★★★★ **Lady Alice Méthode Cap Classique Rosé** Oystershell & raspberry on lively, fresh **18** ⑧⑧ pinot noir sparkler. Good energy & tang, creamy brioche backing from 2 years on lees.

Alberta Annemarie Merlot ★★★★ Gentle, light-bodied & easy **19** ⑧⑤ offers plum succulence & subtle spice from oak, 20% new, 14 months, which also aids structure, length. **Melck's Sauvignon Blanc** ★★★★ Granadilla tropicality with dusty pebble typicity on light, fresh & zesty **22** ⑧⑤. Dry but nicely fleshed from part natural ferment. WO Stellenbosch, as Pinot Noir, Blended Red & Blended White. Not tasted: **Mr May Grenache Noir**, **Ronnie Melck Shiraz**, **Johanna Dry Rosé**.

Fortified Wines

★★★★ **Amber Forever** Jasmine & honeysuckle seduction on **NV** ⑧⑦ fortified muscat. Light & supple with toned sweetness (93 g/L sugar), broad pecan nuttiness from 18 months in older oak. 375 ml.

★★★★ **Ben Prins Cape Vintage** ⍟ Drying, spicy grip adds edge to richly sweet & dark-fruited **20** ⑧⑨'port'. Field blend of 5 Portuguese varieties, traditionally foot-trodden. Good judgment & integration of spirit aids nuance & counters richness for delightful winter warmer.

★★★★ **The Senator Late Bottled Vintage** ⍟ ⍟ 'Port' made in select vintages from 1977 low-yield Portuguese vines. **16** ★★★★☆ ⑨⓪ goes up a notch on **15** ⑧⑦ in its black cherry compote & spice charm, clean, spirity balance & intensity. Less wood (60 months vs 72, none new) yet richer, nuttier & more nuanced. Balanced & bright, lengthy finish.— FM

Location/map: Stellenbosch ▪ Map grid reference: F3 ▪ WO: Simonsberg-Stellenbosch/Stellenbosch ▪ Est 1685 ▪ 1stB ca 1920 ▪ Tasting & sales daily 9-5 (extended summer hours), pub hols 8.30-5 ▪ Tasting fees: R100/premium, R150/flagship, R100 pairing experience, R450/heritage tasting experience - by appt only ▪ Closed Good Fri, Dec 25 & Jan 1 ▪ Farm Kitchen Mon/Tue (seasonal) Wed-Sun 9-3.30 - dine@muratie.co.za ▪ Cellar tours by appt ▪ Group bookings by appt only ▪ Cheese platters ▪ Muratie Canvas - weddings/corporate events - events@muratiecanvas.co.za ▪ MOK art gallery/exhibit ▪ Farm shop ▪ Harvest festival ▪ Live music ▪ MTB ▪ Trail running ▪ Wine club ▪ Owner(s) Melck Family Trust ▪ Winemaker(s) Hattingh de Villiers (Jul 2014) ▪ Viticulturist(s) Etienne Terblanche (Vinpro) ▪ 110ha/44ha (cabs s/f, grenache, merlot, mourv, p verdot, pinot, shiraz, chard, chenin, hanepoot, port, verdelho) ▪ 300t/25,000cs own label 70% red 20% white 1% rosé 9% other ▪ IPW ▪ PO Box 133 Koelenhof 7605 ▪ info@muratie.co.za ▪ www.muratie.co.za ▪ **T +27 (0)21-865-2330/2336**

Muse

Automobile enthusiast, businessman and Cape Wine Master Mark Philp is allowing his boutique wines to age a little longer, hence no new vintages made from mostly Stellenbosch grapes in a Devon Valley cellar shared with Andy Roediger's Boschheim, where visitors are welcome by appointment.

Cabernet Sauvignon Ⓥ ★★★★ More cassis fruit than last, but **20** ⑧⑤'s opulence is reined in by a herbaceous thread & fairly stern tannins in youth. Not tasted: **Shiraz**, **Chenin Blanc**. — DS

Location/WO: Stellenbosch ▪ Est/1stB 2008 ▪ Tasting & sales by appt only ▪ Owner(s) Selford Holdings (Pty) Ltd ▪ Cellarmaster(s)/winemaker(s) Mark Philp ▪ 14t bought-in grapes 85% red 15% white ▪ PO Box 84 Stellenbosch 7599 ▪ mark@selfords.co.za ▪ **T +27 (0)82-566-6315**

Musgrave Crafted Spirits

New owner Halewood SA is running with the baton created by brandy-market disruptor Simóne Musgrave in emphasising flavour over age in the pair of premium offerings, one infused with Zambian dark honey, the other with Indian Ocean island vanilla, both 'luxurious and made to mingle'. New blends tasted this edition.

★★★★☆ **Copper Black Honey** ⓐ Head-turning 5-year old potstill ⑨③ gains breadth & depth to dried apricot & pear, roast nut, chocolate & spice with the infusion of dark honey for a rich, mouthfilling taste. Complex & balanced, long, warm spiced finish. Simply delicious. Also in 200 ml, as sibling.

★★★★ **Copper Vanilla** A much lighter 3 year old potstill ⑧⑨ with bright yellow-gold hue, fresh orchard fruit & citrus flavours, & sweet vanilla lingering sexily on the finish. Perfect for cocktails.— WB

Location: Benoni ▪ Est 2015 ▪ Owner(s) Halewood South Africa ▪ www.musgravespirits.com ▪ **T +27 (0)11-746-4200**

☐ **Music by D'Aria** *see D'Aria Winery*

Mvemve Raats

There never is much news regarding this focused collaboration between Bruwer Raats and Mzokhona Mvemve, except another example or two of international acclaim. The partnership began two decades back when the two were making wine at Delaire, and the methodology has always been the same: to vinify the five main red Bordeaux grapes, sourced from granitic sites in Stellenbosch, and then, after a year, taste them and prepare the best possible blend for this 'Field of Stars' label. The wine is made with Raats Family Wines' winemaker-viticulturalist Gavin Bruwer Slabbert.

★★★★☆ **MR de Compostella** ⓐ Bold, intense & concentrated **20** ⑨④ - elegance is not the only point of this 5-variety Bordeaux-style blend. The impact has gracefulness though, thanks to excellent balance of fine acidity, mouthcoating tannins & deep, ripe fruit. 50% new oak is still obvious, but this is very youthful wine, deserving many years in bottle. Last made was **18** ★★★★★ ⑨⑥.— TJ

Location/map/WO: Stellenbosch ▪ Map grid reference: B6 ▪ Est/1stB 2004 ▪ Tasting & sales Mon-Fri 9-5 by appt only ▪ Closed all pub hols ▪ Owner(s) Bruwer Raats & Mzokhona Mvemve ▪ Cellarmaster(s)/viticulturist(s) Bruwer Raats & Mzokhona Mvemve (both Jan 2004) ▪ Winemaker(s) Bruwer Raats & Mzokhona Mvemve (both Jan 2004), with Gavin Bruwer Slabbert (Feb 2010) ▪ (cabs s/f, malbec, merlot, p verdot) ▪ 10t/900cs own label 100% red ▪ PO Box 2068 Dennesig Stellenbosch 7601 ▪ office@raats.co.za ▪ www.raatswines.co.za ▪ **T +27 (0)21-881-3078**

MVH Signature Wines

A Diners Club Young Winemaker of the Year, Stellenbosch boutique vintner Matthew van Heerden wants his wines to have 'an elegant style of fruit purity, authentic expression and ageability'. He sources grapes locally and in Elgin from sustainably farmed vines, with hand harvesting into small baskets, gentle bunch-pressing and natural ferment in small, open vessels promoting freshness, fruity and floral aromas. His new collection explores pockets of old dryland bushvines, low yields producing 'fantastic, concentrated fruit flavours'.

MVH Signature Wines range

★★★★★ **Cabernet Sauvignon** ⓝⓔⓦ ⓐ Makes a distinguished debut in **21** ⑨⑤. More opulent & concentrated than Dryland sibling, a dense core of cassis is underpinned by authoritative but fine, chalky tannins polished 2 years in old oak. Streamlined & sophisticated, this is pure class, with a rewarding future. Helderberg sourced, as all unless noted, from a single block.

★★★★☆ **Pinot Noir** ⓠ Glamorous & perfumed **20** ㉔'s Elgin-grown red fruit - cherry & strawberry - subtly toned with complex layers of spice & savouriness. In used oak 12 months, tannins are sleek & downy.

★★★★☆ **Chardonnay** ⓐ Shows producer's restrained styling even in warmer **22** ★★★★★ ㉝ vintage. Grapes from old vines bunch pressed & naturally fermented/11 months in oak, 50% new, show the hallmark lime & stonefruit purity, freshness & elegance. Graceful & lingering, will continue to improve as it unfurls - true also of **21** ㉔.

Vine & Co range ⓝⓔⓦ

★★★★ **Dryland Cabernet Sauvignon** ⓐ From various parcels of low-yield, unirrigated vines. **21** ⑧⑧ vibrant berry fruit, some earth & dark chocolate too, all in svelte dry tannin framework. Bunch pressed & wild yeast fermented (as Chenin), 18 months in 60% new oak. Harmonious, with good potential.

★★★★ **Bushvine Chenin Blanc** Ex 42 year old vines on cooler mountain slopes. Small portion fermented in amphora imparts a vibrant freshness to the bright stonefruit & citrus flavours. **22** ⑧⑧ unoaked, allowing fruit purity to shine. Ready to enjoy, though some potential to age.— MW

Location: Stellenbosch • WO: Stellenbosch/Elgin • Est/1stB 2013 • Tasting by appt only • Owner(s) Matthew van Heerden • Winemaker(s)/viticulturist(s) Matthew van Heerden (Jan 2013) • 5t/400cs own label 50% red 50% white • IPW • PO Box 2134 Dennesig Stellenbosch 7601 • mvhwines@gmail.com • **T +27 (0)82-771-7969/+27 (0)82-520-9338**

☐ **My Best Friend** *see* Zandvliet Wine Estate

Myburgh Bros ⓠ

Separate from their larger Joostenberg venture, siblings Tyrrel and Philip Myburgh here recreate the winemaking collaboration between their great-grandfather and his brother. A listing with UK fine-wine company Corney & Barrow is a proud achievement for the collection, handcrafted with minimal manipulations chiefly from heritage varieties, sourced next door or nearby, dry-farmed as bushvines and 25 to 39 years old.

★★★★ **Little J Red** ⊘ Blend change for **22** ⑧⑥ from **21** ★★★★ ⑧⑤'s syrah plus cinsaut, cab & merlot to 55/45 cinsaut & syrah. Fresher, as flavoursome, for equally satisfying dry everyday drinking.

★★★★☆ **Kaalgat Steen** ⓥ ⓦ Previously in sibling Joostenberg's portfolio. **22** ★★★★ ⑧⑥ from chenin, marries 2 skin-fermented batches (57% for 12 days, 28% for 6) with wholebunch grapes. Not as arresting as last **18** ㉔, more bruised apple skin than pineapple, though as dry & vinous at just 9.5% alc.

★★★★ **Old Vine Chenin Blanc** ⓦ Unoaked, to showcase vineyard's electric natural acidity. Effortless density in **22** ⑧⑦, range of ripeness from apple to yellow peach, umami lift on finish.

Ex-Africa Muscat d'Alexandrie ⓠ ★★★★'Ex-Africa' added to name since we tasted **21** ⑧⑤, rare dry & barrel-fermented version of variety, worth seeking out. Pops with grape & litchi aromas & flavours, perfect partner for spicy Malay dishes. In abeyance: **Cinsaut**. — CvZ

Location/map/WO: Paarl • Map grid reference: A7 • Est/1stB 2017 • Tasting & sales Sat-Sun 10-4; weekdays by appt • Owner(s) Tyrrel & Philip Myburgh • Cellarmaster(s)/viticulturist(s) Tyrrel Myburgh (2017) • Winemaker(s) Tyrrel Myburgh (2017), with Mia Burger (2023) • ±4,000cs own label 50% red 50% white • IPW • PO Box 82 Elsenburg 7607 • tyrrel@joostenberg.co.za, winery@joostenberg.co.za • **T +27 (0)21-200-9903**

☐ **My Cosmic Hand** *see* Elemental Bob
☐ **Mystery of Nature** *see* Olivedale Private Vineyards
☐ **My Way** *see* Klein Roosboom Boutique Winery

My Wyn ⓠ ⓟ

The 'smallest winery with the biggest view in Franschhoek' was created by Jacoline Haasbroek with husband Johan at the turn of the millennium, building a loyal following for characterful wines and by-appointment personalised tastings. Latterly Hugo Brink has been the stylist, sourcing small parcels around the valley.

Les Grandes Horizontales range

★★★★ **Rouge** ⓠ Always a multi-blend, **20** ⑧⑦ cab franc & petit verdot dominant, 4 others, Bordeaux varieties accounting for 75%. Crafted for long ageing, palate lithe but tannin perceptible in dry finish.

★★★★ **Blanc** ⓠ Viognier & 20% chardonnay, oaked 10 months, nice comparison with sibling. Vivid peach lifted by zesty citrus acid, giving **20** ⑧⑧ almost a dual personality, but it works.

My Wyn range

★★★★ Cabernet Franc ⓥ Dab of merlot, but **20 ★★★★★** ⑨⓪ has a classic profile, red berries, graphite, a lovely savoury seam, all following on to the palate. Lovely crafting. Last rated was **16** ⑧⑧.

★★★★ Petit Verdot ⓥ Ripe & muscular, dark-toned **16** ⑧⑦ shows variety-true plum & hedgerow fruit, some scrub, ripe but firm tannin promising a future. Unfiltered. More to offer than **15 ★★★★** ⑧③.

★★★★ Cape Blend ⓥ Pinotage with cab franc, 3 other Bordeaux varieties. **20** ⑧⑧ highly complex & involving. Palate elegant, polished, nicely combines fruit & spice, tannins a supple support.

★★★★ Cap Classique Extra Brut ⓥ Chardonnay & 39% pinot noir. Green-gold hue, toasted brioche & preserved citrus, a red berry nuance, **15** ⑧⑨ has flavour depth & surprising lemony freshness for its age.

Shiraz ⓥ **★★★☆** Tasty, juicy drinkability in **20** ⑧⑤, has 7.5% cab franc but character is all shiraz. Plush dark berries, smoky spice, texture smooth & streamlined, tannins ripe. **Viognier-Chardonnay** ⓥ **★★★★** Noteworthy aromatics in **20** ⑧④, peach blossom & fruit, given ginger biscuit seam by oaking. Equal partnership, nicely done. Not tasted: **Shiraz-Viognier, Chardonnay, Viognier, Sauviognier, Cap Classique Brut Rosé, Cap Classique Blanc de Blancs Brut Nature, My Robyn, My Amber.** — CR

Location/map/WO: Franschhoek ▪ Map grid reference: B1 ▪ Est 2001 ▪ Vintner-hosted lunch & dinner events by appt ▪ Owner(s) Jacoline Haasbroek ▪ Vintner Hugo Brink (2019) ▪ info@mywynfranschhoek.com ▪ www. mywynfranschhoek.com ▪ T +27 (0)76-072-7850 Hugo Brink

Nabygelegen Private Cellar   ⓥ ⌂ ⓞ

Infusing fresh energy into this historic Wellington estate is formerly Stellenbosch-based seasoned wine man Jacques Erasmus, who feels his brief to care for both vineyard and cellar is 'a dream come true'. Other causes for enthusiasm are the maturity of the vineyards, resulting in naturally low yield, perfectly designed cellar, to bring in grapes at optimal ripeness, and the experience of his team members, some having been raised on Nabygelegen. With a reputation based on mostly white-wine making, and a special love for chenin, Jacques is gratified to have the merlot as well as the chenin earn places in their respective Top 10s. An access road upgrade will allow farm visits at set hours; for now they are by appointment (but very welcome).

Nabygelegen range

★★★★ Cabernet Sauvignon ⓥ Attention-grabbing inky hue courtesy 12% malbec, **22** ⑧⑥ obvious woody overlay to black & blue fruit from 14 months in 15% new barrique, but lively, with shapely tannins & good persistence.

★★★★ Seventeen Twelve Unspecified proportions cab & merlot in **21** ⑧⑦, neatly dry with firm tannin frame for sweetly ripe plum & date fruit. Whiff of mint mingles with fragrant spices from 14 months in 30% new wood.

★★★★ Scaramanga Red ⓥ Unusual combo cab, merlot, malbec & tempranillo, year in 80/20 French & American barrels, 10% new for **22** ⑧⑦. Tangy red fruit, cherry, berry & plum, adds lovely lift to oak vanilla & sweet smoothness of the finish.

★★★★ Chenin Blanc ⓥ From old vines, average age 35 years, 20% portion wooded. **23** ⑧⑥ takes time to unfurl & peach, apricot & citrus fruit to shine through oak overlay.

★★★★ Lady Anna ⓥ Various ferment vessels including 'egg' for easygoing **22** ⑧⑥ from 70% old vine chenin, equal sauvignon & semillon. Just-picked peach & apricot flavours & aromas, good palate weight & breadth at modest 12.6% alc.

★★★★ Scaramanga White Chenin & verdelho, 10% wooded, in feisty **21** ⑧⑥. Creamy, from 'as much lees work as possible', with appealing spice top note & satisfying dry finish.

Malbec ⓝⒺⓌ **★★★★** With splashes cab & merlot, **21** ⑧⑤ savoury biltong & juniper nuances to dense plum fruit, 30% American oak adds a vanilla sheen & contributes to sweet impression on the finish. WO W Cape, as White. **Merlot ★★★★** Just 5% new oak for soft & plummy **22** ⑧④, lightly coloured, faintly spicy, with friendly tannins. Like most of the reds, few grams sugar smooth the finish. **Sauvignon Blanc ★★★** Guava, gooseberry & fresh apple appeal on **23** ⑧②, brisk acidity to waken the palate, extend the farewell.

Jacquéren range ⓝⒺⓌ

Introvert Merlot ★★★★ Shy-ish **21** ⑧③ gets extra tannin oomph to its soft plum fruit from splashes malbec & cab, seasoning from 13 months in 30% new barriques. WO Coastal, as Lady Anna. **Extrovert**

Sauvignon Blanc ★★★★ Plenty of white asparagus & creamy texture on quietly confident **21** ⑧⑤, courtesy few years in bottle & finishing the ferment in old barrels with lees contact. — PS, CvZ

Location/map: Wellington ▪ Map grid reference: C3 ▪ WO: Wellington/Western Cape/Coastal ▪ Est 2001 ▪ 1stB 2002 ▪ Tasting & cellar tours by appt ▪ Sales Mon-Fri 10-4 Sat by appt ▪ Closed all pub hols ▪ Tour groups ▪ Walks/hikes ▪ MTB trail ▪ Self-catering luxury accommodation ▪ Owner(s) Avalon Vineyards (Pty) Ltd ▪ Cellarmaster(s)/viticulturist(s) Jacques Erasmus (Jan 2021) ▪ 35ha/17ha (cab, malbec, merlot, tempranillo, chenin, sauv, verdelho) ▪ 180t/24,000cs own label 50% red 50% white ▪ PO Box 302 Wellington 7654 ▪ marketing@nabygelegen.co.za ▪ www.nabygelegen.co.za ▪ **T +27 (0)21-873-7534**

☐ **Naked Truth** see Picardi ReBEL

Namaqua Wines ⓟ ⑪ ⓐ ⓑ

Founded at Vredendal in the mid-1940s, with two extensive cellars producing branded and bulk wines for over 50 territories worldwide, Namaqua takes its name from the Namaqua West Coast region, also famous for spring wildflowers. The 200 grower-shareholders have almost 5,000 ha under vine, and the soil and climatic diversity, including the influence of the bordering cold Atlantic, allows for the production of varietal wines in various packaging formats, as well as blends and fortifieds, all sold on a value-for-money platform.

Cape West Limited Releases

★★★★ **The Blend** ⊘ Mainly Bordeaux grapes with shiraz, tempranillo & other tweaks, **21** ⑧⑥ overall just a very tasty wine. Ripe blackberries, touch of liquorice & some tannin grip aided by 16 months in old oak all add up to plenty of drinking pleasure.

Stoneflower ★★★ Last time a preview (as Sandveld), **21** ⑧② from pinotage & shiraz (65/35) soft & juicy mouthful with plummy black fruit & perfumed spicy top notes. Perfect for a weekend braai. **Sandveld** ★★★★ Attractive **22** ⑧③ harmonious mouthful of peach, pear & light citrus. 25% new oak adds creamy texture & fresh spice to very drinkable wine. From chardonnay with sauvignon & chenin.

Namaqua range

★★★★ **Red Muscadel** Warming **23** ⑧⑥ has good muscat typicity of fresh & raisined grapes, lifted by pronounced floral character. Less sugar than White but slightly less intensity as well. WO Olifants River.

★★★★ **White Muscadel** Packing a powerful punch of concentration & luscious sweetness, **22** ★★★★★ ⑨⓪'s abundant flavours (grapes, apricot jam, flowers & honey) reined in by acid & alc. Like last **20** ★★★★★ ⑨⓪, lengthy finish to delicious wine. No ferment, fortified after overnight skin contact, as Hanepoot & Red sibling.

Pinotage ☺ ★★★ Pleasant **22** ⑧⓪ shows variety's tarry black & red plums with smooth tannins & soft fruity finish. **Shiraz** ☺ ★★★ Enjoyable **22** ⑧⓪ with cheerful peppery spice & juicy mouthful of mixed black berries. Half American oak.

Cabernet Sauvignon ★★☆ Simple fruity **22** ⑦⑧, dusty, herbal overlay to black cherry ripeness. 3 months staves, as all these reds. **Merlot** ★★★ Everyday tipple **22** ⑦⑦'s light & fruity character ends on smoky note. **Sauvignon Blanc** ★★☆ Grapefruit & lemon on slender **23** ⑦⑨, for easy summer drinking. **Hanepoot Jerepigo** ★★★★ Showy display of perfumed fruit & flowers on **22** ⑧④, fiery alc & concentrated grapey finish. Occasional release: **Noble Late Harvest**. Discontinued: **Chenin Blanc, Cape Vintage**.

Gôiya range

Shiraz-Pinotage ★★★ Chunky & cheerful **22** ⑧① an equal blend showing soft tannins, smoky overtones & smooth, fruity finish aided by gram sugar. **Sauvignon Blanc-Chardonnay** ★★☆ Easy-drinking **23** ⑦⑦, rounded palate & fresh citrus-fruity finish, touch of sweetness at end.

3L Box range

Cabernet Sauvignon ★★☆ Black cherry fruit, **22** ⑦⑧ smoky, dusty notes & hint of smoke from ageing on staves, as Merlot. **Merlot** ★★★ Soft & smooth **22** ⑦⑦, cherry-berry fruit & charry finish. Some American oak. **Sauvignon Blanc** ★★☆ Eminently quaffable **23** ⑦⑨, crisp, fresh & light for everyday. Discontinued: **Cellar Door range**. — CM

Location: Vredendal ▪ Map: Olifants River ▪ Map grid reference: B4 ▪ WO: Western Cape/Olifants River ▪ Est/1stB 1947 ▪ Tasting & sales at Die Keldery Restaurant T +27 (0)27-213-3699/8, Mon-Sat 9-5 & dinner Wed-Fri 7-10; pub hols (seasonal) please call ahead ▪ Closed Easter Fri-Mon, Ascension day & Dec 25/26 ▪

Cellar tours to be booked in advance ▪ Facilities for children ▪ Conferences & Weddings ▪ Owner(s) 200 members ▪ Cellarmaster(s) Driaan van der Merwe (Vredendal Kelder & Spruitdrift Kelder) ▪ Winemaker(s) Rudi de Wet & Alwyn Maass (Vredendal Kelder); Koos Thiart, Louwritz Louw & Jaco Louw (Spruitdrift Kelder) ▪ Viticulturist(s) Johan Weideman ▪ 4,990ha ▪ PO Box 75 Vredendal 8160 ▪ info@namaquawines.com ▪ www.namaquawines.com ▪ T +27 (0)27-213-1080

Natasha Williams Signature Wines ⓠ

Natasha Williams was winemaker at Bosman Family Vineyards when she sourced the grapes for this small-scale personal venture from the Bosmans' De Bos vine garden and vineyards in Upper Hemel-en-Aarde. She's now full-time in that cool-climate ward, crafting the Hasher Family Estate wines. Her Jade range is a showcase for new vineyards, blends and/or techniques while reflecting her natural and hands-off approach.

Lelie van Saron range
★★★★☆ **Syrah** Adroitly handled, with a light & elegant touch (as all), **21** ⑨① has Rhône-like scrub, convincing black berry & cherry fruit, satin tannins. 50% spent year in mostly older barrels, rest concrete 'egg'.

★★★★☆ **Chardonnay** ⓐ Deliciously fruity yet intricately detailed, **22** ⑨④ shows heft as well as finesse & refinement in its subtle citrus zest & marmalade, creamy texture, vibrant acid & lingering finish. Wild yeast fermented (as all), 50% year on lees in mostly older barrels.

Jade range
★★★★ **Red** Unusual & creative blend, syrah & 33% durif/petite sirah, **22** ⑧⑨ is lithe & supple, suede textured. Red berry fruit, hints of scrub & herbal perfume. 8 months in older barrels. No **21**.

★★★★ **Méthode Ancestrale** Creamy & finely balanced single-ferment sparkling. **22** ⑧⑧ from revamped mix of chardonnay & 17% pinot blanc, disgorged, unusually, after 6 months to clarify. Gentle bubbles retain typical yeasty appeal, fresh-baked biscuit aromas for anytime sipping enjoyment.— GdB

Location: Wellington ▪ WO: Upper Hemel-en-Aarde Valley ▪ 1stB 2017 ▪ Tasting & cellar tours by appt ▪ Closed all pub hols ▪ Owner(s)/winemaker(s) Natasha Williams ▪ 10-12t/1,800cs own label 40% red 60% white ▪ IPW ▪ info@lelievansaron.co.za, natasha@lelievansaron.co.za ▪ T +27 (0)73-034-4846

☐ **Nativo** see Hughes Family Wines
☐ **Natura** see Leopard's Leap Family Vineyards
☐ **Nature** see Bonnievale Wines
☐ **Nature Reserve** see Cape Wine Company
☐ **Natuurlik Organic** see Perdeberg Wines
☐ **Naudé Old Vines** see Naudé Wines

Naudé Wines

The last white blend Ian Naudé released was 2010, and he had no intention of making another. Then, while harvesting his colombard near Vredendal on the West Coast, he noticed an adjacent block of chenin 'which blew me away with its quality'. Encouragement from a Greek friend, who believes the varieties are made for each other, led to Soutbos, named for the hardy and pervasive shrub, old man saltbush. Both vineyards qualify for Old Vine Project certification. Why his passion for old vines? 'Their grapes are storied, complex and unique. Each year they represent something different, whatever nature allows them - and with any luck I do not get in the way.' Ever modest, the eminent Stellenbosch boutique winegrower's enthusiasm for discovering and working with gnarled vines never diminishes. Another abiding love, his sheepdogs, are always at his side - currently only a couple, but the search is on to complete the usual family of four.

Naudé Old Vines range
★★★★☆ **Werfdans Cinsault** ⓦ Gentle & pure, soft raspberry fruit is focused & wrapped in finest tannins. With some development of complexity, Darling-sourced **17** ⑨② enjoys a natural freshness lending great length & a still-youthful profile. Such balance & harmony suggest many years to go.

★★★★☆ **Grenache** ⓖ Stylish, sophisticated **20** ⑨④ reflects the Naudé dexterity & light touch. Naturally fermented (as all) Paardeberg grapes, nimble (11% alc), smooth pure fruit on the palate, fine tannins that will cosset wine for intended 6-10 years.

★★★★★ **Oupa Willem** ⓖ Accomplished homage to winemaker's grandfather & a traditional Cape blend, cinsaut & cab, 82/12 in **20** ★★★★★ ⑨③, plus dash cab franc. Perfumed, concentrated yet weightless, superbly elegant & balanced at a remarkably modest 11.5% alc, same as fine **19** (95). Darling & Bottelary vines, very old oak, 16 months. Will last decades.

★★★★★ **Chenin Blanc** (②) (⊛) Venerable vines in Stellenbosch, expressed with minimum intervention, as all. 10 months on lees in 5-8 year old barrels. **21** (93) achieves a riveting balance among fragrant fruit, cream & vibrant acid. Palate full of flavour & energy, finish mineral, concluding note of wet stone.

★★★★★ **Langpad** (⊛) (⊛) 'Long Road' from Vredendal to Stellenbosch for grapes from old colombard vines. **23** (93) brims with freshness in its ripe pear & lime concentration; lees-enriched creaminess anchors & adds breadth, leading to mouthwatering salty finish. 11.5% alc. Just 500 cases & some magnums.

★★★★★ **Soutbos White Blend** (NEW) (⊛) (⊛) 2 old-vine Vredendal stalwarts, chenin & 16% colombard. Mix of ripe red apples & pears with squeeze of zesty lemon is lees-enriched for texture. **23** (94) refreshing & dry, lingering salty tang as name suggests. Cellaring is a given & will be rewarded. 360 cases.— AL

Location: Stellenbosch ▪ WO: Western Cape ▪ Est 2017 ▪ 1stB 2000 ▪ Closed to public ▪ Owner(s)/winemaker(s) Ian Naudé ▪ 50% red 50% white ▪ PO Box 982 Stellenbosch 7599 ▪ hello@naudewines.co.za, ian@naudewines.co.za ▪ www.naudewines.co.za ▪ **T +27 (0)83-630-3794**

☐ **Neat** *see* Bonnievale Wines

Nederburg Wines   (②) (⑪) (◎) (④) (⑤)

A grand and much-loved name in the world of wine, with two centuries of heritage, owned by Heineken Beverages and now run by general manager Kate Jackson, Nederburg 'with equal commitment' produces 2-million cases of handcrafted gems for cellaring as well as accessible wines to sip every day. With Samuel Viljoen as cellarmaster, the emphasis on, and international success with cabernet and cabernet blends continues, while the vineyardists led by Isabel Teubes care for 1,680 ha of Paarl home-farm vines and independently audited and accredited grower-owned vineyards across the winelands. Ongoing sustainability efforts include regenerative viticulture, water stewardship and solar power use and, in the social realm, support for ethical employment practices on partner farms, and ongoing in-house talent drives and mentorship programmes. The visitor offering is never overlooked, and the large hall beside the manor is being transformed into a wine shop, tasting facility, family eatery and events area. Beyond the welcoming estate, winelovers are invited join Taste, Learn & Discover journeys that are continually refreshed and updated.

Private Bin range

★★★★★ **Two Centuries Cabernet Sauvignon** (⊛) Enthralls from the first sip, **19** (95) sumptuously rich & concentrated yet has a svelte tannin structure from 29 months in new oak. Like **18** ★★★★★ (93), complex & effortlessly balanced, with fresh herbaceous seam & lingering farewell, this statement wine continues its impressive form. WO Coastal, as other Cab & red blends.

Not tasted: **R163 Cabernet Sauvignon**. Occasional release: **Edelkeur**, **Eminence**.

Heritage Heroes range

★★★★★ **The Brew Master** (⊘) (⊛) Tribute to owner from 1937, Johann Graue, **20** (94) cab-led 5-way Bordeaux blend. Richer & more generously styled, with good depth of fruit, fine foil for 29 months new French & American oak. Full, balanced & appealing now, with further ageing potential.

★★★★★ **The Motorcycle Marvel** (⊘) (⊛) Dapper 5-way Rhône blend references legendary winemaker Günter Brözel's preferred method of vineyard inspection: on a 1954 BSA. Red & dark berries, some savouriness & similar dry spice from 28 months in oak on tad riper **20** (94) barrel selection. Still firmly structured for long & rewarding future.

★★★★★ **The Anchorman** (⊘) (⊛) Graceful chenin from 39 year old vines honours estate founder Philippus Wolvaart. Usual complex making in **22** (91): third each fermented in tank, clay amphora & oak barrel, 9 months on lees. Touch fresher & cleaner, crisper apple, greengage & kiwi, lighter 12.8% alc. Lingering lemony farewell.

Manor House range

★★★★★ **Cabernet Sauvignon** (⊛) Fuller bodied, opulent & sleeker in **20** (93), though still good fruit concentration, some liquorice & inky minerality. Similar 25 months oaking to **19** ★★★★★ (95) ensures supple tannin structure & balance, though not quite as impressive.

★★★★ **Shiraz** Structured & still quite tight, has splash carignan in **19** ⑧⑨. Red fruit, savouriness & some tobacco with neat cedary framework from 28 months in barrel. All elements in place, youthful & fresh, good prospects.

Not tasted: **Chardonnay**.

Winemasters range

★★★★ **Cabernet Sauvignon** ⊘ Repeats classic styling in **21** ⑧⑧. Blackcurrant & some leafiness in firm but svelte framework & dry cedar spicing. Oak treatment well integrated (staves, as all varietal reds in range). Appealing drinkability, with potential.

★★★★ **Merlot** ⊘ Good varietal red berry fruit, fully ripe & well structured in **21** ⑧⑥, supple tannins & sleek vanilla sheen from oak, balanced dry farewell. Step up on **20** ★★★ ⑧②, deserves a dinner date.

★★★★ **Pinotage** ⊘ Lots to like in **21** ⑧⑥, similar clean mulberry & plum flavours in sync with sweet oak spice. More gravitas than **20** ★★★★ ⑧⑤, though still accessibly styled, ends clean & dry.

★★★★ **Shiraz** ⊘ Substantial core of dense, dark, spicy fruit with savoury overlay & subtle oaking in **21** ⑧⑧. More balanced & suave than last, ends respectably dry.

★★★★ **Double Barrel Reserve** ⊘ Similar five-way Bordeaux blend, cab with merlot & cab franc (49/20/18) in **21** ⑧⑨. Components oak-aged 15 months, blend further 3, showing better integration of dark berry fruit, pervasive freshness & elegant structure. Already appealing, many years ahead.

★★★★ **Chardonnay** ⊘ Bright stonefruit & lime in mostly unwooded **22** ⑧⑥, also has splash chenin. Balanced & crisp, with creamy nuance from 8 months lees enhancement.

Edelrood ⊘ ★★★★ Consistent cab & merlot partnership more restrained in **21** ⑧⑤. Leafy piquancy to red & black berries, dry cedar spicing from 15 months on staves. Chalky tannins better paired with food though year/2 may allow solo sipping. **Grenache-Carignan Rosé** ⊘ ★★★ Subtle strawberry, cherry & some floral notes in 90% grenache **23** ⑧②. Nip acid freshens, so it appears lighter than 13.5% alc. Alfresco partner or sunset tipple. **Sauvignon Blanc** ⊘ ★★★★ Unwooded in **23** ⑧⑤, though retains splash semillon, adding a little fatness to otherwise crunchy green apple, herb & tangy lime flavours. Perfect with seafood & light lunches. Not tasted: **Pinot Gris**, **Noble Late Harvest**.

Classic range

Baronne ⊘ ★★★ Celebrating 50 years of this bold & hearty steakhouse standard in **22** ⑧②. Mostly cab & shiraz, shows smoky red fruit & good squeeze of firm dry tannin from oak staves. Also in 250 ml.

Sparkling range

Not tasted: **Méthode Cap Classique Brut**, **Cuvée Brut**. — MW

Location/map: Paarl ▪ Map grid reference: F5 ▪ WO: Western Cape/Coastal ▪ Est 1791 ▪ 1stB ca 1940 ▪ Wine tasting, sales & The Manor Restaurant Mon-Sun 9-4 (except Tuesdays when The Manor is closed; open until 6 on weekend days in the case of live music) pub hols (seasonal) please call ahead ▪ Various tasting fees, waived on purchase of R500+ ▪ Closed Dec 25 & Jan 1 ▪ Large groups by appt only ▪ Historic manor house (national monument) ▪ Tour groups ▪ Gifts ▪ Conferences ▪ Conservation area ▪ Play area for kids ▪ Live music on some Saturdays & Sundays ▪ Picnic & music concert in November ▪ Special events & weddings ▪ Owner(s) Heineken Beverages ▪ Cellarmaster(s) Samuel Viljoen (Apr 2021) ▪ Winemaker(s) Zinaschke Steyn (Jul 2021) & Pieter Badenhorst (Jan 2019), with Jamie Williams (Jul 2018) & Imellia Prins (Dec 2021) ▪ Viticulturist(s) Isabel Teubes (Dec 2019) ▪ 1,680ha (cab, carignan, grenache, malbec, merlot, p verdot, ptage, shiraz, tannat, tempranillo, chard, chenin, riesling, sauv, sem) ▪ 13,000t/2m cs own label ▪ ISO 0001:2008, ISO 14001:2004, HACCP, IPW, BRC, SGS organic, WWF-SA Conservation Champion ▪ Private Bag X3006 Paarl 7620 ▪ info@nederburg.com ▪ www.nederburg.com ▪ **T +27 (0)21-877-5155**

Neethlingshof Estate   ⓛ ⑪ ◎ ⑤ ⑥

Historic Neethlingshof has transitioned into the ownership of the Helfrich family, owners of GCF, France's largest private wine company, through its local subsidiary, Iwayini. The new custodians have lost no time in modernising vineyards and production facilities, intent on propelling the brand to new heights. Unchanged are the strong emphases on sustainability and nature preservation, evidenced in WWF-SA Conservation Champion status, or the warm welcome extended to visitors who enter through the unique avenue of stone pines, with wine pairings and a wine garden serving light meals among many amenities.

Short Story Collection

★★★★☆ **The Owl Post** Single-site pinotage acknowledging property's rodent-controlling owls. Change in oaking in **21** ⑨⓪ to include 40% American barrels with usual French & Hungarian, giving sweet vanilla edge to restrained black & blue berry fruit.

★★★★☆ **The Caracal** (☕) Cab-led (51%) Bordeaux blend adds malbec to merlot & petit verdot in **20** ⑨⓪. Black fruit densely packed yet well restrained by firm, focused tannins. Tobacco & milk chocolate whiffs from year in oak add detail on satisfying dry finish.

★★★★☆ **The Duiker Cadenza** (NEW) ⊘ (☕) (☕) Just 500 cases of single-vineyard sauvignon blanc. **23** ⑨① engaging & unforced, with vibrant white-fleshed fruit, succulent acid, dry fantail finish. Weight & breadth from part barrel ferment/3 months well judged to preserve purity & fine structure.

★★★★ **The Jackal's Dance** Single-vineyard sauvignon planted at altitude in 1997. Graceful, stylish **22** ⑧⑦ slightly riper than last, white asparagus & peach joining Cape gooseberry & green fig, comfortable moderate acid.

★★★★ **The Six Flowers** Carefully crafted, characterful blend of 6 white varieties, portion few months in new oak. **23** ⑧⑨ sees chardonnay-chenin take lead from chenin-sauvignon, deliver tad less palate richness than last **21** ★★★★☆ ⑨⓪.

★★★★☆ **Maria Noble Late Harvest** (☕) Riesling vines planted in 1986 deliver light-footed & very fruity unoaked botrytised dessert in **23** ⑨②. Delicious, sweet, with usual quickening limy acid, fraction less concentration & vinosity at just 9.4% alc. 375ml.

Estate range

★★★★☆ **Cabernet Sauvignon** ⊘ Consistently offers good character, inky depth & long grip. **21** ★★★★ ⑧⑧ graphite detail on varietal black fruit, balanced form-giving tannins. Great value, like last-tasted **19** ⑨⓪.

★★★★ **Malbec** ⊘ Fruit-sweet finish & dusty spice from 9 months in older oak, **22** ⑧⑥ meaty nuance to black cherry fruit.

★★★★ **Merlot** ⊘ Jaunty **21** ⑧⑥ has appealing sugared plum flavour, smooth, supple tannin structure from 18 months in seasoned oak.

★★★★☆ **Pinotage** ⊘ Signature grip & sweetness from French & American oak combo (60/4) shade obvious, not as integrated in **22** ★★★★ ⑧⑧. Fruit vivacity also slightly dialled back compared with **21** ⑨⓪, still a delicious & rewarding glassful.

★★★★ **Shiraz** (☕) Supple **21** ⑧⑦ offers blueberry & spiced plum in a charming & friendly body, 6 months in seasoned oak add a chalky grip on the finish.

Chardonnay Unwooded ★★★ Ready-now **23** ⑧②'s gentle lemon & peach tones, light body for uncomplicated patio enjoyment. **Chenin Blanc** ★★★☆ Tasty, with engaging verve, **23** ⑧⑤ offers white peaches, hay & flowers, easy drinkability. **Gewürztraminer** ★★★★ If this wine were a person, she would have an opinion & stand by it. **23** ⑧⑤ characterful, true to variety & style. Rose petals & Turkish Delight bouquet, litchi palate, smidgen sugar lifted by zesty acidity. **Sauvignon Blanc** ★★★☆ Lovely blackcurrant & white peach combo on **23** ⑧③, vibrant & dry, sleek textured if a little brief.

Cap Classique range (NEW)

★★★★ **Brut** Chardonnay & pinot noir (70/30) **NV** ⑧⑦, white gold hue, racy freshness & electric mousse the immediate attractions. Lemon lift, bracing dry finish & savoury persistence seal the deal.

Brut Rosé ★★★★ Pale salmon **NV** ⑧⑤ softly frothy & creamy with attractive red & black berry aromas & flavours, subtle brioche complexity. Pinot noir, pinotage & meunier with 30% chardonnay.

Ode To Nature range

Occasional release: **Weisser Riesling**. — CvZ

Location/map/WO: Stellenbosch ▪ Map grid reference: D5 ▪ Est 1692 ▪ 1stB 1880 ▪ Tasting & sales Mon-Fri 9-5 Sat/Sun/pub hols 10-4 ▪ Tasting fees: R75/5 Estate wines; R110/5 Short Story Collection wines; R90/5 Selection wines ▪ Closed Good Fri & Dec 25 ▪ Cellar tours by appt R60pp ▪ Flash Food & Slow Wine pairing R170pp, booking recommended for 6+ ▪ Chocolate & Wine pairing R90pp ▪ Kiddies pairing R70pp ▪ The Salt Road at Neethlingshof serving pizza & light meals at the Winegarden Wed-Sun ▪ Jungle gym ▪ Tour groups ▪ Conferences ▪ Conservation area ▪ Wednesday night live music (summer) ▪ Wine club ▪ Owner(s) GCF ▪ Winemaker(s) Mika Engelbrecht (since 2023) ▪ Viticulturist(s) Hannes van Zyl ▪ 278ha/101.58ha (cabs s/f, malbec, merlot, p verdot, ptage, shiraz, chard, chenin, gewürz, riesling, sauv, viog) ▪ 900-930t/120,000cs own label 58% red 42% white ▪ WIETA, WWF-SA Conservation Champion ▪ PO Box 104 Stellenbosch 7599 ▪ info@neethlingshof.co.za ▪ www.neethlingshof.co.za ▪ **T +27 (0)21-883-8988**

Neil Ellis Wines　　　　　　　　　　　　　　　⚲ ⑪ ⓫

Founder Neil Ellis, a stalwart member of the Cape Winemakers Guild since its early days, was a pioneer of negotiant winemaking in the Cape, trawling the winelands for special vineyard parcels, first in home base Stellenbosch, then cool pockets to the north and south. These still reflect in the Site Specific range of single mostly blocks and the Premium range of regional specialities, along with sites added in recent years, seeking to express their unique character. Latterly the venture has had an elegant home on the lower reaches of Helshoogte Pass, and Neil has handed the winemaking reins to son Warren, one of a growing band of 2nd-generation CWG members. Visitors to the winery are offered a range of sit-down tasting options as well as cheese and charcuterie platters. Tour groups and functions are also catered for.

Site Specific range

★★★★☆ **Jonkershoek Valley Cabernet Sauvignon** ⚲ ⚘ SA classic from prime terroir, built for 10+ years. Liquorice, cedar & fresh herb overlay to pure cassis fruit, precise acid & fine-boned tannin, **18** ⑨⑷ tightly focused exemplar of this wine's signature elegance, harmony, latent power. All-new oak, 18 months, like standout **17** ★★★★★ ⑨⑺. In 1.5L, 3L, 5L too, as most of these.

★★★★☆ **Groenekloof Cinsaut** Delicate & understated, **20** ⑨⓪ offers floral-perfumed red berries & sweet vanilla nuance from 14 months in oak. Savoury undertone shows on mid-palate, with baked quince & sleek, suede-textured tannins. Riper, fuller than last-tasted **18** ★★★★ ⑧⑧.

★★★★☆ **Piekenierskloof Grenache** ⚘ Maintains impressive form with outstanding varietal expression in **19** ⑨⑷. Sweetly succulent raspberry-cranberry compote, subtle Ribena cordial note, cosseting velvet tannins & bright acid. Polish from 14 months in oak, 25% new.

★★★★☆ **Bottelary Hills Pinotage** ⚘ Charm lies in restraint, satin texture & lithe body prevailing over raw power. **20** ⑨⑷ succulent dark berries & hedonistic spicing, partly from 14 months in 50% new oak, combine for unique varietal expression. Finish is long & intricate, with a savoury-mineral twist at the end. Follows vivacious **19** ★★★★★ ⑨⑸.

★★★★☆ **Rodanos** ⚘ Engaging & elegant Rhône-styled blend of 65% shiraz with cinsault & grenache, **20** ⑨⑷ supple & vibrant cherry & blackberry fruit spiced with dainty scrub & tobacco notes. 30% wholebunch ferment adds floral scents, heightened aromatics, unobscured by 14 months in 25% new oak. WO W Cape. **18** & **19** untasted.

★★★★☆ **Whitehall Chardonnay** ⚲ Elegant **21** ⑨⑷, from Elgin vines, cooler, less intense expression than previous. White peach, pear & subtle citrus, almond nuance from judicious oak ferment/9 months ageing, 30% new. Energy & freshness from mostly suppressed malo & restrained 12.7% alc.

★★★★☆ **Amica** ⚘ Seriously conceived & richly rewarding sauvignon blanc, **21** ★★★★★ ⑨⑸ takes the road less travelled: free-run juice from Jonkershoek vines, wild yeast fermented/9 months in barrel, 20% new. Finely poised, melding vivid acid with the fullness of lees contact, layered citrus & greengage fruit, rounded hazelnut & lime cordial accents. Follows assured **20** ⑨③.

★★★★☆ **Op Sy Moer** ⚘ As Afrikaans name ('on its lees') implies, **22** ⑨③ bottled with fine lees, evident in slight cloudiness. Near-equal Piekenierskloof palomino & chenin show overt, almost visceral ferment character, with ginger & nutmeg, notable palate weight. Should develop interestingly. **21** untasted.

★★★★☆ **Semillon Noble Late Harvest** ⚲ Lovely light-footed **16** ⑨⓪ botrytis dessert from bunch-pressed, barrel-fermented Elgin fruit. Delicate floral & roasted nut flavours & aromas, fine structure & 'cool' balancing acidity. First since **11**, untasted by us. 375 ml.

Premium range

★★★★☆ **Stellenbosch Cabernet Sauvignon** ⚲ Generous cassis fruit, densely packed fine-grained tannins & crisp acid backbone - cab's DNA is well-expressed in **20** ⑨⓪, including its ageing potential &, in this winemaker's hands, early accessibility. Commendable freshness added by 15% dab of petit verdot, malbec & cab franc.

★★★★☆ **Groenekloof Syrah** ⊘ Previewed last edition, **21** ⑨② vindicates rating with heady scrub wafts lacing through Morello cherries & blackberries, delightful meat & tobacco highlights. 15% cinsault adds fragrance & brightness. 14 months in mostly seasoned barrels. Already approachable, but has legs for several more years.

★★★★ **Stellenbosch Cabernet Sauvignon-Merlot** Ⓥ Equal partners in well-composed **20** ⑧⑧. Juicy red plum & leaf accents on black plum & berry body, hint chocolate from 30% new wood, exceedingly pleasant dry finish for food or solo enjoyment.

★★★★☆ **Groenekloof Sauvignon Blanc** ⊘ Always-impressive expression of a cool site. Previewed **23** ㉑ carries the baton with poise, striking depth & length. Herbal notes weave into solid greengage & berry fruit on appealing mineral-earthy substrate. Vibrant acid emphasises palate breadth & lingering finish. Similarly styled **22** ㉒, now bottled, fulfills early promise.

Discontinued: **Aenigma**. — GdB

Location/map: Stellenbosch ▪ Map grid reference: G5 ▪ WO: Groenekloof/Jonkershoek Valley/Piekenierskloof/Elgin/Stellenbosch/Bottelary/Western Cape ▪ Est 1986 ▪ 1stB 1984 ▪ Tasting & sales Mon-Fri 9.30-4.30 Sat/pub hols 10-5 ▪ Closed Good Fri, Dec 25/26 & Jan 1 ▪ Antipasto platters ▪ Tour groups ▪ Wine club ▪ Owner(s) Neil Ellis Wines (Pty) Ltd ▪ Winemaker(s) Warren Ellis (2006) & Christiaan van der Merwe (2016) ▪ Viticulturist(s) Warren Ellis (2006) ▪ Brands for clients: Woolworths ▪ PO Box 917 Stellenbosch 7599 ▪ info@neilellis.com ▪ www.neilellis.com ▪ **T +27 (0)21-887-0649**

☐ **Nelson Estate** *see* Nelson Family Vineyards

Nelson Family Vineyards

The two riverside farms that make up the family estate between Paarl and Wellington were acquired in 1987 by paterfamilias Alan Nelson, and developed over the years into a wine and lifestyle destination with varied attractions. Daughter and Cape Wine Master Lisha is the winecrafter, working with long-term vineyardist Petrus de Villiers and applying 'a minimalist approach' to achieve elegant and pure-fruited results.

Lisha Nelson Signature Wines

★★★★☆ **Cabernet Franc** Ⓥ Serious oaking, 20 months, 80% new, of elegant harvest **19** ⑨⓪ means palate features still cloaked in barrel character & firm dry tannins. Deserves cellaring to fully reveal the fruit.

★★★★☆ **Chenin Blanc** Ⓥ Natural ferment in 50% new barrels, followed by 10 months on lees amplifies **20** ⑨⓪'s substantial fruit, adds oatmeal enticement to the complex layers, long & dry finish.

Discontinued: **Dad's Blend**.

Nelson Family Vineyards range

★★★★ **Cabernet Sauvignon-Merlot** Ⓥ The 55/45 blend in **19** ⑧⑥ shows dusty herbaceous nuance, 80% new oak still integrating mid-2022. Cellaring should liberate the fruit & resolve the tannins.

Rosé Ⓥ ★★★★ Electric pink hue & perfumed red berry flavours in **22** ⑧④ from shiraz & petit verdot, splash cab. Fresh & succulent for sunset/alfresco quaffing. Not tasted: **Chardonnay**, **Sauvignon Blanc**.

Nelson's Creek range

Not tasted: **Chenin Blanc**, **Rosé**. Discontinued: **Shiraz**.

Nelson Estate range

Not tasted: **Shiraz**, **Noble Late Harvest**. — DS

Location/map/WO: Paarl ▪ Map grid reference: D3 ▪ Tasting, sales & cellar tours by appt only ▪ Closed all pub hols ▪ Facilities for children ▪ Tour groups ▪ Conferences ▪ Weddings ▪ Walks/hikes ▪ MTB trails ▪ Guest accommodation ▪ Owner(s) Alan Nelson ▪ Cellarmaster(s)/winemaker(s) Lisha Nelson CWM (Nov 2007) ▪ Viticulturist(s) Petrus de Villiers ▪ 142ha/41ha (cabs s/f, merlot, p verdot, ptage, shiraz, chard, chenin, sauv, sem) ▪ 210t/9,340cs own label 30% red 60% white 10% rosé ▪ IPW ▪ PO Box 2009 Windmeul 7630 ▪ lisha@nelsonscreek.co.za ▪ www.nelsonscreek.co.za ▪ **T +27 (0)73-164-1968**

☐ **Nelson's Creek** *see* Nelson Family Vineyards
☐ **Nero** *see* Bosman Family Vineyards
☐ **Nest Egg** *see* The Fledge & Co
☐ **New Cape Wines** *see* Eagle's Cliff Wines-New Cape Wines

Newstead Lund Family Vineyards

Wines still being finalised mean there's nothing for us to taste from Doug and Sue Lund, boutique wine-growers near oceanside resort town Plettenberg Bay on the tourist Garden Route, recently making waves with top-league cap classique bubblies produced with local consultant Anton Smal.

Location: Plettenberg Bay ▪ Map: Klein Karoo & Garden Route ▪ Map grid reference: C1 ▪ Est 2008 ▪ 1stB 2012 ▪ Open daily 11-4 (high season) Wed-Sun 11-4 (low season) ▪ Wine & cap classique tastings ▪ Vineyard restaurant ▪ Polo ▪ Celebrations ▪ Luxury accommodation ▪ Tour groups ▪ Owner(s) Doug & Sue Lund ▪ Cellarmaster(s)/winemaker(s) Anton Smal (Jan 2011, consultant) ▪ Viticulturist(s) Doug Lund ▪ 11ha/6.5ha (pinot, chard, sauv) ▪ 24t/4,500cs own label white, rosé & MCC ▪ PO Box 295 The Crags 6602 ▪ info@newsteadwines.com ▪ www.newsteadwines.com ▪ **T +27 (0)76-300-9740 (office)**

Newton Johnson Vineyards

New new vintages for us to taste from this internationally acclaimed family business in Upper Hemel-en-Aarde Valley. We look forward to sampling them next time.

Location: Hermanus ▪ Map: Walker Bay & Bot River ▪ Map grid reference: B4 ▪ Est 1996 ▪ 1stB 1997 ▪ Tasting & sales Mon-Fri 9-4 Sat 10-3 ▪ Closed all pub hols ▪ Restaurant @ Newton Johnson lunch 12-3 Wed-Sun (Apr-Nov)/Tue-Sun (Dec-Mar) ▪ Owner(s) Newton Johnson Family Trust ▪ Winemaker(s)/viticulturist(s) Gordon Newton Johnson (Jan 2001) ▪ 14oha/18ha (grenache, mourv, pinot, shiraz, albariño, chard) ▪ 240t/20,000cs own label 50% red 50% white ▪ PO Box 225 Hermanus 7200 ▪ wine@newtonjohnson.com ▪ www.newton-johnson.com ▪ **T +27 (0)28-312-3862**

☐ **NG Kerk Die Paarl** see Strooidak

Nicholson Smith

These are the proprietary wines of substantial Johannesburg drinks business Nicholson Smith. All are non-vintage, a strategic choice which allows consultant winemaker James McKenzie to source wines from different areas, cellars, varieties and even vintages for styling as the various amiably packaged and accessible ranges require. The overarching goal is to 'way over-deliver on the wine at the price point'.

Pandora's Box range

The Persian Connection Shiraz ☺ ★★★ American staves in half the wine to fit the spicing to the name & style: cinnamon & vanilla coat **NV** ⑧₂'s rich plush fruit. Curvaceous & succulent, very easy to like. **The Wheat Fields Chenin Blanc** (NEW) ☺ ★★★ Citrus (lemon & grapefruit) plus apple, **NV** ⑧₂'s fresh & fruity styling with its acid structure is delightful everyday drinking. Touch of oak adds palate weight.

The Bell Pepper Cabernet Sauvignon ⊘ ★★★ Carefully crafted reds for easy but flavourful drinking, just 30% oaking for 9 months unless specified. As the name suggests, a slight green note can be part of cab's character, in **NV** ⑧₀ coupled with berries & plums. **The Black Bird Merlot** ⊘ ★★★ Fruit's the hero in **NV** ⑧₁, oak gives a smoky note, leaving the smooth berry & plum flavours to entice. **The Professor's Pinotage** ⊘ ★★★ Dark-toned, **NV** ⑧₂ has savoury spice, salty liquorice, modest oaking (all American) gives the fruit & smooth texture centre stage. **Lock 1855 Merlot-Cabernet Sauvignon** ⊘ ★★★ Varieties work in tandem to supply **NV** ⑧₁'s cassis & cherries, lightly dusted with spice. Appealing fresh note in the flavours. **The Italian Job Red Blend** ⊘ ★★★ Unspecified varieties, supple texture from 20% oak, the spicing savoury, good for food matching. **NV** ⑧₀ shows berries, some charcuterie tones. **All Day Rosé** ⊘ ★★★ Which it is, for drinking solo or at table. Pale pink & trim (12.5% alc), **NV** ⑧₂ is a berry mix with just a touch of minerality. Its tangy freshness wakens the taste buds. **The High Tea Chardonnay-Pinot Noir** (NEW) ⊘ ★★★ Attractive pink flower-decked bottle (great gift for a favourite aunt), **NV** ⑧₂ dry rosé has citrus tones, red berry top note, showcasing both varieties. Flavourful. **La Dolce Vita Moscato Semi-Sweet** ⊘ ★★★ **NV** ⑦₈'s touch of sugar fits the style, aromatic & muscatty, it's light (12% alc) & easy. **The Godfather Pinot Grigio** ⊘ ★★★ Trim figure of **NV** ⑧₁ (11% alc) fits the variety; apple & winter melon flavour, lime-tinged finish all declare the drinkability. **The Gooseberry Sauvignon Blanc** ⊘ ★★★ Style change for latest **NV** ⑧₁, greenpepper, some grassy nuances, but it's what you'd expect from sauvignon. Sleek, ends crisp & dry. **The Honeysuckle Sweet Red** ★★★ Enough red fruit to appeal, but it's **NV** ⑦₇'s texture, succulently sweet & smooth, that's the prime attraction.

Pandora's Box Sparkling range

The Cherry Blossom Sparkling Rosé Nectar ★★★ Svelte (10.5% alc) but the sweetness gives the impression of full-bodied richness. Pale pink carbonated NV ⑦⑧ has exuberant bubbles, lifting the cherry & strawberry flavours. **The Biscuit Tin Sparkling Brut** ⊘ ★★★ Name tells you what to expect, carbonated NV ⑧① has Lemon Cream biscuit tones, is elegantly fresh, the touch of sugar giving a tangy effect.

Bob's Your Uncle range

Once In A Blue Moon Merlot ⊘ ★★★ Smoky berries, NV ⑧⓪'s 12-month stave oaking for 70% of the wine shows in the perfume & flavours, a dry finish, promising some ageing potential. **Head Over Heels Cabernet Sauvignon-Merlot** ⊘ ★★★ Same oaking as Merlot, similar spice & tannin profile, here alongside cassis & plums, giving NV ⑧⓪ tasty drinkability. **The Fat Cat Chenin Blanc** ⊘ ★★★ Slender (12.5% alc) but no shortage of fruit or flavour in NV ⑧⓪: bruised apple, juicy pear, nice crisp finish. **A Perfect Storm Sauvignon Blanc** ⊘ ★★★ Some greenpepper, whiff of grass, NV ⑧① is classic sauvignon blanc, elegantly crisp & dry.

Bella Vino range

Sultry Red ⊘ ★★★ Unspecified varieties, as most of these. Unwooded NV ⑦⑧ offers dark-toned berries, an intriguing smoky nuance; ends dry, food-friendly. **Sublime White Sauvignon Blanc** ⊘ ★★★ Some meadowgrass notes alongside crunchy appley freshness in NV ⑧②, ends long & zesty. Nice food partner. **Sassy Sweet Red** ⊘ ★★★ Fruit's the focus here, dense red berries, NV ⑦⑦'s body smooth textured, the sweetness mouthfilling. **Perky Pink Natural Sweet Rosé** ⊘ ★★★ Pale salmon-hued NV ⑦⑦ shows red berries & fruit pastilles, is full-sweet & curvaceous despite the modest 12.5% alc. **Seductively Sweet White** ★★★ Restrained alc (11.5%) but NV ⑦⑦'s fruity sweetness adds texture & body, is smoothly round.

Smith & Co range

The Plum Box Soft Smooth Dry Red ⊘ ★★★ Unspecified varieties, attractive & colourful graphics reflecting the name, as all these. NV ⑧⓪ is unwooded, & yes, offers plummy fruit, soft & smooth. Not complex but gives pleasure. Also in 3L & 5L bag-in-box, as all. **The Citrus Box Dazzling Dry White** ⊘ ★★★ Packaging & name tells it like it is, sleek & lemony NV ⑧②, dry & zesty, tightly focused. **The Cherry Box Silky Sweet Red** ⊘ ★★★ No oak, just sweetness & silky texture, NV ⑦⑧ is curvy, the cherry fruit a big part of the appeal. **The Strawberry Box Pretty Pink Natural Sweet Rosé** ⊘ ★★★ The sweetest of these, pale pink & streamlined (12.5% alc), NV ⑦⑧ is aptly named, a combo of fresh & macerated cherries, finishes tangy. **The Honey Box Sensual Sweet White** ⊘ ★★★ Stonefruit, rich & honeyed, NV ⑦⑦ makes no apologies for for its 'sensual' description, has curves & plenty of sweetness. — CR

Location: Johannesburg ▪ WO: Western Cape ▪ Est 1997 ▪ 1stB 2012 ▪ Closed to public ▪ Owner(s) Jason Neal ▪ Winemaker(s)/viticulturist(s) James McKenzie (2012) ▪ 396,000cs own label 70% red 20% white 10% other ▪ PO Box 1659 Jukskei Park 2153 ▪ jason@nicholsonsmith.co.za ▪ www.nicholsonsmith.co.za ▪ T +27 (0)11-496-2947

Nick & Forti's Wines ⓥ

Nick van Huyssteen, founder of acclaimed Saronsberg winery in Tulbagh, and Fortunato 'Forti' Mazzone, entrepreneurial restaurateur based in Pretoria, launched their 'project about food, wine, family and friendship' 20 years ago to offer 'European-style wines with quality and depth at a truly affordable price'. The original pair of red wines are now part of the Signature Range of the Forti Group of hospitality establishments, and available for tasting and sale at Forti Too wine bar and emporium in Lynnwood Bridge Centre.

★★★★ **Shiraz** ⊘ Generous as ever, 21 ⑧⑨ ample bramble, mulberry, cured meet & fynbos flavours. Rich, rounded yet lively, fruit in harmony with vanilla & spice from 18 months in 30% new barrels.

★★★★ **Epicentre** Succulent 21 ⑧⑨ 5-way Bordeaux blend, mostly cab. Lovely scrub undertone & fine tannin support for plums, chocolate & warm spice. Also in magnum, as Shiraz. **20** untasted. WO Tulbagh.

Artspace Chenin Blanc ⑧ ★★★★ Fresh-&-fruity styled 22 ⑧⑤ is pure sunshiny sipping pleasure. Undemanding but very satisfying, with pineapple & peach highlights. WO Coastal. — WB

Location: Tulbagh/Pretoria ▪ WO: Western Cape/Tulbagh/Coastal ▪ Est/1stB 2004 ▪ Tasting ▪ Vee and Forti Wine Bar, Lynnwood Bridge, Pretoria ▪ Owner(s) Fortunato Mazzone & Saronsberg ▪ Winemaker(s) Daniela Jansen (2019) ▪ 4,000cs own label 85% red 15% white ▪ 389 Mackenzie Str, Brooklyn 0181 ▪ forti@fortitoo.co.za ▪ www.saronsberg.com, www.fortitoo.co.za ▪ T +27 (0)83-467-2588

Nicky Versfeld Wines

His Semillon on hold for now, Somerset West winemaker and consultant Nicky Versfeld focuses on a varietal Sauvignon and red blend for his private boutique label, launched in 2016 with knowledge accumulated over many years at well-known wineries and in vineyard sites around the winelands.

★★★★ **Galaxy** ⓥ Unusual shiraz & petit verdot blend (85/15). **19** ⑧⑨ restrained, elegant, in lighter framework of fine dry tannin from year in old oak. Youthful, balanced, but needs time, as previous. No **18**.

★★★★☆ **Sauvignon Blanc** ⓐ Alluringly fresh, with delicate whiteflower, citrus & stonefruit, **23** ⑨③ shows benefit of sourcing cool-grown Coastal fruit. Effortless grace, subtle lees enrichment, so cleanly balanced, could be enjoyed solo or with a light meal. No **22**.

In abeyance: **Semillon.** — MW

Location: Somerset West ▪ WO: Stellenbosch/Coastal ▪ Est 2016 ▪ 1stB 2015 ▪ Closed to public ▪ Winemaker(s) Nicky Versfeld ▪ 1,000cs own label 100% white ▪ Building No 8, Fairways Office Park, 5 Niblick Way, Somerset West 7130 ▪ ncversfeld@gmail.com ▪ **T** +27 (0)21-850-0160/1, +27 (0)83-675-8436

☐ **Nicolas van der Merwe** *see* Nico van der Merwe Wines

Nico van der Merwe Wines   ⓥ

Nico and Petra van der Merwe launched their small venture 25 years ago on Stellenbosch's prime Polkadraai Hills while Nico was making wine at nearby Saxenburg, the estate he put on the map in the 1990s. Priorities are different now, and reducing the business impact of ongoing power outages is number one. 'It's costing a lot of money, but we're nearly there.' Ever forthright, Nico says his philosophy has no truck with old vines, whole bunches, clay pots or concrete tanks. 'Just normal winemaking that's affordable and sustainable.'

Flagship range

★★★★ **Mas Nicolas Stellenbosch** ⓥ Gentle giant, usual cab-shiraz duo. Beguiling dark tarry layers on a fine structure, **17** ⑨④ unfolding flavour profile with great depth, complexity. 100 magnums too. No **16**.

Nicolas van der Merwe range

★★★★☆ **Cabernet Sauvignon** ⓥ Nico van der Merwe's 'ego project in exceptional **17** ⑨④ vintage'. A barrel-selected blockbuster that vibrates with energy. A triumph. Just 600 bottles sold ex cellardoor only.

★★★★☆ **Syrah** ⓐ As appealing in **20** ⑨④, albeit slightly riper & richer than previous. Similar fruit purity & freshness, some subtle sweet spicing from small oaked portion, 20% new. All elements streamlined into elegant balance, already tempting but will certainly benefit from few years in cellar.

★★★★☆ **Merlot-Cabernet Sauvignon-Cabernet Franc** ⓐ Classically styled (as all wines from this producer), **21** ⑨④ a 64/32/4 blend, showing cooler vintage's restraint & structure. Scented red & dark berries with subtle cedary nuance from 15 months oak, 5% new. Already harmonious, will age beautifully.

★★★★☆ **Geelbos Steen** Yellowbush, a local medicinal plant, names this striking chenin from high-elevation vines. **20** ⑨① even richer, with delicious piquancy, cling peach & stewed quince flavours. Vibrant, mouthfilling, with creamy oatmeal substrate from barrel-fermented portion & 6 months on lees.

★★★★ **Five To Nine Sauvignon Blanc** References cool, early morning harvest time, to capture signature herbaceous & green fruit flavours. Five months lees contact provide rich substrate in **23** ⑧⑦, all zested through with lime. First tasted since **20**.

★★★★☆ **White** ⓥ Classically styled white Bordeaux from unwooded sauvignon (67%) & oak-fermented semillon in **19** ⑨③. Medium bodied & focused, vibrant acidity leavened by semillon's waxy texture.

★★★★☆ **Méthode Cap Classique Extra Brut** ⓥ Latest **NV** ⑨⓪ sparkler from chardonnay back to 5 years on lees. Luxurious texture of butter melting into warm bread, well measured & elegant, bone-dry.

Robert Alexander range

★★★★ **Merlot** ⓥ 'Everybody's darling' - & no wonder - versatile, bright as a berry **20** ⑧⑦ exudes juicy vitality. A savoury nuance from year old oak checks the exuberance. Better than last-tasted **17** ★★★★ ⑧④.

★★★★ **Shiraz** ⓞ Plumper in **20** ⑧⑥, with older oak in supple support. Balanced freshness & grip for current enjoyment with a good few years to spare.

Cape Elements range

★★★★ **Shiraz-Grenache** ⊘ Similar smoky, savoury impression, with some riper plummy notes in **20** ⑧⑥, shiraz dominant at 87%. Sappy, juicy blend, lightly oaked with respectable structure & clean dry finish. More fruit depth than **19** ★★★★ ⑧⑤. WO W Cape.

La Polka range

In abeyance: **Rosé**. — MW

Location/map: Stellenbosch ▪ Map grid reference: B6 ▪ WO: Stellenbosch/Western Cape ▪ Est/1stB 1999 ▪ Tasting always available, just call ahead ▪ Owner(s) Nico & Petra van der Merwe ▪ Winemaker(s) Nico van der Merwe ▪ 50t/4,000cs own label 80% red 20% white ▪ PO Box 12200 Stellenbosch 7613 ▪ admin@nvdmwines.com ▪ www.nvdmwines.com ▪ T +27 (0)21-881-3063

Nico Vermeulen Wines ℗

Veteran Paarl wine-maker, -adviser and -trader Nico Vermeulen created this private label just over 20 years ago, and dedicated it to his family, wife Judith and children 'NC', Izelle and Judy; they've responded with unstinting help and support. Latterly Nico crafts his tiny batches in the Goede Hoop cellar near Stellenbosch.

Electos range

★★★★ **Cabernet Sauvignon-Merlot-Cabernet Franc-Petit Verdot-Malbec** Styled differently to its Cape Bordeaux sibling: **19** ⑧⑨ seductive, silky & supple, the Xmas cake spice & fruit set in a frame that's well integrated after 18 months in older barrels, ready to enjoy, in magnums too.

Discontinued: **Sauvignon Blanc**.

The Right Choice range

★★★★ **The Right Two Reds** Blend slightly tweaked in **19** ⑧⑥, cab upped to 52%, still partnering merlot. Dark ripe cherry & plum fruit framed by dry oak & robust tannins. Needs time to meld.

The Right White ⊘ ★★★★ Fig & gooseberry pungency of **23** ⑧⑤ matched by vivid freshness. Taut & bright, good intensity throughout. Sauvignon & 10% semillon. WO Cape Town. Not tasted: **The Right Red**, **Rosé**, **Life From Old Wood**, **Pinot Noir Sparkling Rosé**, **Sauvignon Blanc Sparkling**, **Wit Muskadel**. — FM

Location: Paarl ▪ WO: Stellenbosch/Cape Town/Coastal ▪ Est/1stB 2003 ▪ Tasting by appt only ▪ Owner(s)/viticulturist(s) Nico Vermeulen ▪ Winemaker(s) Nico Vermeulen, with Judy, NC & Izelle Vermeulen ▪ 1,500cs own label & 24,000L bulk export ▪ 3 Pieter Hugo Str, Courtrai, Suider-Paarl 7646 ▪ nicovermeulenwines@gmail.com ▪ T +27 (0)82-553-2024

Niel Joubert Estate ℗

Tucked away in the Paarl foothills of Simonsberg is Klein Simonsvlei, where five generations of the Joubert family have farmed and, since the early 1990s, made wine under their label. At 160,000 cases, volumes match the 1,000-ha extent of the farm, but the winery slogan, 'every bottle filled with pride for your enjoyment', speaks of care and attention to detail. The brand's many fans have commented positively about recent 'exotics' like grüner veltliner, and have the first cabernet franc ('so suited to our slopes') to look forward to.

Reserve range

★★★★☆ **Cabernet Sauvignon** ⓥ Though aged remarkable 72 months in small barrels, all new, **16** ⑨⓪ bustles with berries & spice, & has good few years in store.

★★★★☆ **Shiraz** ⊘ Beguiling heather & spice introduce deliciously mature mulberry flavours of **17** ⑨⓪. Generous 14.5% alc harmonious, 4 years in oak, 40% new, well integrated. Polished, ready to enjoy. No **16**.

★★★★☆ **Tempranillo** ⓥ Accessible, almost gulpable in youth, **20** ⑨⓪ has enough substance, oak & variety's svelte dry tannins to reward cellaring a decade.

★★★★ **Chardonnay** ⓥ Pear & lime fruit given heft & some assertiveness by oaking in **19** ⑧⑧. 20% unwooded portion ensures the whole is poised, the smooth texture makes it moreish.

★★★★ **Chenin Blanc** ⓥ Aromatic **19** ⑧⑧ offers spiced apple & citrus, 22 months in 30% new cask a toasty embellishment. More weight & viscosity than last, though alc remains moderate at 13%. No **18**.

★★★★ **Grenache Blanc** ⓥ Bold & beautiful **19** ⑧⑨ folds fig & baked quince fruit into layers of cream & wood, added richness from grain sugar. Good acid seam lifts.

Proprietor range

★★★★ **Malbec** ⓦ Opulent & bold **15** ⑧⑦, ripe & dried dark fruit, mixed herbs & savoury game hint, liquorice & clove from 100% new oak, plush tannins - all balanced by fresh acid.

Christine-Marié range

★★★★ **Brut Méthode Cap Classique** ⓥ Chardonnay **NV** ⑧⑨ bubbly now lighter, less time on lees for fresh, finessed style. The core is citrus, bright, dry & refreshing with lunchtime-friendly 10.8% alc.

First Kiss Fortified Chenin Blanc ⓦ ★★★★ Creamy honey & ginger flavours on oak-matured **12** ⑧④, warming, delightful nightcap & alternative to 'port'. WO W Cape.

Niel Joubert Estate range

Shiraz ⓥ ⓦ ★★★★ Fresh **19** ⑧⑤ lifted by toasted spice, interleaved with red berry fruit, smoke & white pepper. Soft, supple, glides down with alarming ease... & speed!

Cabernet Sauvignon ⓦ ★★★★ Pure summer berry enjoyment in **19** ⑧⑤, fresh & accessible, 75% unoaked portion adding to the elegance. **Merlot** ⓥ ★★★★ Lighter-styled, ruby-hued **21** ⑧④ has pomegranate tang to savoury core, less meaty, tarry than last. **Pinotage** ⓦ ★★★★ Juicy raspberries, mulberries & plums to the fore in unwooded **18** ⑧③, no jammy or sweet-fruit characters this vintage, ends bone-dry for easy enjoyment. **Chardonnay** ⓥ ★★★★ Piquant **22** ⑧④ embroidered with oatmeal & vanilla from 15% oaked portion, vibrates with bright citrus & crunchy white pear fruit. **Chenin Blanc** ⓥ ★★★★ Cornucopia of ripe pears & guavas yet **23** ⑧③ ends lipsmackingly dry, with some grip. Fuller bodied than last. **Sauvignon Blanc** ⓥ ★★★ Packs a tropical punch of passionfruit & pineapple in **23** ⑧⓪. Clean & fresh, moderate 13% alc.

Lifestyle range

Grüner Veltliner ☺ ★★★ One of only 2 of this Austrian grape in the guide, **23** ⑧② a delicious alternative for jaded palates. Honeysuckle aroma, pick-me-up green apple crunch in flinty dry finish.

Cinsault-Grenache ⓦ ★★★★ Gentle pink colour & earthy forest-floor fruit on 51/49 blend give no hint of the big tannin 14.7% alc in **20** ⑧③. **Blanc de Noir** ★★★ Light & breezy **23** ⑦⑨ is mostly pinotage, pervaded with sweet-sour berries & apricot; modest 12% alc to match the bone-dry finish. — DS

Location/map: Paarl ▪ Map grid reference: C8 ▪ WO: Paarl/Western Cape ▪ Est 1898 ▪ 1stB 1996 ▪ Tasting & sales by appt Mon-Thu 8.30-5 Fri 8.30-3 ▪ Closed all pub hols ▪ Online shop ▪ Owner(s) Joubert family ▪ Cellarmaster(s) Ernst Leicht (Oct 2000) ▪ Winemaker(s) Ernst Leicht, with Niel Joubert jnr (May 2011) ▪ Viticulturist(s) Daan Joubert ▪ 1,000ha/300ha (cab, cinsaut, grenache n/b, malbec, merlot, ptage, shiraz, tempranillo, touriga nacional, chard, chenin, grüner veltliner, sauv) ▪ 1,953t/±160,000cs own label 49% red 50% white 1% rosé ▪ Other export brand: Kleinkloof ▪ GlobalGAP, IPW ▪ PO Box 17 Klapmuts 7625 ▪ wine@ nieljoubert.co.za ▪ www.nieljoubert.co.za ▪ **T +27 (0)21-875-5936**

☐ **Niels Verburg** see Luddite Wines

Nietgegund ⓠ

A liquor licence has been issued at long last, and Jan Dreyer has lost no time converting a farmshed on Nietgegund on Stellenbosch's Blaauwklippen Road into a visitor lounge. He's also pulling out citrus to make room for vines, and revamping the packaging. In the process, the name of the blend is changing, but Jan assures that the intention behind the old one, Pro Amico, is unchanged, and it's still 'made for our friends'.

★★★★ **Nietgegund** ⓥ 70% merlot, with cab & cab franc, **21** ⑧⑦ precise & well structured, tannins refined after year in old oak, supporting cassis & leafy flavours to long, savoury finish. Will keep. No **18 - 20**.

Merlot ⓝⓔⓦ ⓥ ★★★★ Unadorned by oak, **21** ⑧④ redcurrants & cherries, bright acid with sprinkling of Xmas spice & sugar. Easy, fresh, can be lightly chilled. — WB

Location/map/WO: Stellenbosch ▪ Map grid reference: F7 ▪ Est 2004 ▪ 1stB 2008 ▪ Tasting by appt ▪ Owner(s) Nietgegund Boerdery (Edms) Bpk ▪ Winemaker(s) Ronell Wiid (Jan 2013, consultant) ▪ Viticulturist(s) Francois Hanekom (Sep 2006, consultant) ▪ 3.4ha/1ha (cabs s/f, merlot) ▪ 4t/100cs own label 100% red ▪ IPW ▪ PO Box 12684 Die Boord 7613 ▪ info.wine@nietgegund.com, jan@nietgegund.com ▪ www.nietgegund. com ▪ **T +27 (0)21-880-0738/+27 (0)82-990-0621/+27 (0)82-491-2652**

Nieuwedrift Vineyards ⓠ ⑾ ⌂ ◎ ⑧

Seventh-generation farmer and vintner Johan Mostert sells most of his small output from the on-site tasting venue, restaurant and guest house near Piketberg, so he's able to judge the uptake of the cap classique and make enough for two years. But such was demand for the recent sibling (single-ferment) bubblies that no skipping was possible, and more was duly crafted - as naturally as possible, per his longtime philosophy.

★★★★ **Méthode Cap Classique** ⓠ From chardonnay, with a sunny lemon hue, **21** ⑧⑦ has lazy, mouthfilling bubbles that deliver apple pie mixed with vanilla from oaked portion of the base wine.

★★★★ **Méthode Ancestrale Rosé** Bright salmon hue draws you in, ample florals & berries on vigorous mousse please & satisfy in **23** ⑧⑧ from shiraz. Expect some harmless sediment on these well-made single-ferment bubblies, it's aligned with the wine style & artisanal approach.

★★★★ **Méthode Ancestrale Chenin Blanc** Effusive apple, citrus & stonefruit on traditionally crafted **23** ⑧⑧. Perfectly dry & waxy, good lemon-lime cleanout on lingering farewell. Only 100 cases of this, 80 of Rosé - maybe do bit more next vintage?

Shiraz ★★★ Big in every way, **21** ⑧⑤ packed with dark berries, spice, chocolate from 2 years in 25% new oak, & 14.6% alc. Nicely rounded, though, a balancing savouriness at finish. **Blanc de Noir** ★★★ Pale pink **23** ⑧② from shiraz will quench a summer's thirst with its strawberry freshness, bone-dryness, inviting another spicy sip. **Chardonnay** ★★★ Lemon & lime in a creamy body from gentle oak-staving 12 months, **22** ⑧② light & breezy for anytime. Not tasted: **Chenin Blanc**. — WB

Location: Piketberg ▪ Map/WO: Swartland ▪ Map grid reference: C2 ▪ Est/1stB 2002 ▪ Tasting, sales & cellar tours Tue-Thu 9.30-4 Fri 9.30-9 Sat 9.30-5 Sun 9.30-3; pub hols (seasonal) please call ahead ▪ Tasting fee R60/5 wines ▪ Closed Easter Fri/Sun, Dec 25/26 & Jan 1 ▪ Nieuwedrift Wine Estate Restaurant: lunch Mon-Sun 11-3; dinner Fri/Sat 6-9 ▪ Facilities for children ▪ Tour groups ▪ Conferences ▪ Nieuwedrift Cottage ▪ Owner(s)/viticulturist(s) Johan Mostert ▪ Cellarmaster(s) Johan Mostert (Jan 2002) ▪ 15.1ha/15ha (shiraz, chard, chenin) ▪ 200t total 18t/1,560cs own label 14% red 38% white 25% rosé 23% MCC ▪ PO Box 492 Piketberg 7320 ▪ nieuwedrift@patat.co.za ▪ **T +27 (0)22-913-1966/+27 (0)82-824-8104**

☐ **Nieuwe Haarlem** see Cape Wine Company

☐ **Nine Fields** see Ashton Winery

☐ **900 Series** see Idiom Wines

☐ **1945 Reserve** see Simonsvlei International

☐ **1900** see Spioenkop Wines

☐ **19th Wines** see Ernst Gouws & Co Wines

Nitida Cellars ⓠ ⑾ ◎ ⑧ ⑤

A vineyard planted in spare time on Durbanville's smallest farm has blossomed into a multifaceted wine and lifestyle destination, with a further dimension set to be added in the form of a new boutique hotel. Nature and care for the environment has been a feature from the outset: the brand name honours the magnificent namesake protea species, and fynbos provides the theme for the engaging label designs, including the revamped Golden Orb and Coronata livery. What's inside the packaging is the central concern, and here winemaker Etienne Louw has the single, long-held goal of producing 'wines that people enjoy drinking'.

Artisanal range

★★★★☆ **Calligraphy** ⊘ ⓐ A consumer favourite, glossy 5-way blend in **20** ⑨③, mostly merlot, delivers typical Cape Bordeaux flavours of black plums & currants with savoury, leathery overtones. Spice & cedar from year in old oak. Assured & elegant wine.

★★★★☆ **Wild Child** ⊘ Riot of flavour on excellent **22** ⑨⓪ from sauvignon, from green nettle & grass to pineapple & orange, laced together with smooth acid. 50% in seasoned wood adds texture & palate weight. Superior partner for a posh fish pie. **21** untasted.

★★★★☆ **Golden Orb** ⓠ Unoaked flagship single-vineyard sauvignon blanc. **21** ⑨① beautiful expression of exceptional fruit, year on lees lends fatness & texture in harmony with precise acid.

★★★★☆ **Coronata Integration** ⓐ Outstanding Bordeaux white. **22** ⑨④ reverberates with flavour - apple, pear, greengage - on orange peel acidity. Thoughtful winemaking blends barrelled semillon with creamy tank-vinified, lees-aged sauvignon before final wine spends 4 months harmonising in older oak.

★★★★☆ **The Grande Matriarch Méthode Cap Classique** Soft gold **19** (91) from pinot noir has gentle bubbles highlighting crisp redcurrant fruit, almond brioche & mid-palate earthiness. Enriching 20 months on lees add hay & nuts to lengthy finish. Perfect now.

★★★★ **The Matriarch Méthode Cap Classique** Deft **21** (89) from equal chardonnay & pinot noir delivers crisp yellow fruit with tangy acid & salty yeast notes from year on lees. Dry, lively finish completes satisfying wine.

The Tinkery ★★★☆ Experimental, occasional label. **19** ★★★★☆ (92) sumptuous riesling botrytis dessert; **21** (85) classic pinotage with notes of black cherry, fragrant tobacco & tarry intensity. Firm tannins honed by old oak, good dry finish. Occasional release: **Modjadji Semillon Noble Late Harvest**.

Classical range

★★★★☆ **Cabernet Sauvignon** Forthright **20** ★★★★ (89) has rich & dense blackcurrant fruit with perfume & liquorice accent. Cedar oak adds nuance & some freshness to 15.2% alc, but warmer than **19** (91).

★★★★ **Merlot** ⊘ Classic **21** ★★★★☆ (90) marries cool-climate herbal freshness with fully ripe black plum & mulberry fruit, soft tannins give backbone & length. More harmonious & intense than **20** (89). A lot of wine for the money. Year seasoned small-oak.

★★★★ **Pinot Noir** ⊘ Bright **21** (86), now from Franschhoek grapes, typical red cherry fruit with floral hint & earthy undertone. Lively acid bustles through slightly hollow mid-palate. **20** (87) ex Elgin.

★★★★ **Riesling** Excellent balance of limy acid & mere touch of sugar on **22** (89) complement fresh pear & orange peel fruit, signature lily & petrol high notes. Lovely palate weight, cries out for spicy food.

★★★★ **Sauvignon Blanc** ⊘ Everything you'd want from a sauvignon in **23** (87). Vibrant tropicality, granadilla & guava, melded with green herbal sappiness. Fresh acid & zesty clean finish.

★★★★ **Semillon** ⊘ Horticultural encyclopedia of dandelion, grass & nettle on **22** ★★★★★ (90), tamed & smoothed by time in old oak, also adding richness & cream. Sweet green melon, perky acid & long finish complete benchmark example, more intense than **21** (89).— CM

Location: Durbanville ▪ Map: Durbanville, Philadelphia & Darling ▪ Map grid reference: C7 ▪ WO: Durbanville/ Western Cape ▪ Est/1stB 1995 ▪ Tasting & sales Mon-Fri 9-5 Sat 11-4 Sun/pub hols 11-3 ▪ Fee R80-R120 various options ▪ Closed Good Fri, Dec 25/26 & Jan 1 ▪ Cassia Restaurant T +27 (0)21-976-0640; conference & function venue at Cassia (200 pax) ▪ Tables at Nitida T +27 (0)21-975-9357 ▪ Facilities for children ▪ Pet-friendly ▪ MTB, part of Hillcrest/Majik forest trail (www.tygerbergmtb.co.za) ▪ Conservation area ▪ Wine club ▪ Owner(s) Bernhard Veller ▪ Winemaker(s) Etienne Louw (Aug 2020) ▪ 35ha/16ha (cabs s/f, p verdot, riesling, sauv, sem) ▪ 220t/20,000cs own label 30% red 70% white + 6,000cs for clients ▪ Brands for clients: Woolworths, Checkers ▪ Tygerbergvalley Rd Durbanville 7550 ▪ info@nitida.co.za ▪ www.nitida.co.za ▪ **T +27 (0)21-976-1467**

Noble Hill Wine Estate

(wine glass) (food) (camera) (wheelchair)

'Lighter, lower-extraction, delicate wines' are the aspiration at this hospitable estate on the northern slope of Noble Hill, aka the regal Simonsberg, owned by a family with roots in the US. Son, Harvard economics graduate and latterly winemaker-viticulturist Kristopher keeps abreast of every major winegrowing trend, not only lighter-styled wines but also terroir expression through minimal interference, old-vine vinification, sparing or non-use of oak, and environmental impact reduction, manifest in the recently completed conversion to organic agriculture. Through his co-ferment red, Kristopher is even current with trendy field blends.

★★★★☆ **Cabernet Sauvignon** Lithe, aromatic take on variety, **20** ★★★★ (89) generous cassis fruit with earthy-mineral nuance, fine leathery tannins, note of tealeaf. Small dabs cab franc & petit verdot aid heft & form at modest 12.5% alc. Touch less fine than **18** (92) but should benefit from time in cellar. No **19**.

★★★★☆ **Field Atlas** ⊘ Syrah-led (81%), 4-way Rhône-style blend, co-fermented, 20% wholebunch. **21** (91) has meaty-savoury platform for cherry, plum & elegant floral & scrub scents. 18 months older barrels & large concrete tanks impart minimal oak influence, spotlighting concentrated fruit core. **20** untasted.

★★★★☆ **Estate Reserve** ⊘ (leaf) Supple, lithe Cape Bordeaux, cab & merlot plus dabs 2 others, **21** (94) focuses on balance & fruit purity rather than muscle. Thrilling, racy cassis & cherry fruit, subtle white nut & tobacco scents, oak (mostly seasoned barrels, 18 months), in elegant harmony. 1.5, 3 & 6L also available.

★★★★ **Mourvèdre Rosé** Light & blithe, with distinct salty note, pale coral **22** (86) is dry, crisp & refreshing, avoids strawberry clichés. Delivers appealing anytime enjoyment.

★★★★☆ **Simonskop Chenin Blanc** Rich & spicy, with complex tapestry of floral & dried fruit threads, **22** (92) impressive reflection of 35 year old dryland vines farmed organically. 9 months on lees in older barrels & clay amphoras add polish & creamy texture. Generous & full bodied despite low 11.5% alc.

★★★★ **Sur Lie Chenin Blanc** Ripe, wholesome & sunny, with apricot & pineapple fruit, **22** (88) aged on lees in concrete tanks, small portion on skins in clay amphoras for poised & elegant varietal expression.

★★★★ **Viognier** Now 100% viognier (previous had splash grenache blanc), **22** (86) rich & weighty despite modest 12.5% alc. Wild yeast, leesiness from 80% barrel-matured portion, add spice & texture.

★★★★☆ **Estate Reserve White** Lighter, fresher **22** (90) is lemon & lime accented, with faint floral scent, distinct minerality. Marsanne, grenache blanc & chenin with 2% viognier, mostly fermented/9 months in seasoned oak, tad less forthcoming than last.

★★★★☆ **Blanc de Blancs Brut Nature** Structured & elegant, zero-dosage **20** (94) cap classique from chardonnay has yeasty brioche aromas from 36 months on lees, with baked apple & nutmeg notes. Fine, vigorous bubble adds creamy texture & freshness.

Occasional release: **Cruxes Mataro Nova**. — GdB

Location: Paarl ▪ Map: Franschhoek ▪ Map grid reference: B7 ▪ WO: Simonsberg-Paarl ▪ Est/1stB 2001 ▪ Tasting & sales Mon-Sun 9-5 ▪ Fee R80, waived on R400 purchase ▪ Cellar tours by appt only ▪ Food & wine pairing option ▪ Cosecha Restaurant ▪ Farm-produced extra virgin olive oil ▪ Conservation area ▪ Hitachino Nest Japanese craft beer available at winery ▪ Owner(s) Noble Hill Trust ▪ Winemaker(s) Kristopher Tillery ▪ Viticulturist(s) Kristopher Tillery & Stiaan Heyns ▪ 62ha/40ha (cabs s/f, merlot, mourv, p verdot, shiraz, chard, chenin, grenache blanc, marsanne, viog) ▪ Organic (EOS & NOP standards) from 2023 vintage ▪ PO Box 111 Simondium 7670 ▪ info@noblehill.com ▪ www.noblehill.com ▪ **T +27 (0)21-874-3844**

☐ **Noble Nomad** *see* Rosendal Wines

Noble Savage

With this playful younger sibling to their more serious Bartinney Private Cellar, vintners Rose and Michael Jordaan aim for 'approachable, quality-driven wines at an accessible price point'. Made on the family farm in Banhoek Valley, the wines are available at the Bartinney Wine & Champagne Bar in Stellenbosch town.

★★★★ **Cabernet Sauvignon-Shiraz** Lovely, varietally expressive 60/40 blend, **20** (86) juicy, smooth, balanced, tannins gentle after 18 months in older barrels, finish is long & savoury. Banghoek WO.

Rosé ★★★☆ From mostly cab, **23** (84) ticks the drinkability box with bright, sappy strawberry fruit, zesty dry finish. **Sauvignon Blanc** ★★★☆ Tropical fruit in abundance on vibrant **23** (85), flavourful & harmonious for a pool party. — WB

Location/map: Stellenbosch ▪ Map grid reference: F5 ▪ WO: Western Cape/Banghoek ▪ Est 2006 ▪ 1stB 2008 ▪ Sales Tue-Sat 1-9 at Bartinney Wine & Champagne Bar T +27 (0)76-348-5374, 5 Bird Str, Stellenbosch ▪ Closed Dec 25/26/31 & Jan 1 ▪ Owner(s) Rose & Michael Jordaan ▪ Winemaker(s) Ronell Wiid (2012, consultant) ▪ Farm manager Heinright Prins ▪ 13,000cs own label 50% red 50% white ▪ Postnet Suite 231 Private Bag X5061 Stellenbosch 7599 ▪ info@bartinney.co.za ▪ www.noblesavage.co.za ▪ **T +27 (0)21-885-1013**

☐ **No House Wine** *see* Stellar Winery
☐ **Noisy Grape** *see* Camberley Wines

Nomad Wines

Based in Germany, owner and winemaker Kosie van der Merwe remotely controls his namesake father to do the crafting in an old apple store of a pair of wines 'celebrating Elgin Valley'. The Kosies have changed grape growers to ones who work regeneratively, and slightly raised production, to still tiny 1,700 cases. For Nomad Germany, less than half that quantity of Mosel old-vine riesling is bottled under the names Rhizo and Phyllo.

★★★★ **Franc Cabernet Franc** Early picking & some bunch pressing shows in even more leafy freshness & fynbos scrub nuance in **22** (86). Light (12.6% alc), leaner than **21** (88), understated red fruit & perfume. Still a tad unknit, begs time, like Syrah.

★★★★ **Sarel Syrah** Yet more restrained in **22** ★★★☆ (85) than **21** (89), piquant red fruit bound up in herbaceous tannins & brisk acid from greater wholebunch portion (80% vs 50). Similar subtle cedar spicing after 9 months in old oak. Tightly coiled, needs time & hearty fare. — MW

Location/map/WO: Elgin ▪ Map grid reference: C2 ▪ Est/1stB 2019 ▪ Tasting, sales & cellar tours by appt ▪ Owner(s) Kosie van der Merwe ▪ Winemaker(s) Kosie van der Merwe (Oct 2019) & Kola van der Merwe (2022) ▪ 12t/1,700cs own label 100% red ▪ Glen Fruin Farm, Glen Fruin Rd off N2, Elgin 7180 ▪ kosie@ nomadwines.co ▪ www.nomadwines.co ▪ **T +27 (0)76-037-9507**

Nomoya Wines

Michela Sfiligoi and Attilio Dalpiaz, Italian co-founders of this young Paarl boutique winery, make their wines 'clean, fresh and elegant, as they can be in Italy, but with a touch of South African sun in their soul'. Unsurprisingly, varieties from the old country feature in the line-up, including vermentino, first brought into the Cape by the enterprising pair while at nearish-by Ayama. Tasting is at The Wine Hive in the town centre.

★★★★ **Chenin Blanc Old Vine 1982** ⓥ Characterful barrel-fermented **21** ⑧⑧ from 41 year old vines. Ripe yellow peach, honeyed concentration threaded by balanced acid; dry, with good length.

★★★★ **Grenache Blanc** Unoaked **22** ★★★★ ⑧⑤'s subtle citrus blossom develops a pithier grapefruit nuance, leavened by variety's waxiness. Less expressive than **21** ⑧⑦, still balanced in easier-drinking style.

★★★★ **Pinot Blanc** ⓥ Varietal rarity in the Cape, **22** ⑧⑦ from Voor Paardeberg promises much with time. High-toned lemony aromas, ripe, juicy & bright flavours. Short rest should see better integration.

★★★★☆ **Vermentino** ⓥ. From Paarl fruit, **21** ⑨⓪ offers intriguing floral-salty aromatics; flavours ripely & silkily mouthfilling, freshened by 50% unoaked portion. Herby tang ensures balanced conclusion.

Cinsault ⒩ⒺⓌ ★★★★ Sweet red-berry jam fruit, juicy succulence & freshness in **22** ⑧⑧④. Poised & cheerful sipper, also good chilled, with a picnic or light meal. **Grenache Noir** ★★★ Aromatic spice & red fruit notes give way to chalky tannins in **22** ⑧①, unoaked (as Cinsaut). Quite piquant, with drier farewell than last, for meal partnering. Not tasted: **Barbera, Carignan, Nebbiolo, Pinotage Old Vine 1973, Sangiovese, Shiraz, Chenin Blanc.** — MW

Location/map: Paarl ▪ Map grid reference: E5 ▪ WO: Swartland/Voor Paardeberg/Paarl ▪ Est/1stB 2021 ▪ Tasting Wed-Sat 11-7; pub hols 11-6; closed Sun-Tue ▪ Fee R200/5 wines, R360/10 wines ▪ Closed Easter Sun, Dec 25/26 & Jan 1 ▪ Italian cold meats, cheese, breads, pizza & pasta ▪ Farm produce ▪ Wine club ▪ Owner(s) Nomoya World (Pty) Ltd - 3 shareholders ▪ Winemaker(s) Sheree Nothnagel (Nov 2021, consultant), with Michela Sfiligoi (Aug 2021) ▪ Viticulturist(s) Attilio Dalpiaz & Talia Engelbrecht (Aug 2021) ▪ WIETA ▪ 161 Main Rd Paarl 7646 ▪ info@nomoyaworld.com ▪ www.nomoyaworld.com ▪ **T +27 (0)72-357-8417**

Normandie Est. 1693

17th-century Franschhoek farm Normandie is the birthplace of this mostly exported portfolio of high-end wines in appropriately impressive and classic packaging, crafted for new owners Virginie and Juergen Geissinger by wine and vine men Johan Viljoen and Bennie Booysen. Sustaining top quality being paramount, the mature vines on the estate are being scrutinised and uneconomic parcels replaced.

★★★★ **Anno 1693** Classic Cape Bordeaux, cab fleshed out with 10% merlot in **18** ⑧⑧. Year in oak, 10% new, adds vanilla & spice to ripe cherries & berries. Gentle evolution, with notes of cigarbox & Xmas cake.

★★★★☆ **Eisen & Viljoen** ⓐ For this sibling Bordeaux blend, 15% inky petit verdot joins near-equal cab & merlot. Remarkable freshness for a **16** ⑨②, some savoury nuances but still quite primary cassis & cherry fruit. Firm tannin structure well tailored after 22 months in barriques, 50% new.

★★★★ **Karen** Lovely seashell hue on rosé from merlot. Nicely dry, with toffee apple & melon scents & flavours in **19** ⑧⑦. Name given as 'karen.' on minimalist label. — ML

Location/WO: Franschhoek ▪ Est 2008 ▪ 1stB 2009 ▪ Closed to public ▪ Owner(s) Virginie & Juergen Geissinger ▪ Cellarmaster(s)/winemaker(s) Johan Viljoen (Feb 2008) ▪ Viticulturist(s) Johan Viljoen & Bennie Booysen (both Feb 2008) ▪ 47ha/17ha (cab, merlot, p verdot) ▪ ±130t/12,000cs own label 90% red 10% rosé ▪ WIETA ▪ PO Box 398 Pniel 7681 ▪ info@normandie1693.com ▪ www.normandie1693.com ▪ **T +27 (0)21-874-1039**

☐ **Nova Zonnestraal** *see* Constantia Royale
☐ **Ntsiki Biyela Wines** *see* Aslina Wines

Nuiba Wines

Happy childhood memories of Nuiba family ranch in Namibia and its cattle drinking posts inspired boutique vigneronne Suzanne Coetzee in creating her brand. She sources from parcels around Stellenbosch and old dryland vines in Piekenierskloof, and works in Clos Malverne's cellar, which she ran for some time, taking care to 'retain the grape characters and use oak supportively'. Tastings are at The Woodmill in Stellenbosch.

★★★★ **Second Post** From shiraz, harmonious **21** (88) dark berry fruit & leathery note in a good frame after 22 months in barrel, none new (as Third). Appealing, will remain so for a good few years. **20** untasted.

★★★★☆ **Third Post** (⊛) Elegant & fragrant **19** ★★★★★ (95) Cape Blend, pinotage (56%), grenache noir & cab, unveiling glossy black & blue berries, graphite & an earthy core. Well rounded, integrated & complex, the long savoury finish part of good augury for extended cellaring - also true of **18** (94).

★★★★ **Fourth Post** Onion skin **22** (87) rosé delights with fragrant & fruity dry mouthful with touch of earth on a waxy texture. Creative combo barrel-fermented semillon & 2% malbec, balanced & moreish.

★★★★ **First Post** Powerful Bordeaux white, 75% sauvignon & barrique-fermented semillon. Just-dry **22** (88) oozes stonefruit, lemon, crème brûlée in rich coat of vanilla. Delicious now, well-balanced & -structured for a long life. WO Stellenbosch, as Fourth.— WB

Location/map: Stellenbosch ▪ Map grid reference: D5 ▪ WO: Piekenierskloof/Stellenbosch ▪ Est/1stB 2016 ▪ Tasting room & shop: Mon-Fri 9-5; pub hols (seasonal) please call ahead; private tastings by arrangement only ▪ Owner(s) Suzanne Coetzee ▪ Winemaker(s) Suzanne Coetzee (Jan 2016) ▪ 350cs own label 70% red 15% white 15% rosé ▪ Woodmill Centre, Stellenbosch 7600 ▪ suzanne@nuibabrands.co.za ▪ www. nuibabrands.co.za ▪ **T +27 (0)21-883-3617**

☐ **Nuwehoop** *see* Daschbosch

Nuy Wine Cellar

Longevity is in the DNA of this grower-owned winery in Nuy Valley near Worcester, evident in the business itself, which enters its 7th decade this year, and its cellarmasters - Christo Pienaar, the incumbent, is leaving after 20 years; his predecessor, Wilhelm Linde, directed winemaking for 32 years, starting shortly after the founding. Christo's last vintage had its own challenges, delivering a smaller crop but of good quality, thanks to the team's focus on getting the best from their vineyards, which now include durif and petit verdot.

Legacy range
★★★★ **Argilla** (⑨) Majority pinotage (as for last-made **15** (86)), with shiraz & cab. **20** (86) complex, flavourful, well balanced with firm but accommodating tannins, mostly new oak & 14.8% alc not obtrusive.

★★★★☆ **Calcareo** (⑨) Understated notes of peach & thatch on **21** ★★★★ (87) chenin. Rich silky texture & ripe flavours well supported by oak, 50% new, dryness & firm acid giving a generous succulence. Last tasted was **18** (90).

★★★★☆ **Barbieri Idro** (⑨) More than 5 years in barrel give **15** (93) fortified muscadel a unique, rather elegant fascination - the usual muscat grapiness combining with the complexity of developed toffee & savoury notes, recalling tawny port. 16.5% alc & 220 g/L sugar finely balanced with freshness.

Celine Méthode Cap Classique (⑨) ★★★☆ Fresh, ripe apple aromas & plentiful flavour on latest **NV** (85) sparkling from chardonnay & pinot noir. Juicy, tasty & fairly dry.

Mastery range
Pinotage (⑨) ★★★☆ Big, fruit-forward **19** (84) complements its sweet plummy, berry flavour & aroma with hint of old-fashioned acetone. **Shiraz** (⑨) ★★★☆ Bold, rich & smooth **21** (84) with plenty of sweet fruit pastille berry flavour to match. Solidly structured, oak well integrated. **Piekfyn Rosé** (NEW) ★★★ Fragrant strawberry aromas & flavours on juicy **22** (80) from shiraz. Firm & dry, its build allows for many food options. Not tasted: **Cabernet Sauvignon**, **Chardonnay**, **Sauvignon Blanc**.

Inspiration range
★★★★ **Red Muscadel** Fresher & more refined of the fortified pair. The muscat grapiness of **22** (89) rather than sweetness remains a delightful memory.

★★★★ **White Muscadel** (⊘) Full-sweet yet uncloying fortified thanks to balanced acidity. **22** (87) enjoys fresh grapey, tealeaf aromas & flavours, clean spirit smoothly integrated for current enjoyment & cellaring many years. 17% alc, 16% for Red.

Cabernet Sauvignon ★★☆ Pleasant ripe berry juiciness; a few grams of sugar & moderate acid lessen effect of dry tannins in **22** (79). **Merlot** ★★ Tomato, leaf & herbal notes on **22** (75) softened by grain sugar & new-oak staving, effect of big 14.6% alc less so. **Koffiepit Pinotage** ★★☆ Strong roast coffee bean, some red-fruit juiciness & tannin trim in new bottling of equally approachable **22** (79). **Shiraz ★★★** Red berries rather than spice & hint oak vanilla brighten big 15% alc in **21** (80). Few grams sugar make for easy drinking. **Chenin Blanc ★★☆** Ripe guava & peachy flavours on quaffable, dry **23** (79). **Colombar Semi-Sweet ★★☆** Gentle lime & fynbos notes on fresh, sprightly **23** (77). Sun-filled fruity sweetness for happy sipping. **Sauvignon Blanc ★★** Green peas & zesty limes on **23** (75), assertive acid emphasised by dry finish. **Chant de Nuit ★★** Long-time favourite **NV** (75) blend. Latest has prominent ripe pineapple, musk & grapey features. Fullish, with slight bitterness. **Muscat Sparkling Wine** (2) **★★** Coppery pink **22** (75) less charmingly grapey than sometimes; frothy & sweetly fruity. **Sauvignon Blanc Sparkling Wine ★★☆** Brisk bubble & limy freshness on **23** (79), off-dry but flavoursome rather than sweet.

Brandy range
★★★★ Copper Potstilled (2) Mostly 3- & 5-year components on this brandy (87) but also dab 20 year old for complexity. Super-smooth, lightish, but sufficient pale fire for moreish satisfaction.— AL, TJ

Location/map: Worcester ▪ Map grid reference: C4 ▪ WO: Nuy ▪ Est 1963 ▪ Tasting & sales Mon-Fri 9-5 Sat/ Sun 9-4; pub hols (seasonal) please call ahead ▪ Closed Good Fri & Dec 25 ▪ Bistro & deli ▪ MTB ▪ Potstill brandy & craft gin also available for tasting/sale at Nuy on the Hill wine centre, fee R15/tasting ▪ Owner(s) 19 members ▪ CEO Daniel Fourie ▪ Cellarmaster(s) Christo Basson (Oct 2023) ▪ Winemaker(s) Paul Burger (Nov 2016) ▪ Viticulturist(s) Callie Coetzee (Vinpro) ▪ 770ha (cab, merlot, muscadel, ptage, shiraz, chard, chenin, cbard, nouvelle, sauv) ▪ 18,200t/20,000cs own label ▪ PO Box 5225 Worcester 6849 ▪ wines@nuywinery.co.za ▪ www.nuywinery.co.za ▪ **T +27 (0)23-347-0272**

☐ **Oak Lane** *see* Beau Joubert Wines

Oak Valley Estate   (2) (11) (10) (5)
Wine forms part of an extensive, diverse and dynamic agribusiness on the Oak Valley estate in Elgin, under Rawbone-Viljoen family ownership for more than 125 years. Their site on the slope of Groenlandberg is characterised by cool growing conditions and shale soils, and the 2.4 ha of pinot noir clone 115 being established there by viticulturist-winemaker Jacques du Plessis raises pinot to 27% of the 32-ha total plantings; with chardonnay at 25%, both now have a bigger footprint than sauvignon, in line with longer-term strategy. Another large foudre has been added to the cellar for the chardonnay which, like its Burgundy sibling, shows a natural delicacy and freshness that benefits from lighter oaking. Follow-up vintages of the clonal showcase project Tabula Rasa are being held back for further ageing. Recently awarded Melting Pot tapas restaurant is one of several attractions on the estate, recognised by WWF-SA for its conservation efforts.

Groenlandberg range
★★★★☆ Pinot Noir (✓) (🐝) Whole berries from multiple clones in high (±430 m) south-facing blocks have 5-day cold soak ahead of gentle ferment without stalks, 10 months mostly 2nd-fill oak for supple tannins & succulent red fruit. **22** (94) floral spice bouquet ahead of layered, well-weighted delight on the palate. Sensual & long lingering.

★★★★★ Chardonnay (🐝) Bunch pressed & naturally barrel-fermented to preserve fresh grape acid; only 29% new oak, no malo or bâtonnage. Fabulous **22** (95) has concentrated citrus & steely flint vitality, subtle oatmeal, hazelnut & orange peel nuances after 10 months in 300L barrels.

Discovery range
★★★★☆ Sounds of Silence Pinot Noir (✓) Deceptively pale **22** (91) wholeberry fermented after 5-day cold sold to gently extract flavour & structure, 9 months in 87% seasoned oak. Textbook cherry & red berry fruit, hint of mushroom adding savoury/umami intrigue. WO Cape South Coast.

★★★★☆ Beneath The Clouds Chardonnay (✓) Grapes from Elgin & Overberg for **22** (92), 100% oaked (previous had 25% tank component) but just 17% new & malo discouraged to preserve freshness; lemon & lime underpin fleshy pear, oatmeal richness balanced by flint.

★★★★☆ Stone & Steel Riesling (✓) Aptly named, given lipsmacking tension between acid & sugar (7.5 & 8.1 g/L) on **23** (92), & pure rapier-like green-apple & lime flavours, dry mineral finish. Gorgeous tangerine blossom aroma. Super aperitif & table companion.

★★★★☆ Fountain of Youth Sauvignon Blanc (✓) (🐝) Thrilling **23** (94) tingles with oystershell freshness & vibrancy, redolent with scrubby fynbos & grapefruit, ends with lingering pinch of white pepper. Three months on lees add breadth, texture.— DS

Location/map: Elgin ▪ Map grid reference: B1 ▪ WO: Elgin/Cape South Coast ▪ Est 1898 ▪ 1stB 2003 ▪ Tasting & sales Mon-Fri 9-5 Sat/Sun/pub hols 10-4 ▪ Closed Easter Mon, Dec 25/26 & Jan 1 ▪ The Pool Room tasting facility & The Melting Pot restaurant ▪ Picnics ▪ MTB trails ▪ Conservation area ▪ Wine club ▪ Owner(s) AG Rawbone-Viljoen Trust ▪ Winemaker(s) Jacques du Plessis (Oct 2018) ▪ Viticulturist(s) Jacques du Plessis (Oct 2018), assisted by Kevin Watt ▪ 32ha (pinot, chard, riesling, sauv) ▪ ±249t/±33,000cs own label 25% red 75% white ▪ GlobalGAP, IPW, SIZA, WIETA, WWF-SA Conservation Champion ▪ PO Box 30 Elgin 7180 ▪ wines@oak-valley.co.za ▪ www.oakvalley.co.za ▪ T +27 (0)21-859-4110

☐ **Obscura** see Klein Amoskuil

O'Connell's

Paarl-based negociant Lukas O'Connell ships a substantial 300,000 cases under various labels to local and overseas markets, the bottlings all driven by the styles his customers prefer to drink, and made to be extremely smooth and effortlessly drinkable, 'contrary to the usual "chalky" expectations'.

Shirro range (NEW)
Shiraz ✓ ★★★★ Generous, rounded **22** (84) abounds with blackberry, dark plum & meat spice, ends with a pleasant touch of dried herbs. Unoaked, as all.

O'Connell's Private Selection
. . . .
Chenin Blanc ☺ ★★★ 'Sunshine wine', the vintner aptly says, **22** (81) is all ripe pineapple & nectarine, bright & generous, joined by citrus in the mouthwatering finish.
. . . .
Cabernet Sauvignon ★★★ Effortless **22** (82), blackcurrants & plums, waft of mocha at the end. **Merlot** ★★★ Lively, amiable **22** (81) has had any edges smoothed, so the juicy red plum & spice cake flavours drink easily. **Shiraz** (NEW) ★★★ Glassful of dark berries, cherries & warm spice, **22** (82) great with a burger or boerewors roll. **Sauvignon Blanc** ★★★ Uncomplicated, fresh & grassy **22** (81) shows green plum & gooseberry extras on a trim body (12% alc).

Rara Sunt Cara Chairman's Reserve range
Merlot-Pinotage ✓ ★★★ Red plum fruit sprinkled with spice on soft & easy **NV** (78). Name change from 'Vin Rouge Sec/Blanc' for these. **Chenin Blanc-Colombard** ✓ ★★★ Compatible **NV** (78) blend slips down easily thanks to fleshy orchard fruit & a lively, well-judged acidity.

Sparkling Brotherhood Collection
Not tasted: **Geoffrey O'Connell Vin Doux Red, Lukas O'Connell Vin Doux White**. — WB

Location: Paarl ▪ WO: Western Cape ▪ Est 1995 ▪ 1stB 2016 ▪ Closed to public ▪ Owner(s) Lukas O'Connell ▪ 311,720cs own label 54% red 46% white + 94,400cs for clients ▪ PO Box 7206 Noorder-Paarl Paarl 7623 ▪ lukasoconnell34@gmail.com ▪ www.ibnnegociants.co.za ▪ T +27 (0)82-499-4995

☐ **Ode To Nature** see Neethlingshof Estate
☐ **Oesland** see Hofstraat Kelder

Off The Record Wines Ⓠ ⓖ

The hobby project of full-time wine-making siblings Mark and Bobby Wallace has grown into a proper brand, with unique vineyards as its theme. Chenin, the original wine, is from one of only three parcels of the variety in the home terroir of Elgin; the syrah from winter-snow-blanketed vines in Ceres. Bobby is fully responsible for the venture, as his older brother is now based in Australia. (Aussie counterparts of the pair of SA wines have been mooted.) Tastings are in Elgin at Paul Wallace Wines, owned by parents Paul and Nicky.

★★★★☆ **Syrah** Masterly combination of Ceres Plateau dark berries & oak's cigarbox spicing, lush & supple **22** (90) is very easy to like but don't underestimate it, can age. Boldly styled, has presence.

★★★★☆ **Chenin Blanc** ⓐ Elgin cool-climate **22** (93) created from half each skin contact grapes & whole bunch for character & freshness. Natural ferment 10 months in barrel. Thatch & bruised apple styling, ending mineral & long. Sophisticated & pure.— CR

Location/map: Elgin ▪ Map grid reference: C3 ▪ WO: Ceres Plateau/Elgin ▪ Est/1stB 2018 ▪ Tasting Mon-Fri/ Sun by appt Sat 10.30-5 ▪ Sales Mon-Fri 9-5 Sat 10.30-4.30 ▪ Closed Easter Sun, Dec 25 & Jan 1 ▪ Self-catering guest cottages ▪ Owner(s)/winemaker(s) Bobby Wallace ▪ ±1,100cs own label 40% red 60% white ▪ PO Box 141 Elgin 7180 ▪ bobby@offtherecord.co.za ▪ www.offtherecord.co.za ▪ **T +27 (0)76-876-9970**

☐ **Old Brown** *see* Sedgwick's Old Brown

Oldenburg Vineyards

Switzerland-based, yet 'intricately involved' owners Adrian and Vanessa Vanderspuy's vision of producing 'exceptional wines from an extraordinary place, sustainably and with a light touch', latterly has involved the third planting of the site in 60 years. In a multi-year project, Generation 3, viticulturist Christo Crous has worked closely with winemaker Nic van Aarde to optimise site-to-variety matching, trellising methods and more. The young vineyards are beginning to produce, and the results, according to brand manager Stefan Reinmuth, are worth investigating, notably at the vine-circled, glass-fronted visitor venue, where a team of SASA-graded sommeliers under George Young offer pre-booked tastings. For private clients and Rondekop Wine Club members, certified sommelier Stefan leads bespoke and curated sampling experiences.

Rondekop range

★★★★☆ **Per Se** ⓐ Splash merlot added to single-site cab lends some flesh & bounce to classic cedar & blackcurrant. For **21** ⑨③, new oak trimmed to 35% from 55%, allowing juicy fruit-coated tannins & black cherry flavour to shine. Fine structure from 18 months in barrique. Larger bottle formats for this range.

★★★★☆ **Stone Axe** ⓐ Syrah from select parcels gets 1st dash grenache noir in **21** ★★★★★ ⑨⑤, adding floral perfume & damsons. Foot-treading of the whole berries & 18% whole bunches, & ageing in only older, large foudre, 18 months, to enhance fruit purity. Goes up a notch on **20** ⑨③ with perfectly dry finish & mineral backbone.

★★★★☆ **Rhodium** ⓐ Characteristic tealeaf entry on **21** ⑨③ 3-way Bordeaux blend. Barrel-selected cab franc, merlot & cab (55/35/10) follow with savoury delicacy & finesse. Succulent red fruits meld with 38% new oak, 18 months, for satin texture & cranberry-toned finish.

Oldenburg range

★★★★☆ **Cabernet Sauvignon** ⓐ Perfectly ripe red fruit & fynbos unfurl on **21** ⑨④'s lithe structure of tannin & oak, duration still 18 months but portion new reduced to 40%, allowing lush, delicately spiced fruit to shine. A lifting freshness completes a wine of contained power that will go the distance.

★★★★☆ **Cabernet Franc** ⓐ Estate making a name for itself with this variety, & **21** ⑨③ doesn't disappoint. Careful harvesting (lug boxes, hand sorting) followed by 18 months in barrel, 17% new, rounds any angles, polishes curves & adds cardamom spice to the berries, all supported with finest tannin.

★★★★☆ **Grenache Noir** Single plot of bushvines reflects its 410m elevation in pure, bright line of acid. Florals, spice & crunchy red berries add to **21** ⑨①'s vivid profile, gracefully aided by 16 months in older barrels. Rung up on already improved **20** ⑨⓪.

★★★★☆ **Merlot** ⓐ Careful sorting & wholeberry ferment of estate grapes in **21** ⑨⓪ sees generous plums & cherries matched with a firm acid structure, cushioned by soft tannins from 18 months of barrel ageing, 33% new portion adding vanilla & cocoa.

★★★★☆ **Syrah** ⓐ Pinpoint precision on **21** ⑨① takes it up a rung. Vinified wholebunch with wild yeast from single parcel to showcase striking, pepper-spiced red berries & cherries. Delicate aromatics preserved by eschewing new oak for 16-month maturation.

★★★★★ **Chardonnay** ⓐ Simply stunning **22** ⑨⑤ is a Cape classic, full of sunshine yet mountain-crisp & fresh. Supreme balance further achieved by considered winemaking, combo of bâtonnage & barrel roll-ing creates a lacy texture, adding creamy lemons to vanilla, toast & spice from 11 months in oak, 29% new.

★★★★☆ **Chenin Blanc** ⓐ Bunch pressed & wild fermented in foudre, hailing from single block, aged between 40 & 50 years. During 11-month maturation, **22** ⑨③ gets the barrel-rolling treatment (as White), imbuing a savoury nuttiness. Yellow stonefruit on a backbone of lime & gentle acid.

CL range

★★★★ **Red** ⓥ Easy, fruit-filled **21** ⑧⑥ delivers raspberry, hint cassis & chocolate. Generous & juicy, well-judged 16 months oak, 26% new for spice & slippery tannins. 54% merlot with cab, dab cab franc.

★★★★ **White** Reverts to majority chardonnay (78%), rest chenin, in **22** ⑧⑦. Brisk acid tempered with lees, adding creamy texture to lemon & apple fruit. 11 months in oak, 78% new, & concrete 'egg' further enhance mouthfeel. Stellenbosch WO, as Cab Franc, Chardonnay & Chenin.— ML

Location/map: Stellenbosch ▪ Map grid reference: H5 ▪ WO: Banghoek/Stellenbosch ▪ Est 1960s ▪ 1stB 2007 ▪ Tasting & sales Mon-Sat & pub hols 10-5 Sun closed ▪ Reservations essential ▪ Closed Dec 25 & Jan 1 ▪ Luxury accommodation in The Homestead (exclusive use, sleeps up to 12 in 6 bedrooms) ▪ Wine club ▪ Owner(s) Adrian & Vanessa Vanderspuy ▪ MD Nic van Aarde ▪ Winemaker(s) Nic van Aarde (Nov 2018) ▪ Viticulturist(s) Christo Crous (May 2021), with Etienne Terblanche (consultant) ▪ 55ha/26ha (cabs s/f, grenache, merlot, shiraz, chard, chenin) ▪ 160t/17,000cs own label 51% red 49% white ▪ PO Box 2246 Dennesig 7601 ▪ thetastingroom@oldenburgvineyards.com ▪ www.oldenburgvineyards.com ▪ **T +27 (0)21-885-1618 (winery/tasting room/office), +27 (0)87-057-4515 (homestead reservations)**

☐ **Old Harbour** *see* Whalehaven Wines
☐ **Old Man's Blend** *see* Groote Post Vineyards

Old Road Wine Company

Old Road is company-owned but boutique-minded, winemaker Ryan Puttick and viticulturist Heinie Nel keen to emphasise the effort invested in finding special small pockets, some heritage-certified, increasingly in areas beyond the label's original locus. They work with older oak, whole bunches and wild ferments, among others, to bring out the best of each parcel. Tastings are at the brand home on Franschhoek's old (main) road, beside the cellar inaugurated at the end of WW2, an heirloom in its own right.

Single Vineyard range
★★★★☆ **Pepper Wind Syrah** Maintains quality & styling in **22** ⑨①through overt varietal black pepper perfume & ripe red plum, meaty & leathery aromas, unusual but attractive pine needle finish. Glossy, polished tannins after 10 months in 600L barrel, 15% new. No **21**.
★★★★☆ **Grand-Mère Semillon** 🅐 🅦 From vines planted when grandma was a toddler, **21** ★★★★★ ⑨⑤ pumps up the rating again; like **20** ⑨④, it's packed with waxy, lemon-honey varietal character, just more sumptuous, mellowed by 8 months in 500L barrel, 15% new, yet ringing with freshness.
Not tasted: **Stone Trail Chenin Blanc**.

The Elite range
★★★★ **12 Mile Syrah** Swartland grapes for this sibling syrah, **22** ★★★★☆ ⑨⓪ saw no new oak yet mirrors Pepper Wind's striking, well-expressed varietal character, black pepper, dark fruit & supple leathery tannins. Longer-lived than **21** ⑧⑧.
★★★★☆ **Anemos Chenin Blanc** Back after skipping a vintage with a Swartland focus in **22** ⑨①, after widely sourced **20** ⑨⓪. As lovely, with similar oatmeal texture & soft marzipan finish. 10 months in 20% new oak reflect ever more serious intent of recent releases.

The Quirky Ones range
Not tasted: **Pardonnez-Moi Cinsaut**, **Elgin Pinot Noir**, **The Butcher & Cleaver Cape Blend**, **Spotted Hound Red Blend**, **Juliette Sauvignon Blanc**. — DS

Location/map: Franschhoek ▪ Map grid reference: C2 ▪ WO: Franschhoek/Swartland ▪ 1stB 2015 ▪ Tasting Mon-Sat 11-10 Sun 11-9; pub hols (seasonal) please call ahead ▪ Sales Tue-Sat 11-5 ▪ Closed Easter Sun & Dec 25 ▪ Restaurant open for lunch & dinner ▪ Tour groups ▪ Gift shop ▪ Farm produce ▪ Online shop ▪ Owner(s) Artisanal Brands ▪ Winemaker(s) Ryan Puttick (Sep 2017) ▪ Viticulturist(s) Heinie Nel (Jul 2018) ▪ 7ha/14ha (shiraz, chenin, sem) ▪ 40% red 60% white ▪ info@orwc.co.za ▪ www.oldroadwinecompany.com ▪ **T +27 (0)21-271-0379**

☐ **Old Vine Series** *see* Sadie Family Wines
☐ **Old Ways** *see* Cederberg Private Cellar

Olifantsberg Family Vineyards

On the rocky slopes of the Olifantsberg that gives its name to these wines, the Leeuweriks' windy vineyards (in shale, schist and sandstone soils with underlying clay) look out over the wide Breedekloof Valley. Elizma Visser nurtures the vines and vinifies their fruit, with husband Ferdi, carefully, intricately and 'very gently', using natural ferments and a variety of oak and concrete vessels. They ask of their wine that it 'evoke a mental and sensory picture that will do this special place justice'. The wines are also elegant, fresh and characterful (and excellent value), many released with a few beneficial years on them. Care extends to the environment too, with a solar-powered winery and state-of-the-art waste water treatment.

Soul Of The Mountain range

★★★★☆ **The Bull** ⓐ Good to have these released with some development. **19** ⑨④, 38% syrah plus grenache noir, mourvèdre & carignan, subtly fragrant, with complex aromas & flavours - mostly red fruit, but darker, savoury depths. Fresh & intense, with good tannic structure. From 15 mountain sites, blend compiled after separate year in 10% new oak. 14% alc. Ready, but a keeper.

★★★★☆ **The Matriarch** ⓐ Pickings at different ripeness of roussanne (67%), grenache blanc & chenin in **20** ⑨④. Matured separately on lees 9 months in oak (just 8% new, but fairly obvious still), then blended. Less fruit-rich than the varietal wines but gains in developed interest, texture, depth & complexity. 13.5% alc.

Olifantsberg Varietal range

★★★★☆ **Grenache Noir** ⓐ Complex harvesting & vinification, including some wholebunch in the small-batch ferments. 10 months older oak. Result is perfumed, pure-fruited **22** ⑨③, with elegant but substantial seriousness, succulence, subtler tannins than previously. Deliciously rewarding now, should develop.

★★★★☆ **Pinotage** ⓔ Serious & structured **20** ⑨⓪ marginally improves on **19** ★★★★ ⑧⑨. Still affable, with raspberry succulence tempered by spice & concentration from wholeberry ferment. Well-knit oak, 10 months, all old.

★★★★☆ **Syrah** ⊘ ⓐ Quite ripely powerful & intense at 14% alc, characterful **19** ⑨③ goes from fragrantly complex aroma to succulently savoury, firmly structured & incisive palate & lingering finish. Still fairly youthful. From an array of clones & sites; different barrel formats 14 months, 8% new.

★★★★☆ **Lark Chenin Blanc** From a single block on the home-farm.

★★★★☆ 2022 has a serene loveliness, less obviously fruity than Old Vine (and more harmoniously balanced), but rich & interesting, with core of sweet peachiness. 10 months in oak, majority in 2,000L foudre, 7% new.

★★★★ **Old Vine Chenin Blanc** ⊘ ⓦ From 1982 bushvines in Rawsonville town. 74% of **22** ★★★★☆ ⑨⓪ on lees in foudre & barrel 8 months, adding to richness of ripe fruit. Fresh & lively, with forceful lemony sharpness & more powerful flavour & affect than in **21** ⑧⑧.

★★★★☆ **Grenache Blanc** ⓐ Charmingly scented **22** ⑨③, pure-fruited & delicately forceful. 14% alc in balance. Most of 6 pickings fermented in foudre & barrel, final one in concrete. Complex, intricate winemaking, including natural ferment, pays off here & in all these elegant wines.

★★★★☆ **Roussanne** Vibrant, pear-fruit succulence on mostly oaked (all older) **22** ⑨②. Fresh, lively but integrated acidity. Perhaps less intensity than previous, but enough fruit for a lingering finish. Not overt fruitiness, as in all these, primary flavours part of the characterful, expressive whole.

Discontinued: **Carignan**, **Grenache Noir Rosé**. — TJ

Location: Worcester ▪ Map/WO: Breedekloof ▪ Map grid reference: C4 ▪ Est 2003 ▪ 1stB 2005 ▪ Tasting & sales by appt only ▪ Owner(s) Paul J Leeuwerik ▪ Winemaker(s) Elizma Visser (Jun 2015) & Ferdi Visser (Jul 2020) ▪ Viticulturist(s) Elizma Visser (Jun 2015) ▪ 95ha/14ha (carignan, grenache n/b, mourv, ptage, shiraz, chenin, rouss) ▪ 140t/±10,000cs own label 60% red 40% white ▪ PO Box 942 Worcester 6849 ▪ winemaker@olifantsberg.com ▪ www.olifantsberg.com ▪ **T +27 (0)71-301-9440/+27 (0)83-977-9201**

Olivedale Private Vineyards ⓠ

After 'a lot of challenges these past 3 years', says winemaker Jolene le Roux, things are looking positive at this Swellendam farm. Olivedale (named for the local rural community and ultimately the wild olive tree) is moving into a new phase, she adds. It will become an estate winery, 'everything from growing to bottling, respecting each process, all under one roof'. She and part-owner Carl van Wyk in the vineyard will continue to honour Olivedale's mantra 'Respect for nature', allowing the wines 'to claim their own uniqueness'.

Mystery of Nature range

★★★★ **Roobernet** ⓥ Rare bottling of this cab-alicante bouschet cross. **20** ⑧⑥ has enticingly fresh, bright aromas & deep sweet fruit fleshing out a firm, dry structure. Modest oaking & 13% alc.

★★★★ **Wild Melody** ⓥ Charming name for blend of viognier, roussanne, semillon, verdelho &, for **20** ⑧⑨, chardonnay. Fermented under pressure with skins for 40 days, but rather gorgeous & scarcely funky.

Respect for Nature range

★★★★ **Shiraz** ⓥ Savoury fruit, alluding to the effective 20% new oak, alongside good sweet flavours & dry finish, the whole well balanced, **19** ⑧⑥ impressing more than **18** ★★★★ ⑧⑤.

★★★★ **Touriga Nacional** ⓥ Attractively forward berry fruitiness & tobacco undertones from this (mostly) port variety in **20** ⑧⑥. Full of lipsmacking ripe flavour. Should develop, but approachable early, like **19** ★★★★ ⑧⑤.

★★★★ **Sauvignon Blanc** Previewed **23** ⑧⑥ promises plenty of stonefruit & tropical aroma & flavour (but nothing too overt), succulence & good finish. Old oak, 6 months on lees, add texture & complexity, as in last **21** ⑧⑥.

Malbec ⓥ ★★★★ Full, dark-berried **19** ⑧⑤ in fairly serious style but not forbidding at all, though dry tannins control the fruit. 14% alc like most of these reds. **Tempranillo** ⓥ ★★★★ A little spicy oak (25% new, 18 months) shows with the cherries on **19** ⑧④. Nicely dry grip of acid & tannin; the flavours somewhat brief. **Carignan Rosé** ★★★★ Naturally fermented, salmon-hued **23** ⑧⑤ is altogether charming, from the fruity aromas to the full flavour & dry finish. Fresh, lively & lightly structured. Easygoing 12.5% alc. **Chardonnay** ⓥ ★★★★ Ripe & fruit-driven, **21** ⑧⑤ has voluptuous aromas & flavours, mostly tropical, but also preserved lemon; all unobscured by restrained oaking.

Impressions of Nature range

Mystique Mountain ⓥ ★★★ Shiraz, mourvèdre & grenache, part-oaked for early drinkability. **18** ⑧① greenpepper nuance, tannins in need of tad more polish. **River Secrets** ⓥ ★★★★ Another creative blend, verdelho with semillon & chardonnay in unoaked **19** ⑧⑤. Fruitier, creamier than last, tad more freshness, complexity & palate weight.

Masterpiece of Nature range

Occasional release: **Syrah**, **Muscat Rouge**.

Queen of Africa range

★★★★★ **Edel Laat Oes** ⓥ Classic Noble Late Harvest dessert from Darling semillon, **15** ⑨④ has stone-fruit & pineapple richness, brief oaking giving almond shading; acid freshens the sweetness. 375 ml.— TJ

Location/WO: Swellendam ▪ Map: Southern Cape ▪ Map grid reference: D1 ▪ 1stB 2016 ▪ Tasting & cellar tours by appt only ▪ Fee R100pp ▪ Closed all pub hols ▪ Owner(s) 5 shareholders ▪ Winemaker(s) Jolene le Roux (Jan 2016) ▪ Viticulturist(s) Carl van Wyk ▪ 20ha (carignan, grenache, malbec, mourv, p verdot, red muscadel, roobernet, shiraz, tannat, tempranillo, touriga, chard, riesling, rouss, sauv, sem, verdelho, viog, weisser riesling) ▪ 130t total, 50t own labels 60% red 40% white ▪ Buffeljagsrivier, Olivedale, Swellendam 6740 ▪ jolene@olivedalevineyards.com ▪ www.olivedalevineyards.com ▪ **T +27 (0)28-007-0087/+27 (0)82-789-3800**

Olof Bergh Solera

This Heineken Beverages blended brandy has a greater fraction of cask-aged distillate than the norm, thanks to its locally unique ageing in a solera, where batches are racked down tiers of barrels in a dedicated cellar.

Olof Bergh Solera ⓥ ★★★ Straightforward, balanced blended brandy ⑧① for cocktails & mixing (43% alc). Fruity & fresh, with caramel & nut notes. — WB

Olsen Private Vineyards   ⓥ ⓞ

The labels of this Paarl boutique collection strikingly allude to brand co-owner and US national Greg Olsen being only the third civilian in space. He's latterly been joined in the venture by daughters Kimberly and Krista, with Armand Botha as maker of the bold and generous wines. Technical consultant Loftie Ellis is known industry-wide for his phenomenal palate, so the blend that bears his name can only be special.

★★★★ **Cabernet Sauvignon** ⓥ First since **12** ★★★ ⑧⓪, improved **17** ⑧⑥ offers classic cassis, dried herb & cedar aromas & flavours in a firm, lingering body, handles 2 years in 100% new oak with aplomb.

★★★★ **Shiraz** ② Estate's generous body & alc delivered with poise in **17** ⑧⑧. Good varietal fruit & perfume (cured meat, violet, dabs pepper & clove), silky tannins, ending firm.

★★★★ **Lofti's Choice** ⑩ ⊘ Textured, structured **18** ⑧⑧ Cape Blend of pinotage (31%), equal shiraz, merlot & dab cab. Big black fruit generosity & spice with backing of new oak, 30 months, adds to plush appeal & length.

★★★★ **Chardonnay** Creamy, rich **20** ⑧⑥ improves on last **18** ★★★★ ⑧⑤. Typical citrus & vanilla flavours are bright & juicy, year in new barrels adds structure, length. Alc of 14.4% is higher than before.

★★★★ **Chenin Blanc Reserve** ⑩ Confident, composed & substantial **21** ⑧⑦ retains vibrancy of stonefruit while buttressed by richer oatmeal & nut flavours from year in older oak. Deft & nimble, with lime twist on the finish.

Merlot ② ★★★★ Delightful **17** ⑧⑤ takes 15.5% alc ripeness in its stride, tucks sprig of thyme into black-fruited body along with dark chocolate & mocha derived from all-new oak. **Pinotage** ★★★★ Similar attractive berry succulence & spice on **19** ⑧⑤ as last, but drier tannins from house's extensive oak regime, 2 years, all new. **Chenin Blanc** ⊘ ★★★★ Light elderflower & nectarine lift to **22** ⑧④, fresh acid keeps palate dry & bright. Good summertime sipping. Not tasted: **Cape Blend**, **Gregory Hammond Méthode Cap Classique**. — FM

Location/map/WO: Paarl ▪ Map grid reference: G5 ▪ Est/1stB 2002 ▪ Tasting by appt only ▪ Cheese platter & estate olive oil for sale ▪ Owner(s) Greg Olsen & daughters ▪ Cellarmaster(s)/viticulturist(s) Armand Botha (2000) ▪ Winemaker(s) Armand Botha (2007) & Loftie Ellis (consultant) ▪ 15ha ▪ 1,500cs own label 80% red 20% white ▪ PO Box 9052 Huguenot 7645 ▪ admin@olsenprivatevineyards.co.za ▪ www.olsenprivatevineyards.co.za ▪ T +27 (0)21-862-3653/+27 (0)83-400-1909

☐ **On Borrowed Time** see False Bay Vineyards

Onderkloof   ② ⓞ

Originally a grape and milk venture, Onderkloof on the slope of Schapenberg Hill was acquired by Swiss-born Beat Musfeld and wife Heidi in 1997. Son Yves welcomes visitors to the tasting room and, in the attached cellar, makes the wines that now include a pair of kosher bottlings named for his daughter.

Onderkloof range

★★★★ **Cabernet Franc** ⊘ Quite funky, entirely delicious **20** ⑧⑧ shows deep dark-berry flavours with nutty & mocha edge, supple after 18 months in seasoned oak, slides down easily. **17** ⑧⑧ was last tasted.

★★★★ **Sir Lowry** ⊘ Crafty balance of mulberry-fruited cab franc & herbaceous, structured cab, merlot in support. **20** ⑧⑨, like last-tasted **17** ⑧⑧, textured & rich, long cocoa finish from 18 months old oak.

Cabernet Sauvignon ★★★★ Herby, leafy **20** ⑧⑤ in rustic mould, redolent of leather & musk, well structured but needs more flesh for higher rating. **Bottleneck Rosé** ★★★ Several tons of cab franc arrived late, only option was to make rosé. Onion skin blush on **23** ⑧① followed by apricot flavour, touch of mint, thrilling dry finish. **Sauvignon Blanc** ★★★ From Elgin, **23** ⑧⓪ balances cool-climate greenness with juicy tropical depth for pleasant, easy sipping. Not tasted: **Chardonnay**.

Carina Kosher For Passover range ⑩

Cabernet Franc Rosé ★★★★ Pomegranate-hued **22** ⑧③ more herbaceous than Onderkloof bottling. Drier still & perhaps a bit more serious. **Chardonnay** ★★★★ Very fruity **22** ⑧④ has pineapple, peach & pear flavours packed into a chalky, unoaked frame. — DS

Location: Somerset West ▪ Map: Helderberg ▪ Map grid reference: F7 ▪ WO: Stellenbosch/Elgin ▪ Est 1998 ▪ 1stB 1999 ▪ Tasting, sales & cellar tours by appt ▪ Conservation area ▪ Winemaker(s) Yves Musfeld (Jan 2012) ▪ 200t ▪ 17 Old Sir Lowry's Pass Rd, Sir Lowry's Pass 7130 ▪ info@onderkloof.com ▪ www.onderkloof.com ▪ T +27 (0)76-073-3390

☐ **Ondine** see Ormonde Wines
☐ **One Formation** see Boland Cellar
☐ **100 Reserve** see Oude Molen Distillery
☐ **One Man Band** see Iona Vineyards

Onoma Private Cellar

The amphora on this boutique label is a symbol of family roots on the Aegean island of Lemnos, and the years of effort the late patriarch, Com Yiannakis, invested into making the Stellenbosch home-farm Felicia a grape supplier to top labels. This edition's debut wine is the winery's first commercial blend and a tribute to Com, as cabernet-merlot was his 'blend of choice when making wine for family and friends'.

★★★★☆ **Cabernet Sauvignon** ⓥ Sleek, supple & seductive **18** ⑨⓪ edges **17** ★★★★ ⑧⑧ in intensity. Ample fruitcake & spice but structured, with good density, fine tannin from 2 years in older oak.

★★★★☆ **Syrah** ⓥ Peppery **21** ★★★★ ⑧⑨ preview displays signature restraint & cohesion of fruit & seasoned oak, 18 months. Portion wholebunch adds power to the layered, supple whole. Last was **14** ⑨①.

★★★★ **Chardonnay** Unwooded & unpretentious, **22** ⑧⑥ has limy lees richness, restrained lemon zestiness & appealing salty-bitter twist on finish. Attractively lighter & leaner than **21** ⑧⑧.

Legacy Blend ⓝⒺⓦ ★★★ Medium-bodied, sappy & fresh, with leathery tannins & plummy fruit, **22** ⑧② is equal parts cab & merlot, aged 16 months in old barrels. — GdB

Location/WO: Stellenbosch ▪ Est 2016 ▪ 1stB 2015 ▪ Entire villa available on Airbnb ▪ Wine club ▪ Owner(s) Full Imput 146 (Pty) Ltd (shareholder Com Yiannakis Family Trust) ▪ Winemaker(s) Matthew van Heerden (consultant) ▪ 31ha/17.5ha (cab, merlot, shiraz, chard) ▪ 140t/1,350cs own label 60% red 40% white ▪ WIETA ▪ blaise@onomawines.com ▪ www.onomawines.com ▪ **T +27 (0)82-468-3788**

☐ **Openers** *see* Stellenview Premium Wines

Openwine ⓨ ⑪

Marta Gobbo and Raphael Paterniti of Cape Town wine bar Openwine were still working on new releases at press time, and we look forward to tasting them for the next edition.

Location: Cape Town ▪ Map: Cape Peninsula ▪ Map grid reference: B1 ▪ Tasting & sales Mon-Fri 12-10; wine & food pairing ▪ Owner(s) Raphael Paterniti & Marta Gobbo ▪ 72 Wale Str, Cape Town 8001 ▪ info@openwineza. co.za ▪ **T +27 (0)21-422-0800**

Opstal Estate ⓨ ⑪ ⌂ ◎ ⑧ ⑥

Seventh-generation winemaker and prime mover in Slanghoek Valley, Attie Louw doesn't rest on his laurels: there are 4 new wines this edition, including two premium chenins, his big passion. Family features strongly here (brother Zak is one of the viticulturists), as does the celebration of heritage, Carl Everson being the 4th-generation farmer who kept the estate going in the tough postwar years, and The Barber the 5th-generation Attie Louw, a barber in Worcester who married Opstal heiress Ansie Everson and moved to the farm. His contemporary namesake believes wines should have drinkability, which is why he was persuaded to vinify for like-minded Tinashe Nyamudoka, founder of Kumusha Wines, listed separately.

Single Site range ⓝⒺⓦ

★★★★☆ **Bergsteen** ⓐ Chenin from highest vineyard, no irrigation, always first harvested. Preserved melon richness in **22** ⑨④, 10 months in older oak part of the perfume & flavours, intriguing ginger biscuit tone. Palate full & round, thanks to ripeness & lees contact. Impressive, has standout character.

★★★★☆ **Wenblok** ⓐ ⓦ Chenin planted 1982, only concrete tank used, to preserve purity of fruit & site expression. Thatch & quince in **22** ⑨③, an earthy nuance; individual, totally different to estate's other chenins. Definitely savoury on the palate, whiff of charcuterie. Sleek, dry, memorable, likely to be long-lived. Just 100 cases of each of these wines.

Heritage range

★★★★★ **Carl Everson Cape Blend** ⊘ ⓐ Near-equal cab, pinotage & carignan, with 11% cinsaut, **21** ⑨⑥ proves how good this singular partnership is: glossy fruit well-spiced by 20 months in barrel & foudre, seamless texture with a fresh lift, keeping it youthfully appealing. Admirable crafting. Follows light-treading **20** ★★★★★ ⑨③.

★★★★☆ **Carl Everson Chenin Blanc** ⓐ ⓦ Vines rooted 1982, wild ferment, minimal cellar handling, 10 months older barrel & foudre, which **22** ⑨③ expresses as stonefruit & sliced Bosc pear. Oak character subservient, a gentle melba toast tone in the flavours. Noteworthy palate weight & length, ending mineral, as all these.

★★★★☆ **The Barber Semillon** ⊛ Recalls 5th-generation ancestor, hair- turned wine-styler after marrying Opstal heiress. Barrel ferment/10 months which 22 ★★★★★ ⑨⑤'s fruit takes in its stride: richly perfumed citrus & stonefruit; palate reveals built-in ageing potential: intense lemony focus, taut, zinging freshness. Savoury thread throughout. As last 20 ⑨③, wonderful focus, precision.

★★★★☆ **The Barber Verdelho** (NEW) ⊛ Wild ferment/10 months barrel & foudre, which left 22 ⑨③'s fruit intact: stonefruit & floral highlights. Freshness one of variety's attributes, lemony & salty, keeping it all vibrant & eminently appealing. Oak shows as biscuit tone on palate. Worthy addition to range. WO W Cape.

Opstal Estate range

★★★★ **Cinsault** (NEW) ⊘ Thoughtfully handled for a particular fruit profile & freshness, aided by just 11% alc. Pale ruby 22 ⑧⑦ vivid cranberry & cherry, 6 months older foudre adding gentle savouriness without influencing overall character. Shows purity, focus.

★★★★ **Cabernet Sauvignon-Cinsault** ⊘ Cab at 75%, with cinsaut, dash carignan, 9 months older barrel & foudre. Wonderfully perfumed 22 ★★★★★ ⑨⓪ boasts cassis, glacé cherry & cigarbox, deeply layered, reflection of handling change (no oak in 21 ⑧⑨) & riper fruit. Curvaceous, with juicy freshness.

★★★★☆ **Chenin Blanc** ⊘ A fine job of capturing typicity in 22 ⑨⓪, white peach & apple, a subtle savoury seam from 6 months in barrel & foudre for 25% of the wine, the fruit rules. Lees contact gives palate weight, enough freshness ensures lift & vibrancy.

★★★★ **Dessert Muscat** Not discontinued as we thought. From 1987 muscat d'Alexandrie, 21 ★★★★★ ⑨⓪ fortified & full-sweet, shows multiple scents of sultana & fruit pastille, melon & ginger preserve, ends tangy. Hard not to be seduced by the flavours & richness. Dab colombard 'for extra cheerfulness'. In 375 ml, sadly just 125 cases. Last was 18 ⑧⑨.

Syrah-Colombard Blush ★★★★ Co-harvested & -vinified, bright pink 23 ⑧④'s 75/25 blend dictates the styling: red berries with a fresh underpin of the white grape. Dry, perfect for food, good enough to drink solo too. Not tasted: **Southern Secco**.

Sixpence range

Cabernet Sauvignon ⊘ ★★★☆ Partial oaking, 8 months, just enough to add gentle spice without overwhelming 22 ⑧④'s vibrant cherry & cassis fruit. Slight tannin grip but palate smooth, streamlined. WO Breedekloof for these. **Sauvignon Blanc-Semillon** ★★★ Nice combo green apple & pear in unoaked 23 ⑧②'s 60/40 blend, dry & fresh. Has tasty drinkability, as intended. WO Breedekloof. — CR

Location: Rawsonville ▪ Map: Breedekloof ▪ Map grid reference: A5 ▪ WO: Slanghoek/Breedekloof/Western Cape ▪ Est 1847 ▪ 1stB 1978 ▪ Tasting, sales & cellar tours Mon-Fri 9-5 Sat 11-4 Sun 12-3; pub hols (seasonal) please call ahead ▪ Closed Easter Fri-Mon, Dec 25/26 & Jan 1 ▪ Cheese platters ▪ Restaurant Mon-Sun 9-5 ▪ Facilities for children ▪ Tour groups ▪ Farm produce ▪ Conferences ▪ Weddings ▪ Conservation area ▪ MTB trail ▪ Opstal Stay (5 exclusive self-catering units) ▪ Wine club ▪ Owner(s) Louw Family Trust ▪ Winemaker(s) Attie Louw (Sep 2010) ▪ Viticulturist(s) Gerhard Theron (Jan 2002) & Zak Louw (Jan 2016) ▪ 419ha/101ha (cab, cinsaut, grenache, ptage, shiraz, chard, chenin, muscat d'A, rouss, sauv, sem) ▪ 1,600t/50,000cs (x12-btl) own label 30% red 60% white 10% rosé ▪ IPW, WIETA ▪ PO Box 27 Rawsonville 6845 ▪ info@opstal.co.za ▪ www.opstal.co.za ▪ **T +27 (0)23-344-3001**

Orange River Cellars ⑨ ⑪ ⑤

The scale is impressive: ±142 shareholder-growers with 1,100 ha of vines on the banks of South Africa's main river in Northern Cape province, producing 18-million litres of wine for their own labels, and a further 6-million for clients and the bulk trade. Yet the team led by wine production head Chris Venter, cellarmaster Philani Gumede and viticulturist Natasja Combrink are also immersed in crafting small batches of premium wine - the Cellar Master collection allowing free rein for creative expression - and proud that while the white and dessert wines maintain their well-established trajectory, 'our red wines perform better year on year'. Primary production is being centralised in Upington and the main cellar there expanded accordingly.

Reserve range

★★★★ **Lyra Nebula** ⊘ From shiraz, 20 ⑧⑥ shows a smoked bacon richness & intriguing tropical nuance under cloak of oak, has more to offer than Omstaan sibling. First since 17 ⑧⑥. Serious wooding, as the other dry wines here: 18 months, 50-60% new, 40-60% American.

★★★★☆ **Lyra Vega** ⊘ Ambitious **20** ⑨⓪ blend, near-equal shiraz & petit verdot, both adding power & ripeness of blue- & black-berried fruit. Sweet vanilla tone of new oak is threaded through the supple, spicy body, 14% alc in balance.

★★★★ **Lyra Quasar** ⊘ Sauvignon blanc given house's generous oak treatment of 3 months, **22** ⑧⑥ handles it well, retains grassy gooseberry fruitiness for a satisfying drop. WO Greater Cape. Like Nebula, not discontinued as we thought.

★★★★ **Straw Wine** ⓐ Scintillating dessert wine from air-dried chenin. **23** ⑨③'s brilliant amber hue introduces luscious peach & apricot flavours, vibrant acid ensures delicious, uncloying glassful. Fermented/2 months in old oak. 11.5% alc. 375 ml. **22** untasted.

Lyra Irsai Olivér Demi-Sec Sparkling ⊘ ★★★☆ Something different, bubbly from Hungarian variety, low in alc (10%) & carbonated. **22** ⑧⑤ highly aromatic, unusual coconut & pineapple combo, balanced sweetness.

Cellar Master range

★★★★ **Bontstaan Premium Cape Brandy** ⓧ Sunset hued, brimful of peaches, pears & raisins, lively yet smooth, spicy & warming (40% alc), potstill ⑨⓪ with 5-10 year old components ticks the boxes.

Omstaan Cabernet Franc ⓧ ★★★ Lavished with oak, 50% new, combo French & American, 18 months (as all this range unless noted), **19** ⑧② just starting to show sappy varietal fruit flavours & herbaceous notes. **Die Kerkmuis Pinotage** ⊘ ★★★☆ Different oaking to sibling, mainly staves in tank, 50% new, adding vanilla to mix of plum, clove, coconut & mocha on **21** ⑧⑤. **Sterkstaan Pinotage** ★★★☆ Plum pudding flavours of **22** ⑧⑤ more tightly structured by 18 months in 60% new oak than last, reining in the exuberance a little. Alc now more moderate 13%. **Omstaan Shiraz** ⓃⒺⓌ ★★★ Richly fruited **20** ⑧⓪ gets house-style enthusiastic oaking, responds with coconut whiffs over brambles & mulberries. Would benefit from time to settle, as all the wooded wines. **Omstaan Shiraz-Petit Verdot** ★★★★ Less high-aiming sibling to Vega still sees plenty of oak, which encases blue & black berry fruit of **21** ⑧⑤. Time will reveal underlying succulence. **Omstaan Colombard** ★★★ Inherently delicate fruit of **22** ⑦⑨ stumbles under the weight of wood, 80% new. **Regopstaan Colombard** ⓧ ★★ This & sibling similar vinification as sauvignons, 60% oaked, 60% new. **21** ⑦⑤ lightish on fruit & alc (11.9%), leaving wood & bracing acid more exposed. **Omstaan Sauvignon Blanc** ★★★★ Oak shows as thick patina of vanilla, masking **22** ⑧⑤'s fruit mid-2023. Bone-dry finish & modest 12.3% alc are pluses. **Regopstaan Sauvignon Blanc** ⓧ ★★★★ Grassy greengage fruit of **21** ⑧⑤ polished by sweet note from oaked portion. **Die Kerkmuis Sauvignon Blanc** ⓧ ★★★☆ The unoaked & most enjoyable sauvignon, **22** ⑧⑤ has clean green-fruit aromas & a refreshing flavour.

The Hedgehog range

Cabernet Sauvignon ★★★ Promising graphite & cedar features tussle with gruff wood tannins in **21** ⑧②. Mostly American oak, as all these reds. **Pinotage** ★★ Nutmeg & banana fruit of **22** ⑦② shrouded in oak mid-2023. Needs to soften & meld. **Ruby Cabernet** ★★ Second bottling of **20** ⑦⑥ a juicy mouthful, mixed red berries infused with smoke. Combo oak staves & barrels for these reds. **Shiraz** ★★★ Further bottling of **20** ⑧⓪ light but not quiet, meaty red-berry flavour lifted by spice, oak more integrated mid-2023. Also in 2L bag-in-box. **Dry Rosé** ⓃⒺⓌ ★★ Muted floral notes of **23** ⑦④ from pinotage perked up on palate by cranberry piquancy. WO Greater Cape, as Sauvignon. **Chenin Blanc** ⊘ ★★★ Fresh, sunny peach & pear flavours on **23** ⑧⓪. As charming as last, touch more substantial. **Chenin Blanc Organic** ⓧ ⊘ ★★★★ Has more body & gravitas in **21** ⑧③ than sibling of same vintage, attractive bone-dry finish. **Colombard** ★★ Dried herbal features of **23** ⑦⑥ plumped by granadilla & guava ripeness, few grams sugar. **Sauvignon Blanc** ★★ Modest tropical fruit with waxy edge lifted by balanced acid in **23** ⑦②. Also in 2L pack. **Rosé Natural Sweet** ★★ Chenin & morio muscat gain colour & spine from 10% cab in carnival pink **23** ⑦③. Luscious & sweet. Low ±9% alc, as Blanc. **Nouveau Blanc Natural Sweet** ★★ Honeyed fruit sweetness so well balanced by cleansing acid that **23** ⑦③ is versatile before & with meals.

Orange River Cellars range

★★★★ **Die Opsitkers Rooi Muskadel** ⓧ Lovely shimmering hues on **19** ⑧⑨, lush raisin aromas & flavours with fruitcake spice & warming spirit, enduring balanced sweetness.

★★★★★ **Omstaan Rooi Muskadel XO** ⓐ Fortified muscat de Frontignan is the red version of stellar pair of 'precision selections' from multiple harvests - 10 in this **NV** ⑨⑤, hence XO on label. Latest has teak hue, spicy, floral & musky aromas precede mellow, intensely sweet muscat flavours. 299 g/L sugar, 16.8% alc. Many years in neutral barrel. Mere 266 cases of 500 ml, as XI partner.

★★★★ **Red Muscadel** Flame-licked hue invites engagement with **23** ⑧⑨, ample mix of raisin, candied citrus peel & spice, enriched with warming 18% alc. Sweet, smoky & persistent.

★★★★☆ **Die Opsitkers Wit Muskadel** ⚲ Muscat de Frontignan fortified **20** ⑨③ seamlessly merges grape, spice & citrus with deftly judged spirit. On-point sugar-acid finishes clean, invites another sip.

★★★★☆ **Omstaan Wit Muskadel XI** ⚲ Sublime fortified muscat, **NV** ⑨④ a blend of 11 vintages, hence XI on label. Latest version is old gold with amber flecks, offers spicy, floral, musky aromas leading to intense yet poised palate, echoing conclusion. Very special. 319 g/L sugar, 17.4% alc.

★★★★☆ **White Muscadel** ⊘ Fortified muscat de Frontignan with track record of fresh, spiced citrus peel flavours adroitly melded with warming, not fierce spirit. **23** ⑨② has typical grapey sweetness perfectly balanced by a whistle-clean finish.

★★★★ **White Jerepigo** Fortified colombard, **22** ⑧⑥ offers honeysuckle & roast nut nuances with rich, fruity sweetness & lingering finish. Delicious over crushed ice. **21** sold out untasted.

Gwave ⒩ ⊘ ★★★ Creative name & look to emphasise guava character of cellar stalwart colombard. **23** ⑧② has plenty of the advertised fruit, plus few grams sugar offset by brisk acid. **Sparkling Rosé** ★★★ Cherry-toned sweet pink fizz from chenin, morio muscat & pinotage. Previous sold out untasted; cheery, low-alc **22** ⑦⑦ also likely to fly off the shelves. **Sparkling Brut** ⊘ ★★★ Fruity, softly dry bubbly from chenin. **22** ⑧⓪ a fresh pick-me-up. **Sparkling Doux** ⊘ ★★★ From chenin & morio muscat, **22** ⑧⓪'s floral & litchi flavours invigorated by fizz to appeal to those who don't have a sweet tooth. **Hanepoot** ★★★ Fortified **22** ⑧⑤ has pineapple attractions in a grapey mouthful that's super-sweet at 170 g/L sugar. **Red Jerepigo** ★★★★ Ruby cabernet & shiraz make up very fruity, sweet fortified. **22** ⑧⑤ shows its 17.7% alc, warms & comforts with plum & Xmas cake flavours albeit not quite as sleek as **21** ★★★★ ⑧⑥. **Cape Ruby** ⊘ ★★★ 'Port' from unoaked **21** ⑧⓪ ruby cab. Smooth, warming & light, to drink early. **Old Brown Fortified Wine** ⒩ ★★★ Inspired by oloroso sherry, 'old brown' a favoured style of legions of students, here crafted from colombard & chenin. **NV** ⑦⑨ nutty, grapey, sweet & strong. — DS, WB

Location: Upington ▪ Map: Northern Cape, Free State & North West ▪ Map grid reference: B8 ▪ WO: Northern Cape/Greater Cape ▪ Est 1965 ▪ 1stB 1968 ▪ Tasting & sales at Upington: Die Kerkmuis restaurant & tasting centre, virtual cellar tours, tasting & sales Mon-Tue 9-5 Wed-Fri 9-9 Sat 9-4 & at Kakamas Mon-Fri 9-9pm Sat 9-10pm ▪ Pub hols (seasonal) please call ahead ▪ Closed Sun, Good Fri, Dec 25 & Jan 1 ▪ Owner(s) ±142 producer shareholders ▪ Head of wine production Chris Venter ▪ Cellarmaster(s) Philani Gumede ▪ Cellar managers George Kruger, Johan Dippenaar, Johan Esterhuizen ▪ Winemaker(s) Marko Pentz, Willie Biggs, Frikkie du Plessis ▪ Viticulturist(s) Natasja Combrink ▪ 1,100ha (cabs s/f, p verdot, ptage, ruby cab, shiraz, chard, chenin, cbard, muscat varieties, sauv) ▪ 30,000t/18M L own label 10% red 50% white 25% rosé 15% other + 6m L for clients/bulk ▪ PO Box 544 Upington 8800 ▪ info@orangeriverwines.com ▪ www.orangeriverwines.com ▪ **T** +27 (0)54-337-8800

☐ **Oranjerivier Wynkelders** *see* Orange River Cellars
☐ **Oranjezicht** *see* Rogge Cloof
☐ **Organic Wine by Sophie Germanier** *see* Germanier Wines

Org de Rac ⚲ 🍴 ⒶⒷⒸ

'The time for organic wine has arrived in the post-Covid world, with sustainability being the overriding issue in the world of wine,' say the family owners of this substantial certified-organic estate in Swartland, quietly proud of 'having recognised the importance of organic agriculture by implementing this ethos 23 years ago.' They hasten to add that terroir expression, varietal nuance and quality are non-negotiable, and this sees cellarmaster Lizelle Gerber presiding over the commissioning of a new destemmer and press.

Die Waghuis range

★★★★☆ **Red** ⊘ Mostly shiraz with grenache noir & mourvèdre (30/15) in **21** ★★★★ ⑧⑨. Enticing spice & savouriness in a firm, dry tannic embrace. Quite feisty too, less expressive in youth than **19** ⑨⓪, a different blend, needs more time to fully reveal its flavours. **20** untasted.

★★★★☆ **White** ⊘ Chenin plus dabs roussanne & verdelho in **22** ⑨⓪ show similar subtly scented floral notes, freshness & poise. Deft, mostly older oak, year, doesn't obscure the fruit purity, but adds breadth & texture. Ends clean & dry. Fairtrade certified, as all wines tasted this edition.

Reserve range

★★★★ **Merlot** ⓩ ⓥ With ripe fruit, plus dark chocolate & spice from 50% new oak. **17** ⑧⑦ more intense & structured than **15** ★★★☆ ⑧④ & Org de Rac version. Sweetish finish detracts. **16** untasted.

★★★★ **Shiraz** ⓩ ⓥ Chewy, grippy & powerful **17** ⑧⑥ has good fruit, with forward smoky, tobacco notes evidencing all-new French/American oaking. More intense than standard bottling. Should develop.

★★★★☆ **Cabernet Sauvignon-Merlot** ⓩ ⓥ Forward, classic aromas of berry fruit & cigarbox on **17** ⑨②. House-style ripe richness & compensating acidity, plenty of flavour. 2 years in mostly French oak add some austere dry tannins to the balance - should harmonise with the deserved few years ageing.

★★★★ **Chardonnay** ⓥ ⓥ Pleasantly but modestly flavoured **18** ⑧⑥, introduced by nutty, toasty, limy aromas. Silky texture, oak integrated on palate, with bright, balanced acid & lingering citric finish.

Discontinued: **Cabernet Sauvignon**.

Org de Rac range

★★★★ **Chenin Blanc** ⓥ ⓥ Return to form in **23** ⑧⑥. Unoaked, like **22** ★★★☆ ⑧⑤, but has ample ripe apple & dried peach flavours. Natural ferment & lengthy lees infusion provide the earthy, creamy substrate, the whole zested through with acid for balance & quaffability. WO W Cape, as Sauvignon Blanc.

★★★★ **Roussanne** ⓥ Alluring floral- & ginger-scented **22** ⑧⑨ has a delicate intensity characteristic of this variety, & lovely freshness, appearing much lighter than 14% alc. Part old-oak, part amphora aged, all elements in harmony for a very appealing drink.

★★★★ **La Verne Méthode Cap Classique Chardonnay-Pinot Noir** ⓥ Gentle apple & some honey on **21** ⑧⑥ chardonnay-led (68%) sparkler. Styled for versatility: dry, clean & light (12% alc), hint of creaminess from year on lees. Step up on last **19** ★★★★ ⑧⑤.

Cabernet Sauvignon ⓥ ★★★★ Dark berries & leafy notes in **20** ⑧③ from best-performing clones & sites on the home-farm. Quite a firm structure of dry, chalky tannins & brisk acid, tightly coiled in youth. Allow more time to unwind. **Merlot** ⓩ ⓥ ★★★★ Mingles fruitcake, chocolate & tobacco notes on the aroma of **20** ⑧③. Nice combination of juicy approachability with firm structure, though the acid a bit jarring. 13.6% alc lower than last. **Shiraz** ⓥ ★★★ More structure in **21** ⑧②, along with bright & spicy red fruit, full body but alc well tucked into the firmer tannins & finishing respectably dry. A hearty food wine. WO Coastal. **Cabernet Sauvignon-Merlot** ⓩ ⓥ ★★★ Fruity, pastille aromas on **18** ⑧②. Easygoing, but a little useful grip. Notably sweet finish will not please everybody. **Shiraz-Cabernet Sauvignon-Merlot** ⓥ ★★★★ Preview of **23** ⑧④ blend is riper & fuller than previous at 14.5% alc; plush, dark fruit has a mocha nuance from older-oak maturation. Supple styling for uncomplicated enjoyment. **Rosé** ⓥ ★★★ Coppery-hued **23** ⑦⑨ preview from shiraz has a hint of berries & a savoury edge. WO W Cape. **Chardonnay** ⓥ ★★★★ Pre-bottled unwooded **23** ⑧④ has ample ripe stonefruit, lively acid & some leesy breadth adding succulence. Fuller bodied than previous, in popular quaffable style. **Sauvignon Blanc** ⓥ ★★★★ Bright & juicy **23** ⑧③ shows greener fruit flavours, hint of passionfruit & zesty lemony acidity for light & breezy summer tippling. **The Old Pumphouse Cape Ruby Port** ⓩ ⓥ ★★★ From cab & shiraz, **NV** ⑧① pleasingly sweet, cooked plum fruit & raisins, sufficient tannic grip & lively acidity. In abeyance: **Verdelho**. Discontinued: **La Verne Méthode Cap Classique Chardonnay**.

Husk Spirit range

★★★★ **il Genio** ⓩ ⓥ Water-white **17** ⑧⑦ from merlot, fine balance & complexity, delicious length & spicy spirit bite; strawberries & cream on the nose, smooth & husk-y on palate. 500 ml. — MW, TJ

Location: Piketberg ▪ Map: Swartland ▪ Map grid reference: C2 ▪ WO: Swartland/Western Cape/Coastal ▪ Est 2001 ▪ 1stB 2005 ▪ Tasting, sales & tours Mon-Fri 9-5 Sat 9-2 pub hols 10-3 ▪ Closed Good Fri, Dec 25 & Jan 1 ▪ Meals/ refreshments/cheese platters by prior arrangement ▪ Org de Rac merchandise ▪ Facilities for children ▪ Tour groups ▪ Farm produce ▪ Weddings/functions (150 pax) ▪ Conferences ▪ Conservation area ▪ Owner(s) Bacon & Hartzenberg families ▪ GM Johan Gerber ▪ Winemaker(s) Lizelle Gerber (Jul 2021) ▪ Viticulturist(s) Heini Grobler (Jan 2019) ▪ 220ha/54ha (cab, grenache, malbec, merlot, mourv, p verdot, pinot, shiraz, tempranillo, chard, chenin, rouss, verdelho) ▪ 500t/62,500cs own label 80% red 20% white ▪ BSCI, Control Union (organic), Fairtrade, IPW, WIETA ▪ PO Box 268 Piketberg 7320 ▪ wine@orgderac.com ▪ www.orgderac.com ▪ **T** +27 (0)22-913-2397

Ormonde Wines

This venture on the cool Darling hills is fronted by winemaker-viticulturist Theo Basson, whose family planted deep roots here over generations, and established a prized dairy stud, yet in the 1990s Theo decided to focus on vines. The plan was to make a small amount of wine and sell the rest of the grapes from the ±300 ha, yet it became a big business with multiple labels, including Alexanderfontein, listed separately.

Ormonde Heritage Collection

★★★★☆ **Vernon Basson** ⓥ First since **08** ⑨⑨, **13** ⑨⑨ from cab & 30% cab franc maturing nicely; tannins still youthful & all-new oak shows on tobacco-fruitcake aromas & palate, with herbal element. Touch sweet on finish. Flavourful & rich but not over-bold at 14.2% alc. Still many years to go.

★★★★☆ **Theodore Eksteen** ⓥ Ripe & rewardingly succulent, oak well-integrated with rich fruit & spice highlights from 2 years each in new French oak & bottle. **17** ⑨⑨ structured yet restrained, grenache (35%) supports shiraz. First made since **13** ⑨⑨.

★★★★☆ **Noble Late Harvest** ⓥ Charming delicacy as well as delicious but subtle fullness of fruit on **15** ⑨⑨ botrytis dessert from chenin. Lovely balance: light (just over 11% alcohol) but not lacking in presence. Only older oak barrels used. 184 g/L sugar leaves no cloy at all on lingering finish. 375 ml.

Ormonde Barrel Selected range

★★★★ **Cabernet Sauvignon** ⓥ Berry aromas & flavours mingle with tobacco-oak layer on **15** ⑧⑦. Succulent acid balanced by sweet element & firm but integrated tannin. Juicy & drinkable, but will keep.

★★★★ **Shiraz** ⓥ Plush, ripe **15** ⑧⑥ has tobacco, spice & expressive fruit, with chocolate note on the palate. Softly textured, lingering & not too challenging.

Merlot ⓥ ★★★★ Oaky tobacco notes & dark berries on **15** ⑧⑤. Ripe flavours but also a minty, herbal element. Burly 14.7% alc. Dry, grippy tannins, slightly edgy acidity. Not tasted: **Chardonnay**.

Ondine Specialities

★★★★ **Cabernet Franc** ⓥ **17** ⑧⑥ picks up where last-tasted **15** ⑧⑥ left off: perfumed, cocoa-tinged dark berries, same 14.4% alc well knit with fruit & oak, just 15% new, year.

★★★★ **Grenache** ⓥ Lovely vibrancy to **17** ⑧⑦, which improves on **16** ★★★★ ⑧⑤ & lowers alc to 13.4%. Chalky texture & tannin balance out peppery red & blue fruit. Year mainly older oak adds support.

★★★★ **Malbec** ⓥ Plush, spicy & vivacious **19** ⑧⑦ shows hike in quality over gentle **18** ★★★★ ⑧⑤. Frame of oak, 15% new, cradles ripe plum fruit.

★★★★ **Sauvignon Blanc** ⓥ Pre-bottling last time, **17** ⑧⑧ now less overtly fruity, but still with clear passionfruit & a succulent grassy greenness; refreshing acidity part of a pleasing example of the style.

Chardonnay ⓥ ★★★★ Only half barrel-fermented, hence the pleasing freshness on **19** ⑧⑤. Ripe stonefruit, citrus verve set against creamy finish from year in oak, 25% new. Alc just 11.8%. Last-tasted **15** ★★★★ ⑧⑥ was a preview. **Chenin Blanc** ⓥ ★★★★ Pear drop generosity on **18** ⑧⑤. Ripe yet fresh, lively & crisp, it's unwooded with a dry conclusion. Not tasted: **Pinot Noir**.

Single-Vineyard Chip Off The Old Block Collection

★★★★ **Shiraz** ⓥ Improving on **15** ★★★ ⑧②, **17** ⑧⑥'s soft plummy entry belies brooding depths of smoky black fruit, dried herb & structure of well-meshed oak (9 months, 15% new). No **16**.

Cabernet Sauvignon ⓥ ★★★★ Medium-bodied **15** ⑧⑤ has inviting dark fruit, spice & cedar notes, is approachable after 9 months polishing in 15% new oak. From registered single-vineyard, as all these.

Chenin Blanc ⓥ ★★★★ Nectarine & kumquat succulence to unwooded **20** ⑧⑤, light, fresh & full of energy. Not tasted: **Sauvignon Blanc**.

Basson Collection

★★★★☆ **Merlot** ⓥ Hedgerow fruit & spice on seductive **15** ⑨⓪. Layered, rich & sumptuous, it is lithe, supple & powerful. Soft textured & silky too. Well-knit oak, 15% new, 14-16 months, lends support.

★★★★ **Proprietor's Blend** ⓥ Appealing fruitcake & spice typicity on **15** ⑧⑥ Bordeaux blend. Cab leads cab franc & malbec. Well-structured & -defined body, rich long finish.

Not tasted: **Pinotage**, **Cape Blend**. — FM

Location/WO: Darling ▪ Map: Durbanville, Philadelphia & Darling ▪ Map grid reference: A1 ▪ 1stB 1999 ▪ Tasting & sales Mon-Fri 9-4 Sat/pub hols 9-3 ▪ Closed Good Fri, Dec 25/26 & Jan 1 ▪ Chocolate/soup & wine pairings by appt ▪ Facilities for children ▪ Walks ▪ Owner(s) Basson family ▪ Winemaker(s)/viticulturist(s) Theo Basson ▪ ±300ha (cabs s/f, merlot, mourv, p verdot, pinot, shiraz, chard, chenin, sauv, sem) ▪ 1,000t/70,000cs own label 40% red 60% white ▪ PO Box 201 Darling 7345 ▪ info@ormonde.co.za ▪ www.ormonde.co.za ▪ **T +27 (0)22-492-3540**

☐ **Orpheus & The Raven** *see* The Vinoneers
☐ **Oshun** *see* Zidela Wines
☐ **Oude Compagnies Post** *see* Swanepoel Wines
☐ **Oude Kaap** *see* DGB (Pty) Ltd

Oude Molen Distillery

This famous distillery was founded over a century ago in Stellenbosch but is now sited in Elgin. Here, apart from an own range of highly regarded brandies, Oude Molen makes spirits for many other labels, both local and foreign. Their original distiller, French-born René Santhagens, played a crucial role in the history of Cape firewater, encouraging superior brandy-making based on double distillation in copper pots. He was known for an ability to sniff out the finest barrel in a batch, and now (no doubt alongside the angels who'd taken their share) would note with pleasure the release of a highly limited brandy, from a single American cask.

Cape Brandy range

★★★★☆ **Oude Molen XO** Ⓟ Longer ageing (minimum 10 years, partly in bourbon barrels) of the XO adds lighter, more refined fruit (peach, pear) & floral, walnut & cedar notes to the bouquet. Latest bottling ⑨④ from pinotage as well as chenin & colombard. Elegant & fresh, the 40% alc beautifully in sync.

★★★★☆ **Oude Molen Single Cask** ⑭ Just 360 bottles made of this VSOP-grade (minimum of 5 years age) potstilled brandy ⑨② from a single, selected American oak barrel. Sweet wood, spicy notes come through, along with apple, pear & stonefruit. Generously, richly warm, but with smooth elegance.

★★★★☆ **Oude Molen VSOP** Ⓟ From potstill brandies aged 5-9 years. Extra time gives this ⑨⓪ more complexity & elegance than VS. Aromatic power, with sherry-like nutty overtones to the prune & dried peach, but the oak influence well integrated. Smooth & luscious.

★★★★ **Oude Molen VS** Ⓟ All potstill ⑧⑥, 3-6 years old, part in solera system of ex-sherry casks. Like VSOP & Single Cask, from chenin & colombard. Nutty, cedary notes, restrained fruitiness. Refined, light-feeling &, at balanced 40% alc, very much for sipping.

100 Reserve range

Premium Brandy Ⓟ ★★★★ Always one of the most perfumed, smoothest & most sippable blended brandies, despite 43% alc. Rather delectable sweetness on latest ⑧④. Wine spirit with 30% 3 to 5 year potstill, the blend matured in a solera system. — TJ

Location/map: Elgin ▪ Map grid reference: B1 ▪ Tasting & sales by appt only ▪ MD Andre Simonis ▪ Brandy master(s) Kobus Gelderblom (Jun 2013, consultant), with Mark Middleton & Andy Neil ▪ PO Box 494 Grabouw 7160 ▪ info@oudemolen.co.za ▪ www.oudemolen.co.za ▪ **T +27 (0)21-859-2517**

Ouwater Wyne

Arresting front-label art adorns this exceptional boutique wine by Petri de Beer, on a mission to bring to light 'many uncut gems' he's found during his decade as winemaker. In this he's tapping 'some of the finest minds in the industry' to help craft, in hands-off fashion, wines from neglected and undiscovered varieties and terroirs, such that grape and site 'truly shine'. Petri says the sauvignon block is in the Roggeveld near Sutherland, beside a dry riverbed in a small valley at 1,500 m altitude, making it one of the highest in SA.

★★★★☆ **Sutherland-Karoo Sauvignon Blanc** ⊛ Oxidatively made to temper green notes. Mineral & fynbos scents, **22** ⑨③'s sleek (12.5% alc) styling fits the flinty citrus flavours & acid-driven finish to a T. Tightly held, more Old World than New.— CR, CvZ

Location: Kuils River ▪ WO: Sutherland-Karoo ▪ Est/1stB 2022 ▪ Closed to public ▪ Owner(s) Petri de Beer ▪ Winemaker(s) Petri de Beer (Jan 2022), with Lisa Carlse (Jan 2023) ▪ Viticulturist(s) Petri de Beer (Jan 2022) ▪ 3t own label 30% red 60% white ▪ petridb@gmail.com ▪ **T +27 (0)82-389-6590**

Overgaauw Wine Estate

The Van Velden family have been farming their estate for almost 120 years, and making own-label wine for around half of those. Believing 'the key to greatness is preserving the unique', they've blazed trails in many significant areas of Cape wine, including the first and still only commercial bottling of sylvaner in 1971, and the first standalone merlot. The latter variety is the focus of a drive by 4th-generation owner and winemaker David to scale new heights, harnessing their Stellenboschkloof terroir and virus-free vines 'to produce merlot of outstanding quality'. Based on the grape's showing in his stellar Bordeaux blend, the sky's the limit.

★★★★ **Merlot** Smoky, savoury spice in pre-bottling sample's cassis & plummy fruit from 18 months in barrel (as Tria Corda). Youthful tannins on **21** ⑧⑨ still a feature but should meld with time, provide good ageing ability. Demands to be taken seriously.

★★★★★ **Tria Corda** Classic 3-part Bordeaux blend, **20** ⑨⑤ preview cab with merlot, cab franc, 80% new barriques, crafted to age, as its track record shows. Vivid cassis reflects fruit quality, the firm dry tannins its foundation. Deserved flagship, has depth & heft, follows admirable **19** ⑨⑤.

★★★★ **Abraham Sauvignon Blanc** Small portion oak-fermented, but **22** ⑧⑧ preview celebrates fruit, vibrant greengage & winter melon, the flavours revealing herbal nuances. Overall effect of typicity, limy-fresh at the end. No **21**.

★★★★ **Sylvaner** Unique bottling from single-vineyard, tiny quantity. **23** ⑧⑨ presents array of scents, tarragon, fennel, lanolin, hint of spearmint, hard to pin down. Vibrant, complex, has personality. No **21, 22**.

★★★★☆ **Cape Vintage** ⓥ Classic, superbly dry, vibrantly spicy & rich **98** ★★★★★ ⑨⑤ 'port' calls on touriga nacional & equal tintas barocca & roriz, touriga franca, souzão & cornifesto for complexity. Bold & nutty, it's structured from 30 months in 1,300L vats. Good for further half-decade. Last tasted was **96** ⑨⓪.

Occasional release: **Touriga Nacional, DC Classic**. — CR

Location/map/WO: Stellenbosch ▪ Map grid reference: D5 ▪ Est 1905 ▪ 1stB 1970 ▪ Tasting by appt on weekdays ▪ Closed Easter Fri-Mon, Dec 25/26 & Jan 1 ▪ Owner(s) David van Velden ▪ Winemaker(s) David van Velden (Jan 2003) ▪ Viticulturist(s) Jaco Engelbrecht (2016) ▪ 13ha (cabs s/f, merlot, touriga, sauv, sylvaner) ▪ 60% red 40% white ▪ IPW ▪ Stellenboschkloof Rd Vlottenburg 7604 ▪ info@overgaauw.co.za ▪ www. overgaauw.co.za ▪ **T** +27 (0)21-881-3815

Overhex Wines International   ⓥ ♿

Homed near Worcester but sourcing grapes from selected regions in the Cape, Overhex is owned by the Van der Wath family. It's a major industry player and large exporter of bottled wine, yet its brand persona is refreshingly accessible and un-corporate, with a lightness of touch and underlying sense of fun that's widely appealing to wine newcomers in particular. There's a new design and sustainability emphasis for the Balance brand, and creativity and innovation, like the (untasted by us) sparkling orange wine in the new iconoclastic Get Lost range, plus a focus on quality and value for money across the board.

The Mooring range

★★★★ **Syrah-Grenache** ⊘ Demonstrating how well-matched these varieties are, **22** ⑧⑥ barrel sample is a spicy, red-fruited delight; harmonious, with smoothly rounded texture & suave oak tannins.

Sauvignon Blanc ★★★★ Ex tank, reductively made for optimum fruit expression, **23** ⑧③ displays green fig & capsicum, appetisingly zesty freshness. WO Coastal for these.

Get Lost range (NEW)

Premium Red Blend ⊘ ★★★★ Creative, anti-establishment labels befit the range name. Equal syrah & pinotage, **22** ⑧③'s 8 months in French & American barrels give a chocolate tone to the fruit, luscious & smooth. **Rosé** ★★★ Light & delightful, dry **23** ⑧⓪ combines chenin with dabs of pinotage & shiraz. **Chardonnay-Semillon** ★★★ 10% semillon's seasoned oak adds a savoury food-friendly note to elegantly dry **22** ⑧②'s stonefruit. **Chenin Blanc-Pinot Grigio** ★★★ Crunchy fruit salad from dominant chenin, **23** ⑧② finishes crisply dry.

Mensa range

Cabernet Sauvignon ⊘ ★★★★ Pre-bottled sample, as rest of range. **22** ⑧④ already showing oak's smokiness, well matched by dark-toned fruit, plush texture. **Shiraz-Malbec** ⊘ ★★★★ Malbec at 10%, uncommon pairing but no denying **22** ⑧④ works: sweet-spiced brambleberries with ripe tannins, harmonious body. **Sauvignon Blanc** ⊘ ★★★★ **23** ⑧⑤ gives layers of interest, creatively combines green tones & minerality, a refreshing salty finish. **Chenin Blanc-Pinot Grigio** ⊘ ★★★★ Unusual combo, lighter textured than previous but **22** ⑧④ still offers tasty melon flavour, sleek freshness.

Balance Winemaker's Selection
★★★★ **Chenin Blanc** ⊘ Lovely & true to variety, sleek, dry **23** ⑧⑥ winter melon & apple, shot through with a seam of minerality, finishing long.

.....

Pinot Noir ⊘ 🏵 ★★★★ Previewed **23** ⑧⑤ stylistic change from last, oaking adds to the fruit layers, streamlined & smooth. Well crafted. **Shiraz** ⊘ 🏵 ★★★★ Admirable typicity in **22** ⑧⑤ tank sample, scrub, tobacco & brambleberries, succulent & nicely rounded.

.....

Cabernet Sauvignon ⊘ ★★★★ Cassis & cherry welcome from **22** ⑧⑤, cab at its popular best, already approachable, supple. All these reds oak staves 10 months. **Merlot** ⊘ ★★★★ Red-fruited with oak's savoury topnote, **22** ⑧⑤ is satisfyingly balanced, streamlined. **Chardonnay** ⊘ ★★★★ Tasted ex tank, lightly oaked **23** ⑧⑤ has biscuit spicing in its citrus flavours, a lithe & zesty mouthful. **Pinot Grigio** ★★★ Fresh & dry **23** ⑧① displays gentle mineral & lemon notes. **Sauvignon Blanc** ⊘ ★★★★ Layered fruit & meadow grasses, **23** ⑧⑤ provides a lot of interest, including a brisk limy finish.

Balance Classic range

.....

Sauvignon Blanc ⊘ 🏵 ★★★★ Well-priced range, offering good quality. With fig & hay, **23** ⑧③ lifted by zesty acid, finishes dry.

.....

Cabernet Sauvignon-Merlot ⊘ ★★★★ Unwooded, as all, **22** ⑧③'s classic combo offers satisfying berry-rich enjoyment, streamlined texture. **Pinotage-Shiraz** ⊘ ★★★ Equal blend **22** ⑧② is bright fruited, smoothly succulent. **Shiraz-Merlot** ★★★ Light-textured equal blend, **22** ⑦⑨ is designed for everyday quaffing. **Rosé** ⊘ ★★★ **23** ⑧① is off-dry, perfectly matching the pinotage berry tones. A welcome return, last tasted was **19** ★★★ ⑦⑨. **Chenin Blanc-Colombar** ⊘ ★★★ With apple-rich fruit salad, crisp & dry **23** ⑧① shows how compatible this mix is.

Balance Sparklings
Sweet Temptation Sparkling ⑨ ★★★ From pinotage, **NV** ⑧⓪ rosé is berry-sweet, with low 8% alc. Carbonated, as sibling. **Boldly Brut** ⑨ ★★★ Fruity & unpretentious **NV** ⑧⓪ from sauvignon is just-dry. Early harvest ensures crisp acid & reined-in 12% alc.

Balance Natural Sweet range
Red ⑨ ★★ Fruity lift on **NV** ⑦⑤ from generous 31 g/L sugar & use of 3 fruity varieties, ruby cab, pinotage & chenin. **Rosé** ⑨ ★★ Moderate 26 g/L sugar heightens berry fruit on **NV** ⑧⓪, from chenin with dashes pinotage & muscat. **White** ⑨ ★★★ Tank sample of **NV** ⑦⑧ from majority chenin is modestly sweet, fruity, with floral lift ex drop of muscat.

Big Mouth range
Sassy Red ⊘ ★★★ Unoaked shiraz & pinotage, **NV** ⑧① designed for fruity off-dry quaffing. 3L bag-in-box previewed ex tank, as all these. **Blushing Rosé** ⊘ ★★★ Pale-hued **NV** ⑦⑧'s chenin dominance (3% pinotage) dictates the appley character, a slight sweetness enhancing the effect. **Luscious White** ⊘ ★★★ **NV** ⑧① chenin offering exuberant fruit, a touch of sugar for added appeal. — CR

Location/map: Worcester ▪ Map grid reference: B3 ▪ WO: Western Cape/Coastal ▪ Est/1stB 2006 ▪ Winery, tasting & sales Mon-Fri 10-4.30 ▪ Closed all pub hols ▪ Owner(s) G van der Wath ▪ MD Gert van Wyk ▪ Winemaker(s) Ben Snyman (Dec 2010) & Willie Malan (2002) ▪ Viticulturist(s) Hennie Visser & Hanno van Schalkwyk ▪ ISO 22000, Fairtrade, IPW, WIETA ▪ PO Box 139 Worcester 6849 ▪ marketing@overhex.com ▪ www.overhex.com ▪ **T +27 (0)23-347-5012**

.....

☐ **Overmeer Cellars** see Heineken Beverages
☐ **Over the Mountain** see Seven Springs Vineyards
☐ **Paarl Families** see Kaapse Familie Wingerde
☐ **Paarl Perlé** see Heineken Beverages
☐ **Pack** see Painted Wolf Wines

Packwood Wines
⑨ 🍴 🏠 📷
The cool climate of Plettenberg Bay is reflected in the bright fruit, freshness and notably modest alcohol of these small batches, from the forest-fringed wine and hospitality estate owned by UK émigrés Vicky and

Peter Gent. Viticulturist Vicky and winemaker Sollie Sauerman do their crafting with minimal interference and care for sustainability, evident in the recent switch to solar and the use of recycled bottles.

★★★★ **Pinot Noir** ⓠ Captures variety's vibrant red fruit in an earthy body with a kiss of spice. **19** ⑧⑦ significant improvement on last-made **13** ★★★ ⑧⑴.

★★★★ **Sauvignon Blanc Wooded** Lean, cool-climate **22** ⑧⑥ is taut & edgy, with dusty pebble, grassy herb & lime cordial fruit profile. Ferment/11 months in seasoned barrels held well in check, lending shape & polish without intruding.

★★★★ **Semillon** ⒩ Bursts with varietal charm & character: lanolin, beeswax & steely minerality over gentle acid. 5-day skin contact, ferment/11 months in older oak are reflected in **22** ⑧⑦'s weight, texture & polish. Added allure of modest 9.5% alc.

★★★★ **Cap Classique Brut Nature Rosé** ⓠ After year on lees, pinot noir softens partner sauvignon to yield charming sparkler, desert-dry & searingly fresh in **20** ⑧⑦.

Shiraz ⒩ ★★★★ Pale-hued & demure **21** ⑧③, with pomegranate juiciness, mineral notes & gentle tannins. Year barrique oaking doesn't intrude. **Chardonnay** ⓠ ★★★★ Old-oak-fermented & -aged **20** ⑧④ has many layers of flavour in its elegant body, lemon & orange blossom, lively acid & creamy finish from stirring the lees. Low 10% alc for lunchtime. **Cap Classique Brut Nature Sauvignon Blanc** ⓠ ★★★★ Though trenchant nettle character dominates the leesiness after 12 months ageing, & there's near-zero sugar to act as buffer, **20** ⑧⑤ works as a lipsmacking, steely-fresh pick-me-up. Occasional release: **Gent Cap Classique Brut**. In abeyance: **Blanc de Noir**, **Sauvignon Blanc**. — GdB

Location/WO: Plettenberg Bay ▪ Map: Klein Karoo & Garden Route ▪ Map grid reference: C1 ▪ Est 2006 ▪ 1stB 2009 ▪ Tasting & sales Tue-Fri 10-4 Sat & pub hols 10-3 ▪ Homemade cheese lunches ▪ Small tour groups by appt ▪ Farm produce ▪ Hikes ▪ MTB trails ▪ Country house & self-catering cottages ▪ Wine club ▪ Owner(s) Peter & Vicky Gent ▪ Winemaker(s) Sollie Sauerman ▪ Viticulturist(s) Vicky Gent (Jan 2006) ▪ 380ha/3.5ha (pinot, chard, sauv) ▪ 15t/2,000cs own label 30% red 70% white ▪ PO Box 622 Knysna 6570 ▪ vicky@ packwood.co.za ▪ www.packwood.co.za ▪ **T +27 (0)82-253-9621**

☐ **Paddagang** see Tulbagh Winery
☐ **Painted Dog** see Painted Wolf Wines

Painted Wolf Wines ⓠ ⓜ ⓒ

Jeremy Borg, wife Emma and their 16 co-owners, whose winemaking supports conservation projects throughout southern Africa, notably preservation of the African wild dog aka painted wolf, had the application to use their new cellar granted mere weeks before the start of harvest. Despite minor challenges, they pronounce the experience 'such a joy', and plan to move the white-wine making over to the new facility at Simondium Guild, beside the 'den' (tasting room and office) and a collection of other craft businesses. The 'pack members' focus on warmer-climate viticulture and drought-resistant varieties, and work with select growers in different regions to produce wines that 'respect the individual sites'. Their longer-term aim of being the world's leading conservation wine is strengthened by the recent involvement of Greg Garden, former marketing director of Nedbank, and Chris du Toit, ex Graham Beck CEO.

Lycaon Pictus range

★★★★ **Lycaon Grenache** Nod to the Rhône in aromatic, pepper-spiced **21** ★★★★☆ ⑨② from dryland bushvines. Supple, juicy, wholebunch ferment adds freshness, old barrels & staves in FlexCube ensure polished, balanced drinkability. Wellington WO, as **19** ⑧⑦. No **20**.

★★★★☆ **Lycaon Pinotage** ⓐ Cornucopia of dark spiced fruit in bright yet succulent & rich **21** ⑨③ from Breedekloof. Full but fresh (part bunch-pressed), firm yet undaunting tannins in refined balance courtesy lengthy oaking, 18 months, 40% new.

★★★★☆ **Pictus IX** ⓠ Food-styled Rhône red, **21** ⑨⓪ young but already pleasingly integrated & savoury. Mostly equal syrah & mourvèdre ex organic & heritage vines in Swartland & Wellington.

★★★★☆ **Pictus VIII** ⓠ Refined blend, red & blue berry interplay & yielding tannins, elegant finish. **18** ⑨③ chiefly carignan (31%) & 4 others from old vines in Wellington, Voor Paardeberg & Swartland.

Not tasted: **Lycaon Chenin Blanc**. Discontinued: **Pictus VII**, **Pictus VI**.

The Pack range

★★★★ **Darius Carignan** (Ⓩ) Tasty, different & worth seeking out, **21** (88) array of soft fruit from mature Wellington vines, plus dab grenache noir, wild yeast fermented/4 months in new oak & FlexCube.

★★★★☆ **Black Tip Mourvèdre** Tiny 3 t/ha yield of organic, dry-farmed Swartland grapes & 5% syrah, **22** (90) tad richer than last **20** (90) but alc a modest 12.5%. Smoky dark plum & some savoury notes, svelte tannin & deftly integrated oak, year, some American, 20% new. Deliciously balanced, has potential.

★★★★ **Black Pack Syrah** (NEW) From Walker Bay, **22** (88) leafy red fruit mingled with subtler dark spice. Elegant, light but not insubstantial; dry tannins from part wholebunch natural ferment/year mostly old oak. Dry, peppery conclusion.

★★★★ **Scarlet Syrah** Organic Swartland grapes, **20** ★★★★★ (91) vinified as for Black Pack, plus some gumboot treading to release juice. Effort rewarded with ample perfumed dark berry fruit, spice & freshness. Svelte tannins & meshed oak, further polished by 30 months in bottle. All at pleasing 12.5%. **19** (87) was from Walker Bay.

★★★★☆ **Black Pack Chenin Blanc** (Ⓩ) Stylish **21** (90) confirms uptick in rating of last **19** (90). Intense tropical fruit, rich & creamy yet firm, with subtle citrus extra. Precision & delight above its price point.

★★★★☆ **Solo Roussanne** Same Voor Paardeberg source, previewed **23** (92) echoes previous' floral, stonefruit aromas, clean minerality & silky texture from ferment/8 months in barrel & amphora (60/40). Graceful in its rich fruit purity & length.

★★★★☆ **Lightning Sauvignon Blanc** (Ⓩ) A clay amphora joins 2 older barrels for making of **22** (94), ex Stanford vines on gravel-like soil. Canned pea & white asparagus, 5% semillon adds lemon nuance to reverberating salty palate.

★★★★ **Teardrop Viognier** Pre-bottling, **23** (89) ex high-lying Breedekloof vines as alluring as last. Shows grape's aromatic peach, apricot & almond flavours, nutty opulence from part natural ferment in older oak & polymer 'egg'. Dry, with fresh acid, perfect with spicy/Eastern food.

★★★★ **Peloton Blanc** (Ⓩ) Delicious **19** (87) padded with stonefruit, cream & spice, lovely bone-dry finish. Chenin (59%), viognier & roussanne, part-oaked. Supports Children in the Wilderness upliftment & education programmes, as Rouge. W Cape WO.

Peloton Rouge (Ⓩ) ★★★★ Unusual mix pinotage, shiraz & durif. **19** (84) succulent red berry & cherry fruit, appealing vanilla sweetness. Really interesting & satisfying. WO W Cape. **Lapalala White** (Ⓩ) ★★★★ Tank sample **21** (84) offers intense grassiness leavened by lanolin breadth, touch of old oak. 50/50 sauvignon & semillon ex Breedekloof. Not tasted: **Guillermo Swartland Pinotage**. In abeyance: **Lapalala Red**. Discontinued: **Walker Bay Pinot Noir**, **Breede Valley Pinotage**, **Swartland Syrah**, **Penny Viognier**.

The Den range

★★★★ **Chenin Blanc** (✓) Two vintages tasted, both from Swartland with 10% dab viognier, wild fermented in tank with some supportive oak-staving. **22** ★★★★ (85), now bottled, ample peach & some tropicality, light, fresh & dry. Previewed **23** (86) very similar, though seems tad fresher & brighter.

Cabernet Sauvignon ★★★ Approachable & juicy **22** (82) offers smoky cassis honed by oak stave treatment, easy drinking with family & friends. **Pinotage** (Ⓩ) ★★★ Chocolate aroma, baked plums & vanilla gloss on **22** (80), a pleasing combo of fruit & oak characters. **Shiraz** (Ⓩ) ★★★★ Bright berries, plums & cocoa in **21** (83) from Wellington & Stanford, with 12% mourvèdre. Polished & savoury, more oomphy than last. **Pinotage Rosé** ★★★ Usual tangy, lipsmacking style in **23** (82). Blush of pink, dry, fresh & food friendly, with piquant cranberry juiciness, ready to quaff at a restrained 12.3% alc, as other whites here. WO Paarl. **Sauvignon Blanc** ★★★★ Stellenbosch fruit with dash chenin in **23** (84). Crunchy apple freshness, green fig & light lees shading make this a pleasant quaffer or tablemate.

Cape 'Hunting' Blends

In abeyance: **Madach**. — MW

Location: Simondium ▪ Map: Franschhoek ▪ Map grid reference: C7 ▪ WO: Coastal/Swartland/Breedekloof/Western Cape/Wellington/Walker Bay/Voor Paardeberg/Paarl/Stellenbosch ▪ Est/1stB 2007 ▪ Tasting, wine by the glass & sales: Wed-Fri 9-5 Sat/Sun 10-5 Mon/Tue by appt; pub hols (seasonal) please call ahead ▪ Fee various; 5% of sales donated to conservation & social upliftment ▪ The Guild Bistro ▪ Soul Barrel Brewing ▪ Stillman Distillery ▪ Fanglasstic Glass Studio ▪ Owner(s) Jeremy & Emma Borg, & 16 'pack members' ▪ Cellarmaster(s) Jeremy Borg, with Fred Loffner ▪ 20ha (grenache, mourv, ptage, shiraz, viog) ▪ 30t/18,000cs

own label 75% red 20% white 5% rosé ▪ Other export brands: Jemma ▪ Simondium Guild, R45, Simondium
▪ sales@paintedwolfwines.com ▪ www.paintedwolfwines.com ▪ **T +27 (0)21-863-2492**

☐ **Palesa Fairtrade** *see* Daschbosch
☐ **Pandora's Box** *see* Nicholson Smith
☐ **Papenkuils** *see* Merwida Wines (Huis Te Merwede)
☐ **Papillon** *see* Van Loveren Family Vineyards
☐ **Pardus** *see* Leopard's Leap Family Vineyards

Parow Brandy

Afrikaans rapper Jack Parow is a keen brandy drinker, like his 'fan demographic'. 'Brandy should be a fun and
edgy drink' the thinking goes, so the packaging is wild and funny and brilliant. The contents of both the
Parow potstill and newer, equally distinctive but less edgy sibling are produced by Oude Molen in Grabouw.
Black Bull Brandy ⓠ ★★★ Hard to challenge alliterative back label description: 'big, bad, bold &
boisterous'. Fruity too, but not too sweet. Blended brandy ⑧① touch cruder than its partner in label design
& character. Needs a mixer. **Parow Brandy** ⓠ ★★★★ 30% potstill brandy ⑧④ from colombard & chenin
(as Bull), smooth, flavourful & unfiery enough to sip solo. Mostly destined for mixing, however. — TJ
Location: Cape Town ▪ Closed to public ▪ Owner(s) Natures Own Beverages (Pty) Ltd ▪ Brandy master Kobus
Gelderblom (Oude Molen Distillery) ▪ PO Box 369 Bonnievale 6730 ▪ info@parowbrandy.co.za ▪ www.
parowbrandy.co.za ▪ **T +27 (0)23-616-2010**

☐ **Pas de Nom** *see* Beau Constantia

Paserene   ⓠ ⑪

Luxurious wine, for connoisseurs and collectors to cellar and invest in, is the intent of owners Martin Smith
and Ndabe Mareda at their boutique winery with two loci: Franschhoek, where the elegant glass-and-steel
tasting and conference/function venue is, and some vines, to be augmented with chardonnay; and Tulbagh,
where the vineyard will soon feature rare carmenère. Noteworthy among the ranges is The Shiner, whose
presentation includes a serialised mystery novel by Martin and famed crime fiction author Deon Meyer.

Paserene range

★★★★☆ **Marathon** ⓐ Regal **20** ⑨③ from cab & 40% petit verdot offers deep, complex flavours of
cassis, leather, dried herbs & flowers, graphite in a supple structure. Excellent depth & length, finishing on
a balsamic note. Barrel fermented/22 months older oak, unfined. Made to last. Tulbagh vines, as Union.

★★★★☆ **Union** ⓠ Changes to 100% syrah for expressive **19** ⑨④, glossy dark fruit, loads of spice, some
dried herbs, curvaceous lines with just enough tannin for food, cellaring. Mostly seasoned oak.

★★★★☆ **Chardonnay** ⓐ Rich yet beautifully structured & textured **20** ⑨③ from Elgin has unfolding
layers of fruit & oak-derived flavours, lemon crème brûlée, poached quince & brioche, coated with vanilla
from 30% new wood, 16 months. Reined-in 13% alc part of the elegance. Only 240 cases that will keep.

The Shiner range

★★★★ **Red** Rich, rounded **NV** ⑧⑨, equal cab & petit verdot, 4% carmenère, brooding dark berries,
fynbos & chocolate. Oak well-judged (50% new, 22 months) & in good balance with fruit & spice.

★★★★ **White** ⓠ Mainly sauvignon, with semillon, unoaked. Gooseberries, greengage, touch of lime,
18 ⑧⑨ is sleek & crisply dry.

Elements range

★★★★ **Midnight** From cab, **21** ⑧⑨ red & black plum & vanilla spice from 10% new oak, 22 months.
Gentle handling gives smooth, juicy tannins, fresh fruit expression & lifted berry crunch on finish.

★★★★ **Rosie** Rosé has lovely melange of apples & red berries, with freshness, balance & lively flavour
taking **22** ⑧⑦ a notch up on last **19** ★★★☆ ⑧⑤. From chardonnay & mourvèdre, year in older oak.

★★★★ **Bright** Franschhoek chardonnay shines with lightly seasoned baked apple, fresh pear & warm
cinnamon. **21** ⑧⑨ good complexity & intensity before a lingering spice-laden finish. Older oak, year.

★★★★ **Emerald** ⓠ Striking labels in this range, names to capture the wine styles. Pure, bright, focused
19 ⑧⑧ sauvignon fruit, minerality & a green flavour element. 50% oak more texture than taste.

Dark ⓥ ★★★★ Apt name, **18** ⑧④ richly fruited shiraz despite svelte structure (12.5% alcohol). Sweet spice notes from older oak; succulent, ends savoury. — WB

Location/map: Franschhoek ▪ Map grid reference: C4 ▪ WO: Western Cape/Tulbagh/Elgin/Franschhoek ▪ Est/1stB 2013 ▪ Tasting Mon-Sun 10–5; pub hols (seasonal) please call ahead ▪ Small-plate offering ▪ Wine club ▪ Conference & function facility (up to 20 pax) ▪ Owner(s) Martin Smith & Ndabe Mareda ▪ Cellarmaster(s)/winemaker(s) Martin Smith (Jan 2013) ▪ Viticulturist(s) Martin Smith ▪ 60t/1,400cs own label 60% red 40% white ▪ Farm 1665, on R45 Franschhoek 7690 ▪ info@paserene.co.za ▪ www.paserene.co.za ▪ **T +27 (0)21-876-2714**

Patatsfontein

Three Stellenbosch friends own this boutique wine brand, 'Sweet Potato Spring', which is also the name of the Montagu farm and source of the white wines. Partner and winemaker Reenen Borman vinifies in his family's Boschkloof cellar. The distinctive syrah, grown by Jozua Joubert on his Karibib farm close by, is bunch fermented in concrete and unoaked. 'Sugarland is a unique combination of vineyard and technique,' Reenen explains. 'Some vineyards are receptive to wholebunch, others prefer addition of some stems, while concrete preserves the aromatics.' Ongoing success attests to Reenen's deep understanding of the variety.

★★★★★ **Sons of Sugarland Syrah** ⓐ Same Stellenbosch vines, same wholebunch ferment/ageing in concrete only, **22** ⑨⑥ same stellar quality. Penetrating scents of pepper spice & dark berries, great energy in supple, sweet fruit, crunchy grape tannins & resonating length. Will age, if allowed. 12.9% alc.

★★★★☆ **Patatsfontein Steen** ⓐ Sleek, with early harmony between lees-weighted texture & steely tension affording tapered length in **22** ⑨③. Time should give greater expression to present quiet pear tones. Spontaneous ferment, older oak 10 months.

★★★★☆ **Patatsfontein Wit Versnit** Was 'Patatsblanc'. **22** ⑨① bit more sedate than last, without loss of individuality; maintains colombard's wild herb, chenin's juiciness, overall fruit-lifting freshness & concluding grip. Older-oak fermented, on lees 10 months.

Discontinued: **Patatsfontein Doortjie**. — AL

Location: Stellenbosch ▪ WO: Montagu/Stellenbosch ▪ 1stB 2014 ▪ Closed to public ▪ Owner(s) Fritz Schoon, Reenen Borman & Henk Kotze ▪ Winemaker(s) Reenen Borman ▪ 1,500cs own label ▪ reenen@boschkloofwines.com

☐ **Patina** see Boekenhoutskloof Winery

Paul Clüver Family Wines   ⓥ ⑪ ⊚ ⓖ

Elgin's oldest chardonnay vineyard was planted on the pioneering home of Paul Clüver Wines in 1987, and the Seven Flags Chardonnay now bears the Certified Heritage Vineyard seal. This and the other great Burgundian variety, pinot noir, are the focus here, with the 'fervent commitment' of both MD Paul Clüver jnr and cellarmaster Andries Burger, who married into the 2nd-generation of winemaking Clüvers, making this a fully family affair. Andries has now added concrete 'eggs' to the range of large oak foudres and Burgundian barrels in his cellar. Beyond it, on the varied slopes of the estate are substantial vineyards, as well as 1,000 ha under conservation, further expressing the values of what is proudly claimed as 'a beacon for the integral relationship between wine, family, and sustainability'.

CWG Auction range

★★★★☆ **The Wagon Trail Chardonnay** ⓐ ⓦ From Elgin's oldest chardonnay vines, planted 1987. Intense pure fruit on **22** ⑨④ allows for 50% new oak. Piercing freshness gives elegant austerity, tempered by rich generosity & silky texture. Like Seven Flags, no yeast inoculation, on lees 9 months, no malo to retain natural acidity, thus giving great vibrancy.

Estate range

★★★★ **Pinot Noir** ⊘ Ripe strawberry fragrance on **22** ★★★★★ ⑨⓪, note of undergrowth adding complexity to persisting sweet-fruited charm. Notably more depth than Village version. Fresh succulence & tannic touch make for good balance. Altogether moreish, even in youth. Year oak, 16% new, gives support, adds texture. **21** ⑧⑧ a little leaner.

★★★★☆ **Seven Flags Pinot Noir** ⓐ Only best barrels for this flagship red, & best years - no **19** made. **20** ⑨④ part natural ferment; the whole in oak 12 months, 37% new, which shows in youth. Plenty of red & darker cherry & berry character. Silky, with depth & complexity & fine integrated acidity balancing some lightly grippy tannins. Still young; well worth keeping.

★★★★☆ **Chardonnay** ⚫ More intense character than on Village version in **21** ★★★★★ ⑨⑤. All the chardonnays spontaneously fermented, this one in 26% new oak barrels, giving a nutty element to the aroma also noted on **20** ⑨④. On lees 9 months. Good depth of citrusy fruit with the oak integrated. Creamy texture well cut by an infusing ripe acidity. Should still develop well.

★★★★☆ **Seven Flags Chardonnay** ⚫ ⚫ From estate's most mature vineyards. Complex aromas & flavours, including citrus & stonefruit, still-flourishing oaky notes on very youthful **22** ⑨④, but these will harmonise in a few years. Intense & rounded, with fine, luscious acidic thread; lingering lemon-lime finish. All the chardonnays around 12.8% alc. Last tasted was **20** ⑨③.

★★★★☆ **Village Chardonnay** ⊘ Most modest of estate's basic trio is not without seriousness, but most easily delightful in youth, partly thanks to only older oak being used, along with small portions in tank & concrete adding to purity & freshness. Beautifully balanced, fresh & succulent **22** ⑨⓪.

★★★★ **Riesling** ⊘ Charming, easy balance of off-dry softness (17.5 g/L sugar) & fresh acidity on **23** ⑧⑦, with notes of stonefruit, apple & pineapple. Partly fermented/2 months in large oak vat. 11.6% alc part of the pleasant approachability.

★★★★☆ **Sauvignon Blanc** ⊘ Succulent, poised & handsome **23** ⑨② is also beautifully fresh. 5% lightly oaked semillon addition adds to the breadth & interest, but the stony minerality & passionfruit intensity is all sauvignon. A fine & vibrant cool-climate example.

Village Pinot Noir ⊘ ★★★★ Mostly younger vines, giving bright red-berry character, also a lightness (almost leanness) on **22** ⑧⑤. Undistinguished, but pleasing & balanced, fruit untrammelled by oaking, various size barrels & vat, none new. Not tasted: **Riesling Noble Late Harvest**. — TJ

Location/map/WO: Elgin ▪ Map grid reference: C2 ▪ Est 1896 ▪ 1997 1st vintage in own cellar ▪ Tasting centre open 7 days a week, Mon-Thu 8-5 Fri 8-4 Sat/Sun 9-4; pub hols (seasonal) please call ahead ▪ Restaurant open daily, dinner Fri evenings ▪ See website or social media for special events ▪ Larger groups by appt only 7+ people ▪ Cluver Jack craft cider ▪ Owner(s) Clüver family ▪ Cellarmaster(s) Andries Burger (Nov 1996) ▪ Winemaker(s) Anné van Heerden (Dec 2016) ▪ Viticulturist(s) Christiaan Cloete (Dec 2019) ▪ 80ha (pinot, chard, riesling, sauv) ▪ WWF-SA Conservation Champion ▪ Conservation area (part of Kogelberg Biosphere UNESCO heritage site) ▪ PO Box 48 Grabouw 7160 ▪ info@cluver.com ▪ www.cluver.com ▪ **T +27 (0)21-844-0605 Restaurant Dineplan or +27 (0)21-844-0607**

☐ **Paul de Villiers** see Landskroon Wines
☐ **Paulina's Reserve** see Rickety Bridge Winery

Paul René Cap Classique ⓛ

From modest beginnings in the mid-2010s in an underground store sometimes used for processing honey, this classically styled sparkling-wine brand based on family farm Wonderfontein is flying high, on the wings of careful crafting by Henk van Niekerk and Stefan Bruwer, conducive Robertson terroir and creative packaging designed by Henk's wife Monique, featuring 'treasure chest' cartons and stylish 'handbags'. Ideally sited pinot noir and chardonnay, bunch pressing and 'good lees ageing' form the foundation, with tweaks such as maturing the basewine in new barrels from vintage 2023 being added to keep raising the quality.

★★★★☆ **Brut Rosé** Classically styled **19** ⑨② sparkler from 75% pinot noir & chardonnay has creamy-salty substance with convincing berry fruit. 42 months on lees add chalky texture, borne on vigorous mousse. Poised, with deliciously piercing acid, just misses stature of exceptional **18** ⑨④.

★★★★☆ **Brut** ⚫ Impressive chardonnay bubbly, **19** ⑨④ follows recent stellar form, with sweetly aromatic yeasty-bready bouquet, honeysuckle & almond highlights, silky mousse & pinpoint acid. Balanced & assured, sleek from 44 months on lees, should improve several years.

★★★★ **Nectar** Pleasantly creamy **20** ⑧⑦ sparkling is 75% pinot noir with chardonnay. Overtly sweet at 37.8 g/L sugar, but retains appealing shortbread notes, fullness from 36 months on lees, clean but fairly brief finish. No **18**, **19**. — GdB

Location/map: Robertson ▪ Map grid reference: B6 ▪ WO: Western Cape ▪ Est ca 1884 ▪ Tasting Mon-Fri 9-4 Sat/Sun & pub hols by appt only ▪ Sales Mon-Fri 9-4.30 Sat 9-1 ▪ Tour groups ▪ Owner(s) Paul René Marais ▪ Winemaker(s) Stefan Bruwer & Henk van Niekerk ▪ (pinot, chard) ▪ PO Box 4 Robertson 6705 ▪ admin@paulrenemcc.co.za ▪ www.paulrenemcc.co.za ▪ **T +27 (0)23-626-2212**

Paul Roos Farming

An educational empowerment project involving the 5th-generation Roos brothers and grape growers on their farm Rust en Vrede in Stellenbosch, who in 2015 launched this range with a local winemaker to support the rebuilding of a crèche for the children of estate personnel. Rugby legend and educator Paul Roos was born on the property in 1880, making his name the perfect choice for the branding.

★★★★☆ **Die Filantroop** ⓟ Bright aromas on **17** ⑨① blend of 72% shiraz with cab & pinotage. 13.5% alc & touch richer & riper than last, but properly dry & still a feeling of restraint.

★★★★☆ **Susan** ⓟ This **16** ⑨① a once-off tribute to Susan Roos, with Filantroop's varieties but cab now in the lead (64%). Perhaps more immediately charming but still a very serious structure.

★★★★☆ **Die Skoolhoof** ⓟ Chenin with 18% chardonnay adding a lemony note in **17** ⑨②, but maintaining distinctive earthy tinge to the good fruit. Lively & fresh, with fine acidity. Native yeast, as all.— TJ

Location/WO: Stellenbosch ▪ Map: Helderberg ▪ Map grid reference: C1 ▪ Est 2008 ▪ 1stB 2014 ▪ Tasting, sales & cellar tours by appt ▪ Owner(s) Tjuks & Johan Roos, Paul Roos Farming Trust ▪ Winemaker(s) Ricardo Adams (1998) ▪ Viticulturist(s) Piet Adams (1974), with Jan Julius ▪ 24ha/18ha (cab, merlot, ptage, shiraz, chard, chenin) ▪ 7t/±800cs own label 40% red 60% white ▪ IPW, GlobalGAP, WIETA ▪ PO Box 397 Stellenbosch 7599 ▪ info@paulrooswine.com ▪ www.paulrooswine.com ▪ **T +27 (0)21-855-3628**

Paulus Wine Co

Paul Jordaan, Sadie Family Wines winemaker, and partner Pauline Roux, a French vigneronne (see Vino pH for her other vinous collaboration), continue their focused exploration of chenin blanc. The winemaking, designed to express their vineyards as clearly as possible, will get a tweak with the 2023 vintage: partial ferment and maturing in an egg-shaped concrete vessel for Bosberaad, 'adding another dimension'. Grapes from another Paardeberg vineyard will also go into that wine. Basically, says Pauline, we 'apply what we are learning year after year, and just keep on repeating that process... Learn, apply, repeat!'

★★★★★ **Bartas** These chenins made identically: wholebunch natural ferment in old oak; on lees 10 months. Difference is vineyard - this an old Helderberg block. **22** ⑨④ delicately full aromas & flavours, a hint of fragrant floral charm to the fruit. Fresh & pure, silky grip. Also in magnum.

★★★★★ **Bosberaad** From 40+ year old Paardeberg chenin bushvines. **22** ⑨④ presents as uncompromisingly dry & firm but not severe at all. Touch fuller & richer than Bartas, with great vitality & understated intensity of aroma & long-lingering flavour (dried herbs, dried peach) & stoniness. Again, lovely silkiness. These both eminently ageworthy.— TJ

Location: Paarl ▪ WO: Stellenbosch/Swartland ▪ Est 2017 ▪ 1stB 2018 ▪ Closed to public ▪ Owner(s)/winemaker(s) Paul Jordaan & Pauline Roux ▪ 7t/900cs own label 100% white ▪ Old Paarl Rd, Paarl 7646 ▪ hello@pauluswineco.com ▪ **T +27 (0)81-388-1670**

Paul Wallace Wines ⓟ ⌂

Top viticultural adviser Paul Wallace and wife Nicky launched this small family venture 20 years ago by planting vines on their farm Wallovale in Elgin and unveiling a standalone malbec from bought-in fruit. The accent on Bordeaux grapes continues (Nicky's passion for 'her' Bordeaux blend a possible factor), as younger son Bobby now joins the business, bringing extensive area-experience in both winemaking and viticulture. 'Letting the fruit shine and the wine be a charming expression of its terroir' has earned them critical success and a loyal following, and is likely to keep serving them well, with Paul remaining 'king of the vineyard' - and ongoing hope for an angel investor to fund a longed-for red-wine cellar. See also Off The Record Wines.

★★★★☆ **Black Dog Malbec** ⓟ Lots going on in dark-toned, elegant **19** ⑨⓪ from 3 blocks, all managed uniquely. Small portion concrete 'egg', rest older barrique; layered fruit, liquorice, herbaceous nuance, supported by smooth-textured succulence. Cellarworthy, as always.

★★★★ **Brave Heart Pinot Noir** ⓟ Delicious, with admirable typicity, from **20** ★★★★★ ⑨⓪'s light ruby to its elegance (13% alc) & red cherry-berry fruit, having more grip than **19** ⑧⑧. Oaking well-judged, 10 months, adds gentle umami notes.

★★★★☆ **Crackerjack** Merlot-led 4-part Bordeaux blend, **20** ⑨⓪ contains 18 months of 23% new oak without suffocating fruit. Piquant berry mix, sturdy tannin reserves for cellaring but already drinking smoothly. **19** ⑨⓪ spent longer in cask.

★★★★☆ **Reflection Chardonnay** Ⓐ In the groove hewn by previous, citrus styled **22** Ⓨ boasts orange & mandarin in plush, upholstered finery; 10 months in barrel (20% new) the perfect accessory, adding interest & savouriness yet allowing fruit to shine & impress.

★★★★ **Little Flirt Sauvignon Blanc** Shows Elgin's fresh tension, crunchy green apple & passionfruit, but **23** Ⓧ adds a flinty, salty seam to mix. Racy acidity tempered by extended skin contact & 8 months on lees which broaden complexity. The quintessential energizer! No **22**.

★★★★★ **The Nix Noble Late Harvest** Ⓐ Back with **21** Ⓨ after a hiatus since tangerine **17** Ⓨ, consistently botrytised sauvignon, latest in older barrels 16 months. Vividly perfumed, candied lemon peel & rich honeysuckle profile. Stern acidity gives intense, mouthfilling sweetness a tangy offset. 375 ml. — DS

Location/map/WO: Elgin ▪ Map grid reference: C3 ▪ Est 2004 (vineyard)/2013 (brand) ▪ 1stB 2004 ▪ Tasting room open Saturdays 10.30–5, other days by appt or when open sign is displayed ▪ Tasting fee R90, waived on purchase ▪ Self-catering accommodation ▪ Owner(s) Paul & Nicky Wallace ▪ Winemaker(s) Bobby Wallace ▪ Viticulturist(s) Paul Wallace ▪ 25ha/12.5ha (cab f, malbec, pinot, chard, sauv) ▪ 120t/7,000cs own label 60% red 40% white ▪ IPW ▪ PO Box 141 Elgin 7180 ▪ nicky@paulwallacewines.co.za ▪ www.paulwallacewines.co.za ▪ **T +27 (0)21-848-9744/+27 (0)83-255-1884/+27 (0)82-572-1406**

☐ **Peacock Wild Ferment** *see* False Bay Vineyards

☐ **Pearce Predhomme** *see* Radford Dale

☐ **Pearly Bay** *see* KWV Wines

☐ **Pecan Stream** *see* Waterford Estate

☐ **Pella** *see* Super Single Vineyards

☐ **Perdebee** *see* Groote Post Vineyards

☐ **Perdebee Wines** *see* Groote Post Vineyards

Perdeberg Wines   Ⓨ Ⓨ Ⓐ Ⓐ

Founded in 1941, this extensive Paarl winery stresses its advantages in slogan and range names, notably The Dry Land Collection drawing attention to unirrigated vineyards that predominate in the owner-farmers' holdings, supported by new viticulturist Johann Smit. 'Tough conditions,' says Albertus Louw, who heads the winemaking team, but with 'sweet reward': the smaller berries that result give higher flavour concentration, he says. Meanwhile, the popular Cellar Collection is having its packaging refreshed. As for the trademarked phrase 'the home of chenin blanc', the claim is supported by the numerous varietal expressions noted below, with a range of stylistic and quality distinctions. Amenities for visitors to the winery are not neglected either.

Iconic Wines range

★★★★☆ **Rex Equus** Ⓧ Dark-fruited **19** Ⓨ blends best barrels of malbec & cab with merlot & petit verdot. Plenty of flavour, but also a sense of restraint & even elegance, oak supportive, 14.1% alc in balance. Approachable in youth but should keep a good many years. WO Paarl, as Cape Blend.

★★★★☆ **Endura Winemaker's Selection Cape Blend** Ⓐ Just over half pinotage in **20** Ⓨ, with cab & malbec. Enticing, complex aromas, then a lighter-feeling freshness & elegance on palate, not at expense of juicy flavour. With rounded but informing tannins, 13.7% alc, & supportive but unobtrusive oaking, well balanced & should mature for a good many years, as last-tasted **18** Ⓨ.

★★★★☆ **Endura Single Vineyard Chenin Blanc** From Swartland single site on top of Paardeberg, **21** Ⓨ made in mix of tank, oak & clay pot, as last-made **19** ★★★★ Ⓨ, but this fresher. Ripe peachy, thatch aromas & lingering, intense flavours, richly textured, firmly built & dry. Well balanced & harmonious.

The Dry Land Collection

★★★★ **Conqueror Cabernet Sauvignon** As usual, **21** Ⓨ offers classic blackcurrant & cedar, good depth of flavour. Ripe & rich, lingering, but it carries its 14.4% alc without being too imposing, 18 months oak supportive & integrated. Coastal WO.

★★★★ **Resolve Pinotage** Forward aromas & attractive clean fruitiness on **21** Ⓨ, assertive but not too big & bold at 14.1% alc. Sweet ripe flavours well supported by oak & smooth, firm tannins, for a bright, juicy whole.

★★★★ **Tenacious Shiraz** Warm, ripe aromas & flavours on **20** ★★★★ Ⓨ tinged with tobacco & spice from 20% new oak. Decently structured, with same gently firm grip as **19** Ⓨ, but touch too sweet for seriousness, the flavours without much concentration. 14% alc.

★★★★ **Joseph's Legacy 20** ⑧⑥ blends 60% shiraz with grenache, mourvèdre & cinsaut, attains some complexity & interest. Richness & power of ripe 14.5% alc carried well, though plushness is there & finish rather sweet. Easygoing but effective grip allows for pleasing early drinking.

★★★★ **Courageous Old Vine Barrel Fermented Chenin Blanc** ⊛ Ripe, generous dried peachiness on aromatic **22** ⑧⑥, fermented/10 months in oak, which adds supple broadness & spice. Ready appeal will not be much diminished by enriching, smoothing bit of sweetness. 14% alc.

★★★★☆ **Rossouw's Heritage** ⊘ Marsanne joins apricotty viognier & floral grenache blanc in support of chenin (53%) in delicious, gently perfumed **21** ⑨①, 30% oaked portion not detracting from light-feeling, fresh & pure-flavoured charm. Hard to resist now, but should mature well a few years. 13.5% alc. WO W Cape.

★★★★☆ **Longevity Natural Sweet Chenin Blanc** ⊗ Rich gold hue on gorgeously decadent **19** ⑨②, packed with aroma & flavour, & silky, but well enough balanced that the sweetness is far from cloying in its contribution to the overall deliciousness. Light oak maturation & bottle age harmonise. 375 ml.

★★★★ **Fortitude Fortified Chenin Blanc** ⊗ Grape & pineapple notes dominate succulent flavoursomeness of **21** ⑧⑦. Richly sweet & velvety but well enough balanced to be not excessively so. 500 ml.

The Vineyard Collection

★★★★ **Grenache Blanc** ⊘ Delicate, interesting aromas & restrained but pleasing flavour on **23**
★★★☆ ⑧⑤. As with **22** ⑧⑥, 30% oaked portion & lees ageing add to breadth, but this has notably sweeter balance while retaining freshness.

Cinsault ⊘ ★★★☆ Attractively lively, red-fruited & aromatic **22** ⑧③, with just 30% old-oaked, remainder in stainless steel to retain freshness that's part of its lightly fruity charm. Nice bit of grip too. **Grenache Noir** ⒩ⓔⓦ ⊘ ★★★☆ The most interesting of the reds in this range, perfumed **22** ⑧⑤ does not have intensity, but the red & darker fruit is balanced by elegant structure & 13.5% alc. **Malbec** ★★★ Forward dark fruitiness on **22** ⑧②. Fairly lightweight flavours but pleasant drinking. Structured more by very bright acidity than modest tannins, as with many of these reds. **Pinotage** ⊘ ★★★☆ Rather more stuffing on this easygoing **21** ⑧③ than the Cellar version. Balanced, juicy grippiness with sweet fruit. 14.3% alc. WO Coastal, as Pinot-Chardonnay, Grenache Blanc, Rosé Reserve. **Pinot Noir-Chardonnay** ★★★ Aromatic, flavourful, lightly rosy **23** ⑧② has red berry character from the 70% pinot. Bright, creamy & smooth. **Chenin Blanc** ⊘ ★★★★ Lots of guava character on ripely flavourful, attractively laid-back, fresh & balanced (though not very interesting!) **23** ⑧④. **Sauvignon Blanc** ★★★ Tropical & citrus notes on **23** ⑧②, full of typically straightforward aroma & flavour. Brightly tart as usual. Cape Coast WO. **Méthode Cap Classique Pinot Noir Rosé Reserve** ⊘ ★★★★ Copper-tinged pink **20** ⑧③ sparkler offers modest berry charm on nose & pretty flavours. Relaxed, fairly dry. **Méthode Cap Classique Chenin Blanc** ⊘ ⊛ ★★★☆ Some apple as well as varietal dried peach & melon on **20** ⑧④ bubbly. Crisp, fresh & dry-finishing but pleasantly, tastily fruity. 18 months on lees, as rosé version. WO Agter Paarl.

Natuurlik Organic range

Chenin Blanc ⊗ ★★★★ Quiet but more interesting & characterful varietal aromas & flavours on **22** ⑧⑤ than on Cellar & Vineyard versions. Organic yeast. Succulent stony note to the peachy fruit. WO W Cape.

Perdeberg Cellar Collection

. . . .

Chenin Blanc ☺ ★★★ Like previous, **23** ⑧② the flavourful & generously balanced bargain you'd expect from a chenin specialist. Ripely delicious, softly textured.

. . . .

Cabernet Sauvignon ⊘ ★★★ Effective varietal blackcurrant aroma & flavour on rich but gently grippy **22** ⑧②. As all reds in range, lightly oaked & showing some sweetness. **Merlot** ★★★ Ripe fruitcake notes on undemanding **22** ⑦⑨, though it's a little thin. 14%+ alc, as all these reds. **Pinotage** ⊘ ★★★ Aromatic & flavourful **22** ⑧①, fruity & juicy, all in bright balance with a modest structure. **Shiraz** ★★★ Friendly, soft-hearted **22** ⑦⑨, with acidic grip to cope with the sweet fruit. **Pinotage Rosé** ⊘ ★★★ Gleaming salmon-pink **23** ⑧② is full of berry flavour, with a rich velvety smoothness dry & light enough at 12.7% alc to make a good food companion. **Sauvignon Blanc** ★★★ Forward, full-flavoured tropicality on **23** ⑦⑨. Firmly crisp acidity but nicely rounded & not too dry, for easy drinking. Coastal WO for these. Discontinued: **Sparkling Rosé, Sparkling White**.

Perdeberg Soft Smooth range

Rosé ★★ Pinotage gives berries on sweetish **23** (72), muscat gives light grapey perfume. **White ★★** Mostly chenin on off-dry **23** (73), but muscat adds perfumed grapey character. **Red ★★** Soft & smooth indeed, with forward ripeness & sweet finish on **21** (72). 14% alc. WO W Cape for these & Can Red.

Perdeberg Soft Smooth Can range

Red ★★ Sweetish, soft, unoaked **21** (72) gives in with no resistance. Discontinued: **Rosé, White**.

Lighthearted Lower In Alcohol range

Pinotage ★★★ Lightly oaked **21** (77) has attractive perfume, nice fruit weight, very light grip & bright acidity. Cleverly avoids insipidity at 9.5% alc. Pretty packaging too, as all these. **Cinsault Rosé** ⊘ **★★★** The most successful of this range, with a pleasing forward cranberry fruitiness on **23** (78). Full, flavoursome, bright & nearly dry. From Paarl, like Pinotage & Chenin. Others WO W Cape. **Chenin Blanc ★★★** Clean, tight green boiled sweet character on **23** (77). 8.8% alc & nearly dry. Some fruit weight gives substance. **Sparkling Rosé** (NEW) **★★★** Pinotage gives berry notes to pale salmon-pink **NV** (77), & a sweetly simple charm. 9.2% alc. **Sparkling White** (NEW) **★★★** Off-dry **NV** (77) mostly from sauvignon, but it's muscat that dominates. Flavourful & fresh, & a touch insipid. 9.6% alc. — TJ

Location/map: Paarl ▪ Map grid reference: B2 ▪ WO: Paarl/Coastal/Western Cape/Paardeberg/Cape Coast/Agter Paarl ▪ Est 1941 ▪ 1stB 1942 ▪ Tasting & sales Mon-Fri 9-5 Sat/Sun 10-5 ▪ Closed Good Fri, Dec 25/26 & Jan 1 ▪ Light meals, book for groups of 10+ ▪ Child friendly ▪ Eat @ Perdeberg restaurant open Wed-Sat 9-4 Sun/pub hols 10-5 ▪ Function venue (up to 200 pax) ▪ Weddings ▪ Conferences ▪ Tutored tastings ▪ Wine pairings ▪ Wine club ▪ Owner(s) 27 shareholders ▪ Cellarmaster(s) Albertus Louw (Oct 2008) ▪ Winemaker(s) Andri le Roux (Jun 2019), Natalie Kühne (Dec 2015), Lodewyk Botha (Oct 2017) & Arthur Basson (Dec 2017) ▪ Viticulturist(s) Johann Smit (May 2023) ▪ 6,000ha/2,564ha (cab, cinsaut, merlot, ptage, shiraz, chard, chenin, sauv) ▪ 23,000t/300,000cs own label 60% red 40% white ▪ Fairtrade, HACCP, IPW, Organic, WIETA ▪ PO Box 214 Paarl 7620 ▪ info@perdeberg.co.za ▪ www.perdeberg.co.za ▪ **T +27 (0)21-869-8244**

☐ **Perfect Couple** see Simonsvlei International

Peter Bayly Wines   ℗

In Groenfontein Valley just north of Calitzdorp, small-scale vintners Peter and Yvonne Bayly grow Portuguese varieties exclusively, including recently planted white grape albariño, as these are 'best suited to our shale and quartz terrain', and they strive to make 'fine wines with minimal intervention'.

★★★★☆ Peter Bayly III (℗) Unfortified trio of Portuguese grapes, mostly touriga, with souzão & tinta. Aromas of mince pie & raisin give expectation of rich flavour & high alc, but **17 ★★★** (80)'s palate leaner, less generous than **16** (90). Both older-oaked 18 months.

★★★★ Cape Vintage (℗) Charmingly packaged **15 ★★★★** (85)'port' similar specs - touriga-led, 18 months old 500L oak, 19% alc - but smooth & comforting, ready now, with less fire & complexity than last-tasted **12** (88). 375 ml, as White.

Cape White (℗) **★★★★** Latest **NV** (85)'port' from chenin rings the changes: more tawny in colour & style than last, nutty & umami characters vs golden raisins & candied peel. Not tasted: **Chenin Blanc**. Discontinued: **Tinta Barocca**. — CvZ

Location/WO: Calitzdorp ▪ Map: Klein Karoo & Garden Route ▪ Map grid reference: B5 ▪ Est 2002 ▪ 1stB 2004 ▪ Tasting, sales & tours by appt ▪ Owner(s) Peter Bayly Wines (Pty) Ltd ▪ Winemaker(s)/viticulturist(s) Peter Bayly ▪ 7.9ha/1.4ha (souzão, tinta, touriga, albariño) ▪ ±8t/±1,320cs own label ▪ PO Box 187 Calitzdorp 6660 ▪ info@baylys.co.za ▪ www.peterbayly.co.za ▪ **T +27 (0)44-213-3702/+27 (0)83-457-5037**

☐ **Peter Clarke Collection** see PaardenKloof

Peter Falke Wines   ℗ ⑪

Fascinating contrast between the Old World elegance of the chandeliered tasting venue and the powerful, full-bodied New World wines in visitors' glasses at this German-owned winery on the farm Groenvlei, part of the original 17th-century land grant on the Helderberg's north slope. But the estate forms part of the famed 'golden triangle' of Stellenbosch, admired for its muscular wines, so winemaker-viticulturist Werner Schrenk and advisor Louis Nel are simply expressing the terroir, albeit at a high octane. Said locale, geared especially for alfresco tasting in summer, is gaining winter allure with 'a nice fireplace and cosy seating'.

Signature range

★★★★☆ **Kailani Cabernet Sauvignon** ⓐ Ever-improving premium bottling shines brightly in superior vintage, **19** ⓞ94 deep, dense & textured, blackcurrant fruit accented with earthy mineral, sanguine & ferrous notes. 22 months in barrel, 20% new, 30 more in bottle, yet demands more time.

★★★★ **Alani Syrah** ⓩ Fine ripe cherry & cranberry fruit, hefty tannin backbone, satisfying savoury notes in **19** ⓞ87, 18 months in oak, 20% new. Step up from **18 ★★★☆** ⓞ85 but allow time to show best.

★★★★ **Kanoa Exclusive Blend** 77% cab with cab franc, **18** ⓞ86 juicier & more supple than Kailani, offers pleasurable drinking while sibling matures. Black fruit is plush & ripe, tannin robust but manageable. Similar barrique ageing, but only 18 months.

★★★★ **Leilani Muscat d'Alexandrie** Jerepigo-style **NV** ⓞ88, juice fortified to 16.5%, year oaked. Beneficially light & steely even at 165 g/L sugar, honeyed grape-raisin fruit toned-down, consonant with svelte 500-ml presentation.

Not tasted: **Noelina Méthode Cap Classique.**

PF range

★★★★ **Cabernet Sauvignon** House-style ripeness & concentration on both vintages tasted, yet **21 ★★★★☆** ⓞ90 also shows refinement in its taut tannin structure, shapely blackcurrant fruit, earthy-mineral substrate. Youthful, should benefit from cellaring. 18 months new oak adds just enough spice, while it's more overt in **20** ⓞ88, with same weight & texture, touch too-ripe fruit.

★★★★ **Chardonnay** Elegant, characterful **22** ⓞ87 more attractive than **21 ★★★★** ⓞ85. Roast nut, honey & baking spice notes, rounded body, lively acid. Ferment/year seasoned oak impart unobtrusive structure.

Pinot Noir ★★★★ Somewhat attenuated red berries on **20** ⓞ84, taut, sullen, with leather note, dusty tannin. Tad less to offer than **19 ★★★★** ⓞ87. **Ruby** ⓩ **★★★★** Equal cab & shiraz, **18** ⓞ85 saw 18 months in seasoned barriques, reflects that in prominent spice on juicy blackcurrants & cherries. **Blanc de Noir ★★★★** Very pale amber hue on **22** ⓞ84 from minimal skin contact with cab grapes. Light, crisp, with prickle of acid, strawberry marshmallow fruit notes. **Sauvignon Blanc ★★★★** Pungent, aromatic **22** ⓞ83, wafts of nettle & guava underpinned by ripe tropical fruit & crisp acid. — GdB

Location/map/WO: Stellenbosch ▪ Map grid reference: E8 ▪ 1stB 2003 ▪ Tasting & sales Mon-Sun 11-7; pub hols (seasonal) please call ahead ▪ Fee R100, R130 & R230 ▪ Closed Good Fri, Dec 24/25/31 & Jan 1 ▪ Cheese platters, charcuterie, flat breads, nachos & salads ▪ Owner(s) Franz-Peter Falke ▪ GM Werner Schrenk ▪ Winemaker(s) Werner Schrenk (2007) & Louis Nel (2013, consultant) ▪ Viticulturist(s) Werner Schrenk (2007) ▪ 24ha/9ha under vine ▪ PO Box 12605 Stellenbosch 7613 ▪ tasting@peterfalkewines.co.za, marketing@peterfalkewines.co.za ▪ www.peterfalkewines.com ▪ **T +27 (0)21-881-3677**

☐ **Petit** see Ken Forrester Wines
☐ **Philip Jonker** see Weltevrede Estate
☐ **Phoenix** see Stellenbosch Family Wines
☐ **Phumla** see House of Mandela

Picardi ReBEL

Nationwide drinks retailer Picardi Rebel ticks the affordable, easy-drinking boxes with these house brands.

Picardi ReBEL range

Classic Red ★★★ Five-way **NV** ⓞ77 blend. Ripe berry jam flavour, supple tannin, ends on a charry note. In 5L bag-in-box (as all these), there's plenty for friends around the BBQ. Uncertified & unoaked, like both ranges. **Blanc de Blanc ★★★** Clean, fruity green apple & kiwi flavours in semi-dry **NV** ⓞ79 from chenin & colombard. Balanced & easy. **Rosé ★★** For the sweeter toothed from unspecified cultivars, **NV** ⓞ74 low 10% alc decadently unctuous & smooth, with grapey & petally flavours.

Naked Truth range

Old Brown ★★ Fiery & sweet **NV** ⓞ75 sherry-style fortified, aromatic tobacco & dried fruit, rustic & winter warming. Discontinued: **Soetes.** — MW

Est 1994 ▪ PO Box 1868 Cape Town 8000 ▪ **T +27 (0)21-469-3301**

☐ **Pick's Pick** see The Butcher Shop & Grill
☐ **Pictus** see Painted Wolf Wines

Piekenierskloof Wine Company

There's a new team in the Citrusdal-town cellar of Piekenierskloof, with Alecia Boshoff arriving as cellarmaster in time to take in the 2023 harvest, winemaker Wouter Loubser joining soon after. Many of the vineyards in the beautiful Piekenierskloof plateau are a great deal longer established, notably the grenache noir that's just celebrated its half-century and provides fruit for one of the Old Vine Collection wines. The striking labels on it and most of the wines feature the pike-bearing old-time soldiers that give the area (and the wine ward) its name. They (and Carmién rooibos teas and fynbos-infused gins) are available from De Tol farmstall on the crest of Piekenierskloof Pass.

Old Vine Collection

★★★★☆ **Heidedal Cinsault** More savoury than many of this variety, with fynbos & dried herb notes & a little floral perfume on velvety **19** ★★★★ (89). 30% new oak, a little more than **18** (93).

★★★★☆ **Carel Van Zyl Grenache Noir** Perfumed **20** (92) has fuller fruit, savoury depth & flavour than standard version. Sterner & less early-approachable than previous but balanced, should age well.

★★★★☆ **Johan Van Zyl Pinotage** As previously, 50% new oak supports dark ripe & redder fruit on **20** (90), but this beneficially drier & less powerful at 14% alc, though the tannic structure is firmly shaping, & there's a sweet richness to the palate.

★★★★☆ **Bergendal Chenin Blanc** Low-yielding, high-lying 1962 ungrafted bushvines give serene intensity of aromatic fruit on **22** (94), at just 12% alc. Dry, succulent & confident, with stony, thatchy & fynbos notes complementing the fruitier ones, all supported by integrated oak, 30% new. Drinking well now, but should develop a few years.

★★★★ **Samson Straw Wine** Now **NV** ★★★★ (86). Old-oaked dessert wine named for worker who planted muscat de Frontigan vines in 1962. Latest with very sweet (& unmistakable) grapey, slightly raisiny flavours balanced by subtly effective acidity. Silk texture. Last tasted was **20** (86). 375 ml.

Reserve range

★★★★ **Heirloom Red** Another charming & successful blend of 60% shiraz with grenache & mourvèdre. **21** (88) lightly perfumed, charming & supple. A little sweetness adds to friendliness but doesn't detract from balanced, well-structured seriousness. 40% new oak supportive; easy 13% alc.

★★★★ **Heirloom White** From chenin, grenache blanc & minority contribution from aromatically influential viognier in **23** (88). Oak, 15% new, adds texture, as well as spice to floral peachiness. Fresh & light-feeling at 13% alc, but not lacking generosity. Last tasted was **21** (88).

Piekenierskloof range

★★★★ **Cinsault** Charm abounds on **21** (88) from its ripe & fruity aroma onwards. Less drily austere than previous, gently firm tannic grip making this more serious-minded than many modern cinsaults.

★★★★ **Grenache Noir** Dark & red perfumed fruit on **21** (86). As usual, pleasingly restrained, with effective but gentle grip controlling the sweet fruit flavours in a good balance. Older oak, modest 13.1% alc.

★★★★ **Shiraz** Appealing, friendly **21** (88) offers loads of pure, sweet-fruited aroma & flavour, but enough juicy firmness & grip (friendly 13.6% alc) helps to keep a sense of happy restraint. 15% new oak supportive.

★★★★ **Tannat** Dark & savoury **22** (88) with cherry & spice notes. 14.5% alc points to ripeness but in balance with flavour & variety's emphatic dry tannins. Few grams of sugar common to the reds in range are not too noticeable, but add to the richness & underline the fruit.

★★★★ **Chenin Blanc** Panoply of varietal aroma & flavour on **23** (86) - thatch, melon, dried peach. Small oaked portion & some lees contact add breadth, & there's good intensity of flavour & length at modest 13% alc. Last tasted **21** ★★★★ (85).

★★★★ **Grenache Blanc** Delicately forthcoming floral & stonefruit notes on **23** ★★★★ (85). Nice lightness at 12.5–13% alc (like other whites in range), & unobtrusive old-oaking. Pleasing, but light fruit intensity, some sugar & assertive compensating acidity give tart-sweet character that makes for less satisfactory balance than on last-tasted **21** (86).

★★★★ **Wilhelmina Brut Rosé** Copper-tinted light pink on latest **NV** (88) sparkling from grenache noir. Exuberant & characterful red appley aromas & flavours, & refined, fresh, bone-dry & grippy palate making for classier MCC than packaging might suggest. Less intense than previous, but also delicious & moreish.

Cabernet Sauvignon ★★★☆ Ripe, well-flavoured **21** (85) with cedar & spice notes. Touch sweet, & less harmonious than others in range, with more structural power than fruit substance, but approachable now.

30% new oak; 14.5% alc. **Pinotage** ★★★☆ At 14% alc & with brusque dry tannins, **21** ⑧④ less elegantly balanced than some other reds in range. Ripely fruity, though, & plush textured. 30% new oak. **Grenache Rosé** ★★★★ Pretty light pink, copper-tinged **23** ⑧⑤ offering red berry perfume & flavour. Fresh, refined & dry enough. 13% alc. **Chardonnay** ★★★☆ Quiet aromas including toasty note from new oak on flavourful (if straightforwardly so) **22** ⑧⑤. Fairly rich, but good vein of lemony acid. Touch off quality of **21** ★★★★ ⑧⑥.

Stonedance range

Hutton Red ⊘ ★★★★ Unlike previous, grenache in majority in slightly more serious **21** ⑧④ blend, shiraz the minor partner at 20%. Generally easygoing & without great intensity, lightly oaked & well balanced. 13.5% alc. **Granite White** ⊘ ★★★★ As usual, peachy chenin (85%) dominates blend with perfumed viognier in **22** ⑧⑤. Bright & harmonious, with plenty of lipsmacking flavour; lightish at 13% alc. Both in range WO Swartland & Fairtrade.

Six Hats Fairtrade range

Cabernet Sauvignon ⑧ ★★★ Ripe, fruity, rather thickly textured **21** ⑦⑧ beneficially less sweet than previous but juicy & balanced. W Cape WO, as all these. **Pinotage** ★★★ Juicy & smooth, friendly, lightly oaked **22** ⑧② raises standard from sweeter, more powerful previous. **Shiraz** ★★★ Plenty of smoke-tinged red fruit aromas & flavours on **21** ⑧②. Not greatly substantial, but laid-back & tasty. 13.3% alc. **Rosé** ⑧ ★★★ Salmon-hued **22** ⑧⓪ from mourvèdre has modest flavours, but is light-feeling, fresh & dry. **Chardonnay** ★★★ Pleasant, unassuming **23** ⑦⑨ is clean, bright, balanced & dry - & fairly neutral. **Sauvignon Blanc** ⑧ ★★★ Tropical aromas on **22** ⑧⓪. Nice fruity flavours & grippy, zippy dryness. **Viognier** ★★★ Typical floral, apricot notes on gently perfumed **22** ⑧⓪, nicely balanced for approachability, its flavourful easiness enriched by few grams sugar. Not tasted: **Chenin Blanc**. — TJ

Location: Citrusdal ▪ Map: Olifants River ▪ Map grid reference: D7 ▪ WO: Piekenierskloof/Western Cape/ Swartland ▪ Est/1stB 2017 ▪ Tasting Mon-Sat & pub hols 9-5 Sun 9-3 at De Tol, Piekenierskloof Pass, N7 ▪ Deli ▪ Wine pairing ▪ Winery tours by appt only ▪ Owner(s) Majority shareholding Oubaas & Potgieter van Zyl ▪ Cellarmaster(s) Alecia Boshoff (Dec 2022) ▪ Winemaker(s) Wouter Loubser (May 2023) ▪ Fairtrade, HACCP, IPW, WIETA ▪ PO Box 41 Citrusdal 7340 ▪ info@pkwc.co.za ▪ www.piekenierskloofwines.co.za ▪ **T +27 (0)22-921-2233**

Pienaar & Son Distilling Co   ⑨ ⓞ

No new bottling of Bread & Butter, the exciting and offbeat XO brandy by the Cape Town-based Pienaar craft distilling family for us to review. We look forward tasting its unique buttered toast flavour profile next time.

Location: Cape Town ▪ Map: Cape Peninsula ▪ Map grid reference: B1 ▪ Est 2015 ▪ 1stB 2016 ▪ Tasting Fri-Sun 10-6; distillery tours Mon-Fri by appt Sat 10-2; sales 10-4 ▪ Craft gin, vodka, whisky ▪ Owner(s) André Pienaar ▪ Makers Landing, The Cruise Terminal, Victoria & Alfred Waterfront, Cape Town 8001 ▪ info@pienaarandson.co.za ▪ www.pienaarandson.co.za ▪ **T +27 (0)72-759-9928**

☐ **Pierneef Collection** see La Motte
☐ **Pierre Jourdan** see Haute Cabrière
☐ **Pieter Carstens** see Carstens Wines
☐ **Pieter Cruythoff** see Riebeek Valley Wine Co

Pieter Ferreira Cap Classique

For ever, it seems, Pieter 'Bubbles' Ferreira has been deeply and passionately involved in making, and propagandising for, fine sparkling wine, including over 30 years at Graham Beck, where he is now chief operating officer, but also giving help to anyone that asked (and most have). He and wife Ann, also formidably knowledgeable about bubbly, founded this specialist venture more than a decade ago, but its range is still evolving. Champagne remains a benchmark for their purist ambition, despite the commitment to local terroir and conditions, and they've been vinously exploring the 'heritage' varieties found in that heartland of the style, bottling a cap classique from pinot blanc, as well as a blanc de noir from meunier and pinot noir.

★★★★☆ **Rosé** ⊛ Refined coppery-pink **16** ⑨④ at extra brut level. Floral & red fruit (redcurrant & strawberry) notes from pinot noir, brioche & citrus hovering in the background. Elegant, texture like silk brocade. Lingering fruit, but a touch less nervy than the others. 54 months on lees.

★★★★☆ **Birdsong Extra Brut** ⓐ Pale gold **18** ㉝ mostly chardonnay, like **17** ㉝, 31% pinot noir. Yeasty aromas, pinot adding berry notes & core of sweet cherry within palate's limy citrus. Fine example of Ferreira's wines staying brilliantly, youthfully fresh for longer than most - here development from 54 months on lees is subtle. Seriously dry, with some chalky texture. Touch creamier, richer than BdB.

★★★★☆ **Blanc de Blancs** ⓐ Thrillingly dry **17** ㉞ chardonnay shows remarkably youthful freshness of character & pale hue despite 6 years before disgorgement, though there are brioche notes along with stony, lemony citrus. Bright, lively, with a fine persistent bubble but also breadth & depth of flavour along with precision. Altogether a lovely balance. Robertson grapes, small part oaked.— TJ

Location: Franschhoek ▪ WO: Western Cape ▪ Est/1stB 2012 ▪ Closed to public ▪ Owner(s) Pieter Ferreira Wines (Pty) Ltd - Ann Ferreira ▪ Cellarmaster(s) Pieter Ferreira (Graham Beck) ▪ 300cs own label 100% cap classique ▪ PO Box 102 La Motte 7691 ▪ ann@pieterferreira.co.za ▪ www.pieterferreira.co.za ▪ **T +27 (0)82-909-1116**

☐ **Pieter Willem & Sol** *see* Yerden Eksteen

Pilgrim Wines ⓥ

Riëtte Kotzé, owner of this boutique winery, and viticulturist-winemaker husband Henry launched the venture seven years ago, intending 'to inspire, teach and surprise', yet they themselves have learned many things. 'The main one: it takes time to discover the personalities of varieties new to this country; one has to be patient and, in a way, unassuming in winemaking,' Henry notes. 'I have to follow the style, not direct it; it's hard not to be in control!' The couple has also discovered viura with prolonged skin contact can take a long time to open, thus the latest is made in the freshest possible style. Bastardo do Castello's initial elegance and earthy spice gets even better, delivering opulence with effortless grace. The wines may be tasted, by appointment, at the brand home on Mulderbosch, where Henry is winemaker.

★★★★ **Bastardo do Castello** Intriguing example of variety called trousseau in France's Jura. **22** ㉙ high-toned red berry & wildflower perfume, sweet fruit bound by uncompromising dry tannins. Individual, fresh & light-feeling, more harmonious than **21** ㉘. Foot-trodden by whole Kotzé family, wholebunch fermented, older-oaked 15 months. Unfined/filtered.

★★★★☆ **Shiraz** More medium bodied, less bold than last, allowing wider expression of red fruits, florals & spice. **21** ㉙ gentle & supple in texture, freshness & squeeze of tannin bring everything into focus. Natural ferment, 25% wholebunch, older oak, 5% American, 18 months.

★★★★☆ **Chenin Blanc** ⊘ ⓐ Follows previous with texture as a central focus. **22** ㉞ flowing silky breadth, firming acidity & dense yet unharsh grip harbour attractive & persistent red apple, earth & wild herb medley. Good now, possibly better after year/2. Voor Paardeberg grapes, spontaneous ferment, 75% wholebunch, balance skin contact, 8 months older oak.

★★★★ **Viura** Ultra-rare solo bottling. Gentle & a little exotic, **23** ★★★★☆ ㉙ ex Breedekloof adds spice to fresh lime & pear flavours giving them intensity & memorable length. Pillow-soft texture extra note of interest. Has **22** ㉖'s charm with more personality.— AL

Location/map: Stellenbosch ▪ Map grid reference: C5 ▪ WO: Stellenbosch/Voor Paardeberg/Goudini ▪ Est/1stB 2017 ▪ Tasting strictly by appt only ▪ Owner(s) Riëtte Kotzé ▪ Winemaker(s) Henry Kotzé (2017) ▪ Viticulturist(s) Riëtte Kotzé (2017) ▪ 50% red 50% white ▪ info@pilgrimwines.co.za ▪ www.pilgrimwines. co.za ▪ **T +27 (0)83-296-0890**

☐ **Pillar & Post** *see* Stellenrust

Pink Valley Wines ⓥ ⓜ ⓒ ⓑ

This French-owned winery on the Helderberg is unique in the Cape, being dedicated to crafting a single rosé, itself notably southern French-inspired in its sophisticated styling. The estate and boutique cellar lie just below the owners' other mountain venture, Taaibosch (see that listing). Sangiovese increases in importance here: a new block has been planted, and the grape has come to dominate the wine. In the cellar, egg-shaped concrete tanks have now been introduced.

★★★★☆ **Rosé** Now established as a leading local example of the sophisticated, palely gleaming Provençal style. **22** ㉙ tweaks the blend to 73% sangiovese, with grenache noir. Delicate finesse yet full flavour, light 12% alc yet vinous substance, helped by 11 months on lees in stainless steel. Succulent acidity, fresh, grippy & bone-dry. Also magnums.— TJ

Location: Stellenbosch ▪ Map: Helderberg ▪ Map grid reference: C3 ▪ Map: Stellenbosch ▪ Map grid reference: F5 ▪ WO: Stellenbosch ▪ Est/1stB 2019 ▪ Tasting & sales Tue-Thu 11-4 Fri-Sat 11-10 Sun 11-4, closed on Mondays; pub hols (seasonal) please call ahead ▪ Closed Dec 25 & Jan 1 ▪ Cellar tours by reservation ▪ Restaurant ▪ Facilities for children ▪ MTB trail ▪ Wines also available for tasting at Le Chant Wine Bar, 7 Church Str, Stellenbosch: phone ahead for opening hours ▪ Owner(s) Oddo Vins et Domaines ▪ Winemaker(s) Petri Venter (Jan 2021) ▪ Viticulturist(s) Andre Smit (Dec 2018) ▪ 7ha under vine ▪ 100% rosé ▪ IPW, WIETA ▪ PO Box 5609 Helderberg Somerset West 7135 ▪ info@pinkvalleywines.com ▪ www.pinkvalleywines.com ▪ T +27 (0)21-855-3744

Plaisir ⓨ ⓐ ⓞ ⓖ

At 974 hectares, 255 of which planted with vines, the Simonsberg-Paarl estate recently acquired by Rose and Michael Jordaan is large by any measure, and farm manager Alec Versveld is working on multiple fronts to implement the owners' vision relating to biodiversity and environmental sustainability, inter alia. On the wine and branding side, Fred Fismer took charge of the cellar in December 2022 and produced 'exquisite flavours' from the vintage; two impressive new wines were released; and various branding tweaks were done to give the ranges an identity distinct from their Plaisir de Merle predecessors. No change to the intrinsics: 'exceptional wines that capture the essence of their terroir and bring joy to every wine lover's palate'.

Flagship range

★★★★☆ **Grand Plaisir Red** ⓐ Classic 5-way Bordeaux blend led by 41% cab in **18** ⑨⓪, cigarbox, cassis, plum & dried herbs. Generous 14.6% alc is well balanced by nervy freshness, velvet tannins & spice from 18 months in new barrels, softened by further 6 months in 3rd fill.

★★★★★ **Grand Plaisir White** ⓝⓔⓦ ⓐ Stunning **22** ⑨⑤ epitome of Simonsberg chardonnay, rich yet fresh with firm acid. Detailed winemaking: hand-harvest of separate parcels, barrel rolling to stir lees for complexity (as all whites), barrel selection. 60% new, for 11 months, oak maturation gives breadth & depth to honeyed stonefruit, hazelnut & citrus.

Estate range

★★★★☆ **Cabernet Sauvignon** ⓐ Full-bodied & powerful expression of Simonsberg cab in celebrated vintage. Careful sorting & skin contact, 18 months in small-oak, 55% new. Brooding blackberries, cherries in muscular structure with lift of redcurrant tang. A spine of minerals & tannin supports & adds dimension to multifaceted & complex **19** ⑨④.

★★★★☆ **Merlot** ⓐ Pleasure in abundance from unashamedly opulent **20** ⑨④, showing floral, plum & cocoa scents & flavours. 12-16 months in oak polish tannins to a silky sheen, the 35% new-wood component seasons with cinnamon & clove.

★★★★ **Red** ⓐ Was 'Petit Plaisir Red'. Blend of 7 estate reds, cab leading at 51%. **20** ⑧⑨'s black cherries & berries harmonised 16-22 months in mix new & older barrels, enhanced with svelte tannins for accessible drinking in youth, though will go the distance, too.

★★★★ **Chardonnay** Burst of vanilla opens **22** ⑧⑨, lemony & fresh with intriguing gooseberry zing, tamed somewhat by 11 months in oak, 40% new, also bringing in spice & toasted nut. No **21**.

★★★★ **Chenin Blanc** ⓝⓔⓦ Picked at different ripeness levels, **22** ⑧⑧ slips down easily with its seamless marriage of citrus verve, oak, all older, 9 months, & moderate alc of 12.6%.

Not tasted: **Sauvignon Blanc**.

Cap Classique range

★★★★ **Grand Brut** ⓨ Pinot noir with 40% chardonnay, no oaking for **18** ⑧⑦ bubbly, unlike previous, 36 months on lees in bottle. Elegant, vibrates with freshness. WO W Cape.

Discontinued: **Griffin range**. — ML

Location: Simondium ▪ Map: Franschhoek ▪ Map grid reference: C6 ▪ WO: Simonsberg-Paarl/Western Cape ▪ Est 1693 ▪ Tasting & sales Mon-Sun 10-5; pub hols (seasonal) please call ahead ▪ Closed Dec 25 & Jan 1 ▪ Accommodation ▪ Plaisir Market ▪ MTB trails ▪ Owner(s) Rose & Michael Jordaan ▪ Winemaker(s) Fred Fismer (Dec 2022) ▪ Farm manager Alec Versveld ▪ 974ha/255ha (cab, merlot, chard, sauv) ▪ 350t/35,000cs own label 70% red 30% white ▪ WIETA, WWF-SA Conservation Champion ▪ Postnet Suite 231 Private Bag X5061 Stellenbosch 7599 ▪ info@plaisir.co.za ▪ www.plaisir.co.za ▪ T +27 (0)21-488-9977/+27 (0)82-303-8071

Plettenvale Wines ⚲

Practical considerations meant we were unable to taste the new cool-climate releases crafted by Gloria Strack van Schyndel in her boutique cellar near Plettenberg Bay. We hope to sample them next time.

Location: Plettenberg Bay ▪ Map: Klein Karoo & Garden Route ▪ Map grid reference: C1 ▪ Est 2008 ▪ 1stB 2011 ▪ Tasting & sales every Sat 10-1, all other times by appt ▪ Short tour of cellar available with tasting ▪ Owner(s)/winemaker(s) Gloria Strack van Schyndel ▪ Viticulturist(s) Paul Wallace (Nov 2007, consultant) ▪ 5.3ha/2.5ha (pinot, shiraz, chard, viog) ▪ PO Box 2103 Plettenberg Bay 6600 ▪ info@plettenvalewines.co.za ▪ www.plettenvalewines.co.za ▪ **T +27 (0)82-322-0765**

☐ **Poetique** see Idun
☐ **Poetry** see Flagstone Winery
☐ **Polkadraai** see Stellenbosch Hills Wines
☐ **Polo Club** see Val de Vie & Polo Club Wines
☐ **Pomüla** see Imbuko Wines

Pongrácz

Demand for these enduringly popular champagne-method sparklings is such that owner Heineken Beverages is investigating further vine planting on the various farms from which it draws the grapes. With knowledge gained last harvest, new winemaker Matthys Botes understands the vineyards and the contribution of each to the final blend, and how to achieve the desired consistency of quality and character.

★★★★☆ **Blanc de Blancs** ⚲ Serious & cellarworthy extra-dry sparkler from chardonnay, NV ⑨2 36 months on lees, no oaked fraction but usual lemon with honeyed brioche, subtle iodine pique of interest.

★★★★☆ **Brut** Toast, honey & umami touch on NV ⑧6, same blend & ageing as dry rosé, touch lower sugar (7.7 g/L vs 8.1). Could do with dash more freshness.

★★★★☆ **Desiderius** ⚲ Elegant extra-brut sparkler, 15 ⑨3 with 69 months on lees, giving almond nougat & brioche complexity to chardonnay's freshness & verve, pinot noir's weight & richness.

★★★★ **Noble Nectar** ⊘ Attractive old gold hue & tiny racing bubbles on NV ⑧8, succulent acid & perfectly judged 40 g/L sugar ensure mere suggestion of sweetness in the warmed honey & baked quince flavours. Same blend & lees time as Brut Rosé.

Brut Rosé ★★★★ Salad of grapes - near-equal pinot noir & chardonnay, dabs meunier, riesling & chenin - deliver salad of smells & tastes on cheery NV ⑧5, along with pale blush, soft mousse & rounded finish. 12 months on lees, tad less than last. **Nectar Rosé Light** ⚲ ★★★★ Pinot noir takes the lead (67%) with chardonnay & splash meunier in fragrant NV ⑧5. Faint strawberry, more overt ginger wafts, good presence given alc is just 8.3%. — CvZ

Location: Stellenbosch ▪ WO: Western Cape ▪ Owner(s) Heineken Beverages ▪ Winemaker(s) Matthys Botes ▪ 27ha own vyds ▪ 20% red 80% white ▪ ISO 9200 ▪ PO Box 184 Stellenbosch 7599 ▪ www.pongracz.co.za

Porcupine Ridge

Adorned with a drawing of the indigenous crested porcupine by wildlife artist Zakkie Eloff, this Boekenhoutskloof-owned brand was launched with the 1997 vintage. Now an extensive, globally exported label, it's been unwaveringly 'honest, true to type and cultivar' as well as friendly in style and price. A commitment to producing the wines using only plant-based products sees them certified vegan by V-Label.

★★★★ **Syrah** ⊘ Regularly the top performer in this line-up, with commendable varietal expression & complexity. Magenta 22 ⑧6 from Swartland usual fynbos & spice on expressive red fruit, tangy acid lift.
Cabernet Sauvignon ⊘ ★★★★ Dab cab franc added for perfume & structure in 22 ⑧4. Sweet black fruit, friendly tannin & piquant finish. 20% unoaked for freshness, rest older barrel & tank with staves, as all the reds. **Merlot** ⊘ ★★★ Gentle oak seasoning on juicy, plummy 22 ⑧2, smooth, berry-laden finish. Certified vegan, as all. **Chardonnay** ★★★ Yellow & green citrus, nutty whisper from 5% aged in barrel, 22 ⑧2 easy to like & sip, soft acid & well-judged 13.5% alc. **Sauvignon Blanc** ⊘ ★★★★ Various picking dates for freshness & complexity, 23 ⑧4 abundant green & tropical fruit, appealing pithy texture, friendly 12% alc. WO W Cape, rest Coastal unless noted. Not tasted: **Rosé, Chenin Blanc.** — CvZ

Porseleinberg

The epitome of terroir expression, Porseleinberg is a single wine from a single variety, crafted since debut in 2010 by the same pair of hands, from a small, rocky parcel certified organic from 2023, in a namesake Wine of Origin ward in Swartland, adorned with an embossed label that's printed on-site by the winemaker on a 1940s press which he restored. Winemaker-viticulturist Callie Louw does his careful crafting according to Swartland Independent Producer guidelines from the oldest vineyards exclusively, the remainder, also Rhône black grapes, go to Boekenhoutskloof in Franschhoek, the owner

★★★★☆ **Porseleinberg** ⓐ From syrah, opulent layers of dark, baked fruit, savoury & black cherry notes, richer & riper in **21** ⑨② than **20** ⑨④, also tighter in youth, deserves cellar time to show its full complexity & more benevolent persona. Both vintages naturally bunch-fermented, year in older 2,500L foudre & 10% in concrete 'egg'. — MW

Location: Riebeek-Kasteel ▪ WO: Swartland ▪ Est 2009 ▪ 1stB 2010 ▪ Closed to public ▪ Owner(s) Boekenhoutskloof Winery (Pty) Ltd ▪ Winemaker(s)/viticulturist(s) Callie Louw (Jun 2009) ▪ 130ha/90ha (cinsaut, grenache, shiraz) ▪ 90t/4,000cs own label 100% red ▪ PO Box 433 Franschhoek 7690 ▪ callie@ porseleinberg.com ▪ www.porseleinberg.com ▪ **T +27 (0)79-884-2309**

☐ **Portuguese Inspired** *see* Simonsvlei International
☐ **Postcard** *see* Post House Vineyards

Post House Vineyards

ⓟ ⓐ ⓒ ⓖ

The philatelic theme of these ranges stems from the location of the cellar in the old post office of the mission station Raithby between Stellenbosch and Somerset West. The marginal Helderberg foothills soils are ideal for crafting terroir wines, owner-cellarmaster Nick Gebers believes, and he and new assistant Dané Wolmarans work with natural yeasts and traditional tools, handling and intervening as little as possible.

Reserve range

★★★★ **Holy Grail Malbec** ⓐ New to the guide (as Stormy), still fairly rare solo bottling of Bordeaux grape is thick piled in **20** ⑧⑨, 2 years in oak, 5% new, framing dense floral fruit, ensuring measured finish.

★★★★☆ **Stormy Hope Petit Verdot** ⊘ ⓐ Welcome addition to small number of varietal bottlings of Bordeaux blend stalwart. Youthfully intense purple colour on **21** ⑨⓪, clean, elegant lines, less earthy, more svelte than other reds. Oak as Holy Grail, 30% new, & similarly worth keeping.

★★★★ **Treskilling Yellow** ⓐ Lovely, lively botrytis dessert from chenin, named for world's most expensive stamp. **18** ★★★★★ ⑨③ jasmine & honeysuckle billows, marmalade & dried apricot sweetness paired with acid freshness undimmed after 4 years in old oak, twice that for **17** ⑧⑧. 375 ml.

Premium range

★★★★ **Bulls Eye Cabernet Sauvignon** Lighter oaking evident on recent releases of these reds. Honest **21** ⑧⑦'s spicy cassis & fruitcake generosity reined in on dry, structured palate.

★★★★ **Black Mail Merlot** Prominent blackberry fruit & notes of scrubby fynbos on **21** ⑧⑥, subtle oak tannin from 10% new barriques, 18 months, down from 24 previous vintage.

★★★★ **Merry Widow Shiraz** Magenta-hued & vibrant **21** ⑧⑦'s bouquet spiced with whiffs of white pepper, berry fruit still in firm grip of tannin, wood dialled back to 20% new, 18 months, none American.

★★★★ **Missing Virgin** Virgin Islands stamp printed without image of Islands; namesake wine is complete, however, & unusual in its mix of pinotage & dab petit verdot. **21** ⑧⑥ graphite depth to plum & cherry fruit, elegantly spiced by 18 months oak, modest 10% new.

★★★★☆ **Penny Black** ⊘ Creative blend shiraz, cab, merlot & petit verdot, splash chenin blanc, maintains improved form of previous in **21** ⑨⓪. Attractive chalky foundation for perfectly ripe fruit, firm dry tannin polished 18 months in 20% new oak.

★★★★ **Stamp Of Chenin** ⊘ Ferment in old French oak, full malo & weekly lees stirring, 2 months, create **22** ★★★★★ ⑨⓪'s broad, powerful palate of melon & peach, its lively acid just matches rich texture & 15% alc. **21** ⑧⑧ was slighter; unusually for chenin, saw 30% American oak.

Postcard range

Golden Monkey ⊘ 🏵 ★★★★ Perfumed Rhône blend, 64% shiraz with grenache noir & mourvèdre in **22** ⑧⑤, is scrumptious & supple, for carefree early drinking.

Admirals Pinotage ⊘ ★★★★ Satisfying, mediumweight **21** ⑧③ has appealing tannin grip to ripe, mulberry-toned fruit, slides down easily, uncumbered by new oak. **Blueish Black** ⊘ ★★★★ Soft-textured **21** ⑧④ blend of shiraz, pinotage, merlot & cab exposed to oak in large tanks only, so succulent blueberry & cherry fruit shines through. **Three Pearls Grenache Rosé** ★★★ Pale salmon **23** ⑧① preview adds nutty note from barrel ferment to pomegranate profile, fresh acid assures crisp, bone-dry finish. **Cameo Chenin Blanc** ⊘ ★★★★ From 3 decade old vines. Green apple crunch enlivens pre-release **23** ⑧④'s appealing richness, brisk acid freshens the unwooded finish. **Mailing May Sauvignon Blanc** ⊘ ★★★★ From old Stellenbosch vines, **23** ⑧③ offers variety-true blackcurrant flavour in rounded & light body, pleasing fruitiness for easy drinking. — DS

Location/WO: Stellenbosch ▪ Map: Helderberg ▪ Map grid reference: C1 ▪ Est/1stB 1997 ▪ Tasting & sales Mon-Fri 10-4 Sat/Sun by appt ▪ Fee R100 for 5 wines ▪ Closed all pub hols ▪ BYO picnic ▪ Function/wedding venue (up to 150 pax) ▪ Wine club ▪ Owner(s) Nicholas Gebers ▪ Cellarmaster(s) Nick Gebers ▪ Winemaker(s) Nick Gebers, with Dané Wolmarans ▪ 70ha/37ha (cabs s/f, grenache, malbec, merlot, mourv, p verdot, ptage, shiraz, chenin, sauv) ▪ 200t/16,000cs own label 65% red 35% white ▪ PO Box 5635 Helderberg 7135 ▪ nick@posthousewines.co.za ▪ www.posthousewines.co.za ▪ **T +27 (0)21-842-2409**

☐ **Potato Shed** see Bé a Daisy
☐ **Pot Luck Club** see Almenkerk Wine Estate

Pounding Grape Wines

Based in Cape Town's northern suburbs, multifaceted wine man Chris Groenewald uses a back-to-basics approach to creating 'high-quality, variety-true wines' in tiny volumes - currently only 100 cases.

★★★★ **Bringing Back The Joy** 🏵 Characterful skin-contact sauvignon, wild fermented & aged few months in PVC 'egg'. Last release was vintage-dated (**20** ⑧⑧), follow-up is **NV** ⑧⑨, has similar unusual unshelled peanut & pea aromas, & tannin tug, offers tad more freshness & verve, good vinosity at 12% alc.
Not tasted: **Fairies In The Garden**. — CvZ

Location: Bellville ▪ WO: Polkadraai Hills ▪ Est/1stB 2019 ▪ Closed to public ▪ Owner(s) Chris Groenewald ▪ Cellarmaster(s)/winemaker(s) Chris Groenewald (Feb 2019) ▪ 100cs own label 100% white ▪ 70 Gladstone Str, Boston, Bellville 7530 ▪ chrisgroenewald23@gmail.com ▪ www.poundinggrape.co.za ▪ **T +27 (0)83-333-8323**

Prévoir Wines ⑨

For this aptly named brand, Robertson accountant and part-time vintner Tertius de Villiers has taken over the tending of what he calls 'weggooi wingerde' (blocks discarded by others), all single-vineyards, and contracted local small-batch specialist Lourens van der Westhuizen to vinify the grapes as naturally as possible. **Cabernet Sauvignon-Merlot** 🏵 ★★★ Spice-dusted & leather-seamed **19** ⑦⑧'s juicy palate tempered by drying tannins. **Chardonnay** 🏵 ★★★★ Same 7 months in older barrels as last, but **19** ⑧⑤ shows less oak, more lees character, attractive waxy citrus & tropical fruit. **Unwooded Chardonnay** 🏵 ★★★★ Oatmeal & yoghurt hints on **20** ⑧④, palate more intense, citrus, fruit salad & glacé notes, some lees fatness & pleasing tang. Not tasted: **Cabernet Sauvignon**, **Merlot**, **Shiraz**. — DS

Location/WO: Robertson ▪ Est 2012 ▪ 1stB 2015 ▪ Tasting by appt ▪ Wines also available for tasting at La Verne, Platform 62 & Stilbaai Kelders ▪ Owner(s) Bastion Boerdery t/a Prévoir Wines ▪ Winemaker(s) Lourens van der Westhuizen (Arendsig) ▪ 10ha/2.7ha (chard) ▪ 26t/10,000cs own label 37% red 63% white ▪ PO Box 340 Robertson 6705 ▪ tertius@tdva.co.za ▪ **T +27 (0)83-441-0140**

☐ **Pride of Kings** see Stellenview Premium Wines
☐ **Prince** see Bayede!
☐ **Princess** see Bayede!
☐ **Printer's Devil** see Rickety Bridge Winery
☐ **Private Collection** see Saxenburg Wine Farm
☐ **Professor Black** see Warwick Wine Estate

☐ **Prohibition** *see* Camberley Wines
☐ **Project Z** *see* Kleine Zalze Wines
☐ **Prospect** *see* Diemersdal Estate
☐ **Protea** *see* Anthonij Rupert Wyne
☐ **Provenance** *see* L'Avenir Wine Estate

Pulpit Rock Winery

The imposingly large, gabled cellar is near Riebeek West, at the foot of Kasteelberg (a craggy outcrop on the mountain gives Pulpit Rock Winery its name), and here the Brink family makes three ranges of easy-drinking and modestly priced wines from their extensive, well-reputed Swartland properties, De Gift and Panorama. They also have a piggery, and sell pork products from De Gift Farm Butchery & Deli at the visitor venue.

Louisa range

★★★★ **Cape Red Blend** 50% pinotage plus cab & shiraz in **19** ⑧⑧. Plush (15% alc), with good red & black berry combo, supple powdery tannins. Oak spice touch prominent from 18 months in 30% new French & American barriques, but should integrate with time.

★★★★ **Cape White Blend** ⓃⒺⓌ ⊘ Characterful chenin mix with chardonnay, drop viognier, **23** ⑧⑧ round, ripe & spicy, delicious peach-apricot fruit, leesy richness. Fermented & aged in equal parts new oak, amphora & FlexCube.

★★★★ **Méthode Cap Classique Brut** ⊘ Bubbly from chardonnay, **21** ⑧⑦ tangy green apple, lemon curd hint & satisfying fresh-baked yeastiness. Acid tad fresh though, lacking creaminess of last **19** ⑧⑨.

★★★★☆ **Dessert Wine** 🐝 Reimagined 21 ★★★★ ⑧⑧ is fortified red muscat de Frontignan, matured in older barrels. Honeyed raisin fruit core, rich & spicy, but mega-sweet at 240 g/L sugar. Last **19** ⑨⓪ was fortified chardonnay.

Brink Family Vineyards range

★★★★ **Shiraz** ⊘ Uber-ripe **21** ⑧⑥ has honest black cherry & plum fruit, prominent vanilla & cedar aromas from year in barrel, 15% American. Smooth & easy flowing despite near 15% alc.

★★★★ **Barrel Fermented Chardonnay** ⊘ Oak is restrained in **22** ⑧⑧, allowing fuller expression of juicy citrus fruit. Focused, with pleasantly plump body, lees breadth & texture. Improves on **21** ⑧⑥.

Chenin Blanc ⊘ 🍇 ★★★★ Bursting with ripe, sunny tropical fruit, **23** ⑧⑤ is pure summer sipping pleasure, underpinned by mineral lees texture, salty nuance. Bargain priced too.

Cabernet Sauvignon ⊘ ★★★★ Weighty, tad ponderous **21** ⑧④ shows obvious 15.5% alc, thick ripe tannins, muted black fruit & leathery aromas. **Merlot** ⊘ ★★★☆ Medium bodied, with smooth, gentle tannins & striking tobacco aroma, **21** ⑧⑤ has savoury black fruit & hint of rhubarb. **Pinotage** ⊘ ★★★☆ Juicy, expressive **21** ⑧⑤ offers sweetly ripe mulberry & bramble fruit with scented highlights aided by portion American oak. **Chardonnay** ⊘ ★★★☆ Unwooded & vibrantly fruity, **23** ⑧⑤ shows tangy lemon & tangerine citrus notes, fresh acid. Attractive current drinking. **Sauvignon Blanc** ⊘ ★★★☆ Asparagus & dried grass on **23** ⑧⑤ from Darling vines, bolstered by gooseberry & green fig fruitiness.

Stories range

Cinsaut ⊘ ★★★☆ Light & breezy, **22** ⑧⑤ has pretty, scented red berry fruit, sleek body & gentle tannins. Easygoing everyday tipple. Lightly chill & try with sushi, say the Brinks. **Shiraz-Pinotage-Grenache** ★★★ No-frills, easy-drinking **22** ⑦⑨ has plummy red fruit, generous body. **Pinotage Rosé** ⊘ ★★★ Light, mild-mannered & dry, with varietal wild berry appeal, **23** ⑧② is unpretentious poolside refreshment. **Chenin Blanc-Viognier** ⊘ ★★★★ Genial, undemanding **23** ⑧③ is 80% chenin, with appealing hint of salt, pert acid on cheerful yellow stonefruit. — GdB

Location: Riebeek West ▪ Map: Swartland ▪ Map grid reference: D6 ▪ WO: Swartland/Coastal ▪ Est 2003 ▪ 1stB 2004 ▪ Tasting & sales Mon-Fri 9-5 Sat 9-1; pub hols (seasonal) please call ahead ▪ Closed Dec 25 to Jan 1 ▪ Cellar tours by appt ▪ BYO picnic ▪ Owner(s) Brink family ▪ Winemaker(s) Dewald Huisamen (Dec 2016) ▪ 600ha/475ha (cab, grenache, merlot, mourv, p verdot, ptage, shiraz, chard, chenin) ▪ 100,000cs own label 70% red 29% white 1% rosé + 3.5m L bulk ▪ Other export brand: Cape Haven ▪ PO Box 1 Riebeek West 7306 ▪ info@pulpitrock.co.za ▪ www.pulpitrock.co.za ▪ **T +27 (0)22-461-2025**

☐ **Purebred** *see* Excelsior Estate

Quando Vineyards & Winery   ⓠ

Brothers and Robertson vignerons Fanus and Martin Bruwer launched their boutique brand in the early 2000s after endlessly being asked when they'd make wine from their own grapes. They debuted with a sauvignon and added various reds, whites and the current blush, all made with a light touch to reflect their Breede River alluvial terroir. The new pinotage continues that reined-in styling, and is very much on-trend.

Pinotage (NEW) ★★★★ Intended as lighter-styled, chillable red, but no lack of black fruit flavour or substance on **22** ⑧③. Restrained alc (13.4%) & tannin fit the relaxed summery vibe. **Mourvèdre Rosé** ⊘ ★★★★ Variety's orange-pink glow accompanies strawberry & raspberry scents & flavours on **23** ⑧③, touch of confection yet palate is dry, ready for table, picnic or party. **Sauvignon Blanc** ⊘ ★★★★ Single riverside block picked in stages over 3 weeks, delivering desired spectrum of green, yellow & tropical fruit in **23** ⑧⑤, plus signature balance of flavour & freshness. — CvZ

Location: Bonnievale ▪ Map/WO: Robertson ▪ Map grid reference: D4 ▪ Est/1stB 2001 ▪ Tasting & sales by appt ▪ Closed all pub hols ▪ Owner(s) FM Bruwer cc ▪ Cellarmaster(s)/winemaker(s) Fanus Bruwer (Jan 1991) ▪ Viticulturist(s) Martin Bruwer (Jan 1991) ▪ 190ha/80ha (mourv, chenin, sauv) ▪ 3,000cs own label 10% red 90% white ▪ PO Box 82 Bonnievale 6730 ▪ info@quando.co.za ▪ www.quando.co.za ▪ **T +27 (0)82-926-0805**

☐ **Quartet** see Wine-of-the-Month Club
☐ **Queen of Africa** see Olivedale Private Vineyards

Quest Wines

The quest for the purest fruit to make a perfect blend from the Cape's most renowned appellations began in 2010 with a pair of wines, Bordeaux- and Rhône-style, since joined by sparkling and chenin in an expanded line-up. Just 500 cases are crafted annually by Du Toitskloof's Willie Stofberg and Swiss-born Alain Cajeux.

★★★★ **Two** ⓠ Dark-fruited **20** ⑧⑦'s comfortable feel freshened & brightened with florals, softish tannin adds to drinkability. Shiraz with 3 others. 100% new oak, 15 months, well absorbed.

★★★★☆ **One** ⓠ Pleasing balance of flesh & freshness, but quieter in **20** ★★★★ ⑧⑦; softish, touch sweetness allows for current drinking. Echoes **18** ⑨②'s petit verdot (66%), merlot, cab blend. Oak as Two.

★★★★ **Old Vine Chenin Blanc** ⊘ ⓦ Breedekloof 1985 block imparts haunting, honeyed red-apple fragrance & finish. **22** ★★★★☆ ⑨① fresh, fluid, showcases old-vine concentration without heaviness. Light grip, sound structure augur well. New oak & amphora ferment/8 months. Improves on last-tasted **20** ⑧⑧.

Brut Rosé Méthode Cap Classique ★★★ From chardonnay, 12% cinsaut adding coppery lights & soft red berries to creamy mousse on softly dry NV ⑧②. **Brut Méthode Cap Classique** ★★★ Ripe lemon & whisper of biscuit, creamy undertone from year on lees. **NV** ⑧② from chardonnay, brisk & dry. — AL

Location: Rawsonville ▪ WO: Western Cape/Breedekloof ▪ Est 2010 ▪ 1stB 2011 ▪ Closed to public ▪ Owner(s) DTK Wines ▪ Cellarmaster(s) Willie Stofberg (2010) ▪ Winemaker(s) Willie Stofberg & Alain Cajeux (both 2010) ▪ 500cs ▪ info@dtkwines.com ▪ www.questwines.co.za ▪ **T +27 (0)23-349-1601**

☐ **Quinta do Sul** see Lieben Wines

Quoin Rock Wines   ⓠ ⓔ ⓖ ⓞ

This well-established, family-owned winery gets its name from Quoin Point, the rocky, second-most southerly tip of Africa, and it's on the nearby cold Agulhas Plain where vines on the farm Boskloof supply grapes for some of the white wines. The balance of fruit is from very different but also cooler terrain on Stellenbosch's Simonsberg, where winemaker Schalk Opperman works in a modern, unusually large cellar, bordered by vines that reach skyward and enjoy a view that long-serving viticulturist Nico Walters never seems to tire of. The visitor centre has a fine-dining restaurant and wedding/function venue, and there are luxury guest lodgings on-site. Qbars in Stellenbosch and Johannesburg extend the estate experience, and pre-booked cellar tours give glimpses of future directions still under wraps.

Quoin Rock range

★★★★☆ **Red Blend** ⓐ Some gentle development on **17** ⑨⓪ Cape Bordeaux, cab at 75%, dashes of other 4. Light, fragrant intro of flowers, cherries & berries belies fullness of dark-fruited body (15% alc), balanced by bright acid & juicy tannins. 22 months in barrel, 55% new, add savoury undercurrent of spice. Stellenbosch WO.

★★★★ **Simonsberg Blend** (NEW) (🍇) Simonsberg parcels of shiraz & cab, dabs merlot, malbec & cab franc deliver powerful, spicy **18** (89). Complex mix foudre, concrete, tank & barrel for ferment, then 20 months in latter 2, 43 in bottle. Still-sumptuous red & black cherries, smooth tannins & vibrant structure can age many years yet.

★★★★☆ **Chardonnay** (🍇) Maintaining form, **20** (94)'s opulence encouraged by ferment/9 months in 45% new barrels with regular lees stirring, adding lemon cream & brioche to honeyed stonefruit. Well-judged acid heightens citrus undertone & appetising grapefruit pith finish.

★★★★ **Sauvignon Blanc** Two vintages tasted, both semillon dabbed. Cape Coast WO for super-fresh **21** (89), intricately textured from light oak & lees stirring, apple, fig & lime, quite weighty for just 12.5% alc. Vibrant melon, nettle & gooseberry prelude to Elim-grown **23** (86) preview. Freshness intensified by racy acid, same modest alc, lipsmacking dryness. No **22**.

★★★★ **White Blend** Energetic **22** (86) from Elim & Stellenbosch sauvignon blanc (96%) & semillon given extra curves from small barrel-fermented & lees-stirred portion. Also-tasted **20** (88) same sources, similar blend, touch longer in wood (8 months), smidge new, & on lees for a well-balanced expression, its successor showing more tension. No **21**.

★★★★☆ **Black Series Méthode Cap Classique** (🍇) Rich-styled **17** (93), honeyed oats & blanched almonds first impressions. As last **15** (94), grapes (54/46 pinot noir & chardonnay) part-fermented in barrel with bâtonnage for extra butteriness, before 62 months on lees, intensifying autolytic toast & honey. Hint sweetness livened with crunchy apple & grapefruit, steely acid.

★★★★ **Festive Méthode Cap Classique** (NEW) Cool green fruit, blackcurrant undercurrent & snappy acid define **20** (88) elegant party starter from pinot noir (70%) & chardonnay. 18 months on lees weave in biscuit nuance, 14.6 g/L sugar give extra richness. Cape South Coast WO.

★★★★☆ **Vine Dried Sauvignon Blanc** (🌸) Gorgeous clarity of white citrus fruit, ripe green fig & smoky lemon balm on exotic **22** (91). Part-desiccated grapes from Simonsberg no longer aged in old oak, rather freshness is celebrated with 3 months in tank before bottling. 375 ml. No **21**.

Not tasted: **Shiraz, Husk Spirit Sauvignon Blanc**.

Tribute range
Not tasted: **Namysto Shiraz-Cabernet Sauvignon, Namysto Rosé, Namysto Sauvignon Blanc**. — ML
Location/map: Stellenbosch ▪ Map grid reference: F3 ▪ WO: Western Cape/Cape Coast/Simonsberg-Stellenbosch/Stellenbosch/Cape South Coast/Elim ▪ Est 1998 ▪ 1stB 2001 ▪ Tasting & sales Mon-Sun 10-4 ▪ Closed Good Fri, Dec 25 & Jan 1 ▪ Meals/refreshments ▪ Function venue ▪ Gâte Restaurant ▪ Accommodation ▪ Owner(s) Quoin Rock Wines (Pty) Ltd ▪ Winemaker(s) Schalk Willem Opperman (Aug 2020) ▪ Viticulturist(s) Nico Walters ▪ PO Box 23 Elsenburg 7607 ▪ info@quoinrock.co.za ▪ www.quoinrock.co.za ▪ **T +27 (0)21-888-4740**

☐ **Route 43** *see* Aan de Doorns Cellar
☐ **Raar Small Batch** *see* Riebeek Valley Wine Co

Raats Family Wines

This fine producer specialising in cab franc and chenin is based in the small and increasingly prestigious Stellenbosch ward named for the granitic Polkadraai Hills. It was here that Bruwer Raats bought a smallholding with neglected vines, reconditioned the soil and planted just 0.2 ha of cab franc and 0.6 ha of chenin, unusually closely planted and trained up individual poles. The two superb (and pricey!) Eden wines are eloquent as to the quality of both care and terroir. Much of the rest of the fruit taken in by Bruwer and winemaker cousin Gavin Bruwer Slabbert to the shared Karibib Wine Craft cellar comes from the area, via joint ventures with neighbour farms. Now most of the labels proudly declare 'Wine of Origin Polkadraai Hills'.

CWG Auction range

★★★★★ **Stella Nova Cabernet Franc** (🍇) Despite few more years than the other cab francs, **19** (95) shows more primary fruit aromas & flavours, intensely & with purity & freshness. Lovely generosity, youthful tannic severity starting to relax. Working with the succulence of the bright acidity, makes for delicious approachability. Even finer than **18** ★★★★★ (93).

★★★★★ **The Fountain Terroir Specific Chenin Blanc** (🍇) Particularly intense aromas & flavours on **22** ★★★★★ (94), including spicy & herbal (fennel) ones, partly from oak, though only 50% in barrel, to enhance fruit purity. As with **21** Ⓐ, concentration, which leads to long-lingering finish, balanced by ripe, succulent acidity. Trademark Raats delicacy maintained.

Raats Family Wines range

★★★★★ **Cabernet Franc** Ⓐ Less powerful than **20** ★★★★☆ Ⓐ, with balanced 13.5% alc (in line with other cab francs of vintage), yet **21** Ⓐ perhaps more densely fruited & intense. Deeper, more complex than Dolomite, with supple richness. Unquestionably serious & intense, with firm dry tannins. Needs decanting to allow fruit to emerge but preferably at least half-decade in bottle. 30% new oak, 18 months.

★★★★☆ **Dolomite Cabernet Franc** ⊘ Shares a seriousness with grander, pricier bottlings, but **21** Ⓐ has, as usual, no new oak, so leafy-spicy, berried fragrance & deep-fruited flavour shine more approachably in youth, despite firm structure. But aeration (& bottle age) are useful.

★★★★☆ **Eden High Density Single Vineyard Cabernet Franc** Ⓐ Perfumed aromas, bright & lifted, showcase red & darker fruit on particularly fine **21** ★★★★★ Ⓐ. If **20** Ⓐ had some leafiness, herbal edge here, in great vintage, subtler & perfect counterpoint to the berries. Usual vibrancy & notably succulent tannins, already less severe than Family version, more harmonious, though finish laudably drier.

★★★★☆ **Jasper Red Blend** Ⓐ At 53%, cab franc leads **21** Ⓐ 5-way Bordeaux-style blend. Immediately appealing, with ripe but lively cedar-inflected aromas & flavours. Subtle oaking (none new) in support of sweet fruit, tannins juicy, the balance effective. With a good future ahead, it's already delicious. WO Stellenbosch, like Dolomite.

★★★★☆ **Eden High Density Single Vineyard Chenin Blanc** Ⓐ Contemplative **22** Ⓐ, uniquely from rare 'Montpellier' clone, evokes delight. From understatedly insistent aromas to extraordinarily long finish, a subtle, unfolding complexity. Texture silky, balance unquestionable, confident delicacy triumphant. Wholebunch natural ferment, 11 months in concrete 'egg' (65%) or oak, 10% new. Long future but gorgeous in youth.

★★★★☆ **Old Vine Chenin Blanc** Ⓐ As always with this wine & all Raats chenin, delicacy controls richness & intensity of **22** Ⓐ. Stony & savoury notes complement pure citrus & peachy fruit - 50% fermented in stainless steel to accentuate bright purity, remainder in older oak for texture & lusciousness. Poised & balanced. Components blended after 11 months, left together on lees for 2 more.

★★★★☆ **Original Chenin Blanc** ⊘ This more modestly priced, unoaked version shares the virtues of its seniors: freshness, delicacy & balance. Deliciousness too, of course, in **22** Ⓐ. Appley-fruity, well balanced & sufficiently concentrated. — TJ

Location/map: Stellenbosch ▪ Map grid reference: B6 ▪ WO: Polkadraai Hills/Stellenbosch ▪ Est/1stB 2000 ▪ Tasting & sales Mon-Fri 9-5 by appt only ▪ Fee R500 per group (2-10 pax) ▪ Closed all pub hols ▪ Owner(s) Bruwer Raats ▪ Cellarmaster(s) Bruwer Raats (Jan 2000) ▪ Winemaker(s) Gavin Bruwer Slabbert (Feb 2010) ▪ Viticulturist(s) Bruwer Raats (Jan 2000) & Gavin Bruwer Slabbert (Feb 2010) ▪ 30ha (cab f, chenin) ▪ 150t/20,000cs own label 40% red 60% white ▪ PO Box 2068 Dennesig Stellenbosch 7601 ▪ office@raats. co.za ▪ www.raatswines.co.za ▪ **T +27 (0)21-881-3078**

Radford Dale   Ⓠ

Founded just over a quarter-century ago by Briton Alex Dale and Australian Ben Radford, this globally represented, sustainability-orientated Stellenbosch winery was formed around the philosophy of single vineyards and varieties. Later, ownership drew in other international and local wine people; current director of viticulture and winemaking Jacques de Klerk joined in 2008. The wine line-up is ever evolving, but now emphasis is on two specific ranges: Organic, from their Ecocert-approved Elgin vineyards, vinified in an on-site cellar which has never seen commercial yeast, to highlight origin and individuality; and mostly Stellenbosch-sourced Vinum, where quality with drinkability is the goal. The latter range includes long-championed gamay noir, which Alex describes as 'one of the Cape's best natural fits' for a lighter red style. Early plantings are coming on-stream; more are in the pipeline. The portfolio as a whole is one of quality and character.

Radford Dale range

★★★★☆ **Frankenstein Pinotage** One of earliest in lighter, more pinot noir-like style, refrained in pure dark-berry perfume, silky feel of **21** Ⓐ. Closes with tug of finest, freshening tannin. Power with elegance at modest 11.5% alc. Wholebunch/berry ferment in 7,000L vessel; ageing 10 months in old small-oak.

★★★★☆ **Syrah** 🐝 Intensity with style in **21** ⑨⑭'s dark berry & black pepper depths, substantial supple texture. Firmly clasped by ripe tannins with savoury length, this serious wine will reward ageing. 30% wholebunch for freshness, older oak, 18 months, restrained 13% alc. Also in 1.5L, as Gravity.

★★★★☆ **Gravity** 🐝 First since **15** ⑨⑭; **20** ⑨③ from cab franc, mourvèdre, shiraz & cab (34/25/22/19), eclectic yet homogenous blend with natural energy in its dark-fruited, savoury substance. Gravity-drain of juice from skins after lengthy maceration creates purity & refinement with resolutely firm grip for ageing. Older oak, 18 months. Only in finest years. WO W Cape, as Frankenstein.

Not tasted: **The Antidote Gamay Noir**, **Black Rock**, **Chardonnay**, **The Renaissance of Chenin Blanc**. Occasional release: **Vine Dried Chenin Blanc**. Discontinued: **Freedom Pinot Noir**, **Nudity Syrah**.

Radford Dale Vinum range

★★★★ **Gamay** Attracts with brilliant youthful hue, spicy red fruit succulence & mouthwateringly fresh, dry finish. **22** ⑧⑧ delicious now, will continue to give pleasure for a few years. Wholeberry natural ferment, as all in range, 7,000L oak fermenters, ageing in older oak barrels.

★★★★ **Grenache** Sprightly **22** ⑧⑧ shows purity & concentration of red berry, wild herb spiced flavours. Light footed, the densely meshed tannins provide freshness & flavourful resonance. Improves on **21** ★★★★☆ ⑧④. Fermented/6 months older oak.

★★★★ **Pinot Noir** ⊘ Variety with which team has much experience, as elegant, silky & beguiling **22** ⑧⑨ confirms. Delicacy in black cherry fragrance, also depth of sweet fruit trimmed by gentle firmness. Older oak, 9 months. Great value. WO W Cape.

★★★★ **Pinotage** As other reds here, wholeberry ferment highlights purity of varietal fruit. **22** ⑧⑦ has floral element to sweet raspberry fragrance. Palate fleshy, with abundant sweet fruit, rounds off with pinotage's tannin twang. 600L oak fermenters, 6 months older cask.

★★★★ **Chardonnay** Needs coaxing to get beyond initial struck match character & reveal bright lemon-lime flavours on comfortable, bouncy **22** ⑧⑦. Sparing use of older oak (50%) adds a little spice & grip to reach goal of class with drinkability.

★★★★ **Chenin Blanc** Red apple, pear & touch of oak spice complexity on **22** ⑧⑦, lees-enriched palate & some skin contact add verve & gentle grip. Styled for satisfying easy drinking.

Radford Dale Organic range

★★★★☆ **Higher Purpose Cabernet Franc** 🆕 ⊘ 🐝 More Loire than Bordeaux, **22** ⑨③ had 2 weeks' carbonic maceration in clay pots to show off variety's perfumed red fruit, leafy spice & finely woven tannins. Purity, freshness & gentle flesh do this to great effect. Already provides characterful drinking, & substance for few years. Completed ferment/10 months older oak. Elgin WO for these.

★★★★☆ **Freedom Pinot Noir** 🍷 ⊘ Charms & intrigues with whispered berry fragrance, crushed velvet texture & languid freshness. More emphatic on **21** ⑨③ is elegant fantail of red cherries & fine-knit tannins. Wholeberry ferment, 20% new oak, 11 months.

★★★★ **Touchstone Chardonnay** 🆕 ⊘ Has Elgin's cool profile, & like Semillon, ample natural vigour. **22** ⑧⑨'s lemon & more prominent earthy flavours are ripe, further broadened by lees ageing. Just enough supportive acidity suggests more medium- than long-term prospect. Bunch press, natural ferment in oak, 7% new.

★★★★☆ **Revelation Semillon** 🆕 ⊘ 🐝 More flavour than fruit, a twist of ginger spice, texture being main feature of **22** ⑨④. Pure & deep, silkiness threaded with inherent vitality, fuelling the fantail savoury length. Wild ferment, 10 months older oak.

Pearce Predhomme range

★★★★ **Cinsault-Syrah** Exuberant **22** ⑧⑦ 51/49 blend offers spice, red berries & wild herb hint, good depth of flavour & spirited dry tail. Cinsaut's wholebunch ferment imbues freshness, undimmed by older-oak ageing. Moreish. Collaboration with Canadian sommeliers, as Chenin.

★★★★☆ **Chenin Blanc** Intriguing ginger spice note, scented ripe peach too on individual **22** ⑨⓪. More youthfully forthcoming than last, lighter bodied (11.5% vs 12.5%), maintains zest & satisfying length. Wild ferment, 8 months older oak.

Radford Dale Thirst range

★★★★ **Clairette Blanche** Attractive take on rarely bottled variety. Spontaneously fermented **22** ⑧⑥ has expressive pear & earth flavours on a softish core, firmed & enlivened by a few hours' skin contact.

Cinsault ★★★☆ Wild strawberries & spice perfume on **22** (83), succulent & bright with an upbeat, freshening tang. Like Gamay, made with carbonic maceration & best lightly chilled. **Gamay Noir ★★★☆** Soft, succulent plums & strawberries, fruity freshness the hallmark of nouveau-style **22** (84). Mouthwatering, lightish red, quaffably modest 11.5% alc. — AL

Location/map: Elgin ▪ Map grid reference: B3 ▪ WO: Stellenbosch/Elgin/Western Cape ▪ Est/1stB 1998 ▪ Tasting by appt at cellar door; sales Mon-Fri 9-5 ▪ Closed all pub hols ▪ Owner(s) Alex Dale, Andy Openshaw, Robert Hill-Smith (Yalumba), Edouard Labeye, Cliff Roberson, Ben Radford, Heather Whitman, Kathleen Krone & Jacques de Klerk ▪ Director of viticulture & winemaking Jacques de Klerk ▪ Winemaker(s) Jacques de Klerk (Nov 2008), with Gerhard Joubert (Jun 2016) & Petroné Thomas (Oct 2021) ▪ Viticulturist(s) Edouard Labeye, Jacques de Klerk & Gerhard Joubert ▪ ±100ha (cab, carignan, cinsaut, gamay, grenache, mourv, ptage, pinot, shiraz, chard, chenin, clairette) ▪ 700t/40,000cs own label 55% red 45% white ▪ IPW, Organic, WIETA ▪ Postnet Suite 124 Private Bag X15 Somerset West 7129 ▪ thirsty@radforddale.com ▪ www.radforddale.com ▪ **T +27 (0)21-855-5528**

Rainbow's End Wine Estate ⓘ ⓜ ⓒ

The pride of a maximum five-star rating from us this edition for the Malan family's Reserve blend, to add to the satisfaction of their gaining new listings at not one but two Michelin two-star restaurants, in Belgium and Singapore. In their home-valley of Banghoek, with 'arguably one of the best views in country', the recently opened tasting lounge is 'operating very successfully', and offering build-your-own cheese and charcuterie platters to partner the mostly Bordeaux varietal wines grown by Francois Malan and handcrafted alongside his brother Anton. Their bottlings 'celebrate terroir and varietal character, and won't disappoint'.

Reserve range

★★★★☆ Family Reserve ⓐ Merlot-led (33%) 4-way Bordeaux blend captures cooler Banghoek refinement. Multi-layered **20** ★★★★★ (95) reveals deep black cherry, cassis & mulberry fruit, complexity enhanced by enticing dried sage & dark chocolate from 2 years in oak, 60% new, as in **19** (93).

Estate range

★★★★☆ Cabernet Sauvignon ⓐ Dark-fruit-nuanced **21** (93), with graphite minerality & oak spice (40% new, year), the epitome of sophisticated cab. Less exuberant than previous, but showing an athlete's build, with nimble tannins making it approachable now, & intensity to last a decade.

★★★★ Cabernet Franc Deliciously opulent, **21** ★★★★★ (90)'s fine tannin structure polished by year in 40% new oak. Greater fruit focus than Limited Release, mulberry, blackcurrant & plum notes combine well with fynbos & thyme undertones. More penetrating than **20** (89).

★★★★☆ Cabernet Franc Limited Release ⓐ Fruit of single 0.75-ha block of Bordeaux clone 312, expresses more red than black fruit & less of variety's aromatic tealeaf. 5% more new oak than sibling, smaller quantity (±580-660 cases). **21** (94) full bodied, with firm, long-haul tannins & savoury finish.

★★★★☆ Merlot Handsome as ever, with a fine build from serious oaking (third new, year); **21** (90) has vigour in youth with poised tannin for ageing up to a decade, especially in magnum (available for all reds except Shiraz & Mystical). Dark chocolate, plum & spiced cherry, evident on **20** (90) too.

★★★★☆ Syrah Was 'Shiraz'. **21** (90) sees twirls of heady spice interwoven with meaty flavours, textured & generous as previous. Year 25% new barrels adds attractive piquancy & black pepper aftertaste.

★★★★ Mystical Corner ⊘ Charming Bordeaux blend for current drinking without breaking the bank, **22** (86) loaded with juicy fruit, finishes savoury. More cab (54%) than merlot, like **21** ★★★★ (85).

Rosé ★★★ Ripe-fruited **22** (81) offers zesty pomegranate flavour profile & cinnamon spice farewell (though unoaked). Quintet of Bordeaux black grapes with shiraz. **Chenin Blanc ★★★★** Enticing tropical melon, papaya & pineapple on **22** (84) good-value quaffer. Unwooded, whereas last **20** (85) saw 10% aged in old barrels. WO W Cape. Not tasted: **Cabernet Franc Rosé.** — DS

Location/map: Stellenbosch ▪ Map grid reference: H6 ▪ WO: Banghoek/Western Cape ▪ Est 1978 ▪ 1stB 2002 ▪ Tasting & sales Tue-Sat 9.30-5 ▪ Sales also via website, delivery free of charge to most areas ▪ Cheese & charcuterie boards available ▪ Conservation area ▪ Owner(s) Malan family ▪ Cellarmaster(s) Anton Malan (Nov 2000) ▪ Winemaker(s) Anton Malan (Nov 2000) & Francois Malan (Jan 2005) ▪ Viticulturist(s) Francois Malan (Jan 2005) ▪ 15ha (cabs s/f, malbec, merlot, p verdot, shiraz) ▪ 100t/13,000cs ▪ IPW ▪ PO Box 2253 Dennesig 7601 ▪ info@rainbowsend.co.za ▪ www.rainbowsend.co.za ▪ **T +27 (0)21-885-1719/+27 (0)83-411-0170/+27 (0)82-404-1085**

Raka

'Family' has been an abiding theme and underpin of this now sizeable venture in a lovely glen in the cool Klein River mountains near Stanford. Never more so than on the 70th birthday of paterfamilias Piet Dreyer, with wife Elna, four children and seven grandchildren gathered to celebrate the former fisherman who around 20 years ago swapped his career on the freezer vessel Raka for a life of wine, joined in time by daughter and marketer Jorika, and winemaker son Josef and his brother, viticulturist Pieter. Values like caring and working hard, coupled with 'putting as much excellent wine as possible in the bottle and keeping the price affordable' have brought much success while keeping a sense of handcrafting and a familial touch.

Erica range

★★★★☆ **Cabernet Sauvignon** ⓥ Rounded, spicy & pliable **16** ⑨⓪. Fruit bold enough to counter 3 years all-new oak. Juicy & fresh, with a long, piquant finish, nicely integrated tannin. 15% alc.

★★★★☆ **Shiraz** ⓥ Premium-priced limited release. Sleek, soft-textured palate offers ripe plum & spice, along with nutty nuance. Revisited mid-2020, **16** ⑨①'s extra time in bottle had smoothed firm, dry tannins from all-new oak (36 months). Persistent rich finish.

Raka range

★★★★☆ **Cabernet Sauvignon** ⊘ Showing cab at its best, **21** ⑨⓪ has cassis & cigarbox lines, a meaty note, hint of mint in the flavours. Lots going on, all of it good, including masterly oaking, tannins present but fine.

★★★★ **Cabernet Franc** ⊘ Red berries with interleaved lead pencils, white pepper, smooth & supple **21** ★★★★☆ ⑨⓪ shows nothing overt, just admirable finesse & style, as this variety can do in good hands. Classic, a notch up on **20** ⑧⑨.

★★★★ **Barrel Select Merlot** There's depth & richness in **21** ⑧⑨, cassis & tobacco, speaking of quality grapes & cellar care. Gets the palate right too, just enough tannin grip as definition, foundation, leaving the plush fruit intact.

★★★★ **Sangiovese** ⊘ Wonderfully expressive fruit, cherries & red berries, which **21** ⑧⑧'s oaking has savoury-spiced; the palate succulent, showing freshness & length. Does the variety proud. No **20**.

★★★★☆ **Biography Shiraz** ⓥ Moving from house-style ripeness of **19** ⑨⓪ to hedgerow fruit, some scrub & dried herb top notes, **20** ⑨③'s oaking contribution a smoky seam, giving a delicious savoury effect. Classic shiraz profile, has controlled power & concentration. Also in 3L & 5L.

★★★★ **Quinary** ⓥ Name indicates 5 parts to classic Bordeaux blend, cab with merlot, dabs of the rest. **20** ★★★★☆ ⑨⓪ plummy depths, well spiced by oak's cloves, white pepper, hints of dried herbs. Masterly tannin handling, supple, with just enough grip at the end for food, but hidden strength for some ageing. Improves on less layered **19** ⑧⑨. In larger bottle formats up to 18L.

★★★★ **Figurehead** ⓥ Bordeaux varieties, cab-led, with 15% pinotage, **19** ⑧⑨ has fruitcake richness & intensity with a firm but ripe tannin base for some ageing, but allowing earlier access. Last was **17** ⑧⑨.

....

Spliced ⊘ ⊕ ★★★★ Blend always creative, **21** ⑧⑤ changed to 54% shiraz with cab & 3 others. Year in different age barrels, perfectly judged for the fruit; tobacco & cedar, vivid red berries & cherries. Smooth & round, tannin nibble at the end. **Rosé** ⊘ ⊕ ★★★★ Never an ordinary rosé, **22** ⑧④ changes to 40% mourvèdre, equal petit verdot & viognier. Trim & bone-dry, flavours perfect for food: berry mix, touch of watermelon, savoury note at the end.

....

Malbec ★★★★ Dark-toned, with a whiff of green brush, **21** ⑧⑤'s year in barrel (25% new, as all reds) adds a smoky note, white pepper. Complex & involving, the palate doesn't disappoint either, succulent, with a fresh seam & polished tannins. **Pinotage** ★★★★ Grape sorting & skin contact, oaking includes some American, a lot of care went into **21** ⑧⑤. Luscious dark berries, vanilla spiced, grip at the end but no barrier to enjoyment. **Sauvignon Blanc** ⊘ ★★★★ Extended lees contact for both vintages tasted this edition, to extract flavour & give body. Previewed **23** ⑧④ shows youthful limy intensity, some flintiness on the finish. **22** ⑧④, now bottled, gooseberry & lemon attractions. Both attest to the diversity of the 4 different vineyards on the farm. **Happiness** ★★★ Carbonated sauvignon blanc bubbly, **NV** ⑧⓪ has a fruitier expression than last, kiwi & litchi, touch of sugar in support. Fine mousse. Not tasted: **Petit Verdot, Five Maidens**. — CR

Location: Stanford ▪ Map: Walker Bay & Bot River ▪ Map grid reference: C8 ▪ WO: Klein River ▪ Est/1stB 2002 ▪ Tasting & sales Mon-Fri 9-5 Sat/pub hols 10-3 ▪ Tasting fee: R60/8 wines on daily tasting list, or R15 for other wines in our range ▪ Closed Sun, Good Fri & Dec 25 ▪ Cellar tours & large groups by appt ▪ BYO picnic ▪ Kiddies play area ▪ Conservation area ▪ Owner(s) Piet Dreyer ▪ Winemaker(s) Josef Dreyer (Jan 2007) ▪ Viticulturist(s) Pieter Dreyer (Jan 2007) ▪ 760ha/62ha (5 Bdx, mourv, ptage, sangio, shiraz, sauv, viog) ▪ 600t/75,000cs own label 75% red 17% white 8% rosé ▪ IPW ▪ PO Box 124 Caledon 7230 ▪ info@rakawine. co.za ▪ www.rakawine.co.za ▪ **T +27 (0)28-341-0676**

Rall Wines ⓦ

'Wines that speak of the site rather than the winemaker's philosophy or style, and are fresh and ageworthy, and not overly ripe, bold or alcoholic' has been internationally hailed Donovan Rall's aspiration since his first signature bottling in 2008. It has continued to be reflected in his wines while his initial and still primary focus on Swartland broadened to other include other areas, and his talents were enlisted by vintners in Stellenbosch and Ceres. To keep meeting his stylistic and uncompromising quality goals, he's taken over the management of more of the vineyards he sources from, and, in the renovated cellar near Riebeek West, added yet more concrete vessels 'as the combination with oak seems to work well for our style of wines'.

★★★★★ **Cinsault** ⓐ **21** ⑨⑤ equal portions Darling & Swartland fruit, **22** ★★★★☆ ⑨④ majority the former for kaleidoscopic array wild flowers, roses, sour cherries, fynbos & earth, nervy freshness. Old oak, 10 months, & 20% Swartland grapes give weight to intricate tannins & luminous structure.

★★★★★ **Ava Syrah** ⓐ 3 weeks on skins & wholebunch ferment in concrete add fruity tannins to **22** ★★★★☆ ⑨④'s fine structure. Texture from 11 months in foudre, dense red cherry & plum core lifted by fresh mineral acid. Like **21** ⑨⑥, from two low-yield schist sites.

★★★★☆ **Rall Syrah** ⓐ Charming **22** ⑨④ expression of Swartland's schist soils invites with savoury smoked meat, wax & graphite aromas. Fermented/aged in concrete to preserve the savoury-spicy character; succulent fruit nipped by slight chew of tannins. 12.5% alc.

★★★★★ **Red** ⓐ Violets & St Joseph lilies aplenty thanks to more syrah (78%) & usual harmonising grenache noir & carignan, dash cinsault in **21** ★★★★★ ⑨⑤. Lively red berries & plums on velvet tannins ex foudre & old barriques, 11 months. Like **20** ⑨③, released a year later than others. Also in 1.5L, as White.

★★★★★ **Ava Chenin Blanc** ⓐ Utterly compelling **22** ★★★★☆ ⑨④, powerful but oh so detailed. Weighty fruit (peach, nectarine, mandarin & pear) imbued with tangy freshness. From schist-grown vines &, like confident **21** ⑨⑤, wholebunch wild fermented, 10 months older oak.

★★★★☆ **Noa Chenin Blanc** ⓐ As usual, **22** ⑨④ off 1960s Paardeberg site & delicate, its white peach purity woven through with lime, enlivened by sense of freshness. Natural ferment, 8 months in concrete 'egg' & 12% alc enhance featherweight mouthfeel.

★★★★☆ **Grenache Blanc** From Piekenierskloof ungrafted vines. Energetic **22** ⑨① spotlights variety's bright lime & lemon fruit, natural ferment/ageing on lees in concrete 'egg' & 12% alc further enhance gossamer texture & light, fresh feel.

★★★★★ **White** ⓐ Consistently excellent blend of chenin, verdelho & drop viognier, **22** ⑨⑤ whispers salty sea breeze & apple blossom. Real tension on palate, cut with white citrus purity. This essence preserved via older oak ageing (80%) & concrete, 10 months. Long & unfolding. WO Coastal.

Occasional release: **Cinsault Blanc**. — ML

Location: Riebeek West ▪ Map: Swartland ▪ Map grid reference: D6 ▪ WO: Swartland/Coastal/Piekenierskloof ▪ Est/1stB 2008 ▪ Tasting, sales & cellar tours by appt ▪ Owner(s)/winemaker(s)/viticulturist(s) Donovan Rall ▪ 50t/3,500cs own label 50% red 50% white ▪ info@rallwines.co.za ▪ www.rallwines.co.za ▪ **T +27 (0)72-182-7571**

Rannoch Farm

Loch Rannoch in the Scottish highlands lends its name to the estate and wine brand of Rory and Ricky Antrobus, the lake and scenery in general of their Helderberg farm reminding them of their ancestors' homeland. There's a small parcel of cabernet, tended by Rory, whose wine is vinified off-site by consultants.

★★★★ **Cabernet Sauvignon** ⓦ Lovely, pure expression of blackcurrant fruit, subtle tobacco & cedar, **15** ⑧⑨'s seamless integration of new French oak, 18 months, aided by 3 years bottle ageing at cellar. — ML

Location/WO: Stellenbosch ▪ Est 1999 ▪ 1stB 2003 ▪ Closed to public ▪ Owner(s) Rory & Ricky Antrobus ▪ Winemaker(s) Corné Marais, with Ivan September (both Jan 2010, Avondale) ▪ Viticulturist(s) Rory Antrobus (Mar 1999) ▪ 8ha/1ha (cab) ▪ 6t/500cs own label 100% white ▪ PO Box 5667 Helderberg 7135 ▪ rory@gmint. co.za ▪ **T +27 (0)82-570-3106**

☐ **Raptor Post** *see* Tulbagh Mountain Vineyards
☐ **Rara Chairman's Reserve** *see* O'Connell's
☐ **Rare Sightings** *see* The Fledge & Co

Rascallion Wines

℗

Savvy marketer and now sole owner of this venture launched in 2017 to demystify wine, Ross Sleet has formed a joint venture with Wellington Wines, supplying Rascallion with 'long-sought-after scalability and Wellington with a sharpened, marketing-driven brand to showcase the remarkable array of wines they have available'. An expansion drive is underway, with major listings in Canada and plans for the UK and Asia well developed. The local focus will be on 'growing the brand from its current base into a major presence'.

Winemakers' Collection

★★★★☆ **The Devonian** ℗ ☻ Luscious stonefruit & citrus in 21 ⑨2 from chenin. Natural ferment & ageing on lees in older oak add personality & creamy breadth. Affirmation for Swartland's affinity with this variety, lovely fresh intensity, concentration & length. No 20.

In abeyance: **A Mother's Journey, Edward Ross**.

Word Collection

★★★★ **Pandiculation** ℗ Rich & savoury 20 ⑧7, dark berries with spicy cured meat & vanilla courtesy 18 months in barrel. Smooth & satisfying. From shiraz & grenache noir (85/15). No 19.

★★★★ **Aquiver** ℗ Chenin (80%), naturally fermented, partly oaked grenache blanc & sauvignon, all ex Swartland. Vibrates with fresh tension, & a crisp, tangy interplay with honeyed tropical fruit. 22 ⑧7 elegant, flavoursome return to form & step up on last 19 ★★★★ ⑧5.

Discontinued: **Bombinate, Susurrous**.

Vinyl Collection

45 RPM ★★★ Vintage skipped & blend changed, like 33 1/3 RPM. 22 ⑧0 is wooded, cinsault-led with splashes of grenache noir & pinotage. Thatchy red fruit with some jaunty acidity & dry tannins. One for the BBQ with some retro vinyl vibes. **33 1/3 RPM** ☻ ★★★ Latest is an easy-drinking chenin-led blend with chardonnay. 23 ⑧1 warm & plumper, less fresh than last, with baked apple, almond notes & brush of oak.

With Love From The Cape Collection

Cabernet Sauvignon ⊘ ★★★★ Black berry compote & mocha in firm, supple tannin framework, 22 ⑧4 most balanced & flavoursome of the reds, aided by some sweet-spiced oak. Rich, crowd-pleasing style. **Pinotage** ★★★ Ripe plum & earthy notes in 22 ⑧1, from new source. Warming fruit core, reined-in fresh acid & some tannin grip, partly from 100% oak ageing. For hearty fare. **Chenin Blanc** ★★★ Bursts with bright crunchy apple & hint tropical fruit. Now unoaked, 23 ⑧2 riper than last, a welcoming, friendly summer quaffer. **Sauvignon Blanc** ★★★ Drier, leaner in 23 ⑦9. Dusty pebble nuance, hint of fig. Different vineyard source to previous, better with a fish platter. Discontinued: **Rosé**.

Art Collection

Not tasted: **Impress Rouge, Impress Blanc**. — MW

Location: Wellington ▪ WO: Western Cape/Swartland ▪ Est/1stB 2017 ▪ Tasting & sales at Wellington Wines by appt ▪ Wine club ▪ Owner(s) Ross Sleet, Wellington Wines ▪ Winemaker(s) Daniel Slabber (reds), Christo Smit (white & rosé) ▪ 20,000cs own label 40% red 60% white ▪ Stokery Rd Wellington 7655 ▪ ross@rascallionwines.co.za ▪ www.rascallionwines.co.za ▪ **T +27 (0)78-886-2246**

☐ **Rebelle** *see* Belle Rebelle

Rebel Rebel Wines

℗

Having fallen in love with a pair of high-lying vineyards on Stellenbosch's Bottelary Hills, Kaapzicht wine-maker (and David Bowie fan) Kayleigh Hattingh used an area of the cellar dedicated to natural winemaking to craft the debut wine for this own small-batch label in 2020. Latterly she's been focused on improving soil health and pruning methods, and systematic replanting 'to ensure the longevity of the vines and brand'.

★★★★☆ **Syrah** Loses splash cinsault of previous but not its on-trend lighter styling. Wholeberry-fermented 21 ⑨0 appealing fynbos & quarry dust accents; real attraction is tempered tannin structure, aided by 15 months in older barrels. Also in magnum.

★★★★☆ **Old Vine Colombar** ⊛ Smoky, pithy, trenchant - **22** ⑨⓪ will divide the room, & lovers of unfruity whites will want another glass, to savour the deep umami undertone & seam of natural acidity. From 1986 vines, 8 hours skin contact, ferment/7 months in old oak, some Hungarian.

★★★★ **Méthode Ancestrale** ⑭ Energy in these wines is palpable, especially this single-ferment sparkler from cinsault. Sunset pink **23** ⑧⑦ shot through with tiny bubbles, clean strawberry fruit with rosepetal & orange zest notes, dry, slightly nutty finish.— CvZ

Location/map: Stellenbosch ▪ Map grid reference: B4 ▪ WO: Bottelary ▪ Est/1stB 2020 ▪ Tasting, sales & cellar tours by appt only ▪ Owner(s) Kayleigh Hattingh ▪ Winemaker(s) Kayleigh Hattingh (Jun 2020) ▪ 10-15t/600-800cs own label 55% red 40% white 5% rosé ▪ wine@rebelrebelwine.com ▪ **T +27 (0)79-436-0210**

☐ **Rebourne Fairtrade** see Imbuko Wines

Redamancy Vineyards

With long experience in the development aid sector, and golden retrievers Brave and Maisha at their side, Marc van Uytvanck and Antoinette Rapitsi chose 'Reciprocal Love' as their brand name to describe both the relationship among them, their desire to grow wine ethically, using organic principles, for the benefit of all involved in the production, and the 'deep affection' they hope their small range will inspire in the consumer.

★★★★ **Chardonnay** From single-vineyard near coastal hamlet Vermaaklikheid, **22** ★★★★☆ ⑨⓪'s natural ferment/year in oak, 25% new, give a tighter, more elegant structure than **21** ⑧⑧, thrilling contrast between creamy lees & vivid acid, lime piquancy & bone-dry finish.

Not tasted: **Cabernet Sauvignon**, **Cabernet Sauvignon Premium**, **Cabernet Sauvignon Reserve**. — ML

Location: Stellenbosch ▪ WO: Cape South Coast ▪ Est 2014 ▪ 1stB 2022 ▪ Closed to public ▪ Online shop ▪ Owner(s) Marc van Uytvanck & Antoinette Rapitsi ▪ Winemaker(s)/viticulturist(s) Guillaume Nell (Feb 2021, consultant) ▪ 4.5ha/2.2ha (cab) ▪ ±12t/1,500cs own label 75% red 25% white ▪ PO Box 658 Stellenbosch 7599 ▪ info@redamancy.co.za ▪ www.redamancy.co.za ▪ **T +27 (0)83-580-1461**

☐ **Red Chair** see Rooiberg Winery
☐ **Reino Thiart Wines** see Thiart Wines
☐ **Releaf Organic** see Imbuko Wines

Remhoogte Wine Estate

Founded in the mid-1990s by Murray Boustred as a means of escaping the Johannesburg rat race, Remhoogte embodies the very best of a family-run business. Son Chris, viticulturist since 2007, also took over winemaking in 2011, running the unpretentious cellar on truly artisanal lines, his brother Rob handling marketing. A safari theme seems to be taking hold, with bushveld wildlife meandering between the vineyards (Rob yearns for a giraffe), and Vuur, the gourmet braai offered by chef Shaun Scrooby in the miniature converted stable, concentrating on fine-dining venison dishes. To cater for demand, a shared-table version of the experience is under construction on an island in the adjacent dam. Petit verdot, cabernet franc and chenin are replacing older merlot blocks, and the cellar is undergoing extension.

Reserve range

★★★★☆ **Cabernet Sauvignon** ⊛ Brawny, concentrated single-site **19** ⑨⓪ shows serious intent in deep & dark fruit, thick tannin cloak, brooding earthy minerality. Spontaneous ferment in open 500L barrels, 2 years in 75% new barriques. Promises rewards for cellaring.

★★★★☆ **Syrah** ⊛ From 5 special rows of single north-facing parcel, **19** ⑨④ has might as well as charm, rippling muscles adorned with delicate floral perfume, baking spices & sweetly aromatic tobacco. 20% whole-bunch ferment adds lighter facets, 2 years in 40% new oak give lustre & platform for improvement over decade or more.

★★★★☆ **Sir Thomas Cullinan** ⊛ Refined merlot-led Cape Bordeaux with cab &, debuting in the blend, cab franc, 2 years in barrique, 60% new. Finds perfect pitch in **19** ★★★★★ ⑨⑥, reflected in velvet tannins, sweet-ripe & compact fruit core, precise, lingering finish. Edges excellent **18** ⑨④.

★★★★☆ **Honeybunch Chenin Blanc** From official 1987 single-vineyard, sweetly succulent, barrel-fermented **22** ⑨ is full bodied, supple & simply delicious, with ripe stonefruit & pineapple, subtle floral whiff. Name derives from selection of sun-exposed clusters, adding honeyed richness.

Premium range

★★★★ **Aspect Merlot** ⊘ High-lying vines on shale; wild yeast ferment in oak tank, 2 years in barrel. **18** ★★★★★ ⑨⓪'s inky liquorice, tar & tobacco are in harmony with weighty black cherry & blackcurrant fruit. All nicely integrated with cocoa & oak spice on robust but ripe tannins. Pips **17** ⑧⑨.

★★★★ **Vantage Pinotage** ⊘ From 20 year old bushvines, **20** ⑨⓪ radiates health & ripeness, with dense black fruit, sombre tarry vein & ripe, sleek tannins. 18 months in small barrels, 15% new, add gloss & integration.

★★★★ **Chronicle Red Blend** ⊘ Merlot & syrah, with 12% pinotage, splash cab, **20** ⑧⑨ blends all 17 red blocks on the estate. Typical cellar techniques, including some carbonic maceration, wild yeast, produce sultry, juicy & moreish results. Delicious now, should benefit from cellaring.

★★★★ **First Light Chenin Blanc** ⊘ Unpretentious, honest & satisfying, **23** ⑧⑦ is sunny, fruit-filled drinking pleasure: pineapple & peach, subtle orange blossom scent. Ripe & rounded at modest 12% alc.

Free To Be range

★★★★☆ **Red** ⊘ Range theme is adventurous winemaking, here carbonic maceration of syrah, ageing 10 months in concrete tank, giving typical Nouveau-like sour cherry fruit, floral & exaggerated white pepper aromatics in **22** ⑨⓪. Stellenbosch WO, as First Light.

Not tasted: Cabernet Sauvignon-Cinsault, Orange, White. — GdB

Location/map: Stellenbosch ▪ Map grid reference: F3 ▪ WO: Simonsberg-Stellenbosch/Stellenbosch ▪ Est 1812 ▪ 1stB 1995 ▪ Tasting & sales Mon-Fri 9-5 Sat 10-4 ▪ Closed Easter Fri-Sun, Dec 25 & Jan 1 ▪ Cellar tours by appt ▪ Flatbreads ▪ Wine & gourmet braai experience ▪ Functions ▪ Walks/hikes ▪ Game ▪ Guest cottage ▪ Wine club ▪ Owner(s) Murray Boustred Trust ▪ Cellarmaster(s) Chris Boustred (Jan 2011) ▪ Winemaker(s)/viticulturist(s) Chris Boustred (Jan 2007) ▪ 55ha/25ha (cabs s/f, cinsaut, merlot, p verdot, ptage, shiraz, chenin) ▪ 180t/12,000cs own label 80% red 20% white ▪ IPW ▪ PO Box 2032 Dennesig 7601 ▪ info@remhoogte.co.za ▪ www.remhoogte.co.za ▪ **T +27 (0)21-889-5005**

☐ **Renaissance Of Our Heritage** *see* Lammershoek Winery

Renegade Wines

Co-owners Jaap Pijl and Francois Haasbroek locally pioneered wine in aluminium cans, adopting the CanCan name and design based on the risqué French cabaret stars of the late 19th century. Exports to the Americas, Europe and Asia have grown, encouraging a new syrah, vinified in the cellar where Francois crafts his own Blackwater wines. Their philosophy reflects 'minimal intervention in wines that bridge the gap between new wave and old school, are varietally correct and just happen to be packaged in a can'.

CanCan range

Limited Edition Syrah 🆕 🍷 ★★★★ Unoaked **21** ⑧⑤ includes 15% grenache noir to lighten & freshen the rich, smooth dark berry flavours. Gentle grip adds form, completes easy-drinking satisfaction.

Valentin le Désossé Grenache Noir 🥂 🍷 ★★★ Lightly perfumed **21** ⑧⓪ is unoaked, has sweet-fruited charm, gentle squeeze of grip & dry finish for ready pleasure. From Breedekloof. **Satine Rosé** 🥂 ★★★ In pretty 250 ml can, as all these, delightful onion skin **22** ⑧⓪ from grenache noir is fresh, dry, berry-fruity & light (11.9% alc) for elegant picnics. **La Goulue Chenin Blanc** ★★★★ Attractive fresh apple fragrance with well-sustained flavours on **22** ⑧④. Plump & juicy, with balanced freshness, round dryness. **La Mélinite Bubbly White Perlé Wine** ★★★ Lightly sparkling **NV** ⑦⑨, mainly chardonnay, splash pinot noir. Flavoursome, short-lived froth with briskly dry finish. — AL

Location: Stellenbosch ▪ WO: Swartland/Breedekloof ▪ Est/1stB 2019 ▪ Closed to public ▪ Owner(s) Jaap Pijl & Francois Haasbroek ▪ Winemaker(s) Francois Haasbroek (Dec 2018) ▪ 2,000cs own label 20% red 40% white 40% other + 5,000cs for clients ▪ Brands for clients: Banks Brothers, First Crush, Liberator, Riverine ▪ PO Box 12754 Die Boord Stellenbosch 7613 ▪ hello@cancan.wine ▪ www.cancan.wine

☐ **Renosterbos** *see* Hofstraat Kelder
☐ **Respect for Nature** *see* Olivedale Private Vineyards

Restless River Wines

'Young, hungry and strong' is the team update from the Wessels and Fourie families in Upper Hemel-en-Aarde Valley, who set out around 20 years ago with a dream that's materialised in a celebrated wine estate, with 21 ha under vine, understood to be more than any grower in the ward, and exports to 15 countries. 'It has been a lot of work and financial commitment,' say Anne Wessels and winemaker husband Craig, the venture's charming public faces, 'but we could not have done it any other way. Ownership of the vineyards, and therefore security and control, was imperative, no matter how long it took.' Capacity is being expanded, and Anne and Craig acknowledge the contribution of David Cross in the vineyards and Hylton Gibson in the cellar to the goal of 'growing and producing some of the finest wines this special valley has to offer'.

★★★★★ **Main Road & Dignity** ⊛ Fascinating comparison between this rare-in-region cabernet & its pinot noir sibling. From 2 eponymous blocks on granite & clay, **20** ⑭ lean, athletic & textured, with steely graphite nuance, 22 months in 30% new oak add gravitas, cedar scent & a final polish. Needs & deserves extended cellaring, like **19** ★★★★★ ⑮, 1.5L-5L bottle formats ideal for that.

★★★★☆ **Le Luc** ⊛ Pinot noir, named for Wessels son, **21** ⑭ light in tone & alc (13%) yet full flavoured, its savoury dark cherry palate imbued with substance & memorable length without heaviness. Portion wholebunch, year in cask, 25% new. Also in 1.5L. No **20**.

★★★★★ **Ava Marie** ⊛ Arresting, ageworthy chardonnay from 1999 2-ha single-vineyard. Natural bunch-ferment & year on lees in 10% new oak, plus 10% amphora component deliver riveting tension, lime & spice complexity, flinty, limy persistence. Artful crafting of **21** ⑮ gives subtle, effortless power with balance, as in **20** ★★★★★ ⑭.— DS

Location: Hermanus ▪ Map: Walker Bay & Bot River ▪ Map grid reference: B4 ▪ WO: Upper Hemel-en-Aarde Valley ▪ Est 1999 ▪ 1stB 2005 ▪ Tasting & sales by appt ▪ Closed all pub hols ▪ Owner(s) Wessels & Fourie families ▪ Winemaker(s) Craig Wessels (Jan 2005) ▪ Viticulturist(s) Kevin Watt (2012) ▪ 30ha/21ha (cab, pinot, chard) ▪ 70t/10,000cs own label 66% red 33% white ▪ PO Box 1739 Hermanus 7200 ▪ anne@restlessriver.com ▪ www.restlessriver.com ▪ T +27 (0)28-313-2881

☐ **Retief Reserve** *see* Van Loveren Family Vineyards
☐ **Retro Series** *see* Elemental Bob
☐ **Reverie** *see* Idun

Reyneke Wines

The fight against aliens is real! Certified biodynamic producer Reyneke Wines spent much of the past year developing the 40-ha neighbour property on Stellenbosch's rising star Polkadraai Hills, removing vegetation, rehabilitating fynbos and planting vines, including filling gaps in the 1974 chenin vineyard. Environmental philosophy graduate and viticulturist Johan Reyneke believes in the holistic natural system, with the place, plants, animals and people all interlinked, especially the people working the land, the true foundation of the business. Proceeds from Cornerstone sales have bought the fifth house for the team members, the principle being that 'good grapes make good wine, and good people ensure good grapes'. The latter, in turn, are handled as gently and naturally as possible by cellarmaster Rudiger Gretschel and winemaker Barbara Melck.

Biodynamic Reserve range

★★★★☆ **Reyneke Reserve Red** ◎ ⊛ Restraint typifies **20** ⑬ syrah. A third wholebunch & foot crushed in open concrete tank; wild ferment (as all wines), followed by 18 months in old oak. Tangy succulence to plum vibrancy. Deep, concentrated, savoury & cohesive. For the long haul.

★★★★★ **Reyneke Reserve White** ◎ ⊛ Interplay of elements on **21** ⑬ sauvignon blanc: lively grapefruit zest set against integrated broad, creamy richness. Lovely tension & complexity. Ferment in barrel, 80% new, 10 months on lees.

Occasional release: **Cabernet Sauvignon, Natural Chenin Blanc**.

Biodynamic range

★★★★☆ **Syrah** ◎ ⊛ Inky liquorice & graphite mingle with scrub & herb on powerful but nimble & rewarding **21** ⑭. Complex making involves 30% whole bunches, ferment in concrete tank & 14 months in seasoned oak. Svelte & sleek, with lean muscularity & fine tannin.

★★★★ **Cornerstone** ⊘ Cab (14%) again in the minority in **20** ⑧⑨ blend with cab franc. Dark fruitcake, cocoa & herb sheen. After ferment in open kuipe, former has all-new oak while latter has seasoned barrels, 18 months in all. Like **19** ★★★★☆ ⑨①, cohesive & long.

★★★★☆ **Chenin Blanc** ◎ ⊛ Rounded, ripe nectarine & quince on elegant & restrained but confident **22** ⑨①. Bunch press, 10 months in combo barrel & foudre. Like **21** ⑨⓪, lees & oak provide support for lively fruit with creamy breadth.

★★★★ **Sauvignon Blanc** ◎ Where last was gently succulent, **22** ⑧⑧ taut & zingy, with slatey flavours & texture from combo destemmed & wholebunch pressings, fermented in oak, 30% new, on lees for 8 months. Good frame & substance to balance zippy acid.

Vinehugger range

Syrah ⑭ᴱʷ ⊘ ★★★★ Light, fruity **22** ⑧④ debuts with gentle grip & rounded body. Ferment in concrete & open stainless tanks. 12% aged year in older oak. WO W Cape, as Cab-Merlot & Chenin. **Cabernet Sauvignon-Merlot** ⊘ ★★★★ Appealing cocoa-dusted cherry compote on 53/44 blend in **21** ⑧⑤. Bright, juicy, with good core & focus from ferment in concrete & stainless tanks, only a third aged in old, large oak, lending body. **Rosé** ⑭ᴱʷ ⊘ ★★★★ Peppery fynbos & raspberry on perky **23** ⑧③ pink from mourvèdre & shiraz. Cohesive, unfussy & great for summer. **Chenin Blanc** ⊘ ★★★★ Ripe honeyed pear notes on **23** ⑧④, fermented/3 months on lees in stainless tank. Poised, broad & long, to enjoy every day. **Sauvignon Blanc** ⊘ ★★★★ Citrus & white pepper zip & tang on light, unpretentious **23** ⑧③. Half unoaked, rest 6 months in well-seasoned barrels. Discontinued: **Shiraz-Cabernet Sauvignon**. — FM

Location/map: Stellenbosch ▪ Map grid reference: B6 ▪ WO: Stellenbosch/Western Cape ▪ Est 1863 ▪ 1stB 1998 ▪ Tasting by appt only ▪ Fee R75/R150pp ▪ VIP tasting & vineyard walk with viticulturist and/or winemaker at R250pp (max 20), booking essential ▪ Sales Tue-Thu 10-4 Fri 10-3 Sat by appt only 10-3 + online sales ▪ Owner(s) Reyneke Wines (Pty) Ltd ▪ Cellarmaster(s) Rudiger Gretschel ▪ Winemaker(s) Barbara Melck (Dec 2021) ▪ Viticulturist(s) Johan Reyneke, guided by Rosa Kruger ▪ 120ha/70ha (cabs s/f, merlot, shiraz, chenin, sauv) ▪ 50,000cs own label 70% red 30% white ▪ CERES (organic), Demeter (biodynamic), IPW ▪ PO Box 61 Vlottenburg 7604 ▪ lizanne@reynekewines.co.za ▪ www.reynekewines.co.za ▪ **T +27 (0)21-881-3451/ WhatsApp +27 (0)71-137-4869**

Rhebokskloof Wine Estate   ⑨ ⑪ ◎ ⑤ ⑤

Scenic Rhebokskloof on Paarl Mountain's north slope offers a warm welcome and varied experience, including a pairing of chocolate and selected wines made by the team headed by Rolanie Lotz, whose presence in the cellar since 2007 has provided continuity during the transition from family venture to today's corporate-owned multifaceted function, business and leisure venue. While pinnacle Black Marble undoubtedly is the most impressive and showy, all ranges emphasise 'expression, complexity and balance'.

Black Marble Hill range

★★★★☆ **Syrah** ⑧ Lush yet refined **19** ⑨③, plums & berries with pepper lift. Well crafted, harmonious, achieves depth & breadth without weight. Naturally fermented (as Chardonnay), built to last 10+ years.

★★★★★ **Chardonnay** ⑧ Showcases pristine fruit & spice in sumptuous yet graceful body. Like last-tasted **19** ⑨⑥, **21** ★★★★★ ⑨④ expertly oaked & lees aged for textured mouthful of lasting flavour.

★★★★ **Méthode Cap Classique** ⑧ Light gold **16** ⑧⑧ from chardonnay, delicious notes of vanilla & lemon curd in a fine, creamy, melt-in-the-mouth mousse. 20% barrel fermented, 52 months on lees.

Rhebokskloof range

★★★★☆ **Pinotage** ⊘ Generous, smooth black fruit & spice with savoury dried herbs from 16 months in 30% new oak. **20** ★★★★ ⑧⑧ flavoursome but misses the gravitas of **19** ⑨⓪, for earlier drinking.

★★★★ **Shiraz** ⊘ Pleasing typicity in its berry fruit & savoury spice, **20** ⑧⑧'s body rounded after 18 months oak, 30% new. Pinch dried coriander joins usual white pepper in farewell. No viognier this time.

★★★★ **Chardonnay** ⑧ Barrel ferment in older oak, 11 months with regular lees stirring produce delightful **21** ⑧⑧, the wood-derived notes in balance with succulent fruit, giving a clean, lifted finish.

Chenin Blanc ★★★★ Succulent **22** ⑧④'s apple & citrus gain dimension & higher rating from splash grenache blanc, 20% wild-yeast, barrel-fermented portion, & extended lees ageing. Not tasted: **The Rhebok**.

Flatrock range

Red ⊘ ⊚ ★★★★ Unusual but compatible combo, shiraz, pinotage & petite sirah, proportions tweaked for **20** ⑧⑤ but still engaging, full of berried cheer. Subtle oak backbone means no rush to drink up.

Chenin Blanc ★★★ Was 'White'. Vibrant & flavourful **23** ⑧②, abundant apple & tropical fruit, to chill well & enjoy every day. WO Coastal, as siblings. **Sparkle** ⊘ ★★★★ Fragrant party-starting **NV** ⑧③ carbonated fizz pairs viognier & dabs chenin & chardonnay for a fluteful of peach melba & spice. — WB

Location/map: Paarl ▪ Map grid reference: D3 ▪ WO: Paarl/Coastal ▪ 1stB 1975 ▪ Tasting, sales & restaurant Mon-Sun 9-5, open 365 days/year ▪ Fee R50/5 wines, waived on purchase ▪ Chocolate & wine tasting R100pp/5 wines ▪ Rhebokskloof restaurant: serves breakfast, lunch, pizza, picnic ▪ Facilities for children ▪ Tour groups ▪ Weddings, functions & conferences ▪ MTB & hiking trails ▪ Online shop ▪ Wine club ▪ Owner(s) ASLA Group ▪ GM Martin Gebers ▪ Global sales manager Jani Phiri ▪ Cellarmaster(s) Rolanie Lotz (Jan 2007) ▪ Viticulturist(s) André Rousseau (2017) ▪ 180ha/35ha (cab, carignan, durif, mourv, p verdot, ptage, shiraz, chard, chenin, grenache b, viog) ▪ 30,000cs own label 70% red 30% white ▪ WIETA ▪ PO Box 2637 Paarl 7620 ▪ info@rhebokskloof.co.za ▪ www.rhebokskloof.co.za ▪ **T +27 (0)21-869-8386**

☐ **Rhino Run** *see* Van Loveren Family Vineyards
☐ **Rhino Tears** *see* Mount Vernon Estate

Richard Hilton Vineyards

After 'Covid sidestepping', Stellenbosch minimal-intervention vintner and luxury travel specialist Richard Hilton feels his boutique wine brand is moving forward, with the first Carolus chardonnay - 'from a fabulous site' - released at last. The Bounty syrah, unready for tasting by us last time, turns out to be as delicious as he described. Elgin and Helderberg remain his grape sources (he's teasing a pinot noir from there 'if I can get my hands on the right site, clone and quality'), and clarity, balance and terroir reflection his main drivers.

★★★★ **Ironstone** ⊘ This & Dalmatian are a pair, same Helderberg syrah grower, similar vinification, this sees only older oak. **19** ⑧⑧ lavender scented & savoury, more approachable than its partner.

★★★★☆ **The Dalmatian** ⊘ With 30% new barrique & 18 months ageing, **19** ⑨④ from Stellenbosch engineered for 11+ years ageing. Harmonious layers of fruit, spice & charcuterie, elegant savoury finish.

★★★★☆ **The Bounty** Lovely violet wafts entice on lean cool-climate shiraz. **20** ⑨⓪ mulberry (fruit & leaf), white pepper & dab nutmeg on trim palate (12.5% alc), dry structure with fresh plum uplift on finish.

★★★★☆ **The Unyielding** ⊘ From syrah, gains heft & ageing potential from new oak & barrel time, 30%, 16 months. **19** ⑨④ great fruit purity & minerality, savoury tannin. Richly spiced, concentrated & deep.

★★★★☆ **Carolus Magnus Rex** (NEW) Elegant, effortless chardonnay, **22** ⑨① beautifully balanced, smooth textured, with subtle complexity & length, echoing citrus & apple meringue, gentle vanilla & clove accents. Will reward the patient, though so tempting now.

★★★★☆ **The Emperor Probus Viognier** Luscious, rich **19** ⑨② ripe stonefruit, fragrant honeysuckle & vanilla aromas. Mouthfilling & rounded with long spicy farewell. Good balance & presence, cleansing grip.

★★★★ **Clay Shales** (NEW) Viognier, companion to Probus (& oriental food), touch less serious, to enjoy earlier. **22** ⑧⑧ well made, though, voluptuously fruited yet fresh, peach & apricot well spiced & lively.

Not tasted: **Cartref**. Discontinued: **Rose Quartz**. — WB

Location: Stellenbosch ▪ WO: Elgin/Stellenbosch ▪ Est 2003 ▪ Closed to public ▪ Wine club ▪ Owner(s) Richard Hilton ▪ Cellarmaster(s)/winemaker(s) Richard Hilton (2003) ▪ Viticulturist(s) Francois Hanekom ▪ (shiraz, viog) ▪ 20t/2,700cs own label 55% red 45% white ▪ info@hiltonvineyards.co.za ▪ www.hiltonvineyards.co.za ▪ **T +27 (0)83-650-5661**

☐ **Richard Kershaw** *see* Kershaw Wines
☐ **Richard's** *see* Kershaw Wines

Richelieu

Owned by Heineken Beverages, this famous brand pays tribute to the French origins of fine SA brandy though its name and distinctive flavour profile.

★★★★ **10 Year Vintage Brandy** Ⓥ Only Vintage brandy (89) in the guide. Per the category, minimum 30% potstill & brandy spirit aged ten years. Elegant & complex, rich, smooth & floral. Also in 50ml.

★★★★☆ **8 Year Sauvignon Blanc Limited Edition** (NEW) ⊘ Light amber glow on potstill brandy (92), delicately fragranced with apple, dried pear & quince, richly flavoured with creamy cashew & vibrant citrus, well-judged 38% alc warming the finish. All beautifully harmonious & lingering.

Richelieu International Ⓥ ★★★ Blended brandy (82), upbeat peach caramel flavours, rich & robust (43% alc) for mixing. Also in 50ml, 200ml, 375ml & 1L. — WB

Rickety Bridge Winery   Ⓥ 🍴 🏠 📷 👤 ♿

A small block of bushvine cabernet is taking shape on the side of Dassenberg Mountain, overlooking the railway-sleeper bridge over the Franschhoek River that's long been rid of any instability, and nowadays provides access to a modern and extensive wine, lifestyle and hospitality venture. Under British custodianship, the past has not been forgotten, however, and the historic farm buildings have been restored, and founder in 1797, Paulina de Villiers, memorialised in the Reserve range and eatery. Heritage is also reflected in the ancient vines cellarmaster Donovan Ackermann works with for some of the wines. A complex grape sourcing operation includes the home-farm, multiple pockets in the area and as far flung as Swartland and Robertson, for wines that are 'pure, clean and elegant' and, in the premium ranges, well worth cellaring.

Icon range

★★★★☆ **The Bridge** Ⓥ Brooding, concentrated dark fruit from estate & another site perfect foil for serious oaking in **20** ★★★★★ (95). Complexity & structure befitting a top-tier cab, perfect balance for a long future. Sophisticated step up on **19** (93). These in magnum, too, unless noted.

★★★★☆ **The Crossover** Ⓥ This **20** (92) bushvine pinotage more serious than Rickety sibling. Boldly structured & ageworthy, firm dry tannins & bright acid enlivening the dense liquorice-spiced fruit.

★★★★☆ **The Sleeper** Ⓥ Appealing smoky shiraz laced with white pepper, adding a lovely freshness to **20** (94)'s layers of flavour. More time in barrel & new oak add polish to already sophisticated wine.

★★★★★ **The Pilgrimage Old Vine Semillon** 🍇 🌸 Vibrant & exhilarating **21** (95) from venerable 1905 semillon vines on La Brie farm. Hallmark elegance, silk texture & structure, subtly persistent honeyed beeswax, almond & melon, as always seamed with lemony freshness. Wholebunch wild ferment, now 100% oaked, older Austrian foudre, 11 months.

★★★★☆ **The Gateway Old Vine Colombar Straw Wine** (NEW) 🌸 From 46 year old bushvines, straw-dried bunches, half oak aged. **NV** (92) from two vintages unfolds with smooth glacé pineapple, subtle citrus & almond notes; burnt caramel sweetness well balanced by pervasive tangy seam of acid. Refined layers of flavour & persistence. 375 ml.

Niche range (NEW)

★★★★ **The 1905 Semillon** Same 1905 parcel as Pilgrimage, 6% of vines show rare red-skinned mutation, giving colour to **21** (89). Half bunch-pressed, wild yeast fermented & aged in older oak, allowing subtle cranberry, lemon & honeycomb flavours to shine. Gracefully styled, delicate & light (10.7% alc) yet lingering, finishing with grapefruit pithiness.

Paulina's Reserve range

★★★★ **Cabernet Sauvignon** 🍇 Alluringly scented black fruit pastilles & violets in **21** ★★★★★ (94) from two vineyards. Sheathed power, palate attractions still bound up in fine, fruit & oak tannin framework (20 months, 30% new). Better potential than **20** (89), one for the cellar.

★★★★☆ **Old Vine Cinsault** 🌸 Venerable 69 year old Paarl dryland bushvines continue to reward with signature black cherry, sweet clove & polished leather nuances, though more subtly so in **22** (92). Some stems during ferment enhance texture & delicate fruit flavours, deftly underpinned by ageing in old oak & amphora, 6 months. Fresh, elegant, but shade off **21** ★★★★★ (95).

★★★★ **Chenin Blanc** 🍇 From 2 old blocks in Paarl & Swartland, bunch pressed, fermented/10 months in barrel (now 500L), 20% new. **21** ★★★★☆ (93) exudes freshness & vibrancy. Light 12.4% alc but lovely fruit intensity: layers of preserved quince, dried apricot & lime, subtle toasted nut undertone, all lingering to very satisfactory conclusion. Elegant step up on **20** (88).

★★★★☆ **Sauvignon Blanc** ⓐ Textured, understated **22** ⑨③ from home & Bot River grapes, & splash semillon from 1905 Franschhoek vines. Subtle greengage & lime woven into richer waxy substrate. Part tank ferment, completed & 10 months in oak, 50% new. Touch riper than last but still fresh & engaging.

★★★★★ **Semillon** ⓐ Two vintages tasted, both from same, old (33 & 34 years) home vineyards, tank fermented & aged in older oak. **21** ⑨③ vibrates with pure joie de vivre, has layers of nut praline, honey & almond, silky texture zested through with clean citrus acid. **22** ⑨② as flavoursome but does slower seductive tango, succulent & rounded, also touch more alc (13.2%).

Rickety Bridge range

★★★★ **Cabernet Sauvignon** ⓝⓔⓦ Crimson **21** ⑧⑥ quite muscular & compact, keeping its cassis core closely guarded. Mostly old-oak matured, 12 months, shows variety's firm dry tannins. Better with time.

★★★★ **Merlot** Touch more fresh piquancy to **21** ⑧⑧, lively red fruit & brisk acid partly cushioned by mostly older-oak maturation. A youthful tablemate that would also benefit from some cellar time.

★★★★ **Shiraz** Fresher, brighter in **21** ⑧⑨, more on red-berry spectrum but similar perfumed lift from dried stems during ferment. Oak as last, 12 months, 15% new, in supple support. Good few years in store.

★★★★ **Chardonnay** Two vintages tasted, identically made: tank ferment & ageing mostly in larger Austrian foudre & older barrel for subtle brush of oak. Lemon & lime whet appetite, crisp & zesty finish fulfils promise in **21** ★★★★★ ⑨①. Drier, lighter (12.3% alc) but more intense & long-lived than **22** ⑧⑨, which has similar bright citrus but touch riper (13.1% alc) more rounded, already inviting.

★★★★ **Méthode Cap Classique Brut Rosé** Rose gold hue to latest vibrant & piquant **NV** ⑧⑥ sparkling. More savoury, charcuterie nuanced than last, mere hint of brioche after 12 months on lees. Majority chardonnay this time, pinot noir down to 40%. Balanced & ready to celebrate.

★★★★ **Méthode Cap Classique Blanc de Blancs** Latest **NV** ⑧⑧ from chardonnay richer than last courtesy extra 8 months on cork after 12 on lees. Lovely clean green-apple & citrus, subtle brioche, dry & appealing, a versatile sparkler for any occasion.

★★★★ **Noble Late Harvest** From Robertson riesling, **23** ⑧⑦ botrytis dessert on riper side, smooth & supple, candied fruit, some floral notes & touch of lime. Light 9.5% alc, finishes with refreshing lemon barley lift. 375 ml.

....

Chenin Blanc ⓥ ★★★★ Juicy tropical & stonefruit in unwooded **22** ⑧⑤. Widely sourced & now all-chenin, a delicious, cheerful, lees-enriched mouthful.

....

Pinotage ⓥ ★★★★ Some savoury notes to **20** ⑧⑤. Year old oak adds spice to muscular tannin structure. Riper, dark-fruited style, drinking well with a few years in store. WO W Cape, as Chenin & Sauvignon.
Sauvignon Blanc ★★★ Ripe papaya aromas give way to racy acid, greener spectrum fruits & bone-dry styling in **22** ⑧⓪. Tangy & light at 12% alc, for salads & seafood. Not tasted: **Méthode Cap Classique Blanc de Blancs Vintage**.

Foundation Stone range

★★★★ **White** ⓥ Majority chenin in **20** ⑧⑦ with grenache blanc, roussanne & 4 others, half in large oak, rest in concrete tanks. Ripe & succulent apple, almond & hint of ginger, pervasive fresh acid.
Red ⓥ ★★★★ Plump, perfumed red fruit in this varying blend, mostly shiraz & cinsaut, 3 others in **19** ⑧④. Retains alluring spice-laden profile, enhanced by year older oak. WO W Cape, as White. **Rosé** ★★★★ Mourvèdre leads **23** ⑧⑤'s 5-part Rhône varietal mix. Tangy red berries & earthy-savoury notes, similar bone-dry style, but touch more alc (12.5%) than last adds breadth for appealing solo or lunchtime enjoyment. WO Coastal.

Discontinued: **Printer's Devil range**. — MW

Location/map: Franschhoek ▪ Map grid reference: C2 ▪ WO: Franschhoek/Western Cape/Coastal/Paarl/ Robertson ▪ Est 1990 ▪ Tasting, sales & cellar tours Mon-Sun 10-5; pub hols (seasonal) please call ahead ▪ Closed Dec 25 & Jan 1 ▪ Fee R75/5 wines ▪ Panna cotta & wine pairing, kiddies pairing ▪ Wine blending ▪ Cheese & wine pairing ▪ Non-alcoholic pairing ▪ Potjiekos experience ▪ Paulina's Restaurant at Rickety Bridge ▪ Facilities for children ▪ Gift shop ▪ Conferences ▪ Weddings ▪ Rickety Bridge Manor House ▪ Wine club ▪ Owner(s) Duncan Spence ▪ Cellarmaster(s) Donovan Ackermann (Dec 2018) ▪ Winemaker(s) Mari Kotze (Nov 2018) ▪ Viticulturist(s) Rayno White ▪ 50ha/19ha (cab, grenache n/b, merlot, mourv, shiraz, chard, marsanne, rouss, sauv, sem) ▪ 500t/60,000cs own label 60% red 30% white 10% rosé ▪ PO Box 455 Franschhoek 7690 ▪ info@ricketybridge.com ▪ www.ricketybridge.com ▪ **T +27 (0)21-876-2129**

Ridgeback

The potential of this winery on the northern foothills of Paarl Mountain was realised with the release of its debut '01 Shiraz, awarded five stars in this guide. The new owner, a German investor, aims to build on the foundations laid by the Zimbabwean founders, and upgrades to the cellar and further refinements in the vineyards are planned. Toit Wessels, a central presence here since 2000, now cellarmaster-winemaker, viticulturist and general manager, has the satisfaction of working with mature vines ranging between 17 and 23 years. His particular passion is cabernet franc, bottled as a varietal wine and 'the backbone to our blends'. Wearing his winemaker hat, Toit focuses on using only vegan products and fining with grape skin tannins to reduce allergens, his ultimate goal being 'guiding nature into a bottle'.

His Master's Choice range

★★★★★ **Signature C** Impressive, ageworthy Bordeaux blend, mainly cab franc, important input from merlot, cab & petit verdot fusing a complexity of silk-textured spice & ripe blackberries with a graphite mineral core in **19** (95). Poised & balanced, oak, 85% new, refining extra.

★★★★☆ **Signature S** 85% shiraz with splashes mourvèdre, grenache noir augmenting floral, dark berry fragrance, layered texture. **19** ★★★★★ (95) rich & concentrated, also sleek & seamless for drinking now & future. Oak, 85% new - just 50% in **18** (94) - 17 months, adds extra class.

Ridgeback range

★★★★☆ **Cabernet Sauvignon** Splendid **20** (93) has house-style power with finesse. Great depth of colour; cashmere texture with densely layered plush berry & chocolate tones, threaded by freshening acidity & held by finest of tannins.

★★★★☆ **Cabernet Franc** Full-bodied **20** (93) shows precision, detail in its leafy spice features, mineral thread. Supple feel, finely textured tannins provide a fresh, seamless touch & satisfying length. Oak, 44% new, 15 months, a non-intrusive enhancement.

★★★★☆ **Merlot** Rich & muscular, the plush plum & blackberry flavours wrapped in densely layered, ripe tannin. **20** (90) harmonised in barriques, 26% new, 18 months.

★★★★☆ **Shiraz** Excellent balance in **19** (91)'s full body, concentrated ripe fruit & dense grip; notes of clean leather, spice, dark berries complemented by 17 months oak, 36% new. Requires, warrants good number of years.

★★★★☆ **Journey** Bordeaux quartet in homogeneous **20** (90). Bright spice, juicy plums & blackberries form tasty interplay, tannins in zesty yet refined support. 13 months in oak, just 2% new, for dash cedary extra.

★★★★ **Ember** Shiraz-based **19** (86) with grenache noir, mourvèdre adding spicy ripe-fruit interest. Rich & savoury, comfortably rounded for current enjoyment. Older oak.

★★★★☆ **Chenin Blanc** Finely crafted, characterful **21** (94) from 31 year old bushvines shows deft oaking, allowing sweetly ripe tropical & stonefruit to show. Seductively textural & rich, for longer run.

★★★★☆ **Viognier** Among SA's best, regularly awarded; **22** (93) confidently aromatic, toasty oak, peachy fragrance, sweet fruit lifted & lengthened by juicy acidity. Barrel fermented, 24% new.— AL

Location/map/WO: Paarl ▪ Map grid reference: D3 ▪ Est 1997 ▪ 1stB 2001 ▪ Tasting & sales Tue-Sat 8-5 Sun 9-4 ▪ Fee R50pp/lifestyle, R60/premium, R100/master tasting ▪ Closed Good Fri, Dec 25 & Jan 1 ▪ Cellar tours by appt ▪ Hiking & MTB trails ▪ Children's play area ▪ Wine club ▪ Owner(s) Elleke Hospitality (Pty) Ltd ▪ Cellarmaster(s)/winemaker(s) Toit Wessels (Jan 2007) ▪ Viticulturist(s) Toit Wessels (Mar 2000) ▪ 65ha/35ha (cabs s/f, grenache, merlot, mourv, p verdot, shiraz, sauv, viog) ▪ 300t/30,000cs own label 60% red 40% white ▪ WIETA ▪ PO Box 2076 Windmeul Paarl 7630 ▪ info@ridgeback.co.za ▪ www.ridgebackwines.co.za ▪ T +27 (0)21-869-8068

☐ **Riebeek Cellars** *see* Riebeek Valley Wine Co

Riebeek Valley Wine Co

Located in Riebeek-Kasteel, the heart of the Swartland, this 30-shareholder winery is committed to preserving special old parcels, adding 6 ha of chenin to the Old Vine Project's roster of certified heritage vineyards, bringing the winery's total to 41 ha. CEO Werner Engelbrecht and his team are 'undergoing an evolution in winemaking to produce wines that better reflect our passion for Swartland terroir' while showcasing lesser-known varieties alongside mainstream ones. For the Raar and Kasteelberg limited releases, the approach is to intervene minimally, use natural ferments and subtle oaking to express the site. In the core ranges, continuity, drinkability and freshness are goals. The Tasting Emporium now offers a wine tram experience, connecting visitors with wine and olive destinations throughout the valley.

22 Families range (NEW)

★★★★ **Old Vine Project Chenin Blanc Bush Vine** ⊛ Range named for winery's founding families, **22** ⑧⑥ is from 35 year old vines. Its spicy, baked apple juiciness gains depth from time on lees; bright acid freshens & enhances the lingering, sunny fruit. Portion older-oak matured, 6 months.

Kasteelberg range

★★★★ **Shiraz** Lovely reflection of Swartland's signature red grape; **22** ★★★★★ ⑨⑨② perfumed dark berries, spice & suggestion of warm red earth wrapped in supple silkiness & rumble of tannin. Fresh lift gives sense of lightness, maintains concentration, length. 30% wholebunch, natural ferment, older oak, 9 months. 13.8% alc. Different league from **21** ★★★★ ⑧⑤.

★★★★☆ **Chenin Blanc** ⑧ ⊛ From 1969 dryland bushvines, **22** ⑨③ has old vine concentration in its red apple & honeyed richness, hint of oak spice adding interest, the sunny flavours lasting long & memorably. Fresh, dry & well balanced, allows for current & future pleasure. Natural ferment, 6 months oak. **20** untasted, **21** not made.

Discontinued: **Pinotage**, **Méthode Cap Classique**.

Raar Small Batch Limited Releases

★★★★ **Petite Sirah** Dark & dense in colour & brooding character, **22** ⑧⑧ has languid richness with liquorice & plum flavours. Finely meshed tannins provide necessary freshness to harmonise & offset 14.5% alc. 30% wholebunch, wild ferment, older oak 8 months. 14.5% alc.

★★★★ **Carbonic Shiraz** Freshness & purity distinguish **22** ⑧⑦. Aromatic red berries & spice matched by rich, sweet & concentrated flavours in a supple texture; fine tannins effectively freshen & bring balance. 30% wholebunch, wild ferment, older oak 8 months.

★★★★☆ **Chenin Blanc Skin Contact** ⊘ ⑧ ⊛ Textured, with creamy lees, **22** ⑨③'s ripe, earthy, honeyed flavours are lengthened by freshness & firm, but unintimidating tug of tannin. Wild ferment in older oak, 6 months. Follows debut **21** ★★★★ ⑧⑤.

★★★★★ **Grenache Blanc** ⊘ ⑧ A little oak spice adds to complexity & extra dimension on **22** ⑨⑤. Expressive, harmonious & sleek, well weighted with persistent limy freshness. Wholebunch press, wild ferment in older oak, 6 months. **19** ★★★★ ⑧③ was last tasted.

Not tasted: **Grenache Noir**. In abeyance: **Cinsaut**. Discontinued: **Shiraz-Mourvèdre**.

Klein Kasteelberg range

Grenache Noir-Mourvèdre ☺ ★★★ Comfortably smooth partnership offers fresh blackberry flavours & savoury length, brightened by grenache's light, lively spice. Like sibling, **22** ⑧② combines charm, interest with ready satisfaction. **Chenin Blanc-Grenache Blanc** ☺ ★★★ Chenin's fresh appley scents & flavours augmented with 35% grenache & its limy zest, **22** ⑧② gains breadth from lees ageing & is roundly dry. Delightful, interesting & easy to drink.

In abeyance: **Brut Vonkelwijn**.

Riebeek Cellars Collection

★★★★ **Cape Ruby** ⑫ Delicious 'port' from touriga, year in old barrels. **NV** ⑧⑥ true-to-style rich fruitcake & floral aromas & flavours; not too sweet, well-integrated 19.7% alc allows for lengthy aftertaste. **Cabernet Sauvignon** ⊘ ★★★★ Understated yet clear cab blackberry aromas & flavours on **22** ⑧③; a little oak spice, tweak of tannin & freshness provide interest, approachability. **Merlot** ⑫ ★★★ Full-bodied **21** ⑧⓪ has sweet, plummy flavours yet no jamminess thanks to sappy freshening tannins. **Pinotage** ★★★ Full in plum & red berry flavours, with an oak-spice edge, **22** ⑧② has a freshening kick of tannin. **Shiraz** ★★★ Despite much muted dark berries & spice on Swartland's signature grape, **22** ⑧② is supple, smooth & agreeable drinking. **Pinotage Rosé** ⊘ ★★★ Wild, piquant berries on fresh & flavoursome **23** ⑧②, ending with a fruity tang. **Chenin Blanc** ⊘ ★★★★ Sun-filled apple & pear scents, juicy flavours, **23** ⑧⑤ is lively & fresh; a delightful summer sipper & terrific value. **Sauvignon Blanc** ★★★ Softish, with tropical juicy fruit, fresh & dry in **23** ⑧⓪. Discontinued: **Chardonnay**.

Pieter Cruythoff range

Brut Rosè ★★★ Salmon pink carbonated **NV** ⑦⑨ fizz from chardonnay, pinot noir & shiraz. Lively bubble, plentiful sweet red berry flavours; brisk, fruitily dry finish. **Brut** ★★★ **NV** ⑦⑨ carbonated dry bubbly from chardonnay, splash pinot noir. Creamy mousse refreshed by lemony tang.

Montino range

Moscato Light Perlé ⓠ ★★★ Gentle sparkle & light grapey flavours on **NV** ⑦⑦ from muscadel.
Petillant Rosé ⓠ ★★ Raspberry & muscat hints on very sweet **NV** ⑦③ with sherbety prickle of bubbles. Muscadel & pinotage. Both wines low in alc (±7-9%) & best enjoyed well-chilled. — AL

Location: Riebeek-Kasteel ▪ Map: Swartland ▪ Map grid reference: D6 ▪ Map: Swartland ▪ Map grid reference: D6 ▪ WO: Swartland ▪ Est 1941 ▪ Cellardoor: tasting & sales Mon-Fri 9-5 ▪ Closed Good Fri, Dec 25 & Jan 1 ▪ Cellar tours by appt ▪ Tasting Emporium: Mon-Thu 9-5 Fri-Sat 10-6 Sun 10-3; selection of wines, craft beer/gin; cheese, olives & cured meats; various wine pairings; signature wine blending sessions & wine tram experience - booking essential, tastingroom@riebeekwineco.co.za ▪ Owner(s) 30 shareholders ▪ CEO Werner Engelbrecht ▪ Winemaker(s) Boutique cellar: Sheree Nothnagel (Dec 2019) & Rashaad George (Mar 2020); Main cellar: Jacques Theron (Dec 2017) & Christoph Blake (Dec 2022), with Thembile Ntloko (Nov 2016) & Themba Msitho (Nov 2020) ▪ Viticulturist(s) WP Dreyer (Dec 2021) ▪ 900ha (cab, cinsaut, grenache n/b, merlot, mourv, petite sirah, ptage, shiraz, touriga nacional, chard, chenin, marsanne, sauv, viog) ▪ ±100,000cs own label 30% red 60% white 10% rosé ▪ PO Box 13 Riebeek-Kasteel 7307 ▪ info@ riebeekwineco.co.za ▪ www.riebeekvalleywineco.com ▪ **T +27 (0)22-448-1213**

Rietvallei Wine Estate   ⓠ ⑪ ⑤

It's a remarkable 160 years ago that Rietvallei came into the hands of the Burger family, when Alewyn bought the Robertson Valley farm for his son Jacobus Francois. Koos, as he was known, was 70 when he planted muscadel vines in 1908, today farmed by namesake and 6th-generation owner Kobus, who this edition reaches the milestone of 21 years as winemaker, during which the portfolio has expanded (the Burger Family Vineyards and John B brands untasted by us) and grown in volume to a significant 80,000 cases.

Heritage Collection

★★★★ **JMB Cabernet Franc** Savoury, leafy tomato note mingles with mint, dried herbs & hint pepper on fine **19** ★★★★★ ⑨⓪, wild fermented, 26 months in new small-oak & showing ample spice. Gravelly tannins & striking acid add to muscular profile, which will benefit from cellaring. Last tasted was **14** ⑧⑦.

★★★★ **Dark Cin** Different, attractive take on red-fruited variety, warmer ferment & regular pump-overs deliver black cherries, rosepetals & lavender in **21** ⑧⑥. Brooding character underscored by 8 months in old oak, refreshed with buchu scent, crisp acid & juicy tannins. Last reviewed was **16** ⑧⑦.

★★★★ **Estéanna Cabernet Sauvignon-Cabernet Franc** ⓐ 51% cab & its partner spent 2 years in new oak, adding bold spice to plum, violet & tangy num num fruit. Robust structure of tannin & brisk acid will carry **19** ⑧⑧ for good few more years. Last-tasted **15** ★★★★ ⑧④ has splash petit verdot.

★★★★ **Estate 2016** Blend of estate's black grapes in proportion to hectarage, co-fermented & 36 months in oak, 80% new, further 12 in bottle before release. **16** ⑧⑧ savoury overlay to cherry fruit, good weight & silk texture in dainty tannin frame intended for further lengthy ageing.

★★★★ **JMB Chardonnay** Ferment completed in barrel, 50% new, 8 months aged, malo prohibited to retain vivid acid, **22** ★★★★★ ⑨⓪ rich, with caramelised pineapple, brioche & roasted nuts, all vanilla spiced, generous 15.5 alc integrated & balanced with zingy citrus. Also-tasted **23** ⑧⑥ preview same treatment in cellar, similar vivacious citric profile at more modest 13.5% alc.

★★★★☆ **1908 Red Muscadel** ⓐ Stunning dessert wine from SA's oldest red muscadel (bush) vines. Naturally fermented, fortified to 15% alc, aged 17 months in very old large barrels. Rosewater, quince & ginger on subtly aromatic **21** ⑨③, 169.5 g/L sugar gracefully balanced by acid on the long-lingering finish. Simply delicious, as last-tasted **15** ⑨④. 375 ml.

Not tasted: **Estéanna Sauvignon Blanc**. Discontinued: **Estéanna Chardonnay-Sauvignon Blanc-Chenin Blanc-Viognier-Nouvelle.**

Classic Collection

★★★★ **Shiraz** Abundant aromas of mixed red berries & black pepper on **21** ⑧⑥, oak, a quarter new, amplifying spicy seam that runs though to finish.

★★★★ **Chardonnay** Combo tank & 50% new barrel ferment, 6 months regular bâtonnage for **22** ⑧⑨, adding creamy depth & weight to orange citrus fruit, along with almond & buttered toast notes. Vibrant acid keeps balance, as for previewed **23** ★★★★ ⑧⑤, same treatment though lighter tones of pickled ginger & white citrus.

★★★★ **Red Muscadel** After-dinner treat **19** ⑧⑧'s Xmas cake & sultana partner red berries, appleskin & rhubarb. Warmth & spice from 16% alc fortification, plus year harmonising in tank add balance & freshness to luscious 175.6 g/L sugar. Notch up on last-reviewed **17** ★★★★ ⑧④. 500 ml.

- -

Calcrete Chardonnay (NEW) ⓥ ★★★★ Unwooded sibling named for Robertson's limestone soils. Malo avoided to reflect vibrancy of **23** ⑧④'s fruit - green apple & just-ripe pear. Combined with oystershell nuance & modest alc of 12.5%, effect is of almost startling steeliness. Worth seeking out. **Sauvignon Blanc** ⓥ ★★★★ Classic varietal notes of fig, leafy lime & nettle on **23** ⑧③, well-crafted from staggered pickings. 3 months lees contact add breadth & texture.

- -

Cabernet Sauvignon ★★★☆ Naturally fermented **21** ⑧④ has appetising biltong, cocoa, cassia & red cherry aromatics, plummy fruit in pleasantly tight grip of tannin. Year in oak, as Shiraz. **Chenin Blanc** ★★★★ Sun-kissed pineapple & mango on oak-fermented **23** ⑧③. 5 months lees-contact adds whipped cream to tropics. Improves from **18** ★★★ ⑧①. Discontinued: **Shiraz-Petit Verdot-Viognier, Natural Chardonnay**. — ML, PS

Location/map/WO: Robertson ▪ Map grid reference: B4 ▪ Est 1864 ▪ 1stB 1976 ▪ Tasting & sales Mon-Fri 8-5 Sat/pub hols 10-2 ▪ Tasting fee standard ▪ Closed Easter Fri/Sat, Dec 16/25/26 & Jan 1 ▪ Cheese platters, book ahead for groups of 6+ ▪ Wine club ▪ Owner(s) Kobus Burger ▪ Winemaker(s) Kobus Burger (2003) ▪ 215ha/100ha (cabs s/f, cinsaut, merlot, p verdot, red muscadel, shiraz, tinta barocca, chard, chenin, sauv) ▪ 1,000t/80,000cs own label 56% red 42% white 1.5% rosé 0.5% fortified ▪ PO Box 386 Robertson 6705 ▪ info@rietvallei.co.za ▪ www.rietvallei.co.za ▪ **T +27 (0)23-626-3596**

- -

☐ **Rifle Range** *see* Kanu Wines

Rijk's

Lately run by Tiger Dorrington, this is a relatively young vineyard site and wine venture, born in the mid-1990s with plantings on virgin soil by father and founder Neville. He started with a wide range of varieties, and whittled them down over the years to the current chenin and pinotage. Narrow specialisation allows focus on getting the best possible quality and character from the vines, now aided by guidance from consultant Jaco Engelbrecht. The direction is increasingly towards organic practices and working in harmony with nature. The estate offers visitors Cape Dutch-themed luxury hotel accommodation and traditional cuisine in a beautiful mountain setting.

Reserve range

★★★★☆ **Pinotage** ⓐ Almost 2 years in 60% new oak, then selection of finest 20 barrels for plush, succulent **18** ⑨④. Intense blueberry & blackcurrant spiced with nutmeg, cocoa & pimento. Underlying musculature & ripe, leathery structure suggest further cellaring but already approachable. **17** untasted.

★★★★☆ **Chenin Blanc** ⓐ Befitting a Reserve wine, bold & confident **21** ★★★★★ ⑨⑥ commands attention, its sleek body, astonishingly deep tropical & stonefruit flavours all cosseted in fine, leesy cloak. Mostly wild-yeast ferment/year in oak, 40% new, add restrained spice & polish. Notch up on also-impressive **19** ⑨③. **20** untasted.

Not tasted: **Pinotage 888 Gold**.

Private Cellar range

★★★★☆ **Pinotage** Perfectly ripe, healthy fruit finds expression in **19** ⑨②, supple, juicy, layered with exotic red & black berries, rich oak spice (22 months in barrel, some American), silky tannin. Less brooding than last-tasted **17** ⑨②.

★★★★☆ **Chenin Blanc** Sumptuous flavour, richness & weight delivered with finesse. **21** ⑨⓪ seductively creamy & round, lemon curd & shortbread subtly spiced with nutmeg & caramel. Citrus edginess assures balance, drinkability. Mostly barrel fermented/11 months, portion Hungarian, 40% wild yeast. **20** untasted.

Not tasted: **Méthode Cap Classique Brut**.

Touch range

★★★★ **Pinotage** This WO Coastal line-up lighter only on the wallet, flavours still satisfyingly rich, ripe & variety-true. **21** (87), 20 months older oak, plump wild berries & plums, appealing aromatic highlights, smooth tannins & precise acid. **20** untasted.

★★★★ **Chenin Blanc** Exuberantly fresh **22** (89) explodes with bright, sunny tropical fruit, gains honeyed spiciness from 20% old-barrel-fermented portion, fatness & body from 11 months on lees.— GdB

Location/map: Tulbagh ▪ Map grid reference: F5 ▪ WO: Tulbagh/Coastal ▪ Est 1996 ▪ 1stB 2000 ▪ Tasting & sales Tue-Sat 10-4; pub hols (seasonal) please call ahead ▪ Fee R120/5 wines ▪ Cellar tours by appt ▪ Rijk's Hotel ▪ Conferences ▪ Owner(s) Rijk's Cellar (Pty) Ltd ▪ Winemaker(s) Adriaan Jacobs (Jan 2022) ▪ Viticulturist(s) Neville Dorrington, Daniel Pienaar ▪ 89ha/26ha (ptage, chenin) ▪ 180t/20,000cs own label 60% red 40% white ▪ PO Box 400 Tulbagh 6820 ▪ office@rijks.co.za ▪ www.rijks.co.za ▪ **T +27 (0)23-230-1622**

☐ **Rikus Neethling** *see* Bizoe Wines

Rivendell Boutique Wine Farm

Shiraz and sauvignon vines on the boutique estate overlooking Bot River Lagoon have been supplying the grapes for crafting by a small team of consultants. The wines featured here are still selling from the on-site visitor venue, and customers are advised to call ahead for opening times.

Rivendell range

★★★★ **Sauvignon Blanc** (②) Primary herbaceous, nectarine flavours on **20** (87). Crisp & crunchy, less textured than previous, very bright & tangy. Good ageing potential.

Shiraz (②) ★★★☆ An improvement on previous, **17** (84) has better structure, freshness, some grip supporting very ripe dark berries, spice. Oak, 25% new, complementary. **Shiraz Rosé** (②) ★★★ Eye-catching tourmaline pink, **22** (82) has softer, juicy, spiced candy flavours, fruity dryness.

Reserve range

Not tasted: **Shiraz**, **Sauvignon Blanc**. — AL

Location/WO: Bot River ▪ Est 2008 ▪ 1stB 2011 ▪ PO Box 570 Onrusrivier 7201 ▪ office@rivendell-estate.co.za ▪ www.rivendell-estate.co.za ▪ **T +27 (0)28-284-9185 (sales)**

☐ **River Collection** *see* Bonnievale Wines
☐ **River Garden** *see* Lourensford Wine Estate

RiverGold Private Cellar   (②) (⊖) (◎)

Inspired by sunset hues on tranquil water, the Naidoo family's boutique wine brand has a home on the Breede River bank near Bonnievale. Nesting for a time, the label is spreading its wings with wines handcrafted by small-batch and single-site specialist Lourens van der Westhuizen of neighbour winery Arendsig.

RiverGold range

★★★★ **Chardonnay** (⊘) Shows region's limestone freshness in **22** ★★★★★ (91), citrus, apple & pear on backdrop of 10 months older oak, line of creamy lees complements vivid acid, bettering **21** (89).

★★★★☆ **Chenin Blanc** Like **21** (91), single-vineyard, **22** ★★★★ (89) sun-ripe character with good pear & peach fruit & weight yet moderate 13.3 alc. Wild ferment, as Chardonnay, same oak regimen.

★★★★ **Sauvignon Blanc** (⊘) For lovers of classic, high-toned sauvignon, nettle & lime joined on palate by touch of litchi. Modest alc of 12% adds to light, fresh feel on **22** (86).

Not tasted: **Merlot**, **Shiraz**.

Reserve range

Not tasted: **Merlot**, **Chenin Blanc**. — ML

Location: Bonnievale ▪ Map/WO: Robertson ▪ Map grid reference: C4 ▪ Est/1stB 2010 ▪ Tasting by appt ▪ Closed Sun, Dec 25 & Jan 1 ▪ BYO picnic ▪ Conference facilities ▪ Owner(s) Boyce Naidoo ▪ Cellarmaster(s)/winemaker(s) Lourens van der Westhuizen (2009, consultant) ▪ Viticulturist(s) Lourens van der Westhuizen (2019, consultant) ▪ 30ha/8ha (merlot, shiraz, chard, chenin, sauv) ▪ 25t/2,500cs own label 40% red 60% white ▪ WIETA ▪ PO Box 1065 Robertson 6705 ▪ info@rivergold.co.za ▪ www.rivergold.co.za ▪ **T +27 (0)23-616-2218**

☐ **River Grandeur** *see* Viljoensdrift Fine Wines & River Cruises
☐ **Riverine** *see* Renegade Wines
☐ **The River's End** *see* Stellar Winery
☐ **Robert Alexander** *see* Nico van der Merwe Wines

Robertson Winery   Ⓨ ⓞ ⓑ

His second harvest as cellarmaster of this large, long-established and enterprising winery in Robertson town was 'interesting', Rianco van Rooyen says, 'due to the large volumes of rain that fell in March'. However, earlier expansions of red-wine fermentation capacity, storage space and filtration facilities meant his team could 'easily handle the inclement weather thrown at them'. The scale of production at the cellar complex at No 1 Constitution Road is matched by the size of the export market and the legions of loyal local fans who love the 'crowd-pleasing', well-priced wines in their varied, convenient packaging. A revamp of the visitor locale beside the cellar has been so well received, opening times have been extended to include Sundays.

Constitution Road range

★★★★★ **Shiraz** Warm, rounded & smooth **21** (90) mingles dark plums with liquorice on plush tannins, making for eminently satisfying mouthful. New oak dialled back to just 10%, portion American, adding soft spice to elegant finish.

★★★★☆ **Chardonnay** Peaches-&-cream **22** (90) impresses with layers of flavour (spiced apricot, oatmeal & touch of honey) aided by barrel ferment, 60% new. Fresh acid livens lengthy finish on an excellent expression of Robertson fruit.

Cultivar range

Chardonnay ⊘ ⊕ ★★★★ Oodles of flavour on **23** (84), confected peachy fruit balanced by subtle spicy oaking of only 33% of the wine. Fresh & lively acid for a hugely drinkable drop.

Cabernet Sauvignon ★★★ Light & fruity **22** (80) has modest 12.5% alc, aiding quaffability. Black cherries & ripe strawberries, some woody spice add up to pleasant everyday enjoyment. 10 months new oak, as all reds in this range. **Merlot** ★★★ Bouncy red-fruited **22** (81) with soft tannins & light body constituting a refreshing summer red. **Pinotage** ★★★ Roasted coffee & chicory notes on **22** (80), rich black fruit & fresh herbal finish. **Ruby Cabernet** ★★☆ Easy structure on **22** (77) with some soft berry fruit & slight stalky note at finish. **Shiraz** ⊘ ★★★★ Lots of happy drinking here. **22** (83) pepper, floral & smoky charcuterie notes, lively & fresh. **The Blend** ★★★ From cab & shiraz **22** (80), soft & ripe black fruit, smoothing touch sugar at the finish. **Chenin Blanc** ⊘ ★★★★ Cheery pears & pineapples on **23** (83), crisp acid & brisk, clean finish. Perfect pool wine. **Gewürztraminer** ★★★ The few grams sugar on lime- & lemon sherbet-toned **22** (81) offset by fresh acid on light (11% alc), floral finish. **Sauvignon Blanc** ★★★ Grapefruit & gooseberry on tangy **23** (81). Crisp, dry, with brisk acidity & clean finish. **Beaukett** ★★★ Floral aromas with hints of aniseed & tropical fruit, **23** (79) light & slight with semi-sweet sugar at finish. Some of these wines also available in 1L, 2L & 3L.

Light Cultivar range

Merlot ★★★ Cherry & berry fun in **22** (78), light in body & alc (9%, as all these), fresh sappy finish. **Pinotage Rosé** ★★★ Confected red fruit **23** (77) with crisp, sherbetty, almost-dry finish. **Sauvignon Blanc** ★★☆ Brisk & clean **23** (77), zesty citrus notes & light floral finish. Also available in 3L. Not tasted: **Chenin Blanc**.

Chapel range

Dry Red ☺ ★★★ Highly quaffable **22** (80) from cab with merlot & pinotage. Cheery blackberry jam fruit, soft tannins & just-dry finish.

Dry White ⊘ ★★★ Fruity little number, **23** (80) from chenin & colombard, tropical whiffs with bouncy acid & off-dry finish. Some of these wines also available in 500ml, 1.5L & 5L. **Sweet Red** ★★ Rounded & warm **NV** (73) with black berry fruit & pleasing low alc of 7.5%, as all these Natural Sweet wines. **Sweet Rosé** ★★ Candyfloss hue & confection on **NV** (74) with light strawberry & cherry fruit sweetness. **Sweet White** ★★☆ Grapey sweetness on **NV** (78), along with some floral whiffs & clean finish. Discontinued: **Extra Light**.

1-Litre Blended Combibloc range

Smooth Dry Red ⊘ ★★☆ Soft & juicy NV ⑦ packed with red & black fruit for enjoyable everyday quaffing. Some of these wines also available in 500ml, 1L, 3L & 5L. **Crisp Light White** ★★ Citrussy NV ⑦ with lower alc of 9.5% for carefree sipping. **Crisp Dry White** ⊘ ★★★ Touch of tropical fruit & lemon sherbet on zesty NV ⑧, bone-dry & easygoing. **Golden Nectar Late Harvest** ⊘ ★★★ Floral highlights on NV ⑦ semi-sweet mouthful of fresh grapey fruit, finishing clean. **Natural Sweet Red** ★★ Mixed berry NV ⑦ with succulent texture & sweet finish. **Natural Sweet Rosé** ★★ Strawberry & candyfloss confection from light & fresh NV ⑦. **Natural Sweet White** ★★ Grapey & floral NV ⑦ with easy low alc (7.5%, as all the Natural Sweet wines). Not tasted: **Selected Stein.**

3-Litre Blended Slimline range

Smooth Dry Red ⊘ ★★★ For youthful enjoyment, abundant red & black fruit, easy & juicy NV ⑦ ticks all the boxes. **Crisp Dry White** ★★★ Bright & zippy NV ⑧ boasts tropical fruit & lemon sherbet; engages further with satisfying dry finish. **Crisp Light White** ★★ From colombard & just 9.5% alc, citrus-toned NV ⑦ delivers uncomplicated imbibing. **Johannisberger Semi-Sweet White** ⊘ ★★★ Fresh off-dry NV ⑦ with melange of stone & tropical fruit, modest 10.5% alc & crisp finish. **Golden Nectar Late Harvest** (NEW) ★★★ Charming NV ⑦ semi-sweet ends neatly clean, showcases fresh grapey fruit & floral perfume. **Natural Sweet Rosé** ★★ Delicate candyfloss & light strawberry appeal on very quaffable NV ⑦. **Johannisberger Semi-Sweet Red** ★★ Stewed black & red berries on off-dry NV ⑦, lighter alc (11%), clean finish.

Sparkling Wines

Sweet Red ★★ Mixed fruit jam flavours on bubbly NV ⑦. Carbonated & with low ±7% alc, as pink & white siblings. **Sweet Rosé** ★★ Rosepetal freshness on sweet NV ⑦ fizz. **Sweet White** ★★ From colombard, NV ⑦ citrussy & sweet, with frothy bubbles. Not tasted: **Brut Rosé**, **Brut.**

Non-Alcoholic Sparkling range

Dry Rosé ★★ Bright strawberry fruit on NV ⑦, fresh & dry enough for family celebrations. **Sweet Rosé** (NEW) ★★ Grapey sweetness on NV ⑦ with slightly sticky finish. **Dry White** ★★ Simple & fruity NV ⑦ with light citrus notes & foamy fizz. Not tasted: **Sweet White.** — CM

Location/map/WO: Robertson ▪ Map grid reference: B5 ▪ Est 1941 ▪ 1stB 1987 ▪ Tasting & sales Mon-Fri 9-5.30 Sat 9-3 Sun 11-3; pub hols (seasonal) please call ahead ▪ Closed Good Fri, Dec 25/26 & Jan 1 ▪ Cellar tours by appt ▪ Conferences ▪ Cellarmaster(s) Rianco van Rooyen (Oct 2019) ▪ Winemaker(s) Francois Weich (Sep 1997), Thys Loubser (Jan 2012) ▪ Viticulturist(s) Briaan Stipp (May 2005) ▪ 2,400ha under vine ▪ 39,500t ▪ BRC, FSSC 22000, WIETA ▪ PO Box 566 Robertson 6705 ▪ info@robertsonwinery.co.za, sales@robertsonwinery. co.za, customercare@robertsonwinery.co.za ▪ www.robertsonwinery.co.za ▪ **T +27 (0)23-626-3059/+27 (0)23-626-8817 (sales)**

Robin Hood Legendary Wine Series

Elgin brand owner Mark Simpson's wine quartet matches a figure from Sherwood Forest legend with a course in a four-part meal. Maid Marian rosé, for example, pairs with the starter and Friar Tuck 'port' the cheese. Available from Mark's Grabouw wine shop; his more serious Arumdale wines are listed separately.

Rockbelt Ridge

This collection is the realisation of a dream for Dan Mosia, proudly of the Basotho nation, to farm in Robertson Valley, produce wine grapes, and craft his own wine from the rocky soil. In this he is aided by a local farmer and winemaker. The name of the range references one of the bird species which flourish on the land, underlaid by the valley's signature limestone-rich soil.

Rockbelt Ridge range

★★★★ **The Ridge Cabernet Sauvignon** Moderate 13% alc yet **21** ⑧ has presence. Perfumes of lavender & mint, deep flavours of dark fruit accented with red berries, neatly dry finish. 18 months in oak, some rooibos tannins added.

★★★★ **The Rock Chardonnay** 18 months in older oak imbue **21** ⑧'s yellow stonefruit bouquet with vanilla sweetness, yet full, round palate is pleasantly drier than expected.

The Black Korhaan range

★★★★ **Cabernet Sauvignon** Classic tomato, leaf & berry notes on juicy, vibrant **22** ⑧⑦. Drinks easily with deftly done dab sugar (as most of these). Equal old-oak, stave & unwooded portions, as all the reds.

★★★★ **Merlot** Black tea-like tannins give **22** ⑧⑥ noticeable structure to well-fruited plummy body. Steps lightly but is nicely vinous (13.7% alc, as Sauvignon, rest ±12.7%). Year oak, as Pinotage & Merlot.

★★★★ **The Black Blend** Cab & shiraz equal partners in attractive **22** ⑧⑧, latter showing slight lead in the black pepper, earth & red plum characters. Elegant 12.3% alc.

Pinotage ★★★★ On-trend, **22** ⑧④ eschews heavy oaking for fruit succulence & vivacity. Savoury toned, with charcuterie & Provençal herbs. **Shiraz** ★★★☆ Tart raspberry & cherry fruit, pink peppercorn spiciness, tight young tannins, **22** ⑧⑤ ticks the boxes for piquancy & freshness. **Chardonnay** ★★★★ Creamy tone to aperitif-style **23** ⑧④'s winter melon fruit from barest brush of oak. Delicate, if a little brief. **Chenin Blanc** ★★★ Exemplifies range's easy-to-enjoy styling. **23** ⑧② comfortable & packed with Golden Delicious apple flavours. **Sauvignon Blanc** ★★★ Plenty of lemon, lime, gooseberry, green apple & grass attractions, texture & weight from few months on lees (like Chenin) & 13.7% alc on **23** ⑧②. **Méthode Cap Classique** ★★★★ Chardonnay (60%) & pinot noir sparkler **20** ⑧⑤ radiates freshness & satisfying dryness. — ML, PS

Location/WO: Robertson ▪ info@rockbeltridge.co.za ▪ www.rockbeltridge.co.za ▪ **T +27 (0)64-525-3738**

☐ **Rockpool** *see* Lomond

Rogge Cloof

At 1,550-m altitude, these vines in the Sutherland-Karoo district of the Northern Cape are some of the country's highest, and exposed to 'droughts, snow and freezing winds'. From a base on Rogge Cloof farm (meaning 'wild rye ravine'), wine manager Ulrich Gerntholtz works with grapes from two parcels: Kanolfontein, planted in the 2000s and heretofore channelled into other brands. Just 1 ton was picked last season, to be bottled under the 'De Knolle Fonteyn' label; and the Rogge Cloof home-farm, where chardonnay and pinot noir will come into production this year. All are looked after by eminent consultant Rosa Kruger, and their minuscule crops vinified by Johan Kruger of Kruger Family Wines. Visitors are extensively catered for.

Rogge Cloof range

★★★★☆ **De Knolle Fonteyn** ⓐ Ultra-cool, highland syrah vineyards deliver charming fynbos scrub, white pepper aromas & pure red-fruited flavours in **22** ⑨①. Part wholebunch ferment ups the freshness, old oak buffs the firm, supple tannins. Classy tablemate that will reward cellaring. WO Sutherland-Karoo.

In abeyance: **Salpeterkop, Joachim Scholtz, Sneeukop**.

Cape to Cairo range

★★★★ **Letaba** ⓐ From pinot noir, **19** ⑧⑥ pliable, textured & lifted by fresh acid thread. Soft red-fruit character with hint of undergrowth, gentle grip & moderate 13% alc. Older oak 16 months.

★★★★ **Timbavati** ⓐ Intense pale gold hue & oatmeal, nutty features on **20** ⑧⑦ chardonnay, also note of oak spice. Riper, richer flavours are well-balanced & focused by freshening acid. Good now & for year/2.

In abeyance: **Syrah**.

Discontinued: **Emineo range**. — MW

Location: Sutherland ▪ WO: Western Cape/Sutherland-Karoo ▪ Est 1756 ▪ 1stB 2006 ▪ Tasting, sales & cellar tours by appt ▪ Meals & picnics available ▪ Facilities for children ▪ Tour groups ▪ Gift shop ▪ Farm produce ▪ Walks/hikes ▪ Conservation area ▪ 4x4 trail ▪ MTB trail ▪ Museum ▪ Guest house ▪ Stargazing ▪ Nature reserve ▪ Winemaker(s) Johan Kruger (consultant) ▪ Viticulturist(s) Rosa Kruger (consultant) ▪ Wine manager Ulrich Gerntholtz ▪ 80% red 20% white ▪ Other brands: Cape to Cairo, De Knolle Fonteyn, Emineo, Fair Karoo, Joachim Scholtz, Letaba, Oranjezicht, Salpeterkop, Sneeukop, Timbavati ▪ Off the R354, Roggeveld Karoo, Sutherland 6920 ▪ info@roggecloof.com ▪ www.roggecloof.com ▪ **T +27 (0)23-004-1161**

☐ **Romansrivier** *see* Mountain Ridge Wines
☐ **Rondekop** *see* Oldenburg Vineyards
☐ **Roodeberg** *see* KWV Wines

Roodekrantz Wines

This splendid, characterful and elegant range was established by the Burgers of Roodekrantz farm and the Morkels of Diemerskraal to save the grapes of fine old vines from the vast blending vats of big brands. The Old Vine selection is dominated by a unique array of widely sourced chenin blancs, the 2023 vintage including yet another, as well as a second cinsault. Danie Morkel makes the wines in a cellar on Diemerskraal, with the lightest of touches, aiming 'to capture the terroir of each specific wine' and inviting winelovers to 'discover the different personalities of each site.' 'Our main focus at present,' says marketing manager Marius Burger, 'is soil health, cover crops and adding hay for water retention in Swartland vineyards.'

Old Vine range

★★★★☆ Cinsault 1954 🏅 There's a little perfume on **22** ⑧⑥, helped by 20% wholebunch, but less pretty than many in the lighter style. Elegantly & not unpleasingly lean, gently gripping, but without much stuffing. 12.4% alc. Paarl vines unless noted.

★★★★☆ 1974 Old Bush Vine Chenin Blanc 🏅 Moderate intensity of thatch & dried peach & not a great deal of concentration on **22** ⑨⓪, but very well balanced & very appealing, with light richness from 6 months on lees. Part spontaneous ferment & older barrels for 9–11 months, as all these.

★★★★☆ Brand se Berg Chenin Blanc 🏅🏅 Quietly serene loveliness of aroma on **22** ⑨③. Textured, subtly intense with light-feeling balance & complexity. Older oak softens texture, as does easy acidity. 13% alc a little higher than last. These chenins of this vintage already very approachable. Whether all will develop many years is uncertain, but excellent drinking now.

★★★★☆ Die Kliphuis 🏅🏅 Appropriate stoniness along with the fruit of **22** ⑨③, adding to complexity. Bright & fresh, with firm, succulent acidity bringing fine touch of austerity to richness & core of sweet, lingering fruit, all this despite just 12.3% alc. 1968 chenin on Swartland granite.

★★★★☆ Donkermaan 🏅 From 1967 Stellenbosch chenin bushvines on fine form again in **22** ⑨② after less complex **21 ★★★★** ⑧⑧. Suavely balanced & lightly rich, with fynbos tinges to ripe, pure peachy aromas & flavours that belie modest 12.4% alc.

★★★★ Rhenosterbosrug 🏅 More reclusive aromas than most here, though the fruit does come through better on palate of **22** ⑧⑨, whose textural richness also a little less vibrant. Nonetheless, very attractive. 12.6% alc. 1983 Swartland chenin.

Not tasted: **Die Mona, 1983 Old Bush Vine Chenin Blanc**.

Vineyard Selection range

★★★★ Die Filosoof (NEW) Modern, fresh, light-styled & eminently drinkable Swartland **21** ⑧⑨ syrah. Some wholebunch pressing adds to delicate aroma, which, like the flavour, balances modest fruit with a pleasingly savoury element. 13.1% alc.

★★★★ Die Messelaar Blend tweaked again in **22 ★★★★** ⑧⑤, chenin at just 25%, semillon & sauvignon the majority players. Fruity, though not much intensity & balancing the lowish 12% alc satisfactorily. Grippy & rounded **21** ⑧⑦ had 60% chenin.

Barrel Selections

Not tasted: **Coronet, Hemelbos Bordeaux Blend**.

Life Style range

Not tasted: **Pinotage, Pinotage Rosé, Chardonnay**. — TJ

Location: Wellington ▪ Map: Paarl ▪ Map grid reference: D1 ▪ WO: Swartland/Paarl/Stellenbosch ▪ Est 2005 ▪ 1stB 2013 ▪ Tasting, sales & cellar tours by appt ▪ Meals/refreshments by prior arrangement ▪ Owner(s) Burger family (Roodekrantz), Morkel family (Diemerskraal) ▪ Cellarmaster(s) Danie Morkel (2020, Diemerskraal) ▪ Viticulturist(s) Anton Laas ▪ 50t/4,000cs own label 40% red 40% white 20% rosé ▪ WIETA ▪ PO Box 12314 Die Boord 7613 ▪ marketing@roodekrantzwines.co.za ▪ www.roodekrantzwines.co.za ▪ **T +27 (0)82-565-6746**

☐ **Roodezandt** see McGregor Winery

Rooiberg Winery

Situated on one of the country's major tourist routes, the Rooiberg team near Robertson naturally are keen to maximise footfall at their bistro, deli and tasting lounge. Thus all were updated lately, and the resulting industrial-chic vibe deemed sufficiently attractive to be featured in several national lifestyle TV clips, 'which for sure have impacted positively on our visitor numbers'. A substantial 60,000 cases are produced for the branded labels from the total 740 ha of vines in red soils on farms along the Vink, Noree and Breede rivers. All angles are covered and boxes ticked, including Game Reserve eco-themed bottlings that bolster the Wilderness Foundation, as part of a broad accent on 'clean and green production practices and conservation'.

Reserve range

★★★★ Cabernet Sauvignon ⓦ Bold black fruit & spice on improved **20** ⑧⑨. Tweaked oaking (50% new, 18 months vs 100% new, 6 months for **19** ⑧⑦) is better knit. 20% American wood; combo barrel & FlexCube. Similar maturation for all these reds.

★★★★ Pinotage Ripe & plump **22** ⑧⑦ shade less exciting than last **20** ★★★★★ ⑨⓪ but still a fruity mouthful of blueberries & brambles, sweet cherry tobacco oak & tarry tannins.

★★★★ Shiraz ⊘ Warming & rich **22** ⑧⑨ ripples with layers of fruit, black plums & damsons, spicy-sweet oak & peppery top note. Eminently drinkable with creamy vanilla finish. No **21**.

★★★★ Cape Blend ⊘ 50% pinotage with cab & shiraz, **21** ⑧⑨ well rounded & supple, blackberries & blueberries, hints of coffee & tar, nice juicy vanilla finish. Very pleasant stuff.

Chardonnay ★★★☆ Strong oaky opening **22** ⑧③ from ferment in barrel, 50% new, somewhat veiling delicate peach & blossom fruit. Some elegance & restraint but lacks overall intensity & balance.

The Game Reserve range

★★★★ Cabernet Sauvignon ⊘ Bouncy blackcurrant & berry fruit on **22** ⑧⑥, soft & pliable on palate with nicely perfumed cedar oak (none new, year, as all reds in this range). Improved intensity on **21** ★★★☆ ⑧⑤. WO W Cape, as all these.

Merlot ★★★★ Barrel sample **22** ⑧④ looks set to follow **21** ⑧⑤ as mouthful of ripe red & black fruit, juicy tannins & bright, snappy acidity. Year old oak adds attractive whiffs of smoke & meat to both vintages tasted this edition. **Pinotage** ⓦ **★★★★** Light blueberry & plum on **21** ⑧⑤, rounded & appealing, gets gentle oak assist from older barrels, year. Notch up on previous. **Shiraz ★★★★** Real interest & character in pre-bottling **22** ⑧⑤, fresh plummy fruit, spicy peppered salami & firm ripe tannins. Seems set to improve on also-tasted **21** ⑧④ with greater intensity overall. **Chardonnay** ⊘ **★★★★** Ripe & sappy **23** ⑧④ is unwooded, showcasing ample peachy fruit, hints of litchi & lime, dry peach-pip finish. **Chenin Blanc** ⊘ **★★★★** Grapefruit, guava & granadilla on perky **23** ★★★★ ⑧⑤. Unwooded fruit purity with bouncy acid & brisk finish. **Sauvignon Blanc** ⊘ **★★★★** Pungent flavours of citrus, nettle & asparagus on uncomplicated **23** ⑧③, finishes with crisp acid zing.

Rooiberg range

★★★★ Red Muscadel ⓦ Trademark jasmine, barley sugar & muscat perfumes on **22** ⑧⑥ fortified dessert. Richly flavoured yet uncloying courtesy touch less sugar than last. Enduring clean finish.

......

Cabernet Sauvignon ⊘ ⓣ **★★★★** Nicely done **22** ⑧③ mixes sweet blackberry fruit with freshening herbal edge in pleasant everyday sipper.

......

Chenin Blanc ☺ **★★★** Touch of sugar on **23** ⑧② rounds out fruity palate, good acid ensures balanced summer tippling. **Colombar** ☺ **★★★** Zesty acid on **23** ⑧⓪ balances the sweetness, giving attractive jammy grapefruit note on an easy-drinker with more oomph than last.

......

Merlot ⊘ **★★★★** Smoky oak overtones of **22** ⑧③ support soft red plum fruit, hint of chocolate on refreshing finish. Staves & barrels, 15% American, 6-9 months, as all these reds. **Pinotage** ⊘ **★★★** Uncomplicated drinking in **22** ⑧⓪, soft red fruit, gentle tannins & oak. **Shiraz** ⊘ **★★★** Straightforward **22** ⑧⓪ a tad shy, blackberries & smoked meat, hints of spice & leather. **Cabernet Sauvignon-Merlot** ⊘ **★★★★** Pleasant **22** ⑧③ 60/40 blend with dark berries & chocolate, touch of perfume & smoky, charry finish. **Mountain Red** ⊘ **★★★** Unwooded & just-dry **22** ⑧⓪ Cape Blend from pinotage & cab (60/40). Lots of black & red fruit, touch of confection, soft supple texture. **Pinotage Rosé** ⊘ **★★★** Just-dry **22** ⑧① pale pink, with strawberries & cranberries, crisp juicy finish. **Chardonnay** ⊘ **★★★** Tropical mix on **23** ⑧①, mangoes & peaches, fresh acid, unoaked & undemanding. **Sauvignon Blanc** ⊘ **★★★** Pineapple & grapefruit on flinty **23** ⑧⓪, made for early, easy drinking. **Flamingo Sparkling** ⊘ **★★★** Frothy, grapey **NV** ⑦⑨ pink fizz balances 50 g/L sugar with nice acid & modest 9% alc. Breakfast wine. **Brut Sparkling** ⊘ **★★★** Mix of fruit on dry **NV** ⑧⓪ sparkler with apple, litchi & touch of peach at finish. **Red Natural Sweet** ⊘ **★★★** Nice concentration on **22** ⑧⓪ from pinotage & cab (60/40) with tarry note & balancing sweetness. Modest alc. **Rosé Natural Sweet** ⊘ ★★★ Charming **23** (80) cherry compote confection with fresh herbs, crisp acid & modest sweetness. Low 9.5% alc. **Blanc Natural Sweet** ⊘ ★★★ Light (9.8% alc) & fresh **23** (80) from muscadel. Floral, grapey, rounded sweetness for everyday drinking.

Red Chair range
Pinotage ⊘ ★★★ Friendly quick-quaff **22** (79) adds smoky coffee notes ex 25% American staves to mixed-berry jam flavours. Discontinued: **Sauvignon Blanc**.

3L Bag-In-Box range
Pinotage ⊘ ★★★ Succulent, fresh & fruit-driven **22** (80) has soft tannins & rounded mouthfeel. WO W Cape. **Sauvignon Blanc** ⊘ ★★★ Light-intensity **23** (79) laced with brisk acid, lemon & granadilla aromas & flavours. — CM

Location/map: Robertson ▪ Map grid reference: A7 ▪ WO: Robertson/Western Cape ▪ Est 1964 ▪ 1stB 1974 ▪ Tasting & sales Mon-Fri 9-5.30 Sat 9-3 Sun 10-2 ▪ Fee R20pp for tour groups ▪ Closed Good Fri, Dec 25 & Jan 1 ▪ Red Chair Bistro & Deli Mon-Fri 8-4 Sat/Sun 9-3 ▪ Craft beer, craft gin ▪ Facilities for children ▪ Dog-friendly garden ▪ Tour groups ▪ Rooiberg Conservancy ▪ Owner(s) 18 shareholders ▪ Cellarmaster(s) André van Dyk (Oct 2002) ▪ Winemaker(s) André Scriven (Jan 2008), with JJ Simonis (Nov 2021) ▪ Viticulturist(s) Hennie Visser (2007, Vinpro) ▪ 743ha (cab, merlot, ptage, ruby cab, shiraz, chard, chenin, cbard, sauv) ▪ 12,000t/60,000cs own label 35% red 65% white ▪ Brands for clients: Cape Dreams, Zikomo ▪ ISO 9001:2015, HACCP (SANS 10330:2007), IPW, WIETA ▪ PO Box 358 Robertson 6705 ▪ info@rooiberg.co.za ▪ www.rooiberg.co.za ▪ **T +27 (0)23-626-1663**

☐ **Rooibos Ridge** see Fairview
☐ **Rooi Kalahari** see Die Mas van Kakamas

Roos Family Vineyards ⓠ
Spot-on names and attention-grabbing labels give winelovers a foretaste of the fruit profiles expressed in this characterful range, made in the Roos family cellar to offer 'outstanding-quality New World-style wines at a reasonable price'. Available for sampling at Mooiplaas, their estate in Stellenbosch's Bottelary Hills.

The Collection
The Coco ★★★ Light-bodied **22** (81) preview has signature cocoa note from merlot spending time on oak staves. Gentle body & length. **The Bean** ★★★ As name suggests, pre-bottled **22** (82) is a coffee-styled pinotage. Bold mocha notes but light & easy to like. **The Strawberry** ⊘ ★★★ Fruity, fresh & tasty **23** (81) pink from pinotage. Pleasant body & frame, dry finish. WO Stellenbosch, rest W Cape. **The Peach** ★★★ Unfussy, easy citrus & trademark peach notes on **23** (82) chenin blanc. Light, sappy & fresh for everyday enjoyment. **The Lemongrass** ★★★ Cheery, zesty **23** (82) sauvignon blanc is aptly named. Succulent, with lemony verve, it's perfect for summer. **The Mulberry** (ⓠ) ★★★ Unwooded shiraz, **21** (81)'s bit of sugar plumps the body, gives juicy drinkability. — FM

☐ **Rooster** see Middelvlei Estate
☐ **Rose House** see Mile High Vineyards

Rosendal Wines ⓠ ◎ ⓛ
Founded 20 years ago by Norwegian partners, Durbanville-based Rosendal helped prove the viability of a then-novel concept: selling directly to the winelover via electronic channels, with pre-booked corporate and private home tastings as value adds. Recent acquisition by Frogitt & Vonkel Private Wine Merchants unlocks a much larger customer base and new winemaking avenues, while 'continuing with all the firm favourites'.

Reserve range
★★★★ **Aquitaine** (ⓠ) Cab-led Bordeaux blend offers fresh dark-berry fruit in a firm frame of 35% new oak. Compact, athletic **19** (89) shows tautness of the vintage, decant or age a few years.
★★★★ **Cape Francolin** (ⓠ) Cabernet-led 4-way Bordeaux blend **19** (89) from Stellenbosch has fine structure, firm tannins supporting ripe cherry fruit; good acid, length & oak. Dab cab franc. Will keep.
★★★★ **Black Spice** Piquant **20** (88)'s black olive fruit given zip by 18 months oak, gentle 10% new. Soft, juicy & smooth, a delicious drop from equal shiraz & grenache, like last **18** (86).

Not tasted: **Cape Ruby**. Occasional release: **Hilltop Cabernet Sauvignon, Hilltop Merlot, Hilltop Pinot Noir, Hilltop Shiraz, Blue Mountain, Red Rock, Vexator, Black Eagle, Mistral, Classic Cuvée, Serenity Chardonnay**.

Rosendal range

★★★★ **Merlot** Elegant, lingering **21** ⑧⑥ redolent of mulberries, plums & spice with fresh meat notes. Full flavoured, tannins satin-textured after 18 months in older cask.

Sauvignon Blanc ⊘ ★★★★ Greenpepper, fig, cut grass & tropical abundance in **21** ⑧⑤. Fleshy & broad, with an assertive acid backbone & food-friendly salty nuance. Not tasted: **Pinotage Rosé**. Occasional release: **Syrah, Chenin Blanc, HVIT**.

Barony range

★★★★ **Skadi Grenache Noir** ⊘ Stellenbosch fruit delivers earthy flavours & red berries in **21** ★★★★ ⑧⑤, shyer than mouthfilling last-tasted **17** ⑧⑧. Red plums & spice ex 18 months used oak, fresh finish.

Bønne Pinotage ⊘ ★★★★ Bold **21** ⑧④ offers vivacious plum fruit & spice, ground coffee & char notes from oak staving, which not quite as overt as last. **Røsslyng Chardonnay** ⊘ ★★★★ Latterly less oak & lighter, more refreshing styling, & **21** ⑧⑤ has mere hint of vanilla on the applecake & lemon curd flavours. Creaminess from lees ageing. Occasional release: **August Cabernet Sauvignon, Freyja Malbec, Candelabra, Heidi Shiraz, Sophie, Harmoni Cabernet Franc Rosé, Cecile Sauvignon Blanc**.

Noble Nomad range

He Stole My Horse Shiraz-Cabernet Sauvignon ★★★★ Label of easy & fun equal blend refers to 'legendary thief' Claus Voigts, whose wine brims with crunchy vanilla-tinged red berries in **21** ⑧⑤. — DS

Location: Durbanville ▪ WO: Western Cape ▪ Est 2004 ▪ 1stB 2003 ▪ Sales Mon-Fri 8-5 ▪ Home & corporate tastings 20+ pax - client to supply pairing options ▪ Online store ▪ Conferences ▪ VIP club ▪ Owner(s) Froggit & Vonkel cc (John Woodward, Stephen Lee, Alexander Woodward) ▪ Winemaker(s) Therese de Beer (Jan 2012) ▪ 76 Edward Str, Edward Building II, Durbanville 7530 ▪ gm@rosendalwinery.com ▪ www.rosendal-wines.com ▪ **T +27 (0)21-424-4498 (sales), +27 (0)72-075-2583 (WhatsApp)**

☐ **Rough Diamond** *see* Sanniesrust Wines
☐ **Roundstone** *see* Mullineux

Rudera Wines

For almost 25 years, Rudera Wines has specialised in cabernet, syrah and chenin, generously styled and chiefly exported around the world. Most of the wines from Stellenbosch-based owner Riana Hall's portfolio were temporarily sold out or awaiting release this edition. We look forward to reviewing them next time.

★★★★ **Cabernet Sauvignon** Flamboyant, like **17** ⑧⑨, similar cooked dark fruit, **20** ⑧⑥ adds a meaty note, loses some alc & sugar for more measured, bone-dry mouthful. **18** untasted, **19** not made.

★★★★☆ **Noble Late Harvest** ⊘ Old gold **17** ★★★★ ⑧⑨, oaked botrytis dessert from chenin, honeyed aromas, luscious sweetness very well balanced by apricot tang. Last tasted was **10** ⑨②. 375 ml.

Not tasted: **Platinum Cabernet Sauvignon, Syrah, De Tradisie Chenin Blanc, Platinum Chenin Blanc, Robusto Chenin Blanc**. — DS

Location/WO: Stellenbosch ▪ Est 1999 ▪ 1stB 2000 ▪ Closed to public ▪ Owner(s) Riana Hall ▪ Winemaker(s) Riana Hall (2017) ▪ 15ha/10ha (cab, shiraz, chenin) ▪ ±160t/20,000cs own label & BOB 70% red 30% white ▪ IPW ▪ PO Box 589 Stellenbosch 7599 ▪ riana@rudera.co.za ▪ www.rudera.co.za ▪ **T +27 (0)83-287-6364**

☐ **Rudi Schultz Wines** *see* Schultz Family Wines
☐ **Rueda Family Wines** *see* Torero Wine Co
☐ **Runner Duck** *see* Vergenoegd Löw The Wine Estate
☐ **Running Duck** *see* Stellar Winery

Running Stream Wines

On their farm near Ashton in Robertson Valley, sixth-generation Eugene Malherbe and wife Nicole in 2019 ventured beyond the grape-supplier paradigm when they handcrafted a chardonnay for an own-label, later adding a red blend, their chosen style being 'fuller bodied, for the more sophisticated palate'.

★★★★ **Chardonnay** ⓥ Debut **19** ⑧⑨ followed by similar lemony, chalky complexity, Robertson's zesty brightness on **21** ⑧⑦. 50% oak balances, broadens fruity vigour into characterful whole. No **20**.

Cape Blend ⓥ ★★★★ Sweet & soft-fruited **21** ⑧④ preview, headed by pinotage with its piquant raspberry tones, cab & syrah add flesh & structure without disturbing juicy freshness, easy pleasure. — AL

Location: Ashton ▪ WO: Robertson ▪ Est 2016 ▪ 1stB 2019 ▪ Closed to public ▪ Owner(s) Malherbe family ▪ Winemaker(s) Eugene Malherbe ▪ 220ha/25ha (ptage, chard) ▪ 20t/4,950L own label 50% red 50% white ▪ WIETA ▪ PO Box 21 Ashton 6715 ▪ info@runningstream.co.za ▪ www.blackfalls.co.za ▪ **T +27 (0)23-426-0004**

☐ **Rupert Wines** *see Anthonij Rupert Wyne*

Rustenberg Wines

With a gloriously scenic home on the Simonsberg-Stellenbosch mountainside, three centuries of heritage, more than 80 of which under custodianship of one family, the Barlows, and a reputation for producing some of the Cape's finest wine, Rustenberg truly is a Cape grande dame. Yet even an icon the past 12 months has had to deal with the twin challenges of 'intense load-shedding' and 'weather pressure during harvest', the former leading to accelerated solar energy plans, 'which will ultimately benefit our business and the environment'. The latter was approached with 'dedicated focus' to successfully manage picking and processing in the cellar, and attain the aimed-for 'world-class wines using traditional methods with modern improvements, beginning from the very first bud on the vine, to the last drop of wine in the bottle'.

Flagship range

★★★★★ **John X Merriman** ⓥ ⓐ Sophisticated, sumptuous & beautifully balanced, this Cape Bordeaux, renowned for consistent style & quality, shows true distinction in **21** ★★★★★ ⑨⑥. Mostly cab, with merlot, malbec & petit verdot (20/11/6). Concentrated dark fruit, sleek but firm tannins & an oak polishing (20 months, 35% new) already tempt broaching but a decade in the cellar will be handsomely rewarded, as for **20** ⑨③. WO Simonsberg-Stellenbosch.

★★★★☆ **Stellenbosch Chardonnay** Similar dried apricot, marmalade & almond flavour profile to previous, though a touch riper & less intense in **22** ⑨①. Natural ferment/8 months in oak, 25% new, impart creamy breadth, make for earlier accessibility though enough freshness & structure for development.

Site Specific range

Not tasted: **Peter Barlow, Five Soldiers Chardonnay**.

Regional range

★★★★☆ **Stellenbosch Cabernet Sauvignon** ⓥ ⓐ Reverts to the more muscular style in **21** ⑨②. Has all the hallmarks of fine Stellenbosch cabernet: dense core of blackcurrant fruit in a fine tannin framework. Similar oaking to previous (20% new, 15 months) well integrated, though this is built for the longer haul, has good prospects.

★★★★ **Stellenbosch Malbec** ⓥ Robust styling in **22** ⑧⑥ fleshed out with the variety's ample scented berry, savoury & liquorice flavours. Less structured & more accessible than previous but will be a perfect match for a hearty meal. Oak aged 15 months, 10% new.

★★★★ **Stellenbosch Merlot** ⓥ With more gravitas than **20** ⑧⑧, full-bodied **21** ★★★★★ ⑨⓪ has black cherries in the mix alongside juicy plum & herbal notes. Lithe fruit & oak tannins from 11 months in 20% new barrels provide the structure for a lengthy, pleasurable future.

★★★★ **Stellenbosch RM Nicholson** ⓥ Merlot takes the lead in **21** ⑧⑥ with cab & shiraz (58/22/20) in this tribute blend. Quite feisty, shows tighter tannins, savoury dark fruit & some dry cedary backing from oak, 20% new, 10 months. Restrained, needing time & food accompaniment.

★★★★ **Stellenbosch Grenache Blanc** Lighter, unoaked **23** ★★★★ ⑧⑤ has fresh green-fruit flavours, zested through with clean acid. Despite some lees ageing, less texture & intensity than **22** ⑧⑥ but perfect for summer picnics.

Not tasted: **Wild Ferment Unwooded Chardonnay, Stellenbosch Chenin Blanc, Wild Ferment Sauvignon Blanc, Stellenbosch Sauvignon Blanc, Fortified Old Vine Muscat of Alexandria**. Discontinued: **Stellenbosch Grenache, Red Muscadel**. — MW

Location/map: Stellenbosch ▪ Map grid reference: F4 ▪ WO: Stellenbosch/Simonsberg-Stellenbosch ▪ Est 1682 ▪ 1stB 1892 ▪ Tasting & sales Mon-Fri 9-4.30 Sat 10-4 Sun/pub hols 10-3 ▪ Closed Good Fri, Dec

25 & Jan 1 ▪ Gardens ▪ Cattle ▪ Filming ▪ Owner(s) Simon Barlow ▪ Cellarmaster(s) Murray Barlow (Nov 2011) ▪ Winemaker(s) Craig Christians (head, Jun 2012) & Natalia Danilowicz (Jan 2020), with Narissa Pieters ▪ Viticulturist(s) Simon Barlow (Aug 1987), with Tessa Moffat (Nov 2013) & Nick van Zyl (Nov 2015) ▪ 880ha/±120ha (cabs s/f, grenache n/b, malbec, merlot, p verdot, shiraz, chard, rouss, sauv) ▪ ±1,200t/120,000cs own label 51% red 47% white 2% other ▪ IPW, WIETA ▪ PO Box 33 Stellenbosch 7599 ▪ wine@rustenberg.co.za ▪ www.rustenberg.co.za ▪ T +27 (0)21-809-1200

Rust en Vrede Wine Estate

Stately Rust en Vrede in Stellenbosch's 'golden triangle' was returned to former glory in the early 1970s by Springbok rugby legend Jannie Engelbrecht, and cosseted since the mid-2000s by his son Jean, its status in the top echelon of Cape wine entrenched with generous yet impeccably crafted reds from mostly cabernet and syrah plantings. Gabled buildings, heritage sites dating from 1780, still preside over the vineyards, cellar, tasting venue and celebrated fine-dining restaurant. Fitting, then, that the brandy uncorked this edition is a work of time, involving winemaking, distilling and maturation since 2007. And, being grown on the estate and aged in its barrels, a natural, welcome and suitably stylish enhancement of the portfolio. See under Afrikaans, Cirrus, Donkiesbaai, Guardian Peak and Stellenbosch Reserve for the younger sibling brands.

★★★★☆ **Estate Vineyards Cabernet Sauvignon** Intriguing **21** ⑨② promises much (blackcurrants, vanilla, dried herbs), delivers pleasing mouthful of flavour with firm tannins & bright acid. Controlled 13.8% alc aids freshness on touch lighterweight expression than last. 18 months in small barrels, 20% new.

★★★★☆ **Estate Vineyards Syrah** ⓐ Quietly refined **21** ⑨④ grows in stature with aeration, gaining earthy complexity & adding richness to fine red plum & cherry fruit, 15% wholebunch adds fresh, zesty appeal. Chewy tannin, serious oaking, 18 months mainly large older barrels, 16% new, & well-integrated 15% alc all suggest this is styled for the long term, with plenty of drinking pleasure to come.

★★★★★ **Single Vineyard Syrah** ⓖ Intense but balanced **18** ★★★★★ ⑨④ has new oak dialled up to 50% vs 25% in **17** ⑨⑤. Smoky, seductive, vivacious, tight acid provides spring for cherry-raspberry fruit, some whole clusters add herbal/lavender zing.

★★★★★ **1694 Classification** ⓖ Limited bottling of estate's flagship varieties syrah & 37% cab. The former shines in **18** ⑨⑦, violet, rose, incense & saltiness, latter brings backbone & herbal freshness. Long, rich finish layered with liquorice & spice from 18 months in oak, 50% new.

★★★★★ **Estate** ⓖ Reputed blend of cab & shiraz (64/28), dab merlot shows its pedigree in **20** ★★★★☆ ⑨④, enticing notes of gravel, cassis & an iodine, black-fruited core wrapped in sumptuous tannins & good dry finish. Supreme balance. 40% new oak, 22 months.

★★★★☆ **Estate Potstill Brandy** ⓝ ⓐ 12 year old brandy ⑨③ from cab grapes & finished in barrels used for R&V Cab, but distilled in Elgin. Balanced aromas & flavours, with fruit, floral & refined cedary, spicy oak. Drier & more restrained in its fruitiness than many, though a ripe richness (but differing from the common apricot flavours) does come through. Satisfying sipping at 38% alc.

In abeyance: **Single Vineyard Cabernet Sauvignon**. — CM, TJ

Location/map/WO: Stellenbosch ▪ Map grid reference: E8 ▪ Est 1694 ▪ 1stB 1979 ▪ Tasting & sales Mon-Sat 9-5 Sun 10-4 ▪ Various tasting options - fee waived on purchase ▪ Closed Good Fri & Dec 25 ▪ Rust en Vrede Restaurant (fine dining, evenings only) ▪ Rust en Vrede Winemaker's Lunch ▪ Merchandise available ▪ Owner(s) Jean Engelbrecht ▪ Winemaker(s) Danielle le Roux (Dec 2021), with Chris Kruger (2023) ▪ Viticulturist(s) Dirkie Mouton (Jun 2010) ▪ 50ha/34ha (cab, merlot, shiraz) ▪ ±250t/40,000cs own label 100% red ▪ IPW, WWF-SA Conservation Champion ▪ PO Box 473 Stellenbosch 7599 ▪ info@rustenvrede.com ▪ www.rustenvrede.com ▪ T +27 (0)21-881-3881

☐ **Ruyter's Bin** *see* Stellenrust

Saam Mountain Vineyards

The name, meaning 'Together', hints at the desire of brand owner Perdeberg Winery to work with players in the value chain and market, as well as nature and society, to expand the footprint through Fairtrade accreditation and sustainable packaging while making the world a 'better place for all of us'.

Cellar Selection

Cabernet Sauvignon (Ⓥ) ★★★ Pleasant, mildly fruity aromas on **20** (80). Nicely grippy with flavour to match. Simple & friendly, but not trivially styled. **Pinotage** (Ⓥ) ★★★ Forward, sweetly ripe aromas & flavours on part-oaked **20** (77), a touch at odds with the firm dry tannins. **Chenin Blanc** ★★★ Flavourful & generously balanced with a little sweetness. **23** (80) ripely delicious, softly textured, easygoing pleasure. Discontinued: **Sauvignon Blanc**. — TJ

☐ **Saartjie Single Vineyard Selections** *see* Arno Smith Wine Company
☐ **Sabi Sabi** *see* Stellenrust

Sadie Family Wines   (Ⓥ)

Awards - both local and international - multiply for this remarkable winery, and we're pleased to add, for the fourth time, our award for Top Performing Winery of the Year. It's perhaps worth noting that no wine in the whole current range, including the seven that attained our five-star rating, has an alcohol level higher than 13.6%. Eben Sadie has a big footprint in the Swartland and Cape wine as a whole, as one of the earliest and most influential advocates for the region and for the fresh, hands-off yet precisely managed winemaking that has won him a reputation wherever fine wine is drunk. Home-base of his brand, Rotsvas farm on the Paardeberg, continues to be developed, following the planting of vines and the acquisition of neighbouring land in recent years. The first addition to the iconic Old Vines Series in over a decade, Rotsbank, off one of those acquired vineyards, finally brings a Swartland chenin to this collection, and the first Sadie wine from own vines. 2024 sees the maiden crop of the Sonvang experimental block (the farm's viticulture is all organic), including near-extinct pontac and cinsaut blanc. And a splendid new building, including cellar, maturation space and offices (and more), is taking impressive shape as we go to press, the whole complex solar-powered. A tranche of older bottles from the vinothèque was made available in 2023 for wine club members, a release intended to be an annual event.

Signature Series

★★★★★ **Columella** (🐝) Flag bearer for this stunning portfolio, **21** ★★★★★ (93) blends syrah, mourvèdre, grenache noir, carignan & cinsault, with dash tinta barocca, from 10 Swartland vineyards. Sumptuous & refined, with scented black fruit, aromatic spices. Suede textured & sleek, with endless finish. Year in oak, 5% new, another in foudres. Like **20** (98), approachable in youth, but 'time is your friend for this one' says Eben Sadie. Also in 1.5L & 3L, as Palladius.

★★★★★ **Palladius** (🐝) Complex & intricate assembly of 11 varieties from 17 vineyards across the Swartland, **21** (95) had wild ferment & year in concrete 'egg' & clay amphora, another year in old oak foudres. Strikingly full-bodied & magisterial, complex & intense, rich & textural at 13.7% alc. Bone-dry, like all the wines. Tight & focused in youth, it will gain in substance with some deserved maturation in bottle.

Old Vine Series

★★★★☆ **Pofadder** (🐝) (🦋) From old Riebeeks River cinsault, **22** (93) more complex & intense than first seems. Opening rush of exuberantly ripe red berries evolves quickly to reveal exotic, aromatic core, with floral scents, surprisingly full tannins & vibrant acidity. Whole-bunch & -berry ferment; 11 months oak.

★★★★☆ **Soldaat** (🐝) (🦋) Voluptuous & radiantly ripe, **22** (93) grenache noir from old Piekenierskloof vines intense cherry, raspberry & pomegranate fruit, brushed with suede tannins. Whole-bunch & -berry ferment, entire maturation in concrete tank. Just 13% alc, but weightier than last vintage. Delicious drinking now, should develop.

★★★★☆ **Treinspoor** (🐝) (🦋) Restrained handling of 48 year old dryland Swartland tinta barocca shows in succulence & sleekness of **22** (93). Perfumed wafts of waxy walnut mingle with 'porty' brambleberry; big, ripe, powdery tannins lend shape & texture, carrying to lingering finish. Half wholebunch, half destemmed; year old foudre. Characterful & ageworthy.

★★★★★ **Mev. Kirsten** (🐝) (🦋) Statuesque aristocrat of the chenin world, **22** (96) follows form, with great purity of fruit on aroma & palate, grippy lees texture, impressive extract & weight yet it's near-weightless in its delicate refinement. Year on lees in foudre & cask (latter for the younger-vine fruit). Historic Jonkershoek vines, many 100+ years old, have been nurtured to fine condition, reflected in intensity & finesse. At 13.6%, the highest alc level of the Series this year.

★★★★★ **Rotsbank** (NEW) (🍇) (🍷) New to range & its first Swartland chenin. Approximately 40 year old Paardeberg vines in shallow granite (the name means 'rock shelf') produce rich, intensely honeyed peach & citrus fruit, cut through with oystershell minerality. Year in foudre. **22** (96) stately & assured, grippy & vital, with silk texture. Stunning now & built to age.

★★★★★ **Skurfberg** (🍇) (🍷) From old chenin vines, designated WO Citrusdal Mountain since **21** ★★★★★ (93), **22** (96) expresses lean minerality, with vivid acid seam & emerging stonefruit on richly textured palate, along with delicate traces of green apple & melon. Year in large, old oak. Like Rotsbank, just 13% alc in what was generally a low-alcohol year.

★★★★★ **Kokerboom** (🍇) (🍷) From sub-hectare Citrusdal Mountain semillon, 80% blanc & 20% mutated to gris, **22** (95) expresses itself with waxy lanolin, white nut & nougat. Wholesome & generous, with lime cordial, sweet jasmine & echoing finish, promising great cellaring, as **21** ★★★★☆ (93).

★★★★★ **'T Voetpad** (🍇) (🍷) From a small isolated vineyard in a hot northern Swartland valley, parts of it 130 years old, those vines ungrafted: field blend of semillons blanc & gris, palomino, chenin & drop muscat d'Alexandrie. **22** (95) has waxy lanolin entry, with lime cordial, melon & hay, sweet spices & fragrant floral finish. Textured & svelte, with gently cossetting acidity. 13.3% alc in 'dry & desolate vintage'.

★★★★★ **Skerpioen** (🍇) (🍷) From remote Swartland vines, dry & wind-battered, just 2 km from the coast, the pure limestone soil producing an exquisite & unique treasure. **22** (95) is 50/50 chenin & palomino, wild yeast fermented like all these, & after wholebunch pressing left year on lees in old oak & acacia foudre. Wafts of jasmine & chamomile, succulent citrus & chiselled salty minerality.— GdB

Location: Malmesbury ▪ Map: Swartland ▪ Map grid reference: C8 ▪ WO: Swartland/Citrusdal Mountain/
Piekenierskloof/Stellenbosch ▪ Est 1999 ▪ 1stB 2000 ▪ Only scheduled tastings - bookings essential, contact
office@thesadiefamily.com ▪ Owner(s) The Sadie Family (Pty) Ltd ▪ Winemaker(s) Eben Sadie (1999), Paul
Jordaan (2017) ▪ Viticulturist(s) Morné Steyn (2019) ▪ ±40ha (cinsaut, grenache n/b, mourv, shiraz, tinta barocca,
chenin, clairette, palomino, rouss, sem, verdelho, viog) ▪ 90t/14,380cs own label 50% red 50% white ▪ PO Box
1019 Malmesbury 7299 ▪ office@thesadiefamily.com ▪ www.thesadiefamily.com ▪ **T +27 (0)22-125-0085**

☐ **Safari** see Frater Family Wines

☐ **Sainsbury** see Bosman Family Vineyards

☐ **Saints** see DGB (Pty) Ltd

Sakkie Mouton Family Wines

'Unconventional' would be a good descriptor for both the critically acclaimed young vintner, Izak 'Sakkie' Mouton, and his wines and labels, but being Vredendal-born and -raised, he also has a deep knowledge of, and love for the maritime vineyards from which he sources, some within just 5 km of the cool influence of the Atlantic. Where, as we learned when he launched his attention-grabbing chenin a few years back, he engages in another passion, crayfish diving. Above all, he's a serious, Elsenburg-trained winemaker, and there's no doubting the quality he produces with his small-scale, minimalistic approach, designed to reflect 'West Coast uniqueness and personality as honestly as possible'.

★★★★★ **Dawn Of The Salty Tongues Syrah** (NEW) (🍇) Doesn't put a foot wrong. Highly perfumed **22** (95)'s glacé cherries & violets draw you in, seduce. But on the palate the musculature becomes apparent, a firm backbone & dry finish, without the trap of harshness. Long life ahead. WO Olifants River, as Vloedvlak.

★★★★★ **Revenge Of The Crayfish** (🍇) Bunch pressed & wild fermented (as all whites) in 50% tank, 9 months on lees in large old barrels; unfined/filtered (as rest). Cool-climate chenin, multi-layered **22** (95) shows thatch, bruised apple, nectarine, shot through with salty acid. Intensely focused.

★★★★☆ **Vloedvlak Colombar** (NEW) Pre-bottled **23** (90) as individual as you'd expect from this winemaker. Tiny yield, 4 months older small barrels. Grown-up colombard: winter melon, limy-fresh, sleek, pulsates with life. Great prospects. Just 160 cases.

★★★★☆ **Sand Erf** (🍇) From rare-in-SA vermentino, ex-tank **23** (93) is sleek & nervy, with kelp & Bosc pear styling, the fruit showing more in the flavours. Distinctive & complex, doesn't have a mean bone in its body. Just 75 cases.

★★★★☆ **Full On Misfit** (🍇) Idiosyncratic changing blend (name says it all), 54% chenin with colombard, macabeo & hanepoot. **22** (93) spent 9 months in older barrels, its biscuity savoury notes accompany preserved melon, dried pear. Then there's the palate surprise, zinging fresh flavours of cucumber & capsicum. An original. WO W Cape.— CR

Location: Vredendal ▪ WO: Koekenaap/Olifants River/Western Cape ▪ Est 2019 ▪ 1stB 2018 ▪ Closed to public ▪ Owner(s) Sakkie Mouton Family Wines (Pty) Ltd ▪ Winemaker(s)/viticulturist(s) Sakkie Mouton ▪ 16t/1,000cs own label 10% red 90% white ▪ kreefsak88@gmail.com ▪ **T +27 (0)83-622-4470**

☐ **Salpeterkop** *see* Rogge Cloof

Saltare

Cap classique is the speciality of Carla Pauw, owner with husband Christoff of this Stellenbosch boutique winery which also crafts a limited number of still wines. In particular, Carla is drawn to wines that reflect terroir, heightened awareness of this coming from a Cap Classique Association basewine tasting. She especially enjoys trialling pinot noir from different areas, to date Robertson, and Faure and Vlaeberg in Stellenbosch. She seeks the unique vineyard footprint in wines 'that embody clarity, delicacy and natural authenticity'.

★★★★☆ **Syrah** Full-bodied syrah, **20** ⑨② has generous ripe dark berries & spice with soft, supple feel, neatly firmed by squeeze of tannin. Better balanced than last. Harmonious, with freshness to counteract 14.9% alc. Swartland grapes, as Chenin, wholeberry older-oak ferment/24 months.

★★★★☆ **Old Vines Chenin Blanc** Old-vine depth & concentration announce **20** ⑨⓪. Earthy tones & green apples decorate the creamy texture, for now somewhat curtailed by an overly piquant acidity. Greater harmony may be achieved as the fruit richness develops. Wholebunch natural ferment, older oak.

★★★★ **Méthode Cap Classique Brut Rosé** From Stellenbosch pinot noir. **NV** ⑧⑦ exuberant fresh red cherry aromas matched by lively, creamy mousse, 7.5 g/L sugar extending fruitily dry tail. Previous, from Robertson fruit, had more gravitas. Also in 1.5L, as sibling sparklers.

★★★★☆ **Méthode Cap Classique Brut Nature** Chardonnay's lemony zest strikes clean, refreshing & lingering note on latest **NV** ⑨⓪. 15% oaked portion adds depth & enhances creamy bubbles without detracting from overall lightness & energy. Bone-dry. Previous added pinot noir.

★★★★ **Méthode Cap Classique Brut Reserve** Latest **NV** ⑧⑨ 100% Robertson chardonnay. Quite a developed bouquet, more lively lemon zest flavours enhanced by 15% barrel-fermented portion. Initial bright bubble fades somewhat quickly. Not in same league as previous with 55% pinot noir. 25% reserve wine, 72 months on lees.

Occasional release: **Méthode Cap Classique Blanc de Noirs Cuvée Camille**. In abeyance: **Méthode Cap Classique Brut Blanc de Blancs**. Discontinued: **Specialis, Single Vineyard Chenin Blanc**. — AL

Location/map: Stellenbosch ▪ Map grid reference: F5 ▪ WO: Western Cape/Swartland ▪ 1stB 2005 ▪ Tasting & cellar tour by appt ▪ Olive oil ▪ Owner(s) Christoff & Carla Pauw ▪ Cellarmaster(s)/winemaker(s) Carla Pauw (2005) ▪ 25t/2,500cs own label 7% red 8% white 85% MCC ▪ 30 Die Laan, Stellenbosch 7600 ▪ info@saltare.co.za ▪ www.saltare.co.za ▪ **T +27 (0)21-883-9568**

Samesyn Wines

Lawyer Sarah Marx, Canadian marketing consultant Kara Hobby, and vlogger and curator of wine club HanDrinksSolo Jono Le Feuvre are 'wine adventurers from Stellenbosch' looking to 'explore emerging regions and unusual cultivars, and expressing them in liquid form'. The debut limited release was crafted by Angus Paul (see listing) and features a delightful label evoking the brand name, 'Togetherness'.

★★★★ **Syrah** Cool origin shows in **22** ⑧⑧'s pure fruit, blackberries, cherries, spice dusted from 10 months older oak. Succulent, streamlined, this is sophisticated syrah, with lithe muscle tone.— CR, CvZ

Location: Stellenbosch ▪ WO: Cape Agulhas ▪ Est 2001 ▪ 1stB 2022 ▪ Closed to public ▪ Owner(s) K2023787195 (SA) (Pty) Ltd t/a Samesyn Wines (3 shareholders) ▪ Winemaker(s) Angus Paul (Jan 2022, consultant) ▪ 700cs own label 100% red ▪ Karibib Wine Craft, Karibib Vineyards, Polkadraai Rd, Stellenbosch 7600 ▪ hello@samesynwines.com ▪ www.samesynwines.com ▪ **T +27 (0)84-351-2044**

Sandstone

These wines travel from the stony mountains of the Cape to the sandy shores of the Maldives, where they are intended to offer delicious, fresh and well-priced options to guests of the Villa Resorts collection of award-winning, family-owned island destinations. Curator Kent Scheermeyer selects the portfolio, which will grow to around 12 wines, for compatibility with the local weather, cuisine and lifestyle.

★★★★☆ **Chardonnay** Balanced, fresh & succulent **22** ⑨⓪ delightful in youth, partly thanks to only older oak in combo with small portions in tank & concrete for purity & freshness. WO Elgin, as Sauvignon.

★★★★☆ **Sauvignon Blanc** Commendable & vibrant cool-climate expression, **22** ⑨② has 9% oaked semillon & 2 months lees contact to add breadth to poised, intense & granadilla-rich palate.

★★★★☆ **Méthode Cap Classique Brut Rosé Pinot Noir** Fruit & freshness centre stage on salmon-hued, strawberry-toned **NV** ⑨⓪ from 18 months on lees. Appealing & flavoursome with fine mousse.

★★★★☆ **Méthode Cap Classique Brut Chardonnay** Stylish, with purity & presence, **NV** ⑨⓪ brims with vivacity. 18 months on lees for nice savoury note on lemony, elegantly dry conclusion.

Merlot ★★★☆ Expressive cassis & cherries, **18** ⑧⑤ is tobacco spiced from 2 years in barriques; firmly structured, a tannin foundation to provide further ageing, but already approachable. **Rosé** ★★★ From shiraz, strawberry-scented **21** ⑧⓪ is light & dry, has appealing delicacy. — Various tasters

WO: Western Cape/Elgin ▪ Est 2011 ▪ Closed to public ▪ Cellarmaster(s) Andries Burger (Paul Clüver Family Wines) & Elunda Basson (Steenberg Vineyards) ▪ 20,000cs own label 40% red 40% white 10% rosé 10% MCC ▪ Curated by Kent Scheermeyer, ksconsult@icloud.com ▪ T +27 (0)83-484-8781 ▪ hello@villaresorts. com ▪ www.villaresorts.com ▪ **T +960-334-4777**

☐ **Sandveld** *see* Tierhoek
☐ **Sani Wines** *see* Groot Parys Estate

Sanniesrust Wines   ⓛ

'It's hip, but you can drink it' may be a way of thinking about this collection of handcrafted wines by Pieter van der Merwe, previously a collaboration with David Finlayson, now wholly owned by Pieter and his wife Amelia. There's plenty of interest and trendiness on offer, heirloom and rare varieties, modest alcohol, a natural approach, but 'made with as little pretence as possible, to be enjoyed by everyone'.

Sanniesrust range

★★★★ **Cinsaut** ⊘ Charming & intensely fragrant **22** ★★★★★ ⑨① raises bar on last **18** ⑧⑥. Deeper flavour - Turkish delight, redcurrants & florals - yet beautifully poised & fresh, lithe despite 14.4% alc, ends clean & dry. Natural ferment, some wholebunch, old oak in support. WO Simonsberg-Paarl.

★★★★★ **Grenache Noir** Subtle red-fruit pastille flavours & a savoury nuance in less expressive though riper **22** ★★★★ ⑧⑦. Understated, almost reclusive in youth though freshly balanced & dry, old oak (12 months) unnoticeable. May unfurl with time though a shade off more flavoursome **21** ⑨⓪.

Cinsaut Rosé ⑩ₑw ★★★ Flamingo pink & light (10.6% alc) **23** ⑦⑦ is piquant & bone-dry, with hint of red fruit. Summery slimmer's delight. Not tasted: **Pinotage**. In abeyance: **Grenache Blanc**.

Rough Diamond range

Tempranillo ⑦ ★★★★ Perfumed sweet flowers, peach melba & honey complexity, **17** ⑧③'s light oaking & dash sugar add to voluptuousness on palate, touch more freshness would rate higher. — MW

Location: Stellenbosch ▪ WO: Stellenbosch/Simonsberg-Paarl ▪ Est/1stB 2016 ▪ Tasting by appt only ▪ Closed all pub hols ▪ Owner(s) Pieter & Amelia van der Merwe ▪ Winemaker(s) Pieter van der Merwe (Jan 2016) ▪ 4t/250cs own label 75% red 25% rosé ▪ sanniesrust@gmail.com ▪ **T +27 (0)84-512-5266**

☐ **Sarel Roussouw Signature** *see* Simonsvlei International

Saronsberg Cellar   ⓛ ⌂ ⊚

In the first significant winemaker change in 20 years, assistant for the past five years, Elsenburg-trained Daniela Jansen steps into the lead role, with Dimitri Vermeulen beside her in the cellar, while former deputy viticulturist Roux Conradie becomes vine carer-in-chief, tasked with ongoing planting of mostly shiraz on some of the Tulbagh estate's best sites. These are spread over two farms, formerly Waveren and Welgegund and, executive Christiaan van Huyssteen explains, it's the sites that drive the style of the wines, 'from elegant and subtle to concentrated and powerful'. Hand sorting of the entire 600-ton crop, gentle handling and restraint in the winemaking contribute to an enviably consistent harvest of awards and professional ratings.

★★★★☆ **Grenache** ⓢ Unapologetically delicious, with supple, juicy berries & currants oozing charm, **20** ⑨② sleek, silky tannins but focus is totally on fruit purity & nuance.

★★★★ **Provenance Shiraz** ⓥ Dependable over-deliverer. Round, rich **21** ⑧⑨ a riot of berries, meaty smoke & tobacco on supple bed of tannin & melded oak, 30% new. Long, satisfying finish. Also in 1.5L, as Seismic. WO W Cape.

★★★★☆ **Shiraz** ⓐ Captain of this team, confident & expressive, ripe yet nuanced & harmonious with staying power. Vanilla from 85% new oak more than a backdrop in **21** ⑨④ but part of the personality, doesn't overpower the florals, berry fruit or scrub aromas & flavours.

★★★★☆ **Seismic** ⓥ Estate's nod to Bordeaux, expectedly bold but controlled in **21** ⑨⓪, 42% cab with the 4 others, older oak only, 20 months. Classic cassis, graphite & dried tealeaf in supple body with liquorice & wet earth finish. Revisit in 5 years for more drinking pleasure.

★★★★☆ **Seismic Reserve** ⓃⒺⓌ ⓐ Only the 2 cabs represent Bordeaux in this older vintage, same deft oaking as sibling but darker, more brooding character & bigger albeit well-hidden 15.2% alc. The style's hallmarks - blackcurrant, leafy tomato, crushed herb - present in **18** ⑨③'s rounded, harmonious body, along with stamina you'd expect from 75% cab sauvignon.

★★★★☆ **Full Circle** ⓐ Restrained opulence in this Rhône blend, with hidden muscles to see in the mid-2030s. Outspoken dark berry fruit, meat spice & lavender perfume in a cloak of velvet. **21** ⑨④ shiraz, mourvèdre & grenache noir (66/17/13), dabs viognier & recent partner roussanne.

★★★★☆ **Roussanne** ⓥ ⓐ Yet more complex & beguiling than **20** ⑨③, **21** ★★★★★ ⑨⑤ expresses dew-fresh nectarine & apricot flavours with subtlety & grace, older oak ferment/11 months preserves delicate nuances like wet hay & peach melba. Mere 274 cases. From cellardoor & online only, as Grenache.

★★★★ **Sauvignon Blanc** Night harvested for freshness, from estate's oldest vines. **23** ⑧⑦ greengage, nettle & grass aromas in a body that's racy yet well balanced with creaminess from 6 months on the lees. Fragrant fynbos farewell.

★★★★ **Viognier** As seriously conceived & sophisticated as last, **21** ⑧⑧ picked early to preserve natural acidity yet richly endowed with orchard fruit layered with dried herbs pot-pourri perfume. Ample texture from 11 months in seasoned 500L barrels, some Hungarian.

★★★★☆ **Brut Méthode Cap Classique** ⓥ Elegant **20** ⑨⓪ from chardonnay continues improved form of previous. Rich, rounded, with fine, mouthfilling mousse & flavours of fresh apple, pie crust & crème brûlée, a savoury minerality in the persistent conclusion.

. . . .

Shiraz Rosé ⓟ ★★★★ Lovely summery dry glassful of red cherries & plums, pale salmon glints & spice on smooth finish of **23** ⑧⑤. **Earth in Motion** ⓟ ★★★★ Named for 1969 major area quake, **23** ⑧⑤ chenin generous & fun, stirs the taste buds with orchard fruit & freshness, carrying to long grapefruit farewell.

. . . .

Not tasted: **Mourvèdre**. — WB

Location/map: Tulbagh ▪ Map grid reference: F4 ▪ WO: Tulbagh/Western Cape ▪ Est 2002 ▪ 1stB 2004 ▪ Tasting & sales Mon-Fri 8.30-4.30 Sat/pub hols 10-2 Sun 10-1 ▪ Fee R120pp ▪ Closed Good Fri, Ascension day & Dec 25 ▪ Cellar tours by appt ▪ Olive oil ▪ Artworks & sculptures on display ▪ Christmas in Winter Tulbagh festival (Jun) ▪ Self-catering guest cottages ▪ Wedding venue ▪ Conference facilities ▪ Owner(s) Saronsberg Cellar (Pty) Ltd ▪ Winemaker(s) Daniela Jansen (2019), with Dimitri Vermeulen ▪ Viticulturist(s) Roux Conradie (2022) ▪ 550ha/63ha under vine ▪ 550t own label 70% red 30% white ▪ WIETA ▪ PO Box 361 Tulbagh 6820 ▪ info@saronsberg.com ▪ www.saronsberg.com ▪ **T +27 (0)23-230-0707**

Saurwein Wines

Jessica Saurwein crafts her wines on Waterval Farm near Standford on the Cape South Coast. Currently her chosen pinot noir and riesling are sourced elsewhere but both varieties are scheduled to be planted this year on the home-farm, where the philosophy of regenerative and sustainable farming is practised. Also planned is solar power for the cellar, avoiding the need for a generator. 'Challenging, fairly wet' 2023 saw all four vineyards ripening at once, and some technical difficulties, yet was 'good overall', especially the riesling.

★★★★☆ **Nom Pinot Noir** ⓥ ⓐ Cool, penetrating tones on **22** ⑨④ from 700m Elandskloof vines. Still tight, vigorous, the rich dark fruit yet to reveal its full generosity. Like **21** ⑨④, combines power without weight. Nombulelo in Xhosa means 'gratitude', which this wine will demand over time.

★★★★☆ **Om Pinot Noir** ⊘ ⊛ Light of foot **22** ⑨④ has a silky flow to its ripe dark cherry flavours, memorably sustained by fine, lively tannins. Careful oaking, 25% new, furthers complexity, no hindrance to current enjoyment or future pleasure. Hemel-en-Aarde Ridge grapes.

★★★★☆ **Chi Riesling** ⊛ Two vintages tasted: **23** ⑨① has usual delicacy & zest, with riper lime & gentle spice flavours; a hint of sweetness too, neatly swept along by invigorating acidity. Still a baby. **22** ⑨④ has more thrilling tension & dryness, with mouthwatering spicy limes lengthened by beautifully balanced sugar & acid. Promising future.— AL

Location: Stanford ▪ WO: Elgin/Elandskloof/Hemel-en-Aarde Ridge ▪ 1stB 2015 ▪ No tastings; sales online only ▪ Owner(s)/winemaker(s) Jessica Saurwein ▪ 21t/2,700cs own label 50% red 50% white ▪ Waterval Farm, Stanford 7210 ▪ jessica@saurwein.co.za ▪ www.saurwein.co.za ▪ **T +27 (0)76-228-3116**

Savage Wines

CWG member Duncan Savage's current range of wines couldn't be more different to Cape Point Vineyards' which he put on the wine map. It's now a personal journey for him, exploring the Cape's vineyards to find 'interesting sites', including some 'blocks that are being planted on pretty extreme slopes', to be released only from 2025. Sourcing for wines of 'elegance and purity' is with the help of consultant viticulturist Jaco Engelbrecht, and ranges from Piekenierskloof to Malgas and points in-between. The wine names are unusual and personal, with label line-drawings of evocative countryside scenes. The natural-as-possible winemaking happens with the assistance of Banele Vakele in a Cape Town cellar, busy being expanded.

CWG Auction Wines

★★★★★ **Syrah** ⊛ Wild ferment, as rest, here in open fermenters, different oaking to syrah siblings, 22 months older barriques. Always impressive, the cellar's definitive syrah: **21** ⑨⑧ has the expected power & concentration yet with lithe muscle tone, glossy fruit layered with spice, scrub, smoked meat. Firm tannins are ripe, built for a future but hard to resist. WO Coastal.

Savage Wines

★★★★★ **Follow The Line** ⊛ ⊛ Got plenty of cellar attention: ferment in foudre & open fermenters, 50% wholebunch, skin contact, 10 months in older foudre & barrels. Yet **22** ⑨⑤'s fruit is there: red berries, lightly spice-dusted, white pepper, the svelte structure showcasing varietal typicity, with juicy freshness, amenable tannins. Cinsault taken to a higher level. **21** ★★★★★ ⑨④ the first all-cinsault from Darling.

★★★★☆ **Thief In The Night** ⊛ Grenache noir from Piekenierskloof spent 6 months in seasoned foudre, allowing the variety full expression: piquant red berries, subtle oak spicing. One of **22** ⑨④'s main attractions is the texture, supple, sleek, yet full of flavour, a demonstration of how a light-textured variety can impress without losing its character.

★★★★★ **Girl Next Door** ⊛ Three syrahs in the ranges, all distinctive, this Cape Town fruit, remains true to its style; less oak, just 10 months older barrels & foudre, for earlier drinking, no hardship, & without sacrificing quality. **22** ★★★★★ ⑨④ layered, complex, plush fruit & violets, scrub, a spice array including pepper. Tannins supple, & there's welcome freshness in the streamlined body. **21** ⑨⑤ similarly styled.

★★★★★ **Red** ⊛ 70% wholebunch syrah, ferment open fermenters & foudre, year older barrel plus 10 months foudre, care taken for **21** ★★★★★ ⑨④'s fruit expression while creating a serious wine. Spice is tobacco, black pepper, seamed through the brambly fruit, texture smoothly approachable, tannins in place for long ageing. Best lies ahead, don't rush it - as with **20** ⑨⑤. WO Stellenbosch.

★★★★☆ **Are We There Yet?** ⊛ Unusual blend, touriga & syrah (67/33) from maritime Malgas, but enough wildness in both for compatibility: hedgerow berries, scrub, healthy dose of spice from 10 months older barrels, savoury, peppery, even a charcuterie nuance. **22** ★★★★★ ⑨⑤ sleekly accessible, tannins supple, texture smooth, with plenty of flavour. A blending triumph, following elegant **21** ⑨③.

★★★★★ **Never Been Asked To Dance** ⊛ ⊛ From 66 year old Paarl vines. Aged in 600L barrels, all seasoned, **22** ⑨⑦ about respecting fruit but allowing it to display its versatility: chenin's response to oak in the right hands. Peach, apricot & melon, roasted almond savoury notes, & then the unexpected minerality on the palate. Beautifully crafted, complex & sophisticated.

★★★★★ **White** ⊛ Sauvignon with 25% semillon, barrel fermented, 20% new, 14 months on lees, **22** ★★★★☆ ⑨④ a symbiosis of fruit & oak, striking the perfect balance. Leafy-green notes, some gooseberry, lightly brushed with biscuit tones. Many layers, changes in the glass, ending fresh & long, providing lift & vitality to the flavours. Follows highly complex **21** ⑨⑤. WO W Cape.

★★★★★ **Not Tonight Josephine** 🌿 Traditionally made chenin straw wine ex Piekenierskloof: foot-trodden bunches over 1 week, aged demijohns & old barrels 14 months. Full-sweet (295 g/L sugar), low 8.5% alc, gold-hued **22** ⑨⑥ richly impressive apricot & pineapple, its concentration a reflection of masterly crafting. Very special, one to savour. **21** ★★★★☆ ⑨④ touch sweeter, with lower alc. 375 ml.— CR

Location: Cape Town ▪ WO: Piekenierskloof/Coastal/Darling/Cape Town/Stellenbosch/Malgas/Paarl/ Western Cape ▪ Est 2006 ▪ 1stB 2011 ▪ Closed to public ▪ Owner(s) Duncan Savage ▪ Winemaker(s) Duncan Savage (Jan 2006), with Banele Vakele (Oct 2019) ▪ Viticulturist(s) Duncan Savage, with Jaco Engelbrecht (consultant) ▪ 90t/10,000cs own label 75% red 25% white ▪ 6 Spencer Rd, Salt River, Cape Town 7925 ▪ info@savagewines.com ▪ www.savagewines.com

---

☐ **Savanha** *see* Spier

Saxenburg Wine Farm

Further changes see eldest daughter Fiona Bührer, previously partnered with her brother Vincent, take sole ownership of the Polkadraai Hills estate revitalised from 1989 by parents Adrian and Birgit. Fiona and recent winemaker Brendan Smith are pursuing the stylistic changes began in 2020 with the 2nd Generation Syrah, while keeping the focus on that flagship variety and cabernet. Mapping of altitude, aspect, soil, temperature and solar radiation aids identification of sites that will best reflect both the farm and the appellation. In the cellar, the many pickings of each block are treated individually with the same goal, showcasing the terroir. Already the wines show more freshness and dimension, and developments are being watched with interest.

Saxenburg Select range

★★★★☆ **Syrah** The flagship, most contained & currently unrevealing of syrah trio. Rich & savoury, mere glimpse of dark spice. **20** ⑨⓪'s fine, layered tannins freshen, offset full body. Sensitively oaked, 30% new. Promises good evolution with time. 14.2% alc. Small portion bunch-fermented.

Limited Releases

★★★★☆ **Sauvignon Blanc-Semillon** ⑫ Quiet introduction to serene **21** ⑨⓪, texture currently emphasised over fruit, sauvignon injecting a little pizazz into semillon's languid silkiness. A little skin contact, portion natural ferment & older oak, 10 months, add dimension, ageability to these classic partners.

La Rêve ⑫ ★★★★ From botrytised semillon, unwooded **17** ⑧⑤ dessert wine has an elegant honey & wax character, its gentle plumpness energised by balanced acid. Just 10.3% alc & not overly sweet, good solo & at table. 375 ml. Stellenbosch WO.

Private Collection

★★★★☆ **Cabernet Sauvignon** Cedary oak spice & ripe, brambly fruit distinction on soundly built **21** ⑨①. Drops of cab franc & malbec add to texture, complexity. Mainly 21 year old block with some younger vines to augment fruit. Still young; will harmonise, evolve with time. 21% new oak, 18 months.

★★★★ **Pinotage** Ex-tank, **22** ⑧⑥ perfumed & sweet-fruited, complemented by supple texture. Variety's tannin nip no hindrance to early drinking. Also-tasted **21** ⑧⑦ noteworthy for freshness & spicy red fruit purity; approachability enhanced by firm yet rounded build, light body (13% alc). Short wholeberry ferment to accent fruit; year older oak.

★★★★☆ **Syrah** ⊘ 🌿 Step-up in density & structure on 2nd Generation version, **21** ★★★★★ ⑨⑤'s sonorous aromas, sweet-fruited flesh just as enticing, plus whisper of new oak (10%) for extra complexity. Vigorous grape tannins add vitality, alleviate heaviness of 14.3% alc, ensure promising future. 20% wholebunch ferment; year oak. Continues improvement shown in **20** ⑨①.

★★★★ **Chardonnay** Notably tuned-down oak (10% new vs 23% in **20** ⑧⑧) in both vintages tasted this edition. **22** ⑧⑥ greater focus on ripe lime flavours, bolstered by gentle creaminess. Pleasant but lacks structure for long keeping, unlike **21** ⑧⑨, concentrated, complex & ageworthy. Bunch press, portion natural ferment, 11 months larger oak.

★★★★ **Sauvignon Blanc** Reverts to 100% sauvignon in **23** ⑧⑧ (**22** ⑧⑧ had dash semillon). Tasted pre-bottling, usual ripe tropical flavours enriched with tiny oaked portion & lees ageing; full bodied & well-proportioned. On par with previous.

★★★★ Méthode Cap Classique Brut Previously **NV ★★★★** ⑧⑦, **19** ⑧⑦ sparkler mainly chardonnay, 34% pinot noir. Quiet nutty brioche tones, creamy texture contrasted by lively, assertive bubble. Refreshingly dry. Barrel-fermented; 34 months on lees. Stellenbosch WO.

Family Series

★★★★ 2nd Generation Syrah Modern-style **21** ⑧⑧ immediately entices with aromatic spice, dark-berry fruit richness; frisson of vibrant tannins & freshness bring whole into focus. Already so enjoyable. 55% wholebunch ferment, year older oak. **20** ⑧⑦ reflects initial style change.

★★★★ Winemaker's Blend Red ⑫ Shows shiraz & cab's compatibility. **20** ⑧⑥ spice, suppleness with rounded grip & savoury length. Dabs cab franc & malbec add richness, fresh tang. Older oak, year.

★★★★ Winemaker's Blend White Plentiful lemony vigour in **22** ⑧⑥, equal partnership chenin & chardonnay with 10% semillon. All old-oak ferment, lees-ageing 11 months for extra depth, offset by still-edgy acid; should resolve over few months.

Guinea Fowl range

★★★★ Red ⊘ Bright-fruited & fresh **21** ⑧⑥ from usual cab-based Bordeaux blend; malbec's tangy energy influences mouthwatering quality. Year older oak. Great value.

....

White ⊘ ⑫ **★★★★** Previously a blend, **23** ⑧⑤ from chenin, brightly fresh, dry, with ripe tropical intensity, tiny oaked portion adds breadth. — AL

....

Location: Kuils River ▪ Map: Stellenbosch ▪ Map grid reference: A5 ▪ WO: Polkadraai Hills/Stellenbosch ▪ Est 1693 ▪ 1stB 1990 ▪ Tasting & sales Mon-Sun 10-6 ▪ Wine tasting fee R65/R85 ▪ Chocolate & wine pairing R110/4 wines ▪ biltong & wine pairing R110/4 wines ▪ Safari tasting R650pp (incl all wines, glass of MCC, cheese platter with biltong & nuts) - to book in advance, minimum 4 guests ▪ Closed Dec 25 & Jan 1 ▪ Cattle Baron Grill Room restaurant T +27 (0)21-906-5232, www.cattlebaron.co.za ▪ Gifts ▪ Game park ▪ Guest cottages ▪ Wine club ▪ Owner(s) Fiona Bührer ▪ Winemaker(s) Brendan Smith (Nov 2022) ▪ Viticulturist(s) Donovan Diedericks (Apr 2008) ▪ 195ha/60ha (cabs s/f, malbec, merlot, ptage, shiraz, chard, chenin, sauv) ▪ 450t/100,000cs own label 80% red 20% white ▪ Polkadraai Rd, Kuils River 7580 ▪ tastingroom@saxenburg.co.za ▪ www.saxenburg.co.za ▪ **T +27 (0)21-903-6113**

Scali

⑫

Willie and Tania de Waal launched their small-scale venture a quarter-century ago on the Voor Paardeberg family farm, and named it for the shale vineyard soils, skalie in Afrikaans. It's now based, in spirit at least, on a yacht, the lovers of the ocean and travel describing themselves as 'sailing winemakers', with plans to voyage to foreign lands to craft wines 'in the most natural way possible, to reflect terroir and grape variety'.

Scali range

★★★★☆ Pinotage ⑫ Previewed **21** ⑨⓪ from Paardeberg echoes buoyant personality of last **16** ⑨③. Smooth dark plum, red cherry cola & dried coriander notes, lifted cranberry finish. Older oak, as all these.

★★★★☆ Syrah ⑫ Swartland grapes in **21** ⑨⓪ barrel sample provide fragrant array of berries, spice & dark chocolate. Supple, harmonious, savoury dried herb finish. Natural ferment, as all. First since **16** ⑨①.

★★★★☆ Blanc ⑫ Switches from viognier blend to solo chenin in delightful **22** ⑨① preview from Paardeberg. Silky, fresh & balanced, shows benefit of oaking only half the wine. Last was **17** ⑨④.

★★★★ Ancestor ⑫ Méthode ancestrale (single-ferment) sparkling **16** ⑧⑦ from Voor Paardeberg merlot has bready aroma, smooth, creamy texture after remarkable 6 years on lees. Finishes savoury & dry.

Sirkel range

★★★★ Pinotage ⑫ Unadorned by oak, in a fresh, slightly spritzy carbonic style, **20** ⑧⑦ abundant concentrated red berries & gentle spice. Juicy & fun, whereas last-reviewed **16 ★★★** ⑦⑧ was tad chewy.

★★★★ Shiraz-Viognier ⊘ Light **22** ⑧⑥, juicy berry fruit, supple body & perfumed lift. For early drinking, with an x-factor that makes it more than a simple quaffer. Unoaked, like last-tasted **20**. WO W Cape.

Chenin Blanc ★★★★ Easy, wild-fermented **22** ⑧⑤, sunshiny tropical fruit & creamy texture, hint of citrus freshens the finish. Discontinued: **Syrah**.

Anker range

Occasional release: **Cape Vintage**. — WB

Location/map: Paarl ▪ Map grid reference: C1 ▪ WO: Swartland/Paardeberg/Voor Paardeberg/Western Cape ▪ Est/1stB 1999 ▪ Tasting & sales Mon-Sat by appt ▪ Closed all pub hols ▪ Wine club ▪ Owner(s) Willie & Tania de Waal ▪ Cellarmaster(s)/winemaker(s) Willie & Tania de Waal (Aug 1999) ▪ Viticulturist(s) Willie de Waal (Feb 1991) ▪ 45t/6,000cs own label 67% red 33% white ▪ PO Box 7143 Paarl 7620 ▪ info@scali.co.za ▪ www. scali.co.za ▪ **T +27 (0)82-854-9005/+27 (0)82-563-8304**

☐ **Schaap** see Skaap Wines

Schalkenbosch Wines

Four properties make up this large, diverse Tulbagh estate, dating from the 18th century. Fruit from vineyards on the Witzenberg slopes in ordinary years is styled into 'honest, easy-drinking wines for any occasion', but the past vintage had to be skipped, unfortunately. 'Hopefully we will have a better harvest next year'.

Location/map: Tulbagh ▪ Map grid reference: G5 ▪ Est 1792 ▪ 1stB 2002 ▪ Tasting, sales & tours by appt ▪ Closed all pub hols ▪ Tour groups ▪ Weddings/functions ▪ Walking/hiking & MTB trails ▪ Conservation area ▪ Self-catering cottages ▪ Owner(s) Platinum Mile Investments ▪ Winemaker(s) Carl Allen (consultant) ▪ Viticulturist(s) Johan Wiese & Andrew Teubes ▪ 1,800ha/30ha (cabs s/f, grenache, malbec, merlot, mourv, p verdot, shiraz, nouvelle, sauv, viog) ▪ 150t/20,000cs own label 80% red 18% white 2% rosé ▪ WWF-SA Conservation Champion ▪ PO Box 95 Tulbagh 6820 ▪ info@schalkenbosch.co.za ▪ www.schalkenbosch.co.za ▪ **T +27 (0)23-230-0654/1488**

☐ **Schneider Rooi Olifant** see Kaapzicht Wine Estate

Schotia Wines

Schotia brachypetala, the indigenous weeping boer-bean tree, with its showy flowers, is the inspiration for the name of this boutique brand and the Schotia Junction in Hoedspruit, Limpopo Province, where it joins a restaurant, art gallery and other allures at the gateway to the famous Kruger National Park. Portfolio owners Trevor and Caroline Carnaby are well known in the area, and want their wines to have a 'homegrown flavour' to showcase to the many locals and visitors to the Lowveld'. The current line-up, made by Swanepoel Wines in Tulbagh, will diversify and gain a multifaceted tasting-pairing experience. See also Duikersdrift listing.

★★★★ **Shiraz** Both vintages tasted saw 10 months older barrels, as all wines unless noted. **21 ★★★★** ⑧③ red & black fruit, good complexity, open texture with meshed tannins. **22** ⑧⑥ pepper & oak spice dusted, leaner & tighter yet with better prospects than sibling.

★★★★ **Cabernet Sauvignon-Shiraz** Two vintages tasted, both with 67% cab. **22 ★★★★** ⑧⑤ ripe at 14% alc but less fruit-sweet thanks to lift from leafy top note. **21** ⑧⑥ less broad shouldered (12.5% alc) yet densely packed with blue & black fruit, ripe-fruited finish.

★★★★ **Chenin Blanc** Old Citrusdal vines, **22** ⑧⑦ unexpectedly shy on nose & palate, structurally more impressive, rapier-like acid, generous 14% alc, weight & length from natural barrel ferment/6 months on lees with regular stirring.

Cape Ruby ★★★★ Youthful **22** ⑧⑤ 'port' has a firm tannin structure, is less sweet & spirity at 18.5% than also-tasted **21** ⑧⑤, with 20% alc warmth, easier grip of tannin. Both from shiraz, with mince-pie flavour in abundance, per the style. — PS, CvZ

Location: Hoedspruit ▪ WO: Tulbagh/Western Cape ▪ Est/1stB 2022 ▪ Tasting Mon-Fri 11-4.30 Sat/Sun 11-5.30 ▪ Fee R15 per wine ▪ Sales Mon-Fri 9-8 Sat 9-5 Sun no sales ▪ Restaurant Mon-Sat 8-9.30pm for breakfast, lunch & dinners ▪ Coffee shop ▪ Bakery ▪ Farm produce ▪ Gift shop ▪ Playground ▪ Sports facilities ▪ Art gallery ▪ Owner(s) Trevor & Caroline Carnaby ▪ Cellarmaster(s) Swanepoel Wines (Jan 2019) ▪ Winemaker(s)/viticulturist(s) Dirk Swanepoel (Jan 2019, consultant) ▪ 800cs own label 50% red 45% white 5% rosé ▪ Postnet Suite 42, Private Bag X3008, Hoedspruit, Limpopo 1380 ▪ trevor@beataboutthebush.co.za ▪ www. schotia.com ▪ **T +27 (0)83-442-0652**

Schultz Family Wines

Seasoned and widely acclaimed winemaker Rudi Schultz launched this signature label just over 20 years ago, soon after joining Stellenbosch icon Thelema. He later began sourcing more widely, and recently highlighted his love for surfing by adding favourite marine 'terroirs' to the names of the wines. The winemaking approach has remained unchanged throughout: 'I believe in the "essence of site", selecting special vineyards and interpreting them to a wine. It's a very pure form of parenting!'

★★★★☆ **Dungeons Cabernet Sauvignon** (Ⓐ) Like its namesake legendary Cape Town big wave, **19** (94) exudes concentrated power. Dense & sheathed, with similar herbal nuance to dark-berried flavours. Wholeberry ferment, 18 months in barrique (as all reds), this 30% new. Structured to age a decade.

★★★★☆ **Pepper Street Syrah** (Ⓐ) Billows dark fruit, clove & pepper in **20** (90). Natural ferment, 20% wholebunch, 18 months oak, 10% new. Concentrated fruit in a velvet tannin framework. Big-boned & bold but balanced, good few years in store. WO Paarl, though name refers to road to Jeffreys Bay surfing spot.

★★★★☆ **Boneyards** (Ⓐ) Same named J-Bay surf magnet as **18** (94), but the waves not as structured in **19** ★★★★ (89)'s blend of malbec & petit verdot (64/36), misses cab's gravitas & concentration. Less new oak, 40%, in more voluptuous & accessible style, courtesy malbec's ample fruit & savoury spice.

★★★★☆ **Skeleton Bay Chenin Blanc** (Ⓐ) World's longest left-handed surfing wave names **21** (93) from 62 year old Paarl bushvines. Lemony notes whet the appetite, crisp & zesty finish slakes it. Bunch pressed, naturally fermented & 9 months in old oak allow refined but vibrant fruit to shine. — MW

Location: Stellenbosch ▪ WO: Stellenbosch/Paarl ▪ Est 2002 ▪ Tasting by appt ▪ Closed all pub hols ▪ Owner(s)/viticulturist(s) Rudi Schultz ▪ Cellarmaster(s)/winemaker(s) Rudi Schultz (Jan 2002) ▪ 10t/700cs own label 70% red 30% white ▪ 8 Fraser Rd, Somerset West 7130 ▪ rudischultz9@gmail.com ▪ **T +27 (0)82-928-1841**

Scions of Sinai

You get an idea of how deep boutique vintner Bernhard Bredell's passion for the vine runs when you ask for a brand update and he responds with phrases like 'soil observations' and 'understanding cover crops', while the only reference to the bottled product is 'ensure a pure expression in the wines'. Mostly clustered around a Helderberg hill known locally as Sinai, his largely bushvine and dry-farmed single-vineyards have now gained the attention of the Old Vine Project and 'vine whisperer' Rosa Kruger. With her and new assistant Thabo Olifant, Bernhard intends farming in a way that coaxes more of each site's character from the vines.

Single Vineyard Collection

★★★★☆ **Heldervallei** (Ⓐ) Producer's hallmark complex vinification for all wines involves various natural ferments, some whole bunches & stems, old-oak ageing, bottling without fining or filtration. **22** (94) from venerable cinsault, showing its cherries & raspberries, well balanced, with fine mineral persistence.

★★★★☆ **Féniks** (Ⓐ) From registered single-vineyard, as all these, pinotage planted 1979, **22** ★★★★ (88) most fruit-forward of the red trio. Expressive mulberry & sugared plum perfume, black fruit pastille flavour. Very dry, shade less acid/tannin structure than **21** (90).

★★★★☆ **Swanesang** (Ⓐ) Beautifully constructed & harmonious syrah, from twice-picked block, mostly large-format concrete aged. **22** (94) impressive fruit intensity balanced with vivacious mineral acid, thrilling austerity & tension - a contrast with Heldervallei's approachability.

★★★★☆ **Granietsteen** (Ⓐ)(Ⓐ) Pristine fruit from 45 year old vines, a large concrete tank & little else went into **22** (94). Chenin unplugged, with an uncompromising soul. White peach profile touch riper than **21** ★★★★★ (95) yet feisty natural acid very much intact.

★★★★☆ **Gramadoelas** Afrikaans for wild & remote country. **22** (90) grenache blanc on Klein Karoo schist & slate, old-oak fermented/9 months on lees. Somewhat richer, smoother than last, with rounding 12.4% alc vs 11.5%, retains signature pithy finish.

Vineyard Collaboration range

★★★★ **Atlantikas** No oak & partial carbonic ferment, **22** (86) pinotage crafted to tread lightly & full-fruitedly. Does so with style, marrying real vinosity & presence with impressive purity at just 12.5% alc.

★★★★ **Nomadis** (Ⓐ) Cinsault & 12% pinotage, each ex single-vineyard, in **22** ★★★★ (85), bone-dry & trim (12% alc), mostly semi-carbonic fermented for piquant black- & red-berry fruit. Slight farmyard extra, same lovely unforced feel as **21** (86).

★★★★ **Rocinante** 3 single-vineyards provide near-equal chenin, grenache blanc & roussanne in fruity, energetic **22** (87). Emphatically dry, with peach stone savoury overlay, spice from older barrels. Voor Paardeberg contribution.

★★★★ **Señor Tallos** Brassy hue, funky whiff of skin ferment, salty tang, tannic tug - 22 ⑧⑦ delightfully brazen & probably divisive - but many love it. Flor-aged chenin & macerated grenache blanc, on lees 11 months in old oak.— CvZ

Location: Stellenbosch ▪ WO: Stellenbosch/Klein Karoo/Coastal ▪ Est 2016 ▪ 1stB 2017 ▪ Closed to public ▪ Owner(s) Bernhard Bredell ▪ Winemaker(s)/viticulturist(s) Bernhard Bredell (Jun 2016), with Thabo Olifant (Oct 2022) ▪ 35t/2,600cs own label 50% red 40% white 10% skin macerated white ▪ bredell@sofs-wine. com ▪ www.scionsofsinai.com ▪ **T +27 (0)82-772-8657**

☐ **Seaward** *see* Spier
☐ **Secateurs** *see* AA Badenhorst Family Wines
☐ **Sedgwick's Old Brown** *see* Heineken Beverages
☐ **Seerowers** *see* Villion Family Wines
☐ **Selection Vivante** *see* The House of JC le Roux
☐ **Semara** *see* Wine-of-the-Month Club
☐ **Sense of Place** *see* Stellenbosch Hills Wines
☐ **Sentinel** *see* Wine-of-the-Month Club
☐ **Serengeti** *see* Swartland Winery
☐ **Series Privée Unfiltered** *see* Fleur du Cap
☐ **SeriesRARE** *see* ArtiSons
☐ **Seriously Cool** *see* Waterkloof

Ses'Fikile   ⓠ

Nondumiso Pikashe is proud to have her winery, which just turned 15, represented at The Wine Arc, the brand home for black-owned wine labels and entrepreneurs in Stellenbosch. Her substantial production of 50,000 cases, made with top-ranked Leeuwenkuil, is a proud achievement for the Cape Town former teacher. **Matriarch Pinotage** ⓠ ★★★★ Ex Paarl, modern **18** ⑧④ has good freshness to balance 14.5% alc, show off bright, spiced raspberry flavours. Punchy tannins will benefit from year/2. **Chenin Blanc-Roussanne** ⓠ ★★★ Sunny, light & ripe, **21** ⑧② pineapple & stonefruit, appealing texture & perky acid. Not tasted: **Cabernet Sauvignon-Merlot**, **Shiraz-Cinsault**, **Matriarch Méthode Cap Classique**. — GdB

Location: Cape Town ▪ WO: Paarl/Western Cape ▪ Est 2008 ▪ Tasting by arrangement in Gugulethu ▪ Wines also available at the Wine Arc at Nietvoorbij, Stellenbosch ▪ Owner(s) Ses'Fikile Wine Services ▪ Winemaker(s) Madré van der Walt (Leeuwenkuil Family Vineyards) ▪ 50,000cs own label 70% red 30% white ▪ sesfikile@gmail.com ▪ www.sesfikile.co.za ▪ **T +27 (0)83-431-0254**

☐ **7even** *see* Zevenwacht
☐ **7 Icon Wines** *see* Bayede!

Seven Sisters Vineyards   ⓠ ⑪ ◎

Paternoster, a village on the West Coast, is the birth-home of the Brutus family siblings but their brand-home is in Stellenbosch, on the bank of the Eerste River. Tireless efforts over more than a decade, led by sister and prime mover Vivian (Kleynhans), resulted in the land being planted with vines, and a tasting and function venue built. Latterly a non-profit foundation was created to aid disadvantaged and abused women. **Cabernet Sauvignon** ★★★ After last **19** ⑧① 's succulent ripeness, **22** ⑧① is more linear, but winemaker's suggested hearty food accompaniments (stews, steaks, pasta) should turn austerity into a virtue. **Merlot** ⓥ ★★★★ Pair of skipped vintages mean **22** ⑧③ is the current release, offering fleshy black cherries which carry few months of oak-stave contact well. Finish is tad green, though. **Pinotage** ★★★ Blueberry & red fruit of **22** ⑦⑦ freshen house-style coffee sheen from brief brush with new oak. **Chardonnay** ⓥ ★★★★ Typical citrus nuance to mediumweight **22** ⑧③. Soft & succulent, creamy oatmeal breadth from small oaked portion (20%) & 6 months on lees. **Chenin Blanc** ★★★ Guava & melon flavours on sweet-fruited **23** ⑧① cut by fresh acid. For summertime sipping. **Moscato Perlé** ★★ Lightly fizzy **NV** ⑦⑤, sweet & grapey with whiffs of muscat perfume, light acid & low alc (10%). **Sauvignon Blanc** ★★★ Greenpepper & lemon frame to fresh **23** ⑧⓪. Bright & brief with sharp nettle note. Discontinued: **Shiraz**, **John Brutus**, **Chardonnay**. — DS

Location/map: Stellenbosch ▪ Map grid reference: C7 ▪ WO: Western Cape ▪ Wine & food pairings/wine tasting Mon-Sat 9-4 - prior booking required ▪ Tours & groups ▪ Weddings & events ▪ Conferences ▪ Online shop ▪ Owner(s) African Roots Wine (Pty) Ltd ▪ Winemaker(s) Vivian Kleynhans ▪ 468/132 Welmoed Rd, off Annandale Rd, Lynedoch, Stellenbosch 7600 ▪ bookings@sevensisters.co.za, info@sevensisters.co.za ▪ www. sevensisters.co.za ▪ T +27 (0)21-879-1996

Seven Springs Vineyards ⓘ

Between Shaw's Mountain and the Teslaarsdal Mountain range, just beyond Hemel-en-Aarde Ridge in the Overberg, the Seven Springs vines on Bokkeveld shale-derived soils experience a cool oceanic influence, giving freshness to the wines, made according to minimal-intervention principles. Britons Tim and Vaughan Pearson (who have described their wine journey as 'an emotional roller coaster') have again 'welcomed into the winery a number of small producers, giving the business an additional, very positive dimension'.

Seven Springs range

★★★★ **Pinot Noir** ⊘ Different clones fermented & oaked (10% new) separately, then a barrel selection made for this **18** ⑧⑥. Charming, pretty fragrance, fresh & clean, though the dark-fruited palate a touch more severe, with firm acid & tannin. 13.5% alc.

★★★★ **Syrah** Attractive ripe aromas & flavours on wild fermented **20** ⑧⑥. Everything makes for agreeable medium-term drinking: fruit depth, modest oaking, texture & gently firm grip. 14% alc in balance.

★★★★ **Syrah Rosé** ⓘ Pretty ripe berry & spice aroma & flavour on salmon-hued **22** ★★★★ ⑧⑤, with fresh, earthy edge to sweet fruit. Bone-dry, with good grip. Like **21** ⑧⑥, more serious than most.

Chardonnay ★★★★ Natural ferment took 40 days to complete on **20** ⑧⑤, then 10 months in barrel, 10% new. Nutty & limy aromas lead to dry, fresh palate with bright lemony acidity. As with **19** ★★★★ ⑧⑥, more intense fruit than unoaked version. 12.5% alc. **Unoaked Chardonnay** ★★★ Pleasant, clean fruit aromas & flavours on **21** ⑧②. Less acidly balanced than oaked version, but still a little lemony-tart. Both of them admirably dry. This 13% alc. **Sauvignon Blanc** ★★★★ Typical but light cooler-climate aromas - floral, blackcurrant - on **21** ⑧⑤. Silky texture & core of good fruit. As previously, aeration (& time) helps the dominant acidity.

Art Series

★★★★ **Syrah** ⓘ Tasted out of vintage sequence, **12** ⑧⑨ opens in glass to Xmas spice & tapenade, chewy tannins yet backed by juicy fruit, promising a good future. Limited release in magnum ex farm.

★★★★★ **Sauvignon Blanc Fumé** ⓘ Tantalises with heady blackcurrant fragrance, rich flavours shot through with mineral energy. **15** ⑨④, precise & memorably long. 6 months on lees in old oak.— TJ

Location: Hermanus ▪ Map: Walker Bay & Bot River ▪ Map grid reference: C5 ▪ WO: Overberg ▪ Est 2007 ▪ 1stB 2010 ▪ Tasting & sales Mon-Sun 11-4 pub hols (Sep-Jun) 11-4 ▪ Cellar tours by appt ▪ Owner(s) Tim & Vaughan Pearson ▪ Winemaker(s) to be appointed ▪ ±45t/7,000cs own label 60% red 35% white 5% rosé ▪ Other export brand: Over the Mountain ▪ Sandfontein Farm, R320 Hemel en Aarde Rd, Caledon 7230 ▪ info@7springs.co.za ▪ www.7springs.co.za ▪ T +27 (0)28-316-4994

☐ **1707 Reserve** *see* Stellenbosch Hills Wines

Shannon Vineyards ⓘ ⓐ

This Elgin family venture is set on a beautiful hillside and valley property, managed by James Downes, who also oversees the vineyard, working with consultant Kevin Watt, and is partnered by his brother Stuart. The focus is on Bordeaux and Burgundy varieties, and there has been 'meticulous focus' specifically on nurturing younger chardonnay and pinot noir to ensure they yield top-quality grapes. 'Huge excitement', therefore, when the first small batch of pinot noir was vinified in 2023 and showed as much potential as the chardonnay, also double-Guyot pruned, to further strengthen the exceptional portfolio. The wines have long been made at the Newton Johnson cellar in Hemel-en-Aarde, where there is a commitment to 'maximise the expression of a sense of place through minimal intervention'.

★★★★★ **Mount Bullet Merlot** ⓐ Richer in **20** ⑨④, though similar fragrant dark fruit & silky, seductive texture from a mix of clones in 3-ha vineyard, picked at selected ripeness levels. Quite sumptuous but still fresh & balanced. Like sibling, natural ferment, but less time in barrel & new oak (20 months, 25%), all in sync. Deserves & will reward cellaring.

★★★★☆ **The Shannon Black** ⊛ Best-performing clone chosen for each vintage within same merlot block as sibling, 50% new oak, 22 months. **19** ⑭ concentrated dark fruit & pure chocolate, very confident, composed. Despite 14.7% alc, effortlessly balanced, with variety's fresh, leafy acid. This & sibling evolving into Cape benchmarks, unshowy, sophisticated, with pedigree for drinking pleasure in a decade or more.

★★★★☆ **RocknRolla** ⊛ Farm's oldest pinot vineyard, Dijon 113 clone. Highly acclaimed since **16** ⑨③ debut, **21** ★★★★★ ⑨⑤ even finer than **20** ⑨③, takes this label to next level. Intense & layered with dark, perfumed fruit yet inherently bright, thanks to firm yet supremely supple tannin structure. Natural ferment, portion whole bunches, 12 months in oak, as sibling, but this 50% new. More depth & complexity.

★★★★☆ **Rockview Ridge Pinot Noir** ⊘ ⊛ Exudes pinot joy in **21** ⑨④: raspberry, cherry & polished leather from a range of soils & mix of new & older Dijon clones. Harmonious barrel-ageing, 20% new, giving svelte & smooth body. So beautifully fresh & balanced, a delight to drink now plus structure for future development (for the strong-willed).

★★★★☆ **Oscar Browne Chardonnay** ⊛ From eponymous single block, **22** ⑨④ riper than previous, toasty hazelnut notes from natural ferment & 11 months in barrel, 23% new, showing a little more in youth. Zested through with limy acid, hallmark of Elgin's cooler provenance, & clean citrus blossom & fruit flavours. Better with a year or two to fully meld.

★★★★☆ **Sanctuary Peak Sauvignon Blanc** ⊘ Bright passionfruit & scented elderflower notes in unoaked **22** ★★★★ ⑧⑨ mingle with crisp acidity. Ripe but with lively balance & some subtle creamy lees backing. Vivacious summer tablemate, though shade off **21** ⑨⓪.

★★★★☆ **Triangle Block Semillon** ⊛ Alluringly expressive though refined in **21** ★★★★★ ⑨⑤. Silky smooth lanolin texture with layers of flavour: honey, marmelade & white peach, with persistent seam of vibrant acid. Wholebunch natural ferment. Ageing in 500L barrels, 30% new, is a supportive, integrated player in this class act, raising the bar on **20** ⑨②.

Discontinued: **Capall Bán**. — MW

Location/map/WO: Elgin ▪ Map grid reference: A2 ▪ Est 2000 ▪ 1stB 2003 ▪ Tasting by appt Mon-Fri 10-3 ▪ Owner(s) Stuart & James Downes ▪ Winemaker(s) Gordon & Nadia Newton Johnson ▪ Viticulturist(s) Kevin Watt (consultant) ▪ 75ha/11.5ha (merlot, pinot, chard, sauv, sem) ▪ 100t/10,000cs own label 66% red 34% white ▪ GlobalGAP, IPW, Tesco's Natures Choice ▪ PO Box 20 Elgin 7180 ▪ james@shannonwines.com ▪ www. shannonwines.com ▪ **T +27 (0)21-859-2491**

☐ **She** see Cape Wine Crafters

☐ **Shelter** see Atlas Swift

☐ **Shiner** see Paserene

☐ **Ship** see Heineken Beverages

☐ **Shirro** see O'Connell's

☐ **Short Story** see Neethlingshof Estate

☐ **Shortwood** see Imbuko Wines

☐ **SHZ Cilliers/Kuün Wyne** see Stellendrift - SHZ Cilliers/Kuün Wyne

---

Signal Gun Wines   ⓘ ⑪

Hooggelegen is one of the original Durbanville family farms, its altitude singling it out as a site for the chain of cannons installed around the Cape by the Dutch East India Company to muster its defenders. MJ de Wit has run the estate since 2010, adding allures for all ages, including the old signal gun, fired on 'joyous occasions'. Premiumisation will see the wine range focused on the flagships and the brand positioning upgraded.

De Wit Family Reserves

★★★★ **Sea Smoke Sauvignon Blanc** ⊘ From high-lying recognised single-vineyard, **22** ⑧⑨ richer, rounder than sibling yet with fine citrus-zest seam. Subtly part-oaked (20%), giving toasted hazelnut shading to ample stonefruit flavours. **20** ⑧⑧ was last tasted.

★★★★ **B Loved Méthode Cap Classique** ⊘ Classic chardonnay (70%) & pinot noir combo in golden-hued **16** ⑧⑥ dry sparkler. Peach, lemon cream, honey & distinct toasty infusion from extended 6 years on lees ageing, creating more opulence than **15** ★★★★ ⑧④, but tad low on acid, best served well chilled.

Gun Smoke Merlot ★★★★ Mouthfilling, rich & flavoursome **20** ⑧⑤ exudes cassis & sweet tobacco, ripe but not overblown 14.9% alc, still shows some freshness, smooth tannins that invite a leg of lamb.

Signal Gun range

★★★★ **Sauvignon Blanc** ⊘ Showcases Durbanville's signature dust & wet pebble nuances in **23** ⑧⑦. Tangy & dry, quite full but gracefully balanced for mealtime or solo enjoyment.

Pinotage ⊘ ★★★★ Interesting spread of dark chocolate, mulberry & Turkish delight on **20** ⑧③. Bold, robust, with matching 14.9% alc, partly reined in by 20% new oak yet still needs hearty fare. **Blanc de Noir** ⊘ ★★★ Bright as a button red berry flavours in **23** ⑧② from merlot. Nicely crisp, fresh & dry, perfect sunset tipple. **Chardonnay** ⊗ ★★★★ Oak barrels & staves for 14 months, **20** ⑧③ is approachable & cheerful, showing baked pear, peach & citrus. Just 13% alc. Discontinued: **Shiraz**. — MW

Location/WO: Durbanville ▪ Map: Durbanville, Philadelphia & Darling ▪ Map grid reference: C7 ▪ Est/1stB 2006 ▪ Tasting room & restaurant closed for renovations, please refer to website for updates ▪ Online shop ▪ Owner(s) MJ de Wit ▪ Winemaker(s) Etienne Louw (2023, consultant) ▪ Viticulturist(s) Walter Smith ▪ 210ha/70ha (cab, merlot, p verdot, ptage, chard, chenin, sauv) ▪ 30t/4,000cs own label 40% red 60% white ▪ PO Box 364 Durbanville 7551 ▪ sales@signalgun.com ▪ www.signalgun.com ▪ **T +27 (0)21-976-0770**

Signal Hill Wines Ⓦ

As sommelier, judge and educator, to name a few roles, Frenchman Jean-Vincent Ridon is a tireless ambassador and cheerleader for SA wine. He also makes wine for this own-label, a syrah from a tiny parcel of ungrafted vines in residential Cape Town. Unfortunately, the block has succumbed to disease and won't be replanted, meaning vintage '22 will be the last Clos d'Oranje, its place to be taken by a negociant line-up.

★★★★ **Clos d'Oranje** Two vintages tasted of this unique syrah, both similar to previous in their aromatic savouriness, dry firm tannins & black pepper detail. Hallmark charcuterie, too, meatier in **20**, which also less grippy courtesy only 50% bunch ferment. **21** ⑧⑨, back to 100% wholebunch, beautifully ungenerous. **19** ★★★★★ ⑨⓪'s racy acid & 13.4% alc absent in both, 11.5% enhancing leaner feel.— CvZ

Location/WO: Cape Town ▪ 1stB 1997 ▪ Closed to public; only the city vineyard can be visited by appt ▪ Sales online: www.flyingsommelier.co.za ▪ Wine club ▪ Owner(s)/cellarmaster(s) Jean-Vincent Ridon ▪ 1ha ▪ PO Box 12481 Cape Town 8010 ▪ info@winery.co.za ▪ www.winery.co.za ▪ **T +27 (0)21-422-5206**

☐ **Signatures of Doolhof** *see* Doolhof Wine Estate

Sijnn Ⓦ ⑪

Showing true pioneer spirit, Charla Bosman, incumbent winemaker since the on-site cellar's construction in the mid-2010s, has embraced the challenges posed by the rugged terrain with flair and enthusiasm. Set high above the snaking Breede River, the 'first growth' of Malgas (the only one, actually) is an exercise in extreme viticulture, where the rocky ground has small pockets chiselled out to plant individual vines, relief watering is severely limited and yields are tiny. Probably inspired by the stony fields, founder and co-owner David Trafford concentrated on varieties from the Rhône and Douro valleys, but has also introduced cabernet, chenin, vermentino and assyrtiko. These produce an array of small-volume wines, both blended and varietal, with distinctive character and excellent maturation potential.

Sijnn range

★★★★☆ **Free Reign** ⓐ Co-proprietor David Trafford takes the winemaking rei(g)ns for this convention-challenging range-topper. **18** ★★★★★ ⑨⑤ 65% syrah with touriga, mostly carbonic ferment (6 weeks in sealed tank with wild yeast), then 2 years in new 700L barrel. Assertive & deeply impressive, despite modest 13% alc. Previously was **NV** ★★★★☆ ⑨④.

★★★★☆ **Low Profile** 'Entry-level', cosmopolitan red blend, syrah with touriga & 4 others in **21** ⑨⓪, typically rich & satisfying, scrub-spiced red & black berry fruit, hints of smoked meat & liquorice. 18 months older French, American & Hungarian barrels.

★★★★☆ **Sijnn Red** ⓐ Blend in **20** ⑨④ trimmed from 5 to 4 varieties: 58% syrah, equal cab, touriga & tinta amarela, remains big, plush & imposing. Concentrated black cherry fruit with aromatic tobacco note, intricate spicing & svelte, silky texture, promising beneficial cellaring. Follows meatier **19** ⑨④.

★★★★☆ **Sijnn White** ⓐ Beautifully shaped & succulently delicious **22** ⑨④ is 81% chenin with splashes viognier, roussanne & verdelho. Lithe & supple, with scented stonefruit & honeysuckle, creamy texture from year on lees in large older barrels.

★★★★☆ **Cape Vintage** Previewed **21** (93) is 100% tempranillo (tinta roriz in port-speak), offering sombre, tarry black berry fruit, appealing spirit grip, thickly layered tannins. Burly, emphatic, per Vintage style, & quite delicious, with huge ageing potential. Modest 17.5% alc, 105 g/L sugar. 375 ml.
Occasional release: **Saignée**. In abeyance: **Off-Centre**.

Varietal Series

★★★★☆ **Cabernet Sauvignon** Uncompromisingly lean & mineral, with undertones of tarry liquorice & damp earth, **21** (91) is an unadorned, visceral varietal expression. Unevolved blackcurrant & cherry fruit lurks in the wings, sure to come into play in future years. Worth waiting for.

★★★★☆ **Grenache** Seductively juicy **22** (93) has a pitch-perfect raspberry & cherry fruit profile, gently textured tannins. Ample extract & colour from 25% wholebunch, wild-yeast ferment, yet delicate & nuanced. 18 months in large barrel & foudre; unfined/unfiltered, as Mourvèdre.

★★★★☆ **Mourvèdre** Sappy, silky **22** (90) has delicate Rhône-like scrub note, black berry compote & hint of iodine minerality. Full bodied yet restrained (13.5% alc), with pepper highlight from 20% wholebunch ferment, 18 months in older barrels.

★★★★ **Tempranillo** Rioja's treasure finds another spiritual home in Malgas, where **22** ★★★★☆ (90) shows authentic weight, spice & cherry-raspberry fruit, subtle tealeaf note & vibrant acid. Youthful & still melding, but showing potential. 18 months in French barrels, half new; previous **20** (88) 24 months American oak, all new.

★★★★ **Touriga Nacional** Royalty of the Douro Valley finds expression in this unique, experimental terroir, **21** (88) is dense & concentrated, showing distinctive plum-jam fruit, dark chocolate & tarry notes on finish. Brooding & sullen, but should open up in time. 18 months in barrel, 50% new.

★★★★ **Tinta Amarella** Was 'Trincadeira', different name for the same traditional Douro Valley port variety. **22** (86) has grapey rhubarb fruit, lightish body & modest extract. A little unsure as a standalone. Hands-off winemaking, as all in this range, ageing in neutral oak.

★★★★ **Chenin Blanc** Reins in the oak in **22** ★★★★☆ (90), using single older 1,000L foudre, emphasising luscious honeysuckle-scented peach & pear fruit. Spontaneous ferment, malo & year on lees lend weight & class, upstaging spicier **21** (87). Only 100 cases; rest used in Sijnn White.

★★★★☆ **Roussanne** Welcome addition to varietal range. Micro-batch **22** (91) bunch pressed, fermented/15 months in single 5 year old 400L barrel. Rich & creamy, delicate oxidative notes adding appeal to dried apricot fruit. Perhaps an acquired taste, but well worth exploring.

Not tasted: **Carignan**, **Syrah**. Occasional release: **Vermentino**, **Viognier**. — GdB

Location/WO: Malgas ▪ Map: Southern Cape ▪ Map grid reference: D1 ▪ Est 2003 ▪ 1stB 2007 ▪ Tasting, sales & cellar tours at Sijnn Mon-Sat 10-3; pub hols (seasonal) please call ahead ▪ Vintners platters ▪ Wines are also sold at De Trafford ▪ Owner(s) David & Rita Trafford, Simon Farr ▪ Estate manager Rijk Scholtz ▪ Winemaker(s) Charla Bosman (née Haasbroek, Dec 2014) ▪ Viticulturist(s) Etienne Terblanche (Jan 2020, Vinpro) ▪ 125ha/23ha (cab, grenache, mourv, shiraz, tempranillo, touriga nacional, trincadeira, chenin, rouss, viog); 1.5ha olives ▪ 60t/5,400cs own label 52% red 48% white ▪ PO Box 495 Stellenbosch 7599 ▪ info@sijnn.co.za ▪ www.sijnn.co.za ▪ **T +27 (0)21-880-1398**

Silkbush Mountain Vineyards

This large US-owned estate is on the lower mountain slopes of the Breedekloof district, where most vineyards are on the valley floor. Plenty of wildness remains, but a planting (and replanting) programme since 2000 now sees 87 of the 143 hectares planted to a range of varieties, much of the fruit going elsewhere. Chris du Toit of Bergsig is the longtime winemaking consultant.

Reserve range

★★★★☆ **Pinotage Single Vineyard** Deeper hue & tone than Selection version, **21** (90) more complex & harmonious, similar perfume. Sweet fruit, power & density. Deserves time in bottle.

Winemakers Selection

★★★★ **Grenache Noir** Charming pure, perfumed aromas, with savoury & dried notes on **21** (87). Bright & cool-feeling, neither intense nor complex, but very drinkable already.

★★★★ **Pinot Noir** Generously aromatic **21** (89), full of flavour, silky & succulent, with the gentlest of tannins & a slightly over-bright freshness. Feels lighter than the 14.2% alc suggests. Altogether charming.

★★★★ **Pinotage** ⓧ Perfumed & purple, **21** ⑧⑦ offers ripely pretty but not concentrated fruit, moderate dry tannins, & a soft texture complemented by a bright acidity. 50% new oak well absorbed.

★★★★ **Hillside Red** ⊘ Further bottling of **18** ⑧⑥, half malbec with shiraz & petit verdot. Plenty of ripe, sweet fruit with a spicy edge (but only older barrels). Smooth tannins; bright acidity to balance the enriching body. Attractive, ready, but no rush to drink. WO W Cape, rest of these Breedekloof.

★★★★ **Semillon-Sauvignon Blanc** ⓧ Forward tropical, citrus, blackcurrant aromas & flavours on **21** ⑧⑥. No great intensity but an elegant balanced freshness & a stony quality from 50% ferment in clay pot.

Chenin Blanc ★★★ Usual pleasant dried-peachy notes on **22** ⑧⓪. Smooth texture, with tart lemony acidity giving it a bright balance.

Silkbush range

★★★★ **Pinotage** ⊘ Pure, aromatic fruit on **22** ⑧⑧ making for charming if not complex wine, well balanced, with restrained but effective tannins. Lots of early pleasure on offer, but should keep well. Last tasted was very ripe **20** ★★★ ⑦⑦; this, at 13.7% alc, a big quality jump.

★★★★ **Altitude** ⊘ No pinotage in **19** ⑧⑦, unlike **18** ★★★★ ⑧⑤, just petit verdot, malbec & shiraz. Clean, pure fruit, supple & almost elegant at 13.6% alc. As often at Silkbush, there's sugar - 4.8 g/L - compensating big acidity, but here the balance works better than some. Drinking nicely now, but no rush.

Shiraz ★★★★ Much as previous, **20** ⑧③ sweetly ripe, flavoursome & soft textured, with big, rather unharmonious acidity in some sort of compensation. **Rosé** ★★★ Light salmon-hued **23** ⑧⓪ with berry aroma & taste; flavourful, dry & easygoing - just a little sharp. **Chenin Blanc** ⓧ ★★★ Pleasant peachy notes on **21** ⑧⓪. Soft texture, lipsmacking lemon acidity keeping it in bright balance. WO Breedekloof. **Sauvignon Blanc** ★★★★ Lively, fresh & dry **23** ⑧③ pouring forth typical tropical aromas & flavours, with a lemony juiciness. **Viognier** ★★★★ Quite restrained but delicious version of sometimes showy & blowsy variety. **22** ⑧⑤ typical peach-apricot character, silk-smooth roundness. Spontaneous ferment, half in clay pot, rest older oak. Discontinued: **Hillside Red, Summer White**. — TJ

Location: Wolseley ▪ WO: Western Cape/Breedekloof ▪ Est 2000 ▪ 1stB 2007 ▪ Closed to public ▪ Kingsbury Cottage (self-catering), www.silkbush.com/guest-house ▪ Owner(s) Silkbush Holdings LP ▪ Cellarmaster(s) Anton Roos ▪ Viticulturist(s) Francois Roos (2021) ▪ 143ha/87ha (cabs s/f, malbec, merlot, mourv, p verdot, ptage, shiraz, sauv, sem, viog) ▪ 1,200t/10,000cs own label 100% red ▪ Other export brand: Lion's Drift ▪ PO Box 91 Breërivier 6858 ▪ anton@silkbush.co.za ▪ www.silkbush.com ▪ **T +27 (0)83-629-1735**

Silvermist Organic Wine Estate   ⓧ ⑪ ⌂ ⓒ

Boutique Silvermist at the crest of Constantia Nek remains the only certified-organic winery on the local wine route, its cellar manned and vineyards tended by the same winegrower who established them almost 20 years ago, Gregory Brink Louw. Complementing attractions like the famed fine-dining retaurant La Colombe, a boutique hotel and 2.3 km of mountain ziplines, is Drumstruck @ Silvermist, the acclaimed interactive African drumming experience combined with a tasting of the estate's wines.

★★★★ **Cabernet Sauvignon** ⓧ ⓢ At 15.5% alc, **17** ⑧⑦ ripe & rich, shows dense blackcurrant, chocolate & liquorice notes. Perhaps not classically 'cool climate', delicious nonetheless.

★★★★ **Sauvignon Blanc** ⓧ ⓢ Unoaked **20** ⑧⑦ richer & riper than last, more tropical in character, flavours range from granadilla to papaya, equally intense but tad less exhilarating. Constantia WO.

Not tasted: **Constantia Reserve**. Discontinued: **Rocket Dog Red**. — JG

Location: Constantia ▪ Map: Cape Peninsula ▪ Map grid reference: B3 ▪ WO: Cape Town/Constantia ▪ Est 1984 ▪ 1stB 2010 ▪ Wine tasting & sales Mon–Fri by appt Sat/Sun/pub hols 8-5; pub hols (seasonal) please call ahead ▪ Silvermist Boutique Hotel: hotel@silvermisthotel.co.za ▪ Walks & hikes ▪ Conservation area ▪ La Colombe Restaurant: www.lacolombe.co.za / reservations@lacolombe.co.za ▪ Ziplines (2.3km) bookings: +27(0)21-795-0225, www.saforestadventures.co.za ▪ Drumstruck @ Silvermist: music, culture & wine entertainment ▪ Owner(s) Constantia Ridge Estates (Pty) Ltd ▪ Cellarmaster(s)/winemaker(s)/viticulturist(s) Gregory Brink Louw (Jan 2005) ▪ 22ha/6ha (cab, shiraz, sauv) ▪ 5.2t/580cs own label 30% red 70% white ▪ CERES organic ▪ PO Box 608 Constantia 7848 ▪ silvermistvineyards@gmail.com ▪ www.silvermistestate.co.za ▪ **T +27 (0)21-110-5420**

☐ **Silver Myn** see Zorgvliet Wines

Silverthorn Wines

John and Karen Loubser have been working on the 'quest to create incredible cap classique' for a quarter-century. They established their 'little paradise on the banks of the Breede River' in Robertson in 1998; the maiden vintage (the first Green Man) came exactly 20 years ago. The grapes were trucked to Steenberg in Constantia, where John was cellarmaster. Much development since, and the pesticide- and herbicide-free vineyards on 'unique shale and limestone soils' are benefiting from an interplanting programme to keep them productive. The oldest vineyard, of colombard, is now approaching 40. The bubbly made from it and the rosé from shiraz constitute a rare cap classique tribute to local traditions. And the 'little paradise' will now have a luxury guest cottage on a cliff above the river.

Cap Classique range

★★★★ **The Genie** Old-rose tint to this rosé made - unusually - from shiraz. Berried charm on aromas & gently rich, though dry & sufficiently fresh palate of **NV** (89), but touch less incisive & complex than previous. To accompany 'sushi, sundowners, breakfast' says winemaker. 18 months on lees this time.

★★★★★ **CWG Auction Big Dog IX** (🐝) The latest, 18 ★★★★★ (94), Auction version of Jewel Box - both 70% oaked chardonnay, 30% pinot noir. This longer on lees (53 months) & touch less sweet dosage (mere 4 g/L sugar). Also straw-gold, it's a little fresher-feeling, with rather more yeasty aromas. As with 17 (95), a fine-tuned elegance & lingering mousse.

★★★★☆ **Jewel Box** (🐝) Notes of brioche & apple pie on 18 (94) along with ripe strawberry, which comes through more on complex, dry & refined palate. Quite broad but balanced, with hint of honeyed development. Version of 17 ★★★★★ (95) tasted last year had 53 months on lees, this 48 months before disgorgement, less than Big Dog IX.

★★★★ **River Dragon** From old colombard vines, the variety - & ferment 8 months in acacia barrels for half of the wine - giving an unusual character. Latest **NV** (87) dry & fresh as usual, with floral-fruit upfront but not long-lingering. 12 months on lees.

★★★★☆ **The Green Man** (🐝) Citrus, nuts & baked apples with brioche notes from 27 months on lees for **20** (94), with a green glint to its pale straw. From chardonnay, just 15% fermented in oak. Fine, beaded balance, lively & fresh. Also tasted, late disgorgement (5 years; in magnum only) of **17** ★★★★★ (95). Still youthful & vigorous, still tinged with green, but more character & hazelnut-biscuit complexity to aroma & citrus core. Fine, fresh mineral bite. — TJ

Location/map/WO: Robertson ▪ Map grid reference: C4 ▪ Est 1998 ▪ 1stB 2004 ▪ Tasting & cellar tours by appt Mon-Fri 12-3 Sat & select pub hols 10-2 ▪ Closed Good Fri, 3 weeks for annual vacation (to be announced on social media), Dec 25/26 & Jan 1 ▪ Wine club ▪ Owner(s) Silverthorn Wines (Pty) Ltd ▪ Cellarmaster(s)/winemaker(s)/viticulturist(s) John Loubser (1998) ▪ 10.5ha/4ha (cab, shiraz, chard, cbard) ▪ 60t/6,000cs own label 60% white 40% rosé ▪ IPW ▪ PO Box 381 Robertson 6705 ▪ john@silverthornwines.co.za, karen@silverthornwines.co.za ▪ www.silverthornwines.co.za ▪ **T +27 (0)21-788-1706**

☐ **Silver Tree** *see* VinGlo Wines
☐ **Silwervis** *see* Terracura Wines

Simelia Wines

Woestkloof, the high-lying 19th-century Hoogenhout family farm and vine nursery in Wellington, is the source of the boutique wines of German Simon Obholzer and wife Celia (née Hoogenhout). The portfolio, which debuted just over ten years ago, is vinified with consultant Louis Nel in accordance with Old World principles, and features fruit from younger vines as well as established ones, including four-decade-old syrah, which is now in the registers of the Old Vine Project and provides the grapes for the pink wine.

Reserve range

★★★★☆ **Fluvius Single Vineyard Merlot** (🐝) Pitch-perfect **19** ★★★★★ (95) delivers promise suggested by **18** (94) with a real sense of luxury: great depth of velvet fruit, black cherries & plums, tannins smoothed by 4 years in oak, refreshment from brisk acidity, satisfying dryness, too. Will continue to seduce for many years. Also in 1.5L, 3L & 6L, as Syrah.

★★★★☆ **Senectus Old Vine Single Vineyard Syrah** (🐝) (🍸) Restrained aromas of pressed flowers & dried herbs belie **19** (93)'s opulence: blackberry compote, cinnamon-laced prune & roast meat, tailored 4 years in barrel, 10% new, tempered by well-judged acidity. Groenberg WO, like sibling.

Simelia range

★★★★ **Merlot** ⓥ Two years in oak, 43% new, lend smoothness & texture to **20** ★★★★★ ⑨⑩'s succulent black fruit, supported by fine-grained tannin. Notch above last-tasted **18** ⑧⑧. Also in 1.5L, as Syrah.

★★★★ **Syrah** ⓥ Same site & vinification as Woestkloof sibling, touch less new oak (27%), **20** ⑧⑨ shows sappy red fruit & meaty edge to finish. Good balance. First sampled since **15** ★★★★★ ⑨①.

Not tasted: **Skurwekop Family Reserve**.

Woestkloof by Simelia range

★★★★★ **Merlot** ⓥ Accomplished **20** ⑨②, black cherry & plum fruit given 55% new oak over 2 years, effortlessly absorbed; adds a cocoa layer & smooths the lightweight tannins. Wellington WO for these.

★★★★☆ **Syrah** ⓥ From single block planted in 1980, violet-fragranced **20** ⑨⓪ spent two years in barrel, 35% new, giving scented smokiness & savoury ending to abundant blackberries & cherries.

Delucius range

★★★★ **Merlot** Red & black berries on expressive **20** ⑧⑦. Dusty tannins complement the juicy character, given curves of vanilla richness by careful oaking, 2 years, 28% new. Touch riper than last.

★★★★☆ **Syrah** 🍊 Hints of chopped herbs & salt on **20** ★★★★ ⑧⑨'s blackberries. Majority older barrels (24 months) allows the fruit to shine while 18% new portion provides subtle grip to manage house's generosity, just a tad less successfully than in **19** ⑨①.

★★★★ **Single Vineyard Old Vine Syrah Blanc de Noir** 🍊 Just half-hour skin contact for trendily pale pink **23** ★★★★★ ⑨⓪ from 1980 parcel. Pleases palate, too, with refreshing spicy watermelon, redcurrant & melon. Good drinkability yet not unserious. Betters **22** ⑧⑨.

Casa Simelia range

Not tasted: **Syrah**, **Merlot-Cabernet Sauvignon**. — ML

Location: Wellington • WO: Groenberg/Wellington • Est 1837 (Woestkloof farm) 2012 (Simelia brand) • 1stB 2013 • Access by invitation only • Simelia Country House luxury self-catering • Owner(s) Simon A Obholzer & Celia Hoogenhout-Obholzer • Winemaker(s) Louis Nel (Nov 2012) & Simon A Obholzer • 42ha/5.5ha (cab, malbec, merlot, p verdot, shiraz) • 8t/ha total ±5,000cs/ha plus ±500 magnum btls/ha 100% red • OVP • PO Box 15587 Vlaeberg Cape Town 8018 • info@simelia.co.za • www.simelia.co.za • **T +27 (0)21-300-5025**

☐ **Simonay** *see* Simonsvlei International

Simonsig Wine Estate ⓥ ⑪ ⓒ ⓐ ⓑ

A significant year for the Malan family on their substantial Stellenbosch estate, producer of the first cap classique and co-pioneer of the wine route concept at the Cape. In only the third leadership change, 3rd-generation Michael has taken the rein as cellarmaster, and welcomed two newcomers, both originally from Namibia, to the cellar: Danna de Jongh, responsible for white wines and sparkling, and Frank Slabbert, who will also assist Michael in his ongoing red-wine maker role. After 42 years in both the MD's office and the vineyard, Francois Malan hands over the former to his brother and former cellarmaster Johan, and the latter to Tommie Corbett, veteran of 16 seasons on the land. Both men will know each vine in the special parcel of chenin that produces the debut Old Vine Project wine, planted in 1964 by estate founder Frans Malan, who went on to bottle Simonsig's first vintage, using chenin's other name, steen, four years later.

The Garland range

★★★★★ **Cabernet Sauvignon** 🍊 Label shows magnificent Simonsberg mountain, source of this site-specific, all-cabernet flagship. **18** ★★★★★ ⑨④ as densely fruited & balanced as **17** ⑨⑤, opulent flavours an equal match for longer oaking (19 months vs 16), 100% new. So tempting, but handsome rewards in store for the patient. WO Simonsberg-Stellenbosch.

Malan Family Selection

★★★★☆ **Redhill Pinotage** ⓥ Named for colour of bushvines' soil. **20** ⑨④ restrained in youth but with potential to grow. Registered vineyard, as Garland, Merindol, Langbult & Borio. Also in 3 & 5L.

★★★★☆ **Merindol Syrah** 🍊 27 year old vines on weathered granite, **20** ⑨③ shows consistent graceful & refined styling. Fragrant white pepper, polished leather savouriness & tangy red fruit, underscored by fine dry tannins from oak, 58% new, 18 months. Lingering farewell.

★★★★☆ **Tiara** ⓥ Polished Cape Bordeaux, mainly cab & merlot. Tightly coiled in **19** ⑨③, reflecting cooler year, worth ageing decade or more. Also in 1.5 & 3L, as Kaapse Vonkel Brut.

★★★★★ **Frans Malan Cape Blend** ⓦ Named for patriarch & estate founder, **19** ⑨④ pinotage (58%), cab & merlot blend even more muscular & coiled than last, structured for a rewarding future. No **18**.

★★★★★ **Langbult Steen** ⓦ Change in **22** ⑨② from 'Chenin Avec Chêne' to reference old-vine (chenin) block, name meaning Long Hill, planted 1964 & redeveloped 1986/7. Tangy preserved quince, honey & almond flavours from staggered picking; some buttered toast breadth & structure ex natural ferment/11 months in mostly old wood. Lingering freshness. **21** untasted.

Cultivar Selection

★★★★ **Labyrinth Cabernet Sauvignon** ⓐ Dense, rich cassis with customary dab fragrant cab franc in riper **20** ⑧⑨, underpinned by confident dry tannins & deft oaking, 26% new, 18 months. Though less serious than Garland, beautifully balanced, juicy & inviting, yet ageworthy too.

★★★★ **Cape Fox Chardonnay** ⓥ Urbane **21** ⑧⑧'s lemon curd & green apple gain subtle creamy underpin from ferment/9 months in oak. Still tight, though, needs time to show fully as fine table wine.

★★★★ **Jamala Gewürztraminer** ⓥ Adds 'Beauty' to name. Late Harvest-style **23** ⑧⑦ doesn't disappoint. Lemon barley acid balances sugar & variety's signature litchi, rosepetal & Turkish delight opulence for a perfect accompaniment to spicy foods.

. . . .

Cabernet Sauvignon-Shiraz ⓥ ⓥ ★★★★ Pocket-friendly, dapper & flavoursome 60/40 duo has some older oak backing in **21** ⑧⑤. Adds structure while retaining balance & approachability. Worthy of a dinner date. **Chenin Blanc** ⓥ ⓥ ★★★★ Maintains 50+ year track record of balanced & crowd-pleasing styling in **23** ⑧⑤. Zesty tropical flavours, fresh & dry, perfect for summer. Also in 187 ml, as Cab-Shiraz.

Pick Of The Bunch Pinotage ★★★★ Mostly unoaked, **21** ⑧⑤ showcases grape's mulberry exuberance. Well made & juicy, not overly stern tannins, ready to entertain solo or with a meal. **Mr Borio's Shiraz** ★★★★ Red berry & fragrant lily in **20** ⑧⑤. Part wholebunch helps retain freshness & vibrancy in riper vintage, older oak provides balanced framework. Ready to enjoy. **Needless To Say Rosé** ⓝⓔⓦ ★★★ From chenin & pinotage, **23** ⑧① sports ripe apple & cheery red berries, offers succulent, dry & friendly sunset quaffing. WO W Cape, as Export sibling. **Sunbird Sauvignon Blanc** ★★★★ Piquantly fresh, bone-dry & crisp in **23** ⑧⑤, with gooseberry, citrus flavours. As previous, a good lunchtime partner.

Export Market range

Rosé Chenin Blanc-Pinotage ★★★ Onion-skin-hued **23** ⑧① is a bright, berry & red apple flavoured summer quaffer. Dry & crisp but friendly styling, perfect for the picnic basket. Discontinued: **Cabernet Sauvignon-Merlot, Sauvignon Blanc-Semillon**.

Cap Classique range

★★★★☆ **Cuvée Royale** House's most esteemed sparkler, brut-styled from chardonnay, has lees-enhanced base wine & further 58 months pre-disgorgement, longer than siblings. Shows laudable green apple, lime & mineral freshness in **18** ⑨①, underscored by lingering biscuity richness & breadth.

★★★★ **Kaapse Vonkel Brut Rosé** Pinot noir at 83% more dominant in **21** ⑧⑦, with pinotage & meunier. Distinct savoury edge to tangy red fruit, creamy shortbread from 14 months on lees. Quite elegant, refreshing & dry. A more balanced, versatile palate than **20** ★★★★ ⑧⑤.

★★★★ **Kaapse Vonkel Brut** Pioneered cap classique in SA in 1971. Much more piquant in **21** ★★★★ ⑧⑤, though part-oaked chardonnay, pinot noir (54/45) & meunier combo similar. Zestier lemony acid, less lees creaminess (16 months vs 20) favours savoury food pairing & ageing. Misses balance of **20** ⑧⑦.

★★★★ **Kaapse Vonkel Satin Nectar Rosé** Pinot noir & pinotage, 77/23, slightly tweaked in demi-sec **22** ⑧⑥. Drier, fresher than Satin sibling, red berry & cherry lifted by brilliant sparkle. More verve than lasttasted **20** ★★★★ ⑧④. Enjoy solo or with aromatic foods/desserts. WO W Cape for the Nectars & Brut Rosé.

★★★★ **Kaapse Vonkel Satin Nectar** Retains poised & consistently charming semi-dry styling in **22** ⑧⑥, similar proportions of chardonnay, pinot noir (66/33). Rich glacé fruit & lemon cream pastry seamed with fresh acid & burst of fine bubbles. Serve icy cold with fruity desserts or soft cheeses. **12** untasted.

Dessert Wines & Digestifs

★★★★ **Vin de Liza** ⓥ Light-footed & perfectly balanced **19** ★★★★☆ ⑨⓪ Noble Late Harvest from sauvignon & semillon (80/20). Lipsmacking, decadently delicious & a notch up on last **17** ⑧⑥. 375 ml.

★★★★☆ **Straw Wine** ② Occasional release, last in guide was **11** ★★★★ ⑧④. From sun-dried muscat ottonel, **15** ⑨① has variety supplying sublime grapiness, oak adding savoury touch for clean finish. 500 ml.

★★★★ **Cape Vintage Reserve** ② Sumptuous yet refined **15** ⑧⑧ 'port' has big satin tannins, savoury black fruit. Rich & broad, lingering Xmas cake finish. Shiraz, 2 years in oak. 19.4% alc.— MW

Location/map: Stellenbosch ▪ Map grid reference: E2 ▪ WO: Stellenbosch/Western Cape/Simonsberg-Stellenbosch ▪ Est 1953 ▪ 1stB 1968 ▪ Tasting & sales Sat-Wed/pub hols 10-5 Thu-Fri 10-6 (winter hours may vary) ▪ Closed Good Fri, Dec 25 & Jan 1 ▪ Cellar tours by appt ▪ Platters are served ▪ Fireplace ▪ Facilities for children ▪ Tour groups ▪ Conferences ▪ Wine club ▪ Owner(s) Francois & Johan Malan ▪ MD Johan Malan ▪ Cellarmaster(s) Michael Malan (reds, Oct 2017) ▪ Winemaker(s) Danna de Jongh (whites & cap classique, Nov 2022), with Frank Slabbert (Sep 2022) ▪ Viticulturist(s) Tommie Corbett (Nov 2008) ▪ 210ha (cab, merlot, ptage, pinot, shiraz, chard, chenin, sauv) ▪ 2,100t own label 25% red 25% white 50% cap classique ▪ Fairtrade, HACCP, IPW, SANAS, WIETA ▪ PO Box 6 Koelenhof 7605 ▪ tastingroom@simonsig.co.za ▪ www.simonsig.co.za ▪ **T +27 (0)21-888-4900 (general)/+27 (0)21-888-4915 (tasting)**

Simonsvlei International   ② ⑪ ◎ ⑧ ⑤

Buoyed by recent European investment, this stalwart winery on the Old Paarl Road/R101 is rejuvenating its brand to give old favourites a fresh feel, but also introduce more varieties and expand the portfolio to include a comprehensive range of spirits, beer and even cider, head of sales Bennie van Rensburg says. The aim is to 'satisfy every taste and delight every palate' while adhering to the guideline provided by co-founder Sonny le Roux back in 1945, 'offer quality wines at affordable prices'. We look forward to sampling them next time.

Location/map: Paarl ▪ Map grid reference: D7 ▪ Est/1stB 1945 ▪ Tasting & sales Mon-Fri 9-5 Sat/Sun/pub hols 9-3; last tasting 30 minutes prior to closing ▪ Fee R75pp/6 wines; kiddies pairing ▪ Cellar tours by prior arrangement ▪ Kids indoor & outdoor play areas ▪ Restaurant ▪ Conference & function venue ▪ Karoo Craft Breweries (www.kcbrew.co.za) ▪ Cellarmaster(s) Helena Senekal (Oct 2016) ▪ PO Box 584 Suider-Paarl 7624 ▪ winetasting@simonsvlei.co.za ▪ www.simonsvlei.co.za ▪ **T +27 (0)21-863-3040 (tasting/venue)**

☐ **Simplicity Collection** see Cape Wine Crafters
☐ **Since 1922** see Villiersdorp Winery
☐ **Sir George** see Napier Vineyards
☐ **Sirkel** see Scali

Sir Lambert Wines   ②

Veteran viticulturist Johan Teubes and fellow vine-man John Hayes own this boutique brand, bottled since 2007 to showcase oceanside vines in the Lamberts Bay wine ward.

★★★★ **Sauvignon Blanc** ② Some attractive smoky development on pea- & white asparagus-toned **20** ⑧⑥. Light phenolic touch adds dimension & tension to bright, breezy palate.— CvZ

Location/WO: Lamberts Bay ▪ Map: Olifants River ▪ Map grid reference: B5 ▪ Est 2004 ▪ 1stB 2007 ▪ Tasting & sales at Teubes Family Wines ▪ Owner(s) John Hayes & Johan Teubes ▪ Cellarmaster(s) Sybrand Teubes ▪ Winemaker(s) Sybrand Teubes, with Mariska Teubes ▪ Viticulturist(s) John Hayes ▪ 10ha (shiraz, sauv) ▪ PO Box 791 Vredendal 8160 ▪ info@teubeswines.co.za ▪ www.teubeswines.co.za ▪ **T +27 (0)27-213-2377**

☐ **Six Hats** see Piekenierskloof Wine Company
☐ **Sixpence** see Opstal Estate
☐ **1685** see Boschendal Wines
☐ **16 Mile Beach** see Blake Family Wines

Skaap Wines   ② ⑪ ⓐ ◎ ⑧

The Dutch Schaap family and co-owner and compatriot Rutger Siersma want to be represented by 'beautiful and natural wines', and from vintage 2023, their sheep-themed boutique range will be focused on just four labels, made by contractors from mostly own foothills vines. Children's Foodure, their social-care foundation for the local Sir Lowry's Pass community, continues to assist 60 children attain their educational goals.

★★★★☆ **Eline Reserve Sauvignon Blanc** Echoes previous aromatic greeting, ferment & 6 months mostly in new oak lend a distinctly perfumed top note in **22** ★★★★ ⑧⑧. Drier & tad less fruit-rich than **21** ⑨⓪, still brightly balanced & an appealing tablemate.

★★★★ **Sauvignon Blanc** Fresh herb, greengage & a hint of tropical in 22 ★★★★ ⑧③. Some lees enrichment but less fruit depth & intensity than last-tasted 20 ⑧⑥. Poised & ready to entertain.

Shiraz ★★★★ Warm (14.9% alc) dark-fruit & liquorice expression in 21 ⑧④, oak (18 months, 20% new) adding some spicy structure. Dry & savoury for hearty fare. Not tasted: **Rosalie Reserve**, **In Je Sasje Rosé**, **Okuphinki Rosé**. Discontinued: **Nathan Blend**, **Méthode Cap Classique Brut**. — MW

Location: Sir Lowry's Pass ▪ WO: Stellenbosch ▪ Est/1stB 2011 ▪ Wine sales during weekdays only ▪ DIY wine tasting by arrangement; R250pp includes small cheese board ▪ Local art on display & for sale ▪ Conferences (up to 15 pax) ▪ Walks/hikes ▪ Conservation area ▪ 5-bedroom guest house & 2 self-catering lodges plus villa ▪ Caters for weddings up to 24 guests ▪ Swimming pool ▪ Owner(s) Thierry Schaap & Rutger Siersma ▪ Cellarmaster(s)/winemaker(s) Riaan Oosthuizen (Jan 2011) ▪ 17ha/4ha (shiraz, sauv) ▪ 1,700cs own label 50% red 50% white ▪ IPW ▪ PO Box 1393 Somerset West 7130 ▪ marie@skaapwines.com ▪ www.skaapwines.com ▪ T +27 (0)83-452-2083

☐ **Sketchbook** *see* Carrol Boyes Collection

Skilpadvlei Wines

A colony of long-ago resident water tortoises is remembered in the branding of this small range, homed on the Joubert family farm in Stellenbosch along with bountiful hospitality allures and vines supplying contract buyers as well as the own wines, vinified off-site by consultants.

ML Joubert ⓥ ★★★★ Equal cab & merlot in oak-spiced & decently dry 20 ⑧⑤, the latter's ripeness adding dark-fruit appeal, the former's tighter tannins some gravitas & extension of the finish.

Merlot ★★★ Subtle meaty top note on 21 ⑧②'s plum & prune aromas; palate bright & fruity, grippy tannins reined in by 15 months in oak, smidgen new. **Sauvignon Blanc** ★★★ Pre-bottling, 23 ⑦⑨ bright & bouncy, with leafy blackcurrant overlay, zesty acid. Not tasted: **Grenache Rosé**. Discontinued: **Grenache Noir**, **Pinotage**, **Shiraz**, **Chenin Blanc**. — CvZ

Location/map/WO: Stellenbosch ▪ Map grid reference: C6 ▪ Est 2004 ▪ 1stB 2001 ▪ Tasting & sales Mon-Sat 8-5 Sun/pub hols 8-4; pub hols (seasonal) please call ahead ▪ R100pp cheesecake & wine pairing, R40pp standard tasting of 4 wines ▪ Food & wine pairings; kiddies tasting ▪ Closed Dec 25/26 & Jan 1/2 ▪ Restaurant Mon-Sat 8-9 Sun 8-4 ▪ Facilities for children ▪ Gift/decor shop ▪ Deli ▪ Conferences ▪ Weddings & functions ▪ B&B guest house & self-catering cottages ▪ Owner(s) WD Joubert ▪ Cellarmaster(s) Kowie du Toit (consultant) ▪ Viticulturist(s) Dawid Saayman (consultant) ▪ 34ha (cabs s/f, grenache, merlot, ptage, chard) ▪ 652t/12,000cs own label 80% red 20% white ▪ PO Box 17 Vlottenburg 7604 ▪ wines@skilpadvlei.co.za ▪ www.skilpadvlei.co.za ▪ T +27 (0)21-881-3237

Skipskop Wines

These wines are from very different parcels owned by UK geologist and boutique vintner Jonathan de Thierry: one in his garden in Napier town on the Cape South Coast, very near the ship-wrecking point named Skipskop; the other, marginally larger one on Voorbaat Farm in warmer Klein Karoo. The 'fickle' maritime terroir has its risks, and there will be no '23 Nebbiolo, but reward, too, as the rest of the crop was 'good'.

Nebbiolo ⓝⓔⓦ ★★★ Dark toned, meaty nuanced, 21 ⑦⑨ has character despite the low 11.5% alc. Ends dry & firm, a varietal attribute, reinforced by oaking. Would have benefited from more ripeness. WO Napier, as Semillon. **Petit Verdot** ⓥ ★★★★ Same Napier & Klein Karoo grape sources for latest **NV** ⑧⑤. Scented cherry fruit-pastille flavours muted by spice from 50% new oak. Touch trimmer than last, with stalky nuance, finishes dry & food friendly. **Sangiovese** ★★★ With 14% petit verdot, 22 ⑧① has varietal cherry tones, beefed up by savoury oak spice. Light textured (12% alc), allowing tannin to show but without harsh notes. A good food wine. WO Klein Karoo. **JdT Blend** ★★★★ Eclectic mix, equal sangiovese, pinot noir, shiraz plus 2 others, 10 months in portion Hungarian barrels, so expect something different. Sleek (12.5% alc) 22 ⑧③ has interwoven glacé cherries, raspberries & sweet spice, juicy texture, finishing dry but tannins amenable. WO W Cape. **Semillon** ★★★ Elegantly styled oaked version (8 months barriques), 22 ⑧① has savoury, waxy perfume richness, becomes fresher on palate due to racy acid. Better varietal expression than last. **Muscat Blanc** ★★★★ Fortified & oaked muscat de Frontignan, 22 ⑧③ has pungent sultana perfume & flavours, a biscuit savoury seam, but the main attraction is the full sweetness. **Ruby Red** ⓝⓔⓦ ★★★ Port-style wine from petit verdot & 30% shiraz, 22 ⑧⑩'s sweetness already apparent in the richly fruity, touch confected perfume. Palate luscious, with fruit pastille flavours, tannins subservient. Not tasted: **Petit Verdot Rosé, Sauvignon Blanc, Sauvignon Blanc-Semillon**. — CR

Location: Napier ▪ Map: Southern Cape ▪ Map grid reference: C6 ▪ WO: Klein Karoo/Western Cape/Napier ▪ Est 2012 ▪ 1stB 2014 ▪ Tasting by appt only ▪ Craft brandy still ▪ Owner(s) Tweedal Estate cc ▪ Winemaker(s) Jonathan de Thierry ▪ Viticulturist(s) Dirk Viljoen ▪ Napier 2ha (nebb, p verdot, pinot, shiraz, sauv, sem, shz) + Voorbaat (Klein Karoo) 2.5ha (p verdot, sangio, shiraz, white muscadel) ▪ 33t/1,000cs own label 80% red 20% white ▪ Meul Str, Napier 7270 ▪ skipskopwines@gmail.com ▪ www.skipskopwines.com ▪ **T +27 (0)82-093-1791**

☐ **Skyline** *see* Van Loveren Family Vineyards

Slaley

'Along with the highs of new endeavours,' say the 3rd generation Hunting family running the Slaley wine and hospitality estate, 'sadly come the lows' after the passing of the custodian, Lindsay, early last year. The younger vintners will take encouragement from the quality of their prime Simonsberg site, an 'exciting' label refresh, release of the first cap classique, a top seller, and plans 'to take our wines to new consumer spaces'.

Slaley range
★★★★ **Cabernet Sauvignon** ⓠ Unashamedly bold styling in **20** ⑧⑦, ample dark fruit compote, liquorice & bitter black chocolate flavours. 20 months 2nd-fill barrel ageing (as Merlot & Pinotage) & firm, chalky tannins give just enough structure to check hearty 15% alc.

★★★★ **Merlot** ⓠ Ripe, robust **20** ★★★★ ⑧⑤, savoury-smoky plum compote in warm-hearted alc embrace (15.5%), less gracefully balanced than last-tasted **08** ⑧⑦. For fans of swashbuckling reds.

★★★★ **Pinotage** ⓠ ⓦ Shows good typicity in **20** ⑧⑦, ample mouthfilling mulberry flavour & juicy tannins honed in older oak. Generous 14.5% alc in balance with fruit. Last tasted was **08** ★★★☆ ⑧④.

★★★★ **Chardonnay** ⓠ Ripe pear & lime flavours in medium-bodied **21** ⑧⑥, with subtly integrated toasty nuance from maturation in old oak, 16 months. Balanced & flavoursome, ready to enjoy.

In abeyance: **Shiraz**.

Broken Stone range
Red ⓠ ★★★ Old-oak-aged mix of cab & shiraz (60/40) in **20** ⑧⓪, touch less approachable than previous pinotage blend, with tannins still quite chunky. **Rosé** ⓠ ★★★ Just a hint of colour & delicate, savoury berry nuance in **22** ⑦⑧ from cab. Dry & trim (12% alc) with a tweak of tannin on the finish. **White** ⓠ ⓦ ★★★★ A bright & juicy union of sauvignon & chardonnay in **22** ⑧⑤ with lemon barley & greengage flavours. Lightish, balanced & super-quaffable. — MW

Location/map: Stellenbosch ▪ Map grid reference: E2 ▪ WO: Simonsberg-Stellenbosch ▪ Est 1955 ▪ Tasting & sales Mon-Thu 9-5 Fri-Sun 10-4; pub hols (seasonal) please call ahead ▪ Fee R70 ▪ Guest house ▪ Owner(s) Hunting family ▪ Winemaker(s) Wynand Pienaar & Jacques Fourie (consultants) ▪ Viticulturist(s) Stephen Chihwehwete ▪ 183ha/20ha (cab, merlot, ptage, shiraz, chard, sauv) ▪ 150t 67% red 33% white ▪ PO Box 119 Koelenhof 7605 ▪ info@slaley.co.za ▪ www.slaley.co.za ▪ **T +27 (0)21-865-2123**

Slanghoek Winery

Remarkable that any work gets done in this tucked-away corner of the winelands near Rawsonville, given the spellbinding panorama of high crags and serried vines, and the bounty of alluring outdoor activities, festivals and events. But of course there is industry, the team vinifying 30,000 tons of grapes from 25 growers, setting aside a sizeable 80,000 cases' worth for their own characterful and appealingly priced ranges.

Legends range
★★★★ **Barrel Fermented Chenin Blanc** Tasted shortly after bottling, **21** ⑧⑧ in quieter phase, cloaked with spicy oak (100%, previously 50%), subduing the rich stonefruit & citrus core. Should unfurl, just needs time, but one for fans of amply wooded whites. No **20**.

Private Selection
★★★★ **Cabernet Sauvignon** ⓥ Delicious dark berries with well-melded oak spicing (85% new, 14 months) in **21** ⑧⑥, raising the bar on **20** ★★★★ ⑧③. Lipsmacking, light (12.4% alc) & balanced; a pleasure to drink at an equally pleasing price.

★★★★ **Camerca** ⓥ Appealing **22** ⑧⑥ cab-merlot blend, even richer than **21** ★★★☆ ⑧④, with juicy black fruits & firm tannin grip, aided by 9 months in 20% new oak. Dapper & ready to entertain over the next few years.

★★★★ **Crème de Chenin** ⓧ Honeyed marmalade notes of **20** ⑧⑧ Natural Sweet show perfume of 8% muscat d'Alexandrie, 65 g/L sugar countered by fresh acidity for a well-balanced & -resolved dessert wine. Textured & fresh, like last-tasted **16** ⑧⑦. 375 ml.

★★★★ **Noble Late Harvest** ⓧ Acid freshness counters sweetness on consistently delicious chenin botrytis dessert, **18** ⑧⑦ with usual dab muscat (8%). Marmalade, apricot & brûlée remain light yet rich, & perfectly poised. Oaked 9 months, half new. 12.6% alc. 375 ml. No **17**.

Merlot ⓥ ★★★★ Bright plummy flavours in a firm & fresh framework, with well-managed tannins & 30% new oak in harmony. **21** ⑧⑤ respectably juicy & balanced for solo or mealtime enjoyment. **Pinotage** ⓥ ★★★★ Engagingly forward & drinkable, with spicy raspberry notes on **20** ⑧③, oak (80% new, 15 months) in supple support. **Shiraz** ⓧ ★★★★ Well-textured & persistent **20** ⑧⑤ matches previous in dried herb & black fruit, supported by unheavy oak frame, 70% new, 14 months. **Chardonnay** ⓧ ★★★ Oatmeal & biscuit nuances to uncomplicated **22** ⑧② preview. Fresh, light & easy to enjoy everyday. **Chenin Blanc** ⓥ ★★★☆ Sleeker texture than perky 3L sibling, tropical flavours zested through with lime in **23** ⑧③. Balanced for even more summer drinking pleasure than previous. **Sauvignon Blanc** ⓥ ★★★ Crisp & crunchy **23** ⑧② has a tropical top note to add to the easy-drinking pleasure.

Slanghoek range

Cuvée Brut ⓥ ★★★ Zesty carbonated **NV** ⑧⓪ fizz, light & undemanding with neutral green fruits & beeswax nuance; perfect with orange juice for breakfast. **Vin Doux** ★★★ Frothy **NV** ⑦⑧ carbonated bubbly from muscat d'Alexandrie, for the sweeter tooth. Latest softer, with ample floral grapiness & modest 11.3% alc. **Hanepoot Jerepigo** ★★★★ Seductive honeysuckle-, caramel- & sultana-infused **23** ⑧⑤ fortified dessert. Tangy balancing acidity & integrated spirit lift the whole, for an uncloying fireside treat. **Red Muscadel** ★★★★ Electric pink **23** ⑧⑤ brimming with dried raisin & jasmine flavours. Not over-sweet, 233 g/L sugar well tucked into bright acid. Both delicate & intense, perfect foil for wintery weather. **Cape Ruby** ⓥ ★★★☆ From touriga nacional, improved **22** ⑧④ 'port' is true to style: approachable, ample berry flavours, not too sweet or alcoholic (16.2%). A winter warmer with appealing drier farewell.

Vinay range

Chenin Blanc ☺ ★★★ Charming from the first sip, even more so at the price. Crisp, tropical-toned **NV** ⑧② is balanced & light; plenty to share in 3L cask.

Smooth Red ⓥ ★★★ Echoes Vin Rouge in all respects, the same blend & vinification, also **NV** ⑦⑨, but in 3L cask. **Vin Rouge** ⓥ ★★★ Ripe & warm choc-cherry/berry notes in friendly & approachable **NV** ⑦⑨ from near-equal pinotage, malbec & petit verdot. One for the BBQ & laidback enjoyment. **Vin Blanc** ⓥ ★★★ Clean green fruit in latest **NV** ⑧⓪ from equal chenin & sauvignon with dash colombard. Moderate alc (12.17%), gentle styling. **Vin Semi-Doux** ★★★ Delicate, perfumed **NV** ⑦⑦ semi-sweet from muscat (70%) & chenin. Feather-light at 9.2% alc. **Vin Rosé** ★★★ Rosepetal hue & aroma on light (9.5% alc) **NV** ⑦⑦ Natural Sweet from red muscadel. Soft & uncloying. — MW

Location: Rawsonville ▪ Map: Breedekloof ▪ Map grid reference: A5 ▪ WO: Slanghoek ▪ Est 1951 ▪ 1stB 1970 ▪ Tasting & sales Mon-Fri 9-5 Sat/pub hols 10-2; pub hols (seasonal) please call ahead ▪ Closed Easter Fri/Sun, Dec 25 & Jan 1 ▪ Cellar tours by appt ▪ Slanghoek MTB Route, fee R30 - visit website for route map ▪ Loyalty club ▪ Owner(s) 25 producers ▪ Cellarmaster(s) Pieter Carstens (Aug 2002) ▪ Winemaker(s) Nico Grundling (Dec 2002) & Werner du Plessis (Aug 2014), with Jacques de Goede (Dec 2001) & Elaine Conradie (Nov 2016) ▪ Viticulturist(s) Callie Coetzee (Nov 2010) ▪ 1,830ha ▪ 30,000t/80,000cs own label 25% red 55% white 10% rosé 10% fortified ▪ Other export brand: Zonneweelde ▪ ISO 22000, IPW ▪ PO Box 75 Rawsonville 6845 ▪ info@slanghoek.co.za ▪ www.slanghoek.co.za ▪ **T +27 (0)23-344-3026**

☐ **Slent** *see* Ayama Wines
☐ **Slowine** *see* Villiersdorp Winery
☐ **Smiley** *see* Terracura Wines
☐ **Smith & Co** *see* Nicholson Smith
☐ **Smuggler's Boot** *see* Kershaw Wines

☐ **Sneeukop** see Rogge Cloof
☐ **Soek Die Geluk** see Goedverwacht Wine Estate

Soif de Vivre Wines ⓥ

With Soif the golden retriever ever at her side, consultant winemaker Helanie Olivier expresses her thirst for life and trying new, exciting things in this boutique brand emphasising sustainability and naturalness. Her base is Stellenbosch, where for the current release she sourced syrah to co-ferment with Franschhoek petit verdot to 'reflect the true nature of the season'. Next up is a varietal petit verdot from a Stellenbosch vineyard.

★★★★ Soif de Vivre Deep & dark toned, plush fruited, an unusual blend of syrah with 45% petit verdot. Dried herbs & oak spice from year in barrel, half new, **20** (88) is voluptuous & generously flavoured, rich; the tannins amenable. Also in magnum.— CR

Location: Stellenbosch ▪ WO: Coastal ▪ Est/1stB 2019 ▪ Tasting by appt ▪ Owner(s)/winemaker(s) Helanie Olivier ▪ Bought in grapes ▪ 145cs own label 100% red ▪ soifdevivrewines@gmail.com ▪ www.soifdevivrewines.co.za ▪ **T +27 (0)83-639-1528**

Somerbosch Wines ⓥ ⓔ ⓸ ⓹ ⓺

Marius and Japie Roux have been winemaker and viticulturist at Die Fonteine, the property named for its equidistance from Somerset West and Stellenbosch, for almost 30 years now, proudly following their father's 'unpretentious and traditional' style of making 'good-quality wine at an affordable price'. They've built the farm into a multifarious tourist attraction, with everything from breakfasts to business meetings catered for.
Pinot Noir ⓥ ★★★ Nicely dry, with dark berry scents & flavours, subtle oak char (30% new, 12 months), **19** (82)'s 15% alc adds noticeable warmth on finish. **Shiraz** ⓥ ★★★ Brings back American oak (50%), drops alc to less burly 14.5% & ups drinking pleasure in **20** (82). Supple, hints of game & shrub adding complexity to fresh red berries. **Kylix** ⓥ ★★★★ Commendable flagship, again blends cab, merlot & shiraz in **16** (84), stays true to usual flavour profile with dark fruit, some forest floor development. Ready now.
Steen ⓥ ★★★★ Deft oak-staved chenin, **21** (84) has appealing nutty waxiness overlaying peach, pear & floral notes. Bright & fresh, pleasingly vinous from fairly high (14.5%) but balanced alc. **Late Bottled Vintage Port** ⓥ ★★★ From cab, aged 2 years in old barrels, **NV** (81) decadently sweet with spiced fruitcake richness. Not tasted: **Cabernet Sauvignon, Merlot, Pinotage, Shiraz-Merlot, Rosé, Chenin Blanc, Sauvignon Blanc, Sauvignon Blanc-Semillon.** — CvZ

Location/WO: Stellenbosch ▪ Map: Helderberg ▪ Map grid reference: C1 ▪ Est 1950 ▪ 1stB 1995 ▪ Tasting & sales daily 9-5 ▪ Fee R80/6 wines, waived on purchase of any 3 btls; R100pp/ice cream & red wine tasting ▪ Closed Dec 24/25 ▪ Cellar tours by appt ▪ Somerbosch Bistro breakfast 9-11 & lunch 12-4 daily ▪ Facilities for children ▪ Farm produce ▪ Conferences ▪ Craft beer ▪ Owner(s) Somerbosch Wines cc ▪ Cellarmaster(s)/winemaker(s)/viticulturist(s) Marius & Japie Roux (both 1995) ▪ 55ha/43ha (cab, merlot, ptage, pinot, shiraz, chenin, sauv, sem) ▪ 350t 55% red 45% white ▪ PO Box 12181 Die Boord 7613 ▪ sales@somerbosch.co.za ▪ www.somerbosch.co.za ▪ **T +27 (0)21-855-3615**

☐ **Sonkop** see Dragonridge

Son of the Soil Wines ⓥ

Son of the Soil was established in 2016 by Denzel Swarts as a private, non-profit fund-raising venture to help young people living on farms complete their schooling, through a programme of mentorship, lifeskills and leadership. The wines, untasted this edition, are made by consultants, and styled 'by people, for people'.

Location: Cape Town ▪ Map: Cape Peninsula ▪ Map grid reference: C1 ▪ Est 2016 ▪ 1stB 2021 ▪ Tasting & sales Mon-Sat 10-4.30; pub hols 11-7 (seasonal) please call ahead ▪ Fee R150 ▪ Owner(s) Son of the Soil Wines (Pty) Ltd ▪ Winemaker(s)/viticulturist(s) consultants ▪ 750cs own label 35% red 65% white ▪ Unit C3, Salt Orchard, 45 Yew Str, Salt River, Cape Town 7925 ▪ denzel@sosfoundation.org.za ▪ www.sosfoundation.org.za ▪ **T +27 (0)82-789-6332**

☐ **Sonop** see Germanier Wines

Sophie

It's 15 years since the reputed Iona Vineyards team launched this lifestyle brand, showcasing Elgin and other selected cool-grown fruit, and saw it take off on a wave of quality, value, charming packaging and a backstory involving Sophie Te'blanche, better known as 'sauvignon blanc', the 'most famous lady never to exist'. Her beau, Mr P, also hale and hearty, can be found in the bargain pinot noir section of the Iona listing.

★★★★ **Sophie Te'blanche** ⊘ Appetising **23** 86 sauvignon's acid enlivens the creamy centre (ex 4 months on lees), a foil for fresh herb, ruby grapefruit & nectarine flavours. **22** untasted.

Sophie Le Rose ★★★★ Pale salmon pink **23** 85 sophisticated aperitif or alfresco companion. Crisply dry, piquant red berry notes from shiraz & pinotage (70/30), both picked in stages. Lees contact adds satisfying weight. Not tasted: **Sophie Le Rouge**. — CvZ

Location: Elgin ▪ WO: Cape South Coast ▪ Est/1stB 2009 ▪ Closed to public ▪ Owner(s) Andrew Gunn ▪ Cellarmaster(s) Werner Muller (May 2011) ▪ (ptage, pinot, shiraz, sauv, sem) ▪ 300t/35,000cs own label 4% red 80% white 16% rosé ▪ PO Box 527 Grabouw 7160 ▪ orders@iona.co.za ▪ www.sophie.co.za ▪ **T +27 (0)28-284-9678**

☐ **Soul Of The Mountain** *see* Olifantsberg Family Vineyards

Southern Right

There has been remarkable continuity over the three decades of this Hemel-en-Aarde-based brand, co-founded by Anthony Hamilton Russell, also co-owner of top labels Hamilton Russell Vineyards and Ashbourne. Just two varieties, pinotage and sauvignon blanc, have been the focus, and thus it will remain as volumes rise to meet demand, and select new fruit sources are added, Swartland and Polkadraai Hills for the former, Elgin the latter. Anthony is quietly proud that the styling since inception, more classic, nuanced and refined, 'played an early and important role in the current direction' of winemaking in both categories.

★★★★☆ **Pinotage** 🐝 Cool provenance evident in brightness of fruit, plum & red cherry, on **22** 92. Well-judged oak, 14% new, 10 months, provides & aids savoury spice, succulence & lightness; yet a lovely intensity & length, too, with herb & pepper on sustained finish. Worth keeping.

★★★★ **Sauvignon Blanc** Bright, lively, with lovely mouthfeel, dimension & texture from 8% older-oaked portion & lees ageing. Grapes from 27 blocks, wild & inoculated organic yeasts for green & tropical flavours, concluding salty tang. **23** 89 an all-rounder for summer. — WB

Location: Hermanus ▪ Map: Walker Bay & Bot River ▪ Map grid reference: A3 ▪ WO: Cape Coast ▪ Est 1994 ▪ 1stB 1995 ▪ Tasting by appt ▪ Cellar tours by appt ▪ Fynbos reserve, renosterveld reserve & 3 wetlands ▪ Owner(s) Anthony Hamilton Russell, Neil Wessels, Talita Engelbrecht ▪ Winemaker(s) Emul Ross (2014) ▪ Viticulturist(s) Johan Montgomery (2005) ▪ ±46ha (ptage, sauv) ▪ 17,500cs own label 18% red 82% white ▪ PO Box 158 Hermanus 7200 ▪ info@southernright.co.za ▪ www.southernright.co.za ▪ **T +27 (0)28-312-3595**

Southern Treasures

Gifted a small parcel of vines with a southerly aspect on the Akkedisberg mountain range near cool-climate Stanford, the men and women of the Akkedisberg Wine Worker's Trust led by Andrew Moos, and supported by Raka winemaker Josef Dreyer, craft a limited quantity of fine pinotage 'with great care for the land, water, indigenous fynbos, animals and birdlife', in a style intended to be ripe-fruited and complex.

★★★★ **Pinotage** Piquant raspberries, sweetly spiced by year in oak, 40% new, hints fynbos & mint in the flavours, sleek & amenable tannins. **21** 86 respectfully handled, ensuring good typicity. — CR, CvZ

Location: Stanford ▪ Map: Walker Bay & Bot River ▪ Map grid reference: C8 ▪ WO: Klein River ▪ Est 2013 ▪ 1stB 2021 ▪ Tasting & sales Mon-Fri 8-5 Sat 10-3 ▪ Closed Good Fri & Dec 25 ▪ Facilities for children ▪ Deli ▪ Owner(s) Akkedisberg Boerdery (Pty) Ltd ▪ Winemaker(s) Andrew Moos (Jan 2003), with Josef Dreyer (Jan 2007) ▪ 16ha under vine ▪ 80t/1,280cs own label 100% red ▪ PO Box 124 Caledon 7230 ▪ info@southerntreasure.co.za ▪ www.southerntreasureswine.co.za ▪ **T +27 (0)28-341-0676**

☐ **Sparkling Brotherhood Collection** *see* O'Connell's

Spice Route ⓨ ⓘ ◎ ⓰

The brand name, evoking 15th-century mariners who went in search of exotic spice, also alludes to entrepreneurial vintner Charles Back's 1990s venture into Swartland in search of exceptional vineyards, and the setting up of a cellar and expanded vineyards on the farm Klein Amoskuil, now listed separately in this guide. After a recent tweak, the wines featured here are positioned and packaged to better align with their home, the tourist-friendly Spice Route Destination on Paarl Mountain, not far from sibling venture Fairview. Fans will find all their favourites here, with the usual palate appeal, keen prices and, of course, spice.

★★★★☆ Bushvine Grenache ⓥ Less expressive than last, though **21** ⑨⓪ from dryland vines does show clean freshness, seems more elegant than 14% alc. Just a hint of signature red berry & white pepper, should unfurl nicely in a few years. Ferment in concrete 'kuipe'/16 months older oak.

★★★★ Bushvine Mourvèdre ⓥ Not discontinued as we thought. Subtle dark cherry, dry scrub & savoury nuances from low-crop dryland vines. Lengthy 18-month stay in older barrels helps streamline **21** ⑧⑨ but tannins & flavours tightly coiled. Will reveal more charm after a few years. No **20**.

★★★★ Pinotage ⓠ From 28 year old dryland bushvine parcel. Red & black fruit, white pepper on **21** ★★★★☆ ⑨①, vanilla & clove from American oak, 30% new, like **20**, but lower alc (14%) & sugar.

★★★★☆ Malabar ⓠ Brilliant syrah-driven has depth, detail & elegance in **15** ⑨③. Supple & succulent, unfurling layers of spice, cherry fruit, herbal scrub & tobacco.

★★★★☆ Chakalaka ⓥ ⓰ Consistent 6-way varietal mix, just proportions vary, **21** ⑨④ mostly grenache noir. Dense heart of spicy dark fruit, sleek & well toned, finely structured after 20 months mostly older oak. Quality in place, just needs time to show best. No **20**. Fairtrade, as all tasted this edition.

Not tasted: **Saffron Rosé**, **Chenin Blanc**. — MW

Location/map: Paarl ▪ Map grid reference: D6 ▪ WO: Swartland ▪ Tasting & sales Mon-Sun 9-5, last tasting 30min before closing ▪ Standard tasting/wine & charcuterie pairing (applicable fees apply) ▪ Closed Dec 25 & Jan 1 ▪ Jewell's Restaurant ▪ Red Hot Glass Studio ▪ Pilates for Life ▪ Moi Goeters pottery café ▪ De Villiers Chocolate ▪ Jem Coffee Roastery ▪ Barley & Biltong Emporium ▪ Brenda's Deli ▪ The Trading Company ▪ Wilderer's Distillery & La Grapperia Restaurant ▪ Cape Brewing Company ▪ Owner(s) Charles Back ▪ Winemaker(s) Charl du Plessis (Dec 2001), with Licia Solomons (Jan 2006) ▪ Fairtrade, HACCP, IPW, WIETA ▪ PO Box 583 Suider-Paarl 7624 ▪ info@spiceroute.co.za ▪ www.spiceroutewines.co.za ▪ **T +27 (0)21-863-5200**

Spider Pig Wines ⓨ

The brand name and mostly light-hearted packaging, recalling Homer Simpson's parody of the Spiderman theme song, is part of Cape Town wine-entrepreneur and -curator David Wibberley's strategy to offer unintimidating and deliciously drinkable wines, by a crème of Cape winemakers, that serious palates will also love. Most of his selections were unready for tasting; we're looking forward to sampling them next time.

★★★★☆ The Black Pig ⓰ 64% cinsaut with cab, wild fermented, **21** ⑨② elegant & pure, red cherries & silky texture buffed by year in older barrels, mix 225L & 600L, fennel lift to superb dry finish. 50/50 whole-bunch & -berry for cinsaut. — ML

Location: Cape Town ▪ Map: Cape Peninsula ▪ Map grid reference: D1 ▪ WO: Stellenbosch ▪ Est/1stB 2015 ▪ Tasting by appt only ▪ Owner(s) David Wibberley ▪ Winemaker(s) various ▪ 6,000cs own label 60% red 20% white 20% rosé ▪ Unit 8, The Old Timber Yard, 27 7th Ave, Maitland, Cape Town 7405 ▪ david@spiderpig-wines.com ▪ www.spiderpigwines.com ▪ **T +27 (0)72-117-2147**

Spier ⓨ ⓘ ⓖ ◎ ⓑ ⓰

This large and hospitable estate just outside Stellenbosch town traces a complicated history back to 1692. A plethora of owners - and eventual dereliction - followed. The property was restored and revived in 1965. Then in 1993 the part including the cellar and old buildings was acquired by businessman Dick Enthoven, who later also succeeded in reuniting the property with the lost name Spier in 2001. A grand development was already under way, and now visitors have a great variety of experiences offered at the riverside spread. The wide range of wines is remarkable, sourced partly from Spier's own substantial vineyard holdings, and including a number of organic (and certified vegan) wines. The range has a rare reputation for quality at both the rarefied and volume ends of the market. Notable too is Spier's concern for sustainability, the environment, and employee well-being, which won it the Drinks Business Green Awards Ethical Award in 2022.

Its Growing for Good projects and partnerships 'empower communities to create positive social and environmental change'. A focus on regenerative farming is linked to Spier's commitment to 'a net-zero aligned carbon emission target by 2030' - reducing and optimising emissions, and transitioning to renewables.

Frans K. Smit

★★★★★ **Frans K. Smit Red** ⓧ Big & powerful as ever, yet with fine velvet tannins & ripe fruit complexity & depth to beguile even in youth (if you decant; best left 5 years or more). **18** ★★★★☆ ⑨③ hedonistic, as **17** ⑨⑥. 61% cab, with merlot, cab franc & malbec, all ex Stellenbosch.

★★★★☆ **Frans K. Smit White** ⓢ Sauvignon (86%) dominates **20** ⑨④ with array from blackcurrant & fig to grass, though semillon's lemon guides long finish. Spicy oak beautifully absorbed, adds savoury depth. Cape Town, Darling & Stellenbosch grapes, as **19** ★★★★★ ⑨⑥. These certified vegan (by Control Union), other instances noted below.

21 Gables

★★★★☆ **Cabernet Sauvignon** Cedary, dark-berried aromas & flavours on **20** ⑨① preview, with some spicy savoury notes from 60% new oak not too intrusive (20 months, less than last & less drying) but adding to complexity, as no doubt do smidgens cab franc & petit verdot. Usual rounded tannic structure, & lower alc (13.5%) than on most top Spier reds. Stellenbosch WO, as Pinotage & Chenin.

★★★★☆ **Pinotage** ⓐ Plentiful pure fruit (dark cherry, berry) on **20** ⑨③ from Stellenbosch, with the contribution from 40% new oak integrated. Smooth but structuring tannins, & fresher & lighter feeling than seems likely from 14.5% alc, thanks to the good balance. Also in 1.5L, as all these except Sauvignon.

★★★★☆ **Chenin Blanc** ⓦ Bright, ripe aromas of thatch & melon lead to bold, flavourful palate. As usual, some sugar (5.6 g/L) adds to texture, counterposed by firm citric acidity. **22** ⑨② in oak up to year, 40% new, integrated but adding to richness & complexity. Wholebunch & wild ferment components. WO Stellenbosch.

★★★★☆ **Sauvignon Blanc** ⓐ Intense tropical fruit, gooseberry & blackcurrant nuances on work-in-progress **23** ⑨④. Impressive flavour power allied with bright, lipsmacking juiciness. Partial wholebunch pressing. WO Cape Town, as Chenin. Certified vegan, like others in range.

Creative Block

★★★★☆ **Five** ⓥ ⓐ Ripe, sweet-fruited **20** ⑨④ 5-way Bordeaux blend, as usual led by cab & merlot to give classic berry aromas with subtle cedar & tobacco spicing. All integrating well, with molten tannins. At 14.5% alc certainly big, but so well balanced one scarcely notices. 30% new oak. WO Stellenbosch.

★★★★ **Eight** ⓥ ⓐ Pinotage at 37% largest component of 8-grape **20** ★★★★★ ⑨④, followed by shiraz, cab & merlot. No pushover at 14.5%, & fairly plush, but approaches closer to elegant than the others, perhaps thanks to more bright red fruit & less new oak (25%). Delicious even in youth, but should also mature further. Impresses more than last-tasted **17** ⑧⑨.

★★★★☆ **Three** ⓥ Largely from shiraz, with a little mourvèdre & viognier, the last certainly adding to the fragrance. **20** ⑨⓪ warmly generous, sweet fruited, but restrained in feeling despite 14.5% alc. Rounded tannic structure; 40% new oak. Larger formats available, as for Five.

★★★★☆ **Two** ⓥ There's always a different flavour profile from FK Smit version of the blend, lashings of granadilla from 86% sauvignon on ex-tank **23** ⑨⓪, tempered by semillon contributing to the lemon notes of the almost tart acidity (it should settle somewhat after bottling). Incisive, crisp & juicy, the fruit untrammelled by oak. Certified vegan, as all these.

First Stone Organic

★★★★☆ **Red** ⓥ Stellenbosch merlot (62%) & cab on **20** ⑨② Pure ripe fruit - blackberries, mulberries - with year in 65% new oak contributing mostly to structure & texture. Tannins rounded but firm, acid a little obvious, but the whole juicy & approachable. 13.9% alc a little higher than last but also in balance.

Farm House Organic

★★★★☆ **Red** ⓥ ⓐ Classic aromas of blackcurrant & cedar on flavourful **20** ⑨③ from merlot & 30% cab. Less oak than on First Stone version (none new here), & acidity better balanced. Rounded ripe tannins & general feeling of restraint a pleasure. Ready, should age well. Natural ferment a sign of the lower-intervention policy for the organically grown wines. This, Chenin Blanc, WO Stellenbosch.

★★★★☆ **Rosé** ⊘ From 61% merlot with shiraz & sauvignon & drops of cab & chenin. **21** ★★★★ ⑧⑨ rounded & quite soft; beautifully dry with good & not overstated fruit flavours. But touch less interesting & stony-grippy than **20** ⑨⓪ from shiraz. WO Coastal, rest Stellenbosch.

★★★★☆ **Chenin Blanc** ⊘ ⊘ Mid-gold **21** ⑨② showing some attractive early development in a honeyed edge to complex deep fruit & florals. Ripely rich (13.9% alc) & smooth but still fresh, lively & grippy with a phenolic touch. Natural ferment & ageing in mix of oak & ceramic 'egg', as Rosé.

The Yellowwood Organic

★★★★ **Red** ⊘ ⊘ Merlot & malbec with 14% shiraz on **20** ⑧⑦ give ripe berries & spicy tobacco. Smooth, dry, undemanding but effective tannic structure. Supportive oaking. Delicious now, but no hurry.

★★★★ **White** ⊘ As usual, **23** ⑧⑥ mostly from chenin, with viognier to augment the peachy aroma & flavour. Core of sweet ripe fruit, richness from lees ageing, & good balance with succulent acidity make for even more youthful juicy charm than on **22** ★★★★ ⑧④. Light oak influence.

Rosé ⊘ ⊘ ★★★★ From mostly merlot, shiraz, malbec, salmon-hued **22** ⑧⑤ nicely fruity, with a hint of spice. Balanced, light-feeling & fresh. Mildly oaked.

Good Natured Organic

★★★★ **Chenin Blanc** ⊘ ⊘ Lives up to previewed promise of last year. **22** ⑧⑥ lively & characterful, flavourful with core of sweet dried peach, succulent & balanced. Generous texture not depending on sugar, so a good dry finish.

★★★★ **Sauvignon Blanc** ⊘ ⊘ Now-bottled **22** ⑧⑦ shows character & some complexity, avoiding easy clichés of variety in its herb-tinged full aroma & flavours, but not lacking in a range from floral & tropical to citrus. Fresh, with some weight from lees contact.

Shiraz ⊘ ★★★★ Now bottled & showing benefit of another year. **21** ⑧④ ripe, pure aromas & flavours lightly but effectively oaked with staves in tank. Flavourful & fresh, not complex but deliciously drinkable. WO W Cape. **Shiraz-Cabernet Sauvignon** ⊘ ★★★★ Now bottled & just as fresh, juicy & cheerful. **21** ⑧④ soft textured & smooth, but respectably structured. A certain sweetness does no harm to the easygoing charm. WO W Cape, as Shiraz. **Rosé** (NEW) ⊘ ★★★ Easygoing but nicely dry **22** ⑧② from mixed varieties is deeper coloured than many. Clean, slightly earthy fruitiness; silky soft & a bit less than bracing.

Seaward

★★★★ **Pinotage** ⊘ Offers clean, bright ripe fruit for a flavourful juiciness, more depth & structure than the Signature version, supported by 30% new oak. **21** ⑧⑥ better balanced than **20** ★★★★ ⑧④.

★★★★ **Chardonnay** Only 40% oak-fermented on **22** ⑧⑥, giving hint of toasty, nutty complexity to the citrus notes. Silky palate threaded by firm acidity, leading to good lingering finish. Up on **21** ★★★★ ⑧⑤.

★★★★ **Chenin Blanc** More characterful & intense than Signature, **22** ⑧⑥ thatch & melon plus lingering peachiness. Textured, ripely rich & balanced. 14% alc. 10% fermented in tank for extra fruit & freshness.

★★★★ **Sauvignon Blanc** Plenty of passionfruit aroma & flavour on **23** ⑧⑥, some stonefruit & fig notes too. Silk texture, vibrant succulent acidity, 13.6% alc all in balance. More interesting than **22** ★★★★ ⑧⑤.

Cabernet Sauvignon ★★★☆ Classic cedary, dark-berried aromas & flavours on ripe but sufficiently restrained **21** ⑧⑤. Balanced & modestly oaked for early approachability but with good, smooth tannic grip. 14.1% alc. **Shiraz** ★★★★ Spice & ripe berries on **21** ⑧③. Easygoing & undistinguished, decently balanced, gentle tannic grip & sweetness on finish. Supportively oaked, 20% new. 14.2% alc.

Signature

Cabernet Sauvignon ⊘ ★★★☆ Lightly oaked **22** ⑧④, well balanced & structured for approachability but with nice bit of grip. All these reds up to 5 g/L of sugar (technically dry), adding richness & smoothness rather than overt sweetness. WO W Cape, as rest unless noted. **Merlot** ★★★ Quietly ripe, fruitcake character on **22** ⑧② with pleasant herbal edge. Modest grip, sweetish finish. At 13.8% alc, as usual a little lighter than other reds here. **Pinotage** ⊘ ★★★★ Clean, bright, fruit-rich **22** ⑧③. Smoothly friendly, but touch of tannin there; sweet edge but juicy as well as flavourful. **Shiraz** ★★★ Quiet aromas & flavours on **22** ⑧②, with some spice & smoked meat. Plump & easy, smoothed by hint of sweetness. **Cabernet Sauvignon-Merlot-Shiraz** ★★★ Fruit-driven **22** ⑧① , flavourful & juicy enough, deftly balanced for undemanding drinking. **Chardonnay-Pinot Noir** ★★★ Gleaming salmon-pink **23** ⑧① fairly dry, softly textured & inviting blend with some fragrant charm for easy drinking. **Albariño** (NEW) ★★★★ Iberian variety, one of few local bottlings. Attractive character on **22** ⑧④, combining riper stonefruit & some greener notes; brightly fresh, fairly intense if not lengthy or complex. WO Stellenbosch. **Chardonnay ★★★** Tiny part of **23** ⑧⑦ oaked to add interest to the straightforward fruit. Clean & fresh, balanced & friendly, with good citrus flavour & finish. **Chenin Blanc ★★★** Ripe notes of peach & guava on lightly rich **23** ⑧⑦, the sweet note counterpointed by firm acidity. **Sauvignon Blanc** ⊘ **★★★★** As usual, some green notes emerge, indicating some cooler origins amongst the W Cape blend of **23** ⑧④. But passionfruit & some guava dominate the flavourfulness. Brightly balanced, dry & fresh.

Cap Classique

★★★★ Brut Rosé ⊘ Fresher, drier & more incisively elegant than many local rosé sparklers. **21** ⑧⑥ no exception. Fruit rather light, but in balance with lively whole, & it lingers on the cool, dry finish. From pinot noir, 14 months before disgorging. WO W Cape.

★★★★ Brut ⊘ Baked apple notes predominate on flavoursome, dry & fresh **20** ⑧⑧ bubbly from Stellenbosch chardonnay (68%) & pinot. 2 years on lees leave it well balanced, lively drinking.

★★★★☆ Brut RD ⑫ 84 months on lees, **13** ★★★★★ ⑨⑤ disgorged November 2020. Near-equal chardonnay & pinot noir, tiny portion oaked; fine mousse, bruised apple & brioche showing the lees & maturity effect yet still vibrant, in perfect condition. Last was **09** ⑨③.

Ideology

Not tasted: **Cinsaut, Shiraz-Mourvèdre, Albariño, Chenin Blanc, Riesling, Sauvignon Blanc, Chardonnay-Chenin Blanc-Viognier.**

Discontinued: **Spier 5.5%, Spier De-alcoholised 0.5%, Drakenskloof.** — TJ

Location/map: Stellenbosch ▪ Map grid reference: C7 ▪ WO: Coastal/Western Cape/Stellenbosch/Cape Town ▪ Est 1692 ▪ 1stB 1770 ▪ Tasting & sales Mon-Sun 9-5 (seasonal times apply) ▪ Tasting from R45 ▪ Facilities for children ▪ Tour groups ▪ Farm produce ▪ Picnics ▪ Meeting rooms ▪ Manor House & Heritage Walk ▪ Conservation area ▪ Spier Hotel ▪ Spier Farm Café & Spier Hotel Restaurant ▪ Vadas Smokehouse & Bakery ▪ Online shop ▪ Owner(s) Enthoven family ▪ MD Frans Smit ▪ Cellarmaster(s) Johan Jordaan ▪ Winemaker(s) Heidi Dietstein (reds & cap classique), Anthony Kock (whites), Tania Kleintjes (organic wine) ▪ Wine procurement/winemaker(s) Anton Swarts (CWM), Lizanne Jordaan ▪ Viticulturist(s) Bennie Liebenberg ▪ 650ha (cabs s/f, malbec, merlot, mourv, p verdot, ptage, shiraz, chard, chenin, sauv, sem, viog) ▪ 7,400t own label 65% red 31% white 3% rosé 1% MCC ▪ BSCI, FSSC 22000, IPW, Organic, WIETA, WWF-SA Conservation Champion ▪ PO Box 99 Lynedoch 7603 ▪ info@spier.co.za ▪ www.spier.co.za ▪ **T +27 (0)21-809-1100 (wine tasting)**

Spijkerbessie Wyne

For her appealingly packaged Spijker and Bessie boutique wines (in life, a bull and cow), career viticulturist and lately grape buyer Annelie Viljoen sources best-quality wine and blends it to show 'personality and true Stellenbosch character'. The new Börls sparkler is a nice wordplay, 'borrels' being bubbles in Afrikaans.

★★★★ Bessie Sauvignon Blanc ⊘ Perfume leaps out the glass, lime & lemongrass, **23** ⑧⑦ clearly cool-grown, reductive winemaking intensifies the flavours. Mouthfilling, with zesty acid lift.

Spijker Malbec ⑫ **★★★★** Supple & juicy **21** ⑧⑤, with meaty-savoury notes. Appealing red berry fruit, smooth powdery tannin attesting to year in barrel. **Börls Cap Classique Brut** (NEW) **★★★★** From pinot noir, **NV** ⑧④ sleek, bone-dry, relatively brief 18 months on lees, so freshness & youth abound. Gentle biscuit shading to the red berry fruit. Not tasted: **Pinotage.** — CR

Location/WO: Stellenbosch ▪ Est/1stB 2020 ▪ Closed to public ▪ Online sales ▪ Owner(s)/winemaker(s)/viticulturist(s) Annelie Viljoen ▪ 20t/3,333cs own label 50% red 50% white + 1,000 btls MCC ▪ info@spijkerbessie.co.za ▪ www.spijkerbessie.co.za

Spioenkop Wines ⊘

When a serious car accident prevented winemaker Koen Roose from completing the 2022 harvest at this Belgian-family-owned boutique property in Elgin, few in the industry doubted that he would return. And he has, as witty, passionate and committed to the vineyard on the nutrient-poor plateau but without his 'ladies', the rare-in-Elgin chenin blancs named for Boer War figures Johanna Brandt and Sarah Raal. We hope they return next year. In the meantime, there are the estate-grown Pinotage and Riesling to enjoy plus the 1900 wines, more affordable but as carefully crafted from other Elgin and Stellenbosch fruit.

Spioenkop range

★★★★☆ **Pinotage** Celebrates both the variety, in its vibrant mulberry & raspberry fruit purity, & Elgin's cool climate, in its modest 12.8% alc. **21** ⑨ⓛ fresh, satisfyingly dry & for earlier enjoyment than previous.

★★★★☆ **Riesling** Different mould to stellar **18** ⑨④, **19** ⑨ⓛ has gram sugar softening signature arresting acid & dryness. Attractive lime & peach still there, but as understudies to developed kerosene character.

Not tasted: **Johanna Brandt**, **Sarah Raal**.

1900 range

★★★★ **Pinot Noir** ⊘ Drops 'GLB' from name. Energetic & very satisfying **18** ⑧⑧ has good depth of dark fruit & appealing undergrowth nuance, smooth, savoury tannins ably supported by 15% new oak. Structured to improve a few years.

★★★★ **Pinot Noir M.G.** ⊘ 'Prettier, more delicate' of the pinots, ex single-vineyard named Mahatma Gandhi. **18** ⑧⑦ subtle earthy tones over cranberry & raspberry fruit, smoky touch from 20% new oak. Good now & for a few years.

★★★★ **Pinotage** Treading lightly with 13% alc, **20** ⑨② abundant ripe as well as slightly unripe mulberry fruit (adding welcome piquancy), bracing dryness, supple tannins & 40% new oak in unobtrusive support. WO Stellenbosch.

★★★★ **Sauvignon Blanc** Last tasted was **17** ⑧⑥, **21** ⑧⑥ slightly bigger (13.5% alc vs 12.6%) & rounded by few grams sugar but no less charming. Creamy & subtle, with delicate white florals, blackcurrant & leaf accents, signature stony acid lengthening the finish.

★★★★☆ **Queen Manthatisi** Change from sauvignon, chenin & riesling in last **18** ⑨⓪ to sauvignon & chardonnay in **20** ★★★★ ⑧⑦. The Loire grape dominates the Burgundy one, bringing cool green fruit to the blend, easy to drink but shade less thrilling. 10% new oak.— CvZ

Location/map: Elgin ▪ Map grid reference: C4 ▪ WO: Elgin/Stellenbosch ▪ Est 2008 ▪ 1stB 2010 ▪ Tasting & sales by appt only ▪ Tasting fee R150pp, waived on purchase ▪ Pre-booking required for: tasting & cellar tour R150pp; speciality tasting, exclusive vineyard walk with winemaker R250pp ▪ Closed all pub hols ▪ Owner(s) Valuline 119 (Pty) Ltd, 5 shareholders ▪ Cellarmaster(s)/winemaker(s)/viticulturist(s) Koen Roose-Vandenbroucke (2008) ▪ ±47ha/12ha (ptage, pinot, chenin, riesling, sauv, sem) ▪ 60t/8,000cs own label 63% red 37% white ▪ PO Box 340 Grabouw 7160 ▪ info@spioenkopwines.co.za ▪ www.spioenkopwines.co.za ▪ T +27 (0)72-440-2944

Spookfontein Wines ⓥ ⑪ ⌂ ⎙

Among the longer-established ventures in Upper Hemel-en-Aarde Valley, Spookfontein was acquired by the Davis family more than two decades ago as a weekend getaway and developed into today's multifaceted destination, with a vineyard and portfolio differentiated from others in the area in their accent on Bordeaux grapes. Andries Gotze, viticulturist since inception, has now been joined by Dewald Grobler in the cellar.

★★★★ **Cabernet Sauvignon** Concentrated blackcurrant flavour & fresh leafiness on **21** ⑧⑧, dusty tannin & cedar from 16 months in small barrels. Enlivening acid adds length to brisk finish.

★★★★☆ **Cabernet Franc** ⊘ Lovely cool-climate example entices with perfume & herbaceous tang of greenpepper lifting the ripe blackberry fruit of **20** ⑨ⓛ. Tarry well-integrated tannin & clean zesty length complete a well-executed wine.

★★★★ **Merlot** ⓧ Balanced & fresh **21** ⑧⑦ from 3 Hemel-en-Aarde soil types. Approachably supple, well-judged oak adds structure & weight. Good potential, raises bar on last-tasted **18** ★★★ ⑧②.

★★★★ **Syrah** Warm, spicy **22** ⑧⑨ mixes red & black plums & cherries with top notes of perfume & pepper. 15% new barrels add smoked meat & tar, time in old foudres mellow the elegant tannins. WO Cape South Coast, last-tasted **20** ⑧⑦ was Hemel-en-Aarde Valley.

★★★★ **Phantom** Attractive & rounded black-fruited **21** ★★★★☆ ⑨⓪ Bordeaux blend shows freshness & spice of leading cab components (45% sauvignon, 31% franc) wrapping the sweetness of merlot. Pliable tannin structure creates accessible wine, brighter than merlot-led **20** ⑧⑧.

★★★★ **Chardonnay** Citrus fruit cocktail (orange, grapefruit) **22** ⑧⑦ wrapped in toasty, creamy oak, 10 months, none new. Oatmeal graininess in centre, lacks some freshness of previous. Hemel-en-Aarde Ridge fruit, as next.

★★★★ **Sauvignon Blanc** Greengage & orange zest on bone-dry 23 (86), on the zesty side of this grape, eschewing tropical notes. Savoury edge from lees contact adds interest to finish.

★★★★ **Full Moon** Savoury & weighty 23 (89) from chardonnay & chenin, 15% sauvignon adding brisk acid to white peach, green apple & soft apricot fruit. 61% in old oak, plastic 'egg' making up balance. Very satisfying partner for creamy seafood pasta. WO Cape South Coast.

Pinot Noir ★★★★ Red cherry fruit on slender 21 (84) just handles charry oak, year, none new, adding meaty spice. Lovely acid, as all the reds, but this needs more punch of fruit for higher rating. **Rosé** ★★★★ Fresh & crisp 23 (84) from merlot, splashes pinot noir & chardonnay. Savoury-edged cranberry fruit shows smoothness from old-oak ferment & dry finish. Not tasted: **Méthode Cap Classique**, **Cape Ruby**. — CM

Location: Hermanus ▪ Map: Walker Bay & Bot River ▪ Map grid reference: B4 ▪ WO: Upper Hemel-en-Aarde Valley/Cape South Coast/Hemel-en-Aarde Ridge ▪ Est 2000 ▪ 1stB 2004 ▪ Tasting & sales Mon-Sat 10-4.30 Sun/ pub hols 10-4; pub hols (seasonal) please call ahead ▪ Closed Dec 25/26 & Jan 1 ▪ Restaurant @ Spookfontein open for lunch ▪ Functions ▪ Two self-catering guest cottages ▪ Conservation area ▪ Owner(s) Spookfontein Wines cc ▪ Winemaker(s) Dewald Grobler (2023) ▪ Viticulturist(s) Andries Gotze (Jan 2000) ▪ 313ha/±12ha (cabs s/f, merlot, pinot, chard) ▪ 50t/2,000cs own label 85% red 10% white 5% rosé ▪ PO Box 12031 Mill Str Cape Town 8010 ▪ info@spookfontein.co.za ▪ www.spookfontein.co.za ▪ **T +27 (0)28-125-0128**

Spotswood Wines (♀)

The Spotswoods, Bill and son Nick, based their boutique winery on the family farm Down The Road in Stellenbosch's Blaauwklippen Valley after moving south from Polokwane over 15 years ago. They chose the road less travelled in working with some niche varieties like durif/petite sirah for their 'high-quality, easy-drinking and affordable' wines, made from grapes mostly grown by Bill, so for them it's especially satisfying that for the first time they have both the red and pink versions of durif on release simultaneously.

★★★★ **Durif** With dash shiraz, inky 22 (87) very young & showing ample perfumed plum & mulberry fruit, firm tannin & savoury-spicy finish. Well-structured for ageing, best decanted in youth. No 21.

★★★★ **Sauvignon Blanc** Gentle tropical flavours on 22 ★★★★ (85), balanced & moreish, with a citrus lift at the end. Lighter styled than last 20 (86) for pleasurable early enjoyment.

Shiraz (♀) ★★★★ Soft black fruit on 21 (83) along with firmer, grainier tannins than 20 ★★★★ (89), also missing some of the balance & length noted last time. **Durif Dry Rosé** ★★★★ Refreshing cranberry & red plum flavours on deep pink 23 (85). Softly dry, easy, with a savoury aftertaste. **Shiraz Dry Rosé** (♀) ★★★ Bunch pressed & briefly oaked, juicy & fun 22 (82) is rosepetal pink with red berry & spice notes. Chill well. **Chardonnay** (♀) ★★★ Delicate apple & pear flavours on a light body, now-unoaked 21 (80) as easygoing as last. **Viognier** (⊘) ★★★★ Previewed last time & noted as less engaging than 21 ★★★★ (86), now-bottled 22 (85) has settled & continues to offer peach blossom perfume, nectarine & vanilla spice from ferment/8 months in barrel. In abeyance: **Chenin Blanc**. — WB

Location/map/WO: Stellenbosch ▪ Map grid reference: F7 ▪ Est 2007 ▪ 1stB 2008 ▪ Tasting & sales by appt ▪ Owner(s) Spotswood family ▪ Winemaker(s) various (from 2018) ▪ Viticulturist(s) Bill Spotswood (Sep 2007) ▪ 7.05ha/3ha (durif, shiraz, chard, viog) ▪ 28t/3,000cs own label 56% red 19% white 25% rosé ▪ Suite 200 Private Bag X4 Die Boord 7613 ▪ spotswoodwines@gmail.com ▪ www.spotswoodwines.com ▪ **T +27 (0)83-395-5566**

Springfontein Wine Estate (♀) (¶¶) (⌂) (◎)

A radical, passionate originality rules on this patch of maritime limestone soil near Stanford. Springfontein Rim is the name of the Wine of Origin ward, with Springfontein its sole estate. Organic principles govern the approach of Jeanne Vito and her team in both cellar and vineyards, along with the consonance of winemaking and viticulture - spontaneous ferment, for example. The unique focus is on 'terroir-specific expression' of South Africa's varietal calling cards, chenin blanc and pinotage; the rare white grape chenel, a local crossing, is sharpening the strategy: the first bottled Chenel has now been released. The approach continues in the fine-dining restaurant, Wortelgat, with 'terroir-driven wine and food pairings'. There are also the Ulumbaza Wine Bar(n) and other attractions, and the accommodation offering is being further developed.

Limestone Rocks range

★★★★☆ **Gadda da Vida** (♀) (🐝) There's a powerful, characterful vitality on 18 (94) from pinotage with 30% petit verdot, from aromatic opening to dense, firmly structured palate with its sweet fruit core, & dry finish. All-new wood integrating well by now, tannic structure very firm but in tune with impressive fruit. 14% alc. Drinking well now, but no hurry. An original contribution to the Cape Blend, like Lotta.

★★★★ **Child in Time** ② Muscle-bound, dense **17** ⑧⑧ reverses Vida: petit verdot with 15% pinotage, but here oak is 80% new, creating a spice backdrop to almost overwhelming extract & fruit intensity.

★★★★☆ **Whole Lotta Love** ♡ ⓐ Half from previous vintage - its dark fruit permeating the whole - with petit verdot, shiraz & a little chenin blanc. **18** ⑨④ full, intense & succulent, fruit moving into tertiary, more savoury phase, though the wine still developing. 40% new oak well absorbed. Firm but cushiony structure, dry finish. Big, muscular wine, perhaps rather rustic in best sense but also with some elegance.

★★★★☆ **Dark Side of The Moon** ② Unlikely but successful blend of skin-contact chenin & chardonnay with pinotage vinified as white, all wild-yeast fermented. **17** ⑨① fresher, brighter than last, retaining charming marmalade notes, plump roundness. 18 months in oak don't intrude. Walker Bay WO, as Child.

Single Vineyard range

★★★★☆ **Jonathan's Ridge Pinotage** ② Perfumed **18** ⑨⓪ a serious, vibrant wine that manages big varietal tannins well & handles 14.8% alc without suggesting excess. Bunch pressing, indigenous yeast.

★★★★ **Jil's Dune Chenin Blanc** ② 70% oaked component, 30% new, 10 months, a notable presence on **18** ⑧⑧, but some ripe fruit intensity too, stonefruit & a tropical note. **17** ★★★★☆ ⑨⓪ more restrained with wood influence, unlike **16** ★★★★ ⑧④.

Daredevils' Drums range

★★★★ **Blushes Inverse** ♡ Light red-gold **21** ★★★★☆ ⑨⓪ from carefully vinified pinotage, making for what amounts to unusual, attractive & intensely flavourful white wine. Textured richness helped by some unobvious sweetness & grippy acidic structure, supported by oaking, 25% new. 13% alc. Altogether well balanced. **20** ⑧⑨ equally idiosyncratic.

Terroir Selection

★★★★ **Pinotage** ♡ Dark & red fruit on perfumed **20** ⑧⑨. Velvet texture, tannins gentle but dry, succulent & informing, bright acidity a useful part of the good balance. Drinking very well now, thanks to generously late release, as all these wines. 13% alc.

★★★★ **Chenin Blanc** ♡ Confident, full aromas of peach, fynbos, melon on **21** ⑧⑧. Fairly rich, part in old oak helps here; remainder in tank for freshness. Overall, lively & fresh but softly textured. 13% alc.

★★★★☆ **Ikhalezi Noble Late Harvest** ② Botrytised chenin **13** ⑨⓪, first since **09** ⑨⓪, 46 months in barrel, shows advanced development, caramel toffee rounding out dried apricot. 375 ml. WO Walker Bay.

★★★★ **Chenel** (NEW) ② Seriously treated, perhaps unique varietal example of local chenin & ugni blanc crossing. Aromas of **20** ⑧⑥ recall peachy chenin, but flavours more distinctive. Oaking, 25% new, adds spice & vanilla. A pleasing, dry wine, quite grippy, enriched by 8 months on lees.

Ulumbaza range

★★★★ **Red of Springfontein** ♡ Shiraz in the lead for **20** ⑧⑥, usual partners merlot, cab & pinotage. Plenty of ripe, darker, spicy fruit on offer, untrammelled by older oak. Fresh, succulent & balanced; friendly & charming but no pushover.

★★★★ **White of Springfontein** ② ♡ Sauvignon & semillon lead chardonnay & pinotage on light gold **20** ⑧⑥, lovely forward character, soft, slightly chalky texture. Tangy & dry, like **19** ★★★★ ⑧④.

Pink of Springfontein ② ♡ ★★★ Pinotage & merlot in salmon-hued **20** ⑧②. Flavourful though not lingering, bone-dry & brightly balanced. — TJ

Location: Stanford ▪ Map: Walker Bay & Bot River ▪ Map grid reference: B5 ▪ WO: Springfontein Rim/Walker Bay ▪ Est 1996 ▪ 1stB 2004 ▪ Ulumbaza Wine Bar(n) @ Springfontein: bistro & wine tasting/sales 11am-9pm daily; pub hols (seasonal) please call ahead ▪ Wortelgat @ Springfontein: wine & food pairing fine dining (booking essential) ▪ Cellar tours ▪ Klein River cruises & tasting onboard African Queen of Springfontein and the River Rat cruises ▪ Walking/hiking trail ▪ B&B accommodation: Milkwood Cottage, Fisherman's Cottage, Riverside suites, River Lodge rooms ▪ Owner(s) Johst Weber with family, friends & employees ▪ Vigneron(ne) team: Jeanne Vito, with Schalk van der Westhuizen, Jaack Louw, Brian Ntonya, supported by Juan Louw et al ▪ 300ha/30ha (predominantly ptage, chenel, chenin) ▪ 100t/12,500cs own label 70% red 25% white 5% rosé ▪ Certified organic by Ecocert (vyds & cellar) ▪ PO Box 71 Stanford 7210 ▪ info@springfontein.co.za ▪ www.springfontein.co.za ▪ **T +27 (0)28-341-0651**

☐ **Stablemate** *see* Excelsior Estate
☐ **Staggerwing** *see* Fuselage Wines

Stamboom

Strandveld winemaker Conrad Vlok first bottled this own-wine from windswept Elim 20 years ago, naming it 'Family Tree' to reflect both the familial nature of the blend and the involvement of his nearest and dearest, wife Suzán and children Nicholas and Marié, in crafting the handful of barrels with care and dedication.

★★★★ **Stamboom** The child, pinotage, & its parents, pinot noir & cinsaut (33/19). Prominent red fruit from all, the 10 month oaking keeping it serious, focused, but without edges. **20** ⑧⑨ cool-climate Cape Blend, with touch of vinous history.— CR

Location/WO: Elim ▪ 1stB 2004 ▪ Tasting by appt only ▪ Winemaker(s) Conrad Vlok ▪ info@vlokfamilywines.co.za ▪ www.vlokfamilywines.co.za ▪ **T +27 (0)82-328-3824**

Stanford Hills Winery

'We use ducks and cattle in the vineyards, and natural products as far as we can,' say owners Peter and Jami Kastner of the regenerative viticulture and minimalist vinification they have been practicing at their cool-climate farm near Stanford the past few years, under the guidance of viticulturist and assistant winemaker Mark Stephens. 'The results are really starting to show. Life is returning to the soil, and vitality is showing in the vines and wines.' The latter can be sampled on-site, as part of a notably varied visitor offering.

Stanford Hills range

★★★★ **Sauvignon Blanc** ⊘ From 3 separate pickings, **23** ⑧⑥ fig, flint & capsicum typicity with rounded breadth. Lees adds palate weight & presence to lively freshness.

★★★★ **Méthode Cap Classique** ⊗ Characterful, vivacious **17** ⑧⑧ dry fizz from chardonnay (60%) & pinotage, intense red apple scents & flavours, 48 months on lees add pleasing richness, abundant brioche.

Jacksons Pinotage ★★★★ Youngberry & raspberry vivacity on engaging **20** ⑧⑤, improves on previous in absence of slight acetone element. **Reserve Shiraz** ★★★★ Pretty **21** ⑧⑤ improves on last, ripe plum & blueberry fruit, succulence & vanilla. Light footed despite 20 months in oak, 15% new, aided by 20% wholebunch portion. **Shiraz Rosé** ★★★★ Appealing pomegranate hue on **23** ⑧④. Bright, fresh & light, with juicy cherries & chalky, satisfyingly dry finish. **Chardonnay** ★★★★ Fresh citrus tang on **22** ⑧④, wild yeast fermented in older oak. Creamy lees breadth & light, dry conclusion. Improves on previous.

Veldfire range

Pinotage ⊘ ★★★★ Spicy blueberry- & plum-toned **22** ⑧⑤ is unoaked, soft & fruity, easy to like. WO Walker Bay. **Cape Blend** ⊘ ★★★★ Shiraz holds sway over third pinotage in **22** ⑧⑤. Inky black fruit with density & grip courtesy of 65% oaking, all old, 10 months. Matches previous in body & length. **Rosé** ★★★★ Cranberry zip on **23** ⑧④ pink from pinotage, vivid acid & lemon tang counter berry ripeness. Modest 11.5% alc. Not tasted: **White Pinotage**. — FM

Location: Stanford ▪ Map: Walker Bay & Bot River ▪ Map grid reference: B6 ▪ WO: Stanford Foothills/Walker Bay ▪ Est 1856 ▪ 1stB 2002 ▪ Tasting, sales & restaurant Mon-Sun 8.30-5; pub hols 8-5 ▪ Grappa, preserves ▪ Restaurant: breakfast & deli, picnic baskets ▪ Functions & events (up to 180 pax) ▪ Hiking/MTB trails ▪ Horse riding ▪ Fishing ▪ Whale watching flights from own airfield ▪ 2 self-catering cottages & main farmhouse (sleeps up to 22 pax) plus AfriCamps at Stanford Hills (up to 25 guests) ▪ Owner(s) Stanford Hills Estate (Pty) Ltd ▪ Cellarmaster(s) Peter Kastner (Apr 2005) ▪ Winemaker(s) Peter Kastner (Apr 2005), with Mark Stephens (Feb 2019) ▪ Viticulturist(s) Mark Stephens ▪ 131ha/12ha (ptage, shiraz, chard, sauv) ▪ 60t/4,000cs own label 66% red 34% white ▪ PO Box 1052 Stanford 7210 ▪ info@stanfordhills.co.za, living.vineyards@gmail.com, peter@stanfordhills.co.za ▪ www.stanfordhills.co.za ▪ **T +27 (0)28-341-0841**

Stanford Valley Wines

Reinder Nauta's extensive estate near Stanford is home to a luxury country lodge, whose guests can now not only drink in the natural beauty of the surrounds but also sip on debut wines from young vines that flank the guest amenities. The Rhône blend and chenin, untasted by us, were styled by winemaker-viticulturist Helanie Olivier to be pure, elegant and balanced, for food pairing. A cap classique is the next release.

Location: Stanford ▪ Est 2022 ▪ Wines available at the Manor House Restaurant (Wed-Sun), Stanford Valley Country Lodge ▪ Gift shop ▪ Walking/hiking trails ▪ MTB ▪ Art gallery ▪ Spa treatments ▪ Swimming ▪ Owner(s) Reinder Nauta ▪ Winemaker(s) Helanie Olivier (Jan 2022, consultant) ▪ Vineyard manager Gary Snyders (Jan 2022, consultant) ▪ Viticulturist(s) Helanie Olivier & Juan Louw (Jan 2022, consultants) ▪ 440ha/3ha (grenache, pinot, shiraz, chard, chenin) ▪ 17t own label 29% red 24% white 47% MCC ▪ stanfordvalley.co.za

☐ **Star Catcher** *see Stellar Winery*

Stark-Condé Wines   ⓦ ⓟ ⓑ

Founded in 1998 on the historic Oude Nektar estate in Stellenbosch's Jonkershoek Valley, and latterly part of the MAN Vintners portfolio, Stark-Condé is one of SA's most-awarded cabernet producers. A mid-harvest mountain fire in 2021 thankfully avoided damaging vines but did cause the loss of the flagship Three Pines cabernet vintage (and its syrah sibling) due to smoke taint. Fortunately some blocks used for the Stellenbosch range version were unaffected and, supplemented with brought-in grapes, bottled for a limited release. The cabernet accent continues at the tasting room in the middle of the farm lake, where guests are invited to compare three distinct expressions, grown at different altitudes. The Postcard Café remains a popular destination for locals and foreign visitors, who enjoy the relaxed atmosphere and stunning views.

High Altitude range

★★★★☆ **Oude Nektar Cabernet Sauvignon** ⓐ Unfined/filtered, as all reds, indicative of the traditional handcrafting. **20** ⑨③ is 100% cab, eschewing **19** ★★★★★ ⑨⑤'s dab petit verdot. From highest vineyard on estate, hence fresh herb & citrus lift to seamless & harmonious palate, its depth & breadth exquisitely supported by fine tannins & oak, 22 months, 50% new.

★★★★☆ **Three Pines Cabernet Sauvignon** ⓥ Following regal **19** ★★★★★ ⑨⑤, **20** ⑨③ from 31 year old vines, perfumed, pure & berry-fruited, full bodied yet retains elegance through inherent energy, tempered by silky tannins & 22 months in 50% new oak. Dabs petit verdot, cab franc & malbec add complexity. Hand harvested, wild fermented, basket pressed & made for the long haul, like most of the reds.

★★★★☆ **Three Pines Syrah** ⓥ Oldest syrah parcel on property shows remarkable restrained power & concentration, combined with suppleness in **20** ⑨④. Ample fruit, spice & well-judged oak, 15% new, 22 months. Gentle white pepper sprinkle on finish.

Stellenbosch range

★★★★☆ **Cabernet Sauvignon** ⓐ From 7 blocks in Jonkershoek & Helderberg, dabs cab franc & petit verdot for depth & interest. **21** ⑨③ rich, rounded, with firmly structured tannin & oak, 30% new barrels, 20 months. Violet-perfumed blackcurrant, crushed green herb & tealeaf, gentle mocha carry to finish.

★★★★☆ **Petite Sirah** ⓥ Dark ruby **20** ⑨⓪ from small block on home-farm. Gentle handling of concentrated fruit produces a lovely redolence of dark plum & mulberry, & a balanced acid structure. 10% American oak in sync with the fruit character. Stellenbosch WO, as Cab & Syrah.

★★★★☆ **Syrah** ⓥ Components from 3 different elevations & 1% each co-fermented viognier & roussanne create silky, curvaceous & moreish **20** ⑨④, with perfumes of violet & lavender, brooding dark berries, spice & smoke. 22 months in oak, 10% new.

★★★★★ **Monk Stone Chenin Blanc** ⓐ Perfect follow-up to **21** ⑨⑤ debut, **22** ⑨⑥ from same elevated 15 year old Jonkershoek vines. Lovely interplay of fresh & baked apple & quince, steely minerality, acid & cream from 9 months lees-ageing in amphora & barrel, plus portion wholebunch. Intriguing, with deceptive lightness to flavour intensity. Needs time to fully reveal its charms.

★★★★☆ **Round Mountain Sauvignon Blanc** ⓐ An individual, with abundant tropical, green herb & citrus flavours & aromas, lipsmacking grapefruit finish. **22** ⑨③ concentrated, creamy & textured from barrel ferment & extended lees ageing of grapes from mature 30 year old vineyard. Will age gracefully.

★★★★★ **The Field Blend** ⓐ Rich, rounded & harmonious, **22** ★★★★★ ⑨④'s array of scents & tastes run gamut from florals to peach & to earthiness. 58% roussanne with chenin, viognier & verdelho intricately vinified: barrel, 'egg' & amphora (10/5) co-ferment & lees stirring, 9 months. Made for ageing, though as irresistible as **21** ⑨⑤. — WB

Location/map: Stellenbosch ▪ Map grid reference: G6 ▪ WO: Jonkershoek Valley/Stellenbosch ▪ Est/1stB 1998 ▪ Tasting room & wine sales open daily 9-4 ▪ Fee from R95pp ▪ Closed Dec 25 & Jan 1 ▪ Postcard Café open daily 9-4 ▪ Owner(s) MAN Vintners (Pty) Ltd ▪ Cellarmaster(s) José Conde (1998) ▪ Winemaker(s) Rüdger van Wyk (2017) ▪ Viticulturist(s) Andrew Klinck ▪ 250ha/40ha (cabs s/f, p verdot, shiraz) ▪ 250t/12,000cs own label 80% red 20% white ▪ PO Box 389 Stellenbosch 7599 ▪ info@stark-conde.co.za ▪ www.stark-conde.co.za ▪ **T +27 (0)21-861-7700**

☐ **Starlette** *see Allée Bleue Wines*

Steel Wines

For his young boutique brand, Jason Steel sources grapes from special sites around Robertson Valley to handcraft 'interesting wines with as little intervention as possible and showcase the terroir'.

★★★★☆ **Chenin Blanc** (NEW) Robertson sunshine reflected in expressive pineapple, melon & lime flavours, balanced by clean mineral acid. **22** (92), like Colombard, 14 months in old Vin de Constance barrels, adding fine texture to generous fruit.

★★★★ **Colombard** More tropical toned & touch riper in **22** (89) than **21** ★★★★★ (91) (13% alc vs 11.5%) though both vintages from same 1987 parcel. Core of sweet fruit (guava, mango) kept in check by 9 months in large oak.

Not tasted: **Cinsault**, **Red**. In abeyance: **Cabernet Sauvignon**. — ML

Location/WO: Robertson ▪ Est 2019 ▪ 1stB 2020 ▪ Closed to public ▪ Owner(s) Jason Steel ▪ Winemaker(s) Jason Steel (Feb 2019) ▪ 3t/195cs own label 47% red 53% white ▪ jasonsteel100@gmail.com ▪ **T +27 (0)84-519-5324**

Steenberg Vineyards   (Ⓠ) (Ⓜ) (🏠) (◎) (♿)

Steenberg is the most southerly of the Constantia winefarms, thus more open to the cooling winds off False Bay. This, coupled with decomposed granite soils, giving minerality, and different vineyard slopes, including south-east, contribute to cool-climate wines. It follows that the focus is on sauvignon, in six varietal bottlings and blends. Viticulturally, much effort is spent on ensuring perfect matches of clones to soils to climate, with an emphasis on natural, sustainable practices. Recent activities on the estate include refurbishment of the restaurants, and the tasting room and spa/hotel terraces. There has also been an upgrade of irrigation, dam maintenance and replanting of old sauvignon vineyards, plus the installation of more riddling racks. On the ownership side, David Burford has been appointed new CEO of Beck Family Estates.

Icon range

★★★★☆ **Magna Carta** (🐝) Admirable Bordeaux white, seriously styled & intended for ageing a decade. Sauvignon with 30% semillon, fermented/8 months in 400-600L barrels, 40% new. **21** ★★★★★ (95) shows melba toast & winter melon, lemongrass, with a rounded texture, mouthfilling flavours, great length & freshness. Last tasted was **17** (94).

Flagship range

★★★★★ **Nebbiolo** (🐝) One of only a few standalone bottlings in SA, **18** (91) is meaty, savoury, the fruit black plums, an expected tannin foundation but well managed (24 months, 30% new barrels), firm but ripe. Destined to age but already accessible with robust food. Something different & hugely appealing. Back on track after **17** ★★★★ (89).

★★★★★ **Catharina** (🐝) Flagship Bordeaux red from merlot (59%), cab & malbec, & treated accordingly: 2 years in barriques, 60% new, then best-barrel selection. Full-ripe **20** (94) is power-packed with cassis & cherries, dusted with cedar, an intriguing mint chocolate seam. Complex, involving, plenty to applaud including the fine tannins, a hidden strength.

★★★★★ **The Black Swan Sauvignon Blanc** (🐝) Best fruit selection from top 2 vineyards, unwooded. Same handling as predecessors, skin contact plus 9 months on lees, **22** (93) is quintessential cool-climate sauvignon & Steenberg's pièce de résistance. Complex minerality & green notes, including fig, crisply dry yet textured. Great purity & focus, as also noted on **21** ★★★★★ (95).

★★★★☆ **Semillon** (🐝) Ideal terroir for semillon, ripe-picked, oak fermented/3 months on lees, then barrel-matured 10 months. **22** ★★★★★ (96) responded with lanolin & honey biscuit tones, brightened by lemon thyme. Full & round, a long textured finish. Similar winemaking on **21** (94).

Occasional release: **Sauvignon Blanc-Semillon**.

Classic range

★★★★☆ **Merlot** ⊘ 🐝 Like all reds, crafted to age, with concentrated dark fruit interleaved with cigarbox spice from 2 years in seasoned barriques. **20** ⑨⓪'s tannins are masked by succulence to allow current enjoyment, but are there as an ageing backbone.

★★★★ **Chardonnay** Sourced from Robertson, bunch pressed, 7 months in barriques, half new, plus large-format oak. Lots of care taken to preserve fruit, **22** ⑧⑦ has expressive citrus, especially ruby grapefruit & lemon, a toasty top note. Finishes fruity-fresh & long.

★★★★☆ **Barrel Fermented Sauvignon Blanc** ⊘ Selected blocks, barrel fermented/7 months larger oak plus concrete 'egg'. Pea & greengage, some grassy notes but **22** ⑨⓪ shows its oak influence in a gentle smoky nuance, long savoury flavours & finish. Beautifully crafted, the perfect wood-fruit marriage.

★★★★☆ **Sauvignon Blanc** ⊘ In an area renowned for sauvignon, it's fitting that Steenberg should have 4 in its range, including a bubbly. **23** ⑨⓪ in the house style: from different blocks, picked at different times, long slow ferment, very long lees contact. It all shows in multiple layers of grapefruit & fennel, with a tropical seam, vibrantly fresh.

Ruby Rosé ☺ ★★★ From syrah, pale pink **23** ⑧⓪ is dry, zesty & obviously cool-grown, with just-picked strawberry appeal for enjoyment solo or at table.

Discontinued: **Five Lives Red Blend**.

Sparkling Wines

★★★★☆ **1682 Pinot Noir Cap Classique** Salmon-hued, strawberry-toned **NV** ⑨⓪ spent 18 months on lees, allowing the fruit & freshness centre stage without the usual honey ageing effect. Elegant, dry, with a fine mousse, the flavours are pronounced, with extended length. WO W Cape, as all these.

★★★★☆ **1682 Chardonnay Cap Classique** Latest **NV** ⑨⓪ had 18 months on lees, giving freshness & verve, intense lemon-infused flavours, nice savoury note on the elegantly dry finish. Stylish, has purity & presence.

★★★★☆ **Lady R Méthode Cap Classique** 🐝 Longest on lees of the bubblies, 52 months, classic blend of pinot noir with 30% barrel-fermented chardonnay, which **18** ⑨④ reflects as toasted brioche & mellow fruit. There's richness & depth, rounded mouthfeel, yet it's dry, with salty acid adding brightness. For those very special occasions.

Sparkling Sauvignon Blanc ⊘ 🍷 ★★★★ 2nd ferment in bottle, but **NV** ⑧④ quickly disgorged to retain sauvignon's freshness. **NV** ⑧④'s kiwi & litchi fit the touch of sugar, altogether satisfyingly tasty. — CR

Location: Constantia ▪ Map: Cape Peninsula ▪ Map grid reference: B4 ▪ WO: Constantia/Western Cape ▪ Est 1990 ▪ 1stB 1996 ▪ Tasting Mon-Sun 10-4.30 & sales 10-6 ▪ Trading hour variation on 1 January: 12-4.30 (tasting) & 12-6 (sales) ▪ Tasting from R120-R200pp subject to availability ▪ Closed Dec 25 ▪ Bistro Sixteen82; Tryn Restaurant ▪ Steenberg Hotel & Spa; conferences, weddings, functions; access to a world-class golf course, walking trail ▪ Extensive merchandising area ▪ Wine club ▪ Owner(s) Beck Family Estates ▪ CEO David Burford ▪ Cellarmaster(s) Elunda Basson (Jun 2019) ▪ 60ha (cab, malbec, merlot, nebbiolo, shiraz, sauv, sem) ▪ 990t own label 30% red 70% white ▪ WIETA ▪ PO Box 224 Steenberg 7947 ▪ info@steenbergfarm.com ▪ www.steenbergfarm.com ▪ **T +27 (0)21-713-2211**

☐ **Steenhuis** see Wine-of-the-Month Club
☐ **Steenkamp** see Groenland

Steilpad   ⓟ ⒩ⓔⓦ

'Out of this world' is estimable Jorrie du Plessis' assessment of the grape source for his debut chenin: venerable vines 'in the very heart of Swartland'. Raised on a family farm in Paarl, with fond memories of mucking in during school holidays, Jorrie's experience with Donkiesbaai and Lammershoek fruit in particular sparked his desire to work with chenin for this own label. Excitingly, the birth-farm has its own ancient 'hidden gems', not just chenin. None have been bottled solo, and the hope is to redress that missed opportunity in future releases, 'which will be quite remarkable given the wait of more than 35 years'. The ultimate dream is an on-site cellar in which to craft, naturally and carefully, wines that reveal both terroir and vintage.

★★★★☆ **Chenin Blanc** 1970s Paardeberg vines disclose their charm slowly in **22** (90), beginning with barrel-derived honey nougat & vanilla, then a tight steeliness, unfurling to peach, apricot & quince, oak refraining supportively through the memorable finish.— CR, CvZ

Location: Wellington ▪ WO: Swartland ▪ Est/1stB 2022 ▪ Tasting & sales by appt only from Mon-Fri ▪ Closed most pub hols ▪ Wine club ▪ Owner(s) Jorrie du Plessis ▪ Winemaker(s)/viticulturist(s) Jorrie du Plessis (Jan 2022) ▪ 3t/ha 220cs own label 100% white ▪ PO Box 1104 Wellington 7654 ▪ steilpadwines@gmail.com ▪ www.steilpadwines.co.za ▪ **T +27 (0)82-555-8138**

☐ **STELL** *see* Stellenrust
☐ **Stellar Organics** *see* Stellar Winery

Stellar Winery ⓘ

Established at the turn of the millennium, Stellar Winery is focused on producing quality wine that is sustainable and impacts the environment as little as possible, and on caring for its staff. Hence organic certification for all the wines; Fairtrade accreditation for both the cellar and the independent farms from which it receives organic grapes; multiple developmental initiatives; and ownership shared among an empowerment trust, the Rossouw family and others. The largest producer of certified-organic Fairtrade wines in SA, Stellar is also the biggest producer of no-added-sulphur wines in the world, exporting to markets in Europe, Asia, Africa and North America from its base at Kys Halte near Vredendal on the West Coast.

The River's End range

Pinot Noir ⓐ ⓑ ★★★ Crushed strawberry & forest floor, coffee overlay from 12 months in 25% new oak, just 11.6% alc on **19** (80) from Koekenaap grapes. Fairtrade certified, as all ranges. Not tasted: **Chenin Blanc, Sauvignon Blanc**.

The Storyteller range

NSA Cabernet Sauvignon ⓐ ⓑ ★★★☆ Intense plum, cranberry & graphite on no-sulphur-added **19** (85). Year in 25% new oak adds touch of vanilla & tannin squeeze to the medium body. Olifants River WO.

The Sensory Collection

★★★★ **Grande Reserve Shiraz** ⓐ ⓑ Barrel aged 18-24 months, half new, as next, compatible with **17** (88)'s dark fruit; has layered interest, scrub, chocolate. Whole effect richly savoury, characterful.

Grande Reserve Pinotage ⓐ ⓑ ★★★☆ Rich, bold **18** (85) less sweet, ripe than chocolate-dipped banana & cherry aromas suggest, oak rounding out muscular tannins, built to last. **Grande Reserve Chardonnay** ⓐ ⓑ ★★★☆ After year in oak, 10% new, **18** (85) makes a statement with its butterscotch aroma, creamy texture, dried peach & citrus peel flavours. Restrained alc, as all the wines. WO Koekenaap.

Stellar Organics No-Sulphur-Added range

Cabernet Sauvignon ⓐ ⓑ ★★★ Cassis & herbal aromas & flavours brushed with vanilla oak (as all these reds) in easy **21** (79). **Merlot** ⓐ ⓑ ★★★ Pulpy red berries & pleasant veneer of oak spice on smooth & easy **21** (79). **Pinotage** ⓐ ⓑ ★★★ Cappuccino waft, ripe plum & scrub in silky **21** (80), for everyday enjoyment, as all these. **Shiraz** ⓐ ⓑ ★★★ Wild herbs, spice & liquorice bathed in juicy dark berry fruit. **21** (79) supple & gluggable. **Rosé** ⓐ ⓑ ★★★ A drop of shiraz gives pink colour in fresh, orchard-fruited, zippy **22** (80) from colombard. A summer must. Koekenaap WO, as next. **Blanc de Blanc** ⓐ ⓑ ★★★ From chardonnay, showing stonefruit & hints of spice in demure **21** (78).

Running Duck range

Merlot ⓐ ⓑ ★★★ Just-dry **21** (78) is undemanding, red & black plums spiced with oak. **Shiraz** ⓐ ⓑ ★★★ Welcoming & smooth **21** (81) has ripe blueberry appeal, spice & few grams of sugar, slips down oh so easily. **Reserve Cabernet Sauvignon-Pinotage** ⓐ ⓑ ★★★ 15% pinotage in **20** (78), only 50% wooded for juicy, slightly piquant black berry & plum fruit. Koekenaap WO, as next 2. **Chardonnay** ⓐ ⓑ ★★★ Plump melon & apple flavours in nimble **21** (78). Unwooded, as next. **Chenin Blanc** ⓐ ⓑ ★★★ Abundant tropical fruit of **21** (80) served with dab of cream & wedge of lemon. **Sauvignon Blanc** ⓐ ⓑ ★★★ Crisp & dry **21** (80), greenpepper & herb flavours, fresh lime finish. **Reserve Sauvignon Blanc-Semillon** ⓐ ⓑ ★★★ Attractively lean & defined, sauvignon lending grassy aroma, 15% semillon pleasant waxiness. Unwooded **21** (82) smooth & touch salty. Discontinued: **Reserve Malbec**.

Live-A-Little range
Really Ravishing Red ⓥ ⓥ ★★★ Playful names & labels for this collection of easy-drinkers. Dry & light **NV** ⑦⑧ from shiraz & merlot offers a little red fruit & dab oak spice. Less forthcoming than name implies. **Rather Revealing Rosé** ⓥ ⓥ ★★★ Delightful pretty-in-pink **NV** ⑧⓪ is bone-dry yet rounded & fruity, gets apple tone ex chenin & plummy nuance & colour from dash pinotage. **Wildly Wicked White** ⓥ ⓥ ★★★ Faint apple & citrus flavours in barely-there, dry **NV** ⑦⑧ chenin & sauvignon combo. **Slightly Sweet & Shameless** ⓥ ⓥ ★★★ Fragrant apple blossom, melon & apricot in semi-sweet **NV** ⑦⑧ chenin & sauvignon blend. Serve well-chilled. **Somewhat Sweet & Soulful** ⓥ ⓥ ★★★ Semi-dry **NV** ⑦⑨ from shiraz & merlot adds mocha & spice from oak to its juicy red & black plum fruit.

Stellar Organics range
Chardonnay-Pinot Noir Sparkling ⓥ ⓥ ★★★ Salmon pink **NV** ⑧⓪ dry party starter has soft bubbles delivering fresh strawberry & crunchy apple flavours & texture. 50/50 pinot noir & chardonnay. Carbonated & Koekenaap WO, as sibling. **Brut Sparkling** ⓥ ⓥ ★★★ From chenin, **NV** ⑧⓪ is friendly & fun, fragrant apple & citrus flavours, creamy mousse before a dry finish.

Heaven on Earth range
★★★★☆ **Muscat d'Alexandrie** ⓥ ⓥ Consistently exceptional dessert wine from sun-dried Koekenaap muscat d'Alexandrie fermented & aged in tank. **NV** ⑨④ unctuously sweet at 150 g/L sugar, with broad, ripe & rich yellow peach, toasted almond, honey & Oriental spice tones. Yet elegant, too, with just 9.1% alc & impeccable balance, unending & intense finish. — WB

Location: Vredendal ▪ Map: Olifants River ▪ Map grid reference: B4 ▪ WO: Western Cape/Koekenaap/Olifants River ▪ Est 2000 ▪ 1stB 2001 ▪ Tasting & sales Mon-Fri 8-5 ▪ Closed all pub hols ▪ Cellar tours by appt ▪ Owner(s) Rossouw family, Stellar Empowerment Trust & others ▪ Market development Johan Grobler ▪ Winemaker(s) Derick Koegelenberg (Jan 2020) ▪ Viticulturist(s) Wilhelm Steenkamp ▪ ±68ha Stellar Farming, ±149ha independent organic producers (cab, merlot, ptage, pinot, ruby cab, shiraz, chenin, chard, muscat d'A, sauv) ▪ 11,900t ▪ Other export brands: Dig This!, Firefly, Moonlight Organics, No House Wine, Star Catcher ▪ PO Box 308 Vredendal 8160 ▪ info@stellarorganics.co.za ▪ www.stellarorganics.co.za ▪ **T +27 (0)27-216-1310**

Stellekaya Winery ⓥ
Founded just over 25 years ago by Dave and Jane Lello, with a name meaning 'home of the stars', Stellekaya has gained an international following as a boutique producer of wines from black grapes exclusively, including some locally rare ones. The owners feel their success rests on that focus, along with 'a passion for engaging what is possible, and giving our winemaker an inspiring platform for expression'. Grapes are drawn from the home-farm high on Stellenbosch Mountain and elsewhere in the 'golden triangle', and crafted by Rose Kruger in the cellar at Bosman's Crossing, on the edge of Stellenbosch town.

Limited Releases
★★★★ **Malbec** ⓥ Serious-minded single-vineyard bottling. **12** ⑧⑦'s generous mulberry & plum fruit in harmony with gripping yet ripe tannins, but will reward few years patience. Only 700 numbered bottles.
★★★★ **Orion Reserve** ⓥ Cab with merlot plus drops cab franc, malbec. Retasted mid-2018, **12** ⑧⑨'s developed character brings complexity, oxidative, savoury notes to the dark fruit. Fine tannins - tad dry from 44 months in oak. Should hold few more years.

Stellekaya range
★★★★ **Cabernet Sauvignon** ⓥ Fruitcake on **19** ⑧⑥ with tealeaf nuance. Notable acid freshness & oak, countered by flavour intensity & concentration. 30 months in older wood, touch longer than previous.
★★★★ **Malbec** Attractive lifted aromas on **20** ⑧⑧, raspberry joining plum, cherry & hint cinnamon. Palate has good freshness, too, tannins more chalky than sinewy, though still quite muscular. 28 months in barrique. Back on track after **19** ★★★★ ⑧④.
★★★★ **Merlot** ⓥ ⓐ Rich yet fresh **20** ⑧⑨ benefits from 10% perfumed cab franc, improves on last. 2 years in older oak, lemon acid & fruit-coated tannins nip & tuck ebullient berries in all the right places.
★★★★ **Hercules** ⓥ Sangiovese shows its chewy tannins & incense perfume in **21** ⑧⑦. 2 in old oak smooths any edges & glosses sweet cherry core. No splash cab this vintage.

★★★★☆ **Aquarius Reserve** ⓐ Inky graphite & herb notes of **19** ⑨¹ indicative of equal cab, cab franc & merlot portions. Dab malbec too. Layered, textured & seductive. 22 months in oak, 32% new.

★★★★☆ **Orion** ⓐ Powerful 4-way Bordeaux blend, again led by cab for **21** ⑨⁰. Has house's vibrant acid lifting dark, brooding fruit & firm tannin grip. 15% alc well integrated after 2 years in barrel.

Cygnus ⓐ ★★★☆ Delightful **23** ⑧⁵ rosé from sangiovese packed with crunchy stonefruit in a gentle tannin grip. Tasted pre-bottling. — ML

Location/map/WO: Stellenbosch ▪ Map grid reference: E5 ▪ Est 1998 ▪ 1stB 1999 ▪ Tasting by appt only, sales & cellar tours Mon-Fri 10-5; best to schedule in advance ▪ Closed all pub hols ▪ Owner(s) Dave & Jane Lello ▪ Winemaker(s) Rose Kruger (Jan 2018) ▪ Viticulturist(s) Wynand Pienaar ▪ 23ha/15ha under vine ▪ 12,000cs own label ▪ IPW ▪ PO Box 12426 Die Boord Stellenbosch 7613 ▪ info@stellekaya.com ▪ www.stellekaya.com ▪ **T +27 (0)21-883-3873**

☐ **Stellenbosch 1679** see Koelenhof Winery
☐ **Stellenbosch Drive** see Origin Wine

Stellenbosch Family Wines ⓐ

The beautiful rising phoenix labels of the international range of this boutique Stellenbosch venture are joined by a collection aimed at the local market, named Glorious, featuring equally creative packaging by artist Michelle-Lize van Wyk, a member of one of the three families behind the brand. Vinification is at Koelenhof Winery by the youthful Carlo de Vries, just 19 years old, his father Andrew, a seasoned winemaker and Koelenhof's managing director, joined by brother and son Andro, an even younger 15.

Phoenix range

★★★★ **Family Blend** ⓐ Seamless mix merlot & cab, **19** ⑧⁶'s red & dark fruit elegantly shaped by 9-12 months in old oak. Touch of Xmas cake spice on plummy finish. Big improvement on last **13** ★★ ⑦⁵.
Cabernet Sauvignon ⓐ ★★★★ Salted black liquorice opens **19** ⑧³, brambles & smoky black cherry follow; the core is pure & open, woven with fine tannins to a black-fruited finish. Step up from previous.
Merlot ⓐ ★★★ Hint of dried mint on **19** ⑧⁰, flavours of cherry coulis scented with cocoa, decent palate weight & good, firm acid. **Pinot Noir** ⓐ ★★★☆ Intriguing sumac spice on **21** ⑧⁴ joins hint clove from year in older oak. Medium body, with mixed cherries tapering easily to dry finish. Much improved from last.
Pinotage ⓐ ★★★☆ Juicy raspberry fruit on attractive & fragrant **19** ⑧⁵, polished tannins support red berries, touch of smoke on finish. **Chardonnay** ⓐ ★★★☆ Combo tank & barrel ferment for **21** ⑧³ preserves soft, tropical character, older barrels give savouriness & leesy touch. Not tasted: **CMP Legacy Red**.

Glorious range

Cabernet Sauvignon ⓐ ★★★☆ Juicy black cherries & leafy cassis for **19** ⑧³. Honest & fruity, with finespun tannins & fresh finish. **Merlot** ⓐ ★★★ Intense plum & raspberry on **20** ⑧² neatly restrained by oak, friendly choc-cherry finish. Improves on previous. **Pinot Noir** ⓐ ★★★☆ Same spicy profile & vinous weight as sibling, identical winemaking in **21** ⑧⁴ for an equally supple wine. Big step up. **Pinotage** ⓐ ★★★☆ Forest berries on lithe **19** ⑧⁵. Refreshing green herbs to red-fruited palate, cherries, raspberries, plums; all that juice cradled in soft, ripe tannins. **Family Blend** ⓐ ★★★☆ Merlot (51%) unites with blackberry-scented cab on **20** ⑧⁵. Plummy palate, with rounded tannins & seam of spice. Smooth ride ensured by buffing in old oak. More refined than last. **CMP Legacy Red** ⓐ ★★★ Mainly cab with merlot & pinot noir, **15** ⑧⁰ mouthcoating tannins & brisk acidity for beefy stews & potjies. **Chardonnay** ⓐ ★★★☆ Graceful **19** ⑧⁴ is packed with citrus freshness, a line of saltiness lifts the flavours. — ML

Location/map/WO: Stellenbosch ▪ Map grid reference: D1 ▪ Est/1stB 2013 ▪ Tasting by appt ▪ Fee R100/6 wines ▪ Sales Mon-Sat 8-6 by appt ▪ Owner(s) Renata de Vries & Michelle-Lize van Wyk ▪ Winemaker(s) Carlo de Vries, Andrew de Vries (both Jan 2013, consultants), with Andro de Vries (2019) ▪ 2,900cs own label 90% red 10% white ▪ c/o PO Box 1 Koelenhof 7605 ▪ info@stellenboschfamilywines.co.za ▪ www.stellenboschfamilywines.co.za ▪ **T +27 (0)82-835-7107**

☐ **Stellenbosch Gold** see Koelenhof Winery

Stellenbosch Hills Wines

A jauntily polka-dotted facade identifies the dynamic winery founded beside the Eerste River just short of 80 years ago under the banner Vlottenburg Cellar, after the area of Stellenbosch where the processing facility and modern-day tasting venue sit. Cellarmaster-viticulturist PG Slabbert has been here for 26 of those years, channelling fruit from today's 12 owner-growers into wines that 'exceed on quality at a reasonable price'.

Sense of Place range

★★★★☆ **Suikerboschrand** (🐝) Pinotage leads shiraz, cab & merlot on previewed **20** (93) exceptional Cape Blend. Inky, deep, concentrated & structured yet also rounded, approachable, tannins finessed by combo French & American barrels, 18 months, touch shorter duration than last **17** (94).

★★★★ **Kastanjeberg** Registered single-vineyard chenin, **21** (89) maintains form in its baked quince, spice & stonefruit flavour, lovely line of fresh acid. Year new barrels provides integrated support & creamy richness, refinement.

★★★★ **Anna Christina Méthode Cap Classique** (⊘) All-chardonnay sparkling in **20** (88) improves on **18** ★★★ (81) with vivid citrus & apple tang balanced by creamy mid-palate from 12 months on lees.

1707 Reserve range

★★★★ **Red** (⊘) Spicy, ripe & pliable syrah blend with cab, merlot & petit verdot in **18** ★★★★☆ (90). 18 months in French & American oak mute some fruit in youth, yet still better than **16** (89).

★★★★ **White** (⊘) The **21** (89) blend echoes **20** ★★★★☆ (92) in chardonnay, semillon & viognier components & ratio but oak upped to 80% new, obvious in vanilla, butterscotch dominance of peachy florality.

Stellenbosch Hills range

★★★★ **Cabernet Sauvignon** (⊘) Cab's naturally firmer tannin bolstered by 15% new oak but the wood is in sync with the juicy flavours. **18** (87) youthful, balanced & bright, better than **17** ★★★★ (84).

★★★★ **Merlot** (⊘) Supple, elegant **18** (87) raises the bar on **17** ★★★ (81). Riper blue berry, cherry aromas & flavours enhanced by sweet American oak (20%) in 14-month maturation. Clean dry farewell.

★★★★ **Bushvine Pinotage** (⊘) **20** (87) improves on last **18** ★★★★ (85) in body, structure & oak integration. Tealeaf & spice edge to raspberry, cherry vibrancy, good texture & length.

★★★★ **Shiraz** (⊘) Evolution continues with **20** (88) raising the bar on last **18** (87). Ripe succulence & spice tempered by balanced wooding, this time 30% new, 16 months, 85/15 split French & American.

★★★★ **Muscat de Hambourg** (⊘) Balanced single-vineyard **22** (87) fortified dessert seduces with litchi-toned sweetness & well-knit spirit. Clean, light textured & supple, uncloying. 500 ml.

Chenin Blanc (⊘) ★★★★ Fresh, perky & light, with melon & nectarine appeal. **23** (84) ideal summer sipper. **Sauvignon Blanc** (⊘) ★★★★ Fig & tropical notes plus vivid grapefruit on **23** (85). Tangier fruit & more body, texture than Polkadraai sibling.

Polkadraai range

Sauvignon Blanc (☺) ★★★ Lemon zest typicity & brightness to light & tangy **23** (81). Ultra-quaffable & great value (as all) in 3L cask.

Pinotage-Merlot (⊘) ★★★ Cheery berry appeal of pinotage leads the way on **21** (82) 70/30 blend. 6 months in old oak, half American, lends support. WO Polkadraai Hills for these. **Merlot-Shiraz** (⊘) ★★★★ Equal billing for **22** (83) blend partners makes for a rounded yet bright raspberry- & blueberry-toned mouthful. Light, sappy & easy to like, with the convenience of 3L cask. **Rosé** (⊘) ★★★ Plum & berry succulence on **23** (82) from shiraz. Clean & dry, with focused finish. **Chenin Blanc-Sauvignon Blanc** (⊘) ★★★ Chenin leads its blend buddy 70/30 in **23** (82), offering melon & lemon freshness in light, tasty mouthful. Also in 250-ml can for easy enjoyment, as Pinotage-Merlot & Rosé. **Pinot Noir Sparkling Rosé** ★★★ Not discontinued as we thought. Raspberry & strawberry sherbet flavours on bright, carbonated pink fizz. **22** (80) uncomplicated & pleasant for the sweeter toothed. **Sauvignon Blanc Sparkling Brut** (NEW) ★★★ Dry, tangy, lemon-hued carbonated sparkler. **22** (80) light & unfussy with good acid freshness. — FM

Location/map: Stellenbosch ▪ Map grid reference: D6 ▪ WO: Stellenbosch/Polkadraai Hills ▪ Est 1945 ▪ 1stB 1972 ▪ Tasting & sales Mon-Fri 9-5 Sat 10-3 ▪ Wine tasting options: R50pp/standard tasting; R100pp/biltong & droëwors pairing ▪ Closed Sun & all pub hols ▪ Owner(s) 12 members ▪ Cellarmaster(s) PG Slabbert (Jan 1997) ▪ Winemaker(s) Charl Myburgh (Sep 2021) ▪ Viticulturist(s) PG Slabbert ▪ 635ha (cab, cinsaut, merlot, ptage, shiraz, chard, chenin, muscat de Hambourg, sauv) ▪ 6,000t/20,000cs own label 68% red 30% white 2% other ▪ IPW ▪ PO Box 40 Vlottenburg 7604 ▪ info@stbhills.co.za ▪ www.stellenbosch-hills.co.za ▪ T +27 (0)21-881-3828

☐ **Stellenbosch Manor** *see* Stellenrust

Stellenbosch Reserve ⓠ ⓟ

This collection of attractive, approachable wines is offered by esteemed vigneron Jean Engelbrecht as a tribute to his birthplace, 'a small town that has become the epicentre for SA viticulture'. Recent changes see the brand home move from sibling winery Guardian Peak to the property formerly known as Haskell, next to the flagship of the Engelbrecht portfolio, Rust en Vrede, in the heart of Stellenbosch's famed 'golden triangle'.

★★★★☆ **Cabernet Sauvignon** Classic Stellenbosch cab 21 ★★★★ ⑧⑧ shows clarity & direction with firm blackcurrant core enlivened with leafy freshness & tarry edge from year in old oak. Very pleasant drinking, shade less intense than 20 ⑨③.

★★★★ **Cinsault** Bright, cheery 22 ⑧⑧. Cherry & berry melange, hint of marzipan, zingy freshness & no tannins to speak of. Wholebunch/berry bounce, touch of old-oak spice. Stick it in the fridge & enjoy.

★★★★ **Merlot** Easy-drinking 21 ★★★★ ⑧⑤ offers plump mulberry fruit, hints of dark chocolate & dried herbs. Soft tannins & fresh acid round out very pleasant wine, style change from more serious 19 ⑧⑧.

★★★★ **Syrah** Continuing affable yet unfrivolous styling of previous, 21 ⑧⑦ delivers variety's perfume, iodine, black plum fruit & touch of earthiness. Spicy freshness from stem-fermented portion & hint of toffee from 16 months in old oak.

★★★★☆ **Vanderstel** ⊘ ⓐ 5-way Bordeaux blend 21 ⑨④, cab (68%) & co-leader merlot leally hit the spot with sweet blackberry fruit, silky tannin & appealing vanilla spice from year in small oak. An over-deliverer of note, almost worryingly drinkable yet worthy of its top rating.

★★★★ **Chardonnay** Crisp, fresh 22 ⑧⑥ mingles grapefruit, peach & white blossom, adds pithy texture & vanilla cream from part ferment & ageing in barrel, 15% new. Well balanced & characterful.

★★★★ **Chenin Blanc** Heady perfume followed by soft pineapple & green apple fruit, spicy note from part barrel-ferment/ageing, which also adds texture but 22 ★★★★ ⑧⑤ misses intensity of 21 ⑧⑥. — CM

Location/map/WO: Stellenbosch ▪ Map grid reference: F8 ▪ Est 2004 ▪ 1stB 2005 ▪ Tasting & sales Mon-Sat 9-5 Sun 10-4 ▪ Various tasting options - fee waived on purchase ▪ Closed Good Fri & Dec 25 ▪ Restaurant ▪ Owner(s) Jean Engelbrecht ▪ Winemaker(s) Duran Cornhill (Dec 2021) ▪ ±160t/25,000cs own label 90% red 10% white ▪ IPW ▪ PO Box 473 Stellenbosch 7599 ▪ info@thestellenboschreserve.com ▪ www.thestellenboschreserve.com ▪ T +27 (0)21-881-3895

☐ **Stellenbosch Uitsig** *see* Friesland Wines

Stellenbosch University Welgevallen Cellar ⓠ

The university in the heart of SA's winelands has not only a renowned oenology faculty and a cellar (with tasting venue) dating to the birth of its home town (1680), but also its own boutique ranges. They are crafted by Riaan Wassüng, resident winemaker for 20 years, from grapes grown on the Welgevallen experimental farm and estates around Stellenbosch.

Die Laan range

★★★★ **Merlot Reserve** ⓠ More restrained & savoury than standard version, but also a little sweetly ripe, with 14.3% alc. Gentle but informing tannins. 17% new oak supportive. 20 ★★★★ ⑧③ has 15% petit verdot, where 19 ⑧⑦ had cab.

★★★★ **Shiraz** ⓠ Darkly ripe & spicy aromas & flavour on 19 ★★★ ⑦⑨ show evidence of 25% new oak. Big acidity as counterweight to some residual sugar & 14.7% alc. Less successful than last-made 17 ⑧⑦.

Cabernet Sauvignon ⓠ ★★★★ Includes a little petit verdot in 20 ⑧③. Plenty of fruit, boiled sweet hint untrammelled by the 25% new oak. Some residual sugar balanced with 14.4% alc & firm acidity. **Merlot** ⓠ ★★★ Ripe dark notes on approachable 20 ⑧⑩. Richly sweet-fruited, with formidable counterbalancing acidity & modest tannins. Older oak. **Pinotage Blanc de Noir** ⓠ ★★★ Palely gleaming 22 ⑧② has small oaked component for breadth. Pleasant boiled-sweet notes & bright freshness. Juicy, flavourful & dry. **Chenin Blanc** ⓠ ★★★ Forward fruit on fresh, dry & tastily very drinkable 22 ⑧②. Texture & grip helped by otherwise undetectable oaked portion. **Sauvignon Blanc** ⓠ ★★★ Ebullient tropical aroma & flavour on **22** (82), with grassy undertone. Fresh & bone-dry, juicy & full of flavour. Not tasted: **Malbec, Pinotage, Rector's Reserve Pinotage, Cabernet Sauvignon-Shiraz, Chenin Blanc Reserve**.

Maties range
Not tasted: **Rooiplein**. — TJ

Location/map/WO: Stellenbosch ▪ Map grid reference: F5 ▪ Est 2001 ▪ 1stB 2009 ▪ Tasting Mon-Fri 9-4 ▪ Fee R45pp ▪ Closed all pub hols & Dec 15-Jan 10 ▪ Owner(s) Stellenbosch University ▪ Cellarmaster(s)/winemaker(s) Riaan Wassüng (Jan 2004) ▪ 11ha/1.5ha (cab, ptage) ▪ 4,600cs own label 68% red 32% white ▪ Faculty AgriSciences Private Bag X1 Matieland 7602 ▪ winesales@sun.ac.za, rfw@sun.ac.za ▪ http://academic.sun.ac.za/viti_oenol/ ▪ **T +27 (0)21-808-2925/+27 (0)83-622-6394**

Stellenbosch Vineyards   (♀)(♨)(🛝)

From its home on 17th-century farm Welmoed beside the Eerste River, where the past year has seen the already cavernous warehouse extended, French-owned Stellenbosch Vineyards vinifies 5,500 tons and sends 85% of the resulting 'wines of great excellence' to overseas markets, mostly in Europe and the US. An 'elite group' of area growers supply the grapes, their vineyards managed by Francois de Villiers, whose son Abraham is the general manager and winemaker, alongside equally long-serving cellar colleague Bernard Claassen, now joined by Marnich Aucamp. Single-site and niche bottlings help make the crafted ranges featured here so compelling, while high quality-to-price ratios up the appeal of separately listed commercial brands Arniston Bay and Welmoed. The plan is to revamp and enlarge the visitor area, and host more events.

The Flagship range
★★★★☆ **Cabernet Franc** (♀) Beguiling perfumed red berries, wild mint & vanilla nuances in **18** (94), similar firm, chalky tannins though less new oak (40% vs 100% previously, 28 months) enfold this youthful beauty. Piquantly fresh & tightly coiled, handsome rewards in time. No **17**.

★★★★☆ **Petit Verdot** (♨) Infrequent release & no wonder, the quest is for the best grapes, treated with due care & respect. Inky-coloured **18** (94) spent 48 months in 300L barrels, 40% new, which show as cigarbox, a fine-grained tannin backbone. But there's no doubt the fruit is in charge: cherry & mulberry, a note of crystallised violet, deep & seductively layered. Standout example. Last was **15** ★★★★★ (95).

★★★★☆ **Right Bank** (♀) Restrained merlot-led **18** (94) with cab, petit verdot & cab franc (55/27/14/4). Rich & ripe layers of dark-berried fruit & cedar, firm, dry tealeaf tannins. 40% new oak (100% previously), 28 months, supportive & well judged. Still youthful; fine prospects. No **17**.

Limited Release range
★★★★☆ **Cinsault** (♀) Like **17** (93), cherry-toned **18** (90) in modern, lightly oaked, medium-intensity style. Attractive gentle stalky grip, house's impressive acid-tannin balance. Only older wood.

★★★★☆ **Grenache** (♀) Riper, with more savoury, peppery nuances in **20** (90) five-barrel selection. Similar old-oak ageing, but less fresh vitality than **19** (94). Tad reserved & heavier, despite medium 13.2% alc. May just need time to show more fully.

★★★★☆ **Single Vineyard Chenin Blanc** Like Credo version, some cellar changes: wild ferment in older barrels, 3 months on lees, then racked & oaked another 9 months, 30% new. Stonefruit & bruised apple, melba toast, but **22** (90)'s main attraction is the palate, limy, tangy, with mouthcoating freshness, long-lingering finish. Only in exceptional vintages for the vineyard; **18** (90) was last made.

★★★★☆ **Therona** Uniquely SA variety, **22** (90) produced from last remaining vines in Stellenbosch, just 116 cases. Winter melon & kiwi, the 5 months in older barrels a biscuit tone in the flavours. Distinctive, noteworthy. Last made in **20** (91).

★★★★☆ **Verdelho** (♨) **22** (94) fermented/10 months in 60% new barrels, then best 8 barrels selected. Full-ripe, with candied stonefruit, lovely richness given further expression by oak's shortbread tone. But then the contrast of a limy flick of the tail, adding vibrancy. Admirable example of rare variety in SA. Discontinued: **Darling Sauvignon Blanc**.

Credo range
★★★★☆ **Pinotage** (NEW)(✓)(♨) More complex & sophisticated than sibling, longer life ahead. **21** (90) basket press, 18 months small-oak, 30% new, 8 barrels selected, ensuring polished tannins part of the structure. Dried herbs, dark berries, tobacco & salty liquorice, sleek & silky; lots going on, all good.

★★★★☆ **Shiraz** ⊘ ⊛ Same winemaking as its sibling but in **21** ⑨④ fruit more vivid, forthcoming, plush berries, cherries, the oak a secondary perfume & flavour element. Noteworthy succulence & freshness, seam of fine tannins masked by the fruit.

★★★★ **SMV** ⊛ Shiraz (79%) with merlot (not the more usual M!) & viognier, the most serious of the shiraz wines. 26 months in oak, 30% new, then best barrels selected. As expected, **20** ⑧⑨ is quite savoury, with woodsmoke & meaty notes, dried herbs, enough plummy fruit to offset the tannin. Crafted to cellar.

★★★★☆ **Chardonnay** ⊘ ⊛ Cellar regimen well handled: barrel ferment, 8 months on lees, further 3-month oak ageing, 60% new. **22** ⑨④ rewards this with prominent, vibrant citrus & ginger biscuit captivating the senses. Acid gives lift, definition. A very long finish. Has presence.

★★★★☆ **Chenin Blanc** ⊘ ⊛ **22** ★★★★★ ⑨⑤ remains richly impressive, though different oak handling to **21** ⑨③: still wild ferment in barrel, but just 30% new instead of 80%. Marmalade & glacé fruit tones underpinned by crisp acid, a lipsmacking finish.

Stellenbosch Vineyards range

★★★★ **Bushvine Pinotage** ⊘ Variety given voice: wild ferment, whole berries, 16 months oaking. **22** ⑧⑧ piquant red fruit, an earthy note; fleshy & smooth textured, appealing, tannins a hidden strength.

★★★★ **Shiraz** ⊘ ⊛ Barrel selection after 14 months, some new, giving **21** ⑧⑧ cigarbox & white pepper spicing; vibrant fruit in harmony with discernable but supple tannins. Delicious, & will reward ageing. No **20**.

★★★★ **Bushvine Chenin Blanc** ⊛ Similar ripe apple & stonefruit in **22** ⑧⑥. Bunch pressing, natural ferment & 5 months in older oak add breadth. Mouthfilling yet balanced & fresh.

★★★★ **Sauvignon Blanc** ⊘ Litchi & passionfruit, showy **23** ⑧⑧ has Stellenbosch's ripeness, but also spent 6 months on the lees to give it body & texture. Ends zinging fresh to waken the tastebuds.

Cabernet Sauvignon ⊘ ★★★★ Bright-fruited **21** ⑧⑤ is cassis toned, the tannins a supple foundation, no barrier to current enjoyment. Just enough grip for some ageing, robust food. **Unwooded Chardonnay** ⊘ ★★★★ Shows that unoaked chardonnay can stand on its own. Wholebunch, wild ferment, 6 months on the lees to bring out the best in **22** ⑧⑤: citrus preserve, lime freshness at the end. — CR

Location/map/WO: Stellenbosch ▪ Map grid reference: C7 ▪ Est 1997 ▪ Tasting & sales Tue-Fri 9-5 Sat & pub hols (seasonal) 10-4 ▪ Tasting fee R100 ▪ Closed Good Fri, Dec 25 & Jan 1 ▪ Facilities for children ▪ Wine club ▪ Owner(s) AdVini ▪ Winemaker(s) Abraham de Villiers (Dec 2004) & Bernard Claassen (Feb 2005), with Duan Engelbrecht (Oct 2020) & Marnich Aucamp (2022) ▪ Viticulturist(s) Francois de Villiers (1998) ▪ 5,500t 45% red 45% white 10% rosé ▪ Fairtrade, FSSC 22000, IPW, Vegan, WIETA ▪ PO Box 465 Stellenbosch 7599 ▪ info@ stellvine.co.za ▪ www.stellenboschvineyards.co.za ▪ **T +27 (0)21-881-3870**

Stellenrust   ⓠ ⑪ ⓞ

Its history may stretch back 95 years, but it's the modern revival almost 25 years ago at the hands of viti-culturist Kobie van der Westhuizen and cellarmaster Tertius Boshoff that's seen Stellenrust grow into one of South Africa's foremost producers, notably of chenin blanc. This is evident in not just that Stellenrust has fea-tured in the annual Chenin Blanc Top 10 for 9 of the past 10 years, but in 2023 it occupied an unprecedented four spots. Blessed with venerable vines on its Bottelary and Helderberg properties, where the tasting room lies, Stellenrust also draws on own Devon Valley vines for a range as broad and deep as it is commercially successful with, among others, many international supermarkets sourcing wine for their own brands from the cellar. Assisting Tertius are Herman du Preez, twice a Diners Club laureate, and Barend Erasmus.

Super Premium range

★★★★☆ **Reserve Cabernet Sauvignon** ⊛ Supple, sleek **19** ★★★★★ ⑨⑤ follows gentler **18** ⑨④, from same 1942 vineyard. Trademark cassis & cedar richness with silky texture, restrained intensity given complexity & structure by 2 years in new oak, further year in bottle. Fresh & immensely rewarding.

★★★★☆ **Barrel Selection Cabernet Franc** ⊘ ⊛ Signature poise & confidence on **20** ⑨③ from Helderberg vines, along with backbone & structure of fresh acid & judicious oak, 30% new, 18 months. Spice-tinged Black Forest gateau character layered with brush of herbs, nuanced & harmonious.

★★★★☆ **Old Bush Vine Cinsaut** ⊘ Juicy & engaging **22** ⑨⓪ touch lighter, less intense than last but shares its berry-toned cheer, approachability & gentle structure from portions wholebunch & open ferment, year in oak, 20% new.

★★★★☆ **Cornerstone Pinotage** ✓ ⊛ Swarthy **21** ㉝ reflects vintage in concentration & leashed power. Blueberry & cherry vibrancy matched by muscular frame from year in combo French & 5% American oak, 34% new, after open ferment. Small wholebunch portion aids vivacity. •

★★★★☆ **Peppergrinder's Shiraz** ✓ ⊛ Big on the advertised spice in **20** ㉜ from shy-bearing old Helderberg vines, showing freshness & density in equal measure. 38% wholebunch ferment plus year in 35% new oak, portion American, contribute to muscular but nimble & suave body.

★★★★☆ **Timeless** ✓ ⊛ Merlot at 41% nearly on par with cab in 3-way blend with cab franc in **20** ㉞. Xmas pudding, tobacco & cocoa richness gently squeezed by oak tannin from 24 months in barrique, 30% new. Refined, smooth & cohesive, like **19** ★★★★★ ㉟.

★★★★☆ **Barrel Fermented Chardonnay** ⊛ Taut lime vibrancy riffs off creamy cashew on broad but focused **22** ㉝, reflecting influence of Bottelary limestone soils in precision & structure. Complexity from natural ferment & 28% new oak, year, freshness aided by suppressed malo.

★★★★★ **58 Barrel Fermented Chenin Blanc** ⊛ ⊛ Single-parcel bottling, 58 year old vines, Stellenbosch's 2nd-oldest, impresses with vivacity in **22** ㉞, 7.2 g/L acid countering ripe apricot & honeyed richness. Juicy, composed & elegant. Natural ferment, combo oxidative & reductive winemaking plus 9 months in 17% new oak, 10% Hungarian, deliver complexity & precision, as in **21** ★★★★★ ㉝.

★★★★★ **Old Bushvine Chenin Blanc** ⊛ Chalky mouthfeel on structured & serious **22** ㉞, the younger (46 year old) sibling also from Bottelary. Crisp green apple & taut lime nuances. Harmonious & confident. Natural ferment & 7 months on lees in older oak lend breadth, length & creamy richness.

★★★★☆ **Chenin d'Muscat** ⊛ Dried pineapple & barley sugar sweetness from late-harvested, vine-dried muscat d'Alexandrie & botrytised chenin (33/67). Barrel-fermented **21** ㉞'s abundant (134 g/L) sugar brightened & livened by acid of 7.8 g/L for an ambrosial old-vine dessert wine in 375 ml. Just 11% alc.

Not tasted: **Chenin Blanc Brut Spumante Magnifico.**

Premium range

★★★★ **Cabernet Sauvignon** ✓ Pleasant round-bodied, blueberry- & cherry-toned **22** ㊆ shows good depth & length, velvet texture after year in 30% new oak. Over-delivers.

★★★★ **Merlot** ✓ Good core of dark berry fruit on pillowy & succulent **22** ㊅. Has darker cocoa nuance but remains gentle, with subtle grip from year in oak, third new. Lingering & fresh.

★★★★ **Pinotage** ✓ Smoky nuance to spicy blueberry fruit on **22** ㊆ from Helderberg & Bottelary grapes. Lively & juicy with soft texture. Year in barrel, 20% new. Easy to like.

★★★★☆ **Shiraz** ✓ Fynbos scent to intense dark fruit on **22** ㉛. Rounded, succulent & lively with power reined in, more refined than **21** ㉚. Selected yeast & portion wholebunch ferment. Year oak, 20% new, included American & Hungarian barrels.

★★★★ **Simplicity** ✓ Shiraz (56%) & near-equal cab & merlot in **22** ㊆. From three soils & regions, smooth, friendly & harmonious, it offers lingering cigarbox & fruitcake flavour. Year oak, 25% new, portion American.

★★★★ **Chardonnay** Skin contact & partial oxidation, tank & 17% barrel ferment for **23** ㊆. Succulent citrus apparent before broad creaminess sweeps in, framed by harmonious oak. Longer & more rewarding than **22** ★★★★ ㊄.

★★★★ **Chenin Blanc** ✓ Pineapple & nectarine on tangy **23** ㊇ from bushvines, some 45 years old. Natural ferment in 16% old oak & steel tank, 5 months on lees. Ripe but crisp & composed. Lots to love.

★★★★ **Sauvignon Blanc** ✓ Zesty & crisp **23** ㊅ the result of fractional harvest, mix of yeasts & lees contact. Composed & deliciously flinty with ample appeal, also in 375 ml.

Kleine Rust range

Pinotage-Shiraz ✓ ★★★☆ Plum & berry vigour on **22** ㊄ with pinotage at 47% & dab cinsaut adding sappy cheer. Fresh & satisfying, just enough structure from 8 months older oak. Fairtrade, as all these. **Pinotage Rosé** ✓ ★★★★ Luscious yet dry **23** ㊃ offers strawberry flavour plus a cranberry crunch. Vivacious & fun. **Chenin Blanc-Sauvignon Blanc** ✓ ★★★★ Sauvignon (24%) adds zip to chenin's ripe citrus & stonefruit charm in **23** ㊄. Compact, brisk & upbeat for summer enjoyment. **Semi-Sweet** ★★★ Appealing **23** ㊁ has a light sweetness balanced by fresh acid. Tasty & lingering fruit salad flavours from 76% chenin with sauvignon & muscat d'Alexandrie. — FM

Location/map/WO: Stellenbosch ▪ Map grid reference: E7, C3 ▪ Est/1stB 1928 ▪ Tasting & sales (Hberg & Btlry) Mon-Fri 9-5 Sat/pub hols 10-3 ▪ Closed Ash Wednesday, Easter Fri-Mon, Ascension day, Dec 25/26 & Jan 1 ▪ Cellar tours by appt ▪ Farm-style platters & pre-arranged lunches/dinners ▪ Picnic platters ▪ Tour groups ▪ Grape stomping/make your own wine ▪ Gifts ▪ Conferences ▪ Weddings/functions (300+ pax) ▪ Walking/ hiking & MTB trails ▪ Art exhibition ▪ Wine club ▪ Owner(s) Stellenrust Family Trust ▪ Cellarmaster(s) Tertius Boshoff (Jan 2004) ▪ Winemaker(s) Herman du Preez (2014), with Barend Erasmus (2022) ▪ Viticulturist(s) Kobie van der Westhuizen (Jan 2000) ▪ 200ha (cabs s/f, carignan, cinsaut, grenache noir, merlot, ptage, shiraz, chard, chenin, muscat d'A, sauv) ▪ 2,000t/300,000cs own label 50% red 40% white 10% rosé + 100,000cs for clients ▪ Other export brands: Pillar & Post, STELL, Stellenbosch Manor, Steynsrust, Xaro ▪ Brands for clients: Embrace, Lion's Pride, Ruyter's Bin, Sabi Sabi Private Game Lodge ▪ Fairtrade, FSSC, WIETA ▪ PO Box 26 Koelenhof 7605 ▪ info@stellenrust.co.za ▪ www.stellenrust.co.za ▪ **T +27 (0)21-880-2283**

Stellenview Premium Wines ⓠ ⑪

A significant player, with half a million cases of wine under a number of labels, many Africa-themed, the business end of the venture is just outside Stellenbosch in Devon Valley, where owner Reino Kruger helms the cellar, working alongside Debbie Thompson and newcomer Juanita Lategan, and by-appointment tours of the facilities are available. The fun side, however, is in the town centre, where brand-home Le Grand Domaine Enoteca includes a 'wine library' of over thirty bottlings for 'side-by-side tasting and comparison'.

Kruger Family Reserve range

★★★★ **Cabernet Sauvignon** ⓐ Long, satisfying flavours & aromas of bramble, black plum & fynbos before a firm, well-considered tannin structure. **20** ★★★★☆ (90) is more serious & stately than **19** (88), has better ageing prospects. 30% new oak, 16 months, for the reds.

★★★★ **Shiraz** Balanced, full-fruited **20** ★★★★☆ (90) impresses more than **19** (88) in its dark fruit compote, dried herbs & succulent tannin frame, supple enough for current drinking & medium-term cellaring.

★★★★☆ **Sauvignon Blanc** Exuberant **23** (86) shows tropical fruit & green herb flavours mingling with creamy lees for a well-balanced palate, citrus hint on perky finish.

★★★★☆ **Méthode Cap Classique Marguerite** (ⁿᵉʷ) Chardonnay & pinot noir (81/19) combine for a balanced, echoing mouthful of green & baked apple, citrus zest & baked pie crust. A lovely interplay of fresh fruit & creamy mousse on **19** (91).

Rosé (ⁿᵉʷ) ★★★★ Lovely fruity blackberry & subtle spice on **22** (85), juicy & fragrant to the last dry drop. From shiraz. **Chardonnay** ⓠ ★★★★ Stonefruit, ripe apple & citrus announce **21** (85). Balanced, with cream texture thanks to lees ageing in barrel, 40% new, 9 months. WO Stellenbosch, as all these.

Great Five Reserve range

★★★★ **Cabernet Sauvignon** ⓠ ⓐ Slick, polished & very approachable **19** (87). Fragrant fruit, tobacco & dark chocolate balanced by fine savoury tannins. Up a notch from **18** ★★★ (81).

★★★★ **Pinotage** ⓠ Delights with ripe, fragrant dark fruit flavours, creamy cappuccino nuance & dusting of cocoa in **19** (86). Balanced & delicious. More substantial & satisfying than **18** ★★★ (80).

★★★★ **Shiraz** ⓠ Rich **19** (87) has intense plum, dark cherry, olive tapenade, pepper & toasty herb flavours. The palate is supple, the finish savoury, the whole an improvement on last **17** ★★★ (80).

Merlot ⓠ ★★★★ Subtle mulled wine & spice cake aromas & flavours abound in easy-drinking **19** (84), ends with a mint chocolate kiss. **Cape Premier Red** ⓠ ★★★ Back to shiraz & merlot (60/40) duo in improved **19** (82), packed with dark fruit, touch of smoke & savoury spice, slips down easily. Previous was 100% cab. 20% new oak, 12-14 months, for these.

Cape Five Reserve range

★★★★ **Cabernet Sauvignon** ⊘ Cassis & graphite pave the way for a succulent, well-expressed **19** (88). Good balance & depth, with a long dried herb finish. Notch above **18** ★★★★☆ (84).

★★★★ **Pinotage** ⊘ More depth & structure in **20** (87) than **19** ★★★★ (85). Juicier fruit, too, with dark plums & berries underpinned by warm spice & integrated tannins. 20% new barrels, 12-14 months for these unless noted.

★★★★ **Shiraz** ⊘ Bold, somewhat brooding yet not unbalanced **20** (88). Mulberry & hedgerow fruit mingle with creamy tapenade & liquorice on a smooth tannin base.

Merlot Ⓐ ★★★ Polished & inviting Xmas cake flavours mingle with milk chocolate & warm spice in **18** ⑧②. **Red Reserve Organic** ♡ ★★★★ Shiraz & cab with dab pinotage, **20** ⑧⑤ deep fruited, spice laced, with a dark chocolate farewell. **Cape Premier Red** Ⓐ ★★★★ Violet & peach blossom perfumes are giveaways for shiraz & dab viognier on generous **15** ⑧⑤, which saw half the new oak of its siblings.

Sunkloof Reserve range
★★★★ **Shiraz** ⊘ Light hearted, balanced, with soft spicy dark fruit for a generous mouthful in **20** ⑧⑥. In same vein, also-tasted **21** ⑧⑥ shows freshness & cheer. Lovely to drink now, can age a few years.

Stellenview Reserve range
★★★★☆ **Shiraz** Ⓐ Elegant & structured **17** ⑨① improves on **16** ★★★★ ⑧④ with perfume, flavour & integrated tannins that invite another sip. WO Stellenbosch, as Cab.

Cabernet Sauvignon Ⓐ ★★★★ Intense cassis, black cherry & savoury herbs on **18** ⑧⑤. Smooth & rounded, firm grip to finish. Should keep a few more years. 30% new oak, 12-24 months, as sibling.

KFK Reserve range
★★★★ **Pinotage** ⊘ From lower-yield vines, **20** ⑧⑥ dense & dark fruited with touches of chocolate & scrub, grippy tannins on long finish. Needs time, unlike accessible **17** ★★★ ⑦⑨, the last tasted.
Not tasted: **Shiraz**. — WB

Location/map: Stellenbosch ▪ Map grid reference: D4 ▪ Map: Stellenbosch ▪ Map grid reference: F5 ▪ WO: Coastal/Stellenbosch ▪ Est/1stB 2015 ▪ Cellar tours Mon-Fri 8-5 Sat/Sun by appt ▪ Closed all pub hols ▪ Online shop ▪ Tasting & sales at Le Grand Domaine Enoteca, 7 Church Str, Oude Bank Building, Stellenbosch Tue-Sat 12-10 Sun 12-6; pub hols (seasonal) please call ahead: T +27 (0)21-300-3297, enoteca@granddomaine.co.za ▪ Owner(s) Reino Kruger ▪ Cellarmaster(s) Reino Kruger (Apr 2015) ▪ Winemaker(s) Debbie Thompson (Dec 2019), Juanita Lategan (Jan 2023) ▪ 12ha (cabs s/f, merlot, p verdot) ▪ 450t/500,000cs own label 80% red 20% white ▪ Other export brands: Africa Five, Cape Discovery, Openers, Pride of Kings, Top Five, Wild Instinct ▪ PO Box 7177 Stellenbosch 7599 ▪ info@stellenviewwines.com ▪ www.stellenviewwines.com ▪ T +27 (0)87-152-0997/+27 (0)76-248-4739

Stellenzicht Wines Ⓨ

In the heart of Stellenbosch's 'golden triangle', and owned since 2017 by German businessman Hans von Staff-Reitzenstein (also owner/part-proprietor of nearby Alto Estate and Ernie Els Wines), Stellenzicht's branding the past few years has been inspired by geology and soil science, emphasising the centrality of the steeply sloping terrain on the Helderberg mountainside, where considerable rejuvenation has taken place. This continues under viticulturist Nico Nortjé with the planting of more syrah, including a clone drawn from an old top block. The first own chardonnay has been brought into the cellar for crafting by L'Ré Hughes, and the first cap classique bottled for 2025 release. The Wine Pod visitor venue has received further refinements.

★★★★ **Tristone Cabernet Sauvignon** Ⓐ Classic core of dark fruit, minerality & cedar showing home-farm's affinity for cab. Firm, dry chalky tannins from wholeberry ferment, skin contact & 16 months in oak, 30% new. **19** ★★★★★ ⑨① youthful & well-structured step up on **18** ⑧⑧, deserves ageing.

★★★★ **Arenite Syrah** Ⓐ White pepper, red-berry & liquorice flavours in tightly buttoned **19** ⑧⑨. Half bunch-ferment adds structure & freshness, bolstered by 15 months in mostly older oak. Good potential.

★★★★★ **Acheulean Red** Ⓐ Flagship crafted to impress & structured for decade hence. Near-equal cabernet & shiraz with 15% cinsaut in **18** ⑨④, gains stylish vanilla & spice overlay from 40% new oak, this also ensuring greater grip & firmer structure than siblings. Also in magnum.

★★★★☆ **Thunderstone Red** ⊘ All Stellenbosch grapes in **19** ⑨⓪ blend of cinsaut, shiraz & cabernet (35/25). Like previous (which had Voor Paardeberg component), older-oak aged, some whole bunches, some co-ferment. Svelte tannin structure, quite succulent, with rich red fruit & a delicious savouriness.

★★★★☆ **Acheulean Chardonnay** More understated honeyed beeswax, some stonefruit & lime flavours & aroma in **22** ⑨⓪. Bunch pressed, like sibling, but 35% fermented/12 months in barrel, 100% new, rest in amphora. Clean elegant lines, quite closed in youth, with good potential, but shade off the depth & intensity of **21** ⑨①.

★★★★ **Thunderstone Chardonnay** ⊘ Creamy shortbread nuance from partial oak ferment/year in older barrels underpins luscious pear & lime flavours in supple & expansive **22** ⑧⑧. Lovely fresh balance, succulence & length.

Thunderstone Rosé ★★★★ Two vintages tasted, both 2-4 months in old oak. **22 ⑧③** from shiraz & cinsaut more savoury & crisp. **23 ⑧④** adds grenache & is more delicate, with pale pink hue & light floral aromas & flavour. Both attractively dry for easy sunset sipping. WO W Cape. Not tasted: **Silcrete Cinsault**. — MW

Location/map: Stellenbosch ▪ Map grid reference: F8 ▪ WO: Stellenbosch/Western Cape ▪ Est 1982 ▪ 1stB 1989 ▪ Wine pod tasting facility Wed-Fri 10-6 Sat/Sun 9-5 ▪ Sales online ▪ Owner(s) Stellenzicht Wines ▪ Winemaker(s) L'Ré Hughes, with Shannon Jacobs ▪ Viticulturist(s) Nico Nortjé ▪ 218ha/55ha (cab, cinsaut, shiraz, chard) ▪ PO Box 7595 Stellenbosch 7599 ▪ info@stellenzicht.com ▪ www.stellenzicht.com ▪ **T +27 (0)21-880-1103 (office)/+27 (0)21-569-0362 (Wine Pod)**

Stettyn Family Vineyards ⓟ ⑪ ⓞ ⓖ

Marking 60 years since cellar foundations were laid on land between Worcester and Villiersdorp, this dynamic venture owned by local growers and a BEE entity involving Adama Wines produces mostly for mighty export brand FirstCape, which it part owns, but increasingly for its proprietary bottled lines, where a premiumisation strategy is in place. Always much to report, including new amphoras for wines set to join the Signature range, registration with Skillogical to ensure optimal staff skills training, a new gin and dark rum, and extra allures such as MTB and walking routes at the visitor venue, to add to the valley panorama.

Signature range

★★★★ Shackleton Old Vine Chenin Blanc ⑯ Antique military aircraft names this premium bottling from venerated 37 year old vines, producing tangy dried peach & some tropical flavours, balancing acid brightness in **22 ⑧⑧**. Tad riper than last, plumped by touch sugar & succulence from lees contact in oak, halved from 50% new. Appealing now, with potential.

★★★★ The Deed Cap Classique Brut sparkler from chardonnay (70%) & pinot noir celebrates granting of Stettyn farm in 1714. Ripe apple & honey, subtle nutty brioche from year on lees (half as long as last **NV ⑧⑥**). Drier & more serious than carbonated sibling though still vivaciously fresh & versatile. WO W Cape.

★★★★☆ Cape Vintage ⊘ ⓫ New blend from **17 ⑨⓪** vintage a trio of souzão, tinta & touriga (50/25/25) that exudes ripe black fruit, chocolate & sweet Xmas spices. Spirit well integrated, 19.5% alc keeps the higher sugar (118 g/L) in check. Tannins firm, befitting this style of port. As fine & cellarworthy as previous tinta-led version. 500 ml.

....

Babelki Sparkling Rosé Brut ⊘ ⓫ **★★★★** Refreshing dry carbonated **NV ⑧⑤** from 60% chardonnay & pinot noir. Pale vermillion hue, bright mandarin flavours & subtle leesy undertone. Few grams sugar give tangy effect for satisfying everyday quaffing.

....

Guardian ⓧ **★★★★** Opulent shiraz, cab & durif combo (45/35/20), **20 ⑧⑤**'s plummy fruit overlaid with spice from 50% oaked portion. Plushness freshened by present but not assertive tannin & balanced acid.

Stettyn Family Vineyards range

Chardonnay-Pinot Noir ☺ **★★★** Vibrant **23 ⑧②** duo has a coral hue, subtle strawberry & pear flavours & bright acid that teases with a sweet-sour tussle. Cheerful, pocket-friendly summer rosé.

....

Cabernet Sauvignon ⊘ **★★★★** Similar mouthfilling cassis & blackberry fruit on **21 ⑧⑤**, though oak reined in (to only 5% new, 12 months, some Hungarian, as all these reds unless noted). Supple tannins approachable now & for good few years. Very good value, as most from this producer. **Merlot** ⊘ **★★★★** Full ripeness of **21 ⑧④** ensures plush red fruit in a bright, balanced tannin framework. Just a wisp of smoke from part oak-ageing. Structured, fresh & flavoursome step up on previous. **Pinotage** ⊘ **★★★★** Dapper **21 ⑧④** a friendly melange of berries & touch of ripe banana. Good nip of tannin keeps the form & 15% new oak adds a little toast. As last, lots to like & ready to enjoy solo or with a meal. **Shiraz ★★★** Dense core with smoky dark berries & black pepper in more concentrated **21 ⑧②**. Full, muscular build but tannins are supple, new oak beneficially reduced to 15%. Afterglow from higher alc (15.5%) invites robust fare. **Chenin Blanc** ⊘ **★★★★** Clean pineapple & stonefruit, zested through with lime in **23 ⑧③** from a single block. Medium body with nice palate weight & length make a fine lunchtime partner. **Sauvignon Blanc ★★★** Crisp **23 ⑧①** has ample passionfruit flavours & crunchy capsicum & lemon freshness. 14.5% alc, but balanced & better than previous.

Stone range

Red Ⓠ ★★★ Mostly lightly oaked shiraz with 20% viognier in **19** ⑲. Fruity & mouthfilling, red plum jam flavour, subtle charcuterie whiff, bold 14.4% alc. Not tasted: **White.** Discontinued: **Rosé.** — MW

Location: Villiersdorp ▪ Map: Worcester ▪ Map grid reference: A6 ▪ WO: Stettyn/Western Cape ▪ Est 1964 ▪ 1stB 1984 ▪ Tasting & sales Mon-Fri 9-4.30 Sat/Sun 10-3; pub hols (seasonal) please call ahead ▪ Cheese platters ▪ Deli products ▪ Coffee bar ▪ MTB & walking trails ▪ Owner(s) 4 major producers (3 family-owned), Glenrosa Vineyards (BEE partnership with Adama Wines) ▪ Executive manager Sarel Meyer ▪ Winemaker(s) JM Crafford (Nov 2012), with Ronwan Griffiths (Jan 2022) ▪ Viticulturist(s) Pierre Snyman (Vinpro) ▪ 400ha (cab, merlot, ptage, shiraz, chard, chenin, sauv) ▪ 7,500t/23,000cs own label 25% red 75% white ▪ ARA, BEE, HACCP, IPW, WIETA ▪ PO Box 1520 Worcester 6849 ▪ info@stettyncellar.co.za ▪ www.stettyncellar.co.za ▪ **T +27 (0)23-340-4220**

☐ **Steynsrust** see Stellenrust

☐ **Steytler** see Kaapzicht Wine Estate

St Leger Wines

Charles Searle's ambitious but tiny winery - amongst the Cape's smallest by volume - is sited on part of an original Constantia farm granted in 1702. The block of muscat de Frontignan there goes into the dessert wine (no new vintage for us to taste this year), but the chardonnay is sourced from Elgin. The wines are crafted by a local consultant in an on-site, engineer-designed underground cellar.

★★★★☆ **Chardonnay** 🅰 Oak more obvious on **22** ⑨③ than previously, though only half new, & clay pot still contributing. Otherwise finely balanced: intense, sweet fruit gleams & lingers, along with vibrant cooler-climate acidity & lovely silkiness. Elegantly structured at 13.1% alc.

★★★★☆ **Le Marais** Ⓠ Deep gold dessert wine from muscat de Frontignan in historic Constantia style. Grapey muscat aromas dominate **17** ⑨①, palate a touch more complex, with new oak support. Elegantly fresh, delightfully free from cloy thanks to firm integrated acid. Pretty 375-ml teardrop bottle. — TJ

Location: Constantia ▪ WO: Elgin/Constantia ▪ Est 2013 ▪ 1stB 2016 ▪ Closed to public ▪ Owner(s) Charles Searle ▪ Winemaker(s)/viticulturist(s) consultant (2014) ▪ 1.5ha/1ha (muscat de F) & bought-in grapes ▪ 3t/1,000 btls (x 375ml) + 1,000 btls (x 750ml) own label 100% white ▪ 5 Suzanne Rd, Constantia, Cape Town 7806 ▪ enquiries@stleger.com ▪ www.stleger.com ▪ **T +27 (0)72-574-9597/Whatsapp +852 9028 9562**

Stoep   Ⓠ

Boutique label Stoep is owned by SA asset manager Gerrit Mars and Swiss partners, and the Red produced with a contract winemaker. The current vintage has been long aged at cellar and is a pleasure to drink now.

★★★★ **Red** Ⓠ Rare older vintage, **09** ⑧⑧ Bordeaux blend, cab (60%), cab franc, dab merlot. Black plums & liquorice, Mint Crisp, sweet spice. Silk texture, tannins seamless - a lot to like.— CR, CvZ

Location/WO: Stellenbosch ▪ Est/1stB 2001 ▪ Tasting, sales & tours by appt ▪ Owner(s) Zelpy 1023 (Pty) Ltd: 3 shareholders Gerrit Mars (SA), Sven Haefner & Daniel Hofer (both Swiss) ▪ Cellarmaster(s)/winemaker(s) Gerrit Mars & Petri Venter ▪ 850cs own label 100% red ▪ PO Box 216 Stellenbosch 7599 ▪ gerritmars@mweb. co.za ▪ **T +27 (0)82-352-5583**

☐ **Stofberg Family Vineyards** see Belle Rebelle

Stofberg Wine Estate   Ⓠ

Du Toitskloof Mountain foothills farm Klipdrift near Rawsonville in Breedekloof has been home to Stofberg family winecrafting since the late 1800s, and the first in the district, it is thought, to introduce cold fermentations. Current winemaker-viticulturist Pieter intends his wines to be tributes to his immediate predecessors as well as the first of his line in the Cape, Jacobus Stofberg, who arrived on the ship Het Hoop.

Border Stone Chenin Blanc ★★★★ Green-hued, appley **19** ⑧⑤, lemon biscuit & luxurious texture from 8 months on lees in oak, melon note throughout, giving richness & weight. Ends crisp, dry. — CR, CvZ

Location: Rawsonville ▪ Map/WO: Breedekloof ▪ Map grid reference: C5 ▪ Est 1878 ▪ 1stB 2013 ▪ Tasting strictly by appt only - see website for options ▪ Online sales ▪ Owner(s) J Du T Stofberg ▪ Cellarmaster(s)/winemaker(s)/viticulturist(s) Pieter Stofberg (Jan 2017) ▪ (merlot, ruby cab, chard, chenin, cbard, crouchen blanc, hanepoot, sauv, sem) ▪ 204cs own label 100% white ▪ IPW, WIETA ▪ PO Box 21, Klipdrift, R101, Rawsonville 6845 ▪ info@stofbergwines.co.za ▪ www.stofbergwines.co.za ▪ **T +27 (0)82-928-4943**

Stokkiesdraai Wines

'Simply assisting nature to do what she does best' is key to Cape Town winemaker Lieze Norval's approach for her young label, along with unhurried handcrafting of small batches and, for the wine debuting here, 'using as much of the grape as possible, not wasting the skins'. She thanks friend Lola Nicholls of Mitre's Edge for grapes, cellar space, equipment 'and extra hands when needed' in creating the wine, marketed to chiefly wine clubs and restaurants via private tastings. By-appointment public samplings are also available.

Chenin Blanc ★★★★ Three-part tank/barrel ferment for **23** (84), portion skin contact, which shows as melon preserve & thatch. Has underlying stonefruit, lots going on, fruit-acid juxtaposition giving a tangy effect. Previewed & provisionally rated. — CR, CvZ

Location: Cape Town ▪ WO: Simonsberg-Paarl ▪ Est/1stB 2023 ▪ Private tastings by arrangement ▪ Owner(s) Lieze Norval ▪ Winemaker(s) Lieze Norval (Jan 2023) ▪ Viticulturist(s) Bertus de Clerk (Jan 2023, consultant) ▪ 2t/250cs own label 100% white ▪ 20A Queens Rd, Cape Town 8005 ▪ lieze@stokkiesdraaiwines.co.za ▪ www. stokkiesdraaiwines.co.za ▪ **T +27 (0)82-828-5249**

☐ **Stone** see Stettyn Family Vineyards
☐ **Stonedance** see Piekenierskloof Wine Company
☐ **Stone Road** see Louisvale Wines
☐ **Stone Town** see Spice Route

Stonewall Wines

An Instagram-perfect Cape Dutch wine estate, with elegant gabled homestead, oak-shaded yard and white-washed stone perimeter wall, Helderberg home-farm Happy Vale has been in the De Waal family for over 150 years. Current custodian De Waal Koch tends the vines (recently planting more merlot for the blend) and makes the boutique wines alongside his namesake son, guided by Diners Club-lauded Ronell Wiid.

★★★★ Rubér ⊘ Cape Bordeaux from near-equal merlot & cab franc, 10% cab, **21** (87) back to form after **20 ★★★★** (85) with lovely complexity & brightness, savoury fruit & cool, leafy finish. Oak as Cab.
Cabernet Sauvignon ★★★★ Dark plums & cherries on a sturdy tannin base, 60% new oak, 18 months adds dark chocolate to finish in **21** (85). Give it time or decant in youth. In abeyance: **Chardonnay**. — WB

Location/WO: Stellenbosch ▪ Map: Helderberg ▪ Map grid reference: C2 ▪ Est 1828 ▪ 1stB 1997 ▪ Tasting & sales by appt Mon-Fri 10-5 Sat 10-1 ▪ Closed Easter Fri-Sun, Dec 25/26 & Jan 1 ▪ Refreshments by appt ▪ Accommodation ▪ Owner(s) De Waal Koch ▪ Cellarmaster(s) Ronell Wiid (Jan 2000, consultant) ▪ Winemaker(s) De Waal Koch (Jan 2000) ▪ Viticulturist(s) De Waal Koch (Jun 1984) ▪ 90ha/65ha (cabs s/f, merlot, ptage, shiraz, chard, pinot gris, sauv) ▪ 300t/4,000cs own label 80% red 20% white ▪ PO Box 5145 Helderberg 7135 ▪ stonewall@mweb.co.za ▪ www.stonewallwines.co.za ▪ **T +27 (0)83-527-7778/+27 (0)83-310-2407**

Stony Brook

Changes at the small venture founded in the mid-1990s by Nigel and Joy McNaught, with Eckhard and Stephanie Schultz taking the reins as owners, and Bev and Neill Erickson joining as tasting lounge assistant, and manager of the farm and grounds respectively. Supplying continuity are the McNaughts' son Craig, winemaker since 2011, and the house emphasis on traditional techniques, texture and ageing (potential and duration), the latter's importance underlined by the new maturation cellar nearing completion at press time. Grapes are sourced from the farm, home-base Franschhoek and more widely for mostly red wines of character and substance, with extra interest from local rarities like tempranillo and a smashing cap classique.

★★★★☆ Ghost Gum Cabernet Sauvignon From single block farmed for small, concentrated berries, house styled for the long haul. Deep, dark fruit woven with graphite, pencil lead & cigarbox from 28 months in 70% new oak. Latter also polishes **20** (94)'s bold tannins to augur well for the future.
★★★★ Cabernet Franc Single block delivers concentrated **20 ★★★★★** (90), which ups the intensity of **19** (88); same opulence & persistence of layered savoury-scrubby mulberry & cassis flavour, solid tannin grip, deftly integrated oak, none new, 19 months. 15% alc just a touch warming.

★★★★ **Pinot Noir** ⊘ Just three barrels of fruit-rich yet elegant & savoury **21** (88), the wood (third new) lending spice to bright sour cherry & berry fruit, powdery tannin in gentle support. No **20**.

★★★★☆ **Syrah Reserve** Aim is power & longevity, added piquancy of 25% whole-cluster ferment. **20** (91) has somewhat wild, meaty & organic character, as intense as biltong savouriness of more elegant **19** (91). 25 months in barrel, 20% new, add gravitas. Tame with cellar time or food accompaniment.

★★★★ **Ovidius** Quintessential expression of Spanish flag-bearer tempranillo in **21** (89): black cherry, dried fig & raspberry, emphatic grainy tannins demanding cellaring or food pairing. 2 years in 60% new oak add tobacco, cocoa & spice layers to dark & brooding body.

★★★★ **Camissa** ⊘ Khoisan for 'place of sweet waters', an occasional blend, ever changing. **20** (87) from cab & cab franc, dab petit verdot. Elegant, rather linear blackcurrant profile, tannins pliable after 2 years in cask, 30% new. **18** (87) was 40% shiraz & 3 Bordeaux grapes.

★★★★☆ **The Max** ⦾ Fine, cellarworthy Bordeaux red again a 4-way blend, cab led, in **19** ★★★★★ (95). Full, firm body, smoothly delicious after 26 months in 40% new oak, which also give cedar & dark chocolate overlay to blackcurrant, mulberry & plum fruit. Firmly in tradition of **18** (93).

★★★★ **Shiraz-Mourvèdre-Viognier** ⊘ Welcoming Rhône blend, mostly shiraz & splash co-fermented viognier, 30% wholebunch for freshness, plus 37% mourvèdre, all 26 months in older oak. Earthy style of previous reprised in smoke, bacon & meat notes of **20** (87). For the braai.

★★★★☆ **Ghost Gum White** ⦾ Home-farm's 2 best chardonnay blocks. Like last, weighty **21** (93) packed with yellow stonefruit & citrus, a nutty note & creamy texture from ferment/year in 60% new barrels, full malo & limited lees stirring. Crisp acid assures balance.

★★★★ **Sauvignon Blanc** Walker Bay grapes get year on lees in tank, with occasional stirring, in **22** (86). Bright & zesty greengage fruit flavours, fig & gooseberry grip in echoing finish.

★★★★ **The 'J'** ⊘ A white blend to light up the room when the power fails. Mainstay chardonnay (56%) & smidgen semillon, co-fermented & year in 2nd-fill oak, join forces with 38% unwooded viognier in **22** (86) for an explosive mouthful. Last tasted **19** (86) was chenin & viognier.

★★★★☆ **Lyle** ⦾ Poised, stately dry sparkler from single parcel of home-farm chardonnay, given 4 years on lees for subtle brioche & fine mousse. **18** (93) utterly delicious, with oystershell complexity on seamless citrus palate. As previous, no oaked reserve wine.— DS

Location/map: Franschhoek ▪ Map grid reference: D1 ▪ WO: Franschhoek/Walker Bay ▪ Est 1995 ▪ 1stB 1996 ▪ Tasting & sales Mon-Fri 10-5 Sat 10-1; pub hols (seasonal) please call ahead ▪ Fee R100 ▪ Self-catering cottages ▪ Owner(s) Eckhard & Stephanie Schultz ▪ Manager Neill Erickson (May 2023, farm & grounds) ▪ Winemaker(s) Craig McNaught (2011), with Michael Blaauw (Jan 2008) ▪ 23ha/14ha (cabs s/f, mourv, p verdot, shiraz, tempranillo, chard, sem, viog) ▪ 120t/8,000cs own label 65% red 35% white ▪ Green Valley Rd, Franschhoek 7690 ▪ info@stonybrook.co.za ▪ www.stonybrook.co.za ▪ **T +27 (0)21-876-2182**

☐ **Stories** see Pulpit Rock Winery
☐ **Stormhoek** see Origin Wine

Storm Wines ⦾

Storm Wines is a true specialist, crafting only Hemel-en-Aarde pinot noir and chardonnay, from just three sites so different in soil, aspect and location that each wine is individual and distinctive. Hannes Storm was working at Hamilton Russell when he discovered the small Vrede and Ignis vineyards 'with particularly exceptional terroirs'. He made the first pinots in 2012, and was inspired to eventually go out on his own to make site-specific wines, with 'careful viticulture, minimal intervention in the cellar and a constant nod to the Old World'. A Hemel-en-Aarde Ridge site was added, along with a pair of chardonnays and later small parcels of both varieties on Vrede. Latterly joined by wife Nathalia, Hannes is honoured to be invited to join the Cape Winemakers Guild and 'excited to be part of their upliftment initiatives'.

★★★★★ **Ignis Pinot Noir** ⦾ Registered single-vineyard, as rest, all reflecting individual terroir; same cellar treatment, hand harvested, wild ferment, reds 11 months in barrel, only difference is portion new oak, here 33%. Upper Hemel-en-Aarde's decomposed granite gives **22** (95) minerality, an earthy note, but there's fruit aplenty, red berries, oak a subtle savoury note, tannins harmonious. Exudes poise & refinement. Great ageability, as for **21** ★★★★★ (93).

★★★★★ **Vrede Pinot Noir** From Hemel-en-Aarde Valley. Clay-rich, low-vigour Bokkeveld soil, **22** ★★★★☆ ⑨④ had 35% new oak, more than the others, giving a toasty, white pepper note to the red berry-plummy fruit, the tannins firm but ripe. An intriguing violet nuance adds to the complexity; this has more heft than its siblings, a reined-in power. Follows complex **21** ⑨⑤.

★★★★☆ **Ridge Pinot Noir** Clay-rich, low-crop Hemel-en-Aarde Ridge soil dictates style, vivid red berries & cherries, **22** ⑨④'s texture lithe, with tannin edge for food & some ageing. Savoury interplay from the oaking, but done with restraint, balance maintained. Like this range, not showy but nothing lacking, has complexity & admirable class. Also in 1.5L, as all.

★★★★★ **Vrede Chardonnay** Making a pleasing comparison, 2 site-specific chardonnays, this **22** ⑨⑤ from Hemel-en-Aarde Valley. Intense lemon & lime throughout, 8 months in small barrels, 30% new, masterly judged, fruit reigns supreme, with a subtle savoury seam. Sleek, its freshness fitting the character, has purity & focus, admirable breeding. **21** ★★★★★ ⑨④ similar character.

★★★★★ **Ridge Chardonnay** Same treatment as Vrede, except oak 32% new, plus 10% terracotta clay amphora. **22** ⑨⑤ from its Hemel-en-Aarde Ridge site shows lemon & ruby grapefruit bolstered by racy acid, flavours more mineral than citrus. Shortbread tone on the finish another reflection of its impressive complexity.— CR

Location: Hermanus ▪ Map: Walker Bay & Bot River ▪ Map grid reference: B4 ▪ WO: Hemel-en-Aarde Valley/Hemel-en-Aarde Ridge/Upper Hemel-en-Aarde Valley ▪ Est 2011 ▪ 1stB 2012 ▪ Tasting by appt ▪ Closed Easter Fri/Sun, Ascension day, Dec 25/26 & Jan 1 ▪ Owner(s) Hannes Storm ▪ Winemaker(s)/viticulturist(s) Hannes Storm (Dec 2011) ▪ 9.5ha (pinot, chard) ▪ 40t/6,000cs own label 70% red 30% white ▪ IPW ▪ PO Box 431 Hermanus 7200 ▪ info@stormwines.co.za ▪ www.stormwines.co.za ▪ **T +27 (0)28-125-0073**

Strandveld Wines

Close to windswept Cape Agulhas, Strandveld is Africa's southernmost winery, established just over 20 years ago by a group of friends on the ribbon of coastal land that names the venture. Conrad Vlok, Diners Club 2023 laureate and winemaker almost since inception, and viticulturist Dehan Veldsman have harvested the first crops from the young Ribbokrand vineyard, and are excited about the potential of the pinot noir, sauvignon and albariño planted there the past year for providing future building blocks for their 'terroir-true, cool-climate wines showing elegance, complexity and restraint'.

Strandveld range

★★★★☆ **Grenache** With 14% syrah, third wholebunch, 10 months older barrels. Piquant berries in **22** ⑨① , lighter crafting (13% alc) than full-ripe **21** ★★★★ ⑧⑨, sleeker, more refined. Tannins threaded through aid definition & provide foundation for ageing. WO Cape South Coast.

★★★★☆ **Syrah** Just a dab of viognier but overall **21** ⑨③ more serious than sibling, starting with 20 months oaking, 35% new. Enough berry fruit to assimilate the tannins with ease, welcome the savoury spicing. Succulent & streamlined, already drinking well, with a future from the hidden muscle tone.

★★★★☆ **The Navigator** Syrah-led (69%) 4-part Rhône blend, a proven partnership, offering brambly fruit, spice, scrub & smoky oak from 19 months in barrels, 35% new. **20** ⑨④'s plush texture easily handles the supple tannins, but dry finish attests to their underlying strength & function to enable a future.

★★★★★ **Pofadderbos Sauvignon Blanc** ⊘ Single-block sauvignon noted for expressive cool-climate character. With more minerality than its sibling & **21** ⑨④, plus salty freshness, without abandoning the varietal green notes, **22** ★★★★★ ⑨⑤ has a lemongrass & fennel underpin. So zesty, it wakens the taste buds, likely to remain in perfect health for years to come.

★★★★☆ **Adamastor** Sauvignon with 45% semillon, which was barrel fermented/aged 10 months, 40% new. **21** ⑨⓪ has site-influenced intensity & youthfulness, the oaking giving a waxy, wild honey savoury tone to the lemongrass flavours. Taut, complex, individual.

Not tasted: **Skaamgesiggie Méthode Cap Classique.** Occasional release: **Anders Sparrman Pinot Noir, Viognier.**

First Sighting range

★★★★ **Syrah** ⊘ Was 'Shiraz'. Fruit-forward dark berries & plums, **21** ⑧⑧'s 12-month oaking contributes smoky tones, white pepper & spice, adding to the attraction. Juicy, with amenable tannins, in perfect drinking nick, has flavour & interest. WO Cape South Coast.

★★★★ **Sauvignon Blanc** ⊘ Has 14% semillon but sauvignon dictates: green fig, winter melon, some chopped herbs, the piercing acid keeping it fresh & vibrant. **23** ⑧⑨ a good reflection of its cool-climate terroir, shows precision & focus.

Rosé ⊘ ★★★★ Shiraz with 37% grenache, pale salmon hue, trim figured (12.5% alc) but 5 months on lees ensure compensating palate weight. Year later, dry **22** ⑧④'s red berry styling has an intriguing spicy dried herb nuance, offers tasty appeal. — CR

Location: Elim ▪ Map: Southern Cape ▪ Map grid reference: D7 ▪ WO: Elim/Cape South Coast ▪ Est 2002 ▪ 1stB 2003 ▪ Tasting, sales & cellar tours Mon-Fri 8-4 Sat 10-3 pub hols 10-4 (seasonal) please call ahead ▪ Closed Good Fri, Dec 25 & Jan 1 ▪ Farm produce ▪ BYO picnic ▪ Walks/hikes ▪ MTB ▪ Conservation area ▪ Two self-catering cottages ▪ Wine club ▪ Owner(s) Strandveld Vineyards & Rietfontein Trust ▪ Winemaker(s) Conrad Vlok (Dec 2004) ▪ Viticulturist(s) Dehan Veldsman (Dec 2020) ▪ 82ha (grenache, mourv, pinot, shiraz, sauv, sem, viog) ▪ 350t/52,000cs own label 45% red 55% white ▪ IPW ▪ PO Box 1020 Bredasdorp 7280 ▪ info@strandveld.co.za ▪ www.strandveld.co.za ▪ **T +27 (0)28-482-1902/6**

☐ **Strange Kompanjie** *see* Wildeberg Wines

Strydom Family Wine

Louis and Rianie Strydom are CWG members who carved stellar careers at top Helderberg wineries Ernie Els and Haskell (respectively) while building their own brand since 2012, with mostly leased vineyards and rented facilities. French varieties planted in 2020 and nurtured by their elder son, Elsenburg-trained Jean-Louis, at the home-farm on prime Simonsberg foothills are producing fuller crops from which to craft their 'elegant, well-balanced and -structured' wines, reflecting personal involvement 'in every drop we make'. An old shed is being upgraded and the hope is to open a tasting facility in the near future.

CWG Auction range

★★★★☆ **The Game Changer** ⊛ Strydom known for cab sauvignon, so this cab franc-based wine is a departure. With touch more merlot (22%) than previous, **18** ⑨③ is sophisticated, seductive & subtly perfumed, silk textured & effortlessly balanced. Part natural, part inoculated ferment & harmonious oaking (50% new, 18 months) subsumed into the rich depth of fruit. Shows family's mastery of Bordeaux.

Artisan range

★★★★☆ **Rex Cabernet Sauvignon** ⊛ Emphatic yet refined **20** ⑨③ from Helderberg vines. Signature blackcurrant with lead pencil & cigarbox notes from 25% new oak, 18 months. Sappy, dry tannin structure, youthful but inherently poised, augurs well for a decade's development. No **19**.

★★★★ **Rock Star Syrah** ⊘ Intricate vinification in **21** ⑧⑨, 20% wholebunch, 33% aged in amphora, balance in old oak, allows vivid red fruit, savouriness & sprinkling of white pepper centre stage. Refined, not showy as name suggests, with dry tannins, balance & potential to develop. First since **17** ⑧⑨.

★★★★ **Danièle Chenin Blanc** As bright & vivacious as previous, **22** ⑧⑧ offers similar starfruit & green-gage flavours, freshening seam of acid. Tank ferment completed in amphora, aged 10 months in mostly old oak. Delicious now, with a few years to go.

★★★★ **Siblings White** ⊕ Aromatic stonefruit flavours in **22** ⑧⑥ from tiny first harvest of chenin, marsanne & roussanne (83/10/7). Co-ferment & ageing 7 months on lees in amphora preserve delicately balanced flavours, succulence & freshness. Lipsmackingly drinkable.

Legends & Myths Cinsault ⊕ ★★★ First crop in **22** ⑧② shows variety's thatchy red berry fruit, given some breadth from old oak. A plump & amiable sipper.

Premium range

★★★★ **Cabernet Sauvignon-Cinsault** ⊘ Even juicier in **21** ⑧⑦ ex Stellenbosch fruit, from these pioneers of fashionable cab & cinsaut heritage blends. As previous, labelled 'Retro', cab provides dark fruit & gravitas, cinsaut (15%) vivid red fruit. Older oak, 16 months, in support. Ready to enjoy.

Not tasted: **Sauvignon Blanc**. — MW

Location/WO: Stellenbosch ▪ Est 2012 ▪ 1stB 2009 ▪ Tasting by appt only ▪ Owner(s) Louis & Rianie Strydom ▪ Cellarmaster(s) Rianie Strydom ▪ 8.5ha/4.5ha (cab f, cinsaut, shiraz, chenin, marsanne, rouss) ▪ 1,000cs own label 70% red 30% white ▪ IPW ▪ PO Box 1290 Stellenbosch 7599 ▪ rianie@strydomvineyards.com ▪ www.strydomvineyards.com ▪ **T +27 (0)21-889-8553/+27 (0)82-290-6399**

Sugarbird Distillery

The sugarbird in the name and on the label of the brandy here suggests the striking, long-tailed animal's natural habitat, the aromatic vegetation endemic to the Cape known as fynbos, which is used as an infusion and filter during production. Brand owner True Kindred Spirits (see separate listing) also markets Sugarbird & Friends, an innovative collection of mini-bottles showcasing other top South African handmade brandies.

★★★★ **XO Brandy** ⓧ From Paarl & Robertson colombard & chenin, 14 year old potstill (89) has lovely fragrance, as expected, the botanicals & infusion manifesting more on the finish, as subtle dried herbs & honey, with peach, pear drop & chocolate among the other scents & smooth flavours.— WB

Location: Cape Town ▪ Est 2017 (Sugarbird Gin) ▪ Closed to public ▪ Owner(s) True Kindred Spirits (Pty) Ltd ▪ Director Matt Bresler ▪ Distiller Edmund Paulsen (Aug 2017) ▪ Unit E18, Prime Park, Mocke Rd, Diep River, Cape Town 7945 ▪ andre@kindredspirits.co.za ▪ www.sugarbirddistillery.com, www.kindredspirits.co.za ▪ **T** +27 (0)87-057-9651

Sumaridge Wines ⓠ

The wine estate of Britons Holly and Simon Bellingham-Turner has new owners (see Hasher Family), but many of their Sumaridge wines are still available, including some well-matured vintages, styled to be 'distinctively elegant, ample in body and complex in flavour'. Tastings are available by appointment.

★★★★ **Merlot** ⓧ With full dark-fruited ripeness, **16** (87) is curvaceous, confident, has much to give. Well spiced, some cocoa, rich chocolate notes from 18 months in barrel, tannins firm but accessible.

★★★★ **Pinot Noir** ⓧ Darker hued than expected, mirroring the charry oak overlaying cherry, raspberry & lifted floral notes. **17** ★★★★☆ (85) firm & sturdy body, with good support from 30% new oak, 11 months. Unlike **16** (89), ready on release.

★★★★ **Pinotage** ⓧ High-toned aroma & slightly bitter finish to **18** ★★★ (82)'s sweet mulberry & strawberry body, tannins touch rustic. Last was **16** ★★★★☆ (90), which improved on **15** (88).

★★★★ **Syrah** ⓧ Hedgerow fruit with charcuterie notes, savoury spice, **15** ★★★★★ (90)'s opulent perfume draws you in. Smooth texture, tannins from 18 months in barrel (30% new) fully integrated. Delicious, & notch up on **13** (88). No **14**.

★★★★ **Bushell** ⓧ Usual blend, merlot-led with malbec & cab franc, but **17** (88) now from Upper Hemel-en-Aarde grapes. Fleshy & fruit expressive, berry melange supported by 14 months French/Hungarian barrels, 20% new.

★★★★ **Epitome** ⓧ Cape Blend **16** (87), 60% shiraz & pinotage, confident & well matured. Spice & floral detail on red & black fruit, neatly resolved tannins & lively acidity to up refreshment.

★★★★☆ **Chardonnay** ⓧ Like **18** (93), satisfying **19** ★★★★ (89) offers toast & butter richness, 70% in small barrel, 30% new, creating thick, creamy texture which fans of this style will enjoy. Tad less acid verve, though, fruit not as expressive.

★★★★ **Sauvignon Blanc** ⓧ Precise & detailed **20** ★★★★☆ (90), full-spectrum sauvignon character - from cool green fruit & herbs to tropical passionfruit & papaya. Like last-tasted **18** (89), foundation of succulent acid, bracing dryness & persistent savoury oystershell minerality.

★★★★ **Klip Kop** ⓧ Now from Upper Hemel-en-Aarde fruit & unoaked, **20** (87) harmonious blend sauvignon & semillon (79/21) shows former's granadilla & fig characters, latter's wax & lemon. Some attractive nutty character from bottle-age, crisply dry yet rounded.

★★★★☆ **Maritimus** ⓧ After 5 years in bottle, **16** (90) is ready to drink, shows nut & honey development backing its lemon, papaya & Golden Delicious apple fruit. Mostly sauvignon, near equal chardonnay & semillon, unoaked.

Tara Rosé ⓧ ★★★★ Mainly merlot for its red berries but also malbec & cab franc, giving **19** (83) more serious dimensions, slate, a touch of fynbos. Nice food wine. WO Walker Bay. **The Wayfarer** ⓧ ★★★★☆ From pinot noir, 42 months on lees, **17** (85) pink dry cap classique sparkler has strawberry & candyfloss, a leafy note, some meatiness & texture for food. — CvZ

Location: Hermanus ▪ WO: Upper Hemel-en-Aarde Valley/Walker Bay ▪ Tasting by appt only (info@sumaridge.co.za) ▪ Owner(s) Holly & Simon Bellingham-Turner ▪ 20,000cs own label 45% red 50% white 5% rosé ▪ info@sumaridge.co.za ▪ www.sumaridge.co.za

Summerhill Wines

Tying the knot in a stained-glass vineyard chapel, and catching a live show at the Orgasmic Music Gallery are just some of the buffet of attractions served by Charles and Ingrid Hunting on the Summerhill home-farm in Stellenbosch. Wine isn't neglected, however, and in addition to the small range of branded bottlings on offer, there are two tasting venues, one on terra firma, the other floating languidly on the farm dam.

Merlot ⓥ ★★★★ Bold blue- & black-fruited **19** ⑭ improves on last in body, restraint & length. Cocoa & cedar notes from oak, 25% new, 14.2% alc less warm on palate. **Shiraz** ⓥ ★★★ Lively blackberries & brambles mingle with spice on savoury & juicy **17** ⑫. Friendly & moreish. Stellenbosch WO. **Rosé** ★★★ Pale pink hue on **23** ⑧⓪, subtle cherry & lemon flavours, lightly succulent & gently dry. **Chardonnay** ★★★ Marmalade & vanilla on light, tangy **22** ⑫. Ferment & ageing in new barrels masks the fruit mid-2023. **Chenin Blanc** ★★★ Light, melon & citrus on sappy **23** ⑧①, straightforward & somewhat short lived. Not tasted: **Pinot Noir Rosé Sparkling Wine**. Occasional release: **Red Blend**. — FM

Location/map: Stellenbosch ▪ Map grid reference: E3 ▪ WO: Simonsberg-Stellenbosch/Stellenbosch ▪ 1stB 2008 ▪ Tasting & sales daily 9-5 ▪ Pizzeria ▪ Craft beer & gin ▪ Orgasmic Music Gallery ▪ Vineyard chapel (seating 160 pax) ▪ Owner(s) Summerhill Wines cc, Charles R Hunting ▪ Winemaker(s) Mike Dobrovic ▪ Viticulturist(s) Chris Pieters (consultant) ▪ 15ha/10ha (cab, grenache, malbec, merlot, pinot, shiraz, chard, chenin) ▪ 24t/2,500cs own label 40% red 60% white ▪ PO Box 12448 Die Boord 7613 ▪ charles@summerhill-wines.co.za, manager@summerhillwines.co.za, wine@summerhillwines.co.za ▪ www.summerhillwines.co.za ▪ **T +27 (0)21-889-5015**

Sun International Wines

These branded wines are selected for versatility and wide palate appeal by the Food & Beverage team at Sun International, one of SA's foremost hotel groups, working with a 'by appointment' winery.

Cabernet Sauvignon ★★★ Designed to partner a wide variety of dishes through its aromatic blackberry, savoury & meaty tones, **22** ⑧① has a comforting mocha nuance to the fruit. **Chenin Blanc** ★★★ Fresh & appetising **23** ⑧⓪ has guava, green apple & herbal charm with 14.2% alc well tucked away. Discontinued: **Blanc de Noir Red Muscadel**. — DS

WO: Robertson ▪ Sales daily at Sun International Hotel Group venues ▪ Hotels ▪ Restaurants (à la carte/buffet) ▪ Casino bars ▪ Conference venues ▪ Facilities for children ▪ Tour groups ▪ Festivals ▪ Concerts ▪ Owner(s) Sun International Management Limited ▪ www.suninternational.com ▪ **T +27 (0)11-780-7000**

☐ **Sunkissed** *see* Douglas Green

☐ **Sunkloof Reserve** *see* Stellenview Premium Wines

Super Single Vineyards

Daniël de Waal this year celebrates two decades of wine under his own label, based on Canettevallei, an old family wine and lavender farm in Stellenboschkloof. Wider Stellenbosch supplies single-vineyard grapes for his largest range (under the Pella label) and the top-level cabernet-merlot blend, and for some of the Heritage Vineyards line-up. Most of the wines Daniël makes are red - in a style that often successfully straddles traditional Stellenbosch winemaking and a fresher, lighter approach - but there's now a fascinating new semillon, serious but unoaked.

Superior Vineyard

★★★★☆ **The King & I** ⓐ Understated as usual, **18** ⑭ blend has 60% cab lifted by sweet merlot, the whole showing persuasive savoury, cedary edge to dark fruit, which is ripe but restrained. Bonus to have half a decade in bottle before release, giving greater harmony though firm tannins touch drying. 30% new oak & 14% alc, as Granietbult.

Coastal Vineyards

★★★★☆ **Pella Granietbult Cabernet Sauvignon** ⓐ Always classic-styled, elegant cab, with cigarbox & dark berries. Somewhat less intense fruit on **18** ⑭ exposes tannic structure more, but early development integrating it all well, & making for impressive though still restrained wine. Approachable now, but these serious reds will benefit from further bottle age.

★★★★ **Pella Oukliprant Malbec** Plenty of delicious ripe fruit - loganberry, cherry - on **20** ⑧⑨. Soft textured, with gently smooth tannic grip & firm, properly dry finish that characterises these reds.

★★★★☆ **Pella Verlatenkloof Merlot** Matches concentrated complexity & serious, firm structure with generous approachability of sweetly ripe, dark fruit at its core. **19** (94) elegantly balanced & not too powerful at 14% alc, 20% new oak not intrusive but adding spicy tobacco notes. There's even a light-feeling freshness.

★★★★☆ **Pella Thomas Se Dolland Pinotage 21** (91) again winningly finds a mid-point between new-wave, pure-fruited fresh charm & serious, firmly structured ageability of riper, more extracted traditional approaches. 13.5% alc, only older oak. Good now, will develop.

★★★★☆ **Pella Kanniedood Chenin Blanc** (2) (🌼) Quince, pear & lemon vibrancy on **20** (90) reprises exceptional form of previous. Creamy oak frame from 8 months in 20% new Hungarian barrels, ripe richness lingers long. Recognised single-vineyard, as most.

★★★★★ **Pella White Granite Semillon** (NEW) (✓) (🐝) Preserved lemon notes (with lanolin) on **21** (95), made more savoury by 2 days on skins before ferment, mutate into riper, tangerine quality on lingering palate. Also a delicious granadilla tropicality in the subtle complexity. Unoaked, fresh & lively, with gentle phenolic grip. Should develop well.

Not tasted: **Pella Die Hang Sangiovese**.

Continental Vineyards

★★★★★ **Mount Sutherland Syrah** (2) From vines at 1,500 m altitude, seductive **18** (97) shows effortless elegance & poise. Subtle & restrained, complex & fine. 18 months in old oak followed by 12 in bottle. No **17**. WO Sutherland-Karoo.

Heritage Vineyards

★★★★☆ **Voorloper** (🐝) (🌼) Off a 1985 syrah vineyard, lightly perfumed **20** (93) has both dark & red fruit. Fine, firm musculature but also flavourful juiciness untrammelled by new oak. Overall sense is of fresh, inviting lightness, not precluding a significant future.

★★★★☆ **Swaartekrag** (2) (🌼) Chenin blanc from 1968 Swartland vines. **20** (90) mid-gold, with sunny ripe apple & peach flavours balanced by fresh acid on lightly rich, oxidatively broad palate. 13% alc.

Discontinued: **Saamloop**. — TJ

Location/map: Stellenbosch ▪ Map grid reference: C5 ▪ WO: Stellenbosch/Sutherland-Karoo/Swartland ▪ Est/1stB 2004 ▪ Tasting Mon-Sat 10-5 ▪ Closed all pub hols ▪ Owner(s)/viticulturist(s) Daniël de Waal ▪ Winemaker(s) Daniël de Waal, with Suzanne Fourie (also marketing/sales) ▪ 60ha Canettevallei farm (cab, malbec, ptage, pinot, sangio, shiraz, chenin) ▪ 4,000cs own label 80% red 20% white ▪ PO Box 89 Vlottenburg 7604 ▪ marketing@ssvineyards.co.za ▪ www.supersinglevineyards.co.za ▪ **T +27 (0)72-200-5552 (Daniël)/+27 (0)82-331-9866 (Suzanne)/+27 (0)72-730-9811 (office)**

☐ **Supréme** *see* La RicMal

Survivor Wines ⓠ

The story of a resolute Nguni cow named Survivor informs this premium brand, now under the guidance of cellarmaster and CWG member Pierre Wahl, who brings decades of acclaim to the range. Grapes are selected from five regions 'to express unique terroir characteristics and show great complexity'. Tradouw is a focus area, with plans to plant more vines there. Tastings and sales are available by appointment at Overhex.

Reserve range

★★★★★ **Pinotage** (🐝) Power-packed with dense dark fruit, cocoa- & tobacco-seamed from 20 months in oak, 50% new, **21** (95) is bold & impressive, as intended, just 10 best barrels selected. Yet surprisingly accessible, the tannins ripe, providing platform for some ageing.

★★★★☆ **Chenin Blanc** (2) Bold, self-assured **21** (92) has loads of heft & extract, shows sweetly spiced dried apricot, honey & marzipan. 80% was wild-yeast fermented in new oak, remained there for 11 months, & wood still a presence but should settle with cellar time.

Cellar Master Series

★★★★☆ **Pendulum** (2) Cab franc & 15% merlot, **19** (91) has lead pencil & cedarwood aromas, focused black cherry & currant fruit, earthy minerality. Elegant & supple, with lovely ripe tannins that gained gloss & smoothness during 2 years in 20% new oak.

★★★★☆ **Chardonnay** (NEW) Different handling to its sibling, third tank ferment, rest in barrels & on staves. The savoury biscuit seam is an intrinsic part of **22** (90), with fresh & dried stonefruit accompaniment, livening acidity. There's palate weight, richness & power. This range from Tradouw vines.

Terroir range

★★★★ **Cabernet Sauvignon** Herbaceous thread in the blackcurrant fruit, **21** (89) lacks the palate concentration of **20** ★★★★☆ (91) but gets the tannins right, firm but ripe, a support. Spent 15 months in barrel, nice extraction of spice. WO Stellenbosch.

★★★★ **Pinotage** ⊘ (🏵) Change in style, fruit less ripe, 18 months in barrels, 20% new, no American, there's more restraint, focus, without quality loss. Dark-toned fruit, cocoa & smoky spice, **21** ★★★★★ (90) has muscle tone for cellaring, more depth & complexity than **20** (88).

★★★★☆ **Syrah** ⊘ Ripe & full-flavoured, with brambly fruit, scrub & dried herbs, **21** (90)'s 18 months in barrel a spicy top note, bed of amenable tannins. Can age but already delicious, the texture smooth & round, with great mouthfeel.

★★★★☆ **Chardonnay** Boldly styled, fresh & preserved citrus, plus spice from 11 months in barrel, 33% new, after wild ferment: **22** (90) expects to be taken seriously. Elgin imparts fruit depth & intensity, a racy limy freshness to finish.

★★★★☆ **Chenin Blanc** ⊘ Partial tank, 40% oak ferment/8 months, giving **22** (90) layered appeal: apple & pear, some white peach, with melba toast savouriness. Dry, streamlined & fruity-fresh, has heaps of personality.

★★★★☆ **Sauvignon Blanc** ⊘ Cool-climate styling from Elgin, **22** (90) is essentially mineral with green notes in the perfume & flavour; textbook sauvignon. Gets the finish right too, limy, intense, long.

★★★★ **Cap Classique** (NEW) From Darling chardonnay, **20** (88) had a touch of oak which manifests as Lemon Cream biscuit. Spent 16 months on lees, lovely richness of flavour despite the elegant structure (11.5% alc). Vibrantly fresh.— CR

Location: Worcester ▪ WO: Swartland/Tradouw/Elgin/Stellenbosch/Darling ▪ Tasting & sales at Overhex Wines International Mon-Fri 10-4.30 ▪ Closed all pub hols ▪ Cellarmaster(s) Pierre Wahl ▪ pierre@survivor-wines.com, marketing@survivorwines.com ▪ www.survivorwines.com ▪ **T +27 (0)23-347-5012**

☐ **Sutherland** *see* Thelema Mountain Vineyards
☐ **Sutherland Continental** *see* Super Single Vineyards
☐ **Swallow** *see* Natte Valleij Wines

Swanepoel Wines   (𝒬) (⌂)

Previously vinifying under the banner Oude Compagnies Post, Dirk Swanepoel now makes his boutique terroir wines under the family name in the cellar established by parents Jerry and Henriette on a fynbos-carpeted mountain slope in Tulbagh in the 1990s. Dirk has planted more pinotage as well as locally rare white variety assyrtiko, and plans to focus on improving grape quality while attracting more visitors to the farm.

★★★★ **Pinotage** Vibrant & attractively wild, **22** (86) dense & concentrated brambleberry fruit, solid hit of oak spice, powerful tannin grip. Unyielding despite 18 months in oak, needs time.

★★★★ **Shiraz** (🏵) Muscular, intense **21** (89) shows admirable focus & linearity in its morello fruit, tarry tobacco savouriness. Full, chalky tannins underscore heavy extraction, suggest lengthy cellaring.

★★★★ **SMG** Rhône-style blend shiraz & mourvèdre (42/42), splash viognier, **21** ★★★★☆ (85) generous & full, leathery nuance to tangy black cherries, hint of vanilla caramel on thick, chewy tannins which may meld with cellaring. Tad less together than **20** (86).

★★★★ **SMG Rosé** Pale, floral-toned **23** (86) is 87% shiraz, wild yeast co-fermented with mourvèdre & viognier, 4 months on lees. Fresh & focused, weight & acid well-judged, appealing summer refreshment.

★★★★ **White Pinotage** Unusual take on black grape, tank sample **23** (86) is silvery lemon coloured, spice & herb laden, the citrus body pierced with bright acid. Light oak adds dimension without intruding.

★★★★ **Grenache Noir Méthode Cap Classique** (𝒬) Admirably refined & characterful zero-dosage sparkling **20** (88), water-white in hue, spent 6 months in older oak, then 15 months on lees, building body & structure. Creamy strawberry shortbread, pithy lemon & ginger notes.

★★★★ **Vassileon GPS Cape Ruby** 'Port' from mostly grenache noir, **22** ⑧⑦ preview shows better balance & refinement than **21** ★★★★ ⑧⑤ in its honeyed plum & cherry fruit, satisfying spirit grip (17.5% alc). **Cabernet Sauvignon** ★★★ Concentrated, full-bodied **20** ⑧① has impressive extract & generous black fruit, somewhat high-toned aromas. **Grenache Noir** ★★★★ Ripe & forthcoming **21** ⑧⑤, convincing piquant raspberry fruit, prominent acid grip, grainy tannins. Offers juicy, fruity drinking enjoyment whereas **20** ★★★★ ⑧⑥ showed touch more seriousness. **Mourvèdre** ★★★ Rather unsettled **21** ⑧② has tanned leather & oak spice notes, subdued berry & plum fruit, robust, lingering tannic finish. Not tasted: **The Buchu Trail**. — GdB

Location/map/WO: Tulbagh ▪ Map grid reference: F4 ▪ Est 1995 ▪ 1stB 2003 ▪ Tasting & sales Mon-Sat 11-4 Sun 11-2; pub hols (seasonal) please call ahead ▪ Guest accommodation ▪ Owner(s) Oude Compagnies Post (Pty) Ltd ▪ Cellarmaster(s)/winemaker(s)/viticulturist(s) Dirk Swanepoel ▪ 235ha/11ha (cab, grenache, mourv, ptage, shiraz, assyrtiko) ▪ 50t own label 60% red 30% white 10% rosé ▪ Other export brand: Buchu Trail ▪ PO Box 111 Tulbagh 6820 ▪ swanepoel@compagnies.co.za ▪ www.oudecompagnies.com ▪ **T +27 (0)76-013-8613/+27 (0)76-183-0083**

Swartberg Wingerde

This own brand of Rudiger Gretschel, production director for major wine company Vinimark and cellarmaster at Reyneke Wines, now has its own home, after the recent purchase of Swartberg farm in Piekenierskloof. Since inception, Rudiger has been making wine exclusively from these grapes and two neighbours'. Now he has the opportunity to plant more vines and make wines reflecting this singular, harsh landscape, where all vineyards are above 600 metres altitude, grown as bushvines and unirrigated. Some were planted as long ago as 1965. A non-interventionist approach in vineyard and cellar results in wines of purity and freshness.

Swartberg range

★★★★☆ **Sangiro** Ⓥ Perfumed, pure-fruited & characterful **21** ⑨④ pinotage. At just 12.5% alc, it's light, stony-dry, supple & subtle - most beautifully balanced & fresh. 9 months in oak, some new for the first time, adding to the fine texture & supporting an increased seriousness. Last made was **19** ⑨③.

Miracle Bush range

★★★★☆ **Red** Ⓐ As in previous syrah, grenache noir, pinotage blend, there's perfume & fruit purity, but their delicacy more emphatically & lengthily felt in **21** ⑨③'s sweet succulence. Gentle squeeze of tannin lends form to general light feel. Barrel & foudre matured, 9% new.

★★★★☆ **White** Ⓐ Adds 56% grenache blanc to chenin & drop palomino in **22** ⑨④, enhancing freshness, subtle peach & limy complexity, & steely grip. Extra textural dimension from natural ferment in 20% amphora, large & smaller oak, 15% new. Lees ageing adds its own note of distinction. 13.5% alc.

Holism range

★★★★☆ **Garnacha** Ⓥ Lighter colour & fragrance of grenache noir with understated & refined but sweet fruit expressiveness on **21** ⑨②. 20% in oak, rest steel & concrete to maximise fresh purity. Harmonious, as all these wines, making for early approachability but helping to guarantee some ageability.

★★★★ **Palomino** Wild & sea breeze freshness, complemented by light salty farewell, **22** ⑧⑦'s gently firm build & light 11% alc make attractive, interesting if uncomplex drinking. Spontaneous ferment, 9 months 2,500L older oak.— AL

Location: Stellenbosch ▪ WO: Piekenierskloof ▪ Est/1stB 2017 ▪ Closed to public ▪ Owner(s) Swartberg Wingerde (Pty) Ltd ▪ Cellarmaster(s)/winemaker(s) Rudiger Gretschel (2017) ▪ Viticulturist(s) Rudiger Gretschel ▪ 1,000ha/3.4ha (grenache n/b, ptage, shiraz, chenin, palomino) ▪ 2,500cs own label 40% red 60% white ▪ rudiger@swartbergwingerde.co.za

Swartland Winery   Ⓥ Ⓨ ⓘ Ⓐ Ⓖ

Established at Malmesbury in 1948 by 15 farmers, this Swartland pioneer today has 68 producer-shareholders and 3,600 ha of vines spread over many microclimates, some cooled by the Atlantic. Diverse varieties are grown and bottled, and lesser-known ones introduced, confirming winemaker Marius Prins' claim there's 'something to enjoy for everyone's taste'. Styles are also varied: oak-aged Idelia, Bush Vine and Limited Release ranges are from ±45-year-old blocks and vinified for ageing; Winemakers Collection is unwooded, more fruit driven and immediately drinkable. The emphasis across the line-up is on quality at a fair price.

Idelia range

★★★★☆ Idelia ② Pinotage with shiraz & cab from 40+ year old dryland bushvines. Complex berry, spice mix, complemented by freshness & fine tannins. **20** ⑨ drinks well now, has good potential.

Bush Vine range

★★★★ Pinotage ⊘ Presents modern face of variety in appealing raspberry perfume matched by sweet-fruited, smooth palate, fine tannins in **21** ⑧. Oak supportive. Improves on **19 ★★★★** ⑧; no **20**.

★★★★ Syrah ⊘ Dark soft berries & spice in **21** ⑧'s comfortably rounded body; gentle tannin rumble, freshness & savoury conclusion add to drinking pleasure. Better balanced than **20 ★★★★** ⑧.

★★★★ Chenin Blanc ⊘ Fresh, intense apple & pear fragrance bolstered by old-vine concentration & fine, fruity acid. 40% older-oak ferment & lees ageing add depth, interest to **22** ⑧. Great value.

Cabernet Sauvignon ★★★☆ Quiet dark berry, chocolate aromas, lifted on palate by few grams sugar; firm, round tannins provide freshness, drinkability on release in **21** ⑧. Year in oak, 25% new, as all these reds.

Limited Release range

★★★★ Roussanne ⊘ Floral & waxy generosity on **22** ⑧, lees richness adds depth, smooth palate shows fruit weight without heaviness (12.7% alc). 20% older-oak ferment adds dimension. More distinctive than **21 ★★★★** ⑧.

Carignan ★★★ Pruney, ripe & rather sombre. Dash of zest enlivens softish & short palate. **21** ⑧ less attractive than last. **Cinsault** ⑩ ⊘ **★★★☆** Highlights sweet cherry & spice fruit; **21** ⑧ fresh & juicy, gently rounded grip. **Grenache Noir** ⑩ ⊘ **★★★☆** Lively & light textured, **21** ⑧ brims with bright, juicy red berries, tangy grip. Can benefit from light chilling. 10% fermented in older oak. **Mourvèdre** ⊘ **★★★☆** Violets & dark berry fragrance introduce **22** ⑧, ripely rich texture & solid tannin balanced by gentle freshness. Extra dimension from 15% portion older-oak aged. **Pinotage** ② **★★★☆** Echoes generous fruit & focus of previous. Freshness & gentlest of tannins make for ready enjoyment. 10% of **21** ⑧ saw older oak. **Cabernet Sauvignon-Merlot ★★★** Straightforward equal partnership, **22** ⑧ has squeeze of soft, ripe plum fruit, gentle tannin for current enjoyment. **Viognier** ⊘ **★★★☆** Muted aromas on **22** ⑧, mere whiff spice & apricot; fresh, lively palate with concluding bitter nip has more appeal. 20% older-oak fermented.

Winemakers Collection

Syrah ⊘ ⑩ **★★★☆** Richly textured, with liquorice & black pepper, **22** ⑧ has comfortable, chunky grip, savoury finish.

Bukettraube ☺ **★★★** Welcome sighting of rare white grape. Full of spice & muscat grapey fragrance, luscious but uncloying flavours. Partner **23** ⑧ with well-spiced dishes. **Chardonnay** ☺ **★★★** Ripe lemon, nuts & light creaminess offer characterful sipping on dry **23** ⑦. **Chenin Blanc** ☺ **★★★** Mouthwatering red apple & pear attractions on **23** ⑧, fruitily dry & long.

Cabernet Sauvignon ⊘ **★★★** Uncomplicated sweet, dark berry flavours, pinch of tannin make for early enjoyment on **21** ⑧. Unoaked, as all these reds. **Merlot** ⊘ **★★★** Plentiful fleshy, sweet plums, neat tannin trim & freshness offer immediate satisfaction on **22** ⑧. **Pinotage** ② **★★★** Sweet raspberry flavours on **21** ⑧, ripe & juicy, pleasing tangy conclusion. **Tinta Barocca ★★★** Full pruny, earthy fruit on **22** ⑦, smooth, sweetish, with minimal tannin grip. **Dry Red** ② **★★★** No-frills equal cab & merlot **NV** ⑦, smooth, fruity & great value. **Pinotage Rosé** ② **★★★** Bright salmon pink, **23** ⑦ bursts with tangy cherry flavours highlighted by few grams sugar. Appealing sundowner. WO W Cape. **Sauvignon Blanc ★★★** Generous tropical flavours backed by sprightly zest, **23** ⑧ has an extended & fruitily dry aftertaste. **Sparkling Semi-Sweet Rosé** ② **★★★** Ripe red berries, creamy mousse & fruity sweetness in **NV** ⑦ bubbly from pinotage. Carbonated. WO W Cape, as next 5 wines. **Cuvée Brut** ② **★★★** Carbonated sparkling from sauvignon. **NV** ⑦ muted tropical fruit, zesty & dry. **Hanepoot** ② **★★★** Grapey & unctuously sweet, **NV** ⑧ fortified makes a satisfying winter warmer. **Red Jerepigo** ② **★★★** Latest **NV** ⑧ fortified from ruby cab echoes berry-cherry piquant appeal of last. Not too heavy or sweet. **White Jerepigo** ② **★★★★** Fortified grenache blanc. **NV** ⑧ smooth, not overly sweet, with characterful melon & nectarine preserve flavours. **Cape Ruby** ② **★★★** Fresh, clean & not over-sweet **NV** ⑧ 'port' from touriga national, showcasing its plummy floral flavours. In abeyance: **Blanc de Noir**. — AL

Location: Malmesbury ▪ Map: Swartland ▪ Map grid reference: C7 ▪ WO: Swartland/Western Cape ▪ Est/1stB 1948 ▪ Tasting & sales Mon-Thu 9-5 Fri 9-4 Sat/pub hols 9-2 Sun closed; pub hols (seasonal) please call ahead ▪ Closed Easter Fri/Sun, Dec 25/26 & Jan 1 ▪ Light meals, cheese platters ▪ Facilities for children ▪ Tour groups ▪ Farm produce ▪ Online shop ▪ Owner(s) 68 producers ▪ Winemaker(s) Marius Prins ▪ 3,600ha (cab, carignan, merlot, mourv, ptage, shiraz, chard, chenin, rouss, sauv, viog) ▪ 20,000t 38% red 55% white 5% rosé 2% sparkling ▪ BRC, IFS, IPW, WIETA ▪ PO Box 95 Malmesbury 7299 ▪ info@swwines.co.za ▪ www.swartlandwinery.co.za ▪ T +27 (0)22-482-1134

☐ **Sweet Darling** *see* Darling Cellars
☐ **Swepie Selection** *see* Domein Doornkraal
☐ **Swerwer** *see* JC Wickens Wines
☐ **Sweven** *see* Zidela Wines
☐ **Sydney Back Kosher Wines** *see* Backsberg Family Wines

Taaibosch Wines   ⓨ ⌂

'It's our sole purpose to continue building on a rich legacy and safeguard this terroir,' say the Oddo family of French wine specialist Oddo Vins et Domaines, who in 2017 bought the property then known as Cordoba, renowned for its Crescendo blend, and began revitalising it. (Pink Valley and Le Chant are also in the stable.) Now certified organic, the high-lying, steep-sloped Helderberg farm remains under the capable stewardship of Schalk Willem Joubert, who strives to craft 'wine that embodies its origin' while respecting and preserving nature, including the fragrant indigenous shrubs that circle the cellar and lend their name to the venture.

★★★★☆ **Crescendo** ⊘ ⍟ Refined, lithe & rewarding Cape Bordeaux, showing leashed power in **20** ⑨④. Blend tweaked to add more cab to cab franc & merlot (49/36) partnership. Effortless melange of fruitcake & cigarbox, subtle fynbos & cocoa. Elegant, dry & silky after 2 years in small & large oak, 30% new, & concrete 'egg'.— FM

Location/WO: Stellenbosch ▪ Map: Helderberg ▪ Map grid reference: D2 ▪ Est 2017 ▪ 1stB 2018 ▪ Tasting & cellar tours Mon-Fri by appt for Club members only ▪ Closed all pub hols & weekends ▪ Wine club ▪ Luxury accommodation ▪ Owner(s) Oddo Vins et Domaines ▪ Cellarmaster(s)/winemaker(s) Schalk Willem Joubert (Jun 2018) ▪ Viticulturist(s) Andre Smit (Dec 2018) ▪ 25ha under vine ▪ 300t capacity; own label 100% red ▪ IPW, Organic (Ecocert), WIETA ▪ PO Box 5609 Helderberg Somerset West 7135 ▪ info@taaiboschwines.com ▪ www.taaiboschwines.com ▪ T +27 (0)21-855-3744

☐ **Tabula Rasa** *see* Oak Valley Estate
☐ **Tale Series** *see* Journey's End Vineyards
☐ **Tall Horse** *see* DGB (Pty) Ltd

Tamboerskloof Wine - Kleinood Farm   ⓨ ⑪ ◎

Trained engineer and sought-after wine-cellar designer Gerard de Villiers and his wife Libby over more than two decades have developed and run a compact jewel of a farm, Kleinood, in Stellenbosch's Blaauwklippen Valley. A balance between science, accrued knowledge and experience guides the crafting of mostly Rhône-style boutique wines by winemaker-viticulturist Reynie Oosthuizen, who occasionally creates interesting new ones for the Kleinood Tafel wine club. A rich and varied visitor experience, based on the 'cozy' tasting room and summer alfresco area, is central to the brand, with many embellishments like seasonal platters, the house's De Boerin olive oil and artisan foods, walking paths and a native forest on the riverbank.

★★★★ **John Spicer Syrah** ⍟ Flagship named for owner's son, portion of a single block, stylishly & informatively presented. **17** ★★★★★ ⑨④ dense, dark, wild berry fruit, black pepper & wisp of perfumed violets. Layers of complexity, similar oaking to sibling, 18 months, 15% new, much more concentrated, with fine tannins & svelte texture courtesy 4 years in bottle. Long & promising future. Last tasted was **09** ⑧⑨.

★★★★☆ **Syrah** ⍟ Dark berry fruit, savoury polished leather nuance, splashes mourvèdre & viognier absorbed into **19** ⑨④'s dense core. Oaking & 2 years in bottle polish the whole, but still youthfully restrained, worth ageing, also in magnum.

★★★★ **Katharien Syrah Rosé** Piquant red fruit, brioche & hint of savouriness in **23** ⑧⑧. Mouthfilling breadth & texture from 15% oak-fermented portion & 4 months on lees. Dry, fresh, enough substance to summon the canapé platter at pleasingly modest 12.3% alc.

★★★★☆ **Viognier** Cornucopia of sweet spice, citrus blossom & dried stonefruit in **23** (92). Staggered pick ensures tangy freshness & flavour, part oak-ferment & lees contact add succulent base. Lively & charming to last lingering drop. Perfect with spicy food.— MW

Location/map/WO: Stellenbosch ▪ Map grid reference: F7 ▪ Est 2000 ▪ 1stB 2002 ▪ Tasting, sales & cellar tours Mon-Sat 10-4 ▪ Closed Easter & Dec 25/26 ▪ Wine, olive oil, honey, harvest platters, bespoke handmade products for sale ▪ Tree identification route ▪ Wine club ▪ Owner(s) Gerard & Libby de Villiers ▪ Winemaker(s) Reynie Oosthuizen (Oct 2018), with Julio Willemse (Jan 2008) ▪ Viticulturist(s) Reynie Oosthuizen (Oct 2018) ▪ 22ha/10ha (mourv, shiraz, rouss, viog) ▪ 100t/12,000cs own label 70% red 15% white 15% rosé ▪ IPW, WIETA ▪ PO Box 12584 Die Boord 7613 ▪ office@kleinood.com ▪ www.kleinood.com ▪ **T +27 (0)21-880-2527**

Tanagra Winery & Distillery

German couple Anette and Robert Rosenbach are mentored by eminent wine man and fellow Robertson Valley resident John Loubser in their 'handcrafting of wines exclusively from grapes grown on the farm, in certified single-vineyards, sustainably farmed'. Their recently inaugurated on-site cellar also serves as the base for producing 'grappa', eau de vie de lie and fruit spirits in a combined pot-column still from Germany, in quantities that reflect their motto 'klein aber fein' ('small but exquisite'). A recent highlight was the WWF Conservation Pioneer Award for their commitment to responsible cultivation and wine tourism.

Tanagra range

★★★★ **Cabernet Franc** Attractively perfumed, well-balanced **20** (89) combines a light feel with good intensity, depth & length of flavour. Will keep a few years. Natural ferment/10 months older oak, as Syrah.

★★★★ **Syrah** Renamed from 'Shiraz' to signal emphasis on elegance from **21** (89) vintage, here & generally. No compromise on flavour or ageability, ample succulent fruit, perfume & spice, smooth structure.

★★★★ **Heavenly Chaos** (ℚ) Luscious yet refined merlot & cab franc (70/30) in **20** (89) is flavourful & moreish. Ripe plums, Xmas cake & crushed herbs in a silky vanilla robe.

Cabernet Franc Blanc de Noir ★★★★ Pretty salmon pink **22** (85), light & dry, red berry & herbal aromatics, gentle spicy finish to partner with food. **Colombard** ★★★☆ One of few wooded examples, 10 months in older barrique yet retains fruit focus, mostly tropical with wisp of hay. Lovely depth & lifted length to **22** (84).

Husk Spirit range

★★★★ **Marc de Cabernet Sauvignon** (ℚ) This line-up distilled from pressed grapes (pomace aka marc), from own grapes here & for Hanepoot & 8 Years, rest ex Robertson. **15** (89) vibrant, creamy & balanced, protracted silky finish.

★★★★☆ **Marc de Cabernet Sauvignon 8 Years Reserve** (NEW) (✓) (🐝) Seamless & very special **15** (93), perfumed, showing delicate cranberry, red plum & chocolate flavours, lovely herbal undertone. Elegant, silky & creamy, beautifully clean finish. Aged in a red wine barrel. 40% alc.

★★★★☆ **Marc de Chardonnay** (ℚ) Satin **15** (90) oozes baked apple, marmalade & light cinnamon spice aromas & flavours. Full, with lingering vanilla cake farewell. 500 ml, as both ranges.

★★★★☆ **Marc de Hanepoot** (ℚ) Unmatured **16** (91), beautiful glint & exotic spice perfume. Delicate yet rich & round, with raisin, barley sugar & fine fresh-herb notes on long warming finish.

★★★★☆ **Marc de Hanepoot 3 Years Reserve** (ℚ) Aged in old muscat barrel. Vibrant amber hue, fragrant muscat, exotic spice & roasted nut aromas. **14** (90) rich, rounded & smooth, long satisfying finish.

★★★★ **Marc de Sauvignon Blanc** (ℚ) Intense orchard fruit & fresh-cut grass flavours, **15** (89) velvety on palate to long mineral finish. Lovely with espresso.

★★★★☆ **TanaGrappa** (ℚ) Distillation of Heavenly Chaos from 2015 harvest but marketed as non-vintage (91). Delightfully smooth with balanced 43% alc, distinctly 'husk spirit' in character, lingering farewell. Not tasted: **Marc de Chardonnay Barrique**.

Lees Spirit range

★★★★☆ **Cabernet Sauvignon Hefebrand** (✓) Range distilled from Robertson-sourced lees, racked from wine after ferment; may contain some yeast cells. **17** (91) structured & intense yet smooth, creamy, a gentle warmth to the farewell. Briefly tank aged before bottling at 43% alc.

★★★★☆ **Cabernet Sauvignon Hefebrand 5 Years Reserve** (ℚ) Sophisticated sipping in yellow-gold **17** (92), sleek & smooth, seductively perfumed. Aged in a bourbon barrel. First since **12** (92). Well worth seeking out, as all the spirits.

★★★★☆ **Sauvignon Blanc Hefebrand** ⓧ Shares sauvignon character with Marc sibling, but more complexity, intense creaminess on palate from extended lees ageing, lift **15** ⑨⓪ a notch higher.— WB

Location/WO: McGregor ▪ Map: Robertson ▪ Map grid reference: C6 ▪ Est/1stB 2003 ▪ Tasting (wine/grappa), sales & cellar/distillery tours daily by appt ▪ Fee R50pp ▪ Farm produce ▪ Luxury farm accommodation in 6 cottages (self-catering); farm trails/walks, bird watching, mountain biking ▪ Adjoining Vrolijkheid Nature Reserve ▪ Craft distillery ▪ Owner(s) Robert & Anette Rosenbach ▪ Distiller(s) Robert Rosenbach ▪ Cellarmaster(s)/winemaker(s) Robert Rosenbach, mentored by John Loubser ▪ Viticulturist(s) Robert Rosenbach ▪ 78ha/6ha (cab f, merlot, shiraz, cbard) ▪ ±25t/2,000-2,500cs own label 60% red 25% white 15% blanc de noir; 600cs spirits ▪ IPW, WWF-SA Conservation Champion ▪ PO Box 92 McGregor 6708 ▪ tanagra@tanagra.co.za ▪ www.tanagra.co.za ▪ **T +27 (0)23-625-1780**

Tangled Tree

This solo brand of Van Loveren Family Vineyards depicts entwined karee trees on its labels, a reference to the passion for gardening shared by winery founders Hennie and Jean Retief. Apt, given the wines' eco focus, being packaged in light, recyclable and lower-carbon PET, perfect for like-minded, outdoorsy winelovers. **Spicy Shiraz** ★★ Deep red fruit on **21** ⑦⑤ improves on last vintage. Mocha, more than spice, from time on oak. Also in 3L cask, as most. **Rose Petal Moscato Rosé** ⓧ ★★★ Vibrant rose & grapey aromas, semi-sweet **21** ⑦⑧ provides easy, fruity drinking at low 9.5% alc. **Butterscotch Chardonnay** ⊘ ★★★ 5 months on caramel oak staves imbue **22** ⑦⑦ with rich toffee & butterscotch, complementing glacé pineapple & mango but missing some of previous' citrus zing. **Tropical Sauvignon Blanc** ⊘ ★★★ Tangy, citrussy **23** ⑧⓪ is well judged, gaining body from extended lees contact at modest 12.9% alc. Not tasted: **Chocolate Cabernet Sauvignon**. — ML

☐ **Tangram** *see* Durbanville Hills

Tanzanite Wines ⓠ

Captivated by the magical transformation of grapes into stars, Melanie van der Merwe has been crafting sparkling wine for 30 years, over half of which as co-owner of this highly regarded boutique specialist cap classique venture based in Worcester and named for the gemstone associated with her birth month. Early experience at the top champagne houses continues to inspire her traditional varietal choices and methods, and classic styling. The blanc de blancs promised last edition was still on the lees at press time.

Tanzanite range

★★★★ **Cap Classique Brut Rosé** Joyful pink **NV** ⑧⑨ from 60% pinot noir & chardonnay, perfect as a welcome drink. Red berries, including cranberries on a velvet mousse. Appetite awakening, with good tension between crisp acid & 8.9 g/L touch of sugar.

★★★★☆ **Cap Classique Brut** Vivacious & beguiling **NV** ⑨⓪ from 80% chardonnay & pinot noir with well-integrated, floaty mousse from 30 months on the lees, elegant poise between racy acidity & suggestion of appley sweetness.

Limited Editions

In abeyance: **Cap Classique Limited Edition**. — ML

Location: Worcester ▪ Map: Franschhoek ▪ Map grid reference: A7 ▪ WO: Western Cape ▪ Est 2006 ▪ Tasting Mon-Fri by appt ▪ Owner(s) Wentzel & Melanie van der Merwe ▪ Cellarmaster(s) Melanie van der Merwe (Apr 2006) ▪ 2,000cs own label ▪ PO Box 5102 Worcester 6850 ▪ melanie@tanzanitewines.co.za ▪ www.tanzanitewines.co.za ▪ **T +27 (0)82-555-8105**

☐ **Tassenberg** *see* Heineken Beverages
☐ **Taste** *see* Truter Family Wines

Tembela Wines ⓠ

Honouring his mother Tembela, whose name means 'faith, hope and belief', Banele Vakele sources small parcels of sustainably farmed grapes around the Cape and, with least intervention, crafts 'food wines with elegance and finesse' in Savage Wines' Cape Town cellar, where he's been assistant winemaker since 2019.

★★★★☆ **Syrah** Similar aromatic dark fruit & pepper profile to previous, though tad feistier in **22** ⑨1. 40% portion stems in ferment freshens & adds tannic grip, but shade less gravitas & integration than last, needing some cellar time to meld.

★★★★ **Verdelho** Unusual single bottling, from Stellenbosch fruit. The single barrel of **22** ⑧6 shows hallmark vibrant, zesty acid with creamier element from natural ferment & ageing in old 600L cask. Clean, sappy & lipsmacking, with green fruit & some herbaceousness. Last was **20** ⑧8.

Occasional release: **Chenin Blanc**. — MW

Location: Cape Town ▪ WO: Stellenbosch ▪ 1stB 2020 ▪ Tasting by appt only ▪ Closed all pub hols ▪ Owner(s) Banele Vakele ▪ Winemaker(s) Banele Vakele (Jan 2020) ▪ 200cs own label 50% red 50% white ▪ vbanele@gmail.com ▪ **T +27 (0)82-403-1542**

Tempel Wines

To 'let the grapes do the talking' is how Tom Heeremans and Tatjana Holkina see their role at their Paarl wine and hospitality estate, once a Jewish place of worship and extensively redeveloped under the Belgian couple's latter ownership. After being trained for several years by resident winemaker Neil Marais, and gaining experience in France and Spain, Tom has taken the reins of the boutique cellar, working with consultant Marko Roux to apply organic principles and techniques where possible for the estate vines and the select pockets in other areas - some with 35+ year-old-vines - for the character- and interest-packed range.

★★★★☆ **Skemerdans Grenache** Light, aromatic & plush, **21** ⑨0 from Piekenierskloof & Wellington vines shows fine varietal form. Smooth, chalky tannin grip enhances crushed-berry charm, year in seasoned oak polishes without intruding. Enjoy young & vibrant.

★★★★ **Oogwink Shiraz** Supple & racy, **21** ⑧9 oozes black-fruited charm, with layers of smoky aromas, sweet spice & Morello cherries. Ripe & generous, its full, leathery tannins polished by year in oak, 15% new. Stellenbosch grapes.

★★★★☆ **Tydsaam Tempranillo** Commendable rendering of Spain's great red grape, **21** ⑨1 succulently ripe & expressive. Powdery ripe tannins lend texture, with well-judged acid & restrained oak (year in 33% new, lightly toasted barrels). Poised & impressive. WO Wellington.

★★★★★ **Kattemaai Chenin Blanc-Semillon** Ⓔ Remarkable fatness on **22** ★★★★☆ ⑨2, with wild-yeast ferment in barrel & 9 months on lees lending creamy texture, oatmeal richness & dusty oak spice - all countered by lemon-citrus tang & finely poised acid. 7% semillon adds a waxy veneer. Follows standout **21** ⑨5, also ex Wellington & Franschhoek.

Not tasted: **Sorgvry Cinsault**. — GdB

Location/map: Paarl ▪ Map grid reference: E3 ▪ WO: Coastal/Western Cape/Wellington ▪ Est 2000 ▪ 1stB 2003 ▪ Tasting, sales & cellar tours by appt ▪ Fee R200 ▪ Wine & tasting platters available ▪ Guest house/B&B (5-star) ▪ Wine club ▪ Owner(s) Tom Heeremans & Tatjana Holkina ▪ Winemaker(s) Tom Heeremans ▪ Viticulturist(s) Marko Roux (Mar 2018, consultant) ▪ 6ha ▪ 50t own label 60% red 40% white ▪ Suite 12 Private Bag X3041 Paarl 7620 ▪ info@tempelwines.com ▪ www.tempelwines.com ▪ **T +27 (0)79-833-9617**

☐ **Tenacity** see Hartenberg Estate

☐ **Tendai Mtawarira Wines** see The Beast Wine Collection

Terrabosch Wines

Per its tag line, 'expressive by design', this young Stellenbosch boutique venture is focused on wines that 'reflect their origins and honour where they're from'. Having debuted last edition with a Bordeaux red from Simonsberg-Paarl, made with Anura Vineyards, owners Mac Mabidilala and Ziviwe Bubu are exploring other styles and terroirs, in collaboration with Hidden Valley (Helderberg) and Seven Springs (Overberg).

★★★★ **Gabrielle Jordan Overberg Pinot Noir** ⒩ⓔ ⊘ Bright red-berry fruit with classic notes of cumin & earth **22** ⑧6 shows much promise. Charry grip from 9 months in old oak already settling & developing an appealing fresh chalkiness.

★★★★ **Continuum** ⒩Ⓔ Vibrant Helderberg red from mostly cab with syrah & merlot shows juicy black cherry sweetness of fruit, creamy texture & toasty, smoky oak. **21** ⑧9 needs time to assimilate & soften but promising debut & interesting wine.

Not tasted: **Ultima**. — CM

Location: Stellenbosch ▪ WO: Stellenbosch/Overberg ▪ Est 2020 ▪ 1stB 2022 ▪ Closed to public ▪ Owner(s) Mac Mabidilala, Ziviwe Bubu ▪ Cellarmaster(s) Mac Mabidilala (Feb 2020) ▪ Winemaker(s) Annalie van Dyk & Alexandra McFarlane (consultants) ▪ 600cs own label 100% red ▪ 43 Andringa Str, 3rd Floor Office 301, Stellenbosch 7600 ▪ info@terrabosch.com ▪ www.terrabosch.com ▪ **T +27 (0)21-808-1677**

Terracura Wines

There have been some radical changes here in the past few years, in response to a few challenges. But with wine-man Chris Groenewald (importer, distributor and maker) joining Terracura's founder, Michael Roets, as joint owner and cellarmaster, things are being re-established. Concentration has recently been on the Smiley range - light, characterful, occasionally quirky and frequently thought-provoking - but the Silwervis and Terracura wines are to emerge again. Nothing new ready for us to taste this year, unfortunately.

Smiley range

★★★★ Fresh/Vars Ⓥ A multi-year **NV** ⑧⑦ Swartland blend of chenin & grenache blanc, mostly in old oak, but dabs skin-contact & sun wine give hint of funkiness & add grip. Delightful, fresh & light.

★★★★ White Ⓥ Similar vintage & Swartland varietal mix as Fresh, but more grenache blanc, skin-contact & sun wine, making it more savoury. **NV** ⑧⑨ flavoursome & sufficiently vinous at just 12%.

Red Ⓥ **★★★☆** Latest **NV** ⑧⑤ from 2021 syrah with touriga, grenache, cinsaut, lightly oaked. Juicy & ripely fruited, moderate dry tannins & freshness. Not tasted: **Schizo, Spesiale Dry White**.

Terracura range

★★★★☆ Syrah Ⓥ Aim is 'old school', in tradition of northern Rhône'. Ticks that box in **17** ⑨③ with expressive violets, generous black & red fruit, pepper & scrub nuances. Bone-dry, with sleek tannins & 13% alc perfectly aligned. Paardeberg & Kasteelberg fruit, older oak.

Not tasted: **Trinity Syrah, Chenin Blanc**.

Silwervis range

Not tasted: **Cinsault, Chenin Blanc**. — TJ

Location: Hermon ▪ Map: Tulbagh ▪ Map grid reference: A7 ▪ WO: Western Cape/Swartland ▪ Est 2010 ▪ 1stB 2011 ▪ Tasting, sales & cellar tours by appt only ▪ Closed all pub hols ▪ Owner(s) Michael Roets & Chris Groenewald ▪ Winemaker(s) Chris Groenewald (Feb 2022) ▪ Viticulturist(s) various ▪ 45ha (cinsaut, mourv, shiraz, tinta barocca, chenin, sem) ▪ 40t 50% red 50% white ▪ Hermon 7308 ▪ chris@terracura.co.za ▪ www. terracura.co.za, www.silwervis.com ▪ **T +27 (0)84-804-0880**

☐ **Terra Del Capo** see Anthonij Rupert Wyne

Tesselaarsdal Wines

Exciting progress on the ±17 ha of land acquired by Berene Sauls near Tesselaarsdal, her home village the Overberg, not far from eminent Hamilton Russell Vineyards, where she's a longtime team member. Trials with pinot noir grafted on different rootstocks to determine how they would perform on the challenging site were successful, and soil and irrigation preparations are underway for the planting of 2 ha of vines. Berene's father, Brian Sauls, and sons Darren and Calem are responsible for the work, advised by Dean Leppan. Meanwhile grapes are sourced from Hemel-en-Aarde Ridge for Berene's colleague Emul Ross to craft into 'graceful and ageworthy' wines.

★★★★☆ Pinot Noir 🐝 Elegant & dainty yet deeply flavoured in **22** ⑨③. Perfumed rosepetal, wet soil, subtle spiced strawberry & raspberry mingle with balanced, fine tannins from 9 months in 228L barrel, 35% new. Vibrancy added by 10% whole berries. These also available in magnum.

★★★★☆ Chardonnay Understated & classic cool-climate expression. Ex-tank **23** ⑨⓪ bunch pressed, part fermented in older barrels to cosset delicate apple blossom, green apple & vanilla aromas, mineral undertone courtesy of some clay-amphora ferment & lees ageing, balanced by roundness & depth. — WB

Location: Hermanus ▪ WO: Hemel-en-Aarde Ridge ▪ Est/1stB 2015 ▪ Tasting by appt ▪ Owner(s) Berene Sauls ▪ Winemaker(s) Emul Ross (Jan 2015, Hamilton Russell Vineyards) ▪ Viticulturist(s) Dean Leppan (consultant) ▪ 2,300cs own label 40% red 60% white ▪ PO Box 158 Hermanus 7200 ▪ berene@tesselaarsdalwines.co.za ▪ www.tesselaarsdalwines.co.za ▪ **T +27 (0)73-322-9499**

☐ **Testflight** see Fuselage Wines

Teubes Family Wines

The family members behind this boutique winery are Johan Teubes, owner and respected viticultural adviser, and his son Sybrand, winemaker, with wife Mariska alongside him in the cellar. For their 'Old and New World-style' wines, they cover a wide area: from the newer Nieuwoudtville ward in Northern Cape, to Lambert's Bay on the Atlantic coast, where they have a joint venture, Sir Lambert (see listing), with the Hayes family, to inland home, Vredendal. Sustainable farming and organic practices are strong emphases.

Malkopbaai range

Shiraz-Grenache-Mourvèdre-Viognier ⓐ ⓢ ★★★ Faint white pepper & fynbos notes on **20** ⑧②'s sweet black fruit. Fleshy, with hint of warmth from 14.5% alc, robust tannins. **Sauvignon Blanc** ⓐ ★★★ Shy green-fruit aromas, soft acid & transitory flavours, **21** ⑧⓪ touch less sparky than last.

Teubes Signature Organic range

★★★★ **Sauvignon Blanc** ⓐ Lively acid & satisfying vinosity from 14% alc, **20** ⑧⑦ greengage & unusual starfruit notes, creamy finish. WO Nieuwoudtville.

Syrah-Grenache ⓐ ⓢ ★★★ Ripe dark fruit with upfront coffee & chocolate attractions from year in oak, gram sugar rounds out **20** ⑧②'s 80/20 blend. Not tasted: **Cabernet Sauvignon**.

Karoobossie range

Not tasted: **Kap Klassiek Brut Rosé, Kap Klassiek Brut**. — CvZ

Location: Vredendal ▪ Map: Olifants River ▪ Map grid reference: B4 B5 ▪ WO: Coastal/Nieuwoudtville ▪ Est 2010 ▪ 1stB 2011 ▪ Tasting & sales Mon-Fri 8-5 Sat 9.30-5; Lambert's Bay tasting venue Mon-Sat 10-5 ▪ Tasting fee ▪ Cellar tours ▪ Tour groups ▪ Facilities for children ▪ Farm produce ▪ Cheese platters & pizza ▪ Conferences/ functions ▪ Walks/hikes ▪ MTB ▪ Conservation area ▪ Guest cottages ▪ Owner(s) Johan & Ella Teubes ▪ Cellarmaster(s) Sybrand Teubes ▪ Winemaker(s) Sybrand Teubes, with Mariska Teubes ▪ Viticulturist(s) Johan Teubes ▪ (cab, ptage, shiraz, sauv) ▪ 300t ▪ Organic, WIETA ▪ PO Box 791 Vredendal 8160 ▪ info@teubeswines. co.za, sybrand@teubeswines.co.za ▪ www.teubeswines.co.za ▪ **T +27 (0)27-213-2377**

Thamnus Wines

Adam and Karen Potter's boutique wine venture centres on a small vineyard in the Overberg, acquired in 2019 and tended by seasoned viticulturist-winemaker PJ Geyer. Currently there are 10 ha of pinor noir and chardonnay, farmed sustainably and, ultimately, organically. Small parcels of wine are made in rented space, but the plan is to construct an on-site cellar in the near future.

★★★★ **Pinot Noir** ⓐ A newcomer to watch. **21** ⑧⑧ light & delicate, but sweetly perfumed & exuberantly ripe, with earthy mineral finish. 35% wholebunch, 10 months in oak, 36% new.

★★★★ **Chardonnay** ⓐ Though big & solid, **21** ⑧⑧ shows impressive nuance & layering of lemon zest fruit & buttered toast from barrel ferment, 50% with wild yeast, & 9 months in oak, 33% new.— GdB

Location: Caledon ▪ Map: Walker Bay & Bot River ▪ Map grid reference: C5 ▪ WO: Overberg ▪ Est 2019 ▪ 1stB 2020 ▪ Tasting & sales by appt only ▪ Olive press ▪ BYO picnic ▪ Hiking & MTB trails ▪ Conservation area ▪ Owner(s) Adam & Karen Potter ▪ Cellarmaster(s)/winemaker(s) PJ Geyer (Feb 2020) ▪ Viticulturist(s) PJ Geyer (Feb 2021) ▪ 1,176.82ha/10ha (pinot, chard) ▪ 80t/±2,000cs own label 50% red 50% white ▪ info@ thamnuswines.co.za ▪ www.thamnuswines.co.za ▪ **T +27 (0)83-327-3887 (PJ Geyer), +27 (0)76-632-8002 (office)**

That Wine Demesne

At their tiny vineyard in cool Plettenberg Bay, David and Joanna Butler have had to invest considerable time and effort, and do deep dives into the details of vine culture to make their winery viable, but the result speaks for itself, and it clearly inspires them to continue crafting their lovely wine with devoted care.

★★★★ **Take Root Pinot Noir** ⓢ Quietly alluring **22** ⑧⑥ charms with delicate red berry fruit, light texture & comforting farmyard/forest floor nuances. Fleecy tannin & modest 12.5% alc. Year old oak.— DS

Location/WO: Plettenberg Bay ▪ Est 2012 ▪ 1stB 2016 ▪ Closed to public ▪ Tastings can be had at Beau de Jour Café @ Bramon tasting centre ▪ Owner(s) David & Joanna Butler ▪ Winemaker(s) Anton Smal (Bramon Wines) ▪ 1.5ha (pinot) ▪ ±213cs own label 100% red ▪ PO Box 197 The Crags 6602 ▪ thatwine@thatplace.co.za ▪ www.thatwine.co.za ▪ **T +27 (0)82-578-1939**

The Ahrens Family ⓛ ⒨

Albert Ahrens was one of the original Swartland 'revolutionaries' during his residency at Lammershoek in the early 2000s, later gaining experience in France and Spain before moving into a cellar in Paarl. He sources locally, in his former home-base and more widely, aiming for 'the best possible natural expression of site, appellation and vintage'. He's looking forward to launching a pair of new wines, the house's first vintage-dated cap classique, and an old-vine chenin from vintage 2022 to join the current trio of OVCs.

★★★★☆ **Black** Shiraz & carignan blend from, & named for, Swartland; **21** ⑨② ups latter to 30% from 20%. Notes of quarry dust, wild berry, hint of spicy raisin, long, neatly dry & smooth finish. Open-top natural ferment, some whole bunches, 15-16 months mostly older barrel & foudre, as all reds.

★★★★☆ **Kasteel-Neef** Darker toned & touch riper than other reds, still has minerality & iodine core. **21** ⑨⓪ exudes violet, brambleberry & fennel. Usual partners grenache noir, carignan (60/30) & shiraz from 15-20 year old Voor Paardeberg vines.

★★★★☆ **Paarl Rooiwijn** ⓐ Northern Paarl or southern Rhône? **21** ⑨④ multi-vineyard blend of grenache noir & cinsaut (30/30), equal carignan & syrah, on shale with quartz. Absolutely sings of red berries & spice, tantalisingly light-footed without sacrificing fruit depth or palate appeal.

★★★★ **Seventy** ⓐ Modern take on traditional Cape blend, significantly more cab in **21** ⑧⑨ at 90% than last 68%, yet finds the balance between fine cab dryness & sappy red fruit of cinsaut. Old Bottelary vines on quartz bring right amount of freshness.

★★★★☆ **Hometown OVC** ⓐ ⓦ Fruit from 1979 Wellington vines. **21** ⑨④ improves on previous with its tighter body, showing just-ripe melon & juicy citrus array with salty nuance. Natural ferment, 9 months on lees in large oak, as all whites.

★★★★☆ **Koffieklip OVC** ⓐ ⓦ Like **20** ⑨④, **21** ★★★★★ ⑨⑤ a stunner from 1984 Swartland chenin bushvines in sandy soil over ferricrete. Delivers flint, yellow apple & whisper of cool melon. Beautifully dry, hallmark chalky texture pierced by steely acidity.

★★★★☆ **Kwarts Van Die Paarl OVC** ⓐ ⓦ Named for quartz rocks scattered over 1977 chenin bushvine site. More tension on **21** ⑨④ than last, pure apple & white pear with some flesh & density from 10% interplanted palomino.

★★★★★ **The WhiteBlack** ⓐ Consistently brilliant equal blend marsanne, roussanne & grenache blanc from mature vines on Voor Paardeberg decomposed granite, which gives freshness & verve. **21** ⑨⑤ intricate white citrus, pear & grapefruit pith; more citrus on palate with nut oil hint at the edges. — ML

Location/map: Paarl ▪ Map grid reference: G6 ▪ WO: Swartland/Voor Paardeberg/Paarl/Stellenbosch/ Wellington ▪ Est/1stB 2008 ▪ Tasting & sales by appt only ▪ Cellar tastings with either lunch or dinner by appt only; limited private tastings in Gauteng & KZN ▪ Owner(s) Albert & Heidi Ahrens ▪ Cellarmaster(s)/ winemaker(s)/viticulturist(s) Albert Ahrens (2008) ▪ 6ot/7,000cs own label 45% red 50% white 5% MCC ▪ tastewine@theahrensfamily.co.za ▪ **T +27 (0)79-196-6887**

☐ **The Amos Block** see Klein Amoskuil
☐ **Theater of Wine** see Val du Charron
☐ **The Back Roads** see Black Elephant Vintners
☐ **The Bald Ibis** see Mile High Vineyards
☐ **The Bernard Series** see Bellingham

The Berrio Wines ⓛ

This boutique label helped bring the southernmost wine ward of Flim to the world's attention in the early 2000s. First crafted as a joint venture between winemaker and entrepreneur Bruce Jack and longtime friend and vineyard owner Francis Pratt, it's still made from Francis' Modderfontein Farm grapes but brand ownership now rests wholly with Bruce. See also The Drift Estate listing.

★★★★☆ **Sauvignon Blanc** Typical nettle, grapefruit & fig of cool-grown grapes on **22** ⑨⓪ with dab semillon. Rounded, succulent & lively, good tangy, taut core of zesty acid. Structured & concentrated, will keep good few years, like last-tasted **19** ⑨②. — FM

☐ **The Black Korhaan** see Rockbelt Ridge

The Butcher Shop & Grill

A local restaurant-industry institution, The Butcher Shop & Grill has been 'raising the steaks since 1961' at its outlets in Sandton's Nelson Mandela Square and Cape Town's Mouille Point. The housewines are a cut above, being sourced from top producers, including members of the esteemed Cape Winemakers Guild.

Pick's Pick Gold Label range

★★★★☆ **Cabernet Sauvignon** Quite brooding & powerful **18** ⑨② from Ernie Els includes splashes shiraz & petit verdot. Increased oaking, to 20% new, 18 months, in support, adds a dry cedar nuance, tempering some of the ripeness.

★★★★ **Reserve Pinot Noir** By Iona, **22** quiet herb & earthy tones, lively raspberry fruit & grape tannin both supported by older oak. Ready now, good few years to go.

★★★★ **Pinotage** ⓥ Previewed **18** ⑧⑨ has pinotage's lively mulberry flavours & acid, sleek tannins that allow early drinking with some ageability. By Kanonkop.

★★★★ **Sauvignon Blanc** By Iona, **23**'s vibrant acidity lifts the creamy centre, ex 4 months on lees, focuses attention on the fresh herb, ruby grapefruit & nectarine flavours.

Merlot ⓥ ★★★★ Glacé cherries & raspberries matched by savoury oak notes. Streamlined **18** ⑧④ by Morgenster for earlier drinking. Not tasted: **Shiraz**.

Pick's Pick range

★★★★ **Merlot** By Jordan. Hedgerow fruit with leafy tomato typicity on **20** ★★★★★ ⑨① . Lovely integration & length aided by tannin grip from 18 months in oak, 70% new. No **19**, **18**.

★★★★ **Shiraz** ⓥ Smoke & dark fruit, pepper spicing, scrub & dried herbs, **18** ⑧⑨ from Zevenwacht packs a lot into its muscular frame. Savoury end, with well-integrated 14 months mainly older oak.

★★★★ **Chenin Blanc** ⓥ Ripe red apples spiced with a little oak, **21** ⑧⑥ by Saxenburg is rich in flavour, creamy lees adding further dimension. Natural acid & dry finish bring balance & freshness.

★★★★ **Sauvignon Blanc** Made for early drinking, taut **22** ⑧⑦ is lively but focused, with a crisp tang of grapefruit & dry conclusion. By Jordan.

Pinotage ⓥ ★★★★ Smooth, fruity & plummy, 20% touch of oak smooths any edges. Widely sourced **18** ⑧③ by Beyerskloof is highly drinkable. **Rosé** ★★★☆ Plum & cranberry succulence on **21** ⑧③ by Jordan. Shiraz & merlot partner 50/50 for crisp, light-bodied quaffability. Not tasted: **Selection Rouge**, **Unoaked Chardonnay**.

Pick's Pick Platinum range

Not tasted: **Cabernet Sauvignon**. — Various tasters

Location: Cape Town/Sandton ▪ WO: Various ▪ Open Mon-Sat 12-10.30 Sun 12-9.30; pub hols (seasonal) ▪ Owner(s) Alan Pick ▪ Beach Rd, Mouille Point (opposite lighthouse) Cape Town 8005; Shop 30, Nelson Mandela Square, Sandton 2196 ▪ thebutchershop@mweb.co.za ▪ **T +27 (0)11-784-8676/7**

☐ **The Cape** *see* Zidela Wines
☐ **The Chapters** *see* Miles Mossop Wines
☐ **The Cinsault Collective** *see* Natte Valleij Wines
☐ **The Collection** *see* Roos Family Vineyards
☐ **The Cooperative** *see* Bosman Family Vineyards
☐ **The Crags** *see* Bramon Wines
☐ **The Cross Collection** *see* Dieu Donné Vineyards
☐ **The Den** *see* Painted Wolf Wines
☐ **The Dome** *see* Lourensford Wine Estate

The Drift Estate

'The mountain on which we sit was formed 330-m years ago when Antarctica crashed into ancient Africa... At altitude, so far south, the cold, ocean-borne winds scour our slopes and batter our vines, encouraging tiny, mightily concentrated berries. These in turn lead to unique, delicious wine.' This is articulate and charismatic winegrower Bruce Jack's characterisation of the Appelsdrift home-farm, on a hillside near Napier in the Overberg. Since the 1990s, he and his family have faced off everything from wildfires to baboon raids to develop the beautiful and largely organic estate, with its rare mix of varieties on steep slopes and marginal soils, just 45 km from Africa's southernmost tip. International publications have named Bruce and his larger portfolio, Bruce Jack Wines, one of the world's Top 100 winemakers and Most Admired Wine Brands on multiple occasions. See listings for Bruce Jack Wines, Mary Le Bow and The Berrio.

★★★★☆ **There Are Still Mysteries Single Vineyard Pinot Noir** Ⓐ Seemingly straightforward cranberry & spice to start, then the ninja surprise: a palate of tremendous depth, density & sinewy suppleness, power with an ethereal lightness. **19** ⑨⑶ Hemel-en-Aarde, Elim & Overberg grapes naturally vinified under CO2 blanket, much care taken with oaking, 40% new. 13% alc.

★★★★☆ **Moveable Feast Red Blend** Ⓐ Exquisite harmony of pure fruit & oak on estate's signature wine, mostly shiraz & malbec, dabs touriga, barbera, tannat & tinta in **19** ⑨⑶. Composed, focused & seamless, sprinkle of herbs & spices over fresh plum bounty. Complex wholebunch & natural ferment, 26 months barrelled, some American, 20% new.

★★★★ **Penelope Méthode Cap Classique Rosé** Ⓥ Strawberry pink **17** ⑧⑨ named for Bruce Jack's wife, switches from **16** ★★★★ ⑻⑷'s malbec to, uniquely, touriga franca. Lively fizz with tangy cherry. Vivacious, balanced, long creamy finish from 48 months on lees & primary ferment in old oak.

Not tasted: **Gift Horse Single Vineyard Barbera**. In abeyance: **Bonfire Hill Red**, **Bonfire Hill White**. Discontinued: **Over The Moon Red Blend**, **Year of the Rooster Rosé**. — FM

Location: Napier ▪ Map: Southern Cape ▪ Map grid reference: B7 ▪ WO: Overberg/Cape South Coast ▪ 1stB 2005 ▪ Tasting by appt only ▪ Wine sales via website ▪ Owner(s) Bruce Jack ▪ Winemaker(s) Bruce Jack & Marlize Beyers ▪ Viticulturist(s) Andre Purdy ▪ WIETA ▪ PO Box 55 Napier 7270 ▪ info@thedrift.co.za ▪ www.thedrift.co.za ▪ **T +27 (0)21-180-3668**

☐ **The Dry Land Collection** *see* Perdeberg Wines
☐ **The Duckitt Collection** *see* Cloof Wine Estate

The Earth Beneath Our Feet   Ⓥ

Care for the land, empowerment for those who work it, and crafting of wines with a sense of place remain the ideals of this Franschhoek boutique venture, with added accent on a regenerative approach in the vineyards and increasing use of wild and bunch ferments, and larger-format oak. Participating farm employees are allocated small, special pockets of vines to manage, with training and support if needed, and their crops are bought at market value for vinification by specialists. The growers and their stories appear on the labels.

★★★★ **Cinsault** ⓃⒺⓌ Welcome newcomer from 1976 Piekenierskloof dryland bushvines, 14 months older barrels. **22** ⑧⑧ vibrant, juicy, deliciously crunchy raspberry fruit, light body & silky tannins.

★★★★ **Pinotage** Ⓥ Bold, expressive **16** ⑧⑦ from 40 year old ungrafted Piekenierskloof bushvines has muscle & fruit to spare. Mulberry & black cherry with toasty spicing from 14 months in barrel, 25% new.

★★★★ **Syrah** Supple, peppery **20** ⑧⑥, juicy red berry & plum fruit, refined tannins & robust acid. Medium body & spice, pleasant oak notes from 14 months in older barrels.

★★★★ **Field Blend** Chenin with 40% grenache blanc & roussanne, wild-yeast, barrel-fermented **22** ⑧⑦ richer, spicier than sibling 'Blanc'. Bright acid & sweetly ripe stonefruit, lees fatness from 9 months in oak.

Blanc ★★★☆ Unwooded version of Field Blend, **22** ⑻⑸ light, fresh & undemanding yet subtly charming, with generous stonefruit. — GdB

Location: Franschhoek ▪ WO: Franschhoek/Piekenierskloof ▪ Est 2020 ▪ 1stB 2012 ▪ Tasting by appt only ▪ Sales online ▪ Owner(s) Rob Meihuizen ▪ Winemaker(s) Donovan Ackermann (Rickety Bridge Winery) ▪ Viticulturist(s) Sam Hatfield ▪ 2ha (shiraz, chenin, grenache b, rouss) ▪ 20t/2,000cs ▪ info@theearthbeneathourfeet.com ▪ www.theearthbeneathourfeet.com

---

☐ **The Elite** *see* Old Road Wine Company

Theescombe Estate Wine   Ⓥ ⑪ Ⓒ

This family boutique venture revolves around just 1 ha of vines, planted with five varieties, on the edge of Port Elizabeth city in Eastern Cape province. It's run by Roger Futter as vineyard tender and wife Sandra as winemaker and welcomer of visitors, who are accorded various pre-booked tasting, tour and refreshment alternatives, plus the option of hiring the venue for functions.

Semillon ⓧ ★★ Tiny yield, as all. **18** ⑭ has dabs chenin & sauvignon, just 10% alc. Dried apple & pear, a ginger ale note. Very high acid helps keep wine fresh but it's not balanced with the fruit. **Blanc Blend** ⓧ ★★ Semillon with 20% chenin. Powerful waxy note in **19** ⑭'s scents alongside baked apple, stonefruit, gives impression of maturity but palate is fresh due to bracing acid which overrides the fruit. Unoaked, as all. Not tasted: **Cabernet Sauvignon**, **Pinotage**, **Rosé**, **Chenin Blanc**, **White Muscadel Dry**. — CR

Location: Port Elizabeth ▪ Map: Eastern Cape ▪ Map grid reference: D5 ▪ Est/1stB 2010 ▪ Tasting, sales & cellar tours by appt ▪ Full package R260pp (tour, talk on wine making, tutored tasting of 4 wines, cheese platter); Sunshine package R180pp (tasting of 4 wines, cheese platter) ▪ Closed Sundays ▪ Meals/platters (cheese, olives & biltong) to be pre-booked ▪ Functions ▪ Card facilities available ▪ Venue hire ± 20-60 people (with/without food) is available ▪ Owner(s) Futter family ▪ Winemaker(s) Sandra Futter (Oct 2007) ▪ Viticulturist(s) Roger Futter (Jun 2006) & Craig Futter (May 2022) ▪ 1.94ha/1ha (cab, ptage, chenin, sem, white muscadel) ▪ 1-4t ▪ theescombewines@hotmail.co.za ▪ www.theescombewines.wixsite.com/wine, www.theescombe-wines.yolasite.com ▪ **T +27 (0)73-889-6663**

☐ **The Fair Trade** see Koopmanskloof Vineyards
☐ **The Family Tree** see Backsberg Family Wines
☐ **The Fifth Generation** see Backsberg Family Wines
☐ **The First XI** see De Kleine Wijn Koöp

The Fishwives Club Boutique Winery

'An orchid among daisies' is Cape Town's Patrick James Robertson characterisation of the winery he created to target women specifically with whimsically packaged wines styled by collaborator since inception, Imbuko Wines, to deliver balanced drinkability on release. A webstore offers complementary merchandise.

The Fishwives Club range
Cabernet Sauvignon ⓝⒺⓦ ★★★ Grape's blackcurrant aroma, hint of cedar oak & tannins eased by sweet fruit, **21** ⑧⓪ is ready to go. **Merlot** ★★★ Juicy, ripe plummy fruit on **21** ⑦⑨, freshness & a little sweetness curb generous 14% alc. **Pinotage Rosé** ★★★ Gently fresh, with quiet red berry flavours & fruitily dry finish, **23** ⑦⑧ is for friendly everyday drinking. **Chardonnay** ⓧ ★★★ Peach & lemon with a little vanilla butter dressing from light oaking, **22** ⑧① ends with flattering sweet hint. **Sauvignon Blanc** ★★★ Ripe, sappy tropical fruit balanced by lively but not harsh acid make **23** ⑧② a crowd pleaser.

Alu Can range
Magnificent Merlot ★★★ Lively **21** ⑧⓪ has hint of oak spice, succulent berries rounded for ready drinking. **Pastel Pinotage Rosé** ★★☆ Pleasingly understated **23** ⑦⑧, softly dry & red berry toned, undemanding, with nice freshness. **Sensational Sauvignon Blanc** ★★★ Ripe tropical flavours enlivened by balanced natural acidity, **23** ⑧② ticks the box for easy, satisfying sipping. 250-ml can for this & Green range.

The Green Collection Alu Can range
Magical Merlot ⓧ ★★ No sulphur added version, contributes to ocean conservation. **19** ⑦⑥ nicely fleshed but boldly oaked, best with food. — AL

Location: Cape Town ▪ WO: Western Cape ▪ Est/1stB 2013 ▪ Closed to public ▪ Sales online ▪ Owner(s) / CEO Patrick James Robertson ▪ Winemaker(s) Theunis van Zyl (Imbuko Wines) ▪ 40,000cs ▪ WIETA ▪ www.thefishwivesclub.co.za, thefishwivesclubboutique.com

☐ **The Flagship** see Stellenbosch Vineyards

The Fledge & Co
ⓧ

Husband-and-wife vintners Leon Coetzee and Margaux Nel say they have 'Iberian aspirations', meaning the grapes that most excite and inspire their crafting in a Calitzdorp boutique cellar originate from that Mediterranean peninsula, currently albariño, which they recently made for the first time, palomino and tinta barocca, plus as yet unexplored varieties lurking in far-flung sites. They remain 'proudly terroir by truck', bringing in some 27 varieties from over 50 selected pockets for their ±20 labels (the number varies). They work with 'passionately courageous' growers who share their vision of allowing the diversity of the Cape to speak through naturally made wines. Ongoing trials cover a panoply of techniques and directions.

Rare Sightings range

★★★★ **Veld Versnit / Field Blend** Like 20 (88), notch-up 21 ★★★★★ (90) co-planted & -fermented cinsaut (70%), cab franc & alicante bouschet on Stellenbosch granite. Lively cherry fruit, gentle tannins & supple old oak make for light-feeling summer red to serve slightly chilled.

★★★★ **Constantia Riesling** (⬢) Single-site grapes part barrel-fermented, a splash of demijohn-aged 'reserve' blended in after 7 months in old oak. 22 (89) lovely stonefruit, lemongrass & lime scents, then a bone-dry palate shot through with nervy acid for an electrifying mouthful.

Not tasted: **Red Blend, Hatchi**. In abeyance: **U-Velaphi? Stellenbosch Cabernet Sauvignon, Pinot Noir Elgin, U-Velaphi? Elgin Chardonnay**.

Nest Egg range

★★★★ **Katvis Pinot Noir** (⊘) Luminous hue matches bright cherry, berry & currant fruit in 21 (89). Ferment completed in old barrel, matured 11 months for good structure & tannin grip. Unfined/filtered.

★★★★★ **Syrah** (⊘)(⬢) Limpid red fruit & pepper showcase cool terroirs of Elgin & Agulhas in refined 20 (94). Some wholeberry & combo tank, barrel & 'egg' ferment with judicious oaking, 18 months, 20% new, providing a scaffold for weightless yet complex body.

★★★★ **Fumé Blanc** (⊘)(⬢) Multi-region sauvignon off old bushvines with 10% semillon for lemony depth & stony acidity in 22 ★★★★★ (90). Ageing in older wood adds smoky nuance to the flinty limes. Improves on 21 (89).

★★★★☆ **Vagabond** (⬢) Chenin-led, multi-region, multi-variety blend; 21 (94) 1st first time for bukettraube, grenache gris & marsanne. This added complexity, extra time on lees, moderate 12.8% alc & gentle old-oaking elevate it over previous.

Occasional release: **Red/Tinto, Klipspringer Swartland Steen**. In abeyance: **Hoeksteen Stellenbosch Chenin Blanc**.

Jikken Barrels / Experimental Barrels range

★★★★ **Nel & Coetzee Steen** (⊘) Sunshiny 23 (88) chenin from 1968 Swartland block's concentrated peach, pineapple poached pear supported & focused by acidity, savoury lees & faintest caress of old oak, just 6% for 1 month.

★★★★☆ **Redemption Of A Rogue Elgin Viognier** Some botrytised grapes, as usual, in pithy yet elegant 22 (91). Fermented & aged in 500 & 600L Hungarian barrels for breadth & depth, peach with quinine & fynbos, steely acid refreshment. Only 206 cases.

Not tasted: **Praeteritus Bosstok Tinta Barocca, Sauvignon Blanc**. In abeyance: **Touriga Franca, Skn 'n Bnz Steen, Skn 'n Bnz Colombar**. — ML

Location: Calitzdorp/Riebeek West ▪ WO: Elgin/Western Cape/Stellenbosch/Constantia/Elgin-Agulhas/ Swartland ▪ Est 2007 ▪ 1stB 2010 ▪ Tasting by app wine@thefledge.co.za & sales/tastings at Boplaas, Calitzdorp ▪ Closed all pub hols ▪ Wine club ▪ Owner(s) Margaux Nel & Leon Coetzee ▪ Winemaker(s) Margaux Nel & Leon Coetzee (both Jan 2007) ▪ Viticulturist(s) Margaux Nel (Jan 2007) & Leon Coetzee (Jan 2015) ▪ 45% red 55% white ▪ IPW ▪ wine@thefledge.co.za ▪ www.thefledge.co.za ▪ **T +27 (0)82-828-8416/+27 (0)72-385-6503**

☐ **The Flemish Masters** see Almenkerk Wine Estate
☐ **The Founders Series** see Bellingham

The Foundry ⓠ

Since Chris Williams' move into the tiny renovated cellar on the Voor Paardeberg farm of James Reid, his partner in this top-rated venture, detailed daily work plans are a necessity: there's barely room for tanks, barrels, 'eggs' and pots, let alone fellow workers. The schedules are mapped out on the daily 50-minute drive from his Stellenbosch home. Today, fewer of the white grapes make the same journey, as grenache blanc and roussanne, as well as syrah planted in 2018, come into full production. Chris admits harvest 2023 was tough, thanks to ramping up of loadshedding as well as him going down with Covid. He remains up about 'the small, perfectly ripe crop of healthy grapes, and the wines now showing promise in the cellar'.

The Foundry range

★★★★☆ **Grenache Noir** Ⓐ Concentration without heaviness, **21** ⑨③'s rich, spiced dark fruit lifted by freshening, insistent tannins. Laying down year/2 will benefit greater harmony. 40% wholebunch, fermented/13 months, half older oak, rest terracotta dolium (pot).

★★★★☆ **Syrah** Ⓐ From home vines, **21** ⑨④ delicate & graceful. Lilies, red fruit & spice form an enticing complexity layered within supple flesh. Harmonious, with polished, flowing feel, sound structure allows for further ageing. 50% wholebunch, initial spontaneous ferment, 50% unoaked, balance older barrels, year.

★★★★☆ **Grenache Blanc** Ⓐ One of SA's most characterful examples. **22** ★★★★★ ⑨⑤ excellent structure & texture, its fresh hay & limy flavours, lively & intense, underpinned by 8 months on lees, & frisson of grip. Like **21** ⑨③, part natural ferment, 66% older oak, rest terracotta dolium (pot) & amphora.

★★★★☆ **Roussanne** Ⓐ Broad, waxy, with rounded, firm finish, texture is important part of **22** ⑨④. Floral & dried peach flavours weave through this, highlighted by natural freshness, & are lengthily sustained. Wholebunch press, 58% older oak fermented, rest dolium & amphora, 9 months.

★★★★☆ **Viognier** Ⓐ So delicate, & with fine thread of acid focusing fresh apricot & honeysuckle purity. **22** ⑨③'s flesh is succulent, flavours ripe, with an expansive conclusion. Stellenbosch grapes, part spontaneous ferment, older oak, lees aged 7 months.

Geographica range

★★★★☆ **Thoreau Cabernet Franc** Ⓥ Lively **20** ⑨③ has fragrant spice, red fruit & tealeaf complexity, sweet flesh freshened, lengthened by tiny insistent tannins. Part wholebunch & spontaneous ferment; older oak & dolium (80/20), 15 months. Stellenbosch WO.

★★★★☆ **Bonsai Chenin Blanc** Ⓥ Named for pea-size berries off 1957 Helderberg vines. Sense of ripeness rather than overt fruit on fabulously textured **20** ⑨④; rich, viscous, thrilling mineral thread provides energy, expansive length & potential. Wholebunch, older oak & dolium, 10 months. — AL

Location/map: Paarl ▪ Map grid reference: C2 ▪ WO: Voor Paardeberg/Stellenbosch ▪ Est 2000 ▪ 1stB 2001 ▪ Tasting, sales & cellar tours by appt ▪ Closed all pub hols ▪ Owner(s) Chris Williams & James Reid ▪ Cellarmaster(s)/winemaker(s) Chris Williams (Nov 2000) ▪ Viticulturist(s) Chris Williams (Nov 2000), with growers ▪ 15ha (grenache, shiraz, rouss, viog) ▪ ±30t/6,000cs own label 40% red 60% white ▪ PO Box 12423 Die Boord 7613 ▪ chris@thefoundry.co.za ▪ www.thefoundry.co.za ▪ **T +27 (0)82-577-0491**

☐ **The Front Row** see Hirst Wines
☐ **The Game Reserve** see Rooiberg Winery

The Garajeest ⓠ

On track for a career in the performing arts, Zimbabwe-born, now Cape-Town-based Callan Williams changed course and for the past decade has been expressing herself through the vine, Elgin being her studio and small parcels of cab franc and semillon her palette, to which she's planning to add syrah and riesling. Creative and awarded packaging, and homage to favourite rock singers have been features since the start.

★★★★ **Bruce Cabernet Franc** Fresh, leafy **19** ★★★★★ ⑨⓪ steps up on **18** ⑧⑧ with vibrant black plum, cherry & damson fruit energised by cool-grown Elgin acid & juicy tannins. Additional grip from smidgen new oak.

★★★★ **Jim Semillon** Ⓐ Vivacious **20** ★★★★★ ⑨④, redolent of thatch, crab apple & ripe lemon, notch up on **19** ⑧⑨. Full fruited, few grams sugar well balanced by brisk acidity. Half barrel fermented, cream textured from 9 months on lees.— ML

Location: Cape Town ▪ WO: Elgin ▪ Est 2014 ▪ 1stB 2015 ▪ Tasting by appt ▪ Owner(s) Callan Williams ▪ Winemaker(s) Callan Williams (May 2014) ▪ 12t/±1,800cs own label 50% red 50% white ▪ IPW, Vegan ▪ callan@thegarajeest.co.za ▪ www.thegarajeest.co.za ▪ **T +27 (0)72-524-2921**

☐ **The Garland** see Simonsig Wine Estate

The Giant Periwinkle

The small vineyard on the home-farm is planted with only three varieties, pinotage, semillon and sauvi-gnon, other grapes are brought in for terroir-focused, hands-off crafting by Pierre Rabie, owner with Robert

Stelzner and Karen van Helden, in the on-site cellar near Baardskeerdersbos on the cold Agulhas Plain. Much development has been done since the founding 15 years ago, recently a deck beside the farm dam.

★★★★ **Coenraad de Buys** ⊘ Multi-origin blend 50% cinsaut with shiraz, viognier, **20** ⑧⑥ spent year in foudre, is a better balance of ripeness & alc (13%) than **19** ★★★☆ ⑧③, showcases plush red berries & tailored tannins in a streamlined body. Drink in next year/2, no hardship.

★★★★☆ **Blanc Fumé** ⑧ Oaked sauvignon, 6 months, nice contrast to the cool-climate terroir's passionfruit, has weight-giving lees contact, shows melba toast savouriness. **21** ⑨④ vibrates with nervous tension, racy acid fits the trim 12.5% alc. Finishes salty, a great food match. No **20**.

★★★★☆ **Wind Scorpion** ⊘ ⑧ Unoaked sauvignon from Africa's most southerly vineyards, aptly named **22** ★★★★★ ⑨⑤ perfectly captures the site, shows the green side: fynbos, fennel, lemongrass, underpinned by minerality, salty acidity. As **21** ⑨③, has precision & verve.

★★★★☆ **The Bard** ⊘ Skilful unwooded blend of 40% semillon, with significant portions nouvelle, viognier, dab sauvignon, designed to capture floral aromatic notes plus green & sage nuances, which it does with style. **22** ⑨⓪ involving, complex, & as all whites, ends savoury, giving appetite appeal.

Not tasted: **Sun Spider Pinotage**, **Kelp Forest Syrah**, **Baardbek**, **South Cape White**. — CR

Location: Baardskeerdersbos ▪ Map: Southern Cape ▪ Map grid reference: A3 ▪ WO: Cape Agulhas/Western Cape ▪ Est 2009 ▪ 1stB 2012 ▪ Tasting by appt only T +27 (0)82-465-8350 or +27 (0)82-821-2301 ▪ Owner(s) Pierre Jacques Rabie, Robert Stelzner & Karen van Helden ▪ Winemaker(s) Pierre Jacques Rabie ▪ 2.4ha (Baardskeerdersbos: ptage, sauv, sem) ▪ pierre@giantperiwinkle.co.za ▪ www.giantperiwinkle.co.za ▪ **T +27 (0)21-426-2653**

The Goose Wines   ⑦ ⑪ ⑧

The seldom-seen Wine of Origin Upper Langkloof certification of most of these wines testifies to their origins in one of SA's coolest viticultural zones, the Outeniqua mountains near George, in the heart of the Garden Route. Here, at 800-m altitude, lies the home-farm Ganzekraal ('Goose Pen'), owned by renowned professional golfer Retief 'The Goose' Goosen, as is the widely exported brand, with long-term business partner Werner Roux. Alwyn Liebenberg, winemaker at inception in 2005, returned in 2022, just after the limited-release Reserve Sauvignon was made. It's available only from the winery (see email address below).

★★★★ **Cabernet Sauvignon** Harvested quite ripe, **20** ★★★☆ ⑧③ has less of variety's fruit expression & more of its mouthcoating tannins, needing time. Touch less elegant than **19** ⑧⑦.

★★★★ **Owners Reserve Sauvignon Blanc** ⑧ Picked riper than sibling, from low-yield dryland vines, hence tropical nuances, slightly fruitier palate. **22** ⑧⑨'s judicious acid lends freshness & poise.

★★★★ **Sauvignon Blanc** ⊘ Muted aromas but good fennel, greenpepper & Golden Delicious flavours on **23** ★★★★ ⑧⑤. Poised, bright, gram sugar extends finish, as on more engaging **22** ⑧⑦. WO W Cape.

Shiraz ★★★★ Lightly dusted with oak spice, **19** ⑧⑤ now bottled, shows its ripeness in jammy, raisined blackberry & plum fruit. Tannins, while firm & not harsh, tad unsettled mid-2023. Allow more time.

Chardonnay ⊘ ★★★★ Elegant shape & pleasing vinosity, with cool lemon & lime aromas, delicate nuttiness & creamy finish aided by smidgen sugar in **22** ⑧⑤. Coastal WO. Not tasted: **Expression**. — CvZ

Location: George ▪ Map: Klein Karoo & Garden Route ▪ Map grid reference: C3 ▪ WO: Upper Langkloof/Coastal/Western Cape ▪ Est 2005 ▪ Tasting by appt in season ▪ Meals/refreshments by appt in season ▪ Family friendly ▪ Owner(s) Retief Goosen & Werner Roux ▪ GM & financial manager Michéle Botha (May 2010) ▪ Winemaker(s) Alwyn Liebenberg (Sep 2022) ▪ Viticulturist(s) Bennie Botha (Jan 2010) ▪ 500ha/17ha (cab, shiraz, sauv) ▪ 120t/18,666cs own label 66% red 34% white ▪ HACCP ▪ PO Box 2053 George 6530/The Goose Office, 20 Herold Str Stellenbosch 7600 ▪ michele@thegoosewines.com ▪ www.thegoosewines.com ▪ **T +27 (0)82-610-2276**

The Grape Grinder

Oliver Kirsten and Johan du Toit's Paarl-based, export-orientated venture from modest beginnings in 2010 has grown into a substantial business, latterly with an acclaimed craft gin, and now a premium shiraz and collection of perlé wines in cans added. The founding goal of 'showcasing the creative energy present in the modern SA wine industry to an international wine-consuming audience' keeps serving them well.

The Wild Bouquet range (NEW)
★★★★ **Shiraz** Svelte & sophisticated **21** ⑧⑨ ex Swartland, silky tannins, plush ripe black fruit & subtle scrub & herbal notes. 8-week skin maceration, year in large barrels & small foudres, none new, lend refinement & integration.

The Wild Olive range
★★★★ **Old Vines Chenin Blanc** ⊘ Remarkable value in **23** ⑧⑥ from Swartland dryland vineyards. Rich, leesy pineapple & cling peach fruit, firm but yielding acid. Fresh & vibrant for current enjoyment.

The Milkwood range
★★★★ **Shiraz-Viognier** ⊘ Light, supple & fragrant, with scrub & pepper, **21** ⑧⑥ smooth, quaffable yet shows pleasing varietal character & charm. 40% barrelled, rest on staves, lending exotic spice lift.

The Grinder range
★★★★ **Chenin Blanc** ⊘ Very appealing fruit-driven **23** ⑧⑥ from Swartland vines is a conspicuous over-achiever, with lively tropical flavours, commendable mouthfeel & body from 6 months on lees in tank. **Merlot** ⑧ ★★★★ Unoaked **21** ⑧④ shows clarity & brightness, with convincing fruit tannins. Great anytime drinking. **Pinotage** ⊘ ★★★★ Welcome toning down of mocha from heavily toasted staves, sees mulberry & bramble fruit centre stage in **21** ⑧④. **Shiraz** ⑧ ★★★★ Better structure & ripeness in **21** ⑧③, tobacco spices on black cherry fruit, meaty savouriness & hint of liquorice. **Rosé** ⊘ ★★★★ With strawberry cordial fruit, lively acid, dry **22** ⑧④ is Swartland cinsaut, crisp, light & refreshing. **Chardonnay** ⑧ ★★★★ In character of siblings, **22** ⑧④ jam-packed with sunny fruit, balanced & fresh, at rock-bottom price.

Blue Moose range
....
Cabernet Sauvignon-Shiraz ⊘ ⑦ ★★★★ **21** ⑧⑤ has 77% cab, showing solid, succulent black berry fruit, hint of spice from 10 months in seasoned barrels.
....

Cape Fynbos range
....
Chenin Blanc ⊘ ⑦ ★★★★ Chenin with real attitude at bargain price, **23** ⑧④ from Riebeek-Kasteel vineyard delivers classy weight, texture & tropical fruit.
....

Bubbly Chardonnay (NEW) ☺ ★★★ Thoroughly enjoyable **NV** ⑧② picnic fare in 250-ml can, dry, with perky acid, modest bubble, tangy citrus fruit.

Bubbly Merlot (NEW) ★★★ Gentle fizz in **NV** ⑧② can is unfamiliar but pleasant, adding tang to vivid red fruit. Dry, unwooded. WO W Cape, as 3L sibling, rest Coastal. **Merlot** ⊘ ★★★ Previewed last edition, unwooded **22** ⑧① shows staying power, remains fresh & fruit-forward for everyday sipping. 3L bag-in-box, as the other stillwines. **Bubbly Rosé** (NEW) ⊘ ★★★ Similar to still version, lightly sparkling **NV** ⑧① cinsault in 250-ml can shows as drier, more austere, with lower 12.3% alc. **Rosé** ⊘ ★★★★ Likeable, fragrant & fruity, with gentle acid, **22** ⑧④ from Swartland cinsault over-delivers. — GdB

Location: Paarl ▪ WO: Western Cape/Swartland/Coastal ▪ Est/1stB 2010 ▪ Closed to public ▪ Owner(s) Oliver Kirsten & Johan du Toit ▪ Cellarmaster(s) Pieter Carstens (Dec 2010, consultant) ▪ Winemaker(s) Madré van der Walt (Jul 2015, consultant) ▪ Viticulturist(s) Koos van der Merwe (Dec 2010, consultant) ▪ 70,000cs own label 75% red 20% white 5% rosé ▪ ISO 2009, BRC, WIETA ▪ PO Box 606 Paarl 7624 ▪ oliver@grapegrinder. com ▪ www.grapegrinder.com ▪ **T +27 (0)21-863-3943**

The Grapesmith
The awarded Simonsig team see this sibling small-batch label as a blank canvas on which to create, experiment and learn, previously through the prism of white Mediterranean varieties, but the 'surprise' hinted at last edition now adds black grapes to the line-up. 15th- and 16th-century Portuguese mariners and the stone pillars they erected inspired the name and label design, dovetailing with the range's 'cross' theme.

★★★★☆ **Maritimo** (NEW) Mostly mourvèdre (39%) for **21** ⑨② grenache noir, dashes shiraz & rare marselan. As siblings, natural ferment & ageing using complex combo techniques & vessels (here older oak, tank, concrete 'egg', 14 months). Harmonious, nimble (12.5%), & though restrained, an intensity that augurs well. Stellenbosch WO unless noted.

★★★★☆ **Die Kluisenaar** Consistently fine-tuned, ageworthy blend of bunch-pressed & old-oak fermented marsanne & 42% roussanne in **20** (94). As **19** ★★★★★ (95), inhibited maloloctic fermentation ensures freshness, lees ageing & ripeness add waxy texture. Bone-dry, with delicate citrus blossom, lemon & hazelnut.

★★★★☆ **Mediterraneo** Marsanne in **21** ★★★★★ (95) blend with roussanne (68/21), dabs grenache blanc & verdelho. Intricate, persistent & pure quince & citrus, subtly enhanced by ferment & ageing in mix of older oak, tank & amphora. As seamless & succulent, but even brighter & more vivacious than **20** (94). WO W Cape. — MW

- ☐ **The Grinder** *see* The Grape Grinder
- ☐ **The Haute Collection** *see* Haute Cabrière
- ☐ **The Haven Collection** *see* Glen Carlou
- ☐ **The Hedgehog** *see* Orange River Cellars

The High Road

Businessmen Les Sweidan and Mike Church founded their boutique winery with the intention of taking the high road in four main areas of focus: grape variety, origin, use of French oak and honest business practice. Hence their emphasis on cabernet and blends, with the 'king' of red-wine grapes, sourced from Stellenbosch, an area synonymous with the variety. One of the industry's most respected names, Miles Mossop crafts the wines using traditional French small-oak in classic, ageworthy style. Helping 'keep our business transparent' is general manager Lyzette Tanski, joining the venture on its 21st anniversary.

★★★★ **Cabernet Sauvignon** Attractive herbaceous edge to classic Stellenbosch dark-fruit core in **21** (88). Taut, dry tannin framework supported by seasoned oak - everything in place, just needs few years to settle & unfurl.

★★★★☆ **Cabernet Sauvignon Reserve** Regal **19** ★★★★★ (96) enthroned exclusively in magnum, opulent blackcurrant fruit beautifully balanced with effortlessly assimilated oak, all new, 22 months. From a fine vintage, still youthful & will age with distinction, like **18** (93).

★★★★☆ **Classique** Plusher styling for this Cape Bordeaux continues in **20** (92), 41% merlot with cab, cab franc, petit verdot & malbec. Rounded flavours complemented by svelte tannins from adroit barrelling, 10% new. Silky texture & satisfying farewell.

★★★★☆ **Director's Reserve** The cab-based (74%) Bordeaux blend, with merlot & cab franc, dash petit verdot in **20** (93). Seriously oaked, 100% new, 20 months, then 22 months in bottle, creating a fine, already well-meshed structure for the rich dark-berry fruit. Notch up on last.— DS

Location/map/WO: Stellenbosch ▪ Map grid reference: E5 ▪ Est/1stB 2003 ▪ Tasting by appt only ▪ Closed all pub hols ▪ Online wine shop ▪ Boardroom facilities ▪ Wine club ▪ Owner(s) Les Sweidan & Mike Church ▪ GM Lyzette Tanski ▪ Winemaker(s) Miles Mossop (2018, consultant) ▪ 40t own label 100% red ▪ 7D Lower Dorp Str/Distillery Rd, Bosman's Crossing, Stellenbosch 7600 ▪ wine@thehighroad.co.za ▪ www.thehighroad.co.za ▪ T +27 (0)21-886-4288

The Hills

The Hills family has owned Chimanimani boutique farm in Stellenbosch for over five decades, and for almost two of them a small portion of the home-grown fruit has been made for this own-label by consultants. Two fallow blocks have undergone soil regeneration and preparation for replanting with merlot and cabernet franc, while revitalisation continues on two further parcels, including the planting of winter cover crops.

★★★★ **Cabernet Sauvignon** The best fruit substance & structure of the vintage's red in **18** (86). Cedar & cassis, with a tobacco note from 33% new oak, as for Ensemble & Shiraz. Modest 13% alc makes for lightness. Like **17** ★★★★ (85) - & in fact all these wines - genuinely & pleasingly dry.

★★★★ **Pinot Noir** **20** (86) the best vintage yet. Charming ripe & pure cherry & raspberry, with a savoury note too. Continues delicate tradition, with gentle tannins, but has substance & length of flavour.

Dry Red ★★★ Appealing aromas on **16** (79) from undeclared varieties, but a touch light for the dry tannins. WO Devon Valley. **Shiraz** ★★★★ Spicy, dark-berried **18** (85) has silky texture & very restrained but informing tannins. Not much complexity or intensity but rather elegant in its lightness. **Ensemble** ★★★★ Pleasant but unconcentrated fruit on **18** (85) cab-shiraz. Bright, light-feeling, fairly easygoing but drying tannins. **17 ★★★★** ⑧⑥ richer in flavour from similar blend. **Chenin Blanc ★★★** Unassumingly pleasant **22** ⑧② with peach & thatchy notes. A little dilute but flavoursome. — TJ

Location/map: Stellenbosch ▪ Map grid reference: D4 ▪ WO: Stellenbosch/Devon Valley ▪ Est/1stB 2006 ▪ Tasting & sales by appt ▪ Owner(s) The Victor Hills Family Trust ▪ Winemaker(s) Nicky Claasens (2016-2020, consultant), Jacques de Klerk & Danie Steytler (consultants) ▪ Viticulturist(s) Vic Hills (Jan 1998) ▪ 6ha/5ha (cab, pinot, shiraz, chenin) ▪ 40t/600cs own label 80% red 20% white ▪ PO Box 12012 Die Boord Stellenbosch 7613 ▪ vwhills@iafrica.com ▪ www.thehillswine.co.za ▪ **T +27 (0)21-865-2939/+27 (0)82-493-6837**

The Hill Vineyard

Planted exclusively with cabernet by Nederburg some 50 years ago, this is one of the highest sites in Paarl, at 300-320 m altitude on the windy west slope of Hawequa Mountain. Replanted by two shareholders from 2015/6 to echo the original, the older vines yielded the first viable crop in 2019; the youngest ones came into fruit last year. The ratings below speak of the potential to be realised, and the owners are 'looking forward to the benefits that the increasing maturity of our vines will bring'. Vinification is off-site by consultants.

★★★★ Cabernet Sauvignon ⊘ Pair of vintages tasted, **20** ⑧⑦ forthright, even bold at 14.4% alc, with dark savoury notes, berries & a little tobacco. Balanced, if not yet harmonious, firm tannins & acidity. **21** ⑧⑦, the alc a touch higher, is riper-fruited; still youthful & needs time to integrate.— TJ, AL

Location/WO: Paarl ▪ Est 2015/16 ▪ 1stB 2019 ▪ Closed to public ▪ Owner(s) The Hill 590B Property CC (2 members) ▪ Winemaker(s) Schalk van der Westhuizen & Samantha de Morney-Hughes (Aug 2019, consultants) ▪ Viticulturist(s) Hanno van Schalkwyk (Jul 2017, consultant) ▪ 14ha/1.5ha (cab) ▪ 6t/700cs own label 100% red + 300cs for clients ▪ Brands for clients: Hawksmoor at Matjieskuil ▪ IPW ▪ Postnet Suite 354 Private Bag X025 Lynnwood Ridge 0040 ▪ info@thehillvineyard.com ▪ www.thehillvineyard.com ▪ **T +27 (0)82-779-2552**

☐ **The Homestead Series** *see* Bellingham

The House of GM&AHRENS ⑨ ⑪

High-end cap classique specialist GM&AHRENS annually produces a limited quantity of vintage-dated spar-kling, some of which spends up to six years on the lees. Since inception in 2007, grapes have been sourced from the same 13 Western Cape pockets to ensure high quality and consistency. The bubblies are produced off-site and aged in 30,000-bottle underground facilities in Franschhoek town, where tastings are presented by Gerrit Maritz, co-founder and manager of the company.

★★★★☆ Vintage III Always a serious-minded brut sparkler. Plenty going on in **19** ⑨① from equal chardonnay & pinot noir. Year in oak adds spice to ripe peach & dried pear fruit, 24 months on lees give pastry & brioche breadth. Gentle bubbles, fine seam of acid & lengthy apple pie finish.

Not tasted: **Vintage Cuvée**. — CM

Location/map: Franschhoek ▪ Map grid reference: C1 ▪ WO: Western Cape ▪ Est 2007 ▪ 1stB 2008 ▪ Tasting, sales & cellar tours by appt ▪ Closed all pub hols ▪ Meals/refreshments by appt ▪ Owner(s) Provence Village (Pty) Ltd ▪ Bubbly maker Gerrit Maritz (production at Avondale since Jan 2023) ▪ 100% MCC; 1st limited unique 5xbottle cases released annually ▪ PO Box 478 Franschhoek 7690 ▪ aw@gmahrens.com ▪ www.gmahrens.com ▪ **T +27 (0)83-348-1230**

The House of JC le Roux ⑨ ⑪ ⑩ ⑧ ⑤

Owned by Heineken Beverages, JC le Roux has a large and popular range of champagne-method and carbonated bubblies, in a variety of packaging and styles, the core range having a new look. This was SA's first dedicated sparkling-wine cellar, and the multi-function brand-home in Stellenbosch's Devon Valley invites both conferencing and general popping in... and much more popping once there. It's been recently refurbished, and offers everything from misting for hot summer days to a fireplace for winter cosiness.

Cap Classique range

★★★★ Scintilla ⑨ Chardonnay & pinot noir (60/40) sparkler, **15** ⑧⑨ brioche & nut aromas speak of 6+ years on lees. With lemony freshness, it's tight, zippy & properly dry.

Nectar range

Rosé Demi-Sec (Ⓩ) ★★★ Off-dry pink fizz, **NV** ⑧⓪ from combo white & black grapes, delightful character & balance. Fruity, frothy & fun. Carbonated, as all Nectar & Vivante bubbles. **White Demi-Sec** (Ⓩ) ★★ Shy **NV** ⑦④ sparkle with musky sweetness & soft almond finish. From sauvignon & muscadel.

Sélection Vivante

La Chanson (Ⓩ) ★★★ Appetising **NV** ⑦⑧ sparkler, deep ruby colour & tasty red-berry mix. Mainly pinotage. **La Fleurette** (Ⓩ) ★★ Summery pink bubbles, **NV** ⑦⑥ typical muscat grapey floral aromas with strawberries & cream. Great with pavlova. **La Fleurette Non-Alcoholic** (Ⓩ) ★★ Cherry-berry confection on **NV** ⑦⑤ de-alc full-sweet rosé bubbles from sauvignon, muscadel & pinotage. **Sauvignon Blanc** (Ⓩ) ★★ Lower alc (11.5%) on shy **NV** ⑦⑥, missing varietal character of last. Just-dry, crisp citrus notes. **Le Domaine** (Ⓩ) ★★★ Spritzy **NV** ⑦⑦ from sauvignon & muscat with pronounced grape & floral character, strong tinned pineapple finish. Sweet & fresh. **Le Domaine Non-Alcoholic** (Ⓩ) ★★ Floral **NV** ⑦⑥ de-alc full-sweet white fizz packed with grapey aromas, balanced sugar & fresh acid. — TJ

Location/map: Stellenbosch ▪ Map grid reference: D4 ▪ WO: Western Cape ▪ 1stB 1983 ▪ Tasting & sales Mon-Thu/Sun 10-4 Fri-Sat/pub hols 10-5 booking essential; pub hols (seasonal) please call ahead ▪ Fee R95-R195 ▪ Closed Dec 25 & Jan 1 ▪ Nougat, cheesecake & pizza-&-bubbly experiences ▪ Self-tour available during opening hrs ▪ Gifts ▪ Cucina di Giovanni restaurant open for breakfast & lunch, booking essential ▪ Conference facilities ▪ Child friendly ▪ Owner(s) Heineken Beverages ▪ Winemaker(s) Ulrich Hohnes & Matthys Botes ▪ 27ha own vyds ▪ 20% red 80% white ▪ ISO 9200 ▪ PO Box 184 Stellenbosch 7599 ▪ info@jcleroux.co.za, jcleroux@giovannicapetown.co.za ▪ www.jcleroux.co.za ▪ **T +27 (0)21-865-8201 (winery)/+27 (0)21-865-8222 (restaurant)**

☐ **The House of Krone** *see* Krone
☐ **The House of Mandela** *see* House of Mandela
☐ **The Innocent** *see* Lammershoek Winery
☐ **The Introduction** *see* Miles Mossop Wines

The Inventer

Johan Venter's reference to his surname in this boutique spirit venture's branding speaks of 'a man who is following his passion and embracing his creativity to shape something new, rare and remarkable'. In an illustrious career at Distell/Heineken Beverages, he developed some of SA's most prestigious and loved brands. As The Inventer, he's crafting niched and once-off limited editions and selling them directly to customers. The brandies featured here fit his ethos, in being entirely from either black or white grapes.

★★★★★ **XO Rosso** (Ⓩ) A luxurious indulgence, 100% potstill ⑨④ is velvet textured & opulently scented & flavoured, the richness foretold by the golden amber hue, yet the controlled fire of 40% alc assures elegance. From Stellenbosch & Durbanville cabernet & merlot. Only 820 bottles of these brandies.

★★★★☆ **XO Blanco** (Ⓩ) In contrast to its sibling, this white-grape-only potstill ⑨④ is delicate, with fine florals & lifted citrus mirrored in its jewel-like appearance. Textured & mellow, it finishes with the lingering glow of 40% alc. From chenin, sauvignon, ugni blanc & hanepoot ex Stellenbosch & Robertson.— WB

Location: Stellenbosch ▪ Est 2021 ▪ 1stB 2022 ▪ Closed to public ▪ Spirits club ▪ Owner(s) Spirits Master Journey - Johan Venter ▪ Brandy master Johan Venter (2021) ▪ PO Box 12883 Die Boord Stellenbosch 7613 ▪ discover@theinventer.co.za ▪ www.theinventer.co.za

☐ **The Journal** *see* Diemersdal Estate
☐ **The Kin** *see* Beaumont Family Wines

The Kitchen Sink (Ⓩ)

A label in the Somerset West-based Metzer & Holfeld Family Wines portfolio, designed to express 'distinctive vineyard parcels'. Minimalist winemaker Wade Metzer crafts the blends from maritime Helderberg grapes, and bottles them with no or very light filtration 'to retain as much terroir and fruit character as possible'.

★★★★ **Red** Cornucopia of exuberant red fruit, wild-fermented (as White) **22** ⑧⑨ gets extra verve from 20% wholebunch portion. Now cinsaut (60%), equal shiraz & cab, 11 months old oak, some American. Grip of chalky tannin before gently savoury finish. **21** untasted.

★★★★★ **White** ⊛ Beguiling aromas of nettle, acacia flower & citrus touched with flinty smoke on **22** ⑧⑨. 100% sauvignon blanc vs last **16** ⑧⑧'s chenin, vineyard near False Bay, planted 1981. Fermented/7 months in old oak.— ML

Location: Somerset West ▪ WO: Stellenbosch ▪ Tasting by appt ▪ Owner(s) Wade Metzer & Barry Holfeld ▪ Winemaker(s) Wade Metzer ▪ info@kitchensinkwine.com ▪ www.kitchensinkwine.com ▪ **T +27 (0)72-279-7645**

☐ **The Legend Collection** *see* Windmeul Cellar

Thelema Mountain Vineyards ⓆⒸ

Themed on the works of French 16th-century writer François Rabelais, the Webb family's immaculate estate at the apex of Helshoogte Pass on Simonberg Mountain has set and maintained the highest standards for viticulture and modern yet classically styled wines. The property was acquired in 1983 by Gyles Webb and his in-laws, the McLeans, signalling a change from his accounting career. In 2002, they acquired a second property, Sutherland, on the Elgin highlands, to produce a range of cool-climate wines, also made in the Thelema cellar by long-time incumbents Rudi Schultz and Duncan Clarke, but marketed as a standalone brand. This edition sees another Rabelais character, Gargantua, celebrated in a unique dessert offering, and the return of The Mint Cabernet from new plantings in the same eucalyptus-influenced block.

Thelema range

★★★★☆ **Cabernet Sauvignon** ⊛ Individual, distinctive Cape aristocrat in classic Bordeaux style, **20** ★★★★★ ⑨⑤ struts its class. Concentrated, sombre yet sleek & silky, with heavenly layers of cassis, earth, iodine & leafy minerals. Proven track record for beneficial ageing. Pips excellent **19** ⑨④.

★★★★ **The Mint Cabernet Sauvignon** ⊛ Distinctive mint highlight, reputedly from bluegum residue in vineyard, very much in evidence in **21** ★★★★☆ ⑨③. Rich, structured & muscular, with charming cocoa & tilled earth aromas, an exercise in balance, poise & elegance, though tautness & track record suggest extended cellaring. First tasted since **14** ⑧⑧.

★★★★★ **Merlot** Refined **20** ⑨① carries wine's enviable reputation forward, with lithe body, silky tannins & delicious spiced plum & cherry fruit. Leafy notes with cocoa wafts add nuance & charm.

★★★★☆ **Merlot Reserve** ⊛ Perennial high-flyer with stunning varietal expression, **21** ⑨④ follows form, ceding weight & power for elegance. Richly ripe & wholesome, with fine, powdery tannins, flavoursome black fruit threaded with oak spices from 18 months in new barrels.

★★★★☆ **Shiraz** ⊛ Succulent red berry fruit tempered with meat & tobacco savoury notes, hints of scrub & wild herbs. **19** ⑨⓪ full & dense but retaining supple body cloaked in ripe tannin. 30% new barriques, 18 months.

★★★★☆ **Rabelais** ⊛ Flag-bearing label exudes class & finesse in **21** ⑨④, cab with 10% petit verdot offer notable heft but sleekly cloaked in velvet tannins. Impossibly concentrated blackcurrant fruit has delicate iodine & tar mineral wafts, sweet spicing from 18 months in new oak. Follows standout **20** ★★★★★ ⑨⑤.

★★★★☆ **The Abbey** Referencing Rabelais' abbey of pleasures, **21** ⑨⓪ is 72% shiraz, equal grenache noir & petit verdot, offering sweetly ripe plum & cherry fruit spiced with pepper & scrub. Sleek tannins burnished by 18 months in seasoned oak.

★★★★☆ **Chardonnay** Bold & forthright, showing benefit of time in bottle, **20** ⑨② has prominent oak spice, showing in buttered nut & nougat, balanced by delicate lemon zest & frangipani scents. Fermented/10 months on lees in barriques.

★★★★☆ **Riesling** ⊘ Antithesis of Elgin sibling, **19** ⑨① shows bottle development in prominent terpene whiff, rounded citrus marmalade palate, gentle but effective acid & just-dry 6 g/L sugar. Ripe & generous style, added body from 6 months on lees.

★★★★☆ **Sauvignon Blanc** ⊘ ⊛ Again showcases brilliant varietal definition, with chiseled herbal-stony minerality, intense gooseberry & granadilla fruit, lingering to salty finish. Remarkable finesse & value in **23** ⑨③. No dab verdelho this vintage.

★★★★☆ **Cap Classique Brut** Rich, evolved & silky from 63 months on lees, **17** ⑨⓪ exudes charm & refinement. 76% chardonnay with pinot noir, showing savoury baked apple, yeasty grip & lovely sweet biscuit notes. From Elgin fruit.

★★★★☆ **Vin de Hel Muscat Late Harvest** Honeyed, hedonistic Natural Sweet from muscat de Frontignan, **21** ⑨ shows typical raisin-grapey fruit on a sleek frame. Unctuous 149 g/L sugar well restrained by steely, piercing acidity. Unwooded, after brief skin contact. 375 ml.

★★★★★ **Gargantua Muscadel** 🆕 🍸 Named after Rabelais' hero in Five Books, **NV** ⑨④ muscadel is truly unique. Unfermented, fortified muscat de Frontignan spent 19 years in barrel, producing immensely sweet (307 g/L) tawny port-like dessert wine with layers of honeyed confection, nutty nuances & lingering caramel finish. 500 ml.

Mountain Red ★★★☆ Dependable everyday enjoyment, **20** ㉕ shiraz blend made with house flair & care. Ripe, luscious berry compote on ripe, smooth tannins. 18 months older oak. WO W Cape for these.

Mountain White ★★★☆ Sauvignon with 10% viognier, **23** ㉕ commendable body & vibrant gooseberry fruit. Youthful & cheerful, for anytime refreshment. Occasional release: **Verdelho**. Discontinued: **Ed's Reserve Chardonnay**.

Sutherland Reserve range

★★★★★ **Emily Petit Verdot** 🍸 Variety's typical brawn & muscle is tempered by cool site, rendering more finesse & detail to **21** ㉟ (which adds Emily to the name). Solid black plum & currant fruit has subtle notes of anise, violet & cedar, robust but ripe tannins, all integrated by 18 months in new barrels. Back to form after **20** ★★★★★ ㉔.

★★★★★ **Sarah Red** Refined Cab-based Bordeaux blend in **18** ㉜, with merlot & petit verdot. Opulently ripe cherry & currant fruit shaped & restrained with suede tannins, hints of cocoa & cedar from 18 months in 37% new barrels. **17** ㉝, tasted as 'Red', was 100% cab in all-new oak.

★★★★★ **Anna Chardonnay** 🍸 Adds Anna to the name of 12 best barrels selected from 5 sites. Big & bold, with astonishing depth & concentration, **18** ㉔ fermented/10 months in new oak, further 4 years in bottle. Shows benefits of age, with beautifully integrated lemon & chamomile, creamy lees fatness.

Not tasted: **Lisa Grenache**. Occasional release: **Pinot Noir**.

Sutherland range

★★★★☆ **Cabernet Sauvignon** ✓ 🍸 Cool climate finds expression in leafy herbaceousness, adding appeal to perfectly ripe fruit but tempering weight & extract. Alluring & elegant, with gentle tannin grip. Petit verdot fraction in **19** ㉚ omitted in **20** ㉜, showing in suppleness. 18 months in 35% new oak.

★★★★☆ **Pinot Noir** ✓ Subtle, pretty, with sweetly ripe red berry fruit, **21** ㉚ has delicate charm & elegance. Silky tannins, honed by 10 months in barrel, offer gentle support. Notable regional character for the price. **20** untasted.

★★★★☆ **Syrah** ✓ Supple & juicy **21** ㉛ with 14% grenache noir has intense ripe black fruit core, Rhône-like scrub & pepper mingling harmoniously with aromatic spices & subtle smoked meat. 18 months in oak barriques, 30% new. **20** untasted.

★★★★ **Chardonnay** Extroverted & characterful, barrel-fermented **21** ㉙ has sweetly aromatic lemon blossom & zest, gently highlighted with well-judged oak spices. Full, generous, with fine-tuned acid, perfect match for creamy seafood.

★★★★ **Riesling** Lean & resolutely dry, with steely acid & minerality, **23** ㉘ shows delicate hint of terpene, deliciously aromatic citrus fruit. Vibrant acid seam & leesy richness add to appeal. **22** untasted.

★★★★☆ **Sauvignon Blanc** ✓ Racy, piquant & refreshing, **23** ㉛ combines dusty minerality with succulent, ripe tropical fruit in a convincing reflection of cool origins. Youthful & expressive, should develop.

★★★★☆ **Viognier-Roussanne** 🍸 Rhône's white aristocrats unite to produce unusual but harmonious blend. **22** ★★★★★ ㉟ has exotic aromatics & rich, buttery palate, pierced by thrilling acid. Hints of anise & chamomile meld with peach & pear, gently touched by oak from 9 months in older barrels. Even more satisfying than last-tasted **20** ㉝.

Grenache Rosé ★★★☆ Invitingly rose scented, dry & fragrant, **23** ㉕ offers vibrant tangy raspberry, noteworthy lees weight & lingering finish to pair with romantic sunsets. — GdB

Location/map: Stellenbosch ▪ Map grid reference: G4 ▪ WO: Simonsberg-Stellenbosch/Elgin/Western Cape ▪ Est 1983 ▪ 1stB 1988 ▪ Tasting & sales Mon-Fri 9-5 Sat/pub hols 10-3 ▪ Tasting fee: Premium tasting R120/6 wines, waived on purchase; Reserve tasting R250/5 wines, waived on purchase ▪ Owner(s) McLean & Webb family trusts ▪ Cellarmaster(s) Gyles Webb (1983) ▪ Winemaker(s) Rudi Schultz (Dec 2000), with Duncan Clarke (Jan 2010) ▪ Thelema: 157ha/46ha (cabs s/f, grenache, merlot, p verdot, shiraz, chard, muscat, sauv, verdelho); Sutherland: 60ha/42ha (cab, grenache, merlot, p verdot, pinot, syrah, chard, riesling, rouss, sauv, viog = 790t/60,000cs own label 60% red 40% white = PO Box 2234 Dennesig Stellenbosch 7601 = info@ thelema.co.za = www.thelema.co.za = **T +27 (0)21-885-1924**

The Liberator

Nothing to taste from Rick the Liberator, aka UK fine-wine importer and Master of Wine Richard Kelley. On regular visits to SA since 2010, he's saved many vinous gems from being blended away or disposed of in bulk, giving each once-off Episode or Special Release a quirky name and backstory on the label.

Est 2010 = 1stB 2008 = Closed to public = Owner(s) Richard Kelley MW & Eduard Haumann = 50% red 50% white = richard@dreyfus-ashby.co.uk = www.theliberatorwine.co.uk = **T +44 (0)7753-722-085**

☐ **The Lion Hound** see Ridgeback
☐ **The Love Story Collection** see Matthew Krone Wines
☐ **Thembu** see House of Mandela
☐ **The Mentors** see KWV Wines
☐ **The Merchant** see Cape Wine Company

Themika

On the slopes of Saronsberg Mountain near Tulbagh, Themika is a fruit, olive, wine and guest farm owned by medical doctors Paul and Dagmar Whitaker. Paul plans to add a few rows to the block of old chenin, and plant roussanne and grenache blanc for the blend he crafts in the small cellar beside the recently upgraded and now carbon-neutral stay-over facilities. Made as naturally as possible, his wines are unfined/filtered.

Barrel Select range

★★★★ **Chenin Blanc** 2 vintages tasted, both barrel fermented, 20% new, 11 months on lees. **21** (89) attractive stonefruit & pear, light oak spicing (all fruit went into wood vs 80% for sibling), acid touch more vibrant & precise than on **22** (86). Peanut shell & herb notes on similar fruit profile & bone-dryness.

★★★★ **White Blend** Chenin & viognier (60/40) combo, natural ferment/11 months in older barrels, 100% malo. **21** ★★★★★ (90) ginger & apricot stone nuances on yellow & orange citrus & white peach. Calm & composed, viognier's expression more elegant than for last-tasted **16** (88).— PS, CvZ

Location/map/WO: Tulbagh = Map grid reference: F4 = 1stB 2013 = Tasting by appt only = Themika Trails (MTB) & Adventure Lodge (farm house & self-catering cottages) T +27 (0)72-646-9951 = Owner(s) Paul & Dagmar Whitaker = Winemaker(s)/viticulturist(s) Paul Whitaker = 64ha/2ha (chenin) = 4.5t/220cs own label 100% white = ansec166@docswhitaker.co.za = www.themika.com = **T +27 (0)82-781-9211**

☐ **The Misfits** see Ken Forrester Wines
☐ **The Mooring** see Overhex Wines International
☐ **The Mysteries** see Lammershoek Winery
☐ **The Nature Reserve** see Cape Wine Company
☐ **The Old Man's Blend** see Groote Post Vineyards
☐ **Theo's Ark** see VinGlo Wines
☐ **The Pack** see Painted Wolf Wines
☐ **The Patriarch** see Backsberg Family Wines
☐ **The Pierneef Collection** see La Motte
☐ **The Pledge** see Le Grand Domaine
☐ **The Quirky Ones** see Old Road Wine Company
☐ **The Raptor Post** see Tulbagh Mountain Vineyards
☐ **The Rhino Run** see Van Loveren Family Vineyards
☐ **The Right Choice** see Nico Vermeulen Wines
☐ **The River Collection** see Bonnievale Wines
☐ **The Rose House** see Mile High Vineyards
☐ **The Sadie Family** see Sadie Family Wines
☐ **The Saints** see DGB (Pty) Ltd
☐ **The Sensory Collection** see Stellar Winery
☐ **The Shiner** see Paserene

☐ **The Spice Route Winery** *see* Spice Route
☐ **The Stellenbosch Reserve** *see* Stellenbosch Reserve
☐ **The Storyteller** *see* Stellar Winery
☐ **The Tea Leaf** *see* Wildeberg Wines
☐ **The Tin Mine** *see* Zevenwacht
☐ **The Township Winery** *see* Township Winery
☐ **The Vale** *see* Bonnievale Wines
☐ **The Valley** *see* La Brune Wines
☐ **The Vine Guys** *see* Mischa Estate

The Vineyard Party

Cape Town winemaker Jolette Steyn's boutique venture specialises in semillon. Since debut vintage 2018 her search for biodiverse vineyards with a healthy ecosystem, capable of expressing their terroir, has taken her to various areas, but now she's secured a long-term source in Bot River. A new wine, Daisy If You Do, joins Huckleberry this year. Common to them are the inspiration for the name, the Western film Tombstone, area of origin - Constantia, and handling - minimal intervention with wild yeasts and older oak. The main differentiator is skin contact for Huckleberry. 'I have no doubt people will have strong opinions about which they prefer,' the vigneronne says. 'That is what wine is about, a conversation, robust discussion, an engagement.'

★★★★☆ **Daisy If You Do** (NEW) Pure **20** (92) has bright citrus flavours, hints of lanolin & spice, carried on a texture like ripples of liquid silk to a zestily dry conclusion. Delicate yet intense, deserves time to blossom. 100% wholebunch, ferment/11 months in older oak.

★★★★★ **I'm Your Huckleberry** (🐝) Immediate attraction on **20** (93) is the expressive spiced lemon aromas & flavours, dense silk texture & emphatic tannic grip. Spontaneous ferment in plastic tank, 100% on skins, 50% wholebunch, 50% destemmed & crushed, then older oak, 10 months, deliver defined, abundant character. Cosiderable potential too, like **19** ★★★★★ (95).

Discontinued: Here Be Dragons. — AL

Location: Cape Town ▪ WO: Constantia ▪ Est/1stB 2018 ▪ Closed to public ▪ Owner(s)/winemaker(s) Jolette Steyn ▪ 2t/230cs own label 100% white ▪ info@thevineyardparty.com ▪ www.thevineyardparty.com ▪ **T +27 (0)72-973-8133**

The Vinoneers

Having recently invested in two concrete 'eggs', co-owners Brenden Schwartz and Etienne Louw are taking delivery of two more, and preparing to release a concrete-aged cinsaut - this being the second 'deconstruction' of their Cape Blend; the first, from pinot noir, debuts below. A former chemical engineer and trained classical musician, Etienne (aka Orpheus) is now full-time with the brand he and graphic designer 'The Raven' founded in 2016, with a single barrel as asset, as 'a pure expression of the love for fine wine and art'. The latter is represented by the opulent and award-winning packaging, a key feature since inception.

Orpheus & The Raven range

★★★★☆ **Conspiracy of Ravens Pinot Noir** (NEW) (✓) Translucent **21** (91) from Franschhoek has sweet earth, red fruit & wonderful purity, malo in barrel & ageing in concrete 'egg' smooth the edges. Light 12.7% alc, graceful & fresh, ready to enjoy though will continue to improve.

★★★★ **No. 7 Pinotage** Boldly rich & ripe (14.7% alc) **22** (88) has abundant plush dark fruit to savour. Oak, 40% new, provides some structural restraint, fresh acid ensures pleasurable drinking. **21** untasted.

★★★★★ **Old Bush Vine Chenin Blanc** More expressive in riper **22** ★★★★ (88) than **21** (90), mostly old-oak-matured fruit of 49 year old Durbanville parcel. Ample fresh yellow peach & preserved quince, smooth nutty overlay. Sweeter, bigger than sibling, styled for broader appeal yet balanced, succulent.

★★★★ **Eye Of The Tiger Chenin Blanc** (NEW) Subtle poached pear, waxy lanolin & almond in **21** (87), tighter, more classically styled than sibling. Textured & pervaded with zesty acid, fruit unobscured by 7 months in concrete 'egg'. Still introverted, deserves time to unfurl. WO Cape Town.

Not tasted: **No. 42 Cape Blend**, **The Swansong**. In abeyance: **Silke**. — MW

Location: Durbanville ▪ WO: Western Cape/Cape Town ▪ Est/1stB 2016 ▪ Closed to public ▪ Owner(s) Etienne Louw & Brenden Schwartz ▪ Winemaker(s) Etienne Louw (2015) ▪ 65,000 btls own label 80% red 20% white ▪ etienne@vinoneers.com ▪ www.orpheusandtheraven.com ▪ **T +27 (0)21-109-0030**

☐ **The Vinoteque** *see* Heineken Beverages
☐ **The Wallace Brothers** *see* Off The Record Wines
☐ **The Wedge** *see* Babylon's Peak Private Cellar
☐ **The Wild Bouquet** *see* The Grape Grinder
☐ **The Wine Bank** *see* Heineken Beverages

The Winery of Good Hope

The team at Radford Dale adhere to the same style and philosophy when crafting these everyday braai or restaurant by-the-glass wines as the senior brand's premium offerings, to ensure quality while using less expensive packaging options and older barrels to maintain affordable prices.

★★★★ **Full Berry Fermentation Pinotage** Nouveau-style carbonic maceration for **22** ★★★☆ (84), result is expected perfumed, sweet & juicy black cherry & mulberries; finishing bite of tannin reminds of varietal origin. Touch lighter-feeling than **21** (86), both best in youth & lightly chilled.

★★★★ **Mountainside Syrah** ✓ Abundant energy & peppery spice in **22** (86), softer red fruit fills supple texture, lingering pleasantly. Freshness the focus from start to finishing kick of grape tannin, unhindered by depth from 50% oak. WO Stellenbosch unless noted.

Oceanside Cabernet Sauvignon-Merlot ★★★☆ Bright plummy fruit, crunchy tannins & juicy flesh, partly oaked to round but not dim tasty flavours on **21** (85). Coastal WO. Not tasted: **Unoaked Chardonnay, Bush Vine Chenin Blanc**. Occasional release: **Granite Ridge Reserve**. — AL

The Wolftrap

It's 20 years since the first Wolftrap appeared on shelves, its enigmatic backstory - involving the discovery of a namesake snare on the Franschhoek home-farm of brand owner Boekenhoutskloof, despite there never having been wolves in the Cape - playing into the amazement over how so much flavour gets packed into a bottle at what remains a seriously modest price (answer: sophisticated winegrowing and lots of TLC).

Red ✓ ★★★☆ Mostly syrah with mourvèdre & viognier (11/1), latter 2 bring meaty tone, heft & floral lift to abundant red fruit & black pepper in **22** (85). People's favourite: 200,000 cases of 750-ml bottles made; 1.5L too. WO W Cape for these. **White** ✓ ★★★☆ Glides down smoothly after sharing floral, peach & green apple aromas & flavours in **22** (85). Small oaked portion adds richness & weight to viognier & grenache blanc (48/6), chenin lends sparky acidity. These certified vegan. Not tasted: **Rosé**. — CvZ

☐ **The Wrapper Series** *see* Cape Collective
☐ **The Yacht Club** *see* Cape Wine Company
☐ **The Yellowwood Organic** *see* Spier
☐ **The Zahir** *see* Lateganskop Winery

Thiart Wines

Long-standing winemaker for the Bottega family's Idiom and Whalehaven brands, Reino Thiart works after-hours in the latter's Hermanus cellar using traditional methods to celebrate three generations of Marié in his family via Rhône-inspired boutique wines that 'reflect their variety yet are truly South African'.

★★★★ **The Pope's New Crib** ✓ Playful name for grenache noir, referencing French heartland of Châteauneuf-du-Pape. **22** (88) fleshier than last, more sour cherry & raspberry substance yet still light-feeling at reined-in 12.6% alc. Fine, dry tannins firm up structure.

★★★★☆ **Marié** Roussanne & marsanne ex Voor Paardeberg & Stellenbosch demonstrate their compatibility in **20** (91), enlivened with splash floral viognier. Well integrated after 10 months in old oak.— ML

Location: Hermanus ▪ WO: Upper Hemel-en-Aarde Valley/Western Cape ▪ Est/1stB 2016 ▪ Closed to public ▪ Owner(s) Thiart family ▪ Winemaker(s) Reino Thiart (Jan 2016) ▪ 600cs own label 50% red 50% white ▪ wines@thiartwines.co.za ▪ www.thiartwines.co.za ▪ **T +27 (0)83-485-6431**

☐ **Thierry & Guy** *see* Fat Bastard
☐ **Thirst** *see* Radford Dale

Thistle & Weed

Winemaker Stephanie Wiid and viticulturist Etienne Terblanche have been collaborating for close to 10 years, and while their growing number of fans will have their favourite/s in the stellar line-up named for well-known vineyard pests, they continue to see themselves as chenin blanc specialists. They even describe their wine-style as 'chenin' (if pressed for an alternative description, they go with 'honest, simple winemaking'). Though they've changed cellar a few times, and are doing so again at press time, they're pleased that 'vineyard expression is evident, and a golden thread in the wines'. They're putting yet more effort into the vineyards and working with their growers to ensure a mutually beneficial and sustainable relationship.

★★★★☆ **Knapsekêrel** Sophisticated **22** ⑨② cab franc from 7 biodynamically farmed rows on Polkadraai Hills. Well-expressed varietal perfume of rose & crushed herb over soft plum, cherry & graphite. 30% bunch pressed, naturally fermented, 10 months in older barrels, as all unless noted.

★★★★☆ **Nastergal** ⓐ Now-bottled, **21** ⑨④ much more settled & delicious. Fresh, with spiced black plum, chocolate & hint fynbos, savoury finish. Name, Black Nightshade, reflected in inky hue from red-fleshed alicante bouschet, with 36% tempranillo & 5 others, 20 months in oak. WO W Cape.

★★★★☆ **Brandnetel** ⓐ First of trio of chenins, this from tiny 1980 trial rootstock block on Stellenbosch Mountain foothills. **22** ⑨④ good varietal expression of poached quince, baked apple & creamy curd. Impeccably structured for ageing. 100% bunch pressed.

★★★★☆ **Duwweltjie** ⓐ ⓦ Restrained, elegant & ageworthy **22** ⑨④ from 1961 Paarl vines, named for devil's thorn in vineyard. Bright, with citrus, candied pineapple & vanilla. Well-structured & harmonious to the last spice-laden drop.

★★★★☆ **Springdoring** ⓐ ⓦ Newly certified by Old Vine Project. Swartland granitic soil gives a unique minerality & energy to **22** ⑨③, tropical fruit tempered by dried herb savouriness & crisp acid. Complex & impressive, will reward cellaring.

★★★★☆ **Khakibos** ⓐ Iberian white varieties, traditional & more recent, plus chenin in always-superb multi-region blend. **22** ⑨④ seamless, sumptuous, array of tropical flavours alongside hay, earth & fynbos. Textured, endless farewell. Deserves time to fully reveal its charms. 100% bunch pressed, year aged.— WB

Location: Paarl ▪ Map: Stellenbosch ▪ Map grid reference: G6 ▪ WO: Stellenbosch/Western Cape/Paarl/Swartland ▪ Est 2015 ▪ 1stB 2016 ▪ Tasting by appt only ▪ Wines available online ▪ Wine club ▪ Owner(s) Etienne Terblanche & Stephanie Wiid ▪ Winemaker(s) Stephanie Wiid (Sep 2015) ▪ Viticulturist(s) Etienne Terblanche (Sep 2015) ▪ 1,500cs own label 30% red 70% white ▪ Klein Drakenstein Rd/Lustigan Rd, Paarl 7646 ▪ info@thistleandweed.co.za ▪ www.thistleandweed.co.za

Thokozani Wines

Founded almost 20 years ago as a transformation venture between David and Sue Sonnenberg of Diemersfontein and the staff on that Wellington estate, Thokozani has grown into a multifaceted business, with offices and visitor amenities on Diemersfontein and, since 2021, a 55% share of its trading arm. This proprietary wine brand, too, has prospered since debuting in 2005, and now tops a significant 25,000 cases.

★★★★ **Cabernet Franc** ⊘ Now bottled, **21** ⑧⑧ fulfils promise of last year's preview, more distinct cab franc perfume & herbaceous lift than also-tasted **22** ⑧⑥ barrel sample. Tannins also firmer, finer-grained from vintage & more time in oak. More vitality than riper, plumper sibling, though already balanced.

★★★★ **Shiraz-Mourvèdre-Viognier** ⊘ Opulent mouthful of dark fruit, clove & mocha in **22** ⑧⑦ with mostly American oaking. Similar blend of shiraz, mourvèdre & viognier (82/17/1) to last, similarly svelte & accessible, with some ageing potential. **21** untasted.— MW

Location/map/WO: Wellington ▪ Map grid reference: B4 ▪ Est/1stB 2005 ▪ Tasting & sales daily 10-5 ▪ Closed Dec 25 ▪ Cellar tours by appt ▪ HOPE restaurant ▪ Tour groups ▪ Conferences ▪ Walks/hikes ▪ 4-star Thokozani Cottages ▪ Owner(s) Diemersfontein employees & Diemersfontein Wines ▪ Winemaker(s) Francois Roode (Sep 2003), with Lauren Hulsman (Nov 2011) ▪ Viticulturist(s) Francois Roode (Jul 2021) ▪ 180ha/45ha (cabs s/f, grenache, malbec, mourv, p verdot, ptage, roobernet, shiraz, chenin, viog) ▪ 25,000cs 100% red ▪ WIETA ▪ PO Box 41 Wellington 7654 ▪ denisestubbs@thokozani.co.za ▪ www.thokozani.co.za ▪ **T +27 (0)21-864-5050**

Thorne & Daughters Wines

'No major changes' at this top-rank boutique winery founded just over a decade ago by John Seccombe and wife Tasha, who chose 'Thorne' for the branding because it's John's middle name, linked to the family for some four centuries, and the theme of childhood play for the names of the wines, suggestive of the sense of purity in their flavours and the lack of artifice in their making. This still happens in the Gabriëlskloof cellar near Bot River, using grapes from sites across the winelands and a 'simple, honest and gentle' approach, the goal being 'putting together old vineyard parcels with new grape varieties, and making wines with old-school simplicity and a modern edge, that tell a story of the Cape of Good Hope'.

Thorne & Daughters range

★★★★☆ **Cat's Cradle** ⊛ ⊛ Dried pear, sage & fennel notes mark quietly expressive **22** ⑨③ from Swartland heritage chenin. More reined in than **21** ⑨③, both have signature seaside freshness & dry grip in fine balance, lingering finish.

★★★★★ **Snakes & Ladders** ⊛ Compelling rendition of trendy blanc fumé ex Citrusdal Mountain, sauvignon's blackcurrant & basil notes evident but any green features subdued by natural ferment & old oak. **22** ⑨⑤ ample sweet fruit with salty malt richness well countered by firm acidity.

★★★★☆ **Tin Soldier** ⊛ Semillon gris from Swartland granite soils, 50% given week's skin contact to yield onion skin colour, fragrant black tea & dried flower notes in singular **22** ⑨③. Ginger biscuit richness leavens the subtle tannin grip, which works well with food in tandem with restrained 13% alc.

★★★★★ **Paper Kite** ⊛ ⊛ Wonderfully refined Swartland semillon, **22** ★★★★☆ ⑨④ parades hallmark substance & depth of fruit at moderate 13% alc, plus the smooth, ethereal flow that makes the wine so compelling. Savoury nuances piqued by toasted nori tang, lemon zest, nuts & spice with a salty persistence. Natural ferment & 9 months in oak, 15% new as in **21** ⑨⑥, now 500L Austrian barrels.

★★★★★ **Rocking Horse** ⊛ Outstanding example of new-wave Cape white blend, **22** ⑨⑤ fascinating medley of roussanne, semillon, chenin, chardonnay & clairette. Aromatic & multifaceted, like **21** ★★★★☆ ⑨④ & previous, with stonefruit depth & breadth, fine texture & an elegant, dry limy grip. Swartland, Stellenbosch & Franschhoek grapes, 9 months in seasoned oak.

Not tasted: **Wanderer's Heart**.

Copper Pot range

★★★★☆ **Pinot Noir** ⊘ Cherry aromas & raspberry flavours with medium grip, **22** ⑨⓪ continues the uptick in quality from **21** ⑨⓪ & **20** ★★★★ ⑧⑨). 60-80% wholebunch ferment with minimal extraction preserves elegance. Super value, now ex Overberg, Elgin & Stellenbosch.— DS

Location: Bot River ▪ WO: Swartland/Western Cape/Citrusdal Mountain ▪ Est 2012 ▪ 1stB 2013 ▪ Tastings by prior arrangement ▪ Owner(s) John & Tasha Seccombe ▪ Cellarmaster(s)/viticulturist(s) John Seccombe (Dec 2012) ▪ Winemaker(s) John Seccombe (Dec 2012), with Albert van Niekerk (consultant) ▪ 70t/4,000cs own label 30% red 70% white ▪ 36 Main Rd, Onrus 7201 ▪ john@thorneanddaughters.com ▪ www.thorneand-daughters.com ▪ **T +27 (0)76-036-7116**

Thor Vintners

It was tenacity that enabled the young Emile Gentis to finally add the elusive Thor to his superhero trading card collection, and, says the adult winemaker, the same quality applies to his quest for the perfect blend. Based in Durbanville, he works and sources in Swartland, and ranges more widely for small-batch wines that reflect another facet of his personality, the maverick who likes to 'play around and break the norm'.

Iconic range

★★★★ **The Phoenix** ⊛ From petite sirah/durif, rare variety. Inky coloured, full-ripe **22** ⑧⑧ layers of plush, dark-toned berries & plums, well spiced, including black pepper from 18 months oak. Curvaceous, tannins perceptible at the end, firm but ripe, an assured future. Ex Swartland, as Wind Song.

★★★★☆ **The Bishop** (NEW) Usually Bordeaux blend partner, petit verdot shown here in all its opulence; 15% alc, 28 months older barriques. Deep & dark-toned, hints of green scrub, body voluptuous, succulent, tannins supple. **20** ⑨⓪ bold & showy, but tasty. WO Franschhoek.

★★★★☆ **Wind Song** (NEW) ⊛ Cape Blend, 50% pinotage with durif, dash touriga, barrels & staves, half new, 18 months. **22** ⑨③ blueberries & salty liquorice, savoury spice, some scrub notes, then an inspired palate: luscious, smooth, fresh too, tannins firm but ripe. Well crafted, lots to offer. Good potential.

Badlands range

★★★★ **Shiraz** With 10% touriga, full-ripe **22** ⑧⑥ had year's stave oaking, shows smoky notes, brambly fruit, some scrub, classic shiraz attributes. Tannins suppler than **21** ★★★★ ⑧④, still youthful but already showing potential. WO Swartland.

★★★★ **Sauvignon Blanc** ⑭ Prominent, vivid perfume in **23** ⑧⑨, fresh pea, fennel & lemongrass, highlight of lime, textbook sauvignon; palate more grassy, with salty freshness. Tightly held & focused, as expected from maritime Koekenaap vines.

★★★★ **Sauvignon Blanc-Nouvelle-Colombard** ⑫ Creative blend of Swartland & Koekenaap grapes, unoaked. Flinty & vibrant **22** ⑧⑧ ample zesty tang of acid but toned body & structure to balance. Discontinued: **Chenin Blanc**.

Regional Selection

★★★★☆ **Megan-Mari** Bordeaux blend, 60/40 cab franc & petit verdot, wild fermented/2 years 30% new oak, which shows in **21** ⑨⑩ as cocoa & spice, plush berries willing participants in creating a smoothly rounded, classy wine. Layers of interest, lovely harmony & polish. **20** ⑨⑩, cab franc & merlot, still selling.

Lara ★★★★☆ Semillon, tank fermented with staves, lovely waxy top note, underlying melon, orange zest, whiff of sage, **22** ⑧④ becoming generally fruity on palate. For drinking young. WO Franschhoek for these.

Signature & Family range

★★★★ **Gentis Red** ⊘ Now bottled, **21** ⑧⑦ shiraz with cab franc, 2 others, showing better: plush berries, good tannin foundation from barrels & staves. Gentle smoky tone adding complexity & interest.

Gentis White ⑭ ★★★ Equal sauvignon & nouvelle, a rare SA cross. **23** ⑧② has fruit salad aromas, following through to the crisply fresh flavours. Tasty, not complex, for early consumption. — CR

Location: Durbanville ▪ WO: Coastal/Swartland/Franschhoek ▪ Est 2016 ▪ 1stB 2010 ▪ Private tastings for groups by arrangement only ▪ Office hours Mon–Thu 9-4 Fri 9-3 ▪ Closed all pub hols ▪ Cellarmaster(s) Emile Gentis ▪ Other export ranges: Gecko Ridge, Long Mountain, Origiin of Kamma-Kan Kamma ▪ PO Box 46140 Durbanville 7550 ▪ emile@thorvintners.com, jeanne@thorvintners.com, emile@stella.wine, jeanne@stella.wine ▪ www.thorvintners.com ▪ **T +27 (0)76-190-9196**

☐ **Three Peaks** *see* Mount Vernon Estate
☐ **Three Pines** *see* Stark-Condé Wines
☐ **Three Rivers** *see* Bon Courage Estate

Thunderchild

Now in its 3rd decade, this praiseworthy initiative of sympathetic local wineries aims to brighten 'dark and threatening clouds' for the 'thunderchildren' of Die Herberg Children's Home in Robertson. Grapes from on-site vines are vinified pro bono and sold from cellardoors and more widely, and profits used to meet the full range of educational needs, from tutelage through extracurricular activities to tertiary education.

★★★★ **Thunderchild** ⊘ Near-equal cab franc, cab & merlot in harmony on well-realised **21** ⑧⑥, first tasted since **17** ⑧⑧. Smoky black tea aroma adds plum & cherry on palate, laced with lemony acid. Year in old oak, unfiltered/fined.— ML, PS

Location/WO: Robertson ▪ Est 2003 ▪ 1stB 2008 ▪ Wines available from La Verne Wine Boutique & online shop, Platform 62 & online shop, Springfield Estate & online shop, Woolworths, Norman Good Fellows, Ultra Liquors ▪ Owner(s) Thunderchild Wingerd Trust ▪ Cellarmaster(s) Various Robertson winegrowers ▪ 5ha (cabs s/f, merlot) ▪ PO Box 770 Robertson 6705 ▪ info@thunderchild.co.za ▪ www.thunderchild.co.za ▪ **T +27 (0)23-626-3661**

Tierhoek

The Tierhoek home-farm, an elevated 800-m in the Piekenierskloof mountains, was purchased by Shelley Sandell and her late husband Tony in 2001. After completing his studies at Elsenburg, 2nd-generation family member, Harry, has now joined the team. New winemaker and farm manager Charl van Schalkwyk will continue the winery's philosophy of using sustainable practices to create exceptional wines, reflecting respect for the land and craftsmanship. In the hope that more people will be encouraged to visit this beautiful remote area, a campsite has been developed on the edge of the dam.

Tierhoek range

★★★★ **Grenache** Pleasant, if rather light, juicy red fruit on **22** ⑧⑥; lively & fresh but lack of concentration throws focus on grippy grape tannin. May resolve with year/2 but misses appeal of **21** ⑧⑧. Older oak, 8 months, as all the reds.

★★★★☆ **Heritage Vineyard Grenache** ⊘ ⊛ Impressive example from 1977 single parcel. **22** ⑨③ enjoys depth & concentration in rich spice & dark-berry fruit but no sense of heaviness. Carefully judged tannins, freshening acid offer sound support to delicious & ageworthy youngster.

★★★★ **Mourvèdre** Attractive solo version of this variety. **22** ⑧⑧ big but well-proportioned in its full body, rich texture & dense, tiny tannins. Fragrant blue berry flavours are lengthily sustained by freshness.

★★★★ **Syrah-Mourvèdre-Grenache** ⊘ **22** ⑧⑥ flavoursome blend, mourvèdre & grenache noir add blue berry & spice extras. Tweak of tannin provides freshness & form without hindering approachability.

★★★★ **Chenin Blanc** **22** ★★★★ ⑧⑤ full bodied with quiet apple, earth aromas; greater, if short impact on palate thanks to a little sweetness & arresting acidity. Finishes a bit hot. 20% oaked portion, 6 months. Less attractive than **21** ⑧⑨.

★★★★☆ **Heritage Vineyard Chenin Blanc** ⊘ ⊛ Piekenierskloof vines planted 1977. Touches honey, spice & fynbos lend usual distinction to light-footed **22** ⑨①. Touch less concentrated than **21** ⑨③ but racy acid ensures decent length. Soundly build for few years' ageing too. Natural ferment, 6 months oak.

★★★★ **Sauvignon Blanc** ⊘ Bold & ripe **22** ⑧⑥, sumptuous tropical fruit spiced with a little oak & cut by firm acid. Bone-dry. Lacks freshness, length of **21** ★★★★★ ⑨⓪. 10% portion older-oaked 6 months.

★★★★☆ **Méthode Cap Classique** ⓠ Steely & very dry **NV** ⑨⓪ from chardonnay. 5 years on lees give a little biscuity complexity to apple & citrus fruit. Invigorating pick-me-up bubbly.

★★★★☆ **Straw Wine** ⊛ Latest bottling of **NV** ⑨④ straw wine from chenin dazzling red gold; equally arresting honeyed peach succulence & sweetness yet uncloying thanks to sustained cutting acidity. Made in solera, third new wine each bottling. Older oak. 12.5% alc.

Rosé ★★★★ **22** ⑧⑤ an individual; mainly sauvignon, drops grenache noice for coppery tinge & viognier straw wine for peachy flavours, sweetness countered by racy acid. **Chardonnay** ★★★★ Ripe, juicy citrus flavours on **22** ⑧⑤; big but better balanced than last, with subtle older oak, 6 months, adding interest. Occasional release: **Chenin Blanc**. In abeyance: **Grenache Private Reserve**.

Sandveld range

Occasional release: **Sauvignon Blanc**. — AL

Location: Citrusdal ▪ Map: Olifants River ▪ Map grid reference: C6 ▪ WO: Piekenierskloof ▪ Est 2001 ▪ 1stB 2003 ▪ Tasting, sales & cellar tours on the farm by appt Mon-Sat 9-4 Sun 9-3 ▪ Tasting fee applicable ▪ Closed all pub hols ▪ BYO picnic ▪ Walks/hikes/dam ▪ Conservation area ▪ Guest houses & campsite ▪ Wine club ▪ Owner(s) Shelley Sandell ▪ Winemaker(s) Charl van Schalkwyk (Sep 2022), with Basie Snyers (Oct 2006) ▪ Viticulturist(s) Charl van Schalkwyk (Sep 2022), assisted by Harry Sandell ▪ 700ha/16ha (grenache, mourv, shiraz, chard, chenin, sauv) ▪ 85t/6,000cs own label 40% red 60% white ▪ IPW ▪ PO Box 53372 Kenilworth 7745 ▪ info@tierhoek.com ▪ www.tierhoek.com ▪ **T** +27 (0)21-674-3041 **(office)**, +27 (0)82-536-7132 **(Shelley)**, +27 (0)22-125-0249 **(farm)**, +27 (0)71-388-8944 **(Charl)**

☐ **Timbavati** *see* Rogge Cloof
☐ **Timepiece** *see* Jordan Wine Estate

Tim Hillock Wines

ⓠ

Renting space on Swartland's Kasteelberg, 'one-man show' Tim Hillock sources grapes locally and keeps the winemaking simple and traditional, with foot-treading, open concrete tanks and large old vats part of a regime intended to let the 'intrinsic properties of each vineyard, variety or soil shine through'.

★★★★☆ **Paradiso Syrah** Lighter styling with modest 12.9% alc for **22** ⑨⓪, zesty acid & fresh red plum fruit, whiffs smoked meat, iodine & dried herbs. Surprisingly firm tannins frame very satisfying wine. Limited magnums available, as Chenin.

★★★★☆ **La Cosmica Chenin Blanc** Pure pineapple & apple crispness with honey & wool layers on **22** ⑨②. Tang of wet stone & salt from lees contact, toffee hint from 10 months in old foudre. Well-balanced mouthful with good length.

Not tasted: **Pinot Noir**. — CM

Location: Riebeek West ▪ WO: Swartland ▪ Est 2021 ▪ 1stB 2022 ▪ Tasting by appt only ▪ Winemaker(s) Tim Hillock ▪ 9t/7,100btls own label 58% red 42% white ▪ Yellowwood Winery, Riebeeks River Rd, Riebeek West 7306 ▪ tim@timhillock.com ▪ www.timhillock.com

☐ **Tin Cups** *see* Wineways Marketing
☐ **Tin Mine** *see* Zevenwacht
☐ **Title Deed** *see* Croydon Vineyard Residential Estate

Tokara

GT Ferreira, owner with wife Anne-Marie, often quips that the best vineyard sites at Tokara are under olive trees. And it's true that their substantial and acclaimed venture on the crest of Stellenbosch's Helshoogte Pass is about more than just wine. There's a fine-dining restaurant with a panorama that includes the olive groves that produce oils and other crafted products, an exquisite 'estate' brandy, and art, a shared love of the Ferreiras. Patience has informed all developments here: it was years before the first eponymous wines appeared, though the market delighted in the forerunner brand, Zondernaam. Viticulturist since inception Aidan Morton knows every vine, while Stuart Botha displays no itchiness after seven years at the cellar's helm. GM Karl Lambour ensures local and international markets are supplied with long-gestated, meticulously made wines, which benefit from cool-grown fruit from their vineyards in Elgin.

Flagship range

★★★★☆ **Director's Reserve Red** Dab malbec joins petit verdot, merlot, cab franc as partners with 71% cab in **20** ⑨③. Elegant, seamless & velvet textured, with succulent hedgerow fruit layered with cocoa in inky density. Structured & cohesive after 22 months in barrique, portion new down to 44% from 54%.

★★★★★ **Director's Reserve White** Sauvignon (72%) leads semillon on rich & rewarding **20** ⑨④, comprising 'best of the best' vineyards & barrels (25% new, 9 months). Beautiful texture & harmony of creamy cashew from oak ferment & ageing, acid & vibrant citrus & stonefruit. Will age well.

Reserve Collection

★★★★☆ **Cabernet Sauvignon** Burnishes fine reputation for variety. **20** ⑨③ suave, supple, underlying power well-controlled, richness of dark berry fruit seamlessly framed by sympathetic oak, 49% new, 22 months. Like **18** ★★★★★ ⑨⑥, has dabs petit verdot & malbec. Long farewell shows spicy grip of cedar.

★★★★☆ **Syrah** Complex construction of **20** ⑨④ mimics that of also-tasted **19** ⑨④: 25% wholebunch, naturally ferment, extended cold maceration & time on lees. Oak, 66% new, 21 months, lends structure. Muscular yet refined, silky, with spicy dark-fruit succulence & layers of interest.

★★★★☆ **Chardonnay** Like **21** ★★★★★ ⑨⑤, **22** ⑨④ statuesque, structured & rich from lees stirring during ageing, plus oak, 28% new, lending oatmeal nuance. But also focused & energetic courtesy lime freshness from malo for only part of the wine. Harmonious & satisfying.

★★★★☆ **Sauvignon Blanc** ⊘ Vivid granadilla & grapefruit zip with flinty backing on **22** ⑨① from cool-grown Elgin grapes. Taut & lipsmacking, with dry textured mouthfeel. Bright & focused.

Discontinued: **Noble Late Harvest**.

Limited Release Collection

★★★★☆ **Pinotage** Slight brooding nuance to spicy plum- & raspberry-toned **21** ⑨⓪. Refined & succulent but with firm oak tannin squeeze from 22 months in 78% new barrique. Sleeker **20** ⑨①, also tasted, had only 43% new oak for the same period, reflecting lighter vintage.

★★★★ **Chardonnay** ⑧④ Savoury **22** ⑧⑨ preview shows light floral & kumquat notes. Rounded & downy, with gentle nutty cream from 100% malo & 9 months in 28% new oak. Harmonious, with lingering succulent finish.

★★★★☆ **Méthode Cap Classique** Well-structured & graceful chardonnay bubbly from Elgin, **16** ⑨④ shows strings of pearly bubbles & taut, tangy lime & grapefruit zest before broader macadamia & orange notes unfurl & persist. Portion oaked, 84 months on lees. No **15**.

Premium range

★★★★☆ Cabernet Sauvignon ⊘ 🐝 Signature fruitcake & tobacco on **21** (90), supple, ripe & seductive with structure & gentle grip from 19 months in 25% new oak. Harmonious, with elegant finish. Exceptional value.

★★★★ Shiraz ⊘ Where **20 ★★★★★** (90) was swarthy & intense, **21** (89) is curvaceous & pillowy though it retains the juicy blue & black fruit charm along with structure & length. Also similar squeeze of dry tannin & mostly older oak, upped from 10 to 15 months.

★★★★ Chardonnay ⊘ Light & gentle **22** (86) has both orange tang & creamy breadth, a supple texture from barrel ferment/8 months on lees for a balanced & very enjoyable drop.

★★★★ Sauvignon Blanc White pepper & blackcurrant on rounded, flavoursome **23 ★★★★** (85), a balanced fresh acidity lends vigour & liveliness. Like **22** (86), has summer enjoyment written all over it.

Rosé ★★★★ Characterful, bright & fresh **23** (85) from shiraz packed with pomegranate & plum succulence, plus lees breadth, balanced by dry, defined finish.

Brandy range

★★★★★ XO Potstill Brandy 🐝 Glistening light-gold 10 year old potstill (95) in striking, elegant packaging to match the serious, velvety & complex contents. Sumptuous ripe orchard fruit & roast almond nuances, the lingering finish warmed by perfectly judged 40% alc. From chenin, grown, distilled & matured in Limousin casks on the estate. Contains components up to 16 years.— FM, WB

Location/map: Stellenbosch ▪ Map grid reference: G4 ▪ WO: Stellenbosch/Elgin ▪ 1stB 2001 ▪ Tasting & sales Mon-Sun 10-6 ▪ Closed Dec 25 & Jan 1 ▪ Tokara Restaurant: lunch & dinner ▪ Delicatessen: breakfast & lunch ▪ Facilities for children ▪ Gift shop ▪ Art exhibitions ▪ Owner(s) GT & Anne-Marie Ferreira ▪ GM Karl Lambour ▪ Winemaker(s) Stuart Botha (Sep 2017) ▪ Viticulturist(s) Aidan Morton (Nov 2000) ▪ Vineyard manager Gerald Fortuin ▪ 88ha (cabs s/f, malbec, merlot, mourv, p verdot, ptage, shiraz, chard, chenin, sauv, sem) ▪ 700t/100,000cs own label 40% red 59% white 1% rosé ▪ PO Box 12788 Die Boord Stellenbosch 7613 ▪ wine@tokara.com ▪ www.tokara.com ▪ **T +27 (0)21-808-5900**

Too Much Truth Wines ⑅

Vineyard owners in Stellenbosch's Ida's Valley, Michael Böll and Julia Medcalf, joined by good friend and Belgian importer of SA wine Sebastian Vannevel want to 'take the BS out of wine' and offer 'a great glass to enjoy without feeling intimidated'. A trial 2020 chardonnay 'blew them away' and encouraged the creation of a boutique brand and label, to be joined by a blend of the three black grapes on the property.

Location/map: Stellenbosch ▪ Map grid reference: G4 ▪ Est/1stB 2021 ▪ Tasting, sales & cellar tours by prior arrangement only ▪ Closed all pub hols ▪ Owner(s) Michael Böll & Julia Medcalf ▪ Winemaker(s) Sebastian Vannevel (Jan 2020) ▪ 5ha/3ha (cab, malbec, sangio, chard) ▪ 20t/600cs own label 40% red 60% white ▪ PO Box 1177 Somerset West 7129 ▪ seba@elvama.be ▪ www.toomuchtruth.co.za

☐ **Top Five** see Stellenview Premium Wines

Topiary Wine Estate 🍷🍴🏠📷🅰♿

On the lower slopes of Franschhoek's Wemmershoek mountains, Topiary has been owned by Burgundy vigneron Philippe Colin for ten years now, his philosophy of 'letting nature grow by itself in the fields', matched with laissez-faire in the cellar are unchanged. Associated with fabled Chassagne-Montrachet, any chardonnay debut from Philippe is a noteworthy event, and the new Sandstone, from a section of the home-farm vineyard where 'acid and minerality meet in a perfect balance' doesn't disappoint. Afro-fusion restaurant Hari Kitchen joins picnics, hikes, stay-overs and fresh-shucked oysters in the list of reasons to visit.

★★★★ Innocence Contrasts syrah's rich savoury features with 65% cabernet's brighter berry flavours & neat tannin trim. **20** (88) compatible & tasty marriage, where freshness introduces a note of elegance.

★★★★ Rosé ⊘ Coppery pink **22** (87) from syrah. Succulent, savoury, with spicy lift to dry finish, freshness adds welcome delicacy & length. Delicious before & with the meal.

★★★★☆ Chardonnay Sandstone ⑅ Elegant **21** (92) shows clarity & poise. Lees complexity partnered by lemon freshness & minerality forge harmonious whole. Subtle toasty note from ferment/year in barrel, same duration in tank. Modest 13% alc. Documented single-vineyard, as most of the wines.

Cabernet Sauvignon ★★★★ Softly spoken **20** ⑧⑤ has modest, gentle dark fruit, supple feel & well-rounded tannins. Dry with natural freshness; good now, for 2/3 years. French oak, 6 months paced to balance. Less complex than last-tasted **16 ★★★★** ⑧⑥. **Syrah** ⑨ **★★★★** Softish **20** ⑧⑤, lively red fruit, gentle squeeze tannin, savoury dry finish. Year older oak. Not tasted: **Chardonnay**. In abeyance: **Méthode Cap Classique**. — AL

Location/map/WO: Franschhoek ▪ Map grid reference: C4 ▪ Est 2005 ▪ 1stB 2006 ▪ Tasting & sales Mon-Sun 10-5; pub hols (seasonal) please call ahead ▪ Tasting fee R60/4 wines ▪ Cellar tour on booking ▪ Hari Kitchen restaurant Mon-Sun ▪ Oyster bar ▪ Picnic available on request ▪ Child friendly ▪ 2.8km fynbos hiking trail on the farm ▪ Accommodation: deluxe suite & 2 self-catering cottages with swimming pool & braai ▪ Owner(s)/cellarmaster(s)/winemaker(s) Philippe Colin (Aug 2014) ▪ Viticulturist(s) / farm manager Carlo Popolillo (Jun 2019) ▪ 20ha (cab, shiraz, chard) ▪ IPW ▪ Wemmershoek Rd (R301), Franschhoek 7690 ▪ sales@topiarywines.co.za ▪ www.topiarywines.co.za ▪ T +27 (0)21-867-0258

Torero Wine Co ⑨ ⑪

Previously listed in this guide under Rueda Family Wines, this personal project of Fernando Rueda is an impossible dream made reality partly with the guidance of Ian Naudé of Naudé Wines. 'Incredibly passionate' about wine for many years, Fernando works in rented cellar space in Stellenbosch, aiming to craft 'true and pure' expressions of carignan and, now, syrah, as he feels they are the varieties that have evolved to best deliver the 'subtle density, intensity and power' he seeks in his wines. He's tweaked the vinification to make the process of extraction even lighter and gentler, to allow for 'more complex and cerebral wines'.

★★★★☆ The Suit of Lights Carignan ⑧ Striking blood & iron minerality underpins focused, intense candied berry fruit in **22** ⑨③. Elegant & sleek, appealingly juicy yet a firm tannin backbone that signals serious intent. Wellington grapes, 50% wholebunch & foot-trodden; 10 months seasoned oak.

★★★★☆ Pasiphaë Syrah 🆕 ⑧ Referencing mother of mythological Cretan Minotaur, **22** ⑨③ from high altitude Polkadraai vines shows impressive fynbos scent, sappy black berry fruit & smooth, dry tannins. Refined & elegant, promising a fine future. 10 months older barrels. Both wines also in 1.5L. — GdB

Location/map: Stellenbosch ▪ WO: Western Cape ▪ Est/1stB 2021 ▪ Tasting & cellar tours by appt only; sales Mon-Fri 9-5, pub hols (seasonal) please call ahead ▪ Closed Easter Fri/Sun, Dec 25 & Jan 1 ▪ Meals/refreshments on request ▪ Owner(s) Fernando P Rueda ▪ Winemaker(s) Fernando P Rueda (Jan 2021) ▪ 3t/410cs own label 100% red ▪ Karibib Wine Craft, Polkadraai Rd, Stellenbosch 7600 ▪ torero@ruedawine.com ▪ www.ruedawine.com ▪ T +27 (0)79-307-6668

☐ **Touch** see Rijk's
☐ **Touch of Dutch** see WineWolf Foundation

Township Winery ⑨

This community project was launched in 2009 by Cape Town low-income housing developer, the late Kate Jambela, to encourage householders in economically challenged townships and tenants on winefarms to benefit from premium vineyards, individually or communally. Today it is headed by activist Madoda Mahlutshana and career project manager Christelle September. Recent results include vines being established in several Khayelitsha secondary schools, along with the addition of Agricultural Science to the curriculum. The Mailbox and Argument wines help improve educational opportunities for children of tenants.

★★★★ Philippi Cabernet Sauvignon ⑨ Cab's classic cassis & cigarbox aromas in **19** ⑧⑥, 11 months in seasoned barrels result in tannins that are tamed & smooth. A perfect steak companion.

★★★★ Philippi Cabernet Sauvignon-Merlot ⊘ Touch more piquancy, red berries & some herbaceousness in the dark fruit mix in **19** ⑧⑥, cab at 55%. Older oak helps soften the tannins, though still firmly structured for the table.

★★★★ The Argument Corner Field Blend 🆕 Row selections of shiraz, cab & merlot (40/30/30) from 3 adjacent blocks in Wellington. **21** ⑧⑧. Rich, savoury, with red & dark berries, leather nuance, svelte fruit & oak tannins from 33% new barrels. Harmonious, despite name, ready to savour, many years in store.

★★★★ The Mailbox Block Chenin Blanc ⊛ Golden Delicious apple & some preserved quince, shot through with lemony acid in **22** ⑧⑧ from Stellenbosch. Oaking, 14 months, 33% new, provides rich, creamy toasted nut substrate. Flavoursome & balanced step up on **21 ★★★** ⑧② ex Philippi.

Philippi Sauvignon Blanc ★★★★ Familiar bright & tangy styling in **23** ⑧⑤, asparagus & passionfruit flavours with some leesy breadth. — MW

Location: Philippi ▪ Map: Cape Peninsula ▪ Map grid reference: D3 ▪ WO: Coastal/Stellenbosch/Cape Town/ Wellington ▪ Est 2009 ▪ 1stB 2010 ▪ Tasting by appt only ▪ Owner(s) The Township Winery cc ▪ Cellarmaster(s) Wayne Arendse ▪ 800cs own label 50% red 50% white ▪ 13 Arnold Str Observatory 7925 ▪ graham@ townshipwinery.com ▪ T +27 (0)83-625-2865

☐ **Tread Lightly by Backsberg Family Wines** see Backsberg Family Wines
☐ **Treasures of South Africa** see Simonsvlei International
☐ **Tree of Knowledge** see Wijnskool
☐ **Founders Series** see Bellingham

Trizanne Signature Wines

Gliding down the face of a curling wave looks easy when surfing winemaker Trizanne Barnard does it. The same holds true for the ease with which she juggles her eponymous range of wines from both cool, maritime-influenced Cape South Coast and Hemel-en-Aarde, and warmer Swartland, making bulk wine for export, and being on the cutting edge of the canned-wine game with her Dawn Patrol brand, listed separately. All this while based in Kommetjie on the Cape Peninsula. She revels in diversity - of site, expression and execution - with the ultimate aim of making elegant wines with drinkability, freshness and distinctiveness. Face-lifted labels memorably reflect the ocean's beauty, which provides her with endless inspiration.

Reserve range

★★★★☆ **Semillon-Sauvignon Blanc** ⓥ Signature cool Elim flint character, with grapefruit, fig & white pepper on **20** ⑨②. Taut & vivid, poised structure from ferment, part natural, in old barrels.

Seascape range

★★★★ **Hemel-en-Aarde Ridge Barbera** ⑭ Long & rewarding **22** ⑧⑨ shows grape's signature high acid but also cherry succulence. Countering that vibrancy is a darker, graphite & ink nuance. Good body & concentration, with structure from 10 months in seasoned oak.

★★★★☆ **Hemel-en-Aarde Ridge Pinot Noir** ⑭ ⊘ Elusive wisps of raspberry & cherry with bright, spicy life on **22** ⑨①. Leaner style but yielding & focused, precision & poise apparent. Elegant, with drying sheen of oak from 10 months ageing, just 10% new.

★★★★☆ **Elim Syrah** ⓐ Savoury-salty nuance shows cool-climate origins of **22** ⑨③. Deep, concentrated & layered, the spicy plum & blackberry in a chalky tannin grip. Despite this, feels fresh & weightless. Natural open-top ferment/10 months in 20% new oak. No **20**, **21**.

★★★★☆ **Benede-Duivenhoksrivier Chardonnay** ⓐ Slight name change from 'Onderduivenhoksrivier' for **22** ⑨④ but subtle citrus notes remain, along with underlying power that's offset by fresh acid brightness for a seamless, gently poised palate. Bunch pressed & fermented naturally in combo new & old oak, no malo, 10 months aged.

★★★★★ **Sondagskloof White** ⓐ Textural **22** ★★★★★ ⑨③ sauvignon blanc from Sunday's Glen showing vivacious lime & granadilla, tempered by creamy oak. Like **21** ⑨⑤, complex construction involving 50/50 skin & barrel ferment, basket pressing of bunches & berries, blended after 6 months & aged 10 more. Refined, elegant yet lively & long.

★★★★☆ **Groendruif Skin Fermented Semillon** ⑭ ⓐ Nettle typicity to **22** ⑨③ from Elim. Skin ferment lends texture & breadth to tangy, bright & flinty palate with chalky grip, as do 10 months in well-seasoned oak. Seriously styled, with good potential. Modest alc of 11%.

In abeyance: **Elim Semillon**. Discontinued: **Darling Barbera**, **Sondagskloof Syrah**.

TSW range

★★★★ **Cinsault** ⊘ Contained ripe blueberry, cherry & plum liveliness on **22** ⑧⑦ from old dryland bushvines. Textured & appealing, with gentle body & length matching fruitiness.

★★★★ **Syrah** ⊘ Herb-dusted berry compote on juicy, bright **22** ⑧⑦ from older dryland vines. Rounded & textured with dry tannin from year in seasoned oak. WO Swartland, as Cinsault.

★★★★ **Sauvignon Blanc** ⊘ Grapes from 20 year old vines deliver **22** ⑧⑥'s fig & granadilla flavour, with crisp acid & cool-climate dustiness typical of Cape South Coast.— FM

Location: Cape Town ▪ WO: Elim/Swartland/Hemel-en-Aarde Ridge/Lower Duivenhoks River/Sunday's Glen/ Cape South Coast ▪ Est 2008 ▪ 1stB 2009 ▪ Wine sales via website ▪ Owner(s)/winemaker(s) Trizanne Barnard ▪ 15,000cs own label 50% red 50% white + 8m L bulk wine export ▪ Other brands: Dawn Patrol ▪ 6 Minke Close, Klein Slangkop Estate, Kommetjie 7975 ▪ info@trizanne.co.za ▪ www.trizanne.co.za ▪ T +27 (0)82-383-6664

True Kindred Spirits

Cheekily named and marketed as a pick-me-up and antidote to life's challenges, Ja Nee Fok brandy is the sibling to the sophisticated XO marketed under the separately listed Sugarbird label, both distilled for brand owner True Kindred Spirits by KWV. A new brandy, named Stadsjapie, will soon join this range.

Ja Nee Fok Brandy ⓥ ★★★★ Versatile cocktail companion ⑧⑤, with its spread of fruit & savoury tones, pleasing fire. Blended brandy, with 5-year potstill component, from chenin & colombard, 43% alc. — WB

Truter Family Wines

Marketing and sales for this boutique venture are now in the hands of Pretoria-based Rialien Brand, joining Wellington owners, winemakers and spouses Hugo and Celeste Truter in what happily remains a 'virtual wine company', without an own cellar or vineyards. Recent tweaks to the Cape Fern collection winemaking will aid the unchanged goal of 'delighting and satisfying casual wine drinkers as well as connoisseurs'.

Agaat range

★★★★ **John David** ⓥ Cape Blend, pinotage & cab, 3 others, **21** ⑧⑧ smooth plums & berries, long savoury end, fragrant spice & dried herbs from 18 months oak. Drinks well now, will reward some ageing.
★★★★ **Christina** Bright, aromatic unoaked **23** ⑧⑥ shows good balance & depth of ripe orchard fruit & citrus, lifted floral farewell. Sauvignon & chenin (60/25), dabs nouvelle & viognier.

Cape Fern range

★★★★ **Shiraz** ⓥ Habitual over-deliverer, **21** ⑧⑦ no exception. Lets ripe berry & plum fruit shine, adds a creamy chocolate touch. Only 15% oaked (8 months) for extra complexity & suppleness.
Sauvignon Blanc ★★★ Lively lemon & lime on firm, dry **23** ⑧②, zesty, with a pleasing grapefruit bite.

Taste range

Shiraz-Cabernet Sauvignon ☺ ★★★ Equal blend is balanced & cheerful, **21** ⑧② creamy plums & spice with hint of vanilla courtesy 15% stave seasoning.

Rosé ⓥ ★★★ Very gluggable **23** ⑧②, salmon pink easy-drinker from pinotage, light, with perfumed red berry fruit, tangy dry finish. **Chenin Blanc** ★★★ Easy sipper **23** ⑧② packed with tropical fruit & preserved lemon, bright & fresh for picnics. **Sauvignon Blanc** ★★★ Fruit salad & grass flavours on crisp & breezy **23** ⑧②. Chill well & drink easily. — WB

Location: Wellington ▪ WO: Western Cape ▪ Est 2008 ▪ 1stB 2010 ▪ Closed to public ▪ Owner(s)/winemaker(s) Hugo & Celeste Truter ▪ 5,000cs own label 50% red 50% white ▪ hugo@truterfamilywines.co.za ▪ www. truterfamilywines.co.za ▪ T +27 (0)83-639-6288

TTT Cellar Calitzdorp   ⓥ ⓐ ⓑ

Having bought the Things Take Time boutique cellar and Portuguese-origin vines in Calitzdorp with wife Cheryl, and taken up artisan winecrafting as a retirement venture, Graham Anley seems to have having the time of his life, launching a slew of new tiny batches made with sustainable, where possible organic methods, and introducing tiers. There's more to come: a Cape Vintage for the flagship Cellar Reserve Series.

Cellar Reserve Series

★★★★ **Time In A Bottle Field Blend** ⓃⒺⓌ Rounded, ripe **22** ⑧⑥ preview hints at Portuguese-origin components in its plum & blueberry spiciness. Gentle tannin from 18 months in old oak, good persistence & body. From own touriga, tinta & souzão; most other wines partly or wholly from neighbours.

Signature range

Time Keeper ★★★★ Ruby cab & shiraz (36/24) lead on previewed **23** ⑧⑤, dab pinotage & 2 others. Previous was unwooded, this 14 months in old oak. Spicy, chunky black fruit, cocoa & herbs, pleasant & long. **Time Traveller** ⓃⒺⓌ ★★★ Pear, melon & lees mingle on succulent palate of 7-grape blend led by chenin & colombard. Ex-tank **23** ⑧② unfussy & easy.

Portuguese range

Tinta Barocca (NEW) ★★★☆ Lively, perfumed blueberry on soft-textured **22** (84). 20% wholeberry ferment & manual basket pressing part of its making, along with time in seasoned oak. **Touriga Nacional** (NEW) ★★★ Port grape, like tinta sibling, carefully constructed. Light-bodied **22** (82) spiced plum & blue fruit notes, dusty cocoa finish. **A Tempo** (NEW) ★★★ Touriga & tinta given equal billing in **22** (82). Cherry, berry & plum spice as expected from the varieties, dry chalky grip from year in older oak. **Palomino** ★★☆ Heirloom variety giving subtle lemon & pear crispness on uncomplicated, trim (10% alc) **23** (79), with light lees farewell. **Verdelho** (NEW) ⊘ ★★★☆ Fruit salad vivacity on **23** (83) from seldom-seen grape. Light, tangy & crisp, with subtle lees breadth, reined-in 11% alc.

TTT Cellar range

Pinotage (NEW) ★★★☆ Ripe plum appeal to **22** (84). Lively, with good density & body. Gentle 18 months oak frames fruit & adds length. **Ruby Cabernet** (②) ★★★☆ Succulent & fresh **22** (83) saw no oak, so the red plum, sour cherry & herbaceous fruitcake flavours are unfettered & typical. **Shiraz** (NEW) ★★★☆ Wisp of smoky coffee on bold, juicy black-fruited **22** (84). Good grip & structure from 16 months in older oak. **Time & Again** (NEW) ★★★ Equal shiraz & pinotage join 20% ruby cab in **22** (82). Liquorice & herb mingle with fynbos on dry, clean frame from year in older oak. **Summer Time** (NEW) ★★★☆ Nouveau-style carbonic maceration of **23** (85) shiraz (78%) & 3 others results in authentic vivid purple & red fruit, perky plum brightness. Supple & light, gentle grip from older oak. **Pinotage Dry Rosé** ★★★ Pomegranate & cherry ease on **23** (82) pink. Fresh, with zippy acid balance & dry finish. Light 11% alc. **Chardonnay** ★★★ Sappy orange & lemon notes on straightforward **23** (82), ex tank (where it gestated) shows subtle lees nuance. **Chenin Blanc** ★★★ Quince & chamomile on lightly succulent **23** (81) pre-release sample. **Colombard** ★★★ Guava, pear & lemon on **23** (82). Tasted before bottling it's fresh, light & for everyday enjoyment. **Dry Muscat d'Alexandrie** ★★★ Uncommon unfortified version of traditional variety. **23** (82) shows signature jasmine florality on dry palate with lees edge. Would benefit from crisper acid. **Nick Of Time** ★★★ Chenin, colombard & palomino trio delivers pear & melon on airy, soft palate, makes no demands in **23** (80).

Fortified range

Hanepoot ★★★★ Honeysuckle & barley sugar on muscat d'Alexandrie jerepiko. **23** (85) deftly fortified to 16% alc with unaged spirit, settled 14 weeks for light-feeling, clean-finishing drop in 375 ml. **Touriga Red Dessert Wine** ★★★★ Spice & lavender edge to plum fruit with notable spirit nibble on **23** (83), improves on last but remains sweeter, lighter (16.5% alc) & unoaked version of port. 375 ml. **Cape Ruby** ⊘ ★★★ Maintains equal tinta, touriga & ruby cab formula in **23** (81)'port'. Clean raisin, plum & spice typicity but lighter styled at 76 g/L sugar & 17.5% alc. **Cape Pink** ★★★ Now same varieties as Ruby sibling, ruby cab having been added. **23** (81) caramelly cassis & plum sweetness, same light fire as other 'ports' despite highest alc (18.5%). 375 ml. **Time To Dance** ★★★★ Exotic autumn leaves & dry cumin spice on **22** (85) unusual palomino 'port'. Waffle cone, caramel & marmalade flavours well integrated with spirit. Good body & length from 6 months in old oak. 375 ml. Not tasted: **Cape Vintage**. — FM

Location/WO: Calitzdorp ▪ Map: Klein Karoo & Garden Route ▪ Map grid reference: B5 ▪ 1stB 2003 ▪ Tasting, sales & tours Mon-Fri 9-5 Sat 10-5 Sun 10-2; pub hols (seasonal) please call ahead ▪ Closed Good Fri & Dec 25/26 ▪ Facilities for children ▪ Owner(s) Graham & Cheryl Anley ▪ Winemaker(s) Graham Anley ▪ 41 Voortrekker Rd, Calitzdorp 6660 ▪ graham@tttcellars.co.za, admin@tttcellars.co.za ▪ www.tttcellars.co.za ▪ **T** +27 (0)82-491-0529

☐ **Tucana** see Zidela Wines

Tulbagh Mountain Vineyards ⓠ ⓒ

The private partnership of local businessmen that recently took the reins is also taking Tulbagh Mountain Vineyards to back its roots, reinstating its original name to better reflect the position of the cellar and vineyards on an extensive (±180-ha) stretch of Witzenberg Mountain near Tulbagh town. Werner Wessels is back as farm-vineyard manager, working with the cellar team guided by Francois Haasbroek of Blackwater Wine. The focus is a single red, Rhône styled, with possible varietal releases of exceptional syrah. The site is marginal, and its aspect results in morning shade, combined with the steep slope, produce grapes that deliver a coiled energy, exactly what's reflected in the debut 2022 vintage.

★★★★☆ **Estate Red Wine** ⊘ Tightly structured **22** ⑨⓪, 72% syrah 20% wholebunch fermented, grenache noir & mourvèdre destemmed, year old 500L oak. Sweet red berry fruit gains dimension from earthy, meaty notes, supple tannins close out vibrant mouthful.— DS

Location/WO: Tulbagh ▪ Est 1989 ▪ 1stB 2009 ▪ Tasting by appt only (Mon-Fri) ▪ Conservation area ▪ Wine club ▪ Owner(s) Private partnership of local businessmen ▪ Winemaker(s) Francois Haasbroek (Jan 2022) ▪ Vineyard & farm manager Werner Wessels (Jan 2022) ▪ 179ha/28ha (grenache, mourv, shiraz) ▪ PO Box 12817 Die Boord 7613 ▪ francois@blackwaterwine.com ▪ **T +27 (0)82-329-8849**

Tulbagh Winery ⚲ ◎ ♿

At 118 years, grower-owned Tulbagh Winery is a Cape institution and enduring presence on the Tulbagh town fringe, mostly active in the bulk-wine arena but with a substantial proprietary line-up. A surprise this edition is the debut merlot, not quite as old at age 9, but fully mature and ready to entertain. Younger are the Flippenice bottlings, making wine accessible via fun names and on-trend, crowd-pleasing styling.

Groot Tulbagh range
Cabernet Sauvignon ★★★ Dark berry fruit with vanilla & savoury dried herb finish. **20** ⑧② for current enjoyment, as all ranges. **Merlot** 🆕 ★★★ Spicy mulberry & plum compote alongside leathery tones in soft, gentle **15** ⑧②. **Chenin Blanc** ⊘ ★★★ Vibrant tropical fruit on dry **23** ⑧②. Slim body (12.4% alc) & a zippy finish for poolside sipping. Not tasted: **Pinotage**, **Shiraz**.

CCM range
Red ⓥ ★★★ Unchallenging cab (60%), equal cab franc & merlot mix. **15** ⑧②'s flavours flow easily & smoothly, cassis, dark chocolate & spice cake ready to drink. Not tasted: **White**.

Flippenice range
Cabernet Sauvignon-Merlot ⓥ ★★★ Equal blend **NV** ⑦⑨ is fruity, slips down easily trailing coffee-tinged black plums. **Shiraz-Pinotage** ⓥ ★★★ Off-dry, like Cab-Merlot, **NV** ⑦⑨ 60/40 blend is bright & fruit forward, with cappuccino waft from oaking. **Lite** ⓥ ★★★ Name changed from 'Xtra Lite' since we tasted waist- & pocket-friendly **NV** ⑦⑦. Dry, with barely-there orchard fruit aromas & 9% alc. **Chenin Blanc-Sauvignon Blanc** ⓥ ★★★ Tropical-toned 50/50 mix **NV** ⑦⑧ is off-dry & light, like last, maintains balance through zippy acid. Good with light curries. **Sauvignon Blanc Brut** ⓥ ★★★ Apple & lemon flavours in frothy dry **NV** ⑦⑦ carbonated bubbly is the ticket to get the party started. **Lite Natural Sweet Rosé** ⓥ ★★ Was named 'XLight' when we tasted smooth & fresh **NV** ⑦⑥. Light pink, sweet red berries & easy-drinking 9% alc. **Njoy Sweet Red** ⓥ ★★★ Very sweet & bursting with ripe red berries, **NV** ⑦⑦ could do with touch more acid to balance. **Red Jeripiko** ⓥ ★★★ Copper-coloured fortified **NV** ⑧② is full-sweet yet shows good lift & vigour, raisin, spice & boiled sweet flavours end lipsmackingly fresh. 500 ml.

Paddagang range
Paddapoot Hanepoot ⓥ ★★★ Frog-themed label alone worth a buy, but intrinsics of fortified **NV** ⑧② are charming too, full of floral-grapey sweetness & sunny melon flavour. WO W Cape.
Discontinued: **Klein Tulbagh range**, **Tulbagh range**. — WB

Location/map: Tulbagh ▪ Map grid reference: F5 ▪ WO: Coastal/Western Cape ▪ Est 1906 ▪ 1stB 1910 ▪ Tasting & sales Mon-Fri 9-5 Sat/pub hols 9-1 ▪ Closed Good Fri, Dec 25/26 & Jan 1 ▪ Gifts ▪ Farm produce ▪ MTB in the area ▪ Online shop ▪ Owner(s) 86 members ▪ Production manager/senior winemaker Naude Bruwer (Jan 2010) ▪ 740ha (cab, merlot, ptage, shiraz, chenin, chard, sauv) ▪ 9,600t own label 65% red 30% white 5% rosé & 8m L bulk + 40,000cs for clients ▪ PO Box 85 Tulbagh 6820 ▪ info@tulbaghwine.co.za ▪ www.tulbaghwine.co.za ▪ **T +27 (0)23-230-1001**

Twee Jonge Gezellen ◎

A venerable name in local wine, 300-year-old Twee Jonge Gezellen in the north-west corner of Tulbagh latterly is company owned and also home of the reputed Krone sparklings (see listing). A five-year replanting of 50 ha on the property has seen the addition of several varieties, including seldom-seen piquepoul blanc, to the pinot noir and chardonnay needed for the bubblies. Till the young vines produce sufficient quality, most grapes for the stillwines are brought in and crafted in South Africa's first underground cellar.

★★★★☆ **Red** 🐾 Grenache noir joined by syrah (90/10) in **21** ⑨③, both from Piekenierskloof. Natural ferment in open cement tanks, 30% whole bunches, ensures aromatic fruit purity & delicate yet supple structure. The whole 18 months in small & larger old oak. Understated & effortless, with lingering earthy, liquorice & cranberry flavours.

★★★★☆ **White** Finely crafted, **22** ⑨① blend of 72% chenin, mostly from Swartland, some from home-farm, as for rare-in-SA piquepoul component, & grenache blanc from Piekenierskloof. Natural ferment, small-oak for chenin, 2,500L foudre for the othersg. Delicately perfumed, almond, earth, green herb nuances with creamy texture & modest 12.34% alc.— MW

Location: Tulbagh ▪ WO: Piekenierskloof/Western Cape ▪ Est 1710 = 1stB 1937 ▪ Cellar tours Mon-Sat ▪ Closed all pub hols ▪ Annual festival: Christmas in Winter (Jun) ▪ Art gallery ▪ Owner(s) TJG Estate (Pty) Ltd ▪ Winemaker(s) Rudiger Gretschel & Stephan de Beer ▪ Viticulturist(s) Rosa Kruger ▪ PO Box 16 Tulbagh 6820 ▪ info@tjg.co.za ▪ www.tweejongegezellen.co.za ▪ **T +27 (0)23-230-0680**

Twelve Apostles Winery ⓠ

Civil engineer Chris Lourens and winemaker son Charles have run their after-hours, natural-as-possible passion project for 15 years now, revelling in the fact that the constraints imposed by the smallness of the venture in terms of techniques and options, also provide 'the opportunities for making unique wines'.

★★★★ **Merlot** ⓃⒺⓦ ⊘ Well-crafted, silky **21** ⑧⑥, abundance of plums, raspberries, spices & gentle vanilla from 15 months in older barrels. Approachable, should give drinking pleasure for good few years.

★★★★ **Shiraz** ⓥ Harmonious & delicious **20** ⑧⑦ is abundantly fruited with ripe plum & hedgerow berries, reined in by savoury meat spice & dried herbs. Supple, with supportive tannin structure & oaking.

★★★★ **Peter** ⓃⒺⓦ Chocolate, plum & spice cake on succulent, smooth Bordeaux blend. **21** ⑧⑧ rounded, with gentle tannins courtesy of 15 months in 25% new barrels. 50% cab, equal cab franc & merlot.

Not tasted: **Sauvignon Blanc**. In abeyance: **Cabernet Sauvignon, Grenache, Malbec, Mourvèdre, Pinot Noir**. Discontinued: **James, Thomas**. — WB

Location: Cape Town ▪ WO: Stellenbosch ▪ Est/1stB 2009 ▪ Tasting by appt only ▪ Owner(s)/winemaker(s) Chris & Charles Lourens ▪ 3-4t/±500cs own label 60% red 40% white ▪ Brands for clients: Kanah Winery ▪ SAWIS ▪ PO Box 16007 Panorama 7506 ▪ info@twelveapostleswinery.co.za ▪ www.twelveapostleswinery.co.za ▪ **T +27 (0)82-375-2884**

☐ **21 Gables** *see* Spier

☐ **22 Families** *see* Riebeek Valley Wine Co

Twin Wine Collective

A group of wine experts under the banner Twin Wine Collective edition before last launched a shiraz made for Karen Zoid, SA's queen of rock for over two decades, by De Kleine Wijn Koöp. We look forward to taste the new release of 'She Roars' and any other 'excellent wines involving different areas, cellars and backgrounds'.

Location: Wellington ▪ Est 2019 ▪ 1stB 2020 ▪ Closed to public ▪ Sales online ▪ Owner(s) Strive Capital Holdings (Pty) Ltd (shareholder Anelma le Roux) ▪ Cellarmaster(s)/winemaker(s) Wynand Grobler (Apr 2020, consultant) ▪ Bought in grapes ▪ Own label 100% red ▪ wine@strivecapital.co.za ▪ www.twin-wine-collective.co.za ▪ **T +27 (0)81-280-1698**

Two Oceans

Launched in the early 1990s, Heineken Beverages' global brand is styled for affordable early enjoyment, hence some wines also being available in convenient, easy-opening and recyclable bag-in-box.

Pinotage ⊘ ★★★ Ripe mulberry & banana in **22** ⑧⓪, cinnamon & toasty notes too from wood treatment. Juicy tannins, plumped by grain sugar yet finishes dry. WO W Cape, as all. **Shiraz** ⊘ ★★★ Spicy & rounded **22** ⑧② has earthy, sweet tobacco & brambleberry flavours. Smooth & accessible, ready to enjoy. **Cabernet Sauvignon-Merlot** ⊘ ★★★★ Ample cassis & spice in friendly **22** ⑧⑤. More generous & balanced than last, juicy tannins from well-meshed oak enhancement (staves, as all reds). Also in 3L bag-in-box. **Soft & Fruity Red** ★★★ Appealingly ripe berry flavours, plus gram sugar in **22** ⑦⑨ for smooth, uncomplicated quaffing. **Chardonnay** ⊘ ★★★ Pear, lime & brush of oak in succulent & balanced **23** ⑧① preview. Genial sipper, solo or with a meal. **Moscato** ★★ Perfumed, delicate liquid raisin & strawberry cordial sweetness in **23** ⑦② muscat de Frontignan. Light 8% alc & slight spritz. **Pinot Grigio** ⊘ ★★★ Bright, tangy passionfruit & herbaceous notes in more zesty & refreshing **23** ⑧①. **Fresh & Fruity White** ★★★

Equal chenin & colombard in **23** (79) deliver on fresh & fruity promise. Light & semi-dry but balanced for carefree enjoyment. Not tasted: **Chenin Blanc, Sauvignon Blanc**. Discontinued: **Shiraz Rosé**. — MW

- ☐ **221** *see* Alvi's Drift Private Cellar
- ☐ **Uitvlucht** *see* Montagu Wine & Spirits Co
- ☐ **Ukuzala** *see* Mountain River Wines
- ☐ **Ulumbaza** *see* Springfontein Wine Estate
- ☐ **Unbelievable** *see* Mount Vernon Estate

Under Oaks

A fun class in home-winemaking in the early 2000s evolved into a serious wine brand based on the Britz family farm, with historically mostly red wines from Bordeaux and Rhône varieties but now also a pinot noir that shares a name with consultant winemaker since inception, Bertus Fourie. As the brand name suggests, there is a lifestyle element too, and visitors will find actual oaks lending their shade to alfresco wine pairings, light meals and luxury guest accommodation on a scenic slope of Paarl Mountain.

Under Oaks range

★★★★ **Cabernet Sauvignon Reserve** (g) Cassis purity of **18** (89) improves on still-available **17** (87). Rounded spicy cedar from 16 months wooding well integrated with gentle ripe black fruit. Approachable & appealing. New oak in FlexCube, as all reds unless noted.

★★★★ **Merlot** (g) Savoury & supple **17** (86) is lighter than last but retains abundant fruit charm & appeal. Typical graphite & herb sheen to end.

★★★★ **Bertus Pinot Noir** (NEW) (✓) Unabashedly warm-climate **20** (88) ex single parcel has muscle & intensity, its opulently ripe berry fruit & 15% alc perked by acid & ripe leathery tannins. Refined oak spicing from year in new barrels.

★★★★ **Pinotage Reserve** (g) Lively raspberry & cinnamon vibrancy to **18** (86). Improves on firm **17** ★★★☆ (85) in harmony of oak, charming succulence.

★★★★ **Shiraz Reserve** (g) Brush of herbs & fynbos on inky **17** (87). Focused palate shows ripe black fruit, gentle body & soft finish. Good balance.

★★★★ **Gemini** (g) Squeeze of dry tannin on **18** (86) equal mix of cab & shiraz from 15 months oak still integrating with ripe, spicy soft plum & cherry fruit. Like previous, needs time.

★★★★ **Chenin Blanc** (✓) Cheerfully ripe & fruity **22** (86) offers uncomplicated drinking pleasure. Unoaked, fresh & vibrant, with appealing acid twist at finish.

Chardonnay (g) ★★★★ Unwooded **22** (85) is appealingly sleek & rounded, with convincing citrus zest & lime cordial fruit. Fine everyday fare.

Malbec (g) ★★★★ Full & meaty, with subtle spicing, black cherry & cocoa notes, chewy tannins, **21** (85) is first since **17** (83). **Petite Sirah** (g) ★★★★ Inky blue & blackberry of spicy **17** (84) not quite meshed with dry tannic grip from 15 months wooding. **Bla Bla Bla** ★★★ Proudly flippant petite sirah & malbec blend, **19** (82) has potent charred oak overtones to its juicy red berry fruit. **Sauvignon Blanc** ★★★★ Light & breezy **22** (85) delivers upfront juicy stonefruit & grapefruit, well-judged acid & restrained aromas. WO Coastal, as Pinotage Reserve, Shiraz Reserve, Chardonnay & Chenin Blanc.

Britz Brothers range

★★★★ **The Dark Secret** (g) Alluring, deep **19** (89) is rounded & rich, hedgerow fruits well-meshed with creamy oak (12 months). Good density & freshness, long, rewarding salty finish. Coastal WO.

The Bold Secret (g) ★★★★ Blueberry & plum appeal to **18** (84). Approachable & easy, with cocoa undertone & good platform of oak. From undisclosed (red) variety/ies, as sibling. — GdB

Location/map: Paarl • Map grid reference: E3 • WO: Paarl/Coastal • 1stB 2003 • Tasting & sales Tue–Sun 11–4; pub hols (seasonal) please call ahead • Fee R75pp standard tasting, various seasonal pairings • Cellar tours/ private tastings by appt only • Pizzeria (Sep–Apr) Tue–Sat 11.30–9 Sun 12–3.30; (May–Aug) Wed–Sat 11.30–8 Sun 12–3.30 • 4-star country house • Winemaker(s) Bertus Fourie (2002, consultant) • wine@underoaks.co.za • www.underoaks.co.za • **T +27 (0)21-869-8045**

☐ **Underworld** *see* Wildeberg Wines

☐ **Unorthodox** *see* Backsberg Family Wines
☐ **Upington** *see* Orange River Cellars

Upland Organic Estate   ♀ ◎

Edmund Oettlé was a veterinarian, but turned to winemaking and distilling, as well as caring for the vines on his Wellington estate, where he and wife Elsie have cultivated fruit organically since the 1990s. His portfolio of brandies and 'grappas' (not to mention the liqueurs not listed here) reveals his long interest in exploring the possibilities of spirits, but there's an equally characterful range of wines in support.

Estate range

★★★★ **Cape Ruby** ♀ ⊘ From cabernet, individual, less obviously fruity than many Ruby 'ports'. **16** ⑧⑧ 3 years in oak & 1 in bottle give seamless melding of fruit & spirit; firm, dry-seeming finish.

★★★★★ **Cape Tawny Port** ♀ ⊘ Ex cab yet classic; 5 years in barrel. Shimmering russet hues set the scene for exquisitely light nutty fruitcake- & tobacco-styled **14** ⑨⑥, sensual finish aided by smooth spirit.

Not Extinct Cabernet Sauvignon ♀ ⊘ ★★★☆ Balanced, modest & rather nice **17** ⑧③, herby, tomato notes part of savouriness from 3 years older oak, also giving drying tannins; ready now. **Intuition Pinot Noir** ♀ ⊘ ★★★☆ Bright, lively, dusty plum & cherry on pleasant **20** ⑧③, characterful & with unusually firm dry tannins, no doubt abetted by year in new oak. **Earth Song** ♀ ⊘ ★★★☆ Crown-capped **21** ⑧④ méthode ancestrale (single-ferment) bubbly from chenin. Hardly classic or complex, but delightfully light, a genuine pleasure. **Stucki Kaap Cape Ruby** ♀ ⊘ ★★★☆ From cab, fortified with estate's brandy, adding peachy citrus to **21** ⑧④'s stewed plum. Unusual but rather good, with clean finish.

Brandy range

★★★★☆ **Drakenwijn** ♀ ⊘ 15 year old brandy ⑨⓪ from chenin & crouchen. Fine floral & prune notes; on palate great intensity of fruit, warm spice & roasted nuts, creamy dark chocolate on long finish.

★★★★☆ **Pure Pot-still Brandy XO** ♀ ⊘ 10 year old ⑨① offering concentrated flavours of dried fig & peach, apricot kernel. Silky, rounded, hint of dark chocolate on finish. Ex chenin, crouchen & colombard.

★★★★☆ **Rakia** ♀ ⊘ Inspired by Balkan fruit brandy, this potstilled, unmatured chenin ⑨⓪ intended to show intense fruitiness - & it does. Velvet smooth even at 43% alc, lingering honey finish. 375 ml.

★★★★ **Undiluted Cask Strength Potstill Brandy** ♀ ⊘ SA's only cask-strength brandy ⑧⑨, 10 years oaked. Intense, perfumed, powerful yet smooth. 62% alc, small sips only! Chenin & crouchen. 375 ml.

Husk Spirit range

★★★★ **Grapé** ♀ ⊘ Fragrant dried herbs, wildflower notes on 15 year old ⑧⑧ from pinot noir & cabernet husks. Smooth, raisin & gentle nut notes, rounded & perfect for after a rich dinner. 375 ml.— TJ

Location/map/WO: Wellington ▪ Map grid reference: C4 ▪ Est 1990 ▪ 1stB 1996 ▪ Tasting, sales & tours by appt ▪ Closed Easter Fri-Mon & Dec 25 ▪ Organic olives, olive oil, dried fruit & nuts ▪ Craft workshop ▪ Distillery: brandy, grappa, rakia, limoncello, gin ▪ Owner(s) Edmund & Elsie Oettlé ▪ Cellarmaster(s) / brandy master(s) Edmund Oettlé ▪ Winemaker(s)/viticulturist(s) Edmund Oettlé ▪ 46ha/10ha (cab, pinot, chenin, cbard) ▪ 20t/1,200cs own label 70% red 30% white MCC & 2,000L brandy ▪ Ecocert organic ▪ PO Box 152 Wellington 7654 ▪ info@organicwine.co.za ▪ www.organicwine.co.za ▪ **T +27 (0)82-731-4774**

☐ **Usana Wines** *see* Winshaw Vineyards

Val de Vie & Polo Club Wines   ♀ ◎ ♿

Bottled in a renovated 180-year-old cellar, and homed in the L'Huguenot Venue & Vinoteque on luxury Paarl residential estate Val de Vie, these wines are tiered and priced to provide 'a perfect match for any palate'. A wine bar, restaurants and deli supplement the pre-booked tastings and Monday-Saturday sales.

Val de Vie range

★★★★ **Valley of Life** ♀ Bordeaux blend driven by cab & merlot (52/36), splashes malbec for back-bone & petit verdot for freshness. **17** ⑧⑥ ready now. Improves on last **14** ★★★★☆ ⑧⑤.

★★★★ **Ryk Neethling** ♀ Sleek Rhône blend of mostly grenache with shiraz & cinsaut. **18** ⑧⑥ lively red fruit, white pepper & farmyard accents; structure & 40% new oak for ageing a few years. No **17**.

★★★★ **Méthode Cap Classique Cuvée de Vie** ⊘ As versatile, but even fresher than last, **NV** ⑧⑦ brut-style sparkler balanced & ready to celebrate. Chardonnay with pinot noir & meunier showing crunchy red apple & lime, creamy biscuit shading from lees-aged base wine & bottle ageing.

Perfect Host ⑧ ★★★★ Handsomely packaged chenin. **17** ⑧④ peach & apple notes, piquant green-apple acidity, roasted nuts from 10 months oaking, subtle breadth & generosity from 20% new wood.

Polo Club range

Chardonnay-Pinot Noir ⊘ ⊕ ★★★★ Rosé **23** ⑧③ a 70/30 mix, touch lighter but as bright & poised as last. Soupçon sugar highlights red berry flavours, some savouriness too, lees contact adds creamy breadth.

Merlot ★★★ Dark berry, chocolate & smoky nutmeg flavours in **22** ⑧①). Dry, dusty tannins from oak (staves & barrels) still unknit, need hearty meal to resolve. **Sauvignon Blanc** ⊘ ★★★★ Zesty acid & bright fruit in **23** ⑧③, lees-enriched ruby grapefruit & tangy gooseberry make it a refreshing summer quaffer. — MW

Location: Paarl ▪ Map: Franschhoek ▪ Map grid reference: A7 ▪ WO: Western Cape ▪ Est 2003 ▪ 1stB 2004 ▪ Tasting by appt ▪ Sales Mon-Thu 10-5 Fri 10-7 Sat 11-2 ▪ Closed Sun & pub hols ▪ L'Huguenot Vineyards at Val de Vie ▪ Fleet Coffee Roastery ▪ Wijnbar ▪ Village Deli ▪ Owner(s) Val de Vie Wines (Pty) Ltd ▪ Jan van Riebeeck Dr, Paarl 7646 ▪ orders@lhuguenot.com ▪ www.valdevie.co.za ▪ **T +27 (0)21-876-8037**

Val du Charron ⓟ ⑪ ⌂ ◎ ⑧ ⑤

Where Wellington meets its dramatic mountain fringe lies the Bovlei ward, and in it, this beautiful wine and leisure venture, where the family owners are thankful that visitor numbers are rising, and looking forward to adding new menu items on the hospitality side while returning to vintage continuity after some Covid skips. Fifteen mostly red-wine varieties are rooted in rich soils on southerly, hence cooler, aspects, and seasoned vine and wine men Heinie Nel and Hugo Truter are tasked with expressing 'the true spirit of the place'.

Estate Reserve range

★★★★ **Cabernet Sauvignon** ⑧ Blackcurrant & mulberry tones of **19** ⑧⑦ overlaid with graphite & cedar. Rounded yet firm tannins from 9 months with new oak. Last tasted was **14** ★★★★ ⑧③. WO W Cape.

★★★★ **Merlot** ⑧ Deep, dark- & red-fruit core followed by layer of cocoa & spice from 8 months with new oak. **20** ⑧⑦ is juicy, with nimble tannins.

★★★★ **Syrah** ⑧ Mulberry & plum fruit interwoven with new leather & savoury spice. Fine tannins in **20** ⑧⑥ provide elegance & charm. Spiced fruit farewell.

★★★★ **Chardonnay** Preview of **23** ⑧⑥ has same zesty, juicy array of citrus as last **20** ⑧⑥, plus a cheeky pithy twist. Now unoaked, but there is some creamy breadth from 6 months on the lees.

★★★★ **Pinot Gris** Succulent texture interwoven with subtle kiwi & green melon in pre-bottled **23** ★★★★ ⑧⑤. Lighter bodied (11.5% alc), more demure than **20** ⑧⑥, also has hint of saltiness, in similar approachable style for upbeat summer quaffing.

Malbec ⑧ ★★★★ Alluring milk chocolate, perfumed red fruit & sweet spice in **20** ⑧⑤. Well-tamed tannin for a velvet texture. **Chenin Blanc** ★★★★ Now-bottled **22** ⑧⑤ & also-tasted tank sample of **23** ⑧⑤ both reflect the same inviting fresh pineapple, quince & pear flavours, some citrus too. Unoaked but plumped by 6 months on lees.

Theater of Wine range

★★★★ **Erasmus** ⊘ Potential return to form & change to a Bordeaux blend in **22** ⑧⑧ barrel sample of cab, merlot, malbec, petit verdot (48/30/15/7). Dense, rich & ripe black fruit in a bigger structure than range sibling. Svelte, spicy dry tannins from 14 months on well-meshed oak staves ensure delicious approachability in youth. Improves on last **20** ★★★★ ⑧⑤.

★★★★ **Black Countess** ⊘ Similar blend components (shiraz with pinotage, mourvèdre, 2 others) in unbottled **22** ⑧⑥, but riper & rounder, a full-bore, spiced-berry fruit bomb. Succulent & smooth, plus mocha veneer from oak staves in FlexCube (as reds in all ranges), 16 months. Seductively approachable.

Four White Legs ★★★★ Viognier leads, its lilting perfume providing the top note to the succulent textures of grenache blanc & chardonnay, roussanne adds the fresh lift in unoaked preview of **23** ⑧⑤.

Aphaea range

....

Red ☺ ★★★ Petit verdot & pinotage (83/17) in the mix in semi-dry **22** (82). Smoky berries & hint of mocha in supple, easy-drinking style. Will be popular among those who don't like drier red wine.

....

Silk Rosé ★★★ Aptly named semi-dry tank sample of **23** (81) from pinot grigio & 5% splash of pinotage is temptingly smooth, with sweetly spiced floral notes. **White** ★★★ Now bottled, **22** ★★★★ (85) from chardonnay, pinot gris & viognier more vibrant than both previous & also-tasted **23** (82) preview. A zesty ruby grapefruit thread lifts the floral-peachy flavours. The lighter (12% alc) pinot gris-led tank sample has more delicate herb & floral tone along with a pithy twist & plumpness from 4 months on lees. — MW

Location/map: Wellington ▪ Map grid reference: C3 ▪ WO: Wellington/Western Cape ▪ Est 2007 ▪ 1stB 2009 ▪ Tasting daily 10-4 ▪ Sales Mon-Fri 8-5 Sat/Sun 10-4; pub hols 8am-9pm daily (seasonal), please call ahead ▪ Cellar tours by appt ▪ The Grillroom; Pizza Vista ▪ Children play area ▪ Tour groups ▪ Conferences ▪ Spa ▪ 4 & 5 star guest house (stay@vdcwines.com) ▪ Wild Boar MTB & trail runs ▪ Wine club ▪ Owner(s) Val du Charron Wines (Pty) Ltd ▪ Winemaker(s) Hugo Truter (Sep 2020) ▪ Viticulturist(s) Heinie Nel (Apr 2010, consultant) ▪ 43ha/21ha (cab, ptage, shiraz, chard, chenin) ▪ ±300t ▪ IPW ▪ PO Box 890 Wellington 7654 ▪ ce@vdcwines. com ▪ www.vdcwines.com ▪ **T +27 (0)21-873-1256**

☐ **Vale** *see* Bonnievale Wines

Van Biljon Wines ⓠ

On their False-Bay-cooled Polkadraai Hills boutique farm, Tarentaal, just 4 ha of well-drained granite soil are planted with the five ('cinq' in French) classic Bordeaux black grapes, from which owners Anton and Julia van Biljon produce only one, appropriately named wine. 'Perfectionist' consultant Chris Keet is both viticulturist and winemaker, with Anton at his side in the cellar. As a team they can boast an enviable quality record, including in this guide, reflected in listings in 1, 2 and 3-star Michelin restaurants in Europe, and prestigious occasions like the finals of the Royal Windsor Cup polo tournament three years running.

★★★★★ **Cinq** (⊛) Exceptional, cellarworthy Bordeaux blend, cab-led (51%) in **19** ★★★★★ (94). Another classy showing, with finest, supplest tannins coalescing with gorgeous dark fruit & tailing to a gently gripping finish. Like **18** (95), 18 months in barrique, just 10% new.— ML

Location/map/WO: Stellenbosch ▪ Map grid reference: B6 ▪ Est 2004 ▪ 1stB 2013 ▪ Tasting, sales & cellar tours Mon-Sat by appt ▪ Closed all pub hols ▪ Owner(s) Anton & Julia van Biljon ▪ Winemaker(s) Christopher Keet (Oct 2008, consultant), with Anton van Biljon (Jan 2011) ▪ Viticulturist(s) Christopher Keet (Oct 2008, consultant) ▪ 5ha/4ha (cabs s/f, malbec, merlot, p verdot) ▪ 15t/500cs own label 100% red ▪ IPW ▪ PO Box 1292 Hermanus 7200 ▪ wine@vanbiljon.co.za ▪ www.vanbiljonwines.co.za ▪ **T +27 (0)21-882-8445**

Van Hunks Drinks

A rum-fuelled pipe-smoking competition between Jan van Hunks, an 18th-century retired pirate, and the Devil is said to have created the clouds that spill over Cape Town's Table Mountain when the south-easterly is up. The bubblies inspired by the tale are boldly packaged 'to stand out and look different on shelf', says Tom Gamborg, founder of brand owner Van Hunks Drinks, and styled to be 'not too dry and not too sweet'.

Cap Classique Brut Rosé (ⓠ) ★★★★ Pale pink dry sparkler from chardonnay (70%), dashes pinot noir, pinotage & meunier. Piquant & sweet red berries, hint dustiness on characterful **NV** (84). **Cap Classique Brut** (ⓠ) ★★★★ Chardonnay & pinot noir (70/30) **NV** (84) bubbly shows apple pie & honey of bottle age. Rich, with seam of freshness, satisfying dry finish. For current drinking, as Rosé. — CR, CvZ

Location/WO: Stellenbosch ▪ Est 2021 ▪ 1stB 2019 ▪ Owner(s) Skal Drinks t/a Van Hunks Drinks ▪ Winemaker(s) Matthew Krone ▪ info@vanhunksdrinks.com ▪ www.vanhunksdrinks.com

---

Van Loggerenberg Wines ⓠ

Paarl-based Lukas van Loggerenberg established his eponymous winery in 2016 and immediately made an impact with critics and consumers alike, and the eight years since have only burnished his reputation. Vintage vagaries, and their attendant trials and triumphs, are a reality he acknowledges and embraces, and he has no problem sharing his experiences. Harvest 2022, common to all the wines featured this edition, was especially difficult. Several heatwaves required severe bunch and grape sorting, reducing yield and leaving the usual concrete tank for the Lotter cinsaut undesirably less than full. This prompted an on-the-hoof switch to a smaller format, oak barrel, for the ferment and ageing, producing a stellar result. Likewise eschewing the standard concrete component for the Breton cab franc, 'giving it the driest, most Old World profile of all'. No matter what the conditions, Lukas' wines are elegant and pure, and have a lovely freshness.

Van Loggerenberg range

★★★★★ **Breton** ⊛ Local benchmark named & styled after cab franc of France's Loire, earlier picked to emphasise leafy, herbal tones. **22** ⑨④ also amplified by sweet, red-fruited succulence. Balanced for youthful enjoyment, yet freshness & fine grape tannins provide assured future. Grows in gravitas every vintage. Older oak, 10 months, as all the wooded wines unless noted.

★★★★☆ **Geronimo** ⊛ ⊛ Cinsaut ex Stellenbosch, **22** ⑨④ plusher than Lotter sibling, no less expressive in its Eastern spice, fleshy red-berry complexity. Sufficient harmony for current enjoyment & frisson of tannin for future. Good partner for well-flavoured dishes.

★★★★★ **Lotter** ⊛ Franschhoek old-vine cinsaut, **22** ★★★★★ ⑨⑤ full of joie de vivre. Exudes captivating peppery spice, red-berry perfume & flavours; bright, racy feel, zesty tannins provide mouthwatering fantail length. Oaked, & more complex than unwooded **21** ⑨⓪. Lovely now, more so with few years.

★★★★★ **Graft** ⊛ From Polkadraai Hills site acclaimed for syrah. **22** ⑨⑥ has characteristic punchy pepper spice & a silky, supple texture reflective of this exposed, cool vineyard. Fine tannins add energy & irresistible mouthwatering quality for now or few years. At 14.3% alc, biggest wine here. Always among SA's best syrahs, including **21** ★★★★★ ⑨④.

★★★★☆ **High Hopes** Smooth, savoury blend from Swartland. **22** ⑨② mostly syrah with drops grenache, cinsaut brightening the spicy, dark-berry complexity. Fine, integrated grip gives form to rich, supple flesh, enhances balance for current pleasure.

★★★★☆ **Kameraderie** ⊛ ⊛ From Swartland chenin planted 1976, **22** ⑨③ is concentrated, taut. Characteristic warm earth, red apple flavours still youthfully restrained; a little finishing grip adds freshness, structure & future potential. Deserving of several years' ageing.

★★★★☆ **Trust Your Gut** ⊛ ⊛ From chenin, Swartland's sunny generosity meets Polkadraai Hills' cool, steely tension in happy partnership. Oak adds textured breadth, extends spice & honey features on **22** ⑨③. Usual distinction, potential.

Break A Leg range

★★★★ **Merlot** Rich & juicy, the sumptuous dark berry, chocolate features enlivened by bright acid, tannin trim. Oak harmonises, adds extra dimension. Improving on **21** ★★★★ ⑧⑤, **22** ⑧⑥ is more than easy drinking, for few years too.

★★★★ **Blanc de Noir** From cinsaut, **22** ⑨⓪ spiced with 17% grenache, usual portion (45%) oaked. Plentiful spicy-savoury breadth & intensity, memorable length too. Refined & classy. Just 11.5% alc. Versatile as aperitif or at table. Previous was 100% cinsaut.

Unwooded Chardonnay ★★★☆ Easy to drink but creamy texture, limy-nutty richness & crisp dry finish provide satisfaction & interest on **22** ⑧⑤. — AL

Location/map: Paarl ▪ Map grid reference: D6 ▪ WO: Stellenbosch/Swartland/Franschhoek/Polkadraai Hills/ Western Cape ▪ Est/1stB 2016 ▪ Tasting by appt only ▪ Closed all pub hols ▪ Owner(s) Lukas & Roxanne van Loggerenberg ▪ Winemaker(s) Lukas van Loggerenberg (Jan 2016) ▪ 90t/10,000cs own label 45% red 30% white 25% rosé ▪ PO Box 94 Somerset Mall 7137 ▪ lukas@vanloggerenbergwines.co.za ▪ www.vanloggerenbergwines.co.za ▪ T +27 (0)82-093-8091

Van Loveren Family Vineyards

Christiena van Loveren, an ancestor of co-founder Jean Retief, lends her name to this powerhouse of SA wine, producing a remarkable 2-million cases annually, a number that justifies the claim to be 'Africa's leading family-owned private wine business'. The 3rd-generation cousins currently running the venture from its canna-fringed home-farm in Robertson - marketer Phillip, cellarmaster Bussell, and viticulturists Neil and Hennie - build on past success through strategic alliances like the one with Blaauwklippen, Stellenbosch's original wine farm, which enables the partners to expand vineyards, increase capacity and introduce new products. Joint ventures aren't limited to wine: a link-up with Loxtonia opens opportunities in the cider industry. Sustainability and ethical practice are central concerns, as evidenced by Fairtrade accreditation since 2011, and there was much pride when Van Loveren won the international Breaking the Bias award for achievements around gender equality at a recent Fairtrade event. See also Tangled Tree listing.

Christiena Trousseau range

★★★★ **Cabernet Sauvignon** ⓠ Youthful black cherries on **20** ⑧⑧ from single parcel (as most of these varietal wines). Blackcurrant trimmed in glossy tannins & wood spice from 15 months in new oak.

★★★★★ **Pinotage** ⓐ Iron fist in a velvet glove, **21** ⑨③ received regular heavy punch-downs during ferment, all-new oak during 18 months' ageing. While sumptuous, with black cherry, plum & allspice on robust structure, luxurious rather than blockbuckerish, with silky tannin structure & a fine future.

★★★★★ **Shiraz** ⓥ Treated to 18 months in oak, 30% new, 10% American, which **21** ⑨① wears lightly, adding cigarbox detail to smoked meat, olive & white flower notes, latter from viognier skins added to ferment. Attractive fine tannins. **20** untasted.

★★★★☆ **Chardonnay** ⓥ ⓐ Peach & poached pear with vanilla & clove fragrance, creamy salted caramel flavours, all courtesy 100% new-oak maturation, 5 months lees stirring. A stony acid balances the richness of **22** ⑨② , lends freshness for beneficial ageing.

★★★★ **Sauvignon Blanc** Night-picked & cold-fermented to retain aromatics, 30% taken to concrete 'egg' for texture, **22** ⑧⑨ inviting glassful. More tropical fruit than **21** ★★★★★ ⑨①'s citrus, as lively & lifted.

★★★★ **Méthode Cap Classique Brut Rosé** ⓥ Vibrant berries & cream on pale antique pink **NV** ⑧⑥ from pinot noir. Hint sweetness balanced by citrus-toned acid. Similar basewine treatment as sibling, fairly brief 14 months on lees helps retain fruitiness.

★★★★ **Méthode Cap Classique Brut** ⓥ Impressive depth from 8 months lees-ageing of basewine, 22 months in bottle pre-disgorgement. 80% chardonnay with pinot noir, **NV** ⑧⑧ abundant apple in a lemony mousse, with sweet biscuit crumb adding richness.

★★★★ **10 Year Old Brandy** ⓠ Small release of potstill ⑧⑦ from chenin, only ex cellardoor. Delicate bouquet of caramel & nuts, with fresher peach & apricot, plus chocolate note, on restrained palate.

Retief Reserve range

Cape Blend ★★★★ Deep mulberry & sweet black cherry core, some fennel on combo pinotage (51%) with near-equal cab & shiraz. **22** ⑧④ spent year in oak, 30% new, adding hints of roasted spice. **Cape White** ⓠ ★★★★ From best blocks of chenin, colombard & chardonnay, 80% in barrel, 10% new, 8-12 months. **21** ⑧③ generously fruity, guava toned, touch more chenin than last & suggestion of sweetness.

Van Loveren range

....

Blue Velvet Pinot Noir ⓥ ⓦ ★★★ These made for easy-drinking pleasure, with varying levels of sweetness. Open-fermented **22** ⑧② aged in large, old vats to preserve strawberry & subtle earthy scents & flavours. Outstanding value. **Neil's Pick Colombar** ⓥ ⓦ ★★★ Rich & weighty thanks to few grams sugar, punchy **23** ⑧② has variety's guava & tropical fruit, balanced with tangy acid. **Special Late Harvest Gewürztraminer Nectar** ⓦ ★★★★ Rosepetal, litchi & poached pear on **23** ⑧④ , gently sweet yet lithe & refreshing thanks to good acid-sugar balance & restrained 11.2% alc.

....

Blanc de Blanc ☺ ★★★ Bracingly dry & thirst-quenching **23** ⑧② uses colombard's tropical fruit & energetic acid, amplifies it with 20% nervy sauvignon. Also in 500 ml.

....

Cabernet Sauvignon ★★★ Cherry cola & balsamic touch on **22** ⑦⑨ . Smooth, seductive thanks to few grams sugar & 10 months in oak. **Merlot** ⓥ ★★★ Affable **22** ⑧① exudes plum, chocolate & cherry, all neatly held in featherweight oak tannins from 8 months in older barrel. **African Java Pinotage** ★★★ Consistent mocha styling. Off-dry **22** ⑦⑨ displays all the coffee, choc & cream you expect from clever mix French & American staves. **Cabernet Sauvignon-Merlot** ★★★ Now bottled, **21** ⑦⑨ shows herbal zing & classic cassis at the centre. 8 months in old oak. **River Red Shiraz-Pinotage** ⓥ ★★★ Unoaked 60/40 blend, also in 500ml & 1.5L. **23** ⑧⓪ friendly & juicy, with whiff of peppery spice. **Blanc de Noir Red Muscadel** ⓥ ★★★ Free-run juice (& addition of grape juice concentrate for sweetness) keeps semi-sweet **23** ⑦⑦ fruity & floral. Modest 11.7% alc for poolside sipping. **Daydream Chardonnay-Pinot Noir** ⓥ ★★★ Seashell-hued rosé **23** ⑧⓪ is a 80/20 blend, its touch more sugar than last merely accentuates its pretty strawberries. **Chardonnay** ★★★ Unwooded **23** ⑧② improves on previous with flinty lemon aromas, nicely weighted body (14% alc) & bone-dry finish. **Chenin No 5** ★★★ No wood, **23** ⑧⓪'s flesh & density come from ripe tropical fruit & yellow apples, smidgen sugar. **Sauvignon Blanc ★★★** Tinned asparagus & grassy-lemony herbs on **23** (80) have core of sweet fruit without the appetising pithiness of previous. **Chardonnay-Pinot Noir Brut Sparkling ★★★** Party-starting carbonated NV (80) showcases pretty Pink Lady apple. More off-dry than last, with balancing lemony acid. **Red Muscadel ★★★★** Pomegranate, rosepetal & black tea aromas, faintly savoury red fruit, decadent sweetness on **22** (85), spiced with warming fortification of 16% alc. Delicious now with potential for development.

Perlé du Jean range

Pinot Grigio ⊕ **★★★** Effervescent, fruity & just-dry **23** (82) from night-harvested grapes gets its pink flush & grapey fragrance from 10% red muscadel. 30% aged in concrete 'egg' for extra texture.

Four Cousins Director's Reserve (NEW)

Merlot ★★★ Part-American oak treatment for off-dry **21** (79) adds sweet chocolate & lashings of vanilla to glossy cherry & plum fruit, so it slips down easily.

Discontinued: **Rhino Run Organic range**. — ML, TJ

Location/map/WO: Robertson ▪ Map grid reference: B5 C4 ▪ Est 1937 ▪ 1stB 1980 ▪ Tasting & sales: Van Loveren wines (only at home-farm) Mon-Fri 8-5 Sat/pub hols 9.30-4 Sun 11-3; Four Cousins wines (only at @Four Cousins venue, Robertson) Mon-Fri 8-5.30 Sat/pub hols 8-4 Sun 11-3 ▪ Closed Easter Fri/Sun, Dec 25 & Jan 1 ▪ Cellar tours by appt ▪ Garden tours ▪ Food & wine tasting platters ▪ Fish Eagle hiking trail ▪ MTB trails ▪ Christina's @ Van Loveren bistro open daily ▪ Amenities @Four Cousins: food & wine pairings; craft Boet Beer tasting; whiskey pairings ▪ Tasting platters; gin, 10YO brandy, any other 4 wines - fee applicable ▪ @Four Cousins restaurant open daily ▪ Owner(s) Nico, Wynand, Phillip, Hennie, Bussell & Neil Retief ▪ Cellarmaster(s) Bussell Retief ▪ Winemaker(s) Chris Crafford, Danelle Conradie & Jacques Cilliers, with Jakob Pieterse ▪ Viticulturist(s) Neil & Hennie Retief ▪ 847ha (cab, malbec, merlot, mourv, muscadel r/w, ptage, pinot noir/gris, roobernet, ruby cab, shiraz, touriga nacional, chard, chenin, cbard, gewürz, irsai olivér, morio muscat, nouvelle, sauv, sem, viog) ▪ 17,100t/2m cs own label 40% red 30% white 30% rosé ▪ Brands for clients: Liquor City ▪ Fairtrade, HACCP, IPW, WIETA ▪ PO Box 19 Klaasvoogds 6707 ▪ info@vanloveren.co.za ▪ www.vanloveren.co.za ▪ **T +27 (0)23-615-1505**

Van Niekerk Vintners

Honouring family history and farming tradition in the southern Cape, Crystallum assistant winemaker Albert van Niekerk is now joined by wife Anmar in crafting this boutique range simply and with minimal interference in the Gabriëlskloof cellar near Bot River. They source locally for the red, inspired by a justly rebellious 17th-century ancestor, and Swartland for the white, sparked by world-famous 'heritage' blend Lieberstein.

★★★★ Rebellie Charming, lighter-styled but not lightweight grenache noir, **21 ★★★★★** (90)'s bone-dry palate frames piquant red berries & scrub, gentle tannin from 40% bunch ferment, destemmed berries on top. 100% wholebunch **20** (89) was firmer.

★★★★☆ Sonwater ⊛ Apt name ('Sun-Water') given summer-in-a-bottle styling of chenin & 10% clairette blend ex Swartland. **22** (94) bunch pressed, wild fermented (as Rebellie), 10 months older oak which give creaminess but also gravity, as does bone-dry finish. — DS

Location: Bot River ▪ WO: Bot River/Swartland ▪ Est/1stB 2019 ▪ Closed to public ▪ Winemaker(s) Albert & Anmar van Niekerk (Jan 2019) ▪ albert@vnvintners.com ▪ www.vnvintners.com ▪ **T +27 (0)73-259-0049**

Van Ryn Ⓨ ⓞ

Owned by Heineken Beverages, Van Ryn distillery lies on the banks of the Eerste River just outside Stellenbosch town, and its origin lies in the mid-19th century, when Jan van Ryn arrived at the Cape. Past and present are continuous here: among its variety of copper potstills, the distillery has one that's over 200 years old and still in use. And, most unusually, there's a cooperage on site, where ancient maturation barrels are painstakingly repaired. A remarkable number of prestigious international accolades and awards testify to the continuing excellence of Van Ryn traditions, with only very serious, aged brandies bearing the name. The carefully curated venue receives commensurate attention, and is an obligatory stop for any lover of firewater.

★★★★★ 20 Year Old Potstill Ⓨ Ⓐ A light mahogany gleam at the heart of this exceptional brandy (97). The most refined & subtle bouquet in the range & the darkest; the complex, smooth & silky palate with cigarbox & spice recalling the many years in oak, but still reverberating echoes of pure dried fruit.

★★★★★ **15 Year Old Potstill** ⓥ This ⑨⑥ a touch silkier & richer than the 12 year old, but maybe less ethereal, with a delicate spicy tobacco becoming more obvious. The fruit (citrus, dried peach & prune) underplayed as in all these, part of a savoury complexity that includes chocolate & spice.

★★★★★ **12 Year Old Potstill** ⓥ Always a particularly successful bottling ⑨⑦. A remarkable leap in complexity & subtlety from the 10 year old, announcing the sublimation of fruit into the refined but rich style of the house. Here the power plays especially well with delicacy. Fresh, balanced, complete.

★★★★☆ **10 Year Old Potstill** ⓥ An excellent introduction, ⑨⓪, to the combination of flavourful, lightly fiery power with finesse that characterises the whole range. This just less subtle by comparison & a little sweeter & fruitier, though clean & fine. All from chenin and colombard, widely sourced.— TJ

Location/map: Stellenbosch ▪ Map grid reference: D6 ▪ Est 1905 ▪ Tasting & sales Tue-Sun 10-5; closed Mondays unless it is a public holiday ▪ Tasting options: Brandy & Chocolate, Decadent Delight ▪ Closed Good Fri, Dec 25 & Jan 1 ▪ Cellar tours: Tue-Fri 11 & 3 Sat/pub hols 11 & 1 - booking essential ▪ Tour groups ▪ Gift shop ▪ Conference & boardroom facilities ▪ Exhibitions & special events ▪ Museum collection of historical brandies on display ▪ Online sales www.brandycollective.co.za ▪ Owner(s) Heineken Beverages ▪ Brandy master(s) Marlene Bester (Jul 2009) ▪ ISO 9001:2015 ▪ Van Ryn Rd Vlottenburg Stellenbosch 7604 ▪ info@ vanryns.co.za ▪ www.vanryns.co.za ▪ **T +27 (0)21-881-3875**

☐ **Vansha** *see* Ridgeback

Van Wyk Family Wines   ⓥ

Since 2016, winemaker Justin van Wyk has sourced grapes from unique parcels, some older than he, across the winelands for this small signature collection, crafted with gentle, natural techniques 'to allow the inner quality and character of the grapes to shine through'. He enjoys this project so much because it allows him to work with varieties and soils that he wouldn't be able to for Constantia Glen, where he is cellarmaster. The windmill and sheep motif on the labels references his family's farm in the Karoo.

★★★★☆ **Syrah** ⓐ Exceptional cool-climate expression showing violet, pot-pourri, black fruit pastille, exotic herbs & white pepper perfumes in **21** ⑨②. Smooth, with silky tannins, bright fruit, crunchy texture & savoury finish. Elgin grapes, 50% wholebunch, 22% new oak, 15 months.

★★★★☆ **Rebecca May** ⓥ Cinsaut, grenache noir & syrah (56/22/22), **21** ★★★★★ ⑨⑤ dark & red plum, raspberry, exotic spice & wisp of smoke in lithe body, crunchy cranberry finish. Like **20** ⑨④, mostly wholebunch, some carbonic maceration & 8 months in older oak for best-ever vintage of this tribute wine.

★★★★☆ **Chenin Blanc** ⓐ Prime Polkadraai grapes given suitably serious cellar treatment in **22** ⑨④: bunch-pressed into older small-oak, 8 months on lees with malo suppressed to preserve freshness, balance the mouthfilling tropical fruit & subtle creaminess. Lovely lemon & baked apple nuances, excellent depth & length. Hard to resist, but do keep some.

★★★★☆ **Riesling** Unusual treatment of the variety: 80% fermented/8 months on lees in old 600L barrels, rest in a 300L clay amphora. **22** ⑨② very subtle dried rosepetal perfume, preserved stonefruit & lime leaf with a mineral undertone. Poised, composed & excellent with food. WO Stellenbosch.

★★★★☆ **Olivia Grace** ⓐ Rich, ageworthy multi-site blend of chenin, roussanne, riesling & viognier (63/21/14/2), **21** ⑨④ is almost lavish in its orchard fruit abundance yet retains hallmark refinement through a mineral seam, salty note in the farewell & gorgeous spring blossom scents. Bunch pressed & fermented in mostly older barrels, riesling in amphora.— WB

Location: Constantia ▪ WO: Western Cape/Stellenbosch/Elgin ▪ Est/1stB 2016 ▪ Wines available for tasting & sale from Constantia Glen tasting room ▪ Owner(s) Van Wyk Family Wines (Pty) Ltd ▪ Winemaker(s)/viti-culturist(s) Justin van Wyk (Jan 2016) ▪ 18t/2,400cs own label 40% red 60% white ▪ PO Box 780 Constantia 7848 ▪ justin@vanwykfamilywines.co.za ▪ www.vanwykfamilywines.co.za ▪ **T +27 (0)84-582-0107**

☐ **Van Zijl Family Vintners** *see* Imbuko Wines
☐ **Veldfire** *see* Stanford Hills Winery
☐ **Velo** *see* Wildehurst Wines
☐ **Vera Cruz Estate** *see* Delheim Wines

Vergelegen Wines

There's a general air of change at corporate-owned Vergelegen, one of the Cape's historic estates, to enhance the quality of what is already in place rather than a change of direction. With Luke O'Cuinneagain's arrival as winemaker, the range is being consolidated and new labels designed to appeal to younger wine drinkers. As one of the most popular tourist destinations, hospitality plays an important role. Nguni Café, launched as a pop-up in 2021, has again opened, and there are plans for a coffee shop near the rose garden. The environment and sustainability remain a central focus for this extensive estate, a WWF-SA Conservation Champion. Beehives and 4 ha of carbon-sequestering spekboom are being established. Installation at the cellar of a large solar plant has taken it off the grid, achieving both environmental and financial saving.

Flagship range

★★★★☆ **Vergelegen V** Powerful & grand, **17** ⑨④ lives up to great vintage, achieving lovely harmony, full maturity still many years away. Cab plus 13% merlot filling out palate; rich & more savoury than fruit-sweet, to balance big, dense tannins, also spiced with cedar from 100% new oak.

★★★★★ **Vergelegen GVB Red** Supple, bright blend has 22% merlot & 12% cab franc with cab. **17** ★★★★☆ ⑨③ already with some maturing finesse, there's ripe fruit & cedar trimming. Concentrated & dense, with persistent flavour & superfine tannins. 14.5% alc (up on **16** ⑨⑤) not obtrusive. Deserves time.

★★★★☆ **Vergelegen GVB White** Classic semillon, sauvignon blend (56/45) in **22** ⑨③. Unshowy yet precise blackcurrant, honeyed lemon harmony, sleek & silky. Oak, 35% new, important if unobtrusive accessory. Worthy of cellaring minimum 5 years. **21** untasted.

Reserve range

★★★★☆ **Cabernet Sauvignon** Classic cab from Stellenbosch's cooler hilltops, less dense, powerful than warmer areas, still soundly built to permit ageing. **18** ⑨① matches ripe dark fruit with cedary oak, 40% new; finishing sweetness curtailed by just enough freshening acid. Possibly not as long-lived as **17** ⑨③ but worth good few years.

★★★★☆ **Merlot** Stern & robust, **18** ⑨⓪ is not without sweet, plummy flesh or freshness; at present, dense grainy tannins & 14.5% alc take a lead. Oak support, 40% new, well-handled. Touch less complex, elegant than last.

★★★★☆ **Shiraz** Ripe & sumptuous in house style. Savoury dark fruit & meaty concentration in **19** ⑨④'s supple texture, rounded grip. Oak, 25% new, subtle toasty extra. Despite 14.5% alc & fruit richness, sense of freshness is maintained.

★★★★☆ **Chardonnay** Pure citrusy bite & steely backbone on **22** ⑨④ fleshed out by creaminess from lees ageing & subtle oak, 30 % new. Ripe yet bone-dry, still shows youthful reticence but well-structured to benefit from few years' cellaring.

★★★★☆ **Semillon** Barrel-fermented **20** ⑨③ offers typical lemon & wax notes & great depth of flavour, lingering but subtly expressed, development in bottle will bring great benefit. Lovely silky texture shot with fine acid. 25% new oak, a little less than fine **19** ★★★★★ ⑨⑤.

★★★★☆ **MMV Brut** Cap classique from chardonnay, 4 years on lees, **18** ⑨⓪ shows some early nutty development & appley overtones sustained by nicely judged 6.7 g/L sugar. Fine, creamily rich mousse also lingers, enhancing overall elegance & freshness. Primary ferment in older oak.

Not tasted: **Sauvignon Blanc SV Schaapenberg**. Occasional release: **Semillon Straw Wine**. Discontinued: **DNA**.

Premium range

★★★★☆ **Shiraz** Pleasing spicy fruit on **20** ⑨⓪, ripely rounded & grippy. Small wholebunch portion adds perfume. Firm structure balanced with flavour & 14% alc. Earlier drinking than Reserve, but can age.

★★★★ **Cabernet Sauvignon-Merlot** One of more accessible cab-based wines here. Classy **20** ⑧⑨ attractive dark-fruit scents, fine & firm but undaunting structure, fleshed out by merlot; a little cab franc seasoning for freshness & added interest. **19** sold out untasted.

★★★★ **Chardonnay** Gently fresh **22** ⑧⑥ has modest, brief oatmeal & ripe citrus flavours, with a little toasty oak, 25% new, leaving brisk acid as lasting memory.

★★★★☆ **Sauvignon Blanc** Vivid blackcurrant, granadilla & florals, **23** ⑨① fresh & lively, lees-ageing tempering the acidity & adding gentle cream. 100% sauvignon, last-tasted **21** ⑨① included splash semillon.

Discontinued: **Vineyard range**. — AL

Location: Somerset West ▪ Map: Helderberg ▪ Map grid reference: F5 ▪ WO: Stellenbosch ▪ Est 1987 ▪ 1stB 1991 ▪ Tasting & sales daily 9–5 (last entry at 4) ▪ Estate closed Good Fri, May 1 & Dec 25 ▪ Daily heritage & gardens tour at 9.30; cellar tours at 11 & 3 ▪ Tours from R60pp (reservations advised) ▪ Tastings from R55pp ▪ Stables Bistro & Forest Picnic (child-friendly) ▪ Vinoteque ▪ Historic Cape Dutch homestead ▪ Library ▪ Exhibition corridor ▪ Ancient camphor trees (National Monuments since 1942) ▪ Conservation area ▪ 17 gardens including Camellia garden of excellence & children's adventure garden & maze ▪ Wine club ▪ Owner(s) Anglo American plc ▪ Winemaker(s) Luke O'Cuinneagain (Sep 2022) ▪ Viticulturist(s) Rudolf Kriel (Aug 2019) ▪ 3,000ha/126ha (cab, merlot, sauv) ▪ 900t/60,000cs own label 58% red 42% white ▪ ISO 14001, FSSC22001, ISO 45001, FairTrade, IPW, WIETA, WWF-SA Conservation Champion ▪ PO Box 17 Somerset West 7129 ▪ info@vergelegen.co.za ▪ www.vergelegen.co.za ▪ **T +27 (0)21-847-2111**

Vergenoegd Löw The Wine Estate

Sweeping revitalisation since 2015 under Peter Löw of German investment group Livia has left no detail of this 300-year-old property on Stellenbosch's False Bay coast unexamined, from the 54 ha of land 'strategically designated' to viticulture, to the remarkable flock of Indian runner ducks which assists with vine pest control. 'Innovation while preserving our historic identity' has been the guiding principle behind new plantings, refreshed packaging, renovation and added visitor allures, soon to include 5-star guest lodgings.

Vergenoegd Löw range

★★★★ **Lara Cabernet Sauvignon** Bright **21** ⑧⑨ brims with harmonious blackcurrant, dark plum, graphite & chocolate on bed of supple tannin. Delicious now, will improve over next few years. 30% new oak, 15 months, as all these reds. Also in magnum.

★★★★ **Valentina Malbec** Rich soft plums & brambles on well-structured **21** ⑧⑧, touches of black pepper & forest floor, smooth tannins & long, satisfying farewell.

★★★★ **Amalie Merlot** Succulent & generous dark plum, mulberry & hint of milk chocolate in **21** ⑧⑧. Rounded, smooth, long spicy vanilla-oak finish.

★★★★ **Florian Shiraz** Expressive & flavoursome **21** ⑧⑨ offers floral perfume, luscious hedgerow fruit & olive tapenade savoury note on well-meshed tannin base. Balanced for current & medium-term drinking.

★★★★ **Sauvignon Blanc** Asparagus mingles with tropical fruit on bright, zesty **23** ⑧⑨. Mouthfilling flavours paired with creamy texture from lees ageing, lifted lemony conclusion. Super summer sipper.

★★★★ **Méthode Cap Classique Brut Chenin Blanc** ⊘ Was 'Little Flower'. Rush of ripe apple & pineapple aromas on **22** ⑧⑧ followed by soft, rounded yet vibrant mousse, exotically spiced farewell. Pleasing complexity from 13 months on lees.

Not tasted: **Chardonnay**. Discontinued: **Chenin Blanc, Territra Cape Vintage**.

Runner Duck range

Red ★★★ Easy & juicy blend of mainly malbec & petit verdot, 3 others. **20** ⑧① bright berry flavours lightly seasoned with old oak. **Sauvignon Blanc** ⓧ ★★★ These for everyday enjoyment. Breezy **22** ⑧① pleases with apple & gooseberry flavours, bids a zippy farewell. Discontinued: **Rosé, Chenin Blanc**. — WB

Location/map/WO: Stellenbosch ▪ Map grid reference: B8 ▪ Est 1696 ▪ 1stB 1972 ▪ Open throughout the year, except Good Fri, Dec 25 & Jan 1 ▪ Tasting Wed–Sun 10–4; pub hols 9–4 (seasonal) please call ahead ▪ Wine bar & picnic area ▪ Clara's Barn Restaurant ▪ Cellar & vineyard tours by appt ▪ Wine-related gifts ▪ Waterbird habitat project ▪ Accommodation ▪ Owner(s) Livia Investment Group ▪ MD Corius Visser ▪ Winemaker(s) Vusi Dalicuba (May 2021) ▪ 161ha/42ha (cabs s/f, malbec, merlot, p verdot, shiraz, tinta barocca, touriga nacional, chard, chenin, sauv, viog) ▪ 230t/8,300cs 70% red 20% white 10% rosé ▪ IPW, WIETA, WWF-SA Conservation Champion ▪ PO Box 1 Faure 7131 ▪ info@vergenoegd.co.za ▪ www.vergenoegd.co.za ▪ **T +27 (0)21-843-3248**

☐ **Versus** see Stellenbosch Vineyards

Viceroy

With mid-1800s ties to the Van Ryn Wine & Spirit Company, Viceroy ranks among SA's most enduring brandies, now made by Heineken Beverages. The original blended product, which set a category standard with five years' barrelling, is partnered with a 100% potstill that is both stellar and exceptional value.

★★★★☆ **10 Year Old** ⓖ Rich, lingering & complex flavours on amber-hued potstill ⑨⓪ from chenin & colombard: ripe peach, apricot, pear drop & vanilla, layered with honey & gingerbread.

5 Year Old ⓖ ★★★★ Blended brandy ⑧⑤ is fairly serious-minded but 43% alc inclines it more towards mixing than solo. A pepperiness makes it perfect for ginger ale & ice. Also in 375 ml & 200 ml. — WB

☐ **Vigne d'Or** see Terre Paisible

Viljoensdrift Fine Wines & River Cruises ⓖ ⑪ ⊚

The fifth generation to grow wine in Robertson, brothers Manie and Fred Viljoen restored the old cellar on the family farm, where forebears produced sweet wines and brandy, and made the first Viljoensdrift wines in 1998. They also launched an innovative venue on the banks of the Breede, offering cruises on riverboat Uncle Ben and, latterly, a self-help deli for lazy picnics, which have proved enduringly popular.

Cellarmasters Selection

★★★★★ **Villion Pinot Noir Rosé Méthode Cap Classique** ⓖ Copper-hued **17** ★★★★★ ⑨⓪ sparkler spent 60 months on lees, exudes cherry & red berry confit scents & flavours. Has a remarkable intensity, reinforced by the racy acidity, sparks with more vitality & flavour than **16** ⑧⑧.

★★★★ **Moscato Blanco** ⓖ Sweet fortified dessert ex muscat de Frontignan, **16** ⑧⑥'s glacé fruit, barley sugar & honey add interest to the richness. Full yet amazingly easy (& delicious) to drink. 375 ml.

Cape Vintage Reserve Touriga Nacional ⓖ ★★★★ Different variety, was tinta barocca, for **16** ⑧④ 'port', 51 months in seasoned barriques, ultra-smooth, spirit adding vivacity to the richness.

River Grandeur range

★★★★ **Pinotage Single Vineyard** ⓖ Registered single block, something special deserving of care: half each French & American barriques, 24 months, 80% new, giving **20** ⑧⑨ vanilla-infused fruitcake richness, tannins a lithe seam lending ageing potential. Opulent, polished.

★★★★ **Shiraz** ⓖ **20** ⑧⑨ 2nd-fill barriques, 20 months, half American, adding vanilla spicing to glossy dark fruit. Palate supple & succulent, tannins integrated, overall effect delicious drinkability.

Cabernet Sauvignon ★★★ Delightfully accessible **21** ⑧② cherries on a toasty backbone from 15 months in barrel, 70% new. Good balancing freshness. **Chardonnay** ⓖ ★★★ Unwooded but **22** ⑧⓪ preview's grapefruit styling offers enough elegant freshness to please most palates. **Crispy Sauvignon Blanc** ⓥ ★★★☆ As name implies, good acid delivers a brisk **23** ⑧④, heightens sweet lemon, lime & gooseberry flavours. Just 12.5% alc aids freshness, light feel. Not tasted: **Merlot**, **Cape Blend**.

Viljoensdrift range

Muskapino Sweet Pink Sparkling Wine ⓖ ★★★ Muscadel & 23% pinotage, **22** ⑧⓪ is a sweet, bright pink, frothy delight; red berries & raisins in fresh, trim (8% alc) body. Not tasted: **Anchor Drift Dry Red**, **Dry White**. — ML

Location/map/WO: Robertson ▪ Map grid reference: C5 ▪ Est/1stB 1998 ▪ Tasting, sales & river cruises at riverside venue Tue-Fri 9-5 Sat/pub hols 10-4 Sun (1st & last/month) 10-3; open 7 days/week Dec-Mar ▪ Closed Good Fri, Dec 25 & Jan 1 ▪ Self-help deli - create your own picnic basket ▪ Tour groups ▪ Owner(s) Fred & Manie Viljoen ▪ Winemaker(s) Fred Viljoen, with Zonia Lategan ▪ Viticulturist(s) Manie Viljoen ▪ 240ha/120ha (cab, merlot, ptage, shiraz, chard, sauv) ▪ 2,000t/±160,000cs own label 55% red 40% white 4% rosé 1% port + 15,000L for clients ▪ IPW, WIETA ▪ PO Box 653 Robertson 6705 ▪ rivercruises@viljoensdrift.co.za ▪ www.viljoensdrift.co.za ▪ **T +27 (0)23-615-1901 (cellar)/+27 (0)23-615-1017 (tasting/cruises)**

☐ **Villa Esposto** see Klawer Wine Cellars
☐ **Village Walk** see Franschhoek Cellar

Villiera Wines ⓖ ⑪ ⊚ ⓰

Chickens, more recently the male of the species, are entwined with the story of this acclaimed Stellenbosch venture long associated with the Grier family. The 2nd generation was instrumental in developing County Fair Chickens and, when 3rd-generation Jeff applied to study agricultural management with a view to joining the family firm, only to be told it wasn't being offered that year, he opted for winemaking instead. This led to him and cousin Simon establishing Villiera Wines in 1983. Now the family has sold to Iwayini, local subsidiary of Les Grands Chais de France. Ex-Saronsberg cellarmaster Dewaldt Heyns takes over as executive manager and, while the senior Griers stay on for a 3-year transition, there are plans to focus on cap clas-sique, which will see vineyards replanted to chardonnay and pinot noir, and production facilities expanded. Critically, the Griers' philosophy of natural winemaking and environmental sustainability will remain.

Villiera range

★★★★ **Cabernet Sauvignon** ⊘ 🐝 Pleasantly lean thanks to moderate 13.2% alc & few grams rounding sugar, **21** ⑧⑦ opens with dark fruit, then unfurls morello cherry. Usual cedar & vanilla overlay from 90/10 French & American oak less overt courtesy fewer new barrels (10% vs 25% in **20** ⑧⑦).

★★★★ **Bush Vine Gamay Noir** 🌝 Was 'Stand Alone Gamay'. Impressive weight & seriousness from 1981 single-vineyard. **22** ⑧⑧ loses some of **21** ⑧⑧'s dryness but keeps its red cherries & berries, stemmy grip & cleansing acid. 30% wholebunch natural ferment, 10 months amphora & older oak.

★★★★ **Merlot** ⊘ Lightly oaked **21** ⑧⑧ signature plum & cherry notes, light hedgerow & leaf tones. Subtle savouriness on the finish ups the appeal, mealtime friendliness.

★★★★☆ **Monro Merlot** ⊘ 🐝 Deftly done **21** ★★★★★ ⑨⑤, modern with touch of restraint. Black fruit pastille intensity corralled by tangy cranberry acid & fine, form-giving tannin, like accomplished **20** ⑨②, accented by vanilla from 65% new oak/18 months.

★★★★☆ **Punchion Pinot Noir** ⊘ 🐝 Was 'Stand Alone Pinot Noir'. Now named for & fermented in open 400L Burgundy casks. **22** ⑨⓪'s immediate appeal is sun-kissed cherry & berry fruit, smoky spice from 20% new oak, silky tannins. Similar depth & weight as last, shade less tangy refreshment. WO Overberg.

★★★★☆ **The Clan** 🐝 With its sumptuous fruit, lively acid backbone & firm tannin frame, **18** ⑨③ an exercise in precision crafting to reward cellaring decade or more. 85% cab franc & carignan, supported by 18 months oak, 60% new. **17** ★★★★★ ⑨⑤ similar blend.

★★★★ **Barrel Fermented Chenin Blanc** 🌝 Richly textured & complex, full bodied (14.6% alc), **22** ⑧⑧ result of complex winemaking: 4 hours skin contact, no malo, 10 months in oak, 26% new, lees stirring. Dry, with pineapple & honey flavours, dark toast finish.

★★★★ **Sauvignon Blanc** ⊘ Much care taken to preserve **23** ⑧⑥'s range of aromas & flavours, from cool capsicum to riper granadilla & papaya, all nicely complemented by smoke from 15% oaked fraction & weight from some old-vine fruit.

★★★★☆ **Dakwijn** Version of vin doux naturel wines of the area near Griers' estate in France. **21** ★★★★ ⑧⑧ very ripe chenin part-fermented before fortification to 16.7% alc, aged 8 months under flor veil in demijohn on tasting room roof before year in old barrels. Idiosyncratic & worth seeking out, if shade more brown appleskin oxidative notes, less umami & tang than **20** ⑨⓪ to balance the sugar. 500 ml.

Pinotage ⊘ ★★★★ Attractive **20** ⑧⑤ juicy mulberry fruit but tauter than last, needs year/2 to settle, allow tannins to mellow. 10 months oak, 25% new. **Chenin Blanc** ⊘ ★★★★ Vibrant pear- & apple-toned glassful with seductive smoky whisper courtesy 30% barrel-fermented portion. Smidgen sugar aids drinkability in **23** ⑧⑤. **Jasmine** ★★★ Off-dry **23** ⑧② from near-equal muscat & riesling, 25% gewürztraminer, is grapey & subtly spicy, with apricot & rosewater scents. Confidently walks the acid-sugar tightrope. In abeyance: **Bush Vine Sauvignon Blanc**. Discontinued: **Stand Alone Pinotage**.

Cap Classique range

★★★★ **Tradition Brut Rosé** Pale sunset hue on this sparkler, tangy raspberry acid, gentle toast & honey from 18 months on lees. Masterly **NV** ⑧⑧ blend with pinot noir leading, 30% each chardonnay & pinotage, 5% meunier. Also in 1.5L.

★★★★ **Brut Natural** Bottled without sulphur addition, **18** ⑧⑥ sparkling from chardonnay in great shape. Bone-dry, as zero-dosage style dictates, obtaining its weight, texture & savoury complexity from 42 months on the lees.

★★★★☆ **Monro Brut** 🐝 Jewel in the crown of this sparkling line-up thanks to its ability to balance richness & freshness, deliver complexity yet appear so effortless. **16** ⑨④ from chardonnay & 35% pinot noir, myriad apple flavours, salty caramel & savouriness from 66 months on lees.

★★★★ **Shooting Star Light Brut** ⊘ Was 'Starlight Brut'. Pinot noir & pinotage (30/20) ensure satisfying **NV** ⑧⑥ bubbly has body & texture at just 9.6% alc, chardonnay adds freshness, green apple & lemon appeal.

★★★★ **Tradition Brut** If 'the sun is shining somewhere' is your reason pop a cork, this reliably delicious fizz for you. NV ⑧⑨ keeps winning 70/30 chardonnay & pinot noir combo, 18 months on lees. Also in 375 ml & 1.5L.

★★★★ **Pearls of Nectar** (NEW) Seriously styled demi-sec celebrator from chardonnay, 18 months on lees. Rich gold hue on NV ⑧⑧, strawberry candyfloss bouquet with matching delicate mousse & well-judged sweetness & generous appley flavour.

Down to Earth range
Red ⊘ ★★★★ Friendly 21 ⑧⑭'s sweet dark fruit brushed with touriga's florals & orange rind, spice from 10% new oak. Juicy enough to drink now & over next few years. 35% shiraz. **White** ⊘ ★★★★ Mostly sauvignon, with 25% lightly oaked semillon giving whisper smoke to intense grass & passionfruit. 23 ⑧⑭ full bodied (14% alc) & quite plush. — CvZ

Location/map: Stellenbosch ▪ Map grid reference: D1 ▪ WO: Stellenbosch/Overberg ▪ Est/1stB 1983 ▪ Tasting, sales & self-guided cellar tours Mon-Fri 9-5 Sat/pub hols 9-3 ▪ Closed Good Fri, Dec 25 & Jan 1 ▪ MCC & nougat pairing; cheese boards ▪ Wildlife sanctuary ▪ Game drive safaris & birding (incl tasting & self-guided tour of cellar), phone for cost and to book ahead ▪ Wine club ▪ Owner(s) Iwayini (subsidiary of Grands Chais de France) ▪ Cellarmaster(s) Jeff Grier (1983) ▪ Winemaker(s) Nathan Valentine (reds/whites) & Xander Grier (MCC/reserve wines) ▪ Viticulturist(s) Simon Grier ▪ 180ha (cab, merlot, ptage, pinot, shiraz, chard, chenin, sauv) ▪ 1,600t/110,000cs own label 25% red 30% white 45% MCC ▪ Brands for clients: Woolworths (local); Marks & Spencer (export) ▪ B-BBEE, HACCP, IPW, WIETA ▪ Cnr Old Paarl & R304 Roads, Koelenhof 7605 ▪ wine@villiera.com ▪ www.villiera.com ▪ **T +27 (0)21-865-2002/3**

Villiersdorp Winery
A feature of Villiersdorp's townscape for over a century, the production facilities on the main street were built for grape must jam (moskonfyt) and grape juice concentrate, graduating to wine exactly 50 years ago. Upgrades to infrastructure and equipment, and new technology for the pressing hall specifically, are ongoing. The 'easy-drinking, fruit-driven wines' can be sampled at the Kelkiewyn venue across the road.

Since 1922 range
★★★★ **Kiara** ⓖ Stylish pinotage & shiraz Cape Blend, 19 ⑧⑧ exuberantly ripe & sweetly spicy berry fruit in a supple body, satin tannins polished in small oak. No dash viognier this release.

Not tasted: **Mosko**. In abeyance: **Last Straw**.

Villiersdorp Winery range
Pinotage ⓖ ★★★★ Honest, juicy berry fruit in 21 ⑧⑭, gentle mocha & cocoa hints from combo oak staves & barrels. Lightish body for early enjoyment, as all these. **Shiraz** ⓖ ★★★★ Sappy & supple, with spicy black cherry fruit, 20 ⑧⑭ has no-nonsense appeal, for braai-side enjoyment. Oak as Pinotage. **Chardonnay** ⊘ ★★★★ Crisp 23 ⑧⑤ preview pleasant & well made, fresh & light body showing subtle cream from 6 months oak on tiny portion of the wine. **Sauvignon Blanc** ⊘ ★★★★ Taut, citrus-tangy 23 ⑧⑭ tank sample ticks the vibrancy & refreshment boxes. Focused, clean & dry. **Treintjiewyn Hanepoot Jerepigo** ★★★★ Rich, seductive honeysuckle & barley sugar on NV ⑧⑤, bold 191 g/L sweetness countered by fortification to 17.2% alc for balanced, clean sipping, with nothing overplayed. **Cape Ruby** ⊘ ★★★ Light NV ⑧⓪ 'port' from tinta barocca shows raisins, spice & plums but less concentration & fire than expected of the style. WO W Cape, as Treintjie.

Slow range
Merlot ⓖ ★★★ Competent, unfinicky 20 ⑧⓪ represents good value, has spiced raspberry fruit from oak staving, gentle tannins. **Rosé** ⊘ ★★★★ Pinotage & chenin add dash shiraz in 23 ⑧③, keep their strawberry & plum succulence. Fruity, crisp & dry, ideal for summer. Also in 3L & WO W Cape, as Van Der Stel. **Chenin Blanc** ⊘ ★★★★ Melon & quince flavours & aromas on 23 ⑧③ tank sample. Light, bright & unpretentious. **Van Der Stel** ★★★ Chenin plays senior partner to 16% colombard in 23 ⑧② Vivid lemon & quince notes on light, pleasant quaffer. Not tasted: **Bossieveld**. — FM

Location/map: Villiersdorp ▪ Map grid reference: C1 ▪ WO: Cape South Coast/Western Cape ▪ Est 1922 ▪ 1stB 1974 ▪ Tasting & sales Mon-Fri 8-5 Sat 9-1; pub hols (seasonal) please call ahead ▪ Fee R10 for groups of 7+ ▪ Closed Easter Fri-Mon & Dec 25/26 ▪ Cellar tours by appt ▪ Kelkiewyn restaurant ▪ Owner(s) 37 shareholders ▪ GM Christo Versfeld ▪ Winemaker(s)/viticulturist(s) Christo Versfeld ▪ 141ha under vine ▪ IPW ▪ PO Box 151 Villiersdorp 6848 ▪ admin@villiersdorpwinery.co.za ▪ www.villiersdorpwinery.co.za ▪ **T +27 (0)28-840-0083**

Villion Family Wines ⓠ

'Detailed and focused winemaking is our passion,' says vintner Kobie Viljoen, now joined by Lawrie Moore in the Barton Vineyards cellar near Bot River, where tastings are offered, and 'eco-friendly and traditional' methods used to craft a boutique range. Parcels are selected locally and elsewhere in the Cape South Coast region according to a variety of criteria to express the cool-climate terroir as authentically as possible.

★★★★☆ **Cabernet Sauvignon** ⓠ Classic varietal character in **20** ㉝: cassis, graphite minerality, leather & tealeaf, all tightly woven with firm tannin, a dusty grip on the finish. Well crafted for ageing.

★★★★☆ **Cabernet Franc** (NEW) ⚘ In bottle 72 months, after 18 in barrel, 38% new, **15** ㉝ shows graceful development & great complexity - plush dark plums, fynbos fragrance, tealeaves & graphite among the layers - in an elegant structure. Drinks beautifully now & will do for several more years.

★★★★☆ **Grenache** ⓠ Earthy mulberry & dark plum in generous **21** ㉙. Fresh, vibrant, with smoky meat complexity on palate extending to long, savoury exit. 30% wholebunch, 11 months old oak, as Pinot.

★★★★ **Pinot Noir** ⓠ Delicate **21** ㉘ offers fresh strawberry & earthy forest floor aromas, balanced & rounded flavours. Naturally fermented Walker Bay grapes.

★★★★ **Syrah** ⓠ Brooding sweet dark berries on naturally bunch-fermented **19** ㉘, splashes viognier, grenache noir & mourvèdre, & 11 months in neutral barrels adding dimension.

★★★★ **Chardonnay** ⊘ Mouthfilling & broad, with unfolding layers of fruit & spice, lengthy citrus farewell, **22** ★★★★★ improves on **21** ㉘ in lemon, lime & apple brightness & intensity, vanilla oak creaminess. Elgin fruit, 50% wholebunch fermented/10 months in 20% new barrel.

★★★★ **Henning Chenin Blanc** ⚘ From almost 40 year old vines, textured & concentrated **22** ★★★★★ ㉛ shows terrific depth & length of tropical fruit, cashew creaminess & endless savoury farewell. Similar intricate regime as **21** ㉘, 45% wholebunch & 5% skin ferments, 10% new oak, 10 months.

★★★★☆ **Sauvignon Blanc** ⚘ Venerable vines deliver green herbs, citrus & orchard fruit in substantial yet vivacious mouthful. **22** ㉙ reflects deft crafting, free-run juice fermented/9 months in older barrels, adding to texture, density & complexity. Exceptional example of the variety. Unfiltered.

★★★★ **Blanc de l'Atlantique** Lipsmacking, harmonious & joyful viognier (60%) blend with 3 others, **22** ㉘ sees floral fragrance & tropical fruit leap out the glass. Ferment/10 months in 15% new barrel add roundness & delicious vanilla crème brûlée undertone. WO Cape South Coast, as Cabernet & Syrah.— WB

Location: Bot River ▪ Map: Walker Bay & Bot River ▪ Map grid reference: B2 ▪ WO: Bot River/Cape South Coast/Walker Bay/Elgin ▪ Est 2015 ▪ 1stB 2012 ▪ Tasting Mon-Fri 10-5 Sat & pub hols 10-3 ▪ Owner(s) Kobie Viljoen ▪ Winemaker(s) Kobie Viljoen & Lawrie Moore ▪ 70t/5,000cs own label 45% red 55% white ▪ R43/Hermanus Rd, Bot River 7185 ▪ elnette@villionwines.com, kobie@villionwines.com ▪ www.villionwines.com ▪ T +27 (0)28-284-9248

☐ **Vinay** see Slanghoek Winery

Vinette Wine ⓠ

The stylised elephant raising a glass on the front label speaks to the relaxed and convivial nature of this Stellenbosch brand and its wines, sold in 250-ml aluminium cans due to the owners' belief that this packaging type 'is one of the best containers for wine', given its light weight, recyclability and other benefits.

Merlot ★★★ Easy-sipping **22** ㉘ packed with plum fruit, deftly handled & unwooded so there are no rough edges. **Rosé** ★★★ A drop of red gives pink tinge & a pretty berry note to chenin on **23** ㉗. Just about dry, just about charming. **Sweet Sparkle** ★★★ Perlé from Paarl... **23** ㉗ a pale pink, low-alc (8.5%), gently bubbly wine redolent of muscat. Sweetly, lightly delightful. Hard to imagine a picnic without it. **Chenin Blanc** ★★★ Forward fruitiness on nicely balanced **23** ㉘; greenish bite adds freshness, keeps it dryish. — TJ

Location: Stellenbosch ▪ WO: Western Cape ▪ Est 2019 ▪ 1stB 2018 ▪ Tasting by appt only ▪ Closed all pub hols ▪ Owner(s) 3 shareholders ▪ Winemaker(s) Michael van Niekerk (Nov 2018) ▪ 20% red 40% white 40% rosé ▪ 1 Villa Al Sole, Polkadraai Rd, Stellenbosch 7600 ▪ info@vinettewine.co ▪ www.vinettewine.co ▪ T +27 (0)82-346-4655

Vinevenom

Based in the heart of Swartland, Samantha Suddons' current releases are from grapes on one Paardeberg farm, which she crafts in 'natural, hands-off, low-intervention' fashion. She's fascinated by the development of flor yeast on a wine's surface, and inspired by the light-styled red wines of southern Italy.

★★★★☆ **Spektra** 🆕 Single high-lying parcel of syrah, bunch fermented, 18 months in old oak, giving delicious salty olive savouriness to **21** ⑨⑴. Delicate floral nuance to plums & cherries sprinkled with peppery spice. Paardeberg grapes, as all.

★★★★ **Satellites** Light & juicy **NV** ⑧⑺ red from touriga & grenache (65/20), dabs shiraz & cinsault, older oaked. Strawberry coulis with intriguing hibiscus nuance, wholebunch ferment magnifies attractive spicy top notes.

★★★★☆ **Shining** Exotic **NV** ⑨⑵ dry rosé from carignan & touriga is complex & engaging, opens with nougat, nectarine & peach, adds pickled ginger, nutty & salty notes, latter courtesy oxidative maturation under flor & maderised component.

★★★★☆ **Silence** 2nd release of **NV** ⑨⓪ chenin features 2020, 2021 & 2022 vintages aged in 300L old oak under a wild flor yeast veil, then fractionally blended for a riveting combo of lemon, sourdough & nut flavours, ending with a salty tang. Modest 12.3% alc & lively acid.

★★★★☆ **Skin** 🆕 ⊘ 🐝 Single-parcel **NV** ⑨⑶ chenin macerated on skins 27 days in stainless steel tank, oxidatively aged in old barriques. Citrus, ginger & peach opulence kept in check by lemon acidity, tug of fruit tannin & bone-dry finish. 'A wine for whisky lovers.'— ML

Location: Riebeek West ▪ Map/WO: Swartland ▪ Map grid reference: D6 ▪ Est 2020 ▪ 1stB 2015 ▪ Tasting by appt only ▪ Wine club ▪ Owner(s)/winemaker(s) Samantha Suddons ▪ 12t/2,500cs own label 20% red 50% white 30% rosé ▪ PO Box 87 Riebeek Wes 7306 ▪ samantha@vinevenom.com ▪ www.vinevenom.com ▪
T +27 (0)76-392-4301

☐ **Vineyard Friends** *see* DGB (Pty) Ltd

VinGlo Wines

While the wines featured here form part of VinGlo's own boutique portfolio, Cape Town-based Grant Davis and his team specialise in producing bespoke wines for clients around the world.

Eighth Wonder range

★★★★ **Cape Cauldron Cabernet Sauvignon** ⓥ Substantial, dark & brooding **18** ⑧⑻, berry fruit, dried herbs & chocolate on a velvet tannin bed, long savoury finish. 2 years in oak, as Merlot.

Cape Cauldron Merlot ⓥ ★★★★ Inky colour, lively berries, touch of spice & gentle tannins in juicy & friendly **20** ⑧⑸. Stellenbosch WO, as Cab. **Pinotage** 🆕 ★★★ Dark plums touch overshadowed by hefty tannins, a charred coffee finish on **21** ⑧⓪ from year in oak. Not tasted: **Silver Tree Reserve**, **Silver Tree Red**, **Cabernet Sauvignon**, **Shiraz**, **Cabernet Sauvignon-Merlot**. — WB

Location: Cape Town ▪ WO: Stellenbosch/Coastal ▪ Est/1stB 2012 ▪ Tasting by appt ▪ Winemaker(s) Hendrien de Munck ▪ 7–10t/ha ▪ 8,000cs own label 80% red 20% white ▪ 50 Esme Rd, Newlands, Cape Town 7700 ▪ grant@vinglo.co.za ▪ www.vinglowines.co.za ▪ **T +27 (0)21-671-7905**

Vinimark

The largest independent wine-specialist company in SA, distributing and marketing over 60 well-known brands, including wholly owned ones, many listed in these pages.

Location: Stellenbosch ▪ Closed to public ▪ Directors Eckhardt Gerber (CEO), Rudiger Gretschel, Guy Pause & Jeannie Olsen ▪ PO Box 441 Stellenbosch 7599 ▪ info@vinimark.co.za ▪ www.vinimark.co.za ▪ **T +27 (0)21-883-8043/4**

☐ **Vinography** *see* Benguela Cove Lagoon Wine Estate
☐ **Vinoneers** *see* The Vinoneers

Vino pH

'An adventure in wine by a French and African girl team,' say Pauline Roux and Hanneke Krüger. It's one that's evolving, with their bukettraube-based méthode ancestrale trying out some varietal additions, and a 'slow but sure' move to making wine on the Piketberg farm of Hanneke and her husband Thinus of Fram Wines. The two reds, however, noted last year as 'one-off experiments', were so well received that they seem to be becoming a happily permanent feature.

Red Series

★★★★ **Barbera** One of a handful of varietal barbera bottlings. **22** ★★★★☆ ⑨⓪ from Paardeberg offers gorgeous dark cherry aromas & flavours (lifted by wholebunch ferment; 5 days carbonic maceration) - a little wild, perhaps. Fresh, bright, light-feeling but more vinous than ethereal **21** ⑧⑥. Just 6 months in old oak to preserve the pure fruit character.

★★★★ **Pinot Noir** ⊘ Flavoursome but elegant **22** ★★★★☆ ⑨⓪ from Ceres Plateau, with aromatic depth but not facilely fruity - there's a touch of fresh earth. Soft texture & subtlest of tannin. Balanced for earlyish drinking - certainly delicious in youth. 15% wholebunch; 16 months old oak, unfined/filtered. 13.5% alc. Like **21** ⑧⑨ but touch more convincing.

pH range

★★★★ **Palomino** Mid-gold **22** ★★★ ⑧② pleasant enough but rather neutral aroma & flavour - much less vibrant, intense & characterful than **21** ⑧⑥; little vinosity at 11% alc. 50% on skin for light grippiness; all aged in old oak. WO Piekenierskloof.

PhD Méthode Ancestrale ★★★★ Mildly aromatic **22** ⑧④ (some honey, floral, grapey) from bukettraube plus chenin & sauvignon. Refreshing & dry but a touch insipid. Paardeberg grapes. — TJ

Location: Malmesbury ▪ WO: Paardeberg/Ceres Plateau/Piekenierskloof/Swartland ▪ Est/1stB 2019 ▪ Closed to public ▪ Owner(s)/winemaker(s) Hanneke Krüger & Pauline Roux ▪ 6t/ha 1,700cs own label 15% red 35% white 50% pet nat ▪ HB Projekte, PO Box 657 Riebeek West 7306 ▪ sales@vinoph.co.za ▪ **T +27 (0)76-642-1336/+27 (0)81-388-1670**

- ☐ **Vino Pronto** *see* Hirst Wines
- ☐ **Vino Sacci** *see* Klawer Wine Cellars
- ☐ **Vinoteque** *see* Heineken Beverages
- ☐ **Vintage Mashup** *see* De Wet Cellar
- ☐ **Vinum** *see* Radford Dale
- ☐ **Vinyl Collection** *see* Rascallion Wines

Visio Vintners ⑨

Founded in 2018 and owned by the Kleine Zalze Empowerment Trust, Visio Vintners has ±22 ha in Stellenbosch under long-term lease, where it sustainably farms around 14 ha of mostly red-wine varieties. Top-ranked Kleine Zalze provides multidisciplinary guidance and facilitates production, in its cellar, of small parcels of 'quality, characterful wine that appeals to the modern consumer', available locally and in Europe.

★★★★☆ **Alliance** ⑨ Cabs sauvignon & franc lead **20** ⑨⓪ blend with 2 partners. Ripe & supple, big alc adds touch of warmth on finish but no major distraction. Potential to age. WO Stellenbosch.

Pinotage ⑨ ★★★★ Smoky mocha edge to **20** ⑧⑤, spicy blueberry vibrancy backed by frame of seasoned oak. **Cinsault Rosé** ⑨ ★★★★ Instant appeal of succulent raspberry & cherry on **22** ⑧③. Fresh, light & dry, great for summer. **Sauvignon Blanc** ⊘ ★★★★ Taut, bright grapefruit & granadilla on **22** ⑧⑤, portion cooler-grown fruit lends flint nuance to dry, zesty finish. WO W Cape. — FM

Location: Stellenbosch ▪ WO: Coastal/Stellenbosch/Western Cape ▪ Est 2018 ▪ 1stB 2020 ▪ Tasting at Kleine Zalze Wines tasting facility ▪ Wine club ▪ Owner(s) Liciacept (Pty) Ltd t/a Visio Vintners (shareholders Kleine Zalze Empowerment Trust & Kleine Zalze Wines) ▪ Cellarmaster(s) RJ Botha (consultant) ▪ Viticulturist(s) Henning Retief (consultant) ▪ 22.6ha/14.6ha (cabs s/f, shiraz) ▪ 63t/4,000cs own label 30% red 45% white 25% rosé ▪ IPW, WIETA ▪ cgous@kleinezalze.co.za ▪ www.visiovintners.co.za ▪ **T +27 (0)21-880-0717**

- ☐ **Vlok Family Wines** *see* Stamboom
- ☐ **Voetspore** *see* Arendskloof-New Cape Wines

Vondeling ⑨ ⑪ ◎ ⑤

Owners Julian Johnsen and Anthony Ward and their team say their wish is to 'nurture our environment so as to produce exquisite wines with a special sense of place, using only our own grapes, fermented and bottled on the premises'. At the extensive home-farm, on the south-east slopes of Paardeberg Mountain, a number of projects are ongoing, including the renewal of virus-infected vines, and removal of alien vegetation on the mountain. Visitor wise, on-site St Clement's chapel and wedding, function and conference venue remain, but the tasting locale is now more conveniently sited at Vrymansfontein on the side of Paarl Mountain. It now also features a lunch and dinner restaurant, outdoor bar and terrace, and landscaped gardens. Nearby on the mountainside is a recently acquired farm where almond orchards and vineyards are being planted.

Flagship Wines

★★★★☆ **Monsonia** Substantial yet refined blend of 60% shiraz with mourvèdre, carignan & grenache noir, **19** ⑨② opulently ripe & fruit driven yet layered & nuanced, poised, tannins plush & smooth. Whole-bunch & -berry ferment, 16 months in barrel.

★★★★☆ **Babiana** Ⓐ Sumptuous, stately chenin blend, **22** ⑨④ adds chardonnay to **21** ⑨③'s viognier, grenache blanc & roussanne. Bold, succulent & assertive, proudly wearing nutty sweet spices from ferment/year in oak, 33% new.

Limited Releases

★★★★☆ **Bowwood Pinotage** Eight barrels selected from special block, **20** ⑨① richly ripe & full, plush, sweet red-berry fruit, caramel & butterscotch notes from 14 months in American oak. Wholeberry ferment lends brightness & perfume. Also-tasted **19** ⑨① similar character, same fine quality.

★★★★★ **Philosophie** Ⓐ Massive structure & muscle of **19** ⑨⑦ Cape Bordeaux tempered by intricately detailed spice & minerals. Fruit is ripe, concentrated yet sweetly aromatic, tobacco & tilled earth among the myriad scents. 65% cab with merlot & cab franc, 18 months in 75% new barrels. No **18**.

★★★★☆ **Bowwood Chenin Blanc** Bold, assertive, barrel-fermented **22** ⑨② first since **19** ⑨②, shows presence & gravity in layers of ripe stonefruit, vanilla biscuit & lemon rind. Rich, textured & lingering, showing well now but good for several years.

★★★★☆ **Rurale Méthode Ancestrale** Ⓐ Riper grapes & single bottle ferment, started in tank with wild yeast, differentiate this pioneer of the style from cap classique. **19** ⑨④ ex chardonnay & pinotage is dry yet rich, creamy, with vigorous mousse, primary green apple fruit & appealing savoury yeastiness.

★★★★☆ **Sweet Carolyn** Ⓐ Unctuous, mega-sweet dessert from vine-dried muscat de Frontignan, **22** ⑨② fermented on skins, barrelled 11 months. Typical grapey-raisined fruit has layers of baked confectionery, honey & citrus peel, tempered by fine linear acid. 500 ml. Last was **18** ⑨②.

Barrel Selection range

★★★★☆ **Cabernet Sauvignon** Full & rich, with burly tannins, cedary oak spice & supple, sweet-ripe fruit, **21** ★★★★ ⑧⑨ has presence but also charm - though not fully melded mid-2023, needed time. 18 months in 25% new barrels. Shade off **20** ⑨①.

★★★★☆ **Merlot** ⊘ Brooding **21** ⑨⓪ has impressive fruit concentration paired with subtle earthy minerality. Blackcurrant & cherry, fragrantly oak spiced from 18 months in 30% new barrels. Robust leathery tannins suggest cellaring.

★★★★ **Chardonnay** Prominent oak of **21** ⑧⑦ reined in for **22** ⑧⑨, allowing fruit to take centre stage. Fine textured & sleek from well-managed lees contact, notes of pear, red apple & citrus, all elegantly spiced during 11 months barrel time, 30% new.

Vondeling range

★★★★ **Baldrick Shiraz** ⊘ Unpretentious yet more serious than entry-level tier & price suggest. **21** ⑧⑥ ripe, succulent, showing plum, cherry & bramble fruit, hints of pepper & scrub. Fullish body & assertive tannins smoothed by 14 months in older barrels.

....

Petit Rouge Merlot ⊘ Ⓣ ★★★★ Modestly pitched but generously fruity, **22** ⑧⑤ is pure everyday drinking pleasure, offers juicy black cherries, plums & damsons. **Petit Blanc Chenin Blanc** Ⓣ ★★★★ Cheerful, uncomplicated refreshment, **23** ⑧⑤ delivers upfront tropical fruit, satisfying lees texture & presence on palate.

....

Rosé ★★★★ From mainly merlot, dry **23** ⑧⑤ has tantalizingly fragrant berries, wholesome fruit & leesy palate weight. **Sauvignon Blanc** ★★★★ Fruit-driven, juicy **23** ⑧⑤ offers honest granadilla & gooseberry flavours, appealing lees body & texture, reined-in aromatics. **Little Sparkle** ★★★★ Chardonnay **NV** ⑧③ carbonated bubbly has energetic mousse, piquant acid & pleasant, just-dry citrus fruit. — GdB

Location/map: Paarl ▪ Map grid reference: D6 ▪ WO: Voor Paardeberg ▪ Est 2001 ▪ 1stB 2005 ▪ Tasting & sales at Vrymansfontein Wed-Sun 10-6 ▪ Scape à la carte restaurant open for lunch & dinner ▪ Tree Bar: outdoor bar & terrace ▪ Wedding/function/conference venue ▪ St Clement's chapel ▪ Wine club ▪ Owner(s) Julian Johnsen & Anthony Ward ▪ Winemaker(s) Matthew Copeland (Jul 2007), with Emile van der Merwe (Dec 2011) ▪ Viticulturist(s) Magnus Joubert (Jul 2012) & Basson Potgieter (May 2021) ▪ 100ha (cabs s/f, carignan, grenache r/w, malbec, merlot, mourv, p verdot, shiraz, chard, chenin, muscat de F, rouss, sauv, sem, viog) ▪ 900t/100,000cs own label 40% red 40% white 20% rosé ▪ WWF-SA Conservation Champion ▪ PO Box 57 Wellington 7654 ▪ admin@vondelingwines.co.za, info@vrymansfontein.co.za ▪ www.vondelingwines.co.za, www.vrymansfontein.co.za ▪ **T +27 (0)21-869-8595 (Vondeling)/+27 (0)82-617-4903 (Vrymansfontein)**

Vredenheim Wines

On the Bezuidenhout family's 17th-century estate near Stellenbosch, wine is made as unfussily as possible, to showcase the character of the grapes. Receiving finishing touches at press time were a wooded chardonnay and a port-style wine. Novel among the wealth of attractions is a Big Cats Park, the legacy of matriarch and 'gracious lady' Rikie Bezuidenhout and late husband 'M'Lord' Coen's previous residency on a game farm.

★★★★ **Cabernet Sauvignon** Blackcurrant & meaty, savoury seam, **20** (88) has heft, is built on firm foundation yet without hard edges. 18 months older oak give structure for ageing or food matching. No **19.**

Gracious Lady ★★★★ Changing blend, cab with shiraz & merlot, 14 months smaller barrels, 20% new. Vibrant cassis, some dried herbs & tobacco, supple tannins, **20** (85) remains alluring, true to the name.

Merlot ★★★ Plumply ripe **21** (81) shows vanilla-spiced berry confit, sure to please its audience. Not complex but very likeable. **Rosé** ★★★ From sauvignon, with 5% cab for the light pink hue, **NV** (81)'s gooseberry & passionfruit flavours augmented by the touch of sugar. **Chenin Blanc** ★★★ Light oaking fits **22** (80)'s apple & pear styling, the gentle melba toast overlay making it food-friendly. Ends crisply dry. **Sauvignon Blanc** ★★★ More character & ripeness than last, with winter melon & greengage, **23** (81) finishes with crisp green notes, shows typicity. **Vredenvonkel Rosé** ★★★ Pale straw coloured **NV** (80) bubbly is 95% sauvignon with 5% cab for colour, like Rosé. Winter melon & apple throughout, slight touch of sweetness fitting the style. Not tasted: **Pinotage, Shiraz.** — CR

Location/map/WO: Stellenbosch ▪ Map grid reference: D6 ▪ Tasting, sales & cellar tours Mon-Sat 9-4.30; pub hols 9-5 (seasonal) please call ahead ▪ Closed Good Fri, Dec 25 & Jan 1 ▪ Hudson's Restaurant T +27 (0)21-881-3590 ▪ Conferences/functions ▪ Vredenheim Angus Stud ▪ Big Cats Park ▪ Curio shop ▪ De Boerderijwinkel ▪ Guest house ▪ Gin distillery: tasting Fri-Sun 12-5 ▪ Owner(s) Bezuidenhout family ▪ Winemaker(s) Elzabé Bezuidenhout / Jaco Bezuidenhout ▪ Viticulturist(s) Kalie Kirsten ▪ 80ha under vine ▪ 20,000cs own label 60% red 40% white ▪ PO Box 369 Stellenbosch 7599 ▪ wine@vredenheim.co.za ▪ www.vredenheim.co.za ▪ **T +27 (0)21-881-3878**

Vriesenhof Vineyards

Well-respected and widely seasoned Adam Mason is listed as winemaker this edition, reflecting the changes underway at the Stellenbosch Mountain farm bought in 1980 and developed by wine and rugby hero Jan 'Boland' Coetzee. At press time there were building works at the tasting venue, and visitors are very welcome but advised to phone ahead to confirm opening times.

★★★★ **Cabernet Sauvignon** ⊘ Delicate **21** (88) shows classic blackcurrant, cedar & vanilla nuances from considered oaking, 9 months in older barrels, further 6 in mix new (10%) & old. Sweet plummy fruit with glossy tannin & gentle acid support for good drinkability. No **20.**

★★★★ **Grenache** ⊛ Exceptional **22** ★★★★★ (94), from own grapes, enchants with rose, black cherry & plum notes in seductive velvet tannins. Year in large oak gives texture & structure without wood flavour. Beautifully dry. Also-tasted **20** (89), from Piekenierskloof, cooler toned & red fruited, with chalky tannins & spice from 18 months in 20% new oak. No **21.**

★★★★ **Pinot Noir** ⊘ ⊛ Earth, mushrooms, brambleberries, **22** ★★★★★ (92) a walk in the forest. Fine-boned structure aided by 10 months in barrel, 25% new, just the faintest grip on the juicy raspberry finish. Step up on last **18** (87).

★★★★ **Jan Boland Coetzee** (NEW) ⊘ Honours estate founder, & wine & rugby legend. Charming cab franc-led blend **20** (87), with dashes merlot & cab (29/20), 18 months in old oak, adding perfume & elegance to the light-footed raspberry & plum fruit.

★★★★ **Kallista** Refined & classic Cape Bordeaux, **20** ★★★★☆ ⑩ cab & cab franc (54/29) with merlot, judiciously raised in older oak for 12 months, further 12 in mix old & 50% new, adding layers of baking spice, cedar & pencil shavings. Lovely Old World feel improves on last **17** ⑱.

★★★★ **Rosé** ⊘ Grenache & mourvèdre seasoned with spicy shiraz for **23** ⑱. Dry, crisp melon & berries shot through with lively acid, upping the refreshment value. Last was **20** ★★★★ ⑧.

★★★★☆ **Chardonnay** Bunch-pressed **21** ⑭ so fine & ethereal, it seems fashioned from air. Just 10% new wood, 10 months, lends depth to lime pithiness & extends steely mineral length. Also-tasted **22** ⑫, 15% new oak & touch toastier, broader, a cream nuance accompanying the citrus. No **19**, **20**.

Unwooded Chardonnay ★★★★ Pithy, lifted **23** ⑧, pure & streamlined pear & lemon drop flavours for elegant lunchtimes. Discontinued: **Pinotage, Grenache-Shiraz-Mourvèdre.** — ML

Location/map: Stellenbosch ▪ Map grid reference: F7 ▪ WO: Stellenbosch/Piekenierskloof ▪ Est 1980 ▪ 1stB 1981 ▪ Tasting & sales: please phone to confirm opening times ▪ Fee R150 ▪ Closed all pub hols ▪ Cellar tours by appt ▪ Owner(s) Landgoed Vriesenhof (Pty) Ltd ▪ Winemaker(s) Adam Mason ▪ 85% red 15% white ▪ PO Box 155 Stellenbosch 7599 ▪ info@vriesenhof.co.za ▪ www.vriesenhof.co.za ▪ **T +27 (0)21-880-0284**

Vriesenhuijs Wines

From his Durbanville base, founder and curator Ian Vries works with select winemakers to source bottlings that exemplify the variety, style and flavour of their particular area to add to his Vriesenhuijs Collection. A lightish Stellenbosch pinotage and mature Paardeberg syrah are the first of 'many more regional treasures'.

Reserve range

★★★★ **Pinotage** Showing varietal typicity, blueberries, hint of banana, **22** ⑱ has appealing luscious texture, the tannins in support, allowing the fruit to shine. Has purity & elegance (12.5% alc).

Syrah ★★★★ Something unusual, release of an older vintage, **17** ⑧ has Swartland's ripeness & depth, the dark-toned brambly fruit upscaled by dry scrub & peppery spice. Tannins amenable, lipsmacking succulence, lifting freshness for current enjoyment. — CR, CvZ

Location: Durbanville ▪ WO: Swartland/Stellenbosch ▪ Est 2015 ▪ 1stB 2017 ▪ Closed to public ▪ Owner(s) Ian Vries (founder & curator) ▪ 3 Edwards Str, Vygeboom 7550 ▪ orders@vriesenhuijswines.co.za ▪ vriesenhuijswines.co.za

☐ **Vry Burgher** *see* Group CDV
☐ **King Vusani** *see* House of Mandela

Vuurberg

Renovations are taking place at the boutique cellar on Netherlander Sebastiaan Klaassen's steep-sloped estate in Banhoek Valley, under the eye of celebrated Donovan Rall, cellarmaster since 2010. During his tenure, Donovan has produced only two wines here, a consistently excellent red and white blend, from grapes from own vines supplemented with fruit from around and beyond Stellenbosch. Now there's the possibility of a chenin returning to the line-up in the next few years, alongside a carbernet franc. The house style remains natural wines that are textured and generous but also fresh and focused, for cellaring.

★★★★☆ **Reserve Red** Generous & inky **20** ⑨ ups cab & petit verdot to 95%, drops cinsaut from **19** ⑨'s 13% to 5%, giving a richer, riper & chewier profile, the dark fruit raised 18 months in older oak for layers of spice. 15% alc well integrated. Own & Swartland grapes, as White. Worth keeping good few years.

★★★★★ **White** Usual chenin-led combo with 12% viognier, equal portions 3 others in **22** ★★★★★ ⑭. Enticing seashell & ocean spray notes over yellow plums & peaches, 10% new oak, 20 months, lightly embraces the sweetly ripe fruit & its tingly acid. 8% saw no new oak.— ML

Location/map: Stellenbosch ▪ Map grid reference: H4 ▪ WO: Coastal ▪ Tasting, sales & cellar tours by appt ▪ Closed all pub hols ▪ Owner(s) Sebastiaan Klaassen ▪ Cellarmaster(s) Donovan Rall ▪ Winemaker(s) Donovan Rall (Oct 2010) ▪ 8ha (cabs s/f, malbec, merlot, p verdot, chenin, viog) ▪ 3,000cs own label 40% red 60% white ▪ PO Box 449 Stellenbosch 7599 ▪ info@vuurberg.co.za ▪ www.vuurberg.co.za ▪ **T +27 (0)72-182-7571**

Waboomsrivier Winery

A challenging past year for these mostly bulk-wine-focused Breedekloof shareholder-growers and their team, with a reduced crop, personnel changes and fire damage to the offices and visitor venue. On the plus side, a new solar array helps with power outages; the cellar, described as 'a leader in its use of technology', continues to produce the aimed-for 'fresh and fruity' wines; and public tastings will resume asap.

Wagenboom range

Pinotage ⓥ ★★★ Supple tannin & year in oak hold juicy plums & dark berries in check, giving **20** ⑧⓪ both a structure for food pairing & succulence to savour fireside. **Pinotage-Shiraz** ⊘ ★★★ Sappy **NV** ⑧② blend in which plum dominates fragrant dark berry, woodsmoke laces the caramelised, punchy palate (14.6% alc). **Sauvignon Blanc** ⊘ ★★★ Ripe tropical body nicely balanced with grass, green apple & lime notes in fresh, dry **23** ⑧② summer sipper. **Wit Muskadel** ⓥ ★★ Fortified dessert wine changes from hanepoot to muscadel in **21** ⑦④, retains charming pineapple & papaya flavours but not enough spirit zing to be truly moreish. Not tasted: **Arborea**, **Cape Vintage**. In abeyance: **Cabernet Sauvignon-Shiraz**.

3L Bag-in-Box range

Kaapse Wit ☺ ★★★ Fresh & floral **23** ⑧② chenin blanc bursts with sun-ripe fruit, has loads of everyday drinking appeal. Offers incredible value, too. — DS

Location: Worcester ▪ Map/WO: Breedekloof ▪ Map grid reference: A3 ▪ Est 1949 ▪ Tasting & sales Mon-Fri 9-5 (tasting to resume on completion of new tasting room) ▪ Closed all pub hols ▪ Cellar tours by appt only ▪ Cellarmaster(s) Bennie Wannenburg (Sep 2005-Aug 2023) ▪ Winemaker(s) To be appointed; assistant winemaker Lara Prins (Nov 2016) ▪ 934.33ha ▪ 15,289t ▪ ISO 22000:2018 ▪ PO Box 24 Breërivier 6858 ▪ sales@ wabooms.co.za ▪ www.waboomsrivier.com ▪ **T +27 (0)23-355-1730**

Wade Bales Wine Co ⓠ

Constantia based and well established, Wade Bales is a specialist wine merchant who sources fine wines from producers and sells them directly to private clients, adding the convenience of buying wine monthly through membership of his Wade Bales Wine Club. Wade is also a negociant, bottling and marketing exclusive and limited-release wines under his Regional and Winemaker Selection labels.

Wade Bales Regional Series

★★★★★ **Stellenbosch Cabernet Sauvignon** ⓥ Effortlessly suave & sleek multi-producer blend, **19** ⑨⑤ as stellar as last. Deep, enticing fruit harmoniously knit with tannin & oak, just 40% new, French. Firm but not overbearing structure from 15 months in barrel. Excellent density & concentration.

★★★★☆ **Breedekloof Chenin Blanc** ⓐ Six wineries combine to create **22** ⑨③, which includes fruit from a 1982 vineyard. Vinification differs from **21** ★★★★★ ⑨⑤, this bunch pressed, naturally fermented in older oak & lees aged 9 months. Harmonious, succulent, but not quite as complex, the baked apple, earth & brioche flavours more demure.

★★★★☆ **Franschhoek Semillon** ⓝⒺⓦ ⓐ In a unique collaboration, 4 producers each contribute one of their best barrels for very elegant, understated **21** ⑨③. Subtle starfruit, delicate white blossom & honey, a vibrant thread of acid binding incipient flavours. Tightly knit in youth, greater rewards with time.

★★★★★ **Constantia White** ⓐ Was 'Sauvignon Blanc-Semillon'. Same varieties in **22** ★★★★★ ⑨④'s 69/31 blend from 7 winegrowers, touch riper than **21** ⑨⑤, still shows area's hallmark cooler nuance in greengage & kiwi fruit, honey & beeswax a subtle contribution from old oak. Some minerality & a lovely freshness melded into a refined offering that would grace a table & be worth cellaring.— MW

Location: Constantia ▪ Map: Cape Peninsula ▪ Map grid reference: B3 ▪ WO: Stellenbosch/Breedekloof/ Constantia/Franschhoek ▪ Est 1992 ▪ Tasting & sales Mon-Fri 8.30-5 ▪ Closed all pub hols ▪ Wine club ▪ Owner(s) Wade Bales ▪ 15,000cs own label ▪ Private Bag X2 Constantia 7848 ▪ info@wadebales.co.za ▪ www. wadebales.co.za ▪ **T +27 (0)21-794-2151**

☐ **Wade Bales Winemaker Selection** *see* Wade Bales Wine Co
☐ **Wagenboom** *see* Waboomsrivier Winery

Walker Bay Estate ⓠ ⓜ ⊙ ⓐ ⓑ

On the cool, maritime slope overlooking Stanford town, where vines and barrels share space with family meals and bottles of craft beer, winemaker-viticulturist Anneke Steenkamp and the team have decided to display their most-planted varieties in a fruitier, lighter new line-up named for the small Welsh town where two of the winery owners met and became engaged. In both ranges, Anneke aims for balance, finesse and elegance, by picking optimally ripe, handling the fruit softly and ageing on the lees for as long as possible.

Estate range

★★★★ **Cabernet Sauvignon** Like Syrah, **22** ⑧⑥ only older oak, 18 months, well-crafted & -poised at moderate 13% alc, with ripe, almost compote black & blue fruit. Preview rated tentatively. Last was **16** ⑧⑦.

★★★★ **Pinot Noir** Similar flavour profile in **22** ★★★★ ⑧⑤, maraschino cherry & earth, yet shade less confident & complex than last **19** ⑧⑥, slight stemmy nuance at the end.

★★★★ **Syrah** ⊘ Name change to reflect style tweak since last **18** ★★★★ ⑧⑤, labelled 'Shiraz'. Deeper fruit & more serious intent but not over-worked or -oaked. Decently dry **22** ⑧⑧ pre-bottling sample has black pepper detail, supple yet forming tannins, succulent & savoury end.

★★★★ **Sauvignon Blanc** Now bottled, **22** ⑧⑥ as fresh & fruity as last time. Passionfruit & cassis plus gooseberry & papaya, exciting balance between bone-dry finish, softer acid & mouthfilling 13.6% alc.

★★★★ **Pinot Noir-Chardonnay** ⑭ Dark yellow rather than usual pink, **23** ⑧⑥ tank sample one of few to pair these varieties as a white blend. Both put best foot forward: enticing lemon & lime, zingy raspberry acid, super balance.

★★★★ **Semillon-Sauvignon Blanc** Now-bottled **22** ⑧⑦ improves on tentative rating in 2023 edition. Composed & elegant, noticeable white asparagus nuance from sauvignon, gentle grip from lees ageing, richness & depth to wine's dry persistence ex 70% semillon.

Amesteca ★★★★ Five-way Cape Bordeaux, though merlot led, the cabs play bigger role in **21** ⑧③, giving satisfying dryness despite generous & sweet fruit. Tannins less defined than on varietal siblings. Year oak, 15% new. **Rosé** ★★★★ Now bottled, **22** ⑧③ from sauvignon, shiraz & petit verdot, deep orange-pink hue, candyfloss & petit four flavours & aromas, dry & ready for brunch. **Chardonnay** ★★★★ Ferment finished in older barrel for **22** ⑧⑤, perky yellow & green citrus contrast with decadent butter & cream ex 13 months on lees & full malo. Ticks the boxes for the style, some may prefer tad more freshness. Occasional release: **Red Chardonnay**. In abeyance: **Pinot Noir Rosé, Shiraz Rosé, Méthode Cap Classique**. Discontinued: **Merlot, Petit Verdot, Barrel Fermented Sauvignon Blanc, Limestone Sauvignon Blanc**.

Llyswen range ⑭

Syrah ⊘ ⑲ ★★★★ Lovely purity of red berry & hedgerow fruit on **22** ⑧⑤, quite precise tannin management (year older barrels), satisfying weight & density. Punches above its weight.

Sauvignon Blanc ★★★★ Water white, with house's cassis & blackcurrant signature, straightforward **23** ⑧③ not as complex or rich as big/older sibling but lively & ready to enjoy. — CvZ

Location: Stanford ▪ Map: Walker Bay & Bot River ▪ Map grid reference: B6 ▪ WO: Walker Bay ▪ Est 1997 ▪ 1stB 2007 ▪ Tasting & sales Mon-Sun 10-5 ▪ Tasting fee applicable ▪ Closed Dec 25 ▪ Cellar tours by appt ▪ Restaurant ▪ Facilities for children ▪ Tour groups ▪ Craft beer brewery ▪ Winemaker(s) Anneke Steenkamp (Jul 2021) ▪ Viticulturist(s) Anneke Steenkamp (Jul 2021), mentored by Theo Brink ▪ 300ha/24ha (cab, merlot, p verdot, pinot, shiraz, chard, sauv, sem) ▪ 100t/14,000cs own label 40% red 60% white ▪ PO Box 530 Stanford 7210 ▪ walkerbayvineyards@birkenhead.co.za ▪ www.walkerbayestate.com ▪ **T +27 (0)28-341-0013**

☐ **Wallace Brothers** see Off The Record Wines

Wandering Cellars ♀

After 30 years in Silicon Valley, Bill Thompson 'finally figured out what I want to do when I grow up': roll up his sleeves and handcraft thimblefuls of eco-friendly wine around the world. In the Cape, he and wife Chris base themselves at Overgaauw in Stellenbosch, where the grapes for their new release are from.

Cabernet Franc ⑭ ★★★ Rum-&-raisin scented **21** ⑧② is big, bold & densely fruited with glacé plums, mouthcoating tannins, commendable dry finish. **Chenin Blanc** ⑲ ★★★★ Several micro ferments for **22** ⑧③ from Bottelary vines, old 350L & 400L barrels, small demijohns, aged on lees with regular stirring. Attractive white peach & quince flavours, noticeable oak flavour. Boutique ±150 cases of each wine. — CvZ

Location: Stellenbosch ▪ WO: Stellenbosch/Bottelary ▪ Est 2015 ▪ 1stB 2020 ▪ Tasting, sales & cellar tours by appt ▪ Closed all pub hols ▪ Owner(s)/winemaker(s) Bill & Chris Thompson ▪ Cellarmaster(s) Bill Thompson ▪ 300cs own label 40% red 60% white ▪ bill@wanderingcellars.com ▪ www.wanderingcellars.com ▪ **T +1 612 817 0630 WhatsApp**

Warwick Wine Estate

The title deed for this prime Simonsberg-Stellenbosch foothills land was issued in 1771. It was only in the 1960s that Stan and Norma Ratcliffe introduced vines to the farm, today known as Warwick, producing acclaimed wines from 1983. Under owners Charles Marston and Kishore Bopardikar of San Francisco investment company Eileses Capital since 2017, exports have expanded to markets such as Tanzania, Kenya, Australia and Spain. Focus at home is replanting virused vines with clean ones. 'Leading varieties, cabernets sauvignon and franc form the majority,' confirms winemaker JD Pretorius, 'with a little merlot and chardonnay.' If cabernet franc is mentioned as the farm's calling card, JD confirms site is 90% of its success. 'It's warm enough to achieve ripeness with true varietal character before it becomes over-ripe and porty.'

Site Specific range

★★★★☆ **Blue Lady Cabernet Sauvignon** 🏵 Classic Simonsberg dark fruit & muscular flesh on **20** ⑨③, all underscored by resilient tannins & freshness necessary for lengthy ageing. Barriques, 38% new, 22 months perfect complement.

★★★★★ **Cabernet Franc** 🏵 One of SA's earliest varietal bottlings & regularly awarded since 1988. **20** ★★★★★ ⑨③ fine & precise, fresh plum & spice flavours delicate & encased in dense tannin weave. Tad less rich than **19** ⑨⑥ but so well balanced, time will reveal its undoubted promise. Oak, 35% new, 22 months.

★★★★☆ **Trilogy** 🏵 Cab franc (50%) shines through **20** ⑨④ with its energy, spice intensity; partners, cab (44%) & merlot, provide shoulder & ripe flesh, creating a trilogy of refinement & class. Oak, 43% new, beneficial accessory.

★★★★★ **White Lady Chardonnay** 🏵 Pure yet complex array of ripe citrus, toasted nuts & lees-enriched texture, fine acid seam lengthens, binds **22** ★★★★★ ⑨③ into complete, elegant whole. Burgundy 228L barrels, 33% new, 10 months - similar regime to **21** ⑨⑤ - adds further class. From home farm, 3 other Stellenbosch sites.

Heritage Wines

★★★★☆ **Three Cape Ladies** Change of blend, style in **21** ★★★★ ⑧⑥. Pinotage now partnered with merlot 22% for some fruity flesh, cab 17% firming structure (previous included cab franc). Ripe, good freshness to balance but lacks depth of **20** ⑨④, hint bitterness in grippy tannins. WO Stellenbosch.

★★★★☆ **Old Vine Chenin Blanc** 🏵 1978 vines offer delicate pear & earthy tones woven into gentle silkiness. Precision & a dry, lengthy conclusion are ensured by quiet yet effective acid. **22** ⑨⓪ harmonious but less concentration, depth than last. Wholebunch press; natural ferment in older oak.

In abeyance: **Black Lady Cinsault**.

Professor Black range

★★★★☆ **Pitch Black** ⊘ Strong cab presence in **21** ⑨⓪ donates cedar, graphite & chain mail tannins. Partners merlot, cab franc & cinsaut play important bit parts, bring a lightness of touch & spice, also necessary flesh. Enjoyable now & better built than **20** ★★★★ ⑧⑦ for medium term. 12% new oak, year. WO Stellenbosch.

★★★★☆ **Sauvignon Blanc** ⊘ Plenty of drama on **23** ⑨⓪: pungent figgy, tropical aromas, a scythe of steely acid concluding emphatically dry with great length. Lees ageing forges harmony & weight, which should allow for further few years. Big improvement on **22** ★★★★ ⑧⑤.

First Lady range

Cabernet Sauvignon ★★★☆ Appeals with sweet blackberry flesh, energy & lively, fine tannins, all assembled for youthful enjoyment. **22** ⑧⑤ can also go a few years. 12 months oak, 12% new. **Pinotage** ★★★☆ With splash cinsaut, **22** ⑧⑤ fresh & fruity style for youthful enjoyment, also has structure. The spicy red berries are juicy & sweet, & backed by tangy grape tannin. Oak, 8% new, year. **Rosé** ★★★☆ Lightish & sprightly, spiced wild strawberry flavours linger well on roundly dry finish. **23** ⑧⑤ from Swartland pinotage. 11.5% alc. **Chardonnay** ★★★☆ Fullish **23** ⑧⑤, tasted ex tank, has ripe citrus flavours, firm dryness. Lees ageing, tiny portion oak-ferment, add spice & breadth. **Sauvignon Blanc** ★★★ Confident ripe tropical & fig flavours, bright fruity acids tempered by a little sweetness on ex-tank **23** ⑧②. WO W Cape for these. — AL

Location/map: Stellenbosch ▪ Map grid reference: F1 ▪ WO: Simonsberg-Stellenbosch/Western Cape/ Stellenbosch ▪ Est 1964 ▪ 1stB 1983 ▪ Tasting & sales daily 9-5; pub hols (seasonal) please call ahead ▪ Cellar tours by appt ▪ Vineyard safari ▪ Gourmet picnics in summer; à la carte winter menu ▪ Facilities for children ▪ Furry friends welcome ▪ Gifts ▪ Club Warwick ▪ Owner(s) Charles Marston & Kishore Bopardikar ▪ CEO

Christiane von Arnim ▪ Winemaker(s) JD Pretorius (May 2019) & Estelle Lourens (May 2018) ▪ Viticulturist(s) Marko Roux ▪ 65ha (cabs s/f, merlot, ptage, chard, chenin, sauv) ▪ 700t/300,000cs own label 60% red 40% white ▪ IPW, WIETA, WWF-SA Conservation Champion ▪ PO Box 2 Elsenburg 7607 ▪ info@warwickwine.com ▪ www.warwickwine.com ▪ T +27 (0)21-884-4410

Waterford Estate

IT businessman Jeremy Ord and his wife Leigh brought a fresh perspective on winelands architecture in the late 1990s when they drew inspiration from Tuscany rather than Cape vernacular for their splendid winery on the Helderberg foothills. A visitor-friendly destination, it offers dining at chef Craig Cormack's Salt Restaurant in the impressive central fountain courtyard, safaris on an authentic game-viewing 4x4, mountain trail picnics and a variety of winetasting options. While cabernet has been their calling card, many other grapes appear across the varietal wines and in the blends, including ones sourced off-site, all vinified the past 15 years by Mark le Roux, laterly as cellarmaster and COO. The Library range showcases experimental bottlings.

Waterford Estate range

★★★★☆ **Cabernet Sauvignon** Statuesque **19** (94) returns to form after lighter **18** ★★★★ (89). Classically styled, seriously oaked, lean & muscular, with delightful earthy core, rich cassis alongside hints of cocoa & tar. Everything cab should be. Needs time for full expression, but worth the wait.

★★★★ **Grenache Noir** Juicy & sweet-berry fruity, **21** (87) light & supple, with gently cosseting tannin. 60% spent 16 months in old barrels, rest in porcelain. Young, vibrant, yet structured to improve.

★★★★★ **The Jem** Aspirational flagship blend, cab & shiraz with 6 others, **16** ★★★★★ (94) is youthful & muscular yet supple, complex, with densely packed black fruit wrapped in massive, leathery tannins. Highlights of oak spice, aromatic tobacco & iodine add to appeal. 21 months in 30% new small barrels, as Cabernet. One for the long road, as with **15** (96). Also in larger bottle formats.

★★★★ **Single Vineyard Chardonnay** Textured & mineral, **20** ★★★★★ (90) from official single-vineyard (as Grenache) planted 1988 shows generous but understated citrus fruit, subtle oak nuance from 11 months in 12% new barrels. Refined & taut, has good potential. **19** (88) similar but less intense.

Library Collection

★★★★★ **Sangiovese** (NEW) Plush & savoury, with sun-dried tomato highlights, **18** (91) evokes the hills of Chianti, showing dark cherries, earthy minerality & hints of leather & rosepetal. Ripe powdery tannins add texture & muscle. Complementary 19 months in mostly seasoned barrels.

★★★★☆ **Sonop Chenin** (NEW) Very special chenin from venerable 1966 vines, **20** (93) complex, expressive, unencumbered by oak (90% raised in concrete 'egg'), allowing intensely honeyed fruit to shine. Succulent & textured, with mineral salty twist in extended finish.

Occasional release: **Barbera**, **Cabernet Sauvignon #1**, **Cabernet Sauvignon #2**, **Petit Verdot**.

Waterford range

★★★★★ **Kevin Arnold Shiraz** Supple, athletic style in **19** (92) eschews muscle for elegance, with charming scrub, aromatic tobacco & raw meat laced into wholesome black cherry fruit. 6% mourvèdre, reined-in oaking - 22 months, older barrels - add focus & linearity. Also in 1.5L.

★★★★ **Antigo** Less serious take on classic Bordeaux blend, **20** (87) is 79% cab with merlot, cab franc. Fruity, sleek & elegant, with convincing currants & plums, deliciously ripe tannins. 20 months in barrel, 20% new, add spice & aromatic notes.

★★★★☆ **Chenin Blanc** Rich & creamy **22** (91) has delightfully typical Stellenbosch yellow stone-fruit borne on satin-textured lees. Lithe, with gentle acid, showing honey, floral & white nut highlights. No oak this vintage (last-made **20** (91) had 15%): fermented & aged in concrete 'eggs'.

★★★★ **Elgin Sauvignon Blanc** Bold & assertive **22** (88) has khaki bush pungency & overt granadilla fruit, evolving to sweetly ripe, textured palate with herbaceous highlights. Vivid acid & lingering aftertaste up the attraction.

★★★★☆ **Méthode Cap Classique Brut** Classy, poised & richly textured from 7 years on lees, **15** (94) chardonnay shows lively acid & gentle, fine bead, refreshing lime minerality & just-baked brioche. Drinking beautifully now, could be cellared a few years.

★★★★ **Heatherleigh** From 55% muscat d'Alexandrie with chardonnay, viognier & chenin, **NV** ⑧⑨ vine-dried Natural Sweet has typical muscat spice, honey & charm. Full-sweet at 96 g/L sugar yet uncloying, courtesy nicely balanced acid, clean finish. 18 month in older barrels. 375 ml.

Rose-Mary ★★★ Multinational array of varieties in **23** ⑧① produces neutral but pleasantly quaffable summertime rosé. Discontinued: **Elgin Pinot Noir**.

Pecan Stream range

Pebble Hill ★★★★ Seemingly arbitrary 11-part blend, medium-bodied, smooth & juicy **21** ⑧④ delivers satisfying, easygoing everyday drinking nonetheless. **Chenin Blanc** ⊘ ★★★★ Bursting with stonefruit & pear, **22** ⑧⑤ is sunny & charming, tempered acid adding to quaffing appeal. 25% lightly oaked. WO W Cape.
Sauvignon Blanc ⊘ ★★★★ Juicy, zesty & undemanding, passionfruit & acid nicely balanced, **22** ⑧⑤ has toned-down khaki bush presence, clean finish. Mostly Elgin grapes. — GdB

Location/map: Stellenbosch ▪ Map grid reference: F8 ▪ WO: Stellenbosch/Western Cape/Elgin ▪ Est/1stB 1998 ▪ Tasting, sales & cellar tours Mon-Sun 10-5; pub hols 10-5 (seasonal) please call ahead ▪ Tasting fees: R150/portfolio; R135/chocolate; R185/Experience; R150/The Jem (current vintage only); R790/wine walk & R1,760/wine drive, pre-booking essential ▪ Closed Dec 25 & Jan 1 ▪ SALT Restaurant lunch Tue-Sun 11.30-3 ▪ Wine & salt food pairing Tue-Sun 11.30-3 ▪ Tea, coffee, soft drinks & chocolates ▪ Olive oil ▪ Wine club ▪ Owner(s) Jeremy & Leigh Ord ▪ COO & cellarmaster Mark le Roux (Jul 2009) ▪ Viticulturist(s) David van Schalkwyk (Jun 2014) ▪ 120ha/60ha (barbera, cabs s/f, grenache, malbec, merlot, mourv, p verdot, sangio, shiraz, tempranillo, chard); 27.3ha conserved land ▪ 550t/54,000cs own label 70% red 30% white ▪ WWF-SA Conservation Champion ▪ PO Box 635 Stellenbosch 7599 ▪ info@waterfordestate.co.za ▪ www.waterfordestate.co.za ▪ **T +27 (0)21-880-5300**

Waterkloof   ⑪ ⑤

Briton Paul Boutinot bought Waterkloof just over two decades ago, and has led its development into one of the Cape's top estates, with 90 ha of vines, farmed according to biodynamic principles and a regenerative approach by a team headed by veteran Christiaan Loots, and cellar on windswept Schapenberg Hill overlooking False Bay, where Nadia Langenegger has crafted wine in minimal-intervention fashion since 2009. Officially winemaker since 2013, she's introduced 'evolutionary rather than revolutionary' changes, notably foot-treading of the grapes for gentler extraction, a labour of love given there are 20 fermenters to work through. The visitor venue beside the cellar has closed for public tastings, its glass-walled, spectacularly cantilevered space now occupied by Chorus fine-dining restaurant and lounge headed by chef Bertus Basson.

Waterkloof range

★★★★☆ **Syrah** ⑧ ⑨ First red under this label, ex single block. Elegant & pure, supple textured, **20** ⑨③'s light touch & fine tannin ensure smooth flow & lingering savouriness. Delicious cool-climate wine.
★★★★☆ **Boreas** 🆕 ⑨ 🐝 4-way Cape Bordeaux from best parcels of mainly cab franc with merlot, petit verdot & cab, **20** ⑨④ strides confidently onto the stage with inky blackcurrant fruit from very low-yield vines (2 t/ha) lifted with perfume & dried rosemary & thyme. Firm grip of tannin supported by vanilla oak, 10% new, excellent acid & endless finish.
★★★★☆ **Chenin Blanc** ⑨ Quiet, steely **22** ★★★★ ⑧⑨ shows fine intensity from low-crop vines in gravelly mouthful of appleskin, peach stone & herbal honey. Wild ferment in barrel, 10% new, adds texture, as do 10 months on lees, but missing clean vibrancy of **21** ⑨⓪.
★★★★☆ **Sauvignon Blanc** ⑨ 🐝 From single block of old low-harvest vines, exceptional **22** ★★★★★ ⑨⑤ delivers elegance & finesse along with concentration of fruit - a melange of peach & pear, tangy nettle & pea. Wholebunch wild ferment in old, large oak plus 10 months on lees all add layers of texture, taste & interest, lengthening the absorbing finish. **21** ⑨① in less-fruity style.

Circle of Life range

★★★★☆ **Red** ⑧ Tasted ex barrel & provisionally rated, **20** ⑨② intrigues with spices & wild herbs, underpinned by soft, dark berries & freshening fine tannins. Blended to reflect farm's terroir: syrah, cab franc, merlot & petit verdot. Small/larger oak, 10% new, 17 months vs 32 months for **19** ★★★★★ ⑨⑥.
★★★★☆ **White** ⊘ 🐝 Over-delivering **22** ⑨③ sees sauvignon & chenin, 10% semillon combine to create complete & satisfying glassful of apple, pineapple, quince & fresh herbs. Creamy oatmeal texture from oak, 15% new, long evolving finish.

Seriously Cool range
★★★★ Chenin Blanc ⊘ Strong minerality on **22** ⑧⑥ from old bushvines. Apple & pear palate tingles with acid, shows texture from time in old oak & concrete 'egg', finish slightly warmed by 14% alc.

Cinsault ★★★☆ Sappy, snappy **22** ⑧③ offers bright red-cherry confection & attractive herbal whiffs. Part semi-carbonic ferment & old-oak ageing add complexity to slightly short finish.

Circumstance range
★★★★ Cabernet Sauvignon Refined **20** ⑧⑦ shows cool-climate origin in fragrant blackcurrant tone. Firm tannin, smoky tobacco from oak, 10% new, complete restrained rather than rich, ripe wine.

★★★★ Cabernet Franc ⊘ Wholebunch ferment for **21** ⑧⑧ gives spicy freshness but also slightly astringent tannins, offset by polished black cherry & berry fruit. Vanilla from oak, 11% new, add dimension to bold wine, needing time to fully knit (like **20**, still ageing at cellar).

★★★★ Merlot ⑳ ⊘ Big but with sound acid spine to focus strong dark plum, cassis fruit & oak spice (11% new). **18** ⑧⑦'s structure also in tune, needs time to settle, harmonise.

★★★★☆ Mourvèdre ⊘ Perfectly suited to windy conditions, variety thrives on stony slopes as bushvines, giving meaty mouthful with cooked plum & blackberry fruit in **20** ⑨⓪. Slight wild herbal note, fresh acid & well-managed tannins all create fascinating & unusual wine.

★★★★ Petit Verdot ⑳ Lively & scented **18** ⑧⑥ has silky feel, sweet fruit lifted & lengthened by easy freshness. Nip of fine tannin no barrier to current enjoyment.

★★★★☆ Syrah ⊘ 🐝 Huge peppery aromas on **21** ⑨⓪ aided by wholebunch ferment, also giving silk texture. Dark chocolate & salami vie with ripe black plums & slightly stalky tannins. Needs time & food but should get there. 24 months in old 600L barrels. **20** held back for ageing.

★★★★ Chenin Blanc ⊘ Ripeness & restraint unusual bedfellows but **22** ⑧⑨ effortlessly tames glossy apple & pineapple fruit by adding subtle creamy spice from barrel ferment, all carried through to finish by lively acid in thoroughly enjoyable wine.

★★★★ Sauvignon Blanc Fermented in large old oak with wild yeasts, **22** ⑧⑥ isn't your normal sauvignon, yet subtle cooked quince & pear notes, & well-integrated acid create a fine, balanced & flavourful vintage.

★★★★ Viognier ⊘ Showing house's signature reserve, **22** ⑧⑨ is supple & balanced yet not short of varietal apricot & ginger, white blossoms & touch of talc. Just-dry finish rounds off an elegant expression.

Cape Coral Mourvèdre Rosé ⑳ **★★★** Delicate blush on **22** ⑧②, the dry, savoury flavours smooth & long. Versatile aperitif, food partner. In abeyance: **Chardonnay**.

Astraeus range
★★★★ Méthode Cap Classique Reserve Pinot Noir Organically farmed Elgin grapes (as sibling) create a light-hued **NV** ⑧⑧, heady & perfumed with red appleskin & toasty biscuit. Lively mousse, delicate texture, perfect for a seafood feast. 9 months on lees in old oak, 11 months in bottle.

★★★★☆ Méthode Cap Classique Reserve Chardonnay Brut Extra attention shows in notch-up **NV** ⑨⓪, classic mix of apple & fresh lemon, creamy biscuit & marzipan. Touch of richness from 15% **09** MCC & 2 years on lees. Bone-dryness rounds off exciting, elegant & savoury wine with long future.— CM

Location: Somerset West ▪ WO: Stellenbosch/Elgin/Western Cape ▪ Est 2003 ▪ 1stB 2005 ▪ Tasting lounge closed ▪ Online wine sales; retail sales through warehouse ▪ Wine club ▪ Chorus restaurant open for lunch Tue-Sun & dinner Thu-Sat; email info@chorusrestaurant.com to book your table ▪ Owner(s) Paul Boutinot ▪ Cellarmaster(s)/winemaker(s) Nadia Langenegger (Jan 2013) ▪ Viticulturist(s) Christiaan Loots (Jan 2010) ▪ 189ha/90ha (cabs s/f, grenache, merlot, mourv, p verdot, shiraz, chenin, sauv, sem, viog) ▪ 450t/20,000cs own label 50% red 45% white 5% rosé ▪ Ecocert organic, IPW, WIETA, WWF-SA Conservation Champion ▪ PO Box 2093 Somerset West 7129 ▪ info@waterkloofwines.co.za ▪ www.waterkloofwines.co.za ▪ **T +27 (0)21-858-1292**

Waterleliefontein
Jo and Tessa Neser's Bot River farm Waterleliefontein is planted mostly with olives, but the tiny blocks of grenache noir and syrah are the realisation of a cherished dream to make a Rhône-style blend. Proportions may vary from year to year, but growing and making only one wine, 'as naturally as possible', remains the goal.

★★★★☆ **Shiraz-Grenache Noir** Reverses the blend in **20 ★★★★** ⑧⑨ with shiraz (58%) to the fore, giving meaty, spicy succulence over **19** ⑨①'s brighter profile. Charry smoke from 11 months old oak surrounds sweet black cherry fruit, 40% wholebunch adding to juicy overall appeal.— CM

Location: Bot River ▪ Map: Walker Bay & Bot River ▪ Map grid reference: D2 ▪ WO: Walker Bay ▪ Est 1996 ▪ 1stB 2019 ▪ Tasting by appt only ▪ Owner(s) Waterleliefontein (Pty) Ltd - shareholders Jo & Tessa Neser ▪ Winemaker(s) Albert van Niekerk (Jan 2019, consultant) ▪ Viticulturist(s) Johan Hugo (Nov 2014, consultant) ▪ ±45ha/3ha (grenache, shiraz) ▪ 14t/800cs own label 100% red ▪ PO Box 124 Botriver 7185 ▪ jo.neser@icloud.com ▪ www.waterleliefontein.co.za ▪ **T +27 (0)82-577-3199**

☐ **Waterlily** *see* Bloemendal Wine Estate
☐ **Waterval Single Vineyards** *see* JC Wickens Wines

Waverley Hills Organic Wines & Olives

These characterful bottlings, many with long ageing in barrel and/or bottle at cellar for suave texture and buffed tannins, and including SA's first commercial marselan, are certified organic and grown near Wolseley on a conservation- and sustainability-minded family estate with 2,000 ha of mountain reserve - its sea of fynbos mirrored in what cellarmaster Johan Delport characterises as a 'robust garrigue' top note in the wines.

Premium range

★★★★ **Grenache** Bursts with red berry fruit, laced with earthy & floral hints, all finely balanced. **18 ★★★★☆** ⑨⓪, with drop mourvèdre, fresh & supple, silky. Tops charming **17** ⑧⑨.

★★★★☆ **Marselan** 2nd edition of only SA bottling of this cab-grenache noir cross, **21 ★★★★** ⑧⑧ lighter, fruitier than **20** ⑨⓪, offers strawberry & blackberry fruit, sappy acid & juicy length. With modest 12.3% alc, makes ideal summer drinking. 13 months 2nd-fill oak.

★★★★☆ **CW Reserve Shiraz** Powerful & muscular **18** ⑨③ handles 46 months in new oak with aplomb, adds vanilla & smoke to dense blackcurrant fruit, topped off with lashings of liquorice, pepper, smoked meat & spice. Firm tannins suggest plenty more to come.

★★★★ **De Huijsbosch** Bordeaux blend of 50% cab, equal cab franc & merlot, 27 months in barriques, 50% new. **19** ⑧⑥ solid black fruit tinged with mint, full, ripe tannins.

★★★★ **Shiraz-Mourvèdre-Viognier** Return to form for **17** ⑧⑦ after oaky **16 ★★★★** ⑧③. Melange of black & red plums & cherries with spice & pepper fragrance. Co-fermented red grapes spent remarkable 65 months in oak, 50% new, before being freshened with unwooded viognier.

★★★★ **Chardonnay** Thoroughly steeped in oak after barrel ferment & 2 years ageing, **19** ⑧⑥ has nutty overtone with burnt butter, citrus fruit compote, nutmeg & clove on lees-rich texture.

Grenache Rosé ★★★★ Characterful salmon-hued **20** ⑧⑤ avoids the strawberry cliché, offers ripe, evolved stonefruit & steely minerality. **Méthode Cap Classique Brut** ★★★★ From chardonnay, **19** ⑧⑤ pithy apple fruit, delicate mousse, vibrant acid. Resolutely dry, with prominent yeastiness.

Estate range

★★★★ **Shiraz** Well-judged, harmonious **18** ⑧⑦ shows black cherry fruit, mixed spices, smooth tannins with firm acidity & lingering finish. 17 months in older small barrels. Step up from **17 ★★★★** ⑧⑤.

Pinotage ★★★ Light, unconcentrated **19** ⑦⑦ shows minty notes on red berry fruit. **Cabernet Sauvignon-Shiraz** ★★★ Undemanding, medium-bodied **21** ⑧② has forward red berry fruit, mild toffee-vanilla spicing, light tannins. **Pinot Grigio** ★★★★ Returns with **22** ⑧④ preview after skipping a vintage. Now totally dry, with bracing acidity, lean & fresh, food friendly. **Sauvignon Blanc-Semillon** ★★★ Trim & grassy **21** ⑧② offers gooseberry & green apple fruit, prominent acid. Light & crisp, for early drinking.

No Added Sulphites range

Cabernet Sauvignon ★★★ Redolent of caramel toffee with medicinal nuance in **21** ⑦⑨. — CM
Location/map/WO: Tulbagh ▪ Map grid reference: G6 ▪ Est 2006 ▪ 1stB 2004 ▪ Tasting & cellar tours by appt ▪ Facilities for children ▪ Tour groups ▪ Conferences ▪ Wedding venue & chapel ▪ Walks/hikes ▪ Conservation area ▪ Wine club ▪ Owner(s) Waverley Hill Wines (Pty) Ltd ▪ Cellarmaster(s)/viticulturist(s) Johan Delport (Oct 2008) ▪ Winemaker(s) Lebohang Pitso (Jan 2021) ▪ 80ha/24ha (grenache, marselan, merlot, mourv, ptage, shiraz, chard, pinot gris, sauv, sem, viog) ▪ 200t/18,000cs own label 80% red 15% white 5% MCC ▪

Cape Nature Stewardship, Ecocert, WIETA, WWF-SA Conservation Champion ▪ PO Box 185 Wolseley 6830 ▪ info@waverleyhills.co.za ▪ www.waverleyhills.co.za ▪ T +27 (0)23-231-0002

Wavescape Wines

Steve Pike, Cape Town freelance journalist and surfing forecaster, and Jeremy Walker, owner-cellarmaster at Grangehurst, are the 'board members' behind this brand, seriously conceived but easy to drink, and seriously good value for money. No wines for us to taste this time, hopefully next edition we'll catch a break.

Location: Stellenbosch ▪ Est 2014 ▪ 1stB 2009 ▪ Closed to public ▪ Sales by telephone or websites ▪ Owner(s) Grangehurst Winery (Jeremy Walker) & Wavescape (Steve Pike) ▪ Cellarmaster(s) Jeremy Walker ▪ 70% red 30% white ▪ PO Box 206 Stellenbosch 7599 ▪ jeremy@grangehurst.co.za, spike.wavescape@gmail.com ▪ www.wavescape.co.za, www.grangehurst.co.za ▪ T +27 (0)21-855-3625

☐ **Weathered Hands** *see* Dewaldt Heyns Family Wines

Weather Report

'All the fine and natural details, from the root to the fruit' are what concern Christopher Keet (nephew of Chris Keet of Keet Wines). The focus of the Weather Report team - now including wife Katherine - remains on exploring cabernet franc, with new-found sites joining the roster of reporters and, coming up, the planting of their own vineyard in the Overberg. And a possible bit of divergence, as 'there may just be a white wine on the horizon.' The wines are made ('minimal intervention with maximum attention' is the mantra) at Gabriëlskloof, where Chris is viticulturist.

★★★★☆ **Flight Farm** (⚘) Cab franc bottling named for the Elgin farm that is its source. Aromatic **21** (93) shares scrubby, dried herb notes (especially rosemary) with the blended wine, but is more intense, focused & deep fruited, with firmer structure - & a little sterner in youth. 13.7% alc. No **20**.

★★★★☆ **Weather Report** Was 'Atlas'. **21** (90) adds a little cinsault to the cab franc, augmenting perfumed charm & approachability, though maintains increased depth & seriousness noted last year. Delicious & juicy, with refined tannic structure; lightish in feel despite 14.1% alc. Widely sourced fruit. These wines wholebunch ferment, 14 months in old oak, & properly bone-dry.

Not tasted: **Sands**. — TJ

Location: Bot River ▪ WO: Western Cape/Elgin ▪ Est 2018 ▪ 1stB 2019 ▪ Tasting by appt ▪ Owner(s) Christopher (jnr) & Katherine Keet ▪ Winemaker(s) Christopher Keet (Aug 2018) ▪ 12t own label 100% red ▪ chris@ weatherreport.wine ▪ www.weatherreport.wine ▪ T +27 (0)72-841-6483

Webersburg Wines

'Unhurried' has been a keyword at this portion of the venerable Helderberg farm Groenerivier, since owner and businessman Fred Weber engaged then Meerlust winemaker and Cape Bordeaux pioneer Giorgio Dalla Cia, just short of 30 years ago, to guide the creation of a premium winery. Giorgio urged time in bottle, and his advice echoes in the maturity of the current release reds, all likely to reward further cellaring. The estate, with its lovingly modernised 17th-century core, is well worth a visit and/or stay.

Family Reserve range
★★★★☆ **Shobi Cabernet Sauvignon** (⚘) Only 200 cases of **19** (94) from farm's best cab blocks. Again deserving of full new-barrel ageing, 30 months, then 12-24 in bottle. Sheathed power, less ripe than **18** (90) (13.5% alc vs 14.7), fresher & more sophisticated, youthful black fruit poised to evolve with distinction.

Webersburg range
★★★★☆ **Cabernet Sauvignon** Richer, plusher textured in **18** (90), ample dark fruit & sweet tobacco, supple tannins, increased new oak (70% vs 50%, 18 months) reins in opulence. Inviting, will charm for many more years, though less long lived than last.

★★★★ **Bastiaan Blend** Still majority cab but more merlot & petit verdot (36/25) in **19** (89). Fuller than last, respectably structured with a good concentration of cocoa-dusted dark fruit & cedar from 70% new oak, 18 months. One for the table & cellar.

Rosé ★★★ Preview of flamingo-hued **23** (82) from shiraz is piquantly fresh, crisp & dry. Perfect for sunset sipping, or to pop in the picnic basket. **Sauvignon Blanc** ★★★★ Tangy passionfruit & citrus in **23** (83), plumped by some lees breadth. Dry & easy-drinking for summer. Not tasted: **Méthode Cap Classique Brut Rosé, Méthode Cap Classique Brut**. — MW

Location/map/WO: Stellenbosch ▪ Map grid reference: E8 ▪ Est 1995 ▪ 1stB 1996 ▪ Tasting, sales & cellar tours Mon-Fri 10-5 Sat/Sun 10-4 pub hols 11-5 ▪ Closed for lunch on Mondays ▪ Bistro: breakfast 8-10.30 lunch 12-5 ▪ Tour groups ▪ Historic buildings: manor house 1786; cellar & jonkershuis 1796 ▪ 5-star Cape Dutch guest house ▪ Conferences ▪ Weddings/functions ▪ Owner(s) Fred Weber ▪ 20ha under vine ▪ 30t/4,000cs own label 80% red 20% white ▪ PO Box 3428 Somerset West 7129 ▪ info@webersburg.co.za ▪ www.webersburg. co.za ▪ **T +27 (0)21-881-3636**

Wederom Boutique Winery   (ⓦ) (🍴) (🏠) (◎)
In addition to a small vineyard, the Robertson winefarm owned by the Meyer and Viljoen families includes a wedding venue, guest houses and, fascinatingly, an on-site museum representing the Italian prisoners of war sent here as labourers during WW II, including officer Giovanni Salvadori.

Merlot (ⓦ) ★★★★ Sweet aromas of prune, milk chocolate & vanilla joined on **19** (84) palate by few grams sugar; these combine with 15 months polishing in older oak for delightful velvet softness. **Giovanni Salvadori Shiraz** (ⓦ) ★★★★ Smooth, rounded **18** (85) calls for an Italian feast with its glossy red fruit, pepper & spice. Lightly wooded for easy-drinking pleasure at moderate 13% alc. Bargain priced. — JG

Location/map/WO: Robertson ▪ Map grid reference: B7 ▪ Tasting, sales & cellar tours by appt ▪ Fee R60pp tasting/tour ▪ Meals by appt ▪ Weddings, conferences, tours ▪ Italian Prisoners of War Museum ▪ Wederom Guest House ▪ Owner(s) Meyer & Viljoen families ▪ Winemaker(s) Ferdie Viljoen ▪ 3ha (merlot, shiraz) ▪ IPW ▪ Goree Rd Robertson 6705 ▪ info@wederom.co.za, bookings@wederom.co.za ▪ www.wederom.co.za ▪ **T +27 (0)23-626-4139**

Welbedacht Wine Estate   (ⓦ) (🍴) (◎) (👤) (♿)
Originally part of the farm Driefontein, Welbedacht ('Well Thought Out') in the Wellington ward of Groenberg, is owned by one of SA's best-known rugby families, the Burgers. Son, general manager and marketer Tiaan is impressed and gratified by what 'genuine artisan winemaker' Christiaan Nigrini has achieved in the short time since starting to work in the on-site cellar, custom built 'to suit our unique fruit'. Both are upbeat about the new single-site bottlings, the 'big things to come' from the 2023 crush currently in barrel, and the larger pack size for the Meerkat family of easy-drinkers, 'making them even more gregarious'.

Schalk Burger & Sons Proprietors Reserve range
★★★★✩ **No. 6** (ⓦ) Only best barrels from premium blocks for a limited release. Bold but balanced **16** (91) continues '6' theme in sextet of varieties, 2 years in oak, 20% new. Wellington WO.

Discontinued: **Myra, Mon René**.

Single Vineyard range (NEW)
★★★★ **Bakleiblok Cinsault** Appealing example of SA's lighter-style reds. **22** (87) orange zest & piquant berries, sweet fruit, stemmy tug on the finish. 12.2% alc. From 32 year old vines, pride of the vineyard team.

Skoolblok Chenin Blanc ★★★★ Delicate but promising **23** (85) rather reserved, with faint peach & apple aromas & flavours. Some texture & presence from few weeks lees ageing, emphatic dryness a real treat.

Welbedacht Estate range
★★★★ **Barrique Select Pinotage** Was 'Old Bush Vine' when we tasted **18** (86). **22** ★★★★ (85) barrel sample a little old-fashioned in a comfortable, good way. Dark berries, high-toned whiff & variety's signature acid softened by smidgen sugar.

★★★★ **Cricket Pitch** Old-oak-aged (2 years) Bordeaux blend, **22** (88) preview is 42% merlot with 3 others. Similar maraschino nuance as Merlot but reined in, some orange zest. Vibrant, unforced & fresh.

★★★★ **Bohemian SMV** Last tasted in **18** (89) as 'Bohemian Syrah'. Pre-bottling & rated & provisionally, **21** ★★★★ (85) adds dabs mourvèdre & viognier. Brooding red & black fruit under veil dusty (older) oak, enlivened by tangy acid, peach stone nudge on finish. Like Pinotage, some sweetness & 14.9% alc.

★★★★ **Barrel Fermented Chenin Blanc** (ⓦ) Was 'Old Bush Vine', still is from venerable vines. **18** (86) most successful of the barrel-fermented whites. Attractive white peach & almond, oak, 15 months, none new, in supportive role.

Merlot Barrique Select ★★★☆ Generous plum & liqueur cherry ripeness of **21** (84) set in firm tannin frame, accented by subtle vanilla, mellowed by 18 months in older oak (as Pinotage). **Barrel Fermented Chardonnay** ★★★☆ Buttered popcorn, dark toast & oak spice, **18** (83)'s ferment/15 months in old oak to the fore, but seamed on the palate by intense lemon flavours, acidity. Steps lightly at 11.9% alc. **Sauvignon Banc** (NEW) ★★★☆ Peach- & blackcurrant-toned **23** (83) ideal for alfresco lunchtimes at modest 12.4% alc. Body from 40% lightly wooded portion. **Barrel Fermented Viognier** (NEW) ★★★☆ Confident **22** (85) boasts sweet-savoury complexity in its array of apricot & peach, curry leaf & cardamom. Nicely dry, but 13.8% alc a tad hefty for the fruit. Not tasted: **Cabernet Sauvignon Barrique Select**. In abeyance: **Hat Trick**. Discontinued: **Patriot**.

Meerkat range
Pinotage ★★★ Raspberry & rosepetal on **22** (78), only half oaked (with staves & old oak, as Burrow) for body & grip. Bright & friendly. WO W Cape for these, all also in 3L bag-in-box. **Burrow Blend** ★★★ Sweetsour **22** (80) gentle grip from 70% oaked portion, plump red & black fruit from near-equal shiraz & merlot, splashes mourvèdre, viognier & 2 others. **Pinotage Rosé** ★★★ Pale orange hue, sweet berries & patisserie cream, **23** (77) from pinotage is dry, generous 14.2% alc in balance. **Chenin Blanc** ★★★ Bone-dry & racy, **23** (78) packed with apples - Granny Smith, Golden Delicious & Pink Lady, but brief. Discontinued: **Sauvignon Blanc, Sun Angel Semi-Sweet**. — NK, CvZ

Location/map: Wellington ▪ Map grid reference: B1 ▪ WO: Groenberg/Western Cape/Wellington ▪ Est/1stB 2005 ▪ Tasting, sales & cellar tours Mon-Fri 9-5 Sat 10-2 Sun/pub hols by appt only ▪ Fee R60 ▪ Closed Easter Fri & Mon, Dec 25/26 & Jan 1 ▪ Echt Bistro & Restaurant @ Welbedacht ▪ Picnics ▪ Facilities for children ▪ Tour groups ▪ Conferences ▪ Functions ▪ Welbedacht cricket oval ▪ Owner(s) Schalk Burger Family Trust ▪ Winemaker(s) Christiaan Nigrini (Oct 2022), with Whaney Eiman (Apr 2023) ▪ 140ha/92ha (12 varieties r/w) ▪ 500t 75% red 20% white 5% rosé ▪ OVP ▪ PO Box 51 Wellington 7654 ▪ info@welbedacht.co.za ▪ www. welbedacht.co.za ▪ **T +27 (0)21-873-1877**

Welgegund Heritage Wines (Ⓟ) (◎)

The Brimacombe family show appreciation of heritage regarding all aspects of their 18th-century Wellington estate. Old farm buildings have been sensitively converted into guest suites, and gardens have been replanted. Vini-viti man Friedrich Kühne nurtures vines that include cinsaut, carignan and chenin registered as heirloom vineyards. Old-vine grapes, gently and minimally handled, deliver richly fruited yet nuanced boutique wines, with small, newer parcels of grenache noir and syrah adding to Friedrich's palette.

★★★★☆ **Cinsault** (Ⓟ) (🌠) Range is beautifully packaged. **19** (93) drinks well too, with notes of bright raspberry & sour cherry, tannins integrated for a lovely backbone. Two-thirds unoaked. No **18**.

★★★★ **Grenache Noir** (Ⓟ) Lighter bodied (13.5% alc), with fresh, youthful tannins, **19** (86) as charming & engaging as last. Bushvine fruit, wholebunch fermented, only 50% in older/larger barrels to spotlight wild strawberry flavour with touch of red appleskin. **18** skipped.

★★★★ **Providence** (Ⓟ) Red fruit melange, lovely freshness & supple tannins, **15** (86) shiraz with 30% old-vine (42 years) cinsaut, dash carignan, adroitly oaked, 30% new.

★★★★ **Chenin Blanc** (Ⓟ) (🌠) From senior vines, producing rich, ripe tropical & fresh citrus aromas & flavours in **19** (89), unlike savoury 'unfruity' **17** (89). Similar cellar regime, just 33% oaked, 14 months, after bunch-pressing & partial wild ferment. 13% alc. No **18**.— PS

Location/map/WO: Wellington ▪ Map grid reference: C4 ▪ Est 1777 ▪ 1stB 1997 ▪ Tasting & sales by appt ▪ Olive oil ▪ Owner(s) Brimacombe family ▪ Winemaker & vineyard manager Friedrich Kühne ▪ 42ha/20ha (carignan, cinsaut, grenache, shiraz, chenin) ▪ 1,550cs 80% red 20% white ▪ PO Box 683 Wellington 7654 ▪ wine@welgegund.co.za ▪ www.welgegund.co.za ▪ **T +27 (0)82-891-5459**

☐ **Welgelegen** see Friesland Wines

Welgesind Kelder (Ⓟ) (⌂) (◎) (NEW)

A retirement project has grown into a small but fully fledged wine business for Chris and Amanda de Wit on their cool-climate Welgesind Farm overlooking the Klein River and Stanford town. Some foothills land was cleared of fynbos and shiraz planted in 2011, and a few rows of malbec added later. Consultant Mark Stephens helps care for the vines while Chris does the handcrafting, with help from wife and friends, in the cellar below the family home, using natural processes and a light touch when it comes to the wine style.

★★★★ **Director's Reserve Shiraz** Mature aromas of leather & cigarbox with coffee top note complement **16** (86)'s still-fresh & -succulent plum & maraschino cherry fruit for ready-to-drink fireside red.

★★★★ **Mechanic Shiraz** Trio of vintages tasted. **18** ★★★★ (85) plum nuance, a little earth & appealing chalky tannin. **19** (87) hibiscus & cherry whiffs, opulent damsons & blueberries but not overdone. **20** ★★★★ (83) least expressive, more unfruity tones of talc, wax & musk. Older barrels, 23-60 months.

Limited Release Shiraz ★★★☆ More complexity than Mechanic thanks to longer oaking, 60 months, none new, but very ripe. Plums & prunes, signature maraschino cherries, **18** (84) would benefit from more freshness. **Romanse Blanc de Noir** ★★★☆ 2 vintages reviewed, both from shiraz & pale salmon pink hue, very dry but **23** (77) with noticeable acid. Orange zest & candied strawberry on both, **22** (78) some beetroot & earth. **De Wit Sauvignon Blanc** ⊘ ★★★★ Juicy & still very primary, with passionfruit, blackcurrant & citrus aromas, mango on palate. **22** (85) not overly persistent, benefits from chilling. — ML, CvZ

Location: Stanford ▪ Map: Walker Bay & Bot River ▪ Map grid reference: B6 ▪ WO: Walker Bay ▪ Est 2011 ▪ 1stB 2013 ▪ Tasting & cellar tours Mon-Sat 10-5 ▪ Closed Easter Fri/Sun & Dec 25 ▪ BYO picnic ▪ Refreshments for large groups by prior arrangement only ▪ Walking/hiking trails ▪ Owner(s) Chris & Amanda de Wit ▪ Winemaker(s) Chris de Wit ▪ Viticulturist(s) Mark Stephens (Jan 2021, consultant) ▪ 6sha/2ha (malbec, shiraz) ▪ 6-9t/±980cs ▪ PO Box 213 Stanford 7210 ▪ chris@multi-loads.co.za ▪ www.welgesind.co.za ▪ **T +27 (0)82-572-5856**

☐ **Welgevallen Cellar-Stellenbosch University** *see* Stellenbosch University Welgevallen Cellar

---

Wellington Wines

(wine glass) (utensils) (camera) (accessibility)

A substantial and significant producer, and a presence in Wellington town for almost 120 years, Wellington Wines has 2,400 ha of vines owned by 60 member-farmers around Wellington and in Paarl and Swartland, and a global customer base. The venture supplies retailers' private labels and buyers' own brands, as well as its proprietary bottled brands, Hari sparkling wine aperitif, Imprint muscat-based, low-alcohol perlé, Duke easy-drinking lifestyle and La Cave pinnacle single-site. All can be sampled (with cheese platters) at the venue on a hill just outside town, also a 'convenient departure or "wine-down" spot' for hikers and bikers.

La Cave range

★★★★ **Cabernet Sauvignon** Opulent yet well-structured **20** (89), herbal richness to the cassis & graphite tones, balanced with bright acid & powdery tannin grip. Lengthy finish.

★★★★☆ **Pinotage** ⊘ (organic) One of the best to date, **20** (93) sumptuously flavoured with refinement & balance in the form of violet perfume, & savouriness from coriander spice & fynbos. Lovely pure fruit in a layered structure of dusty tannins, hint of cream on unflagging farewell.

★★★★ **Shiraz** Uninhibited **20** (89) loaded with hedgerow fruit, spicy vanilla & earth borne on a liqueur-like texture, melded tannins holding it all together. Quite something.

★★★★ **Cape Blend** ⊘ (organic) Loses roobernet in **20** ★★★★★ (93) for a pinotage (65%), cab & merlot mix that improves on **19** (88) in depth & breadth. Lashings of dark fruit, dried herbs & meat spice held in check by firm yet supple grip that will last a good few years. Again, attractive pristine fruit, undimmed by the oak, all new, 18 months, like all these reds.

★★★★ **Chenin Blanc** Tropical fruit & crème brûlée richness turning savoury on the palate of **21** (89). Creamy vanilla overlay from year in 70% new oak, which also aids texture & extends the good dry finish.

Duke range

Pinotage ⊘ (award) ★★★★ Forward plum & berry fruit with earthy spice, **21** (85) bright, balanced & full of joie de vivre, no wonder **19**, **20** sold out untasted.

Cabernet Sauvignon ⊘ ★★★★ Easy, balanced **20** (84), youthful ruby hue matched by liveliness of the herby-peppery plum flavour. Year seasoned oak, as other reds. **Merlot** ★★★ Xmas cake & spiced plum in juicy, just-dry **20** (82), rounded for comfortable everyday sipping. **Shiraz** ⊘ ★★★★ Opaque, with ruby glints, dark berries & pot-pourri fragrance in **20** (85). Touch brooding but generous & friendly, made for the BBQ. **Chenin Blanc** ⊘ ★★★ Fresh apple, tropical fruit & a touch of cream on easygoing **23** (82). **Sauvignon Blanc** ★★★ Grass, lemon & lime cordial on light, zippy **22** (82) for summer fun times. **White Pinotage** ★★★ Gentle plum & subtle spice on a lean body in **22** (78).

Imprint Frizzanté range
Blush ★★★ Fragrant lightly carbonated fizz from Natural Sweet chenin, muscat & pinotage. **NV** ⑦⑨ palest pink with plum & exotic spice flavours. **Blanc** ★★★ Fruitily sweet party starter from chenin & muscat. **NV** ⑦⑧ rounded, with apple & melon flavours, prickle of tiny bubbles. Low 8% alc, as Blush. — WB
Location/map/WO: Wellington ▪ Map grid reference: B3 C3 ▪ Est 1906 ▪ Tasting & sales Mon-Fri 9-5 Sat/pub hols (only Bovlei tasting room) 10-3; pub hols (seasonal) please call ahead ▪ Sun closed ▪ Cheese platters available ▪ Three winetasting options ▪ Boardroom bookings available ▪ Winemaker(s) Production team: Francois van Niekerk (2014), Erik van Wyk (2015), Daniel Slabber (2019), Johan Hurter (2019), Christo Smit (2022) ▪ Viticulturist(s) Nikey van Zyl (2017) ▪ 2,400ha ▪ 32,000t 60% red 40% white ▪ BRC, Fairtrade, HACCP, IPW, WIETA ▪ PO Box 509 Wellington 7654 ▪ tasting@wellingtonwines.com ▪ www.wellingtonwines.com ▪ **T** +27 (0)21-873-1582

Welmoed

Well-priced, easy-drinking and widely exported collection named for the property whose 17th-century owner, Jacobus van der Heyden, resisted government corruption and earned the people's admiration for his 'moed' (courage). The site is now home to brand owner Stellenbosch Vineyards.

Chardonnay ⊘ ⊛ ★★★★ Partial oak ferment allows **22** ⑧⑤ the ability to showcase its intense citrus, while adding a gently savoury top note.

Cabernet Sauvignon ⊘ ★★★★ Care taken in **21** ⑧④ for varietal expression & drinking pleasure. Sleek, with supple tannins from well-managed oaking, tobacco overlay another point of interest. Stellenbosch WO, as all. **Merlot** ⊘ ★★★ Cassis & plums, savoury dusted by light oaking, **22** ⑧①'s tannin grip proclaims it's not a pushover, can be aged or enjoyed with food. **Pinotage** ⊘ ★★★ Variety-true dark berries, an attractive forthcoming fruitiness, **21** ⑧②'s light oaking shows on the finish, a dry grip. **Shiraz** ⓥ ★★★ Brusquer **21** ⑦⑨ has just-ripe red berries with a generous sprinkling of white pepper to freshen. Brush of oak (staves) adds a smoky note. Endorsed by The Vegan Society, as all. **Rosé** ⊘ ★★★ Strawberry-hued & -toned, cheerfully light & dry **23** ⑧② offers satisfying drinking enjoyment. **Chenin Blanc** ⊘ ★★★★ Unoaked yet has a thatch underpin to the appley fruit. Good lees contact offsets **23** ⑧④'s 12.5% alc, giving palate weight & substance. **Pinot Grigio** ⊘ ★★★★ Not discontinued, as we thought (like Chardonnay). Floral, with winter melon appeal, **23** ⑧④ ends with mouthwatering tanginess. Rare solo bottling. **Sauvignon Blanc** ⊘ ★★★★ Crunchy fresh apple, **23** ⑧④ has hints of green, ticks all the sauvignon boxes, including finishing crisply dry. **Sparkling Pinot Grigio Brut** ⓥ ★★★ Subtle floral & greengage in effortless carbonated **NV** ⑧⓪. Dry, but gentle fizz & softish acidity make it appear sweeter. Chill well. — CR

Weltevrede Estate ⓟ ⑪ ⊚ ⓑ

Blessed with the ideal medium, limestone soil, the Jonkers are now focused on growing mineral-driven world-class chardonnay and cap classique exclusively under the banner of Weltevrede, the Bonnievale estate they've had for more than a century, and one of SA's oldest wine brands owned and run by the same family. Underlying the realignment is co-owner and cellarmaster Philip Jonker's desire to turn his passion for one of Burgundy's signature grapes into a legacy. He's doing much more, including adding visitor experiences like garden tours. He's also created a brand home on the estate for Cape Wine Crafters, listed separately in this guide, which showcases favourites such as Cherrychoc Merlot and muscadels dedicated to oupa and ouma.

Chardonnay Collection

★★★★ **Place of Rocks Chardonnay** ⊛ Hand-picked, bunch-pressed grapes (as all) ex old vines on broken shale slope. **22** ★★★★★ ⑨⓪'s lemon, orange peel & mandarin gain toast & spice from barrel, 25% new, 8 months, complementary creaminess enhanced by weekly bâtonnage. Rich yet light-feeling at 12.4% alc. Improves on **21** ⑧⑨.

★★★★ **Poet's Prayer Chardonnay** ⊛ Keen balance on old-vine, fruit-filled **22** ⑧⑦, nut, toast & cedar nuances from year in new wood. Compact & dense, unfolding to more savoury flavours, with potential to show more with time.

★★★★ **Calcrete Chardonnay** ⊘ Named for area's limestone soils, **23** ⑧⑥ unencumbered by oak, its flinty acid offsetting lemon-lime freshness, texture from 3 months on lees. Modest 12% alc.

Philip Jonker Cap Classique Collection

★★★★☆ **Brut Entheos** ⊘ &⃝ Pearskin & spiced Golden Delicious apple on fragrant **NV** ⑨⑨, 60% chardonnay & pinot noir, woven through with fine bubbles. Touch of sugar balances striking acidity, 24 months on lees add toast & lemon cream.

★★★★☆ **Brut The Ring Blanc de Blancs** ⑦ Long-aged chardonnay sparkler, **13** ⑨③ among the best yet. Mature, honeyed yet fresh, crisp, with a creamy biscuit finish. Last tasted was **10** ⑨⓪. — ML

Location: Bonnievale ▪ Map: Robertson ▪ Map grid reference: D3 ▪ WO: Robertson/Bonnievale ▪ Est 1912 ▪ 1stB 1945 ▪ Tasting & sales Mon-Sat 8.30-5 ▪ Closed Good Fri, Dec 25/26 & Jan 1 ▪ Restaurant Tue-Sun 12-4 ▪ Weddings/functions ▪ Underground cellar tour experiences - online booking available ▪ Walks/hikes ▪ Conservation area ▪ Owner(s) Philip & Lourens Jonker ▪ Cellarmaster(s) Philip Jonker (Jan 1997) ▪ Viticulturist(s) Francois Viljoen (consultant) ▪ PO Box 6 Bonnievale 6730 ▪ reception@weltevrede.com ▪ www.weltevrede.com ▪ **T +27 (0)23-616-2141**

☐ **Weltevreden Estate** *see* Bertha Wines

Welvanpas

Custodian and cellarmaster Dan Retief celebrates the 320th anniversary of Welvanpas this year, as well as 10 generations of his family on the Wellington site, today an extensive and wide-ranging agribusiness as well as a winefarm and vine nursery. Aiming for 'easy-drinking, fruitful, natural wines', he's planning upgrades to the old cellar once the public road that passes it has been moved, to protect the clay walls from damage. **Daniel Pinotage** ⑦ ★★★ Generous ripe cherry & berry fruit with robust tannin structure, lightish body. **19** ⑧② for braai-time enjoyment. **Revival Red** ★★★ Unwooded & unpretentious co-fermented cab, merlot & shiraz, **21** ⑧⓪ has vibrant mulberry & bramble fruit, gentle tannins. **Suzanne Pinotage Rosé** ⑦ ★★★ Easygoing, affable **19** ⑧② is dry & liberally fruited, with gentle acid nudge to add refreshment value. **Heritage Chenin Blanc** ⑦ ★★★ Light, easy-drinking **21** ⑦⑧ has modest tropical fruit, hint of beeswax. **Legacy Sauvignon Blanc** ⑦ ★★ Light & lean **21** ⑦④ has green apple notes, gentle acid. In abeyance: **De Krakeelhoek Rood**, **Chardonnay**. — GdB

Location/map/WO: Wellington ▪ Map grid reference: C3 ▪ Est 1704 ▪ 1stB 1994 ▪ Tasting & sales Tue-Fri 10-4 Sat/pub hols 10-3 ▪ Fee R50pp ▪ Closed Easter Fri-Mon, Dec 24-Jan 2 ▪ Die Ou Meul coffee shop Tue-Fri 9-4 Sat 8-3 ▪ Tour groups ▪ History Package incl lunch, tasting & talk on Piet Retief family, booking required ▪ Farm produce ▪ Walks/hikes ▪ Wild Boar MTB trails ▪ Owner(s)/viticulturist(s) Dan Retief ▪ Cellarmaster(s) Dan Retief (Jan 1993) ▪ Winemaker(s) Dan Retief (Jan 1990), with Neels Samuels (Jan 1999) ▪ 210ha/40ha (12 varieties r/w) ▪ 25t own label 80% red 15% white 5% rosé ▪ PO Box 75 Wellington 7654 ▪ welvanpas@gmail. com ▪ www.welvanpas.co.za ▪ **T +27 (0)21-300-5708/+27 (0)83-231-2149**

Whalehaven Wines

A trailblazer of winemaking on the Cape's cool southern coast, Bottega-family-owned Whalehaven continues to draw fruit from maritime vineyard areas, supplemented with grapes from sibling property Idiom near Sir Lowry's Pass Village in the Helderberg. At the cellar and tasting venue in the Village precinct of Hermanus, Reino Thiart makes the wines of both brands, plus his newer boutique own-label, Thiart Wines.

Reserve range

★★★★☆ **Pinot Noir** ⊘ Rich, earthy **20** ⑨⓪ fragrant & open, appetisingly dry. Ripe raspberry, rhubarb & pomegranate on supple tannins, polished year in oak, 30% new.

★★★★☆ **Seascape Chardonnay** &⃝ Lemon balm, pear & crushed stone nuances, supreme balance on **20** ⑨④, which adds 'Seascape' to name. Characteristic coastal chardonnay with cool-toned fruit, delicately accented with roast nut & toast from 12 months in barrique, 30% new.

Terroir range

★★★★ **Cabernet Franc** ⊘ Graceful **16** ⑧⑥ shows herbal & leafy varietal character acquiring tertiary tobacco, prune & fennel nuances. Acid stil lively, edged with spice from year in oak, 25% new.

★★★★ **Pinot Noir** ⑦ Dried herb & mint on engaging **20** ★★★★★ ⑨⓪. Bright cherry fruit courtesy 15% wholebunch ferment, feathery tannins moulded year in older oak. Good dry finish. Betters last **18** ⑧⑧.

★★★★ **Chardonnay** ⑦ Clean lemon & lime on **20** ⑧⑨, elegant, flinty acid melded harmoniously with yellow apple, melon & peach, creamy-buttery nuances from 36 months older oak.

★★★★ **Sauvignon Blanc** ⊘ Remarkable sense of place on **23** ★★★★★ ⑨①'s fynbos, green fig & white citrus notes. Textured, long, driven with energetic acid. Even more delicious than **22** ⑧⑨.

Not tasted: **Unwooded Viognier**.

Old Harbour range
Merlot-Pinotage ★★★ Adds splash mourvèdre in **19** ⑦⑦, sweet fruit overlaid with leather & farmyard notes. Ready now. WO Coastal, as Cab Franc. — ML, CvZ

Location: Hermanus ▪ Map: Walker Bay & Bot River ▪ Map grid reference: A3 ▪ WO: Upper Hemel-en-Aarde Valley/Coastal ▪ Est/1stB 1995 ▪ Tasting & sales Mon-Sat 10-5 Sun 10-3 ▪ Wine tastings ▪ Tour groups (up to 40 pax) ▪ Private tasting room can be booked for small functions/corporate events (up to 14 pax) ▪ Owner(s) Bottega family ▪ Winemaker(s) Reino Thiart ▪ 120t capacity ▪ Private Bag X14 Hermanus 7200 ▪ experience@ whalehaven.co.za ▪ www.whalehaven.co.za ▪ **T +27 (0)28-050-1301**

Whiley Wines
Kenneth Whiley makes his small-batch wines in Swartland's Riebeek-Kasteel from grapes sourced not far distant from there. Both the debut Red and its sold-out sibling are blends, and Kenneth doesn't see that changing in future releases.

Foxtrot range
Red ⓠ ★★★★ Lightish, with zesty red-fruit juiciness, rounded & ready, easy to drink. **21** ⑧⑤ equal cinsaut & cab with grenache, shiraz. Not tasted: **White**. — TJ, AL

Location: Riebeek-Kasteel ▪ WO: Swartland ▪ Est/1stB 2020 ▪ Closed to public ▪ Owner(s) Kenneth Whiley ▪ Winemaker(s) Kenneth Whiley (Jan 2020) ▪ 2t/200cs own label 22% red 78% white ▪ Fairtrade, WIETA ▪ kenneth@whileywines.co.za ▪ www.whileywines.co.za ▪ **T +27 (0)71-383-3868**

Wightman & Sons Wine Co ⓠ
Andrew Wightman's Paardeberg farm covers 42 hectares; vines account for half, most of their fruit going to well-known wineries. The rest is crafted for the boutique family brand by Andrew and son Brandon. They hope a viura will join in a few years. Half the block planted in 2016 perished in the drought, but canes from survivors were grafted by a nursery and, once planted, will made up a hectare of this locally rare variety.

Top Tier Wines
★★★★☆ **Old Bushvine Chenin Blanc** ⓠ 1965 single-vineyard. **21** ⑨③ intense, steely & aromatic, flavours linger memorably. Bone-dry, as all the wines; wild ferment, older oak, 9 months as all unless noted.
Not tasted: **Skin Contact Chenin Blanc**. In abeyance: **The Hedge**.

Lifestyle Wines
★★★★ **Chenin Blanc** Gold brilliance of **21** ⑧⑦ refrained in **22** ★★★★ ⑧⑤ plus bruised apple & yellow peach attractions. Softish, with oxidative suggestion, savoury conclusion but tad less concentration.

Clairette Blanche ⓝⓔⓦ ⑨ ★★★★ Rare varietal example. Bright yellow-gold **22** ⑧⑤, restrained earth & wild herb character with tasty oxidative, savoury flavours & freshening tannin to complement spectrum of dishes. 9 months oak.

Syrah ★★★ Lightish & fresh, **22** ⑧② modest pepper, red berry fruit, modicum of tannin for current drinking.
Pinotage Rosé ⓝⓔⓦ ★★★ Sunset pink hue on **22** ⑧⓪ is striking, soft berry flavours less so; 6 months older oak & lipsmacking finish add some structure. In abeyance: **A&B's Blend**. — AL

Location: Malmesbury ▪ Map/WO: Swartland ▪ Map grid reference: C8 ▪ Est/1stB 2015 ▪ Tasting by appt only ▪ Owner(s) Andrew Wightman ▪ Winemaker(s) Andrew & Brandon Wightman ▪ 42ha/22ha (carignan, ptage, shiraz, tinta barocca, chenin, clairette) ▪ 90-100t/2,000cs own label 35% red 65% white ▪ PO Box 1133 Malmesbury 7299 ▪ andrew@wswines.co.za ▪ www.wightmanandsons.co.za ▪ **T +27 (0)82-658-1101**

Wijnskool ⓠ
The name means 'Wine School', and the aim is to enable high school students to make a career choice by 'conveying the understanding of terroir and the art of making wine'. The small batches featured here are crafted in Hemel-en-Aarde Valley by the learners, guided by acclaimed winemaker and academy co-founder

(with wife Suné) Bartho Eksteen and his son Pieter Willem, recently joined by Dewald Grobler. Proceeds from sales fund the operations. See also Bartho Eksteen Estate Wine and Yerden Eksteen listings.

★★★★ **Tree of Knowledge Shiraz** Lively red fruit of **21** ★★★★ ⑧⑤ lightly dusted with oak spice from 18 months in older barrels. Perhaps not as complex as **19** ⑧⑦ (which included dabs grenache noir & viognier) but friendly tannins & touch liquorice still deliver satisfying glassful.

★★★★ **Tree of Knowledge Sauvignon Blanc** Previewed & provisionally rated **23** ⑧⑥'s tad muted by lingering ferment notes but well balanced, firm filled & dry, with granadilla flavours & pithy tug.

Occasional release: **Tree of Knowledge SMGV.** — CvZ

Location: Hermanus ▪ WO: Western Cape ▪ Est/1stB 2011 ▪ Tasting, sales & cellar tours at Bartho Eksteen ▪ Owner(s) Bartho & Suné Eksteen ▪ Winemaker(s) Bartho Eksteen (Feb 2011), with Pieter Willem Eksteen (Jan 2012), Dewald Grobler (May 2022) & young entrepreneurs ▪ Viticulturist(s) Johan Viljoen, Pieter Willem Eksteen - bought-in grapes ▪ 30t/3,680cs own label 50% red 50% white ▪ PO Box 1999 Hermanus 7200 ▪ bartho@hermanus.co.za, sune@hermanus.co.za ▪ www.barthoeksteen.co.za ▪ **T +27 (0)82-920-7108 (Bartho), +27 (0)72-323-5060 (Suné)**

Wild Air ⓛ

Storm Wines' owner and crafter Hannes Storm is behind this boutique project launched in 2016 with a focus on sauvignon blanc from an old, low-crop parcel in Hemel-en-Aarde Valley on shale-derived clay soils. Most of the 1,000 cases go to six countries, with local listings limited to a handful of restaurants and other outlets.

★★★★ **Sauvignon Blanc** Early picked, wild fermented/8 months small barrels. Gooseberry & lime in **22** ★★★★★ ⑨⓪, intense salty acid giving vibrancy, ageing ability, oak's contribution gentle biscuit throughout, plus palate weight despite the elegance (12.5% alc.) More typicity than last-tasted **19** ⑧⑨. — CR

Location: Hermanus ▪ Map: Walker Bay & Bot River ▪ Map grid reference: B4 ▪ WO: Hemel-en-Aarde Valley ▪ Est/1stB 2016 ▪ Tasting by appt ▪ Closed Easter Fri/Sun, Ascension day, Dec 25/26 & Jan 1 ▪ Owner(s)/winemaker(s)/viticulturist(s) Hannes Storm ▪ 2.2ha (sauv) ▪ 6t/1,000cs own label 100% white ▪ IPW ▪ PO Box 431 Hermanus 7200 ▪ info@stormwines.co.za ▪ **T +27 (0)28-125-0073**

☐ **Wild Bouquet** see The Grape Grinder
☐ **Wild Card** see Le Sueur Wines
☐ **Wildebeest Brandewyn** see Bundu Brands

Wildeberg Wines ⓛ ⓗ ⓞ

Franschhoek-based Wildeberg, owned by Manchester wine company Boutinot, over the past eight years has been building its brand, reputation and tiers of characterful wines. In the current line-up, Wildeberg White and Red represent the best of Franschhoek; Terroirs expresses origins and gems outside Franschhoek; Coterie, 'a love child between the two', quips winemaker JD Rossouw, houses blends from the wider Coastal region; and Wild House, wild-fermented wines of high quality at affordable prices. More blocks are being established on the home-farm, bushvine chenin and cabernet franc being the latest. What JD describes as a 'tough' vintage, 2023 was the 2nd in their new cellar. They're now dreaming of a new, bigger barrel facility.

Wildeberg range

★★★★ **Terroirs Cinsault** ⓝⒺⓦ ⓦ From 1974 Wellington vines, **22** ⑧⑨ bright, succulent spicy red berries, concentrated but unheavy, brisk, ripe tannins leaving a mouthwatering finish. Clever oaking, 30% new, 8 months, adds shoulder while allowing current enjoyment. 13.5% alc

★★★★☆ **Red** ⓦ As last, all Franschhoek grapes in **22** ⑨③; syrah with 10% cab franc. Fragrant & flavourful mix white pepper spice & dark fruit; supple feel brightened by lively, fine grip providing delicious lipsmacking quality to lingering savouriness. Oak, 40% new, supportive. 13% alc.

★★★★☆ **Terroirs Chenin Blanc** ⓦ Paarl bushvines' age reflected in **22** ⑨⓪'s concentration & lingering memory of scented honey & baked apple. Full textural richness & weight from lees ageing currently restrained by steely natural acidity, worth few months' wait for pleasurable harmony. Oak, 20% new, 9 months, well judged.

★★★★☆ **Terroirs Sauvignon Blanc** ⓦ From elevated dryland Banghoek parcel, intensity without showiness, **22** ⑨③'s granadilla & blackcurrant carried seamlessly on taut acid through sleek, lees-enriched body with memorable length. This style of unoaked sauvignon deserves & will reward ageing.

★★★★☆ **White** (ⓦ) (ⓨ) From Franschhoek heirloom variety semillon & venerable 1905 vines. Earthy, waxy flavours, silky breadth lifted by lemony acid in weighty but elegant 22 ★★★★★ (95). Individual with its own personality & wonderful, worthwhile ageing potential. Natural ferment, 50% new oak vs only older wood for 21 (93).

★★★★ **Meteorique Méthode Cap Classique** Bone-dry sparkling from Stellenbosch chardonnay, 22 (88) still edgily brisk, underlying lemony & creamy tones plus the oak dimension promise future greater complexity along lines of 19 (89). Barrel fermented/5 months, 10% new. 20 untasted, no 21.

Coterie by Wildeberg range

★★★★ **Cabernet Franc-Malbec** (✓) Maintains 20 (88)'s successful 67/33 combo with more distinction, complexity in 21 ★★★★☆ (92). Zingy bite to expressive leafy spice & fleshy red berry flavours, concluding savouriness. Freshening tannins lend necessary form & balance, as well as mitigating effects of 14.5% alc. Positive influence of 30% new oak, 20 months. WO Coastal as all these.

★★★★ **Grenache-Syrah** In 22 (89), 67% grenache noir brings a light feel, fresh red berries & liveliness to syrah's darker, richer & more savoury tones in tasty, compatible partnership. Silk texture & squeeze of resistant tannins allow for both current & few years' enjoyment. 20% new oak, 10 months.

★★★★ **Cinsault Rosé** Seriously conceived 22 (88) flavoursome rather than fruity, palate is spicy, concentrated & long thanks to sound acid & firm build. Bone-dry but unharsh. Natural ferment in older oak, 6 months on lees.

★★★★ **Chenin Blanc-Grenache Blanc** (ⓨ) Barrel-fermented 22 (89) 67/33 blend has ginger spice & appley zest distinction in its rich concentration, firm & dry finish. Few more years could reveal greater interest. Like white sibling, 20% new oak, 9 months.

★★★★ **Semillon-Sauvignon Blanc** (✓) (ⓦ) Rich, waxy concentration with toasty extra, showing of barrel-fermented semillon's dominance on 22 ★★★★☆ (94). Just 10% tank-raised sauvignon freshens, tightens, forming cohesive, savoury whole. Classic partnership worth cellaring. Step up on 21 (86).

Wild House range

★★★★ **Shiraz** (✓) Packs good punch of rich, spicy dark fruit, lively grip, yet nothing overdone to disturb balance or youthful enjoyment. 20% whisper of new oak adds to structure. 22 (86) different quality-agea-bility level to 21 ★★★ (80). Spontaneous ferment, as all these.

Pinotage (✓) ★★★★ Ripe dark fruit & smooth body framed by merest squeeze of tannin, 22 (85)'s savoury ending has light spicing from 10 months in oak, 35% new. More serious than last. Previewed, may rate higher once bottled. **Grenache Rosé** (✓) ★★★★ Rose pink 23 (84) has light spicing to creamy soft red berries; bright acid freshens & lifts, lends savoury length. Attractively modest 11.5% alc. **Chardonnay** (NEW) ★★★★ Lemons & tropical fruit, unwooded 23 (82) pre-bottling sample is plump, concludes with a pithy tang. **Chenin Blanc** (✓) ★★★★ Lively 23 (85) offers easy-sipping value in its ripe peachy flesh & briskly dry finish. **Sauvignon Blanc** (NEW) (✓) ★★★★ Ripe granadilla fragrance & flavours, juicy acidity & round dryness, pre-bottling 23 (85) in less aggressive style. Has charm & great value. — AL

Location/map: Franschhoek ▪ Map grid reference: D1 ▪ WO: Western Cape/Coastal/Franschhoek/Stellenbosch/Paarl/Wellington ▪ Est/1stB 2016 ▪ Tasting, sales & cellar tours by invitation; also open to public on selected calendar days; closed all pub hols ▪ Wine club ▪ Function venue ▪ Accommodation ▪ Trail runs, hikes & walks ▪ Owner(s) Wildeberg & Kompanjie ▪ Winemaker(s) JD Rossouw, with Abigail Buckenham (May 2023) ▪ 300t own label 30% red 70% white ▪ jd@wildeberg.co.za ▪ www.wildeberg.co.za ▪ **T +27 (0)82-895-4111**

Wildehurst Wines

(ⓞ)

The insight that everything needed to make the best wine is already present when the grapes are harvested guides the organics-based farming and hands-off winemaking at Joanne Hurst's boutique winery at Koringberg in the Swartland heartland. This is matched with a hands-on approach once the wines are bottled, with every process, from labelling to applying the wax closure, done by hand.

Wildehurst range

★★★★ **Cinsaut** (ⓞ) Sour cherry tang of now-bottled 19 (88) delivers delight promised last year. Light on its feet, rosemary & thyme flavours interleaved with fine tannins. Tiny production & only older oak, as all.

★★★★☆ **Petit Wilde** ⓥ Harvest experiments, offered as 'something for consumers to look forward to'. Previewed **18** ★★★★ ⑧⑨ first tasted since **15** ⑨①, both from petite sirah (durif), enticing spicy chocolate & cherry notes, herby, savoury finish. 2 years oak.

★★★★☆ **Chenin Blanc** ⓥ Quintessential pure-fruited Swartland chenin, sensual sunshine-in-a-glass style but melon fruit of **20** ⑨③ is finessed & textured, with hint of sweetness. Serious enough to contemplate, easy enough to quaff. Old Paardeberg bushvines; barrel fermented/6 months.

★★★★ **Semillon** ⓥ Scintillating debut, worthy addition to cellar's ranks. **19** ⑧⑨ spicy, richly textured, enviable length of flavour. Wild ferment/6 months in barrique. 11.8% alc.

★★★★☆ **The Wilde Le Premier Or** ⓥ 'The Wilde' a witty name for experimental wines. **19** ⑨⓪ 1-week skin-macerated chenin. Truly special wine, delivers sumptuous flavour in an unforced way.

★★★★ **Viognier** ⓥ From Paardeberg & Malmesbury vines, elegant **19** ⑧⑨ peach intensity, pleasing slim 12% alc & hint of pineapple in farewell.

★★★★ **Méthode Cap Classique Chenin Blanc-Chardonnay** ⓥ 69% chenin, dry **17** ⑧⑥ offers drinking pleasure & interest. Creamy citrus & apple notes, mouthwatering acidity, good complexity.

★★★★ **Méthode Cap Classique Colombar** ⓥ Natural ferment, year on lees, **19** ⑧⑨ has resolute strings of fine bubbles delivering variety's signature guava fragrance, stonefruit & creamy lemon curd to nose & rounded, delicious palate. Seriously crafted but lots of fun too.

★★★★ **Straw Wine** ⓥ **19** ⑧⑦ from chenin, 8 months oaked. Amber hues light the stage for honeysuckle & tangerine peel richness, thrilling acidity tames eye-watering sugar, 6% al. 330 ml.

Discontinued: **Red**, **Méthode Cap Classique Cinsaut**.

Velo range

★★★★ **Red** ⓥ Grenache noir (69%) leads syrah & dab cinsaut in delectable **18** ⑧⑥. Red berry profile has seasoned oak (18 months) & bottle-age breadth; full of flavour for uncomplicated drinking.

Blanc ⓥ ★★★★ Colombard & chenin gets oomph from oaked viognier in **18** ⑧⑤ summer white. — WB

Location: Koringberg ▪ Map/WO: Swartland ▪ Map grid reference: B2 ▪ Est 2006 ▪ 1stB 2009 ▪ Cellar tours & tasting by appt at 1 Main Rd, Koringberg ▪ Owner(s) Joanne Hurst ▪ Winemaker(s) Sheree Nothnagel ▪ 1.1ha (carignan, cinsaut, grenache, mourv, shiraz, viog) ▪ 24t own label 50% red 50% white ▪ PO Box 103 Koringberg 7312 ▪ wildehurst@gmail.com ▪ www.wildehurst.com ▪ **T +27 (0)22-913-2397**

Wildekrans Wine Estate ⓩ ⓜ ⓖ ⓞ ⓛ

'Wine is made in the vineyard' is a phrase repeated endlessly in wine country, but at the Harlow family estate near Bot River there's a conscious and ongoing programme to produce 'excellent' grapes and thus intervene less in the cellar. Hence the uprooting of a further 14 ha of vines and planned replanting of most with varieties suited to the cool climate. 'Elegant and tight wines of purity and complexity' remains the goal.

Barrel Select Reserve range

★★★★☆ **Cabernet Franc** 🆕 ⓐ Mainly older-barrel aged, 18 months (as Pinotage) so variety's personality prevails: red berries, graphite & cigarbox, some dried meat tones. Despite **21** ⑨⓪'s 14% alc, effect is streamlined, packed with delicious fruit, structure harmonious. Hidden muscles promise ageing.

★★★★☆ **Pinotage** ⓐ Riper than Estate version, **21** ⑨④ is deeply layered: smoky spice, black pepper, dark-toned berries giving sufficient succulence for balance. Tannins a lithe strength for long cellaring. Impressive presence & stature.

★★★★☆ **Shiraz** With some tempranillo, as Estate, here 10%, plus less oaking, 18 months, giving better balance. Dried herbs, peppery notes, charcuterie, all vie with the plum & berry fruit, **20** ⑨⓪'s palate's juiciness particularly appealing. Tannins allow both ageing current access. **19** untasted.

★★★★ **Cape Blend** ⓐ Pinotage-led at 45% with shiraz, 2 cabs (different ratio to Estate), 2 years mainly older barrels. **21** ⑧⑨ has plummy depths, expected savoury spicing, the tannin structure still youthfully grippy, geared for a long future, needing decanting for earlier consumption.

★★★★☆ **Chenin Blanc** ⓐ Ferment started in tank, moved to barrel & amphora, aged 8 months. Gentle biscuit seamed through the appley fruit, a nuance of preserved lemon, the flavours quite savoury, food apt. **22** ⑨④ softer acid than siblings, but fits this richer styling. Grown-up chenin.

★★★★ **Grenache Blanc-Chenin Blanc** (NEW) Split 60/40, same cellar treatment as Chenin. Ginger biscuit & melon, yellow apple in **22** (87), scents already draw you in, flavours don't disappoint. Fruit has a tang from acid interaction, finishes crisply fresh & long.

Estate range

★★★★ **Cape Blend** (✓) Pinotage at 58% with 2 cabs & shiraz, 2 years older small barrels, leaving tannins amenable. Plum-fruited **21** (88) proudly wears its savoury coat: spice, meaty tones, liquorice, lots to appeal to the drinker who likes streamlined, juicy texture, yet appreciates crafting. **20** untasted.

★★★★ **Deep Purple** (⊘) Make-up of 6-way blend of Rhône, Burgundy, Bordeaux & SA grapes changes in latest **NV** (86), shiraz (48%) dominant. Good intensity, length, structured dry tannin from oak ageing.

★★★★ **Sauvignon Blanc** (✓) With 8% semillon, **22** (89) has a cool-site-influenced distinctive character: sea spray & wild herbs, racy acid giving focus & verve. Dry, elegant, some plumping from 7 months on lees. Again shows sauvignon's potential here after **21** ★★★★ (84).

. . . .

Shiraz (🍇) ★★★ With 5% tempranillo, **20** (81) 2 years mainly older barrels, giving strong savoury focus, spicy, smoked meat, some scrub, plummy fruit shows more in the flavours. Ideal food wine.

. . . .

Pinotage ★★★★ Mainly older barrels, 2 years, but no shortage of fruit, blueberries, mulberries, **21** (84)'s tannin firm but ripe platform for some ageing. Savoury, peppery, nice food match. **Chenin Blanc** (✓) ★★★★ Melon & quince, yellow apple, **23** (84) plenty of flavour, perked up by zesty acid, giving fruity-fresh appeal. Also-tasted **22** ★★★★ (88), different style & class, crunchy green apple & kiwi, winter melon, brisk salty acid giving backbone, promising a future. Sleek muscle tone of an athlete. Not tasted: **Rosé**.

Méthode Cap Classique range

★★★★ **Brut Rosé** (⊘) Tang of green apple & strawberry on **19** (87) pink dry sparkler from pinot noir, chardonnay, dab chenin. Lively freshness gives way to richer sourdough toast ex 30 months on lees.

★★★★ **Brut Chenin Blanc** Change since last vintage of this satisfying dry sparkler, on lees 53 months vs 20, **17** (88) honeyed melon tones, attractive richness, touch sugar giving tangy effect with the acid.— CR

Location/WO: Bot River ▪ Map: Walker Bay & Bot River ▪ Map grid reference: B1 ▪ Est/1stB 1993 ▪ Tasting room Wed-Sun & pub hols 10-4 ▪ Cellar tours by appt ▪ Olive oil ▪ Restaurant ▪ Conferences ▪ Weddings ▪ Celebrations ▪ Farm cottage accommodation ▪ Wine club ▪ Tour groups ▪ MTB ▪ Horse riding ▪ Walks ▪ Birding ▪ Conservation area ▪ Owner(s) Gary & Amanda Harlow ▪ Winemaker(s) Maryke Botha (Dec 2021) ▪ Viticulturist(s) / farm manager Stefan Rust (May 2022) ▪ 1,015ha/45ha (cabs s/f, merlot, ptage, pinot, shiraz, chard, chenin, grenache b, hanepoot, riesling, sauv, sem) ▪ 220t own label 55% red 40% white 5% rosé; ±13,200cs for clients ▪ OVP, SIZA, WIETA, WWF-SA Conservation Champion ▪ PO Box 31 Botriver 7185 ▪ sales@wildekrans.com ▪ www.wildekrans.com ▪ **T +27 (0)28-284-9902**

Wildeloot Wines (NEW)

The Nel family's tiny parcel of chardonnay, deep in Stellenbosch's Jonkershoek Valley, cooled by the 'angry' southeaster, was planted in 2005 but waited till 2020 for cultivar specialist Simon Smith of Louisvale to craft a lightly oaked, single-site wine for the own label. A 'wildeloot' is an unproductive vine shoot that's always removed yet reappears the next season. The Nel parents combine this peculiarity with the Afrikaans 'wilde' to celebrate their children, who they see as 'resilient, different... and somewhat on the wild side'.

Chardonnay ★★★★ More 'white wine' than 'chardonnay', yet with ample appeal & charm. Floral bouquet follows to white peach & pineapple on palate, joined by subtle smoke from daub oak. Good weight & appley acid lift on **23** (85). — NK, CvZ

Location/WO: Stellenbosch ▪ Est 2005 ▪ 1stB 2020 ▪ Closed to public ▪ Owner(s) Nel family ▪ Winemaker(s) Simon Smith (Louisvale Wines) ▪ 1.5ha (chard) ▪ sales@wildelootwines.com ▪ **T +27 (0)82-339-2501**

Wilderer Distilleries (🍷)(🍴)(📷)(👤)

Christian Wilderer's late father Helmut, a German restaurateur, founded South Africa's first private husk spirit distillery, in the 1990s, and became a leading producer of fruit-based eaux de vie. Latterly a wide, innovative range of spirits and liqueurs is made at the Paarl distillery, and there's a second tasting and dining location at Spice Route Destination, with new Pasta Pasta eatery. Despite such successes as Fynbos Gin, the oak-matured grappas remain what the team recognises as 'the foundation spirits on which the company is built'.

★★★★☆ Grappa Muscato ⊘ You can't keep muscat hidden even when distilled, & its grapey, floral charm shines through here (from muscats ottonel & morio) though in refined fashion. **22** ⑨ notably silky-smooth as well as flavourful. 43% alc & 500 ml, as all. No **21**.

★★★★ Grappa Pinotage ⊘ Lighter red-gold hue on **22 ★★★★★** ⑨ than last-tasted (and slightly less refined) **20** ⑧. Similar roasting coffee & chocolate notes from ageing in ex-pinotage casks, with a complex sweet fruitiness too. Piercing clarity, fine & fiery.

★★★★☆ Grappa Shiraz ⊘ Mid-straw-gold **22** ⑨ shows subtle smoky oak characters as well as the usual intriguing note of peppermint. Lively, fresh, aromatic & clean, in the sophisticated & elegant modern Italian style common to all these. Last was **19** ⑨.— TJ

Location/map: Paarl • Map grid reference: D7 • Est/1stB 1995 • Tasting & sales daily 10-5 (Wilderer Distillery at Wilderer Estate) & 10-6 (Wilderer Distillery at Spice Route Destination) • Fee R60-R120pp • Closed Dec 25 & Jan 1 • Restaurants (Ristorante Pappa Grappa at Wilderer Estate & La Grapperia Pizza & Bistro at Spice Route Destination) open for lunch & dinner Mon-Sun • Restaurant (Ristorante Pasta Pasta at Spice Route Destination) open for breakfast & lunch Mon-Sun • Facilities for children • Tasting room sales • Gin blending experiences available during tasting room hours & group bookings • Owner(s) Christian Wilderer • Distiller André Pretorius (2021) • 2ha • ±22,000cs (6x500ml) • PO Box 150 Paarl-Simondium 7670 • info@wilderer.co.za • www.wilderer.co.za • **T +27 (0)21-863-3555 (Wilderer Distillery & Ristorante Pappa Grappa)** • **T +27 (0)21-863-4367 (Wilderer Distillery & La Grapperia Pizza & Bistro)** • **T+27(0)21-863-4367 (Ristorante Pasta Pasta)**

☐ **Wildflower** *see* Darling Cellars
☐ **Wild House** *see* Wildeberg Wines
☐ **Wild Instinct** *see* Stellenview Premium Wines
☐ **Wild Olive** *see* The Grape Grinder

William Everson Wines ⓥ ⌂

Winecrafting with 'an artisan approach', based on tiny batches and little intervention, at his home-cellar in Elgin has been William Everson's passion for almost 25 years. He's experimenting with pet-nat sparkling, and though he's sold his cider-making venture, keeping his hand in with a trial bottle-fermented version.

★★★★ Shiraz Fresh, red-fruited **22** ⑧ early picking giving lightness & vigour but perhaps detracting from intensity & depth of fruit. Dry, bright & moderately structured. Only old oak barrels.

★★★★ Semillon Yellow-gold **22** ⑧ fermented on skins 7 days to give austerely flavourful wine with savoury component to lemon & apple fruit, gentle tannic grip. Light but sufficiently vinous at ±11% alc, & significantly up on insubstantial **21 ★★★** ⑧.

Cabernet Sauvignon ⓥ **★★★** Berries on pre-bottled **19** ⑦ from Durbanville but more savoury notes & a little bubblegum, grippy tannins, bright acidity, all a bit awkward. — TJ

Location: Grabouw • Map: Elgin • Map grid reference: B2 • WO: Elgin/Durbanville • Est/1stB 2001 • Tasting, sales & tours by appt • Self-catering accommodation • Owner(s)/winemaker(s) William Everson • 4t/800cs own label 60% red 40% white • 2281 Essenhout Ave, Klipkop, Grabouw 7160 • william@williameverson-wines.com • www.williameverson-wines.com • **T +27 (0)82-554-6357**

☐ **Willowbrook** *see* Wine-of-the-Month Club
☐ **Wind Band** *see* Cecilia Wines

Windfall Wine Farm ⓥ ⌂ ◎

The late Eddie Barlow, founding owner and famed cricketer, was inspired in the naming of this boutique venture in secluded Agterkliphoogte by low clouds cascading over the mountains into the valley. The Alexander family acquired it in 2000, later joined by long-time resident viticulturist Jaco de Wet. Later additions to the palette, cap classique and potstill brandy, have been a success, like the colourful guest cottages.

Windfall Wine range

★★★★ Barrel 41 Equal cab, shiraz & merlot, 3 others, previewed **21** ⑧'s oaking increased since last **19 ★★★★** ⑧, which it proudly displays. Vivid cassis, mulberries, peppery-meaty spice in a succulent frame. Already delicious, clearly good fruit well handled, tannins a hidden strength.

Shiraz ⚥ ★★★★ Tasted pre-bottling, **21** ⑧⑤'s oaking shows as spice array seamed through the plush fruit. There's a brightness, this is modern shiraz, the texture smooth, succulent, a nice fresh note at the end.

Cabernet Sauvignon ★★★★ Small portions cab franc & shiraz, **21** ⑧⑤ preview wholeberry fermented (as rest), 24 months in older barriques (as all reds). Savoury shading, juicy berries, some mintiness adding interest, tannins supple. **Pinotage** ★★★ Not discontinued as we thought. Ex barrel, **23** ⑧② piquant mulberry & blueberry fruit, savoury spiced from older oak, palate fresh & juicy. Firm grip on finish, which might settle with time. **Chardonnay** ⑩④ ★★★ Unoaked **22** ⑧② nicely combines stonefruit & citrus, crisp acid keeping it fresh, adding lift & length. **Chenin Blanc** ★★★ Sleek tank sample **23** ⑧② shows the guava & melon characteristics of a young wine, zesty acid there to keep it in good health & appealing drinking mode. **Sauvignon Blanc** ★★★★ Tank sample **23** ⑧③ has lemon & lime intensity, some underlying winter melon. Vibrates with freshness, wakens the taste buds. Subsequent bottling of **22** ⑧③, also tasted, has house-style citrus but acid more restrained than before, allows other fruit to appear, apple, pear. Elegant, dry. Discontinued: **Pinot Noir.**

Mendola Cap Classique range
★★★★ **Brut Pinot Noir Rosé** Change from **16** ⑧⑥'s chardonnay-pinot noir, **17** ★★★★★ ⑨⓪ also longer on lees (66 months) & better for it. Pale salmon hue, red berry perfume, dry, but its the freshness, remarkable youthfulness that strike you, refinement (12% alc) part of the character too. Aromatic brioche reminds of time spent on lees, but it's woven with the fruit, yet another thing to admire.

★★★★★ **Brut Blanc De Blanc** ⑧ Chardonnay dry sparkler lavished with 66 months on lees, **17** ⑨③ follows in style of last **15** ⑨⓪ in its elegance, brioche & citrus tones. Has admirable freshness, no age showing, in perfect, stylish condition. More purity & finesse than previous.

Brandy range
★★★★☆ **The Hunter** ⑧ Gorgeous depth of flavour on 10 year old potstill ⑨⓪ from chenin - dried peach & pear, cinnamon & vanilla emerging on smooth finish. Concentrated & elegant. 500 ml.— CR, WB

Location/map/WO: Robertson ▪ Map grid reference: C8 ▪ Est 1998 ▪ 1stB 2006 ▪ Tasting, sales & tours by appt ▪ Closed all pub hols ▪ 5 self-catering cottages (sleeps between 2 & 4 people) R500pp/n ▪ Olive oil ▪ Owner(s) Rob Alexander & Jaco de Wet ▪ Cellarmaster(s) Kobus van der Merwe (Jan 2006, consultant) & Jaco de Wet ▪ Winemaker(s) Kobus van der Merwe (Jan 2006, consultant), with Van Zyl de Wet (Jan 2009, consultant) ▪ Viticulturist(s) Jaco de Wet (Jan 2003) ▪ 300ha/63ha (cabs s/f, grenache, merlot, mourv, ptage, pinot, shiraz, chard, chenin, sauv) ▪ 2,000cs own label 70% red 30% white ▪ PO Box 22 Robertson 6705 ▪ info@windfallwine.co.za ▪ www.windfallwine.co.za ▪ **T +27 (0)83-320-8473**

Windmeul Cellar ⑧ ⑪ ⓐ ⓐ ⓑ

It's 80 years since Windmeul was founded as a cooperative on the lower slopes of Paarl Mountain, and named for the windmill that was once the hub of the region's economic activity. It seems that the quality of wine produced was not exactly great back then, but today's 34 grower-owners and the cellar team under veteran Danie Marais produce wines with a well-established reputation. Pinotage is something of a specialty here, the line-up led by the imposing Legend Collection example.

The Legend Collection
★★★★☆ **Pinotage** ⑧ Splendid **20** ⑨③ honours ex Windmeul director & rugby Springbok TPD Briers. Intense, long lingering, tannins well managed, oaking supportive, alc fairly modest. WO Paarl, as Reserves. Not tasted: **Chenin Blanc.** Discontinued: **Left Wing.**

Reserve range
★★★★☆ **Pinotage** ⊘ ⓐ Savoury, dark ripe fruit aromas & flavour on **19** ⑨⓪, tobacco notes from all-new oak adding to the complexity. Bold 14.7% alc & firmly tannic structure too, yet with all this power the wine is well balanced & not too imposing. A model of the grape's grander style.

★★★★☆ **Cape Blend** ⑧ Composition of **19** ⑨⓪, 60% pinotage with cab, petit verdot & merlot, repeats that of **18** ★★★★ ⑧⑨ - the Bordeaux varieties influential, with fruitcake & cedar notes, the 100% new oak well absorbed.

★★★★ **Chenin Blanc** ⊘ ⓦ First since **16** ⑧⑨, **21** ★★★★ ⑧⑤ needs time or decanting to soften & show better. Now new oak too dominant on aroma & flavour, big acid also makes for some awkwardness. But there's succulence & good fruit too.

Not tasted: **VSOP Brandy**. Discontinued: **Cabernet Sauvignon**, **Shiraz**.

Cellar range

Cabernet Sauvignon ⊘ ★★★ Good varietal notes on **21** ⑧⑴, with herbal overtones. A decent grippiness & firm dry finish, yet a welcome approachability. **Merlot** ⑧ ★★★ Fruitcake & herbaceousness on sufficiently flavoursome **20** ⑺⑼, light but grippy structure, 14.1% alc. Modest oaking, as other reds in range. **Pinotage** ⊘ ★★★★ As always, **21** ⑻⑶ a pleasure, with its juicy, tasty fruitiness yet dry finish. 14.5% alc doesn't impose. **Shiraz** ⊘ ★★★ Ripely fruity & meaty aromas & flavours on **21** ⑻⑴. Grippy & juicy, & handles its 14.5% alc well. **Cabernet Sauvignon-Merlot** ⊘ ★★★ Appealing berry charm on **20** ⑻⑵, with usual 70% cab. Flavourful, succulent & welcomely dry (like all these reds). A bonus that these are released with a few years maturity. **Pinotage Rosé** ⊘ ★★★ Fashionably pale **23** ⑻⓪ has pleasing berry character; softly textured, balanced & dry. **Chenin Blanc** ★★★ Tasted soon after bottling, **23** ⑺⑺ has some bright fruity charm, though the whack of acidity is a touch brutal. **Sauvignon Blanc** ★★★ Pre-bottling, **23** ⑺⑼ promises its usual fruity exuberance & drinkability, with a notably bright acidity. — TJ

Location/map: Paarl ▪ Map grid reference: D3 ▪ WO: Coastal/Paarl ▪ Est 1944 ▪ 1stB 1945 ▪ Tasting & sales Mon-Fri 9-5 Sat 9-3 ▪ Closed all pub hols ▪ Cellar tours by appt ▪ Parskuip Neighbourhood Marketplace Mon-Fri 8-5 Sat 9-3 ▪ Farmers' market every 1st Sat of each month (excl Jan) ▪ Function/tasting area ▪ Facilities for children ▪ Wine club ▪ Owner(s) 34 members ▪ Cellarmaster(s) Danie Marais (Oct 1999) ▪ Winemaker(s) Abraham van Heerden (Nov 2014), with Michael Kotzé (Jan 2022) ▪ Viticulturist(s) Anton Laas (Oct 2007) ▪ 1,700ha ▪ 11,000t/20,000cs own label 54% red 44% white 2% rosé ▪ PO Box 2013 Paarl 7620 ▪ windmeul@iafrica.com ▪ www.windmeul.com ▪ **T +27 (0)21-869-8100/8043**

☐ **Wine Bank** *see* Heineken Beverages

Wine-of-the-Month Club

Wine-of-the-Month is SA's longest-standing and largest wine club, offering members panel-selected wine with nationwide delivery and a money-back guarantee. Wine Tonight?, their boutique fine-wine and spirits retail outlets in Cape Town, offer customers the unique opportunity to taste any wine in store. They also host complimentary Friday afternoon tastings, and by-appointment private tastings and events. The club also has several proprietary labels, including Berg en Dal, Boschenheuwel, Jakkalskloof, Klaasenbosch, Lakehurst, Martindale, Mortons, Quartet, Semara, Sentinel, Steenhuis and Willowbrook.

Location: Cape Town ▪ Est 1986 ▪ MD Cliff Collard ▪ Private Bag X2 Glosderry 7702 ▪ cheers@wineofthemonth.co.za ▪ www.wineofthemonth.co.za ▪ **T +27 (0)21-492-4100**

☐ **Winery of Good Hope** *see* The Winery of Good Hope

Wines of Brocha

⑨ ◎

Previously listed under Iona Vineyards, this separate showcase for the varietal syrah and blend brings into focus the lower-lying sibling Elgin farm of Brocha. It's the site of a new syrah vineyard-in-the-making, designed and laid out by consultant Jaco Engelbrecht, using the staked-vine (echalas) system and a 'serpentine' shape to accommodate the steep gradient without the need for terracing. The team of Iona winemaker Werner Muller and Brocha viticulturist Bobby Wallace are overseeing the planting, and will nurture the completed block as naturally as possible to ensure the resulting wine is 'sincere and genuinely representative of the site'.

★★★★★ **Solace** ⑧ Syrah from two parcels on stony, north-facing sites on Brocha farm, sensitively oaked, 10% new, mostly French. **20** ⑼⑶ white pepper dusted, finely structured & tightly coiled, with elegance & thrilling purity of black cherry & red plum fruit.

★★★★☆ **One Man Band** ⑧ Syrah 46% leads eclectic 'band' in masterly **19** ⑼⑷, with 22% petit verdot, splashes 4 others including last-tasted **17** ⑼⑴'s frontman, cab. Fleshy but firm, savoury & dry, with spicy oak tannins & hallmark muscles best decanted now or preferably cellared few years.— CvZ

Location/map/WO: Elgin ▪ Map grid reference: C4 ▪ Est 2002 ▪ 1stB 2001 ▪ Tasting, sales & tours Mon-Fri 9-4 Sat by appt ▪ Walks/hikes ▪ MTB ▪ Conservation area ▪ Owner(s) Rozanne Gunn ▪ Winemaker(s) Werner Muller (May 2011) ▪ Vineyard manager(s) Bobby Wallace (May 2017) ▪ Viticulturist(s) Bobby Wallace ▪ 10ha (mourv, p verdot, shiraz, sauv, sem) ▪ PO Box 527 Grabouw 7160 ▪ orders@iona.co.za ▪ www.iona.co.za ▪ **T +27 (0)28-284-9678**

Wine Village-Hermanus

With over a quarter-century as a fine-wine store, and an international customer base, Wine Village under recent owner Jean-Pierre Rossouw offers over 4,500 curated South African wines, gins and brandies under one roof in Hermanus, including the house label Are We Having Fun Yet?, not ready for tasting this time.

Location: Hermanus ▪ Map: Walker Bay & Bot River ▪ Map grid reference: A3 ▪ Est 1998 ▪ 1stB 2004 ▪ Open Mon-Fri 9-6 Sat 9-5 Sun 10-3 ▪ Closed Dec 25 ▪ Tasting of wine, gin & brandy ▪ Owner(s) Jean-Pierre Rossouw ▪ ±2,000cs 50% red 50% white ▪ PO Box 465 Hermanus 7200 ▪ info@winevillage.co.za ▪ www. winevillage.co.za ▪ **T +27 (0)28-316-3988**

Wineways Marketing

Extensive negociant business Wineways Marketing sources fruit widely for vinification by Leeuwenkuil and Stellenbosch Vineyards, and marketing under a variety of brand names. The wines, some in bag-in-box, offer good value, and are available locally and in many export markets. Kuils River-based Wineways also distributes the De Villiers Wines range; see separate listing for wine descriptions and winery details.

Black Box range

Merlot ⊘ ★★★ Cassis & plums, fruit-driven NV ⑧⑴ has a matching palate, smooth & tasty. Unoaked & easy drinking, as all ranges. **Pinotage** ⊘ ★★★ No shortage of fruit in NV ⑧⑴, succulent & rounded body, ends tasty-fresh. **Shiraz** ⊘ ★★★ Dark-toned fruit, suggestion of scrub, NV ⑧⑴ has great drinkability thanks to the freshness & fleshy body, unaided by sugar this time. **Cabernet Sauvignon-Merlot** ⊘ ★★★ Cab the leader at 55%, but both partners contribute to NV ⑧⑴'s cassis-driven, lipsmacking succulence, suede-textured body. 5L pack for all in this range.

Black Tie range

Cabernet Sauvignon ⊘ ★★★ True to the variety, 22 ⑧⑵ has prominent cassis perfume & flavours, sleek texture, fresh end. **Merlot** ⊘ ★★★ Aromatic cassis & cherries draw you in to 22 ⑧⑴'s unruffled palate, juicy freshness. **Pinotage** ⊘ ★★★ Forthcoming berry & cherry fruit, 22 ⑧⑴ has buffed texture & freshness, upping the appetite appeal. **Cabernet Sauvignon-Merlot** ⊘ ★★★ Beneficiary of 3 months lees contact for the curvaceous body, but 22 ⑧⑵ offers more than that: vivid red berries & plums, tasty freshness. **Semi-Sweet Shiraz** ⊘ ★★☆ Brambly fruit typicity, 22 ⑦⑻ streamlined, the sweetness giving fullness, enhancing the fruit. Nice drinkability. Discontinued: **Sauvignon Blanc**.

Coral Reef range

Cabernet Sauvignon ⊘ ★★★ With forthcoming variety-true cassis perfume & flavours, svelte 22 ⑧⑵ ends fresh. **Merlot** ⊘ ★★★ Smooth & open-textured 22 ⑧⑴ has appealingly aromatic cassis & cherries, sappy flavours. **Pinotage** ⊘ ★★★ 22 ⑧⑴ offers expressive berry & cherry fruit, unaggressive tannins & good mouthfeel. **Cabernet Sauvignon-Merlot** ⊘ ★★★ Showing vivid red berries & plums, a well-shaped body from few months on the lees, 22 ⑧⑵ is lively & moreish. **Sauvignon Blanc** ⊘ ★★★ Expressive kiwi & litchi, dry 23 ⑧⑵ oozes freshness, is trim (12.5% alc) but has no shortage of flavour. **Semi-Sweet Shiraz** ⊘ ★★☆ True to the variety, 22 ⑦⑻ has brambly aromas & flavours, a streamlined body which the sweetness has plumped out, enhancing the fruit.

Leipoldt 1880 range

Cabernet Sauvignon-Merlot ⊘ ★★★ Has multiple attractions in 22 ⑧⑵: red berries & plums, ample flavour & verve, mellow texture from brief lees ageing in tank. **Smooth Red** ⊘ ★★★ Unspecified blend, with touch of fattening sweetness, fruity NV ⑦⑼ hints at fruit pastille richness, drinks easily. **Sauvignon Blanc** ⊘ ★★★ Slender build (12.5% alc) but generous tropical fruit flavours on 23 ⑧⑵, backed by zinging freshness. **Semi-Sweet Shiraz** ⊘ ★★☆ Part of 22 ⑦⑻'s appeal is the brambly fruit, typical of the variety, the sweetness giving fullness, enhancing the fruit. Discontinued: **Fruity Dry White**.

Tin Cups Screw Cap range

Smooth Red ⊘ ★★★ Undisclosed variety/ies, with a few grams of sugar, NV ⑦⑼ fruity, with some pastille richness. Goes down easily. Discontinued: **Cabernet Sauvignon-Merlot**, **Fruity Dry White**. — CR

Location: Kuils River ▪ WO: Western Cape ▪ Est 2000 ▪ Closed to public ▪ Owner(s) Carl Schmidt, Stephen Vermeulen & Fanie Marais ▪ Winemaker(s) Pieter Carstens & Corrien Basson (Leeuwenkuil), Bernard Claassen (Stellenbosch Vineyards) ▪ 400,000cs own label 80% red 20% white ▪ Plot 689, Zinfandel Str, Saxenburg Park 2, Blackheath 7580 ▪ info@wine-ways.co.za ▪ www.wine-ways.co.za ▪ **T +27 (0)21-905-7713/6/9**

Winshaw Vineyards

At their extensive Stellenbosch farm, 'family' and 'heritage' are keywords for JP Winshaw and sibling Pierre, also part-owner, winemaker and viticulturist, who celebrate their grandfather Charles and great-grandfather Bill in these Bordeaux-accented craft ranges (Usana previously listed separately). An American doctor who arrived in the Cape at the turn of the 20th century, Bill went on to create Stellenbosch Farmers' Winery, founder member of today's giant Heineken Beverages. With 'the utmost work in the vineyard' and 'a soft hand in the cellar', the brothers want their wines 'to tell a story about the vintage and the farm's terroir'.

Winshaw Heritage range

★★★★☆ **Malbec** Wholebunch & wild ferment for all, reds in open tanks, whites in barrel. **22** ⑨④ lighter oaking than companions, just 12 months, to showcase dark-toned fruit, streamlined texture while adding cocoa, peppery spice. Lovely drinkability with serious intent, ageability. Also-tasted **21** ⑨③, same oak, showing standout dark fruit seamed by savoury spice, a scrub nuance. Finishes firm & dry but not harsh, the credentials for a long life.

★★★★☆ **Bill Winshaw** Cape Bordeaux **19** ⑨④ is 82% cab franc, equal dabs 3 others, 20 months in small barrels (as all reds except malbec), 61% new, beneficially tad less than **18** ⑨④ so fruit not overwhelmed, instead shows red berries, some cassis, graphite & hint of dried herbs, the classic cab franc profile. Texture succulent, grip at the end, attesting to cellaring potential.

★★★★☆ **Charles Winshaw** This a different take on red Bordeaux. Serious wine in composition & cellar handling: 61% cab with malbec, cab franc & merlot, barrels 53% new, but fruit good enough to handle it. Vivid cassis in **19** ⑨③, savoury spice & cured meat notes threaded through, the firm dry finish confirming the ageing potential.

Winshaw Usana Story range

★★★★ **The Fox Cabernet Sauvignon** Better fruit-oak balance in **19** ⑧⑦ than **18** ★★★★ ⑧⑤, cassis shines through, the 25% new barrels a dry savoury seam in the flavours, ensuring a future.

★★★★ **Gold Dust To Grapes Chardonnay** Same oaking as chenin, but **22** ⑧⑧ much lighter (12.5% alc) & the savoury notes are more prominent in the citrus. Lovely salty freshness perks it up, ends limy.

★★★★ **Swashbuckler Chenin Blanc** Riper chenin, 9-month oaking assimilated as shortbread overlay to melon preserve & quince, **22** ⑧⑧ has aroma & flavour richness; palate weight makes it a pleasure.

★★★★ **The Queen's Horses Pinot Gris** Differs from sibling in being fully oaked: barrel ferment, 5 months on lees, then further 9 months ageing, giving **22** ⑧⑨ buttered toast top note to greengage & green apple. More complex than Runaway, perfectly suited to food pairing. No **21**.

★★★★ **The Runaway Pinot Gris** Particular care taken, picked in 3 batches as sibling), **22** ⑧⑧ fermented/7 months stainless steel & 40% old barrels, long lees contact. Fruit stands out, greengage & apple, trim (13% alc) & bone-dry, gentle oat biscuit savoury notes at the end.

★★★★ **The Doctor's Journey Sauvignon Blanc** Combo seasoned barrels, 7 months, for half of **22** ⑧⑨, rest plastic eggs, leaving fruit & freshness intact. Gooseberry & winter melon, ending mineral & long. Sauvignon with the added interest of delicate savoury notes.

Not tasted: **Luck Of The Gambler Pinot Gris.** — CR

Location/map/WO: Stellenbosch ▪ Map grid reference: C8 ▪ Est/1stB 2017 ▪ Tasting & sales open Wed-Sun 10-5 ▪ Farm produce ▪ Weddings & functions ▪ Deli ▪ Restaurant ▪ Butchery ▪ Owner(s) JP & Pierre Winshaw ▪ Winemaker(s)/viticulturist(s) Pierre Winshaw ▪ 300ha/45ha (cabs s/f, malbec, merlot, chard, chenin, pinot gris) ▪ 35t/5,000cs own label 50% red 50% white ▪ PO Box 68 Lynedoch 7603 ▪ jp@winshaw.co.za, pierre@winshaw.co.za ▪ www.winshaw.co.za ▪ **T +27 (0)83-650-9528**

Withington

Based in Darling, Charles Withington owns and runs a fine-wine shop and small merchant label, the latter featuring his lauded contribution to the Cape Brandy category. This, he's pleased to note, 'is at last becoming recognised as comparable to the best in the world'. About his pair of wines, Malbec and Roan Ranger, unready for tasting by us, he chuckles: 'Like the groundsman at Lord's, we just keep rolling that pitch...'

Cape Brandy range
★★★★ **Voorkamer VSOP** Latest blend ⑧⑨ contains only 6 & 8 year old potstill brandies for usual sophisticated but friendly (even seductive) charm. Floral & fruity bouquet with nutty & spicy undertones, palate rich with sweet apricot, 40% alc fully harmonious, the whole as smooth as ever.— TJ

Location: Darling ▪ Map: Durbanville, Philadelphia & Darling ▪ Map grid reference: A1 ▪ Est 2001 ▪ 1stB 2003 ▪ Tasting & sales at Darling Wine Shop Mon-Sat 10-6 (10-7 in summer) Sun 11-2; pub hols (seasonal) please call ahead ▪ Closed Mar 21, Easter Fri/Sun & Dec 25/26 ▪ Fresh West Coast mussels on order every Friday ▪ Owner(s) Withington family ▪ 2,000cs own label 90% red 10% Cape brandy ▪ 5 Main Str Darling 7345 ▪ taste@withington.co.za ▪ www.withington.co.za ▪ **T +27 (0)22-492-3971/+27 (0)74-194-1711**

☐ **With Love From The Cape** see Rascallion Wines
☐ **Witklip** see Eerste Hoop Wine Cellar
☐ **Woestkloof** see Simelia Wines
☐ **Wolfgat** see Gedeelte Wines
☐ **Wolftrap** see The Wolftrap

Wolf & Woman Wines

The labels feature a memorable juxtaposition of a wolf and a woman. The latter is Jolandie Fouché, making a small range of 'honest and sincere' wines, working minimalistically and lightly with grapes from selected old Swartland vineyards 'that tell the stories of their seasons and unveil their unique personalities in unexpected ways'. In this she's inspired by the wolf, 'fierce, untamed and glorious'.

★★★★☆ **Pinotage** ⊛ ⊛ Paardeberg 1973 vines spotlit in new-generation style, 22 ⑨④ as flavoursome & engaging as before. Well crafted, 15% wholebunch ferment, rest wholeberry, old-oak aged, 300 & 500L barrels, 10 months, allowing fruit purity to shine. Lovely vibrancy & freshness, an elegant nod to grape's pinot noir parentage.

★★★★★ **Syrah** ⊛ ⊛ Riper & richer in 22 ★★★★☆ ⑨④, with similar infusion of white & black pepper to freshen dark-berried fruit. Naturally fermented whole bunches provide firm, supple structure; fuller bodied (13.8% alc) than 21 ⑨⑤ but balanced, lovely spicy undertone to complex layers. Old oak, 10 months.

★★★★☆ **Chenin Blanc** ⊛ ⊛ As composed, understated yet persistent in 22 ⑨③, from bushvines planted 1971-1981. Similar savoury nuance to subtle dried pineapple & stonefruit, silky texture from natural ferment & lees ageing in older oak. Effortlessly elegant & balanced.

★★★★ **Grenache Blanc** Tad less expressive in 22 ⑧⑦ from a different fruit source, now WO W Cape. Still very appealing, with more muted baked apple & quince flavours, waxy texture; less viscous than last courtesy freshening twist of lime.

Not tasted: **Grenache Rosé**. — MW

Location: Malmesbury ▪ WO: Swartland/Western Cape ▪ Est/1stB 2018 ▪ Closed to public ▪ Owner(s) Jolandie Fouché ▪ Winemaker(s) Jolandie Fouché (Jan 2018) ▪ 5t 40% red 60% white ▪ jolandie@wolfandwoman-wines.com ▪ www.wolfandwomanwines.com ▪ **T +27 (0)83-602-5602**

Wolvenhoek Vineyards ⓛ ⑪ ⊖ ⊚

The Belgian Sas family acquired the Wolvenhoek property in Wellington's Groenberg ward in 2018, and a consultant made the first small quantity of low-intervention wine two years later. The on-site cellar is complete, and now there are inter-range movements, renamings and new releases, with more debuts promised.

Single Vineyard range
★★★★☆ **Impisi Old Vine Chenin Blanc** ⊛ ⊛ Adds 'Impisi' to name. More oak (90%, 7 months, none new) than other chenin, plays a savoury role in 22 ⑨⓪, adding richness to marmalade styling, giving palate weight despite modest 12.5% alc. Bold, makes a statement.

Not tasted: **Shiraz**.

Premium range
★★★★☆ **Takaya** ⑭ ⊛ Shiraz dictates at 55% but 3 Bordeaux varieties add layers, depth. Spiced fruit-cake, cocoa, 21 ⑨⓪'s perfume seduces while palate earns respect with ripe tannin backbone for cellaring. Crafted for both appeal & structure, 70% in barrique 14 months.

★★★★ **The Emerald Hill**  Pared-down cellar handling & just shiraz (80%) & cab in **22** (88), but nothing lost, attraction remains. Bright fruit, spice array, lovely succulence & texture, tannin seam from 14 months in barrique adds definition. Nice contrast to Baba Yeto blend.

Baba Yetu range

★★★★ **Cabernet Sauvignon-Shiraz** (NEW) ⊘ Near-equal blend, **22** (88) proof of how well it works: plush dark fruit, spiced by time in oak. Delicious, has silky succulence, concentrated flavour, good length.

★★★★ **Old Vine Chenin Blanc** ⊘ ✹ Just 10% oaked, imparts thatch note to **22** (87)'s apple & pear. Trim figured at 12% alc but has mouthfeel, plenty of personality.

Shiraz Rosé ★★★ Strawberry tones of **22** (82) spark with life, freshness. Bone-dry, for food or solo. — CR

Location/map: Wellington ▪ Map grid reference: C2 ▪ WO: Groenberg ▪ Est 2018 ▪ 1stB 2020 ▪ Tasting, sales & cellar tours Mon-Sat 10-4 Sun/pub hols by appt only ▪ Tasting fee R50 ▪ Closed Easter Sun, Dec 25/26 & Jan 1 ▪ Breakfast & lunch; dinner by appt ▪ Farm produce ▪ BYO picnic ▪ Conference facility ▪ Walks/hikes ▪ 4x4 trail ▪ MTB trail ▪ Wine club ▪ Owner(s) Wolvenhoek Beleggings (Pty) Ltd ▪ Viticulturist(s) Ronald Spiers (Aug 2020, consultant) ▪ 84ha/21ha (cab, grenache n/b, shiraz, chenin) ▪ 160t/8,000cs own label 55% red 30% white 7% rosé 8% MCC ▪ Other export brand: Baba Yetu ▪ WIETA ▪ Wolvenhoek Farm, 38 Slangrivier Rd, Wellington 7655 ▪ info@wolvenhoekvineyards.com ▪ www.wolvenhoekvineyards.com ▪ **T +27 (0)60-820-6482**

☐ **Wonderfontein** see Paul René Cap Classique

Woolworths

Upmarket, nationwide retail giant Woolworths for more than 35 years has treated winelovers with an exceptionally wide, knowledgeably curated and merchandised collection of wines specially selected for the brand everyone knows as 'Woolies'. The current buying team continue the sterling work with the latest menu of around 200 wines, offering quality, value and off-the-shelf drinkability for special and everyday occasions.

Cabernet Sauvignon range

★★★★☆ **Alto Cabernet Sauvignon** (NEW) ⊘ Convincing varietal character & muscle in **18** (90), with tarry-earthy notes & succulent black fruit. Ripe & confident, tannins powdery & gripping, showing well, with potential for several years' cellaring. 18 months in oak.

★★★★ **Diemersdal Reserve Collection Cabernet Sauvignon** ⊘ Succulent **22** (88) weaves ripe cassis fruit & spice of seasoned oak into a rich yet elegantly dry glassful. Savoury, like last-tasted **20** (87), ready to grace the dinner table.

★★★★ **Kleine Zalze Cabernet Sauvignon** ⊘ Fruitcake, tobacco & cedar on **20** (86). Though light & pliable, with gentle grip, has more depth, body & length than **19** ★★★★ (85), aided by year in old oak.

★★★★ **Signature Cabernet Sauvignon** ⊘ By Thelema, showing distinctive depth & muscle, **20** (90) has noble bearing, fine balance too. Cassis, leather & roast meat, some tarry liquorice, all wrapped in full, ripe tannins. 18 months older oak. 100% cab, **19** ★★★★ (88) had dabs merlot & petit verdot.

★★★★ **Spier Private Collection Cabernet Sauvignon** Classic aromas of blackcurrant & cedar on **21** (86). Ripe, rich, juicy fruit is the focus, well supported by integrated oak & tannins both grippy & rounded. Good drinking now, but no hurry.

★★★★ **Thelema Cool Climate Cabernet Sauvignon** ⊘ Leaner than house style but still distinctively herbaceous & refined, **21** (88) offers supple, juicy black fruit beefed up with 9% petit verdot. Vibrant, nervy, tannins smoothed by 18 months oak, 35% new.

★★★★ **Villiera Cabernet Sauvignon** Usual splash cab franc for additional freshness, leafy top note to **21** (87)'s deep cassis & black pastille. Sweet-oak spice from 10% American oak, rounded tannins, yet enough grip for food.

Blackberry Cabernet Sauvignon (🍇) ★★★ Super-juicy **21** (81) abounds with blue- & black-berries, tailored with 3 months in older oak. Great braai companion. By Cape Wine Crafters. **House Cabernet Sauvignon** ⊘ ★★★ A touch riper in **22** (82), softening the herby nuance. Dry tannins, with toasty top note from oaking; one for the table. By Koopmanskloof. **Organic No Added Sulphites Cabernet Sauvignon** (🍇) ⊘ ★★★ Undemanding everyday quaffing in **21** (79) by Stellar Winery, offering vanilla-scented cassis & herbal aromas & flavours. Fairtrade certified. **Spier Cabernet Sauvignon** ★★★ Only lightly oaked to keep the pure ripe fruit character, **22** (82) balanced for easy, softly textured, early drinking, but well structured, pretty dry & varietally true. **Warwick Cape Lady Cabernet Sauvignon** (🍇) ★★★★

Youthful **20** (85) delivers abundant ripe blackberry fruit, freshness, & enough structure for immediate & few years' pleasure. Year oak, 10% new, mainly staves.

Merlot range

★★★★ Ladybird Organic Merlot (Ⓥ) (Ⓨ) Succulent plum & cassis on **20** (88), food-friendly meatiness with spice overlay from year in oak, 5% new. By Ladybird Vineyards.

★★★★ Reserve Collection Merlot (Ⓨ) Hartenberg's **21** (86) has chocolate-coated cherries, fine notes of scrub & spice, a white pepper undertone on ripe, grainy tannins, honed 18 months in older oak.

★★★★ Thelema Cool Climate Merlot (Ⓨ) Mild in manner & body, **21** (87) appeals with ripe plum & redcurrant fruit. Soft, leathery tannins & sweetly spiced finish add to charm. 18 months oak, 25% new.

★★★★ Tokara Merlot (Ⓨ) Bags of cocoa & hedgerow fruit on supple **21** (88). Plush, rounded & appealing, with harmonious spicy grip from 20 months in oak, 15% new. Balanced & rewarding.

★★★★ Villiera Merlot Tiny drop touriga for colour, 20% new oak neatly enhance **21** (87)'s fleshy dark orchard fruit. Inviting raspberry top note & tang, densely packed tannins for food or cellaring few years.

Blackcherry Merlot ★★☆ Espresso, cocoa & black cherry in harmony on well-judged **22** (79). Easy to drink, kiss of fruity sweetness on finish. By Cape Wine Crafters. **Durbanville Hills Merlot ★★★☆** Previewed **21** (83) attractive deep purple hue with forward red & black plums, fleshy body & sweet vanilla overlay from year in oak, 50% new, rounding very dry finish. **House Merlot** (Ⓨ) **★★★** Spicy, perfumed red fruit in **22** (81), with distinctly toasty nuance. Slightly edgy in youth, better with a meal. By Koopmanskloof. **La Motte Platinum Merlot ★★★★** Juicy, friendly & bright **21** (85), with abundant vanilla-dipped red plum & spice-laden farewell from year in older barrels. **Light Merlot ★★** Fruitcake notes on **22** (73) from Spier; soft, nearly dry & a touch insipid. 9% alc. **Organic No Added Sulphites Merlot** (Ⓥ) (Ⓨ) **★★☆** Stellar Winery's easy, smooth **21** (79) delivers succulent vanilla-coated red berry flavour. Fairtrade certified. **Spier Merlot ★★★** Modest fruitcake charm on **22** (82). Smooth & easygoing with a bit of grip, just about dry. Last tasted was **19** (82).

Pinot Noir range

★★★★☆ Catherine Marshall Reserve Collection Pinot Noir (Ⓨ) Fragrant, forthcoming **22** (90) is sultry, smoky & seductive, earthy strands running through fragrant red berry fruit. Sleek tannins & gentle acid maintain balance & poise. Seasoned oak, 10 months, in sync.

★★★★ Iona Ten Barrels Pinot Noir (Ⓨ) Deftly oaked, just 4% new, to showcase fruit purity & freshness, **22** (89) smooth, with piquant raspberry & cranberry fruit, whiff of clean earth. Intended for early drinking but will improve over few years. **20**, **21** untasted.

DMZ Pinot Noir (Ⓨ) **★★★** Light & fruit forward, **22** (84) by DeMorgenzon offers hints of earthiness with honest red berry fruit. Unoaked, for early drinking.

Pinotage range

★★★★ Bellevue Reserve Collection Pinotage (Ⓨ) Fuller bodied than last, **20** (86) retains juicy wildberry fruit, unshowy elegance, fine tannins. Spice from year in French & American oak.

★★★★ Diemersfontein Pinotage Reserve Continues fine form in **22** (89), even more delicious dark chocolate, black cherry & mulberry fruit. Tannin & oak, 50% new, 16 months, deftly integrated, help to streamline opulent fruit. Very moreish.

★★★★ Signature Pinotage (Ⓥ) By Beyerskloof, serious wine for dinner parties & special occasions, **19** (89) fine intensity of plum pudding & blackberry, succulent & round, spice from 15 months in 15% new oak. **Beyerskloof Reserve Collection Pinotage ★★★☆** Melange of plums, cherries, berries & spice on lightly oaked **20** (85). Rounded, agile & smooth for everyday enjoyment. **Organic No Added Sulphites Pinotage** (Ⓥ) (Ⓨ) **★★★** Oak treatment lends a coffee nuance to **21** (80)'s velvety ripe plum palate, fynbos perfume adds interest. For current drinking by Stellar Winery. Fairtrade certified. **Plum Pinotage ★★★** Smoky plums & mulberries in **22** (82), ripe & cheerful, more balanced than last. By Diemersfontein.

Shiraz range

★★★★☆ Neil Ellis Groenekloof Bush Vine Shiraz (Ⓨ) Charming, rich & sleek, **20** (90) offers scrub & pepper woven with succulent black cherries. Scented highlights from whole-bunch & -berry ferments, 14 months in mostly seasoned oak. Good now, but legs for several more years. Certified vegan.

★★★★ **Reserve Collection Shiraz** ⊘ Previewed last time, sleek, classy **20** ⑧⑦ by shiraz specialist Hartenberg has meaty-savoury notes, hints of tobacco & fynbos, opulent black cherry fruit. Rich, satisfying, polished by 18 months in seasoned oak.

★★★★ **Saronsberg Life Is Fine Shiraz** Full, rounded **21** ⑧⑦ shows dark fruit, meat spice & dark choc-olate on a supple frame of tannin, ends on a delicious roasted nut & raisin note. 20 months older barrels.

★★★★ **Woolworths Signature Shiraz** From Hartenberg, showing typical flair for variety, **20** ⑧⑨ plush & juicy, with loads of extract. Black cherry & plum fruit has notes of roast meat & tobacco, delicate scrub flowers, on ripe, smooth tannins.

Diemersdal Syrah (NEW) ★★★☆ Layered & textured **22** ⑧⑤, generous dark-berry compote, spice & cured meat attractions paired with an earthiness from dab grenache noir. Super BBQ partner. **House Shiraz** ⊘ ★★★☆ Preview of **21** ⑧④ from Diemersfontein fills the glass with savoury tapenade & sweet oak spice, has a good structure, too, for mealtime enjoyment. Ticks the typicity box as well. **Kleine Zalze Shiraz** ⊘ ★★★☆ Supple, rounded & easy to like, **21** ⑧⑤'s inky spice & plum plushness gently countered by chalky tannin grip. Year in older oak. **Mocha Shiraz** ★★★ Aptly named **23** ⑧② pre-bottling sample exudes dark chocolate & sweet clove. Supple tannin & toasty top note from oak stave treatment. By Diemersfontein.

Organic No Added Sulphites Shiraz ⑳ ⊘ ★★★ Accessible **21** ⑦⑨ by Stellar Winery ticks the drink-ability box with sappy dark berries, with wild herbs, spice & liquorice adding allure. Fairtrade certified.

Niche Red Cultivars

★★★★☆ **Raats Granite Blocks Cabernet Franc** ⊘ From a cab franc master, serious, firmly structured **21** ⑨② which is approachable but would benefit from decanting or few years in bottle. Fragrant, with herbal tinge, supple, bright full-fruited palate. Only older oak.

★★★★ **Woolworths Cherry Cinsault** ⊘ Showing variety's prettiness & delicacy, supple & juicy **22** ⑧⑥ from Adama gushes red berry fruit, its sleek body has gentle tannins & scented finish. Partly oaked, whereas last-tasted **20** ⑧⑥ was unwooded.

★★★★ **Bellevue Reserve Collection Malbec** ⊘ Vivacious & fruit-packed **21** ⑧⑥ starts with pulpy red berries & blackcurrants, ends with piquant raspberries. Ripe tannins provide texture & support, year in 25% new oak adds spice & volume.

★★★★ **Diemersfontein Malbec Reserve** Mouthfilling & succulent, previewed **22** ⑧⑧ dark berries & meaty savouriness with supple dry tannins after 14 months in oak, half new. Fresh & bursting with flavour.

★★★★ **Terra Del Capo Reserve Collection Sangiovese** ⊘ Anthonij Rupert's **21** ⑧⑥ adds dab cinsaut fruitiness to main variety's slightly earthy sour cherry character, dry tannin & acid bite for a piquant aperitif or dinner partner. 15 months in oak.

★★★★ **Touriga Nacional** ⊘ Up a notch on last release, **22** ⑧⑦ by Boplaas is appealing, approachable & lively, offers cherries & aromatic spice from 10 months seasoned oak, light squeeze of tannin.

Ken Forrester Reserve Collection Grenache ⊘ ★★★☆ Gentle **22** ⑧⑤ from old Stellenbosch vines. Year in seasoned barrels polishes the sappy berries & plums. **Boplaas Tinta Barocca** ⑳ ★★★☆ Raspberry & blueberry charm on spicy **21** ⑧④. Sappy, balanced & enduring flavours, squeeze of dry tannin.

Red Blends

★★★★ **Delheim Reserve Collection Cabernet Sauvignon-Merlot** Recently more serious yet still delightful & thoroughly drinkable. **21** ⑧⑧ has dark-berry fruit intensity & elegant cedar perfume.

★★★★ **Ladybird Red** ⊘ Bordeaux blend invariably scores high in both drinkability & quality. **20** ⑧⑨ cherry flavours & some earth, dried herbs & spice, pleasingly firm on the palate.

★★★★ **Neil Ellis Reserve Collection Cabernet Sauvignon-Merlot** ⊘ Plush & juicy, **21** ⑧⑧ has substance, polish & style, offering spice-laced blackcurrants with tarry tobacco notes, hints of liquorice & iodine. Splashes malbec & cab franc add interest. Oaked 17 months, 25% new. Certified vegan.

★★★★ **Warwick Cape Lady Cape Blend** ⑳ Fragrant, red-berry & rose-scented blend, pinotage, merlot & cab (70/17/13). **20** ⑧⑥ ripe & juicily soft, cab's rounded tannins giving just enough form without hindering ready drinkability. Older oak, 70% barrel, balance staves. No **19**.

★★★★ **Reserve Collection Shiraz-Grenache-Mourvèdre** ⊘ Sappy & vibrant **21** ⑧⑥ preview is 65% shiraz, seamlessly integrated with its partners after 18 months in older oak, rounded & ready for satisfying drinking. By Ken Forrester.

★★★★ **Saronsberg SGM** Shiraz & roughly equal grenache noir & mourvèdre, 19 months in oak, 10% new. 21 ⑧⑥ bright, juicy, packed with dark berries & scents of fynbos, hedgerows & earth.

★★★★ **Alto 1693** ⊘ Blackcurrant- & liquorice-toned 21 ⑧⑦ full & ripe, very satisfying mouthful. Near-identical Bordeaux-shiraz blend to Alto Estate's enduring Rouge.

★★★★ **Fairview Roaming Goat** ⊘ Juicy & flavoursome 8-way blend, 22 ⑧⑦ spicy red berries, dusting of pepper & sweet cinnamon from light oaking. Silky tannins, balanced freshness & grip for attractive easy drinking.

Diemersdal Reserve Collection Merlot-Malbec ★★★★ Abundant red & black berries mingle in meaty 23 ⑧④, leading to firm savoury finish. Seasoned oaked adds dark chocolate nuance for even more interest. **House Cabernet Sauvignon-Merlot** ★★★ A 70/30 blend by Koopmanskloof in 22 ⑧①. Ample dark fruit, sweet & toasty oak, still a tad edgy, with brisk acidity & firmish tannins. Needs a hearty meal. **La Motte Platinum Cabernet Sauvignon-Merlot** ★★★★ Friendly & juicy for any occasion, 21 ⑧⑤ sees plums, Xmas cake & warm spice leap out the glass, silky smooth from year in older barrels. **Porcupine Ridge Cabernet Sauvignon-Merlot** ⊘ ★★★★ Equal combo 22 ⑧③ punches above its price with good varietal expression of plums & black berries, melded oak from well-judged seasoned barrels & staves. Certified vegan. **Light Red** ★★ Spier's unwooded shiraz-pinotage 22 ⑦⑤ has a dilute fruitiness & a vinous touch at 9% alc. **Diemersfontein Cabernet Sauvignon-Shiraz** ⊘ ★★★★ Dark berries & dusting of pepper in 75/25 blend. 21 ⑧⑤ well structured, with older oak in solid support. A tablemate ending respectably dry. **Grand Rouge** ⊘ ★★★★ Easygoing 21 ⑧④ cab & merlot combo with juicy black & red fruit well-seasoned with savoury herbs from year in oak. By La Motte. **Hartenberg Cabernet Sauvignon-Shiraz** ★★★★ One of this range's perennial favourites for solo fireside sipping or the table. Unpretentious 21 ⑧⑤ ripe & bright berry-currant fruit, decent structure: very satisfying glassful.

Rosé Wines

David Nieuwoudt Cinsault Rosé ⊘ ★★★★ Rose-scented strawberry delight, 23 ⑧⑤ light, sunny & inviting, for poolside refreshment or seafood pairing. **Diemersdal Reserve Collection Grenache Rosé** ⊘ ★★★ Candy cane pink 23 ⑧① exudes damp earth aromas & zesty cranberry flavour, a lemony touch at the dry end. **Light Rosé** ★★★ From pinotage & pinot noir, 23 ⑧② pale sunset hue, fresh berries & lively acid, just-dry & less than 10% alc. Ideal summer poolside sipper by Villiera. **Strawberry Rosé** ★★★ Full, sweet-ripe fruit & hint candyfloss on 23 ⑦⑨, 77% chardonnay, pinot noir & dab shiraz. Strawberry to the core, juicy dry finish. By Cape Wine Crafters. **Warwick Cape Lady Rosé** ⑧ ★★★★ From Swartland pinotage, 22 ⑧④ bright & appealingly light, with delicate, juicy strawberry flavours, softly dry. Modest 11.5% alc. **Natural Sweet Rosé** ★★ Pleasant enough boiled-sweet character on 23 ⑦④ from Spier. Sweet but uncloying; 8.5% alc.

Chardonnay range

★★★★☆ **Iona Ten Barrels Chardonnay** Refined & flavoursome cool-climate expression. 22 ⑨① lemon, lemon blossom & lemongrass perfume, satisfying weight & vinosity at less than 13% alc, oak barely a whisper, just there in support.

★★★★★ **Ladybird Chardonnay** ⊘ Aided by dab chenin, 22 ⑨⓪ will complement all manner of foods given its textured mouthfeel & inviting flavours & aromas of citrus, spanspek, spice & flowers.

★★★★☆ **Neil Ellis Barrel Fermented Chardonnay** ⑧ Confident & approachable 21 ⑨① almost carbon copy of previous. Seamlessly combines & balances bright lemon & lime fruit, oak-derived almond nougat flavours, vigorous acid. Fermented/8 months in barrique, 20% new. Certified vegan.

★★★★ **Reserve Collection Chardonnay** Hartenberg's distinctive house style subtly stamped on lithe, lightly oaked 22 ⑧⑥ (just 40% saw older barrels). Supple, nicely rounded, generously citrus-fruited, finishes with lemon twist.

★★★★ **Thelema Cool Climate Chardonnay** Lithe & linear, richly seamed with citrus acid, 22 ⑧⑨ from Sutherland vines in Elgin oozes charm. Creamy texture highlights limes & lemons, suggesting seafood pairing. 10 months 35% new barrels lend subtle smoothness.

Spier Chardonnay ★★★ A touch of bubblegum along with varietal character on 23 ⑧②. Flavourful & nicely rounded, with a fresh lemony tartness. Slight brush of oak. **Vanilla Chardonnay** ★★★ Vanilla-infusing American oak marries rich pineapple & mango in 22 ⑦⑧, finishes with touch sweetness. **Warwick Cape Lady Chardonnay** ⑧ ★★★★ Two months on lees, tiny oaked portion add breadth, drinkability to fresh citrusy & floral fruit on 22 ⑧③. **House Chardonnay** ★★★ Good weight on 23 ⑧② though unoaked, fleshy stonefruit & baking apples balanced by citrus acid. By Cape Wine Crafters, as Vanilla sibling. **Organic Chardonnay** Ⓐ Ⓥ ★★★ Bouncy & fresh **21** ⑦⑧ is unwooded, spotlighting its melon & apple flavours. Shows Stellar Winery's signature modest alc (±12%). Fairtrade certified.

Chenin Blanc range

★★★★ **DMZ Chenin Blanc** Wild yeast fermented in older barrels & tank, **23** ⑧⑥ plump & well rounded, appealing honeyed peach & apricot fruit, subtle oak spicing, impressive weight & balance.

★★★★ **Ken Forrester Reserve Collection Chenin Blanc** Ⓥ Peach blossom & lime alongside exotic cardamom & gingery quince notes on **22** ⑧⑧, which goes up a notch with its lithe, complex body & silken finish from tiny oaked component.

★★★★☆ **Signature Chenin Blanc By Ken Forrester** Ⓥ Hallmark salty oystershell nuance on **22** ⑨② from Piekenierskloof & Swartland fruit, year in old oak, adding breadth & touch of creamy lees to white pear, green apple & melon.

★★★★ **Spier Private Collection Chenin Blanc** Ripely, richly flavourful but refined & firm **22** ⑧⑥. Some spicy oak influence, but balanced & bright, to be easily approachable.

Villiera Chenin Blanc ★★★★ 35% new oak gives peach- & pear-toned **23** ⑧⑤ a nutty vanilla overlay & firm structure. Lively & persistent for satisfying solo sipping or with food. **House Chenin Blanc** Ⓥ ★★★★ By Koopmanskloof, **23** ⑧③ is a bright & flavoursome everyday sipper. Smooth lemon cream texture, with fresh & ripe apple crunch. **Kleine Zalze Chenin Blanc** Ⓥ ★★★★ Crisp liveliness to pear- & quince-toned **23** ⑧④. Light, juicy & fresh for everyday enjoyment. **Light Chenin Blanc** Ⓐ ★★★ Modest 9% alc on peach-driven **22** ⑦⑨, blend of low-alc & riper portions giving flavour & some vinosity. Sweet but balanced to be lipsmacking & fresh. By Spier. **Organic Chenin Blanc** Ⓐ Ⓥ ★★★ By Stellar Winery, offering generous tropical fruit flavours with a touch of lemon cream in **21** ⑧① Fairtrade certified. **Peachy Chenin Blanc** ★★★ Pretty & undeniably peachy aromas & flavours on **23** ⑦⑦, made by Spier from widely sourced grapes. Rich, just off-dry & rather charming.

Sauvignon Blanc range

★★★★ **Cape Point Vineyards Sauvignon Blanc** Ⓥ Fynbos note woven with citrus, stonefruit & hint of bubblegum on unoaked **23** ⑧⑥ preview. Tight & steely-dry grip leavened by 8% semillon & 4 months on lees. Lingering finish.

★★★★ **Diemersdal Reserve Collection Sauvignon Blanc** Ⓥ Bright orchard fruit & crunchy green apple add flesh to tightly wound lemon-zest core of **23** ⑧⑥. Green herbs & wet stone minerality on balanced finish. Quite a serious sauvignon but very easy to drink.

★★★★☆ **Signature Sauvignon Blanc By Diemersdal** Occasional release. Dryland Cape Town vines yield concentrated fruit, **23** ★★★★ ⑧⑦ more tropical than green in style. Like **20** ⑨⓪, a big wine, with 14% alc & touch of sugar, but no girth from oak.

★★★★ **Thelema Cool Climate Sauvignon Blanc** Ⓥ Poised, accomplished **23** ⑧⑧ shows fine, vibrant acid, generously ripe tropical fruit, toned-down aromatics. Lees contact adds heft to palate.

Durbanville Hills Sauvignon Blanc ★★★ Pre-bottling, **23** ⑧① summer sipper reticent on nose, mere whisper of blackcurrant, palate more forthcoming & substantial at 14% alc. **Fairview Sauvignon Blanc** Ⓥ ★★★★ More tropical than mineral flavours in crisply balanced **23** ⑧⑤ from Paarl & Darling grapes. Dry & juicy, lots of refreshing summer appeal. **Kleine Zalze Sauvignon Blanc** Ⓥ ★★★★ Tropical **23** ⑧④ has fig & zest vivacity on textured palate. Light & fresh, with ample appeal. **Light Sauvignon Blanc** Ⓐ ★★★ By Spier, **22** ⑦⑦ cleverly manages to bring some nearly-dry charm & fresh structure at just 9% alc. **Organic Sauvignon Blanc** Ⓐ Ⓥ ★★★ Stellar Winery's crisply dry **21** ⑧⓪ has typical herby greenpep-per aromas & flavours, joined by lime on the fresh finish. Fairtrade certified. **Passion Fruit Sauvignon Blanc** ★★★ Inviting, friendly **23** ⑧① has spadefuls of promised granadilla tempered by lemon acidity. By Diemersdal. **Spier Sauvignon Blanc** Ⓥ ★★★★ Forward aromas & flavours, blending passionfruit & guava smoothly on **23** ⑧③. Some enriching sugar but nicely balanced by acidity for freshness.

Niche White Cultivars

★★★★ **Noble Late Harvest** Ⓐ Luscious yet fresh botrytis dessert by chenin specialist Ken Forrester. **21** ★★★★☆ ⑨⓪ delicate apple blossom, apricot & dried pear notes follow onto honeyed palate where generous 112.3 g/L sugar is enlivened by streak of acid. 375 ml. Last **18** ⑧⑦ was from viognier.

House Moscato ★★★ Sweet, grapey & fragrant **23** (82) from muscat d'Alexandrie begs spicy food pairings. By Adama Wines. **Terra Del Capo Reserve Collection Pinot Grigio** ⊘ ★★★★ By Anthonij Rupert, **23** (85) shows familiar macadamia nougat character mixed with apples - yellow ones for flavour, green for piquant acid - cushioned by brief lie-in on lees. **Ken Forrester Reserve Collection Viognier** ★★★☆ Full of fruit & flavour at reined-in 12% alc, previewed **23** (85) offers lemon, just-ripe peach & blossoms plus a hint of oak.

White Blends

★★★★ **Saronsberg Earth & Sky** (NEW) Juicy & delicious melange of orchard fruit, honeydew melon, fynbos, warm hay & toasted nuts. **22** (87) intricately crafted & unusual blend of chenin (65%), viognier, verdelho & roussanne, portion unoaked for freshness.

★★★★ **Nitida The Bush Baby Sauvignon Blanc-Semillon** Pungent & forthright **23** ★★★★ (85) is crisp & fresh with plenty of citrus (mandarin & lime), touch of hay, poached guava at the finish. Follows **22** (87), also a 50/50 blend.

★★★★ **Villiera Carte Blanche** Unoaked, vivacious summer sipper. Sauvignon's cool green aromas & capsicum flavours to the fore in **23** (86), 19% old-vine, skin-fermented chenin adding weight & complexity, early-picked pinot grigio upping freshness.

Chardonnay-Pinot Noir ★★★★ Pioneer blend & a signature of Haute Cabrière since 1994. **23** (85) puts best foot forward: lovely peach & citrus, palate weight & matching freshness, modest 12.5% alc for picnics & patio parties. **House Chardonnay-Pinot Noir** (Ⓥ) ★★★★ Exuberantly youthful, light & fresh, previewed **21** (84) offers bright apple fruit, gentle acid hug. By Adama Wines. **Porcupine Ridge Sauvignon Blanc-Semillon** ⊘ ★★★ For easy everyday drinking, **22** (81) 70/30 blend picked in stages for balanced freshness & a salad of fruit flavours which could linger longer. Vegan certified. **Simonsig Reserve Collection Chenin Blanc-Pinotage** ★★★ Picnic-perfect **23** (81) packs lively berry & apple flavours into a satisfyingly dry, crisp & friendly body. **Spier Chardonnay-Pinot Noir** ★★★ Inviting aromatic charm on salmon-hued **23** (81). Flavours a little less generous, but soft textured, dry & pleasantly easygoing. Modest 12.5% alc.

Méthode Cap Classique Sparkling range

★★★★ **Simonsig Pinot Noir Rosé NSA** ⊘ Coral-hued, no-sulphur-added **22** (86) bubbly is refreshingly dry, lively & ready to celebrate. Delicate yet persistent cranberries, rosepetals & some savouriness, gentle biscuit note from year on lees.

★★★★ **Villiera Brut Rosé** Distinctive salmon hue on elegant, characterful **NV** (88) from chardonnay & pinotage (40/30), dashes pinot noir & meunier. Strawberry sherbet flavour & creamy mousse from 18 months on lees, tangy raspberry finish. Also in 375 ml.

★★★★ **Kleine Zalze Brut** (NEW) Focused, taut **NV** (87) sparkler from chardonnay & pinot noir (60/40). Chalk grip followed by fantail of sourdough & lemon on broad palate. Richly rewarding, crisp & succulent. 18 months on lees.

★★★★☆ **Signature Vintage Reserve Brut** ⊘ (≋) Villiera's masterly, confident **16** (94) walks tightrope between richness & freshness. Classic apple tart aromas & flavours from part oaking of the basewine & 66 months on lees; vivacity from the unoaked chardonnay component, red apple note & complexity from pinot noir & meunier.

★★★★ **Villiera Brut** Stalwart **NV** (89) 'golden' in every way: in glass, where tiny bubbles dart to surface, on nose, with honey overlay, on palate where its richness lingers. From chardonnay, pinot noir & pinotage (60/30/10), 18 months on lees.

★★★★ **Villiera Brut Natural** Vibrancy & leanness the hallmarks of zero-dosage **18** (87) sparkler. Lithe, with chardonnay's citrus fruit & zip, 42 months on lees adding attractive umami yeastiness.

Kleine Zalze Nectar (NEW) ★★★☆ Marmalade & lemongrass on **NV** (85) sparkler from 60% chardonnay & pinot noir. Sweet-&-sour lime tang with honeyed mather than sweet farewell, richness from 18 months on lees. **Light Brut** ★★★☆ Crisp & flavoursome at less than 10% alc, Villiera's **NV** (85) party starter boasts clean lime & lemon of chardonnay (60%), decent weight from pinot noir & pinotage, smooth finish from 18 months on lees. **Nectar Royale** ★★★☆ Delicate savoury notes enhance the honeysuckle & apple appeal of **NV** (85)'s gentle sweetness. Quite frothy yet with a serious, firm backbone. From chardonnay & 20% pinot noir, 18 months on lees. By Villiera.

Sparkling Wines

Tranquille Blush Sparkling ★★★ Dry carbonated **NV** ⑧② from pinot noir & chardonnay (60/40) by Haute Cabrière. Lightest of pinky orange hues, frothy bubbles & happy tropical flavours of litchi & mango. **Organic Sparkling Chardonnay-Pinot Noir** Ⓥ ♡ ★★★ Equal parts pinot noir & chardonnay in salmon pink **NV** ⑧⓪, dry & softly effervescent, redolent of strawberries & crisp apples. **Organic Sparkling Sauvignon Blanc** Ⓥ ♡ ★★★ Zesty & light-hearted **NV** ⑦⑨, crisp apple & riper pineapple flavours, bone-dry but comfortable finish. **Steenberg Sparkling Sauvignon Blanc** ♡ ★★★★ Altogether satisfyingly tasty **NV** ⑧④ whose short time on lees in bottle keeps pristine sauvignon character. Kiwi & litchi notes fit the touch of sugar, ends with livening acidity.

1L Box range

Dry Red ★★★ Unwooded, cellar handling designed to highlight fruit, forthcoming berries in **NV** ⑧⓪, with tasty smooth succulence. **Light Red** ★★★ Unspecified varieties, **NV** ⑦⑧ with its 9.5% alc is designed for youthful, easy drinking. Piquant red berries, no oak, juicy & fresh. By Darling Cellars, as all these. **Crisp White** ★★★ Multi-variety **NV** ⑧① blend, focusing on freshness & texture, tropical, pineapple flavours, a few aromatic notes. Crunchy, dry & satisfyingly fruity. **Light White** ★★★ Same blend as Crisp White, with lower alc, 9.5%. Also tropical toned, but **NV** ⑦⑧ has a bit less flavour, body. **Sweet Red** ★★★ Well-judged sweetness plumps up the red berries in this unoaked **NV** ⑦⑦ red blend, drinks easily, smoothly. **Natural Sweet Rosé** ★★ Mainly white varieties, dash of red for colour, palely blushing **NV** ⑦③ is the sweetest of the boxed wines, packed with fruit.

2L Box range

★★★★ **Alto 1693** ♡ Near-identical Bordeaux-shiraz blend to Alto Estate's enduring Rouge, **21** ⑧⑦ satisfyingly full-bodied & ripe, with convincing blackcurrant & liquorice highlights.

★★★★ **Diemersdal Sauvignon Blanc** A fine bargain, **23** ⑧⑥ has all the winning aromas & flavours - apple, lemon zest, green herbs - plus the usual pleasing firmness & stony minerality on the palate.

Spier Cabernet Sauvignon ★★ Pleasantly fruit-driven **22** ⑦⑥, smoothed by a little sugar & then balanced by some tart acidity & touch of tannin. **House Merlot** ★★★ 10% other varieties but merlot is in charge. Red berries, touch of herbaceousness, no oak, **NV** ⑦⑨ a good match with food. By Darling Cellars. **Beyerskloof Pinotage** ★★★★ Blackberry, plum & light dusting of cocoa on juicy, rounded **21** ⑧⑤. Supple & cheery, with gentle oak frame. **Cabernet Sauvignon-Merlot** ★★★ Cab with 30% merlot & 15% cinsaut, unwooded **NV** ⑧② proudly shows its berry fruit, is smooth textured & fresh for early enjoyment. From Darling Cellars. **House Cabernet Sauvignon-Merlot** (NEW) ★★★ With 30% merlot, 15% cinsaut, unwooded **NV** ⑧② ex Darling Cellars proudly shows its berry fruit; smooth textured & fresh, for youthful enjoyment. **Organic Red** Ⓥ ♡ ★★★ Succulent red berries & touch of spice on **NV** ⑧⓪ pinotage & shiraz combo by Stellar Winery. Fairtrade certified. **Tranquille Blush** ♡ ★★★★ Very pale salmon dry rosé. **NV** ⑧④ 60/40 pinot noir & chardonnay with firm, food-friendly texture to its lemons & berries, easily manageable 11.5% alc. By Haute Cabrière. **Kleine Zalze Chenin Blanc** ♡ ★★★ Light & juicy every day sipper, **23** ⑧④ has crisp liveliness to bright pear & quince tones. **House Sauvignon Blanc** ★★★ With a touch of nouvelle, **NV** ⑧① is leafy, with gooseberries, hint of fennel, all the characteristics you'd expect from sauvignon. By Darling Cellars. **Organic White** Ⓥ ♡ ★★★ Fragrant orchard fruit & touch of spice on **NV** ⑧⓪ colombard & chenin partnership. Unoaked, dry & charming. By Stellar Winery. Fairtrade certified.

3L Box range

Dry Red ★★★ By Darling Cellars, as all these. **NV** ⑧⓪'s upfront berries are untrammelled by wood, deliver satisfying flavour in a silky body. **Light Red** ★★★ No oak used, so tangy red berries are the stars of this sappy, youthful easy-drinker with low 9.5% alc. **NV** ⑦⑧ from unspecified varieties. **Crisp White** ★★★ Aptly named crunchy **NV** ⑧① offers tropical fruit flavour & freshness along with a perfumed nuance from riesling in the multi-variety blend. **Light White** ★★★ Lower in alc (9.5%) than Crisp White but same varieties & similar tropical tones; **NV** ⑦⑧ touch lighter in flavour & body. **Natural Sweet Red** ★★★ Made for effortless sweet quaffing without cloy, this **NV** ⑦⑦ blend has ripe red berry flavours in a rounded body. **Natural Sweet Rosé** ★★ Delicate blush on **NV** ⑦③ from splash red in the otherwise white blend, fruity, luscious yet not over-sweet. **Sweet White** ♡ ★★★ Five-way blend, including a few aromatic varieties, **NV** ⑦⑦ offers floral & fruity tones in a slim 10.5% alc package. Sweet but fits the style.

5L Box range

Dry Red Wine ★★★ By Darling Cellars, as all these. Ample berry fruit packed into unoaked **NV** ⑧⓪, sappy & forthcoming, a tasty anytime quaffer. **Crisp White Wine** ★★★ Per the name, **NV** ⑧① has a pleasant bite of acid adding verve to mostly tropical flavours, ends dry & clean with a lift from aromatic grapes in the multi-part blend. **Sweet Red Wine** ★★★ Smooth, rather than sweet, thanks to deft balance of sugar & acid in **NV** ⑦ blend. Red-berry flavours are bright & easy to like. **Natural Sweet Rosé** ★★ As previous, **NV** ⑦ is for the sweeter-toothed winelover but, again, well balanced & clean through to the fruity finish.

De-Alcoholised Wine range
Merlot ★★ Lightly wooded **NV** ⑦ improves on last with good concentration of merlot's plummy flavour. By Holder Vineyard & Wines, as all these; all under 0.5% alc, sugar around 20 g/L. **Cabernet Sauvignon-Merlot** (NEW) ★★★ Cab's cassis merges with merlot's plump berries in **NV** ⑦, hint of oak for structure. **Moscato Rosé** ★★ Pretty & pink **NV** ⑦ from muscadel is fragrant with roses & sun-ripe grapes. Good freshness here, too. **Chenin Blanc** ★★★ Variety's apples & pears underscored by racy acidity. Latest **NV** ⑦ betters last. **Sauvignon Blanc** ★★★ Well-pitched **NV** ⑦ notch up on last with its tangy character & fresh, clean finish. **Sparkling Rosé** ★★★ Pinotage lends strawberry freshness to **NV** ⑦ carbonated bubbly. Pleasing to the eye, too, with salmon hue. **Sparkling Brut** (NEW) ★★★ Crisp & frothy carbonated **NV** ⑦ starts the party with engaging appley freshness. — Various tasters

WO: Various ▪ Senior Buyer: Rob Gower; Buyers: Charles Pohl & Tshepo Mashile ▪ Owner(s) Woolworths Holdings ▪ Woolworths House, 93 Longmarket Str, Cape Town 8000 ▪ www.woolworths.co.za ▪ **T +27 (0)21-407-9111**

☐ **#WO Prieska** *see* Lowerland

☐ **Word Collection** *see* Rascallion Wines

☐ **Workhorse** *see* Ken Forrester Wines

☐ **Wrapper Series** *see* Cape Collective

☐ **Xaro** *see* Stellenrust

☐ **Yacht Club** *see* Cape Wine Company

☐ **Yellowwood Organic** *see* Spier

Yerden Eksteen ⓠ ⑪

Winemaking couple Pieter Willem Eksteen and Sol Yerden Eksteen are focused on malbec, probably the signature of Sol's native Argentina, still largely off-radar locally. Based in Hemel-en-Aarde, they've switched to warmer Stellenbosch vines for 'a more typical style', along with a name change from 'Pieter Willem & Sol'.

★★★★☆ **Nosotros Malbec** (🐝) Deeply coloured **22** ⑨'s higher alc (14.5%) carefully managed to retain bright plum fruit & satisfying dryness. Obvious succulence, too, controlled by dense tannins for overall sense of restraint. Minuscule 315 cases from Vlottenburg grapes. — CvZ

Location: Hermanus ▪ WO: Stellenbosch ▪ Est/1stB 2018 ▪ Tasting & sales at Bartho Eksteen ▪ Owner(s)/winemaker(s) Pieter Willem Eksteen & Sol Yerden Eksteen ▪ 0.5ha ▪ 330cs own label 100% red ▪ PO Box 199 Hermanus 7200 ▪ pieterwillem@hermanus.co.za ▪ **T +27 (0)79-506-8613**

☐ **Yes, You Can** *see* Black Elephant Vintners

Yonder Hill ⓠ ⑪ ⓞ ⓑ

The Naudé family's 'fascination' with Ankole cattle sees an eponymous pinnacle wine, namesake craft beer on-tap at the multi-allure cellardoor, and herd of the magnificent longhorned animals roaming the boutique estate, overlooked by the equally impressive, 1,000 m-high 'hill' better known as Helderberg Mountain. Janette van Lill styles the recently pared line-up, working with seasoned vine man Francois Hanekom.

Premium range
★★★★ **Ella** (ⓥ) Back to 100% merlot for silky **21** ⑧⑦, cocoa-dusted damsons & crushed raspberries anchored by fine tannins for 15 months in old oak.

★★★★ **Ankole** (ⓥ) The flagship, a Bordeaux blend, like Nicola, same varieties but cab (47%) in charge here, in composition, structure & flavour. **18** ⑧⑧ vibrant & delicious now, even better in 5 years.

★★★★ **Nicola** (ⓥ) 4-way Bordeaux blend, merlot (40%) leads in **18** ⑧⑧ displaying ripe red fruits housed in graceful structure. Herbal lift from partner grapes.

★★★★ **Danilo** (✓) Seductive seashell pink rosé, **23** ⑧⑥ mixes grenache noir & merlot, latter partly saignée. Wisps strawberry & melon, crisp dry finish, even lighter at 12.4% alc than **22** ★★★☆ ⑧⑤.

Benjamin ☺ ★★★ Classic gooseberry, green fig & nettle tones, medium body refreshed with lemony acid, bargain-priced **23** (82) checks the boxes for sauvignon lovers & value seekers alike. — ML

Location/WO: Stellenbosch ▪ Map: Helderberg ▪ Map grid reference: C3 ▪ Est 1989 ▪ 1stB 1993 ▪ Tasting & sales Tue-Fri 9-4 Sat 10-2 ▪ Closed Sun & all pub hols ▪ Cellar tours by appt only ▪ Function & conference venue ▪ Tour groups ▪ Gift shop ▪ Food-and-wine pairings ▪ Olives & olive products ▪ Ankole craft beer ▪ Owner(s) Naudé family ▪ Winemaker(s) Janette van Lill (2022) ▪ Viticulturist(s) Francois Hanekom (2022) ▪ 12ha/5ha (cabs s/f, merlot, p verdot) ▪ 40t/3,000cs own label 50% red 30% white 20% rosé ▪ PO Box 914 Stellenbosch 7599 ▪ wines@yonderhill.co.za ▪ www.yonderhill.co.za ▪ **T +27 (0)21-855-1008**

☐ **Zahir** see Lateganskop Winery
☐ **Zakkie Bester** see Bester Family Wines

Zandvliet Wine Estate ⓠⓑ

The larger Zandvliet farm, near Ashton in the Breede River Valley, was proclaimed in 1838, with the current property a later subdivision. Another significant development came in 2015 when it was bought by a major citrus producer, who converted some of the poorer vineyards but continued to grow the wine. The brands were sold to Van Loveren Family Vineyards in 2019, and that substantial winery also leases the cellar and vineyards (on 'kalkveld' soil, pocketed with chalky limestone). So the Zandvliet traditions continue - most notably the place of shiraz, which has long had a 'truly special relationship' with the farm.

Hill of Enon range
★★★★☆ **Small Berry Pick Shiraz** Generous but quite restrained aromas & flavours, with both fruit & more savoury notes, on **20** (90). Everything works well together - the ripe character, firm but balanced tannins, supportive oaking, 60% new. Well textured & balanced, but less depth & character than last.

Kalkveld range
★★★★ **Shiraz** 20 (86) more complex & grippy than Estate version, with the ripe, plummy fruit complementary with spice & tobacco notes from 30% new oak. Firmly built. Last tasted was **18** (86).

Zandvliet Estate range
Shiraz ★★★★ Ripe, dark aroma (with tobacco hints) & flavour on **21** (83). 20% new oak in support. Gently gripping tannins but acid rather prominent for balance. Also in 375ml to 12L bottles. 14% alc, like all the shirazes. **Syrah Rosé** ★★★ Previously 'Shiraz Rosé'. Fashionably pale **23** (82) has fragrant berry charm with an earthy edge. Dry, not a great deal of substance but a pleasant balance. **Chardonnay** ★★★★ Full, buttery aromas with the lemon & lime notes that persist throughout **22** (83). Straightforward, balanced & flavourful, supported by old-oak barrelling. **Muscat** ★★★ Natural Sweet **23** (80) from white muscat giving unmistakeable & delightful aroma & flavour in all its charming simplicity. Balanced & not unctuous, with 85 g/L sugar, low 8.5% alc. **Cape Vintage Reserve Shiraz** ★★★★ Port-style wine from Zandvliet's signature grape. Rich & flavourful **17** (85), though light for style at 65 g/L sugar & 18% alc, & the tannic structure modest (firm acidity though). 5 years in old barrels. Touch less impressive than last-tasted **14** ★★★★ (86).

My Best Friend range
Cape Red ★★★ Ripely inviting **22** (78). Friendly (though acidity touch stern, as White) & just-dry. 13.5% alc. **Cape White** ★★★ Lightly fragrant, flavourful & easy **23** (78) from unnamed varieties, as Red. — TJ

Location: Ashton ▪ Map/WO: Robertson ▪ Map grid reference: C4 ▪ Est 1867 ▪ 1stB 1975 ▪ Tasting & sales Mon-Sat 10-3; pub hols (seasonal) please call ahead ▪ Private tastings by appt ▪ Sales currently at Kalkveld Lounge on Zandvliet & online ▪ Winemaker(s) Jacques Cilliers (Dec 2011) ▪ PO Box 19 Klaasvoogds Robertson 6707 ▪ zandvliet@vanloveren.co.za ▪ www.zandvliet.co.za, www.vanloveren.co.za ▪ **T +27 (0)23-615-1505**

☐ **Zaràfa** see Mountain River Wines
☐ **Z-Collection** see Zevenwacht
☐ **Zeffer** see Simonsvlei International
☐ **Zenzela** see Simonsvlei International

Zevenwacht ⓠⓘⓐⓞⓑ

There's continuing emphasis on the flagship Z-Collection at the Johnson family's extensive wine and hospitality venture near Kuils River, with investment in new amphoras for the chenin and sauvignon, and

Wine of Origin certification that highlights the estate's location within the increasingly rated Polkadraai Hills appellation. The current Estate releases are all varietal wines and, while not certified as Polkadraai Hills, do focus on expressing that terroir. The blended wines feature some fruit from the higher-lying sister property Zevenrivieren in Banhoek Valley. Vineyard expansion sees more mouvrèdre planted for the Tin Mine red, and soil preparations for establishing additional blocks of syrah and chenin during this year.

Z-Collection

★★★★☆ **Syrah** Always special handling, 70% wholebunch of which half carbonic maceration, year older foudre, all designed to showcase **22** ⑨⓪'s plush fruit. Wild berries, some peppery notes, tannins supple but with hidden musculature. Can age, already eminently drinkable.

★★★★☆ **Reserve** ⓐ Exceptional Cape Bordeaux, cab with 15% petit verdot, 18 months in barrel, now 60% new, for both vintages tasted. Showing depth & intensity, **21** ⑨③ packed with fruit, tannins firm, befitting wine of its class. Made for ageing but already showing its credentials, the fine crafting. **20** ⑨⓪, same blend, more prominent cassis in perfume & flavours, the oaking a tobacco seam. Tannins firm, ensure a good future, but texture succulent enough for earlier enjoyment. Also in 1.5L. Last was **17** ⑨⓪.

★★★★ **Chenin Blanc** ⓦ Heritage vines planted 1981. Wild bunch-ferment, half each concrete 'egg' & barrel, 9 months on lees which **22** ★★★★★ ⑨⓪ shows as quince & melon preserves; there's flavour richness, which includes a melba toast top note, limy-fresh finish. Has style & presence, a notch up on **21** ⑧⑧. WO Polkadraai Hills, as all except Reserve.

★★★★☆ **Sauvignon Blanc** ⓐ Blanc fumé style, fully oaked, 9 months on lees, with 15% semillon, yet another admirable version of the variety from this cellar. Lime cordial, Lemon Cream biscuit, especially on the palate, **22** ★★★★★ ⑨⑤ not a big wine but impresses with concentration, presence & understated power. As all these, wonderful freshness & length. Long lived, like **21** ⑨③.

Estate range

★★★★ **Cabernet Sauvignon** More restrained oaking than Z-Collection, 14 months, 20% new, which allows **20** ⑧⑧ to showcase its fruit, plush cassis, smoothly rounded & juicy. For earlier enjoyment but still cellar-worthy.

★★★★ **Chardonnay** Wholebunch, as next two, barrel ferment/9 months, some new, 16% concrete 'egg'. Forthcoming citrus in **22** ⑧⑧, also a savoury biscuit note which deepens on the palate & gives an extended finish. Proudly displays its oaking but enough fruit to balance.

★★★★ **Chenin Blanc** ⓦ Lots of care taken with chenins to produce something special. **23** ⑧⑧ barrel ferment/5 months, 10% amphora, contains some old-vine fruit. Displays layered apple & quince, oak spice a subtle seam, lovely freshness throughout. Has palate weight & length.

★★★★☆ **Old Vine Chenin Blanc** ⊘ ⓐ ⓦ From dryland vines planted 1981, diffent handling to Z: **22** ⑨④ barrel ferment/7 months, 15% concrete 'egg'. More limy than siblings, winter melon as an underpin, the palate revealing trademark varietal minerality. Lots to offer, multifaceted & wonderful typicity.

★★★★☆ **Sauvignon Blanc** ⊘ With 6% oaked semillon, 5 months on lees, different character to its siblings; reductively made **23** ⑨⓪ has green notes vying with minerality, some kiwi appearing in the flavours. All upheld by zesty freshness, promising youth & health for years to come.

Not tasted: **Merlot**, **Syrah**. Occasional release: **Vine Dried Muscat Blanc**.

The Tin Mine Collection

★★★★☆ **Syrah-Mourvèdre-Grenache** ⊘ Same varieties as previous 'Tin Mine Red' but shiraz in charge of **21** ⑨⓪, & boldly so. Brambly fruit, smoky spice from 12-month oaking, some scrub, tannins firm but ripe. Has depth & heft, makes a statement. Improves on sterner **20** ★★★★ ⑧⑧.

★★★★ **Cape White Blend** ⊘ Chenin, chardonnay & 3 others, wholebunch, barrel fermented/7 months, **22** ⑨⓪ showcases both main varieties, grapefruit & stonefruit, becoming limy in the flavours & finish. Great drinkability, always a creative success.

7even range

Rood ⊘ ⓥ ★★★★ Commonplace name ('Red') but no ordinary wine: shiraz, dabs zinfandel & grenache, wholeberry ferment, year older barrels. Vivid mixed berries, smoked meat & liquorice, **20** ⑧⑤ packed with flavour & tasty succulence. **Sauvignon Blanc** ⊘ ⓥ ★★★★ Reflecting house-style intensity, **23** ⑧⑤'s passionfruit & lime scents & flavours backed by salty acid, keeping it vibrantly alive.

Pinotage ★★★ Year later, **21** ⑧²'s blueberry fruit forthcoming, thanks to wholeberry ferment, oak spicing from older barrels subservient, tannins pliable. In tasty drinking mode. **Rosé ★★★** Near-equal cab & cab franc blend creates **23** ⑧¹'s berry-fresh dry wine with tangy flavours. Good enough to drink solo or with food. **Bouquet Blanc ★★★** Creative blend designed to live up to its name, 40% gewürztraminer with muscat blanc, viognier, dash chenin, off-dry, fitting the aromatics. **23** ⑧² floral & rosewater perfume, piquant, grapey flavours nicely backed by acid. — CR

Location: Kuils River ▪ Map: Stellenbosch ▪ Map grid reference: B5 ▪ WO: Stellenbosch/Polkadraai Hills ▪ Est 1980 ▪ 1stB 1983 ▪ Tasting & sales Mon-Fri 8.30-5 Sat/Sun/pub hols 9.30-5 ▪ Tasting options: international R45pp/5 wines (excl Z collection); executive R70pp/6 wines; chocolate truffle & wine pairing R75pp (4 wines paired with 4 chocolate truffles); cheese and wine tasting: cheese platter R55 shared by 2 guests, with 4 pre-selected wines R38pp ▪ Off-Road Vineyard Safari: francois@allterrain4x4.co.za - booking essential ▪ Closed Dec 25 ▪ Cellar tours by appt ▪ Restaurant ▪ Picnics in summer ▪ Facilities for children ▪ Conferences ▪ Weddings/banqueting ▪ Walking & MTB trails ▪ Conservation area ▪ Bakwena Spa ▪ 4-star Country Inn ▪ Wine club ▪ Owner(s) Harold Johnson & family ▪ Winemaker(s) Hagen Viljoen (Aug 2018), with Charles Lourens (Jun 2014) ▪ Viticulturist(s) Eduard van den Berg (Jan 2001) ▪ 473ha/100ha (cabs s/f, grenache, merlot, mourv, ptage, primitivo, shiraz, chard, chenin, gewürz, muscat de F, rouss, sauv, sem, viog) ▪ 657t/100,000cs own label 48% red 48% white 4% rosé ▪ IPW ▪ PO Box 387 Kuils River 7579 ▪ info@zevenwacht.co.za ▪ www.zevenwacht.co.za ▪ **T +27 (0)21-900-5700**

Zidela Wines

The tagline, 'Worldwide wines', speaks of the focus, extent and reach of the well-established Stellenbosch venture owned and run by Danie Kritzinger with sons Erik and Jaco. 'Putting wine in bottle as directed by our clients', including supermarkets and restaurant chains, is a strong emphasis and source of growth, notably in the US and Asia. Some of the private labels recently became available for purchase online.

African King range
Pinotage ⊘ **★★★** Raspberry simplicity to juicy, fresh **23** ⑦⁸. Unoaked, for current drinking, as all ranges.
Chenin Blanc ★★★ Pear & melon intro to **23** ⑦⁸, shows decent succulence & length.

Black Bird range
Natural Sweet Red Ⓩ **★★★** Sweet, soft & rounded **NV** ⑦⁸, light & touch jammy. **Natural Sweet Rosé** Ⓩ **★★★** Candyfloss & plum jam sweetness to straightforward yet fresh **NV** ⑦⁹ pink. Restrained alc in all ranges, here 12%. **Natural Sweet White** Ⓩ **★★★** Ripe apple on **NV** ⑦⁸, tang of lemon zest to balance the sweetness.

Mbali range
Chenin Blanc-Viognier ⊘ **★★★** Guava & nectarine with honey drizzle on **23** ⑧⁰ airy poolside sipper.

Oshun range (NEW)
Sweet Rosé ★★ Trim, light & sweet with some strawberry notes on **23** ⑦⁶. **Natural Sweet White ★★** Tropical fruit salad sweetness on **23** ⑦⁶, clean & uncloying.

Sweven range (NEW)
Chardonnay ★★★ Trim-figured **23** ⑦⁸ shows subtle lees edge to fresh lemon nuance. **Chenin Blanc ★★★** Melon & guava with lemony zing, **23** ⑦⁹ carefree anytime sipper. **Sauvignon Blanc ★★★** Flint typicity **23** ⑦⁸. Flavour tad short-lived, hint white pepper at the end.

The Cape range (NEW)
Pinotage ★★★ Meaty nuance to red-fruited **21** ⑧². Notable spice & dry tannin matched by body & length. **Shiraz-Pinotage ★★★** Earthy black fruit on **21** ⑧², quite muscular, with dry tannin squeeze, lingering berries & plums. Made for pizza & pasta.

Tucana range
Cabernet Sauvignon ⊘ **★★★** Black-fruited **22** ⑧¹ is fresh & light, has flattering few grams of sugar, as all these. **Merlot** (NEW) ⊘ **★★★** Leafy hedgerow fruit & dry grip on **22** ⑦⁹, dusting of cocoa on finish. **Pinotage** (NEW) ⊘ **★★★** Sappy berries & boiled sweets of **22** ⑦⁸ followed by brief chalky grip. **Shiraz** ⊘ **★★★** Uncomplicated quaffer, **22** ⑧⁰ offers black berry fruit & light hint of herb. **Cabernet Sauvignon-Pinotage** Ⓩ **★★★** Subtle grip on medium-bodied 60/40 blend, **20** ⑧⁰ appealing blackberry flavour, fresh & lively. **Shiraz-Merlot** Ⓩ **★★★** Soft, squishy blueberry, cherry & plum on **21** ⑧². Rounded, light

& easy to like. Good pizza partner. **Rosé** (NEW) ⊘ ★★★ Candyfloss & berry notes on softly dry **23** (77) pink. Fresh & light. **Chardonnay** ⊘ ★★★ Shows some guava & lemon zip on light-bodied frame in **23** (81). **Chenin Blanc** ⊘ ★★★ Accessible melon & guava flavours in **23** (80) everyday sipper. **Sauvignon Blanc** ★★★ Brief flash of flint on **23** (78), light & lemony, ends with sweet-sour tang.

Zidela range

Shiraz-Merlot ⊘ ★★★ Smoky black fruit aromas on **23** (80) 60/40 blend, juicy plums coming through on palate. **Chenin Blanc-Viognier** ⊘ ★★★ Sweet melon & peach succulence on **23** (80), light & easy. Discontinued: **Boschheuvel range**. — FM

Location: Stellenbosch ▪ WO: Western Cape ▪ Est 2001 ▪ 1stB 2002 ▪ Closed to public ▪ Online sales ▪ Owner(s) Danie, Erik & Jaco Kritzinger ▪ 50% red 40% white 10% rosé ▪ 13-million litres for clients ▪ PO Box 3021 Matieland 7602 ▪ info@zidelawines.co.za ▪ www.zidelawines.co.za, shop.zidelawines.co.za ▪ **T +27 (0)21-880-2936**

☐ **Zikomo** *see* Rooiberg Winery

Zoetendal Wines

Zoetendal was a pioneer of winegrowing in cool, windy Elim near Africa's southern tip, but has seen some rejuvenation - including a more generous array of visitor amenities - since a fairly recent change of ownership. The aim, says new sales and brand executive Denzel Swarts, is to position the wine brand at a luxury level. They are, he adds, 'looking at upgrading Zoetendal's facility to include a boutique cellar', but meanwhile vinification happens with other producers.

★★★★☆ **Shiraz Single Vineyard** (NEW) Gorgeous fragrance on **22** (90) from Elim grapes, with bright red fruit. Light-feeling at just 13% alc, even a little lean in its dry freshness, but charming, the fruit purity unchallenged by old-oak maturation.

★★★★ **The Monarch 18** ★★★★☆ (90) red blends aromatic shiraz with the red Bordeaux varieties for fruitcake richness. More generously built & firmly structured than the straight Shiraz, but still elegant & fairly light-feeling at 14% alc, with good dry finish. Impresses more than **17**.

★★★★ **Sauvignon Blanc Limited Release** More intensity of aroma & flavour than standard bottling on **23** (86) tasted ex tank, a touch more complex, with the green element more expressive. Both sauvignons telling of the bracing Elim coolness.

Chenin Blanc ★★★★ Attractively forward ripe aromas & flavours on **21** (85). Sweet fruit core & a soft texture for easy approachability. WO Coastal, as The Monarch. **Sauvignon Blanc** ★★★★ The usual medley of grassy, tropical & blackcurrant notes on pre-bottled **23** (84). Soft textured yet bone-dry & with bright acidity. — TJ

Location: Elim ▪ Map: Southern Cape ▪ Map grid reference: C7 ▪ WO: Elim/Coastal ▪ Est 2002 ▪ 1stB 2004 ▪ Tasting & sales Wed-Sun 10-4; pub hols (seasonal) please call ahead ▪ Closed Good Fri, Dec 25 & Jan 1 ▪ Restaurant & venue (up to 40 pax) ▪ Kayaking, fishing, bird viewing ▪ Conservation area ▪ Owner(s) Meli Capital (Pty) Ltd ▪ 125ha/10.3ha (shiraz, sauv) ▪ 39t/4,000cs own label 15% red 85% white ▪ IPW ▪ PO Box 22 Elim 7284 ▪ hospitality@zoetendal.co.za ▪ www.zoetendal.co.za ▪ **T +27 (0)72-854-1720**

Zonnebloem

You could lay them down, as some still-strong examples from earlier decades attest, but the wines named for the sunflower are made for tasty current drinking, at an affordable price. The all-women team currently styling the range in the Heineken Beverages cellars are custodians of one of the Cape's oldest wine brands, gaining fame and legend status after entering the Stellenbosch Farmers' Winery stable in the late 1940s.

★★★★ **Cabernet Sauvignon** ⊘ Notch above an everyday sipper, but highly sippable, **21** (86) offers convincing cassis fruit with sweet baking spices, pleasantly robust tannins & decent weight.

★★★★ **Pinotage** ⊘ Unmistakable varietal character of brambles & mulberries on **21** (86), plus a steely mineral vein & vanilla-toned oak spice from staves & barrels, half American.

★★★★ **Lauréat** Meaty, earthy cab & merlot with petit verdot, **20** (89) wholesome & savoury, with stewed fruit & forest-floor minerality, full leathery tannins, commendable heft & length. 24-36 months in 50% new oak reflects in rounded, polished structure.

★★★★ **Shiraz-Mourvèdre-Viognier** 85% shiraz in **20** ★★★★ ⑧⑤, sweetly ripe, offering oak-spiced berry compote, decent weight & gentle tannins. 18-24 months in mixed-origin barrels, 40% new. Similar make-up & profile to last-tasted **18** ⑧⑥.

Not tasted: **Merlot, Shiraz, Chardonnay, Sauvignon Blanc, Blanc de Blanc**. — GdB

Location/WO: Stellenbosch ▪ Est 1893 ▪ Owner(s) Heineken Beverages ▪ Cellarmaster(s) Elize Coetzee ▪ Winemaker(s) Bonny van Niekerk (reds) & Kelly-Marie Jacobs (whites) ▪ Viticulturist(s) Isabel Habets ▪ (cab, merlot, shiraz, chard, sauv, sem) ▪ 9,500t/±109,000cs own label 60% red 40% white ▪ ISO 9002, Fairtrade ▪ PO Box 184 Stellenbosch 7599 ▪ info@zonnebloem.co.za ▪ www.zonnebloem.co.za ▪ **T +27 (0)21-809-7000**

☐ **Zonneweelde** *see* Slanghoek Winery

Zorgvliet Wines

In the mountainous wine ward of Banghoek, named for the fear instilled in early travellers by the slopes, vagabonds and predators, lies the pristine, whitewashed domain created by developer and entrepreneur Mac van der Merwe, with its precipitous vineyards and meticulously restored Cape Dutch buildings. The wines, with the emphasis on Bordeaux varieties and blends, are the responsibility of Bernard le Roux, assisted by Ruben Adams and Richelle Wille, née Van der Merwe, the third generation, whose name adorns the flagship red wine. The estate incorporates a luxury country lodge, perfect for exploring these breathtaking surroundings, wedding and function facilities as well as a restaurant in the historic 1692 Herenhuis.

Grand Cuvée range

★★★★★ **Simoné** Statuesque flagship white, **22** ⑨② sauvignon & semillon (52/48) follows form with mineral core, perfect balance, satisfyingly lingering finish. Gently spiced from barrel ferment with some whole berries, 10 months older 500L barrels.

Not tasted: **Richelle**.

Zorgvliet range

★★★★☆ **Cabernet Sauvignon** ⊘ 🐝 Classy **21** ⑨② hits the spot again, typical earthy minerality underpinning succulent, inky blackcurrant fruit, leafy herbal notes & ripe, leathery tannins. Still youthfully muscular after 20 months in barrel, should reward cellaring.

★★★★☆ **Cabernet Franc** ⊘ 🐝 Imposing, heavyweight **21** ⑨③ in Bordeaux Right Bank style has pitch-perfect varietal character: layers of graphite minerality with iodine, liquorice & cassis, wrapped in velvet tannins, easily coping with 20 months in barrel.

★★★★☆ **Merlot** ⊘ 🐝 Showing meaty savouriness typical of Banghoek, **21** ⑨① is brawny & concentrated, has thick, ripe tannins. Black plum & currant fruit has appealing spiced highlights, gentle oak influence from 20 months in barrel, 18% new. Best cellared for a while.

★★★★☆ **Petit Verdot** ⊘ 🐝 Biggest & most powerful of all, **21** ⑨⓪ not for the faint-hearted. Echoes previous years with impossibly dense blackcurrant palate, tarry & sombre, with cocoa & herbal highlights, formidable tannins, hints of oak spice. Best revisited several years hence.

★★★★ **Cabernet Franc Rosé** Noteworthy example, previewed **23** ⑧⑦ is delicate silver-rose, clear & bright, with varietal earthiness, crisp acid, elegant floral scent. Resolutely dry, appealing saltiness on finish.

★★★★☆ **Single Vineyard Sauvignon Blanc** Switches to unwooded in **22** ★★★★ ⑧⑧ yet shows leesy weight & texture, reined-in aromatics, striking lime-mineral tone & refined passionfruit. Shade off more extroverted **21** ⑨①.

★★★★ **Semillon** Characterful, wild-yeast barrel-fermented **22** ⑧⑦ had some skin contact, 10 months in older oak. Rich, wholesome & leesy, appealing honeyed wax, baked apple & lemon cream notes. First tasted since **19** ⑧⑧.

Silver Myn range

★★★★ **Argentum** ⊘ Preview of sophisticated **22** ⑧⑥ merlot-led 4-way Bordeaux blend punches above its weight. Full palate of black fruit, tar & anise on elegant backdrop of leafy freshness. 10 months older barrels & foudres. WO Stellenbosch.

Rosé ⊘ ★★★ Pale tinsel-pink **23** ⑧② from sauvignon & 4 others has vibrant acid, appealing strawberry cordial flavour & floral accents. **Sauvignon Blanc** ★★★ Light, unpretentious **23** ⑧② with 10% semillon offers waves of aromas, herbal grassiness & ripe gooseberry fruit. Touch of oak this vintage. — GdB

Location/map: Stellenbosch ▪ Map grid reference: H4 ▪ WO: Banghoek/Stellenbosch ▪ Est/1stB 2002 ▪ Tasting & sales Mon-Sat 10-6 Sun/pub hols 11-5; pub hols (seasonal) please call ahead ▪ Closed Good Fri, Dec 25 & Jan 1 ▪ Tasting fee, waived on purchase ▪ Herenhuis 1692 Restaurant Wed-Sat 11.30-4.30 ▪ Cellar tours by appt ▪ Zorgvliet picnic Sep-Apr ▪ Facilities for children ▪ Tour groups ▪ Gifts ▪ Conferences ▪ Walks/hikes ▪ Zorgvliet Country Lodge (18 rooms) ▪ Owner(s) Stephan & Izelle van der Merwe ▪ Winemaker(s) Bernard le Roux (Dec 2013), with Ruben Adams & Richelle Wille ▪ Viticulturist(s) Hannes Jansen van Vuuren ▪ 58ha/25ha (cabs s/f, merlot, p verdot, sauv, sem) ▪ 350t/35,000cs own label 32% red 64% white 4% rosé ▪ PO Box 1595 Stellenbosch 7599 ▪ winecellar@zorgvliet.com ▪ www.zorgvliet.com ▪ **T +27 (0)21-885-1399**

This Year's Ratings Summarised

Here we summarise the wines featured in the A-Z section, with their ratings, sorted first by wine style, in alphabetical order, and then by producer or brand. New wines in **bolder type**. **NS** = no star; **NT** = not tasted; **NR** = tasted but not rated; **D** = discontinued. Where wineries produce more than one version of a particular style, the number of versions is indicated in brackets after the name. A number of wines were tasted as pre-bottling barrel or tank samples, and therefore ratings are provisional. Refer to the A-Z for details.

Albariño
★★★★★ Botanica
★★★★☆ Kleine Zalze
★★★★ Boplaas
★★★☆ Spier NT Newton Johnson; Spier

Alternative white/red
★★★★☆ Neil Ellis (White blends, wooded, dry); **Deep Rooted** (3) (Shiraz/syrah; Sauvignon blanc wooded; Verdelho); Thorne & Daughters (Semillon gris); ArtiSons (Cabernet sauvignon)
★★★★ Olivedale (2) (Rooibernet; White blends, wooded, dry; Skin-macerated white); Mount Abora (Cinsaut); Scions of Sinai (Pinotage)
★★★ Wightman & Sons (2) (Shiraz/syrah; Rosé dry)

Assyrtiko
★★★★ Jordan
NT Mullineux

Barbarossa
★★★★ Gedeelte

Barbera
★★★★☆ Merwida; Vino pH
★★★★ Trizanne
★★★☆ Esona; Idiom NT Hofstraat; Idiom; **Nomoya**; The Drift; Waterford **D** Trizanne

Bastardo do Castello
★★★★ Pilgrim

Biodynamic
★★★★★ Reyneke (4) (Shiraz/syrah; Sauvignon blanc wooded; Shiraz/syrah; Chenin blanc wooded, dry; Old Vines)
★★★★ Reyneke (Sauvignon blanc wooded)

Blanc de noir
★★★★☆ Simelia (Old Vines); Van Loggerenberg
★★★★ Aaldering; Maison
★★★☆ Arra; Elgin Vintners; Lynx; Meerendal; Peter Falke; Tanagra ★★★ Calitzdorp; Deux Frères; Dieu Donné; Esona; **Hazendal**; Landskroon; Lemberg; Nieuwedrift; Signal Gun; Stellenbosch University ★★★☆ Niel Joubert; Van Loveren; **Welgesind** (2)
★★ Botha; Lovane NT Aan't Vette; Beau Constantia; Bezalel; deKaap; **Migliarina**; Packwood; Swartland **D** Doolhof; Hazendal; Sun International

Brandy
★★★★★ Boplaas; **KWV Brandies** (7); Tokara; Van Ryn (3)
★★★★☆ Anthonij Rupert; Avontuur; Blaauwklippen; Boplaas; Die Mas (2); Diemersfontein; Durbanville Hills; Groot Constantia; Joseph Barry; **KWV Brandies**; **Metanoia**; **Mimosa**; Musgrave; **Oude Molen** (3); **Richelieu**; **Rust en Vrede**; The Inventer (2); Upland (3) (Organic); Van Ryn; Viceroy; Windfall
★★★★ Boschendal; **Bundu**; Copeland; Dalla Cia; Die Mas (2); Eendracht; Flight of the Fish Eagle; Joseph Barry (2); Kaapse Liqueurs; Karo; KWV Brandies (2); Lemberg; Mimosa; Montagu Wine & Spirits; Musgrave; Nuy; Orange River; Oude Molen; Richelieu; Sugarbird; Upland (Organic); Van Loveren; Withington
★★★☆ **Bundu**; Die Mas; Fynbos; Grundheim (2); Joseph Barry; Klipdrift (2); KWV Brandies; Oude Molen; Parow; True Kindred Spirits; Viceroy ★★★ Commando; Grundheim; Landzicht; Olof Bergh; Parow; Richelieu★★★ Grundheim; Wellington VO **NT** AA Badenhorst; Backsberg (3); Bayede!; Bezalel (3); Boplaas (4); D'Aria; De Vry; **Eendracht**; Jorgensen's; Kaapzicht; Kingna (2); Oude Wellington (2); Pienaar & Son; **Simonsvlei** (2) (Skin-macerated white); Windmeul

Bukettraube
★★★★ Cederberg
★★★ Swartland **NT** Darling Cellars **D** Darling Cellars

Cabernet franc
★★★★★ Beaumont; De Trafford; Hogan; Raats (3)
★★★★☆ Anthonij Rupert; Backsberg; Botanica; Buitenverwachting; Chamonix; ?David Finlayson; Gabriëlskloof; Glenelly; **Great Heart**; Hermanuspietersfontein; Holden Manz; Jordan; Joubert-Tradauw; Journey's End; KWV; **Leeu Passant**; Lokaia; Marklew; Mischa; Mulderbosch; My Wyn; Nelson; Oldenburg; Raats; **Radford Dale** (Organic); Rainbow's End (2); Raka; Ridgeback;

Rietvallei; Spookfontein; Stellenbosch Vineyards; Stellenrust; Stony Brook; The Foundry; The Garajeest; Thistle & Weed; Van Loggerenberg; **Villion**; Warwick; Weather Report (2); **Wildekrans**; Woolworths; Zorgvliet

★★★★ Anthology; Blaauwklippen; Bushmanspad; Cape Collective; Doolhof; **Ghost In The Machine**; **Hasher**; Hawksmoor (2); Jakkalsvlei; Keermont; Le Pommier; Lozärn; Lynx (2); Mont du Toit; Morgenster; Nomad; Onderkloof; Ormonde; Tanagra; Thokozani (2); Waterkloof (Organic); Whalehaven

★★★ Aden's Star; Orange River; **Wandering NT** Annandale; Arno Smith; Avontuur; Benguela Cove; Berry Wines; Camberley; Eikendal; Glen Carlou; Idiom; Kaapzicht; Lovane; Mitre's Edge; Snow Mountain; Weather Report **D** Lieben; Môreson; Morgenhof; Mount Abora

Cabernet sauvignon

★★★★★ Beyerskloof; Boekenhoutskloof; Cederberg; ?David Finlayson; Diemersdal; Erika Obermeyer; Hartenberg; Kanonkop; Le Riche; Mooiplaas; **MVH Signature Wines**; Nederburg; Rickety Bridge; Stellenrust; The High Road; Thelema; ?Trade Winds; Wade Bales

★★★★☆ Alto; Anthonij Rupert; Anura; Arendsig; Aristea; ArtiSons (Alternative white/red); **Atlas Swift**; Avontuur; Bartinney (2); Bayede!; Bellevue; Benguela Cove (2); Bergsig; Black Elephant; Black Pearl; Boekenhoutskloof; Boschendal; Cape Collective; Capelands; Cavalli; Cederberg; Dalla Cia; ?David Finlayson (2); **De Trafford** (2); Delaire Graff (2); Deux Frères; Dornier; Eikendal; Ernie Els; Excelsior; Flagstone; Friesland; Glen Carlou; Glenelly; Grangehurst; Great Heart; Groenland; Groot Constantia; Groot Phesantekraal (2); **Hartenberg** (2); Holden Manz; Jakob's Vineyards; Joostenberg (Organic); Jordan; Journey's End; Keermont; **Kleine Zalze** (3); Koelenhof; KWV; La Bri; Le Bonheur (2); Le Grand Domaine (2); Le Riche; Leeu Passant; Lievland; Lyngrove; Malanot; Marianne; Meerlust; Middelvlei; Miles Mossop (2); Mooiplaas; Muratie (2); Nederburg; Neil Ellis (2); Nico van der Merwe; Niel Joubert; Oldenburg (2); Onoma; Paserene; Peter Falke (2); Plaisir; Rainbow's End; Raka (2); Remhoogte; Restless River; Rickety Bridge; Ridgeback; Rust en Vrede; Rustenberg; Saxenburg; Schultz Family; Sijnn; Simonsig; Spier; Stark-Condé (3); Stellenview; Stellenzicht; Stony Brook; Strydom; Super Single Vineyards; The Butcher Shop; Thelema (2); Tokara (2); Vergelegen (2); Villion; Warwick; Waterford; Webersburg (2); **Woolworths** (2); Zorgvliet

★★★★ Allesverloren; Annandale; Anthology; Anura (2); Arra; Asara; Aslina; Audacia; Babylonstoren; Backsberg; Belle Rebelle; Bloemendal; Boland; Bon Courage; Bonnievale; Boplaas; Boschheim; Boschkloof; Botanica; Bushmanspad; Camberley; Capelands; **Cloof**; Darling Cellars; De Wet; Delheim; DeWaal (2); Diemersfontein; Dieu Donné; Doolhof; Durbanville Hills; Ernie Els; Ernst Gouws; Fairview; **Gabriel & Gysbert**; Glen Carlou; Goedverwacht; Grande Provence; Groenland; Guillaumé; Haskell; Havana Hills; Hawksmoor; Hazendal; Hoopenburg; House of Mandela; Jakkalsvlei; Kaapzicht; Kanonkop; Klein DasBosch; **Klein Goederust**; Kleine Zalze; Knorhoek (2); Kranskop; Kruger Family; Kusafiri (Organic); Kyburg; La Motte; La Petite Ferme; Landskroon; Lanzerac; Le Grand Chasseur; Leipzig; Lomond; Longridge (Organic); Louisvale (2); Lowerland; **Lozärn**; Lutzville; Lynx; Maastricht; Manley; **Marcology**; Marklew; Meinert; Mellasat; Miravel; Mischa; Mitre's Edge; Mont du Toit; Mont Rochelle; Morgenhof; Morgenster; Mount Vernon; **MVH Signature Wines**; Nabygelegen; Nederburg; Neethlingshof; Nitida; Noble Hill; Olsen; Ormonde; Paserene; Perdeberg; Peter Falke; Post House; Rannoch; **Rickety Bridge**; **Rockbelt** (2); Rooiberg (2); Rudera; Silvermist (Organic); Simonsig; Slaley; Slanghoek; Spookfontein; Stellekaya; Stellenbosch Hills; Stellenbosch Reserve; Stellenrust; Stellenview (2); Survivor; The High Road; The Hill Vineyard (2); The Hills; Township Winery; Under Oaks; Val du Charron; Van Loveren; Vergenoegd; Villiera; VinGlo; Vondeling; Vredenheim; Vriesenhof; Walker Bay Estate; Waterkloof; Wellington Winery; Winshaw; Woolworths (5); Zevenwacht; Zonnebloem

★★★★ Abbottshill; Akkerdraai; Anthonij Rupert; Bayede!; Bé a Daisy; Beau Joubert; Bergsig; Blaauwklippen; Black Oystercatcher; Boland; Bon Courage; Boplaas; Bosman Family; Brampton; Calitzdorp; Cape Classics; Cape Wine Crafters; Chennells; Clairvaux; Cloof; Clos Malverne; Contreberg; Darling Cellars; Daschbosch; Durbanville Hills; Excelsior; Flagstone; Fleur du Cap; **Frater**; House of Mandela; Imbuko; Jason's Hill; Kanu; Koopmanskloof (Fairtrade); Kumusha; KWV; La Petite Provence; Land of Hope (Skin-macerated white); Landskroon; Langverwacht; Late Bloomer; Lutzville; Lynx; M'hudi (2); MAN Family; Maske; **McGregor**; Mimosa; Miravel; Mischa; MolenVliet; Mont Blois; Muse; Niel Joubert; Onderkloof; Opstal; Org de Rac (Fairtrade; Organic); Ormonde; Overhex (2); Piekenierskloof; Porcupine Ridge; Pulpit Rock; Rascallion; Riebeek Valley; Rietvallei; Rooiberg; Spier (2); Stellar (Fairtrade; Organic);

Stellenbosch Family Wines (2); Stellenbosch University; Stellenbosch Vineyards; Stellenview; Stettyn; Stonewall; Swartland; The Goose; Topiary; Upland (Organic); Warwick; Wellington Winery; Welmoed; Windfall; Woolworths ★★★ Aan de Doorns; Asara; Ayama (Old Vines); Bonnievale; Botha; Breëland; Cape Dreams; De Krans; De Villiers; Du Toitskloof; False Bay; Fat Bastard; **Germanier** (Organic); Goedvenwacht; Guardian Peak; Imbuko; **Joubert Family**; Ken Forrester; Koopmanskloof (Fairtrade); La Couronne; Landzicht; Le Manoir de Brendel; Leopard's Leap; Louisvale; Merwida; Nicholson Smith; O'Connell's; Orange River; Painted Wolf; Perdeberg; Robertson; Saam; Seven Sisters; Sun International; Swanepoel; Swartland; **The Fishwives Club**; Tulbagh Winery; Viljoensdrift; Windmeul; Wineways (2); Woolworths (3); Zidela ★★★ Ashton; Eagle's Cliff; Group CDV; Klawer; KWV (2); Landzicht; Louisvale; **Mile High**; Namaqua (2); Nuy; Piekenierskloof (Fairtrade); Stellar (Fairtrade; Organic); Van Loveren; Waverley Hills (Organic); William Everson; Woolworths ★★ Woolworths **NT** Absolute Style; Alexanderfontein; Arendskloof; Beau Joubert; Bemind; Berry Wines; Black Elephant; Boschrivier; Brampton; Buitenverwachting; Cape Wine Crafters; Charla Haasbroek; Chennells; Cloof; Croydon; De Kleine Wijn Koöp; Die Mas; Diemersdal; Du Preez (2); Eerste Hoop; Eikehof; **Elethu**; Franschhoek Cellar; Gun Bay; Hofstraat (2); Idiom; Jan Harmsgat; Kaapse Familie Wingerde; Klein Roosboom; La RicMal; Late Bloomer; Libby's Pride; Lovane (Skin-macerated white); Lutzville; Lyngrove; Mark le Roux; Meerendal; Meerhof; Metzer; Mitre's Edge (2); Mooi Bly; Mountain Ridge; Mountain River (2); Nederburg; Nuy; Pearl Mountain; Prévoir; **Redamancy** (3); Reyneke (Organic); Rietvallei; Robertson (3); Rosendal (2); Rudera; Rust en Vrede; Rustenberg; Safriel (2); Sarah's; Schalkenbosch (2) (Fairtrade); **Simonsvlei** (3); Somersbosch; Steel; Stellendrift (3); Stone Ridge; Strooidak; Tangled Tree; Teubes (Organic); The Butcher Shop; The Fledge; Theescombe (Lower in Alcohol); Twelve Apostles; VinGlo (2); Waterford (2); Welbedacht; Women in Wine (2) **D** Breëland; Cape Dreams; Cape Rock; Fairvalley; Fleur du Cap; Grangehurst; KWV (2); Le Riche (3); McGregor; Mont du Toit; Mooiplaas (Lower in Alcohol); Mountain Ridge (2); Org de Rac (Organic); Safriel; Tulbagh Winery; Vergelegen (2); Windmeul; Woolworths (2)

Carignan

★★★★☆ ArtiSons; Ayama; Blackwater; **De Kleine Wijn Koöp**; Torero

★★★★ Hazendal; Painted Wolf

★★★ Swartland **NT** Cape Rock; Kloovenburg; Mullineux; **Nomoya**; Sijnn; The Horsemen **D** Anura; Fairview (Old Vines); Olifantsberg

Carmenère

★★★★☆ Lozärn

Chardonnay unwooded

★★★★☆ Bouchard Finlayson; **Dalsig**; Haute Cabrière (Old Vines); Jasper Raats; Lokaia; Lourensford; Môreson

★★★★ Chamonix; Clouds; Constantia Uitsig; Diemersdal; Eikendal; Glenelly; GlenWood; Hartenberg; Jordan; Kruger Family; La Vierge; Onoma; Val du Charron; Weltevrede

★★★★ **Arendskloof**; Bellpost; Blue Owl; Compagniesdrift; De Krans; Eerste Hoop; Group CDV; Hill & Dale; Hoopenburg; Klein Roosboom; Kleine Zalze; Kruger Family; La Petite Ferme; Langverwacht; Le Grand Chasseur; Louisvale; Meerhof; Middelvlei; **Morgenhof**; **Onderkloof** (Kosher); Org de Rac (Fairtrade; Organic); Prévoir; Pulpit Rock; **Rietvallei**; Robertson; Rooiberg; Stellenbosch Vineyards; The Goose; The Grape Grinder; Under Oaks; Van Loggerenberg; Vriesenhof ★★★ Cape Dreams; Dieu Donné; **Du Preez**; False Bay; Haute Cabrière; Ken Forrester; Landskroon; Leeuwenberg; Leopard's Leap; Less; McGregor; Merwida; Neethlingshof; Rooiberg; Seven Springs; Spotswood; **The Grape Grinder** (Perlé); Van Loveren; Vendôme; Viljoensdrift; **Wildeberg**; **Windfall**; Woolworths; Zidela★★★ Bon Courage; Cape Wine Crafters; Duma; Flagstone; Klawer; Kloovenburg; Lutzville; Piekenierskloof (Fairtrade); Stellar (2) (Fairtrade; Organic); Swartland; Woolworths (Fairtrade; Organic); **Zidela** ★★ Du'SwaRoo **NT** AA Badenhorst; Absolute Style; Alexanderfontein; Ashton; Bé a Daisy; Brampton; Brunia; Eikehof; Ernst Gouws; Franschhoek Cellar; Libby's Pride; Lynx; Mountain River; Pearl Mountain; Plettenvale; Robertson; Roodekrantz; Rustenberg; Sarah's; Stone Ridge; The Butcher Shop; The Winery of Good Hope; VinGlo; Women in Wine; Woolworths (3) **D** Cloof; Daschbosch; Doolhof; Frater; Groote Post; Idun; Jordan; Meerendal (2); Riebeek Valley; Rietvallei; Welbedacht; Woolworths

Chardonnay wooded

★★★★★ Bartinney; Cap Maritime; Capensis; Creation; ?David Finlayson; Delaire Graff; **Draaiboek** (2); GlenWood; Haskell; Hogan; Kershaw (3); La Bri; Lanzerac; Leeu Passant (2) (Extended-barrel-aged white/gris); MVH Signature Wines; Oak Valley; Oldenburg; Paul Clüver; **Plaisir**; Restless River; Storm (2)

★★★★★ Akkerdal; Almenkerk; Alvi's Drift; Anthonij Rupert; Arendsig; Aristea; **Asara**; Atlas Swift (3); Babylonstoren; Baleia; Bartinney; Benguela Cove (2); Boschendal; Bosman Hermanus; Bouchard Finlayson (2); Brew Cru; Bruce Jack; Buitenverwachting; Callender; Canto; **Cap Maritime**; Capensis (2); Cavalli; Chamonix (2); Clouds; Constantia Uitsig; Creation (3); Crystallum (3); ?David Finlayson; De Grendel (Skin-macerated white); Delaire Graff; Delheim; DeMorgenzon; Die Kat; Doolhof; Dorrance; Eikendal (2); Epicurean; Fairview; Fleur du Cap; Glen Carlou; Glenelly; GlenWood; Great Heart; Groot Constantia; Hamilton Russell; Hartenberg; Highlands Road; Holden Manz; Iona (3); Jakkalsvlei; Jayne's; **Jordan** (2); Joubert-Tradauw; Journey's End; Julien Schaal; Kara-Tara; Kershaw (3); Klein Constantia; Kleine Zalze; Kruger Family (3) (Old Vines); La Bri; La Couronne; La Vierge (2); Ladybird (Organic); Le Riche; Leeuwenberg; Longridge (Organic); Lourensford (2); Maison; Meerlust; Mont Rochelle; **Mooiplaas**; Môreson (2); Natasha Williams; Neil Ellis; Oak Valley; Paserene; Paul Clüver (3) (Old Vines); Paul Wallace; Quoin Rock; Redamancy; Rhebokskloof; **Richard Hilton**; Rickety Bridge; Rietvallei; RiverGold; Robertson; Rustenberg; **Sandstone**; Shannon; St Leger; Stellenbosch Vineyards; Stellenrust; Stellenzicht; Stony Brook; **Survivor** (2); Tesselaarsdal; Thelema (2); Tokara; **Topiary**; Trizanne; Van Loveren; Vergelegen; Villion; Vriesenhof (2); Warwick; Waterford; Weltevrede; Whalehaven; Woolworths (3) (Organic)

★★★★ Aaldering; Allée Bleue; Alvi's Drift; Anthology; Aslina; Atlas Swift (2); **Bacco**; Backsberg; Bellevue; Bellingham; Bergsig; Bizoe; **Blaauwklippen**; Bloemendal; Boland; Bonnievale; Boschendal; Boschkloof; Bruce Jack; Cape Point; Dalla Cia; Delaire Graff; DeMorgenzon; Domaine des Dieux; Donegal; Eerste Hoop; Elgin Vintners; False Bay; Fram; **Gabriel & Gysbert**; **Ghost In The Machine**; Goedverwacht; Grande Provence; Hartenberg; Hasher; Haskell; Haute Cabrière (2) (Old Vines); Havana Hills; Holden Manz; Hoopenburg; Idun; Jordan; Journey's End; Julien Schaal; Kershaw; Klein Constantia; Klein DasBosch; Koelfontein; Kranskop; Kruger Family; KWV; La Couronne; La Motte; La Petite Ferme; Lanzerac; Le Bonheur; Le Grand Domaine; **Le Pommier**; Longridge (Organic); Lozärn; Lutzville; Lyngrove; MAN Family; Mellasat; Migliarina; **Mimosa**; Mont Blois (2); Mont Rochelle; Mount Vernon; Mulderbosch; Muratie; Nederburg; Niel Joubert; Olsen; Org de Rac (Organic); Paserene;

Peter Falke; Plaisir; Pulpit Rock; **Radford Dale** (2) (Organic); Rhebokskloof; Rickety Bridge; Rietvallei (2); **Rockbelt**; Rogge Cloof; Running Stream; Saxenburg (2); Simonsig; Slaley; Spier; Spookfontein; Steenberg; Stellenbosch Reserve; Stellenrust; Stellenzicht; Sumaridge; Thamnus Wines; Thelema; Thorngrove; **Tokara** (2); Vergelegen; Vondeling; Waverley Hills (Organic); Weltevrede; Whalehaven; Winshaw; Woolworths (2); Zevenwacht

★★★★ Anthonij Rupert; Anura; Arendskloof; Asara; Ashton; Badsberg; Baleia; Bergsig; Bon Courage; Botha; Breëland; Calitzdorp; Cape Classics; Cape Moby; Cape Wine Crafters; Darling Cellars; De Wet; Delphin; **Dickens Family**; Dieu Donné; Esona; Excelsior; Flagstone; Germanier (Organic); Glen Carlou; Journey's End; Kloovenburg; Koopmanskloof (Fairtrade); KWV (2); Land of Hope; Lomond; Lord's; Louisvale; **Mama Afrika**; Marcology; Merwida; Miss Molly; Morgenhof; Niel Joubert; Olivedale; Ormonde; Overhex; Packwood; Piekenierskloof; Prévoir; Rietvallei (Skin-macerated white); **Rockbelt**; Rooiberg; Rosendal; Seven Sisters; Seven Springs; Signal Gun; Stanford Hills; Stellar (Fairtrade; Organic); Stellenbosch Family Wines (2); Stellenview; Tierhoek; Villiersdorp; Walker Bay Estate; Warwick; Welbedacht; Welmoed; **Wildeloot**; Woolworths; Zandvliet ★★★ Boland; Bonnievale; Cilmor; Clos Malverne; Die Mas; Drostdy-Hof; Du Toitskloof; Durbanville Hills; Excelsior; Fat Bastard; **Gabriel & Gysbert**; Goedverwacht; **Klein Goederust**; Louisvale; Mimosa; Nieuwedrift; Porcupine Ridge; Slanghoek; Spier; Summerhill; The Fishwives Club; Two Oceans; Woolworths★★★ Cape Wine Crafters; **Lautus** (De-Alcoholised); Tangled Tree; Woolworths **NT** Anthonij Rupert; Anura; Atlas Swift; Avontuur; Backsberg; Bosjes; Burgershof; Cape Collective; Capelands; Draaiboek; Dragonridge; Durbanville Hills; Eikendal; Fairvalley (2); Fleur du Cap; Foothills; Goedverwacht; Hazendal; Jan Harmsgat; Kumala; Laarman; Lazanou (Organic); Lieben; Lodestone; Lynx; Maison de Teijger; Malanot; Marklew; Middelvlei; Migliarina; Mooi Bly; Mountain River; My Wyn; Nederburg; Nelson; Newton Johnson (3); Nuy; Oak Valley (2); Onderkloof; Ormonde; Pearl Mountain; Radford Dale; Rietvallei; Robertson; Rosendal; Rustenberg; Simonsvlei; Snow Mountain; Stonewall; The Fledge; Topiary; Varkenskraal; Vergenoegd; Waterkloof; Welvanpas; Women in Wine; Woolworths; Zonnebloem **D** Bayedel; Botanica; Cape Town Wine Co; Groote Post; Hillock; Jordan; Kruger Family; Le Manoir de Brendel; Maastricht; Safriel; Seven Sisters; Thelema; Tulbagh Winery

Chenel

★★★★ Springfontein

Chenin blanc off-dry/semi-sweet (w & u/w)

★★★★☆ Longridge

★★★★ Beaumont

★★★ Mara; **Rockbelt**★★★☆ Landzicht; Woolworths (2) **NT** Ashton (Perlé); Ken Forrester; Robertson (2); Valley Vineyards **D** Hillock; Spier (2) (Lower in Alcohol)

Chenin blanc unwooded dry

★★★★☆ Anthonij Rupert (Old Vines); Black Pearl; **Creation** (Old Vines); Grande Provence; Great Heart; House of Hier; Kings Kloof; Kleine Zalze (2); Kruger Family (Old Vines); Mount Abora; Raats; Rall; Rascallion (Old Vines); Scions of Sinai (Old Vines); Super Single Vineyards (Old Vines); Waterford

★★★★ Adama; Aslina (Skin-macerated white); Beaumont; **Bizoe**; Black Elephant; Blackwater; Bosman Family; Cederberg; Clouds; Croydon; Darling Cellars; Fairview; False Bay; Jakkalsvlei; Lubanzi; Maison; Malanot; MAN Family; Mischa (Old Vines); Mooiplaas (Old Vines); **MVH Signature Wines**; Myburgh Bros (Old Vines); Nieuwedrift; Noble Hill; Org de Rac (Fairtrade; Organic); Overhex; Piekenierskloof; Remhoogte; Spier (Organic); The Grape Grinder (2); **The Vinoneers**; Under Oaks; Wildekrans

★★★☆ Aaldering; Aan de Doorns; Allesverloren; Anthonij Rupert; Asara; Babylon's Peak; Badsberg; Belle Rebelle; Bemind; Bergheim; Blaauwklippen; Bonnievale; **Camberley**; Cape Dreams; Cape Fold; Cape Wine Company; Cavalli; Chameleon; Cilmor; Dawn Patrol (2); Denneboom; **Du Preez**; Durbanville Hills; False Bay; Groot Phesantekraal; Groote Post; Hill & Dale; Kaapzicht; Kanu; Klawer (2) (Old Vines); Kleine Zalze; Koopmanskloof (Fairtrade); KWV; L'Avenir; Landskroon; Leeuwenkuil; Lemberg; Leopard's Leap; Lyngrove; M'hudi; Meerhof; Merwida; Neethlingshof; Nick & Forti's; Niel Joubert; Olsen; Orange River (Organic); Ormonde (2); Perdeberg (2); Post House; Pulpit Rock; Rainbow's End; Renegade; Reyneke (Organic); Rhebokskloof; Rickety Bridge; Riebeek Valley; Robertson; Rooiberg; Saronsberg; Scali; Simonsig; Slanghoek; Stellenbosch Hills; Stettyn; The Grape Grinder; Val du Charron (2); Villiersdorp; Vondeling; **Welbedacht**; Welmoed; Wildeberg; Wildekrans; Woolworths (3); Zoetendal ★★★ Ayama (Old Vines); Bé a Daisy; Bergsig; Boland; Boschendal; Breëland; Calitzdorp; Darling Cellars; Daschbosch (2) (Fairtrade); De Krans; De Wet; DeWaal; Diemersfontein; Domein Doornkraal; Du Toitskloof; Eagle's Cliff; Ernie Els; Ernst

Gouws; Goedverwacht (2); Groenland; Guardian Peak; Hawksmoor; Imbuko (3); Ken Forrester; **Kirabo**; Koelenhof; La Capra; Langverwacht; Late Bloomer; Lutzville; McGregor; **Mellasat**; Mont Blois; Montagu Wine & Spirits (2); Mountain Ridge; Nicholson Smith (2); O'Connell's; Orange River; Perdeberg; Piekenierskloof (Fairtrade); Rascallion; Rooiberg; Roos Family; Saam (Fairtrade); Seven Sisters; Silkbush; Slanghoek; Spier; Stellar (Fairtrade; Organic); Summerhill; Sun International; Swartland; The Hills; Truter Family; TTT Cellar; Tulbagh Winery; Van Loveren; Waboomsrivier; Wellington Winery; Windfall; Woolworths (Fairtrade; Organic); Zidela ★★★ Ashton; Bayede!; Boland (Lower in Alcohol); Bon Courage; Du'SwaRoo; Durbanville Hills (Lower in Alcohol); Fleur du Cap (Lower in Alcohol); House of Mandela; La Couronne; Nuy; Perdeberg (Lower in Alcohol); Vinette; Welbedacht; Welvanpas; Windmeul; Woolworths (Lower in Alcohol); **Zidela** (2) ★★ Botha **NT** AA Badenhorst (4) (Old Vines); Alexanderfontein; Ashton; Audacia; Backsberg; Badger; Bayede!; Blue Crane; Cape Wine Company (Fairtrade); Darling Cellars (Old Vines); Dorrance (Fairtrade); Dragonridge (Organic); Drostdy-Hof; DuVon; Ernst Gouws; Fairvalley; Fish Hoek (Fairtrade); Flagstone; Franschhoek Cellar; Friesland; Groot Parys (2) (Organic); Hoopenburg; Jacaranda; Joostenberg (Organic); Klawer; Kranskop; Kumala (2); Lazanou (Organic); **Libby's Pride**; Lieben; Lion's Kop; Mitre's Edge; Mooi Bly; Mother Rock (3); Mountain River; Nelson; Nieuwedrift; Nomoya; Pearl Mountain; Peter Bayly; Porcupine Ridge; Reyneke (Organic); Rietvallei; Robertson (Lower in Alcohol); Rosendal; Rustenberg; Schalkenbosch; **Simonsvlei** (3); Somersbosch; Son of the Soil; Spier; Terracura; The Winery of Good Hope; Theescombe; Two Oceans; Valley Vineyards (2); Varkenskraal; **WineWolf**; Women in Wine; Woolworths **D** Bayede!; Boland; Cloof (Old Vines); Daschbosch; Le Manoir de Brendel; Namaqua; Plaisir; Silkbush; Skilpadvlei; Vergenoegd; Woolworths (2); Zidela

Chenin blanc wooded, dry

★★★★★ ArtiSons; Asara; Beaumont (Old Vines); Bellingham (Old Vines); Bosman Family (Old Vines); Botanica (Old Vines); Carinus Family; Cederberg; Charla Haasbroek; **City on a Hill**; Daschbosch (Old Vines); **David & Nadia** (2) (Old Vines); DeMorgenzon (2) (Old Vines); Eenzaamheid (Old Vines); Huis van Chevallerie; Ken Forrester (Old Vines); Leeuwenkuil; Metzer; Mullineux (2) (Old Vines); Rijk's; **Sadie** (3) (Old Vines); Sakkie Mouton; Savage (Old Vines); Stark-Condé; Stellenbosch

Vineyards; Stellenrust (2) (Old Vines); The Ahrens Family

★★★★★ Alheit (5) (Old Vines); Alvi's Drift; Angus Paul (2); Anthonij Rupert (2) (Old Vines); Arendsig; Asara; Axle (Old Vines); Belle Rebelle (2); Bellevue (Old Vines); Bellingham (Old Vines); **Black Elephant**; Blackwater; Boschkloof; Brookdale (Old Vines); Bruce Jack; Buitenverwachting; Cape Collective; Carinus Family; Catherine Marshall; Cecilia (Old Vines); Chamonix (Old Vines); **City on a Hill** (2); Dalkeith (2) (Old Vines); Darling Cellars (Old Vines); David & Nadia (4) (Old Vines); ?David Finlayson; De Trafford (3) (Skin-macerated white); De Wet; Delheim (2) (Old Vines); DewaldtHeyns; Diemersfontein (Old Vines); Donkiesbaai; Doolhof; Dornier; Erika Obermeyer; Esona; Flagstone (Old Vines); Gabriëlskloof (Old Vines); **Groenland** (Old Vines); Groot Phesantekraal; Harry Hartman (2); Hogan; Holden Manz (2) (Old Vines); Illimis; JC Wickens (2); Jean Daneel; Joostenberg (Old Vines; Organic); Jordan (Old Vines); Julien Schaal (Organic); Kaapzicht (2) (Old Vines); Kanu (Old Vines); Keermont (Old Vines); Ken Forrester (2) (Old Vines); Kleine Zalze (2) (Old Vines); Koelenhof (Old Vines); KWV; Kyburg; L'Avenir (Old Vines); Ladybird (Organic); Le Sueur; Leeuwenkuil; Lievland (Old Vines); Lourens Family; Luddite (Skin-macerated white); Maison; McFarlane; **Metzer** (2); Michaella; Miles Mossop (Old Vines); Mont Blois; Mooiplaas (Old Vines); Mulderbosch (Old Vines); Naudé (Old Vines); Nederburg (Old Vines); Nelson; Nico van der Merwe; Noble Hill; Off The Record; Old Road; Oldenburg; Olifantsberg (2) (Old Vines); **Opstal** (4) (Old Vines); Painted Wolf; Patatsfontein; Paulus (2); Perdeberg; Piekenierskloof (Old Vines); Pilgrim; Post House; Quest (Old Vines); Raats (3); Radford Dale; Rall; Remhoogte; Reyneke (Biodynamic; Old Vines); Rickety Bridge; Ridgeback; Riebeek Valley (2) (Old Vines); Rijk's; Roodekrantz (4) (Old Vines); Saltare; Scali; Schultz Family; Sijnn; Simonsig; Spier (2) (Old Vines; Organic); **Steel**; **Steilpad**; Stellenbosch Vineyards; Super Single Vineyards (Old Vines); Survivor (2); The Ahrens Family (2) (Old Vines); The Foundry; Thistle & Weed (3) (Old Vines); Thorne & Daughters (Old Vines); Tierhoek (Old Vines); Tim Hillock; Van Loggerenberg (2) (Old Vines); Van Wyk; Villion (Old Vines); **Vinevenom** (2); Vondeling; Wade Bales; Warwick (Old Vines); **Waterford** (Old Vines); Wightman & Sons (Skin-macerated white); Wildeberg (Old Vines); Wildekrans; Wolf & Woman (Old Vines); Wolvenhoek (Old Vines); Woolworths; Zevenwacht (2) (Old Vines)

★★★★ Alvi's Drift; Badsberg; Beau Joubert; Belle Rebelle; Bellingham; Bergsig; Bester Family; Blake; Boland; Boschheim; Botha; Brookdale; Cage Wine; **Cape Dreams**; Carinus Family; Catherine Marshall; Cavalli; DA Hanekom; DeMorgenzon; Dorrance; **Duikersdrift**; Durbanville Hills; Flagstone; Fram; Friesland; Gabriëlskloof; Ghost In The Machine; **Groot Parys** (2) (Old Vines; Skin-macerated white); Hawksmoor (Old Vines); Holder; Jacaranda (Skin-macerated white); Jordan; Kanu; Kirabo; Knorhoek (Old Vines); Kruger Family (2) (Old Vines); L'Avenir; Le Chant; **Le Grand Domaine** (Old Vines); Leipzig; Lomond; Longridge (Organic); Lourensford; Lyngrove (Old Vines); M'hudi; Malanot; Manley; Maree Family; Merwida; Migliarina; Miles Mossop; Morgenhof; Mosi; Mulderbosch; Mullineux (Old Vines); Myburgh Bros (Old Vines; Organic; Skin-macerated white); Nabygelegen; Niel Joubert; Nomoya; Nuy; **Olsen**; Painted Wolf; Perdeberg (Old Vines); **Plaisir**; Radford Dale; **Riebeek Valley** (Old Vines); Rijk's; RiverGold; Roodekrantz (Old Vines); **Schotia**; Slanghoek; Spier; Springfontein (2) (Organic); Stellenbosch Hills; Stellenbosch Vineyards; Stellenrust; Stettyn (Old Vines); Strydom; Swartland; The Butcher Shop; The Fledge; The Vinoneers; Themika (2); Township Winery (Old Vines); Villiera (Old Vines); Waterkloof (3) (Organic); Welbedacht (Old Vines); Welgegund (Old Vines); Wellington Winery; Winshaw; Wolvenhoek (Old Vines); Woolworths (3); Zevenwacht

★★★★ Axe Hill; Babylonstoren; Cape Classics (2); Cilmor; **Doolhof**; Doran; Dragonridge; Eerste Hoop; Fat Bastard; **Fram**; Fryer's Cove; **Gabriel & Gysbert**; Grande Provence; **House of Hlela** (Fairtrade; Old Vines); **Klein Goederust**; Kumusha; KWV; Land of Hope; Lord's; Maison de Teijger; Manley; Meerendal; Mimosa; Mountain Ridge; Rietvallei; Saxenburg; Somersbosch; Stellenbosch Reserve; **Stofberg**; **Stokkiesdraai**; Tierhoek (2); Val de Vie; Villiera; Wandering (Old Vines); Waterford; Wightman & Sons (Natural/non-fortified pale); Windmeul (Old Vines); Woolworths ★★★ Botha; Dornier; Fleur du Cap; **Nicholson Smith**; Silkbush; Stellenbosch University; Vredenheim **NT** AA Badenhorst (5) (Old Vines); Alheit (Old Vines); Allée Bleue; Anura; Arendskloof; Axe Hill; Babylon's Peak; Cape Fold; Capelands; Creation; Equitana; Fuselage (2) (Old Vines); Glen Carlou; Goedverwacht; Groot Parys (Skin-macerated white); Hawksmoor (2) (Old Vines); Hazendal; Hermit on the Hill; Hirst; Hogan; Jan Harmsgat; Jason's Hill; Jean Daneel; Joostenberg (Organic); Leopard's Leap; Lutzville; Mark le Roux; McFarlane; Miles Mossop; Mountain Ridge; Mullineux (2); Muse;

Nico Vermeulen; Old Road (Old Vines); Openwine;
Painted Wolf (2) (Old Vines); Pearl Mountain;
Radford Dale; Remhoogte; RiverGold; Rogge Cloof;
Roodekrantz (Old Vines); Rudera (3); Safriel (Old
Vines); Snow Mountain; Spice Route (Old Vines);
Spider Pig; Spioenkop (2); Spotswood; **Stanford
Valley**; Stellar (Fairtrade; Organic); Stellenbosch
University; Stone Ridge; Tembela; Terracura (2); The
Fledge (3) (Old Vines); The Horsemen; Wightman &
Sons (Skin-macerated white); Wildehurst; Windmeul
D City on a Hill; Cloof (Old Vines); Doran; Frater; Land
of Hope; Lieben; Mountain Ridge; Saltare; Thor (Old
Vines; Skin-macerated white); Vergenoegd

Cinsaut

★★★★★ ArtiSons; Eenzaamheid; Kleine Zalze;
Savage (Old Vines); Van Loggerenberg

★★★★☆ Bellevue (Old Vines); Blackwater;
Bosman Family; Bruwer Vintners; Darling Cellars
(Old Vines); Fram; Illimis; Jasper Raats (Old Vines);
Kaapzicht; Lanzerac; Leeu Passant (Old Vines);
McFarlane; Metzer (Old Vines); Mischa (Old Vines);
Naudé (Old Vines); Neil Ellis; Rall; Rickety Bridge
(Old Vines); Sadie (Old Vines); Sanniesrust; Scions
of Sinai; Stellenbosch Vineyards; Stellenrust; Van
Loggerenberg (Old Vines); Welgegund

★★★★ Angus Paul; Babylon's Peak; Bellevue;
City on a Hill; Daschbosch; Die Kat; Donkiesbaai
(Old Vines); Dorrance; House of Hier; **Ken Forrester;**
Kruger Family (2) (Old Vines); Landskroon;
McFarlane; Miles Mossop; Mount Abora
(Alternative white/red); **Opstal;** Piekenierskloof
(2) (Old Vines); Rietvallei; Roodekrantz (Old Vines);
Stellenbosch Reserve; **The Earth Beneath Our
Feet;** Trizanne; **Welbedacht; Wildeberg** (Old
Vines); Wildehurst; Woolworths

★★★★ AD Wines; Axe Hill; Bemind; Erika
Obermeyer; Mitre's Edge; **Nomoya;** Perdeberg;
Pulpit Rock; Radford Dale (Nouveau); **Swartland;**
Waterkloof ★★★ Darling Cellars; Dawn Patrol;
Strydom★★★ Jason's Hill **NT** AA Badenhorst
(2) (Old Vines); Cape Fold; De Kleine Wijn Koöp
(2) (Old Vines); De Trafford; Elemental Bob; Enfin;
Fairview; Fuselage; Laarman; Myburgh Bros; Old
Road; Riebeek Valley; **Simonsvlei;** Spider Pig; Spier;
Steel; Stellenzicht; Tempel; Terracura; Warwick **D**
Bonnievale; Du'SwaRoo; Leeu Passant; Spider Pig

Cinsaut blanc
NT Rall

Clairette blanche
★★★★☆ Daschbosch

★★★★ **Ghost In The Machine;** Radford Dale
★★★★☆ Wightman & Sons

Colombard

★★★★☆ Beaumont; Naudé (Old Vines); Rebel
Rebel (Old Vines); **Sakkie Mouton**

★★★★ Mont Blois; Steel

★★★☆ Bon Courage; Goedwacht; Langverwacht;
Mont Blois; Tanagra ★★★ Esona; Landzicht;
McGregor; **Orange River;** Robertson; Rooiberg;
TTT Cellar; Van Loveren★★★ Nuy; Orange River;
Robertson ★★ Aan de Doorns; Orange River
(2); Robertson (2) **NT** Arendsig; Bezalel; Cape
Dreams; Lowerland; Micu Narunsky; The Fledge **D**
Patatsfontein; Robertson

De-Alcoholised

★★★ Darling Cellars (Sauvignon blanc unwooded);
Leopard's Leap (2) (Red blends, other; White blends,
unwooded, dry); **Woolworths** (5) (Red blends,
Cape Bordeaux; Chenin blanc off-dry/semi-sweet
(w & u/w); Sauvignon blanc unwooded; Sparkling,
Non-MCC, rosé, off-dry/semi-sweet; Sparkling,
Non-MCC, white, dry); **Lautus** (4) (Rosé off-dry/
semi-sweet; Chardonnay wooded; Sauvignon
blanc unwooded; Sparkling, Non-MCC, white,
dry); Bonnievale (Sauvignon blanc unwooded)
★★ Robertson (2) (Sparkling, Non-MCC, rosé, dry;
Sparkling, Non-MCC, white, dry); Darling Cellars
(2) (Shiraz/syrah; Rosé off-dry/semi-sweet);
Woolworths (2) (Merlot; Rosé off-dry/semi-sweet);
Lautus (Red blends, with pinotage) ★★ Darling
Cellars (Sparkling, Non-MCC, rosé, off-dry/semi-
sweet) **NT** Robertson

Fairtrade

★★★★☆ Bosman Family (Red blends, shiraz/
syrah-based); Org de Rac (White blends, wooded,
dry; Organic); Asara (Red blends, Cape Bordeaux);
Spice Route (Grenache noir); Stellar (Vin de paille/
straw wine)

★★★★ Stellar (Shiraz/syrah; Organic); Bosman
Family (White blends, wooded, dry; Organic); Org
de Rac (Red blends, shiraz/syrah-based; Organic);
Imbuko (Red blends, Cape Bordeaux); Du Toitskloof
(2) (Hanepoot fortified; Muscadel, red, fortified);
Org de Rac (5) (Merlot; Shiraz/syrah; Chenin blanc
unwooded dry; Roussanne; Sparkling, Méthode
cap classique, rosé, dry; Organic); Spice Route
(Mourvèdre); **Le Grand Domaine** (2) (Red blends,
shiraz/syrah-based; White blends, wooded, dry;
Organic); Goats do Roam (Red blends, shiraz/
syrah-based); Kyburg (Red blends, other); Klein
Amoskuil (White blends, unwooded, dry)

★★★★ Stellar (3) (Cabernet sauvignon; Pinotage;
Chardonnay wooded; Organic); Org de Rac
(4) (Cabernet sauvignon; Red blends, shiraz/

syrah-based; Chardonnay unwooded; Sauvignon blanc unwooded; Organic); Koopmanskloof (2) (Cabernet sauvignon; Pinotage); Piekenierskloof (2) (Red blends, other; White blends, unwooded, dry); Stellenrust (3) (Red blends, with pinotage; Rosé dry; White blends, unwooded, dry); Koopmanskloof (3) (Shiraz/syrah; Chardonnay unwooded; Chenin blanc unwooded dry); Daschbosch (Pinotage); Arniston Bay (Sauvignon blanc unwooded); **House of Hlela** (2) (Pinotage; Chenin blanc wooded, dry; Old Vines); Klein Amoskuil (Red blends, shiraz/syrah-based); Havana Hills (Rosé dry); Lubanzi (Rosé dry) ★★★ Woolworths (Pinotage; Organic); Stellar (Pinot noir; Organic); Woolworths (2) (Chenin blanc unwooded dry; Sauvignon blanc unwooded; Organic); Stellar (7) (Pinotage; Rosé dry; Shiraz/syrah; Chenin blanc unwooded dry; Sauvignon blanc unwooded; White blends, unwooded, dry; Rosé dry; Organic); Woolworths (Sparkling, Non-MCC, white, dry; Organic); Org de Rac (Shiraz/syrah; Organic); Woolworths (2) (Red blends, shiraz/syrah-based; White blends, unwooded, dry; Organic); Asara (White from red/black grapes (not Blanc de noir)); Saam (Chenin blanc unwooded dry); Stellar (2) (Sparkling, Non-MCC, rosé, dry; Sparkling, Non-MCC, white, dry; Organic); Stellenrust (White blends, off-dry/semi-sweet (w & u/w)); Koopmanskloof (4) (Cabernet sauvignon; Merlot; Rosé dry; Sauvignon blanc unwooded); Daschbosch (Chenin blanc unwooded dry); Piekenierskloof (6) (Pinotage; Shiraz/syrah; Rosé dry; Chenin blanc unwooded dry; Sauvignon blanc unwooded; Viognier); Arniston Bay (2) (Shiraz/syrah; Rosé dry) ★★★ Woolworths (4) (Cabernet sauvignon; Merlot; Shiraz/syrah; Chardonnay unwooded; Organic); Stellar (11) (Cabernet sauvignon; Merlot; Shiraz/syrah; Chardonnay unwooded; Merlot; Red blends, with pinotage; Chardonnay unwooded; Red blends, shiraz/syrah-based; White blends, unwooded, dry; White blends, off-dry/semi-sweet (w & u/w); Sweet red; Organic); Woolworths (Sparkling, Non-MCC, white, dry; Organic); Org de Rac (Rosé dry; Organic); Saam (Pinotage); Koopmanskloof (Pinotage); Piekenierskloof (2) (Cabernet sauvignon; Chardonnay unwooded) **NT** Stellar (2) (Chenin blanc wooded, dry; Sauvignon blanc wooded; Organic); Imbuko (Red blends, other); Cape Wine Company (8) (Grenache noir; Merlot; Pinotage; Shiraz/syrah; Red blends, shiraz/syrah-based; Rosé dry; Chenin blanc unwooded dry; Sauvignon blanc unwooded); Koopmanskloof (Pinotage); Imbuko (4) (Muscadel, red, unfortified; Muscadel, white, unfortified; Muscadel, white, unfortified; White blends, off-dry/

semi-sweet (w & u/w); Lower in Alcohol; Perlé); Cape Wine Company (Red blends, Cape Bordeaux); Dorrance (Chenin blanc unwooded dry); Fish Hoek (6) (Merlot; Pinotage; Shiraz/syrah; Rosé dry; Chenin blanc unwooded dry; Sauvignon blanc unwooded); Schalkenbosch (2) (Cabernet sauvignon; Shiraz/syrah); Lubanzi (Red blends, shiraz/syrah-based) **Cape Wine Company** (2) (Red blends, Cape Bordeaux; White blends, unwooded, dry; Organic) **D** Stellar (Malbec)

Extended-barrel-aged white/gris
★★★★★ Leeu Passant (Chardonnay wooded)

Gamay noir
★★★★ Asara; Radford Dale; Villiera
★★★★ Radford Dale **NT** Radford Dale

Gewürztraminer
★★★★ Buitenverwachting; Elemental Bob; Simonsig
★★★★ Bergsig; Bon Courage; Delheim; **Morgenhof**; Neethlingshof ★★★ Robertson **NT** Koelenhof **D** ArtiSons; Migliarina

Grenache blanc
★★★★★ Riebeek Valley; The Foundry
★★★★☆ Bosman Family; De Kleine Wijn Koöp; Donkiesbaai; **Edouard Labeye**; Fairview; Glen Heatlie; KWV; Momento; Mont Blois; Olifantsberg; Rall; Scions of Sinai
★★★★ Arbeidsgenot; Ayama; Huis van Chevallerie; Niel Joubert; Wolf & Woman
★★★★ KWV; Nomoya; Perdeberg; Piekenierskloof; Rustenberg **NT** Doran; Klein Amoskuil (Skin-macerated white); Sanniesrust (Skin-macerated white); **Simonsvlei** (Perlé); The Horsemen **D** Ayama

Grenache gris
★★★★☆ Fram; Momento

Grenache noir
★★★★★ Elemental Bob; Kleine Zalze; Kruger Family
★★★★☆ ArtiSons; Blackwater; Catherine Marshall; David & Nadia; Illimis; **Ken Forrester**; Kleine Zalze; Lourens Family; Migliarina; Mischa; Momento; Naudé; Neil Ellis; Oldenburg; Olifantsberg; Painted Wolf; Piekenierskloof (Old Vines); Sadie (Old Vines); Saronsberg; Savage; Sijnn; Spice Route (Fairtrade); Stellenbosch Vineyards; Strandveld; Swartberg; Tempel; The Foundry; Tierhoek; Twee Jonge Gezellen; Van Niekerk Vintners; Villion; Vriesenhof; Waverley Hills
★★★★ Arbeidsgenot; **Arno Smith**; **Badger**; Bartho Eksteen; Beaumont; Boland; Cage Wine; Cape Wine Company; **City on a Hill**; DeMorgenzon;

Die Kat; Donkiesbaai; Doran; Dunstone; **Edouard Labeye**; Fairview (2); Franki's; Idun; La Petite Ferme; Ormonde; Piekenierskloof; Radford Dale; Sanniesrust; Silkbush; Thiart; Tierhoek; Vriesenhof; Waterford; Welgegund

★★★★ Anura; Cape Rock; Donegal; Esona; Kloovenburg; Lemberg; Lynx; **Perdeberg**; Rosendal; Swanepoel; **Swartland**; Woolworths ★★★ Nomoya; Renegade NT AA Badenhorst (Old Vines); Alphabetical; Babylon's Peak; Black Elephant; Cape Wine Company (Fairtrade); De Kleine Wijn Koöp (Old Vines); Dunstone; Elemental Bob; Enfin; Fuselage; Glen Carlou; Joostenberg (Organic); Muratie; Pearl Mountain; Riebeek Valley; Schalkenbosch; Spider Pig; The Horsemen; Thelema; Tierhoek; Twelve Apostles **D** Anura; Arendsig; Creation; Kleine Zalze; Rustenberg; Skilpadvlei

Grüner veltliner
★★★ Niel Joubert NT Diemersdal

Hanepoot fortified
★★★★☆ Boplaas; Daschbosch (Old Vines); Jakkalsvlei; Opstal

★★★★ Clairvaux; Du Preez; Du Toitskloof (Fairtrade); Klawer; Muratie; Peter Falke

★★★★ Badsberg; Boplaas; Domein Doornkraal; Orange River; Slanghoek; TTT Cellar; Villiersdorp ★★★ De Wet; Du'SwaRoo; Landzicht; Swartland; Tulbagh Winery NT Breëland; Calitzdorp; Die Mas; Rustenberg

Hanepoot unfortified
★★★★ Compagniesdrift; Glen Carlou

★★★★ KWV; Myburgh Bros ★★★ Calitzdorp (Perlé); Cape Classics; TTT Cellar; Woolworths ★★★ Du'SwaRoo (Lower in Alcohol); Riebeek Valley NT Meerhof; Openwine **D** City on a Hill; Zidela

Hárslevelü
★★★★☆ Lemberg

Husk spirit/grappa-styles
★★★★★ Dalla Cia

★★★★☆ Bartho Eksteen; **Dalla Cia**; **Tanagra** (8); Wilderer (3)

★★★★ Blackwood (2); Dalla Cia (3) (Organic); Delaire Graff; **Metanoia**; Org de Rac (Organic); Tanagra (2); Upland

★★★ Dalla Cia; Fynbos; Kaapzicht ★★★ Fynbos NT Dalla Cia; Quoin Rock; Tanagra

Jerepigo red
★★★★ Badsberg; Blaauwklippen; Domein Doornkraal; Orange River ★★★ Domein Doornkraal; Landzicht; Montagu Wine & Spirits; Swartland ★★★ Botha NT Grundheim; Simonsvlei **D** Camberley

Jerepigo white
★★★★ Calitzdorp; Darling Cellars; Orange River; Perdeberg

★★★★ Haute Cabrière; Namaqua; Niel Joubert; Swartland ★★★ Botha; Montagu Wine & Spirits NT Aufwaerts; Backsberg

Kosher
★★★★ Onderkloof (2) (Rosé dry; Chardonnay unwooded)

Late Harvest
★★★★★☆ Thelema

★★★★ Grande Provence ★★★ Robertson (2) NT Bergsig; Drostdy-Hof; Hoopenburg **D** Gabriëlskloof

Lledoner Pelut/Grenache Poilu
★★★★ Kloovenburg

Lower in Alcohol
★★★★★ Mullineux (Vin de paille/straw wine); Savage (Vin de paille/straw wine)

★★★★★ Neethlingshof (Noble Late Harvest; Old Vines); Klawer (Vin de paille/straw wine; Old Vines); Stellar (Vin de paille/straw wine; Fairtrade; Organic); Bouchard Finlayson (Vin de paille/straw wine)

★★★★ Meerendal (Natural Sweet, white); Glen Carlou (Natural Sweet, white); Rickety Bridge (Noble Late Harvest); Villiera (Sparkling, Méthode cap classique, white, dry); **Packwood** (Semillon wooded); Wildehurst (Vin de paille/straw wine)

★★★★ Escape (Rosé dry); Woolworths (Sparkling, Méthode cap classique, white, dry); Durbanville Hills (Noble Late Harvest); Pongrácz (Sparkling, Méthode cap classique, rosé, off-dry/semi-sweet) ★★★ Woolworths (Rosé dry); Daschbosch (Natural Sweet, rosé; Perlé); Overhex (Sparkling, Non-MCC, rosé, off-dry/semi-sweet); **Boplaas** (Rosé off-dry/semi-sweet; Perlé); Rooiberg (2) (Natural Sweet, rosé; Natural Sweet, white); De Krans (3) (Natural Sweet, red; Natural Sweet, rosé; Natural Sweet, white; Perlé); Zandvliet (Natural Sweet, white); Landzicht (Rosé off-dry/semi-sweet); Viljoensdrift (Sparkling, Non-MCC, rosé, off-dry/semi-sweet); Badsberg (3) (Rosé off-dry/semi-sweet; Muscadel, white, unfortified; Sparkling, Non-MCC, white, off-dry/semi-sweet; Perlé); Orange River (Sparkling, Non-MCC, white, off-dry/semi-sweet) ★★★ Robertson (4) (Merlot; Rosé dry; Sauvignon blanc unwooded; Natural Sweet, white); Woolworths (4) (Chenin blanc unwooded dry; Sauvignon blanc unwooded; Red blends, other; White blends, unwooded, dry); Durbanville Hills (Chenin blanc unwooded dry); Lutzville (4) (Sparkling, Non-MCC, rosé, off-dry/semi-sweet; Natural Sweet, red; Natural Sweet, rosé;

Natural Sweet, white); Daschbosch (Natural Sweet, white; Perlé); Fairview (Verdelho; Perlé); Tulbagh Winery (White blends, unwooded, dry); Rooiberg (Sparkling, Non-MCC, rosé, off-dry/semi-sweet); Woolworths (2) (Red blends, other; White blends, unwooded, dry); Breëland (Natural Sweet, rosé; Perlé); Fleur du Cap (Chenin blanc unwooded dry); Elgin Vintners (Red blends, other; White blends, wooded, dry); **Landzicht** (2) (White blends, off-dry/semi-sweet (w & u/w); Sparkling, Non-MCC, rosé, off-dry/semi-sweet); **Perdeberg** (5) (Pinotage; Rosé dry; Chenin blanc unwooded dry; Sparkling, Non-MCC, rosé, off-dry/semi-sweet; Sparkling, Non-MCC, white, off-dry/semi-sweet); Riebeek Valley (Hanepoot unfortified; Perlé); The House of JC le Roux (2) (Sparkling, Non-MCC, red, dry; Sparkling, Non-MCC, white, off-dry/semi-sweet); Slanghoek (2) (White blends, off-dry/semi-sweet (w & u/w); Natural Sweet, rosé); Domein Doornkraal (Sparkling, Non-MCC, rosé, off-dry/semi-sweet); Du'SwaRoo (Hanepoot unfortified); Tangled Tree (Rosé off-dry/semi-sweet); Vinette (Rosé off-dry/semi-sweet; Perlé); Wellington Winery (2) (Natural Sweet, rosé; Natural Sweet, white; Perlé); Boland (2) (Pinotage; Chenin blanc unwooded dry) ★★ Woolworths (3) (Merlot; Red blends, with pinotage; Natural Sweet, rosé); Robertson (12) (Natural Sweet, red; Natural Sweet, rosé; Natural Sweet, red; Natural Sweet, rosé; Natural Sweet, white; Colombard; Natural Sweet, red; Natural Sweet, rosé; Natural Sweet, white; Sparkling, Non-MCC, red, off-dry/semi-sweet; Sparkling, Non-MCC, rosé, off-dry/semi-sweet; Sparkling, Non-MCC, white, off-dry/semi-sweet); Bonnievale (Rosé off-dry/semi-sweet; Perlé); Tulbagh Winery (Natural Sweet, rosé); De Wet (Muscadel, white, unfortified; Perlé); KWV (2) (Sparkling, Non-MCC, rosé, off-dry/semi-sweet; Sparkling, Non-MCC, white, off-dry/semi-sweet); Seven Sisters (Muscadel, white, unfortified; Perlé); Riebeek Valley (Natural Sweet, rosé; Perlé); The House of JC le Roux (Sparkling, Non-MCC, rosé, off-dry/semi-sweet); Orange River (2) (Natural Sweet, rosé; Natural Sweet, white); Mara (2) (Rosé off-dry/semi-sweet; Sweet red; Perlé); KWV (Sparkling, Non-MCC, rosé, off-dry/semi-sweet); Jakkalsvlei (Muscadel, red, unfortied) ★★ Two Oceans (Muscadel, white, unfortified) **NT** Robertson (Chenin blanc unwooded dry); Woolworths (6) (Natural Sweet, red; Sweet red; Chardonnay unwooded; White blends, unwooded, dry; Natural Sweet, white; Natural Sweet, white); Namaqua (Noble Late Harvest); Robertson (Sparkling, Non-MCC, rosé, dry); Paul Clüver (Noble Late Harvest);

Mullineux (2) (Vin de paille/straw wine; Vin de paille/straw wine); Imbuko (4) (Muscadel, red, unfortified; Muscadel, white, unfortified; Muscadel, white, unfortified; White blends, off-dry/semi-sweet (w & u/w); Fairtrade; Perlé); O'Connell's (2) (Sparkling, Non-MCC, red, off-dry/semi-sweet; Sparkling, Non-MCC, white, off-dry/semi-sweet); Angus Paul (Vin de paille/straw wine); Skaap (Rosé dry); Arcangeli (Nebbiolo); Drostdy-Hof (2) (Rosé dry; White blends, unwooded, dry); Jakkalsvlei (2) (Rosé off-dry/semi-sweet; Muscadel, white, unfortified; Perlé); Drostdy-Hof (3) (Natural Sweet, red; Natural Sweet, rosé; Natural Sweet, white); Theescombe (2) (Cabernet sauvignon; Muscadel, white, unfortified) **D** Robertson (Colombard); Durbanville Hills (Shiraz/syrah); Hazendal (Sparkling, Méthode cap classique, white, dry); Spier (2) (Shiraz/syrah; Chenin blanc off-dry/semi-sweet (w & u/w)); Mooiplaas (Cabernet sauvignon); Alheit (Vin de paille/straw wine)

Low Alcohol

★★★★☆ Black Elephant (Sparkling, Méthode cap classique, white, dry)

★★ The House of JC le Roux (2) (Sparkling, Non-MCC, rosé, off-dry/semi-sweet; Sparkling, Non-MCC, white, off-dry/semi-sweet); KWV (Sparkling, Non-MCC, rosé, off-dry/semi-sweet) **D** Spier (2) (Shiraz/syrah; Chenin blanc off-dry/semi-sweet (w & u/w))

Malbec

★★★★☆ Anura; Diemersfontein; Doolhof; Glen Carlou; Malanot; Mischa; Mitre's Edge; Morgenhof; Paul Wallace; Winshaw (2); Yerden Eksteen

★★★★ Akkerdal; Bellevue; Bizoe; Blaauwklippen; Blake; **Boschheim**; **Capelands**; DA Hanekom; Doolhof; Dornier; La Couronne; Lanzerac; Le Pommier; **Lozärn**; Maison; Neethlingshof; Niel Joubert; Ormonde; Post House; Rustenberg; Stellekaya (2); Super Single Vineyards; Vergenoegd; Woolworths (2)

★★★☆ Bloemendal; Bushmanspad; Diemersdal; **Leipzig**; **Mama Afrika**; Mount Vernon; **Nabygelegen**; Olivedale; Raka; Spijkerbessie; Under Oaks; Val du Charron ★★★ Daschbosch; Perdeberg **NT** Arno Smith; Bitou; Enfin; Hartenberg; Idiom; Lovane; Mooi Bly; Rosendal; Schalkenbosch; Stellenbosch University; Twelve Apostles; Withington **D** Stellar

Marselan

★★★★ Waverley Hills

Merlot

★★★★★ Simelia; Villiera

★★★★☆ Anthonij Rupert (2); Anura (2); Bein (2); Botanica; Canto; Creation; De Trafford; **Diemersdal**; Durbanville Hills; Excelsior; Fleur du Cap; Groenland; Groot Constantia; Groote Post; Hartenberg; Holden Manz; Jordan; Keermont; Kruger Family; Ladybird (Organic); Longridge (Organic); Marianne; Meerlust; Nitida; Oldenburg; Ormonde; Plaisir; Rainbow's End; Remhoogte; Ridgeback; Rustenberg; Shannon (2); Simelia (2); Steenberg; Super Single Vineyards; The Butcher Shop; Thelema (2); Vergelegen; Vondeling; Zorgvliet

★★★★ Almenkerk; Arendsig; Asara; Bayede!; Bein (2); Bloemendal; Boland; Bon Courage; Boschendal; Boschheim; Bosman Family; Catherine Marshall; De Grendel; Delaire Graff; Dornier; Eagles' Nest; Elgin Vintners (2); Ernie Els; Fairview; Glenelly; GlenWood; Groote Post; Haskell; Havana Hills; Hillcrest; Jason's Hill; Journey's End; Kings Kloof; Kleine Zalze; Kloovenburg; Kyburg; La Bri; La Petite Ferme; Landskroon; Lanzerac; Le Bonheur (Old Vines); Lieben; Lomond; Longridge (Organic); Lourensford; Marklew; Meerendal; Meinert; Mischa; Morgenhof; Morgenster; Nederburg; Neethlingshof; Nico van der Merwe; Org de Rac (Fairtrade; Organic); Overgaauw; Post House; Raka; Rickety Bridge; **Rockbelt**; Rosendal; Simelia; Spookfontein; Stellekaya; Stellenbosch Hills; Stellenrust; Sumaridge; **Twelve Apostles**; Under Oaks; Val du Charron; Van Loggerenberg; Vergenoegd; Villiera; Waterkloof (Organic); Woolworths (5) (Organic); Yonder Hill

★★★★ **Amperbo**; Anura; Audacia; Ayama; Backsberg; Badsberg; Bellpost; **Blaauwklippen**; Blue Owl; Boplaas; **Bosjes**; Botha; Cape Classics; Chameleon; Clos Malverne; Croydon; D'Aria; Daschbosch; ?David Finlayson; **De Wet**; Delheim; DeWaal; Diemersdal; Dieu Donné; Domein Doornkraal; Doolhof; Du Toitskloof; Durbanville Hills; Eikehof; Excelsior; False Bay; Fleur du Cap; Glen Carlou; Grande Provence; Hill & Dale; Hoopenburg; Hout Bay; Kirabo; Klein DasBosch; Koelenhof; L'Avenir; La Couronne; La Petite Provence; Landskroon; Leeuwenberg; Lomond; Louisvale; **Lozärn**; Lyngrove; Maastricht; MAN Family; Middelvlei; Mischa; Mont du Toit; Muratie; Nabygelegen; Niel Joubert; **Nietgegund**; Olsen; Org de Rac (Organic); Ormonde; Overhex; Pulpit Rock; Rooiberg (3); **Sandstone**; Seven Sisters; Signal Gun; Slaley; Slanghoek; Stellenbosch Reserve; Stellenbosch University; Stellenview; Stettyn; Summerhill; The Butcher Shop; The Grape Grinder; VinGlo; Vondeling; Wederom; Welbedacht; Woolworths (2) ★★★ Anthonij

Rupert; Bayede! (2); Boland; Bonnievale; Cloof; Darling Cellars; Daschbosch; De Villiers; Dornier; Drostdy-Hof; Du Preez; Ernst Gouws; Fat Bastard; Flagstone; Goedverwacht; Guardian Peak; Hillock; Imbuko; Jakkalsvlei; Kanu; Ken Forrester; Klawer; Koopmanskloof (Fairtrade); KWV (2); La Capra; La RicMal; Landzicht; Le Sueur; Leopard's Leap; Lutzville; Meerhof; MolenVliet; Nicholson Smith (2); O'Connell's; Porcupine Ridge; Riebeek Valley; Robertson; Roos Family; Skilpadvlei; Spier; Stellenbosch Family Wines (2); Stellenbosch University; Stellenview; Swartland; The Fishwives Club; **The Grape Grinder** (2) (Perlé); **Tulbagh Winery**; Val de Vie; Van Loveren; Villiersdorp; Vredenheim; Wellington Winery; Welmoed; Wineways (3); Woolworths (2) ★★☆ Ashton; Bon Courage; Burgershof; Hoopenburg; KWV; Landzicht; Le Manoir de Brendel; Libby's Pride; Louisvale; Namaqua (2); Perdeberg; Robertson (Lower in Alcohol); Stellar (2) (Fairtrade; Organic); The Fishwives Club; Vinette; Windmeul; Woolworths (3) (Fairtrade; Organic); **Zidela** ★★ Cape Wine Crafters; Nuy; The Fishwives Club; Woolworths (2) (Lower in Alcohol) **NT** AA Badenhorst; Absolute Style; Alexanderfontein; Annandale; Audacia; Bergsig; Bushmanspad; Calitzdorp; **Canetsfontein**; Cape Dreams; Cape Wine Company (Fairtrade); Creation; Die Mas; Fish Hoek (Fairtrade); Franschhoek Cellar; Glen Carlou; Hidden Valley; Idiom; JP Bredell; Klawer; Klein Roosboom; Kranskop; Kumala; Kusafiri (Organic); Louis 57; Marklew; Mitre's Edge (2); Montagu Wine & Spirits; Mountain Ridge; Pearl Mountain (2); Prévoir; Rietvallei; RiverGold (2); Robertson (3); Rosendal; Sarah's; Simonsvlei (2); Somersbosch; Stellendrift (2); Stone Ridge; Varkenskraal; Viljoensdrift; Women in Wine; Woolworths (4); Zevenwacht; Zonnebloem **D** Boschkloof; Camberley; Cloof; Daschbosch; Eikendal; Meerendal (2); Miravel; Mont du Toit; Namaqua; Tulbagh Winery (2); Vergelegen; Walker Bay Estate; Woolworths (5)

Morio Muscat fortified
★★★★ Ashton

Mourvèdre
★★★★☆ Beaumont; Painted Wolf; Sijnn; Waterkloof

★★★★ Deux Frères; Joostenberg (Organic); Spice Route (Fairtrade); Tierhoek

★★★★ **Esona**; Swartland ★★★ Swanepoel **NT** Black Pearl; De Kleine Wijn Koöp; Hartenberg; Hawksmoor (2); Hughes Family (Organic); Idiom; Lomond; Noble Hill (Nouveau); Saronsberg; Twelve Apostles

Muscadel, red, fortified

★★★★★ Orange River

★★★★☆ Nuy; Rietvallei

★★★★ Aan de Doorns; Badsberg; Boplaas; Burgershof; Clairvaux; De Wet; Die Mas; Domein Doornkraal; Du Toitskloof (Fairtrade); Excelsior Vlakteplaas; Jakkalsvlei; Klawer (2); Namaqua; Nuy; Orange River (2); Pulpit Rock; Rietvallei; Rooiberg

★★★★ Bon Courage; Calitzdorp; Cape Wine Crafters; Darling Cellars; Excelsior Vlakteplaas; KWV; McGregor; Slanghoek; Van Loveren ★★★ Du'SwaRoo; Landzicht; Montagu Wine & Spirits; Tulbagh Winery ★★ Landzicht NT Allesverloren; Ashton; Grundheim; Olivedale D Picardi; Rustenberg

Muscadel, red, unfortified

★★ Jakkalsvlei NT Imbuko

Muscadel, white, fortified

★★★★☆ Bon Courage; Boplaas; De Krans; De Wet; Mont Blois (2); Namaqua; Orange River (3); Thelema

★★★★ Boplaas; Clairvaux; Die Mas; Le Grand Chasseur; Nuy; Viljoensdrift

★★★★ Cape Wine Crafters; Klawer; McGregor; Merwida; Skipskop ★★★ Montagu Wine & Spirits ★★ Waboomsrivier NT Calitzdorp; Grundheim; La Couronne; Landzicht; Lutzville; Nico Vermeulen

Muscadel, white, unfortied

★★★★★ Alvi's Drift

★★★ Badsberg (Lower in Alcohol; Perlé); Boplaas ★★★☆ Nicholson Smith ★★ De Wet (Lower in Alcohol; Perlé); Seven Sisters ★★ Two Oceans NT Fuselage; Imbuko (2) (Lower in Alcohol; Fairtrade; Perlé); Jakkalsvlei (Lower in Alcohol; Perlé); The Fledge; Theescombe (Lower in Alcohol)

Muscat de Hambourg fortified

★★★★ Stellenbosch Hills

Natural Sweet, fortified

★★★★☆ Kleine Zalze

Natural Sweet, red

★★★ Bonnievale; Cape Dreams; De Krans (Lower in Alcohol; Perlé); Rooiberg★★★☆ Arra; Lutzville (Lower in Alcohol); Nicholson Smith (3); Wineways; Woolworths (3); Zidela ★★ Overhex; Robertson (3) (Lower in Alcohol) NT Drostdy-Hof (Lower in Alcohol); Kanu; Libby's Pride; Simonsvlei; Woolworths

Natural Sweet, rosé

★★★ Daschbosch (Lower in Alcohol; Perlé); De Krans (Lower in Alcohol; Perlé); Overhex; Rooiberg ★★★ Breëland (Lower in Alcohol; Perlé); Lutzville (Lower in Alcohol); Nicholson Smith (2); Slanghoek (Lower in Alcohol); Wellington Winery (Lower in Alcohol; Perlé); Zidela ★★ Orange River (Lower in Alcohol); Picardi; Riebeek Valley (Lower in Alcohol; Perlé); Robertson (3) (Lower in Alcohol); Tulbagh Winery (Lower in Alcohol); Woolworths (4); Zidela NT Absolute Style; Drostdy-Hof (Lower in Alcohol); Libby's Pride; Nelson; Simonsvlei; Woolworths

Natural Sweet, white

★★★★★ Klein Constantia (2)

★★★★☆ Badsberg; Constantia Uitsig; Groot Constantia; Jordan; Perdeberg; Quoin Rock (Old Vines); St Leger; Stellenrust

★★★★ Glen Carlou (Lower in Alcohol); Meerendal (Lower in Alcohol); Slanghoek; Waterford

★★★☆ Cape Dreams; Havana Hills ★★★ Arra; Calitzdorp (Perlé); Clos Malverne; De Krans (Lower in Alcohol; Perlé); Rooiberg (Lower in Alcohol); Zandvliet★★★ Daschbosch (Lower in Alcohol; Perlé); Domein Doornkraal; Lutzville (Lower in Alcohol); Nicholson Smith (2); Overhex; Robertson (Lower in Alcohol; Perlé); Woolworths; Zidela ★★ Orange River (Lower in Alcohol); Robertson (2) (Lower in Alcohol); Zidela NT Absolute Style; Constantia Nectar; Delheim; Dornier; Drostdy-Hof (Lower in Alcohol); Herold; Ken Forrester; Mimosa; Safriel; Simonsvlei; Woolworths (2) (Lower in Alcohol) D Black Elephant

Natural/non-fortified pale

★★★★ Wightman & Sons (2) (Chenin blanc wooded, dry; Clairette blanche)

Nebbiolo

★★★★☆ Elemental Bob; Iona; Morgenster; Steenberg

★★★★ Anura; Hofstraat; Idiom

★★★☆ Du Toitskloof; Mama Afrika; Thorngrove ★★★ Skipskop NT Arcangeli (Lower in Alcohol); Nomoya

Nero d'Avola

★★★★ Ayama; Bosman Family

Noble Late Harvest

★★★★★ Boschendal; Buitenverwachting; Delheim

★★★★☆ Badsberg; Beaumont; Benguela Cove; Boekenhoutskloof (Organic); Bon Courage; Boschendal; De Grendel; Diemersdal; GlenWood; Highlands Road; Iona; Joostenberg (Organic); Ken Forrester; Kranskop; Neethlingshof (Lower in Alcohol; Old Vines); Neil Ellis; Olivedale; Ormonde;

Paul Wallace; Post House; Simonsig; Springfontein; Woolworths

★★★★ Asara; Bartho Eksteen; Bloemendal; Delaire Graff; Koelenhof (Old Vines); Longridge; Mooiplaas; Rickety Bridge (Lower in Alcohol); Rudera; Slanghoek

★★★★ Durbanville Hills (Lower in Alcohol); Kanu; Saxenburg **NT** Aaldering; Bergsig; Bizoe; Cape Point; Hartenberg; Lomond; Lutzville; Miles Mossop (Old Vines); Namaqua (Lower in Alcohol); Nederburg (3); Nelson; Nitida; Paul Clüver **D** D'Aria; Tokara

Non-muscat, red, fortified
★★★★ TTT Cellar

Non-muscat, white, fortified
★★★★ Villiera

Nouveau
★★★★★ Remhoogte (Shiraz/syrah)

★★★★ TTT Cellar (Red blends, shiraz/syrah-based); Radford Dale (2) (Cinsaut; Gamay noir); The Winery of Good Hope (Pinotage) **NT** Noble Hill (Mourvèdre); Hasher (Pinot noir)

Nouvelle
★★★ Morgenhof **NT** Koueberg

Organic
★★★★★ Waterkloof (Sauvignon blanc wooded); Upland (Port-style, red)

★★★★ Springfontein (3) (Red blends, with pinotage; Red blends, with pinotage; White from red/black grapes (not Blanc de noir)); Woolworths (Chardonnay wooded); Spier (3) (Red blends, Cape Bordeaux; Red blends, Cape Bordeaux; Chenin blanc wooded, dry); Org de Rac (2) (White blends, wooded, dry; Red blends, Cape Bordeaux; Fairtrade); Longridge (5) (Merlot; Pinotage; Red blends, Cape Bordeaux; Chardonnay wooded; Chenin blanc off-dry/semi-sweet (w & u/w); Old Vines); Joostenberg (6) (Cabernet sauvignon; Shiraz/syrah; Red blends, shiraz/syrah-based; Chenin blanc wooded, dry; White blends, wooded, dry; Noble Late Harvest; Old Vines); Ladybird (2) (Merlot; Chenin blanc wooded, dry); **Waterkloof** (2) (Shiraz/syrah; Red blends, Cape Bordeaux); Waverley Hills (2) (Grenache noir; Shiraz/syrah); **Radford Dale** (3) (Cabernet franc; Pinot noir; Semillon wooded); Boekenhoutskloof (Noble Late Harvest); Ladybird (Chardonnay wooded); Meerendal (Sauvignon blanc unwooded); Waterkloof (2) (Mourvèdre; Shiraz/syrah); Stellar (Vin de paille/straw wine; Lower in Alcohol; Fairtrade); Jasper Raats (2) (Sauvignon blanc wooded; Verdelho); Hughes Family (2) (Red blends,

with pinotage; White blends, wooded, dry); Taaibosch (Red blends, Cape Bordeaux); Upland (3) (Brandy; Brandy; Brandy); Hughes Family (3) (Tempranillo/tinta roriz; White blends, wooded, dry; White blends, wooded, dry); Julien Schaal (2) (Shiraz/syrah; Chenin blanc wooded, dry)

★★★★ Springfontein (4) (Pinotage; Chenin blanc wooded, dry; Red blends, with pinotage; White blends, unwooded, dry); Woolworths (2) (Merlot; Red blends, Cape Bordeaux); Spier (5) (Rosé dry; Red blends, other; White blends, wooded, dry; Chenin blanc unwooded dry; Sauvignon blanc unwooded); Stellar (Shiraz/syrah; Fairtrade); Bosman Family (White blends, wooded, dry; Fairtrade); Org de Rac (4) (Red blends, shiraz/syrah-based; Merlot; Shiraz/syrah; Chardonnay wooded; Fairtrade); Joostenberg (Red blends, shiraz/syrah-based); Waterkloof (Chenin blanc wooded, dry); Org de Rac (3) (Chenin blanc unwooded dry; Roussanne; Sparkling, Méthode cap classique, rosé, dry; Fairtrade); Longridge (Cabernet sauvignon); Waverley Hills (Marselan); Longridge (Merlot); Waverley Hills (3) (Red blends, Cape Bordeaux; Red blends, shiraz/syrah-based; Chardonnay wooded); Longridge (2) (Chardonnay wooded; Chenin blanc wooded, dry); **Radford Dale** (Chardonnay wooded); Waverley Hills (Shiraz/syrah); Longridge (Sparkling, Méthode cap classique, white, dry); Reyneke (Red blends, Cape Bordeaux); Dalla Cia (Husk spirit/grappa-styles); Ladybird (Red blends, Cape Bordeaux); Joostenberg (Mourvèdre); **Springfontein** (Chenel); De Grendel (Viognier); Waterkloof (4) (Cabernet franc; Merlot; Chenin blanc wooded, dry; Viognier); Org de Rac (Husk spirit/grappa-styles); **Le Grand Domaine** (2) (Red blends, shiraz/syrah-based; White blends, wooded, dry; Fairtrade); Upland (Port-style, red); **Haskell** (Rosé dry); Kusafiri (Cabernet sauvignon); Myburgh Bros (Chenin blanc wooded, dry; Old Vines; Skin-macerated white); Silvermist (2) (Cabernet sauvignon; Sauvignon blanc unwooded); Upland (2) (Brandy; Husk spirit/grappa-styles); Hughes Family (Viognier); Klein Amoskuil (Sauvignon blanc wooded)

★★★★ Stellar (Cabernet sauvignon; Fairtrade); Spier (3) (Rosé dry; Shiraz/syrah; Red blends, shiraz/syrah-based); Stellar (2) (Pinotage; Chardonnay wooded; Fairtrade); **Germanier** (4) (Red blends, shiraz/syrah-based; Red blends, shiraz/syrah-based; Chardonnay wooded; Red blends, other); Stellenview (Red blends, with pinotage); Org de Rac (5) (Cabernet sauvignon; Merlot; Red blends, shiraz/syrah-based; Chardonnay unwooded; Sauvignon blanc unwooded; Fairtrade); Waverley Hills (3) (Rosé dry; Sparkling, Méthode cap classique, white, dry; Pinot gris/grigio); Longridge (Sparkling, Méthode cap classique, white, dry); Orange River (Chenin blanc unwooded dry); Upland (4) (Cabernet sauvignon; Pinot noir; Sparkling, Méthode ancestrale; Port-style, red); **Kusafiri** (4) (Shiraz/syrah; Sauvignon blanc unwooded; Viognier; Sauvignon blanc unwooded); **Reyneke** (5) (Shiraz/syrah; Red blends, Cape Bordeaux; Rosé dry; Chenin blanc unwooded dry; Sauvignon blanc wooded) ★★★ Springfontein (Rosé dry); Woolworths (Pinotage; Fairtrade); Stellar (Pinot noir; Fairtrade); Woolworths (2) (Chenin blanc unwooded dry; Sauvignon blanc unwooded; Fairtrade); **Spier** (Rosé dry); Stellar (6) (Pinotage; Rosé dry; Shiraz/syrah; Chenin blanc unwooded dry; Sauvignon blanc unwooded; White blends, unwooded, dry; Fairtrade); **Germanier** (5) (Cabernet sauvignon; Pinotage; Pinotage; Rosé dry; White blends, unwooded, dry); Stellar (Rosé dry; Fairtrade); Woolworths (Sparkling, Non-MCC, white, dry; Fairtrade); **Germanier** (White blends, unwooded, dry); Org de Rac (2) (Shiraz/syrah; Port-style, red; Fairtrade); Woolworths (2) (Red blends, shiraz/syrah-based; White blends, unwooded, dry; Fairtrade); Waverley Hills (2) (Red blends, other; White blends, unwooded, dry); Teubes (2) (Red blends, shiraz/syrah-based; Red blends, shiraz/syrah-based); Stellar (2) (Sparkling, Non-MCC, rosé, dry; Sparkling, Non-MCC, white, dry; Fairtrade) ★★★ Woolworths (4) (Cabernet sauvignon; Merlot; Shiraz/syrah; Chardonnay unwooded; Fairtrade); Stellar (7) (Cabernet sauvignon; Merlot; Shiraz/syrah; Chardonnay unwooded; Merlot; Red blends, with pinotage; Chardonnay unwooded; Fairtrade); Germanier (Red blends, other); Stellar (4) (Red blends, shiraz/syrah-based; White blends, unwooded, dry; White blends, off-dry/semi-sweet (w & u/w); Sweet red; Fairtrade); Woolworths (Sparkling, Non-MCC, white, dry; Fairtrade); Org de Rac (Rosé dry; Fairtrade); Waverley Hills (2) (Pinotage; Cabernet sauvignon); Kusafiri (Pinotage) **NT** Groot Parys (Chenin blanc unwooded dry); Stellar (2) (Chenin blanc wooded, dry; Sauvignon blanc wooded; Fairtrade); Joostenberg (Chenin blanc unwooded dry); Org de Rac (Verdelho); Reyneke (2) (Cabernet sauvignon; Chenin blanc unwooded dry); Germanier (Red blends, with pinotage); Teubes (Cabernet sauvignon); Germanier (Red blends, Cape Bordeaux); Joostenberg (4) (Grenache noir; Shiraz/syrah; Touriga nacional; Chenin blanc wooded, dry); Germanier (2) (Red blends, Cape Bordeaux; Red blends, with pinotage); **Canetsfontein** (Red

blends, other); Constantia Mist (Sauvignon blanc unwooded); Dragonridge (Chenin blanc unwooded dry); Kusafiri (5) (Merlot; Pinotage; Shiraz/syrah; Red blends, Cape Bordeaux; White blends, wooded, dry); Lazanou (8) (Shiraz/syrah; Red blends, shiraz/syrah-based; Red blends, shiraz/syrah-based; Chardonnay wooded; Chenin blanc unwooded dry; Viognier; White blends, unwooded, dry; Sparkling, Méthode cap classique, white, dry); Silvermist (Sauvignon blanc wooded); Solara (2) (Sauvignon blanc unwooded; Sparkling, Non-MCC, white, dry); Hughes Family (5) (Mourvèdre; Pinotage; Shiraz/syrah; Red blends, shiraz/syrah-based; Red blends, other); **Cape Wine Company** (2) (Red blends, Cape Bordeaux; White blends, unwooded, dry; Fairtrade) **D** Woolworths (Rosé dry); Van Loveren (Sauvignon blanc unwooded); Stellar (Malbec; Fairtrade); Org de Rac (Cabernet sauvignon); Woolworths (3) (Sparkling, Non-MCC, rosé, off-dry/semi-sweet; Sparkling, Non-MCC, white, dry; Sparkling, Non-MCC, white, off-dry/semi-sweet); Org de Rac (Sparkling, Méthode cap classique, white, dry); Silvermist (Red blends, other); Reyneke (Red blends, shiraz/syrah-based)

Old Vines

★★★★★ DeMorgenzon (Chenin blanc wooded, dry); Daschbosch (Chenin blanc wooded, dry); Rickety Bridge (Semillon wooded); Bosman Family (Chenin blanc wooded, dry); Ken Forrester (Chenin blanc wooded, dry); Mullineux (Semillon gris); Bellevue (Pinotage); Botanica (Chenin blanc wooded, dry); Mullineux (Chenin blanc wooded, dry); Stellenrust (Chenin blanc wooded, dry); Old Road (Semillon wooded); **David & Nadia** (Chenin blanc wooded, dry); Bellingham (Chenin blanc wooded, dry); Wildeberg (Semillon wooded); Mullineux (White blends, wooded, dry); David & Nadia (Chenin blanc wooded, dry); Beaumont (Chenin blanc wooded, dry); Delheim (Noble Late Harvest); Eenzaamheid (Chenin blanc wooded, dry); Kruger Family (Grenache noir); The Ahrens Family (Chenin blanc wooded, dry); Van Loggerenberg (Cinsaut); **Sadie** (6) (Chenin blanc wooded, dry; Chenin blanc wooded, dry; Chenin blanc wooded, dry; Semillon wooded; White blends, wooded, dry; White blends, wooded, dry); Savage (2) (Cinsaut; Chenin blanc wooded, dry)

★★★★☆ Simonsig (Chenin blanc wooded, dry); Miles Mossop (Chenin blanc wooded, dry); Spier (Chenin blanc wooded, dry); Darling Cellars (2) (Cinsaut; Chenin blanc wooded, dry); Kleine Zalze (Chenin blanc wooded, dry); Daschbosch (2) (Clairette blanche; Hanepoot fortified); **Rickety**

Bridge (Vin de paille/straw wine); Riebeek Valley (Chenin blanc wooded, dry); Nederburg (Chenin blanc wooded, dry); Mischa (Cinsaut); Jordan (2) (Chenin blanc wooded, dry; Sauvignon blanc wooded); Simelia (Shiraz/syrah); L'Avenir (Chenin blanc wooded, dry); Kaapzicht (Chenin blanc wooded, dry); Flagstone (Chenin blanc wooded, dry); Anthonij Rupert (2) (Chenin blanc wooded, dry; Semillon wooded); Piekenierskloof (3) (Grenache noir; Pinotage; Chenin blanc wooded, dry); Riebeek Valley (Chenin blanc wooded, dry); Longridge (2) (Pinotage; Chenin blanc off-dry/semi-sweet (w & u/w); Organic); Kleine Zalze (Chenin blanc wooded, dry); Rascallion (Chenin blanc unwooded dry); Zevenwacht (Chenin blanc wooded, dry); Joostenberg (Chenin blanc wooded, dry; Organic); Zevenwacht (Chenin blanc wooded, dry); **Bellevue** (Cinsaut); Gabriëlskloof (Chenin blanc wooded, dry); Roodekrantz (4) (Chenin blanc wooded, dry; Chenin blanc wooded, dry; Chenin blanc wooded, dry; Chenin blanc wooded, dry); Muratie (Shiraz/syrah); Holden Manz (Chenin blanc wooded, dry); **Groenland** (Chenin blanc wooded, dry); Ken Forrester (Chenin blanc wooded, dry); Paul Clüver (Chardonnay wooded); Warwick (Chenin blanc wooded, dry); Rickety Bridge (Cinsaut); **Neethlingshof** (2) (Sauvignon blanc wooded; Noble Late Harvest); **Opstal** (Chenin blanc wooded, dry); Klawer (Vin de paille/straw wine; Lower in Alcohol); Boekenhoutskloof (Semillon wooded); Diemersfontein (Chenin blanc wooded, dry); Super Single Vineyards (Chenin blanc wooded, dry); Opstal (Chenin blanc wooded, dry); Mooiplaas (Chenin blanc wooded, dry); Noble Hill (Chenin blanc wooded, dry); Meerendal (Pinotage); Wolvenhoek (Chenin blanc wooded, dry); Tierhoek (Chenin blanc wôoded, dry); Kanu (Chenin blanc wooded, dry); Holden Manz (Chenin blanc wooded, dry); Paul Clüver (Chardonnay wooded); Muratie (Port-style, red); Haute Cabrière (Chardonnay unwooded); Anthonij Rupert (Chenin blanc unwooded dry); **Waterford** (Chenin blanc wooded, dry); Bellevue (Chenin blanc wooded, dry); Koelenhof (2) (Pinotage; Chenin blanc wooded, dry); Kaapzicht (Chenin blanc wooded, dry); Bellingham (Rosé dry); Scions of Sinai (Chenin blanc unwooded dry); Bellingham (Chenin blanc wooded, dry); Wildeberg (Chenin blanc wooded, dry); Reyneke (Chenin blanc wooded, dry; Biodynamic); Simelia (Blanc de noir); **Naudé** (4) (Cinsaut; Chenin blanc wooded, dry; Colombard; White blends, unwooded, dry); Mulderbosch (Chenin blanc wooded, dry); David & Nadia (3)

(Chenin blanc wooded, dry; Chenin blanc wooded, dry; Chenin blanc wooded, dry); Keermont (Chenin blanc wooded, dry); Waterford (Chenin blanc unwooded dry); David & Nadia (Chenin blanc wooded, dry); **Creation** (Chenin blanc unwooded dry); Super Single Vineyards (2) (Shiraz/syrah; Chenin blanc unwooded dry); Olifantsberg (Chenin blanc wooded, dry); Alheit (5) (Chenin blanc wooded, dry; Chenin blanc wooded, dry; Chenin blanc wooded, dry; Chenin blanc wooded, dry; Semillon wooded); Axle (Chenin blanc wooded, dry); Cecilia (2) (Pinotage; Chenin blanc wooded, dry); Dalkeith (Chenin blanc wooded, dry); Delheim (2) (Chenin blanc wooded, dry; Chenin blanc wooded, dry); DeWaal (Pinotage); Huis van Chevallerie (Sparkling, Méthode cap classique, white, dry); Jasper Raats (Cinsaut); Kruger Family (Chenin blanc unwooded dry); Leeu Passant (Cinsaut); Metzer (Cinsaut); Quoin Rock (Natural Sweet, white); Rebel Rebel (Colombard); Chamonix (Chenin blanc wooded, dry); The Ahrens Family (2) (Chenin blanc wooded, dry; Chenin blanc wooded, dry); Thistle & Weed (2) (Chenin blanc wooded, dry; Chenin blanc wooded, dry); Thorne & Daughters (2) (Chenin blanc wooded, dry; Semillon wooded); Van Loggerenberg (3) (Cinsaut; Chenin blanc wooded, dry; Chenin blanc wooded, dry); Villion (2) (Chenin blanc wooded, dry; Sauvignon blanc wooded); Wolf & Woman (2) (Pinotage; Chenin blanc wooded, dry); Allée Bleue (Pinotage); Brookdale (Chenin blanc wooded, dry); Lievland (Chenin blanc wooded, dry); Kruger Family (Chardonnay wooded); Sadie (3) (Cinsaut; Grenache noir; Tinta barocca); Quest (Chenin blanc wooded, dry); ArtiSons (White from red/black grapes (not Blanc de noir)); Tempel (White blends, wooded, dry); Klein Amoskuil (Sherry-style wines); Welgegund (Cinsaut)

★★★★ Groot Parys (Chenin blanc wooded, dry; Skin-macerated white); Miles Mossop (Sauvignon blanc wooded); **Riebeek Valley** (Chenin blanc wooded, dry); Perdeberg (Chenin blanc wooded, dry); Bosman Family (Sparkling, Méthode cap classique, white, dry); Du Toitskloof (Sauvignon blanc wooded); Mischa (Chenin blanc unwooded dry); **Jordan** (Riesling); Piekenierskloof (2) (Cinsaut; Vin de paille/straw wine); Zevenwacht (Chenin blanc wooded, dry); Roodekrantz (2) (Cinsaut; Chenin blanc wooded, dry); Lyngrove (Chenin blanc wooded, dry); Villiera (2) (Gamay noir; Chenin blanc wooded, dry); Ken Forrester (Sparkling, Méthode cap classique, white, dry); Knorhoek (Chenin blanc wooded, dry); Haute

Cabrière (Chardonnay wooded); Stettyn (Chenin blanc wooded, dry); Slaley (Pinotage); Koelenhof (Noble Late Harvest); Scions of Sinai (Pinotage); **Wildeberg** (Cinsaut); Hawksmoor (Chenin blanc wooded, dry); Le Bonheur (Sauvignon blanc wooded); Mooiplaas (Chenin blanc unwooded dry); Welbedacht (Chenin blanc wooded, dry); Le Bonheur (2) (Merlot; Sauvignon blanc wooded); Township Winery (Chenin blanc wooded, dry); Wolvenhoek (Chenin blanc wooded, dry); Wildeberg (White blends, wooded, dry); Mullineux (Chenin blanc wooded, dry); **Le Grand Domaine** (Chenin blanc wooded, dry); Donkiesbaai (Cinsaut); Kruger Family (2) (Cinsaut; Palomino/malvasia rei); Myburgh Bros (2) (Chenin blanc wooded, dry; Chenin blanc unwooded dry; Organic; Skin-macerated white); Kruger Family (4) (Cinsaut; Tinta barocca; Chenin blanc wooded, dry; Chenin blanc wooded, dry); Klein Amoskuil (Sauvignon blanc wooded; Organic); Welgegund (Chenin blanc wooded, dry)

★★★★ Perdeberg (Sparkling, Méthode cap classique, white, dry); Klawer (Chenin blanc unwooded dry); Windmeul (Chenin blanc wooded, dry); Slaley (White blends, unwooded, dry); Wandering (Chenin blanc wooded, dry); **House of Hlela** (Chenin blanc wooded, dry; Fairtrade); Imvini Wethu (Red blends, other); Scions of Sinai (Red blends, with pinotage) ★★★ Ayama (2) (Cabernet sauvignon; Chenin blanc unwooded dry); Rascallion (White blends, unwooded, dry); Renegade (Grenache noir); Deux Frères (Sauvignon blanc unwooded) **NT** Miles Mossop (Noble Late Harvest); Darling Cellars (Chenin blanc unwooded dry); Painted Wolf (Chenin blanc wooded, dry); Roodekrantz (2) (Pinotage; Chenin blanc wooded, dry); Villiera (Sauvignon blanc wooded); De Kleine Wijn Koöp (Cinsaut); Old Road (Chenin blanc wooded, dry); AA Badenhorst (6) (Cinsaut; Grenache noir; Tinta barocca; Chenin blanc wooded, dry; Chenin blanc wooded, dry; Chenin blanc unwooded dry); De Kleine Wijn Koöp (Grenache noir); Fuselage (2) (Rosé dry; Chenin blanc wooded, dry); Hawksmoor (Chenin blanc wooded, dry); The Fledge (Chenin blanc wooded, dry); De Kleine Wijn Koöp (Cinsaut); Spice Route (Chenin blanc wooded, dry); The Fledge (Tinta barocca); Rustenberg (Hanepoot fortified); Alheit (Chenin blanc wooded, dry); Safriel (Chenin blanc wooded, dry) **D** Cloof (Chenin blanc wooded, dry); Thor (Chenin blanc wooded, dry; Skin-macerated white); Villiera (Pinotage); Fairview (Carignan); Cloof (Chenin blanc unwooded dry); Super Single

Vineyards (Rosé dry); Alheit (Vin de paille/straw wine)

Palomino/malvasia rei

★★★★☆ Blackwater; Gedeelte; Huis van Chevallerie

★★★★ Kruger Family (Old Vines); Swartberg

★★★ Vino pH ★★★ TTT Cellar **NT** AA Badenhorst

Perlé Wines

★★★★ Elemental Bob (Sparkling, Méthode ancestrale) ★★★ Van Loveren (Pinot gris/grigio; Perlé); Daschbosch (Natural Sweet, rosé; Lower in Alcohol; Perlé); **Boplaas** (2) (Rosé off-dry/semi-sweet; Muscadel, white, unfortified; Lower in Alcohol; Perlé); De Krans (3) (Natural Sweet, red; Natural Sweet, rosé; Natural Sweet, white; Lower in Alcohol; Perlé); **The Grape Grinder** (3) (Merlot; Rosé dry; Chardonnay unwooded; Perlé); Badsberg (2) (Rosé off-dry/semi-sweet; Muscadel, white, unfortified; Lower in Alcohol; Perlé); House of BNG (Sparkling, Non-MCC, white, off-dry/semi-sweet; Perlé); **Calitzdorp** (2) (Hanepoot unfortified; Natural Sweet, white; Perlé) ★★★ Daschbosch (Natural Sweet, white; Lower in Alcohol; Perlé); Fairview (Verdelho; Lower in Alcohol; Perlé); De Wet (Rosé off-dry/semi-sweet; Perlé); Breëland (Natural Sweet, rosé; Lower in Alcohol; Perlé); Riebeek Valley (Hanepoot unfortified; Lower in Alcohol; Perlé); Renegade (White blends, unwooded, dry; Perlé); Vinette (Rosé off-dry/semi-sweet; Lower in Alcohol; Perlé); Wellington Winery (2) (Natural Sweet, rosé; Natural Sweet, white; Lower in Alcohol; Perlé) ★★ Bonnievale (Rosé off-dry/semi-sweet; Lower in Alcohol; Perlé); De Wet (Muscadel, white, unfortified; Lower in Alcohol; Perlé); Seven Sisters (Muscadel, white, unfortified; Lower in Alcohol; Perlé); Riebeek Valley (Natural Sweet, rosé; Lower in Alcohol; Perlé); Mara (2) (Rosé off-dry/semi-sweet; Sweet red; Lower in Alcohol; Perlé); Jakkalsvlei (Muscadel, red, unfortified) ★★ Two Oceans (Muscadel, white, unfortified) **NT Simonsvlei** (Grenache blanc; Perlé); Ashton (Chenin blanc off-dry/semi-sweet (w & u/w); Imbuko (4) (Muscadel, red, unfortified; Muscadel, white, unfortified; Muscadel, white, unfortified; White blends, off-dry/semi-sweet (w & u/w); Lower in Alcohol; Fairtrade; Perlé); Jakkalsvlei (2) (Rosé off-dry/semi-sweet; Muscadel, white, unfortified; Lower in Alcohol; Perlé)

Petit verdot

★★★★★ Benguela Cove; Thelema

★★★★☆ De Trafford; **Hidden Valley**; KWV; La Bri; Le Bonheur; Post House; Stellenbosch Vineyards; **Thor**; Zorgvliet

★★★★ Anura; Botanica; Definitum; Dornier; Kirabo; Miravel; My Wyn; Waterkloof

★★★☆ Du Preez; Jason's Hill; KWV; Landzicht; Skipskop **NT** Arno Smith; Buitenverwachting; Du'SwaRoo; Jordan; Lovane; Mitre's Edge; Raka; Waterford **D** Kirabo; Walker Bay Estate

Petite sirah/durif

★★★★☆ Fairview; Mischa; Stark-Condé

★★★★ Arendskloof; Lourensford; Riebeek Valley; Spotswood; Thor; Wildehurst

★★★☆ Ayama; Under Oaks **NT** Black Elephant; Glen Carlou

Pinot blanc

★★★★ Belle Rebelle; **Black Elephant**; Lanzerac; Nomoya

Pinot gris/grigio

★★★★ Idiom; Winshaw (2)

★★★☆ Anthonij Rupert (2); **Esona**; iL Geco; **Morgenhof**; Val du Charron; Waverley Hills (Organic); Welmoed; Woolworths ★★★ Anura; Eagle's Cliff; Merwida; Nicholson Smith; Overhex; Two Oceans; Van Loveren★★★ La Capra **NT** Nederburg; Simonsvlei; Winshaw **D** Woolworths

Pinot noir

★★★★★ Crystallum; ?David Finlayson; Iona; Kara-Tara; Shannon; Storm

★★★★☆ Anthonij Rupert; Benguela Cove; Blackwater; Boschendal; Bosman Hermanus; Botanica; Bouchard Finlayson (2); Brew Cru; Cap Maritime; Cape Elevation; Catherine Marshall (3); Cederberg; Cirrus; Clouds; Creation (4); Crystallum (3); Dalla Cia; ?David Finlayson (2); De Grendel; Domaine des Dieux (2); Driehoek; Elgin Vintners; **Great Heart**; Hamilton Russell; Hasher; Haute Cabrière; Highlands Road; Iona (2); Jasper Raats; Jayne's; Kershaw (4); Kruger Family; La Vierge (2); Lieben; Litigo; Meerlust; Mooiplaas; Moya's; **Mulderbosch**; MVH Signature Wines; Oak Valley (2); Paul Clüver (2); Paul Wallace; Radford Dale (Organic); Restless River; Saurwein; Shannon; Storm (2); Tesselaarsdal; The Drift; **The Vinoneers**; Thelema; Thorne & Thoughters; **Trizanne**; Villiera; Vino pH; Vriesenhof; Whalehaven (2); Woolworths

★★★★ Aristea; Baleia; Bartho Eksteen; Bosman Hermanus; Brew Cru; Buitenverwachting; **Cap Maritime**; Chamonix; Die Kat; Dorrance; Eerste Hoop; Elgin Vintners; Esona; Flagstone; **Groote Post**; **Harry Hartman**; Haute Cabrière; Havana Hills; Herold; Hoopenburg; House of Hier; Idun; Iona; Jakkalsvlei; Kara-Tara; Kershaw (2); Kranskop; La Vierge; Lemberg; Leopard's Leap; Lodestone; Lourensford; Lynx; Meerendal; Muratie; Nitida; Packwood; Radford Dale; Rogge Cloof; Seven Springs; Silkbush; Spioenkop (2); Stony Brook; **Terrabosch**; Thamnus Wines; That Wine Demesne; The Butcher Shop; The Fledge; The Hills; **Under Oaks**; Villion; Woolworths

★★★★ Arendskloof; Bon Courage; Chamonix; Ernst Gouws; Foothills; Glen Carlou; Haute Cabrière; La Vierge; Lord's; Overhex; Paul Clüver; Peter Falke; Spookfontein; Stellenbosch Family Wines (2); Sumaridge; Upland (Organic); Walker Bay Estate; Woolworths ★★★ Cape Moby; Herold; **McGregor**; Somersbosch; Stellar (Fairtrade; Organic); Van Loveren **NT** AA Badenhorst; Arendsig; Benguela Cove; Bezalel; Black Elephant; Brunia; De Kleine Wijn Koöp; Draaiboek; Elemental Bob; Enfin; Fryer's Cove; Hasher (Nouveau); Hazendal; Herold (2); Hoopenburg; Jan Harmsgat; Kruger Family; La Vierge; Land of Hope; Lomond; Maastricht; **Mama Afrika**; Mark le Roux; Meinert; Mile High; Newton Johnson (5); Oak Valley (4); Old Road; Ormonde; Rosendal; Snow Mountain (2); Spider Pig; Strandveld; The Fledge; Thelema; Tim Hillock; Twelve Apostles; VinGlo; Woolworths **D** Avontuur; Botanica; Bruce Jack; Joubert-Tradauw; Khayelitsha's Finest; Kruger Family; Painted Wolf; Radford Dale; Waterford; Windfall

Pinotage

★★★★★ Bellevue (Old Vines); Fairview; Flagstone; Francois van Niekerk; Kaapzicht; Kanonkop (2); L'Avenir; **Lanzerac**; Survivor

★★★★☆ Aaldering; Allée Bleue (2) (Old Vines); Alvi's Drift; Angus Paul; Anthonij Rupert; Anura (2); Ashbourne; Beeslaar; Bellevue; Bellingham; **Beyerskloof** (3); **Bruce Jack**; Bruwer Vintners; Cecilia (Old Vines); Chamonix; De Grendel; Delheim; DeWaal (2) (Old Vines); DewaldtHeyns; Diemersdal (2); Diemersfontein; Eenzaamheid; False Bay; Flagstone; Fram; Grangehurst; Groot Constantia; Groot Phesantekraal; **Hasher**; Holder; Illimis; Koelenhof (2) (Old Vines); KWV; Lanzerac; Longridge (Old Vines; Organic); Lyngrove; **McFarlane**; Meerendal (2) (Old Vines); Middelvlei; Môreson; Neethlingshof; Neil Ellis; Olifantsberg; Painted Wolf; Piekenierskloof (Old Vines); Radford Dale; Remhoogte; Rickety Bridge; Rijk's (2); Scali; Silkbush; Simonsig; Southern Right; Spice Route; Spier; Spioenkop (2); Springfontein; **Stellenbosch Vineyards**; Stellenrust; Super Single Vineyards; Survivor; Swartberg; Tokara (2); Van Loveren;

Vondeling (2); Wellington Winery; Wildekrans; Windmeul (2); Wolf & Woman

★★★★ Aaldering; Anura; **Arendsig**; Asara (2); Babylon's Peak; Barista; Beaumont; Bellevue; Bellingham; Beyerskloof; Bruce Jack; Camberley; Canto; **Cape Collective**; **Cloof** (2); Clos Malverne; Croydon; DA Hanekom; Darling Cellars; Diemersdal; Doolhof; Dornier; Durbanville Hills; Fairview; **Fram**; Glen Carlou; Grangehurst; Groot Phesantekraal; Huis van Chevallerie; Kaapzicht (2); Kanonkop; Kanu; Kleine Zalze; Kumusha; KWV; **L'Avenir** (2); Lanzerac; Le Grand Domaine; Lemberg; Leopard's Leap; Lievland; Lomond; Longridge; Lutzville (2); Maastricht; MAN Family; Marianne; Marklew; Meerendal; Meinert; Mooiplaas; Nederburg; Neethlingshof; Perdeberg; Radford Dale; Rhebokskloof; Rijk's; Rooiberg; Saxenburg (2); Scali; Scions of Sinai (2) (Alternative white/red); Old Vines); Silkbush (2); Slaley (Old Vines); **Southern Treasures**; Spier; Springfontein (Organic); Stellenbosch Hills; Stellenbosch Vineyards; Stellenrust; Stellenview (3); Swanepoel; Swartland; The Butcher Shop; The Earth Beneath Our Feet; The Vinoneers; Under Oaks; Viljoensdrift; **Vriesenhuijs**; Woolworths (3); Zonnebloem

★★★★ Adama; Alvi's Drift; **Amperbo**; Arra; At se Wyn; Ayama; Backsberg; Beyerskloof; Bloemendal; Blue Crane; Boplaas; Camberley; Cape Classics; Cape Wine Company; Cloof; Clos Malverne; Darling Cellars; Daschbosch (Fairtrade); Delheim; DeWaal; Doran; Du Toitskloof; Ernst Gouws; False Bay; Fat Bastard; Flagstone; Hazendal; Hill & Dale; **House of Hlela** (Fairtrade); House of Mandela; Imbuko; Ken Forrester; Klawer; Koelenhof; Koopmanskloof (Fairtrade); Kruger Family; KWV; L'Avenir; La Capra; Landskroon; Le Grand Chasseur; Leipzig; Lemberg; Less; Lyngrove; M'hudi; Manley; Meerhof; Merwida; Middelvlei; Mont Blois; Niel Joubert; Nitida; Nuy; Olsen; Orange River (2); Perdeberg; Piekenierskloof; Post House; Pulpit Rock; **Quando**; Raka; Rickety Bridge; **Rockbelt**; Rooiberg; Rosendal; Ses'Fikile; Signal Gun; Simonsig; Slanghoek; Spier; Stanford Hills (2); Stellar (Fairtrade; Organic); Stellenbosch Family Wines (2); Stettyn; Swartland; The Butcher Shop; The Grape Grinder; The Winery of Good Hope (Nouveau); **TTT Cellar**; Villiera; Villiersdorp; Visio; Warwick; Welbedacht; Wellington Winery; Wildeberg; Wildekrans; Windmeul; **Women in Wine**; Woolworths (2) ★★★ Aan de Doorns; Badsberg; Bayede! (2); Bergsig; Boland; Bon Courage; Breëland; Cape Dreams; Cape Wine Company; Cilmor; Darling Cellars (2); Daschbosch; De Villiers; Diemersfontein (2); Durbanville Hills;

Eagle's Cliff; Flagstone; **Germanier** (2) (Organic); Grande Provence; Imbuko (2); Klawer; Koelenhof; **Landzicht**; Leopard's Leap; Libby's Pride; Lutzville; M'hudi; McGregor; Namaqua; Nicholson Smith; Painted Wolf; Perdeberg; Piekenierskloof (Fairtrade); Rascallion; Riebeek Valley; Robertson; Rooiberg (2); Roos Family; Stellar (Fairtrade; Organic); Sumaridge; Swartland; Two Oceans; **VinGlo**; Waboomsrivier; Welmoed; Welvanpas; Windfall; Wineways (3); Woolworths (2) (Fairtrade; Organic); Zevenwacht; **Zidela** ★★★ Ashton; Barista; Boland (Lower in Alcohol); Bonnievale; Botha; Calitzdorp; Goedvertwacht; Jakkalsvlei; Koopmanskloof (Fairtrade); Kusafiri (Organic); Le Manoir de Brendel; Mile High; Nuy; Perdeberg (Lower in Alcohol); Rooiberg; Saam (Fairtrade); Seven Sisters; Van Loveren; Waverley Hills (Organic); Welbedacht; **Zidela** (2) ★★ KWV ★★ Orange River **NT** AA Badenhorst; Allée Bleue; Angus Paul; Arendskloof; Ashton; Babylon's Peak; Bayede!; Blue Owl; Brampton; Burgershof; Camberley; Cape Wine Company (Fairtrade); Die Mas; Diemersdal; Dragonridge; Drostdy-Hof; Du'SwaRoo; Ernst Gouws; Fairvalley; Fish Hoek (Fairtrade); Franschhoek Cellar; Frater; Friesland; Groot Parys; Gun Bay; Hawksmoor (2); Hofstraat; Hoopenburg; Hughes Family (Organic); Idiom; Jan Harmsgat; Koopmanskloof (Fairtrade); Kumala (2); Kusafiri (Organic); Kuypers Kraal; Lion's Kop; Liz Ogumbo; Mimosa; Mont Blois; Mountain River (3); Nomoya; Ormonde; Painted Wolf; Rijk's; Robertson; Roodekrantz (2) (Old Vines); Sanniesrust; Sarah's (2); Schalkenbosch (2); **Simonsvlei** (4); Somerbosch; Son of the Soil; Spijkerbessie; Stellenbosch University (2); Stellendrift; The Giant Periwinkle; Theescombe; **Tulbagh Winery**; Valley Vineyards; VinGlo; Vredenheim; Woolworths **D** Avontuur; Badsberg; Bayede!; Cape Dreams; Grangehurst; Kleine Zalze; Liz Ogumbo; Meerendal; Mountain Ridge; Namaqua; Painted Wolf; Riebeek Valley; Skilpadvlei; Spier; Tulbagh Winery (2); Villiera (Old Vines); Vriesenhof; Woolworths

Port-style, pink
★★★ De Krans; TTT Cellar ★★ Du'SwaRoo

Port-style, red
★★★★★ De Krans; Delaire Graff; KWV; Overgaauw; Upland

★★★★☆ Allesverloren; Anthonij Rupert; Beaumont; Boplaas (6); De Krans (2); Groot Constantia; Lieben; Morgenhof; Muratie (Old Vines); Sijnn; Stettyn

★★★★ Axe Hill; Badsberg; Beyerskloof; Boplaas; ?David Finlayson; De Krans; Du'SwaRoo; Fairview;

Hout Bay; Jakkalsvlei; KWV; Landskroon; Muratie; Riebeek Valley; Simonsig; Swanepoel; Upland

★★★★ Aan de Doorns; Beau Joubert; Bon Courage; Botha; Calitzdorp (2); Darling Cellars; De Wet; Domein Doornkraal; **Duikersdrift** (2); KWV; Peter Bayly; **Schotia** (2); Slanghoek; Upland (Organic); Viljoensdrift; Zandvliet ★★★ Clairvaux; Domein Doornkraal; Du'SwaRoo; Frater; Klawer; Koelenhof; Orange River; Org de Rac (Organic); **Skipskop**; Somersbosch; Swartland; TTT Cellar; Villiersdorp ★★★ Landzicht; Montagu Wine & Spirits **NT** Allesverloren; Alto; Annandale; Arra; Axe Hill (3); Bergsig (3); Bezalel; Die Mas; Eikehof; Grundheim (3); Holden Manz; JP Bredell (2); Lovane; Lutzville; Micu Narunsky; Miles Mossop; My Wyn; Robin Hood; Rosendal; Scali; Spookfontein; TTT Cellar; Waboomsrivier **D** Baleia; De Krans; Du Toitskloof; Namaqua; Vergenoegd

Port-style, white
★★★★ Peter Bayly; TTT Cellar **NT** Axe Hill; Beaumont; Lourensford; My Wyn

Red blends, Cape Bordeaux
★★★★★ Babylonstoren; **Bacco**; Constantia Glen; Darling Cellars; Diemersdal; Ernie Els; Glenelly; Jordan; Keet; Marianne; Meerlust; Overgaauw; Rainbow's End; Remhoogte; Ridgeback; Rustenberg; Stony Brook; Vondeling

★★★★★ Allée Bleue; Alto; Anthonij Rupert (2); Anura; Arcangeli; Asara (Fairtrade); Aslina; Atlas Swift; Beau Constantia; Bellingham; Benguela Cove; Botanica; Buitenverwachting (4); Capelands; Catherine Marshall; Cavalli; Chamonix; Constantia Glen; Constantia Uitsig; Dalla Cia; **?David Finlayson**; Delaire Graff (2); Delheim; Dieu Donné; Dornier (2); Durbanville Hills; Eikendal; Epicurean; Fleur du Cap; Franschhoek Cellar; Gabriëlskloof; Glen Carlou; Grande Provence; Grangehurst; Groenland; Groot Constantia; Guillaumé; Harry Hartman (2); Hartenberg; Haskell; Havana Hills; Hermanuspietersfontein; Hidden Valley; Hillcrest; Holden Manz; Hoopenburg; Idiom; Jean Daneel (2); Jordan (2); Journey's End; Kaapzicht; Kanonkop; Klein Constantia; Koelenhof; Kumusha; KWV; La Petite Ferme; La Vierge; Landskroon; Lanzerac; Le Bonheur (2); Le Grand Domaine; Leipzig; Longridge (Organic); Louisvale; Lourensford; Lynx; Meerlust; Miles Mossop; Mimosa; Mischa; Mitre's Edge (2); Mont Blois; Mooiplaas (2); Morgenster (2); **Mulderbosch** (3); Muratie; Mvemve Raats; Nederburg; Neethlingshof; Nico van der Merwe; Nitida; Noble Hill; Normandie; Oldenburg; Org de Rac (Organic); Ormonde; Paul Wallace; Perdeberg; Plaisir; Quoin Rock; Raats;

Raka; Ridgeback; **Saronsberg** (2); Simonsig; Spier (4) (Organic); Spookfontein; Steenberg; Stellekaya (2); Stellenbosch Reserve; Stellenbosch Vineyards; Stellenrust; Strydom; Super Single Vineyards; Survivor; Taaibosch (Organic); The High Road (2); Thelema (2); Thor; Tokara; Van Biljon; Vergelegen; Vriesenhof; Warwick; **Waterkloof** (2); Wildeberg; Winshaw (2); Zevenwacht (2)

★★★★ Aaldering; **Amperbo**; Anura; Audacia; Avontuur; Bacco (2); Backsberg; Beau Joubert; Bellevue; Blaauwklippen (2); Boschkloof; Buitenverwachting; Camberley; Chameleon; Cloof; Clouds; Constantia Uitsig; D'Aria; Definitum; **Dickens Family**; **Doolhof**; Dornier; Eikendal; Equitania; Flagstone; Grande Provence; Guillaumé; Hillcrest; Imbuko (Fairtrade); Jason's Hill; Kanu; Klein DasBosch; Klein Gustrouw; Kleine Zalze; Kruger Family (2); La Bri (2); La Motte; La Vierge; Ladybird (Organic); Le Pommier; Leopard's Leap (2); Louis 57; Marklew; Mount Vernon; Nabygelegen; Nederburg; Neil Ellis; Nelson; Nick & Forti's; Nico Vermeulen (2); Nietgegund; Normandie; Oldenburg; Onderkloof; Ormonde; Peter Falke; Quest; Rainbow's End; Reyneke (Organic); Rietvallei; Rosendal (2); Saxenburg; Schultz Family; Slanghoek; Stellekaya; Stellenbosch Family Wines; Stoep; Stonewall; Stony Brook; Sumaridge; Tanagra; Thorngrove; Thunderchild; Township Winery; **Twelve Apostles**; Val de Vie; Val du Charron (Skin-macerated white); Vergelegen; **Vriesenhof**; Waterford; Waverley Hills (Organic); Webersburg; Welbedacht; Woolworths (3) (Organic); Yonder Hill (2); Zonnebloem; Zorgvliet

★★★★ Bellascene; Beyerskloof; Birthmark of Africa; Bushmanspad; Camberley (3); Capaia; Cape Classics; Cape Town Wine Co; Chamonix; Compagniesdrift; CvD Wines; Diemersdal; Fat Bastard; Friesland; Goedverwacht; Hartenberg; Klawer; Klein Constantia; KWV (2); Landskroon; Louisvale; Lourensford; Lynx (2); Marklew; McGregor; Meinert; Miravel; MolenVliet (2); Morgenhof; Mountain Ridge; **Nabygelegen**; Nederburg; Overhex; Reyneke (Organic); Rooiberg; Skilpadvlei; Stellenbosch Family Wines; The Winery of Good Hope; Two Oceans; Walker Bay Estate; Woolworths (3) ★★★ Ashton; Bayede!; Beau Joubert; Bonnievale; Cloof; Clos Malverne; De Wet; deKaap; **Gun Bay**; Hoopenburg; Jacaranda; Le Grand Chasseur; Leopard's Leap; Nicholson Smith (2); **Onoma**; Org de Rac; Swartland; Tulbagh Winery; Windmeul; Wineways (4); **Woolworths** (3) ★★★ Excelsior; Mara; Prévoir; Swartland; Tulbagh Winery; Van Loveren; **Woolworths** ★★ Bon Courage **NT**

AA Badenhorst; Akkerdraai; **André van Rensburg**; Arcangeli; Arid; Backsberg; Berry Wines; Black Elephant; **Cape Wine Company** (2) (Fairtrade; Organic); Creation; De Grendel; De Trafford; Doran; Ernst Gouws; Frater; Germanier (2) (Organic); Glen Carlou; Grangehurst (2); Gun Bay; Havana Hills; Hirst; Idiom; Jacaranda; Journey's End; Kanu; Ken Forrester; Klein Roosboom; Kusafiri (Organic); La Petite Provence; Leeuwenberg; Louis 57; Lovane; Mischa (2); MolenVliet (2); Morgenhof; Overgaauw; Raka; Robin Hood; Roodekrantz (2); Rosendal (4); Rousseau; Schalkenbosch; Ses'Fikile; Sherwood; Simelia; **Simonsvlei**; Somfula; Stellendrift (4); Terrabosch; The Butcher Shop; The Vinoneers; Véraison; Villiersdorp; VinGlo (4); Zorgvliet **D** Black Oystercatcher; De Wet; Deux Frères; Eagle's Cliff; Kershaw; Môreson; Nelson; Rogge Cloof; Saltare; Seven Sisters; Simonsig; Skaap; Spider Pig; Steenberg; Twelve Apostles (2); Vergelegen; Windmeul; Wineways; Woolworths (3)

Red blends, other

★★★★★ Alto; Anysbos; Boschendal; De Trafford; Hogan; Leeu Passant; Van Wyk

★★★★☆ Afrikaans; Allesverloren; Anwilka; Bergsig; Bester Family; Blackwater; Boplaas; Boschendal; Boschkloof (2); Bosman Family; Bouchard Finlayson; Cape Wine Company; **Charla Haasbroek**; **City on a Hill**; Dalla Cia; David & Nadia; De Krans; DeMorgenzon; Donkiesbaai; Ernie Els (2); Fairview (2); Glenelly; Hartenberg; Haskell; Idun; JC Wickens; Keermont; Ken Forrester (2); KWV (3); Kyburg; Lanzerac (2); Le Chant; **Le Riche** (2); Le Sueur; Leopard's Leap; Lourens Family; Lowerland; Marianne (2); Mary le Bow; Morgenster; Naudé; Nederburg; Nico van der Merwe; Opstal; Painted Wolf (2); Progressive Inebriation; Radford Dale; Rust en Vrede; Spice Route; Spider Pig; Stellenzicht (2); **The Ahrens Family** (2); The Drift; The Fledge; **The Grapesmith**; Thistle & Weed; Thorngrove; Villiera; Vuurberg; Warwick; Waterford; Zoetendal

★★★★ Akkerdal (2); Alto; Annandale; Anthonij Rupert; Anura; Arumdale; Axe Hill; Badsberg; Baleia; **Bizoe**; **Boekenhoutskloof**; **Brookdale**; Bushmanspad; Capaia; Cape Collective; Cecilia; Cederberg; Chennells; **Duikersdrift**; Four Paws; Fryer's Cove; **Ghost In The Machine**; Groote Post; Holden Manz (2); Idiom; Idun; Joubert-Tradauw; Kanu; Kershaw; **Kindred Coast**; Kranskop; Kumusha; **KWV** (2); Kyburg (Fairtrade); La Couronne; Late Bloomer; Lowerland; Lozärn; Lynx; Miles Mossop; Mont du Toit (3); Mother Rock; Muratie; My Wyn; Nabygelegen; Namaqua; Noble Savage; Paserene; Plaisir; Radford Dale; Rietvallei;

Rockbelt; Rosendal; Rustenberg; **Schotia**; Silkbush (2); Spier (Organic); Strydom; **Terrabosch**; The Ahrens Family; The Giant Periwinkle; Topiary; **TTT Cellar**; Under Oaks (2); Val de Vie; Vinevenom; Wildehurst; Windfall; **Wolvenhoek**; Woolworths (3)

★★★★ Aan de Doorns; Audacia; Avontuur; Axe Hill; Bon Courage; Bushmanspad; Cape Rock; De Krans; Dieu Donné; Donegal; Dornier; Dragonridge; **Duikersdrift** (Skin-macerated white); Elgin Vintners; **Franki's**; **Germanier** (Organic); Goats do Roam; Hartenberg; Hill & Dale; Imvini Wethu (Old Vines); Kaapzicht; **Kloovenburg**; **KWV**; Mont du Toit; Mont Rochelle; Niel Joubert; Peter Falke; Piekenierskloof (Fairtrade); Rosendal; **Schotia** (Skin-macerated white); Simonsvlei; Skipskop; Somerbosch; Stellenbosch Hills; Stettyn; The Grape Grinder; The Hills; Under Oaks; Villiera; Vredenheim; Waterford; Whiley; Woolworths (3) ★★★ Axe Hill; Calitzdorp; Chateau Libertas; Clos Malverne; Darling Cellars; **Du Toitskloof** (2) (Skin-macerated white); **Grande Provence** (2); Koelenhof; KWV; Landskroon (2); Late Bloomer; Nederburg; Nicholson Smith (2); Peter Bayly; Riebeek Valley; Robertson; Spier; **TTT Cellar**; Under Oaks; Vergenoegd; Waverley Hills (Organic); Welvanpas; Woolworths (3) ★★★ **Du'SwaRoo** (2); Elgin Vintners (Lower in Alcohol); Germanier (Organic); Leopard's Leap (De-Alcoholised); Nicholson Smith; Picardi; Robertson (2); Wineways (2); Woolworths (2) (Lower in Alcohol) ★★ Botha **NT** AA Badenhorst; Allée Bleue; Alphabetical; Arendskloof; **Ashton**; Aufwaerts; Axe Hill; Boschheim; Brampton (2); Burgerhof; **Canetsfontein** (2) (Organic); Cape Collective; De Kleine Wijn Koöp; Dornier (2); Durbanville Hills; Franki's; Hermanuspietersfontein; Hughes Family (Organic); Idiom; Imbuko (Fairtrade); La RicMal; Lingen; Malanot; Mischa; Mountain River; Old Road; Remhoogte; Rhebokskloof; Rietvallei (2); Rogge Cloof; Rosendal; **Safriel**; Schalkenbosch; Sijnn (2); Simonsvlei; Snow Mountain; Spider Pig; Stellenbosch Family Wines (2); Stellenbosch University; Summerhill; Terracura; The Drift; The Fledge (2); The Goose; Thorne & Daughters; Véraison; VinGlo; Waboomsrivier; Welvanpas; **WineWolf**; Withington; Woolworths; Zanddrift **D** Allesverloren; Bergsig; Kumala; Lynx (2); M'hudi; Painted Wolf; Plaisir; Plettenvale; Rickety Bridge; Silvermist (Organic); Vriesenhof; Woolworths

Red blends, shiraz/syrah-based

★★★★★ Boekenhoutskloof; Ellerman House; Fairview (2); Rall; Ridgeback; Rust en Rede; Savage; Sijnn

★★★★☆ Akkerdal; Anthonij Rupert (2); Anura; ArtiSons; Bartho Eksteen; Beau Constantia; Bellingham; Black Pearl; Boschendal (3); Bosman Family (Fairtrade); Cape Rock; Creation; De Kleine Wijn Koöp; DeMorgenzon; Deux Frères; Eikendal; Elemental Bob; **Erika Obermeyer** (2); Flagstone; Great Heart; Groote Post; Hermanuspietersfontein; Hidden Valley; Holden Manz; Idiom; JAN Wines; Joostenberg (Organic); Ken Forrester; Kronendal; KWV; Lomond; Lourensford; Luddite; Meerhof; Metzer; **Mullineux** (2); Neil Ellis; Olifantsberg; Orange River; Ormonde; Post House; Sadie; Saronsberg; Sijnn (2); Spice Route; Spier; Stellenbosch Hills; Strandveld; The Ahrens Family; Thelema; Tulbagh Mountain Vineyards; Van Loggerenberg; Vondeling; Waterkloof; Welbedacht; Wildeberg; Wines of Brocha; **Wolvenhoek**; Zevenwacht

★★★★ Anwilka; Arendskloof; Babylon's Peak (2); Bartho Eksteen; Bergheim; Bezuidenhout Family; Biodynamix; Birthmark of Africa; Bizoe; Blackwater; Boland; Boplaas; Carstens; De Kleine Wijn Koöp; **Delphin**; Domaine des Dieux; Doran; Du Toitskloof; Eerste Hoop; Ernie Els; Esona; Friesland; Goats do Roam (Fairtrade); Groenland; Guardian Peak; **Harry Hartman**; Haute Cabrière; Hawksmoor; Hoopenburg; Hout Bay; Idun; Joostenberg (Organic); Kanu; Kleine Zalze; Kloovenburg; Kruger Family; La Petite Ferme; **Le Grand Domaine** (Fairtrade; Organic); Leipzig; Lemberg; Leopard's Leap; Lomond; **Lozärn**; MAN Family; Mimosa; Myburgh Bros; Natasha Williams; Nicky Versfeld; Nico van der Merwe; Org de Rac (Fairtrade; Organic); Overhex; Perdeberg; Piekenierskloof; **Quoin Rock**; Rascallion; Ridgeback; Saxenburg; Scali; Soif de Vivre; Stellenbosch Vineyards; Stellenrust; Stony Brook; The Grape Grinder; The Kitchen Sink; Thokozani; Tierhoek; **Township Winery**; Waterleliefontein; Waverley Hills (Organic); Welgegund; Wildeberg; Wolvenhoek; Woolworths (2)

★★★★ **Adama**; Anura; Cape Collective; D'Aria; ?David Finlayson; Delheim; Delphin; **Dickens Family**; Doran; **Germanier** (2) (Organic); Hartenberg; Herold; Imbuko; Jacaranda; Journey's End; Kaapzicht; Kay & Monty; Khayelitsha's Finest; Klein Amoskuil (Fairtrade); Lynx; M'hudi; Montagu Wine & Spirits; Orange River; Org de Rac (Fairtrade; Organic); Overhex; Post House; Raka; Rickety Bridge; Spier (Organic); Stellenview; Swanepoel; Terracura; The Wolftrap; Thelema; **TTT Cellar** (Nouveau); Vendôme; Welbedacht; Zevenwacht; Zonnebloem

★★★ Arra; Beau Joubert; **Cape Fold**; Darling Cellars;

Drostdy-Hof; Groenland; Kirabo; Klawer; Olivedale; Stellenview; Teubes (2) (Organic); Truter Family; Welbedacht; Woolworths (Fairtrade; Organic); Zidela (2) (Skin-macerated white) ★★★ Overhex; Stellar (Fairtrade; Organic); Stettyn; Two Oceans **NT** AA Badenhorst (2); Abbottshill; African Pride; Arra; Babylon's Peak; Bezuidenhout Family; Blue Crane; Cape Wine Company (Fairtrade); Charla Haasbroek; De Grendel; De Kleine Wijn Koöp; Delphin; Dunstone; Flagstone; Fuselage; Glen Heatlie; Gun Bay; Havana Hills; Hawksmoor (2); Hughes Family (Organic); Lazanou (2) (Organic); Lodestone; Lubanzi (Fairtrade); Maree Family; Migliarina; Mile High; My Wyn; Newton Johnson (2); Openwine; Quoin Rock; Radford Dale; Rascallion; Rosendal (2); Schalkenbosch; Ses'Fikile; Simelia; Simonsvlei; Somerbosch; Spier; **Stanford Valley**; Swanepoel; The Giant Periwinkle; The Winery of Good Hope; Valley Vineyards (3); Vendôme; VinGlo; Wightman & Sons; Wijnskool; Wine Village-Hermanus; Woolworths **D** City on a Hill; Deux Frères; Excelsior; Frater; Neil Ellis; Rascallion; Reyneke (Organic); Riebeek Valley; Rietvallei; Rogge Cloof; The Ahrens Family; Wildehurst; Woolworths; Zidela

Red blends, with pinotage

★★★★★ Beaumont; Beyerskloof (2); Nuiba; Opstal

★★★★☆ Alvi's Drift (2); Anura; Bartho Eksteen; Beaumont; **Bellingham**; Cape Collective; Grangehurst; Groot Constantia; Hughes Family (Organic); Kaapzicht; KWV; Lyngrove; Maanschijn; Marianne; Meerendal; Meinert; Middelvlei; **Mimosa**; Paul Roos (2); Perdeberg; Simonsig; Spier; Springfontein (2) (Organic); Stellenbosch Hills; Swartberg; Swartland; **Thor**; Visio; Wellington Winery; Windmeul

★★★★ Aaldering; Asara; **Ashton**; Babylonstoren; Bellevue; Beyerskloof (2); Botha; Cape Dreams; Cilmor; Clos Malverne; Darling Cellars; Daschbosch; DeWaal; Dragonridge; Flagstone; Herold; Hofstraat; Idiom; Jakkalsvlei; Jasper Raats; Kanonkop; Kirabo; Koelenhof; L'Avenir; Leipzig (2); Lemberg; Lutzville; Lyngrove; **Mimosa**; My Wyn; Nuy; **Olsen**; Post House; Pulpit Rock; Raka; Remhoogte; Rooiberg; Springfontein (2) (Organic); Stamboom; Sumaridge; Thor; Truter Family; Val du Charron; Villiersdorp; Warwick; Wildekrans (3); Woolworths

★★★★ Alvi's Drift; **Amperbo** (2); Anura; Arra; Asara; Ashton; Blake; Blue Crane; Cape Moby; Cilmor; Cloof; Croydon; De Wet; Du Preez; Eagle's Cliff; **Groot Phesantekraal**; **Hazendal**; Jason's Hill; Konkelberg; Meerhof; Middelvlei; **Overhex**; Painted Wolf; Post House; Rhebokskloof; Running Stream;

Scions of Sinai (Old Vines); Stanford Hills; Stellenrust (Fairtrade); Stellenview (Organic); TTT Cellar; Van Loveren ★★★ Clos Malverne; Diemersfontein; Imbuko; Mellasat; Namaqua (2); Overhex (2); Rascallion; Robertson; Rooiberg; Slaley; Stellenbosch Hills; **TTT Cellar**; Val du Charron; Van Loveren; Waboomsrivier; **Zidela** (2) ★★★ Aan de Doorns; Blake; Du Toitskloof; Leopard's Leap; O'Connell's; Pulpit Rock; Slanghoek (2); Stellar (Fairtrade; Organic); Tulbagh Winery; Whalehaven; Zandvliet ★★ KWV; Lautus (De-Alcoholised); Woolworths **NT** Ashton; Badger; Beaumont; Cape Fold; Definitum; Drostdy-Hof; Fuselage; Germanier (2) (Organic); Grangehurst; Hillock; Kruger Family; Liz Ogumbo; Lovane; Merwida; Mile High; Old Road; Olsen; Ormonde; Painted Wolf (2); Rascallion; Robertson; **Simonsvlei** (3); Sophie; Stellenbosch University; Stellendrift (2); The Vinoneers; Valley Vineyards; Viljoensdrift (2); Waboomsrivier; Wavescape; Welbedacht **D** Ayama; Cloof (2); D'Aria; De Wet; Du'SwaRoo; Groot Constantia; Hazendal; Kumala; Meerendal (2); Mooiplaas; Namaqua; Rogge Cloof; Silkbush; The Drift; Welbedacht; Woolworths

Riesling

★★★★☆ Cape Collective; Catherine Marshall; Klein Constantia; Oak Valley; Saurwein (2); Spioenkop; Thelema; Van Wyk

★★★★ Bergsig; Cape Collective; **Elemental Bob**; Fairview; Groote Post; Hartenberg; Herold; **Jordan** (2) (Old Vines); La Vierge; Meinert; Nitida; Paul Clüver; The Fledge; Thelema

★★★☆ Delheim & Hammel ★★☆ Bosjes **NT** Hartenberg; Illimis; Neethlingshof; Remhoogte; Rietvallei; Spier; The Vinoneers; Woolworths **D** Groote Post

Roobernet

★★★★ Olivedale

Rosé dry

★★★★☆ Anthonij Rupert; Bartho Eksteen; Bellingham (Old Vines); Ken Forrester; L'Avenir; Pink Valley; Vinevenom

★★★★ Akkerdal; Bacco; Bosman Family; Creation; De Grendel; Delaire Graff; Dorrance; **Eenzaamheid**; False Bay; Groot Constantia; **Haskell** (Organic); Holden Manz; Huis van Chevallerie (Skin-macerated white); Kanonkop; La Motte; Leeuwenkuil; Lievland; **McFarlane**; Noble Hill; Normandie; Nuiba; Paserene; Spier (Organic); Swanepoel; Tamboerskloof; Topiary; Vriesenhof; Wildeberg; Yonder Hill; Zorgvliet

★★★☆ Aaldering; Allesverloren; Anthonij Rupert; Asara; At se Wyn; Babylonstoren; Baleia; Bein; Beyerskloof; Blaauwklippen; Black Elephant; Bloemendal; Blue Crane; Bon Courage; Boplaas; **Bosjes**; Botanica; Brookdale; Camberley; Capaia; Cape Collective; Cederberg; Chamonix; Clouds; Compagniesdrift; Constantia Uitsig; Croydon; Dawn Patrol (2); De Wet; DeMorgenzon; Domaine des Dieux; Doran; Dunstone; Eerste Hoop (2); Eikendal; **Escape** (Lower in Alcohol); Fairview; Flagstone; Foothills; Goats do Roam; Groot Phesantekraal; Groote Post; Haute Cabrière (2); Havana Hills (2) (Fairtrade); Hawksmoor (2); Hidden Valley; Hout Bay (2); **Jordan**; Ken Forrester; Klawer; Klein DasBosch; Kleine Zalze; Kranskop; L'Avenir; La Bri; La Petite Ferme; Lanzerac; Le Grand Domaine; Leeuwenberg; Leopard's Leap (2); Lomond; Longridge; Lord's; Lourensford; Lozärn; Lubanzi (Fairtrade); Maastricht; Meerendal; Meerhof; Misty Mountains; **Mont Rochelle**; Mooi Bly; Morgenhof; Morgenster; Nelson; Noble Savage; Olivedale; **Onderkloof** (Kosher); Opstal; Piekenierskloof; Quando; Raka; **Reyneke** (Organic); Rickety Bridge; Saronsberg; Seven Springs; Sophie; Spier (Organic); Spookfontein; Spotswood; Stanford Hills (2); Stellekaya; Stellenrust (Fairtrade); **Stellenview**; Stellenzicht (2); Strandveld; Sumaridge; The Butcher Shop; The Grape Grinder; Thelema; Tokara; Val de Vie; Villiersdorp; Visio; Vondeling; Walker Bay Estate; Warwick; Waverley Hills (Organic); Wildeberg; Woolworths (3) ★★★ Allée Bleue (2); Anura; **Arbeidsgenot**; Arendskloof; Ariston Bay (Fairtrade); Arumdale; Asara; Avontuur; **Bé a Daisy**; Bertha; Blake; **Blue Crane**; Buitenverwachting; Bushmanspad; D'Aria; Darling Cellars (3); De Krans; Delheim; Denneboom; Die Mas; Diemersfontein; Dornier; Du Toitskloof; Duma; Durbanville Hills; Eagle's Cliff; Excelsior; Fat Bastard; Franki's; **Germanier** (Organic); Goedverwacht (2); Grande Provence; Groenland; Herold; Hill & Dale; Hillcrest; Imbuko; Jakkalsvlei; Kaapzicht; Kanu; Koelenhof; Koopmanskloof (Fairtrade); Kumusha; KWV (3); Late Bloomer; Le Pommier; Leipzig; Lodestone; Lutzville; Lyngrove; Marianne; Mellasat; Merwida; Middelvlei; Mont du Toit; Mountain Ridge; Mulderbosch; Nederburg; **Nicholson Smith** (2); **Nuy**; Onderkloof; **Overhex**; Painted Wolf; Perdeberg (2); Piekenierskloof (Fairtrade); Post House; Pulpit Rock; Rainbow's End; Riebeek Valley; Rivendell; Roos Family; **Sandstone**; Silkbush; **Simonsig** (2); **Spier** (2) (Organic); Spotswood; Springfontein (Organic); Steenberg; Stellar (2) (Fairtrade; Organic); Stellenbosch Hills; Stettyn; Summerhill; **The Grape Grinder** (Perlé); Truter Family; TTT Cellar; Vredenheim; Waterford; Waterkloof; Webersburg;

Welmoed; Welvanpas; **Wightman & Sons** (Alternative white/red); Windmeul; Wolvenhoek; Woolworths (2); Zandvliet; Zevenwacht; Zorgvliet ★★★ **Amperbo**; Boschheim; Boschrivier; Cape Town Wine Co; **Cape Wine Crafters**; Clos Malverne; Diemersdal; **Hillock**; Imbuko; **Joubert Family**; Kay & Monty; Klein Roosboom; La Couronne; Leopard's Leap; Meerhof; Org de Rac (Fairtrade; Organic); Perdeberg (Lower in Alcohol); Robertson (Lower in Alcohol); Slaley; **Swartland**; The Fishwives Club (2); Vinette; Welbedacht; Woolworths; **Zidela** ★★ Darling Cellars; **Kirabo; Orange River NT** AA Badenhorst (2); Aaldering; Akkerdal; Arid; Backsberg; Badger; Bergsig; Bezuidenhout Family; **Bitou**; Black Elephant; Black Oystercatcher; Boschendal; Brampton; Buitenverwachting; Cape Rock; Cape Wine Company (Fairtrade); Cecilia; Coucou; De Kleine Wijn Koöp; Dragonridge; Driehoek; Drostdy-Hof (2); Du'SwaRoo; Eagle's Cliff; Eikehof; Ernie Els; Fish Hoek (Fairtrade); Franschhoek Cellar; Frater; Fryer's Cove; Fuselage (Old Vines); Gabriëlskloof; Grangehurst; Guillaumé; Hermanuspietersfontein; Herold; Highlands Road; Holden Manz; Hoopenburg; Jacaranda; Klein Amoskuil; La Petite Ferme; **Libby's Pride**; Louis 57; Louisvale; Lynx; Malanot; Manley; Mitre's Edge; Mother Rock; Mountain River; Muratie; Newstead; Nico van der Merwe; Nico Vermeulen; Pearl Mountain; Plettenvale; Porcupine Ridge; Quoin Rock; Rainbow's End; Renegade; Rietvallei; Roodekrantz; Rosendal (2); Safriel (2); Schalkenbosch; **Simonsvlei** (3); Skaap (2) (Lower in Alcohol); Skipskop; Snow Mountain; Somerbosch; Spice Route; Spider Pig; Strooidak; The Wolftrap; Vendôme; Walker Bay Estate (3); Wildekrans; Wolf & Woman; Woolworths; Zanddrift **D** Bayede!; Bellevue; Chameleon; Cloof (2); Daschbosch; Fleur du Cap; Haskell; Kruger Family; Mooiplaas; Olifantsberg; Rascallion; Rickety Bridge; Stettyn; Super Single Vineyards (Old Vines); The Drift; Two Oceans; Vergenoegd; Woolworths (3) (Organic); Zidela

Rosé off-dry/semi-sweet

★★★★ Tierhoek ★★★ Badsberg (Lower in Alcohol; Perlé); **Boplaas** (Lower in Alcohol; Perlé); Cape Dreams; Landzicht (Lower in Alcohol); Overhex; Rooiberg; Val du Charron; Van Loveren ★★★ Bon Courage; Bonnievale; Cape Classics; Darling Cellars; De Wet (Perlé); Klawer; Lautus (De-Alcoholised); Montagu Wine & Spirits; Overhex; Tangled Tree (Lower in Alcohol); Vinette ★★ Bonnievale (Lower in Alcohol; Perlé); Cape Wine Crafters; Darling · Cellars (De-Alcoholised); Mara (Lower in Alcohol; Perlé); Woolworths ★★ Perdeberg **NT** Ashton (2);

Backsberg; Bezalel; Jakkalsvlei (Lower in Alcohol; Perlé); Kumala; Leopard's Leap; Rietvallei; Robin Hood; Skilpadvlei; Theescombe; Women in Wine **D** Meerendal; Perdeberg

Roussanne

★★★★★ Saronsberg

★★★★☆ Ken Forrester; Mischa; Olifantsberg; Painted Wolf; **Sijnn**; The Foundry

★★★★ **Arbeidsgenot**; La Bri; Org de Rac (Fairtrade; Organic); Swartland

NT Doran; Hazendal; Lourensford

Ruby cabernet

★★★★ Badsberg

★★★★ Bellpost; TTT Cellar ★★★ Langverwacht ★★★ Robertson; Du'SwaRoo; Orange River **NT** Robertson; VinGlo

Sacramental Wines

★★☆ Landzicht (Muscadel, red, fortified)

Sangiovese

★★★★☆ Waterford

★★★★ Anthonij Rupert; Anura; Domaine des Dieux; Idiom; **iL Geco**; La Vierge; Morgenster; Raka; Stellekaya; Woolworths

★★★★ **Esona**; Idiom; Jasper Raats; La Capra ★★★ Havana Hills; Koelenhof; Skipskop **NT** Bezalel; Idiom; **Nomoya**; Super Single Vineyards

Sauvignon blanc unwooded

★★★★★ Anthonij Rupert; Buitenverwachting; Diemersdal; Lomond; Strandveld; The Giant Periwinkle

★★★★☆ Aaldering; Arendsig; Bartho Eksteen; Bosman Hermanus; Callender; Catherine Marshall; Cederberg; Constantia Glen; Constantia Uitsig; Diemersdal (2); Erika Obermeyer; Flagstone; Gabriëlskloof; Garden Route; Groot Constantia; Iona; Kleine Zalze; La Motte; Lievland; Lomond; Meerendal (Organic); Moya's; Neil Ellis (2); Nicky Versfeld; Nitida; Oak Valley; **Ouwater**; Spier; Steenberg (2); Sumaridge; Survivor; The Berrio; Thelema (2); ?Trade Winds; Vergelegen; Warwick; Whalehaven; Wildeberg

★★★★ Allée Bleue; Asara; Beau Joubert; Bitou; Black Elephant; Black Oystercatcher; Blackwater; Boplaas; Boschendal; Boschkloof; Bruce Jack; Buitenverwachting; Cape Elevation; **Cape Moby**; Cape Point; Cape Town Wine Co; Cederberg; Chamonix; Clouds; **Darling Cellars** (2); ?David Finlayson; De Grendel; DeMorgenzon; Diemersdal; Driehoek; Durbanville Hills; Eikendal; Elgin Vintners (2); **Escape** (2); Fairview; False Bay; Flagstone; Friesland; Fryer's Cove; Goedvertrouw; Groote

Post; Harry Hartman; Haskell; Hidden Valley; Hillcrest; Idun; Izak van der Vyver; Jakkalsvlei; Jordan; Journey's End; Kay & Monty; Ken Forrester; Kershaw; Kings Kloof; Kruger Family; KWV; La Vierge; Land's End; Lanzerac; Le Grand Domaine (3); Le Sueur; Lomond; Mark le Roux; Marklew; Meerendal; Mischa; **Misty Mountains** (2); Mont Blois; Mooiplaas; Morgenster; Neethlingshof; Nico van der Merwe; Nitida; Ormonde; Paul Wallace; Pounding Grape (Skin-macerated white); Quoin Rock; Rivendell; RiverGold; Saronsberg; Shannon; Signal Gun; Silvermist (Organic); Sophie; Spier (2) (Organic); Spijkerbessie; Spioenkop; Spookfontein; Stanford Hills; Stellenbosch Vineyards; Stellenrust; Stellenview; Stony Brook; Strandveld; Teubes; The Butcher Shop (2); The Goose; **Thor**; Trizanne; Van Loveren; Vergenoegd; Walker Bay Estate; Waterford; Wijnskool; Wildekrans; Woolworths (5); Zoetendal ★★★★ **Adama** (2); Anura; Arendskloof; Arniston Bay (Fairtrade); Aslina; Bé a Daisy; Bellevue; Bellingham; Bergsig; Blaauwklippen; Bloemendal; Boplaas; Breëland; Buitenverwachting; Calitzdorp; Canto; Capaia; Cape Classics; **Chameleon**; Contreberg; Croydon; D'Aria (2); Dalla Cia; Darling Cellars (2); Daschbosch; Dawn Patrol (2); Delheim; Delphin; DeWaal; Diemersfontein; Dieu Donné; Domaine des Dieux; Du Preez; False Bay; Fat Bastard; Foothills; Fryer's Cove; Gabriëlskloof; Glen Carlou; GlenWood; Grande Provence; Groenland; Groot Phesantekraal; Hartenberg; Herold; Hout Bay; Imbuko (3); Kaapzicht; Kanu; Klein Constantia; Klein Roosboom; Kleine Zalze; Kranskop; Kruger Family; Kumusha; Kusafiri (2) (Organic); KWV; L'Avenir; La Motte; La Petite Ferme; Land's End; Le Grand Chasseur; Leeuwenberg; Lemberg; Lodestone; Louisvale; Lutzville; Lyngrove; Maastricht; MAN Family; Meinert; Miravel; Miss Molly; Mont Blois; Morgenhof; Muratie; **Nabygelegen**; Nederburg; Neethlingshof; Nico Vermeulen; Noble Savage; Orange River; Org de Rac (Fairtrade; Organic); Overhex (4); Painted Wolf; Peter Falke; Porcupine Ridge; Post House; Pulpit Rock; Quando; Raka (2); Rietvallei; Rooiberg; Rosendal; Seven Springs; Silkbush; Simonsig; Skaap; Spier; Spotswood; Stellenbosch Hills; The Goose; Township Winery; Under Oaks; Val de Vie; Viljoensdrift; Villiersdorp; Visio; **Walker Bay Estate**; Waterford; Webersburg; **Welgesind**; Welmoed; **Wildeberg**; Windfall (2); Woolworths (3); Zevenwacht; Zoetendal ★★★ Aan de Doorns; Anthonij Rupert; Arumdale; Ashton; Avontuur; Badsberg; Bertha; **Bizoe**; Boland; Bon Courage; Bushmanspad; Cape Classics; Cilmor; Clairvaux; Clos Malverne (2); Daschbosch (2);

Deux Frères (Old Vines); DeWaal; **Doran**; Dornier; Drostdy-Hof; Durbanville Hills; Eagle's Cliff; Esona; Excelsior; Fleur du Cap; **Grande Provence** (2); Guardian Peak; Gun Bay; House of Mandela; **Joubert Family**; Journey's End; Ken Forrester; Koelenhof (2); Konkelberg; Koopmanskloof (Fairtrade); KWV; La Capra; Landskroon; Langverwacht; Le Pommier; Leipzig; Leopard's Leap; Lord's; Louisvale; Lovane; Lozärn; Lutzville; McGregor; Merwida; Mont du Toit; Mountain Ridge; Nabygelegen; Nicholson Smith (3); Niel Joubert; O'Connell's; Onderkloof; Perdeberg; Piekenierskloof (Fairtrade); Rickety Bridge; Riebeek Valley; Robertson; Rooiberg; Roos Family; Seven Sisters; Slanghoek; Stellar (Fairtrade; Organic); Stellenbosch Hills; Stellenbosch University; Stettyn; Swartland; Tangled Tree; Teubes; The Fishwives Club (2); Truter Family (2); Van Loveren; Vergenoegd; Vredenheim; Waboomsrivier; Warwick; Wellington Winery; Wineways (2); Woolworths (4) (Fairtrade; Organic); Yonder Hill ★★☆ Bonnievale (2); Boschrivier; Bosjes; Cloof; Darling Cellars (De-Alcoholised); De Wet; Du Toitskloof; Hill & Dale; Hillock; Hoopenburg; **Klawer** (2); Kloovenburg; KWV; Landzicht; Late Bloomer; Lautus (De-Alcoholised); Libby's Pride; Namaqua (2); Perdeberg; Rascallion; Robertson (Lower in Alcohol); Rooiberg; Skilpadvlei; Windmeul; Woolworths (2) (Lower in Alcohol); **Zidela** (2) ★★ Die Mas; Nuy; Welvanpas ★★ Orange River **NT** AA Badenhorst (3); Akkerdal; Alexanderfontein; Alphabetical; Aufwaerts; Backsberg; Bayede!; Belle Rebelle; Bezalel; Black Elephant; Blue Crane; Brampton; Burgershof; Cape Collective; Cape Dreams; Cape Wine Company (Fairtrade); Constantia Mist (Organic); Coucou; Creation; Duma; Eikehof; Ernst Gouws; Excelsior; Fairvalley; Fish Hoek (Fairtrade); Flagstone; Franschhoek Cellar; Fryer's Cove; Havana Hills (2); Hermanuspietersfontein; Hoopenburg; **House of Hlela**; Jan Harmsgat; Kaapse Familie Wingerde; Klein Gustrouw; Klein Roosboom; Kleine Zalze; Koueberg; Kumala; Kuypers Kraal; La RicMal; Libby's Pride; Lieben; Liz Ogumbo; Louis 57; Maison de Teijger; Malanot; Meerhof; Middelvlei; Midgard; Mimosa; Mischa; Misty Mountains; MolenVliet; Mosi; Mountain River (2); Nelson; Newstead; Nuy; Old Road; Ormonde; Packwood; Plaisir; Quoin Rock; Rietvallei (3); Robertson (4); Robin Hood; Rosendal; Rustenberg; Sarah's; Schalkenbosch; **Simonsvlei** (3); Sir Lambert; Skipskop; Solara (Organic); Somerbosch; Stellendrift; Strydom; The Fledge; Two Oceans; Valley Vineyards; Wine Village-Hermanus; Women in Wine; Zonnebloem **D** Bayede!; Breëland; Cloof (2); Daschbosch; Doolhof; Kumala; Land of

Hope; Le Manoir de Brendel; Meerendal; Montagu Wine & Spirits; Rooibosg; Saam; Stellenbosch Vineyards; Van Loveren (Organic); Walker Bay Estate; Welbedacht; Wineways; Woolworths (4)

Sauvignon blanc wooded

★★★★★ Bartho Eksteen; Buitenverwachting; Cederberg; Die Kat; Diemersdal (2); Hasher; Klein Constantia (2); Neil Ellis; Thorne & Daughters; Waterkloof (Organic); Zevenwacht

★★★★☆ Almenkerk; Alvi's Drift; Bartho Eksteen; Benguela Cove (2); Bloemendal; Cape Point (2); Constantia Royale; D'Aria; Deep Rooted (Alternative white/red); Delaire Graff; Eagles' Nest; Elgin Vintners; Erika Obermeyer; Fryer's Cove; Gedeelte; Groot Phesantekraal; Groote Post; Hermanuspietersfontein; Highlands Road (2); Hillcrest; Idiom; Idun; Iona; Jasper Raats (Organic); Jordan (2) (Old Vines); **Kirabo; Klein Constantia** (6); Kleine Zalze; Kumusha; Lomond; Marianne; Mellish; **Neethlingshof** (Old Vines); Nitida; Painted Wolf; Paul Clüver; Reyneke (Biodynamic); Rickety Bridge; **Sandstone**; Seven Springs; Stark-Condé; Steenberg; The Fledge; The Giant Periwinkle; Tokara; Trizanne; Villion (Old Vines); Wild Air; Zevenwacht

★★★★ Alvi's Drift; Baleia; Boschendal; Bouchard Finlayson; Cilmor; DA Hanekom; Domaine des Dieux; Du Toitskloof (Old Vines); Fortes (2); Gedeelte; **Ghost In The Machine**; Klein Amoskuil (Old Vines; Organic); KleinSering; Kruger Family; Le Bonheur (2) (Old Vines); Lourensford; Maastricht; Meinert; Miles Mossop (Old Vines); Miravel; Misty Mountains; Mulderbosch; Olivedale; Orange River; Overgaauw; Packwood; Paserene; Quoin Rock; Reyneke (Biodynamic); Saxenburg; Signal Gun; Skaap; Southern Right; The Kitchen Sink; Tierhoek; Villiera; Waterkloof; Winshaw; Zorgvliet

★★★★☆ Cilmor; KleinSering; Orange River (2); Reyneke (Organic); Tokara; Vondeling; **Welbedacht**

★★★ Botha; **Rockbelt**; Vendôme; Zorgvliet **NT** Brunia; Capelands; D'Aria; De Grendel; Enfin; Klein Constantia (2); Maison de Teijger; Newton Johnson; Rietvallei; Rivendell; Rousseau (2); Rustenberg; Safriel; Silvermist (Organic); Spier; Stellar (Fairtrade; Organic); Stone Ridge; Tierhoek; Twelve Apostles; Vergelegen; Villiera (Old Vines); Woolworths **D** Avontuur; D'Aria; Namaqua; Nico Vermeulen; Walker Bay Estate; Woolworths

Semillon gris

★★★★★ Mullineux

★★★★☆ **Cederberg**; JC Wickens; Thorne & Daughters

★★★★ Rickety Bridge

Semillon unwooded

★★★★★ Super Single Vineyards

★★★★☆ Bizoe (3); Haute Cabrière; Lokaia

★★★★ Arcangeli; GD1 Project

★★★☆ **Cape Moby**; Mont Rochelle ★★ Theescombe **NT** Kings Kloof; Mother Rock **D** The Vineyard Party

Semillon wooded

★★★★★ Benguela Cove; Old Road (Old Vines); Opstal; Rickety Bridge (Old Vines); Sadie (Old Vines); Shannon; Steenberg; Wildeberg

★★★★☆ Alheit (Old Vines); Anthonij Rupert (Old Vines); Belle Rebelle; Black Elephant; Bloemendal; Boekenhoutskloof (Old Vines); Cederberg; Constantia Uitsig; De Kleine Wijn Koöp (2); Dornier; **Elemental Bob** (2); Foothills; Gabriëlskloof; Highlands Road; Holden Manz; JC Wickens; **Leeu Passant**; Lomond; Nitida; **Radford Dale** (Organic); Rickety Bridge (2); The Garajeest; **The Vineyard Party** (2) (Skin-macerated white); Thorne & Daughters (Old Vines); **Trizanne**; Vergelegen; **Wade Bales**; Wildehurst

★★★★ Akkerdal; **Bruwer Vintners**; Idiom; KleinSering; **Packwood** (Lower in Alcohol); William Everson; Zorgvliet

★★★☆ Herold; Thor ★★★ Bertha; Eikehof; Skipskop **NT** Arno Smith; Beaumont; Brunia; Celestina; Eikehof; Hartenberg; La Bri; Nicky Versfeld; Trizanne; Wildehurst; **WineWolf D** Black Oystercatcher; Botanica; Elgin Vintners

Sherry-style wines

★★★★☆ Klein Amoskuil

★★★★ Monis

★★★★ Monis (2) ★★★ Landzicht ★★★☆ Orange River ★★ Picardi

Shiraz/syrah

★★★★★ ArtiSons; Boschkloof; De Grendel; **Diemersdal**; Driehoek; La Bri; Metzer; Mullineux; Oldenburg; Patatsfontein; **Sakkie Mouton**; Savage; Saxenburg; Super Single Vineyards; Van Loggerenberg

★★★★☆ Allée Bleue; Allesverloren; Alto; Annandale; Anthonij Rupert (2); Arcangeli; ArtiSons; Babylonstoren; Baleia; Beau Constantia; Beaumont; Belle Rebelle; Bellingham; Benguela Cove; Bizoe; Black Pearl; Blackwater; Bloemendal; Boekenhoutskloof; Boschendal; Boschheim; Boschkloof; Bruce Jack; Carinus Family; Cecilia; **Cederberg** (2); Creation; D'Aria; De Grendel (2); **De Trafford** (3); **Deep Rooted** (Alternative white/red); DeMorgenzon; DewaldtHeyns; Dieu Donné; Dornier; Dorrance; Eagles' Nest; Eenzaamheid; Elgin

Vintners; Erika Obermeyer; Ernie Els; Excelsior; Fairview (2); Flagstone; Fram; Gabriëlskloof (3); Glenelly; GlenWood (2); Groenland; Groot Constantia; Harry Hartman; Hartenberg (3); Haskell; Highlands Road; Hirst; Holden Manz (2); Idun; Jasper Raats; JC Wickens; **Jean Daneel**; Joostenberg (Organic); Jordan; Journey's End; Julien Schaal (Organic); Keermont (3); Kershaw (5); Kleine Zalze (3); Kloovenburg; **Kruger Family**; KWV; La Bri; La Motte (2); La Petite Ferme; Leeuwenkuil (2); Lievland; Lomond (2); Luddite; Malanot; Marianne; Mellish; Michaella; Mont Rochelle (2); Mosi; Mullineux (3); Muratie (Old Vines); Natasha Williams; Neil Ellis; Nico van der Merwe; Niel Joubert; Noble Hill; Off The Record; Old Road (2); Oldenburg; Olifantsberg; Painted Wolf; Paserene; Pilgrim; Porseleinberg; Radford Dale; Rainbow's End; Raka (2); Rall (2); Rebel Rebel; Remhoogte (2) (Nouveau); Reyneke (2) (Biodynamic); Rhebokskloof; Richard Hilton (3); Rickety Bridge; Ridgeback; Riebeek Valley; Robertson; Rogge Cloof; Rust en Vrede (2); Saltare; Saronsberg; Savage (2); Saxenburg; Scali; Schultz Family; Scions of Sinai; Simelia (2) (Old Vines); Simonsig; Stark-Condé (2); Stellenbosch Vineyards; Stellenrust (2); Stellenview (2); Stony Brook; Strandveld; Sumaridge; Super Single Vineyards (Old Vines); Survivor; Tamboerskloof (2); Tembela; Terracura; The Fledge; The Foundry; Thelema (2); Tim Hillock; Tokara (2); **Torero**; Trizanne; Van Loveren; Van Wyk; Vergelegen (2); **Vinevenom**; Waterford; Waterkloof (2) (Organic); Waverley Hills (Organic); Wildekrans; Wines of Brocha; Wolf & Woman; Woolworths; Zandvliet; Zevenwacht; **Zoetendal**

★★★★ Aaldering; Adama; Andreas (2); Anura; Arbeidsgenot; Arendsig; Arendskloof; Arra; Asara; Audacia; Backsberg; **Baleia**; Bayede!; Bellingham; Bernind; Blaauwklippen; Black Oystercatcher; Bloemendal; Boland; Bon Courage; Capaia; Cape Wine Company; **Cloof** (3); Clouds; Constantia Uitsig; D'Aria; Darling Cellars; DeMorgenzon; Denneboom; Dieu Donné; Donegal; **Duikersdrift**; Dunstone; Durbanville Hills; Elana; Elgin Vintners; **Escape**; Fairview; Foothills (2); Gabriëlskloof; Garden Route; **Ghost In The Machine**; Grande Provence; Groot Phesantekraal; Groote Post; Gun Bay; Hartenberg; Haskell; Havana Hills; Hermit on the Hill; Imbuko; Jacaranda; Joubert-Tradauw; Journey's End; Kanu; **Ken Forrester**; Kings Kloof; **Klein Goederust**; Kleine Schuur; Kloovenburg; Koelfontein; Kranskop; KWV; Kyburg; La Couronne; Land of Hope; Land's End (2); Landskroon; Leeuwenberg; Leeuwenkuil; Lemberg;

Lomond; Lord's; **Lourensford**; Lutzville; Lynx; Maison; MAN Family; Maree Family; Meerendal; Meinert; Mellasat; Migliarina; Mischa; Mitre's Edge; Mont du Toit; Nederburg (2); Neethlingshof; Nick & Forti's; Nico van der Merwe; Nuiba; Olivedale; Olsen; Onoma; Orange River; Org de Rac (Fairtrade) (Organic); Ormonde (2); **Painted Wolf**; Peter Falke; Piekenierskloof; Porcupine Ridge; Post House; Pulpit Rock; Quest; Rhebokskloof; Richard Hilton; Rickety Bridge; Riebeek Valley; Rietvallei; **Roodekrantz**; Rooiberg; **Samesyn**; Saronsberg; Saxenburg; **Schotia**; Seven Springs (2); Signal Hill (2); Simelia (2); Spookfontein; Stellar (Fairtrade) (Organic); Stellenbosch Hills; Stellenbosch Reserve; Stellenbosch Vineyards; Stellenview (4); Stellenzicht; Strandveld; Strydom; Swanepoel; Swartland; Tanagra; Tempel; The Butcher Shop; The Earth Beneath Our Feet; **The Grape Grinder**; The Winery of Good Hope; Thor; Thorngrove; Tokara; Trizanne; Truter Family; Twelve Apostles; Under Oaks; Val du Charron; Vergenoegd; Viljoensdrift; Villion; Vondeling; Walker Bay Estate; Waverley Hills (Organic); **Welgesind**; Wellington Winery; Wildeberg; William Everson; Woolworths (3); Zandvliet

★★★★ Aan de Doorns; Abbottshill; Allée Bleue; Bacco; Bayede! (2); Bellascene; Belle Rebelle; Bellevue; Blue Crane; Bon Courage; Boschendal; Bosman Family; Brookdale; Bushmanspad; Calitzdorp; Camberley; Cape Collective; Cape Dreams; Cape Fold; Cape Wine Crafters (2); Cavalli; Chameleon; Contreberg; Croydon; Darling Cellars (2); Daschbosch; Dawn Patrol (2); Delaire Graff; DeWaal; Diemersdal; Diemersfontein; Du Toitskloof; Du'SwaRoo; **Duikersdrift**; Durbanville Hills; Eerste Hoop; Excelsior; False Bay; Glen Carlou; Goedvertwacht; Groenland; Guardian Peak; Hawksmoor (2); Herold; Hoopenburg; House of Mandela (2); Hout Bay; Imbuko; Kaapzicht; Klawer; Koelenhof; Koopmanskloof (Fairtrade); Kranskop; Kusafiri (Organic); KWV (2); La Vierge; Landskroon; **Landzicht**; Langverwacht; Late Bloomer; Le Grand Chasseur; Le Manoir de Brendel; Lemberg; Lord's; Lozärn; Lynx; Manley; McGregor; Meerhof; Middelvlei; Mimosa; **Misty Mountains**; Montegray; Mount Pleasant; Mountain Ridge; My Wyn; Niel Joubert; Nieuwedrift; Nomad; Nuy; **O'Connell's**; Overhex; **Packwood**; Painted Wolf; Paserene; Perdeberg; **Renegade**; **Reyneke** (Organic); Rivendell; Robertson; **Rockbelt**; Rooiberg (2); **Schotia**; Silkbush; Simonsig; Skaap; Slanghoek; Spier (2) (Organic); Spotswood; Stanford Hills; Swartland; The Goose; The Grape

Grinder; The Hills; Topiary; **TTT Cellar**; Villiersdorp; **Vriesenhuijs**; **Walker Bay Estate**; Wederom; **Welgesind** (3); Wellington Winery; Wijnskool; Windfall; **Woolworths** (3); Zandvliet ★★★ Aan't Vette; Anthonij Rupert; Arniston Bay (Fairtrade); Ayama; Bellpost; Bertha; Bonnievale; Cilmor; Clairvaux; Clos Malverne; De Wet; Du Preez; Eagle's Cliff; Esona; False Bay; Fat Bastard; Hazendal; Hillock; Kirabo; KWV; La RicMal; Leipzig; Leopard's Leap; Libby's Pride; Louisvale; Lutzville; Lyngrove; M'hudi; **Mile High** (2); Misty Mountains; Montagu Wine & Spirits; Namaqua; Nicholson Smith; Nuy; **O'Connell's**; **Orange River** (2); Org de Rac (Fairtrade; Organic); Piekenierskloof (Fairtrade); Riebeek Valley; Rooiberg; Somersbosch; Spier; Stellar (Fairtrade; Organic); Stettyn; Summerhill; Two Oceans; Wightman & Sons (Alternative white/red); Wildekrans; Windmeul; Wineways; Woolworths; Zidela ★★★ Botha; Cape Wine Crafters; Le Manoir de Brendel; **Misty Mountains**; Perdeberg; Stellar (Fairtrade; Organic); Stellenbosch University; The Hills; Welmoed; Woolworths ★★ Ashton; Bonnievale; Darling Cellars (De-Alcoholised); Jason's Hill; Tangled Tree **NT** Aan't Vette; Absolute Style; Alexanderfontein; Alphabetical; Anura; Arid; Avontuur; Axe Hill; Badger; Benguela Cove; Bezalel; Boschrivier; Bosjes; Brampton; Brunia; Cape Rock; Cape Wine Company (Fairtrade); Chennells; Cloof; **Coltrane's**; ?David Finlayson; De Kleine Wijn Koöp (2); Delphin; Die Mas; Diemersdal; Doran; Dunstone; DuVon; Eenzaamheid; Eikehof; Enfin (3); Fish Hoek (Fairtrade); Franschhoek Cellar (2); Frater; Fuselage; Groote Post; Grundheim; Hawksmoor; Hofstraat; Hughes Family (Organic); Idiom; Jan Harmsgat; Joostenberg (Organic); JP Bredell; Klein Roosboom; Kumala (2); Kusafiri (Organic); Lazanou (Organic); Liz Ogumbo (2); Louis 57; Lovane; Marklew; Mason's; Montagu Wine & Spirits; Mooi Bly; Mountain Ridge; Mountain River (2); Muratie; Muse; Nelson; Nico Vermeulen; Nomoya; Olivedale; Pearl Mountain; Prévoir; Quoin Rock; Rascallion; Richard Hilton; Rietvallei; Rivendell; RiverGold; Robertson (2); Rogge Cloof (2); Rosendal (4); Rudera; Safriel; Sarah's (2); Schalkenbosch (Fairtrade); Sijnn; Simelia; **Simonsvlei** (4); Skaap; Slaley; Sluk Jou Woorde; Snow Mountain; Spider Pig; Stellendrift; Stellenview; Stone Ridge (2); Terracura; The Butcher Shop; The Giant Periwinkle; **Tulbagh Winery**; Twin; Valley Vineyards; Véraison; VinGlo (2); Vredenheim; Wolvenhoek; Women in Wine; Woolworths (2); Zevenwacht; Zonnebloem **D** Boland; Cape Dreams; Cape Town Wine Co; Carstens; City on a Hill; Daschbosch; Durbanville Hills (Lower in Alcohol);

Ernst Gouws; KWV; Lanzerac; Meerendal; Mountain Ridge (2); Nelson; Painted Wolf; Radford Dale; Scali; Seven Sisters; Signal Gun; Skilpadvlei; Spier (2) (Lower in Alcohol); Trizanne; Tulbagh Winery (2); Windmeul

Skin-macerated white

★★★★☆ Wightman & Sons (Chenin blanc wooded, dry); De Grendel (Chardonnay wooded); De Trafford (Chenin blanc wooded, dry); Luddite (Chenin blanc wooded, dry); The Vineyard Party (Semillon wooded); Wildehurst (Semillon wooded)

★★★★ Groot Parys (Chenin blanc wooded, dry; Old Vines); Olivedale (White blends, wooded, dry; Alternative white/red); Jacaranda (Chenin blanc wooded, dry); Val du Charron (Red blends, Cape Bordeaux); Aslina (Chenin blanc unwooded dry); Huis van Chevallerie (Rosé dry); Myburgh Bros (Chenin blanc wooded, dry; Old Vines; Organic); Pounding Grape (Sauvignon blanc unwooded); Scions of Sinai (White blends, wooded, dry)

★★★★ Rietvallei (Chardonnay wooded); Jacaranda (White blends, wooded, dry); Land of Hope (Cabernet sauvignon); **Duikersdrift** (Red blends, other); **Schotia** (Red blends, other) ★★★ Du Toitskloof (Red blends, other); Zidela (Red blends, shiraz/syrah-based) **NT** Groot Parys (Chenin blanc wooded, dry); Wightman & Sons (Chenin blanc wooded, dry); Sanniesrust (Grenache blanc); AA Badenhorst (White blends, unwooded, dry); **Simonsvlei** (Brandy); Lovane (Cabernet sauvignon); Klein Amoskuil (Grenache blanc) **D** Thor (Chenin blanc wooded, dry)

Sparkling, Méthode ancestrale

★★★★★☆ Vondeling

★★★★ Bushmanspad; Cage Wine; **Camberley**; Deep Rooted; Ken Forrester; Metzer; Natasha Williams; Nieuwedrift; **Rebel Rebel**; Scali

★★★★ **Bushmanspad** (5); Elemental Bob (Perlé); Upland (Organic); Vino pH ★★★ Bushmanspad (2) **NT** AA Badenhorst; Bushmanspad (5); Daschbosch; Lubanzi **D** Botanica (2)

Sparkling, Méthode cap classique, red, dry

NT Camberley; Mount Babylon

Sparkling, Méthode cap classique, red, off-dry/semi-sweet

★★★★ Kleine Zalze

Sparkling, Méthode cap classique, rosé, dry

★★★★★☆ Ambeloui (2); Anthonij Rupert (2); Aristea; Bon Courage; Canto; Colmant; De Grendel; Domaine des Dieux; Graham Beck; Hidden Valley; Krone; Le Lude; Lourensford; Matthew Krone;

Nitida; Paul René; Pieter Ferreira; **Sandstone**; Steenberg; Viljoensdrift; Windfall

★★★★ Anthonij Rupert; Aurelia; Belle Rebelle; Bellevue; Black Elephant; Black Oystercatcher; Boschendal; Canto; Esona; Graham Beck; Groote Post; Haute Cabrière; House of BNG; Klein Roosboom; Kleine Zalze; KWV; L'Avenir; Lomond; Louisvale; Maison de Teijger; Miss Molly; Muratie; Org de Rac (Fairtrade; Organic); Packwood; Piekenierskloof; Rickety Bridge; Saltare; Silverthorn; Simonsig; Spier; Tanzanite; The Drift; Van Loveren; Villiera; Waterkloof; Wildekrans; Woolworths (2)

★★★☆ Bein; **Cape Dreams**; Clos Malverne; Darling Cellars; Dieu Donné; Hoopenburg; Kanu; Kruger Family; Longridge; Lord's; Maastricht; Mimosa; **Neethlingshof**; Perdeberg; Pongrácz; Sumaridge; Van Hunks ★★★ Bemind; Koelenhof; Misty Mountains; Quest **NT** Allée Bleue; Bayede!; Charles Fox (3); Dainty Bess; Franschhoek Cellar; Genevieve; Graham Beck; Grande Provence; Groot Constantia; Lodestone; Lovane; My Wyn; Newstead; Plettenvale; **Simonsvlei**; **Slaley**; Strandveld; Teubes; Webersburg **D** African Pride; Cape Town Wine Co; Graham Beck; Hazendal; Hillock; Lievland; Wildehurst

Sparkling, Méthode cap classique, rosé, off-dry/semi-sweet

★★★★ Graham Beck; Krone; Simonsig
★★★☆ **Kleine Zalze**; Pongrácz (Lower in Alcohol); Woolworths

Sparkling, Méthode cap classique, white, dry

★★★★★ Anthonij Rupert; Babylonstoren; **Graham Beck** (2); Le Lude (2); Silverthorn; Spier
★★★★☆ Alvi's Drift; Ambeloui; Anura; Aristea; Bartho Eksteen; Belle Rebelle; Benguela Cove; Black Elephant (4); Bon Courage (2); Boschendal (2); Canto; Cederberg; Chamonix; Chantelle; Charles Fox; Colmant (4); DeMorgenzon; Domaine des Dieux; Graham Beck (3); Haute Cabrière; Hidden Valley; House of BNG; Huis van Chevallerie (Old Vines); Jordan; Kay & Monty; Klein Constantia; Klein Roosboom; **Krone** (6); KWV; La Bri; La Motte; Le Grand Domaine; **Le Lude** (4); Lourensford (2); Maison; Maison de Teijger; Matthew Krone; Mount Babylon; Mulderbosch; Nico van der Merwe; Noble Hill; Paul René; Pieter Ferreira (2); Pongrácz (2); Quoin Rock; Saltare; **Sandstone**; Saronsberg; Silverthorn (3); Simonsig; Steenberg (2); **Stellenview**; Stony Brook; Tanzanite; The House of GM&AHRENS; Thelema; Tierhoek; Tokara; Vergelegen; Villiera; Waterford; Waterkloof; Weltevrede (2); Windfall; Woolworths

★★★★ Allée Bleue; Alvi's Drift; Ambeloui; Anthonij Rupert; Aurelia; Birthmark of Africa; Bitou; Boschendal; Bosman Family (Old Vines); Cavalli; Clouds; **Constantia Uitsig**; Darling Cellars (2); De Grendel; Delaire Graff; Du Preez; Durbanville Hills; Fairview; Gabriëlskloof; Glen Carlou; Graham Beck; Groot Phesantekraal; Groote Post; Haute Cabrière; Hawksmoor; **Hermit on the Hill**; Hillock; Hoopenburg; House of BNG; Hout Bay; Idun (2); **Jakkalsvlei**; **Jason's Hill**; Jean Daneel; Kanu; Ken Forrester (Old Vines); **Klein Goederust**; Klein Roosboom; Kleine Zalze (2); Krone; KWV; Lanzerac; **Lomond** (2); Longridge (Organic); Lord's (2); Louisvale; Lyngrove; Marklew; Meerendal; Miss Molly; Morgenhof; My Wyn; **Neethlingshof**; Niel Joubert; Nieuwedrift; Nitida; Plaisir; Pongrácz; Pulpit Rock; **Quoin Rock**; Rhebokskloof; Rickety Bridge; Saltare; Saxenburg; Signal Gun; Silverthorn; Spier; Stanford Hills; Stellenbosch Hills; Stettyn; **Survivor**; The House of JC le Roux; Val de Vie; Van Loveren; Vergenoegd; Villiera (3); Wildeberg; Wildehurst (2); Wildekrans; **Woolworths** (3)

★★★☆ Arendskloof; Asara; Avontuur; **Bé a Daisy**; Blaauwklippen; Bloemendal; CvD Wines; Dieu Donné; Four Paws; **iL Geco**; **Khulu**; Koelenhof; Leopard's Leap; Longridge (Organic); **Merwida**; Mooiplaas; Nuy; Packwood; Perdeberg (Old Vines); **Rockbelt**; Simonsig; **Spijkerbessie**; Van Hunks; Waverley Hills (Organic); Woolworths

★★★ Bemind; Dragonridge; **Hillock**; Quest **NT** Arendskloof; **Camberley** (2); Canto; Charles Fox (4); Constantia Uitsig; Croydon; De Wet; Delheim; Die Mas; Dragonridge; Foothills; Franschhoek Cellar; Genevieve (2); Graham Beck (4); Grande Provence; Huis van Chevallerie (2); Imbuko; Kay & Monty; Klein Constantia; Lazanou (Organic); Lowerland; Mellasat; Miss Molly; My Wyn; Nederburg; Newstead; Olsen; Packwood; Peter Falke; Rickety Bridge; Rijk's; Saltare (2); Ses'Fikile; **Simonsvlei**; Snow Mountain; Son of the Soil; Spookfontein; Swanepoel; Tanzanite; Teubes; The House of GM&AHRENS; Topiary; Walker Bay Estate; Webersburg **D** Beau Joubert; Boland; Botanica; Cape Town Wine Co; Graham Beck (3); Hazendal (Lower in Alcohol); Knorhoek; Maison de Teijger; Org de Rac (Organic); Riebeek Valley; Skaap; Welbedacht; Woolworths

Sparkling, Méthode cap classique, white, off-dry/semi-sweet

★★★★☆ Krone

★★★★ Darling Cellars; Haute Cabrière; KWV; Pongrácz; Simonsig; **Villiera**
★★★☆ Boschendal; Graham Beck; Havana Hills; Woolworths

Sparkling, Non-MCC, red, dry
★★☆ The House of JC le Roux **D** D'Aria

Sparkling, Non-MCC, red, off-dry/semi-sweet
★★ Robertson **NT** O'Connell's

Sparkling, Non-MCC, rosé, dry
★★★★ Alvi's Drift

★★★☆ Belle Rebelle; Boplaas; **Daschbosch**;
Hill & Dale; Kloovenburg; Mulderbosch; Stettyn
★★★ D'Aria; Durbanville Hills; **Haute Cabrière**;
Hoopenburg; Stellar (Fairtrade; Organic);
Stellenbosch Hills; Van Loveren; Vredenheim;
Woolworths★★★ **Riebeek Valley** ★★ Bonnievale;
Robertson **NT** Huis van Chevallerie; Nico Vermeulen;
Robertson (Lower in Alcohol); **Simonsvlei**;
Summerhill **D** Graham Beck

**Sparkling, Non-MCC, rosé, off-dry/
semi-sweet**
★★★ Goedverwacht; Overhex (Lower in Alcohol);
The House of JC le Roux; Viljoensdrift★★★ Bon
Courage; Domein Doornkraal (Lower in Alcohol);
House of BNG; Klawer; Koelenhof; **Landzicht**
(Lower in Alcohol); Lutzville (Lower in Alcohol);
Nicholson Smith; Orange River; **Perdeberg** (Lower
in Alcohol); Rooiberg (Lower in Alcohol); Swartland;
Woolworths ★★ KWV (3) (Low Alcohol); Nuy;
Robertson (Lower in Alcohol); The House of JC
le Roux (2) (Low Alcohol) ★★ Darling Cellars
(De-Alcoholised); **Robertson NT** Ashton; Rietvallei
D Perdeberg; Woolworths

Sparkling, Non-MCC, white, dry
★★★★ Alvi's Drift; Botha; MAN Family

★★★☆ Belle Rebelle; Dalla Cia; Lyngrove;
Mulderbosch; Rhebokskloof; Steenberg; Vondeling;
Woolworths ★★★ **Daschbosch; Du**
Toitskloof; Hill & Dale; Leopard's Leap (2); Merwida;
Nicholson Smith; Orange River; Overhex; Raka;
Rooiberg; Slanghoek; Stellar (Fairtrade; Organic);
Stellenbosch Hills; Welmoed; Woolworths★★★☆
KWV; Lautus (De-Alcoholised); Riebeek Valley;
Swartland; Tulbagh Winery; **Woolworths** (2)
(De-Alcoholised; Fairtrade; Organic) ★★ Bonnievale;
Robertson (De-Alcoholised); The House of JC le Roux
NT Absolute Style; Ashton; D'Aria; Durbanville Hills;
Foothills; Havana Hills; **Libby's Pride**; Nederburg;
Nico Vermeulen; Opstal; Riebeek Valley; Rietvallei;
Robertson; **Simonsvlei**; Solara (Organic); Stellenrust
D Daschbosch; Diemersdal; Woolworths (2)
(Organic)

**Sparkling, Non-MCC, white, off-dry/
semi-sweet**
★★★★ Krone; Paul René

★★★☆ Orange River ★★★ Badsberg (Lower in
Alcohol); House of BNG (Perlé); Orange River★★☆
Breëland; Koelenhof; KWV; Nuy; **Perdeberg** (Lower
in Alcohol); Slanghoek; The House of JC le Roux
★★ KWV (Lower in Alcohol); Robertson (Lower in
Alcohol); The House of JC le Roux (2) (Low Alcohol)
NT Durbanville Hills; O'Connell's (Lower in Alcohol);
Sarah's; **Simonsvlei D** Perdeberg; Woolworths

Special Late Harvest
★★★☆ Bon Courage; Van Loveren ★★★ De Wet
NT Meerhof

Sun wine
★★★★☆ Tierhoek (Vin de paille/straw wine)
★★★★ Diemersfontein (Vin de paille/straw wine)

Sweet red
★★★ Cape Classics (2); De Villiers; Kirabo; Roos
Family★★★ Darling Cellars; Imbuko; La RicMal;
Stellar (Fairtrade; Organic); Tulbagh Winery;
Wineways (2) ★★ Mara (Lower in Alcohol; Perlé);
Robertson ★★ Perdeberg (2) **NT** Ashton; Aufwaerts;
Sarah's (2); Woolworths

Sylvaner
★★★★ Overgaauw

Tannat
★★★★☆ Lieben; Lowerland

★★★★ Arendskloof; Kranskop; **Landzicht**; Mooi
Bly; Piekenierskloof

★★★ **Landzicht NT** Du'SwaRoo; Glen Carlou

Tempranillo/tinta roriz
★★★★☆ Hughes Family (Organic); Niel Joubert;
Sijnn; Tempel

★★★★ Anura; **Atlas Swift; Baleia**; Mellasat;
Stony Brook; Thorngrove

★★★☆ Axe Hill; Olivedale; Sanniesrust **NT** De
Krans; Dornier

Therona
★★★★☆ Stellenbosch Vineyards

Tinta barocca
★★★★☆ Momento; Sadie

★★★★ Allesverloren; **City on a Hill**; Dornier;
Kruger Family

★★★☆ Boplaas; Hofstraat; **TTT Cellar**; Woolworths
★★★ Du'SwaRoo★★★ Swartland **NT** AA
Badenhorst (Old Vines); Calitzdorp; Micu Narunsky;
The Fledge **D** Cape Collective; City on a Hill;
Elemental Bob; Peter Bayly

Touriga franca
NT The Fledge

Touriga nacional

★★★★☆ Boplaas; De Krans; JC Wickens

★★★★ Axe Hill; Boplaas; Micu Narunsky; Olivedale; Sijnn; Woolworths

★★★☆ Bergsig ★★★ Du'SwaRoo; **TTT Cellar NT** Allesverloren; Calitzdorp; Joostenberg (Organic); Overgaauw

Trincadeira/tinta amarela

★★★★ Sijnn

NT Charla Haasbroek

Vegan

★★★★★ Cap Maritime (Chardonnay wooded); Fairview (Red blends, shiraz/syrah-based); Boekenhoutskloof (2) (Cabernet sauvignon; Red blends, shiraz/syrah-based)

★★★★☆ Cap Maritime (Pinot noir); Woolworths (Shiraz/syrah); Spier (10) (Red blends, Cape Bordeaux; White blends, wooded, dry; Cabernet sauvignon; Pinotage; Chenin blanc wooded, dry; Sauvignon blanc unwooded; Red blends, Cape Bordeaux; Red blends, with pinotage; Red blends, shiraz/syrah-based; White blends, unwooded, dry; Old Vines); Woolworths (Chardonnay wooded); Perdeberg (2) (Red blends, Cape Bordeaux; Red blends, with pinotage); Groote Post (2) (Merlot; Red blends, shiraz/syrah-based); Stellenbosch Vineyards (Therona); Fairview (Red blends, other); Flagstone (2) (Chenin blanc wooded, dry; Sauvignon blanc unwooded; Old Vines); Paul Clüver (Chardonnay wooded; Old Vines); Flagstone (3) (Cabernet sauvignon; Pinotage; Shiraz/syrah); Boekenhoutskloof (4) (Cabernet sauvignon; Shiraz/syrah; Semillon wooded; Noble Late Harvest; Old Vines; Organic); La Motte (2) (Shiraz/syrah; Sauvignon blanc unwooded); Flagstone (2) (Viognier; White blends, wooded, dry); Paul Clüver (Sauvignon blanc wooded); Baleia (Shiraz/syrah); La Motte (2) (Shiraz/syrah; Sparkling, Méthode cap classique, white, dry); Keermont (9) (Shiraz/syrah; Shiraz/syrah; Chenin blanc wooded, dry; Cabernet sauvignon; Merlot; Shiraz/syrah; Red blends, other; White blends, wooded, dry; Vin de paille/straw wine; Old Vines); Neil Ellis (4) (Cabernet sauvignon; Shiraz/syrah; Sauvignon blanc unwooded; Sauvignon blanc unwooded); Cecilia (Shiraz/syrah); Lievland (2) (Cabernet sauvignon; Shiraz/syrah)

★★★★ Woolworths (3) (Red blends, Cape Bordeaux; Red blends, other; Chenin blanc wooded, dry); Spier (5) (Rosé dry; Chenin blanc unwooded dry; Sauvignon blanc unwooded; Pinotage; Chardonnay wooded; Organic); Perdeberg (3) (Cabernet sauvignon; Pinotage; Red blends, shiraz/syrah-based); **Groote Post** (Pinot noir); Spier (2) (Sparkling, Méthode cap classique, rosé, dry; Sparkling, Méthode cap classique, white, dry); Groote Post (4) (Merlot; Shiraz/syrah; Riesling; Sauvignon blanc unwooded); Flagstone (5) (Pinot noir; Red blends, Cape Bordeaux; Red blends, with pinotage; Chenin blanc wooded, dry; Sauvignon blanc unwooded); Stellenbosch Vineyards (Chenin blanc wooded, dry); Groote Post (Red blends, other); Idun (2) (Sparkling, Méthode cap classique, white, dry; Sparkling, Méthode cap classique, white, dry); Swanepoel (4) (Pinotage; Shiraz/syrah; Rosé dry; White from red/black grapes (not Blanc de noir)); Kershaw (Pinot noir); La Motte (Chardonnay wooded); Keermont (Cabernet franc); La Motte (3) (Cabernet sauvignon; Red blends, Cape Bordeaux; Rosé dry); Groote Post (2) (Sparkling, Méthode cap classique, rosé, dry; Sparkling, Méthode cap classique, white, dry); Aurelia (2) (Sparkling, Méthode cap classique, rosé, dry; Sparkling, Méthode cap classique, white, dry); Lievland (2) (Pinotage; Rosé dry)

★★★★ Woolworths (5) (Merlot; Red blends, Cape Bordeaux; Red blends, Cape Bordeaux; Red blends, other; Sauvignon blanc unwooded); Spier (4) (Shiraz/syrah; Red blends, shiraz/syrah-based; Cabernet sauvignon; Shiraz/syrah; Organic); Perdeberg (Shiraz/syrah); Spier (Sauvignon blanc unwooded); **Perdeberg** (3) (Cinsaut; Grenache noir; Pinotage); **Germanier** (3) (Red blends, shiraz/syrah-based; Chardonnay wooded; Red blends, other; Organic); Groote Post (2) (Rosé dry; Chenin blanc unwooded dry); Flagstone (2) (Pinotage; Chardonnay wooded); Cape Wine Company (Pinotage); Stellenbosch Vineyards (Chardonnay unwooded); Groote Post (White blends, unwooded, dry); Swanepoel (2) (Grenache noir; Red blends, shiraz/syrah-based); La Motte (Sauvignon blanc unwooded); Leeuwenberg (Sauvignon blanc unwooded); Arniston Bay (Sauvignon blanc unwooded; Fairtrade); Upland (Pinot noir; Organic); Konkelberg (Red blends, with pinotage); Porcupine Ridge (2) (Cabernet sauvignon; Sauvignon blanc unwooded); The Wolftrap (2) (Red blends, shiraz/syrah-based; White blends, wooded, dry); Welmoed (5) (Cabernet sauvignon; Chardonnay wooded; Chenin blanc unwooded dry; Pinot gris/grigio; Sauvignon blanc unwooded) ★★★ Woolworths (White blends, unwooded, dry); Spier (2) (Chardonnay wooded; Chenin blanc unwooded dry); Perdeberg (Malbec); **Germanier** (5) (Cabernet sauvignon; Pinotage; Pinotage; Rosé dry; White blends, unwooded, dry; Organic); Cape Wine Company (Pinotage); **Germanier** (White blends, unwooded, dry; Organic); Durbanville Hills (2) (Pinotage; Rosé dry); Perdeberg (2) (Cabernet sauvignon; Pinotage);

Swanepoel (2) (Cabernet sauvignon; Mourvèdre);
Arniston Bay (2) (Shiraz/syrah; Rosé dry; Fairtrade);
Konkelberg (Sauvignon blanc unwooded); Porcupine
Ridge (2) (Merlot; Chardonnay wooded); Welmoed
(4) (Merlot; Pinotage; Rosé dry; Sparkling, Non-MCC,
white, dry)★★★ Perdeberg (4) (Merlot; Shiraz/syrah;
Sauvignon blanc unwooded; Pinotage) ★★ Perdeberg
(3) (Rosé off-dry/semi-sweet; Sweet red; Sweet red)
NT Woolworths (2) (Shiraz/syrah; Sauvignon blanc
wooded); Spier (4) (Cinsaut; Albariño; Chenin blanc
unwooded dry; Riesling); Woolworths (Merlot); Paul
Clüver (Noble Late Harvest; Lower in Alcohol); Cape
Wine Company (8) (Grenache noir; Merlot; Pinotage;
Shiraz/syrah; Red blends, shiraz-syrah-based; Rosé
dry; Chenin blanc unwooded dry; Sauvignon blanc
unwooded; Fairtrade); The Fledge (2) (Touriga franca;
Colombard); Porcupine Ridge (Chenin blanc unwooded
dry); **Cape Wine Company** (2) (Red blends, Cape
Bordeaux; White blends, unwooded, dry; Fairtrade;
Organic) **D** Woolworths (3) (Cabernet sauvignon; Rosé
dry; Sauvignon blanc unwooded); Groote Post (2)
(Chardonnay wooded; Chardonnay unwooded)

Verdelho
★★★★☆ De Krans; Deep Rooted (Alternative
white/red); Jasper Raats (Organic); Kirabo; **Opstal**;
Stellenbosch Vineyards

★★★★ Arbeidsgenot; **Arno Smith**; Tembela
★★★☆ Boplaas; **TTT Cellar**★★★ Fairview ★★
Du'SwaRoo **NT** Arcangeli; Glen Carlou; Org de Rac
(Organic); Thelema

Vermentino
★★★★☆ Ayama; Morgenster; Nomoya; Sakkie
Mouton

★★★★ Bacco

★★★☆ Ayama **NT** Sijnn

Vin de paille/straw wine
★★★★★ Mullineux (Lower in Alcohol); Savage
★★★★☆ Botanica; Bouchard Finlayson (Lower
in Alcohol); De Trafford; Donkiesbaai; Flagstone;
Foothills; Keermont; Klawer (Lower in Alcohol; Old
Vines); Meerhof; Orange River; **Rickety Bridge**
(Old Vines); Simonsig; Stellar (Lower in Alcohol;
Fairtrade; Organic); Tierhoek (Sun wine); Vondeling
★★★★ Asara; Diemersfontein (Sun wine);
Meinert; Piekenierskloof (Old Vines); Wildehurst
★★★☆ Darling Cellars; Elgin Vintners; Fairview
★★★ Dragonridge **NT** Angus Paul (Lower in
Alcohol); Boplaas; DeMorgenzon; Fairview; Maison;
Môreson; Mullineux (2) (Lower in Alcohol); Radford
Dale; Vergelegen; Villiersdorp; Zevenwacht **D** Alheit
(Lower in Alcohol; Old Vines); Clairvaux; Mellasat

Viognier
★★★★★ Lourensford
★★★★☆ Asara; Beau Constantia;
Buitenverwachting; Flagstone; Idiom; La Bri;
Marianne; Mary le Bow; Richard Hilton; Ridgeback;
Tamboerskloof; The Fledge; The Foundry
★★★★ Arendsig; Arra; Babylonstoren; **Bruce
Jack**; Capelands; De Grendel (Organic); Eagles' Nest;
Fairview; Franki's; Hughes Family (Fairtrade); Kanu;
La Petite Ferme; Lynx; Maison; Mellasat; Noble
Hill; Painted Wolf; **Richard Hilton**; Saronsberg;
Waterkloof (Organic); Wildehurst
★★★☆ Axe Hill; **Esona**; Excelsior; **Kusafiri**
(Organic); Lynx; Mont du Toit; **Morgenhof**; Silkbush;
Spotswood; Swartland; **Welbedacht**; Woolworths
★★★ Ayama; Chennells; Manley; Piekenierskloof
NT Bezalel; Black Elephant; Blue Crane; Charla
Haasbroek; Chennells; Creation; Diemersdal; Dieu
Donné; Dragonridge; Dunstone; Eerste Hoop;
Foothills; Koueberg; Kranskop; Lazanou (Organic);
Leipzig; Lomond; Lowerland; Mitre's Edge; My Wyn;
Schalkenbosch (2); Sijnn; Strandveld; Whalehaven
D Bellingham; Mountain Ridge; Painted Wolf;
Richard Hilton

Viura/macabeo/macabeu/maccabéo
★★★★☆ Pilgrim

White blends, off-dry/semi-sweet (w & u/w)
★★★ Du Toitskloof; Leopard's Leap; Overhex;
Stellenrust (Fairtrade); Villiera; Zevenwacht★★★
Darling Cellars; Landzicht (Lower in Alcohol);
Leopard's Leap; Picardi; Robertson; Slanghoek
(Lower in Alcohol); Stellar (Fairtrade; Organic);
Tulbagh Winery; Two Oceans ★★ Perdeberg **NT**
Aufwaerts; Bitou; Imbuko (Lower in Alcohol;
Fairtrade; Perlé); Robertson **D** Perdeberg;
Welbedacht

White blends, unwooded, dry
★★★★☆ **Creation**; Daschbosch; Kleine Zalze;
Naudé (Old Vines); Spier; Sumaridge; The Giant
Periwinkle

★★★★ Bouchard Finlayson; Cape Moby;
Eenzaamheid; Klein Amoskuil (Fairtrade); MAN
Family; Paserene; Springfontein (Organic);
Strydom; Sumaridge; Thor; Truter Family; **Walker
Bay Estate** (2); Woolworths

★★★☆ Aaldering; Beyerskloof; Blue Crane; Bon
Courage; Camberley; Cecilia; Doran; Four Paws;
Goats do Roam; Groote Post; Haute Cabrière;
Imbuko; Mont Rochelle; Olivedale; Overhex;
Piekenierskloof (Fairtrade); Pulpit Rock; Slaley (Old
Vines); Stellenrust (Fairtrade); The Earth Beneath
Our Feet; Thelema; Val du Charron (2); Villiera;

Wildehurst; Woolworths (3) ★★★ Allée Bleue; Darling Cellars; **Du'SwaRoo**; Flagstone; **Germanier** (2) (Organic); KWV; Opstal; **Overhex** (2); Rascallion (Old Vines); Rhebokskloof; Riebeek Valley; Robertson (2); Ses'Fikile; Slanghoek; Stellar (Fairtrade; Organic); Stellenbosch Hills; **Thor**; TTT Cellar; Val du Charron; Van Loveren; Villiersdorp; Waverley Hills (Organic); Woolworths (7) (Fairtrade; Organic); Zidela (2) ★★☆ Aan de Doorns; Blake; Leopard's Leap (2); Namaqua; O'Connell's; Renegade (Perlé); Stellar (Fairtrade; Organic); Tulbagh Winery (Lower in Alcohol); Woolworths (2) (Lower in Alcohol); Zandvliet ★★ Nuy; Theescombe **NT** AA Badenhorst (Skin-macerated white); **Ashton**; Babylon's Peak; Badger; Beau Joubert; Bezuidenhout Family (2); **Cape Wine Company** (Fairtrade; Organic); Chameleon; Darling Cellars; **De Wet**; Drostdy-Hof (Lower in Alcohol); Foothills; Kanu; La RicMal; Lazanou (Organic); Lodestone; Merwida; Mountain River; Pounding Grape; **Rascallion**; Rosendal; Simonsvlei (2); Skipskop; Somersbosch; Stellendrift; Stettyn; Viljoensdrift; Wavescape; Woolworths (3); Zonnebloem **D** Drostdy-Hof; Frater; GlenWood; Hazendal; Kumala; Le Manoir de Brendel; Mellasat; Mooiplaas; Simonsig; Welbedacht; Wineways (2)

White blends, wooded, dry

★★★★★ Beaumont; Bellingham; Brookdale; Constantia Glen; Delaire Graff; Fairview; Groot Constantia; Kershaw; Mullineux (Old Vines); Rall; Sadie (3) (Old Vines); Steenberg; The Ahrens Family; The Grapesmith; Thelema; Thorne & Daughters

★★★★☆ Alheit; Alvi's Drift; Anthonij Rupert; Anysbos; Aristea; Asara; Ashbourne; Babylon's Peak; Beau Constantia; Bizoe; Black Oystercatcher; Boplaas; **Brookdale**; Bruwer Vintners; **Cape Point** (2); Carstens; Cavalli; Cederberg; Celestina; Chamonix; Cilmor; Constantia Royale; Constantia Uitsig; Creation; David & Nadia; De Grendel; DeMorgenzon; Durbanville Hills; Flagstone; Grande Provence; Highlands Road; Holden Manz; Hughes Family (3) (Organic); Jean Daneel; Joostenberg (Organic); Keermont; **Kindred Coast**; Kloovenburg; Kumusha; Lemberg; Lomond; Lourens Family; Lourensford; Luddite; Maanschijn; McFarlane; Meerhof; Miles Mossop; Momento; Morgenster; **Mullineux**; Neil Ellis (Alternative white/red); Nico van der Merwe; Nitida; Noble Hill; Olifantsberg; Org de Rac (Fairtrade; Organic); Patatsfontein; Paul Roos; Perdeberg; Sakkie Mouton; Savage; Saxenburg; Sijnn; Spier; Springfontein; Stark-Condé; Strandveld; Swartberg; Tempel (Old Vines); The Fledge; The Grapesmith; Themika; Thiart; Thistle & Weed; Tokara; Trizanne; Twee Jonge Gezellen; Van

Niekerk Vintners; Van Wyk; Vergelegen; Vondeling; Vuurberg; Wade Bales; Waterkloof; Wildeberg; Zevenwacht; Zorgvliet

★★★★ Afrikaans; Asara; At se Wyn; Babylonstoren; Badsberg; Beau Constantia; Bergsig; Blackwater; Blake; Bloemendal; Boland; Boschendal; Bosman Family (Fairtrade; Organic); Buitenverwachting; Cage Wine; Cape Collective; Capelands; Cilmor; Eerste Hoop; Elgin Vintners; Fram; **Hazendal**; Huis van Chevallerie; Jakkalsvlei; JAN Wines; Khayelitsha's Finest; KleinSering; KWV; Lanzerac; **Le Grand Domaine** (Fairtrade; Organic); Leipzig; **Lomond** (2); Lowerland; Muratie (2); My Wyn; Nabygelegen (2); Neethlingshof; Nuiba; Oldenburg; Olivedale (Alternative white/red; Skin-macerated white); Painted Wolf; Piekenierskloof; **Pulpit Rock**; Quoin Rock (2); Rascallion; Rickety Bridge; Saxenburg; Scions of Sinai (2) (Skin-macerated white); Silkbush; Spier (Organic); Spioenkop; Spookfontein; Stellenbosch Hills; Stony Brook; Terracura (2); The Earth Beneath Our Feet; Villion; Wildeberg (Old Vines); **Wildekrans**; **Woolworths**

★★★☆ Axe Hill; Cape Rock; **Caravel**; Darling Cellars; Jacaranda (Skin-macerated white); Kruger Family; **La Bri**; My Wyn; Namaqua; Painted Wolf; Roodekrantz; The Wolftrap; Van Loveren ★★★ Bellpost; **Overhex**; TTT Cellar★★☆ Elgin Vintners ★★ Late Bloomer **NT** AA Badenhorst; African Pride; Alphabetical (2); **André van Rensburg**; Benguela Cove; Bitou; Brunia; Cape Rock; Creation; Croydon; Darling Cellars; ?David Finlayson; De Kleine Wijn Koöp; De Wet; Dornier; Dragonridge; Durbanville Hills; Fuselage (2); Glen Carlou (2); Hazendal; Kusafiri (Organic); La Petite Ferme; Malanot; Mother Rock; Mullineux; My Wyn; Openwine; Safriel; **Simonsvlei** (2); Spier; Steenberg; The Drift; The Giant Periwinkle; Tulbagh Winery; Villiersdorp; Whiley; Wightman & Sons **D** City on a Hill; Drostdy-Hof; Elemental Bob; Hidden Valley; Liz Ogumbo; Painted Wolf; Rascallion; Rickety Bridge; Rietvallei; Shannon

White from red/black grapes (not Blanc de noir)

★★★★☆ ArtiSons (Old Vines); Springfontein

★★★★ Meinert; Swanepoel

★★★☆ Mellasat ★★★ Asara ★★☆ Wellington Winery **NT** Libby's Pride; Stanford Hills

Zinfandel/Primitivo

★★★★ Blaauwklippen

★★★☆ Idiom

The Industry

Overview

South Africa in 2022 retained the 8th position on the International Organisation of Vine & Wine (OIV) ranking of the leading wine-producing nations by volume, ahead of Germany and Portugal but behind New World rivals Australia, Chile and Argentina. Italy, with a stable 19.3% share of global production, remained the number one producer, again followed by France with a much-increased 17.7%, Spain near-unchanged at 13.8% and the US, whose output dipped slightly to 8.7%. South Africa, with 1,020 m litres, in 2022 contributed 3.9% to global volume, compared with 4.1% the year before.

The number of wine-grape growers in South Africa continued to decline in 2022 (2,487 vs 2,613 in 2021), along with the hectares under vine (89,384 vs 90,512). The overall number of wine cellars crushing grapes dipped to 524 after a slight rise last count, though the total of private cellars was effectively unchanged at 458, as was producing wholesalers crushing grapes, at 23, mirroring the co-operative – officially 'producer cellar' – sector which remained level at 43.

Boutique ventures, vinifying less than 100 tons, slipped from 224 to 213 yet remained the largest single category at 40.7% and a major driver in the industry.

Vineyards

According to adjusted official numbers, the hectares established in 2022 were 1,865, a little more than

last. Planting for red wine again outstripped white, this time by a bigger margin (1,023 ha vs 843), with shiraz (208 ha) now the first-choice black grape for planting, followed by cabernet sauvignon (179), pinotage (170), and merlot (131).

Chenin blanc (204) lost its long-term spot as most-planted white variety to sauvignon blanc (268) in 2022, followed by chardonnay (202), colombard (72) and pinot gris (32). Adding insult to injury, chenin (669) also regained its longtime place from colombard (564) as most-uprooted variety, yet continued to have the largest footprint overall, with a largely steady 18.4% of the national vineyard's 89,384 ha. Cabernet remained the leading red, with a near-unchanged 10.6% share.

The percentage of very young vines (under 4 years) continued to rise, from 9.5 to 10.1, mirrored by an increase in the portion older than 20 years, from 31.5 to 33.5.

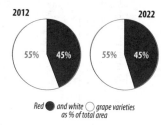

Red ⬤ and white ⬤ grape varieties as % of total area

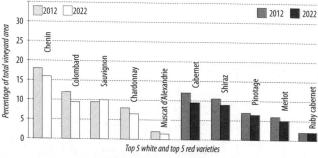

Top 5 white and top 5 red varieties

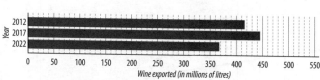

Wine exported (in millions of litres)

South African Wine Industry – Ten-Year Overview

	2013	2014	2015	2016	2017	2018	2019	2020	2021	2022
Number of wineries	564	559	566	568	546	542	533	529	536	524
Total vine area (excl sultana) (hectares)	99 687	99 472	98 594	95 775	94 545	93 021	92 067	92 005	90 512	89 384
Producing area 4 yrs & older (excl sultana) (hectares)	89 045	88 900	88 633	86 076	85 950	85 094	84 088	83 849	81 934	80 343
Avg yield (tons/hectare)	16.83	17.09	16.67	16.33	16.72	14.61	14.84	16.01	17.81	17.13
Grapes crushed (millions of tons)	1.50	1.52	1.48	1.41	1.44	1.24	1.25	1.34	1.46	1.38
Total production (millions of litres)	1 156.9	1 181.1	1 154.0	1 089.0	1 120.0	966.0	974.0	1 042.0	1 133.4	1 068.4
Domestic sales (millions of litres)	363.5	390.8	422.1	434.6	447.0	429.2	407.8	316.0	392.9	453.4
Consumption per capita (litres SA wine)	6.79	7.19	7.65	7.76	7.87	7.44	6.91	5.31	6.53	7.48
Export volume (millions of litres)	525.6	422.7	420.0	428.3	448.4	420.2	319.8	318.0	388.0	368.7

Exports

Exports of 369 m litres represented a slight dip below 2021's 388 m yet a satisfying improvement on the lows of 2019 and 2020. Some 40.4% of SA's total wine production went offshore in 2022, the 12-year average being 45% and the high 57.4% in 2013.

Sauvignon and chenin continued their reign as most-exported varietal wines (bottled and bulk), with chardonnay continuing its much-improved performance at 33 m. Red and white blends as well as pinks completed the top 5 spots. The UK, long the biggest consumer of SA wine (packaged and bulk), retained its thirst in 2022, followed by Germany, Canada, topping the US, and France, moving ahead of the Netherlands. For packaged wine only, once again it was the UK, followed by the Netherlands, Germany, turning the tables on Sweden, and the US.

Local wine consumption

According to revised statistics, SA's per-capita wine consumption recovered further to 7.48L in 2022 after plunging to 5.31L in 2020 amid Covid-induced alcohol bans and restrictions. As a result, wine's combined share (natural, fortified and sparkling) of the alcoholic beverages market edged higher to 16.7%. Whisky lost 0.5% share to end at 4.5%, the lowest in 17 years, while brandy also dipped, to 4%. Beer was more or less stable at 51.8% after dropping sharply in 2021.

For comparison, the top five wine-consuming nations (OIV figures for 2020, latest available) are: Portugal (51.9L per capita), Italy (46.6), France (46.0), Switzerland (35.7) and Austria (29.9).

Of natural wine sold domestically in 2022 (including locally bottled imports, de-alcoholised and low-alcohol wines), 36.5% was in glass (extending a downward trend), and of that 63.2% was in the standard 750-ml bottle. Burgeoning

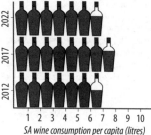

SA wine consumption per capita (litres)

bag-in-box rose to 48.6% of total sales, while plastic containers accounted for 9.7% and Tetra packs a much-increased 4.7%.

Sales of wine in aluminium cans, authorised as packaging in 2019, more than doubled in 2022 for a total of 1.4 m litres.

Note

Statistical data provided by SAWIS NPC.

Industry Organisations

Agricultural Ethical Trade Initiative See Wine & Agricultural Ethical Trade Association.

ARC Infruitec-Nietvoorbij Senior manager, research: prof Bongani Ndimba ▪ Winemaker: Craig Paulsen ▪ **T +27 (0)21-809-3091** ▪ PaulsenC@arc. agric.za ▪ Marketing & communications: Derusha Crank ▪ **T +27 (0)21-809-3100** ▪ PaulsenC@arc. agric.za, CrankD@arc.agric.za ▪ www.arc.agric.za

ARC Infruitec-Nietvoorbij focuses on research and development as well as technology transfer on the breeding, cultivation, protection and post-harvest technology of deciduous fruit, grape vines, alternative crops and indigenous herbal teas. Nietvoorbij, ARC's internationally acclaimed

research farm, is synonymous with quality research in oenology and viticulture. Annually, 1,000 small-batch wines are made for research purposes, along with commercial wines for sale to the public.

Biodiversity & Wine Initiative (BWI) See WWF-SA Conservation Champion Programme

Biodynamic & Organic Wines of South Africa (BOWSA) Chair: Alex Dale ▪ jeanne@radforddale. com ▪ **T +27 (0)21-846-8060** ▪ www.bowsa. co.za

Association aiming to help consumers and media easily see which local wine producers and grape growers are officially certified as biodynamic and organic.

Cap Classique Producers Association (CCPA)

Chair: Pieter Ferreira ▪ Marketing & info: Caroline van Schalkwyk ▪ marketing@capclassique.co.za ▪ www.capclassique.co.za

Established in 1992 by producers who share a passion for bottle-fermented sparkling wines, made according to the traditional method (méthode champenoise). The mandate of the CCPA is to promote South Africa's premium cap classique wines, as well as the common interests of the producers.

Cape Brandy Distillers Guild (CBDG) Founder:

Dave Hughes ▪ Trustees: Kobus Gelderblom & Charles Withington ▪ info@capebrandy.co.za ▪ www.capebrandy.co.za

Communication and promotion platform for positioning Cape Brandy which, since 2021, is the official descriptor for a brandy grown and made in the Cape using a process that mirrors that established by Cognac centuries ago. Rare and sought after, Cape Brandy accounts for less than 5% of brandy produced in SA. Members enjoy access to skills and expertise, and benefit from collective marketing and exposure under the Cape Brandy banner.

Cape Port Producers' Association (CAPPA)

Chair: Margaux Nel ▪ T +27 (0)44-213-3326 ▪ info@boplaas.co.za

Producer group aiming to further improve the quality and market for Cape 'ports' and Portuguese-variety table wines in SA.

Cape Winemakers Guild (CWG) Chair: Gordon

Newton Johnson ▪ General manager: Kate Jonker ▪ T +27 (0)21-852-0408 ▪ info@capewinemakersguild.com ▪ www.capewinemakersguild.com

Independent, invitation-only association, founded in 1982 to promote winemaking excellence among its members. Since 1985, the CWG has held an annual public auction of rare and unique wines, produced by its members exclusively for the auction. The Nedbank CWG Development Trust, established in 1999, supports social development in the winelands through its oenology and viticulture protégé programmes, Billy Hofmeyr AgriSeta bursaries and support of Wine Training South Africa.

Chardonnay Forum of South Africa Chair:

Johann de Wet ▪ johanndewet@dewetshof.com ▪ T +27 (0)23-615-1853

Producers and people creating awareness and stimulating interest in SA chardonnay among consumers, buyers, media and producers locally and internationally.

Chenin Blanc Association (CBA) Chair: Ken

Forrester ▪ T +27 (0)21-855-2374 / +27 (0)82-783-7203 ▪ ken@kenforresterwines.com ▪ www.chenin.co.za ▪ Manager: Christina Harvett +27 (0)76-523-8999 ▪ cheninblancasso@gmail.com ▪ Manager special projects: Ina Smith T +27 (0)82-467-4331 ▪ ina.smith.chenin@gmail.com ▪ @CheninBlancAsso

Formed in 2000 by a few concerned winemakers in response to dramatic decreases in plantings. The focus is to promote the variety and raise the image of chenin blanc.

Fairtrade Africa - Southern Africa Network

(FTA-SAN) Regional head: Zinhle Dlamini Ndlovu ▪ T +265 (0)99-374-7361 ▪ z.dlamini@fairtradeafrica.net ▪ www.fairtradeafrica.net

Fairtrade Africa (FTA) is the independent non-profit umbrella organisation representing all Fairtrade-certified producers in Africa. FTA is owned by its members, who are African producer organisations certified against international Fairtrade standards. The Southern Africa Network (SAN), located in Blantyre and Cape Town, is one of four FTA regional networks which represent Fairtrade-certified producers (smallholder farmers, farm-workers and -owners) in southern Africa. SAN provides technical support on Fairtrade standards; facilitates trade linkages and market access opportunities; advocates on behalf of and with its producers on relevant issues; and enhances knowledge and capacity around social and environmental issues.

Institute of Cape Wine Masters (ICWM)

Chai: Jacques Steyn ▪ T +27 (0)76-161-4600 ▪ Vice-chair: Mark Philp ▪ T +27 (0)82-566-6315 ▪ Secretary: Raymond Noppé ▪ T +27 (0)82-335-2020 ▪ info@icwm.co.za ▪ www.icwm.co.za

First instituted in 1983, Cape Wine Master is one of the most sought-after formal qualifications in SA wine. To date 110 candidates have qualified, and a further 3 have been awarded the title Honorary Cape Wine Master. The purpose of the ICWM is to harness the collective ability of CWMs to open the world of wine and brandy to others through education, and a deep understanding and passion for the wine industry.

Integrated Production of Wine (IPW) Manager:

Daniël Schietekat ▪ T +27 (0)21-889-6555 ▪ daniel@ipw.co.za ▪ www.ipw.co.za

Innovative, internationally recognised and widely supported initiative of the South African wine industry aimed at producing in an environmentally sustainable, profitable way by providing guidelines for both farm and cellar, embracing all aspects of grape production, winemaking, and biodiversity conservation. See also Sustainable Wine South Africa.

Méthode Cap Classique Producers' Association
See Cap Classique Producers Association

Muscadel SA Chair: Henri Swiegers ▪ T +27 (0)23-344-3021 ▪ henri@badsberg.co.za ▪ Vice-chair: André Scriven ▪ T +27 (0)23-626-1664 ▪ andres@rooiberg.co.za

Old Vine Project (OVP) Manager, marketing, communications: André Morgenthal ▪ T +27 (0)82-658-3883 ▪ andre@oldvineproject.co.za ▪ www.oldvineproject.co.za

Believing that old vines produce wines with a unique character – pure and delicate yet powerful – OVP strives to preserve as many of SA's 4,292 gnarled-vine hectares as possible, while creating a culture of helping young vineyards mature into stellar seniors. The Certified Heritage Vineyards seal which, affixed to a bottle, assures winelovers these wines are from genuinely venerable vines (35+ years) and reflects authenticity, traceability and integrity.

Pinotage Association Chair: Beyers Truter ▪ T +27 (0)21-865-1235 ▪ reception@beyerskloof.co.za ▪ Manager: Elsabé Ferreira ▪ T +27 (0)21-863-1599 ▪ admin@pinotage.co.za ▪ Marketing manager: Belinda Jacobs ▪ T +27 (0)79-879-9705 ▪ brand@pinotage.co.za ▪ www.pinotage.co.za

The Pinotage Association has, through the following aims, accepted responsibility to maintain South Africa's leading role in the production of quality pinotage wines: increasing the knowledge of its members about all aspects of cultivating pinotage grapes and vinifying pinotage wines; serving as a forum for exchanging ideas on producing and marketing pinotage; identifying problems relating to growing and making pinotage; and prioritising research needs regarding pinotage.

Sauvignon Blanc South Africa Chair: RJ Botha ▪ T +27 (0)21-880-0717 ▪ RJBotha@kleinezalze.co.za ▪ Contact: Eunice Joubert ▪ T +27 (0)82-808-1114 ▪ admin@sauvignonblanc.comm

Fosters excellence in making and marketing SA sauvignon blanc locally and internationally via members' networking, information exchange and wine competitions, including the annual FNB Sauvignon Blanc SA Top 10.

Shiraz South Africa Chair: Edmund Terblanche ▪ T +27 (0)82-770-2929 ▪ et.cellar@la-motte.co.za ▪

Secretary: Sandra Lotz ▪ T +27 (0)82-924-7254 ▪ info@shirazsa.co.za

Founded in 2008, and today representing more than 200 producers including all the wine routes, Shiraz SA aims to promote the image of wine produced from this noble grape, with the purpose of establishing acceptance and enjoyment of South African shiraz locally and internationally.

South Africa Wine Chair: Ronald Ramabulana ▪ CEO: Rico Basson ▪ Communications & brand manager: Wanda Augustyn ▪ T +27 (0)21-276-0429 ▪ wanda@sawine.co.za ▪ www.sawine.co.za

Newly established non-profit company that provides essential support services to the wine and brandy value chain with the vision to enable it to become more robust, transformed, agile and competitive. The purpose is to optimise diverse resources to deliver sustainable value to all stakeholders.

South African Brandy Foundation (SABF) Director: Christelle Reade-Jahn ▪ T +27 (0)64-754-6552 ▪ christelle@sabrandy.co.za ▪ www.sabrandy.co.za

A registered non-profit organisation representing more than 95% of local brandy producers, SABF facilitates long-term growth and helps preserve the integrity and heritage of the SA brandy industry.

South African Pinot Noir Association Chair: Andries Burger ▪ pinotnoirass@gmail.com ▪ T +27 (0)28-312-3515 ▪ Admin: Vanessa Hoek ▪ vanessa@wmg.co.za

Producer group aiming to further improve the general quality of local pinot noir still-wines by sharing ideas, and ultimately finding an identity for the variety in South Africa.

South African Sommeliers Association (SASA) Chair: Spencer Fondaumiere ▪ info@sommeliers.org.za

Non-profit organisation established in 2010 to promote a culture of fine wine, food and service, and provide a network portal for industry professionals. SASA offers four levels of certification to sommeliers, from Introductory to Diploma, to promote continuous development of professional standards at the highest level. SASA's services are available to sommeliers locally and internationally, and the organisation is dedicated to promoting excellence in the field of sommellerie.

SA Wine Industry Information & Systems NPC (SAWIS) Executive manager: Yvette van der Merwe ▪ T +27 (0)21-807-5700 ▪ info@sawis.co.za

Responsible for the collection, processing and dissemination of industry information. Administers the Wine of Origin (WO) system.

Southern Africa Fairtrade Network (SAFN) See Fairtrade Africa-Southern Africa Network

Stellenbosch Cabernet Collective (SCC) ▪ T +27(0)21-886-4310 ▪ wine@stellenboschcabernet.co.za ▪ www.stellenboschcabernet.co.za

A collective of producers who wish to promote and market Stellenbosch cabernet sauvignon locally and on the global stage. Through participation in and facilitation of key events, the SCC aims to allow Stellenbosch to compete against some of the world's leading cabernet-producing regions.

Sustainable Wine South Africa (SWSA) www.swsa.co.za ▪ Contact details as for individual organisations.

Alliance between the Wine & Spirit Board (WSB), Integrated Production of Wine (IPW), WWF-SA Conservation Champion Programme (CCP) and Wines of South Africa (WOSA), driving the industry's commitment to sustainable, eco-friendly production.

Swartland Independent Producers (SIP) Chair: Jasper Wickens ▪ T +27 (0)72-461-4249 ▪ swartland.independent@gmail.com ▪ www.swartlandindependent.co.za

Alliance of like-minded Swartland producers seeking to make wines that are a true expression of their Swartland origin. SIP members share a number of core values, such as natural vinification and minimal intervention, and follow an evolving set of guidelines covering vineyard and cellar practices.

Wine & Agricultural Ethical Trade Association (WIETA) CEO: Linda Lipparoni ▪ T +27 (0)21-880-0580 ▪ linda@wieta.org.za, info@wieta.org.za ▪ www.wieta.org.za

Multi-stakeholder, non-profit, voluntary organisation established in 2002 to promote ethical trade in wine and general agriculture. WIETA's members have adopted a code of ethical and labour standards for the wine industry. WIETA's main task is to support, enhance and promote members' ethical performance, encourage best practice and promote improved working conditions on farm and at the cellar through training, capacity-building projects and third-party ethical auditing. WIETA also issues a Fair Labour Certification seal on individual wines, which has been endorsed by the wine industry in recognition of wine supply chains' ethical commitment to good working conditions on farms and in cellars.

Wine & Spirit Board Chair: Matome Mbatha ▪ Executive manager: Olivia Poonah ▪ T +27 (0)21-889-6555 ▪ olivia@wsb.org.za

Administers the Wine of Origin, Estate Brandy and Integrated Production of Wine (IPW) schemes.

Wines of South Africa (WOSA) CEO: Siobhan Thompson ▪ Non-executive chair: Carina Gous ▪ info@wosa.co.za ▪ T +27 (0)21-883-3860 ▪ www.wosa.co.za

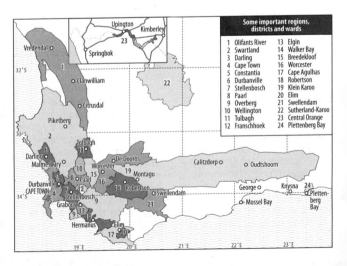

Some important regions, districts and wards	
1 Olifants River	13 Elgin
2 Swartland	14 Walker Bay
3 Darling	15 Breedekloof
4 Cape Town	16 Worcester
5 Constantia	17 Cape Agulhas
6 Durbanville	18 Robertson
7 Stellenbosch	19 Klein Karoo
8 Paarl	20 Elim
9 Overberg	21 Swellendam
10 Wellington	22 Sutherland-Karoo
11 Tulbagh	23 Central Orange
12 Franschhoek	24 Plettenberg Bay

Generic marketing organisation, responsible for raising the profile of SA wine in key export markets.

Wine Industry Network of Expertise & Technology (WINETECH) See South Africa Wine

WWF-SA Biodiversity & Wine Initiative See WWF-SA Conservation Champion Programme.

WWF-SA Conservation Champion Programme manager: Shelly Fuller ▪ T +27 (0)21-881-3086 ▪ sfuller@wwf.org.za ▪ Head of extension: Jacques van Rensburg ▪ T +27 (0) 21-881-3086 ▪ jvrensburg@wwf.org.za

In 2005 the Biodiversity & Wine Initiative (BWI) started as a world-leading partnership between the SA wine industry and the conservation sector to minimise further loss of threatened natural habitat in the Cape Floral Kingdom, and contribute to sustainable wine production through better environmental management practices on farm and in cellar. After 10 years of successful implementation, the needs of the membership base shifted to a more holistic approach of managing environmental risk. The BWI name fell away, and today consumers can support WWF-SA Conservation Champions by buying wines displaying the colourful sugarbird and protea logo, recognising industry leaders who have a strong commitment to biodiversity conservation and show continual improvement of production practices, energy-efficiency measures and water stewardship.

Winegrowing Areas

From modest beginnings in the Dutch East India Company's 17th-century gardens at the foot of Table Mountain, South Africa's vineyards now cover 89,384 ha and more than 100 official appellations.

Changes to the Wine of Origin (WO) scheme of 1972/3 saw 'geographical units' incorporated into the WO classification alongside 'regions', 'districts' and 'wards' (the latter have the smallest footprint of the WO areas, following earlier amendments to the 'estate' legislation). Recently these demarcations have been extended by the inclusion of 'overarching' geographical units and regions, and subregions.

Below are brief notes on the most noteworthy grape cultivation zones. Information is supplied by Wines of South Africa (WOSA) and SA Wine Industry Information & Systems NPC (SAWIS), and reflects 2022 data for the WO areas. Note: Area maps are not to the same scale.

Breedekloof Large (12,719 ha) Breede River Valley district producing mainly for the brandy industry and merchant trade, but also featuring some quality-focused boutiques, family estates and grower-owned ventures with ever-greater ambitions for pinotage, chenin, chardonnay and

Cape Town

1 Philadelphia 3 Cape Town 5 Constantia
2 Durbanville 4 Hout Bay

Paarl, Wellington & Franschhoek

1 Mid-Berg River 6 Blouvlei
2 Limietberg 7 Agter Paarl
3 Voor Paardeberg 8 Paarl
4 Groenberg 9 Simonsberg-Paarl
5 Bovlei 10 Franschhoek

Cape Agulhas, Elgin, Overberg & Walker Bay

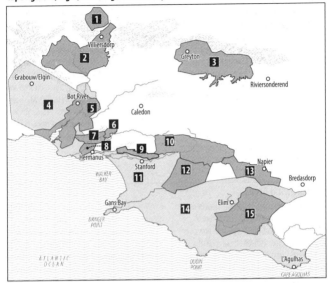

1 Elandskloof
2 Theewater
3 Greyton
4 Elgin

5 Bot River
6 Hemel-en-Aarde Ridge
7 Upper Hemel-en-Aarde
8 Hemel-en-Aarde Valley

9 Stanford Foothills
10 Klein River
11 Walker Bay
12 Sunday's Glen

13 Napier
14 Cape Agulhas
15 Elim

semillon, particularly from old vines. Major varieties (ha): chenin (2,803), colombard (1,782), sauvignon (1,465), pinotage (912), chardonnay (819). See under Robertson for climate, geology etc.

Cape Coast Overarching appellation for Cape South Coast and Coastal regions.

Cape South Coast 'Umbrella' region (2,611 ha) for Cape Agulhas, Elgin, Lower Duivenhoks River, Overberg, Plettenberg Bay, Swellendam and Walker Bay districts, and Herbertsdale, Napier and Stilbaai East wards.

Cape Town Maritime district (2,598 ha) incorporating Constantia, Durbanville, Hout Bay and Philadelphia wards, and vines in Cape Town city.

Cape West Coast First and only official subregion, part of the Coastal area, containing Darling and Lutzville Valley districts, and Bamboes Bay, Lamberts Bay and a portion of St Helena Bay wards.

Cederberg 102-ha standlone ward in the Cederberg Mountain range, with some of SA's remotest and highest vineyards (950-1,100 m). Mean February Temperature (MFT) 22.8°C; rain total/summer: 473/147 mm; geology: sandstone-derived alluvium

and colluvium. Best known for shiraz (18), chenin (17), sauvignon (16), cab (12) and bukettraube (11).

Central Orange River District (2,149 ha) on the Orange River (Gariep) banks in the Northern Cape Geographical Unit with wards Groblershoop, Grootdrink, Kakamas, Keimoes and Upington. Altitude: 500-1,000 m; temp 25.3°C; rain: 250/208 mm; granite, dolorite, shale, alluvial. Overwhelmingly a white-grape area but red plantings are increasing. Sultana (4,035), colombard (1,117), chenin (618), villard blanc (117), muscat d'Alexandrie (64).

Constantia Premium viticultural ward (422 ha) and cradle of SA winemaking on the eastern slopes of the Cape Peninsula, cooled by south-easterly sea breezes. Recognised for whites generally, notably sauvignon, semillon and muscat. Altitude: 100-300 m; temp 20.6°C; rain: 1,056/335 mm; geology: granite and sandstone. Major varieties: sauvignon (186), cab (40), merlot (30), shiraz (28), muscat blanc (25).

Darling District (2,557 ha) encircling the eponymous West Coast town, best known for the wines from higher-lying ward Groenekloof, long the source of top sauvignon; also a reputation for full-flavoured reds, especially shiraz; source of interesting young-gun bottlings. Altitude: 110 m; temp 22.7°C; rain: 586/173 mm; geology: granite. Groenekloof: sauvignon (475), cab (387), shiraz (328), pinotage (196), merlot (185).

Durbanville Ocean-tempered hilly ward (1,369 ha) in Cape Town district with reputation for sauvignon (540) and merlot (175). Cab (192), shiraz (139) and pinotage (110). Altitude: 150–350 m; temp 22.4°C; rain: 481/140 mm; geology: shale.

Elgin Cool upland district (721 ha) in Cape South Coast region producing many stellar aromatic whites and elegant reds. Altitude: 200–250 m; temp 19.7°C; rain: 1,011/366 mm; geology: shale (sandstone). Sauvignon (273), chardonnay (129), pinot noir (119), shiraz (47), cab (34).

Elim Maritime ward in Cape Agulhas district, its 154 ha of windswept vineyards arrayed around the old mission village of Elim near Africa's most southerly point. Sauvignon (87), shiraz (39), semillon (14), pinot noir (10), viognier (2).

Franschhoek Increasingly dynamic, and stylistically diverse, Coastal district with 1,153 ha under vine, perhaps best known for cab (173) and semillon (74), latter among SA's oldest vines. Chardonnay (178), sauvignon (171), shiraz (155), merlot (111).

Greater Cape Overarching Geographical Unit encompassing Eastern, Northern and Western Cape.

Hemel-en-Aarde See Walker Bay.

Klein Karoo Mostly scrubby semi-arid region (1,985 ha), reliant on irrigation. Recognised for 'ports' and fortifieds generally; increasingly a hunting ground for young terroirists. Calitzdorp district: colombard (62), muscat d'Alexandrie (59), chenin (44), tinta (13) and touriga (12). Tradouw ward: merlot (7), sauvignon (5), chardonnay and colombard (3), and shiraz (2). Groenfontein, a

Olifants River & Standalone Wards

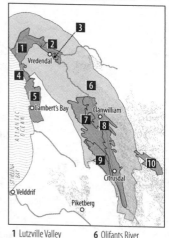

1 Lutzville Valley
2 Vredendal
3 Spruitdrift
4 Bamboes Bay
5 Lamberts Bay
6 Olifants River
7 Citrusdal Mountain
8 Citrusdal Valley
9 Piekenierskloof
10 Cederberg

ward in the foothills north of Calitzdorp town, was recently demarcated; still no official data available. Boutique-scale plantings in Langeberg-Garcia district (43), and the standalone wards of Cango Valley (9), Outeniqua (20) Upper Langkloof (51) and newer Koo Plateau (4).

Lutzville Valley This district (2,670) in the Coastal region, with toes in the Atlantic, is best known for zingy whites from its Koekenaap ward: chenin (218), sauvignon (217), colombard (164), cab (49), pinotage (45).

Northern Cape Quality moves are afoot in this geographical unit, particularly in Sutherland-Karoo,

Klein Karoo, Lower Duivenhoks River, Plettenberg Bay & Swellendam

1 Prince Albert Valley
2 Swartberg
3 Cango Valley
4 Montagu
5 Klein Karoo
6 Calitzdorp
7 Tradouw Highlands
8 Langeberg-Garcia
9 Outeniqua
10 Upper Langkloof
11 Stormsvlei
12 Tradouw
13 Herbertsdale
14 Plettenberg Bay
15 Swellendam
16 Malgas
17 Buffeljags
18 Lower Duivenhoks River
19 Stilbaai East

Stellenbosch

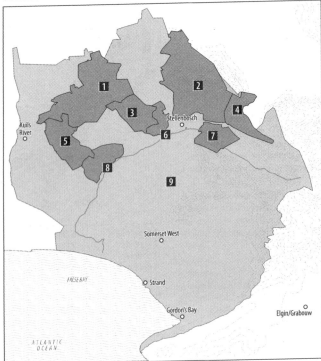

1 Bottelary
2 Simonsberg-Stellenbosch
3 Devon Valley
4 Banghoek
5 Polkadraai Hills
6 Papegaaiberg
7 Jonkershoek Valley
8 Vlottenburg
9 Stellenbosch

a high-altitude (1,450 m), semi-arid district around Sutherland, SA's coldest town. The smallest SA district by far (5 ha, mostly pinot noir, shiraz, chardonnay), but big on character, quality. Also-exciting ward Prieska (neighbour of Central Orange River) continues to expand: it now covers 148 ha and is headed by colombard, chenin blanc, merlot, sauvignon and rare villard blanc.

Olifants River Fruit for SA's highest-rated wines increasingly originates from this north-westerly region (5,749 ha), particularly the Citrusdal Mountain district (608) and cool upland ward of Piekenierskloof (512). On the valley floor, a climate conducive to organic cultivation is exploited to that end. Altitude: 20–100 m; temp 23°C; rain: 139/47 mm; geology: mainly schist and alluvial deposits. Citrusdal Mountain: grenache noir (96), chenin (85), pinotage (81), cinsaut (45) and sauvignon (43). Piekenierskloof: grenache noir

(74), pinotage (72), chenin (49), palomino (41), cinsaut (38).

Orange River See Central Orange River.

Paarl This district (8,533) has many meso-climates, soils and aspects, and thus succeeds with a variety of styles and grapes. Altitude: 100–300 m; temp 23.2°C; rain: 945/273 mm; geology: granite and shale. Paarl proper is recognised for shiraz and, more recently, viognier and mourvèdre grown on warmer slopes. Chenin (794), shiraz (621), cab (520), pinotage (342), chardonnay (272). The following are wards: Agter Paarl covers a portion of Paarl Mountain and its western foothills: chenin (511), shiraz (254), pinotage (223), cab (215) and cinsaut (204); Simonsberg-Paarl, on the warmer slopes of the Simonsberg, recognised for red blends, shiraz and chardonnay. Cab (226), chardonnay (185), shiraz (146), sauvignon (137), chenin (122); Voor Paardeberg, long an

Wine of Origin-defined production areas
(New appellation/s in **bold**.)

Overarching Geographical Unit	Geographical Unit	Overarching Region	Region	Subregion	District	Ward
—	Free State	—	—	—	—	Rietrivier FS
—	KwaZulu-Natal	—	—	—	Central Drakensberg	—
			—	—	Lions River	—
—	Limpopo	—	—	—	—	—
Greater Cape	Eastern Cape	—	—	—	—	St Francis Bay
	Northern Cape	—	—	—	Central Orange River	Groblershoop
						Grootdrink
						Kakamas
						Keimoes
						Upington
			—	—	Douglas	—
			—	—	Sutherland-Karoo	—
			—	—	—	Hartswater
			—	—	—	Prieska
	Western Cape	—	—	—	Ceres Plateau	Ceres
			—	—	—	Cederberg
			—	—	—	Leipoldtville-Sandveld
			—	—	—	Nieuwoudtville
			—	—	—	Kweekvallei
			—	—	Prince Albert	Prince Albert Valley
			—	—	—	Swartberg

Overarching Geographical Unit	Geographical Unit	Overarching Region	Region	Subregion	District	Ward
Greater Cape (continued)	Western Cape (continued)	—	Breede River Valley	—	Breedekloof	Goudini
		—		—	Robertson	Slanghoek
						Agterkliphoogte
						Ashton
						Boesmansrivier
						Bonnievale
						Eilandia
						Goedemoed
						Goree
						Goudmyn
						Hoopsrivier
						Klaasvoogds
						Le Chasseur
						McGregor
						Vinkrivier
						Zandrivier
				—	Worcester	Hex River Valley
						Nuy
						Scherpenheuwel
						Stettyn

Overarching Geographical Unit (continued)	Geographical Unit	Overarching Region	Region	Subregion	District	Ward
Greater Cape (continued)	Western Cape (continued)	—	Klein Karoo	—	Calitzdorp	Groenfontein
				—	Langeberg-Garcia	—
				—	—	Cango Valley
				—	—	Koo Plateau
				—	—	Montagu
				—	—	Outeniqua
				—	—	Tradouw
				—	—	Tradouw Highlands
				—	—	Upper Langkloof
		—	Olifants River	—	Citrusdal Mountain	Piekenierskloof
				—	Citrusdal Valley	—
				—	—	Spruitdrift
				—	—	Vredendal
		Cape Coast	Cape South Coast	—	Cape Agulhas	Elim
				—	Elgin	—
				—	Lower Duivenhoks River	—
				—	Overberg	Elandskloof
						Greyton
						Klein River
						Theewater
				—	Plettenberg Bay	—
				—	Swellendam	Buffeljags
						Malgas
						Stormsvlei

Overarching Geographical Unit	Geographical Unit	Overarching Region	Region	Subregion	District	Ward
Greater Cape (continued)	Western Cape (continued)	Cape Coast (continued)	Cape South Coast (continued)	—	Walker Bay	Bot River
						Hemel-en-Aarde Ridge
						Hemel-en-Aarde Valley
						Springfontein Rim
						Stanford Foothills
						Sunday's Glen
						Upper Hemel-en-Aarde Valley
				—	—	Herbertsdale
				—	—	Napier
				—	—	Stilbaai East
			Coastal	—	Cape Town	Constantia
						Durbanville
						Hout Bay
						Philadelphia
				—	Franschhoek	—
				—	Paarl	Agter Paarl
						Simonsberg-Paarl
						Voor Paardeberg
				—	Stellenbosch	Banghoek
						Bottelary
						Devon Valley
						Jonkershoek Valley

Overarching Geographical Unit	Geographical Unit	Overarching Region	Region	Subregion	District	Ward
Greater Cape (continued)	Western Cape (continued)	Cape Coast (continued)	Coastal (continued)	—	Stellenbosch (continued)	Papegaaiberg
						Polkadraai Hills
						Simonsberg-Stellenbosch
						Vlottenburg
					Swartland	Malmesbury
						Paardeberg
						Paardeberg South
						Piket-Bo-Berg
						Porseleinberg
						Riebeekberg
						Riebeeksrivier
						St Helena Bay
				—	Tulbagh	—
				—	Wellington	Blouvlei
						Bovlei
						Groenberg
						Limietberg
						Mid-Berg River
				Cape West Coast	Darling	Groenekloof
					Lutzville Valley	Koekenaap
					—	St Helena Bay (portion)
					—	Bamboes Bay
					—	Lamberts Bay

Source: Vinpro/SAWIS

Darling, Swartland & Tulbagh

1 Swartland 2 Darling 5 Riebeekberg
3 Malmesbury 6 Porseleinberg
4 Riebeeksrivier 7 Tulbagh

Breedekloof, Ceres & Worcester

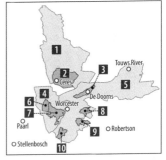

1 Ceres Plateau 4 Breedekloof 8 Nuy
2 Ceres 5 Worcester 9 Scherpen-
3 Hex River 6 Slanghoek heuvel
  Valley 7 Goudini 10 Stettyn

uncredited source of top-quality grapes, now a star in own right: cab (366), shiraz (295), chenin (240), merlot (213), pinotage (147).

Robertson Traditionally a white-wine district (12,889), latterly also recognised for shiraz and cab though chardonnay, sauvignon and sparkling remain standouts. Has the highest number of wards (14). Altitude: 150-250 m; temp 23℃; rain: 280/116 mm; geology: shale and alluvial. Colombard (1,847), chardonnay (1,710), sauvignon (1,655), chenin (1,488), cab (1,333).

Stellenbosch To many, this intensively farmed district (12,192) is the wine capital of SA. Key contributors to quality are the cooler mountain slopes, varied soil types and breezes off False Bay which moderate summer temperatures. Altitude: 200-400 m; temp 21.5℃; rain: 713/229 mm; geology: granite (sandstone). Jonkershoek Valley, a ward east of Stellenbosch town, is recognised for cab and cab blends. Cab (54), chardonnay (23), pinotage (20), shiraz (15) and merlot (14). Simonsberg-Stellenbosch, in the south-western foothills of the Simonsberg Mountain, especially recognised for cab, cab blends and pinotage, and reds generally. Cab (313), sauvignon (158), merlot (154), chardonnay (119), shiraz (114). Banghoek, the most

Robertson

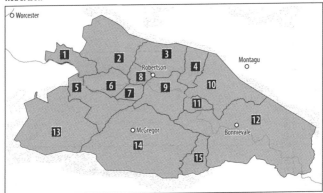

1 Eilandia
2 Vinkrivier
3 Hoopsrivier
4 Klaasvoogds
5 Le Chasseur
6 Goree
7 Robertson
8 Zandrivier
9 Goedemoed
10 Ashton
11 Goudmyn
12 Bonnievale
13 Agterkliphoogte
14 McGregor
15 Boesmansrivier

easterly of these wards, is a mountain amphitheatre above the village of Pniel - cab (46), shiraz (36), chardonnay and merlot (28), and sauvignon (22). North-west of Stellenbosch town are five adjoining wards: Papegaaiberg - sauvignon (27), chenin (21), chardonnay (12), pinotage (11), cab (8); Devon Valley, recognised mainly for red blends - merlot (121), sauvignon (87), cab (75), pinotage (67) shiraz (43); Bottelary, noted for chenin, pinotage, shiraz and warm-blooded blends - chenin (376), cab (320), pinotage (256), shiraz (231), sauvignon (215); the most westerly ward, Polkadraai Hills - sauvignon (138), cab (118), shiraz (110), merlot (88), chenin (66); Vlottenburg, the most recent of these wards, sits on the south-eastern border of Polkadraai Hills - cab (106), sauvignon (99), pinotage (77), chenin (72), merlot (70). The remainder of the Stellenbosch district, as yet officially undemarcated, includes Stellenboschberg, Helderberg and Faure, recognised for red blends, chenin and sauvignon. Cab (1,404), shiraz (908), sauvignon (857), merlot (778), chenin (654).

Sutherland-Karoo See Northen Cape.

Swartland Traditionally associated with hearty wines, but latterly with elegant, personality-packed chenins, Mediterranean-style reds and whites, and revived heirloom varieties, this fashionable district (9,561) north of Cape Town has eight wards (the newest being Piket-Bo-Berg, demarcated in 2021/22) plus a large unappellated area. Altitude: 100-300 m; temp 23.3℃; rain: 523/154 mm; geology: mostly granite and shale. Malmesbury: cab (569), shiraz (557), chenin (494), pinotage (397), sauvignon (315); Paardeberg: chenin (405), pinotage (207), shiraz (189), cab (145), sauvignon (87); Paardeberg South: chenin (47), semillon (24), cab (21), sauvignon (18), chardonnay (13); Porseleinberg: shiraz (122), chenin (60), pinotage (48), chardonnay (32), cab (22); Riebeekberg: chenin (197), shiraz (175), pinotage

(127), cab (72), chardonnay (66); Riebeeksrivier: shiraz (16), chenin (9), cinsaut and grenache (5), mourvèdre, clairette, marsanne, colombard, roussanne, petite sirah/durif, grenache blanc and viognier (1); St Helena Bay: sauvignon (13), chenin and semillon (4), shiraz and muscat d'Alexandrie (3). 'Swartland': chenin (1,0251), shiraz (518), cab (406), pinotage (337), chardonnay (173).

Tulbagh Inland district (861) traditionally known for sparkling and lightish whites, more recently also for quality reds and serious white blends. Altitude: 160-400 m; temp 24℃; rain: 551/175 mm; geology: sandstone boulderbeds and shale. Chenin (170), shiraz (124), colombard (87), cab (78), chardonnay (72).

Walker Bay Highly regarded maritime district (1,022) south-east of Cape Town, recognised for pinot noir, pinotage, sauvignon and chardonnay. Altitude: 100-250 m; temp 20.3℃; rain: 722/322 mm; geology: shale, granite and sandstone. Sauvignon (256), pinot noir (156), shiraz (139), chardonnay (130), cab (72). Bot River, Hemel-en-Aarde Ridge, Hemel-en-Aarde Valley, Springfontein Rim, Stanford Foothills, Sunday's Glen and Upper Hemel-en-Aarde Valley are wards.

Wellington District (3,785) in the Coastal region increasingly reputed for shiraz, gutsy red blends and chenin. Altitude: 100-500 m; temp 23.2℃; rain: 741/104 mm; geology: shale and granite. Chenin (799), cab (572), shiraz (549), pinotage (433), chardonnay (325).

Worcester District (6,336) producing chiefly for the brandy industry and merchant trade, but small quantities bottled under own labels are increasingly impressive. Recognised for red and white blends, chenin and fortifieds. Chenin (1,761), colombard (1,069), sauvignon (694), chardonnay (435), pinotage (416). See under Robertson for climate, geology etc.

Grape Varieties

Below are brief notes on the grape varieties mentioned in the guide, and their contribution to the national vineyard (statistics from SAWIS NPC). See under Winegrowing Areas for details of the most widely planted and best-performing varieties in the major vine cultivation zones.

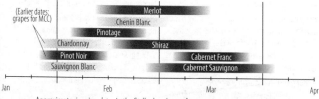

Approximate ripening dates in the Stellenbosch area for some important grape varieties

Red-wine varieties

Alicante Bouschet Vigorous variety created in 19th-century France by Henri Bouschet from grenache (alicante) and petit bouschet. One of few red-fleshed grapes, producing vividly hued wines with lower acid. No solo bottlings in this guide. 0.04% of total vineyard area.

Barbarossa Name for a variety of grapes in Italy, and in SA assumed to be an import from there but the few rows planted locally are in fact the French table grape danugue aka gros guillaume. Just one solo bottling.

Barbera Piedmont's second grape (after nebbiolo), its natural high acidity suiting warm climates; sought after, too, for low tannins, good colour. (0.04%)

Bastardo do Castello Aka trousseau, a vine from Jura in eastern France producing aromatic, racy and potentially ageworthy wines. Less than 1 ha planted in SA; just one varietal bottling listed in this guide.

Cabernet franc Like its descendant cabernet sauvignon, with which it is often partnered, a classic part of the Bordeaux blend, but in SA and elsewhere – particularly in the Loire – also used for varietal wines. (0.92%)

Cabernet sauvignon Adaptable and internationally planted black grape making some of the world's finest and longest-lasting wines. And retaining some of its inherent qualities even when over-cropped in less suitable soils and climates. Can stand alone triumphantly, but frequently blended with a wide range of other varieties: traditionally, as in Bordeaux, with cab franc, merlot and a few minor others, but also in SA sometimes partnering varieties such as shiraz and pinotage. Number of different clones, with differing characteristics. (10.64%)

Carignan Hugely planted in the south of France, where it is not much respected. But there, as in SA, older, low-yielding vines can produce pleasant surprises. (0.14%)

Carmenère Dark-skinned, late-ripening parent of cabernet franc; once important in Bordeaux, today most significant in Chile. Deep-hued/flavoured wines if picked fully ripe. Handful of bottlings in SA - varietals as well as blends. (0.01%)

Chambourcin Disease-resistant, productive French hybrid available commercially since the 1960s but approved for winemaking in SA only in 2021. About 10 ha, mostly in Olifants River region. Yet to debut as a standalone wine in this guide.

Cinsaut (noir) 'Cinsault' in France. Another of the mass, undistinguished plantings of southern France,

which only occasionally comes up trumps. Used to be known locally as hermitage, the name reflected in its offspring (with pinot noir), pinotage. (1.89%)

Counoise Native of southern Rhône and permitted for Châteauneuf-du-Pape, to which it adds freshness and spice. Locally, limited to few rows in Olifants River, Swartland and Tulbagh. No solo bottling in the guide.

Durif *See Petite sirah.*

Gamay noir Although it produces some serious long-lived wines in Beaujolais, its use for (mainly) early- and easy-drinking 'nouveau' wines there, often using carbonic maceration, is the model mostly copied in SA. (0.01%)

Grenache (noir) The international (i.e. French) name for the Spanish grape garnacha. Widespread in Spain and southern France, generally used in blends (as in Rioja and Châteauneuf), but occasionally solo. A favourite for rosés. When vigour restrained, capable of greatness, but this is rare. (0.62%) White/pink versions also occur.

Malbec Once a significant part of Bordeaux's blend, now most important in Cahors in western France (where it is known as cot), and as Argentina's signature variety. In SA a small but rising number of varietal and some blended examples. (0.82%)

Marselan Cab sauvignon-grenache noir cross developed in early 1960s with France's Languedoc in mind. Fewer than 7 ha in SA, mostly in Breede River Valley. First bottled solo in 2020 from tiny echalas (staked-vine) block in Tulbagh.

Mataro See Mourvèdre.

Merlot Classic blending partner (as in Bordeaux) for cabernet, fashionable around the world, where it tends to be seen as an 'easier' version of cab – although this is perhaps because it is often made in a less ambitious manner. Merlot varietal wines increasingly common in SA too. (5.93%)

Meunier Aka pinot meunier, a mutation of pinot noir and, like pinot noir and chardonnay, significant in France's Champagne region where it adds fruitiness to blended sparklings. Rare in SA; also mostly for bubbly, lone varietal bottling in this guide. (0.02%)

Mourvèdre Internationally known by its French name, though originally Spanish (monastrell). In South Africa officially called mataro; also known as that in Australia and California. Particularly successful in some serious southern French blends, and increasingly modish internationally. (0.54%)

Nebbiolo Perhaps the greatest red grape to have scarcely ventured from its home – Piedmont in this case, where it makes massive, tannic, long-lived wines. Tiny (0.02%) footprint here.

Nero d'Avola Sicily's major red grape, aka calabrese, of interest to SA because of heat tolerance and ability to produce full-flavoured/coloured wines. Handful of local bottlings.

Petite sirah/durif Originally from southern France, a cross of peloursin and syrah/shiraz. Produces tannic, densely fruited wines. (0.46%)

Petit verdot Use of this excellent variety in the Médoc limited by its late ripening. Recently appearing in some local blends, and a few varietals. (0.80%)

Pinotage A 1920s cross between pinot noir and cinsaut ('hermitage'). Made in a range of styles, from simply fruity to ambitious, well-oaked examples. (7.4%)

Pinot Meunier See Meunier.

Pinot noir Notoriously difficult grape to succeed with outside its native Burgundy, but SA, along with the rest of the New World, now produces some excellent examples. (1.31%)

Pontac One of SA's original varieties, now insignificant with mere ±4 ha under vine. Outside SA known as teinturier (du cher), one of few red-fleshed grapes, delivering deep-coloured/flavoured wines.

Roobernet Relatively recent local crossing of cabernet sauvignon and what was thought to be pontac, in fact alicante bouschet. Mostly blended. (0.39%)

Ruby cabernet US cross between cabernet sauvignon and carignan, designed for heat tolerance. In South Africa, rather rustic, used mostly in cheaper blends. (2.09%)

Sangiovese Tuscany's signature black grape, producing light or big wines, depending on how it is grown. Can be unacceptably acidic and tannic with little colour unless well managed in the vineyard. (0.09%)

Shiraz Better known as syrah outside SA and Australia (and on some local labels too). Internationally increasing in popularity, with northern Rhône and now also Australia as its major domiciles. Made here in a variety of styles – generally wooded. (9.95%)

Souzão Portuguese vine giving wines with deeply dark looks and flavours; stalwart of local 'port' category. No solo versions in the guide. (0.04%)

Syrah See Shiraz.

Tannat From France's Basque region, recently Uruguay's calling card but still little more than a curiosity in SA. Known for deep colour and high tannin. (0.15%)

Tempranillo Aka tinta roriz. The soul of Spain's storied Rioja and Ribera del Duero. Low tannin, balanced acidity and plush fruit; suited to warm climates but hardly on the SA radar – yet. (0.12%)

Tinta amarela See Trincadeira.

Tinta barocca Elsewhere spelt 'barroca'. One of the important Portuguese port-making grapes, which is its primary role in SA, usually blended. Also used for some varietal unfortified wines, and namelessly in some 'dry reds'. (0.17%)

Touriga franca Formerly known as touriga francesa. Most-planted grape in Portugal's Douro Valley, used for port as well as unfortified reds. Only a few hectares in SA.

Touriga francesa See Touriga franca.

Touriga nacional Important Portuguese port-making grape, usefully grown here for similar ends, along with tinta barocca, tinta roriz (tempranillo) and souzão. (0.11%)

Trincadeira Also 'tinta amarela/amarella'; from Portugal, deep coloured with good black fruit and big tannins. (0.02%)

Trousseau See Bastardo do Castello.

Zinfandel The quintessential California grape (of European origin, and the same as Italy's primitivo), used here in a small way. (0.02%)

White-wine varieties

Albariño Aromatic, high-acid white grape from Spain's damp north-west (also grown in Portugal, as alvarinho), recently fashionable in New World. Mostly varietals, occasionally oaked, potentially ageworthy. Handful of varietal bottlings in SA. (0.04%)

Bourboulenc Just 0.69 ha of this French vine planted here, with no varietal bottling featured in this guide to date. Best Provençal and southern Rhône examples are lively, fresh and fragrant.

Bukettraube Light and acidic German variety, mostly used to add zing to white blends. (0.05%)

Chardonnay In SA, as elsewhere, many new vineyards of this grape have come on-stream, with wines showing a wide range of styles, quality and price. Generally used varietally, but also in blends, and for sparkling. Wooded, lately with a lighter touch, in more ambitious wines. (7.32%)

Cape Riesling See Riesling

Chenel First white-grape crossing in SA, released 1974. Robust and productive vine, near-impervious to rot. Ripens touch later than chenin blanc but much earlier than its other parent, trebbiano/ugni blanc. One solo bottling in this guide. (0.03%)

Chenin blanc SA has more chenin (locally also called steen) than even France's Loire Valley, the variety's home. Used here for everything from generic 'dry white' to ambitious sweet wines, to brandy. Increasing numbers of table-wine successes in recent years, as well as inexpensive but flavoursome easy-drinkers. (18.44%)

Clairette blanche High-alcohol, low-acid, musky component of southern Rhône white blends; bottled as single variety only off superior sites. In SA, also mainly used in blends. (0.16%)

Colombar(d) One of the mainstays of brandy production in SA, colombard (usually without the 'd' in SA) is also used for numerous varietal and blended wines, ranging from dry to sweet – seldom wooded. (10.73%)

Crouchen Blanc See Riesling

Fernão pires Aromatic workhorse from Portugal; can be used for wide range of wine styles. (0.04%)

Gewürztraminer Readily identifiable from its rosepetal fragrance, best known in its (dry) Alsatian guise. In SA usually made off-dry. (0.09%)

Grenache blanc Staple of Rhône white blends, finding adherents in SA, particularly when given skin contact, oak ferment/ageing. Needs careful handling. (0.18%) Also very rare gris plantings/vinifications.

Grüner veltliner Austria's no. 1 white grape (by hectare and repute) venturing west (to America), east (Australasia) and south to SA, where plantings are still tiny and vinification follows dry, full, aromatic style of home country's top examples. (0.01%)

Hanepoot Traditional Afrikaans name for muscat d'Alexandrie, SA's most common muscat variety (see also muscadel below). (1.59%, some for raisins and table grapes). Also minuscule red plantings.

Hárslevelü From Tokaj, Hungary; delicate when fermented dry, fat and smoky in sweeter styles. Only 10 ha in SA (0.01%).

Marsanne Rhône grape, more widely planted than 'twin' roussanne. Dependable, but flabby in too-warm terroir, bland in too-cool. (0.03%)

Muscadel Name used here for both muscat de Frontignan and muscat blanc à petits grains (both red and white versions). The grape associated with the famous Constantia dessert wines of the 18th century today is used chiefly for dessert and fortified wines and for touching up blends. (1.26% red and white). Morio muscat, muscat de Hambourg and muscat Ottonel also bottled on small scale, mostly as fortifieds.

Muscat See Hanepoot and Muscadel.

Nouvelle Local crossing of semillon and neutral ugni blanc/trebbiano, produces intense grass and greenpepper characters. Typically blended. (0.45%)

Palomino Aka malvasia rei, fransdruif, white french. Once important in Spain's sherry industry and locally for distilling, palomino fino is now just 0.10% of the total SA vineholding. Roles in some hipster bottlings may help raise the profile.

Piquepoul blanc High-acid grape (literally 'lip stinger') indigenous to southern France. Mere 1.4 ha in SA, no varietal bottling in the guide as yet. No official record here of the rare noir and gris variants.

Pinot blanc Import from north-east Italy; just 2.7 ha and very few examples locally.

Pinot gris/grigio In north-east Italy prized for acidity, France's Alsace for plump richness. Tiny quantities in SA, named 'gris' or 'grigio' depending on style. (0.49%)

Riesling The name by itself now refers to the great German grape (as it does in this guide). Previously, the variety by law had to carry the prefix 'Rhine' or 'weisser', and the 'riesling' was an official SA synonym for the crouchen blanc, also known as Cape riesling and mostly used anonymously in blends, occasionally varietally. Rhine riesling often off-dry here, in blends or varietally, some excellent botrytised dessert examples. (Rhine: 0.13%; crouchen: 0.15%)

Roussanne Like frequent blending partner marsanne, from the northern Rhône. Also aromatic component of Châteauneuf du Pape. Gaining a following in SA. (0.09%)

Sauvignon blanc Prestigious vine most associated with eastern Loire regions, Bordeaux and New Zealand – whose wines have helped restore fashionability to the grape. The SA version not a poor relation of these. Usually dry, but some sweet wines; increasingly wooded and occasionally called fumé blanc/blanc fumé. (11.17%)

Sauvignon gris Distinct from sauvignon blanc, pink skinned, as alias sauvignon rose suggests. Just under ±10 ha locally and no solo bottlings in the guide.

Semillon Spelt sémillon in French. Sometimes heavily wooded, sometimes sweet, more often in blends but some spectacular old-vine varietal examples. (1.04%, including rare red-skinned version)

Sylvaner Native of Germany's Franken, more about style and texture than flavour. Just 1 ha and one varietal bottling in SA.

Therona 1950s cross of chenin blanc and crouchen blanc/Cape riesling, named for local viticulturist CJ Theron. Only solo bottling in the guide is from 100 select vines on Stellenbosch Mountain. (0.02%)

Trebbiano High-cropping, acidic and somewhat low-character grape used for blending and distilling. Officially known in SA as ugni blanc. (0.16%)

Ugni blanc See *Trebbiano*.

Verdelho From Portugal (not to be confused with Spain's verdejo). Both a grape and a (sweet) fortified style in Madeira; mostly dry in the southern hemisphere. (0.09%)

Vermentino Sardinia and Corsica's premier white grape is recent in SA but holds potential to deliver aroma, flavour and verve in a warming climate. Seven bottlings in the guide, most by Italians. (0.01%)

Villard blanc High-yielding, disease-resistant hybrid from France with a small footprint here - 245 ha of the white variant and 10.14 ha of the red.

Viognier Homed in the northern Rhône, long established locally but still niched. Mostly oaked. (0.74%)

Viura Aka macabeo, macabeu and maccabéo, it is widely planted in Spain and, as in SA, used for both still and sparkling styles. Locally just 5.62 ha.

Competitions, Challenges & Awards

An increasing number of wine competitions, awards and challenges are run by liquor industry bodies, independent companies, publishing houses and individuals. Below are the main national events.

Absa Top 10 Pinotage Competition Run annually by the Pinotage Association and a major financial institution to help set international quality targets for growers of pinotage. The recent Vintage Class category aims to demonstrate that top pinotage wines are fulfilling their promise of great ageability. Local judges. See under Industry Organisations for contact details.

Absa Vintage Class Competition See Absa Top 10 Pinotage Competition.

Amorim Cap Classique Challenge Annual competition to appoint SA's top cap classique sparkling wines. Mostly local judges. ▪ admin@ capclassique.co.za ▪ www.capclassique.co.za ▪ T +27 (0)21-863-1599

Cabernet Franc Challenge Annual competition aimed at raising public awareness and rewarding quality in the production of cabernet franc varietal wines and blends. 'Museum' category spotlights maturation potential; Best Value category rewards value-for-money entries. Local judges. ▪ celia@ eventsbycelia.com bjorn@cvomarketing.co.za ▪ T+27 (0)84-511-1806 / +27 (0)82-782-1977

Cabernet Sauvignon Challenge Annual competition aimed at raising public awareness and rewarding quality in the production of cabernet sauvignon wines. Local judges ▪ celia@eventsbycelia. com ▪ T +27 (0)82-782-1977

CAPPA Cape Port & Wine Challenge Organised by the Cape Port Producers' Association to award best in class and gold medals in each of the port categories, and select the Top 10 Portuguese-style wines. Local judges. ▪ info@boplaas.co.za ▪ www. capeportproducers.co.za ▪ T +27 (0)44-213-3326

Chenin Blanc Top 10 Challenge See Standard Bank Chenin Blanc Top 10 Challenge.

Diners Club Winemaker of the Year Inaugurated in 1981, this prestigious competition features a different category each year. The Young Winemaker of the Year recognises the winning entrant aged 30 years or younger. Local panel with some overseas representation.

Winemaker of the Year since inception

1981 Walter Finlayson, Blaauwklippen Zinfandel 1980

1982 Walter Finlayson, Blaauwklippen Cabernet Sauvignon 1980

1983 Günter Brözel, Nederburg Rhine Riesling 1983

1984 Manie Rossouw, Eersterivier Sauvignon Blanc 1984

1985 Günter Brözel, Nederburg Gewürztraminer 1985

1986 Sydney Back, Backsberg Chardonnay 1985

1987 Beyers Truter, Kanonkop Pinotage 1985

1988 Wilhelm Linde, Nuy White Muscadel 1985

1989 Peter Finlayson, Hamilton Russell Pinot Noir 1986

1990 André Bruwer, Bon Courage Gewürztraminer Special Late Harvest 1989

1991 Wilhelm Linde, Nuy Riesling 1991

1992 Jean Daneel, Buitenverwachting Reserve Merlot 1991

1993 Danie de Wet, De Wetshof Finesse Chardonnay 1993

1994 Gyles Webb, Thelema Cabernet Sauvignon-Merlot 1992

1995 Nicky Krone, Twee Jonge Gezellen Krone Borealis Brut 1993

1996 Gyles Webb, Thelema Cabernet Sauvignon 1994

1997 Jeff Grier, Villiera Bush Vine Sauvignon Blanc 1997

1998 Danie Malan, Allesverloren Shiraz 1996

1999 Ronell Wiid, Hazendal Shiraz-Cabernet Sauvignon 1998

2000 Paul de Villiers, Landskroon Port 1997

2001 Teddy Hall, Kanu Chenin Blanc 2001

2002 Danie de Waal, Uiterwyk De Waal Top of the Hill Pinotage 2001

2003 John Loubser, Constantia Uitsig Reserve Semillon 2002

2004 Pieter Ferreira, Graham Beck Brut Blanc de Blancs 1999

2005 Carl Schultz, Hartenberg Merlot 2004

2006 Gottfried Möcke, Chamonix Reserve Chardonnay 2005

2007 Marc Kent, Boekenhoutskloof Syrah 2005

2008 Not awarded

2009 Coenie Snyman, Rust en Vrede Cabernet Sauvignon 2007

2010 Bartho Eksteen, Hermanuspietersfontein Nr. 5 Sauvignon Blanc 2009

2011 Johan Jordaan, Spier Creative Block 5 2009

2012 Razvan Macici, Nederburg Private Bin Eminence 2007

2013 Christiaan Groenewald, Arendskloof Voetspoere Tannat-Syrah 2011

2014 Jacques Erasmus, Spier Creative Block 2 2014

2015 Johann Fourie, KWV The Mentors Pinotage 2013

2016 Pierre Wahl, Rijk's Chenin Blanc 2014

2017 Christiaan Groenewald, Eagle's Cliff Pinotage 2017

2018 Clayton Reabow, Môreson Mercator Chardonnay 2017

2019 Daniel Keulder, Nitida Pinot Noir 2017

2020 Johan Malan, Simonsig Kaapse Vonkel Brut 2015

2021 Justin van Wyk, Constantia Glen Five 2017

2022 Conrad Vlok, Strandveld Poffaderbos Sauvignon Blanc 2021

Young Winemaker of the Year since inception

2001 Henri Swiegers, Slanghoek Noble Late Harvest 2001

2002 Boela Gerber, Groot Constantia Merlot 2001

2003 Ivy du Toit, Jason's Hill Sauvignon Blanc 2003

2004 Johan Nesenberend, For My Friends Shiraz 2002

2005 Johan Kruger, Sterhuis Chardonnay 2004

2006 Francois Agenbag, Mountain Ridge Seven Oaks 6+1 Reserve Cabernet Sauvignon-Shiraz 2004

2007 Ruth Penfold, Steenberg Semillon 2007

2008 Ossie Sauermann, La Vigne Single Vineyard Shiraz 2007

2009 Clayton Reabow, Môreson Premium Chardonnay 2007

2010 RJ Botha, Nitida Calligraphy 2009

2011 Matthew van Heerden, Uva Mira Chardonnay 2009

2012 Anri Truter, Beyerskloof Diesel Pinotage 2010

2013 Murray Barlow, Rustenberg Stellenbosch Chardonnay 2012

2014 JD Pretorius, Steenberg Merlot 2012

2015 Phillip Viljoen, Bon Courage Noble Late Harvest 2015

2016 Murray Barlow, Rustenberg RM Nicholson 2015

2017 Wade Roger-Lund, Jordan Blanc de Blancs Méthode Cap Classique 2015

2018 Rüdger van Wyk, Stark-Condé Stellenbosch Syrah 2016

2019 Herman du Preez, ArtiSons The Apprentice White Cinsault 2018

2020 Philip Theron, Glen Carlou Collection Tannat 2018

2021 Herman du Preez, ArtiSons The Apprentice White Cinsault 2020

2022 Jerome van Rooi, Cederberg Five Generations Cabernet Sauvignon 2020

▪ winemaker@dinersclub.co.za ▪ www.dinersclub.co.za ▪ T +27 (0)86-034-6377

FNB Sauvignon Blanc SA Top 10 Annual competition hosted by Sauvignon Blanc South Africa since 2007 to promote innovation and excellence of the sauvignon blanc cultivar, and reward those making wines of true distinction. Local judges. ▪ admin@sauvignonblanc.com ▪ www.sauvignon-blanc.com ▪ T +27 (0)21-975-4440

Lumo Awards (previously SA Woman's Wine & Spirit Awards) Annual competition since 2015, open to all winemakers and distillers. Trophies are awarded for Woman Distiller of the year, Woman Winemaker of the Year, Red Wine of the Year and Cap Classique of the Year. Local judges. ▪ Contact Sanet van Heerden ▪ hello@lumoawards.com ▪ www.lumoawards.com ▪ T +27 (0)84-446-0412

Malbec Challenge Annually seeks to raise public awareness and reward quality in the production of malbec wines. The overall highest-scoring wine receives a French oak barrel to the winery's specifications. Local judges ▪ celia@eventsbycelia.com ▪ T +27 (0)82-782-1977

Michelangelo International Wine & Spirits Awards Said to be the largest international drinks competition in the southern hemisphere, Michelangelo celebrated 25 years in 2021. Winners are awarded trophies, as well as Platinum, Gran d'Or, Gold and Silver medals. New categories include ready-to-drink products, low- and non-alcohol wines and spirits, and Old Vine Project-certified wines. Predominantly international panel. ▪ dirk@michelangeloawards.com ▪ www.michelange-loawards.com ▪ T +27 (0)82-394-3280

Mosaic Top 5 Pinot Noir Wine Awards The awards identify five wines to serve as a benchmark for the development of distinctive South African pinot noir red wines, and illustrate the quality of such wines to the world. Wines that score 90 or more points, but do not make it into the top five, receive a 90+ Award. Local judges ▪ info@top5.co.za ▪ www.top5.co.za

Muscadel Award for Excellence Annual competition aimed at raising consumer awareness and recognising quality in the creation, packaging and promotion of SA's muscadel wines. Local judges. ▪ henri@badsberg.co.za, andres@rooiberg.co.za ▪ T +27 (0)23-344-3021 / +27 (0)23-626-1664

National Wine Challenge Fine-wine-only competition incorporating Top 100 SA Wines. Uses key international and local judges with a focus on Master of Wine qualifications. Blind-tasted audited results yield Double Platinum/Top 100 status for the top-scoring 100 wines. Four unique awards include: National Champion for top-scoring red, white, bubbly and sweet wine; 'Grand Cru' for best-in-class wines; Wine Consistency for most single wine wins over 13 years; Vineyard Consistency for most overall wins over 13 years. Either Double Gold or Double Silver awarded for the next two tiers of high-scoring wines. Winning wines are showcased in various ways. ▪ accounts@buybetterwine.com ▪ www.buybetterwine.com ▪ www.thenationalwinechal-lenge.com

Niche Variety Challenge Annual competition aimed at raising public awareness and rewarding quality in the production of wines from South Africa's lesser-known grape varieties. Local judges ▪ celia@eventsbycelia.com ▪ T +27 (0)82-782-1977

Perold Absa Cape Blend Competition Launched in 2011 and aimed at creating a signature style for Cape Blends (see SA Wine Styles section). Reflecting the growing value and popularity of pink wines made from pinotage, the newer Pinotage Rosé Competition reiterates the vision of the contest as a whole: to showcase the versatility of pinotage. Local judges. Contacts as for Absa Top Ten Pinotage.

Pinotage Rosé Competition See Perold Absa Cape Blend Competition.

Red Blends Challenge Annual competition aimed at raising public awareness and rewarding quality in the production of the complete range of red blends. Local judges. ▪ celia@eventsbycelia.com ▪ T +27 (0)82-782-1977

Shiraz SA Wine Challenge Annual competition to identify the 12 best varietal shiraz wines, 3 best shiraz blends and one rosé across all regions and styles. Local/international judges. ▪ info@shirazsa.co.za ▪ www.shirazsa.co.za ▪ T +27 (0)82 924-7254

SA National Bottled Wine Show See Veritas.

Semillon Challenge Annual competition aimed at raising public awareness and rewarding quality in the production of semillon wines. Local judges ▪ celia@eventsbycelia.com ▪ T +27 (0)82-782-1977

South African Terroir Wine Awards Established 17 years ago and now run by the SA National Wine Show Association (also responsible for the SA Young Wine Show and Veritas), the Terroir Wine Awards focus on soil and climatic factors in narrowly defined cultivation areas. Only wines certified as originating from single vineyards, units registered for the production of estate wine, wards or districts (last-mentioned not divided into more than one ward) may be entered, making this one of the most exclusive wine competitions in the world. Top Wine, Top Single-Vineyard Wine, Top Wine Area, Top Wine Estate and Top Producer trophies also awarded. Five local judges ▪ entries@terroirwineawards.co.za ▪ www.terroirwineawards.co.za ▪ T +27 (0)21-863-1599

South African Wine Tasting Championship (SAWTC) In the spirit of ongoing education, and in an attempt to encourage new converts to wine, SAWTC offers all winelovers the chance to put their talents to the test and be the centre of a local wine event, with an opportunity to compete internationally. ▪ info@sawtc.co.za ▪ www.sawtc.co.za ▪ T +27 (0)21-422-5206

South African Young Wine Show Inaugurated in 1975 to gauge the quality of embryo wines, prior to finishing and bottling, thereby also recognising wineries which sell their products in bulk. The grand champion receives the General Smuts Trophy. Local judges. ▪ info@veritas.co.za ▪ www.youngwineshow.co.za ▪ T +27 (0)21-863-1599

Standard Bank Chenin Blanc Top 10 Challenge Annual event in which varietal chenins and chenin-dominated (85%) blends in the drier spectrum (max 12 g/L sugar) are assessed by a panel of five judges and an associate. The ten winners each receive R25,000, to be used to reinforce economic and social benefits in the workplace. ▪ cheninblancasso@gmail.com ▪ www.chenin.co.za ▪ T +27 (0)82-467-4331

The Intercontinental Spirits Challenge The Intercontinental Challenge aims to raise professionalism in the drinks industry. Tastings occur on different continents under one umbrella to find the best drinks worldwide. By not having one centralised event, industry experts can better assess products regionally, lower the cost of entry, and significantly reduce the carbon footprint by hosting tastings on different continents. International judges. info@interspiritchallenge.africa ▪ Interspiritchallenge.com ▪ T +27 (0)84-446-0412

The Intercontinental Wine Challenge Sibling to The Intercontinental Spirit Challenge. See listing. ▪ info@interspiritchallenge.africa ▪ Interwinechallenge.com ▪ T +27 (0)84-446-0412

The Rosé Wine & Spirit Challenge Annually raises public awareness and rewards quality in the production of rosé wines and pink spirits. Local judges. Contact Sanet van Heerden ▪ info@rosechallenge.co.za ▪ www.rosechallenge.co.za ▪ T +27 (0)84-446-0412

Top 100 South African Wines See National Wine Challenge.

Trophy Spirits Show Brought To You By Investec Inaugural event in 2019. Convened by Michael Fridjhon and sponsored by Investec. Seeks to identify the best spirits available in SA and award trophies to the top gold medal winners. Local and international judges. ▪ alex@outsorceress.co.za ▪ www.trophyspiritshow.co.za ▪ T +27 (0)11-482-5936

Trophy Wine Show Brought To You By Investec Convened by Michael Fridjhon and sponsored by Investec. Seeks to identify the best wines in SA and award trophies to the top gold medal winners, as well as the top producer overall. Local and international judges. ▪ alex@outsorceress.co.za ▪ www.trophywineshow.co.za ▪ T +27 (0)11-482-5936

Ultra Value Wine Challenge Provides an objective, independent and professional annual rating of SA wines selling for under R130/bottle. Wines are tasted unsighted, in order to assess quality. Thereafter an algorithm takes into account price attractiveness. Resultant top-performing wines are awarded Double-Gold, Gold or Silver medals. SA judges. ▪ accounts@buybetterwine.com ▪ www.ultravaluewines.com ▪ www.buybetterwine.com

Veritas South Africa's biggest competition for market-ready wines, awarding double-gold, gold, silver and bronze medals across a wide range of categories. Since 2017 the overall champion wine has received the Duimpie Bayly Veritas Vertex award. The VinoVeritas by CTP app was launched in 2020 to enable the public to order awarded wines directly and have them delivered. Local palates with some overseas input. ▪ info@veritas.co.za ▪ www.veritas.co.za ▪ T +27 (0)21-863-1599

Viognier Challenge Annual competition aimed at raising public awareness and rewarding quality in the production of viognier wines. Local judges ▪ celia@eventsbycelia.com ▪ T +27 (0)82-782-1977

Vitis Vinifera Awards Annual competition since 2012, celebrating the noble species of vine, Vitis vinifera. The Anchor Oenology Trophy goes to the best wine or spirit on the show, with a prize worth R30,000 for the winning winemaker or distiller to travel to any wine destination in the world. Local panel of Masters of Wine, Cape Wine Masters, sommeliers and industry experts. Contact Sanet van Heerden ▪ support@vitisawards.com ▪ www.vitisawards.com ▪ T +27 (0)84-446-0412

White Blends Challenge Annual competition aimed at raising public awareness and rewarding quality in the production of white blends of all types. Local judges. ▪ celia@eventsbycelia.com ▪ T +27 (0)82-782-1977

Wine & Brandy Education

Brandy Course for Hospitality Staff Underwritten by the Cape Wine Academy (CWA) and subsidised by the SA Brandy Foundation, this quarterly training programme is aimed specifically at tasting room and other hospitality staff. Topics covered include the history of brandy, brandy production and conducting a brandy tasting. Successful students receive a CWA certificate. T +27 (0)64-754-6552 ▪ christelle@sabrandy.co.za

Cape Wine Academy Recognised leader in wine education and appreciation in SA for over 40

years, CWA focuses on the development of skills and knowledge for all sectors of the wine and related industries, tertiary institutions as well as private wine enthusiasts and corporates. Educational, training and experiential classroom sessions, as well as virtually presented and online self-study courses are offered and presented by wine industry experts, winemakers and Cape Wine Masters. Everyone is welcome. ▪ info@capewineacademy.co.za ▪ www.capewineacademy.co.za ▪ Stellenbosch: **T +27 (0)21-889-8844** ▪ Johannesburg: **T +27 (0)11-024-3616**

Sommeliers Academy Founded in 2016, with campuses in Johannesburg, Durban, Cape Town and, recently, Harare. Provides wine and hospitality education for local (SASA) and international (ASI) qualifications. Also runs exchange programs with counterparts in France and Switzerland. Online learning available. ▪ info@sommellerie.co.za ▪ www.sommeliers.academy ▪ **T +27 (0)21-422-5206**

University of Stellenbosch Garagiste Winemaking Course See under Make Your Own Wine or Brandy

Wine Judging Academy Run by Michael Fridjhon in association with the University of Cape Town's Graduate School of Business, this intensive 3-day tasting and wine judging course aims to increase the number of competent wine judges at work in the local industry. ▪ crossley@reciprocal.co.za

WSET in South Africa with the International Wine Education Centre Led by WSET Educator of the Year, Cathy Marston, IWEC was the first provider of the UK-based Wine & Spirit Education Trust's (WSET) courses in SA, catering for enthusiastic amateurs and wine industry professionals alike. WSET wine and spirit qualifications are recognised as the industry standard in over 70 countries. The IWEC offers all WSET wine and spirit courses, and is the only provider of the flagship qualification, WSET Level 4, in Africa and the Middle East. In-house training and ad hoc courses are also offered, and for those wanting to take their wine education to the highest level, WSET is the direct path to Master of Wine (MW) and Master Sommelier (MS). ▪ courses@thewinecentre.co.za ▪ www.thewinecentre.co.za ▪ **T +27 (0)82-764-0680**

Make Your Own Wine or Brandy

Hofstraat Kelder Wim Smit, owner and winemaker at Malmesbury's Hofstraat Kelder, acts as a mentor to aspirant winemakers by arrangement, facilitating grape sourcing through to labelling. See listing in A-Z directory.

Create Your Own Cap Classique at Weltevrede Wine Estate Gain an insight into the intricate and rewarding art of cap classique at Weltevrede, home of the highly regarded Philip Jonker sparkling-wine portfolio. You'll not only learn about the process of making bottle-fermented bubbly, you'll also craft your own by doing the disgorging, dosaging, corking, foiling and labelling of the bottle yourself. You get to take your handiwork home to share with the special person in your life. Book your cap classique-making experience online at weltevrede.com.

Sign Your Name in Wine at Stellenrust Stellenrust wine farm near Stellenbosch offers groups of 20 or more the

opportunity to pick grapes, crush them in 3-ton open-tank fermenters and put a personal signature on their very own wine. Packages include a full-day excursion followed by traditional braai lunch and bottles of participants' handcrafted wine (after proper barrel maturation in the boutique cellar). info@stellenrust.co.za ▪ www.stellenrust.co.za ▪ T +27 (0)21-880-2283

University of Stellenbosch Garagiste Winemaking Course The premium short course for people interested in producing quality small-scale wines at home or simply expanding their wine knowledge. Attendees receive a set of notes; observe the use of garagiste winemaking equipment; taste different vinifications; bottle their own wine; and receive a certificate from Stellenbosch University. A follow-on, advanced course was introduced in 2016. ▪ wdutoit@sun.ac.za ▪ **T +27 (0)21-808-2022**

A-Code Numbers & Certification Codes

Many wines appear on the market under brand names, with, at first glance, no reference to their producers or purveyors. However, consumers need not buy 'blind', and may trace a wine's provenance by checking the official 'A-number' which appears on the bottle or pack. This identity code tells you either who produced the wine, or who sourced it for resale. In the latter case, an enquiry to the merchant should elicit the source. The list keeps growing and being revised, and is too lengthy to reproduce in this guide. Via the Wine Online page **www.sawis.co.za/sealsearch.php**, it is possible however to search the list of A-codes, as well as the certification codes issued for each wine by the Wine & Spirit Board, for details about the production area, variety and vintage.

Styles & Vintages

Recent South African Vintages

South African wines do not exhibit the major vintage variations seen in some other winegrowing areas. There are, nevertheless, perceptible differences from year to year. Dry, hot summers are the norm but a variety of factors make generalisations difficult and possibly misleading.

2023 Clement early season with freshness and energy, followed by cool, wet spells needing steady hands and nerves, and yielding generally lighter-toned, possibly earlier-drinking wines.

2022 Cool pre-season and moderate weather slowed ripening, giving reds and whites of excellent quality with good acidity.

2021 Bumper crop, exceptional both for reds and whites thanks to cool temperatures, unusually high rainfall and a late harvest.

2020 Hailed for concentration, freshness, svelte tannins and modest alcohol. Higher volumes too.

2019 Like 2017, bone-dry but cool, small but pristine crop showing freshness and concentration. Likely longer-lived than 2018.

2018 Challenging year, lingering drought requiring particular focus on optimal picking times. Sound, concentrated if perhaps earlier-peaking wines.

2017 Dry but surprisingly cool, resulting in smaller but excellent crop with vivacity and fine flavour concentration on reds as well as whites.

2016 Exceptionally hot and dry, later-ripening varieties benefiting from lower temperatures. In cool climates, healthy fruit yielded some stellar wines.

2015 Near-ideal conditions produced less but perfect fruit. One of the great vintages, possibly surpassing 2009.

2014 Later, slightly smaller and unusually cool. Lighter, less powerful wines; potential for fine concentration with elegance if picked judiciously.

2013 Biggest crop to date; moderate conditions yielded good to very good reds and whites, lighter alcohol levels.

2012 Unusually dry, hot January strained unirrigated vineyards; otherwise good to very good vintage for both reds and whites; moderate alcohol levels.

2011 Yet more variable than the last, impossible to generalise. As in 2010, producer's track record should guide the buying/cellaring decision.

2010 A real test of the winegrower's savvy, and one of the toughest recent harvests to call. Be guided by producer's track record.

2009 Perhaps one of the greatest vintages. Late, gruelling, but whites and reds both stellar.

2008 Long, wet, late and challenging but also unusually cool, favouring elegance in reds and whites.

Older Vintages

2007 Elegant, structured whites; smaller red-grape berries gave intense colour and fruit concentration. **2006** Perhaps the best white-wine vintage in a decade. Fleshy, mild-tannined reds, lower alcohols. **2005** Concentrated if alcoholic reds; mostly average whites. **2004** Cooler dry conditions yielded elegant, often ageworthy wines with lower alcohols, softer tannins. **2003** Outstanding, especially for reds — concentrated and structured, and often slow to show their best. **2002** Challenging and patchy, but top producers show fine concentration and moderate alcohols. **2001** Fruity and concentrated, best are long lived. Flavourful if alcoholic whites. **2000** Powerful reds, befitting a hot year; the best have kept very well. Whites generally less impressive. **1999** Fat, alcoholic reds with ripe fruit for earlier drinking. Generally not much excitement among the whites. **1998** Excellent red vintage with enough fruit for extended cellaring; whites generally not for keeping. **1997** Among coolest and latest vintages on record. Supple, elegant reds; some excellent and stylish whites. **1996** Generally awkward reds, like whites, except for top NLHs, best drunk up. **1995** For many, the vintage of the 90s. Concentrated reds, some still maturing well. **1994** Hottest, driest vintage in decades; variable quality; new-clone cabs and early ripening reds fared well. **1993** Some excellent sauvignons; above-average reds. **1992** Coolish season, favouring whites; the reds (notably pinotage) very good; **1991** Dry, warm to hot, favouring early to mid-season ripeners; some long-lasting reds. **1990** Uneven year, alternately cool and warm; average whites and reds. **1980**s: even years ('82, '84, '86) usually more favourable for reds; uneven years, marginally cooler, favoured whites, but 'white' years '87 and '89 produced remarkable reds. **1970**s: again, even years generally favoured reds. Best was '74; but some other vintages are still delicious. **1960**s and earlier yielded some long-lived wines.

South African Wine Styles

Agrafe/agraffe See Sparkling wine.

Air-dried See Straw wine.

Alcohol-free wine See De-alcoholised wine

Alternative white/red Intended to allow for greater flexibility within the official certification framework, recent category provides for dry (≤4 g/L), lower-sulphur wines with colours ranging from light gold to amber (white) and light red to purple (red). Certification is mandatory.

Amber wine See Orange wine.

Biodynamic See Winemaking Terms section.

Blanc de blancs White wine made from white grapes only; also used for champagne and cap classique. Alternative name is 'vin gris'.

Blanc de noir A pink wine (shades range from off-white through peach to pink) made from red grapes. See also Rosé.

Blanc fumé or **fumé blanc** Dry white from sauvignon, usually but not necessarily wooded (nor smoked, smoky).

Blend See Varietal wine, and Cape Blend.

Brut See Sugar or sweetness, and Sparkling wine.

Can (aluminium) Authorised in 2019 as packaging for certified wine. Can itself must have max volume of 340ml, internal protective coating and sealant. Product must have min 12-month shelf life, and filling date must be stated.

Cap classique See Sparkling wine.

Cape Blend Usually denotes a (red) blend with pinotage, the 'local' grape making up a significant part of the assemblage (the Pinotage Association stipulates min 30% and max 70% pinotage for entries in its Cape Blend competition); sometimes simply a blend showing a distinct 'Cape' character; occasionally used for chenin-based blends.

Cape Heritage Blend Sometimes (unofficially) denotes a modern version of the traditional cabernet-cinsaut blend; also a blend of traditional varieties generally.

Carbonated See Sparkling wine.

Cultivar Grape variety (a contraction of 'cultivated variety').

Cuvée French term for the blend of a wine.

De-alcoholised wine One of four classes of low/no alcohol wines now officially recognised: **Lower in Alcohol** was 'Low Alcohol', now wine with alcohol by volume > 4.5% and < 10%; **Low Alcohol** has ABV > 0.5% and < 4.5%; **De-Alcoholised** (approved synonyms: 'Non-Alcoholic' and 'Alcohol Removed') has < 0.5% ABV; **Alcohol Free** has ABV of < 0.05%.

Demi-sec See Sugar or sweetness.

Dessert wine A sweet wine, often to accompany the dessert but sometimes pleasurably prior, as in the famous Sauternes/foie gras combo.

Dry to sweet See Sugar or sweetness.

Estate wine Term reserved for wine originating from an officially registered 'unit for the production of estate wine' (see www.sawis.co.za/cert/about. php for current list).

Extended barrel-aged white/gris Category of vintage-dated, dry (≤4 g/L) wine from white/gris grapes, light gold to amber in colour, matured in oak for at least 2 years and showing a nutty/oxidative character.

Fortified wines Increased in alcoholic strength by the addition of spirit, by SA law to minimum 15% alcohol by volume.

Grand cru See Premier Grand Cru.

Ice wine Intensely sweet wine from ripe grapes picked and pressed while frozen. Not an official category.

Jerepiko or **jerepigo** Red or white wine produced without fermentation; grape juice is fortified with grape spirit, preventing fermentation; very sweet, with considerable unfermented grape flavours.

Kosher See Winemaking Terms section.

Late Harvest Unfortified wine from late-harvested and therefore sweeter grapes. Alcohol by volume (ABV) must exceed 10%. See also Sugar or sweetness.

Low/lower-alcohol wine See De-alcoholised wine

Méthode ancestrale There are two official classes of this bottle-fermented bubbly: perlé (pressure in bottle is ≤ 300 kPa) and sparkling (> 300 kPa). The perlé style may also be labelled as 'pétillant natural/natura'. See Sparkling wine.

Méthode cap classique (**MCC**) See Sparkling wine.

Natural pale/non-fortified pale Class of white wines oak-matured (under a film of flor yeast, for minimum of 2 years) with discernible almond, flor yeast and wood characters.

Natural Sweet Aka Sweet Natural. Unfortified wine with residual sugar greater than 20 g/L. See also Sugar or sweetness.

Noble Late Harvest (NLH) Sweet dessert wine (still, perlé or sparkling) exhibiting a noble rot (botrytis) character, from grapes infected by the botrytis cinerea fungus. This mould, in warm, misty autumn weather, attacks the skins of ripe grapes, causing much of the juice to evaporate.

As the berries wither, their sweetness and flavour become powerfully concentrated. SA law dictates that grapes for NLH must be harvested at a minimum of 28° Balling and residual sugar must exceed 50 g/L.

Nouveau Term originated in Beaujolais for fruity young and light red, usually from gamay and made by the carbonic maceration method. Bottled soon after vintage to capture the youthful, fresh flavour of fruit and yeasty fermentation.

Orange wine Officially recognised (since 2020) name for fashionable style of white-wine making using extended skin contact (see Winemaking Terms section), as for red wine, resulting in darker hues and greater flavour/aroma intensity, sometimes with an (attractive) oxidative character and/or noticeable tannins. See also Skin-macerated white.

Organic See Winemaking Terms section.

Perlant, perlé, pétillant Lightly sparkling, usually carbonated wine.

Pétillant natural/natura See Méthode ancestrale.

Port Fortified dessert with excellent quality record in SA since late 1980s, partly through efforts of Cape Port Producers' Association which has adopted 'Cape' to identify the local product. Following are CAPPA-defined styles: **Cape White**: non-muscat grapes, oak-aged min 6 months, any size vessel, drier to full-sweet; **Cape Pink**: non-muscat varieties, pink hue, barrel/tank-aged min 6 months; **Cape Ruby**: full bodied, fruity; min 50% barrel/tank-aged 6-36 months; can be vintage dated; **Cape Vintage**: fruit of one harvest; dark, full-bodied; tank/cask-aged min 1 year; must be certified, sold in glass, vintage dated; **Cape Vintage Reserve**: as for Vintage, but 'superior quality'; **Cape Late Bottled Vintage** (LBV): fruit of single year, full-bodied, slightly tawny colour, barrel/bottle aged min 3 years (of which min 2 years in oak); **Cape Tawny**: min 80% wood matured, amber-orange (tawny) colour, smooth, slightly nutty taste; **Cape Dated Tawny**: single-vintage tawny.

Premier Grand Cru Unlike in France, not a quality rating in SA – usually an austerely dry white.

Residual sugar See Sugar or sweetness.

Rosé Pink wine, made from red or a blend of red and white grapes. The red grape skins are removed before the wine takes up too much colour.

Single-vineyard wine Classification for wines from officially registered vineyards, no larger than 6ha in size and planted with a single variety.

Skin-macerated white Dry (≤4 g/L) white wine, light gold to deep orange in colour, macerated on-skin for at least 96 hours. See also Orange wine.

Sparkling wine Bubbly, or 'champagne', usually white but sometimes rosé and even red, given its effervescence by carbon dioxide – allowed to escape in the normal winemaking process. **Carbonated** sparklers are made by the injection of carbon dioxide bubbles (as in fizzy soft drinks). **Charmat** undergoes its second, bubble-forming fermentation in a tank and is bottled under pressure. **Méthode ancestrale** results from a single ferment, spontaneously initiated in tank and completed in bottle. From harvest 2023, the classes of bottle-fermented bubblies, which undergo a second ferment in bottle, are: **Bottle-fermented sparking** Fermented in a bottle and spends min 3 months on the lees; **Traditional method sparkling** Min 9 months on lees and, like **Méthode cap classique sparkling (MCC)**, fermented in the bottle in which it's sold. MCC has min 12 months ageing and is certified. A newer class of MCC, with **Extended lees ageing**, is made from chardonnay, pinot noir and/or meunier only, and spends min 36 months on lees. **Champagne** also undergoes its second fermentation in the bottle. However, under an agreement with France, SA does not use the term, which describes the sparkling wines from the Champagne area. **Agrafe** (or agraffe) bubbly undergoes bottle-ferment under cork instead of the usual metal crown cap. See also Sugar or sweetness.

Special Late Harvest (SLH) SA designation for a lighter dessert-style wine. There is no legal stipulation for residual sugar content, but if the RS is below 20 g/L, the label must state 'extra dry', 'dry', 'semi-dry' or 'sweet', as the case may be. The minimum alcohol content is 11% by volume.

Spirit-barrel-aged wine Wine matured in spirit barrels for min 3 months. Label must state name of relevant spirit.

Stein Semi-sweet white wine, usually a blend and often confused with steen, a grape variety (chenin blanc), though most steins are at least made partly from steen grapes.

Straw wine Vin de paille in French; sweet, unfortified wine from ripe grapes that are 'naturally dried' (optionally on straw mats). Minimum ABV is 16%.

Sugar or sweetness In still wines: extra-dry or bone-dry wines have less than 2.5 g/L residual sugar, undetectable to the taster. A wine legally is dry up to 5 g/L*. Taste buds will begin picking up a slight sweetness, or softness, in a wine – depending on its acidity – at about 6 g/L, when it is still off-dry. By about 8–9 g/L a definite sweetness can usually be noticed. However, an acidity of 8–9 g/L can render a sweet wine fairly crisp even with a sugar content of 20 g/L plus. Official sweetness levels in SA wine are listed in the table below.

Wine	Sugar (g/L)
Still wines	
Extra-dry	≤ 2.5
Dry*	≤ 5
Semi-dry*	> 5 ≤ 12
Semi-sweet	> 5 < 30
Late Harvest	≥ 20
Special Late Harvest (SLH)	—
Natural Sweet (or Sweet Natural)	> 20
Noble Late Harvest (NLH)	> 50
Naturally dried grape wine (straw wine)	> 30
Sparkling wines	
Brut nature	< 3
Extra brut	< 6
Brut	< 12
Extra-dry	12–17
Dry	17–32
Semi-sweet	32–50
Sweet	> 50

* Amendments allow for higher sugar levels for dry (9 g/L) and semi-dry (18 g/L) if the total acidity is within 2 g/L or 10 g/L respectively of the sugar level.

Sun wine Bottlings in this fortified category must be from white grapes, pale to deep gold in colour and show a maderised character (see under Winetasting Terms section). Must be certified and vintage dated.

Sweet Natural See Natural Sweet.

Uncertified wine Does not claim origin, variety and/or vintage year.

Varietal wine From a single variety of grape. Legislation requires the presence in the wine of 85% of the stated variety or vintage. Blends may name component parts only if those components were vinified separately, prior to blending; then they are listed with the larger contributor(s) named first. If any one of the blend partners is less than 20%, percentages for all the varieties must be given. Blends may be vinified separately in any recognised WO area; component areas may be named, as above except the threshold is 30%.

Vin de paille See Straw wine.

Vine-dried wine Often – but not necessarily – sweet, from grapes desiccated on the vine.

Vintage In SA primarily used to denote year of harvest. Not a quality classification (a 'vintage' port in Europe means one from an officially declared great port-grape year).

Wine in cans See Cans

South African Brandy, Husk Spirit & Sherry-Style Wines

Brandy and Husk Spirit

SA brandy is divided into three main stylistic categories. Put simply and reductively, these are as follows:

- **Blended brandy** must by law contain at least 30% per LAA (litres absolute alcohol) brandy distilled in a potstill and aged for at least three years in oak barrels smaller than 340L each. The remaining component will be of wine spirit (made in a continuous still). More often than not, these brandies are intended to partner mixers or to play a role in cocktails. The alcohol by volume (ABV) must be at least 43% (in practice it usually is 43%).

- **Vintage brandy** (a small category) must have at least 30% potstill brandy, but not more than 80%, aged minimum eight years. Up to 70% wine spirit, but not less than 20%, is permitted but it too must be matured at least eight years.

- **Potstill brandy** must be 100% potstilled and matured at least three years in oak barrels. The

ABV is a minimum of 38%, as for Vintage brandy. Since 2020, may also be labelled 'Cape Brandy'.

Estate brandy is brandy in any of the above categories in which all stages of production, from vineyard to maturation, took place on one property (as for 'estate' wine).

Not (yet) regulated locally, the following official French (cognac) designations are increasingly used here, with minimum age adjustments for VS to comply with local legislation:

- **VS (Very Special)** - youngest component is at least 3 years old (2 for cognac).
- **VSOP (Very Superior Old Pale)** - youngest component is at least 4 years old.
- **XO (Extra Old)** - youngest component is at least 10 years old.
- **XXO (Extra Extra Old)** - youngest component is at least 14 years old.

Husk Spirit will have an ABV level of at least 43% and not be matured; **Premium Husk Spirit** must be at least 40% ABV, and be matured in oak for between three and six months.

Sherry-Style Fortified Wines

There are eight classes of sherry-style wines described in South Africa's Liquor Products Act. The colour of these wines must range – depending on the class – from pale straw to amber. Their aromas and flavours must be 'nutty' and 'woody'. Five of the eight classes must have a discernible flor yeast and/or wood character. In addition:

- In the case of **Fino**, the residual sugar shall not exceed 20 g/L, and the alcohol content must not exceed 16%. It should have an almond flavour.
- The alcohol content of an **Amontillado** must be at least 16%, and it should have a flavour of hazelnuts.
- **Oloroso** must have rich, nutty flavours, a minimum of 50 g/L residual sugar, and at least 16% alcohol by volume.
- The residual sugar content of a **Pale Dry** wine cannot exceed 30 g/L, and its alcohol content should exceed 16%.

- Similarly, the alcohol content of a **Pale Cream** must exceed 16%, but its residual sugar must range between 30 g/L and 80 g/L.
- The remaining three classes need only exhibit a discernible wood character.
- In addition, the residual sugar and alcohol content of a **Medium Cream** must be between 80 g/L and 115 g/L, and above 16% respectively.
- A **Full Cream** wine must have at least 115 g/L residual sugar, and an alcohol content above 16%.
- A muscat character and an aldehyde content of at least 80 mg/L, a residual sugar content of at least 100 g/L, and at least 16% alcohol by volume is necessary for an **Old Brown**. This may also only be sweetened with concentrated must, or with fortified wine with a residual sugar content of at least 180 g/L.

Words & Phrases

Winetasting Terms

Short of a ready description? Here are a few frequently used words, phrases and explanations that may be helpful. See also Winemaking Terms, and SA Wine Styles.

Accessible, approachable Flavours and feel of the wine are harmonious, easily recognised; it is ready to drink.

Aftertaste The lingering flavours and impressions of a wine; its persistence – the longer, the better.

Alcoholic 'Hot' or, in excess, burning character caused by imbalanced or excessive alcohol. Also simply spirituous.

Astringent Mouth-puckering sensation, associated with high tannin (and sometimes acid); also bitter, sharp.

Aroma Smells in the bouquet, or nose, especially the odours associated with the grape rather than the winemaking process.

Attack First sensations on palate/nose – pungent, aggressive, quiet etc.

Austere Usually meaning unyielding, sometimes harsh. Sometimes, more favourably, to imply a notable restraint/refinement.

Backbone The wine is well formed, firm, not flabby or insipid.

Baked 'Hot', earthy quality. Usually from scorched/shrivelled grapes which have been exposed too long to the sun, or from too warm a ferment, especially in some whites.

Balance Desirable attribute. The wine's chief constituents – alcohol, acid, tannin, fruit and wood (where used) – are in harmony.

Bead Bubbles in sparkling wine; a fine, long-lasting bead is the most desirable. See also Mousse.

Big Expansive in the mouth, weighty, full-bodied, as a result of high alcohol and/or fruit concentration.

Bite or **grip** Imparted by tannin, acid and/or alcohol, important in young wines designed for ageing. If overdone can impart undesirable bitterness, harshness or spiry 'glow'.

Bitter Sensation perceived mainly on the back of the tongue, and in the finish of the wine. Usually unpleasant, though an accepted if not immediately admired character of certain Italian wines. Sometimes more positively associated with the taste of a specific fruit or nut, such as cherry-kernel or almond.

Body Fullness on the palate.

Botrytis/ed Exhibits a noble rot/botrytis character, from grapes infected by the *botrytis cinerea* fungus.

Bottle-age Negative or positive, depending on context. Positively describes development of aromas/flavours (i.e. complexity) as wine moves from youth to maturity. Much-prized attribute in fine whites and reds. Negatively, bottle age results in a wine with stale, empty or even off odours.

Buttery Flavour and texture associated with barrel-fermented white wines, especially chardonnays; rich, creamy smoothness.

Claret Another name for a dry red Bordeaux or Bordeaux-like red.

Classic Showing characteristics of the classics of Bordeaux, Burgundy etc; usually implying balance, elegance, subtlety.

Coarse Rough, unbalanced tannins, acid, alcohol or oak.

Complexity Strong recommendation. A complex wine has several layers of flavour, usually developing with age/maturation. See Bottle-age.

Concentration See Intensity.

Confected Over-elaborately constructed, artificial, forced; sometimes overly sweet.

Corked, corky Wine is faulty; its flavours have been tainted by yeast, fungal or bacterial infections, often but not necessarily from the cork. It smells damp and mouldy in its worst stages – but sometimes it's barely detectable. In a restaurant, a corked wine should be rejected and returned immediately; producers are honour-bound to replace corked wine.

Creamy Not literally creamy, of course; more a silky, buttery feel and texture.

Crisp Refers to acidity. Positively, means fresh, clean; negatively, too tart, sharp.

Deep and **depth** Having many layers; intense; also descriptive of a serious wine.

Dense Well-padded texture, flavour packed.

Deposits (also sediment or crust) Tasteless and harmless tartrates, acid crystals or tannin in older red wines. Evidence that wine has not been harshly fined, filtered or cold-stabilised.

Dried out Bereft of fruit, harder constituents remaining; tired.

Earthy Usually positive, wine showing its origins from soil, minerals, damp leaves, mushrooms etc.

Easy Undemanding (and hopefully inexpensive).

Elegant Stylish, refined, 'classic'.

Esters Scents and smells usually generated by alcohols and acids in wine. A wine may be 'estery' when these characteristics are prominent.

Extract An indication of the 'substance' of a wine, expressed as sugar-free or total extract (which would include some sugars). 18 g/L would be low, light; anything much above 23 g/L in whites is significant; the corresponding threshold for reds is around 30g/L.

Fat Big, full, ample in the mouth.

Finesse/d Graceful, polished. Nothing excessive.

Finish The residual sensations – tastes and textures – after swallowing. Should be pleasant (crisp, lively) and enduring, not short, dull or flat. See also Aftertaste and Length.

Firm Compact, has good backbone.

Flabby Usually lacking backbone, especially acid.

Flat Characterless, unexciting, lacks acid. Or bubbly which has lost its fizz.

Fleshy Very positive, meaning a wine is well fleshed out with texture and grape flavours.

Flowery, floral Flower-like (i.e. smell of rose, honeysuckle, jasmine etc.). Distinct from 'fruity' (i.e. smell/taste of papaya, cantaloupe, grape! etc.).

Forward rather than shy; advancing in age too; mature.

Fresh Lively, youthful, invigorating. Closely related to the amount of acid in the wine and absence of oxidative character: a big, intensely sweet dessert without a backbone of acidity will taste flat and sickly; enough acid and the taste is fresh and uncloying.

Fruity See Flowery.

Full High in alcohol and extract.

Gamey Overripe, decadent, not universally unattractive; also meaty, 'wild'.

Gravel/ly With suggestions of mineral, earthy quality; also firm texture.

Green Usually unripe, sour; also herbaceous; sometimes simply youthful.

Grip Gripping, firm on palate, in finish. Acid, tannin, alcohol are contributors.

Heady Usually refers to the smell of a wine. High in alcohol; intense, high-toned.

Herbaceous Grassy, hay-like, heathery; can also indicate under-ripeness.

Hollow Lacking substance, flavours.

Honey or honeyed Sometimes literally a honey/beeswax taste or flavour; a sign of developing maturity in some varieties or more generally a sign of bottle age.

Hot Burning sensation of alcohol in finish.

Intensity No flab, plenty of driving flavour; also deep colour.

Lean Thin, mean, lacking charm of ample fruit; also, more positively, compact, sinewy.

Lees/leesy Taste-imparting dead yeast cells (with grape skins and other solid matter) remaining with wine in tank/barrel (or bottle in the case of méthode champenoise sparkling wines) after fermentation. The longer the wine is 'on its lees' (sur lie) the more richness and flavour it should absorb.

Light/lite Officially wines under 10% alcohol by volume; also light in body (and often short on taste); a health-conscious trend in both reds and whites.

Lively Bouncy, fresh flavours.

Long or length Enduring; wine's flavours reverberate on the palate long after swallowing.

Maderised Oxidised and flat; colour is often brownish. Over-mature. More positively, a madeira-like oxidative quality, with 'cooked'/caramelised flavours.

Meaty Sometimes suggesting a general savouriness; but also literally the aroma of meat – raw, smoked etc.

Mousse Fizz in sparkling wines; usually refers also to quality, size and effervescence of the bubbles. See also Bead.

Mouthfeel, mouthfilling Texture, feel; racy, crispness (fine with appropriate dishes) or generous, supple, smooth.

Neutral What it says, neither here nor there.

New World Generally implies accessible, bold, often extrovert (in terms of fruit and use of oak). **Old World** embraces terms like subtle, complex, less oaky, more varied and generally more vinous (than fruity). See also Classic.

Oaky Having exaggerated oak aromas/flavours (vanilla, spice, char, woodsmoke etc.). Oak balanced by fruit in young wines may lessen with age, but over-oaked young wines (where fruit is not in balance) will become over-oaked old wines.

Palate Combination of flavour, taste and texture of a wine.

Pebbly See Gravelly.

Perfumed or scented Strong fragrances (fruity, flowery, animal etc)

Phenolic Astringency or bitterness, usually in white wine, attributed to excessive phenolic compounds.

Plump Well fleshed in a charming, cherubic way.

Porty Heavy, over-ripe, stewed; a negative in unfortified wine.

Rich Flavourful, intense, generous. Not necessarily sweet.

Robust Strapping, full-bodied (but not aggressive).

Rough Bull-in-a-china-shop wine, or throat sand-papering quality.

Round Well balanced, without gawkiness or jagged edges.

Sharp or **tart** All about acid, usually unbalanced. But occasionally sharpish, fresh wine is right for the occasion.

Short or **quick** Insubstantial wine, leaving little impression.

Simple One-dimensional or no flavour excitement.

Stalky Unripe, bitter, stemmy.

Stewed Over-ripe, cooked, soft, soggy fruit.

Structure The wine's make up (fruit, acid, tannin, alcohol etc), also in relation to its ageing ability; if a wine is deemed to have 'the structure to age' it suggests these principal elements are in place.

Stylish Classy, distinguished; also voguish.

Supple Very desirable (not necessarily subtle), yielding, refined texture and flavours. See also Mouthfeel.

Tannic Tannins are prominent in the wine, imparting, positively, a mouth-puckering, grippy, tangy quality; negatively, a harsh, unyielding character.

Tension Racy, nervy fruit-acid play on the palate.

Terpene(s)/terpenoid Strong, floral compounds influencing the aromas of especially riesling, gewürztraminer and the muscats; with bottle-age, terpenes can develop a pungent resinous oiliness.

Texture Tactile 'feel' in the mouth: hard, acidic, coarse and alcoholic; or, smooth, velvety, 'warm'.

Toasty Often used for barrel-fermented or -aged wines showing a pleasant biscuity, charry character.

Vegetal Grassy, leafy, herby – in contrast to fruity, flowery, oaky. Overdone, a no-no.

Yeasty Warm bakery smells, often evident in barrel-fermented whites and méthode champenoise sparkling wines, where yeasts stay in contact with the wine after fermentation.

Winemaking Terms

A few brief reference explanations. See also sections on Winetasting Terms and SA Wine Styles.

Acid and **acidity** The fresh – or, in excess, sharp or tart – taste of wine. Too little acid and the wine tastes dull and flat. In SA, winemakers are permitted to adjust acidity either by adding acid – at any stage before bottling – or by lowering the acid level with a de-acidifier. See also Volatile acid and Malolactic.

Alcohol Essential component of wine, providing fullness, richness and, at higher levels, sometimes an impression of sweetness. Also a preservative, helping keep wines in good condition. Produced by yeasts fermenting the sugars in the grape. Measured by volume of the total liquid. Most unfortified table wines in SA have between 11% and 14.5% alc by vol; fortifieds range from ±15% to 21%. A variation of up to 1% between the strength stated on the label and the laboratory analysis is permitted by local law. Various techniques (such as reverse osmosis and 'spinning cone', also the addition of water) exist to address the increasingly important issue of high alcohol levels in wine, and some are legal in SA (though not for export to, e.g., Europe).

Barrels (**barrel-aged**; **barrel-fermented**) Wines are transferred to barrels to age, pick up oaky flavours etc. When must or fermenting must is put into barrels, the resulting wine is called barrel-fermented. A barrel or cask is generally a 225–500L oak container; barrique is a French word for a 225-L barrel; pipe, adapted from the Portuguese pipa, usually indicates a vessel of 530–630L; vat and foudre are terms generally used for larger (2,000–5,000L) wooden vessels.

Bâtonnage See Lees.

Biodynamic See Organic.

Blend A wine made from two or more different grape varieties, vintages, vineyards or containers. Some of the world's finest wines are blends.

Bottles While the 750-ml (75-cl) bottle is now the most widely used size of container for wine, it is by no means the only one. Smaller bottles (375 and 500 ml) are popular with restaurants and airlines, and larger sizes are prized by collectors because of their novelty value and/or their tendency to promote slower wine ageing. The following are the larger bottle sizes (note: some no longer in production):

Capacity		Bordeaux	Champagne/Burgundy
litres	bottles		
1.5	2	Magnum	Magnum
3	4	Double magnum	Jéroboam
4.5	6	Jéroboam	Rehoboam
6	8	Impériale	Methuselah

Capacity		Bordeaux	Champagne/ Burgundy
litres	bottles		
9	12	—	Salmanazar
12	16	—	Balthazar
15	20	—	Nebuchadnezzar

Brettanomyces or **'brett'** Naturally occurring yeast, usually associated with red wine and regarded as a spoilage factor, because its growth triggers the formation of volatile acids, phenols and other compounds which, in sufficient concentration, impart a range of unpleasant characters, from barnyard to sweat to cheese. At low concentrations, can enhance complexity and character.

Carbonic maceration or **maceration carbonique** Method of fermenting wine without first crushing the grapes. Whole clusters with stalks etc. are put into closed vat; intracellular fermentation occurs within the grape berries, which then burst.

Chaptalisation Originally French term for the addition of sugar to grape must to raise the alcohol of a wine. Selectively legal in northern Europe, where acid adjustments are not allowed as they are in SA.

Charmat Method of making sparkling wine in a sealed tank (cuvée close) under pressure. Easier, cheaper than méthode champenoise.

Chips See Oak chips.

Cold ferment 'Cold' is a relative term; applied to ferment of mainly white wines in temperature-controlled tanks, it refers to a temperature around usually 13–16°C. The benefits, especially important in a warm country, include conserving the primary fruit aromas and ensuring fermentation is carried out steadily and thoroughly.

Cold soak or **cold maceration**. Red-wine making method carried out prior to fermentation. Skins and juice are held, usually for a few days, at a sufficiently cool temperature to prevent fermentation. The theory is that this extracts more favourable colour and aromas than after fermentation.

Cold stabilisation Keeping a wine at about -4°C for a week or more to precipitate tartaric acid and 'clean up' the wine, preventing later formation of (harmless) tartrate crystals in bottle. Some winemakers believe this process damages flavour and prefer to avoid it.

Concrete Traditionally the preferred construction material for larger fermentation and storage containers, largely superseded since the 1970s by stainless steel. More recently concrete 'eggs', their shape reminiscent of the amphoras of antiquity, have found favour for reasons varying from more-uniform fermentations to improved wine structure, texture and flavour.

Disgorgement (dégorgement in French) Important stage in the production of traditionally fermented sparkling where accumulated sediment (or lees), which could cloud the finished wine, is removed from the neck of the bottle.

Dosage The sugar added to sparkling wine after the second fermentation.

Fermentation The conversion of sugar in grapes into alcohol and carbon dioxide, a function of enzymes secreted by yeasts. In modern SA winemaking, cultured yeasts are normally added to secure the process, but along with the growth of the natural winemaking movement, ferments using wild yeasts (which occur both in vineyard and cellar) are increasing. Beyond about 15% of alcohol, yeasts are overwhelmed and fermentation ceases, although it usually is stopped (for instance by cooling, filtration or the addition of alcohol) before this stage. See also Malolactic.

Filtration Removes last impurities including yeast cells. Done excessively, can thin a wine. Some traditionalists bottle without cold- or protein-stabilisation or filtration.

Fining and **protein stabilisation** Fining is ridding wine of suspended particles by adding substances that attract and draw the particles from the wine.

Flash-pasteurisation See Kosher.

Free run After grapes have been de-stalked and crushed, juice runs freely.

Garage wine Generic term for wine made in minuscule quantities, sometimes literally in a garage; a grower of such wine is sometimes called a garagiste.

Glycerol Minor product of alcoholic fermentation; from the Greek for sweet. Has an apparent sweetening effect on even dry wines and also gives a viscous, mouthfilling character.

Icewine Sweet, concentrated wine from grapes picked and pressed while frozen. Not a recognised category for SA wine production.

Kosher Wine made 'correctly', ie under rabbinical supervision, to be suitable for use by religious Jews. Vinification and any initial movement of the wine must be done by an observant Jew. Flash-pasteurisation, increasingly by means of flavour-preserving processes such as Thermoflash, renders the resulting meshuval wine (literally 'boiled' or 'cooked') fit for handling by non-Jews.

Leafroll virus Virus (or complex of viruses), widespread throughout the winegrowing world, which causes the vine to perform below its potential and thereby produce wine which is lower in colour, body and flavour than that derived from virus-free or 'cleaned-up' plants.

Lees Spent yeast cells and other matter which collect at the bottom of any container in winemaking. Yeast autolysis, or decomposition, can impart richness and flavour to a wine, sometimes referred to as leesy. Lees stirring or bâtonnage involves mixing the bed of lees in a barrel or tank through the wine, which is said to be sur lie; it is employed primarily on barrel-fermented white wines. The main effects of mixing lees and wine are to prevent off-odours developing from lack of oxygen, to limit the amount of wood tannin and oak character extracted, and to increase flavour.

Malolactic fermentation (malo) Occurs when bacteria convert malic into lactic acids. This reduces the acidity of a wine, a normal and healthy process, especially in reds — provided, of course, it occurs before bottling.

Maturation Ageing properties are closely related to tannin and/or fixed acid content of a wine. A relatively full red wine with tannin has lasting power. With age, it may develop complexity, subtlety and smooth mellowness. Lighter wines with lower tannins are drinkable sooner but probably will not reach the same level of complexity. A rising number of SA whites mature well over several years, but most are best drunk in their fruity youth, up to 18 months.

Méthode champenoise Classic method of making champagne by inducing secondary fermentation in the bottle and producing fine bubbles. Due to French restrictions on terminology, local wines made in this way are called bottle-fermented sparkling, traditional method sparkling or (méthode) cap classique sparkling. See Sparkling wine in Styles & Vintages section.

Micro-oxygenation Technique enabling introduction of precise, controlled doses of oxygen to must/wine. Advocates claim softer tannins, more stable colours and other advantages.

Oak chips, either in older barrels or stainless steel tanks, are widely used in SA, as are oak **staves**. Still frowned on by some purists, the 'additives' approximate the flavour effects of a new barrel, far more cheaply, more easily handled.

Oak-matured See Barrels.

Organic viticulture/winemaking Increasingly popular alternative to 'conventional' or 'industrialised' winegrowing, emphasising natural and sustainable farming methods and cellar techniques. A variant is biodynamic viticulture, influenced by anthroposophy, focused on improving wine quality through harmony with nature and its rhythms.

Oxidation Change (usually for the worse) due to exposure to air, in whites often producing dark yellow or yellowish colour (called maderisation), altering, 'ageing' the taste. Controlled oxidation can be used to produce positive development in wine (see next entry).

Oxidative winemaking Intentional exposure to oxygen during vinification, imparting in a nutty/biscuity quality to the wine. Contrast with protective winemaking, where contact with oxygen is avoided as much as possible.

Pasteurisation See Kosher.

pH A chemical notation, used in winemaking and evaluation. The pH of a wine is its effective, active acidity — not in volume but by strength or degree. The reading provides a guide to a wine's keepability. The optimum pH in a wine is somewhere between 3.1 and 3.4 — which significantly improves a wine's protection from bacterial spoilage, so permitting it to mature and develop if properly stored.

Racking Drawing or pumping wine off from one cask or tank to another, to leave behind the deposit or lees.

Reductive Wine in an unevolved, unoxidised state is said to be 'reductive'; usually with a tight, sometimes unyielding character. The absence of air (in a bottled wine) or the presence of substantial sulphur dioxide (anti-oxidant) levels, will inhibit both oxidation and reduction processes, which are linked and complementary.

Reverse osmosis A specialised filtration technique, permitted in SA for various purposes, including the removal of water from wine. See also Alcohol.

Skin contact After crushing and de-stemming, white grapes may be left for a period with the juice, remaining in contact with skins (before being moved into the press, from which the grape juice is squeezed). Some winemakers believe the colours and flavours in and under the grape skins should be maximised in this way; others believe extended (or any) contact can lead to coarseness, even bitterness.

Sulphur dioxide (SO$_2$) Sterilising agent and preservative, near-ubiquitous in winemaking since antiquity, now strictly controlled. In SA, max total

SO_2 level for dry wines is 150–160 mg/L; for wines with 5+ g/L sugar it is 200 mg/L; and botryt-is-style wines 300 mg/L. Any wine with more than 10 mg/L total SO_2 must carry the warning 'Contains sulphites' (or 'sulfites') on the label.

Sur lie See Lees.

Tannin Vital preservative in wine, derives primarily from the grape skins. Necessary for a red wine's longevity. A young wine's raw tannin can give it a harshness, but no red wine matures into a great one without tannin, which itself undergoes change, combines with other substances and mellows. Tannin leaves a mouth-puckering dryness about the gums, gives 'grip' to a wine. A wooded wine will usually also contain some wood tannin.

Tartrates Harmless crystals formed by tartaric acid precipitating in non-cold-stabilised wine. Because of lack of public acceptance, usually avoided through cold stabilisation.

Terroir Important, controversial (and in SA over-used) French term embracing soil, climate, topography and other elements which constitute the natural environment of a vineyard site and give it a unique character.

Thermovinification/Thermoflash See Kosher.

Unfiltered See Filtration.

Virus or **virused** See Leafroll.

Volatile acid (VA) The part of the acidity which can become volatile. A high reading indicates a wine is prone to spoilage. Recognised at high levels by a sharp, 'hot', vinegary smell. In SA, most wines must by law be below 1.2 g/L of VA; in practice, the majority are well below 1 g/L.

Wholebunch pressing or **cluster pressing** Some SA cellars use this age-old process of placing whole bunches directly in the press and gently squeezing. The more usual method is to de-stem and crush the berries before pressing. Wholebunch pressing is said to yield fresher, cleaner must, and wine lower in polyphenols which, in excess, tend to age wines faster and render them coarser.

Wood-fermented/matured See Barrels.

Yeasts Micro-organisms that secrete enzymes which convert or ferment sugar into alcohol. See Fermentation.

Touring Wine Country

Wine Routes, Trusts & Associations

For localised information about regional official wine routes and wineries, contact these organisations:

Agulhas Wine Triangle ▪ T +27 (0)82-658-3883 (André Morgenthal) ▪ andre@agulhaswinetriangle.co.za ▪ www.agulhaswinetriangle.co.za

Breedekloof Wine & Tourism ▪ T +27 (0)23-349-1791 ▪ info@breedekloof.com ▪ www.breedekloof.com

Constantia Wine Route ▪ info@constantiawineroute.com ▪ www.constantiawineroute.com

Darling Wine & Food Experience ▪ +27 (0)22-492-3971 ▪ taste@darlingwine.co.za ▪ www.hellodarling.org.za

Wines of Elgin ▪ info@winesofelgin.co.za ▪ www.winesofelgin.co.za

Franschhoek See Vignerons de Franschhoek.

Helderberg See Stellenbosch.

Hemel-en-Aarde Winegrowers Association ▪ T +27 (0)84-498-0779 (Bernice Baumgarten) ▪ info@hemelenaardewines.com ▪ www.hemel-enaardewines.com

Klein Karoo Wine Route ▪ T +27 (0)82-214-5910 (Ellen Marais) ▪ info@kleinkaroowines.co.za ▪ www.kleinkaroowines.co.za

Northern Cape Wine Association See Orange River Wine Route

Olifants River Vodacom Wine Route See West Coast Wine Route

Orange River Wine Route ▪ T +27 (0)54-337-8800 (Maderé Liebenberg) ▪ info@orangeriver-wines.com / madere@owk.co.za

Paarl Wine Route ▪ T +27 (0)21-872-4842 ▪ info@paarlwine.co.za ▪ www.paarlwine.co.za

Plett Winelands (Plettenberg Bay) ▪ info@plettwinelands.com ▪ www.plettwinelands.com

Robertson Wine Valley ▪ manager@robertsonwinevalley.com ▪ www.robertsonwinevalley.com

Stanford Wine Route ▪ T +27 (0)82-572-5856 / +27 (0)82-927-0979 ▪ stanfordwr@gmail.com

Stellenbosch Wine Routes ▪ T +27 (0)21-886-4310 ▪ info@wineroute.co.za ▪ www.wineroute.co.za

Swartland Wine & Olive Route ▪ T +27 (0)22-487-1133 ▪ swartlandinfo@westc.co.za ▪ www.swartlandwineandolives.co.za

Tulbagh Wine Route ▪ T +27 (0)23-230-1348/75 ▪ info@tulbaghtourism.co.za ▪ www.tulbaghwineroute.com ▪ www.tulbaghtourism.co.za

Vignerons de Franschhoek ▪ T +27 (0)66-224-6360 / +27 (0)73-688-9894 ▪ infodesk@franschhoek.org.za ▪ www.franschhoek.org.za

Walker Bay Wine Wander ▪ T +27 (0)28-316-3988 ▪ info@hermanus.co.za

Wellington Wine Route ▪ T +27 (0)21-864-1378 ▪ wine@wellington.co.za ▪ www.wellington.co.za

West Coast Wine Route ▪ T+27 (0)82-608-7554 / +27 (0)27-201-3376 ▪ wine@visitnwc.com ▪ www.visitnwc.com

Worcester Wine & Olive Route ▪ T+27 (0)23-342-6244 / +27 (0)76-200-8742 ▪ info@worcesterwineroute.com ▪ www.worcesterwineroute.com

Winelands Tourism Offices

For additional accommodation options, brochures and local advice, contact the information offices and/or publicity associations of the wine areas you plan to visit.

Breedekloof Wine & Tourism ▪ T +27 (0)23-349-1791 ▪ info@breedekloof.com ▪ www.breedekloof.com

Calitzdorp Tourism ▪ info@visitcalitzdorp.co.za ▪ www.visitcalitzdorp.co.za

Elgin Grabouw Tourism ▪ T +27 (0)71-267-9785 ▪ info@elgingrabouw.co.za ▪ www.elgingrabouw.co.za

Franschhoek Wine Valley ▪ T +27 (0)66-224-6360 / +27 (0)73-688-9894 ▪ infodesk@franschhoek.org.za ▪ www.franschhoek.org.za

McGregor Tourism ▪ T +27 (0)23-625-1954 ▪ info@tourismmcgregor.co.za ▪ www.tourismmcgregor.co.za

Paarl Visitor Information Centre See Visit Paarl

Route 62 ▪ info@route62.co.za ▪ www.route62.co.za

Tulbagh Tourism ▪ T +27 (0)23-230-1348/75 ▪ info@tulbaghtourism.co.za ▪ www.tulbaghwineroute.com ▪ www.tulbaghtourism.co.za

Visit Paarl ▪ T +27 (0)21-872-4842 ▪ info@paarlonline.com ▪ www.paarlonline.com

Visit Stellenbosch ▪ T +27 (0) 21-886-4310 ▪ info@visitstellenbosch.org ▪ www.visitstellenbosch.org

Visit Wellington ▪ T +27 (0)21-864-1378 ▪ info@
wellington.co.za ▪ www.wellington.co.za
Wellington Visitor Information Centre See
Visit Wellington

Worcester Tourism Association ▪ T+27 (0)23-
342-6244 / +27 (0)76-200-8742 ▪ info@worces-
tertourism.com / manager@worcestertourism.
com ▪ www.worcestertourism.com

Specialist Wine Tours

Below are some specialist wine tour guides operating in Cape Town and the winelands. These are paid
entries. The guides supplied information on their services, which was then edited for consistency of style.

African Story Wine Tours Contact Bruce Storey ▪
info@africanstorytours.com ▪ www.africanstory-
tours.com ▪ English spoken ▪ **T +27 (0)73-755-
0444 / +27 (0)79-694-7915** ▪ Tour times: about
8.30am-5.30pm daily, pick-up/drop-off in Cape
Town city centre ▪ Closed Christmas & New Year
▪ Facebook/Twitter/Flickr/YouTube: African Story
Tours ▪ Son Vida Flats, 79 Somerset Rd, Green Point ▪
PostNet Cape Quarter, PostNet Suite 029, Private Bag
X100, Cape Town 8000 ▪ Special/unique facilities &
features: private and group tours also offered.

The scheduled tour leaves from Cape Town city
centre and is fun but informative, visiting Paarl,
Franschhoek and Stellenbosch wine regions. The
day includes four wineries and a delicious gourmet
lunch. Also cheese-and-wine pairings and, for the
adventurous, occasionally more exotic matches like
wine and chocolate. Cellar tours are included.

African Wine Tour info@africanwinetour.com
▪ www.africanwinetour.com ▪ English spoken ▪
Facebook: Wine Tours South Africa ▪ Instagram:
Winetour.co.za ▪ **T +27 (0)82-229-8865** ▪ 12
Market Str, Stellenbosch ▪ Special/unique facilities
& features: group tours & private tours, plus shuttle
services, departing daily from Cape Town and
Stellenbosch.

Creating memories for international visitors and
locals since 1994, African Wine Tour provides tours
and shuttles to suit every taste, requirement and
budget. Full-day group tours and bespoke private
tours tailored to your individual preferences are
offered, along with shuttle services between Cape
Town and the winelands' premier destinations,
Stellenbosch and Franschhoek. All designed with
a focus on wine and its culture. Qualified and
registered guides are top-rated, and always keen to
share their local knowledge.

Cape Fine Wine Tours Contact John Lawrence ▪
john@capefinewinetours.com ▪ www.capefinew-
inetours.com ▪ English, German, Italian spoken ▪
T +27 (0)82-258-2951 ▪ 41 Loresta, St Andrews Rd,
Rondebosch, Cape Town ▪ Special/unique facilities &
features: introductions to winemakers.

Cape Fine Wine Tours' winelands excursions are
private and customised, and include cellar tours,
vineyard walks, barrel tastings and library tastings.
Overnight tours are a speciality, and feature fine
wines and fine dining.

Percy Tours Hermanus Contact Percy Heywood
▪ travel@percytours.com ▪ www.percytours.com ▪
www.hermanuswinetours.com ▪ English, Afrikaans,
some French ▪ **T +27 (0)72-062-8500** ▪ WhatsApp/
Instagram/Facebook: Percy Tours Hermanus ▪ PO Box
488, Hermanus 7200 ▪ Special/unique facilities &
features: registered and accredited with Cape Wine
Academy; Cape Town and Hermanus & Overberg
tourism boards; registered tour guides and PDP
professional chauffeurs; insured to the highest levels
(Passenger Liability and General Liability policies).

Established in 2004, Percy Tours specialise in fully
tailor-made, personalised, door-to-door wine tours
of Hermanus, recently named a UNESCO Creative City
of Gastronomy, as well as Stellenbosch, Franschhoek
and the Cape winelands in all their remarkable
diversity. A fleet of spacious and luxurious minibuses
(and cars) with knowledgeable chauffeur wine-tour
guides collect you from your accommodation and
supply many comforts on board. The guides have
completed Cape Wine Academy courses, so they will
discuss many wine topics - and much more - while
you sip delicious wines. Flexibility is key, meaning
individuals or groups of any size can be hosted.
Wine-and-food pairings, and restaurant lunches at
scenic wineries are increasingly popular and highly
recommended, and Percy Tours can easily advise
you and make the necessary reservations. Visit
Percy Tours' TripAdvisor page for reviews by many
delighted clients.

R44 Tours ExperienceTheWinelands@yahoo.com
▪ English & Afrikaans spoken ▪ Facebook: R44 Wine
Tours ▪ **T +27 (0)65-564-0731 / +27(0)83-312-
9544 (WhatsApp only)** ▪ Special/unique facilities
& features: servicing local and international guests
the Helderberg area with visits to wine estates from
Stellenbosch to Elgin.

Departing at 10 am from guests' accommodation
in the Helderberg environs, each approximately

4-hour tour covers the area that surrounds the R44 route between Stellenbosch and Elgin, giving local and international visitors the opportunity to explore one of the most beautiful and alluring parts of the Cape's winelands. Gertrude Mcstay, qualified cultural guide, leads each tour herself, ensuring a personal, authentic and informative experience.

Sipper Club Contact Sasha van Zyl ▪ hellosipper-club@gmail.com ▪ www.sipperclub.co.za ▪ English spoken ▪ **T +27 (0)79-815-9020** ▪ Instagram: @ sipper.club ▪ Dawson Street, Onrus 7201 ▪ Special/unique facilities & features: hosted by a sommelier. Meet and taste with winemakers. Cellar & vineyard tour. Personalised itinerary.

Explore South Africa's coolest wine regions, Bot River, Hemel-en-Aarde and Stanford, hosted by local sommelier Sasha van Zyl, who believes wine is an art, a story and an adventure. You'll be immersed in the world of winemaking, walking alongside the passionate winemakers, exploring private cellars and picturesque vineyards, and savouring vintage wines opened exclusively for you, ensuring every experience is extraordinary.

Vineyard Ventures (Glen Christie) Contact Glen Christie ▪ vinven@iafrica.com ▪ www.vineyard-ventures.co.za ▪ English, Afrikaans, German spoken; other languages on request ▪ **T +27 (0)21-434-8888 / +27 (0)82-920-2825** ▪ A82 Punta Del Mar, Milton Rd, Sea Point ▪ PO Box 554, Sea Point 8060

Vineyard Ventures creates private, all-inclusive tours of Cape Town, the winelands and southern Africa tailored to clients' personal interests and preferences. Glen Christie and her team are wine and food specialists, and with more than 30 years' experience, their knowledge, expertise and contacts in the industry can't be matched. They deal with the widest range of travel requirements when arranging itineraries or travel bookings, combining this with personal attention and flexibility. Their forte is introducing clients to the captivating world of South African wines while facilitating unforgettable adventures and experiences beyond the expected.

Restaurants in the Winelands and Cape Town

Below are some dining out options in Cape Town and the winelands. These are paid entries. The venues supplied information on their cuisine, menus and attractions, which was then edited for consistency of style. For more restaurants among the vines, consult the A–Z section of the guide for wineries that offer light lunches, picnics etc. Look for the (🍴) symbol beside the individual entries. Unless stated to the contrary, all allow you to bring your own (BYO) wine – the corkage fee is indicated at the start of each entry. Should you wish to know about wheelchair access, please discuss with the relevant restaurant.

INDEX OF RESTAURANTS

CAMPS BAY

Azure The Twelve Apostles Hotel & Spa, Victoria Rd, Camps Bay, Cape Town ▪ Contemporary South African cuisine with global culinary influences ▪ Open daily for breakfast 7am-10.30am, lunch 12.30pm-3.30pm & dinner 6pm-10pm ▪ Booking advised ▪ Children welcome ▪ No BYO ▪ Major credit cards accepted ▪ Owners Tollman family/Red Carnation Hotels ▪ Executive chef Christo Pretorius ▪ restaurants@12apostles. co.za ▪ www.12apostleshotel. com ▪ **T +27 (0)21-437-9000**

Azure is the fine-dining restaurant at Cape Town's Twelve Apostles Hotel & Spa, where mesmer-ising ocean views vie for attention with executive chef Christo Pretorius' creations. Azure offers leisurely breakfasts that include fresh oysters and sparkling wine, degustation dinners, food-and-wine dinners, à la carte lunches and dinners, special tasting menus, fly-in helicopter culinary journeys, a vegan offering and buffet lunches on the Atlantic-facing terrace or stylish Leopard Bar – perfect for spectacular sunsets and cocktails. (See also The Twelve Apostles Hotel & Spa in the Accommodation section.)

DORING BAY

The Jetty Restaurant at Fryer's Cove Fryer's Cove Vineyards, Portion #1, Old Fish Factory, Hawe Rd, Doringbaai ▪ Seafood/West Coast cuisine ▪ Specialities: fish & chips, abalone ▪ Open daily 10am-6pm ▪ Open pub hols ▪ Closed Good Fri & 25 Dec ▪ Booking advised ▪ Children welcome ▪ All major credit cards accepted ▪ No BYO ▪ admin@ fryerscove.co.za ▪ www.fryerscove.co.za ▪ **T +27 (0)76-290-4372**

Some 300 km from Cape Town on the picturesque and largely unspoiled West Coast lies Doring Bay, home to a small but hardy fishing community and arguably the most unique winery, with vineyards 500m from the icy Atlantic Ocean. At The Jetty Restaurant the uniqueness of the vines truly shines - paired with delicious West Coast favourites such as snoekkoekies, kerrievis, roosterkoek, and fresh fish and chips. (See also Backsberg Family Wines, Brampton Wine Studio, Franschhoek Cellar Restaurant and Old Road Wine Co. in the Restaurants section, Franschhoek Cellar – Rose & Protea Cottages in the Accommodation section, and Backsberg Family Wines, Brampton, Franschhoek Cellar, Fryer's Cove Vineyards and Old Road Wine Co. in the A-Z section.)

FRANSCHHOEK

Backsberg Family Wines Main Rd R45, Franschhoek ▪ Sustainable South African tapas-style fare with Lithuanian influences ▪ Open Wed-Sun 10am-6pm ▪ Hours may differ on pub hols, call ahead ▪ Closed Mon, Tue, Good Fri & 25 Dec ▪ Booking advised ▪ Children welcome ▪ Private functions & micro-conferencing ▪ All major cards & SnapScan accepted ▪ No BYO ▪ backsbergwine@ dgb.co.za ▪ www.backsberg.co.za ▪ **T +27 (0)21-876-2086**

Now situated in Franschhoek overlooking the majestic Mont Rochelle mountain range, the revitalised and re-imagined Backsberg brand home invites winelovers to enjoy the refreshed portfolio of awarded Backberg wines, browse memorabilia and soak up the beauty of the surroundings. To complement the winetasting experience, a selection of pairings, both sweet and savoury, as well as grazing boards and gourmet barbecue platters in the summer months are on offer. Expect delightful dishes with local flavours, such as black West Coast mussels, smoked snoek samosas, seasonal salads and an exciting wine jelly pairing, to name but a few. (See also Brampton Wine Studio, Franschhoek Cellar Restaurant, Old Road Wine Co. and The Jetty Restaurant at Fryer's Cove in the Restaurants section, Franschhoek Cellar – Rose & Protea Cottages in the Accommodation section, and Backsberg Family Wines, Brampton, Franschhoek Cellar, Fryer's Cove Vineyards and Old Road Wine Co. in the A-Z section.)

Franschhoek Cellar Restaurant Franschhoek Cellar, R45/Franschhoek Main Rd, Franschhoek ▪ Bistro cuisine ▪ Mon-Fri 10am-6pm, Sat 9am-6pm, Sun 9am-5pm ▪ Open pub hols ▪ Closed Good Fri & 25 Dec ▪ Booking advised ▪ Children welcome ▪ VISA & MasterCard accepted ▪ No BYO ▪ Chef Karen du Toit ▪ fhccellardoor@dgb.co.za ▪ www.franschhoekcellar. co.za ▪ **T +27 (0)21-876-2086**

The kitchen opens at 11am and serves light snacks, lunches and cakes throughout the day. Expect hearty and delicious artisanal food using home-grown ingredients and fresh produce from local markets and suppliers in Franschhoek Valley. Chef Karen du Toit garners inspiration from the natural goodness of farm life, and expertly combines modern and traditional techniques to produce a menu that is as exciting as it is wholesome. (See also Backsberg Family Wines, Brampton Wine Studio, Old Road Wine Co. and The Jetty Restaurant at Fryer's Cove in the Restaurants section, Franschhoek Cellar – Rose & Protea Cottages in the Accommodation section, and Backsberg Family Wines, Brampton, Franschhoek Cellar, Fryer's Cove Vineyards and Old Road Wine Co. in the A-Z section.)

Haute Cabrière Restaurant Lambrechts Rd, Franschhoek ▪ French-inspired South African cuisine ▪ Hours: see website ▪ Booking advised, walk-ins welcome ▪ Children welcome ▪ Corkage R100/btl ▪ All major credit cards accepted ▪ Cashless payments only ▪ reservations@cabriere.co.za ▪ www.cabriere. co.za ▪ **T +27 (0)21-876-8500**

With the best view of Franschhoek Valley, dining at Haute Cabrière is as beautiful as it is delicious. The glass-enclosed restaurant terrace's seasonal à la carte lunch and suggested wine pairings offer guests a food-and-wine experience to remember. Don't miss out on the Bakery, which offers freshly baked breads, pastries and preserves to enjoy on the estate or at home. (See also Haute Cabrière in the A-Z section.)

Old Road Wine Co. R45, Main Rd, Franschhoek ▪ International fusion cuisine (specialities: wood-fired oven pizzas) ▪ Open Mon 10am-6pm Tue-Sun 10am-10pm ▪ Closed Easter Fri & 25 Dec ▪ Booking advised ▪ Children welcome (but no kids' menu) ▪ VISA &

MasterCard accepted ▪ No BYO ▪ Head chef Marlin Clayton ▪ info@orwc.co.za ▪ www.oldroadwinecompany.com ▪ T +27 (0)21-876-2086 / 7

With a beautiful, historically significant location between Franschhoek's old main road and railway line, the Old Road Wine Co. winery and restaurant are colourful visual tributes to the village artisans of the past. Guests enjoy sundowner wines on a deck with views of the Franschhoek mountains, followed by delicious contemporary cuisine prepared under the creative watch of chef Marlin Clayton. (See also Backsberg Family Wines, Brampton Wine Studio and The Jetty Restaurant at Fryer's Cove in the Restaurants section, Franschhoek Cellar – Rose & Protea Cottages in the Accommodation section, and Backsberg Family Wines, Brampton, Franschhoek Cellar, Fryer's Cove Vineyards and Old Road Wine Co. in the A-Z section.)

The Restaurant at La Petite Ferme Pass Rd, Franschhoek ▪ Country contemporary cuisine ▪ Open daily 12pm-3pm, dinners in season 6.30pm-9pm (Nov-Apr), winter 6pm-8.30pm (Fri & Sat) ▪ Booking advised ▪ Children welcome ▪ No BYO ▪ Major credit cards accepted ▪ Owners The Nest Estate ▪ reception@lapetiteferme.co.za ▪ www. lapetiteferme.co.za ▪ T +27 (0)21-876-3016

The Restaurant at La Petite Ferme Boutique Hotel & Winery offers a culinary experience like no other. The best and freshest ingredients are sourced locally in Franschhoek and a combination of international methods are used to deliver flavours in a unique country contemporary style. (See also La Petite Ferme in the Accommodation section and La Petite Ferme Winery in the A-Z section.)

HERMANUS

B's Stro@Lavierge R320, Hemel-en-Aarde Valley, Hermanus ▪ Traditional South African steak & local twists to popular cuisines ▪ Lunch Tue-Sun, dinner Sat ▪ Open pub hols ▪ Closed Mon & sometime in July 2021 but please check with tasting room ▪ Booking advised ▪ Children welcome ▪ Major credit cards accepted ▪ No BYO ▪ Owner/head chef Bruce Henderson ▪ bruce@lavierge.co.za ▪ www.lavierge. co.za ▪ T +27 (0)28-313-2007

At the summit of an infamous cycling hill, with a superb view over Hemel-en-Aarde Valley, B's Stro@Lavierge continues where local legend B's Steakhouse left off, serving exceptional grain-fed South African beef, game in season and plenty of other traditional - and different - fare to please all palates (speciality dish: 350g sirloin with foraged mushroom sauce). Acclaimed La Vierge and Domaine des Dieux wines complement the experience. Excellent venue for weddings, corporate functions, private parties, product launches and more. Charcuterie, local cheese, home-made biltong, in-house pâte platters and an exciting seasonal tapas menu available too. (See also La Vierge Private Cellar in A-Z section.)

KUILS RIVER

Zevenwacht Restaurant Zevenwacht Wine Estate, Langverwacht Rd, Kuils River, Cape Town ▪ Contemporary country cuisine ▪ Breakfast Mon-Sun 7.30am-10.30am, à la carte available 12pm–10pm, Sunday à la carte available 12pm–5pm ▪ Booking advised ▪ Children welcome ▪ Major credit cards accepted ▪ No BYO ▪ restaurant@zevenwacht.co.za ▪ www.zevenwacht.co.za ▪ T +27 (0)21-900-5800

Decorated with finesse and charm, Zevenwacht Restaurant is located within a turn-of-the-19th century Cape Dutch manor house with views of a tranquil lake and park-like gardens. Open for breakfast, lunch and dinner, the restaurant offers contemporary country cuisine, perfectly prepared, as well as a range of picnic baskets (including a braai basket) served on tree-shaded lawns around the lake. (See also Zevenwacht Country Inn under Accommodation and Zevenwacht in A-Z section.)

MONTAGU

BluVines District (Café Blu[es] and The Fire Kitchen) 12 Long Str, Montagu ▪ Contemporary fusion ▪ Open Fri-Tue 9am-10pm ▪ Closed Wed & Thu ▪ Booking advised ▪ Vegan friendly ▪ Children welcome ▪ Dog friendly ▪ Major credit cards accepted ▪ No BYO ▪ Executive chef Sean Bassett ▪ info@ bluvines.co.za ▪ www.bluvines.co.za ▪ T +27 (0)23-614-1663 / (0)23-614-1512

Café Blu[es] is a passion project that combines excellent food, quality wine and top-notch coffee with social development and responsible job creation. In a glamorously refurbished old farmhouse, the restaurant offers a gastronomic encounter unlike any other on Route 62. A uniquely designed menu with dishes like picanha and new-age sashimi happily coexist with popular favourites like all-day breakfasts, gourmet burgers and steaming cups of Truth coffee. **The Fire Kitchen**'s elevated approach to open-flame cooking is inspired by shisha nyama and Argentinian asado. Smoke and fire give unique character and complexity to every dish, individually cooked to order. Local supplier collaborations, thoughtfully selected produce, and the art of cooking with natural heat ensures each meal is multi-sensory and unforgettable. Open evenings only. (See also Mimosa Wines in the A-Z section.)

SOMERSET WEST

Vergelegen Vergelegen Wine Estate, Lourensford Rd, Somerset West ▪ **Stables Bistro at Vergelegen** open Mon-Sun for breakfast 8.30-11.30, lunch 12.00-3.30, tea/coffee & cakes 8.30-16.30; **Forest Picnic** (luxury/'white tablecloth' picnic) pre-booked baskets available Nov-Apr between 12.15-1.30 ▪ Estate closed Good Fri, May 1 & Dec 25 ▪ Booking advised ▪ Child-friendly ▪ Major credit cards accepted ▪ No dogs, cycling or BYO ▪ Owners Anglo American plc ▪ info@vergelegen.co.za ▪ www.vergelegen.co.za ▪ T+27(0)21-847-2111 ▪ **Forest Picnic** T+27(0)21-847-2137; **Stables Bistro** T+27(0)21-847-2156

With award-winning wines, history spanning over 300 years, heritage, exquisite gardens and cuisine to suit all tastes, it comes as no surprise that Vergelegen Estate continues to be the choice of the discerning visitor seeking a total sensory experience. Think of Vergelegen to spend quality time with family and friends – winetasting, heritage, environmental and cellar tours, Stables Bistro and seasonal luxury picnic in the camphor forest are only a few of a myriad of enjoyable activities at Vergelegen. (See also Vergelegen in A-Z section.)

STELLENBOSCH

Brampton Wine Studio 11 Church Str, Stellenbosch ▪ Continental & tapas ▪ Specialities: flatbreads ▪ Open Mon-Fri 10am-10pm, Sat 11am-10pm, Sun & pub hols 11am-6pm ▪ Closed some pub hols ▪ Booking advised ▪ Children welcome (no kids' menu) ▪ No BYO ▪ Major credit cards accepted ▪ bramptonstudio@dgb.co.za ▪ www.brampton.co.za ▪ T +27 (0)21-883-9097

In the heart of vibey Stellenbosch, Brampton Wine Studio is a unique urban winery where you can taste and buy Brampton's award-winning wines, nibble on delectable tapas or flatbreads, and sip refreshing house beer on tap. The Studio is always buzzing with creativity and fun, including a social calendar featuring epic quiz nights and food-and-wine sessions with a difference. (See also Backsberg Family Wines, Franschhoek Cellar Restaurant, Old Road Wine Co and The Jetty Restaurant at Fryer's Cove in the Restaurants section, Franschhoek Cellar – Rose & Protea Cottages in the Accommodation section, and Backsberg Family Wines, Franschhoek Cellar, Fryer's Cove Vineyards and Old Road Wine Co in the A-Z section.)

Delaire Graff Restaurant Delaire Graff Estate, Helshoogte Pass, Stellenbosch ▪ Bistro-chic cuisine ▪ Open daily for lunch, certain evenings for dinner (times change according to the season) ▪ Booking advised ▪ Children welcome during lunch only ▪ Major credit cards accepted ▪ Corkage fee ▪ Owner Laurence Graff ▪ Head chef Clinton Jacobs ▪ reservations@delaire.co.za ▪ www.delaire.co.za ▪ T +27 (0)21-885-8160

The dining experience here on the exquisite Delaire Graff Estate is an expression of the seasons, underpinned by the belief that the best food starts with the best ingredients. Classic bistro favourites are served with the finest South African touches, enriched by the restaurant's high-altitude location, affording unique views from the terrace of Simonsberg Mountain and its mantle of vines and olives, down into the steep-sloped Banhoek Valley. Inside, the David Collins Studio designed interiors include curving orange leather banquettes and handpicked art. (See also Indochine Restaurant under Restaurants, Delaire Graff Lodges & Spa under Accommodation and Delaire Graff Estate in A-Z section.)

Guardian Peak Winery & Grill Guardian Peak Wines, Annandale Rd (off R44), Stellenbosch ▪ Grill house ▪ Open Mon-Sun 12pm-3.30pm, Tue-Sat 6pm-10pm (summer) / Wed-Sat 6pm-10pm (winter) ▪ Closed Good Friday & Dec 25 ▪ Reservations advised ▪ Children welcome ▪ Major credit cards accepted ▪ No BYO ▪ Owner Jean Engelbrecht ▪ Executive chef Willie Mostert ▪ info@guardianpeak.com ▪ www.guardianpeak.com ▪ T +27 (0)21-881-3899

A relaxed Stellenbosch winelands experience with vineyard and mountain vistas, appreciated from a wide veranda and adjacent deck. Generous lunches and dinners, with focus on prime-quality beef and venison, enjoyed with Guardian Peak wines, as well as other family wine brands Stellenbosch Reserve, Donkiesbaai, Cirrus and Afrikaans. (See also Rust en Vrede Restaurant (Dinner Only)/Winemaker's Lunch under Restaurants, and Guardian Peak Wines and Rust en Vrede Estate in A-Z section.)

Indochine Restaurant Delaire Graff Estate, Helshoogte Pass, Stellenbosch ▪ Afro-Asian-influenced cuisine ▪ Open daily for lunch 12pm-2.30pm & dinner 6pm-8.30pm ▪ Booking advised ▪ Dineplan affiliated ▪ Children of all ages welcome for lunch; dinner for children over the age of 10 ▪ Major credit cards accepted ▪ Corkage fee R110 per btl ▪ Owner Laurence Graff ▪ Head chef Virgil Kahn ▪ indochine.res@delaire.co.za ▪ www.delaire.co.za ▪ T +27 (0)21-885-8160

Indochine is more than a restaurant: it's a fine-dining food theatre where all elements are handcrafted to create a multi-sensory dining experience, including an intimate setting featuring a calming blue and copper colour palette. Flavours are delicate, balanced yet vibrant, and menus are inspired by fresh, organic produce grown on the estate. Savour signature dishes with influences from across Asia and Africa. Indochine's ideal of turning cuisine into art is reflected in the stunning aerial installation by Lionel Smit and André Stead, with over 1,000 swallows becoming part of the experience and panorama stretching to distant Table Mountain.(See also Delaire Graff Restaurant under Restaurants, Delaire Graff Lodges & Spa under Accommodation and Delaire Graff Estate in A-Z section.)

Jordan Restaurant with Marthinus Ferreira Jordan Wine Estate, Stellenbosch Kloof Rd, Stellenbosch ▪ Contemporary fare ▪ Open for lunch daily 12-3pm, dinner Thu, Fri & Sat from 6:30pm Dec to Apr. Closed Mon & Tue May to Nov ▪ Open pub hols ▪ Booking essential ▪ No under 12s at dinner unless by prior arrangement ▪ Major credit cards accepted ▪ BYO allowed if not on winelist (corkage R120, 1 bottle/table) ▪ Owner & chef Marthinus Ferreira ▪ reservations@jordanwines.com ▪ www.jordanwines.com ▪ T +27 (0)21-881-3441

Jordan Restaurant with Marthinus Ferreira opened in October 2022 after extensive renovations, elevating the space with a more modern feel but keeping the uninterrupted panoramic views of Stellenbosch Kloof Valley. Having taken the helm, Marthinus Ferreira, of dw eleven – 13 in Johannesburg, continues to use his finely tuned skills in combination with a strong home-grown farm-to-table focus, with ethically sourced meat from local farmers and the freshest seasonal ingredients. (See also The Cellar Door in the Restaurants section, Jordan Luxury Suites and Ted's Villa in the Accommodation section, and Jordan Wine Estate in the A-Z section.)

Lanzerac – Dining Lanzerac Rd, Stellenbosch ▪ Culinary classics reimagined ▪ Open daily for breakfast 7am-10am & dinner 6pm-10pm; afternoon tea Sat 2pm-5pm; seven-course experience Fri & Sat 6pm-10pm ▪ Booking essential ▪ Children welcome ▪ Corkage R95 ▪ Major credit cards accepted ▪ Executive chef Stephen Fraser ▪ restaurants@lanzerac.co.za ▪ www.lanzerac.co.za ▪ T +27 (0)21-887-1132

The Manor Kitchen, the main à la carte restaurant at Lanzerac, opens daily to welcome guests with contemporary and seasonal dishes, served with the estate's own award-winning wines. Generous continental and full English breakfasts, appetising lunches and delicious dinners are served daily on the estate, with gourmet sharing dishes offered on the outdoor terrace of the Taphuis, overlooking the historic manor house. Light meals and platters are served at the Tasting Room & Deli. (See also Lanzerac - Hotel in the Accommodation section Lanzerac in the A-Z section.)

Rust en Vrede Restaurant (Dinner Only) Rust en Vrede Wine Estate, Annandale Rd (off R44), Stellenbosch ▪ Fine dining ▪ Tue-Sat 6.30pm till late ▪ Closed Good Friday, 25 Dec ▪ Reservations essential ▪ Major credit cards accepted ▪ No BYO ▪ Owner Jean Engelbrecht ▪ Executive chef Fabio Daniel ▪ dining@rustenvrede.com ▪ www.rustenvrede.com ▪ T +27 (0)21-881-3757

Contemporary fine dining within Rust en Vrede Wine Estate's historic former cellar (also a provincial heritage site), where the front-and-centre kitchen, fine stemware and bespoke crockery enhance the creative menu. A comprehensive winelist carries wide local and international selections, leaving little to be desired. (See also Guardian Peak Winery & Grill and Rust en Vrede Restaurant Winemaker's Lunch under Restaurants, and Guardian Peak Wines and Rust en Vrede Estate in the A-Z section.)

Rust en Vrede Winemaker's Lunch Rust en Vrede Wine Estate, Annandale Rd (off R44), Stellenbosch ▪ Set menu ▪ Open Mon-Sun 12pm-3pm ▪ Closed Good Friday, 25 Dec ▪ No reservations; first come, first served ▪ Major credit cards accepted ▪ No BYO ▪ Owner Jean Engelbrecht ▪ Executive chef Fabio Daniel ▪ tastingroom@rustenvrede.com ▪ www.rustenvrede.com ▪ T +27 (0)21-881-3881

Comprising a three-item set menu, salmon, sirloin and fillet, historic Stellenbosch estate Rust en Vrede's lunch experience is a no-fuss version of its celebrated fine-dining dinner. Tables set under ancient oaks suggest a laid-back approach, yet the linen is classily crisp and white, the cookery flawless and the service impeccable. Enjoy your choice of meal with a glass of red or white. (See also Guardian Peak Winery & Grill and Rust en Vrede Restaurant (Dinner Only) under Restaurants, and Guardian Peak Wines and Rust en Vrede Estate in the A-Z section.)

Stellenbosch Reserve 1 Annandale Rd, Stellenbosch ▪ Mediterranean cuisine ▪ Open Tue-Sat for winetasting 8am-5pm, lunch 12pm-3pm, dinner 6.30pm-9pm ▪ Closed Sun & Mon ▪ Reservations recommended ▪ Major credit cards accepted ▪ No BYO ▪ Children welcome ▪ Owner Jean Engelbrecht ▪ visit@thestellenboschreserve.com ▪ T +27 (0)74-420-0073

Located on the slopes of the Helderberg at a slightly higher elevation than neighbouring Rust en

Vrede, the new Stellenbosch Reserve Tasting Room & Restaurant overlooks the rolling vineyards of the winelands and is embraced by the surrounding mountains.

Nestled next to the cellar, the space has rustic contours which add character to the clean, contemporary decor, with a nod to the winery's ties to Stellenbosch town at its viticultural heritage. The flagstone patio covered in dappled shade invites visitors to linger and enjoy a refreshing glass of wine while soaking up the views and the countryside ambience of the winelands.

On the menu, the sophistication of Mediterranean cuisine is combined with the rustic charm of home cooking. Aromatic & flavourful dishes have a focus on local ingredients and sustainable sourcing. The main attractions are the wood-fired oven and rotisserie, around which the menu has been built. Think authentic Neapolitan pizza, and baby chicken roasted to perfection, ready to devour.

The Cellar Door Jordan Wine Estate, Stellenbosch Kloof Rd, Stellenbosch ▪ Continental cuisine ▪ Open Mon-Sun & pub hols 8am-4pm ▪ Booking advised ▪ Children welcome ▪ No BYO ▪ VISA & MasterCard accepted ▪ Breakfast, lunch & picnics (picnics to be booked 48 hrs in advance) ▪ Owners Gary & Kathy Jordan ▪ Executive chef Thys Esterhuysen ▪ reservations@jordanwines.com ▪ www.jordanwines.com ▪ **T +27 (0)21-881-3441**

Combining award-winning estate wines at farm prices with fresh seasonal dishes, The Cellar Door at Jordan offers exciting winetasting experiences that can be enjoyed with the casual all-day menu seven days a week. (See also Jordan Restaurant with Marthinus Ferreira under Restaurants, Jordan Luxury Suites and Ted's Villa under Accommodation, and Jordan Wine Estate in the A-Z section.)

The Stellenbosch Wine Bar 8 Church Str, Stellenbosch ▪ Wine bar & tapas ▪ Open Mon-Sun 10am-10pm ▪ Closed Good Friday & 25 Dec ▪ Major credit cards accepted ▪ No BYO ▪ Owner Jean Engelbrecht ▪ winebar@thestellenboschcollection.com ▪ **T +27 (0)63-646-3207**

A sophisticated wine bar in the heart of wine country, with a focus on wines from the acclaimed Stellenbosch Collection, including Rust en Vrede, Donkiesbaai, Stellenbosch Reserve, Guardian Peak, Cirrus and Afrikaans. Guests enjoy true Stellenbosch hospitality in an elegant village setting, with attention to stemware and comfort, and nibbles to accompany the variety of wines.

Accommodation in the Winelands and Cape Town

Featured below are some guest lodges, hotels, country inns, B&Bs and self-catering cottages in Cape Town and the winelands, many of them on wine farms (look for the 🏠 symbol beside the individual entries in the A-Z section of this guide). These are paid entries. The venues supplied information on their facilities and attractions, which was then edited for consistency of style. Unless stated to the contrary, all speak English and Afrikaans, and have parking and gardens/terraces. Rates are for standard double rooms unless otherwise specified — for example per person (pp) or breakfast included (B&B). Tourism Grading Council of South Africa (TGCSA) ratings where provided. Should you wish to know about wheelchair access, please discuss with the relevant venue.

INDEX OF ACCOMMODATION

CAMPS BAY

The Twelve Apostles Hotel & Spa Victoria Rd, Camps Bay, Cape Town ▪ TGCSA 5-star hotel ▪ 70 rooms ▪ Best available seasonal rates B&B ▪ Major credit cards accepted ▪ Azure and Café Grill restaurants with Sushi@12A sushi bar ▪ Leopard Bar for light meals, high tea by the sea & sundowners ▪ Conferences ▪ Weddings/functions ▪ Spa & hydrotherapy pools ▪ Gym ▪ Walks/hikes ▪ Wine, gin & craft beer tasting ▪ Secure parking ▪ Complimentary shuttle service to Waterfront ▪ Laundry service ▪ Air-conditioning ▪ TV ▪ DStv ▪ DVD player ▪ Wifi ▪ Safe ▪ French, Mandarin & Dutch spoken ▪ Owners Tollman family/Red Carnation Hotels ▪

reservations1@12apostles.co.za ▪ www.12apostleshotel.
com ▪ **T +27 (0)21-437- 9000**

Award-winning Twelve Apostles Hotel & Spa is
situated on Cape Town's most scenic route, flanking
Table Mountain National Park and overlooking the
Atlantic Ocean. Part of the family-run Red Carnation
Hotel Collection, it offers 55 deluxe guest rooms and
15 luxurious suites, not to mention a holistic spa and
private cinema, with Azure Restaurant serving up
breathtaking views in addition to legendary local
cuisine and Sushi@12A in The Café Grill offering
delicious sushi specialities. (See also Azure under
Restaurants.)

FRANSCHHOEK

Franschhoek Cellar – Rose & Protea
Cottages Franschhoek Cellar, R45, Franschhoek
Main Rd, Franschhoek ▪ 2 cottages sleeping 4 pax
per cottage ▪ R1,750-R2,000 per cottage ▪ VISA &
MasterCard accepted ▪ Restaurant ▪ Conference facilities
▪ Weddings/functions ▪ Winetasting ▪ Secure parking
▪ Air-conditioning ▪ Fireplace ▪ Safe ▪ TV ▪ DStv ▪ Wifi
▪ accommodation@franschhoekcellar.co.za ▪ www.
franschhoekcellar.co.za ▪ **T +27 (0)21-876-2086**
Ideal for winelovers wanting to be close to the action,
Rose and Protea cottages are situated beside the
production cellar on the premises in the heart of
Franschhoek. Both cottages have been remodelled
to match the contemporary-chic styling of the visitor
venue, which is also on the property. The self-catering
homes each sleep four adults and have been fitted
with all modern conveniences to ensure you have a
relaxing stay in one of South Africa's food capitals. (See
also Backsberg Family Wines, Brampton Wine Studio,
Franschhoek Cellar Restaurant, Old Road Wine Co and
The Jetty Restaurant at Fryer's Cove in the Restaurants
section, and Backsberg Family Wines, Brampton,
Franschhoek Cellar, Fryer's Cove Vineyards and Old Road
Wine Co in the A-Z section.)

La Petite Ferme Pass Road, Franschhoek ▪
TGCSA 4-star boutique hotel ▪ 15 rooms ▪ Rates
from R8,910-R15,365 per room ▪ Breakfast included
▪ Major credit cards accepted ▪ Restaurant ▪ Vine
Orientation tours ▪ Winetasting ▪ Secure parking
▪ Air-conditioning ▪ Ceiling fans ▪ Fireplace ▪
Under-floor heating ▪ Safe ▪ TV ▪ DStv ▪ Wifi ▪ Some
rooms have plunge pools ▪ Owners The Nest Estate
▪ accommodation@lapetiteferme.co.za ▪ www.
lapetiteferme.co.za ▪ **T +27 (0)21-876-3016**
La Petite Ferme Boutique Hotel & Winery offers
the perfect combination of private, contemporary
country-style accommodation, luxury amenities
and heart-warming hospitality. Situated on the
Oliphants Pass high on the Middagkrans Mountain

slopes, the Manor House, Vineyard Suites and
Winery Suites each have all the creature comforts
you'd expect plus spectacular views of Franschhoek
Valley – a picture-perfect paradise in which to relax.
(See also The Restaurant at La Petite Ferme in the
Restaurants section and La Petite Ferme Winery in
the A-Z section.)

Leeu Estates Dassenberg Rd, Franschhoek ▪
TGCSA 5-star premium boutique hotel ▪ 24 rooms ▪
Rates from R15,400 per room per night ▪ Breakfast
included ▪ All major credit cards accepted ▪ 1 hour
from Cape Town ▪ Restaurants ▪ Spa & Gym ▪
Swimming pool ▪ Walks/hikes ▪ Wine tasting ▪
Picnics ▪ Shuttle service ▪ Secure parking ▪ Laundry
service ▪ Fully air-conditioned ▪ Ceiling fans &
fireplaces (selected rooms) ▪ Under-floor heating
▪ Apple TV ▪ Safe ▪ Wifi ▪ Owner Leeu Collection ▪
reservations@leeucollection.com ▪ www.leeucollec-
tion.com ▪ **T +27 (0)21-492-2222**
One of three properties in Leeu Collection
Franschhoek, Leeu Estates is an exclusive boutique
hotel and winery in scenic Franschhoek Valley, just
an hour from Cape Town. The focal point of this
elegant and sophisticated private hideaway is the
refurbished 19th-century manor house with its six
guest rooms, in-house restaurant and bar with a
living room. Adjacent is Leeu Spa & Gym, plus spacious cottages scattered among gardens, oak trees
and vineyards. Guests can enjoy The Dining Room,
La Petite Colombe, Mullineux & Leeu Family Wines
Wine Studio, Leeu Spa by Healing Earth, and Everard
Read - Leeu Estates. (See also Leeu House and Le
Quartier Français in the Accommodation section.)

Leeu House 12 Huguenot Str, Franschhoek ▪
TGCSA 5-star boutique hotel ▪ 13 rooms ▪ Rates from
R10,500 per room per night ▪ Breakfast included ▪
All major credit cards accepted ▪ 1 hour from Cape
Town ▪ In-house restaurant ▪ Spa & Gym ▪ Guest
lounge ▪ Swimming pool ▪ Wine tasting ▪ Shuttle
service ▪ Secure parking ▪ Laundry service ▪ Fully
air-conditioned ▪ Ceiling fans (selected rooms) ▪
Under-floor heating ▪ Apple TV ▪ Safe ▪ Wifi ▪ Owner
Leeu Collection ▪ reservations@leeucollection.com ▪
www.leeucollection.com ▪ **T +27 (0)21-492-2222**
Leeu House is an oasis of tranquillity and
comfort, exclusively offered to adults of 18 and above
in the heart of Franschhoek, a mere hour from Cape
Town. Leeu House's special appeal is its country
ambience despite being located on the village's
vibrant main street, very near award-winning
restaurants, art galleries and boutiques. The hotel's
stylish interiors are a contemporary take on Cape
Dutch heritage, with its strong French influences.

This unique hotel also offers sole use of the property options. (See also Leeu Estates and Le Quartier Français in the Accommodation section.)

Le Quartier Français Cnr Wilhelmina & Berg Str, Franschhoek ▪ TGCSA 5-star ▪ 25 rooms ▪ Rates from R10,500 per room per night ▪ Breakfast included ▪ All major credit cards accepted ▪ 1 hour from Cape Town ▪ Restaurants ▪ Spa & Gym ▪ Guest lounge ▪ Swimming pool ▪ Wine tasting ▪ Secure parking ▪ Shuttle service ▪ Laundry service ▪ Fully air-conditioned ▪ Ceiling fans & fireplaces (selected rooms) ▪ Under-floor heating ▪ Apple TV ▪ Safe ▪ Wifi ▪ Owner Leeu Collection ▪ reservations@leeucollection.com ▪ www.leeucollection.com ▪ **T +27 (0)21-492-2222**

Tucked away in the heart of Franschhoek, just an hour from Cape Town, Le Quartier Français is an exclusive and romantic 25-room boutique hotel, and revered culinary landmark with two exceptional restaurants – Protégé, offering casual dining, and fine-dining establishment Épice. It also features the Everard Read Franschhoek Art Gallery and the Great Heart Wine Boutique. This peaceful auberge's ideal location makes it easy to wander out from its scented gardens to explore the quaint charms of the village and the wonders of the winelands beyond. (See also Leeu Estates and Leeu House in the Accommodation section.)

HERMANUS

High Season Farm Cottages Hemel-en-Aarde Valley, Hermanus ▪ TGCSA 4-star self-catering ▪ Rates from R360 pp (low season) to R500 pp (high season) ▪ 8 cottages ▪ VISA, MasterCard, Diners Club & Amex accepted ▪ Weddings/functions ▪ Pool ▪ Mountain biking ▪ Walks/hikes ▪ Birding ▪ Cellar tours ▪ Winetasting ▪ Secure parking ▪ Laundry service ▪ Air-conditioning ▪ Ceiling fans ▪ Fireplace ▪ Under-floor heating ▪ Safe ▪ TV ▪ DStv ▪ Wifi ▪ info@highseasonfarm.co.za ▪ www.highseasonfarm.co.za ▪ **T +27 (0)21-200-2514**

High Season Farm is ideally located near the whale-watching hotspot of Hermanus, and within walking distance of all the top pinot noir vineyards of the Upper Hemel-en-Aarde Valley. Beautifully decorated 4-star farm cottages are ideal for groups or couples travelling to this internationally hailed and wonderfully scenic wine region.

KUILS RIVER

Zevenwacht Country Inn Zevenwacht Wine Estate, Langverwacht Rd, Kuils River ▪ TGCSA 4-star country house ▪ Total 38 rooms: 1 honeymoon suite (deluxe), 12 Country Inn luxury suites, ungraded 7 x 3-bedroom cottages, 1 x 4-bedroom self-catering chalet ▪ Low season from R610 pps B&B, high season from R800 pps B&B ▪ Major credit cards accepted ▪ Restaurant ▪ Conferences ▪ Weddings/functions ▪ Spa ▪ Sauna ▪ Pool ▪ Mountain biking ▪ Walks/hikes ▪ Birding ▪ Cellar tours ▪ Winetasting ▪ Secure parking ▪ Shuttle service ▪ Laundry service ▪ Air-conditioning ▪ TV ▪ DStv ▪ Wifi ▪ Owners Harold & Denise Johnson ▪ reservations@zevenwacht.co.za ▪ www. zevenwacht. co.za ▪ **T +27 (0)21-900-5700**

Meaning 'Seven Expectations', the name Zevenwacht encapsulates several delights that await visitors at this historic estate. Choose between the Country Inn, offering four-star accommodation in luxuriously appointed air-conditioned suites; ungraded three-bedroom Vineyard Cottages; or self-catering four-bedroom chalet. (See also Zevenwacht Restaurant under Restaurants and Zevenwacht in A-Z section.)

PAARL

Under Oaks Guest House Noord Agter Paarl Rd, Paarl ▪ TGCSA 4-star country house ▪ Rates from R1,400 single/R1,700 double (low season) to R1,800/R2,700 (high season), breakfast included ▪ 7 bedrooms ▪ VISA, MasterCard & Amex accepted ▪ Pizzeria ▪ Conference facilities ▪ Pool ▪ Winetasting ▪ Secure parking ▪ Air-conditioning ▪ Safe ▪ TV ▪ DStv ▪ Wifi ▪ Coffee & tea station ▪ Iron plus ironing board ▪ Owners The Britz family ▪ accommodation@underoaks.co.za ▪ www.underoaks.co.za ▪ **T +27 (0)21-869-8535 ext 1**

Four-star graded, newly built and limited to seven spacious en suite rooms, the suites on working farm Under Oaks are stylish and luxurious, with personalised designs and decor ensuring exclusivity in a vine-fringed, tranquil setting. All suites feature a private patio and uplifting vistas of vineyards and mountains. Historic Paarl town and the Cape winelands' myriad allures are within easy reach. (See also Under Oaks in A-Z section.)

STELLENBOSCH

Delaire Graff Lodges & Spa Helshoogte Pass, Stellenbosch ▪ Owner's Villa, Presidential, Superior, Luxury & Garden lodges ▪ Rates from R28,800 pp ▪ Breakfast included ▪ VISA, MasterCard & international money transfer accepted (Diners Club card not accepted) ▪ Delaire Graff & Indochine restaurants ▪ Functions ▪ Spa ▪ Sauna ▪ Gym ▪ Pool ▪ Jacuzzi ▪ Walks/hikes ▪ Cellar tours ▪ Wine tasting ▪ Secure parking ▪ Shuttle service ▪ Helipad ▪ In-room tea & coffee facilities ▪ Laundry service ▪ Air-conditioning ▪ Under-floor heating ▪ Safe ▪ TV ▪

DStv ▪ Netflix ▪ Wifi ▪ Condé Nast Traveller Gold List - Top 20 Best Hotels in the World (Feb 2018) ▪ lodge. reservations@delaire.co.za ▪ www.delaire.co.za ▪ **T +27 (0)21-885-8160**

A magnificent Cape winelands property flanked by majestic mountain ranges, Delaire Graff Estate is a unique destination offering exceptional experiences born of exclusive lodges and villa, a destination spa, two outstanding restaurants, state-of-the-art winery and wine lounge where guests are hosted for a complimentary tasting, and luxury boutiques. (See also Delaire Graff Restaurant and Indochine Restaurant under Restaurants and Delaire Graff Estate in A-Z section.)

Jordan Luxury Suites Jordan Wine Estate, Stellenbosch Kloof Rd, Stellenbosch ▪ Klink Award best accommodation on a wine estate ▪ 13 rooms ▪ Rates on request (breakfast included) ▪ Major credit cards accepted ▪ Restaurant ▪ Conference facilities ▪ Functions ▪ Cellar tours ▪ Winetasting ▪ Secure parking ▪ Laundry service ▪ Air-conditioning ▪ Fireplace ▪ Safe ▪ TV ▪ Wifi ▪ English & Afrikaans spoken ▪ Owners Gary & Kathy Jordan ▪ reservations@jordanwines.com ▪ www.jordanwines.com ▪ **T +27 (0)21-881-3441**

Tucked away close to the wine cellar, Jordan Restaurant and The Cellar Door, the luxury suites on Jordan Wine Estate offer panoramic views of the vineyards and Stellenbosch mountains. Each suite has spacious interiors that are individually designed and uniquely decorated, making Jordan Luxury Suites an ideal choice for a perfect winelands getaway. (See also Jordan Restaurant with Marthinus Ferreira and The Cellar Door in the Restaurants section, Ted's Villa in the Accommodation section, and Jordan Wine Estate in the A-Z section.)

Ladybird Vineyards Lodge Ladybird Vineyards, R44 Elsenburg, Stellenbosch ▪ 8 rooms ▪ Swimming pool ▪ Braai area ▪ Secure parking ▪ TV ▪ DStv ▪ Wifi ▪ Walks/hikes ▪ Cycling ▪ Winetasting ▪ Managed by Touch Down Africa ▪ reservations@touchdown-africa.com ▪ www.ladybirdwinestays.co.za ▪ **T +27 (0)800-008-710 *1 / WhatsApp +27 (0)82-234-6540**

Ladybird Vineyards Lodge is nestled in the centre of a sea of organic vines on a 50-hectare working vineyard, only a few kilometres north of Stellenbosch. The lodge offers eight spacious, elegant hotel-style rooms with magnificent Table Mountain views. The Indian and Atlantic Ocean beaches are just 45 minutes away. There are several golf courses nearby, as well as a variety of superb restaurants and world-renowned wine estates. (See also Ladybird Vineyards in the A-Z section.)

Lanzerac – Hotel Lanzerac Rd, Stellenbosch ▪ TGCSA 5-star premium boutique hotel ▪ 53 rooms ▪ Seasonal rates on request ▪ Major credit cards accepted ▪ Main restaurant & cigar bar ▪ Tasting Room & Deli ▪ Conferences ▪ Weddings/functions ▪ Day spa ▪ Sauna ▪ Gym ▪ Pool ▪ Jacuzzi ▪ Helipad ▪ Horse riding ▪ Mountain biking ▪ Walks/hikes ▪ Birding ▪ Cellar tours ▪ Winetasting on-site ▪ Secure parking ▪ Shuttle service ▪ Laundry service ▪ Air-conditioning ▪ Under-floor heating ▪ TV ▪ DStv ▪ Wifi ▪ In-room tea & coffee facilities ▪ Safe ▪ info@lanzerac.co.za ▪ www.lanzerac.co.za ▪ **T +27 (0)21-887-1132**

Steeped in history, and nestled in Stellenbosch's idyllic Jonkershoek Valley, 331-year-old Lanzerac is synonymous with Old World charm and rich Cape heritage. Staying in exquisitely styled rooms, blending period grandeur with contemporary style, guests are indulged with warm and passionate service, and the best wine and cuisine – in short, the finest hospitality the Cape winelands has to offer. (See also Lanzerac - Dining in the Restaurants section and Lanzerac in the A-Z section.)

Ted's Villa at Jordan Wine Estate Jordan Estate, Stellenbosch Kloof Rd, Stellenbosch ▪ 5 rooms ▪ Rates on request (breakfast included) ▪ Visa & Mastercard accepted ▪ Swimming pool ▪ Mountain biking ▪ Birding ▪ Cellar tours ▪ Winetasting ▪ Secure parking ▪ Laundry service ▪ Air-conditioning ▪ Safe ▪ TV ▪ Chromecast ▪ Wifi ▪ English & Afrikaans spoken ▪ Owners Gary & Kathy Jordan ▪ reservations@jordanwines.com ▪ www.jordanwines.com ▪ **T +27 (0)21-881-3441**

Overlooking the Nine Yards vineyard, Ted's Villa is currently being upgraded to form the pinnacle of the offering on Jordan Wine Estate. Poised on the ridge that separates the western and eastern portions of the estate, the villa faces the latter and affords spectacular views, perhaps no more so than from the pool, while being protected from the False Bay breezes by a forested hillside. Designed for long-term stays and decorated to complete the contemporary, farmhouse feel, Ted's Villa is enhanced with optional extras and fully serviced by a housekeeping team. (See also Jordan Restaurant with Marthinus Ferreira and The Cellar Door in the Restaurants section, Jordan Luxury Suites in the Accommodation section, and Jordan Wine Estate in the A-Z section.)

The Homestead at Oldenburg Vineyards Zevenrivieren Rd, Banghoek, Stellenbosch ▪ Luxury guest villa sleeping max 12 persons ▪ 6 bedrooms ▪ Exclusive use ▪ Rates from R67,000 ▪ Breakfast included ▪ Major credit cards accepted ▪ Guests staying min 3 nights treated to complimentary gourmet SA braai or 3-course dinner ▪ Complimentary winetasting ▪ Daily fruit & snacks ▪ Gym ▪ Pool ▪ Mobile spa & yoga sessions (extra cost) ▪ Mountain biking (extra cost for hiring bikes) ▪ Walks/hikes ▪ Birding ▪ Secure parking ▪ Shuttle & transfer service (extra cost) ▪ Laundry service ▪ Safe ▪ Air-conditioning ▪ Open fireplaces in common areas ▪ Under-floor heating in bathrooms ▪ TV ▪ DStv ▪ Free wifi ▪ homestead@oldenburgvineyards.com ▪ www.oldenburgvineyards.com ▪ **T +27 (0)87-057-4515 / +27 (0)21-885-1618 / +27 (0)76-909-1377**

Spacious and elegantly proportioned, the 200-year-old Oldenburg homestead has been meticulously restored and modernised to create a seamless flow of indoor and outdoor spaces for relaxed family living and sophisticated entertaining. The Homestead is well suited to a multi-generational family, party of friends or corporate team. Fringed by a well-established garden, olive groves and vineyards, the two-level house has deep verandas, large swimming pool and gym. It comes with housekeeping and personalised service. (See also Oldenburg Vineyards in A-Z section.)

Winelands Maps

The maps in this section show locales where wine is available for tasting/sale either at set times or by appointment. The larger-scale map below shows the areas covered by the maps, and the table starting on the next page lists some details for prospective visitors.

Areas covered by the maps

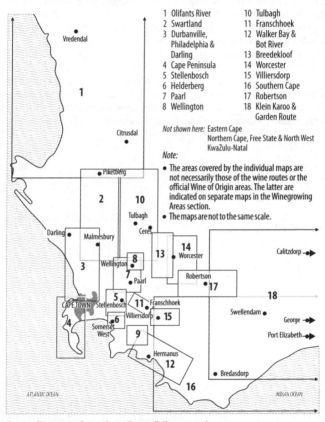

1 Olifants River
2 Swartland
3 Durbanville, Philadelphia & Darling
4 Cape Peninsula
5 Stellenbosch
6 Helderberg
7 Paarl
8 Wellington
9
10 Tulbagh
11 Franschhoek
12 Walker Bay & Bot River
13 Breedekloof
14 Worcester
15 Villiersdorp
16 Southern Cape
17 Robertson
18 Klein Karoo & Garden Route

Not shown here: Eastern Cape
Northern Cape, Free State & North West
KwaZulu-Natal

Note:
• The areas covered by the individual maps are not necessarily those of the wine routes or the official Wine of Origin areas. The latter are indicated on separate maps in the Winegrowing Areas section.
• The maps are not to the same scale.

Some distances from Cape Town (kilometres)

Calitzdorp	370	Paarl	60	Tulbagh	125
Franschhoek	80	Plettenberg Bay	520	Upington	800
Hermanus	120	Robertson	160	Vredendal	300
Malmesbury	70	Stellenbosch	50	Worcester	110

Key for maps

═══ Main access roads
═══ Roads
······· Gravel roads

─R62─ ─R60─ Road numbers
● Towns

Details of Locales Shown on Maps

The tables below are intended to facilitate winery visits by providing summary information about all the winetasting venues which are open to the public, either at set times or by appointment, and appear on our winelands maps. Venues are listed by region, and details provided include a **map grid-reference**; whether the particular venue is **open only by appointment** (T); **open on Saturdays and/or Sundays** (✓ = at set times; T = by appointment); **open on public holidays** (× = closed all public holidays; otherwise assume open all or some holidays); and whether **meals/refreshments are available** (BYO = bring your own picnic). Other details include availability of **accommodation**, **cellar tours** and **facilities friendly to individuals with reduced mobility**, as audited by our disability consultants, are highlighted. **Other languages spoken** (besides English and Afrikaans) are also noted (Danish = da, Dutch/Flemish = nl, French = fr, German = de, Hebrew = he, Hungarian = hu, Indian = in, Italian = it, Japanese = ja, Latvian = lv, Luo = luo, Mandarin = mdr, Norwegian = nn, Portuguese = pt, Romanian = ro, Russian = ru, Sesotho = st, Setswana = tn, Spanish = sp, Swahili = sw, Swedish = sv, Swiss = gsw, isiXhosa = xh, isiZulu = zu). For more information, **particularly items marked with an asterisk**, see the A–Z and Restaurants/Accommodation sections.

	Grid reference	Open by appt. only	Open Saturdays	Open Sundays	Open public holidays	Meals/refreshments	Accommodation	Cellar tours	Disabled friendly	Child friendly	Languages spoken
Breedekloof Map (page 714)											
Aufwaerts	B6	T									
Badsberg	B5		✓			✓*		T	✓	✓	
Belle Rebelle	C5		✓	✓		✓		T		✓	
Bergsig	A3		✓			✓	✓	T	✓	✓	
Bosjes	B3		✓	✓		✓	✓			✓	
Botha	B3		✓			✓*		T	✓	✓	
Breëland	A5		✓				✓	T			
Cecilia	C6	T									
Daschbosch	C6		✓							✓	
Du Preez	B6		✓		×			T*	✓		
Du Toitskloof	B6		✓	✓		✓		T	✓		de
Jason's Hill	A5		✓						✓	✓	
Kirabo	C6		✓			✓*		✓*		✓	
Merwida	C6		✓			✓		✓			
Mountain Ridge	A2		✓					T	✓		
Olifantsberg	C4	T									
Opstal	A5		✓	T		✓*	✓	✓*	✓	✓	
Slanghoek	A5		✓					T	✓		
Stofberg	C5	T									sp
Waboomsrivier	A3				×			T			
Cape Peninsula Map (page 703)											
Beau Constantia	B3		✓	✓		✓					
Blackwood	A3	T*			×			T*			de/nl
Buitenverwachting	B3		✓		×	✓			✓		

	Grid reference	Open by appt. only	Open Saturdays	Open Sundays	Open public holidays	Meals/refreshments	Accommodation	Cellar tours	Disabled friendly	Child friendly	Languages spoken
Cape Point	B4		✓	✓		✓*			✓	✓	
Cape Town Wine Co	A4		✓	✓							
Constantia Glen	B3		✓	✓		✓*					
Constantia Royale	B3	T			X						
Constantia Uitsig	B3		✓*	✓*		✓					
Dorrance	B1					✓		✓			fr
Ellerman House	B1		✓*	✓*		✓	✓				fr/sp/xh
Groot Constantia	B3		✓	✓		✓		✓	✓		fr
Hout Bay	A3	T						T		✓	de
Klein Constantia	B3		✓	✓		✓*			✓		fr/sv
Openwine	B1					✓*					
Pienaar & Son	B1	T*						T*			
Silvermist	B3	T*	✓	✓		✓*	✓				
Son of the Soil	C1		✓								
Spider Pig	D1	T									
Steenberg	B4		✓	✓		✓	✓	✓			
Township Winery	D3	T									
Wade Bales	B3				X						
Durbanville, Philadelphia & Darling Map (page 702)											
Arno Smith	C7		✓	✓							
Blake	A1		✓	✓		✓*					
Bloemendal	C7		✓	✓		✓			✓	✓	
Canto	C7		✓	✓		✓*				✓	
Capaia	C5		✓*	✓*		✓		✓		✓	de
Cloof	B3	T*						T	✓	✓	
Contreberg	A2	T*	✓	✓			✓				
DA Hanekom	C7	T*									
D'Aria	C7		✓	✓		✓	✓			✓	nl
Darling Cellars	B2		✓			✓*		T	✓	✓	xh
De Grendel	C8		✓	✓		✓		T	✓		
Diemersdal	D7		✓	✓		✓					
Durbanville Hills	C7		✓	✓		✓*		✓*	✓	✓	
Groot Phesantekraal	D7		✓	✓		✓					
Groote Post	A3		✓	✓		✓*		✓	✓	✓	
Havana Hills	C5	T						T			
Hermit on the Hill	C8	T									
Hillcrest	C7		✓	✓		✓		T			
House of Mandela	C7	T									
Klein Roosboom	C7		✓	✓		✓			✓	✓	
Kronendal	C7	T*							✓		
Maastricht	C7		✓	✓		✓*					
Maison de Teijger	D7	T									
Meerendal	C7		✓	✓		✓*	✓	T	✓	✓	xh/zu
Nitida	C7		✓	✓		✓			✓	✓	
Ormonde	A1		✓							✓	
Signal Gun	C7		✓*			✓*					
Withington	A1		✓	✓					✓		

	Grid reference	Open by appt. only	Open Saturdays	Open Sundays	Open public holidays	Meals/refreshments	Accommodation	Cellar tours	Disabled friendly	Child friendly	Languages spoken
Eastern Cape Map (page 720)											
Theescombe	D5	T				T*		T			
Elgin Map (page 710)											
Almenkerk	B2		✓			✓/BYO*		✓*			nl/fr
Arumdale	B1				T						
Charles Fox	C3							✓		✓	
Elgin Vintners	B2		✓	✓		✓*	✓				
Highlands Road	C3		✓	✓		✓*		✓	✓	✓	
Iona	C4		T		×			✓			
Kershaw	B2	T			×						fr
Nomad	C2	T						T			de
Oak Valley	B1		✓	✓		✓			✓		it/fr
Off The Record	C3	T*	✓	T			✓				
Oude Molen	B1	T									
Paul Clüver	C2		✓	✓		✓*			✓		
Paul Wallace	C3	T*	✓				✓				
Radford Dale	B3	T*			×						fr/sv
Shannon	A2	T*							✓		de/sp
Spioenkop	C4	T			×			T*			fr/nl
William Everson	B2	T					T	T			
Wines of Brocha	C4		T					✓			
Franschhoek Map (page 712)											
Akkerdal	C4	T*			×		✓				
Allée Bleue	C6		✓	✓		✓*			✓		de
Anthonij Rupert	C5	T*				✓			✓		
Atlas Swift	C3		✓	✓		✓*		✓			
Babylonstoren	B8		✓	✓		✓*		✓*	✓		
Bacco	A8		✓	✓		✓*		✓			pt
Backsberg	C2		✓	✓		✓*		✓	✓		
Bellingham	C2		✓	✓		✓*				✓	
Black Elephant	C1	T*									
Boekenhoutskloof	D1	T			×				✓		xh
Boschendal	D6		✓	✓		✓	✓		✓	✓	
Chamonix	C1		✓	✓		✓	✓	T			
Chantelle	C2	T						T			
Colmant	C1		✓					✓*	✓		fr
Dieu Donné	C1		✓	✓		✓		T*			
Eikehof	C3		✓	✓		✓*					
Enfin	C1	T									
Franschhoek Cellar	C2		✓	✓		✓*	✓		✓	✓	
GlenWood	C2		✓	✓		✓			✓		
Grande Provence	C2		✓	✓		✓	✓	T	✓	✓	
Great Heart	C1	T*									
Haute Cabrière	C1		✓	✓		✓		✓	✓		fr/de
Holden Manz	D1		✓	✓		✓	✓	T	✓		de
Klein Goederust	C2		✓	✓		✓*					xh
La Bri	C1		✓	✓		✓*					

	Grid reference	Open by appt. only	Open Saturdays	Open Sundays	Open public holidays	Meals/refreshments	Accommodation	Cellar tours	Disabled friendly	Child friendly	Languages spoken
La Motte	C3		✓	✓		✓*			✓		xh
La Petite Ferme	C1	T*				✓	✓				
Le Lude	C1		✓	✓		✓	✓	✓			
Le Manoir de Brendel	C3		✓	✓			✓			✓	
Leeu Passant	C2		✓	✓							
Leopard's Leap	C3		✓	✓		✓*				✓	
Lynx	C4		✓	✓							de/sp
Maison	C3		✓	✓		✓*					
Mont Rochelle	C2		✓	✓		✓	✓	✓*			
Môreson	C3	T			×						
Mullineux	C2		✓	✓							
My Wyn	B1	T*				T*					
Noble Hill	B7		✓	✓		✓		T	✓		fr
Old Road	C2		✓	✓*		✓					
Painted Wolf	C7		✓*			✓					fr
Paserene	C4		✓	✓		✓*					
Plaisir	C6		✓	✓			✓		✓		de
Rickety Bridge	C2		✓	✓		✓	✓	✓	✓	✓	
Stony Brook	D1	T*	✓				✓		✓		
Tanzanite	A7	T*									
The House of GM&AHRENS	C1	T			×	T		T			
Topiary	C4		✓	✓		✓*	✓	✓*	✓	✓	fr
Val de Vie	A7	T*			×				✓		
Wildeberg	D1	T*			×			T	T*		
Helderberg Map (pages 706–707)											
Avontuur	C2		✓	✓		✓	✓		✓		de/pt
Cape Classics	F4	T									
Capelands	F7	T				✓*	✓				
Cavalli	C1		✓	✓		✓*			✓		
Chennells	C2	T*			×			T			de/sp
Croydon	A3							T	✓	✓	
Eikendal	C1		✓	✓		✓*		✓	✓	✓	de
Equitania	C3	T*			×						
Flagstone	B6		✓			✓*		T	✓		
Foothills	B1	T*				T	✓				
Grangehurst	C1		✓*				✓				
Idiom	H7		✓	✓		✓*					it
Jasper Raats	C1		✓	✓							
Journey's End	G7	T									
Ken Forrester	C2 B2		✓	✓*		✓*					
Kings Kloof	E4	T									
Konkelberg	C1		✓	✓							
Le Riche	B1	T*			×						de
Longridge	C1		✓	✓		✓	✓	T	✓	✓	
Lourensford	F4		✓	✓		✓		✓	✓		
Lyngrove	B1	T					✓				
Miravel	A3	T			T						nl/fr
Morgenster	F5		✓	✓		✓					

	Grid reference	Open by appt. only	Open Saturdays	Open Sundays	Open public holidays	Meals/refreshments	Accommodation	Cellar tours	Disabled friendly	Child friendly	Languages spoken
Onderkloof	F7	T						T			
Paul Roos	C1	T						T			fr
Pink Valley	C3		✓	✓		✓		T		✓	
Post House	C1		T	T	X	X			✓		
Somerbosch	C1		✓	✓		✓		T	✓	✓	
Stonewall	C2	T*				T	✓				
Taaibosch	D2	T*			X		✓	T			
Vergelegen	F5		✓	✓		✓		✓*	✓	✓	
Yonder Hill	C3		✓		X	✓*		T	✓		
Klein Karoo & Garden Route Map (page 718)											
Aan't Vette	C6	T			X	✓*	✓	T			
Axe Hill	B5	T*		T		✓		T			
Baleia	C6		✓			X	✓	✓		✓	
Bitou	C1		✓	✓		✓					
Boplaas	B5		✓	✓				T		✓	
Boplaas	C3										
Boplaas	C1										
Calitzdorp	B5		✓	✓					✓		
De Krans	B5		✓	✓		✓*			✓	✓	
Domein Doornkraal	B3		✓	✓*		✓*	✓				
Donegal	C3		✓*			✓/BYO*		✓*		✓	
Du'SwaRoo	B5		✓					✓			
Excelsior Vlakteplaas	B3	T									
Garden Route	C3 B5		✓*						✓		
Grundheim	B4		T*						✓		
Herold	C3		✓			✓*	✓	✓	✓	✓	
Hillock	B6		✓	✓		✓	✓	✓			
Jakkalsvlei	C5		✓	✓		✓				✓	
Joseph Barry	C7		✓	✓							
Joubert-Tradauw	C7		✓			✓	✓	✓	✓	✓	
JP Bredell	C5	T									
Kay & Monty	C1		✓	✓		✓*					
Kingna	C8	T*						T*			de
Le Sueur	C5	T*									
Louis 57	C4					✓					
Metanoia	C7		✓	✓							
Mimosa	B8		✓	✓		✓*				✓	de/gsw
Montagu Wine & Spirits	B8		✓							✓	
Newstead	C1		✓	✓		✓	✓				zu
Packwood	C1		✓	✓		✓*					
Peter Bayly	B5	T						T			
Plettenvale	C1	T*						T*			
The Goose	C3	T*				T*				✓	
TTT Cellar	B5		✓	✓				✓	✓	✓	
Northern Cape, Free State & North West Map (page 719)											
Bezalel	B8			✓		✓*	✓	✓		✓	nl
Die Mas	B8			✓		✓*	✓	✓		✓	

	Grid reference	Open by appt. only	Open Saturdays	Open Sundays	Open public holidays	Meals/refreshments	Accommodation	Cellar tours	Disabled friendly	Child friendly	Languages spoken
Landzicht	C5				X			T			
Lowerland	C6	T						T			
Orange River	B8		✓			✓*		✓*	✓		
Olifants River Map (page 700)											
Bellpost	B3	T*						T			
Cape Rock	B4	T				X		T			
Cederberg	D7		✓	✓*			✓				
Driehoek	D6		✓	✓			✓			✓	
Fryer's Cove	A4		✓	✓		✓*		✓	✓	✓	
Gedeelte	B7	T									
Klawer	B4		✓			X			✓		
Lutzville	B3		✓			✓		T	✓		
Namaqua	B4		✓			✓*		T*		✓	
Piekenierskloof	D7		✓			T*		T			
Sir Lambert	B5										
Stellar	B4				X			T			
Teubes	B4 B5		✓			✓*	✓	✓	✓	✓	
Tierhoek	C6	T*			X	X	✓	T*			
Paarl Map (pages 708–709)											
Anura	C7		✓	✓		✓*			✓		de
Arra	C8		✓	✓							
Ayama	B2		✓	✓		✓*	✓			✓	it
Bayede!	E6	T*									
Bergheim	E6	T									
Black Pearl	D5	T*					*	T*	✓		
Boland	E4		✓								
Brookdale	G5		✓	✓		✓*	✓				
Denneboom	C2	T*					✓				
Doran	C1	T*						T	✓		
Eenzaamheid	B5	T									
Fairview	D6		✓	✓		✓			✓		
Fuselage	D1	T						T			
Germanier	C1	T									fr
Glen Carlou	D7		✓	✓		✓		T	✓	✓	de
Groot Parys	E5	T									nl
Hawksmoor	A7	T*				T*	✓				fr/de/ja
Jacaranda	F1		✓			T*	✓				fr/de/mdr
Joostenberg	A7	T*	✓	✓		✓*				✓	
Kusafiri	F4	T					✓	T			
KWV	E6		✓	✓		✓*		✓	✓		de
Landskroon	D6		✓*			X	✓	T*	✓		
Mason's	E6	T				✓*					
Mellasat	G5		✓	✓		T*	✓	T	✓		
Mitre's Edge	C8	T*					✓	T			
Mooi Bly	F4	T					✓	T			nl
Mount Vernon	C7	T									
Myburgh Bros	A7	T*	✓	✓							de
Nederburg	F5		✓	✓		✓*			✓	✓	de

	Grid reference	Open by appt. only	Open Saturdays	Open Sundays	Open public holidays	Meals/refreshments	Accommodation	Cellar tours	Disabled friendly	Child friendly	Languages spoken
Nelson	D3	T			×		✓	T	✓	✓	
Niel Joubert	C8	T*			×						
Nomoya	E5		✓			✓*					it
Olsen	G5	T									
Perdeberg	B2		✓	✓		✓*				✓	
Rhebokskloof	D3		✓	✓		✓			✓	✓	
Ridgeback	D3		✓	✓				T	✓	✓	
Roodekrantz	D1	T				T*					
Scali	C1	T*			×						
Simonsvlei	D7		✓			✓		T	✓	✓	
Spice Route	D6		✓	✓		✓			✓		
Tempel	E3	T				T*	✓	T			fr/lv/nl/ru
The Ahrens Family	G6	T				T*					
The Foundry	C2	T			×			T			
Under Oaks	E3		✓	✓		✓*	✓	T			
Van Loggerenberg	D6	T			×						
Vondeling	D6		✓	✓		✓*			✓		
Wilderer	D7		✓	✓		✓*				✓	de
Windmeul	D3		✓		×	✓*		T	✓	✓	
Robertson Map (page 717)											
Arendsig	C4	T					✓				
Ashton	B4		✓			T*			✓	✓	
Bemind	D6		✓			T*		✓			
Bon Courage	B5		✓			✓			✓	✓	
Bonnievale	D3		✓						✓		
Bushmanspad	C1				×	T/BYO*	✓				nl
Cape Dreams	A6	T						T			
Cape Wine Crafters	D3		✓			✓		✓		✓	
Clairvaux	B6				×	×		T	✓		
deKaap	C5		✓	✓	×	✓*					
DuVon	B7	T					✓	T			
Esona	C4		✓			✓*					
Excelsior	C4		✓			✓*				✓	
Goedverwacht	C4					×		✓			
Graham Beck	B6		✓	✓		✓*			✓		
Jan Harmsgat	C2		✓	✓		✓	✓				
Kranskop	B4		✓			✓*		✓			de
Langverwacht	D4				×			✓	✓		
Le Grand Chasseur	B7	T			×			✓			
Lord's	D7		✓	✓		✓				✓	
Lozärn	D3	T						T			
McGregor	B5				×				✓		
McGregor	D6		✓							✓	
Mont Blois	A5	T									fr
Paul René	B6		✓*	T	T						
Quando	D4	T			×						de
Rietvallei	B4		✓			✓*			✓		
RiverGold	C4	T			T	×					

	Grid reference	Open by appt. only	Open Saturdays	Open Sundays	Open public holidays	Meals/refreshments	Accommodation	Cellar tours	Disabled friendly	Child friendly	Languages spoken
Robertson	B5		✓	✓				T	✓		
Rooiberg	A7		✓	✓		✓			✓	✓	
Silverthorn	C4	T*						T*			
Tanagra	C6	T*					✓	T			de
Van Loveren	B5 C4		✓	✓		✓		T	✓		
Viljoensdrift	C5		✓	✓*		✓*					fr
Wederom	B7	T			T	T	✓	T			de
Weltevrede	D3		✓			✓*		✓*	✓		
Windfall	C8	T			×		✓	T			
Zandvliet	C4		✓						✓		
Southern Cape Map (page 716)											
Black Oystercatcher	B3		✓			✓*	✓		✓	✓	
Brunia	B2	T			×						
Delphin	A7		✓	✓	T	✓*		✓			
Fortes	B2	T*			×	×	*	T			
Lomond	C8		✓	✓		✓*					
Olivedale	D1	T			×			✓			
Sijnn	D1		✓			✓*		✓			
Skipskop	C6	T									
Strandveld	D7		✓			×		✓			
The Drift	B7	T									
The Giant Periwinkle	A3	T*									
Zoetendal	C7		✓	✓		✓					
Stellenbosch Map (pages 704–705)											
Aalderling	D4		✓*		×		✓	T	✓		
Akkerdraai	E8	T			×						de
Alto	E8		✓	✓							
Annandale	E8		✓			✓*			✓		
ArtiSons	C3	T			×			T			
Asara	D6		✓	✓		✓	✓	T*		✓	de
Aslina	D3	T									
Audacia	E8	T*			×						
Bartinney	H5		✓	✓		✓*	✓		✓		
Bein	B6	T						T			de/fr
Bellevue	C3		✓	✓		✓*				✓	
Bertha	E4		✓	✓		✓*	✓			✓	
Beyerskloof	E3		✓	✓		✓		T	✓		
Bezuidenhout Family	E5	T					T				
Blaauwklippen	E7		✓	✓		✓		✓*	✓	✓	de
Boschheim	E5	T									de
Boschkloof	C6					✓/BYO		✓			
Botanica	D4	T*				✓*	✓				
Brampton	F5		✓	✓							
Bruwer Vintners	B6	T*			×						
Camberley	H4		✓	✓			✓				
Capensis	H5	T									
Catherine Marshall	B6							✓			
Clos Malverne	D4		✓	✓		✓	✓	✓*	✓	✓	

	Grid reference	Open by appt. only	Open Saturdays	Open Sundays	Open public holidays	Meals/refreshments	Accommodation	Cellar tours	Disabled friendly	Child friendly	Languages spoken
Clouds	H5	T				✓*	✓	T			
Dalla Cia	E5		✓		×	✓		T*	✓		it
David Finlayson	E3	T									
De Trafford	G8	T*	✓		×			T*			
Delaire Graff	H5		✓	✓		✓	✓	T*	✓		
Delheim	F2		✓	✓		✓			✓		de
DeMorgenzon	C5		✓	✓		✓*		T			
Deux Frères	E3		✓			T*	✓	✓			
DeWaal	C5		✓								de
Domaine Coutelier	D4	T			×		✓	T			fr
Dornier	F7		✓	✓				T	✓		
Ernie Els	E8					✓*			✓		
Ernst Gouws	D1		✓						✓	✓	de
Friesland	B3	T*				T*					
Glenelly	F4		✓	✓		✓		T	✓		de/fr
Groenland	B3		✓					T	✓		
Guardian Peak	E8		✓	✓		✓			✓		
Hartenberg	C4		✓	✓		✓*		T	✓	✓	de
Hazendal	B3		✓	✓		✓	✓	T	✓	✓	de/ru
Hidden Valley	E8		✓	✓		✓*	✓	T	✓		
Hoopenburg	E1					×	✓	✓			
Illimis	B6										
Jordan	C5		✓	✓		✓*	✓	T*			
Joubert Family	E2		✓		×	T/BYO				✓	
Kaapzicht	B4		✓								de
Kanonkop	F2		✓			T/BYO*			✓		
Kanu	E3		✓	✓		✓*			✓		
Karo	E5	T*									
Keermont	G8	T*	✓*		×		✓	T			
Klein DasBosch	F7	T*				✓					
Kleine Zalze	E7		✓	✓					✓		
Knorhoek	F3		✓	✓		✓*	✓		✓	✓	
Koelenhof	D1		✓			✓*		✓	✓	✓	de
Kyburg	D4	T						✓			fr/de
Ladybird	F1		✓					✓			
Lanzerac	G5		✓	✓		✓	✓	✓*	✓		
L'Avenir	E3		✓	✓		✓	✓	T	✓	✓	fr
Le Bonheur	F1	T									
Le Chant	F5	T*									
Le Grand Domaine	D4	T*									
Le Grand Domaine	F5		✓	✓		✓*					
Le Pommier	H4		✓	✓		✓	✓			✓	
Lievland	F1		✓	✓		✓*			✓		
Louisvale	D4		✓			✓			✓		
Lovane	D6		✓	✓				✓	✓		
Marianne	G1		✓	✓		✓*	✓	✓	✓	✓	de/fr
Marklew	F1	T						T			
Meerlust	C8		✓		×		✓	T			

	Grid reference	Open by appt. only	Open Saturdays	Open Sundays	Open public holidays	Meals/refreshments	Accommodation	Cellar tours	Disabled friendly	Child friendly	Languages spoken
Meinert	D4	T*			X						de
M'hudi	B1					✓					tn/xh/zu
Middelvlei	E4		✓	✓		✓*	✓	T	✓	✓	
MolenVliet	H4	T*					✓				
Mooiplaas	B4		✓	✓*		✓*				✓	
Morgenhof	F3		✓	✓		✓	✓	T*	✓	✓	de
Mulderbosch	C5		✓	✓		✓*			✓	✓	fr
Muratie	F3		✓	✓		✓*		T			
Mvemve Raats	B6	T*			X						
Neethlingshof	D5		✓	✓		✓*		T	✓	✓	de
Neil Ellis	G5		✓			✓*			✓		
Nico van der Merwe	B6	T*									fr/de
Nietgegund	F7	T									
Noble Savage	F5		✓								
Nuiba	D5										
Oldenburg	H5		✓				*		✓		
Overgaauw	D5	T*							✓		
Peter Falke	E8		✓	✓		✓*					
Pilgrim	C5	T									de
Pink Valley	F5	T*									
Quoin Rock	F3		✓	✓		✓	T				
Raats	B6	T*			X						
Rainbow's End	H6		✓			✓*					
Rebel Rebel	B4	T						T			
Remhoogte	F3		✓			✓*	✓	T	✓		
Reyneke	B6	T*						T			
Rust en Vrede	E8		✓	✓		✓*					
Rustenberg	F4		✓	✓							
Saltare	F5	T						T			
Saxenburg	A5		✓	✓		✓	✓				
Seven Sisters	C7		✓*			✓*					
Simonsig	E2		✓	✓		✓*		T	✓	✓	
Skilpadvlei	C6		✓	✓		✓	✓		✓	✓	
Slaley	E2		✓	✓			✓				
Spier	C7		✓	✓		✓	✓		✓	✓	de/xh
Spotswood	F7	T									
Stark-Condé	G6		✓	✓	X	✓			✓		ja
Stellekaya	E5	T*			X			✓*			zu
Stellenbosch Family Wines	D1	T									
Stellenbosch Hills	D6		✓		X				✓		
Stellenbosch Reserve	F8		✓	✓		✓					
Stellenbosch University	F5				X						
Stellenbosch Vineyards	C7		✓						✓	✓	xh
Stellenrust	E7, C3		✓		X	✓*		T			xh
Stellenview	D4		T	T	X			✓*			
Stellenview	F5		✓	✓		✓*					
Stellenzicht	F8		✓	✓							
Summerhill	E3					✓					

	Grid reference	Open by appt. only	Open Saturdays	Open Sundays	Open public holidays	Meals/refreshments	Accommodation	Cellar tours	Disabled friendly	Child friendly	Languages spoken
Super Single Vineyards	C5		✓		✗						
Tamboerskloof	F7		✓			✓*		✓			de/fr
The High Road	E5	T			✗				✓		
The Hills	D4	T									
The House of JC le Roux	D4		✓	✓		✓*		✓*	✓	✓	
Thelema	G4		✓					✓			
Thistle & Weed	G6	T*									
Tokara	G4		✓	✓		✓					
Too Much Truth	G4	T			✗			T			de/nl
Torero	B6	T*				T*		T			sp
Van Biljon	B6	T			✗			T			
Van Ryn	D6		✓	✓				✓*			
Vergenoegd	B8		✓	✓		✓*	✓	T	✓		xh
Villiera	D1					✓*		✓	✓		fr
Vredenheim	D6		✓			✓	✓	✓	✓		
Vriesenhof	F7	T*			✗			T			
Vuurberg	H4	T			✗			T			
Warwick	F1		✓	✓		✓*		T	✓	✓	
Waterford	F8		✓	✓		✓*		✓	✓		
Webersburg	E8		✓	✓		✓*	✓	✓			
Winshaw	C8		✓	✓		✓					
Zevenwacht	B5		✓	✓		✓*	✓	T	✓	✓	xh
Zorgvliet	H4		✓	✓		✓*	✓	T	✓	✓	
Swartland Map (page 701)											
AA Badenhorst	C8	T*			✗	✓*	T	T*			
Abbottshill	B7	T				✗	T	T			
Allesverloren	D6		✓	✓		✓*		T	✓	✓	
Arbeidsgenot	D6		✓	✓		✓*					
Babylon's Peak	C8	T							✓		
Badger	C8	T			✗			T			
Cage Wine	C8	T						T			ja
City on a Hill	C8	T									
David & Nadia	C8	T			✗						
Dragonridge	C8	T				T*	✓	T		✓	
Franki's	A6	T*			✗	✗*	✓	T*			
Hofstraat	C7	T*				✓*		T			
Hughes Family	C6	T									sp
Hunneyball	B7	T					✓				
JC Wickens	C8	T									
Kloovenburg	D6		✓	✓		✓*			✓	✓	
Kloovenburg	D6		✓	✓		✓*					
Lammershoek	C8	T			✗			T			de
Meerhof	D6		✓	✓		✓*					
Mullineux	D6	T*									
Nieuwedrift	C2		✓	✓		✓*	✓	✓		✓	
Org de Rac	C2		✓			✓*		✓	✓	✓	de
Pulpit Rock	D6		✓			✗		T	✓		
Rall	D6	T						T			

	Grid reference	Open by appt. only	Open Saturdays	Open Sundays	Open public holidays	Meals/refreshments	Accommodation	Cellar tours	Disabled friendly	Child friendly	Languages spoken
Riebeek Valley	D6							T	✓		
Riebeek Valley	D6		✓	✓		✓*					
Sadie	C8	T*									
Swartland	C7		✓			✓*			✓	✓	
Vinevenom	D6	T									
Wightman & Sons	C8	T									
Wildehurst	B2	T*						T*			
Tulbagh Map (page 711)											
Blackwater	C6	T									
Duikersdrift	B5		✓	✓		✓*	✓			✓	
Koelfontein	H5		T		X		✓				
Krone	F4		✓		X			✓			pt/sp
Lemberg	F5		✓	✓		✓/BYO*	✓	✓	✓		
Manley	B5		✓				✓	T			
Rijk's	F5		✓				✓	T	✓		
Saronsberg	F4		✓	✓			✓	✓			
Schalkenbosch	G5	T			X		✓	T			de
Swanepoel	F4		✓	✓			✓				
Terracura	A7	T			X						
Themika	F4	T					✓				
Tulbagh Winery	F5		✓						✓		
Waverley Hills	G6	T						T	✓	✓	
Villiersdorp Map (page 715)											
Bundu	C1		✓	✓							
Eerste Hoop	A2	T						T			
Villiersdorp	C1		✓			✓		T	✓		
Walker Bay & Bot River Map (page 713)											
Anysbos	C3	T						T			
Arcangeli	C3	T				✓	✓				
Bartho Eksteen	A3		✓			✓*		T		✓	fr/xh
Beaumont	C2		✓	✓		✓*	✓		✓	✓	
Benguela Cove	B2		✓	✓		✓*		✓	✓	✓	
Boschrivier	C8		✓	✓*		✓/BYO	✓		✓		
Bosman Hermanus	B3		✓	✓		✓*					
Bouchard Finlayson	B4		✓	✓		✓*		✓	✓		de/fr
Bruce Jack	B6										
Cape Moby	B5		✓	✓							
Creation	C4		✓	✓		✓		✓	✓	✓	de/fr
Deep Rooted	B6	T			T			T			fr
Domaine des Dieux	C4		✓	✓		✓*				✓	
Escape	B2	T									
Fynbos	B6		✓	✓		✓		✓		✓	
Gabriëlskloof	C3		✓	✓		✓		✓	✓		
Genevieve	C2		✓*								
Hamilton Russell	B4		✓					T			tn/xh
Hasher	B4		✓*								
Hermanuspietersfontein	A3		✓				✓	✓*	✓		
Jakob's Vineyards	C4	T									

	Grid reference	Open by appt. only	Open Saturdays	Open Sundays	Open public holidays	Meals/refreshments	Accommodation	Cellar tours	Disabled friendly	Child friendly	Languages spoken
La Vierge	B4		✓	✓		✓			✓		
Luddite	D2		T	T				T	✓		nl
Maanschijn	B5	T						T			
McFarlane	C5	T						T			
Misty Mountains	B5		✓	✓		✓	✓	T			
Mount Babylon	C4	T*									
Newton Johnson	B4		✓		×	✓			✓		
Raka	C8		✓			×		T	✓	✓	
Restless River	B4	T			×						
Seven Springs	C5		✓	✓				T			
Southern Right	A3	T*						T	✓		
Southern Treasures	C8		✓			✓				✓	
Spookfontein	B4		✓	✓		✓	✓				
Springfontein	B5		✓	✓		✓*	✓	✓			
Stanford Hills	B6		✓	✓		✓	✓		✓		
Storm	B4	T									
Thamnus Wines	C5	T				×					
Villion	B2		✓								
Walker Bay Estate	B6		✓	✓		✓		T	✓	✓	
Waterleliefontein	D2										
Welgesind	B6		✓			×*		✓			
Whalehaven	A3		✓	✓							
Wild Air	B4	T									
Wildekrans	B1		✓	✓		✓	✓	T	✓		
Wine Village – Hermanus	A3		✓	✓					✓		
Wellington Map (page 710)											
Andreas	C3	T*			×		✓	T			sv
Bosman Family	C3	T*				✓*		T*			
De Kleine Wijn Koöp	C3	T									
Diemersfontein	B4		✓	✓		✓*	✓	T			
Doolhof	D3		✓	✓		✓*	✓	T	✓		
Dunstone	C3	T*				✓	✓		✓	✓	
Imbuko	B4		✓			✓*		T		✓	
Lazanou	B2	T*				T*					
Maske	C4	T									de
Mischa	B2	T*			×	T*		T*			
Mont du Toit	C4	T			×			T	✓		de
Nabygelegen	C3	T*			×		✓	T			
Thokozani	B4		✓	✓		✓	✓	T			
Upland	C4	T			T			T			de
Val du Charron	C3		✓	✓		✓	✓	T	✓	✓	
Welbedacht	B1		✓	T*		✓		✓	✓	✓	de
Welgegund	C4	T									
Wellington Winery	B3 C3		✓*			✓*			✓		
Welvanpas	C3		✓			✓*					nl
Wolvenhoek	C2		✓	T	T	✓/BYO*		✓			de/fr/nl

	Grid reference	Open by appt. only	Open Saturdays	Open Sundays	Open public holidays	Meals/refreshments	Accommodation	Cellar tours	Disabled friendly	Child friendly	Languages spoken
Worcester Map (page 715)											
Aan de Doorns	B4		✓		✗			T*	✓		
Alvi's Drift	B5	T*			✗						
Cilmor	B4		T	T	✗						
De Wet	B3		✓		✗	✓/BYO*		T	✓		
Eagle's Cliff	A6				✗	✓*			✓		
Leipzig	C3		✓			T*	✓	✓*		✓	ru
Nuy	C4		✓	✓		✓			✓		
Overhex	B3				✗				✓		
Stettyn	A6		✓	✓		✓*			✓		

Olifants River & West Coast

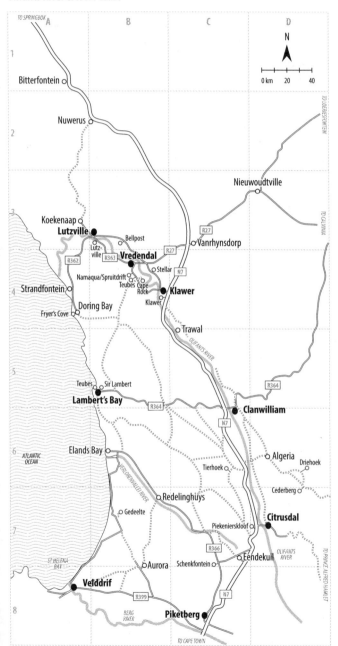

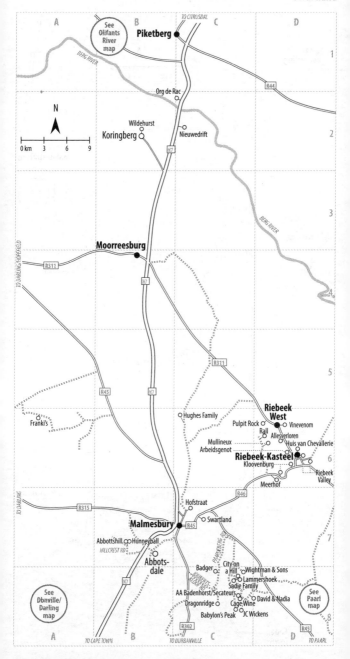

Durbanville, Philadelphia & Darling

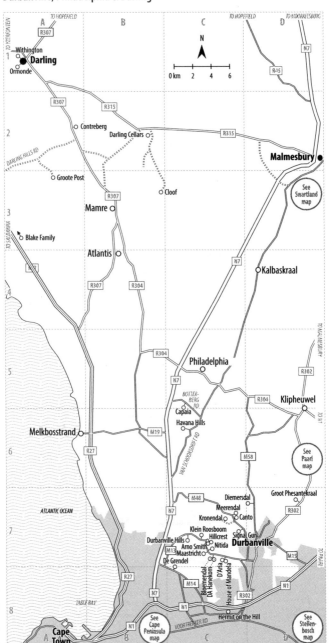

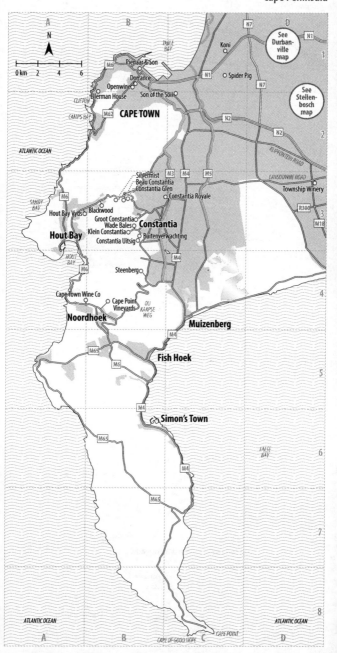

N

0 km   2   4   6

TABLE BAY

See Durban-
ville
map

N7

N1

Koni

N1

Spider Pig

N7

M6

Pienaar & Son

Dorrance

CLIFTON

Openwine

Ellerman House

Son of the Soil

See Stellen-
bosch
map

CAMPS BAY

M62

CAPE TOWN

N2

ATLANTIC OCEAN

N2

KLIPFONTEIN ROAD

LANDSDOWNE ROAD

M3

Silvermist
Beau Constantia
Constantia Glen

M4

M5

Township Winery

Constantia Royale

R300

SANDY BAY

M6

Blackwood

Hout Bay Vyds

Groot Constantia
Wade Bales
Klein Constantia
Constantia Uitsig

Constantia

M18

Hout Bay

Buitenverwachting

HOUT BAY

M6

Steenberg

M4

Cape Town Wine Co

Cape Point
Vineyards

OU KAAPSE WEG

Noordhoek

Muizenberg

M4

M65

M6

Fish Hoek

M4

Simon's Town

M65

FALSE BAY

M4

M65

ATLANTIC OCEAN

ATLANTIC OCEAN

CAPE OF GOOD HOPE

CAPE POINT

Stellenbosch

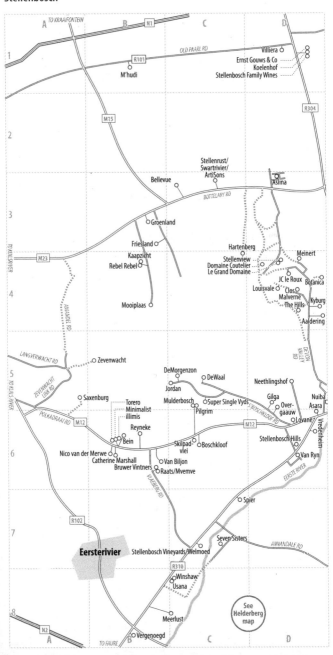

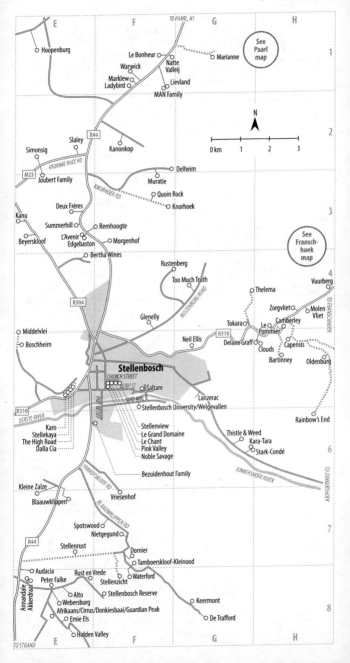

See Paarl map

See Franschhoek map

TO PAARL, N1

N

0 km   1   2   3

Hoopenburg

Le Bonheur

Warwick

Natte Valleij

Marklew

Lievland

Ladybird

MAN Family

Marianne

Slaley

R44

Kanonkop

Simonsig

KROMME RHEE RD

M23

Joubert Family

Delheim

Muratie

KNORHOEK RD

Quoin Rock

Knorhoek

Deux Frères

Kanu

Summerhill

Remhoogte

Beyerskloof

L'Avenir

Edgebaston

Morgenhof

Bertha Wines

Rustenberg

Too Much Truth

Thelema

Vuurberg

RUSTENBURG ROAD

Zorgvliet

Molen Vliet

Camberley

R304

Glenelly

Tokara

Le Pommier

Capensis

Middelvlei

R310

Delaire Graff

Boschheim

Neil Ellis

Clouds

Bartinney

Oldenburg

Stellenbosch

CHURCH STREET

DORP ST

Saltare

Lanzerac

Rainbow's End

PLEIN ST

SUID WAL

Stellenbosch University/Welgevallen

EERSTE RIVER

R310

Karo

Stellekaya

The High Road

Dalla Cia

Stellenview

Le Grand Domaine

Le Chant

Pink Valley

Noble Savage

Thistle & Weed

Kara-Tara

Stark-Condé

PIET RETIEF

Bezuidenhout Family

JONKERSHOEK RIVER

TO JONKERSHOEK

Kleine Zalze

Blaauwklippen

Vriesenhof

PARADYSKLOOF RD

Spotswood

Nietgegund

R44

Stellenrust

Dornier

BLAAUWKLIPPEN RD

Tamboerskloof-Kleinood

Audacia

Peter Falke

Rust en Vrede

Annandale

Akkerdraai

Stellenzicht

Waterford

Alto

Webersburg

Stellenbosch Reserve

Keermont

Afrikaans/Cirrus/Donkiesbaai/Guardian Peak

Ernie Els

De Trafford

Hidden Valley

TO STRAND

Helderberg

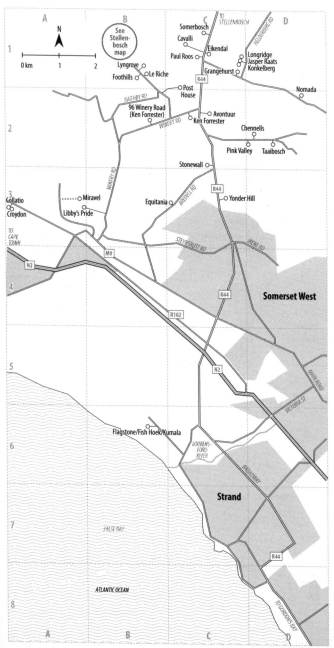

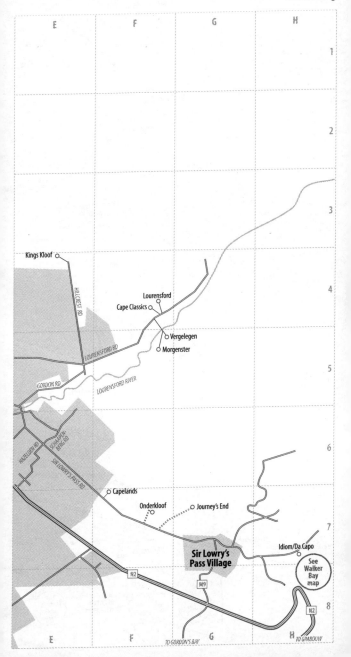

Paarl

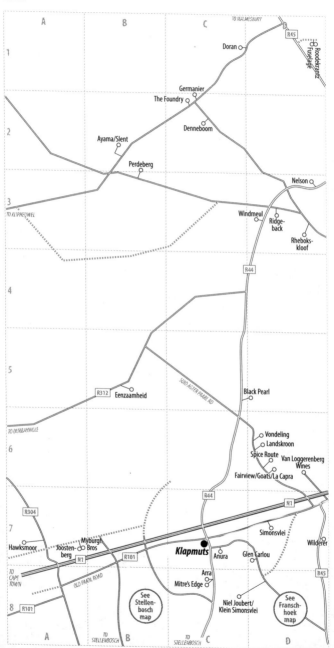

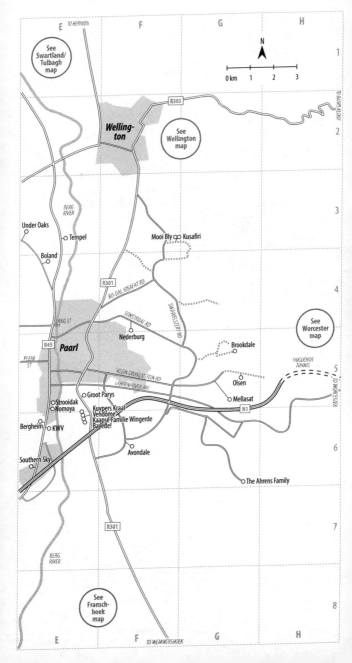

Wellington

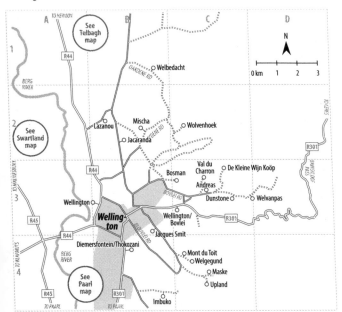

Elgin

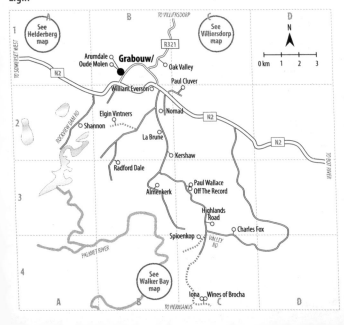

Tulbagh

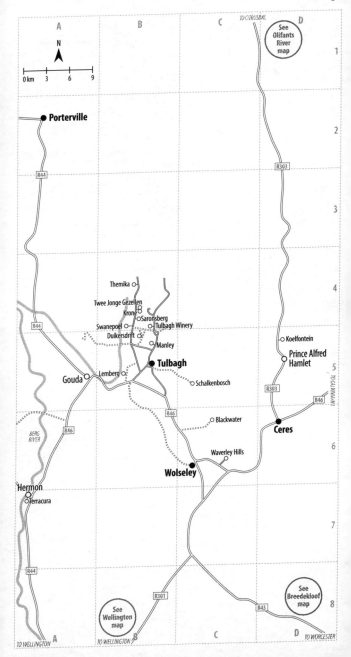

Franschhoek

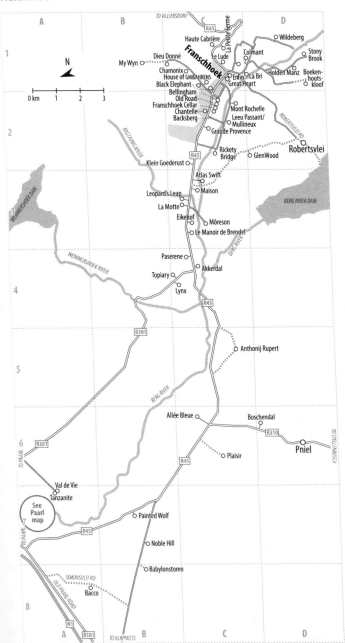

N

0 km   1   2   3

TO VILLIERSDORP

Franschhoek

R45

TO PAARL

TO KLAPMUTS

KASTEELBERG RIVER
WEMMERSHOEK DAM
WEMMERSHOEK RIVER
BERG RIVER
BERG RIVER DAM
ROBERTSVLEI RD
HOSPITAALSKLOOF RD
SIMONSVLEI RD
OLD PAARL ROAD

Haute Cabrière
La Petite Ferme
Wildeberg
My Wyn
Dieu Donné
Le Lude
Colmant
Stony Brook
Holden Manz
Boekenhoutskloof
Chamonix
House of GM&AHRENS
Black Elephant
Enfin
La Bri
Great Heart
Bellingham
Old Road
Franschhoek Cellar
Chantelle
Backsberg
Mont Rochelle
Leeu Passant/
Mullineux
Grande Provence
Rickety Bridge
GlenWood
Robertsvlei
Klein Goederust
Atlas Swift
Maison
Leopard's Leap
La Motte
Eikehof
Môreson
Le Manoir de Brendel
Paserene
Akkerdal
Topiary
Lynx
Anthonij Rupert
Allée Bleue
Boschendal
Pniel
Plaisir
Val de Vie
Tanzanite
See Paarl map
Painted Wolf
Noble Hill
Babylonstoren
Bacco

R45
R301
R310
R101
N1

Walker Bay & Bot River

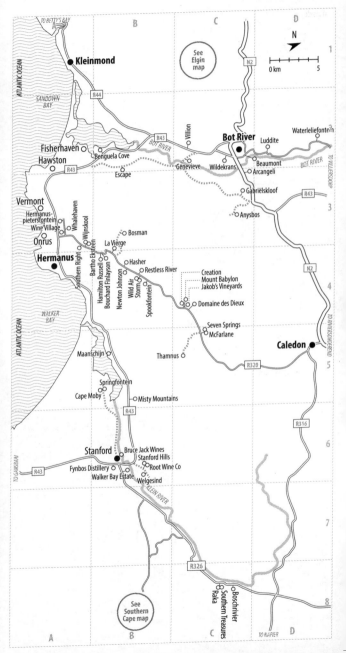

Breedekloof

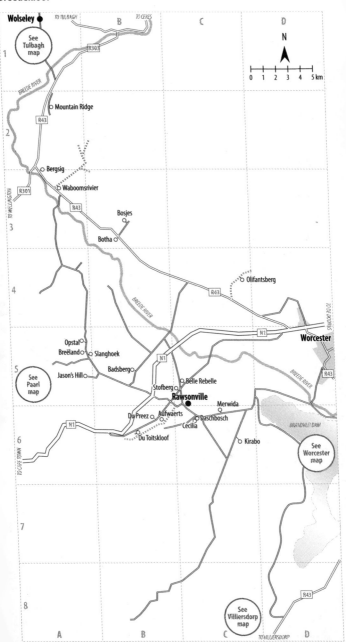

Worcester

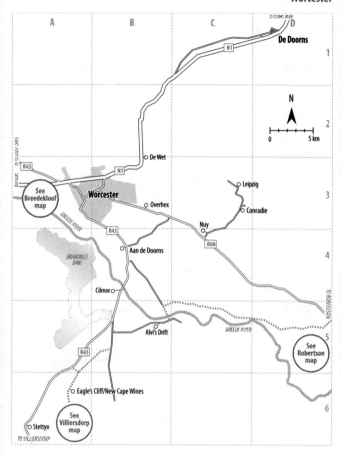

Villiersdorp

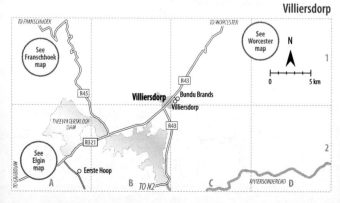

Southern Cape

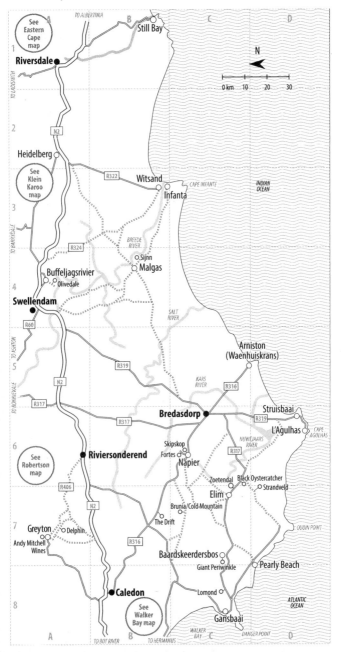

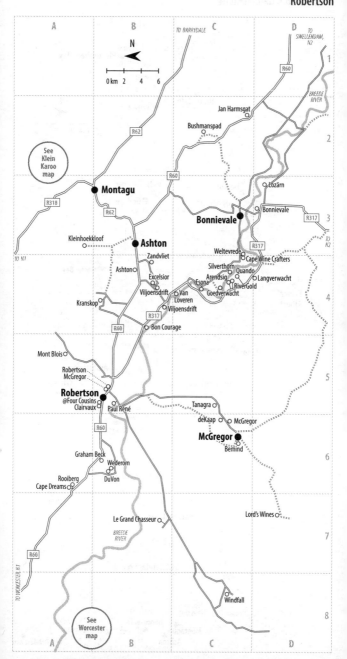

N

0 km 2 4 6

TO BARRYDALE

TO SWELLENDAM, N2

R60

BREEDE RIVER

R62

See Klein Karoo map

R318

Montagu

R62

Jan Harmsgat

Bushmanspad

R60

Lozärn

Bonnievale

Bonnievale

R317

Kleinhoekkloof

Ashton

Zandvliet

Weltevrede

Cape Wine Crafters

R317

TO N1

Ashton

Excelsior

Viljoensdrift

Silverthorn

Quando

Langverwacht

Esona

Arendsig

RiverGold

Goedverwacht

Van Loveren

Viljoensdrift

Kranskop

R317

Bon Courage

R60

Mont Blois

Robertson McGregor

Robertson

@Four Cousins

Clairvaux

Paul René

Tanagra

deKaap

McGregor

McGregor

Bemind

R60

Graham Beck

Wederom

Rooiberg

DuVon

Cape Dreams

Lord's Wines

Le Grand Chasseur

BREEDE RIVER

TO WORCESTER, N1

R60

Windfall

See Worcester map

Klein Karoo & Garden Route

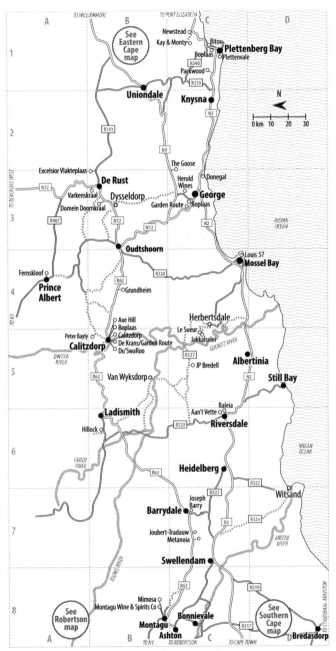